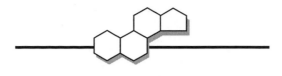

HORMONES, BRAIN and BEHAVIOR

VOLUME ONE

CHAPTERS 1–15

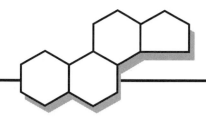

HORMONES, BRAIN and BEHAVIOR

VOLUME ONE
CHAPTERS 1–15

Edited by

Donald W. Pfaff
The Rockefeller University
New York, New York

Arthur P. Arnold
Department of Physiological Science
University of California, Los Angeles
Los Angeles, California

Anne M. Etgen
Department of Neuroscience
Albert Einstein College of Medicine
Bronx, New York

Susan E. Fahrbach
Department of Entomology
University of Illinois at Urbana-Champaign
Urbana, Illinois

Robert T. Rubin
Allegheny General Hospital
Pittsburgh, Pennsylvania

ACADEMIC PRESS
An imprint of Elsevier Science

Amsterdam   Boston   London   New York   Oxford   Paris   San Diego   San Francisco
Singapore   Sydney   Tokyo

This book is printed on acid-free paper. ∞

Academic Press
An imprint of Elsevier Science.
525 B Street, Suite 1900, San Diego, California 92101-4495, USA
http://www.academicpress.com

Academic Press
84 Theobalds Road, London WC1X 8RR, UK
http://www.academicpress.com

Library of Congress Catalog Card Number: 2002104386

International Standard Book Number: 0-12-532104-X (set)
International Standard Book Number: 0-12-532105-8 (volume 1)
International Standard Book Number: 0-12-532106-6 (volume 2)
International Standard Book Number: 0-12-532107-4 (volume 3)
International Standard Book Number: 0-12-532108-2 (volume 4)
International Standard Book Number: 0-12-532109-0 (volume 5)

PRINTED IN THE UNITED STATES OF AMERICA
02   03   04   05   06   07   MM   9   8   7   6   5   4   3   2   1

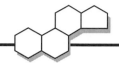

Brief Contents of All Volumes

Contents of Volume One

Contents of Volume Two

PART II
NONMAMMALIAN HORMONE-BEHAVIOR SYSTEMS
A. NONMAMMALIAN VERTEBRATES

Contents of Volume Three

PART III

CELLULAR AND MOLECULAR MECHANISMS OF HORMONE ACTIONS ON BEHAVIOR

Contents of Volume Four

PART IV

DEVELOPMENT OF HORMONE-DEPENDENT NEURONAL SYSTEMS

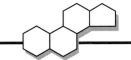

Contents of This Volume

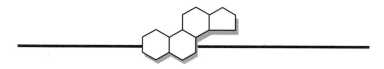

Contributors

Volume numbers are boldfaced, separated from the chapter number with a colon.

Elizabeth Adkins-Regan (**4**: 66)
Department of Psychology
Cornell University
Ithaca, New York 14853

H. Elliott Albers (**1**: 6)
Departments of Biology amd Psychology
Center for Behavioral Neuroscience
Georgia State University
Atlanta, Georgia 30303

Grant W. Anderson (**3**: 50)
Department of Medicine
Division of Endocrinology and Diabetes
University of Minnesota
Minneapolis, Minnesota 55455

Arthur P. Arnold (**4**: 63)
Department of Physiological Science
University of California, Los Angeles
Los Angeles, California 90095

Gordon J. Atkins (**3**: 39)
Biology Department
Andrews University
Berrien Springs, Michigan 49104

Gregory F. Ball (**2**: 32)
Department of Psychological and Brain Sciences
Johns Hopkins University
Baltimore, Maryland 21218

Jacques Balthazart (**2**: 32; **4**: 66)
Center for Cellular and Molecular Neurobiology
Research Group in Behavioral Neurobiology
University of Liege
B-4020 Liege
Belgium

Andrew H. Bass (**2**: 23)
Department of Neurobiology and Behavior
Cornell University
Ithaca, New York 14853

Michael Bauer (**2**: 21)
Neuropsychiatric Institute and Hospital
Department of Psychiatry and Biobehavioral
  Sciences
University of California at Los Angeles
Los Angeles, California 90095

Michael J. Baum (**4**: 69)
Department of Biology
Boston University
Boston, Massachusetts 02215

Nancy E. Beckage (**3**: 42)
Departments of Entomology and Cell Biology
  and Neuroscience
University of California, Riverside
Riverside, California 92521

M. E. Bell (**1**: 9)
Department of Physiology
University of California at San Francisco
San Francisco, California 94143

Nira Ben-Jonathan (5: 86)
Department of Cell Biology, Neurobiology, and
Anatomy
University of Cincinnati
Cincinatti, Ohio 45267

Sarah L. Berga (5: 99)
Departments of Obstetrics-Gynecology,
Reproductive Sciences,
and Psychiatry
Division of Reproductive Endocrinology and
Fertility
McGee Women's Hospital
Pittsburgh, Pennsylvania 15213

Karen Berkley (5: 95)
Program in Neuroscience
Florida State University
Tallahassee, Florida 32306

Juan Bernal (4: 74)
Instituto de Investigaciones Biomedicas Alberto Sols
CSIC-UAM
28029 Madrid
Spain

Seema Bhatnagar (1: 9)
Department of Biopsychology
University of Michigan
Ann Arbor, Michigan 48104

Mariel Birnbaumer (3: 58)
Departments of Anesthesiology amd Physiology
Molecular Biology Institute
UCLA School of Medicine
Los Angeles, California 90095

Per Björntorp (5: 102)
Department of Heart and Lung Diseases
Salhgren's Hospital
University of Göteborg
S-41345 Göteborg
Sweden

D. Caroline Blanchard (1: 13)
Department of Genetics and Molecular Biology
John A. Burns School of Medicine
Pacific Biomedical Research Center
Honolulu, Hawaii 96822

Robert J. Blanchard (1: 13)
Department of Psychology
University of Hawaii Manoa
Honolulu, Hawaii 96822

Jeffrey D. Blaustein (1: 2)
Center for Neuroscience Studies
Neuroscience and Behavior Program
University of Massachusetts
Amherst, Massachusetts 01003

Guy Bloch (3: 40)
Department of Entomology
University of Illinois
Urbana, Illinois 61801

Graham C. Boorse (2: 28)
Department of Biology
University of Michigan
Ann Arbor, Michigan 48109

Lisa Borg (5: 106)
Laboratory of the Biology of Addictive
Diseases
The Rockefeller University
New York, New York 10021

Cherif Boudaba (3: 59)
Department of Cell and Molecular
Biology
Division of Neurobiology
Tulane University
New Orleans, Louisiana 70118

Stephen Marc Breedlove (4: 65)
Department of Psychology
University of California
Berkeley, California 94720

Eliot A. Brenowitz (2: 33)
Departments of Psychology and Zoology
Virginia Merrill Bloedel Hearing
Research Center
University of Washington
Seattle, Washington 98195

Greagh Breuner (3: 51)
Department of Integrative Biology
University of Texas
Austin, Texas 78712

Michael Bronsert (3: 39)
Biology Department
Andrews University
Berrien Springs, Michigan 49104

Karen Bulloch (1: 14)
Laboratory of Neuroendocrinology
The Rockefeller University
New York, New York 10021

C. Sue Carter (1: 4)
Brain-Body Center
Department of Psychiatry
University of Illinois at Chicago
Chicago, Illinois 60612

George P. Chrousos (4: 81)
Pediatric and Reproductive Endocrinology
Branch
Intramural Research Program
National Institute of Child Health and Human
Development
National Institutes of Health
Bethesda, Maryland 20892

Rochelle S. Cohen (4: 77)
Department of Anatomy and Cell
Biology
University of Illinois at Chicago
Chicago, Illinois 60612

P. Michael Conn (4: 61)
Oregon Regional Primate Research Center
Beaverton, Oregon 97006

David Crews (2: 30)
Institute for Cellular and Molecular Biology
University of Texas
Austin, Texas 78712

Mary F. Dallman (1: 9)
Department of Physiology
University of California, San Francisco
San Francisco, California 94143

Robert C. Daly (5: 84)
Behavioral Endocrinology Branch
National Institute of Mental Health
Bethesda, Maryland 20892

Martin Daly (5: 94)
Department of Psychology
McMaster University
Hamilton, Ontario, L8S 4K1
Canada

E. Ronald De Kloet (3: 52)
Sylvius Laboratories
Leiden University
2300 RA Leiden
The Netherlands

Geert J. De Vries (4: 64)
Center for Neuroendocrine Studies
University of Massachusetts
Amherst, Massachusetts 01003

Robert J. Denver (2: 28)
Department of Molecular, Cellular,
and Developmental Biology
Department of Ecology and Evolutionary
Biology
University of Michigan
Ann Arbor, Michigan 48109

Timothy G. Dinan (5: 97)
Department of Pharmacology and
Therapeutics
University College Cork
Cork University Hospital
Wilton, Cork
Ireland

Hugh Dingle (3: 41)
Department of Entomology
Center for Population Biology
University of California, Davis
Davis, California 95616

Gary P. Dohanich (2: 22)
Department of Psychology
Neuroscience Program
Tulane Unviersity
New Orleans, Louisiana 70118

Richard E. J. Dyball (4: 60)
Department of Anatomy
University of Cambridge
Cambridge CB2 3DY
United Kingdom

Mary S. Erskine (1: 2)
Department of Biology
Boston University
Boston, Massachusetts 02215

Anne M. Etgen (3: 46)
Department of Neuroscience and Psychiatry
Albert Einstein College of Medicine
Bronx, New York 10461

John Ewer (3: 35)
Department of Entomology
Cornell University
Ithaca, New York 14853

Susan E. Fahrbach (3: 44)
Department of Entomology
University of Illinois at Urbana-Champaign
Urbana, Illinois 61801

Russell D. Fernald (2: 26)
Program in Neuroscience
Department of Psychology
Stanford University
Stanford, California 94305

Caleb E. Finch (4: 79)
Andrus Gerontology Center
Department of Biological Sciences
University of Southern California
Los Angeles, California 90089

Steven J. Fluharty (1: 8; **3**: 53)
Department of Animal Biology
   and Pharmacology
Institute of Neurological Science
University of Pennsylvania
Schools of Medicine and Veterinary Medicine
Philadelphia, Pennsylvania 19104

Jonathan Frohlich (3: 47)
Department of Neurobiology and Behavior
The Rockefeller University
New York, New York 10021

K. Eddie Gabry (4: 81)
Clinical Neuroendocrinology Branch
National Institute of Mental Health
National Institutes of Health
Bethesda, Maryland 20892

Paul Gasser (3: 51)
Department of Biology
Arizona State University
Tempe, Arizona 85287

Thomas D. Geracioti, Jr. (5: 89)
Department of Psychiatry
University of Cincinnati Medical Center
Veterans Affairs Medical Center
Cincinnati, Ohio 45267

Elizabeth S. Ginsburg (5: 105)
Department of Obstetrics and Gynecology
Brigham and Women's Hospital
Boston, Massachusetts 02115

Karen A. Glennemeier (2: 28)
Department of Biology
University of Michigan
Ann Arbor, Michigan 48109

John Godwin (2: 30)
Department of Zoology
North Carolina State University
Raleigh, North Carolina 27695

Philip W. Gold (4: 81)
Clinical Neuroendocrinology Branch
National Institute of Mental Health
National Institutes of Health
Bethesda, Maryland 20892

Francisca Gomez (1: 9)
Department of Physiology
University of California at San Francisco
San Francisco, California 94143

Gabriela González-Mariscal (1: 3)
Centro de Investigación en Reproducción Animal
Centro de Investigación y Estudios Avanzdos–
Universidad Autónoma de Tlaxcala
90120 Tlaxcala
Mexico

Elizabeth Gould (4: 78)
Department of Psychology
Princeton University
Princeton, New Jersey 08543

Richard Green (4: 71)
Department of Psychiatry
Imperial College School of Medicine at
   Charing Cross
Gender Identity Clinic
Charing Cross Hospital
London W6 8RF
United Kingdom

Matthew S. Grober (2: 23)
Center for Behavioral Neuroscience
Department of Biology
Georgia State University
Atlanta, Georgia 30303

Melvin M. Grumbach (4: 76)
Department of Pediatrics
University of California, San Francisco
San Francisco, California 94143

Jane F. Gumnick (5: 90)
Moccasin Bend Mental Health
   Institute
Chattanooga, Tennessee 37405

Toshiyuki Hamada (2: 18)
Department of Psychology
Columbia University
New York, New York 10027

Jing Hao (3: 39)
Cardiovascular Medicine
School of Medicine
Vanderbilt University
Nashville, Tennessee 37232

Matthew P. Hardy (1: 13)
The Population Council
New York, New York 10021

Nicholas B. Hastings (4: 78)
Department of Psychology
Princeton University
Princeton, New Jersey 08543

David A. Heath (5: 101)
University Hospital
Birmingham NHS Trust
Selly Oak Hospital
Birmingham B29 6JD
United Kingdom

Victor W. Henderson (4: 80)
Donald W. Reynolds Center on Aging
Departments of Geriatrics, Neurology,
    Pharmacology and Toxicology,
    and Epidemiology
University of Arkansas for Medical
    Sciences
Little Rock, Arkansas 72205

Joe Herbert (1: 11)
Department of Anatomy
University of Cambridge
Cambridge CB2 3DY
United Kingdom

James P. Herman (3: 53)
Department of Psychiatry
University of Cincinnati Medical Center
Cincinnati, Ohio 45267

Melissa Hines (4: 70)
Department of Psychology
City University London
London EC1V 0HB
United Kingdom

Robert Hnasko (5: 86)
Department of Cell Biology, Neurobiology,
    and Anatomy
University of Cincinnati
Cincinatti, Ohio 45267

Gloria E. Hoffman (5: 95)
Department of Anatomy and
    Neurobiology
University of Maryland
Baltimore, Maryland 21201

Anita Holdcroft (5: 95)
Magill Department of Anaesthesia
Chelsea and Westminster Hospital
Imperial College School of Medicine
London SW10 9NH
United Kingdom

Florian Holsboer (5: 91)
Max Planck Institute of Psychiatry
D-80404 Munich
Germany

Kim L. Huhman (1: 6)
Department of Psychology
Center for Behavioral Neuroscience
Georgia State University
Atlanta, Georgia 30303

Elaine M. Hull (1: 1)
Department of Psychology
State University of New York at Buffalo
Amherst, New York 14260

Julianne Imperato-McGinley (5: 92)
Department of Medicine
Weill Medical College of Cornell University
New York, New York 10021

Lothar H. Jennes (4: 61)
Department of Anatomy and Neurobiology
University of Kentucky
Lexington, Kentucky 40536

Marian Joëls (3: 52)
Swammerdan Institute for the Life Sciences
University of Amsterdam
1098 GB Amsterdam
The Netherlands

Russell T. Joffe (4: 82)
Department of Psychiatry
New Jersey Medical School
Newark, New Jersey 07103

Cynthia L. Jordan (4: 65)
Department of Psychology
University of California
Berkeley, California 94720

John Kasckow (5: 89)
Department of Psychiatry
University of Cincinnati Medical Center
Veterans Affairs Medical Center
Cincinnati, Ohio 45267

Makoto Kashiwayanagi (2: 16)
Graduate School of Pharmaceutical Sciences
Hokkaido University
060-0812 Sapporo
Japan

Martin E. Keck (5: 91)
Max Planck Institute of Psychiatry
D-80404 Munich
Germany

Darcy B. Kelley (2: 27; 3: 49; 4: 65)
Department of Biological Science
Columbia University
New York, New York 10027

Martin J. Kelly (3: 45)
Department of Physiology and Pharmacology
Oregon Health & Science University
Portland, Oregon 97201

Keith M. Kendrick (3: 48)
Department of Neurobiology
The Babraham Institute
Cambridge CB2 4AT
United Kingdom

Eric B. Keverne (1: 4)
University of Cambridge
Department of Animal Behaviour
Cambridge CB3 8AA
United Kingdom

Sudha Khurana (5: 86)
Department of Cell Biology, Neurobiology,
and Anatomy
University of Cincinnati
Cincinatti, Ohio 45267

Kami Kia (3: 47)
Department of Neurobiology and Behavior
The Rockefeller University
New York, New York 10021

Karel S. Kits (3: 43)
Department of Neurophysiology
Research Institute Neurosciences
Vrije University
1081 HV Amsterdam
The Netherlands

Lee-Ming Kow (3: 47)
Department of Neurobiology and Behavior
The Rockefeller University
New York, New York 10021

Christopher Krebs (3: 47)
Department of Neurobiology and Behavior
The Rockefeller University
New York, New York 10021

Mary Jeanne Kreek (5: 106)
Laboratory of the Biology of Addictive
Diseases
The Rockefeller University
The Rockefeller University Hospital
New York, New York 10021

Lance J. Kriegsfeld (2: 18)
Department of Psychology
Columbia University
New York, New York 10027

Harm J. Krugers (3: 52)
Swammerdan Institute for the Life Sciences
University of Amsterdam
1098 SM Amsterdam
The Netherlands

Delores J. Lamb (5: 93)
Scott Department of Urology
Baylor College of Medicine
Houston, Texas 77030

Zvi Laron (5: 85)
Endocrinology and Diabetes Research Unit
WHO Collaborating Center for the Study of
Diabetes in Youth
Schneider Children's Medical Center
Tel Aviv University
Israel

Kevin Laugero (1: 9)
Department of Physiology
University of California at San Francisco
San Francisco, California 94143

Sandra M. Leal (3: 38)
Department of Pharmacological
and Physiological Science
St. Louis University School of Medicine
St. Louis, Missouri 63104

Ronald Michael Lechan (2: 20)
  Tupper Research Institute
  Department of Medicine
  Department of Neuroscience
  Division of Endocrinology
  Tufts University School of Medicine
  Boston, Massachusetts 02111

Joseph LeSauter (2: 18)
  Department of Psychology
  Barnard College
  New York, New York 10027

Seymour Levine (4: 73)
  Department of Psychiatry
  Center for Neuroscience
  University of California, Davis
  Davis, California 95616

Alfred J. Lewy (5: 87)
  Department of Psychiatry
  Oregon Health & Science University
  Portland, Oregon 97201

Israel Liberzon (5: 96)
  Mental Health Research Institute
  University of Michigan School of Medicine
  Ann Arbor, Michigan 48109

Julio Licinio (5: 98)
  Departments of Psychiatry, Medicine,
    and Pharmacology
  Laboratory of Pharmacogenomics
  Interdepartmental Clincial Pharmacology
    Center
  UCLA School of Medicine
    and Neuropsychiatric Institute
  Los Angeles, California 90095

Lucia Magliulo-Cepriano (4: 67)
  Department of Biology
  State University of New York
  Farmingdale, New York 11735

Shaila K. Mani (3: 54)
  Department of Molecular and Cellular Biology
  Baylor College of Medicine
  Houston, Texas 77030

Marco Marcelli (5: 93)
  Department of Molecular and Cellular Biology
  Baylor College of Medicine
  Houston, Texas 77073

Cary N. Mariash (3: 50)
  Division of Endocrinology and Diabetes
  Department of Medicine
  University of Minnesota
  Minneapolis, Minnesota 55455

Martha K. McClintock (1: 15)
  Department of Psychology
  Institute for Mind and Biology
  University of Chicago
  Chicago, Illinois 60637

Bruce S. McEwen (1: 14)
  Laboratory of Neuroendocrinology
  The Rockefeller University
  New York, New York 10021

Marilyn Y. McGinnis (5: 93)
  Department of Cell Biology and Anatomy
  Mt. Sinai School of Medicine
  New York, New York 10029

Christina R. McKittrick (1: 13)
  Center for Molecular and Behavioral
    Neuroscience
  Rutgers University
  Newark, New Jersey 07102

Robert L. Meisel (1: 1, 6)
  Department of Physiological Sciences
  Purdue University
  West Lafayette, Indiana 47907

Nancy K. Mello (5: 104, 105)
  Alcohol and Drug Abuse Research Center
  McLean Hospital
  Harvard Medical School
  Belmont, Massachusetts 02478

Jack H. Mendelson (5: 104, 105)
  Alcohol and Drug Abuse Research Center
  McLean Hospital
  Harvard Medical School
  Belmont, Massachusetts 02478

Andrew H. Miller (5: 90)
  Department of Psychiatry and Behavioral
    Sciences
  Emory University School of Medicine
  Atlanta, Georgia 30322

Frank L. Moore (2: 29)
  Department of Zoology
  Oregon State University
  Corvallis, Oregon 97331

Marianne B. Müller (**5**: 91)
Max Planck Institute of Psychiatry
D-80404 Munich
Germany

Anne Z. Murphy (**5**: 95)
Department of Anatomy and Neurobiology
University of Maryland
Baltimore, Maryland 21201

Wendi S. Neckameyer (**3**: 38)
Department of Pharmacological
and Physiological Science
St. Louis University School of Medicine
St. Louis, Missouri 63104

André B. Negrão (**5**: 98)
Departmento de Psicobiologia
Universidade Federal de São Paulo
04023-062 São Paulo
Brazil

Randy J. Nelson (**2**: 19)
Department of Psychology
The Ohio State University
Columbus, Ohio 43210

Sarah Winans Newman (**2**: 17)
Department of Psychology
Cornell University
Ithaca, New York 14853

Bert W. O'Malley (**3**: 54)
Department of Molecular and Cellular Biology
Baylor College of Medicine
Houston, Texas 77030

Sonoko Ogawa (**3**: 47)
Department of Neurobiology and Behavior
The Rockefeller University
New York, New York 10021

Sergio R. Ojeda (**4**: 75)
Division of Neuroscience
Oregon Regional Primate Center
Oregon Health & Science University
Beaverton, Oregon 97006

Miles Orchinik (**3**: 51)
Department of Biology
Arizona State University
Tempe, Arizona 85287

Mary Ann Ottinger (**4**: 68)
Department of Animal and Avian Sciences
University of Maryland
College Park, Maryland 20742

Barbara L. Parry (**5**: 99)
Department of Psychiatry
University of California, San Diego
Women's Mood Disorders Clinic
La Jolla, California 92093

Elaine R. Peskind (**5**: 103)
VA Puget Sound Health Care
System Mental Illness
Research Education and Clinical Center
Department of Psychiatry and Behavioral
Sciences
University of Washington School of Medicine
Seattle, Washington 98108

Donald Pfaff (**3**: 47)
Department of Neurobiology and Behavior
The Rockefeller University
New York, New York 10021

SiNae M. Pitts (**2**: 18)
Department of Psychology
Columbia University
New York, New York 10027

Paul M. Plotsky (**4**: 72)
Stress Neurobiology Laboratory
Department of Psychiatry and Behavioral Sciences
Emory University School of Medicine
Atlanta, Georgia 30222

Pascal Poindron (**1**: 3)
Centro de Neurobiologia
Universidad Autónoma de México
76001 Querétaro
Mexico

Dominique A. Poulain (**3**: 59)
Laboratoire de Neurobiologie Morphofonctionnelle
INSERM U 378
Institut François Magendie
Université Victor Segalen Bordeaux 2
France

Nicholas Pound (**5**: 94)
School of Biological Sciences
University of East Anglia
Norwich NR4 7TJ
United Kingdom

Brian J. Prendergast (**2**: 19)
Department of Psychology
The Ohio State University
Columbus, Ohio 43210

Ryszard Przewłocki (1: 12)
Department of Molecular Neuropharmacology
Institute of Pharmacology
Polish Academy of Sciences
31-343 Krakow
Poland

Charles L. Raison (5: 90)
Department of Psychiatry and Behavioral Sciences
Emory University School of Medicine
Atlanta, Georgia 30322

Murray A. Raskind (5: 103)
VA Puget Sound Health Care System Mental
 Illness Research, Education and Clinical Center
Department of Psychiatry and Behavioral Sciences
University of Washington School of Medicine
Seattle, Washington 98108

Donald W. Reynolds (4: 80)
Center on Aging
University of Arkansas for Medical Sciences
Little Rock, Arkansas 72205

Stuart E. Reynolds (3: 35)
Department of Biology and Biochemistry
University of Bath
Bath BA2 7AY
United Kingdom

Lynn M. Riddiford (2: 34)
Department of Zoology
University of Washington
Seattle, Washington 98195

John M. Ringo (3: 36)
Department of Biological Sciences
University of Maine
Orono, Maine 04469

Françoise Robert (3: 55)
Laboratoires Nervous Systems
INSERM U 488
94276 Kremlin-Bicêtre
France

Gene E. Robinson (3: 40)
Department of Entomology and Neuroscience
 Program
University of Illinois
Urbana, Illinois 61801

Catherine A. Roca (5: 84)
Behavioral Endocrinology Branch
National Institute of Mental Health
Bethesda, Maryland 20892

Oline K. Rønnekleiv (3: 45)
Department of Physiology and Pharmacology
Division of Neurosciences
Oregon Regional Primate Research Center
Oregon Health & Science University
Portland, Oregon 97201

James D. Rose (2: 29)
Department of Psychology and Zoology-Physiology
University of Wyoming
Laramie, Wyoming 82071

Robert T. Rubin (5: 97)
Center for Neurosciences Research
MCP Hahnemann University School of Medicine
Allegheny General Hospital
Pittsburgh, Pennsylvania 15212

David R. Rubinow (5: 84)
Behavioral Endocrinology Branch
National Institute of Mental Health
Bethesda, Maryland 20892

Chistopher M. Ryan (5: 100)
Department of Psychiatry
Western Psychiatric Institute and Clinic
University of Pittsburgh School of Medicine
Pittsburgh, Pennsylvania 15213

Benjamin D. Sachs (1: 1)
Department of Psychology
University of Connecticut
Storrs, Connecticut 06269

Randall R. Sakai (3: 53)
Department of Psychiatry
University of Cincinnati Medical Center
Cincinnati, Ohio 45267

Barney A. Schlinger (2: 33)
Department of Physiological Science
Laboratory of Neuroendocrinology
Brain Research Institute
University of California, Los Angeles
Los Angeles, California 90095

James Schluger (5: 106)
Laboratory of the Biology of Addictive Diseases
The Rockefeller University
New York, New York 10021

Peter J. Schmidt (5: 84)
Behavioral Endocrinology Branch
National Institute of Mental Health
Bethesda, Maryland 20892

Alan G. Watts (1: 7)
Department of Biological Sciences
Program in Neuroscience
University of Southern California
Los Angeles, California 90089

Janis C. Weeks (3: 44)
Institute of Neuroscience
University of Oregon
Eugene, Oregon 97403

Leonie A. M. Welberg (4: 72)
Stress Neurobiology Laboratory
Department of Psychiatry and Behavioral Sciences
Emory University School of Medicine
Atlanta, Georgia 30222

Diana E. Wheeler (3: 40)
Department of Entomology
University of Arizona
Tucson, Arizona 85721

Ruth E. White (5: 101)
Worcestershire Community and Mental Health
Newtown Hospital
Worcester WR5 1JG
United Kingdom

Peter C. Whybrow (2: 21)
Neuropsychiatric Institute and Hospital
Department of Psychiatry and Biobehavioral
    Sciences
University of California at Los Angeles
Los Angeles, California 90095

Charles W. Wilkinson (5: 103)
VA Puget Sound Health Care System Geriatric
    Research, Education and Clinical Center
Department of Psychiatry and Behavioral
    Sciences
University of Washington School of Medicine
Seattle, Washington 98195

Margo Wilson (5: 94)
Department of Psychology
McMaster University
Hamilton, Ontario, L8S 4K1
Canada

John C. Wingfield (2: 31)
Department of Zoology
University of Washington
Seattle, Washington 98195

Catherine S. Woolley (4: 77)
Department of Neurobiology and Physiology
Northwestern University
Evanstown, Illinois 60208

Hiroshi Yamashita (4: 60)
Department of Physiology, School of Medicine
University of Occupational and Environmental
    Health
807-8555 Kitakyushu
Japan

Elizabeth A. Young (5: 96)
Mental Health Research Institute
University of Michigan School of Medicine
Ann Arbor, Michigan 48109

Harold H. Zakon (2: 24)
Section of Neurobiology
Institute for Neuroscience
University of Texas
Austin, Texas 78712

Yan Zhou (5: 106)
Laboratory of the Biology of Addictive Diseases
The Rockefeller University
New York, New York 10021

Yuan-Shan Zhu (5: 92)
Department of Medicine
Weill Medical College of Cornell University
New York, New York 10021

Hans H. Zingg (3: 57)
Laboratory of Molecular Endocrinology
McGill University Health Center
Royal Victoria Hospital
Montreal, H3A 1A1
Canada

Irving Zucker (2: 19)
Departments of Psychology and Integrative Biology
University of California, Berkeley
Berkeley, California 94720

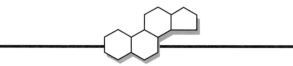

Dedication

These volumes are dedicated first and foremost to the three generations of productive scientists in our field who have lifted our state of knowledge from the elementary proofs of hormone–behavior relationships by Frank Beach and his students. Now, the accomplishments of these three generations of dedicated scientists not only have extended the range of our knowledge over a tremendous zoologic spectrum, but also have provided us with detailed mechanisms of behaviorally relevant hormone actions at the molecular, biophysical, and genetic levels. Because of the ability of workers in our field to incorporate all the tools of experimental, chemical, and molecular endocrinology, as well as the insights of clinical endocrinology, into our investigations of hormone–brain–behavior relations, it is fair to say that our field has achieved a depth of knowledge and understanding unique in neurobiology at the beginning of the twenty-first century.

Second, the editors fondly dedicate this treatise to the memory of Professor Robert Moss, late of the Department of Physiology at the Southwestern Medical School in Dallas, Texas. An insightful and productive neuroendocrinologist, Bob Moss fearlessly pursued membrane mechanisms of hormone action when everyone else was concentrating on different levels of cellular activities. On a personal note, one of us (D. P.) was sometimes described by superficial acquaintances as Bob's "rival" in science. They didn't know that we were good friends, or even that papers from our laboratories, which could have been considered competitive, actually supported each other. For example, our two 1973 papers in *Science*, which demonstrated effects of LHRH (GnRH) on female rat reproductive behavior, complemented each other because the range of controls used in each paper was different. Bob and I (D. P.) understood that the word "competition" comes from the Latin words meaning "seek with," and refers, among scientists and others, to a "competitive" search for excellence.

Finally, the editor-in-chief would like to pay tribute to his doctoral advisor, Professor Joseph Altman, who gave excellent advice during our years at MIT. In those years, Joe Altman was discovering postnatal neurogenesis in the rat brain. More or less ignored at the time, more than three decades later Altman's work was being recognized as having been so far ahead of its time that he did not receive the credit he deserved. In addition, he launched D.P.'s entire career with a seven-word sentence spoken in 1961: "I'd like to do something with hormones." So, if any students are reading this book, please listen to your advisors, especially when they speak in seven-word sentences.

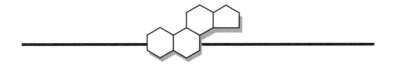

Preface

Because of the large number of neuroactive substances discovered by chemical endocrinologists and the prominent roles of nuclear hormone receptors as ligand-activated transcription factors, scientists studying hormone–brain–behavior relations have made discoveries and achieved explanations of behavior that place their field foremost in neurobiology. The purpose of these volumes is to review the current state of this knowledge inclusively. That means covering true molecular genetic approaches as well as neuroanatomical, electrophysiological, zoological, neurochemical, developmental, and behavioral studies. The medical importance of this work is clear from the last section of this treatise. The editors intend these reviews to be comprehensive; if there are any gaps in the coverage, a second edition will correct them.

ACKNOWLEDGMENTS

Lucy Frank and Carol Oliver, at The Rockefeller University, organized all the volumes. Noelle Gracy and Mica Haley handled things efficiently at Academic Press. Jasna Markovac at Academic Press presided over all stages of this project. The editors thank all of these folks for their intelligent and gracious efforts.

Donald Pfaff
The Rockefeller University, New York

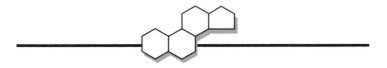

About the Editors

DONALD W. PFAFF heads the Laboratory of Neurobiology and Behavior at The Rockefeller University. He received his scientific training at Harvard University and MIT and is a member of the National Academy of Science and a Fellow of the American Academy of Arts and Sciences. Pfaff's laboratory focuses on steroid hormones and brain function, interactions among transcription factors, luteinizing-hormone-releasing-hormone neurons, and genes influencing neuronal functions. He is the author or coauthor of over 10 books and more than 600 research publications.

ARTHUR P. ARNOLD, professor of physiological science at UCLA, was educated at Grinnell College and The Rockefeller University. He has been named a Fellow of the John Simon Guggenheim Foundation and of the American Association for the Advancement of Science, and was the inaugural president of the Society for Behavioral Neuroendocrinology. Arnold's laboratory studies sexual differentiation of the brain and the effects of steroid hormones on neurons. Recently, the focus of his research has been on the role of the sex chromosomes in brain development. Much of his work has been on two neural systems that are sensitive to gonadal steroids—the neural circuit for song in Passerine birds and the spinal nucleus of the bulbocavernosus.

ANNE M. ETGEN is professor in the Departments of Neuroscience and Psychiatry at the Albert Einstein College of Medicine. She received her scientific training at the University of California, Irvine, and Columbia University. She is a two-time recipient of Research Scientist Development Awards and MERIT Awards from NIMH. Etgen served as director of the Sue Golding Graduate Division on Biomedical Sciences at the Albert Einstein College of Medicine (1997–2000) and has been on the External Advisory Committee for the Minority Fellowship Program in the Neurosciences since 1999. Her laboratory focuses on the mechanisms underlying ovarian steroid hormone regulation of female reproductive physiology and behavior, with a particular emphasis on the hormonal regulation of neurotransmission. She is the author or coauthor of approximately 100 research publications.

SUSAN E. FAHRBACH is professor in the Department of Entomology and a member of the Neuroscience Program at the University of Illinois at Urbana-Champaign. She was named University Scholar and is the director of the Howard Hughes Program for Undergraduate Education in the Life Sciences at Illinois. She has received numerous awards for teaching, including being named an Illinois Vice-Chancellor's Teaching Fellow, and is a mentor in the College of Liberal Arts and Sciences Teaching Academy. She was introduced to the study of the mechanisms of behavior as an undergraduate at the University of Pennsylvania. She then studied physiology at Oxford University with the goal of becoming a physiological psychologist. Her studies of the endocrine mediation of maternal behavior in rodents as a graduate student at The Rockefeller University led to her current broad interests in the hormonal regulation of behavior, while postdoctoral work at the

University of Washington stimulated an interest in insect models.

ROBERT T. RUBIN, M.D., Ph.D., is Highmark Blue Cross Blue Shield Professor of Neurosciences and professor of psychiatry at the MCP Hahnemann University School of Medicine, Allegheny General Hospital, Pittsburgh, Pennsylvania. Prior to joining Allegheny General Hospital in 1992, he was professor of psychiatry and biobehavioral sciences at the UCLA School of Medicine. He is certified in psychiatry by the American Board of Psychiatry and Neurology, and he has a Ph.D. in physiology. For more than 30 years, his research has focused on the neuroendocrinology of stress and depression. Currently, he is studying the influence of acetylcholine neurotransmission in the brain on the activity of the hypothalamic-pituitary-adrenal cortical axis. Rubin also has a clinical practice in adult psychiatry, specializing in the treatment of bipolar disease, depressive disorders, and anxiety disorders.

PART I

MAMMALIAN
HORMONE-BEHAVIOR SYSTEMS

Chapters 1–22

1

Male Sexual Behavior

Elaine M. Hull
Department of Psychology
University at Buffalo
State University of New York
Buffalo, New York 14260-4110

Robert L. Meisel
Department of Psychological Sciences
Purdue University
West Lafayette, Indiana 47906

Benjamin D. Sachs
Department of Psychology
University of Connecticut
Storrs, Connecticut 06269-1020

"Long before the human species appeared, the pinnacle of evolution was already the brain—as it had been before mammals appeared, before land vertebrates, before vertebrates. From this point of view, everything else in the multicellular animal world was evolved to maintain and reproduce nervous systems—that is, to mediate behavior, to cause animals to do things. Animals with simple and primitive or no nervous system have been champions at surviving, reproducing, and distributing themselves but they have limited behavioral repertoires. The essence of evolution is the production and replication of diversity—and more than anything else, diversity in behavior."

—Theodore Bullock (1984)

The sexual behavior of animals, including copulation and the courtship that precedes it, is among the most diverse behaviors. That diversity, a product of natural and sexual selection, helps assure that mating will occur with the right partner at the right time in the right place. The measure of a "successful" mating, in most species, is whether progeny result to carry the parental genotypes to the next generation. Thus, we subscribe to the often-expressed view that a chicken is an egg's way of making another egg. However, we do not subscribe to another often-expressed view—that animals, unlike humans, have sexual interactions only for reproduction, not for pleasure. On the contrary, in all likelihood humans are the only species that understand the reproductive consequences of sex. Animals can be presumed to engage in sex primarily for pleasure, although there is some evidence that social factors, such as dominance or access to resources such as food, contribute to sexual motivation in some species.

Sexual behavior is an expression of the organism's reproductive physiology, a system whose fundamental structure developed often many months or years earlier through a complex series of neuroendocrine events. Because this chapter deals with the physiology of mating in the male mammal, we will focus necessarily on his behavior. However, the contribution of the female to the sexual interaction cannot be overemphasized: mating is an activity that requires two participants, and when the temporal organization of mating behavior is viewed from the female's perspective, a rather different picture often emerges (see Chapter 2 on female sexual behavior in this volume). Nonetheless, an androcentric perspective is warranted in the present circumstances, so long as one keeps in mind that neither this perspective nor a gynocentric perspective gives a full description of the complexity of the interaction.

In this chapter, we summarize the progress that has been made in understanding how hormones, the central nervous system, and the periphery interact to regulate male sexual behavior, focusing on how that understanding developed and where it is incomplete. We summarize recent research on the neural mechanisms by which males integrate hormonal and sensory inputs to produce adaptive behavioral and physiological responses, especially in the context of mating but also in other contexts. We begin by describing the copulatory behaviors of species commonly studied in the laboratory, the paradigms and measures used to study them, and the conceptual contexts in which the research takes place. We then review the behavioral effects of gonadal steroids and systemically or intraventricularly administered drugs. We next summarize information about the functions of the brain areas implicated in the control of male sexual behavior, including effects of lesions and stimulation, local hormonal and pharmacological manipulations, and measures of neural activity. Finally, we describe the interconnections among the neural structures that mediate sexual behavior. We conclude with a series of questions that remain unanswered and that may form a basis for future research. This chapter is an updating of Meisel and Sachs (1994). We have expanded the coverage of neuropharmacology and of measures of neural activity in areas throughout the central and peripheral nervous systems. However, we have decreased the coverage of penile innervation and of psychosexual influences on hormone-behavior interactions; readers wishing a more in-depth coverage of these topics are encouraged to consult Meisel and Sachs (1994).

I. PATTERNS OF SEXUAL BEHAVIOR OF MALE MAMMALS

A. Description of Common Behavioral Elements

1. Precopulatory Behaviors

Species-specific displays highlight secondary sex characteristics that signal a male's appropriateness as a mate and his desirability relative to other males. Since males are usually larger and more aggressive than females, a courting male must also make clear that it is safe for the female to allow him to approach her. In monogamous species, the female may also look for signs that the male does not have another partner and that he is willing to commit resources to her and to their potential offspring. While approaching the female,

the male also acquires additional information about her suitability and desirability and can continue or abort the courtship accordingly. In the species commonly used in neurobiology, as in many other mammals, a male's attempts to copulate with a female are often preceded by his investigation of her anogenital region, which can expose him to stimuli that arouse him sexually or that help him to determine whether the female will be receptive to his advances. Among rodents, both partners may emit ultrasonic vocalizations, which may further arouse the partner, as well as themselves (Floody and Pfaff, 1977; Floody *et al.*, 1977; Geyer and Barfield, 1978; Geyer *et al.*, 1978; McIntosh and Barfield, 1980; Nyby and Whitney, 1978; Pomerantz and Clemens, 1981; Sales, 1972; White *et al.*, 1990; Whitney *et al.*, 1973).

2. Mounting

A receptive female may remain immobile while the male investigates her and allow him to initiate a mount by lifting his forebody over her hindquarters, clasping her flanks with his forepaws, and beginning a series of rapid, shallow thrusts with his pelvis. (See Fig. 1.) During this thrusting, the male's penis is usually at least partially erect. In response to the flank contact at the beginning of a mount or to the ensuing perineal contact, the female may display lordosis, a more rigid posture in which her back is flat or concave and her tail is deflected. By exposing the vagina, lordosis makes it possible for the male to achieve intromission, which is the defining event of copulation. Females of other species, such as swine, exhibit kyphosis, the opposite of lordosis, as their receptive posture. One or both of the male's hindfeet usually remain on the ground during mounting. However, male macaques use a "double foot-clasp mount" in which the male's hindfeet grasp the female's hindlegs above the ankles (Chevalier-Skolnikoff, 1975; Estep *et al.*, 1984; Nadler and Rosenblum, 1973). In other species, including the felids (Lanier and Dewsbury, 1976; Rosenblatt and Aronson, 1958; Whalen, 1963) and mustelids (Carroll *et al.*, 1985), the male grasps the female's neck with his teeth before or during the mount, and he may retain this grip for the duration of the copulatory episode.

Instead of remaining immobile, a receptive female may dart away when investigated; but then, she may stop just as abruptly. This sequence of darting and

FIGURE 1   Three views of copulating rats. Usually, as in (A) one is unable to see the genitals. Therefore, without some technical means of detecting intromission, the scoring of copulatory behavior in rats and many other small mammals relies upon recognition of relatively subtle differences in the patterns of movement to discriminate among mounts, intromissions, and ejaculations. On rare occasions the genitals can be seen. In (B) it is clear that insertion is in progress, and the tight clasp suggests that this is an ejaculatory intromission. In (C) the engorged glans penis can be seen extending forward just in front of the male's right hindleg. The position of his forelegs indicates that he is dismounting after ejaculation. In all three figures the female is in the characteristic receptive posture of lordosis, with body lowered and rump and head elevated. [We thank Ronald J. Barfield for contributing these photographs.]

stopping can promote mounting by provoking the male to chase and run into her. If an inexperienced male fails to respond to her overtures, the female may nudge his side, which may stimulate him to mount (Madlafousek

and Hlinak, 1983; McClintock and Adler, 1978). Even a receptive female may reject a male, particularly if his approaches are not optimal. Her rejecting behaviors can include escape, keeping her tail and hindquarters low, kicking the male in the face with her hindlegs, or turning around to threaten or attack the male.

3. Intromission

Presumably, every mount involving pelvic thrusts is an attempt to achieve intromission. However, if the male does not detect the vagina with his penis relatively soon after he begins thrusting, he usually dismounts and re-approaches the female or turns to other activities. If a male rat or other rodent does detect the vagina, he typically performs a deeper, intravaginal thrust, followed immediately by a springing dismount. In fact, this "intromission pattern" of movement is usually taken as the measure of intromission in rats and many other rodents, because of its reliable association with penile insertion (Pollak and Sachs, 1975a). In other species, such as mice, the male maintains the intromission and shows repeated intravaginal thrusting (McGill, 1962; Mosig and Dewsbury, 1976). In ungulates, penile insertion may entail only a brief genital contact with immediate ejaculation (Bermant *et al.*, 1969; Lott, 1981). After an intromission, it is common for the male to groom his genitalia.

4. Ejaculation

Most male mammals ejaculate in the context of copulation only after they have received the stimulation derived from a series of intravaginal thrusts. For species such as rats, gerbils, and hamsters, this requires multiple intromissions. At ejaculation, the male often displays a deeper and longer thrust, during which he lifts his torso and lifts and opens his forelegs, thus releasing his grasp on the female. This is followed by a slower, more relaxed dismount than the one seen after an intromission without ejaculation. As with intromission, the behavioral pattern associated with ejaculation, rather than seminal expulsion per se, is usually taken as the operational definition of the physical event. Among dogs and other canids, ejaculation commonly begins immediately after insertion and before the swelling of the base of the penis results in a "lock" of the male to the female that may last 30 minutes or more (Beach, 1969; Hart and Kitchell, 1966). Technically, ejaculation refers to the often very forceful expulsion of the ejaculate from the distal urethra, whereas seminal emission refers to the movement of the ejaculate into the proximal urethra. Ejaculation is usually accompanied by spasmodic contractions of skeletal muscles, as well as the striated muscles of the perineal area, including the ischiocavernosus, bulbospongiosus, and anal sphincter. In the human male this constellation of events is associated with orgasm, a term best restricted to the experiential or cognitive correlates of ejaculation in men or, more generally, the correlates of the culmination of sexual excitement for both men and women.

5. Postejaculatory Behavior

Ejaculation is typically followed by genital grooming and a period of sexual quiescence. The postejaculatory interval may last for less than 30 seconds in Syrian hamsters (Bunnell *et al.*, 1976), for 5 to 10 minutes in rats, or hours or days in other species (Dewsbury, 1972). During the otherwise quiescent stage, the male may produce some distinctive sounds. For example, male rats make ultrasonic calls and male gerbils foot stomp. The ultrasonic (22 kHz) vocalizations of male rats are typically restricted to the first 50 to 75% of the postejaculatory interval, as are synchronized EEG waves characteristic of sleep (Barfield and Geyer, 1975). During this time, sometimes referred to as the absolute refractory period, no amount of stimulation can induce the male to resume copulation. Blumberg and Moltz (1987, 1988) have suggested that the function of the ultrasonic vocalizations is to cool the lower forebrain (including the medial preoptic area and hypothalamus) by initiating hemodynamic events that redirect blood flow from the brain to the nose at the same time that air is being deeply inhaled and then forcefully exhaled, thereby producing the vocalization. They measured a consistent increase in temperature of about 1°C in the medial preoptic area during copulation, followed by a rapid cooling following ejaculation. They suggested that the vocalization may be an artifact of the process of restoring normal brain temperature. Although the male is less responsive to many other stimuli during the absolute refractory interval (Barfield and Sachs, 1968; Pollak and Sachs, 1975b), he is even more likely than usual to initiate an attack against a male intruder (Flannelly *et al.*, 1982; Thor and Flannelly, 1979). The relative refractory period occupies the re-

mainder of the postejaculatory interval; during this time, painful stimuli or introduction of a novel female may elicit renewed copulation. Sexual refractoriness during the postejaculatory interval does not result from a failure of erectile function, at least in some species. In rats, for example, *ex copula* touch-based erections are maintained, or actually enhanced, after ejaculation (O'Hanlon and Sachs, 1980). Erections evoked by remote cues from the female are usually evident before 22 kHz vocalization ends, a finding that casts doubt on the use of vocalization to measure the refractory periods and perhaps on the utility of those concepts (Sachs and Bialy, 2000). Following the postejaculatory interval, the sequence of approach, mounting, intromission, and ejaculation is likely to occur again.

6. Sexual Satiety

If a male rat is allowed to copulate freely, he may achieve up to seven or eight ejaculations before reaching sexual satiety lasting for several days. The second and third ejaculations typically occur with shorter latencies and fewer intromissions than the first; however, subsequent ejaculations take progressively longer and require more intromissions (Larsson, 1979). However, the postejaculatory interval increases monotonically after the first ejaculation, suggesting that different factors regulate the progression to ejaculation and the resumption of copulation. After reaching sexual satiety with one female, some males can be induced to reinitiate copulation with a novel female. The phenomenon is sometimes referred to as the "Coolidge effect," a reference to an apocryphal incident involving President and Mrs. Calvin Coolidge. When visiting a farm, Mrs. Coolidge was impressed that one rooster mated repeatedly during her visit to the poultry house and asked the farmer to call Mr. Coolidge's attention to the rooster's prowess when the president visited the facility. When the farmer obliged later in the day, Mr. Coolidge noted that the repeated activity was directed to many different hens, and asked the farmer to point that out to Mrs. Coolidge.

B. Functional Significance of Copulatory Elements

In addition to providing the male with the genital stimulation needed to elicit ejaculation, and hence to fertilize the female's eggs, the mating behavior of the male can affect the female's reproductive physiology and his own. For example, females of some species, such as rabbits and cats, do not ovulate unless they receive the cervical stimulation associated with mating. This enables them to avoid egg wastage when males are not available and to proceed opportunistically when they are. Females of other species, such as rats, ovulate without mating but do not secrete enough progesterone to support implantation of a fertilized egg, unless they receive the number of intromissions normally displayed before the first ejaculation. When female rats mate postpartum, even that amount of stimulation is inadequate, which may help to explain why male rats resume mating after fertilization has presumably occurred (reviewed in Dewsbury, 1990; Dewsbury *et al.*, 1979).

Multiple intromissions or intravaginal thrusting may also facilitate sperm transport (Adler and Toner, 1986), or promote male-female bonding, or both (reviewed in Carter *et al.*, 1995; Dewsbury, 1987). Delaying ejaculation until the male has displayed a sufficient number of intromissions can also increase the number of sperm in the ejaculate, which may enhance its fertilizing capacity (Adler and Toner, 1985, 1986; Toner and Adler, 1986; Toner *et al.*, 1987). However, male sexual behavior is energetically expensive, and prolonging copulation can put both partners at risk for predation. Thus, the copulatory behavior of males, like that of females, must reflect a balance of selection pressures imposed by their physical, biological, and social environments (see reviews of this issue in Wallen and Schneider, 2000). (See Table 1.)

C. Species Used to Study the Neurobiology of Male Sexual Behavior

As in other areas of mammalian biology, most research on the neuroendocrine basis of male sexual behavior has been done on a limited number of species, most of them rodents. Because it is commonly used in neurobiology and endocrinology in general, the rat is also a common model for behavioral neuroendocrinology. Other rodents used routinely to study male sexual behavior are hamsters, gerbils, mice, voles, and guinea pigs. Carnivores are represented primarily by ferrets. Among the larger species, primates are the best represented. Those particularly interested in primate sexual

behavior may wish to see the fine review by Dixson (1998). For neurobiological analyses of male sexual behavior, one must study species that reliably display the behavior under conditions in which it can be observed and quantified, before and after various manipulations of the nervous or endocrine systems. For neurobiological manipulations, it is also useful to have a published stereotaxic atlas of the adult brain. There are also advantages to studying species for which pertinent neural or endocrine data can be gleaned from studies undertaken on different neural or behavioral questions. The disadvantage of focusing on a limited range of species is that it limits the opportunities to identify the interesting variations that almost certainly exist and to correlate those neural and behavioral variations with each other.

D. Standard Tests of Copulation: Their Purposes, Impact on the Data Obtained, and Their Interpretation

Laboratory tests of male copulatory behavior are usually designed to optimize the male's opportunity to mate. To ensure that the measures recorded reflect the state of the male, not the female, researchers provide the males with receptive test partners, just as they try to make the conditions favorable for mating by maintaining the animals under favorable photoperiods and testing them during favorable parts of the light-dark cycle. It is also common for the male to be given time to adapt to the test arena before the female is introduced to ensure that his latency to initiate sexual interaction is not artificially prolonged by the effects of novel surroundings. While the male is usually not given a choice of females, the female he is given usually is not allowed to escape his presence. It is also common for him to be given a different female if he does not initiate copulation within a prescribed period. This helps take into account the possibility that his initial failure to mate was a result of his indifference to the original partner. Although the features of the test situation may distort some aspects of a pair's interaction, they do allow display of the full range of copulatory behavior.

Test length is usually determined by both behavioral and temporal measures, so that experimental effects on the initiation of sexual behavior can be distinguished from effects on the male's ability to copulate to ejaculation once he has begun to mate. For example, a male

TABLE 1
Classification System for Patterns of Copulation in Mammals[a]

Lock?	Intravaginal thrusting?	Multiple intromissions?	Multiple ejaculations?	Pattern number	Examples (common names)
Yes	Yes	Yes	Yes	1	
Yes	Yes	Yes	No	2	
Yes	Yes	No	Yes	3	Dog, wolf, climbing rat
Yes	Yes	No	No	4	
Yes	No	Yes	Yes	5	
Yes	No	Yes	No	6	*Akodon molinae*
Yes	No	No	Yes	7	Golden mouse, southern grasshopper mouse
Yes	No	No	No	8	Northern pygmy mouse
No	Yes	Yes	Yes	9	Rhesus macaque, house mouse, montane vole
No	Yes	Yes	No	10	Mole rat (?)
No	Yes	No	Yes	11	Human, chimpanzee, Japanese macaque, meadow vole
No	Yes	No	No	12	Vervet monkey
No	No	Yes	Yes	13	Norway rat, Mongolian gerbil
No	No	Yes	No	14	
No	No	No	Yes	15	Bison, domestic cat
No	No	No	No	16	Black-tailed deer

[a] Adapted from Dewsbury (1972, 1978). The fourfold dichotomization is based on the presence or absence of (a) a lock between penis and vagina, (b) intravaginal thrusting, (c) multiple intromissions prior to ejaculation, and (d) multiple ejaculations prior to the male's sexual satiety. Examples are selected to show that closely related species may have the same or very different patterns, whereas distantly related species may have similar patterns. Locks are rare except in canids and some rodents, so there are few species that exemplify patterns 1–8. Some other pattern classes, such as 10 and 14, are also empty or rare, whereas classes such as 9, 11, and 13 are rather common.

is usually allowed a specific amount of time to begin mating (e.g., 30 minutes to achieve intromission). If he begins to mate, he is allowed a specific amount of time to complete mating (e.g., 30 minutes to ejaculate once the first intromission has been attained), and if he meets that criterion, he is allowed a specific amount of time to resume mating (e.g., 15 minutes to intromit after ejaculation). Often the test is ended at that point, but strictly time-limited tests allow the male to go on to additional ejaculatory series. Other paradigms allow the male to mate until he displays sexual satiety, which is defined as failure to resume mating within a specified time after the last ejaculation. Typically, male rats do not resume copulation for several days after achieving satiety.

Mounting behavior is usually scored by counting the number of properly oriented mounts that involve pelvic thrusting. If the mount is misdirected or does not include thrusting, it is usually not scored or is scored separately as an ectopic or simple mount, respectively. For intromission and ejaculation, the data are usually collected on the basis of the gross motor patterns, as noted above (see Sachs and Barfield, 1970).

E. Theoretical Constructs: Motivation vs Performance

1. Measures of Sexual Motivation

It is often useful to distinguish between the motivation for sexual activity and performance of the behavior. However, both sexual motivation and copulatory performance may be difficult to quantify, because other factors may inhibit the male's ability to express his motivation or perform copulatory motor patterns. For example, lesion- or drug-induced changes in sexual behavior may reflect changes in the male's ability to detect or interpret stimuli, perform the movements being assayed, remember stimuli associated with previous sexual encounters, or link those processes. Drugs or lesions can also cause general malaise. Furthermore, alteration of stimuli from the male may reduce the proceptive or receptive behavior of the female, thereby compounding the male's deficits.

The motivation-performance distinction in some respects mirrors the classical ethological distinction between appetitive and consummatory behavior (Tinbergen, 1951). Thus, appetitive behavior is that engaged in by motivated animals to bring them into contact with an appropriate stimulus, a *releaser,* which will then trigger a consummatory response. In the context of sexual behavior, courtship or movement toward a potential mate might be considered appetitive, whereas copulation per se would be considered the consummatory act. Classically, too, appetitive behavior was considered to be more variable, whereas consummatory acts were viewed as highly stereotyped "fixed action patterns." In time, this distinction (and its underlying theoretical basis) became suspect and was largely abandoned by ethologists. However, it has been retained by some psychologists who value it as a pedagogical device. For example, Pfaus (1996) used this device to identify certain interesting similarities and differences among species and between the sexes in respect to their precopulatory and copulatory behavior and the underlying neuroendocrine regulation. Pfaus views sexual consummatory behaviors as highly stereotyped, sexually differentiated, and species-specific, whereas appetitive behaviors are more flexible, less sexually differentiated, and less species-specific. However, the line between appetitive and consummatory behaviors is fuzzy; in logical terms, they are fuzzy sets. For example, sniffing and following the female are frequently regarded as appetitive behaviors; yet, they are as stereotypic in form as most copulatory acts, and they usually blend seamlessly into a sequence of behavioral elements that may end in ejaculation, genital grooming, and postejaculatory vocalizations (see discussion by Sachs, 1983). All of these elements are fixed action patterns, and may therefore be considered to be "consummatory." However, each element may be thought of as a precursor to the next, and therefore "appetitive." For example, an intromission may be viewed as a consummatory act, the goal of the "appetitive" approach and mount that preceded it, but also as an appetitive behavior, bringing the male to the threshold for triggering ejaculation. Because a considerable body of research has addressed the distinction between motivation and performance and between appetitive and consummatory behaviors, we review that literature briefly here, but we add the caveat that it is not always easy to differentiate the respective classes.

Male sexual behavior itself has been used to infer motivational state. The latencies to mount or intromit after presentation of the female are the most common measures of sexual motivation. However, intromission latency confounds motivation with the ability to achieve an erection, which may be impaired by some drug treatments or lesions without affecting motivation. Therefore, mount latency is the better measure of sexual motivation, although even mount latency may be increased by treatments that impair motor behavior. Therefore, it is preferable to test motivation by using a measure specifically designed for that purpose and that does not confound motor activity or learning ability with motivation per se.

There are several tests of sexual motivation that do not rely directly on copulatory performance. In place preference tests the male is initially allowed to copulate with a female in one of two interconnected areas and to spend time alone in the other area. He is later placed into the center of the apparatus and allowed to spend time in either the side previously associated with copulation, or the one that he inhabited alone. This technique has the advantage that motor ability is not confounded with motivation, since little effort is required to access and remain in the preferred goal box. In addition, any drugs administered during the training phase will not affect the test phase. However, the male must be able to remember the stimuli associated with copulation and associate them with the reinforcement of mating. A second technique is the obstruction apparatus, in which the male must cross an electrified grid or other obstruction in order to reach the female. This test is easy to perform, but it confounds motor ability and motivation. A third test is the X-maze or cross-maze, in which an estrous female is placed in one of four interconnected goal boxes, and other objects are placed in the other three goal boxes, or they remain empty. The male is placed into the central area and his latency to reach a goal box is measured on each of 10 trials. The average latencies to reach each goal box, the number of no-choice trials, and the percentage of trials on which the male chooses the female's goal box are tabulated. This has the advantage of dissociating motor activity (assessed by latencies to reach each goal box and number of trials on which the male fails to leave the start area) from specifically sexual motivation (percentage of trials on which the female's goal box is chosen). Another technique for measuring sexual motivation is the bilevel apparatus, in which a male and female are allowed to copulate during the training phase (Mendelson and Pfaus, 1989). Then during the test phase, the number of times the male changes levels, presumably in search of the female, is tabulated. This provides an easy, readily quantifiable measure, but it has the disadvantage of confounding motor and motivational factors. Finally, lever pressing for a secondary reinforcer that has been paired with copulation has been studied (reviewed in Everitt, 1990). The advantage of this test is that the task can be made harder by simply increasing the number of bar presses required for presentation of the secondary reinforcer. In addition, successive presentations of the reinforcer are not subject to the changes in motivation that occur if the male is allowed to ejaculate. However, motoric ability and the ability to learn the secondary reinforcement task are again confounded with motivational factors.

2. Factor Analysis of Copulation

Copulation has been conceptually dissected into numerous measures: the latency to mount (ML) or intromit (IL), the latency from the first intromission to the first ejaculation (EL), the inter-intromission interval (III), the time from an ejaculation to the following intromission (postejaculatory interval, PEI), the time from an ejaculation to the termination of ultrasonic vocalization (VT), the number of mounts (NM, sometimes referred to as mount frequency, MF) and intromissions (NI, or intromission frequency, IF) preceding ejaculation, and the total numbers of mounts, intromissions, and ejaculations in the test. Also commonly calculated is the intromission ratio [IR = NI/(NM + NI)], sometimes referred to as "copulatory efficiency" or "hit rate."

Copulatory behavior of male rats has been factor analyzed into four weakly correlated factors (Sachs, 1978). First, a copulatory rate factor comprises the III, EL, VT, and PEI. Although these four measures are highly correlated in standardized tests of normal males, they may be dissociated from one another by experimental treatments; therefore, they may not be controlled by a single physiological mechanism. This factor accounted for approximately 40% of the total variance of the samples analyzed.

Three other factors accounted for roughly equal portions of the remaining variance. An initiation factor included primarily ML and IL, but also the time from VT to the first intromission of the next ejaculatory series. The inclusion of both the initial copulatory acts and the resumption after VT in a single factor suggests that similar physiological mechanisms may promote copulation in both situations. An intromission ratio factor reflected the number of mounts preceding ejaculation and the intromission ratio. This measure may reflect the ease with which the male achieves an erection. It is assumed that every mount is an attempt to intromit. Therefore, many nonintromissive mounts decrease the intromission ratio. Finally, an intromission count factor was based primarily on the number of intromissions preceding ejaculation (NI). The relative independence of NI from temporal factors suggests that the amount of genital stimulation is more important for triggering ejaculation than time since the beginning of copulation, although timing also plays a role.

A subsequent factor analysis, based on copulation tests in bilevel chambers, identified five factors that accounted for 95% of the variance (Pfaus et al., 1990a). Four of these conceptual mechanisms were essentially identical to those proposed by Sachs (1978). However, an anticipatory factor, based on the number of times the male changed levels, was relatively independent of the remaining four factors. The emergence of separate anticipatory and initiation factors suggests that they may be controlled by at least partially distinct neural mechanisms.

F. Measures of Penile Function

1. Observations during Copulation

Erection and intromission are readily observable in studies of the sexual behavior of monkeys, dogs, cats, and many other species, and of course in humans. However, in research on rodents and many other small mammals, these penile components of copulation, as well as ejaculation, are more often inferred than observed. In some cases an angled mirror has been placed beneath a clear floor of a test cage in order to observe penile actions, and in other experiments the female's vagina has been inspected immediately after copulation for evidence of sperm. Some experiments have relied on the presence of a copulatory plug of coagulated semen on the floor of the cage as evidence of previous copulation to ejaculation. However, males of many species ejaculate spontaneously one or more times each day (Beach, 1975; Orbach, 1961; Stefanick and Davidson, 1987), and some primates may masturbate to ejaculation more than once per day (Phoenix and Jensen, 1973; Slimp *et al.*, 1978). Conversely, such plugs may underestimate the number of ejaculations, because males often eat their ejaculate in the process of grooming their genitalia during or immediately after spontaneous or copulation-induced ejaculation (Orbach, 1961). Because genital reflexes are difficult to measure while the male is copulating, paradigms have been developed for monitoring them *ex copula*. The evidence for different physiological controls among these contexts (reviewed in Sachs, 2000) implies that none of these tests can be assumed to assess whether the male would have similar erectile competence *in copula*.

2. Ex copula Measures of Penile Function

a) Spontaneous or Drug-Induced Erections First, erections can occasionally be observed when a male is alone in his home cage or a neutral arena. These erections are referred to as spontaneous, a term meaning that they have no apparent extrinsic cause. Such "unstimulated" erections can be increased by administration of various drugs, in which case they are referred to as drug-induced erections. They are usually characterized by extension of the engorged glans beyond the sheath and by genital grooming coincident with or immediately after erection. Some descriptions (e.g., Bertolini *et al.*, 1978) indicate that each erectile episode is accompanied by ejaculation, but there is no evidence to support that observation. Occasionally slight hip movements may also accompany erection, but these movements and the whole motor pattern bear little similarity to those occurring during copulation.

Nonetheless, antecedent copulation changes the probability of drug-induced erections (Sachs *et al.*, 1994a). The mechanical and neuroendocrine bases for these and related responses are considered further in the section, "The Role of the Penis in Male Sexual Behavior."

b) Noncontact Erections The number of spontaneous erections increases considerably if an inaccessible estrous female is present (Sachs *et al.*, 1994b) or if the male is exposed to the volatile odors of an estrous female (Sachs, 1997; Kondo *et al.*, 1999a). These "noncontact" erections, whose motor pattern appears to be identical to spontaneous and drug-induced erections, have been considered to be a model for psychogenic erections in humans. Noncontact erections may be accompanied by genital grooming, hip thrusts or constrictions, and raising of the heels of the hindfeet (Sachs, 2000).

c) Touch-Based Erections, Anteroflexions, and Seminal Emissions Reflexive, or touch-based, erections have been elicited by manually stimulating the penis of dogs (Beach, 1984; Hart, 1967a) or other species. However, tactile stimulation of the penis in rats and other rodents tends to inhibit erection, rather than stimulate it (Hart, 1968c). To overcome this problem, Hart (1968c) developed a technique that exerts pressure at the base of the penis of rats. This technique has also been used in mice (Sachs, 1980). The male is restrained on his back and the penile sheath is retracted, exposing the glans penis. The continuing pressure of the sheath around the base of the penis gives rise to a series of erections, which are seen as tumescence of the glans penis due to engorgement of the corpus spongiosum. Penile anteroflexions (previously called "flips") also occur; they result from erection of the penile body and ischiocavernosus muscle contractions, causing the glans to straighten from its normal posteroflexed position. Occasionally a seminal emission occurs, usually as a result of drug administration. There are three gradations of glans erection: in the first, the penile body elongates and rises; in the second, the glans becomes engorged and slightly flared; and in the third, the glans flares intensely into a cup. (See Fig. 2.) During copulation the cup is important for depositing the ejaculated semen around the cervix, where it coagulates to form a "copulatory plug." Without this plug, much of the semen seeps out of the vagina, and pregnancy rarely

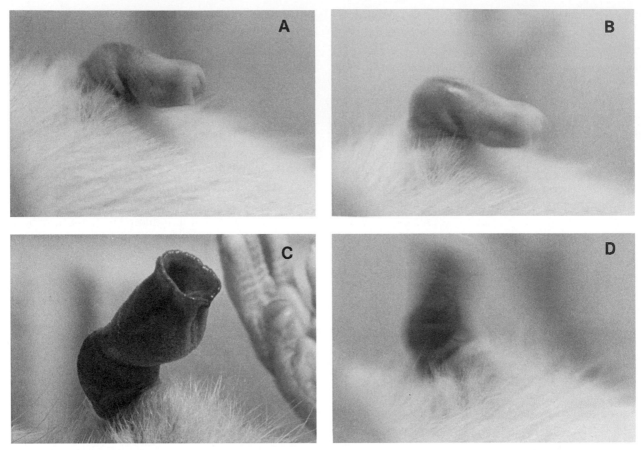

FIGURE 2 Reflexive erections displayed by supine male rats after retraction of the penile sheath. Several days earlier the suspensory ligaments had been surgically removed, thereby preventing retraction of the penis during the test and permitting better visualization of the distal penile body [perpendicular to the torso in (B)] and of the entire glans [parallel to the torso in (B)]. In (A)–(C), the glans is directed toward the tail, its normal orientation. In (D) the glans points rostrally, the orientation necessary to achieve intromission. (A) The quiescent (flaccid) penis. (B) Tumescence and elevation of the penile body without glans erection. (C) Intense erection of the glans ("cup") and of the penile body. (D) Anteroflexion ("flip") of the penis due to a straightening of the penile body. The blurring is due to the speed of the response relative to the shutter speed (1/30 sec). [The photographs are from Leipheimer and Sachs, 1988.]

occurs (Sachs, 1983). The similarity in form and mechanical basis between these responses as they occur *ex copula* and *in copula* has been established by behavioral (Hart, 1968c; Sachs and Garinello, 1978) and electromyographic (Holmes *et al.*, 1991; Wallach and Hart, 1983) techniques, but the temporal relations are different, as are aspects of their neuroendocrine regulation (Sachs, 1983; see below).

d) Urethrogenital Reflex Another *ex copula* genital response is the urethrogenital reflex, which has been proposed as a model for the orgasmic reflex in humans. This reflex can be elicited in both male and female spinally transected anesthetized rats (McKenna *et al.*, 1991) by pressure-filling the urethra with saline and then rapidly releasing the pressure. The reflex consists of a series of clonic contractions of the pelvic muscles, with approximately the same timing as human orgasm. The motor pattern is generated by neurons in the lower spinal cord, which are under tonic inhibitory control by the brain, primarily the nucleus paragigantocellularis (nPGi) of the ventral medulla (see below).

II. THE ROLE OF THE PENIS IN MALE SEXUAL BEHAVIOR

Two ways in which hormones can influence behavior are by increasing the sensitivity of sensory systems that detect pertinent stimuli and by enhancing the effectiveness of tissues used to perform the behavior. The somatosensory stimuli received by the male during copulation are important for determining the timing of intromissions and ejaculation and, in most species, enable the male to identify the vaginal opening when it is contacted.

A. Anatomy of the Penis and the Mechanics of Erection

In mammalian species the erect penis is essential for delivering sperm into the reproductive tract of the female. In some species that have fibroelastic penises, such as sheep and goats, erection occurs primarily by extrusion of the penis, with little increase in its diameter. In others, erection involves penile enlargement and stiffening. In most species, the increase in size involves coordinated vascular and striated muscle activity. However, the relative importance of these components differs across species.

The general plan of the penis is common among all mammalian species. (See Fig. 3.) The erectile structures of the penis consist of the paired corpora cavernosa, which occupy most of the body of the penis, and the corpus spongiosum, which surrounds the urethra and is expanded proximally as the penile bulb and distally as the glans penis. The penile corpora are composed in part of smooth muscle and vascular tissue, and each of the corpora is more or less paired in its function with a set of striated muscles. That is, the bulbospongiosus muscle (also known as the ventral bulbocavernosus muscle) encloses and inserts on the penile bulb, which is the origin of the corpus spongiosum. The ischiocavernosus muscles surround the crura, which lie on either side of the root of the penis and are continuous with the corpora cavernosa. A bone (os penis) may lie centrally in the body and extend forward to the glans.

The two sets of corpora are usually coordinated in their erection and detumescence, but they may act quite independently, in part because there is at least some

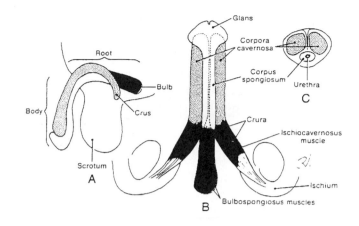

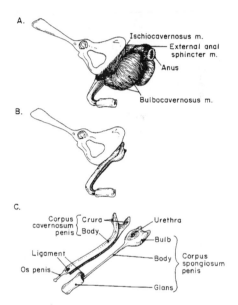

FIGURE 3 Some basic structural similarities in penile anatomy illustrated from the human [top: (A) lateral view, (B) inferior view with penile body lifted, (C) cross section] and rat [bottom: (A) lateral view including all muscles, (B) lateral view with muscles removed, (C) "exploded" view]. In both species, the penile crura, attached to the ischium, are covered by the ischiocavernosus muscles and are continuous with the body of the penis, composed primarily of the paired corpora cavernosa. The penile bulb, wrapped by the bulbospongiosus (bulbocavernosus) muscles, gives rise to the corpus spongiosum, which terminates in the glans penis. The rat muscle identified as the external anal sphincter is also known as the levator ani or the dorsal bulbospongiosus. [Figures of human penis from Wilson and Wilson (1978) are reprinted by permission of Oxford University Press. Those of the rat penis from Hart and Melese-d' Hospital (1983) are reprinted by permission of Pergamon Press.]

independence of their vascular (Fernandez *et al.*, 1991) and neural (Chapelle *et al.*, 1980; Sachs and Liu, 1991) effector systems. Hence, the term "erection" by itself, without reference to which of the corpora is erect, is often inadequate to describe or interpret processes occurring in the penis. This distinction is particularly important for making species comparisons. In the literature on humans, erection almost always refers only to the penile body. When referring to rats and other rodents, erection commonly refers only to actions of the glans, whereas changes in the penile body are termed anteroflexions.

The mechanical basis for erection in most species lies in a combination of vascular, smooth muscle, and striated muscle actions, although the relative contribution (or even the very presence) of each of these effector systems varies from one species to another. Thus, damage to the striated penile muscles or their innervation would seriously compromise erection in a rat, whereas humans and other species that rely less on striated muscles may continue to have strictly vascular erections after such damage. In addition, the physiology of erection may vary somewhat among species as a function of the normal duration of erection, i.e., very brief, as in rats, in which the duration is measured in fractions of a second, or long, as in canids, in which erection may continue for as long as an hour.

The intracorporal actions involve the relaxation of the smooth muscles, thereby allowing their expansion and an increased inflow of blood that fills the corporal interstices. The increased intracavernous pressure compresses and occludes the venous outflow, trapping blood in the corpora. Coordinated with these vascular actions, the striated muscles overlying the vascular reservoirs (penile bulb and crura) contract, increasing penile rigidity (Gerstenberg *et al.*, 1990; Lavoisier *et al.*, 1986). In some species, including the ungulates and many carnivores, the retractor penis, a smooth muscle that is tonically contracted, relaxes, thus allowing extension of the penis. As Sjöstrand (1981, p. 374) has put it, "Erection is a matter of relaxation of these [smooth] muscles, while their contraction keeps the penis in the 'relaxed state.'"

B. Neural Innervation of the Penis

The pelvic nerves (primarily parasympathetic and proerectile), hypogastric nerves (primarily sympathetic

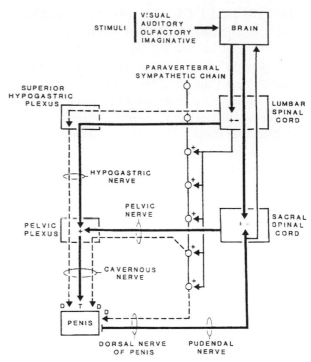

FIGURE 4 Schematic diagram of the excitatory (+) and inhibitory (−) innervation of the penis for the regulation of tumescence (T) and detumescence (D). Note that the motor branch of the pudendal nerve is not depicted, nor are the striated muscles to which the pudendal nerve projects. Also, the penis is shown as a single structure, although recent evidence suggests that the innervation of the penile body and glans are not identical. The depicted innervation may better represent that of the body than that of the glans. [Diagram is from de Groat and Steers (1988) and is reprinted by permission of Lippincott Williams & Wilkins.]

and antierectile), and pudendal nerves (sensory and somatomotor) comprise the three major pathways for the regulation of penile erection. (See Fig. 4.) Most fibers in the pelvic nerve derive from the lumbosacral spinal cord and travel via the pelvic plexus and cavernous nerve to the penile corpora and vasculature. Although this path is primarily parasympathetic, it apparently also carries some sympathetic fibers, at least in rats (Dail and Minorsky, 1986; Dail *et al.*, 1985, 1986). This is the major proerectile pathway in all mammals studied so far (Giuliano and Rampin, 2000; Giuliano *et al.*, 1995, 1997). The pudendal nerve (again, at least in rats) divides into distinct sensory and motor branches near the ischium, where the branches course ventrally toward their perineal targets (McKenna and Nadelhaft, 1986; Ueyama *et al.*, 1987). Figure 4 depicts only the sensory branch of the pudendal nerve. Both branches of the pudendal nerve also carry sympathetic efferent fibers (Hulsebosch and Coggeshall, 1982; McKenna and Nadelhaft, 1986). The motor branch of this nerve has primarily somatic fibers that originate in the lumbosacral cord and innervate the striated penile muscles (Breedlove, 1984, 1985; Sato *et al.*, 1978; Schroder, 1980; Ueyama *et al.*, 1984, 1985). The third pathway is thought to be entirely sympathetic. It arises from the thoracolumbar spinal cord and reaches the penis via two routes (Booth, 1976; Dail *et al.*, 1985, 1986; Dail and Minorsky, 1986; Giuliano *et al.*, 1995; Giuliano and Rampin, 2000). The prevertebral outflow passes through the superior hypogastric plexus and is carried distally by the hypogastric and cavernous nerves. The second route utilizes the paravertebral sympathetic chain, which contributes fibers that travel in the pudendal, pelvic, and cavernous nerves.

A potential proerectile role of sympathetic axons in the hypogastric nerve has been debated. Electrical stimulation of the hypogastric nerve decreased penile blood flow in intact anesthetized rabbits (Langley and Anderson, 1895) but increased penile volume if the sympathetic chain had been cut before the experiment began (Sjöstrand and Klinge, 1979). In anesthetized rats (Dail *et al.*, 1989) and dogs (Carati *et al.*, 1987; Diederichs *et al.*, 1991) stimulation of the hypogastric nerve had no effect on intracavernous pressure unless the pelvic nerve had been cut previously (Dail *et al.*, 1989). However, stimulation of the hypogastric nerve in anesthetized cats increased penile volume (Andersson *et al.*, 1987). In some studies, erections persisted following lesions of the sacral spinal cord or the parasympathetic outflow in cats (Root and Bard, 1947). Thus, various efferent fibers with opposing roles may run in the hypogastric nerve (Giuliano and Rampin, 2000). Section of the hypogastric nerve in male rats produced inconsistent impairments of copulation (lower intromission ratios and longer ejaculation latencies) but no decrement in the facilitation of touch-based erections occasioned by exposure to an inaccessible receptive female (Sachs and Liu, 1998). Noncontact erections were also unaffected (Cruz *et al.*, 1999).

There are two potential ways in which sympathetic fibers could produce partial erections. First, normal erection results from a combination of increased parasympathetic and decreased sympathetic activity.

Even after lesions of parasympathetic innervation, a decrease in sympathetic outflow to the penis, elicited by "proerectile" stimulation, could still allow blood to fill the penis and produce at least partial erection (Giuliano and Rampin, 2000). Second, some sympathetically controlled arteries may increase vascular tone in other pelvic structures, thereby diverting blood flow away from those structures and toward the penis (Giuliano *et al.*, 1997).

Giuliano *et al.* (1997) provided evidence for a proerectile role of sympathetic fibers in male rats. As noted above, sympathetic input to the pelvis reaches the penis via two routes: the prevertebral outflow, carried by the hypogastric and cavernous nerves; and the paravertebral sympathetic chain, axons from which travel in the pudendal, pelvic, and cavernous nerves. Removal of the second pathway, achieved by acute or chronic section of the paravertebral sympathetic chain or by the use of the catecholamine neurotoxin 6-hydroxydopamine (6-OHDA), resulted in a significant decrease in the effectiveness of electrical stimulation of the medial preoptic area (MPOA) in increasing erection. Bilateral section of the hypogastric nerve produced a slight, nonsignificant decrease in MPOA-stimulated erection. (See Fig. 5.) Therefore, the paravertebral chain of sympathetic ganglia, and possibly the hypogastric nerve, contribute proerectile input to the penis. However, bilateral section of the parasympathetic input to the penis abolished the erectile response. These data confirm that the primary proerectile influence is via the parasympathetic innervation; however, sympathetic fibers also contribute to erectile function. Giuliano *et al.* suggested that the previous lack of support for a proerectile role of sympathetic neurons arose because electrical stimulation of a given peripheral nerve activates both pro- and antierectile fibers, which may cancel each other's effects. Also, the stimulus parameters that were used may preferentially recruit one population of fibers or the other in different proportions. However, stimulation of the MPOA activates a coordinated response that is mediated by both parasympathetic and sympathetic outflow. A potential role of the striated penile muscles in MPOA stimulation-elicited erection was ruled out by the demonstration that administration of a muscle relaxant (gallamine triethiodide) did not affect the erections elicited by MPOA stimulation. Therefore, the erectile response coordinated by the MPOA

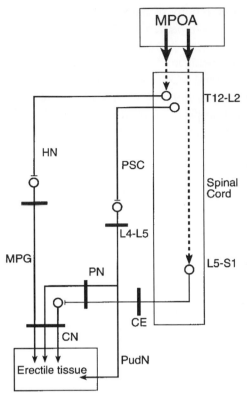

FIGURE 5 Diagrammatic representation of peripheral autonomic pathways potentially involved in erectile response elicited by medial preoptic area (MPOA) stimulation. Sites of neural lesions are represented by black bars. No direct projections from MPOA to spinal autonomic nuclei have been reported; dotted lines represent hypothetical pathways. CE, cauda equina; CN, cavernous nerve; HN, hypogastric nerve; L4–L5, fourth and fifth lumbar levels of the paravertebral sympathetic chain; L6-S1, sixth lumbar and first sacral level of the spinal cord; MPG, major pelvic ganglion; PN, pelvic nerve; PSC, paravertebral sympathetic chain; PudN, pudendal nerve; T12-L2, twelfth thoracic to second lumbar level of the spinal cord. [Figure is from Giuliano *et al.* (1997) and is reproduced with permission from the American Physiological Association.]

includes activation of both parasympathetic and sympathetic neurons but not motoneurons that innervate striated penile muscles. Men with lower spinal cord injuries can have "psychogenic" erections, presumably mediated by sympathetic neurons that leave the spinal cord above the level of the lesion (reviewed in Comarr, 1992). Although the role of sympathetic influence in "psychogenic" erections in spinally intact men is not clear, the demonstration of proerectile sympathetic

influence in spinally intact rats suggests that similar mechanisms could contribute to such erections in men.

The dorsal penile nerve is the main terminus of the sensory pudendal nerve and is the sole identified route for tactile sensory information from the penis. Other genital afferent fibers are carried to the spinal cord by the pelvic nerve (Nadelhaft and Booth, 1984; Purinton *et al.*, 1981; Richard *et al.*, 1991), and the genitofemoral nerve may carry afferents from the perigenital skin, but no role has been discovered for these afferents in erection (Sachs and Liu, 1992). The dorsal penile nerve originates in the same spinal segments—and projects in the cord to spinal laminae—containing autonomic and somatic motoneurons projecting to penile muscles (Núñez *et al.*, 1986). The overlapping pudendal and pelvic afferent and efferent spinal projections (Roppolo *et al.*, 1985) may represent the structural basis for the rapid sensorimotor coordination (Núñez *et al.*, 1986; Roppolo *et al.*, 1985; Rose and Collins, 1985) implicit in an intromission pattern that, as in rats, has preintromission "contact-detection" thrusts lasting only a few milliseconds and an intromission duration of only 200 to 400 msec.

The pudendal motor neurons innervate the bulbocavernosus and ischiocavernosus muscles, which play a critical role in mammalian copulation (reviewed in Giuliano and Rampin, 2000; Sachs, 1983). The ischiocavernosus muscle produces penile elongation and anteroflexion. Excising this muscle in rats dramatically decreases intromissions and essentially eliminates ejaculation (Monaghan and Breedlove, 1992; Sachs, 1982; Wallach and Hart, 1983). However, castrated males can still intromit during copulation when given hormonal treatments that stimulate copulation but that do not maintain the mass of this muscle (Sachs, 1983). The bulbocavernosus muscle is responsible for the formation of the cup, in which the tip of the glans dilates to a cup or bell-like form wider than the rest of the glans penis. Removal of this muscle in rats did not affect other types of erections. The bulbocavernosus muscle is also important for erecting the spines on the surface of a male rat's penis (Phoenix *et al.*, 1976), which may play a role in promoting the progestational state in the female (Adler, 1978; Dewsbury, 1981; Milligan, 1979) and in dislodging a previously placed plug (Hartung and Dewsbury, 1978; Mosig and

Dewsbury, 1970; O'Hanlon and Sachs, 1986). Because rats mate in groups, the male that provides the second ejaculation is not necessarily the one that provided the first (McClintock *et al.,* 1984). If the second male can dislodge the plug from the first mating, his sperm will have a competitive advantage.

The pelvic ganglion (PG, or pelvic plexus) provides sympathetic and parasympathetic innervation to the penis via the cavernous nerve. The PG of rats is sexually dimorphic; the male ganglion contains two to four times as many neurons as the female's (Greenwood *et al.,* 1985). The amount of immunoreactivity (ir) for Fos, the protein product of the immediate-early gene *c-fos,* in the PG of male rats was positively correlated with the amount of both genital and noncontact stimulation (Fang *et al.,* 2000). Ejaculation produced the greatest increase in Fos-ir. The increase in Fos-ir following noncontact erections may have resulted from sensory stimulation from the erection itself or from the genital grooming that normally accompanies such erections.

C. Sympathetic and Somatic Control of Ejaculation

The ejaculatory reflex is initiated primarily by sensory receptors in the glabrous skin of the glans penis, which discharge when sufficient excitation has been achieved (reviewed in Hendry *et al.,* 2000). However, ejaculation occurring during nocturnal penile tumescence or certain other conditions may not require direct stimulation of the glans. Sensory input travels via the sensory fibers of the dorsal penile nerve and pudendal nerve to the spinal cord and also via the hypogastric nerve to the paravertebral chain of sympathetic ganglia. Seminal emission is controlled by sympathetic neurons in the T12-L2 region of the human spinal cord, which send axons through the hypogastric nerve and hypogastric plexus to the pelvic plexus, where they synapse. Postganglionic neurons from the pelvic plexus produce closure of the bladder neck (to prevent retrograde ejaculation), stimulate movement of sperm through the vas deferens, and release seminal fluids from the seminal vesicles, prostate, and Cowper's glands. Normal activation of the vas deferens requires both adenosine triphosphate (ATP) and norepinephrine, which are stored in small and large synaptic vesicles in the sympathetic

terminals (Kasakov *et al.,* 1988; Sneddon and Westfall, 1984; von Kugelgen and Starke, 1991). Expulsion of semen is controlled by somatic fibers from the ventral horn of S2–S4 spinal segments, which travel in the motor branch of the pudendal nerve to the muscles of the pelvic floor, including the bulbocavernosus and ischiocavernosus muscles.

D. Tactile Receptors on the Penis

The mammalian penis is equipped with both slowly adapting (SA) and rapidly adapting (RA) mechanoreceptors, which are differentially distributed on the glans and may have different functions. Both types of receptors were found throughout the length of the glans of cats, but the SA type predominated at the distal end, and RA receptors were concentrated at the proximal end, just distal to the anterior margin of preputial attachment (Johnson *et al.,* 1986). It has been proposed (Aronson and Cooper, 1968; Hart, 1978) that the mechanoreceptors of the glans serve to detect the vagina, but Johnson *et al.* suggested that SA receptors could also serve to transmit information concerning skin movement, pressure, and state of erection. They also suggested that RA receptors contribute to sexual excitability and that penile spines increase their activation. Penile mechanoreceptors are more responsive when the penis is erect (Johnson, 1988) or near core body temperature (Johnson and Kitchell, 1987). Therefore, diversion of blood into the penis not only produces erection, but may also warm and distend the skin sufficiently to increase the responsiveness of the mechanoreceptors. The role of the penile spines in sensory processes is unclear. Male marmosets whose penile spines had been removed with a depilatory required more thrusts to achieve intromission, presumably because of difficulty in detecting the vaginal orifice (Dixson, 1991). Neither intravaginal thrusting nor ejaculation was significantly affected. However, a sensory role for penile spines in the copulatory behavior of rats is unlikely. Castrated male rats whose penile spines have regressed but whose copulation is maintained by estradiol display the ejaculatory pattern after the normal number of intromissions, rather than the increase that would be expected if the spines have an important sensory role (Baumgardner and Dewsbury, 1980; O'Hanlon, *et al.,* 1981; Södersten, 1973).

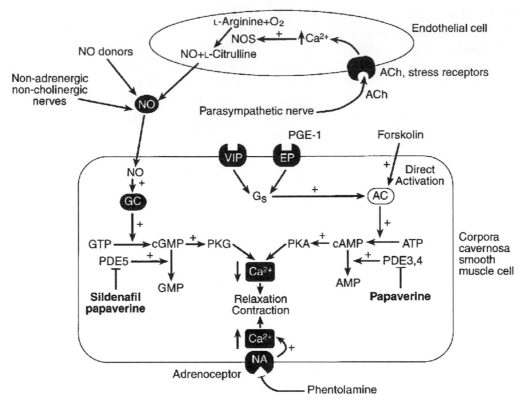

FIGURE 6 Mechanisms and pharmacological therapies involved in regulation of corpora cavernosa smooth muscle tone and penile erection. All pharmacological agents are shown in bold. Prostaglandin E_1 (PGE_1) and vasoactive intestinal peptide (VIP) activate adenylyl cyclase and increase intracellular levels of cAMP, thereby resulting in cavernosal smooth muscle relaxation and penile erection. Type-3 and type-4 phosphodiesterase (PDE) inhibitors prevent the breakdown of cAMP to AMP. Papaverine, a nonselective PDE inhibitor, prevents the breakdown of both cAMP and cGMP cyclic nucleotides, a result that leads to enhanced smooth muscle relaxation and penile erection. Forskolin activates adenylyl cyclase directly, thus increasing intracellular cAMP levels. Nitric oxide (NO), synthesized by nonadrenergic, noncholinergic (NANC) nerves and endothelial cells, diffuses into the smooth muscle cell, thus activating guanylyl cyclase and increasing intracellular cGMP synthesis and resulting in cavernosal smooth muscle relaxation and penile erection. Sildenafil, the orally active type-5 PDE inhibitor, inhibits the breakdown of cGMP to GMP. Phentolamine, a nonselective β-adrenoceptor blocker, blocks the increase in intracellular Ca^{2+} by inhibiting the activation of protein kinase C (PKC) and inositol triphosphate, thus resulting in decreased intracellular Ca^{2+} and cavernosal smooth muscle relaxation. Abbreviations: ACh, acetylcholine; EP, prostaglandin receptor, NOS, nitric oxide synthase. [Reprinted from Bivalacqua *et al.* (2000) with permission of *Trends in Pharmacological Sciences.*]

E. Cellular Mediators of Erection

Nitric oxide (NO) is the primary mediator of vascular relaxation of the corpora cavernosa (reviewed in Bivalacqua *et al.*, 2000). (See Fig 6.) Parasympathetic nerves release acetylcholine (ACh) onto muscarinic receptors on endothelial cells lining the cavernosal cisternae and blood vessels. These muscarinic receptors increase intracellular calcium, which activates NO synthase. As a result, NO is released from the endothelial cells; NO is also released from nonadrenergic, noncholinergic (NANC) nerve terminals. NO diffuses into smooth muscle cells and activates guanylyl cyclase to produce cGMP. The cGMP induces smooth muscle relaxation via several mechanisms: (1) activation of protein kinase G (PKG); (2) activation of ion channels that extrude or sequester calcium; (3) opening of potassium channels to hyperpolarize smooth muscle cells; and (4) activation of myosin light-chain kinases (Lee *et al.*, 1997; Moreland *et al.*, 1999; Stief *et al.*, 1997). The activity of cGMP is terminated by type-5 phosphodiesterase (PDE5); sildenafil citrate (Viagra) prolongs cGMP activity by inhibiting PDE5. Other processes that may contribute to erection include activation of adenylyl cyclase by vasoactive intestinal peptide (VIP), calcitonin gene related peptide (CGRP), and prostaglandin E_1 (PGE_1) (reviewed in Andersson and Wagner, 1995; Bivalacqua *et al.*, 2000). At least some of the acute proerectile effects of PGE_1 are mediated by an increase in the production of NO, and repeated administration of PGE_1 increases the content of both neuronal and endothelial forms of NOS (Escrig *et al.*, 1999b). Finally, gap junctions in the membranes of cavernosal smooth muscle cells allow passage of ions and second messengers from cell to cell, thereby promoting unified relaxation or contraction of the smooth muscle tissue in erection or detumescence (Christ *et al.*, 1999). (The dependence of NO synthase on testosterone is discussed below, in Section IV.H on NO.)

Detumescence of the penis is induced and maintained by sympathetic adrenergic nerves, whose stimulation of α_1 receptors on smooth muscle cells in the corpora cavernosa results in increased intracellular calcium (reviewed in Andersson and Stief, 1997; Christ, 1995). This calcium in turn leads to contraction of the smooth muscle cells, decreased blood inflow, and detumescence. Stimulation of α_1 receptors can also increase the sensitivity of smooth muscle to calcium, without affecting calcium levels, via the Rho-kinase pathway (Somlyo and Somlyo, 2000). A rho-kinase antagonist [(+)-(R)-*trans*-4-(1-aminoethyl)-*N*-(4-pyridyl) cyclohexanecarboxamide dihydrochloride monohydrate, Y-27632] applied to strips of human or rabbit corpus cavernosum inhibited smooth muscle contraction that had been elicited by either the α receptor agonist phenylephrine or electrical field stimulation (Rees *et al.*, 2001). Y-27632 also stimulated penile erection in rats (Chitaley *et al.*, 2001). Therefore, inhibition of rho-kinase may provide a new treatment for erectile dysfunction. Other factors that contribute to detumescence include endothelin, angiotensin, and thromboxane A_2.

III. ROLE OF GONADAL STEROIDS IN THE CONTROL OF MALE SEXUAL BEHAVIOR

A. Dependence of Copulation on Recent Exposure to Testosterone

Male sexual behavior is heavily dependent on testosterone (T) and its metabolites. T is secreted by the Leydig cells of the testes and reaches its nontesticular targets via the blood. In all mammals studied, the display of mating behavior in adult males is promoted by circulating T or its metabolites, estradiol (E) and dihydrotestosterone (DHT). Increasing production of T at puberty underlies the increased sexual activity of maturing males, and if the source of T is removed by surgical castration, sex drive and sexual activity typically decline. However, in some species, such as the big brown bat (*Eptesicus fuscus*), the display of sexual behavior occurs during autumn and during periodic arousals from hibernation, when testes are regressed and hormones are at basal levels (Mendonca *et al.*, 1996). Even in these bats gonadectomy several months before the mating season inhibited mating in a large flight cage with numerous other animals, though not in staged tests in a small cage (Mendonca *et al.*, 1996). The stimulatory effects of T on sexual behavior of adult males are called activational or concurrent effects, to distinguish them from T's organizational effects during sexual differentiation (see Chapter 63, by Art Arnold, in Volume 4). T is usually present in considerably greater quantities than is necessary to stimulate sexual behavior (Davidson *et al.*, 1978). The excess production of T is apparently necessary for normal testicular function. Therefore, relatively small reductions of T levels should not affect behavior. (See below for studies of humans.)

1. Time Course of Changes in Copulation Following Castration

Although plasma hormone levels decline to unmeasurable levels within 24 hours after castration (Krey and McGinnis, 1990), male rats may continue to exhibit the complete copulatory pattern for days or weeks (Davidson, 1966b). Indeed, the ejaculatory threshold actually decreases in the early days after castration (Davidson, 1966b), as indicated by the number of intromissions preceding ejaculation. However, intromission latency begins to lengthen soon after castration. Therefore, one of the normal functions of T may be to increase the number of intromissions preceding ejaculation, thereby increasing the number of sperm in the ejaculate, facilitating sperm transport, and triggering a progestational state in the female (Toner and Adler, 1986; Toner *et al.,* 1987).

The changes in behavior produced by castration follow a distinct sequence. Ejaculation stops first, then intromission, and later mounting (Beach and Pauker, 1949; Davidson, 1966b; Grunt and Young, 1953; Michael and Wilson, 1974; Rosenblatt and Aronson, 1958). This pattern of decline is consistent across species (Larsson, 1979). The consistency is understandable, because a loss of mounting would necessarily include the elimination of intromissions and ejaculations. Elimination of mounts with intromission precludes the expression of ejaculation. Although all of the motor patterns of copulation could be lost simultaneously, any sequence of loss of these motor patterns could occur only in the order described. The differential loss of copulatory elements following castration occurs, in part, because the different elements depend on different peripheral target cells or mechanisms. For example, mounting does not depend on the tactile sensitivity of the penis or its ability to become erect, as intromission does, and ejaculation requires even more penile sensory input and motor output than does intromission. The various behaviors may also depend on different neuronal circuits in the central nervous system, which have different degrees of dependence on hormones.

There are mixed reports of the effects of castration on sexual desire and copulation in men. Based on anecdotal accounts, Kinsey (Kinsey *et al.,* 1948) concluded that there was little basis for the assertion that castration impaired sexual function in most men. Subsequently, more detailed reports revealed considerable variability. Heim and Hursch (1979) reviewed the results of prospective studies of men who had been castrated as "treatment" for sexual offenses. In these studies, half to two-thirds of the men reported a rapid loss of sexual desire and interest, whereas in the remaining men sexual activity waned gradually, with as many as 10% reporting sexual intercourse for up to 20 years after castration. Depending on the individual, castration would either eliminate intercourse immediately, produce a progressive loss of sexual activity over the

period of a year, or in some cases have little effect on sexual behavior. There was a greater effect the older the individual was at the time of castration (Heim and Hursch, 1979).

2. Time Course of Changes in Copulation Following T Restoration

After complete loss of the behavior, exogenous T restores the behavioral elements in the reverse order in which they were lost, with mounting occurring first, followed by intromission, and finally ejaculation (Larsson, 1979). As noted for castration, these responses could not return in any other order, although there is no physical reason that these responses could not return simultaneously. The effectiveness of T replacement suggests that it is the loss of T that leads to a reduction in sexual activity, rather than other effects of castration, such as the consequent rise in pituitary gonadotropins. Higher doses of hormone are required to restore copulatory behavior if it has been completely lost than if hormones are administered soon after castration to maintain the behavior (Davidson, 1966b). Presumably, continuity in the exposure of neural and peripheral tissues to T maintains the responsiveness of these tissues, whereas a greater input is needed to reactivate the diminished activity in males castrated for a long time.

In long-term castrates, copulation is restored over a period of 5 to 10 days after exogenous T treatment has begun (Beach and Holz-Tucker, 1949; Davidson, 1966b; Goldfoot and Baum, 1972; McGinnis and Mirth, 1986; McGinnis *et al.,* 1989; Putnam *et al.,* 2001). However, T increased neural firing in the MPOA within minutes (Pfaff and Pfaffmann, 1969) or even seconds (Yamada, 1979). Therefore, longer-term genomic effects are necessary for the restoration of copulatory behavior. This conclusion was supported by the finding that the protein synthesis inhibitor anisomycin blocked the effects of T on copulatory behavior (McGinnis and Kahn, 1997). But anisomycin did not disrupt, and in some conditions actually facilitated, the restoration of touch-based erections by T (Meisel *et al.,* 1986). (See section III B below.)

Increasing doses of T produce greater levels of copulatory activity (Davidson, 1966b). This increase in sexual activity can be expressed as an increase in the proportion of males that display a given response (i.e., mount, intromission, or ejaculation) or in the attainment of copulatory parameters comparable to those measured prior to castration (Hlinak and Madlafousek, 1982). Although individual males vary widely in their copulatory performance, once an individual's precastration copulatory level is reached, additional T treatment produces little benefit (Grunt and Young, 1953; Larsson, 1966).

3. The Role of T Metabolites in Maintaining and Restoring Copulation

T differs from most steroid hormones in that it seldom stimulates target cells directly. Instead, its target cells metabolize T to one or more steroids that bind more avidly than T to intracellular steroid receptors. One such metabolite is estradiol (E), which is formed by aromatase, a P450 enzyme. E acts by binding to estrogen receptors (ERs), of which there are at least two types, ERα and ERβ. The other common T metabolite is 5α-dihydrotestosterone (DHT), which is formed by the enzyme 5α-reductase. (See Chapter 92, by Imperato-McGinley and Zhu, in this volume concerning human disorders resulting from deficiency of 5α-reductase.) DHT is the preferred ligand of the androgen receptor (AR), possessing approximately five-fold greater affinity than T for the AR (Wilbert *et al.*, 1983). Unlike T, DHT cannot be aromatized to E; therefore, it is frequently used to differentiate androgenic vs estrogenic effects of T administration. Some target cells may produce both metabolites and have both types of receptors.

E and DHT are differentially effective in maintaining copulation and *ex copula* reflexes. E may be necessary and sufficient to maintain or restore most elements of copulatory behavior of male rats (Christensen and Clemens, 1975; Davidson, 1969; Södersten, 1973; reviewed in Larsson, 1979). Not only is E administration sufficient to reverse most of the effects of castration on copulation by male rats, but systemic administration of aromatase inhibitors or ER antagonists to castrates inhibits or prevents the subsequent restoration of copulation by T administration (Bonsall *et al.*, 1992; Beyer *et al.*, 1976; Vagell and McGinnis, 1997). Similar inhibitory effects of the nonsteroidal aromatase inhibitor fadrozole was found in castrated, T-treated monkeys (Zumpe *et al.*, 1996). Fadrozole, administered to gonadally intact male rats that were treated with exoge-

nous T to "clamp" T levels, decreased anticipatory level changing, increased the latencies to mount, intromit, and ejaculate, and decreased the numbers of these behaviors (Roselli *et al.*, 2001). Replacement E restored anticipatory behavior, mounts, and intromissions, but not ejaculations.

Neither DHT (Beyer *et al.*, 1973; McDonald *et al.*, 1970; Whalen and Luttge, 1971) nor the nonaromatizable androgen methyltrienolone (R1881) (Baum *et al.*, 1987) was effective in restoring or maintaining copulation in castrated male rats. DHT and R1881 were also ineffective in stimulating copulation in male gerbils, hamsters, pigs, rams, or sheep (Christensen *et al.*, 1973; DeBold and Clemens, 1978; Levis and Ford, 1989; Lisk and Greenwald, 1983; Parrott, 1986; Yahr and Stephens, 1987). In further support of the lack of importance of AR stimulation, several synthetic androgens (5α-androstanediols) that can be aromatized to E, but not 5α-reduced to DHT, were even more effective than T in restoring sexual behavior in castrated rats (Morali *et al.*, 1993) or mice (Ogawa *et al.*, 1996). The effectiveness of E, and the ineffectiveness of DHT, in restoring or maintaining copulation have given rise to the "aromatization hypothesis," which states that it is the aromatization of T to E that is critical for maintaining or restoring copulation in male rats.

Support for the importance of E for copulation has been obtained from studies of genetically altered mice. Two forms of the ER have been cloned, ERα and ERβ; both forms are expressed in the brain (Shughrue *et al.*, 1997). Gonadally intact male mice lacking the ERα (ERα "knock out" mice, or ERα KO) mounted normally, but had fewer intromissions than wild-type mice, and almost no ejaculations (Ogawa *et al.*, 1997, 1998). However, ERα KO mice secrete more T than do wild-type mice, due to diminished ER-mediated negative feedback (Wersinger *et al.*, 1997). Castration of ERα KO males and replacement with normal levels of T (Wersinger *et al.*, 1997) or with higher than normal levels of DHT (Ogawa *et al.*, 1998) resulted in deficits similar to those in gonadally intact ERα KO males. There appeared to be no compensation by up-regulation of other steroid receptors, because AR immunoreactivity (Ogawa *et al.*, 1997) and ERβ mRNA (Couse *et al.*, 1997) were comparable in ERα KO and in wild-type mice. These data suggest that stimulation of AR and perhaps ERβ is sufficient to permit normal sexual motivation and mounting behavior in mice, but is not sufficient for normal intromissions and ejaculations.

However, E is not sufficient to maintain full copulatory behavior. Frequently, availability of E alone was unable to maintain any behavioral ejaculatory patterns or resulted in fewer ejaculatory patterns than when both metabolites were present (Feder et al., 1974; Kaplan and McGinnis, 1989; McGinnis and Dreifuss, 1989, Putnam et al., 2002a,b; Roselli; et al., 2001; Södersten and Gustafsson, 1980; Vagell and McGinnis, 1997; but see Roselli; et al., 2001, discussed above). The lack of estrogenic effects on partner preference was shown by the inability of E alone to restore partner preference and the inability of the nonsteroidal aromatization inhibitor fadrozole to block the effects of T on that measure (Vagell and McGinnis, 1997). The ER antagonist RU-58668 also failed to block copulation or partner preference in male rats but did inhibit the restoration of scent marking and 50 kHz vocalizations (Vagell and McGinnis, 1998). Similar findings were reported for male hamsters; fadrozole administered chronically for 5 or 8 weeks failed to inhibit copulation or anogenital investigation of a receptive female (Cooper et al., 2000). There was differential ability of several anabolic androgens to maintain copulation in castrated male rats. Stanozolol and oxymetholone were ineffective in restoring ejaculatory behavior patterns and in maintaining sex accessory tissues, whereas testosterone cypionate was fully effective in both regards (Clark and Harrold, 1997). The ability of these compounds to restore ejaculatory patterns reflected their relative binding to peripheral ARs (Saartok et al., 1984). It is not clear whether binding to brain ARs or peripheral ARs was more important for the maintenance of ejaculatory behavior patterns. Together, the above experiments suggest that activation of ERs is not always sufficient to maintain copulation or partner preference in male rats or hamsters, and blocking of ER does not always render applications of T ineffective.

In contrast to the relative ineffectiveness of E-alone and of ER antagonists, AR antagonists inhibited T's effects in several experiments, suggesting that stimulation of ARs does contribute to T's effects. For example, administration of the nonsteroidal antiandrogen flutamide reduced the ability of T to restore copulation in castrated male rats (Gladue and Clemens, 1980; Gray, 1977; Vagell and McGinnis,

1998). Flutamide also blocked the expression of partner preference, scent marking, and 50 kHz ("attraction") ultrasonic vocalizations. Therefore, blockade of ARs appeared to be more disruptive of copulation than blockade of ERs. An antiandrogen with greater affinity for the AR ($\alpha\alpha\alpha$-trifluoro-2-methyl-4'-nitro-m-lactoluidide, SCH-16423) eliminated all mating behavior, including mounting, in 80% of male rats treated with a dose of T that restored ejaculation in all of the control males (McGinnis and Mirth, 1986). Therefore, stimulation of ER is not sufficient, and in some cases may not be necessary, to restore or maintain full copulatory behavior in male rats or Syrian hamsters. Rather, conversion of T to DHT, and subsequent binding to AR, may be necessary to promote central integrative processes and to maintain peripheral sensory and motor functions that contribute to copulatory performance. Thus, stimulation of both ERs and ARs may be necessary for full restoration of copulatory behavior.

In a number of species other than rats, the aromatization hypothesis has little or no support. DHT is able to maintain or restore copulation in rabbits (Ågmo and Södersten, 1975), guinea pigs (Alsum and Goy, 1974; Butera and Czaja, 1989b), deer mice (Clemens and Pomerantz, 1982), monkeys (Cochran and Perachio, 1977; Michael et al., 1986; Phoenix, 1974), and mice (Luttge and Hall, 1973).

B. Effects of Castration and Hormonal Replacement on ex copula Penile Responses

There are differences in hormonal regulation of copulation and of ex copula penile responses. Both the postcastration loss of ex copula reflexes and the post-replacement restoration are more rapid than the loss and restoration of copulation. In addition, different metabolites appear to mediate the hormonal effects.

1. Animal Studies

In spinally transected male rats, castration reduced touch-based erections within 24 hours, reaching an asymptote over the next 12 days (Hart et al., 1983). In an earlier report, however, erections and anteroflexions (penile body erections) continued to decline for up to 8 days after T withdrawal (Hart, 1967b). In spinally intact males a reduction in penile reflexes was observed 4 days after castration, the earliest time examined (Meisel et al.,

1984a). At this time, castrated males had a lower proportion of males displaying penile cups (intense erections of the glans). By 7 days after castration the proportion of males showing anteroflexions significantly declined, but a reduction in glans erections was not seen until 11 days after castration. Davidson *et al.* (1978) also reported that the loss of penile reflexes in spinally intact males followed the sequence of cups, then anteroflexions, and finally less intense glans erections. Because cups are intense glans erections, it is clear why castration should affect these responses before lesser erections, but it is not obvious why castration effects on anteroflexions (penile body erections) should be intermediate.

Normal levels of touch-based penile erections can be maintained in animals receiving T replacement at the time of castration (Davidson *et al.,* 1978; Hart, 1973; Meisel *et al.,* 1984a), and reflex activity can be restored by T treatments in males that had been castrated for some time (Gray *et al.,* 1980; Hart, 1973; Hart *et al.,* 1983; Rodgers and Alheid, 1972). In castrated males T-filled Silastic capsules, 6 or 18 mm in length, maintained touch-based erections at the level of intact males, despite the fact that these treatments produced plasma levels (6 mm: 0.79 ng/ml; 18 mm: 1.09 ng/ml) considerably lower than that measured in intact males (1.95 ng/ml) (Davidson *et al.,* 1978). As is the case with copulation, plasma T levels in adult male rats are well above the threshold levels needed to activate penile reflexes.

Unlike the time course of restoration of copulation, touch-based reflexes could be reinstated rather rapidly (Hart, 1967b). On the first test of spinally transected, castrated male rats, 2 days after T injection, the number of erections doubled, and the number of anteroflexions tripled, compared to the day before T treatment. In a subsequent experiment, a significant facilitation of erections was already evident 6 hours after implantation of a T-containing capsule, with maximal stimulation of erections reached by 24 hours (Hart *et al.,* 1983). In spinally intact male rats, a significant facilitation of touch-based erections was detected 24 hours after T replacement, with normal levels of erections reached by 48 hours (Gray *et al.,* 1980). The same males were tested for copulation at 52 hours, and only 1 of 10 males mounted. Thus, not only do penile reflexes decline at a faster rate in spinally transected males than in spinally intact males, but they are also apparently restored more rapidly in transected males. One is tempted to speculate that, in general, T influences on the brain accumulate and decay more slowly than comparable actions on the spinal cord (and possibly the periphery). The slower restoration of reflexes in spinally intact male rats may reflect the time required for T to reduce supraspinal inhibition to a level at which the already primed spinal effector systems can act.

Noncontact erections also show a more rapid rate of loss following castration and of restoration following hormone treatments, compared to the loss and restoration of copulation (Manzo *et al.,* 1999). On the first test, 3 days after castration, noncontact erections had been completely lost, and on the first test, 3 days after hormone restoration, the numbers of noncontact erections were comparable to those before castration. Therefore, the hormonal mechanisms controlling noncontact and touch-based erections may be similar, and they may differ from hormonal mechanisms that control copulation, at least with regard to temporal factors.

As with copulation, T is not the critical molecule for the activation of penile reflexes. However, in contrast to its effects on copulation, E is completely ineffective in restoring or maintaining *ex copula* reflexes in male rats, whereas DHT is fully effective in this regard (Gray *et al.,* 1980; Hart, 1973, 1979; Meisel *et al.,* 1984a). (See Fig. 7.) In addition, DHT was the active androgen that maintained nitric oxide-mediated erection in rats (Lugg *et al.,* 1995; see below.). The DHT regimens that maintained or restored reflexes were no more effective than control treatments (empty Silastic capsules) in maintaining or restoring mounting, a finding that emphasizes the difference in hormonal control of these two behaviors (Gray *et al.,* 1980; Meisel *et al.,* 1984a). Further evidence for the importance of AR for the activation of *ex copula* penile reflexes was marshaled by studies showing that concurrent treatment of T-replaced castrated male rats with either the AR antagonist flutamide (Gray *et al.,* 1980) or a 5α-reductase inhibitor (Bradshaw *et al.,* 1981) blocked the restorative effects of T. Therefore, the aromatization of T to E maintains or restores most aspects of copulatory behavior in male rats, whereas 5α-reduction of T to DHT maintains or restores penile reflexes and sensitivity to tactile stimuli.

DHT was as effective as T in maintaining noncontact erections in castrated male rats, whereas E was

blocker or an aromatase inhibitor had no effect on sexual function (Gooren, 1985). An exception to this finding comes from an unusual case study of a man receiving a combination of E and progesterone (P) to alleviate menopausal-like symptoms after undergoing castration (Davidson *et al.*, 1979). In this individual a normal level of sexual activity was maintained in the absence of androgen treatment. However, P is a precursor of T; therefore, it is possible that some increase in T occurred and was sufficient to stimulate sexual function.

In studies of "psychogenic" erectile dysfunction there was generally no difference between T levels in normal and impotent men (Pirke *et al.*, 1979; Schwartz *et al.*, 1980). [See Sachs (2000) for a critique of the conventional distinction between "psychogenic" and "organic" erectile dysfunction.] Furthermore, among normal men, there was no relation between T levels and frequency of sexual activity (Brown *et al.*, 1978). Similarly, no differences in sexual activity were found between normal men and men with reduced plasma T levels as a result of Klinefelter's syndrome (Raboch and Starka, 1973). An exception to the generalization that no relation exists between plasma T and sexual function was reported by Lange et al. (1980), who found that T levels correlated negatively with latency to maximum erectability in men viewing erotic films.

C. The Role of Progesterone in Male Sexual Behavior

There has been renewed interest in the effects of progesterone (P), which is secreted by both the adrenals and the testes, on male sexual behavior. This was prompted by the observation that P stimulates mounting in unisexual lizards (Grassman and Crews, 1986) and in some males of the ancestral species (Lindzey and Crews, 1988). In sexually naive male rats, P implants that produced physiological levels of P partially overcame the effects of castration on intromissive behavior but not ejaculation (Witt *et al.*, 1994, 1995). Furthermore, sexually naive male mice that were homozygous for a P receptor knockout (PRKO) allele showed copulatory deficits on the first test but not on subsequent tests (Phelps *et al.*, 1998). However, in sexually experienced male mice, restoring physiological P levels neither restored mating after castration nor altered the behavioral response to T in wild-type males or those that

were heterozygous for the PRKO allele (Phelps *et al.*, 1998).

In male primates P appears to have inhibitory effects on sexual behavior. The synthetic progestin Depo-Provera (medroxyprogesterone acetate) is sometimes used to decrease sexual interest in male sex offenders. Both P and Depo-Provera decreased sexual motivation and performance in male cynomolgus monkeys (Zumpe *et al.*, 1996, 1997). Whereas Depo-Provera decreased both plasma T and binding to androgen receptors, P did not affect either measure; therefore, P may be preferable to Depo-Provera for treatment of male sex offenders. It is not clear whether the effects of the PR on male sexual behavior are mediated by classic genomic processes, by which P-bound PR dimerizes and acts as a transcription factor, or by "ligand-independent" activation of PR by dopamine (DA) acting through D1 receptors via the cAMP system, as in female rats and mice (Mani *et al.*, 1994a,b, 1996, 1997, 2000). Because in the latter method the PR is activated by phosphorylation following an intracellular cascade of enzyme actions, and not by binding with its usual ligand (P), this method of activation has been referred to as "ligand independent." In support of the possibility that DA may activate the PR in "ligand-independent" fashion in castrated male rats, the PR antagonist RU-58486 blocked the ability of the DA agonist apomorphine to restore mounting behavior in long-term castrated male rats (Du *et al.*, 1997). The ER antagonist tamoxifen and the AR antagonist flutamide had similar inhibitory effects. Thus, although the male rats had been castrated for approximately two months, and had not mounted for at least two consecutive weeks before the DA agonist was administered, apomorphine restored some mounting, and blocking the steroid receptors rendered apomorphine ineffective.

D. Possible Role of Membrane Effects of Steroid Hormones

Steroid effects on protein synthesis are apparently necessary for T's facilitation of copulation (Hlinak and Madlafousek, 1982; McGinnis and Kahn, 1997; Yahr and Ulibarri, 1987). However, E has been reported to have very rapid effects on ion channels in neuron membranes (Clarke *et al.*, 2000; Kelly *et al.*, 1999; Mermelstein *et al.*, 1996; Norfleet *et al.*, 2000; Watters and Dorsa, 1998; Xiao and Becker, 1998). In addition, P and its metabolites enhance the functioning of GABA$_A$ receptors in an agonist-like manner (Majewska *et al.*, 1986), thereby increasing chloride influx and hyperpolarizing neurons. (See Chapter 69.) There have been reports of effects of T on cell firing within the medial preoptic area (MPOA) within minutes (Pfaff and Pfaffmann, 1969) or seconds (Yamada, 1979) in castrated male rats. It is possible that these effects were mediated via aromatization of T to E within the target tissues. However, neurons maintained in MPOA slices and perfused with solutions containing either T or E showed increases, or more rarely decreases, in firing rate within minutes of hormone administration (Silva and Boulant, 1986). These neurons typically responded to either T or E, but not both, and the distributions of T-sensitive and E-sensitive neurons tended to be different, with T-sensitive neurons located in the middle slice and more ventral and medial than E-sensitive neurons, and the E-sensitive neurons distributed more evenly throughout the three slices. Many of these same neurons also responded rapidly to changes in temperature, especially to warming. Therefore, MPOA neurons can respond rapidly to androgen administration, and those responses appear not to arise from aromatization to E. Yet it is clear that the behaviorally important effects of steroid hormones require hours, in the case of restoration of *ex copula* reflexes, or days, in the case of copulation. Therefore, rapid membrane effects of steroid hormones are clearly not sufficient for behavioral facilitation of male copulatory behavior. However, it is not known whether they may contribute to such facilitation.

There is evidence for a rapid onset of the action of T on erectile function (Sachs and Leipheimer, 1988). EMG recordings were made of bulbospongiosus muscle activity during tests of touch-based erections in male rats castrated several weeks earlier. Animals were tested immediately after injections of T or oil vehicle. Although none of the males displayed any erections, penile muscle activity was observed in significantly more of the androgen-treated males, sometimes within 5 minutes after injection. The rapid action on penile muscle contractions suggested that this effect of T did not depend on genomic activation. In a related study (Meisel *et al.*, 1986), administration of the antibiotic anisomycin, a potent inhibitor of protein synthesis, to

male rats did not affect the short-latency (within 24 hours) activation by T of touch-based erections, their maintenance by T, or their waning following castration. Thus, protein synthesis did not seem to be a necessary component of the activation of touch-based erections by T.

E. Individual Differences

1. Hormone Levels

There is great individual variability in sexual motivation and copulatory ability. As noted above, hormonal levels may be one factor in the variable restoration of copulation or *ex copula* erections in castrated male rats or in hypogonadal men. However, while hormone levels may account for some variability, individual differences in responsiveness to hormones are probably more important. Hormone levels are typically well above the threshold levels necessary to stimulate sexual interest and copulatory ability. The individual differences in hormone responsiveness were demonstrated in experiments on guinea pigs (Grunt and Young, 1952, 1953) and, later, in rats (Larsson, 1966). Animals were classified as having high, medium, or low sex drive before castration. Following castration, the animals with low drive were the first to lose copulatory behavior, and those with high drive were the last. (See Fig. 9.) Furthermore, upon replacement with a standard low dose of T, the animals fell into the same classification as before castration, even though all had the same amount of hormone replacement. Therefore, responsiveness to hormones, rather than hormone levels themselves, appear to be more important in determining sex drive.

A similar conclusion was derived from a study in which plasma levels of T were determined for male rats that were classified as copulators or noncopulators (Damassa *et al.*, 1977). The known copulators, whose T levels ranged between 2 and 3 ng/ml of plasma, were then castrated. They next received T-containing Silastic implants of different lengths, which resulted in different plasma levels of T. Normal copulatory behavior was restored in most animals, including those with very low T levels. These data confirm the earlier findings that responsiveness to T is more important than hormone levels in determining copulatory ability (Grunt and Young, 1952, 1953; Larsson, 1966). As noted above, high T

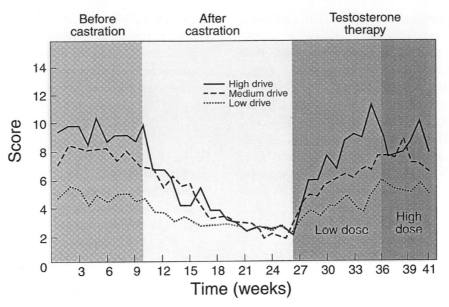

FIGURE 9 Individual differences in sex drive in guinea pigs before and after castration and testosterone restoration. Guinea pigs were classified as having high, medium, or low sex drive, based on behavioral assessments. They were then castrated, and all animals showed a gradual decline, eventually reaching similar low levels of sexual behavior. Both low- and high-dose testosterone replacement restored copulatory behavior; each group displayed behavior similar to that shown before castration. There was not a close correspondence between blood androgen levels and copulatory ability. Therefore, individual differences in sexual behavior are more likely related to variation in target-tissue sensitivity to androgens. [Figure is reprinted from Grunt and Young (1952).]

levels in the testes are important for sperm formation and maturation; high T levels also contribute to the maintenance of other masculine traits, including aggression and the secondary sex characteristics according to which females choose their mates (Andersson, 1994; Short, 1979).

2. Characteristics of the Target Tissues

One mechanism that may account for some individual differences in copulatory ability is the number of ERs in the MPOA (A. S. Clark *et al.*, 1985). Although uptake and metabolism of T in the MPOA was not different in sexually active and inactive male rats, the sexually inactive males had fewer ERs in the MPOA, compared to the active males. Other potential factors include differences in the metabolizing enzymes (aromatase and 5α-reductase) in brain, spinal cord, or peripheral tissue and differences in capacities of affected cells to synthesize the requisite proteins.

3. Sexual and Social Experience

Repeated sexual experience of male rats confers an increase in copulatory "efficiency," including fewer mounts and intromissions before ejaculation and shorter latencies to mount, intromit, and ejaculate, compared to sexually naive animals (Dewsbury, 1969; Larsson, 1978). (Note the previous caveat that decreased numbers of intromissions before ejaculation may, in fact, be less effective in promoting a progestational state in female rats.) In addition, sexually experienced male rats (Claro *et al.*, 1995; de Jonge *et al.*, 1989; Kondo, 1992; Pfaus and Wilkins, 1995; Saito and Moltz, 1986), hamsters (Lisk and Heimann, 1980; Meredith, 1986), and cats (Rosenblatt and Aronson, 1958) have shown reduced susceptibility to the effects of castration, various brain lesions, and other manipulations. However, prior experience did not prolong copulation after castration in some rats (Bloch and Davidson, 1968) or dogs (Hart, 1968b). Furthermore, differences due to experience in male hamsters in the Lisk and Heimann (1980) study may have been exaggerated by the brief (10 minute) test duration. Therefore, sexual experience sometimes, but not always, protects against surgical or other insults.

Previous pairing of a neutral odor (almond or lemon) with sexual activity resulted in preferential ejaculation with a female bearing that odor, despite indiscriminate copulation with scented and unscented females (Kippin *et al.*, 1998). Both ejaculation and the postejaculatory refractory interval were necessary unconditioned stimuli for this association (reviewed in Pfaus, 1999). Random presentation of the odor did not result in such preferential behavior, and pairing the odor with a nonreceptive female resulted in avoidance of females scented with that odor. Furthermore, presentation of the odor on a cotton ball activated the expression of Fos, the protein product of the immediate-early gene *c-fos,* in several brain areas associated with mating (MPOA, nucleus accumbens, and lateral hypothalamus; see below).

In sexually experienced, but not inexperienced males, exposure to an inaccessible receptive female resulted in an increase in touch-based erections and in decreased erection latencies (Sachs and Liu, 1998). Furthermore, this facilitative effect increased during a 10-minute interval following exposure to the female. Section of the hypogastric nerve, which has been suggested to mediate "psychogenic" erections (see section on innervation of the penis), did not diminish the facilitative effect of female exposure on touch-based erections, although it did produce inconsistent impairments of copulation.

4. Age

The development of copulation in pubertal rats is quite variable, with the first mount appearing between 40 and 50 days, the first intromission between 44 and 75 days, and the first ejaculation between 48 and 75 days (reviewed in Meisel and Sachs, 1994). This behavioral development is clearly hormone dependent, since prepubertal castration prevents the appearance of sexual behavior (Beach and Holz-Tucker, 1949; Larsson, 1967). Furthermore, administration of exogenous T (Baum, 1972; Carr *et al.,* 1970; Södersten *et al.,* 1985) or E (Baum, 1972; Södersten *et al.,* 1985) significantly accelerated the onset of copulation, with E hav-

ing much more potent effects. However, the onset of copulation preceded the pubertal surge of T by several days (Sachs and Meisel, 1979; Södersten *et al.,* 1977).

The development of touch-based erections also appeared prior to the T surge (Sachs and Meisel, 1979). An unexpected outcome of this study was the coincidence in the development of mounts and erections (41 vs 40 days), intromission and anteroflexions (both 44 days), and ejaculation and cups (both 48 days). Unlike the constraints on the developmental sequence observed for copulation, the expression of erections (including cups) and anteroflexions are independent events. Thus, there were no a priori reasons to expect that the motor patterns for copulation and the individual penile responses should have a coincident development.

Maturation of the effector systems appears not to be the limiting factor in the expression of penile reflexes. Spinally transected males showed penile erections on the first test, at 28 days of age, 10 days earlier than control males (Meisel and Sachs, 1980). Anteroflexions were first seen at 30 days of age in transected males, but at 41 days in control males. Therefore, as with copulation, the maturation of the motor systems for penile reflexes predates the actual appearance of the behavior.

Early in development the penile sheath is attached to the penis so that the penis cannot be extruded from the sheath. Androgens stimulate cornification of the epithelial cells connecting the penis to the sheath, a process leading to preputial sheath separation (Korenbrot *et al.,* 1977). However, sheath separation occurs before the pubertal surge of T (Korenbrot *et al.,* 1977) and after the onset of mounting and touch-based erections (Sachs and Meisel, 1979). Furthermore, some animals also exhibited intromission patterns and ex copula penile anteroflexions before preputial separation. Therefore, it seems unlikely that the motor patterns associated with intromission or anteroflexions depend on preputial separation. In contrast, preputial separation antedated the development of cups and ejaculation by several days. A similar dissociation of sheath separation and copulation was observed in bulls, with mounting preceding, and ejaculation following, sheath separation (Ashdown, 1962; Folman and Volcani, 1966; Price and Wallach, 1991). Preputial separation may afford the degree of penile extensibility necessary for the glans to receive sufficient stimulation for ejaculation to occur. However, the fact that female rats can display the behavioral pattern of ejaculation (Emery and Sachs, 1975), despite their very small and minimally extensible phallus, is a reminder of our limited knowledge of the sensory and mechanical prerequisites of some sexual responses.

There is great variation in the ability of aged males to copulate. In one study aged (30 months old) male mice had lower gonadal mass, rates of spermatogenesis, and plasma T levels than did younger (6 months old) mice (Bronson and Desjardins, 1982). However, some aged males could copulate, whereas others could not, despite similar plasma T levels. Therefore, neither age nor plasma T levels could fully account for the differences in behavior.

A similar dissociation between hormone levels and copulation was observed in old male monkeys (Chambers and Phoenix, 1981; Chambers *et al.,* 1981). T levels in old (20 years old) males were similar to those of younger (10 years old) males. However, old males had higher binding of T to T-binding globulin (67%) than did young males (57%). Sexual activity was not correlated with total or free T levels in the blood of old males, but there was a significant negative correlation between their mean percentage T binding and six major indices of sexual performance. However, T treatment did not bring castrated old rhesus monkeys to higher levels of performance than intact age mates (Phoenix and Chambers, 1986), nor did it improve the sexual performance of gonadally intact old males relative to that of young monkeys (Phoenix and Chambers, 1988).

5. Developmental Influences

Because this topic is covered in detail in Chapter 70, we will mention these influences only briefly here. Prenatal stress or alcohol can decrease the ability of adult male rats to copulate to ejaculation (Ward *et al.,* 1996; Ward and Weisz, 1980). The effects of stress and alcohol exposure were maximal if they occurred during the prenatal peak of T secretion, on days 18 and 19 of gestation (Ward and Weisz, 1980). In addition, maternal licking of the male genitalia contributes to later sexual competence (Moore, 1984).

6. Genotype

There are substantial differences among species, genetic strains, and individuals in behavioral responsiveness to hormones. The classic paradigm for demonstrating the effects of gonadal hormones on behavior is to trace the consequences of castration and hormone replacement. This removal and reinstatement of androgen may be accomplished surgically or functionally, e.g., by natural or experimental variation in photoperiod known to result in gonadal regression and recrudescence. However, sexual behavior does not invariably wane rapidly following castration: in some species, e.g., dogs, cats, rhesus monkeys, and humans, males have been known to copulate for years after castration (Aronson, 1959; Beach, 1947, 1948; Hart, 1974a). Conversely, androgen replacement does not guarantee behavioral restoration. In some species, e.g., red deer (Lincoln *et al.,* 1972), there is a time, following the regression of the testes due to changes in photoperiod, that males are insensitive to the usual restorative effects of testosterone injections. What are the sources of this variability among species?

Among the earliest to consider this question systematically was Beach (1947). The evidence then at hand suggested that after castration, male sexual behavior declines rapidly in rodents and lagomorphs, more slowly in carnivores and ungulates, and slower yet in primates. This pattern was interpreted by Beach as reflecting the evolution of progressive encephalization of the regulation of sexual behavior, with a consequent decline in the strict control of the behavior by hormones. A corollary of this hypothesis was that with greater cortical control should come a greater influence of sexual experience on the postcastration retention of copulatory potential.

In 1959 Aronson reviewed Beach's hypotheses and found the evidence less than compelling. His review of the literature on fishes, amphibians, reptiles, birds, and mammals revealed that within each of these phyletic groups there were species in which the decline of mating behavior was abrupt after gonadectomy (the decline generally being far more rapid for females than for males), and other species in which at least the male's mating behavior was commonly retained for a period of weeks, months, or longer. Furthermore, considerable individual differences in postcastration potential for copulation have contributed to the difficulty of understanding the phyletic differences. Aronson emphasized the importance of avoiding unitary conceptions of sexual behavior and, instead, of attending to the complexity of the acts, including somewhat separate—but not independent—mechanisms regulating attraction to the female from a distance, the proximal stimulation of penile erection, and the accumulation of ejaculatory excitation.

Hart (1974a) undertook a comprehensive review of copulation, aggression, and scent marking by examining androgenic effects on central neural and peripheral nonneural structures and the social, experiential, and environmental milieu of different species. Hart rejected Beach's progressive encephalization hypothesis on the strong grounds that the differences among humans, rhesus monkeys, cats, dogs, and rats in retention of copulatory behavior after castration were poorly correlated with the proportion of neocortex to cerebral cortex in these species. Furthermore, although prior copulatory experience has a major effect on retention of copulation after castration in cats (Rosenblatt and Aronson, 1958), such an effect has been weak or absent for dogs (Hart, 1968b), rats (Bloch and Davidson, 1968), and other species. Thus, among different species neither the degree of precastration sexual experience nor the size of the cortex predicts the duration of retention of copulatory potential after castration. Fewer data were available to Hart on the effects of castration on aggression and scent marking, but in general these effects seemed to parallel the data from copulation and the conclusions drawn from them.

Hart proposed two complementary hypotheses to account for these species differences. First, he assumed that the effects of castration on a behavior should reflect the relation between the natural waxing and waning of gonadal hormones and the behaviors that are sensitive to those hormones. Accordingly, in species that breed seasonally but that maintain a dominance hierarchy throughout the year (e.g., rhesus monkeys), one would expect a relatively rapid waning of heterosexual copulatory behavior after castration but, perhaps, an indefinite retention of aggressive behavior. In rhesus as in many species, however, the picture is complicated by the noncopulatory contexts in which mounting and sexual presenting are performed.

Hart's second hypothesis concerned the relative dependence on early (organizing) and concurrent (activating) hormone levels. Hart considered that the species whose mating behavior "survived" castration are those that require only early organizational influ-

ences, whereas species whose sexual behavior was lost after castration are those that require both organizational and activational influences. However, postcastrational loss of function is a graded effect, which may occur over days, weeks, or years, and which has large individual differences within species. Therefore in at least this application the organizational-activational typology may better be viewed in terms of continua rather than discrete classes.

Since most effects of hormones on behavior are mediated through genomic action in the nervous system, genetic differences within species, as well as between species, should predict differences in their responses to hormonal manipulations (Vale *et al.,* 1973). Research with inbred and hybrid strains of mice, guinea pigs, and rats amply confirms this prediction. Some of the earliest work with guinea pigs, summarized by Young (1969), documented a number of important effects. For example, strain differences in the mean age of first appearance of mounts, intromissions, and ejaculations could not be overcome by injecting the slower strains with androgen, thereby suggesting that differences in neural development, rather than in androgen titers or androgen sensitivity, were responsible for the different rates of behavioral puberty. Similarly, strain differences in the amount of male sexual behavior displayed during a test persisted after males of those strains were castrated and injected daily with 5 mg/kg of testosterone propionate. The most sexually vigorous population was derived from heterogeneous stock. Sounding a now familiar note, Young (1969, p. 16) commented, "The mating behavior of the male guinea pig is not inherited as a unitary trait. The elements composing the pattern of behavior show a considerable degree of independence from one another." Presumably, the different elements could have differential sensitivity to gonadal steroids in their organization and activation.

This last point was addressed in research on inbred mouse strains (Vale *et al.,* 1973). The three-day-old offspring of three strains of mice were injected with 1 mg testosterone propionate, 0.5 mg estradiol benzoate, or oil vehicle. The treated animals were tested as adults for male and female sexual behavior, with or without the injection of ovarian steroids. For most behavioral variables reliable effects were found due to treatment, strain, and the interaction of treatment and strain. The authors concluded that because of the interactions, "the effects of neonatal hormone treatment cannot be considered separately from those of genotype" (Vale *et al.*, 1973, p. 324).

Other research with inbred strains of guinea pigs and mice addressed the question of why species vary so much in their retention of male sexual behavior after castration (McGill, 1977; McGill and Tucker, 1964; Young, 1969). Rather consistently in these studies, males of inbred strains lost their copulatory potential after castration more rapidly than did male offspring of crosses between the strains. These results led to the inference that heterozygosity may promote retention of copulatory behavior after castration (McGill and Haynes, 1973; McGill and Tucker, 1964). One asset of this hypothesis was that it could be invoked to account for some of the observed species differences: perhaps monkeys, dogs, and cats retained mating behavior after castration longer than rats, mice, and rabbits because the laboratory population of rodents and lagomorphs were more highly inbred than the populations of primates and carnivores.

A trilogy of papers (Manning and Thompson, 1976; McGill and Manning, 1976; Thompson *et al.*, 1976) cast doubt on this hypothesis while generating further evidence for the influence of genotype on hormone-behavior interactions. The first of these papers (McGill and Manning, 1976) used a number of diallele crosses of inbred strains in a predictive study of copulatory retention after castration. Neither total genetic heterozygosity, nor heterozygosity at any particular locus, predicted the average performance of the several strains and their crosses. Within strains there were substantial individual differences. For example, in weekly postcastration mating tests of 22 B6D2F1 (BDF1) males in one treatment condition (injected with oil neonatally), four males never ejaculated more than one week after castration (noncontinuers), whereas nine males continued to show the ejaculatory pattern in most tests more than a year after castration (continuers). Males of the reciprocal cross (D2B6F1), which were genetically identical on the autosomes, tended to stop mating much sooner, thereby suggesting sex linkage or maternal influences on the resistance to castration. The differential effects of castration were cast in terms of differential sensitivity of the "arousal" and "copulatory" mechanisms posited by Beach (1956), a sensitivity regulated by the in-

teraction of the genotype with hormones and experience.

The second paper of the trilogy (Thompson *et al.*, 1976) combined adrenalectomy with castration to help establish that the retention of sexual behavior in castrated BDF1 males was not due to unusually large production of androgen by the adrenal glands. In the final paper (Manning and Thompson, 1976), the postcastration sexual behavior of males of this strain was characterized more precisely: in contrast to castrated rats, male BDF1 mice required more mounts, more intromissions, and more time to achieve ejaculation after castration than before. An additional study demonstrated that the postweaning social experience of these males prior to castration influenced their postcastration sexual performance. As a whole the three papers further established the essential roles of genotype, hormonal status, social experience, and individual differences of undetermined origin in the retention of sexual behavior after castration.

More recently, the ejaculatory reflex of castrated BDF1 continuer males was inhibited by administration of the aromatase inhibitor androst-1,4,6-triene-3,17-dione (ATD) (Sinchak and Clemens, 1989). Furthermore, administration of E to castrated noncontinuers resulted in restoration of copulation to precastration levels (Wee *et al.*, 1988). Therefore, the ability of BDF1 males to copulate following castration appears to be dependent on E. However, a subsequent study found no decrease in E titers following castration, although T declined to very low levels (Sinchak *et al.*, 1996). Furthermore, there were no differences between continuers and noncontinuers in plasma levels of T or E or in either aromatase activity or ERs in the preoptic area (POA), amygdala, or hypothalamus. The authors suggested that nongonadal E is important for the maintenance of copulation in these animals, but that differences in response to external stimuli or other processes in the cascade of ER-initiated events, besides aromatization and presence of ERs, may account for the difference between continuers and noncontinuers.

The number and size of neurons in the sexually dimorphic spinal nucleus of the bulbocavernosus (SNB) varied according to both genotype and hormonal condition (Wee and Clemens, 1987). Gonadally intact DBA/2J males had fewer SNB motoneurons than did C57B1/6J or B6D2F1 hybrids, but there were no strain differences in soma size of these cells. However, following castration the number of SNB neurons, but not their size, was decreased in C57 males (the maternal strain), whereas the size, but not the number, of SNB neurons was decreased in the BDA males (the paternal strain). Both the size and number of neurons were decreased in the BDF1 hybrids. Therefore, both genotype and hormonal state influenced neurons in the SNB.

IV. EFFECTS OF SYSTEMICALLY OR INTRACEREBROVENTRICULARLY ADMINISTERED DRUGS

Steroid hormones influence sexual behavior primarily by relatively slow effects on gene transcription. However, sexual behavior comprises rapid, highly interactive behavioral elements. Therefore, the slow effects of hormones must be translated into rapid, moment-to-moment neural patterns. Hormones bias neural responding so that sexually relevant sensory input is processed efficiently and linked to appropriate, well-organized motor output. Thus, hormones can increase the sensitivity of sensory structures, the CNS connectivity, and the strength and innervation of certain muscles. A major step in the translation process is the up- (or down-) regulation of neurotransmitter or neuromodulator synthesis, release, receptors, second-messenger systems, or degradation. In order to determine which neurotransmitters influence behavior, the most common procedure is to administer agonists or antagonists of certain neurotransmitter receptors or drugs that affect synthesis, degradation, or release of neurotransmitters. Because no drug is entirely selective for its nominal effect, it is necessary to block the effect of an agonist with an appropriate antagonist to show that the effect was mediated by the particular receptor and to replicate the effect with a drug of different chemical composition that targets the same receptor.

There are advantages to systemic or intracerebroventricular administration of drugs. First, neurotransmitters may act synergistically in numerous brain areas; therefore, to understand the role of the neurotransmitter throughout the nervous system, drugs must be distributed broadly. In addition, the sites of drug action may not be known a priori. Finally, drugs designed for clinical treatment must be given systemically. However, drugs may produce opposing or interfering effects at different sites. To understand the effects of a neurotransmitter within a given site one must target a drug at that site. Therefore, a full understanding of a neurotransmitter's influence will require drugs to be both targeted to specific sites and, in other experiments, available widely throughout the system. (Table 2 summarizes the effects of systemically or intraventricularly administered drugs on sexual behavior.)

A. Dopamine

The catecholamines, dopamine (DA), norepinephrine (NE), and epinephrine, are formed from tyrosine by the rate-limiting enzyme, tyrosine hydroxylase, producing L-DOPA, which is in turn decarboxylated by aromatic amino acid decarboxylase to DA. In noradrenergic neurons NE is formed from DA by dopamine-β-hydroxylase. In a few neurons, phenylethanolamine N-methyl transferase converts NE to epinephrine. The major dopaminergic cell groups are those in the substantia nigra (A9) and ventral tegmental area (A10), which ascend, respectively, to the caudate-putamen (dorsal striatum) in the nigrostriatal tract and to the nucleus accumbens, prefrontal cortex, and other limbic sites in the mesocorticolimbic tract (reviewed in Fallon, 1988). Several cell groups also reside in the hypothalamus, including the periventricular (A14) perikarya, which are distributed along the length of the third ventricle (reviewed in Moore and Lookingland, 1995). The rostral periventricular neurons send axons laterally into the adjacent medial preoptic nucleus and anterior hypothalamus.

DA has been recognized since the late 1960s and early 1970s as a pro-sexual neurotransmitter. Soon after L-DOPA, the precursor of DA, became a common treatment for Parkinson's disease, notable side effects, including increased libido and sexual potency, were reported (Barbeau, 1969; Bowers *et al.*, 1971). The classic DA agonist apomorphine has been used for some years to treat erectile dysfunction (Lal *et al.*, 1984, 1987), and a new sublingual formulation of apomorphine has been effective clinically with fewer side effects, such as nausea (Dula *et al.*, 2000; Padma-Nathan *et al.*, 1999; reviewed in Padma-Nathan and Giuliano, 2001). In rats, too, systemic administration of L-DOPA

TABLE 2
Summary of Effects on Male Sexual Behavior of Systemically or Intraventricularly Administered Drugs[a]

Transmitter	Drug	Motiv.	Cop.	Ejac.	Rev. Sat.	T-B Er.	S.Em.	NCE	Drug-Ind.	U-G	Cavern.	Other
DA	Mixed ag.	↑	↑	↑	↑	↑	↑		↑			
	Mixed antag.	↓	↓	↓		↓						
	D₁ ag.		↑						↓?↑?			
	D₁ antag.			↓		↓						
	D₂ ag.		Lo ↑, Hi ↓	↑					↑?↓?			
	D₂ antag.		↓	↓					↑?↓?			
NE	Precursor or symp. stim.		↑	↑		↑				↑		
	Lesions		↑↓			↑↓	↓			↓		
	α₂ ag.		↓			↑						
	α₂ antag.		↑	↓		↓	↓				↓	
	α₁ ag.		↓		↑	↑	↑					
	α₁ antag.		↑↓ ↔									
	β ag. or antag.		↔									
5-HT	5-HT or precursor, SSRI	↓	↓	↑						↑		
	Lesions or depletion		↑[b]							↓		
	5-HT₁ₐ ag.		↑	↓	↑	↑↓						
	5-HT₁ᵦ ag.		↓	↑		↓		↓				
	5-HT₂C ag.		↓	↓								
	5-HT₂ (nonselective) ag.		↓					↑	↑		↑	
	5-HT₂ antag.		↓						↑			
ACh	Nonspec. ag.		↓	↓								
	Nonspec. antag.		↓						↑			
	Musc. ag.		↑	↑								
	Musc. antag.		↓	↓								
GABA	Gen. ↑ (↓ catabolism)		↓									↓ ischio. muscle
	GABAₐ ag.		↓									
	GABAₐ antag.		↔									
	GABAᵦ ag.		↓									
	GABAᵦ antag.		↔									

Continued

Transmitter	Drug	Motiv.	Cop.	Ejac.	Rev. Sat.	T-B Er.	S.Em.	NCE	Drug-Ind.	U-G	Cavern.	Other
Opioids	Mixed antag.	↓	↑↓	↑	↑	(↓)						↑ bonding
	μ ag.		→			→	→					
	κ ag.		→									
	δ ag.		→	↑								
OT	OT		lo↑, hi↓	↑		↓			↑			
	OT antag.		→						→			
NO	L-Arg/donors	↔↓	↑	↑		↑					↔ (↑)	↓ fertil.
	NOS inhib.	↑	↓	↑		→	↑					
GnRH	GnRH	↑	↑↓ ↔	↑								
PRL	Pit. transplants, PRL-tumors, drugs ↑ PRL		↓ (↑)			→						↓DA in MPOA/AH
CRF			→	→								
CCK				↔↑								
VIP			↓								↑	
GAL	GAL	↓	→									
	GAL antag.		↑↔									
NPY			→			↔						
PGE₂			↑									↑temp.
ANG II			→	↑								

[a] *Abbreviations*: Motiv., motivation; Cop., copulation; Ejac., ejaculation; Rev. Sat., reverse satiety; T-B Er., touch-based erection; S.Em., seminal emission; NCE, noncontact erection; Drug-Ind., drug-induced erection; U-G, urethro-genital reflex; Cavern., cavernous nerve firing or intracavernous pressure; DA, dopamine; NE, norepinephrine; 5-HT, serotonin; ACh, acetylcholine; GABA, gamma amino butyric acid; OT, oxytocin; NO, nitric oxide; GnRH, gonadotropin releasing hormone; PRL, prolactin; CRF, corticotropin releasing factor; CCK, cholecystokinin; VIP, vasoactive intestinal peptide; GAL, galanin; NPY, neuropeptide Y; PGE₂, prostaglandin E₂; ANG II, angiotensin II; ag., agonist; antag., antagonist; Symp. stim., stimulation of sympathetic nervous system; Musc., muscarinic; ischio., ischiocavernosus; L-Arg, L-arginine; NOS, nitric oxide synthase; Pit., pituitary; MPOA/AH, medial preoptic area/anterior hypothalamus; fertil., fertility; temp., temperature.

Arrows in different directions for the same measure indicate contrasting findings from different researchers. *Question marks* indicate that there is disagreement about the interpretation or reliability of the effect.

Arrows in parentheses indicate that the effect was found only with one drug dose or only in one group of animals.

[b] Effect reported only in ferrets.

and of DA agonists facilitated copulation and increased touch-based and drug-induced erections (reviewed in Bitran and Hull, 1987; Guiliano and Alland, 2001; Melis and Argiolas, 1995). Sexually sluggish males were induced to copulate, the time and the number of intromissions preceding ejaculation were reduced, and the numbers of ejaculations were increased by L-DOPA and/or apomorphine. Apomorphine has more recently restored copulation in sexually satiated rats (Mas *et al.,* 1995a; Rodriguez-Manzo, 1999) or socially stressed mice (Sugiura *et al.,* 1997). Similarly, DA releasers have decreased the very long mount and intromission latencies that resulted from damage to the medial frontal cortex (Ågmo and Villalpando, 1995). Even in short-term (Malmnas, 1976) and long-term (Scaletta and Hull, 1990) castrated male rats, and in castrates with suboptimal T replacement (Malmnas, 1973), apomorphine partially restored copulation. Indeed, apomorphine injected systemically in male mice lacking the gene for the estrogen receptor alpha (ERα) fully restored copulation (Wersinger and Rissman, (2000). (See Fig. 10.) These ERα "knockout" (ERα KO) males usually exhibit little or no copulatory behavior (Ogawa *et al.,* 1997, 1998; Wersinger *et al.,* 1997). Even female ERα KO mice mounted other females when injected with apomorphine (Wersinger and Rissman, 2000). This is the

first report of full restoration of male sexual behavior by a DA agonist in animals lacking either T or the ERα receptor. Furthermore, it demonstrates that the ERα receptor is not necessary, either during early sex differentiation or during adulthood, for normal masculine sexual behavior.

Daily injections of amphetamine (which elicits DA release) result in sensitization of amphetamine's motor activational effects. After sensitizaton has occurred, animals show greater locomotor response to low doses of amphetamine that were previously ineffective. This type of sensitization regimen also resulted in facilitation of sexual behavior of sexually naive male rats, without additional amphetamine on the day of testing (Fiorino and Phillips, 1999b). Thus, the same (presumably dopaminergic) mechanisms that result in drug sensitization also "cross-sensitize" to a natural motivated behavior. This finding suggests that the enhancement of copulatory efficiency that results from repeated sexual experience (see above) may also be mediated, in part, by sensitization of dopaminergic activity.

In confirmation of the facilitative actions of endogenous DA, various systemically injected antagonists have inhibited copulatory behavior of sexually experienced rats (Ågmo and Fernandez, 1989; Ahlenius and Larsson, 1984a, 1990; Malmnas, 1973; Pfaus and Phillips, 1989; Tagliamonte *et al.,* 1974). Some antagonist-treated males were unable copulate, while those that did copulate exhibited longer latencies to intromit and to ejaculate. Two DA antagonists (pimozide and cis-flupenthixol) decreased the number of sexually naive males that initiated copulation on their first encounter with a female, and fewer males that did copulate were able to achieve ejaculation (Ågmo and Picker, 1990). Haloperidol decreased the numbers of touch-based erections; however, domperidone, which does not cross the blood-brain barrier, had no effect (Pehek *et al.,* 1988a).

Mild tail pinch has been used to promote copulation in sexually inactive male rats. Tail pinch increased the percentage of castrated males, maintained on low doses of T, that copulated (Leyton and Stewart, 1996). Systemic administration of a DA antagonist (pimozide) blocked that facilitation, suggesting that the effect was mediated by activation of DA receptors. An opioid antagonist (naloxone) was similarly effective; thus, tail pinch may have activated the midbrain DA systems via

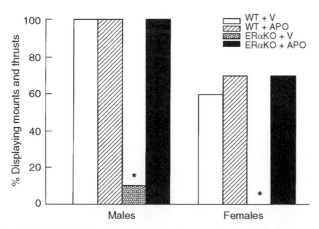

FIGURE 10 The percentage of wild-type (WT) and estrogen receptor α knock-out (ERαKO) mice treated with either vehicle (V) or apomorphine (APO) that show mounting and thrusting behavior toward a receptive female. *Significantly lower than the other groups, $p < .05$. [Figure reprinted from Wersinger and Rissman (2000) with permission.]

an opioid mechanism, resulting in behavioral activation.

Mice with a deletion of the gene for tyrosine hydroxylase in dopaminergic, but not noradrenergic, neurons required daily administration of L-DOPA for survival (Szczypka *et al.*, 1998). Male DA−/− mice exhibited greater aggressive mounting of intruder males and nonestrous females following their daily injection of L-DOPA. These DA-deficient males were less dependent on T than wild-type males; they continued to mount receptive females up to 21 days postcastration, whereas wild-type males stopped mounting after one week. Furthermore, lower doses of T were sufficient to restore the behavior 7 days after beginning hormone restoration. Similarly, a low dose of L-DOPA stimulated more mounting of nonestrous females by DA−/− males, compared to wild-type males. Therefore, DA−/− males were more sensitive to both T and DA than were wild-type males, perhaps because of more efficient coupling of DA receptors to their second messenger systems.

DA receptors have been classified into two families. The D_1 family consists of D_1 and D_5 subtypes, and the D_2 family includes the D_2, D_3, and D_4 subtypes. D_1 receptors were originally defined as those that stimulate adenylyl cyclase, whereas D_2 receptors inhibit adenylyl cyclase and also influence certain ion channels and the phosphoinositide system. DA and apomorphine stimulate both receptor families; their behavioral and physiological effects depend on the ratio, affinity, and efficacy of the receptors available to the agonist. However, drugs have been designed to bind with greater affinity to certain subtypes than to others. Such selective agonists and antagonists have been used to analyze the roles of the different subtypes in different aspects of copulation.

Stimulation of D_2-like receptors has frequently been associated with enhancement of ejaculatory processes. D_2/D_3 agonists (SND 919 and B-HT 920) and a selective D_3 agonist (7-OH-DPAT) decreased the time and numbers of intromissions before ejaculation in sexually active rats but were ineffective in sexually inactive males (Ferrari and Giuliani, 1995, 1996a,b; Giuliani and Ferrari, 1996). A D_2/D_3 antagonist (eticlopride) blocked the premature ejaculation elicited by a D_2/D_3 (SND 919) (Ferrari and Giuliani, 1994) or a D_3 (7-OH-DPAT) (Ahlenius and Larsson, 1995) agonist, thereby

confirming the receptor specificity. The stimulation of ejaculation by D_2 activity may be mediated by cholinergic effects, because the muscarinic antagonist atropine inhibited the pro-ejaculation effects of both dopaminergic and cholinergic agonists (Zarrindast *et al.*, 1994). However, the effectiveness of DA agonists is very dose-dependent. For example, a D_3/D_2 agonist (quinelorane) facilitated copulation when administered in low doses but impaired the behavior when higher doses were used (Foreman and Hall, 1987). Apparently, stereotyped behavior elicited by the higher doses interfered with copulation. Administration of a D_1 agonist (SKF-81297) to the DA-deficient mice described above increased their mounting, whereas a D_2 agonist (quinpirole) stimulated little mounting, perhaps because it elicited considerable stereotyped behavior, even at very low doses (Szczypka *et al.*, 1998).

The roles of D_1 and D_2 receptors in *ex copula* penile erection are unclear. One series of experiments suggested that stimulation of D_2-like receptors mediated drug-induced erections in unrestrained males in a neutral arena, whereas stimulation of D_1-like receptors inhibited such erections (Zarrindast *et al.*, 1992). However, a D_2/D_3 antagonist [(−) eticlopride], administered with either cocaine or several presumed-selective D_2 agonists actually increased drug-induced erections in unrestrained males, thus suggesting that stimulation of D_2 receptors may, instead, inhibit those erections (Ferrari and Giuliani, 1996b, 1997). It now seems likely that those presumed-selective D_2 agonists have substantial activity at D_1 receptors, as would cocaine indirectly, by increasing extracellular DA. Thus, blocking D_2 receptors may have uncovered proerectile effects due to stimulation of D_1 receptors. Touch-based erections in restrained, supine male rats also appear to be inhibited by D_2-like receptors. The D_3/D_2 agonist quinelorane, administered either systemically or into the MPOA, decreased the number of touch-based erections (Bitran *et al.*, 1989). As discussed below, intense stimulation of D_2 receptors in certain brain areas can shift autonomic balance away from parasympathetically mediated erection toward sympathetically mediated ejaculation.

The role of DA in the regulation of male sexual behavior is highly conserved. Systemic administration of a D_1 agonist (SKF-81297) in gonadectomized, P- or E-treated lizards of two species increased the proportion of individuals mounting and decreased mount latencies (Woolley *et al.*, 2001). *Cnemidophorine inornatus* is a diploid sexual species and the ancestral species of *C. uniparens,* a triploid, all-female, parthenogenetic species. The triploid parthenogenetic species, tested following E injections, was more sensitive to the D_1 agonist than was the diploid ancestral species, which was tested without concurrent hormonal treatment. The authors suggested that the E pretreatment may have upregulated D_1 receptors in sexually relevant brain areas. E has been shown to increase D_1 receptor gene transcription in cell cultures of neuroblastoma cells (Lee and Mouradian, 1999).

Additional evidence for evolutionary conservation of dopaminergic facilitation of male sexual behavior was obtained in castrated, T-replaced male Japanese quail. The D_1 agonist SKF-38393 and the D_2 antagonist spipirone stimulated copulatory performance but did not affect the amount of time spent in the proximity of a receptive female (Balthazart *et al.*, 1997). The D_1 antagonist SCH-23390 and the D_2 agonist quinpirole inhibited copulatory behavior, and quinpirole also decreased the time spent near a receptive female. Therefore, copulatory behavior in Japanese quail appears to be stimulated by activation of D_1 receptors and inhibited by stimulation of D_2 receptors.

B. Norepinephrine

Central noradrenergic neurons are located primarily in the locus coeruleus (A6) and cell groups (A1–5,7) scattered through the medulla and pons (reviewed in Kuhar *et al.*, 1999). The locus coeruleus projects via the dorsal noradrenergic bundle to the cerebral cortex and hippocampus, and the remaining cell groups project via the ventral noradrenergic bundle to the hypothalamus, amygdala, and septum. In addition, norepinephrine (NE) is the postganglionic neurotransmitter of most of the sympathetic nervous system.

There are apparently contradictory effects of noradrenergic drugs and lesions of NE pathways. Electrolytic lesions that included the ascending dorsal noradrenergic bundle in the midbrain produced facilitative effects in two studies, decreasing postejaculatory intervals and increasing the numbers of ejaculations in a 1-hr test (Clark, 1975, 1980). However, 6-OHDA lesions of the same area did not affect copu-

latory parameters (Clark, 1980). Electrolytic lesions of the locus coeruleus, a major site of NE cell bodies in the pons, or systemic inhibition of NE synthesis, using diethyl-dithiocarbamate (DDC), inhibited copulation in one study (McIntosh and Barfield, 1984) but not in a more recent one (Fernandez-Guasti and Rodriguez-Manzo, 1997). However, locus coeruleus lesions did block the facilitative effects of introduction of a novel female to sexually satiated males (the "Coolidge effect") and also decreased the facilitative effects of the serotonin 5-HT$_{1A}$ agonist 8-OH-DPAT in both satiated and nonsatiated males (Fernandez-Guasti and Rodriguez-Manzo, 1997).

NE release is under tonic inhibitory control by presynaptic α_2 autoreceptors. Inhibiting α_2 receptors with yohimbine resulted in increases in mounting, intromission, or both by sexually sluggish males (Clark *et al.*, 1984; Smith *et al.*, 1987), castrated males (J. T. Clark *et al.*, 1985b), and males with anesthetized genitals (Clark *et al.*, 1984). Yohimbine was also able to reverse sexual satiety (Rodriguez-Manzo and Fernandez-Guasti, 1994, 1995; Rodriguez-Manzo, 1999); however, yohimbine's effects were blocked by the DA antagonist haloperidol, thus suggesting that its effects were ultimately mediated via the DA system (Rodriguez-Manzo, 1999). However, a more selective α_2 antagonist (delaquamine) increased the sexual behavior score [which was devised by Tallentire *et al.* (1996) and was based on whether males mounted, intromitted, or ejaculated] in naive, gonadally intact males (Tallentire *et al.*, 1996). This α_2 antagonist also increased the numbers of castrates that mounted. Two other α_2 antagonists also facilitated copulatory behavior; rauwolscine decreased the intercopulatory interval and postejaculatory interval, and phentolamine decreased the ejaculation threshold (number of intromissions and time preceding ejaculation) (Clark, 1995). Therefore, blocking α_2 autoreceptors, thereby promoting NE release, appears to increase sexual performance.

Stimulating α_2 receptors with clonidine had effects opposite those of yohimbine: It inhibited copulation and touch-based *ex copula* erections (J. T. Clark *et al.*, 1985b; Clark and Smith, 1990). Similar inhibitory effects were observed with two other α_2 agonists, guanabenz and guanfacine (Clark, 1995). But high doses of yohimbine inhibited copulation (Sala *et al.*, 1990). Similarly, the NE precursor *dl*-threodihydroxyphenylserine, combined with a peripheral decarboxylase inhibitor (to restrict drug action to the CNS), increased mount and intromission latencies in both intact male rats and those with prefrontal cortex lesions (Ågmo and Villalpando, 1995). Thus, increased noradrenergic activity may not always facilitate copulation. The facilitative effects of moderate doses of yohimbine on sexual behavior may result via increased NE release and consequent stimulation of α_1 receptors; blocking α_1 receptors with prazosin or methoxamine impaired copulation and potentiated the suppressive effects of clonidine (J. T. Clark *et al.*, 1985b, 1987).

In keeping with NE's role in penile detumescence, high levels of peripheral sympathetic activity inhibited penile reflexes (Stefanick *et al.*, 1983). Also, in contrast to its generally facilitative effects on copulation, yohimbine inhibited touch-based erections and seminal emissions in *ex copula* tests (Smith *et al.*, 1987). However, stimulation of α_2 receptors with clonidine also inhibited the pro-erectile effect of electrical stimulation of the cavernous nerves (Lin *et al.*, 1988) and inhibited touch-based erections, as noted above (Clark and Smith, 1990). Thus, both stimulating and blocking α_2 receptors had similar inhibitory effects. These results suggest that low to moderate levels of NE activity facilitate erection but that excess activity is inhibitory. However, stimulating α_1 receptors with methoxamine inhibited touch-based *ex copula* erections (under parasympathetic influence) but promoted seminal emission (sympathetically controlled) (Clark *et al.*, 1987). The effects of β receptors are unclear, since stimulation of β_2 receptors with clenbuterol inhibited copulation in active rats but facilitated it in sluggish rats; the nonselective β antagonist propranolol blocked the effects of clenbuterol but was ineffective when administered alone (Benelli *et al.*, 1990).

It is not possible to distinguish between the possible central and peripheral effects of the noradrenergic agents on penile reflexes in the studies just summarized. Two approaches have been taken to examine directly the peripheral involvement of norepinephrine in penile function. Selective peripheral depletion of adrenergic nerve terminals through treatment with guanethidine had marked effects on penile reflexes (Stefanick *et al.*, 1985). A single injection of guanethidine increased anteroflexions; longer treatments of 4 to 8 weeks decreased the number of erections. The sup-

pression of seminal emission was especially marked. Presumably, these effects of guanethidine reflect a depression of peripheral sympathetic neural activity.

A second approach highlighted in a study on dogs demonstrated that yohimbine and clonidine can act at the periphery, where they exert antagonistic influence on erection, as measured by pressure in the corpus cavernosum (Lin *et al.*, 1988). Erection was induced in anesthetized animals by electrical stimulation of the cavernous nerves. When injected into the internal pudendal artery, clonidine progressively reduced the erectile effect of cavernous nerve stimulation, even at accumulated doses (0.02–0.4 μg/kg) too small to change systemic blood pressure. The inhibitory effect of the highest dose of clonidine (0.4 μg/kg) was blocked by 0.25–0.50 μg/kg yohimbine. Any effects on cavernous pressure paralleled effects on blood flow in the internal pudendal artery, leaving unresolved the question of whether clonidine acted in this preparation on the vasculature, the corporal smooth muscles, or both. Also not resolved is the question of why clonidine and yohimbine had similar rather than opposite effects on touch-based erections in rats (see Clark and Smith, 1990).

The mixed facilitative and inhibitory influences of NE on male sexual behavior may have relevance for human sexual function. For an overview of the complex interaction between excitatory and inhibitory influences in the regulation of erection, see Bancroft and Janssen's insightful review (2000).

C. Serotonin

Serotonin (5-hydroxytryptamine, 5-HT) is synthesized from tryptophan by the rate-limiting enzyme tryptophan hydroxylase, producing 5-hydroxytryptophan, which is then converted to 5-HT by aromatic acid decarboxylase. Serotonergic cell bodies are located largely in nine groups (B1–9) throughout the medulla, pons, and midbrain. Axons from these raphe nuclei ascend and descend to innervate nearly every area of the CNS. However, some cell bodies lie outside these groups, and less than half the neurons within these groups are serotonergic (reviewed in Frazer and Hensler, 1999).

5-HT is generally inhibitory to sexual behavior. Lesions of the median, but not the dorsal, raphe nucleus

(Albinsson et al., 1996; Kondo and Yamanouchi, 1997), a major source of 5-HT in the brain, or drugs that deplete 5-HT (Ahlenius et al., 1971; Mitler et al., 1972; Salis and Dewsbury, 1971) have been reported to facilitate copulation. Facilitative effects were most notable in animals that were initially noncopulators (Dallo, 1977; Salis and Dewsbury, 1971; Ginton, 1976), in castrates maintained on suboptimal hormone replacement (Larsson et al., 1978; Luttge, 1975; Malmnas and Meyerson, 1971; Södersten et al., 1976, 1977; Rodriguez et al., 1984), or in sexually naive males (Rodriguez et al., 1984). Ex copula penile reflexes were also facilitated by depletion of 5-HT. Specifically, radiofrequency lesions of the median and pontine raphe nuclei potentiated the expression of cups (intense, flared erections) and anteroflexions (penile body erections) (Monaghan et al.,1993), and neurotoxic lesions of serotonin terminals in the brain or spinal cord released the urethrogenital reflex from tonic inhibition (Marson and McKenna, 1994a). Depletion of 5-HT by the 5-HT-synthesis inhibitor, p-chlorophenylalanine (pCPA) decreased the latency to the first touch-based erection but also decreased the number of erections (Matsumoto et al., 1997). Males treated with pCPA were more likely to exhibit noncontact erections; however, pCPA did not elicit erections in the absence of an estrous female (Matsumoto et al., 1997). Therefore, 5-HT may have both facilitative and inhibitory effects on touch-based erections, whereas it inhibits responsiveness to the stimuli that normally elicit noncontact erections. In further support of 5-HT's inhibitory effects on copulation, administration of its precursor, 5-hydroxytryptophan, increased both intromission and ejaculation latencies and increased the number of intromissions prior to ejaculation (Ahlenius and Larsson, 1991). Similarly, intrathecal administration of 5-HT abolished the urethrogenital reflex, an effect that was blocked by systemic injection of the 5-HT antagonist methysergide (Marson and McKenna, 1992).

Increasing extracellular 5-HT by means of a selective serotonin reuptake inhibitor (SSRI) impairs sexual behavior in both humans and rats. A common side effect of SSRI antidepressants is difficulty achieving orgasm or ejaculation, sometimes accompanied by diminished sexual interest (reviewed in Rosen et al., 1999; Seagraves, 1990). Typically, these inhibitory effects increase over approximately the same time as the an-

tidepressant effects occur. The means by which SSRIs inhibit sexual behavior is unclear but may include an increase in prolactin secretion, anticholinergic effects, and inhibition of nitric oxide synthase (Rosen et al., 1999), or an increase in penile sensory thresholds (Yilmaz et al., 1999). The propensity of SSRIs to inhibit ejaculation has been used to treat premature ejaculation (e.g., Haensel et al., 1995; Kim and Seo, 1998; McMahon and Touma, 1999; Waldinger et al., 1998; Yilmaz et al., 1999). Unwanted side effects include anorgasmia and decreased libido, particularly with higher doses and chronic treatment as opposed to "on demand" use (McMahon and Touma, 1999).

In rats, too, chronic administration of the SSRI fluoxetine inhibited both sexual motivation and ejaculation (Cantor et al., 1999; Taylor et al., 1996; Vega Matusczyk et al., 1998). Administration of oxytocin reversed the inhibition of ejaculation but had no effect on the inhibition of sexual motivation (Cantor et al., 1999). One means by which SSRIs may inhibit ejaculation is by reducing the pressure response of the seminal vesicle to splanchnic nerve stimulation (Hsieh et al., 1998). Acute, as opposed to chronic, administration of fluoxetine did not inhibit ejaculation in most studies (Cantor et al., 1999; Mos et al., 1999; Vega Matusczyk et al., 1998). However, one study found a slowing of copulation by acute injections of fluoxetine, which was reversed by an NE releaser (amantadine), thereby suggesting an interaction between 5-HT and NE in the control of temporal patterning of copulation (Yells et al., 1995). One measure of sexual motivation (time spent near a receptive female) showed no effect of acute administration of fluoxetine (Vega Matusczyk et al., 1998), but another measure (level changing in search of a female) showed inhibition (Cantor et al., 1999).

Although 5-HT is generally inhibitory to copulation, stimulation of one class of receptor, 5-HT$_{1A}$, promotes ejaculation. The 5-HT$_{1A}$ agonist, 8-hydroxy-2-(di-n-propylamino)tetralin (8-OH-DPAT), decreased the time and number of intromissions preceding ejaculation (Ahlenius and Larsson, 1984b; Ahlenius et al., 1981, 1989; Schnur et al., 1989). Indeed, some rats ejaculated on the first intromission (Ahlenius and Larsson, 1991; Ahlenius et al., 1981; Coolen et al., 1997a; Haensel and Slob, 1997). A different 5-HT$_{1A}$ agonist, flesinoxan, produced effects similar to those of 8-OH-DPAT, except that no males ejaculated on the first or second intromission (Haensel and Slob, 1997). Because this facilitation of ejaculation is the opposite of the typical effects of the 5-HT precursor, 8-OH-DPAT may work by stimulating inhibitory autoreceptors on cell bodies in the raphe nuclei. However, lesions of the raphe nuclei did not diminish the facilitative effects of 8-OH-DPAT, thus suggesting that at least some of its effects are mediated by postsynaptic receptors (Fernandez-Guasti and Escalante, 1991). This conclusion was supported by the facilitative effects of injections into terminal fields (MPOA and nucleus accumbens) (Fernandez-Guasti *et al.*, 1992), where the only 5-HT_{1A} receptors are postsynaptic (Verge *et al.*, 1985).

The facilitative effects of 8-OH-DPAT are dependent on both T and previous sexual experience (Rowland and Houtsmuller, 1998). Castrates with subnormal T replacement showed no facilitation by 8-OH-DPAT; in those with threshold T replacement, only sexually experienced animals showed facilitation. High levels of hormone replacement resulted in a strong effect of 8-OH-DPAT.

8-OH-DPAT, as well as the α_2 adrenoceptor antagonist, yohimbine, and the opioid antagonist, naloxone, increased the percentage of males that copulated 24 hours after copulating to sexual satiety (Rodriguez-Manzo and Fernandez-Guasti, 1994;1995). Neurotoxic lesions of the noradrenergic system blocked the facilitative effects of 8-OH-DPAT and naloxone in sated males, but not the facilitation by yohimbine (Rodriguez-Manzo and Fernandez-Guasti, 1995). Noradrenergic lesions also decreased the facilitation of ejaculation by 8-OH-DPAT in nonexhausted males (Fernandez-Guasti and Rodriguez-Manzo, 1997). These data suggest that one mechanism of 8-OH-DPAT's facilitation is an increase in noradrenergic activity in one or more brain areas.

The most commonly reported effect of 8-OH-DPAT is facilitation of ejaculation, mediated in part by the sympathetic nervous system. In agreement with a prosympathetic effect, administration of 8-OH-DPAT decreased the numbers of touch-based erections, cups, and anteroflexions and lengthened the latency to the first erection (Rehman *et al.*, 1999). The same doses also decreased the time and number of intromissions preceding ejaculation in copulation tests and decreased the length of intromissions. Thus, ejaculation was promoted and erection was impaired by 8-OH-DPAT.

Similar effects were observed in monkeys; moderate doses of 8-OH-DPAT decreased noncontact erections (Pomerantz *et al.*, 1993a) but facilitated ejaculation (Pomerantz *et al.*, 1993b).

The effects of 8-OH-DPAT on copulation in monkeys were biphasic (Pomerantz *et al.*, 1993b). A moderate dose shortened ejaculation latency and decreased the number of intromissions preceding ejaculation. However, a high dose lengthened ejaculation latency. Therefore, moderate stimulation of 5-HT_{1A} receptors lowered the ejaculatory threshold of monkeys, as it does in rats. But 8-OH-DPAT had inhibitory effects in ferrets (Paredes *et al.*, 1994). The same doses that facilitated ejaculation in rats inhibited copulation in male ferrets. Furthermore, those same doses facilitated receptive behavior in female ferrets, in contrast to the drug's typical inhibition of female sexual behavior in rats (Uphouse *et al.*, 1991). Lower doses had no effects in either male or female ferrets. Therefore, there appear to be important species differences in the effects of 8-OH-DPAT on copulatory behavior.

Consistent with the generally inhibitory nature of 5-HT influence, stimulation of other 5-HT receptor subtypes has inhibited various aspects of copulation. In rats stimulation of 5-HT_{1B} receptors appears to inhibit ejaculation. The 5-HT_{1B} agonist, anpirtoline, produced a dose-dependent impairment of ejaculation, an effect that was blocked by two selective 5-HT_{1B} antagonists (Hillegaart and Ahlenius, 1998). In addition, co-administration of an SSRI (citalopram) together with a 5-HT_{1A} antagonist increased ejaculation latency, an effect that was blocked by a 5-HT_{1B} antagonist (Ahlenius and Larsson, 1999). The authors suggested that blocking the inhibitory 5-HT_{1A} autoreceptors had disclosed inhibitory effects of the SSRI that were mediated by stimulation of 5-HT_{1B} receptors. Similarly, administration of the 5-HT precursor, 5-hydroxytryptophan, together with a peripheral 5-HT decarboxylase inhibitor (to confine effects to the CNS) increased ejaculation latency (Ahlenius and Larsson, 1998). This inhibitory effect was blocked by a 5-HT_{1B} antagonist but was enhanced by a 5-HT_{1A} antagonist. Therefore, stimulation of 5-HT_{1A} receptors promotes ejaculation, whereas stimulation of 5-HT_{1B} receptors inhibits it.

Stimulation of 5-HT_{2C} receptors, however, may facilitate erection but inhibit ejaculation, the opposite of 8-OH-DPAT's effects. In monkeys the $5\text{-HT}_{2C/1D}$

agonist mCPP decreased the numbers of males that initiated copulation and that ejaculated; however, the same doses increased the number of males that had drug-induced and noncontact erections (Pomerantz *et al.,* 1993a). [At the time these experiments were conducted, mCPP was classified as a 5-HT$_{1C/1D}$ agonist. However, the 5-HT$_{1C}$ receptor has more recently been renamed the 5-HT$_{2C}$ receptor (Hoyer *et al.,* 1994). Therefore, we have changed the published nomenclature to agree with the currently accepted terminology.] Further evidence of a facilitative effect of mCPP on erection was provided by a study showing increased firing of the cavernous nerves, accompanied by an increase in intracavernous pressure in urethan-anesthetized rats (Steers and de Groat, 1989). Drug-induced erections were also observed in awake rats following administration of mCPP (Berendsen *et al.,* 1990) or a more selective 5-HT$_{2C}$ agonist, RO60-0175 (Millan *et al.,* 1997). The opposing effects of 5-HT$_{1A}$ agonists and of 5-HT$_{2C/1D}$ agonists on erection vs ejaculation strongly suggest that 5-HT$_{1A}$ agonists promote sympathetic nervous system mediation of ejaculation, whereas 5-HT$_{2C}$ agonists promote parasympathetically mediated erection, at the expense of ejaculation.

Stimulation of other 5-HT$_2$ receptors appears to be inhibitory to male copulatory behavior. DOI, a relatively nonselective 5-HT$_2$ agonist, inhibited copulation in male rats (Foreman *et al.,* 1989; Gonzalez *et al.,* 1994; Klint and Larsson, 1995; Padoin and Lucion, 1995), whereas ritanserin, a 5-HT$_2$ antagonist, facilitated copulation (Gonzalez *et al.,* 1994). In summary, stimulation of 5-HT$_{1B}$, 5-HT$_{2C}$, or other 5-HT$_2$ receptors may raise the ejaculatory threshold and, in some cases, interfere with copulation, although stimulation of 5-HT$_{2C}$ receptors may also facilitate erection. Stimulation of 5-HT$_{1A}$ receptors primarily promotes ejaculation. However, 5-HT$_3$ receptors may have little role in the regulation of male sexual behavior (Tanco *et al.,* 1994).

D. Acetylcholine

Acetylcholine (ACh) is formed from choline and acetyl coenzyme A by the action of choline acetyltransferase. There are eight major groups of cholinergic neurons in the CNS (Ch1-8), primarily in the basal forebrain and brainstem; however, in these areas,

cholinergic neurons are intermixed with noncholinergic neurons (reviewed in Mesulam, 1995). In addition, all peripheral motor nerves, preganglionic autonomic neurons, and postganglionic parasympathetic neurons are cholinergic. Five subtypes of muscarinic receptors have been identified; they are coupled to either G$_{q/11}$ or G$_{i/o}$ G-proteins (Alexander and Peters, 2000). Muscarinic receptors may have either excitatory or inhibitory effects, depending on the tissue (Taylor and Brown, 1999). Nine subtypes of nicotinic receptors have been described (Alexander and Peters, 2000); nicotinic receptors are linked to sodium channels and are excitatory (Taylor and Brown, 1999).

The effects of systemic administration of cholinergic drugs are confounded by the drugs' effects on striated muscle and on the parasympathetic nervous system. Indeed, both the ACh receptor agonist pilocarpine (Ågmo, 1976) and several antagonists (Ågmo, 1976; Bignami, 1966) inhibited copulation. The fact that one of the antagonists (methscopolamine) that does not cross the blood-brain barrier was as effective as one that does (scopolamine) suggests that the effects were mediated peripherally, possibly at the penis. However, administration of the acetylcholinesterase antagonist, physostigmine (which would have slowed degradation of ACh), or the muscarinic agonist, pilocarpine, increased the number of ejaculations, an effect that was inhibited by the muscarinic antagonist atropine (Zarrindast *et al.,* 1994). Similarly, the muscarinic agonist, oxotremorine, facilitated copulatory performance in both experienced and inexperienced castrates treated with T, but not before T replacement (Retana-Marquez and Velasquez-Moctezuma, 1997). Spontaneous erections were also increased by the muscarinic agonist pilocarpine (Maeda *et al.,* 1990). Therefore, systemic administration of muscarinic agonists may facilitate both copulation and spontaneous erections, but contradictory results have also been obtained, and the effects may be at least partially mediated by peripheral actions on the autonomic nervous system and/or striated penile muscles.

E. Gamma Amino Butyric Acid

Gamma amino butyric acid (GABA) is a ubiquitous neurotransmitter in the brain. The majority of the neurons in the brain use either GABA or its excitatory amino acid counterpart, glutamate, as their primary neurotransmitters (reviewed in Paul, 1995). It is formed by decarboxylation of glutamate by glutamic acid decarboxylase (GAD). Glutamate, in turn, is formed from α-ketoglutarate, a product of glucose metabolism, via the Krebs cycle. Stimulation of $GABA_A$ receptors opens chloride channels, resulting in hyperpolarization of the cell. Stimulation of $GABA_B$ receptors inhibits various intracellular processes via the $G_{i/o}$.

Systemic administration of $GABA_A$ (Ågmo *et al.*, 1997) and $GABA_B$ (Paredes and Ågmo, 1995) agonists inhibited male rat sexual behavior without impairing motor function. Similar copulatory, and not motor, impairment was seen in male rabbits treated with a $GABA_A$ agonist; GABA antagonists had no effect (Paredes *et al.*, 1998a). However, another $GABA_A$ agonist, an inhibitor of GABA synthesis, and an inhibitor of GABA catabolism all inhibited sexual, social, and drinking behaviors, thus leading to the suggestion that altered GABA neurotransmission had reduced sensitivity to environmental stimuli and had thereby inhibited motivated behaviors in a nonspecific manner (Paredes *et al.*, 1997). Because GABA is an inhibitory neurotransmitter in many different neural sites, it is not clear that systemically administered drugs targeting its receptors influence sexual behavior in a specific manner. Sodium valproate, an inhibitor of GABA transaminase, the enzyme that degrades GABA, decreased intromission ratios without affecting thrusting (Ågmo *et al.*, 1987). This apparent decrease in erectile function may have resulted in part from its ability to decrease EMG activity in ischiocavernosus muscles during thrusting (Paredes *et al.*, 1993b). Thus, some GABAergic inhibition of copulation may arise in part from peripherally mediated effects.

F. Opioids

Endogenous opioids are classified into three major groups: endorphins, enkephalins, and dynorphins (reviewed in Mains and Eipper, 1999). Endorphins are derived from proopiomelanocortin (POMC) in the anterior pituitary, intermediate lobe of the pituitary, and the hypothalamus. Met- and Leu-enkephalin are more pervasively located throughout the central and peripheral nervous systems. There are four major dynorphin peptides—dynorphins A and B and neoendorphins α and β—which also are widely distributed throughout the central and peripheral nervous systems. In addition, a newly discovered peptide, orphanin FQ or nociceptin, binds to an orphan receptor that is classified as opioid-like on the basis of its structural homology to the conventional opioid receptors. Neuropeptides are often colocalized with conventional neurotransmitters. There are three classes of opioid receptors—δ, κ, and μ—in addition to the orphanin FQ receptor. β-Endorphin is the best endogenous ligand for the μ receptor; the enkephalins have greatest affinity for δ receptors; and dynorphins are best at κ receptors (Mains and Eipper, 1999).

Endogenous opioids are generally thought to inhibit male sexual behavior (reviewed in van Furth *et al.*, 1995b). However, systemic injections of the opiate antagonists naloxone or naltrexone have produced a constellation of effects, including both facilitative and inhibitory influences: decreased intromissions preceding ejaculation (Myers and Baum, 1979, 1980; Pellegrini-Quarantotti *et al.*, 1979; van Furth *et al.*, 1994; Wu and Noble, 1986), decreased intromission latency (McIntosh *et al.*, 1980; Myers and Baum, 1979), increased (Myers and Baum, 1979; Pellegrini-Quarantotti *et al.*, 1979) or decreased (McIntosh *et al.*, 1980) interintromission interval, increased postejaculatory interval (Lieblich *et al.*, 1985; McConnell *et al.*, 1981; Sachs *et al.*, 1981; van Furth and van Ree, 1994), and decreased ability of tail pinch to activate copulation in castrates with subnormal T (Leyton and Stewart, 1996). Meisel and Sachs (1994) note that some of these effects may be similar to those of recent castration or the enforced-interval effect, in which increased inter-intromission intervals decrease the number of intromissions preceding ejaculation. However, naloxone has more consistent facilitative effects in sexually sluggish males (Gessa *et al.*, 1979), sexually naive males tested in a novel environment (Pfaus and Wilkins, 1995), and sexually satiated males (Rodriguez-Manzo and Fernandez-Guasti, 1995).

Systemic administration of either morphine or the κ-receptor agonists U-50,488H or bremazocine inhibited copulation in sexually active rats (Ågmo and Paredes, 1988; Ågmo *et al.*, 1994b; Leyton and Stewart,

1992). However, naloxone also inhibited copulation (Ågmo *et al.*, 1994b), thus suggesting that at least some activity at opioid receptors facilitates, but excess stimulation may impair, sexual behavior. Ågmo *et al.* (1994b) concluded that the effects of morphine were centrally mediated, because a peripherally active opioid antagonist (i.e., one that is administered peripherally and does not cross the blood-brain barrier), methylnaloxone, did not inhibit morphine's effects, and because a peripherally active opiate agonist, loperamide, had only marginal effects.

Some of the inhibitory effects of morphine on copulation may be mediated by inhibition of genital reflexes. Seminal emission was especially sensitive to opiate inhibition, being suppressed by all doses of morphine (0.1, 0.5, 1, and 5 mg/kg, ip), although touch-based erections were also decreased in dose-related fashion (Gomez-Marrero *et al.*, 1988). However, the opiate antagonist, naloxone, also decreased erections at the lowest dose (0.1 mg/kg, ip). In addition, anticipatory level changes were inhibited by naloxone in a sexual motivation test (van Furth and van Ree, 1994, 1996; van Furth *et al.*, 1994). Therefore, interference with endogenous opioid activity may impair both reflexive and motivational aspects of sexual behavior. Some of the facilitative effects of endogenous opioids may be mediated by enkephalins. Intraventricular administration of an enkephalinase inhibitor, which would have slowed the breakdown of enkephalins, reduced the time and number of intromissions before ejaculation but also increased mount and intromission latencies (Ågmo *et al.*, 1994a). In summary, low to moderate levels of endogenous opioids may facilitate sexual motivation and genital reflexes; however, exogenous opiates or high levels of endogenous opioids may interfere with sexual function.

G. Oxytocin and Arginine Vasopressin

Oxytocin (OT) and arginine vasopressin (AVP) are nonapeptides that are released from the posterior pituitary and are also neurotransmitters in the central nervous system. OT stimulates smooth muscles, which in turn results in seminal emission and, in humans, accompanies orgasm. As would be expected, levels of OT were elevated in rabbit plasma (Stoneham *et al.*, 1985) and in rat cerebrospinal fluid (Hughes *et al.*, 1987b) fol-

lowing ejaculation. Copulation increased plasma OT in sexually naive male rats but not in sexually experienced animals (Hillegaart *et al.*, 1998). Furthermore, plasma OT levels were highly correlated with the intensity of copulatory performance in the naive animals. As noted above, systemically administered OT restored ejaculatory behavior in chronic fluoxetine-treated males without affecting level changing (Cantor *et al.*, 1999). However, the effects of peripheral or intracerebroventricular administration of exogenous OT appear to be dose dependent; high doses impaired copulation in prairie voles (Mahalati *et al.*, 1991) or rats (Stoneham *et al.*, 1985), and lower doses facilitated copulation in rats (Arletti *et al.*, 1985) and dominant squirrel monkeys (Winslow and Insel, 1991; see Witt, 1995, for review). The hypothesis that endogenous OT has a facilitative effect on copulation is supported by the dose-related inhibition of copulation in male rats by intracerebroventricular administration of an OT antagonist (Argiolas *et al.*, 1988a).

Intracerebroventricular injections of OT increased spontaneous erections (reviewed in Argiolas and Gessa, 1991). This effect was blocked by an anticholinergic drug (atropine), but not by a DA antagonist (haloperidol) (Argiolas *et al.*, 1986, 1988b). Furthermore, an OT antagonist blocked erections elicited by either OT or the DA agonist apomorphine (Argiolas *et al.*, 1988a). Thus, in the cascade of neural and neurochemical bases of erection, DA is "upstream" of OT, which in turn is "upstream" of a cholinergic influence on drug-induced erections. However, there is also feedback from "downstream" structures back to "upstream" ones.

Male and female prairie voles form stable preferences to spend time with a member of the opposite sex with which they have copulated for one to several hours (reviewed in Carter *et al.*, 1995; Dewsbury, 1987). OT and AVP are released during sexual behavior, and administration of either peptide can promote bonding in either sex, although it is likely that endogenous vasopressin is more important in males and oxytocin in females (Cho *et al.*, 1999). Although vasopressin may promote bonding in prairie voles, systemic injection of lysine vasopressin decreased the number of ejaculations and increased mount and intromission latencies in male rabbits (Kihlström and Ågmo, 1974). No effects of vasopressin were found in rats following systemic injection of the analog, desglycinamide-lysine vasopressin

(Bohus, 1977). Therefore, effects of vasopressin may be species- and context-specific.

H. Nitric Oxide

Nitric oxide (NO) is a gaseous molecule given off when NO synthase (NOS) converts arginine to citrulline. There is considerable evidence that NO promotes parasympathetic function, including vasodilation, by both peripheral and central actions. Both endothelial (eNOS) and neuronal (nNOS) isoforms of NOS are present in the penis. Electrical stimulation of the cavernous nerve increased the production of NO and also increased intracavernosal pressure (Escrig *et al.*, 1999a). Both eNOS, and nNOS are upregulated by androgens. Specifically, castration decreased, and T restored, NOS, as measured by NADPH-diaphorase histochemistry (Baba *et al.*, 2000; Zvara *et al.*, 1995), nNOS mRNA (Reilly *et al.*, 1997), or nNOS and eNOS immunoreactivity (Marin *et al.*, 1999) in the corpus cavernosum and dorsal penile nerves. The production of NO in the corpora was similarly affected (Marin *et al.*, 1999; Lugg *et al.*, 1995). Furthermore, castration decreased, and T replacement restored, the erectile responses elicited by systemic apomorphine, papaverine injection into the penis, and/or cavernous nerve electrostimulation (Baba *et al.*, 2000; Lugg *et al.*, 1995; Marin *et al.*, 1999; Mills *et al.*, 1992, 1994; Zvara *et al.*, 1995; reviewed in Mills *et al.*, 1996). Papaverine is a nonspecific inhibitor of phosphodiesterases that normally inactivate cGMP, the most common second messenger of NO. Thus, one means by which T enhances erectile ability may be up regulation of NOS in the corpus cavernosum and dorsal penile nerves.

DHT is the active androgen that maintains NOS activity and the erectile response to cavernous nerve stimulation (Lugg *et al.*, 1995). However, castration differentially affects NOS activity in other parts of the reproductive system. Whereas NOS activity was decreased in the penis and epididymis of castrates compared to T-replaced males, NOS activity was higher in seminal vesicles and lateral prostate (Chamness *et al.*, 1995). T's reduction of NOS activity in the seminal vesicles and prostate suggests that NO may impair some aspect of ejaculation or sperm function. Indeed, systemic injection of 200 mg/kg of L-arginine inhibited the fertility of male rats without affecting copulatory behavior (Ratnasooriya and Dharmasiri, 2001). The authors suggested that the infertility may have resulted from hyperactivated sperm motility and capacitation. Thus, excessive NO production in some parts of the reproductive tract may be detrimental to male fertility.

Systemic administration of NOS inhibitors has decreased the number of males that ejaculated, decreased the number of intromissions, and increased the number of mounts in sexually experienced (Bialy *et al.*, 1996; Hull *et al.*, 1994) or sexually naive (Benelli *et al.*, 1995) males. NOS inhibitors also inhibited touch-based erections and increased the number of seminal emissions (Hull *et al.*, 1994), thus suggesting that NO normally increases parasympathetic and decreases sympathetic activity. NOS inhibitors did not affect sexual motivation, measured by choice of the female's goal box in an X-maze (Hull *et al.*, 1994), or mount latency (Bialy *et al.*, 1996). However, another study reported a decrease in sexual motivation, measured by decreased precoital activity and failure of most rats to mount (Ratnasooriya *et al.*, 2000). In those males that did ejaculate, spermatozoa were present in normal numbers, but the numbers of pregnancies and implants per pregnancy were reduced. One possible explanation for the decreased fertility is that NO injected by the sperm into the egg is required to activate the egg to release internal stores of calcium, which then triggers cell division (Kuo *et al.*, 2000). Although this report concerned sea urchin sperm and eggs, the eggs of many other species also release calcium when contacted by sperm. Therefore, the NO-stimulated calcium release may be a widespread trigger for oocyte division.

Deletion of the gene for nNOS (nNOS–/–) resulted in increased aggression and inappropriate mounting of non-receptive females (Nelson *et al.*, 1995). However, penile function was maintained in nNOS–/– mice by increased production of eNOS in the penis (Burnett *et al.*, 1996). Mice with a deletion of the gene for eNOS (eNOS–/–) showed an increased ability to ejaculate, requiring fewer mounts and intromissions to ejaculate, compared to wild-type mice (Kriegsfeld *et al.*, 1999). This provides further support for NO's normal promotion of parasympathetically mediated erection and inhibition of sympathetically mediated seminal emission and ejaculation, which perhaps prevent "premature ejaculation."

Although systemic inhibition of NOS activity has produced relatively consistent impairment of erectile function and copulation, systemic administration of the precursor L-arginine or NO donors has had less consistent results. L-arginine did increase the percentage of naive males that copulated and improved copulatory performance in experienced males (Benelli et al., 1995). It also increased the production of NO in the corpus cavernosum (Escrig et al., 1999a). However, other studies found only marginal facilitation of touch-based erections in gonadally intact males (Hull et al., 1994) or no effects on intracavernosal pressure elicited by electrical stimulation in either untreated or T-replaced castrates. (Reilly et al., 1997). Systemic administration of the NO donor sodium nitroprusside did increase intracavernosal pressure in untreated castrates, but not in T-replaced animals (Reilly et al., 1997). Thus, it appears that many gonadally intact males have sufficient NOS activity for efficient copulation and erectile function, and that supplying excess precursor or NO itself may yield little benefit.

However, prolonging the effects of NO on its most common second messenger, cGMP, is clinically useful for treating erectile dysfunction (e.g., Christiansen et al., 2000; Giuliano et al., 2000; Goldstein et al., 1998; Meuleman et al., 2001; Porst et al., 2001). Both sildenafil (Viagra) and vardenafil selectively inhibit phosphodiesterase V, which hydrolyzes (inactivates) cGMP, thereby allowing cGMP to accumulate in endothelial cells and prolonging its action (Moreland et al., 1999; Porst et al., 2001). Sildenafil had no effect on either erections or semen quality in normal healthy men, but it did decrease the postejaculatory interval before resumption of erections (Aversa et al., 2000). Thus, enhancement of NO's effect on the penile vasculature can increase erections in men with erectile dysfunction and can also promote postejaculatory, but not pre-ejaculatory, erections in healthy men.

I. Gonadotropin-Releasing Hormone

Gonadotropin-releasing hormone (GnRH) is a decapeptide produced in several hypothalamic nuclei and released in the median eminence to stimulate gonadotropin release from the anterior pituitary. Within the brain it also serves as a neuromodulator, particularly in the MPOA and the amygdala (Barry et al.,

1985; Kostarczyk, 1986). The greatest numbers of GnRH-containing perikarya are found in the mediobasal hypothalamus, the lamina terminalis, and the MPOA (Barry et al., 1985).

Moss and his coworkers were the first to examine a role for GnRH in copulation in male rats (Moss et al., 1975). Castrated males were given daily injections of a low dose of T (10 or 25 μg T propionate per day). Whereas this dose of T maintained copulation in all males, animals also treated systemically with an injection of GnRH had shorter intromission and ejaculation latencies than did males injected with saline. Other parameters of copulation were not affected by GnRH treatment. This shortening of copulatory latencies by GnRH was not seen in gonadally intact male rats, presumably because these males showed high levels of copulatory activity even without treatment. Myers and Baum (1980) also found effects of GnRH in male rats, although their specific findings differed somewhat from those of Moss' group. In this study, GnRH decreased ejaculation latency, but only in intact males, not in castrated, T-treated males. For T-treated males, the only effect of GnRH injection was an increase in the postejaculatory interval. No significant effects of GnRH on copulation in male rats were detected by Ryan and Frankel (1978). In male rats whose genitalia had been anesthetized to prevent intromission and ejaculation, GnRH infused into the cerebral ventricles increased the rate of mounting (Dorsa and Smith, 1980). Gray-tailed voles also responded to GnRH treatment, primarily with shortened intromission and ejaculation latencies and an increased number of mounts in the 10-min tests (Boyd and Moore, 1985).

GnRH promoted sexual behavior in hypogonadal men with reduced luteinizing hormone (LH) release (Mortimer et al., 1974). However, improved sexual function in men with erectile disorder was modest (Benkert, 1975; Davies et al., 1976; Evans and Distiller, 1979; Ehrensing et al., 1981) or nonexistent (Perras et al., 2001). GnRH administered to old rhesus macaques actually decreased the intromission rate, whereas similar treatment of young males had no effect (Phoenix and Chambers, 1990). This lack of facilitation did not result from failure of GnRH to produce a physiological response, because both old and young macaques showed increased plasma levels of LH and T following GnRH treatment. Although several facilitative effects of

GnRH in male rats and voles and in men have been reported, the lack of consistency among studies in the measures affected, or indeed whether any effects were observed, makes it difficult to infer how endogenous GnRH might regulate copulation.

This problem of interpretation is compounded by the results of a study in which chronic administration of a synthetic GnRH agonist ([6-D-(2-napthyl)-alanine] GnRH) disrupted copulation in male rats (Dorsa *et al.,* 1981). Chronic treatment of gonadally intact males with this GnRH analog increased their mount and intromission latencies relative to control males. As the treatment with the GnRH analog reduced serum T levels, the changes in behavior in the treated males could be attributed to the loss of endogenous T. Not so easily explained was the finding that in castrated males the GnRH analog hastened the loss of copulation compared with control castrated males. A similar problem of interpretation involved the effects of the GnRH analog given to castrated male rats treated with T. Males treated with a low dose of T (mean plasma level of 0.5 ng/ml) and the GnRH analog had longer intromission latencies than did control males. The GnRH analog had no effect on copulation in males given a higher dose of T (mean plasma level of about 1.0 ng/ml). The results of this study would indicate that chronic GnRH stimulation is inhibitory to male sexual behavior, and that maintaining plasma T levels in the physiological range can circumvent the effects of GnRH on copulation.

The findings summarized above are further tempered by studies finding little evidence for a role of GnRH in the regulation of copulation in males. Systemic administration of GnRH to either intact male rhesus monkeys (Phoenix *et al.,* 1976) or to geldings, with or without concurrent T supplements (McDonnell *et al.,* 1989), failed to exert any potentiating effects on copulation. Female, but not male, rats showed a copulation-induced increase in GnRH-positive neurons that coexpressed Fos, the protein product of the immediate-early gene *c-fos* (Lambert *et al.,* 1992). For male rats, the inhibitory effects on copulation of systemic treatments with a GnRH antagonist having potent antigonadal effects appeared to result from reduced T secretion (Bhasin *et al.,* 1988; Fielder *et al.,* 1989). However, a more recent study found that icv administration of GnRH to inexperienced male hamsters restored their mating behavior, which had been impaired

by removal of their vomeronasal organs (Meredith and Fernandez-Fewell, 1994). An analog of GnRH (Ac5-10LHRH), which does not lead to LH release from the pituitary, produced similar results, thus suggesting that central effects, rather than LH or T release, mediated the facilitation. Therefore, GnRH may act centrally to promote male sexual behavior, especially in sexually naive males or those whose copulatory ability is compromised by sensory or hormonal impairment.

J. Prolactin

The effects of prolactin on copulatory behavior in male rodents have been examined largely through treatments designed to produce chronically elevated levels of prolactin. The procedures used to elevate prolactin levels have been of three types: transplants of two to four pituitaries into the kidney capsule of the male (Bailey and Herbert, 1982; Bailey *et al.,* 1984; Doherty *et al.,* 1981, 1982, 1985a,b; Drago *et al.,* 1981; Svare, *et al.,* 1979), injection of cells from prolactin-secreting pituitary tumors (Clark and Kalra, 1985; Kalra *et al.,* 1983; Kooy *et al.,* 1988; Weber *et al.,* 1982), or drug treatments designed to stimulate prolactin release (Bailey *et al.,* 1984; Bailey and Herbert, 1982; Bartke *et al.,* 1984). In only one study has serum prolactin been elevated through direct injection (Doherty *et al.,* 1989).

Although few studies investigating the effects of elevated prolactin levels (hyperprolactinemia) on male sexual behavior have reported a reduction (Doherty *et al.,* 1985a; Svare *et al.,* 1979) or elimination (Kalra *et al.,* 1983) of ejaculatory potential, a disruption of other parameters of copulatory performance is consistently obtained. Depending on the particular experiment, different measures of copulatory activity have been affected, although the ability of males to initiate copulation, as measured by increased intromission latencies, seems particularly susceptible to hyperprolactinemia (Bailey *et al.,* 1984; Bartke *et al.,* 1984; Doherty *et al.,* 1981, 1982, 1985a,b; Kalra *et al.,* 1983; Svare *et al.,* 1979). Once copulation is initiated, hyperprolactinemic males generally take longer to ejaculate than do control males (Bailey *et al.,* 1984; Bailey and Herbert, 1982; Doherty *et al.,* 1985a,b; Kalra *et al.,* 1983; Svare *et al.,* 1979; Weber *et al.,* 1982). This increased ejaculation latency appears to result primarily from a slower pacing of copulation

(Bartke *et al.,* 1984; Doherty *et al.,* 1982, 1985a,b). Although an increase in the numbers of intromissions to ejaculation was reported in one study (Bailey *et al.,* 1984), the number of mounts and intromissions are usually not affected by hyperprolactinemia. When altered, the number of mounts increases (Doherty *et al.,* 1982, 1985b; Weber *et al.,* 1982), whereas the number of intromissions decreases (Doherty *et al.,* 1981, 1982; Svare *et al.,* 1979). The resumption of copulation following ejaculation (postejaculatory interval) was delayed in only one study (Doherty *et al.,* 1982).

It is typical in these experiments to allow a month or more to elapse between the onset of prolactin treatment and the first test for sexual behavior. However, two notable studies examined the time-course of behavioral changes following the elevation of prolactin levels. In one experiment (Doherty *et al.,* 1985b), behavioral testing was conducted every four days following implantation of pituitary pars distalis grafts. In as few as eight days after implantation, significant elevations in intromission latency, ejaculation latency, and mount frequency and a decrease in the number of intromissions per minute were observed. Prolactin levels were maximally elevated one week after pituitary implantation, the earliest time examined. In a second study (Weber *et al.,* 1982), injection of a suspension of pituitary tumor cells did not alter copulatory activity compared with control males until about three to four weeks later. Although the time course was longer in this study, as compared with that by Doherty *et al.,* (1985b), it still corresponded to the time course of elevation in prolactin levels. Consistent with these findings are the results of daily injections of prolactin, which produce significant changes in intromission latency and intromission rate within 9 to 15 days after the start of the injections (Doherty *et al.,* 1985b).

Besides the effects on copulatory behavior, high levels of prolactin can also disrupt touch-based genital reflexes. In one study (Doherty *et al.,* 1986), a significant reduction in the number of erections was observed as early as one week after pituitary implantation. In a second study (Clark and Kalra, 1985), erections were eliminated in all but one rat inoculated with fragments of a pituitary tumor secreting prolactin (and growth hormone), although the erectile dysfunction was not apparent until 34 days after inoculation. Following spinal transection, hyperprolactinemic males initially

showed fewer erections; by 10 days after transection, erection frequency was equivalent to that of transected control males (Doherty *et al.,* 1986). These studies indicate that hyperprolactinemia may disrupt genital reflex components of copulation independently of prolactin's inhibitory actions on other aspects of copulatory function.

In contrast to the studies just summarized, there is one report of a facilitation of male copulatory behavior following pituitary implants (Drago *et al.,* 1981). Sexually experienced male rats receiving implants of two whole pituitaries had lower postoperative mount and intromission latencies, reduced interintromission intervals, and a higher number of mounts and intromissions preceding ejaculation than did control males. The differences, although statistically significant, were rather small, probably due to the high levels of sexual activity in the control males. For example, pituitary-implanted males had an intromission latency of about 20 seconds vs about 85 seconds for the control males. Serum prolactin levels of implanted males, measured after the copulation test (five days after surgery), were only about 61 ng/ml, values comparable to those of control males in many studies (Bailey *et al.,* 1984; Bartke *et al.,* 1984; Doherty *et al.,* 1981, 1982, 1985a,b; Svare *et al.,* 1979; Weber *et al.,* 1982). Control males in this study had serum prolactin levels of about 25 ng/ml. One problem with interpreting the results of this study is the absence of preoperative copulatory data from these animals. Thus, it is not known to what extent the postoperative differences were due to group assignment as opposed to the treatment variable. Before we speculate that the effects of prolactin on copulation in male rats may depend on the resultant serum levels (i.e., low levels facilitate copulation, whereas high levels inhibit copulation), replication of the effects of low levels of prolactin on sexual behavior are needed.

The mechanism through which prolactin may inhibit copulation in male rats has focused on alterations in brain DA. Prolactin increases turnover while decreasing concentrations (Füxe *et al.,* 1977; Kalra *et al.,* 1983) of DA in a number of brain regions, the most notable with regard to sexual behavior being the MPOA-anterior hypothalamic region (Kalra *et al.,* 1981). The parallel alterations in preoptic area DA and sexual behavior induced by hyperprolactinemia have prompted the suggestion that the effects of prolactin on male copulatory behavior are a result of DA depletion (Kalra *et al.*, 1983). This suggestion has received further support from observations that DA depletion produces copulatory disruptions similar to those seen in hyperprolactinemic animals (see review by Drago, 1984). While prolactin's effects on DA may contribute to the copulatory dysfunction in male rats, it does not account for all the effects of prolactin, since hyperprolactinemia can also inhibit sexual behavior in the absence of changes in preoptic area DA activity (Doherty *et al.*, 1989).

A role for endogenous prolactin in the regulation of copulation in male rats is, so far, circumstantial. Prolactin is released in normal male rats following exposure to an estrous female rat, both with and without copulation (Kamel *et al.*, 1977). Kamel and Frankel (1978) observed that lesions of the MPOA, which leave basal levels of prolactin unaffected, prevented the surge of prolactin normally occurring after contact with an estrous female. As these authors pointed out, it is not clear whether the loss of the mating-induced surge after MPOA lesions simply reflects the absence of mating, or whether the effects of the lesion on prolactin secretion contribute to the failure to mate. The inference, however, is that prolactin release during mating contributes to copulatory performance (Kamel and Frankel, 1978). In any event, no studies have been done to determine whether specifically blocking the mating-induced surge in prolactin has any effect on copulation.

Although these studies do not adequately address the issue of whether endogenous prolactin influences copulation in rats, the hyperprolactinemic rat may be a useful animal model of some effects of hyperprolactinemia in men. Disorders that produce chronically high levels of prolactin in men are associated with impotence (Drago, 1984). Although low T levels measured in these men undoubtedly contribute to their impotence, the studies on rats clearly demonstrate that the chronically elevated prolactin also contributes to sexual dysfunction.

K. Corticotropin-Releasing Hormone

Third ventricle infusions of corticotropin-releasing factor (CRH) in sexually experienced male rats delayed the initiation of copulation (both mount and intromission latencies) and increased the numbers of mounts and intromissions leading to ejaculation (Siri-nathsinghji, 1987). The greater numbers of mounts and intromissions also contributed to a longer ejaculation latency. No effect of CRH on the postejaculatory intromission interval was observed. Because the males were not tested for a second ejaculatory series, it is not possible to determine whether CRH actually did not have any effect on the postejaculatory interval or the effects of the CRH were too short-lived to be manifest during that interval. The effects of CRH on copulation were attenuated by combined treatment with naloxone, thus suggesting that CRH may affect copulation through interactions with endogenous opioid systems. Furthermore, CRH can inhibit GnRH release, possibly through effects on endogenous opioids (Almeida *et al.*, 1988), a finding that suggests that decreased GnRH secretion may be the ultimate pathway through which CRH affects copulation.

L. Cholecystokinin

Based on observations that castration of male rats reduces the number of cholecystokinin (CCK)-immunoreactive cells in forebrain areas regulating copulation (Simerly and Swanson, 1986), several studies have examined the effects of CCK on male sexual behavior, with mixed results. Pfaus and Phillips (1987) found that systemic administration of 8 μg/kg body weight of sulfated CCK reduced the number of intromissions and the latency to ejaculate. Lower doses of CCK were ineffective. The effects of CCK on copulation could be reversed with concurrent administration of proglumide, a CCK receptor antagonist. In other studies, neither systemic (Bloch *et al.*, 1988; Lindén *et al.*, 1987) nor intracranial (Bloch *et al.*, 1988; Dornan and Malsbury, 1989) administration of CCK had any effects on copulation in male rats. However, although Lindén et al. (1987) did not find any effect of systemically administered CCK on sexual behavior, they did observe an increase in plasma CCK levels following ejaculation. There are at least two receptor subtypes for CCK (Altar, 1989), which may have antagonistic effects even within a single nucleus (Dauge *et al.*, 1989; Minabe *et al.*, 1991; Vaccarino and Rankin, 1989). Perhaps the failure to find effects of CCK on copulation in males results from the simultaneous activation of excitatory and inhibitory systems. (See Section V. I. 4.ii on mesolimbic DA system.)

M. Vasoactive Intestinal Polypeptide

Vasoactive intestinal polypeptide (VIP) is reported to have a role in the maintenance of erection through actions on the corpus cavernosum. Relaxation of the smooth muscle in this structure is necessary to maintain erection (see Section II, above). VIP relaxes the corpus cavernosum in several species, either in muscle-bath preparations [dogs (Andersson *et al.,* 1984), humans (Hedlund and Andersson, 1985; Steers *et al.,* 1984), rabbits (Willis *et al.,* 1981, 1983), monkeys (Steers *et al.,* 1984)] or *in vivo* [wallaby (Dixson *et al.,* 1984)]. This effect is usually seen *in vitro* only after contraction of the corpus induced by either direct electrical stimulation or NE stimulation. Manually stimulated erection in the wallaby (Dixson *et al.,* 1984) or electrical stimulation of the pelvic nerve in dogs (Andersson *et al.,* 1984) promotes the release of VIP in the penis. These results have been interpreted as indicating a direct neurotransmitter role for VIP in penile erection. However, since VIP increases ACh binding by 10,000 fold (Lundberg *et al.,* 1980), it is possible that the effects of VIP may have more to do with altering synaptic efficacy of another transmitter.

There is some evidence that VIP may affect copulation in males, quite apart from its effects on penile erection (Gozes *et al.,* 1989). Sexual behavior in castrated male rats was maintained through daily injections of T (4 μg/100 g body weight). Compared with the effects of saline injection, systemic treatment with 5 μg of VIP significantly reduced intromission latency and interintromission interval. Both of these effects of VIP on copulation were blocked when a synthetic antagonist was administered with the VIP.

N. Galanin

There are contradictory reports concerning the effects of galanin on male sexual behavior. Intracerebroventricular (icv) infusion of galanin inhibited mounting and intromission behaviors in male rats (Poggioli *et al.,* 1992), and a galanin antagonist (galantide) facilitated those behaviors (Benelli *et al.,* 1994). These inhibitory effects of galanin are opposed to the facilitative effects on copulation of preoptic area infusions of galanin in castrated, T-replaced male rats (Bloch *et al.,* 1993). Icv infusions of a galanin antagonist

(M-40) in male ferrets decreased their preference to spend time near a receptive female in a T-maze but did not affect their copulatory performance (Park and Baum, 1999). It is not clear whether site and species differences account for these apparent contradictions.

O. Neuropeptide Y

Neuropeptide Y (NPY) is a substance that has been found to have one of the most extensive distributions of cell bodies and fibers in the rat brain (Allen *et al.,* 1983). Administration of NPY to the cerebral ventricular system of male rats increased mount and intromission latencies and reduced the percentage of male rats copulating to ejaculation (J. T. Clark *et al.,* 1985a; Poggioli *et al.,* 1990). No disruptive effects of systemically delivered NPY on reflexive erections were detected (J. T. Clark *et al.,* 1985a).

P. Prostaglandin E$_2$

The effects of prostaglandin E$_2$ on sexual behavior of male rats have been investigated in two paradigms. The facilitative effects of microinjections into the MPOA are described later, in Section V.D.4.viii on drug injections into the MPOA. Blumberg (1991) tested the effects of fourth ventricle infusions of prostaglandin E$_2$ (8–12 μg) on sexual behavior of intact, sexually experienced male rats. In this case the primary effect of prostaglandin E$_2$ was a reduction in the postejaculatory mount and intromission intervals. This prostaglandin treatment raised basal forebrain temperature (measured in the MPOA) by 2–3°C. It is not known whether this increase in temperature influenced copulation or the behavioral effect of prostaglandin E$_2$ was mediated directly on behaviorally important neurons. However, Blumberg and his colleagues (Blumberg and Moltz, 1987, 1988; Blumberg *et al.,* 1987) reported an increase in core and MPOA temperature during copulation, followed by rapid cooling of the MPOA during the postejaculatory interval (see Section I.A.5. on the postejaculatory interval). Moltz (1990) suggested that the increase in MPOA temperature elicited by prostaglandin E$_2$ may itself affect copulation. About half of the temperature-sensitive (primarily warm-sensitive) neurons in MPOA slices also responded to addition of either T or E (but not both) to the bath medium; T affected about twice as many neurons as E (Silva and Boulant, 1986). (See Section III.D on membrane effects of steroids.) Silva and Boulant (1986) suggested that these responses to MPOA warming are likely to initiate physiological changes that promote cooling, including redirection of blood flow to the periphery. It seems likely that some of this blood flow is redirected to the penis during sexual encounters.

Q. Angiotensin II

There is one study in which the effects of central administration of angiotensin II on copulation in males has been examined (Clark, 1989). Angiotensin II, at one of two dosages (0.5 μg or 5.0 μg), was infused into the third ventricle of sexually experienced male rats. Each rat served as its own control, receiving the saline vehicle. The low dose of angiotensin II significantly increased intromission latency, whereas the higher dose increased the number of intromissions to ejaculation and postejaculatory interval, as well as intromission latency. Water was available during the copulation test, and the higher dose of angiotensin II stimulated drinking in nine out of 13 animals. None of the rats drank in other treatment conditions. Whether angiotensin II exerts specific effects on copulation remains to be determined.

V. BRAIN AREAS AND CIRCUITRY IMPLICATED IN THE CONTROL OF MASCULINE SEXUAL BEHAVIOR

The initial attempts to understand the neural organization of copulation were based on the results of removing large areas of the brain. However, more recent studies have limited the extent of the lesions to nuclei classically identified from Nissl-stained material, subsets of such nuclei, or discrete fiber pathways. In addition, electrophysiological stimulation and recording, direct hormonal and drug manipulations, microdialysis, and measures of cellular activation have been employed. Because the MPOA appears to be an integral component of this system, we will organize our presentation in terms of afferent and efferent pathways of the MPOA, starting most rostrally. However, it should be noted that sensory and motor pathways not described here do contribute to the neural organization of male sexual behavior. Visual and auditory stimuli clearly contribute to the elicitation of male sexual behavior, and somatomotor pathways are necessary for the patterned motor output. But relatively little research has been devoted to these connections; therefore, we will focus on the primary directions of research in this area. Effects of manipulations of each brain area, together with evidence of its functional activity, will be summarized first, followed by an integrative summary of the most important interconnections.

A. Olfactory Bulbs

The olfactory bulbs play an important role in the neural regulation of copulation. The initial rationale for removing the olfactory bulbs was a purely sensory one: to induce a loss of olfaction. The resulting behavioral deficits were attributed only to the resultant anosmia. However, it has been effectively argued that the olfactory bulbs have integrative functions other than simple sensory processing (e.g., Cain, 1974). Undoubtedly, both olfactory and nonsensory influences are important.

1. Effects of Lesions

Damage to the olfactory system of male hamsters produces severe copulatory deficits. Bilateral removal of the olfactory bulbs in male Syrian hamsters has completely eliminated copulation (Devor, 1973; Doty *et al.,* 1971; Lisk *et al.,* 1972; Murphy, 1980; Murphy and Schneider, 1970; Winans and Powers, 1974). The olfactory bulbs consist of two anatomically distinct components, the main and accessory olfactory bulbs, which receive innervation from the receptors of the nasal epithelium and vomeronasal organ (see Fig. 11), respectively. The contributions of lesions in each of these systems to the copulatory deficit following olfactory bulbectomy have been studied. Irrigation of the nasal cavity with zinc sulfate, a procedure designed to induce anosmia by destroying the receptors of the nasal epithelium (Winans and Powers, 1974), severely disrupted copulation in hamsters in some studies (Devor and Murphy, 1973; Lisk *et al.,* 1972), but in other studies no effect of this treatment has been found (O'Connell and Meredith, 1984; Powers and Winans, 1973, 1975; Winans and Powers, 1977). Some of the variability in outcomes may

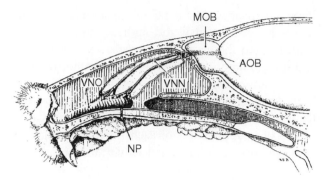

FIGURE 11 Relation between the vomeronasal organ and the olfactory bulbs of the Syrian hamster. The vomeronasal organ (VNO) projects to the accessory olfactory bulb (AOB) via the vomeronasal nerve (VNN). The vomeronasal nerve travels medial to the main olfactory bulb on the way to the accessory olfactory bulb. Olfactory information is presumed to reach the vomeronasal organ through the nasopalatine duct. In contrast, the main olfactory bulb receives innervation from the olfactory nerve originating from receptors in the nasal mucosa (pathway not shown). Efferent connections of the main and accessory olfactory bulbs as they relate to copulation are illustrated in Figs. 14 and 16. Abbreviations: AOB, accessory olfactory bulb; MOB, main olfactory bulb; NP, nasopalatine duct; VNN, vomeronasal nerve; VNO, vomeronasal organ. [We appreciate the generosity of Sarah W. Newman for providing this illustration adapted from one previously published (Winans and Powers, 1977).]

stem from the ineffectiveness of zinc sulfate in producing complete destruction of the nasal epithelium (Slotnick *et al.*, 2001). Denervating the accessory olfactory bulb by cutting the vomeronasal nerve or removal of the vomeronasal organ resulted in copulatory deficits affecting between 0 and 44% of the males, depending on the particular study, with the majority of the males copulating normally following surgery (Meredith, 1986; O'Connell and Meredith, 1984; Powers *et al.*, 1979; Powers and Winans, 1975; Winans and Powers, 1977). In contrast to the variable results of deafferenting either the main or the accessory olfactory systems, simultaneously interfering with both these systems on a peripheral level resulted in the elimination of copulation seen following bilateral olfactory bulbectomy. That is, when zinc sulfate treatment was combined with vomeronasal nerve cuts, copulation in male hamsters was eliminated (Meredith *et al.*, 1980; Powers and Winans, 1975; Winans and Powers, 1977). In addition, deafferenting the vomeronasal pump, the system that

draws chemosensory stimuli into the vomeronasal cavity, severely disrupted copulation in hamsters that were also treated intranasally with zinc sulfate (Meredith *et al.*, 1980). Because the elimination of copulation depends on the deafferentation of both the main and accessory olfactory systems, it is possible that the inconsistencies in the effects of zinc sulfate treatments on mating relate to the degree to which the zinc sulfate affected both the nasal epithelium and the vomeronasal organ (Winans and Powers, 1977).

As does olfactory bulbectomy, cutting the efferent pathways of the olfactory bulbs by transecting the lateral olfactory tract eliminates copulation in male hamsters (Devor, 1973). The results of these studies in hamsters have largely been taken to mean that interrupting olfaction is responsible for the observed copulatory deficits. However, several aspects of research with transections of the lateral olfactory tracts point to a neural contribution, in addition to the resultant anosmia. In one study (Devor, 1973), cuts of the caudal lateral olfactory tract eliminated copulation, whereas the incidence of vaginal licking was unaffected, suggesting that receipt of pheromones was unimpaired. In other studies, simultaneous lateral olfactory tract lesions yielded a delayed copulatory deficit (Macrides *et al.*, 1976; Marques *et al.*, 1982), whereas similar cuts in which the right and left sides were severed at different times produced an immediate disruption of copulation following the second cut (Macrides *et al.*, 1976). The delayed copulatory deficits indicate that neural changes secondary to the transection of the olfactory tracts were responsible for the deficits in copulation and that these secondary changes required time to develop. In the second case, the time between the first and second olfactory tract cuts could have permitted some secondary degeneration to occur, so that by the time the second cut was made, sufficient alterations had occurred to disrupt copulation immediately.

The primary effect of olfactory bulb removal in the male rat is a reduction in the percentage of males that copulate to ejaculation (Larsson, 1969, 1975; Lumia *et al.*, 1987; Meisel *et al.*, 1980, 1982; Wang and Hull, 1980; Wilhelmsson and Larsson, 1973; reviewed in Meisel *et al.*, 1984b). This failure to ejaculate stems from both an inability of some males to initiate copulation (Edwards *et al.*, 1990; Larsson, 1969, 1975; Meisel *et al.*, 1980; Wang and Hull, 1980; Wilhelmsson and

Larsson, 1973), as well as an inability to sustain copulation, once initiated (Meisel *et al.*, 1980). After olfactory bulbectomy or surgical deafferentation of the bulbs, many male rats retained the ability to copulate to ejaculation, but these males took longer to intromit and, subsequently, to ejaculate than did control males (Bermant and Taylor, 1969; Cain and Paxinos, 1974; Edwards and Davis, 1997; Edwards *et al.*, 1996; Heimer and Larsson, 1967; Larsson, 1969). Surgical deafferentation also decreased anogenital investigation of a female, but did not decrease the preference for a receptive female over a nonreceptive female (Edwards *et al.*, 1996). There is some indication that prior sexual experience may reduce the degree of the behavioral deficit in male rats (Bermant and Taylor, 1969), although severe copulatory dysfunction has also been reported for olfactory bulbectomized male rats previously screened for sexual vigor (Larsson, 1969; Meisel *et al.*, 1980; Wang and Hull, 1980). Administration of exogenous gonadotropin or T did not alter the effects of olfactory bulbectomy on copulation (Larsson, 1969, 1975; Meisel *et al.*, 1980), thus suggesting that the copulatory impairment was not a secondary consequence of diminished gonadal output.

The longer intromission latencies of male rats after olfactory bulbectomy can be taken as an indication of reduced sexual arousal, an interpretation supported by the failure of these males to show a preference for estrous females over nonestrous female rats (Edwards *et al.*, 1990). Procedures designed to increase levels of general arousal have been effective in activating copulation in male rats following olfactory bulbectomy (Barfield and Sachs, 1968; Caggiula *et al.*, 1976). The administration of either mildly painful flank shock (Meisel *et al.*, 1980) or tail pinch (Wang and Hull, 1980) to olfactory bulbectomized male rats stimulated these males to copulate to ejaculation, but they still exhibited longer intromission latencies and ejaculation latencies than did similarly stimulated males without lesions (Meisel *et al.*, 1980). Tail pinch and flank shock produced only a temporary restoration of copulation, as olfactory bulbectomized males were unable to copulate when tested the following week without such exogenous stimulation (Meisel *et al.*, 1980; Wang and Hull, 1980).

Much less has been done in the rat to determine the role of peripheral denervation of the olfactory system on copulation. Zinc sulfate treatment reduced the percentage of isolated male rats that copulated in one study (Thor and Flannelly, 1977), yet group-housed male rats in other studies were unaffected by such treatment (Cain and Paxinos, 1974; Thor and Flannelly, 1977). The amount of prior copulatory experience may determine the severity of the effects of zinc sulfate treatment, since males with no prior copulatory experience were affected to a greater degree than were sexually experienced male rats. The degree to which the zinc sulfate treatments in these experiments affected both the nasal epithelium and the vomeronasal organ was not assessed. The effect of vomeronasal organ removal on copulation in male rats has also been examined (Saito and Moltz, 1986). In sexually experienced males this surgery increased the latency to the first intromission as well as decreasing intromission rate, leading to longer ejaculation latencies, but all males copulated to ejaculation (Saito and Moltz, 1986). As with hamsters, damaging only the vomeronasal system produced a less severe copulatory disruption than interrupting both the main and vomeronasal systems.

Noncontact erections in male rats were eliminated by olfactory bulbectomy (Kondo *et al.*, 1999a). Lavage of the nasal epithelium with zinc sulfate significantly decreased noncontact erections; however, removal of the vomeronasal organ had no effect. Fresh urine, but not fresh feces, from estrous females elicited noncontact erections. Neither removal of auditory cues by devocalizing the females nor removal of visual cues by placing an opaque barrier between the subjects affected noncontact erections. Therefore, stimuli processed by the main olfactory system are the primary stimuli that elicit noncontact erections.

A few studies have explored the effects of damaging the efferents of the olfactory bulbs on copulation in male rats. Lesions of the olfactory tubercle had no effect on copulation or the male's investigation of the female rat's genital region (Perkins *et al.*, 1980). In contrast, olfactory peduncle lesions produced a slight, but statistically significant, reduction in the percentage of male rats copulating to ejaculation (Larsson, 1971). Males that ejaculated had longer ejaculation latencies than did control males (Larsson, 1971), findings consistent with the reported effects of olfactory bulbectomy in the male rat.

The role of the olfactory system in other rodent species has been studied to a much lesser degree than in the hamster and rat. Complete olfactory bulbectomy produced variable deficits in the male guinea pig (Beauchamp *et al.,* 1977), and vomeronasal organ removal had no effect on copulation (Beauchamp *et al.,* 1982). Nothing is known about the effects of bulbectomy on copulatory behavior in mating tests for male gerbils, but these animals could inseminate females when housed with them for extended periods (Cheal and Domesick, 1979). Olfactory bulbectomy eliminated mounting in essentially all male mice (Edwards and Burge, 1973; Rowe and Edwards, 1972; Rowe and Smith, 1973), although zinc sulfate treatment was without effect (Edwards and Burge, 1973). Removal of the vomeronasal organ in male mice sharply decreased the proportion of males that intromitted and subsequently ejaculated (Clancy *et al.,* 1984). Since in mice the effects of olfactory bulbectomy are more closely matched by damage to the vomeronasal system than to the primary olfactory epithelium, copulation in this species seems to be more dependent on an intact vomeronasal/accessory system than on the main olfactory system. In contrast, for the rat and hamster the vomeronasal system has an important, but not critical, role in copulation.

For nonrodent species, the olfactory system may not be as important for copulation. Olfactory bulbectomy or damage to the nasal epithelium had no effect on copulation in male dogs (Hart and Haugen, 1972), cats (Aronson and Cooper, 1974), rhesus monkeys (Goldfoot *et al.,* 1978), or sheep (Fletcher and Lindsay, 1968).

2. Activation of c-fos or Other Immediate-Early Genes

Although lesions provide information about areas that are critical for behavior, they may fail to identify other areas that contribute to behavioral performance. This difficulty may arise from either post-lesion recovery of function or tests that lack sensitivity to some behavioral parameters. As a result, some researchers have used activation of immediate-early genes to map pathways that are activated by behavior (reviewed in Pfaus and Heeb, 1997). (See Fig. 12 for brain areas showing activation of immediate-early genes.) Immediate-early genes are expressed transiently in response to stimulation (reviewed in Dragunow and Faull, 1989). Their

protein products serve as transcription regulators for other genes, which may in turn affect neural activity or responsiveness to certain stimuli.

There are notable similarities, but also some differences, among species in the responses of the main and accessory olfactory bulbs and their downstream connections to chemosensory cues from a female and to copulation. Copulation in male hamsters increased immunoreactivity (ir) to Fos, the protein product of the immediate-early gene *c-fos,* in their accessory olfactory bulbs, even in males whose main olfactory system had been ablated with zinc sulfate (Fernandez-Fewell and Meredith, 1994). There was no increase in Fos-ir in the main olfactory system of those animals. Therefore, pheromonal stimulation of the vomeronasal organ and accessory olfactory bulb is necessary and sufficient for Fos induction in the central vomeronasal pathways of male hamsters.

Either copulation or exposure of male rats to estrous female bedding elicited increased Fos-ir in their accessory olfactory bulbs and downstream structures; mating elicited more Fos-ir than did chemosensory stimulation alone (Kelliher *et al.,* 1999). However, the Fos-ir change was not affected by the occurrence or nonoccurrence of noncontact erections in response to the distal cues from a receptive female. Exposure to bedding from estrous females was sufficient to elicit Fos-ir, but not noncontact erections. As in hamsters in the previous study, there was no increase in Fos-ir in the main olfactory pathway. In male musk shrews both exposure to chemosensory cues from a receptive female and copulation increased Fos-ir in the same structures that were activated in rats and hamsters; however, unlike those species, musk shrews did not show increased Fos-ir in response to pheromones in structures caudal to the olfactory bulbs (Gill *et al.,* 1998).

Although the vomeronasal system appears to be more important than the main olfactory system for Fos induction in rodents, male ferrets, which are carnivores, rely on the main olfactory system (Kelliher *et al.,* 1998). Both estrous female bedding and an artificial peppermint odor increased Fos-ir in the main olfactory bulb of castrated male ferrets. Furthermore, T treatment increased the Fos response to female odors but not to peppermint. There was no difference in the amount of sniffing displayed by T-treated compared to vehicle-treated ferrets, thereby indicating that T's facilitation of

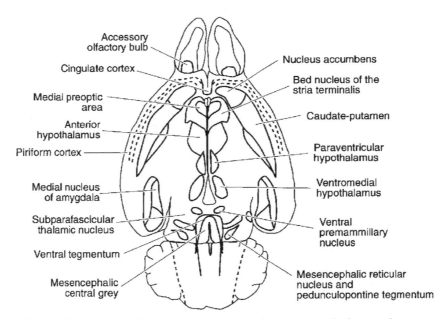

FIGURE 12   Regions within a horizontal section of rat brain in which Fos induction is observed after sexual stimulation in females and males. With some notable exceptions, Fos has been observed in similar regions in hamsters and gerbils. [Figure is reprinted from Pfaus and Heeb (1997) with permission.]

the response to female odors could not be attributed to increased scent gathering. Female pheromones failed to increase Fos-ir in the accessory olfactory bulb. Immunoreactivity to AR, but not ER, was present in both the main and accessory olfactory bulbs. Thus, T may act directly on neurons in the main olfactory bulb of ferrets to increase their responsiveness to female pheromones. The importance of the main olfactory system was further demonstrated by blocking the nares of both male and female ferrets (Kelliher and Baum, 2001). Neither males nor females with such occlusion preferred to approach the odor or combined odor, visual, and auditory cues from the opposite sex, compared to same-sex cues. Animals with sham occlusion did express a preference for the opposite-sex cues. Therefore the processing of odor cues by the main olfactory system is necessary for heterosexual mate choice in ferrets.

B. Amygdala

Several amygdaloid nuclei show sex differences in size, neurochemistry, and neuronal structure. The posterodorsal region of the medial nucleus, and also the encapsulated area of the bed nucleus of the stria terminalis (BNST), are approximately twice as large in males

as in females and contain more substance P, CCK, and vasopressin (Hines *et al.*, 1992). The posteromedial region of the cortical amygdaloid nucleus is also larger in males (VinanderCaerols *et al.*, 1998). The medial nucleus of male rats also shows a different pattern of synaptic contacts, compared to females (Nishizuka and Arai, 1981, 1983).

Modern neuroanatomical techniques have shown far more functional subdivisions of the amygdala than previously recognized (reviewed in Newman, 1999). There is controversy as to whether the amygdala should be considered an entity at all, rather than a conglomeration of dissimilar areas that may be more closely related to the cortex (cortical and basolateral divisions) or the striatum (medial and central nuclei) (Canteras *et al.*, 1995; Swanson and Petrovich, 1998). However, the interconnections of certain amygdaloid nuclei with sources of chemo- and genitosensory input and with output to the BNST and MPOA are very important for the control of male sexual behavior.

1. Effects of Radio-Frequency or Cell-Body Lesions

The role of the amygdala in the control of copulation in rodents has been assessed by lesions of two regions of the amygdala, one encompassing the cortical and

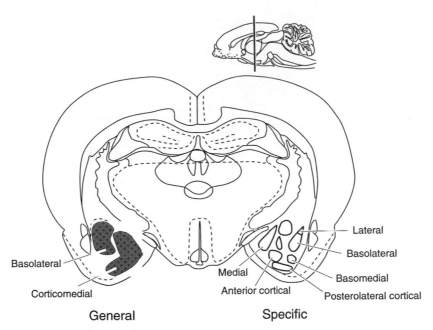

FIGURE 13 The amygdala, an almond-shaped structure located in each temporal lobe, seen in a schematic drawing of a coronal section of the rat brain. Two general amygdaloid regions, the basolateral and corticomedial nuclei (left), have been studied extensively. Destruction of the corticomedial nuclei, but not the basolateral nuclei, severely affects male copulatory behavior in rodents. The specific nuclei of the basolateral and corticomedial amygdala are depicted (right). [Figure is reprinted from Nelson (2000) with permission.]

medial nuclei (corticomedial amygdala), the other including the basal and lateral nuclei (basolateral amygdala). (See Fig. 13.) Lesions of the basolateral amygdala have not been found to have any disruptive effects on copulation in either male rats (Giantonio *et al.,* 1970; Harris and Sachs, 1975; Kondo, 1992) or hamsters (Lehman and Winans, 1982), and there has been indication that male rats with basolateral amygdaloid lesions copulate more rapidly than control males (Harris and Sachs, 1975). However, basolateral amygdala lesions abolished bar-pressing for a secondary reinforcer that had previously been paired with access to a receptive female (Everitt, 1990). Everitt (1990) suggested that the basolateral amygdala is important for sexual motivation, although, as noted above, this bar-pressing task may confound motivation with motor ability and ability to remember learned associations.

In contrast to basolateral lesions, those of the corticomedial amygdala impair copulation. Male rats (de Jonge *et al.,* 1992; Dominguez *et al.,* 2001; Giantonio

et al., 1970; Harris and Sachs, 1975; Kondo, 1992; McGregor and Herbert, 1992; Tsutsui *et al.,* 1994), hamsters (Lehman *et al.,* 1980), or gerbils (Heeb and Yahr, 2000) with these lesions had longer mount and ejaculation latencies, more intromissions preceding ejaculation, longer inter-intromission intervals, and fewer ejaculations to sexual exhaustion than did control males. Lesions restricted to the dorsolateral part of the medial amygdala of male rats reduced the number of ejaculations and increased ejaculation latency but did not affect mounting (Giantonio *et al.,* 1970; Harris and Sachs, 1975), thereby suggesting that this subregion is especially important for the control of ejaculation. However, such lesions did decrease mounting and delay ejaculation in gerbils (Heeb and Yahr, 2000).

The effects of corticomedial amygdala lesions may depend on the stimulus properties of the female rat. When males with lesions were tested with females brought into heat through injections of E alone, reliable effects on ejaculation latency, intromission frequency, and interintromission interval were found (Perkins *et al.*, 1980). However, when stimulus females treated with both E and P were used to test the males, there were no differences between lesion and control males. It is not known which stimulus properties or behavior of female rats treated only with E are important to uncovering the copulatory deficit of males with corticomedial amygdala lesions. Although the amygdala receives information from the sensory nerves of the genital region (Carrer, 1978), inadequate genital sensitivity can probably be excluded as a contributing factor, since the intromissions of males with lesions were intravaginal, and the proportion of mounts with and without intromission (intromission ratio) was normal (Sachs, 1978). Perhaps female rats treated with both E and P are more sexually arousing and control the pacing of the copulatory interactions more effectively than females treated with E alone.

Large excitotoxic lesions encompassing much of the amygdala abolished mating in most rats; however, as discussed below, microinjections of the classic DA agonist apomorphine into the MPOA restored behavior, thus suggesting that amygdala lesions may somehow disrupt DA release in the MPOA and thereby inhibit copulation (Dominguez *et al.*, 2001). This hypothesis was supported by the results of smaller radio frequency lesions restricted to the medial amygdala. These lesions resulted in increased intromissions and time preceding ejaculation and fewer ejaculations per test, compared to males with sham lesions. Furthermore, although basal DA levels in the MPOA were not different from those of control males, there was no DA increase in response to a receptive female or during copulation (Dominguez *et al.*, 2001). Because there are no DA-containing neurons in the medial amygdala of rats, amygdala efferents apparently synapse, either directly or indirectly, on dopaminergic cell bodies or terminals in the MPOA.

Unilateral lesions of the MPOA impaired but did not eliminate mounting behavior of male rats (Kondo and Arai, 1995). When a contralateral but not an ipsilateral lesion of the medial amygdala was added, copulatory behavior was severely disrupted. Therefore, the medial amygdala and MPOA may function as a unitary system controlling male copulatory behavior.

In another demonstration of the contextual specificity of the physiological mechanisms mediating erec-

tions, radiofrequency lesions of the medial amygdala abolished noncontact erections, but had no effect on touch-based erections and actually increased the number of anteroflexions (Kondo *et al.*, 1997). In copulation tests, these animals had lower intromission ratios, longer inter-intromission intervals, and no ejaculations in the 20 minutes after the first intromission. Lesions in the posterodorsal area of the medial amygdala are especially damaging to noncontact erections, but some of this effect may result from impairment of the detection or processing of the relevant odors, rather than from impairment of attention to receptive females or sexual arousal per se (Kondo *et al.*, 1999b).

2. Activation of c-fos or Other Immediate-Early Genes

Anterior cortical and medial nuclei of the amygdala receive major projections from the main and accessory olfactory bulbs (McDonald, 1998). Therefore, it was of interest to determine the effects of various types of olfactory input on the expression of *c-fos*. The two earliest studies to map the activation of Fos expression by copulation found a circuit of Fos immunoreactivity in structures receiving olfactory and genital somatosensory input (Baum and Everitt, 1992; Robertson *et al.*, 1991). Sites activated by copulation included the medial amygdala, as well as the BNST, the MPOA, and the central tegmental field of male rats. Increasing amounts of copulation, from mounting to several ejaculations, elicited increasing amounts of Fos-ir in these sites (Baum and Everitt, 1992; Coolen *et al.*, 1996; Veening and Coolen, 1998). A similar pattern was observed in male hamsters (Kollack and Newman, 1992; Kollack-Walker and Newman, 1995, 1997), gerbils (Heeb and Yahr, 1996), prairie voles (Wang *et al.*, 1997), and musk shrews (Gill *et al.*, 1998). However, administration of lidocaine anesthetic to the penis of male rats resulted in few intromissions but a significant increase in Fos-ir in both the medial amygdala and the MPOA (Oboh *et al.*, 1995). The authors suggested that chemosensory stimuli were the primary determinants of the mounting-induced increments in neuronal Fos-ir.

The importance of chemosensory input for activation of Fos-ir in the medial amygdala has been investigated directly. Exposure of male rats to bedding from estrous females increased Fos-ir at each level of the vomeronasal circuit, including the posterodorsal portion of the

medial amygdala (Bressler and Baum, 1996; Coolen
et al., 1997b). Heeb and Yahr (1996) found that it was
the medial part of the posterodorsal medial amygdala
of gerbils that was activated by exposure to sex-related
odors, whereas the lateral portion was activated only
following ejaculation (see Section VI on circuitry below). However, both anterior and posterior portions
of the medial amygdala of male rats were activated by
exposure to bedding from estrous females or by noncontact erections in the presence of an estrous female
behind a barrier (Kelliher *et al.,* 1999). The authors
suggested that although these odors did not increase
Fos-ir in areas of the main olfactory bulb that they examined, the stimuli important for noncontact erection
are probably mediated by the main olfactory system.

The main olfactory system contributes input primarily to the anterior corticomedial amygdala, whereas the
vomeronasal system sends projections to both the anterior and posterior corticomedial amygdala (reviewed
in Wood and Newman, 1995b). (See Fig. 14.) The
vomeronasal projections are more medial than those of
the main olfactory system. In agreement with the differential distribution of main olfactory and vomeronasal
system inputs, intranasal zinc sulfate treatment, which
made male hamsters anosmic but left the vomeronasal
system intact, decreased copulation-induced Fos-ir in
the anterior medial amygdala (Fernandez-Fewell and
Meredith, 1998), a finding that suggests that input from
the main olfactory system contributes to the activation
of neurons in this area. In ferrets pheromones derived
from estrous females activated Fos-ir only in the main
olfactory system, although the authors acknowledged
that other biologically relevant odors may activate the
ferret's vomeronasal system (Kelliher *et al.,* 1998).

Fos-ir was colocalized with AR in the dorsal medial
amygdala and numerous other sites in male rats (Gréco
et al., 1998b). Furthermore, a tract-tracing experiment
showed that neurons that colocalized Fos-ir and AR-
ir were interconnected (Gréco *et al.,* 1998b; see Section VI on circuitry below). Although both chemosensory and hormonal forms of stimulation are necessary
for activation of male hamster mating, the circuits that
detect these two types of cues may be separate but interactive (Wood, 1997; Wood and Coolen, 1997; Wood
and Newman, 1995c). However, male rats that had
been castrated seven days earlier and treated with T,
E, or no steroid showed equivalent amounts of Fos-ir

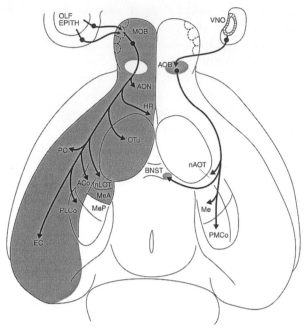

FIGURE 14   Diagram of the ventral surface of the hamster
brain. Shaded areas indicate brain regions that receive efferent
projections of the olfactory system, via the main olfactory bulb
(left), and of the vomeronasal system, via the accessory olfactory bulb (right). Abbreviations: ACo, anterior cortical nucleus
of the amygdala; AOB, accessory olfactory bulb; AON, anterior
olfactory nucleus; BNST, bed nucleus of the stria terminalis; EC,
entorhinal cortex; HR, hippocampal rudiment; Me, medial nucleus of the amygdala; MeA, medial nucleus of the amygdala,
anterior division; MeP, medial nucleus of the amygdala, posterior division; MOB, main olfactory bulb; nAOT, nucleus of the
accessory olfactory tract; nLOT, nucleus of the lateral olfactory
tract; OLF EPITH, olfactory epithelium; OTu, olfactory tubercle;
PC, piriform cortex; PLCo, posterolateral cortical nucleus of the
amygdala; PMCo, posteromedial cortical nucleus of the amygdala; VNO, vomeronasal organ. [Figure is reprinted from Wood
and Newman (1995b) with permission.]

in the medial amygdala, bed nucleus of the stria terminalis, and MPOA following eight intromissions (Baum
and Wersinger, 1993). Therefore, circulating gonadal
steroids have little effect on copulation-induced Fos-ir.
Instead, the hormones present before castration initiated long-term changes that allowed both copulation
and Fos expression to occur one week after castration.

Fos-ir in the medial amygdala, but not in the MPOA,
was positively correlated with the duration of the postejaculatory interval, thus suggesting that this area may

contribute to postejaculatory quiescence (Lumley and Hull, 1999). As reviewed below (Section VI), a lateral subregion of the posterodorsal medial amygdala appears to be associated with ejaculation and approaching sexual satiety. Indeed, lesions of this area increased the number of ejaculations that preceded satiety (Parfitt *et al.*, 1996). Furthermore, approximately one-third of the ejaculation-related (Fos-ir) neurons also showed staining for nicotinamide adenine dinucleotide phosphate diaphorase (NADPHd), a marker for NOS, suggesting that NO may contribute to the regulation of neurons in this area (Simmons and Yahr, 2001).

3. Effects of Hormone Implants

There is considerable evidence that hormone implants in the medial amygdala can contribute to the maintenance or restoration of male sexual behavior. Bilateral T implants into the medial amygdala of castrated male rats delayed the loss of both copulation and noncontact erections (Bialy and Sachs, 2000). Similarly, either T (Wood, 1996) or E (Wood and Coolen, 1997; Coolen and Wood, 1999) implants into the medial amygdala restored copulatory behavior in castrated male hamsters. However, DHT implants were ineffective, thereby suggesting that activation of androgen receptors in the medial amygdala is insufficient for behavioral restoration in male hamsters (Wood, 1996). But DHT implants into the medial amygdala were sufficient for behavioral activation in castrated rats that were given subthreshold systemic injections of E (Baum *et al.*, 1982). Unfortunately, the effects of DHT in the medial amygdala without systemic E were not assessed in this (or any other) study, so the contribution of the systemic E treatment to copulation in these animals is uncertain. Implants of the AR antagonist, hydroxyflutamide, into the medial amygdala of T-replaced castrated male rats were only partially effective in inhibiting copulation (McGinnis *et al.*, 1996). Therefore, stimulation of ARs in the medial amygdala contributes to the elicitation of male copulatory behavior in both rats and hamsters; however, such stimulation is not necessary and may not be sufficient for copulation in male rats or hamsters.

A series of studies probed the interactions between hormonal and chemosensory stimulation. Olfactory bulbectomy in male hamsters, either ipsilateral or contralateral to a T implant into the medial amygdala, rendered the implant ineffective (Wood and Coolen, 1997). (See Fig. 15.) Similar implants into the MPOA were less susceptible to the loss of olfactory input. Cottingham and Pfaff (1986) suggested that steroid-responsive networks should exhibit redundancy amplification, stability, and selective filtering. Because both the medial amygdala and the MPOA transduce steroid cues and receive chemosensory input, Coolen and Wood (1999) tested whether steroid implants into these two areas exhibit steroid amplification. Although there is some redundancy, in that steroid implants into either area were sufficient to activate copulation, there appears to be no amplification, in that males with dual implants into the medial amygdala and MPOA showed no greater copulatory ability than did males with single implants.

The posterodorsal medial amygdala (MeApd) is larger in males than in females; however, castration in adulthood caused the MeApd to shrink to a female-typical size within four weeks (Cooke *et al.*, 1999). Androgen treatment of adult females for the same period enlarged the MeApd to male-typical sizes. The size difference arose from changes in soma size. Therefore, hormone treatments in adulthood can completely reverse a sexual dimorphism in a brain area important for sexual behavior. Castration also led to smaller neurons in the anterodorsal amygdala (MeAad); restoration of either DHT or E independently increased soma size in the MeApd but not in the MeAad (Cooke *et al.*, 2001). In addition, castration decreased immunoreactivity for CCK in the MeApd as well as in sexually dimorphic areas of the BNST and medial preoptic nucleus (Simerly and Swanson, 1987). T treatment restored CCK-ir in all three areas.

4. Amygdaloid Efferents

Efferents of the corticomedial amygdala of rats travel via the stria terminalis, innervating the BNST as well as the MPOA (Krettek and Price, 1978). In the hamster, the caudal corticomedial amygdala projects to the MPOA via the stria terminalis (Kevetter and Winans, 1981). The rostral corticomedial amygdala projects to the caudal medial BNST via a ventral fiber pathway (Lehman and Winans, 1983). Cutting the stria terminalis in the male hamster increased mount latency, ejaculation latency, and interintromission interval for two weeks postoperatively (Lehman *et al.*, 1983). Three weeks after surgery, the ejaculation latency was still

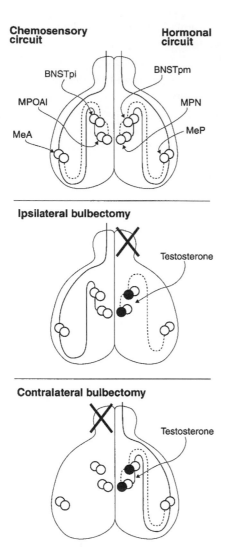

Chemosensory circuit   **Hormonal circuit**

BNSTpi   BNSTpm

MPOAl   MPN

MeA   MeP

Ipsilateral bulbectomy

Testosterone

Contralateral bulbectomy

Testosterone

FIGURE 15 Schematic diagram of mating behavior circuitry through the medial amygdaloid nucleus (Me), bed nucleus of the stria terminalis (BNST), and medial preoptic area (MPOA) in the male Syrian hamster brain, illustrating the separate pathways for receipt of chemosensory and hormonal cues. (Top) Normal male. Elements of the chemosensory circuit (*left*) include the anterior subdivision of the Me (MeA), posterointermediate subdivision of BNST (BNSTpi), and the lateral subdivision of MPOA (MPOAl). The hormonal circuit (*right*) consists of the posterior subdivision of the Me (MeP), the posteromedial subdivition of BNST (BNSTpm), and the medial preoptic nucleus (MPN). (Middle) Testosterone stimulation of BNSTpm and MPN (solid circles), combined with removal of the ipsilateral olfactory bulb, prevents communication between the chemosensory and hormonal circuits. (Bottom) Removal of the contralateral olfactory bulb permits chemosensory and hormonal integration. [Figure reprinted from Wood and Newman (1995c) with permission.]

lengthened, and the number of intromissions before ejaculation was significantly increased. These effects parallel those following lesions of the caudal corticomedial amygdala, a source of the strial fibers. Knife cuts of the ventral pathway that interrupted fibers arising from the rostral corticomedial amygdala produced a less severe loss of mating behavior (Lehman, 1982). Combined knife cuts of both the strial and ventral outputs of the corticomedial amygdala eliminated copulation in male hamsters (Lehman *et al.*, 1983). In rats, too, a possible role of a nonstrial output from the medial amygdala was suggested by the observation that lesions of the medial amygdala were more disruptive of copulation than were cuts of the stria terminalis (Kondo and Yamanouchi, 1995).

C. Bed Nucleus of the Stria Terminalis

The BNST has reciprocal connections with the medial amygdala and the MPOA (Canteras *et al.*, 1992; Gomez and Newman, 1992; Wood, 1997; Wood and Newman, 1995b). It also contains a high concentration of ARs (Doherty and Sheridan, 1981; Simerly *et al.*, 1990; Wood and Newman, 1993; Wood *et al.*, 1992).

1. Effects of Radio-Frequency or Cell-Body Lesions

Lesions of either the stria terminalis or the BNST in rats have produced copulatory deficits in male rats similar to those seen following corticomedial amygdala lesions. Giantonio *et al.* (1970) reported that lesions of the stria terminalis significantly increased the ejaculation latencies of male rats and that these males displayed a "distinct, though nonsignificant" (p. 42) increase in the number of mounts and intromissions prior to ejaculation. In subsequent studies of male rats, lesions of the stria terminalis (Paxinos, 1976), or BNST (Emery and Sachs, 1976; Valcourt and Sachs, 1979) significantly increased the number of intromissions preceding ejaculation, the interintromission interval, and consequently the ejaculation latency. The similarity of the effects of lesions of the BNST and corticomedial amygdala in particular suggests that little or no processing of copulatory information occurs in the BNST of male rats, and that this nucleus serves primarily to relay information from the amygdala to other areas, such as the medial preoptic nucleus.

Large lesions of the BNST resulted in a greater number of intromissions preceding ejaculation, longer inter-intromission intervals, longer postejaculatory refractory periods, and a reduction in ejaculations (Valcourt and Sachs, 1979). However, touch-based erections were not affected. But smaller radiofrequency lesions of the BNST greatly decreased the number of noncontact erections (Liu *et al.*, 1997b). These lesions also slowed the rate of copulation but did not affect intromission ratio, thus suggesting that *in copula* erections were not affected. These results are in dramatic contrast to the effects of lesions of the MPOA, which had little effect on noncontact erections but dramatically impaired copulation.

In male gerbils bilateral lesions of either the caudal medial BNST or the sexually dimorphic area (SDA) of the preoptic area severely impaired copulation (Sayag *et al.*, 1994). Furthermore, unilateral lesions of the caudal medial BNST and the contralateral SDA also produced severe detrimental effects on copulation. However, ipsilateral lesions of the medial amygdala and SDA produced much less impairment. Therefore, the caudal medial BNST does not simply relay input from the medial amygdala to the SDA of gerbils. Rather, it appears to perform an important integrative function. It is not clear whether the different conclusions regarding the importance of the BNST in rats (Paxinos, 1976; Emery and Sachs, 1976; Valcourt and Sachs, 1979) and gerbils (Sayag *et al.*, 1994) reflects a species difference or a difference in experimental procedures.

2. Activation of c-fos or Other Immediate-Early Genes

As in the amygdala, Fos-ir in the BNST of male rats was increased by mating, noncontact erections, or estrous female bedding (Kelliher *et al.*, 1999). Exposure of male hamsters to female hamster vaginal fluid increased Fos-ir in the BNST (Fernandez-Fewell and Meredith, 1994). In addition, entering an arena containing sex-related odors, in which the males had previously copulated, elicited an increase in Fos-ir in the posteromedial area of the BNST of male gerbils (Heeb and Yahr, 1996). Coolen et al. (1996) also identified the posteromedial portion of the BNST of male rats as responding to chemosensory investigation; however, specific subregions within the posteromedial BNST were

activated only following ejaculation. Mating, but not aggressive behavior, increased Fos-ir in the MPOA and the posteroventral portion of the posteromedial BNST of male Syrian hamsters (Kollack-Walker and Newman, 1995). Both mating and aggressive behavior elicited Fos-ir in several other areas; thus, the MPOA and a portion of the BNST are more directly related to sexual than aggressive behavior in Syrian hamsters. In contrast to the chemosensory activation of Fos responses in the BNST of rodents, there was no increase in Fos-ir in the BNST of male ferrets exposed to estrous female bedding (Kelliher *et al.*, 1998).

3. Role of Vasopressin

There are more neurons that are immunoreactive for arginine vasopressin (AVP) in the BNST of male prairie voles, which are monogamous, and in male mountain voles, which are not monogamous, than in females of the same species (Wang, 1995). Furthermore, three days of cohabitation with a female dramatically reduced the density of AVP-ir fibers in two projection areas (lateral septum and lateral habenular nucleus) of male prairie voles, suggesting an increase in release of this peptide (Wang *et al.*, 1994). Cohabitation increased the number of BNST cells labeled for AVP mRNA and also raised plasma T levels in male prairie voles. However, no changes in AVP mRNA were found in female prairie voles or in mountain voles of either sex. Therefore, cohabitation may result in increased synthesis and release of AVP in male prairie voles, which may contribute to pair-bonding in this species.

4. Hormonal Control of CCK

In the sexually dimorphic encapsulated part of the BNST, castration decreased immunoreactivity for CCK (Simerly and Swanson, 1987). T treatment restored CCK-ir to normal. Similar effects were observed in sexually dimorphic areas of the medial amygdala and medial preoptic nucleus.

D. Medial Preoptic Area

The MPOA is a critical integrative site for male sexual behavior in all vertebrate species that have been tested. Because there is great variability among species in the stimuli that elicit copulation and the motor patterns that express it, the universal regulatory role of the MPOA confirms its importance as a central integrative node. However, as discussed below, it has been difficult to pinpoint the precise function of the MPOA. For example, large lesions of the MPOA completely abolish copulation in males of numerous species, yet similar lesions have less catastrophic effects on measures of sexual motivation and almost no effect on noncontact erections (see Section V.D.1). The MPOA receives indirect input from every sensory modality and sends reciprocal connections back to those sources (Simerly and Swanson, 1986). These reciprocal connections allow the MPOA to modify the processing of sensory input. Furthermore, the MPOA and its afferent connections contain steroid receptors, which provide the means to bias sensory input to favor sexually relevant stimuli. Efferent connections from the MPOA are critical for the initiation and patterning of copulation. They project to hypothalamic, midbrain, and brain stem nuclei that regulate autonomic or somatomotor patterns and motivational states (reviewed in Simerly and Swanson, 1988; Yahr, 1995). (See Section VI.)

1. Effects of Electrolytic and Cell-Body Lesions

Lesions of the MPOA severely impair copulation in male rats (Ågmo *et al.*, 1977; Bermond, 1982; Brackett and Edwards, 1984; Chen and Bliss, 1974; de Jonge *et al.*, 1989; Edwards and Einhorn, 1986; Giantonio *et al.*, 1970; Ginton and Merari, 1977; Hansen and Hagelsrum, 1984; Heimer and Larsson, 1966/1967; Hendricks and Sheetz, 1973; Kamel and Frankel, 1978; Kondo *et al.*, 1990; Larsson and Heimer, 1964; Meisel, 1982, 1983; Ryan and Frankel, 1978; Singer, 1968; Twiggs *et al.*, 1978; van de Poll and van Dis, 1979), hamsters (Floody, 1989; Powers *et al.*, 1987), mice (Bean *et al.*, 1981), guinea pigs (Phoenix, 1961), gerbils (Commins and Yahr, 1984c; Yahr *et al.*, 1982, 1984), dogs (Hart, 1974b), cats (Hart *et al.*, 1973), ferrets (Cherry and Baum, 1990), goats (Hart, 1986), marmosets (Lloyd and Dixson, 1988), rhesus monkeys (Slimp *et al.*, 1978), birds (Balthazart and Surlemont, 1990), lizards (Wheeler and Crews, 1978), snakes (Krohmer and Crews, 1987) and fish (Macey *et al.*, 1974). Most of the research on the effects of MPOA lesions on copulation in males has been done in rats. Heimer and Larsson (1964, 1966/1967) published

the first comprehensive analysis. Large lesions of the MPOA, extending into the rostral anterior hypothalamus, eliminated copulation in sexually experienced male rats. Indeed, none of the males with lesions even mounted a receptive female rat in periodic tests given as long as three months after surgery. Attempts to arouse these males during testing by handling them or exposing them to different females were ineffective in stimulating copulation. Chronic T administration was similarly ineffective, an indication that the effects of the MPOA lesions were not an indirect result of diminished gonadal output. Smaller lesions of the MPOA typically produced less severe deficits (Heimer and Larsson, 1966/1967), and the results of these smaller lesions on copulation will be considered later in this section.

Van de Poll and van Dis (1979) discovered a relation between the location of the lesion and the severity of the subsequent copulatory deficit. Damage to the caudal part of the MPOA, including the rostral anterior hypothalamus [much like the lesions in the Heimer and Larsson study (1966/1967)], was associated with a severe copulatory deficit. Male rats with lesions placed in the rostral MPOA had much less severe copulatory deficits; many of the males copulated to ejaculation.

Although we refer to these lesions as MPOA lesions, we have noted that additional damage extending into the rostral anterior hypothalamus enhances the copulatory deficit in rats. Similarly, lesions confined to the MPOA of marmosets decreased parameters of copulation; lesions at the junction of the MPOA and anterior hypothalamus eliminated intromission and ejaculation (Lloyd and Dixson, 1988). The MPOA and anterior hypothalamus of rats can be delineated on the basis of cytoarchitecture, connectivity, and distribution of cells containing steroid receptors (Conrad and Pfaff, 1975, 1976a,b; Pfaff and Keiner, 1973; Simerly *et al.*, 1990; Simerly and Swanson, 1988), yet it has not been determined that this anatomical distinction can be generalized to other vertebrate species, nor do we know the location of the functional boundaries for neurons in this area involved in the regulation of copulation. However, the similarity of effects of electrolytic lesions, which destroy both cell bodies and fibers of passage, and excitotoxic lesions, which destroy cell bodies but spare passing fibers, indicates that neurons within the MPOA play a critical role in the activation of copulation in male rats (Hansen *et al.*, 1982a). (See Fig. 16

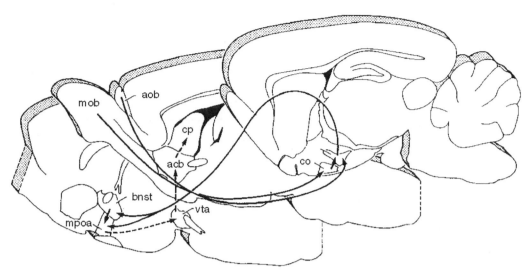

FIGURE 16 Some of the neural pathways regulating male copulatory behavior, depicted in three parasagittal sections (most medial on the left, most lateral on the right) of a rodent brain. Only a few of the relevant inputs to the preoptic area have been indicated, primarily those arising from the medial amygdala. Abbreviations: acb, nucleus accumbens; aob, accessory olfactory bulb; bnst, bed nucleus of the stria terminalis; co, cortical amygdala; cp, caudate-putamen; me, medial amygdala; mob, main olfactory bulb; mpoa, medial preoptic area; vta, ventral tegmental area. [Figure is reprinted from Meisel and Sachs (1994).]

for a summary of some afferent and efferent pathways relevant for copulation.)

A number of attempts have been made to reactivate copulation in male rats that have MPOA lesions. We have already noted that handling the male rat or replacing the estrous female during testing, procedures that can stimulate copulation in intact male rats, had no effect on copulation in males with MPOA lesions in the Heimer and Larsson study (1966/1967). Even more extreme forms of excitation, such as repeated flank shock, could not compensate for MPOA damage (Meisel, 1983). The only procedure that has been shown to promote copulation in adult males receiving medial preoptic lesions has been a pharmacological manipulation. Systemic injection of lisuride in male rats, a nonspecific monoamine receptor agonist, transiently activated copulation in 100% of the animals with MPOA lesions; 50% copulated to ejaculation (Hansen *et al.*, 1982a). When these animals were subsequently treated with saline, they once again failed to copulate. The success of manipulations of the monoamine systems to overcome the effects of the MPOA damage contrasts with the inefficacy of administration of GnRH (Ryan and Frankel, 1978) or naloxone (Hansen *et al.*, 1982a) under similar conditions.

For many brain lesions behavioral recovery occurs simply as a function of time after the lesion. However, there were no signs of recovery following MPOA lesions in male rats either three (Heimer and Larsson, 1966/1967) or eight (Ginton and Merari, 1977) months after surgery. Furthermore, two-stage lesions of the MPOA in male cats, with time for recovery between the lesions on the two sides, produced just as severe copulatory deficits as did bilateral lesions made at the same time (Hart, 1980). Therefore, reorganization in other brain areas appears to be unable to compensate for the loss of the MPOA.

Considering the resistance of animals with MPOA lesions to the numerous therapeutic actions that improve behavior after other lesions, it was surprising that MPOA lesions in juvenile male rats produced only minimal copulatory deficits when these animals were tested as adults (Leedy *et al.*, 1980; Twiggs *et al.*, 1978). When these males were reared in isosexual or heterosexual groups, normal levels of copulatory behavior were observed for the first ejaculatory series (Klaric, 1990; Twiggs *et al.*, 1978). There were two respects in which the behavior of these animals differed from that of control animals: they had fewer ejaculations before sexual exhaustion, and they showed a more rapid decline in copulation following castration than did control males (Leedy *et al.,* 1980). In contrast, males receiving lesions as juveniles and reared in social isolation did not copulate as adults (Klaric, 1990; Twiggs *et al.,* 1978). This result is difficult to interpret, however, as similar detrimental effects of social isolation on male rats without brain damage are also found (e.g., Gerall *et al.,* 1967). Furthermore, behavioral recovery was observed in male rats that received lesions as juveniles and were socially isolated but were handled daily until adulthood (Meisel, 1982), thus suggesting that specific interactions with their peers are not critical for the development of copulatory behavior in these animals.

Two other studies also yielded evidence of behavioral recovery following MPOA lesions in juvenile male rats, although these males still had a deficit relative to control males (Meisel, 1982, 1983). The MPOA lesions in these studies were probably larger and more caudally placed (including the rostral anterior hypothalamus) than those in the earlier studies. Because such large lesions, including the anterior hypothalamus, would be expected to produce the most severe deficits in adult male rats, this might explain the incomplete recovery. So far, the plasticity in copulatory behavior exhibited by males receiving MPOA lesions seems to be specific to rats, as MPOA lesions eliminated copulation in dogs (Hart and Ladewig, 1979, 1980) and cats (Leedy and Hart, 1986) operated on as juveniles, despite extensive social experience.

Compared with large lesions, the effects of small lesions of the MPOA on copulation in males are much more variable. These restricted lesions are of potential interest because the MPOA can be partitioned into several subnuclei, based on Nissl-stained material, with some of the subregions showing different patterns of connectivity (Maragos *et al.,* 1989; Simerly and Swanson, 1986) and neurotransmitter content (Simerly *et al.,* 1986). Smaller lesions of the MPOA spared copulation in male rats, in that most of the males were able to at least initiate copulation, and the majority of these ejaculated (Arendash and Gorski, 1983; Ginton and Merari, 1977; Heimer and Larsson, 1966/1967). Heimer and Larsson (1966/1967) were unable to attribute the most severe deficits of restricted lesions to damage within a particular subregion of the MPOA. Arendash and Gorski (1983), paying particular atten-

tion to the medial preoptic subregions, found that lesions in the dorsal parastrial area reduced the percentage of male rats that ejaculated; lesions in other subregions spared copulation. In another study (Kondo *et al.,* 1990) either dorsal or ventral MPOA lesions essentially eliminated ejaculation, but only the ventral lesions disrupted the initiation of copulation. Small lesions in the region of the sexually dimorphic nucleus of the MPOA (Gorski *et al.,* 1978) had no effect on copulation in experienced male rats (Arendash and Gorski, 1983) and produced only a transient increase (evident only on the first postoperative test) in latencies to mount, intromit, and ejaculate in previously inexperienced male rats (de Jonge *et al.,* 1989). In general, male rats that were still able to copulate after small preoptic lesions had prolonged intromission and ejaculation latencies (Arendash and Gorski, 1983), were inconsistent from test to test (Heimer and Larsson, 1966/1967), and in some cases recovered normal copulatory ability over time (Ginton and Merari, 1977).

The conclusion that lesions of the MPOA must be large to result in the elimination of copulation may be limited to rats. Small lesions of the MPOA in male hamsters, confined to the peristrial region that receives terminals from the caudal medial amygdala, eliminated copulation (Powers *et al.,* 1987). In male gerbils, small lesions of the MPOA produced copulatory deficits just as severe as those seen following large lesions, when small bilateral lesions were localized to either of two regions of the sexually dimorphic area (SDA) (Commins and Yahr, 1984b). Both the medial (mSDA) and lateral (lSDA) cell groups are sexually dimorphic with regard to size (Commins and Yahr, 1984a), density of ARs and ERs (Commins and Yahr, 1985), and acetylcholinesterase immunoreactivity (Commins and Yahr, 1984b). Furthermore, these cell groups are interconnected (De Vries *et al.,* 1988; Finn *et al.,* 1993; reviewed in Yahr, 1995). Small excitotoxic lesions of the left or right mSDA, paired with similar lesions of the contralateral lSDA, were as effective as bilateral lesions of each (Yahr and Gregory, 1993). Therefore, these two areas are part of a critical circuit for the control of male sexual behavior. Small lesions targeting the posterodorsal preoptic nucleus, which is selectively activated by ejaculation in male gerbils (Heeb and Yahr, 1996), decreased mounting and delayed ejaculation, thereby suggesting that this area normally facilitates copulation, rather than simply responding to sensory stimulation (Heeb and Yahr, 2000).

The inability of male rats with large MPOA lesions to initiate copulation has been taken to mean that the source of the behavioral impairment is a reduction in sexual arousal or motivation (e.g., Chen and Bliss, 1974; Edwards and Einhorn, 1986; Ginton and Merari, 1977). However, male rats with MPOA lesions pursue estrous female rats and investigate their anogenital region, climb over them, and occasionally clasp and mount them without thrusting (Hansen and Hagelsrum,1984; Heimer and Larsson, 1966/1967; Meisel, 1983). A similar pattern of behavior has been described for male cats (Hart *et al.*, 1973) and dogs (Hart, 1974b) with MPOA lesions. Indeed, male dogs with such lesions mounted and sometimes showed shallow thrusting, but they did not copulate effectively (Hart, 1974b). Although monkeys or rats with preoptic lesions rarely showed female-directed sexual contact, they would press a bar for access to a receptive female (Everitt and Stacey, 1987; Slimp *et al.*, 1978) or for a secondary reinforcer that had previously been associated with a receptive female (reviewed in Everitt, 1990). Furthermore, the frequency of masturbation by the monkeys was unaffected by MPOA lesion; although they were clearly sexually aroused, they did not appear to recognize or respond to the female as a sexual partner. Similarly, MPOA lesions that dramatically impaired copulation had little or no effect on noncontact erections (Liu *et al.*, 1997b). Based on this apparent dissociation between sexual motivation and copulatory performance, Everitt (1990) has suggested that the MPOA controls only copulatory performance and does not influence sexual motivation.

However, lesions of the MPOA have diminished sexual motivation in other contexts, including the preference for a female partner in rats (Edwards and Einhorn, 1986; Edwards *et al.*, 1996; Paredes *et al.*, 1998b) and ferrets (Baum *et al.*, 1996; Kindon *et al.*, 1996; Paredes and Baum, 1995), pursuit of a female by male rats (Paredes *et al.*, 1993a), or precopulatory behavior (anticipatory erections, tongue flicking, and anogenital investigations) in marmosets (Lloyd and Dixson, 1988). Therefore, while sexual motivation is not eliminated by MPOA lesions, as is copulation, it is clearly diminished. The evolutionary conservation of MPOA influence on both sexual motivation and performance

is apparent in studies of Japanese quail (Balthazart *et al.*, 1998). Small lesions of subregions of the MPOA differentially impaired copulatory performance and sexual motivation, measured as time spent in front of a window through which the male could view a female.

The specificity of effects of MPOA lesions is highlighted by contrast with the effects of lesions in the lateral preoptic area (LPOA). Like humans, rats have erections during episodes of paradoxical sleep (Schmidt *et al.*, 1994). Schmidt *et al.* (2000) showed that rats with MPOA lesions experience no disruption of sleep or erections during sleep. In contrast, LPOA lesions dramatically reduced the occurrence of erection during paradoxical sleep, whereas erections during the waking state were unchanged. The reduction in erections was not attributable to impaired paradoxical sleep, which was normal in males with LPOA lesions, though the males had extended insomnia and less slow-wave sleep. Although most of the affected males also had some damage to the ventral BNST, case analysis suggested that it was LPOA damage that contributed most to the observed effects. This study also exemplifies the context-specificity of the regulation of erection: a question of the sort, "Is [brain structure X] important to the regulation of erection?" cannot be answered without first asking, "Erection in which context?"

2. Effects of Electrical or Chemical Stimulation

Theoretically, one would expect that electrical stimulation of a given brain region should have an effect opposite to lesions of that region, and indeed electrical stimulation of the MPOA of male rats (Malsbury, 1971; Merari and Ginton, 1975; Rodriguez-Manzo *et al.*, 2000; van Dis and Larsson, 1971), guinea pigs (Martin, 1976), or opossum (Bergquist, 1970; Roberts *et al.*, 1967) facilitated the expression of copulatory behavior. In the rat, electrical stimulation of the MPOA accelerated copulation by reducing mounts and intromissions preceding ejaculation, ejaculation latency, and postejaculatory interval (Malsbury, 1971; Merari and Ginton, 1975). Electrical stimulation of the lateral preoptic area generally was without effect on copulation in males (Malsbury, 1971; Merari and Ginton, 1975; Roberts *et al.*, 1967), although some facilitative effects were found in one study (Madlafousek *et al.*, 1970).

Damaging the medial forebrain bundle interfered with the effects of electrical stimulation of the MPOA in the opossum (Roberts *et al.*, 1967).

Repeated electrical stimulation of the MPOA (four per day, separated by two hours) elicited local afterdischarges, which increased over days and eventually resulted in a general seizure ("kindling") (Paredes *et al.*, 1990). Most (78%) of previously noncopulating rats, tested on days with no electrical stimulation, began copulating after the kindling procedure, and 56% ejaculated. Kindling had no effect on previously copulating rats. Therefore, long-lasting changes in preoptic area activity reduced the threshold for initiating copulation but had little effect on normal copulatory performance.

Similar facilitation of copulation has been reported with stimulation of the hypothalamus encompassing the medial forebrain bundle, which carries efferents from the MPOA. In these studies, electrical stimulation reduced intromissions preceding ejaculation, interintromission interval, ejaculation latency, and postejaculatory interval (Caggiula and Hoebel, 1966; Caggiula and Szechtman, 1972; Stephan *et al.*, 1971; Vaughan and Fisher, 1962). These findings complement the lesion studies summarized above, establishing the idea that the MPOA and its efferent pathways are important for the initiation and execution of copulation in males.

Electrical stimulation of the MPOA did not restore copulation in sexually satiated males (Rodriguez-Manzo *et al.*, 2000). Neither electrical stimulation alone nor the combination of stimulation and subthreshold systemic apomorphine (a DA agonist) or yohimbine (an α_2-adrenoceptor antagonist) restored copulation 24 hours after copulation to sexual exhaustion. However, several copulatory measures showed facilitation in nonsatiated rats. Higher doses of both drugs had previously been shown to facilitate copulation and to restore copulation in satiated males (Rodriguez-Manzo, 1999). The authors suggested that sexual satiety does not represent a prolonged extension of the postejaculatory interval, and that stimulation of an excitatory site does not overcome the inhibitory effects of satiety.

An additional sex-related effect of electrical stimulation of the MPOA and medial forebrain bundle has been reported. In monkeys, stimulation of these areas elicited penile erection, and sometimes ejaculation, without applying tactile stimulation to the penis (MacLean *et al.*, 1963; MacLean and Ploog, 1962; Robinson and

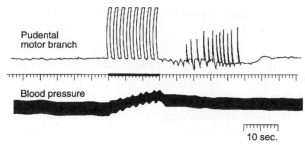

FIGURE 17 Polygraph tracing illustrating that in many trials the urethrogenital (UG) reflex was initiated by hypothalamic stimulation in the absence of any genital stimulation. Bilateral stimulation of the MPOA (400 μA/0.2 ms pulses delivered at 50 Hz, 1 sec on/off) is indicated by the black bar on the timer trace. After termination of the stimulus, the UG reflex was elicited as shown by the rhythmic activity in the pudendal motor branch. Increases in blood pressure often accompanied hypothalamic stimulation. [Figure reprinted from Marson and McKenna (1994b) with permission.]

Mishkin, 1966). In rats, seminal emission in the absence of any erection followed electrical stimulation of the preoptic area or medial forebrain bundle regions (Herberg, 1963; van Dis and Larsson, 1970), although other researchers (Courtois and MacDougall, 1988), using different parameters of stimulation, noted erections occurring immediately after the offset of each stimulus train. Either electrical or L-glutamate stimulation of the MPOA elicited erectile responses in anesthetized male rats (Giuliano *et al.*, 1996). Electrical or chemical stimulation of the MPOA also elicited the urethrogenital reflex in the absence of genital stimulation (Marson and McKenna, 1994b). (See Fig. 17.) MPOA neurons do not project directly to the lumbosacral spinal cord, where genital reflexes are organized. Therefore, MPOA neurons presumably activate other sites that in turn project to spinal nuclei mediating erection and ejaculation. It is unlikely, however, that the MPOA is necessary for penile erection or seminal emission, at least in rats and in some contexts, since damage to this region has little or no effect on spontaneous seminal emission (Ågmo *et al.*, 1977), noncontact erections (Liu *et al.*, 1997b), or touch-based erections (Szechtman *et al.*, 1978).

3. Effects of Direct Applications of Steroids or Steroid Antagonists

Fisher (1956) first tested the brain localization of T effects on copulation by using a water-soluble form of T. Although detailed methods and data are not available, Fisher indicated that the preoptic area was the most effective site for the activation of copulation in castrated male rats. A more detailed study, using crystalline T implants, also found the MPOA to be the most effective implant site; 100% of the males receiving MPOA implants copulated to ejaculation (Davidson, 1966a). Several other hypothalamic, hippocampal, and "other" sites yielded 0 to 81% of animals copulating to ejaculation. Cholesterol control implants were ineffective. The effectiveness of MPOA implants of T was later confirmed by other studies of castrated male rats (Christensen and Clemens, 1974; Johnston and Davidson, 1972; Kierniesky and Gerall, 1973; Lisk, 1967), ferrets (Tang and Sisk, 1991), birds (Barfield, 1969, 1971; Hutchison, 1978; Watson and Adkins-Regan, 1989), and anoles (Morgantaler and Crews, 1978). Therefore, androgenic mechanisms in the MPOA that stimulate copulation are highly conserved in evolution.

The interpretation of the behavioral responsiveness of castrated male rats to brain implants of T is complicated by the test-to-test variability for individual animals. For instance, although 100% of the males implanted with T in the MPOA copulated to ejaculation in one study (Davidson, 1966a), these males ejaculated in only 57% of the tests. Unlike the behavior of most intact male rats, the fact that an individual male was able to copulate during one test session did not guarantee copulation on subsequent tests. In addition, even among males that copulated to ejaculation, the parameters of copulation for these males were not always normal (e.g., Johnston and Davidson, 1972). This finding appears to extend to the behavior of male hamsters, as MPOA or hypothalamic implants of T can activate copulation, but not restore copulation to levels equivalent to those of intact males (Lisk and Bezier, 1980). T implants in the MPOA of male mice were even less effective than those in male rats or hamsters. Such implants increased several measures of sexual motivation—ultrasonic vocalizations and urine marking in response to female urine and investigation of a female rather than a male—however, little copulation was observed (Matochik *et al.,* 1994; Nyby *et al.,* 1992). The decrease in effectiveness of brain, as opposed to systemic, implants is probably attributable to the activation of only a limited portion of the neural circuitry by the brain implants.

An obvious requirement for localizing the effects of T implants to specific brain regions is the ability to limit the spread of the steroid. In almost all studies in which T implants were applied to the brains of castrated males, some stimulation of androgen-sensitive peripheral tissues occurred. Significant stimulation of penile spines occurred in several studies, compared with cholesterol-implanted animals, although not enough stimulation to approximate intact males (Christensen and Clemens, 1974; Kierniesky and Gerall, 1973; Lisk and Bezier, 1980). In one study (Smith *et al.,* 1977), plasma T levels were measured following implants of T into the cerebral cortex or the MPOA. Substantial leakage into the peripheral circulation occurred, as levels of up to 0.5 ng of T per ml of serum were measured. It is unlikely that the peripheral leakage of T from intracranial implants is a factor in the activation of copulation, because similar implants placed subcutaneously had no effect on copulation (Johnston and Davidson, 1972), and because there was no correlation between indices of peripheral T leakage (e.g., plasma T levels) and levels of copulatory behavior (Smith *et al.,* 1977; Tang and Sisk, 1991). However, it is also possible that steroid from the implant could affect other brain sites without entering the peripheral circulation.

E and DHT are the principal metabolites of T that have been investigated with respect to their ability to activate copulation when implanted intracranially. In the hamster, implants of E in the rostral anterior hypothalamus stimulated mounting but not intromission or ejaculation (Lisk and Bezier, 1980). Davis and Barfield (1979) implanted small-gauge cannulae containing E into male rats in the MPOA–anterior hypothalamus of male rats in an attempt to limit diffusion from the implant site. Only 20% (2/10) of the males receiving these E implants ejaculated, a proportion not different from castrated, untreated males. Christensen and Clemens (1974) compared the efficacy of pellets of T or E implanted in the MPOA to activate copulation. Only 30% (6/20) of the males implanted with T copulated to ejaculation, whereas 70% of the males implanted with E ejaculated. In a subsequent study, Christensen and Clemens (1975) infused solutions containing controlled doses of T (10 μg/day) or E (5 μg/day) into the rostral anterior hypothalamus. These treatments stimulated only mounting in these animals. Concurrent treatment with ATD (an aromatization inhibitor) blocked the increase in mounting induced by T infusion, without affecting mounting activated by E treatment. Collectively, these results are consistent with the idea that E is able to stimulate copulation in males, and that the effects of T on behavior require the conversion of T to E within cells of the central nervous system. In addition, an intracranial E treatment affecting a region larger than just the MPOA–anterior hypothalamus may be needed to activate copulation.

There have been relatively few experiments in which implants of DHT were used to activate male sexual behavior. In one study, male rats received DHT in implants distributed throughout the extent of the MPOA and anterior hypothalamus (Johnston and Davidson, 1972). Only 35% (6/17) of these males copulated to ejaculation, a percentage not significantly different from the 9% (1/11) of the cholesterol-treated males that ejaculated. For the implanted males that copulated to ejaculation, intromission latency and the number of mounts to intromission were significantly elevated compared with precastration levels, although other measures of copulation were normal. Like similar T implants, DHT implants stimulated the development of penile spines. Baum *et al.* (1982) were somewhat more successful in stimulating copulation with DHT implants in the MPOA–anterior hypothalamus. In this study, castrated males ejaculated on about 35% of the tests prior to implantation, whereas after the males received intracranial DHT the percentage increased to about 70%. Again, substantial stimulation of penile spines was related to the activation of copulation. Male guinea pigs have been shown to be particularly responsive to intrapreoptic area implants of DHT; full copulatory behavior was restored in virtually all males tested (Butera and Czaja, 1989b). In contrast, implantation of DHT into the anterior hypothalamus of male hamsters had no detectable effect on copulation (Lisk and Bezier, 1980).

Another approach taken to study the effects of intracranial steroid administration on copulation has been to combine the brain implant with a systemic hormone treatment that, by itself, is subthreshold for the elicitation of behavior. In one study, preoptic area implants of DHT in castrated male rats promoted ejaculation in 40% of males receiving a concurrent systemic DHT regimen that, by itself, was behaviorally ineffective (Butera and Czaja, 1989a). Davis and Barfield (1979) gave brain implants of E to castrated male rats treated systemically with DHT. Of 42 males receiving implants in the MPOA–anterior hypothalamus, 25 males (60%) copulated to ejaculation. Posterior hypothalamic implants of E had little effect on copulation; 4/18 (22%) of these males ejaculated. Also, E implants in the MPOA–anterior hypothalamus (AH) alone (20% ejaculated, 2/10), or just systemic DHT treatment (33% ejaculating, 3/9) were much less effective than the combined treatments. The complementary experiment was performed by Baum *et al.* (1982), who implanted DHT into the brain of male rats receiving E systemically. However, DHT implants in the MPOA-AH were ineffective, as were implants into the caudate-putamen and substantia nigra-ventral tegmentum. This study provides evidence for extrahypothalamic sites of action of androgen on copulation, as DHT implants were effective only when placed in the lateral septum or the medial amygdala. Unfortunately, the effects of DHT in the lateral septum or medial amygdala without systemic E were not assessed in this (or any other) study, so the contribution of the systemic E treatment on copulation in these animals is uncertain.

A nonsteroidal aromatase inhibitor, fadrozole, which blocks conversion of T to E but does not directly affect steroid receptors, impaired sexual behavior when delivered into the MPOA (Clancy *et al.,* 1995) or the lateral ventricle (Vagell and McGinnis, 1997). In an interesting twist on those studies, Clancy *et al.* (2000) implanted E into the MPOA of gonadally intact males that were treated systemically with an aromatase inhibitor. Thus, E was available only to the MPOA, although androgens were available throughout the body. After a steep postsurgical decline, E-treated animals regained about half the numbers of mounts, intromissions, and ejaculations that they had exhibited before surgery; copulatory behavior of controls remained low. Therefore, E in the MPOA, combined with systemically available androgen, is sufficient to maintain at least some copulatory and ejaculatory behavior; however, the fact that behavior was not fully maintained suggests that estrogenic effects in other brain areas contribute to copulatory behavior. The aromatization of T to E in the MPOA may be important for rams, as well as for rats. Rams that prefer to mate with other rams, rather than with females, have reduced capacity to aromatize T to E in the POA and anterior hypothalamus, in addition to lower levels of T and estrogens in serum (Resko *et al.*, 1999).

In addition, high sexually performing rams had more ERs than did low sexually performing rams (Alexander *et al.,* 1993).

Castration decreased immunoreactivity of CCK in the sexually dimorphic central part of the medial preoptic nucleus (Simerly and Swanson, 1987). T treatment restored CCK-ir to normal levels. Similar effects were seen in sexually dimorphic regions of the medial amygdala and BNST.

4. Effects of Direct Applications of Drugs Affecting Specific Transmitters

Because of the central role of the MPOA in organizing the many facets of copulatory behavior, it is not surprising that local administration of drugs has influenced a variety of behavioral measures. In general, locally applied drugs have had effects similar to those of the same drug injected systemically. However, there are several site-dependent differences. (See Table 3 for a summary of effects of drugs administered into various neural sites).

a) Dopamine DA in the MPOA has a major facilitative role in male sexual behavior. DA input to the MPOA arises from neurons in the periventricular nucleus along the whole length of the third ventricle; laterally directed axons branch widely into the MPOA and anterior hypothalamus (reviewed in Moore and Lookingland, 1995). Microinjection of the classic D_1/D_2 agonist apomorphine facilitated copulation in both gonadally intact (Hull *et al.,* 1986) and long-term castrated (Scaletta and Hull, 1990) male rats. Apomorphine microinjections also increased the number of touch-based erections and seminal emissions in restrained supine males (Pehek *et al.,* 1989b). Conversely, microinjections of the classic D_1/D_2 antagonist cis-flupenthixol impaired copulation (Pehek *et al.,* 1988b) and decreased touch-based *ex copula* erections (Warner *et al.,* 1991). Cis-flupenthixol also decreased the percentage of trials on which a male chose the X-maze goal box containing a receptive female, without affecting running speed or the number of no-choice trials (Warner *et al.,* 1991). Thus, DA in the MPOA appears to facilitate genital reflexes and the motor patterning of copulation and to enhance sexual motivation, without altering general motor activation. Neurotoxic lesions of MPOA DA neurons by 6-hydroxydopamine (6-OHDA) impaired

copulation only if tests occurred within 24 hours of the lesion (Bazzett *et al.,* 1992) or if an otherwise subthreshold dose of a DA synthesis inhibitor was administered (Bitran *et al.,* 1988a). DA levels were depleted by only 23%, perhaps because the MPOA contains few DA transporters, which are necessary to transport the toxin into the axon terminals. These findings suggest that within 24 hours of 6-OHDA administration into the MPOA, increased DA synthesis in remaining neurons can restore copulation to normal.

There is consistent evidence that stimulation of D_1 receptors in the MPOA facilitates copulation and touch-based *ex copula* erections, whereas stimulation of D_2 receptors has biphasic effects. Microinjection of a low dose of the D_3/D_2 agonist quinelorane decreased the latency to the first genital reflex, without affecting the numbers of glans erections, anteroflexions, or seminal emissions, thereby suggesting that small increases of DA in the MPOA may disinhibit genital reflexes via D_2-like receptors (Bazzett *et al.,* 1991). However, microinjection of a high dose of quinelorane or of the D_1 antagonist SCH-23390 decreased the number of erections but increased the number of seminal emissions. Therefore, either intense stimulation of D_2 receptors or blockade of D_1 receptors promoted seminal emission at the expense of erectile function. Furthermore, microinjection of a selective D_1 agonist (tetrahydrothienopyridene, THP) into the MPOA increased touch-based erections and inhibited seminal emissions (Markowski *et al.,* 1994). The suggestion that D_1 stimulation facilitates erection and D_2 stimulation promotes seminal emission was supported by studies using microinjections of the mixed D_1/D_2 agonist apomorphine alone or together with selective antagonists (Hull *et al.,* 1992). A low dose ($1\mu g$) of apomorphine increased the number of touch-based erections but not seminal emissions; that increase was blocked by $5\mu g$ of both D_1 (SCH-23390) and D_2 (raclopride) antagonists, suggesting that both disinhibition by D_2 receptors and direct facilitation by D_1 receptors contributed to the increase in erections (Hull *et al.,* 1992; Fig. 18A). However, a high dose (10 μg) of apomorphine did not increase the number of erections when administered alone. Co-administration of the D_2 antagonist with the high dose did increase erections, a finding that suggests that intense stimulation of D_2 receptors by the high dose alone had inhibited erections. Thus, co-administration of the D_2 antagonist

TABLE 3

Summary of the Effects on Male Sexual Behavior of Drugs Administered into Specific Brain Areas

Transmitter	Drug	Activ.	Motiv.	Cop.	Ejac.	Rev. Sat.	T-B Er.	S.Em.	NCE	Drug-Ind.	U-G	Cavern.	Other
MPOA													
DA	Mixed ag.	↔		↑				↑					
	Mixed antag.	↔	↓	↓			↓						
	D₁ ag.			↑			↑	↑					
	D₁ antag.	↔	↓	↓	↑		↓	↑					
	D₂ ag.		Hi↓	Hi↓	↑		Lo↑,Hi↓	↑					
	D₂ antag.						(↑)	↓					
5-HT	Precursor, 5-HT												↑DA,5-HT
	5-HT₁A ag.		↓	↓	↑								
	5-HT₁B ag.			↓									
GABA	GABAₐ ag.			↓									
	GABAₐ antag.			↑	↑	↕							
Opioids	Nonspec. antag.		↓										
	μ ag.			Hi↓	Lo↑								
	κ ag.				Lo↑								
NE	NE			↑									
	Nonspec. α antag.			↓									
	Nonspec. β antag.			↓									
	α₂ ag.			↓	(↓)(↑)								
	α₂ antag.			↑									
NO	l-Arg, donor			↑									
	NOS antag.			↓				↑					
ACh	Nonspec. ag.				↑								
	Musc. ag.			↓	↑								
	Musc. antag.				↓								
PGE₂											↑		
Glu	NMDA			↑			↑						
PVN													
DA	Mixed ag.			↕			↑	↑		↑			↑NO syn
	D₂ ag.			↓↕			↑	↑		↑			↑NO syn
OT	OT									↑			
	Antag.									↓			
NO	l-Arg.						↑		↓				↑NO syn
	NOS antag.						↓	↑					↓NO syn
Glu	NMDA									↑			↑NO syn

Continued

Transmitter	Drug	Activ.	Motiv.	Cop.	Ejac.	Rev. Sat.	T-B Er.	S.Em.	NCE	Drug-Ind.	U-G	Cavern.	Other
GABA	GABA$_A$ ag.									↓			
	GABA$_B$ ag.									↕			
ACTH										↑			
Opioid	μ ag.			↓									↓NO syn
Mesolimbic DA Tract													
DA	↑ DA activ.	↑	(↑)										
	↓ DA activ.	↓	↕										
	D$_2$ ag. (NAcc)	↓	↕				↕						
CCK	CCKA or B antag.												↓ eff. of VTA stim.
5-HT	5-HT (NAcc)				↓								
	5-HT$_{1A}$ ag. (NAcc)				↓								
Opioids	Mixed antag. (VTA)		↓	↕									
	μ ag. (VTA)			↕									
Spinal Cord													
DA	Mixed ag.	↑		↓	↑		↓						
5-HT	5-HT			↓	↑			↕			↓	↑	↑
	5-HT$_{1A}$ ag.				↑		↓	↓			↑		
	5,7-DHT lesion												
TRH				↓			↓						
GABA	GABA$_A$ ag.						(↓)						
	GABA$_B$ ag.			↕	↕		↓						
NE	NE			↑ thrust freq.									
	α$_2$ ag.			↓ thrust freq.									
	β ag.			↓ thrust freq.									
OT												↑	
Opioids	μ ag.				↓								
	Mixed antag.				↑								

Abbreviations: Activ., activity; Motiv., motivation; Cop., copulation; Ejac., ejaculation; Rev. Sat., reverse satiety; T-B Er, touch-based erection; S.Em, seminal emission; NCE, noncontact erection; Drug-Ind., drug-induced erection; U-G, urethro-genital reflex; Cavern., cavernous nerve firing or intracavernous pressure; DA, dopamine; NE, norepinephrine; 5-HT, serotonin; ACh, acetylcholine; GABA, gamma amino butyric acid; OT, oxytocin; NO, nitric oxide; GnRH, gonadotropin releasing hormone; PRL, prolactin; CRH, corticotropin releasing hormone; CCK, cholecystokinin; VIP, vasoactive intestinal peptide; GAL, galanin; NPY, neuropeptide Y; PGE$_2$, prostaglandin E$_2$; ANG II, angiotensin II; ag., agonist; antag., antagonist; Musc., muscarinic; ischio., ischiocavernosus; ENK, enkephalin; L-Arg, L-arginine; NOS, nitric oxide synthase; 5,7-DHT, 5,7-dihydroxytryptamine, a selective 5-HT neurotoxin.

Arrows in parentheses indicate that the effect was found only with one drug dose or only in one group of animals. Arrows in different directions for the same measure indicate contrasting findings from different researchers. Question marks indicate that there is disagreement about the interpretation or reliability of the effect.

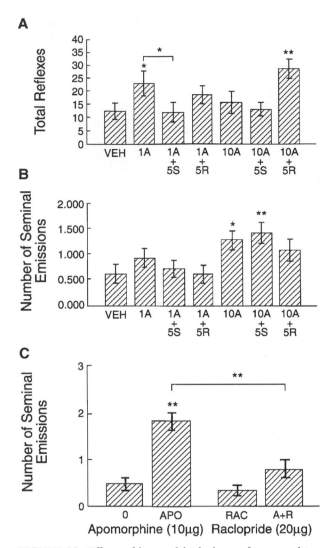

unmasked the facilitative effect of apomorphine's stimulation of D_1 receptors. The high dose of apomorphine did increase the number of seminal emissions, an effect that was enhanced by 5 μg of the D_1 antagonist, diminished by 5 μg of the D_2 antagonist (Fig. 18B) and blocked by 20 μg or the D_2 antagonist (Fig. 18C). Therefore, stimulation of D_1 receptors in the MPOA appears to facilitate parasympathetically mediated erections and inhibit seminal emission, whereas intense stimulation of D_2 receptors may shift the autonomic balance to favor sympathetically mediated seminal emission and inhibit erections.

The differential association of D_1 stimulation with the early stages of copulation, characterized by the presence of erections, and of intense D_2 stimulation with ejaculation, was supported by tests of copulation. Microinjection of the D_1 agonist THP into the MPOA speeded copulation, resulting in more ejaculations per test (Markowski *et al.*, 1994), whereas microinjection of a D_1 antagonist (SCH-23390) into the MPOA delayed the onset of copulation and decreased the ejaculatory threshold (Hull *et al.*, 1989). It also decreased the percentage of trials on which the male chose the female's goal box in an X-maze, a measure of sexual motivation (Moses *et al.*,1995). However, microinjection of a high dose of the D_3/D_2 agonist quinelorane increased the latency to reach the female's goal box (Moses *et al.*, 1995) and delayed the start of copulation, as though the male had recently ejaculated, but then decreased both the time and number of intromissions preceding ejaculation (Hull *et al.*, 1989; Moses *et al.*, 1995). Therefore, D_1 and D_2 receptors in the MPOA appear to exert reciprocal influences on copulation: stimulation of D_1 receptors promotes erection and copulation, and stimulation of D_2 receptors facilitates ejaculation and the postejaculatory state.

FIGURE 18 Effects of low and high doses of apomorphine, alone or with a D_1 or D_2 antagonist, on *ex copula* genital reflexes. (A) Effects on touch-based erections and anteroflexions (total reflexes). The low dose (1 μg) of apomorphine (1A) increased total erections plus anteroflexions. Addition of 5 μg of the D_1 antagonist SCH-23390 (1A + 5S) blocked this effect. Addition of 5 μg of the D_2 antagonist raclopride partially blocked the effect. The high dose (10 μg) of apomorphine alone (10A) did not facilitate this measure; addition of 5 μg of the D_2 antagonist raclopride to apomorphine (10A + 5R) significantly increased erections plus anteroflexions. (B) Effects on seminal emissions. The high dose (10 μg) of apomorphine (10A) increased the number of seminal emissions. Addition of 5 μg of the D_1 antagonist SCH-23390 (1A + 5S) resulted in slightly more seminal emissions than did apomorphine alone. Addition of 5 μg of the D_2 antagonist raclopride to 10 μg apomorphine (10A + 5R) reduced the effect of apomorphine. (C) Effects of the high dose (10 μg) of

apomorphine and a high dose (20 μg) of the D_2 antagonist raclopride, alone or together, on seminal emissions. Apomorphine again increased seminal emissions, and that increase was blocked by coadministration of the high dose of the D_2 antagonist raclopride. [Figure reprinted from Hull *et al.* (1992) with permission.]

b) Serotonin In accord with the generally inhibitory effects of 5-HT on male sexual behavior, microinjections of large doses of 5-HT into the MPOA impaired male sexual behavior (Fernandez-Guasti *et al.*, 1992; Verma *et al.*, 1989). Similarly, a 5-HT_{1B} agonist microinjected into the MPOA increased ejaculation latency (Fernandez-Guasti *et al.*,1992). However, microinjections of the 5-HT_{1A} agonist 8-OH-DPAT into the MPOA facilitated ejaculation, similar to the effects of systemic administration of the drug (Fernandez-Guasti and Escalante, 1991). More recently, 8-OH-DPAT, dialyzed into the MPOA through a microdialysis probe, also facilitated copulation (Matuszewich *et al.*, 1999) and increased extracellular levels of both DA and 5-HT (Lorrain *et al.*, 1998). Some of the facilitative effects of 8-OH-DPAT were inhibited by the D_2 antagonist raclopride, but not by the 5-HT_{1A} antagonist p-MPPI, thereby suggesting that the elevation of DA levels, rather than stimulation of 5-HT_{1A} receptors, was responsible for much of the behavioral facilitation (Matuszewich *et al.*, 1999).

c) GABA GABA has almost universally inhibitory postsynaptic effects in adult mammals. Because stimulation of the MPOA facilitates male sexual behavior, it is not surprising that administration of GABAergic drugs into the MPOA inhibits behavior. Drugs that increased GABAergic activity (muscimol or ethanolamine-O-sulfate) in the MPOA decreased the numbers of males that mounted, intromitted, and ejaculated, whereas inhibitors of GABA activity (bicuculline or 3-mercaptopropionic acid, 3-MPA) dramatically shortened both the postejaculatory interval and ejaculation latency (Fernandez-Guasti *et al.*, 1985, 1986). These $GABA_A$ antagonists also decreased the number of intromissions preceding ejaculation (Fernandez-Guasti *et al.*, 1985, 1986). However, MPOA microinjections of the same two $GABA_A$ antagonists failed to reverse sexual satiety (Rodriguez-Manzo *et al.*, 2000).

d) Opioids Exogenous opiates are usually inhibitory to copulation, though, as noted above, low to moderate levels of endogenous opioids may facilitate sexual motivation and ejaculation. Microinjections of both morphine (a μ agonist) and dynorphin (1–13) (a naturally occurring κ agonist) into the MPOA

had dose-dependent effects; the lowest doses decreased the time and number of intromissions preceding ejaculation and the highest dose of morphine produced a failure to resume copulation after the second ejaculation (Band and Hull, 1990). However, the selective μ agonist morphiceptin delayed the start of copulation (Matuszewich and Dornan, 1992; Matuszewich *et al.*, 1995) but did not affect copulatory performance, genital reflexes, sexual motivation, or general motor activity (Matuszewich *et al.*, 1995). Microinjections of β-endorphin (a naturally occurring μ agonist) impaired the initiation of copulation and also inhibited copulatory performance (Hughes *et al.*, 1987a; van Furth *et al.*, 1995a). However, naloxone microinjected into the MPOA blocked the induction of sexual reinforcement (Ågmo and Gomez, 1993). Therefore, endogenous opioids or very low doses of opioid agonists may facilitate copulation and sexual motivation, but high levels of endogenous or exogenous opioids in the MPOA inhibit sexual behavior.

e) Norepinephrine Microinjection of NE into the MPOA increased sexual arousal and copulatory performance, whereas the β-noradrenergic receptor antagonist propranolol and the α-receptor antagonist phenoxybenzamine inhibited sexual behavior, with propranolol having more potent effects (Mallick *et al.*, 1996). Stimulating α_2-receptors with clonidine (which would have stimulated inhibitory autoreceptors and thereby decreased NE release) decreased the numbers of males that mounted, intromitted, or ejaculated (Clark, 1991). Clonidine also increased ejaculation latency and interintromission interval but decreased the ejaculatory threshold (numbers of intromissions preceding ejaculation). Administration of yohimbine (an α_2-receptor antagonist) into the MPOA blocked the inhibitory effects of systemically administered clonidine, whereas systemic administration of yohimbine blocked the inhibitory effects of clonidine injected into the MPOA (Clark, 1991). Therefore, stimulation of α_2 receptors in the MPOA impairs copulation in male rats, whereas blocking those receptors facilitates the behavior. (Although there are postsynaptic, as well as presynaptic, α_2 receptors, Clark interpreted these results as being due to alterations in NE release, consequent to stimulating or blocking presynaptic autoreceptors.)

f) Nitric Oxide   Manipulation of NO production in the MPOA produces effects that are generally congruent with those of systemic manipulations. The NO precursor L-arginine, dialyzed into the MPOA, increased the rate of mounting estrous females, and the NOS inhibitor N(G)-monomethyl-L-arginine(L-NMMA) decreased mounting rate (Sato *et al.*, 1998). In addition, L-NMMA microinjected into the MPOA increased the number of seminal emissions in an *ex copula* genital reflex test and decreased the number of sexually naive males that initiated copulation, though it did not affect sexually experienced males (Moses and Hull, 1994, 1999).

NOS in the MPOA is hormonally regulated. Castration decreased the production of cGMP, the most common second messenger of NO, and blocked the ability of NMDA to increase cGMP in MPOA slices and to increase plasma luteinizing hormone (Pu *et al.*, 1996). Furthermore, castration decreased NOS immunoreactivity (NOS-ir) in the medial preoptic nucleus (MPN) of male hamsters (Hadeishi and Wood, 1996) and rats (Du and Hull, 1999; Putnam *et al.*, 2002b). Many NOS-ir neurons also contained androgen receptors (Hadeishi and Wood, 1996). However, only E or T was able to restore NOS-ir after castration; DHT (which, unlike T, cannot be aromatized to estrogen) was ineffective (Putnam *et al.*, 2002b).

In contrast to the above studies, Singh *et al.* (2000) reported that castration increased, and androgens decreased, NOS activity in the brain. The conversion of L-arginine to L-citrulline (with the consequent production of NO), the transcription of NOS mRNA, and the number of NOS-ir cells were all increased by castration and decreased by administration of T or DHT in hypothalamic tissue. However, there are several puzzling aspects of these data. First, enzyme activity in the cerebellum was also increased by castration, although there are few androgen receptors there, and exogenous T did not return activity to normal. Second, T replacement had the same effect on enzyme activity as did DHT, although T is aromatized to E in the hypothalamus, and E has been shown to upregulate NOS-ir in the hypothalamus (Rachman *et al.*, 1998; Warembourg *et al.*, 1999). Thus, it is not clear why the effects of the two metabo-

lites of T (E and DHT) did not tend to cancel each other. In addition, it is possible that the sections of the posterior sexually dimorphic nucleus of the preoptic area (pSDN-POA) that were counted for NOS-ir in the Singh et al. (2000) experiment were posterior to those examined by Hadeishi and Wood (1996), Du and Hull (1999), and Putnam *et al.* (2002b). Indeed, Singh *et al.* reported that there were very few nNOS-ir cells in the pSDN-POA, whereas there were numerous labeled cells in the MPN sections examined by Hadeishi and Wood (1996), Du and Hull (1999), and Putnam *et al.*(2002b). It is also possible that differences in antibodies used in the immunohistochemistry accounted for some of the differences. In summary, NO in the MPOA promotes male sexual behavior and increases GnRH release; however, there is disagreement as to whether T increases NOS activity in the MPOA.

g) Acetylcholine   Microinjections of the nonspecific ACh agonist carbachol or the muscarinic agonist oxotremorine into the MPOA decreased the number of intromissions preceding ejaculation (Hull *et al.*, 1988a). Microinjections of either drug into the lateral ventricle delayed the start of copulation but did not affect ejaculatory threshold. The muscarinic antagonist scopolomine, microinjected into the MPOA together with oxotremorine, blocked oxotremorine's reduction of ejaculatory threshold (Hull *et al.*, 1988b). Scopolomine microinjected alone into the MPOA decreased the percentage of animals that mounted, intromitted, or ejaculated; similar microinjections into the lateral ventricle delayed the onset of mounts and intromissions, as had carbachol in the previous experiment. Therefore, activation of muscarinic receptors in the MPOA may regulate ejaculation threshold and copulatory ability, whereas cholinergic influences in another structure near the ventricles may affect sexual arousal.

In male gerbils, immunoreactivity for acetylcholinesterase in the SDA was more dense than in females (Commins and Yahr, 1984b). Gonadectomy decreased, and T replacement restored, staining intensity. These findings suggest that ACh in this area contributes to the control of hormone-stimulated behavior.

h) Prostaglandin E_2   Clemens and Gladue (1977) administered prostaglandin E_2(PGE$_2$) (10 μg per side) directly into the MPOA of long-term castrated male rats given daily T treatments that were ineffective in maintaining copulation. Treatment with prostaglandin E_2 activated copulation within 30 min of infusion; 50% of the males intromitted and 40% of the males copulated to ejaculation. Therefore, activation of receptors for PGE_2 in the MPOA facilitates copulation in male rats, possibly by increasing MPOA temperature. (See Section IV.P on systemic manipulation of PGE_2.)

5. Electrophysiological Recordings

There is electrophysiological evidence for participation of the MPOA in both the motivational and the performance aspects of male sexual behavior. Some MPOA neurons in male rats showed increased activity only before the male began to copulate, whereas others had increased activity only during copulation (Shimura *et al.*, 1994). Similarly, in male monkeys neuronal activity was highest when the animal was bar pressing to bring a female into close proximity; activity decreased somewhat during copulation, and ceased after ejaculation (Oomura *et al.*, 1988). Therefore, neural activity in the MPOA may promote both the motivational and performance aspects of male sexual behavior. These data illustrate the heterogeneity of function of MPOA neurons.

6. Chemical Changes Detected by Microdialysis

As predicted by the microinjection data, there is a close association between extracellular DA in the MPOA and male sexual behavior. There was an increase in extracellular DA in the MPOA as soon as a male rat was presented with a receptive female behind a barrier (Hull *et al.*, 1995) (See Fig. 19.) DA levels remained high, or increased further, when the animals were allowed to copulate (Hull *et al.*, 1995; Sato *et al.*, 1995). The recent presence of T is permissive for this effect; most one-week castrates showed a DA increase in response to the female behind the barrier and copulated after the barrier was removed (Hull *et al.*, 1995). The remaining one-week castrates, and all two-week castrates, failed to show the DA response to the female and failed to copulate. The DA response was behaviorally specific; exercise and presentation of a male instead of a female (Hull *et al.*, 1995) or eating a palatable food (Hull *et al.*, 1993) did not elicit a significant response. Probes placed anterior or lateral to the MPOA did not reveal a response.

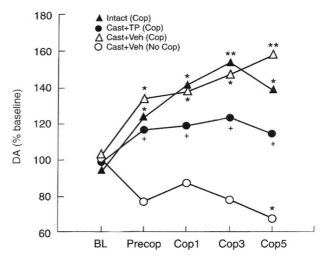

FIGURE 19 Extracellular dopamine in the MPOA of male rats during baseline, a precopulatory period (estrous female behind a perforated barrier), and three six-minute periods after the barrier was removed and the animals were free to copulate. All gonadally intact males and all castrates treated with testosterone propionate (200 μg/day) showed a significant increase in dopamine during the precopulatory period and during copulation; all these animals did copulate. A total of nine of 14 oil-treated one-week castrates also showed the precopulatory dopamine response and copulated after the barrier was removed. The remaining one-week and all four two-week oil-treated castrates failed to show the precopulatory dopamine response and failed to copulate; data from these two groups are combined. *$P < .05$ compared to final baseline for intact males or for one-week vehicle-treated castrates that copulated. **$P < .01$ compared to final baseline for intact males or for one-week vehicle-treated castrates that copulated. $^+P < .05$ compared to baseline for testosterone-treated castrates. $^\#P < .05$ compared to final baseline for vehicle-treated castrates that failed to copulate. [Figure reprinted from Hull *et al.* (1995) with permission.]

No-net-flux analyses were used to test whether basal levels of DA, as opposed to the increase in response to a female, were hormone-dependent (Du *et al.*, 1998). The no-net-flux technique uses different concentrations of DA in the dialysate; if there is more DA in the dialysate than in brain, the loss can be detected, and if there is less, the gain can be detected (Olson and Justice, 1993). A regression line is drawn, and the point at which the line crosses from loss to gain represents the absolute extracellular level of DA. The absolute levels of extracellular DA in the MPOA of castrates were only about one-fifth those of intact males (0.3 vs 1.3 nM,

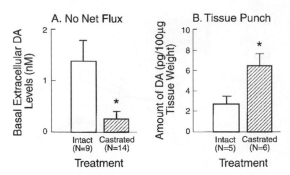

FIGURE 20 (A) Basal levels of extracellular dopamine in MPOA of one-month castrates and gonadally intact males. Absolute levels were determined by using the no-net-flux method (see text). Intact males had significantly higher dopamine levels than did castrates. (B) Dopamine levels in tissue punches from the MPOA of one-month castrates or gonadally intact males. Castrates had significantly more dopamine in tissue than did intact males. Because almost all dopamine in tissue is stored in vesicles, this suggests that castrates synthesize and store dopamine normally, or even excessively; the deficit in extracellular dopamine of castrates may be due to decreased release. [Data from Du et al. (1998); figure from Hull et al. (1997) with permission.]

respectively), thus indicating that the deficit in MPOA DA release is a general one, not limited to the sexual context. (See Fig. 20.) However, amphetamine released more DA from castrates than from intact males, and there was more DA in tissue punches from the MPOA of castrates than in those from gonadally intact males (Du et al., 1998). Therefore, castrates synthesized and stored at least as much DA as did intact males, but they were unable to release it.

The association between MPOA DA release and the ability to copulate was further strengthened by a study of restoration of copulation by T in long-term castrates (Putnam et al., 2001). None of the six two-day-T-treated castrates showed a DA response to the female and none copulated. Eight of the nine five-day-T-treated castrates copulated, with five of these ejaculating; all but the one noncopulator showed a precopulatory DA increase. All of the 10-day-T-treated castrates showed the precopulatory DA increase and all copulated. Therefore, all animals that showed the DA response to the female were able to copulate, whereas none that failed to show the response copulated. Furthermore, there were numerous significant correlations between DA increases and behavioral measures of copulation. Thus,

hormonal restoration of copulation is closely linked to female-elicited DA release in the MPOA, as is loss of copulation following castration.

One factor regulating DA release in the MPOA is NO. Both basal (Lorrain and Hull, 1993) and copulation-induced (Lorrain et al., 1996) DA levels in the MPOA were dependent, in part, on NO. Furthermore, castration decreased, and T replacement restored, NOS-ir in the MPOA (Ceccatelli et al., 1996; Du and Hull, 1999; Hadeishi and Wood, 1996; Putnam et al., 2002b; but see Singh et al., 2000). Thus, one means by which T maintains both basal and female-stimulated DA levels may be by upregulating NOS in the MPOA.

The metabolites of T were differentially effective in restoring basal and female-stimulated DA release in castrated male rats (Putnam et al., 2002a). E restored high basal DA levels; however, DA levels in these animals declined throughout the afternoon, and there was no DA increase in response to an estrous female. See Fig. 21.) All E-treated males intromitted, but none showed a

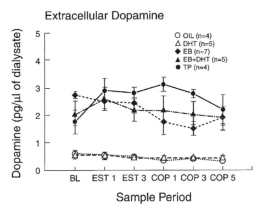

FIGURE 21 Levels of extracellular dopamine in six-minute microdialysate samples from the MPOA of male rats during baseline conditions (BL), during exposure to an estrous female behind a barrier (EST), and during copulation testing (COP). Castrates treated with testosterone propionate (TP) or with estradiol benzoate plus dihydrotestosterone (EB + DHT) showed increased extracellular dopamine during EST or COP conditions. All these males copulated to ejaculation. Castrates treated with EB alone showed high basal levels of dopamine but no increase in response to the female or during copulation. All these males intromitted, but none ejaculated. Castrates treated with DHT alone or with vehicle had low basal levels of extracellular dopamine and no increase during EST or COP conditions; none of these animals copulated. [Figure from Putnam et al. (2002a).]

behavioral ejaculatory pattern. DHT was no more effective than oil vehicle in restoring either basal or female-stimulated DA levels or copulation. Both T and E Plus DHT treatments restored both basal and female-stimulated DA levels and copulation. Thus, E restored basal levels of extracellular DA, which was sufficient to promote intromissions; however, E did not restore the female-stimulated increase in DA, which appears to be related to the ability to ejaculate. Furthermore, while DHT alone was completely unable to promote DA release in the MPOA or the ability to copulate, the combination of E and DHT was effective.

Whereas extracellular DA levels correlated positively with several copulatory measures, tissue (stored) levels of DA were negatively correlated with those measures (Putnam *et al.*, 2002b). The three hormonal regimens that supported copulation (E, E Plus DHT, and T) all resulted in tissue DA levels that were lower than those of the noncopulating groups (DHT and oil). Thus, the noncopulating animals were able to synthesize and store DA, but not to release it. Again, the difficulty in releasing DA may be at least partially due to decreased NOS. The three groups that were able to copulate had higher levels of NOS-ir in the MPOA than the two groups that did not.

Another factor regulating the DA response to a female is input from the medial amygdala (Dominguez *et al.*, 2001). Small radio-frequency lesions of the medial amygdala resulted in the typical increases in intromissions preceding ejaculation and ejaculation latency, and decreases in the number of ejaculations, that have previously been reported (reviewed in Section V. B.1). Furthermore, these lesions abolished the MPOA DA response to a female but had no effect on basal DA levels. Therefore, as with E treatments in castrated male rats (Putnam *et al.*, 2002a), normal basal DA levels appear to be compatible with at least some copulatory ability. However, the increase in DA before and during copulation appears to foster the ability to ejaculate. The link between amygdala input and MPOA DA activity was confirmed by a microinjection study. Larger excitotoxic lesions removing most of the amygdala severely impaired the ability of male rats to copulate (Dominguez *et al.*, 2001). However, copulatory ability was restored to prelesion levels by microinjections of the DA agonist apomorphine into the MPOA. Thus, the impairment of copulation resulting from amygdala lesions appears

to be mediated, in part, by a decrease in the normal female-stimulated release of DA in the MPOA.

The signal provided by the amygdala apparently originates in the olfactory bulbs. Presentation of a receptive female increased extracellular DA in the MPOA of male hamsters with sham or contralateral olfactory bulbectomy (Nagatani and Wood, 2001). Bilateral or ipsilateral bulbectomy inhibited the increase in extracellular DA and also inhibited sexual behavior. These results are very similar to those of Dominguez *et al.* (2001) from male rats with medial amygdala lesions and suggest that olfactory input processed by the amygdala leads to the increase in MPOA DA that facilitates copulatory behavior.

Mas and his colleagues suggested that serotonin (5-HT) was released in the preoptic area at the time of ejaculation, and that these high levels of 5-HT may contribute to postejaculatory sexual quiescence (Fumero *et al.*, 1994; Mas *et al.*, 1987, 1995b). This suggestion was based on increased levels of 5-HT in POA homogenates following ejaculation, and on a postejaculatory increase in 5-HIAA, the major metabolite of serotonin, in dialysate; 5-HT in dialysate was below the detection limits of the assay. However, a more recent study was able to detect 5-HT and found that extracellular 5-HT in the MPOA, POA, or LPOA remained constant during copulation and after ejaculation (Lorrain *et al.*, 1997). However, 5-HT was released in the anterior lateral hypothalamus (LHA) at the time of ejaculation, as reviewed in Section V. G. The increase in 5-HIAA observed by Mas and his colleagues (1987; Fumero *et al.*,1994) may have resulted from diffusion from the LHA. Therefore, it appears to be unlikely that 5-HT in the MPOA contributes significantly to postejaculatory refractoriness.

7. Expression of c-fos or Other Immediate-Early Genes

Increasing numbers of Fos-immunoreactive (Fos-ir) neurons were observed in the MPN following exposure of male rats to the odor of an estrous female and following mounts, intromissions, and ejaculations (Baum and Everitt, 1992; Robertson *et al.*, 1991; Veening and Coolen, 1998). Furthermore, combined bilateral lesions of the medial amygdala and the central tegmental field blocked the copulation-induced Fos-ir in the MPN, though lesions of only one site did not affect the induction of Fos-ir (Baum and Everitt, 1992). Male rats that displayed noncontact erections or were exposed to the bedding of an estrous female also showed increased Fos-ir in the MPN and in several other sites; however, these conditions elicited less Fos-ir than did copulation (Kelliher et al., 1999). Mating, but not aggressive behavior, increased Fos-ir in the MPOA and the posteroventral portion of the posteromedial BNST of male Syrian hamsters (Kollack-Walker and Newman, 1995). Both mating and aggressive behavior elicited Fos-ir in several other areas; thus, the MPOA and a portion of the BNST are more directly related to sexual than aggressive behavior.

It appears that nonvolatile odors of a female are more effective in inducing a Fos response in male rats than are volatile odors. Sexually experienced male rats that were exposed to estrous females but did not mount (Baum and Everitt, 1992), or were exposed to estrous-female bedding that had been stored in air-tight containers (Bressler and Baum, 1996), showed an increase in Fos-ir in the MPOA. However, when sexually experienced males were presented with an estrous female and her volatile odors but not given access to her, Fos induction did not occur (Baum and Everitt, 1992). Coolen et al. (1996, 1997b) did not observe an increase in Fos-ir in the MPN of sexually experienced males following anogenital investigation of an anestrous female rat. Therefore, nonvolatile pheromones associated with estrus may be more effective in activating Fos expression than are volatile odors of estrous females or any odors of anestrous females. Alternatively, the variability in chemosensory induction of Fos-ir in the MPOA may result from the relatively small increases observed, compared with the striking increases that result from copulation and from differences in the specific areas examined.

Sexually experienced male gerbils also showed increased Fos-ir in the MPOA in response to sex-related odors in the absence of a female (Heeb and Yahr, 1996). In male macaques mating elicited no more Fos-ir in the MPOA and eight other areas than did exposure to an inaccessible female (Michael et al., 1999), thus suggesting that stimuli from the female, rather than mating itself, was important for Fos induction. There are apparently contradictory reports on the induction of Fos-ir in the MPOA of male hamsters. On one hand, Fiber et al. (1993) found an increase in Fos response to female hamster vaginal fluid in the magnocellular portion of the MPN of male Syrian hamsters. On the other hand, Fernandez-Fewell and Meredith (1994) found no increase in Fos-ir in the MPOA of inexperienced male hamsters in response to female hamster vaginal fluid, although Fos-ir was increased in several other sites in the vomeronasal system. However, mating elicited dense staining in the MPOA of these hamsters, a finding that suggests that Fos activation in the MPOA is more closely related to copulatory performance than to the chemosensory stimuli that trigger copulation. There was also no increase in Fos-ir in the MPOA of male ferrets exposed to estrous female bedding (Kelliher et al., 1998).

Several brain areas of male mammals show increased Fos-immunoreactivity that appears to be relatively specific to ejaculation, including the posterodorsal preoptic nucleus (PdPN), the lateral part of the posterodorsal medial amygdala (MeApd), and the subparafascicular nucleus (SPFp) of hamsters (Kollack-Walker and Newman, 1997), gerbils (Heeb and Yahr, 1996), and rats (Coolen et al., 1996). The PdPN is part of a pathway that includes the MeApd and that facilitates copulation and ejaculation, rather than responding passively to the stimuli of ejaculation (Heeb and Yahr, 2000). Approximately half of the ejaculation-related (Fos-ir) neurons in PdPN also showed staining for NADPHd, similar to findings in the MeApd, suggesting that NO may contribute to the regulation of neurons in both of these components of the ejaculation circuit (Simmons and Yahr, 2001).

Previous sexual experience increased the number of Fos-ir neurons in the MPN following one ejaculation (Lumley and Hull, 1999). Furthermore, the sexually experienced males ejaculated after fewer intromissions than required for the sexually naive males. Therefore, the increased Fos-ir did not result from increased copulatory activity preceding ejaculation. In addition, administration of a DA D_1 antagonist before copulation decreased ejaculation-induced Fos-ir (Lumley and Hull, 1999), similar to its ability to decrease amphetamine-induced Fos-ir in the striatum (Graybiel et al., 1990; Young et al., 1991). Therefore, previous sexual experience may prime MPOA neurons to be more responsive to sexual stimuli, and at least some of the copulation-induced Fos-ir may result from stimulation of D_1 receptors.

8. Effects of Intracerebral Grafts

Declines in sexual arousal and copulatory ability occur in male rats with advancing age. Suspensions of fetal MPOA neurons into the MPOA of aged (19 to 24 months old) male rats that displayed no ejaculations showed increased sexual motivation and copulatory activity (Hung *et al.*, 1997). Copulatory behavior was restored between 21 and 45 days after graft implantation and persisted for 2 to 4.5 months (until the end of observation). Neither grafts from the cerebral cortex into the MPOA nor from the MPOA into the ventromedial hypothalamus resulted in sexual improvement. Improvement was also observed in two hormonal measures, serum T and the postcastration increase in luteinizing hormone. The authors suggested that some age-related decreases in copulatory ability, sexual motivation, and neuroendocrine functions may be at least partially due to dysfunction of the MPOA.

9. Cell Size

Rams are heterogeneous in their copulatory performance (Perkins *et al.*, 1992) and in their preferences to mate with a female rather than another male (Perkins and Fitzgerald, 1992). A discriminant function analysis of soma sizes in the MPOA and the medial amygdala, bed nucleus of the stria terminalis, and ventromedial hypothalamus differentiated between low sexually performing males and high-performing rams but did not differentiate male-oriented rams from either of the other groups (Alexander *et al.*, 2001). Low-performing males had somewhat larger cells in the medial amygdala and somewhat smaller cells in the MPOA than high-performing or male-oriented rams.

E. Paraventricular Nucleus of the Hypothalamus

The paraventricular nucleus (PVN) consists of a magnocellular division, whose neurons contain oxytocin and vasopressin and project to the posterior pituitary, and a parvocellular division, which projects to the median eminence, the brain stem, including the dorsal vagal complex, and the spinal cord (reviewed in Swanson and Sawchenko, 1980). Some of the axons projecting to the spinal cord contain oxytocin, vasopressin, somatostatin, or DA, although the neurotransmitters of other axons have not been determined. The parvocellular division is innervated by adrenergic and noradrenergic axons from the brain stem and by axons from the dorsal vagal complex. This pattern of connections suggests that the PVN plays an important integrative role in autonomic and neuroendocrine regulation.

1. Effects of Electrolytic or Cell Body Lesions

Lesions of the PVN have decreased the numbers of noncontact erections but have produced inconsistent effects on touch-based erections and copulation. Electrolytic lesions of the PVN decreased the latency to the first touch-based *ex copula* erection (i.e., facilitated erection) (Monaghan *et al.*, 1993). However, excitotoxic lesions restricted to the parvocellular PVN inhibited noncontact erections but did not affect copulation (Liu *et al.*, 1997a). Similarly, excitotoxic lesions of the parvocellular PVN failed to affect copulatory behavior but did decrease the quantity of seminal emission at the time of ejaculation and also decreased the number of oxytocin-immunoreactive fibers in the lower lumbar spinal cord (Ackerman *et al.*, 1997). Therefore, oxytocin-containing neurons originating in the PVN may contribute to the release of seminal fluid at the time of ejaculation. Radiofrequency lesions that destroyed both parvocellular and magnocellular neurons inhibited both noncontact and touch-based erections and also decreased intromission ratios and increased ejaculation latencies in copulation tests (Liu *et al.*, 1997a). (Touch-based erections were not assessed in animals with excitotoxic lesions.) Therefore, the PVN appears to contribute to both touch-based and noncontact erections and to ejaculation but has relatively little influence on copulatory behavior.

Lesions of the lateral parvocellular subnucleus of the PVN abolished neurophysin-containing efferents to the sexually dimorphic spinal nucleus of the bulbocavernosus (SNB) (Wagner and Clemens, 1993). Neurophysin is the coproduct of oxytocin and vasopressin, and is therefore a marker for the presence of oxytocin. Neurophysin-containing terminals appeared to contact the somas and dendrites of the SNB. The loss of these terminals after PVN lesions suggests that the PVN is the source of oxytocinergic input to the SNB, which in turn promotes seminal emission and ejaculation.

2. Effects of Direct Applications of Drugs Affecting Specific Transmitters

a) DA and Oxytocin   Administration of drugs into the PVN has provided a consistent picture in which DA, via D_2 receptors, increases NO production in oxytocin-containing neurons, which then increases oxytocin release, probably from axon terminals in the hippocampus, which in turn promotes drug-induced and non-contact erections (reviewed in Argiolas and Gessa, 1991; Argiolas and Melis, 1995). Microinjection of apomorphine (Melis *et al.,* 1987), the D_2 agonist quinpirole, or oxytocin (Argiolas *et al.,* 1987) into the PVN elicited drug-induced erections, which were blocked by an intraventricular oxytocin antagonist (Melis *et al.,* 1989). PVN microinjections of apomorphine (Pehek *et al.,* 1989a) or the D_3/D_2 agonist quinelorane (Eaton *et al.,* 1991) also increased touch-based erections and seminal emissions. Intraventricular, but not PVN, administration of an oxytocin antagonist inhibited noncontact erection (Melis *et al.,* 1999b), thereby suggesting that axon terminals from the PVN ending elsewhere, probably the hippocampus (Melis *et al.,* 1992), facilitate noncontact erections.

b) NO   The NOS inhibitor N(G)-nitro-L-arginine methyl ester (L-NAME), microinjected into the PVN, decreased the number of noncontact erections and impaired copulatory behavior (Melis *et al.,* 1998). A different NOS inhibitor, N(G)-monomethyl L-arginine (L-NMMA), dialyzed into the PVN, decreased the number of touch-based erections, and the NO precursor, L-arginine, increased erections; however, copulatory behavior was not affected by either L-arginine or L-NMMA (Sato *et al.,* 1999). These authors contrasted the effects of PVN administration of L-NMMA, which did not affect copulation, with those of MPOA administration, which did decrease the rate of mounting (Sato *et al.,* 1998). Thus, both drug-induced and noncontact erections are influenced by DA and NO in the PVN and by oxytocin released elsewhere from neurons with cell bodies in the PVN. However, manipulations of NO in the PVN have had inconsistent effects on copulation.

c) Amino Acids   Microinjection of *N*-methyl-D-aspartic acid (NMDA) into the PVN increased erections (Melis *et al.,* 1997). This increase was blocked by the NMDA antagonist dizocilpine (MK-801) and by the NOS antagonist L-NAME. Therefore, activation of NMDA receptors by glutamate appears to result in activation of NOS, probably by opening calcium channels, thereby allowing calcium to activate calcium-calmodulin kinase (CAM kinase), which in turn activates NOS. PVN microinjections of the $GABA_A$ agonist muscimol, but not the $GABA_B$ agonist baclofen, reduced the erections elicited by apomorphine, oxytocin, or NMDA microinjections into the PVN (Melis *et al.,* 2000). Therefore, inhibition of PVN neurons by GABA, acting via $GABA_A$ receptors, reduces the effectiveness of dopaminergic, oxytocinergic, and glutamatergic stimulation of erections.

d) Adrenocorticotropin   Adrenocorticotropin [ACTH(1-24)] increased penile erection when microinjected into the periventricular hypothalamus, including the PVN (Argiolas *et al.,* 2000). However, it was ineffective when administered into the POA, caudate nucleus, or hippocampus (Argiolas *et al.,* 2000).

3. Chemical Changes Detected by Microdialysis

Not only does manipulation of NO production affect erection, but erection is associated with the production of endogenous NO. Both noncontact erections and copulation increased NO in dialysate from the PVN, as detected by an increase in NO_2 and NO_3 (Melis *et al.,* 1998, 1999a). The increase in NO production was blocked by prior intraventricular injection of hemoglobin, which scavenges extracellular NO, but hemoglobin injected into the PVN failed to affect the number of noncontact erections (Melis *et al.,* 1998). Therefore, NO apparently works intracellularly in PVN neurons and is also transmitted to neurons in other areas to promote erection. Morphine microinjected into the PVN blocked the production of NO and impaired copulation (Melis *et al.,* 1999a). Reverse dialysis of the NO precursor L-arginine into the PVN increased the production of NO as it increased touch-based erections, and similar administration of L-NMMA decreased NO and erections (Sato *et al.,* 1999). Systemic injection of apomorphine or of the D_2 agonist LY-171555, but not of the D_1 agonist SKF-38393, increased NO production in the PVN and also increased erections (Melis *et al.,* 1996). The increase in NO production was blocked by the mixed D_1/D_2 antagonist haloperidol and the

D_2 antagonist L-sulpiride but not by the D_1 antagonist SCH-23390. However, the increase in penile erections was blocked by all three antagonists, suggesting that stimulation of D_1 receptors was necessary, but not sufficient, for apomorphine-stimulated erections. The microinjections of NMDA that increased erections (see above) also increased the production of NO in the PVN (Melis *et al.*, 1997). Finally, intra-PVN microinjection of omega-conotoxin, a potent blocker of N-type voltage-activated calcium channels, prevented the increases in NO production and penile erection that were otherwise elicited by apomorphine or oxytocin (Succu *et al.*, 1998). The conotoxin did not block responses to the NO donors sodium nitroprusside or hydroxylamine, thereby suggesting that the calcium entry normally promoted by apomorphine or oxytocin injections was necessary to activate NOS. Thus, exogenous provision of NO overcame effects of the toxin-induced blocking of NOS activity. Conotoxin also did not block the effects of NMDA microinjections on either erection or NO production; this lack of effectiveness would be expected, because the calcium channels activated by NMDA are ligand-activated, not voltage-activated.

NOS and oxytocin are colocalized in the PVN (Yamada *et al.*, 1996). Therefore, activation of NOS/oxytocin neurons in the PVN facilitates *ex copula* erections and may also contribute to copulation. It is likely that these neurons release their oxytocin in the hippocampus, where it promotes noncontact and touch-based erections (Melis *et al.*, 1992), and in the spinal cord, where it promotes seminal emission (Ackerman *et al.*, 1997).

4. Presence of Steroid Receptors

Retrograde fluorescent tract tracing from the L5–L6 region of the spinal cord, combined with steroid autoradiography, revealed that the majority of double-labeled cells were located in the lateral parvocellular subnucleus of the PVN (Wagner *et al.*, 1993). Approximately 30% of the neurons in that subnucleus that projected to the lower spinal cord concentrated E, and almost half of the E-concentrating neurons projected to the lumbar spinal cord. Therefore, at least some of the effects of gonadal steroids on the sexually dimorphic spinal nucleus of the bulbocavernosus (SNB), located in the L5–L6 segments of the spinal cord, may be indirect, via steroid-sensitive afferents.

5. Expression of c-fos and Other Immediate-Early Genes

The numbers of Fos-ir neurons in the parvocellular regions of the PVN increased following intromission or ejaculation; ejaculation elicited about 2.5 times as many Fos-ir neurons as intromission (Witt and Insel, 1994). Significant but less striking increases in Fos-ir neurons were found in the magnocellular regions, where ejaculation again elicited several times as much Fos-ir as did intromissions. Furthermore, even in noncopulating males approximately half the Fos-ir neurons also contained oxytocin. The percentage of double-labeled cells was not altered by copulation, except in lateral parvocellular regions in the caudal-most PVN, where a third of cells were double-labeled following ejaculation but where no cells were double-labeled in control males. In male gerbils exposure to an arena not previously associated with copulation was as effective in eliciting Fos expression as exposure to an arena in which males had previously copulated (Heeb and Yahr, 1996). Copulation did not elicit a further increase in Fos-ir in the PVN of gerbils.

6. Expression of mRNA for Neuropeptides

Another study suggesting the importance of oxytocin in the PVN found that sexually impotent male rats had a reduced expression of oxytocin mRNA and an increased expression of proenkephalin and prodynorphin mRNA (Arletti *et al.*, 1997). This finding is consistent with the report that morphine in the PVN inhibited both the production of NO and copulation (Melis *et al.*, 1999a).

7. Projections from the PVN

The retrograde tracer wheat germ aglutinin, attached to horseradish peroxidase (WGA-HRP) and injected into the lumbar (L5–L6) region of the male rat spinal cord, labeled neurons in the parvocellular subnucleus of the PVN, as well as regions of the lateral and dorsal areas of the hypothalamus (Wagner and Clemens, 1991). This projection could modulate the activity of motoneurons in the lumbar spinal cord that are sexually dimorphic and androgen-dependent.

F. Ventromedial Hypothalamus

The ventromedial hypothalamus (VMH) is recognized primarily for its role in the control of female rat sexual behavior. (See Chapter 2 on female sexual behavior in this volume.) However, it may also influence male sexual behavior.

1. Effects of Electrolytic or Cell Body Lesions

Small electrolytic lesions of the VMH of castrated male rats, treated with exogenous T, resulted in significantly higher levels of male sexual behavior and shorter latencies. These results suggest that the VMH may normally inhibit some aspects of male sexual behavior (Christensen *et al.*, 1977).

2. Effects of Hormonal Manipulations

Both ARs and ERs are present in the VMH of male rats (Simerly *et al.*, 1990) and hamsters (Wood *et al.*, 1992). Cannulae that contained T and were implanted bilaterally in the VMH restored partner preference, but not copulation, in castrated male rats (Harding and McGinnis, 2001). Implants of the AR antagonist hydroxyflutamide into the VMH were even more effective in preventing the restoration of sexual behavior in castrated, T-replaced male rats than were implants into the MPOA (McGinnis *et al.*, 1996). Therefore, ARs in the VMH may be more important for male sexual behavior than was previously recognized. These inhibitory effects of hydroxyflutamide in the VMH stand in contrast to the facilitative effects of VMH lesions (Christensen *et al.*, 1977). One possible resolution to this apparent contradiction would be that AR-containing neurons may inhibit other VMH neurons, or may themselves be inhibited during male copulatory behavior. Thus, androgens may contribute to inhibition in certain VMH neurons, as do lesions, and may thereby facilitate male copulatory behavior.

3. Expression of c-fos or Other Immediate-Early Genes

Distinct clusters of cells in the VMH were Fos-immunoreactive following copulation in male rats (Coolen *et al.*,1996). Heeb and Yahr (1996) identified a specific area in the ventrolateral part of the VMH in which Fos-ir was present whenever male gerbils were with receptive females; thus, copulatory activity was not required for the increase in Fos expression. Mating increased Fos-ir in the ventrolateral VMH of both male and female rats that had been gonadectomized and given seven days of E treatment and four hours of P

(Wersinger *et al.*, 1993). Pelvic nerve section in those E-P-treated females significantly attenuated the Fos-ir response in the VMH; however pelvic nerve section in E-P-treated males did not affect Fos-ir in the VMN. The lack of effect of nerve section in males suggests that Fos expression in the VMH of males is more dependent on chemosensory input or genitosensory input carried in other pathways, such as the pudendal nerve. However, bedding from estrous females failed to increase Fos-ir in the VMH of other male rats, thus suggesting that other cues from the female or from mating are required to activate Fos expression in male rats (Bressler and Baum, 1996). In contrast to the mating-induced increase in Fos-ir in the VMH of rats and gerbils, there was no increase in Fos-ir in the VMH of male musk shrews following mating, although Fos-ir was significantly increased in the VMH of females (Gill *et al.*, 1998). There was also no mating-induced increase in Fos-ir in the VMH of male ferrets (Kelliher *et al.*, 1998; Lambert *et al.*, 1992). In male macaques, mating actually elicited less Fos-ir in the VMH, BNST, lateral mammillary area, and arcuate nucleus than did exposure to an inaccessible female (Michael *et al.*, 1999). Therefore, mating may inhibit neural activity in some brain areas, including the VMH, in macaques.

G. Lateral Hypothalamus

Major reciprocal connections between the MPOA and numerous more caudal structures pass through the lateral hypothalamus (LH) in the medial forebrain bundle (Simerly and Swanson, 1988). As reviewed in Section VI on circuitry, lesions that sever these connections abolish copulatory behavior, as do lesions of the MPOA itself. However, cell bodies in the LH may also influence copulation.

1. Effects of Direct Applications of Drugs Affecting Specific Transmitters

Microinjection of a selective serotonin reuptake inhibitor (SSRI) into the anterior lateral hypothalamus (LHA) increased the latencies of male rats to mount, intromit, and ejaculate (Lorrain *et al.*, 1997). Thus, both sexual motivation and ejaculatory ability may be compromised by increased 5-HT in the LHA. These effects are similar to the side effects of SSRI antidepressants in humans (reviewed in Rosen *et al.*, 1999).

2. Changes Detected by Microdialysis

5-HT is released in the LHA at the time of ejaculation (Lorrain et al., 1997). (See Fig. 22.) Furthermore, reverse dialysis of 5-HT into the LHA decreased DA levels in the nucleus accumbens (NAcc), a major terminus of the mesolimbic DA system (Lorrain et al., 1999). In control animals DA in the NAcc rose during copulation and decreased during each postejaculatory interval. However, 5-HT dialyzed into the LHA immediately decreased basal NAcc DA and prevented the usual copulation-induced rise. Copulation was not affected, perhaps because the 5-HT was administered only unilaterally. Because mesolimbic DA energizes numerous motivated behaviors, including sexual behavior, a decline in DA in the NAcc may at least partially account for SSRI-induced decreases in sexual motivation that have been reported clinically (reviewed in Rosen et al., 1999) and may have relevance for other motivated behaviors.

H. Ventral Premammillary Nucleus

The ventral premammillary nucleus has connections with several areas that are important for the regulation of male sexual behavior, including the medial preoptic nucleus, the VMH, and the posterodorsal part of the medial amygdala (Canteras et al., 1992).

1. Presence of Steroid Receptors

The ventral premammillary nucleus of both rats (Simerly et al., 1990; Yokosuka and Hayashi, 1996; Yokosuka et al., 1997) and Syrian hamsters (Wood and Newman, 1995a) contains ARs.

2. Expression of c-fos or Other Immediate-Early Genes

Copulation increased Fos-ir in the ventral premammillary nucleus of male rats (Coolen et al., 1996).

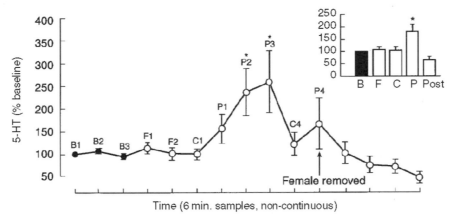

FIGURE 22 Temporal changes in extracellular serotonin (5-HT) collected from the lateral hypothalamic area (LHA) of male rats before and during copulation. Each data point is the mean ($\pm$ SE) for six-minute dialysate samples collected during baseline (B), in the presence of an estrous female (F), during copulation (C), during the postejaculatory interval (P), and after the female was removed (expressed as a percentage of mean baseline levels). A total of four samples were analyzed after the female was removed, at 30-minute intervals. 5-HT levels increased during the second (P2) and third (P3) postejaculatory intervals, compared to final baseline (B3), female behind barrier (F2), and first copulation period (C1). 5-HT during P3 was also higher than during the fourth copulation interval (C4). Samples collected during the second and third copulation series were not analyzed, because most males ejaculated before a full six-minute sample could be collected. The summary graph (inset) represents the mean ($\pm$ SE) for data from the 15 sample periods collapsed into five groups, based on behavioral condition. Samples collected during the postejaculatory intervals showed higher 5-HT levels compared to all other conditions. Basal extracellular concentrations of 5-HT in the LHA were calculated to be 1.6 ± 0.1 nM. [Figure from Lorrain et al. (1997) with permission.]

Furthermore, Fos-ir neurons were also immunoreactive for ARs, a finding that suggests that androgens may contribute to the responsiveness of those neurons (Gréco *et al.*, 1998b). However, male gerbils showed no greater increase in Fos-ir in this nucleus following copulation or exposure to an arena in which the male had previously copulated than following exposure to a nonsexual context (Heeb and Yahr, 1996). In male mice female-soiled bedding elicited a Fos response in the ventral premammillary nucleus, but not in the VMH, posterodorsal part of the medial amygdala, or posteromedial part of the cortical amygdala (Yokosuka *et al.*, 1999). In male hamsters both mating and agonistic behavior activated Fos expression in the ventral premammillary nucleus (Kollack-Walker and Newman, 1995).

I. Mesocorticolimbic DA Tract

The mesocorticolimbic DA tract arises from cell bodies in the ventral tegmental area (VTA) and projects to the nucleus accumbens (NAcc), septal area, olfactory tubercle, BNST, amygdala, the ventral part of the dorsal striatum and the frontal cortex (Domesick, 1988). This tract has been implicated in behavioral activation, reward, and incentive learning related to numerous motivated behaviors (reviewed in DiChiara, 1995). Because most studies of motivated behaviors have focused on the projection to the NAcc, this review will also concentrate on the NAcc and VTA components of this tract.

1. Effects of Electrolytic or Cell Body Lesions

Radiofrequency or DA-depleting (6-OHDA) lesions of the NAcc increased the latency to the first noncontact erection; in addition, 6-OHDA lesions decreased the number of noncontact and apomorphine-induced erections (Liu *et al.*, 1998). Copulation was normal after both types of lesion, except for increased intromission latency in the 6-OHDA-treated males, who also showed less amphetamine-induced locomotion. These data suggest that the mesocorticolimbic projection to the NAcc promotes arousal in response to remote cues from estrous females but has relatively little to do with copulatory performance. On the other hand, bilateral lesions of the VTA increased the postejaculatory interval but did not affect other copulatory measures (Brackett *et al.*, 1986).

2. Effects of Electrical Stimulation

Electrical stimulation of the VTA decreased mount, intromission, and ejaculation latencies and postejaculatory interval (Eibergen and Caggiula, 1973; Markowski and Hull, 1995). Stimulation also increased the number of ejaculations in a 30-min test (Markowski and Hull, 1995).

3. Effects of Castration or of Direct Applications of Hormones

Early studies reported no binding of hormones to classic steroid receptors in the VTA, though low levels of binding were found in the NAcc (Pfaff and Keiner, 1973; Sar and Stumpf, 1975). However, a more recent study found small patches of AR-ir neurons in the VTA that were also immunoreactive for tyrosine hydroxylase, the rate-limiting enzyme for catecholamine synthesis (Kritzer, 1997). There are apparently contradictory reports of the effects of castration on NAcc DA levels. Castration in adulthood decreased DA and its major metabolite DOPAC in NAcc tissue homogenates; these changes coincided with changes in sexual arousal (Mitchell and Stewart, 1989). However, amphetamine released more DA in dialysate from prepubertally castrated males, thereby suggesting that there was more DA stored in tissue (Hernandez *et al.*, 1994b). It is not clear whether the time of castration or other factors account for this difference. Bilateral implants of T into the VTA of castrated male house mice were ineffective in restoring mounting, ultrasonic vocalizations, urine marking, or attraction to female urine (Sipos and Nyby, 1996). However, the combined application of T to the MPOA and VTA was more effective than implants in the MPOA alone. Implants that missed their intended sites were ineffective, thus indicating that the quantity of steroid implanted could not account for the facilitative effects of the VTA implants. Therefore, ARs in the VTA may contribute to the activation of male sexual behavior, possibly by increasing activity of dopaminergic neurons.

4. Effects of Direct Applications of Drugs Affecting Specific Transmitters

a) DA Microinjection of the DA agonist apomorphine into the VTA delayed the start of copulation and slowed its rate, presumably by stimulating impulse-regulating autoreceptors on cell bodies (Hull *et al.*, 1990). Similar injections also slowed the speed of running to all four arms of an X-maze and increased the number of trials on which the male remained in the start box but failed to affect the percentage of trials on which the female's goal box was chosen or the numbers of touch-based genital reflexes (Hull *et al.*, 1991). Thus, inhibition of mesocorticolimbic activity reduced behavioral activation but did not affect specifically sexual motivation or reflexes.

A similar conclusion was supported by the application of drugs to the NAcc. Amphetamine speeded the onset of copulation, whereas the DA antagonist cis-flupenthixol or the DA neurotoxin 6-OHDA delayed it (reviewed in Everitt, 1990). Amphetamine also increased responding for a secondary reinforcer that had been paired with access to a female (Everitt, 1990). The D_3/D_2 agonist quinelorane increased the number of times that the male failed to leave the start area of an X-maze but did not affect the percentage of trials that the male chose the female if he did run and did not affect copulation once he reached the female (Moses *et al.*, 1995). It is not clear whether quinelorane's effects resulted from stimulation of inhibitory autoreceptors on DA axon terminals or from stimulation of postsynaptic receptors. However, there is a consistent pattern of mesolimbic drug effects on general activation, with little influence on specifically sexual motivation or on copulatory performance.

b) CCK Microinjection of a cholecystokinin type A (CCK_A) receptor antagonist into the posteromedian NAcc attenuated the facilitation produced by electrical stimulation of the VTA, as did microinjection of either a CCK_A or CCK_B antagonist into the anterolateral NAcc (Markowski and Hull, 1995). CCK is colocalized in dopaminergic neurons of the VTA that project to the posteromedian NAcc but is in nondopaminergic terminals in the anterolateral portion (Hokfelt *et al.*, 1980). These results suggest that the facilitative effects of the mesocorticolimbic DA tract are potentiated by CCK in the NAcc.

c) 5-HT Microinjections of 5-HT (0–40 μg) into the NAcc increased the number of mounts and intromissions preceding ejaculation and ejaculation latency (Hillegaart *et al.*, 1991). Microinjections of 8-OH-DPAT

decreased these same measures. Injections of either compound into the dorsal striatum had no effect. The authors suggested that the effects of 8-OH-DPAT may have resulted from a blockade of $5-HT_2$ receptors.

d) Opioids The opioid antagonist naloxone microinjected into the VTA decreased anticipatory level changing but did not affect sexual performance; β-endorphin had no effect (van Furth and van Ree, 1996). Therefore, stimulation of opioid receptors in the VTA may increase behavioral activation but not copulatory performance.

5. Chemical Changes Detected by Microdialysis or Voltammetry

Extracellular DA in the NAcc increased when a male rat was exposed to the odor of a receptive female but not to a nonreceptive female or a male (Damsma *et al.*, 1992; Fumero *et al.*, 1994; Louilot *et al.*, 1991; Mas *et al.*, 1990; Mitchell and Gratton, 1991; Pfaus *et al.*, 1990b; Wenkstern *et al.*, 1993). DA levels also increased during copulation (Fumero *et al.*, 1994; Mas *et al.*, 1990; Pleim *et al.*, 1990; Wenkstern *et al.*, 1993). The increase in response to estrous female odor occurred during the first exposure to that odor (Wenkstern *et al.*, 1993) and was attenuated by systemically administered naloxone (Mitchell and Gratton, 1991). Mitchell and Gratton suggested that stimulation of opioid receptors in the VTA may result in increased firing of VTA neurons, which would promote behavioral activation. Finer temporal analysis, achieved with *in vivo* voltammetry (Mas *et al.*, 1990; Blackburn *et al.*, 1992) or with microdialysis combined with capillary chromatography (Lorrain *et al.*, 1999), revealed that extracellular DA in the NAcc rose when the female was first presented, increased further during copulation, fell after each ejaculation, and rose again as the male resumed copulation. (See Fig. 23.) Furthermore, reverse dialysis of 5-HT into the anterior lateral hypothalamic area (LHA) depressed basal DA levels and prevented the DA increase during copulation (Lorrain *et al.*, 1999). Because 5-HT is released in the LHA at the time of ejaculation (Lorrain *et al.*, 1997), these data suggest that one factor in the sexual quiescence of the postejaculatory interval may be reduced DA release in the NAcc, consequent to 5-HT release in the LHA.

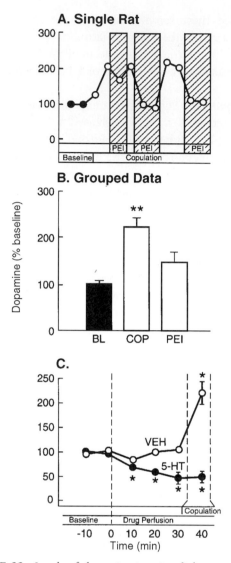

A. Single Rat

B. Grouped Data

C.

FIGURE 23 Levels of dopamine in microdialysate collected from the nucleus accumbens (NAcc) of male rats during sexual behavior sessions. (A) Representative example of temporal changes in a single rat. (B) Mean change in DA levels (± SE) for a group of six rats. Samples were collected at three-minute intervals during three ejaculatory series and are designated precopulatory baseline (BL; *filled circles*), copulation (COP; *open circles*), or postejaculatory interval (PEI; *hatched circles*). Dopamine content was significantly greater in samples collected during copulation, compared with samples collected under baseline and postejaculatory conditions (**$P < .01$). (C) Temporal change in dopamine concentration of the dialysates collected from the NAcc before and during 40 minutes of 5-HT perfusion into the LHA of six male rats. Samples were collected at 10-minute intervals. An estrous female was introduced to the male, and copulation was allowed during collection of the final sample

Sexually satiated males, presented with a novel receptive female behind a barrier, showed a slight increase in NAcc DA, which rose significantly during renewed copulation with the novel female (Fiorino *et al.*, 1997). Furthermore, repeated administration of amphetamine, which resulted in sensitization to the motor-activating effects of amphetamine, also increased the DA response to a receptive female behind a barrier and resulted in shorter latencies to copulate and more copulatory behaviors (Fiorino and Phillips, 1999a). Thus, sensitization to a psychostimulant drug can cross-sensitize to a natural behavior. Prenatal stress decreased the number of rats that were able to copulate; however, the NAcc DA release in response to an inaccessible female and during copulation did not differ between those stressed and nonstressed males that did copulate (Wang *et al.*, 1995).

6. Expression of c-fos or Other Immediate-Early Genes

Copulatory behavior elicited a pronounced increase in Fos-ir in the NAcc of male rats (Robertson *et al.*, 1991). In addition, exposure to an almond odor, which had previously been associated with copulation to ejaculation, increased Fos-ir in both the NAcc and VTA, as well as in the MPOA, posterodorsal medial amygdala, and piriform cortex (Kippin *et al.*, 1996). Tail pinch, a nonspecific arousing stimulus that can promote copulation in sexually sluggish or noncopulating rats, also increased Fos-ir in the VTA, as well as the MPOA, BNST, PVN, medial amygdala, and several sites not usually associated with copulation (Smith *et al.*, 1997).

7. Immunocytochemistry for Specific Neurotransmitters

Confocal microscopy revealed that μ opioid receptors were present on GABA interneurons in the rostral VTA; in more caudal areas of the VTA these receptors were located on presynaptic terminals that contacted GABAergic neurons (Balfour *et al.*, 2001). In turn,

during 5-HT perfusion. A significant decrease in dopamine occurred throughout the entire 5-HT perfusion period. This treatment blocked the increase in NAcc DA seen in control animals [*$P < .05$, perfusion times vs time 0 (baseline)]. [Figure is from Lorrain *et al.* (1999) with permission.]

GABA-containing terminals were in close apposition to DA neurons. Therefore, DA neurons may be disinhibited by morphine's inhibition of GABA neurons. Furthermore, the μ opioid receptors were internalized in the VTA of male rats that had ejaculated 1 hour earlier. (Receptor internalization is an indication of previous activation by neurotransmitters.) Finally, copulation increased Fos-ir in the VTA, and a subset of Fos-ir neurons contained tyrosine hydroxylase (TH-ir) and therefore were dopaminergic. These data provide an integrated picture in which copulation elicits the release of endogenous opioids in the VTA, which inhibit GABA interneurons, thereby releasing DA-containing cells from tonic inhibition.

J. Nigrostriatal DA Tract

The nigrostriatal DA tract ascends from the substantia nigra (A9 cell group) to the dorsal striatum (caudate-putamen). Activity in this tract enhances the readiness to respond to external stimuli (Robbins and Everitt, 1992). Loss of nigrostriatal DA in Parkinson's disease results in difficulty initiating movements and general slowing of movement. Nigrostriatal neurons respond with short latencies to a variety of stimuli that have "alerting, arousing, and attention-grabbing properties," but do not provide specific information about those stimuli (Schultz, 1992).

1. Effects of Electrolytic or Cell Body Lesions

Consistent with its importance for initiating motor movements, the nigrostriatal tract has been suggested to promote the somatomotor patterns required for pursuit and mounting of the female (Robbins and Everitt, 1992; Hull *et al.*, 1999). Bilateral lesions of the substantia nigra slowed the rate of copulation and decreased the number of ejaculations per test (Brackett *et al.*, 1986).

2. Chemical Changes Detected by Microdialysis or Voltammetry

In contrast to the release of DA in the NAcc and MPOA immediately after introduction of a receptive female (reviewed in Sections V.D.6 and V.I.5), DA was released in the dorsal striatum only after the male began to copulate (Damsma *et al.*, 1992). This temporal pattern suggests that DA in the dorsal striatum

is more concerned with motor activation than with the motivational aspects of copulation.

3. Expression of c-fos or Other Immediate-Early Genes

In contrast to the striking copulation-induced increase in Fos-ir in the NAcc, MPOA, BNST, and piriform cortex, there was no increase in Fos expression in the dorsal striatum (Robertson *et al.*, 1991).

K. Subparafascicular Nucleus of the Thalamus

The medial parvocellular portion of the subparafascicular nucleus of the thalamus (SPFp) has been implicated as part of an ejaculation circuit in rats, hamsters, and gerbils (see Circuitry section below).

1. Effects of Electrolytic or Cell Body Lesions

Bilateral lesions of the SPFp of gerbils did not affect their copulatory behavior, suggesting that their activation (measured as increased Fos-ir) by ejaculation represents a response to ejaculation-related stimuli, rather than participation in the control of the behavior (Heeb and Yahr, 2000).

2. Location of Steroid Receptors

AR immunoreactivity was observed in the SPFp, as well as in other areas previously reported to contain ARs (Gréco *et al.*, 1996). Furthermore, the distributions of cells containing AR-ir and Fos-ir were largely overlapping.

3. Expression of c-fos or Other Immediate-Early Genes

Ejaculation, but not other copulatory behaviors or chemosensory investigation, increased Fos-ir in the SPFp of rats (Coolen *et al.*, 1996, 1997a,b), gerbils (Heeb and Yahr, 1996), and hamsters (Kollack-Walker and Newman, 1997). To test whether the ejaculation-specific increase was due simply to the number of intromissions required to trigger ejaculation, Coolen *et al.* (1997a) administered the 5-HT$_{1A}$ agonist, 8-OH-DPAT, before copulation. This drug dramatically decreased the number of intromissions preceding ejaculation. Indeed, some animals ejaculated on their first intromission. Males that ejaculated after few or no mounts or intromissions had almost as many Fos-ir neurons in the SPFp and other parts of the "ejaculation-related subcircuit" as did those that ejaculated following the normal numbers of mounts and intromissions. Additional support for the suggestion that the SPFp responds to sensory input but does not contribute to the motor control of ejaculation comes from the observation that female rats have a very similar pattern of Fos-ir following ejaculation by the male (Veening and Coolen, 1998).

4. Immunocytochemistry for Specific Neurotransmitters

The SPFp consists of medial and lateral subdivisions. The medial portion contained a high concentration of galanin-ir fibers (Veening *et al.*, 1997). Furthermore, mating-induced Fos-ir neurons were also located in the medial subdivision and were surrounded by galanin-ir fibers. Therefore, projections from the lumbosacral spinal cord to the medial SPFp may contain galanin and may transmit sensory information related to ejaculation.

L. Central Tegmental Field and Dorsolateral Tegmentum

The midbrain tegmentum is reciprocally connected to the MPOA and anterior hypothalamus (Coolen *et al.*, 1998; Gréco *et al.*, 1998b, 1999; Murphy *et al.*, 1999a; Simerly and Swanson, 1986, 1988). Subregions of the midbrain tegmentum have been referred to as the central tegmental field (CTF) (e.g., Baum and Everitt, 1992; Gréco *et al.*, 1996, 1998b,c, 1999; Simerly and Swanson, 1986) or the dorsolateral tegmentum (DLT) (e.g., Brackett and Edwards, 1984; Brackett *et. al.*, 1986; Edwards and Einhorn, 1986; Giordano *et al.*, 1998; Maillard and Edwards, 1991; Paredes *et al.*, 1993c). This region lies immediately dorsal to the lateral half of the substantia nigra and includes the SPFp, part of the caudal zona incerta, the peripeduncular nucleus, the mesencephalic reticular nucleus, and the anterior pretectal nucleus. (See Fig. 24.) Portions of this region supply somatosensory input from the genitals to the MPOA, whereas other subareas provide important efferent connections.

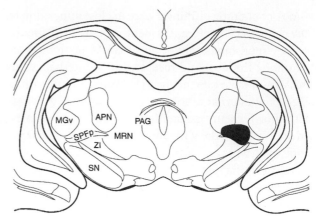

FIGURE 24 Site of Fluorogold (FG) injection into the lateral central tegmental field (CTF) (*black area* on *right* side of section). The site of injection was defined as the area of brilliant FG surrounding the region of necrosis induced by the injection. APN, anterior pretectal nucleus; MGv, venral medial geniculate nucleus of the thalamus; MRN, median raphe nucleus; PAG, periaqueductal gray; SN, substantia nigra; SPFp, parvocellular portion of the subparafascicular nucleus; ZI, zona incerta. [Figure is redrawn from Gréco *et al.*, 1999, with permission.]

1. Effects of Electrolytic or Cell Body Lesions

Combined ipsilateral lesions of the CTF and the medial amygdala abolished copulation-induced Fos-expression in the MPOA (Baum and Everitt, 1992). However, unilateral lesions of either the CTF or medial amygdala alone did not affect Fos-ir in the MPOA. Unilateral MPOA lesions did not affect Fos-ir in the CTF or medial amygdala, thus suggesting that the major direction of information flow that elicits Fos-ir is from the CTF to the MPOA (for genital sensory input) and from the medial amygdala to the MPOA (for chemosensory input). Similarly, as noted above, bilateral lesions of the SPFp, a major component of the CTF, did not affect copulatory behavior of male gerbils (Heeb and Yahr, 2000). Thus, portions of the midbrain tegmentum may be more important for sensory input than for motor output.

In contrast to the primarily sensory function of the CTF, the DLT is implicated in the motor expression of copulation. Bilateral lesions of the area referred to as the DLT virtually eliminated the mating behavior of male rats (Brackett and Edwards, 1984; Brackett *et al.*, 1986; Hansen and Gummesson, 1982). Furthermore, bilateral lesions of the MPOA or of the DLT inhibited both copulation and the preference for an estrous female (Edwards and Einhorn, 1986). Similar effects were observed following unilateral lesions of the MPOA and the contralateral DLT, a finding that suggests that connections between these two areas are essential for copulation (Brackett and Edwards, 1984). Furthermore, implantation of fetal hypothalamic grafts into males that had lost copulatory ability as a result of MPOA lesions resulted in gradual recovery of sexual behavior over a course of 15 weeks (Paredes *et al.*, 1993c). Injections of the retrograde tracer Fluorogold into the DLT resulted in labeling of neurons in the MPOA, thus suggesting that the fetal neurons had made connections with DLT neurons of the host. Fetal grafts of cortical tissue did not restore sexual behavior and did not form connections to the DLT. Therefore, both tissue specificity and the formation of connections with the host brain, including the DLT, appear to be important for recovery from MPOA lesions. In a more recent study, bilateral electrolytic lesions of the DLT resulted in copulatory impairment for 15 weeks following the lesion (Giordano *et al.*, 1998). In addition, sniffing, pursuit, and genital exploration of the female were also decreased, as was postcopulatory self-grooming. The impairment of socio-sexual interactions (Giordano *et al.*, 1998), together with the decrease in preference for an estrous female (Edwards and Einhorn, 1986), suggests that both sexual motivation and copulatory performance are affected by an output pathway from the MPOA to the DLT.

Either electrolytic or excitotoxin-induced lesions of a different region of the dorsal tegmentum dramatically shortened the postejaculatory interval of male rats (Hansen *et al.*, 1982b). However, lesions of NE cell bodies in the region, using the NE neurotoxin DSP4, decreased copulatory rate (i.e., impaired copulation). Therefore, noradrenergic cell bodies in the dorsal tegmentum appear to increase copulatory performance, whereas non-noradrenergic neurons contribute to the active inhibition of copulation after ejaculation.

2. Expression of c-fos or Other Immediate-Early Genes

Copulation to ejaculation elicited increased Fos-ir in the CTF of male rats (Baum and Everitt, 1992; Wersinger *et al.*, 1993) and male musk shrews (Gill *et al.*, 1998). Immunofluorescence studies showed that

AR-containing neurons in the CTF and several other structures showed increased Fos-ir following copulation (Gréco *et al.*, 1998b). Therefore, androgens may contribute to neuronal activation in the CTF.

3. Presence of Steroid Receptors

The CTF exhibits AR-ir, but not ER-ir (Gréco *et al.*, 1998a).

4. Connections of the CTF

Injections of the retrograde tracer Fluorogold into the CTF labeled numerous neurons in the dorsal and ventral parts of Lamina X in the L5-S1 segments of the rat spinal cord (Gréco *et al.*, 1999). Some of these projection neurons also contained AR-ir and mating-induced Fos-ir. Fluorogold-labeled neurons were also found in the MPOA, immediately dorsolateral to the MPN; some of these neurons also contained both AR-ir and Fos-ir. The BNST also contained numerous Fluorogold-labeled neurons, some of which contained both AR-ir and Fos-ir. Therefore, the lateral tegmentum appears to receive input from neurons in the spinal cord, MPOA, and BNST, some of which are androgen-sensitive and are activated by mating.

M. Midbrain Periaqueductal Gray (PAG)

The MPOA has extensive reciprocal projections to the midbrain periaqueductal gray (PAG) (Simerly and Swanson, 1986; Holstege, 1987; Murphy and Hoffman, 2001; Rizvi *et al.*, 1992, 1996).

1. Effects of Electrolytic or Cell Body Lesions

Bilateral lesions of the central gray of male rats greatly facilitated copulation by increasing mounting rate, decreasing ejaculation latency, and increasing the number of ejaculations per test (Brackett *et al.*, 1986). However, combined unilateral lesions of the ventrolateral PAG and the contralateral sexually dimorphic area (SDA) of the medial preoptic area of male gerbils did not affect behavior (Finn and Yahr, 1994).

2. Presence of Steroid Receptors

The caudal two-thirds of the PAG contains a large population of ERα and AR receptors (Murphy *et al.*, 1999b). In the middle third of the structure, the steroid concentrating neurons were distributed primarily in the dorsomedial and lateral PAG, whereas in the caudal third, immunoreactive cells were located primarily in the dorsal half. The distributions of ERα and AR receptors were quite similar, and the authors suggested that it is likely that some PAG neurons contain both types of receptors. Furthermore, afferents from the MPOA terminated in close apposition to ERα-ir and AR-ir neurons in the PAG, and between 17 and 54% of PAG neurons that projected to the nucleus paragigantocellularis (nPGi) (see below) were also immunoreactive for ERα or AR (Murphy and Hoffman, 2001).

N. Nucleus Paragigantocellularis of the Medulla

Spinal mechanisms that control erection are under tonic inhibitory control. In rats (Hart, 1968a; Sachs and Garinello, 1979, 1980), mice (Sachs, 1980), and dogs (Hart, 1967a; Hart and Kitchell, 1966) spinal transection results in an increase in the number or intensity of erections or urethrogenital reflexes or a decrease in the amount of stimulation required to elicit such responses. There is increasing evidence that a major source of that inhibition is the nPGi, located in the ventrolateral medulla.

1. Effects of Electrolytic or Cell Body Lesions

Bilateral electrolytic lesions of the nPGi in sexually naive male rats increased the number of animals that ejaculated on their first exposure to an estrous female (Yells *et al.*, 1992). In the males that did ejaculate, nPGi lesions decreased the time and the numbers of mounts and intromissions preceding ejaculation and increased copulatory efficiency. In sexually experienced males nPGi lesions increased the latency to sexual satiety and increased the number of ejaculations preceding satiety (Yells *et al.*, 1992). Similar lesions decreased the latency to the onset of touch-based penile reflexes and increased the number of anteroflexions (Marson *et al.*, 1992). Lesions of the nPGi also allowed the urethrogenital reflex to be elicited without spinal transection (Marson and McKenna, 1990). Indeed, nPGi lesions were as effective as spinal transection in disinhibiting the urethrogenital reflex, suggesting that the nPGi is a major source of the tonic inhibition.

2. Effects of Electrical Stimulation

Electrical stimulation of the nPGi of male rats elicited field potentials in the lumbosacral cord near the motor neurons of the pudendal nerve (Tanaka and Arnold, 1993b), thus suggesting that nPGi efferents could affect perineal muscles.

3. Immunocytochemistry

A majority (78%) of nPGi neurons projecting to the lumbosacral spinal cord contain 5-HT (Marson and McKenna, 1992). Therefore, serotonergic input could mediate the tonic inhibition of genital reflexes.

O. Other Brain Areas

Electrical stimulation of the cingulate gyrus, the medial dorsal nucleus of the thalamus, the periventricular region, and the VTA elicited erections in conscious monkeys (MacLean and Ploog, 1962). In anesthetized rats stimulation of the hippocampus elicited increases in intracavernosal pressure (Chen *et al.*, 1992). Oxytocin pathways from the PVN may activate the hippocampus (Argiolas and Melis, 1995), as may cholinergic input from the septum. The hippocampus also receives serotonergic input from the raphe nuclei (Maeda *et al.*, 1990, 1994).

Lesions of the lateral septum of male rats resulted in markedly lower numbers of mounts and intromissions, compared to intact controls (Kondo *et al.*, 1993). However, implantation of the AR antagonist hydroxyflutamide into the lateral septum of male rats did not prevent the restoration by T of copulation in male rat castrates, whereas similar implants into the MPOA did prevent restoration (McGinnis *et al.*, 1996). Therefore, the lateral septum facilitates male sexual behavior, but activation of ARs in the lateral septum appears to be unnecessary for its facilitative effects.

Vasopressin in the lateral septum may promote pair bonding in male prairie voles. Microinjection of vasopressin into the lateral septum of male prairie voles increased the time spent with a partner, as opposed to a stranger, whereas both a vasopressin antagonist and an oxytocin antagonist in the lateral septum blocked the formation of pair bonds induced by either mating or microinjection of vasopressin (Liu *et al.*, 2001). Therefore, vasopressin in the lateral septum regulates

1. Male Sexual Behavior

the formation of pair bonds through both vasopressin and oxytocin receptors.

Lesions of the caudal zona incerta, in the subthalamic region, eliminated mating in male rats, but did not affect preference for a receptive female over a nonreceptive female (Edwards and Isaacs, 1991; Maillard and Edwards, 1991). The zona incerta has reciprocal connections with the DLT (Ricardo, 1981) and receives somatosensory input from the trigeminal complex, dorsal column nuclei, and primary somatosensory cortex (Berkeley, 1986). Furthermore, bilateral transections of the pontine tegmentum reduced mating, and the combination of a unilateral tegmental cut and a contralateral lesion of either the MPOA or subthalamus almost completely eliminated copulation (Maillard-Gutekunst and Edwards, 1994). The elimination of copulation by zona incerta lesions suggests that it is an important node in the control of copulation, but little is known of its specific contributions. However, it appears to be a part of a critical circuit for the expression of copulatory behavior.

Several regions of the cerebral cortex showed increased activity in positron emission tomography (PET) scans when men were presented with sexually explicit films compared to humorous or emotionally neutral films (Stoleru *et al.,* 1999). The inferior temporal cortex, a visual association area, was activated bilaterally. The right insula and right inferior frontal cortex were also activated; these are paralimbic areas that are thought to associate highly processed sensory information with motivational states. Finally, the left anterior cingulate cortex, which is associated with autonomic and neuroendocrine functions, showed increased activity. Plasma T levels were positively correlated with the degree of activation of some of those areas. This type of imaging research will prove the more valuable when controls are added that provide additional nonsexual emotional content. At present, one cannot know which brain areas are particularly active during sexual arousal and which are active in several emotional contexts.

P. Spinal Cord

The spinal cord contains the autonomic and somatic nuclei that control the hemodynamic and striated muscle effectors of erection, ejaculation, and detumescence and that provide initial processing of somatic and visceral information from the genital region. Both descending axons from the brain and local reflex loops are important for these processes (see Giuliano and Rampin, 2000 for review).

1. Effects of Lesions or Transections

There is convincing evidence of descending inhibition from supraspinal sources, which can be eliminated by transection of the spinal cord. Spinal cord transection releases the urethrogenital reflex from descending inhibition, allowing it to be elicited by urethral stimulation (McKenna *et al.,* 1991). Early postnatal spinal cord transection also accelerates the developmental expression of touch-based erections in male rats from about 38 to about 28 days of age, without altering androgen titers or their morphological correlates (Meisel and Sachs, 1980). Spinal cord transection also reversed the reduction of penile reflex potential that resulted from severing of the dorsal penile nerves (Sachs and Garinello, 1980), application of a topical anesthetic to the glans penis (Stefanick *et al.,* 1983), or excision of the penile sheath, which removes the tonic stimulation necessary for penile reflexes in neurally intact rats (Lumia *et al.,* 1980).

2. Effects of Direct Application of Drugs Selective for a Neurotransmitter

The need for caution in interpreting the effects of spinal transection is emphasized by a study in which spinal anesthesia was induced in rats at the thoracic level via an intrathecal cannula (Sachs and Bitran, 1990). After induction of spinal block, supine males exhibited the abbreviated erection latencies characteristic of spinally transected males, but unlike transected males, they had fewer and weaker erections. The reduction in erection latency may truly be due to the removal of inhibitory influences from the brain, but the decreased number and intensity of erections in spinally blocked males implies interference with excitatory influences from the brain. The increase in touch-based erections after surgical transection may therefore be secondary to neural reorganization within the cord, rather than a direct effect of removing supraspinal inhibition.

a) 5-HT The urethrogenital reflex typically cannot be elicited unless the spinal cord is transected (McKenna *et al.,* 1991), the nPGi is ablated (Marson and McKenna, 1990; Marson *et al.,* 1992), or the MPOA is stimulated (Marson and McKenna, 1994b). However, either intrathecal or intracerebroventricular (icv) administration of the 5-HT neurotoxin 5,7-DHT allowed the urethrogenital reflex to be elicited without spinal transection or nPGi ablation or MPOA stimulation (Marson and McKenna, 1994a). This suggests that descending serotonergic axons are responsible for a major part of the central inhibition of this reflex. A majority (78% ipsilateral) of the axons from the nPGi contain 5-HT (Marson and McKenna, 1992). Intrathecal administration of 5-HT abolished the urethrogenital reflex, and the 5-HT antagonist methysergide prevented the 5-HT-induced blockade of the reflex (Marson and McKenna, 1992). In addition, lesions of the median raphe nuclei (a major source of serotonergic neurons) significantly increased the numbers of anteroflexions (penile body erections) and cups (intense glans erections) in tests of touch-based erections (Monaghan *et al.,* 1993).

Intrathecal administration of either 5-HT or thyrotropin releasing hormone (TRH) resulted in only slight increases in mount and intromission latencies; however, co-administration of 5-HT and TRH caused a marked increase in mount and intromission latencies (Hansen *et al.,* 1983). However, in a test of touch-based penile reflexes, intrathecal administration of TRH alone decreased the proportion of responders, decreased the numbers of reflexes, and increased their latencies (Holmes *et al.,* 1997). TRH and 5-HT are colocalized in some spinal neurons (Hokfelt *et al.,* 1986). Furthermore, methiothepin, a relatively nonspecific 5-HT antagonist, partially blocked some of the inhibitory effects of TRH (Holmes *et al.,* 2001). Therefore, either 5-HT or TRH may inhibit copulation and genital reflexes, but their effects may be enhanced by co-administration or endogenous co-release.

Intrathecal administration of 8-OH-DPAT decreased the percentage of male rats displaying touch-based erections and seminal emissions (Lee *et al.,* 1990). This is in dramatic contrast to the facilitative effects of intrathecally administered 8-OH-DPAT on copulation, and especially ejaculatory threshold. In the copulation tests 8-OH-DPAT decreased ejaculation latency, intercopulatory interval, and the number of intromissions preceding ejaculation (Lee *et al.,* 1990). The basis for the apparent discrepancy between *in copula* and *ex copula*

measures is not clear. However, a similar discrepancy was observed with intrathecal apomorphine (Pehek *et al.,* 1989b, summarized below).

b) GABA   In the lower spinal cord GABA, as well as 5-HT, inhibits sexual reflexes. Intrathecal injection of the GABA$_B$ agonist baclofen into the lumbosacral (L5-S1) area decreased the number of touch-based erections and increased the latency to the first glans erection; the highest dose completely blocked penile responses (Bitran *et al.,* 1988b). However, none of the doses used (0.2, 0.4, or 0.8 μg) prevented males from copulating to ejaculation. *In copula* ejaculation shortly before the reflex test facilitated the onset of touch-based erections in saline controls and also blocked the inhibitory effects of the lower two doses of baclofen, but not the highest dose. Therefore, as in the experiment using 8-OH-DPAT (Lee *et al.,* 1990), different neural mechanisms appear to control copulation and *ex copula* reflexes. In contrast to the inhibitory effects of intrathecal baclofen on *ex copula* reflexes, the GABA$_A$ agonist THIP (0.5, 1 or 2 μg) produced only slight inhibitory effects at the highest dose. Therefore, stimulation of spinal GABA$_B$, but not GABA$_A$, receptors inhibits *ex copula* reflexes.

c) DA   Intrathecal infusion of lisuride, a nonspecific monoamine agonist, into the region of the rostral lumbar spinal cord of male rats produced the same effects on copulation as seen following systemic injection, namely, decreased time and number of intromissions preceding ejaculation (Hansen, 1982). Therefore, stimulation of some type(s) of monoamine receptors appears to facilitate ejaculation, perhaps by increasing sensitivity to peripheral stimulation. Furthermore, intrathecal administration of the catecholamine neurotoxin 6-OHDA increased postejaculatory intervals of male rats and rendered the animals more sensitive to androgen deprivation (Hansen and Ross, 1983).

Intrathecal administration of the DA agonist apomorphine also decreased the number of intromissions preceding ejaculation, suggesting that stimulation of spinal cord DA receptors facilitated ejaculation (Pehek *et al.,* 1989b). However, intrathecal apomorphine also increased the interintromission interval, the ejaculation latency, and the postejaculatory interval. In touch-based reflex tests the highest dose of intrathecal apomorphine (50 μg) decreased the numbers of touch-based erections and anteroflexions but did not affect seminal emissions; a lower dose (10 μg) was ineffective (Pehek *et al.*, 1989b). These data stand in contrast to the effects of systemic injection of apomorphine, which facilitated erections at low doses, inhibited erections at high doses, and facilitated seminal emissions at both low and high doses (Pehek *et al.*, 1988a). However, intracavernous pressure was increased by 30 μg apomorphine administered intrathecally (Giuliano *et al.*, 2001a). It is not clear whether the differences between the findings of Pehek *et al.* (1989b) and those of Giuliano *et al.* (2001a) are due to differences in dosage or in the test paradigms.

d) NE   Intrathecal administration of NE increased the frequency of pelvic thrusting during intromission; similar administration of both the α_2 agonist clonidine and the β agonist isoproterenol decreased the frequency of thrusting (Hernandez *et al.*, 1994a). It is likely that clonidine's inhibitory effect resulted from stimulation of α_2 autoreceptors, thereby decreasing NE release. These results are consistent with the findings that α_1 receptors probably mediate NE's facilitative effects on copulation (see earlier Section IV. B on NE).

e) Oxytocin   Oxytocinergic axons from the PVN densely innervate clusters of sympathetic preganglionic neurons in the intermediolateral cell column of the thoracolumbar spinal cord (Millan *et al.*, 1984; Swanson and McKellar, 1979). There is also sparse immunoreactivity for oxytocin in the sacral parasympathetic nucleus of the rat spinal cord; furthermore, those fibers make synaptic contacts on preganglionic neurons in the sacral parasympathetic nucleus (Schoenen *et al.*, 1985; Swanson and McKellar, 1979; Tang *et al.*, 1998). Oxytocin-receptor immunoreactivity was found in the superficial dorsal horn, sacral parasympathetic nucleus, and dorsal gray commissure of the male rat lumbosacral spinal cord (Vérronneau-Longueville *et al.*, 1999).

Administration of oxytocin at the lumbosacral, but not the thoracolumbar, level increased intracavernous pressure in dose-dependent fashion (Giuliano *et al.*, 2001). The proerectile effects of intrathecal oxytocin were blocked by an oxytocin antagonist, pelvic nerve section, and a nicotinic antagonist, which blocked transmission between the pre- and postganglionic parasympathetic nerves. An oxytocin agonist also produced proerectile effects, although with less efficacy on the number of increases in intracavernosal pressure and with a right-shifted dose-response curve. Vasopressin, a nonapeptide that differs from oxytocin by only one amino acid, was ineffective, as were lumbosacral NaCl and systemic oxytocin. Blockade of striated muscle activation failed to inhibit oxytocin's facilitative effects, suggesting that oxytocin's effects were mediated by the parasympathetic nervous system, and not by striated penile muscles. These data provide compelling evidence for the proerectile role of oxytocin-containing fibers descending from the PVN to the lumbosacral cord and for the mediation of oxytocin's effects by parasympathetic fibers in the pelvic nerve.

f) Opiates   Intrathecally administered naloxone decreased the number of intromissions preceding ejaculation, whereas morphine administered in a similar manner increased the number of intromissions (Wiesenfeld-Hallin and Södersten, 1984). These treatments had no other effects on copulation. The authors suggested that naloxone and morphine influenced the strength of the sensory signal from each intromission.

3. Chemical Changes Detected by Analysis of Cerebrospinal Fluid

The concentration of GABA in cerebrospinal fluid of male rats increased by more than 1,000% following ejaculation; concentrations of aspartate and glutamate increased by about 200% (Qureshi and Södersten, 1986). Therefore, the concentration of a major inhibitory neurotransmitter increased markedly during the absolute refractory interval.

4. Presence of Steroid Receptors

AR-ir was found in three areas of the male rat lumbosacral spinal cord: the spinal nucleus of the bulbocavernosus (SNB), dorsolateral nucleus (DLN), and retrodorsolateral nucleus (RDLN) (Freeman *et al.*, 1995). Virtually no AR-ir was seen in long-term castrated males or males with the Tfm mutation, which renders the AR inactive. Furthermore, unilateral capsules filled with T and placed next to the bulbocavernosus and levator ani muscle complex, increased the dendritic arborization of SNB neurons of castrated male rats, compared to contralateral SNB neurons treated locally with the antiandrogen, hydroxyflutamide (Rand

and Breedlove, 1995). Thus, in adult male rats androgens promoted the growth of dendritic connections in areas that control genital reflexes.

Gréco et al. (1998c), also found dense labeling for AR in the L5-S1 segments of the spinal cord, especially in the dorsal part of Lamina X. Furthermore, mating-induced Fos-ir was predominantly located in AR-ir neurons. Therefore, the lumbosacral neurons that are activated by mating are androgen sensitive.

5. Immunocytochemistry

In contrast to the demonstrated inhibitory effects of 5-HT on genital reflexes, stimulation of one receptor subtype, the $5-HT_{2C}$ receptor, appears to facilitate erectile function. (See Section IV.D on systemically or intraventricularly administered serotonergic drugs.) Consistent with such a facilitative effect, $5-HT_{2C}$ receptor immunoreactivity was found on motoneurons of the sacral parasympathetic nucleus, the dorsal gray commissure, and the motoneurons of the ventral horn (Bancila et al., 1999). Furthermore, $5-HT_{2C}$ receptor immunoreactivity was exhibited by all neurons retrogradely labeled from the corpus cavernosum to the sacral parasympathetic nucleus and the dorsal gray commissure of L5–L6, and in ventral horn motoneurons retrogradely labeled from the ischiocavernosus and bulbocavernosus muscles. Therefore, the neurons that are known to promote erection possess $5-HT_{2C}$ receptors, and a systemically administered $5-HT_{2C}$ agonist (mCPP) facilitated erections in monkeys (Pomerantz et al., 1993a) and rats (Berendsen and Broekkamp, 1987; Berendsen et al., 1990; Steers and DeGroat, 1989; Millan et al., 1997) and increased cavernous nerve firing and intracavernous pressure in anesthetized rats (Steers and DeGroat, 1989).

Neurons in segments L3 and L4 of the lumbar spinal cord contain both galanin and CCK (Ju et al., 1987) and project to the SPFp (Truitt and Coolen, 2001a; Veening et al., 1998; Wells and Coolen, 2001). These neurons are thought to relay somatosensory information from the genitals to the brain. Galanin and CCK-immunoreactive neurons showed increased Fos expression only in males that had ejaculated one or two times and not in animals that only mounted or intromitted (except for a few Fos-ir neurons in one male that only intromitted) (Truitt and Coolen, 2001a). Furthermore, lesions of galanin-containing neurons in L3 and

L4 severely impaired ejaculatory ability of male rats (Truitt and Coolen, 2001b). Therefore, these neurons not only relay ejaculation-specific sensory information to the brain, but also contribute to the execution of the behavior.

VI. CIRCUITRY AND ANATOMICAL INTERCONNECTIONS

There are two major sources of sensory input to the MPOA of male rodents, one carrying chemosensory information and the other, somatosensory input from the genitals. There are also excitatory and disinhibitory pathways from the MPOA to the midbrain and brain stem, from which neurons descend to the spinal cord nuclei that regulate genital reflexes and copulatory motor patterns.

A. The Chemosensory Circuits

Both the main and accessory olfactory systems provide input to the medial amygdala, with the relative importance of these two systems varying for different species (see section on amygdala above). In the rat (Canteras et al., 1992) and hamster (Gomez and Newman, 1992; Coolen and Wood, 1998), efferents from the medial amygdala to the BNST form two separate, reciprocal pathways; both travel through the stria terminalis and the ventral amygdalofugal pathway. The anterior pathway proceeds from the anterodorsal medial amygdala (MeAad) to a lateral area in the posterior BNST, which in the hamster has been called the posterointermediate BNST (BNSTpi) (Gomez and Newman, 1992). (See Fig. 25.) This anterior pathway shows similarly increased Fos-ir in response to both mating and aggressive encounters (Kollack-Walker and Newman, 1995). Therefore, the anterior pathway may be associated with nonspecific activation of social behaviors (Newman, 1999). However, the posterior pathway, which passes from the posterodorsal medial amygdala (MeApd) to the posteromedial area of the BNST (BNSTpm), responds more selectively to specific chemosensory inputs and to stimuli associated with ejaculation. There are a greater number of steroid hormone receptors in the posterior circuit than the anterior one in rats, hamsters, and gerbils (Simerly et al., 1990;

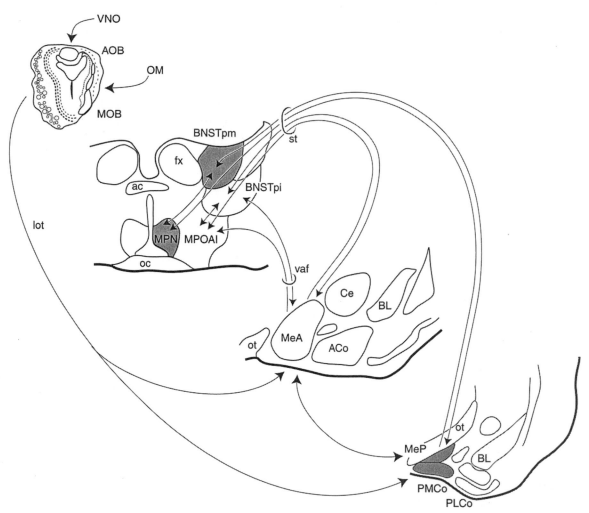

FIGURE 25 Schematic diagram of principal limbic nuclei and connections in hamster brain that transmit chemosensory and hormonal cues to control male sexual behavior. Shading indicates areas with abundant steroid receptor-containing neurons. ac, anterior commissure; ACo, anterior cortical amygdaloid nucleus; AOB, accessory olfactory bulb; BL, basolateral amygdaloid nucleus; BNST, bed nucleus of the stria terminalis; BNSTpi, posterointermediate subdivision of BNST; BNSTpm, posteromedial subdivision of BNST; Ce, central amygdaloid nucleus; fx, fornix; lot, lateral olfactory tract; Me, medial amygdaloid nucleus; MeA, anterior subdivision; MeP, posterior subdivision; MOB, main olfactory bulb; MPN, medial preoptic nucleus; MPOAl, lateral subdivision of the medial preoptic area; oc, optic chiasm; OM, olfactory mucosa; ot, optic tract; PLCo, posterolateral cortical amygdaloid nucleus; PMCo, posteromedial cortical amygdaloid nucleus; st, stria terminalis; vaf, ventral amygdalofugal pathway; VNO, vomeronasal organ. [Reprinted from Wood (1997) with permission.]

Chen and Tu, 1992; Wood and Newman, 1993, 1995a; Commins and Yahr, 1985).

Lesions of the MeAD resulted in a failure of mating and a severe deficit in chemosensory investigatory behavior (Lehman *et al.*, 1980; Lehman and Winans, 1982). In contrast, males with lesions of the caudal half of the medial amygdala mated to ejaculation;

however, they had longer latencies to begin copulating and required more intromissions to trigger ejaculation (Lehman *et al.*, 1983). They also had a more modest inhibition of chemosensory investigatory behavior. In those studies no groups had lesions restricted to the BNSTpi or BNSTpm. However, lesions that included the BNSTpi, which is connected to the MeAad, produced effects that were similar to those of the MeAad, whereas lesions that included the BNSTpm, which is connected to the MeApd, resulted in the more modest impairments characteristic of MeApd lesions (reviewed in Newman, 1999). Reciprocal connections link both the anterior and posterior pathways with the MPOA.

B. Somatosensory Input from the Genitals

The dorsal nerve of the penis (DNP), a branch of the pudendal nerve, carries sensory input from the penile skin, prepuce, and glans penis (Steers, 2000). It is the major source of afferent input from the penis, although the cavernous nerve also contributes input from deeper structures (Steers, 2000). These nerves transmit information to the spinal cord, especially the dorsal gray commissure, intermediate zone, and sacral parasympathetic nucleus (Tang *et al.*, 1999). Electrical stimulation of the DNP elicited activity in the nPGi, the PVN, the MPOA, and the cortex (Haldeman *et al.*, 1982; reviewed in Giuliano and Rampin, 2000). The CTF of male rats (Baum and Everitt, 1992) and SPFp of rats (Coolen *et al.*, 1996, 1997a,b), gerbils (Heeb and Yahr, 1996), and hamsters (Kollack-Walker and Newman, 1997) show increased Fos-ir following copulation and also project to the MPOA. (See below). Finally, a combined anterograde and retrograde tracer study revealed that axons from the L3 and L4 segments of the lumbar spinal cord terminated in close proximity to neurons that projected to the MPOA or BNSTpm (Wells and Coolen, 2001).

C. An Ejaculation-Related Circuit

Ejaculation, but not copulation without ejaculation, elicited small clusters of Fos-ir in the MeApd, the BNSTpm, posterodorsal preoptic nucleus (PD or PdPN), and the SPFp of rats (Coolen *et al.*, 1996, 1997a,b, 1998), hamsters (Fernandez-Fewell and Meredith, 1994; Parfitt and Newman, 1998; Kollack-Walker and Newman, 1997), and gerbils (Heeb and Yahr, 1996). (See Fig. 26.) These subdivisions are reciprocally connected to the MPN. (See Fig. 27.) However, it was not clear whether the Fos-ir represented primarily sensory input to these structures or activation of motor patterns leading to ejaculation. The similar distribution of Fos-ir in female rats following ejaculation by the male

(Pfaus *et al.*, 1993; Rowe and Erskine, 1993; Coolen *et al.*, 1996) suggests that activation of these neurons represents receipt of sensory input, rather than programming of motor output. However, cell-body lesions of the PdPN and MeApd decreased mounting and delayed ejaculation, thus suggesting that these areas contribute to the motor output, as well as receiving sensory input (Heeb and Yahr, 2000). Furthermore, unilateral lesions of the MeApd and the contralateral PdPN mimicked both effects, a result that indicates that they are part of a circuit that influences mounting and ejaculation. In contrast, lesions of the SPFp did not affect copulation; therefore, it may be primarily a recipient of sensory input related to ejaculation. The SPFp receives ascending sensory inputs, either directly or indirectly, from the lumbosacral and cervical regions of the spinal cord (Ju *et al.*, 1987; LeDoux *et al.*, 1987). The SPFp, in turn, projects to the BNSTpm and MeApd (Coolen *et al.*, 1997c; Yasui *et al.*, 1991). Male hamsters show Fos activation in the BNSTpm and MeApd only after multiple ejaculations, or when they are reaching sexual satiety after only a few ejaculations, due to mating on previous consecutive days (Parfitt and Newman, 1998). Furthermore, small lesions of the lateral MeApd in male hamsters increased the number of ejaculations before satiety (Parfitt *et al.*, 1996). Therefore, subsets of neurons within the MeApd may contribute to ejaculatory behavior and promote sexual satiety.

D. Efferents from the MPOA

The primary efferents of the MPOA project to the midbrain via the medial forebrain bundle (Swanson, 1976). Our organization of the nervous system into structures that form afferent and efferent pathways of the MPOA is somewhat arbitrary, since most of the interactions of the MPOA with other brain regions involve reciprocal connections (Simerly and Swanson, 1986). For example, horizontal knife cuts dorsal to the MPOA in rats produce copulatory deficits (Szechtman *et al.*, 1978) similar to those seen following lesions of the bed nucleus of the stria terminalis, the stria terminalis itself, or the corticomedial amygdala, i.e., longer intromission and ejaculation latencies, longer interintromission intervals, and more intromissions preceding ejaculation. Because these dorsal knife cuts would probably

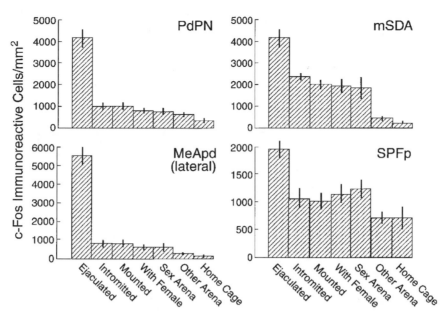

FIGURE 26 Increased densities of Fos-ir cells in the PdPN, mSDA, lateral MeApd, and SPFp of male gerbils that copulated to ejaculation. In the mSDA and SPFp, Fos-ir densities also increased when males were placed in the sex arena. Bar heights indicate group means. Vertical lines denote standard errors. $N = 7$ in all four areas for the Home Cage group and in the SPFp for the ejaculated group. In all other cases, $n = 8$. Fos-ir, immunoreactivity to Fos, the protein product of the immediate-early gene *c-fos*; PdPN, Posterodorsal preoptic nucleus; mSDA, medial sexually dimorphic area; MeApd, posterodorsal region of the medial amygdala; SPFp, subparafascicular nucleus, parvocellular portion. [Reprinted from Heeb and Yahr (1996) with permission.]

interrupt efferent connections from the MPOA to the BNST as well as efferents to the corticomedial amygdala (Simerly and Swanson, 1986), it would also be legitimate to interpret the consequences of these lesions as damaging a common efferent, or reciprocal pathway, of the MPOA. Presently, we are not able to distinguish experimentally among these alternatives.

The elimination of copulation by lesions of the MPOA generally is considered to result from an interruption of efferents to the midbrain. Knife cuts just lateral to the MPOA also eliminated copulation in male rats (Scouten *et al.*, 1980; Szechtman *et al.*, 1978). The effects of knife cuts just dorsal to the MPOA were discussed in the previous paragraph, and knife cuts either rostral or caudal to the MPOA had no effect on copulation (Szechtman *et al.*, 1978). These results were interpreted to indicate that the copulatory disruption was due to the severing of MPOA efferents coursing laterally to join the medial forebrain bundle. This interpretation is supported by

a number of studies showing that lesions of the medial forebrain bundle rostral to the MPOA had no effect on copulation (Hendricks and Scheetz, 1973), whereas lesions along the extent of this fiber pathway caudally all eliminated copulation (Caggiula *et al.*, 1973, 1974, 1975; Hendricks and Scheetz, 1973; Hitt *et al.*, 1970, 1973; Modianos *et al.*, 1973). Also consistent with this interpretation are findings that asymmetrical lesions damaging the MPOA unilaterally, as well as the contralateral medial forebrain bundle, produced the same effects as bilateral lesions in either of these areas separately (Hendricks and Scheetz, 1973). The effects of medial forebrain bundle lesions in rats seem to be permanent, and as with MPOA lesions, arousing stimuli were unable to activate copulation in these males (Caggiula *et al.*, 1974).

The critical neurons of the medial forebrain bundle include reciprocal connections between the MPOA and the ventral pons and medulla (Murphy *et al.*, 1999a).

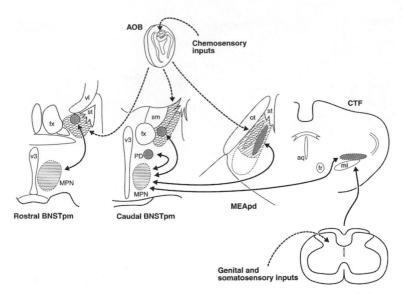

FIGURE 27 Schematic overview of neural activation in circuits underlying male sexual behavior. Areas where Fos is induced following chemosensory cues or chemosensory investigation are illustrated by diagonal stripes from upper left to lower right. Areas where Fos is induced primarily following ejaculation are illustrated in dark shading. Areas where Fos is induced by all consummatory elements of behavior are illustrated by diagonal stripes from lower left to upper right. AOB, accessory olfactory bulbs; MPN, medial preoptic nucleus; PD, posterodorsal preoptic nucleus; BNSTpm, posteromedial bed nucleus of the stria terminalis; MEApd, posterodorsal medial amygdala; CTF, central tegmental field; LSSC, lumbosacral spinal cord; v3, third ventricle; fx, fornix; vl, lateral ventricle; st, stria terminalis; sm, stria medularis; ot, optic tract; aq, aqueduct; Fr, fasciculus retroflexus; ml, medial lemniscus. [Figure courtesy of Lique Coolen.]

(See Fig. 28.) Dense projections from the MPOA were directed to the nPGi and the midline raphe nuclei, both of which are thought to exert inhibitory influence on male sexual behavior. Lesions of the nPGi facilitated both copulation (Yells *et al.,* 1992) and *ex copula* genital reflexes (Marson and McKenna, 1994a). Furthermore, 5-HT from the raphe nuclei is generally inhibitory to sexual behavior (reviewed in Hillegaart, 1991). Therefore, one way in which the MPOA may facilitate copulation is by inhibiting these two sites. However, reciprocal input from these sites may inhibit copulation by inhibiting activity in the MPOA. The MPOA also sends a dense projection to the PAG, which in turn projects to the nPGi; thus, the MPOA has both direct and indirect connections to the nPGi. The PAG contains a large number of cells that contain ARs, ERs, or both (Murphy *et al.,* 1999b). Both MPOA efferents to the PAG and PAG efferents to the nPGi contain ERα and/or AR, and MPOA axons end in close apposition to efferents from PAG to nPGi (Murphy and Hoffman, 2001). Therefore, hormones could influence the ability of the MPOA to disinhibit sexual behavior via the nPGi. However, disinhibiting behavior by inhibiting the nPGi does not account for the actual elicitation of reflexes that has resulted from electrical or chemical stimulation of the MPOA (Giuliano *et al.,* 1996, 1997; Marson and McKenna, 1994b; MacLean *et al.,* 1963; MacLean and Ploog, 1962; Robinson and Mishkin, 1966). There must be an additional pathway that delivers excitation to the lumbosacral neurons that control the reflexes.

The peripheral pathways mediating that excitatory effect have recently been elucidated (Giuliano *et al.,* 1997). The proerectile response appears to result from activation of both parasympathetic outflow, via the pelvic and cavernous nerves, and sympathetic efferents in the paravertebral sympathetic chain and possibly the

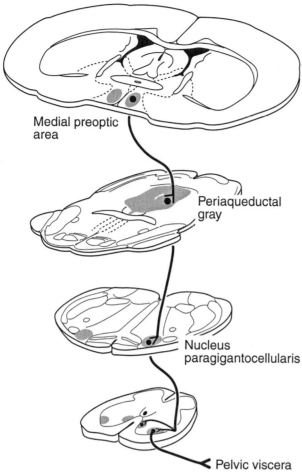

Medial preoptic area

Periaqueductal gray

Nucleus paragigantocellularis

Pelvic viscera

FIGURE 28 Summary figure showing the MPOA-PAG-nPGi-spinal cord circuit. MPOA projections to the periaqueductal gray (PAG) terminate preferentially among PAG neurons projecting to the nucleus paragigantocellularis (nPGi). Descending projections from the nPGi terminate within the dorsomedial and dorsolateral motor pools of the ventral horn of the lumbosacral spinal cord. Motoneurons from these pools innervate the bulbocavernosus and ishiocavernosus muscles, which are essential for penile erection and ejaculation. [Figure is from Murphy and Marson (2000) and Murphy and Hoffman (2001).]

hypogastric nerve. The parasympathetic input has long been recognized as the major proerectile force, and the sympathetic system has usually been considered to be antierectile. However, stimulation of the hypogastric nerve elicited partial erection in male rabbits whose sympathetic chain had been cut before the experiment began (Sjöstrand and Klinge, 1979) and in male cats (Andersson *et al.*, 1987). Giuliano *et al.* (1997) sug-

gested that sympathetic fibers may produce vasoconstriction in nonpenile areas, and thereby divert blood flow to the penis. In addition, a decrease in sympathetic outflow to the penis, elicited by "proerectile" stimulation, could produce at least partial erection. (See Section II.B on neural innervation of the penis).

E. Sexual Behavior in the Context of Mammalian Social Behavior

Neurons within the same brain areas that mediate male sexual behavior also contribute to female sexual behavior, maternal behavior, aggressive behavior, and territorial marking (reviewed in Newman, 1999). Newman (1999) suggests that these structures form an integrated circuit that subserves mammalian social behaviors. Specifically, the corticomedial amygdala/BNST, MPOA, anterior hypothalamus, ventromedial hypothalamus, lateral septum, and midbrain are richly and reciprocally interconnected; all but the midbrain are richly endowed with steroid hormone receptors; and each area participates in the control of more than one behavior. As a result of perinatal and adult steroid influences, the network becomes sexually dimorphic; thus, the network may be predisposed to produce particular patterns of behavior. Furthermore, minicircuits within this network may regulate specific elements characteristic of only one behavior. However, the "ejaculation circuit" described for male rats (Coolen *et al.*, 1996,1997a), hamsters (Kollack-Walker and Newman, 1997; Parfitt and Newman, 1998), and gerbils (Heeb and Yahr, 1996) is also activated in female rats following ejaculation by the male (Dudley *et al.*, 1996; Erskine and Hanrahan, 1997; Pfaus *et al.*, 1993). Thus, this circuit may regulate the timing of both male and female sexual behaviors in order to promote achievement of a successful pregnancy. It is not clear whether individual cell groups have multiple functions or whether individual labeled-line neurons are intermingled with those in the same structure that serve other functions. Diversity in the network may be conferred by the specificity of sensory stimuli that drive them, and this specificity may derive from organizational and activational effects of steroid hormones. Although progress in understanding each behavior may require more analytic methods, it may be wise to focus also on the common themes underlying diverse social behaviors.

VII. UNANSWERED QUESTIONS AND FUTURE DIRECTIONS

In spite of, and also perhaps because of, the great progress that has been made in analyzing the neural and hormonal bases of male sexual behavior, there are many questions that remain unanswered or incompletely answered. These fall into several categories: anatomical interconnections, neurotransmitter interactions, electrophysiological responses, roles of intracellular messengers and gene transcription, relations among the components of male sexual behavior within and between species, and, finally, the relation of mechanisms underlying male sexual behavior to the control of other behaviors. The questions below represent only a small subset of these remaining perplexities.

There are several questions relating to anatomical interconnections. What are the pathways by which the main and accessory olfactory systems promote sexual arousal? What are the similarities and differences among pathways that mediate *in copula,* noncontact, and touch-based erections, and the urethrogenital reflex? Which neural pathway(s) account for the excitatory, as opposed to disinhibitory, effects of MPOA stimulation on genital reflexes? Which pathways mediate the sympathetic proerectile effects of MPOA stimulation? Which neural connections from the dorsal tegmentum contribute to the postejaculatory interval?

Questions concerning neurotransmitter interactions include the following: What neurotransmitters are released at each step in the pathways from sensory input to motor output? What neuropeptides are coreleased, and under what conditions? Are changes in neurotransmitter release a result of altered cell firing or of presynaptic influences on the axon terminals? What receptor subtypes mediate these various effects?

Issues concerning intracellular mediators of hormonal and neurotransmitter effects include the following: What changes in gene transcription are produced by hormones binding to steroid receptors? Do rapid membrane effects of steroids contribute to the control of sexual behavior, and if so, in what way? What changes in gene transcription mediate the effects of sexual experience? Does sexual experience recruit new neurons and pathways, or merely strengthen previous connections? What are the roles of *c-fos* and other immediate-

early genes in the control of sexual behavior? Which second messenger systems contribute to the immediate and long-term effects of neurotransmitters? What can we learn from the patterns of electrophysiological responses?

Finally, broader questions include, How do motivational systems mesh with those that produce the behavior? What, exactly, *does* the MPOA do? What neuroanatomical and physiological differences among species account for the differences in their reproductive behavior patterns? How do these differences relate to their different ecological niches? How are the neural elements underlying male sexual behavior similar to, and different from, elements underlying other mammalian social behaviors?

Acknowledgments

Research for this chapter was conducted with the support of various grants, including awards to E.M.H. from NIMH: R01MH40826 and K02MH01714; to R.L.M. from NIH: HD21478 and NSF: IBN 9723876; and to B.D.S. from NIH: HD-08933 and NSF: IBN-9603917. The authors are grateful to Dr. Pauline Yahr, the University of California at Irvine, for her contributions to the planning and early sections of this chapter. Thanks also to Juan M. Dominguez and Satoru Sato, University at Buffalo, State University of New York, for valuable assistance researching various topics, and to Drs. David A. Edwards at Emory University and Andrew Clancy at Georgia State University for sharing their insights about the midbrain tegmentum. We also thank Dr. Lique Coolen for constructing Figure 27 for this chapter. Special thanks go to Dr. Richard T. Hull for dogged, but not tireless, assistance with references. Finally, we gratefully acknowledge financial support from the Dean of Arts and Sciences, University at Buffalo.

Correspondence should be addressed to Dr. Elaine M. Hull, Department of Psychology, University at Buffalo, State University of New York, Park Hall, Buffalo, NY 14260-4110.

References

Ackerman, A. E., Lange, G. M., and Clemens, L. G. (1997). Effects of paraventricular lesions on sex behavior and seminal emissions in male rats. *Physiol. Behav.* **63**, 49–53.

Adler, N. T. (1978). Social and environmental control of reproductive processes in animals. *In* "Sex and Behavior" (T. E. McGill, D. A. Dewsbury, and B. D. Sachs, eds.), pp. 115–160. Plenum Press, New York.

Adler, N. T., and Toner, J. P. (1986). The effects of copulatory behavior on sperm transport and fertility in rats. *Ann. N. Y. Acad. Sci.* **474**, 21–32.

Ågmo, A. (1976). Cholinergic mechanisms and sexual behavior in the male rabbit. *Psychopharmacology* **51**, 43–45.

Ågmo, A., and Fernandez, H. (1989). Dopamine and sexual behavior in the male rat: A reevaluation. *J. Neural Transm.* **77**, 21–37.

Ågmo, A., and Gomez, M. (1993). Sexual reinforcement is blocked by infusion of naloxone into the medial preoptic area. *Behav. Neurosci.* **107**, 812–818.

Ågmo, A., and Paredes, R. (1988). Opioids and sexual behavior in the male rat. *Pharmacol., Biochem. Behav.* **30**, 1021–1034.

Ågmo, A., and Picker, Z. (1990). Catecholamines and the initiation of sexual behavior in male rats without sexual experience. *Pharmacol., Biochem. Behav.* **35**, 327–334.

Ågmo, A., and Södersten, P. (1975). Sexual behaviour in castrated rabbits treated with testosterone, oestradiol, dihydrotestosterone or oestradiol in combination with dihydrotestosterone. *J. Endocrinol.* **67**, 327–332.

Ågmo, A., and Villalpando, A. (1995). Central nervous stimulants facilitate sexual behavior in male rats with medial prefrontal cortex lesions. *Brain Res.* **696**, 187–193.

Ågmo, A., Soulairac, M.-L., and Soulairac, A. (1977). Preoptic lesions, sexual behavior, and spontaneous ejaculation in the rat. *Scand. J. Psychol.* **18**, 345–347.

Ågmo, A., Paredes, R., and Fernandez, H. (1987). Differential effects of GABA transaminase inhibitors on sexual behavior, locomotor activity, and motor execution in the male rat. *Pharmacol., Biochem. Behav.* **28**, 47–52.

Ågmo, A., Gomez, M., and Irazabal, Y. (1994a). Enkephalinase inhibition facilitates sexual behavior in the male rat but does not produce conditioned place preference. *Pharmacol., Biochem. Behav.* **47**, 771–778.

Ågmo, A., Paredes, R. G., and Contreras, J. L. (1994b). Opioids and sexual behaviors in the male rabbit: The role of central and peripheral opioid receptors. *J. Neural Transm.—Gen. Sec.* **97**, 211–223.

Ågmo, A., Paredes, R. G., Sierra, L., and Garces, I. (1997). The inhibitory effects on sexual behavior and ambulatory activity of the mixed $GABA_A$/$GABA_B$ agonist progabide are differentially blocked by GABA receptor antagonists. *Psychopharmacology* **129**, 27–34.

Ahlenius, S., and Larsson, K. (1984a). Apomorphine and haloperidol-induced effects on male rat sexual behavior: No evidence for actions due to stimulation of central dopamine autoreceptors. *Pharmacol., Biochem. Behav.* **21**, 463–466.

Ahlenius, S., and Larsson, K. (1984b). Lisuride, LY-141865, and 8-OH-DPAT facilitate male rat sexual behavior via a nondopaminergic system. *Psychopharmacology* **83**, 330–334.

Ahlenius, S., and Larsson, K. (1990). Effects of selective D_1 and D_2 antagonists on male rat sexual behavior. *Experientia* **46**, 1026–1028.

Ahlenius, S., and Larsson, K. (1991). Opposite effects of 5-methoxy-N, N-di-methyl-tryptamine and 5-hydroxytryptophan on male rat sexual behavior. *Pharmacol., Biochem. Behav.* **38**, 201–205.

Ahlenius, S., and Larsson, K. (1995). Effects of the dopamine D_3 receptor ligand 7-OH-DPAT on male rat ejaculatory behavior. *Pharmacol., Biochem. Behav.* **51**, 545–547.

Ahlenius, S., and Larsson, K. (1998). Evidence for an involvement of 5-HT_{1B} receptors in the inhibition of male rat ejaculatory behavior produced by 5-HTP. *Psychopharmacology* **137**, 374–382.

Ahlenius, S., and Larsson, K. (1999). Synergistic actions of the 5-HT_{1A} receptor antagonist WAY-100635 and citalopram on male rat ejaculatory behavior. *Eur. J. Pharmacol.* **379**, 1–6.

Ahlenius, S., Eriksson, H., Larsson, K., Modigh, K., and Södersten, P. (1971). Mating behavior in the male rat treated with p-chlorophenylalanine methyl ester alone and in combination with pargyline. *Psychopharmacologia* **20**, 383–388.

Ahlenius, S., Larsson, K., Svensson, L., Hjorth, S., Carlsson, A., Lindberg, P., Wikstrom, H., Sanchez, D., Arvidsson, L. E., Hacksell, U., and Nilsson, J. L. (1981). Effects of a new type of 5-HT receptor agonist on male rat sexual behavior. *Pharmacol., Biochem. Behav.* **15**, 785–792.

Ahlenius, S., Larsson, K., and Arvidsson, L. E. (1989). Effects of stereoselective 5-HT_{1A} agonists on male rat sexual behavior. *Pharmacol., Biochem. Behav.* **33**, 691–695.

Albinsson, A., Andersson, G., Andersson, K., Vega-Matuszczyk, J., and Larsson, K. (1996). The effects of lesions in the mesencephalic raphe systems on male rat sexual behavior and locomotor activity. *Behav. Brain Res.* **80**, 57–63.

Alexander, B. M., Perkins, A., Van Kirk, E. A., Moss, G. E., and Fitzgerald, J. A. (1993). Hypothalamic and hypophyseal receptors for estradiol in high and low sexually performing rams. *Horm. Behav.* **27**, 296–307.

Alexander, B. M., Rose, J. D., Stellflug, J. N., Fitzgerald, J. A., and Moss, G. E. (2001). Low-sexually performing rams but not male-oriented rams can be discriminated by cell size in the amygdala and preoptic area: A morphometric study. *Behav. Brain Res.* **119**, 15–21.

Alexander, G. M., Swerdloff, R. S., Wang, C., Davidson, T. McDonald, V., Steiner, B., and Hines, M. (1997). Androgen-behavior correlations in hypogonadal men and eugonadal men: I. Mood and response to auditory sexual stimuli. *Horm. Behav.* **31**, 110–119.

Alexander, S. P. H., and Peters, J. A., eds. (2000). "TiPS Receptor and Ion Channel Nomenclature," Suppl. 11. Elsevier, Amsterdam.

Allen, Y. S., Adrian, T. E., Allen, J. M., Tatemoto, K., Crow, T. J., Bloom, S. R., and Polak, J. M. (1983). Neuropeptide Y distribution in the rat brain. *Science* **221**, 877–879.

Almeida, O. F. X., Nikolarakis, K. E., and Herz, A. (1988). Evidence for the involvement of endogenous opioids in the inhibition of luteinizing hormone by corticotropin-releasing factor. *Endocrinology (Baltimore)* **122**, 1034–1041.

Alsum, P., and Goy, R. (1974). Actions of esters of testosterone, dihydrotestosterone, or estradiol on sexual behavior in castrated male guinea pigs. *Horm. Behav.* **5**, 207–217.

Altar, C. A. (1989). Cholecystokinin receptor subtypes and neuromodulation. *Prog. Neuro-Psychopharmacol. Biol. Psychiatry* **13**, 381–393.

Andersson, K. E., and Stief, C. G. (1997). Neurotransmission and the contraction and relaxation of penile erectile tissues. *World J. Urol.* **15**, 14–20.

Andersson, K. E., and Wagner, G. (1995). Physiology of penile erection. *Physiol. Rev.* **75**, 191–236.

Andersson, M. (1994). "Sexual Selection." Princeton University Press, Princeton, NJ.

Andersson, P.-O., Bloom, S. R., and Mellander, S. (1984). Haemodynamics of pelvic nerve induced penile erection in the dog: Possible mediation by vasoactive intestinal polypeptide. *J. Physiol. (London)* **350**, 209–224.

Andersson, P. O., Björnberg, J., Bloom, S. R., and Mellander, S. (1987). Vasoactive intestinal polypeptide in relation to penile erection in the cat evoked by pelvic and by hypogastric nerve stimulation. *J. Urol.* **138**, 419–422.

Ansari, J. M. (1975). A study of 65 impotent males. *J. Psychiatry* **127**, 337–341.

Arendash, G. W., and Gorski, R. A. (1983). Effects of discrete lesions of the sexually dimorphic nucleus of the preoptic area or other medial preoptic regions on the sexual behavior of male rats. *Brain Res. Bull.* **10**, 147–154.

Argiolas, A., and Gessa, G. L. (1991). Central functions of oxytocin. *Neurosci. Biobehav. Rev.* **15**, 217–231.

Argiolas, A., and Melis, M. R. (1995). Neuromodulation of penile erection: An overview of the role of neurotransmitters and neuropeptides. *Prog. Neurobiol.* **47**, 235–255.

Argiolas, A., Melis, M. R., and Gessa, G. L. (1986). Oxytocin: An extremely potent inducer of penile erection and yawning in male rats. *Eur. J. Pharmacol.* **130**, 265–272.

Argiolas, A., Melis, M. R., Mauri, A., and Gessa, G. L. (1987). Paraventricular nucleus lesion prevents yawning and penile erection induced by apomorphine and oxytocin, but not by ACTH in rats. *Brain Res.* **421**, 349–352.

Argiolas, A., Collu, M., Gessa, G. L., Melis, M. R., and Serra, G. (1988a). The oxytocin antagonist d(CH2)5Tyr(Me)-Om8-vasotocin inhibits male copulatory behaviour in rats. *Eur. J. Pharmacol.* **149**, 389–392.

Argiolas, A., Melis, M. R., and Gessa, G. L. (1988b). Yawning and penile erection: Central dopamine-oxytocin-adrenocorticotropin connection. *Ann. N. Y. Acad. Sci.* **525**, 330–337.

Argiolas, A., Melis, M. R., Murgia, S., and Schioth, H. B. (2000). ACTH- and alpha-MSH-induced grooming, stretching, yawning and penile erection in male rats: Site of action in the brain and role of melanocortin receptors. *Brain Res. Bull.* **51**, 425–431.

Arletti, R., Bazzani, C., Castelli, M., and Bertolini, A. (1985). Oxytocin improves male copulatory performance in rats. *Horm. Behav.* **19**, 14–20.

Arletti, R., Calza, L., Giardino, L., Benelli, A., Cavazzuti, E., and Bertolini, A. (1997). Sexual impotence is associated with a reduced production of oxytocin and with an increased production of opioid peptides in the paraventricular nucleus of male rats. *Neurosci. Lett.* **233**, 65–68.

Aronson, L. R. (1959). Hormones and reproductive behavior: Some phylogenetic considerations. *In* "Comparative Endocrinology" (A. Gorbman, ed.), pp. 98–120. Wiley, New York.

Aronson, L. R., and Cooper, M. L. (1968). Desensitization of the glans penis and sexual behavior in cats. *In* "Reproduction and Sexual Behavior" (M. Diamond, ed.), pp. 51–82. Indiana University Press, Bloomington.

Aronson, L. R., and Cooper, M. L. (1974). Olfactory deprivation and mating behavior in sexually experienced male cats. *Behav. Biol.* **11**, 459–480.

Ashdown, R. R. (1962). Development of penis end sheath in young dairy bulls and its relationship to age and body weight. *J. Agric. Sci.* **58**, 65–69.

Aversa, A., Mazzilli, F., Rossi, T., Delfino, M., Isidori, A. M., and Fabbri, A. (2000). Effects of sildenafil (Viagra) administration on seminal parameters and post-ejaculatory refractory time in normal males. *Hum. Reprod.* **15**, 131–134.

Baba, K., Yajima, M., Carrier, S., Akkus, E., Reman, J., Nunes, L., Lue, T. F., and Iwamoto, T. (2000). Effect of testosterone on the number of NADPH diaphorase-stained nerve fibers in the rat corpus cavernosum-dorsal nerve. *Urology* **56**, 533–538.

Bailey, D. J., and Herbert, J. (1982). Impaired copulatory behaviour of male rats with hyperprolactinaemia induced by domperidone or pituitary graft. *Neuroendocrinology* **35**, 186–193.

Bailey, D. J., Dolan, A. L., Pharoah, P. D., and Herbert, J. (1984). Role of gonadal and adrenal steroids in the impairment of the male rat's sexual behaviour by hyperprolactinaemia. *Neuroendocrinology* **39**, 555–562.

Balfour, M. E., Yu, L., and Coolen, L. (2001). Activation of ventral tegmental neurons following sexual behavior in male rats. *Soc. Behav. Neuroendocrinol. Abst.* **5**, 324.

Balthazart, J., and Surlemont, C. (1990). Copulatory behavior is controlled by the sexually dimorphic nucleus of the quail POA. *Brain Res. Bull.* **25**, 7–14.

Balthazart, J., Castagna, C., and Ball, G. F. (1997). Differential effects of D_1 and D_2 dopamine-receptor agonists and antagonists on appetitive and consummatory aspects of male sexual behavior in Japanese quail. *Physiol. Behav.* **62**, 571–580.

Balthazart, J., Absil, P., Gerard, M., Appeltants, D., and Ball, G. F. (1998). Appetitive and consummatory male sexual behavior in Japanese quail are differentially regulated by subregions of the preoptic medial nucleus. *J. Neurosci.* **18**, 6512–6527.

Bancila, M., Verge, D., Rampin, O., Backstrom, J. R., Sanders-Bush, E., McKenna, K. E., Marson, L., Calas, A., and Giuliano, F. (1999). 5-Hydroxytryptamine2C receptors on spinal neurons controlling penile erection in the rat. *Neuroscience* **92**, 1523–1537.

Bancroft, J., and Janssen, E. (2000). The dual control model of male sexual response: A theoretical approach to centrally mediated erectile dysfunction. *Neurosci. Biobehav. Rev.* **24**, 571–579.

Bancroft, J., and Wu, F. C. (1983). Changes in erectile responsiveness during androgen replacement therapy. *Arch. Sex. Behav.* **12**, 59–66.

Band, L. C., and Hull, E. M. (1990). Morphine and dynorphin (1–13) microinjected into the medial preoptic area and nucleus accumbens: Effects on sexual behavior in male rats. *Brain Res.* **524**, 77–84.

Barbeau, A. (1969). L-DOPA therapy in Parkinson's disease: A critical review of nine years' experience. *Can. Med. Assoc. J.* **101**, 791–800.

Barfield, R. J. (1969). Activation of copulatory behavior by androgen implanted into the preoptic area of the male fowl. *Horm. Behav.* **1**, 37–52.

Barfield, R. J. (1971). Activation of sexual and aggressive behavior by androgen implanted into the male ring dove brain. *Endocrinology (Baltimore)* **89**, 1470–1476.

Barfield, R. J., and Geyer, L. A. (1975). The ultrasonic postejaculatory vocalization and the postejaculatory refractory period of the male rat. *J. Comp. Physiol. Psychol.* **88**, 723–734.

Barfield, R. J., and Sachs, B. D. (1968). Sexual behavior: Stimulation by painful electrical shock to skin in male rats. *Science* **161**, 392–395.

Barry, J., Hoffman, G. E., and Wray, S. (1985). LHRH containing systems. *In* "Handbook of Chemical Neuroanatomy" (A. Björklund and T. Hökfelt, eds.), pp. 116–215. Elsevier, Amsterdam.

Bartke, A., Doherty, P. C., Steger, R. W., Morgan, W. W., Amador, A. G., Herbert, D. C., Siler-Khodr, T. M., Smith, M. S., Klemcke, H. G., and Hymer, W. C. (1984). Effects of estrogen-induced hyperprolactinemia on endocrine and sexual functions in adult male rats. *Neuroendocrinology* **39**, 126–135.

Baum, M. J. (1972). Precocious mating in male rats following treatment with androgen or estrogen. *J. Comp. Physiol. Psychol.* **78**, 356–367.

Baum, M. J., and Everitt, B. J. (1992). Increased expression of *c-fos* in the medial preoptic area after mating in male rats: Role of afferent inputs from the medial amygdala and midbrain central tegmental field. *Neuroscience* **50**, 627–646.

Baum, M. J., and Wersinger, S. R. (1993). Equivalent levels of mating-induced neural *c-fos* immunoreactivity in castrated male rats given androgen, estrogen, or no steroid replacement. *Biol. Reprod.* **48**, 1341–1347.

Baum, M. J., Tobet, S. A., Starr, M. S., and Bradshaw, W. G. (1982). Implantation of dihydrotestosterone propionate into the lateral septum or medial amygdala facilitates copulation in castrated male rats given estradiol systemically. *Horm. Behav.* **16**, 208–223.

Baum, M. J., Kingsbury, P. A., and Erskine, M. S. (1987). Failure of the synthetic androgen 17 beta-hydroxy-17alpha-methyl-estra-4,9,11-triene-3-one (methyltrienolone, R1881) to duplicate the activational effect of testosterone on mating in castrated male rats. *J. Endocrinol.* **113**, 15–20.

Baumgardner, D. J., and Dewsbury, D. A. (1980). Pseudopregnancy in female rats: Effects of hormonal manipulations of the male. *Physiol. Behav.* **24**, 693–697.

Bazzett, T. J., Eaton, R. C., Thompson, J. T., Markowski, V. P., Lumley, L. A., and Hull, E. M. (1991). Dose dependent D_2 effects on genital reflexes after MPOA injections of quinelorane and apomorphine. *Life Sci.* **48**, 2309–2315.

Bazzett, T. J., Lumley, L. A., Bitran, D., Markowski, V. P., Warner, R. K., and Hull, E. M. (1992). Male rat copulation following 6-OHDA lesions of the medial preoptic area: Resistance to repeated administration and rapid behavioral recovery. *Brain Res.* **580**, 164–170.

Beach, F. A. (1947). Evolutionary changes in the physiological control of mating behavior in mammals. *Psychol. Rev.* **54**, 297–315.

Beach, F. A. (1948). "Hormones and Behavior." Hoeber, New York.

Beach, F. A. (1956). Characteristics of masculine "sex drive." *In* "The Nebraska Symposium on Motivation" (M. R. Jones, ed.), pp. 1–32. University of Nebraska Press, Lincoln.

Beach, F. A. (1969). Locks and beagles. *Am. Psychol.* **24**, 971–989.

Beach, F. A. (1975). Variables affecting "spontaneous" seminal emission in rats. *Physiol. Behav.* **15**, 91–95.

Beach, F. A. (1984). Hormonal modulation of genital reflexes in male and masculinized female dogs. *Behav. Neurosci.* **98**, 325–332.

Beach, F. A., and Holz-Tucker, A. M. (1949). Effects of different concentrations of androgen upon sexual behavior in castrated male rats. *J. Comp. Physiol. Psychol.* **42**, 433–453.

Beach, F. A., and Pauker, R. S. (1949). Effects of castration and subsequent androgen administration upon mating behavior in the male hamster (*Cricetus auratus*). *Endocrinology (Baltimore)* **45**, 211–221.

Bean, N. J., Núñez, A. A., and Conner, R. (1981). Effects of medial preoptic lesions on male mouse ultrasonic vocalizations and copulatory behavior. *Brain Res. Bull.* **6**, 109–112.

Beauchamp, G. K., Magnus, J. G., Shmunes, N. T., and Durham, T. (1977). Effects of olfactory bulbectomy on social behavior of male guinea pigs (*Cavia porcellus*). *J. Comp. Physiol. Psychol.* **91**, 336–346.

Beauchamp, G. K., Martin, I. G., Wysocki, C. J., and Wellington, J. L. (1982). Chemoinvestigatory and sexual behavior of male guinea pigs following vomeronasal organ removal. *Physiol. Behav.* **29**, 329–336.

Benelli, A., Zanoli, P., and Bertolini, A. (1990). Effect of clenbuterol on sexual behavior in male rats. *Physiol. Behav.* **47**, 373–376.

Benelli, A., Arletti, R., Bertolini, A., Menozzi, B., Basaglia, R., and Poggioli, R. (1994). Galantide stimulates sexual behavior in male rats. *Eur. J. Pharmacol.* **260**, 279–282.

Benelli, A., Bertolini, A., Poggioli, R., Cavazzuti, E., Calza, L., Giardino, L., and Arletti, R. (1995). Nitric oxide is involved in male sexual behavior of rats. *Eur. J. Pharmacol.* **294**, 505–510.

Benkert, O. (1975). Effects of hypothalamic releasing hormones in depression and sexual impotence. *In* "Neuropsychopharmacology" (J. R. Boissier, H. Hippius, and P. Pichot, eds.), pp. 663–671. Excerpta Medica, Amsterdam.

Berendsen, H. H., and Broekkamp, C. L. (1987). Drug-induced penile erections in rats: Indications of serotonin$_{1B}$ receptor mediation. *Eur. J. Pharmacol.* **135**, 279–287.

Berendsen, H. H., Jenck, F., and Broekkamp, C. L. (1990). Involvement of 5-HT$_{1C}$-receptors in drug-induced penile erections in rats. *Psychopharmacology* **101**, 57–61.

Bergquist, E. H. (1970). Output pathways of hypothalamic mechanisms for sexual, aggressive, and other motivated behaviors in opossum. *J. Comp. Physiol. Psychol.* **70**, 389–398.

Berkeley, K. J. (1986). Specific somatic sensory relays in the mammalian diencephalon. *Rev. Neurol.* **142**, 283–290.

Bermant, G., and Taylor, L. (1969). Interactive effects of experience and olfactory bulb lesions in male rat copulation. *Physiol. Behav.* **4**, 13–17.

Bermant, G., Clegg, M. T., and Beamer, W. (1969). Copulatory behaviour of the ram, *Ovis aries*: I. A normative study. *Anim. Behav.* **17**, 700–705.

Bermond, B. (1982). Effects of medial preoptic hypothalamus anterior lesions on three kinds of behavior in the rat: Intermale aggressive, male sexual, and mouse killing behavior. *Aggress. Behav.* **8**, 335–354.

Bertolini, A., Genedani, S., and Castelli, M. (1978). Behavioural effects of naloxone in rats. *Experientia* **34**, 771–772.

Beyer, C., Larsson, K., Perez-Palacios, G., and Morali, G. (1973). Androgen structure and male sexual behavior in the castrated rat. *Horm. Behav.* **4**, 99–108.

Beyer, C., Morali, G., Naftolin, F., Larsson, K., and Perez-Palacios, G. (1976). Effect of some antiestrogens and aromatase inhibitors on androgen induced sexual behavior in castrated male rats. *Horm. Behav.* **7**, 353–363.

Bhasin, S., Fielder, Y., Peacock, N., Sod-Moriah, U. A., and Swerdloff, R. S. (1988). Dissociating antifertility effects of GnRH-antagonist from its adverse effects on mating behavior in male rats. *Am. J. Physiol.* **254**, E84–E91.

Bialy, M., and Sachs, B. D. (2000). Androgen implants in medial amygdala briefly maintain noncontact erection in castrated male rats. *Soc. Behav. Neuroendocrinol. Abstr.* **4**, 268.

Bialy, M., Beck, J., Abramczyk, P., Trzebski, A., and Przybylski, J. (1996). Sexual behavior in male rats after nitric oxide synthesis inhibition. *Physiol. Behav.* **60**, 139–143.

Bignami, G. (1966). Pharmacologic influences on mating behavior in the male rat: Effects of d-amphetamine, LSD-25, strychnine, nicotine, and various anticholinergic agents. *Psychopharmacologia* **10**, 44–58.

Bitran, D., and Hull, E. M. (1987). Pharmacological analysis of male rat sexual behavior. *Neurosci. Biobehav. Rev.* **11**, 365–389.

Bitran, D., Hull, E. M., Holmes, G. M., and Lookingland, K. J. (1988a). Regulation of male rat copulatory behavior by preoptic incertohypothalamic dopamine neurons. *Brain Res. Bull.* **20**, 323–331.

Bitran, D., Miller, S. A., McQuade, D. B., Leipheimer, R. E., and Sachs, B. D. (1988b). Inhibition of sexual reflexes by lumbosacral injection of a GABA$_B$ agonist in the male rat. *Pharmacol., Biochem. Behav.* **31**, 657–666.

Bitran, D., Thompson, J. T., Hull, E. M., and Sachs, B. D. (1989). Quinelorane (LY163502), a D$_2$ dopamine receptor agonist, facilitates seminal emission but inhibits penile erection in the rat. *Pharmacol., Biochem. Behav.* **34**, 453–458.

Bivalacqua, T. J., Champion, H. C., Hellstrom, W. J. G., and Kadowitz, P. J. (2000). Pharmacotherapy for erectile dysfunction. *Trends Pharmacol. Sci.* **21**, 484–489.

Blackburn, J. R., Pfaus, J. G., and Phillips, A. G. (1992). Dopamine functions in appetitive and defensive behaviors. *Prog. Neurobiol.* **39**, 247–279.

Bloch, G. J., and Davidson, J. M. (1968). Effects of adrenalectomy and experience on postcastration sex behavior in the male rat. *Physiol. Behav.* **3**, 461–465.

Bloch, G. J., Babcock, A. M., Gorski, R. A., and Micevych, P. E. (1988). Effects of cholecystokinin on male copulatory behavior and lordosis behavior in male rats. *Physiol. Behav.* **43**, 351–357.

Bloch, G. J., Butler, P. C., Kohlert, J. G., and Bloch, D. A. (1993). Microinjection of galanin into the medial preoptic nucleus facilitates copulatory behavior in the male rat. *Physiol. Behav.* **54**, 615–624.

Blumberg, M. S. (1991), Prostaglandin E accelerates sexual behavior in male rats. *Physiol. Behav.* **50**, 95–99.

Blumberg, M. S., and Moltz, H. (1987). Hypothalamic temperature and the 22 kHz vocalization of the male rat. *Physiol. Behav.* **40**, 637–640.

Blumberg, M. S., and Moltz, H. (1988). How the nose cools the brain during copulation in the male rat. *Physiol. Behav.* **43**, 173–176.

Blumberg, M. S., Mennella, J. A., and Moltz, H. (1987). Hypothalamic temperature and deep body temperature during copulation in the male rat. *Physiol. Behav.* **39**, 367–370.

Bohus, B. (1977). Effect of desglycinamide-lysine vasopressin (DG-LVP) on sexually motivated T-maze behavior of the male rat. *Horm. Behav.* **8**, 52–61.

Bonsall, R. W., Clancy, A. N., and Michael, R. P. (1992). Effects of the nonsteroidal aromatase inhibitor, Fadrozole, on sexual behavior in male rats. *Horm. Behav.* **26**, 240–254.

Booth, A. M., Jr. (1976). Nervous control of penile erection and copulatory behavior in the rat. Unpublished Doctoral Dissertation, University of Pittsburgh, Pittsburgh.

Bowers, M. B., Jr., Van Woert, M., and Davis, L. (1971). Sexual behavior during L-dopa treatment for Parkinsonism. *Am. J. Psychiatry* **127**, 1691–1693.

Boyd, S. K., and Moore, F. L. (1985). Luteinizing hormone-releasing hormone facilitates the display of sexual behavior in male voles (*Microtus canicaudus*). *Horm. Behav.* **19**, 252–264.

Brackett, N. L., and Edwards, D. A. (1984). Medial preoptic connections with the midbrain tegmentum are essential for male sexual behavior. *Physiol. Behav.* **32**, 79–84.

Brackett, N. L., Iuvone, P. M., and Edwards, D. A. (1986). Midbrain lesions, dopamine and male sexual behavior. *Behav. Brain Res.* **20**, 231–240.

Bradshaw, W. G., Baum, M. J., and Awh, C. C. (1981). Attenuation by a 5α-reductase inhibitor of the activational effect of testosterone propionate on penile erections in castrated male rats. *Endocrinology (Baltimore)* **109**, 1047–1051.

Breedlove, S. M. (1984). Steroid influences on the development and function of a neuromotor system. *Prog. Brain Res.* **61**, 147–170.

Breedlove, S. M. (1985). Hormonal control of the anatomical specificity of motoneuron-muscle innervation in rats. *Science* **227**, 1357–1359.

Bressler, S. C., and Baum, M. J. (1996). Sex comparison of neuronal Fos immunoreactivity in the rat vomeronasal projection circuit after chemosensory stimulation. *Neuroscience* **71**, 1063–1072.

Bronson, F. H., and Desjardins, C. (1982). Endocrine responses to sexual arousal in male mice. *Endocrinology (Baltimore)* **111**, 1286–1291.

Brown, W. A., Monti, P. M., and Corriveau, D. P. (1978). Serum testosterone and sexual activity and interest in men. *Arch. Sex. Behav.* **7**, 97–103.

Bullock, T. H. (1984). Understanding brains by comparing taxa. *Perspect. Biol. Med.* **27**, 510–524.

Bunnell, B. N., Boland, B. D., and Dewsbury, D. A. (1976). Copulatory behavior of golden hamsters (*Mesocricetus auratus*). *Behaviour* **61**, 180–206.

Burnett, A. L., Nelson, R. J., Calvin, D. C., Liu, J. X., Demas, G. E., Klein, S. L., Kriegsfeld, L. J., Dawson, T. M., and Snyder, S. H. (1996). Nitric oxide-dependent penile erection in mice lacking neuronal nitric oxide synthase. *Mol. Med.* **2**, 288–296.

Butera, P. C., and Czaja, J. A. (1989a). Activation of sexual behavior in male rats by combined subcutaneous and intracranial treatments of 5α-dihydrotestosterone. *Horm. Behav.* **23**, 92–105.

Butera, P. C., and Czaja, J. A. (1989b). Effects of intracranial implants of dihydrotestosterone on the reproductive physiology and behavior of male guinea pigs. *Horm. Behav.* **23**, 424–431.

Caggiula, A. R., and Hoebel, B. (1966). "Copulation-reward site" in the posterior hypothalamus. *Science* **153**, 1284–1285.

Caggiula, A. R., and Szechtman, H. (1972). Hypothalamic stimulation: A biphasic influence on copulation of the male rat. *Behav. Biol.* **7**, 591–598.

Caggiula, A. R., Antelman, S. M., and Zigmond, M. J. (1973). Disruption of copulation in male rats after hypothalamic lesions: A behavioral, anatomical and neurochemical analysis. *Brain Res.* **59**, 273–287.

Caggiula, A. R., Antelman, S. M., and Zigmond, M. J. (1974). Ineffectiveness of sexually arousing stimulation after hypothalamic lesions in the rat. *Physiol. Behav.* **12**, 313–316.

Caggiula, A. R., Gay, V. L., Antelman, S. M., and Leggens, J. (1975). Disruption of copulation in male rats after hypothalamic lesions: A neuroendocrine analysis. *Neuroendocrinology* **17**, 193–202.

Caggiula, A. R., Shaw, D. H., Antelman, S. M., and Edwards, D. J. (1976). Interactive effects of brain catecholamines and variations in sexual and non-sexual arousal on copulatory behavior of male rats. *Brain Res.* **111**, 321–336.

Cain, D. P. (1974). The role of the olfactory bulb in limbic mechanisms. *Psychol. Bull.* **81**, 654–671.

Cain, D. P., and Paxinos, G. (1974). Olfactory bulbectomy and mucosa damage: Effects on copulation, irritability, and interspecific aggression in male rats. *J. Comp. Physiol. Psychol.* **86,** 202–212.

Canteras, N. S., Simerly, R. B., and Swanson, L. W. (1992). Connections of the posterior nucleus of the amygdala. *J. Comp. Neurol.* **324,** 143–179.

Canteras, N. S., Simerly, R. B., and Swanson, L. W. (1995). Organization of projections from the medial nucleus of the amygdala: A PHAL study in the rat. *J. Comp. Neurol.* **360,** 213–245, published erratum: *Ibid.* **369,** 328–330 (1996).

Cantor, J. M., Binik, Y. M., and Pfaus, J. G. (1999). Chronic fluoxetine inhibits sexual behavior in the male rat: Reversal with oxytocin. *Psychopharmacology* **144,** 355–362.

Carati, C. J., Creed, K. E., and Keogh, E. J. (1987). Autonomic control of penile erection in the dog. *J. Physiol. (London)* **384,** 525–538.

Carr, W. J., Wylie, N. R., and Loeb, L. S. (1970). Responses of adult and immature rats to sex odors. *J. Comp. Physiol. Psychol.* **72,** 51–59.

Carrer, H. F. (1978). Mesencephalic participation in the control of sexual behavior in the female rat. *J. Comp. Physiol. Psychol.* **92,** 877–887.

Carroll, R. S., Erskine, M. S., Doherty, P. C., Lundell, L. A., and Baum, M. J. (1985). Coital stimuli controlling luteinizing hormone secretion and ovulation in the female ferret. *Biol. Reprod.* **32,** 925–933.

Carter, C. S., DeVries, A. C., and Getz, L. L. (1995). Physiological substrates of mammalian monogamy: The prairie vole model. *Neurosci. Biobehav. Rev.* **19,** 303–314.

Chambers, K. C., and Phoenix, C. H. (1981). Diurnal patterns of testosterone, dihydrotestosterone, estradiol, and cortisol in serum of rhesus males: Relationship to sexual behavior in aging males. *Horm. Behav.* **15,** 416–426.

Chambers, K. C., Hess, D. L., and Phoenix, C. H. (1981). Relationship of free and bound testosterone to sexual behavior in old rhesus males. *Physiol. Behav.* **27,** 615–620.

Chamness, S. L., Ricker, D. D., Crone, J. K., Dembeck, C. L., Maguire, M. P., Burnett, A. L., and Chang, T. S. (1995). The effect of androgen on nitric oxide synthase in the male reproductive tract of the rat. *Fertil. Steril.* **63,** 1101–1107.

Chapelle, P. A., Durand, J., and Lacert, P. (1980). Penile erection following complete spinal cord injury in man. *Br. J. Urol.* **52,** 216–219.

Cheal, M., and Domesick, V. B. (1979). Mating in male Mongolian gerbils after olfactory bulbectomy. *Physiol. Behav.* **22,** 199–202.

Chen, J. J., and Bliss, D. K. (1974). Effects of sequential preoptic and mammillary lesions on male rat sexual behavior. *J. Comp. Physiol. Psychol.* **87,** 841–847.

Chen, K. K., Chan, J. Y. H., Chang, L. S., Chen, M. T., and Chan, S. H. H. (1992). Elicitation of penile erection following activation of the hippocampal formation in the rat. *Neurosci. Lett.* **141,** 218–222.

Chen, T. J., and Tu, W. W. (1992). Sex differences in estrogen and androgen receptors in hamster brain. *Life Sci.* **50,** 1639–1647.

Cherry, J. A., and Baum, M. J. (1990). Effects of lesions of a sexually dimorphic nucleus in the preoptic/anterior hypothalamic area on the expression of androgen- and estrogen-dependent sexual behaviors in male ferrets. *Brain Res.* **522,** 191–203.

Chevalier-Skolnikoff, S. (1975). Heterosexual copulatory patterns in stumptail macaques (*Macaca arctoides*) and in other macaque species. *Arch. Sex. Behav.* **4,** 199–220.

Chitaley, K., Wingard, C. J., Webb, R. C., Branam, H., Stopper, V. S., Lewis, R. W., and Mills, T. M. (2001). Antagonism of Rho-kinase stimulates rat penile erection via a nitric oxide-independent pathway. *Nature Med.* **7,** 199–122.

Cho, M. M., DeVries, A. C., Williams, J. R., and Carter, C. S. (1999). The effects of oxytocin and vasopressin on partner preferences in male and female prairie voles (*Microtus ochrogaster*). *Behav. Neurosci.* **113,** 1071–1079.

Christ, G. J. (1995). The penis as a vascular organ: The importance of corporal smooth muscle tone in the control of erection. *Urol. Clin. North Am.* **22,** 727–745.

Christ, G. J., Wang, H. Z., Venkateswarlu, K., Zhao, W., and Day, N. S. (1999). Ion channels and gap junctions: Their role in erectile physiology, dysfunction, and future therapy. *Mol. Urol.* **3,** 61–73.

Christensen, L. W., and Clemens, L. G. (1974). Intrahypothalamic implants of testosterone or estradiol and resumption of masculine sexual behavior in long-term castrated male rats. *Endocrinology (Baltimore)* **95,** 984–990.

Christensen, L. W., and Clemens, L. G. (1975). Blockade of testosterone-induced mounting behavior in the male rat with intracranial application of the aromatization inhibitor, androst-triene-dione. *Endocrinology (Baltimore)* **97,** 1545–1551.

Christensen, L. W., Coniglio, L. P., Paup, D. C., and Clemens, L. C. (1973). Sexual behavior of male golden hamsters receiving diverse androgen treatments. *Horm. Behav.* **4,** 223–229.

Christensen, L. W., Nance, D. M., and Gorski, R. A. (1977). Effects of hypothalamic and preoptic lesions on reproductive behavior in male rats. *Brain Res. Bull.* **2,** 137–141.

Christiansen, E., Guirguis, W. R., Cox, D., and Osterloh, I. H. (2000). Long-term efficacy and safety of oral Viagra (sildenafil citrate) in men with erectile dysfunction and the effect of randomized treatment withdrawal. *Int. J. Impotence Res.* **12,** 177–182.

Clancy, A. N., Coquelin, A., Macrides, F., Gorski, R. A., and Noble, E. P. (1984). Sexual behavior and aggression in male mice: Involvement of the vomeronasal system. *J. Neurosci.* **4**, 2222–2229.

Clancy, A. N., Zumpe, D., and Michael, R. P. (1995). Intracerebral infusion of an aromatase inhibitor, sexual behavior and brain estrogen receptor-like immunoreactivity in intact male rats. *Neuroendocrinology* **61**, 98–111.

Clancy, A. N., Zumpe, D., and Michael, R. P. (2000). Estrogen in the medial preoptic area of male rats facilitates copulatory behavior. *Horm. Behav.* **38**, 86–93.

Clark, A. S., and Harrold, E. V. (1997). Comparison of the effects of stanozolol, oxymetholone, and testosterone cypionate on the sexual behavior of castrated male rats. *Behav. Neurosci.* **111**, 1368–1374.

Clark, A. S., Davis, L. A., and Roy, E. J. (1985). A possible physiological basis for the dud-stud phenomenon. *Horm. Behav.* **19**, 227–230.

Clark, J. T. (1989). A possible role for angiotensin II in the regulation of male sexual behavior in rats. *Physiol. Behav.* **45**, 221–246.

Clark, J. T. (1991). Suppression of copulatory behavior in male rats following central administration of clonidine. *Neuropharmacology* **30**, 373–382.

Clark, J. T. (1995). Sexual arousal and performance are modulated by adrenergic-neuropeptide-steroid interactions. *In* "The Pharmacology of Sexual Function and Dysfunction" (J. Bancroft, ed.), pp. 55–68. Excerpta Medica, Amsterdam.

Clark, J. T., and Kalra, P. S. (1985). Effects on penile reflexes and plasma hormones of hyperprolactinemia induced by MtTW 15 tumors. *Horm. Behav.* **19**, 304–310.

Clark, J. T., and Smith, E. R. (1990). Clonidine suppresses copulatory behavior and erectile reflexes in male rats: Lack of effect of naloxone pretreatment. *Neuroendocrinology* **51**, 357–364.

Clark, J. T., Smith, E. R., and Davidson, J. M. (1984). Enhancement of sexual motivation in male rats by yohimbine. *Science* **225**, 847–849.

Clark, J. T., Kalra, P. S., and Kalra, S. P. (1985a). Neuropeptide Y stimulates feeding but inhibits sexual behavior in rats. *Endocrinology (Baltimore)* **117**, 2435–2442.

Clark, J. T., Smith, E. R., and Davidson, J. M. (1985b). Evidence for the modulation of sexual behavior by α-adrenoceptors in male rats. *Neuroendocrinology* **41**, 36–43.

Clark, J. T., Kalra, S. P., and Kalra, P. S. (1987). Effects of a selective alpha-1-adrenoceptor agonist, methoxamine, on sexual behavior and penile reflexes. *Physiol. Behav.* **40**, 747–753.

Clark, T. K. (1975). Sexual inhibition is reduced by rostral midbrain lesions in the male rat. *Science* **190**, 169–171.

Clark, T. K. (1980). Male rat sexual behavior compared after 6-OHDA and electrolytic lesions in the dorsal NA bundle region of the midbrain. *Brain Res.* **202**, 429–443.

Clarke, C. H., Norfleet, A. M., Clarke, M. S., Watson, C. S., Cunningham, K. A., and Thomas, M. L. (2000). Perimembrane localization of the estrogen receptor alpha protein in neuronal processes of cultured hippocampal neurons. *Neuroendocrinology* **71**, 34–42.

Claro, F., Segovia, S., Guillamon, A., and Del Abril, A. (1995). Lesions in the medial posterior region of the BST impair sexual behavior in sexually experienced and inexperienced male rats. *Brain Res. Bull.* **36**, 1–10.

Clemens, L. G., and Gladue, B. A. (1977). Effect of prostaglandin E2 on masculine sexual behavior in the rat. *J. Endocrinol.* **75**, 383–389.

Clemens, L. G., and Pomerantz, S. M. (1982). Testosterone acts as a prohormone to stimulate male copulatory behavior in male deer mice (*Peromyscus maniculatus bairdi*). *J. Comp. Physiol. Psychol.* **96**, 114–122.

Cochran, C. A., and Perachio, A. A. (1977). Dihydrotestosterone propionate effects on dominance and sexual behaviors in gonadectomized male and female rhesus monkeys. *Horm. Behav.* **8**, 175–187.

Comarr, A. E. (1992). Neurology of spinal cord-injured patients. *Semin. Urol.* **10**, 74–82.

Commins, D., and Yahr, P. (1984a). Acetylcholinesterase activity in the sexually dimorphic area of the gerbil grain: Sex differences and influences of adult gonadal steroids. *J. Comp Neurol.* **224**, 123–131.

Commins, D., and Yahr, P. (1984b). Adult testosterone levels influence the morphology of a sexually dimorphic area in the Mongolian gerbil brain. *J. Comp. Neurol.* **224**, 132–140.

Commins, D., and Yahr, P. (1984c). Lesions of the sexually dimorphic area disrupt mating and marking in male gerbils. *Brain Res. Bull.* **13**, 185–193.

Commins, D., and Yahr, P. (1985). Autoradiographic localization of estrogen and androgen receptors in the sexually dimorphic area and other regions of the gerbil brain. *J. Comp. Neurol.* **231**, 473–489.

Conrad, L. C., and Pfaff, D. W. (1975). Axonal projections of medial preoptic and anterior hypothalamic neurons. *Science* **190**, 1112–1114.

Conrad, L. C., and Pfaff, D. W. (1976a). Efferents from medial basal forebrain and hypothalamus in the rat. I. An autoradiographic study of the medial preoptic area. *J. Comp. Neurol.* **169**, 185–220.

Conrad, L. C., and Pfaff, D. W. (1976b). Efferents from medial basal forebrain and hypothalamus in the rat. II. An autoradiographic study of the anterior hypothalamus. *J. Comp. Neurol.* **169**, 221–262.

Cooke, B. M., Tabibnia, G., and Breedlove, S. M. (1999). A brain sexual dimorphism controlled by adult circulating androgens. *Proc. Nat. Acad. Sci. U.S.A.* **96**, 7538–7540.

Cooke, B. M., Jordan, C., and Breedlove, S. M. (2001). The effect of androgen metabolites on sexual arousal and neuronal phenotype in the medial amygdala. *Soc. Behav. Neuroendocrinol. Abst.* **5**, 328.

Coolen, L. M., and Wood, R. I. (1998). Bidirectional connections of the medial amygdaloid nucleus in the Syrian hamster brain: Simultaneous anterograde and retrograde tract tracing. *J. Comp. Neurol.* **399**, 189–209.

Coolen, L. M., and Wood, R. I. (1999). Testosterone stimulation of the medial preoptic area and medial amygdala in the control of male hamster sexual behavior: Redundancy without amplification. *Behav. Brain Res.* **98**, 143–153.

Coolen, L. M., Peters, H. J., and Veening, J. G. (1996). Fos immunoreactivity in the rat brain following consummatory elements of sexual behavior: A sex comparison. *Brain Res.* **738**, 67–82.

Coolen, L. M., Olivier, B., Peters, H. J., and Veening, J. G. (1997a). Demonstration of ejaculation-induced neural activity in the male rat brain using 5-HT$_{1A}$ agonist 8-OH-DPAT. *Physiol. Behav.* **62**, 881–891.

Coolen, L. M., Peters, H. J., and Veening, J. G. (1997b). Distribution of Fos immunoreactivity following mating versus anogenital investigation in the male rat brain. *Neuroscience* **77**, 1151–1161.

Coolen, L. M., Veening, J. G., Murphy, A. Z., and Shipley, M. T. (1997c). Projections of subparafascicular nucleus: Evidence for a discrete spino-thalamo-forebrain circuit activated by mating. *Soc. Neurosci. Abst.* **27**, No. 532.3.

Coolen, L. M., Peters, H. J., and Veening, J. G. (1998). Anatomical interrelationships of the medial preoptic area and other brain regions activated following male sexual behavior: A combined *c-fos* and tract-tracing study. *J. Comp. Neurol.* **397**, 421–435.

Cooper, T. T., Clancy, A. N., Karom, M., Moore, T. O., and Albers, H. E. (2000). Conversion of testosterone to estradiol may not be necessary for the expression of mating behavior in male Syrian hamsters (*Mesocricetus auratus*). *Horm. Behav.* **37**, 237–245.

Cottingham, S. L., and Pfaff, D. W. (1986). Interconnectedness of steroid hormone-binding neurons: Existence and implications. *Curr. Top. Neuroendocrinol.* **7**, 223–250.

Courtois, F. J., and MacDougall, J. C. (1988). Higher CNS control of penile responses in rats: The effect of hypothalamic stimulation. *Physiol. Behav.* **44**, 165–171.

Couse, J. F., Lindzey, J., Grandien, K., Gustafsson, J. A., and Korach, K. S. (1997). Tissue distribution and quantitative analysis of estrogen receptor-alpha (ERalpha) and estrogen receptor-beta (ERbeta) messenger ribonucleic acid in the wild-type and ERalpha-knockout mouse. *Endocrinology (Baltimore)* **138**, 4613–4621.

Cruz, M. R., Liu, Y. C., Manzo, J., Pacheco, P., and Sachs, B. D. (1999). Peripheral nerves mediating penile erection in the rat. *J. Auton. Nerv. Syst.* **76**, 15–27.

Dail, W. G., and Minorsky, N. (1986). Composition of the pelvic nerve. *Exp. Neurol.* **92**, 278–283.

Dail, W. G., Manzanares, K., Moll, M. A., and Minorsky, N. (1985). The hypogastric nerve innervates a population of penile neurons in the pelvic plexus. *Neuroscience* **16**, 1041–1046.

Dail, W. G., Minorsky, N., Moll, M. A., and Manzanares, K. (1986). The hypogastric nerve pathway to penile erectile tissue: Histochemical evidence supporting a vasodilator role. *J. Auton. Nerv. Syst.* **15**, 341–349.

Dail, W. G., Walton, G., and Olmstead, M. P. (1989). Penile erection in the rat: Stimulation of the hypogastric nerve elicits increases in penile pressure after chronic interruption of the sacral parasympathetic outflow. *J. Auton. Nerv. Syst.* **28**, 251–258.

Dallo, J. (1977). Effect of two brain serotonin depletors on the sexual behavior of male rats. *Pol. J. Pharmacol. Pharm.* **29**, 247–251.

Damassa, D. A., Davidson, J. M., and Smith, E. R. (1977). The relationship between circulating testosterone levels and male sexual behavior in rats. *Horm. Behav.* **8**, 275–286.

Damsma, G., Pfaus, J. G., Wenkstern, D., Phillips, A. G., and Fibiger, H. C. (1992). Sexual behavior increases dopamine transmission in the nucleus accumbens and striatum of male rats: A comparison with novelty and locomotion. *Behav. Neurosci.* **106**, 181–191.

Dauge, V., Steimes, P., Derrien, M., Beau, N., Roques, B. P., and Feger, J. (1989). CCK8 effects on motivational and emotional states of rats involve CCKA receptors of the postero-median part of the nucleus accumbens. *Pharmacol., Biochem. Behav.* **34**, 157–163.

Davidson, J. M. (1966a). Activation of the male rat's sexual behavior by intracerebral implantation of androgen. *Endocrinology (Baltimore)* **79**, 783–794.

Davidson, J. M. (1966b). Characteristics of sex behaviour in male rats following castration. *Anim. Behav.* **14**, 266–272.

Davidson, J. M. (1969). Effects of estrogen on the sexual behavior of male rats. *Endocrinology (Baltimore)* **84**, 1365–1372.

Davidson, J. M., Stefanick, M. L., Sachs, B. D., and Smith, E. R. (1978). Role of androgen in sexual reflexes of the male rat. *Physiol. Behav.* **21**, 141–146.

Davidson, J. M., Camargo, C. A., and Smith, E. R. (1979). Effects of androgen on sexual behavior in hypogonadal men. *J. Clin. Endocrinol. Metab.* **48**, 955–958.

Davidson, J. M., Kwan, M., and Greenleaf, W. J. (1982). Hormonal replacement and sexuality in men. *J. Clin. Endocrinol. Metab.* **11**, 599–623.

Davies, T. F., Mountjoy, L. Q., Gomez-Pan, A., Watson, M. J., Hanker, J. P., Hall, R., and Bessey, G. M. (1976). A double blind cross over trial of gonadotrophin releasing hormone (LHRH) in sexually impotent men. *Clin. Endocrinol. (Oxford)* **5**, 601–607.

Davis, P. G., and Barfield, R. J. (1979). Activation of masculine sexual behavior by intracranial estradiol benzoate implants in male rats. *Neuroendocrinology* **28**, 217–227.

DeBold, J. F., and Clemens, L. G. (1978). Aromatization and the induction of male sexual behavior in male, female, and androgenized female hamsters. *Horm. Behav.* **11**, 401–413.

de Groat, W. C., and Steers, W. D. (1998). Neuroanatomy and neurophysiology of penile erection. *In* "Contemporary Management of Impotence and Infertility" (E. A. Tanagho, T. F. Lue, and R. D. McClure, eds.), pp. 3–27. Williams & Wilkins, Baltimore, MD.

de Jonge, F. H., Louwerse, A. L., Ooms, M. P., Evers, P., Endert, E., and van de Poll, N. E. (1989). Lesions of the SDN-POA inhibit sexual behavior of male Wistar rats. *Brain Res. Bull.* **23**, 483–492.

de Jonge, F. H., Oldenburger, W. P., Louwerse, A. L., and van de Poll, N. E. (1992). Changes in male copulatory behavior after sexual exciting stimuli: Effects of medial amygdala lesions. *Physiol. Behav.* **52**, 327–332.

Devor, M. (1973). Components of mating dissociated by lateral olfactory tract transection in male hamsters. *Brain Res.* **64**, 437–441.

Devor, M., and Murphy, M. R. (1973). The effect of peripheral olfactory blockade on the social behavior of the male golden hamster. *Behav. Biol.* **9**, 31–42.

De Vries, G. J., Gonzales, C. L., and Yahr, P. (1988). Afferent connections of the sexually dimorphic area of the hypothalamus of male and female gerbils. *J. Comp. Neurol.* **271**, 91–105.

Dewsbury, D. A. (1969). Copulatory behaviour of rats (*Rattus norvegicus*) as a function of prior copulatory experience. *Anim. Behav.* **17**, 217–223.

Dewsbury, D. A. (1972). Patterns of copulatory behavior in male mammals. *Q. Rev. Biol.* **47**, 1–33.

Dewsbury, D. A. (1978). The comparative method in studies of reproductive behavior. *In* "Sex and Behavior" (T. E. McGill, D. A. Dewsbury, and B. D. Sachs, eds.), pp. 83–114. Plenum Press, New York.

Dewsbury, D. A. (1981). On the function of the multiple-intromission, multiple-ejaculation copulatory patterns of rodents. *Bull. Psychon. Soc.* **18**, 221–223.

Dewsbury, D. A. (1987). The comparative psychology of monogamy. *In* "Nebraska Symposium on Motivation" (D. W. Leger, ed.), Vol. 35, pp. 1–50. University of Nebraska Press, Lincoln.

Dewsbury, D. A. (1990). Modes of estrus induction as a factor in studies of the reproductive behavior of rodents. *Neurosci. Biobehav. Rev.* **14**, 147–155.

Dewsbury, D. A., Evans, R. L., and Webster, D. G. (1979). Pregnancy initiation in postpartum estrus in three species of muroid rodents. *Horm. Behav.* **13**, 1–8.

DiChiara, G. (1995). The role of dopamine in drug abuse viewed from the perspective of its role in motivation. *Drug Alcohol Depend* **38**, 95–137.

Diederichs, W., Stief, C. G., Benard, F., Bosch, R., Lue, T. F., and Tanagho, E. A. (1991). The sympathetic role as an antagonist of erection. *Urol. Res.* **19**, 123–126.

Dixson, A. F. (1991). Sexual selection, natural selection and copulatory patterns in male primates. *Folia Primatol.* **57**, 96–101.

Dixson, A. F. (1998). "Primate Sexuality: Comparative Studies of the Prosimians, Monkeys, Apes and Human Beings." Oxford University Press, Oxford.

Dixson, A. F., Kendrick, K. M., Blank, M. A., and Bloom, S. R. (1984). Effects of tactile and electrical stimuli upon release of vasoactive intestinal polypeptide in the mammalian penis. *J. Endocrinol.* **100**, 249–252.

Doherty, P. C., and Sheridan, P. J. (1981). Uptake and retention of androgen in neurons of the brain of the golden hamster. *Brain Res.* **219**, 327–334.

Doherty, P. C., Bartke, A., and Smith, M. S. (1981). Differential effects of bromocriptine treatment on LH release and copulatory behavior in hyperprolactinemic male rats. *Horm. Behav.* **15**, 436–450.

Doherty, P. C., Bartke, A., Hogan, M. P., Klemcke, H., and Smith, M. S. (1982). Effects of hyperprolactinemia on copulatory behavior and testicular human chorionic gonadotropin binding in adrenalectomized rats. *Endocrinology (Baltimore)* **111**, 820–826.

Doherty, P. C., Bartke, A., and Smith, M. S. (1985a). Hyperprolactinemia and male sexual behavior: Effects of steroid replacement with estrogen plus dihydrotestosterone. *Physiol. Behav.* **35**, 99–104.

Doherty, P. C., Bartke, A., Smith, M. S., and Davis, S. L. (1985b). Increased serum prolactin levels mediate the suppressive effects of ectopic pituitary grafts on copulatory behavior in male rats. *Horm. Behav.* **19**, 111–121.

Doherty, P. C., Baum, M. J., and Todd, R. B. (1986). Effects of chronic hyperprolactinemia on sexual arousal and erectile function in male rats. *Neuroendocrinology.* **42**, 368–375.

Doherty, P. C., Lane, S. J., Pfeil, K. A., Morgan, W. W., Bartke, A., and Smith, M. S. (1989). Extra-hypothalamic dopamine is not involved in the effects of hyperprolactinemia on male copulatory behavior. *Physiol. Behav.* **45**, 1101–1105.

Domesick, V. B. (1988). Neuroanatomical organization of dopamine neurons in the ventral tegmental area. *Ann. N. Y. Acad. Sci.* **537**, 10–26.

Dominguez, J., Riolo, J. V., Xu, Z., and Hull, E. M. (2001). Regulation by the medial amygdala of copulation and medial preoptic dopamine release. *J. Neurosci.* **21**, 349–355.

Dornan, W. A., and Malsbury, C. W. (1989). Peptidergic control of male rat sexual behavior: The effects of intracerebral injections of substance P and cholecystokinin. *Physiol. Behav.* **46**, 547–556.

Dorsa, D. M., and Smith, E. R. (1980). Facilitation of mounting behavior in male rats by intracranial injections of luteinizing hormone-releasing hormone. *Peptides (N.Y.)* **1**, 147–155.

Dorsa, D. M., Smith, E. R., and Davidson, J. M. (1981). Endocrine and behavioral effects of continuous exposure of male rats to a potent luteinizing hormone-releasing hormone (LHRH) agonist: Evidence for central nervous system actions of LHRH. *Endocrinology (Baltimore)* **109**, 729–735.

Doty, R. L., Carter, C. S., and Clemens, L. G. (1971). Olfactory control of sexual behavior in the male and early androgenized female hamster. *Horm. Behav.* **2**, 325–335.

Drago, F. (1984). Prolactin and sexual behavior: A review. *Neurosci. Biobehav. Rev.* **8**, 433–439.

Drago, F., Pellegrini-Quarantotti, B., Scapagnini, U., and Gessa, G. L. (1981). Short-term endogenous hyperprolactinaemia and sexual behavior of male rats. *Physiol. Behav.* **26**, 277–279.

Dragunow, M., and Faull, R. (1989). The use of *c-fos* as a metabolic marker in neuronal pathway tracing. *J. Neurosci. Methods* **29**, 261–265.

Du, J., and Hull, E. M. (1999). Effects of testosterone on neuronal nitric oxide synthase and tyrosine hydroxylase. *Brain Res.* **836**, 90–98.

Du, J., Dominguez, J., Wang, J., Putnam, S., and Hull, E. M. (1997). Dopamine facilitation of copulation in castrates depends on steroid hormone receptors. *Soc. Behav. Neuroendocrinol. Abstr.* **1**, 81.

Du, J., Lorrain, D. S., and Hull, E. M. (1998). Castration decreases extracellular, but increases intracellular, dopamine in medial preoptic area of male rats. *Brain Res.* **782**, 11–17.

Dudley, A., Rajendren, G., and Moss, R. L. (1996). Signal processing in the vomeronasal system: Modulation of sexual behavior in the female rat. *Crit. Rev. Neurobiol.* **10**, 265–290.

Dula, E., Keating, W., Siami, P. F., Edmonds, A., O'Neil, J., and Buttler, S. (2000). Efficacy and safety of fixed-dose and dose-optimization regimens of sublingual apomorphine versus placebo in men with erectile dysfunction. The Apomorphine Study Group. *Urology* **56**, 130–135.

Eaton, R. C., Markowski, V. P., Lumley, L. A., Thompson, J. T., Moses, J., and Hull, E. M. (1991). D_2 receptors in the paraventicular nucleus regulate genital responses and copulation in male rats. *Pharmacol., Biochem. Behav.* **39**, 177–181.

Edwards, D. A., and Burge, K. G. (1973). Olfactory control of the sexual behavior of male and female mice. *Physiol. Behav.* **11**, 867–872.

Edwards, D. A., and Davis, A. B. (1997). Deafferentation of the olfactory bulbs of male rats reduces erection to remote cues from females. *Physiol. Behav.* **62**, 145–149.

Edwards, D. A., and Einhorn, L. C. (1986). Preoptic and midbrain control of sexual motivation. *Physiol. Behav.* **37**, 329–335.

Edwards, D. A., and Isaacs, S. (1991). Zona incerta lesions: Effects on copulation, partner-preference and other socio-sexual behaviors. *Behav. Brain Res.* **44**, 145–150.

Edwards, D. A., Griffis, K. T., and Tardival, C. (1990). Olfactory bulb removal: Effects on sexual behavior and partner-preference in male rats. *Physiol. Behav.* **48**, 447–450.

Edwards, D. A., Walter, B., and Liang, P. (1996). Hypothalamic and olfactory control of sexual behavior and partner preference in male rats. *Physiol. Behav.* **60**, 1347–1354.

Ehrensing, R. H., Kastin, A. J., and Schally, A. V. (1981). Behavioral and hormonal effects of prolonged high doses of LHRH in male impotency. *Peptides (N.Y.)* **1**, 147–155.

Eibergen, R. D., and Caggiula, A. R. (1973). Ventral midbrain involvement in copulatory behavior of the male rat. *Physiol. Behav.* **10**, 435–441.

Emery, D. E., and Sachs, B. D. (1975). Ejaculatory pattern in female rats without androgen treatment. *Science* **190**, 484–486.

Emery, D. E., and Sachs, B. D. (1976). Copulatory behavior in male rats with lesions in the bed nucleus of the stria terminalis. *Physiol. Behav.* **17**, 803–806.

Erskine, M. S., and Hanrahan, S. B. (1997). Effects of paced mating on *c-fos* gene expression in the female rat brain. *J. Neuroendocrinol.* **9**, 903–912.

Escrig, A., Gonzalez-Mora, J. L., and Mas, M. (1999a). Nitric oxide release in penile corpora cavernosa in a rat model of erection. *J. Physiol.* **516**, 261–269.

Escrig, A., Marin, R., and Mas, M. (1999b). Repeated PGE1 treatment enhances nitric oxide and erection responses to nerve stimulation in the rat penis by upregulating constitutive NOS isoforms. *J. Urol.* **162**, 2205–2210.

Estep, D. Q., Bruce, K. E. M., Johnston, M. E., and Gordon, T. P. (1984). Sexual behavior of group-housed stumptail macaques (*Macaca arctoides*): Temporal, demographic and sociosexual relationships. *Folia Primatol.* **42**, 115–126.

Evans, I. M., and Distiller, L. A. (1979). Effects of lutenizing hormone-releasing hormone on sexual arousal in normal men. *Arch. Sex. Behav.* **8**, 385–395.

Everitt, B. J. (1990). Sexual motivation: A neural and behavioral analysis of the mechanisms underlying appetitive and copulatory responses of male rats. *Neurosci. Biobehav. Rev.* **14**, 217–232.

Everitt, B. J., and Stacey, P. (1987). Studies of instrumental behavior with sexual reinforcement in male rats (*Rattus norvegicus*): II. Effects of preoptic lesions, castration, and testosterone. *J. Comp. Psychol.* **101**, 407–419.

Fallon, J. H. (1988). Topographic organization of ascending dopaminergic projections. *Ann. N. Y. Acad. Sci.* **537**, 1–9.

Fang, J., Chung, Y.-W., and Clemens, L. G. (2000). Relation of Fos-IR expression in the pelvic ganglion to sexual behavior in laboratory rats. *Behav. Neurosci.* **114**, 543–552.

Feder, H. H., Naftolin, F., and Ryan, K. J. (1974). Male and female sexual responses in male rats given estradiol benzoate and 5 alpha-androstan-17 beta-ol-3-one propionate. *Endocrinology (Baltimore)* **94**, 136–141.

Fernandez, E., Dail, W. G., Walton, G., and Martinez, G. (1991). The vasculature of the rat penis: A scanning electron microscopic and histologic study. *Am. J. Anat.* **192**, 307–318.

Fernandez-Fewell, G. D., and Meredith, M. (1994). *C-fos* Expression in vomeronasal pathways of mated or pheromone-stimulated male golden hamsters: Contribution from vomeronasal sensory input and expression related to mating performance. *J. Neurosci.* **14**, 3643–3654.

Fernandez-Fewell, G. D., and Meredith, M. (1998). Olfactory contribution to Fos expression during mating in inexperienced male hamsters. *Chem. Senses* **23**, 257–267.

Fernandez-Guasti, A., and Escalante, A. L. (1991). Role of presynaptic serotonergic receptors on the mechanism of action of 5-HT$_{1A}$ and 5-HT$_{1B}$ agonists on masculine sexual behavior: Physiological and pharmacological implications. *J. Neural Transm.* **85**, 95–107.

Fernandez-Guasti, A., and Rodriguez-Manzo, G. (1997). 8-OH-DPAT and male rat sexual behavior: Partial blockade by noradrenergic lesion and sexual exhaustion. *Pharmacol., Biochem. Behav.* **56**, 111–116.

Fernandez-Guasti, A., Larsson, K., and Beyer, C. (1985). Comparison of the effects of different isomers of bicuculline infused in the preoptic area on male rat sexual behavior. *Experientia* **41**, 1414–1416.

Fernandez-Guasti, A., Larsson, K., and Beyer, C. (1986). GABAergic control of masculine sexual behavior. *Pharmacol., Biochem. Behav.* **24**, 1065–1070.

Fernandez-Guasti, A., Escalante, A. L., Ahlenius, S., Hillegaart, V., and Larsson, K. (1992). Stimulation of 5-HT$_{1A}$ and 5-HT$_{1B}$ receptors in brain regions and its effects on male rat sexual behavior. *Eur. J. Pharmacol.* **210**, 121–129.

Ferrari, F., and Giuliani, D. (1994). The selective D$_2$ dopamine receptor antagonist eticlopride counteracts the *ejaculatio praecox* induced by the selective D$_2$ dopamine agonist SND 919 in the rat. *Life Sci.* **55**, 1155–1162.

Ferrari, F., and Giuliani, D. (1995). Sexual attraction and copulation in male rats: Effects of the dopamine agonist SND 919. *Pharmacol., Biochem. Behav.* **50**, 29–34.

Ferrari, F., and Giuliani, D. (1996a). Behavioral effects induced by the dopamine D$_3$ agonist 7-OH-DPAT in sexually-active and -inactive male rats. *Neuropharmacology* **35**, 279–284.

Ferrari, F., and Giuliani, D. (1996b). Influence of eticlopride on cocaine and DA D$_2$ agonist-induced behavioral effects in rats. *Pharmacol., Biochem. Behav.* **53**, 525–530.

Ferrari, F., and Giuliani, D. (1997). Involvement of dopamine D$_2$ receptors in the effect of cocaine on sexual behaviour and stretch-yawning of male rats. *Neuropharmacology* **36**, 769–777.

Fiber, J. M., Adages, P., and Swann, J. M. (1993). Pheromones induce c-fos in limbic areas regulating male hamster mating behavior. *Neuro Report* **4**, 871–874.

Fielder, T. J., Peacock, N. R., McGivern, R. F., Swerdloff, R. S., and Bhasin, S. (1989). Testosterone dose-dependency of sexual and nonsexual behaviors in the gonadotropin-releasing hormone antagonist-treated male rat. *J. Androl.* **10**, 167–173.

Finn, P. D., and Yahr, P. (1994). Projection of the sexually dimorphic area of the gerbil hypothalamus to the retrorubral field is essential for male sexual behavior: Role of A8 and other cells. *Behav. Neurosci.* **108**, 362–378.

Finn, P. D., De Vries, G. J., and Yahr, P. (1993). Efferent projections of the sexually dimorphic area of the gerbil hypothalamus: Anterograde identification and retrograde verification in males and females. *J. Comp. Neurol.* **338**, 491–520.

Fiorino, D. F., and Phillips, A. G. (1999a). Facilitation of sexual behavior and enhanced dopamine efflux in the nucleus accumbens of male rats after D-amphetamine-induced behavioral sensitization. *J. Neurosci.* **19**, 456–463.

Fiorino, D. F., and Phillips, A. G. (1999b). Facilitation of sexual behavior in male rats following D-amphetamine-induced behavioral sensitization. *Psychopharmacology* **142**, 200–208.

Fiorino, D. F., Coury, A., and Phillips, A. G. (1997). Dynamic changes in nucleus accumbens dopamine efflux during the Coolidge effect in male rats. *J. Neurosci.* **17**, 4849–4855.

Fisher, A. E. (1956). Maternal and sexual behavior induced by intracranial chemical stimulation. *Science* **124**, 228–229.

Flannelly, K. J., Blanchard, R. J., Muraoka, M. Y., and Flannelly, L. (1982). Copulation increases offensive attack in male rats. *Physiol. Behav.* **29**, 381–385.

Fletcher, I. C., and Lindsay, D. R. (1968). Sensory involvement in the mating behaviour of domestic sheep. *Anim. Behav.* **16**, 410–414.

Floody, O. R. (1989). Dissociation of hypothalamic effects on ultrasound production and copulation. *Physiol. Behav.* **46**, 299–307.

Floody, O. R., and Pfaff, D. W. (1977). Communication among hamsters by high-frequency acoustic signals: III. Responses evoked by natural and synthetic ultrasounds. *J. Comp. Physiol. Psychol.* **91**, 820–829.

Floody, O. R., Pfaff, D. W., and Lewis, C. D. (1977). Communication among hamsters by high-frequency acoustic signals: II. Determinants of calling by females and males. *J. Comp. Physiol. Psychol.* **91**, 807–819.

Folman, Y., and Volcani, R. (1966). Copulatory behaviour of the prepubertally castrated bull. *Anim. Behav.* **14**, 572–573.

Foreman, M. M., and Hall, J. L. (1987). Effects of D_2-dopaminergic receptor stimulation on male rat sexual behavior. *J. Neural Transm.* **68**, 153–170.

Foreman, M. M., Hall, J. L., and Love, R. L. (1989). The role of the 5-HT_2 receptor in the regulation of sexual performance of male rats. *Life Sci.* **45**, 1263–1270.

Frazer, A., and Hensler, J. G. (1999). Serotonin. *In* "Basic Neurochemistry, Sixth Ed." (G. J. Siegel, B. W. Agranoff, R. W. Albers, S. K. Fisher, and M. D. Uhler, Eds.), pp. 263–292. Lippencott-Raven Press, Philadelphia.

Freeman, L. M., Padgett, B. A., Prins, G. S., and Breedlove, S. M. (1995). Distribution of androgen receptor immunoreactivity in the spinal cord of wild-type, androgen-insensitivity and gonadectomized male rats. *J. Neurobiol.* **27**, 51–59.

Fumero, B., Fernandez-Vera, J. R., Gonzalez-Mora, J. L., and Mas, M. (1994). Changes in monoamine turnover in forebrain areas associated with masculine sexual behavior: A microdialysis study. *Brain Res.* **662**, 233–239.

Füxe, K., Eneroth, P., Gustafsson, J.-A., Lofstrom, A., and Skett, A. (1977). Dopamine in the nucleus accumbens: Preferential increase of DA turnover by rat prolactin. *Brain Res.* **122**, 177–182.

Gerall, H. D., Ward, I. L., and Gerall, A. A. (1967). Disruption of the male rat's sexual behavior induced by social isolation. *Anim. Behav.* **15**, 54–58.

Gerstenberg, T. C., Levin, R. J., and Wagner, G. (1990). Erection and ejaculation in Man. Assessment of the electromyographic activity of the bulbocavernosus and ischiocavernosus muscles. *Br. J. Urol.* **65**, 395–402.

Gessa, G. L., Paglietti, E., and Quarantotti, B. P. (1979). Induction of copulatory behavior in sexually inactive rats by naloxone. *Science* **204**, 203–205.

Geyer, L. A., and Barfield, R. J. (1978). Influence of gonadal hormones and sexual behavior on ultrasonic vocalization in rats: I. Treatment of females. *J. Comp. Physiol. Psychol.* **92**, 438–446.

Geyer, L. A., Barfield, R. J., and McIntosh, T. K. (1978). Influence of gonadal hormones aud sexual behavior on ultrasonic vocalization in rats: II. Treatment of males. *J. Comp. Physiol. Psychol.* **92**, 447–456.

Giantonio, G. W., Lund, N. L., and Gerall, A. A. (1970). Effect of diencephalic and rhinencephalic lesions on the male rat's sexual behavior. *J. Comp. Physiol. Psychol.* **73**, 38–46.

Gill, C. J., Wersinger, S. R., Veney, S. L., and Rissman, E. F. (1998). Induction of *c-fos*-like immunoreactivity in musk shrews after mating. *Brain Res.* **811**, 21–28.

Ginton, A. (1976). Copulation in noncopulators: Effect of PCPA in male rats. *Pharmacol., Biochem. Behav.* **4**, 357–359.

Ginton, A., and Merari, A. (1977). Long range effects of MPOA lesion on mating behavior in the male rat. *Brain Res.* **120**, 158–163.

Giordano, M., Guemes, M., Lopez-Arias, V., and Paredes, R. G. (1998). Socio-sexual behavior in male rats after lesions of the dorsolateral tegmentum. *Physiol. Behav.* **65**, 89–94.

Giuliani, D., and Ferrari, F. (1996). Differential behavioral response to dopamine D_2 agonists by sexually naïve, sexually active, and sexually inactive male rats. *Behav. Neurosci.* **110**, 802–808.

Giuliano, F., and Allard, J. (2001). Dopamine and sexual function. *Intl. J. Impotence Res.* **13** Suppl. 3, S18–S28.

Giuliano, F., and Rampin, O. (2000). Central neural regulation of penile erection. *Neurosci. Biobehav. Rev.* **24**, 517–533.

Giuliano, F., Rampin, O., Bernabé, J., and Rousseau, J. P. (1995). Neural control of penile erection in the rat. *J. Auton. Nerv. Syst.* **55**, 36–44.

Giuliano, F., Rampin, O., Brown, K., Courtois, F., Benoit, G., and Jardin, A. (1996). Stimulation of the medial preoptic area of the hypothalamus in the rat elicits increases in intracavernous pressure. *Neurosci. Lett.* **209**, 1–4.

Giuliano, F., Bernabé, J., Brown, K., Droupy, S. Benoit, G., and Rampin, O. (1997). Erectile response to hypothalamic stimulation in rats: Role of peripheral nerves. *Am. J. Physiol.* **273**, R1990–R1997.

Giuliano, F., Montorsi, F., Mirone, V., Rossi, D., and Sweeney, M. (2000). Switching from intracavernous prostaglandin E1 injections to oral sildenafil citrate in patients with erectile dysfunction: Results of a multicenter European study. *J. Urol.* **164**, 708–711.

Giuliano, F., Allard, J., Rampin, O., Droupy, S., Benoit, G., Alexandre, L., Bernabé, J. (2001a). Spinal proerectile effect of apomorphine in the anesthetized rat. *Intl. J. Impotence Res.* **13**, 110–115.

Giuliano, F., Bernabé, J., McKenna, K., Longueville, F., and Rampin, O. (2001b). Spinal proerectile effect of oxytocin in anesthetized rats. *Am. J. Physiol.* **280**, R1870–R1877.

Gladue, B. A., and Clemens, L. G. (1980). Flutamide inhibits testosterone-induced masculine sexual behavior in male and female rats. *Endocrinology (Baltimore)* **106**, 1917–1922.

Goldfoot, D. A., and Baum, M. J. (1972). Initiation of mating behavior in developing male rats following peripheral electric shock. *Physiol. Behav.* **8**, 857–863.

Goldfoot, D. A., Essock-Vitale, S. M., Asa, C., Thornton, J. E., and Leshner, A. L. (1978). Anosmia in male rhesus monkeys does not alter copulatory activity with cycling females. *Science* **199**, 1095–1096.

Goldstein, I., Lue, T. F., Padma-Nathan, H., Rosen, R. C., Steers, W. D., and Wicker, P. A. (1998). Oral sildenafil in the treatment of erectile dysfunction. *N. Engl. J. Med.* **338**, 1397–1404.

Gomez, D. M., and Newman, S. W. (1992). Differential projections of the anterior and posterior regions of the medial amygdaloid nucleus in the Syrian hamster. *J. Comp. Neurol.* **317**, 195–218.

Gomez-Marrero, J., Feria, M., and Mas, M. (1988). Stimulation of opioid receptors suppresses penile erectile reflexes and seminal emission in rats. *Pharmacol., Biochem. Behav.* **31**, 393–396.

Gonzalez, M. I., Farabollini, F., Albonetti, E., and Wilson, C. A. (1994). Interactions between 5-hydroxytryptamine (5-HT) and testosterone in the control of sexual and nonsexual behavior in male and female rats. *Pharmacol., Biochem. Behav.* **47**, 591–601.

Gooren, L. J. (1985). Human male sexual functions do not require aromatization of testosterone: A study using tamoxifen, testolactone, and dihydrotestosterone. *Arch. Sex. Behav.* **14**, 539–548.

Gorski, R. A., Gordon, J. H., Shryne, J. E., and Southam, A. M. (1978). Evidence for a morphological sex difference within the medial preoptic area of the rat brain. *Brain Res.* **148**, 333–346.

Gozes, I., Meltzer, E., Rubinrout, S., Brenneman, D. E., and Fridkin, M. (1989). Vasoactive intestinal peptide potentiates sexual behavior: Inhibition by a novel antagonist. *Endocrinology (Baltimore)* **125**, 2945–2949.

Grassman, M., and Crews, D. (1986). Progesterone induction of pseudocopulatory behavior and stimulus-response complementarity in an all-female lizard species. *Horm. Behav.* **20**, 327–335.

Gray, G. D. (1977). Differential effects of the antiandrogen flutamide on aspects of sexual behavior in castrated, androgen-treated male rats. *Psychoneuroendocrinology* **2**, 315–320.

Gray, G. D., Smith, E. R., and Davidson, J. M. (1980). Hormonal regulation of penile erection in castrated male rats. *Physiol. Behav.* **24**, 463–468.

Graybiel, A. M., Moratalla, R., and Robertson, H. A. (1990). Amphetamine and cocaine induce drug-specific activation of the *c-fos* gene in striosome-matrix compartments and limbic subdivisions of the striatum. *Proc. Natl. Acad. Sci. U.S.A.* **87**, 6912–6916.

Gréco, B., Edwards, D. A., Michael, R. P., and Clancy, A. N. (1996). Androgen receptor immunoreactivity and mating-induced Fos expression in the forebrain and midbrain structures in the male rat. *Neuroscience* **75**, 161–171.

Gréco, B., Edwards, D. A., Michael, R. P., and Clancy, A. N. (1998a). Androgen receptors and estrogen receptors are colocalized in male rat hypothalamic and limbic neurons that express Fos immunoreactivity induced by mating. *Neuroendocrinology* **67**, 18–28.

Gréco, B., Edwards, D. A., Zumpe, D., and Clancy, A. N. (1998b). Androgen receptor and mating-induced Fos immunoreactivity are co-localized in limbic and midbrain neurons that project to the male rat medial preoptic area. *Brain Res.* **781**, 15–24.

Gréco, B., Edwards, D. A., Zumpe, D., Michael, R. P., and Clancy, A. N. (1998c). Fos induced by mating or noncontact sociosexual interaction is colocalized with androgen receptors in neurons within the forebrain, midbrain, and lumbosacral spinal cord of male rats. *Horm. Behav.* **33**, 125–138.

Gréco, B., Edwards, D. A., Michael, R. P., Zumpe, D., and Clancy, A. N. (1999). Colocalization of androgen receptors and mating-induced FOS immunoreactivity in neurons that project to the central tegmental field in male rats. *J. Comp. Neurol.* **408**, 220–236.

Greenwood, D., Coggeshall, R. E., and Hulsebosch, C. E. (1985). Sexual dimorphism in the numbers of neurons in the pelvic ganglia of adult rats. *Brain Res.* **340**, 160–162.

Grunt, J. A., and Young, W. C. (1952). Differential reactivity of individuals and the response of the male guinea pig to testosterone propionate. *Endocrinology (Baltimore)* **51**, 237–248.

Grunt, J. A., and Young, W. C. (1953). Consistency of sexual behavior patterns in individual male guinea pigs following castration and androgen therapy. *J. Comp. Physiol. Psychol.* **46**, 138–144.

Hadeishi, Y., and Wood, R. I. (1996). Nitric oxide synthase in mating behavior circuitry of male Syrian hamster brain. *J. Neurobiol.* **30**, 480–492.

Haensel, S. M., and Slob, A. K. (1997). Flesinoxan: A prosexual drug for male rats. *Eur. J. Pharmacol.* **330**, 1–9.

Haensel, S. M., Rowland, D. L., and Slob, A. K. (1995). Serotonergic drugs and masculine sexual behavior in laboratory rats and men. *In* "The Pharmacology of Sexual Function and Dysfunction" (J. Bancroft, ed.), pp. 235–247. Excerpta Medica, Amsterdam.

Haldeman, S., Bradley, W. E., Bhatia, N. N., and Johnson, B. K. (1982). Pudendal evoked responses. *Arch. Neurol. (Chicago)* **39**, 280–283.

Hansen, S. (1982). Spinal control of sexual behavior: Effects of intrathecal administration of lisuride. *Neurosci. Lett.* **33**, 329–332.

Hansen, S., and Gummesson, B. M. (1982). Participation of the lateral midbrain tegmentum in the neuroendocrine control of sexual behavior and lactation in the rat. *Brain Res.* **251**, 319–325.

Hansen, S., and af Hagelsrum, L. J. (1984). Emergence of displacement activities in the male rat following thwarting of sexual behavior. *Behav. Neurosci.* **98**, 868–883.

Hansen, S., and Ross, S. B. (1983). Role of descending monoaminergic neurons in the control of sexual behavior: Effects of intrathecal infusions of 6-hydroxydopamine and 5,7-dihydroxytryptamine. *Brain Res.* **268**, 285–290.

Hansen, S., Köhler, C., Goldstein, M., and Steinbusch, H. V. (1982a). Effects of ibotenic acid-induced neuronal degeneration in the medial preoptic area and the lateral hypothalamic area on sexual behavior in the male rat. *Brain Res.* **239**, 213–232.

Hansen, S., Köhler, C., and Ross, S. B. (1982b). On the role of the dorsal mesencephalic tegmentum in the control of masculine sexual behavior in the rat: Effects of electrolytic lesions, ibotenic acid and DSP 4. *Brain Res.* **240**, 311–320.

Hansen, S., Svensson, L., Hokfelt, T., and Everitt, B. J. (1983). 5-Hydroxytryptamine-thyrotropin releasing hormone interactions in the spinal cord: Effects on parameters of sexual behaviour in the male rat. *Neurosci. Lett.* **42**, 299–304.

Harding, S. M., and McGinnis, M. Y. (2001). Testosterone propionate in the VMN of the hypothalamus is sufficient to restore partner preference in castrated male rats. *Soc. Behav. Neuroendocrinol. Abst.* **5**, 332.

Harris, V. S., and Sachs, B. D. (1975). Copulatory behavior in male rats following amygdaloid lesions. *Brain Res.* **86**, 514–518.

Hart, B. L. (1967a). Sexual reflexes and mating behavior in the male dog. *J. Comp. Physiol. Psychol.* **64**, 388–399.

Hart, B. L. (1967b). Testosterone regulation of sexual reflexes in spinal male rats. *Science* **155**, 1283–1284.

Hart, B. L. (1968a). Sexual reflexes and mating behavior in the male rat. *J. Comp. Physiol. Psychol.* **65**, 453–460.

Hart, B. L. (1968b). Role of prior experience in the effects of castration on sexual behavior of male dogs. *J. Comp. Physiol. Psychol.* **66**, 719–725.

Hart, B. L. (1968c). Alteration of quantitative aspects of sexual reflexes in spinal male dogs by testosterone. *J. Comp. Physiol. Psychol.* **66**, 726–730.

Hart, B. L. (1973). Effects of testosterone propionate and dihydrotestosterone on penile morphology and sexual reflexes of spinal male rats. *Horm. Behav.* **4**, 239–246.

Hart, B. L. (1974a). Gonadal androgen and sociosexual behavior of male mammals: A comparative analysis. *Psychol. Bull.* **7**, 383–400.

Hart, B. L. (1974b). The medial preoptic-anterior hypothalamic area and sociosexual behavior of male dogs: A comparative neuropsychological analysis. *J. Comp. Physiol. Psychol.* **86**, 328–349.

Hart, B. L. (1978). Hormones, spinal reflexes, and sexual behavior. *In* "Biological Determinants of Sexual Behaviour" (J. B. Hutchison, ed.), pp. 319–347. Wiley, Chichester.

Hart, B. L. (1979). Activation of sexual reflexes of male rats by dihydrotestosterone but not estrogen. *Physiol. Behav.* **23**, 107–109.

Hart, B. L. (1980). Sequential medial preoptic-anterior hypothalamic lesions have the same effect on copulatory behavior of male cats as simultaneous lesions. *Brain Res.* **185**, 423–428.

Hart, B. L. (1986). Medial preoptic-anterior hypothalamic lesions and sociosexual behavior of male goats. *Physiol. Behav.* **36**, 301–305.

Hart, B. L., and Haugen, C. M. (1972). Scent marking and sexual behavior maintained in anosmic dogs. *Commun. Behav. Biol.* **6**, 131–135.

Hart, B. L., and Kitchell, R. L. (1966). Penile erection and contraction of penile muscles in the spinal and intact dog . *Am. J. Physiol.* **210**, 257–262.

Hart, B. L., and Ladewig, J. (1979). Effects of medial preoptic-anterior hypothalamic lesions on development of sociosexual behavior in dogs. *J. Comp. Physiol. Psychol.* **93**, 566–573.

Hart, B. L., and Ladewig, J. (1980). Accelerated and enhanced testosterone secretion in juvenile male dogs following medial preoptic-anteriorhypothalamic lesions. *Neuroendocrinology* **30**, 20–24.

Hart, B. L., and Melese-d'Hospital, P. (1983). Penile mechanisms and the role of the striated penile muscles in penile reflexes. *Physiol. Behav.* **31**, 807–813.

Hart, B. L., Haugen, C. M., and Peterson, D. M. (1973). Effects of medial preoptic-anterior hypothalamic lesions on mating behavior of male cats. *Brain Res.* **54**, 177–191.

Hart, B. L., Wallach, S. J. R., and Melese-d'Hospital, P. Y. (1983). Differences in responsiveness to testosterone of penile reflexes and copulatory behavior of male rats. *Horm. Behav.* **17**, 274–283.

Hartung, T. G., and Dewsbury, D. A. (1978). A comparative analysis of copulatory plugs in muroid rodents and their relationship to copulatory behavior. *J. Mammal.* **59**, 717–723.

Hedlund, H., and Andersson, K.-E. (1985). Effects of some peptides on isolated human penile erectile tissue and cavernous artery. *Acta Physiol. Scand.* **124**, 413–419.

Heeb, M. M., and Yahr, P. (1996). *c-fos* immunoreactivity in the sexually dimorphic area of the hypothalamus and related brain regions of male gerbils after exposure to sex-related stimuli or performance of specific sexual behaviors. *Neuroscience* **72**, 1049–1071.

Heeb, M. M., and Yahr, P. (2000). Cell-body lesions of the posterodorsal preoptic nucleus or posterodorsal medial amygdala, but not the parvicellular subparafascicular thalamus, disrupt mating in male gerbils. *Physiol. Behav.* **68**, 317–331.

Heim, N., and Hursch, C. J. (1979). Castration for sex offenders: Treatment or punishment? A review and critique of recent European literature. *Arch. Sex. Behav.* **8**, 281–304.

Heimer, L., and Larsson, K. (1964). Drastic changes in the mating behavior of male rats following lesions in the junction of diencephalon and mesencephalon. *Experientia* **20**, 460–461.

Heimer, L., and Larsson, K. (1966/1967). Impairment of mating behavior in male rats following lesions in the preoptic-anterior hypothalamic continuum. *Brain Res.* **3**, 248–263.

Heimer, L., and Larsson, K. (1967). Mating behavior of male rats after olfactory bulb lesions. *Physiol. Behav.* **2**, 207–209.

Hendricks, S. E., and Scheetz, H. A. (1973). Interaction of hypothalamic structures in the mediation of male sexual behavior. *Physiol. Behav.* **10**, 711–716.

Hendry, W. F., Althof, S. E., Benson, G. S., Haensel, S. M., Hull, E. M., Kihara, K., and Opsomer, R. J. (2000). Male orgasmic and ejaculatory disorders. *In* "Erectile Dysfunction" (A. Jardin, G. Wagner, S. Khoury, F. Giuliano, H. Padma-Nathan, and R. Rosen, eds.), pp. 477–506. World Health Organization, Geneva.

Herberg, L. J. (1963). Seminal ejaculation following positively reinforcing electrical stimulation of the rat hypothalamus. *J. Comp. Physiol. Psychol.* **56**, 679–685.

Hernandez, L., Gonzalez, M., Oropeza, M. V., Guevara, M. A., Cervantes, M., and Morali, G. (1994a). Effects of intrathecal administration of adrenergic agonists on the frequency of copulatory pelvic thrusting of the male rat. *Arch. Med. Res.* **25**, 419–425.

Hernandez, L., Gonzalez, L., Murzi, E., Paez, X., Gottberg, E., and Baptista, T. (1994b). Testosterone modulates mesolimbic dopaminergic activity in male rats. *Neurosci. Lett.* **171**, 172–174.

Hillegaart, V. (1991). Functional topography of brain serotonergic pathways in the rat. *Acta Physiol. Scand., Suppl.* **598**, 1–54.

Hillegaart, V., and Ahlenius, S. (1998). Facilitation and inhibition of male rat ejaculatory behavior by the respective 5-HT$_{1A}$ and 5-HT$_{1B}$ receptor agonists 8-OH-DPAT and anpirtoline, as evidenced by use of the corresponding new and selective receptor antagonists NAD-299 and NAS-181. *Br. J. Pharmacol* **125**, 1733–1743.

Hillegaart, V., Ahlenius, S., and Larsson, K. (1991). Region-selective inhibition of male rat sexual behavior and motor performance by localized forebrain 5-HT injections: A comparison with effects produced by 8-OH-DPAT. *Behav. Brain Res.* **42**, 169–180.

Hillegaart, V., Alster, P., Uvnas-Moberg, K., and Ahlenius, S. (1998). Sexual motivation promotes oxytocin secretion in male rats. *Peptides (N.Y.)* **19**, 39–45.

Hines, M., Allen, L. S., and Gorski, R. A. (1992). Sex differences in subregions of the medial nucleus of the amygdala and the bed nucleus of the stria terminalis of the rat. *Brain Res.* **579**, 321–326.

Hitt, J. C., Hendricks, S. E., Ginsberg, S. I., and Lewis, J. H. (1970). Disruption of male, but not female, sexual behavior in rats by medial forebrain bundle lesions. *J. Comp. Physiol. Psychol.* **73**, 377–384.

Hitt, J. C., Bryon, D. M., and Modianos, D. T. (1973). Effects of rostral medial forebrain bundle and olfactory tubercle lesions upon sexual behavior of male rats. *J. Comp. Physiol. Psychol.* **82**, 30–36.

Hlinak Z., and Madlafousek, J. (1982). Initiation of copulatory behaviour in castrated male rats implanted with very small testosterone-filled silastic capsules. *Endokrinologie* **79**, 35–43.

Hokfelt, T., Skirboll, L., Rehfeld, J. F., Goldstein, M., Markey, K., and Dann, O. (1980). A subpopulation of mesencephalic dopamine neurons projecting to limbic areas contains a cholecystokinin-like peptide: Evidence from immunohistochemistry combined with retrograde tracing. *Neuroscience* **5**, 2093–2124.

Hokfelt, T., Fried, G., Hansen, S., Holets, V., Lundberg, J. M., and Skirboll, L. (1986). Neurons with multiple messengers: Distribution and possible functional significance. *Prog. Brain Res.* **65**, 115–137.

Holmes, G. M., and Sachs, B. D. (1992). Erectile function and bulbospongiosus EMG activity in estrogen-maintained castrated rats vary with behavioral context. *Horm. Behav.* **26**, 406–419.

Holmes, G. M., Chapple, W. D., Leipheimer, R. E., and Sachs, B. D. (1991). Electromyographic analysis of male rat perineal muscles during copulation and reflexive erections. *Physiol. Behav.* **49**, 1235–1246.

Holmes, G. M., Rogers, R. C., Bresnahan, J. C., and Beattie, M. S. (1997). Differential effects of intrathecal thyrotropin-releasing hormone (TRH) on perineal reflexes in male rats. *Physiol. Behav.* **61**, 57–63.

Holmes, G. M., Stephens, R. L., Breshnahan, J. C., and Beattie, M. S. (2001). Intrathecal methiothepin and thyrotropin-releasing hormone (TRH): Effects on penile erection. *Physiol. Behav.* **73**, 59–64.

Holstege, G. (1987). Some anatomical observations on the projections from the hypothalamus to brainstem and spinal cord: An HRP and autoradiographic tracing study in the cat. *J. Comp. Neurol.* **260**, 98–126.

Hoyer, D., Clarke, D. E., Fozard, J. R., Hartig, P. R., Martin, G. R., Mylecharane, E. J., Saxena, P. R., and Humphrey, P. P. (1994). International Union of Pharmacology classification of receptors for 5-hydroxytryptamine (serotonin). *Pharmacol. Rev.* **46**, 157–203.

Hsieh, J. T., Chang, H. C., Law, H. S., Hsieh, C. H., and Cheng, J. T. (1998). In vivo evaluation of serotonergic agents and alpha-adrenergic blockers on premature ejaculation by inhibiting the seminal vesicle pressure response to electrical nerve stimulation. *Br. J. Urol.* **82**, 237–240.

Hughes, A. M., Everitt, B. J., and Herbert, J. (1987a). Selective effects of beta-endorphin infused into the hypothalamus, preoptic area and bed nucleus of the stria terminalis on the sexual and ingestive behavior of male rats. *Neuroscience* **23**, 1063–1073.

Hughes, A. M., Everitt, B. J., Lightman, S. L., and Todd, K. (1987b). Oxytocin in the central nervous system and sexual behavior in male rats. *Brain Res.* **414**, 133–137.

Hull, E. M., Bitran, D., Pehek, E. A., Warner, R. K., and Band, L. C. (1986). Dopaminergic control of male sex behavior in rats: Effects of an intracerebrally infused agonist. *Brain Res.* **370**, 73–81.

Hull, E. M., Bitran, D., Pehek, E. A., Holmes, G. M., Warner, R. K., Band, L. C., and Clemens, L. G. (1988a). Brain localization of cholinergic influence on male sex behavior in rats: Antagonists. *Pharmacol., Biochem. Behav.* **31**, 169–174.

Hull, E. M., Pehek, E. A., Bitran, D., Holmes, G. M., Warner, R. K., Band, L. C., Bazzett, T., and Clemens, L. G. (1988b). Brain localizations of cholinergic influence on male sex behavior in rats: Agonists. *Pharmacol., Biochem. Behav.* **31**, 175–178.

Hull, E. M., Warner, R. K., Bazzett, T. J., Eaton, R. C., Thompson, J. T., and Scaletta, L. L. (1989). D_2/D_1 ratio in the medial preoptic area affects copulation of male rats. *J. Pharmacol. Exp. Ther.* **251**, 422–427.

Hull, E. M., Bazzett, T. J., Warner, R. K., Eaton, R. C., and Thompson, J. T. (1990). Dopamine receptors in the ventral tegmental area modulate male sexual behavior in rats. *Brain Res.* **512**, 1–6.

Hull, E. M., Weber, M. S., Eaton, R. C., Dua, R., Markowski, V. P., Lumley, L., and Moses, J. (1991). Dopamine receptors in the ventral tegmental area affect motor, but not motivational or reflexive, components of copulation in male rats. *Brain Res.* **554**, 72–76.

Hull, E. M., Eaton, R. C., Markowski, V. P., Moses, J., Lumley, L. A., and Loucks, J. A. (1992). Opposite influence of medial preoptic D_1 and D_2 receptors on genital reflexes: Implications for copulation. *Life Sci.* **51**, 1705–1713.

Hull, E. M., Eaton, R. C., Moses, J., and Lorrain, D. (1993). Copulation increases dopamine activity in the medial preoptic area of male rats. *Life Sci.* **52**, 935–940.

Hull, E. M., Lumley, L. A., Matuszewich, L., Dominguez, J., Moses, J., and Lorrain, D. S. (1994). The roles of nitric oxide in sexual function of male rats. *Neuropharmacology* **33**, 1499–1504.

Hull, E. M., Du, J., Lorrain, D. S., and Matuszewich, L. (1995). Extracellular dopamine in the medial preoptic area: Implications for sexual motivation and hormonal control of copulation. *J. Neurosci.* **15**, 7465–7471.

Hull, E. M., Du, J., Lorrain, D. S., and Matuszewich, L. (1997). Testosterone, preoptic dopamine, and copulation in male rats. *Brain Res. Bull.* **44**, 327–333.

Hull, E. M., Lorrain, D. S., Du, J., Matuszewich, L., Lumley, L. A., Putnam, S. K., and Moses, J. (1999). Hormone-neurotransmitter interactions in the control of sexual behavior. *Behav. Brain Res.* **105**, 105–116.

Hulsebosch, C. E., and Coggeshall, R. E. (1982). An analysis of the axon populations in the nerves to the pelvic viscera in the rat. *J. Comp. Neurol.* **211**, 1–10.

Hung, S. H., Pi, W. P., Tsai, Y. F., and Peng, M. T. (1997). Restoration of sexual behavior in aged male rats by intracerebral grafts of fetal preoptic area neurons. *J. Formosan. Med. Assoc.* **96**, 812–818.

Hutchison, J. B. (1978). Hypothalamic regulation of male sexual responsiveness to androgen. In "Biological Determinants of Sexual behavior" (J. B. Hutchison, ed.), pp. 277–317. Wiley, Chichester.

Johnson, R. D. (1988). Efferent modulation of penile mechanoreceptor activity. *Prog. Brain Res.* **74**, 319–324.

Johnson, R. D., and Kitchell, R. L. (1987). Mechanoreceptor response to mechanical and thermal stimuli in the glans penis of the dog. *J. Neurophysiol.* **57**, 1813–1836.

Johnson, R. D., Kitchell, R. L., and Gilanpour, H. (1986). Rapidly and slowly adapting mechanoreceptors in the glans penis of the cat. *Physiol. Behav.* **37**, 69–78.

Johnston, P., and Davidson, J. M. (1972). Intracerebral androgens and sexual behavior in the male rat. *Horm. Behav.* **3**, 345–357.

Ju, G., Melander, T., Ceccatelli, S., Hokfelt, T., and Frey, P. (1987). Immunohistochemical evidence for a spinothalamic pathway co-containing cholecystokinin- and galanin-like immunoreactivities in the rat. *Neuroscience* **20**, 439–456.

Kalra, P. S., Simpkins, J. W., and Kalra, S. P. (1981). Hyperprolactinemia counteracts the testosterone-induced inhibition of the preoptic area dopamine turnover. *Neuroendocrinology* **33**, 118–122.

Kalra, P. S., Simpkins, J. W., Luttge, W. G., and Kalra, S. P. (1983). Effects on male sex behavior and preoptic dopamine neurons of hyperprolactinemia induced by MtTW15 pituitary tumors. *Endocrinology (Baltimore)* **113**, 2065–2071.

Kamel, F., and Frankel, A. I. (1978). The effect of medial preoptic area lesions on sexually stimulated hormone release in the male rat. *Horm. Behav.* **10**, 10–21.

Kamel, F., Wright, W. W., Mock, E. J., and Frankel, A. I. (1977). The influence of mating and related stimuli on plasma levels of luteinizing hormone, follicle stimulating hormone, prolactin, and testosterone in the male rat. *Endocrinology (Baltimore)* **101**, 421–429.

Kaplan, M. E., and McGinnis, M. Y. (1989). Effects of ATD on male sexual behavior and androgen receptor binding: A reexamination of the aromatization hypothesis. *Horm. Behav.* **23**, 10–26.

Kasakov, L., Ellis, J., Kirkpatrick, P., Milner, P., and Burnstock, G. (1988). Direct evidence for concomitant release of noradrenaline, adenosine 5'-triphosphate and neuropeptide Y from sympathetic nerve supplying the guinea pig *vas deferens. J. Auton. Nerv. Syst.* **22**, 75–82.

Kelliher, K. R., and Baum, M. J. (2001). Nares occlusion eliminates heterosexual partner selection without disrupting coitus in ferrets of both sexes. *J. Neurosci.* **21**, 5832–5840.

Kelliher, K. R., Chang, Y.-M., Wersinger, S. R., and Baum, M. J. (1998). Sex difference and testosterone modulation of pheromone-induced neuronal Fos in the ferret's main olfactory bulb and hypothalamus. *Biol. Reprod.* **59**, 1454–1463.

Kelliher, K. R., Liu, Y. C., Baum, M. J., and Sachs, B. D. (1999). Neuronal Fos activation in olfactory bulb and forebrain of male rats having erections in the presence of inaccessible estrous females. *Neuroscience* **92**, 1025–1033.

Kelly, M. J., Lagrange, A. H., Wagner, E. J., and Ronnekleiv, O. K. (1999). Rapid effects of estrogen to modulate G protein-coupled receptors via activation of protein kinase A and protein kinase C pathways. *Steroids* **64**, 64–75.

Kevetter, G. A., and Winans, S. S. (1981). Efferents of the corticomedial amygdala in the golden hamster: I. Efferents of the 'vomeronasal amygdala.' *J. Comp. Neurol.* **197**, 81–98.

Kierniesky, N. C., and Gerall, A. A. (1973). Effects of testosterone propionate implants in the brain on the sexual behavior and peripheral tissue of the male rat. *Physiol. Behav.* **11**, 633–640.

Kihlström, J. E., and Ågmo, A. (1974). Some effects of vasopressin on sexual behaviour and seminal characteristics in intact and castrated rabbits. *J. Endocrinol.* **60**, 445–453.

Kim, S. C., and Seo, K. K. (1998). Efficacy and safety of fluoxetine, sertraline and clomipramine in patients with premature ejaculation: A double-blind, placebo controlled study. *J. Urol.* **159**, 425–427.

Kindon, H. A., Baum, M. J., and Paredes, R. J. (1996). Medial preoptic/anterior hypothalamic lesions induce a female-typical profile of sexual partner preference in male ferrets. *Horm. Behav.* **30**, 514–527.

Kinsey, A. C., Pomeroy, W. B., and Martin, C. E. (1948). "Sexual Behavior in the Human Male." Saunders, Philadelphia.

Kippin, T. E., Manitt, C., Talianakis, S., and Pfaus, J. G. (1996). Fos immunoreactivity in male rat brain following exposure to conditioned and unconditioned sex odors. *Soc. Neurosci. Abstr.* **22**, 154.

Kippin, T. E., Talianakis, S., Schattmann, L., Bartholomew, S., and Pfaus, J. G. (1998). Olfactory conditioning of sexual behavior in the male rat. *J. Comp. Psychol.* **112**, 389–399.

Klaric, J. S. (1990). Prepubertal MPOA lesions and housing condition: Effects on rats' male sex behaviors. *Physiol. Behav.* **47**, 1287–1289.

Klint, T., and Larsson, K. (1995). Clozapine acts as a $5\text{-}HT_2$ antagonist by attenuating DOI-induced inhibition of male rat sexual behavior. *Psychopharmacology* **119**, 291–294.

Kollack, S. S., and Newman, S. W. (1992). Mating behavior induces selective expression of Fos protein within the chemosensory pathways of the male Syrian hamster brain. *Neurosci. Lett.* **143**, 223–228.

Kollack-Walker, S., and Newman, S. W. (1995). Mating and agonistic behavior produce different patterns of Fos immunolabeling in the male Syrian hamster brain. *Neuroscience* **66**, 721–736.

Kollack-Walker, S., and Newman, S. W. (1997). Mating-induced expression of *c-fos* in the male Syrian hamster brain: Role of experience, pheromones, and ejaculations. *J. Neurobiol.* **32**, 481–501.

Kondo, Y. (1992). Lesions of the medial amygdala produce severe impairment of copulatory behavior in sexually inexperienced male rats. *Physiol. Behav.* **51**, 939–943.

Kondo, Y., and Arai, Y. (1995). Functional association between the medial amygdala and the medial preoptic area in regulation of mating behavior in the male rat. *Physiol. Behav.* **57**, 69–73.

Kondo, Y., and Yamanouchi, K. (1995). The possible involvement of the nonstrial pathway of the amygdala in neural control of sexual behavior in male rats. *Brain Res. Bull.* **38**, 37–40.

Kondo, Y., and Yamanouchi, K. (1997). Potentiation of ejaculatory activity by median raphe nucleus lesions in male rats: Effect of p-chlorophenylalanine. *Endocrinol. Jpn.* **44**, 873–879.

Kondo, Y., Shinoda, A., Yamanouchi, K., and Arai, Y. (1990). Role of septum and preoptic area in regulating masculine and feminine sexual behavior in male rats. *Horm. Behav.* **24**, 421–434.

Kondo, Y., Yamanouchi, K., and Arai, Y. (1993). P-chlorophenylalanine facilitates copulatory behavior in septal lesioned but not in preoptic lesioned male rats. *J. Neuroendocrinol.* **5**, 629–633.

Kondo, Y., Sachs, B. D., and Sakuma, Y. (1997). Importance of the medial amygdala in rat penile erection evoked by remote stimuli from estrous females. *Behav. Brain Res.* **88**, 153–160; corrected and republished: *Ibid.* **91**, 215–221 (1998).

Kondo, Y., Tomihara, K., and Sakuma, Y. (1999a). Sensory requirements for noncontact penile erection in the rat. *Behav. Neurosci.* **113**, 1062–1070.

Kondo, Y., Jordan, P. G., and Sachs, B. D. (1999b). Small medial amygdala lesions prevent noncontact erections in rats without impairing copulation or partner preference. *Soc. Neurosci. Abstr.* **25**, No. 137.8, 345.

Kooy, A., Weber, R. F. A., Ooms, M. P., and Vreeburg, J. T. M. (1988). Deterioration of male sexual behavior in rats by the new prolactin-secreting tumor 7315b. *Horm. Behav.* **22**, 351–361.

Korenbrot, C. C., Huhtaniemi, I. T., and Weiner, R. I. (1977). Preputial separation as an external sign of pubertal development in the male rat. *Biol. Reprod.* **17**, 298–303.

Kostarczyk, E. M. (1986). The amygdala and male reproductive functions: I. Anatomical and endocrine bases. *Neurosci. Biobehav. Rev.* **10**, 67–77.

Kraemer, H. C., Becker, H. B., Brodie, H. K. H., Doering, C. H., Moos, R. H., and Hamburg, D. A. (1976). Orgasmic frequency and plasma testosterone levels in normal human males. *Arch. Sex. Behav.* **5**, 125–132.

Krettek, J. E., and Price, J. L. (1978). Amygdaloid projections to subcortical structures within the basal forebrain and brainstem in the rat and cat. *J. Comp. Neurol.* **178**, 225–254.

Krey, L. C., and McGinnis, M. Y. (1990). Time-courses of the appearance/disappearance of nuclear androgen + receptor complexes in the brain and adenohypophysis following testosterone administration/withdrawal to castrated male rats: Relationships with gonadotropin secretion. *J. Steroid Biochem.* **35**, 403–408.

Kriegsfeld, L. J., Demas, G. E., Huang, P. L., Burnett, A. L., and Nelson, R. J. (1999). Ejaculatory abnormalities in mice lacking the gene for endothelial nitric oxide synthase (eNOS-/-). *Physiol. Behav.* **67**, 561–566.

Kritzer, M. F. (1997). Selective colocalization of immunoreactivity for intracellular gonadal hormone receptors and tyrosine hydroxylase in the ventral tegmental area, substantia nigra, and retrorubral fields in the rat. *J. Comp. Neurol.* **379**, 247–260.

Krohmer, R. W., and Crews, D. (1987). Temperature activation of courtship behavior in the male red-sided garter snake (*Thamnophis sirtalis parietalis*): Role of the anterior hypothalamus-preoptic area. *Behav. Neurosci.* **101**, 228–236.

Kuhar, M. J., Couceyro, P. R., and Lambert, P. D. (1999). Catecholamines. *In* "Basic Neurochemistry: Molecular, Cellular and Medical Aspects" (G. J. Siegel, B. W. Agranoff, R. W. Albers, S. K. Fisher, and M. D. Uhler, eds.), 6th ed., pp. 243–262. Lippincott-Raven, Philadelphia.

Kuo, R. C., Baxter, G. T., Thompson, S. H., Stricker, S. A., Patton, C., Bonaventura, J., and Epel, D. (2000). NO is necessary and sufficient for egg activation at fertilization. *Nature (London)* **406**, 633–636.

LaFerla, J. L., Anderson, D. L., and Schalch, D. S. (1978). Psychoendocrine response to sexual arousal in human males. *Psychosom. Med.* **40**, 166–172.

Lal, S., Ackman, D., Thavundayil, J. X., Kiely, M. E., and Etienne, P. (1984). Effect of apomorphine, a dopamine receptor agonist, on penile tumescence in normal subjects. *Prog. Neuropsychopharmacol. Biol. Psychiatry* **8**, 695–699.

Lal, S., Laryea, E., Thavundayil, J. X., Nair, N. P., Negrete, J., Ackman, D., Blundell, P., and Gardiner, R. J. (1987). Apomorphine-induced penile tumescence in impotent patients: Preliminary findings. *Prog. Neuropsychopharmacol. Biol. Psychiatry* **11**, 235–242.

Lambert, G. M., Rubin, B. S., and Baum, M. J. (1992). Sex difference in the effect of mating on *c-fos* expression in luteinizing hormone-releasing hormone neurons of the ferret forebrain. *Endocrinology (Baltimore)* **131**, 1473–1480.

Lange, J. D., Brown, W. A., Wincze, J. P., and Zwick, W. (1980). Serum testosterone concentration and penile tumescence changes in men. *Horm. Behav.* **14**, 267–270.

Langley, J. N., and Anderson, H. K. (1895). The innervation of the pelvic and adjoining viscera. *J. Physiol. (London)* **19**, 71–130.

Lanier, D. L., and Dewsbury, D. A. (1976). A quantitative study of copulatory behavior of large *felidae. Behav. Processes* **1**, 327–333.

Larsson, K. (1966). Individual differences in reactivity to androgen in male rats. *Physiol. Behav.* **1**, 255–258.

Larsson, K. (1967). Testicular hormone and developmental changes in mating behavior of the male rat . *J. Comp. Physiol. Psychol.* **63**, 223–230.

Larsson, K. (1969). Failure of gonadal and gonadotrophic hormones to compensate for an impaired sexual function in anosmic male rats. *Physiol. Behav.* **4**, 733–737.

Larsson, K. (1971). Impaired mating performances in male rats after anosmia induced peripherally or centrally. *Brain Behav. Evol.* **4**, 463–471.

Larsson, K. (1975). Sexual impairment of inexperienced male rats following pre- and postpubertal olfactory bulbectomy. *Physiol. Behav.* **14**, 195–199.

Larsson, K. (1978). Experiential factors in the development of sexual behavior. *In* "Biological Determinants of Sexual Behaviour" (J. B. Hutchison, ed.), pp. 55–86. Wiley, New York.

Larsson, K. (1979). Features of the neuroendocrine regulation of masculine sexual behavior. *In* "Endocrine Control of Sexual Behavior" (C. Beyer, ed.), pp. 77–163. Raven Press, New York.

Larsson, K., and Heimer, L. (1964). Mating behavior of male rats after lesions in the preoptic area. *Nature (London)* **202**, 413–414.

Larsson, K., Füxe, K., Everitt, B. J., Holmgren, M., and Södersten, P. (1978). Sexual behavior in male rats after intracerebral injection of 5,7-dihydroxytryptamine. *Brain Res.* **141**, 293–303.

Lavoisier, P., Courtois, F., Barres, D., and Blanchard, M. (1986). Correlation between intracavernous pressure and contraction of the ischiocavernosus muscle in man. *J. Urol.* **136**, 936–939.

Lawrence, D. M., and Sawyer, G. I. M. (1974). Plasma testosterone and testosterone binding affinities in men with impotence, oligospermia and hypogonadism. *Br. Med. J.* **1**, 349–351.

LeDoux, J. E., Ruggiero, D. A., Forest, R., Stornetta, R., and Reis, D. J. (1987). Topographic organization of convergent projections to the thalamus from the inferior colliculus and spinal cord in the rat. *J. Comp. Neurol.* **264**, 123–146.

Lee, M. R., Li, L., and Kitazawa, T. (1997). Cyclic GMP causes Ca^{2+} desensitization in vascular smooth muscle by activating the myosin light chain phosphatase. *J. Biol. Chem.* **272**, 5063–5068.

Lee, R. L., Smith, E. R., Mas, M., and Davidson, J. M. (1990). Effects of intrathecal administration of 8-OH-DPAT on genital reflexes and mating behavior in male rats. *Physiol. Behav.* **47**, 665–669.

Lee, S. H., and Mouradian, M. M. (1999). Up-regulation of D_{1A} dopamine receptor gene transcription by estrogen. *Mol. Cell. Endocrinol.* **156**, 151–157.

Leedy, M. G., and Hart, B. L. (1986). Medial preoptic-anterior hypothalamic lesions in prepubertal male cats: Effects on juvenile and adult sociosexual behaviors. *Physiol. Behav.* **36**, 501–506.

Leedy, M. G., Vela, E. A., Popolow, H. B., and Gerall, A. A. (1980). Effect of prepuberal medial preoptic area lesions on male rat sexual behavior. *Physiol. Behav.* **24**, 341–346.

Lehman, M. N. (1982). Neural pathways of the vomeronasal and olfactory systems controlling sexual behavior in the male golden hamster. Unpublished Ph.D. Dissertation, University of Michigan, Ann Arbor.

Lehman, M. N., and Winans, S. S. (1982). Vomeronasal and olfactory pathways to the amygdala controlling male hamster sexual behavior: Autoradiographic and behavioral analyses. *Brain Res.* **240**, 27–41.

Lehman, M. N., and Winans, S. S. (1983). Evidence for a ventral non-strial pathway from the amygdala to the bed nucleus of the stria terminalis in the male golden hamster. *Brain Res.* **268**, 139–146.

Lehman, M. N., Winans, S. S., and Powers, J. B. (1980). Medial nucleus of the amygdala mediates chemosensory control of male hamster sexual behavior. *Science* **210**, 557–560.

Lehman, M. N., Powers, J. B., and Winans, S. S. (1983). Stria terminalis lesions alter the temporal pattern of copulatory behavior in the male golden hamster. *Behav. Brain Res.* **8**, 109–128.

Leipheimer, R. E., and Sachs, B. D. (1988). GABAergic regulation of penile reflexes and copulation in rats. *Physiol. Behav.* **42**, 351–357.

Levis, D. G., and Ford, J. J. (1989). The influence of androgenic and estrogenic hormones on sexual behavior in castrated adult male pigs. *Horm. Behav.* **23**, 393–411.

Leyton, M., and Stewart, J. (1992). The stimulation of central kappa opioid receptors decreases male sexual behavior and locomotor activity. *Brain Res.* **594**, 56–74.

Leyton, M., and Stewart, J. (1996). Acute and repeated activation of male sexual behavior by tail pinch: Opioid and dopaminergic mechanisms. *Physiol. Behav.* **60**, 77–85.

Lieblich, I., Baum, M. J., Diamond, P., Goldblum, N., Iser, C., and Pick, C. G. (1985). Inhibition of mating by naloxone or morphine in recently castrated, but not intact male rats. *Pharmacol., Biochem. Behav.* **22**, 361–364.

Lin, S. N., Yu, P. C., Yang, M. C., Chang, L. S., Chiang, B. N., and Kuo, J. S. (1988). Local suppressive effect of clonidine on penile erection in the dog. *J. Urol.* **139**, 849–852.

Lincoln, G. A., Guinness, F., and Short, R. V. (1972). The way in which testosterone controls the social and sexual behavior of the red deer stag (*Cervus elaphus*). *Horm. Behav.* **3**, 375–396.

Lindén, A., Hansen, S., Bednar, I., Forsberg, G., Södersten, P., and Uvnas-Moberg, K. (1987). Sexual activity increases plasma concentrations of cholecystokinin octapeptide and offsets hunger in male rats. *J. Endocrinol.* **115**, 91–95.

Lindzey, J., and Crews, D. (1988). Effects of progestins on sexual behaviour in castrated lizards (*Cnemidophorus inornatus*). *J. Endocrinol.* **119**, 265–273.

Lisk, R. D. (1967). Neural localization for androgen activation of copulatory behavior in the male rat. *Endocrinology (Baltimore)* **80**, 754–761.

Lisk, R. D., and Bezier, J. L. (1980). Intrahypothalamic hormone implantation and activation of sexual behavior in the male hamster. *Neuroendocrinology* **30**, 220–227.

Lisk, R. D., and Greenwald, D. P. (1983). Central plus peripheral stimulation by androgen is necessary for complete restoration of copulatory behavior in the male hamster. *Neuroendocrinology* **36**, 211–217.

Lisk, R. D., and Heimann, J. (1980). The effects of sexual experience and frequency of testing on retention of copulatory behavior following castration in the male hamster. *Behav. Neural Biol.* **28**, 156–171.

Lisk, R. D., Zeiss, J., and Ciaccio, L. A. (1972). The influence of olfaction on sexual behavior in the male golden hamster (*Mesocricetus auratus*). *J. Exp. Zool.* **181**, 69–78.

Liu, Y., Curtis, J. T., and Wang, Z. (2001). Vasopressin in the lateral septum regulates pair bond formation in male prairie voles (*Microtus ochrogaster*). *Horm. Behav.* **115**, 910–919.

Liu, Y. C., Salamone, J. D., and Sachs, B. D. (1997a). Impaired sexual response after lesions of the paraventricular nucleus of the hypothalamus in male rats. *Behav. Neurosci.* **111**, 1361–1367.

Liu, Y. C., Salamone, J. D., and Sachs, B. D. (1997b). Lesions in medial preoptic area and bed nucleus of stria terminalis: Differential effects on copulatory behavior and noncontact erection in male rats. *J. Neurosci.* **17**, 5245–5253.

Liu, Y. C., Sachs, B. D., and Salamone, J. D. (1998). Sexual behavior in male rats after radiofrequency or dopamine-depleting lesions in nucleus accumbens. *Pharmacol., Biochem. Behav.* **60**, 585–592.

Lloyd, S. A., and Dixson, A. F. (1988). Effects of hypothalamic lesions upon the sexual and social behaviour of the male common marmoset (*Callithrix jacchus*). *Brain Res.* **463**, 317–329.

Lorrain, D. S., and Hull, E. M. (1993) Nitric oxide increases dopamine and serotonin release in the medial preoptic area. *NeuroReport* **5**, 87–89.

Lorrain, D. S., Matuszewich, L., Howard, R. V., Du, J., and Hull, E. M. (1996). Nitric oxide promotes medial preoptic dopamine release during male rat copulation. *NeuroReport* **8**, 31–34.

Lorrain, D. S., Matuszewich, L., Friedman, R. D., and Hull, E. M. (1997). Extracellular serotonin in the lateral hypothalamic area is increased during postejaculatory interval and impairs copulation in male rats . *J. Neurosci.* **17**, 9361–9366.

Lorrain, D. S., Matuszewich, L., and Hull, E. M. (1998). 8-OH-DPAT influences extracellular levels of serotonin and dopamine in the medial preoptic area of male rats. *Brain Res.* **790**, 217–223.

Lorrain, D. S., Riolo, J. V., Matuszewich, L., and Hull, E. M. (1999) Lateral hypothalamic serotonin inhibits nucleus accumbens dopamine: Implications for sexual refractoriness. *J. Neurosci.* **19**, 7648–7652.

Lott, D. F. (1981). Sexual behavior and intersexual strategies in American bison . *Z. Tierpsychol.* **56**, 97–114.

Louilot, A., Gonzalez-Mora, J. L., Guadalupe, T., and Mas, M. (1991). Sex-related olfactory stimuli induce a selective increase in dopamine release in the nucleus accumbens of male rats: A voltammetric study. *Brain Res.* **553**, 313–317.

Lugg, J. A., Rajfer, J., and Gonzalez-Cadavid, N. F. (1995). Dihydrotestosterone is the active androgen in the maintenance of nitric oxide-mediated penile erection in the rat. *Endocrinology (Baltimore)* **136**, 1495–1501.

Lumia, A. R., Sachs, B. D., and Meisel, R. L. (1980). Spinal transection restores sexual reflexes of rats following suppression by penile sheath removal. *Physiol. Behav.* **25**, 89–92.

Lumia, A. R., Zebrowski, A. F., and McGinnis, M. Y. (1987). Olfactory bulb removal decreases androgen receptor binding in amygdala and hypothalamus and disrupts masculine sexual behavior. *Brain Res.* **404**, 121–126.

Lumley, L. A., and Hull, E. M. (1999). Effects of a D$_1$ antagonist and of sexual experience on copulation-induced Fos-like immunoreactivity in the medial preoptic nucleus. *Brain Res.* **829**, 55–68.

Lundberg, J. M., Anggard, A., Fahrenkrug, J., Hokfelt, T., and Mutt, V. (1980). Vasoactive intestinal polypeptide in cholinergic neurons of exocrine glands: Functional significance of coexisting transmitters for vasodilation and secretion. *Proc. Natl. Acad. Sci. U.S.A.* **77**, 1651–1655.

Luttge, W. G. (1975). Effects of anti-estrogens on testosterone stimulated male sexual behavior and peripheral target tissues in the castrate male rat. *Physiol. Behav.* **14**, 839–846.

Luttge, W. G., and Hall, N. R. (1973). Differential effectiveness of testosterone and its metabolites in the induction of male sexual behavior in two strains of albino mice. *Horm. Behav.* **4**, 31–43.

Macey, M. J., Pickford, G. E., and Peter, R. E. (1974). Forebrain localization of the spawning reflex response to exogenous neurohypophysial hormones in the killifish, *Fundulus heteroclitus. J. Exp. Zool.* **190**, 269–280.

MacLean, P. D., and Ploog, D. W. (1962). Cerebral representation of penile erection . *J. Neurophysiol.* **25**, 29–55.

MacLean, P. D., Dua, S., and Denniston, R. H. (1963). Cerebral localization for scratching and seminal discharge . *Arch. Neurol. (Chicago)* **9**, 485–497.

Macrides, F., Firl, A. C., Jr., Schneider, S. P., Bartke, A., and Stein, D. G. (1976). Effects of one-stage or serial transections of the lateral olfactory tracts on behavior and plasma testosterone levels in male hamsters. *Brain Res.* **109**, 97–110.

Madlafousek, J., and Hlinak, Z. (1983). Importance of female's precopulatory behaviour for the primary initiation of male's copulatory behavior in the laboratory rat. *Behaviour* **86**, 237–249.

Madlafousek, J., Freund, K., and Grofova, I. (1970). Variables determining the effect of electrostimulation in the lateral preoptic area on the sexual behavior of male rats. *J. Comp. Physiol. Psychol.* **72**, 28–44.

Maeda, N., Matsuoka, N., and Yamaguchi, I. (1990). Septohippocampal cholinergic pathway and penile erections induced by dopaminergic and cholinergic stimulants. *Brain Res.* **537,** 163–168.

Maeda, N., Matsuoka, N., and Yamaguchi, I. (1994). Role of the dopaminergic, serotonergic and cholinergic link in the expression of penile erection in rats. *Jpn. J. Pharmacol.* **66,** 59–66.

Mahalati, K., Okanoya, K., Witt, D. M., and Carter, C. S. (1991). Oxytocin inhibits male sexual behavior in prairie voles. *Pharmacol., Biochem. Behav.* **39,** 219–222.

Maillard, C. A., and Edwards, D. A. (1991). Excitotoxin lesions of the zona incerta/lateral tegmentum continuum: Effects on male sexual behavior in rats. *Behav. Brain Res.* **46,** 143–149.

Maillard-Gutekunst, C. A., and Edwards, D. A. (1994). Preoptic and subthalamic connections with the caudal brainstem are important for copulation in the male rat. *Behav. Neurosci.* **108,** 758–766.

Mains, R. E., and Eipper, B. A. (1999). Peptides. *In* "Basic Neurochemistry: Molecular, Cellular and Medical Aspects" (G. J. Siegel, B. W. Agranoff, R. W. Albers, S. K. Fisher, and M. E. Uhler, eds.), 6th ed., pp. 363–382. Lippincott-Raven, Philadelphia.

Majewska, M. D., Harrison, N. L., Schwartz, R. D., Barker, J. L., and Paul, S. M. (1986). Steroid hormone metabolites are barbiturate-like modulators of the GABA receptor. *Science* **232,** 1004–1007.

Mallick, H., Manchanda, S. K., and Kumar, V. M. (1996). Beta-adrenergic modulation of male sexual behavior elicited from the medial preoptic area in rats. *Behav. Brain Res.* **74,** 181–187.

Malmnas, C. O. (1973). Monoaminergic influence on testosterone-activated copulatory behavior in the castrated male rat. *Acta Physiol. Scand., Suppl.* **395,** 1–128.

Malmnas, C. O. (1976). The significance of dopamine, versus other catecholamines, for L-dopa induced facilitation of sexual behavior in the castrated male rat. *Pharmacol., Biochem. Behav.* **4,** 521–526.

Malmnas, C. O., and Meyerson, B. J. (1971). p-Chlorophenylalanine and copulatory behavior in the male rat. *Nature (London)* **232,** 398–400.

Malsbury, C. W. (1971). Facilitation of male rat copulatory behavior by electrical stimulation of the medial preoptic area. *Physiol. Behav.* **7,** 797–805.

Mani, S. K., Allen, J. M., Clark, J. H., Blaustein, J. D., and O'Malley, B. W. (1994a). Convergent pathways for steroid hormone- and neurotransmitter-induced rat sexual behavior. *Science* **265,** 1246–1249, published erratum: *Ibid.* **268,** 1833 (1995).

Mani, S. K., Blaustein, J. D., Allen, J. M., Law, S. W., O'Malley, B. W., and Clark, J. H. (1994b). Inhibition of rat sexual behavior by antisense oligonucleotides to the progesterone receptor. *Endocrinology (Baltimore)* **135,** 1409–1414.

Mani, S. K., Allen, J. M., Lydon, J. P., Mulac-Jericevic, B., Blaustein, J. D., DeMayo, F. J., Conneely, O., and O'Malley, B. W. (1996). Dopamine requires the unoccupied progesterone receptor to induce sexual behavior in mice. *Mol. Endocrinol.* **10,** 1728–1737, published erratum: *Ibid.* **11,** 423 (1997).

Mani, S. K., Blaustein, J. D., and O'Malley, B. W. (1997). Progesterone receptor function from a behavioral perspective. *Horm. Behav.* **31,** 244–255.

Mani, S. K., Fienberg, A. A., O'Callaghan, J. P., Snyder, G. L., Allen, P. B., Dash, P. K., Moore, A. N., Mitchell, A. J., Bibb, J., Greengard, P., and O'Malley, B. W. (2000). Requirement for DARPP-32 in progesterone-facilitated sexual receptivity in female rats and mice. *Science* **287,** 1053–1056.

Manning, A., and Thompson, M. L. (1976). Postcastration retention of sexual behavior in the male BDF$_1$ mouse: The role of experience. *Anim. Behav.* **24,** 523–533.

Manzo, J., Cruz, M. R., Hernandez, M. E., Pacheco, P., and Sachs, B. D. (1999). Regulation of noncontact erection in rats by gonadal steroids. *Horm. Behav.* **35,** 264–270.

Maragos, W. F., Newman, S. W., Lehman, M. N., and Powers, J. B. (1989). Neurons of origin and fiber trajectory of amygdalofugal projections to the medial preoptic area in Syrian hamsters. *J. Comp. Neurol.* **280,** 59–71.

Marin, R., Escrig, A., Abreu, P., and Mas, M. (1999). Androgen-dependent nitric oxide release in rat penis correlates with levels of constitutive nitric oxide synthase isoenzymes. *Biol. Reprod.* **61,** 1012–1016.

Markowski, V. P., and Hull, E. M. (1995). Cholecystokinin modulates mesolimbic dopaminergic influences on male rat copulatory behavior. *Brain Res.* **699,** 266–274.

Markowski, V. P., Eaton, R. C., Lumley, L. A., Moses, J., and Hull, E. M. (1994) A D$_1$ agonist in the MPOA facilitates copulation of male rats. *Pharmacol., Biochem. Behav.* **47,** 483–486.

Marques, D. M., O'Connell, R. J., Benimoff, N., and Macrides, F. (1982). Delayed deficits in behavior after transection of the olfactory tracts in hamsters. *Physiol. Behav.* **28,** 353–365.

Marson, L., and McKenna, K. E. (1990). The identification of a brainstem site controlling spinal sexual reflexes in male rats. *Brain Res.* **515,** 303–308.

Marson, L., and McKenna, K. E. (1992). A role for 5-hydroxytryptamine in descending inhibition of spinal sexual reflexes. *Exp. Brain Res.* **88,** 313–320.

Marson, L., and McKenna, K. E. (1994a). Serotonergic neurotoxic lesions facilitate male sexual reflexes. *Pharmacol., Biochem. Behav.* **47,** 883–888.

Marson, L., and McKenna, K. E. (1994b). Stimulation of the hypothalamus initiates the urethrogenital reflex in male rats. *Brain Res.* **638,** 103–108.

Marson, L., List, M. S., and McKenna, K. E. (1992). Lesions of the nucleus paragigantocellularis alter ex copula penile reflexes. *Brain Res.* **592**, 187–192.

Martin, J. R. (1976). Motivated behaviors elicited from hypothalamus, midbrain, and pons of guinea pig (*Cavia porcellus*). *J. Comp. Physiol. Psychol.* **90**, 1011–1034.

Mas, M., Rodriguez del Castillo, A., Guerra, M., Davidson, J. M., and Battaner, E. (1987). Neurochemicals correlates of male sexual behavior. *Physiol. Behav.* **41**, 341–345.

Mas, M., Gonzalez-Mora, J. L., Louilot, A., Sole, C., and Guadalupe, T. (1990). Increased dopamine release in the nucleus accumbens of copulating male rats as evidenced by in vivo voltammetry. *Neurosci. Lett.* **110**, 303–308.

Mas, M., Fumero, B., and Perez-Rodriguez, I. (1995a). Induction of mating behavior by apomorphine in sexually sated rats. *Eur. J. Pharmacol.* **280**, 331–334.

Mas, M., Fernandez-Vera, J. R., and Gonzalez-Mora, J. L. (1995b). Neurochemical correlates of sexual exhaustion and recovery as assessed by in vivo microdialysis. *Brain Res.* **675**, 13–19.

Matochik, J. A., Sipos, M. L., Nyby, J. G., and Barfield, R. J. (1994). Intracranial androgenic activation of male-typical behaviors in house mice: Motivation versus performance. *Behav. Brain Res.* **60**, 141–149.

Matsumoto, T., Kondo, Y., Sachs, B. D., and Yamanouchi, I. (1997). Effects of p-chlorophenylalanine on reflexive and noncontact penile erections in male rats. *Physiol. Behav.* **61**, 165–168.

Matuszewich, L., and Dornan, W. A. (1992). Bilateral injections of a selective mu-receptor agonist (morphiceptin) into the medial preoptic nucleus produces a marked delay in the initiation of sexual behavior in the male rat. *Psychopharmacology* **106**, 391–396.

Matuszewich, L., Ormsby, J. L., Moses, J., Lorrain, D. S., and Hull, E. M. (1995) Effects of morphiceptin in the medial preoptic area on male sexual behavior. *Psychopharmacology* **122**, 330–335.

Matuszewich, L., Lorrain, D. S., Trujillo, R., Dominguez, J., Putnam, S. K., and Hull, E. M. (1999) Partial antagonism of 8-OH-DPAT's effects on male rat sexual behavior with a D_2, but not a $5\text{-}HT_{1A}$, antagonist. *Brain Res.* **820**, 55–62.

McClintock, M. K., and Adler, N. T. (1978). The role of the female during copulation in wild and domestic Norway rats (*Rattus norvegicus*). *Behaviour* **67**, 67–96.

McClintock, M. K., Anisko, J. J., and Adler, N. T. (1984). Group mating among Norway rats. II. The social dynamics of copulation: Competition, cooperation, and mate choice. *Anim. Behav.* **30**, 410–425.

McConnell, S. K., Baum, M. J., and Badger, T. M. (1981). Lack of correlation between naloxone-induced changes in sexual behavior and serum LH in male rats. *Horm. Behav.* **15**, 16–35.

McDonald, A. J. (1998). Cortical pathways to the mammalian amygdala. *Prog. Neurobiol.* **55**, 257–332

McDonald, P. G., Beyer, C., Newton, F., Brien, B., Baker, R., Tan, H. S., Sampson, C., Kitching, P., Greenhill, R., and Pritchard, D. (1970). Failure of 5α-dihydrotestosterone to initiate sexual behavior in the castrated male rat. *Nature (London)* **227**, 964–965.

McDonnell, S. M., Diehl, N. K., Garcia, M. C., and Kenny, R. M. (1989). Gonadotropin releasing hormone (GnRH) affects precopulatory behavior in testosterone-treated geldings. *Physiol. Behav.* **45**, 145–149.

McGill, T. E. (1962). Sexual behavior in three inbred strains of mice. *Behaviour* **19**, 341–350.

McGill, T. E. (1977). Reproductive isolation, behavioral genetics, and function of sexual behavior in rodents. *In* "Reproductive Behavior and Evolution" (J. S. Rosenblatt and B. R. Komisaruk, eds.), pp. 73–109. Plenum Press, New York.

McGill, T. E., and Haynes, C. M. (1973). Heterozygosity and retention of ejaculatory reflex after castration in male mice. *J. Comp. Physiol. Psychol.* **84**, 423–429.

McGill, T. E., and Manning, A. (1976). Genotype and retention of the ejaculatory reflex in castrated male mice. *Anim. Behav.* **24**, 507–518.

McGill, T. E., and Tucker, G. R. (1964). Genotype and sex drive in intact and in castrated male mice. *Science* **145**, 514–515.

McGinnis, M. Y., and Dreifuss, R. M. (1989). Evidence for a role of testosterone-androgen receptor interactions in mediating masculine sexual behavior in male rats. *Endocrinology (Baltimore)* **124**, 618–626.

McGinnis, M. Y., and Kahn, D. F. (1997). Inhibition of male sexual behavior by intracranial implants of the protein synthesis inhibitor anisomycin into the medial preoptic area of the rat. *Horm Behav.* **31**, 15–23.

McGinnis, M. Y., and Mirth, M. C. (1986). Inhibition of cell nuclear androgen receptor binding and copulation in male rats by an antiandrogen, Sch 16423. *Neuroendocrinology* **43**, 63–68.

McGinnis, M. Y., Mirth, M. C., Zebrowski, A. F., and Dreifuss, R. M. (1989). Critical exposure time for androgen activation of male sexual behavior in rats. *Physiol. Behav.* **46**, 159–165.

McGinnis, M. Y., Williams, G. W., and Lumia, A. R. (1996). Inhibition of male sex behavior by androgen receptor blockade in preoptic area or hypothalamus, but not amygdala or septum. *Physiol. Behav.* **60**, 783–789.

McGregor, A., and Herbert, J. (1992). Differential effects of excitotoxic basolateral and corticomedial lesions of the amygdala on the behavioural and endocrine responses to either sexual or aggression-promoting stimuli in the male rat. *Brain Res.* **574**, 9–20.

McIntosh, T. K., and Barfield, R. J. (1980). The temporal patterning of 40–60 kHz ultrasonic vocalizations and copulation in the rat (*Rattus norvegicus*). *Behav. Neural Biol.* **29**, 349–358.

McIntosh, T. K., and Barfield, R. J. (1984). Brain monoaminergic control of male reproductive behavior. III. Norepinephrine and the post-ejaculatory refractory period. *Behav. Brain Res.* **12**, 275–281.

McIntosh, T. K., Vallano, M. L., and Barfield, R. J. (1980). Effects of morphine, beta-endorphin and naloxone on catecholamine levels and sexual behavior in the male rat. *Pharmacol., Biochem. Behav.* **13**, 435–441.

McKenna, K. E., and Nadelhaft, I. (1986). The organization of the pudendal nerve in the male and female rat. *J. Comp. Neurol.* **248**, 532–549.

McKenna, K. E., Chung, S. K., and McVary, K. T. (1991). A model for the study of sexual function in anesthetized male and female rats. *Am. J. Physiol.* **30**, R1276–R1285.

McMahon, C. G., and Touma, K. (1999). Treatment of premature ejaculation with paroxetine hydrochloride. *Int. J. Impotence Res.* **11**, 241–245.

Meisel, R. L. (1982). Effects of postweaning rearing condition on recovery of copulatory behavior from lesions of the medial preoptic area in rats. *Dev. Psychobiol.* **15**, 331–338.

Meisel, R. L. (1983). Recovery of masculine copulatory behavior from lesions of the medial preoptic area: Effects of age versus hormonal state. *Behav. Neurosci.* **97**, 785–793.

Meisel, R. L., and Sachs, B. D. (1980). Spinal transection accelerates the developmental expression of penile reflexes in male rats. *Physiol. Behav.* **24**, 289–292.

Meisel, R. L., and Sachs, B. D. (1994). The physiology of male sexual behavior. *In* "The Physiology of Reproduction" (E. Knobil and J. D. Neill, eds.), 2nd ed., pp. 3–106. Raven Press, New York.

Meisel, R. L., Lumia, A. R., and Sachs, B. D. (1980). Effects of olfactory bulb removal and flank shock on copulation in male rats. *Physiol. Behav.* **25**, 383–387.

Meisel, R. L., Lumia, A. R., and Sachs, B. D. (1982). Disruption of copulatory behavior of male rats by olfactory bulbectomy at two, but not ten days of age. *Exp. Neurol.* **77**, 612–624.

Meisel, R. L., O'Hanlon, J. K., and Sachs, B. D. (1984a). Differential maintenance of penile responses and copulatory behavior by gonadal hormones in castrated male rats. *Horm. Behav.* **18**, 56–64.

Meisel, R. L., Sachs, B. D., and Lumia, A. R. (1984b). Olfactory bulb control of sexual function. *In* "Early Brain Damage" (S. Finger and C. R. Almli, eds.), Vol. 2, pp. 253–268. Academic Press, Orlando, FL.

Meisel, R. L., Leipheimer, R. E., and Sachs, B. D. (1986). Ani-

somycin does not disrupt the activation of penile reflexes by testosterone in rats. *Physiol. Behav.* **37**, 951–956.

Melis, M. R., and Argiolas, A. (1995). Dopamine and sexual behavior. *Neurosci. Biobehav. Rev.* **19**, 19–38.

Melis, M. R., Argiolas, A., and Gessa, G. L. (1987). Apomorphine-induced penile erection and yawning: Site of action in brain. *Brain Res.* **415**, 98–104.

Melis, M. R., Argiolas, A., and Gessa, G. L. (1989). Evidence that apomorphine induces penile erection and yawning by releasing oxytocin in the central nervous system. *Eur. J. Pharmacol.* **164**, 565–572.

Melis, M. R., Stancampiano, R., and Argiolas, A. (1992). Hippocampal oxytocin mediates apomorphine-induced penile erection and yawning. *Pharmacol., Biochem. Behav.* **42**, 61–66.

Melis, M. R., Succu, S., and Argiolas, A. (1996). Dopamine agonists increase nitric oxide production in the paraventricular nucleus of the hypothalamus: Correlation with penile erection and yawning. *Eur. J. Neurosci.* **8**, 2056–2063.

Melis, M. R., Succu, S., Iannucci, U., and Argiolas, A. (1997). N-methyl-D-aspartic acid-induced penile erection and yawning: Role of hypothalamic paraventricular nitric oxide. *Eur. J. Pharmacol.* **328**, 115–123.

Melis, M. R., Succu, S., Mauri, A., and Argiolas, A. (1998). Nitric oxide production is increased in the paraventricular nucleus of the hypothalamus of male rats during non-contact penile erections and copulation. *Eur. J. Neurosci.* **10**, 1968–1974.

Melis, M. R., Succu, S., Spano, M. S., and Argiolas, A. (1999a). Morphine injected into the paraventricular nucleus of the hypothalamus prevents noncontact penile erections and impairs copulation: Involvement of nitric oxide. *Eur. J. Neurosci.* **11**, 1857–1864.

Melis, M. R., Succu, S., Spano, M. S., and Argiolas, A. (1999b). The oxytocin antagonist d(CH2)5Tyr(ME)2-Om8-vasotocin reduces non-contact penile erections in male rats. *Neurosci. Lett.* **265**, 171–174.

Melis, M. R., Spano, M. S., Succu, S., and Argiolas, A. (2000). Activation of gamma-aminobutyric acid(A) receptors in the paraventricular nucleus of the hypothalamus reduces apomorphine-, N-methyl-D-aspartic acid- and oxytocin-induced penile erection and yawning in male rats. *Neurosci. Lett.* **281**, 127–130.

Mendelson, S. D., and Pfaus, J. G. (1989). Level searching: A new assay of sexual motivation in the male rat. *Physiol. Behav.* **45**, 337–341.

Mendonca, M. T., Chemetsky, S. D., Nester, K. E., and Gardner, G. L. (1996). Effects of gonadal sex steroids on sexual behavior in the big brown bat, *Eptesicus fuscus,* upon arousal from hibernation. *Horm. Behav.* **30**, 153–161.

Merari, A., and Ginton, A. (1975). Characteristics of exaggerated sexual behavior induced by electrical stimulation of the medial preoptic area in male rats. *Brain Res.* **86**, 97–108.

Meredith, M. (1986). Vomeronasal organ removal before sexual experience impairs male hamster mating behavior. *Physiol. Behav.* **36**, 737–743.

Meredith, M., and Fernandez-Fewell, G. (1994). Vomeronasal system, LHRH, and sex behavior. *Psychoneuroendocrinology* **19**, 657–672.

Meredith, M., Marques, D. M., O'Connell, R. J., and Stem, F. L. (1980). Vomeronasal pump: Significance for male hamster sexual behavior. *Science* **207**, 1224–1226.

Mermelstein, P. G., Becker, J. B., and Surmeier, D. J. (1996). Estradiol reduces calcium currents in rat neostriatal neurons via a membrane receptor. *J. Neurosci.* **16**, 595–604.

Mesulam, M.-M. (1995). Structure and function of cholinergic pathways in the cerebral cortex, limbic system, basal ganglia, and thalamus of the human brain. *In* "Psychopharmacology: The Fourth Generation of Progress" (F. E. Bloom and D. J. Kupfer, eds.), pp. 135–146. Raven Press, New York.

Meuleman, E., Cuzin, B., Opsomer, R. J., Hartmann, U., Bailey, M. J., Maytom, M. C., Smith, M. D., and Osterloh, I. H. (2001). A dose-escalation study to assess the efficacy and safety of sildenafil citrate in men with erectile dysfunction. *Bju Int.* **87**, 75–81.

Michael, R. P., and Wilson, M. (1974). Effects of castration and hormone replacement in fully adult male rhesus monkeys (*Macaca mulatta*). *Endocrinology (Baltimore)* **95**, 150–159.

Michael, R. P., Zumpe, D., and Bonsall, R. W. (1986). Comparison of the effects of testosterone and dihydrotestosterone on the behavior of male cynomologus monkeys (*Macaca fascicularis*). *Physiol. Behav.* **36**, 349–355.

Michael, R. P., Clancy, A. N., and Zumpe, D. (1999). Effects of mating on *c-fos* expression in the brains of male macaques. *Physiol. Behav.* **66**, 591–597.

Millan, M. J., Millan, M. H., Czlonkowski, A., and Herz, A. (1984). Vasopressin and oxytocin in the rat spinal cord: Distribution and origins in comparison to [Met]enkephalin, dynorphin and related opioids and their irresponsiveness to stimuli modulating neurohypophyseal secretion. *Neuroscience* **13**, 179–187.

Millan, M. J., Peglion, J. L, Lavielle, G., and Perrin-Monneyron, S. (1997). 5-HT$_{2C}$ receptors mediate penile erections in rats: Actions of novel and selective agonists and antagonists. *Eur. J. Pharmacol.* **325**, 9–12.

Milligan, S. R. (1979). The copulatory pattern of the bank vole (*Clethrionomys glareolus*) and speculation on the role of penile spines. *J. Zool.* **188**, 279–283.

Mills, T. M., Wiedmeier, V. T., and Stopper, V. S. (1992). Androgen maintenance of erectile function in the rat penis . *Biol. Reprod.* **46**, 342–348.

Mills, T. M., Stopper, V. S., and Wiedmeier, V. T. (1994). Effect of castration and androgen replacement on the hemodynamics of penile erection in the rat. *Biol. Reprod.* **51**, 234–238.

Mills, T. M., Reilly, C. M., Lewis, R. W. (1996). Androgens and penile erection: A review. *J. Androl.* **17**, 633–638.

Minabe, Y., Ashby, C. R., Jr., and Wang, R. Y. (1991). The CCK-A receptor antagonist devazepide but not the CCK-B antagonist L-365,260 reverses the effects of chronic clozapine and haloperidol on midbrain dopamine neurons. *Brain Res.* **549**, 151–154.

Mitchell, J. B., and Gratton, A. (1991). Opioid modulation and sensitization of dopamine release elicited by sexually relevant stimuli: A high speed chronoamperometric study in freely behaving rats. *Brain Res.* **551**, 20–27.

Mitchell, J. B., and Stewart, J. (1989). Effects of castration, steroid replacement, and sexual experience on mesolimbic dopamine and sexual behaviors in the male rat. *Brain Res.* **491**, 116–127.

Mitler, M. M., Morden, B., Levine, S., and Dement, W. (1972). The effects of parachlorophenylalanine on the mating behavior of male rats. *Physiol. Behav.* **8**, 1147–1150.

Modianos, D. T., Flexman, J. E., and Hitt, J. C. (1973). Rostral medial forebrain bundle lesions produce decrements in masculine, but not feminine, sexual behavior in spayed female rats. *Behav. Biol.* **8**, 629–636.

Moltz, H. (1990). E-series prostaglandins and arginine vasopressin in the modulation of male sexual behavior. *Neurosci. Biobehav. Rev.* **14**, 109–115.

Monaghan, E. P., and Breedlove, S. M. (1992). The role of the bulbocavernosus in penile reflex behavior in rats. *Brain Res.* **587**, 178–180.

Monaghan, E. P., Arjomand, J., and Breedlove, S. M. (1993). Brain lesions affect penile reflexes. *Horm. Behav.* **27**, 122–131.

Moore, C. L. (1984). Maternal contributions to the development of masculine sexual behavior in laboratory rats. *Dev. Psychobiol.* **17**, 347–356.

Moore, K. E., and Lookingland, K. J. (1995). Dopaminergic neuronal systems in the hypothalamus. *In* "Psychopharmacology: The Fourth Generation of Progress" (F. E. Bloom and D. J. Kupfer, eds.), pp. 245–246. Raven Press, New York.

Morali, G., Lemus, A. E., Munguia, R., Arteaga, M., Perez-Palacios, G., Sundaram, K., Kumar, N., and Bardin, C. W. (1993). Induction of male sexual behavior in the rat by 7 alpha-methyl-19-nortestosterone, an androgen that does not undergo 5 alpha-reduction. *Biol. Reprod.* **49**, 577–581.

Moreland, R. B., Goldstein, I., Kim, N. N., and Traish, A. (1999). Sildenafil citrate, a selective phosphodiesterase type

5 inhibitor: Research and clinical implications in erectile dysfunction. *Trends Endocrinol. Metab.* **10**, 97–104.

Morgantaler, A., and Crews, D. (1978). Role of the anterior hypothalamus-preoptic area in the regulation of reproductive behavior in the lizard, *Anolis carolinensis*: Implantation studies. *Horm. Behav.* **11**, 61–73.

Mortimer, C. H., McNeilly, A. S., Fisher, R. A., Murray, M. A. F., and Besser, G. M. (1974). Gonadotrophin-releasing hormone therapy in hypogonadal males with hypothalamic or pituitary dysfunction. *Br. Med. J.* **4**, 617–621.

Mos, J., Mollet, I., Tolboom, J. T., Waldinger, M. D., and Olivier, B. (1999). A comparison of the effects of different serotonin reuptake blockers on sexual behaviour of the male rat. *Eur. J. Neuropsychopharmacol.* **9**, 123–135.

Moses, J., and Hull, E. M. (1994). Inhibition of nitric oxide synthase in the MPOA increases seminal emissions in restrained supine rats and reduces the incidence of copulation in the copulation test. *Conf. Reprod. Behav. Abstr.* **26**, 37.

Moses, J., and Hull, E. M. (1999). A nitric oxide synthesis inhibitor administered into the medial preoptic area increases seminal emissions in an *ex copula* reflex test. *Pharmacol., Biochem. Behav.* **63**, 345–348.

Moses, J., Loucks, J. A., Watson, H. L., Matuszewich, L., and Hull, E. M. (1995). Dopaminergic drugs in the medial preoptic area and nucleus accumbens: Effects on motor activity, sexual motivation, and sexual performance. *Pharmacol., Biochem. Behav.* **51**, 681–686.

Mosig, D. W., and Dewsbury, D. A. (1970). Plug fate in the copulatory behavior of rats. *Psychonom. Sci.* **20**, 315–316.

Mosig, D. W., and Dewsbury, D. A. (1976). Studies of the copulatory behavior of house mice (*Mus musculus*). *Behav. Biol.* **16**, 463–473.

Moss, R. L., McCann, S. M., and Dudley, C. A. (1975). Releasing hormones and sexual behavior. *Prog. Brain. Res.* **42**, 37–46.

Murphy, A. Z., and Hoffman, G. E. (2001). Distribution of gonadal steroid receptor containing neurons in the preoptic-periaqueductal gray-brainstem pathway: A potential circuit for the initiation of male sexual behavior. *J. Comp. Neurol.* **438**, 191–212.

Murphy, A. Z., and Marson, L. (2000). Identification of neural circuits underlying male reproductive behavior: Combined viral and traditional tract tracing studies. *Soc. Neurosci. Abstr.* **26**, No. 760.25.

Murphy, A. Z., Rizvi, T. A., Ennis, M., and Shipley, M. T. (1999a). The organization of preopticmedullary circuits in the male rat, evidence for interconnectivity of neural structures involved in reproductive behavior, antinociception and cardiovascular regulation. *Neuroscience* **91**, 1103–1116.

Murphy, A. Z., Shupnik, M. A., and Hoffman, G. E. (1999b). Androgen and estrogen (alpha) receptor distribution in the periaqueductal gray of the male rat. *Horm. Behav.* **36**, 98–108.

Murphy, M. R. (1980). Sexual preferences of male hamsters: Importance of preweaning and adult experience, vaginal secretion, and olfactory or vomeronasal sensation. *Behav. Neural Biol.* **30**, 323–340.

Murphy, M. R., and Schneider, G. E. (1970). Olfactory bulb removal eliminates mating behavior in the male golden hamster. *Science* **167**, 302–304.

Myers, B. M., and Baum, M. J. (1979). Facilitation by opiate antagonists of sexual performance in the male rat. *Pharmacol., Biochem. Behav.* **10**, 615–618.

Myers, B. M., and Baum, M. J. (1980). Facilitation of copulatory performance in male rats by naloxone: Effects of hypophysectomy, 17 alpha-estradiol, and luteinizing hormone releasing hormone. *Pharmacol., Biochem. Behav.* **12**, 365–370.

Nadelhaft, I., and Booth A. M. (1984). The location and morphology of preganglionic neurons and the distribution of visceral afferents from the rat pelvic nerve: A horseradish peroxidase study. *J. Comp. Neurol.* **226**, 238–245.

Nadler, R. D., and Rosenblum, L. A. (1973). Sexual behavior during successive ejaculations in bonnet and pigtail macaques. *Am. J. Phys. Anthropol.* **38**, 217–220.

Nagatani, S., and Wood, R. I. (2001). Chemosensory regulation of medial preoptic area dopamine release in male hamsters. *Soc. Behav. Neuroendocrinol. Abst.* **5**, 341.

Nelson, R. J. (2000). "An Introduction to Behavioral Endocrinology," Second Ed., p. 224. Sinauer Assoc., Sunderland, MA.

Nelson, R. J., Demas, G. E., Huang, P. L., Fishman, M. C., Dawson, T. M., and Snyder, S. H. (1995). Behavioral abnormalities in male mice lacking neuronal nitric oxide synthase. *Nature (London)* **378**, 383–386.

Newman, S. W. (1999). The medial extended amygdala in male reproductive behavior: A node in the mammalian social behavior network. *Ann. N. Y. Acad. Sci.* **877**, 242–257.

Nishizuka, M., and Arai, Y. (1981) Sexual dimorphism in synaptic organization in the amygdala and its dependence on neonatal hormone environment. *Brain Res.* **212**, 31–38.

Nishizuka, M., and Arai, Y. (1983). Regional difference in sexually dimorphic synaptic organization of the medial amygdala. *Exp. Brain Res.* **49**, 462–465.

Norfleet, A. M., Clark, C. H., Gametchu, B., and Watson, C. S. (2000). Antibodies to the estrogen receptor-alpha modulate rapid prolactin release from rat pituitary tumor cells through plasma membrane estrogen receptors. *FASEB J.* **14**, 157–165.

Núñez, R., Gross, G. H., and Sachs, B. D. (1986). Origin and central projections of rat dorsal penile nerve: Possible direct projection to autonomic and somatic neurons by primary afferents of nonmuscle origin. *J. Comp. Neurol.* **247**, 417–429.

Nyby, J., and Whitney, G. (1978). Ultrasonic communication of adult myomorph rodents. *Neurosci. Biobehav. Rev.* **2**, 1–14.

Nyby, J., Matochik, J. A., and Barfield, R. J. (1992). Intracranial androgenic and estrogenic stimulation of male-typical behaviors in house mice (*Mus domesticus*). *Horm. Behav.* **26**, 24–45.

Oboh, A. M., Paredes, R. G., and Baum M. J. (1995). A sex comparison of increments in Fos immunoreactivity in forebrain neurons of gonadectomized, testosterone-treated rats after mounting an estrous female. *Neurobiol. Learn. Mem.* **63**, 66–73.

O'Carroll, R., Shapiro, C., and Bancroft, J. (1985). Androgens, behaviour and nocturnal erection in hypogonadal men: The effects of varying the replacement dose. *Clin. Endocrinol. (Oxford)* **23**, 527–538.

O'Connell, R. J., and Meredith, M. (1984). Effects of volatile and nonvolatile chemical signals on male sex behaviors mediated by the main and accessory olfactory systems. *Behav. Neurosci.* **98**, 1083–1093.

Ogawa, S., Robbins, A., Kumar, N., Pfaff, D. W., Sundaram, K., and Bardin, C. W. (1996). Effects of testosterone and 7 alpha-methyl-19-nortestosterone (MENT) on sexual and aggressive behaviors in two inbred strains of male mice. *Horm. Behav.* **30**, 74–84.

Ogawa, S., Lubahn, D. B., Korach, K. S., and Pfaff, D. W. (1997). Behavioral effects of estrogen receptor gene disruption in male mice. *Proc. Natl. Acad. Sci. U.S.A.* **94**, 1476–1481.

Ogawa, S., Washburn, T. F., Taylor, J., Lubahn, D. B., Korach, K. S., and Pfaff, D. W. (1998). Modification of testosterone-dependent behaviors by estrogen receptor-alpha gene disruption in male mice. *Endocrinology (Baltimore)* **139**, 5058–5069.

O'Hanlon, J. K., and Sachs, B. D. (1980). Penile reflexes in rats after different numbers of ejaculations. *Behav. Neural Biol.* **29**, 338–348.

O'Hanlon, J. K., and Sachs, B. D. (1986). Fertility of mating in rats (*Rattus norvegicus*). Contributions of androgen-dependent morphology and actions of the penis. *J. Comp. Psychol.* **100**, 178–187.

O'Hanlon, J. K., Meisel, R. L., and Sachs, B. D. (1981). Estradiol maintains castrated male rats' sexual reflexes in copula, but not ex copula. *Behav. Neural Biol.* **32**, 269–273.

Olson, R. J., and Justice, J. B., Jr. (1993). Quantitative microdialysis under transient conditions. *Anal. Chem.* **65**, 1017–1022.

Oomura, Y., Aou, S., Koyama, Y., and Yoshimatsu, H. (1988). Central control of sexual behavior. *Brain Res. Bull.* **20**, 863–870.

Orbach, J. (1961). Spontaneous ejaculation in rat. *Science* **134**, 1072–1073.

Padma-Nathan, H., Auerbach, S., Lewis, R., Lewand, M., and Perdok, R. (1999). The apomorphine study group. Efficacy and safety of apomorphine SL vs. placebo for male erectile dysfunction. *J. Urol.* **161**, S214.

Padoin, M. J., and Lucion, A. B. (1995). The effect of testosterone and DOI (1-(2,5-dimethoxy-4-iodophenyl)-2-aminopropane) on male sexual behavior of rats. *Eur. J. Pharmacol.* **277**, 1–6.

Paredes, R. G., and Ågmo, A. (1995). The GABA$_B$ antagonist CGP 35348 inhibits the effects of baclofen on sexual behavior and motor coordination. *Brain Res. Bull.* **36**, 495–497.

Paredes, R. G., and Baum, M. J. (1995). Altered sexual partner preference in male ferrets given excitotoxic lesions of the preoptic area/anterior hypothalamus . *J. Neurosci.* **15**, 6619–6630.

Paredes, R. G., Haller, A. E., Manero, M. C., Alvaradom, R., and Ågmo, A. (1990). Medial preoptic area kindling induces sexual behavior in sexually inactive male rats. *Brain Res.* **515**, 20–26.

Paredes, R. G., Highland, L., and Karam, P. (1993a). Socio-sexual behavior in male rats after lesions of the medial preoptic area: Evidence for reduced sexual motivation. *Brain Res.* **618**, 271–276.

Paredes, R. G., Holmes, G. M., Sachs, B. D., and Ågmo, A. (1993b). Electromyographic activity of rat ischiocavernosus muscles during copulation after treatment with a GABA-transaminase inhibitor. *Behav. Neural. Biol.* **60**, 118–122.

Paredes, R. G., Pina, A. L., and Bermudez-Rattoni, F. (1993c). Hypothalamic but not cortical grafts induce recovery of sexual behavior and connectivity in medial preoptic area-lesioned rats. *Brain Res.* **620**, 351–355.

Paredes, R. G., Kica, E., and Baum, M. J. (1994). Differential effects of the serotonin 1A agonist, 8-OH-DPAT, on masculine and feminine sexual behavior of the ferret. *Psychopharmacology* **114**, 591–596.

Paredes, R. G., Karam, P., Highland, L., and Ågmo, A. (1997). GABAergic drugs and socio-sexual behavior. *Pharmacol., Biochem. Behav.* **58**, 291–298.

Paredes, R. G., Contreras, J. L., and Ågmo, A. (1998a). GABAergic drugs and sexual behavior in the rabbit: Evidence for species-specific effects. *J. Psychopharmacol.* **12**, 186–191.

Paredes, R. G., Tzschentke, T., and Nakach, N. (1998b). Lesions of the medial preoptic area/anterior hypothalamus (MPOA/AH) modify partner preference in male rats. *Brain Res.* **813**, 81–83.

Parfitt, D. B., and Newman, S. W. (1998). Fos-immunoreactivity within the extended amygdala is correlated with the onset of sexual satiety. *Horm. Behav.* **34**, 17–29.

Parfitt, D. B., Coolen, L. M., Newman, S. W., and Wood, R. I. (1996). Lesions of the posterior medial nucleus of the amygdala delay sexual satiety. *Soc. Neurosci Abstr.* **22**, 155.

Park, J.-J., and Baum, M. J. (1999). Intracerebroventricular infusion of the galanin antagonist M40 attenuates heterosexual partner preferences in ferrets. *Behav. Neurosci.* **113**, 391–400.

Parrott, R. F. (1986). Minimal effects of 17 beta-hydroxy-17 alpha-methyl-estra-4,9,11-triene-3-one (R1881) on sexual behavior in prepubertally castrated rams. *J. Endocrinol.* **110**, 481–487.

Paul, S. M. (1995). GABA and glycine. *In* "Psychopharmacology: The Fourth Generation of Progress" (F. E. Bloom and D. J. Kupfer, eds.), pp. 87–94. Raven Press, New York.

Paxinos, G. (1976). Interruption of septal connections: Effects on drinking, irritability, and copulation. *Physiol. Behav.* **17**, 81–88.

Pehek, E. A., Thompson, J. T., Eaton, R. C., Bazzett, T. J., and Hull, E. M. (1988a). Apomorphine and haloperidol, but not domperidone, affect penile reflexes in rats. *Pharmacol., Biochem. Behav.* **31**, 201–208.

Pehek, E. A., Warner, R. K., Bazzett, T., Bitran, D., Band, L. C., Eaton, R. C., and Hull, E. M. (1988b). Microinjection of cis-flupenthixol, a dopamine antagonist, into the medial preoptic area impairs sexual behavior of male rats. *Brain Res.* **443**, 70–76.

Pehek, E. A., Thompson, J. T., and Hull, E. M. (1989a). The effects of intracranial administration of the dopamine agonist apomorphine on penile reflexes and seminal emission in the rat. *Brain Res.* **500**, 325–332.

Pehek, E. A., Thompson, J. T., and Hull, E. M. (1989b). The effects of intrathecal administration of the dopamine agonist apomorphine on penile reflexes and copulation in the male rat. *Psychopharmacology* **99**, 304–308.

Pellegrini-Quarantotti, B., Paglietti, E., Banana, A., Petra, M., and Gessa, G. I. (1979). Naloxone shortens ejaculation latency in male rats. *Experientia* **35**, 524–525.

Perkins, A., and Fitzgerald, J. A. (1992). Luteinizing hormone, testosterone, and behavioral response of male-oriented rams to estrous ewes and rams. *J. Anim. Sci.* **70**, 1787–1794.

Perkins, A., Fitzgerald, J. A., Price, E. O. (1992). Sexual performance of rams in serving capacity tests predicts success in pen breeding. *J. Anim. Sci.* **70**, 2722–2725.

Perkins, M. S., Perkins, M. N., and Hitt, J. C. (1980). Effects of stimulus female on sexual behavior of male rats given olfactory tubercle and corticomedial amygdaloid lesions. *Physiol. Behav.* **25**, 495–500.

Perras, B., Smolnik, R., Fehm, H. L., and Born, J. (2001). Signs of sexual behaviour are not increased after subchronic treatment with LHRH in young men. *Psychoneuroendocrinology* **26**, 1–15.

Pfaff, D., and Keiner, M. (1973). Atlas of estradiol-concentrating cells in the central nervous system of the female rat. *J. Comp. Neurol.* **151**, 121–158.

Pfaff, D. W., and Pfaffmann, C. (1969). Olfactory and hormonal influences on the basal forebrain of the male rat. *Brain Res.* **15**, 137–156.

Pfaus, J. G. (1996). Frank A. Beach award. Homologies of animal and human sexual behaviors. *Horm. Behav.* **30**, 187–200.

Pfaus, J. G. (1999). Neurobiology of sexual behavior. *Curr. Opin. Neurobiol.* **9**, 751–758.

Pfaus, J. G., and Heeb, M. M. (1997). Implications of immediate-early gene induction in the brain following sexual stimulation of female and male rodents. *Brain Res. Bull.* **44**, 397–407.

Pfaus, J. G., and Phillips, A. G. (1987). Cholecystokinin facilitates ejaculation in male rats: Blockade with proglumide and apomorphine. *Eur. J. Pharmacol.* **141**, 331–338.

Pfaus, J. G., and Phillips, A. G. (1989). Differential effects of dopamine receptor antagonists on the sexual behavior of male rats. *Psychopharmacology* **98**, 363–368.

Pfaus, J. G., and Wilkins, M. F. (1995). A novel environment disrupts copulation in sexually naïve but not experienced male rats: Reversal with naloxone. *Physiol. Behav.* **57**, 1045–1049.

Pfaus, J. G., Mendelson, S. D., and Phillips, A. G. (1990a). A correlational and factor analysis of anticipatory and consummatory measures of sexual behavior in the male rat. *Psychoneuroendocrinology* **15**, 329–340.

Pfaus, J. G., Damsma, G., Nomikos, G. G., Wenkstern, D. G., Blaha, C. D., Philips, A. G., and Fibiger, H. C. (1990b). Sexual behavior enhances central dopamine transmission in the rat. *Brain Res.* **530**, 345–348.

Pfaus, J. G., Kleopoulus, S. P., Mobbs, C. V., Gibbs, R. B., and Pfaff, D. W. (1993). Sexual stimulation activates *c-fos* within estrogen-concentrating regions of the female rat forebrain. *Brain Res.* **624**, 253–267.

Phelps, S. M., Lydon, J. P., O'Malley, B. W., and Crews, D. (1998). Regulation of male sexual behavior by progesterone receptor, sexual experience, and androgen. *Horm. Behav.* **34**, 294–302.

Phoenix, C. H. (1961). Hypothalamic regulation of sexual behavior in male guinea pigs. *J. Comp. Physiol. Psychol.* **54**, 72–77.

Phoenix, C. H. (1974). Effects of dihydrotestosterone on sexual behavior of castrated male rhesus monkeys. *Physiol. Behav.* **12**, 1045–1055.

Phoenix, C. H., and Chambers, K. C. (1986). Threshold for behavioral response to testosterone in old castrated male rhesus monkeys. *Biol. Reprod.* **35**, 918–926.

Phoenix, C. H., and Chambers, K. C. (1988). Testosterone therapy in young and old rhesus males that display low levels of sexual activity. *Physiol. Behav.* **43**, 479–484.

Phoenix, C. H., and Chambers, K. C. (1990). Sexual performance of old and young male rhesus macaques following treatment with GnRH. *Physiol. Behav.* **47**, 513–517.

Phoenix, C. H., and Jensen, J. N. (1973). Ejaculation by male rhesus in the absence of female partners. *Horm. Behav.* **4**, 231–238.

Phoenix, C. H., Copenhaver, K. H., and Brenner, R. M. (1976). Scanning electron microscopy of penile papillae in intact and castrated rats. *Horm. Behav.* **7**, 217–227.

Pirke, K. M., Kockott, G., Aldenhoff, J., Besinger, U., and Feil, W. (1979). Pituitary gonadal system function in patients with erectile impotence and premature ejaculation. *Arch. Sex. Behav.* **8**, 41–48.

Pleim, E. T., Matochik, J. A., Barfield, R. J., and Auerbach, S. B. (1990). Correlation of dopamine release in the nucleus accumbens with masculine sexual behavior in rats. *Brain Res.* **524**, 160–163.

Poggioli, R., Vergoni, A. V., Marrama, D., Giuliani, D., and Bertolini, A. (1990). NPY-induced inhibition of male copulatory activity is a direct behavioral effect. *Neuropeptides* **16**, 169–172.

Poggioli, R., Rasori, E., and Bertolini, A. (1992). Galanin inhibits sexual behavior in male rats. *Eur. J. Pharmacol.* **213**, 87–90.

Pollak, E. I., and Sachs, B. D. (1975a). Masculine sexual behavior and morphology: Paradoxical effects of perinatal androgen treatment in male and female rats. *Behav. Biol.* **13**, 401–411.

Pollak, E. I., and Sachs, B. D. (1975b). Excitatory and inhibitory effects of stimulation applied during the postejaculatory interval of the male rat. *Behav. Biol.* **15**, 449–461.

Pomerantz, S. M., and Clemens, L. G. (1981). Ultrasonic vocalizations in male deer mice (*Peromyscus maniculatus bairdi*), their role in male sexual behavior. *Physiol. Behav.* **27**, 869–872.

Pomerantz, S. M., Hepner, B. C., and Wertz, J. M. (1993a). 5-HT$_{1A}$ and 5-HT$_{1C/1D}$ receptor agonists produce reciprocal effects on male sexual behavior of rhesus monkeys. *Eur. J. Pharmacol.* **243**, 227–234.

Pomerantz, S. M., Hepner, B. C., and Wertz, J. M. (1993b). Serotonergic influences on male sexual behavior of rhesus monkeys: Effects of serotonin agonists. *Psychopharmacology* **111**, 47–54.

Porst, H., Rosen, R., Padma-Nathan, H., Goldstein, I., Giuliano, F., Ulbrich, E., and Bandel, T. (2001). The efficacy and tolerability of vardenafil, a new, oral, selective phosphodiesterase type 5 inhibitor, in patients with erectile dysfunction: The first at-home clinical trial. *Int. J. Impotence Res.* **13**, 192–199.

Powers, J. B., and Winans, S. S. (1973). Sexual behavior in peripherally anosmic male hamsters. *Physiol. Behav.* **10**, 361–368.

Powers, J. B., and Winans, S. S. (1975). Vomeronasal organ: Critical role in mediating sexual behavior of the male hamster. *Science* **187**, 961–963.

Powers, J. B., Fields, R. B., and Winans, S. S. (1979). Olfactory and vomeronasal system participation in male hamsters' attraction to female vaginal secretions. *Physiol. Behav.* **22**, 77–84.

Powers, J. B., Newman, S. W., and Bergondy, M. L. (1987). MPOA and BNST lesions in male Syrian hamsters: Differential effects on copulatory and chemoinvestigatory behaviors. *Behav. Brain Res.* **23**, 181–195.

Price, E. O., and Wallach, S. J. R. (1991). Development of sexual and aggressive behaviors in Hereford bulls. *J. Anim. Sci.* **69**, 1019–1027.

Pu, S., Xu, B., Kalra, S. P., and Kalra, P. S. (1996). Evidence that gonadal steroids modulate nitric oxide efflux in the medial preoptic area: Effects of N-methyl-D-aspartate and correlation with luteinizing hormone secretion. *Endocrinology (Baltimore)* **137**, 1949–1955.

Purinton, P. T., Oliver, J. E., Jr., and Bradley, W. E. (1981). Differences in routing of pelvic visceral afferent fibers in the dog and cat. *Exp. Neurol.* **73**, 725–731.

Putnam, S. K., Du, J., Sato, S., and Hull, E. M. (2001). Testosterone restoration of copulatory behavior correlates with medial preoptic dopamine release in castrated male rats. *Horm. Behav.* **39**, 225–231.

Putnam, S. K., Sato, S., and Hull, E. M. (2002a). Effects of testosterone metabolites on copulation and extracellular dopamine in the medial preoptic area. Submitted.

Putnam, S. K., Sato, S., and Hull, E. M. (2002b). Effects of testosterone metabolites on copulation and preoptic tissue dopamine and nitric oxide synthase. Submitted.

Quershi, G. A., and Södersten, P. (1986). Sexual activity alters the concentration of amino acids in cerebrospinal fluid of male rat. *Neurosci. Lett.* **70**, 374–378.

Raboch, J., and Starka, L. (1973). Reported coital activity of men and levels of plasma testosterone. *Arch. Sex. Behav.* **2**, 309–315.

Raboch, J., Mellan, J., and Starka, L. (1975). Plasma testosterone in male patients with sexual dysfunction. *Arch. Sex. Behav.* **4**, 541–545.

Racey, P. A., Ansari, M. A., Rowe, P. H., and Glover, T. D. (1973). Proceedings: Testosterone in impotent men. *J. Endocrinol.* **59**, 23.

Rachman, I. M., Unnerstall, J. R., Pfaff, D. W., and Cohen, R. S. (1998). Regulation of neuronal nitric oxide synthase mRNA in lordosis-relevant neurons of the ventromedial hypothalamus following short-term estrogen treatment. *Brain Res.* **59**, 105–108.

Rand, M. N., and Breedlove, S. M. (1995). Androgen alters the dendritic arbors of SNB motoneurons by acting upon their target muscles. *J. Neurosci.* **15**, 4408–4416.

Ratnasooriya, W. D., and Dharmasiri, M. G. (2001). L-arginine, the substrate of nitric oxide synthase, inhibits fertility of male rats. *Asian J. Androl.* **3**, 97–103.

Ratnasooriya, W. D., Dharmasiri, M. G., and Wadsworth, R. M. (2000). Reduction in libido and fertility of male rats by administration of the nitric oxide (NO) synthase inhibitor N-nitro-L-arginine methylester. *Int. J. Androl.* **23**, 187–191.

Rees, R. W., Ralph, D. J., Royle, M., Moncada, S., and Cellek, S. (2001). Y-27632, an inhibitor of Rhokinase, antagonizes noradrenergic contractions in the rabbit and human corpus cavernosum. *Brit. J. Pharmacol.* **133**, 455–458.

Rehman, J., Kaynan, A., Christ, G., Valcic, M., Maayani, S., and Melman, A. (1999). Modification of sexual behavior of Long-Evans male rats by drugs acting on the 5-HT$_{1A}$ receptor. *Brain Res.* **821**, 414–425.

Reilly, C. M., Zamorano, P., Stopper, V. S., and Mills, T. M. (1997). Androgenic regulation of NO availability in rat penile erection. *J. Androl.* **18**, 110–115.

Resko, J. A., Perkins, A., Roselli, C. E., Stellflug, J. N., and Stormshak, F. K. (1999). Sexual behaviour of rams: Male orientation and its endocrine correlates. *J. Reprod. Fertil, Suppl.* **54**, 259–269.

Retana-Marquez, S., and Velazquez-Moctezuma, J. (1997). Cholinergic-androgenic interaction in the regulation of male sexual behavior in rats. *Pharmacol., Biochem. Behav.* **56**, 373–378.

Ricardo, J. A. (1981). Efferent connections of the subthalamic region in the rat. II. The zona incerta. *Brain Res.* **214**, 43–60.

Richard, P., Moos, F., and Freund-Mercier, M. J. (1991). Central effects of oxytocin. *Physiol. Rev.* **71**, 331–370.

Rizvi, T. A., Ennis, M., and Shipley, M. T. (1992). Reciprocal connections between the medial preoptic area and the midbrain periaqueductal gray in rat: A WGA-HRP and PHA-L study. *J. Comp. Neurol.* **315**, 1–15.

Rizvi, T. A., Murphy, A. Z., Ennis, M., Behbehani, M. M., and Shipley, M. T. (1996). Medial preoptic area afferents to periaqueductal gray medullo-output neurons: A combined Fos and tract tracing study. *J. Neurosci.* **16**, 333–344.

Robbins, T. W., and Everitt, B. J. (1992). Functions of dopamine in the dorsal and ventral striatum. *Semin. Neurosci.* **4**, 119–128.

Roberts, W. W., Steinberg, M. L., and Means, L. W. (1967). Hypothalamic mechanisms for sexual, aggressive, and other motivational behaviors in the opossum, *Didelphis virginiana. J. Comp. Physiol. Psychol.* **64**, 1–15.

Robertson, G. S., Pfaus, J. G., Atkinson, L. J., Matsumura, H., Phillips, A. G., and Fibiger, H. C. (1991). Sexual behavior increases *c-fos* expression in the forebrain of the male rat. *Brain Res.* **564**, 352–357.

Robinson, B. W., and Mishkin, M. (1966). Ejaculation evoked by stimulation of the preoptic area in monkeys. *Physiol. Behav.* **1**, 269–272.

Rodgers, C. H., and Alheid, G. (1972). Relationship of sexual behavior and castration to tumescence in the male rat. *Physiol. Behav.* **9**, 581–584.

Rodriguez, M., Castro, R., Hernandez, G., and Mas, M. (1984). Different roles of catecholaminergic and serotoninergic neurons of the medial forebrain bundle on male rat sexual behavior. *Physiol. Behav.* **33**, 5–11.

Rodriguez-Manzo, G. (1999). Yohimbine interacts with the dopaminergic system to reverse sexual satiation: Further evidence for a role of sexual motivation in sexual exhaustion. *Eur. J. Pharmacol.* **372**, 1–8.

Rodriguez-Manzo, G., and Fernandez-Guasti, A. (1994). Reversal of sexual exhaustion by serotonergic and noradrenergic agents. *Behav. Brain Res.* **62**, 127–134.

Rodriguez-Manzo, G., and Fernandez-Guasti, A. (1995). Participation of the central noradrenergic system in the reestablishment of copulatory behavior of sexually exhausted rats by yohimbine, naloxone, and 8-OH-DPAT. *Brain Res. Bull.* **38**, 399–404.

Rodríguez-Manzo, G., Pellicer, F., Larsson, K. and Fernandez-Guasti, A. (2000). Stimulation of the medial preoptic area facilitates sexual behavior but does not reverse sexual satiation. *Behav. Neurosci.* **114**, 553–560.

Root, W. S., and Bard, P. (1947). The mediation of feline erection through sympathetic pathways with some remarks on sexual behavior after deafferentation of the genitalia. *Am. J. Physiol.* **151**, 80–90.

Roppolo, J. R., Nadelhaft, I., and de Groat, W. C. (1985). The organization of pudendal motoneurons and primary afferent projections in the spinal cord of the rhesus monkey revealed by horseradish peroxidase. *J. Comp. Neurol.* **234**, 475–488.

Rose, R. D., and Collins, W. F., III (1985). Crossing dendrites may be a substrate for synchronized activation of penile motoneurons. *Brain Res.* **337**, 373–377.

Roselli, C. E., Cross, E., Poonyagariyagorn, H. K., and Stadelman, H. L. (2001). Role of aromatization in anticipatory and consummatory aspects of sexual behavior in male rats. *Soc. Behav. Neuroendocrinol. Abst.* **5**, 346.

Rosen, R. C., Lane, R. M., and Menza, M. (1999). Effects of SSRIs on sexual function: A critical review. *J. Clin. Psychopharmacol.* **19**, 67–85.

Rosenblatt, J. S., and Aronson, L. R. (1958). The decline of sexual behavior in male cats after castration with special reference to the role of prior sexual experience. *Behaviour* **12**, 285–338.

Rowe, D. W., and Erskine, M. S. (1993). *c-fos* proto-oncogene activity induced by mating in the preoptic area, hypothalamus and amygdala in the female rat: Role of afferent input via the pelvic nerve. *Brain Res.* **621**, 25–34.

Rowe, F. A., and Edwards, D. A. (1972). Olfactory bulb removal: Influences on the mating behavior of male mice. *Physiol. Behav.* **8**, 37–41.

Rowe, F. A., and Smith, W. E. (1973). Simultaneous and successive olfactory bulb removal: Influences on the mating behaviour of male mice. *Physiol. Behav.* **10**, 443–449.

Rowland, D. L. and Houtsmuller, E. J. (1998). 8-OH-DPAT interacts with sexual experience and testosterone to affect ejaculatory response in rats. *Pharmacol., Biochem. Behav.* **60**, 143–149.

Ryan, E. L., and Frankel, A. I. (1978). Studies on the role of the medial preoptic area in sexual behavior and hormonal response to sexual behavior in the mature male laboratory rat. *Biol. Reprod.* **19**, 971–983.

Saartok, T., Dahlberg, E., and Gustafsson, J. A. (1984). Relative binding affinity of anabolic-androgenic steroids: Comparison of the binding to the androgen receptors in skeletal muscle and in prostate, as well as to sex hormone-binding globulin. *Endocrinology (Baltimore)* **114**, 2100–2106.

Sachs, B. D. (1978). Conceptual and neural mechanisms of masculine copulatory behavior. *In* "Sex and Behavior" (T. E. McGill, D. A. Dewsbury, and B. D. Sachs, eds.), pp. 267–295. Plenum Press, New York.

Sachs, B. D. (1980). Sexual reflexes of spinal male house mice. *Physiol. Behav.* **24**, 489–492.

Sachs, B. D. (1982). Role of striated penile muscles in penile reflexes, copulation, and induction of pregnancy in the rat. *J. Reprod. Fertil.* **66**, 433–443.

Sachs, B. D. (1983). Potency and fertility: Hormonal and mechanical causes and effects of penile actions in rats. *In* "Hormones and Behavior in Higher Vertebrates" (J. Balthazart, E. Pröve, and R. Gilles, eds.), pp. 86–110. Springer-Verlag, Berlin.

Sachs, B. D. (1997). Erection evoked in male rats by airborne scent from estrous females. *Physiol. Behav.* **62**, 921–924.

Sachs, B. D. (2000). Contextual approaches to the physiology and classification of erectile function, erectile dysfunction, and sexual arousal. *Neurosci. Biobehav. Rev.* **24**, 541–560.

Sachs, B. D., and Barfield, R. J. (1970). Temporal patterning of sexual behavior in the male rat. *J. Comp. Physiol. Psychol.* **73**, 359–364.

Sachs, B. D., and Bialy, M. (2000). Female presence during the postejaculatory interval facilitates penile erection and 22 kHz vocalization in male rats. *Behav. Neurosci.* **114**, 1203–1208.

Sachs, B. D., and Bitran, D. (1990). Spinal block reveals roles for brain and spinal cord in the mediation of reflexive erection in rats. *Brain Res.* **528**, 99–108.

Sachs, B. D., and Garinello, L. D. (1978). Interaction between penile reflexes and copulation in male rats. *J. Comp. Physiol. Psychol.* **92**, 759–767.

Sachs, B. D., and Garinello, L. D. (1979). Spinal pacemaker controlling sexual reflexes in male rats. *Brain Res.* **171**, 152–156.

Sachs, B. D., and Garinello, L. D. (1980). Hypothetical spinal pacemaker regulating penile reflexes in rats: Evidence from transection of spinal cord and dorsal penile nerves. *J. Comp. Physiol. Psychol.* **94**, 530–535.

Sachs, B. D., and Leipheimer, R. E. (1988). Rapid effect of testosterone on striated muscle activity in rats. *Neuroendocrinology* **48**, 453–458.

Sachs, B. D., and Liu, Y.-C. (1991). Maintenance of erection of penile glans, but not penile body, after transection of rat cavernous nerves. *J. Urol.* **146**, 900–905.

Sachs, B. D., and Liu, Y.-C. (1992). Copulatory behavior and reflexive penile erection in rats after section of the pudendal and genitofemoral nerves. *Physiol. Behav.* **51**, 673–680.

Sachs, B. D., and Liu, Y.-C. (1998). Mounting and brief noncontact exposure of males to receptive females facilitate reflexive erection in rats, even after hypogastric nerve section. *Physiol. Behav.* **65**, 413–421.

Sachs, B. D., and Meisel, R. L. (1979). Pubertal development of penile reflexes and copulation in male rats. *Psychoneuroendocrinology* **4**, 287–296.

Sachs, B. D., Valcourt, R. J., and Flagg, H. C. (1981). Copulatory behavior and sexual reflexes of male rats treated with naloxone. *Pharmacol., Biochem. Behav.* **14**, 251–253.

Sachs, B. D., Akasofu, K., and McEldowney, S. (1994a). Effects of copulation on apomorphine-induced erection in rats. *Pharmacol., Biochem. Behav.* **48**, 423–428.

Sachs, B. D., Akasofu, K., Citron, J. H., Daniels, S. B., and Natoli, J. H. (1994b). Noncontact stimulation from estrous females evokes penile erection in rats. *Physiol. Behav.* **55**, 1073–1079.

Saito, T. R., and Moltz, H. (1986). Copulatory behavior of sexually naïve and sexually experienced male rats following removal of the vomeronasal organ. *Physiol. Behav.* **37**, 507–510.

Sala, M., Braida, D., Leone, M. P., Calcaterra, P., Monti, S., and Gori, E. (1990). Central effect of yohimbine on sexual behavior in the rat. *Physiol. Behav.* **47**, 165–173.

Sales, G. D. (1972). Ultrasound and mating behavior in rodents with some observations on other behavioural situations. *J. Zool.* **168**, 149–164.

Salis, P. S., and Dewsbury, D. A. (1971). p-Chlorophenylalanine facilitates copulatory behavior in male rats. *Nature (London)* **232**, 400–401.

Salmimies, P., Kockott, G., Pirke, K. M., Vogt, H. J., and Schill, W. B. (1982). Effects of testosterone replacement on sexual behavior in hypogonadal men. *Arch. Sex. Behav.* **11**, 345–353.

Sar, M., and Stumpf, W. E. (1975). Distribution of androgen-concentrating neurons in rat brain. *In* "Anatomical Neuroendocrinology" (W. E. Stumpf and L. D. Grant, eds.), pp. 120–133. Karger, Basel.

Sato, M., Mizuno, N., and Konishi, A. (1978). Localization of motoneurons innervating perineal muscles: A HRP study in cat. *Brain Res.* **140**, 149–154.

Sato, Y., Wada, H., Horita, H., Suzuki, N., Shibuya, A., Adachi, H., Kato, R., Tsukamoto, T., and Kumamoto, Y. (1995). Dopamine release in the medial preoptic area during male copulatory behavior in rats. *Brain Res.* **692**, 66–70.

Sato, Y., Horita, H., Kurohata, T., Adachi, H., and Tsukamoto, T. (1998). Effect of the nitric oxide level in the medial preoptic area on male copulatory behavior in rats. *Am. J. Physiol.* **274**, R243–R247.

Sato, Y., Christ, G. J., Horita, H., Adachi, H., Suzuki, N., and Tsukamoto, T. (1999). The effects of alterations in nitric oxide levels in the paraventricular nucleus on copulatory behavior and reflexive erections in male rats. *J. Urol.* **162**, 2182–2185.

Sayag, N., Hoffman, N. W., and Yahr, P. (1994). Telencephalic connections of the sexually dimorphic area of the gerbil hypothalamus that influence male sexual behavior. *Behav. Neurosci.* **108**, 743–757.

Scaletta L. L., and Hull, E. M. (1990). Systemic or intracranial apomorphine increases copulation in long-term castrated male rats. *Pharmacol., Biochem. Behav.* **37**, 471–475.

Schmidt, M. H., Valatx, J. L., Schmidt, H. S., Wauquier, A., and Jouvet, M. (1994). Experimental evidence of penile erections during paradoxical sleep in the rat. *NeuroReport* **5**, 561–564.

Schmidt, M. H., Valatx, J. L., Sakai, K., Fort, P., and Jouvet, M. (2000). Role of the lateral preoptic area in sleep-related erectile mechanisms and sleep generation in the rat. *J. Neurosci.* **20**, 6640–6647.

Schnur, S. L., Smith, E. R., Lee, R. L., Mas, M., and Davidson, J. M. (1989). A component analysis of the effects of DPAT on male rat sexual behavior. *Physiol. Behav.* **45**, 897–901.

Schoenen, J., Lotstra, F., Vierendeels, G., Reznik, M., and Vanderhaeghen, J. J. (1985). Substance P, enkephalins, somatostatin, cholecystokinin, oxytocin, and vasopressin in human spinal cord. *Neurology* **35**, 881–890.

Schroder, H. D. (1980). Organization of the motoneurons innervating the pelvic muscles of the male rat. *J. Comp. Neurol.* **192**, 567–587.

Schultz, W. (1992). Activity of dopamine neurons in the behaving primate. *Semin. Neurosci.* **4**, 129–138.

Schwartz, M. F., Kolodny, R. C., and Masters, W. H. (1980).

Plasma testosterone levels of sexually functional and dysfunctional men. *Arch. Sex. Behav.* **9**, 355–366.

Scouten, C. W., Burrell, L., Palmer, T., and Cegavske, C. F. (1980). Lateral projections of the medial preoptic area are necessary for androgenic influence on urine marking and copulation in rats. *Physiol. Behav.* **25**, 237–243.

Seagraves, R. T. (1990). Effects of psychotropic drugs on human erection and ejaculation. *Arch. Gen. Psychiatry* **46**, 275–284.

Shimura, T., Yamamoto, T., and Shimokochi, M. (1994). The medial preoptic area is involved in both sexual arousal and performance in male rats: Re-evaluation of neuron activity in freely moving animals. *Brain Res.* **640**, 215–222.

Short, R. V. (1979). Sexual selection and its component parts, somatic and genital selection, as illustrated by man and the great apes. *Adv. Study Behav.* **9**, 131–158.

Shugrue, P. J., Lane, M. V., and Merchenthaler, I. (1997). Comparative distribution of estrogen receptor-alpha and -beta mRNA in the rat central nervous system. *J. Comp. Neurol.* **388**, 507–525.

Silva, N. L., and Boulant, J. A. (1986). Effects of testosterone, estradiol, and temperature on neurons in preoptic tissue slices. *Am. J. Physiol.* **250**, R625–R632.

Simerly, R. B., and Swanson, L. W. (1986). The organization of neural inputs to the medial preoptic nucleus of the rat. *J. Comp. Neurol.* **246**, 312–342.

Simerly, R. B., and Swanson, L. W. (1987). Castration reversibly alters levels of cholecystokinin immunoreactivity in cells of three interconnected sexually dimorphic forebrain nuclei in the rat. *Proc. Natl. Acad. Sci. U.S.A.* **84**, 2087–2091.

Simerly, R. B., and Swanson, L. W. (1988). Projections of the medial preoptic nucleus: A *Phaseolis vulgaris* leucoagglutinin anterograde tract-tracing study in the rat. *J. Comp. Neurol.* **270**, 209–242.

Simerly, R. B., Gorski, R. A., and Swanson, L. W. (1986). Neurotransmitter specificity of cells and fibers in the medial preoptic nucleus: An immunohistochemical study in the rat. *J. Comp. Neurol.* **246**, 343–363.

Simerly, R. B., Chang, C., Muramatsu, M., and Swanson, L. W. (1990). Distribution of androgen and estrogen mRNA-containing cells in the rat brain: An in situ hybridization study. *J. Comp. Neurol.* **294**, 76–95.

Simmons, D., and Yahr, P. (2001). Posterodorsal preoptic nucleus (PdPN) and posterodorsal medial amygdala (MeApd) cells that are activated with ejaculation: Additional projections and presence of nitric oxide synthase (NOS). *Soc. Behav. Neuroendocrinol. Abst.* **5**, 349.

Sinchak, K., and Clemens, L. G. (1989). Expression of the ejaculatory reflex in castrated male B6D2F1 hybrid house mouse (*Mus musculus*) is reduced by the aromatase inhibitor ATD. *Soc. Neurosci. Abstr.* **15**, No. 155.16.

Sinchak, K., Roselli, C. E., and Clemens, L. G. (1996). Levels of serum steroids, aromatase activity, and estrogen receptors in preoptic area, hypothalamus, and amygdala of B6D2F1 male house mice that differ in the display of copulatory behavior after castration. *Behav. Neurosci.* **110**, 593–602.

Singer, J. J. (1968). Hypothalamic control of male and female sexual behavior in female rats. *J. Comp. Physiol. Psychol.* **66**, 738–742.

Singh, R., Pervin, S., Shryne, J., Gorski, R., and Chaudhuri, G. (2000). Castration increases and androgens decrease nitric oxide synthase activity in the brain: Physiologic implications. *Proc. Natl. Acad. Sci. U.S.A.* **97**, 3672–3677.

Sipos, M. L., and Nyby, J. G. (1996). Concurrent androgenic stimulation of the ventral tegmental area and medial preoptic area: Synergistic effects on male-typical reproductive behaviors in house mice. *Brain Res.* **729**, 29–44.

Sirinathsinghji, D. J. (1987). Inhibitory influence of corticotropin releasing factor on components of sexual behavior in the male rat. *Brain Res.* **407**, 185–190.

Sjöstrand, N. O. (1981). Smooth muscles of vas deferens and other organs in the male reproductive tract. *In* "Smooth Muscle: An Assessment of Current Knowledge" (E. Bülbring, A. F. Brading, A. W. Jones, and T. Lomita, eds.), pp. 367–549. University of Texas Press, Austin.

Sjöstrand, N. O., and Klinge, E. (1979). Principal mechanisms controlling penile retraction and protrusion in rabbits. *Acta Physiol. Scand.* **106**, 199–214.

Slimp, J. C., Hart, B. L., and Goy, R. W. (1978). Heterosexual, autosexual and social behavior of adult male rhesus monkeys with medial preoptic-anterior hypothalamic lesions. *Brain Res.* **142**, 105–122.

Slotnick, B., Glover, P., and Bodyak, N. (2001). Does intranasal application of zinc sulfate produce anosmia in the rat? *Behav. Neurosci.* **114**, 814–29.

Smith, E. R., Damassa, D. A., and Davidson, J. M. (1977). Plasma testosterone and sexual behavior following intracerebral implantation of testosterone propionate in the castrated male rat. *Horm. Behav.* **8**, 77–87.

Smith, E. R., Lee, R. L., Schnur, S. L., and Davidson, J. M. (1987). Alpha 2-adrenoceptor antagonists and male sexual behavior: I. Mating behavior. *Physiol. Behav.* **41**, 7–14.

Smith, W. J., Stewart, J., and Pfaus, J. G. (1997). Tail pinch induces Fos immunoreactivity within several regions of the male rat brain: Effects of age. *Physiol. Behav.* **61**, 717–723.

Sneddon, P., and Westfall, D. P. (1984). Pharmacological evidence that adenosine triphosphate and noradrenaline are cotransmitters in the guinea pig *vas deferens. J. Physiol. (London)* **347**, 561–580.

Södersten, P. (1973). Estrogen-activated sexual behavior in male rats. *Horm. Behav.* **4**, 247–256.

Södersten, P., and Gustafsson, J. A. (1980). Activation of sexual behavior in castrated rats with the synthetic androgen 17 beta-hydroxy-17 alpha-methyl-estra-4,9,11-triene-3-one (R 1881). *J. Endocrinol.* **87**, 279–283.

Södersten, P., Larsson, K., Ahlenius, S., and Engel, J. (1976). Stimulation of mounting behavior but not lordosis behavior in ovariectomized female rats by p-chlorophenylalanine. *Pharmacol. Biochem. Behav.* **5**, 329–333.

Södersten, P., Damassa, D. A., and Smith, E. R. (1977). Sexual behavior in developing male rats. *Horm. Behav.* **8**, 320–341.

Södersten, P., Eneroth, P., Mode, A., and Gustafsson, J.-A. (1985). Mechanisms of androgen-activated sexual behavior in rats. *In* "Neurobiology" (R. Gilles and J. Balthazart, eds.), pp. 48–59. Springer-Verlag, Berlin.

Somlyo, A. P., and Somlyo, A. V. (2000). Signal transduction by G-proteins, rho-kinase and protein phosphatase to smooth muscle and non-muscle myosin II. *J. Physiol. (Lond)* **522**, 177–185.

Steers, W. D. (2000). Neural pathways and central sites involved in penile erection: Neuroanatomy and clinical implications. *Neurosci. Biobehav. Rev.* **24**, 507–516.

Steers, W. D., and de Groat, W. C. (1989). Effects of m-chlorophenylpiperazine on penile and bladder function in rats. *Am. J. Physiol.* **257**, R1441–R1449.

Steers, W. D., McConnell, J., and Benson, G. S. (1984). Anatomical localization and some pharmacological effects of vasoactive intestinal polypeptide in human and monkey corpus cavernosum. *J. Urol.* **132**, 1048–1053.

Stefanick, M. L., and Davidson, J. M. (1987). Genital responses in noncopulators and rats with lesions in the medial preoptic area or midthoracic spinal cord. *Physiol. Behav.* **41**, 439–444.

Stefanick, M. L., Smith, E. R., and Davidson, J. M. (1983). Penile reflexes in intact rats following anesthetization of the penis and ejaculation. *Physiol. Behav.* **31**, 63–65.

Stefanick, M. L., Smith, E. R., Szumowski, D. A., and Davidson, J. M. (1985). Reproductive physiological behavior in the male rat following acute and chronic peripheral adrenergic depletion by guanethidine. *Pharmacol., Biochem. Behav.* **23**, 55–63.

Stephan, F. K., Valenstein, E. S., and Zucker, 1. (1971). Copulation and eating during electrical stimulation of the rat hypothalamus. *Physiol. Behav.* **7**, 587–593.

Stief, C. G., Noack, T., and Andersson, K. E. (1997). Signal transduction in cavernous smooth muscle. *World J. Urol.* **15**, 27–31.

Stoleru, S., Grégoire, M. C., Gerard, D., Decety, J., Lafarge, E., Cinotti, L., Lavenne, F., Le Bars, D., Vernet-Maury, E., Rada, H., Collet, C., Mazoyer, B., Forest, M. G., Magnin, F., Spira, A., and Comar, D. (1999). Neuroanatomical correlates of visually evoked sexual arousal in human males. *Arch. Sex. Behav.* **28**, 1–21.

Stoneham, M. D., Everitt, B. J., Hansen, S., Lightman, S. L., and Todd, K. (1985). Oxytocin and sexual behavior in the male rat and rabbit. *J. Endocrinol.* **107**, 97–106.

Succu, S., Spano, M. S., Melis, M. R., and Argiolas, A. (1998). Different effects of omega-conotoxin on penile erection, yawning and paraventricular nitric oxide in male rats. *Eur. J. Pharmacol.* **359**, 19–26.

Sugiura, K., Yoshimura, H., and Yokoyama, M. (1997). An animal model of copulatory disorder induced by social stress in male mice: Effects of apomorphine and L-dopa. *Psychopharmacology* **133**, 249–255.

Svare, B., Bartke, A., Doherty, P., Mason, I., Michael, S. D., and Smith, M. S. (1979). Hyperprolactinemia suppresses copulatory behavior in male rats and mice. *Biol. Reprod.* **21**, 529–535.

Swanson, L. W. (1976). An autoradiographic study of the efferent connections of the preoptic region in the rat. *J. Comp. Neurol.* **167**, 227–256.

Swanson, L. W., and McKellar, S. (1979). The distribution of oxytocin- and neurophysin-stained fibers in the spinal cord of the rat and monkey. *J. Comp. Neurol.* **188**, 87–106.

Swanson, L. W., and Petrovich, G. D. (1998). What is the amygdala? *Trends Neurosci.* **21**, 323–331.

Swanson, L. W., and Sawchenko, P. E. (1980). Paraventricular nucleus: A site for the integration of neuroendocrine and autonomic mechanisms. *Neuroendocrinology* **31**, 410–417.

Szczypka, M. S., Zhou, Q. Y., and Palmiter, R. D. (1998). Dopamine-stimulated sexual behavior is testosterone dependent in mice. *Behav. Neurosci.* **112**, 1229–1235.

Szechtman, H., Caggiula, A. R., and Wulkan, D. (1978). Preoptic knife cuts and sexual behavior in male rats. *Brain Res.* **150**, 569–591.

Tagliamonte, A., Fratta, W., Del Fiacco, M., and Gessa, G. L. (1974). Possible stimulatory role of brain dopamine in the copulatory behavior of male rats. *Pharmacol., Biochem. Behav.* **2**, 257–260.

Tallentire, D., McRae, G., Spedding, R., Clark, R., and Vickery, B. (1996). Modulation of sexual behaviour in the rat by a potent and selective α-2-adrenoceptor antagonist, delequamine (RS-15385-197). *Br. J. Pharmacol.* **118**, 63–72.

Tanaka, J., and Arnold, A. P. (1993b). An electrophysiological study of descending projections to the lumbar spinal cord in adult male rats. *Exp. Brain Res.* **96**, 117–124.

Tanco, S. A., Watson, N. V., and Gorzalka, B. B. (1994). Effects of 5-HT$_3$ agonists on reproductive behaviors in rats. *Psychopharmacology* **115**, 245–248.

Tang, Y., Rampin, O., Calas, A., Facchinetti, P., and Giuliano, F. (1998). Oxytocinergic and serotonergic innervation of identi-

fied lumbosacral nuclei controlling penile erection in the male rat. *Neuroscience* **82**, 241–254.

Tang, Y., Rampin, O., Giuliano, F., and Ugolini, G. (1999). Spinal and brain circuits to motoneurons of the bulbospongiosus muscle: Retrograde transneuronal tracing with rabies virus. *J. Comp. Neurol.* **414**, 167–192.

Tang, Y. P., and Sisk, C. L. (1991). Testosterone in MPOA elicits behavioral but not neuroendocrine responses in ferrets. *Brain Res. Bull.* **26**, 373–378.

Taylor, G., Bardgett, M., Csernansky, J., Early, T., Haller, J., Scherrer, J., and Womack, S. (1996). Male reproductive systems under chronic fluoxetine or trimipramine treatment. *Physiol. Behav.* **59**, 479–485.

Taylor, P., and Brown, J. H. (1999). Acetycholine. *In* "Basic Neurochemistry: Molecular, Cellular and Medical Aspects" (G. J. Siegel, B. W. Agranoff, R. W. Albers, S. K. Fisher, and M. D. Uhler, eds.), 6th ed., pp. 213–242. Lippincott-Raven, Philadelphia.

Thompson, M. L., McGill, T. E., McIntosh, S. M., and Manning, A. (1976). The effects of adrenalectomy on the sexual behavior of castrated and intact BDF$_1$ mice. *Anim. Behav.* **24**, 519–522.

Thor, D. H., and Flannelly, K. J. (1977). Social-olfactory experience and initiation of copulation in the virgin male rat. *Physiol. Behav.* **19**, 411–417.

Thor, D. H., and Flannelly, K. J. (1979). Copulation and inter-male aggression in rats. *J. Comp. Physiol. Psychol.* **93**, 223–228.

Tinbergen, N. (1951). "The Study of Instinct." Oxford University Press, Oxford.

Toner, J. P., and Adler, N. T. (1985). Potency of rat ejaculations varies with their order and with male age. *Physiol. Behav.* **35**, 113–115.

Toner, J. P., and Adler, N. T. (1986). The pre-ejaculatory behavior of male and female rats affects the number of sperm in the vagina and uterus. *Physiol. Behav.* **36**, 363–367.

Toner, J. P., Attas, A. I., and Adler, N. T. (1987). Transcervical sperm transport in the rat: The roles of pre-ejaculatory behavior and copulatory plug fit. *Physiol. Behav.* **39**, 371–375.

Truitt, W. A., and Coolen, L. M. (2001a). Ejaculation-induced neural activation in lumbar spinal cord of the rat. *Soc. Behav. Neuroendocrinol. Abst.* **5**, 352.

Truitt, W. A., and Coolen, L. M. (2001b). Targeted lesions of Substance P receptor cells in L3–4 lumbar spinal cord severely impair male ejaculatory behavior. *Soc. Neurosci Abst.* **31**, 352.

Tsutsui, Y., Shinoda, A., and Kondo, Y. (1994). Facilitation of copulatory behavior by pCPA treatments following stria terminalis transection but not medial amygdala lesion in the male rat. *Physiol. Behav.* **56**, 603–608.

Twiggs, D. G., Popolow, H. B., and Gerall, A. A. (1978). Medial preoptic lesions and male sexual behavior: Age and environmental interactions. *Science* **200**, 1414–1415.

Ueyama, T., Mizuno, N., Nomura, S., Konishi, A., Itoh, K., and Arakawa, H. (1984). Central distribution of afferent and efferent components of the pudendal nerve in cat. *J. Comp. Neurol.* **222**, 38–46.

Ueyama, T., Arakawa, H., and Mizuno, N. (1985). Contralateral termination of pudendal nerve fibers in the gracile nucleus of the rat. *Neurosci. Lett.* **62**, 113–117.

Ueyama, T., Arakawa, H., and Mizuno, N. (1987). Central distribution of efferent and afferent components of the pudendal nerve in rat. *Anat. Embryol.* **177**, 37–49.

Uphouse, L., Montanez, S., Richards-Hill, R., Caldarola-Pastuszka, M., and Droge, M. (1991). Effects of the 5-HT$_{1A}$ agonist, 8-OH-DPAT, on sexual behaviors of the proestrous rat. *Pharmacol., Biochem. Behav.* **39**, 635–640.

Vaccarino, F. J., and Rankin, J. (1989). Nucleus accumbens cholecystokinin (CCK) can either attenuate or potentiate amphetamine-induced locomotor activity: Evidence for rostral-caudal differences in accumbens function. *Behav. Neurosci.* **103**, 831–836.

Vagell, M. E., and McGinnis, M. Y. (1997). The role of aromatization in the restoration of male rat reproductive behavior. *J. Neuroendocrinol.* **9**, 415–421.

Vagell, M. E., and McGinnis, M. Y. (1998). The role of gonadal steroid receptor activation in the restoration of sociosexual behavior in adult male rats. *Horm. Behav.* **33**, 163–179.

Valcourt, R. J., and Sachs, B. D. (1979). Penile reflexes and copulatory behavior in male rats following lesions in the bed nucleus of the stria terminalis. *Brain Res. Bull.* **4**, 131–133.

Vale, J. R., Ray, D., and Vale, C. A. (1973). The interaction of genotype and exogenous neonatal androgen and estrogen: Sex behavior in female mice. *Dev. Psychobiol.* **6**, 319–327.

van de Poll, N. E., and van Dis, H. (1979). The effect of medial preoptic-anterior hypothalamic lesions on bisexual behavior of the male rat. *Brain Res. Bull.* **4**, 505–511.

van Dis, H., and Larsson, K. (1970). Seminal discharge following intracranial electrical stimulation. *Brain Res.* **23**, 381–386.

van Dis, H., and Larsson, K. (1971). Induction of sexual arousal in the castrated male rat by intracranial stimulation. *Physiol. Behav.* **6**, 85–86.

van Furth, W. R., and van Ree, J. M. (1994). Endogenous opioids and sexual motivation and performance during the light phase of the diurnal cycle. *Brain Res.* **636**, 175–179.

van Furth, W. R., and van Ree, J. M. (1996). Sexual motivation: Involvement of endogenous opioids in the ventral tegmental area. *Brain Res.* **729**, 20–28.

van Furth, W. R., Wolterink-Donselaar, I. G., and van Ree, J. M. (1994). Endogenous opioids are differentially involved in appetitive and consummatory aspects of sexual behavior of male rats. *Am. J. Physiol.* **266**, R606–R613.

van Furth, W. R., van Ernst, M. G., and van Ree, J. M. (1995a). Opioids and sexual behavior of male rats: Involvement of the medial preoptic area. *Behav. Neurosci.* **109**, 123–134.

van Furth, W. R., Wolterink, G., and van Ree, J. M. (1995b). Regulation of masculine sexual behavior: Involvement of brain opioids and dopamine. *Brain Res. Rev.* **21**, 162–184.

Vaughan, E., and Fisher, A. E. (1962). Male sexual behavior induced by intracranial electrical stimulation. *Science* **137**, 758–760.

Veening, J. G., and Coolen, L. M. (1998). Neural activation following sexual behavior in the male and female rat brain. *Behav. Brain Res.* **92**, 181–193.

Veening, J. G., Coolen, L. M., Murphy, A. Z., and Shipley, M. T. (1997). Ejaculation, but not pelvic nerve stimulation, activates galanin-IR pathways between lumbosacral spinal cord and subparafascicular thalamic nucleus, in the male rat. *Soc. Neurosci. Abstr.* **23** (No. 532.2), 1354.

Vega Matuszcyk, J., Larsson, K., and Eriksson, E. (1998). The selective serotonin reuptake inhibitor fluoxetine reduces sexual motivation in male rats. *Pharmacol., Biochem. Behav.* **60**, 527–532.

Verge, D., Daval, G., Patey, A., Gozlan, H., el Mestikawy, S., and Hamon, M. (1985). Presynaptic 5-HT autoreceptors on serotonergic cell bodies and/or dendrites but not terminals are of the 5-HT$_{1A}$ subtype. *Eur. J. Pharmacol.* **113**, 463–464.

Verma, S., Chhina, G. S., Kumar, M. V., and Singh, B. (1989). Inhibition of male sexual behavior by serotonin application in the medial preoptic area. *Physiol Behav.* **46**, 327–330.

Véronneau-Longueville, F., Rampin, O., Freund-Mercier, M. J., Tang, Y., Calas, A., Marson, L., McKenna, K. E., Stoeckel, M. E., Benoit, G., and Giuliano, F. (1999). Oxytocinergic innervation of automatic nuclei controlling penile erection in the rat. *Neuroscience* **93**, 1437–1447.

VinanderCaerols, C., Collado, P., Segovia, S., and Guillamon, A. (1998). Sex differences in the posteromedial cortical nucleus of the amygdala in the rat. *NeuroReport* **9**, 2653–2656.

von Kugelgen, I., and Starke, K. (1991). Release of noradrenaline and ATP by electrical stimulation and nicotine in guinea pig *vas deferens. Naunyn-Schmiedeberg's Arch. Pharmacol.* **344**, 419–429.

Wagner, C. K., and Clemens, L. G. (1991). Projections of the paraventricular nucleus of the hypothalamus to the sexually dimorphic lumbosacral region of the spinal cord. *Brain Res.* **539**, 254–262.

Wagner, C. K., and Clemens, L. G. (1993). Neurophysin-containing pathway from the paraventricular nucleus of the hypothalamus to a sexually dimorphic motor nucleus in lumbar spinal cord. *J. Comp. Neurol.* **336**, 106–116.

Wagner, C. K., Sisk, C. L., and Clemens, L. G. (1993). Neurons in the paraventricular nucleus of the hypothalamus that project to the sexually dimorphic lower lumbar spinal cord concentrate 3H-estradiol in the male rat. *J. Neuroendocrinol.* **5**, 545–551.

Waldinger, M. D., Hengeveld, M. W., Zwinderman, A. H., and Olivier, B. (1998). Effects of SSRI antidepressants on ejaculation: A double-blind, randomized, placebo-controlled study with fluoxetine, fluvoxamine, paroxetine, and sertraline. *J. Clin. Psychopharmacol.* **18**, 274–281.

Wallach, S. J. R., and Hart, B. L. (1983). The role of the striated penile muscles of the male rat in seminal plug dislodgement and deposition. *Physiol. Behav.* **31**, 815–821.

Wallen, K., and Schneider, J. E. (2000). "Reproduction in Context: Social and Environmental Influences on Reproduction." MIT Press, Cambridge, MA.

Wang, C. T., Huang, R. L., Tai, M. Y., Tsai, Y. F., and Peng, M. T. (1995). Dopamine release in the nucleus accumbens during sexual behavior in prenatally stressed adult male rats. *Neurosci. Lett.* **200**, 29–32.

Wang, L., and Hull, E. M. (1980). Tail pinch induces sexual behavior in olfactory bulbectomized male rats. *Physiol. Behav.* **24**, 211–215.

Wang, Z. (1995). Species differences in the vasopressin-immunoreactive pathways in the bed nucleus of the stria terminalis and medial amygdaloid nucleus in prairie voles (*Microtus ochrogaster*) and meadow voles (*Microtus pennsylvanicus*). *Behav. Neurosci.* **109**, 305–311.

Wang, Z., Smith, W., Major, D. E., and De Vries, G. J. (1994). Sex and species differences in the effects of cohabitation on vasopressin messenger RNA expression in the bed nucleus of the stria terminalis in prairie voles (*Microtus ochrogaster*) and meadow voles (*Microtus pennsylvanicus*). *Brain Res.* **650**, 212–218.

Wang, Z., Hulihan, T. J., and Insel, T. R. (1997). Sexual and social experience is associated with different patterns of behavior and neural activation in male prairie voles. *Brain Res.* **767**, 321–332.

Ward, I. L., and Weisz, J. (1980). Maternal stress alters plasma testosterone in fetal males. *Science* **207**, 328–329.

Ward, I. L., Ward, O. B., French, J. A., Hendricks, S. E., Mehan, D., and Winn, R. J. (1996). Prenatal alcohol and stress interact to attenuate ejaculatory behavior, but not serum testosterone or LH in adult male rats. *Behav. Neurosi.* **110**, 1469–1477.

Warembourg, M., Leroy, D., and Jolivet, A. (1999). Nitric oxide synthase in the guinea pig preoptic area and hypothalamus: Distribution, effect of estrogen, and colocalization with progesterone receptor. *J. Comp. Neurol.* **407**, 207–227.

Warner, R. K., Thompson, J. T., Markowski, V. P., Loucks, J. A., Bazzett, T. J., Eaton, R. C., and Hull, E. M. (1991). Microinjection of the dopamine antagonist cis-flupenthixol into the MPOA impairs copulation, penile reflexes and sexual motivation in male rats. *Brain Res.* **540**, 177–182.

Watson, J. T., and Adkins-Regan, E. (1989). Activation of sexual behavior by implantation of testosterone propionate and estradiol benzoate into the preoptic area of the male Japanese quail (*Coturnix japonica*). *Horm. Behav.* **23**, 251–268.

Watters, J. J., and Dorsa, D. M. (1998). Transcriptional effects of estrogen on neuronal neurotensin gene expression involve cAMP/protein kinase A-dependent signaling mechanisms. *J. Neurosci.* **18**, 6672–6680.

Weber, R. F. A., Ooms, M. P., and Vreeburg, J. T. M. (1982). Effects of a prolactin-secreting tumour on copulatory behavior in male rats. *J. Endocrinol.* **93**, 223–229.

Wee, B. E., and Clemens, L. G. (1987). Characteristics of the spinal nucleus of the bulbocavernosus are influenced by genotype in the house mouse. *Brain Res.* **424**, 305–310.

Wee, B. E., Weaver, D. R., and Clemens, L. G. (1988). Hormonal restoration of masculine sexual behavior in long-term castrated B6D2F1 mice. *Physiol. Behav.* **42**, 77–82.

Wells, A. B., and Coolen, L. M. (2001). Lumbar spinal cord efferents directly contact thalamic neurons that project to MPOA or BNST. *Soc. Behav. Neuroendocrinol. Abst.* **5**, 354.

Wenkstern, D., Pfaus, J. G., and Fibiger, H. C. (1993). Dopamine transmission increases in the nucleus accumbens of male rats during their first exposure to sexually receptive female rats. *Brain Res.* **618**, 41–46.

Wersinger, S. R., and Rissman, E. F. (2000). Dopamine activates masculine sexual behavior independent of the estrogen receptor alpha . *J. Neurosci.* **20**, 4248–4254.

Wersinger, S. R., Baum, M. J., and Erskine, M. S. (1993). Mating-induced FOS-like immunoreactivity in the rat forebrain, a sex comparison and a dimorphic effect of pelvic nerve transection. *J. Neuroendocrinol.* **5**, 557–568.

Wersinger, S. R., Sannen, K., Villalba, C., Lubahn, D. B., Rissman, E. F., and De Vries, G. J. (1997). Masculine sexual behavior is disrupted in male and female mice lacking a functional estrogen receptor alpha gene. *Horm. Behav.* **32**, 176–183.

Whalen, R. E. (1963). Sexual behavior of cats. *Behaviour* **20**, 321–342.

Whalen, R. E., and Luttge, W. G. (1971). Testosterone, androstenedione and dihydrotestosterone: Effects on mating behavior of male rats. *Horm. Behav.* **2**, 117–125.

Wheeler, J. M., and Crews, D. (1978). The role of the anterior hypothalamus-preoptic area in the regulation of male reproductive behavior in the lizard, *Anolis carolinensis*: Lesion studies. *Horm. Behav.* **11**, 42–60.

White, N. R., Cagiano, R., Moises, A. U., and Barfield, R. J. (1990). Changes in mating vocalizations over the ejaculatory series in rats (*Rattus norvegicus*). *J. Comp. Psychol.* **104**, 255–262.

Whitney, G., Coble, J. R., Stockton, M. D., and Tilson, E. F. (1973). Ultrasonic emissions: Do they facilitate courtship in mice? *J. Comp. Physiol. Psychol.* **84**, 445–452.

Wiesenfeld-Hallin, Z., and Södersten, P. (1984). Spinal opiates affect sexual behavior in rats. *Nature (London)* **309**, 257–258.

Wilbert, D. M., Griffin, J. E., and Wilson, J. D. (1983). Characterization of the cytosol androgen receptor of the human prostate. *J. Clin. Endocrinol. Metab.* **56**, 113–120.

Wilhelmsson, M., and Larsson, K. (1973). The development of sexual behavior in anosmic male rats reared under various social conditions. *Physiol. Behav.* **11**, 227–232.

Willis, E. A., Ottesen, B., Wagner, G., Sundler, F., and Fahrenkrug, J. (1981). Vasoactive intestinal polypeptide (VIP) as a possible neurotransmitter involved in penile erection. *Acta Physiol. Scand.* **113**, 545–547.

Willis, E. A., Ottesen, B., Wagner, G., Sundler, F., and Fahrenkrug, J. (1983). Vasoactive intestinal polypeptide (VIP) as a putative neurotransmitter in penile erection. *Life Sci.* **33**, 383–391.

Wilson, D. B., and Wilson, W. J. (1978). "Human Anatomy." Oxford University Press, New York.

Winans, S. S., and Powers, J. B. (1974). Neonatal and two-stage olfactory bulbectomy: Effects on male hamster sexual behavior. *Behav. Biol.* **10**, 461–471.

Winans, S. S., and Powers, J. B. (1977). Olfactory and vomeronasal deafferentation of male hamsters: Histological and behavioral analyses. *Brain Res.* **126**, 325–344.

Winslow, J. T., and Insel, T. R. (1991). Social status in pairs of male squirrel monkeys determines the behavioral response to central oxytocin administration. *J. Neurosci.* **24**, 761–765.

Witt, D. M. (1995). Oxytocin and rodent sociosexual responses: From behavior to gene expression. *Neurosci. Biobehav. Rev.* **19**, 315–324.

Witt, D. M., and Insel, T. R. (1994). Increased Fos expression in oxytocin neurons following masculine sexual behavior. *J. Neuroendocrinol.* **6**, 13–18.

Witt, D. M., Young, L. J., and Crews, D. (1994). Progesterone and sexual behavior in males. *Psychoneuroendocrinology* **19**, 553–562.

Witt, D. M., Young, L. J., and Crews, D. (1995). Progesterone modulation of androgen-dependent sexual behavior in male rats. *Physiol. Behav.* **57**, 307–313.

Wood, R. I. (1996). Estradiol, but not dihydrotestosterone, in the medial amygdala facilitates male hamster sex behavior. *Physiol. Behav.* **59**, 833–841.

Wood, R. I. (1997). Thinking about networks in the control of male hamster sexual behavior. *Horm. Behav.* **32**, 40–45.

Wood, R. I., and Coolen, L. M. (1997). Integration of chemosensory and hormonal cues is essential for sexual behavior in the male Syrian hamster: Role of the medial amygdaloid nucleus. *Neuroscience* **78**, 1027–1035.

Wood, R. I., and Newman, S. W. (1993). Mating activates androgen receptor-containing neurons in the chemosensory pathways of the male Syrian hamster brain. *Brain Res.* **614**, 65–77.

Wood, R. I., and Newman, S. W. (1995a). Androgen and estrogen receptors coexist within individual neurons in the brain of the Syrian hamster. *Neuroendocrinology* **62**, 487–497.

Wood, R. I., and Newman, S. W. (1995b). Hormonal influence on neurons of the mating behavior pathway in male hamsters. *In* "Neurobiological Effects of Sex Steroid Hormones" (P. E. Micevych and R. P. Hammer, Jr., eds.), pp. 3–39. Cambridge University Press, New York.

Wood, R. I., and Newman, S. W. (1995c). Integration of chemosensory and hormonal cues is essential for mating in the male Syrian hamster. *J. Neurosci.* **15**, 7261–7269.

Wood, R. I., Brabec, R. K., Swain, J. M., and Newman, S. W. (1992). Androgen and estrogen receptor concentrating neurons in chemosensory pathways of the male Syrian hamster brain. *Brain Res.* **596**, 89–98.

Woolley, S. C., Sakata, J. T., Gupta, A., and Crews, D. (2001). Evolutionary changes in dopaminergic modulation of courtship behaviors in *Cnemidophorus* whiptail lizards. *Horm. Behav.* **40**, 483–489.

Wu, F. M., and Noble, R. G. (1986). Opiate antagonists and copulatory behavior of male hamsters. *Physiol. Behav.* **38**, 817–825.

Xiao, L., and Becker, J. B. (1998). Effects of estrogen agonists on amphetamine-stimulated striatal dopamine release. *Synapse* **29**, 379–391.

Yahr, P. (1995). Neural circuitry for the hormonal control of male sexual behavior. *In* "Neurobiological Effects of Sex Steroid Hormones" (P. E. Micevych and R. P. Hammer, Jr., eds.), pp. 40–56. Cambridge University Press, New York.

Yahr, P., and Gregory, J. E. (1993). The medial and lateral cell groups of the sexually dimorphic area of the gerbil hypothalamus are essential for male sex behavior and act via separate pathways. *Brain Res.* **631**, 287–296.

Yahr, P., and Stephens, D. R. (1987). Hormonal control of sexual and scent marking behaviors of male gerbils in relation to the sexually dimorphic area of the hypothalamus. *Horm. Behav.* **21**, 331–346.

Yahr, P., and Ulibarri, C. (1987). Polyadenylated and nonadenylated messenger RNA and androgen control of sexual behavior and scent marking in male gerbils. *Horm. Behav.* **21**, 53–64.

Yahr, P., Commins, D., Jackson, J. C., and Newman, A. (1982). Independent control of sexual and scent marking behaviors of male gerbils by cells in or near the medial preoptic area. *Horm. Behav.* **16**, 304–322.

Yahr, P., Finn, P. D., Hoffman, N. W., and Sayag N. (1994). Sexually dimorphic cell groups in the medial preoptic area that are essential for male sex behavior and the neural pathways needed for their effects. *Psychoneuroendocrinology* **19**, 463–470.

Yamada, K., Emson, P., and Hokfelt, T. (1996). Immunohistochemical mapping of nitric oxide synthase in the rat hypothalamus and colocalization with neuropeptides. *J. Chem. Neuroanat.* **10**, 295–316.

Yamada, Y. (1979). The effects of testosterone on unit activity in rat hypothalamus and septum. *Brain Res.* **172**, 165–169.

Yasui, Y., Saper, C. B., and Cechetto, D. F. (1991). Calcitonin gene-related peptide (CGRP) immunoreactive projections from the thalamus to the striatum and amygdala in the rat. *J. Comp. Neurol.* **308**, 293–310.

Yells, D. P., Hendricks, S. E., and Prendergast, M. A. (1992). Lesions of the nucleus paragigantocellularis effects on mating behavior. in male rats. *Brain Res.* **596**, 73–79.

Yells, D. P., Prendergast, M. A., Hendricks, S. E., and Miller, M. E. (1995). Monoaminergic influences on temporal patterning of sexual behavior in male rats. *Physiol. Behav.* **58**, 847–852.

Yilmaz, U., Tatlisen, A., Turan, H., Arman, F., and Ekmekcioglu, O. (1999). The effects of fluoxetine on several neurophysiological variables in patients with premature ejaculation . *J. Urol.* **161**, 107–111.

Yokosuka, M., and Hayashi, S., (1996). Co-localization of neuronal nitric oxide synthase and androgen receptor immunoreactivity in the premammillary nucleus in rats. *Neurosci. Res.* **26**, 309–314.

Yokosuka, M., Prins, G. S., and Hayashi, S. (1997). Colocalization of androgen receptor and nitric oxide synthase in the ventral premammillary nucleus of the newborn rat: An immunohistochemical study. *Dev. Brain Res.* **99**, 226–233.

Yokosuka, M., Matsuoka, M., Ohtani-Kaneko, R., Iigo, M., Hara, M., Hirata, K., and Ichikawa, M. (1999). Female-soiled bedding induced *c-fos* immunoreactivity in the ventral part of the premammillary nucleus (PMv) of the male mouse. *Physiol. Behav.* **68**, 257–261.

Young, S. T., Porrino, L. J., and Iadarola, M. J. (1991). Cocaine induces striatal *c-fos* immunoreactive proteins via dopaminergic D_1 receptors. *Proc. Natl. Acad. Sci. U.S.A.* **88**, 1291–1295.

Young, W. C. (1969). Psychobiology of sexual behavior in the guinea pig. *Adv. Study Behav.* **2**, 1–110.

Zarrindast, M. R., Shokravi, S., and Samini, M. (1992). Opposite influences of dopaminergic receptor subtypes on penile erection. *Gen. Pharmacol.* **23**, 671–675.

Zarrindast, M. R., Mamanpush, S. M., and Rashidy-Pour, A. (1994). Morphine inhibits dopaminergic and cholinergic induced ejaculation in rats . *Gen. Pharmacol.* **25**, 803–808.

Zumpe, D., Clancy, A. N., Bonsall, R. W., and Michael, R. P. (1996). Behavioral responses to Depo-Provera, Fadrozole, and estradiol in castrated, testosterone-treated cynomolgus monkeys (*Macaca fascicularis*): The involvement of progestin receptors. *Physiol. Behav.* **60**, 531–540.

Zumpe, D., Clancy, A. N., and Michael, R. P. (1997). Effects of progesterone on the sexual behavior of castrated, testosterone-treated male cynomolgus monkeys (*Macaca fascicularis*). *Physiol. Behav.* **62**, 61–67.

Zvara, P., Sioufi, R., Schipper, H. M., Begin, L. R., and Brock, G. B. (1995). Nitric oxide mediated erectile activity is a testosterone dependent event: A rat erection model. *Int. J. Impotence Res.* **7**, 209–219.

2

Feminine Sexual Behavior: Cellular Integration of Hormonal and Afferent Information in the Rodent Forebrain

Jeffrey D. Blaustein
Center for Neuroendocrine Studies
University of Massachusetts
Amherst, Massachusetts 01003-9271

Mary S. Erskine
Department of Biology
Boston University
Boston, Massachusetts 02215

*F*eminine sexual behavior has been used extensively as a model system for understanding the mechanisms by which hormonal and neural signals interact at the cellular level to modulate behavior. Synthesis of much of the early behavioral and neuroendocrine work on this system with new cellular and molecular findings suggests that a fruitful direction to pursue is to examine how behavioral, hormonal, and sensory factors interact to modulate changes in the suite of female sexual behaviors. The neuronal integration of hormonal and neural mechanisms is a major contributor to the control of this behavior. This review offers a revised, theoretical framework with which to approach the study of feminine sexual behavior. Although some of the deficiencies in our knowledge of how the hormonal and mating stimuli are integrated in the brain will be discussed, so too will results of experiments showing the substantial progress made in understanding mechanisms of steroid hormone action, as well as integration of neural input with steroid hormone receptor processes. Collectively these studies are beginning to demonstrate the ways that hormonal and afferent, neuronal sensory inputs are orchestrated to alter brain and behavior.

I. INTRODUCTION: NEW PERSPECTIVES AND APPROACHES

A. The Neuroethological Approach

In the search for explanations to the neurobiological and endocrine bases for behavior, the field has been enormously enriched by the studies carried out on sexual behavior in rodent species. With these model systems, many of the components of sexual behavior are readily observable in the lab, and the simplicity of the behaviors observed make the task of accurate measurement relatively straightforward. Studies examining feminine sexual behavior, for instance, relied historically on the lordosis reflex as a measure of sexual behavior, and the occurrence or intensity of the lordosis response has been particularly useful for questions relating to the hormonal basis of reproductive behavior. The description of feminine sexual behavior using the lordosis response allows us to measure the female's responsiveness to the flank, perineal, and vaginocervical stimuli provided by the male and to explore the cellular and molecular mechanisms that underpin the expression of estrous responsiveness in the brain and periphery. However, one limitation to this approach is that because lordosis is reflexively triggered by stimuli provided by the male, it is difficult to examine motivational and performance aspects of sexual behavior. While data on readiness and willingness to mate are easily extrapolated from data collected on masculine sexual performance, they are not measurable in females via the lordosis measure. The corollary problem is that focusing on lordosis ignores the complexity of behavioral patterns that make up sexual behavior in species commonly used in the lab for mechanistic studies. We know that in the wild or in naturalistic conditions, females display a wide diversity of behaviors to initiate and sustain sexual behavior. Each behavioral component ultimately influences production of offspring. These behaviors are therefore likely to have been molded by evolution and to be controlled by the nervous system in ways that are unique to the female of each species. The use of lordosis as a simple laboratory measure of sexual behavior has been useful in addressing many questions regarding the facilitation and persistence of sexual responsiveness; however, the approach and withdrawal, orientation, and solicitational behaviors displayed by the female during mating may be equally important for understanding the neural basis of behavior. As studies of brain and behavior become more sophisticated, it has become clear that our understanding of the neurobiological mechanisms controlling behavior will be significantly deepened if more naturalistic aspects of the behavior are incorporated into our studies.

A conceptual framework for study of the complexities of behavior is supplied by the interdisciplinary field of neuroethology, in which naturally occurring patterns of behavior are used as a basis for understanding how the nervous system functions. This approach can be useful for examining questions of how the nervous system filters and localizes information about the environment, how it controls motoric aspects of behavior, how it initiates the expression of behaviors, and how it coordinates complex acts. This perspective allows the interdigitation of reductionist questions which can be explored at the cellular and molecular levels with more inclusive questions about the brain's control of behavior. For instance, ethologists have shown that for a particular species, a sign stimulus can trigger a fixed action pattern by perceptual mechanisms that identify and isolate the relevant stimulus from all others. That is, the expression of particular behaviors is dependent upon species-specific filtering of sensory information by the nervous system. Understanding the particular stimuli that trigger or facilitate behavioral expression will direct our attention to aspects of the nervous system that are likely to control that behavior.

B. Levels of Analysis Used to Understand Hormonal Regulation and Functional Consequences of Female Mating Behavior

A major challenge for experimenters looking at the neural and endocrine control of behavior is to bring together and integrate several levels of analysis in concert to demonstrate anatomical, biochemical, and physiological continuity of hypothesized mechanisms. Studies directed at cellular, molecular, and system levels can be used to address questions of locus of action, mechanism of action, and functional consequences of perturbations in neural and behavioral function. At the cellular level, biochemical binding assays and immunocytochemical or immunohistochemical methods can be used to localize the presence of synthesizing enzymes for neurotransmitters, steroid and neurotransmitter receptors, neuropeptides, and neuropeptide mRNA to specific sets of neurons or glia; co-labeling and coexpression of substances within populations of neurons can suggest possible interactions among different neurons and among substances within those neurons. Retrograde, anterograde, and transsynaptic tracers can be used to determine where and how interactions between the populations of neurons occur. These studies can be carried out on the whole animal *in vivo,* or they can be carried out with slice preparations, explants, cell suspensions, or single-cell recording. At the subcellular level, studies of hormone-behavior mechanisms can be carried out by using biochemical assays for measures of metabolic and enzymatic activity. In addition, molecular mechanisms such as gene transcription and translation can be explored as can pre- and postsynaptic mechanisms of signal transduction. Pharmacological and hormonal manipulations can be used to evaluate the importance of synthesis, transport, storage, and receptor binding in the normal and abnormal functions of particular cellular systems or neural circuits. At the systems level, we identify the behavior, learn when and under which conditions it is manifest, study how environmental and social factors alter its expression, and develop hypotheses about brain-behavior relationships that can be tested at the cellular and subcellular levels. We also can use this level of analysis to cross-check our assumptions about how the behavior is generated and regulated at the cellular and molecular levels. Experimental results at each of these levels need to be integrated for a comprehensive understanding of how the nervous system works to modify the expression of a behavior.

II. ELEMENTS OF FEMININE SEXUAL BEHAVIOR

Sexual behavior in both sexes comprises a complex series of motoric events that ensure successful transfer of sperm from the male to the female reproductive tract. Sexual behavior in the female includes postural stances and adjustments required for vaginal intromission by the male and a number of additional behaviors that modulate the occurrence and timing of sexual behavior. The former behaviors are relatively stereotyped and reflexive, while the latter behaviors are integral to the initiation and sequencing of behavioral events during the copulatory session. Practically speaking, the appropriate measure of sexual behavior chosen for any given experiment depends upon the questions being asked. On one hand, if the question centers around whether a given female is displaying estrous behavior, a simple measure of the lordosis posture suffices. On the other hand, a composite of the several solicitational behaviors displayed by the female can be used to ascertain an overall level of sexual readiness as an estimate of the female's motivation to mate. Or, if one wishes to examine the effects of female sexual expression on neuroendocrine function and reproductive success, behaviors involved in induction of pregnancy and facilitation of sperm transport can be obtained. Finally, single measures of different components of sexual behavior can be useful for experimental analysis of neural and endocrine mechanisms controlling their individual expression. As noted above, the experimental measures of female sexual behavior are easily obtained and unambiguous. However, female rats' sexual behavior is far from perfunctory or haphazard, and it is clear that the expression of all of the components of sexual behavior facilitate a complex interplay between females and

males that serves to maximize the likelihood of fertilization in the face of individual differences in sexual arousal or performance.

In 1976, Beach proposed that female sexual behavior comprises three basic elements: attractivity, proceptivity, and receptivity. *Attractivity* was defined as a "female's value as a sexual stimulus" (p 107) and included behavioral as well as nonbehavioral components such as olfactory cues that stimulated the male to engage in sexual behavior with the female. Attractivity, by definition, measured the behavioral responses of the male to the female. *Proceptivity* included a number of solicitational behaviors that were followed by increases in sexual mounts by males. Beach (1976) suggested that these behaviors involved assumption of "female initiative" in sexual interactions with males (Beach, 1976). Therefore, these behaviors in some way reflected the appetitive aspect of sexual behavior and implied a motivation to mate. *Receptivity*, measured largely by the lordosis response, was defined as the behavioral responses by the female to sexual contact with males that resulted in successful insemination. This classic paper acknowledged the multiple components of feminine sexual behavior and the key role that sequential male-female interactions play in the sequencing of sexual behavior. For many years, attractivity, proceptivity, and receptivity provided an adequate structural framework for studying female sexual behavior. More recently, however, recognition of additional behavioral elements of sexual behavior and the recognition that the female is an active rather than a passive participant in male-female sexual interactions has called for a revision of this framework. Below, we present three functional components of female sexual behavior which, though conceptual and not without overlap, are useful in studying the neural and endocrine control of female sexual responsiveness.

A. Copulatory Behaviors

Copulatory behaviors are behaviors that result in successful transfer of sperm from the male to the female. This term is used instead of Beach's "receptivity," because it connotes an active participation by the female, and because it is complementary to the term as it is applied to male sexual behavior. In response to flank and perineal somatosensory stimulation received from the male during copulatory mounts, the female rat displays lordosis, a posture that positions the female genitalia to allow penile intromission by the male. During lordosis, the female becomes immobile and shows extension of the rear legs, dorsiflexion of the spine, elevation of the head, and tail deviation (Pfaff *et al.,* 1973). Additional copulatory behaviors include postural adjustments that occur during lordosis and that are required to facilitate proper orientation and penile insertion by the male. These postural adjustments occur in response to stimulation of the receptive field of the pudendal nerve (Adler *et al.,* 1977) during lordosis.

During estrus, lordosis is reliably induced by the somatosensory stimulation provided by the male copulatory mount and can, in rare instances at least in the rat, be expressed spontaneously in the presence of the male. Lordosis can also be elicited by artificial vaginocervical stimulation (VCS) in anestrous animals (Komisaruk and Diakow, 1973). Both the occurrence of and the magnitude of spinal dorsiflexion have been used as measures of female sexual responsiveness. The proportion of lordosis responses observed in response to a given number of mounts from the male expressed as a percentage (lordosis quotient, LQ; Whalen, 1974) or as a ratio (lordosis to mount ratio, L/M (Dudley *et al.,* 1992) is a measure of the basic level of sexual receptivity. In addition, the lordosis rating (LR), defined as the average intensity of each spinal dorsiflexion based on a four-point scale (0 = no spine dorsiflexion, 1 = marginal dorsiflexion, 2 = normal moderate dorsiflexion with some head or nose elevation, 3 = exaggerated dorsiflexion and head and rump elevation; Hardy and DeBold, 1972), is used to measure the magnitude of the lordosis response. However, there is generally little heuristic value in comparing the LQ and LR measures, as they are so intimately linked that they highly covary under diverse experimental conditions. This is due in part to the reflexive nature of the lordosis response, which is often expressed as a full-blown posture triggered by the perineal and flank stimulation provided by the male (see Pfaff, 1980). In rats, the display of lordosis occurs briefly (approximately 0.5–1.5 sec; Pfaff *et al.,* 1973) beginning at the time of the male mount, while in hamsters, the lordosis posture, once induced, is maintained for seconds to minutes after the male has dismounted, and in guinea pigs, it is held for 10–20 seconds (Goy and Young, 1957). Substantial work

by Pfaff and colleagues (Pfaff, 1980) has elucidated the neural circuit underlying the expression of lordosis in rats, and lordosis has been used as the dependent measure almost exclusively in mechanistic studies of female sexual behavior.

B. Paracopulatory Behaviors

Paracopulatory behaviors are species-typical behaviors displayed by the female that arouse the male and stimulate him to mount. These behaviors have variously been termed proceptive (Beach, 1976), precopulatory (Madlafousek and Hlinak, 1977), or solicitation (Erskine, 1985) behaviors. Paracopulatory behaviors exhibited spontaneously by estrous female rats during the normal course of mating include hopping, darting, and ear wiggling (Beach, 1976; Madlafousek and Hlinak, 1977), a posing or presenting posture (Emery and Moss, 1984a,b), a rapid sequence of approach toward, orientation to and withdrawal from proximity to a sexually active male (McClintock and Adler, 1978), and production of ultrasonic vocalizations known to stimulate mating by the male (White and Barfield, 1989). We propose the term *paracopulatory* behaviors to obviate the assumptions inherent in the older terms about the female's sexual motivation to initiate mating, and because it is not clear whether these behaviors are exclusively solicitational. All these behaviors are expressed prior to and between mounts and occur repetitively during the mating session. The frequency and rate with which these behaviors are expressed are altered by ovarian steroids, by the rate at which the male copulates with the female, and by the specific experimental conditions under which mating is observed (Erskine, 1985).

C. Progestative Behaviors

An additional component of female sexual behavior includes behaviors that maximize the likelihood that pregnancy will occur, which we term *progestative* behaviors. This component includes behaviors separate from copulatory behaviors that allow the male to deposit sperm in the female's reproductive tract but include behaviors that otherwise facilitate or initiate pregnancy. These behaviors regulate the frequency and timing of intromissions and ejaculations from males and include the female's selection of males that are ready to ejaculate (McClintock *et al.*, 1982a), the females' post-ejaculatory interval that enhances sperm transport by preventing rapid displacement of the copulatory plug deposited by the male (McClintock *et al.*, 1982b), and the female's pacing of sexual stimulation, through intermittent approaches toward and withdrawals from the male (Bermant, 1961; Erskine, 1985; Gilman and Hitt, 1978; Krieger *et al.*, 1976; Peirce and Nuttall, 1961). Like the other components of feminine sexual behavior, these patterns of behavior occur throughout mating. They involve progressive short-term behavioral adjustments in the patterning of ongoing sexual contacts with males, which ensure optimal reproductive success.

The recognition that female rat sexual behavior contained elements through which females regulated this pattern of male contact came from observations of feminine sexual behavior under seminatural conditions by McClintock and her colleagues (McClintock and Adler, 1978; McClintock and Anisko, 1982; McClintock *et al.*, 1982a) and under laboratory conditions by several other investigators (Bermant, 1961; Kreiger *et al.*, 1976; Peirce and Nuttall, 1961). Each progestative behavior uncovered to date has as a requirement for its expression a large test chamber or living environment in which the female can avoid contacts with either the single male stimulus animal or an individual male in a multimale-multifemale social grouping. Under the latter circumstances, McClintock *et al.* (1982a) have shown that estrous females preferentially copulate with males that are ready to ejaculate. This increases the overall number of sperm that are transferred to the female by the several males with whom she mates during estrus and effects sperm competition among males (McClintock *et al.*, 1982a). In addition, the ejaculatory stimulus has been demonstrated to be more effective than intromissions or mounts-without-intromission in initiating the vaginocervically induced neuroendocrine changes required for pregnancy (O'Hanlon and Sachs, 1986). This suggests that the female's active selection of imminently ejaculatory males acts to ensure that sufficient VCS is received to induce these changes. The postejaculatory interval that is enforced by the female (as opposed to that enforced by the male; Beach and Whalen, 1959) also is progestative insofar as this interval is long enough to ensure that maximum transport of sperm through the uterine cervix into the uterus has occurred (Adler and Zoloth, 1970).

The most striking of the progestative behaviors include those by which the female controls the timing of the repeated intromissions that she receives from the male during copulation. This control has been observed under seminatural conditions and under experimental conditions that allow the female to escape from the male between intromissions (Gilman and Hitt, 1978; Emery and Moss, 1984b; Erskine, 1985, 1989; Pfaus *et al.*, 1999). During a mating sequence, the female receives a number of mounts without intromission (mounts), mounts with penile intromission (intromissions), and several ejaculations from the male. In addition, the female rat exhibits patterns of approach toward and withdrawal from the male that occur in response to individual copulatory stimuli (mounts, intromissions, and ejaculations) and that serve to regulate, or pace, the types and amounts of VCS received during mating (Erskine, 1989; McClintock *et al.*, 1982a; Bermant, 1961; Gilman *et al.*, 1979; Krieger *et al.*, 1976; Peirce and Nuttall, 1961; McClintock and Anisko, 1982). Under appropriate laboratory conditions, females actively pace their contacts with males by withdrawing to a neutral cage between mounts, intromissions, and ejaculations and approaching the male for renewed copulation at predictable intervals (Bermant, 1961; Gilman *et al.*, 1979; Krieger *et al.*, 1976; Peirce and Nuttall, 1961; McClintock and Anisko, 1982; Frye and Erskine, 1990; Bermant and Westbrook, 1966; Erskine, 1989; Bermant *et al.*, 1969). Females mated in small or undivided test arenas are unable to avoid contact with the male and thus receive nonpaced coital stimulation. The major consequence of paced mating for the female is that sexual contacts with males occur at a slower rate than they do during nonpaced mating tests.

The hallmark of pacing behavior is the differential patterns of approach and withdrawal that occur in response to changes in the intensity of sexual stimulation. Stronger effects on both approaches and withdrawals are seen as the intensity of the coital stimulus increases. As shown in Fig. 1 top, females tested for feminine sexual behavior in an apparatus in which the male is restricted to one compartment withdraw from the chamber containing the male more frequently (percentage exits) after receiving an ejaculation than after receiving an intromission, and withdraw least frequently after receiving a mount-without-intromission

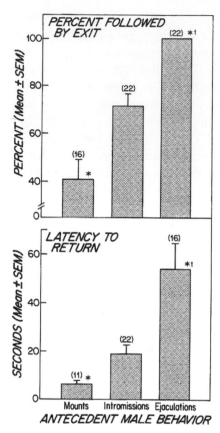

FIGURE 1 Data illustrating the pacing of coital contacts by female rats in an escape-reentry apparatus. (*Top*) The percentage of exits from and (*bottom*) the latency to return to the male compartment following mounts, intromissions, and ejaculations. $*p < 0.001$, significantly different from intromissions. $†p < 0.001$, significantly different from mounts. (From Erskine, 1985.)

(mount). In addition, females actively control the timing of copulatory stimuli by altering the rate at which they return to the male compartment after receiving a mount, intromission, or ejaculation (return latency in seconds; Fig. 1, bottom). Therefore, the rate at which they receive mounts, intromissions, and ejaculations from males is in inverse proportion to the intensity of the specific stimulus, i.e. the interval between an ejaculation and the first succeeding copulatory mount is greater than that following an intromission, and that, in turn, is greater than the interval following a mount (Erskine, 1985). As discussed below, the temporal patterning of VCS that the female receives during mating is a critical determinant of whether the neuroendocrine responses required for pregnancy occur (Erskine, 1995;

Gilman *et al.,* 1979), and pacing behaviors influence the likelihood that sufficient luteal progesterone is secreted for successful implantation. Thus, pacing behavior directly facilitates pregnancy initiation by altering the timing of the coital stimuli received by the estrous female.

III. EXPERIMENTAL MEASURES OF SEXUAL MOTIVATION

In contrast to studies in the male in which the latency to initiate mating is an easily derived measure of masculine sexual motivation, study of female sexual motivation is complicated by the fact that the female displays a varied repertoire of paracopulatory behaviors, only some of which could be linked to a motivation to mate. Naturally occurring behaviors, such as hopping, darting, and ear wiggling, have been used as indices of feminine sexual motivation, because these behaviors serve to stimulate or solicit sexual attention from males (see Erskine, 1985). Likewise, the component of pacing behavior in which the female returns to the male for renewed copulation has been proposed as a measure of sexual readiness (Erskine, 1985). However, the fact that the expression of these behaviors changes over the course of a single mating session makes them problematic for use as unified measures of motivation. Other behaviors expressed under several experimental conditions have furnished measures of female sexual motivation, and these are discussed below.

A. Sexual Preference and Proximity

One of the more common methods for examining female sexual motivation involves measuring whether females will seek proximity to a sexually active male (A. S. Clark *et al.,* 1981; Meyerson and Lindstrom, 1973; Edwards and Pfeifle, 1983) and whether, in a choice paradigm, they will display a preference for a sexually active male over another stimulus animal (Edwards and Pfeifle, 1983; Meyerson and Lindstrom, 1973). In a typical experiment, females are placed in a chamber in which two stimulus animals are positioned at different sites, and the length of time the female spends with each stimulus animal is recorded. The results obtained in these types of tests demonstrate that

(1) the female in estrus will approach and mate with sexually active males; (2) the duration of time the female spends with a male stimulus animal is shorter if she is able to have sexual interactions with the male than if she is not, and (3) estradiol stimulates her to increase selection of a sexually active over a sexually inactive male (Edwards and Pfeifle, 1983; Meyerson and Lindstrom, 1973). In prairie voles (*Microtus ochogaster*), a species in which pair bonding occurs between the female and male, females exhibited a strong preference for a familiar rather than unfamiliar partner (Williams *et al.,* 1992). The results of these tests are very much influenced by whether the female can or cannot mate with the male stimulus animal. In tests in which mating with a stimulus male can occur, females spend less time with the male than in tests in which the mating does not occur. In fact, in tests with two sexually active and interactive stimulus males, ovariectomized rats treated with estradiol benzoate and progesterone to induce estrous behavior avoid contact with both males, spending greater amounts of time in a neutral compartment than in either compartment containing a male (Broekman *et al.,* 1988). In addition, when given a choice between a castrated and an intact male, these same females spent significantly more time with the castrated male than with the intact male. However, females given exposure to males that restricts their sexual interactions (for instance, by keeping the males in a wire cage or by using a vaginal mask to prevent intromissions), spend more time with sexually active than with castrated, inactive males (Meyerson and Lindstrom, 1973; Broekman *et al.,* 1988). These results suggest that females initially seek out contact with sexually active males, but that the mating stimulation they receive results in subsequent avoidance of these same stimulus males. The combination of positive and negative motivation to interact with males is reminiscent of pacing behavior, in which both approach toward and withdrawal from the male occurs.

The steroid hormone background of both the female and the stimulus male and the amount of sexual experience (Williams *et al.,* 1992; Carter and Getz, 1985) are important for the expression of partner preference by the female. Treatment of the female with testosterone propionate rather than estradiol benzoate enhanced the time she spent in proximity to the male, and there was no facilitatory effect of additional proges-

terone treatment (de Jonge *et al.,* 1986). However, the incentive value of the male was greater after treating him with estradiol than after treating him with testosterone (de Bruijn *et al.,* 1988). Because estradiol-treated males showed a reduction in copulatory efficiency compared to TP-treated males, these results are consistent with the hypothesis that females actively avoid prolonged contact with sexually active males and that they choose to spend time with males that provide fewer or less intense vaginocervical stimuli.

B. Operant Tasks

Other tasks that have been used to examine female sexual motivation have been obtained under circumstances in which the female must perform an operant task to gain access to a male. Studies using lever pressing as the operant task for access to a male (Bermant, 1961; French *et al.,* 1972) have not been particularly informative; although such studies have demonstrated that females will bar press for a male, no studies have been attempted that actually compared this behavior between groups thought to have different levels of sexual motivation. Meyerson and Lindstrom (1973), in a classic paper on female sexual motivation, tested the female's willingness to cross an electrified grid to be near a sexually active male. Behavioral measures in this test were the frequency of grid crossings and the latency in seconds to cross the grid to be near an incentive animal located behind a wire mesh screen. The findings obtained with this method demonstrated that estrous-cycling females in estrus were more likely than nonestrous females to cross the grid when the incentive animal was an intact male. In ovariectomized hormone-primed females, estradiol treatment by itself did not alter the response times compared to oil-treated controls when either an estrous female or no animal was in the goal box, a result that suggests that nonspecific effects of estrogens on sensitivity to shock had not occurred. However, in agreement with the data obtained from cycling females, injection of estradiol to these ovariectomized females increased the number of grid-crossings and decreased the hesitation times over oil-treated females, and these changes were dependent upon estradiol dose. In another experiment, females allowed two to three mounts from the male during a 15 second period of interaction after crossing the grid did not decrease the amount of time they hesitated before crossing the grid on a subsequent trial. However, no information is available on the level of sexual responsiveness displayed by the females in this experiment or on the numbers of these mounts that included intromission. In some respects, therefore, the results obtained with the electric grid method are similar to those obtained in the sexual preference tests. Females in estrus that do not mate with the stimulus male show a higher motivation to be with the male than do females who have had some sexual interaction with the stimulus male.

C. Conditioned Place Preference

One additional means to measure female sexual motivation is to determine whether sexual interactions have reward value for the female. A test used to determine this is the conditioned place preference paradigm in which the female mates with a male in one of two sensorally distinct compartments and is exposed without the male incentive to the alternate compartment. After several conditioning trials, the female is placed alone into the place preference apparatus, and the length of time that she spends in each compartment is recorded. If she spends more time in the compartment in which mating previously occurred, then sexual behavior can be said to have been rewarding for the female and to have provided sufficient reward to condition her response to the mating chamber. In fact, ovariectomized females treated with either estradiol or estradiol plus progesterone developed a preference for the compartment in which copulation occurred (Oldenburger et al., 1992). The time that the females spent in the compartment in which sexual behavior occurred was significantly greater than the time spent in compartments in which they had not previously been paired with a male. However, this preference was not expressed until the last third of the 15 minute preference test.

As with the sexual preference and operant tests discussed above, there is clear evidence obtained from conditioned place preference that the vaginocervical stimulation (VCS) received during mating has negatively as well as positively reinforcing properties. Oldenburger et al. (1992) demonstrated that there was a negative correlation between the number of intromissions received by the female during mating in the preference box and the amount of time that the female subsequently spent in that box. In addition, they found that estradiol plus progesterone-treated ovariectomized females paired with a male in one compartment and exposed to an inaccessible caged male in the other tended to spend more time in the compartment in which they had been exposed to the caged male than in the compartment in which they had copulated. In contrast, when these same females received a low number of intromissions in a neutral arena immediately prior to the preference test, they spent significantly more time in the compartment in which they had previously mated than in the other chamber. Presumably, the pretest intromissions stimulated a changed neural state that had occurred during prior matings and had become associated with the earlier mating experience.

In another demonstration that mating stimulation is positively reinforcing to the female, Paredes and Alonso (1997) demonstrated, using conditioned place preference, that paced mating but not nonpaced mating induced a conditioned place preference in ovariectomized hormonally treated females. The rats were given conditioning trials in which they were paired with a sexually active male in either paced or nonpaced mating conditions, and then were immediately placed into the chamber of the place preference apparatus that they had avoided in pretests. At the time of the preference trial, females that had received paced mating stimulation showed an increase in time spent in that chamber, whereas nonpaced and control animals did not distinguish between the chambers. Taken together, the results of the motivational tests demonstrate that mating stimulation is less rewarding than is noncopulatory social exposure to a stimulus male. However, the aversive components of mating stimulation are sufficiently reduced during paced mating to allow development of a conditioned place preference. One question to be tested about this outcome is whether the slower rate at which the female receives intromissions during paced mating accounts for the decrease in perceived aversive nature of the stimulation.

IV. ENDOCRINE ASPECTS

The sexual behavior of most animals is under tight hormonal control. During the estrous cycle of rats and many other species, the sequential secretion of estradiol and progesterone from the ovaries results in a period of sexual behavior that is linked to the time of ovulation (Barfield and Lisk, 1974; Boling and Blandau, 1939; Collins *et al.*, 1938; Powers, 1970). After the period of sexual behavior (heat; behavioral estrus) terminates, sexual behavior is not seen until the proestrous stage of the reproductive cycle returns with its sequential secretion of estradiol and progesterone. Although sex steroid hormones modulate all aspects of sexual behaviors—copulatory, paracopulatory, and progestative—the majority of studies, particularly on cellular processes, have been limited to the regulation of the reflexive lordosis posture in response to copulatory stimulation. Although a limitation of much of the work in one respect, the reflexive, simplistic nature of this response has facilitated the study of its cellular underpinnings.

Much of what we know about the hormonal regulation of female copulatory behavior comes from the pioneering work of W.C. Young and his collaborators. A superb review describing in detail much of the early behavioral work in this field is available (Young, 1969). Ovariectomy abolishes the appearance of sexual behavior by eliminating the cyclic release of sex steroid hormones (Boling and Blandau, 1939; Dempsey *et al.*, 1936). Timed ovariectomy during the proestrous stage of the rat reproductive cycle prevents the preovulatory rise in estradiol level and eliminates the preovulatory progesterone secretion. Ovariectomy during the estrous stage eliminates much of the progesterone surge with little effect on estradiol secretion. Sexual behaviors can be reinstated by mimicking the cyclic release of estradiol and progesterone with exogenous hormone treatments. The behavioral deficits produced by ovariectomy at proestrus (prior to the peak estradiol secretion) can be restored by replacement with estradiol and progesterone, and reversal of the deficits caused by ovariectomy during estrus requires only progesterone treatment (Powers, 1970). These experiments as well as experiments with timed injections of progesterone in guinea pigs (Joslyn *et al.*, 1971) have pointed out the dependence of sexual behavior during the estrous cycle on both estradiol and progesterone. This result stands in contrast to some other behaviors such as ingestive, in which estradiol alone appears to be responsible for the changes observed during the estrous cycle (Wade, 1976).

Although ovariectomized rats and guinea pigs may respond to estradiol alone, sequential treatment with estradiol and progesterone results in more predictable onset and termination of the period of sexual behavior, increases the likelihood of response (Beach, 1942; Boling and Blandau, 1939; Collins *et al.*, 1938; Dempsey *et al.*, 1936), increases lordosis duration in guinea pigs (Wallen and Thomton, 1979), and increases the level of paracopulatory behaviors in rats (e.g., ear-wiggling, darting, and hopping Tennent *et al.*, 1980). Just as the dose of estradiol required for expression of sexual behavior is dependent on progesterone, the dose of progesterone required is dependent on estradiol (Whalen, 1974). Increasing doses of estradiol used for priming allow lower levels of progesterone to be used to facilitate sexual behavior. Thus, estradiol modulates responsiveness to progesterone.

For a short time after exposure to progesterone, animals become refractory to further stimulation of sexual behavior by either progesterone alone (Dempsey *et al.*, 1936) or, in some cases, estradiol and progesterone (Blaustein and Wade, 1977; Goy *et al.*, 1966; Zucker, 1966, 1968). This desensitization, which is most dramatic in guinea pigs, has been referred to as the postestrous refractory period (Morin, 1977), the sequential inhibitory effect of progesterone (Blaustein and Wade, 1977; Feder and Marrone, 1977; Powers and Moreines, 1976), or the biphasic effect of progesterone (Zucker, 1968). Although progesterone induces a refractory period to further facilitation of sexual behavior in the experimental model of ovariectomized rodents, its role during the estrous cycle of rats has been somewhat controversial. Furthermore, whereas it has generally been accepted that progesterone inhibits sexual behavior in guinea pigs under some circumstances (Feder *et al.*, 1968a; Goy *et al.*, 1966), it has been suggested that this not true under physiological conditions in rats (Hansen and Södersten, 1978; Södersten and Eneroth, 1981; Södersten and Hansen, 1977).

The time course of estradiol and progesterone action on sexual behavior is of great interest, particularly inasmuch as it provides additional clues to the underlying cellular processes by which hormones act in the brain. In estrogen-primed ovariectomized rats, maximum levels of lordosis are typically seen within about an hour of intravenous progesterone injection (Glaser *et al.*, 1983; Kubli-Garfias and Whalen, 1977; McGinnis *et al.,* 1981; Meyerson, 1972), and maximum levels of paracopulatory behaviors are seen within about two hours of treatment (Fadem *et al.,* 1979; Glaser *et al.,* 1983). In contrast, estrogen priming of responsiveness to progesterone takes nearly a day (Feder and Marrone, 1977; Green *et al.,* 1970). This difference was originally taken as evidence of a fundamentally different mechanism of action for estradiol and progesterone on sexual behavior (McEwen *et al.,* 1979). However, it is likely that the main difference between the two hormones is the time course of otherwise similar cellular processes. Much of the research done in the past 25 years supports the idea that estradiol and progesterone act by similar cellular mechanisms of action to prime and then facilitate, respectively, the expression of feminine sexual behaviors.

V. STEROID HORMONE RECEPTORS AND HORMONAL REGULATION OF FEMININE SEXUAL BEHAVIOR

A great deal of work on the regulation of feminine sexual behavior has been done within the context of the cellular mechanisms of action of estradiol and progesterone. Because many studies implicate a role for intracellular steroid hormone receptors in this regulation, these will be reviewed in detail, including the history of the study of these binding proteins for estrogens and progestins in the brain.

A. History of Models of Steroid Hormone Action

The field of the mechanisms of action of steroid hormones is rapidly progressing and changing, with frequent challenges to the discipline's dogma. Although it was originally believed that unoccupied receptors are located in the cellular cytoplasm and occupied receptors are located in the cell's nucleus (Jensen and DeSombre, 1972; O'Malley and Means, 1974; Gorski *et al.,* 1968), subsequent experiments refined this idea, as we will discussed. Further, though it was originally believed that neural steroid receptors require cognate ligand for activation, we will present evidence that is consistent with the idea (Power *et al.,* 1991b) that steroid receptors can be activated by compounds other

than steroid hormones, including neurotransmitters (Mani *et al.,* 1994a). Finally, we will present data that suggest that the receptor proteins synthesized from the same gene may function not only in the cell nucleus, but also to signal rapid membrane events (Razandi *et al.,* 1999). There is general agreement that steroid hormones act through steroid hormone receptors functioning as transcriptional regulators, as well as by other mechanisms. Likewise, it is probably safe to say that whereas steroid hormone receptors are often activated by their cognate ligand, they can also be activated by other mechanisms.

It was originally proposed (Gorski *et al.,* 1968; Jensen *et al.,* 1968) that steroid hormone receptors act by a two-step mechanism. Steroid hormones, being extremely lipid soluble, diffuse freely into and out of all cells. However, in target cells for the particular hormone, the hormones bind with high affinity to unoccupied receptors, originally believed to reside exclusively in the cytoplasm. Occupation of the receptor results in a conformational change, activation, and dimerization. It was originally believed that the steroid hormone-receptor complex was then translocated into cell nuclei, where it could bind tightly to nuclear constituents. Once bound to the chromatin, the hormone-receptor complex was thought to cause changes in gene expression, leading to alterations in protein synthesis and consequently to changes in cellular function. Although specific points, such as the molecular structure of the receptor, differ among species and with the class of hormone considered (Grody *et al.,* 1982), it was generally accepted that the occupation of the receptor and the consequent conformational change caused it to acquire a high affinity for binding sites on chromatin (Walters, 1985).

This original two-step model was modified in 1984 based on results of two sets of experiments (King and Greene, 1984; Welshons *et al.,* 1984) that suggested that both unoccupied and occupied estrogen receptors are present almost exclusively in cell nuclei. This model conflicted with the original model, because it proposed that the high concentration of unoccupied receptors typically found in the cytoplasm (actually in cytosol—the high speed supernatant) after cell fractionation and differential centrifugation was an artifact of tissue homogenization.

Despite this apparent conflict with the original two-step model, there is agreement that unoccupied

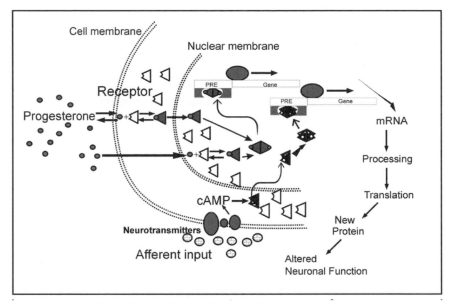

FIGURE 2 Model mechanism of action for steroid hormones in the brain. Binding of the steroid receptor to ligand causes activation and transformation of the receptor, resulting in its binding to hormone response elements on particular genes. This then results in transcription of particular mRNA transcripts and translation of peptides and proteins, which then cause changes in neuronal function. As discussed in Section VI, steroid receptors can also be activated indirectly by membrane receptors for some neurotransmitters.

receptors are not functional until they are activated by binding to steroid hormones and dimerization. Similarly, there is agreement that a principal site of hormone action is at the level of the genome. And over the years, much has been learned about the protein-protein interactions involved in steroid hormone regulation of the transcriptional machinery, including the role of association with various heat shock proteins (Gehring, 1998; Pratt and Toft, 1997; Toft *et al.,* 1987) and co-regulators (McKenna *et al.,* 1999; Tetel, 2000), and about hormone response elements often in the promoter region of target genes in the function of these receptors. Although early work may have been incorrect in the labeling of all of the receptors that are found in the cytosol fraction as "cytoplasmic," a designation that denotes a particular intracellular locus *in vivo,* it is clear that the steroid hormones are likely to have access to the receptors, regardless of their intracellular location. A more important question, which we discuss later, is whether receptors found in various locations within the cytoplasm have functions different from those that act as transcriptional regulators (Blaustein, 1994), and for that reason knowledge of the intracellular sites of steroid receptors is of

crucial importance. It is important to understand the evolution of this model in order to put the early experiments on steroid hormone mechanisms of action into context.

B. Estrogen Receptors

1. History

Shortly after intracellular receptors for estrogens were first characterized in the brain (Eisenfeld, 1969; Kahwanago *et al.,* 1969), biochemical experiments investigating the mechanisms of action of estradiol and progesterone with reference to sexual behavior were conducted (Zigmond and McEwen, 1969). A variety of approaches has been used to determine the role of neural estrogen receptors (ERs) in the induction of sexual behavior and to establish whether, when response to estradiol changes due to physiological intervention, the change in response is mediated by changes in the concentrations of steroid hormone receptors. Some experiments have been designed to determine the neuroanatomical and temporal relationships between receptors and behavior. Another approach has been to study the effects of pharmacological inhibitors on reproductive behaviors to establish the necessity of receptors. Although estradiol also acts by other mechanisms to influence neuronal physiology (e.g., Kelly and Wagner, 1999; Ramirez *et al.*, 1996) the results of many experiments are consistent with the idea that estradiol operates in the brain to influence sexual behavior in large part through intracellular steroid receptors acting as transcriptional regulators. As in peripheral tissues, estradiol binds to unoccupied receptors, causing activation, which then results in changes in transcription and translation and ultimately causes changes in neuronal physiology. Many lines of evidence are consistent with the hypothesis that in many situations, modulation of response to estradiol is due to regulation of concentrations of receptors (Fig. 1).

2. Two Estrogen Receptors

In the 1960s, the existence of an estrogen-specific binding protein that met the criteria for a receptor was documented (Gorski *et al.*, 1968; Jensen *et al.*, 1968), and in 1969, its presence was confirmed in the brain (Eisenfeld, 1969). This estrogen-binding protein was considered a receptor because it was of high affinity, saturable, and steroid-specific; showed tissue specificity; and its presence correlated with biological response—criteria originally described by Clark and Peck (1977). Originally a single ER gene was described (Greene *et al.*, 1986). However, it is clear now that the techniques that were used would not have revealed a second form of the receptor, if that receptor had a similar affinity for estradiol and if that receptor was of similar molecular weight.

In 1996, a second ER gene (ERβ) was discovered in the prostate gland (Kuiper *et al.*, 1996), and then this finding was extended to other tissues, including the brain. ERβ shares a high level of sequence homology with the first ER discovered (and renamed ERα) in some portions of the receptor, and both receptors bind to estradiol with similar binding affinity (Kuiper *et al.*, 1997). Depending on the ligand and the estrogen response elements present in cells, ERβ and ERα can have different transcriptional activities (Hyder *et al.*, 1999; Paech *et al.*, 1997; Zou *et al.*, 1999). Furthermore, ERβ and ERα may heterodimerize, bind to estrogen response elements, and have different transcriptional activity dependent on the particular dimer

(Petersen *et al.*, 1998; Pettersson *et al.*, 1997; Tremblay *et al.*, 1999). Because the responses of cells to estradiol should depend on the presence and abundance of each ER subtype, an understanding of the distribution and the extent of cellular coexpression of ERβ and ERα in different neuroanatomical areas is of critical importance.

Like issues of basic cellular mechanisms of action for steroid hormone receptors, it is important to understand the evolution of this field in order to understand the results of particular experiments. The majority of the studies to be described in this chapter were performed before the discovery of the second ER gene, and therefore they were performed with the assumption that there is *one* ER. However, in earlier binding studies, every assay represented a composite of both receptors. But in immunocytochemical studies, most of the antibodies that have been used are specific for ERα, so half the story was probably missing. This deficiency is being corrected, because probes used for *in situ* hybridization histochemistry and many antibodies now used for immunocytochemistry are specific for each of the receptors, but this is a very recent development.

3. Anatomical Localization of Estrogen Receptors—Relationship to Effects of Estradiol on Feminine Sexual Behavior

Early autoradiographic studies (Pfaff and Keiner, 1973; Pfaff, 1968; Stumpf, 1968; Warembourg, 1977) demonstrated a high density of estradiol-concentrating cells in a variety of hypothalamic, limbic, and to a lesser extent mesencephalic structures. *In vitro* binding assays with microdissected tissues demonstrated that the neural areas with the highest concentrations of estrogen receptors in rats are the periventricular and medial preoptic area, followed by the periventricular anterior hypothalamus, lateral hypothalamus, arcuate nucleus, suprachiasmatic preoptic area, and the ventromedial nucleus of the hypothalamus (Rainbow *et al.*, 1982c). Since these studies were based on ligand binding, they would have described a composite of the sites of ERα and ERβ.

Because the ventromedial nucleus of the hypothalamus has been the subject of so many studies in this field, the distribution of ERs in this area warrants additional discussion. The early autoradiographic studies on ER distribution had described a dense population of ER-containing cells within the ventrolateral aspect of the ventromedial nucleus (Pfaff and Keiner, 1973; Pfaff, 1968; Stumpf, 1970). They also described a population that extended beyond the borders of the nucleus as defined by Nissl staining. However, because the majority of the cells were localized to the actual ventrolateral-ventromedial nucleus, the cells lying outside the nucleus were largely overlooked (Figs. 3 and 4). As will be discussed in Section VII.A on sites of action of estradiol on feminine sexual behavior, an important question is whether the entire area represents a relatively homogeneous population or distinct populations with different anatomical projections and functions. The work that has been done so far suggests that they are not functionally distinct, and perhaps studies of the role of the ventromedial nucleus should routinely be extended to include the *entire* population of ER-containing neurons in the ventromedial nucleus of the hypothalamus

and its surround. In some studies, we have referred to this population of cells as the "ovarian steroid hormone receptor containing area associated with the ventrolateral aspect of the ventromedial hypothalamus" (Auger *et al.*, 1997), a cumbersome but descriptive name. In this chapter, for simplicity, we will refer to them as being localized within the ventromedial hypothalamic *area,* a diffuse area that extends beyond the boundaries of the ventromedial *nucleus.* In guinea pigs, the nomenclature used to describe this population of cells is the ventrolateral hypothalamus.

ERα and ERβ are each present in abundance in a variety of brain regions (Osterlund *et al.*, 1998; Shughrue *et al.*, 1997, 1998; Simerly *et al.*, 1990). ERα mRNA or protein is expressed most densely throughout the bed nucleus of stria terminalis, the posterodorsal part and cortical nucleus of the amygdala, medial and periventricular preoptic area (Fig. 5), arcuate nucleus, ventromedial and periventricular hypothalamus, the ventral part of the lateral septum, and the periaqueductal gray (DonCarlos *et al.*, 1991; Shughrue *et al.*, 1997; Simerly *et al.*, 1990).

The distribution of ERβ mRNA and protein has also been described. ERβ mRNA has been found in substantial quantity in hypothalamic and limbic regions, which are known to contain abundant ERα and PR, as well as in other regions known to express little or no ERα or PR. Although there is overlap of the areas

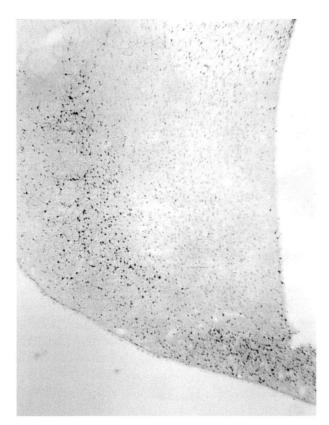

FIGURE 3 Photomicrograph of ERα-ir in rostral ventrolateral hypothalamic area of an ovariectomized female guinea pig illustrating that the ERir cells extend dorsally well beyond the ventromedial-ventrolateral nuclei of the hypothalamus.

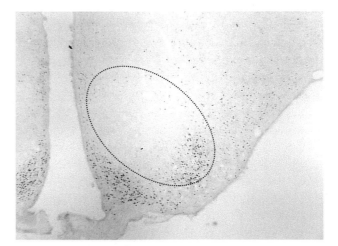

FIGURE 4 Photomicrograph of ERα-ir in the rostral ventromedial hypothalamic area of an ovariectomized female rat illustrating the distribution of ERα-ir cells beyond the limits of the actual ventromedial hypothalamic nucleus.

FIGURE 5 Photomicrograph of ERα-ir in the medial preoptic area of an ovariectomized female rat. Abbreviations: ac, anterior commissure; oc, optic chiasm.

expressing ERβ and ERα mRNA (Shughrue *et al.*, 1996, 1997) or protein (Li *et al.*, 1997; Merchenthaler *et al.*, 2000) in the bed nucleus of stria terminalis, most amygdaloid nuclei, medial and periventricular preoptic area, the distribution of ERβ mRNA or protein extends to some regions containing no detectable or low levels of ERα. Some of the most striking differences in distribution between ERα and ERβ were found in the paraventricular and supraoptic nuclei, which are rich in ERβ mRNA, with almost no detectable ERα mRNA (Alves *et al.*, 1998; LaFlamme *et al.*, 1998; Shughrue *et al.*, 1996, 1998; Simonian and Herbison, 1997), as well as the dentate gyrus, isocortex, accessory olfactory nucleus, anterodorsal portion of the preoptic nucleus, and cerebellum. Although the highest proportion of intracellular coexpression of ERα and ERβ occurs within the principal nucleus of the stria terminalis, the posterodorsal medial amygdala, and the periventricular preoptic nucleus (Gréco *et al.*, 2001; Shughrue *et al.*,

1998), many cells containing only ERα or ERβ were also found in these regions. The differences in ER subtype distribution are consistent with the idea that the role of ERβ may differ from that of ERα (Shughrue *et al.*, 1998). Because genes may be differentially regulated by ERα and ERβ, changes in the coexpression may influence the moment-to-moment response of particular ER-dependent genes.

4. Regulation of Neural Estrogen Receptors by Estradiol

In general, estradiol downregulates ERα mRNA (Lauber *et al.*, 1990; Simerly and Young, 1991), protein (Meredith *et al.*, 1994; Osterlund *et al.*, 1998; Yuri and Kawata, 1991), and [³H]estradiol binding (Brown *et al.*, 1996). However, there are numerous inconsistencies in the literature on regulation of ERs by estradiol, in part due to the recent "complication" of the discovery of the second ER gene.

There is consistency that estradiol downregulates ERα mRNA levels in the arcuate nucleus and ventrolateral-ventromedial nucleus of the hypothalamus (Lauber *et al.*, 1991; Simerly and Young, 1991). However, DonCarlos *et al.* (1995) reported that estradiol treatment caused a decrease in ERα-ir in the guinea pig ventrolateral hypothalamus and the bed nucleus of stria terminalis, but not the periventricular preoptic area, while Gréco *et al.* (2001) reported a decrease in the posterodorsal medial amygdala and paraventricular nucleus, but not the principal nucleus of bed nucleus of stria terminalis. In another study in guinea pigs, estradiol caused downregulation of ERα-ir in all brain areas studied with the exception of the medial preoptic nucleus (Meredith *et al.*, 1994). With respect to ERβ, one study (Patisaul *et al.*, 1999) reported a decrease in ERβ mRNA in the paraventricular nucleus but not other areas (Patisaul *et al.*, 1999), while another (Gréco *et al.*, 2001) reported a decrease in ERβ-ir in the periventricular preoptic area and the bed nucleus of stria terminalis but not the paraventricular nucleus and posterodorsal medial amygdala. In contrast, Osterlund *et al.* (1998) reported a decrease in ERβ mRNA in the posterodorsal medial amygdala but an increase in the arcuate nucleus.

There are many reasons for the inconsistencies that exist in the literature with respect to the regulation of ERs by estradiol. For example, binding studies measure very different things than immunocytochemical or *in situ* hybridization studies, and studies of mRNA may not always be consistent with studies of protein. There are also numerous, important methodological differences, such as doses of estradiol used, time of exposure to hormone, etc. Nevertheless, it is clear that ERα is generally downregulated by estradiol, but ERβ may be more complex. Furthermore, it can be concluded that there is heterogeneity in the regulation of each form of ER, not just among neuroanatomical areas, but also among different neurons in a particular area, and that ERα and ERβ are probably not regulated in parallel at all times.

Long-term deprivation of steroid hormones by ovariectomy decreases the response of rats and guinea pigs to estradiol plus progesterone induction of sexual behavior (Beach and Orndoff, 1974; C.R. Clark *et al.,* 1981; Czaja *et al.,* 1985; Delville and Blaustein, 1989). Long-term ovariectomy (C.R. Clark *et al.,* 1981; Delville and Blaustein, 1989; Parsons *et al.,* 1979) results in a decrease in the concentration of estradiol-induced, hypothalamic progestin receptors (PRs) in rats. Although some biochemical studies have typically shown no change in brain ERs after long-term ovariectomy (C.R. Clark *et al.,* 1981; Parsons *et al.,* 1979), one study suggests that long-term ovariectomy results in an increase in ERα immunoreactivity (Liposits *et al.,* 1990). This apparent increase in ERs after ovariectomy is consistent with downregulation of ER mRNA and proteins by acute estradiol (DonCarlos *et al.,* 1995; Meredith *et al.,* 1994; Simerly and Young, 1991).

At present, it is not known how important physiologically the regulation of ERs by estradiol is over the estrous cycle. In an autoradiographic study of occupation of ERs during proestrus and estrus (Yuan *et al.,* 1995), dramatic changes in the number of occupied receptors were observed, but the total number of receptors changed (declined) only in the ventromedial nucleus of the hypothalamus. A limitation of this study is that the autoradiographic technique assayed all ERs capable of binding estradiol, not each form of ER. Perhaps this estradiol-dependent regulation of ERs by estradiol during other reproductive events, such as after ovariectomy, pregnancy (e.g., Wagner and Morrell, 1996), and lactation, or during menopause in humans has dramatic effects on response of particular genes. Similarly, it has not yet been shown that the regulation of ERs by estradiol has functional consequences in modulat-

ing the sensitivity of particular neurons to estradiol. However, it can be predicted that in cells in which a particular form of ER is downregulated, fewer of that form of ER would be likely to be activated less after a given dose of estradiol. Thus, changes in the relative concentrations of each ER form might have profound effects on ER-regulated genes, and consequently on the effects of estradiol on sexual behaviors.

The role of steroid hormone receptors has often been studied as that of a switch. That is, the presence of receptors in a tissue has often been looked at as being permissive or all-or-none, and it has been assumed that mere presence of receptors should explain response. An attempt has been made in few experiments to relate receptor levels more correctly to *sensitivity* to the hormone. The question is not whether a partial reduction in receptor level prevents the effect of the hormone, but whether changes in concentration of a receptor mediate changes in sensitivity to the hormone.

5. Interference with Estrogen Receptors
The necessity of ERs for estradiol's actions on sexual receptivity has been tested directly in two ways: via estrogen antagonists, which may either block the binding of estradiol to ERs, and via ER gene-disrupted mice (ER knockouts; ERKOs), in which the gene for ERs has been disrupted. While the results of each type of study are consistent with the conclusion that ERs are essential to estradiol's effects on the expression of sexual receptivity, each approach provides different types of information.

a) Estrogen Antagonists Receptor-blocking experiments demonstrated the necessity of the presence of unoccupied ERs and the accumulation of bound receptors in mediating the effects of estradiol on sexual behavior. Although the antagonists used so far do not differentiate the two forms of ERs, treatment with a variety of antiestrogens that block hypothalamic cell nuclear accumulation of (presumably receptor bound) peripherally administered [³H]estradiol (Etgen, 1979; Landau, 1977; Roy and Wade, 1977; Walker and Feder, 1977b) or decrease the concentration of available unoccupied ERs (Vagell and McGinnis, 1996: Wade and Blaustein, 1978) also block the effects of estradiol on the induction of sexual behavior.

Unfortunately, the nature of antiestrogens is not as simple as the name implies. Whereas antiestrogens may act as estrogen antagonists in some cells, under some conditions and in other cells most can also act as estrogen agonists. Perhaps the best example of this is that the antiestrogen tamoxifen and some other antiestrogens are antiestrogenic on breast tissue (Jordan, 1995) but estrogenic on bone metabolism (Jordan, 1999). Likewise, they may block estradiol's effects on feminine sexual behavior but have estrogenic effects on other behaviors (e.g., feeding; Roy and Wade, 1976) or neuronal end points. To complicate matters even more, many antiestrogens can be antagonists or agonists on the same end points, depending on timing and dose (Etgen and Shamamian, 1986; Wade and Blaustein, 1978; Walker and Feder, 1977a; Wilcox and Feder, 1983).

b) Estrogen Receptor-Gene-Disrupted Mice

Because the two ERs are made from independent genes, knockout strains of mice have been developed in which the gene for each of the receptors (Krege *et al.*, 1998) or both receptors (Couse *et al.*, 1999) has been disrupted. Targeted disruption of the ERα gene in a transgenic strain of mouse (αERKO; ERα knockouts) completely eliminates progesterone-facilitated copulatory behavior (Ogawa *et al.*, 1998; Rissman *et al.*, 1997) but appears to be without effect on one paracopulatory behavior (i.e., number of mount attempts by the male; Rissman *et al.*, 1997). Based on the fact that sexual receptivity seems to be completely blocked in the ERα-disrupted mice, it might be predicted that disruption of the β form of the ER would have little if any influence on sexual receptivity. In fact, the first study of this found that there was little effect of disruption of the β form of the ER, except perhaps to lengthen the duration of sexual receptivity during the estrous cycle (Ogawa *et al.*, 1999).

Although the knockout strains of mice provide powerful models for the study of the role of particular proteins in behavior, there are also several potential problems associated with this animal model that must be considered:

1. Although there are numerous similarities between rats and mice, there are many differences as well. Estrogenic regulation of PRs is remarkably similar in rats and wild-type littermates of αERKO (Moffatt *et al.*, 1998) or PR knockout (Mani *et al.*, 1996) mice. Furthermore, the expression of sexual receptivity in female rats and mice requires similar, although not identical, priming regimens. However, mice do not have very much ERβ-mRNA in pituitary and mammary glands, whereas ERβ-mRNA is readily detected in both structures in rats and humans (for a review, see Couse and Korach, 1999). Therefore, species generalizations must be made cautiously.

2. Knockout animals have been deprived of the receptor during the *entire* period of development. Neural and behavioral changes in adult knockouts could reflect a combination of early developmental changes as well as acute deficiencies in adulthood (Rissman *et al.*, 1997).

3. There may be splice variants of the disrupted receptor (Moffatt *et al.*, 1998), which may be transcriptionally active (Couse *et al.*, 1997). However, as long as it is considered that the receptor levels in the knockout may only be drastically reduced, not completely absent, this concern can be dealt with. Corroboration of this work is needed by using antisense oligonucleotides to the two forms of ERs in rats, or at some future time by using conditional knockout models in which ERs can be disrupted only in adulthood.

6. Long-Term Retention of ERs and Behavior

An interesting question that was raised early in the study of the mechanism of action of estradiol in feminine sexual behavior is the role of what was originally referred to as long-term retention of ERs by cell nuclei for behavioral response to estradiol. In modern-day language, we would probably ask what is the role of long-term, continued association of occupied ERs with hormone response elements on the promoters of particular genes. It had been shown that after injection of a behaviorally sufficient dose of estradiol, hypothalamic cell nuclear ER levels (occupied ERs) peak within an hour or two and decline to nondetectable levels within 12 hours (McEwen *et al.*, 1975). This time course had been taken by some as evidence that the estradiol-ER interaction has a strictly priming effect on sexual behavior, perhaps only initiating the transcriptional response that then results in *de novo* protein synthesis by the time of estradiol induction of sexual behavior. However, in later work in which a more sensitive technique was used, a barely detectable level of hypothalamic cell nuclear ERs (0.5% of peak) was still retained in the hypothalamus

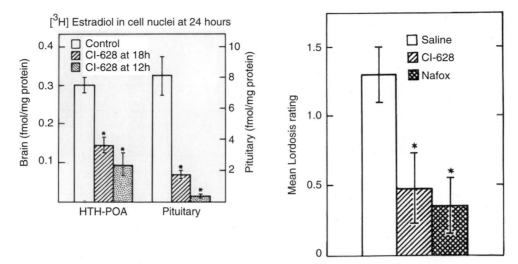

FIGURE 6 Long-term retention of estradiol and lordosis. (A) Effects of antiestrogen, CI-628 treatment on 24 hour retention of [³H]estradiol by cell nuclei from hypothalamus-preoptic area and pituitary gland in ovariectomized rats. Rats received injections of CI-628 or saline 12 or 18 hours after intravenous injection of [³H]estradiol, and were sacrificed at 24 hours. (B) Effect of the antiestrogen on estrous behavior. Rats received intravenous injections of 3 μg unesterified estradiol followed by subcutaneous injection of 0.5 mg progesterone 18 hours later. At 18 hours, rats received intraperitoneal injection of the antiestrogens CI-628, nafoxidine, or saline vehicle, and they were tested for lordosis at 24 hours. (From Blaustein *et al.* (1979), *Brain Res.* **103**, 355–359, © 1979, with permission of Elsevier Science.)

24 hours after estradiol injection (Blaustein *et al.*, 1979) (Fig. 6). Antiestrogen treatment as late as 18 hours after estradiol injection eliminated these few remaining estradiol-occupied cell nuclear receptors, and it also eliminated the expression of sexual behavior when assessed at 24 hours. These findings suggested that ERs must remain occupied, activated, and bound to estrogen response elements on particular genes even as late as the time that sexual behavior is observed. The answer to the question of the importance of long-term receptor occupation and activation lies in the molecular regulation of sexual receptivity by ERs. Once we know the critical steroid receptor-responsive genes involved and the half-life of the relevant proteins, then the necessity of bound ERs at precise times should become clear.

Other experiments have shown that high levels of ERs need not remain bound *continuously* during the entire priming period for sexual receptivity. Two brief pulses of estradiol are far more potent in inducing sexual behavior in response to progesterone than a single large injection (Clark and Roy, 1983; Södersten *et al.*, 1981; Wilcox *et al.*, 1984), and if timed properly, they can be as potent as continuous exposure to estradiol (Parsons *et al.*, 1982a). Although little is known concerning the cellular basis, the behavioral effects of each pulse can be blocked by protein synthesis inhibitors (Parsons and McEwen, 1981) and pentobarbital anesthesia (Roy *et al.*, 1985). Furthermore, there is some evidence that the particular proteins modulated in response to each injection may differ (Jones *et al.*, 1986). It is perhaps most noteworthy that administration of pulses of estradiol nearly abolishes the well-known sex difference in the induction of sexual receptivity in response to estradiol followed by progesterone in rats (Södersten *et al.*, 1983) and guinea pigs (Olster and Blaustein, 1990). Although males of these species do not express lordosis in response to single, large injections of estradiol, oddly they respond readily to pulses of estradiol nearly as reliably as do females (Fig. 7). To date, no explanation has been suggested that would explain this peculiar phenomenon. However, since it is known that males may show high levels of female-like sexual behavior after particular kinds of brain lesions (e.g., preoptic area; Hennessey *et al.*, 1986;

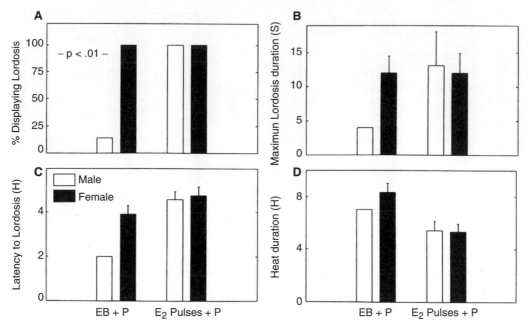

FIGURE 7 Behavioral responses of gonadectomized guinea pigs to estradiol benzoate (10 μg) or unesterified estradiol (E$_2$) pulses [(two injections of 2 μg, 28 hours apart, followed by progesterone (P, 0.5 mg)]. (A) Percentage of animals displaying lordosis, (B) maximum lordosis duration, (C) latency to lordosis (relative to P injection), (D) heat duration. Data in (B), (C) and (D) represent responding animals only. (From Olster and Blaustein (1990), *J. Neuroendocrinol.* **2**, 79–86, Blackwell Science Ltd.)

Rodriguez-Sierra and Terasawa, 1979), one can imagine that a population of estradiol-sensitive neurons in these areas might also be differentially sensitive to this pulse administration. However, if the pioneers in the study of sex differences in feminine sexual behavior had used pulses of estradiol rather than bolus injections, they might never have discovered the tremendous sex difference in behavioral response to estradiol and progesterone. As with the question concerning the need for long-term retention of bound ERs, our understanding of the basis for the exquisite sensitivity to estradiol when using the pulsed estradiol paradigm will probably be clarified by studies performed on the molecular mechanisms of hormone action.

To summarize this section on the involvement of ERs in the regulation of feminine sexual behavior, the experiments on neuroanatomical localization, temporal factors, receptor blocking, and knockout mice, as well as other experiments, are consistent with the idea that estradiol acts through a receptor-mediated, genomic mechanism to regulate feminine sexual behavior. Although ERα is essential for estradiol's ef-

fects on feminine sexual behavior in mice, many questions remain regarding the role of ERβ and perhaps other forms of ER in this regulation. Though much is known about the role of ERs and much is known (but many questions remain) regarding the regulation of different ER forms, it is essential to determine which genes are regulated by ERs, by which mechanisms, and how neuronal function is altered in response to these changes.

7. Genes That Estrogens Regulate in the Brain

One of the next logical steps in the study of the cellular mechanisms of estradiol action on feminine sexual behavior is to tie the effects of estradiol on gene transcription to behavior by studying the regulation of mRNA for specific proteins in neurons involved in sexual behavior. The genes that estradiol modulates that then influence sexual behavior must be determined and their regulation must be understood. This cannot be done yet; although it is clear that estradiol action in neurons is necessary and sufficient for estrogen action on sexual behavior, neither the specific neurons in which estradiol action is necessary nor the phenotype of those neurons has been identified.

The identities are known of many specific genes that are activated by estradiol and believed to require interaction with ERs. Some of the genes that are activated include progestin receptors (see next section), vasopressin (De Vries *et al.,* 1994; Shapiro *et al.,* 2000), vasopressin receptors (De Vries *et al.,* 1994), oxytocin (Miller *et al.,* 1989), oxytocin receptors (Bale *et al.,* 1995; Quinones-Jenab *et al.,* 1997a; Young *et al.,* 1997, 1998), GnRH (Petersen *et al.,* 1993b, 1995), mu-opiod receptors (Eckersell *et al.,* 1998; Quinones-Jenab *et al.,* 1997b; Zhou and Hammer, 1995), preproenkephalin (Quinones-Jenab *et al.,* 1996), cholecystokinin receptors (Popper *et al.,* 1996), neurotensin (Watters and Dorsa, 1998), preprotachykinin (E.R. Brown *et al.,* 1990), and a host of others (e.g., Kaplitt *et al.,* 1993; McEwen and Alves, 1999). In addition, some genes are downregulated by estradiol interaction with ERs, such as ERs themselves (Brown *et al.,* 1996; Lauber *et al.,* 1991; Meredith *et al.,* 1994; Simerly *et al.,* 1996; Simerly and Young, 1991) and proopiomelanocortin (Petersen *et al.,* 1993a; Wilcox and Roberts, 1985). ERs are often, but not always, coexpressed in neurons in which estradiol causes changes in expression of particular genes. In many cases, changes in gene expression occur by estradiol acting via ERs regulating transcription in the same neurons, but in other cases, changes in gene expression are likely to involve trans-synaptic effects on other downstream neurons. The regulation of many of these genes will be discussed elsewhere in this volume, and the possible importance of many of these genes in the regulation of feminine sexual behavior has been discussed in great depth in other reviews (e.g., De Vries, 1990; McCarthy and Pfaus, 1996; Pfaff *et al.,* 1994).

Other ways that estradiol can alter neuronal function may or may not involve regulation of gene expression. For example, estradiol can influence neurotransmission by regulation of binding of other receptors, including monaminergic receptors (Bosse and DiPaolo, 1996; Etgen and Karkanias, 1990; Petitti *et al.,* 1992), coupling of membrane neurotransmitter receptors to G proteins (Etgen *et al.,* 1999; Etgen and Karkanias, 1994; Petitti and Etgen, 1992) or Fos expression (Conde *et al.,* 1996), and release of neurotransmitters (e.g., Becker, 1990). Estradiol also causes changes in Fos

expression (Auger and Blaustein, 1995; Insel, 1990) and results in phosphorylation of cAMP-response element binding protein (CREB) (Zhou *et al.,* 1996) and DARPP-32 (Auger *et al.,* 2001). Each of these hormone-induced changes represents a potential means by which estradiol can potentially modulate feminine sexual behavior.

C. Progestin Receptors (PRs)

1. History

Although it is difficult to imagine, considering the progress of the past 25 years, early attempts to extend the intracellular receptor model of steroid hormone mechanisms to progesterone action in the brain were almost uniformly unsuccessful. At first, there were conflicting reports regarding the presence of neural PRs based on *in vitro* binding techniques (Atger *et al.,* 1974; Seiki *et al.,* 1977; Seiki and Hattori, 1973), and *in vivo* studies showed [³H]progesterone uptake that was not saturable (Luttge *et al.,* 1974; Wade and Feder, 1972; Whalen and Luttge, 1971). Although binding of [³H]progesterone in guinea pig brain was first documented by using autoradiography (Sar and Stumpf, 1973; Warembourg, 1978b), biochemical attempts were mostly unsuccessful (Marrone and Feder, 1977; McEwen *et al.,* 1976). With the development of [³H]progestins with a higher affinity for PRs than [³H]progesterone, it became possible to reliably assay and characterize progestin binding in the brain (Blaustein and Feder, 1979a; Blaustein and Wade, 1978; Kato *et al.,* 1978; Kato and Onouchi, 1977; MacLusky and McEwen, 1978; Moguilewsky and Raynaud, 1979a).

In contrast to the neuroanatomical localization seen with ERs, PRs, as defined by ligand binding, were observed throughout the brain of ovariectomized guinea pigs, rats, and other species (Balthazart *et al.,* 1980; Fraile *et al.,* 1987; Roselli and Snipes, 1983). However, estradiol priming dramatically increased the concentration of PRs in some neuroanatomical areas, including the hypothalamus and medial preoptic area of rats and guinea pigs (Blaustein and Feder, 1979a; MacLusky and McEwen, 1978; Moguilewsky and Raynaud, 1979a) and the midbrain of guinea pigs (Blaustein and Feder, 1979a). With punch microdissection, which provided slightly better spatial resolution (Parsons *et al.,* 1982b;

Thornton *et al.*, 1986a), it was learned that brain regions with the highest abundance of estradiol-induced PRs are the arcuate nucleus, the ventromedial nucleus, periventricular preoptic area, the periventricular hypothalamus, the suprachiasmatic preoptic area, and the medial preoptic area, all areas that also have a high concentration of ERs (Rainbow *et al.*, 1982c).

At first, it was not known whether the PRs present in many sites throughout the brain represented a low level in all cells or a few, scattered cells with an abundance of PRs (Blaustein and Olster, 1989). The immunocytochemical technique (Blaustein *et al.*, 1988; DonCarlos *et al.*, 1989; Warembourg *et al.*, 1986) provided cellular resolution, as well as high sensitivity. The results were consistent with but also extended those obtained with the autoradiographic technique (Sar and Stumpf, 1973; Warembourg, 1978a). In guinea pigs the sites with the highest numbers of estradiol-induced immunoreactive PR (PRir) neurons include the bed nucleus of arcuate nucleus, periventricular preoptic region, medial preoptic nucleus, medial preoptic area, and the ventrolateral hypothalamus, as we have described this area in this chapter. As discussed earlier, the location of the PRir and ERir cells extends beyond the Nissl-defined nuclei within the ventromedial-ventrolateral hypothalamic; this distribution also varies considerably from species to species (e.g., mouse PRir: Fig. 8). Areas with a

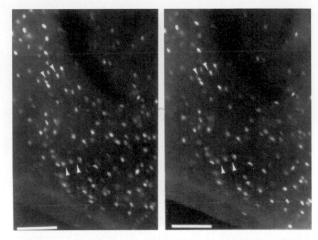

FIGURE 9 Photomicrographs of PRir (*right panel*) and ERα-ir (*left panel*) coexpression in the ventrolateral hypothalamus of an estradiol-primed female guinea pig showing that virtually all estradiol-induced PR cells also coexpress ERα-ir. *Arrowheads* point to cells containing both estradiol-induced PRir and ERα-ir. (From Blaustein and Turcotte (1989b), *Neuroendocrinology* **49**, 454–461, S. Kager AG, Basel.)

lower number of PRir cells include the bed nucleus of stria terminalis, paraventricular nucleus and lateral hypothalamus. Even within most of the PR-rich areas, relatively few neurons are darkly stained, suggesting that relatively few neurons have a high concentration of PRs. Consistent with the idea that most effects of progesterone require priming with estradiol, estradiol-induced PRir is found only in cells containing ERir (Blaustein and Turcotte, 1989b; Warembourg *et al.*, 1989) (Fig. 9).

The neuroanatomical sites containing high concentrations of PR-containing cells are in reasonable agreement in guinea pigs and rats with a few exceptions, including the following. In rats, many of the PRir cells lateral to the ventrolateral-ventromedial nucleus of the hypothalamus are located in a somewhat less dorsal position (Fig. 10). PRs, assessed by either immunocytochemistry (J.C. Turcotte, B. Gréco, and J.D. Blaustein, unpublished; Numan *et al.*, 1999), autoradiography (Sar, 1988) or *in situ* hybridization histochemistry (Blaustein *et al.*, 1999; Hagihara *et al.*, 1992), are also seen in the parts of the amygdala in rats (a site at which PRir is evident in guinea pigs only after colchicine treatment; Blaustein and Olster, 1993. Although there are some discrepancies in other areas, it is not known which of these are due to species differences

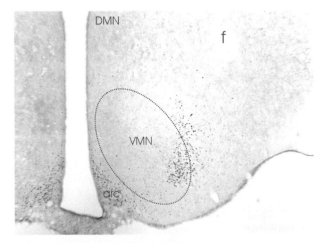

FIGURE 8 Photomicrograph of PRir in the rostral ventrolateral hypothalamic area of an ovariectomized estradiol-primed female rat illustrating the wide distribution of PRir cells beyond the ventrolateral-ventromedial nucleus of the hypothalamus. DMN, dorsomedial nucleus of the hypothalamus; arc, arcuate nucleus: VMN, ventromedial nucleus.

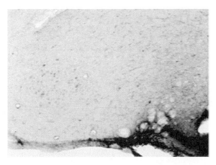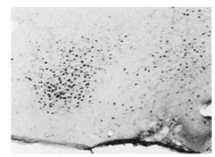

FIGURE 10 Photomicrographs of PRir in the ventromedial hypothalamic area of ovariectomized, estradiol-primed female rats injected with either oil vehicle (*left panel*) or estradiol benzoate (*right panel*) two days earlier.

and which are due to the technique used or the sensitivity of the technique.

In each of these areas, detection of PRs by immunocytochemistry is dependent on prior estrogen priming. In most experiments, regions such as the cerebral cortex, amygdala, and cerebellum show no evidence of estradiol-induced increases in PRir. In fact, early immunocytochemical (Blaustein *et al.*, 1988; Warembourg *et al.*, 1986) and autoradiographic experiments (Warembourg, 1978a) failed to demonstrate any PR-containing neurons in these areas; this finding suggested that although the receptor concentration is sufficient to assay by *in vitro* binding techniques, the cellular concentration of PRs may be too low to be detected immunochemically with the antibodies that were available. However, in many of the studies, antibody concentrations were titrated so that only estradiol-induced PRs were visible (Blaustein *et al.*, 1988). It is well-known that the number of immunoreactive cells in a particular condition can be increased or decreased by titration of the sensitivity of the technique by any of a number of methods (e.g., antibody dilution, chromogen, fixative, etc.; e.g., Auger and Blaustein, 1995; Sar, 1988). At present, the function of the estradiol-uninduced PRs present throughout the brain is unknown.

2. Progestin Receptors and Facilitation of Feminine Sexual Behavior

The characterization of neural PRs led us to propose that PRs are essential in mediating the facilitation of sexual behavior by progesterone, presumably by an interaction of activated hormone-receptor complexes with the genome (Blaustein and Olster, 1989). This hypothesis predicts that sensitivity to progesterone is determined by the concentration of unoccupied PRs available in specific neurons involved in progesterone-facilitated sexual behavior (although not necessarily *all* PR-containing neurons), and response is dependent on accumulation of an adequate concentration of bound PRs in those cells. An increased concentration of PRs (e.g., by estradiol priming) increases the sensitivity of the neural substrate for progesterone, presumably by increasing the concentration of receptors that become activated in response to progesterone treatment. Likewise, a decreased concentration of unoccupied PRs results in decreased sensitivity to progesterone.

3. Temporal Correlations: Induction of Progestin Receptors

The increase in the concentration of hypothalamic PRs after estradiol treatment occurs with a latency that correlates well with behavioral responsiveness to progesterone. After treatment with estradiol, the earliest increase in the concentration of PRs is seen about one day later in both guinea pigs (Blaustein and Feder, 1979a) and rats (Moguilewsky and Raynaud, 1979b; Parsons *et al.*, 1980), as is the first behavioral response to progesterone treatment (Feder *et al.*, 1977; Green *et al.*, 1970; Parsons *et al.*, 1980). The increased concentration of receptors is transient, as is the behavioral response to progesterone, and the duration is dependent upon the species, dose of estradiol, and mode of administration (Blaustein and Feder, 1979a; Clark *et al.*, 1982; Parsons *et al.*, 1980). Although most work has been done in ovariectomized animals in which hormone levels can be controlled the concentration of hypothalamic unoccupied PRs during the estrous cycle increases during proestrus, prior to, and in preparation for the preovulatory release of progesterone (McGinnis *et al.,* 1981)

4. Progestin Antagonists

Just as estrogen antagonists have been used to test the requirement of ER binding in the effects of estradiol on sexual behavior, progesterone antagonists have been used to test the importance of progesterone binding to its receptor. Systemic injection (Brown and Blaustein, 1984b; Richmond and Clemens, 1986) or intrahypothalamic implantation (Etgen and Barfield, 1986) of the progestin antagonist, RU 486, which binds to PRs and decreases the concentration of receptors available to bind progesterone, also inhibits the facilitation of sexual behavior by progesterone in rats and guinea pigs. The fact that RU 486-induced inhibition was overcome by a large injection of progesterone, but not by cortisol, refuted the possibility that the inhibition was due to RU 486's antiglucorticoid activity (Moguilewsky and Philibert, 1984) and suggested that the inhibition by RU 486 was due to specific blockade of PRs (Brown and Blaustein, 1986). The results of one study suggested that the progesterone antagonist, RU 486 (Pleim *et al.,* 1990), has progesterone-like effects. Like estrogen antagonists that can have both antagonistic and agonistic effects, RU 486 has agonist-like effects under particular conditions (e.g., Vegeto *et al.,* 1992).

5. Estrogen Antagonists and Agonists and Progestin Receptors

Experiments using antiestrogens that block the induction of sexual behavior by estradiol or that substitute for estradiol in its priming effects generally are consistent with a role for PRs in the facilitation of sexual behavior. In most cases, antiestrogen treatments that inhibit estradiol's priming actions on sexual behavior block estradiol's induction of PRs in the rat hypothalamus (Etgen and Shamamian, 1986; Roy *et al.,* 1979).

Treatment with enclomiphene, an estrogen antagonist that in some cases can substitute for estradiol in its early priming effects on sexual behavior in guinea pigs, also results in an increase in the concentration of PRs in the hypothalamus (Wilcox and Feder, 1983). The estrogenic effects of many antiestrogens may account for the imperfect correlation of antiestrogen inhibition of sexual behavior and of induction of PRs that has been reported (Etgen and Shamamian, 1986). Results similar to the estrogenic priming of sexual behavior

and PR induction by antiestrogens were obtained with the polychlorinated insecticide 1-(o-chlorophenyl)-1 (p-chlorophenyl)-2,2,2-trichloroethane (o,p-DDT), which has the estrogenic property of inducing behavioral response to progesterone in rats (Etgen, 1982). It is interesting that o,p-DDT also binds to progestin receptors *in vitro,* there by suggesting that o,p-DDT can induce PRs and then bind to these PRs, as well as to ERs (Brown and Blaustein, 1984a).

6. Antisense Oligonucleotides

Further evidence for the importance of PRs in the regulation of progesterone-facilitated sexual behavior comes from infusions of antisense oligonucleotides to PR mRNA, which inhibit PR synthesis, into the cerebral ventricles (Mani *et al.,* 1994a) or ventromedial hypothalamus (Frye *et al.,* 2000; Ogawa *et al.,* 1994; Pollio *et al.,* 1993). The results of these studies support the idea that facilitation of copulatory behavior, as well as paracopulatory behavior (Ogawa *et al.,* 1994), by progesterone in rats is mediated predominantly by estradiol-induced, genomic activation of neural PRs in the ventromedial hypothalamic area. As will be discussed later, other studies also suggest nongenomic effects of progestins on feminine sexual behaviors (e.g., DeBold and Frye, 1994a; Frye *et al.,* 2000).

7. Progestin Receptor Gene Disruptions

A transgenic strain of mouse with a targeted disruption of the PR gene (PR knockouts, PRKOs; Lydon *et al.,* 1995) is completely unresponsive to the effect of progesterone in the facilitation of sexual behavior (Mani *et al.,* 1994c) (Fig. 11). In a parallel study of hypothalamic unoccupied PRs in PRKO mice, a 70% reduction in estradiol-induced PRs was seen in the PRKO females, whereas heterozygous females had a 40% decrease in EB-induced PRs compared to the wild types. Although it cannot be determined whether the binding in the PRKO represents a residual low level of high-affinity binding (i.e., PRs) or the low-affinity binder known to bind [^{3}H]progestin *in vitro,* it is clear that the PRKOs have at least a greatly reduced level of estradiol-induced brain PRs.

8. Multiple Progestin Receptor Isoforms

There are actually two forms of the PR in most species. The heavier form of the receptor (PR-B) typically migrates as a 110–120 kDa protein on western

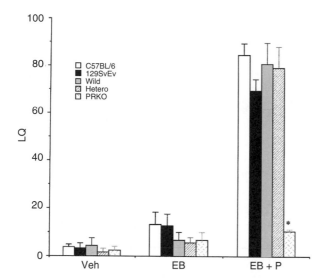

FIGURE 11 Lack of progesterone-facilitated lordosis in PR gene-disrupted (PRKO) mice. Ovariectomized mice from the three genotypes and parental strains were administered 0.5 μg estradiol benzoate followed by progesterone (100 μg) 48 hours later. The hormones were administered weekly for four weeks, and mice were tested weekly for sexual receptivity. Data shown are from the fourth weekly test. Values are mean lordosis quotients (LQ) ± SEM. (From Mani *et al.*, 1997.)

immunoblots, and the smaller form typically migrates as an 80–95 kDa protein (e.g., Ilenchuk and Walters, 1987; Mulac-Jericevic, 2000). Unlike the case with the two forms of ERs, which are synthesized from different genes, these two proteins are synthesized from a single gene and are the result of both transcription from two promoters on that gene (Kastner *et al.*, 1990) and initiation of translation from two sites on the mRNA transcript (Conneely *et al.*, 1989).

Although largely ignored in work on the effects of progesterone in the central nervous system, these isoforms are likely to be of great importance. Experiments *in vitro* have suggested that some genes are preferentially activated by PR-B (Kastner *et al.*, 1990; Tora *et al.*, 1988; Vegeto *et al.*, 1993), whereas other genes are equally responsive to PR-A and PR-B. In yet other cases, PR-A is an inhibitory regulator of PR-B (Vegeto *et al.*, 1993). Studies in transgenic strains of mice demonstrate that normal tissue responses to progesterone are dependent upon appropriate levels of PR-A and PR-B (Mulac-Jericevic *et al.*, 2000; Shyamala *et al.*, 1998). Other studies suggest differential subcellular localization of PR-A and PR-B in a living cell line (Lim *et al.*,

1999), with unoccupied PR-A being more nuclear in its localization than PR-B.

As with the finding of two forms of ERs, it is essential to keep in mind the presence of the two isoforms in interpretation of experiments on PRs. Since progestins bind equally to both isoforms, and most antibodies are not selective for a particular isoform, nearly all experiments on PRs would have assayed a sum of both isoforms. However, a few studies have looked at the presence of PR-A and PR-B in the brain. Kato *et al.* (1993, 1994) first provided evidence for two distinct mRNA transcripts in the brain for PR-A and PR-B that seem to be regulated differentially. Though PR mRNA transcripts are present throughout the brain, the PR-B form is differentially distributed. It is present in very high levels in cerebral cortex and in much lower levels in the hypothalamus–preoptic area. In a more recent study (Camacho-Arroyo *et al.*, 1998), both PR mRNA isoforms were induced and downregulated by estradiol and progesterone, respectively, in the hypothalamus, but in the preoptic area, only the PR-B showed this pattern. In contrast, in the hippocampus PR-A but not PR-B was induced by estradiol, and progesterone was without effect. The authors then reported (Guerra-Araiza *et al.*, 2000) that during the estrous cycle, the PR-B isoform predominated in the hypothalamus, preoptic area, and frontal cerebral cortex and the pattern of regulation differed among these areas. In contrast, no change was observed in the hippocampus. In monkey hypothalamus (Bethea and Widmann, 1998), the relative concentrations of the two isoforms are similar and do not appear to be differentially affected by hormonal treatments. To date, there have been no reports on the differential function of the two PR isoforms on sexual behavior.

9. Estradiol Pulses and Progesterone Facilitation of Sexual Behavior

As discussed earlier, administration of small, discrete pulses of 17β-estradiol are as effective as a much larger single dose of the esterified, longer-acting estradiol benzoate in priming ovariectomized rats (Clark and Roy, 1983; Olster and Blaustein, 1988; Södersten *et al.*, 1981) and guinea pigs (Olster and Blaustein, 1990; Wilcox *et al.*, 1984) to display progesterone-facilitated copulatory behavior. Although it was known that estradiol pulses can induce PRs in the hypothalamus (Parsons et al., 1982a), an immunocytochemical experiment was conducted to determine whether PR-containing cells within particular subareas within the hypothalamus and preoptic area might be differentially responsive to these two estradiol treatments (Olster and Blaustein, 1990). Estradiol pulse treatment induced fewer PRir cells in the arcuate nucleus and medial preoptic-anterior hypothalamic nuclei than estradiol benzoate. In contrast, PRir in the medial preoptic area, the periventricular preoptic area and the ventrolateral hypothalamus did not differ between groups of animals receiving the different estradiol treatments. Therefore, some populations of PRir cells, including those in the area of great importance for hormonal regulation of feminine sexual behavior—the ventrolateral hypothalamus—are quite responsive to the low, behaviorally sufficient, estradiol-pulse treatment, whereas others are not.

10. What Does Progestin Receptor Activation Do to Neurons?

It seems clear that brain PRs are essential for progesterone to facilitate feminine sexual behavior. Though a fair amount is known about which neurotransmitters and neuropeptides are coexpressed in PRir cells and about neuronal changes that result from progesterone administration, relatively little is known about the cellular consequences of progesterone action critical to the facilitation of sexual behavior. However, it is known that this process occurs very quickly—certainly in less than an hour in rats, in some circumstances (Glaser et al., 1983; Lisk, 1960; Meyerson, 1972). It is of great interest to learn what the neurochemical changes are that can occur so quickly yet have such profound effects on the behavioral response of female rats. Like estradiol, progesterone regulates a wide variety of neuronal genes, including the following neurotransmitter-related genes: oxytocin (Thomas et al., 1999), neuropeptide Y1 receptors (Xu et al., 2000), GnRH (Cho et al., 1994; Petersen et al., 1995; Rossmanith et al., 1996), tyrosine hydroxylase (Arbogast and Voogt, 1993, 1994), GAD 67 (Unda et al., 1995), preproopiomelanocortin (Petersen et al., 1993a), mu-opioid receptors (Petersen and LaFlamme, 1997), galanin (Brann et al., 1993), glutamate receptors (Gu et al., 1999), as well as other genes, such as 70-kDA heat shock cognate protein (Krebs et al., 1999) and the membrane-associated progesterone-binding protein, 25-Dx (Krebs et al., 2000). Progesterone also in-

duces Fos protein expression (Auger and Blaustein, 1995), presumably by altering transcription of the c-fos gene, and it downregulates PRs and ERs (Attardi, 1981; Blaustein and Brown, 1984; Brown and MacLusky, 1994).

Like estradiol, the effects of progesterone on neurons are not limited to modulating gene expression. For example, progesterone also causes changes in phosphorylation of CREB (Gu et al., 1996), and it causes changes in neurotransmitter receptor binding as well as coupling of neurotransmitter receptors to G proteins (e.g., Etgen et al., 1999; Etgen and Karkanias, 1994; Petitti and Etgen, 1992). Furthermore, progesterone causes rapid changes in electrophysiological responses in neurons (Havens and Rose, 1988; Kawakami et al., 1979; Kawakami and Sawyer, 1959; Komisaruk et al., 1967; Lincoln, 1969b), and it causes changes in the electrophysiological response to various neurotransmitters (Smith et al., 1987a,b). Much work is needed on the possible relationship of each of these and other progesterone-directed cellular changes to progesterone's effect on sexual behavior.

11. Role of Progestin Receptors in Progesterone-Independent Sexual Behavior ("Estrogen Heats")

Because estradiol binds to PRs in rats with an affinity about 1% that of progesterone (MacLusky and McEwen, 1980; Parsons et al., 1984), it was suggested (Parsons et al., 1984) that the effects of estradiol on estradiol-induced sexual behavior in the absence of progesterone might also involve interaction of estradiol with intracellular PRs, as well as ERs. However, several lines of evidence argue against the notion that estradiol influences sexual behaviors through interaction with PRs:

1. Injection of a protein synthesis inhibitor blocks progesterone-facilitated sexual behavior but not sexual behavior induced by chronic exposure to estradiol (Rainbow et al., 1982c).
2. The progesterone antagonist, RU 486, blocks progesterone-facilitated sexual behavior, but it does not block estradiol-induced or estradiol-facilitated sexual behavior (Blaustein et al., 1987).
3. An injection of progesterone facilitates high levels of paracopulatory behavior, whereas an injection of estradiol does not (Blaustein et al., 1987).

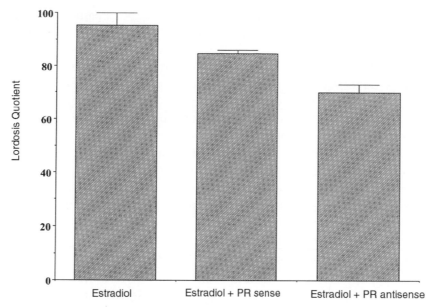

FIGURE 12 Lack of blockade of estradiol-only induced sexual behavior by antisense oligonucleotides to PR mRNA. Ovariectomized rats received 200 μg estradiol benzate two days before testing and either antisense oligonucleotides or sense control icv at the time of the estradiol benzoate injection and 24 hours later. The slight decrease in lordosis is not statistically significant (S.K. mani, unpublished observations).

4. Although estradiol induces sexual behavior in rats (Davidson *et al.*, 1968) and guinea pigs (Landau *et al.*, 1978; Wallen and Thornton, 1979), the hormone binds poorly to PRs in guinea pigs (Blaustein and Feder, 1979a).
5. Estradiol induces lordosis in PRKO mice, as well as wild-type mice, thus demonstrating that the ability of PR-deficient mice to respond and exhibit lordosis is not compromised (Mani *et al.*, 1997).
6. Antisense oligonucleotides to PR mRNA do not block estradiol-induced sexual behavior as they do sexual behavior induced by estradiol and progesterone (Fig. 12).

Therefore, it would seem very unlikely that estradiol-induced sexual behavior is attributable to binding of estradiol to PRs.

VI. OTHER MECHANISMS OF ACTION OF STEROID HORMONES

The emphasis of this chapter has been on the genomic mechanisms involved in hormonal regulation of sexual behavior. This emphasis should not be taken to imply that estradiol and progesterone act *only* in this way to influence sexual behavior. In fact, there is ample evidence that estradiol and progesterone can both act through membrane mechanisms in the brain, and progesterone can influence brain function and sexual behavior through this mechanism. Estradiol has rapid effects on neuronal electrophysiology that are too fast for a transcriptionally mediated mechanism (e.g., Kelly *et al.*, 1977, 1999; Wong and Moss, 1991). Membrane receptors have been reported and characterized in the brain (Ke and Ramirez, 1990; Ramirez *et al.*, 1996; Towle and Sze, 1983). Some steroid hormones bind to the $GABA_A$-benzodiazepine receptor and may influence sex behaviors through these receptors (DeBold and Frye, 1994a; Frye *et al.*, 1998; Frye and Vongher, 1999). Estradiol and progesterone have rapid influences on neuronal responsiveness to amino acids (Smith *et al.*, 1987c; Smith, 1989). Effects of steroid hormones on the release of GnRH that are independent of cell nuclei have been reported (Becker, 1990; Dluzen and Ramirez, 1989; Ke and Ramirez, 1987). Lordosis can be induced in female hamsters by applying bovine serum albumin (BSA)-conjugated progesterone to the ventral tegmentum (DeBold and Frye, 1994b), which presumably is not taken up into cells. Hormonal regulation of behavior and physiology might involve a variety of mechanisms operating at different cellular levels.

Generally, mechanistic studies have either focused on the role of nuclear ERs and PRs acting as transcriptional regulators or on the role of membrane receptors for the steroid receptors in regulation of sexual behavior. A very important recent study suggests that at least some membrane ERs may be synthesized from the same gene as the nuclear receptor (Razandi *et al.*, 1999). *In vitro*, either the ERα or ERβ gene is capable of directing the synthesis of receptors that become associated with membranes and is capable of signaling through the mitogen-activated protein kinase, ERK, pathway. This finding raises an important question about many of the studies that have either used hormone antagonists, antisense oligonucleotides, or targeted gene disruption to test the involvement of steroid receptors acting as transcription factors. If it is found that in the brain, the same ER and PR genes that direct synthesis of the receptors that act as transcription factors also direct synthesis of the membrane receptor, then the conclusions of many of these experiments could be called into question, because these manipulations would have disrupted a membrane receptor as well. It is interesting that antiestrogens have been shown to block some of the rapid effects of estradiol on electrophysiological response (Lagrange *et al.*, 1997). Furthermore, in immunocytochemical studies, ERα (Blaustein *et al.*, 1992; Blaustein, 1992a; Milner *et al.*, 2001; Wagner *et al.*, 1998) and PRs (Blaustein *et al.*, 1988; Clarke *et al.*, 2000; Watson and Gametchu, 1999) have been found in extranuclear locations, including distal dendrites and axon terminals (Blaustein *et al.*, 1992). In some cases, they have been observed to be associated with synaptic densities (Blaustein *et al.*, 1992; Blaustein, 1994).

VII. NEUROANATOMICAL SITES OF REGULATION OF SEXUAL BEHAVIORS BY HORMONES

Studies on the roles of different neuroanatomical areas in the regulation of feminine sexual behavior have used the techniques of lesions (with our without knife cuts) or hormone implants. These studies have asked two related, but independent, questions. Lesion studies ask whether a particular brain area is *necessary* for sexual behavior induced in a particular way (usually hormonally but sometimes by VCS). In contrast, hormone implant studies ask whether hormonal stimulation of a particular area is *sufficient* for the effects of the particular hormone on sexual behavior. Although the two techniques are complementary, they provide different information. It is not hard to imagine wiring diagrams in which a particular area, when lesioned, would decrease the expression of a behavior without itself being hormone-sensitive. While a great deal is known about the neuroanatomical pathways involved in feminine sexual behavior (see Pfaff *et al.*, 1994, for comprehensive review), our focus is on two major forebrain sites of integration of hormonal signals and information from the social environment—the ventromedial hypothalamus and the preoptic area—and we will briefly discuss the role of the midbrain central gray as a contrast.

The emphasis of research over the past decade has been on understanding the cellular and molecular processes involved in hormonal regulation of sexual behaviors, with little emphasis on refining our understanding of the sites at which hormones regulate these behaviors. It has become axiomatic that the ventromedial nucleus of the hypothalamus is the most critical site for hormonal regulation of feminine sexual behavior. Is there strong evidence to support this claim? The issue becomes quite important to resolve, because so many subsequent studies on cellular processes of hormone action on feminine sexual behavior have focused on the molecular processes ongoing in this nucleus to the *exclusion* of other areas. Unfortunately, although this is no longer an intense area of investigation, we still do not have the answers to some of the original questions.

A. Sites That Are Necessary for Hormonal Effects on Sexual Behavior: Lesion Studies

1. Ventromedial Hypothalamic Area

Some of the earliest lesion studies implicated an area within the mediobasal hypothalamus in the regulation of feminine sexual behavior. In these studies, large hypothalamic lesions were often used, and in fact deficits in sexual behavior were seen. However, the fine points of many of these studies have been lost through the years. For example, while it is true that, as often cited, Goy and Phoenix (1963) found that lesions of the ventromedial hypothalamic area decreased lordosis in estradiol plus progesterone-treated, ovariectomized female guinea pigs, the lesions included a wide variety of structures within the hypothalamic region, including the periventricular anterior nucleus, the anterior hypothalamic nucleus and other areas. In referring to the four animals with the most severe deficit in behavior, the authors noted that "the common area of destruction for these brains may be described as lying with the lateral extensions of the arcuate nucleus and ventrolateral portions of the ventromedial." It is interesting that the authors pointed out that the lesions in the brains from the four poorest responders were "localized predominantly in these cell-poor zones, close to or on the ventral surface of the hypothalamus." This region, which is adjacent to the ventromedial nucleus, is the precise region of highest density of ER- and PRir neurons in the ventrolateral-ventromedial hypothalamic area. Although the results do not *directly* support a critical role for the ventromedial nucleus of the hypothalamus per se, they do support an important role for the general steroid-receptor-rich area within the ventromedial-ventrolateral hypothalamus.

Likewise, although Kennedy and his colleagues (Kennedy, 1964; Kennedy and Mitra, 1963) are often cited as providing evidence for a role of the ventromedial hypothalamus in hormonally regulated feminine sexual behavior, these investigators did not really assess the level of sexual receptivity in their lesioned animals; rather they reported the presence or absence of a sperm plug within one hour of testing in gonadally intact (Kennedy and Mitra, 1963) or ovariectomized, hormone-injected (Kennedy, 1964) rats. Changes in any of the sex behaviors—copulatory, paracopulatory, or progestative—could result in the absence of a sperm plug. Also, it is unfortunate that detailed histological results on the extent of the lesions were not reported, as these hypothalamic lesions included, but were not limited to, the ventromedial nucleus.

Later studies using more precise analysis of sites of tissue damage had mixed results with respect to the role of the ventromedial nucleus of the hypothalamus. In landmark studies, Mathews and Edwards (1977a,b) reported deficits in estradiol-alone induced sexual behavior in ovariectomized rats, but not in estradiol plus progesterone–induced sexual behavior. This pattern of interference with estradiol-induced lordosis, but not estradiol plus progesterone-induced was also seen after sagittal knife cuts made laterally to the anterior hypothalamus (Pfeifle *et al.,* 1980). Although these data actually suggested a dissociation in the neuroanatomical substrates of estradiol-only versus estradiol plus progesterone–facilitated sexual receptivity, other studies by this group (A.S. Clark *et al.,* 1981) suggested that ventromedial nucleus lesions inhibited copulatory and paracopulatory behavior induced by either estradiol alone or estradiol and progesterone. The possibility of slight differences in the extent of the lesions cannot be eliminated, especially since the lesions of the earlier papers were quite small, and the lesions in the latter work were rather large (A. Clark, personal communication). Nevertheless, these studies suggested that different sites within the ventromedial nucleus itself might be essential for estradiol-induced versus estradiol plus progesterone–induced sexual behavior.

In a subsequent study, Pfaff and Sakuma (1979) followed the time course of loss of sexual receptivity after ventromedial nucleus lesions in estradiol (only)-primed ovariectomized rats. Lordosis declined over the course of 36 to 60 hours, with a minimum latency of 12 hours, suggesting that whereas this area is critical to estradiol modulation of sexual receptivity, it is not likely to be a part of the actual reflex arc. In contrast, disruption of lordosis occurs within 15 minutes of lesion in hamsters (Gibson and Floody, 1998).

In many experiments, care was taken to limit the extent of the lesion to the ventromedial nucleus of the hypothalamus, as defined by Nissl staining (Mathews and Edwards, 1977a,b). As discussed earlier, many ERir and PRir neurons lie lateral to the ventromedial nucleus of the hypothalamus, particularly at more rostral levels, so these lesions would have spared many of these ERir/PRir neurons. However, parasagittal knife cuts made laterally to the ventromedial nucleus often cut directly through the adjacent area containing a large population of ovarian steroid receptor-containing neurons. These knife-cuts eliminate lordosis in response to either hormonal treatment (Pfeifle *et al.,* 1980), thereby suggesting that perhaps the typical lesions of the ventromedial hypothalamic spare some of the adjacent progesterone-sensitive neurons, and that these neurons or efferent projections of these neurons are critical to progesterone-facilitated sexual receptivity.

Other studies have shown that quite large ventromedial lesions may result in near-total loss of estradiol and progesterone-induced lordosis, whereas lesions that spare 30 to 50% of the nucleus may result in no decrement at all (Richmond and Clemens, 1988). Some studies (e.g., Okada *et al.,* 1980) reported recovery of sexual behavior weeks after lesions, but a subsequent study (Mathews *et al.,* 1983) did not observe this recovery.

Another wrinkle was introduced into the interpretation of these studies by a report (Emery and Moss, 1984a) that ventromedial nucleus-lesioned rats had decreased contact with males when allowed to pace the contacts, although they were quite capable of displaying lordosis when mounted. These authors argued that the decrease in lordosis seen in other studies may be due to avoidance of mounting by the lesioned rats, and it may be due to differences in size of the lesions and to particular damage outside the nucleus. The possibility cannot be excluded that this deficit enters into the results of some of the experiments in this area, and is in fact consistent with the earlier interpretation of LaVaque and Rodgers (1975).

Thus, even after numerous studies on the role of the ventromedial nucleus of the hypothalamus in estradiol-induced and estradiol plus progesterone–induced sexual behavior, one cannot help but wonder whether we really know the *precise* cells that are essential for each. There are large differences among experiments in the extent of damage to the ventromedial nucleus, the ventrolateral aspect of the ventromedial nucleus, the anterior hypothalamus, and the area adjacent to the ventromedial nucleus, so conclusions on the specific cells that mediate estradiol-induced and estradiol plus progesterone–induced copulatory and paracopulatory behaviors are difficult to make with confidence.

In spite of the limitations of these lesion studies, there appear to be a number of conclusions that can be drawn about the role of the ventromedial nucleus from the lesion studies:

1. The ventromedial nucleus of the hypothalamus and/or a nearby population of cells is involved in the action of estradiol on sexual receptivity.
2. This area is not part of the actual reflex arc, since deficits take hours to days to be manifest after its lesion. Furthermore, rats with sagittal knife-cuts made laterally to the ventromedial nucleus do not

show deficits in responding to experimenter-induced, VCS with a probe.
3. Estradiol-induced sexual behavior is more adversely affected by lesions of the small, ventromedial nucleus of the hypothalamus than is sexual receptivity induced by estradiol and progesterone; this suggests that this area may be less critical in the presence of progesterone.
4. Lesions of the ventromedial nucleus always reduce sexual behaviors, but they rarely eliminate them, perhaps because either the entire steroid receptor-containing region associated with the ventromedial hypothalamic area or an as-yet-undefined subpopulation of cells within this region is critical for hormonal regulation of sexual behavior.

2. Preoptic Area and Sites Rostral to the Ventromedial Hypothalamus

Although there are sites in the anterior hypothalamus that appear to be essential for hormonal regulation of feminine sexual behavior (Law and Meagher, 1958; Singer, 1968), the adjacent medial preoptic is inhibitory to the expression of hormonally regulated feminine copulatory behavior (Powers and Valenstein, 1972). Lesions of the medial preoptic area not only result in higher levels of response; they also dramatically decrease the threshold dose of estradiol necessary to induce copulatory behavior in conjunction with progesterone (Powers and Valenstein, 1972). Although few experiments have used the dose-titration technique used by these original investigators, other experiments have confirmed that the preoptic area has an inhibitory role in copulatory behavior in rats (Hoshina *et al.,* 1994) and guinea pigs (Olster, 1998; Rodriguez-Sierra and Terasawa, 1979). In other studies chemical lesions or electrolytic lesions of the medial preoptic area eliminated or reduced proceptive and pacing behaviors (Hoshina *et al.,* 1994, Whitney, 1986, Yang and Clemens, 2000). This surprising finding suggests that this area might have opposite effects on copulatory and paracopulatory-progestative behaviors.

Lesions of the medial forebrain bundle, which would disrupt many of the efferents from the preoptic area (e.g., Conrad and Pfaff, 1975) have a similar facilitative effect on estradiol plus progesterone–induced lordosis (Modianos *et al.,* 1976), doubling the number of days that rats continue to show sexual receptivity after a particular hormonal regimen. Studies of estradiol plus progesterone–induced lordosis in rats that received knife cuts dorsal to the preoptic area (Yamanouchi and Arai, 1990) confirmed earlier findings that the septum may be another site of origin of an inhibitory influence on lordosis rostral to the ventromedial hypothalamus (Nance *et al.*, 1975); lesions of the septum, like the medial preoptic area, increase sensitivity to estradiol in an estradiol plus progesterone–induced sexual behavior paradigm. Based on horizontal knife cuts rostral to the preoptic area (roof cuts), which also result in hypersensitivity to estradiol plus progesterone–induced lordosis, Takeo *et al.* (1993) suggested that the inhibitory effect of the septum is distinguishable from the inhibitory effect of the preoptic area. In contrast, knife cuts of stria terminalis resulted in hyposensitivity to estradiol–induced lordosis (Takeo *et al.*, 1995), perhaps due to interruption of projections from the amygdala.

3. Midbrain Central Gray

The midbrain central gray contains steroid receptor-containing neurons that, in contrast to the neurons of the ventromedial nucleus of the hypothalamus, are likely to be part of the lordosis reflex arc. Like the areas in the forebrain that have been implicated in the hormonal regulation of sexual behavior, the midbrain central gray has ERs (Pfaff and Keiner, 1973; Turcotte and Blaustein, 1993) and estradiol-induced PRs (Blaustein and Feder, 1979a; Turcotte and Blaustein, 1993). Neurons of the ventromedial hypothalamic area (Canteras *et al.*, 1994; Krieger *et al.*, 1979; Sakuma and Pfaff, 1980) and preoptic area (Conrad and Pfaff, 1976), including steroid receptor-containing neurons (Morrell and Pfaff, 1982; Ricciardi *et al.*, 1996), project directly to the midbrain central gray. As was the case with lesions of the ventromedial nucleus of the hypothalamus, lesions of the midbrain central gray disrupt estradiol-induced lordosis (Riskind and Moss, 1983; Sakuma and Pfaff, 1979), but they may not have as large an effect on estradiol plus progesterone–induced lordosis (Riskind and Moss, 1983). However, transection of the projection pathways between the ventromedial hypothalamic area and the midbrain central gray completely eliminates lordosis in response to estradiol and progesterone (Edwards and Pfeifle, 1997; Hennessey *et al.*, 1990).

As has been discussed by Pfaff and colleagues (1994), the midbrain central gray functions very differently than the ventromedial hypothalamus. Whereas deficits in lordosis are delayed after the hypothalamic lesions (Pfaff and Sakuma, 1979), they are immediate after the midbrain lesions (Sakuma and Pfaff, 1979). Although the midbrain central gray is also involved in hormonal regulation of sexual behavior in hamsters (Floody and O'Donohue, 1980), other sites in both dorsal (Muntz *et al.*, 1980) and ventral (DeBold and Malsbury, 1989; Lisciotto and DeBold, 1991) midbrain are important as well.

B. Sites That Are Sufficient for Hormonal Stimulation of Sexual Behaviors: Implants

1. Estradiol

Intracranial hormone implant experiments suggest a number of areas that seem to be critical to the full expression of copulatory behavior. Unfortunately, studies of estradiol application to the brain have rarely looked at more than copulatory behavior (i.e., lordosis). The results of earliest experiments suggested that estradiol, applied to a fairly wide variety of sites, increased the expression of lordosis. These included the midbrain reticular formation (Ross *et al.*, 1971; Yanase and Gorski, 1976), preoptic area (Barfield and Chen, 1977; Lisk, 1962; Morin and Feder, 1974c; Yanase and Gorski, 1973), and the ventromedial hypothalamus (Barfield and Chen, 1977; Morin and Feder, 1974b). However, because of the focus of lesion experiments on the ventromedial hypothalamus and the preoptic area, most of the subsequent implant work also focused on these two areas.

The results of many experiments in which care was taken to control for diffusion of estradiol to other parts of the brain from the implant site singled out the ventromedial nucleus of the hypothalamus as the most sensitive site of action for estradiol priming of sexual behavior in rats (Barfield and Chen, 1977; Davis *et al.*, 1982; Davis and Barfield, 1979; Rubin and Barfield, 1980) and hamsters (DeBold *et al.*, 1982; Floody *et al.*, 1987). Though the results of many experiments point to the ventromedial nucleus of the hypothalamus as the *most* sensitive forebrain site for estradiol action, it is safe to say that other areas have not been as extensively studied as this nucleus.

Because the ventromedial nucleus of the hypothalamus is among the areas of highest density of ERs in the brain, with 40% of the neurons in the ventrolateral subdivision containing ERs (Morrell *et al.,* 1986), this localization also was taken as support for the notion that ERs are involved in mediating the effects of estradiol on feminine sexual behavior. Results of experiments using localized implants of antiestrogens (Howard *et al.,* 1984; Meisel *et al.,* 1987), protein synthesis inhibitors (Glaser and Barfield, 1984; Meisel and Pfaff, 1985; Rainbow *et al.,* 1982a), and transcription inhibitors (Yahr and Ulibarri, 1986) confirm that a site in or near the ventromedial nucleus is a critical site involved in ER-mediated, genomic regulation of sexual behavior by estradiol. It should be noted, however, that compounds implanted or infused into the brain do not stay precisely where they are placed, so the results should not be interpreted as having pinpoint accuracy.

An experiment on the neuroanatomical site of estradiol action in guinea pigs used a different approach. In order to identify a hypothalamic site sufficient for estradiol to prime response to progesterone, Delville and Blaustein (1991) applied small, dilute estradiol-containing cannulae (33 gauge) bilaterally to the ventrolateral hypothalamus (the region analogous to the ventromedial nucleus of the hypothalamus in rats). Animals were injected with progesterone, tested for lordosis responses, and then perfused, and brains were immunostained for the expression of PRs. Because only estradiol-induced PRir was examined, this served as a bioassay for spread of estradiol to other cells capable of expressing estradiol-induced PRir. Only cannulae located at the rostral and ventral aspect of the ventrolateral hypothalamus induced behavioral response to progesterone, and the expression of estradiol-induced PRir in the rostral-ventral ventrolateral hypothalamus correlated with response to progesterone (Fig. 13). Thus, stimulation of a population of ovarian steroid hormone-sensitive neurons within the ventrolateral hypothalamus by very low levels of estradiol may be sufficient to induce sexual behavior in response to progesterone in female guinea pigs. Many of the PRir cells lie outside of the Nissl-defined neuroanatomical nuclear groups in this region in agreement with the earlier discussion that the Nissl-defined nucleus itself may not be the critical site of action of estradiol and progesterone on feminine sexual behavior.

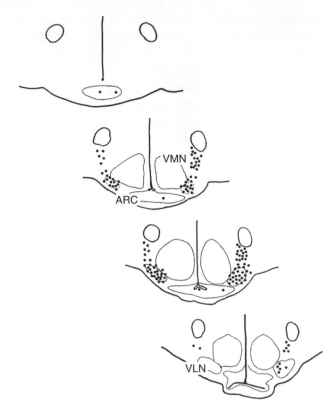

FIGURE 13   Reconstruction of the location of PRir cells observed at different levels of the ventrolateral hypothalamus in guinea pigs that became sexually receptive after implantation of an estradiol cannula in the rostral ventrolateral hypothalamus. VMN, ventromedial nucleus of the hypothalamus; VLN, ventrolateral nucleus of the hypothalamus. (From Delville and Blaustein (1991), *Brain Res.* **559,** 191–199, © 1991, with permission from Elsevier Science.

2. Progesterone

As was the case with estradiol, implantation of progesterone into an array of neuroanatomical areas has been reported to facilitate sexual behavior in estradiol-primed rats and guinea pigs. Among these areas are the caudate (Yanase and Gorski, 1976), hippocampus and amygdala (Franck and Ward, 1981), interpeduncular nucleus (Luttge and Hughes, 1976), habenula (Tennent *et al.,* 1982), reticular formation (Ross *et al.,* 1971; Tennent *et al.,* 1982; Yanase and Gorski, 1976), preoptic area (Rodriguez-Sierra and Komisaruk, 1982; Ward *et al.,* 1975), and mediobasal hypothalamus (Morin and Feder, 1974b; Powers, 1972). The capability of neural progesterone implants to facilitate the expression of lordosis in all these tissues, some of which lack estradiol-induced PRs, is puzzling if estradiol induction of PRs is required for the facilitation by progesterone. However, later work, using intracranial implants of progesterone (Rubin and Barfield, 1983) or a progesterone antagonist (Etgen and Barfield, 1986) suggests that stimulation of the ventromedial nucleus of the hypothalamus by progesterone is *sufficient* for facilitation of sexual behavior. Similar results have been obtained in hamsters (DeBold and Malsbury, 1989) and guinea pigs (Morin and Feder, 1974b). The failure of earlier studies fully to consider the diffusion of progesterone from the implant site to other parts of the brain *may* have contributed to the contradictory findings. However, it is clear that progesterone can have at least a contributory function in other areas, such as the ventral midbrain (Pleim *et al.*, 1991). Though delineating the full network of steroid hormone-sensitive neurons regulating sexual behavior is also essential, the data also justify intensive investigations of the role of the ventromedial nucleus of the hypothalamus and the surrounding area in the regulation of sexual behavior in rats. These implant data can be reconciled with the lesion experiments described earlier, which show that estradiol plus progesterone–induced sexual receptivity often remains even after ventromedial nucleus lesions, because the critical site of action is likely to include the surround of the nucleus, where many ERir and PRir cells are found (see, for example, Figs. 4 and 10).

Studies on the *inhibitory* effects of progesterone on sexual behavior have suggested that the midbrain reticular formation (Morin and Feder, 1974a; Yanase and Gorski, 1976) and the mediobasal hypothalamus (Marrone *et al.*, 1979) are important areas for progesterone action. However, as with the search for the site of facilitation, the work by Rubin and Barfield (1984) suggested that a principal site for progesterone in the progesterone-induced refractory period in rats is the same site as the facilitatory effect—the ventromedial nucleus of the hypothalamus. This is consistent with a reanalysis (Blaustein and Brown, 1985) of earlier data of Morin and Feder (1974a), which suggested that progesterone implants in the mediobasal hypothalamus of guinea pigs at sites that cause facilitation of sexual behavior also cause refractoriness to progesterone. Therefore, the facilitation and refractory period induced by progesterone can occur after implantation of progesterone in the same neuroanatomical site, perhaps in the same neurons.

While other areas have been studied for their roles in hormonal regulation of sexual receptivity, the ventromedial nucleus and the preoptic area have been the most extensively studied. However, many questions remain in addition to the relative role of the ventromedial nucleus and its surround in the hormonal regulation of sexual behaviors. The neural network governing hormonal regulation of sexual receptivity is complex and involves many other areas (e.g., Pfaff *et al.*, 1994). Other neuroanatomical areas respond similarly to mating stimulation (e.g., with Fos expression) and have ERs and PRs that are regulated similarly to those in the ventromedial hypothalamic area. However, relatively little is known about the role of each of these other areas in the mediation of hormonal effects on feminine sexual behavior. For example, little work has been done on the role of the bed nucleus of stria terminalis and posterodorsal medial amygdala in the regulation of copulatory and paracopulatory behaviors or heat duration. Nevertheless, the ventromedial hypothalamic area, if not the ventromedial *nucleus* itself, the medial preoptic area, and the midbrain central gray are clearly important sites. Unfortunately, after forty years of study, neither the precise role of these areas in regulation of feminine sexual behavior nor the *precise* site of the relevant, lordosis-promoting or lordosis-inhibiting cells are known.

VIII. CELLULAR MECHANISMS REGULATING ESTROUS DURATION

A. Down-regulation of PRs Leads to Estrous Termination and the Refractory Period

The period of sexual receptivity for each species is rather tightly regulated. For example, in estrous-cycling guinea pigs, as after estradiol and progesterone treatments, heat lasts about eight hours (Young, 1969) Likewise, rats remain sexually receptive for approximately 14 hours (Blandau *et al.*, 1941), but in ovariectomized rats, the duration is very dependent on hormonal treatment. It has been suggested that this timing of sexual receptivity is referable to the regulation of occupied PRs in particular neurons (Blaustein and Olster, 1989). Injection of a behaviorally effective dose of progesterone in

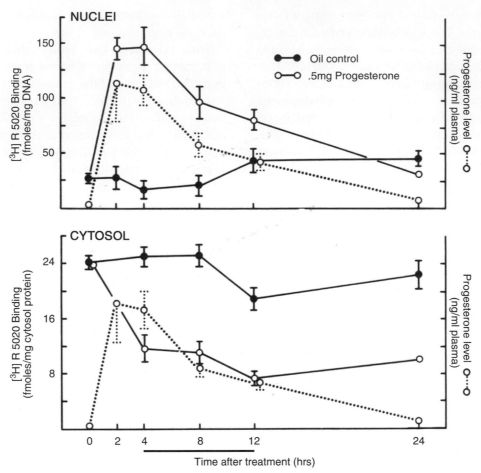

FIGURE 14   Time course of accumulation of occupied PRs (*top panel*) and depletion of cytosol PRs (*bottom panel*) in guinea pig hypothalamus-preoptic area after treatment of estradiol-primed, ovariectomized guinea pigs with 0.5 mg progesterone. *Dotted lines* indicate results of progesterone radioimmunoassay to determine progesterone levels. *Bar* along x-axis denotes approximate time during which similarly treated guinea pigs exhibit sexual behavior. (Adapted from Blaustein and Feder (1980), *Endocrinology* **106**, 1061–1069, © The Endocrine Society.)

estrogen-primed guinea pigs and rats causes the rapid binding to brain PRs, including in the hypothalamus and preoptic area (Blaustein and Feder, 1980; McGinnis *et al.*, 1981; Rainbow *et al.*, 1982b). In rats, the preovulatory secretion of progesterone during the estrous cycle binds to hypothalamic PRs (Rainbow *et al.*, 1982b). In guinea pigs, the presence of occupied PRs after progesterone injection is transient; the level returns to baseline by about 12 hours after injection (Blaustein and Feder, 1980) (Fig. 14). The presence of occupied PRs after progesterone injection correlates well with the expression of sexual behavior. This temporal concordance

first suggested that the expression of lordosis requires maintenance of elevated levels of occupied PRs and that termination of sexual behavior is due to loss of these receptors.

Subsequent experiments support the hypothesis that occupied PRs are essential for the maintenance of sexual behavior. Physiological manipulations that extend the duration of the period of sexual behavior also increase the duration that hypothalamic PRs remain occupied. For example, a supplemental injection of estradiol at the time of a facilitatory progesterone injection in ovariectomized guinea pigs extends heat duration (Blaustein,

1982a; Joslyn and Feder, 1971) and likewise prolongs the duration of occupied, hypothalamic PRs, presumably by increasing the concentration of PRs available to bind progesterone (Blaustein, 1982a). Similarly, supplemental progesterone treatment during the period of sexual behavior increases the duration of behavioral estrus and prolongs the duration of occupied PRs (Brown and Blaustein, 1985).

Although during the estrous cycle, as in ovariectomized animals administered hormones exogenously, a decrease in blood levels of progesterone correlates with the termination of behavioral estrus (Blaustein and Feder, 1980; Feder *et al.,* 1968b), the two events are by no means inextricably linked. Extended maintenance of elevated blood levels of progesterone by supplemental progesterone treatment in guinea pigs prolongs heat duration for two to three hours (Brown and Blaustein, 1985; Morin and Feder, 1973), but heat nevertheless terminates. Similarly, retention of occupied, hypothalamic PRs is only prolonged for a short time by these treatments (Brown and Blaustein, 1985). Failure to prolong retention of cell nuclear PRs for very long may be due to the inevitable progesterone-induced decrease in the concentration of unoccupied PRs in the presence of constantly elevated progesterone levels.

The loss in behavioral response can be caused by either a declining concentration of hypothalamic unoccupied PRs or the absence of a sufficient level of progesterone to interact with the particular level of unoccupied receptors. The decline in the concentration of unoccupied PRs, in turn, can be caused by loss of estradiol priming with its resulting decline in the concentration of unoccupied PRs, previous exposure to progesterone with its resulting downregulation of PRs, or both. Given the complexity of these interactions and the fact that progesterone level has only a contributory role in causing the loss of PRs, it is not surprising that conflicting results concerning progesterone's role in estrous termination have been obtained; some results suggest a role for progesterone (Barfield and Lisk, 1974; Powers and Moreines, 1976) and some suggest no role (Hansen and Södersten, 1978).

The use of the progesterone antagonist, RU 486, provided evidence of a causal relationship between the occupation of PRs and maintenance of progesterone-

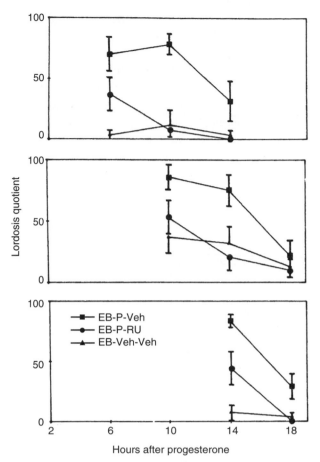

FIGURE 15 RU 486 inhibits ongoing sexual receptivity in rats. Ovariectomized rats were treated with 0.5 mg progesterone 44 hours after receiving 2 μg estradiol benzoate. Rats were treated with RU 486 (EB-P-RU) or oil vehicle (EB-P-Veh) 2 hours, 6 hours, or 10 hours after progesterone injection. A third group of rats treated with EB only (EB-Veh-Veh) was included for comparison. Animals were tested for sexual receptivity 4, 8 and, in some cases 12 hours after RU 486 injection. (From Brown *et al.* (1987), *Endocrinology* **121**, 298–304, © The Endocrine Society.)

facilitated sexual behavior. Injection of RU 486 during the period of sexual behavior shortens the duration of behavioral estrus in guinea pigs (Brown and Blaustein, 1986) and rats (Brown *et al.,* 1987), at the same time causing the rapid displacement of hypothalamic progesterone-occupied PRs (Fig. 15). By whatever mechanism this loss of cell nuclear PRs occurs (Brown and Blaustein, 1986), termination of behavioral estrus seems to be due to loss of neural progesterone-occupied PRs.

Thus, by a variety of experimental paradigms in which estrous duration was either extended or abbreviated, the relationship between the retention of occupied PRs and the duration of behavioral estrus has been confirmed. Although the evidence suggests that the accumulation of occupied PRs is essential, the sequelae of PR action, whatever they may be, are essential as well. Therefore, we should expect to find other proteins, peptides, or neurotransmitters, that are endpoints of PR action, and that also correlate well with facilitation of sexual behavior, heat duration, termination, and lack of further responsiveness.

In an attempt to tease apart a possible active effect of progesterone on termination of behavioral estrus from the effects of declining estradiol, Wallen and Thornton (1979) induced sexual behavior in guinea pigs by daily injections of estradiol alone. When estradiol injections were stopped and animals were treated with progesterone or oil, sexual behavior did not terminate more rapidly in the progesterone-treated animals. The conclusion that termination of heat is not due to progesterone action may have relevance to the process of termination of sexual receptivity induced by estradiol alone. However, because estradiol-induced sexual behavior does not seem to be attributable to interaction with PRs (Section V.C.11), this experimental is probably not relevant to progesterone-facilitated sexual receptivity.

B. Down-regulation of Progestin Receptors and the Progesterone-Induced Refractory Period

Following termination of behavioral estrus in guinea pigs (Goy *et al.*, 1966) and in some circumstances in rats (Blaustein and Wade, 1977; Nadler, 1970), a refractory period occurs during which animals are not responsive to a second exposure to progesterone. Many experiments support the hypothesis that the downregulation of PRs by progesterone is responsible for this phenomenon. First, during the refractory period, the concentration of hypothalamic PRs is depressed (Blaustein and Feder, 1979b; Moguilewsky and Raynaud, 1979b; Parsons *et al.*, 1981), most robustly in guinea pigs in the ventrolateral hypothalamus (Blaustein and Turcotte, 1990), and progesterone treat-

ment results in low levels of occupied PRs (Blaustein, 1982b; Blaustein and Feder, 1980). Second, hormonal treatments that influence responsiveness to progesterone also cause correlated changes in the concentration of PRs. Supplemental estradiol priming (Blaustein and Wade, 1977; Joslyn and Feder, 1971; Nadler, 1970; Shivers *et al.*, 1980) offsets the progesterone-induced refractory period, so that animals regain responsiveness to the second progesterone injection. In guinea pigs, the supplemental estradiol injection also offsets the decrease in the concentration of unoccupied PRs, thereby resulting in high levels of occupied progestin receptors in response to progesterone (Blaustein, 1982b). Third, the refractory period can be overcome by a large dose of progesterone (Blaustein, 1982b; Hansen and Södersten, 1979), despite the presence of low PR levels. This high dose increases progesterone-occupied, hypothalamic PRs, whereas a typical, behaviorally ineffective, lower dose does not (Blaustein, 1982b). Therefore, under a variety of conditions, there is a strong relationship between the level of hypothalamic PRs that become occupied after progesterone treatment and the presence of lordosis. Heat termination and the progesterone-induced refractory period may both be due to a progesterone-induced decrease in the concentration of unoccupied PRs with consequent loss of occupied PRs (heat termination) or failure to accumulate an adequate concentration of occupied PRs in response to progesterone (refractory period).

The results of some pharmacological experiments support the hypothesis that the progesterone-induced refractory period is caused by desensitization specifically to progesterone rather than by inhibition of estradiol's action. In rats that are refractory to progesterone, the neuropeptide, gonadotropin-releasing hormone (Gilchrist and Blaustein, 1984), or the serotonin antagonist, methysergide (Gilchrist and Blaustein, 1984; Rodriguez-Sierra and Davis, 1977), facilitates sexual behavior, even in progesterone-unresponsive rats. These earlier papers suggested that estradiol priming itself is unaffected by the intervening progesterone injection, and that animals seem to be specifically desensitized to progesterone, a finding consistent with a role for downregulation of PRs during the refractory period. However, in a more recent paper (Gonzalez-Mariscal *et al.,* 1993), in which the progestin, norgestrol, was used to induce "sequential inhibition," an opposite conclusion was found. In this experiment, it was reported that animals became refractory to gonadotropin-releasing hormone, prostaglandin E_2, and cAMP, as well as progesterone. The authors suggest that this cannot be explained by depletion of PRs, but by progestins having a depressive effect on the nervous system. In a subsequent experiment (Beyer *et al.,* 1997), however, these authors demonstrated that a progestin antagonist blocks the facilitation by each of these compounds, thereby providing evidence that each may facilitate sexual receptivity by activation of PRs, a concept (Mani *et al.,* 1994a, 1997) that will be discussed later in this chapter.

It was suggested that progesterone induces the refractory period by a protein synthesis-dependent process unrelated to the downregulation of PRs (Parsons and McEwen, 1981). When the protein synthesis inhibitor, anisomycin, was injected into rats around the time of the first progesterone injection, the response to the second progesterone injection appeared to be restored. However, it was subsequently shown that although anisomycin rapidly inhibits ongoing sexual behaviors (Brown *et al.,* 1987), it actually delays termination of behavioral estrus, such that the rats were still sexually receptive from the first progesterone injection at the time of the second progesterone injection (Blaustein *et al.,* 1982). Therefore, these data suggest that the inhibition of protein synthesis, in some conditions, delays heat termination. Although the cellular basis for the delay in termination of sexual behavior in this particular case is unknown, it could be due to interference with the process of downregulation of PRs.

The suggestion that the process of downregulation of PRs results in heat termination and then persists in causing a robust refractory period may explain the difficulties in demonstrating a refractory period in rats. The ease of overcoming the refractory period with progesterone should be related to the ease of extending heat duration with progesterone. Indeed, guinea pigs have a pronounced refractory period (Goy *et al.,* 1966), they respond to supplemental progesterone with a small increase in heat duration (Brown and Blaustein, 1985; Morin and Feder, 1973), and they show dramatic downregulation of PRs with

moderate doses of progesterone (Blaustein and Feder, 1979b). Conversely, in rats in which the refractory period is only seen with very specific hormonal conditions (low estradiol and high progesterone; (Blaustein and Wade, 1977), heat duration is readily extended by a variety of progesterone treatments (Brown and Blaustein, 1984c; Dudley *et al.,* 1980; Hansen and Södersten, 1978), and downregulation of PRs is far less extreme even with high doses of progesterone (Moguilewsky and Raynaud, 1979b; Parsons *et al.,* 1981; Schwartz *et al.,* 1979).

Just as there have been conflicting reports of progesterone involvement in termination of behavioral estrus in rats, there have been questions concerning the presence or absence of a progesterone-induced refractory period during the rat estrous cycle. In fact, rats become hyposensitive to progesterone after termination of behavioral estrus during the estrous cycle as well as in the ovariectomized, hormonally treated model. A typical dose (0.5 mg) of progesterone is only effective in inducing sexual behavior during the proestrous stage of the estrous cycle (Södersten and Hansen, 1979). The fact that a large dose of progesterone is effective immediately after heat termination (Hansen and Södersten, 1979), but a low dose is not (Powers and Zucker, 1969; Södersten and Hansen, 1979; Zucker, 1967), suggests that the animals are hyposensitive at this time to progesterone.

Another cellular event that may be related to estrous termination is the downregulation of ERs by progesterone under some conditions (Attardi, 1981; Bethea *et al.,* 1996; Blaustein and Brown, 1984; Brown and MacLusky, 1994; Smanik *et al.,* 1983) (Fig. 16). Though this presumably decreases the effectiveness of estradiol, downregulation of ERs should then slow the synthesis of PRs, which would then further contribute to the downregulation of PRs.

To summarize, the evidence suggests that termination of the period of sexual receptivity after progesterone treatment results from downregulation of PRs, and the ensuing period of hyposensitivity to progesterone is a consequence of this downregulation. Fewer PRs are available to bind progesterone, so animals tend to be unresponsive. Thus, heat termination and the refractory period can be seen as due to the same cellular underpinnings.

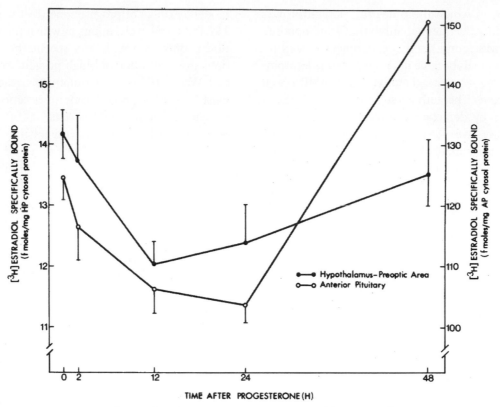

FIGURE 16   Downregulation of ERs by progesterone in rats. Cytosol (unoccupied) ER concentrations in hypothalamus-preoptic area and anterior pituitary gland in rats that were ovariectomized and implanted with a silastic capsule containing estradiol one week earlier, and then injected with 5 mg progesterone at 0 hours (no injection), 2, 12, 24, or 48 hours prior to assay. (From Blaustein and Brown (1984), *Brain Res.* **304**, 225–236, © 1984, with permission from Elsevier Science.)

IX. CROSS-TALK BETWEEN NEUROTRANSMITTERS AND STEROID HORMONE RECEPTORS: ACTIVATION OF STEROID RECEPTORS BY AFFERENT INPUT

A. Neurotransmitters Influence Concentrations of ERs and PRs

Early work by Cardinali (1979) showed that the catecholamines can regulate the concentration of steroid hormone receptors in the pineal gland. This was a very surprising finding, and it raised the possibility that steroid receptors could be regulated by environmental stimuli as well as by steroid hormones. In studies aimed at extending this finding to the hypothalamus, it was reported that catecholaminergic activity influences the concentrations of neural sex steroid receptors in

rat and guinea pig brain (Blaustein, 1992b). Drugs that either inhibit norepinephrine synthesis (dopamine-β-hydroxylase inhibitors) or block noradrenergic receptors (e.g., α-adrenergic antagonists) typically decrease ER concentration (Blaustein *et al.*, 1986; Blaustein, 1987; Blaustein and Letcher, 1987; Blaustein and Turcotte, 1987; cf. Malik *et al.*, 1993) or inhibit estradiol's induction of unoccupied PRs (Clark *et al.*, 1985; Nock *et al.*, 1981; Thornton *et al.*, 1986b) in the hypothalamus or both, and α-adrenergic agonists reverse this suppression. Lesioning noradrenergic cell groups tends to decrease ER concentrations in the hypothalamus (Montemayor *et al.*, 1990), thereby supporting the interpretation that noradrenergic blockade decreases the concentration of functional, biologically active ERs. Finally, under some conditions stimulation of dopamine receptors increases the concentration of ERs in the brain (Blaustein and Turcotte, 1987; Gietzen *et al.,* 1983; Thompson *et al.,* 1983; Woolley *et al.,* 1982).

Use of techniques with cellular resolution provided evidence for direct connections between catecholaminergic neurons and ER and PR-containing neurons, which could provide sites of integration between catecholaminergic neurons and steroid hormone-responsive neurons. [³H]estradiol-concentrating neurons were described that appear to be innervated by catecholaminergic neurons (Heritage *et al.,* 1977, 1980). Further, tyrosine hydroxylase-ir and dopamine-β-hydroxylase-ir (DBH-ir) varicosities closely associated with PRir or ERir neurons in the hypothalamus and preoptic area have been described (Blaustein and Turcotte, 1989a; T. D. Brown *et al.,* 1990). Many of the ERir cells in the ventrolateral hypothalamus of female guinea pigs have closely associated DBH-ir varicosities, suggestive of extensive noradrenergic innervation of ERir neurons (Tetel and Blaustein, 1991), and those with closely associated DBH-ir varicosities stain more darkly than ERir neurons lacking this association, a finding suggestive of noradrenergic regulation of basal cellular ER levels in this area.

The regulation of steroid hormone receptors by neurotransmitters is not limited to regulation of sex steroid receptors by catecholamines. For example, concentrations of ERs are regulated by muscarinic agonists (Lauber, 1988a; Lauber and Whalen, 1988) and antagonists (Lauber, 1988b). And concentrations of glucocorticoid receptors are regulated by social conflict (Johren *et al.,* 1994), perinatal handling (ODonnell *et al.,* 1994), stress (Meaney *et al.,* 1996), norepinephrine (Maccari *et al.,* 1992), and serotonin (Mitchell *et al.,* 1992; Seckl and Fink, 1991).

There are many other examples of this relationship between neurotransmitters and steroid hormone receptors that may be of relevance to the regulation of feminine sexual behavior by sensory or environmental stimuli. For example, the odor of soiled bedding induces Fos-ir in a variety of neuroanatomical areas that contain an abundance of ERir neurons, including the medial amygdala (Dudley *et al.,* 1992), and the removal of the olfactory bulbs results in an increase in the concentration of ERs in the amygdala of female rats (McGinnis *et al.,* 1985). Likewise, anterior roof deafferentation knife cuts increase the level of lordosis in response to estradiol and also increase the concen-

tration of ERs in the mediobasal hypothalamus, but they decrease the concentration in the septum (Chen *et al.,* 1992). Conversely, exposure of female prairie voles to the odors of males induces estrous behavior (Carter and Getz, 1985) and increases the concentration of ERs in the preoptic area (Cohen-Parsons and Roy, 1989). While the increase in the concentration of ERs was not seen at the immunocytochemical level (Hnatczuk *et al.,* 1994), this may have been caused by technical limitations of the procedure (see Blaustein, 1992b). However, not all of the effects of lesions on hormonal response are due to modulation of concentrations of receptors. For example, medial preoptic area lesions in guinea pigs increase behavioral response to estradiol and progesterone, but have no apparent effect on ERs or PRs in the hypothalamus (Olster, 1998).

Thus, although the cellular processes involved have not been elucidated, it is clear that the principle of regulation of steroid hormone receptor concentrations by neurotransmitters is a common means of integration and regulation. The anatomical evidence suggests that this regulation occurs by interaction of particular neurotransmitters with their receptors on steroid receptor-containing neurons. This regulation provides a means by which afferent inputs derived from stimuli coming from the environment, including the social environment, can influence steroid receptor concentrations, which, in turn, can modulate the sensitivity of particular neurons to each steroid hormone.

B. Ligand-Independent Activation of PRs

During the first 25 years of studies of steroid receptors, it had been assumed that binding of receptors to their cognate ligands—the steroid hormones—was necessary for activation of the receptor. However, it is now known that steroid hormone receptors can be activated by a means other than steroid hormones. In 1991, Power *et al.* (1991a) made the startling discovery that the COUP (chick ovalbumin upstream promoter, one of the so-called "orphan" receptors) receptor could be activated *in vitro* in the CV-1 cell line by stimulation with dopamine. These investigators (Power *et al.,* 1991b) then showed that PRs could be activated by dopaminergic agonists in an *in vitro* transfection system as well. The process by which dopamine induces the activation is apparently via a second messenger rather than a direct effect of the agonist on the PR and is referred to as ligand-independent activation. The idea that steroid receptors can be activated indirectly via membrane-related events has now been supported in a wide variety of work, including that on GnRH activation of PRs (Turgeon and Waring, 1994) and growth factor activation of ERs (Aronica and Katzenellenbogen, 1993; Ignar-Trowbridge *et al.,* 1993).

In a behavioral study it was found that dopamine activates PRs in neurons *in vivo*. Intracerebroventricular administration of the D1-specific dopamine agonists were used to substitute for progesterone in the facilitation of sexual behavior in estradiol-primed rats (Mani *et al.,* 1994a), thus confirming and extending earlier work in which dopaminergic agonists were infused into the hypothalamus and preoptic area (Foreman and Moss, 1979a). Like progesterone activation of sexual behavior, facilitation of sexual behavior by dopaminergic agonists was blocked by progesterone antagonists or antisense oligonucleotides directed at the PR mRNA administered intracerebroventricularly. A similar relationship holds for gonadotropin-releasing hormone (GnRH) (Beyer *et al.,* 1997; Mani *et al.,* 1995), as well as prostaglandin E_2 and cAMP (Beyer *et al.,* 1997) facilitation of sexual receptivity; each can be blocked by treatment with a progesterone antagonist. Likewise, nitric oxide (Mani *et al.,* 1994b, p. 6472) and cGMP (Chu *et al.,* 1999) may each facilitate sexual behavior via activation of PRs. Thus, dopamine and other neurotransmitters may activate feminine sexual behavior by indirect activation of neural PRs.

In light of these studies, some experiments that have evaluated the effects of neurotransmitters on facilitation of sexual behaviors may have to be re-assessed. Many of these experiments were performed with the assumption that the pharmacological agents were stimulating or antagonizing output of steroid hormone sensitive systems. However, it is likely that some of the drugs act on *afferents* to progesterone-sensitive neurons, some act on the *efferent projection sites* of these neurons, some act on these *neurons themselves,* some act on a combination, and perhaps others even influence sexual behavior independently of steroid hormone-sensitive neurons.

In experiments in which norepinephrine synthesis was blocked with a dopamine-β-hydroxylase inhibitor,

U-14624, increased accumulation of PRs (Blaustein, 1986b) and ERs (Blaustein, 1986a) was observed in the absence of progesterone or estradiol, suggestive of activation of the receptors. Although in 1986 there was no apparent explanation for this, besides causing a depletion of norephinephrine, this inhibitor increases dopamine levels in the hypothalamus. Perhaps, the increase in dopamine results in the activation of PRs and ERs with consequent accumulation of receptors in the cell nuclear fraction.

Studies on the regulation of GnRH during the rat and mouse estrous cycle are consistent with the idea that activation of PRs may be an intermediate step in the mechanism by which some neurotransmitters and other factors regulate GnRH. For example, blockade of PRs or inhibition of PR synthesis blocks some of the effects of estradiol on GnRH regulation, presumably by inhibiting activation of PRs by a neural consequence of estradiol action (Chappell *et al.,* 1999; Chappell and Levine, 2000; Xu *et al.,* 2000).

In 1986 Whalen and Lauber proposed the hypothesis that many drugs that substitute for progesterone do so by elevating neuronal levels of cGMP. Alternatively, Beyer and his colleagues (1981) showed that drugs that increase cAMP may substitute for progesterone. Although it is not possible to exclude either possibility, the data suggest that some of the drugs that influence sexual behavior do so by modulating second-messenger systems and then by secondarily activating PRs (and perhaps other transcription factors).

This type of influence of afferent input on steroid receptors could come into play in the regulation of reproductive physiology. For example, VCS causes a variety of neuroendocrine changes in female rats, including the induction of pseudopregnancy (Gunnet and Freeman, 1983), increase in LH release (Moss *et al.,* 1977), increase in lordosis intensity (Diakow, 1975), and subsequently termination of the period of sexual behavior (Blandau *et al.,* 1941). Similarly, olfactory stimuli associated with mating have profound effects on reproductive physiology, and many of these could be mediated via afferent influences onto steroid-sensitive neurons.

Many questions remain about the role of ligand-independent activation in regulation of sexual behavior.

First, the two types of regulation of steroid receptors by afferent input discussed here, ligand-independent activation and regulation of concentrations of receptors, have been treated as independent processes. However, activation of PRs by progesterone downregulates PRs. Might appropriate afferent input first activate receptors by ligand-independent activation, and then cause downregulation of the receptor in the same way that ligand-dependent activation does, and then result in decreased sensitivity to progesterone?

A second question is whether "ligand-independent" activation is actually due to afferent regulation of neural progesterone synthesis. Afferent input facilitates sexual receptivity via PRs, and this occurs in the absence of peripheral release of progesterone from the ovaries and adrenal glands. This is a reasonable hypothesis, particularly because the results are consistent with ligand-independent activation seen *in vitro* in transfected cell systems. However, the possibility that these factors may activate progesterone synthesis in the brain (Baulieu *et al.*, 1996; Guennoun *et al.*, 1997; Jungtestas *et al.*, 1989) has not yet been excluded. The fact that estradiol induces progesterone synthesis in the hypothalamus (Micevych *et al.*, 2000) raises the possibility that some of these factors may influence PRs through this route (ligand-dependent activation) rather than by ligand-independent activation. Although one report suggests that this is not the case, further study is warranted (Auger *et al.*, 2000).

X. PHYSIOLOGICAL REGULATION OF RESPONSE TO ESTRADIOL AND PROGESTERONE IS OFTEN DUE TO REGULATION OF ESTROGEN AND PRs: PHYSIOLOGICAL PERTURBATIONS

Reproductive behavior is regulated not only by acute changes in steroid hormones. A variety of influences, including environmental factors, afferent input from other organs, and long-term deprivation of sex steroid hormones, can feed into this. Much of the evidence supports the view that many of the influences that regulate behavioral response to estradiol and progesterone do so by regulation of the concentrations of steroid hormone receptors in particular neurons.

A. Food Deprivation and Metabolic Inhibitors

An important physiological regulator of hormonal responsiveness is the availability of food. Food deprivation and perturbation of availability of nutrients by use of metabolic inhibitors in many species interrupt ovulatory cycles and suppress estrous behavior. Because of an apparent critical role for ERs in the ventromedial hypothalamic area for hormonal regulation of sexual receptivity, the hypothesis was tested that the effects of food deprivation on responsiveness to sex steroid hormones were due to a decrease in ERs in that area. Food deprivation in ovariectomized hamsters decreasd the number of ERir cells in the ventromedial hypothalamic area (Li *et al.*, 1994). There was neuroanatomical specificity to this response: whereas food deprivation decreased ERir in the ventromedial hypothalamic area, it increased the number of detectable ERir neurons in the medial preoptic area. Although subdiaphramatic vagotomy blocked the effects of metabolic inhibitors on ERir in the medial preoptic area, it was without effect on lordosis or ERir in the ventromedial hypothalamus. In contrast, area postrema lesions blocked the effects of metabolic inhibitors on lordosis and ERir in the ventromedial hypothalamic area, but they were without effect on ERir in the medial preoptic area.

In an analogous study to determine whether the effects of food deprivation might be attributable to a decreased induction of PRs in this area, food deprivation decreased estradiol-induced PRs in the medial preoptic area and medial amygdala, but it had no apparent effect in the ventromedial hypothalamus (Du *et al.*, 1996). Although these studies provide an example of regulation of PRs by an afferent influence, they do not follow from the effects of food deprivation on ERs in the ventromedial hypothalamus.

Female rats made diabetic by drugs, such as streptozotocin, that destroy the insulin-secreting β-cells of the pancreas are deficient in hormonally regulated sexual behavior and have reduced levels of ERs in the hypothalamus and preoptic area (Dudley *et al.*, 1981a,b; Gentry *et al.*, 1977; Siegel and Wade, 1979), including a decrease in ERir in the ventromedial hypothalamic area (Li *et al.*, 1994). In addition, estradiol injection results in less induction of PRs (Ahdieh *et al.*, 1983). Insulin replacement in turn restores ER levels as well as hormonally induced sexual behavior. These data suggest that the changes in the concentrations of ERs and PRs are at least partially responsible for the reductions in feminine sexual behavior that accompany diabetes in rats.

B. Photoperiod

When Syrian hamsters are exposed to short, winterlike photoperiods or appropriate nightly melatonin signals, gonadotropin secretion declines, reproduction is completely inhibited, and there is a decreased responsiveness to steroid hormones for the expression of sexual behaviors. Results of several studies suggest that at least a part of the modulation of response is referable to changes in steroid receptor in localized neuroanatomical areas. First, injections of melatonin, which mimicked an inhibitory photoperiod, in ovariectomized hamsters resulted in a decreased number of ERir cells in the medial preoptic area (Hill *et al.*, 1996; Lawson *et al.*, 1992), the hypothalamus (Lawson *et al.*, 1992), or bed nucleus of the stria terminalis (Hill *et al.*, 1996).

In a subsequent study specifically on the the effects of long- and short-photoperiod exposure, ERir and PRir were examined in neuroanatomical areas associated with sexual behaviors of ovariectomized hamsters (Mangels *et al.*, 1998). As expected, exposure to short photoperiods attenuated the lordosis response following sequential treatment with estradiol and progesterone, decreased the immunostaining intensity of ER immunoreactive cells in the medial preoptic area, and increased the number of ERir cells in part of the medial amygdala. Hamsters exposed to short photoperiods had lower levels of PRir in the ventromedial hypothalamic area, the adjacent medial tuberal nucleus, the medial preoptic area, medial amygdala, and arcuate nucleus, consistent with the idea that the behavioral refractoriness caused by exposure to short photoperiods may be attributable to changes in the induction of neural PRs by estradiol.

C. Circadian Effects on Sexual Receptivity

Not all differences in response to estradiol are readily attributable to changes in ER concentration. It had been reported that female rats show higher levels of lordosis during the dark phase of the lighting cycle than during the light phase (Hansen *et al.*, 1979). In an attempt to determine whether this circadian rhythm is referable to fluctuations in ERs, Roy and Wilson (1981) noted a circadian rhythm in the concentration of neural ERs. However, the fact that the behavioral response is optimal when estradiol is administered during the dark phase of the cycle (Hansen *et al.*, 1979; Wilson *et al.*, 1983) but the peak in ERs is in the light phase suggests that the rhythm in neural ERs, although interesting, is unrelated to behavioral response. In fact, it has been suggested that the circadian rhythm in behavior may be due to a circadian variation in the kinetics of estradiol metabolism (Wilson *et al.*, 1983).

D. Hysterectomy

The removal of the uterus (hysterectomy) is an experimental treatment that increases behavioral response to sex steroid hormones (Siegel *et al.*, 1978). Studies of the mechanism of this increased response reveal that hysterectomy increases the concentration of estrogen binding in the hypothalamus (Ahdieh and Wade, 1982). Although it is not known whether this is due to a fundamental modification of ER function or to an altered rate of peripheral estradiol metabolism in hysterectomized rats, female rats are more responsive to estradiol, and they show increased levels of occupied ERs after estradiol injection.

It is not yet known whether hysterectomy influences hormonal response by a humoral route or a direct neural route. Although it is possible that hysterectomy causes changes in hormonal response via changes in the metabolism of sex hormones, it is also possible that hysterectomy causes changes in ER levels by loss of afferent input from the uterus to steroid receptor-containing neurons, a result that in turn can modulate steroid receptor levels.

XI. ROLE OF AFFERENT INPUT FROM SEXUAL STIMULI IN MODULATION OF SEXUAL BEHAVIOR

Changes in the display of individual patterns of behavior as well as the overall level of feminine sexual responsiveness may occur as a consequence of sexual stimuli received by the female during the mating sequence and at the onset and termination of estrus. All aspects of sexual performance have been demonstrated to be wholly or partially influenced by the successive sexual and nonsexual interactions that occur during mating. Endocrine influences initiate the changes that result in the onset of behavioral expression, but both neural and endocrine influences modulate the changing behavior patterns observed during the expression and termination of feminine sexual behavior.

The intensity of copulatory and paracopulatory behaviors and the timing of progestative behaviors are modulated by feedback loops which are activated in response to the sensory stimulation that the female receives from the male during estrus. Such stimulation includes mounts, intromissions, and ejaculations as well as olfactory and auditory inputs. These stimuli have effects on the short-term expression of copulatory, paracopulatory, and progestative behaviors as well as on the length of behavioral estrus.

In other species, including the prairie vole (Carter *et al.,* 1987) and musk shrew (*Suncus murinus;* Rissman, 1987), olfactory and somatosensory stimuli provided by the male induce endocrine changes necessary for the induction of estrous behavior. However, detailed discussion of this topic is beyond the scope of this chapter.

A. Vaginocervical Stimulation

Vaginocervical stimulation is a reproductively relevant, external, environmental stimulus that is an important component of the stimulation received by female rats during mating. Though this in itself does not provide adequate rationale for studying its effects on steroid receptor-containing neurons, there are numerous physiological situations in which VCS influences hormone-sensitive processes. As discussed below, VCS induces luteinizing hormone (LH) release (Moss *et al.,* 1977) and the twice daily surges of prolactin that then result in pseudopregnancy (Gunnet and Freeman, 1983). In the short term, it prolongs lordosis responses (Diakow, 1975), and in the long-term, it decreases lordosis responding, increases rejection (Hardy and DeBold, 1972), and causes abbrevia-

tion of the period of sexual receptivity (Blandau *et al.,* 1941; Reading and Blaustein, 1984), especially when mating stimulation is paced by the female (Erskine, 1989).

The results of many experiments suggest that experimentally-administered VCS in rats can mimic the effects of intromissions by a male rat on reproductive physiology and behavior. This finding is interesting, because the experimental probes that are used are typically smooth glass or plastic, and they provide pressure directly to the cervix with only mild distension pressure on the vaginal wall (and in many cases, electrical stimulation of the cervix has been used; e.g., Gorospe and Freeman, 1981). In contrast, the rat penis is covered with keratinous spines (Sachs *et al.,* 1984; Taylor *et al.,* 1983), and it may not actually contact the cervix directly during an intromission. Although it is unclear whether experimentally induced VCS provides the same crucial element of genitosensory stimulation provided by an intromission, experimentally-administered VCS causes longitudinal stretching of the vaginal wall which appears to cause sufficient vaginal stimulation to induce immobilization similar to that induced by an intromission (Komisaruk and Larsson, 1971). Therefore, experimentally-administered VCS may induce the same behavioral effects as intromissions.

B. Short-Term Effects of Mating Stimulation

Both closed-loop and open-loop feedback regulation (Camhi, 1984) of behavior have been observed. Closed-loop or negative feedback effects can be said to be active when the expression of feminine sexual behavior leads to subsequent decreases in sexual responsiveness. The closed-loop feedback effects on feminine sexual behavior are easily observed during behavioral tests in which the female can pace contact with the male. As indicated above, during paced mating, the likelihood that the female will leave the cage containing the male and the latency for her to return to the male cage after receipt of a copulatory stimulus is influenced by the type of antecedent stimulus that precedes the response. Withdrawals from the male occur more often and the latencies of the female's return to the male's cage are longer when the antecedent stimulus is an intromission or an ejaculation than when the antecedent stimulus is a mount (Bermant, 1961;

Bermant and Westbrook, 1966; Erskine, 1985). Thus, copulatory mounts that include VCS result in a short-term inhibition of sexual responsiveness: that is, intromissions and ejaculations result in lengthier inter-intromission intervals than do copulatory mounts without intromission. There is virtually no understanding of the cellular mechanisms that underlie these rapid and transient changes. Coopersmith *et al.* (1996) showed that over the course of a test in which cycling females in estrus received 30 intromissions, the latency to return to the male's cage increased as a function of the numbers of prior intromissions. As seen in Fig. 17, the inter-intromission interval (III) increased at a significantly greater rate during paced mating tests in which the female could control the timing of contact with males than in tests in which the female could not avoid the male and thus received nonpaced stimulation. As the number of intromissions increased, the latency to return to the male compartment increased. These results demonstrate that when the female is allowed to pace sexual contacts with males, there is a progressive lengthening in the rate at which females receive VCS. Since this graded change is not observed during non-

paced mating tests, the pacing behavior of the female demonstrates that the female is modulating her own behavioral expression in response to the prior stimuli received. Interestingly, this increase in III is revealed by, but not dependent upon, paced mating. As seen in Fig. 17, if a female receives the first 15 intromissions at a nonpaced, i.e., more rapid rate, she will still space the subsequent 15 intromissions in the same way as the group that initially paced intromissions. Therefore, the increasing III over the course of a mating sequence is not dependent upon the prior expression of paced mating, but is solely the consequence of the prior VCS, in whatever pattern it has been received.

C. Mating-Induced Heat Abbreviation

In another form of closed-loop feedback, the receipt of intromissions and ejaculations results in abbreviation of the period of estrus in rats (Boling and Blandau, 1939; Erskine, 1985; Lodder and Zeilmaker, 1976; Pfaus *et al.*, 2000; Reading and Blaustein, 1984), guinea pigs (Goldfoot and Goy, 1970; Roy *et al.*, 1993), hamsters (Carter, 1972,1973; Carter *et al.*, 1973; Carter and Schein, 1971; Ramos and DeBold, 1999), and gerbils (McDermott and Carter, 1980) such that females that receive VCS during mating express copulatory behaviors for a shorter length of time than do females who have not received VCS. Estrous duration in the unmated cycling female rat as measured by manual palpation for occurrence of lordosis was approximately 19 hours in length, whereas the female's receipt of intromissive but not mounts-without-intromissive stimulation significantly reduced the length of estrus to 16 hours (Lodder and Zeilmaker, 1976). In rats, pacing of sexual contacts increases the inhibitory effect of VCS on estrus length (Erskine, 1985; Coopersmith *et al.*, 1996) so that the overall duration of estrus is reduced from approximately 16 hours in females receiving nonpaced intromissive stimulation to approximately 13 hours in females receiving paced mating stimulation. It has been suggested that some of the inhibitory effects of intromissions on subsequent sexual receptivity may be dependent upon trauma to the vagina. Excessive intromissions reduce subsequent sexual receptivity (Hardy and DeBold, 1972), and Rodriguez-Sierra *et al.* (1975) also reported that experimenter-induced VCS resulted in some active rejection behaviors as well. There have

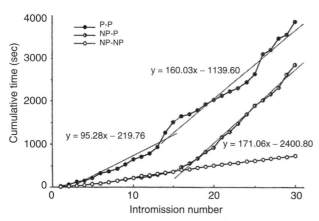

FIGURE 17 Cumulative time in seconds between intromissions during a 30-intromission mating test. P-P females received both the first 15 and the second 15 intromissions under paced mating conditions, and NP-NP females received the first 15 and the second 15 intromissions under nonpaced mating conditions. For NP-P females, the first 15 intromissions were nonpaced and the second 15 intromissions were paced. (From Coopersmith *et al.* (1996), *J. Comp. Psychol.* **110**, 176–186, © 1996 by the American Psychological Association, Reprinted with permission.)

been no comprehensive studies examining effects on the duration of either paracopulatory or progestative estrous behaviors.

There is more to heat abbreviation than these early studies may have appreciated. Early studies defined the period of sexual receptivity as the time during which a female responds to appropriate mating stimulation with the lordosis response. However, in a testing situation that allows the female to passively avoid the male or demonstrate rejection behaviors (and presumably in nature), it appears that heat termination is preceded by the presence of active and passive rejection behaviors. For example, Pfaus *et al.* (2000) studied the effects of administration of 50 vaginocervical stimulations with a glass probe on subsequent sexual behavior in a bilevel testing chamber in which the female can escape from the male. By 16 to 20 hours after the VCS, females displayed both passive (remaining away from the male) and active rejection behavior toward the male. Although van der Schoot *et al.* (1992) failed to find effects of previous copulatory stimulation on heat duration, the study by Pfaus suggests that in the study by van der Schoot, the investigators may not have waited a sufficiently long time to test for abbreviation.

Mating-induced heat abbreviation in rats seems to be mediated by the pelvic nerve, since pelvic neurectomy blocks it (Lodder and Zeilmaker, 1976). However, in guinea pigs, transection of the pelvic, pudendal, and genitofemoral nerves (Slimp, 1977) is without effect. This has been taken as evidence for a nonneural route of travel for the information from the genitals to the brain in guinea pigs. However, it is now known that the vagus nerve also plays a role in conveying sensory information from the vagina and cervix to the brain (Cueva-Rolon *et al.*, 1996; Komisaruk *et al.*, 1996), so the possibility that this route is involved in guinea pigs cannot be excluded. However, Roy *et al.* (1993) showed that whereas an ejaculation by an intact male abbreviated the period of sexual receptivity, an ejaculation by a gonadectomized male with hormone replacement did not. This study suggested that in guinea pigs, unlike rats and hamsters, heat abbreviation may be dependent upon a factor in intact males' ejaculate, but it cannot be excluded that the nature of the mechanical stimulus delivered by the intact male was quantitatively different than that of the gonadectomized male. Furthermore,

this latter study is in conflict with the earlier study (Goldfoot and Goy, 1970) in which it was reported that either a male or vaginocervical probing by the experimenter resulted in heat abbreviation.

D. Enhancement of Sexual Behavior by Mating Stimuli

In addition to these closed-loop feedback effects, there is also open-loop feedback control of feminine sexual behavior. In one type of open-loop feedback, particular stimuli received during mating result in a behavior pattern of enhanced response to repeated input from the same or similar stimuli. Although female rats that are sexually receptive respond to appropriate stimulation of the flanks and perineum with the expression of the lordosis response, the presence of VCS by penile intromission with or without ejaculation results in a greater intensity of the lordosis reflex (Diakow, 1975). VCS administered by a glass probe in conjunction with manual palpation of the flanks and perineum intensifies the lordosis response (as assessed by amount of spinal dorsiflexion; Komisaruk and Diakow, 1973). Ovariectomized rats and ovariectomized rats treated with doses of estrogen that were subthreshold for inducing lordosis showed enhanced lordosis responsiveness to manual palpation immediately following artificially applied mechanosensory stimulation to the cervix and vagina (Komisaruk and Diakow, 1973). This facilitated response to VCS persisted for the subsequent 60 minutes (Rodriguez-Sierra *et al.*, 1975).

Similar facilitation of lordosis responding was demonstrated by using another test paradigm in which females were exposed to sexually active males for 4 to 10 intermittent 15 minute periods of mating tests with males (Foreman and Moss, 1977; Rajendren *et al.*, 1990; Rajendren and Moss, 1993). With repeated exposure to males, the enhancement of lordosis continued throughout the test sequence. This short-term potentiation of lordosis is not dependent upon the presence of gonadal or adrenal steroids (Auger *et al.*, 1997). Although the relative contribution of VCS as compared to flank and perineal stimulation provided by the male was not addressed in these studies, recent experiments (Bennett *et al.*, 2001) show that the mating-induced potentiation is dependent upon VCS. Elimination of

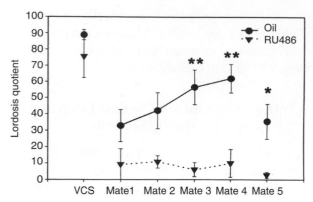

FIGURE 18 Effects of the progesterone antagonist RU 486 on sexual behavior of estradiol-primed female rats following VCS and repeated testing with a male. Although RU 486 was without effect on the lordosis accompanying VCS, it completely inhibited mating-induced potentiation of lordosis. VCS, manual vaginal-cervical stimulation; Mate, 15-minute mating test with a male; Manual, manual stimulation of flanks and perineum by the experimenter. (From Auger *et al.* (1997), *Endocrinology* **138**, 511–514, © The Endocrine Society.)

VCS by placing tape over the vagina blocks the potentiation, whereas experimenter-induced VCS can induce potentiation in the absence of the male.

In an interesting example of cross-talk between mating stimuli and hormone-response mechanisms, it was shown that the potentiation of response was dependent on PRs, because it was blocked by administration of progesterone antagonists (Fig. 18). One mechanism by which mating stimulation might facilitate sexual receptivity is the following. VCS and other mating-related stimuli induce release of dopamine, as well as other neurotransmitters (Kohlert *et al.*, 1997; Matuszewich *et al.*, 2000; Mermelstein and Becker, 1995; Vathy and Etgen, 1989). Dopamine then acts on dopamine receptors in forebrain, which then activates second-messenger pathways. This may include an increase in cAMP, which then causes phosphorylation (Meredith *et al.*, 1998) of DARPP-32 (dopamine, cAMP-regulated phosphoprotein, molecular weight 32; Greengard *et al.*, 1999) (Fig. 19), which in turn may lead to activation of PRs (Auger *et al.*, 1997; Mani *et al.*, 2000) either directly or by activation of co-activators. The possibility that the VCS of mating-induced release of norepinephrine (Crowley *et al.*, 1977; Vathy and Etgen, 1989) is involved has not been studied.

In contrast, Moss and collaborators (Foreman and Moss, 1979b; Moss *et al.*, 1977; Rajendren *et al.*, 1990, 1991, 1993; Rajendren and Moss, 1993) suggested an alternate pathway for at least some of the effects of mating on potentiation of sexual behavior. That is, they suggest that an accessory olfactory system pathway involving the vomeronasal organ, medial amygdals, and the ventromedial nucleus of the hypothalamus and release of GnRH is involved in this potentiation. The mechanism described by these investigators would seem to be independent of the ligand-independent activation of PRs, described above.

Sexual receptivity also increases over the course of extended testing (Clemens *et al.*, 1969; Hardy and DeBold, 1973; Larsson *et al.*, 1974; Rajendren *et al.*, 1990). However, because adrenalectomy can prevent this increase (Larsson *et al.*, 1974) and because mere handling can substitute for mating (Hardy and DeBold, 1973), this increase would not seem to be a consequence of afferent input from the genital region to the brain. In a study on the negative consequences of mating stimulation, Reading and Blaustein (1984) observed that the levels of both progesterone and occupied hypothalamic PRs increased in both female rats receiving intromissions and those in which intromission was blocked by a vaginal mask. Although they concluded that this response of a change in progesterone and PR levels was unrelated to heat abbreviation, it may relate to the facilitation that can occur during extended testing.

Another type of open-loop feedback is the circumstance where one type of behavior stimulates the expression of another type of behavior by the same animal, or a progressive sequence of behaviors are stimulated in both the male and the female by their sexual interactions. An example of this type of open-loop feedback can also be seen in paced mating. In this instance, the female's receipt of a copulatory mount from a male stimulates her actively to withdraw from the male's compartment. As we have seen, such open-loop behavior is then followed by subsequent suppression of the reentry response. The paracopulatory behaviors discussed in Section II.B, such as hopping and darting, are also expressed most often prior to a copulatory mount, and these behaviors stimulate behavioral arousal in and mounting behavior by the males.

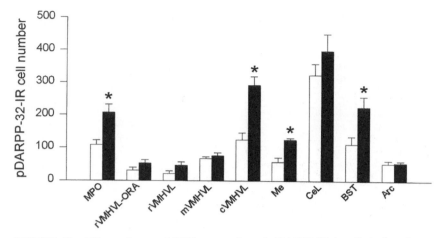

FIGURE 19 Effects of manual VCS on number of pDARPP-32-ir cells in female rat brain. *Open bars,* control stimulation; *filled bars,* VCS. MPO, medial preoptic area; rVMHVL-ORA, ovarian steroid receptor-containing area associated with the rostral ventrolateral aspect of ventromedial nucleus; rVMHVL, mVMHVL, cVMHVL, rostral, mid, caudal ventrolateral-ventromedial nucleus of the hypothalamus; Me, medial amygdaloid nucleus; CeL, central amygdaloid nucleus; BST, bed nucleus of stria terminalis; Arc, arcuate nucleus. (From Meredith *et al., J. Neurosci.* **18,** 10189–10195, © 1998 by the Society for Neuroscience.)

XII. FUNCTIONAL CONSEQUENCES: NEURAL RESPONSES TO SEXUAL BEHAVIOR

In many female mammals, VCS received during mating initiates several neuroendocrine changes that influence reproductive success. In the rat, mating stimulation can stimulate the release of LH (Erskine and Kornberg 1992) and prolactin as well as alter peptidergic and catecholaminergic neurotransmission. In several cases, the progestative aspects of feminine sexual behavior have been shown to play a significant role in initiating these neuroendocrine responses. Paced mating, which has been shown to result in lengthened intervals between intromissions as well as an increase in duration of each individual intromission (Erskine *et al.,* 1989), facilitates the mating-induced changes in both LH and prolactin secretion.

A. Mating-Induced Secretion of Luteinizing Hormone

To examine the effects of progestative behaviors on LH secretion, an experiment was performed in which blood samples were obtained from chronically catheter-ized cycling females prior to mating on proestrus and every 15 minutes following mating for two hours (Erskine and Kornberg, 1992). Groups of females received between 5 and 10 intromissions in paced or nonpaced mating tests or received mounts only by use of a vaginal mask. Circulating LH concentrations were statistically higher in overall samples among the paced animals than among the other two groups (Fig. 20), and significantly higher levels were seen in the paced animals at 15 minutes than in the nonpaced or mounts-only group at this time. No statistically significant increase was seen in the paced group at any other individual time point. The increase in LH observed in the paced group was of short duration, and by 30 minutes, LH levels in the three groups of rats were comparable. The time course of this response is consistent with data demonstrating that hypothalamic GnRH content decreased between 0 and 5 minutes after cervical stimulation in estrous rats (Takahashi *et al.,* 1975) and suggests that paced mating may trigger hypothalamic release of GnRH. Although several previous studies have shown that LH may be released in response to mating or cervical stimulation in rats (Linkie and Niswender, 1972; Moss and Cooper, 1973; Moss *et al.,* 1977; Spies and Niswender, 1971; Taleisnik *et al.,* 1966; Wuttke and

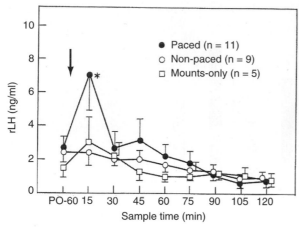

FIGURE 20 Plasma LH concentrations (ng/ml) in cycling rats mated on the evening of proestrus receiving paced, nonpaced, or mounts-only mating stimulation. *$p < 0.05$, significantly higher than the other groups at this time point. (From Erskine and Kornberg (1992), *J. Neuroendocrinol.* **4**, 173–179, Blackwell Science Ltd.)

Meites, 1972), this study showed that particular characteristics of the cervical stimulation received by the estrous female rat during mating can influence the release of LH. Apart from data demonstrating that mating with a male is a more potent stimulus for LH (Taleisnik *et al.*, 1966) release than is artificial cervical stimulation, analysis of the characteristics of the mating stimulation required for LH release in those studies was not carried out. The lack of quantified measures of copulatory stimulation received and the lack of mating controls such as mounts-only groups in many of the previous studies make it difficult to attribute the LH response to specific elements of mating stimulation. The study showing that LH is released selectively after paced mating differed from the earlier studies in that the number of intromissions received by the females was strictly controlled and comparisons were made between paced and nonpaced matings. Under these experimental conditions, when the effects of mating stimulation itself rather than the possible contributions of male exposure and other experimental procedures can be determined, there are clear effects of elements of feminine sexual behavior on LH release. Thus, behavioral regulation of mating stimulation by the female induces an LH response to mating that may not occur under mating conditions in which the male rather than the female controls the occurrence of copulatory stimulation.

The comparison between paced and nonpaced females, groups that received the same numbers of intromissions, established that the frequency of intromission alone was not the determining factor in mating-induced LH release. Other factors such as timing of intromittive stimuli or alterations in arousal during different mating conditions may also contribute to this response. One possible element in the mating stimulation that was effective in inducing LH release may have been the lengthened intervals between intromissions received in the paced as opposed to the nonpaced mating tests (Frye and Erskine, 1990). There was a highly significant positive relationship between the circulating LH concentrations 15 minutes after mating onset and the interval between intromissions in individual animals in the paced and nonpaced groups.

The reproductive consequence of this brief change in circulating LH on the evening of proestrus may be significant. Among females that received mating stimulation from a single ejaculatory series of a male, there was a significant increase in litter size when females were tested under paced conditions rather than under nonpaced conditions (Coopersmith and Erskine, 1994). The mean number of pups born to paced females was 14, whereas the mean number born to nonpaced females was 11; as there were no effects of behavioral treatment on the numbers of nonviable fetuses in utero after day seven of pregnancy (Coopersmith and Erskine, 1994), the effect of paced mating may have been on the number of ova released at the time of mating (Rodgers, 1971) or alterations in sperm transport, or both (Adler and Zoloth, 1970; Agren, 1990).

B. Mating-Induced Prolactin Secretion

Prolactin surge secretion is observed in response to several hormonal and sensory stimuli in the adult female rat. Prolactin levels rise in unmated females in conjunction with the preovulatory LH surge, stimulated during each estrous cycle by rising estrogen levels (Neill, 1988). In mated estrous females, VCS received during copulation results in the secretion of acute prolactin responses that are observed within five minutes of mating and that terminate within an hour (Erskine and Kornberg, 1992; Polston *et al.*, 1998). However, in contrast to the acute LH response, this early prolactin response in not influenced by either paced mating (Erskine and Kornberg, 1992) or the number of intromissions received during the test (Polston and Erskine, 2001). The mean magnitude of the prolactin response seen at 20 minutes after mating did not vary among four groups of animals receiving 5, 10, 15, or 20 intromissions, whereas no prolactin increase was observed among females receiving mounts-only stimulation (Polston *et al.,* 1998). In a separate study, there were no effects of time of day on the mating-induced acute prolactin response (Polston, *et al.,* 1998). Because prolactin responses occur within five minutes of receipt of VCS (Polston *et al.,* 1998), mechanisms involved in transducing afferent sensory information into adenohypophyseal hormone release must be extremely rapid, occurring well before the postmating peak synthesis of immediate-early gene products such as Fos. Acute postmating prolactin release may be due to a rapid decrease in dopamine release from tuberoinfundibular dopamine neurons, resulting in disinhibition of pituitary lactotrophs. Although VCS-induced changes in levels of dopaminergic activity in tuberoinfundibular neurons have not been examined within this short a time postmating, this mechanism is known to be involved in VCS-(De Greef and Neill, 1979; Lerant, *et al.,* 1996), suckling-(Arbogast and Voogt, 1998), and estrogen-induced (DeMaria *et al.,* 1998) prolactin release. Mating-induced changes in opiatergic tone may also stimulate prolactin release (Arbogast and Voogt, 1998; Sirinathsinghji and Audsley, 1985).

The most dramatic neuroendocrine change that is known to be dependent upon the VCS received by the female during mating is that comprising the release of twice-daily surges (called diurnal and nocturnal) of prolactin, which are required for progesterone-dependent changes in the uterus and implantation. These surges are first observed within 36 to 48 hours after mating (Kornberg and Erskine 1994), and they persist for the first 10 to 12 days of pregnancy (Gunnet and Freeman, 1983; Erskine, 1995). Prolactin serves to increase and prolong the ovarian progesterone secretion that comes from the corpus luteum and is required for pregnancy (Smith, *et al.,* 1976; Gunnet and Freeman, 1983; Erskine, 1995). If sufficient mating stimulation is received, these surges are expressed even if pregnancy doesn't ensue, and the resulting period of acyclicity is called pseudopregnancy. One of the most compelling aspects of this neuroendocrine reflex is that the par-

ticular characteristics of the VCS received by the female during mating are critical determinants of whether changes in prolactin secretion will occur (Terkel, 1988; Adler, 1969; Wilson *et al.,* 1965). There is a close correspondence between the VCS that the female requires for initiation of pregnancy and the characteristics of the mating stimulation that she receives from the male during natural mating.

The repetitive and intermittent nature of the intromissive stimulation received by the female contributes to initiation of pseudopregnancy. In particular, it has been known since the now classic studies of Adler and others (Adler, 1969, 1983; Adler *et al.,* 1970; Chester and Zucker, 1970) that intromission frequency and rate are important determinants of whether pseudopregnancy is initiated. Pseudopregnancy occurs with greater frequency when females receive high (approximately 10 to 15) as opposed to low (approximately 3 to 5) numbers of intromissions from males (Adler, 1969; Chester and Zucker, 1970; Terkel and Sawyer, 1978; Wilson *et al.,* 1965), and ejaculation also increases its likelihood (O'Hanlon and Sachs, 1986). We and others (Erskine *et al.,* 1989; Gilman *et al.,* 1979; Frye and Erskine, 1990) have shown a higher incidence of pregnancy or pseudopregnancy following paced than nonpaced mating. Pacing of coital stimuli appears to enhance the effectiveness of the VCS received by the female, since numbers of intromissions usually insufficient to induce pseudopregnancy in nonpaced mating tests (five intromissions) are sufficient for induction of pseudopregnancy in paced mating tests (Erskine *et al.,* 1989; Gilman *et al.,* 1979; Erskine, 1995). Thus, pacing provides a behavioral mechanism by which females maximize the genitosensory stimulation needed for successful reproduction.

It has been clear for many years that differential mating stimulation has profound effects on induction of pseudopregnancy as measured by prolonged vaginal diestrum, but little was known about the effects of particular types of mating stimulation on the secretion of prolactin itself. With very few exceptions, studies on the regulation of the prolactin surges had involved animals that received artificial mechanical or electrical stimulation of the cervix (Gunnet and Freeman, 1983; Neill, 1988; Freeman and Neill, 1972; Smith *et al.,* 1976; Smith and Neill, 1976) and therefore had not measured patterns of prolactin secretion induced by natural mating stimulation. In addition, since low levels of pro-lactin and only the nocturnal surge are required for pro-longed diestrum (Wuttke and Meites, 1972; Peters and Gala, 1975), it is necessary to measure both diurnal and nocturnal surges directly in order to study changes in neural function that subsume each surge. We examined whether varying the number and timing of intro-missions alters the expression of the nocturnal surge in intact animals mated on proestrus (Erskine and Korn-berg, 1992; Kornberg and Erskine, 1994). Our results showed that the first nocturnal surge did not occur until the second day after mating and that no particular type of mating (paced, nonpaced, 5 or 10 intromissions) ad-vanced the onset of the nocturnal surge or altered the peak levels of this prolactin surge. These data support previous data suggesting that the prolactin surges are secreted in an all-or-none fashion once sufficient mat-ing stimulation has been received (Terkel and Sawyer, 1978). The implication of this all-or-none response is that changes in the output arm of this neuroendocrine reflex occur only after a threshold amount of VCS has been received to trigger expression of the surges and that summation of intromissive stimulation occurs in order for the threshold to be reached. The mechanisms involved in establishment of the threshold and summa-tion of intromissions are not yet well understood.

C. Mating-Induced Changes in Oxytocin and Effects of Peripheral Oxytocin on Sexual Behavior

Various mechanosensory stimuli, including suckling and VCS, have the ability to stimulate the synthesis and release of oxytocin in mammals. The mating-induced increases in oxytocin observed in these studies indicate that activation of both central and peripheral oxytocin-ergic systems has occurred. Oxytocin neurons within the parvocellular but not the magnocellular portion of the paraventricular nucleus showed increases in *c-fos* gene expression, a marker of cellular activity, after mat-ing (Polston *et al.*, 1998). This particular population of cells releases oxytocin onto central synapses and into the median eminence (Armstrong, 1995). Cells in the supraoptic nucleus showed similar responses to those seen in the parvocellular paraventricular nu-cleus, in that receipt of 15 intromissions induced a significant increase in both oxytocin-immunoreactive

and Fos/oxytocin-immunoreactive cells above control levels. However, despite the high numbers of magno-cellular neurons within the supraoptic nucleus, which release oxytocin through the posterior pituitary, plasma oxytocin concentrations did not diverge from base-line levels throughout 60 minutes following mating (Polston *et al.*, 1998). These data verify a previous re-port that plasma oxytocin levels are not altered follow-ing mating stimulation in the female rat (Caldwell *et al.*, 1988). Increases in peripheral oxytocin levels follow-ing VCS have been demonstrated in other mammalian species, including sheep (Kendrick *et al.*, 1991) and rabbits (Fuchs *et al.*, 1981).

Interestingly, oxytocin as well as prostaglandin E_2 exert some of their effects on sexual behavior by their actions on the uterus, cervix, or both (Moody *et al.*, 1994; Moody and Adler, 1995). Estradiol-primed fe-male rats respond to intracranial infusion of oxytocin or prostaglandins, suggesting that these hormones act in the brain. However, the response to systemically ad-ministered hormones is dampened by removal of the uterus and/or cervix, as well as by transection of the pelvic nerve (Moody *et al.*, 1994). Because oxytocin and prostaglandins induce contractions of the uterus and cervix, it is likely that the expression of sexual behavior after these hormones are injected systemically is depen-dent on the afferent input to the brain, derived from these contractions and mediated by the pelvic nerve. Related to this, peripheral oxytocin injection also causes norepinephrine release in the hypothalamus (Vincent and Etgen, 1993), but oxytocin, itself, does not appear to act directly on the hypothalamus (Etgen, 1995). This finding led Etgen (1995) to suggest that the release of norepinephrine might be mediated by uterine or cervi-cal contractions.

D. Brain Areas Showing Neuronal Responses to Mating

In females, neurons within several areas of the CNS have been demonstrated to respond to perineal or VCS of the type that is received during mating. Neu-rons within areas of the brain stem and thalamus respond to stimulation of pelvic or pudendal affer-ents and are localized in areas considered to be stan-dard relay areas for afferent sensory information. Other responsive areas are seen within the hypothalamus and limbic system. Several of these areas are of particular relevance to the processes involved in initiation and maintenance of the prolactin surges of pseudopregnancy discussed above. Brain areas that respond to VCS have been demonstrated through cell-recording techniques, measurement of 2-deoxyglucose uptake, and immunocytochemical and in situ hybridization techniques for measurement of immediate early gene expression in specific neurons.

Neurons that show electrophysiological responses to VCS-induced afferent input from the spinal cord are located in areas within the brain stem, including the pons and medulla. Of these, the largest number of VCS-responsive neurons were located in the nucleus reticularis gigantocellularis of the medulla (Hornby and Rose, 1976). VCS resulted in both increases and decreases in firing rate in different cells within this area. Additional cells within the peripeduncular region of the midbrain (Carrer, 1978) show increases in firing rates in response to bilateral stimulation of the pudendal nerve, the sympathetic nerve innervating the perineal area (Pfaff, 1980). More rostrally, neurons within the ventrobasal complex of the thalamus (Berkley *et al.,* 1993; Komisaruk and Wallman, 1977) are sensitive to VCS.

Changes in the characteristiscs of the EEG have been seen following VCS in estrous-cycling rats, notably a sleep-like "afterreaction." During a several-minute period following artificial mechanical stimulation of the cervix and vagina, synchronization of the EEG occurs that resembles that seen during slow-wave sleep (Barraclough, 1960; Ramirez *et al.,* 1967; Sawyer and Kawakami, 1959). This response is observed 100% of the time (Ramirez *et al.,* 1967) when stimulation is given on proestrus, and less frequently (Ramirez *et al.,* 1967) or not at all (Kawakami and Kubo, 1971) on other days of the cycle. The occurrence of a VCS-induced EEG afterreaction on particular days of the estrous cycle does not appear to be correlated with the ability of VCS on those days to induce prolactin surges, as pseudopregnancy is most likely to occur when VCS is given on the days of estrus and diestrus-1 than when it is given on proestrus (Castro-Vasquez and McCann, 1979; Beach *et al.,* 1975). A significant percentage of neurons (in one study about 30% of hypothalamic units studied; Ramirez *et al.,* 1967) exhibited activity patterns that were linked to the EEG. Brain areas containing neu-

rons that respond to VCS in association with changes in EEG activity are the granule layer of the olfactory bulb (Kawakami and Kubo, 1971), midbrain reticular formation, medial amygdala, hippocampus, septum, thalamus, and cortex (Komisaruk *et al.,* 1967; Kawakami and Kubo, 1971). It is not clear whether cells in these areas can be considered to have shown specific responses to VCS or nonspecific responses that are associated with general changes in arousal (Lincoln, 1969a).

Experimenter-induced VCS has been reported to induce alterations in single- and multi-unit activity in anesthetized females in several hypothalamic and limbic areas, although the response direction of these neurons is variable and dependent upon the time after stimulation. Firing rates of neurons within the lateral (Barraclough and Cross, 1963) and rostral (Kawakami and Kubo, 1971; Lincoln, 1969a) hypothalamus, the suprachiasmatic nucleus (Dafny and Terkel, 1990), ventromedial hypothalamic area (Kawakami and Ibuki, 1972; Kawakami and Kubo, 1971), dorsomedial nucleus of the hypothalamus (Kawakami and Ibuki, 1972), arcuate nucleus (Kawakami and Ibuki, 1972; Kawakami and Kubo, 1971), medial preoptic area (Grosvenor *et al.,* 1990; Kawakami and Kubo, 1971; Dafny and Terkel, 1990; Blake and Sawyer, 1972; Haskins and Moss, 1983), median eminence (Blake and Sawyer, 1972), and amygdala (Kawakami and Ibuki, 1972; Kawakami and Kubo, 1971) have been shown to change in anesthetized females in response to VCS. In addition, distension of the vaginal wall altered firing rates in neurons within the paraventricular nucleus (Negoro *et al.,* 1973). Both short-term increases and decreases in unit firing have been observed in different cells within a nucleus, and there are variable results between studies as well. The response latency of the cells in several of these hypothalamic areas ranged from between approximately 30–111 minutes (Dafny and Terkel, 1990; Blake and Sawyer, 1972), although latencies as short as 3.9 sec were seen in ventromedial hypothalamic area cells that responded specifically to VCS (Chan *et al.,* 1984). VCS-induced changes persisted for as long as three hours (Blake and Sawyer, 1972) to two to six days (Kawakami and Ibuki, 1972) after VCS. Cells within the hypothalamus (Barraclough and Cross, 1963) are also often responsive to several other types of stimuli (Komisaruk *et al.,* 1967; Lincoln, 1969a), a finding that suggests a significant amount of convergence of different sensory modalities in these areas.

Ovarian steroids modulate the firing patterns in VCS-responsive neurons; the spontaneous activity (Haskins and Moss, 1983) or the proportion of neurons that show increases or decreases in firing rates in response to VCS change over the days of the estrous cycle (Barraclough and Cross, 1963). Estradiol and progesterone given to ovariectomized females in a regimen that induces sexual reponsiveness resulted in an increase in the percentage of ventromedial hypothalamic area neurons that showed increased activity in response to VCS (Chan et al., 1984). Treatment of ovariectomized rats with estradiol increased spontaneous activity in the medial preoptic area, anterior hypothalamus, and septum (Kawakami and Kubo, 1971). Medial preoptic area neurons responded to iontophoretically applied estradiol with increases in spontaneous firing rate when the steroid was given in the proestrus-estrus phases of the cycle (Haskins and Moss, 1983). However, VCS-induced increases in medial preoptic area firing were not shown to be dependent upon stage of the estrous cycle (Haskins and Moss, 1983), thereby suggesting that VCS and estradiol may increase activity within medial preoptic area neurons independently. Estradiol treatment in vivo similarly increases spontaneous activity of medial amygdala neurons recorded in vitro (Scheiss et al., 1988).

In contrast to the generally excitatory effects of estrogens, progesterone given intravenously to lightly anesthetized females decreases the firing rates in units responsive to VCS (Komisaruk et al., 1967; Ramirez et al., 1967; Barraclough and Cross, 1963; Negoro et al., 1973). There has been some uncertainty about whether the effects of progesterone are selective for neurons that respond to genitosensory stimulation. In the lateral hypothalamus, progesterone was shown specifically to inhibit responses of cells to VCS, while at the same time not inhibiting responses to pain (tail pinch) or cold stimuli (Barraclough and Cross, 1963). However, other studies suggested that the effects of progesterone on single units were correlated with characteristics of the EEG (Komisaruk et al., 1967; Ramirez et al., 1967), an indication that progesterone had an effect on general arousability of neurons, which was not specific to stimulation of the cervix.

In order to localize brain areas responsive to VCS, Allen et al. (1981) measured the brain uptake of

$[^{14}C]$2-deoxy-$_D$-glucose (2-DG), a measure of cellular metabolism and an indirect measure of neural activity. In ovariectomized, estradiol- and progesterone-treated rats, VCS induced a 37% increase in 2-DG uptake in the medial preoptic area and lesser increases in the reticular formation, the bed nucleus of the stria terminalis, locus coeruleus, and lateral preoptic area, among others (Allen et al., 1981). After examining the results of their study, the authors hypothesized that the medial preoptic area is an important relay point for input from the midbrain and that the medial preoptic area acts to process genitosensory stimulation and influence the occurrence of prolactin surges. Unfortunately, the resolution of the 2-DG method is not sufficiently sensitive to warrant its use for more precise neuroanatomical analysis after types and amounts of mating stimulation, which are more or less effective in initiating neuroendocrine or behavioral changes.

A strategy that has been used to identify neurons that respond to either sex steroid hormones or mating stimulation is immunocytochemistry for immediate early gene protein products. Fos, the protein products of the immediate early gene, c-fos, and other immediate early proteins are minimally expressed in cells exhibiting basal levels of activity. Fos expression is then induced genomically within minutes upon extracellular stimulation by a variety of agents, including Ca^{2+} influx, excitatory amino acids, polypeptide growth and differentiation factors, and neurotransmitters (Morgan and Curran, 1995). The immediate early gene proteins may function as transcription factors by regulating genetic transcription, in part via homodimerization or heterodimerization through a common leucine zipper with subsequent binding to AP-1 binding sites on promoters of specific genes. However, immunocytochemical detection of Fos and other immediate early genes can also be used as a marker for neurons that respond to a particular hormonal or environmental stimulus (Morgan and Curran, 1995).

The activation of immediate early genes, as indicated by increases in either immunocytochemically detected gene products or in mRNA for these proteins, has been demonstrated to occur in neurons following increases in firing (Bullitt, 1990; Morgan and Curran, 1991; Sagar et al., 1988), and measurement of the activity of these genes, particularly c-fos, has proven useful in tracing functional pathways involved in processing of sensory information (Hunt et al., 1987; Rusak et al., 1990). This technique has important advantages over both the electrophysiological and 2-DG methods because the technique allows for the staining, localization, and counting of individual cells. In addition, the studies of coexpression of other substances enables the phenotyping of responsive neurons. Several studies have examined the localization of the *c-fos* product, Fos, or Fos mRNA following mating stimulation or artificial VCS in the cycling female during estrus and in ovariectomized rats treated with estradiol and progesterone. Fairly consistent patterns of Fos staining have been seen among the several studies. Fos-ir cells are observed within one to two hours after VCS or mating in the medial preoptic area, ventromedial hypothalamic area, bed nucleus of stria terminalis, paraventricular nucleus, medial amygdala, accessory olfactory bulb, midbrain central grey, and central tegmental field (Dudley *et al.,* 1992; Rowe and Erskine, 1993; Pfaus *et al.,* 1993; Tetel *et al.,* 1993; Wersinger *et al.,* 1993; Dudley and Moss, 1994; Erskine, 1993).

In the first experiments on hormonal regulation of VCS- or mating-induced Fos expression, it was predicted that estradiol plus progesterone priming would increase neuronal response. Although it was unexpected that hormone priming would be without effect on Fos expression (Pfaus *et al.,* 1993), subsequent experiments found a more complicated relationship. In the ventromedial hypothalamic area and bed nucleus of stria terminalis, hormonal priming actually *decreased* the number of Fos-ir cells after a moderate amount of VCS (Pfaus *et al.,* 1996; Tetel *et al.,* 1994b). In contrast, hormonal treatment *increased* Fos expression in other areas, including the medial preoptic area and posterodorsal medial amygdala (Pfaus *et al.,* 1996). Although the relationships are more complicated than was anticipated, these experiments point to these areas as sites of integration of hormonal and mating stimulation.

E. Sites of Neurons That May Integrate Information About Social Environment and Hormonal Milieu

Many of the sites in which Fos is expressed after mating-related stimulation also contain ERs, PRs, or both, so the anatomy suggests obvious sites to be investigated for integration of hormonal signals with afferent

input from the social environment as well. One way that sites of integration have been explored is by mapping of the coexpression of VCS-induced Fos expression with either ERir (Tetel *et al.,* 1994a) or estradiol-induced PRir (Auger *et al.,* 1996). Because of the many issues of sensitivity of immunocytochemistry for each of the proteins, coexpression studies should be interpreted relatively rather than absolutely. With this in mind, extensive coexpression of Fos-ir with ERir is seen in the medial preoptic area, bed nucleus of stria terminalis, posterodorsal medial amygdala, ventromedial hypothalamic area, and midbrain central gray (Tetel *et al.,* 1994a). Extensive coexpression of Fos-ir with PRir is seen in the medial preoptic area, ventromedial hypothalamic area, and the arcuate nucleus (Auger *et al.,* 1996) (other areas were not investigated).

In a test of a novel mechanism of integration of afferent input with the hormone-response systems, Auger *et al.* (1997) tested the idea that ligand-independent activation might be involved in the process by which mating stimulation induces Fos expression. In order to test this hypothesis, estradiol-primed, ovariectomized rats were administered VCS to induce Fos expression. When either of two progesterone antagonists was administered systemically an hour before VCS, Fos expression in some, but not all, neuroanatomical areas was blocked. The progestin antagonists blocked VCS-induced Fos expression in the medial preoptic area, medial bed nucleus of stria terminalis, and caudal ventromedial hypothalamic area, but not other areas, including the medial amygdala, dorsomedial hypothalamus, and paraventricular nucleus. The fact that many cells in these areas that respond to VCS with Fos expression coexpress PRir (Auger *et al.,* 1996) is consistent with the idea that the afferent input is gated by the PR, which may ordinarily undergo ligand-independent activation by the consequences of the VCS. Presumably, this finding relates to the finding that ligand-independent activation of PRs may mediate mating-induced potentiation of sexual behavior, discussed earlier.

Although olfactory stimuli are of profound importance to reproduction and sexual behavior, unlike VCS (Auger *et al.,* 1996), the neurons in which Fos is expressed after exposure to bedding soiled by male rats do not contain PRs (A.L. Bennett, M.E. Blasberg, and J.D. Blaustein, unpublished). Furthermore, unlike the case with VCS-induced Fos expression (Auger *et al.,* 1997), administration of a progesterone antagonist does not block odor-induced Fos expression.

F. Sites of Neurons That Are Involved in Mating-Induced Prolactin Surges

In order to accurately localize areas within the brain that are responsive to VCS and that might be involved in the transduction of mating stimulation into the prolactin surges of pseudopregnancy, we examined the effects of mating on the expression of the immediate early genes, *c-fos* and *egr-1* (KROX-24; Herdegen *et al.,* 1991). Differing amounts of mating stimulation known to be sufficient or less-than-sufficient to produce pseudopregnancy (Rowe and Erskine, 1993; Kornberg and Erskine, 1994) were given and brains were obtained one hour after mating (Polston and Erskine, 1995). Increases in Fos specifically in response to intromissive stimulation were seen in the medial preoptic area, bed nucleus of stria terminalis, ventromedial hypothalamic area, and medial amygdala; control females that received mounts-without-intromission, did not show Fos-ir above the low levels seen in brains of untreated home-cage controls in these areas. Evidence of a graded response to differing numbers of intromissions received by the females was observed in the medial amygdala, but the other Fos responsive areas were not as sensitive to incremental changes in VCS (Polston and Erskine, 1995). The presence of a graded response suggests that the medial amygdala is involved in assimilating and summating afferent stimuli and that this area may be involved in transducing genitosensory stimulation into the prolactin surges of pseudopregnancy.

The forebrain areas showing immunoreactivity for EGR-1, the protein product of *egr-1*, after mating were similar to those seen in the Fos studies (Polston and Erskine, 1995). In general, the numbers of EGR-ir cells present constitutively in the unstimulated animal were lower than those shown for Fos, and the magnitude of the EGR-1 response in mated animals was greater. The comparison of the Fos and EGR-1 responses following intromissive and mounts-only mating stimulation showed that neither the stimuli derived from flank and perineal stimulation nor male exposure alone were responsible for the elevations in immediate-early gene expression seen in the medial preoptic area and me-

dial amygdala; the responses occurred specifically in response to intromissive stimulation. The possibility that the Fos-positive cells seen following intromissions were involved in pseudopregnancy was tested first by measuring mating-induced Fos-ir after pelvic nerve transection (Rowe and Erskine, 1993), a treatment that completely prevents pseudopregnancy (Carlson and DeFeo, 1965). Transection of the pelvic nerve reduced the Fos responses to intromissive stimulation seen in the medial preoptic area and medial amygdala to levels seen following mounts-only stimulation (Rowe and Erskine, 1993). These data show that in the medial preoptic area and medial amygdala the *c-fos* expression occurred specifically in response to genitosensory stimulation associated with and necessary for induction of pseudopregnancy.

In a second test of which brain areas might be involved in processing of VCS for pseudopregnancy, we compared *c-fos* expression following paced and nonpaced mating tests in which females received five or 15 intromissions (Erskine and Hanrahan, 1997). The higher number of intromissions reliably induces pseudopregnancy regardless of whether the female paces her contacts with males. In contrast, females receiving five intromissions during paced mating tests would be expected to show pseudopregnancy, whereas female given five intromissions during nonpaced mating tests would be expected to continue cycling (Erskine *et al.,* 1989). Selective increases one hour after paced mating were observed in the posterodorsal medial amygdala, where significantly more Fos-ir cells were observed in the two groups pacing coital contacts than in the nonpaced groups. Animals receiving five paced intromissions had levels of Fos-ir that were equivalent to animals receiving 15 nonpaced intromissions (Erskine and Hanrahan, 1997). Other brain areas that showed less dramatic but significant effects of paced mating were the ventromedial hypothalamic area and the bed nucleus of stria terminalis. However, the medial amygdala, but not the ventromedial hypothalamic area and bed nucleus of stria terminalis, showed robust Fos responses to mating tests in which the lengthened IIIs characteristic of paced mating were simulated experimentally. Stimulus males were placed with females at prolonged intervals so that the VCS the female received mimicked what she would have received during paced mating. These females showed increased numbers of Fos-ir cells in the medial amygdala than did females receiving intromissions at a rate comparable to nonpaced mating tests, and there was no effect of this treatment on Fos-ir within the ventromedial hypothalamic area and bed nucleus of stria terminalis. These results show that the characteristics of the VCS that the female receives, and not the performance of pacing per se, initiates cellular activity within the medial amygdala.

Colocalization of neuropeptides with Fos has yielded significant amounts of information about the regulation of neuroendocrine function (Hoffman *et al.*, 1990). This approach has been used with some success in the paraventricular nucleus, a complex nucleus composed of several subgroups of parvocellular and magnocellular neurons that are involved in a wide variety of neuroendocrine functions. Because cells within the paraventricular nucleus are known to contain corticotropin releasing factor, vasopressin, and oxytocin (Kiss, 1988; Swanson and Sawchenko, 1983) and to show increases in Fos after stress (Ceccatelli *et al.*, 1989; Kononen *et al.*, 1992), measurement of Fos alone does not allow identification of neurons involved in control of pseudopregnancy in this nucleus. Indeed, in our early studies, we failed to show an increase in paraventricular nucleus Fos-ir that was selective for intromissive stimulation. However, studies examining colocalization of oxytocin with Fos in the paraventricular nucleus indicate that VCS increases activity acutely within oxytocin neurons. An increase in the number of oxytocin cells colabeled with Fos occurred after one hour of mating in the ovariectomized hormone-primed female (Polston *et al.*, 1998; Flanagan *et al.*, 1993), and the largest response occurred at 0600 hours, a time of day when the nocturnal prolactin surge is being expressed (Polston *et al.*, 1998). The numbers of oxytocin cells and cells coexpressing oxytocin and Fos in the mated females in these studies were higher than the number of each reported in the mated male (Witt and Insel, 1994).

XIII. OVERVIEW

In this chapter, we have reviewed a subset of the field of hormonal regulation of feminine sexual behavior in rodents with emphasis on rats. We have been rather selective in our discussion, focusing on the roles of hormones and afferent input from the environment on hormonal response, including input from mating-related stimulation. A great deal of progress has been made in our understanding of how estradiol and progesterone act in the brain and elsewhere at the cellular level, since steroid hormone receptors were first discovered and characterized in the brain in the 1960s and 1970s. However, the discovery of new steroid hormone receptors and mechanisms demonstrates how much there is to learn about these processes. Surprisingly, while much is known about the cellular mechanisms of, and response to, hormones in various neuroanatomical areas, we still have not identified the *precise* sites at which estradiol and progesterone regulate each aspect of these complex behaviors. And although our understanding of hormonal response mechanisms is progressing rapidly, we know far less about how and where behavioral responses to internal and external factors are *integrated* in the brain. Although our knowledge of the brain's response to stimuli from the social environment is certainly advancing, we are just beginning to make progress in identifying the critical sites and cellular processes that mediate the female's response to mating stimuli—from the moment-to-moment changes to the delayed responses. It is clear that we do know that the integration of hormones and mating stimuli in the brain, which then leads to appropriate changes in the suite of copulatory, paracopulatory, and progestative behaviors, ultimately results in female rodents becoming pregnant under appropriate conditions.

Acknowledgments

The research in the authors' laboratories discussed in this review was supported by HD 21802 and Career Development Award MH 01435 to M.S.E. and NS 19327, MH 56187, and Senior Scientist Award MH 01312 to J.D.B. We thank Drs. Beatrice Greco, Laura Lubbers, and Joanne Turcotte for helpful comments on portions of the manuscript, and we thank Dr. Ann Clark for sharing decades-old data from her undergraduate thesis.

References

Adler, N.T. (1969). Effects of the male's copulatory behavior in the initiation of pregnancy in the female rat. *J. Comp. Physiol. Psychol.* **69**, 613–622.

Adler, N.T. (1983). The neuroethology of reproduction. *In* "Advances in Vertebrate Neuroethology" (J. Ewert, R. Capranica, and D. Ingle, eds.), pp. 1033–1061. Plenum Press, London.

Adler, N.T., and Zoloth, S.R. (1970). Copulatory behavior can inhibit pregnancy in female rats. *Science* **168**, 1488.

Adler, N.T., Resko, J.A., and Goy, R.W. (1970). The effect of copulatory behavior on hormonal change in the female rat prior to implantation. *Physiol. Behav.* **5**, 1003–1007.

Adler, N.T., Davis, P.G., and Komisaruk, B.R. (1977). Variation in the size and sensitivity of a genital sensory field in relation to the estrous cycle in rats. *Horm. Behav.* **9**, 334–344.

Agren, G. (1990). Sperm competition, pregnancy initiation and litter size: Influence of the amount of copulatory behavior in Mongolian gerbils, *Meriones unguiculatus*. *Anim. Behav.* **40**, 417–427.

Ahdieh, H.B., and Wade, G.N. (1982). Effects of hysterectomy on sexual receptivity, food intake, running wheel activity, and hypothalamic estrogen and progestin receptors in rats. *J. Comp. Physiol. Psychol.* **96**, 886–892.

Ahdieh, H.B., Hamilton, J.M., and Wade, G.N. (1983). Copulatory behavior and hypothalamic estrogen and progestin receptors in chronically insulin-deficient female rats. *Physiol. Behav.* **31**, 219–223.

Allen, T.O., Adler, N.T., Greenberg, J.H., and Reivich, M. (1981). Vaginocervical stimulation selectively increases metabolic activity in the rat brain. *Science* **211**, 1070–1072.

Alves, S.E., Lopez, V., McEwen, B.S., and Weiland, N.G. (1998). Differential colocalization of estrogen receptor beta (ER beta) with oxytocin and vasopressin in the paraventricular and supraoptic nuclei of the female rat brain: An immunocytochemical study. *Proc. Natl. Acad. Sci. U.S.A.* **95**, 3281–3286.

Arbogast, L.A., and Voogt, J.L. (1993). Progesterone reverses the estradiol-induced decrease in tyrosine hydroxylase messenger RNA levels in the arcuate nucleus. *Neuroendocrinology* **58**, 501–510.

Arbogast, L.A., and Voogt, J.L. (1994). Progesterone suppresses tyrosine hydroxylase messenger ribonucleic acid levels in the arcuate nucleus on proestrus. *Endocrinology (Baltimore)* **135**, 343–350.

Arbogast, L.A., and Voogt, J.L. (1998). Endogenous opioid peptides contribute to suckling-induced prolactin release by suppressing tyrosine hydroxylase activity and messenger ribonuclei acid levels in tuberoinfundibular dopaminergic neurons. *Endocrinology (Baltimore)* **139**, 2857–2862.

Armstrong, W.E. (1995). Morphological and electrophysiological classification of hypothalamic supraoptic neurons. *Prog. Neurobiol.* **47**, 201–339.

Aronica, S.M., and Katzenellenbogen, B.S. (1993). Stimulation of estrogen receptor-mediated transcription and alteration in the phosphorylation state of the rat uterine estrogen receptor by estrogen, cyclic adenosine monophosphate, and insulin-like growth factor-1. *Mol. Endocrinol.* **7**, 743–752.

Atger, M., Baulieu, E.E., and Milgrom, E. (1974). An investigation of progesterone receptors in guinea pig vagina, uterine cervix, mammary glands, pituitary and hypothalamus. *Endocrinology (Baltimore)* **94**, 161–167.

Attardi, B. (1981). Facilitation and inhibition of the estrogen-induced luteinizing hormonesurge in the rat by progesterone: Effects on cytoplasmic and nuclear estrogen receptors in the hypothalamus-preoptic area, pituitary, and uterus. *Endocrinology (Baltimore)* **108**, 1487–1496.

Auger, A.P., and Blaustein, J.D. (1995). Progesterone enhances an estradiol-induced increase in fos immunoreactivity in localized regions of female rat forebrain. *J. Neurosci.* **15**, 2272–2279.

Auger, A.P., Moffatt, C.A., and Blaustein, J.D.(1996). Reproductively-relevant stimuli induce Fos-immunoreactivity within progestin receptor-containing neurons in localized regions of female rat forebrain. *J. Neuroendocrinol.* **8**, 831–838.

Auger, A.P., Moffatt, C.A., and Blaustein, J.D. (1997). Progesterone-independent activation of rat brain progestin receptors by reproductive stimuli. *Endocrinology (Baltimore)* **138**, 511–514.

Auger, A.P., LaRiccia, L.M., Moffatt, C.A., and Blaustein, J.D. (2000). Progesterone, but not progesterone-independent activation of progestin receptors by a mating stimulus, rapidly decreases progestin receptor immunoreactivity in female rat brain. *Horm. Behav.* **37**, 135–144.

Auger, A.P., Meredith, J.M., Snyder, G.L., and Blaustein, J.D. (2001). Oestradiol increases phosphorylation of a dopamine- and cyclic AMP-regulated phosphoprotein (DARPP-32) in female rat brain. *J. Neuroendocrinol.* **13**, 761–768.

Bale, T.L., Pedersen, C.A., and Dorsa, D.M. (1995). CNS oxytocin receptor mRNA expression and regulation by gonadal steroids. *Adv. Exp. Medi. Biol.* **395**, 269–280.

Balthazart, J., Blaustein, J.D., Cheng, M.F., and Feder, H.H. (1980). Hormones modulate the concentration of cytoplasmic progestin receptors in the brain of male ring doves (*Streptopelia risoria*). *J. Endocrinol.* **86**, 251–261.

Barfield, M.A., and Lisk, R.D. (1974). Relative contributions of ovarian and adrenal progesterone to the timing of heat in the 4–day cyclic rat. *Endocrinology (Baltimore)* **94**, 571–575.

Barfield, R.J., and Chen, J.J. (1977). Activation of estrous behavior in ovariectomized rats by intracerebral implants of estradiol benzoate. *Endocrinology (Baltimore)* **101**, 1716–1725.

Barraclough, C.A. (1960). Hypothalamic activation associated with stimulation of the vaginal cervix in proestrous rats. *Anat. Rec.* **136**, 159.

Barraclough, C.A., and Cross, B.A. (1963). Unit activity in the hypothalamus of the cyclic female rat: Effect of genital stimuli and progesterone. *J. Endocrinol.* **26**, 339–359.

Baulieu, E.E., Schumacher, M., Koenig, H., Jungtestas, I., and Akwa, Y. (1996). Progesterone as a neurosteroid: Actions within the nervous system. *Cell. Mol. Neurobiol.* **16**, 143–154.

Beach, F.A. (1942). Importance of progesterone to induction of sexual receptivity in spayed female rats. *Proc. Soc. Exp. Biol. Med.* **51**, 369–371.

Beach, F.A. (1976). Sexual attractivity, proceptivity, and receptivity in female mammals. *Horm. Behav.* **7**, 105–138.

Beach, F.A., and Orndoff, R.K. (1974). Variation in the responsiveness of female rats to ovarian hormones as a function of preceding hormonal deprivation. *Horm. Behav.* **5**, 201–205.

Beach, F.A., and Whalen, R.E. (1959). Effects of ejaculation on sexual behavior in the male rat. *J. Comp. Physiol. Psychol.* **52**, 249–254.

Beach, J.E., Tyrey, L., and Everett, J.W. (1975). Serum prolactin and LH in early phases of delayed versus direct pseudopregnancy in the rat. *Endocrinology (Baltimore)* **96**, 1241–1246.

Becker, J.B. (1990). Direct effect of 17-beta-estradiol on striatum - sex differences in dopamine release. *Synapse* **5**, 157–164.

Bennett, A.L., Blasberg, M.E., and Blaustein, J.D. (2001). Sensory cues mediating mating-induced potentiation of sexual receptivity in female rats. *Hormones Behav.* **40**, 77–83.

Berkley, K.J., Guilbaud, G., Benoist, J.-M., and Gautron, M. (1993). Responses of neurons in and near the thalamic ventrobasal complex of the rat to stimulation of uterus, cervix, vagina, colon and skin. *J. Neurophysiol.* **69**, 557–568.

Bermant, G. (1961). Response latencies of female rats during sexual intercourse. *Science* **133**, 1771–1773.

Bermant, G., and Westbrook, W.H. (1966). Peripheral factors in the regulation of sexual contact by female rats. *J. Comp. Physiol. Psychol.* **61**, 244–250.

Bermant, G., Anderson, L., and Parkinson, S.R. (1969). Copulation in rats: Relations among intromission duration, frequency, and pacing. *Psychon. Sci.* **17**, 293–294.

Bethea, C.L., and Widmann, A.A. (1998). Differential expression of progestin receptor isoforms in the hypothalamus, pituitary, and endometrium of rhesus macaques. *Endocrinology (Baltimore)* **139**, 677–687.

Bethea, C.L., Brown, N.A., and Kohama, S.G. (1996). Steroid regulation of estrogen and progestin receptor messenger ribonucleic acid in monkey hypothalamus and pituitary. *Endocrinology (Baltimore)* **137**, 4372–4383.

Beyer, C., Canchola, E., and Larsson, K. (1981). Facilitation of lordosis behavior in the ovariectomized estrogen primed rat by dibutyryl cAMP. *Physiol. Behav.* **26**, 249–251.

Beyer, C., Gonzalez-Flores, O., and González-Mariscal, G. (1997). Progesterone receptor participates in the stimulatory effect of LHRH, prostaglandin E2, and cyclic AMP on lordosis

and proceptive behaviours in rats. *J. Neuroendocrinol.* **9**, 609–614.

Blake, C.A., and Sawyer, C.H. (1972). Effects of vaginal stimulation on hypothalamic multiple-unit activity and pituitary LH release in the rat. *Neuroendocrinology* **10**, 358–370.

Blandau, R.J., Boling, J.L., and Young, W.C. (1941). The length of heat in the albino rat as determined by the copulatory response. *Anat. Rec.* **79**, 453–463.

Blaustein, J.D. (1982a). Alteration of sensitivity to progesterone facilitation of lordosis in guinea pigs by modulation of hypothalamic progestin receptors. *Brain Res.* **243**, 287–300.

Blaustein, J.D. (1982b). Progesterone in high doses may overcome progesterone's desensitization effect on lordosis by translocation of hypothalamic progestin receptors. *Horm. Behav.* **16**, 175–190.

Blaustein, J.D. (1986a). Cell nuclear accumulation of estrogen receptors in rat brain and pituitary gland after treatment with a dopamine-b-hydroxylase inhibitor. *Neuroendocrinology* **42**, 44–50.

Blaustein, J.D. (1986b). Noradrenergic inhibitors cause accumulation of nuclear progestin receptors in guinea pig hypothalamus. *Brain Res.* **325**, 89–98.

Blaustein, J.D. (1987). The α_1-noradrenergic antagonist prazosin decreases the concentration of estrogen receptors in female hypothalamus. *Brain Res.* **404**, 39–50.

Blaustein, J.D. (1992a). Cytoplasmic estrogen receptors in rat brain: Immunocytochemical evidence using three antibodies with distinct epitopes. *Endocrinology (Baltimore)* **131**, 1336–1342.

Blaustein, J.D. (1992b). Modulation of sex steroid receptors by neurotransmitters: Relevant techniques. *Neuroprotocols* **1**, 42–51.

Blaustein, J.D. (1994). Estrogen receptors in neurons: New subcellular locations and functional implications. *Endocr. J.* **2**, 249–258.

Blaustein, J.D., and Brown, T.J. (1984). Progesterone decreases the concentration of hypothalamic and anterior pituitary estrogen receptors in ovariectomized rats. *Brain Res.* **304**, 225–236.

Blaustein, J.D., and Brown, T.J. (1985). Neural progestin receptors: Regulation of progesterone-facilitated sexual behaviour in female guinea pigs. *In* "Comparative Physiology and Biochemistry" (R. Gilles and J. Balthazart, eds.), Vol. C, pp. 60–76. Springer-Verlag, Berlin.

Blaustein, J.D., and Feder, H.H. (1979a). Cytoplasmic progestin receptors in guinea pig brain: Characteristics and relationship to the induction of sexual behavior. *Brain Res.* **169**, 481–497.

Blaustein, J.D., and Feder, H.H. (1979b). Cytoplasmic progestin receptors in female guinea pig brain and their relationship to refractoriness in expression of female sexual behavior. *Brain Res.* **177**, 489–498.

Blaustein, J.D., and Feder, H.H. (1980). Nuclear progestin receptors in guinea pig brain measured by and in vitro exchange assay after hormonal treatments that affect lordosis. *Endocrinology (Baltimore)* **106**, 1061–1069.

Blaustein, J.D., and Letcher, B. (1987). Noradrenergic regulation of cytosol estrogen receptors in female hypothalamus: Possible role of alpha$_2$-noradrenergic receptors. *Brain Res.* **404**, 51–57.

Blaustein, J.D., and Olster, D.H. (1989). Gonadal steroid hormone receptors and social behaviors. *In* "Advances in Comparative and Environmental Physiology." Vol. 3, (J. Balthazart, ed.), pp. 31–104. Springer-Verlag, Berlin.

Blaustein, J.D., and Olster, D.H. (1993). Colchicine-induced accumulation of estrogen receptor and progestin receptor immunoreactivity in atypical areas in guinea-pig brain. *J. Neuroendocrinol.* **5**, 63–70.

Blaustein, J.D., and Turcotte, J. (1987). Further evidence of noradrenergic regulation of rat hypothalamic estrogen receptor concentration: possible non-functional increase and functional decrease. *Brain Res.* **436**, 253–264.

Blaustein, J.D., and Turcotte, J.C. (1989a). A small population of tyrosine hydroxylase-immunoreactive neurons in the guinea-pig arcuate nucleus contains progestin receptor-immunoreactivity. *J. Neuroendocrinol.* **1**, 333–338.

Blaustein, J.D., and Turcotte, J.C. (1989b). Estradiol-induced progestin receptor immunoreactivity is found only in estrogen receptor-immunoreactive cells in guinea pig brain. *Neuroendocrinology* **49**, 454–461.

Blaustein, J.D., and Turcotte, J.C. (1990). Down-regulation of progestin receptors in guinea pig brain: New findings using an immunocytochemical technique. *J. Neurobiol.* **21**, 675–685.

Blaustein, J.D., and Wade, G.N. (1977). Sequential inhibition of sexual behavior by progesterone in female rats: Comparison with a synthetic antiestrogen. *J. Comp. Physiol. Psychol.* **91**, 752–760.

Blaustein, J.D., and Wade, G.N. (1978). Progestin binding by brain and pituitary cell nuclei and female rat sexual behavior. *Brain Res.* **140**, 360–367.

Blaustein, J.D., Dudley, S.D., Gray, J.M., Roy, E.J., and Wade, G.N. (1979). Long-term retention of estradiol by brain cell nuclei and female rat sexual behavior. *Brain Res.* **103**, 355–359.

Blaustein, J.D., Brown, T.J., and Reading, D.S. (1982). Failure of a protein synthesis inhibitor to block progesterone's desensitization action on lordosis in female rats. *Physiol. Behav.* **29**, 475–481.

Blaustein, J.D., Brown, T.J., and Swearengen, E.S. (1986). Dopamine-β-hydroxylase inhibitors modulate the concentration of functional estrogen receptors in female rat

hypothalamus and pituitary gland. *Neuroendocrinology* **43**, 150–158.

Blaustein, J.D., Finkbohner, R., and Delville, Y. (1987). Estrogen-induced and estrogen-facilitated female sexual behavior is not mediated by progestin receptors. *Neuroendocrinology* **45**, 152–159.

Blaustein, J.D., King, J.C., Toft, D.O., and Turcotte, J. (1988). Immunocytochemical localization of estrogen-induced progestin receptors in guinea pig brain. *Brain Res.* **474**, 1–15.

Blaustein, J.D., Lehman, M.N., Turcotte, J.C., and Greene, G. (1992). Estrogen receptors in dendrites and axon terminals in the guinea pig hypothalamus. *Endocrinology. (Baltimore)* **131**, 281–290.

Blaustein, J.D., Lubbers, L.S., Meredith, J.M., and Wade, G.N. (1999). Dopamine receptor subtypes in progesin-receptor (PR)-rich regions of the hypothalamus in female rats. *Soc. Neurosci. Abstr.* **25**, No. 582.6.

Boling, J.L., and Blandau, R.J. (1939). The estrogen-progesterone induction of mating responses in the spayed female rat. *Endocrinology (Baltimore)* **25**, 359–364.

Bosse, R., and DiPaolo, T. (1996). The modulation of brain dopamine and GABA(A) receptors by estradiol: A clue for CNS changes occurring at menopause. *Cell. Mol. Neurobiol.* **16**, 199–212.

Brann, D.W., Chorich, L.P., and Mahesh, V.B. (1993). Effect of progesterone on galanin messenger RNA levels in the hypothalamus and the pituitary-correlation with the gonadotropin surge. *Neuroendocrinology* **58**, 531–538.

Broekman, M., de Bruin, M., Smeenk, J., Slob, A.K., and van der Schoot, P. (1988). Partner preference behavior of estrous female rats affected by castration of tethered male incentives. *Horm. Behav.* **22**, 324–337.

Brown, E.R., Harlan, R.E., and Krause, J.E. (1990). Gonadal steroid regulation of substance-P (Sp) and Sp-encoding messenger ribonucleic acids in the rat anterior pituitary and hypothalamus. *Endocrinology (Baltimore)* **126**, 330–340.

Brown, T.J., and Blaustein, J.D. (1984a). 1-(o-Chlorophenyl)-1(p-Chlorophenyl)2,2,2,-trichlorothane induces functional progestin receptors in the rat hypothalamus and pituitary gland. *Endocrinology (Baltimore)* **115**, 1052–2058.

Brown, T.J., and Blaustein, J.D. (1984b). Inhibition of sexual behavior in female guinea pigs by a progestin receptor antagonist. *Brain Res.* **301**, 343–349.

Brown, T.J., and Blaustein, J.D. (1984c). Supplemental progesterone delays heat termination and loss of progestin receptors from hypothalamic cell nuclei in female guinea pigs. *Neuroendocrinology* **39**, 384–391.

Brown, T.J., and Blaustein, J.D. (1985). Loss of hypothalamic nuclear-bound progestin receptors: Factors involved and the relationship to heat termination in female guinea pigs. *Brain Res.* **358**, 180–190.

Brown, T.J., and Blaustein, J.D. (1986). Abbreviation of the period of sexual behavior in female guinea pigs by the progesterone antagonist, RU 486. *Brain Res.* **373**, 103–113.

Brown, T.J., and MacLusky, N.J. (1994). Progesterone modulation of estrogen receptors in microdissected regions of the rat hypothalamus. *Mol. Cell. Neurosci.* **5**, 283–290.

Brown, T.J., Moore, M.J., and Blaustein, J.D. (1987). Maintenance of progesterone-facilitated sexual behavior in female rats requires continued hypothalamic protein synthesis and nuclear progestin receptor occupation. *Endocrinology (Baltimore)* **121**, 298–304.

Brown, T.J., MacLusky, N.J., Leranth, C., Shanabrough, M., and Naftolin, F. (1990). Progestin receptor-containing cells in guinea pig hypothalamus: Afferent connections, morphological characteristics, and neurotransmitter content. *Mol. Cell. Neurosci.* **1**, 58–77.

Brown, T.J., Scherz, B., Hochberg, R.B., and MacLusky, N.J. (1996). Regulation of estrogen receptor concentrations in the rat brain: Effects of sustained androgen and estrogen exposure. *Neuroendocrinology* **63**, 53–60.

Bullitt, E. (1990). Expression of C-fos-like protein as a marker for neuronal activity following noxious stimulation in the rat. *J. Comp. Neurol.* **296**, 517–530.

Caldwell, J.D., Jirikowski, G.F., Greer, E.R., Stumpf, W.E., and Pedersen, C.A. (1988). Ovarian steroids and sexual interaction alter oxytocinergic content and distribution in the basal forebrain. *Brain Res.* **446**, 236–244.

Camacho-Arroyo, I., Guerra-Araiza, C., and Cerbon, M. A. (1998). Progesterone receptor isoforms are differentially regulated by sex steroids in the rat forebrain. *NeuroReport* **9**, 3993–3996.

Camhi, J.M. (1984). "Neuroethology." Sinauer, Sunderland, MA.

Canteras, N.S., Simerly, R.B., and Swanson, L.W. (1994). Organization of projections from the ventromedial nucleus of the hypothalamus: A phaseolus vulgaris-leucoagglutinin study in the rat. *J. Comp. Neurol.* **348**, 41–79.

Cardinali, D.P. (1979). Models in neuroendocrinology: Neurohumoral pathways to the pineal gland. *Trends Neurosci.* **2**, 250–253.

Carlson, R.R., and DeFeo, V.J. (1965). Role of the pelvic nerve vs. the abdominal sympathetic nerves in the reproductive function of the female rat. *Endocrinology (Baltimore)* **77**, 1014–1022.

Carrer, H.F. (1978). Mesencephalic participation in the control of sexual behavior in the female rat. *J. Comp. Physiol. Psychol.* **92**, 877–887.

Carter, C.S. (1972). Postcopulatory sexual receptivity in the female hamster: The role of the ovary and adrenal. *Horm. Behav.* **3**, 261–265.

Carter, C.S., and Getz, L.L. (1985). Social and hormonal determinants of reproductive patterns in the prairie vole. In "Neurobiology: Current Comparative, Approaches" (R. Gilles and J. Balthazart, eds.), pp. 18–36. Springer-Verlag, Berlin.

Carter, C.S., and Schein, M.W. (1971). Sexual receptivity and exhaustion in the female golden hamster. *Horm. Behav.* **2**, 191–200.

Carter, C.S., Michael, S.J., and Morris, A.H. (1973). Hormonal induction of female sexual behavior in male and female hamsters. *Horm. Behav.* **4**, 129–141.

Carter, C.S., Landauer, M.R., Tierney, B.M., and Jones, T. (1976). Regulation of female sexual behavior in the golden hamster: Behavioral effects of mating and ovarian hormones. *J. Comp. Physiol. Psychol.* **90**, 839–850.

Carter, C.S., Witt, D.M., Schneider, J., Harris, Z.L., and Volkening, D. (1987). Male stimuli are necessary for female sexual behavior and uterine growth in prairie voles (*Microtus ochrogaster*). *Horm Behav.* **21**, 74–82.

Castro-Vazquez, A., and Carreno, N.B. (1985). Estrogen but not progesterone facilitates the lordosis reaction to cervicovaginal stimulation of ovariectomized rats. *Physiol. Behav.* **35**, 21–24.

Castro-Vazquez, A., and McCann, S.M. (1979). Cyclic changes in the reflex release of prolactin following cervicovaginal stimulation. *Neuroendocrinology* **28**, 3–10.

Ceccatelli, S., Villar, M.J., Goldstein, M., and Hokfelt, T. (1989). Expression of c-Fos immunoreactivity in transmitter-characterized neurons after stress. *Proc. Natl. Acad. Sci. U.S.A.* **8**, 9569–9573.

Chan, A., Dudley, C.A., and Moss, R.L. (1984). Hormonal and chemical modulation of ventromedial hypothalamic neurons responsive to vaginocervical stimulation. *Neuroendocrinology.* **38**, 328–336.

Chappell, P.E., and Levine, J.E. (2000). Stimulation of gonadotropin-releasing hormone surges by estrogen. I. Role of hypothalamic progesterone receptors. *Endocrinology (Baltimore)* **141**, 1477–1485.

Chappell, P.E., Schneider, J.S., Kim, P., Xu, M., Lydon, J.P., O'Malley, B.W., and Levine, J.E. (1999). Absence of gonadotropin surges and gonadotropin-releasing hormone self-priming in ovariectomized (OVX), estrogen (E-2)-treated, progesterone receptor knockout (PRKO) mice. *Endocrinology (Baltimore)* **140**, 3653–3658.

Chen, T.J., Chang, H.C., Hsu, C., and Peng, M.T. (1992). Effects of anterior roof deafferentation on lordosis behavior and estrogen receptors in various brain regions of female rats. *Physiol. Behav.* **52**, 7–11.

Chester, R.V., and Zucker, I. (1970). Influence of male copulatory behavior on sperm transport, pregnancy and pseudopregnancy in female rats.*Physiol. Behav.* **5**, 35–43.

Cho, B.N., Seong, J.Y., Cho, H., and Kim, K. (1994). Progesterone stimulates GnRH gene expression in the hypothalamus of ovariectomized, estrogen treated adult rats. *Brain Res.* **652**, 177–180.

Chu, H.P., Morales, J.C., and Etgen, A.M. (1999). Cyclic GMP may potentiate lordosis behaviour by progesterone receptor activation. *J. Neuroendocrinol.* **11**, 107–113.

Clark, A.S., and Roy, E.J. (1983). Behavioral and cellular responses to pulses of low doses of estradiol-17β. *Physiol. Behav.* **30**, 561–565.

Clark, A.S., Nock, B., Feder, H.H., and Roy, E.J. (1985). α-Noradrenergic receptor blockade decreases nuclear estrogen receptor binding in guinea pig hypothalamus and preoptic area. *Brain Res.* **330**, 197–199.

Clark, A.S., Pfeifle, J.K., and Edwards, D.A. (1981). Ventromedial hypothalamic damage and sexual proceptivity in female rats. *Physiol. Behav.* **27**, 597–602.

Clark, C.R., MacLusky, N.J., and Naftolin, F. (1982). Oestrogen induction of progestin receptors in the rat brain and pituitary gland: Quantitative and kinetic aspects. *J. Endocrinol.* **93**, 339–353.

Clark, C.R., MacLusky, N.J., Parsons, B., and Naftolin, F. (1981). Effects of estrogen deprivation on brain estrogen and progestin receptor levels and the activation of female sexual behavior. *Horm. Behav.* **15**, 289–298.

Clark, J.H., and Peck, E.J., Jr. (1977). Steroid hormone receptors: Basic principles and measurement. *In* "Receptors and Hormone Action" (B.W. O'Malley and L. Birnbaumer, eds.), pp. 383–410. Academic Press, New York.

Clarke, C.H., Norfleet, A.M., Clarke, M.S.F., Watson, C.S., Cunningham, K.A., and Thomas, M.L. (2000). Perimembrane localization of the estrogen receptor alpha protein in neuronal processes of cultured hippocampal neurons. *Neuroendocrinology* **71**, 34–42.

Clemens, L.G., Hiroi, M., and Gorski, R.A. (1969). Induction and facilitation of female mating behavior in rats treated neonatally with low doses of testosterone propionate. *Endocrinology (Baltimore)* **84**, 1430–1438.

Cohen-Parsons, M., and Roy, E.J. (1989). Social stimuli augment estrogen receptor binding in preoptic area of female prairie voles. *Brain Res.* **476**, 363–366.

Collins, V.J., Boling, J.I., Dempsey, E.W., and Young, W.C. (1938). Quantitative studies of experimentally induced sexual receptivity in the spayed guinea pig. *Endocrinology (Baltimore)* **23**, 188–196.

Conde, G.L., Herbison, A.E., Fernandez-Galaz, C., and Bicknell, R.J. (1996). Estrogen uncouples noradrenergic activation of Fos expression in the female rat preoptic area. *Brain Res.* **735**, 197–207.

Conneely, O.M., Kettleberger, D.M., Tsai, M.J., Schrader, W.T., and O'Malley, B.W. (1989). The chicken progesterone receptor A and B isoforms are products of an alternate translation initiation event. *J. Biol. Chem.* **264**, 14062–14064.

Conrad, L.C.A., and Pfaff, D.W. (1975). Axonal projections of medial preoptic and anterior hypothalamic neurons. *Science* **121**, 1112–1114.

Conrad, L.C.A., and Pfaff, D.W. (1976). Efferents from medial basal forebrain and hypothalamus in the rat. *J. Comp. Neurobiol.* **169**, 185–219.

Coopersmith, C., and Erskine, M.S. (1994). Influence of paced mating and number of intromissions on fertility in the laboratory rat. *J. Reprod. Fertil.* **102**, 451–458.

Coopersmith, C., Candurra, C., and Erskine, M.S. (1996). Effects of paced mating and intromissive stimulation on feminine sexual behavior and estrus termination in the cycling rat. *J. Comp. Psychol.* **110**, 176–186.

Couse, J.F. and Korach, K.S. (1999). Estrogen receptor null mice: What have we learned and where will they lead us? *Endocr. Revi.* **20**, 358–417.

Couse, J.F., Lindzey, J., Grandien, K., Gustafsson, J.A., and Korach, K.S. (1997). Tissue distribution and quantitative analysis of estrogen receptor-alpha (ER alpha) and estrogen receptor-beta (ER beta) messenger ribonucleic acid in the wild-type and ER alpha-knockout mouse. *Endocrinology (Baltimore)* **138**, 4613–4621.

Couse, J.F., Hewitt, S.C., Bunch, D.O., Sar, M., Walker, V.R., Davis, B.J., and Korach, K.S. (1999). Postnatal sex reversal of the ovaries in mice lacking estrogen receptors alpha and beta. *Science* **286**, 2328–2331.

Crowley, W.R., Rodriguez-Sierra, J.F., and Komisaruk, B.R. (1977). Monoaminergic mediation of the antinociceptive effect of vaginal stimulation in rats. *Brain Res.* **137**, 67–84.

Cueva-Rolon, R., Sansone, G., Bianca, R., Gomez, L.E., Beyer, C., Whipple, B., and Komisaruk, B.R. (1996). Vagotomy blocks responses to vaginocervical stimulation after genitospinal neurectomy in rats. *Physiol. Behav.* **60**, 19–24.

Czaja, J.A., Butera, P.C., and McCaffrey, T.A. (1985). Duration of hormonal deprivation: Influences on physiological and behavioral responsiveness to estradiol. *Horm. Behav.* **19**, 52–63.

Dafny, N., and Terkel, J. (1990). Hypothalamic neuronal activity associated with the onset of pseudopregnancy in the rat. *Neuroendocrinology* **51**, 459–467.

Davidson, J.M., Rodgers, C.H., Smith, E.R., and Bloch, G.J. (1968). Stimulation of female sex behavior in adrenalectomized rats with estrogen alone. *Endocrinology (Baltimore)* **82**, 193–195.

Davis, P.G., and Barfield, R.J. (1979). Activation of masculine sexual behavior by intracranial estradiol benzoate implants in male rats. *Neuroendocrinology* **28**, 217–227.

Davis, P.G., Krieger, M.S., Barfield, R.J., McEwen, B.S., and Pfaff, D.W. (1982). The site of action in intrahypothalamic estrogen implants in feminine sexual behavior: An autoradiographic analysis. *Endocrinology (Baltimore)* **111**, 1581–1586.

DeBold, J.F., and Frye, C.A. (1994a). Genomic and non-genomic actions of progesterone in the control of female hamster sexual behavior. *Horm. Behav.* **28**, 445–453.

DeBold, J.F., and Frye, C.A. (1994b). Progesterone and the neural mechanisms of hamster sexual behavior. *Psychoneuroendocrinology* **19**, 563–579.

DeBold, J.F., and Malsbury, C.W. (1989). Facilitation of sexual receptivity by hypothalamic and midbrain implants of progesterone in female hamsters. *Physiol. Behav.* **46**, 655–660.

DeBold, J.F., Malsbury, C.W., Harris, V.S., and Malenka, R. (1982). Sexual receptivity: Brain sites of estrogen action in female hamsters. *Physiol. Behav.* **29**, 589–593.

de Bruijn, M., Broekman, M., and van der Schoot, P. (1988). Sexual interactions between estrous female rats and castrated male rats treated with testosterone propionate or estradiol benzoate. *Physiol. Behav.* **43**, 35–39.

De Greef, W.J., and Neill, J.D. (1979). Dopamine levels in hypophyseal stalk plasma of the rat during surges of prolactin secretion induced by cervical stimulation. *Endocrinology (Baltimore)* **105**, 1093–1099.

de Jonge, F.H., Eerland, E.M.J., and van de Poll, N.E. (1986). The influence of estrogen, testosterone and progesterone on partner preference, receptivity and proceptivity. *Physiol. Behav.* **37**, 885–891.

Delville, Y., and Blaustein, J.D. (1989). Long-term ovariectomy and hormone-induced sexual behavior, progestin receptors, and hypothalamic morphology in female rats. *Horm. Behav.* **23**, 269–278.

Delville, Y., and Blaustein, J.D. (1991). A site for estradiol priming of progesterone-facilitated sexual receptivity in the ventrolateral hypothalamus of female guinea pigs. *Brain Res.* **559**, 191–199.

DeMaria, J.E., Livingstone, J.D., and Freeman, M.E. (1998). Characterization of the dopaminergic input to the pituitary gland throughout the estrous cycle of the rat. *Neuroendocrinology* **67**, 377–383.

Dempsey, E.W., Hertz, R., and Young, W.C. (1936). The experimental induction of oestrus (sexual receptivity) in the normal and ovariectomized guinea pig. *Am. J. Physiol.* **116**, 201–209.

De Vries, G.J. (1990). Sex differences in neurotransmitter systems. *J. Neuroendocrinol.* **2**, 1–13.

De Vries, G.J., Wang, Z.X., Bullock, N.A., and Numan, S. (1994). Sex differences in the effects of testosterone and its metabolites on vasopressin messenger RNA levels in the bed nucleus of the stria terminalis of rats. *J. Neurosci.* **14**, 1789–1794.

Diakow, C. (1975). Motion picture analysis of rat mating behavior. *J. Comp. Physiol. Psychol.* **88**, 704–712.

Dluzen, D.E., and Ramirez, V.D. (1989). Progesterone effects upon dopamine release from the corpus striatum of female rats. II. Evidence for a membrane site of action and the role of albumin. *Brain Res.* **476**, 338–334.

DonCarlos, L.L., Greene, G.L., and Morrell, J.I. (1989). Estrogen plus progesterone increases progestin receptor immunoreactivity in the brain of ovariectomized guinea pigs. *Neuroendocrinology* **50**, 613–623.

DonCarlos, L.L., Monroy, E., and Morrell, J.I. (1991). Distribution of estrogen receptor-immunoreactive cells in the forebrain of the female Guinea Pig. *J. Comp. Neurol.* **305**, 591–612.

DonCarlos, L.L., Malik, K., and Morrell, J.I. (1995). Region–specific effects of ovarian hormones on estrogen receptor immunoreactivity. *NeuroReport* **6**, 2054–2058.

Du, Y., Wade, G.N., and Blaustein, J.D. (1996). Effects of food deprivation on induction of neural progestin receptors by estradiol in female Syrian hamsters. *Am. J. Physiol.* **270**, R978–R983.

Dudley, C.A., and Moss, R.L. (1994). Lesions of the accessory olfactory bulb decrease lordotic responsiveness and reduce mating-induced c-fos expression in the accessory olfactory system. *Brain Res.* **642**, 29–37.

Dudley, C.A., Cooper, K.J., and Moss, R.L. (1980). Progesterone-induced mating behavior in rats on the day following spontaneous heat. *Physiol. Behav.* **25**, 759–762.

Dudley, C.A., Rajendren, G., and Moss, R.L. (1992). Induction of FOS immunoreactivity in central accessory olfactory structures of the female rat following exposure to conspecific males. *Mol. Cell. Neurosci.* **3**, 360–369.

Dudley, S.D., Ramirez, I., and Wade, G.N. (1981a). Deficits in pituitary and brain cell nuclear retention of (^{3}H)estradiol in diabetic rats deprived of insulin: Time course and metabolic correlates. *Neuroendocrinology* **33**, 1–6.

Dudley, S.D., Ramirez, I., and Wade, G.N. (1981b). Estrous behavior and pituitary and brain cell nuclear retention of [^{3}H]estradiol in chronically insulin-deficient female rats. *Neuroendocrinology* **33**, 7–11.

Eckersell, C.B., Popper, P., and Micevych, P.E. (1998). Estrogen-induced alteration of mu-opioid receptor immunoreactivity in the medial preoptic nucleus and medial amygdala. *J. Neurosci.* **18**, 3967–3976.

Edwards, D.A., and Pfeifle, J.K. (1983). Hormonal control of receptivity, proceptivity and sexual motivation. *Physiol. Behav.* **30**, 437–443.

Edwards, D.A., and Pfeifle, J.K. (1997). Hypothalamic and midbrain control of sexual receptivity in the female rat. *Physiol. Behav.* **26**, 1061–1067.

Eisenfeld, A.J. (1969). Hypothalamic oestradiol-binding macromolecules. *Nature (London)* **224**, 1202–1203.

Emery, D.E., and Moss, R.L. (1984a). Lesions confined to the ventromedial hypothalamus decrease the frequency of coital contacts in female rats. *Horm. Behav.* **18**, 313–329.

Emery, D.E., and Moss, R.L. (1984b). p-Chlorophenylalanine alters pacing of copulation in female rats. *Pharmacol., Biochem. Behav.* **20**, 337–341.

Erskine, M.S. (1985). Effects of paced coital stimulation on estrous duration in intact cycling rats and ovariectomized and ovariectomized-adrenalectomized hormone-primed rats. *Behav. Neurosci.* **99**, 151–161.

Erskine, M.S. (1989). Solicitation behavior in the estrous female rat: A review. *Horm. Behav.* **23**, 473–502.

Erskine, M.S. (1993). Mating-induced increases in FOS protein in preoptic area and medial amygdala of cycling female rats. *Brain Res. Bull.* **32**, 447–451.

Erskine, M.S. (1995). Prolactin release after mating and genitosensory stimulation in females. *Endocr. Rev.* **16**, 508–528.

Erskine, M.S., and Hanrahan, S.B. (1997). Effects of paced mating on c-fos gene expression in the female rat brain. *J. Neuroendocrinol.* **9**, 903–912.

Erskine, M.S., and Kornberg, E. (1992). Acute luteinizing hormone and prolactin responses to paced mating stimulation in the estrous female rat. *J. Neuroendocrinol.* **4**, 173–179.

Erskine, M.S., Kornberg, E., and Cherry, J.A. (1989). Paced copulation in rats: Effects of intromission frequency and duration on luteal activation and estrus length. *Physiol. Behav.* **45**, 33–39.

Etgen, A.M. (1979). Antiestrogens: Effects of tamoxifen, nafoxidine, and CI-628 on sexual behavior, cytoplasmic receptors, and nuclear binding of estrogen. *Horm. Behav.* **13**, 97–112.

Etgen, A.M. (1982). 1-(o-Chlorophenyl)-1-(p-chlorophenyl) 2,2,2-trichloroethane: A probe for studying estrogen and progestin receptor mediation of female sexual behavior and neuroendocrine responses. *Endocrinology (Baltimore)* **111**, 1498–1504.

Etgen, A.M. (1995). Oxytocin does not act locally in the hypothalamus to elicit norepinephrine release. *Brain Res.* **703**, 242–244.

Etgen, A.M., and Barfield, R.J. (1986). Antagonism of female sexual behavior with intracerebral implants of antiprogestin RU 38486: Correlation with binding to neural progestin receptors. *Endocrinology (Baltimore)* **119**, 1610–1617.

Etgen, A.M., and Karkanias, G.B. (1990). Estradiol regulates the number of alpha-1-noradrenergic receptor but not beta-noradrenergic receptor or alpha-2 noradrenergic receptors in hypothalamus of female rats. *Neurochem. Int.* **16**, 1–9.

Etgen, A.M., and Karkanias, G.B. (1994). Estrogen regulation of noradrenergic signaling in the hypothalamus. *Psychoneuroendocrinology* **19**, 603–610.

Etgen, A.M., and Shamamian, P. (1986). Regulation of estrogen-stimulated lordosis behavior and hypothalamic progestin receptor induction by antiestrogens in female rats. *Horm. Behav.* **20**, 166–180.

Etgen, A.M., Chu, H.P., Fiber, J.M., Karkanias, G.B., and Morales, J.M. (1999). Hormonal integration of neurochemical and sensory signals governing female reproductive behavior. *Behav. Brain Res.* **105**, 93–103.

Fadem, B.H., Barfield, R.J., and Whalen, R.E. (1979). Dose-response and time-response relationships between progesterone and the display of patterns of receptive and proceptive behavior in the female rat. *Horm. Behav.* **13**, 40–48.

Feder, H.H., and Marrone, B.L. (1977). Progesterone: Its role in the central nervous system as a facilitator and inhibitor of sexual behavior and gonadotropin release. *Ann. N.Y. Acad. Sci.* **286**, 331–354.

Feder, H.H., Resko, J.A., and Goy, R.W. (1968a). Progesterone concentrations in the arterial plasma of guinea pigs during the oestrous cycle. *J. Endocrinol.* **40**, 505–513.

Feder, H.H., Resko, J.A., and Goy, R.W. (1968b). Progesterone levels in the arterial plasma of pre-ovulatory and ovariectomized rats. *J. Endocrinol.* **41**, 563–569.

Feder, H.H., Landau, I.T., Marrone, B.L., and Walker, W.A. (1977). Interactions between estrogen and progesterone in neural tissues that mediate sexual behavior of guinea pigs. *Psychoneuroendocrinology* **2**, 337–347.

Flanagan, L.M., Pfaus, J.G., Pfaff, D.W., and McEwen, B.S. (1993). Induction of FOS immunoreactivity in oxytocin neurons after sexual activity in female rats. *Neuroendocrinology* **58**, 352–358.

Floody, O.R., and O'Donohue, T.L. (1980). Lesions of the mesencephalic central gray depress ultrasound production and lordosis by female hamsters. *Physiol. Behav.* **24**, 79–85.

Floody, O.R., Blinn, N.E., Lisk, R.D., and Vomachka, A.J. (1987). Localization of hypothalamic sites for the estrogen-priming of sexual receptivity in female hamsters. *Behav. Neurosci.* **101**, 309–314.

Foreman, M.M., and Moss, R.L. (1977). Effects of subcutaneous injection and intrahypothalamic infusion of releasing hormones upon lordotic response to repetitive coital stimulation. *Horm. Behav.* **8**, 219–234.

Foreman, M.M., and Moss, R.L. (1979a). Role of hypothalamic dopaminergic receptors in the control of lordosis behavior in the female rat. *Physiol. Behav.* **22**, 282–289.

Foreman, M.M., and Moss, R.L. (1979b). Roles of gonadotropins and releasing hormones in hypothalamic control of lordotic behavior in ovariectomized, estrogen-primed rats. *J. Comp. Physiol. Psychol.* **93**, 556–565.

Fraile, I.G., Pfaff, D.W., and McEwen, B.S. (1987). Progestin receptors with and without estrogen induction in male and female hamster brain. *Neuroendocrinology* **45**, 487–491.

Franck, J.A.E., and Ward, I.L. (1981). Intralimbic progesterone and methysergide facilitate lordotic behavior in estrogen-primed female rats. *Neuroendocrinology* **32**, 50–56.

Freeman, M.E., and Neill, J.D. (1972). The pattern of prolactin secretion during pseudopregnancy in the rat: A daily nocturnal surge. *Endocrinology (Baltimore)* **90**, 1292–1294.

French, D., Fitzpatrick, D., and Law, O.T. (1972). Operant investigation of mating preference in female rats. *J. Comp. Physiol. Psychol.* **81**, 226–232.

Frye, C.A., and Erskine, M.S. (1990). Influence of time of mating and paced copulation on induction of pseudopregnancy in cyclic female rats. *J. Reprod. Fertil.* **90**, 375–385.

Frye, C.A., and Vongher, J.M. (1999). Progestins' rapid facilitation of lordosis when applied to the ventral tegmentum corresponds to efficacy at enhancing GABA(A) receptor activity. *J. Neuroendocrinol.* **11**, 829–837.

Frye, C.A., Bayon, L.E., Pursnani, N.K., and Purdy, R.H. (1998). The neurosteroids, progesterone and 3 alpha, 5 alpha-THP, enhance sexual motivation, receptivity, and proceptivity in female rats. *Brain Res.* **808**, 72–83.

Frye, C.A., Murphy, R.E., and Platek, S.M. (2000). Anti-sense oligonucleotides, for progestin receptors in the VMH and glutamic acid decarboxylase in the VTA, attenuate progesterone-induced lordosis in hamsters and rats. *Behav. Brain Res.* **115**, 55–64.

Fuchs, A.R., Cubile, L., and Dawood, M.Y. (1981). Effects of mating on levels of oxytocin and prolactin in the plasma of male and female rabbits. *J. Endocrinol.* **90**, 245–253.

Gehring, U. (1998). Steroid hormone receptors and heat shock proteins. *Vitam. Horm. (N.Y.)* **54**, 167–205.

Gentry, R.T., Wade, G.N., and Blaustein, J.D. (1977). Binding of (^{3}H)estradiol by brain cell nuclei and female rat sexual behavior: Inhibition by experimental diabetes. *Brain Res.* **130**, 135–146.

Gibson, B.M., and Floody, O.R. (1998). Time course of VMN lesion effects on lordosis and ultrasound production in hamsters. *Behav. Neurosci.* **112**, 1236–1246.

Gietzen, D.W., Hope, W.G., and Woolley, D.E. (1983). Dopaminergic agonists increase [^{3}H]estradiol binding in hypothalamus of female rats, but not of males. *Life sci.* **33**, 2221–2228.

Gilchrist, S., and Blaustein, J.D. (1984). The desensitization effect of progesterone on female rat sexual behavior is not due to interference with estrogen priming. *Physiol. Behav.* **32**, 879–882.

Gilman, D.P., and Hitt, J.C. (1978). Effects of gonadal hormones on pacing of sexual contact by female rats. *Behav. Biol.* **24**, 77–87.

Gilman, D.P., Mercer, L.F., and Hitt, J.C. (1979). Influence of female copulatory behavior on the induction of pseudopregnancy in the female rat. *Physiol. Behav.* **22**, 675–678.

Glaser, J.H., and Barfield, R.J. (1984). Blockade of progesterone-activated estrous behavior in rats by intracerebral anisomycin is site specific. *Neuroendocrinology* **38**, 337–343.

Glaser, J.H., Rubin, B.S., and Barfield, R.J. (1983). Onset of the receptive and proceptive components of feminine sexual behavior in rats following the intravenous administration of progesterone. *Horm. Behav.* **17**, 18–27.

Goldfoot, D.A., and Goy, R.W. (1970). Abbreviation of behavioral estrus in guinea pigs by coital and vagino-cervical stimulation. *J. Comp. Physiol. Psychol.* **72**, 426–434.

Gonzalez-Mariscal, G., Melo, A.I., and Beyer, C. (1993). Progesterone, but not lhrh or prostaglandin E$_2$, induces sequential inhibition of lordosis to various lordogenic agents. *Neuroendocrinology* **57**, 940–945.

Gorospe, W.C., and Freeman, M.E. (1981). The effects of various methods of cervical stimulation on continuation of prolactin surges in rats. *Proc. Soc. Exp. Biol. Med.* **167**, 78–82.

Gorski, J., Toft, D., Shyamala, G., Smith, D., and Notides, A. (1968). Hormone receptors: Studies on the interaction of estrogen with the uterus. *Recent Prog. Horm. Res.* **24**, 45–80.

Goy, R.W., and Phoenix, C.H. (1963). Hypothalamic regulation of female sexual behavior, establishment of behavioural oestrus in spayed guinea-pigs following hypothalamic lesions. *J. Reprod. Fertil.* **5**, 23–40.

Goy, R.W., and Young, W.C. (1957). Strain differences in the behavioral responses of female guinea pigs to alpha-estradiol benzoate and progesterone. *Behaviour* **10**, 340–354.

Goy, R.W., Phoenix, C.H., and Young, W.C. (1966). Inhibitory action of the corpus luteum on the hormonal induction of estrous behavior in the guinea pig. *Gen. Comp. Endocrinol.* **6**, 267–275.

Gréco, B., Allegretto, E.A., Tetel, M.J., and Blaustein, J.D. (2001). Coexpression of ERs and progestin receptor proteins in the female rat forebrain: Effects of E$_2$ treatment. *Endocrinology* **142**, S172–S181.

Green, R., Luttge, W.G., and Whalen, R.E. (1970). Induction of receptivity in ovariectomized female rats by a single intravenous injection of estradiol-17β. *Physiol. Behav.* **5**, 137–141.

Greene, G.L., Gilna, P., Waterfield, M., Baker, A., Hort, Y., and Shine, J. (1986). Sequence and expression of human estrogen receptor complementary DNA. *Science* **231**, 1150–1154.

Greengard, P., Allen, P.B., and Nairn, A.C. (1999). Beyond the dopamine receptor: The DARPP-32/Protein phosphatase-1 cascade. *Neuron* **23**, 435–447.

Grody, W.W., Schrader, W.T., and O'Malley, B.W. (1982). Activation, transformation, and subunit structure of steroid hormone receptors. *Endocr. Rev.* **3**, 141–163.

Grosvenor, C.E., Shah, G.V., and Crowley, W.R. (1990). Role of neurogenic stimuli, milk prolactin in the regulation of prolactin secretion during lactation. *In* "Mammalian Parenting: Biochemical, Neurobiological, Behavioral Determinants" (N.A. Krasnegor and R.S. Bridges, eds.), pp. 324–342. Oxford University Press, New York.

Gu, G.B., Rojo, A.A., Zee, M.C., Yu, J.H., and Simerly, R.B. (1996). Hormonal regulation of CREB phosphorylation in the anteroventral periventricular nucleus. *J. Neurosci.* **16**, 3035–3044.

Gu, G.B., Varoqueaux, F., and Simerly, R.B. (1999). Hormonal regulation of glutamate receptor gene expression in the anteroventral periventricular nucleus of the hypothalamus. *J. Neurosci.* **19**, 3213–3222.

Guennoun, R., Schumacher, M., Robert, F., Delespierre, B., Gouezou, M., Eychenne, B., Akwa, Y., Rebel, P., and Baulieu, E.E. (1997). Neurosteroids: Expression of functional 3 beta-hydroxysteroid dehydrogenase by rat sensory neurons and Schwann cells. *Eur. J. Neurosci.* **9**, 2236–2247.

Guerra-Araiza, C., Cerbon, M.A., Morimoto, S., and Camacho-Arroyo, I. (2000). Progesterone receptor isoforms expression pattern in the rat brain during the estrous cycle. *Life Sci.* **66**, 1743–1752.

Gunnet, J.W., and Freeman, M.E. (1983). The mating-induced release of prolactin: A unique neuroendocrine response. *Endocr. Revi.* **4**, 44–61.

Hagihara, K., Hirata, S., Osada, T., Hirai, M., and Kato, J. (1992). Distribution of cells containing progesterone receptor messenger RNA in the female rat dicephalon and telencephalon - An insitu hybridization study. *Mol. Brain Res.* **14**, 239–249.

Hansen, S., and Södersten, P. (1978). Effects of subcutaneous implants of progesterone on the induction and duration of sexual receptivity in ovariectomized rats. *J. Endocrinol.* **77**, 373–379.

Hansen, S., and Södersten, P. (1979). Reversal of progesterone inhibition of sexual behavior in ovariectomized rats by high doses of progesterone. *J. Endocrinol.* **80**, 381–388.

Hansen, S., Södersten, P., Eneroth, P., Srebro, B., and Hole, K. (1979). A sexually dimorphic rhythm in oestradiol-activated lordosis behavior in the rat. *J. Endocrinol.* **83**, 267–274.

Hardy, D.F., and DeBold, J.F. (1972). Effects of coital stimulation upon behavior of the female rat. *J. Comp. Physiol. Psychol.* **78**, 400–408.

Hardy, D.F., and DeBold, J.F. (1973). Effects of repeated testing on sexual behavior of the female rat. *J. Comp. Physiol. Psychol.* **85**, 195–202.

Haskins, J.T., and Moss, R.L. (1983). Action of estrogen and mechanical vaginocervical stimulation on the membrane excitability of hypothalamic and midbrain neurons. *Brain Res. Bull.* **10**, 489–496.

Havens, M.D., and Rose, J.D. (1988). Estrogen-dependent and estrogen-independent effects of progesterone on the electrophysiological excitability of dorsal midbrain neurons in golden hamsters. *Neuroendocrinology* **48**, 120–129.

Hennessey, A.C., Wallen, K., and Edwards, D.A. (1986). Preoptic lesions increase the display of lordosis by male rats. *Brain Res.* **370**, 21–28.

Hennessey, A.C., Camak, L., Gordon, F., and Edwards, D.A. (1990). Connections between the pontine central gray and the ventromedial hypothalamus are essential for lordosis in female rats. *Behav. Neuro.* **104**, 477–488.

Herdegen, T., Kovary, K., Leah, J., and Bravo, R. (1991). Specific temporal and spatial distribution of JUN, FOS, and KROX-24 proteins in spinal neurons following noxious transsynaptic stimulation. *J. Comp. Neurol.* **313**, 178–191.

Heritage, A.S., Grant, L.D., and Stumpf, W.E. (1977). }H}3}h}H estradiol in catecholamine neurons of rat brain stem: Combined localization by autoradiography and formaldehyde-induced fluorescence. *J. Comp. Neurol.* **176**, 607–630.

Heritage, A.S., Stumpf, W.E., Sar, M., and Grant, L.D. (1980). Brainstem catecholamine neurons are target sites for sex steroid hormones. *Science* **207**, 1377–1379.

Hill, S.M., Spriggs, L.L., Lawson, N.O., and Harlan, R.E. (1996). Effects of melatonin on estrogen receptor expression in the forebrain of outbred (Lak.LVG) golden hamsters. *Brain Res.* **742**, 107–114.

Hnatczuk, O.C., Lisciotto, C.A., DonCarlos, L.L., Carter, C.S., and Morrell, J.I. (1994). Estrogen receptor immunoreactivity in specific brain areas of the prairie vole (*Microtus ochrogaster*) is altered by sexual receptivity and genetic sex. *J. Neuroendocrinol.* **6**, 89–100.

Hoffman, G.E., Lee, W.-S., Attardi, B., Yann, V., and Fitzsimmons, M.D. (1990). Luteinizing hormone-releasing hormone neurons express c-fos antigen after steroid activation. *Endocrinology* (*Baltimore*) **126**, 1736–1741.

Hornby, J.B., and Rose, J.D. (1976). Responses of caudal brain stem neurons to vaginal and somatosensory stimulation in the rat and evidence of genital-nociceptive interactions. *Exp. Neurol.* **51**, 363–376.

Hoshina, Y., Takeo, T., Nakano, K., Sato, T., and Sakuma, Y. (1994). Axon-sparing lesion of the preoptic area enhances receptivity and diminishes proceptivity among components of female rat sexual behavior. *Behav. Brain Res.* **61**, 197–204.

Howard, S.B., Etgen, A.M., and Barfield, R.J. (1984). Antagonism of central estrogen action by intracerebral implants of tamoxifen. *Horm. Behav.* **18**, 256–266.

Hunt, S.P., Pini, A., and Evan, G. (1987). Induction of c-fos-like protein in spinal cord neurons following sensory stimulation. *Nature (London)* **328**, 632–634.

Hyder, S.M., Chiappetta, C., and Stancel, G.M. (1999). Interaction of human estrogen receptors alpha and beta with the same naturally occurring estrogen response elements. *Biochem. Pharmacol.* **57**, 597–601.

Ignar-Trowbridge, D.M., Teng, C.T., Ross, K.A., Parker, M.G., Korach, K.S., and McLachlan, J.A. (1993). Peptide growth factors elicit estrogen receptor-dependent transcriptional activation of an estrogen-responsive element. *Mol. Endocrinol.* **7**, 992–998.

Ilenchuk, T.T., and Walters, M.R. (1987). Rat uterine progesterone receptor analyzed by [³H]5020 photoaffinity labeling: Evidence that the A and B subunits are not equimolar. *Endocrinology (Baltimore)* **120**, 1449–1456.

Insel, T.R. (1990). Regional induction of c-fos-like protein in rat brain after estradiol administration. *Endocrinology (Baltimore)* **126**, 1849–1853.

Jensen, E.V., and DeSombre, E.R. (1972). Mechanism of action of the female sex hormones. *Annu. Revi. Biochemi.* **41**, 203–230.

Jensen, E.V., Suzuki, T., Kawasima, T., Stumpf, W.E., Jungblut, P.W., and DeSombre, E.R. (1968). A two-step mechanism for the interaction of estradiol with rat uterus. *Proc. Natl. Acad. Sci. U.S.A.* **59**, 632–638.

Johren, O., Flügge, G., and Fuchs, E. (1994). Hippocampal glucocorticoid receptor expression in the tree shrew: Regulation by psychosocial conflict. *Cell. Mol. Neurobiol.* **14**, 281–296.

Jones, K.J., Chikaraishi, D.M., Harrington, C.A., McEwen, B.S., and Pfaff, D. W. (1986). In situ hybridization of estradiol-induced changes in ribosomal RNA levels in rat brain. *Mol. Brain Res.* **1**, 145–152.

Jordan, V.C. (1995). Long-term tamoxifen treatment for breast cancer. *J. Natl. Cancer Inst.* **87**, 1805–1806.

Jordan, V.C. (1999). Targeted antiestrogens to prevent breast cancer. *Trends Endocrinol. Metab.* **10**, 312–317.

Joslyn, W.D., and Feder, H.H. (1971). Facilitatory and inhibitory effects of supplementary estradiol benzoate given to ovariectomized, estrogen-primed guinea pigs. *Horm. Behav.* **2**, 307–314.

Joslyn, W.D., Wallen, K., and Goy, R.W. (1971). Cyclic changes in sexual response to exogenous progesterone in female guinea pigs. *Physiol. Behav.* **7**, 915–917.

Jungtestas, I., Hu, Z.Y., Baulieu, E.E., and Robel, P. (1989). Neurosteroids—Biosynthesis of pregnenolone and progesterone in primary cultures of rat glial cells. *Endocrinology (Baltimore)* **125**, 2083–2091.

Kahwanago, I., Heinrichs, W.L., and Herrmann, W.L. (1969). Isolation of oestradiol "receptors" from bovine hypothalamus and anterior pituitary gland. *Nature (London)* **223**, 313–314.

Kaplitt, M.G., Kleopoulos, S.P., Pfaff, D.W., and Mobbs, C.V. (1993). Estrogen increases HIP-70/PLC-alpha messenger ribonucleic acid in the rat uterus and hypothalamus. *Endocrinology (Baltimore)* **133**, 99–104.

Kastner, P., Krust, A., Turcotte, B., Stropp, U., Tora, L., Gronemeyer, H., and Chambon, P. (1990). 2 distinct estrogen-regulated promoters generate transcripts encoding the 2 functionally different human progesterone receptor form-A and form-B. *EMBO J.* **9**, 1603–1614.

Kato, J., and Onouchi, T. (1977). Specific progesterone receptors in the hypothalamus and anterior hypophysis of the rat. *Endocrinology (Baltimore)* **101**, 920–928.

Kato, J., Onouchi, T., and Okinaga, S. (1978). Hypothalamic and hypophysial progesterone receptors: Estrogen-priming effect, differential localization, 5a-dihydroprogesterone binding, and nuclear receptors. *J. Steroid. Biochem.* **9**, 419–427.

Kawakami, M., and Ibuki, T. (1972). Multiple unit activity in the brain correlated with induction and maintenance of pseudopregnancy in rats. *Neuroendocrinology* **9**, 2–11.

Kawakami, M., and Kubo, K. (1971). Neuro-correlate of limbic-hypothalamo-pituitary-gonadal axis in the rat: Change in limbic-hypothalamic unit activity induced by vaginal and electrical stimulation. *Neuroendocrinology* **7**, 65–88.

Kawakami, M., and Sawyer, C.H. (1959). Neuroendocrine correlates of changes in brain activity thresholds by sex steroids and pituitary hormones. *Endocrinology (Baltimore)* **65**, 652–668.

Kawakami, M., Akema, T., and Ando, S. (1979). Electrophysiological studies on the neural networks among estrogen and progesterone effective brain areas on lordosis behavior of the rat. *Brain Res.* **169**, 287–301.

Ke, F.-C., and Ramirez, V.D. (1987). Membrane mechanism mediates progesterone stimulatory effect on LHRH release from superfused rat hypothalami in vitro. *Neuroendocrinology* **45**, 514–517.

Ke, F.C., and Ramirez, V.D. (1990). Binding of progesterone to nerve cell membranes of rat brain using progesterone conjugated to I-125-bovine serum albumin as a ligand. *J. Neurochem.* **54**, 467–472.

Kelly, M.J., and Wagner, E.J. (1999). Estrogen modulation of G-protein-coupled receptors. *Trends Endocrinol. Metab* **10**, 369–374.

Kelly, M.J., Moss, R.L., Dudley, C.A., and Fawcett, C.P. (1977). The specificity of the response of preoptic-septal area neurons to estrogen: 17α-estradiol versus 17β-estradiol and the response of extrahypothalamic neurons. *Exp. Brain Res.* **30**, 43–52.

Kelly, M.J., Lagrange, A.H., Wagner, E.J., and Ronnekleiv, O.K. (1999). Rapid effects of estrogen to modulate G protein-coupled receptors via activation of protein kinase A and protein kinase C pathways. *Steroids* **64**, 64–75.

Kendrick, K.M., Keverne, E.B., Hinton, M.R., and Goode, J.A. (1991). Cerebrospinal fluid and plasma concentrations of oxytocin and vasopressin during parturition and vaginocervical stimulation in the sheep. *Brain Res. Bull.* **26**, 803–807.

Kennedy, G.C. (1964). Hypothalamic control of the endocrine and behavioral changes associated with oestrus in the rat. *J. Physiol. (London)* **172**, 383–392.

Kennedy, G.C., and Mitra, J. (1963). Hypothalamic control of energy balance and the reproductive cycle in the rat. *J. Physiol. (London)* **166**, 395–407.

King, W.J., and Greene, G.L. (1984). Monoclonal antibodies localize oestrogen receptor in the nuclei of target cells. *Nature (London)* **307**, 745–747.

Kiss, J.Z. (1988). Dynamism of chemoarchitecture in the hypothalamic paraventricular nucleus. *Brain Res. Bull.* **20**, 699–708.

Kohlert, J.G., Rowe, R.K., and Meisel, R.L. (1997). Intromissive stimulation from the male increases extracellular dopamine release from fluoro-gold-identified neurons within the midbrain of female hamsters. *Horm. Behav.* **32**, 143–154.

Komisaruk, B.R., and Diakow, C. (1973). Lordosis, reflex intensity in rats in relation to the estrous cycle, ovariectomy, estrogen administration and mating behavior. *Endocrinology (Baltimore)* **93**, 548–557.

Komisaruk, B.R., and Larsson, K. (1971). Suppression of a spinal and a cranial reflex by vaginal or rectal probing in rats. *Brain Res.* **35**, 231–235.

Komisaruk, B.R., and Wallman, J. (1977). Antinociceptive effects of vaginal stimulation in rats: Neurophysiological and behavioral studies. *Brain Res.* **137**, 85–107.

Komisaruk, B.R., McDonald, P.G., Whitmoyer, D.I., and Sawyer, C.H. (1967). Effects of progesterone and sensory stimulation on EEG and neuronal activity in the rat. *Exp. Neurol.* **19**, 494–507.

Komisaruk, B.R., Bianca, R., Sansone, G., Gomez, L.E., Cueva-Rolon, R., Beyer, C., and Whipple, B. (1996). Brain-mediated responses to vaginocervical stimulation in spinal cord-transected rats: Role of the vagus nerves. *Brain Res.* **708**, 128–134.

Kononen, J., Honkaniemi, J., Alho, H., Koistinaho, J., Iadarola, M., and Pelto-Huikko, M. (1992). Fos-like immunoreactivity in the rat hypothalamic-pituitary axis after immobilization stress. *Endocrinology (Baltimore)* **130**, 3041–3047.

Kornberg, E., and Erskine, M.S. (1994). Effects of differential mating stimulation on the onset of prolactin surges in pseudopregnant rats. *Psychoneuroendocrinology* **19**, 357–371.

Krebs, C.J., Jarvis, E.D., and Pfaff, D.W. (1999). The 70-kDa heat shock cognate protein (Hsc73) gene is enhanced by ovarian hormones in the ventromedial hypothalamus. *Proc. Natl. Acad. Sci. U.S.A.* **96**, 1686–1691.

Krebs, C.J., Jarvis, E.D., Chan, J., Lydon, J.P., Ogawa, S., and Pfaff, D.W. (2000). A membrane-associated progesterone-binding protein, 25-Dx, is regulated by progesterone in brain regions involved in female reproductive behaviors. *Proc. Natl. Acad. Sci. U.S.A* **97**, 12816–12821.

Krege, J.H., Hodgin, J.B., Couse, J.F., Enmark, E., Warner, M., Mahler, J.F., Sar, M., Korach, K.S., Gustafsson, J.A., and Smithies, O. (1998). Generation and reproductive phenotypes of mice lacking estrogen receptor beta. *Proc. Natl. Acad. Sci. U.S.A.* **95**, 15677–15682.

Krieger, M.S., Orr, D., and Perper, T. (1976). Temporal patterning of sexual behavior in the female rat. *Behav. Biol.* **18**, 379–386.

Krieger, M.S., Conrad, C.A., and Pfaff, D.W. (1979). An autoradiographic study of the efferent connections of the ventromedial nucleus of the hypothalamus. *J. Comp. Neurol.* **183**, 785–815.

Kubli-Garfias, C., and Whalen, R.E. (1977). Induction of lordosis behavior in female rats by intravenous administration of progestins. *Horm. Behav.* **9**, 380–386.

Kuiper, G.G.J.M., Enmark, E., Peltohuikko, M., Nilsson, S., and Gustafsson, J.A. (1996). Cloning of a novel estrogen receptor expressed in rat prostate and ovary. *Proc. Natl. Acad. Sci. U.S.A.* **93**, 5925–5930.

Kuiper, G.G.J.M., Carlsson, B., Grandien, K., Enmark, E., Haggblad, J., Nilsson, S., and Gustafsson, J.A. (1997). Comparison of the ligand binding specificity and transcript tissue distribution of estrogen receptors alpha and beta. *Endocrinology (Baltimore)* **138**, 863–870.

LaFlamme, N., Nappi, R.E., Drolet, G., Labrie, C., and Rivest, S. (1998). Expression and neuropeptidergic characterization of estrogen receptors (ERalpha and ERbeta) throughout the rat brain: Anatomical evidence of distinct roles of each subtype. *J. Neurobiol.* **36**, 357–378.

Lagrange, A.H., Ronnekleiv, O.K., and Kelly, M.J. (1997). Modulation of G protein-coupled receptors by an estrogen receptor that activates protein kinase A. *Mol. Pharmacol.* **51**, 605–612.

Landau, I.T. (1977). Relationships between the effects of the anti-estrogen, CI-628, on sexual behavior, uterine growth, and cell nuclear estrogen retention after estradiol-17β-benzoate administration in the ovariectomized rat. *Brain Res.* **133**, 119–138.

Landau, I.T., Logue, C.M., and Feder, H.H. (1978). Comparison of the effects of estradiol-β and the synthetic estrogen, RU-2858, on lordosis behavior in adult female rats and guinea pigs. *Horm. Behav.* **10**, 143–155.

Larsson, K., Feder, H.H., and Komisaruk, B.R. (1974). Role of the adrenal glands, repeated matings and monoamines in lordosis behavior of rats. *Pharmacol. Biochem. Behav.* **2**, 685–692.

Lauber, A.H. (1988a). Atropine sulfate modulates estrogen binding by female, but not male, rat hypothalamus. *Brain Res. Bull.* **20**, 273–276.

Lauber, A.H. (1988b). Bethanechol-induced increase in hypothalamic estrogen receptor binding in female rats is related to capacity for estrogen-dependent reproductive behavior. *Brain Res.* **456**, 177–182.

Lauber, A.H., and Whalen, R.E. (1988). Muscarinic cholinergic modulation of hypothalamic estrogen binding sites. *Brain Res.* **443**, 21–26.

Lauber, A.H., Romano, G.J., Mobbs, C.V., and Pfaff, D.W. (1990). Estradiol regulation of estrogen receptor messenger ribonucleic acid in rat mediobasal hypothalamus—an *in situ* hybridization study. *J. Neuroendocrinol.* **2**, 605–611.

Lauber, A.H., Mobbs, C.V., Muramatsu, M., and Pfaff, D.W. (1991). Estrogen receptor messenger RNA expression in rat hypothalamus as a function of genetic sex and estrogen dose. *Endocrinology (Baltimore)* **129**, 3180–3186.

LaVaque, T.J., and Rodgers, C.H. (1975). Recovery of mating behavior in the female rat following VMH lesions. *Physiol. Behav.* **14**, 59–63.

Law, T., and Meagher, W. (1958). Hypothalamic lesions and sexual behavior in the female rat. *Science* **128**, 1626–1627.

Lawson, N.O., Wee, B.E.F., Blask, D.E., Castles, C.G., Spriggs, L.L., and Hill, S.M. (1992). Melatonin decreases estrogen receptor expression in the medial preoptic area of inbred (LSH/sslak) golden hamsters. *Biol. Reprod.* **47**, 1082–1090.

Lerant, A., Herman, M.E., and Freeman, M.E. (1996). Dopaminergic neurons of periventricular and arcuate nuclei of pseudopregnant rats: Semicircadian rhythm in FOS-related antigens immunoreactivities and in dopamine concentration. *Endocrinology (Baltimore)* **137**, 3621–3628.

Li, H.Y., Wade, G.N., and Blaustein, J.D. (1994). Manipulations of metabolic fuel availability alter estrous behavior and neural estrogen receptor immunoreactivity in syrian hamsters. *Endocrinology (Baltimore)* **135**, 240–247.

Li, X., Schwartz, P.E., and Rissman, E.F. (1997). Distribution of estrogen receptor-beta-like immunoreactivity in rat forebrain. *Neuroendocrinology* **66**, 63–67.

Lim, C.S., Baumann, C.T., Htun, H., Xian, W.J., Irie, M., Smith, C.L., and Hager, G.L. (1999). Differential localization and activity of the A- and B-forms of the human progesterone receptor using green fluorescent protein chimeras. *Mol. Endocrinol.* **13**, 366–375.

Lincoln, D.W. (1969a). Response of hypothalamic units to stimulation of the vaginal cervix: Specific versus non-specific effects. *J. Endocrinol.* **43**, 683–684.

Lincoln, D.W. (1969b). Effects of progesterone on the electrical activity of the forebrain. *J. Endocrinol.* **45**, 585–596.

Linkie, D.M., and Niswender, G.D. (1972). Serum levels of prolactin, luteinizing hormone, and follicle stimulating hormone during pregnancy in the rat. *Endocrinology (Baltimore)* **90**, 632–637.

Liposits, Z., Kallo, I., Coen, C.W., Paull, W.K., and Flerko, B. (1990). Ultrastructural analysis of estrogen receptor immunoreactive neurons in the medial preoptic area of the female rat brain. *Histochemistry* **93**, 233–239.

Lisciotto, C.A., and DeBold, J.F. (1991). Ventral tegmental lesions impair sexual receptivity in female hamsters. *Brain Res. Bull.* **26**, 877–883.

Lisk, R.D. (1960). A comparison of the effectiveness of intravenous, as opposed to subcutaneous, injection of progesterone for the induction of estrous behavior in the rat. *J. Biochem. Physiol.* **38**, 1381–1383.

Lisk, R.D. (1962). Diencephalic placement of estradiol and sexual receptivity in the female rat. *Am. J. Physiol.* **203**, 493–496.

Lodder, J., and Zeilmaker, G.H. (1976). Role of pelvic nerves in the postcopulatory abbreviation of behavioral estrus in female rats. *J. Comp. Physiol. Psychol.* **90**, 925–929.

Luttge, W.G., and Hughes, J.R. (1976). Intracerebral implantation of progesterone: Reexamination of the brain sites responsible for facilitation of sexual receptivity in estrogen-primed ovariectomized rats. *Physiol. Behav.* **17**, 771–775.

Luttge, W.M., Wallis, C.J., and Hall, N.R. (1974). Effects of pre- and post-treatment with unlabeled steroids on the in vivo uptake of [^{3}H]progestins in selected brain regions, uterus and plasma of the female mouse. *Brain Res.* **71**, 105–115.

Lydon, J.P., DeMayo, F.J., Funk, C.R., Mani, S.K., Hughes, A.R., Montgomery, C.A., Shyamala, G., Conneely, O.M., and O'Malley, B.W. (1995). Mice lacking progesterone receptor exhibit pleiotropic reproductive abnormalities. *Genes Dev.* **9**, 2266–2278.

Maccari, S., Piazza, P.V., Rougepont, F., Angelucci, L., Simon, H., and Lemoal, M. (1992). Noradrenergic regulation of type-i and type-II corticosteroid receptors in amygdala and hypothalamus. *Brain Res.* **587**, 313–318.

MacLusky, N.J., and McEwen, B.S. (1978). Oestrogen modulates progestin receptor concentrations in some rat brain regions but not in others. *Nature (London)* **274**, 276–278.

MacLusky, N.J., and McEwen, B.S. (1980). Progestin receptors in rat brain: Distribution and properties of cytoplasmic progestin-binding sites. *Endocrinology (Baltimore)* **106**, 192–202.

Madlafousek, J., and Hlinak, Z. (1977). Sexual behavior of the female laboratory rat: Inventory, patterning, and measurement. *Behaviour* **63**, 129–174.

Malik, K.F., Feder, H.H., and Morrell, J.I. (1993). Estrogen receptor immunostaining in the preoptic area and medial basal hypothalamus of estradiol benzoate- treated and prazosin-treated female guinea-pigs. *J. Neuroendocrinol.* **5**, 297–306.

Mangels, R.A., Powers, J.B., and Blaustein, J.D. (1998). Effect of photoperiod on neural estrogen and progestin receptor immunoreactivity in female Syrian hamsters. *Brain Res.* **796**, 63–74.

Mani, S.K., Allen, J.M.C., Clark, J.H., Blaustein, J.D., and O'Malley, B. W. (1994a). Convergent pathways for steroid hormone- and neurotransmitter- induced rat sexual behavior. *Science* **265**, 1246–1249.

Mani, S.K., Allen, J.M.C., Rettori, V., McCann, S.M., O'Malley, B.W., and Clark, J.H. (1994b). Nitric oxide mediates sexual behavior in female rats. *Proc. Natl. Acad. Sci. U.S.A.* **91**, 6468–6472.

Mani, S.K., Blaustein, J.D., Allen, J.M., Law, S.W., O'Malley, B.W., and Clark, J.H. (1994c). Inhibition of rat sexual behavior by antisense oligonucleotides to the progesterone receptor. *Endocrinology (Baltimore)* **135**, 1409–1414.

Mani, S.K., Allen, J.M.C., Clark, J.H., and O'Malley, B.W. (1995). Progesterone receptor involvement in the LHRH-facilitated sexual behavior of female rats. *Abstr. 77th Annu. Meet. Endoc. Soc.,* Abstract 440.

Mani, S.K., Allen, J.M.C., Lydon, J.P., Mulac-Jericevic, B., Blaustein, J.D., DeMayo, F.J., Conneely, O., and O'Malley, B.W. (1996). Dopamine requires the unoccupied progesterone receptor to induce sexual behavior in mice. *Mol. Endocrinol.* **10**, 1728–1737.

Mani, S.K., Blaustein, J.D., and O'Malley, B.W. (1997). Progesterone receptor function from a behavioral perspective. *Horm. Behav.* **31**, 244–255.

Mani, S.K., Fienberg, A.A., O'Callaghan, J.P., Snyder, G.L., Allen, P.B., Dash, P.K., Moore, A.N., Mitchell, A.J., Bibb, J., Greengard, P., and O'Malley, B.W. (2000). Requirement for DARPP-32 in progesterone-facilitated sexual receptivity in female rats and mice. *Science* **287**, 1053–1056.

Marrone, B.L., and Feder, H.H. (1977). Characteristics of (³H)estrogen uptake in brain, anterior pituitary and peripheral tissues of male and female guinea pigs. *Biol. Reprod.* **17**, 42–57.

Marrone, B.L., Rodriguez-Sierra, J.F., and Feder, H.H. (1979). Intrahypothalamic implants of progesterone inhibit lordosis behavior in ovariectomized, estrogen-treated rats. *Neuroendocrinology* **28**, 92–102.

Mathews, D., and Edwards, D.A. (1977a). Involvement of the ventromedial and anterior hypothalamic nuclei in the hormonal induction of receptivity in the female rat. *Physiol. Behav.* **19**, 319–326.

Mathews, D., and Edwards, D.A. (1977b). The ventromedial nucleus of the hypothalamus and the hormonal arousal of sexual behaviors in the female rat. *Horm. Behav.* **8**, 40–51.

Mathews, D., Donovan, K.M., Hollingsworth, E.M., Hutson, V.B., and Overstreet, C.T. (1983). Permanent deficits in lordosis behavior in female rats with lesions of the ventromedial nucleus of the hypothalamus. *Exp. Neurol.* **79**, 714–719.

Matuszewich, L., Lorrain, D.S., and Hull, E.M. (2000). Dopamine release in the medial preoptic area of female rats in response to hormonal manipulation and sexual activity. *Behav. Neurosci.* **114**, 772–782.

McCarthy, M.M., and Pfaus, J.G. (1996). Steroid modulation of neurotransmitter function to alter female reproductive behavior. *Trends Endocrinol. Metab.* **7**, 327–333.

McClintock, M.K., and Adler, N.T. (1978). The role of the female during copulation in wild and domestic norway rats (*Rattus norvegicus*). *Behaviour* **67**, 67–96.

McClintock, M.K., and Anisko, J.J. (1982). Group mating among Norway rats. I. Sex differences in the pattern and neuroendocrine consequences of copulation. *Anim. Behav.* **30**, 398–409.

McClintock, M.K., Anisko, J.J., and Adler, N.T. (1982a). Group mating among Norway rats. II. The social dynamics of copulation: Competition, cooperation, and mate choice. *Anim. Behav.* **30**, 410–425.

McClintock, M.K., Toner, J.P., Adler, N.T., and Anisko, J.J. (1982b). Postejaculatory quiescence in female and male rats: Consequences for sperm transport during group mating. *J. Comp. Physiol. Psychol.* **96**, 268–277.

McDermott, J.L., and Carter, C.S. (1980). Ovarian hormones, copulatory stilmuli, and female sexual behavior in the Mongolian gerbil. *Horm. Behav.* **14**, 211–223.

McEwen, B.S., and Alves, S.E. (1999). Estrogen actions in the central nervous system. *Endocr. Rev.* **20**, 279–307.

McEwen, B.S., Pfaff, D.W., Chaptal, C., and Luine, V. (1975). Brain cell nuclear retention of [³H]estradiol doses able to promote lordosis: Temporal and regional aspects. *Brain Res.* **86**, 155–161.

McEwen, B.S., deKloet, R., and Wallach, G. (1976). Interactions in vivo and in vitro of corticoids and progesterone with cell nuclei and soluble macromolecules from rat brain regions and pituitary. *Brain Res.* **105**, 129–136.

McEwen, B.S., Davis, P.G., Parsons, B., and Pfaff, D.W. (1979). The brain as a target for steroid hormone action. *Annu. Rev. Neurosci.* **2**, 65–112.

McGinnis, M.Y., Parsons, B., Rainbow, T.C., Krey, L.C., and McEwen, B.S. (1981). Temporal relationship between cell nuclear progestin receptor levels and sexual receptivity following intravenous progesterone administration. *Brain Res.* **218**, 365–371.

McGinnis, M.Y., Lumia, A.R., and McEwen, B.S. (1985). Increased estrogen receptor binding in amygdala correlates with facilitation of feminine sexual behavior induced by olfactory bulbectomy. *Brain Res.* **334**, 19–25.

McKenna, N.J., Lanz, R.B., and O'Malley, B.W. (1999). Nuclear receptor coregulators: Cellular and molecular biology. *Endocr. Rev.* **20**, 321–344.

Meaney, M.J., Diorio, J., Francis, D., Widdowson, J., LaPlante, P., Caldji, C., Sharma, S., Seckl, J.R., and Plotsky, P.M. (1996). Early environmental regulation of forebrain glucocorticoid receptor gene expression: Implications for adrenocortical responses to stress. *Dev. Neurosci.* **18**, 49–72.

Meisel, R.L., and Pfaff, D.W. (1985). Specificity and neural sites of action of anisomycin in the reduction or facilitation of female sexual behavior in rats. *Horm. Behav.* **19**, 237–251.

Meisel, R.L., Dohanich, G.P., McEwen, B.S., and Pfaff, D.W. (1987). Antagonism of sexual behavior in female rats by ventromedial hypothalamic implants of antiestrogen. *Neuroendocrinology* **45**, 201–207.

Merchenthaler, A., Scrimo, P.J., and Shughrue, P.J. (2000). The distribution of estrogen receptor-b immunoreactivity in the rat brain. *Abstr. Annu. Meet. Soc. Neurosci.,* No. 346.6.

Meredith, J.M., Auger, C.J., and Blaustein, J.D. (1994). Down-regulation of estrogen receptor immunoreactivity by 17 beta-estradiol in the guinea pig forebrain. *J. Neuroendocrinol.* **6**, 639–648.

Meredith, J.M., Moffatt, C.A., Auger, A.P., Snyder, G.L., Greengard, P., and Blaustein, J.D. (1998). Mating-related stimulation induces phosphorylation of dopamine- and cyclic AMP-regulated phosphoprotein-32 in progestin receptor- containing areas in the female rat brain. *J. Neurosci.* **18**, 10189–10195.

Mermelstein, P.G., and Becker, J.B. (1995). Increased extracellular dopamine in the nucleus accumbens and striatum of the female rat during paced copulatory behavior. *Behav. Neurosci.* **109**, 354–365.

Meyerson, B. (1972). Latency between intravenous injection of progestins and the appearance of estrous behavior in estrogen-treated ovariectomized rats. *Horm. Behav.* **3**, 1–9.

Meyerson, B.J., and Lindstrom, L.H. (1973). Sexual motivation in the female rat. A methodological study applied to the investigation of the effect of estradiol benzoate. *Acta Physiol. Scand. Suppl.* **389**, 1–80.

Micevych, P.E., Mills, R.H., Sinchak, K., Chen, J., Tao, L., LaPolt, P., and Lu, J.K.H. (2000). Estrogen increases progesterone expression in young but not old female rat hypothalamus. *Abstr. 30th Annu. Meet. Soc. Neurosci.,* 346. 16.

Miller, F.D., Ozimek, G., Milner, R.J., and Bloom, F.E. (1989). Regulation of neuronal oxytocin mRNA by ovarian steroids in the mature and developing hypothalamus. *Proc. Natl. Acad. Sci. U.S.A.* **86**, 2468–2472.

Milner, T.A., McEwen, B.S., Hayashi, S., Li, C.J., Reagan, L.P., and Alves, S.E. (2001). Ultrastructural evidence that hippocampal alpha estrogen receptors are located at extranuclear sites. *J. Comp. Neurol.* **429**, 355–371.

Mitchell, J.B., Betito, K., Rowe, W., Boksa, P., and Meaney, M.J. (1992). Serotonergic regulation of type-II corticosteroid receptor binding in hippocampal cell cultures—evidence for the importance of serotonin-induced changes in cAMP levels. *Neuroscience* **48**, 631–639.

Modianos, D.T., Delia, H., and Pfaff, D.W. (1976). Lordosis in female rats following medial forebrain bundle lesions. *Behav. Biol.* **18**, 135–141.

Moffatt, C.A., Rissman, E.F., Shupnik, M.A., and Blaustein, J.D. (1998). Induction of progestin receptors by estradiol in the forebrain of estrogen receptor-alpha gene-disrupted mice. *J. Neurosci.* **18**, 9556–9563.

Moguilewsky, M., and Philibert, D. (1984). RU 38486: Potent antiglucocorticoid activity correlated with strong binding to the cytosolic glucocorticoid receptor followed by an impaired activation. *J. Steroid Biochem.* **20**, 271–276.

Moguilewsky, M., and Raynaud, J.P. (1979a). Estrogen-sensitive progestin-binding sites in the female rat brain and pituitary. *Brain Res.* **164**, 165–175.

Moguilewsky, M., and Raynaud, J.P. (1979b). The relevance of hypothalamic and hypophyseal progestin receptor regulation in the induction and inhibition of sexual behavior in the female rat. *Endocrinology (Baltimore)* **105**, 516–522.

Montemayor, M.E., Clark, A.S., Lynn, D.M., and Roy, E.J. (1990). Modulation by norepinephrine of neural responses to estradiol. *Neuroendocrinology* **52**, 473–480.

Moody, K.M., and Adler, N.T. (1995). The role of the uterus and cervix in systemic oxytocin-PGE(2) facilitated lordosis behavior. *Horm. Behav.* **29**, 571–580.

Moody, K.M., Steinman, J.L., Komisaruk, B.R., and Adler, N.T. (1994). Pelvic neurectomy blocks oxytocin-facilitated sexual receptivity in rats. *Physiol. Behav.* **56**, 1057–1060.

Morgan, J.I., and Curran, T. (1991). Stimulus-transcription coupling in the nervous system: Involvement of the inducible proto-oncogenes fos and jun. *Annu. Rev. Neurosci.* **14**, 421–451.

Morgan, J.I., and Curran, T. (1995). The immediate-early gene response and neuronal death and regeneration. *Neuroscientist* **1**, 68–75.

Morin, L.P. (1977). Progesterone: inhibition of rodent sexual behavior. *Physiol. Behav.* **18**, 701–715.

Morin, L.P., and Feder, H.H. (1973). Multiple progesterone injections and the duration of estrus in ovariectomized guinea pigs. *Physiol. Behav.* **11**, 861–865.

Morin, L.P., and Feder, H.H. (1974a). Inhibition of lordosis behavior in ovariectomized guinea pigs by mesencephalic implants of progesterone. *Brain Res.* **70**, 71–80.

Morin, L.P., and Feder, H.H. (1974b). Hypothalamic progesterone implants and facilitation of lordosis behavior in estrogen-primed ovariectomized guinea pigs. *Brain Res.* **70**, 81–93.

Morin, L.P., and Feder, H.H. (1974c). Intracranial estradiol benzoate implants and lordosis behavior of ovariectomized guinea pigs. *Brain Res.* **70**, 95–102.

Morrell, J.I., and Pfaff, D.W. (1982). Characterization of estrogen-concentrating hypothalamic neurons by their axonal projections. *Science* **217**, 1273–1276.

Morrell, J.I., Krieger, M.S., and Pfaff, D.W. (1986). Quantitative autoradiographic analysis of estradiol retention by cells in the preoptic area, hypothalamus and amygdala. *Exp. Brain Res.* **62**, 343–354.

Moss, R.L., and Cooper, K.J. (1973). Temporal relationship of spontaneous and coitus-induced release of luteinizing hormone in the normal cyclic rat. *Endocrinology (Baltimore)* **92**, 1748–1753.

Moss, R.L., Dudley, C.A., and Schwartz, N.B. (1977). Coitus-induced release of luteinizing hormone in the proestrous rat: Fantasy or fact? *Endocrinology (Baltimore)* **100**, 394–397.

Mulac-Jericevic, B., Mullinax, R.A., DeMayo, F.J., Lydon, L.P., and Conneely, O.M. (2000). Subgroup of reproductive functions of progesterone mediated by progesterone receptor-B isoform. *Science* **289**, 1751–1754.

Muntz, J.A., Rose, J.D., and Shults, R.C. (1980). Disruption of lordosis by dorsal midbrain lesions in the golden hamster. *Brain Res. Bull.* **5**, 359–364.

Nadler, R.D. (1970). An improved instrument for implanting micropellets in the brain. *Physiol. Behav.* **5**, 123–124.

Nance, D.M., Shryne, J., and Gorski, R.A. (1975). Effects of septal lesions on behavioral sensitivity of female rats to gonadal hormones. *Horm. Behav.* **6**, 59–64.

Negoro, H., Visessuwan, S., and Holland, R.C. (1973). Reflex activation of paraventricular nucleus units during the reproductive cycle and in ovariectomized rats treated with oestrogen or progesterone. *J. Endocrinol.* **59**, 559–567.

Neill, J.D. (1988). Prolactin secretion and its control. *In* "The Physiology of Reproduction" (E. Knobil and J.D. Neill, eds.), Vol. 1, pp.1379–1390. Raven Press, New York.

Nock, B.L., Blaustein, J.D., and Feder, H.H. (1981). Changes in noradrenergic transmission alter the concentration of cytoplasmic progestin receptors in hypothalamus. *Brain Res.* **207**, 371–396.

Numan, M., Roach, J.K., Del Cerro, M.C.R., Guillamon, A., Segovia, S., Sheehan, T.P., and Numan, M.J. (1999). Expression of intracellular progesterone receptors in rat

brain during different reproductive states, and involvement in maternal behavior. *Brain Res.* **830**, 358–371.

O'Donnell, D., Larocque, S., Seckl, J.R., and Meaney, M.J. (1994). Postnatal handling alters glucocorticoid, but not mineralocorticoid messenger RNA expression in the hippocampus of adult rats. *Mol. Brain Res.* **26**, 242–248.

Ogawa, S., Olazabal, U.E., Parhar, I.S., and Pfaff, D.W. (1994). Effects of intrahypothalamic administration of antisense DNA for progesterone receptor mrna on reproductive behavior and progesterone receptor immunoreactivity in female rat. *J. Neurosci.* **14**, 1766–1774.

Ogawa, S., Eng, V., Taylor, J., Lubahn, D.B., Korach, K.S., and Pfaff, D.W. (1998). Roles of estrogen receptor alpha gene expression in reproduction-related behaviors in female mice. *Endocrinology (Baltimore)* **139**, 5070–5081.

Ogawa, S., Chan, J., Chester, A.E., Gustafsson, J.A., Korach, K.S., and Pfaff, D.W. (1999). Survival of reproductive behaviors in estrogen receptor beta gene-deficient (Beta ERKO) male and female mice. *Proc. Natl. Acad. Sci. U.S.A.* **96**, 12887–12892.

O'Hanlon, J.K., and Sachs, B.D. (1986). Fertility of mating in rats (Rattus norvegicus): contributions of androgen-dependent morphology and actions of the penis. *J. comp. Physiol. Psychol.* **100**, 178–187.

Okada, R., Watanabe, H., Yamanouchi, K., and Arai, Y. (1980). Recovery of sexual receptivity in female rats with lesions of the ventromedial hypothalamus. *Exp. Neurolo.* **68**, 595–600.

Oldenburger, W.P., Everitte B.J., and DeJonge, F.H. (1992). Conditioned place preference induced by sexual interaction in female rats. *Horm. Behav.* **26**, 214–228.

Olster, D.H. (1998). Lordosis-enhancing medial preoptic area lesions do not alter hypothalamic estrogen receptor- or progestin receptor-immunoreactivity in prepubertal female guinea pigs. *Brain Res.* **790**, 254–263.

Olster, D.H., and Blaustein, J.D. (1988). Progesterone facilitation of lordosis in male and female Sprague- Dawley rats following priming with estradiol pulses. *Horm. Behav.* **22**, 294–304.

Olster, D.H., and Blaustein, J.D. (1990). Biochemical and immunocytochemical assessment of neural progestin receptors following estradiol treatments that eliminate the sex difference in progesterone-facilitated lordosis in guinea-pigs. *J. Neuroendocrinol.* **2**, 79–86.

O'Malley, B.W., and Means, A.R. (1974). Female steroid hormones and target cell nuclei. *Science* **183**, 610–620.

Osterlund, M., Kuiper, G.G., Gustafsson, J.A., and Hurd, Y.L. (1998). Differential distribution and regulation of estrogen receptor-alpha and -beta mRNA within the female rat brain. *Mol. Brain Res.* **54**, 175–180.

Paech, K., Webb, P., Kuiper, G.G., Nilsson, S., Gustafsson, J.A., Kushner, P.J., and Scanlan, T.S. (1997). Differential ligand activation of estrogen receptors ER alpha and ER beta at AP1 sites. *Science* **277**, 1508–1510.

Paredes, R.G., and Alonso, A. (1997). Sexual behavior regulated (paced) by the female induces conditioned place preference. *Behav. Neurosci.* **111**, 123–128.

Parsons, B., and McEwen, B.S. (1981). Sequential inhibition of sexual receptivity by progesterone is prevented by a protein synthesis inhibitor and is not causally related to decreased levels of hypothalamic progestin receptors in the female rat. *J. Neurosci.* **1**, 527–531.

Parsons, B., MacLusky, N.J., Krieger, M.S., McEwen, B., and Pfaff, D.W. (1979). The effects of long-term estrogen exposure on the induction of sexual behavior and measurements of brain estrogen and progestin receptors in female the rat. *Horm. Behav.* **13**, 301–313.

Parsons, B., MacLusky, N.J., Krey, L., Pfaff, D.W., and McEwen, B.S. (1980). The temporal relationship between estrogen-inducible progestin receptors in the female rat brain and the time course of estrogen activation of mating behavior. *Endocrinology (Baltimore)* **107**, 774–779.

Parsons, B., McGinnis, M.Y., and McEwen, B.S. (1981). Sequential inhibition by progesterone: Effects on sexual receptivity and associated changes in brain cytosol progestin binding in the female rat. *Brain Res.* **221**, 149–160.

Parsons, B., McEwen, B.S., and Pfaff, D.W. (1982a). A discontinuous schedule of estradiol treatment is sufficient to activate progesterone-facilitated feminine sexual behavior and to increase cytosol receptors for progestins in the hypothalamus of the rat. *Endocrinology (Baltimore)* **110**, 613–624.

Parsons, B., Rainbow, T.C., MacLusky, N.J., and McEwen, B.S. (1982b). Progestin receptor levels in rat hypothalamic and limbic nuclei. *J. Neurosci.* **2**, 1446–1452.

Parsons, B., Rainbow, T.C., Snyder, L., and McEwen, B.S. (1984). Progesterone-like effects of estradiol on reproductive behavior and hypothalamic progestin receptors in the female rat. *Neuroendocrinology* **39**, 25–30.

Patisaul, H.B., Whitten, P.L., and Young, L.J. (1999). Regulation of estrogen receptor beta mRNA in the brain: Opposite effects of 1yβ-estradiol and the phytoestrogen, coumestrol. *Mol. Brain Res.* **67**, 165–171.

Peirce, J.T., and Nuttall, R.L. (1961). Self-paced sexual behavior in the female rat., *J. Comp. Physiol. Psychol.* **54**, 310–313.

Peters, J.A., and Gala, R.R. (1975). Induction of pseudopregnancy in the rat by electrochemical stimulation of the brain. *Horm. Res.* **6**, 36–46.

Petersen, D.N., Tkalcevic, G.T., KozaTaylor, P.H., Turi, T.G., and Brown, T.A. (1998). Identification of estrogen receptor beta(2), a functional variant of estrogen receptor beta expressed in normal rat tissues. *Endocrinology (Baltimore)* **139**, 1082–1092.

Petersen, S.L., and LaFlamme, K.D. (1997). Progesterone increases levels of mu-opioid receptor mRNA in the preoptic area and arcuate nucleus of ovariectomized, estradiol- treated female rats. *Mol. Brain Res.* **52**, 32–37.

Petersen, S.L., Keller, M.L., Carder, S.A., and McCrone, S. (1993a). Differential effects of estrogen and progesterone on levels of POMC messenger RNA levels in the arcuate nucleus-relationship to the timing of LH surge release. *J. Neuroendocrinol.* **5**, 643–648.

Petersen, S.L., McCrone, S., and Shores, S. (1993b). Localized changes in LHRH messenger RNA levels as cellular correlates of the positive feedback effects of estrogen on LHRH neurons. *Am. Zool.* **33**, 255–265.

Petersen, S.L., McCrone, S., Keller, M., and Shores, S. (1995). Effects of estrogen and progesterone on luteinizing hormone-releasing hormone messenger ribonucleic acid levels: Consideration of temporal and neuroanatomical variables. *Endocrinology (Baltimore)* **136**, 3604–3610.

Petitti, N., and Etgen, A.M. (1992). Progesterone promotes rapid desensitization of alpha1-adrenergic receptor augmentation of cAMP formation in rat hypothalamic slices. *Neuroendocrinology* **55**, 1–8.

Petitti, N., Karkanias, G.B., and Etgen, A.M. (1992). Estradiol selectively regulates alpha1b-noradrenergic receptors in the hypothalamus and preoptic area. *J. Neurosci.* **12**, 3869–3876.

Pettersson, K., Grandien, K., Kuiper, G.G., and Gustafsson, J.A. (1997). Mouse estrogen receptor beta forms estrogen response element-binding heterodimers with estrogen receptor alpha. *Mol. Endocrinol.* **11**, 1486–1496.

Pfaff, D.W., (1968). Uptake of ^{3}H-estradiol by the female rat brain. An autoradiographic study. *Endocrinology (Baltimore)* **83**, 1149–1155.

Pfaff, D.W. (1980). "Estrogens and Brain Function." Springer-Verlag, New York.

Pfaff, D.W., and Keiner, M. (1973). Atlas of estradiol-concentrating cells in the central nervous system of the female rat. *J. Comp. Neurol.* **151**, 121–158.

Pfaff, D.W., and Sakuma, Y. (1979). Deficit in the lordosis reflex of female rats caused by lesions in the ventromedial nucleus of the hypothalamus. *J. Physiol. (London)* **288**, 203–210.

Pfaff, D.W., Lewis, C., Diakow, C., and Keiner, M. (1973). Neurophysiological analysis of mating behavior responses as hormone-sensitive reflexes. *Prog. Physiol. Psychol.* **5**, 253–297.

Pfaff, D.W., Schwartz-Giblin, S., McCarthy, M.M., and Kow, L.-M. (1994). Cellular and molecular mechanisms of female reproductive behaviors. *In* "The Physiology of Reproduction" (E. Knobil and J.D. Neill, eds), 2nd ed., pp. 107–220. Raven Press, New York.

Pfaus, J.G., Kleopoulos, S.P., Mobbs, C.V., Gibbs, R.B., and Pfaff, D.W. (1993). Sexual stimulation activates c-fos within estrogen-concentrating regions of the female rat forebrain. *Brain Res.* **624**, 253–267.

Pfaus, J.G., Marcangione, C., Smith, W.J., Manitt, C., and Abillamaa, H. (1996). Differential induction of Fos in the female rat brain following different amounts of vaginocervical stimulation: Modulation by steroid hormones. *Brain Res.* **741**, 314–330.

Pfaus, J.G., Smith, W.J., and Coopersmith, C.B. (1999). Appetitive and consummatory sexual behaviors of female rats in bilevel chambers. I. A correlational and factor analysis and the effects of ovarian hormones. *Horm. Behav.* **35**, 224–240.

Pfaus, J.G., Smith, W.J., Byrne, N., and Stephens, G. (2000). Appetitive and consummatory sexual behaviors of female rats in bilevel chambers. II. Patterns of estrus termination following vaginocervical stimulation. *Horm. Behav.* **37**, 96–107.

Pfeifle, J.K., Shivers, M., and Edwards, D.A. (1980). Parasagittal hypothalamic knife cuts and sexual receptivity in the female rat. *Physiol. Behav.* **24**, 145–150.

Pleim, E.T., Cailliau, P.J., Weinstein, M.A., Etgen, A.M., and Barfield, R.J. (1990). Facilitation of receptive behavior in estrogen-primed female rats by the anti-progestin, RU486. *Horm. Behav.* **24**, 301–310.

Pleim, E.T., Baumann, J., and Barfield, R.J. (1991). A contributory role for midbrain progesterone in the facilitation of female sexual behavior in rats. *Horm. Behav.* **25**, 19–28.

Pollio, G., Xue, P., Zanisi, M., Nicolin, A., and Maggi, A. (1993). Antisense oligonucleotide blocks progesterone-induced lordosis behavior in ovariectomized rats. *Mol. Brain Res.* **19**, 135–139.

Polston, E.K., and Erskine, M.S. (1995). Patterns of induction of the immediate-early genes c-fos and egr-1 in the female rat brain following differential amounts of mating stimulation. *Neuroendocrinology* **62**, 370–384.

Polston, E.K., and Erskine, M.S. (2001). Excitotoxic lesions of the medial amygdala differentially disrupt prolactin secretory responses in cycling and mated female rats. *J. Neuroendocrinol.* **13**, 13–21.

Polston, E.K., Centorino, K.M., and Erskine, M.S. (1998). Diurnal fluctuations in mating-induced oxytocinergic activity within the paraventricular and supraoptic nuclei do not influence prolactin secretion. *Endocrinology (Baltimore)* **139**, 4849–4859.

Popper, P., Priest, C.A., and Micevych, P.E. (1996). Regulation of cholecystokinin receptors in the ventromedial nucleus of the hypothalamus: Sex steroid hormone effects. *Brain Res.* **712**, 335–339.

Power, R.F., Lydon, J.P., Conneely, O.M., and O'Malley, B.W. (1991a). Dopamine activation of an orphan of the steroid receptor superfamily. *Science* **252**, 1546–1548.

Power, R.F., Mani, S.K., Codina, J., Conneely, O.M., and O'Malley, B.W. (1991b). Dopaminergic and ligand-independent activation of steroid hormone receptors. *Science* **254**, 1636–1639.

Powers, J.B. (1970). Hormonal control of sexual receptivity during the estrous cycle of the rat. *Physiol. Behav.* **5**, 831–835.

Powers, J.B. (1972). Facilitation of lordosis in ovariectomized rats by intracerebral implants. *Brain Res.* **48**, 311–325.

Powers, J.B., and Moreines, J. (1976). Progesterone: Examination of its postulated inhibitory actions on lordosis during the rat estrous cycle. *Physiol. Behav.* **17**, 493–498.

Powers, J.B., and Valenstein, E.S. (1972). Sexual receptivity: Facilitation by medial preoptic lesions in female rats. *Science* **175**, 1003–1005.

Powers, J.B., and Zucker, I. (1969). Sexual receptivity in pregnant and pseudopregnant rats. *Endocrinology (Baltimore)* **84**, 820–827.

Pratt, W.B., and Toft, D.O. (1997). Steroid receptor interactions with heat shock protein and immunophilin chaperones. *Endocr. Rev.* **18**, 306–360.

Quinones-Jenab, V., Ogawa, S., Jenab, S., and Pfaff, D.W. (1996). Estrogen regulation of preproenkephalin messenger RNA in the forebrain of female mice. *J. Chem. Neuroanat.* **12**, 29–36.

Quinones-Jenab, V., Jenab, S., Ogawa, S., Adan, R.A.M., Burbach, J.P.H., and Pfaff, D.W. (1997a). Effects of estrogen on oxytocin receptor messenger ribonucleic acid expression in the uterus, pituitary, and forebrain of the female rat. *Neuroendocrinology* **65**, 9–17.

Quinones-Jenab, V., Jenab, S., Ogawa, S., Inturrisi, C., and Pfaff, D.W. (1997b). Estrogen regulation of mu-opioid receptor mRNA in the forebrain of female rats. *Mol. Brain Res.* **47**, 134–138.

Rainbow, T.C., McGinnis, M.Y., Davis, P.G., and McEwen, B.S. (1982a). Application of anisomycin to the lateral ventromedial nucleus of the hypothalamus inhibits the activation of sexual behavior by estradiol and progesterone. *Brain Res.* **233**, 417–423.

Rainbow, T.C., McGinnis, M.Y., Krey, L.C., and McEwen, B.S. (1982b). Nuclear progestin receptors in rat brain and pituitary. *Neuroendocrinology* **34**, 426–432.

Rainbow, T.C., Parsons, B., MacLusky, N.J., and McEwen, B.S. (1982c). Estradiol receptor levels in rat hypothalamic and limbic nuclei. *J. Neurosci.* **2**, 1439–1445.

Rajendren, G., and Moss, R.L. (1993). The role of the medial nucleus of amygdala in the mating-induced enhancement of lordosis in female rats—the interaction with luteinizing hormone-releasing hormone neuronal system. *Brain Res.* **617**, 81–86.

Rajendren, G., Dudley, C.A., and Moss, R.L. (1990). Role of the vomeronasal organ in the male-induced enhancement of sexual receptivity in female rats. *Neuroendocrinology* **52**, 368–372.

Rajendren, G., Dudley, C.A., and Moss, R.L. (1991). Role of the ventromedial nucleus of hypothalamus in the male-induced enhancement of lordosis in female rats. *Physiol. Behav.* **50**, 705–710.

Rajendren, G., Dudley, C.A., and Moss, R.L. (1993). Influence of male rats on the luteinizing hormone-releasing hormone neuronal system in female rats—role of the vomeronasal organ. *Neuroendocrinology* **57**, 898–906.

Ramirez, V.D., Komisaruk, B.R., Whitmoyer, D.I., and Sawyer, C.H. (1967). Effects of hormones and vaginal stimulation on the EEG and hypothalamic units in rats. *Am. J. Physiol.* **212**, 1376–1384.

Ramirez, V.D., Zheng, J.B., and Siddique, K.M. (1996). Membrane receptors for estrogen, progesterone, and testosterone in the rat brain: Fantasy or reality. *Cell. Mol. Neurobiol.* **16**, 175–198.

Ramos, S.M., and DeBold, J.F. (1999). Protein synthesis in the medial preoptic area is important for the mating-induced decrease in estrus duration in hamsters. *Horm. Behav.* **35**, 177–185.

Razandi, M., Pedram, A., Greene, G.L., and Levin, E.R. (1999). Cell membrane and nuclear estrogen receptors (ERs) originate from a single transcript: Studies of ER alpha and ER beta expressed in Chinese hamster ovary cells. *Mol. Endocrinol.* **13**, 307–319.

Reading, D.S., and Blaustein, J.D. (1984). The relationship between heat abbreviation and neural progestin receptors in female rats. *Physiol. Behav.* **32**, 973–981.

Ricciardi, K.H.N., Turcotte, J.C., De Vries, G.J., and Blaustein, J.D. (1996). Efferent projections from the ovarian steroid receptor-containing area of the ventrolateral hypothalamus in female guinea pigs. *J. Neuroendocrinol.* **8**, 673–685.

Richmond, G., and Clemens, L.G. (1986). Cholinergic mediation of feminine sexual receptivity: Demonstration of progesterone independence using a progestin receptor antagonist. *Brain Res.* **373**, 159–163.

Richmond, G., and Clemens, L. (1988). Ventromedial hypothalamic lesions and cholinergic control of female sexual behavior. *Physiol. Behav.* **42**, 179–182.

Riskind, P., and Moss, R.L. (1983). Effects of lesions of putative LHRH-containing pathways and midbrain nuclei on lordotic behavior and luteinizing hormone release in ovariectomized rats. *Brain Res. Bull.* **11**, 493–500.

Rissman, E.F. (1987). Social variables influence female sexual behavior in the musk shrew (*Suncus murinus*). *J. Comp. Psychol.* **101**, 3–6.

Rissman, E.F., Early, A.H., Taylor, J.A., Korach, K.S., and Lubahn, D.B. (1997). Estrogen receptors are essential for female sexual receptivity. *Endocrinology (Baltimore)* **138**, 507–510.

Rodgers, C.H. (1971). Influence of copulation on ovulation in the cycling rat. *Endocrinology (Baltimore)* **88**, 433–436.

Rodriguez-Sierra, J.F., and Davis, G.A. (1977). Progesterone does not inhibit lordosis through interference with estrogen priming. *Life Sci.* **22**, 373–378.

Rodriguez-Sierra, J.F., and Komisaruk, B.R. (1982). Common hypothalamic sites for activation of sexual receptivity in female rats by LHRH, PGE₂ and progesterone. *Neuroendocrinology* **35**, 363–369.

Rodriguez-Sierra, J.F., and Terasawa, E. (1979). Lesions of the preoptic area facilitate lordosis behavior in male and female guinea pigs. *Brain Res. Bull.* **4**, 513–517.

Rodriguez-Sierra, J.F., Crowley, W.R., and Komisaruk, B.R. (1975). Vaginal stimulation in rats induces prolonged lordosis responsiveness and sexual receptivity. *J. Comp. Physiol. Psychol.* **89**, 79–85.

Roselli, C.E., and Snipes, C.A. (1983). Cytoplasmic progesterone receptors in the hypothalamus-preoptic area of the mouse: Effect of estrogen priming. *J. Steroid Biochem.* **19**, 1571–1575.

Ross, J., Claybaugh, C., Clemens, L.G., and Gorski, R.A. (1971). Short latency of estrous behavior with intracerebral gonadal hormones in ovariectomized rats. *Endocrinology (Baltimore)* **89**, 32–38.

Rossmanith, W.G., Marks, D.L., Clifton, D.K., and Steiner, R.A. (1996). Induction of galanin mRNA in GnRH neurons by estradiol and its facilitation by progesterone. *J. Neuroendocrinol.* **8**, 185–191.

Rowe, D.W., and Erskine, M.S. (1993). c-Fos proto-oncogene activity induced by mating in the preoptic area, hypothalamus, and amygdala in the female rat: Role of afferent input via the pelvic nerve. *Brain Res.* **621**, 25–34.

Roy, E.J., and Wade, G.N. (1976). Estrogenic effects of an antiestrogen, MER-25, on eating and body weight in rats. *J. Comp. Physiol. Psychol.* **90**, 156–166.

Roy, E.J., and Wade, G.N. (1977). Binding of [³H]estradiol by brain cell nuclei and female rat sexual behavior: Inhibition by antiestrogens. *Brain Res.* **126**, 73–87.

Roy, E.J., and Wilson, M.A. (1981). Diurnal rhythm of cytoplasmic estrogen receptors in the rat brain in the absence of circulating estrogens. *Science* **213**, 1525–1527.

Roy, E.J., MacLusky, N.J., and McEwen, B.S. (1979). Antiestrogen inhibits the induction of progestin receptors by estradiol in the hypothalamus-preoptic area and pituitary. *Endocrinology (Baltimore)* **104**, 1333–1336.

Roy, E.J., Lynn, D.M., and Clark, A.S. (1985). Inhibition of sexual receptivity by anesthesia during estrogen priming. *Brain Res.* **337**, 163–166.

Roy, M.M., Goldstein, K.L., and Williams, C. (1993). Estrus termination following copulation in female guinea pigs. *Horm. Behav.* **27**, 397–402.

Rubin, B.S., and Barfield, R.J. (1980). Priming of estrous responsiveness by implants of 17-estradiol in the ventromedial hypothalamic nucleus of female rats. *Endocrinology (Baltimore)* **106**, 504–509.

Rubin, B.S., and Barfield, R.J. (1983). Progesterone in the ventromedial hypothalamus facilitates estrous behavior in ovariectomized, estrogen-primed rats. *Endocrinology (Baltimore)* **113**, 797–804.

Rubin, B.S., and Barfield, R.J. (1984). Progesterone in the ventromedial hypothalamus of ovariectomized, estrogen-primed rats inhibits subsequent facilitation of estrous behavior by systemic progesterone. *Brain Res.* **294**, 1–8.

Rusak, B., Roberston, H.A., Wisden, W., and Hunt, S.P. (1990). Light pulses that shift rhythms induce gene expression in the suprachiasmatic nucleus. *Science* **248**, 1237–1239.

Sachs, B.D., Glater, G.B., and O'Hanlon, J.K. (1984). Morphology of the erect glans penis in rats under various gonadal hormone conditions. *Anat. Rec.* **210**, 45–52.

Sagar, S.M., Sharp, F.R., and Curran, T. (1988). Expression of c-fos protein in brain: Metabolic mapping at the cellular level. *Science* **240**, 1328–1330.

Sakuma, Y., and Pfaff, D.W. (1979). Mesencephalic mechanisms for integration of female reproductive behavior in the rat. *Am. J. Physiol.* **R237**, R285–R290.

Sakuma, Y., and Pfaff, D.W. (1980). Covergent effects of lordosis-relevant somatosensory and hypothalamic influences on central gray cells in the rat mesencephalon. *Exp. Neurol.* **70**, 269–281.

Sar, M. (1988). Distribution of progestin-concentrating cells in rat brain: Colocalization of [3H]ORG.2058, a synthetic progestin, and antibodies to tyrosine hydroxylase in hypothalamus by combined autoradiography and immunocytochemistry. *Endocrinology (Baltimore)* **123**, 1110–1118.

Sar, M., and Stumpf, W.E. (1973). Neurons of the hypothalamus concentrate [3H]progesterone or its metabolites. *Science* **183**, 1266–1268.

Sawyer, C.H., and Kawakami, M. (1959). Characteristics of behavioral and electroencephalographic after-reactions to copulation and vaginal stimulation in the female rabbit. *Endocrinology (Baltimore)* **65**, 622–630.

Scheiss, M.C., Joels, M., and Shinnick-Gallagher, P. (1988). Estrogen priming affects active membrane properties of medial amygdala neurons. *Brain Res.* **440**, 380–385.

Schwartz, S.M., Blaustein, J.D., and Wade, G.N. (1979). Inhibition of estrous behavior by progesterone in rats: role of neural estrogen and progestin receptors. *Endocrinology (Baltimore)* **105**, 1078–1082.

Seckl, J.R., and Fink, G. (1991). Use of in situ hybridization to investigate the regulation of hippocampal corticosteroid receptors by monoamines. *J. Steroid Biochem. Mol. Biol.* **40**, 685–688.

Seiki, K., and Hattori, M. (1973). In vivo uptake of progesterone by the hypothalamus and pituitary of the female ovariectomized rat and its relationship to cytoplasmic progesterone-binding protein. *Endocrinology (Baltimore)* **20**, 111–119.

Seiki, K., Haruki, Y., Imanishi, Y., and Enomoto, T. (1977). Further evidence of the presence of progesterone-binding proteins in female rat hypothalamus. *Endocrinol. Jpn.* **24**, 233–238.

Shapiro, R.A., Xu, C., and Dorsa, D.M. (2000). Differential transcriptional regulation of rat vasopressin gene expression by estrogen receptor alpha and beta. *Endocrinology (Baltimore)* **141**, 4056–4064.

Shivers, B.D., Harlan, R.E., Parker, C.R., and Moss, R.L. (1980). Sequential inhibitory effect of progesterone on lordotic responsiveness in rats: Time course, estrogenic nullification, and actinomycin-D insensitivity. *Biol. Reprod.* **23**, 963–973.

Shughrue, P.J., Komm, B., and Merchenthaler, I. (1996). The distribution of estrogen receptor-beta mRNA in the rat hypothalamus. *Steroids* **61**, 678–681.

Shughrue, P.J., Lane, M.V., and Merchenthaler, I. (1997). Comparative distribution of estrogen receptor-alpha and -beta mRNA in the rat central nervous system. *J. Comp. Neurol.* **388**, 507–525.

Shughrue, P.J., Scrimo, P.J., and Merchenthaler, I. (1998). Evidence for the colocalization of estrogen receptor-beta mRNA and estrogen receptor-alpha immunoreactivity in neurons of the rat forebrain. *Endocrinology (Baltimore)* **139**, 5267–5270.

Shyamala, G., Yang, X., Silberstein, G., Barcellos-Hoff, M.H., and Dale, E. (1998). Transgenic mice carrying an imbalance in the native ratio of A to B forms of progesterone receptor exhibit developmental abnormalities in mammary glands. *Proc. Natl. Acad. Sci. U.S.A.* **95**, 696–701.

Siegel, H.I., Ahdieh, H.B., and Rosenblatt, J.S. (1978). Hysterectomy-induced facilitation of lordosis behavior in the rat. *Horm. Behav.* **11**, 273–278.

Siegel, L.I., and Wade, G.N. (1979). Insulin withdrawal impairs sexual receptivity and retention of brain cell nuclear estrogen receptors in diabetic rats. *Neuroendocrinology* **29**, 200–206.

Simerly, R.B., and Young, B.J. (1991). Regulation of estrogen receptor messenger ribonucleic acid in rat hypothalamus by sex steroid hormones. *Mol. Endocrinol.* **5**, 424–432.

Simerly, R.B., Chang, C., Muramatsu, M., and Swanson, L.W. (1990). Distribution of androgen and estrogen receptor messenger RNA-containing cells in the rat brain—an in situ hybridization study. *J. Comp. Neurol.* **294**, 76–95.

Simerly, R.B., Carr, A.M., Zee, M.C., and Lorang, D. (1996). Ovarian steroid regulation of estrogen and progesterone receptor messenger ribonucleic acid in the anteroventral periventricular nucleus of the rat. *J. Neuroendocrinol.* **8**, 45–56.

Simonian, S.X., and Herbison, A.E. (1997). Differential expression of estrogen receptor alpha and beta immunoreactivity by oxytocin neurons of rat paraventricular nucleus. *J. Neuroendocrinol.* **9**, 803–806.

Singer, J.J. (1968). Hypothalamic control of male and female sexual behavior in female rats. *J. Comp. Physiol. Psychol.* **66**, 738–742.

Sirinathsinghji, D.J.S., and Audsley, A.R. (1985). Endogenous opioid peptides participate in the modulation of prolactin release in response to cervicovaginal stimulation in the female rat. *Endocrinology (Baltimore)* **117**, 549–556.

Slimp, J.C. (1977). Reduction of genital sensory input and sexual behavior of female guinea pigs. *Physiol. Behav.* **18**, 1027–1031.

Smanik, E.J., Young, H.K., Muldoon, T.G., and Mahesh, V.B. (1983). Analysis of the effect of progesterone in vivo on estrogen receptor distribution in the rat anterior pituitary and hypothalamus. *Endocrinology (Baltimore)* **113**, 15–22.

Smith, M.S., and Neill, J.D. (1976). Termination at midpregnancy of the two daily surges of plasma prolactin initiated by mating in the rat. *Endocrinology* **98**, 696–701.

Smith, M.S., McLean, B.K., and Neill, J.D. (1976). Prolactin: The initial luteotropic stimulus of pseudopregnancy in the rat. *Endocrinology (Baltimore)* **98**, 1370–1377.

Smith, S.S. (1989). Progesterone enhances inhibitory responses of cerebellar Purkinje cells mediated by the GABAA receptor subtype. *Brain Res. Bull.* **23**, 317–322.

Smith, S.S., Waterhouse, B.D., Chapin, J.K., and Woodward, D.J. (1987a). Progesterone alters GABA and glutamate responsiveness: A possible mechanism for its anxiolytic action. *Brain Res.* **400**, 353–359.

Smith, S.S., Waterhouse, B.D., and Woodward, D.J. (1987b). Locally applied progesterone metabolites alter neuronal responsiveness in the cerebellum. *Brain Res. Bull.* **18**, 739–747.

Smith, S.S., Waterhouse, B.D., and Woodward, D.J. (1987c). Sex steroid effects on extrahypothalamic CNS. II. Progesterone, alone and in combination with estrogen, modulates cerebellar responses to amino acid neurotransmitters. *Brain Res.* **422**, 52–62.

Södersten, P., and Eneroth, P. (1981). Evidence that progesterone does not inhibit the induction of sexual receptivity by oestradiol-17β in the rat. *J. Endocrinol.* **89**, 63–69.

Södersten, P., and Hansen, S. (1977). Effects of oestradiol and progesterone on the induction and duration of sexual receptivity in cyclic female rats. *J. Endocrinol.* **74**, 477–485.

Södersten, P., and Hansen, S. (1979). Induction of sexual receptivity by oestradiol benzoate in cyclic female rats: Influence of ovarian secretions before injection of oestradiol benzoate. *J. Endocrinol.* **80**, 389–395.

Södersten, P., Eneroth, P., and Hansen, S. (1981). Induction of sexual receptivity in ovariectomized rats by pulse administration of oestradiol-17β. *J. Endocrinol.* **89**, 55–62.

Södersten, P., Pettersson, A., and Eneroth, P. (1983). Pulse administration of estradiol-17β cancels sex difference in behavioral estrogen sensitivity. *Endocrinology (Baltimore)* **112**, 1883–1885.

Spies, H.G., and Niswender, G.D. (1971). Levels of prolactin, LH, and FSH in the serum of intact and pelvic neurectomized rats. *Endocrinology (Baltimore)* **88**, 937–943.

Stumpf, W.E. (1968). Estradiol-concentrating neurons: Topography in the hypothalamus by dry-mount autoradiography. *Science* **162**, 1001–1003.

Stumpf, W.E. (1970). Estrogen-neurons and estrogen-neuron systems in the periventricular brain. *Am. J. Anat.* **129**, 207–218.

Swanson, L.W., and Sawchenko, P.E. (1983). Hypothalamic integration: Organization of the paraventricular and supraoptic nuclei. *Annu. Rev. Neurosci.* **6**, 269–324.

Takahashi, M., Ford, J.J., Yoshinaga, K., and Greep, R.O. (1975). Effects of cervical stimulation and anti-LH releasing hormone serum on LH releasing hormone content in the hypothalamus. *Endocrinology (Baltimore)* **96**, 453–457.

Takeo, T., Chiba, Y., and Sakuma, Y. (1993). Suppression of the lordosis reflex of female rats by efferents of the medial preoptic area. *Physiol. Behav.* **53**, 831–838.

Takeo, T., Kudo, M., and Sakuma, Y. (1995). Stria terminalis conveys a facilitatory estrogen effect on female rat lordosis reflex. *Neurosci. Lett.* **184**, 79–81.

Taleisnik, S., Caligaris, L., and Astrada, J.J. (1966). Effect of copulation on the release of pituitary gonadotropins in male and female rats. *Endocrinology (Baltimore)* **79**, 49–54.

Taylor, G.T., Weiss, J., and Komitowski, D. (1983). Reproductive physiology and penile papillae morphology of rats after sexual experience. *J. Endocrinol.* **98**, 155–163.

Tennent, B.J., Smith, E.R., and Davidson, J.M. (1980). The effects of estrogen and progesterone on female rat proceptive behavior. *Horm. Behav.* **14**, 65–75.

Tennent, B.J., Smith, E.R., and Davidson, J.M. (1982). Effects of progesterone implants in the habenula and midbrain on proceptive and receptive behavior in the female rat. *Horm. Behav.* **16**, 352–373.

Terkel, J. (1988). Neuroendocrine processes in the establishment of pregnancy and pseudopregnancy in rats. *Psychoneuroendocrinology.* **13**, 5–28.

Terkel, J., and Sawyer, C.H. (1978). Male copulatory behavior triggers nightly prolactin surges resulting in successful pregnancy in rats. *Horm. Behav.* **11**, 304–309.

Tetel, M.J. (2000). Nuclear receptor coactivators in neuroendocrine function. *J. Neuroendocrinol.* **12**, 927–932.

Tetel, M.J., and Blaustein, J.D. (1991). Immunocytochemical evidence for noradrenergic regulation of estrogen receptor concentrations in the Guinea Pig hypothalamus. *Brain Res.* **565**, 321–329.

Tetel, M.J., Getzinger, M.J., and Blaustein, J.D. (1993). Fos expression in the rat brain following vaginal-cervical stimulation by mating and manual probing. *J. Neuroendocrinol.* **5**, 397–404.

Tetel, M.J., Celentano, D.C., and Blaustein, J.D. (1994a). Intraneuronal convergence of tactile and hormonal stimuli associated with female reproduction in rats. *J. Neuroendocrinol.* **6**, 211–216.

Tetel, M.J., Getzinger, M.J., and Blaustein, J.D. (1994b). Estradiol and progesterone influence the response of ventromedial hypothalamic neurons to tactile stimuli associated with female reproduction. *Brain Res.* **646**, 267–272.

Thomas, A., Shughrue, P.J., Merchenthaler, I., and Amico, J.A. (1999). The effects of progesterone on oxytocin mRNA levels in the paraventricular nucleus of the female rat can be altered by the administration of diazepam or RU486. *J. Neuroendocrinol.* **11**, 137–144.

Thompson, M.A., Woolley, D.E., Gietzen, D.W., and Conway, S. (1983). Catecholamine synthesis inhibitors acutely modulate [^{3}H]estradiol binding by specific brain areas and pituitary in ovariectomized rats. *Endocrinology (Baltimore)* **113**, 855–865.

Thornton, J.E., Nock, B., McEwen, B.S., and Feder, H.H. (1986a). Estrogen induction of progesterone receptors in microdissected hypothalamic and limbic nuclei of female guinea pigs. *Neuroendocrinology* **43**, 182–188.

Thornton, J.E., Nock, B., McEwen, B.S., and Feder, H.H. (1986b). Noradrenergic modulation of hypothalamic progestin receptors in female guinea pigs is specific to the ventromedial nucleus. *Brain Res.* **377**, 155–159.

Toft, D.O., Sullivan, W.P., McCormick, D., and Riehl, M. (1987). Heat shock proteins and steroid hormone receptors. *In* "Biochemical Actions of Hormones" (G. Litwack, ed.) pp. 293–316. Academic Press, Orlando, FL.

Tora, L., Gronemeyer, H., Turcotte, B., Gaub, M.-P., and Chambon, P. (1988). The N-terminal region of the chicken progesterone receptor specifies target gene activation. *Nature (London)* **333**, 185–188.

Towle, A.C., and Sze, P.Y. (1983). Steroid binding to synaptic plasma membrane: Differential binding of glucocorticoids and gonadal steroids. *J. Steroid Biochem.* **18**, 135–143.

Tremblay, G.B., Tremblay, A., Labrie, F., and Giguère, V. (1999). Dominant activity of activation function 1 (AF-1) and differential stoichiometric requirements for AF-1 and -2 in the estrogen receptor alpha-beta heterodimeric complex. *Mol. Cell. Biol.* **19**, 1919–1927.

Turcotte, J.C., and Blaustein, J.D. (1993). Immunocytochemical localization of midbrain estrogen receptor-containing and progestin receptor-containing cells in female guinea pigs. *J. Comp. Neurol.* **328**, 76–87.

Turgeon, J.L., and Waring, D.W. (1994). Activation of the progesterone receptor by the gonadotropin-releasing hormone self-priming signaling pathway. *Mol. Endocrinol.* **8**, 860–869.

Unda, R., Brann, D.W., and Mahesh, V.B. (1995). Progesterone suppression of glutamic acid decarboxylase (GA D 67) mRNA levels in the preoptic area: Correlation to the luteinizing hormone surge. *Neuroendocrinology* **62**, 562–570.

Vagell, M.E., and McGinnis, M.Y. (1996). Effects of the antiestrogen, RU 58668, on female sexual behavior in rats. *Brain Res. Bull.* **41**, 121–124.

van der Schoot, P., Vanophemert, J., and Baumgarten, R. (1992). Copulatory stimuli in rats induce heat abbreviation through effects on genitalia but not through effects on central nervous mechanisms supporting the steroid hormone-induced sexual responsiveness. *Behav. Brain Res.* **49**, 213–223.

Vathy, I., and Etgen, A.M. (1989). Hormonal activation of female sexual behavior is accompanied by hypothalamic norepinephrine release. *J. Neuroendocrinol.* **1**, 383–388.

Vegeto, E., Allan, G.F., Schrader, W.T., Tsai, M.J., McDonnell, D.P., and O'Malley, B.W. (1992). The mechanism of RU 486 antagonism is dependent on the conformation of the carboxy-terminal tail of the human progesterone receptor. *Cell (Cambridge, Mass.)* **69**, 703–713.

Vegeto, E., Shahbaz, M.M., Wen, D.X., Goldman, M.E., O'Malley, B.W., and McDonnell, D.P. (1993). Human progesterone receptor-a form is a cell-specific and promoter-specific repressor of human progesterone receptor-b function. *Mol. Endocrinol.* **7**, 1244–1255.

Vincent, P.A., and Etgen, A.M. (1993). Steroid priming promotes oxytocin-induced norepinephrine release in the ventromedial hypothalamus of female rats. *Brain Res.* **620**, 189–194.

Wade, G.N. (1976). Sex hormones, regulatory behaviors, and body weight. *Adv. Study Behav.* **6**, 201–279.

Wade, G.N., and Blaustein, J.D. (1978). Effects of an antiestrogen on neural estradiol binding and on behaviors in female rats. *Endocrinology (Baltimore)* **102**, 245–251.

Wade, G.N., and Feder, H.H. (1972). [1,2-3]progesterone uptake by guinea pig brain and uterus: Differential localization, time-course of uptake and metabolism, and effects of age, sex, estrogen-priming and competing steroids. *Brain Res.* **45**, 525–543.

Wagner, C.K., and Morrell, J.I. (1996). Levels of estrogen receptor immunoreactivity are altered in behaviorally-relevant brain regions in female rats during pregnancy. *Mol. Brain Res.* **42**, 328–336.

Wagner, C.K., Silverman, A.J., and Morrell, J.I. (1998). Evidence for estrogen receptor in cell nuclei and axon terminals within the lateral habenula of the rat: Regulation during pregnancy. *J. Comp. Neurol.* **392**, 330–342.

Walker, W.A., and Feder, H.H. (1977a). Inhibitory and facilitatory effects of various anti-estrogens on the induction of female sexual behavior by estradiol benzoate in guinea pigs. *Brain Res.* **134**, 455–465.

Walker, W.A., and Feder, H.H. (1977b). Anti-estrogen effects on estrogen accumulation in brain cell nuclei: Neurochemical correlates of estrogen action of female sexual behavior in guinea pigs. *Brain Res.* **134**, 467–478.

Wallen, K., and Thornton, J.E. (1979). Progesterone and duration of heat in estrogen-treated ovariectomized guinea pigs. *Physiol. Behav.* **22**, 95–97.

Walters, M.R. (1985). Steroid hormone receptors and the nucleus. *Endocr. Rev.* **6**, 512–543.

Ward, I.L., Crowley, W.R., Zemlan, F.P., and Margules, D.L. (1975). Monoaminergic mediation of female sexual behavior. *J. Comp. Physiol. Psychol.* **88**, 53–61.

Warembourg, M. (1977). Radiographic localization of estrogen-concentrating cells in the brain and pituitary of the guinea pig. *Brain Res.* **123**, 357–362.

Warembourg, M. (1978a). Radioautographic study of the brain and pituitary after [^{3}H]progesterone injection into estrogen-primed ovariectomized guinea pigs. *Neurosci. Lett.* **7**, 1–5.

Warembourg, M. (1978b). Uptake of ^{3}H labeled synthetic progestin by rat brain and pituitary. A radioautography study. *Neurosci. Lett.* **9**, 329–332.

Warembourg, M., Logeat, F., and Milgrom, E. (1986). Immunocytochemical localization of progesterone receptor in the guinea pig central nervous system. *Brain Res.* **384**, 121–131.

Warembourg, M., Jolivet, A., and Milgrom, E. (1989). Immunohistochemical evidence of the presence of estrogen and progesterone receptors in the same neurons of the guinea pig hypothalamus and preoptic area. *Brain Res.* **480**, 1–15.

Watson, C.S., and Gametchu, B. (1999). Membrane-initiated steroid actions and the proteins that mediate them. *Proc. Soc. Exp. Biol. Med.* **220**, 9–19.

Watters, J.J., and Dorsa, D.M. (1998). Transcriptional effects of estrogen on neuronal neurotensin gene expression involve cAMP/protein kinase A-dependent signaling mechanisms. *J. Neurosci.* **18**, 6672–6680.

Welshons, W.V., Lieberman, M.E., and Gorski, J. (1984). Nuclear localization of unoccupied oestrogen receptors. *Nature (London)* **307**, 747–749.

Wersinger, S.R., Baum, M.J., and Erskine, M.S. (1993). Mating-induced FOS-like immunoreactivity in the rat forebrain: A sex comparison and a dimorphic effect of pelvic nerve transection. *J. Neuroendocrinol.* **5**, 557–568.

Whalen, R.E. (1974). Estrogen-progesterone induction of mating in female rats. *Horm. Behav.* **5**, 157–162.

Whalen, R.E., and Lauber, A.H. (1986). Progesterone substitutes: cGMP mediation. *Neurosci. Biobehavi. Rev.* **10**, 47–53.

Whalen, R.E., and Luttge, W.G. (1971). Differential localization of progesterone uptake in brain, role of sex, estrogen pretreatment and adrenalectomy. *Brain Res.* **33**, 147–155.

White, N.R., and Barfield, R.J. (1989). Playback of female rat ultrasonic vocalizations during sexual behavior. *Physiol. Behav.* **45**, 229–233.

Whitney, J.F. (1986). Effect of medial preoptic lesions on sexual behavior of female rats is determined by test situation. *Behav. Neurosci.* **100**, 230–235.

Wilcox, J.N., and Feder, H.H. (1983). Long-term priming with a low dosage of estradiol benzoate or an antiestrogen (Enclomiphene) increases nuclear progestin receptor levels in brain. *Brain Res.* **266**, 243–251.

Wilcox, J.N., and Roberts, J.L. (1985). Estrogen decreases rat hypothalamic proopiomelanocortin messenger ribonucleic acid levels. *Endocrinology (Baltimore)* **117**, 2392–2396.

Wilcox, J.N., Barclay, S.R., and Feder, H.H. (1984). Administration of estradiol-17β in pulses to guinea pigs: Self-priming effects of estrogen on brain tissues mediating lordosis. *Physiol. Behav.* **32**, 483–488.

Williams, J.R., Catania, K.C., and Carter, C.S. (1992). Development of partner preferences in female prairie voles (microtus-ochrogaster)—the role of social and sexual experience. *Horm. Behav.* **26**, 339–349.

Wilson, J.R., Adler, N., and LeBoeuf, B. (1965). The effects of intromission frequency on successful pregnancy in the rat. *Proc. Natl. Acad. Sci. U.S.A.* **53**, 1392–1395.

Wilson, M.A., Clark, A.S., Clyde, V., and Roy, E.J. (1983). Characterization of a pineal-independent diurnal rhythm in neural estrogen receptors and its possible behavioral consequences. *Neuroendocrinology* **37**, 14–22.

Witt, D.M., and Insel, T.R. (1991). A selective oxytocin antagonist attenuates progesterone facilitation of female sexual behavior. *Endocrinology (Baltimore)* **128**, 3269–3276.

Witt, D.M., and Insel, T.R. (1994). Increased fos expression in oxytocin neurons following masculine sexual behavior. *J. Neuroendocrinol.* **6**, 13–18.

Wong, M., and Moss, R.L. (1991). Electrophysiological evidence for a rapid membrane action of the gonadal steroid, 17-beta-estradiol, on CA1 pyramidal neurons of the rat hippocampus. *Brain Res.* **543**, 148–152.

Woolley, D.E., Hope, W.G., Gietzen, D.W., Thompson, M.T., and Conway, S.B. (1982). Bromocriptine increases ³H-estradiol uptake in brain and pituitary of female, but not of male, gonadectomized adrenalectomized rats. *Proc. West. Pharmacol. Soc.* **25**, 437–441.

Wuttke, W., and Meites, J. (1972). Induction of pseudopregnancy in the rat with no rise in serum prolactin. *Endocrinology (Baltimore)* **90**, 438–443.

Xu, M., Urban, J.H., Hill, J.W., and Levine, J.E. (2000). Regulation of hypothalamic neuropeptide YY1 receptor gene expression during the estrous cycle: Role of progesterone receptors. *Endocrinology (Baltimore)* **141**, 3319–3327.

Yahr, P., and Ulibarri, C. (1986). Estrogen induction of sexual behavior in female rats and synthesis of polyadenylated messenger RNA in the ventromedial nucleus of the hypothalamus. *Mol. Brain Res.* **1**, 153–165.

Yamanouchi, K., and Arai, Y. (1990). The septum as origin of a lordosis-inhibiting influence in female rats: Effect of neural transection. *Physiol. Behav.* **48**, 351–355.

Yanase, M., and Gorski, R.A. (1973). The ability of the intracerebral exposure to progesterone on consecutive days to facilitate lordosis behavior: and interaction between progesterone and estrogen. *Biol. Reprod.* **15**, 544–550.

Yanase, M., and Gorski, R.A. (1976). Sites of estrogen and progesterone facilitation of lordosis behavior in the spayed rat. *Biol. Reprod.* **15**, 536–543.

Yang, L.-Y., and Clemens, L.G. (2000). MPOA lesions affect female pacing of copulation in rats. *Behav. Neurosci.* **114**, 1191–1202.

Young, L.J., Muns, S., Wang, Z.X., and Insel, T.R. (1997). Changes in oxytocin receptor mRNA in rat brain during pregnancy and the effects of estrogen and interleukin-6. *J. Neuroendocrinol.* **9**, 859–865.

Young, L.J., Wang, Z.X., Donaldson, R., and Rissman, E.F. (1998). Estrogen receptor alpha is essential for induction of oxytocin receptor by estrogen. *NeuroReport* **9**, 933–936.

Young, W.C. (1969). Psychobiology of sexual behavior in the guinea pig. *Adv. Study Behav.* 1–110.

Yuan, H., Bowlby, D.A., Brown, T.J., Hochberg, R.B., and MacLusky, N.J. (1995). Distribution of occupied and unoccupied estrogen receptors in the rat brain: Effects of physiological gonadal steroid exposure. *Endocrinology (Baltimore)* **136**, 96–105.

Yuri, K., and Kawata, M. (1991). The effect of estrogen on the estrogen receptor-immunoreactive cells in the Rat medial preoptic nucleus. *Brain Res.* **548**, 50–54.

Zhou, L., and Hammer, R.P. (1995). Gonadal steroid hormones upregulate medial preoptic mu-opioid receptors in the rat. *Eur. J. Pharmacol.* **278**, 271–274.

Zhou, Y., Watters, J.J., and Dorsa, D.M. (1996). Estrogen rapidly induces the phosphorylation of the cAMP response element binding protein in rat brain. *Endocrinology (Baltimore)* **137**, 2163–2166.

Zigmond, R.E., and McEwen, B.S. (1969). Selective retention of oestradiol by cell nuclei in specific brain regions of the ovariectomized rat. *J. Neurobiol.* **17**, 889–899.

Zou, A.H., Marschke, K.B., Arnold, K.E., Berger, E.M., Fitzgerald, P., Mais, D.E., and Allegretto, E.A. (1999). Estrogen receptor beta activates the human retinoic acid receptor alpha-1 promoter in response to tamoxifen and other estrogen receptor antagonists, but not in response to estrogen. *Mol. Endocrinol.* **13**, 418–430.

Zucker, I. (1966). Facilitatory and inhibitory effects of progesterone on sexual responses of spayed guinea pigs. *J. Comp. Physiol. Psychol.* **62**, 376–381.

Zucker, I. (1967). Actions of progesterone in the control of sexual receptivity of the spayed female rat. *J. Comp. Physiol. Psychol.* **63**, 313–316.

Zucker, I. (1968). Biphasic effects of progesterone on sexual receptivity in the female guinea pig. *J. Comp. Physiol. Psychol.* **65**, 472–478.

3

Parental Care in Mammals: Immediate Internal and Sensory Factors of Control

Gabriela González-Mariscal

Centro de Investigación en Reproducción Animal, Centro de Investigación y Estudios Avanzados–Universidad Autónoma de Tlaxcala, Tlaxcala Tlax 90 000, Mexico

Pascal Poindron

Centro de Neurobiología, Universidad Nacional Autónoma de México, Querétaro 76 001, Mexico

I. INTRODUCTION

The strategies by which animals succeed in reproducing and spreading their genes vary greatly across species. Whereas those using the "r" strategy (or opportunistic breeders) tend to produce many small offspring in a short time, "K" breeders (also called stable species) produce fewer but larger offspring at longer intervals. There are numerous internal and environmental factors that influence the type of reproductive strategy that a species will develop. Overall, mammals tend to be "K" breeders: They generally show a relatively long gestation period and give birth to few neonates of reasonable weight compared to the adult (May and Rubenstein, 1984). Nonetheless, within this range, striking differences exist: Some species produce in a single reproductive cycle more young than others do in a lifetime (e.g., rodents versus most large herbivores and primates). In other words, some mammalian species tend to show "r" reproductive strategies. The degree of maturity of the offspring also varies greatly, from a rather underdeveloped larva (marsupials) to a fully developed young, able to follow its dam within less than an hour after birth (ungulates). Given this extraordinary variation in the characteristics of the neonate, it is not surprising that selective pressure by ultimate factors (i.e., those ensur-

ing the successful transmission of the parent's genes) has resulted in a remarkable diversification in the patterns of parental care in mammals (Section II).

What do we mean by parental care? In terms of parental investment, it is anything done by the parent for the offspring that increases the latter's chances of survival while decreasing the parent's ability to invest in other offspring (Trivers, 1974). An important implication of this statement is that the parent-infant interaction is mutually adjusted only up to a point, an important reflection to consider when investigating the evolution of the mechanisms that terminate the parent-infant relationship (i.e., weaning; Section IV; Galef, 1981). Alternative definitions of parental care are those of Rosenblatt and Lehrman (1963), who consider maternal behavior as changes in the mother in ways that correlate with changes in the needs of the developing young, and of Bridges (1996), who speaks of a set of behavioral responses over the course of lactation that help ensure the growth and survival of the offspring. In the present chapter we will be mainly concerned with the immediate control of parental behavior (proximate causes, i.e., hormonal, neural, and sensory factors; Section III). Therefore, we will use the more restrictive definition of direct parental care, which refers to those behaviors performed by the parents and directed to the young (e.g., licking, nursing) or that are commonly regarded as directly advantageous to the young (e.g., nest-building, prepartum isolation, placentophagia, nest-defense, postpartum aggression). By maternal and paternal behavior we will refer to those actions that are part of the normal ethogram of mothers (or females) and fathers (or males), respectively, directed towards their own or alien young. The term *parental behavior* will be used when referring to the care given to the infant (s), regardless of the sex of the care-giver; *alloparental behavior* will be used to denote the care provided by animals other than the mother or father.

Most studies investigating the proximate factors controlling parental behavior have been performed in rodents, more specifically in the laboratory rat. Though studies in this species have proven invaluable for investigating the neurobiological mechanisms controlling maternal behavior, parental care in this species represents only one type of the parent-infant relationship. In the last decade or so, new types of parental care have been investigated and have given us a broader picture of the ways in which ensuring survival of the young has been solved across mammalian species. Typical examples are sheep, rabbits, and prairie voles, which illustrate specific characteristics of parental care; namely, selective bonding, reduced care, and biparental care, respectively. However, advances in methodology (e.g., the "simultaneous" quantification of neuronal activity and behavior, the manipulation of specific genes) are expanding the type of questions we can ask about parental behavior. A growing field of interest is how the display of this activity modifies the parent's subsequent behavior and permanently alters the way in which the growing young respond, as adults, to stress and to their own offspring.

II. CHARACTERISTICS OF MAMMALIAN PARENTAL CARE

Maternal care, as short as it may be in duration, is always present in the initial phase of development of the young. This is obviously linked to the fact that, as opposed to nonmammalian species, the neonate strictly depends on the mother's colostrum and milk to ensure its early survival and adequate growth. Another aspect that influences how mothers care for their

young is the degree of development of the young at birth. The physiological requirements of an altricial neonate (Rheingold, 1963; Rosenblatt and Lehrman, 1963; Schneirla *et al.,* 1963) such as a rat pup, a kitten, or a cub are quite different from those of a precocial neonate lamb or kid (Collias, 1956; Herscher *et al.,* 1963a), and maternal care has to be adjusted accordingly to ensure the survival and proper psychophysiological development of the progeny. Primates, whose young most often show an intermediate stage of maturity, have developed another type of relation called *matricolia,* in which mother-young physical contact associated with the carrying of the infant is a characteristic feature (De Vore, 1963; Harlow *et al.,* 1963; Jay, 1963).

A. Maternal versus Biparental Care

As pointed out by Kleiman and Malcolm (1981), the information about paternal care is far from complete and reliable, for various reasons. In many cases the existence of paternal behavior is mentioned but not described, while in others it is described but not quantified, and the real frequency of occurrence even among closely related species is unknown. Direct paternal care is not specific to particular orders or families and should not be regarded as a taxonomic indicator (Klopfer, 1981). Rather, its display seems to depend on the nature of the habitat, the social structure of the species, and the developmental characteristics of the young (Clutton-Brock, 1991; Spencer-Booth, 1970). Thus, biparental care has been observed more frequently in species that are monogamous, inhabit stable environments with abundant resources, and have young that develop slowly (Klopfer, 1981; Solomon and French, 1997; Wang and Insel, 1996). Moreover, in such species alloparental behavior is frequently observed, i.e., juvenile siblings or nonlactating adult females frequently care for the young. These forms of cooperative breeding have been studied from various perspectives in some species and have revealed the intricate web of connections between individuals and their social and ecological environment that regulates the organization of parental care in mammals.

1. Characteristics of Paternal and Alloparental Behavior

Nine of 30 rodent families (Solomon and Getz, 1997), several species of primates (Yogman, 1990), and virtually every species of canid studied (Asa, 1997) have been reported to show some form of alloparental behavior. Yet this incidence varies much, even among closely related species. For instance, in prosimians of the genus *Lemur,* mothers may transfer the young to "helpers" as early as 72 hours after birth (*L. catta*), at about one month of age (*L. fulvus*), or they may leave the newborn in the nest and almost never carry them (*L. variegatus*) (Klopfer and Boskoff, 1979). Are such differences in behavior immediately adaptive? Do they contribute to preserving or increasing an individual's genotype? If parental care is displayed at a cost to the individual that shows it, there must be some long-term benefits. Before considering the hypotheses proposed to explain the existence of paternal-alloparental care we will describe the hallmarks that define cooperative breeding (Solomon and French, 1997):

1. Philopatry, which refers to the "decision" of an individual to postpone dispersion from the natal group and attempt independent reproduction later on.
2. Reproductive suppression, which consists of the use of behavioral strategies (Asa, 1997) and chemosignals (Carter *et al.,* 1986; Getz *et al.,* 1983; Novotny *et al.,* 1999) by the parents to temporarily arrest gonadal development and prevent mating in their juvenile progeny.
3. Care for other's offspring, which can be *direct and depreciable* (i.e., those behaviors that change as a function of the number of young cared for and have an immediate physical influence on them, e.g., food-provisioning, grooming, playing) or *indirect and nondepreciable* (i.e., those patterns that are independent of the number of young cared for and may be displayed even in their absence, e.g., nest-defense, construction of shelters and runways, warning of predators).

2. Advantages and Benefits of Paternal and Alloparental Care

It has been proposed that a direct benefit of allo-parental care to juveniles is that in caring for their siblings, they acquire and practice the skills of parental behavior to be used later on with their own progeny (Elwood and Broom, 1978; Gubernick and Laskin, 1994; Salo and French, 1989). Indeed, in mongolian

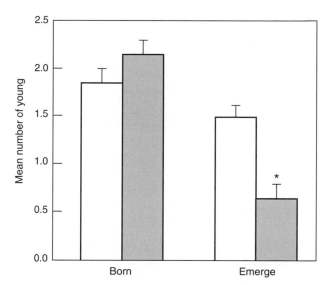

FIGURE 1 Relation between the number of young *Peromyscus californicus* born and those emerging from the nest when the father is present (open bars) versus when it is absent (dashed bars). *$p < 0.01$. (From Gubernick and Teferi (2000), with permission from the Royal Society.)

gerbils, prior experience with younger siblings leads to earlier reproduction and the production of litters that mature faster (Salo and French, 1989). Yet mothers may also benefit from alloparental behavior, as suggested by the observation that the interval between successive litters was reduced in prairie vole mothers in which juveniles were present and helped in rearing their siblings (Solomon, 1991). Moreover, in California mice (*Peromyscus californicus*) living under natural conditions, the proportion of mothers that weaned a whole litter was much greater in families with a father than in those without it (Gubernick and Teferi, 2000; Fig. 1). However, alloparental care may also enhance the inclusive fitness of the fathers because, in prairie voles, the presence of juveniles allowed fathers more time for drinking, feeding, foraging, and presumably for extra-pair copulations (Solomon, 1991).

3. Factors That Determine the Occurrence of Paternal Behavior

A major determinant of paternal behavior is whether or not the female allows the male near the young. As many effects of paternal care are beneficial for the development of the young (see below), the mother may increase her fitness by allowing males to care for the progeny. Yet because infanticide by males is common in many rodents, females may be expected to protect their young from the male until he proves to be non-infanticidal (Dewsbury, 1985). Indeed, female meadow voles are less tolerant of fathers that were removed during pregnancy and returned after the pups were born than of males that stayed across the whole pregnancy. Yet after renewed contact and lack of infanticide, such females were tolerant of fathers and excluded other males from the nest (Storey *et al.*, 1994). The frequency of infanticide varies among rodents and is influenced by the perinatal and the adult hormone environment. Thus, in rats castration of juveniles reduces infanticide in adulthood (Rosenberg, 1974; Rosenberg *et al.*, 1971) and the injection of testosterone to such adult males restores it (Rosenberg and Sherman, 1975). Castration of adult rats, however, does not reduce infanticidal behavior (Rosenberg and Sherman, 1975) but the injection of estrogen (alone or with progesterone) does (Bridges *et al.*, 1973). In mice, infanticide is seen in about 10% of females and 35–40% of males (Gandelman and Vom Saal, 1975). This behavior is reduced by gonadectomy in adulthood and reinstated by testosterone implants in both sexes (Gandelman and Vom Saal, 1975; Svare, 1979; Svare and Mann, 1981). Yet neonatal castration of male mice *increases* infanticide in adults given testosterone and the older the male is at castration the *less* likely he is to kill pups (Gandelman and Vom Saal, 1977; Samuels *et al.*, 1981). Hamsters are very different from rats and mice because males are more likely to care for pups and less likely to kill them than non-lactating females; these differences are not modified by castration or by progesterone injections (Marques and Valenstein, 1976).

From the male point of view, the benefits of remaining with the female and aiding in raising the young must be weighed against the potential benefits and costs of seeking out additional mates. The ability of males to show care of the young depends partly on their intrinsic capacity to respond positively to the presence of young. For example, in the domestic mouse, males have the capacity to show some maternal-like behaviors with a very short latency (Noirot, 1972), although in the field pregnant females may impede the male from approaching them (Noirot *et al.*, 1975; Svare, 1981). Another situation in which paternal care is unlikely to be seen is that of species in which seasonal segregation of the sexes occurs along with seasonal reproduction, as in sheep. Sexual activity initiates in summer or early autumn and it is then that rams join the groups of ewes. When the females give birth at the end of winter and during spring, the males are no longer with them but, rather, stay away in bachelors' groups and thus have no contact with the young until the summertime. In addition, there is no stable pair formation and thus the probability that a given male can invest in behaviors favorable to its own progeny is very low (Jewell and Grubb, 1974). However, it must be noted that no studies have systematically investigated whether rams are able to display some form of paternal care beneficial to the young. Nevertheless, in a study of postpartum anestrus in domestic sheep in which rams were kept with ewes starting at a few days before parturition and continuing for several weeks across lactation (Schirar *et al.*, 1989, 1990), rejection of newborn and week-old lambs by rams was observed in several instances (P. Poindron, unpublished).

4. *"True" Paternal Behavior versus Maternal-like Behavior Displayed by Males*

As stated earlier, "true" paternal behavior is characteristic of many rodent species (De Vries, 1999; Gubernick and Nelson, 1989; King, 1963; Wilson, 1982). Thus, males and females lick, retrieve, huddle over and manipulate pups, and also engage in nest-building. In a study using sexually inexperienced individuals from four *Microtus* species (*M. montanus*, *M. pennsylvanicus*, *M. ochrogaster*, and *M. californicus*) and two species of *Peromyscus* (*P. maniculatus* and *P. leucopus*), sex differences in parental care were found relatively infrequently (except for nursing; Hartung and Dewsbury, 1979). In contrast, male rats (*Rattus norvegicus*) are less responsive to pups than are females, this difference becoming apparent at around 45 days of age (Mayer *et al.*, 1979). Nonetheless, adult male rats can be "sensitized" to show maternal behavior (licking, crouching, retrieving) after repeated pup exposure, as occurs with virgin females (Section IVD; Jakubowski and Terkel, 1985b,c; Leboucher and Lescoat, 1986; Rosenblatt, 1967). The possibility that these differences between male and female rats are a consequence of the action of gonadal hormones during the perinatal or adult periods is supported by the following evidence:

1. Castration on neonatal day 1 increases the likelihood of maternal-like behavior display in adulthood (Quadagno, 1974; Quadagno and Rockwell, 1972; Quadagno *et al.,* 1973) whereas neonatal exposure to testosterone facilitates infanticide and reduces retrieving (Ichikawa and Fujii, 1982; Rosenberg and Herrenkohl, 1976; Rosenberg and Sherman, 1975; Rosenberg *et al.,* 1971).
2. Testosterone injections increase the latency to show such behavior in male rats castrated as adults (Leon *et al.,* 1973).
3. The injection of estrogen, alone or combined with progesterone and prolactin, decreases such latency (Bridges, 1983; Bridges *et al.,* 1973; Lubin *et al.,* 1972).

In mice, the display of maternal-like behavior is facilitated by the action of testicular hormones during the perinatal period: Neonatal castration reduces the proportion of males showing this behavior in adulthood (Gandelman and Vom Saal, 1975) but increases nest-building provoked by the injection of estrogen and progesterone to adult animals (Lisk *et al.,* 1973). Yet testicular hormones are inhibitory to maternal-like behavior in adult animals because the proportion of male mice displaying this behavior is increased by castration during adulthood (Gandelman and Vom Saal, 1975). Also, both in rats and mice, studies on the behavioral effects of the sex of neighboring fetuses indicate that it can influence parental behavior in the female (Kinsley, 1990; but see also Palanza *et al.,* 1995, in wild mice). In prairie voles, males and females are parental, even as adult virgins, upon their first exposure to pups (Lonstein and De Vries, 2000c). Yet a sex difference seems to exist, because males are more parental than females and, though such behavior is not modified by gonadectomy in either sex, estrogen administration increases parental behavior much more in such virgin females (Lonstein and De Vries, 1999b). When tested with their own litter, voles of both sexes from four species (*Microtus montanus, M. pennsylvanicus, M. ochrogaster,* and *M. californicus*) have been found to display the same repertoire of parental behaviors toward the young, including licking and huddling (Hartung and Dewsbury, 1979; Lonstein and De Vries, 1999a; Solomon, 1993). The amount of time spent by males and females in parental activities was practically the same in two studies (Hartung and Dewsbury, 1979; Lonstein and De Vries, 1999a), and slightly larger in female prairie voles in another study (Solomon, 1993). Similarly, male and female mongolian gerbils (*Meriones unguiculatus*) have been found to display the same parental behaviors toward their young, with slight differences in their frequency between the sexes (Elwood, 1975). In this species also intrauterine position is important for the later expression of sexual and parental care: *Male* gerbil fetuses located between two females show reduced male sexual behavior and paternal care is increased by 30–50% (Clark and Galef, 2000). In the rabbit, androgen administration during pregnancy results in a decrease of nest building in females (Anderson *et al.,* 1970). A striking example of true paternal care is that of the Djungarian hamster (*Phodopus campbelli*): Males assist the mother at parturition by consuming the amniotic fluid and placenta, pulling the pups during expulsion, and licking the neonates to stimulate breathing (Jones and Wynne-Edwards, 2000).

5. Parental and Alloparental Contributions to Offspring Development

A number of studies have shown that stimulation from the parents or other members of the social group plays a major role in the development of the offspring. The nature of the investment ranges from huddling with young (thus increasing body temperature and growth rate, as in *Peromyscus californicus;* Dudley, 1974a,b), cleaning and grooming them, ingesting excreta (Kleiman and Malcolm, 1981) to retrieving (common in rodents and carnivores) and transporting young (primates), provisioning food (Knight *et al.,* 1992), baby-sitting, defense, and play (Woodroffe, 1993). Whether this stimulation comes from the mother alone or from both parents (sometimes including siblings) varies across species. For instance, when the development of meadow voles (monoparental; promiscuous) and prairie voles (biparental; monogamous) was compared under different "social units" it was found that the former developed faster when reared only by their mothers whereas the rate of development of the latter was higher when raised in units that included both parents (Wang and Novak, 1992). Moreover, prairie vole pups raised with their juvenile siblings (along with their parents) weighed more at weaning and opened their eyes sooner than those raised only by their parents (Solomon, 1991). The effects of the "extra" stimulation received during infancy persisted into adulthood because female prairie voles reared with their siblings had shorter interlitter intervals and their pups grew faster than those reared without their siblings (Solomon, 1994a).

Conversely, prenatal stress and mother-young separation can induce a wide range of short- and long-term effects that can affect psychological and physiological development of the young, including their ability to cope with social stressors and express maternal care (Clarke and Schneider, 1993; Harlow *et al.,* 1963; Hofer, 1987; Kinsley, 1990; Kraemer, 1992; Kraemer and Clarke, 1997; Levine, 1987; Ruppenthal *et al.,* 1976). Thus, prenatal stress differentially affects the later expression of maternal behavior of male and female rats in adulthood (M. C. Del Cerro, personal communication; Kinsley and Bridges, 1988). Both in rats and primates, mother-young separation induces activation of the hypothalamo-hypophysis-adrenal axis (Byrne and Suomi, 1999; Levine *et al.,* 1978), as well as physiological attachment-related systems (opiates, oxytocin, catecholamines (Hennessy *et al.,* 1997; Kuhn and Schanberg, 1998; Nelson and Panksepp, 1998), and this can affect later endocrine response to stress, emotionality, and brain structures important for maternal behavior expression (Hall *et al.,* 1999; Lehmann *et al.,* 1999; Lephart and Watson, 1999; Workel *et al.,* 1997). Recently, a series of studies have provided evidence that the stimulation provided by the mother can permanently modify specific aspects of the behavior of rat pups as adults. By diverse experimental strategies the groups of Meaney (Caldji *et al.,* 1998; Francis and Meaney, 1999; Francis *et al.,* 1999a; Liu *et al.,* 1997) and Fleming (Fleming *et al.,* 1999; Gonzalez *et al.,* 2000) modified the intensity or quality of maternal stimulation and assessed the impact of such manipulations on the maternal behavior of the female offspring and their reactivity to stress. Their results indicate that a reduced maternal care leads to similar "low maternal responses" in the female offspring toward their own young, an effect that is further transmitted to the next generation. This does not occur by a genetic transmission because pups born to "low maternal" rats but raised by "highly maternal" ones (or vice versa) dis-

play, as adults, the qualities of the adoptive mother. Thus, female offspring reared by "high maternal" rats show not only more licking-grooming and crouching toward their litter but also the decreased levels of fearfulness characteristic of their adoptive mothers. These behavioral changes are accompanied by modifications in the density of some receptors (alpha-2-adrenergic, benzodiazepine, glucocorticoids) in brain areas related with the regulation of stress responses (e.g., hippocampus, central and basolateral amygdala, locus coeruleus; Caldji *et al.,* 1998; Francis *et al.,* 1999b). These results indicate the operation of a mechanism for the intergenerational transfer of behavioral traits that is nongenomic and depends on experiences acquired during the early postnatal period in the context of mother-young interactions.

These results may be paralleled with the adverse long-term impacts of *natural* variations in some aspects of parental behavior in infancy, such as parental aggression or foraging under unpredictable conditions, that have been documented in primates (Coplan *et al.,* 1996; Dettling *et al.,* 1998), thus stressing the possible importance of this type of transmission in natural conditions. Finally, further support for the importance of mother-young interactions on the subsequent behavior of the young comes from studies showing that separation from the mother (leading to a reduction in milk intake and sensory stimulation) provokes alterations in maternal (i.e., nest building, retrieving, and nursing) and nonmaternal (e.g., self-grooming and circling) behaviors in adulthood (Salas *et al.,* 1984). It is interesting that undernourishment without separation from the mother provokes less severe effects, whereas stimulation at critical stages of brain ontogeny can compensate for the detrimental effects associated with severe undernourishment (Regalado *et al.,* 1999).

B. Maternal Behavior Ethogram

1. Prepartum Behaviors

As the pregnant female approaches parturition, several behavioral changes can be noted. Some of these changes are common to many species (e.g., changes in social behavior and aggression), while others are more specific to the ecology of the species or specific needs of the young (e.g., nest-building).

a) Maternal Aggression   Aggression toward adult conspecifics, especially males, is a common feature in various rodents. This has been particularly well documented in mice, rats, and hamsters. In the mouse, late pregnant females may kill strange males that come close to the nest (Brown, 1953). In experimentally controlled conditions, when female mice are put in the presence of an intruder, they usually show very intense attacks with a latency of a few seconds and for a period of about 30 minutes, if under continuous exposure (Green, 1978; Svare and Gandelman, 1973). In the rat the picture is similar, although the latency for aggression to be displayed is longer (a few minutes) and does not differ from that of intermale aggression (Erskine *et al.*, 1978a,b; Price and Bélanger, 1977). In the mouse, aggression increases as early as day 5 of pregnancy (Noirot *et al.*, 1975), while in the rat highest levels of aggression have been reported at around days 18 to 22 (Erskine *et al.*, 1978b) and on day 10 in the hamster (Wise, 1974). In sheep, intraspecific aggression has not been reported but in goats it appears to be an efficient mechanism for defending the birth site and avoiding cross-fostering (Das and Tomer, 1997; Lickliter, 1985; Ramírez *et al.*, 1995). It appears, therefore, that physiological changes associated with pregnancy, parturition, and lactation bring about profound modifications in aggressive behaviors of the female and that these have to be considered as intrinsic components of the behavioral profile of motherhood.

b) Social Isolation and Prepartum Agitation   In sheep and goats, several studies have reported prepartum isolation from the rest of the flock shortly before the birth of the young (sheep: Arnold and Morgan, 1975; Echeverri *et al.*, 1992; Lécrivain and Janeau, 1987; Shackleton and Haywood, 1985; goat: Das and Tomer, 1997; Lickliter, 1985; O'Brien, 1983, 1984; Ramírez *et al.*, 1995; Rudge, 1970). Normally, both species show very strong behavioral responses indicative of agitation and distress when isolated from conspecifics (Carbonaro *et al.*, 1992; Le Neindre *et al.*, 1993; Lyons *et al.*, 1988; Poindron *et al.*, 1994; Price and Thos, 1980). However, across the last 24 hours preceding delivery, and even more intensely at the start of parturition, females show a clear reduction of agitation following separation from their flockmates (Poindron

et al., 1997, 1998a,b). In the wild boar, the female also isolates herself from the other flock members to farrow (Gundlach, 1968; Frädrich, 1974). Similar results have been reported in feral and free-ranging domestic pigs, in which social isolation may extend for one to three weeks postpartum (Jensen, 1986; Jensen *et al.*, 1987; Kurz and Marchinton, 1972; Stangel and Jensen, 1991). Thoroughbred mares also tend to leave the herd a few days before foaling (Barty, 1974). Finally, as parturition becomes imminent females tend to show strong signs of agitation, increased restlessness, locomotion, and vocalisations (sheep and goats: Collias, 1956; Das and Tomer, 1997; Herscher *et al.*, 1963a; Ramírez *et al.*, 1995; Shackleton and Haywood, 1985; Smith, 1965; mare: Barty, 1974; pig: Biensen *et al.*, 1996; Jensen, 1986; Jensen *et al.*, 1987; Meunier-Salaün *et al.*, 1991; cattle: George and Barger, 1974).

c) Nest-Building   Another characteristic of periparturient mammals that give birth to altricial young is providing shelter and thermal protection to the neonates. A good example of this prepartum initiation of maternal care are lagomorphs. Some days before parturition, the female digs several shallow basins (e.g., swamp rabbit, *Sylvilagus aquaticus*; Sorensen *et al.*, 1972) or true underground burrows (e.g., european rabbit, *Oryctolagus cuniculus*; Ross *et al.*, 1963a,b). In this last species, the digging starts to increase at about day 21 of the 30 to 32-day pregnancy, with a peak on days 25 to 27 (González-Mariscal *et al.*, 1994; González-Mariscal and Rosenblatt, 1996; Fig. 2). Straw or grass is then collected and used to build a nest inside the burrow (Denenberg *et al.*, 1963; Sawin and Crary, 1953; Sorensen *et al.*, 1972; Verga *et al.*, 1978). This behavior is maximally expressed on the day before parturition (González-Mariscal *et al.*, 1994). Finally, females select one of the straw nests and line it with hair pulled from their own chest, thus resulting in an elaborate structure in which the pups will be born (Deutsch, 1957; Ross *et al.*, 1956; Sawin *et al.*, 1960; Zarrow *et al.*, 1961, 1962b, 1963). Hair-loosening and hair-plucking are maximally observed around parturition and may continue for a few days afterwards (González-Mariscal *et al.*, 1994). At this stage, periparturient females are also able to distinguish among several materials and various types of hair provided

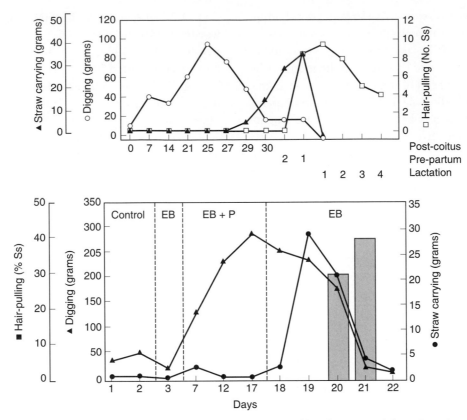

FIGURE 2   Maternal nest-building displayed by pregnant rabbits (upper panel; from González-Mariscal *et al.* (1994), with permission from Elsevier Science) and by ovariectomized females treated with estradiol benzoate (EB; 5 μg/day) and progesterone (P; 10 mg/day; lower panel; from González-Mariscal and Rosenblatt (1996), with permission from Academic Press). Note the similarity in the onset and decline of digging, straw-carrying, and hair-pulling between the two types of animals.

for this purpose and they react differentially to them (González-Mariscal *et al.*, 1998b).

Other lagomorphs, such as snowshoe and european hares, also make a nest, although its structure consists mainly of grass gathered and shaped into the form of a nest in some secluded place above ground (Broekhuizen and Maaskamp, 1980; Rongstad and Tester, 1971). The young of these species are precocious and remain in the nest for only a few days, reuniting daily with their dam at the birth site for nursing (Broekhuizen and Maaskamp, 1980; Rongstad and Tester, 1971). In the rat, burrowing increases in the pregnant female (Calhoun, 1962), but nest-building is initiated only about 24 hours before giving birth and consists merely of a rather loose structure with walls about 2 to 5 cm high, into which the pups will be delivered. Nonetheless, this nest is more elaborate

than the mat usually built by nonpregnant females (Moltz, 1975). In the hamster, digging increases shortly (<4 days) after conception and nest-building rises in the last quarter of gestation (Daly, 1972). Felidae, in which young are born deaf, blind, and unable to thermoregulate, also use nest sites both under solitary and communal care conditions (Feldman, 1993).

Among ungulates, which give birth to precocious young, pawing, scratching, and sniffing the ground are common, as if vestigial of nest-building. Swine, however, differ strikingly from the rest, as they are the only species of ungulates that build an elaborate nest, where a large litter will be delivered. About 24 hours before farrowing the female leaves the group and selects an isolated place to build a nest that consists of a shallow hole rooted out and filled with grass and small branches (Frädrich, 1974; Gundlach, 1968; Hansson and Karstad, 1959; Jensen, 1986; Stangel and Jensen, 1991). Although goats do not build a nest, they do select a protected site for kidding (O'Brien, 1983). This contrasts with sheep, which only seek shelter at the time of parturition if they are cold, and not for the purpose of sheltering the neonate (Alexander *et al.*, 1980; Lynch and Alexander, 1977; Stevens *et al.*, 1981).

2. Postpartum Behaviors

a) Placentophagia and Amniotic Fluid Ingestion

In most mammals, one of the first behaviors that characterize the parturient mother is the cleaning of the neonate and the consumption of amniotic fluids and placenta. Only a few species do not show these behaviors (camelids: Sumar, 1999; swine: Frädrich, 1974; Fraser, 1984; Gundlach, 1968; Jensen, 1986; pinnipeds: Knudston, 1974; see also Kristal, 1980). In sheep, attraction to amniotic fluids begins during the last stage of parturition and disappears within a few hours if ewes are not kept in contact with their lamb (Arnould *et al.*, 1991; Lévy *et al.*, 1983). In rabbits, ingestion of placentas is observed only around parturition (Melo *et al.*, 1998), whereas in rats this behavior is maximal during delivery but also occurs in nonpregnant females (Kristal, 1980). Recently, placentophagia has been found to be displayed at parturition by both males and females of the biparental hamster *Phodopus campbelli* (Jones and Wynne-Edwards, 2000). Placentophagia is also common in other herbivores but its actual frequency of occurrence, onset, and decline have been studied in only a few species (Pinheiro Machado *et al.*, 1997). The biological advantages of placentophagia and amniotic fluid ingestion are not totally understood, but it has been suggested that they could have an important analgesic effect during the peripartum period, especially when combined with vaginal stimulation (Kristal, 1991; Kristal *et al.*, 1985, 1986, 1990). Cleaning the neonate of amniotic fluids is important for young that are likely to be exposed to cold temperatures, such as ungulates that give birth in the winter or early spring (Alexander, 1988). It has also been proposed that the licking stimulation the young receives while being cleaned by its mother stimulates behavioral and learning functions. This has been particularly well documented in the rat (Hofer, 1987; Leon *et al.*, 1987).

b) Emission of Vocalizations

Mothers of many mammals emit characteristic low-amplitude and frequency vocalizations (Boinski and Mitchell, 1995; Kiley, 1972; McCowan and Reiss, 1995) and also show a high sensitivity to calls emitted by the young. In sheep and goats, mothers shift their vocal activity to low-pitch bleats as the young is born (Collias, 1956; Dwyer *et al.*, 1998; Nowak, 1990; Smith, 1965). In rodents that give birth to precocious pups various maternal calls have been identified in several species, including guinea pigs (Berryman, 1974; Eisenberg, 1974; Kleiman, 1972; Kunkel and Kunkel, 1964). In the rat and other altricial rodents, early maternal vocalizations have not been documented, since the pups are deaf and do not respond to ultrasonic vocalizations until about 10 days of age (Porter, 1983). However, when emitted by pups, ultrasonic vocalizations are potent activators of retrieving behavior in the mother (Elwood and McCauley, 1983; King, 1963). In the mouse it has been shown that females respond preferentially to 50 kHz frequencies and that this is influenced by hormones and experience (Ehret and Haack, 1982, 1984; Ehret and Koch, 1989; Koch and Ehret, 1989). These changes in maternal vocalization and responsiveness to the neonate's vocal activity serve as a basis for the development of acoustic communication between mother and young and, in some species, for the individual recognition of offspring at a distance.

c) Nursing

This is undoubtedly the most important and characteristic pattern of maternal behavior in mammals. In fact, regardless of the stage of development of the neonate, nursing generally occurs shortly after the young are born. Even in marsupials, that give birth to a small larva, the neonate immediately crawls from the vagina to the pouch, through the mother's fur, guided by the track of moist hair created by the mother's self-licking. Once inside the pouch, the larva firmly attaches itself to the nipple like a pressure button (Renfree *et al.*, 1989; Rose and MacFayden, 1997; Tyndale-Biscoe and Renfree, 1987). In species that build a nest, the first nursing occurs shortly after the whole litter is delivered and in some cases (rabbits: Hudson *et al.*, 1999; pigs; P. Poindron, personal observation) even earlier, throughout parturition. While nursing the mother rat adopts a characteristic posture, consisting of a high arching of the back (kyphosis), which is triggered by the pups actually attaching to the nipples (De Vries, 1999; Stern, 1989, 1996a; see Section IV.A). In ruminants, the one or two neonates generally get access to the udder between 30 minutes and one hour after they are born (Illmann and Spinka, 1993; Lidfors and Jensen, 1988; Slee and Springbett, 1986). Locating and reaching the udder or the nipple depends on a number of sensory cues provided by the dam (e.g., nipple search pheromone in mother rabbits: Hudson and Distel, 1983, 1984; maternal pheromone and saliva deposited on nipples in mother rats: Hofer *et al.,* 1976; Leon and Moltz, 1972; temperature and texture of body surface in sheep: Vince, 1993).

d) Maternal Aggression and Nest Defense

After parturition, maternal aggression is most intense in the first days of lactation and gradually declines thereafter (mouse: Svare and Gandelman, 1976; rat: Erskine *et al.,* 1978b; hamster: Wise, 1974). In rats and mice, a period of about two days of mother-young contact is necessary for mothers fully to develop a strong defense behavior of the young against adult conspecifics. This behavior reaches a peak at about day 3 of lactation in the mouse, and day 9 in the rat (Erskine *et al.,* 1978b; Gandelman, 1972; Green, 1978) and progressively decreases as lactation advances. Aside from showing conspecific aggression, lactating mice attack juvenile and adult voles (Rowley and Christian, 1976a,b, 1977), whereas lactating rabbits show aggression toward their human handler (Denenberg *et al.,* 1958, 1959), and lactating rats increase frog and mouse-killing (Endröczi *et al.,* 1958; Flandera and Nováková, 1975). Defense of the young has also been reported in rabbits (Ross *et al.,* 1963a,b), squirrels (Taylor, 1966), cats (Schneirla *et al.,* 1963), ungulates (moose: Altmann, 1963; sheep: Herscher *et al.,* 1963a), and primates (De Vore, 1963). In ungulates the most documented form of aggressive behavior is that shown by mothers toward alien young, which is related to the establishment of a selective bond (see next section).

e) Recognition of Young and Selective Nursing

As a rule, parents (especially mothers) invest more in their own young than in alien ones. However, the extent to which a dam will preferentially care for her own or closely related young versus nonkin progeny varies greatly from one species to another. Those giving birth to altricial young, initially confined to a burrow or nest, do not show an early exclusive maternal care. Rather, they respond maternally to any young that is presented to them. Thus, mother rats are able to discriminate their own litter from an alien one but will readily nurse alien young (Beach and Jaynes, 1956a). Mice can build communal nests and nurse pups other than their own (Crowcroft and Rowe, 1963; Manning *et al.,* 1992; Saylor and Salmon, 1969; Southwick, 1969). Rabbits also will nurse alien young in the maternal nest (González-Mariscal *et al.,* 1998b), whereas marsupials accept other joeys than their own if placed in the pouch (Merchant and Sharman, 1966). Ground squirrel mothers do not show discriminative behavior before the young wander out of the burrow (Holmes, 1990). By contrast, domestic sheep, goats, and cattle, which give birth to precocious neonates, rapidly establish an exclusive bond with their infant and thereafter reject any alien young that attempts to suckle (Herscher *et al.,* 1963a,b; Hudson and Mullord, 1977; Klopfer *et al.,* 1964; Smith *et al.,* 1966). However, allomaternal nursing has been reported in wild sheep, water buffaloes, and deer (Ekvall, 1998; Murphey *et al.,* 1990; Paranhos da Costa *et al.,* 2000; Siqueiros *et al.,* 1998). It must be emphasized, however, that often it is not clear whether the reported behavior is true allonursing (with active acceptance by the mother) or "stealing," a strategy developed by young that are reared in high-density conditions (Poindron, 1974, 1976b). The mechanisms by which recognition and exclusive nursing develop will be dealt with in Section IV.C (see also Chapter 4 in this volume). Finally, in species giving birth to large litters (polytocous), preferential care of the young appears to rely more on defense of the nest or burrow, while maternal selectivity is more likely to be observed in monotocous species. For example, although piglets are precocial, sows are generally considered as showing little selective behavior toward alien piglets. Yet the lack or the presence of exclusive care in a given species should not be regarded as an absolute rule; for example, although sheep are very selective, non-negligible occurrence of allomaternal care has been reported, depending on the level of predator pressure (Hass, 1990). Conversely, though cross-fostering is a common practice in commercial pig rearing, in the field, adoption of alien piglets may not be the rule because of the piglets' attachment to their dam (Horrel and Bennet, 1981; Horrel and

Hodgson, 1986, 1992; Morrow-Tesch and McGlone, 1990a,b), the presence of a well-established teat order (Jeppesen, 1982a,b), and the eviction of alien intruders by the sow's own piglets (Jensen, 1986). Therefore, although in this chapter we basically focus on maternal behavior, keep in mind that the selectivity of the relation usually results from a bidirectional process.

f) Postpartum Estrus and Mother-Young Relationships during Lactation Once the intense care of the newborn characteristic of the immediate postpartum period has faded away, nursing becomes the main maternal activity directed to the young, together with heat transfer in altricial species (Galef, 1981). The frequency of nursing varies greatly among species: rats initially spend most of their time in the nest (Grota and Ader, 1969, 1974) and nursing bouts occur at about twice per hour (Price and Bélanger, 1977). Yet maximum milk production in rats occurs at around day 15 of lactation (Babicky et al., 1970). At the other extreme, rabbits nurse their litter only once a day for about three minutes (Drewett et al., 1982; González-Mariscal and Rosenblatt, 1996; Zarrow et al., 1965), and this behavior is displayed with remarkable circadian periodicity (Jilge, 1993, 1995). In sheep (Ewbank, 1964, 1967; Fletcher, 1971; Hess et al., 1974; Hinch, 1989), goats (Delgadillo et al., 1997; Lévy and Alexandre, 1985; Lickliter, 1984a,b; O'Brien, 1984), and pigs (Gustafsson et al., 1999; Jensen, 1986), dams nurse their young once or twice per hour, although in goats this may be reduced during the first days of lactation due to the "hiding" behavior of the kid. The duration of lactation varies greatly, and not always in relation to body size, although larger animals tend to nurse for longer periods (Short, 1984). Thus, one of the shortest nursing phases is that of the hooded seal, lasting only four days (Oftedal, 1997; Oftedal et al., 1993). Marsupials can nurse simultaneously a newborn and an older joey (that has left the pouch and returns only for suckling) due to the capacity of their mammary glands to produce two types of milk (May and Rubenstein, 1984). Rats nurse for 25 to 30 days, whereas sheep wean their young after three to five months (Arnold et al., 1979), and some primates, including humans, lactate for more than a year (Short, 1984).

Another characteristic of motherhood associated with lactation and varying across species is the occurrence of a postpartum estrus. In some species (e.g., rodents, rabbits, horses), the dam comes into heat soon after giving birth and can be fertilized at that time. By contrast, in various ungulates motherhood is characterized by the absence of estrus behavior, even though the hormonal sequence of sex steroids should theoretically promote the expression of female receptivity (Fabre-Nys and Martin, 1991). It is likely that a combination of factors (e.g., photoperiod, food resources, climatic conditions, pregnancy duration) have precluded the expression of an immediate postpartum estrus in ungulates, a condition demanding a high investment on the female. In sheep, the intracerebral liberation of oxytocin occurring during vaginal stimulation could be one of the factors participating in the inhibition of immediate postpartum estrus (Kendrick et al., 1993).

III. THE REGULATION OF PARENTAL BEHAVIOR

A. Endocrine and Proprioceptive Factors

From the previous section it is clear that several aspects of maternal care are displayed during pregnancy and that following parturition a new set of activities directed toward the young emerges and is maintained across lactation. To what extent are these two categories of behaviors regulated by hormones? This question has been investigated by using three main experimental approaches: (a) correlating the levels of hormones (steroids, proteins, peptides) in blood with the expression of specific patterns of maternal behavior; (b) removing the sources of endocrine secretions (e.g., ovary, placenta, pituitary) and assessing the impact of such procedures on the display of maternal care; (c) administering hormonal combinations and quantifying the expression of particular aspects of maternal behavior. By the use of these strategies it has been established that a variety of hormones prime the female and modulate or trigger specific maternal activities. Though most of the work on this topic has been done in rodents, it is clear that the hormonal stimulation of maternal behavior is manifest through a broad spectrum of activities characteristic of each species. Moreover, the relative importance of a given hormone for the onset and expression of specific maternal responses is not universal either: On the one hand redundancy is evident because several hormones can stimulate the same action in a given species and, on the other hand, a hormone clearly associated with the expression of maternal care in one species may be relatively unimportant in another one. In the following section we will present the evidence showing the participation of steroids, peptide hormones, and prostaglandins in the regulation of parental behavior in mammals.

1. Estrogen and Progesterone

As a rule progesterone, produced mainly by the ovaries or the placenta, depending on the species (placental source: guinea pig, sheep, human: Bazer *et al.,* 1998; Solomon, 1994b; ovarian source: rat, rabbit, goat, cow: Bedford *et al.,* 1972; Ramirez and Soufi, 1994), is present at high levels in blood during pregnancy and markedly decreases close to parturition (Table 1). Exceptions are guinea pigs (Challis *et al.,* 1971a; Heap and Deanesly, 1966) and some primates (e.g., chimpanzees: Reyes *et al.,* 1973; humans: Llauro *et al.,* 1968). Estradiol-17β is also present in high concentrations in blood during specific stages of pregnancy in most mammals studied (Table 1). In some species (e.g., rodents, rabbits) the main source of estrogens are the ovaries and in others (e.g., guinea-pig, ewe, cow, primates) the placenta (Bedford *et al.,* 1972). Shortly before parturition, estradiol plasma levels rise in rats (Shaikh, 1971), mice (McCormack and Greenwald, 1974), guinea pigs (Challis and Illingworth, 1972), rabbits (Challis and Lye, 1994; González-Mariscal *et al.,* 1994), ewes (Chamley *et al.,* 1973; Stabenfeldt, 1974; Terqui, 1974), goats (Challis and Linzell, 1971), cows (Hoffman *et al.,* 1973), pigs (Ash and Heap, 1975), dogs (Gräf, 1978), cats (Verhage *et al.,* 1976), marmosets (Pryce, 1996), rhesus monkeys (Weiss *et al.,* 1976), and chimpanzees (Reyes *et al.,* 1973) but decrease in hamsters (Baranczuk and Greenwald, 1974). These observations are consistent with the idea that specific factor(s) in the blood of pregnant and periparturient females or a change in their ratio (independent of the absolute concentrations of the hormones) close to parturition play an important role in facilitating the expression of maternal behavior. Indeed, the now classical studies of Terkel and Rosenblatt (1968, 1972) showed that by cross-transfusing blood between parturient rats and virgins (but not between two virgins), maternal behavior was successfully stimulated in the latter. Though the chemical identity of the factor(s) responsible for this effect was not determined then, such studies indicated that the expression of maternal behavior in rats did not rely on the female's pregnancy per se but, rather, on compound(s) present in its blood. Early studies were unsuccessful in attempting to stimulate maternal behavior in ovariectomized and intact rats by injecting estrogen and progesterone (Beach and Wilson, 1963; Lott, 1962; Riddle *et al.,* 1942). The first studies that successfully stimulated maternal behavior in ovariectomized virgin rats were done by Moltz *et al.* (1970) and Zarrow *et al.* (1971a). The main difference between these and the earlier studies was that they involved a prolonged administration of estradiol (as the benzoate, a long-acting ester), the addition of progesterone for several days, and the withdrawal of this hormone before the end of the estrogen treatment. The stimulatory effects of these treatments consisted of inducing in nonpregnant ovariectomized rats several motor patterns characteristic of the maternal behavior of this species (e.g., retrieving young, crouching over them, etc.; see Section II).

In rabbits, the group of Zarrow and Denenberg was the first to show a participation of hormones in a specific aspect of maternal behavior: nest-building. These authors effectively stimulated maternal nest-building in rabbits by injecting ovariectomized does for several days with estradiol benzoate combined with progesterone, followed by the removal of this hormone and continuation of estradiol (Anderson *et al.,* 1971; Zarrow *et al.,* 1961, 1963, 1971a). These hormones stimulate and time the expression of specific components of the nest-building process (González-Mariscal *et al.,* 1994, 1996b). Thus, digging (into a piece of cardboard, to simulate digging a burrow) steadily rose when both estradiol and progesterone were high, i.e., during midpregnancy or when these hormones were injected together to ovariectomized does. Straw-carrying was expressed only as progesterone levels declined toward the end of pregnancy or following progesterone withdrawal in ovariectomized estrogen-treated animals. In late pregnant does hair-pulling was expressed very close to parturition (and continued for three more days) while in ovariectomized, estrogen-treated animals it occurred three to four days after discontinuing the injection of progesterone (Fig. 2). The emission of the so-called "nipple pheromone" (an olfactory signal that is perceived by rabbit pups and guides them to the mother's nipples) is also under the control of estradiol and progesterone: It is maximally emitted by pregnant mothers (Hudson and Distel, 1983, 1984), abolished by ovariectomy, and reinstated by the combined injection of estradiol and progesterone (Hudson *et al.,* 1990).

In hamsters and mice, estradiol and progesterone also facilitate maternal nest-building. This behavior is maximal when high levels of such hormones are present during pregnancy and can be stimulated following ovariectomy by the combined administration of both steroids (Daly, 1972; Lisk, 1971; Lisk *et al.,* 1969; Richards, 1969; Swanson and Campbell, 1979a). Estrogen also facilitates maternal responsiveness in mice: Intact virgins retrieve pups placed in a novel environment, a response abolished by ovariectomy and restored by estradiol treatment (Koch and Ehret, 1989).

In sheep a facilitatory effect of estrogen on maternal behavior comes from the following evidence:

1. Acceptance of a lamb by non-parturient ewes occurs only when estrogen levels are high, i.e., at estrus and during the last ten days of pregnancy (Poindron and Le Neindre, 1980).
2. When lambing is induced by the injection of estradiol benzoate, maternal responsiveness fades more slowly (in mothers deprived of their neonate) than when lambing is induced by injecting dexamethasone (Poindron *et al.,* 1979).
3. The injection of high doses of estradiol 17β (free or as a benzoate) to nonpregnant, maternally experienced ewes induces maternal responses in a proportion of them (Le Neindre *et al.,* 1979; Poindron and Le Neindre, 1980; Poindron *et al.,* 1988).
4. The stimulatory effect of vaginocervical stimulation on the maternal responsiveness of nonpregnant ewes can only be evidenced in estrogen-treated or in estrogen plus progesterone–primed ewes (Kendrick and Keverne, 1991; Keverne *et al.,* 1983; Poindron *et al.,* 1986, 1988).

An alternative model attempting to simulate the hormonal changes that normally occur around parturition and to assess the impact of such changes on maternal behavior in rats was developed by Rosenblatt,

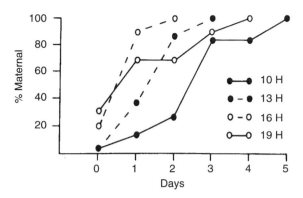

FIGURE 3 Cumulative percentage of pregnant female rats becoming maternal after daily exposure to foster pups, in relation to the day of pregnancy in which hysterectomy (H) was performed. (From Rosenblatt *et al.* (1979), with permission from Academic Press).

based on an earlier finding of Wiesner and Sheard (1933). It consists of terminating pregnancy a few days before parturition by removing the uterus, fetuses, and placentas (hysterectomy) or only the last two (Cesarean section). Both procedures provoke a rise in estradiol and an onset of maternal behavior with latencies that vary from 24–48 hours to 3–4 days (Rosenblatt and Siegel, 1975; Siegel and Rosenblatt, 1975a,c). The shortest latencies are observed in females hysterectomized close to term (i.e., on pregnancy days 16 or 19; Fig. 3). The crucial role of estrogen in this rapid facilitation of maternal behavior is evident from the observation that ovariectomy performed along with hysterectomy significantly delays the onset of this effect. Moreover, the injection of estradiol to such ovariectomized-hysterectomized rats reduces the latency to show maternal behavior to values similar to those observed in hysterectomized only rats (Rosenblatt *et al.,* 1979). Together, these findings indicate that, in rats, the rise in estrogen that normally occurs before parturition exerts a crucial facilitatory influence on the display of maternal behavior. In contrast, hamsters do not respond maternally following hysterectomy or estrogen treatment (Siegel and Rosenblatt 1980; Siegel *et al.,* 1983) and gerbils show a deficient maternal behavior after hysterectomy (accompanied or not by ovariectomy) (Wallace, 1973).

In rabbits, the group of Zarrow and Denenberg found that ovariectomy in midpregnancy (days 15–17), but

TABLE 1
Hormonal Concentrations[a] during Pregnancy in Mammals

Species	Estradiol (E) Pg/ml	days	Progesterone (P) ng/ml	days	Testosterone (T) pg/ml	days	Prolactin (PRL) ng/ml	days	Pregnancy length	References
Rat	130	5	90	5			7	5	22 days	Shaikh, 1971; E;
	120	11	76	11			0	11		Pepe and Rotchild, 1974; P;
	450	21	60	21			28	22		Morishige et al., 1973; PRL
	600	Parturition	0	Parturition			100	Parturition		
Hamster	41	4	29	4			31	4	16 days	Baranczuk and Greenwald, 1974; E, P;
	52	8	29	8			26	8		Bast and Greenwald, 1974; PRL
	52	12	14	12			33	12		
	19	16	17	16			56	14		
							27	16		
Mouse	17	0	10	0	10	0			19–20 days	Murr et al., 1974b; P;
	20, 25	4	40, 1	2	15	4				Barkley et al., 1979; E, P, T;
	24, 13	10	35, 27	10	42	10				McCormack and Greenwald, 1974; E, P;
	45, 29	15	112, 34	15	45	15				Murr et al., 1974a; PRL
	64, 43	17	0, 1	20	12	Parturition				
	60	20	0	Parturition						
	40	Parturition								
Guinea pig	3[b]	20	100	20					65 days	Challis et al., 1971b; E, P
	14[b]	40	300	40						
	30[b]	60	200	60						
Goat	12	Prepartum 3	8	112			4	1	148 days	Irving et al., 1972; P;
	31	Parturition	4	Prepartum 4			15	43		Buttle et al., 1972; PRL;
			1	Parturition			1	127		Currie et al., 1988; E, PRL
							40	Prepartum 3		
							160	Prepartum 1		
							150	Parturition		
Sheep	20	Prepartum 5	12	Prepartum 5			0	Prepartum 4	150 days	Chamley et al., 1973; E, P, PRL
	25	Prepartum 1	6	Prepartum 1			180	Prepartum 1		
	145	Parturition	2	Parturition			170	Parturition		
Pig	25	80	13	40					116 days	Roberston and King, 1974; E, P;
	200	100	10	80						Ash and Heap, 1975; E, P
	3[b]	Prepartum 5	8	Prepartum 5						
	350	Prepartum 1	4	Prepartum 1						
	400, 0–1[b]	Parturition	0	Parturition						

228

Species							Gestation	Reference
Cat	25	20	38	20			65 days	Verhage et al., 1976
	4	40	23	40				
	10	60	12	60				
	20	Prepartum 1	9	Prepartum 1				
Dog	105	7	31, 30	7, 6–10	3	7	65 days	Gräf, 1978; E, P, PRL; Smith and McDonald, 1974; P
	79	14	50	14	18	42		
	63	28	50, 45	21, 21–25	22	56		
	75	63	5	Prepartum 5	30	Parturition		
			10	Parturition				
Puma	500	5	60	5			95 days	Bonney et al., 1981
	63	30	275	30				
	50	60	135	60				
	115	90	5	90				
	71	Parturition	5	Parturition				
Rabbit	55	10	7	10	250	10	30 days	González-Mariscal et al., 1994; E, P, T; González-Mariscal et al., 2000; PRL; McNeilly and Friessen, 1978; PRL
	61	25	6	25	250	25		
	75	30	3	30	300	30		
		Parturition	0	Parturition				
Rhesus monkey	550	Prepartum 20	2	Prepartum 20	15	Prepartum 20	180 days	Weiss et al., 1976
	510	Prepartum 15	3	Prepartum 15	20	Prepartum 15		
	400	Prepartum 10	3	Prepartum 10	35	Prepartum 10		
	695	Prepartum 1	4	Prepartum 1	80	Prepartum 1		
Chimpanzee	0.05[e]	40	30	40	17	40	200–240 days	Reyes et al., 1973
	0.1[e]	120	25	120	20	120		
	0.5[e]	200	60	200	20–100	Parturition		
Marmoset	90[c]	Prepartum 105	32[d]	Prepartum 105			140 days	Fite and French, 2000
	190[c]	Prepartum 70	30[d]	Prepartum 70				
	75[c]	Prepartum 7	8[d]	Prepartum 7				
Gorilla	1[c]	127					255 days	Czekala et al., 1983
	2[c]	204						
	4[c]	255						
Orangutan	4[c]	129					258 days	Czekala et al., 1983
	7[c]	206						
	12[c]	258						

[a] In plasma or serum, unless otherwise indicated.
[b] Total unconjugated estrogen.
[c] As μg/mg creatinine, determined in urine.
[d] As μg pregnanediol glucuronide/mg creatinine, determined in urine.
[e] pg/dl.

not earlier, led to maternal nest-building in 56–100% of cases (Zarrow et al., 1962a) and that Cesarean section, performed between pregnancy days 20–22, provoked nest-building in 59–97% of rabbits (Zarrow et al., 1961). These findings indicate that in rabbits the hormonal changes taking place in late pregnancy and close to parturition facilitate maternal nest-building. In primates, parental behavior depends mainly on ecological, sensory, experiential, and social factors (Benedek, 1970; Coe, 1990; Holman and Goy, 1995; Keverne, 1995; Maestripieri, 1994a,b,c), although the hormonal changes taking place close to parturition may promote maternal responsiveness in inexperienced females (Holman and Goy, 1980, 1995). This is consistent with the frequent occurrence of alloparental care in primates (MacKenna, 1981; Snowdon, 1990; Swartz and Rosenblum, 1981; see Section IIA). Yet new evidence indicates that estrogen does facilitate maternal responsiveness in this mammalian order. Thus, in red-bellied tamarins Pryce et al. (1988, 1995) found a correlation between estradiol blood levels and maternal "motivation": The frequency of bar-pressing to access an infant peaked in the last 10 days of pregnancy, under high levels of such hormone. Thereafter, bar-pressing frequency remained high despite the prepartum decline of progesterone and postpartum decline of estradiol. A similar increase in bar-pressing frequency was induced by the combined administration of estradiol and progesterone (17–20 days) followed by progesterone withdrawal. Evidence for a role of sexual steroids in the facilitation of maternal behavior has also been found in pigtail (Maestripieri and Wallen, 1995) and rhesus (Maestripieri and Zehr, 1998) macaques: (a) maternal interest is highest at the end of pregnancy, associated with an increase in the estrogen/progesterone ratio; (b) infant handling increases in ovariectomized females given estradiol implants. In humans, the pattern of change in the estradiol-progesterone ratio over pregnancy has been related to postpartum attachment feelings (Fleming et al., 1997a). As a whole, these studies are consistent with the idea that endocrine secretions present during pregnancy and parturition promote maternal behavior in primates.

As noted earlier, in practically all mammals studied a dramatic reduction in the concentration of progesterone in blood occurs before parturition. In rats, progesterone levels drop from about 100 ng/ml to around 10 ng/ml between 24 and 48 hours before females initiate maternal behavior (Bridges, 1978). The way in which progesterone participates in regulating maternal behavior has been studied in relation to its interaction with estrogen. Indeed, except for hamsters, the decline in progesterone concentration usually occurs in association with an increase in estrogen plasma levels. Is the decline in progesterone a necessary precondition for the facilitatory effect of estrogen to become evident? In rats, the injection of progesterone on pregnancy day 21 prevents the expression of maternal behavior in 50% of Cesarean-delivered primiparous mothers (Moltz et al., 1969), and the facilitation of this behavior, normally provoked by the injection of estrogen to virgin rats hysterectomized or ovariectomized during late pregnancy, does not occur if progesterone levels are kept high (Bridges and Feder, 1978; Bridges et al., 1978; Numan, 1978; Siegel and Rosenblatt, 1978). If progesterone is given 44 hours after estradiol, the inhibitory effect of progesterone is no longer manifest (Siegel and Rosenblatt, 1975d), thereby suggesting that the antagonistic effect of this hormone occurs only when it is given before estrogen has completed its action. These results, however, do not rule out the possibility that a preexposure to progesterone may in fact facilitate the stimulatory action of estrogen on maternal behavior. Indeed, the administration of progesterone for several days, followed by its removal, decreases the dose of estradiol necessary to stimulate maternal behavior in virgins and reduces the latency for this effect to occur (Bridges and Russell, 1981; Doerr et al., 1981). Moreover, the longer time virgin rats are exposed to a treatment of progesterone (injection followed by withdrawal) and estrogen, the shorter their latencies are to initiate maternal behavior (Bridges, 1984) (Fig. 4). Furthermore, the latencies of females to respond to pups following hysterectomy are smaller as this procedure is performed later in gestation (Bridges et al., 1977; Rosenblatt and Siegel, 1975). In hamsters, the drop in progesterone preceding parturition seems to facilitate maternal responsiveness because retrieving and crouching over foster young are displayed by females only a few hours before delivery (Siegel and Greenwald, 1975).

In rabbits, an inhibitory action of progesterone is also evident because injections of this hormone across

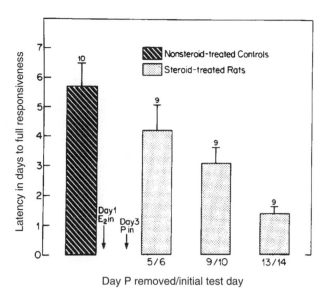

FIGURE 4 Latency to display full maternal behavior in ovariectomized nulliparous rats implanted with estradiol (E₂) and progesterone (P) capsules in relation to the duration of the P treatment. Capsules filled with P were inserted on day 3 (i.e., two days after E₂)and removed on days 5, 9, or 13. Testing for maternal behavior was initiated on the day following P removal. [From Bridges, R. S. *et al.* (1984). *Endocrinology* **114**, 930–940, © The Endocrine Society.]

pregnancy days 28 to 35 inhibit maternal nest-building and delay parturition (Zarrow *et al.*, 1961). The possibility that long-term exposure to progesterone may facilitate maternal responsiveness to pups has not been explored in this species, but a decline in progesterone is a necessary precondition for nest-building to occur in both pregnant and ovariectomized steroid-treated does (González-Mariscal *et al.*, 1994, 1996b; Zarrow *et al.*, 1963).

In sheep, progesterone is not required for the occurrence of maternal behavior in a naturally occurring reproductive cycle. Moreover, it does not seem to be associated with the *absence* of maternal behavior either: Maternal interest for neonates is still observed when progesterone levels are high (Alexander, 1960; Poindron and Le Neindre, 1980). On the contrary, a slight facilitatory (although not statistically significant) effect is observed in nonpregnant females injected with pharmacological doses of progesterone (Poindron and Le Neindre, 1980). In addition, a 14-day treatment with medroxyprogesterone acetate (a synthetic progestin) prior to the injection of estrogen

improves the response induced by vaginocervical stimulation in nonpregnant ewes (Kendrick and Keverne, 1991).

2. Androgens

The role of androgens in maternal behavior has received surprisingly little attention, even though significant levels of testosterone are observed in serum across pregnancy and lactation in rabbits (González-Mariscal *et al.*, 1994), mice (Barkley *et al.*, 1977, 1979), gerbils (Clark *et al.*, 1991, 1993), and primates (Kilinga *et al.*, 1978; Meulenberg and Hofman, 1991; Resko, 1970). In rabbits, the combined injection of 5-alpha-dihydrotestosterone (derived from the reduction of testosterone in carbon 5) plus progesterone, followed by withdrawal of this hormone and continuation of androgen injections, stimulates one aspect of maternal nest-building: hair-loosening, which allows the female to pluck her body hair and thus complete the maternal nest (Jiménez *et al.*, 2000).

The role of androgens in paternal behavior has been investigated mainly in rodents. In voles the display of this activity correlates with changes in androgen and vasopressin (Wang and De Vries, 1993; Wang *et al.*, 1994; see below), whereas in rats the frequency in paternal behavior of males housed with pups for 22 days is positively correlated with high plasma levels of testosterone (Brown and Moger, 1983). In hamsters, a relationship has been found between the display of paternal behavior, high plasma concentrations of prolactin, and low levels of testosterone in the paternal *Phodopus campbelli* but not in the nonpaternal *P. sungorus* (Reburn and Wynne-Edwards, 1999). In the former species, testosterone increased as parturition approached, consistent with the male's behavior of guarding its mate, and decreased following delivery, consistent with a reduction in the aggression of the male toward the pups.

In primates, contact with the young does not modify plasma concentrations of testosterone in marmosets (Dixson and George, 1982), but in male Japanese monkeys androgen levels are lowest when females give birth (Alexander, 1970). In humans, there is a tendency for testosterone levels to be positively correlated with active maternal behaviors in new mothers, possibly associated with the significant correlation between cortisol and behavior (Fleming *et al.*, 1987, 1997a,c).

In fathers, however, the relation appears to be inverse (Fleming *et al.*, 1997b, cited in Maestripieri, 1999).

3. Prolactin and Other Lactogens

Table 1 shows the concentration of prolactin (PRL) in blood across gestation and the peripartum period in several mammalian species. A clear rise in prolactin levels occurs close to parturition, largely as a consequence of the decrease in progesterone and increase in estrogen plasma concentrations that occur at this time (Ben-Jonathan *et al.*, 1989; Neill and Nagy, 1994). A notable exception is the hamster, which shows the highest prolactin levels in early pregnancy and maintains medium levels of this hormone from late gestation into lactation (Bast and Greenwald, 1974). Aside from prolactin (of pituitary origin), other lactogens (of placental origin) have been detected in rats (Soares *et al.*, 1998; Tonkowicz and Voogt, 1983; Voogt *et al.*, 1982), mice (Murr *et al.*, 1974a; Soares and Talamantes, 1982; Soares *et al.*, 1998), hamsters (Bast and Greenwald, 1974), sheep (Talamantes, 1975; Talamantes *et al.*, 1980), and rabbits (Grundker *et al.*, 1993). This temporal coincidence between high levels of prolactin (or placental lactogen) in blood and the expression of maternal behavior prompted the investigation of the role of this hormone in several aspects of maternal care.

The first report of a prolactin effect on maternal behavior was that of Riddle *et al.* (1935). Later studies assessed the influence of prolactin on maternal behavior by injecting this hormone together with sexual steroids or by giving ergot derivates (e.g., ergocryptine, bromocryptine, apomorphine) that prevent prolactin release by stimulating dopamine receptors (Martin and Bateson, 1982; Meltzer *et al.*, 1982a,b). Although a slight facilitatory effect of prolactin was found in the presence of estradiol (Moltz *et al.*, 1970), ergot drugs did not antagonize the expression of maternal behavior normally observed with a short latency in ovariectomized, estrogen-treated virgins daily exposed to pups (Numan *et al.*, 1972; Rodriguez-Sierra and Rosenblatt, 1977). Moreover, the behavior of lactating rats was not modified by injections of ergocryptine (Stern, 1977), and the implantation of pituitaries into ovariectomized virgins did not induce maternal behavior (Baum, 1978). By using a different experimental model, Bridges has obtained evidence to support a facilitatory role of prolactin in rat maternal behavior. His findings can be summarized as follows (Fig. 5). The stimulation of

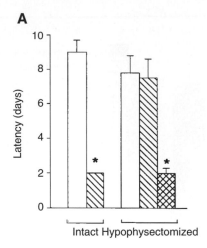

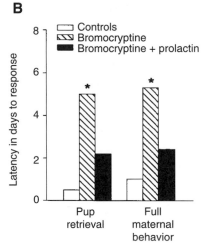

FIGURE 5   (A) Effect of hypophysectomy on the latency to display maternal behavior in ovariectomized nulliparous rats given progesterone and estrogen (dashed bars) or vehicle (open bars). Implantation of pituitary grafts to hypophysectomized females (cross-hatched bar) reduces the latency to become maternal following steroid treatment. *$p < 0.01$ [Reprinted with permission from Bridges, R. S. *et al.* (1985). *Science* **227**, 782–784, Copyright 1985 American Association for the Advancement of Science.] (B) Bromocryptine increases the latency to show maternal responsiveness in ovariectomized nulliparous rats given progesterone and estrogen (dashed bars). Ovine prolactin injected along with bromocryptine reverses such inhibitory effect (black bars). Control group (open bars) received vehicle instead of steroids. *$p < 0.01$ [Modified from Bridges, R. S. *et al.* (1990). *Endocrinology* **126**, 837–848, © The Endocrine Society.]

maternal behavior provoked by injecting virgins with progesterone followed by estrogen is abolished by hypophysectomy (Bridges *et al.*, 1985). This effect is counteracted by grafting donor pituitaries or by injecting ovine prolactin for several days (Bridges *et al.*, 1985;

Loundes and Bridges, 1986). In ovariectomized virgins the implantation of progesterone capsules for several days, followed by the insertion of estradiol-filled capsules and removal of progesterone, provokes a release of prolactin and the expression of maternal behavior. The injection of bromocryptine to such females prevents both effects and the concurrent injection of ovine prolactin restores them (Bridges and Ronsheim, 1990). Maternal behavior can be induced in ovariectomized hypophysectomized, steroid-treated virgins by injecting growth hormone (Bridges and Millard, 1988), a member of the lactogenic hormone family.

It must be noted, however, that the conditions under which a stimulatory effect of prolactin on rat maternal behavior has been found (i.e., ovariectomized virgins given progesterone and then estrogen) are different from those in which prolactin release blockers have had no effect on maternal behavior (i.e., estrogen-primed virgins and lactating mothers). One explanation for these apparently contradictory results is that prolactin exerts a priming (rather than a triggering) action on maternal care, so antagonizing its release once the behavior is initiated has no effect. Support for this possibility has recently been found in rabbits (see below). Moreover, Orpen *et al.* (1987), when investigating the factors that maintain postpartum responsiveness in rats in the absence of pups, found that prolactin (but not estrogen) allowed the expression of nest-building and retrieving up to postpartum day 7, although females could not be considered fully maternal. Regarding males, the frequency of paternal behavior in sires housed with pups for 22 days is positively correlated with increased plasma levels of prolactin (Brown and Moger, 1983).

In mice, prolactin has been shown to facilitate maternal responsiveness in two experimental paradigms: (a) "bar-pressing for pups," a model presumably assessing maternal motivation, is more frequent in prolactin-treated mice (Hauser and Gandelman, 1985); (b) retrieving and crouching over foster pups is more rapid and intense in prolactin-treated virgins (Voci and Carlson, 1973). In contrast, in this species prolactin is apparently unrelated with the stimulation of maternal aggression, although this behavior can be very intense during lactation (Gandelman, 1980; Noirot *et al.,* 1975; Svare and Gandelman, 1973). Thus, no association was found between circulating levels of prolactin,

and the intensity of maternal aggression and the injection of bromocryptine reduced prolactin concentration but did not modify maternal aggression (Broida *et al.,* 1981). Moreover, maternal aggression was not prevented by performing a hypophysectomy on lactation day 9 (Mann *et al.,* 1980; Svare *et al.,* 1982). In *Peromyscus californicus* mice, higher levels of plasma prolactin are found in males acting paternally than in virgin ones or in those living with pregnant females (Gubernick and Nelson, 1989). In hamsters, prolactin may facilitate nest-building, promote maternal aggression, and reduce infanticide because bromocryptine injections reduce the two first activities and promote the last one (McCarthy *et al.,* 1994; Wise and Pryor, 1977).

In rabbits, the following evidence supports a role of prolactin in maternal nest-building: A rise in estrogen levels provoked earlier than normal by injecting estradiol across pregnancy days 20–22, and presumably eliciting an earlier release of prolactin, advances nest-building by 4–5 days (Zarrow *et al.,* 1963). Injections of bromocryptine from pregnancy day 26 until parturition reduce the incidence of nest-building (Anderson *et al.,* 1971; González-Mariscal *et al.,* 2000; Zarrow *et al.,* 1971a). Hypophysectomy (Anderson *et al.,* 1971; Zarrow *et al.,* 1971a) or injections of bromocryptine (González-Mariscal *et al.,* 1996b) prevent the stimulatory effect of estradiol and progesterone on nest-building in ovariectomized does. Stimulation of maternal nest-building provoked in ovariectomized does by the combined injection of estrogen and progesterone, followed by progesterone withdrawal, correlates with the release of prolactin in plasma (González-Mariscal *et al.,* 1996b).

To investigate whether prolactin, released before parturition and across lactation, had any role in the behavior of mother rabbits toward their pups, bromocryptine was injected either across the first week of lactation, from pregnancy day 26 until parturition (which occurred on pregnancy days 30–31), or from pregnancy day 26 to postpartum day 7 (González-Mariscal *et al.,* 2000). Though the first treatment had practically no impact on maternal responsiveness, a clear reduction in this behavior was observed with the last two (Fig. 6). These results indicate that together with the decline in progesterone and rise in estrogen, the rise in prolactin normally occurring close to parturition promotes maternal behavior in rabbits.

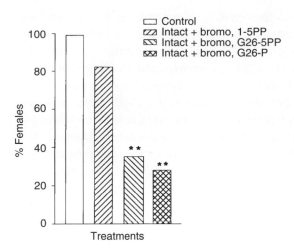

FIGURE 6 Percentage of intact primiparous rabbits that entered the nest box and crouched over the litter on postpartum day 3 following treatment with bromocryptine (bromo) across postpartum days 1–5 (1-5PP), from gestation day 26 to postpartum day 5 (G26-5PP), or from gestation day 26 to Parturition (G26-P). [Modified from González-Mariscal *et al.* (2000), with permission from Blackwell Science Ltd.]

In sheep, the facilitation of maternal behavior provoked by estrogen injections is not mediated by the release of prolactin because the injection of bromocryptine, though effective in antagonizing prolactin release, does not interfere with the lengthening of the sensitive period induced by estradiol treatment (Poindron *et al.,* 1980b). Moreover, daily injections of bromocryptine for a week during the first month postpartum do not provoke major changes in nursing behavior (Poindron and Le Neindre, 1980). Even if bromocryptine injections are initiated before parturition and continued into lactation, no clear-cut effects on maternal responsiveness at parturition or during spontaneous nursing have been observed, except for an increase in nursing frequency, which is likely due to a decreased milk production (Louault, 1983; P. Poindron, unpublished). Finally, icv administration of PRL does not induce maternal behavior in non pregnant ewes (Lévy *et al.,* 1996).

In sows a facilitatory action of PRL on nest-building is uncertain because in preparturient sows prolactin release is associated with both prostaglandin F (PGF) α-induced and spontaneous nest-building, although it is not clear to what an extent this effect is a direct consequence of PGF2α action (Widowski *et al.,* 1990). Yet bromocryptine injections to pseudopregnant gilts do not significantly decrease PGF2α-induced nest-building (Boulton *et al.,* 1998).

In wolves it has been suggested that the increase in prolactin observed during spring in males and females, coinciding with the birth of their pups, may stimulate parental behavior in both sexes (Asa, 1997). In primates, contact with the young increases urinary prolactin levels in marmosets (Dixson and George, 1982), and in cotton-top tamarins (*Saguinus oedipus*), which show extensive paternal care, experienced fathers show higher levels of prolactin and lower levels of cortisol than other males (Ziegler, 2000; Ziegler *et al.,* 1996; but see also Ziegler *et al.,* 2000).

4. Oxytocin

In all mammals studied, oxytocin concentration increases in plasma during parturition, especially during the actual phase of expulsion (Ferguson reflex: Chard, 1972; Garfield *et al.,* 1998). In rabbits, this increase is seen shortly before delivery, and if such prepartum release of oxytocin does not occur, abnormal parturitions are observed (Fuchs and Dawood, 1980). A possible role of oxytocin in the facilitation of maternal behavior was first proposed in the goat by Klopfer (1971). However, because oxytocin does not easily cross the blood-brain barrier in eutherian species (Kendrick *et al.,* 1986; Mens *et al.,* 1983; Zaidi and Heller, 1974), its action on maternal behavior is generally considered to be due to intracerebral release of this peptide provoked by natural (at parturition) or artificial vaginocervical stimulation (see Section III.B). Yet in wild mice, the peripheral injection of oxytocin reduces infanticide and promotes maternal behavior (McCarthy *et al.,* 1986). Due to its uterotonic properties, peripherally injected oxytocin may exert some of its effects by the proprioceptive cues generated from uterine contractions. Alternatively, peripherally injected oxytocin may promote maternal behavior by stimulating the synthesis and release of prostaglandins. Indeed, in the Tasmanian bettong (*Bettongia gaimardi,* an Australian marsupial), the injection of a prostaglandin synthesis inhibitor blocks the expression of birth behavior induced in males and females by oxytocin injection (Rose and MacFayden, 1997). By contrast, in the short-tailed opossum (*Monodelphis domestica,* an american marsupial), oxytocin-induced birth behavior in females appears to be independent of prostaglandins (Rose and Fadem, 2000).

The intracerebroventricular (icv) injection of oxytocin can, under some conditions, stimulate maternal behavior in estrogen-primed rats (Pedersen and Prange 1979; Pedersen *et al.*, 1982). Though later studies, performed under different testing conditions and using other strains of rats, were unable to replicate the above findings (Bolwerk and Swanson, 1984; Fahrbach *et al.*, 1986; Rubin *et al.*, 1983; see also Rosenblatt *et al.*, 1988), there is now good evidence for a stimulatory role of oxytocin in the initiation of maternal behavior in rats:

1. The icv injection of an oxytocin antagonist or antiserum reduces the proportion of females showing maternal behavior following hysterectomy plus ovariectomy on pregnancy day 16 (Fahrbach *et al.*, 1985a,b).
2. Oxytocin antiserum reduces the facilitation of maternal behavior normally provoked by estrogen-progesterone treatments in ovariectomized virgins (Pedersen *et al.*, 1985).
3. Administration of an oxytocin antagonist at parturition increases the latency to pup retrieval by one hour but maternal behavior is expressed normally on the following day (Van Leengoed *et al.*, 1987).
4. An oxytocin antagonist given to lactating females has no effect on ongoing maternal behavior (Fahrbach *et al.*, 1985a,b), thereby suggesting that the stimulatory effect of oxytocin in rats is on the initiation rather than on the maintenance of this behavior. A rapid facilitatory action of icv oxytocin administration on maternal behavior is also well documented in the ewe (Kendrick *et al.*, 1987; Lévy *et al.*, 1992).

5. *Vaginocervical Stimulation*

The importance of vaginocervical stimulation (VCS) for the activation of maternal behavior has been most extensively studied in sheep. The induction of maternal behavior in nonpregnant animals is achieved with some success only by using pharmacological doses of estradiol (Dwyer and Lawrence, 1997; Kendrick and Keverne, 1991; Kendrick *et al.*, 1992a; Le Neindre *et al.*, 1979; Poindron and Le Neindre, 1980). In addition, the type of behaviors induced, their latency and sequence

of appearance, are quite variable, thus suggesting that additional factors are required for the activation of a "normal" maternal behavior. Indeed, by applying artificial VCS for 5 minutes, 80% of nonpregnant multiparous females show maternal behavior within 30 minutes (Keverne *et al.*, 1983). This facilitatory effect of VCS is evident only in multiparous ewes, primed with ovarian steroids (Kendrick and Keverne, 1991; Poindron *et al.*, 1988). In parturient ewes expulsion of the second lamb enhances licking behavior toward any neonate (Poindron *et al.*, 1980a), as does additional vaginal stimulation applied one hour postpartum (Keverne *et al.*, 1983). Conversely, the suppression of the sensory information associated with labor (by applying peridural anesthesia or performing a Cesarean section) results in the failure of parturient mothers to display maternal behavior, especially if they are primiparous (Alexander *et al.*, 1988; Krehbiel *et al.*, 1987). Similar results are obtained in goats (Poindron *et al.*, 1998a,b), although the effects of peridural anesthesia are more variable, possibly due to interindividual variations of genital innervation in this species (Labussière, 1999). Although the nervous pathways that convey the transmission of sensory information from the vagina and uterus to the brain are not known in detail, it is well established that one way by which VCS facilitates maternal behavior in sheep is through the intracerebral release of oxytocin (see Section III.B).

In rats there is also evidence that the proprioceptive stimulation associated with the birth process is important to activate maternal behavior. Indeed, responsiveness to pups is evident already before parturition, being fully developed at about 3.5 hours prepartum (Mayer and Rosenblatt, 1984; Rosenblatt and Siegel, 1975; Rosenblatt *et al.*, 1979; Slotnick *et al.*, 1973), which corresponds to the beginning of labor. This responsiveness is difficult to explain only on the basis of action of estradiol because injections of this hormone stimulate maternal behavior in nonpregnant rats with a latency of 3 to 24 hours or more (Numan *et al.*, 1977; Siegel and Rosenblatt, 1975a–d). VCS applied to steroid primed multiparous nonpregnant females does induce an immediate onset of maternal behavior in a majority of females (Yeo and Keverne, 1986).

In primates there are indications that the birth process is important for the normal expression of maternal care. Cesarean delivery prevents acceptance of the neonate in socially deprived mothers (Meier, 1965). The magnitude of this effect can reach 95% of rejection ($n = 211$) in rhesus and cynomolgus monkeys (Lundblad and Hodgen, 1980). It is not clear, however, whether this is due only to the lack of VCS normally received at parturition, as these authors mention that swabbing the newborn with the mother's vaginal secretions allowed its acceptance within 12 to 24 hours after delivery. Interestingly, preliminary results in primates suggest that icv oxytocin application also stimulates positive infant-directed behaviors in nonpregnant female rhesus monkeys (Holman and Goy, 1995). However, Wagner *et al.* (1989) did not observe negative consequences of peridural anesthesia on initial mother-infant interaction in humans.

6. Opiates

The plasma concentration of beta-endorphin is elevated during parturition in rats (Petraglia *et al.*, 1985) and humans (Goland *et al.*, 1981), mainly as a consequence of secretion from the anterior pituitary. A possible role of opiates in maternal behavior has been studied through the peripheral administration of agonists and antagonists. In rats hysterectomized-ovariectomized on pregnancy day 17, daily morphine injections prevent the onset of maternal behavior normally observed at 2 hours following surgery (Bridges and Grimm, 1982), whereas concurrent injections of naloxone reverse such effect. Injection of opiates that bind to the mu-opiate receptor blocks maternal behavior in lactating females (Grimm and Bridges, 1983; Mann and Bridges, 1992; Mann *et al.*, 1991). However, naloxone (an opiate antagonist) injected in late pregnancy interferes with placentophagia and cleaning of pups, behaviors normally observed at parturition (Mayer *et al.*, 1985). In sheep the intravenous injection of naltrexone (another opiate antagonist) at parturition provokes effects similar to those reported in rats, for it delays the onset of maternal behavior in primiparous and multiparous ewes (Caba *et al.*, 1995). Icv injections of morphine facilitate the induction of maternal behavior in sheep, but only if accompanied by VCS (Keverne and Kendrick, 1991). Conversely, infusions of naltrexone block maternal behavior, though the magnitude of this disruptive effect is smaller than the one provoked by peridural anesthesia (Kendrick and Keverne, 1989; Krehbiel *et al.*, 1987). In monkeys, naltrexone reduces care-giving and

protective behavior toward the infant in group-living rhesus monkeys (Keverne, 1992, 1995; Martel *et al.*, 1993), a finding that agrees with the general hypothesis that the endogenous opiate system promotes "the positive affect arising from maternal behavior" (Dum and Herz, 1987; Keverne *et al.*, 1997; Panksepp, 1981).

7. Cholecystokinin

The peptide cholecystokin facilitates the rapid onset of maternal behavior when it is given systemically to ovariectomized estrogen-primed Wistar but not Sprague-Dawley rats (Lindén *et al.*, 1989; Mann *et al.*, 1995). Because cholecystokinin (CCK) stimulates the release of oxytocin and prolactin (Renaud *et al.*, 1987; Tanimoto *et al.*, 1987), it is possible that these peptides mediate the stimulatory action of CCK on maternal behavior. CCK may also modulate ongoing maternal behavior because systemic injections of a specific antagonist on lactation days 5–6 increased the latency to pup retrieval and decreased the incidence of crouching (Mann *et al.*, 1995), whereas icv CCK infusion blocks the disruptive effect of β-endorphin on these behaviors (Felicio *et al.*, 1991).

8. Prostaglandins

Prostaglandins play an important role in the cascade of events occurring at parturition by facilitating uterine contractility and expulsion of the fetus (Challis and Lye, 1994; Fredriksson, 1985; Karim, 1972; Liggins *et al.*, 1972; Thorburn and Challis, 1979). They can also be released during vaginal stimulation and in response to oxytocin secretion (Flint *et al.*, 1974, 1975). In rats, early onset of maternal behavior can be provoked by inducing a premature parturition through the injection of prostaglandin F2-α, which is normally secreted by the uterus at term (Strauss *et al.*, 1975). When this agent was injected on pregnancy days 16 or 19, parturition occurred approximately 30 hours later, and maternal behavior was expressed shortly thereafter (Rodriguez-Sierra and Rosenblatt, 1982). In rabbits, the injection of a synthetic analogue of prostaglandin F2-α on pregnancy day 29 advanced parturition and did not modify the proportion of young surviving to weaning, thus indicating that maternal behavior was normal (Ubilla and Rodríguez, 1989). In pigs, Blackshaw and Smith (1982) first reported the facilitation of maternal nest-building in nonpregnant sows following the injection of prostaglandin F2-α. In pregnant (Diehl *et al.*, 1974; Wetteman *et al.*, 1977; Widowski and Curtis, 1989; Widowski *et al.*, 1990) and pseudopregnant (Boulton *et al.*, 1997a,b) sows, prostaglandin F2-α induces the sequential expression of rooting the ground, ripping nest material (e.g., grass), carrying it into a hole, and "shaping" the nest by lying down and pushing the body against the carried material, as described in free ranging animals (Jensen, 1989). These effects occur with a short latency (around 15 minutes) and are not a consequence of the luteolytic action of prostaglandin F2-α because nest-building is still observed in ovario-hysterectomized pseudopregnant sows (Burne *et al.*, 2000). In contrast, injections of this agent to pseudopregnant sows do not seem to promote maternal responsiveness to piglets (Gilbert *et al.*, 2000). In marsupials, the injection of prostaglandin F2-α has been shown to induce a typical "birth behavior" in female, adult, nonpregnant tammar wallabies (*Macropus eugenii;* Hinds *et al.*, 1990), brushtail possums (*Trichosurus vulpecula;* Gemmel *et al.*, 1991), bettongs (*Bettongia gaimardi;* Rose and MacFayden, 1997), and gray short-tailed possums (*Monodelphis domestica,* american marsupial; Rose and Fadem, 2000), and this applies also to males. It occurs with a short latency (5–7 min) following prostaglandin F2-α injection and consists of adopting a crouched posture with the hips flexed and the tail placed between the legs (Russell, 1973). It is accompanied by grooming and licking of the urogenital sinus up to the opening of the pouch and cleaning the inside of this structure. It has been proposed that, because prostaglandin F2-α also induces contraction of the pouch, the release of this agent prior to parturition, in a marsupial that is already holding a large young in the pouch, synchronizes pouch vacation with the birth of the new young (Rose and MacFayden, 1997).

B. Neural Control

The investigation of the brain structures, fiber pathways, and neurotransmitters-neuromodulators involved in regulating the expression of the many behavioral patterns characteristic of parental care has involved the use of diverse experimental strategies. By far, most of this work has been done in rats, but recently other nonrodent species (e.g., rabbits, voles, sheep) have

begun to be investigated in this regard. As will be described in detail below, brain lesions to obliterate in the mother the perception of specific cues (olfactory, visual, auditory, tactile) from the young were performed to assess the role of the different senses on the display of maternal behavior. Later on, more refined methods (e.g., chemical lesions, deafferentation of individual brain regions, icv infusion and implantation of hormones, localization of receptors and neuroactive agents in specific brain areas, electrical stimulation of fiber pathways) have provided detailed information on how a complex network of nuclei and tracts may be activated by hormones and organized to coordinate the perception of stimuli from the young with the expression of the appropriate behavioral patterns. Finally, the "active" parental brain has been sampled by the use of methods (e.g., microdyalisis, immunostaining of the c-fos and fos-B proteins, uptake of 2-deoxy-glucose) that allow the detection of ongoing brain activity.

1. Cortex, Trigeminal Complex, and Olfactory Circuit

The first study that began investigating the neural control of maternal behavior was performed by Beach (1937), who found that by destroying more than 40% of the neocortex this behavior was abolished in rats. Subsequent work confirmed these findings (Davis, 1939; Slotnick, 1967; Stamm, 1955; Stone, 1938; Wilsoncroft, 1963). Beach and Jaynes (1956c) determined that no single sensory modality is essential for the performance of retrieving behavior in postpartum rats, i.e., they proposed that this behavior is under multisensorial control because the elimination of either vision, olfaction, or tactile sensitivity of the snout and perioral region did not interfere with the retrieval of pups. Later work (Benuck and Rowe, 1975; Herrenkohl and Rosenberg, 1972; Herrenkohl and Sachs, 1972) has confirmed the lack of effect of anosmia, blindness, and deafness of lactating rats on maternal behavior. More recent studies in which the perioral region was desensitized by either injecting a local anesthetic into the mystacial pads or by sectioning the infraorbital branch of the trigeminal nerve have found that these procedures do interfere with pup retrieval (Kenyon *et al.*, 1981, 1983; Stern and Kolunie, 1989). The discrepancy between these results and those of Beach and Jaynes (1956c) may have been due to the fact that these authors allowed several weeks between the performance of snout desensitization and testing for maternal behavior, a period during which reinnervation of the perioral region may have occurred.

In hamsters, the total removal of the neocortex does not eliminate maternal behavior, but when this procedure is accompanied by lesions of the cingulate cortex and the underlying hippocampus, maternal behavior is abolished (Murphy *et al.*, 1981). In primates, lesions to either the prefrontal cortex or the anterior temporal cortex (performed at around two months postpartum) severely disrupt the mother's active search for her young and provoke a loss of the protective retrieval of the infant faced with threatening situations (Bucher, 1970; Franzen and Myers, 1973; Myers *et al.*, 1973).

Removing the main olfactory bulbs (Fleming and Rosenblatt, 1974a; Pollack and Sachs, 1975; Schlein *et al.*, 1972) or destroying the olfactory epithelium with a $ZnSO_4$ spray (Benuck and Rowe, 1975) during pregnancy provokes very minor alterations in the maternal behavior of rats. In contrast, when anosmia is performed in virgin rats (by severing the lateral olfactory tract or by spraying $ZnSO_4$ on the nasal epithelium), the latency to display maternal behavior by continued exposure to pups is markedly reduced (Fleming and Rosenblatt, 1974b; Mayer and Rosenblatt, 1977). It is interesting that $ZnSO_4$ application does not produce anosmia in all cases; yet it consistently facilitates maternal behavior in virgin rats (Mayer and Rosenblatt, 1975). The combined lesion of the main plus the accessory olfactory system produces a greater facilitation of maternal behavior than the lesion of either one alone (Fleming *et al.*, 1979).

In rabbits, removal of the accessory olfactory bulbs before mating does not modify fertility or the expression of maternal behavior in rabbits (Chirino *et al.*, 1999). In virgins, this procedure provokes a dramatic facilitation of maternal behavior: Although intact females are absolutely indifferent to foster young, even after two weeks of daily exposure to them, lesioned animals enter the nest box and adopt a "nursing" posture over foster young after a few days of exposure (Chirino *et al.*, 2000). In contrast, destroying the olfactory epithelium with $ZnSO_4$ in virgin rabbits provokes anosmia but does not facilitate maternal behavior: On the contrary, 50% of anosmic females show cannibalism (Chirino *et al.*, 2001). In multiparous mice, olfactory bulbectomy

performed during pregnancy eliminates nest-building and maternal behavior (Gandelman *et al.*, 1971a, 1972; Zarrow *et al.*, 1971b) and spraying $ZnSO_4$ into the olfactory epithelium in late pregnancy provokes a high incidence of cannibalism in primiparous, though not in multiparous, mice (Seegal and Denenberg, 1974). Olfactory bulbectomy eliminates maternal behavior in virgin mice, which are spontaneously maternal upon their first exposure to pups (Gandelman *et al.*, 1971a,b, 1972; Zarrow *et al.*, 1971b). In hamsters, olfactory bulbectomy performed neonatally (day 10) provokes cannibalism in 30% of adult females (Leonard, 1972), but vomeronasal deafferentation promotes maternal behavior (Marques, 1979). In sheep and goats, olfactory bulbectomy or $ZnSO_4$-induced anosmia during pregnancy do not disrupt maternal behavior but prevent mothers from recognizing their own young (for sheep: Baldwin and Shillito, 1974; Bouissou, 1968; Morgan *et al.*, 1975; Poindron, 1976a,b); for goats: (Klopfer and Gamble, 1966; Klopfer and Klopfer, 1968; Romeyer *et al.*, 1994b). In contrast, vomeronasal denervation does not appear to affect maternal behavior or selectivity (Lévy *et al.*, 1995b), although this finding has been recently challenged (Booth and Katz, 2000).

However, the finding that anosmia does facilitate maternal behavior induced by the icv infusion of oxytocin in virgin rats (Wamboldt and Insel, 1987) or by VCS in nonpregnant sheep (Poindron *et al.*, 1988) suggests an interaction among VCS-induced release of oxytocin, olfactory function, and the facilitation of maternal behavior. Such a hypothesis is further supported by the following findings. In rats, electrical stimulation of the paraventricular nucleus of the hypothalamus (PVN) induces excitatory and inhibitory responses in mitral and granular cells of the olfactory bulb that depend on the release of oxytocin into the cerebrospinal fluid (Yu *et al.*, 1996a). Infusion of an oxytocin antagonist into the olfactory bulb delays the onset of maternal behavior at parturition (Yu *et al.*, 1996b). Infusion of oxytocin into virgins induces maternal responses within two hours in half the treated females (Yu *et al.*, 1996b). In sheep, oxytocin-immunoreactive terminals have been reported in the main olfactory bulb and the accessory olfactory nucleus (Broad *et al.*, 1993a). Oxytocin is released into the cerebrospinal fluid (CSF) and the main olfactory bulb at parturition and following VCS, together with dopamine and noradrenaline

(Kendrick *et al.,* 1988a,b). The release of oxytocin, no-radrenaline, and acetylcholine is lower in primiparous than in multiparous ewes (Kendrick *et al.,* 1988a,b). The magnitude of the release of noradrenaline and acetylcholine (but not of GABA) observed in the olfactory bulb following the local infusion of oxytocin is dependent on parity (Lévy *et al.,* 1993, 1995a).

Lesions of the amygdala (a structure that receives major input from the main and the accessory olfactory systems) do not disrupt maternal behavior in lactating mice (Slotnick and Nigrosh, 1975), and lesions to the stria terminalis (the major efferent pathway of the amygdala) have no effect on the maternal care of lactating rats (Numan, 1974). By contrast, lesions of the corticomedial amygdala (Fleming *et al.,* 1980; Numan *et al.,* 1993), bed nucleus of the accessory olfactory tract (BAOT) (Del Cerro *et al.,* 1991), or stria terminalis in virgin rats stimulate maternal behavior (Fleming *et al.,* 1980) whereas "kindling"-type electrical stimulation of the medial amygdala delays the onset of maternal responsiveness to foster pups in experienced mother rats (Morgan *et al.,* 1999).

2. Septum and Bed Nucleus of the Stria Terminalis

The septal area has been lesioned in mother rats (Fleischer and Slotnick, 1978; Terlecki and Sainsbury, 1978), mice (Carlson and Thomas, 1968; Slotnick and Nigrosh, 1975), and rabbits (Cruz and Beyer, 1972). In rodents, these lesions do not abolish maternal motivation but provoke a spatial disorganization of maternal behavior: Mothers pick up pups, carry them around, drop them at random (thus altering crouching and nursing), and they may also build several small nests where they retrieve young (Terlecki and Sainsbury, 1978). Excitotoxic amino acid lesions of the bed nucleus of the stria terminalis (BNST) disrupt retrieval behavior in postpartum rats (Numan, 1996). Rats lesioned in the septal region also show increased defensiveness, an alteration proposed to explain the disorganization of maternal behavior (Sheehan *et al.,* 2000). In contrast, the behavior of rabbits is severely altered in all its aspects following septal lesions: Mothers do not build nests and refuse to enter the nest box for nursing (Cruz and Beyer, 1972). In voles, two lines of evidence support the participation of vasopressin neurons in the lateral septum for promoting paternal behavior:

1. A similar number of vasopressin-immunoreactive fibers is observed in the lateral septum of fathers and sexually naive meadow voles (a species not showing paternal behavior), whereas a less dense plexus of such fibers is found in fathers than in virgin male prairie voles (a species showing extensive paternal behavior; Bamshad *et al.,* 1993; Oliveras and Novak, 1986).
2. Vasopressin injections into the lateral septum of sexually naive male prairie voles stimulate paternal behavior, an effect counteracted by the previous injection of an antagonist to the V1a receptor into the same brain region (Wang *et al.,* 1994). Yet no significant changes in V1a receptors are observed between prairie and montane voles under any reproductive condition in the lateral septum, BNST, the ventromedial hypothalamus, or the amygdala (Wang *et al.,* 2000).

Similar comparisons have been made in mice between a monogamous biparental species (*Peromyscus californicus*) and a promiscuous exclusively maternal one (*P. leucopus*). In this case males showing paternal care (*P. californicus*) showed more vasopressin-immunoreactive fibers in the bed nucleus of the stria terminalis (but not in the paraventricular hypothalamic and supraoptic nuclei) than *P. leucopus* (Bester-Meredith *et al.,* 1999). Moreover, *P. californicus* also showed more vasopressin V1a receptors (in septum, cortex, and diagonal band) than *P. leucopus* (Bester-Meredith *et al.,* 1999; Insel *et al.,* 1991). Because these results are opposite those found in voles (see above), the participation of vasopressin in the expression of paternal behavior in mammals is, on the one hand, supported and, on the other, complicated by the possibility that this hormone may act in different ways across mammalian genuses. Indeed, the distribution of the V1a receptor varies greatly, even among closely related species. In addition, the regulation of vasopressin receptors by gonadal steroids is not uniform either: In some mammals such hormones increase the expression of vasopressin (and oxytocin) receptors, whereas in others they exert the opposite effect or none (Young, 1999).

In rats, the following evidence supports an action of oxytocin on the BNST and septum for the facilitation of maternal behavior: (a) oxytocin binding sites increase during lactation in the BNST (Insel, 1986, 1990, 1992);

(b) the number of oxytocin binding sites in the BNST are modified by sex steroids (Kremarik *et al.*, 1991); (c) oxytocin release into the septum increases around parturition (Landgraf *et al.*, 1991).

3. Medial Preoptic Area and Its Connections

a) Studies Using Lesion and Deafferentation Techniques
Much evidence has accumulated to identify the medial preoptic area (MPOA) as a critical site for the expression of maternal behavior. Electrolytic or radiofrequency lesions of this region disrupt retrieving, nest-building, and nursing in lactating rats (Gray and Brooks, 1984; Jacobson *et al.*, 1980; Numan, 1974; Numan *et al.*, 1977; Fig. 7) and hamsters (Marques *et al.*, 1979; Miceli and Malsbury, 1982). A similar effect is provoked by injecting *N*-methyl-D-aspartate (NMDA), which selectively destroys cell bodies but spares fibers of passage, into the MPOA of lactating rats (Numan *et al.*, 1988). Moreover, virgin females (ovariectomized or intact) lesioned in the MPOA do not show maternal behavior despite many days of exposure to pups (Gray and Brooks, 1984; Miceli *et al.*, 1983; Numan

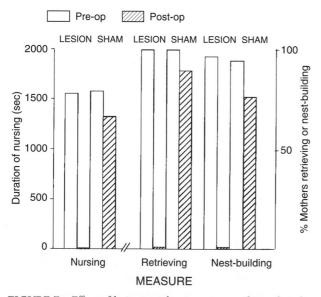

FIGURE 7   Effect of lesions or sham surgery performed in the medial preoptic area (MPOA) of primiparous rats on the duration of nursing and the incidence of retrieving and nest-building. Note that before the operation (pre-op) no differences were evident between the two groups, whereas after the operation (post-op) all maternal responses were abolished in MPOA-lesioned animals. (Modified from Numan, 1974.)

et al., 1977). Furthermore, the facilitation of maternal behavior provoked in virgin rats by lesioning the corticomedial amygdala does not occur if such females have also been lesioned in the MPOA (Fleming *et al.*, 1983). In contrast, by applying "kindling"-type electrical stimulation to the MPOA, maternal responsiveness to foster pups is promoted in both experienced mothers and virgins (Morgan *et al.*, 1999), a finding that supports the idea that activity of this brain structure is critical for the performance of maternal behavior. Furthermore, this brain region also seems to mediate the reinforcing properties of young pups in postpartum and in "sensitized" virgin rats: electrolytic lesions to the MPOA have been recently found to disrupt maternal behavior in the home cage and to decrease the rate of bar-pressing for pups in an operant reinforcement paradigm (Lee *et al.*, 2000; Fig. 8).

A different experimental approach has been used to investigate the connections of the MPOA that may be part of a circuit regulating specific aspects of maternal behavior. By selectively severing the rostral, caudal, lateral, or dorsal connections of the MPOA and assessing the effects of such procedures on the maternal behavior of lactating rats, a series of works (Franz *et al.*, 1986; Miceli *et al.*, 1983; Numan, 1974; Numan and Callahan, 1980; Numan and Corodimas, 1985; Terkel *et al.*, 1979) have revealed that the lateral projections of the MPOA exert the most important influence: Knife cuts interrupting such connections severely disrupt the oral components of maternal behavior (i.e., retrieving and nest-building) and provoke moderate alterations in crouching and nursing. Such deficits are long-lasting, and are still apparent one month after the knife cuts are performed (Jakubowski and Terkel, 1986; Numan, 1990). It is important to note that the observed deficits in pup-retrieval are not a consequence of a general inability to retrieve "anything" because lesioned females readily hoard candy (Numan and Corodimas, 1985). It must also be emphasized that the disruption in maternal behavior that follows MPOA lesions is not an indirect consequence of alterations in pituitary function because (a) this effect occurs even in hormonally primed rats (Numan and Callahan, 1980); (b) such lesions disrupt the *maintenance* of maternal behavior in lactating (Jacobson *et al.*, 1980; Miceli *et al.*, 1983; Numan, 1974; Numan and Callahan, 1980; Terkel

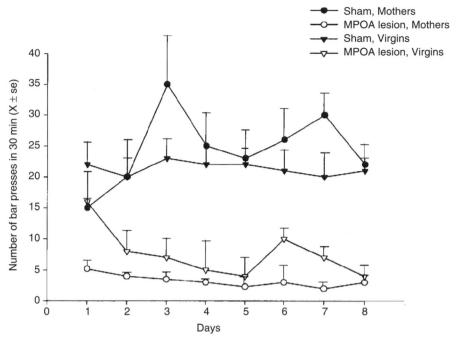

FIGURE 8 Lesions to the medial preoptic area (MPOA; open symbols) decrease maternal motivation in mother rats (circles) and in virgins sensitized to respond maternally by daily pup exposure (triangles), as evidenced by a decrease in the number of bar presses performed to access a pup. Sham surgery (black symbols) provoked no significant effects. Before MPOA lesions both types of females were showing high levels of bar-pressing (data not shown; modified from Lee *et al.* (2000), *Behav. Brain Res.* **108**, 215–231, © 2000 with permission from Elsevier Science.)

et al., 1979) and virgin (i.e., "sensitized"; Gray and Brooks, 1984; Miceli *et al.,* 1983; Numan *et al.,* 1977) rats, known to be largely independent of hormones (see Section IV).

To further define the elements and pathways comprised in a "maternal circuit," the group of Numan has performed a systematic series of studies involving the selective destruction of specific brain areas and neural connections and the determination of their effects on the maternal behavior of lactating rats. As stated earlier, severing the lateral projections of the MPOA disrupts maternal behavior, an effect also seen after lesioning the lateral hypothalamus (Avar and Monos, 1966, 1967, 1969a,b). These lateral MPOA projections travel to the ventral tegmental area (VTA) by one of two routes: a direct one and an indirect one involving a synapse in the lateral preoptic area (LPOA; Barone *et al.,* 1981; Conrad and Pfaff, 1976; Swanson, 1976). Numan has proposed that the VTA may be important in regulating *ongoing* maternal behavior because some of the ascending projections of this region reach the striatum and are

involved in the control of oral motor responses. Indeed, bilateral electrolytic (though *not* NMDA) lesions of the VTA severely disrupt maternal behavior in postpartum rats (Gaffori and Le Moal, 1979; Numan and Smith, 1984). Bilateral knife cuts through the lateral hypothalamus disrupt maternal behavior only when performed at a level (dorsal) in which fibers coming from neurons in the lateral hypothalamus and going to the VTA are severed. When cuts are made ventrally, the connections disrupted are those from MPOA neurons projecting directly to the VTA, and this procedure has no effect on maternal behavior (Numan *et al.,* 1985). Severe alterations in maternal behavior are also obtained when unilateral electrolytic lesions of the VTA are combined with contralateral knife cuts of the lateral projections of the MPOA, thus indicating that intact bilateral connections between the MPOA and the VTA are essential for the adequate display of maternal behavior. To distinguish which of the two routes connecting MPOA and VTA (i.e., the direct one or the one with a relay in the LPOA) is part of the "maternal circuit," Numan *et al.*

(1988) performed radiofrequency or NMDA lesions in the LPOA and found that both procedures provoked severe disruptions in maternal behavior. This was not observed when NMDA lesions were performed in the lateral hypothalamus. These results are consistent with the finding that fibers passing through the lateral hypothalamus (and which are crucial for maternal behavior) come mainly from cell bodies located in the LPOA and BNST (Numan *et al.*, 1985). In summary, these studies support the existence, in rats, of a "maternal circuit" involving the MPOA, LPOA, and afferent fibers passing through the lateral hypothalamus and the VTA.

b) Studies Using Implantation of Hormones and Detection of Their Receptors   As described in Section IIIA1, the "normal" onset of maternal behavior is estrogen-dependent. To assess whether this action of estrogen is exerted on the MPOA, diluted estradiol was implanted into the MPOA of rats that were ovariectomized and hysterectomized on pregnancy day 16 (Numan *et al.*, 1977). This procedure effectively stimulated maternal behavior, and the results were confirmed in a later study (Fahrbach and Pfaff, 1986). These findings coincide with the observation that many cells that concentrate estradiol and project to or through the ventral midbrain are located in the MPOA, LPOA, and BNST, as determined by the combined use of a fluorescent retrograde tracer (injected into the ventral midbrain) plus ^{3}H-estradiol autoradiography (Fahrbach and Pfaff, 1986). Moreover, toward the end of pregnancy there is an increase in the number of estrogen receptors in the MPOA, as determined by the binding of ^{3}H-estradiol to cytosol and nuclear receptors extracted from this region (Giordano *et al.*, 1989, 1990) and by the detection of mRNA specific for the alpha form of the ER (Wagner and Morrell, 1996; Wagner *et al.*, 1998).

In ovariectomized rabbits estradiol implants into the preoptic region stimulate maternal nest-building when combined with the systemic injection and subsequent withdrawal of progesterone (González-Mariscal *et al.*, 1996a), coinciding with the presence of abundant estrogen receptor alpha immunoreactive neurons in this area (Caba *et al.*, 2002). In ovariectomized gerbils estrogen implants into the MPOA stimulate maternal scent-marking of young (Owen *et al.*, 1974; Wallace *et al.*, 1973). In sheep abundant ERα-immunoreactive neurons have been detected in the MPOA during estrus

(Blache *et al.*, 1994; Herbison *et al.*, 1993; Lehmann *et al.*, 1993), but their number is markedly reduced within 30 minutes after parturition (Gonzalez *et al.*, 1998).

The recent identification of a new form of the estrogen receptor, ERβ (Kuiper *et al.*, 1996; Mosselman *et al.*, 1996) has raised the question of its possible role in maternal behavior regulation. Though ERβ has been detected in various regions involved in the control of maternal behavior (rat: Alves *et al.*, 1998; Hrabovszky *et al.*, 1998; Li *et al.*, 1997; Shughrue *et al.*, 1997b; Simonian and Herbison, 1997; mouse: Shughrue *et al.*, 1997a; ram: Hileman *et al.*, 1999), its potential role remains unclear. Recent studies (Hall and McDonnell, 1999) suggest that ERβ may act as a cofactor that regulates the action of ERα in target cells, and consequently the relative concentration of the two isoforms could determine estrogen sensitivity. Future studies are needed to assess the role of this new receptor in the expression of maternal behavior.

It is unclear whether progesterone acts on the MPOA to regulate maternal behavior because implants of the hormone in this region fail to inhibit maternal behavior induced by estradiol injections given to ovariectomized-hysterectomized late pregnant rats (Numan, 1978). Yet progesterone receptors are found at highest levels in late pregnancy in the MPOA and ventral part of the BNST, among other regions (rat: Numan *et al.*, 1999; guinea pig: Blaustein and Turcotte, 1989a,b; Blaustein *et al.*, 1988; Warembourg *et al.*, 1986, 1989). In sheep, recent results indicate that the distribution of progesterone receptors is similar to that of other species (Scott *et al.*, 2000), but their possible role in the control of maternal behavior remains unexplored. In ovariectomized estrogen-treated rabbits, implants of progesterone into the preoptic region facilitate specific aspects of maternal nest-building (digging and straw-carrying; González-Mariscal *et al.*, 1997).

Support for an action of prolactin on the MPOA to facilitate maternal behavior comes from the findings by the group of Bridges. These investigators found that implants of ovine or rat prolactin, placental lactogen-I, or growth hormone into the MPOA of ovariectomized, bromocryptine-treated rats, given progesterone and then estrogen, readily facilitate maternal behavior (Bridges and Freemark, 1995; Bridges and Mann, 1994; Bridges *et al.*, 1990, 1997). MPOA implants of ovine prolactin also facilitate maternal behavior and nest-building in mice (Voci and Carlson, 1973). Prolactin-binding sites were initially detected in the hypothalamus by the binding of ^{125}I-ovine prolactin to neuronal membranes (Muccioli and Di Carlo, 1994). Later studies have detected estrogen-induced prolactin receptors in the MPOA by the use of immunocytochemistry (Pi and Grattan, 1998) and *in situ* hybridization (Pi and Grattan, 1999a). Moreover, the mRNA for this receptor is expressed most abundantly at the end of pregnancy (Bakowska and Morrell, 1997) and during lactation (Pi and Grattan, 1999a,b,c) in several brain regions, including the MPOA. In rabbits, prolactin-binding sites have been detected in (a) the hypothalamus of intact females by measuring the affinity labeling of ^{125}I-ovine prolactin to membranes obtained from the hypothalamus (Di Carlo and Muccioli, 1981); (b) the MPOA and several hypothalamicnuclei (e.g., paraventricular, supraoptic, suprachiasmatic, arcuate) of intact females by autoradiography of ^{125}I-ovine prolactin (Walsh *et al.*, 1990); (c) the paraventricular thalamic nucleus, medial habenula, infundibular nucleus, mesencephalic central gray, and choroid plexus by means of immunocytochemistry (González-Mariscal *et al.*, 1998a).

Various lines of evidence suggest that in rats, the facilitatory action of oxytocin on maternal behavior (see Section III.A.4) may occur in the preoptic region:

1. This region contains oxytocinergic neurons as evidenced by immunocytochemistry and *in situ* hybridization (Brooks, 1992; Jirikowski, 1992).
2. The levels of this peptide increase during lactation in the MPOA (Brooks *et al.*, 1990; Caldwell *et al.*, 1989; Jirikowski *et al.*, 1989).
3. Oxytocin binding is higher in the MPOA during pregnancy and postpartum (Pedersen *et al.*, 1994).
4. Infusion of an oxytocin antagonist into either of these two regions inhibits pup retrieval and nursing at parturition (Pedersen *et al.*, 1994).
5. Maximal stimulation of oxytocin mRNA, determined in the whole hypothalamus, is achieved by long-term administration of estradiol and progesterone, followed by progesterone withdrawal (Amico *et al.*, 1997; Crowley *et al.*, 1995), i.e., by the same hormonal milieu characteristic of pregnancy and the peripartum period.
6. Following parturition and across lactation (i.e., under a different hormonal profile from that of pregnancy), cytoplasmic oxytocin and vasopressin gene transcripts decline in the whole hypothalamus (Crowley *et al.*, 1993; Thomas *et al.*, 1996).

In ewes the disruptive effect of peridural anesthesia on maternal behavior can be partly overcome by the icv injection of oxytocin (Lévy *et al.*, 1992). Also, in multiparous (Kendrick *et al.*, 1987; Keverne and Kendrick, 1991) and nulliparous (Kendrick *et al.*, 1997a) steroid-primed, nonpregnant ewes, the icv injection of oxytocin can stimulate maternal behavior in a way similar to that of vaginocervical stimulation. Though the infusion of oxytocin into the MPOA does not stimulate maternal behavior in nonpregnant steroid-primed ewes, it does reduce the incidence of rejection behaviors (Kendrick *et al.*, 1992b). These results indicate that, in sheep, the abrupt onset of maternal behavior at parturition requires a "triggering" effect exerted by oxytocin on a background of steroid hormones.

The injection of morphine into the MPOA of lactating rats disrupts maternal behavior, an effect prevented by the concurrent administration of naloxone into the same region (Rubin and Bridges, 1984). A similar inhibitory effect is provoked by the icv injection of selective mu-receptor agonists (Mann *et al.*, 1990). The relevance of an inhibitory opiatergic tone for the maternal behavior of intact rats is suggested by the observation that (a) the MPOA is rich in mu-opioid binding sites (Desjardins *et al.*, 1990; Mateo *et al.*, 1992) and (b) the beta-endorphin content and the opioid-binding density in the MPOA rise during pregnancy but decline after parturition and remain low throughout lactation (Bridges and Ronsheim, 1987; Dondi *et al.*, 1991; Hammer and Bridges, 1987).

In contrast to this large amount of information supporting a role of the MPOA in the regulation of maternal behavior, few studies have explored the participation of this brain region in paternal behavior. Over 40 years ago, implants of testosterone into the MPOA were reported to stimulate maternal-like behavior in male rats (Fisher, 1956). More recently, Rosenblatt *et al.* (1996) found that radiofrequency lesions of the MPOA prevented sensitization in male rats and induced severe deficits in maternal behavior. Conversely, estradiol implants into the MPOA of adult castrated male rats stimulate a short latency onset of maternal behavior, as occurs in females (Rosenblatt and Ceus, 1998).

4. Midbrain Tegmentum, Paraventricular Nucleus, and Habenular Complex

The lateral midbrain tegmentum, which includes the peripeduncular nucleus, receives input from descending preoptic efferents and trigeminal sensory pathways that pass through the ventral tegmental area (VTA) and carry input from the perioral region (Nadaud et al., 1984; Smith, 1973). Lesions in this area abolish maternal aggression toward males, block milk ejection, but do not interfere with nursing behavior (Hansen and Ferreira, 1986; Hansen and Gummesson, 1982; Hansen and Kohler, 1984). However, knife cuts made caudal to the VTA (thus disrupting ascending and descending pathways travelling through the mesencephalon) abolish maternal behavior (Numan and Numan, 1991). These results indicate that fibers passing through the VTA and relevant for maternal behavior terminate at levels lower than the mesencephalon (e.g., caudal periaqueductal gray and central tegmental field).

The paraventricular nucleus (PVN) seems to participate in the onset of maternal behavior in several species through the release of oxytocin and its parvocellular extra-hypothalamic projections. Thus, in rats oxytocin is released in the supraoptic nucleus (SON) and the PVN at parturition (Neumann et al., 1993). Ultrastructural changes are observed in the SON and PVN, such as glia retraction and increase in direct neuronal coupling, in the last 24 hours preceding parturition (Hatton and Ellisman, 1982; Perlmutter et al., 1984; Theodosis and Poulain, 1984; Theodosis et al., 1981). Most of these changes disappear within 10 to 30 days after weaning (Modney and Hatton, 1990). Similar changes can be observed in sensitized virgins (Salm et al., 1988) following icv injection of oxytocin (Theodosis et al., 1986) or in response to electrical stimulation of the olfactory pathways in brain slice preparations (Hatton and Yang, 1989, 1990). Isolation of the mediobasal hypothalamus (MBH), a procedure that leaves the PVN and its extra-hypothalamic connections intact but severs pathways between the PVN and the MBH, abolishes milk output but does not affect maternal behavior (Herrenkohl and

Rosenberg, 1974). Lesions to the PVN disrupt rat maternal behavior, although only if performed before its onset (Insel and Harbaugh, 1989; Numan and Corodimas, 1985): If performed after parturition, PVN lesions significantly reduce maternal aggression (Consiglio and Lucion, 1996). Kainic acid-induced lesions of the PVN on pospartum day 2 affect retrieving behavior (but not other maternal behavior components; Olazabal and Ferreira, 1997), whereas lesions performed on day 5 postpartum, with ibotenic acid (a procedure that preferentially lesions parvocellular neurons) or infusion of antisense oligonucleotides against oxytocin, increase maternal aggression (Giovenardi et al., 1997, 1998).

In female prairie and montane voles, the expression of the oxytocin gene is increased in the paraventricular hypothalamic and supraoptic nuclei on postpartum days 1 and 6, relative to virgin females (Wang et al., 2000). Male prairie voles show increased expression of the oxytocin and vasopressin genes in the paraventricular hypothalamic and supraoptic nuclei on postpartum days 1 and 6 (relative to sexually naive animals), whereas male montane voles, which show no paternal care, do not (Wang et al., 2000). In rabbits, the number and size of oxytocin-immunoreactive neurons significantly increases in the lateral hypothalamus and suprachiasmatic and paraventricular nuclei from estrus to late pregnancy and lactation (Caba et al., 1996b). The relevance of these findings for the expression of maternal behavior has not been directly explored, but similar changes in the number and size of oxytocin-immunoreactive neurons can be elicited in ovariectomized rabbits by the same hormonal treatments that stimulate maternal nest-building (Caba et al., 1996a).

In sheep there is strong evidence for the participation of oxytocin from the PVN in the activation of maternal behavior. Oxytocin is released in this structure during parturition and retrodialysis of this peptide induces maternal behavior in nonpregnant steroid-primed females (Da Costa et al., 1996). Birth or VCS activate the PVN (as determined by expression of the FOS protein; see following section), where oxytocinergic neurons and fibers, as well as oxytocin receptors have been found (Kendrick et al., 1997a). The number of oxytocin immunoreactive neurons and mRNA transcripts for the oxytocin receptor are increased in the PVN at parturition and following progesterone or estradiol priming

(Broad *et al.*, 1993a). Previous maternal experience further enhances the expression of oxytocin receptor mRNA in the PVN (Broad *et al.*, 1999). From this evidence it has been proposed that at parturition oxytocin facilitates its own release (by acting on autoreceptors), not only in the PVN itself but also in the brain regions to which it projects, e.g., MPOA and olfactory bulbs (Kendrick *et al.*, 1997a). Along this line, the fact that ERα and ERβ have been found in the sheep PVN (A. Gonzalez, unpublished; Hileman *et al.*, 1999) may partially explain how estradiol and VCS interact to stimulate maternal behavior in this species. In addition, there are also increases in the mRNA expression of CRF, pro-opiomelanocortin and preproenkephalin in the PVN of parturient ewes (Broad *et al.*, 1993b, 1995), a result that has led to the proposition that opiates may be exerting their positive effect on maternal behavior through the modulation of oxytocin release (Kendrick *et al.*, 1997a; Lévy *et al.*, 1996).

The lateral habenular complex is necessary for the hormonal onset of maternal behavior because cytotoxic lesions in this region produce deficits in pup retrieval, nest-building, and nursing in rats that were ovariectomized or hysterectomized and injected with estrogen on pregnancy day 16 (Corodimas *et al.*, 1993; Matthews-Felton *et al.*, 1995). However, implants of estradiol in the lateral habenula fail to stimulate maternal behavior in rats that were ovariectomized-hysterectomized on pregnancy day 16 (Matthews-Felton *et al.*, 1999), despite the fact that estradiol receptors have been found in this region by autoradiography (Pfaff and Keiner, 1973) and *in situ* hybridization (Wagner *et al.*, 1998).

5. Sampling the "Active" Parental Brain

a) The Expression of Immediate Early Genes The protein products of *c-fos, fosB, egr-1, and zif-268* (examples of the so-called immediate early genes) participate in regulating the transcription of "late-responding" genes. A large amount of evidence supports the idea that an increased production of the mRNA or the protein products of such genes indicates neuronal stimulation (Dacoit *et al.*, 1990; Morgan and Curran, 1991; Wisden *et al.*, 1990). Thus, the quantification of such gene products has been used to measure neuronal activity in specific brain regions under a variety of experimental conditions. Because several antibodies for the FOS protein

are readily available, most studies have used the detection of this protein by means of immunocytochemistry to explore the brain regions activated during the display of maternal behavior. By using this approach, Numan and Numan (1994) found that lactating rats exposed to pups (following a three-day separation) showed significantly higher numbers of FOS-immunoreactive (ir) neurons in the MPOA, ventral (though not dorsal) BNST, and anterior cortical and posterodorsal medial amygdaloid nuclei compared with lactating rats that were given candy instead of pups on the day of testing. Very similar changes were observed in virgin rats behaving maternally after having been exposed to pups for several days, with respect to females also given pups for the same number of days but not yet behaving maternally (Fig. 9). No differences in the number of FOS-ir neurons between maternal and nonmaternal rats were noted in other brain regions (e.g., VMN, BAOT, anterior medial or posteroventral medial amygdaloid nuclei). Similarly, Fleming *et al.* (1994b) found that postpartum rats exposed to pups showed many more FOS-ir

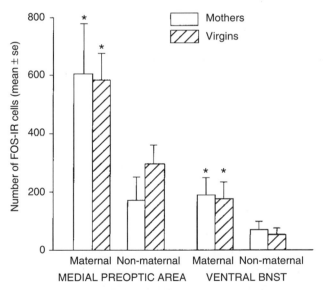

FIGURE 9 A significantly larger number of FOS-immunoreactive cells is observed in the medial preoptic area and ventral bed nucleus of the stria terminalis (BNST) of female rats behaving maternally than in nonmaternal animals. This difference is observed in both postparturient mothers (given candy instead of pups) and in virgin females not yet behaving maternally despite daily exposure to pups. *p < 0.05 vs corresponding nonmaternal animals. (Modified from Numan and Numan, 1994.)

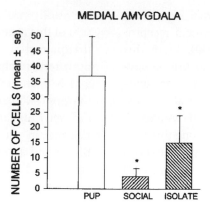

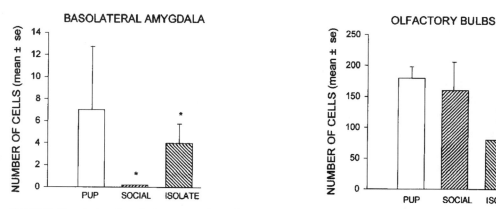

FIGURE 10   A significantly larger number of FOS-immunoreactive cells is observed in the medial and basolateral amygdala following a maternal interaction with pups than after a "social" encounter with a conspecific or no stimulation (isolate). In contrast, a similar number of such cells is observed in the olfactory bulbs following either pup or social contact. *$p < 0.05$. (Modified from Fleming and Walsh (1994), *Psychoneuroendocrinology* **19**, 429–443, with permission from Elsevier Science.)

neurons in MPOA, piriform cortex, and medial and cortical amygdala than mothers exposed to a familiar adult female or to food (Fig. 10). The active display of maternal behavior in lactating rats was also associated with an increase in the number of fosB and egr-1 immunoreactive neurons in the MPOA and ventral BNST, though the temporal course of expression of these proteins was different from that observed with the c-FOS protein (Numan *et al.*, 1998). Recently, the same group of investigators (Stack and Numan, 2000) has shown that immunoreactivity to the c-FOS and fosB proteins is maintained in the MPOA, ventral BNST, and paraventricular hypothalamic nucleus (anterior, magnocellular region) for as long as mothers interact with their pups (maximal time studied was 47 hours). In other

regions explored (e.g., posterodorsal medial amygdala, lateral habenula, posterior paraventricular hypothalamic nucleus, and ventromedial hypothalamic nucleus), immunoreactivity declined over time despite continuous mother-litter interaction (Stack and Numan, 2000). Because the MPOA and ventral BNST are essential for the display of maternal behavior in rats (see previous sections), these authors have proposed that the continuous expression of the c-fos and fosB genes may be necessary to maintain the activity of these areas. In addition, sensitized adult virgin rats also show an increased number of neurons immunoreactive to both c-fos- and fosB-proteins in the MPOA and ventral BNST following a 2-hour interaction with pups (Kalinichev *et al.*, 2000b).

Despite these clear results, the interpretation of changes in the number of FOS-ir neurons is not unequivocal because, in the context of a behavior that is stimulated by pup cues, a given brain region may be activated by either (a) the perception of such cues, (b) the expression of maternal behavior per se, or (c) the occurrence of events not related with maternal behavior (e.g., neuroendocrine secretion). To distinguish among these possibilities, strategies have been used to block selectively the perception of specific cues from the pups and then assess the impact of such manipulations on the expression of FOS in particular brain regions. The removal of nipples (thelectomy) did not modify the number of FOS-ir neurons in the MPOA (Numan and Numan, 1995; Walsh *et al.,* 1996) or ventral BNST (Numan and Numan, 1995), and the application of a local anesthetic in the ventrum reduced FOS expression only in the somatosensory cortex (Walsh *et al.,* 1996). Similarly, the surgical removal of the olfactory bulbs (Numan and Numan, 1995; Walsh *et al.,* 1996) or the spraying of $ZnSO_4$ into the olfactory epithelium (Fleming and Walsh, 1994; Walsh *et al.,* 1996) did not modify the number of FOS-ir neurons in the MPOA of lactating mothers but reduced it in structures related with the olfactory system (e.g., medial amygdala and piriform cortex). Moreover, the number of FOS-ir neurons in the MPOA following an interaction with the litter remained unchanged even after the combined application of local anesthetic to the ventrum plus $ZnSO_4$ to the olfactory epithelium (Fleming and Walsh, 1994; Walsh *et al.,* 1996). However, the combined surgical removal of nipples and main olfactory bulbs reduced but did not eliminate the number of FOS-ir neurons in the MPOA and ventral BNST (Numan and Numan, 1995). From these results it has been proposed that neurons expressing FOS following an interaction with the litter represent mostly the efferent output from the MPOA and are related to the *performance* of maternal behavior (Numan and Numan, 1995; Walsh *et al.,* 1996). In a detailed study involving the quantification of FOS-ir neurons in 20 brain regions Lonstein *et al.* (1998) found that the degree of neuronal activation provoked by interacting with a suckling litter was not significantly different from that observed following an interaction with pups that had their snouts anesthetized and were, therefore, unable to suckle. The single area where FOS expression was significantly greater following suckling (versus nonsuckling) stimulation was the caudal periaqueductal gray (PAG; lateral and ventrolateral portions; Lonstein and Stern, 1997). Because only suckling pups elicit the upright crouch (kyphosis) characteristic of normal nursing (Stern, 1996a), and electrolytic lesions to the caudal PAG disrupt it (Lonstein and Stern, 1997), these authors have suggested that a discrete population of FOS-ir neurons in this region is related to the sensorimotor control of kyphotic nursing. Indeed, unilateral thelectomy reduced both the proportion of time spent in the kyphotic posture (in relation to the total time spent over the litter) and the number of FOS-ir neurons found in the caudal PAG on the side ipsilateral to the thelectomy (Lonstein and Stern, 1999).

To further understand the significance of changes in the number of FOS-ir neurons associated with the display of maternal behavior, Lonstein and De Vries (2000b) recently analyzed brain sections co-stained with FOS and an antiserum against GAD_{67} (an isoform of the rate-limiting synthesizing enzyme for GABA, found in the cytoplasm; Martin and Rimvall, 1993). They found that in lactating rats, interaction with pups increased the number of colabeled neurons in the MPOA, ventral BNST, and caudal periaqueductal gray (ventrolateral region), a result suggesting that GABAergic neurons may promote specific aspects of maternal behavior by removing tonic inhibitory influences. By using a similar experimental strategy, Lonstein *et al.* (2000) reported that lactating rats allowed to interact with pups showed an increased number of neurons co-stained with FOS and an antibody against the ERα than did mothers not given young. These differences were particularly evident in the medial preoptic area, lateral habenula, and ventral BNST.

In virgin Balb/c mice a single brief (30 minute) exposure to pups increased the number of FOS-ir neurons in the MPOA, corticomedial amygdala, entorhinal and piriform cortex, and anterior olfactory nucleus, regardless of whether females were intact or ovariectomized (Calamandrei and Keverne, 1994). It is interesting that the presentation of pups inside a dark, perforated box that allowed females to perceive only olfactory and auditory signals from the young stimulated FOS expression in the olfactory areas but not in the MPOA. In contrast, the depletion of noradrenaline in the olfactory bulb (provoked by injecting 6-hydroxy-dopamine into the medial olfactory stria) reduced FOS expression only in the anterior olfactory nucleus and the piriform cortex. These results coincide with those obtained in rats and support the notion that FOS expression in the MPOA occurs as a result of the active display of maternal behavior.

In multiparous sheep, the interaction between the mother and her lamb for the first thirty minutes after parturition stimulated c-fos mRNA transcription (detected by *in situ* hybridization) in the cerebral cortex (e.g., entorhinal, piriform, somatosensory), habenula, hippocampus (CA3 region, dentate gyrus), limbic system (e.g., BNST, lateral septum, olfactory bulb), MPOA, and several hypothalamic nuclei (e.g., paraventricular, supraoptic). Very similar changes were observed in nonpregnant multiparous ewes treated with estrogen and progesterone and given five minutes of vaginocervical stimulation. In contrast, zif-268 mRNA transcription was noted in only a few areas (entorhinal and orbitofrontal cortex, dentate gyrus) of postpartum sheep (Da Costa *et al.*, 1997).

In the monogamous prairie vole (*Microtus ochrogaster*), a single exposure to pups stimulates the expression of parental behavior in virgin males and females (Bamshad *et al.*, 1994; Lonstein and De Vries, 2000c; Roberts *et al.*, 1992). This brief (three hours) interaction increased the number of FOS-ir neurons in the MPOA, medial amygdala, lateral septum, medial BNST, accessory olfactory bulb, nucleus reuniens, and paraventricular thalamic nucleus in both sexes. The effects seen in the MPOA were much larger in males than in females (Kirkpatrick *et al.*, 1994).

b) Other Methods   The uptake of ^{14}C-2-deoxyglucose (2DG) has been used as an index of activity in neuronal terminals but not cell bodies (Nudo and Masterton, 1986; Sharp *et al.*, 1988). At parturition, mother rats showed an increased uptake of 2DG in the MPOA and ventral tegmental area, whereas in sensitized virgins displaying maternal behavior a decreased 2DG uptake was observed in several structures of the accessory olfactory system (i.e., accessory olfactory bulb, medial amygdaloid nucleus, bed nucleus of the accessory olfactory tract; Del Cerro *et al.*, 1995). These results coincide with the proposition that the facilitation of maternal behavior in virgin rats occurs as a consequence of reducing the impact of aversive olfactory stimulation coming from the pups (see

Section IV.B). To distinguish between excitatory and disinhibitory synaptic relations in specific brain areas associated with the display of maternal behavior, the same group of investigators has recently combined the 2DG method with the immunocytochemical detection of FOS (Komisaruk *et al.*, 2000). In the three models of maternal behavior explored (parturient, sensitized virgins, and rats hysterectomized on pregnancy day 16), the MPOA showed increased uptake of 2DG *and* increased expression of FOS. This indicates that the expression of maternal behavior (regardless of how it is induced) involves excitatory input to the MPOA and excitatory output from it. A different pattern was observed in structures of the olfactory system (e.g., BAOT, medial amygdala). Although parturient rats showed increased 2DG uptake *and* increased FOS expression (i.e., excitatory/excitatory relations), in sensitized virgins 2DG uptake decreased and FOS increased. (Fig. 11). This observation further supports the notion that the expression of maternal behavior through sensitization in virgin rats involves a reduction in the activity of the olfactory system.

To further explore the role of immediate early genes in the expression of maternal behavior, antisense oligodeoxyribonucleotides (ODNs) have been infused into the PVN of periparturient sheep (Da Costa *et al.*, 1999). As described earlier (Section III.B.4), there is evidence that the release of oxytocin from this nucleus at parturition promotes maternal behavior in this species. The bilateral infusion of antisense ODNs against c-fos and c-jun via microdialisis probes placed in the paraventricular nucleus antagonized oxytocin release in this region (but not in plasma) and reduced the expression of mRNA to specific peptides (e.g., oxytocin, CRH, pre-proenkephalin) also in this nucleus. This procedure also decreased the incidence of low-pitch bleats, though only at 10 minutes postpartum. The other components of maternal behavior were not significantly modified, and rejection behaviors toward the neonate were not observed.

A series of studies initiated in the mid 1990s by several independent groups of investigators have used the tools of molecular biology to produce strains of mice lacking specific genes and have assessed the impact of such manipulations on the expression of maternal behavior. By "knocking out" the receptor for prolactin, the group of Kelly (Bole-Feysot *et al.*, 1998;

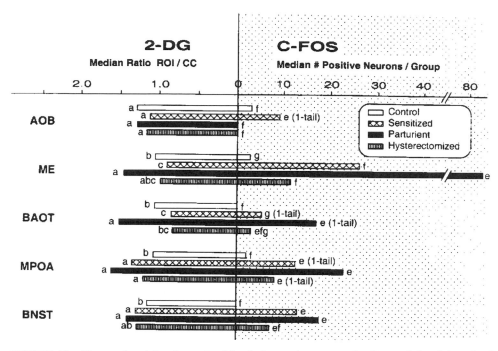

FIGURE 11 Neuronal activity determined by 2-deoxy-glucose uptake (2-DG; left side) and c-fos protein immunoreactivity (c-fos; right side) in the accessory olfactory bulb (AOB), medial amygdala (ME), bed nucleus of the accessory olfactory tract (BAOT), medial preoptic area (MPOA), and bed nucleus of the stria terminalis (BNST) of three groups of rats behaving maternally (sensitized virgins, parturient, or hysterectomized in late pregnancy) and in one (control) group of virgins not exposed to pups. [Modified from Komisaruk *et al.* (2000), *Brain Res.* **859**, 262–272, with permission from Elsevier Science.]

Ormandy *et al.,* 1997) found that heterozygous mothers (homozygous females are infertile) showed minor alterations in maternal behavior: They would often leave a pup outside the nest while suckling the rest of the litter. Yet the litter did not survive because milk was not produced. It is interesting that all these alterations completely disappeared on subsequent pregnancies. Similarly, homozygous oxytocin knockout mice have been found to be normal regarding pregnancy, parturition, nest-building, pup-retrieving, and adoption of crouching over the litter. Milk ejection does not occur, despite the vigorous suckling of the young, but injection of oxytocin provokes milk letdown and allows the litter to survive for as long as such injections are continued (Nishimori *et al.,* 1996). In contrast, major reproductive abnormalities are found in progesterone-receptor null mutant mice: Females are unable to ovulate and show marked alterations in uterine development (Lydon *et al.,* 1995, 1996). Such abnormalities have precluded the use of these mice to

evaluate maternal behavior toward their litter; unfortunately, the responsiveness of these animals to foster pups has not been studied. To assess the participation of specific neurotransmitter systems in the control of maternal behavior, knockout mice for the serotonin 1B receptor and nitric oxide synthase have been generated. Mothers lacking serotonin 1B receptors show clear signs of hyperactivity not seen in wild-type animals (e.g., rearing and climbing to the edge of the cage) and spend 20% more time outside the maternal nest. Yet their maternal performance is normal in terms of retrieving, nest-building, and nursing, and consequently litter weight gain is almost identical to that observed in wild-type pups (Brunner *et al.,* 1999). In contrast, homozygous mothers lacking the variety of nitric oxide synthase present in neurons are deficient in one specific aspect of maternal behavior: maternal aggression toward intruders (Gammie and Nelson, 1999). It is interesting that mothers that are deficient in the variety of nitric oxide synthase present in endothelia do not show

the beha
compon
In agree
tion of a
extende
procedu
output,
  Anotl
pressior
the olfa
parturie
odors tl
treatmei
duce a p
reducin,
et al., 19
a behav
ception
Vernet-l
Togethe
Magnus
that in r
nest be
promot
tum, th
that pre
tion of r
  In sh
quires s
Thus, ta
gion, fr
mobiliz
1993).
mote m
major f
ception
niotic f
ewes ai
become
turition
percept
Poindr
have al
Machac
results i
ternal k
(Lévy a

and Perper, 1979). In cats, the transition from mother-initiated feeding to kitten-initiated feeding occurs gradually in relation to the development of the young. In the final phases of lactation the mother actively avoids the suckling attempts of the kittens and, if given the chance, escapes to a place where they cannot reach her (Rosenblatt *et al.,* 1962). In response, the kittens begin to ingest solid food. These behaviors eventually lead to weaning because when the mother comes back to the young they are no longer hungry, which leads to a reduction in the number of nursing episodes, a reduced milk output, and eventually the cessation of lactation. In dogs, contact with the puppies, nursing, and licking are highest in early lactation but decline after the third or fourth weeks, coinciding with an increase in playing behavior by the young and in the number of episodes during which the mother leaves the litter (Fuller and Du Buis, 1962; Rheingold, 1963; Scott *et al.,* 1958). In ungulates, which have precocial young, mother-initiated nursing generally occurs only during the first ten days of lactation; thereafter, it is the young that look for the mother and attempt to suckle. The termination of suckling episodes, initially determined by the young, is resolved by the mother as lactation advances (Espmark, 1969; Geist, 1971; Lent, 1974; Obregon *et al.,* 1992). In right whales, mother and calf remain in close proximity for the first year, but the initiative to maintain this close contact shifts from the mother to the young as weaning approaches (Taber and Thomas, 1982). In primates, the time of contact between mother and young has been found to decrease as lactation proceeds and the young develop (baboons: Nash, 1978; Rhine *et al.,* 1984; macaques: Chance *et al.,* 1977; Johnson and Southwick, 1984). In contrast, the single daily nursing bout characteristic of rabbits remains unchanged across lactation (lasting around three minutes), despite the fact that milk output decreases from around day 17 onward (González-Mariscal *et al.,* 1994; Hudson *et al.,* 1996). Yet a contribution of the young in the control of nursing in rabbits is supported by the findings that (a) by providing older pups in early lactation or younger pups in midlactation, milk output is reduced or increased, respectively (Mena *et al.,* 1990a) and (b) nursing mothers that are also pregnant (by fertilization at pospartum estrus) show an earlier and more abrupt reduction in milk output than rabbits that are only lactating (Lebas, 1972).

The above evidence suggests that a major factor contributing to the decline in maternal responsiveness across lactation is the changing stimulation the mother receives from the young as they develop. Indeed, by continually replacing older pups with younger ones, maternal responsiveness has been prolonged in rats (Grosvenor and Mena, 1974; Nicoll and Meites, 1959; Rowland, 1981; Wiesner and Sheard, 1933), hamsters (Swanson and Campbell, 1980), gerbils (Elwood, 1981), and mice (Noirot, 1964). In contrast, substituting for older pups (12 days old) in early lactation provokes a decline in the suckling behavior of rats (Grosvenor and Mena, 1974) and a parallel decrease in PRL response to suckling (Shanti *et al.,* 1995). Indeed, the suckling stimuli from the young that initially stimulate release of prolactin and milk production become inhibitory as lactation advances due to an increasing sympathetic influence (Grosvenor and Mena, 1973; Mena *et al.,* 1990b). Moreover, if litters are removed from mother rats on lactation days 9 or 14, maternal responsiveness declines more slowly than if litters are left with their mothers (Rosenblatt and Lehrman, 1963). An additional factor that contributes to weaning in rats is maternal heat: As pup thermoregulation increases, so does heat overload on the mother in the nest, a factor leading to a progressively shorter duration of contact with the pups (Adels and Leon, 1986; Leon *et al.,* 1978, 1985, 1990; Woodside and Jans, 1988).

Together, the above results indicate that (a) younger pups have a higher capacity to stimulate maternal responsiveness than older ones or have a reduced ability to inhibit maternal responsiveness and (b) mothers are sensitive to the type of stimulation they receive from the young and can adapt their behavior accordingly. We must bear in mind, however, that the exchange of litters, and more generally the presence of young, modifies not only the time spent in the nest but also milk output and the release of various hormones. This has led to the investigation of the involvement of hormones in the weaning process. Under normal conditions, the gradual decrease in nursing behavior is accompanied by an increase in gonadotropin secretion and a decrease in prolactin release (McNeilly, 1994). By giving a newborn litter late in lactation, nursing behavior was increased in rats but gonadotropin levels did not decrease and prolactin concentrations increased only slightly (Södersten and Eneroth, 1984). Moreover, neither ovariectomy (Moltz and Wiener, 1966) nor hypophysectomy (Erskine *et al.,* 1980; Obias, 1957) influences the maintenance and gradual decline of retrieving behavior in postpartum rats. Similarly, hamsters given pups 10 days younger than their own litter in midlactation prolonged their nursing behavior by 10 days, despite the fact that prolactin concentrations had declined to low levels at the usual time, i.e., 10 days earlier (Swanson and Campbell, 1981).

In ungulates the presence of the young and the establishment of a selective bond influence the release of prolactin, oxytocin, and, depending on the condition, gonadotropins (Griffith and Williams, 1996; Hernández *et al.,* 1999; Poindron *et al.,* 1998b; Silveira *et al.,* 1993). To what an extent these events are related to the maintenance or fading of maternal responsiveness is unclear. Though Arnold *et al.* (1979) reported that weaning depended on the lactation potential of the sheep mother, inhibiting lactation by blocking prolactin secretion does not suppress maternal responsiveness (Louault, 1983; Poindron and Le Neindre, 1980).

However, a participation of the hormones of pregnancy in the weaning process is suggested in some species by the findings that (a) rats and rabbits mated at postpartum estrus (being, therefore, pregnant and lactating) lose their maternal behavior toward their (first) litter earlier than nonpregnant (i.e., lactating-only) mothers (rats: Gilbert *et al.,* 1983; Rowland, 1981; rabbits: Hudson *et al.,* 1996); (b) Cesarean section, performed in late pregnant rats that were also lactating, reduced the above decline in maternal responsiveness (Rowland, 1981); (c) in precocial species (e.g. moose and elk) the birth of a new young coincides with increasing hostile behavior toward the previous young and weaning of it (Altmann, 1963).

When viewed from a wider perspective, weaning implies the achievement of the adult degree of independence for the acquisition of the necessities of life. This has led to the proposition that other factors, aside from the somatosensory and endocrine ones described above, may also contribute to the weaning process (Galef, 1981). A major determinant is the ingestion of solid food by the young, a multifactorial process that has been shown to involve (a) increased energy requirements, which cannot be satisfied by the sole ingestion of maternal milk (Babicky *et al.,* 1973); (b) de-

ficiency in lactase (the enzyme metabolizing the lactose in milk), which leads to a gradual incapacity to digest milk (Alvarez and Sas, 1961); (c) ability to learn about the types of food that are safe and unsafe in the environment (Bilkó *et al.,* 1994; Hudson and Altbäcker, 1992); (d) maturation of the many physiological processes involved in the ability to ingest and profit from solid food (Babicky *et al.,* 1973; Galef, 1979). Finally, it must be kept in mind that regardless of the multiplicity of factors that contribute to weaning, this process represents a resolution of the conflict between mother and young, in which the reproductive fitness of the former is better met by investing in a new litter than by continuing caring for the current one. Understanding how energetic balance in parents and young is regulated during lactation in mono- and biparental care systems (McInroy *et al.,* 2000; Woodside and Jans, 1995; Woodside *et al.,* 2000) will provide additional information on the proximate factors that participate in the fading of maternal responsiveness at the end of a maternal cycle.

V. CONCLUSIONS AND PERSPECTIVES

When considering the many different forms by which parental care is expressed in mammals and the variety of control mechanisms involved, it becomes quite evident that no general model can be proposed to explain this complex behavior. Even in species occupying the same ecological niches, producing neonates that share the same characteristics (e.g., various rodents that give birth to altricial young) and expressing similar patterns of parental care, the mechanisms that control this behavior are quite different. Typical examples of this are rats and mice: Whereas the former are highly dependent on internal factors (i.e., hormones) for the facilitation of maternal behavior at the first parturition and olfactory cues tonically inhibit maternal responsiveness in virgins, in mice olfactory cues appear to be mostly facilitatory and endocrine factors are not essential for the rapid display of parental care. In other cases, closely related species such as prairie and pine voles on the one hand, and meadow and mountain voles on the other, have clearly different sociosexual strategies and patterns of parental care (i.e., monogamous vs promiscuous; biparental vs monoparental, respectively) associated with different mechanisms of control. Thus, neither similarity in characteristics of parental care nor phylogenetic proximity among species allow us to generalize the results obtained in a given species. Therefore, rather than as *models,* the most extensively studied species should be best regarded as *examples* of a given type of parental care, extremely useful to generate new questions but not allowing us to predict general principles. Indeed, experiments using knockout animals have been done only in mice, thus providing results that are limited to this species (see Keverne, 1997, for a discussion on this point).

However, the above considerations do not mean that no general conclusions can be drawn from the body of knowledge obtained so far, especially given the variety of species studied. Indeed, in all mammals including nonhuman *and* human primates (Fleming *et al.,* 1993, 1997a,c; Maestripieri, 1999; Pryce, 1996; Rosenblatt and Siegel, 1981), a relation has been found between internal physiological events in the peripartum period and the facilitation of maternal behavior (or maternal attitudes). This effect ranges from a clearly activating role (e.g., the action of estrogen in rats; Bridges and Byrnes, 2000) to a permissive one (e.g., estrogen enhancing the effect of vaginocervical stimulation on maternal behavior and oxytocin release in sheep (Kendrick *et al.,* 1997a; Lévy *et al.,* 1996). Although no single hormone can be proposed to be essential for the stimulation of parental responsiveness, perhaps the strongest case can be made for estrogen (see Section IIIA1) because (a) in most species high concentrations of estradiol are present in plasma at the end of pregnancy; (b) estrogen shortens the latency to express maternal behavior after daily pup exposure in rats, facilitates maternal responsiveness in nonpregnant ewes following vaginocervical stimulation, and is required to observe maternal responses following accessory olfactory bulb removal in virgin rabbits; and (c) estrogen receptors are present in brain regions that regulate the expression of maternal behavior in rats, and their concentration increases close to parturition. Yet daily pup exposure can induce maternal behavior in virgin rats that have had their ovaries and pituitary removed; in hamsters estrogen plasma levels decrease before parturition and the injection of this hormone does not facilitate maternal behavior, and exposure to estrogen is insufficient to induce nest-building in rabbits. Rather than ruling out a participation of estrogen, the last two pieces

of evidence may indicate that additional factors are required to stimulate maternal behavior effectively in some species. Indeed, nest-building is effectively stimulated in ovariectomized hamsters and rabbits by the combined administration of estradiol and progesterone. Conversely, the few models in which a facilitatory action of progesterone has been investigated (nest-building in rabbits, responsiveness to foster pups in ovariectomized virgin rats, and acceptance of lambs in response to vaginocervical stimulation in sheep) have shown that estrogen is also required. It is interesting that the withdrawal of progesterone (and presence of estradiol) is essential to stimulate responsiveness to pups in rats and straw-carrying followed by hair-plucking in rabbits. Moreover, the facilitation of maternal behavior by PRL in these two species occurs once females have been exposed to estrogen and progesterone. Together, these results suggest that specific hormonal combinations that may change across pregnancy, rather than a single hormone, facilitate aspects of maternal behavior that are characteristic of a given species.

These hormones act on a set of structures that includes the medial preoptic area, the paraventricular nucleus of the hypothalamus, the septum, amygdala, and bed nucleus of the stria terminalis (some of which pertain to the main or accessory olfactory systems) and are connected as elements of a maternal "web" or "circuit" where they play inhibitory or excitatory functions (Numan, 1994; Sheehan *et al.,* 2000). A question that applies more particularly to the olfactory system is whether hormones activating parental behavior do so by changing the brain of an animal that perceives the young as aversive to one that is accepting of (and even attracted by) them? A striking example of such a change is the processing of olfactory signals coming from the young, the nest, and amniotic fluid. In sheep amniotic fluids loose their usually repulsive character to become strongly stimulatory for maternal behavior expression under the influence of natural (i.e., at parturition) or artificial vaginocervical stimulation (Lévy *et al.,* 1990b; Poindron *et al.,* 1988, 1993). Similarly, in rats, maternal odors become attractive at parturition (Fleming *et al.,* 1989) and play an important role in eliciting pup-directed behaviors (Brouette-Lahlou and Vernet-Maury, 1990; Brouette-Lahlou *et al.,* 1999). In addition, in rabbits, placentophagia occurs only close to parturition (Melo *et al.,* 1998). To what extent an increased interest for odors related with motherhood (e.g., placenta and amniotic fluids) is a common feature to parturient females across mammalian species remains to be determined. Nonetheless, based on the available evidence, we may propose that an important characteristic of the "sensitive period" may be a change in the hedonic value of specific olfactory cues that occurs as a consequence of internal events associated with parturition (e.g., intracerebral release of oxytocin). Similar changes seem to occur in other sensory modalities: The attractiveness of acoustic cues from the pups in mice varies in relation with the hormonal status of the female (Ehret and Haack, 1982; Ehret and Koch, 1989), and the size of the genital area responding to tactile stimulation and of the receptive fields in trigeminal mechanoreceptive neurons is increased by estrogen (Bereiter and Barker, 1980; Komisaruk et al., 1972), a factor that may modify the relevance of somatosensory cues at the time of maternal behavior expression (Stern, 1996a).

Is this change achieved by the removal of inhibitory influences, the activation of circuits that are stimulatory to maternal behavior, or both? In rats it seems that the MPOA of behaving mothers (parturient, sensitized, or hysterectomized in late pregancy) is activated as a consequence of excitatory input impinging on it. However, structures of the olfactory system become activated as a consequence of reduced input to them in sensitized virgins, whereas in parturient rats this occurs as a consequence of excitatory influences on such olfactory structures (Komisaruk et al., 2000). Moreover, the finding that the FOS pattern of expression differs between virgin rats behaving maternally, as a consequence of pup exposure, and those that have not yet become maternal (despite exposure to pups) further supports the notion that both excitatory and inhibitory influences control the activation of maternal behavior. To what extent the main and the accessory olfactory systems differentially contribute to the facilitation of maternal behavior in mammals is not clear, in view of the fact that lesions to either of these systems facilitate maternal behavior in virgin rats, whereas in virgin rabbits only lesions to the accessory olfactory system provoke this effect (see Section III.B.1). As a whole, the above results suggest that maternal behavior may be stimulated by a variety of means that include the simultaneous selective activation and inactivation of different subpopulations of neurons within a same structure. A better knowledge of the chemical identity of such neurons and of their interconnections is crucial to understanding the mechanisms of action of hormones and neurotransmitters for the stimulation of parental behavior.

Another aspect of parental care that has emerged over the years is its dynamic quality. In all species studied experienced mothers are more resistant to conditions that threaten maternal responsiveness and they require less stimulation to respond to young. Neurobiological studies of the sexual differentiation of parental care (Clark and Galef, 2000; Del Cerro, 1998; Lonstein and De Vries, 2000a,c) and of the mechanisms of maternal behavior consolidation during the sensitive period and the longer term (Fleming and Korsmit, 1996; Fleming et al., 1996, 1999; Lévy et al., 1995a) provide us with invaluable information about the neurobiological basis of behavioral plasticity. The experimental data available indicate that acquisition of maternal experience can be seen as a change from a functioning in "series" to a functioning in "parallel," as proposed for memory processing structures (Cobos-Zapiain et al., 1996; Prado-Alcala, 1995). According to this proposition any single or limited combination of sensory or internal factors can become sufficient to activate the complete maternal response in experienced animals, whereas the totality of them is required in naive animals. How this may relate to changes in the cognitive representation of what is a neonate for the naive versus the experienced mother, and how this can be shaped by early experience remains largely unexplored. Further studies of the involvement of higher cortical functions in parental behavior regulation should help clarify this point. Finally, work investigating the neurobiological mechanisms of maternal experience transmission (Caldji et al., 1998; Fleming et al., 1999; Francis et al., 1999a; Gonzalez et al., 2000) has shown that during the early postnatal period contact between mothers and their female offspring may permanently determine how the latter behave toward their own progeny. The above studies illustrate that a multiplicity of factors (genetic, hormonal, sensory) act on the developing mammalian brain to alter permanently the characteristics of a parental response in adulthood. Moreover, recent studies evaluating the influence of cross-species fostering between sheep and goats on later mate selection have shown that the identity of the adoptive mother (i.e., from the same or a different species) strongly influences the adult sexual choice of male kids and lambs, but exerts only a weak influence on the female progeny (Kendrick *et al.,* 1998). These results raise the question of whether a similar process occurs in females concerning the object of filial attachment and whether this representation may be modified with maternal experience acquired during the first maternal cycle.

The overwhelming majority of studies on parental care have been concerned with the neurobiological mechanisms underlying its immediate activation. In contrast, the factors controlling the ongoing expression of maternal behavior, the maintenance of maternal responsiveness across lactation, and the processes leading to the dissolution of the maternal bond remain largely unexplored. Based on the evidence presented in Section IV, it would be interesting to investigate whether the young play a crucial role in maintaining and terminating maternal behavior by mechanisms similar to those proposed for the regulation of lactation (Mena and Grosvenor, 1972; Mena *et al.,* 1990a,b; Modney and Hatton, 1994; Shanti *et al.,* 1995). Finally, investigation of the immediate factors controlling the maintenance and fading of maternal responsiveness should consider the ideas of parent-infant conflict (Trivers, 1972, 1974) and the fact that at this stage we are dealing with a bi- or multidirectional relation, with continuous adjusting and misadjusting between the interests of the young and those of their parents.

Acknowledgments

The authors are grateful to Drs. J. S. Rosenblatt, C. Beyer, and F. Lévy for their comments on an earlier version of the manuscript, N. Serafín and P. Galazza for helping with the search and organization of the bibliography, and O. González-Flores and J. M. Ramírez for the preparation of the illustrations.

References

Abitbol, M. L., and Inglis, S. R. (1997). Role of amniotic fluid in newborn acceptance and bonding in canines. *J. Maternal-Fetal Med.* **6,** 49–52.

Adels, L. E., and Leon, M. (1986). Thermal control of mother-young contact in Norway rats: Factors mediating the chronic elevation of maternal temperature. *Physiol. Behav.* **36,** 183–196.

Alexander, B. K. (1970). Parental behavior of adult male Japanese monkeys. *Behaviour* **36,** 270–285.

Alexander, G. (1960). Maternal behavior in the Merino ewe. *Proc. Aust. Soc. Anim. Prod.* **3,** 105–114.

Alexander, G. (1988). What makes a good mother?: Components and comparative aspects of maternal behavior in Ungulates. *Proc. Aust. Soc. Anim. Prod.* **17,** 25–41.

Alexander, G., and Peterson, J. E. (1961). Intensive observations during lambing in a flock of maiden Merino ewes. *Aust. Vet. J.* **37,** 371–381.

Alexander, G., and Shillito, E. E. (1977a). The importance of odor, appearance and voice in maternal recognition of the young in Merino sheep (*Ovis aries*). *Appl. Anim. Ethol.* **3,** 127–135.

Alexander, G., and Shillito, E. E. (1977b). Importance of visual clues from various body regions in maternal recognition of the young in Merino sheep (*Ovis aries*). *Appl. Anim. Ethol.* **3,** 137–143.

Alexander, G., and Shillito, E. E. (1978). Maternal responses in Merino ewes to artificially coloured lambs. *Appl. Anim. Ethol.* **4,** 141–152.

Alexander, G., Lynch, J. J., Mottershead, B. E., and Donnelly, J. B. (1980). Reduction in lamb mortality by means of grass wind breaks: Results of a five years study. *Proc. Aust. Soc. Anim. Prod.* **13,** 329–332.

Alexander, G., Stevens, D., and Bradley, L. R. (1988). Maternal behaviour in ewes following caesarian section. *Appl. Anim. Ethol.* **19,** 273–277.

Altmann, M. (1963). Naturalistic studies of maternal care in moose and elk. *In* "Maternal Behavior in Mammals" (H. L. Rheingold, ed.), pp. 233–253. Wiley, New York.

Alvarez, A., and Sas, J. (1961). Beta-galactosidase changes in the developing intestinal tract of the rat. *Nature (London)* **190,** 826–827.

Alves, S. E., Lopez, V., McEwen, B. S., and Weiland, N. G. (1998). Differential colocalization of estrogen receptor beta (ERbeta) with oxytocin and vasopressin in the paraventricular and supraoptic nuclei of the female rat brain: An immunocytochemical study. *Proc. Natl. Acad. Sci. U.S.A.* **95,** 3281–3286.

Amico, J. A., Thomas, A., and Hollingshead, D. J. (1997). The duration of estradiol and progesterone exposure prior to progesterone withdrawal regulates oxytocin messenger RNA levels in the paraventricular nucleus of the rat. *Endocr. Res.* **23,** 141–156.

Anderson, C. O., Zarrow, M. X., and Denenberg, V. H. (1970). Maternal behavior in the rabbit: Effects of androgen treatment during gestation upon the nest-building behavior of the mother and her offspring. *Horm. Behav.* **1,** 337–345.

Anderson, C. O., Zarrow, M. X., Fuller, G. B., and Denenberg, V. H. (1971). Pituitary involvement in maternal-nest building in the rabbit. *Horm. Behav.* **2,** 183–189.

Arnold, G. W., and Morgan, P. D. (1975). Behaviour of the ewe and lamb at lambing and its relationship to lamb mortality. *Appl. Anim. Ethol.* **2**, 25–46.

Arnold, G. W., Wallace, S. R., and Maller, R. A. (1979). Some factors involved in natural weaning processes in sheep. *Appl. Anim. Ethol.* **5**, 43–50.

Arnould, C., Piketty, V., and Lévy, F. (1991). Behaviour of ewes at parturition toward amniotic fluids from sheep, cows and goats. *Appl. Anim. Behav. Sci.* **32**, 191–196.

Asa, C. S. (1997). Hormonal and experiential factors in the expression of social and parental behavior in canids. *In* "Cooperative Breeding in Mammals" (N. G. Solomon and J. A. French, eds.), pp. 129–149. Cambridge University Press, Cambridge, UK.

Ash, R. W., and Heap, R. B. (1975). Oestrogen, progesterone and corticosteroid concentrations in peripheral plasma of sows during pregnancy, parturition, lactation and early weaning. *J. Endocrinol.* **64**, 141–154.

Avar, Z., and Monos, E. (1966). Effect of lateral hypothalamic lesion on pregnant rats and fetal mortality. *Acta Med. Acad. Sci. Hung.* **22**, 259–264.

Avar, Z., and Monos, E. (1967). Effect of lateral hypothalamic lesion on maternal behavior and fetal vitality in the rat. *Acta Med. Acad. Sci. Hung.* **23**, 255–261.

Avar, Z., and Monos, E. (1969a). Biological role of lateral hypothalamic structures participating in the control of maternal behavior in the rat. *Acta Physiol. Acad. Sci. Hung.* **35**, 285–294.

Avar, Z., and Monos, E. (1969b). Behavioral changes in pregnant rats following farlateral hypothalamic lesions. *Acta Physiol. Acad. Sci. Hung.* **35**, 295–303.

Babicky, A., Ostadalova, I., Parizek, J., Kolar, J., and Bibr, B. (1970). Use of radioisotope techniques for determining the weaning period in experimental animals. *Physiol. Bohemoslov.* **19**, 457–467.

Babicky, A., Parizek, J., Ostadalova, I., and Kolar, J. (1973). Initial solid food intake and growth of young rats in nests of different sizes. *Physiol. Bohemoslov.* **22**, 557–566.

Bakowska, J. C., and Morrell, J. I. (1997). Atlas of the neurons that express mRNA for the long form of the prolactin receptor in the forebrain of the female rat. *J. Comp. Neurol.* **386**, 161–177.

Balcombe, J. P. (1990). Vocal recognition of pups by mother Mexican free-tailed bats, *Tadarida brasiliensis mexicana. Anim. Behav.* **39**, 960–966.

Baldwin, B. A., and Shillito, E. E. (1974). The effects of ablation of the olfactory bulbs on parturition and maternal behavior in Soay sheep. *Anim. Behav.* **22**, 220–223.

Bamshad, M., Novak, M. A., and De Vries, G. J. (1993). Sex and species differences in the vasopressin innervation of sexually naive and parental prairie voles, *Microtus ochrogaster,* and meadow voles, *Microtus pennsylvanicus. J. Neuroendocrinol.* **5**, 247–255.

Bamshad, M., Novak, M. A., and De Vries, G. J. (1994). Cohabitation alters vasopressin innervation and paternal behavior in prairie voles, *Microtus ochrogaster. Physiol. Behav.* **56**, 751–758.

Baranczuk, R., and Greenwald, G. S. (1974). Plasma levels of oestrogen and progesterone in pregnant and lactating hamsters. *J. Endocrinol.* **63**, 125–135.

Barkley, M. S., Michael, S. D., Geschwing, I. I., and Bradford, G. E. (1977). Plasma testosterone during pregnancy in the mouse. *Endocrinology (Baltimore)* **100**, 1472–1475.

Barkley, M. S., Geschwing, I. I., and Bradford, G. E. (1979). The gestagional pattern of estradiol, testosterone and progesterone secretion in selected strains of mice. *Biol. Reprod.* **20**, 733–738.

Barone, F. C., Weiner, M. J., Scharoun, S. L., Guevarra-Aguilar, R., and Aguilar-Baturoni, H. U. (1981). Afferent connection of the lateral hypothalamus: A horseradish peroxidase study in the rat. *Brain Res. Bull.* **7**, 75–88.

Barty, K. (1974). Observations and procedures at foaling on a thoroughbred stud. *Aust. Vet. J.* **50**, 553–557.

Bast, J. D., and Greenwald, G. S. (1974). The daily concentrations of gonadotrophins and prolactin in the serum of pregnant or lactating hamsters. *J. Endocrinol.* **63**, 527–532.

Bauer, J. H. (1983). Effects of maternal state on the responsiveness to nest odors of hooded rats. *Physiol. Behav.* **30**, 229–232.

Baum, M. J. (1978). Failure of pituitary transplants to facilitate the onset of maternal behavior in ovariectomized virgin rats. *Physiol. Behav.* **20**, 87–89.

Bazer, F. W., Ott, T. L., and Spencer, T. E. (1998). Endocrinology of the transition from recurring estrous cycles to establishment of pregnancy in subprimate mammals. *In* "The Endocrinology of Pregnancy" (F. W. Bazer, ed.), pp. 1–34. Humana Press, Totowa, NJ.

Beach, F. A. (1937). The neural basis of innate behavior. I. Effects of cortical lesions upon the maternal behavior pattern in the rat. *J. Comp. Physiol. Psychol.* **24**, 393–436.

Beach, F. A., and Jaynes, J. (1956a). Studies of maternal retrieving in rats. I. Recognition of young. *J. Mammal.* **37**, 177–180.

Beach, F. A., and Jaynes, J. (1956b). Studies of maternal retrieving in rats. II. Effects of practice and previous parturitions. *Am. Nat.* **90**, 103–109.

Beach, F. A., and Jaynes, J. (1956c). Studies of maternal retrieving in rats. III. Sensory cues involved in the lactating female's response to her young. *Behaviour* **10**, 104–125.

Beach, F. A., and Wilson, J. (1963). Effects of prolactin, progesterone, and estrogen on reactions of non-pregnant rats to foster young. *Psychol. Rep.* **13**, 231–239.

Bedford, C. A., Challis, J. R. G., Harrison, F. A., and Heap, R. B. (1972). The rôle of oestrogens and progesterone in the onset of parturition in various species. *J. Reprod. Fertil.* **16**, 1–23.

Bekoff, M., and Wells, M. C. (1982). Behavioral ecology of coyotes: Social organization, rearing patterns, space use, and resource defense. Z. Tierpsychol. **60**, 281–305.

Benedek, T. (1970). Motherhood and nurturing. In "Parenthood: Its Psychology and Psychopathology" (E. J. Anthony and T. Benedek, eds.), pp. 153–166. Little, Brown, Boston.

Ben-Jonathan, N., Arbogast, L. A., and Hyde, J. (1989). Neuroendocrine regulation of prolactin release. Prog. Neurobiol. **33**, 399–447.

Benuck, I., and Rowe, F. A. (1975). Centrally and peripherally induced anosmia: Influences on maternal behavior in lactating female rats. Physiol. Behav. **14**, 439–447.

Bereiter, D. A., and Barker, D. J. (1980). Hormone-induced enlargement of receptive fields in trigeminal mechanoreceptive neurons. I. Time course, hormone, sex and modality specificity. Brain Res. **184**, 395–410.

Berryman, J. C. (1974). A study of guinea-pig vocalizations with particular reference to mother infant interaction. Ph.D. Thesis, University of Leicester, Leicester.

Bester-Meredith, J. K., Young, L. J., and Marler, C. A. (1999). Species differences in paternal behavior and aggression in Peromyscus and their associations with vasopressin immunoreactivity and receptors. Horm. Behav. **36**, 25–38.

Biensen, N. J., von Borell, E. H., and Ford, S. P. (1996). Effects of space allocation and temperature on periparturient maternal behaviors, steroid concentrations, and piglet growth rates. J. Anim. Sci. **74**, 2641–2648.

Bilkó, A., Altbäcker, V., and Hudson, R. (1994). Transmission of food preference in the rabbit: The means of information transfer. Physiol. Behav. **56**, 907–912.

Blache, D., Batailler, M., and Fabre-Nys, C. (1994). Oestrogen receptors in the preopticohypothalamic continuun: Immunohistochemical study of the distribution and cell density during oestrous cycle in ovariectomized ewe. J. Neuroendocrinol. **6**, 329–339.

Blackshaw, J. K., and Smith, L. D. (1982). Behavioral effects of PGF2alfa in the non-pregnant sow. Appl. Anim. Ethol. **8**, 581–583.

Blaustein, J. D., and Turcotte, J. C. (1989a). Estradiol-induced progestin receptor immunoreactivity is found only in estrogen receptor-inmunoreactive cells in guinea pig brain. Neuroendocrinology **49**, 454–461.

Blaustein, J. D., and Turcotte, J. C. (1989b). Estrogen receptor-immunostaining of neuronal cytoplasmic processes as well as cell nuclei in guinea pig brain. Brain Res. **495**, 75–82.

Blaustein, J. D., King, J. C., Toft, D. O., and Turcotte, J. (1988). Immunocytochemical localization of estrogen-induced progestin receptors in guinea pig brain. Brain Res. **474**, 1–15.

Boinski, S., and Mitchell, C. M. (1995). Wild squirrel monkey (Saimiri sciureus) caregiver calls: Context and acoustic structure. Am. J. Primatol. **35**, 129–137.

Bole-Feysot, C., Goffin, V., Edery, M., Binart, N., and Kelly, P. A. (1998). Prolactin (PRL) and its receptor: Actions, signal transduction pathways and phenotypes observed in prolactin receptor knockout mice. Endocr. Rev. **19**, 225–268.

Bolwerk, E. L. M., and Swanson, H. H. (1984). Does oxytocin play a role in the onset of maternal behavior in the rat? J. Endocrinol. **101**, 353–357.

Bonney, R. C., Moore, H. D. M., and Jones, D. M. (1981). Plasma concentrations of estradiol-17-beta and progesterone, and laparoscopic observations of the ovary in the puma (Felis concolor) during oestrus, pseudopregnancy and pregnancy. J. Reprod. Fertil. **63**, 523–531.

Booth, K. K., and Katz, L. S. (2000). Role of the vomeronasal organ in neonatal offspring recognition in sheep. Biol. Reprod. **63**, 953–958.

Bouissou, M. F. (1968). Effet de l'ablation des bulbes olfactifs sur la reconnaissance du jeune par sa mère chez les Ovins. Rev. Comp. Anim. **2**, 77–83.

Boulton, M. I., Wickens, A., Brown, D., Goode, J. A., and Gilbert, C. L. (1997a). Prostaglandin PGF2α-induced nest-building in pseudopregnant pigs. I. Effects of environment on behaviour and cortisol secretion. Physiol. Behav. **62**, 1071–1078.

Boulton, M. I., Wickens, A., Brown, D., Goode, J. A., and Gilbert, C. L. (1997b). Prostaglandin PGF2α-induced nest-building in pseudopregnant pigs. II. Space restriction stress does not influence secretion of oxytocin, prolactin, oestradiol or progesterone. Physiol. Behav. **62**, 1079–1085.

Boulton, M. I., Wickens, A., Goode, J. A., Lawrence, A. B., and Gilbert, C. L. (1998). Does prolactin mediate induced nest-building behavior in pseudopregnant gilts treated with PGF2α? J. Neuroendocrinol. **10**, 601–609.

Bridges, R. (1996). Biochemical basis of parental behavior in the rat. Adv. Study Behav. **25**, 215–242.

Bridges, R., Zarrow, M. X., Gandelman, R., and Denenberg, V. H. (1972). Differences in maternal responsiveness between lactating and sensitized rats. Dev. Psychobiol. **5**, 123–127.

Bridges, R. S. (1975). Long-term effects of pregnancy and parturition upon maternal responsiveness in the rat. Physiol. Behav. **14**, 245–249.

Bridges, R. S. (1977). Parturition: Its role in the long term retention of maternal behavior in the rat. Physiol. Behav. **18**, 487–490.

Bridges, R. S. (1978). Retention of rapid onset of maternal behavior during pregnancy in primiparous rats. Behav. Biol. **24**, 113–117.

Bridges, R. S. (1983). Sex differences in prolactin secretion in parental male and female rats. Psychoneuroendocrinology **8**, 109–116.

Bridges, R. S. (1984). A quantitative analysis of the roles of dosage, sequence, and duration of estradiol and progesterone exposure in the regulation of maternal behavior in the rat. *Endocrinology (Baltimore)* **114**, 930–940.

Bridges, R. S. (1990). Endocrine regulation of parental behavior in Rodents. *In* "Mammalian Parenting: Biochemical, Neurobiological, and Behavioral Determinant" (N. A. Krasnegor and R. S. Bridges, eds.), pp. 93–117. Oxford University Press, New York.

Bridges, R. S., and Byrnes, E. M. (2000). Neuroendocrine regulation of maternal behavior. *In* "Neuroendocrinology in Physiology and Medicine" (P. M. Conn and M. E. Freeman, eds.), pp. 301–315. Humana Press, Totowa, NJ.

Bridges, R. S., and Feder, H. H. (1978). Inhibitory effects of various progestins and deoxycorticosterone on the rapid onset of maternal behavior induced by ovariectomy-hysterectomy during late pregnancy in rats. *Horm. Behav.* **10**, 30–39.

Bridges, R. S., and Freemark, M. S. (1995). Human placental lactogen infusions into the medial preoptic area stimulate maternal behavior in steroid-primed, nulliparous female rats. *Horm. Behav.* **29**, 216–226.

Bridges, R. S., and Grimm, C. T. (1982). Reversal of morphine disruption of maternal behavior by concurrent treatment with the opiate antagonist naloxone. *Science* **218**, 166–168.

Bridges, R. S., and Mann, P. E. (1994). Prolactin-brain interactions in the induction of material behavior in rats. *Psychoneuroendocrinology* **19**, 611–622.

Bridges, R. S., and Millard, W. J. (1988). Growth hormone is secreted by ectopic pituitary grafts and stimulates maternal behavior in rats. *Horm. Behav.* **22**, 194–206.

Bridges, R. S., and Ronsheim, P. M. (1987). Immunoreactive beta-endorphin concentrations in brain and plasma during pregnancy in rats: Possible modulation by progesterone and estradiol. *Neuroendocrinology* **45**, 381–388.

Bridges, R. S., and Ronsheim, P. M. (1990). Prolactin (PRL) regulation of maternal behavior in rats: bromocriptine treatment delays and PRL promotes the rapid onset of behavior. *Endocrinology (Baltimore)* **126**, 837–848.

Bridges, R. S., and Russell, D. W. (1981). Steroidal interactions in the regulation of maternal behaviour in virgin female rats: effects of testosterone, dihydrotestosterone, oestradiol, progesterone and the aromatase inhibitor, 1,4,6-androstatriene-3,17-dione. *J. Endocrinol.* **90**, 31–40.

Bridges, R. S., Zarrow, M. X., and Denenberg, V. H. (1973). The role of neonatal androgen in the expression of hormonally-induced maternal responsiveness in the adult rat. *Horm. Behav.* **4**, 315–322.

Bridges, R. S., Zarrow, M. X., Goldman, B. D., and Denenberg, V. H. (1974). A developmental study of maternal responsiveness in the rat. *Physiol. Behav.* **12**, 149–151.

Bridges, R. S., Feder, H. H., and Rosenblatt, J. S. (1977). Induction of maternal behaviors in primigravid rats by ovariectomy, hysterectomy, or ovariectomy plus hysterectomy: effect of length of gestation. *Horm. Behav.* **9**, 156–169.

Bridges, R. S., Rosenblatt, J. S., and Feder, H. H. (1978). Serum progesterone concentrations and maternal behavior in rats after pregnancy termination: behavioral stimulation after progesterone withdrawal and inhibition by progesterone maintenance. *Endocrinology (Baltimore)* **102**, 258–267.

Bridges, R. S., DiBiase, R., Loundes, D. D., and Doherty, P. C. (1985). Prolactin stimulation of maternal behavior in female rats. *Science* **227**, 782–784.

Bridges, R. S., Numan, M., Ronsheim, P. M., Mann, P. E., and Lupini, C. E. (1990). Central prolactin infusions stimulate maternal behavior in steroid-treated, nulliparous female rats. *Proc. Natl. Acad. Sci. U.S.A.* **87**, 8003–8007.

Bridges, R. S., Robertson, M. C., Shiu, R. P., Sturgis, J. D., Henriquez, B. M., and Mann, P. E. (1997). Central lactogenic regulation of maternal behavior in rats: Steroid dependence, hormone specificity, and behavioral potencies of rat prolactin and rat placental lactogen I. *Endocrinology (Baltimore)* **138**, 756–763.

Broad, K. D., Kendrick, K. M., Sirinathsinghji, D. J., and Keverne, E. B. (1993a). Changes in oxytocin immunoreactivity and mRNA expression in the sheep brain during pregnancy, parturition and lactation and in response to oestrogen and progesterone. *J. Neuroendocrinol.* **5**, 435–444.

Broad, K. D., Kendrick, K. M., Sirinathsinghji, D. J., and Keverne, E. B. (1993b). Changes in pro-opiomelanocortin and pre-proenkephalin mRNA levels in the ovine brain during pregnancy, parturition and lactation and in response to oestrogen and progesterone. *J. Neuroendocrinol.* **5**, 711–719.

Broad, K. D., Keverne, E. B., and Kendrick, K. M. (1995). Corticotrophin releasing factor mRNA expression in the sheep brain during pregnancy, parturition and lactation and following exogenous progesterone and oestrogen treatment. *Brain Res. Mol. Brain Res.* **29**, 310–316.

Broad, K. D., Lévy, F., Evans, G., Kimura, T., Keverne, E. B., and Kendrick, K. M. (1999). Previous maternal experience potentiates the effect of parturition on oxytocin receptor mRNA expression in the paraventricular nucleus. *Eur. J. Neurosci.* **11**, 3725–3737.

Broekhuizen, S., and Maaskamp, F. (1980). Behaviour of does and leverest of the European hare (*Lepus europaes*) whilst nursing. *J. Zool.* **191**, 487–501.

Broida, J., Michael, S. D., and Svare, B. (1981). Plasma prolactin levels are not related to the initiation, maintenance, and decline of postpartum aggression in mice. *Behav. Neural Biol.* **32**, 121–125.

Brooks, P. J. (1992). The regulation of oxytocin mRNA levels in the medial preoptic area. Relationship to maternal behavior in the rat. _Ann. N.Y. Acad. Sci._ **652,** 271–285.

Brooks, P. J., Lund, P. K., Stumpf, W. E., and Pedersen, C. A. (1990). Oxytocin messenger RNA levels in the medial preoptic area are increased during lactation. _J. Endocrinol._ **2,** 621–626.

Brouette-Lahlou, I., and Vernet-Maury, E. (1990). Amniotic fluid and dodecyl propionate pheromone: influence on the onset and regulation of maternal anogenital licking in the rat. _In_ "Chemical Signals in Vertebrates" (D. W. MacDonald, D. Müller-Schwarze, and S. E. Natynczuk, eds.), Vol. 5, pp. 276–281. Oxford University Press, New York.

Brouette-Lahlou, I., Godinot, F., and Vernet-Maury, E. (1999). The mother rat's vomeronasal organ is involved in detection of dodecyl propionate, the pup's preputial gland pheromone. _Physiol. Behav._ **66,** 427–436.

Brown, J. R., Ye, H., Bronson, R. T., Dikkes, P., and Greenberg, M. E. (1996). A defect in nurturing in mice lacking the immediate early gene fosB. _Cell (Cambridge, Mass.)_ **86,** 297–309.

Brown, R. E., and Moger, W. H. (1983). Hormonal correlates of parental behavior in male rats. _Horm. Behav._ **17,** 356–365.

Brown, R. E., and Schellinck, H. M. (1992). Interactions among the MHC, diet and bacteria in the production of social odors in rodents. _In_ "Chemical Signals in Vertebrates" (R. L. Doty and R. L. Müller-Schwarze, eds.), Vol. 6, pp. 175–181. Plenum Press, New York.

Brown, R. Z. (1953). Social behavior, reproduction, and population changes in the house mouse. _Ecol. Monogr._ **23,** 217–240.

Brunelli, S. A., and Hofer, M. A. (1990). Parental behavior in juvenile rats: Environmental determinants. _In_ "Mammalian Parenting: Biochemical, Neurobiological, and Behavioral Determinant" (N. A. Krasnegor and R. S. Bridges, eds.), pp. 372–399. Oxford University Press, New York.

Brunelli, S. A., Shindledecker, R. D., and Hofer, M. A. (1985). Development of maternal behaviors in prepubertal rats at three ages: Age-characteristic patterns of responses. _Dev. Psychobiol._ **18,** 309–326.

Brunelli, S. A., Shindledecker, R. D., and Hofer, M. A. (1987). Behavioral responses of juvenile rats (_Rattus norvegicus_) to neonates after infusion of maternal blood plasma. _J. Comp. Psychol._ **101,** 47–59.

Brunelli, S. A., Shindledecker, R. D., and Hofer, M. A. (1989). Early experience and maternal behavior in rats. _Dev. Psychobiol._ **22,** 295–314.

Brunner, D., Buhot, M. C., Hen, R., and Hofer, M. (1999). Anxiety, motor activation, and maternal-infant interactions in 5HT1B knockout mice. _Behav. Neurosci._ **113,** 587–601.

Bucher, K. L. (1970). Temporal lobe neocortex and maternal behavior in rhesus monkeys. Ph.D. Thesis, Johns Hopkins University, School of Hygiene and Public Health, Baltimore, MD.

Buntin, J. D., Jaffe, S., and Lisk, R. D. (1984). Changes in responsiveness to newborn pups in pregnant, nulliparous golden hamsters. _Physiol. Behav._ **32,** 437–439.

Burne, T. H. J., Murfitt, P. J. E., and Gilbert, C. L. (2000). Effects of ovariohysterectomy and age on prostaglandin F2-alpha-induced nest-building in female pigs. _Trab. Inst. Cajal_ **7,** 350–352.

Buttle, H. L., Forsyth, I. A., and Knaggs, G. S. (1972). Plasma prolactin measured by radioimmunoassay and bioassay in pregnant and lactating goats and the occurrence of a placental lactogen. _J. Endocrinol._ **53,** 483–491.

Byrne, G., and Suomi, S. J. (1999). Social separation in infant cebus apella: Patterns of behavioral and cortisol response. _Int. J. Dev. Neurosci._ **17,** 265–274.

Caba, M., Poindron, P., Krehbiel, D., Lévy, F., Romeyer, A., and Vénier, G. (1995). Naltrexone delays the onset of maternal behavior in primiparous parturient ewes. _Pharmacol. Biochem. Behav._ **52,** 743–748.

Caba, M., González-Mariscal, G., and Beyer, C. (1996a). Hormonal paradigms activating maternal nest-building in ovariectomized rabbits modify hypothalamic oxytocin immunoreactivity. _26th Annu. Meet. Neurosci.,_ Washington, DC, Abstr. 704, 715.

Caba, M., Silver, R., González-Mariscal, G., Jiménez, A., and Beyer, C. (1996b). Oxytocin and vasopressin immunoreactivity in rabbit hypothalamus during estrus, late pregnancy, and postpartum. _Brain Res._ **720,** 7–16.

Caba, M., Beyer, C., González-Mariscal, G., and Morrell, J. I. (2002). Atlas of neurons that express the estrogen receptor-alpha in the forebrain of female rabbits. _Neuroendocrinology_ (submitted for publication).

Cahill, L., and McGaugh, J. L. (1996). Modulation of memory storage. _Curr. Opin. Neurobiol._ **6,** 237–242.

Calamandrei, G., and Keverne, E. B. (1994). Differential expression of Fos protein in the brain of female mice dependent on pup sensory cues and maternal experience. _Behav. Neurosci._ **108,** 113–120.

Caldji, C., Tannenbaum, B., Sharma, S., Francis, D., Plotsky, P. M., and Meaney, M. J. (1998). Maternal care during infancy regulates the development of neural systems mediating the expression of fearfulness in the rat. _Proc. Natl. Acad. Sci. U.S.A._ **95,** 5335–5340.

Caldwell, J. D., Jirikowski, G. F., Greer, E. R., and Pedersen, C. A. (1989). Medial preoptic area, oxytocin and female sexual receptivity. _Behav. Neurosci._ **103,** 655–662.

Calhoun, J. B. (1962). "The Ecology and Sociology of the Norway Rat." U.S. Department of Health, Education, and Welfare, Bethesda, MD.

Carbonaro, D. A., Friend, T. H., and Dellmeier, G. R. (1992). Behavioral and physiological responses of dairy goats to isolation. *Physiol. Behav.* **51**, 297–301.

Carlson, N. R., and Thomas, G. J. (1968). Maternal behavior of mice with limbic lesions. *J. Comp. Physiol. Psychol.* **66**, 731–737.

Carlson, S. G., Larsson, K., and Schaller, J. (1980). Early mother-child contact and nursing. *Reprod. Nutr. Dev.* **20**, 881–899.

Carter, C. S., Getz, L. L., and Cohen-Parsons, M. (1986). Relationships between social organization and behavioral endocrinology in a monogamous mammal. *Adv. Study Behav.* **16**, 109–145.

Challis, J. R. G., and Linzell, J. L. (1971). The concentration of total unconjugated oestrogens in the plasma of pregnant goats. *J. Reprod. Fertil.* **26**, 401–404.

Challis, J. R. G., and Illingworth, D. V. (1972). Oestrogens in the pregnant guinea-pig. *J. Reprod. Fertil.* **31**, 504–505.

Challis, J. R. G., and Lye, S. J. (1994). Parturition. *In* "The Physiology of Reproduction" (E. Knobil and J. D. Neill, eds.), Vol. 1, pp. 985–1031. Raven Press, New York.

Challis, J. R. G., Harrison, F. A., and Heap, R. B. (1971a). Uterine production of oestrogens and progesterone at parturition in the sheep. *J. Reprod. Fertil.* **25**, 306–307.

Challis, J. R. G., Heap, R. B., and Illingworth, D. V. (1971b). Concentrations of oestrogen and progesterone in the plasma of non pregnant, pregnant and lactating guinea pigs. *J. Endocrinol.* **51**, 333–345.

Chamley, W. A., Buckmaster, J., Cereni, M. E., Cumming, I. A., Goding, J. R., Obst, J. M., Williams, A., and Winfield, C. (1973). Changes in the levels of progesterone, corticosteroids, estrone, oestradiol 17-beta, luteinizing hormone and prolactin in the peripheral plasma of the ewe during late pregnancy and at parturition. *Biol. Reprod.* **9**, 30–35.

Chance, M. R. A., Jones, E., and Shostak, S. (1977). Factors influencing nursing in Macaca fascicularis. *Folia Primatol.* **27**, 28–40.

Chantrey, D. F., and Jenkins, B. A. B. (1982). Sensory processes in the discrimination of pups by female mice (*Mus musculus*). *Anim. Behav.* **30**, 881–885.

Chard, T. (1972). The posterior pituitary in human and animal parturition. *J. Reprod. Fertil.* **16**, 121–138.

Cheney, D. L., and Seyfarth, R. M. (1980). Vocal recognition in free-ranging vervet monkeys. *Anim. Behav.* **28**, 362–367.

Chirino, R., González-Mariscal, G., and Beyer, C. (1999). Efecto de la lesión del bulbo olfatorio accesorio (BOA) sobre diferentes conductas reproductivas de la coneja. *Congr. Nac. Cienc. Fisiol.*, *42nd*, Zacatecas, México, p. O101.

Chirino, R., Beyer, C., Rosenblatt, J. S., and González-Mariscal, G. (2001). Intranasal zinc sulfate spray induces anosmia but does not facilitate maternal behavior in estrous rabbits. *Dev. Psychobiol.* **38**, 197.

Chirino, R., Beyer, C., Rosenblatt, J. S., and González-Mariscal, G. (2000). Virgin female rabbits show pup-induced maternal behavior (MB) only after lesioning the accessory olfactory bulbs. *Dev. Psychobiol.* **36**, 248.

Clark, M. M., and Galef, B. G. J. (2000). Why some male Mongolian gerbils may help at the nest: testosterone, asexuality and alloparenting. *Anim. Behav.* **59**, 801–806.

Clark, M. M., Spencer, C. A., and Galef, B. G. J. (1986). Responses to novel odors mediate maternal behavior and concaveation in gerbils. *Physiol. Behav.* **36**, 845–851.

Clark, M. M., Crews, D., and Galef, B. G. J. (1991). Concentrations of sex steroid hormones in pregnant and fetal Mongolian gerbils. *Physiol. Behav.* **49**, 239–243.

Clark, M. M., Crews, D., and Galef, B. G. J. (1993). Androgen mediated effects of male fetuses on the behavior of dams late in pregnancy. *Dev. Psychobiol.* **26**, 25–35.

Clarke, A. S., and Schneider, M. L. (1993). Prenatal stress has long-term effects on behavioral responses to stress in juvenile rhesus monkeys. *Dev. Psychobiol.* **26**, 293–304.

Clarke, M. R., and Glander, K. E. (1981). Adoption of infant howling monkey. *Am. J. Primatol.* **1**, 469–472.

Clutton-Brock, T. H. (1991). "The Evolution of Parental Care." Princeton Univ. Press, Princeton, NJ.

Cobos-Zapiain, G. G., Salado-Castillo, R., Sanchez-Alvarez, M., Quirate, G. L., Roldan-Roldan, G., and Prado-Alcala, R. A. (1996). High level foot-shock during inhibitory avoidance training prevents amnesia induced by intranigral GABA antagonists. *Neurobiol. Learn. Mem.* **65**, 202–206.

Coe, C. L. (1990). Psychobiology of maternal behavior in nonhuman primates. *In* "Mammalian Parenting: Biochemical, Neurobiological and Behavioral Determinants" (N. A. Krasnegor and R. S. Bridges, eds.), pp. 157–183. Oxford University Press, New York.

Cohen, J., and Bridges, R. S. (1981). Retention of maternal behavior in nulliparous and primiparous rats: effects of duration of previous maternal experience. *J. Comp. Physiol. Psychol.* **95**, 450–459.

Collias, N. E. (1956). The analysis of socialization in sheep and goats. *Ecology* **37**, 228–239.

Conrad, L. C. A., and Pfaff, D. W. (1976). Efferences from medial basal forebrain and hypothalamus in the rat. I. Medial preoptic area. *J. Comp. Neurol.* **169**, 185–220.

Consiglio, A. R., and Lucion, A. B. (1996). Lesion of hypothalamic paraventricular nucleus and maternal aggressive behavior in female rats. *Physiol. Behav.* **59**, 591–596.

Coplan, J. M., Andrews, M. W., Rosenblum, L. A., Owens, M. J., Friedman, S., Gorman, J. M., and Nemeroff, C. B. (1996). Persistent elevations of cerebrospinal fluid concentrations of corticotropin-releasing factor in adult nonhuman primates exposed to early-life stressors: Implications for the pathophysiology of mood and anxiety disorders. *Proc. Natl. Acad. Sci. U.S.A.* **93**, 1619–1623.

Corodimas, K. P., Rosenblatt, J. S., Canfield, M. E., and Morrell, J. I. (1993). Neurons in the lateral subdivision of the habenular complex mediate the hormonal onset of maternal behavior in rats. *Behav. Neurosci.* **107**, 827–843.

Cosnier, J. (1963). Quelques problèmes posés par le "comportement maternel provoqué" chez la ratte. *C. R. Seances Soc. Biol. Ses Fil.* **157**, 1611–1613.

Cosnier, J., and Couturier, C. (1966). Comportement maternel provoqué chez les rattes adultes castrées. *C. R. Seances Soc. Biol. Ses Fil.* **160**, 789–791.

Crowcroft, P., and Rowe, F. P. (1963). Social organization and territorial behavior in the wild house mouse (*Mus musculus* L.). *Proc. Zool. Soc. London* **140**, 517–531.

Crowley, R. S., Insel, T. R., O'Keefe, J. A., and Amico, J. A. (1993). Cytoplasmic oxytocin and vasopressin gene transcripts decline postpartum in the hypothalamus of the lactating rat. *Endocrinology (Baltimore)* **133**, 2704–2710.

Crowley, R. S., Insel, T. R., O'Keefe, J. A., Kim, N. B., and Amico, J. A. (1995). Increased accumulation of oxytocin messenger RNA in the hypothalamus of the female rat: induction by long-term estradiol and progesterone administration and subsequent progesterone withdrawal. *Endocrinology (Baltimore)* **136**, 224–231.

Cruz, M. L., and Beyer, C. (1972). Effects of septal lesions on maternal behavior and lactation in the rabbit. *Physiol. Behav.* **9**, 361–365.

Currie, W. B., Gorewit, R. C., and Michel, F. J. (1988). Endocrine changes, with special reference on estradiol 17-beta, prolactin and oxytocin before and during labour and delivery in goats. *J. Reprod. Fertil.* **82**, 299–308.

Czekala, N. M., Benirschke, K., and McClure, H. (1983). Urinary estrogen excretion during pregnancy in the gorilla (*Gorilla gorilla*), orangutan (*Pongo pygmaeus*) and the human (*Homo sapiens*). *Biol. Reprod.* **28**, 289–294.

Dacoit, J. P., Squinto, S. P., and Bazan, N. G. (1990). Fos-jun and the primary genomic response in the nervous system. *Mol. Neurobiol.* **2**, 27–55.

Da Costa, A. P., Guevara-Guzman, R. G., Ohkura, S., Goode, J. A., and Kendrick, K. M. (1996). The role of oxytocin release in the paraventricular nucleus in the control of maternal behavior in the sheep. *J. Neuroendocrinol.* **8**, 163–177.

Da Costa, A. P., Broad, K. D., and Kendrick, K. M. (1997). Olfactory memory and maternal behavior-induced changes in c-fos and zif/268 mRNA expression in the sheep brain. *Brain Res. Mol. Brain Res.* **46**, 63–76.

Da Costa, A. P., De La Riva, C., Guevara-Guzman, R., and

Kendrick, K. M. (1999). C-fos and c-jun in the paraventricular nucleus play a role in regulating peptide gene expression, oxytocin and glutamate release, and maternal behaviour. *Eur. J. Neurosci.* **11**, 2199–2210.

Daly, M. (1972). The maternal behavior cycle in golden hamsters (*Mesocricetus auratus*). *Z. Tierpsychol.* **31**, 289–299.

Das, N., and Tomer, O. S. (1997). Time pattern on parturition sequences in Beetal goats and crosses: Comparison between primiparous and multiparous does. *Small Rumin. Res.* **26**, 157–161.

Davis, C. D. (1939). The effect of ablations of neocortex on mating, maternal behavior and the production of pseudopregnancy in the female rat and on copulatory activity in the male. *Am. J. Physiol.* **127**, 374–380.

Davis, H. P., and Squire, L. R. (1984). Protein syntheis and memory: A review. *Psychol. Bull.* **96**, 518–559.

De Chateau, P., and Wiberg, B. (1977a). Long term effect on mother-infant behavior of extra-contact during the first hour post-partum. I: First observation at 36 hours. *Acta Paediatr. Scand.* **66**, 137–143.

De Chateau, P., and Wiberg, B. (1977b). Long term effect on mother-infant behavior of extra-contact during the first hour post-partum. II: Follow-up at three months. *Acta Paediatr. Scand.* **66**, 145–151.

Del Cerro, M. C. (1998). Role of the vomeronasal input in maternal behavior. *Psychoneuroendocrinology* **23**, 905–926.

Del Cerro, M. C., Izquierdo, M. A., Collado, P., Segovia, S., and Guillamón, A. (1991). Bilateral lesions of the bed nucleus of the accessory olfactory tract facilitate maternal behavior in virgin female rats. *Physiol. Behav.* **50**, 67–71.

Del Cerro, M. C., Izquierdo, M. A., Rosenblatt, J. S., Johnson, B. M., Pacheco, P., and Komisaruk, B. R. (1995). Brain 2-deoxyglucose levels related to maternal behavior-inducing stimuli in the rat. *Brain Res.* **696**, 213–220.

Delgadillo, J. A., Poindron, P., Krehbiel, D., Duarte, G., and Rosales, E. (1997). Nursing, suckling and postpartum anoestrus of creole goats kidding in January in subtropical Mexico. *Appl. Anim. Behav. Sci.* **55**, 91–101.

Denenberg, V. H., Sawin, P. B., Frommer, G. P., and Ross, S. (1958). Genetic, physiological and behavioral background of reproduction in the rabbit: IV. An analysis of maternal behavior at successive parturitions. *Behaviour* **13**, 131–142.

Denenberg, V. H., Petropolus, S. F., Sawin, P. B., and Ross, S. (1959). Genetic, physiological and behavioral background of the reproduction in the rabbit: VI. Maternal behavior with reference to scattered and cannibalized newborn and mortality. *Behaviour* **15**, 71–76.

Denenberg, V. H., Gota, L. J., and Zarrow, M. X. (1963). Material behavior in the rat: analysis of cross-fostering. *J. Reprod. Fertil.* **5**, 133–141.

Desjardins, G. C., Brawer, J. R., and Beaudet, A. (1990). Distribution of mu, delta, and kappa opioid receptors in the hypothalamus of the rat. *Brain Res.* **536**, 114–123.

Dettling, A., Pryce, C. R., Martin, R. D., and Döbeli, M. (1998). Physiological responses to parental separation and a strange situation are related to parental care received in juvenile Goeldi's monkeys *(Callimico goeldii)*. *Dev. Psychobiol.* **33**, 21–31.

Deutsch, J. A. (1957). Nest building behaviour of domestic rabbits under semi-natural conditions. *Bri. J. Anim. Behav.* **2**, 53–54.

De Vore, I. (1963). Mother-young relationships in free-ranging baboons. *In* "Maternal Behavior in Mammals" (H. L. Rheingold, ed.), pp. 305–335. Wiley, New York.

De Vries, G. J. (1999). Comparison of the parental behavior of pair-bonded female and male prairie voles *(Microtus ochrogaster)*. *Physiol. Behav.* **66**, 33–40.

Dewsbury, D. A. (1985). Paternal behavior in rodents. *Am. Zool.* **25**, 841–852.

Di Carlo, R., and Muccioli, G. (1981). Presence of specific prolactin binding sites in the rabbit hypothalamus. *Life Sci.* **28**, 2299–2307.

Diehl, J. R., Godke, R. A., Killian, D. B., and Day, B. N. (1974). Induction of parturition in swine by prostaglandin F2-alpha. *J. Anim. Sci.* **38**, 1229–1234.

Dixson, A. F., and George, L. (1982). Prolactin and parental behavior in a male New World primate. *Nature (London)* **299**, 551–553.

Doane, H. M., and Porter, R. H. (1978). The role diet in mother-infant reciprocity in the spiny mouse. *Dev. Psychobiol.* **11**, 271–277.

Doerr, H. K., Siegel, H. I., and Rosenblatt, J. S. (1981). Effects of progesterone withdrawal and estrogen on maternal behavior in nulliparous rats. *Behav. Neural Biol.* **32**, 35–44.

Dondi, D., Maggi, R., Panerai, A. E., Piva, F., and Limonta, P. (1991). Hypothalamic opiatergic tone during pregnancy, parturition and lactation in the rat. *Neuroendocrinology* **53**, 460–466.

Drewett, R. F., Kendrick, K. M., Sanders, D. J., and Trew, A. M. (1982). A quantitative analysis of the feeding behavior of suckling rabbits. *Dev. Psychobiol.* **15**, 25632.

Dudley, D. (1974a). Contributions of paternal care to the growth and development of the young in *Peromyscus californicus*. *Behav. Biol.* **11**, 155–166.

Dudley, D. (1974b). Paternal behavior in the California mouse *Peromyscus californicus*. *Behav. Biol.* **11**, 247–252.

Dum, J., and Herz, A. (1987). Opioids and motivation. *Interdiscip. Sci. Rev.* **12**, 180–190.

Dunbar, I., Ranson, E., and Buehler, M. (1981). Pup retrieval and maternal attraction to canine amniotic fluids. *Behav. Processes* **6**, 249–260.

Dwyer, C. M., and Lawrence, A. B. (1997). Induction of maternal behavior in non-pregnant ewes. *Anim. Sci.* **65**, 403–408.

Dwyer, C. M., McLean, K. A., Deans, L. A., Chirnside, J., Calvert, S. K., and Lawrence, A. B. (1998). Vocalizations between mother and young in sheep: Effects of breed and maternal experience. *Appl. Anim. Behav. Sci.* **58**, 105–119.

Echeverri, A. C., Gonyou, H. W., and Ghent, A. W. (1992). Preparturient behavior of confined ewes: Time budgets, frequencies, spatial distribution and sequential analysis. *Appl. Anim. Behav. Sci.* **34**, 329–344.

Ehret, G., and Buckenmaier, J. (1994). Estrogen-receptor occurrence in the female mouse brain: Effects of maternal experience, ovariectomy, estrogen and anosmia. *J. Physiol. (Paris)* **88**, 315–329.

Ehret, G., and Haack, B. (1982). Ultrasound recognition in house mice: Key-stimulus configuration and recognition mechanism. *J. Comp. Physiol.* **148**, 245–251.

Ehret, G., and Haack, B. (1984). Motivation and arousal influence sound-induced maternal pup-retrieving behavior in lactating house mice. *Z. Tierpsychol.* **65**, 25–39.

Ehret, G., and Koch, E. J. (1989). Ultrasound-induced parental behavior in lactating house mice is controlled by female sex hormones and parental experience. *Ethology* **80**, 81–93.

Eisenberg, J. F. (1974). The function and motivational basis of hystricomorph vocalizations. *In* "The Biology of the Hystricomorph Rodents" (I. W. Rowlands and B. J. Weir, eds.), pp. 211–247. Academic Press, London.

Ekvall, K. (1998). Effects of social organization, age and aggressive behavior on allosuckling in wild fallow deer. *Anim. Behav.* **56**, 695–703.

Ellsworth, J. A., and Andersen, C. (1997). Adoption by captive parturient rhesus macaques: Biological vs. adopted infants and the cost of being a twin and rearing twins. *Am. J. Primatol.* **43**, 259–264.

Elwood, R. W. (1975). Paternal and maternal behavior in the Mongolian gerbil. *Anim. Behav.* **23**, 766–772.

Elwood, R. W. (1977). Changes in the responses of male and female gerbils *(Meriones unguiculatus)* towards test pups during the pregnancy of the female. *Anim. Behav.* **25**, 46–51.

Elwood, R. W. (1980). The development, inhibition, and disinhibition of pup-cannibalism in the mongolian gerbil. *Anim. Behav.* **28**, 1188–1194.

Elwood, R. W. (1981). Post-parturitional establishment of pup cannibalism in female gerbils. *Dev. Psychobiol.* **14**, 209–212.

Elwood, R. W., and Broom, D. M. (1978). The influence of litter size and parental behavior on the development of Mongolian gerbil pups. *Anim. Behav.* **26**, 438–454.

Elwood, R. W., and McCauley, P. J. (1983). Communication in rodents: infants to adults. *In* "Parental Behaviour of Rodents" (R. W. Elwood, ed.), pp. 127–149. Wiley, New York.

Endröczi, E., Lissak, K., and Telegdy, G. (1958). Influence of sexual and adrenocortical hormones on the maternal aggressivity. *Acta Physiol. Acad. Sci. Hung.* **15**, 353–357.

Erskine, M. S., Denenberg, V. H., and Goldman, B. D. (1978a). Aggression in the lactating rat: Effects of intruder age and test arena. *Behav. Biol.* **23**, 52–66.

Erskine, M. S., Barfield, R. J., and Goldman, B. D. (1978b). Intraspecific fighting during late pregnancy and lactation in rats and effects of litter removal. *Behav. Biol.* **23**, 206–218.

Erskine, M. S., Barfield, R. J., and Goldman, B. D. (1980). Postpartum aggression in rats: I. Effects of hypophysectomy. *J. Comp. Physiol. Psychol.* **94**, 484–494.

Espmark, Y. (1969). Mother-young relations and development of behavior in roe deer (*Capreolus capreolus* L.). *Viltrey* **6**, 461–540.

Espmark, Y. (1971). Individual recognition by voice in reindeer mother-young relationship. Field observations and playback experiments. *Behaviour* **40**, 295–301.

Espmark, Y. (1975). Individual characteristics in the calls of reindeer calves. *Behaviour* **54**, 50–59.

Ewbank, R. (1964). Observations on the suckling habits of twin lambs. *Anim. Behav.* **12**, 34–37.

Ewbank, R. (1967). Nursing and suckling behavior amongst Clun Forest ewes and lambs. *Anim. Behav.* **15**, 251–258.

Fabre-Nys, C., and Martin, G. B. (1991). Hormonal control of proceptive and receptive sexual behavior and the preovulatory LH surge in the ewe: Reassessment of the respective roles of estradiol, testosterone, and progesterone. *Horm. Behav.* **25**, 295–312.

Fahrbach, S. E., and Pfaff, D. W. (1986). Effect of preoptic region implants of dilute estradiol on the maternal behavior of ovariectomized, nulliparous rats. *Horm. Behav.* **20**, 354–363.

Fahrbach, S. E., Morrell, J. I., and Pfaff, D. W. (1985a). Possible role for endogenous oxytocin in estrogen-facilitated maternal behavior in rats. *Neuroendocrinology* **40**, 526–532.

Fahrbach, S. E., Morrell, J. I., and Pfaff, D. W. (1985b). Role of oxytocin in the onset of estrogen-facilitated maternal behavior. *In* "Oxytocin: Clinical and Laboratory Studies" (J. A. Amico and A. G. Robinson, eds.), pp. 372–388. Am. Elsevier, New York.

Fahrbach, S. E., Morrell, J. I., and Pfaff, D. W. (1986). Effect of varying the duration of pre-test cage habituation on oxytocin induction of short-latency maternal behavior. *Physiol. Behav.* **37**, 135–139.

Featherstone, R. E., Fleming, A. S., and Ivy, G. O. (2000). Plasticity in the maternal circuit: Effects of experience and partum condition on brain astrocyte number in female rats. *Behav. Neurosci.* **114**, 158–172.

Feldman, H. N. (1993). Maternal care and differences in the use of nests in the domestic cat. *Anim. Behav.* **45**, 13–23.

Felicio, L. F., Mann, P. E., and Bridges, R. S. (1991). Intracerebroventricular cholecystokinin infusions block beta-endorphin-induced disruption of maternal behavior. *Pharmacol. Biochem. Behav.* **39**, 201–204.

Ferreira, G., Gervais, R., Durkin, T. P., and Lévy, F. (1999). Postacquisition scopolamine treatments reveal the time course for the formation of lamb odor recognition memory in parturient ewes. *Behav. Neurosci.* **113**, 136–142.

Ferreira, G., Terrazas, A., Poindron, P., Nowak, R., Orgeur, P., and Lévy, F. (2000). Learning of olfactory cues is not necessary for early lamb recognition by the mother. *Physiol. Behav.* **69**, 405–412.

Fisher, A. E. (1956). Maternal and sexual behavior induced by intracranial chemical stimulation. *Science* **124**, 228–229.

Fite, J. E., and French, J. A. (2000). Pre- and postpartum sex steroids in female marmosets (*Callitrhrix kuhlii*): Is there a link with infant survivorship and maternal behavior? *Horm. Behav.* **38**, 1–12.

Flandera, V., and Nováková, V. (1975). Effect of mother on the development of aggressive behavior in rats. *Dev. Psychobiol.* **8**, 49–54.

Fleischer, S., and Slotnick, B. M. (1978). Disruption of maternal behavior in rats with lesions of the septal area. *Physiol. Behav.* **21**, 189–200.

Fleischer, S., Kordower, J. H., Kaplan, B., Dicker, R., Smerling, R., and Ilgner, J. (1981). Olfactory bulbectomy and gender differences in maternal behavior of rats. *Physiol. Behav.* **26**, 957–959.

Fleming, A. S., and Korsmit, M. (1996). Plasticity in the maternal circuit: Effects of maternal experience on Fos-Lir in hypothalamic, limbic, and cortical structures in the postpartum rat. *Behav. Neurosci.* **110**, 567–582.

Fleming, A. S., and Luebke, C. (1981). Timidity prevents the nulliparous female from being a good mother. *Physiol. Behav.* **27**, 863–868.

Fleming, A. S., and Rosenblatt, J. S. (1974a). Olfactory regulation of maternal behavior in rats. I. Effects of olfactory bulb removal in experienced and inexperienced lactating and cycling females. *J. Comp. Physiol. Psychol.* **86**, 221–232.

Fleming, A. S., and Rosenblatt, J. S. (1974b). Olfactory regulation of maternal behavior in rats. II. Effects of peripherally induced anosmia and lesions of the lateral olfactory tract in pup-induced virgins. *J. Comp. Physiol. Psychol.* **86**, 233–246.

Fleming, A. S., and Rosenblatt, J. S. (1974c). Maternal behavior in the virgin and lactating rat. *J. Comp. Physiol. Psychol.* **86**, 957–972.

Fleming, A. S., and Sarker, J. (1990). Experience-hormone interactions and maternal behavior in rats. *Physiol. Behav.* **47**, 1165–1173.

Fleming, A. S., and Walsh, C. (1994). Neuropsychology of maternal behavior in the rat: c-fos expression during mother-litter interactions. *Psychoneuroendocrinology* **19**, 429–443.

Fleming, A.S., Vaccarino, F., Tambosso, L., and Chee, P. (1979). Vomeronasal and olfactory system modulation of maternal behavior in the rat. *Science* **203**, 372–374.

Fleming, A. S., Vaccarino, F., and Luebke, C. (1980). Amygdaloid inhibition of maternal behavior in the nulliparous female rat. *Physiol. Behav.* **25**, 731–743.

Fleming, A. S., Miceli, M., and Moretto, D. (1983). Lesions of the medial preoptic area prevent the facilitation of maternal behavior produced by amygdala lesions. *Physiol. Behav.* **31**, 503–510.

Fleming, A. S., Steiner, M., and Anderson, V. (1987). Hormonal and attitudinal correlates of maternal behavior during the early postpartum period in first-time mothers. *J. Reprod. Inf. Psychol.* **5**, 193–205.

Fleming, A. S., Flett, G. L., Ruble, D., and Shaul, D. L. (1988). Postpartum adjustment in first-time mothers: Relation between mood, maternal attitudes, and mother-infant interactions. *Dev. Psychobiol.* **24**, 71–81.

Fleming, A. S., Cheung, U., Myhal, N., and Kessler, Z. (1989). Effects of maternal hormones on 'timidity' and attraction to pup-related odors in female rats. *Physiol. Behav.* **46**, 440–453.

Fleming, A. S., Cheung, U. S., and Barry, M. (1990). Cycloheximide blocks the retention of maternal experience in postpartum rats. *Behav. Neural Biol.* **53**, 64–73.

Fleming, A. S., Gavarth, K., and Sarker, J. (1992). Effects of transsections to the vomeronasal nerves or to the main olfactory bulbs on the initiation and long-term retention of maternal behavior in primiparous rats. *Behav. Neural Biol.* **57**, 177–188.

Fleming, A. S., Corter, C., Franks, P., Surbey, M., Schneider, B., and Steiner, M. (1993). Postpartum factors related to mother's attraction to newborn infant odors. *Dev. Psychobiol.* **26**, 115–132.

Fleming, A. S., Korsmit, M., and Deller, M. (1994a). Rat pups are potent reinforcers to the maternal animal: Effects of experience, parity, hormones, and dopamine function. *Psychobiology* **22**, 44–53.

Fleming, A. S., Suh, E. J., Korsmit, M., and Rusak, B. (1994b). Activation of Fos-like immunoreactivity in the medial preoptic area and limbic structures by maternal and social interactions in rats. *Behav. Neurosci.* **108**, 724–734.

Fleming, A. S., Morgan, H. D., and Walsh, C. (1996). Experiential factors in postpartum regulation of maternal care. *In* "Parental Care: Evolution, Mechanisms, and Adaptive Sig-

nificance" (J. S. Rosenblatt and C. T. Snowdon, eds.), pp. 295–332. Academic Press, San Diego.

Fleming, A. S., Ruble, D., Krieger, H., and Wong, P. Y. (1997a). Hormonal and experiential correlates of maternal responsiveness during pregnancy and the puerperium in human mothers. *Horm. Behav.* **31**, 145–158.

Fleming, A. S., Stallings, J., Steiner, M., Corter, C., and Worthman, C. (1997b). Cortisol and testosterone correlates of affective responses to infant cry and odor stimuli in new parents. *Annu. Conf. Soc. Behav. Neuroendocrinol.*, Baltimore, MD.

Fleming, A. S., Steiner, M., and Corter, C. (1997c). Cortisol, hedonics, and maternal responsiveness in human mothers. *Horm. Behav.* **32**, 85–98.

Fleming, A. S., O'Day, D. H., and Kraemer, G. W. (1999). Neurobiology of mother-infant interactions: Experience and central nervous system plasticity across development and generations. *Neurosci. Biobehav. Rev.* **23**, 673–683.

Fletcher, I. C. (1971). Relationships between frequency of suckling, lamb growth and post-partum oestrous behavior in ewes. *Anim. Behav.* **19**, 108–111.

Flint, A. P. F., Anderson, A. B. M., Patten, P. T., and Turnbull, A. C. (1974). Control of utero-ovarian venous PGF during labour in the sheep: Acute effects of vaginal and cervical stimulation. *J. Endocrinol.* **63**, 67–87.

Flint, A. P. F., Forsling, M. L., Mitchell, M. D., and Turnbull, A. C. (1975). Temporal relationship between changes in oxytocin and prostaglandin F levels in response to vaginal distention in the pregnant and puerperal ewe. *J. Reprod. Fertil.* **43**, 551–554.

Formby, D. (1967). Maternal recognition of infant's cry. *Dev. Med. Child. Neurol.* **9**, 292–298.

Frädrich, H. (1974). A comparison of behavior in the Suidae. *In* "The Behavior of Ungulates and Its Relation to Management" (V. Geist and F. Walther, eds.), pp. 133–143. IUCN, Morgues, Switzerland.

Francis, D. D., and Meaney, M. J. (1999). Maternal care and the development of stress responses. *Curr. Opin. Neurobiol.* **9**, 128–134.

Francis, D. D., Diorio, J., Liu, D., and Meaney, M. J. (1999a). Nongenomic transmission across generations of maternal behavior and stress responses in the rat. *Science* **286**, 1155–1158.

Francis, D. D., Caldji, C., Champagne, F., Plotsky, P. M., and Meaney, M. J. (1999b). The role of corticotropin-releasing factor-norepinephrine systems in mediating the effects of early experience on the development of behavioral and endocrine responses to stress. *Biol. Psychiatry* **46**, 1153–1166.

Franz, J. R., Leo, R. J., Steuer, M. A., and Kristal, M. B. (1986). Effects of hypothalamic knife cuts and experience on maternal behavior in the rat. *Physiol. Behav.* **38**, 629–640.

Franzen, E. A., and Myers, R. E. (1973). Neural control of social behavior: prefrontal and anterior temporal cortex. *Neuropsychologia* **11**, 141–157.

Fraser, D. (1984). Some factors influencing the availability of colostrum to piglets. *Anim. Prod.* **339**, 115–123.

Fraser, D. G., and Barnett, S. A. (1975). Effects of pregnancy on parental and other activities of laboratory mice. *Horm. Behav.* **2**, 207–215.

Fredriksson, G. (1985). Release of PGF2 alpha during parturition and the postpartum period in the ewe. *Theriogenology* **24**, 331–335.

Fuchs, A. R., and Dawood, M. Y. (1980). Oxytocin release and uterine activation during parturition in rabbits. *Endocrinology (Baltimore)* **107**, 1117–1126.

Fucillo, R., Scucchi, S., Troisi, A., and D'Amato, F. R. (1983). Newborn adoption in a confined group of Japanese macaques. *Am. J. Primatol.* **5**, 257–260.

Fuller, J. L., and Du Buis, E. M. (1962). The behavior of dogs. *In* "The Behavior of Domestic Animals" (E. S. E. Hafez, ed.), pp. 415–452. Baillière, Tindall & Cox, London.

Gaffori, O., and Le Moal, M. (1979). Disruption of maternal behavior and appearance of cannibalism after ventral mesencephalic tegmentum lesions. *Physiol. Behav.* **23**, 317–323.

Galef, B. G. (1985). Social learning in wild Norway rats. *In* "Issues in the Ecological Study of Learning" (T. D. Johnston and A. T. Pietrewicz, eds.), pp. 143–166. Erlbaum, Hillsdale, NJ.

Galef, B. G. J. (1979). Investigation of the functions of coprophagy in juvenile rats. *J. Comp. Physiol. Psychol.* **93**, 295–305.

Galef, B. G. J. (1981). The ecology of weaning: parasitism and the achievement of independence by altricial mammals. *In* "Parental Care in Mammals" (D. J. Gubernick and P. H. Klopfer, eds.), pp. 211–241. Plenum Press, New York.

Gammie, S. C., and Nelson, R. J. (1999). Maternal aggression is reduced in neuronal nitric oxide synthase-deficient mice. *J. Neurosci.* **19**, 8027–8035.

Gammie, S. C., Olaghere-da Silva, U. B., and Nelson, R. J. (2000). 3-bromo-7-nitroindazole, a neuronal nitric oxide synthase inhibitor, impairs maternal aggression and citrulline immunoreactivity in prairie voles. *Brain Res.* **870**, 80–86.

Gandelman, R. (1972). Mice: Postpartum aggression elicited by the presence of an intruder. *Horm. Behav.* **3**, 23–28.

Gandelman, R. (1973). Induction of maternal nest building in virgin female mice by the presentation of young. *Horm. Behav.* **4**, 191–197.

Gandelman, R. (1980). Determinants of maternal aggression in mice. *In* "Maternal Influences and Early Behavior" (R. W. Bell and W. P. Smotherman, eds.), pp. 215–231. Spectrum, New York.

Gandelman, R., and Vom Saal, F. S. (1975). Pup-killing in mice: The effects of gonadectomy and testosterone administration. *Physiol. Behav.* **15**, 647–651.

Gandelman, R., and Vom Saal, F. S. (1977). Exposure to early androgen attenuates androgen-induced pup-killing in male and female mice. *Behav. Biol.* **2**, 252-260.

Gandelman, R., Zarrow, M. X., and Denenberg, V. H. (1970). Maternal behavior: differences between mother and virgin mice as a function of the testing procedure. *Dev. Psychobiol.* **3**, 207–214.

Gandelman, R., Zarrow, M. X., and Denenberg, V. H. (1971a). Stimulus control of cannibalism and maternal behavior in anosmic mice. *Physiol. Behav.* **7**, 583–586.

Gandelman, R., Zarrow, M. X., Denenberg, V. H., and Myers, M. (1971b). Olfactory bulb removal eliminates maternal behavior in the mouse. *Science* **171**, 210–211.

Gandelman, R., Zarrow, M. X., and Denenberg, V. H. (1972). Reproductive and maternal performance in the mouse following removal of the olfactory bulbs. *J. Reprod. Fertil.* **28**, 453–456.

Garfield, R. E., Saade, G., and Chwalisz, K. (1998). Endocrine control of parturition. *In* "The Endocrinology of Pregnancy" (F. W. Bazer, ed.), pp. 407–430. Humana Press, Totowa, NJ.

Geist, V. (1971). Behavior of ewes and lambs. *In* "Mountain Sheep" (G. B. Schaller, ed.), pp. 239–255. University of Chicago Press, Chicago.

Gemmel, R. T., MacFayden, A. S., and Rose, R. W. (1991). The induction of parturient behaviour in possums and bandicoots. *Aust. Mammal.* **14**, 133–136.

George, J. M., and Barger, I. A. (1974). Observations on bovine parturition. *Proc. Aust. Soc. Anim. Prod.* **10**, 314–317.

Getz, L. L., Dluzen, D., and McDermott, J. L. (1983). Suppression of reproductive maturation in male-stimulated virgin female *Microtus* by a female urinary chemosignal. *Behav. Processes* **8**, 59–64.

Gibber, J. R., Piontkewitz, Y., and Terkel, J. (1984). Response of male and female Siberian hamsters towards pups. *Behav. Neural Biol.* **42**, 177–182.

Gilbert, A. N., Burgoon, D. A., Sullivan, K. A., and Adler, N. T. (1983). Mother-weanling interactions in Norway rats in the presence of a successive litter produced by postpartum mating. *Physiol. Behav.* **30**, 267–271.

Gilbert, C. L., Murfitt, P. J. E., and Burne, T. H. J. (2000). Prostaglandin F2-alpha induces nest-building in pseudopregnant pigs but does not affect interactions with newborn piglets. *Trab. Inst. Cajal* **77**, 353–354.

Giordano, A. L., Siegel, H. I., and Rosenblatt, J. S. (1989). Nuclear estrogen receptor binding in the preoptic area and hypothalamus of pregnancy-terminated rats: Correlation with the onset of maternal behavior. *Neuroendocrinology* **50**, 248–258.

Giordano, A. L., Ahdieh, H. B., Mayer, A. D., Siegel, H. I., and Rosenblatt, J. S. (1990). Cytosol and nuclear estrogen receptor binding in the preoptic area and hypothalamus of female rats during pregnancy and ovariectomized, nulliparous rats after steroid priming: correlation with maternal behavior. *Horm. Behav.* **24**, 232–255.

Giovenardi, M., Padoin, M. J., Cadore, L. P., and Lucion, A. B. (1997). Hypothalamic paraventricular nucleus, oxytocin, and maternal aggression in rats. *Ann. N. Y. Acad. Sci.* **807**, 606–609.

Giovenardi, M., Padoin, M. J., Cadore, L. P., and Lucion, A. B. (1998). Hypothalamic paraventricular nucleus modulates maternal aggression in rats: Effects of ibotenic acid lesion and oxytocin antisense. *Physiol. Behav.* **63**, 351–359.

Goland, R. S., Wardlaw, S. L., Stark, R. I., and Frantz, A. G. (1981). Human plasma β-endorphin during pregnancy, labour and delivery. *J. Clin. Endocrinol. Metab.* **52**, 74–78.

Gonzalez, A., Meurisse, M., Lévy, F., Caba, M., and Poindron, P. (1998). Estradiol receptors in the sheep hypothalamic structures in relation with parturition, maternal behavior and maternal experience. *In* "Binational Workshop on Reproductive and Behavioral Neuroendocrinology" (J. Bakker, M. J. Baum, and R. G. Paredes, eds.), p. 49. Universidad Nacional Autonoma de Mexico, Querétaro.

Gonzalez, A., Lovic, V., Ward, G. R., Wainwright, P. E., and Fleming, A. S. (2000). Intergenerational effects of complete maternal deprivation and replacement stimulation on maternal behavior and emotionality in female rats. *Dev. Psychobiol.* **38**, 11–32.

González-Mariscal, G., and Rosenblatt, J. S. (1996). Maternal behavior in rabbits: A historical and multidisciplinary perspective. *In* "Parental Care: Evolution, Mechanisms and Adaptative Significance." (J. S. Rosenblatt and C. T. Snowdon, eds.), Vol. 25, pp. 333–360. Academic Press, San Diego.

González-Mariscal, G., Díaz-Sánchez, V., Melo, A. I., Beyer, C., and Rosenblatt, J. S. (1994). Maternal behavior in New Zealand white rabbits: Quantification of somatic events, motor patterns, and steroid plasma levels. *Physiol. Behav.* **55**, 1081–1089.

González-Mariscal, G., Chirino, R., Beyer, C., and Rosenblatt, J. S. (1996a). Estradiol benzoate in the medial preoptic area facilitates maternal nest-building in ovariectomized rabbits. *Conf. Reprod. Behav.*, Montreal, Canada, p. 58.

González-Mariscal, G., Melo, A. I., Jiménez, P., Beyer, C., and Rosenblatt, J. S. (1996b). Estradiol, progesterone, and prolactin regulate maternal nest-building in rabbits. *J. Neuroendocrinol.* **8**, 901–907.

González-Mariscal, G., Chirino, R., Beyer, C., and Rosenblatt, J. S. (1997). Progesterone in the medial preoptic area facilitates specific aspects of maternal nest-building in ovariectomized,

estrogen primed rabbits. *Conf. Reprod. Behav.*, Baltimore, MD, p. 96.

González-Mariscal, G., Melo, A. I., and Beyer, C. (1998a). Prolactin receptor immunoreactivity in the female rabbit brain: Variations across the reproductive cycle. *Meet. Soc. Neurosci.*, Los Angeles, Abstr. 53, 56.

González-Mariscal, G., Melo, A. I., Chirino, R., Jiménez, P., Beyer, C., and Rosenblatt, J. S. (1998b). Importance of mother/young contact at parturition and across lactation for the expression of maternal behavior in rabbits. *Dev. Psychobiol.* **32**, 101–111.

González-Mariscal, G., Melo, A. I., Parlow, A. F., Beyer, C., and Rosenblatt, J. S. (2000). Pharmacological evidence that prolactin acts from late gestation to promote maternal behavior in rabbits. *J. Neuroendocrinol.* **12**, 983–992.

Gräf, K. J. (1978). Serum oestrogen, progesterone and prolactin concentrations in cyclic, pregnant and lactating beagle dogs. *J. Reprod. Fertil.* **52**, 9–14.

Gray, P., and Brooks, P. J. (1984). Effect of lesion location within the medial preoptic-anterior hypothalamic continuum on maternal and male sexual behaviors in female rats. *Behav. Neurosci.* **98**, 703–711.

Gray, P., and Chesley, S. (1984). Development of maternal behavior in nulliparous rats (*Rattus norvegicus*): Effects of sex and early maternal experience. *J. Comp. Psychol.* **98**, 91–99.

Green, J. A. (1978). Experiential determinants of postpartum aggression in mice. *J. Comp. Physiol. Psychol.* **92**, 1179–1187.

Griffith, M. K., and Williams, G. L. (1996). Roles of maternal vision and olfaction in suckling-mediated inhibition of luteinizing hormone secretion, expression of maternal selectivity, and lactational performance of beef cows. *Biol. Reprod.* **54**, 761–768.

Grimm, C. T., and Bridges, R. S. (1983). Opiate regulation of maternal behavior in the rat. *Pharmacol. Biochem. Behav.* **19**, 609–616.

Grosvenor, C. E., and Mena, F. (1973). Evidence that suckling pups, through and exteroceptive mechanism, inhibit the milk stimulatory effects of prolactin during late lactation. *Horm. Behav.* **4**, 209–222.

Grosvenor, C. E., and Mena, F. (1974). Neural and hormonal control of milk secretion and milk ejection. *In* "Lactation: A Comprehensive Treatise" (B. L. Larson and V. R. Smith, eds.), Vol. 1, pp. 227–276. Academic Press, New York.

Grota, I. J., and Ader, R. (1969). Continuous recording of maternal behavior in *Rattus norvegicus*. *Anim. Behav.* **17**, 722–729.

Grota, L. J., and Ader, R. (1974). Behavior of lactating rats in a dual-chambered maternity cage. *Horm. Behav.* **5**, 275–282.

Grundker, C., Hrabe de Angelis, M., and Kirchner, C. (1993). Placental lactogen-like proteins in the rabbit placenta. *Anat. Embryol.* **188**, 395–399.

Gubernick, D. J. (1980). Maternal "imprinting" or maternal "labelling" in goats. *Anim. Behav.* **28**, 124–129.

Gubernick, D. J. (1981a). Mechanisms of maternal "labelling" in goats. *Anim. Behav.* **29**, 305–306.

Gubernick, D. J. (1981b). Parent and Infant attachment in Mammals. *In* "Parental Care in Mammals" (D. J. Gubernick and P. H. Klopfer, eds.), pp. 243–305. Plenum New York.

Gubernick, D. J., and Laskin, B. (1994). Mechanisms influencing sibling care in the monogamous biparental California mouse, *Peromyscus californicus. Anim. Behav.* **48**, 1235–1237.

Gubernick, D. J., and Nelson, R. J. (1989). Prolactin and paternal behavior in the biparental California mouse, *Peromyscus californicus. Horm. Behav.* **23**, 203–210.

Gubernick, D. J., and Teferi, T. (2000). Adaptive significance of male parental care in a monogamous mammal. *Proc. R. Soc. London B,* Ser. **267**, 147–150.

Gubernick, D. J., Corbeau Jones, K., and Klopfer, P. H. (1979). Maternal imprinting in goats? *Anim. Behav.* **27**, 314–315.

Gundlach, H. (1968). Brutfursorge, brutpflege, verhaltensontogenese und tagesperiodik beim europaischem wildschwein (*Sus scrofa* L.). *Z. Tierpsychol.* **25**, 955–995.

Gustafsson, M., Jensen, P., de Jonge, F. H., Illmann, G., and Spinka, M. (1999). Maternal behavior of domestic sows and crosses between domestic sows and wild boar. *Appl. Anim. Behav. Sci.* **65**, 29–42.

Gustin, M. K., and McCracken, G. F. (1987). Scent recognition between females and pups in the bat *Tadarida brasiliensis mexicana. Anim. Behav.* **35**, 12–19.

Hall, F. S., Wilkinson, L. S., Humby, T., and Robbins, T. W. (1999). Maternal deprivation of neonatal rats produces enduring changes in dopamine function. *Synapse* **32**, 37–43.

Hall, J. M., and McDonnell, D. P. (1999). The estrogen receptor β-isoform (ERβ) of the human estrogen receptor modulates ERα transcriptional activity and is a key regulator of the cellular response to estrogens and antiestrogens. *Endocrinology (Baltimore)* **140**, 5566–5578.

Hammer, R. P. J., and Bridges, R. S. (1987). Preoptic area opioids and opiate receptors increase during pregnancy and decrease during lactation. *Brain Res.* **420**, 48–56.

Hanggi, E. B. (1992). The importance of vocal cues in mother-pup recognition in California sea lion. *Mar. Mamm. Sci.* **8**, 430–432.

Hansen, S., and Ferreira, A. (1986). Food intake, aggression, and fear behavior in the mother rat: Control by neural systems concerned with milk ejection and maternal behavior. *Behav. Neurosci.* **100**, 64–70.

Hansen, S., and Gummesson, B. M. (1982). Participation of the lateral midbrain tegmentum in the neuroendocrine control of sexual behavior and lactation in the rat. *Brain Res.* **251**, 319–325.

Hansen, S., and Kohler, C. (1984). The importance of the peripeduncular nucleus in the neuroendocrine control of sexual behavior and milk ejection in the rat. *Neuroendocrinology* **39**, 563–572.

Hansson, R. P., and Karstad, I. (1959). Feral swine in the southeastern United States. *J. Wildl. Manage.* **23**, 64–79.

Harlow, H. F., Harlow, M. K., and Hansen, E. W. (1963). The maternal affectional system of rhesus monkeys. *In* "Maternal Behavior in Mammals" (H. L. Rheingold, ed.), pp. 254–281. Wiley, New York.

Hartung, T. G., and Dewsbury, D. A. (1979). Paternal behaviour in six species of muroid rodents. *Behav. Neural Biol.* **26**, 446–478.

Hass, C. C. (1990). Alternative maternal-care patterns in two herds of bighorn sheep. *J. Mammal.* **71**, 24–35.

Hatton, G. I., and Ellisman, M. H. (1982). A restructuring of hypothalamic synapses is associated with motherhood. *J. Neurosci.* **2**, 704–707.

Hatton, G. I., and Yang, Q. Z. (1989). Supraoptic nucleus afferents from the main olfactory bulb. II. Intracellularly recorded responses to lateral olfactory tract stimulation in rat brain slices. *Neuroscience* **31**, 289–297.

Hatton, G. I., and Yang, Q. Z. (1990). Activation of excitatory amino acid inputs to supraoptic neurons. I. Induced increases in dye-coupling in lactating, but not virgin or male rats. *Brain Res.* **513**, 264–269.

Hauser, H., and Gandelman, R. (1985). Lever pressing for pups: Evidence for hormonal influence upon maternal behavior of mice. *Horm. Behav.* **19**, 454–468.

Heap, R. B., and Deanesly, R. (1966). Progesterone in systemic blood and placentae of intact and ovariectomized pregnant guinea-pigs. *J. Endocrinol.* **34**, 417.

Hennessy, M. B., McInturf, S. M., and Mazzei, S. J. (1997). Evidence that endogenous corticotropin-releasing factor suppresses behavioral responses of guinea pig pups to brief isolation in novel surroundings. *Dev. Psychobiol.* **31**, 39–47.

Hepper, P. G. (1987). The discrimination of different degrees of relatedness in the rat: evidence for a genetic identifier? *Anim. Behav.* **35**, 549–554.

Herbison, A. E., Robinson, J. E., and Skinner, D. C. (1993). Distribution of estrogen receptor-immunoreactive cells in the preoptic area of the ewe: Co-localization with glutamic acid decarboxylase but not luteinizing hormone-releasing hormone. *Neuroendocrinology* **57**, 751–759.

Hernández, H., Poindron, P., Delgadillo, J. A., Rodriguez, A. D., Kann, G., and Marnet, P. G. (1999). Respuesta hormonal de PRL y GH a la succión en cabras, bajo diferente regimen de contacto madre-cría. *Congr. Soc. Mexi. Cienci. Fisiol., 42nd,* Zacatecas, México, p. Resumen O 50.

Hernández, H., Serafin, N., Rodriguez, A. D., Terrazas, A., Flores, J. A., Delgadillo, J. A., and Poindron, P. (2000). Anosmia does not reduce the duration of postpartum anestrus nursing goats. *Int. Confer. Goats, 7th,* Clermont-Ferrand, France, p. 740.

Herrenkohl, L. R., and Rosenberg, P. A. (1972). Exteroceptive stimulation of maternal behavior in the naive rat. *Physiol. Behav.* **8,** 595–598.

Herrenkohl, L. R., and Rosenberg, P. A. (1974). Effects of hypothalamic deafferentation late in gestation on lactation and nursing behavior in the rat. *Horm. Behav.* **5,** 33–41.

Herrenkohl, L. R., and Sachs, B. D. (1972). Meeting report: Sensory regulation of maternal behavior in mammals. *Physiol. Behav.* **9,** 689–692.

Herscher, L., Moore, A. U., and Richmond, J. B. (1958). Effect of postpartum separation of mother and kid on maternal care in the domestic goat. *Science* **128,** 1342–1343.

Herscher, L., Richmond, J. B., and Moore, A. U. (1963a). Maternal behavior in sheep and goats. *In* "Maternal Behavior in Mammals" (H. L. Rheingold, ed.), pp. 203–232. Wiley, New York.

Herscher, L., Richmond, J. B., and Moore, A. U. (1963b). Modifiability of the critical period for the development of maternal behavior in sheep and goats. *Behaviour* **20,** 311–319.

Hess, C. E., Graves, H. B., and Wilson, L. L. (1974). Individual preweaning suckling behavior of single, twin and triplet lambs. *J. Anim. Sci.* **38,** 1313–1318.

Hileman, S. M., Handa, R. J., and Jackson, G. L. (1999). Distribution of estrogen receptor-beta messenger ribonucleic acid in the male sheep hypothalamus. *Biol. Reprod.* **60,** 1279–1284.

Hinch, G. N. (1989). The sucking behaviour of triplet, twin and single lambs at pasture. *Appl. Anim. Behav. Sci.* **22,** 39–48.

Hinch, G. N., Lécrivain, E., Lynch, J. J., and Erwin, R. L. (1987). Changes in maternal-young associations with increasing age of lambs. *Appl. Anim. Behav. Sci.* **17,** 305–318.

Hinch, G. N., Lynch, J. J., Elwin, R. L., and Green, G. C. (1990). Long term association between Merino ewes and their offspring. *Appl. Anim. Behav. Sci.* **27,** 93–103.

Hinds, L. A., Tyndale-Biscoe, C. H., Shaw, G., Fletcher, T. P., and Renfree, M. B. (1990). Effects of prostaglandin and prolactin on luteolysis and parturient behavior in the non-pregnant tammar, *Macropus eugenii. J. Reprod. Fertil.* **88,** 323–333.

Hofer, M. A. (1987). Shaping forces within early social relationships. *In* "Perinatal Development: A Psychobiological Perspective" (N. A. Krasnegor, E. M. Blass, M. A. Hofer, and W. P. Smotherman, eds.), pp. 251–274. Academic Press, Orlando, FL.

Hofer, M. A., Shair, H., and Singh, P. (1976). Evidence that maternal ventral skin substances promote suckling in infant rats. *Physiol. Behav.* **17,** 131–136.

Hoffman, B., Schans, D., Gimenez, T., Ender, M. L., Herman, C., and Karg, H. (1973). Changes of progesterone, total oestrogens, corticosteroids, prolactin and LH in bovine peripheral plasma around parturition with special reference to the effect of exogenous corticoids and prolactin inhibitor respectively. *Acta Endocrinol. (Copenhagen)* **73,** 385–395.

Holman, S. D., and Goy, R. W. (1980). Behavioral and mammary responses of adult female rhesus to strange infants. *Horm. Behav.* **14,** 348–357.

Holman, S. D., and Goy, R. W. (1995). Experiential and hormonal correlates of care giving in Rhesus macaques. *In* "Motherhood in Human and Nonhuman Primates" (C. R. Pryce, R. D. Martin, and D. Skuse, eds.), pp. 87–93. Karger, Basel.

Holmes, W. G. (1990). Parent-offspring recognition in mammals: A proximate and ultimate perspective. *In* "Mammalian Parenting: Biochemical, Neurobiological, and Behavioral Determinants" (N. A. Krasnegor and R. B. Bridges, eds.), pp. 441–460. Oxford Univ. Press, New York.

Horrell, I., and Bennett, J. (1981). Disruption of teat preferences and retardation of growth following cross-fostering of 1-week-old pigs. *Anim. Prod.* **33,** 99–106.

Horrel, I., and Hodgson, J. (1986). The behavioral effects of fostering in pigs. *In* "Ethology of Domestic Animals" (M. Nichelmann, ed.), pp. 87–92. Privat, Toulouse, France.

Horrel, I., and Hodgson, J. (1992). The bases of sow-piglet identification. 1. The identifications by sows of their own piglets and the presence of intruders. *Appl. Anim. Behav. Sci.* **33,** 319–327.

Hrabovszky, E., Kallo, I., Hajszan, T., Shughrue, P. J., Merchenthaler, I., and Liposits, Z. (1998). Expression of estrogen receptor-beta messenger ribonucleic acid in oxytocin and vasopressin neurons of the rat supraoptic and paraventricular nuclei. *Endocrinology (Baltimore)* **139,** 2600–2604.

Hrdy, S. B. (1977). "The Langurs of Abu." Harvard University Press, Cambridge, MA.

Hudson, R., and Altbäcker, V. (1992). Development of feeding and food preference in the European rabbit: Environmental and maturational determinants. *In* "Ontogeny and Social Transmission of Food Preferences in Mammals: Basic and Applied Research" (B. G. Galef, M. Mainardi, and P. Valsecchi, eds.), pp. 125–145. Harwood Academic Publ., London.

Hudson, R., and Distel, H. (1983). Nipple location by newborn rabbits: Behavioral evidence for pherohomonal guidance. *Behaviour* **85,** 260–275.

Hudson, R., and Distel, H. (1984). Nipple search pheromone in rabbits: Dependence on season and reproductive state. *J. Comp. Physiol., Sect. A* **155,** 13–17.

Hudson, R., Gonzáles-Mariscal, G., and Beyer, C. (1990). Chin-marking behavior, sexual receptivity, and pheromone emission in steroid-treated, ovariectomized rabbits. *Horm. Behav.* **24**, 1–13.

Hudson, R., Bilkó, A., and Altbäcker, V. (1996). Nursing, weaning and the development of independent feeding in the rabbit (*Oryctolagus cuniculus*). *Z. Säugetierk.* **61**, 39–48.

Hudson, R., Cruz, Y., Lucio, R. A., Ninomiya, J., and Martínez-Gómez, M. (1999). Temporal and behavioral patterning of parturition in rabbits and rats. *Physiol. Behav.* **66**, 599–604.

Hudson, S. J., and Mullord, M. M. (1977). Investigations on maternal bonding in dairy cattle. *Appl. Anim. Ethol.* **3**, 271–276.

Ichikawa, J., and Fujii, J. (1982). Effect of prenatal androgen treatment on maternal behavior in the female rat. *Horm. Behav.* **16**, 224–233.

Illmann, G., and Spinka, M. (1993). Maternal behavior of dairy heifers and suckling of their newborn calves in group housing. *Appl. Anim. Behav. Sci.* **36**, 91–98.

Insel, T. R. (1986). Postpartum increases in brain oxytocin binding. *Neuroendocrinology* **44**, 515–518.

Insel, T. R. (1990). Regional changes in brain oxytocin receptors post-partum: Time course and relationship to maternal behavior. *J. Neuroendocrinol.* **2**, 539–545.

Insel, T. R. (1992). Oxytocin-a neuropeptide for affiliation: evidence from behavioral, receptor autoradiographic, and comparative studies. *Psychoneuroendocrinology* **17**, 3–35.

Insel, T. R., and Harbaugh, C. R. (1989). Lesions of the hypothalamic paraventricular nucleus disrupt the initiation of maternal behavior. *Physiol. Behav.* **45**, 1033–1041.

Insel, T. R., Gelhard, R., and Shapiro, L. E. (1991). The comparative distribution of forebrain receptors for neurohypophyseal peptides in monogamous and polygamous mice. *Neuroscience* **43**, 623–630.

Irving, C., Jones, D. E., and Knifton, A. (1972). Progesterone concentrations in the peripheral plasma of pregnant goats. *J. Endocrinol.* **53**, 447–452.

Izquierdo, M. A., Collado, P., Segovia, S., Guillamón, A., and Del Cerro, M. C. (1992). Maternal behavior induced in male rats by bilateral lesions of the bed nucleus of the accessory olfactory tract. *Physiol. Behav.* **52**, 707–712.

Jacobson, C. D., Terkel, J., Gorski, R. A., and Sawyer, C. H. (1980). Effects of small medial preoptic area lesions on maternal behavior: retrieving and nest building in the rat. *Brain Res.* **194**, 471–478.

Jakubowski, M., and Terkel, J. (1982). Infanticide and caretaking in non-lactating *Mus musculus*: Influence of genotype, family group, and sex. *Anim. Behav.* **30**, 1029–1035.

Jakubowski, M., and Terkel, J. (1985a). Establishment and maintenance of maternal responsiveness in postpartum Wistar rats. *Anim. Behav.* **34**, 256–262.

Jakubowski, M., and Terkel, J. (1985b). Incidence of pup killing and parental behavior in virgin female and male rats (*Rattus norvegicus*): Differences between Wistar and Sprague-Dawley stocks. *J. Comp. Psychol.* **99**, 93–97.

Jakubowski, M., and Terkel, J. (1985c). Transition from pup killing to parental behavior in male and virgin female albino rats. *Physiol. Behav.* **34**, 683–686.

Jakubowski, M., and Terkel, J. (1986). Female reproductive function and sexually dimorphic prolactin secretion in rats with lesions in the medial preoptic-anterior hypothalamic continuum. *Neuroendocrinology* **43**, 696–705.

Jay, P. (1963). Mother-infant relations in Langurs. *In* "Maternal Behavior in Mammals" (H. L. Rheingold, ed.), pp. 282–304. Wiley, New York.

Jay, P. (1965). Field studies. *In* "Behavior of Nonhuman Primates" (A. M. Schrier, H. F. Harlow, and F. Stollnitz, eds.), Vol. 2, pp. 525–591. Academic Press, New York.

Jensen, P. (1986). Observations on the maternal behaviour of free-ranging domestic pigs. *Appl. Anim. Behav. Sci.* **16**, 131–142.

Jensen, P. (1989). Nest choice and nest-building of free-ranging domestic pigs due to farrow. *Appl. Anim. Behav. Sci.* **22**, 13–21.

Jensen, P., Florén, K., and Hobroh, B. (1987). Peri-parturient changes in behaviour in free-ranging domestic pigs. *Appl. Anim. Behav. Sci.* **17**, 69–76.

Jeppesen, L. E. (1982a). Teat order in groups of piglets reared on an artificial sow: II. Maintenance of teat-order with some evidence for the use of odour cues. *Appl. Anim. Ethol.* **8**, 347–355.

Jeppesen, L. E. (1982b). Teat order in groups of piglets reared on an artificial sow: I. Formation of teat-order and influence of milk yield on teat preference. *Appl. Anim. Ethol.* **8**, 335–345.

Jewell, P. A., and Grubb, P. (1974). "Island Survivors: The Ecology of the Soay Sheep on St Kilda." Athlone Press, London.

Jilge, B. (1993). The ontogeny of circadian rhythms in the rabbit. *J. Biol. Rhythms* **8**, 247–260.

Jilge, B. (1995). Ontogeny of the rabbit's circadian rhythms without an external zeitgeber. *Physiol. Behav.* **58**, 131–140.

Jiménez, A., Beyer, C., Rosenblatt, J. S., and González-Mariscal, G. (2000). Localización de neuronas inmunorreactivas a la proteína FOS como consecuencia del amamantamiento. *Congr. Latinoamer. Cienci. Fisiol. 20th,* Cancún, México, p. C28.

Jirikowski, G. F. (1992). Oxytocinergic neuronal systems during mating, pregnancy, parturition, and lactation. *Ann. N. Y. Acad. Sci.* **652**, 253–270.

Jirikowski, G. F., Caldwell, J. D., Pilgrim, C., Stumpf, W. E., and Pedersen, C. A. (1989). Changes in immunostaining for oxytocin in the forebrain of the female rat during late pregnancy, parturition and early lactation. *Cell Tissue Res.* **256**, 411–417.

Johnson, R. L., and Southwick, C. H. (1984). Structural diversity and mother-infant relations among rhesus monkeys in India and Nepal. *Folia Primatol.* **43**, 198–215.

Jones, J. S., and Wynne-Edwards, K. E. (2000). Paternal hamsters mechanically assist the delivery, consume amniotic fluid and placenta, remove fetal membranes, and provide parental care during the birth process. *Horm. Behav.* **37**, 116–125.

Kalinichev, M., Rosenblatt, J. S., and Morrell, J. I. (2000a). The medial preoptic area, necessary for adult maternal behavior in rats, is only partially established as a component of the neural circuit that supports maternal behavior in juvenile rats. *Behav. Neurosci.* **114**, 196–210.

Kalinichev, M., Rosenblatt, J. S., Nakabeppu, Y., and Morrell, J. I. (2000b). Induction of c-Fos-Like and FosB-Like immunoreactivity reveals forebrain neuronal populations involved differentially in pup-mediated maternal behavior in juvenile and adult rats. *J. Comp. Neurol.* **416**, 45–78.

Källquist, L., and Mossing, T. (1982). Olfactory recognition between mother and calf in reindeer (*Rangifer tarandus* L.). *Appl. Anim. Ethol.* **8**, 561–565.

Kaplan, J. N., Winship-Ball, A., and Sim, L. (1978). Maternal discrimination of infant vocalizations in squirrel monkeys. *Primates* **19**, 187–193.

Karim, S. M. M. (1972). Physiological rôle of prostaglandins in the control of parturition and menstruation. *J. Reprod. Fertil.* **16**, 105–119.

Kendrick, K. M., and Keverne, E. B. (1989). Effects of intracerebroventricular infusions of naltrexone and phentolamine on central and peripheral oxytocin release and on maternal behaviour induced by vaginocervical stimulation in the ewe. *Brain Res.* **505**, 329–332.

Kendrick, K. M., and Keverne, E. B. (1991). Importance of progesterone and estrogen priming for the induction of maternal behavior by vaginocervical stimulation in sheep: effects of maternal experience. *Physiol. Behav.* **49**, 745–750.

Kendrick, K. M., Keverne, E. B., Baldwin, B. A., and Sharman, D. F. (1986). Cerebrospinal fluid levels of acetylcholinesterase, monoamines and oxytocin during labour, parturition, vaginocervical stimulation, lamb separation and suckling in sheep. *Neuroendocrinology* **44**, 149–156.

Kendrick, K. M., Keverne, E. B., and Baldwin, B. A. (1987). Intracerebroventricular oxytocin stimulates maternal behaviour in the sheep. *Neuroendocrinology* **46**, 56–61.

Kendrick, K. M., Keverne, E. B., Chapman, C., and Baldwin, B. A. (1988a). Intracranial dialysis measurement of oxytocin, monoamine and uric acid release from the olfactory bulb and substantia nigra of sheep during parturition, suckling, separation from lambs and eating. *Brain Res.* **439**, 1–10.

Kendrick, K. M., Keverne, E. B., Shapman, C., and Baldwin, B. A. (1988b). Microdialysis measurement of oxytocin, aspartate, gama-aminobutyric acid and glutamate release from the olfactory bulb of the sheep during vaginocervical stimulation. *Brain Res.* **442**, 171–174.

Kendrick, K. M., Lévy, F., and Keverne, E. B. (1991). Importance of vaginocervical stimulation for the formation of maternal bonding in primiparous and multiparous parturient ewes. *Physiol. Behav.* **50**, 595–600.

Kendrick, K. M., da Costa, A. P., Hinton, M. R., and Keverne, E. B. (1992a). A simple method for fostering lambs using anoestrous ewes with artificially induced lactation and maternal behaviour. *Appl. Anim. Behav. Sci.* **34**, 345–357.

Kendrick, K. M., Keverne, E. B., Hinton, M. R., and Goode, J. A. (1992b). Oxytocin, amino acid and monoamine release in the region of the medial preoptic area and bed nucleus of the stria terminalis of the sheep during parturition and suckling. *Brain Res.* **569**, 199–209.

Kendrick, K. M., Lévy, F., and Keverne, E. B. (1992c). Changes in the sensory processing of olfactory signals induced by birth in sleep. *Science* **256**, 833–836.

Kendrick, K. M., Fabre-Nys, C., Blache, D., Goode, J. A., and Broad, K. D. (1993). The role of oxytocin release in the mediobasal hypothalamus of the sheep in relation to sexual female receptivity. *J. Neuroendocrinol.* **5**, 13–21.

Kendrick, K. M., Atkins, K., Hinton, M. R., Broad, K. D., Fabre-Nys, C., and Keverne, B. (1995). Facial and vocal discrimination in sheep. *Anim. Behav.* **49**, 1665–1676.

Kendrick, K. M., Atkins, K., Hinton, M. R., Heavens, P., and Keverne, B. (1996). Are faces special for sheep? Evidence from facial and object discrimination learning tests showing effects of inversion and social familiarity. *Behav. Processes* **38**, 19–35.

Kendrick, K. M., Da Costa, A. P., Broad, K. D., Ohkura, S., Guevara, R., Lévy, F., and Keverne, E. B. (1997a). Neural control of maternal behaviour and olfactory recognition of offspring. *Brain Res. Bull.* **44**, 383–395.

Kendrick, K. M., Guevara-Guzman, R., Zorrilla, J., Hinton, M. R., Broad, K. D., Mimmack, M., and Ohkura, S. (1997b). Formation of olfactory memories mediated by nitric oxide. *Nature (London)* **388**, 670–674.

Kendrick, K. M., Hinton, M. R., Atkins, K., Haupt, M. A., and Skinner, J. D. (1998). Mothers determine sexual preferences. *Nature (London)* **395**, 229–230.

Kennell, J. H., Jerauld, R., Wolfe, H., Chesler, D., Kreger, N. C., McAlpine, W., Steffa, M., and Klaus, M. H. (1974). Maternal behavior one year after early and extended post-partum contact. *Dev. Med. Child. Neurol.* **16**, 172–179.

Kenyon, P., Cronin, P., and Keeble, S. (1981). Disruption of maternal retrieving by perioral anesthesia. *Physiol. Behav.* **27**, 313–321.

Kenyon, P., Cronin, P., and Keeble, S. (1983). Role of the infraorbital nerve in retrieving behavior in lactating rats. *Behav. Neurosci.* **97**, 255–269.

Keverne, E. B. (1992). Primate social relationships: Their determinants and consequences. *Adv. Study Behav.* **21**, 1–37.

Keverne, E. B. (1995). Neurochemical changes accompanying the reproductive process: Their significance for maternal care in primates and other mammals. *In* "Motherhood in Human and Nonhuman Primates" (C. R. Price, R. D. Martin, and D. Skuse, eds.), pp. 69–77. Karger, Basel.

Keverne, E. B. (1997). An evaluation of what the mouse knockout experiments are telling us about mammalian behavior. *BioEssays* **19**, 1091–1098.

Keverne, E. B., and Kendrick, K. M. (1991). Morphine and corticotrophin-releasing factor potentiate maternal acceptance in multiparous ewes after vaginocervical stimulation. *Brain Res.* **540**, 55–62.

Keverne, E. B., Lévy, F., Poindron, P., and Lindsay, D. R. (1983). Vaginal stimulation: An important determinant of maternal bonding in sheep. *Science* **219**, 81–83.

Keverne, E. B., Lévy, F., Guevara-Guzman, R., and Kendrick, K. M. (1993). Influence of birth and maternal experience on olfactory bulb neurotransmitter release. *Neuroscience* **56**, 557–565.

Keverne, E. B., Nevison, C. M., and Martel, F. L. (1997). Early learning and the social bond. *Ann. N. Y. Acad. Sci.* **807**, 329–339.

Kiley, M. (1972). The vocalizations of ungulates, their causation and function. *Z. Tierpsychol.* **31**, 171–222.

Kilinga, K., Bek, E., and Runnenbaum, B. (1978). Maternal peripheral testosterone levels during the first half of pregnancy. *Am. J. Obstet. Gynecol.* **131**, 60–62.

King, J. A. (1963). Maternal behavior in *Peromyscus. In* "Maternal Behavior in Mammals" (H. L. Rheingold, ed.), pp. 58–93. Wiley, New York.

Kinsley, C. H. (1990). Prenatal and postnatal influences on parental behavior in rodents. *In* "Mammalian Parenting: Biochemical, Neurobiological, and Behavioral Determinants" (N. A. Krasnegor and R. B. Bridges, eds.), pp. 347–371. Oxford University Press, New York.

Kinsley, C. H., and Bridges, R. S. (1988). Prenatal stress and maternal behavior in intact virgin rats: Response latencies are decreased in males and increased in females. *Horm. Behav.* **22**, 76–89.

Kirkpatrick, B., Kim, J. W., and Insel, T. R. (1994). Limbic system fos expression associated with paternal behavior. *Brain Res.* **658**, 112–118.

Kleiman, D. J. (1972). Maternal behavior of the Green acouchi (*Myoprocta pratti),* a South American caviomorph rodent. *Behaviour* **43**, 48–84.

Kleiman, D. J., and Malcolm, J. R. (1981). The evolution of male parental investment in mammals. *In* "Parental Care in Mammals" (D. J. Gubernick and P. H. Klopfer, eds.), pp. 347–387. Plenum Press, New York.

Klopfer, P. H. (1970). Discrimination of young of galalgos. *Folia Primatol.* **13**, 137–143.

Klopfer, P. H. (1971). Mother love: what turns it on? *Am. Sci.* **59**, 404–407.

Klopfer, P. H. (1981). Origins of parental care. *In* "Parental Care in Mammals" (D. J. Gubernick and P. H. Klopfer, eds.), pp. 1–11. Plenum Press, New York.

Klopfer, P. H., and Boskoff, K. J. (1979). Maternal behavior in prosimians. *In* "The Study of Prosimian Behavior" (G. A. Doyle and R. D. Martin, eds.), pp. 123–156. Academic Press, New York.

Klopfer, P. H., and Gamble, J. (1966). Maternal imprinting in goats: the role of chemical senses. *Z. Tierpsychol.* **23**, 588–592.

Klopfer, P. H., and Gilbert, B. K. (1966). A note on retrieval and recognition of young in the elephant seal, *Mirounga angustirostris. Z. Tierpsychol.* **23**, 757–760.

Klopfer, P. H., and Klopfer, M. S. (1968). Maternal "imprinting" in goats: fostering of alien young. *Z. Tierpsychol.* **25**, 862–866.

Klopfer, P. H., Adams, D. K., and Klopfer, M. S. (1964). Maternal imprinting in goats. *Proc. Natl. Acad. Sci. U.S.A.* **52**, 911–914.

Knight, M. H., Van Jaarsveld, A., and Mills, M. G. L. (1992). Allosuckling in spotted hyaenas (*Crocuta crocuta):* An example of behavioural flexibility in carnivores. *Afr. J. Ecol.* **30**, 245–251.

Knudston, P. M. (1974). Birth of a harbor seal. *Nat. Hist.* **83**, 30–37.

Koch, M. (1990). Effects of treatment with estradiol and parental experience on the number and distribution of estrogen-binding neurons in the ovariectomized mouse brain. *Neuroendocrinology* **51**, 505–514.

Koch, M., and Ehret, G. (1989). Estradiol and parental experience, but not prolactin, are necessary for ultrasound recognition and pup-retrieving in the mouse. *Physiol. Behav.* **45**, 771–776.

Komisaruk, B. R., Adler, N. T., and Hutchinson, J. (1972). Genital sensory field: Enlargement by estrogen treatment in female rats. *Science* **178**, 1295–1298.

Komisaruk, B. R., Rosenblatt, J. S., Barona, M. L., Chinapen, S., Nissanov, J., O'Bannon, R. T., III, Johnson, B. M., and Del Cerro, M. C. (2000). Combined c-fos and ^{14}C-2-deoxyglucose method to differentiate site-specific excitation from disinhibition: Analysis of maternal behavior in the rat. *Brain Res.* **859**, 262–272.

Koranyi, L., Lissak, K., Tamasy, V., and Kamaras, L. (1976). Behavioral and electrophysiological attempts to elucidate central nervous system mechanisms responsible for maternal behavior. *Arch. Sex. Behav.* **5**, 503–510.

Kraemer, G. W. (1992). Attachment and psychopathology. *Behav. Brain Sci.* **15**, 512–541.

Kraemer, G. W., and Clarke, A. S. (1997). Social attachment, brain function, and aggression. *Ann. N.Y. Acad. Sci.* **794**, 121–135.

Krehbiel, D., Poindron, P., Lévy, F., and Prud'Homme, M. J. (1987). Peridural anesthesia disturbs maternal behavior in primiparous and multiparous parturient ewes. *Physiol. Behav.* **40**, 463–472.

Krehbiel, D. A., and Le Roy, L. M. (1979). The quality of hormonally stimulated maternal behavior in ovariectomized rats. *Horm. Behav.* **12**, 243–252.

Kremarik, P., Freund-Mercier, M. J., and Stoeckel, M. E. (1991). Autoradiographic detection of oxytocin- and vasopressin-binding sites in various subnuclei of the BNST in the rat. Effect of functional and experimental sexual steroid variations. *J. Neuroendocrinol.* **3**, 689–698.

Kristal, M. B. (1980). Placentophagia: A biobehavioral enigma (or De gustibus non disputandum est). *Neurosci. Biobehav. Rev.* **4**, 141–150.

Kristal, M. B. (1991). Enhancement of opioid-mediated analgesia: A solution to the enigma of placentophagia. *Neurosci. Biobehav. Rev.* **15**, 425–435.

Kristal, M. B., Thompson, A. C., and Grishkat, H. L. (1985). Placenta ingestion enhances opiate analgesia in rats. *Physiol. Behav.* **35**, 481–486.

Kristal, M. B., Thompson, A. C., and Abbott, P. (1986). Ingestion of amniotic fluid enhances opiate analgesia in rats. *Physiol. Behav.* **38**, 809–815.

Kristal, M. B., Tarapacki, J. A., and Barton, D. (1990). Amniotic fluid ingestion enhances opioid-mediated but not nonopioid-mediated analgesia. *Physiol. Behav.* **47**, 79–81.

Kuhn, C. M., and Schanberg, S. M. (1998). Responses to maternal separation: Mechanisms and mediators. *Int. J. Dev. Neurosci.* **16**, 261–270.

Kuiper, G. G. J. M., Enmark, E., Pelto-HuiKko, M., Nilsson, S., and Gustafsson, J.-Å. (1996). Cloning of a novel estrogen receptor expressed in rat prostate and ovary. *Proc. Natl. Acad. Sci. U.S.A.* **93**, 5925–5930.

Kunkel, P., and Kunkel, I. (1964). Beitrage zur ethologie des hausmeerschweinchens, *Cavia apera F. porcellus. Z. Tierpsychol.* **21**, 603–641.

Kurz, J. C., and Marchinton, R. L. (1972). Radiotelemetry studies of feral hogs in South Carolina. *J. Wildl. Manage.* **36**, 1240–1248.

Labussière, J. (1999). The physiology of milk ejection: Consequences on milking techniques. *In* "Biology of Lactation"

(J. Martinet, L. M. Houdebine, and H. H. Head, eds.), pp. 307–343. INRA Editions, Paris.

Landgraf, R., Neumann, I., and Pittman, Q. J. (1991). Septal and hippocampal release of vasopressin and oxytocin during late pregnancy and parturition in the rat. *Neuroendocrinology* **54**, 378–383.

Lebas, F. (1972). Effet de la simultanéité de la lactation et de la gestation sur les performances laitières chez la lapine. *Ann. Zootech.* **21**, 129–131.

Leboucher, G., and Lescoat, G. (1986). Réponses comportementale et surrélienne à l'exposition brève ou chronique à des nouveau-nés chez des rats Wistar adultes. *Biol. Behav.* **11**, 116–129.

Lécrivain, E., and Janeau, G. (1987). Comportement d'isolement et de recherche d'abri de brebis agnelant en plein air dans un système d'élevage à caractère extensif. *Biol. Behav.* **12**, 127–148.

Lee, A., Clancy, S., and Fleming, A. S. (2000). Mother rats bar-press for pups: effects of lesions of the MPOA and limbic sites on matenal behavior and operant responding for pup-reinforcement. *Behav. Brain Res.* **108**, 215–231.

Lefebvre, L., Viville, S., Barton, S. C., Ishino, F., Keverne, E. B., and Surani, M. A. (1998). Abnormal maternal behaviour and growth retardation associated with loss of the imprinted gene Mest. *Nat. Genet.* **20**, 163–169.

Lehmann, J., Pryce, C. R., Bettschen, D., and Feldon, J. (1999). The maternal separation paradigm and adult emotionality and cognition in male and female Wistar Rats. *Pharmacol. Biochem. Behav.* **64**, 705–715.

Lehmann, M. N., Ebling, J. P., Moenter, S. M., and Karsh, F. J. (1993). Distribution of estrogen receptor-inmunoreactive cells in the sheep brain. *Endocrinology (Baltimore)* **133**, 876–886.

Le Neindre, P., and D'Hour, P. (1989). Effects of a postpartum separation on maternal responses in primiparous and multiparous cows. *Anim. Behav.* **37**, 166–167.

Le Neindre, P., and Garel, J. P. (1976). Existence d'une période sensible pour l'établissement du comportement maternel chez la vache après la mise-bas. *Biol. Behav.* **1**, 217–221.

Le Neindre, P., Poindron, P., and Delouis, C. (1979). Hormonal induction of maternal behavior in non-pregnant ewes. *Physiol. Behav.* **22**, 731–734.

Le Neindre, P., Poindron, P., Trillat, G., and Orgeur, P. (1993). Influence of breed on reactivity of sheep to humans. *Genet., Sel., Evol.* **25**, 447–458.

Lent, P. C. (1974). Mother-infant relationship in ungulates. *In* "The Behaviour of Ungulates and Its Relation to Management" (V. Geist and F. Walther, eds.), pp. 14–55. I.U.CN., Morgues, Switzerland.

Leon, M., and Moltz, H. (1972). The development of the pheromonal bond in the albino rat. *Physiol. Behav.* **8**, 683–686.

Leon, M., Numan, M., and Moltz, H. (1973). Maternal behavior in the rat: Facilitation through gonadectomy. *Science* **179**, 1018–1019.

Leon, M. L., Croskerry, P. G., and Smith, G. K. (1978). Thermal control of nurtural behavior. *J. Comp. Physiol. Psychol.* **21**, 793–811.

Leon, M., Adels, L., and Coopersmith, R. (1985). Thermal limitation of mother-young contact in Norway rats. *Dev. Psychobiol.* **18**, 85–105.

Leon, M., Coopersmith, R., Lee, S., Sullivan, R. M., Wilson, D. A., and Woo, C. C. (1987). Neural and behavioral plasticity induced by early olfactory learning. *In* "Perinatal Development: A Psychobiological Perspective" (N. A. Krasnegor, E. M. Blass, M. A. Hofer, and W. P. Smotherman, eds.), pp. 145–167. Academic Press, Orlando, FL.

Leon, M., Coopersmith, R., Beasley, L. J., and Sullivan, R. M. (1990). Thermal aspects of parenting. *In* "Mammalian Parenting: Biochemical, Neurobiological, and Behavioral Determinant" (N. A. Krasnegor and R. B. Bridges, eds.), pp. 400–415. Oxford University Press, New York.

Leonard. (1972). Effects of neonatal (Day 10) olfactory bulb lesions on social behavior of female golden hamsters (*Mesocricetus auratus*). *J. Comp. Physiol. Psychol.* **80**, 208–215.

Lephart, E. D., and Watson, M. A. (1999). Maternal separation: Hypothalamic-preoptic area and hippocampal Calbindin-D-28K and calretinin in male and female infantile rats. *Neurosci. Lett.* **267**, 41–44.

Le Roy, L. M., and Krehbiel, D. A. (1978). Variations in maternal behavior in the rat as a function of sex and gonadal state. *Horm. Behav.* **11**, 232–247.

Levine, S. (1987). Psychobiologic consequences of disruption in mother-infant relationships. *In* "Perinatal Development. A Psychobiological Perspective" (N. A. Krasnegor, E. M. Blass, M. A. Hofer, and W. P. Smotherman, eds.), pp. 359–376. Academic Press, Orlando, FL.

Levine, S., Coe, C. L., and Smotherman, W. P. (1978). Prolonged cortisol elevation in the infant squirrel monkey after reunion with mother. *Physiol. Behav.* **20**, 7–10.

Lévy, F., and Alexandre, G. (1985). Le comportement alimentaire du cabri créole élevé en stabulation libre de la naissance au sevrage. *Ann. Zootech.* **34**, 181–192.

Lévy, F., and Poindron, P. (1984). Influence du liquide amniotique sur la manifestation du comportement maternel chez la brebis parturiente. *Biol. Behav.* **9**, 271–278.

Lévy, F., and Poindron, P. (1987). The importance of amniotic fluids for the establishment of maternal behaviour in experienced and inexperienced ewes. *Anim. Behav.* **35**, 1188–1192.

Lévy, F., Poindron, P., and Le Neindre, P. (1983). Attraction and repulsion by amniotic fluids and their olfactory control in the ewe around parturition. *Physiol. Behav.* **31**, 687–692.

Lévy, F., Gervais, R., Kindermann, U., Orgeur, P., and Piketty, V. (1990a). Importance of beta-noradrenergic receptors in the olfactory bulb of sheep for recognition of lambs. *Behav. Neurosci.* **104**, 464–469.

Lévy, F., Keverne, E. B., Piketty, V., and Poindron, P. (1990b). Physiological determinism of olfactory attraction for amniotic fluids in sheep. *In* "Chemical Signals in Vertebrates" (D. W. MacDonald, D. Müller-Schwarze, and S. E. Natynczuk, eds.), pp. 162–165. Oxford Univ. Press, New York.

Lévy, F., Kendrick, K. M., Keverne, E. B., Piketty, V., and Poindron, P. (1992). Intracerebral oxytocin is important for the onset of maternal behavior in inexperienced ewes delivered under peridural anesthesia. *Behav. Neurosci.* **106**, 427–432.

Lévy, F., Guevara-Guzman, R., Hinton, M. R., Kendrick, K. M., and Keverne, E. B. (1993). Effects of parturition and maternal experience on noradrenaline and acetylcholine release in the olfactory bulb of sheep. *Behav. Neurosci.* **107**, 662–668.

Lévy, F., Kendrick, K. M., Goode, J. A., Guevara-Guzman, R., and Keverne, E. B. (1995a). Oxytocin and vasopressin release in the olfactory bulb of parturient ewes: changes with maternal experience and effects on acetylcholine, gamma-aminobutyric acid, glutamate and noradrenaline release. *Brain Res.* **669**, 197–206.

Lévy, F., Locatelli, A., Piketty, V., Tillet, Y., and Poindron, P. (1995b). Involvement of the main but not the accessory olfactory system in maternal behavior of primiparous and multiparous ewes. *Physiol. Behav.* **57**, 97–104.

Lévy, F., Kendrick, K., Keverne, E. B., Porter, R. H., and Romeyer, A. (1996). Physiological, sensory and experiential factors of parental care in sheep. *Adv. Study Behav.* **25**, 385–473.

Li, L., Keverne, E. B., Aparicio, S. A., Ishino, F., Barton, S. C., and Surani, M. A. (1999). Regulation of maternal behavior and offspring growth by paternally expressed Peg3. *Science* **284**, 330–333.

Li, X., Schwartz, P. E., and Rissman, E. F. (1997). Distribution of estrogen receptor-beta-like immunoreactivity in rat forebrain. *Neuroendocrinology* **66**, 63–67.

Lickliter, R. E. (1982). Effects of a post-partum separation on maternal responsiveness in primiparous and multiparous domestic goats. *Appl. Anim. Ethol.* **8**, 537–542.

Lickliter, R. E. (1984a). Hiding behavior in domestic goat kids. *Appl. Anim. Behav. Sci.* **12**, 245–251.

Lickliter, R. E. (1984b). Mother-infant spatial relationships in domestic goats. *Appl. Anim. Behav. Sci.* **13**, 93–100.

Lickliter, R. E. (1985). Behavior associated with parturition in the domestic goat. *Appl. Anim. Ethol.* **13**, 335–345.

Lidfors, L., and Jensen, P. (1988). Behavior of free-ranging beef cows and calves. *Appl. Anim. Behav. Sci.* **20**, 237–247.

Liggins, G. C., Grieves, S. A., Kendall, J. Z., and Knox, B. S. (1972). The physiological rôles of progesterone, oestradiol-17beta and prostaglandin F-2alfa in the control of ovine parturition. *J. Reprod. Fertil.* **16**, 85–103.

Lindén, A., Uvnäs-Moberg, P., Eneroth, P., and Söderstetn, P. (1989). Stimulation of maternal behavior in rats with cholecystokinin octapeptide. *J. Neuroendocrinol.* **1**, 389–392.

Lindsay, D. R., and Fletcher, I. C. (1968). Sensory involvement in the recognition of lambs by their dams. *Anim. Behav.* **16**, 415–417.

Lisk, R. D. (1971). Oestrogen and progesterone synergism and elicitation of maternal nest-building in the mouse (*Mus musculus*). *Anim. Behav.* **17**, 730–738.

Lisk, R. D., Prelow, R. A., and Friedman, S. A. (1969). Hormonal stimulation necessary for elicitation of maternal nest-building in the mouse. *Anim. Behav.* **17**, 730–738.

Lisk, R. D., Russell, J. A., Kahler, S. G., and Hanks, J. B. (1973). Regulation of hormonally mediated maternal nest structure in the mouse (*Mus musculus*) as a function of neonatal hormone manipulation. *Anim. Behav.* **21**, 296–301.

Liu, D., Diorio, J., Tannenbaum, B., Caldji, C., Francis, D., Freedman, A., Sharma, S., Pearson, D., Plotsky, P. M., and Meaney, M. J. (1997). Maternal care, hippocampal glucocorticoid receptors, and hypothalamic-pituitary-adrenal responses to stress. *Science* **277**, 1659–1662.

Llauro, J. L., Runnebaum, B., and Zander, J. (1968). Progesterone in human peripheral blood before during and after labor. *Am. J. Obstet. Gynecol.* **101**, 867.

Lonstein, J. S., and De Vries, G. J. (1999a). Comparison of the parental behavior of pair-bonded female and male prairie voles (*Microtus ochrogaster*). *Physiol. Behav.* **66**, 33–40.

Lonstein, J. S., and De Vries, G. J. (1999b). Sex differences in the parental behavior of adult virgin prairie voles: Independence from gonadal hormones and vasopressin. *J. Neuroendocrinol.* **11**, 441–449.

Lonstein, J. S., and De Vries, G. J. (2000a). Influence of gonadal hormones on the development of parental behavior in adult virgin prairie voles (*Microtus ochrogaster*). *Behav. Brain Res.* **114**, 79–87.

Lonstein, J. S., and De Vries, G. J. (2000b). Maternal behavior in lactating rats stimulates c-fos in glutamate decarboxylase-synthesizing neurons of the medial preoptic area, ventral bed nucleus of the stria terminalis, and ventrocaudal periaqueductal gray. *Neuroscience* **100**, 557–568.

Lonstein, J. S., and De Vries, G. J. (2000c). Sex differences in the parental behavior of rodents. *Neurosci. Biobehav. Rev.* **24**, 669–686.

Lonstein, J. S., and Stern, J. M. (1997). Role of the midbrain periaqueductal gray in maternal nurturance and aggression: c-fos and electrolytic lesion studies in lactating rats. *J. Neurosci.* **17**, 3364–3378.

Lonstein, J. S., and Stern, J. M. (1999). Effects of unilateral suckling on nursing behavior and c-fos activity in the caudal periaqueductal gray in rats. *Dev. Psychobiol.* **35**, 264–275.

Lonstein, J. S., Simmons, D. A., Swann, J. M., and Stern, J. M. (1998). Forebrain expression of c-fos due to active maternal behavior in lactating rats. *Neuroscience* **82**, 267–281.

Lonstein, J. S., Gréco, B., De Vries, G. J., Stern, J. M., and Blaustein, J. D. (2000). Maternal behavior stimulates c-fos activity within estrogen receptor alpha-containing neurons in lactating rats. *Neuroendocrinology* **72**, 91–101.

Lott, D. (1962). The role of progesterone in the maternal behavior of rodents. *J. Comp. Physiol. Psychol.* **55**, 610–613.

Louault, F. (1983). Comment les relations mère-jeune influencent-t-elles la reprise post-partum de l'activité cyclique de reproduction chez la brebis Préalpes du Sud? Diplôme d'Etudes Approfondies, Ecole Nationale Supérieure Agronomique, Montpellier, France.

Loughry, W. J., and McCracken, G. F. (1991). Factors influencing female-pup scent recognition in mexican free-tailed bats. *J. Mammal.* **72**, 624–626.

Loundes, D. D., and Bridges, R. S. (1986). Length of prolactin priming differentially affects maternal behavior in female rats. *Biol. Reprod.* **34**, 495–501.

Lubin, M., Leon, M., Moltz, H., and Numan, M. (1972). Hormones and maternal behavior in the male rat. *Horm. Behav.* **3**, 369–374.

Lundblad, E. G., and Hodgen, G. D. (1980). Induction of maternal-infant bonding in Rhesus and Cynomolgus monkeys after cesarean delivery. *Lab. Anim. Sci.* **30**, 913.

Lydon, J. P., De Mayo, F. J., Funk, C. R., Mani, S. K., Hughes, C. A., Montgomery, C. A., Shyamala, G., Conneely, O. M., and O'Malley, B. W. (1995). Mice lacking progesterone receptors exhibit pleiotropic reproductive abnormalities. *Genes Dev.* **9**, 2266–2278.

Lydon, J. P., De Mayo, F. J., Conneely, O. M., and O'Malley, B. W. (1996). Reproductive phenotypes of the progesterone receptor null mutant mouse. *J. Steroid Biochem. Mol. Biol.* **56**, 67–77.

Lynch, J. J., and Alexander, G. (1977). Sheltering behavior of lambing Merino sheep in relation to grass hedges and artificial windbreaks. *Aust. J. Agric. Res.* **28**, 691–701.

Lynch, J. J., Hinch, G. N., and Adams, D. B. (1992). "The Behavior of Sheep. Biological Principles and Implications for Production." CAB International, Oxon, UK.

Lyons, D. M., Price, E. O., and Moberg, G. P. (1988). Individual differences in temperament of domestic dairy goats: Consistency and change. *Anim. Behav.* **36**, 1323–1333.

MacKenna, J. J. (1981). Primate infant caregaving behavior: origins, consequences and variability with emphasis on the common indian Langur Monkey. *In* "Parental Care in Mammals" (D. J. Gubernick and P. H. Klopfer, eds.), pp. 389–416. Plenum Press, New York.

Maestripieri, D. (1994a). Mother-infant relationships in three species of macaques (*Macaca mulata, M. nemestrina, M. Arctoides*). I. Development of the mother-infant relationship in the first three months. *Behaviour* **131**, 75–96.

Maestripieri, D. (1994b). Mother-infant relationships in three species of macaques (*Macaca mulata, M. nemestrina, M. Arctoides*). II. The social environment. *Behaviour* **131**, 97–113.

Maestripieri, D. (1994c). Social structure, infant handling, and mothering styles in group-living Old World monkeys. *Int. J. Primatol.* **15**, 531–553.

Maestripieri, D. (1999). The biology of human parenting: insights from nonhuman primates. *Neurosci. Biobehav. Rev.* **23**, 411–422.

Maestripieri, D., and Zehr, J. L. (1998). Maternal responsiveness increases during pregnancy and after estrogen treatment in macaques. *Horm. Behav.* **34**, 223–230.

Magnusson, J. E., and Fleming, A. S. (1995). Rat pups are reinforcing to the maternal rat: Role of sensory cues. *Psychobiology* **23**, 69–75.

Malenfant, S. A., Barry, M., and Fleming, A. S. (1991). Effects of cycloheximide on the retention of olfactory learning and maternal experience effects in postpartum rats. *Physiol. Behav.* **49**, 289–294.

Mann, M., Michael, S. D., and Svare, B. (1980). Ergot drugs suppress plasma prolactin and lactation but not aggression in parturient mice. *Horm. Behav.* **14**, 319–328.

Mann, P. E., and Bridges, R. S. (1992). Neural and endocrine sensitivities to opioids decline as a function of multiparity in the rat. *Brain Res.* **580**, 241–248.

Mann, P. E., Pasternak, G. W., and Bridges, R. S. (1990). Mu 1 opioid receptor involvement in maternal behavior. *Physiol. Behav.* **47**, 133–138.

Mann, P. E., Kinsley, C. H., and Bridges, R. S. (1991). Opioid receptor subtype involvement in maternal behavior in lactating rats. *Neuroendocrinology* **53**, 487–492.

Mann, P. E., Felicio, L. F., and Bridges, R. S. (1995). Investigation into the role of cholecystokinin (CCK) in the induction and maintenance of maternal behavior in rats. *Horm. Behav.* **29**, 392–406.

Manning, C. J., Wakeland, E. K., and Pots, W. K. (1992). Communal nesting patterns in mice implicate MHC genes in kin recognition. *Nature (London)* **360**, 581–583.

Marques, D. M. (1979). Roles of the main olfactory and vomeronasal systems in the response of the female hamster to young. *Behav. Neural Biol.* **26**, 311–329.

Marques, D. M., and Valenstein, E. S. (1976). Another hamster paradox: more males carry pups and fewer kill and cannibalize young than do females. *J. Comp. Physiol. Psychol.* **90**, 653–657.

Marques, D. M., Malsbury, C. W., and Daood, J. (1979). Hypothalamic knife cuts dissociate maternal behaviors, sexual receptivity and estrous cyclicity in female hamsters. *Physiol. Behav.* **23**, 347–355.

Martel, F. L., Nevison, C. M., Rayment, F. D., Simpson, M. J., and Keverne, E. B. (1993). Opioid receptor blockade reduces maternal affect and social grooming in rhesus monkeys. *Psychoneuroendocrinology* **18**, 307–321.

Martin, D. L., and Rimvall, K. (1993). Regulation of gamma-aminobutyric acid synthesis in the brain. *J. Neurochem.* **60**, 395–407.

Martin, P., and Bateson, P. (1982). The lactation-blocking drug bromocriptine and its application to studies of weaning and behavioral development. *Dev. Psychobiol.* **15**, 139–157.

Mateo, A. R., Hijazi, M., and Hammer, R. P. (1992). Dynamic patterns of medial preoptic mu-opiate receptor regulation by gonadal steroid hormones. *Neuroendocrinology* **55**, 51–58.

Matthews-Felton, T., Corodimas, K. P., Rosenblatt, J. S., and Morrell, J. I. (1995). Lateral habenula neurons are necessary for the hormonal onset of maternal behavior and for the display of postpartum estrus in naturally parturient female rats. *Behav. Neurosci.* **109**, 1172–1188.

Matthews-Felton, T., Linton, L. N., Rosenblatt, J. S., and Morrell, J. I. (1999). Estrogen implants in the lateral habenular nucleus do not stimulate the onset of maternal behavior in female rats. *Horm. Behav.* **35**, 71–80.

May, R. M., and Rubenstein, D. I. (1984). Reproductive strategies. *In* "Reproductive Fitness" (C. R. Austin and R. V. Short, eds.), Vol. 4, pp. 1–23. Cambridge University Press, Cambridge, UK.

Mayer, A. D. (1983). The ontogeny of maternal behavior in rodents. *In* "Parental Behavior of Rodents" (R. W. Elwood, ed.), pp. 1–21. Wiley, Chichester.

Mayer, A. D., and Rosenblatt, J. S. (1975). Olfactory basis for the delayed onset of maternal behavior in virgin female rats: Experiential effects. *J. Comp. Physiol. Psychol.* **89**, 701–710.

Mayer, A. D., and Rosenblatt, J. S. (1977). Effects of intranasal zinc sulfate on open field and maternal behavior in female rats. *Physiol. Behav.* **18**, 101–109.

Mayer, A. D., and Rosenblatt, J. S. (1979a). Hormonal influences during the ontogeny of maternal behavior in female rats. *J. Comp. Physiol. Psychol.* **93**, 879–898.

Mayer, A. D., and Rosenblatt, J. S. (1979b). Ontogeny of maternal behavior in the laboratory rat: Early origins in 18- to 27-day-old young. *Dev. Psychobiol.* **12**, 407–424.

Mayer, A. D., and Rosenblatt, J. S. (1984). Prepartum changes in maternal responsiveness and nest defense in *Rattus norvegicus*. *J. Comp. Psychol.* **98,** 177–188.

Mayer, A. D., Freeman, N. C., and Rosenblatt, J. S. (1979). Ontogeny of maternal behavior in the laboratory rat: Factors underlying changes in responsiveness from 30 to 90 days. *Dev. Psychobiol.* **12,** 425–439.

Mayer, A. D., Faris, P. L., Komisaruk, B. R., and Rosenblatt, J. S. (1985). Opiate antagonism reduces placentophagia and pup cleaning by parturient rats. *Pharmacol. Biochem. Behav.* **22,** 1035–1044.

McCarthy, M. M., Bare, J. E., and Vom Saal, F. S. (1986). Infanticide and parental behavior in wild female house mice: effects of ovariectomy, adrenalectomy, and administration of oxytocin and prostaglandin F2-alpha. *Physiol. Behav.* **36,** 17–23.

McCarthy, M. M., Curran, G. H., and Siegel, H. I. (1994). Evidence for the involvement of prolactin in the maternal behavior of the hamster. *Physiol. Behav.* **55,** 181–184.

McCormack, J. T., and Greenwald, G. S. (1974). Concentration of progesterone and estradiol 17-beta in the peripheral plasma during pregnancy in the mouse. *J. Endocrinol.* **62,** 101–107.

McCowan, B., and Reiss, D. (1995). Maternal aggressive contact vocalizations in captive bottlenose dolphins (*Tursiops truncatus*): Wide-band, low-frequency signals during mother/aunt-infant interactions. *Zoo Biol.* **14,** 293–309.

McCracken, G. F. (1984). Communal nursing in Mexican free-tailed bat maternity colonies. *Science* **223,** 1090–1091.

McCracken, G. F., and Gustin, M. K. (1991). Nursing behavior in Mexican free-tailed bat maternity colonies. *Ethology* **89,** 305–321.

McGaugh, J. L. (1992). Neuromodulatory systems and the regulation of memory storage. *In* "Neuropsychology of Memory" (L. R. Squire and N. Butters, eds.), pp. 386–401. Guilford Press, New York.

McInroy, J. K., Brousmiche, D. G., and Wynne-Edwards, K. E. (2000). Fathers, fat, and maternal energetics in a biparental hamster: Paternal presence determines the outcome of a current reproductive effort and adipose tissue limits subsequent reproductive effort. *Horm. Behav.* **37,** 399–409.

McNeilly, A. S. (1994). Suckling and the control of gonadotropin secretion. *In* "The Physiology of Reproduction" (E. Knobil and J. D. Neill, eds.), 2nd ed., pp. 1179–1212. Raven Press, New York.

McNeilly, A. S., and Friessen, H. G. (1978). Prolactin during pregnancy and lactation in the rabbit. *Endocrinology (Baltimore)* **102,** 1548–1554.

Meese, G. B., and Baldwin, B. A. (1975). Effects of olfactory bulb ablation on maternal behavior in sows. *Appl. Anim. Ethol.* **1,** 379–386.

Meier, G. W. (1965). Maternal behaviour of feral- and laboratory-reared monkeys following the surgical delivery of their infants. *Nature (London)* **206,** 492–493.

Melo, A. I., Rosenblatt, J. S., and González-Mariscal, G. (1998). Placentophagia in New Zealand white rabbits. *Dev. Psychobiol.* **32,** 155.

Meltzer, H. Y., Gudelsky, G. A., Simonovic, M., and Fang, V. S. (1982a). Effect of dopamine agonists and antagonists on prolactin and growth hormone secretion. *Psychopharmacology (Berlin)* **28,** 200–218.

Meltzer, H. Y., So, R., and Fang, V. S. (1982b). Effect of benzamide drugs on prolactin secretion: Relation to the dopamine receptor. *Adv. Biochem. Psychopharmacol.* **35,** 61–82.

Mena, F., and Grosvenor, C. E. (1972). Effect of suckling and exteroceptive stimulation upon prolactin release in the rat during late lactation. *J. Endocrinol.* **52,** 11–22.

Mena, F., Clapp, C., and Martinez De La Escalera, G. (1990a). Age related stimulatory and inhibitory effects of suckling regulate lactation in rabbits. *Physiol. Behav.* **48,** 307–310.

Mena, F., Clapp, C., Aguayo, D., and Martínez de la Escalera, G. (1990b). Prolactin and propranolol prevent the suckling-induced inhibition of lactation in rabbits. *Physiol. Behav.* **48,** 311–315.

Mens, W. B. J., Witter, A., and Van Wimersma Greidanus, T. B. (1983). Penetration of neurohypophyseal hormones from plasma into cerebrospinal fluid (CSF): Half-times of disappearance of these neuropeptides from CSF. *Brain Res.* **262,** 143–149.

Merchant, J. C., and Sharman, G. B. (1966). Observation on the attachment of marsupial pouch young to the teats and on the rearing of pouch young by foster-mothers of the same or different species. *Aust. J. Zool.* **14,** 593–609.

Meulenberg, P. M. M., and Hofman, J. A. (1991). Maternal testosterone and fetal sex. *J. Steroid Biochem. Mol. Biol.* **39,** 51–54.

Meunier-Salaün, M. C., Gort, F., Prunier, A., and Schouten, W. P. G. (1991). Behavioral patterns and progesterone, cortisol and prolactin levels around parturition in European (Large-White) and Chinese (Meishan) sows. *Appl. Anim. Behav. Sci.* **31,** 43–59.

Miceli, M. O., and Malsbury, C. W. (1982). Sagittal knife cuts in the near and far lateral preoptic area-hypothalamus disrupt maternal behavior in female hamsters. *Physiol. Behav.* **28,** 857–867.

Miceli, M. O., Fleming, A. S., and Malsbury, C. W. (1983). Disruption of maternal behavior in virgin and postparturient rats following sagittal plane knife cuts in the preoptic area-hypothalamus. *Behav. Brain Res.* **9,** 337–360.

Michener, G. R. (1973). Maternal behaviour in Richardson's ground squirrel (*Spermophilus richardsonii richardsonii*):

Retrieval of young by non-lactating females. *Anim. Behav.* **21**, 157–159.

Michener, G. R. (1974). Development of adult-young identification in Richardson's ground squirrel. *Dev. Psychobiol.* **7**, 375–384.

Modney, B. K., and Hatton, G. I. (1990). Motherhood modifies magnocellular neuronal relationships in functionally meaningful ways. *In* "Mammalian Parenting: Biochemical, Neurobiological, and Behavioral Determinants" (N. A. Krasnegor and R. S. Bridges, eds.), pp. 305–323. Oxford University Press, New York.

Modney, B. K., and Hatton, G. I. (1994). Maternal behaviors: Evidence that they feed back to alter brain morphology and function. *Acta Paediatr., Suppl.* **397**, 29–32.

Moehlman, P. D. (1987). Social organization in jackals. *Am. Sci.* **75**, 366–375.

Moffat, S. T., Suh, E. J., and Fleming, A. S. (1993). Noradrenergic involvement in the consolidation of maternal experience in postpartum rats. *Physiol. Behav.* **53**, 805–811.

Moltz, H. (1975). Maternal behavior: Some hormonal, neural and chemical determinants. *In* "The Behavior of Domestic Animals" 3rd ed. (E. S. E. Hafez, ed.), pp. 146–170. Baillière Tindall, London.

Moltz, H., and Wiener, E. (1966). Effects of ovariectomy on maternal behavior in primiparous and multiparous rats. *J. Comp. Physiol. Psychol.* **62**, 382–387.

Moltz, H., Levin, R., and Leon, M. (1969). Differential effects of progesterone on the maternal behavior of primiparous and multiparous rats. *J. Comp. Physiol. Psychol.* **67**, 36–40.

Moltz, H., Lubin, M., Leon, M., and Numan, M. (1970). Hormonal induction of maternal behavior in the ovariectomized nulliparous rat. *Physiol. Behav.* **5**, 1373–1377.

Montagna, W. A. (1980). A case of adoption. *Primate News* **18**, 20.

Morgan, H. D., Fleming, A. S., and Stern, J. M. (1992). Somatosensory control of the onset and retention of maternal responsiveness in primiparous Sprague-Dawley rats. *Physiol. Behav.* **51**, 549–555.

Morgan, H. D., Watchus, J. A., Milgram, N. W., and Fleming, A. S. (1999). The long lasting effects of electrical simulation of the medial preoptic area and medial amygdala on maternal behavior in female rats. *Behav. Brain Res.* **99**, 61–73.

Morgan, J. I., and Curran, T. (1991). Stimulus-transcription coupling in the nervous system: Involvement of the inducible proto-oncogenes fos and jun. *Annu. Rev. Neurosci.* **14**, 421–451.

Morgan, P. D., Boundy, C. A. P., Arnold, G. W., and Lindsay, D. R. (1975). The roles played by the senses of the ewe in the location and recognition of lambs. *Appl. Anim. Ethol.* **1**, 139–150.

Morishige, W. K., Pepe, G. J., and Rotchild, I. (1973). Serum luteinizing hormone (LH), prolactin and progesterone levels during pregnancy in the rat. *Endocrinology (Baltimore)* **92**, 1527–1530.

Morrow-Tesch, J., and McGlone, J. J. (1990a). Sensory systems and nipple attachment behavior in neonatal pigs. *Physiol. Behav.* **47**, 1–4.

Morrow-Tesch, J., and McGlone, J. J. (1990b). Sources of maternal odors and the development of odor preferences in baby pigs. *J. Anim. Sci.* **68**, 3563–3571.

Mosselman, S., Polman, J., and Dijkema, R. (1996). ER-beta: Identification and characterization of a novel human estrogen receptor. *FEBS Lett.* **392**, 49–53.

Muccioli, G., and Di Carlo, R. (1994). Modulation of prolactin receptors in the rat hypothalamus in response to changes in serum concentration of endogenous prolactin or to ovine prolactin administration. *Brain Res.* **663**, 244–250.

Murphey, R. M., Ruiz-Miranda, C. R., and Moura Duarte, F. A. (1990). Maternal recognition in Gyr (*Bos indicus*) calves. *Appl. Anim. Behav. Sci.* **27**, 183–191.

Murphy, M. R., MacLean, P. D., and Hamilton, S. C. (1981). Species-typical behavior of hasmters deprived from birth of the neocortex. *Science* **213**, 459–461.

Murr, S. M., Bradford, G. E., and Geschwing, I. I. (1974a). Plasma luteinizing hormone, follicle-stimulating hormone and prolactin during pregnancy in the mouse. *Endocrinology (Baltimore)* **94**, 112–116.

Murr, S. M., Stabenfeldt, G. H., Bradford, G. E., and Geschwind, I. I. (1974b). Plasma progesterone during pregnancy in the mouse. *Endocrinology (Baltimore)* **94**, 1209–1211.

Myers, R. E., Swett, C., and Miller, M. (1973). Loss of social group affinity following prefrontal lesions in free-ranging macaques. *Brain Res.* **64**, 257–269.

Mykytowycz, R., and Dudzinski, M. L. (1972). Aggressive and protective behavior of adult rabbits *Oryctolagus cuniculus* (L) towards juveniles. *Behaviour* **43**, 97–119.

Nadaud, D., Simon, H., Herman, J. P., and Le Moal, M. (1984). Contributions of the mesencephalic dopaminergic system and the trigeminal sensory pathway to the ventral tegmental aphagia syndrome in rats. *Physiol. Behav.* **33**, 879–887.

Nash, L. T. (1978). The development of the mother-infant relationship in wild baboons (*Papio anubis*). *Anim. Behav.* **26**, 746–759.

Negayama, K., and Honjo, S. (1986). An experimental study on developmental changes of maternal discrimination of infants in crab-eating monkeys (*Macaca fascicularis*). *Dev. Psychobiol.* **19**, 49–56.

Neill, J. D., and Nagy, G. M. (1994). Prolactin secretion and its control. *In* "The Physiology of Reproduction" (E. Knobil and J. D. Neill, eds.), 2nd ed., Vol. 1, pp. 1833–1860. Raven Press, New York.

Nelson, E. E., and Panksepp, J. (1998). Brain substrates of infant-mother attachment: Contributions of opioids, oxytocin, and norepinephrine. *Neurosci. Biobehav. Rev.* **22**, 437–452.

Neumann, I., Russell, J. A., and Landgraf, R. (1993). Oxytocin and vasopressin release within the supraoptic and paraventricular nuclei of pregnant, parturient and lactating rats: A microdialysis study. *Neuroscience* **53**, 65–75.

Nicoll, C. S., and Meites, J. (1959). Prolongation of lactation in the rat by litter replacement. *Proc. Soc. Exp. Biol. Med.* **101**, 81–82.

Nishimori, K., Young, L. J., Guo, Q., Wang, Z., Insel, T. R., and Matzuk, M. M. (1996). Oxytocin is required for nursing but is not essential for parturition or reproductive behavior. *Proc. Natl. Acad. Sci. U. S. A.* **93**, 11699–11704.

Noirot, E. (1964). Changes in responsiveness to young in the adult mouse. 1. The problematical effect of hormones. *Anim. Behav.* **12**, 52–58.

Noirot, E. (1972). The onset and development of maternal behavior in rats, hamsters and mice. *Adv. Study Behav.* **4**, 107–145.

Noirot, E., and Goyens, J. (1971). Changes in maternal behavior during gestation in the mouse. *Horm. Behav.* **6**, 237–245.

Noirot, E., Goyens, J., and Buhot, M. C. (1975). Aggressive behavior of pregnant mice toward males. *Horm. Behav.* **6**, 9–17.

Novotny, M. V., Ma, W., Zidek, L., and Daev, E. (1999). Recent biochemical insights into puberty acceleration, estrus induction, and puberty delay in the house mouse. *In* "Advances in Chemical Signals in Vertebrates" (R. E. Johnston, D. Müller-Schwarze, and P. Sorensen, eds.), pp. 99–116. Kluwer Academic/Plenum, New York.

Nowak, R. (1990). Lamb's bleats: Important for the establishment of the mother-young bond? *Behaviour* **115**, 14–29.

Nudo, R. J., and Masterton, R. B. (1986). Stimulation-induced 14C-2-deoxyglucose labeling of synaptic activity in the central auditory system. *J. Comp. Neurol.* **245**, 553–565.

Numan, M. (1974). Medial preoptic area and maternal behavior in the female rat. *J. Comp. Physiol. Psychol.* **87**, 746–759.

Numan, M. (1978). Progesterone inhibition of maternal behavior in the rat. *Horm. Behav.* **11**, 209–231.

Numan, M. (1990). Long-term effects of preoptic area knife cuts on the maternal behavior of postpartum rats. *Behav. Neural Biol.* **53**, 284–290.

Numan, M. (1994). Maternal behavior. *In* "The Physiology of Reproduction" (E. Knobil and J. D. Neill, eds.), 2nd ed., Vol. 2, pp. 221–302. Raven Press, New York.

Numan, M. (1996). A lesion and neuroanatomical tract-tracing analysis of the role of the bed nucleus of the stria terminalis in retrieval behavior and other aspects of maternal responsiveness in rats. *Dev. Psychobiol.* **29**, 23–51.

Numan, M., and Callahan, E. C. (1980). The connections of

the medial preoptic region and maternal behavior in the rat. *Physiol. Behav.* **25**, 653–665.

Numan, M., and Corodimas, K. P. (1985). The effects of paraventricular hypothalamic lesions on maternal behavior in rats. *Physiol. Behav.* **35**, 417–425.

Numan, M., and Numan, M. J. (1991). Preoptic-brainstem connections and maternal behavior in rats. *Behav. Neurosci.* **105**, 1013–1029.

Numan, M., and Numan, M. J. (1994). Expression of Fos-like immunoreactivity in the preoptic area of maternally behaving virgin and postpartum rats. *Behav. Neurosci.* **108**, 379–394.

Numan, M., and Numan, M. J. (1995). Importance of pup-related sensory inputs and maternal performance for the expression of Fos-like immunoreactivity in the preoptic area and ventral bed nucleus of the stria terminalis of postpartum rats. *Behav. Neurosci.* **109**, 135–149.

Numan, M., and Smith, H. G. (1984). Maternal behavior in rats: evidence for the involvement of preoptic projections to the ventral tegmental area. *Behav. Neurosci.* **98**, 712–727.

Numan, M., Leon, M., and Moltz, H. (1972). Interference with prolactin release and the maternal behavior of female rats. *Horm. Behav.* **3**, 29–38.

Numan, M., Rosenblatt, J. S., and Komisaruk, B. R. (1977). Medial preoptic area and onset of maternal behavior in the rat. *J. Comp. Physiol. Psychol.* **91**, 146–164.

Numan, M., Morrell, J. I., and Pfaff, D. W. (1985). Anatomical identification of neurons in selected brain regions associated with maternal behavior deficits induced by knife cuts of the lateral hypothalamus in rats. *J. Comp. Neurol.* **237**, 552–564.

Numan, M., Corodimas, K. P., Numan, M. J., Factor, E. M., and Piers, W. D. (1988). Axon-sparing lesions of the preoptic region and substantia innominata disrupt maternal behavior in rats. *Behav. Neurosci.* **102**, 381–396.

Numan, M., Numan, M. J., and English, J. B. (1993). Excitotoxic amino acid injections into the medial amygdala facilitate maternal behavior in virgin female rats. *Horm. Behav.* **27**, 56–81.

Numan, M., Numan, M. J., Marzella, S. R., and Palumbo, A. (1998). Expression of c-fos, fos B, and egr-1 in the medial preoptic area and bed nucleus of the stria terminalis during maternal behavior in rats. *Brain Res.* **792**, 348–352.

Numan, M., Roach, J. K., Del Cerro, M. C., Guillamón, A., Segovia, S., Sheehan, T. P., and Numan, M. J. (1999). Expression of intracellular progesterone receptors in rat brain during different reproductive states, and involvement in maternal behavior. *Brain Res.* **830**, 358–371.

Obias, M. D. (1957). Maternal behavior of hypophysectomized gravid albino rats and the development and performance of their progeny. *J. Comp. Physiol. Psychol.* **62**, 382–387.

Obregon, F., Arias de Reyna, L., and Recuerda, P. (1992). Nursing and suckling behaviour in the mouflon. *Ethol. Ecol. Evol.* **4**, 285–291.

O'Brien, P. H. (1983). Feral goat parturition and lying-out sites: Spatial, physical and meteorological characteristics. *Appl. Anim. Behav. Sci.* **10**, 325–339.

O'Brien, P. H. (1984). Leavers and stayers: Maternal post-partum strategies in feral goats. *Appl. Anim. Behav. Sci.* **12**, 233–243.

Oftedal, O. T. (1997). Lactation in whales and dolphins: Evidence of divergence between baleen- and toothed-species. *J. Mammary Gland Biol. Neopasia* **2**, 205–230.

Oftedal, O. T., Bowen, W. D., and Boness, D. (1993). Energy transfer by lactating hooded seals and nutrient deposition in their pups during the four days from birth to weaning. *Physiol. Zool.* **66**, 412–436.

Olazabal, D. E., and Ferreira, A. (1997). Maternal behavior in rats with kainic acid-induced lesions of the hypothalamic paraventricular nucleus. *Physiol. Behav.* **61**, 779–784.

Oliveras, D., and Novak, M. (1986). A comparison of paternal behavior in the meadow vole, *Microtus pennsylvanicus,* the pine vole, *M. pinetorum,* and the prairie vole, *M. ochrogaster. Anim. Behav.* **34**, 519–526.

Ormandy, C. J., Camus, A., Barra, J., Damotte, D., Lucas, B. K., Buteau, H., Edery, M., Brousse, M., Babinet, C., Binart, N., and Kelly, P. A. (1997). Null mutation of the prolactin receptor gene produces multiple reproductive defects in the mouse. *Genes Dev.* **11**, 167–178.

Orpen, B. G., and Fleming, A. S. (1987). Experience with pups sustains maternal responding in postpartum rats. *Physiol. Behav.* **40**, 47–54.

Orpen, B. G., Furman, N., Wong, P. Y., and Fleming, A. S. (1987). Hormonal influences on the duration of postpartum maternal responsiveness in the rat. *Physiol. Behav.* **40**, 307–315.

Owen, K., Wallace, P., and Thiessen, D. (1974). Effects of intracerebral implants of steroid hormones on scent-marking in the ovariectomized female gerbil *(Meriones unguiculatus). Physiol. Behav.* **12**, 755–760.

Palanza, P., Parmigiani, S., and Vom Saal, F. S. (1995). Urine marking and maternal aggression of wild female mice in relation to anogenital distance at birth. *Physiol. Behav.* **58**, 827–835.

Panksepp, J. (1981). Brain opioids — A neurochemical substrate for narcotic and social dependence. *In* "Theory in Psychopharmacology" (S. J. Cooper, ed.), pp. 149–175. Academic Press, London.

Paranhos da Costa, M. J. R., Andriolo, A., Simplício de Oliveira, J. F., and Schmidek, W. R. (2000). Suckling and allosuckling in river buffalo calves and its relation with weight gain. *Appl. Anim. Behav. Sci.* **66**, 1–10.

Pedersen, C. A., and Prange, A. J. J. (1979). Induction of maternal behavior in virgin rats after intracerebroventricular administration of oxytocin. *Proc. Natl. Acad. Sci. U. S. A.* **76**, 6661–6665.

Pedersen, C. A., Ascher, J. A., Monroe, Y. L., and Prange, A. J. J. (1982). Oxytocin induces maternal behavior in virgin female rats. *Science* **216**, 648–650.

Pedersen, C. A., Caldwell, J. D., Johnson, M. F., Fort, S. A., and Prange, A. J. J. (1985). Oxytocin antiserum delays onset of ovarian steroid-induced maternal behavior. *Neuropeptides* **6**, 175–182.

Pedersen, C. A., Caldwell, J. D., Walker, C., Ayers, G., and Mason, G. A. (1994). Oxytocin activates the postpartum onset of rat maternal behavior in the ventral tegmental and medial preoptic areas. *Behav. Neurosci.* **108**, 1163–1171.

Pepe, G. J., and Rotchild, I. (1974). A comparative study of serum progesterone levels in pregnancy and various types of pseudopregnancy in the rat. *Endocrinology (Baltimore)* **95**, 275–279.

Pereira, M. (1986). Maternal recognition of juvenile offspring coo vocalizations in japanese macaques. *Anim. Behav.* **34**, 935–937.

Perlmutter, L. S., Tweedle, C. D., and Hatton, G. I. (1984). Neuronal-glial plasticity in the supraoptic dendritic zone: Dendritic bundling and double synapse formation at parturition. *Neuroscience* **13**, 769–779.

Petraglia, F., Baraldi, M., Giarre, G. *et al.* (1985). Opioid peptides of the pituitary and hypothalamus: Changes in pregnant and lactating rats. *J. Endocrinol.* **105**, 239–245.

Petrinovich, L. (1974). Individual recognition of pup vocalizations by northern elephant seal mothers. *Z. Tierpsychol.* **34**, 308–312.

Pfaff, D. W., and Keiner, M. (1973). Atlas of estradiol-concentrating cells in the central nervous system of the rat. *J. Comp. Neurol.* **141**, 121–158.

Pi, X. J., and Grattan, D. R. (1998). Distribution of prolactin receptor immunoreactivity in the brain of estrogen-treated, ovariectomized rats. *J. Comp. Neurol.* **394**, 462–474.

Pi, X., and Grattan, D. R. (1999a). Expression of prolactin receptor mRNA is increased in the preoptic area of lactating rats. *Endocrine* **11**, 91–98.

Pi, X. J., and Grattan, D. R. (1999b). Increased expression of both short and long forms of prolactin receptor mRNA in hypothalamic nuclei of lactating rats. *J. Mol. Endocrinol.* **23**, 13–22.

Pi, X. J., and Grattan, D. R. (1999c). Increased prolactin receptor immunoreactivity in the hypothalamus of lactating rats. *J. Neuroendocrinol.* **11**, 693–705.

Pinheiro Machado, L. C., Hurnik, J. F., and King, G. J. (1997). Timing of the attraction towards the placenta and amniotic fluid by the parturient cow. *Appl. Anim. Behav. Sci.* **53**, 183–192.

Pissonnier, D., Thiéry, J. C., Fabre-Nys, C., Poindron, P., and Keverne, E. B. (1985). The importance of olfactory bulb noradrenalin for maternal recognition in sheep. *Physiol. Behav.* **35**, 361–363.

Poindron, P. (1974). Etude de la relation mère-jeune chez des brebis *(Ovis aries)*, lors de l'allaitement. *C. R. Hebd. Seances Acad. Sci., Ser. D* **278**, 2691–2694.

Poindron, P. (1976a). Effets de la suppression de l'odorat, sans lésion des bulbes olfactifs, sur la sélectivité du comportement maternel de la Brebis. *C. R. Hebd. Seances Acad. Sci., Ser. D* **282**, 489–491.

Poindron, P. (1976b). Mother-young relationships in intact or anosmic ewes at the time of suckling. *Biol. Behav.* **2**, 161–177.

Poindron, P. (1981). Contribution à l'étude des mécanismes de régulation du comportement maternel chez la brebis (*Ovis aries* L.)." Université de Provence (Aix-Marseille 1), Marseille.

Poindron, P., and Carrick, M. J. (1976). Hearing recognition of the lamb by its mother. *Anim. Behav.* **24**, 600–602.

Poindron, P., and Le Neindre, P. (1980). Endocrine and sensory regulation of maternal behavior in the ewe. *Adv. Study Behav.* **11**, 75–119.

Poindron, P., and Schmidt, P. (1985). Distance recognition in ewes and lambs kept permanently indoors or at pasture. *Appl. Anim. Behav. Sci.* **13**, 267–273.

Poindron, P., Martin, G. B., and Hooley, R. D. (1979). Effects of lambing induction on the sensitive period for the establishment of maternal behavior in sheep. *Physiol. Behav.* **23**, 1081–1087.

Poindron, P., Le Neindre, P., Raksanyi, I., Trillat, G., and Orgeur, P. (1980a). Importance of the characteristics of the young in the manifestation and establishment of maternal behavior in sheep. *Reprod. Nutr. Dev.* **20**, 817–826.

Poindron, P., Orgeur, P., Le Neindre, P., Kann, G., and Raksanyi, I. (1980b). Influence of the blood concentration of prolactin on the length of the sensitive period for establishing maternal behavior in sheep at parturition. *Horm. Behav.* **14**, 173–177.

Poindron, P., Le Neindre, P., Lévy, F., and Keverne, E. B. (1984a). Les mécanismes physiologiques de l'acceptation du nouveau-né chez la brebis. *Biol. Behav.* **9**, 65–88.

Poindron, P., Raksanyi, I., Orgeur, P., and Le Neindre, P. (1984b). Comparaison du comportement maternel en bergerie à la parturition chez des brebis primipares ou multipares de race Romanov, Préalpes de Sud et Ile-de-France. *Génét. Sél. Evol.* **16**, 503–522.

Poindron, P., Lévy, F., Le Neindre, P., and Keverne, E. B. (1986). The roles of genital stimulation, oestrogens and olfaction in the maternal bonding of sheep and other Mammals. *In* "Hormones and Behaviour" (L. Dennerstein and I. Fraser, eds.), pp. 538–548. Elsevier Science Publishers, Melbourne, Australia.

Poindron, P., Lévy, F., and Krehbiel, D. (1988). Genital, olfactory, and endocrine interactions in the development of maternal

behavior in the parturient ewe. *Psychoneuroendocrinology* **13**, 99–125.

Poindron, P., Nowak, R., Lévy, F., Porter, R. H., and Schaal, B. (1993). Development of exclusive mother-young bonding in sheep and goats. *Oxford Rev. Reprod. Biol.* **15**, 311–364.

Poindron, P., Caba, M., Gomora Arrati, P., Krehbiel, D., and Beyer, C. (1994). Responses of maternal and non-maternal ewes to social and mother-young separation. *Behav. Processes* **31**, 97–110.

Poindron, P., Soto, R., and Romeyer, A. (1997). Decrease of response to social separation in preparturient ewes. *Behav. Processes* **40**, 45–51.

Poindron, P., Hernandez, H., Gonzalez, F., Navarro, M. L., and Delgadillo, J. A. (1998a). Mother-young relationships in goats: Mechanisms of control and possible implications for production. *In* "Proceedings of the 32nd Congress of the International Society for Applied Ethology" (I. Veissier and A. Boissy, eds.), pp. 85. INRA, Clermont-Ferrand, France.

Poindron, P., Hernandez, H., Navarro, M. L., Gonzales, F., Delgadillo, J. A., and Garcia, S. (1998b). Relaciones madrecria en cabras. *Reun. Nac. Sobre Caprinocult.,*. 13th, Universidad Autonoma de San Luis Potosi, San Luis Potosi, Mexico, pp. 48–66.

Pollack, E. I., and Sachs, B. D. (1975). Male copulatory behavior and female maternal behavior in neonatally bulbectomized rats. *Physiol. Behav.* **14**, 337–343.

Porter, R. H. (1983). Communication in rodents: Adults to infants. *In* "Parental Behaviour of Rodents" (R. W. Elwood, ed.), pp. 95–125. Wiley, New York.

Porter, R. H., and Doane, H. M. (1978). Studies of maternal behavior in spiny mice (*Acomis cabirinus*). *Z. Tierpsychol.* **47**, 225–235.

Porter, R. H., Cernoch, J. M., and McLaughlin, F. J. (1983). Maternal recognition of neonates through olfactory cues. *Physiol. Behav.* **30**, 151–154.

Porter, R. H., Lévy, F., Poindron, P., Litterio, M., Schaal, B., and Beyer, C. (1991). Individual olfactory signatures as major determinants of early maternal discrimination in sheep. *Dev. Psychobiol.* **24**, 151–158.

Porter, R. H., Lévy, F., Nowak, R., Orgeur, P., and Schaal, B. (1994a). Lambs' individual odor signatures: Mosaic hypothesis. *Adv. Biosci.* **93**, 233–238.

Porter, R. H., Romeyer, A., Lévy, F., Krehbiel, D., and Nowak, R. (1994b). Investigation of the nature of lamb's individual odour signature. *Behav. Processes* **31**, 301–308.

Prado-Alcala, R. A. (1995). Serial and parallel processing during memory consolidation. *In* "Plasticity in the Central Nervous System. Learning and memory" (J. L. McGaugh, F. Bermudez-Rattoni, and R. A. Prado-Alcala, eds.), pp. 57–65. Erlbaum, Hillsdale, NJ.

Price, E., and Bélanger, P. (1977). Maternal behavior of wild and domestic stocks of norway rats. *Behav. Biol.* **20**, 60–69.

Price, E. G., and Thos, J. (1980). Behavioral responses to short-term isolation in sheep and goat. *Appl. Anim. Ethol.* **6**, 331–339.

Priestnall, R. (1972). Effects of litter size on the behavior of lactating female mice. *Anim. Behav.* **20**, 386–394.

Protomastro, M., and Stern, J. M. (1995). Nursing behavior in lactation-suppressed postpartum Long-Evans rats during and after treatment with bromocriptine. *Dev. Psychobiol.* **28**, 193.

Pryce, C. R. (1996). Socialization, hormones, and the regulation of maternal behavior in nonhuman primates. *Adv. Study Behav.* **25**, 423–473.

Pryce, C. R., Abbott, D. H., Hodges, J. K., and Martin, R. D. (1988). Maternal behavior is related to prepartum urinary estradiol levels in red-bellied tamarin monkeys. *Physiol. Behav.* **44**, 717–726.

Pryce, C. R., Mutschler, T., Döbeli, M., Nievergelt, C., and Martin, R. D. (1995). Prepartum sex steroid hormones and infant-directed behavior in primiparous marmoset mothers (*Callithrix jacchus*). *In* "Motherhood in Human and Nonhuman Primates" (C. R. Pryce, R. D. Martin, and D. Skuse, eds.), pp. 78–86. Karger, Basel.

Putu, I. G., Poindron, P., Oldham, C. M., Gray, S. J., and Ballard, M. (1986). Lamb desertion in primiparous and multiparous Merino ewes induced to lamb with dexamethasone. *Proc. Aust. Soc. Anim. Prod.* **16**, 315–318.

Quadagno, D. M. (1974). Maternal behavior in the rat: Aspects of concaveation and neonatal androgen treatment. *Physiol. Behav.* **12**, 1071–1074.

Quadagno, D. M., and Rockwell, J. (1972). The effect of gonadal hormones in infancy on maternal behavior in the adult rat. *Horm. Behav.* **3**, 55–62.

Quadagno, D. M., McCullough, J., Ho, G. K., and Spevak, A. M. (1973). Neonatal gonadal hormones: Effect on maternal and sexual behavior in the female rat. *Physiol. Behav.* **11**, 251–254.

Ramirez, V., and Soufi, W. L. (1994). Neuroendocrine control of the rabbit ovarian cycle. *In* "The Physiology of Reproduction" (E. Knobil and J. D. Neill, eds.), 2nd ed., Vol. 2, pp. 585–611. Raven Press, New York.

Ramírez, A., Quiles, A., Hevia, M., and Sotillo, F. (1995). Behavior of the Murciano-Granadina goat in the hour before parturition. *Appl. Anim. Behav. Sci.* **44**, 29–35.

Ramírez, A., Quiles, A., Hevia, M. L., Sotillo, F., and Ramírez, M. C. (1996). Effects of immediate and early postpartum separation on maintenance of maternal responsiveness in parturient multiparous goats. *Appl. Anim. Behav. Sci.* **48**, 215–224.

Reburn, C. J., and Wynne-Edwards, K. E. (1999). Hormonal changes in males of a naturally biparental and a uniparental mammal. *Horm. Behav.* **35**, 163–176.

Regalado, M., Torrero, C., and Salas, M. (1999). Maternal responsiveness of neonatally undernourished and sensory stimulated rats: Rehabilitation of maternal behavior. *Nutr. Neurosci.* **2**, 7–18.

Reisbick, S., Rosenblatt, J. S., and Mayer, A. D. (1975). Decline of maternal behavior in the virgin and lactating rat. *J. Comp. Physiol. Psychol.* **89**, 722–732.

Renaud, L. P., Tang, M., McCann, M. J., Stricker, E. M., and Verbalis, J. G. (1987). Cholecystokinin and gastric distention activate oxytocinergic cells in rat hypothalamus. *Am. J. Physiol.* **253**, R661–R665.

Renfree, M. B., Fletcher, T. P., Blanden, D. R., Lewis, P. R., Shaw, G., Gordon, K., Short, R. V., Parer-Cook, E., and Parer, D. (1989). Physiological and behavioral events around the time of birth in macropodid marsupials. *In* "Kangaroos, Wallabies and Rat Kangaroos" (P. Jarman, I. D. Hume, and G. Grigg, eds.), pp. 323–337. Surrey Beatty and Sons, Sydney, Australia.

Resko, J. A. (1970). Androgen secretion by fetal and neonatal rhesus monkeys. *Endocrinology* (Baltimore) **87**, 680–687.

Reyes, F. I., Winter, J. S. D., Faiman, C., and Hobson, W. C. (1973). Serial serum levels of gonadotropins, prolactin and sex steroids in the non pregnant and pregnant chimpanzee. *Endocrinology (Baltimore)* **96**, 1447–1455.

Rheingold, H. L. (1963). Maternal behavior in the dog. *In* "Maternal Behavior in Mammals" (H. L. Rheingold, ed.), pp. 169–202. Wiley, New York.

Rhine, A. J., Norton, G. W., and Westlund, B. J. (1984). The waning of dependence in infant free-ranging yellow baboons (*Papio cynocephalus*). *Am. J. Primatol.* **7**, 213–228.

Richards, M. P. M. (1969). Effects of oestrogen and progesterone on nest-building in the golden hamster. *Anim. Behav.* **17**, 356–361.

Riddle, O., Lahr, E. L., and Bates, R. W. (1935). Maternal behavior induced in virgin rats by prolactin. *Proc. Soc. Exp. Biol. Med.* **32**, 730–734.

Riddle, O., Lahr, E. L., and Bates, R. W. (1942). Maternal behavior induced in virgins by prolactin. *Am. J. Physiol.* **137**, 299–317.

Roberston, H. A., and King, G. J. (1974). Plasma concentrations of progesterone, oestrone, oestradiol-17beta and oestrone sulphate in the pig at implantation, during pregnancy and at parturition. *J. Reprod. Fertil.* **40**, 133–141.

Roberts, R. L., Kearse, A. F., and Carter, C. S. (1992). Helper males attend more to pups than do females in prairie voles. *Abstr. Conf. Reprod. Behav.*, p. 24.

Rodriguez-Sierra, J. F., and Rosenblatt, J. S. (1977). Does prolactin play a role in estrogen-induced maternal behavior in rats: Apomorphine reduction of prolactin release. *Horm. Behav.* **9**, 1–7.

Rodriguez-Sierra, J. F., and Rosenblatt, J. S. (1982). Pregnancy termination by prostaglandin F2 alpha stimulates maternal behavior in the rat. *Horm. Behav.* **16**, 343-351.

Romeyer, A. (1993a). Développement et sélectivité du lien mère-jeune chez la chèvre et la brebis. *Rev. Ecol. (Terre et Vie)* **48**, 143–153.

Romeyer, A. (1993b). Facteurs impliqués dans le développement de la signature olfactive individuelle chez les nouveau-nés ovins et caprins. Doctorate Thesis, Université François Rabelais, Tours, France.

Romeyer, A., and Poindron, P. (1992). Early maternal discrimination of alien kids by post-parturient goats. *Behav. Processes* **26**, 103–112.

Romeyer, A., Porter, R. H., Lévy, F., Nowak, R., Orgeur, P., and Poindron, P. (1993). Maternal labelling is not necessary for the establishment of discrimination between kids by recently parturient goats. *Anim. Behav.* **46**, 705–712.

Romeyer, A., Poindron, P., Porter, R. H., Lévy, F., and Orgeur, P. (1994a). Establishment of maternal bonding and its mediation by vaginocervical stimulation in goats. *Physiol. Behav.* **55**, 395–400.

Romeyer, A., Poindron, P., and Orgeur, P. (1994b). Olfaction mediates the establishment of selective bonding in goats. *Physiol. Behav.* **56**, 693–700.

Romeyer, A., Porter, R. H., Poindron, P., Orgeur, P., Chesné, P., and Poulain, N. (1994c). Recognition of dizygotic and monozygotic twin lambs by ewes. *Behaviour* **127**, 119–139.

Rongstad, O. J., and Tester, J. R. (1971). Behavior and maternal relations of young snowshoe hares. *J. Wildl. Manage.* **35**, 338–346.

Rood, J. P. (1978). Dwarf mongoose helpers at the den. *Z. Tierpsychol.* **48**, 277–287.

Rose, R., and Fadem, B. H. (2000). The hormonal control of birth behavior in the gray short-tailed Opossum. *Horm. Behav.* **37**, 163–167.

Rose, R. W., and MacFayden, A. S. (1997). Oxytocin and prostaglandin F2-alpha induce birth behavior in the bettong, *Bettongia gaimardi*. *Horm. Behav.* **31**, 120–125.

Rosenberg, K. M. (1974). Effects of pre- and post-pubertal castration and testosterone on pup-killing behavior in the male rat. *Physiol. Behav.* **13**, 159–161.

Rosenberg, K. M., and Sherman, G. F. (1975). The role of testosterone in the organization, maintenance, and activation of pup-killing behavior in the male rat. *Horm. Behav.* **6**, 173–179.

Rosenberg, K. M., Denenberg, V. H., Zarrow, M. X., and Frank, B. L. (1971). Effects of neonatal castration and testosterone on the rat's pup-killing behavior and activity. *Physiol. Behav.* **7**, 363–368.

Rosenberg, P. A., and Herrenkohl, L. R. (1976). Maternal behav-ior in male rats: Critical times for the suppressive action of androgens. *Physiol. Behav.* **16**, 293–297.

Rosenblatt, J. S. (1967). Nonhormonal basis of maternal behavior in the rat. *Science* **156**, 1512–1514.

Rosenblatt, J. S., and Ceus, K. (1998). Estrogen implants in the medial preoptic area stimulate maternal behavior in male rats. *Horm. Behav.* **33**, 23–30.

Rosenblatt, J. S., and Lehrman, D. S. (1963). Maternal behavior in the laboratory rat. *In* "Maternal Behavior in Mammals" (H. L. Rheingold, ed.), pp. 8–57. Wiley, New York.

Rosenblatt, J. S., and Siegel, H. I. (1975). Hysterectomy-induced maternal behavior during pregnancy in the rat. *J. Comp. Physiol. Psychol.* **89**, 685–700.

Rosenblatt, J. S., and Siegel, H. I. (1981). Factors governing the onset and maintenance of maternal behavior among non-primate Mammals. *In* "Parental Care in Mammals" (D. J. Gubernick and P. H. Klopfer, eds.), pp. 13–76. Plenum Press, New York.

Rosenblatt, J. S., Turkewitz, G., and Schneirla, T. C. (1962). Development of suckling and related behavior in neonate kittens. *In* "Roots of Behavior" (E. L. Bliss, ed.), pp. 198–210. Hoeber, New York.

Rosenblatt, J. S., Siegel, H. I., and Mayer, A. D. (1979). Progress in the study of maternal behavior in the rat: Hormonal, non-hormonal, sensory, and developmental aspects. *Adv. Study Behav.* **10**, 225–311.

Rosenblatt, J. S., Mayer, A. D., and Siegel, H. I. (1985). Maternal behavior among the non-primate mammals. *In* "Handbook of Behavioral Neurobiology" (N. Adler, D. Pfaff, and R. W. Goy, eds.), Vol. 7, pp. 229–298. Plenum Press, New York.

Rosenblatt, J. S., Mayer, A. D., and Giordano, A. L. (1988). Hormonal basis during pregnancy for the onset of maternal behavior in the rat. *Psychoneuroendocrinology* **13**, 29–46.

Rosenblatt, J. S., Hazelwood, S., and Poole, J. (1996). Maternal behavior in male rats: Effects of medial preoptic area lesions and presence of maternal aggression. *Horm. Behav.* **30**, 201–215.

Rosenblum, L. A. (1972). Sex and age differences in response to infant squirrel monkeys. *Brain, Behav. Evol.* **5**, 30–40.

Rosenson, L. M. (1972). Interaction between infant greater bushbabies (*Galago crassicaudatus crassicaudatus*) and adults other than their mothers under experimental conditions. *Z. Tierpsychol.* **3**, 240–269.

Rosenson, L. M., and Asheroff, A. K. (1975). Maternal aggression in CD-1 mice: Influence of the hormonal condition of the intruder. *Behav. Biol.* **15**, 219–224.

Ross, S., Denenberg, V. H., Sawin, P. B., and Meyer, P. (1956). Changes in nest building behaviour in multiparous rabbits. *Br. J. Anim. Behav.* **4**, 69–74.

Ross, S., Sawin, P. B., Zarrow, M. X., and Denenberg, V. H. (1963a). Maternal behavior in the rabbit. In "Maternal Behavior in Mammals" (H. L. Rheingold, ed.), pp. 94–121. Wiley, New York.

Ross, S., Zarrow, M. X., Sawin, P. B., Denenberg, V. H., and Blumenfield, M. (1963b). Maternal behavior in the rabbit under semi-natural conditions. Anim. Behav. 11, 283–285.

Rowell, T. E. (1960). On the retrieving of young and other behaviour in lactating golden hamsters. Proc. Zool. Soc. London 135, 265–282.

Rowell, T. E. (1961). Maternal behaviour in non-maternal golden hamsters. Anim. Behav. 9, 11–15.

Rowland, D. L. (1981). Effects of pregnancy on the maintenance of maternal behavior in the rat. Behav. Neural Biol. 31, 225–235.

Rowley, M. H., and Christian, J. J. (1976a). Interspecific aggression between Peromyscus and Microtus females: A possible factor in competitive exclusion. Behav. Biol. 16, 521–525.

Rowley, M. H., and Christian, J. J. (1976b). Intraspecific aggression of Peromyscus leucopus. Behav. Biol. 17, 249–253.

Rowley, M. H., and Christian, J. J. (1977). Competition between lactating Peromyscus leucopus and juvenile Micorosus pennsylvanicus Microtus. Behav. Biol. 20, 70–80.

Rubianes, E. (1992). Genital stimulation modifies behavior towards amniotic fluid in oestrus ewes. Appl. Anim. Behav. Sci. 35, 35–40.

Rubin, B. S., and Bridges, R. S. (1984). Disruption of ongoing maternal responsiveness in rats by central administration of morphine sulfate. Brain Res. 307, 91–97.

Rubin, B. S., Menniti, F. S., and Bridges, R. S. (1983). Intracerebroventricular administration of oxytocin and maternal behavior in rats after prolonged and acute steroid pretreatment. Horm. Behav. 17, 45–53.

Rudge, M. R. (1970). Mother and kid behavior in feral goats (Capra hircus L.). Z. Tierpsychol. 27, 687–692.

Ruppenthal, G. C., Arling, G. L., Harlow, H. F., Sackett, G. P., and Suomi, S. J. (1976). A 10-year perspective of motherless-mother monkey behavior. J. Abnorm. Psychol. 85, 341–349.

Russell, E. M. (1973). Mother-young relations and early behavioral development in the marsupials Macropus eugenii and Megaleia rufa. Z. Tierpsychol. 33, 163–203.

Salas, M., Torrero, C., and Pulido, S. (1984). Long-term alterations in the maternal behavior of neonatally undernourished rats. Physiol. Behav. 33, 273–278.

Salm, A. K., Modney, B. K., and Hatton, G. I. (1988). Alterations in supraoptic nucleus ultrastructure of maternally behaving virgin rats. Brain Res. Bull. 21, 685–691.

Salo, A. L., and French, J. A. (1989). Early experience, reproductive success, and the development of parental behavior in Mongolian gerbils. Anim. Behav. 38, 693–702.

Samuels, O., Jason, G., Mann, M., and Svare, B. (1981). Pup-killing behavior in mice: Suppression by early androgen exposure. Physiol. Behav. 26, 473–477.

Sawin, P. B., and Crary, D. D. (1953). Genetic and physiological background of reproduction in the rabbit. II. Some racial differences in the pattern of maternal behavior. Behaviour 6, 128–146.

Sawin, P. B., Denenberg, V. H., Ross, S., Hafter, E., and Zarrow, M. X. (1960). Maternal behavior in the rabbit: Hair loosening during gestation. Am. J. Physiol. 198, 1099–1102.

Saylor, A., and Salmon, M. (1969). Communal nursing in mice: Influence of multiple mothers on the growth of the young. Science 164, 1309–1310.

Schaal, B., and Marlier, L. (1998). Maternal and paternal perception of individual odor signatures in human amniotic fluid—potential role in early bonding? Biol. Neonate 74, 266–273.

Schaal, B., and Porter, R. (1991). "Microsmatic Humans" revisited: The generation and perception of chemical signals. Adv. Study Behav. 20, 135–199.

Schaal, B., Montagner, H., Hertling, E., Bolzoni, D., Moyse, A., and Quinchon, R. (1980). Les stimulations olfactives dans les relations entre l'enfant et la mère. Reprod. Nutr. Dev. 20, 843–858.

Schirar, A., Cognie, Y., Louault, F., Poulin, N., Levasseur, M. C., and Martinet, J. (1989). Resumption of oestrous behavior and cyclic ovarian activity in suckling and non-suckling ewes. J. Reprod. Fertil. 87, 789–794.

Schirar, A., Cognié, Y., Louault, F., Poulin, N., Meusnier, C., Levasseur, M. C., and Martinet, J. (1990). Resumption of gonadotrophin release during the post-partum period in suckling and non-suckling ewes. J. Reprod. Fertil. 88, 593–604.

Schlein, P. A., Zarrow, M. X., Cohen, H. A., Denenberg, V. H., and Johnson, N. P. (1972). The differential effect of anosmia on maternal behavior in the virgin and primiparous rat. J. Reprod. Fertil. 30, 139–142.

Schneirla, T. C., Rosenblatt, J. S., and Tobach, E. (1963). Maternal behavior in the cat. In "Maternal Behavior in Mammals" (H. L. Rheingold, ed.), pp. 122–168. Wiley, New York.

Scott, C. J., Pereira, A. M., Rawson, J. A., Simmons, D. M., Rossmanith, W. G., Ing, N. H., and Clark, I. J. (2000). The distribution of progesterone receptor immunoreactivity in the preoptic area and hypothalamus of the ewe: Upregulation of progesterone receptor mRNA in the mediobasal hypothalamus by oestrogen. J. Neuroendocrinol. 12, 565–575.

Scott, E. M., Smithe, S. J., and Verner, E. L. (1958). Self-selection of diet: VII. The effect of age and pregnancy on selection. J. Nutr. 35, 281–286.

Seegal, R. F., and Denenberg, V. H. (1974). Maternal experience prevents pup-killing in mice induced by peripheral anosmia. *Physiol. Behav.* **13**, 339–341.

Shackleton, D. M., and Haywood, J. (1985). Early mother-young interactions in California bighorn sheep, *Ovis canadensis californiana. Can. J. Zool.* **63**, 868–8752.

Shaikh, A. A. (1971). Estrone and estradiol levels in the ovarian venous blood from rats during the oestrus cycle and pregnancy. *Biol. Reprod.* **5**, 297–307.

Shanti, A. S., Subramanian, M. G., Savoy-Moore, R. T., Kruger, M. L., and Moghissi, K. S. (1995). Attenuation of the magnitude of suckling-induced prolactin release with advancing lactation: Mechanisms. *Life Sci.* **56**, 259–266.

Sharp, J. S., González, M. F., Morton, M. T., Simon, R. P., and Sharp, F. R. (1988). Decreases of cortical and thalamic glucose metabolism produced by parietal cortex stimulation in the rat. *Brain Res.* **438**, 357–362.

Sheehan, T. P., Cirrito, J., Numan, M. J., and Numan, M. (2000). Using c-Fos immunocytochemistry to identify forebrain regions that may inhibit maternal behavior in rats. *Behav. Neurosci.* **114**, 337–352.

Shillito, E. E., and Alexander, G. (1975). Mutual recognition amongst ewes and lambs of four breeds of sheep. *Appl. Anim. Ethol.* **1**, 151–165.

Shillito-Walser, E. E. (1978). A comparison of the role of vision and hearing in ewes finding their own lamb. *Appl. Anim. Ethol.* **4**, 71–79.

Shillito-Walser, E. E., Hague, P., and Walters, E. (1982). Vocal recognition of recorded lambs voices by ewes of three breeds of sheep. *Behaviour* **78**, 261–272.

Short, R. V. (1984). Species differences in reproductive mechanisms. *In* "Reproduction in Mammals" (C. R. Austin and R. V. Short, eds.), pp. 24–61. Cambridge University Press, Cambridge, UK.

Shughrue, P. J., Scrimo, P., Lane, M. V., Askew, R., and Merchenthaler, I. (1997a). The distribution of estrogen receptor-beta mRNA in forebrain regions of the estrogen receptor-alpha knockout mouse. *Endocrinology (Baltimore)* **138**, 5649–5652.

Shughrue, P. J., Lane, M. V., and Merchenthaler, I. (1997b). Comparative distribution of estrogen receptor-alpha and -beta mRNA in the rat central nervous system. *J. Comp. Neurol.* **388**, 507–525.

Siegel, H. I., and Greenwald, G. S. (1975). Prepartum onset of maternal behavior in hamsters and the Effects of estrogen and progesterone. *Horm. Behav.* **6**, 237–245.

Siegel, H. I., and Greenwald, G. S. (1978). Effects of mother-litter separation on later maternal responsiveness in the hamster. *Physiol. Behav.* **21**, 147–149.

Siegel, H. I., and Rosenblatt, J. S. (1975a). Estrogen-induced maternal behavior in hysterectomized-ovariectomized virgin rats. *Physiol. Behav.* **14**, 465–471.

Siegel, H. I., and Rosenblatt, J. S. (1975b). Hormonal basis of hysterectomy-induced maternal behavior during pregnancy in the rat. *Horm. Behav.* **6**, 211–222.

Siegel, H. I., and Rosenblatt, J. S. (1975c). Latency and duration of estrogen induction of maternal behavior in hysterectomized-ovariectomized virgin rats: Effects of pup stimulation. *Physiol. Behav.* **14**, 473–476.

Siegel, H. I., and Rosenblatt, J. S. (1975d). Progesterone inhibition of estrogen-induced maternal behavior in hysterectomized-ovariectomized virgin rats. *Horm. Behav.* **6**, 223–230.

Siegel, H. I., and Rosenblatt, J. S. (1978). Duration of estrogen stimulation and progesterone inhibition of maternal behavior in pregnancy-terminated rats. *Horm. Behav.* **11**, 12–19.

Siegel, H. I., and Rosenblatt, J. S. (1980). Hormonal and behavioral aspects of maternal care in the hamster: a review. *Neurosci. Biobehav. Rev.* **4**, 17–26.

Siegel, H. I., Clark, M. C., and Rosenblatt, J. S. (1983). Maternal responsiveness during pregnancy in the hamster (*Mesocricetus auratus*). *Anim. Behav.* **31**, 497–502.

Silveira, P. A., Spoon, R. A., Ryan, D. P., and Williams, G. L. (1993). Evidence for maternal behavior as a requisite link in suckling-mediated anovulation in cows. *Biol. Reprod.* **49**, 1338–1346.

Simonian, S. X., and Herbison, A. E. (1997). Differential expression of estrogen receptor alpha and beta immunoreactivity by oxytocin neurons of rat paraventricular nucleus. *J. Neuroendocrinol.* **9**, 803–806.

Singh, P. B., Brown, R. E., and Roser, B. (1987). MHC antigens in urine as olfactory recognition cues. *Nature (London)* **327**, 161–164.

Singh, P. B., Herbert, J., Roser, B., Arnott, L., Tucker, D. K., and Brown, R. E. (1990). Rearing rats in a germ-free environment eliminates their odors of individuality. *J. Chem. Ecol.* **16**, 1667–1682.

Siqueiros, Y., Luna, A., Vázquez, C., and Shimada, A. (1998). Suckling and foraging behavior of confined red deer (*Cervus elaphus*) fawns and hinds during lactation. *In* "Advances in Deer Biology. Proceedings of the 4th International Deer Biology Congress" (Z. Zoomborszki, ed.), pp. 49–51. Hungary University, Kaposvar.

Sirevaag, A. M., and Greeough, W. T. (1991). Plasticity of GAP-immunoreactive astrocyte size and number in visual cortex of rats reared in complex environments. *Brain Res.* **540**, 273–278.

Slee, J., and Springbett, A. (1986). Early post-natal behavior in lambs of ten breeds. *Appl. Anim. Behav. Sci.* **15**, 229–240.

Slotnick, B. M. (1967). Disturbances of maternal behavior in the rat following lesions of the cingulate cortex. *Behaviour* **29**, 204–236.

Slotnick, B. M., and Nigrosh, B. J. (1975). Maternal behavior of mice with cingulate cortical, amygdala, or septal lesions. *J. Comp. Physiol. Psychol.* **88**, 118–127.

Slotnick, B. M., Carpenter, M. L., and Fusco, R. (1973). Initiation of maternal behavior in pregnant, nulliparous rats. *Horm. Behav.* **4**, 53–59.

Smith, F. V. (1965). Instinct and learning in the attachment of lamb and ewe. *Anim. Behav.* **13**, 84–86.

Smith, F. V., Van Toller, C., and Boyes, T. (1966). The "critical period" in the attachment of lambs and ewes. *Anim. Behav.* **14**, 120–125.

Smith, M. S., and McDonald, L. E. (1974). Serum levels of LH and progesterone during the estrous cycle, pseudopregnancy, and pregnancy in the dog. *Endocrinology (Baltimore)* **94**, 404–412.

Smith, R. L. (1973). The ascending fibers from the principal trigeminal sensory nucleus in the rat. *J. Comp. Neurol.* **148**, 423–446.

Snowdon, C. T. (1990). Mechanisms maintaining monogamy in monkeys. *In* "Contemporary Issues in Comparative Psychology" (D. A. Dewsbury, ed.), pp. 225–251. Sinauer Assoc., Sunderland, MA.

Soares, M. J., Dai, G., Cohick, C. B., Müller, H., and Orwig, K. E. (1998). The rodent placental prolactin family and pregnancy. *In* "The Endocrinology of Pregnancy" (F. W. Bazer, ed.), pp. 47–176. Humana Press, Totowa, NJ.

Soares, M. M., and Talamantes, F. (1982). Gestational effects on placental and serum androgen, progesterone, and prolactin-like activity in the mouse. *J. Endocrinol.* **95**, 29–36.

Södersten, P., and Eneroth, P. (1984). Suckling and serum prolactin and LH concentrations in lactating rats. *J. Endocrinol.* **102**, 251–256.

Solomon, N. G. (1991). Current indirect fitness benefits associated with philopatry in juvenile prairie voles. *Behav. Ecol. Sociobiol.* **29**, 277–282.

Solomon, N. G. (1993). Comparison of parental behavior in male and female praire voles. *Can. J. Zool.* **71**, 434–437.

Solomon, N. G. (1994a). Effect of the pre-weaning environment on subsequent reproduction in prairie voles, *Microtus ochrogaster. Anim. Behav.* **48**, 331–341.

Solomon, S. (1994b). The placenta as an endocrine organ: Steroids. *In* "The Physiology of Reproduction" (E. Knobil and J. D. Neill, eds.), 2nd ed., Vol. 2, pp. 863–873. Raven Press, New York.

Solomon, N. G., and French, J. A. (1997). The study of mammalian cooperative breeding. *In* "Cooperative Breeding in Mammals" (N. G. Solomon and J. A. French, eds.), pp. 1–10. Cambridge University Press, Cambridge, UK.

Solomon, N. G., and Getz, L. L. (1997). Examination of alternative hypotheses for cooperative breeding in rodents. *In* "Cooperative Breeding in Mammals" (N. G. Solomon and J. A. French, eds.), pp. 199–230. Cambridge University Press, Cambridge, UK.

Sorensen, M. F., Rogers, G. P., and Baskett, T. S. (1972). Parental behavior in swamp rabbits. *J. Mammal.* **53**, 840–849.

Southwick, C. H. (1969). Populations dynamics and social behavior of domestic rodents. *In* "Biology of Populations" (B. K. Sladen and F. B. Bang, eds.), pp. 380–394. Am. Elsevier, New York.

Spencer-Booth, Y. (1970). The relationship between mammalian young and conspecifics other than mothers and peers: A review. *Adv. Study Behav.* **3**, 119–194.

Stabenfeldt, G. H. (1974). The role of progesterone in parturition: premature, normal, prolonged gestation. *In* "Avortement et Parturition provoqués" (M. J. Bosc, R. Palmer, and C. Sureau, eds.), pp. 97–122. Masson, Paris.

Stack, E. C., and Numan, M. (2000). The temporal course of expression of c-Fos and Fos B within the medial preoptic area and other brain regions of postpartum female rats during prolonged mother-young interactions. *Behav. Neurosci.* **114**, 609–622.

Stamm, J. S. (1955). The function of the median cerebral cortex in maternal behavior of rats. *J. Comp. Physiol. Psychol.* **48**, 347–356.

Stangel, G., and Jensen, P. (1991). Behavior of semi-naturally kept sows and piglets (except suckling) during 10 days postpartum. *Appl. Anim. Behav. Sci.* **31**, 211–227.

Stern, J. M. (1977). Effects of ergocryptine on postpartum maternal behavior, ovarian cyclicity, and food intake in rats. *Behav. Biol.* **21**, 134–140.

Stern, J. M. (1983). Maternal behavior priming in virgin and caesarean-delivered Long-Evans rats: Effects of brief contact or continuous exteroceptive pup stimulation. *Physiol. Behav.* **31**, 757–763.

Stern, J. M. (1987). Pubertal decline in maternal responsiveness in Long-Evans rats: Maturational influences. *Physiol. Behav.* **41**, 93–98.

Stern, J. M. (1989). Maternal behavior: Sensory, hormonal, and neural determinants. *In* "Psychoendocrinology" (F. R. Brush and S. Levine, eds.), Vol. 3, pp. 105–196. Academic Press, Orlando, FL.

Stern, J. M. (1991). Nursing posture is elicited rapidly in maternally naive, haloperidol-treated female and male rats in response to ventral trunk stimulation from active pups. *Horm. Behav.* **25**, 504–517.

Stern, J. M. (1996a). Somatosensation and maternal care in Norway rats. *In* "Parental Care: Evolution, Mechanisms and Adaptative Significance" (J. S. Rosenblatt and C. T. Snowdon, eds.), Vol. 25, pp. 243–294. Academic Press, San Diego.

Stern, J. M. (1996b). Trigeminal lesions and maternal behavior in Norway rats: II. Disruption of parturition. *Physiol. Behav.* **60**, 187–190.

Stern, J. M., and Johnson, S. K. (1989). Perioral somatosensory determinants of nursing behavior in Norway rats *(Rattus norvegicu). J. Comp. Psychol.* **103**, 269–280.

Stern, J. M., and Johnson, S. K. (1990). Ventral somatosensory determinants of nursing behavior in Norway rats. I. Effects of variations in the quality and quantity of pup stimuli. *Physiol. Behav.* **47**, 993–1011.

Stern, J. M., and Kolunie, J. M. (1989). Perioral anesthesia disrupts maternal behavior during early lactation in Long-Evans rats. *Behav. Neural Biol.* **52**, 20–38.

Stern, J. M., and Kolunie, J. M. (1991). Trigeminal lesions and maternal behavior in Norway rats: I. Effects of cutaneous rostral snout denervation on maintenance of nurturance and maternal aggression. *Behav. Neurosci.* **105**, 984–997.

Stern, J. M., and Mackinnon, D. A. (1976). Postpartum, hormonal, and nonhormonal induction of maternal behavior in rats: Effects on T-maze retrieval of pups. *Horm. Behav.* **7**, 305–316.

Stern, J. M., and Taylor, L. A. (1991). Haloperidol inhibits maternal retrieval and licking, but enhances nursing behavior and litter weight gains in lactating rats. *J. Neuroendocrinol.* **3**, 591–596.

Stern, J. M., Dix, L., Bellomo, C., and Thramann, C. (1992). Ventral trunk somatosensory determinants of nursing behavior in Norway rats. II. Role of nipple and surrounding sensations. *Psychobiology* **20**, 71–80.

Stern, J. M., Yu, Y. L., and Crockett, D. C. (1993). Spinal pathway mediating suckling-induced nursing behavior and neuroendocrine reflexes. *Soc. Neurosc. Abstr.* **19**, 1610.

Stevens, D., Alexander, G., and Lynch, J. J. (1981). Do Merino ewes seek isolation or shelter at lambing? *Appl. Anim. Ethol.* **7**, 149–155.

Stone, C. P. (1938). Effects of cortical destruction on reproductive behavior and maze learning in albino rats. *J. Comp. Psychol.* **26**, 217–236.

Storey, A. E., Bradbury, C. G., and Joyce, T. L. (1994). Nest attendance in male meadow voles: The role of the female in regulating male interactions with pups. *Anim. Behav.* **47**, 1037–1046.

Strauss, J. F., Sokoloski, J., Caploe, P., Duffy, P., and Mintz, G. (1975). On the role of prostaglandins in parturition in the rat. *Endocrinology (Copenhagen)* **96**, 1040–1043.

Sumar, J. B. (1999). Reproduction in South American domestic camelids. *J. Reprod. Fertil. Supp.* **54**, 169–178.

Svare, B. (1979). Steroidal influences on pup-killing behavior in mice. *Horm. Behav.* **13**, 153–164.

Svare, B., and Gandelman, R. (1973). Postpartum aggression in mice: Experiential and environmental factors. *Horm. Behav.* **4**, 323–334.

Svare, B., and Gandelman, R. (1976). A longitudinal analysis of maternal aggression in Rockland-Swiss albino mice. *Dev. Psychobiol.* **9**, 437–446.

Svare, B., and Mann, M. (1981). Infanticide: Genetic, developmental and hormonal influences in mice. *Physiol. Behav.* **27**, 921–927.

Svare, B., Mann, M. A., Broida, J., and Michael, S. D. (1982). Maternal aggression exhibited by hypophysectomized parturient mice. *Horm. Behav.* **16**, 455–461.

Svare, B. B. (1981). Maternal aggression in Mammals. *In* "Parental Care in Mammals" (D. J. Gubernick and P. H. Klopfer, eds.), pp. 179–210. Plenum Press, New York.

Swanson, L. J., and Campbell, C. S. (1979a). Induction of maternal behavior in nulliparous golden hamsters *(Mesocricetus auratus). Behav. Neural Biol.* **26**, 364–371.

Swanson, L. J., and Campbell, C. S. (1979b). Maternal behavior in the primiparous and multiparous golden hamster. *Z. Tierpsychol.* **50**, 96–104.

Swanson, L. J., and Campbell, C. S. (1980). Weaning in the female hamster: Effect of pup age and days post partum. *Behav. Neural Biol.* **28**, 172–182.

Swanson, L. J., and Campbell, C. S. (1981). The role of the young in the control of the hormonal events during lactation and behavioral weaning in the golden hamster. *Horm. Behav.* **15**, 1–15.

Swanson, L. W. (1976). An autoradiographic study of the efferent connections of the preoptic region in the rat. *J. Comp. Neurol.* **167**, 227–256.

Swartz, K. B., and Rosenblum, L. A. (1981). The social context of parental behavior: A perspective on Primate socialization. *In* "Parental Care in Mammals" (D. J. Gubernick and P. H. Klopfer, eds.), pp. 417–454. Plenum Press, New York.

Symmes, D., and Biben, M. (1985). Maternal recognition of individual infant squirrel monkeys from isolation call playbacks. *Am. J. Primatol.* **9**, 39–46.

Taber, S., and Thomas, P. (1982). Calf development and mother-calf spatial relationships in southern right whales. *Anim. Behav.* **30**, 1073–1083.

Talamantes, F. J. (1975). Comparative study of the occurrence of placental prolactin among mammals. *Gen. Comp. Endocrinol.* **27**, 115–121.

Talamantes, F. J., Ogren, L., Markoff, E., Woodard, S., and Madrid, J. (1980). Phylogenetic distribution, regulation of secretion, and prolactin-like effects of placental lactogen. *Fed. Proc., Fed. Am. Soc. Exp. Biol.* **39**, 2582–2587.

Tanimoto, K., Tamminga, C. A., Chase, T. N., and Nilaver, G. (1987). Intracerebroventricular injection of cholecystokinin octapectide elevates plasma prolactin levels through stimulation of vasoactive intestinal polypeptide. *Endocrinology (Baltimore)* **102**, 115–119.

Taylor, J. C. (1966). Home range and agonistic behavior in the grey squirrel. *In* "Play Exploration, and Territory in Mammals" (P. A. Jewell and C. Loizos, eds.), pp. 229–236. Academic Press, New York.

Terkel, J., and Rosenblatt, J. S. (1968). Maternal behavior induced by maternal blood plasma injected into virgin rats. *J. Comp. Physiol. Psychol.* **65**, 479–482.

Terkel, J., and Rosenblatt, J. S. (1972). Humoral factors underlying maternal behavior at parturition: Cross transfusion between freely moving rats. *J. Comp. Physiol. Psychol.* **80**, 365–371.

Terkel, J., Bridges, R. S., and Sawyer, C. H. (1979). Effects of transecting lateral neural connections of the medial preoptic area on maternal behavior in the rat: Nest building, pup retrieval and prolactin secretion. *Brain Res.* **169**, 369–380.

Terlecki, L. J., and Sainsbury, R. S. (1978). Effects of fimbria lesions on maternal behavior in the rat. *Physiol. Behav.* **21**, 89–97.

Terqui, M. (1974). Les oestrogènes au cours de la gestation et de la parturition chez la truie et la brebis. *In* "Avortement et Parturition provoqués" (M. J. Bosc, R. Palmer, and C. Sureau, eds.), pp. 71–79. Masson, Paris.

Terrazas, A., Ferreira, G., Lévy, F., Nowak, R., Serafin, N., Orgeur, P., Soto, R., and Poindron, P. (1999). Do ewes recognize their lambs within the first day postpartum without the help of olfactory cues? *Behav. Processes* **47**, 19–29.

Theodosis, D. T., and Poulain, D. A. (1984). Evidence for structural plasticity in the supraoptic nucleus of the rat hypothalamus in relation to gestation and lactation. *Neuroscience* **11**, 183–193.

Theodosis, D. T., Poulain, D. A., and Vincent, J.-D. (1981). Possible morphological bases of synchronization of neuronal firing in the rat supraoptic nucleus during lactation. *Neuroscience* **6**, 919–929.

Theodosis, D. T., Montagnese, C., Rodriguez, F., Vincent, J. D., and Poulain, D. A. (1986). Oxytocin induces morphological plasticity in the adult hypothalamo-neurohypophysial system. *Nature (London)* **322**, 738–740.

Thomas, A., Kim, N. B., and Amico, J. A. (1996). Differential regulation of oxytocin and vasopressin messenger RNA levels by gonadal steroids in postpartum rats. *Brain Res.* **738**, 48–52.

Thorburn, G. D., and Challis, J. R. (1979). Endocrine control of parturition. *Physiol. Rev.* **59**, 863–918.

Tonkowicz, P. A., and Voogt, J. L. (1983). Termination of prolactin surges with development of placental lactogen secretion in the pregnant rat. *Endocrinology (Baltimore)* **113**, 1314–1318.

Trillmich, F. (1981). Mutual mother-pup recognition in galápagos fur seals and sea lions: Cues used and functional significance. *Behaviour* **78**, 21–42.

Trivers, R. L. (1972). Parental investment and sexual selection. *In* "Sexual Selection and the Descent of Man" (B. Campbell, ed.), pp. 136–179. Aldine-Atherton, Chicago.

Trivers, R. L. (1974). Parent-infant conflict. *Am. Zool.* **14**, 249–264.

Tucker, H. A. (1994). Lactation and its hormonal control. *In* "The Physiology of Reproduction" (E. Knobil and J. D. Neill, eds.), 2nd ed., Vol. 2, pp. 1065–1098. Raven Press, New York.

Tyndale-Biscoe, C. H., and Renfree, M. B. (1987). "Reproductive Physiology of Marsupials." Cambridge University Press, Cambridge, UK.

Ubilla, E., and Rodríguez, J. M. (1989). Routine grouping of parturitions when using a new synthetic analogue of prostaglandin F2-alpha (Etiproston) administered in rabbits on day 29 of pregnancy. *Anim. Reprod. Sci.* **19**, 299–307.

Van der Steen, H. A. M., Schaeffer, L. R., de Jong, H., and Groot, P. N. (1988). Aggressive behavior of sows at parturition. *J. Anim. Sci.* **66**, 271–279.

Van Leengoed, E., Kerker, E., and Swanson, H. H. (1987). Inhibition of postpartum maternal behavior in the rat by injecting an oxytocin antagonist into the cerebral ventricles. *J. Endocrinol.* **112**, 275–282.

Verga, M., Dell'Orto, V., and Carenzi, C. (1978). A general review and survey of maternal behavior in the rabbit. *Appl. Anim. Ethol.* **4**, 235–252.

Verhage, H. G., Beamer, N. B., and Brenner, R. M. (1976). Plasma levels of estradiol and progesterone in the cat during polyestrus, pregnancy and pseudopregnancy. *Biol. Reprod.* **14**, 579–585.

Vince, M. A. (1987). Tactile communication between ewe and lamb and the onset of suckling. *Behaviour* **101**, 156–176.

Vince, M. A. (1993). Newborn lambs and their dams: The interaction that leads to sucking. *Adv. Study Behav.* **22**, 239–268.

Voci, V. E., and Carlson, N. R. (1973). Enhancement of maternal behavior and nest building following systemic and diencephalic administration of prolactin and progesterone in the mouse. *J. Comp. Physiol. Psychol.* **83**, 388–393.

Voogt, J., Robertson, M., and Friesen, H. (1982). Inverse relationship of prolactin and rat placental lactogen during pregnancy. *Biol. Reprod.* **26**, 800–805.

Wagner, A., Grenom, A., Pierre, F., Soutoul, J. H., Fabre-Nys, C., and Krehbiel, D. (1989). Le comportement de la mère face à son enfant à la naissance. Ses modifications éventuelles par l'analgésie péridurale ou la préparation à la naissance. *Rev. Fr. Gynecol. Obstet.* **84**, 29–35.

Wagner, C. K., and Morrell, J. I. (1996). Levels of estrogen receptor immunoreactivity are altered in behaviorally-relevant brain regions in female rats during pregnancy. *Brain Res. Mol. Brain Res.* **42**, 328–336.

Wagner, C. K., Silverman, A. J., and Morrell, J. I. (1998). Evidence for estrogen receptor in cell nuclei and axon terminals within the lateral habenula of the rat: Regulation during pregnancy. *J. Comp. Neurol.* **392**, 330–342.

Wallace, P. (1973). Hormonal influences on maternal behavior in the female mongolian gerbil (*Meriones unguiculatus*). Ph.D. Thesis, University of Texas, Austin.

Wallace, P., Owen, K., and Thiessen, D. D. (1973). The control and function of maternal scent marking the Mongolian gerbil. *Physiol. Behav.* **10**, 463–466.

Walsh, C. J., Fleming, A. S., Lee, A., and Magnusson, J. E. (1996). The effects of olfactory and somatosensory desensitization on Fos-like immunoreactivity in the brains of pup-exposed postpartum rats. *Behav. Neurosci.* **110**, 134–153.

Walsh, R. J., Mangurian, L. P., and Posner, B. I. (1990). The distribution of lactogen receptors in the mammalian hypothalamus: an in vitro autoradiographic analysis of the rabbit and rat. *Brain Res.* **530**, 1–11.

Wamboldt, M. Z., and Insel, T. R. (1987). The ability of oxytocin to induce short latency maternal behavior is dependent on peripheral anosmia. *Behav. Neurosci.* **101**, 439–441.

Wang, Z., and De Vries, G. J. (1993). Testosterone effects on paternal behavior and vasopressin immunoreactive projections in prairie voles (*Microtus ochrogaster*). *Brain Res.* **631**, 156–160.

Wang, Z., and Insel, T. R. (1996). Parental behavior in voles. *In* "Parental Care: Evolution, Mechanisms and Adaptative Significance" (J. S. Rosenblatt and C. T. Snowdon, eds.), Vol. 25, pp. 361–384. Academic Press, San Diego, CA.

Wang, Z., Ferris, C. F., and De Vries, G. J. (1994). Role of septal vasopressin innervation in paternal behavior in prairie voles (*Microtus ochrogaster*). *Proc. Natl. Acad. Sci. U. S. A.* **91**, 400–404.

Wang, Z. X., and Novak, M. A. (1992). Influence of the social environment on parental behavior and pup development of meadow voles (*Microtus pennsylvanicus*) and prairie voles (*M. ochrogaster*). *J. Comp. Psychol.* **106**, 163–171.

Wang, Z. X., Liu, Y., Young, L. J., and Insel, T. R. (2000). Hypothalamic vasopressin gene expression increases in both males and females postpartum in a biparental rodent. *J. Neuroendocrinol.* **12**, 111–120.

Warembourg, M., Logeat, F., and Milgrom, E. (1986). Immunocytochemical localization of progesterone receptor in the guinea pig central nervous system. *Brain Res.* **384**, 121–131.

Warembourg, M., Jolivet, A., and Milgrom, E. (1989). Immunohistochemical evidence of the presence of estrogen and progesterone receptors in the same neurons of the guinea pig hypothalamus and preoptic area. *Brain Res.* **480**, 1–15.

Waring, A., and Perper, T. (1979). Parental behaviour in the mongolian gerbil (*Meriones unguiculatus*). I. Retrieval. *Anim. Behav.* **27**, 1091–1097.

Weiss, G., Butler, W. R., Hotchkiss, J., Dierschke, D. J., and Knobil, E. (1976). Periparturitional serum concentrations of prolactin, the gonadotrophins, and the gonadal hormones in the rhesus monkey. *Proc. Soc. Exp. Biol. Med.* **153**, 330–331.

Wenzel, J., Lammert, G., Meyer, U., and Krug, M. (1991). The influence of long-term potentiation on the spatial relationship between astrocytic processes and potentiated synapses in the dentate gyrus neuropil of the rat brain. *Brain Res.* **560**, 122–131.

Wetteman, R. P., Hallford, D. M., Kreider, D. L., and Turman, E. J. (1977). Influence of prostaglandin F2-alpha on endocrine changes at parturition in gilts. *J. Anim. Sci.* **44**, 106–111.

Widowski, T. M., and Curtis, S. E. (1989). Behavioral responses of periparturient sows and juvenile pigs to prostaglandin $F_{2\alpha}$. *J. Anim. Sci.* **67**, 3266–3276.

Widowski, T. M., Curtis, S. E., Dzuik, P. J., and Wagner, W. C. (1990). Behavioral and endocrine responses of sows to prostaglandin F2-alpha and cloprostenol. *Biol. Reprod.* **43**, 290–297.

Wiesner, B. P., and Sheard, N. M. (1933). "Maternal Behavior in the Rat." Oliver & Boyd, London.

Williams, C. L., Hall, W. G., and Rosenblatt, J. S. (1980). Changing oral cues in suckling of weaning-age rats: Possible contributions to weaning. *J. Comp. Physiol. Psychol.* **94**, 472–483.

Wilson, S. C. (1982). Parent-young contact in prairie and meadow voles. *J. Mammal.* **63**, 300–305.

Wilsoncroft, W. E. (1963). Effects of median cortex lesions on the maternal behavior of the rat. *Psychol. Repo.* **13**, 835–838.

Wisden, W., Errington, M. L., Williams, S., Dunnett, S. B., Waters, C., Hitchcock, D., Evan, G., Bliss, T. V., and Hunt, S. P. (1990). Differential expression of immediate early genes in the hippocampus and spinal cord. *Neuron* **4**, 603–614.

Wise, D. A. (1974). Aggression in the female golden hamster: Effects of reproductive state and social isolation. *Horm. Behav.* **5**, 235–250.

Wise, D. A., and Pryor, T. L. (1977). Effects of ergocornine and prolactin on aggression in the post-partum golden hamster. *Horm. Behav.* **8**, 30–39.

Wolski, T. R., Houpt, K. A., and Aronson, R. (1980). The role of the senses in mare-foal recognition. *Appl. Anim. Ethol.* **6**, 121–138.

Woodroffe, R. (1993). Alloparental behavior in the European badger. *Anim. Behav.* **46,** 413–415.

Woodside, B., and Jans, J. E. (1988). Neuroendocrine basis of thermally regulated maternal responses to young in the rat. *Psychoneuroendocrinology* **13,** 79–98.

Woodside, B., Abizaid, A., and Walker, C. D. (2000). Changes in leptin levels during lactation: Implications for lactational hyperphagia and anovulation. *Horm. Behav.* **37,** 353–365.

Woodside, C., and Jans, J. E. (1995). Role of the nutritional status of the litter and length and frequency of mother-litter contact bouts in prolonging lactational diestrus in rats. *Horm. Behav.* **29,** 154–176.

Workel, J. O., Oitzl, M. S., Ledeboer, A., and de Kloet, E. R. (1997). The Brown Norway rat displays enhanced stress-induced ACTH reactivity at day 18 after 24-h maternal deprivation at day 3. *Dev. Brain Res.* **103,** 199–203.

Yeo, J. A., and Keverne, E. B. (1986). The importance of vaginal-cervical stimulation for maternal behavior in the rat. *Physiol. Behav.* **37,** 23–26.

Yogman, M. W. (1990). Male parental behavior in humans and nonhuman primates. *In* "Mammalian Parenting: Biochemical, Neurobiological, and Behavioral Determinants" (N. A. Krasnegor and R. S. Bridges, eds.), pp. 461–481. Oxford University Press, New York.

Young, L. J. (1999). Oxytocin and vasopressin receptors and species-typical social behaviors. *Horm. Behav.* **36,** 212–221.

Yu, G. Z., Kaba, H., Okutani, F., Takahashi, S., Higuchi, T., and Seto, K. (1996a). The action of oxytocin originating in the hypothalamic paraventricular nucleus on mitral and granule cells in the rat main olfactory bulb. *Neuroscience* **72,** 1073–1082.

Yu, G. Z., Kaba, H., Okutani, F., Takahashi, S., and Higuchi, T. (1996b). The olfactory bulb: A critical site of action for oxytocin in the induction of maternal behavior in the rat. *Neuroscience* **72,** 1083–1088.

Zaidi, S. M., and Heller, H. (1974). Can neurohypophysial hormones cross the blood-cerebrospinal fluid barrier? *J. Endocrinol.* **60,** 195–196.

Zarrow, M. X., Sawin, P. B., Ross, S., Denenberg, V. H., Crary, D., Wilson, E. D., and Farooq, A. (1961). Maternal behavior in the rabbit: Evidence for an endocrine basis of maternal-nest building and additional data on maternal-nest building in the Dutch-Belted race. *J. Reprod. Fertil.* **2,** 152–162.

Zarrow, M. X., Farooq, A., and Denenberg, V. H. (1962a). Maternal behavior in the rabbit: Critical period for nest-building following castration during pregnancy. *Proc. Soc. Exp. Biol. Med.* **3,** 537–538.

Zarrow, M. X., Sawin, P. B., Ross, S., and Denenberg, V. H. (1962b). Maternal behavior in the rabbit: Evidence for an endocrine basis of maternal-nest building in the Dutch-belted race. *In* "Roots of Behavior" (E. L. Bliss, ed.), pp. 187–197. Hoeber, New York.

Zarrow, M. X., Farooq, A., Denenberg, V. H., Sawin, P. B., and Ross, S. (1963). Maternal behavior in the rabbit: Endocrine control of maternal-nest building. *J. Reprod. Fertil.* **6,** 375–383.

Zarrow, M. X., Denenberg, V. H., and Anderson, C. O. (1965). Rabbit: Frequency of suckling in the pup. *Science* **150,** 1835–1836.

Zarrow, M. X., Gandelman, R., and Denenberg, V. H. (1971b). Lack of nest-building and maternal behavior in the mouse following olfactory bulb removal. *Horm. Behav.* **2,** 227–238.

Zarrow, M. X., Gandelman, R., and Denenberg, V. H. (1971a). Prolactin: Is it an essential hormone for maternal behavior in the mammal? *Horm. Behav.* **2,** 343–354.

Ziegler, T. E. (2000). Hormones associated with non-maternal infant care: A review of mammalian and avian studies. *Folia Primatol.* **71,** 6–21.

Ziegler, T. E., Wegner, F. H., and Snowdon, C. T. (1996). Hormonal responses to parental and non-parental conditions in male cotton-top tamarins, *Saguinus oedipus,* a New World primate. *Horm. Behav.* **30,** 287–297.

Ziegler, T. E., Wegner, F. H., Carlson, A. A., Lazaro-Perea, C., and Snowdon, C. T. (2000). Prolactin levels during the periparturitional period in the biparental cotton-top tamarin (*Saguinus oedipus*): Interactions with gender, androgen levels, and parenting. *Horm. Behav.* **38,** 111–122.

4

The Neurobiology of Social Affiliation and Pair Bonding

C. S. Carter

Department of Psychiatry
University of Illinois at Chicago
Chicago, Illinois 60612

E. B. Keverne

Department of Animal Behaviour
University of Cambridge
Cambridge CB3 8AA, United Kingdom

I. INTRODUCTION

Positive social interactions, including affiliations and social bonds, dominate the behavioral repertoire of humans and many higher vertebrates. Social bonds provide a context for reproduction and can facilitate survival (Table 1). Epidemiological evidence reveals that the presence or absence of positive social experiences and social bonds can have major effects on health and well-being (Ryff and Singer, 1998). However, society and research tend to focus on demanding and often negative issues, such as illness or stress. Even the medical concept of *health* is defined primarily by its absence.

Studies of the neurobiology of social affiliation and pair bonding have been slowed by a general failure to recognized the importance of positive behaviors, as well as difficulties associated with the measurement of social behaviors, and especially social bonds. Thus, in contrast to more easily characterized reproductive or aggressive behaviors, the processes responsible for affiliation and social bonds are less commonly studied, especially from a neurobiological perspective.

Social behaviors involve two or more individuals and require the willingness of animals to aggregate and remain together. Social behaviors are typically identified as positive, including affiliations and social bonds, or agonistic, including aggressive or defensive behaviors.

This review will focus on behavioral and physiological systems that support beneficial or healthful social interactions, conducted for mutual benefit or social support. Selective social behaviors and social bonds are a critical component of long-lasting social interactions. Social behaviors also are inherently species-typical and variable across individuals. Patterns of social behavior are the product of evolution and result from phylogenetic and ontogenetic processes, as well as changes in adulthood.

Research in this area has focused on a limited number of species with natural tendencies to form maternal infant bonds or selective adult pair bonds (Table 2). Selective social bonds are uncommon in laboratory rodents, and the requirement for intraspecific social bonds may be reduced in the process of domestication. Inter- and intraspecific variation, along with the tendency of physiologists to study socially promiscuous species, including rats and mice, has slowed awareness of the neurobiology of social bonding.

The purpose of this review is to examine mechanisms underlying social affiliation and social bonds. Several recent reviews have examined social behavior and social bonding from a behavioral perspective (Kraemer, 1992; Reite and Bocca, 1994; Levine *et al.*, 1997: Hennessy, 1997; Mendoza and Mason, 1997; Panksepp *et al.*, 1997; Mason and Mendoza, 1998;

TABLE 1
Benefits of Pair Bonding

Reproduction	Survival
Availability of mates	Predator defense
Care and protection of young	Homeostasis and energy exchange
	Reduction of stress or perceived stress

TABLE 3
Experiences Associated with Pair Bonding

Birth
Postpartum period and lactation
Sexual behavior
Prolonged cohabitation
Threatening or novel experiences, followed by fear reduction

Nelson and Panksepp, 1998; Keverne, 1992, 1995a; Carter, 1998; Carter *et al.,* 1997). That material is repeated here only as it aids in understanding of the neurobiology of these behaviors.

It is likely that biological systems responsible for many types of positive interactions are based on shared biological processes. For example, the neural and endocrine mechanisms involved in adult social bonding and pair bonding have much in common with mother-infant bonding and maternal behavior. As described in detail here, neuroendocrine systems that incorporate neuropeptides, including oxytocin, vasopressin, opioids, corticotropin-releasing hormone (CRH), and related hormones, play a central role in social bond formation. These peptides also serve to coordinate the physiological and behavioral consequences of positive social experiences.

II. THE NATURAL HISTORY OF PAIR BOND FORMATION

Social bonds may form between a parent and infant, between two adults, and among other members of a social group (Table 3). These apparently very different bonding relationships have a common function—

namely, to enhance reproduction and ensure reproductive success. This is achieved in pair bonding and social group bonding by providing a readily available mate and predator defense, while mother-infant bonding and social group bonding secure the nurture of infants and their protection. Pair bonding is especially favored in mammalian species whose offsprings' survival cannot be assured without the help of mates.

Nurturing an infant places enormous energetic demands on the mother, requiring additional food intake for infant growth during pregnancy and for milk production in the postpartum period. The ability to sustain adequate foraging may be limited by the female's added commitment to the offspring; should these demands pose a threat to mother-infant survival, pair bonding and male parenting may provide support for the offspring.

Selective social bonds may be rare or absent in domestic species—and in some cases are further minimized by the processes of domestication. However, clear examples of pair bonding and the physiological basis for social bond formation are provided from studies on voles, marmosets, and other species that are identified as "monogamous" (Kleiman, 1977).

In promiscuous mammalian species, in which parental males are frequently absent, mother-infant bonding may help guarantee infant survival. This bonding

TABLE 2
Animal Models for Studying the Biological Bases of Pair Bonding

Maternal-infant bonding	Maternal behavior	Adult pair bonding
Most commonly studied in animals in which the mother is selective and cares for only her own young. Example: sheep.	Not selective, but may share physiological substrates with pair bonding. Examples: rats, other rodents.	Most commonly studied in adult monogamous mammals. Examples: prairie voles, titi monkeys.

often involves individual infant recognition. Examples of filial bonding are found among ungulate species. Research on maternal bonding has taken advantage of the fact that precocial ungulates, including sheep, are excellent subjects for neurobiological investigation because they develop selective mother-infant bonding.

In social mammals and especially in primate societies, an alternative strategy for promoting reproductive success through infant survival is seen in the assistance given by other females. Serving as surrogate parents may involve a self-sacrifice for reproductive potential and often is undertaken by females that are genetically related to the offspring. Old World primate societies are frequently referred to as being "female-bonded." Such primate matrilines not only provide for group cohesion and social continuity, but kin also benefit from the learning experience gained when helping the mother. The neurobiology of same-sex social bonds remains largely unexplored but may rely on the underlying neural systems that regulate other forms of social bonding.

Alloparenting and male parental behavior are traits of species, ranging from birds to rodents to canids to New World primates, that are defined as socially monogamous (Solomon and French, 1997). Although both related and unrelated animals may aid in the care of young, alloparenting is most common among genetically related individuals. Selective social behaviors and social bonds are defining characteristics of species that engage in alloparenting or paternal behavior, thus suggesting that common underlying mechanisms may regulate social bonding and other social traits in species that tend to form communal families.

Social bonds also may provide direct benefits to the members of a pair or group by serving to buffer the individual from stress. The physiological mechanisms for stress-buffering are related to those responsible for the formation of pair bonds.

A. Experiences Associated with Pair Bonding

The essential first steps in social bond formation involve proximity and social engagement (Porges, 1998). Potential partners must interact in a species- and gender-appropriate manner. The choice of a social partner, the tendency to engage in social behaviors, and patterns of social behavior differ among species and individuals and between males and females (DeVries et al., 1996). In addition, because the outcome of social interactions can be positive or negative, the emotional experience of a particular social encounter may determine whether that encounter leads to pair bond formation.

Both positive social interactions and social bonds may function to provide a sense of safety and reduce anxiety or the negative feelings associated with stressful experience. In species that do tend to form pair bonds, stressful experiences (such as pregnancy and parturition), anxiety, neophobia, and isolation often precede the formation of long-lasting social attachments (Carter, 1998). Threatening situations may encourage return to a "secure base" or otherwise strengthen social bonds (Bowlby, 1969; Panksepp et al., 1985). These circumstances may increase social "drive" or "motivation" and subsequent social interactions, and thus increase the tendency to form a social attachment.

The association of pair bonding with overcoming stressful experiences also offers clues to the physiology of pair bond formation (Table 3). Hormones can reduce fear or behavioral inhibition and permit the subsequent expression of selective social behaviors, such as those necessary for pair bonding. The neurochemical processes that are capable of overcoming neophobia also may be needed to permit the formation of new social attachments. Although they share some common substrates, the neural substrates for social engagement and selective social bonding are probably not identical (Cho et al., 1999), and it is likely that the processes leading to social interactions differ from those necessary for a bond to form.

B. Measurement of Social Bonding

Social bonds are hypothetical constructs, and thus direct measurements are not possible. However, selective behavioral, hormonal, or autonomic responses to social stimuli, or their absence, may be used to infer social bonds (Table 4). Laboratory analyses of social bonding often involve preference tests in which experimental animals are allowed to choose between or express differential responses to social stimuli.

TABLE 4
Measurements of Pair Bonding

Selective contact or physical proximity in the presence of an
   attachment object
Aggression in defense of the attachment object
Autonomic or endocrine responses or both
Distress after separation
   Crying or vocalization
   Increased release of stress hormones (HPA activation)

Differential responses to the entire animal, visual cues, vocalizations, odors, or visual cues can be used to assess preferences. The most compelling evidence for positive social preference is usually obtained in tests in which an experimental animal is allowed a simultaneous or sequential choice between a familiar animal or an otherwise similar unfamiliar conspecific (or stimuli associated with those individuals). Physical proximity and positive social interactions are commonly used to index preference. Testing conditions in which the experimental animal is allowed elective physical contact with the stimulus animals are especially sensitive (Williams *et al.,* 1992a). In addition, conditions that allow the experimental animal to remain alone are desirable, since voluntary social preferences may differ from forced choices.

Responses to separation or reunion can also be evidence for social bonding. In mammals and birds, "distress" vocalizations may increase following separation and decline following reunion. Secretion of hormones from the hypothalamic-pituitary-adrenal (HPA) axis, usually cortisol or corticosterone or adrenocorticotrophic hormone (ACTH), also follows separation

from the "attachment figure," and HPA activity tends to return to normal upon reunion. However, vocalizations, changes in the HPA axis, and autonomic responses may be triggered by either social or nonsocial stressors. Thus, it is difficult to prove that such changes are related to social bonding. Furthermore, various autonomic, behavioral, and endocrine responses to separation, reunion, or the presence of a stressor may have different time courses or be discordant (Levine *et al.,* 1989; Hennessy, 1997). No single measure of bonding has gained universal acceptance, and existing behavioral and endocrine measures may reflect different, although in some cases related, physiological processes. The most compelling evidence for social bonding is obtained when various measures converge, and when those measures can be interpreted in light of the biology of the entire organism and especially the neuroendocrine system.

III. OXYTOCIN AND VASOPRESSIN: CLASSICAL NEUROENDOCRINE PEPTIDES

Because oxytocin and vasopressin are released during social and sexual interactions, and under conditions that result in pair bonding, the neural systems that incorporate these neuropeptides are potential candidates for a role in the mediation of social behavior and especially social bonding (Table 5). Oxytocin and vasopressin are neuropeptides composed of nine amino acids, including a six-amino acid ring with a three-amino acid tail. Oxytocin and vasopressin differ from each other in two amino acids, one in the ring and one in the tail, and may have evolved from a common

TABLE 5
Endocrine Theories of Pair Bonding

Steroids	*Peptides*
Gonadal steroids—not essential	Oxytocin—may be especially important in females
But may modulate effects of peptides	Vasopressin—may be especially important in males
Adrenal steroids—not essential	CRH—may modulate effects of stress
May modulate effects of peptides	Opioids—modulation of separation responses
Effects may be sexually dimorphic	
Tends to be elevated then decline	

TABLE 6
Behavioral Effects of Oxytocin

Type of Behavior	Direction
Positive social behaviors or contact	Increase
Pair bonding—onset in adults	Increase
Maternal attachment	Increase
Infant attachment	Increase
Exploration or approach to novelty	Increase
Response to stress or pain	Decrease

ancestral peptide (Van Kesteren et al., 1992; Acher et al., 1997). The gene for these two peptides is located on the same chromosome. The stereochemical similarities between these peptides probably allow functional interactions with each other's receptors (Barberis and Tribollet, 1996; Carter et al., 1995; De Wied et al., 1993; Engelmann et al., 1996; Pedersen et al., 1992). Oxytocin and vasopressin are the predominant neurophypohyseal hormones in mammals, although structurally similar peptides, such as vasotocin, mesotocin, and isotocin, have been identified in other vertebrates (Acher et al., 1997). In addition, structurally related peptides are found in invertebrates, a finding that suggests that variations on these molecules appeared prior to the evolution of vertebrates (Van Kesteren et al., 1992).

The major sources of systemic oxytocin and vasopressin in mammals are the magnocellular neurons of the supraoptic nucleus (SON) and paraventricular nucleus of the hypothalamus (PVN) (Russell and Leng, 1998). Oxytocin and vasopressin, in conjunction with neurophysin carrier proteins, are transported from magnocellular neurons in the SON and PVN to the posterior pituitary, where they are secreted into the bloodstream. The release of oxytocin into the systemic circulation is typically pulsatile. In addition, oxytocin and vasopressin are released within the central nervous system (CNS) from smaller, parvocellular neurons, located in the PVN and other brain areas. The release of peptides within the CNS and posterior pituitary can occur independently, although central and peripheral release patterns also may be coordinated (Kendrick et al., 1986).

In addition to the oxytocin that is produced in the SON and PVN, cell bodies producing oxytocinergic fibers also have been identified in the bed nucleus of the stria terminalis (BNST), the anterior commissural nucleus, and the spinal cord (Sofroniew, 1983). The latter fibers terminate within the CNS or release oxytocin into the cerebrospinal fluid. Oxytocin gene expression increases in the PVN and SON during lactation and around birth or under hormonal conditions that mimic birth (Lightman and Young, 1987, 1989; Russell and Leng, 1998). Oxytocin also is produced in other tissues, including the ovary, uterus, placenta, and thymus. The multiple actions of this hormone may integrate a variety of peripheral and central processes, including those involved in reproduction and behavior.

As with oxytocin, the most abundant sources of vasopressin are found in the PVN and SON. Vasopressin is synthesized and released within the nervous system by parvocellular neurons in the PVN. Vasopressinergic cell bodies also have been identified in the suprachiasmatic nucleus (SCN), medial amygdala (mAMY), BNST, and other areas of the caudal brain stem. Androgens facilitate the synthesis of vasopressin, particularly in the mAMY and lateral septum (LS) (Van Leeuwen et al., 1985; DeVries and Villalba, 1997), thereby accounting for clear sex differences in the abundance of vasopressin in the CNS.

A. Oxytocin and Vasopressin Receptors

The oxytocin receptor is a member of the seven transmembrane G-protein coupled receptors and is distinguished by differences in its distribution across different mammalian species. There is at present only evidence for one oxytocin receptor, which is similar across species. However, species differences do exist in the regulation of the oxytocin receptor, thus allowing a variety of other neuroendocrine factors, including steroids, to determine species-typical patterns of receptor distribution (Witt et al., 1991; Insel, 1992, 1997; Insel and Shapiro, 1992; Insel et al., 1991; Young et al., 1996).

Oxytocin receptors have been identified by receptor autoradiography and receptor mRNA expression in several brain areas. Among the areas that contain high concentrations of the oxytocin receptor are the olfactory bulbs, anterior olfactory nucleus (AON), olfactory tubercle, nucleus accumbens (NAcc), prelimbic cortex (PLC), ventral subiculum, BNST, central nucleus of the amygdala (cAMY), ventromedial hypothalamus

(VMH), LS, cingulate cortex (CC), dorsal motor nucleus of the vagus (DMX), and the nucleus tractus solitarius (NTS) (Tribollet *et al.*, 1990; Barberis and Tribollet, 1996; Insel *et al.*, 1993; Young *et al.*, 1996).

Although three isoforms of the vasopressin receptor have been identified, most of the behavioral effects have been attributed to the V1a receptor, which is expressed in the brain. Vasopressin V1a binding has been identified in the granule cell layer of olfactory bulbs, accessory olfactory bulbs, the diagonal band of Broca, cingulate cortex, central and lateral aspects of the amygdala, the dorso-lateral thalamus, and superior colliculus (Insel, 1997). Like oxytocin, the distribution of V1a receptors is highly species-specific and follows a pattern that implicates this receptor in social behavior and pair bonding (Insel and Shapiro, 1992).

IV. MOTHER-INFANT BONDING

The most notable form of an enduring social bond is that between a mother and her infants. Bonding, although integral to maternal behavior, can be distinguished from this. This distinction is most obvious in a postpartum mother that is highly maternal but rejects her offspring through a failure to bond. This dissociation of maternal behavior and infant rejection occurs following failure in the recognition process. Recognition is prerequisite for bonding, and in ungulate species a sensitive period following birth provides the window of opportunity for this recognition bond to occur. A failure to make this recognition within the sensitive period, as sometimes occurs in primiparous mothers, or multiparous mothers if their infant is experimentally removed, results in a rejection of the offspring (Lévy *et al.*, 1991). It might seem counterintuitive that a maternally motivated female, having experienced the hormones of pregnancy and parturition, would reject her genetically related infant. Indeed, this only makes sense when we view maternal rejection behavior in its appropriate biological context. Within minutes after birth in ungulates, the mother starts to lick the newborn, which can usually stand and suckle within two hours of birth (Poindron and Le Neindre, 1980). It is around this same time that maternal care becomes exclusive. Thus in sheep, the ewe, having "bonded," accepts only her own lamb at suckling and rejects, often violently, any strange

lamb that attempts to suckle. Since sheep are seasonal breeders with synchronized multiple births occurring throughout the flock, all within a few weeks, it is important that the mother recognizes and only permits her own lamb to suckle. Nurturing is energetically costly to the mother and "bonding" ensures that this energetic sacrifice is only made to her own genetically related offspring.

The mechanisms that underlie the formation of the mother-infant bond involve the female being in a maternal state, being able to recognize her offspring dependent on unique sensory cues, and having the sensitive window for recognition contingent upon the appearance of the offspring. The recognition window is activated by parturition and delivery of the neonate.

A. Mechanisms Underlying Maternal State

The ovarian hormones of importance in maternal behavior are estrogen and progesterone, and since there is no restriction to the passage of steroid hormones from the vascular to the cerebral compartment, high-affinity binding neurons for these hormones will be activated in all parts of the brain simultaneously (Kendrick and Keverne, 1991). Although studies have tended to focus attention on the hypothalamus as a site of action for steroid hormones, it should be remembered that steroid-binding neurons have a widespread distribution throughout the limbic and olfactory brain. The pattern of secretion of steroid hormones during pregnancy is remarkably similar among all nonprimate mammals and is characterized by high levels of progesterone in the postimplantation period, which decreases prior to parturition with a concomitant increase in estradiol. This prolonged priming of the brain by exposure to high progesterone and low estrogen is important for the suppression of sexual behavior in mammals and for genomic activation promoting the synthesis of hypothalamic peptides (oxytocin, CRH, prolactin and β-endorphin). Progesterone decline followed by the sequential increase in estradiol is important for synthesis of receptors for these peptides in many parts of the limbic brain. In other words, steroid hormones have their action in the brain by binding to DNA motifs on the promoter regions of certain genes, many of which code for neuropeptides and their receptors (Table 7).

TABLE 7
Mechanisms Through Which Steroids and Peptides May Influence Social Bonding

Developmental regulation	*In adulthood*
Species-typical traits	Peptide synthesis or release
Sexual dimorphism in nervous system	Peptide receptors or binding
Alterations in peptide sensitivity or reactivity by altering hormones or neurotransmitters or their receptors	Alteration of behaviors that release peptides
	Peptide-peptide interactions
	Steroid-steroid interactions
	Steroid-peptide-neurotransmitter interactions
	Hormonal effects on the autonomic nervous system

The steroid hormones of pregnancy are integral to the induction of maternal responding but do not exclusively code for these events; they also influence sexual behavior, feeding behavior, and exploratory behavior, and thus have the recruiting capacity for a wide range of neural systems. The ovarian steroids are therefore perhaps best viewed as part of a widely distributed addressing system, provided with a degree of specificity in the context of maternal behavior by the events that occur at parturition (Keverne and Kendrick, 1992). The prolonged action of progesterone throughout pregnancy suppresses estrus, while parturition itself recruits other neural systems for the initiation of maternal behavior, thereby synchronizing maternal care with the birth of infants.

B. Oxytocin, Infant Recognition, and Bonding

Pederson and Prange (1979) first tested the hypothesis that central oxytocin has a role in maternal behavior. It is an attractive idea that both the central and peripheral components of a neuroendocrine system may be activated simultaneously as part of a coordinated behavioral and neuroendocrine response (Table 6). Their experiments involved infusion of this and other peptides via in-dwelling cannulae into the ventricular system of the female rat's brain. These females had been ovariectomized and hormonally primed, and were presented with one or two day-old rat pups and observed for maternal behavior. Infusions of oxytocin and its analogue, tocinoic acid, had a significant effect in promoting maternal behavior within a two-hour period. These findings were followed by studies that revealed

a dose-dependent effect in promoting maternal behavior of oxytocin given directly to the brain (Pederson et al., 1982). Subsequent studies showed that the onset of maternal behavior can be delayed by intracerebroventricular (icv) treatment with oxytocin antisera or a synthetic oxytocin antagonist (Fahrbach et al., 1985).

In the sheep, vaginocervical stimulation and parturition increase the levels of oxytocin within the brain, even though the blood-brain barrier is relatively impermeable to oxytocin (Keverne and Kendrick, 1992). Vaginocervical stimulation can itself promote a rapid onset of maternal behavior in nongestant ewes (Keverne et al., 1983) (Fig. 1), whereas ewes that deliver under epidural anaesthesia show no interest in lambs until they are subsequently given intracerebral oxytocin (Lévy et al., 1992). Also in sheep, administration of oxytocin directly to the brains' ventricular system stimulates a rapid onset of maternal behavior and induces the ewe to maintain proximity with lambs in an open field. Even with the competing stimulus of food in the opposite corner of the field, oxytocin-treated ewes prefer to spend time in proximity with the lamb, a significant change of priority in comparison with untreated ewes (Kendrick et al., 1987).

Direct evidence for the release of oxytocin at sites in the brain known to be involved in maternal behavior have come from microdialysis studies. In the ewe, oxytocin is released during labor, birth, and suckling in both the bed nucleus of the stria terminalis (BNST), medial preoptic area (MPOA), and olfactory bulbs (Kendrick et al., 1992). The BNST and MPOA and olfactory bulbs are rich in oxytocin-binding sites (Insel, 1997) and play an integral part in the induction of maternal behavior (Numan et al., 1988), whereas the

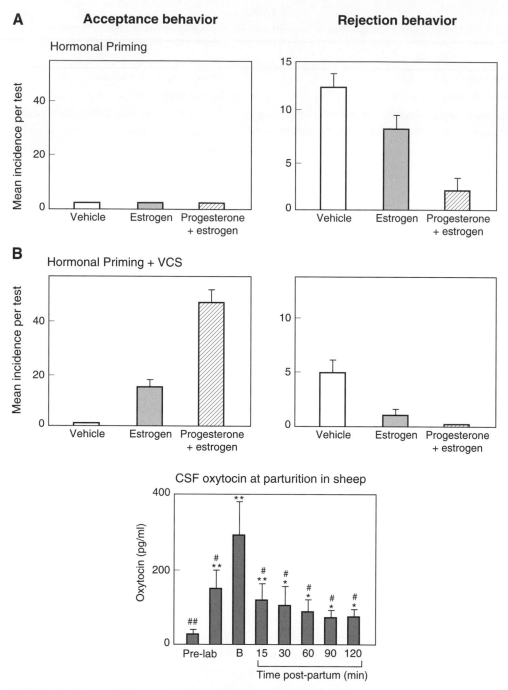

FIGURE 1 Maternal behavior in sheep: hormones of pregnancy and VCS. (A) Administration of pregnancy hormones (estrogen and progesterone) has no effect on maternal acceptance behavior unless accompanied by vaginal-cervical stimulation (VCS). (B) Rejection behavior does decline as a result of hormonal priming (A) and is reduced further when accompanied by VCS. (C) Parturition or VCS evoke large increases of oxytocin in the brain.

olfactory bulbs appear to have no oxytocin terminals but play an important role in maternal recognition of lambs (Kendrick *et al.,* 1992a). Attempts to induce maternal behavior by infusing oxytocin into the MPOA in both rats (Fahrbach *et al.,* 1985) and sheep (Kendrick and Keverne, 1992) have met with little success, other than a reduction of rejection behavior in sheep. However, elimination of rejection behavior is an essential prelude to the proceptive behavioral sequences that follow. It may therefore be the case that the exceptionally high levels of oxytocin released into cerebrospinal fluid (CSF) at parturition act both as a transmitter and neurohumoral factor, thereby orchestrating the maternal responses that require activity throughout widespread areas of the brain, including the olfactory bulbs for integration of the complex sensorimotor programmes (Fig. 1). It is certainly the case that administration of oxytocin to CSF in nonparturient ewes evokes the complete complement of sensorimotor patterns that make up full maternal responsiveness (Kendrick *et al.,* 1987).

For some time anatomists have been confused by the mismatch between neurotransmitter terminals and their receptors in the brain. Indeed, under basal conditions oxytocin may only be effective at terminal areas. During critical life events such as mating and parturition, however, the whole brain may be flooded with the peptide, thus activating receptors where terminals have failed to be located.

The main source of intracerebral oxytocin is the parvocellular neurons in the paraventricular nucleus of the hypothalamus (PVN), which project widely throughout the brain (Sofroniew, 1985) to areas that are important for the control of maternal behavior (Numan, 1994a,b). These include the MPOA, BNST, septum, amygdala, hippocampus, ventral tegmental area, and olfactory bulb. Furthermore, lesioning studies of the PVN in rodents have shown that it is necessary for the induction of maternal behavior in rats (Numan and Corodimas, 1985; Insel and Harbaugh, 1989). Although equivalent lesioning studies have not been performed in sheep, other techniques have shown that in this species the storage and synthesis of oxytocin is greatly increased at birth in the PVN and its terminal projections (Broad *et al.,* 1993). In addition, oxytocin has been shown to be released during the induction of maternal behavior in sheep at most of the sites to which the PVN projects (Kendrick *et al.,* 1988; Kendrick and Keverne, 1992).

Not only is the PVN the main source of intracerebral oxytocin (OT) but it also seems to be one of the targets for OT. Recent studies have shown the presence of cells in the PVN of sheep that express oxytocin receptor mRNA. Similarly, the PVN of rats contains oxytocin receptor binding sites (Freund-Mercier and Stoecket, 1993), and oxytocin is released in the PVN of rats undergoing parturition (Neumann *et al.,* 1993). Finally, oxytocin released by the magnocellular nuclei *in vitro* stimulates the oxytocin cells to facilitate further oxytocin release (Moos *et al.,* 1984). Altogether, these findings indicate that oxytocin itself is part of a positive feedback mechanism to controlling its own release in the brain. The relative importance of this oxytocin feedback for the induction of maternal behavior has been shown following low doses of oxytocin infused directly to the PVN (Da Costa *et al.,* 1996). The consequent induction of behavior was comparable to the induction of maternal behavior by vagino cervical stimulation and by intracerebral infusions of high doses of oxytocin into the ventricles.

As in rats, vasopressin was also capable of inducing maternal behavior, although not as effectively as oxytocin and requiring a tenfold increase in dose (Da Costa *et al.,* 1996). The most likely explanation for this finding is that vasopressin can weakly act on oxytocin receptors, since the two peptides are structurally different at only two amino acids. Oxytocin release in the PVN at parturition probably facilitates a positive feedback on both parvocellular and magnocellular neurons to coordinate the high levels of oxytocin release that are important for the induction of maternal behavior, infant recognition, and bonding.

The half-life of peptides such as oxytocin in CSF is considerably longer than that found in peripheral plasma. Nevertheless, the duration of its behavioral effectiveness is approximately one hour, a finding in parallel with a rapid waning of maternal behavior in parturient ewes that fail to bond because their lambs are removed (Poindron and Le Neindre, 1980). The comparatively short duration for which intracerebral oxytocin stimulates maternal behavior in ewes suggests that its central release may only be important for inducing maternal behavior, unless additional mechanisms are available for increasing central oxytocin release at other times. In this context, it is interesting to note that not only parturition but also suckling increases CSF oxytocin in sheep (Keverne and Kendrick, 1992), whereas chemosensory cues from anogenital licking of pups maintains the efficiency of oxytocin release in rats in response to suckling, and a baby's crying can induce oxytocin release and milk let-down in lactating women. Hence the initiation and maintenance of maternal care appear to differ in important ways. For initiation, oxytocin and its receptor depend largely on steroid hormone priming, but sustained release of oxytocin is evoked by somatosensory stimulation at parturition. During the maintenance of maternal behavior, steroid levels are low and oxytocin sustains its own receptors, whereas its release can be evoked by sucking and other sensory stimuli from the offspring. The duration of the maintenance phase is therefore dependent on the frequency of sensory stimulation from the lamb, which will diminish in both type and frequency as the infant becomes self-sufficient.

C. Opioids, Affiliation, and Bonding

Among the earliest physiological theories of attachment was the opioid-dependency theory of Panksepp and his collaborators (1985, 1997; Nelson and Panksepp, 1998). Based on parallels between narcotic addiction and the phenomenology of attachment and social separation, Panksepp proposed that the brain opioid systems could provide neural substrates for both phenomena. This theory was based on the premise that affiliation and attachment evolved from ancient motivational processes, sharing substrates with neural systems that were involved in pain, thermoregulation, and the formation of place-preferences. According to this hypothesis the release of endogenous opioids might play a role in a social reward system, which could motivate or reinforce the formation of social bonds (Panksepp *et al.,* 1994). However, attempts in adult rats to use naltrexone or naloxone to block the rewarding effects of social behavior have been unsuccessful. Based on research with rats, Panksepp and associates (1997) have concluded, "even though opioids are very powerful in reducing separation-distress, they are apparently not essential for social reward." However, endogenous opioids do have various interactions with oxytocin and vasopressin, including the capacity to regulate peptide release (Keverne and Kendrick, 1991; Russell and Leng,

1998), and thus may have indirect effects on social attachment.

There are a number of findings which have been taken to indicate that endogenous opioids are active during late pregnancy and parturition. Plasma concentrations of β-endorphin increase during labor and birth in humans, and in the rat brain β-endorphin concentrations are elevated in the hypothalamus, midbrain, and amygdala during pregnancy and parturition (Wardlaw and Frantz, 1983). There are three main classes of endogenous opioids: the endorphins, which act predominantly on μ receptors; the enkephalins, which act predominately on delta receptors; and the dynorphins, which act predominately on the kappa receptors (Olson *et al.,* 1990). The terminal areas of distribution for endorphin neurons have much in common with oxytocin neurons, and in certain areas the release of oxytocin is strongly regulated by β-endorphin. However, considerable species differences have been demonstrated with respect to the receptor concentrations in different areas of the brain (Mansour *et al.,* 1988). Proopiomelanocortin, the precursor peptide for β-endorphin, shows an increased synthesis in ewes following estradiol or progesterone replacement therapy, which mimics the effects of pregnancy hormones. In sheep, but not in rats, expression of proopiomelanocortin mRNA during lactation is significantly increased. Also in ewes, levels of preproenkephalin messenger RNA expression are significantly higher during lactation compared to late pregnancy and parturition (Kendrick and Keverne, 1992). Taken together, these findings provide an anatomical basis for opioid-oxytocin interactions during pregnancy and lactation. A functional relationship between these peptides has also been demonstrated in the context of maternal behavior.

Studies with sheep have shown that intracerebral administration of the opioid receptor blocker, naltrexone, reduced the ability of vaginocervical stimulation to stimulate maternal bonding, and ewes continue to be aggressive to the lamb, with head butts and withdrawals, as though they had not received this somatosensory stimulation. The behaviors that result in acceptance of the lamb all decreased when vaginocervical stimulation was preceded by naltrexone treatment, and ewes failed to bond with the lamb. Moreover, central naltrexone administration blocked the release of oxytocin that normally occurs following vaginocervical

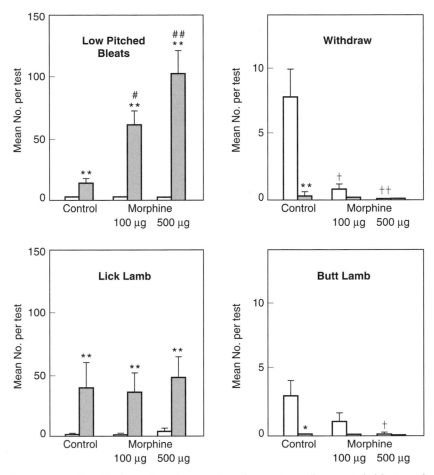

FIGURE 2 Opioids potentiate sheep maternal acceptance (lower pitch bleats and licking of lamb) in the context of VCS. Rejection behavior is reduced by central administration of opioids, and is eliminated in the context of VCS. Opioid administration also induces central but not peripheral release of oxytocin. (Modified after Keverne and Kendrick, 1991.)

stimulation. Hence, although opioid receptor block-ade had little effect on CSF oxytocin during baseline conditions, in the context of parturition (vaginocervical stimulation) similar receptor blockade caused a failure of oxytocin levels to increase in CSF but not in plasma. The failure in maternal responsiveness and bonding could therefore have been due to a failure of oxytocin release and thereby be secondary to the effects of opioid receptor blockade itself. The converse study, namely opiate agonist administration, failed to promote maternal acceptance or bonding when given outside the context of vaginocervical stimulation but did reduce the level of overt aggression (head butts to lambs) (Keverne and Kendrick, 1991). Together with

vaginocervical stimulation, the opioid agonist not only eliminated rejection behavior, but also greatly potentiated the amount of licking and low-pitch bleats the ewe made while with the lamb. Vaginocervical stimulation given to morphine-treated ewes produced an intense and focused display of maternal behavior that was qualitatively and quantitatively indistinguishable from that of the postparturient ewe (Fig. 2). Evidence of firm bonding was seen when the lamb was removed and the ewe protested vocally with high-pitched bleats. This potentiation in bonding is in line with a number of studies that have suggested a role for opioids in social attachment and affiliative behavior (Panksepp *et al.*, 1985, 1994, 1997).

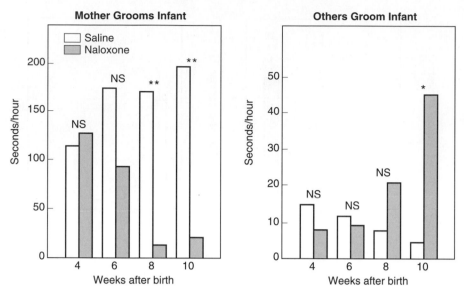

FIGURE 3 Effects of opioid blockade on affiliative behavior of monkey mother. Administration of opioid receptor blocker (naloxone) reduced mother's grooming of infant rhesus monkeys while permitting others in the group to handle and groom her infant more. (Modified after Keverne *et al.,* 1997.)

It has been suggested that the activation of the endogenous opioid system during late pregnancy and suckling promotes the positive affect arising from maternal behavior and the mechanisms subserving this bonding might provide the neural basis from which other socially rewarding systems have evolved (Martel *et al.,* 1993). Studies on naloxone treatment of rhesus monkey mothers living in social groups have addressed the importance of opioids in primate affiliative behavior. Naloxone treatment reduced the mothers' social grooming with other group members, but more significantly, they were less care-giving and protective toward their infants. In the first weeks of life when infant retrieval is normally very high, naloxone-treated mothers neglected their infants and showed little retrieval when the infant moved away. As the infants approached eight weeks of age, when a strong grooming relationship normally develops between mother and infant, mothers treated with naloxone failed to develop such a grooming relationship. Moreover, they permitted other females to groom their infants, but saline-treated controls were very possessive and protective of their infants (Martel *et al.,* 1993) (Fig. 3).

In the postpartum period, a mother's social interactions are predominantly with her infant and, as outlined above, opiate receptor blockade has marked effects on this relationship. The infant is not rejected from suckling, but mother's possessive preoccupation with the infant declines. She is not the normal attentive caregiver, and mother-infant interactions are invariably infant-initiated. It is clear, therefore, that primates are similar to other mammals with respect to opioid involvement in maternal care, although the consequences of opioid blockade in nonprimate mammals are much greater for the biological aspects of maternal behavior. In rodents and sheep, interference with the endogenous opioid system severely impairs maternal behavior, including suckling, whereas monkeys neglect their care-giving but still permit suckling. These differences may reflect the degree of emancipation from endocrine influences that maternal behavior has undergone in primates, together with the accompanying separation of cognitive from affective behavioral control mechanisms.

D. Opioids and Infant Attachment

The early development of monkey social behavior occurs exclusively in the context of interactions with the mother. These early social interactions are almost totally under the mother's control in terms of both the amount and the kinds of interaction permitted. By 40 weeks of age, infants are considerably more independent from their mother, and much of their behavior is oriented toward peers. Nevertheless, mothers continue to monitor their infants and quickly intervene in response to risks arising during play (Simpson *et al.,* 1989). The mother serves as a secure base from which the infant can obtain contact and grooming while developing and strengthening its social bonds with peers or other kin.

Administration of opioids has been shown to reduce the distress shown by diverse species of infants when separated from their mothers. For example, the opiate agonist morphine reduces distress vocalization rates in chicks (Panksepp *et al.,* 1978), guinea pigs (Herman and Panksepp, 1978), puppies, and rhesus monkeys (Kalin *et al.,* 1988). Processes involving opioid reward may therefore play a role in infant attachment and the development of social behavior as well as in maternal bonding. This has been investigated in a study of young rhesus monkeys given acute treatment with the opioid receptor blocker, naloxone, and observed in their natal group (Martel *et al.,* 1995). Naloxone increases the duration of affiliative infant-mother contact and the amount of time the infant spends on the nipple. This occurs even at one year of age when the mothers are no longer lactating. Indeed, feeding is unaffected by naloxone treatment of infants, but play activity decreases and distress vocalizations increases. Moreover, the opioid system in both infant and mother coordinates intimate contact during reunion (Kalin *et al.,* 1995). These results may be interpreted in terms of opiate receptor blockade reducing the positive affect arising from new and developing social relationships with peers, as a result of which the young infant returns to mother as a secure base.

In the first two years of life, no difference is found between male and female infants with respect to the effects of naloxone on increasing their contact with mother. However, at puberty, the picture changes. Males spend equal portions of their time in the group with mother, with others, and alone. Treatment with naloxone results in significant increases in time with mother and decreases in time spent with others and alone (Fig. 4). Females, on the other hand, spend more than half their time alone, usually foraging and eating, and the remaining time is shared equally with mother and with

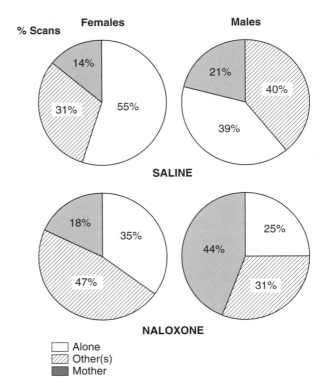

FIGURE 4 Opioid receptor blockade and time infants spend with mother or other monkeys in the social group. Differential effect on social interactions of postpubertal male and female rhesus monkeys when administered the opioid receptor blocker, naloxone. Males return to mother for affiliation and reduce their time alone or with other males. Females also decrease their time alone but seek affiliation from other females in the group rather than mother. (Modified after Keverne *et al.,* 1997.)

others. Treatment with naloxone significantly increases the time spent with others, but not with mother, and decreases the time alone. This suggests that at puberty females have developed other socially meaningful relationships to which they respond when challenged with naloxone, whereas males still depend on mother. Of course, pubertal males running to mother could invite aggression from the dominant males in the group, and the lack of strong social affiliation with others in the group would be a significant driving force to peripheralize such males, and result in the well recognized mobility of males from the natal social group.

E. Opioids and Adult Social Behavior

The effect of opioid antagonism on the developing socialization of monkeys and its differential effects in males and females are maintained in the adult. How the endogenous opioid system is deployed differs in males and females according to differences in intrasexual behavioral strategies. Behavioral interactions in social groups of monkeys cluster into four main categories: investigation, aggression, affiliation, and sexual interaction. Investigation is high among and between males and females and invariably leads to another behavioral category. Among these, grooming is an important affiliative behavior that is influenced by naloxone. Grooming itself produces acute increases in CSF β-endorphin (Keverne *et al.*, 1989), and the receipt of aggression leads to chronic increases in CSF β-endorphin (Martenez *et al.*, 1986). As sexual behavior also has a substantial affiliative grooming component, it too is likely to be accompanied by increases in β-endorphin. Certainly, naloxone treatment in both rhesus and talapoin monkeys blocks sexual activity more effectively and rapidly than castration (Meller *et al.*, 1980; Fabre-Nys *et al.*, 1982).

How social behaviors are deployed is very different between males and females, and within sex it is further different according to rank (Keverne, 1992). Intrasexual aggression is low among females and high among males, while the reverse is true for affiliative behavior, being high among females. No difference exists in chronic levels of β-endorphin in females, but among males, those of lowest rank have significantly higher levels of CSF β-endorphin than do others in the group (Fig. 5). Moreover, the opioid receptor seems to be downregulated in low-ranking males, because challenges with naloxone fail to produce increases in levels of luteinizing hormone or testosterone, which are normally held low by opioid inhibition (Martenez *et al.*, 1986) (Fig. 5). Hence, low-ranking males that receive a little affiliation and high levels of aggression paradoxically have a nonfunctional opioid system because of sustained activity in the system downregulating the receptor. If the endogenous opioids serve as the "glue" for social cohesion, then the attraction of life in the social group for subordinate males is lost, and this may further explain why it is mainly males of low rank that are more likely to leave their natal group in the wild.

These experimental studies with naloxone in primates reveal an important role for the opioid system in a wide variety of social interactions, including mother-infant, infant-peer, and the affiliative, sexual, and ag-

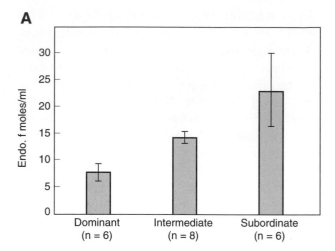

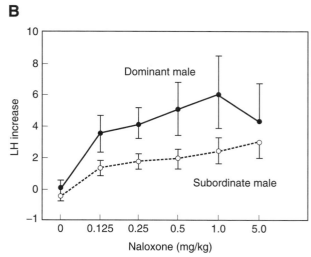

FIGURE 5 (A) Rank-related CSF endorphin in monkeys. CSF β endorphin is related to social rank in male Talapoin monkeys, with subordinate males having chronically high levels compared to dominants. (B) Dose response of LH to naloxone challenged in monkeys. Opioid receptor blockade might be anticipated to produce significant increases in LH, which is suppressed by opioids. Paradoxically these increases are seen in the dominant male but not in the subordinate, thus suggesting a downregulation of the receptors. (Modified after Martenez *et al.*, 1986.)

gressive interactions of adults. Release of central opioids is itself achieved by somotosensory stimulation, but the type of sensory stimulus and the context in which it occurs are very different, ranging from parturition, suckling, and grooming to aggression. Moreover, the way that these life events and behaviors occur also varies according to rank and is very different in males and females. The outcome of these behavioral strategies for social cohesion is therefore very different in males and females. Females engage in the sort of behavior that is likely to acutely activate the opioid system and activate it at intervals contingent on affiliative social interactions. Males are more likely to activate the opioid system in the context of aggressive behavior, which in the case of subordinates is unpredictable and forever a threatening presence. Such chronic activation of the opioid system in males effectively deprives them of any social reward. Subordinate males are therefore more likely to leave their natal group, or if they stay, it is essential that they learn the social rules in order to reduce the aggression they receive from others. These rules for a low-ranking male entail a very low priority in the pecking order for females, food, and the receipt of affiliative behavior.

Studies such as these illustrate the continuing significance of the brain's opioid system for the affective component of relationships, not only throughout early social development, but also into the adult life of primate mammals. In evolutionary terms the mechanisms that underlie "affect" in these contexts have much in common with the mother-infant affect in other mammals. This is not to imply that the endorphins are the only "affectional" peptide, because opioids have themselves been shown to influence the release of other peptide transmitters in the limbic brain (oxytocin, vasopressin), as well as the classical neurotransmitters (noradrenaline, acetylcholine). Oxytocin and vasopressin, in particular, are closely tied to pair bonding in other mammals (Carter *et al.,* 1992; Winslow *et al.,* 1993).

V. ADULT PAIR BONDS

A. Mating Systems and Pair Bonds

One common method for categorizing species is based on mating systems, characterized by the presumed choice or number of sexual partners, and often focused on male behavior. The most common mating system in mammals is called *polygamy* (many mates) or *polygyny* (many wives). The less common alternative, *monogamy* (one mate), is estimated to occur in about 3% of mammalian species (Kleiman, 1977), whereas polyandry (many husbands) is even rarer.

In mammals female reproduction is constrained by gestation, birth, and lactation. In contrast, males have the option to invest less than females in their offspring: the minimal investment is a contribution of sperm and genetic material. It has been conventional to describe mating systems in terms of male fitness or reproductive success. However, defining mating systems in terms of male behavior tends to ignore female fitness, female-female interactions, and the importance of the larger family unit. In addition, within the last two decades DNA fingerprinting has revealed that at least some of the offspring raised by seemingly monogamous partners of most species are in fact due to extra-pair copulations or EPCs. The high incidence of EPCs and extra-pair paternity create a problem for theories that focus on monogamy purely as a mating system, and have encouraged scientists to shift their attention to social systems.

B. Social Systems

A vast array of social systems have been described, many of which are based directly on mating systems (such as polygamy or monogamy), while others may be defined by the living arrangements or genetic relationship among the members of a group. In comparison to mating systems, definitions of social systems are more likely to take into account the role of females and offspring. For example, as described above, many mammalian social systems can be described as matrilinear, and a variety of mammalian species live in groups in which young animals may remain in the natal family. The tendency to form extended families, often but not always based around a monogamous pair, has been termed *communal* or *cooperative breeding* (Solomon and French, 1997).

C. Sexual versus Social Monogamy

Most of what has been written regarding monogamy focuses on sexual monogamy. The recent awareness that, at the species level, sexual exclusivity is rare has created a challenge for the concept of sexual monogamy (Carter *et al.,* 1995). Nonetheless, selective social behaviors and pair bonds between adults do provide a social matrix for reproductive behaviors, including sexual behavior and care of offspring, that support the welfare of individuals, groups, and species.

The traits of mammalian social monogamy typically occur together, forming what has been called a "syndrome" (Kleiman, 1977). The cardinal characteristic of social monogamy is a male-female pair bond, characterized by selective partner preferences and social interactions. Selective aggression is another feature of social monogamy. Monogamous mammals are highly social within their families, although they can show lethal aggression toward strangers (Carter *et al.,* 1995; Bowler *et al.,* 2001). Aggression is most common toward members of the same sex and usually occurs during or after pair bond formation. The capacity of socially monogamous partners to defend their mates, family, or territory may influence reproductive fitness and their own survival. Incest avoidance, a tendency for reproductive suppression of the young, who remain as alloparents in communal families, and a relative absence of physical sexual dimorphism also characterize monogamous mammals.

D. Social Monogamy in Prairie Voles

Prairie voles (*Microtus ochrogaster*) exhibit all the features of social monogamy, including the formation of pair bonds between adult conspecifics. Prairie voles, which are small rodents found in grasslands throughout midwestern North America, have attracted particular interest because they can be studied under both field and laboratory conditions. Field studies begun in the 1960s provided the first evidence that prairie voles form long-lasting pair bonds (McGuire *et al.,* 1993; Getz *et al.,* 1981, 1993). Male and female pairs of this species maintain a common nest and territory and tend to enter live traps together as long as both members of the pair are alive. By contrast, less social, polygamous meadow voles (*Microtus pennysylvanicus*) and montane voles (*Microtus montanus*) show few indications of pair bonding; males and females of these species have separate nests and territories and are usually trapped alone. In the laboratory nonmonogamous species are less likely to engage in social contact and less likely to exhibit selective partner preferences (Dewsbury, 1987; Carter *et al.,* 1995).

Prairie voles live in nature in communal family groups comprising primarily a male and female breeding pair and their offspring. About 70–75% of young voles do not leave their natal family (McGuire *et al.,* 1993; Getz *et al.,* 1993). The original breeding pair within a family has a reproductive advantage, and most other members of the communal groups are reproductively inactive offspring. These offspring serve as helpers at the nest or alloparents, presumably gaining reproductive advantages through inclusive fitness. Familiarity inhibits reproduction in young prairie voles, and incest is avoided through several mechanisms, including reluctance to mate with a family member. Young males remain sexually suppressed within the family nest and must leave the family group to reproduce (Carter *et al.,* 1995). New pairs are most likely to form when previously naive males and females leave their group, meet an unfamiliar member of the opposite sex, develop new pair bonds, mate, and generate their own families.

Pair bond formation in prairie voles commences within hours of meeting. In addition, when young males and females meet strangers of the opposite sex, a cascade of events is initiated that leads to reproductive activation in both sexes and eventual estrus induction in the female (Carter *et al.,* 1995; Dluzen *et al.,* 1981). Female prairie voles do not cycle and spontaneous estrus is rare. Mating usually follows within a day or two. In newly formed pairs, intermittent mating bouts continue for about 24 to 48 hours followed by a 21-day gestation (Carter *et al.,* 1995). After an initial mating and pregnancy, prairie vole females experience a postpartum estrus, allowing females to breed again and nurse one litter while they are pregnant with a second litter (Witt *et al.,* 1989).

Attempts to use sexual preferences as an index of pair bonding have not been successful. However, significant social preferences for physical contact with a new partner can be measured within hours following an initial pairing (Carter *et al.,* 1995; DeVries *et al.,* 1997). The onset of social preferences is facilitated by mating, but can occur in the absence of mating and even in gonadectomized animals, albeit less readily (Williams *et al.,* 1992a).

Females in postpartum estrus that have remained with a male for one or more litters may exhibit a sexual preference for the familiar male. However, even in postpartum estrus, if given an opportunity, a significant proportion of females will mate with an unfamiliar male (Getz *et al.,* 1981). Once females are in oestrus, sexual postures allowing mating are reflexive and may be less selective than social contact (Carter *et al.,* 1995).

Pair-bonded males become highly aggressive following mating and probably patrol the runways that lead to their nest. If successful in defending his partner, the male may father the offspring that his partner delivers. In nature, when one member of the pair dies or abandons the nest, fewer than 20% of the remaining partners form a new pair bond (Getz *et al.,* 1993); thus, for most prairie voles pair bonds last until the pair is separated by death.

E. Experimental Analysis of Partner Preferences

Prairie voles adapt easily to the laboratory and therefore it has been possible to investigate various aspects of the behavioral and neuroendocrine control of pair bonding. Voles may be placed in a large three-chambered apparatus that allows the experimental animal to spend time with either a stimulus animal designated by familiarity as the "partner," or with a comparable "stranger", or elect to be alone in a neutral cage (Williams *et al.,* 1992a). Female stimulus animals are tethered loosely, allowing them to move only within their own chamber, whereas the experimental male is free to explore the entire test apparatus. This testing paradigm yields reliable social preferences that can be studied as a function of physiological and experimental manipulations. In female prairie voles social preferences for the familiar partner are established more quickly if mating occurs prior to testing. Nonsexual cohabitation also is eventually followed by a significant partner preference (DeVries and Carter, 1999). As mentioned above, however, social preference may bias reproduction to favor the familiar or resident male; laboratory studies do not indicate that newly paired females form a strong sexual preference for familiar or unfamiliar males (Carter *et al.,* 1995). In fact, during the early stages of pair bonding, females are equally likely to mate with familiar and unfamiliar males. For this reason social contact is more selective and probably more useful as an index of pair bonding than is sexual preference.

F. Selective Aggression as a Component of Pair Bonding

Sexually naive prairie voles of either sex are rarely aggressive toward conspecifics. By contrast, after ap-

proximately 12 to 24 hours of sexual experience, male prairie voles become extremely aggressive toward unfamiliar males (Winslow *et al.,* 1993). Sexually experienced "breeder" males are socially dominant and drive away or, if necessary, kill male strangers. However, they are usually not aggressive to familiar animals, and breeder males will allow their own offspring to remain in the family, at least as long as these offspring are sexually naive. Cohabitation with a nonreproductive female, even for several days, usually does not produce a reliable increase in male aggression; however, nonsexual cohabitation does cause hormonal changes that are associated with reproductive activation.

Females also become aggressive after mating, but postcopulatory aggression develops more slowly in females than in males, and in females the onset and intensity of aggression is variable (Bowler *et al.,* 2001). If two unrelated females are placed with a male, both may mate with the male (Gavish *et al.,* 1981; Witt *et al.,* 1989). Under these conditions one female becomes socially dominant, and the nondominant female is blocked from social contact with the male (Firestone *et al.,* 1991). During the postmating period and before either female can deliver young, the nondominant female often dies, apparently as the consequence of both direct aggression and the "stress" of remaining in the presence of a dominant female. When corticosterone levels were assessed after three days of living in such trio, the corticosterone levels in both the dominant and subordinate female had declined to approximately half the normal levels; females housed in male-female pairs or trios consisting of two sisters and a male did not show a significant decline (K. B. Firestone and C. S. Carter, unpublished data). Thus, levels of stress hormones, at least at this time, did not predict eventual survival or reproductive success.

In both sexes postpartum aggression is common and may be directed toward both unfamiliar females and unfamiliar males (Getz *et al.,* 1981). However, female prairie voles do not express aggression toward their own offspring. Female-female aggression, sometimes leading to death of one female, is also a feature of the behavior of paired tamarins and other monogamous mammals (Kleiman, 1977).

Partner preferences and selective aggression characterize established pair bonding in prairie voles, whereas sexual and social experiences regulate the onset of the pair bond (Carter *et al.,* 1995). However, partner preferences can develop even in the absence of gonadal hormones. The initial development of a partner preference usually occurs prior to mating during a time when gonadal hormones are comparatively low. Subsequent sexual experience may consolidate the pair bonding process (Williams *et al.,* 1992a). Hormonal events associated with social interactions therefore are likely contributors to pair bond formation. Prior to these studies it was known that neuropeptides, including oxytocin and vasopressin, are released by both sexual (Carter, 1992; Argiolas, 1999) and nonsexual contact (Uvnas-Moberg, 1998). In addition, as described above, oxytocin is implicated in both nonselective maternal behavior and maternal bonding.

Most research on pair bonding has examined factors capable of modulating the formation of a partner preference or selective aggression. Relatively little is known regarding the mechanisms that are involved in the maintenance of these behaviors, although there is reason to believe that the factors responsible for the induction of pair bonding can differ from those involved in its maintenance, since compounds that block vasopressin prevent the development but not the expression of selective aggression (Winslow *et al.,* 1993).

G. Affiliative Behaviors and Positive Sociality

Most socially monogamous mammals show high levels of social contact within the family. Sociality can be either selective, and thus in some cases indicative of social bonds, or nonselective. Oxytocin and vasopressin can increase the tendency to show both selective and nonselective social behaviors. For example, icv treatment with either oxytocin (OT) or vasopressin (AVP) approximately doubles nonselective social contact in male or female prairie voles (Cho *et al.,* 1999). Pretreatment with a selective antagonist for either peptide (OT plus an OTA, or AVP plus an AVPA) reduces social contact. High levels of social behavior are still seen if either of these peptides are combined with an antagonist for the heterologous receptor (OT plus AVPA or AVP plus OTA). However, when animals are treated with either OTA or AVPA they no longer show a selective partner preference. These results indicate that either oxytocin or vasopressin, at least when applied at high doses (100 ng/icv), can stimulate social contact in prairie voles of

either sex; however, it is possible that both types of receptors must be accessible to allow these peptides to facilitate the formation of a selective social preference.

Species specificity in the location of peptide receptors may play a role in species differences in social behavior. For example, in nonmonogamous montane and meadow voles the density of vasopressin receptors is much higher in the lateral septum, lateral habenula, and central gray than in monogamous prairie voles and pine voles (Insel and Shaprio, 1992).

Based on the behavioral effects of vasopressin and species differences in the vasopressin receptor, Young and his associates (1999) created transgenic mice carrying the gene for the vasopressin receptor. These transgenic animals expressed the vasopressin receptor (AVPR) in a pattern that was different from the wild-type mouse and similar in some brain regions to prairie voles. For example, AVPR binding was elevated in transgenic mice in the cingulate cortex, claustrum, laterodorsal and ventroposterior thalamic nuclei, and especially the olfactory bulbs. Oxytocin receptor distribution was not altered in the V1a AVPR transgenic mice. When the AVPR transgenic male animals were treated with exogenous vasopressin, they also showed high levels of social contact with female stimulus animals. However, this social contact was not selective (L. J. Young, personal communication) and thus could not be interpreted as pair bonding. The capacity of the transgenic mice to respond to oxytocin, possibly through effects on the AVPR, has not been explored.

Additional information regarding the neural basis of social behavior comes from studies of knockout mice created with selective genetic lesions. Deletions of the exon that encodes the oxytocin peptide in mice produces an animal (OTKO) capable of all aspects of reproduction except milk ejection (Nishimori *et al.,* 1996). However, the social behavior of OTKO mice also is not normal. OTKO mice tend to be more aggressive than normal mice (Winslow *et al.,* 2000). OTKO mice also have deficiencies in "social memory," which are restored by injections of oxytocin (Ferguson *et al.,* 2000).

H. Selective Social Behavior, a Role for Oxytocin and Vasopressin

Taken together these data suggest that neural systems responsible for the expression of sociality can be stimulated by either vasopressin or oxytocin. However, the formation of social bonds may require peptides or the activation of additional neural systems, or both, beyond those required to facilitate nonselective social behaviors (Cho *et al.*, 1999).

In prairie voles sexual experience can hasten the onset of pair bonding (Williams *et al.*, 1992a) and in males induces aggression toward strangers (Winslow *et al.*, 1993). It is also known that oxytocin and vasopressin can be released during mating (Carter, 1992; Argiolas, 1999). These observations suggested the hypothesis that oxytocin or vasopressin or both could promote social bonding. Oxytocin infusions, when centrally administered, do indeed facilitate the onset of partner preferences in sexually naive female and male prairie voles (Williams *et al.*, 1994; Cho *et al.*, 1999). In addition , when administered in pulses, peripheral oxytocin treatments can also facilitate the formation of a partner preference in female prairie voles (Cushing and Carter, 1999, 2000). However, the effects of such treatments vary by gender and according to the habitat from which voles are derived (Cushing *et al.*, 2001). In this species, oxytocin antagonists reduce the behavioral effects of exogenous oxytocin and also block partner preference formation during prolonged cohabitation. In addition, in male prairie voles, vasopressin is necessary to the onset of stranger-directed aggression (Winslow *et al.*, 1993).

Experimental evidence for a role of vasopressin in males comes from the finding that pretreatment with a V1a vasopressin antagonist inhibited pair bonding that normally results from sexual experience (Winslow *et al.*, 1993). In addition, exogenous vasopressin administration facilitates aggression induction in this species. When tested under comparable conditions, infusions of vasopressin were not effective in facilitating female aggression (C. M. Bowler and C. S. Carter, unpublished data).

VI. STRESS AND PAIR BOND FORMATION

Evidence for a role for hormones of the HPA axis in pair bond formation comes from studies that reveal the repeated association between stressful experiences and social bonding (Carter, 1998; Sachser *et al.*, 1998). More direct evidence can be found in laboratory studies of the effects of stressful stimuli or administration of hormones of the HPA axis on the formation of partner preferences.

Evidence for the formation of an attachment comes from behavioral changes associated with mammalian birth, lactation, and sexual interactions. In addition, novel or stressful experiences may encourage increased social behaviors and attachment. Comparatively high levels of HPA axis activity or indications of sympathetic arousal and the subsequent release of oxytocin have been measured under conditions that commonly precede or are associated with the formation of social bonds.

Mammalian birth is a uniquely stressful experience. In the mother the physiological events preceding and during parturition involve exceptionally high levels of adrenal activity and catecholamines and the subsequent release of peptides, including endogenous opioids, oxytocin, and vasopressin (Keverne and Kendrick, 1992; Kendrick, 2000; Landgraf *et al.*, 1991). Infants also experience parturitional stress or "birth trauma" and probably experience increased exposure to maternal oxytocin during labor. Hormonal experiences associated with birth may affect the tendency of young animals to form social bonds, although such effects remain to be demonstrated.

In species that form heterosexual pair bonds, including prairie voles, sexual interactions are associated with the formation of social attachments (Carter *et al.*, 1995). Sexual behavior also can be physiologically stressful for both sexes. Adrenal steroids, vasopressin, oxytocin, and endogenous opioids are released during sexual behavior (Carter, 1992; Argiolas, 1999).

Stress or corticosterone facilitates pair bond formation in male prairie voles (DeVries *et al.*, 1996). Although female prairie voles did not form pair bonds with familiar males following stressful treatments, stress did encourage the development of preferences for other females, consistent with the communal breeding pattern of this species (A. C. DeVries, A. George and C. S. Carter, unpublished data). Steroid hormones, including glucocorticoids, can influence the synthesis and release of neuropeptides and affect their receptors. In addition, steroid and peptide hormones may regulate or interact with each other to influence behavior.

Hormones can reduce fear or behavioral inhibition and permit the expression of social behaviors, such as those necessary for pair bonding, maternal behavior (Fleming *et al.*, 1989; McCarthy *et al.*, 1992; Numan, 1994a,b), or sexual behavior (Carter, 1992; Argiolas, 1999). The neurochemical processes that are capable of overcoming neophobia also may be needed to permit the formation of new social attachments. Prosocial behavior or social contact is facilitated and aggression is diminished following central oxytocin treatments in estrogen-treated female prairie voles (Witt *et al.*, 1990). Increases in social contact also follow oxytocin treatment in both male and female rats (Witt *et al.*, 1992). In addition, in sexually naive male rats a brief (15 minute) heterosexual interaction is followed by an approximate doubling of serum oxytocin levels; this change was not seen in sexually experienced males for which this situation may have been less novel (Hillegaart *et al.*, 1999). Oxytocin treatments may reduce anxiety as measured by exploration of a novel environment in rats (McCarthy *et al.*, 1992; Uvnas-Moberg, 1997). In humans (Chiodera *et al.*, 1991) and prairie voles (DeVries *et al.*, 1997), oxytocin inhibited the secretion of glucocorticoids. Social contact also can inhibit HPA axis activity in prairie voles (DeVries *et al.*, 1995, 1996). In reproductively naive prairie voles, either oxytocin (icv) or social contact produced a 50% decline in corticosterone, which occurred within 30 to 60 minutes. In male prairie voles, either mating (Insel *et al.*, 1995) or vasopressin treatment (Dharmadhikari *et al.*, 1997) is associated with increased exploration in the open arm of a plus maze, a measure often considered indicative of reduced anxiety.

The unanticipated finding that socially naive prairie voles respond to exposure to a novel stranger of the opposite sex with a decline in corticosterone suggested that pair bonding in prairie voles might be inhibited by hormones of the HPA axis (DeVries *et al.*, 1995). This was shown to be the case when removal of the adrenal glands in naive female prairie voles facilitated the development of a partner preference. Adrenalectomized females formed a significant preference for the familiar male within one hour or less of cohabitation compared with the usual requirement of in excess of three hours. The facilitatory effect of adrenalectomy was reversed by corticosterone replacement prior to female exposure. In addition, increases in corticosterone levels by exogenous injection or pellets of corticosterone in females produced a dose-dependent inhibition of the preference formation.

In contrast, in socially naive male prairie voles the behavioral effects of corticosterone, when examined in experiments that paralleled those in females, produced

strikingly different results (DeVries *et al.*, 1996). Injections of corticosterone, or the stress of swimming, facilitated the development of partner preferences in males. By contrast, removal of the adrenal gland was followed by failure to form a partner preference, which was subsequently restored by corticosterone replacement.

Sex differences in the behavioral effects of oxytocin and vasopressin are consistent with a larger literature implicating oxytocin in various aspects of positive sociality and female reproduction and vasopressin in territoriality and defensive behaviors. As described above, vasopressin is more abundant in males, and vasopressin production, especially within the mAMY and BNST, is increased by androgens. Sex differences also exist in pair bonding (DeVries *et al.*, 1996), and it has been suggested that pair bonding in female prairie voles depends primarily on oxytocin, whereas males rely on vasopressin (Winslow *et al.*, 1993; Insel and Hulihan, 1995).

However, there are no dramatic sex differences in oxytocin or vasopressin receptors in prairie voles (Insel, 1997). As mentioned above, steroid-dependent increases in hypothalamic oxytocin receptors have been reported in rats. In female prairie voles estrogen-dependent changes in hypothalamic oxytocin receptors were not seen; only the anterior olfactory nucleus showed an obvious estrogen dependency (Witt *et al.*, 1991). Furthermore, when given as an exogenous treatment, either oxytocin or vasopressin can facilitate pair bonding in both male and female prairie voles, and receptors for both peptides may need to be available to allow pair bond formation (Cho *et al.*, 1999).

The finding, described elsewhere, that the effects of stressful experiences on prairie vole pair bonding are sexually dimorphic (DeVries *et al.*, 1996) is most easily interpreted in the context of natural history. Male prairie voles must leave the family to breed and must be capable of forming new pair bonds and mating under stressful conditions. In contrast females of this species may respond to stressful conditions by remaining within the natal family (Getz *et al.*, 1993). Thus, sexually different behavioral strategies and the hormonal response to stress from the HPA axis may both reflect and support a sex difference in reproductive strategies.

Corticotropin-releasing hormone (CRH) regulates the release of ACTH, and also is known to have a number of behavioral effects, including increased arousal.

In addition, in rats glucocorticoids are capable of enhancing the behavioral effects of CRH (Schulkin, 1999). CRH, administered icv and in moderate doses, is capable of facilitating pair bond formation in male prairie voles (DeVries *et al.,* 2001). These findings are consistent with the observation in sheep that CRH can facilitate the maternal acceptance of a lamb (Keverne and Kendrick, 1991). In addition, there is evidence in rats that CRH is colocalized with oxytocin (Levin and Sawchenko, 1993), thus suggesting that functional interactions between these peptides are likely.

VII. OLFACTORY RECOGNITION IN PAIR BONDING, MATING, AND MOTHER-INFANT BONDING

Studies on several mammalian species have indicated an important role for experience in establishing effective bonding and affiliative responses. In rodents this experience relies heavily on olfactory cues. For example, mice depend mainly on olfaction to regulate the events that constitute normal maternal responsiveness. Anosmia in primiparous mice, induced either by bulbectomy or by intranasal application of zinc sulphate, leads to a severe impairment of pup-care behavior; anosmic females either cannibalize or desert their pups. In rats, maternal experience abolishes the effects of bulbectomy on cannibalism regardless of whether the experience is obtained in the postpartum period or as a consequence of sensitization by repeated pup exposure prior to birth. It would therefore appear that odor cues from infant rodents are critical to the recognition process and thereby facilitate the onset of maternal affiliation, as opposed to treating the pup as alien or as potential food.

In both mice and rats, social recognition, dependent on olfactory cues, occurs such that familiarity results in less investigation occurring on a subsequent exposure in comparison with investigation of a novel conspecific. The ability of rodents to recognize familiar from strange conspecifics assists the individual in regulating social interactions. Androgen-dependent vasopressinergic neurons have been implicated in this social recognition memory, which in rats and mice lasts for approximately one hour (Bluthé *et al.,* 1990). However, intracerebral administration of AVP prolongs the

social memory, whereas administration of the V1 receptor antagonist blocks the social recognition (Bluthé and Dantzer, 1992). Recent studies have demonstrated that direct infusions of AVP or oxytocin into the olfactory bulbs resulted in prolonged recognition responses (Dluzen *et al.,* 1998a). However, similar infusions of AVP or OT in animals that had been depleted of noradrenaline by 6-hydrodopamine (6-OHDA) infusions to the olfactory bulb were not able to preserve the recognition responses (Dluzen *et al.,* 1998b). These results suggest that there is an interaction of oxytocin and vasopressin neuropeptides with the bulbar noradrenergic system to preserve social recognition.

In sheep, olfactory cues are also important for the onset of maternal recognition and hence bonding with lambs. The smell of amniotic fluids becomes very attractive at the time of birth, and its presence on the newborn's wool is essential for the development of normal maternal behavior (Lévy *et al.,* 1983). Within two hours of parturition the ewe forms an exclusive recognition bond with her infant based on olfactory cues. Once this bond is established, any attempt by alien lambs to suckle is violently resisted. This olfactory selectivity fulfils two requirements. It prevents alien lambs from exploiting the finite lactational resources of the ewe, and enhances bonding in a species that is nomadic and social and rarely remains on a given pasture for anything other than transitory periods.

A marked difference in the importance of amniotic fluids is found between maternally experienced and inexperienced ewes. Washing the lamb delays the onset of maternal responding in multiparous ewes, whereas primiparous ewes display high levels of rejection behavior toward their washed newborn lamb and fail to bond with or accept their lambs at the udder (Lévy and Poindron, 1987). These differences in the capacity for maternal recognition by multiparous versus primiparous ewes are reflected in the neurochemical changes that occur in the brain at birth. Glutamate, γ-aminobutyric acid (GABA), noradrenaline, dopamine, acetylcholine, and oxytocin all show differences in release in the olfactory bulbs at parturition, all being higher in multiparous ewes, with the exception of dopamine, which is higher in primiparous ewes (Lévy *et al.,* 1993, 1995). However, within six hours of birth the response profiles of primiparous ewes have changed to that of multiparous (Keverne *et al.,* 1993). These neurochemical changes represent changes in synaptic efficacy, which result in a greater sensitivity to lamb odors and clearer definition of odor profiles, thus enabling selectivity for the ewe's own lamb to be established (Kendrick et al., 1992).

Artificial induction of maternal behavior by steroid hormones (Kendrick and Keverne, 1991) or by vaginocervical stimulation is less successful in nulliparous ewes than in those with previous maternal experience (Kendrick et al., 1991). It would appear that experience of pregnancy and parturition provokes some reorganization of the neural substrates controlling maternal behavior such that they become more responsive to the consequences of these events on subsequent occasions. During parturition, signals from the stimulation of the vagina and cervix feed back to the brain to induce the ewe both to become maternally responsive toward lambs and to form a selective bond with them (Keverne et al., 1983). Profound neurochemical changes occur in the olfactory bulb of the sheep as a result of parturition or artificial stimulation of the vagina and cervix (Lévy et al., 1993; Kendrick et al., 1992). How the organization of olfactory processing in the brain is altered electrophysiologically and neurochemically to accommodate the animal's behavioral requirement of recognizing its own lambs has therefore been investigated.

Electrophysiological recordings, made from olfactory bulb neurons, revealed a total of 188 cells that responded differentially to the various chemical and biological odors presented (Kendrick et al., 1992). These cells were located mainly in the mitral cell layer. In recordings made during the last two months of pregnancy, none of these cells responded preferentially to lamb or amniotic fluid odors. In only 11 cells (10%) were these odors capable of eliciting any significant change in firing rate. The majority of cells (72%) responded preferentially to food odors, and some responded to wool or amyl acetate. Following birth, there was a dramatic increase in the proportion of cells in the same area of the olfactory bulb that responded preferentially to lamb odors (60%). The majority of those cells that responded to lamb odors (70%) did not differentiate between the odor of the ewe's own lamb and that of an alien lamb and were remarkably resistant to habituation. However, a proportion of the cells (30%) did respond preferentially to the odor of the ewe's own

lamb, and in all cases the smell of the lamb's wool was almost as effective a stimulus as that of the whole lamb. A small proportion of cells was found that responded preferentially to amniotic fluid odors (12%), but a large reduction was found in the number of cells that responded primarily to food odors. The proportion of cells that responded primarily to amyl acetate and adult wool odors remained unchanged. These results indicate that although the odors of lambs have almost no influence on the activity of olfactory bulb neurons during the period before birth, when lambs have no behavioral attraction, they become the most potent olfactory stimulus in the period after birth, when the recognition of lamb odors has a very high behavioral priority. Moreover, a proportion of these neurons responds preferentially to the odor of the lamb with which the ewe has formed a selective bond.

The olfactory bulb is a relatively simple trilaminar structure, and its network comprises three basic neural types. The mitral cells, which show this increased responsiveness to lamb odors after birth, receive and transmit olfactory signals, and their activity is modulated at their apical dendrites by periglomerular cells and at their lateral dendrites by granule cells. Intrinsic connections within this network contain both excitatory and inhibitory amino acid transmitters and dopamine. Transmission among neurons in the network is further influenced by centrifugal projections from noradrenergic and serotonergic neurons that originate from the brain stem and cholinergic neurons from the nucleus basalis (Fig. 6).

To further understand how the mitral cells increase their responsiveness to lamb odors, in vivo microdialysis has been used to measure the effect of lamb odors on the release of acetylcholine (ACH), excitatory and inhibitory amino acid, and monoamine transmitters in the olfactory bulb before and after bonding (Lévy et al., 1993, 1995). After parturition, when ewes have established a selective bond with their lambs, odors of these lambs, but not those of alien ones, increased the release of both the excitatory amino acid glutamate and the inhibitory one, GABA. Release of another intrinsic transmitter, dopamine, was not influenced by lamb odors. These changes in glutamate and GABA release occurred only during the first five minutes of exposure to the lamb. Moreover, the increase of GABA release after bonding was significantly greater than that of

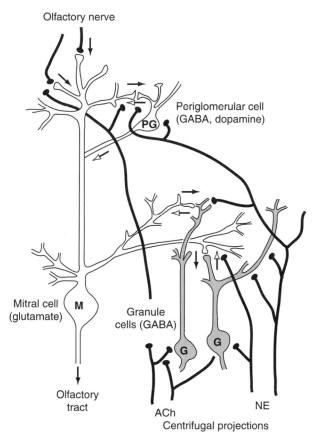

Olfactory nerve

Periglomerular cell
(GABA, dopamine)

PG

Mitral cell
(glutamate)

M

Granule
cells (GABA)

G   G

Olfactory
tract

ACh

NE

Centrifugal projections

FIGURE 6   The synaptic connections and neurotransmitter release in the neurons of the trilaminar olfactory bulb.

glutamate, whereas the basal release of GABA and glutamate in the period after birth was also significantly higher than in the period before birth (Fig. 7).

The GABA-containing granule cells are intrinsic bulbar neurons excited by mitral cells, which thereby provide feedback inhibition to the mitral cells by way of reciprocal dendrodendritic synapses. Hence the proportionately higher release of GABA compared to glutamate can be explained in terms of a changed efficacy of glutamate at the dendrodentritic synapse after birth. Moreover, the overall increase in both glutamate and GABA release in the period after birth is synonymous with more mitral cell activity in response to lamb odors. The significant shift in the ratio of GABA to glutamate release is probably a result of an increased efficacy of glutamate in promoting GABA release from the granule cells. Such enhancement of neurotransmission at the granule to mitral cell synapses after birth, and in re-

sponse to the odor of the animal's own lamb, may not simply produce more inhibition but could also result in a change in the firing frequency of the neurons that are coded for the odor of the bonded lamb. This situation would then produce a bias in the network with respect to these odors to produce the appropriate selective maternal response (Keverne, 1995b).

A. Olfaction and Adult Pair Bond Formation

The formation and expression of social bonds requires individual recognition. Rodents and especially prairie voles are dependent on olfactory cues for such recognition. Pair bond formation, but also high levels of sociality, requires an intact olfactory system (Williams *et al.*, 1992b). After selective lesions of the vomeronasal organ, female prairie voles continue to be highly social but no longer show a partner preference (Curtis *et al.*, 2001). In other species, the olfactory bulb is the target for steroid hormones and peptides (Dluzen *et al.*, 1998a; Engelmann *et al.*, 1996, 1998). In addition, the vomeronasal system, possibly through effects on central vasopressin, plays a role in social recognition in rats (Bluthé and Dantzer, 1993).

The formation of partner preferences in prairie voles requires prolonged cohabitation and can be facilitated by mating (Williams *et al.*, 1994). In that species the olfactory-vomeronasal system and male pheromones also are necessary for estrus induction (Dluzen *et al.*, 1981; Reynolds and Keverne, 1979). Exposure to a novel sexual partner and the resultant sexual behavior promotes the release of neuropeptides, including oxytocin and vasopressin, which may act on receptors in the olfactory system, thereby facilitating mate recognition and consolidation of bonding with the partner following mating. Exposure to estrogen or natural estrus increases oxytocin-receptor binding in the anterior olfactory nucleus in female prairie voles (Witt *et al.*, 1991), thus providing another putative target for the behavioral effects of oxytocin.

By acting at the level of the olfactory system, oxytocin and vasopressin may allow the formation of a long-lasting recognition of the partner, which in turn facilitates selective bonding. Infusion of vasopressin into the olfactory bulbs of male rats is known to facilitate social recognition (Dluzen *et al.*, 1998a; Engelmann *et al.*, 1996, 1998), whereas oxytocin infusion into the

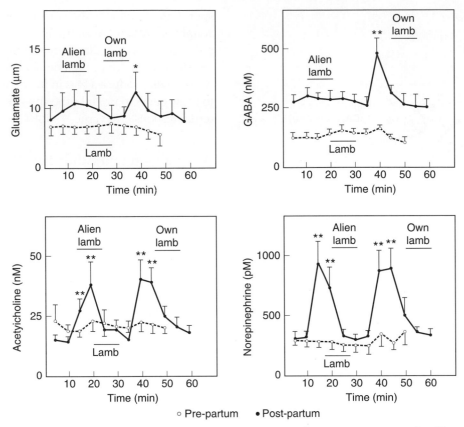

FIGURE 7 Effects of own and alien lamb odors or release of neurotransmitters in the olfactory bulb of mothers. Following parturition, lamb odors induce significant increases in the olfactory bulb compared to prepartum lamb odor exposure. Transmitter release between the mitral (glutamate) and granule (GABA) neurons distinguishes between own and strange lambs. (Modified after Kendrick *et.al.,* 1992b.)

olfactory bulbs of female rats facilitates maternal recognition and pup acceptance in maternal behavior. Oxytocin or vasopressin infusions into the olfactory bulbs may bring about a prolonged release of norepinephrine and acetylcholine, which also are important for enhancing the signal-to-noise ratio in the context of recognition (Kendrick, 2000).

Within a day or so of meeting, especially if the male and female remain in contact, female prairie voles come into behavioral estrus. Subsequent sexual interactions also may activate oxytocin and V1a vasopressin-receptor dependent systems (Carter, 1992; Argiolas, 1999), which can reinforce pair bonding (Williams *et al.,* 1994; Insel and Hulihan, 1995). As described above, in males, sexual experience also promotes aggression toward intruder males (Winslow *et al.,* 1993)

and facilitates subsequent parental behavior (Wang *et al.,* 1993), thus helping to coordinate the expression of the central traits of monogamy.

B. Other Neural Structures and Pair Bonding

There is direct vomeronasal input into the amygdala and bed nucleus of the stria terminalis (BNST). Lesions of the corticomedial and central amygdala (cAMY) interfered with the formation of pair bonds in male prairie voles; however, following these lesions other nonselective social behaviors, including male parental behavior, also were inhibited (Kirkpatrick *et al.,* 1994). These structures also are important targets for oxytocin, vasopressin, and CRH, and peptide binding in these areas is steroid-hormone dependent (Liberzon *et al.,* 1997;

Patchev *et al.*, 1993; Schulkin, 1999), a result that would allow functional modulation by both the HPA and gonadal axes. For example, in prairie voles oxytocin and vasopressin treatments have regionally specific effects on neuronal activation, as indexed by cFOS expression (Gingrich *et al.*, 1997). Treatment with oxytocin increased cFOS expression in the BNST, whereas vasopressin treatment was associated with increased activity in the nucleus accumbens (NAcc). In male, but not female, prairie voles vasopressin injections were associated with increased cFOS in the cAMY (Gingrich *et al.*, 1997). In turn, oxytocin and vasopressin act on the cAMY to regulate autonomic functions (Roozendaal *et al.*, 1993), thereby allowing these peptides to have broad effects on emotional states.

Exposure to a novel partner and subsequent sexual interactions may both enhance arousal and reinforce the formation of new pair bonds, in part through the action of catecholamines. One target for the combined behavioral effects of catecholamines and oxytocin is the NAcc. Experiments in female prairie voles have shown that systemic or central administration of dopaminergic drugs can facilitate the formation of a partner preference (Wang *et al.*, 1999). Compounds that were selective for the dopamine D2-like receptors were most effective, especially when administered directly into the NAcc (Gingrich *et al.*, 2000). In monogamous, but not polygynous, voles the NAcc has an abundance of both oxytocin and dopamine receptors, a finding that possibly accounts for the ability of monogamous species to form selective social bonds.

VIII. RESPONSES TO SEPARATION

One indication of pair bond formation is the degree to which animals show behavioral or autonomic responses to the absence of a familiar or preferred partner. Because responses to separation are species-typical, they are best understood in the context of social organization and ecology.

Separation from an attachment figure may be associated with various behavioral and physiological changes (Reite and Bocca, 1994; Hennessy, 1997; Sachser *et al.*, 1998; Mendoza and Mason, 1997; Mason and Mendoza, 1998). Young animals' vocalizations, in either the audible or ultrasonic range, often increase

following separation. Measurements of these vocalizations have been used as indices of "distress" and may be indicative of attachment (Nelson and Panksepp, 1998). Physiological changes, including increased secretion of glucocorticoids or ACTH, cardiovascular measures, and immune system parameters, also have been described following social separation in primates (Reite and Bocca, 1994). Cortisol responses are sometimes used to assess the intensity of separation "distress" or to examine the hypothesis that the presence of a partner may provide a form of social buffering (Hennessy, 1997; Mendoza and Mason, 1997; Mason and Mendoza, 1998).

Social separation in both male and female prairie voles is followed by an increase in glucocorticoid (corticosterone) levels (J. R. Williams and C. S. Carter, unpublished data). When reunited with a partner, corticosterone levels drop to below baseline in previously paired males and females. However, if previously paired animals and separated animals are placed with an unfamiliar partner of the opposite sex, corticosterone levels remain elevated.

Experiments on separation "distress" have tested the capacity of peptides to prevent behavioral changes during separation. The intense calling behavior of isolated domestic chicks declines following various treatments, including injections of oxytocin-vasotocin, opioids that stimulate μ receptors, and prolactin (Panksepp *et al.*, 1997). Opiate injections also diminish distress vocalizations in guinea pigs (Herman and Panksepp, 1978), but separation cries of infant rats do not show the predicted decline following opiate treatments (Winslow and Insel, 1991). However, in rat pups separation cries are inhibited by central treatments with oxytocin or vasopressin (Insel and Winslow, 1991; Winslow and Insel, 1993). In squirrel monkeys there is evidence that both vasopressin and oxytocin are capable of reducing isolation calling, although the effects are dependent on social status and high doses of the peptides were necessary to obtain behavioral effects (Winslow and Insel, 1991).

Monogamous monkeys, such as titi monkeys (Mendoza and Mason, 1997; Mason and Mendoza, 1998), form social bonds that can be observed in the laboratory. In fact, in this species pairs typically sit in physical contact with their long tails braided together. In titi monkeys increases in cortisol in response to disturbances are attenuated by the presence of a familiar companion. Titi monkeys also respond to the absence of adult partners. In contrast, there is little evidence that titi monkeys differentiate between familiar and unfamiliar infants of comparable ages, and it is reported that this species typically will select their adult mate over their infant. The presence of an adult partner could have survival consequences in this monogamous species, and maintenance of adult social bonds would permit subsequent reproduction.

Squirrel monkeys are small New World primates that usually live in unisex groups. Behavioral changes in squirrel monkeys do occur following the removal of companions, although these responses may reflect general arousal or physiological adjustments to being alone rather than the loss of a particular companion. Although squirrel monkeys appear highly social, physiological measures do not suggest selective pair bonding or stress buffering by companions (Mendoza and Mason, 1997; Hennessy, 1997).

Oxytocin is capable of regulating the HPA axis (DeVries *et al.*, 1997; Uvnas-Moberg, 1998) and may indirectly account for some of the symptoms of social separation. Oxytocin is well positioned to influence both the behavioral (Carter, 1998) and autonomic (Porges, 1998) symptoms that follow the loss of an attachment object, although direct tests of this hypothesis remain to be done.

IX. PHYLOGENETIC AND ONTOGENETIC FACTORS INFLUENCING PAIR BONDING

The expression of attachment behaviors varies widely among species, and the mechanisms responsible for these behaviors also must have species-specific components (Sachser *et al.*, 1998). Peptide hormones, including oxytocin and vasopressin, with species-typical patterns of peptide production, receptor distributions, and functions (Insel and Shapiro, 1992; Insel *et al.*, 1997; Wang, 1995; Wang *et al.*, 1996, 1997; Witt *et al.*, 1991; Young *et al.*, 1996, 1999), are particularly well positioned to influence behaviors, such as pair bonding, that vary among different species (Carter *et al.*, 1995, 1997).

Both general patterns of oxytocin receptor expression and binding and receptor responses to steroids differ among species (Insel and Shapiro, 1992; Insel *et al.*,

1994, 1997; Tribollet *et al.*, 1992; Witt, 1997; Young *et al.*, 1996). For example, estrogen increases oxytocin binding within the ventromedial hypothalamus (VMH) in rats but not in prairie voles (Witt *et al.*, 1991).

Species differences in peptide receptor activity are presumably an important source of interspecific variation in the behavioral effects of oxytocin and vasopressin. Species-typical variations in peptide receptors are apparent in early development. For example, vasopressin-receptor binding increased rapidly in the second week of life in the lateral septum (LS) of nonmonogamous montane voles but not prairie voles (Wang *et al.*, 1997). Insel (1997) and Young *et al.* (1996, 1998) have compared the genes for oxytocin receptors in prairie voles and montane voles and found that these receptors are "virtually identical" in genetic structure. However, promoter elements can regulate the expression of these receptor genes in particular tissues; subtle, but potentially important species differences in base sequences may be responsible for the interspecific variations in peptide receptor distributions. Based on rodent work, especially in voles, Wang and associates (1996) suggest that "neuroendocrine systems may evolve by changes in receptor distribution rather than by restructuring the presynaptic pathway." Comparisons among related vole species with very different patterns of social behavior offer insights into the role of peptides and their receptors in species-typical social behaviors (Insel, 1997).

Among the traits of monogamous mammals is a relative absence of physical sexual dimorphism in appearance (Kleiman, 1997). It is well-known that steroid hormones, including testosterone and dihydrotestosterone, play an important role in the development of masculine genitalia. Thus, the absence of physical sexual dimorphism in monogamous species may reflect a comparative absence of or insensitivity to sex steroids, especially in early life (Carter and Roberts, 1997). It is possible that social behaviors, including the tendency to form pair bonds, that characterize monogamous mammals also emerge in the relative absence of developmental exposure to high levels of androgens. For example, male parental care is a trait of some, but not all, pair-bonding species. There is evidence for a variety of species that exposure to androgens in early life and in some cases in adulthood can inhibit the tendency to be parental.

In the relative absence of high levels of androgens some species may rely more directly on neuropeptides, including vasopressin, to determine "masculine" patterns of physiology and behavior—for example, selective aggression. Neonatal exposure to vasopressin also can facilitate aggression, especially in male prairie voles (Stribley and Carter, 1999). Peptide treatments either in development (Böer, 1993; Swabb and Böer, 1994) or in adulthood (Poulain and Pittman, 1993) may alter the sensitivity of the nervous system to subsequent hormonal experiences. For example, in rats treatment with vasopressin during the first week of life is capable of reducing gene expression for the oxytocin receptor in the PVN during adulthood (Ostrowski, 1998). Since vasopressin is part of the HPA axis and is sensitive to androgens, this finding suggests that developmental changes associated with perinatal stress or gender-dependent androgenization could alter the subsequent sensitivity of the oxytocinergic system.

It is possible that the presence or absence of androgens at various times in the lifespan plays a role in the development of the capacity to form pair bonds; however, this hypothesis remains to be directly tested. It is known that exposure to steroids, including testosterone or corticosterone during perinatal life, can alter the tendency of young prairie voles to prefer a sibling versus a novel stranger (Roberts *et al.*, 1997). In addition, even in prairie voles, there is a sex difference in the initial preference for male or female stimulus animals (DeVries and Carter, 1999), which may reflect the developmental effects of steroids in this species. During development varying exposure to peptides and steroids may "retune" the nervous system by altering thresholds for sociality and aggression; these changes in turn may affect the subsequent tendency of a species or individual to develop social bonds.

Ontogenetic experiences, including levels of perinatal stress and varying amounts of parent-young interaction, can contribute to the development of species-typical patterns of social behavior (Carter, 1998; Francis *et al.*, 1999; Ladd *et al.*, 2000). An example of the consequences of perinatal exposure to stress hormones again comes from work with prairie voles; in this species corticosterone treatments during the perinatal period altered both social and reproductive behaviors. In female prairie voles postnatal treatments with corticosterone were associated with an increased preference

for unfamiliar partners versus siblings, lower levels of alloparenting, and increased masculinization of sexual behavior (indexed by mounting behavior in females). Stressful experiences, including the absence of the father, also inhibit alloparenting in female prairie voles from a population captured in Illinois (Roberts *et al.,* 1997, 1998). However, even within prairie voles, intraspecific population differences exist in social behaviors, including juvenile alloparental behavior and other indices of communal breeding. Prairie voles reared from populations captured in Illinois are both monogamous and communal, whereas those from populations captured in Kansas show some features of monogamy, but are not communal (Roberts *et al.,* 1998). When prairie voles were reared with both parents present, alloparental behavior was much more common in Illinois versus Kansas animals; this behavioral difference in alloparenting disappeared when animals were reared only by their mothers. Animals from both populations formed pair bonds, although voles from the Illinois population were slightly more tolerant of unfamiliar animals than were Kansas voles.

Intraspecific variation provides a model for the analysis of factors that can contribute to sociality, and more specifically to social attachment. In both cases, differences based on developmental experiences would be expressed within genetic constraints. Behavioral flexibility, such as that seen in prairie voles, and possibly mediated by peptide-steroid interactions during development, allows animals individually to adapt their social systems to accommodate early experiences and environmental demands.

X. PEPTIDES AND HUMAN BEHAVIOR

Two aspects of mammalian life, birth and lactation, are clearly associated with the release of oxytocin. Among the neuroendocrine adaptations that accompany both birth and subsequent lactation are hormonal changes that may promote selective social interactions, including high levels of physical contact between parent and offspring and maternal-infant bonding. Although it is likely that the experiences associated with birth facilitate maternal bonding in humans as they do in other animals, studies of the physiology of mother-infant interactions are at present primarily correlational.

Birth is a hormonally complex event that is hard to study. In addition, it is well known that strong social attachments between adults and children can occur in the absence of birth. Thus, the hormonal events of birth are not essential for social bonding. However, as described above, research on bonding in sheep provides strong evidence for a role for vaginocervical stimulation and birth-related hormonal events, and there is no reason to believe these physiological events will differ in humans (Kendrick, 2000).

Lactation is the defining property of mammalian existence, and until modern times was necessary for mammalian reproduction. Oxytocin plays an essential role in milk-let down but not maternal behavior (Nishimori *et al.,* 1996; Russell and Leng, 1998). However, it has been found that lactating women interact more positively with their babies, directing more touching and smiling toward their infants than do bottle-feeding mothers. It also is reported that nursing versus bottle-feeding mothers are more likely to describe positive mood states and be less reactive to stressful experiences (Carter and Altemus, 1997).

Lactating female rodents showed reduced adrenal reactivity, often indexed by reduced secretion of corticosterone, following exposure to stressors such as ether, surgical trauma, and electric shock (Thoman *et al.,* 1970). In women, both ACTH and cortisol levels fall during a bout of breast feeding. There also is evidence that peripheral injections of oxytocin can inhibit ACTH and cortisol release in both men and women. In addition, oxytocin injections can inhibit the release of ACTH or cortisol, which normally follows treatments with CRH, vasopressin plus CRH, or exercise (Carter and Altemus, 1997).

Altemus and associates (1995) have examined the effects of physical stress in lactating versus recently delivered, bottle-feeding women. In that study women were given treadmill exercise to 90% of their VO2 max. The two groups were matched in age and weeks postpartum. The peak blood lactate level, a measure of exercise intensity, was similar in both groups, and lactating and nonlactating subjects had similar basal levels of ACTH and cortisol. ACTH, cortisol, and vasopressin increased following exercise in bottle-feeding women, as would be expected in normal controls. However, the magnitude of the increase in ACTH, cortisol, and vasopressin in response to exercise stress was blunted in the lactating women. Thus, lactating women show a marked inhibition of stress hormone secretion in response to exercise, which was not seen in postpartum women who bottle fed their infants. Taken together these studies suggest for humans and other mammals that lactation, oxytocin, or both can reduce physiological reactivity to various stressors.

Lactation also influences the activity of other neural systems that have been implicated in the management of psychological stress. For example, catecholamine responses to stress are reduced in lactating rats. Suckling also increases central production of GABA in rats and sheep. Lactating females do not show the expected activation in cortical neurons following exposure to an excitatory amino acid, a result that suggests that the functional modifications associated with lactation extend beyond the hypothalamus to include cortical functions (Abbud *et al.,* 1993).

Clinical research also indicates that biological changes associated with pregnancy and lactation may protect some women from mental disorders. In women with a history of panic disorder, panic symptoms tend to decline in pregnancy and remain low during the lactation period (Carter and Altemus, 1997). These results suggest that patterns of infant feeding may influence a mother's mental health and thus her ability to deal with the demands of child rearing. This in turn has consequences for both parents and their offspring.

Lactation may provide additional opportunity for maternal bonding, perhaps allowing oxytocin to reinforce attachments initially formed during parturition. In addition, milk contains comparatively high levels of hormones, including oxytocin (Leake *et al.,* 1981) and prolactin (Grosvenor *et al.,* 1990). In infants the digestive system is more permeable than in adults. There is evidence in rats that milk-borne prolactin has long-term effects on neuroendocrine development. The behavioral effects of milk-borne oxytocin have not been studied, but hormones in milk could provide another level of regulation for the developing nervous system and possibly influence the offspring's subsequent management of stressful experiences (Carter, 1988).

Oxytocin injections given peripherally to the mother can facilitate nipple attachment by young rat pups, a finding that suggests that oxytocin may change the response of a young animal to its mother (Singh and Hofer, 1978). Rats pups also show preferences for specific odors that are associated with exposure to their mothers. Preferences for the mother do not develop in animals that are pretreated with oxytocin antagonists (Nelson and Panksepp, 1996). Thus, oxytocin may act on both the mother and infant to influence the response of young animals, including humans, to their mother.

XI. CLINICAL IMPLICATIONS OF A PEPTIDERGIC THEORY OF SOCIAL ATTACHMENT

The presence or absence of attachments has broad consequences across the lifespan. Like other mammals, humans rely on positive social interactions for both safety and reproduction. It has been argued that the tendency to form pair bonds or social attachments is a universal human characteristic (Money, 1980; Fisher, 1992; Hazan and Shaver, 1987). Social support has documented health benefits, and the absence of positive social interactions or social bonds typically is associated with both physical and mental illness (Reite and Boccia, 1994; Ryff and Singer, 1998; Sperling and Berman, 1994; Henry and Wang, 1998; Knox and Uvnas-Moberg, 1998).

Forced social separations or the absence of social attachments can trigger stress, anxiety, fear and even depression (Sachser *et al.*, 1998). The behaviors and physiological changes associated with bereavement or grief are similar to those used to define depression (Reite and Boccia, 1994). Understanding the nature of physiological processes that regulate social attachment also could be of value in the treatment or prevention of disorders such as depression or schizophrenia that can involve dysfunctional social attachment (Kirkpatrick, 1997; Henry and Wang, 1998).

In primate infants the absence of adequate maternal care has been associated with growth retardation, social withdrawal, inadequate interpersonal relationships, and inhibited verbal communication (Harlow, 1971). This complex of symptoms has even been recognized in human development as a medical syndrome, termed "reactive attachment disorder of infancy" (Shaffer and Campbell, 1994). Although the concept of attachment disorder has begun to generate treatment strategies, the relationship between this "disorder" and normal human attachment remains to be described.

It has been proposed that autism, which can be characterized by atypical social behavior and a failure to form social attachments, may involve abnormal activity in endogenous peptidergic systems. For example, a variety of clinical studies have implicated opioids in autism (Bouvard *et al.*, 1995). Treatment with naltrexone produces some clinical benefits and alters biochemical profiles in a subset of autistic children. More recent studies also have begun to explore the role of oxytocin in autism (Insel, 1997). Studies in autistic adults suggest that deficits in oxytocin may be correlated with some symptoms of autism (Modahl *et al.*, 1998), and there is a report that increased gregariousness may follow oxytocin treatments. However, the possible role for oxytocin, vasopressin, or endogenous opioids in selective human social attachments that are more analogous to pair bonding remains unexplored.

Other neurochemicals, such as catecholamines and serotonin, have effects on behavior and also can influence the release and actions of oxytocin and vasopressin. For example, selective serotonin reuptake inhibitors can influence peptidergic systems (Li *et al.*, 1993; Uvnas-Moberg *et al.*, 1999). The clinical effects of these chemicals in the context of attachment are largely unknown, although drugs that affect these systems could influence social bonding.

Forced isolation, anxiety, fear, and other forms of stressful conditions are associated with increased levels of HPA activity. Such conditions or experiences normally tend to encourage social interactions. Both the human (Simpson and Rholes, 1994) and animal literature (Carter, 1998) suggests an association between HPA activation and stressful experiences and the development of social attachments. The role of hormones of the HPA axis in attachment is probably not linear, since both animals and humans under extreme conditions may become either self-protective or immobilized—conditions that are at odds with the formation of social bonds (Porges, 1998). Excessively stressful conditions, such as those that could compromise survival or that of intense grief, may lead to a breakdown of social relationships (Reite and Boccia, 1994). Thus, chronic or extreme stress could inhibit subsequent attachment. However, research with rodents suggests that within a homeostatic range, stress-related physiological processes, including hormones of the HPA axis, can promote the subsequent development of social bonds, especially in males (DeVries *et al.*, 1996). In addition, positive social interactions, including social bonds, may help create physiological states that are anxiolytic or stress reducing.

Oxytocin, perhaps released by positive social interactions, has the capacity to produce both acute and chronic reductions in the activity of the HPA axis (Carter, 1998; Petersson *et al.*, 1999). Studies of lactating women support this hypothesis in humans (Altemus *et al.*, 1995). Thus, oxytocin, with both central and peripheral processes, is part of an endogenous homeostatic system. This system has the concurrent capacity to increase social attachment and other positive social behaviors, thereby providing the additional indirect benefits of sociality.

The role of vasopressin in human social behavior is more difficult to characterize. Vasopressin is believed to be similar to the ancestral peptide from which oxytocin and vasopressin were derived. Vasopressin binds to several types of receptors, including the oxytocin receptor. Vasopressin has been implicated in territoriality, agonistic behaviors, and HPA arousal and may be part of a more primitive adaptive system for mobilization and self-defense (Carter, 1998; Porges, 1998). In some cases the functions of vasopressin are apparently similar to those of oxytocin. However, under other conditions oxytocin and vasopressin may have antagonistic actions (Engelmann *et al.*, 1996). Dynamic and complex interactions between oxytocin and vasopressin, in the presence of a more slowly changing steroid background, could help regulate underlying human visceral states and emotions.

Awareness of the importance of peptides, including oxytocin and vasopressin, in human behavior is comparatively recent but of considerable importance. Many aspects of daily life can affect the release of the peptides. For example, social or sexual contact, food intake (Uvnas-Moberg, 1994), and the use of steroid hormones, drugs of abuse, or alcohol (Kovacs *et al.*, 1998) are only a few examples of experiences that have been shown to influence the endogenous production, release, or actions of these peptides.

Many components of human behavior, such as motor patterns, are regulated at least in part, by cognitive processes. However, various mood states and the decision to engage in a given behavior are strongly determined by visceral processes or autonomic states, which may

in turn motivate the occurrence of specific behaviors (Porges, 1998). Peptides, including oxytocin and vasopressin, regulate these visceral states or emotional feelings. Steroids, opioids, oxytocin, and vasopressin may induce a physiological process or "social motivation" that increases the probability of social interactions and the formation of social bonds. In addition, oxytocinergic processes, possibly due to their unique central position in the nervous system, may help modulate autonomic and behavioral reactivity. Thus, by understanding the neurobiology of peptides, such as oxytocin, we may gain a better understanding of the processes through which social bonds promote physical and emotional health.

Hormones, including oxytocin and vasopressin, are directly and indirectly manipulated by various medical practices. For example, large doses of Pitocin, a synthetic version of oxytocin, are routinely used to hasten childbirth, with unexplored effects on the social behavior or propensity to attachment of both the mother and child (Böer, 1993). Long labors, Caesarian sections, and the decision to breast or bottle feed are indirectly peptidergic manipulations (Uvnas-Moberg, 1998). Remarkably little attention has been given to the behavioral or hormonal consequences of these peptide-related events that can have profound effects on behavioral, homeostatic, and emotional systems for both the parent and the child.

XII. ATTACHMENT AND BONDING IN PRIMATES: AN EVOLUTIONARY PERSPECTIVE FOR HUMANS

Human infants form attachment bonds with their caregiver, who is usually the mother, for it is she who provides the secure base for fostering exploration, play, and other social behaviors (Klaus *et al.*, 1995). The nature of this attachment figure becomes more visible under conditions that are fearful or novel and threatening to the infant. By seeking protection through attachment, the immature offspring are believed to increase their likelihood of survival. Infant attachment is not independent of caregiving and therefore it is important that mothers should find "satisfaction with the parental role," and across many cultures this appears to be the case. To the extent that such "satisfaction" may help maintain investment in rearing offspring to reproductive age, maternal caregiving behavior must have evolved with infant attachment behavior. Also common to all cultures are the changes in hormonal status during pregnancy and parturition that predispose women to respond to an infant's signals.

The quality of mothering, particularly in times of fear and stress, contributes substantially to the infant's security of attachment. Bowlby (1969) has argued that infant attachment and maternal bonding provide the foundation for human attachment behavior from the cradle to the grave. Although the "internalized" bond is secured by the various forms of attachment behavior that contribute to it, touching and huddling are features of attachment behavior that persist into adult life, particularly in times of distress, fear, and illness.

A question of some importance is how might this relationship engendered by maternal bonding and reciprocated by infant attachment, but extending into adult relationships and bonds, be subserved at the neural level. If, as Bowlby suggests, all meaningful relationships are structured on the foundations of early attachment, are there common underlying mechanisms, and if so how have they evolved? The biology of mammalian bonding, as exemplified by monogamous prairie voles and sheep with their lambs, focuses heavily on the importance of peripheral steroid hormones (estrogen, progesterone, testosterone, and corticosterone), and their effects on central release of peptides, including vasopressin, oxytocin, CRH, opioids, and the synthesis of receptors for these peptides. A principal site of action for these peptides, although not exclusive, may be in olfactory recognition, which is important in the bonding process. It is likely that attachment or bonding in humans is more complex and probably more dependent on cognitive processes and mental representations rather than the olfactory processes that occur in rodents or sheep. However, some insight regarding the processes involved in social bonding in humans may come from studies in nonhuman primates.

Many of the basic features in human infant behavior that helped Bowlby formulate his attachment theory can be observed in the mother-directed behavior of infant monkeys. This sharing of behavioral propensities and emotional labilities of monkey and human infants (sucking, clinging, crying, and following) is consistent with their close evolutionary histories. The first detailed studies of attachment relationships were undertaken in the 1960s on rhesus monkeys and provided descriptions of infant behavioral development that generalize to many primate species (Harlow, 1971; Kraemer, 1992). Primate mothers provide their infants with nourishment, protection, and warmth, protection from predators, and a secure base to which they can retreat when disruptions occur in the social group. The attachment that rhesus monkey infants develop to their mothers is especially enduring in females, lasting a lifetime, whereas in infant males it rarely lasts beyond puberty.

A. The Evolutionary Basis of Bonding

What are the evolutionary developments that have enabled expansion of the affectional system deployed in mother-infant bonding to incorporate other contexts of social-affiliative relationships? In considering primates, strong interrelations are beginning to emerge between the two important features noted earlier, neocortical expansion and matrilineal inheritance. These are common to all mammals that exhibit complex social organizations. The development of a larger neocortex has enabled motivated behavior to occur at will, such that maternal affiliation may take place without pregnancy and parturition. This unique development in primate evolution has matched parturient females with nonparturient females in sustaining the behavioral potential for infant caregiving. Such an emancipation of behavior from endocrine determinants has only been evolutionarily possible with the development of a bigger brain, since decision-making processes, especially in the context of maternal behavior, are complex and need to be strategically correct. Progression away from the syncronization of maternal behavior with the hormones of pregnancy and replacement with a system of cognitive control require exceptional cognitive abilities. These abilities are not inherited, but a larger brain enables social factors to take over from hormonal factors in predicting reproductive success. This would explain the overriding importance of social and maternal experience in order to achieve successful maternal care, experience that is acquired during early social development under the watchful eye of mothers but outside the immediate context of pregnancy and parturition.

From the available fossil records it appears that many mammalian lineages have evolved increased cranial capacity, but because it is claimed that the push for an exceptionally larger neocortex in primates has developed from complex social living, differences in maternal and paternal lifestyles may have subjected brain evolution to differential selection pressures. In Old World monkeys, females provide social stability and group cohesion, are more affiliative than males, and maintain the continuity of the group over successive generations. Females are the primary caregivers: social rank of daughter, but not son is related to the matriline. This kind of matrilineal inheritance is compatible with genomic imprinting, which not only results in the development of a larger forebrain from maternally expressed alleles (Keverne *et al.,* 1996a), but the advantages of genomically imprinted inheritance are transmitted to both sons and daughters. Hence, the differential selection pressures operating through the matriline could have resulted in a larger neocortex, thereby giving greater cognitive control over behavior (Keverne *et al.,* 1996b). For such neocortical control over behavior to be successful, the process of attachment and early learning is essential for the subsequent development of normal affiliative relationships.

The development of a larger brain has been particularly important to enable the lifetime attachments like those that occur in humans. For the operation of "attachments" to sustain relationships and endure a human lifetime requires a brain that can develop growing insights into self as well as the maternal attachment figure. As young children develop, their knowledge base expands especially in regard to the changing ways in which their mother responds to them and, what is more important, how each is likely to respond to the other. This knowledge steadily becomes organized in the form of internal working models of self and mother, encompassing an understanding of both her moods and intentions. Building on this early knowledge provides the infant with an ability to simulate happenings in an expanding world of relationships. Forward planning may occur with the advantages of foresight and security. Because these working models are in constant daily use, their influence on thought, feeling, and behavior becomes routine and all-pervasive.

Deploying our brains in the construction of internalized working models of self and others would be difficult, if not impossible, without an attachment figure, and we would further argue that attachment figures would be extremely scarce without maternal bonding. Those parts of the brain that are characteristically enlarged in humans (neocortex and striatum) develop in the postnatal period (neotany) when infants are forming their internal working models. Important in this context is the availability of exclusive access to mother and her undivided attention. Biology has assisted this possibility by extending the interbirth interval, aided by the contraceptive effects of infant suckling. There can surely be no better way of increasing maternal investment than by reducing the number of infants in which the mother invests.

It is also important to note that in these early years, when the neocortex is forming and makings its connections and associations with other parts of the brain, the limbic emotional brain is well developed. The large emotional repertoire of young infants bears testimony to this. Understanding emotions, curbing these emotions, and channelling these emotions for beneficial purposes must represent an important phase in brain development. These cognitive abilities have surely prospered from experiencing the dynamics of reciprocity in the interplay between mother and child, while the subsequent expansion of social relationships, based on secure attachment, provides a second cushion for the emotional turmoil of puberty. The child's need for an attachment figure and the mother's predisposition to bond provides an optimal social environment in which the human brain can develop. Weaning and expansion of the child's social world have not only coincided, but are made easier by having a secure base from which to explore.

XIII. SUMMARY

Pair bonding is an evolved trait and may play a critical role in reproduction, as well as in individual and species survival. The neurobiology of pair bonding or other forms of social affiliation are most readily understood in this context. The proximate mechanisms underlying various forms of positive social behaviors, including pair bonding and maternal-infant behavior, rely on common neural and endocrine systems. At the heart of pair bonding are neural systems dependent on peptides, including oxytocin, vasopressin, opioids, CRH, and related hormones. Steroid hormones, although probably not essential for pair bonding, may modulate these behaviors. Neuropeptides also serve to coordinate the autonomic and endocrine consequences of positive social experiences with behavioral states that support the formation and maintenance of social bonds.

Acknowledgments

We gratefully acknowledge the many scientists, including our collaborators, whose work has contributed to the understanding of this subject. Studies on maternal bonding in sheep and primate behavior were sponsored by grants to E.B.K. from the BBSRC and the Medical Research Council of the United Kingdom. Studies on pair bonding in prairie voles described in this review were sponsored by grants to C.S.C. from the United States National Institutes of Health (NICHD and NIMH) and National Science Foundation. Studies of human breast feeding were sponsored by a grant from the United States Department of Defense.

References

Abbud, R., Hoffman, G. E., and Smith, M. S. (1993). Cortical refractoriness to N-methyl-D, L-aspartic acid (NMA) stimulation in the lactating rat: Recovery after pup removal and blockade of progesterone receptors. *Brain Res.* **604**, 16–23.

Acher, R., Chauvet, J., Chauvet, M.-T., and Michel, G. (1997). Principles in protein hormone evolution: The neurohypophysial peptides as avian evolutionary tracers. *Poult. Avian Biol. Rev.* **8**, 33–51.

Altemus, M., Deuster, P. A., Gallivan, E., Carter, C. S., and Gold, P. W. (1995). Suppression of hypothalamic-pituitary-adrenal responses to exercise stress in lactating women. *J. Clin. Endocrinol. Metab.* **80**, 2954–2959.

Argiolas, A. (1999). Neuropeptides and sexual behaviour. *Neurosci. Biobehav. Rev.* **23**, 1127–1142.

Barberis, C., and Tribollet, E. (1996). Vasopressin and oxytocin receptors in the central nervous system. *Crit. Rev. Neurobiol.* **10**, 119–154.

Bluthé, R. M., and Dantzer, R. (1992). Chronic intracerebral infusion of vasopressin and vasopressin antagonist modulate social recognition in rats. *Brain Res.* **572**, 261–264.

Bluthé, R. M., and Dantzer, R. (1993). Role of the vomeronasal system in vasopressinergic modulation of social recognition in rats. *Brain Res.* **604**, 205–210.

Bluthé, R. M., Schoenen, J., and Dantzer, R. (1990). Androgen-dependent vasopressinergic neurons are involved in social recognition in rats. *Brain Res.* **519**, 261–264.

Böer, G. J. (1993). Chronic oxytocin treatment during late gestation and lactation impairs development of rat offspring. *Neurotoxicol. Teratol.* **15**, 383–389.

Bouvard, M. P., Leboyer, M., Launay, J.-M., Recasens, C., Plumet, M.-H., Waller-Perotte, D., Tabuteau, F., Bondoux, D., Dugas, M., Lensing, P., and Panksepp, J. (1995). Low-dose naltrexone effects on plasma chemistries and clinical symptoms in autism: A double-blind, placebo-controlled study. *Psychiatry Res.* **58**, 191–201.

Bowlby, J. (1969). "Attachment and Loss," Vol. 1. Hogarth Press, London.

Bowler, C. M., Cushing, B. S., and Carter, C. S. (2002). Social factors regulate female-female aggression and affiliation in prairie voles. (In press.)

Broad, K. D., Kendrick, K. M., Sirinathsinghji, D. J. S., and Keverne, E. B. (1993). Changes in oxytocin immunoreactivity and messenger-RNA expression in the sheep brain during pregnancy, parturition and lactation and in response to estrogen and progesterone. *J. Neuroendocrinol.* **5**, 435–444.

Carter, C. S. (1988). Patterns of infant feeding, the mother-infant interaction and stress management. *In* "Stress and Coping Across Development" (T. M. Field, P. M. McCabe, and N. Schneiderman, eds.), pp. 27–46. Erlbaum, Hillsdale, NJ.

Carter, C. S. (1992). Oxytocin and sexual behavior. *Neurosci. Biobehav. Rev.* **16**, 131–144.

Carter, C. S. (1998). Neuroendocrine perspectives on social attachment and love. *Psychoneuroendocrinology* **23**, 779–818.

Carter, C. S., and Altemus, M. (1997). Integrative functions of lactational hormones in social behavior and stress management. *Ann. N.Y. Acad. Sci.* **807**, 164–174.

Carter, C. S., and Roberts, R. L. (1997). The psychobiological basis of cooperative breeding. *In* "Cooperative Breeding in Mammals" (N. G. Solomon and J. A. French, eds.), pp. 231–266. Cambridge University Press, New York.

Carter, C. S., Williams, J. R., Witt, D., and Insel, T. R. (1992). Oxytocin and social bonding. *Ann. N.Y. Acad. Sci.* **652**, 204–211.

Carter, C. S., DeVries, A. C., and Getz, L. L. (1995). Physiological substrates of mammalian monogamy: the prairie vole model. *Neurosci. Biobehav. Rev.* **19**, 303–314.

Carter, C. S., Lederhendler, I. I., and Kirkpatrick, B., eds. (1997). "The Integrative Neurobiology of Affiliation," Vol. 807. N. Y. Acad. Sci., New York.

Chiodera, P., Salvarani, C., Bacchi-Modena, A., Spallanzani, R., Cigarini, C., Alboni, A., Gardini, E., and Coiro, V. (1991). Relationship between plasma profiles of oxytocin and adrenocorticotropic hormone during suckling or breast stimulation in women. *Horm. Res.* **35**, 119–123.

Cho, M. M., DeVries, A. C., Williams, J. R., and Carter, C. S. (1999). The effects of oxytocin and vasopressin on partner preferences in male and female prairie voles (*Microtus ochrogaster*). *Behav. Neurosci.* **5**, 1071–1080.

Curtis, J. T., Liu, Y., and Wang, Z. (2001). Lesions of the vomeronasal organ disrupt mating-induced pair bonding in female prairie voles (*Microtus ochrogaster*). *Brain Res.* **901**, 167–174.

Cushing, B. C., and Carter, C. S. (1999). Prior exposure to oxytocin mimics the effects of social contact and facilitates sexual behaviour in females. *J. Neuroendocrinol.* **11**, 765–769.

Cushing, B. S., and Carter, C. S. (2000). Peripheral pulses of oxytocin increase partner preferences in female, but not male, prairie voles. *Horm. Behav.* **37**, 49–56.

Cushing, B. C., Martin, J. O., Young, L. J., and Carter, C. S. (2001). The effects of peptides on partner preference formation are predicted by habitat in prairie voles. *Horm. Behav.* **39**, 48–58.

Da Costa, A., Guevara-Guzman, R., Ohkura, S., Goode, J., and Kendrick, K. M. (1996). The role of the paraventricular nucleus in the control of maternal behaviour in sheep. *J. Neuroendocrinol.* **8**, 163–177.

DeVries, A. C., and Carter, C. S. (1999). Sex differences in temporal parameters of partner preference in prairie voles (*Microtus ochrogaster*). *Can. J. Zool.* **77**, 885–889.

DeVries, A. C., DeVries, M. B., Taymans, S. E., and Carter, C. S. (1995). The modulation of pair bonding by corticosterone in female prairie voles (*Microtus ochrogaster*). *Proc. Natl. Acad. Sci. U.S.A.* **92**, 7744–7748.

DeVries, A. C., DeVries, M. B., Taymans, S. E., and Carter, C. S. (1996). The effects of stress on social preferences are sexually dimorphic in prairie voles. *Proc. Natl. Acad. Sci. U.S.A.* **93**, 11980–11984.

DeVries, A. C., Johnson, C. L., and Carter, C. S. (1997). Familiarity and gender influence social preferences in prairie voles (*Microtus ochrogaster*). *Can. J. Zool.* **75**, 295–301.

DeVries, A. C., Guptaa, T., Cardillo, S., Cho, M., and Carter, C. S. (2001). Corticotropin-releasing factor induced social preferences in male prairie roles. *Psychoneuroendocrinology*, in press.

De Vries, G. F., and Villalba, C. (1997). Brain sexual dimorphism and sex differences in parental and other social behaviors. *Ann. N.Y. Acad. Sci.* **807**, 273–286.

De Wied, D., Diamant, M., and Fodor, M. (1993). Central nervous system effects of neurohypophyseal hormones and related peptides. *Front. Neuroendocrinol.* **14**, 251–302.

Dewsbury, D. A. (1987). The comparative psychology of monogamy. *Nebr. Symp. Motiv.* **35**, 1–50.

Dharmadhikari, A., Lee, Y. S., Roberts, R. L., and Carter, C. S. (1997). Exploratory behavior correlates with social organization and is responsive to peptide injections in prairie voles. *Ann. N.Y. Acad. Sci.* **807**, 610–612.

Dluzen, D. E., Ramirez, V. C., Carter, C. S., and Getz, L. L. (1981). Male vole urine changes luteinizing hormone-releasing hormone and norepinephrine in female olfactory bulb. *Science* **212**, 573–575.

Dluzen, D. E., Muraoka, S., Engelmann, M., and Landgraf, R. (1998a). The effects of infusion of arginine vasopressin, oxytocin, or their antagonists into the olfactory bulb upon social recognition responses in male rats. *Peptides (N.Y.)* **19**, 999–1005.

Dluzen, D. E., Muraoka, S., and Landgraf, R. (1998b). Olfactory bulb norepinephrine depletion abolishes vasopressin and oxytocin preservation of social recognition responses in rats. *Neurosci. Lett.* **254**, 161–164.

Engelmann, M., Wotjak, C. T., Neumann, I., Ludwig, M., and Landgraf, R. (1996). Behavioral consequences of intracerebral vasopressin and oxytocin: Focus on learning and memory. *Neurosci. Biobehav. Rev.* **20**, 341–358.

Engelmann, M., Ebner, K., Wotjak, C. T., and Landgraf, R. (1998). Endogenous oxytocin is involved in short-term olfactory memory in female rats. *Behav. Brain Res.* **90**, 89–94.

Fabre-Nys, C., Meller, R. E., and Keverne, E. B. (1982). Opiate antagonists stimulate affiliative behavior in monkeys. *Pharmacol., Biochem. Behav.* **16**, 653–659.

Fahrbach, S. E., Morrell, J. I., and Pfaff, D. W. (1985). Possible role for endogenous oxytocin in estrogen-facilitated maternal behavior in rats. *Neuroendocrinology* **40**, 526–532.

Ferguson, J. N., Young, L. J., Hearn, E. F., Insel, T. R., and Winslow, J. T. (2000). Social amnesia in mice lacking the oxytocin gene. *Nat. Genet.* **25**, 284–288.

Firestone, K. B., Thompson, K., and Carter, C. S. (1991). Female-female interactions and social stress in prairie voles, *Behav. Neural Biol.* **55**, 31–41.

Fisher, H. (1992). "Anatomy of Love." Fawcett Colombine, New York.

Fleming, A. S., Cheung, U., Myhal, N., and Kessler, Z. (1989). Effects of maternal hormones on 'timidity' and attraction to pup-related odors in female rats. *Physiol. Behav.* **46**, 449–453.

Francis, D. D., Liu, D., Daldji, C., and Meaney, M. J. (1999). Variations in maternal care and the development of stress responses. *Int. Congr. Ser. M Experpta Med.* **1185**, 11–28

Freund-Mercier, M. J., and Stoeckel, M. E. (1993). Oxytocin receptors on oxytocin neurons: Histoautoradiographic detection after ICV oxytocin antagonist injection. *J. Endocrinol. Invest.*, Abst. B49.

Gavish, L., Carter, C. S., and Getz, L. L. (1981). Further evidence for monogamy in the prairie vole. *Anim. Behav.* **29**, 955–957.

Getz, L. L., Carter, C. S., and Gavish, L. (1981). The mating system of the prairie vole *Microtus ochrogaster*: Field and laboratory evidence for pair-bonding. *Behav. Ecol. Sociobiol.* **8**, 189–194.

Getz, L. L., McGuire, B., Pizzuto, T., Hormann, J. E., and Frase, B. (1993). Social organization of the prairie vole (*Microtus ochrogaster*). *J. Mammal.* **74**, 44–48.

Gingrich, B. S., Huot, R. L., Wang, Z., and Insel, T. R. (1997). Differential fos expression following microinjection of oxytocin or vasopressin in the prairie vole brain. *Ann. N.Y. Acad. Sci.* **807**, 504–505.

Gingrich, B. S., Liu, Y., Cascio, C., Wang, Z., and Insel, T. R. (2000). Dopamine D2 receptors in the nucleus accumbens are important for social attachment in female prairie voles (*Microtus ochrogaster*). *Behav. Neurosci.* **114**, 173–183.

Grosvenor, C. E., Shah, G. V., and Crowley, W. R. (1990). Role of neurogenic stimuli and milk prolactin in the regulation of prolactin secretion during lactation. *In* "Mammalian Parenting: Biochemical, Neurobiological and Behavioral Determinants" (N. A. Krasnegor and R. S. Bridges, eds.), pp. 324–342. Oxford University Press, New York.

Harlow, H. F. (1971). "Learning to Love." Albion, San Francisco.

Hazan, C., and Shaver, P. R. (1987). Romantic love conceptualized as an attachment. *J. Pers. Soc. Psychol.* **52**, 511–524.

Hennessy, M. B. (1997). Hypothalamic-pituitary-adrenal responses to brief social separation. *Neurosci. Biobehav. Rev.* **21**, 11–29.

Henry, J. P., and Wang, S. (1998). Effects of early stress on adult affiliative behavior. *Psychoneuroendocrinology* **23**, 863–876.

Herman, B. H., and Panksepp, J. (1978). Effects of morphine and naloxone on separation distress and approach attachment: Evidence of opiate mediation of social effect. *Pharmacol., Biochem. Behav.* **9**, 213–220.

Hillegaart, V., Alster, P., Uvnas-Moberg, K., and Ahlenius, S. (1999). Sexual motivation promotes oxytocin secretion in male rats. *Peptides (N.Y.)* **19**, 39–45.

Insel, T. R. (1992). Oxytocin: A neuropeptide for affiliation— evidence from behavioral, receptor autoradiographic, and comparative studies. *Psychoneuroendocrinology* **17**, 3–33.

Insel, T. R. (1997). A neurobiological basis of social attachment. *Am. J. Psychiatry* **154**, 726–735.

Insel, T. R., and Harbaugh, C. R. (1989). Lesions of the hypothalamic paraventricular nucleus disrupt the initiation of maternal behavior. *Physiol. Behav.* **45**, 1033–1041.

Insel, T. R., and Hulihan, T. J. (1995). A gender-specific mechanism for pair bonding: Oxytocin and partner preference formation in monogamous voles. *Behav. Neurosci.* **109**, 782–789.

Insel, T. R., and Shapiro, L. E. (1992). Oxytocin receptor distribution reflects social organization in monogamous and polygamous voles. *Proc. Natl. Acad. Sci. U.S.A.* **89**, 5981–5985.

Insel, T. R., and Winslow, J. T. (1991). Central administration of oxytocin modulates the infant rat's response to social isolation. *Eur. J. Pharmacol.* **203**, 149–152.

Insel, T. R., Gelhard, R. E., and Shapiro, L. E. (1991). The comparative distribution of neurohypophyseal peptide recep-

tors in monogamous and polygamous mice. *Neuroscience* **43**, 623–630.

Insel, T. R., Young, L. J., Witt, D., and Crews, D. (1993). Gonadal steroids have paradoxical effects on brain oxytocin receptors. *J. Neuroendocrinol.* **5**, 619–628.

Insel, T. R., Wang, Z., and Ferris, C. F. (1994). Patterns of brain vasopressin receptor distribution associated with social organization in microtine rodents. *J. Neurosci.* **14**, 5381–5392.

Insel, T. R., Preston, S., and Winslow, J. T. (1995). Mating in the monogamous male: Behavioral consequences. *Physiol. Behav.* **57**, 615–627.

Insel, T. R., Young, L., and Wang, Z. (1997). Molecular aspects of monogamy. *Ann. N.Y. Acad. Sci.* **807**, 302–316.

Kalin, N. H., Shelton, S. E., and Barksdale, C. M. (1988). Opiate modulation of separation-induced distress in nonhuman primates. *Brain Res.* **440**, 285–292.

Kalin, N. H., Sheldon, S. E., and Lynn, D. E. (1995). Opiate systems in mother and infant primates coordinate intimate contact during reunion. *Psychoneuroendocrinology* **7**, 735–742.

Kendrick, K. M. (2000). Oxytocin, motherhood and bonding. *Exp. Physiol.* **85S**, 111S–124S.

Kendrick, K. M., and Keverne, E. B. (1991). Importance of progesterone and estrogen priming for the induction of maternal behavior by vaginocervical stimulation in sheep: Effects of maternal experience. *Physiol. Behav.* **49**, 745–750.

Kendrick, K. M., and Keverne, E. B. (1992). Control of synthesis and release of oxytocin in the sheep brain. *Ann. N.Y. Acad. Sci.* **652**, 102–121.

Kendrick, K. M., Keverne, E. B., Hinton, M. R., and Goode, J. A. (1986). Cerebrospinal fluid levels of acetylcholinesterase, monoamines and oxytocin during labour, parturition, vaginocervical stimulation, lamb separation and suckling in sheep. *Neuroendocrinology* **44**, 149–156.

Kendrick, K. M., Keverne, E. B., and Baldwin, B. A. (1987). Intracerebroventricular oxytocin stimulates maternal behaviour in the sheep. *Neuroendocrinology* **46**, 56–61.

Kendrick, K. M., Keverne, E. B., Chapman, C., and Baldwin, B. A. (1988). Intracranial dialysis measurement of oxytocin, monoamines and uric acid release from the olfactory bulb and substantia nigra of sheep during parturition suckling, separation from lambs and eating. *Brain Res.* **439**, 1–10.

Kendrick, K. M., Lévy, F., and Keverne, E. B. (1991). Importance of vaginocervical stimulation for the formation of maternal bonding in primiparous and multiparous parturient ewes. *Physiol. Behav.* **50**, 595–600.

Kendrick, K. M., Keverne, E. B., and Goode, J. A. (1992a). Changes in the sensory processing of olfactory signals induced by birth in sheep. *Science* **256**, 833–836.

Keverne, E. B. (1992). Primate social relationships: Their determinants and consequences. *Adv. Study Behav.* **21**, 1–37.

Keverne, E. B. (1995a). Olfactory learning. *Curr. Opin. Neurobiol.* **5**, 482–488.

Keverne, E. B. (1995b). Neurochemical changes accompanying the reproductive process: Their significance for maternal care in primates and other mammals. *In* "Motherhood in Human and Nonhuman Primates" (C. R. Pryce, R. D. Martin, and D. Skuse, eds.), pp. 69–77. Karger, Basel.

Keverne, E. B., and Kendrick, K. M. (1991). Morphine and corticotropin releasing factor potentiates maternal acceptance in multiparous ewes after vaginocervical stimulation. *Brain Res.* **540**, 55–62.

Keverne, E. B., and Kendrick K. M. (1992). Oxytocin facilitation of maternal behavior. *Ann. N.Y. Acad. Sci.* **652**, 83–101.

Keverne, E. B., Lévy, F., Poindron, P., and Lindsay, D. R. (1983). Vaginal stimulation: An important determinant of maternal bonding in sheep. *Science* **219**, 81–83.

Keverne, E. B., Martenez, N. D., and Tuite, B. (1989). Beta-endorphin concentrations in cerebrospinal fluid of monkeys are influenced by grooming relationships. *Psychoneuroendocrinology* **14**, 155–161.

Keverne, E. B., Lévy, F., Guevara-Guzman, R., and Kendrick, K. M. (1993). Influence of birth and maternal experience on olfactory bulb neurotransmitter release. *Neuroscience* **107**, 557–565.

Keverne, E. B., Fundele, R., Narashima, M., Barton, S., and Surani, M. A. (1996a). Genomic imprinting and the differential roles of parental genomes in brain development. *Dev. Brain Res.* **92**, 91–100.

Keverne, E. B., Martel, F. L., and Nevison, C. M. (1996b). Primate brain evolution: Genetic and functional considerations. *Proc. R. Soc. London, Ser. B* **262**, 689–696.

Keverne, E. B., Nevison, C. M., and Martel, F. L. (1997). Early learning and the Social bond. *Ann. N.Y. Acad. Sci.* **807**, 329–339.

Kirkpatrick, B. (1997). Affiliation and neuropsychiatric disorders: The deficit syndrome of schizophrenia. *Ann. N.Y. Acad. Sci.* **807**, 455–468.

Kirkpatrick, B., Carter, C. S., Newman, S. W., and Insel, T. R. (1994). Axon-sparing lesions of the medial amygdala decrease affiliative behaviors in the prairie vole (*Microtus ochrogaster*): Behavioral and anatomical specificity. *Behav. Neurosci.* **108**, 501–513.

Klaus, M. H., Kennel, J. H., and Klaus, P. H. (1995). "Bonding." Addison-Wesley, Reading, MA.

Kleiman, D. (1977). Monogamy in Mammals. *Q. Rev. Biol.* **52**, 39–69.

Knox, S. S., and Uvnas-Moberg, K. (1998). Social isolation and cardiovascular disease: An atherosclerotic pathway. *Psychneuroendocrinology* **23**, 877–890.

Kovacs, G. L., Sarnyai, Z., and Szabo, G. (1998). Oxytocin and addiction: A review. *Psychoneuroendocrinology* **23**, 945–962.

Kraemer, G. W. (1992). A psychobiological theory of attachment. *Behav. Brain Sci.* **15**, 493–511.

Ladd, C. O., Huot, R. L., Thrivikraman, K. V., Nemeroff, C. B., Meaney, M. J., and Plotsky, P. M. (2000). Long-term behavioral and neuroendocrine adaptations to adverse early experience. *Prog. Brain Res.* **122**, 81–103.

Landgraf, R., Neumann, I., and Pittman, Q. J. (1991). Septal and hippocampal release of vasopressin and oxytocin during late pregnancy and parturition in the rat. *Neuroendocrinology* **54**, 378–383.

Leake, R. D., Wietzman, R. E., and Fisher, D. A. (1981). Oxytocin concentrations during the neonatal period. *Biol. Neonate* **39**, 127–131.

Levin, M. C., and Sawchenko, P. E. (1993). Neuropeptide co-expression in the magnocellular neurosecretory system of the female rat: Evidence for differential modulation by estrogen. *Neuroscience* **54**, 1001–1018.

Levine, S., Coe, C., and Wiener, S. G. (1989). Psychoneuroendocrinology of stress: A psychobiological perspective. *In* "Psychoendocrinology" (F. R. Brush and S. Levine, eds.), pp 341–380. Academic Press, Orlando, FL.

Levine, S., Lyons, D. M., and Schatzberg, A. F. (1997). Psychobiological consequences of social relationships. *Ann. N.Y. Acad. Sci.* **807**, 210–218.

Lévy, F., and Poindron, P. (1987). Importance of amniotic fluids for the establishment of maternal behaviour in relation with maternal experience in sheep. *Anim. Behav.* **35**, 1188–1192.

Lévy, F., Poindron, P., and Le Neindre, P. (1983). Attraction and repulsion by amniotic fluids and their olfactory control in the ewe around parturition. *Physiol. Behav.* **31**, 687–692.

Lévy, F., Gervais, R., Kindermann, U., Litterio, M., Poindron, P., and Porter R. (1991). Effects of early post-partum separation on maintenance of maternal responsiveness and selectivity in parturient ewes. *Appl. Anim. Behav. Sci.* **31**, 101–110.

Lévy, F., Kendrick, K. M., Keverne, E. B., Piketty, V., and Poindron, P. (1992). Intracerebral oxytocin is important for the onset of maternal behavior in inexperienced ewes delivered under peridural anaesthesia. *Behav. Neurosci.* **106**, 427–432.

Lévy, F., Guevara-Guzman, R., Hinton, M. R., Kendrick, K. M., and Keverne, E. B. (1993). Effects of parturition and maternal experience on noradrenaline and acetylcholine release in the olfactory bulb of sheep. *Behav. Neurosci.* **107**, 662–668.

Lévy, F., Guevara-Guzman, R., Hinton, M. R., Kendrick, K. M., and Keverne, E. B. (1995). Oxytocin and vasopressin release in the olfactory bulb of parturient ewes: Changes with maternal experience and effects on acetylcholine, gamma-aminobutyric acid, glutamate and noradrenaline release. *Brain Res.* **669**, 197–206.

Li, Q., Levy, A. D., Cabrera, T. M., Brownfield, M. S., Battaglia, G., and Van de Kar, L. D. (1993). Long-term fluoxetine, but not desipramine, inhibits the ACTH and oxytocin responses to the 5-HT1a agonist, 8-OH-DPAT, in male rats. *Brain Res.* **630**, 148–156.

Liberzon, I., Trujillo, K. A., Akil, H., and Young, E. A. (1997). Motivational properties of oxytocin in the conditioned place preference paradigm. *Neuropsychopharmacology* **17**, 353–359.

Lightman, S. L., and Young, W. S., III (1987). Vasopressin, oxytocin, dynorphin, enkephalin, and corticotrophin releasing factor mRNA stimulation in the rat. *J. Physiol. (London)* **394**, 23–29.

Lightman, S. L., and Young, W. S., III (1989). Lactation inhibits stress-mediated secretion of corticosterone and oxytocin and hypothalamic accumulation of corticotropin-releasing factor and enkephalin messenger ribonucleic acids. *Endocrinology (Baltimore)* **124**, 2358–2364.

Mansour, A., Khachaturian, H., Lewis, M. E., Akil, H., and Watson, S. J. (1998). Anatomy of CNS opioid receptors. *Trends Neurosci.* **11**, 308–315.

Martel, F. L., Nevison, C. M., Rayment, F. D., Simpson, M. D. A., and Keverne, E. B. (1993). Opioid receptor blockade reduces maternal affect and social grooming in rhesus monkeys. *Psychoneuroendocrinology* **18**, 307–321.

Martel, F. L., Nevison, C. M., Simpson, M. J. A., and Keverne, E. B. (1995). Effects of opioid receptor blockade on the social behavior of rhesus monkeys living in large family groups. *Dev. Psychobiol.* **28**, 71–84.

Martenez, N. D., Vellucci, S. V., Keverne, E. B., and Herbert, J. (1986). β-endorphin levels in the cerebrospinal fluid of male talapoin monkeys in social groups related to dominance status and the luteinizing hormone response to naloxone. *Neuroscience* **3**, 651–658.

Mason, W. A., and Mendoza, S. P. (1998). Generic aspects of primate attachments: Parents, offspring and mates. *Psychoneuroendocrinology* **23**, 765–778.

McCarthy, M. M., Kow, L. M., and Pfaff, D. W. (1992). Speculations concerning the physiological significance of central oxytocin in maternal behavior. *Ann. N.Y. Acad. Sci.* **652**, 70–82.

McGuire, B., Getz, L. L., Hofmann, J. E., Pizzuto, T., and Frase, B. (1993). Natal dispersal and philopatry in prairie voles (*Microtus ochrogaster*) in relation to population density, season, and natal social environment. *Behav. Ecol. Sociobiol.* **32**, 293–302.

Meller, R. E., Keverne, E. B., and Herbert, J. (1980). Behavioral and endocrine effects of naltrexone in male talopoin monkeys. *Pharmacol., Biochem. Behav.* **13**, 663–672.

Mendoza, S. P., and Mason, W. A. (1997). Attachment relationships in New World primates. *Ann. N.Y. Acad. Sci.* **807**, 203–209.

Modahl, C., Green L.-A., Fein, D., Morris, M., Waterhouse, L., Feinstein, C., and Levin, H. (1998). Plasma oxytocin levels in autistic children. *Biol. Psychiatry* **43**, 270–277.

Money, J. (1980). "Love & Love Sickness." Johns Hopkins Press, Baltimore, MD.

Moos, F., Freund-Mercier, M. J., Guerné, Y., Guerné, J. M., Stoeckel, M. E., and Richard, P. H. (1984). Release of oxytocin and vasopressin by magnocellular nuclei *in vitro*: Specific facilitatory effect of oxytocin on its own release. *J. Endocrinol.* **102**, 63–72.

Nelson, E., and Panksepp, J. (1996). Oxytocin mediates acquisition of maternally associated odor preferences in preweanling rat pups. *Behav. Neurosci.* **110**, 583–592.

Nelson, E., and Panksepp, J. (1998). Brain substrates of infant-mother attachment: Contributions of opioids, oxytocin and norepinephrine. *Neurosci. Biobehav. Rev.* **22**, 437–452.

Neumann, I., Russell, J. A., and Landgraf, R. (1993). Oxytocin and vasopressin release within the supraoptic and paraventricular nuclei of pregnant, parturient and lactating rats: A microrodialysis study. *Neuroscience* **53**, 65–75.

Nishimori, K., Young, L. J., Guo, Q., Wang, Z., Insel, T. R., and Matzuk, M. M. (1996). Oxytocin is required for nursing but is not essential for parturition or reproductive behavior. *Proc. Natl. Acad. Sci. U.S.A.* **93**, 11699–11704.

Numan, M. (1994a). A neural circuitry analysis of maternal behavior in the rat. *Acta Paediatr. Scand.* **83**, 19–28.

Numan, M. (1994b). Maternal behavior. *In* "The Physiology of Reproduction" (E. Knobil and J. D. Neill, eds.), 2nd ed., Vol. 2, pp. 221–301. Raven Press, New York.

Numan, M., and Corodimas, K. P. (1985). The effects of paraventricular hypothalamic lesions on maternal behavior in rats. *Physiol. Behav.* **35**, 417–425.

Numan, M., Corodimas, K. P., Jactor, M. J., and Piers, W. D. (1988). Axon-sparing lesions of the preoptic region and substantia innomonata disrupt maternal behavior in rats. *Behav. Neurosci.* **6**, 381–396.

Olson, G. A., Olson, R. D., and Kastin, A. J. (1990). Endogenous opiates. *Peptides (N.Y.)* **11**, 1277–1304.

Ostrowski, N. L. (1998). Oxytocin receptor mRNA expression in rat brain: Implications for behavioral integration and reproductive success. *Psychoneuroendocrinology* **23**, 989–1004.

Panksepp, J., Vilber, T., Bean, N. J., Coy, D. H., and Gaskin, J. (1978). Reduction of distress vocalization in chicks by opiate-like peptide. *Brain Res. Bull.* **3**, 663–667.

Panksepp, J., Siviy, S., and Normansell, L. (1985). Brain opioids and social emotions. *In* "The Psychobiology of Attachment and Separation" (M. Reite and T. Fields, eds.), pp. 3–49. Academic Press, New York.

Panksepp, J., Nelson, E., and Siviy, S. (1994). Brain opioids and mother-infant social motivation. *Acta Paediatr. Scand., Suppl.* **397**, 40–46.

Panksepp, J., Nelson, E., and Bekkedal, M. (1997). Brain systems for the mediation of social separation-distress and social-reward. *Ann. N.Y. Acad. Sci.* **807**, 78–100.

Patchev, V. K., Schlosser, S. F., Hassan, A. H. S., and Almeida, O. F. X. (1993). Oxytocin binding sites in rat limbic and hypothalamic structures: Site specific modulation by adrenal and gonadal steroids. *Neuroscience* **57**, 537–543.

Pedersen, C. A., and Prange, A. J., Jr. (1979). Induction of maternal behavior in virgin rats after intracerebroventricular administration of oxytocin. *Proc. Natl. Acad. Sci. U.S.A.* **76**, 6661–6665.

Pedersen, C. A., Caldwell, J. D., Peterson, G., Walker, C. H., and Mason, G. A. (1992). Oxytocin activation of maternal behavior in the rat. *Ann. N.Y. Acad. Sci.* **652**, 58–69.

Pederson, P. A., Archer, J. A., Monroe, J. A., and Prange, A. J. Jr. (1982). Oxytocin induces maternal behaviour in virgin female rats. *Science* **216**, 648–649.

Petersson, M., Lundeberg, T., and Uvnas-Moberg, K. (1999). Short-term increase and long-term decrease of blood pressure in response to oxytocin-potentiating effect of female steroid hormones. *J. Cardiovasc. Pharmacol.* **33**, 102–108.

Poindron, P., and Le Neindre, P., (1980). Endocrine and sensory regulation of maternal behavior in the ewe. *Adv. Study Behav.* **11**, 75–119.

Porges, S. W. (1998). Love: An emergent property of the mammalian autonomic nervous system. *Psychoneuroendocrinology* **23**, 837–862.

Poulain, P., and Pittman, Q. (1993). Oxytocin pretreatment enhances arginine vasopressin-induced motor disturbances and arginine vasopressin-induced phosphoinositol hydrolysis in rat septum: A cross-sensitization phenomenon. *J. Neuroendocrinol.* **5**, 33–39.

Reite, M., and Bocca, M. L. (1994). Physiological aspects of adult attachment. *In* "Attachment in Adults" (M. B. Sperling and W. H. Berman, eds.), pp. 98–127. Guilford Press, New York.

Reynolds, J., and Keverne, E. B. (1979). The accessory olfactory system and its role in the pheromonally mediated suppression of oestrus in grouped mice. *J. Reprod. Fertil.* **57**, 31–35.

Roberts, R. L., Zullo, A. S., and Carter, C. S. (1997). Sexual differentiation in prairie voles: The effects of corticosterone and testosterone. *Physiol. Behav.* **62**, 1379–1383.

Roberts, R. L., Williams, J.R., Wang, A. K., and Carter, C. S. (1998). Cooperative breeding and monogamy in prairie voles: Influence of the sire and geographic variation. *Anim. Behav.* **55**, 1131–1140.

Roozendaal, B., Schoorlemmer, G. H. M., Koolhaas, J. M., and Bonus, B. (1993). Cardiac, neuroendocrine, and behavioral effects of central amygdaloid vasopressinergic and oxytocinergic mechanisms under stress-free conditions in rats. *Brain Res. Bull.* **32**, 573–579.

Russell, J. A., and Leng, G. (1998). Sex, parturition and motherhood without oxytocin? *J. Endocrinol.* **157**, 343–359.

Ryff, C. S., and Singer, B. (1998). The concept of positive human health. *Psychol. Inquires* **9**, 1–19.

Sachser, N., Durschlag, M., and Hirzel, D. (1998). Social relationships and the management of stress. *Psychoneuroendocrinology* **23**, 891–904.

Schulkin, J. (1999). Corticotropin-releasing hormone signals adversity in both the placenta and the brain: Regulation by glucocorticoids and allostatic overload. *J. Endocrinol.* **161**, 349–356.

Shaffer, D., and Campbell, M. (1994). Reactive attachment disorder of infancy or early childhood. *In* "Diagnostic and Statistical Manual of Mental Disorders: DSM-IV" (A. Frances, H. A. Pincus, and H. B. First, eds.), 4th ed., pp. 116–118. American Psychiatric Association, Washington, DC.

Simpson, J. A., and Rholes, W. S. (1994). Stress and secure base relationships in adulthood. *Adv. Person Relat.* **5**, 181–204.

Simpson, M. J. A., Gore, M. A., Janus, M., and Rayment, F. D. G. (1989). Prior experience of risk and individual differences in enterprise shown by rhesus monkey infants in the second half of their first year. *Primates* **30**, 493–509.

Singh, P. J., and Hofer, M. A. (1978). Oxytocin reinstates maternal olfactory cues for nipple orientation and attachment in rat pups. *Physiol. Behav.* **20**, 385–389.

Sofroniew, M. W. (1983). Vasopressin and oxytocin in the mammalian brain and spinal cord. *Trends Neurosci.* **6**, 467–472.

Sofroniew, M. V. (1985). Vasopressin, oxytocin and their related neurophysins. *In* "Handbook of Chemical Neuroanatomy" (A. Bjorklund and T. Hokfelt, eds.), pp. 93–165. Elsevier, Amsterdam.

Solomon, N. G., and French, J., eds. (1997). "Cooperative Breeding in Mammals." Cambridge University Press, New York.

Sperling, M. B., and Berman, W. H., eds. (1994). "Attachment in Adults." Guilford Press, New York.

Stribley, J. M., and Carter, C. S. (1999). Developmental exposure to vasopressin increases aggression in adult prairie voles. *Proc. Natl. Acad. Sci. U.S.A.* **96**, 12601–12604.

Swabb, D. F., and Böer, G. J. (1994). Neuropeptides and brain development: Current perils and future potential. *J. Dev. Physiol.* **5**, 67–75.

Thoman, E. B., Conner, R. L., and Levine, S. (1970). Lactation suppresses adrenocorticosteroid activity and aggressiveness in rats. *J. Comp. Physiol. Psychol.* **70**, 364–369.

Tribollet, E., Audigier, S., Dubois-Dauphin, M., and Dreifuss, J. J. (1990). Gonadal steroids regulate oxytocin receptors but not vasopressin receptors in the brain of male and female rats. An autoradiographical study. *Brain Res.* **511**, 129–140.

Tribollet, E., Dubois-Dauphin, M., Dreifuss, J. J., Barberis, C., and Jard, S. (1992). Oxytocin receptors in the central nervous system: Distribution, development, and species differences. *Ann. N.Y. Acad. Sci.* **652**, 29–38.

Uvnas-Moberg, K. (1994). Role of efferent and afferent vagal nerve activity during reproduction: Integrating function of oxytocin on metabolism and behavior. *Psychoneuroendocrinology* 19, 687–695.

Uvnas-Moberg, K. (1997). Physiological and endocrine effects of social contact. *Ann. N.Y. Acad. Sci.* 807, 146–163.

Uvnas-Moberg, K. (1998). Oxytocin may mediate the benefits of positive social interaction and emotions. *Psychoneuroendocrinology* 23, 819–836.

Uvnas-Moberg, K., Bjorkstrand, E., Hillegaart, V., and Ahlenius, S. (1999). Oxytocin as a possible mediator of SSRI-induced antidepressant effects. *Psychopharmacology* 142, 95–101.

Van Kesteren, R. E., Smit, A. B., Dirkds, R. W., Dewith, N. D., Deraerts, W. P. M., and Joosse, J. (1992). Evolution of the vasopressin/oxytocin superfamily: Characterization of a cDNA encoding a vasopressin-related precursor, preproconopressin, from the mollusc *Lymnaea stagnalis*. *Proc. Natl. Acad. Sci. U.S.A.* 89, 4593–4597.

Van Leeuwnen, F. W., Caffe, A. R., and De Vries, G. J. (1985). Vasopressin cells in the bed nucleus of the stria terminalis of the rat: Sex differences and the influence of androgens. *Brain Res.* 325, 391–394.

Wang, Z. (1995). Species differences in the vasopressin-immunoreactive pathways in the bed nucleus of the stria terminalis and medial amygdaloid nucleus in prairie voles (*Microtus ochrogaster*) and meadow voles (*Microtus pennsylvanicus*). *Behav. Neurosci.* 109, 305–311.

Wang, Z., Ferris, C. F., and De Vries, G. J. (1993). The role of septal vasopressin innervation in paternal behavior in prairie voles (*Microtus ochrogaster*). *Proc. Natl. Acad. Sci. U.S.A.* 91, 400–404.

Wang, Z., Zhou, L., Hulihan, T., and Insel, T. R. (1996). Immunoreactivity of central vasopressin and oxytocin pathways in microtine rodents: A quantitative comparative study. *J. Comp. Neurol.* 366, 726–737.

Wang, Z., Young, L. J., Liu, Y., and Insel, T. R. (1997). Species differences in vasopressin receptor binding are evident early in development: Comparative anatomic studies in prairie and montane voles. *J. Comp. Neurol.* 378, 535–546.

Wang, Z., Yu, G., Cascio, C., Liu, Y., Gingrich, B., and Insel, T. R. (1999). Dopamine D2 receptor-mediated regulation of partner preferences in female prairie voles (*Microtus ochrogaster*): A mechanism for pair bonding. *Behav. Neurosci.* 113, 602–611.

Wardlaw, S. L., and Franz, A. G. (1983). Brain β-endorphin during pregnancy, parturition, and the post-partum period. *Endocrinology (Baltimore)* 113, 1664–1668.

Williams, J. R., Catania, K. C., and Carter, C. S. (1992a). Development of partner preferences in female praire voles (*Microtus ochrogaster*): The role of social and sexual experience. *Horm. Behav.* 26, 339–349.

Williams, J. R. Slotnick, B. M., Kirkpatrick, B. W., and Carter, C. S. (1992b). Olfactory bulb removal affects partner preference development and estrus induction in female prairie voles. *Physiol. Behav.* 52, 635–639.

Williams, J. R., Insel, T. R., Harbaugh, C. R., and Carter, C. S. (1994). Oxytocin centrally administered facilitates formation of a partner preference in female prairie voles (*Microtus ochrogaster*). *J. Neuroendocrinol.* 6, 247–250.

Winslow, J. T., and Insel, T. R. (1991). Endogenous opioids: Do they modulate the rat pup's response to social isolation? *Behav. Neurosci.* 105, 253–263.

Winslow, J. T., and Insel, T. R. (1993). Effects of central vasopressin administration to infant rats. *Eur. J. Pharmacol.* 233, 101–107.

Winslow, J. T., Hastings, N., Carter, C. S., Harbaugh, C. R., and Insel, T. R. (1993). A role for central vasopressin in pair bonding in monogamous prairie voles. *Nature (London)* 365, 545–548.

Winslow, J. T., Hearn, E. F., Ferguson, J., Young, L. J., Matzuk, M. M., and Insel, T. R. (2000). Infant vocalization, adult aggression, and fear behavior of an oxytocin null mutant mouse. *Horm. Behav.* 37, 145–155.

Witt, D. M. (1997). Regulatory mechanisms of oxytocin-mediated sociosexual behavior. *Ann. N.Y. Acad. Sci.* 807, 22–41.

Witt, D. M., Carter, C. S., Chayer, R., and Adams, K. (1989). Patterns of behavior during postpartum oestrus in prairie voles, *Microtus ochrogaster*. *Anim. Behav.* 39, 528–534.

Witt, D. M., Carter, C. S., and Walton, D. (1990). Central and peripheral effects of oxytocin administration in prairie voles (*Microtus ochrogaster*). *Pharmacol., Biochem. Behav.* 37, 63–69.

Witt, D. M., Carter, C. S., and Insel, T. R. (1991). Oxytocin receptor binding in female prairie voles: Endogenous and exogenous oestradiol stimulation. *J. Neuroendocrinol.* 3, 155–161.

Witt, D. M., Winslow, J. T., and Insel, T. R. (1992). Enhanced social interactions in rats following chronic, centrally infused oxytocin. *Pharmacol., Biochem. Behav.* 43, 855–861.

Young, L. J., Juot, B., Nilsen, R., Wang, Z., and Insel, T. R. (1996). Species differences in central oxytocin receptor gene expression: Comparative analysis of promoter sequences. *J. Neuroendocrinol.* 8, 777–783.

Young, L. J., Wang, Z., and Insel, T. R. (1998). Neuroendocrine bases of monogamy. *Trends Neurosci.* 21, 71–75.

Young, L. J., Lilsen, R., Waymire, K. G., MacGregor, G. R., and Insel, T. R. (1999). Increased affiliative response to vasopressin in mice expressing the V1a receptor from a monogamous vole. *Nature (London)* 400, 766–768.

5

Hormonal Processes in the Development and Expression of Aggressive Behavior

Neal G. Simon

Department of Biological Sciences
Lehigh University
Bethlehem, Pennsylvania 18015

I. INTRODUCTION

Characterizing hormonal processes involved in the development and expression of conspecific offensive aggressive behavior is the broad objective of this chapter. This statement has a specific purpose beyond delineating a primary goal; it also serves as a necessary boundary. The need for limitation in scope is based on the breadth of behaviors subsumed under "aggression" and the potential role of hormones in several of these forms. These circumstances render any single effort to cover the entire field at best cursory, at worst frequently in error, or a multiyear undertaking that would surely require extensive revision immediately on completion. Although the interested reader can turn to Moyer (1974) for descriptions of the various forms of aggression, the most frequently studied model in behavioral neuroendocrinology continues to be testosterone-dependent intermale aggression. This type of aggressive behavior is exhibited between conspecifics and determines dominance status. The interactions generally include investigative, threat, and attack behaviors. The form and extent of these behaviors as well as other related components have been described carefully in numerous species (Grant and Mackintosh, 1963, Marler and Hamilton, 1966; Scott, 1966; Smith, 1977; Wittenberger, 1981). A wealth of information is available about this system, spanning gene expression, development, steroid receptor function, and related processes, allowing in-depth consideration. Considerably less attention has been paid to the potential role of hormonal processes in conspecific interfemale aggressive behavior despite a compelling group of studies conducted in the 1980s that demonstrated that if females were tested in small group settings (e.g., housed in triads), they regularly displayed aggression toward other females, juvenile males, or gonadectomized adult males (Brain and Haug, 1992; Haug *et al.*, 1992). These experiments further established that neurosteroids, which are synthesized in the brains of humans and other mammals (Baulieu, 1997; Compagnone and Mellon, 2000; Robel and Baulieu, 1995), played a major role in the regulation of this female-typical form of aggression. Given the identification of this hormone-behavior relationship, interfemale aggression also will be considered, although substantially less is known about underlying mechanisms compared to males. Several factors contributed to this state of affairs. Among the most prominent were the general observations that females, except when lactating, almost never displayed aggression in typical resident-intruder tests, which generally used individual males that were nonaggressive as a standard opponent, and that if females were to exhibit aggression, its regulation would

---

follow principles that were developed from studies with males. For example, androgen treatment regimens that restored aggressive behavior in males were given to females in several studies during the 1960s and early 1970s; these were ineffective in promoting aggression (Gandelman, 1980; Svare, 1983). Also, removal of the testes was highly effective in reducing male-typical conspecific aggression. These results, plus a host of related findings, led to a dominant interest in testosterone (T) and, as a corollary, an almost exclusive focus on males.

In discussing hormonal function in both male-typical and female-typical offensive aggression, the focus, to a large extent, will be on relatively recent work to highlight developments in biochemistry, cell biology, and molecular biology that have allowed the framing of integrative regulatory models that span gene function through behavioral expression, although not without debate in some areas (Balaban et al., 1996; Crawley and Paylor, 1997; Miczek, 1999). Ultimately, it is likely that advances in proteomics (see discussions in Collins and Jegalian, 1999; Eisenberg et al., 2000; Lockhart and Winzeler, 2000; Vukmirovic and Tilghman, 2000) will be critical for establishing full models of behavioral regulation, although this line of research is clearly in its earliest formative stages with regard to aggression and other behaviors.

A. Three Hypotheses: Causal, Facilitative, and Neuromodulator

Progress in understanding the role of androgens and estrogens in conspecific aggression can be marked through changing perspectives on how these steroids contribute to behavioral expression. Early castration–hormone replacement studies in males were predicated largely on a *causal hypothesis*. Simply put, T, the principal secretion of the testis, was considered the agent directly responsible for the display of aggression. This viewpoint and the abundant studies in numerous species that were interpreted as providing support (Albert et al., 1993; Archer, 1988; Beatty, 1979; Brain, 1979, 1983; Gandelman, 1980; Monaghan and Glickman, 1992; Simon et al., 1993) had a dramatic and ongoing impact beyond their contribution to basic research on behavioral regulation by generating substantial interest among clinical researchers and practitioners about the potential role of T in what might

be termed "murder and mayhem." The focus of these studies was on the possible existence of a positive systematic relationship between circulating levels of T and violent offenses ranging from assault to rape to murder (e.g., Albert et al., 1993; Archer, 1991, 1994; Banks and Dabbs, 1996; Dabbs and Hargrove, 1997; Isaacson et al., 1998; Rada et al., 1983; Simon, 1981; Simon and Coccaro, 1999; Sullivan, 2000; Virkkunen et al., 1996; Yesalis et al., 1993). In general, these studies have produced equivocal results for myriad reasons, with one of the most important being that testosterone-dependent aggression studied in nonhuman mammals and other species is hardly analogous to either planned or spontaneous violent, injurious behavior. Offensive aggression between same sex members within a species is a productive behavior that determines dominance status and, as a result, provides resource access. From this vantage point, it then should be asked if there are analogous behaviors in human males and females. Interestingly, there do appear to be behaviors associated with dominance (e.g., competitive interactions) and the likelihood of an aggressive response to threat that may be related to T in humans; these are discussed here. At the same time, little research has been directed at the potential role of neurosteroids in nonhuman primate or human aggression, an intriguing possibility that awaits experimental attention. On this basis, another aspect of this review is an effort to delineate how and to what extent basic research with animal models of hormone-dependent conspecific aggression can inform our understanding of various types of human aggressive behavior (Albert et al., 1993; Mazur and Booth, 1998; Simon and Coccaro, 1999).

Around 1980, prevailing views of hormone-behavior relationships in the context of aggressive behavior shifted from a casual to a *facilitative hypothesis*. This perspective saw androgens and estrogens as either increasing or decreasing the likelihood that aggressive behavior would be exhibited, largely on the basis of endocrine and physiological status that, at least in male rodents, presumably altered sensitivity to pheromones that served as aggression-eliciting stimuli. This change to a more probabilistic model was an improvement, if for no other reason than it shed the explicit invariance tied to a causal hypothesis. Although the concept of hormones as agents that facilitate aggression remains part of the contemporary literature, it still suffers from a major limitation, notably an almost exclusive focus on the male. On the surface, this seemed rational because females, obviously, have very low T production and investigators were exploring the contribution of testicular hormones in male–male interactions. Nevertheless, several studies with females, including humans, have measured levels of circulating androgens and estrogens to determine potential relationships (e.g., Cashdan, 1995; Dougherty *et al.,* 1997; Dabbs and Hargrove, 1997; Persky *et al.,* 1971, 1982). The conceptual basis for this approach was that aggression displayed by females (other than that displayed during lactation) necessarily would follow the same hormonal regulatory paths that had been identified in males. The general failure to secure data in accord with this *common path* hypothesis was not surprising for several reasons, among the obvious being that the endocrine physiology of males and females is so different. Regardless, as noted earlier, the 1980s saw numerous studies describing conspecific aggression among female rodents in group settings that was not part of maternal behavior (Brain and Haug, 1992; Haug *et al.,* 1981, 1992). The hormonal contribution to this behavior involves a novel class of steroids known as neurosteroids (Baulieu, 1997; Robel and Baulieu, 1995; Young *et al.,* 1995, 1996). Particularly important is the neurosteroid dehydroepiandrosterone (DHEA), a weak androgen that directly modulates γ-amino butyric acid ($GABA_A$), σ_1, and the N-methyl-D-aspartate (NMDA) receptor (Compagnone and Mellon, 2000; Maurice *et al.,* 1989) and that also can serve as a substrate for the production of other, more potent steroids (Labrie *et al.,* 1998; Robel and Baulieu, 1995).

An important theoretical question is whether a construct that bridges androgenic and estrogenic influences on aggressive behavior in both males and females can be framed or whether distinct, sex-constrained models are needed. The position taken in this review is the former, based on the premise that the contribution of androgens and estrogens to the regulation of aggression is through their actions as modulators of neurochemical function. This *neuromodulator hypothesis,* which is a refinement of the facilitation model, was developed by incorporating available data on endocrine, peptidergic, and neurochemical systems that are currently recognized as principal factors in the regulation of conspecific aggression. The potential strength of this model is twofold. First, it

is integrative, stressing a systems perspective; second, it may potentially provide a rational basis for bridging basic and clinical considerations related to hormonal function and aggressive behaviors. The chapter reviews the state of the field and develops the neuromodulator hypothesis. This is accomplished through a consideration of hormonal processes that regulate aggression in adulthood, developmental events that contribute to the establishment of functional pathways, representative major neurochemical systems, and their interactions in the specific context of aggressive behavior.

B. Test Paradigms

The contribution of gonadal steroids to the display of offensive aggression has been assessed in numerous species in controlled laboratory settings, seminaturalistic environments, and field observations, and by a host of methods in humans. Rodents serve as the primary model in lab environments and the most common test paradigms for assessing offensive aggressive behavior are presented. For males, these include the *resident-intruder model* and *isolation-induced offense.* In the first, resident males are housed singly or with a female. The period of individual housing can range from 2–7 days prior to the initial test for aggression. The stimulus intruder, a male, is by intention a low-aggression animal (accomplished by continuous group housing) or completely nonaggressive (produced by anosmia through olfactory bulbectomy or zinc sulfate administration; see Section II.C for additional details). These stimulus preparations are designed to allow any offensive aggression that is displayed to be ascribed to the resident, experimental male. In the second method, which is more common in psychopharmacological investigations, males are housed individually for extended periods (at least 14 days and typically 30 days) prior to testing. It produces highly aggressive males, but is now widely recognized for inducing significant changes in neurotransmitter function, which constrains its utility. In these and other paradigms, scoring systems can vary widely, ranging from ethoexperimental analyses that measure numerous components of offensive behavior to simple measurements of biting attacks (Brain and Haug, 1992; Miczek *et al.,* 1994; Olivier *et al.,* 1995; Simon, 1979; Simon *et al.,* 1983). In females, the test paradigm in which offensive aggression is displayed other than during lactation involves a different social structure than that used with males. Specifically, females are housed in triads. Intruders can be either lactating, intact, or ovariectomized adult females, with lactating females most commonly employed. Latency to first attack and number of attacks are commonly measured as indices of offensive aggression, although numerous other aggression-related behaviors also may be assessed (e.g., Haug *et al.,* 1986; Perché *et al.,* 2000).

Among other nonprimate species, lizards and birds have been employed as subjects with increasing frequency. In lizards, offensive behaviors include raising up, exposing ventral patches if present, and shuddering. Territorial or resident males exhibit combinations of hissing, chasing, snapping, and biting (e.g., Ruby, 1978, Matter *et al.,* 1998). In birds, commonly measured agonistic behaviors include displacements of conspecifics from aerial pursuits, charges, and flying directly at a perched stimulus. These behaviors can be aggregated under the category "chases." Other agonistic behaviors include species-typical displays, postures, and vocalizations, although their diversity precludes a detailed discussion (interested readers can refer for examples to Marler and Hamilton, 1966; Smith, 1977).

In nonhuman primates, a variety of focal sampling methods have been used. Multiple sessions are routinely scored over periods of time that range from weeks to years. Offensive aggressive behaviors include, for example, displacements (forcing a conspecific to move from its position), threats (encompassing a range of facial expressions, gestures, and displays), chases (the object of the chase flees), and physical assaults (bites, hits, or slaps). In humans, indices from paper-and-pencil tests through contest results to violent attacks have been used to indicate aggressiveness or aggressive acts.

The differences among scoring systems and indices represent a substantive issue in the study of hormonal, neurochemical, and other factors that contribute to the display of offensive aggression. This lack of consistency represents an ongoing issue for the field. Investigators should assess the evaluative systems as a source of variation among studies.

II. MALES

The ability of T to facilitate the display of intermale aggressive behavior in a broad range of species is one of the most widely recognized relationships in behavioral neuroendocrinology. This was demonstrated clearly and unequivocally through castration–hormone replacement experiments and studies of seasonal effects on testicular function and behavior (Nelson, 1995), although exceptions have been noted (e.g., Wingfield, 1994; Wingfield *et al.,* 1997). With the establishment of this fundamental relationship, the focus of research shifted to a mechanistic orientation. The elaboration of the genomic mechanism of action of steroids (see any of several excellent reviews, e.g., French *et al.,* 1990; Gorski *et al.,* 1986; Jordan, 1995; McEwen *et al.,* 1979; Muldoon, 1980; Tsai and O'Malley, 1994) defined a number of processes that required investigation to develop a comprehensive model of neuroendocrine regulation. Among the major areas requiring attention were metabolism, particularly the contributions of aromatization and 5α reduction, steroid-receptor binding, nuclear acceptor site interactions, transcriptional regulation, and protein synthesis.

A. Four Research Goals

The bulk of research on the steroidal mechanism(s) regulating aggression has relied primarily on rodent models, although a number of contributing studies have employed species ranging from arctic charr to leopard gecko to various birds (Eloffson *et al.,* 2000; Rhen and Crews, 2000; Simon *et al.,* 1996; Wingfield *et al.,* 1997). Broadly speaking, these investigations have had four goals. The most frequent was to define the pathways in the adult central nervous system (CNS) through which T could promote the display of aggressive behavior. Comparisons of sex and strain differences in the response to this testicular hormone and its major metabolites, estradiol (E_2) and dihydrotestosterone (DHT), as well as pharmacological studies using enzymatic inhibitors and receptor antagonists, were powerful tools in elaborating these pathways (Brain *et al.,* 1991; Brain and Bowden, 1979; Clark and Nowell, 1979a,b; Hau *et al.,* 2000; Simon *et al.,* 1981; Simon and Masters, 1987; Simon and Perry, 1988; Soma *et al.,* 1999; Tokarz, 1986, 1987). The finding of pronounced sex differences in sensitivity to the aggression-promoting property of T, DHT, and E_2, provided the foundation for the second objective, defining the perinatal hormonal conditions that established these functional systems. More precisely, investigators sought to delineate the specific effects of E_2 and DHT on the sexual differentiation of each pathway. To characterize developmental processes, these studies used a variety of perinatal hormone treatments and naturalistic models. Prominent examples of the latter are the uterine position effect in mice and rats and the manipulation of temperature in amphibians (Crews *et al.*, 1998; Vom Saal, 1979, 1984). The third objective was to use these biobehavioral findings as the basis for biochemical and immunochemical studies of steroid receptor function to identify potential cellular mechanisms involved in the hormonal regulation of aggression. The availability of mice with specific steroid receptor and other gene deletions (knockouts) is a relatively recent development that has contributed to progress in this area (Anagnastopoutos *et al.*, 2001; Maxson, 1996, 1998; Nelson, 1997; Nelson and Young, 1998; Ogawa *et al.*, 1997, 1999; Shih *et al.*, 1999; Tecott and Barondes, 1996), although some caution is required in assessing these studies (Balaban *et al.*, 1996; Crawley and Paylor, 1997; Miczek, 1999). The fourth and broadest goal was to integrate these results to describe the cell and molecular processes that regulate sensitivity or insensitivity to the aggression-promoting property of gonadal steroids. To achieve this final objective requires a perspective that extends beyond a strict consideration of only hormonal systems. More specifically, it appears that progress in this area will be tied to defining interactions between steroidal and relevant neurochemical systems. Although there is an abundant literature on the neurochemical regulation of aggression that, not surprisingly, implicates virtually every known neurotransmitter (Kruk, 1991; Miczek *et al.*, 1994; Siegel *et al.*, 1999), attempts to characterize the interface between neuroendocrine and neurochemical systems is a relatively recent development in the aggression literature (Simon *et al.*, 1998). Interestingly, these relationships were addressed at an earlier stage in studies of female-typical aggression than they were in male-typical fighting behavior. The most extensive studies of hormonal modulation to this point have been in regard to serotonin and vasopressin function in males; the modulation of $GABA_A$ receptor function by DHEA has been a major focus of studies in females. These relationships are reviewed here as examples of the neuromodulator hypothesis. In addition, the molecular conservation of steroid receptors, neurochemical systems (Baker, 1997; Hoyle, 1999; Mohr *et al.*, 1995; Peroutka, 1992, 1994; Peroutka and Howell, 1994; Peroutka *et al.*, 1990; Van Kesteren and Geraerts, 1998; Vernier *et al.*, 1993; Whitfield *et al.*, 1999), and their regulation suggests that findings with animal models may help facilitate the development of hypotheses concerning how T and neurosteriods influence the expression of certain forms of aggression in humans.

B. Regulation in the Adult Brain

Understanding how T facilitates the display of aggression requires characterizing the specific contributions of E_2, the product of aromatization, and DHT, the 5α-reduced metabolite of T, in behavioral regulation. While it is widely recognized that aromatization is an important step in the promotion of aggression by T (Brain and Haug, 1992; Callard, 1990a,b; Simon *et al.*, 1996), a small but substantive body of evidence also has demonstrated that androgens can directly induce male-typical fighting behavior (Gravance *et al.*, 1996; Kamis and Brain, 1985; Luttge and Hall, 1973; Simon *et al.*, 1985; Simon and Masters, 1987). Embedded in the process of defining the contributions of each metabolite are related questions about the distribution of relevant enzymes (Celotti *et al.*, 1997; Martini *et al.*, 1993; Melcangi *et al.*, 1998; Negri-Cesi *et al.*, 1996; Sasano *et al.*, 1998; Schlinger, 1997; Silverin *et al.*, 2000) and their relationship to neuroanatomical sites that had been implicated in the regulation of male-typical aggression. A number of approaches, primarily with rodent models, have been employed to address the role of T metabolites. These included behavioral assessments in mice with naturally occurring mutations (e.g., Tfm), targeted disruptions of specific steroid receptor genes (ERα, ERβ), pharmacological manipulations (antagonists, enzyme inhibitors), and comparisons among outbred strains in the response to specifically acting androgens and estrogens after gonadectomy (e.g., diethylstilbestrol, methyltrienolone). These investigations generally used the resident-intruder test paradigm. The results demonstrated that there are four pathways through which T can promote the display of aggression in the adult male brain (Simon and

TABLE 1
Hormonal Pathways Identified in the Adult Male Brain That Facilitate the Display of Offensive Intermale Aggression[a]

Genotype	Estrogen-sensitive	Androgen-sensitive	Synergistic (estrogen + androgen)	Direct T mediated
CF-1	+++	++	−	−
CFW	+++	−	−	−
CD-1	−	++	+++	−
C57BL/6J	−	−	−	++

[a] Plus (+) and minus (−) signs indicate relative sensitivity or insensitivity. Tests for aggressive behavior consisted of introducing an olfactory bulbectomized stimulus male into the home cage of the experimental male for 10 min. Resident males were housed individually for 48 hr prior to the initial test for aggression and tests were given every other day for 10 days. Olfactory bulbectomized males were used because they reliably elicit aggression, but do not fight back in response to attacks. This allows any aggression that is displayed to be reliably ascribed to the resident experimental male. Aggressive behavior was scored as the sum of threats and biting attacks, a statistically derived index (Simon *et al*, 1983). This procedure is typical of the resident-intruder paradigm, which is used extensively in studies of intermale aggression (e.g., Olivier *et al.*, 1994; Simon *et al.*, 1998).

Whalen, 1986; Simon *et al.,* 1996; see Table 1): an androgen-sensitive pathway, which responds to T itself or its 5α-reduced metabolite, DHT; an estrogen-sensitive pathway, which uses E_2 derived by aromatization of T; a synergistic or combined pathway, in which both the androgenic and estrogenic metabolites of T are used to facilitate behavioral expression; and a direct T-mediated pathway that appears to utilize T itself. Not all of these steroid-sensitive systems are present in every male. Rather, the functional pathway appears to be determined by genotype, as seen through castration–hormone replacement studies in which gonadectomized males were treated with specifically acting androgens or estrogens and then tested for aggression. Using the mouse as a model, experiments showed that, for example, CF-1 males have both an androgen- and estrogen-sensitive regulatory pathway. CFW males have only an estrogen-responsive system, whereas CD-1 males evidence both an androgenic and a synergistic pathway (Finney and Erpino, 1976; Simon and Masters, 1987, 1988; Simon and Whalen, 1986; see Table 1). The most commonly recognized system uses E_2 as the active aggression-promoting agent, which supports the importance of aromatization and a major role for the estrogen receptor, a mechanistic step that will be considered in greater detail later. Regardless of the functional system, in males these pathways share the basic feature of high sensitivity. That is, after the postcastration decline in fighting behavior in rats or mice, it takes an average of only 2–3 days of hormone treatment with the appropriate steroid at physiological doses to restore aggression to levels seen in intact males. This is consistent with the importance of a ge-

nomic effect in the activation of conspecific intermale aggression.

Additional insights into these neuroendocrine regulatory systems were obtained through several studies in which androgenic treatments were used successfully to induce male-like aggression in female mice. The female CNS does have an androgen-sensitive pathway that can be activated by chronic exposure to T, DHT, or methyltrienolone (R1881), a nonaromatizeable androgen (Schechter *et al.,* 1981; Simon *et al.,* 1985). This system differs from that seen in males because of its low sensitivity; that is, it takes approximately 16–21 days of androgen exposure after ovariectomy to induce male-like fighting behavior in a mouse model. An even more dramatic difference is that the adult female brain is completely insensitive to the aggression-promoting property of estrogens (Simon *et al.,* 1985; Simon and Gandelman, 1978). Thus, the neural substrate that uses androgen to activate male-typical aggression is present in both sexes, but there is a relative sexual dimorphism in target tissue sensitivity. By contrast, there is an absolute sexual dimorphism in the capacity to respond to the aggression-activating property of estrogen. These observations raise intriguing questions about plasticity in the adult female brain and how androgens and estrogens contribute to these effects.

C. Neuroanatomical Substrates

The finding of distinct hormonal pathways adds an element of complexity to efforts directed at characterizing the neuroanatomical circuitry for testosterone-facilitated offensive aggression. Lesion and implant studies in rodents have identified subregions of the amygdala, lateral septum (LS), bed nucleus of the stria terminalis (BNST), anterior hypothalamus (AHTH), and medial preoptic area (MPOA) as part of a presumptive steroid-sensitive circuit for this behavior (Koolhaas *et al.,* 1998; Lisciotto *et al.,* 1990; McGregor and Herbert, 1992; Owen *et al.,* 1974; Slotnick and McMullen, 1972; Simon *et al.,* 1996, 1998). The interconnections among these regions are well documented, as is the presence of target neurons for estrogen and androgen, which lends further support to their involvement. At the same time, conspecific offensive aggression in rodents is dependent on an olfactory stimulus. Male rodents produce an androgen-dependent aggression-eliciting pheromone, and its critical role has been demonstrated extensively in the mouse (Bean, 1982; Ropartz, 1968; Rowe and Edwards, 1971; Mugford and Nowell, 1970). The capacity to detect this pheromone is a prerequisite for the display of attack behavior (Edwards *et al.,* 1992; Denenberg *et al.,* 1973; Clancy *et al.,* 1984) and cells in the vomeronasal organ and accessory olfactory bulb involved in this response recently were defined using c-fos immunocytochemistry (Kumar *et al.,* 1999). In addition, an as yet undefined pathway in the adult male mouse brain from the olfactory bulbs to the MPOA is part of the circuit for offensive aggression (Edwards *et al.,* 1993). However, the necessary tract-tracing, fos immunoreactivity, and steroid receptor colocalization studies have not yet been conducted to fully define this circuitry in the mouse brain. Greater progress in defining the chemosensitive circuitry linked to conspecific aggression has been made in other rodents. Using c-fos immunoreactivity, a functional pathway from the vomeronasal organ through the olfactory tracts to the medial amygdala (MAMYG), bed nucleus of the stria terminalis, lateral septum, anterior hypothalamus and other relevant structures has been demonstrated in hamsters and rats (Delville *et al.,* 2000; Kollack-Walker and Newman, 1995; Martinez *et al.,* 1998; Newman, 1999).

Other elements, however, constrain progress in defining neuroanatomical substrates. For example, the identification of distinct androgen-sensitive and estrogen-sensitive pathways raises the possibility that these systems are at least partially independent. The fact that the distribution of androgen receptor and estrogen receptor is not identical suggests that this may

well be the case. To date, no studies have addressed the hypothesis of steroid-specific neuroanatomical systems. Next, aggression itself is a complex behavior with multiple components, many of which are non-reflexive. This aspect of conspecific aggression led to a *de facto* strategy in which investigators sought to define regions that were either tied to distinct components of the behavioral sequence or that appeared to serve as major points of integration. Examples of the former include portions of the hypothalamus that, based on detailed electrical stimulation studies in rats, appear to constitute a putative attack area, as well as elegant studies of the neuroanatomy of defensive rage in the cat (Adamec, 1997; Kruk, 1991; Kruk *et al.,* 1998; Shaikh and Siegel, 1994; Siegel *et al.,* 1997, 1999). However, these findings did not seem to be tied to either androgenic or estrogenic effects. Regarding integration, the MAMYG, MPOA, AHTH, and LS seem to represent important sites based on findings in rats, hamsters, and mice (Delville *et al.,* 1996a; Ferris, 2000; Koolhaas *et al.,* 1998; Simon *et al.,* 1998). These investigations bridged findings on the chemical neuroanatomy of offensive aggression, in which serotonin and vasopressin have important regulatory roles, with manipulation of the steroidal environment. Interestingly, putative molecular linkages between androgens, estrogens, and subtypes of vasopressin and serotonin receptors can be identified. Determining whether these linkage are functional and their relationship to the physiology of conspecific aggression would represent a significant step in defining the neuroanatomical substrate(s) for this behavior.

Another approach that may prove valuable for defining the androgen-sensitive system involves the adult female, in which progressive changes in neuroanatomical organization can be assessed as the capacity to display male-typical aggression is induced by chronic androgen treatment. The 16- to 21-day treatment course required for behavioral activation may provide an opportunity to identify androgen-induced changes in neuronal structure and function that may be critical for the display of male-typical aggression.

D. Development of Regulatory Pathways

The presence of robust differences in gonadal steroid sensitivity between males and females in adulthood

Estrogen-Sensitive

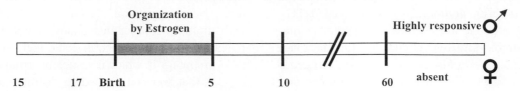

Androgen-Sensitive

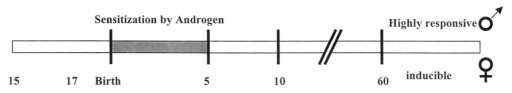

FIGURE 1   A summary of the major hormonal events and their timing in the establishment of androgen-sensitive and estrogen-sensitive regulatory pathways for offensive male-typical aggressive behavior in the mouse. The development of each pathway depends on exposure to specific testosterone metabolites during a restricted period shortly after birth. Reprinted with permission from Simon, N. *et al.* Development and expression of hormonal systems regulating aggression. *Ann. NY Acad. Sci. 794*, 8–17. © 1996 New York Academy of Science.

points to a pivotal role of hormonal events during sexual differentiation in the establishment of androgen-sensitive and estrogen-sensitive pathways. Given the essential role of T in the masculinization of the CNS (e.g., Cooke *et al.*, 1998; Godwin and Crews, 1997), several studies assayed circulating levels of this hormone during perinatal development and then determined whether these influenced either sensitivity to the aggression-promoting property of T or level of aggressiveness later in life (Compaan *et al.*, 1993a, 1994b; de Ruiter *et al.*, 1993). Although some intriguing as well as controversial data have been obtained, the presence of distinct hormonal pathways in the adult brain, combined with the recognized importance of aromatization in differentiation of the CNS (Balthazart, 1997; Hutchison, 1997), indicated that a more refined approach was required to elaborate the specific contributions of T, DHT, and E_2 in the establishment of particular pathways. This issue was addressed through studies that used pharmacological tools such as enzymatic inhibitors and receptor antagonists or through administration of specifically acting androgens and estrogens to characterize the

potential role of the metabolites of T in the development of male-typical androgen-sensitive and estrogen-sensitive regulatory systems. Another important consideration was to narrow the time when each of the systems was established. This necessitated assessments of hormonal effects both late in prenatal development and early in the postnatal period in rodents such as rats and mice. A model based on findings from a series of studies in our laboratory (Cologer-Clifford *et al.*, 1992; Klein and Simon, 1991; Simon and Cologer-Clifford, 1991; Simon and Whalen, 1987) is summarized in Fig. 1.

A more global approach to defining the developmental contributions of T is exemplified in a series of studies that compared aromatase activity and the response to exogenously administered T in short attack latency (SAL) and long attack latency mice (LAL). These lines differ substantially in their propensity for displaying aggressive behavior (Compaan *et al.*, 1992, 1993, 1994a,b; de Ruiter *et al.*, 1992; Koolhaas *et al.*, 1998; Sluyter *et al.*, 1996; van Oortmerssen and Sluyter, 1994). An intriguing feature of these strains is the apparent absence of either prenatal or postnatal maternal effects on the genetically selected characteristic, attack latency, demonstrating both the robustness of the genetic component and the potential for identifying candidate genes linked to this aspect of male-typical aggression. In the aggregate, the results showed that SAL males exhibited higher levels of aromatase activity in the amygdala and lower levels in the preoptic area than LAL males, a different pattern of T secretion between embryonic day 17 and postnatal day 1, and larger mean anogenital distance, an effect indicative of greater target tissue sensitivity to androgen. These observations led the authors to suggest that both enhanced E_2 formation and responsiveness to androgen contributed to differential organization of the neural substrate for aggression.

These and related studies in birds, lizards, and other species (Balthazart, 1997; Hutchison *et al.,* 1999; Rhen and Crews, 2000; Simon *et al.,* 1993) provide a broad view of the factors that establish the neural substrates for conspecific intermale aggression. Important roles for E_2, the product of aromatization, and environmental factors such as temperature have been demonstrated. These findings do not, however, allow for an analysis of how distinct pathways are organized, a process that at a minimum requires examining the specific contributions of the androgenic and estrogenic metabolites of T to each system.

1. Estrogen Response System

The ontogeny of the estrogen-responsive system has been defined using a mouse model (Klein and Simon, 1991; Simon and Gandelman, 1978; Simon and Whalen, 1987; Simon *et al.,* 1993, 1996). This system is organized by an effect of E_2 on neural tissue between days 1 and 4 postpartum (gestation in mice is 19 days). Results that led to this conclusion were: (1) males delivered by cesarean section and castrated immediately were incapable of responding to the aggression-promoting property of E_2 as adults; (2) if gonadectomy occurred on postnatal day 10, the estrogen-sensitive system was fully competent; (3) the administration of diethylstilbestrol (DES), a synthetic, specifically acting estrogen, on day 1 or the aromatizable androgen T on day 1–3 masculinized the subsequent response to E_2, while R1881, a nonaromatizable androgen, was ineffective; and (4) adult female mice are completely insensitive to the ability of E_2 to induce male-like aggression. These observations show

that the prenatal hormonal environment does not contribute to the development of an estrogen-sensitive regulatory pathway, a finding consistent with the existence of a critical period during the first few postpartum days for the establishment of this pathway. An important set of issues that have not been addressed experimentally in the context of aggression involves the cell, molecular, and neuroanatomical effects induced by estradiol during this period that establish the subsequent capacity to display aggression in response to this T metabolite during adulthood. This is a provocative question in behavioral neuroendocrinology because its resolution may provide some insight into the basis for the sexual dimorphism in the response to estradiol during adulthood.

A number of investigators have thoughtfully considered developmental effects of estradiol on neuroanatomical structures, their organization, and neurochemical systems (e.g., Cooke *et al.,* 1998; Gorski, 1985; MacLusky *et al.,* 1997; Segovia *et al.,* 1999; Toran-Allerand, 2000; Toran-Allerand *et al.,* 1999). Several of these effects are considered extensively elsewhere in this volume. One area that has received continuing interest is the possibility of estrogen-induced changes in chromatin organization, a process that potentially represents a mechanism for establishing tissue-specific gene regulation (Badia *et al.,* 2000; Beato *et al.,* 1996; Davie and Spencer, 2000; Elgin and Workman, 2000; Farkas *et al.,* 2000; Gregory and Horz, 1998; Mao and Shapiro, 2000; Truss *et al.,* 1995; Wolffe and Guschin, 2000). This process can lead to enhancement or repression of transcriptional activity in subsets of genes linked to the display of aggression (Fig. 2). The transcriptional activity of the ligand-bound estrogen receptor (ER) is modulated by steroid receptor coactivators and corepressors, which function to relax or condense chromatin, respectively (Delage-Mourroux *et al.,* 2000; DiRenzo *et al.,* 2000; Kalkhoven *et al.,* 1998; Klinge, 2000; Kobayashi *et al.,* 2000; Lazennec *et al.,* 1997; Llopis *et al.,* 2000; Mak *et al.,* 1999; Muramatsu and Inoue, 2000; Shibata *et al.,* 1997; Tetel, 2000). A study by Auger *et al.* (2000) demonstrated that reducing SRC-1 protein levels during sexual differentiation through the use of antisense oligonucleotides interferes with estrogen-mediated defeminization of rat brain. Because SRC-1 can modify the structural and chemical makeup of chromatin (DiRenzo *et al.,* 2000),

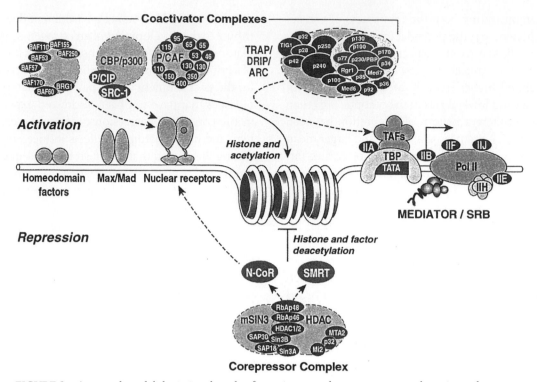

FIGURE 2 A general model depicting the role of coactivator and corepressor complexes in nuclear receptor (NR) transcription. Coactivator complexes include SWI/SNF, CBP/SRC-1/p/CAF, and TRAP/DRIP/ARC. The SWI/SNF complex has ATP-dependent chromatin remodeling activities, whereas CBP and p/CAF complexes possess histone acetyltransferase activities. These complexes may act in concert to relieve chromatin-mediated repression, with the TRAP/DRIP/ARC complex functioning to recruit core transcription factors. Corepressor complexes include the SIN3/HDAC complex, which may be recruited via the NR corepressors N-CoR or SMRT. This complex possesses histone deacetylase activity and is thought to reverse actions of histone acetyltransferase-containing complexes. Reprinted with permission from Glass, C. K., and Rosenfeld, M. G. The coregulator exchange in transcriptional functions of nuclear receptors. *Genes and Development 14,* 121–141. © 2000 Cold Spring Harbor Laboratory Press. **See insert for a color version of this figure.**

this observation potentially supports the role of chromatin remodeling as an active component of sexual differentiation. Whether these changes are enduring or transient and how they relate to the establishment of a regulatory path for conspecific aggression represent significant questions for the field.

2. Androgen Response System

Resolving the hormonal processes involved in the development of the androgen-responsive system appears to be an even more complex undertaking, primarily for two reasons. The first is that the CNS of adult males and females differs only in relative sensitivity to the aggression-promoting property of androgen during adulthood (Simon *et al.,* 1993, 1996). Therefore,

it is likely that more subtle effects are involved in the sensitization of this pathway compared to the estrogen-responsive system, in which there is an absolute dimorphism. The second reason involves timing in the perinatal period because of controversies surrounding the potential role of prenatal androgens in sensitization of this pathway (Cologer-Clifford *et al.,* 1992; Gandelman and Kozak, 1988; Simon and Cologer-Clifford, 1991; vom Saal, 1979, 1984, 1989). Several studies in short-gestation rodents (rats and mice) indicate that maximal and essentially complete sensitization can be accomplished by direct androgenic stimulation in the period shortly after birth. The administration of the androgens R1881 or T, but not the synthetic estrogen DES, led to a male-like response to specifically acting androgen

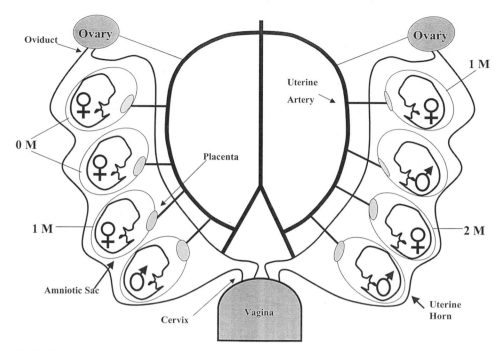

FIGURE 3 A schematic showing the three possible uterine positions that can be occupied by female fetuses relative to males: 0 M, adjacent to no males; 1 M, adjacent to one male; 2 M, between two males. Position is determined after delivery by Cesarean section on the evening of day 18 (in mice) approximately 8–12 hr before normal parturition. Adapted and reprinted with permission from vom Saal, F. S. (1984). The intrauterine position phenomenon: Effects on physiology, aggressive behavior and population dynamics in house mice. *Prog. Clin. Biol. Res. 169,* 135–179, © 1984. Reprinted by permission of Wiley-Liss, Inc., a subsidiary of John Wiley & Sons, Inc.

in adulthood (Simon and Whalen, 1987). Although numerous investigations had shown that T administration shortly after birth resulted in a short-latency male-typical response in adulthood, this study was important because it showed that it was specifically the androgenic metabolites of T that masculinized the response to the aggression-promoting property of androgen. Also supporting this perspective were results with mice that showed that the greater the duration of androgen exposure in females or the later that males were castrated during the postnatal period, the shorter the duration of androgen exposure required during adulthood to induce aggression (Motelica-Heino *et al.,* 1993; vom Saal *et al.,* 1976).

Whether prenatal androgen exposure contributes to the masculinization of the androgen-sensitive system is unclear. Primary support for a prenatal effect came from the description of uterine position effects (vom Saal, 1984, 1989), which suggested that variation in endogenous androgen exposure *in utero* altered subsequent

sensitivity to the aggression-promoting property of androgen later in life in Rockland-Swiss female mice. This effect, which reportedly influences a wide range of phenotypic variables in rodents (Hernandez-Tristan *et al.,* 1999; Houtsmuller *et al.,* 1994; Houtsmuller and Slob, 1990; Rines and vom Saal, 1984; vom Saal and Moyer, 1985; vom Saal, 1981, 1983; vom Saal and Bronson, 1980), is predicated on diffusion of androgens to female fetuses from contiguous or caudal males (Fig. 3). Females positioned between two males (2M) reportedly have higher levels of androgen in the amniotic fluid than females that develop between two females (0M) (Even *et al.,* 1992; vom Saal and Bronson, 1980). This fetal androgen exposure led to a more rapid response to the aggression-activating property of T (2M, 15 days; 0M, 21 days) in adulthood, an effect presumably due to a sensitizing action of prenatal androgen. In subsequent studies, however, no effect of uterine position on T sensitivity or hypothalamic androgen binding was noted in CF-1 female mice (Cologer-Clifford *et al.,*

1992; Simon and Cologer-Clifford, 1991). This raised the possibility that uterine position effects, if present, may be either genetically constrained or not essential for masculinization of the androgenic regulatory pathway.

E. Neural Steroid Receptors

The use of specifically acting androgens and estrogens, as well as other pharmacological methods, has allowed characterization of multiple neuroendocrine pathways through which T can promote aggressive behavior and the necessary hormonal events during sexual differentiation that establish subsequent behavioral sensitivity in the adult male CNS. Beyond providing valuable information about the role of steroid metabolism in the ontogeny and display of male-typical offensive aggression, these observations delineate a framework for investigating the function of androgen receptor (AR) and estrogen receptor (ER) in the regulation of aggression. These receptor proteins are members of the nuclear receptor superfamily and known transcription factors (Beato, 1989; Evans, 1988; Glass, 1994; Glass and Rosenfeld, 2000; Kumar and Tindall, 1998; Mangelsdorf *et al.*, 1995). Their importance in mediating steroidal effects in target cells has been extensively documented through biochemical and molecular biological studies of hormone resistance and through the production of receptor-deficient or knockout mice (Brinkmann *et al.*, 1992; Couse and Korach, 1999; French *et al.*, 1990; Griffen and Wilson, 1989; Linder and Thompson, 1989; Quigley *et al.*, 1995). On this basis, it is abundantly clear that characterization of neural ER and AR functions is an essential step in defining cellular processes that mediate behavioral responsiveness. It is not the intent of this section to provide a comprehensive review of steroid receptor function in the brain. Rather, the focus is specifically on studies that were motivated, at least in part, by an effort to understand processes tied to the regulation of conspecific aggression.

A number of superb reviews covering the genomic and nongenomic mechanisms of action of steroids are available (Compagnone and Mellon, 2000; French *et al.*, 1990; Gorski *et al.*, 1986; Jordan, 1995; McEwen *et al.*, 1979; Muldoon, 1980; Tsai and O'Malley, 1994; Schmidt *et al.*, 2000; Wheling, 1997). The

time frame for the activation of aggressive behavior in gonadectomized male mice and other rodents by hormone treatment following castration (2–3 days) is generally consistent with a genomic effect, and the discussion focuses on this aspect of hormone function. Briefly, the major events in the production of genomic effects are steroid-receptor (S-R) binding, activation of and conformational changes in the S-R complex that enhance affinity for nuclear acceptor sites, S-R binding to nuclear acceptor sites, S-R up- or down-regulation of target genes, and subsequent changes in protein synthesis, which are in turn linked to behavioral expression (Fig. 4). Our understanding of these processes in relation to the steroidal regulation of aggression is not well developed in comparison to, for example, reproductive behaviors. Nevertheless, a number of intriguing observations suggest that there may be differences in the way that AR and ER functions contribute to the regulation of aggression. If these differences can be validated and fully defined, it would further support the existence of distinct regulatory pathways for this behavior.

1. Androgen Receptor

Regarding the androgen-sensitive system, studies in adults have ranged from equilibrium assays that compared sex and strain differences in AR binding characteristics through immunochemical and Western blot analyses that examined the distribution, density, and regulation of AR (Clark and Nowell, 1980; S. Lu *et al.*, 1998, 1999; Simon and Whalen, 1986). These studies were motivated by descriptions of hormone resistance syndromes such as the Tfm mutation and glucocorticoid resistance, which had shown that receptor concentration and the affinity of ligand-receptor interactions were important determinants of target tissue responsiveness (Chrousos *et al.*, 1983, 1984; Fox *et al.*, 1983; Lipsett *et al.*, 1985; Wieland and Fox, 1981). Although differences among genotypes in neural AR concentration and binding affinity were found, neither measure appeared to be systematically related to observed differences in behavioral sensitivity. These findings indicated that other methodological approaches were required to define the relationship between AR and aggression or, alternatively, that different conceptual models would be needed.

Autoradiographic and immunocytochemical methods have permitted the construction of detailed AR

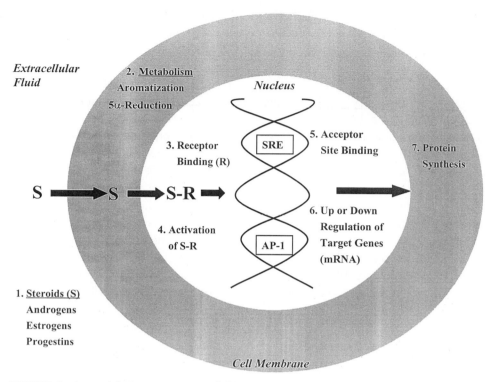

FIGURE 4 A simplified representation of the major steps involved in the genomic mechanism of action of testosterone (T). In target cells, T can be metabolized to E_2 by aromatization or DHT by 5α-reduction. These products, or T itself, bind to cognate steroid receptor proteins that, upon the formation of the steroid-receptor (S-R) complex, undergo a conformational shift that increases affinity for nuclear acceptor sites such as the steroid response elements (SRE) or AP-1 element. This binding interaction up or down regulates transcription of target genes, altering mRNA levels and, as a result, protein sythesis.

distribution maps. Major regions exhibiting positive immunoreactivity include the BNST, LS, MPOA, and MAMYG, regions that constitute part of the neuroanatomical substrate for conspecific aggression based on lesion and implant studies (Lisciotto *et al.,* 1990; Owen *et al.,* 1974; Slotnick and McMullen, 1972; Simon *et al.,* 1993). However, these descriptive findings, while valuable for defining functional circuitry, cannot shed light on how the regulation of AR itself contributes to behavioral expression.

An abundant literature has demonstrated in both peripheral and neural tissue from males that AR expression is decreased by castration and up-regulated by androgen replacement therapy (Freeman *et al.,* 1995; Iqbal and Jacobson, 1995; S. Lu *et al.,* 1999; Menard and Harlan, 1993; Prins and Birch, 1993; Simon *et al.,* 1996; Wood and Newman, 1993; Zhou *et al.,* 1994).

These observations raised the possibility that neural AR regulation might differ between males and females. If this were the case, it could be a contributing mechanism to variation in behavioral sensitivity. Such studies could involve assessments of AR mRNA regulation, using, for example, ribonuclease protection assay, northern analysis, or *in situ* hybridization, which potentially provide direct indices of changes in transcriptional activity; or an examination of alterations in the level of AR protein under differing hormonal conditions, which would provide a more direct measure. At this point in time, the last approach appears to have greater validity because of inconsistencies in studies that focused on the AR message and other concerns about static assessments of mRNA (Maas *et al.,* 1997; Melcher *et al.,* 1996; Ross, 1996; Sachs, 1993). For example, androgenic stimulation reportedly down-regulates AR mRNA in rat prostate and three human cell lines, LNCap, T47D, and MGM323 (Handa *et al.*, 1996; Mora *et al.*, 1996; Krongrad *et al.*, 1991), whereas no effect was observed in rat testis and micropunched brain regions (Wolf *et al.*, 1993). In rat Sertoli cells, transient down-regulation of AR mRNA was followed by up-regulation (Blok *et al.*, 1991), and, in amphibians, up-regulation of AR message by androgens has been described (Hackenberg *et al.*, 1992). Although these intriguing findings require further investigation, measurements that assess changes in protein expression seem to have greater utility, at least until issues surrounding cell and tissue specificity of AR mRNA regulation and stability are better understood.

The effects of castration with or without testosterone propionate (TP) injections on AR protein regulation in several brain regions have been compared in adult male and female CF-1 mice, a strain that has an androgen-sensitive system and is highly aggressive. The results for BNST, which were typical of all regions studied, are shown as an example of the findings (Fig. 5).Gonadectomy led to a rapid loss of immunostaining, while TP replacement led to nearly a twofold increase in AR density in both sexes. Western blot analyses were conducted to confirm these results. Because this technique involves denaturation of all proteins, it avoided a potentially controversial feature of immunochemical studies, which is whether an antibody fully recognizes both liganded and unliganded forms of the receptor. The results, shown in Fig. 6, were consistent with the immunochemical observations.

Common regulation of AR in both male and female neural tissue strongly indicates that the observed rapid increase in AR protein level by itself is not sufficient to produce parallel changes in behavioral responsiveness. This is because the activation of male-typical aggression in ovariectomized females, as noted earlier, requires 16–21 days of androgen treatment, whereas the AR level increased dramatically within 24 hr. Given these findings, increased cellular AR content, which depends on the presence of androgen, probably triggers enhanced (or suppressed) transcription of other androgen-regulated genes, which in combination leads to the expression of aggression. The extended time frame required to induce male-like aggression in females raises intriguing potential mechanisms, with one possibility being that the receptor complex promotes elaboration of an androgen-dependent circuit through interactions with or the regulation of growth factors (Katoh-Semba *et al.*, 1994; Lustig *et al.*, 1994; Tirassa *et al.*, 1997; Yang and Arnold, 2000). A comparable view regarding the lack of a simple relationship between AR immunoreactivity and responsiveness to the masculine sexual behavior-promoting effect of testosterone has been expressed based on findings in hamsters (Meek *et al.*, 1997). The concept of AR-induced circuit remodeling is somewhat analogous to that which has been described in the adult male canary brain, where a testosterone-dependent increase in BDNF appears to play an important role in the viability of neurons in the high vocal center (Rasika *et al.*, 1999). Also consistent with the possibility of AR-induced circuitry are the pronounced sexual dimorphisms in neural pathways mediating reproductive behaviors (Simerly, 1995, 1998; Hutton *et al.*, 1998). Several of these structures, including the vomeronasal organ, accessory olfactory bulbs, medial and posterior nuclei of the amygdala, and BNST, are part of circuits that process pheromonal and other olfactory cues (Segovia and Guillamon, 1993; Simerly, 1998; Hutton *et al.*, 1998; Van den Bergh, 1994). Because intermale aggression is triggered by a pheromonal stimulus, androgenic stimulation may function to establish this pathway in females and maintain it in normal males. Studies testing these concepts are lacking in the context of aggressive behavior and are needed to further refine our understanding of steroid-dependent neuroanatomical substrates.

The augmentation of neural AR levels and the rapid up-regulation of this protein within 7 hr of androgen administration (S. Lu *et al.*, 1999) also may have implications for understanding personality changes associated with anabolic steroid abuse. Exposure to anabolic steroids has been linked to "roid rage" in some individuals (Bahrke *et al.*, 1996; Galligani *et al.*, 1996; Pope *et al.*, 1996, 2000; Yates *et al.*, 1992). Elevated AR seen in response to androgen may represent part of the cellular processes that underlie these changes. In this context, chronic high-level anabolic androgen treatment significantly increased the aggressiveness of pubertal male hamsters and adult rats (Clark and Barber, 1994; Harrison *et al.*, 2000; Melloni *et al.*, 1997) and the density of AR in rat brain (Menard and Harlan, 1993).

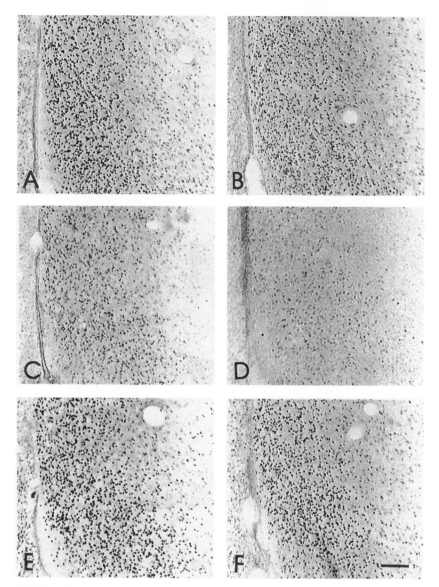

FIGURE 5   Representative ICC sections showing AR immunoreactivity in bed nucleus of the stria terminalis–posterior aspect (BNSTp) in groups of male and female mice that were either intact, gonadectomized (GDX), or gonadectomized and treated with TP (GDX + TP). (A) intact male. (B) intact female. (C) GDX male. (D) GDX female. (E) GDX +TP male. (F) GDX female +TP. This pattern of group differences in AR regulation was seen in all regions examined. Bar = 100 μm. Reprinted with permission from S. Lu *et al.* Androgen receptor in mouse brain: Sex difference and similarities in autoregulation. *Endocrinology 139*, 1594–1601. © 1998 The Endocrine Society.

2. Estrogen Receptor

Defining the potential role of ER in the regulation of aggression potentially became a far more formidable task in 1996 when a novel form of this receptor was cloned from rat and human cDNA libraries (Giguere *et al.*, 1998; Kuiper *et al.*, 1996, 1998; Mosselman *et al.*, 1996). This novel form was termed ERβ (MW = 54,000), and the classical ER was referred to as ERα (MW = 67,000). As shown in Fig. 7, the novel ERβ shares significant amino acid homology with ERα,

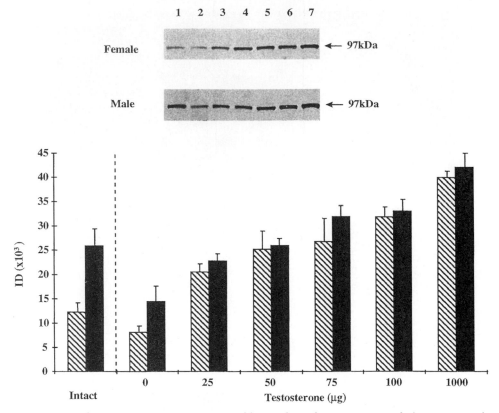

FIGURE 6 A histogram summarizing western blot results and representative gels (upper portion) showing the regulated 97-kDa androgen receptor band in females and males that were intact, gonadectomized, or gonadectomized and treated with 0–1000 μg TP. Data shown are the integrated densities of each band (mean + SEM) of three independent replications in each sex for each condition. Lanes 1–7 on both gels: intact, gonadectomized (0), and 25, 50, 75, 100, or 1000 μg TP, respectively. Females, ▨; males, ■. Reprinted with permission from Lu, S., *et al.* Androgen receptor in mouse brain: Sex differences and similarities in autoregulation. *Endocrinology 139,* 1594–1601. © 1998 The Endocrine Society.

particularly in the DNA-binding and ligand-binding domains (Mosselman *et al.,* 1996; Ogawa *et al.,* 1998a; Petterson *et al.,* 1997; Shughrue *et al.,* 1996; Tremblay *et al.,* 1997). It differs from ERα in two important aspects. First, although many ligands (including some selective ER modulators) bind to both ERα and ERβ with similar affinities, a subset of synthetic or naturally occuring ligands, including estradiol, exhibit differential relative affinity for ERα vs. ERβ (Kuiper *et al.,* 1997; Paige *et al.,* 1999; Sun *et al.,* 1999). Second, both the pattern and level of ERα and ERβ mRNA expression differ in relative tissue distribution and cellular localization (Shughrue *et al.,* 1997, 1998). Remarkably, no reports to date have compared ERα and ERβ expression in neural tissues at the protein level.

The production of ERα and ERβ knockout mice (ERKO and BERKO, respectively) was reviewed (Couse and Korach, 1999). As described by the authors, the availability of these recombinant strains has provided important insights regarding the functions of ER and its mechanism of action in a number of target tissues. In regard to aggression, a series of studies by Ogawa and colleagues (1997, 1998b, 1999) in male mice has demonstrated a primary role for ERα. The initial study assessed aggressive behavior by intact ERKO males in the resident-intruder and homogeneous set designs (for descriptions of these paradigms, see Simon, 1979). Offensive attacks were rarely displayed by ERKO males, whereas wild-type (WT) and heterozygous males showed significantly greater attack durations

Human ERα vs ERβ:
Protein Sequence Homology

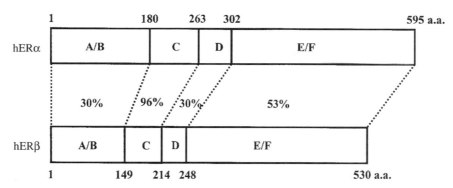

FIGURE 7 A comparison of the protein structure between human estrogen receptors alpha (hERα) and beta (hERβ). Both receptor subtypes are organized into similar functional domain structures (A–F). Percentages indicate the degree of homology between domains, with the highest levels seen in region C (DNA-binding domain) and region E/F (ligand binding domain). Adapted and reprinted with permission from Ogawa, S., *et al.* The complete primary structure of human estrogen receptor-β and its heterodimerization with estrogen receptor-α *in vivo* and *in vitro*. *Biochem. Biophys. Res. Comm. 243,* 122–126. © 1998 Academic Press.

(Ogawa *et al.,* 1997). The second investigation (Ogawa *et al.,* 1998b) included castration–hormone replacement findings, which showed that daily TP injections were ineffective in promoting aggression in ERKO males and highly effective in gonadectomized WT males. These observations confirmed that ERKO males only have an estrogen-responsive regulatory system. The third report assessed aggression in the BERKO mice. In accord with a model that posits ERα as the active receptor form in aggression, these animals exhibited normal or enhanced attack behavior compared to WT males (Ogawa *et al.,* 1999).

Resolving the basis for the sexual dimorphism in response to estrogen requires understanding how ERα can produce such dramatically different effects in male and female neural tissue. It appears this problem might be addressed by analyses at several levels including, for example, organization of the nuclear matrix, interactions with alternative transcription sites such as AP-1 and NFKβ, and ERα structure and function (Barrett and Spelsberg, 1999; Cerillo *et al.,* 1998; Hyder *et al.,* 1999; Katzenellenbogen, 2000; Malayer *et al.,* 1999; Paech *et al.,* 1997; Webb *et al.,* 1999). These potential mechanisms are neither mutually exclusive nor are they meant to represent an exhaustive list, but they can serve as examples.

The nuclear matrix (NM) is a dynamic substructure that has been implicated in the regulation of gene expression due to its role in DNA organization, replication, and transcription; heteronuclear RNA synthesis and processing; the preferential association of actively transcribed genes; and the association of transcription factors and steroid receptors (Barrack, 1987; Barrack and Coffey, 1982; Barrett and Spelsberg, 1999; Metzger *et al.,* 1991; Oesterreich *et al.,* 2000; Stenoien *et al.,* 2000). The existence of tissue-specific NM proteins has been described, suggesting that unique protein content may be responsible for modulating transcription factor access, providing a potential mechanism for tissue-specific gene regulation (Getzenberg, 1994; Getzenberg and Coffey, 1990). Interestingly, some of these tissue-specific NM proteins were found to be hormonally regulated, strengthening the potential link between the NM and hormonal regulation of gene expression. In this context, estrogen-dependent ER binding to hypothalamic matrix from female mice has been observed and confirmed by western analysis (McKenna-Repsher and Simon, 1994, 1995), suggesting that this may be a fruitful line of inquiry for

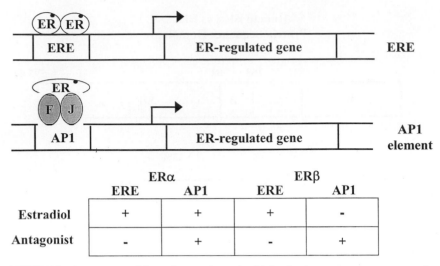

FIGURE 8 A summary of the pathways through which selective estrogen receptor modulators can activate transcription in target cells. Antagonist or agonist effects can be obtained as a function of ER subtype or response element, the classic ERE or the alternative AP-1. (F, fos; J, jun.) Reprinted with permission from Paech, K., *et al.* Differential ligand activation of estrogen receptors α and β at AP1 sites. *Science* 277, 1508–1510. © 1997 American Association for the Advancement of Science.

future studies. In addition, the phenomenon *chromatin memory* has been reported for estrogenic stimulation of several genes in chicken hepatic cells (Barrett and Spelsberg, 1999; Burch and Evans, 1986; Evans *et al.,* 1987), as well as hormone-induced structural modifications in chromatin that alter transcriptional efficiency. Although these effects have not yet been demonstrated in neural tissue, such changes would influence which genes were silenced or accessible in target cells.

Turning to alternative transcription sites, ERα (and ERβ) can enhance or repress transcription through sites other than the classical estrogen response element (ERE). At AP-1 elements, for example, selective estrogen receptor modulators (SERMs) such as tamoxifen exert agonist effects; at the classic ERE it is an antagonist, as shown in Fig. 8 (Paech *et al.,* 1997; Webb *et al.,* 1995; A. Zhou *et al.,* 1999). The extent of involvement of these alternative sites in potentially determining sex-specific effects of ERα remains to be determined. Finally, ERα contains two transcriptional activating functions, AF1 and AF2, located within the N-terminal and C-terminal domains of the receptor, respectively (Gronemeyer *et al.,* 1992). Although these transactivation functions normally act in concert to regulate gene expression (Tzuckerman *et al.,* 1994), their

relative effects are cell- and promoter-specific (Berry *et al.,* 1990; Krishnan *et al.,* 2000; Tzukerman *et al.,* 1994; Watanabe *et al.,* 1997). These findings raise the intriguing possibility that sex-typical responses to estrogen may be a product of differential effects of AF1 and AF2 in the neural substrate for the estrogen-sensitive pathway. Support for this possibility can be found in studies that compared the effects of tamoxifen and estradiol on estrogen-regulated responses in CF-1 mice. Tamoxifen blocks ligand-dependent responses, that is, those mediated primarily through AF2. In some instances, it acts as an agonist by initiating transcription through alternative sites such as an AP-1 element or through constitutive effects of AF-1. This compound suppressed estrogen-induced lordotic behavior and progestin-receptor induction in ovariectomized female mice, but had no effect when given alone (McKenna *et al.,* 1992). In castrated and intact males, however, tamoxifen restored and enhanced aggression as effectively as DES (W. Klein and N. Simon, unpublished observations). These findings suggest that, at least in mice, female-typical responses to estrogen depend on transcription mediated through AF2, whereas male-typical aggression may involve AF1 or alternative response elements. Although further study will be required to assess these possibilities, the observed sexual dimorphisms suggest that the mouse CNS may provide a useful model for determining of the transactivation functions that are critical for the expression of male-typical estrogen-facilitated aggression.

III. HORMONAL MODULATION OF NEUROCHEMICAL FUNCTION: SEROTONIN AND VASOPRESSIN

The 1980s and 1990s have produced refined models of the neurochemical processes involved in the expression of conspecific aggression. Although virtually every known neurotransmitter system has been implicated at some point in the regulation of this behavior, a compelling body of pharmacological and molecular biological studies indicate that serotonin (5-HT), via its action at the 5-HT$_{1A}$ and 5-HT$_{1B}$ receptors, and vasopressin, through the V1a receptor, represent major neurochemical regulators in numerous species (Bell and Hobson, 1994; Ferris, 2000; Koolhaas *et al.*, 1998; Kravitz, 2000; Ramboz *et al.*, 1996; Olivier and Mos, 1990; Olivier *et al.*, 1994, 1995; Simon *et al.*, 1998). In general, serotonin acts as an inhibitor of aggression, whereas vasopressin is facilitative. These findings essentially paralleled advances in defining neuroendocrine pathways. Because it was evident that the hormonal and neurochemical systems functioned in concert to regulate offensive aggression, there was a clear need to integrate observations from both areas. The 1990s saw the beginning of progress in developing these models (see Simon *et al.*, 1998, for a review) and the modulatory effects of androgens and estrogens on each of the aforementioned neurochemical systems can be demonstrated, although it is sometimes necessary to draw on studies other than those specifically focusing on aggression. Collectively, these observations provide the basis for newer comprehensive regulatory models that emphasize neuromodulation as a primary function of androgens and estrogens in the regulation of aggressive behavior.

A. Serotonin

From lobster to lizards through rodents to humans, there has been enormous interest in the contribution of serotonergic function to aggressive behaviors (Berman *et al.*, 1997; Deckel and Fuqua, 1998; Hen, 1996;

Kravitz, 2000; Mann, 1995; Manuck *et al.*, 1999; Simon and Coccaro, 1999; Summers and Greenberg, 1995; Wallman, 1999). These studies have included assessments of dominance interactions in several species (the interest of this chapter); maternal, shock-induced, and predatory aggression in rodents; self-injurious behavior in nonhuman primates; and impulsive aggression, violence, and suicide in humans. Although some inconsistencies and exceptions have been noted (e.g., Berman *et al.*, 1997; Stevenson *et al.*, 2000; Wallman, 1999), a basic conclusion of this research is that diminished or reduced serotonergic function is associated with increased aggression, enhanced serotonergic tone is associated with reduced levels of aggressive behavior. The consistent effects across different behavioral forms strongly argued for the prominent role of 5-HT and for investigation of the underlying mechanisms. Molecular biological and pharmacological findings that identified distinct 5-HT receptor classes and, in several cases, subtypes within these classes (Hoyer and Martin, 1997; Mengod *et al.*, 1996; Middlemiss and Hutson, 1990, Monsma *et al.*, 1993; Pazos and Palacios, 1985; Peroutka, 1991), have established opportunities to more carefully define these mechanisms.

In regard to 5-HT function in intermale aggression, extensive behavioral studies have been conducted using a class of 5-HT agonists termed serenics (Olivier *et al.*, 1994, 1995). The findings consistently demonstrated that drugs with selective affinity for 5-HT$_1$ receptors, particularly mixed 5-HT$_{1A}$ (1A) and 5-HT$_{1B}$ (1B) agonists (e.g., eltoprazine), specifically and selectively reduced offensive aggression. Pharmacological studies have supported this view, with results suggesting that somatodendritic 1A autoreceptors and postsynaptic 1B receptors exert key effects on offensive aggression (De Boer *et al.*, 2000; Miczek, 1999; Sijbesma *et al.*, 1991). The importance of the 1B receptor was further indicated by results demonstrating that males lacking this receptor (1B knockouts) exhibited higher levels of aggressive behaviors compared to WT males (Hen, 1996; Ramboz *et al.*, 1996; Saudou *et al.*, 1994). However, caution is needed in evaluating these findings. More specifically, the WT males exhibited extremely low levels of aggression (Brunner and Hen, 1997; Miczek, 1999). Thus, even the presumably elevated aggression displayed by the 1B knockout males is very low compared to that seen in most genotypes.

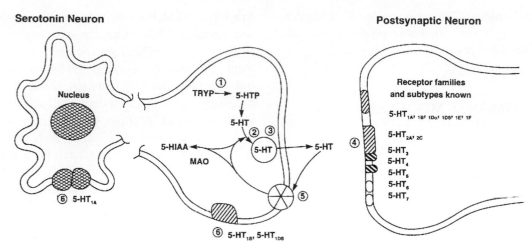

FIGURE 9 A schematic diagram showing the cellular processes in serotonergic cells and synapses. 1. Synthetic pathway (tryptophan, TRYP; 5-hydroxytryptophan, 5-HTP, 5-hydroxytryptamine, 5-HT (serotonin); 5-hydroxyindoleacetic acid, (5-HIAA); 2. Storage; 3. Release; 4. Activation of postsynaptic receptors; 5. Transporter or uptake to terminate 5-HT action; 6. Activation of presynaptic receptors; 7. Degradation by monoamine oxidase, MAO. Reprinted with permission from Wong, D. T., *et al.* Presynaptic regulation of extracellular serotonin concentrations in brain. In A. Takada and G. Curzon (eds.), *Serotonin in the Central Nervous System and Periphery,* pp. 3–15, © 1995 Elsevier Science.

Further, an extended isolation period was employed in the initial studies demonstrating an effect of the gene knockout. This period results in enhanced responsiveness of the 5-HT$_{1B}$ receptor (Frances and Monier, 1991a,b; Frances *et al.*, 1990), which may have led to greater behavioral inhibition in WT males. In combination, these observations can be interpreted as indicating that the effects may be due to a diminution of aggression of WT males rather than an enhancement in the 5-HT$_{1B}$-deficient males. Alternatively, it has been suggested that the knockout males may generally exhibit increased novelty seeking and reactivity (Brunner and Hen, 1997; Zhuang *et al.*, 1999). This raises the possibility that at least some portion of the aggressive behavior exhibited by these males is not analogous to conspecific intermale fighting behavior but rather may be more akin to impulsive aggression.

Gonadal hormones may promote behavioral activation by modulating serotonin function in one or more brain regions that constitute the neuroanatomical substrate for intermale aggression. This is supported by autoradiographic and *in situ* hybridization studies that demonstrated overlapping distributions of androgen-, estrogen-, and serotonin-concentrating neurons and receptor gene expression in these regions (Herbison,

1995; Koch and Ehret, 1989; Lu *et al.*, 1998; Menard and Harlan, 1993; Mengod *et al.*, 1996; Miquel *et al.*, 1992; Palacios *et al.*, 1990; Pazos and Palacios, 1985; Sheridan, 1978; Sijbesma *et al.*, 1990; Simerly *et al.*, 1990; Simon *et al.*, 1996; Wright *et al.*, 1995). However, these observations do not directly test how 5-HT function is affected by gonadal steroids in regard to the regulation of offensive intermale aggression. This requires delineating: (1) whether androgens or estrogens differentially affect the ability of 5-HT$_{1A}$, 5-HT$_{1B}$, or combined agonist treatments to modulate offensive intermale aggression; (2) where in the brain these effects are produced, with a specific focus on the LS, MPOA, AHTH, MAMYG, and dorsal raphe (DR) and median raphe (MR) nuclei based on the aforementioned studies; and (3) whether androgen or estrogen influences 5-HT$_{1A}$ or 5-HT$_{1B}$ function in these regions by altering receptor density or other aspects of serotonin function (Fig. 9).

There have been only two studies that directly addressed specific androgenic and estrogenic effects on 5-HT$_{1A}$ and 5-HT$_{1B}$ function in the context of offensive aggression (Cologer-Clifford *et al.*, 1997, 1999). The findings, shown in Fig. 10, demonstrated that serotonergic agents were far more effective in the presence

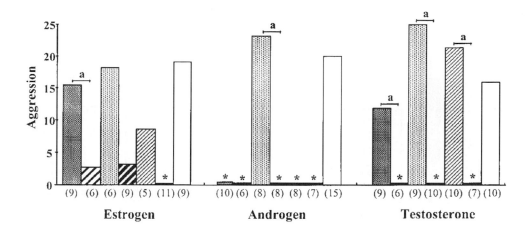

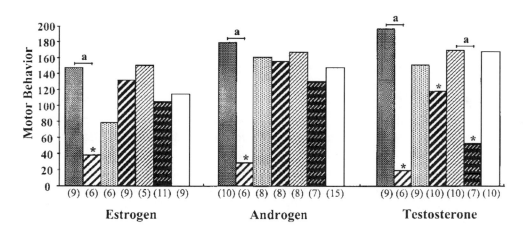

* significantly different from vehicle
(a) significant difference between low and high doses

FIGURE 10 Effects of 8-OH-DPAT (0.1 or 1.0 mg/kg, i.p.) and CGS12066B (4.0 or 8.0 mg/kg, i.p.) given alone or in combination on the frequency of (A) offensive aggression and (B) motor behavior in CF-1 male mice treated with either DES (estrogen), DHT or R1881 (androgen), or TP. Aggression scores are expressed as the median of biting attacks + lateral threats + tail rattling. Motor behavior represents the median of rearing and locomotion (grid crossings in the home cage by the experimental male). Results were analyzed using nonparametric statistics (Kruskal-Wallis; Mann-Whitney for additional comparisons) because of the large number of zero scores. The number of mice in each condition is shown in parentheses; *, significantly different from water vehicle ($p < 0.05$); (a), significant difference between low and high doses. Reprinted with permission from Cologer-Clifford, A., *et al.* Androgens and estrogens modulate 5HT$_{1A}$ and 5HT$_{1B}$ agonist effects on aggression. *Physiol. Behav.* 65, 823–828, © 1999 Elsevier Science.

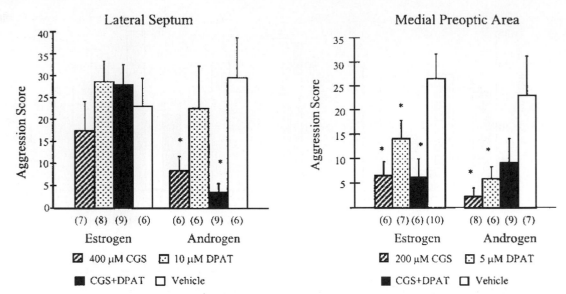

FIGURE 11   Effects of microinjections of 5-HT$_{1A}$ (8-OH-DPAT; 10 μM) and 5-HT$_{1B}$ (CGS12066B; 400 μM) agonists alone or in combination into the lateral septum or medial preoptic area of CF-1 male mice treated with either DES (estrogen) or DHT (androgen). Aggression scores are expressed as the mean + SE$_m$ of biting attacks + lateral threats + tail rattling.*, significantly different from water vehicle ($p < 0.05$). Reprinted with permission from Cologer-Clifford, A., *et al.* Serotonin agonist-induced decrease in intermale aggression are dependent on brain region and receptor subtype. *Pharm. Biochem. Behav. 58*, 425–430. © 1997b Elsevier Science.

of androgen, compared to estrogen, in attenuating the display of fighting behavior. These effects, however, also must be viewed in the context of changes in motor behavior, particularly in regard to the 1A receptor, which mediates the 5-HT syndrome. As seen in the lower portion of the figure, the high dose of CGS12066B consistently decreased locomotion, indicating that changes in aggression in these groups were nonspecific. Taking this into account, it can be suggested that if estrogens are present, either alone or as a product of aromatization, there are restrictive conditions for the inhibition of male-typical offensive aggression by 5-HT$_{1A}$ and 5-HT$_{1B}$ agonists. In contrast, when aggression is promoted by a direct androgenic effect, 1A and 1B agonists are very effective in decreasing the expression of offensive attacks and threats.

The systemic data constituted an initial step in defining the relationship between functional hormonal pathways and the modulation of serotonergic effects on offensive intermale aggression. A second question involved the potential location in the brain where these effects occurred. Likely sites for modulatory actions on 5-HT$_{1A}$ or 5-HT$_{1B}$ agonist effects of gonadal steroids include the LS, MPOA, MAMYG, and DR, based on receptor distribution and our current understanding of neuroanatomical substrates for intermale aggression.

The findings for two representative areas are shown in Fig. 11. Interestingly, there were pronounced differences between the two regions in the effects of the microinjections. In LS, the presence of DES blocked inhibitory effects of either the 1A or 1B agonists. When gonadectomized males were implanted with DHT, aggressive behavior was decreased with CGS12066B alone or in combination with 8-OH-DPAT; the 1A agonist alone was ineffective. The effects of CGS12066B treatment appear to be specific because motor behavior was unaffected in these conditions. These findings demonstrate that at the level of the LS, the androgen-sensitive pathway that facilitates aggression can be attenuated by the action of serotonin at 1B receptor sites.

In the MPOA, effects were more pronounced. Both 1A and 1B agonist microinjections significantly reduced offensive aggression in the presence of either androgen or estrogen without altering motor behavior. These findings suggest that the MPOA may be a major integrative site for hormone–serotonin interactions in the regulation of T-dependent aggression.

The results also suggest refinements in our understanding of the neuroanatomical circuitry underlying T-dependent offensive aggression. In the LS, the presence of estrogen again inhibited 1A, 1B, or combined agonist treatments from attenuating aggression. When androgens provided the steroidal background, the 5-HT_{1B} agonists effectively decreased aggression, as did the combined treatment. However, the 1A agonist alone had no effect, suggesting that androgen–5-HT_{1B} agonist interactions were important in regulating behavioral expression in this region. Regarding the MPOA, both 5-HT_{1A} and 5-HT_{1B} agonists given alone attenuated aggression in the presence of either steroid. Overall, these results indicate that the MPOA is part of both the androgen-dependent and estrogen-dependent circuits and that it is a major locus of testosterone–serotonin interactions in the regulation of offensive aggression.

That the hormonal environment modulates the effects of serotonergic agents on T-dependent intermale aggression is not surprising. These types of interactions have been well documented in other systems, particularly in regard to reproductive behavior (Ahlenius and Larson, 1997; Bitran and Hull, 1987; Dohanich *et al.*, 1985; Etgen *et al.*, 1999; Etgen and Karkanias, 1994; Gonzalez *et al.*, 1997; McCarthy, 1995; McCarthy *et al.*, 1992; Trevino *et al.*, 1999; Uphouse *et al.*, 1992) and their potential role in anxiety and mood disorders (Bethea *et al.*, 2000; Fink *et al.*, 1998, 1999; Flügge *et al.*, 1998; Pecins-Thompson and Bethea, 1998). Rather, it was the differences in the ability of estrogens and androgens to attenuate the aggression-inhibiting effects of 5-HT_{1A} and 5-HT_{1B} agonists, and the regional variation in these effects, that appear to be the most interesting feature of these experiments. When male-typical offensive aggression is regulated via an estrogen-sensitive pathway, there seems to be a restrictive environment for serotonergic effects at 1A and 1B sites. This was particularly evident in the systemic data. Androgens, in contrast to estrogens, did little to inhibit the ability of $5HT_{1A}$ and $5HT_{1B}$ agonists to attenuate aggression, suggesting that this steroid establishes a permissive environment for serotonergic modulation.

Studies that build on these and related results might focus on the mechanisms through which steroids either enhance or repress the ability of 5-HT_{1A} and

5-HT_{1B} agonists to attenuate the display of offensive intermale aggression. The majority of available data in this area has focused on the 1A receptor because of its potential role in anxiety (Ramboz *et al.*, 1998; Parks *et al.*, 1998; Sibille *et al.*, 2000; Scearce-Levie *et al.*, 1999; Zhuang *et al.*, 1999). Estrogens can affect 5-HT_{1A} function in a variety of ways: by altering 5-HT_{1A} gene expression; by exerting nongenomic effects on the receptor; or by indirectly influencing ligand availability through effects on synthesis, reuptake, or metabolism (Bethea *et al.*, 2000; Biegon, 1990; Chang and Chang, 1999; Fischette *et al.*, 1983; Frankfurt *et al.*, 1993; McQueen *et al.*, 1999; Mendelson and Gorzalka, 1985; Mendelson and McEwen, 1990a,b; Mize and Alper, 2000; Osterlund *et al.*, 2000; Raap *et al.*, 2000; Rastegar *et al.*, 1993; Sumner *et al.*, 1999). Conclusive evidence for a direct effect on 5-HT_{1A} gene function requires the identification of an ERE in the promoter region of the 5-HT_{1A} receptor gene. Interestingly, both the mouse and the human 5-HT_{1A} receptor genes appear to contain the classic ERE, as shown in Table 2. The postulated ERE-like motif deviates from the consensus GGTCANNNTGACC ERE only in the length of the intervening spacer element (indicated by N and

TABLE 2
Naturally Occurring Estrogen Response Elements with Variable Spacers

Species and gene	Starting position	DNA sequence
Traditional spacer (n = 3)		
Xenopus vitellogenin A2	−331	**GGTCA**CAG**TGACC**
Chicken vitellogenin II	−625	**GGTCA**GCG**TGACC**
Chicken ovalbumin	−177	**GGTAA**CAA**TGTGT**
Human c-fos	−1209	**CGGCA**GCG**TGACC**
Rat prolactin	−1572	**TGTCA**CTA**TGTCC**
Nontraditional spacer (n > 3)		
Rat LH-β	−1173	**GGACA**[N]$_5$**TGTCC**
Rat BDNF	−1045	**GGTGA**[N]$_9$**TGACC**
Salmon GnRH	−1501	**GGTCA**[N]$_8$**TGTCC**
Salmon GnRH	−1569	**AGTCA**[N]$_9$**TGACC**
Putative h5-HT_{1A} motif	−429	**GGTCA**[N]$_5$**TGACC**
Putative mouse 5-HT_{1A} motif	−426	**GGTCA**[N]$_5$**TGACC**

underlined), which consists of five nucleotides instead of the typical three nucleotides. However, nonconsensus EREs of varying spacer lengths can function effectively to regulate transcription of corresponding target genes (Berry et al., 1989; Klein-Hitpass et al., 1990; Klungland et al., 1994; Martinez et al., 1987; Shupnik and Rosenzweig, 1990; Sohrabji et al., 1995; Tora et al., 1988). For example, both the salmon gonadotrophin-releasing hormone (GnRH) gene (Klungland et al., 1994) and the gene encoding BDNF in the rat (Sohrabji et al., 1995) have ERE motifs with eight- or nine-nucleotide spacers that are functionally active and can bind activated estrogen receptors in vitro. Moreover, Shupnik and Rosenzweig (1990) characterized a functional nonconsensus ERE in the rat LHβ gene that has five intervening nucleotides between the two half-sites. In addition, not all naturally occurring response elements for a given hormone receptor conform strictly to the consensus sequence (Schwabe et al., 1995). These investigators showed that in the promoters of some estrogen-responsive genes it is only possible to identify single isolated half-sites that match the consensus. Regarding indirect influences, estrogen treatment can affect the sensitivity of the 5-HT$_{1A}$ receptor as indicated by hormone-induced decreases in [^{35}S]GTPδS binding or several G proteins (Raap et al., 2000; Mize and Alper, 2000). Estrogen treatment also affects 5-HT$_{1A}$ receptor binding (Osterlund et al., 2000), as well as ligand availability. The latter can be produced through several effects, including changes in transporter gene expression and function or tryptophan hydroxylase activity levels (Bethea et al., 2000; Chang and Chang, 1999; McQueen et al., 1999; Pecins-Thompson and Bethea, 1998; Sumner et al., 1999). Most of these effects, however, have been defined in females. In one of the few studies with males (McQueen et al., 1999), the effects of estrogen treatment on the serotonin transporter were opposite those reported for female rats. Therefore, extrapolating from studies with females about mechanisms related to intermale aggression should be done very cautiously. Nevertheless, these observations demonstrate that in males estrogenic effects on several aspects of 5-HT function require analysis. In addition, ERβ potentially may have direct effects on the function of serotonin in DR (Alves et al., 2000) and also may modulate the regulatory actions of ERα. The latter is suggested by studies demonstrating that the two forms of the recep-

tor form heterodimers, that the presence of ERβ can inhibit transcriptional activation by ERα, and that the ratio of ERα:ERβ affects receptor–response element interactions (Cowley et al., 1997; Hall and McDonnell, 1999; Maruyama et al., 1998; Pennie et al., 1998; Petterson et al., 1997; Tremblay et al., 1999).

B. Vasopressin

The neuropeptide vasopressin (AVP) has received considerable attention for its potential role in a broad spectrum of social behaviors, including intermale aggression (Albers and Bamshad, 1998; Albers and Huhman, this volume; Bester-Meredith et al., 1999; Dantzer, 1998; DeVries and Boyle, 1998; Carter et al., 1995; Ferris, 2000; Goodson, 1998a,b; Insel et al., 1999; Koolhaas et al., 1998; Moore et al., 2000; Young et al., 1998, 1999). The link between testosterone and this neuropeptide was established through numerous demonstrations that the structural and functional integrity of specific aspects of the AVP system in rats, hamsters, and other species was dependent on gonadal steroids (Delville et al., 1996b; De Vries and Miller, 1998; De Vries et al., 1984, 1985; Johnson et al., 1995; Jurkevich et al., 1996; Ota et al., 1999; Panzica et al., 1999a,b; Watters et al., 1998). The most direct evidence for a systematic relationship among AVP, aggression, and testosterone has been obtained from over a decade of studies employing the male Syrian hamster (Mesocricetus auratus) as an experimental model (Delville et al., 1996b; Ferris, 2000). Related investigations in rats, mice, voles, birds, and other species, including humans, have broadened our understanding of these interrelationships by defining the ways that social structure (e.g., territorial vs. colonial birds, monogamous vs. promiscuous voles) interacts with the AVP or vasotocin (AVT) system and by identifying cellular and molecular processes involved in hormonal modulation of AVP synthesis and the V1a receptor. In this section, the Syrian hamster studies are reviewed followed by findings in other species. By employing a comparative perspective, both general principles and limitations associated with efforts to develop comprehensive models of hormone–neurotransmitter interactions in intermale aggression can be illustrated.

In hamsters, AVP innervation to the AHTH plays a fundamental role in the regulation of offensive aggression (i.e., initiation of attacks and bites).

The blockade of V1a receptors with a selective AVP receptor antagonist in this region inhibits offensive aggression by resident male hamsters toward smaller intruders (Ferris and Potegal, 1988) as well as between hamsters tested in a neutral arena for dominant–subordinate behavior (Potegal and Ferris, 1990). Conversely, activation of V1a receptors by microinjection of AVP into the AHTH facilitates offensive aggression (Ferris *et al.*, 1997).

The AHTH has a dense plexus of AVP fibers colocalized with V1a receptors (Ferris *et al.*, 1997). Microdialysis studies in this area show the release of AVP by resident hamsters during agonistic encounters with intruders (C. F. Ferris, personal communication). There is evidence that AVP neurons localized to the medial supraoptic nucleus and nucleus circularis are the source of innervation to the AHTH, releasing neuropeptide and facilitating aggression (Ferris *et al.*, 1991). For example, lesioning the neurons themselves causes a reduction in agonistic behavior (Ferris *et al.*, 1990).

Testosterone is essential for the modulation of aggression by AVP. Microinjections of the neuropeptide into the ventrolateral hypothalamus (VLH) did not activate offensive aggression in castrated males, whereas attack behavior was induced if animals were treated with T implants (Delville *et al.*, 1996b). AVP-induced flank marking, a communicative behavior that contributes to the maintenance of dominance status, also depends on bioavailable testosterone (Albers and Bamshad, 1998). The facilitative effect of T on the AVP system in hamsters appears to involve primarily the maintenance of V1a receptor populations in the AHTH and VLH (Delville and Ferris, 1995; Delville *et al.*, 1996b; Johnson *et al.*, 1995). Whether this is accomplished via a direct effect on V1a receptor gene expression, e.g., through an ARE or ERE, is unknown because the promoter region for the hamster V1a gene has not yet been sequenced.

In rats and mice, the BNST and MAMYG exhibit a robust sexual dimorphism in the number of AVP neurons, which is highly dependent on circulating gonadal steroids (De Vries *et al.*, 1985; De Vries and Boyle, 1998; Koolhaas *et al.*, 1990). Males have two to three times as many AVP cells and denser projections to, among other areas, the LS, periaqueductal gray (PAG), and DR, regions that are considered part of the neuroanatomical substrate for offensive intermale aggression in these species (Koolhaas *et al.*, 1998; Simon *et al.*, 1996, 1998). The sex difference in

AVP content appears to depend on a combined effect of E_2 and DHT based on castration–hormone replacement studies (De Vries and Boyle, 1998; Watters *et al.*, 1998).

Elucidating the relationship among AVP, testosterone, and aggression represents a complex undertaking based on observations in mice genetically selected for aggression and wild rats that varied in attack latency (Compaan *et al.*, 1993a; Everts *et al.*, 1997). Initial reports with rats found that AVP injections into the LS or MAMYG stimulated aggression (Koolhaas *et al.*, 1990, 1991), suggesting a systematic positive relationship. However, mice that are nonaggressive had higher AVP content and more AVP fibers in LS than highly aggressive mice, at least when attack latency was used as a major index (Compaan *et al.*, 1993a; Koolhaas *et al.*, 1998). A similar inverse relationship was found in Norway rats (Everts *et al.*, 1997). Males with shorter attack latencies had lower LS AVP levels than males with long attack latencies. These observations led to the suggestion that LS AVP more broadly influences the response to social challenges rather than only affecting aggression (Koolhaas *et al.*, 1998, Everts *et al.*, 1997), although several alternatives can be put forward. Prominent possibilities include that other regions, for example, the MAMYG, are more sensitive to variation in androgen-dependent AVP level in relation to the facilitation of offensive aggression or that it is the release rather than the cellular content of AVP in the LS that is associated with aggression. It is evident, however, that AVP can promote the display of aggression and that this effect is dependent on the presence of testosterone because both AVP gene expression and AVP immunoreactivity are regulated by this steroid (Watters *et al.*, 1998; De Vries and Miller, 1998).

Modulation of the steroid-sensitive components of the AVP system depends critically on the estrogenic and androgenic metabolites of T. Estrogen treatment alone after castration partially restored AVP immunoreactivity, DHT alone was ineffective, and combined treatment produced the greatest effect (De Vries *et al.*, 1985). A direct effect on AVP gene expression appears to be an important mechanism because AVP mRNA also increases in response to circulating gonadal steroid levels (Brot *et al.*, 1993; Wang and De Vries, 1995; Watters *et al.*, 1998). The recent identification of putative ARE, ERE, and AP-1 elements in the rat AVP gene promoter region strongly supports enhanced AVP gene transcription as a component of steroidal modulation of the AVP system in rats (Murasawa et al., 1995; Shapiro et al., 2000). It also is worth noting that hormonal modulation may be achieved through a mechanism different from that in hamsters, where regulation of the V1a receptor appears to be the primary target for steroidal effects. In keeping with this perspective, Tribollet et al. (1990, 1998) did not find an effect of T on V1a receptor binding in rat brain regions that are part of the gonadal steroid-sensitive circuit.

Species comparisons among monogamous (prairie and pine) and non-monogamous (montane and meadow) voles have provided insights into the relationship between AVP, T, and aggression. In general, monogamous male voles become highly aggressive toward intruders within 24 hr of mating, whereas non-monogamous voles exhibit little if any fighting behavior after engaging in copulatory bouts (Getz et al., 1993; Carter et al., 1995; Wang et al., 1998). The effect in monogamous males is associated with an increase in plasma testosterone, enhanced AVP mRNA in BNST and MAMYG, and reduced AVP fiber density in LS (Wang et al., 1994; De Vries and Boyle, 1998). These mating-induced testosterone-dependent changes are seen in only certain regions because AVP mRNA expression in the supraoptic and periventricular nuclei were not altered (Wang et al., 1998). Although the decrease in LS AVP fiber density may seem inconsistent, this effect has been attributed to increased AVP release in LS (De Vries and Boyle, 1998), a perspective that is in keeping with a general elevation in vasopressinergic tone in response to mating. An essential role for T in this constellation of behavioral and neurochemical effects was demonstrated by results showing that after mating, nonmonogamous males did not exhibit an increase in plasma T, enhanced LS AVP release, or an increase in aggressive behavior (Wang et al., 1994, 1998). In this context, a study by Demas et al. (1999) that showed no effect of T on aggression in prairie voles should be mentioned. The males used were not sexually experienced, thus the mating-induced elevation in T that is linked to increased AVP tone and aggression was not present.

The pronounced difference in behavior and the AVP system between monogamous and nonmonogamous voles has been employed to define the potential

molecular mechanisms that underlie these effects (Young et al., 1998, 1999; Wang et al., 1998). These investigations demonstrated, for example, different patterns of V1a receptor distribution between species. Prairie voles had increased receptor density in MAMYG compared to montane voles, whereas the latter species exhibited higher binding levels in LS (Wang et al., 1998). Perhaps of even greater interest was the identification of heterologous regions of the promoter sequence of the V1a gene (Wang et al., 1998). The importance of this difference was shown through the production of mice transgenic for the V1a receptor gene (Young et al., 1999). These mice showed a V1a receptor binding pattern similar to the prairie vole and, in response to AVP, exhibited behavioral patterns typical of the vole. These findings suggest that the primary link between gonadal steroids and the AVP system in male prairie voles is likely through the regulation of the V1a receptor. By demonstrating the presence of regulatory elements that are responsive to steroid receptors in the heterologous promoter sequence, a mechanism for a direct interface among AVP, T, and aggression could be established. Interestingly, putative ARE and ERE half-sites are present in the promoter region of the rat V1a receptor gene, as shown in Fig. 12 (S. Lu and N. Simon, unpublished observations, Koukoulas et al., 1999).

Studies in birds also are germane for understanding the interrelationship among social structure, testosterone, the vasotocin (AVT, the homolog of mammalian AVP) system, and intermale aggression. In territorial species such as the violet-eared waxbill and field sparrow, AVT infusion into LS of males inhibited aggression as measured by chases and initial attack latency (Goodson, 1998a,b). These findings parallel those

Rat V1a Receptor Gene Promoter Region

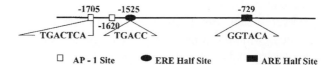

FIGURE 12 The promoter region of rat vasopressin receptor 1A gene contains both ERE and ARE half-site sequences in addition to two AP-1 sites. The presence of these DNA elements suggests the potential for direct regulation of this gene by estrogenic and androgenic hormones. Illustrated according to Genbank sequence search (gi:1217598).

regarding LS AVP levels and aggression in rats and mice (Koolhaas *et al.*, 1998). When zebra finch males, a colonial species, received LS AVT infusions, aggressive behavior increased and when an antagonist was given, chases were reduced (Goodson and Adkins-Regan, 1999). These effects of AVT are comparable to those described earlier for AVP in Syrian hamsters and prairie voles, where increased activity in the vasopressin system was associated with increased aggression (e.g., Ferris, 2000; Wang *et al.*, 1998). Unfortunately, direct demonstrations of a role for testosterone in these studies are missing. However, a number of reports have defined an essential role for testosterone and, more specifically, its aromatized metabolite, estradiol, as a modulator or regulator of the AVT system in birds. A testosterone-dependent sexual dimorphism in AVT immunostaining and AVT mRNA has been identified in several telencephalic and diencephalic nuclei (Jurkevich *et al.*, 1996; Kimura *et al.*, 1999; Panzica *et al.*, 1999a,b). Further, neurons expressing aromatase immunoreactivity (IR) in the sexually dimorphic MPOA, BNST, LS, and ventromedial hypothalamus were located in a robust AVT-IR network (Balthazart, 1997), suggesting that estradiol is an important modulator of the AVT system. How these interactions affect offensive aggressive behavior has not yet been fully defined.

It seems appropriate to conclude that T modulates the AVP and AVT systems. This can be achieved through different pathways, including regulatory effects on the AVP or V1a receptor genes. A specific role for estrogen, the product of aromatization, is indicated, but how the androgenic metabolites contribute has not yet been elucidated. Social structure and seasonality must be overlaid on these effects because they impose boundaries on the extent to which AVP or AVT contribute to offensive aggression. Studies suggest a potential molecular basis for these effects, at least in voles (Young *et al.*, 1999). Characterizing these interrelationships appears to represent one of the important steps in developing an integrative neurobiology of offensive aggression.

IV. FEMALES

There has been a long-standing interest in the possible contribution of T to aggression in females. As discussed in the introduction, these studies appear to have been motivated largely by a belief in a *common path hypothesis,* which holds that aggressive behavior exhibited by females toward conspecifics (other than during lactation) necessarily has the same hormonal determinants that had been identified in males. These studies, not surprisingly, have yielded mixed to outright negative outcomes (e.g., Albert *et al.*, 1993; Batty *et al.*, 1986; Stavisky *et al.*, 1999; von Engelhardt *et al.*, 2000). Overall, the findings suggest that a different conceptual approach to hormone function in female-typical offensive aggression is needed. In this section, a model that focuses on the effects and mechanism of action of the neurosteroid dehydroepiandrosterone (DHEA), which functions as an inhibitor of female-typical aggression, is considered. This behavioral action of DHEA has been extensively documented (Baulieu, 1997; Bayart *et al.*, 1989; Perché *et al.*, 2000; Young *et al.*, 1991, 1995, 1996).

When intact or ovariectomized females are housed in triads, they reliably display intense attack behavior toward intruder females that are intact, ovariectomized, or lactating (Bayart *et al.*, 1989; Brain and Haug, 1992; Haug, 1978; Haug and Brain, 1983; Haug *et al.*, 1980). This same pattern of aggression also is displayed by group-housed gonadectomized males toward intact, ovariectomized, or lactating females. If castrated males are treated with T, however, attack toward females is completely inhibited (Haug and Brain, 1983; Haug *et al.*, 1982, 1986; Paroli *et al.*, 1972; Schlegel *et al.*, 1985). These observations, which have been developed almost exclusively in mice, suggest the existence of a generalized form of offensive aggression in females that is independent of T. This type of aggression on the part of females appears to be under GABAergic control and is modulated by DHEA (Perché *et al.*, 2000; Young *et al.*, 1991, 1995, 1996), a neurosteroid synthesized by local, *in situ* mechanisms the CNS (Baulieu, 1997; Compagnone and Mellon, 2000; Robel and Baulieu, 1995). A prominent role for DHEA was identified in studies that showed that following 15 days of treatment with this neurosteroid (80 μg/day), attack behavior by gonadectomized or intact females toward females or lactating females was significantly reduced (Bayart *et al.*, 1989; Brain and Haug, 1992; Perche *et al.*, 2000). Further, a nonmetabolizable analog of DHEA, 3β-methyl-androst-5-en-7-one (M-DHEA),

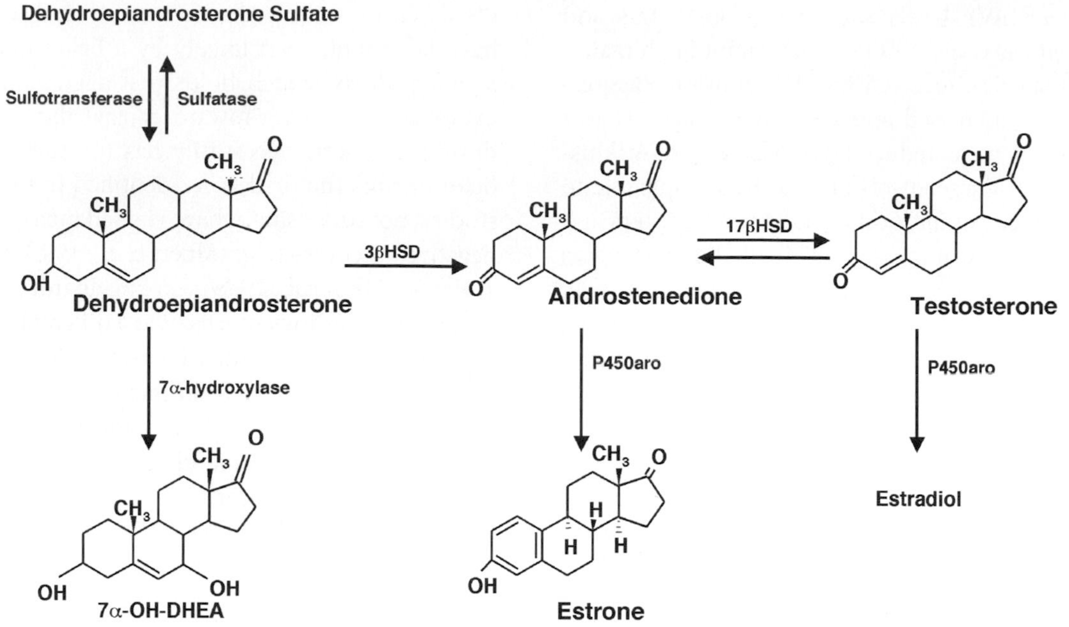

FIGURE 13 A general outline of DHEA metabolism in the central nervous system. The 3β-hydroxysteroid dehydrogenase pathway leads to the formation of androstenedione, which can serve as the substrate for the production of additional androgens and estrogens.

also suppressed attack when given for 15 days (Haug *et al.*, 1989; Robel and Baulieu, 1995), providing evidence that DHEA itself contributed directly to its antiaggressive action. *In situ*, there also may be contributions of other steroidal metabolites to its neuromodulatory actions (Fig. 13), especially in light of the duration of treatment required to reduce aggression and studies demonstrating androgenic effects of DHEA (Hornsby, 1997; Labrie *et al.*, 1998; S. Lu *et al.*, 2001), but these potential mechanisms have not been explored.

A. Neurosteroid DHEA

Dehydroepiandrosterone and other neurosteroids are modulators of GABA$_A$, NMDA, and σ_1 receptors (Compagnone and Mellon, 2000). The dominant focus of the neurosteroid literature, however, has been on effects exerted at the GABA$_A$ receptor complex (see reviews by Baulieu, 1997; Rupprecht and Holsboer, 1999). This is particularly true for DHEA, a potent inhibitor of female-typical aggression (i.e., aggressive behavior that is not androgen-dependent) (Bayart *et al.*, 1989; Brain and Haug, 1992; Haug *et al.*, 1989, 1992;

Paroli *et al.*, 1972; Perché *et al.*, 2000; Schlegel *et al.*, 1985; Young *et al.*, 1996). The emphasis on modulation of GABA$_A$ receptor function in the context of female-typical aggression is appropriate for several reasons. First, numerous studies have shown pronounced specific GABAergic effects on offensive aggression (see reviews by Miczek *et al.*, 1994, 1997; Siegel *et al.*, 1997, 1999). In fact, the 1990s saw over 200 studies (not cited here; see PubMed) on GABA and aggressive behavior. Second, there is no evidence linking the σ_1 receptor to aggression. Third, a smaller number of studies (approximately 30) examined the role of NMDA receptor involvement in aggression (Adamec, 1997, 1998; Adamec *et al.*, 1999; Blanchard *et al.*, 1995; Gould and Cameron, 1997; Siegel *et al.*, 1997) and these strongly indicate that it is primarily linked to defensive, not offensive, behavior. Last, it is worth noting that focusing studies on a single neurotransmitter receptor in a complex behavior can be exceptionally fruitful even when multiple neurotransmitters may be involved. Perhaps the best examples of advances using this approach are in the context of a female-typical behavior, where the elegant studies of Etgen *et al.* (1999) and McCarthy

(1995) have helped define the roles of β-adrenergic and GABA$_A$ function, respectively, in female sexual receptivity.

1. Mechanisms of Action

The finding of a robust antiaggressive effect of DHEA generated efforts to elucidate underlying mechanisms. There has been a singular emphasis on DHEA-induced alterations in brain levels of pregnenolone sulfate (PREG-S), a neurosteroid that is a negative modulator of the GABA$_A$ receptor and reduces GABAergic effects (Majewska and Schwartz, 1987). DHEA decreases PREG-S levels in whole brain, as shown in Fig. 14 (Young *et al.*, 1991, 1995), and this action leads to enhanced GABA function via the GABA$_A$ receptor complex, emphasizing a membrane-level effect of DHEA (Robel and Baulieu, 1995; Young *et al.*, 1991). The increased GABA function then inhibits offensive aggression, a premise strongly supported by numerous studies that demonstrated specific inhibitory effects of GABA on attack behavior (Miczek *et al.*, 1994, 1997; Siegel *et al.*, 1999).

However, observations suggest that additional processes may be involved. One is the description of AR up-regulation by DHEA in mouse brain and GT1-7

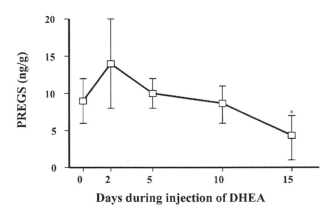

FIGURE 14 Time course of the PREG-S decrease in the brains of castrated male Swiss mice. DHEA was given daily for 15 days (80 μg/day) and groups of GDX males were killed by decapitation 2 hours after the injection on the indicated days.*, significantly lower compared to day 0 ($p < 0.05$) Reprinted with permission from Robel, P., *et al.* Biosynthesis and assay of neurosteroids in rats and mice: Functional correlates. *J. Ster. Biochem. Molec. Biol. 53*, 355–360. © 1995 Elsevier Science.

cells, shown in Fig. 15 (S. Lu *et al.*, 2001). This represents a novel mechanistic finding that also may be a potential component of the antiaggressive mechanism. Intact and T-treated GDX males do not exhibit aggression toward female targets and a 15-day treatment course is required for DHEA to reduce aggression. On this basis, it seems plausible that androgens exert an inhibitory effect and that the time frame is consistent with a genomic mechanism of action involving AR protein regulation. Viewed in combination, it appears reasonable to hypothesize that extended DHEA treatment involves both membrane-level and genomic effects and that both processes contribute to the ability of this neurosteroid to modulate female-typical aggression. This working model is supported by findings with allopregnenolone, a positive allosteric modulator of the GABA$_A$ receptor, where membrane-level and additional genomic effects via progestin receptor have been observed (Rupprecht, 1997; Rupprecht and Holsboer, 1999), although comparabale studies on DHEA are lacking.

Neurosteroids such as DHEA exert profound effects on the GABA$_A$ receptor. This is a complex process involving several sites on this transmembrane protein that can be produced by direct action at the membrane level in a time frame from minutes (a nongenomic effect) to longer-term processes that involve neurosteroid metabolites, steroidal effects, or both on gene function, which, through alterations in protein synthesis, in turn influence membrane receptor function (a genomic effect). In order to define these effects, the following should be taken into account: (1) the nature of the binding sites on GABA$_A$ receptor, (2) the extended-time course of DHEA treatment required to significantly reduce aggression, (3) that PREG-S, which appears to be involved in the reduction of aggression by DHEA, is an antagonist of GABA function through modulation of several sites on GABA$_A$ receptor, and (4) that DHEA itself and its androgenic metabolites, acting via AR, may be involved in the production of effects on the GABA$_A$ receptor (Friedman *et al.*, 1993; Masonis and McCarthy, 1995, 1996; Nett *et al.*, 1999).

The structure and function of the GABA$_A$ receptor are reviewed in Barnard *et al.* (1998) and Mehta and Ticku (1999). For the present purposes, the most salient feature is that it is a ligand-gated chloride channel that can be modulated through neurosteroid effects

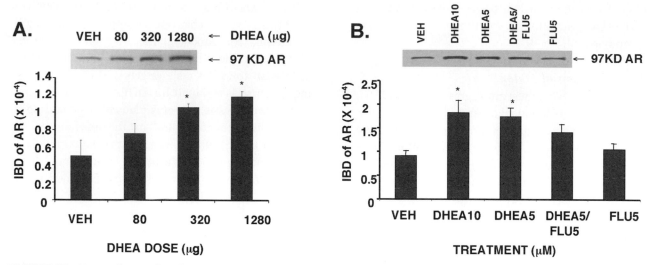

FIGURE 15 Up-regulation of AR by DHEA in mouse brain and GT1-7 cells. A. Female mice were ovariectomized 1 week before being treated with 80, 320, or 1280 μg DHEA or vehicle ($n = 3$/group) for four consecutive days (s.c.). Five hours after the last injection, major limbic system regions were isolated and analyzed by western blot for relative concentrations of AR. DHEA treatment augmented the cellular AR level in a dose-dependent manner. The effect of DHEA dosage is significant ($p < 0.01$; trend analysis). Data shown are mean integrated band densities (IBD + SEM) for 97-kDa AR bands. B. Cultured GT1-7 cells were treated with 5 μM DHEA with or without flutamide (5 μM). Comparisons of AR band densities showed that DHEA significantly increased AR level over vehicle control, whereas concurrent flutamide treatment completely inhibited the DHEA effect. Data shown are mean IBD + (SEM) of 97 kDa AR bands. *, significantly different from vehicle ($p < 0.05$). From Lu *et al.* (2001).

on the GABA (or agonist) site, the benzodiazepine (BZ) site, the Cl$^-$ ionophore (TBPS) site, the barbiturate site, the antagonist site, and an as yet unidentified neurosteroid binding site, as well as by compounds such as ethanol. Fortunately, Majewska (1995), Majewska and Schwartz (1987), and Majewska *et al.* (1990) have shown that PREG-S modulates binding at only two or three of these: the Cl$^-$ ionophore, the BZ site, and the GABA agonist site. DHEA-induced changes in binding need to be assessed at each site in regard to effects at the membrane level as well as in the context of genomic modulation. Regarding the latter, DHEA is metabolized to androstenedione (as well as to other androgens, although in lesser quantities), thus providing an additional steroid substrate that can influence genomic function through intracellular receptors. Changes in GABA$_A$ receptor gene expression that affect subunit structure, for example, represent one possible pathway for steroidal modulation (Canonaco *et al.*, 1993; Herbison and Fenelon, 1995; Mehta and Ticku, 1999; Rupprecht *et al.*, 1993). The androgenic effects of DHEA and its metabolites may represent a cross-talk cellular signaling system (for detailed descriptions,

see Katzenellenbogen, 1996; Rupprecht and Holsboer, 1999) linked to the antiaggressive effect of this neurosteroid. These observations demonstrate the importance of defining the potential interrelationship among DHEA, its androgenic effects, and the GABA$_A$ receptor function to fully understand its mechanism of action as well as how DHEA modulates the expression of female-typical aggression.

The preceding discussion should be viewed as an effort to define a subset of issues that require analysis if the modulatory effects of DHEA on the function of GABA$_A$ receptor are to be characterized. Although these studies are essential for elucidating cellular mechanisms, demonstrating their functional significance in relation to female-typical aggression requires additional steps. Clearly, a functional neuroanatomy for this form of aggression needs to be defined; there are no data available pertaining to this question. The issue is complex, if for no other reason than DHEA–GABA$_A$ interactions can occur through multiple mechanisms that need not be common throughout the brain. For example, the GABA$_A$ receptor subunit structure, which can vary by brain region, is a constraint on steroidal effects (Mehta and Ticku, 1999). In addition, AR distribution and the GABA system only partially overlap. Thus, a cross-talk system may be important in some areas, whereas a DHEA-induced reduction in PREG-S may be a key modulatory effect elsewhere. Pharmacological studies using antiandrogens can help resolve the contributions of AR. Defining the neuroanatomical substrates probably will require chronic microinfusion experiments to assess the regional effects of DHEA on PREG-S and whether these changes are functionally significant.

V. HUMAN CONNECTION

Defining the hormonal contribution to human aggressive behavior has proven to be a formidable challenge. Numerous considerations have hindered progress in this area, some of the most prominent being: (1) wide variation in experimental models, spanning paper and pencil assessments, athletic and staged competitions, and criminal and violent histories including various forms of sexual assault and suicide (e.g., Persky *et al.,* 1971; Meyer-Bahlburg *et al.,* 1974; McCaul *et al.,* 1992; Suay *et al.,* 1999; Gonzalez-Bono *et al.,* 1999; Scaramella and Brown, 1974; Banks and Dabbs, 1996; Virkkunen *et al.,* 1994; Soler *et al.,* 2000; Rada *et al.,* 1983; Brooks and Reddon, 1996; Olweus *et al.,* 1980, 1988; Pope and Katz, 1990; Thiblin *et al.,* 1999); (2) disparities between time of fluid collection for assay and when the dependent measure or index of aggression was committed, including concurrent or near-concurrent sampling through attempts to identify relationships between current hormone profiles and past violent acts (e.g., Gladue *et al.,* 1989; van Honk *et al.,* 1999; Booth *et al.,* 1989; Salvador *et al.,* 1999; Olweus *et al.,* 1988; Finkelstein *et al.,* 1997; Dabbs and Jurkovic, 1991; Brooks and Reddon, 1996; Matthews, 1979; Soler *et al.,* 2000; Virkkunen *et al.,* 1994; Bradford and McClean, 1984; Rada *et al.,* 1983); (3) dependence on assays of systemic T levels as indicators of effects in the brain without an appreciation for the role of intracellular events; (4) a frequent emphasis on violent, assaultive behavior as an end point (e.g., Banks and Dabbs, 1996; Brooks and Reddon, 1996; Choi and Pope, 1994; Isaacsson *et al.,* 1998; Kreuz *et al.,* 1972; Raboch *et al.,* 1987; Rada, *et al.,* 1983; Thiblin *et al.,* 1999; Studer *et al.,* 1997; Virkkunen

et al., 1996) rather than on types of aggressive behavior, such as dominance, that appear to be facilitated by T (Gray *et al.,* 1991; Mazur and Booth, 1998; although see Hines, 1998, for an opposing view); (5) vigorous disagreement regarding definitions of behaviors that constitute various forms of aggression even as the focus of contemporary studies narrows to more specific behaviors or attributes (see Archer, 1988, 1991, 1994; Mazur and Booth, 1998); and (6) the complexity that accrues as developmental, cognitive, social, cultural, economic, and experiential factors interact with physiological systems. Even with these limitations, there appears to have been some progress in assessing how gonadal hormones may influence aggression, at least in human males, if the evolution of conceptual models is emphasized rather than mechanistic advances. The literature is now replete with terms such as hostility, irritability, implusiveness, and dominance, as well as other more specific personality attributes, as possible correlates of circulating T rather than the global construct "aggression." This more refined analytical approach, although still under debate, holds the opportunity for providing clearer direction. From a mechanistic viewpoint, molecular genetic tools have led to the identification of polymorphisms in several genes, including tryptophan hydroxylase, the 5-HT transporter, certain 5-HT receptor subtypes, and monoamine oxidase A (MAO-A), that may be associated with inappropriate or impulsive aggression in some individuals (Brunner *et al.,* 1993; Manuck *et al.,* 1999, 2000; Nielsen *et al.,* 1998; Rotondo *et al.,* 1999; Gorwood *et al.,* 2000). At the same time, other groups have not found these relationships or have raised issues that temper these findings (Furlong *et al.,* 1998; Huang *et al.,* 1999; Hallikainen *et al.,* 2000; Miczek, 1999), demonstrating that caution is needed when assessing these results. This point is worth emphasizing because molecular biological findings related to aggression, when they first appear, have been interpreted by some as defining the cause of inappropriate aggression and violent behavior (e.g., Angier, 1995; summarized chronologically in Ensernik, 2000). Even a cursory historical review finds, for example, the XYY syndrome, the 5-HT$_{1B}$ receptor, and nNOS assigned this status. A detailed consideration of these findings falls outside the scope of this chapter, but the absence of uniform effects associated with any single genetic marker reinforces the need for an integrative systems perspective. Such an approach obviously requires delineation of interrelationships among neuroendocrine and neurochemical functions, paralleling the direction of studies with nonprimate species. Investigations with human populations, however, have not reached this stage.

An initial question, then, is whether a potential relationship between testosterone and aggression in humans can be framed in a way that affords an opportunity for meaningful progress. At the present time, the state of the field makes it premature to directly assess the effects of T or its metabolites in terms of the neuromodulator hypothesis. Rather, there is a need to establish clearly the types of aggressive interactions where T may have a contributory role, an important and no doubt controversial undertaking given the scope of presumptive T-aggression relationships that have been pursued (see reviews by Albert *et al.,* 1993; Archer, 1988, 1991, 1994; Gerra *et al.,* 1996; Mazur and Booth, 1998; Rubinow and Schmidt, 1996; Simon, 1981). To achieve this requires focused behavioral definitions, an understanding that the effects of testosterone (and other hormones) in target tissues including the brain are affected by processes that are not necessarily reflected in systemic measurements (except perhaps in extreme cases such as hypogonadism or the ingestion of large doses of anabolic steroids), and recognition that hormonal effects on behavior in humans may be subtle due to factors such as experience and cognition. The first two points suggest that by carefully drawing from nonprimate behavioral studies and knowledge of the mechanism of action of gonadal steroids, interpretations of existing human data could be improved. For example, it seems reasonable to suggest that dominance interactions and status in males may be influenced by T. This view was put forward by Mazur and Booth (1998), although their definition appears somewhat broad because it also included antisocial and defiant behaviors. Next, there is a need to consider metabolic processes, although this issue has received scant, if any, attention. In addition, it also may well be that the dynamics of T secretion, specifically changes in level in anticipation of and in response to an aggressive interaction and the subsequent effects produced by these changes are more important than absolute levels in circulation. This concept is consistent with an experimental approach that focuses on more subtle aspects of hormone function in

the context of human aggression and also recognizes that normal physiological function in adult males is seen across a range of systemic T values.

A. Males: Dominance and T Dynamics

Looking at the dynamics of systemic T in settings analogous to dominance contests is not new. In human males, competitive interactions that involve physical and nonphysical components show a fairly consistent pattern—T rises in anticipation of competition in participants, with divergence seen when the outcome is determined (Booth *et al.,* 1989; McCaul *et al.,* 1992; Gladue *et al.,* 1989; Elias, 1981). These studies found that T levels are transiently elevated in winners (akin to dominance) and significantly lowered in losers (akin to subordinates). Studies with nonhuman primates complement and extend these findings. For example, when dominance status was established through actual contests, changes in T comparable to those described in humans have been observed (Clarke *et al.,* 1986; Rose, 1975). In stable group structures, it is widely recognized that T secretion is suppressed in subordinates (e.g., Kraus *et al.,* 1999). Interestingly, baboon males that undergo transition to dominant status begin to show elevated T levels (Virgin and Spolsky, 1997). Although studies of stable groups in humans are rare, an investigation with prison populations did find that socially dominant male prisoners exhibited elevated T levels (Ehrenkranz *et al.,* 1974). Although additional studies are needed, these findings are consistent with the idea that it is the dynamics of changes in T seen in response to anticipated or experienced competitive interactions that are most important in primates. This concept is consistent with the challenge hypothesis advanced by Wingfield *et al.* (1990), which proposed that the effects of T on aggressive behavior are greatest during the establishment of dominance relationships (e.g., Cavigelli and Pereira, 2000) and with the neuromodulator hypothesis proposed in this chapter. Regarding the latter, alterations in T in response to dominance interactions or the outcome of competition establish a neuroendocrine environment that could differentially modulate neurochemical systems, with attendant effects on mood and behavior. Although changes in neurochemical function with chronic subordinate status (Blanchard *et al.,* 1993; Ferris, 2000; Fontenot *et al.,* 1995; Kaplan and Manuck, 1999; McKittrick *et al.*, 2000) have been linked to alterations in HPA axis function, the modulatory effects of gonadal steroids in human males on neurochemical systems is a speculative possibility pending direct experimental evidence.

B. Females: An Alternative Perspective

Attempts to demonstrate a systematic relationship between T and various forms of aggression in women, for the most part, have been unsuccessful (Bloch *et al.*, 1998; Cashdan, 1995; Dougherty *et al.*, 1997; Persky *et al.*, 1982; van Goozen *et al.*, 1997; Mazur and Booth, 1998), although positive results were obtained in some instances (e.g., Dabbs and Hargrove, 1997; Banks and Dabbs, 1996; Eriksson *et al.*, 1992). Given the range of behaviors that were assessed, which include delinquency, self-regard, assertiveness, various competitive situations, and feelings of hostility or irritability over the course of the menstrual cycle, the mixed to negative of results should not be surprising. It seems appropriate to ask whether a more focused examination of dominance-related behaviors might provide some insights, an approach that would parallel that taken with human males in the preceding section. Not surprisingly, even this more restrictive perspective is uninformative. Women do not seem to exhibit changes in T dynamics comparable to those seen in men in competitive settings (Mazur *et al.*, 1997; Booth *et al.*, 1989), nor are changes in T levels over the menstrual cycle positively correlated with moods generally associated with aggression (Backstrom *et al.*, 1983; Bloch *et al.*, 1998; Dougherty *et al.*, 1997; van Goozen *et al.*, 1997; although see Eriksson *et al.*, 1992). Nonhuman primate studies are largely consistent with the absence of a systematic, positive relationship between androgens and dominance or aggression in females. Although Batty *et al.* (1986) found lower T and androstenedione (AE) in subordinate vs. dominant talapoin monkeys, the amount of aggression displayed by individuals was not correlated with androgen levels. Even in ring-tailed lemurs, where females are the dominant sex, individual rates of aggression by females toward same-sex individuals were not correlated with circulating androgens (von Engelhardt *et al.*, 2000). A chronic 24-month anabolic steroid treatment regimen also failed to increase aggression in cynomolgus females (Stavisky *et al.*, 1999).

The equivocal to negative results in human and nonhuman primate studies raise several questions about an appropriate perspective on the role of androgens in aggression by human females. Given the continued interest in this potential relationship, it might be appropriate to examine the dynamics of T secretion in females. As discussed earlier, this may be a useful model for defining the potential relationship between T and dominance behavior in human males. However, results obtained in studies of hormonal changes over the menstrual cycle and their relationship to mood suggest this would not be productive. The findings from a small number of studies in which competition among women was involved (Mazur *et al.*, 1997; Booth *et al.*, 1989) also are inconsistent with support for this approach. Alternatively, a sociobiological model based on the nature of competition among females could be applied. From this perspective, whether androgens might be involved would depend on whether female dominance was based on competition for material resources (e.g., food) or whether competition was in regard to securing paternal investment (Daly and Wilson, 1983). Although an appealing aspect of this model is that it narrows the social context in which androgens might contribute to dominance-related behaviors in females, it remains trapped by the common path hypothesis (that the hormonal contribution to dominance-related offensive aggression between females necessarily follows the same principles derived from studies with males). As discussed earlier, the concept suffers from several weaknesses. A different approach to the relationship between hormones and offensive aggression in women seems to be required. The thesis of this chapter in relation to female–female aggressive behavior is that models that are independent of ovarian androgen effects are needed. In Section IV, it was argued that intrasex aggression in females was modulated by the neurosteroid DHEA. Whether this pertains to human or nonhuman primates is undetermined, but it suggests that an emphasis on the GABA system and its steroidal modulation might be fruitful.

VI. CONCLUSION

Summarizing the current understanding of hormonal processes involved in the development and expression of conspecific offensive aggression requires the recognition of concepts that have been clearly established, areas where there are gaps in knowledge, and an appreciation for issues in need of experimental analysis. The development of regulatory systems in males has been characterized in various models in regard to hormonal requirements and timing issues. Neuroanatomical sexual dimorphisms induced by the perinatal hormonal environment also have been defined, although their specific relationship to offensive aggression has not yet been ascertained. Newer lines of inquiry concerning the cellular and molecular effects of gonadal hormones during CNS differentiation, including the role of receptor coactivators and corepressors as well as how steroid receptors may influence chromatin organization, appear to represent important steps in delineating the relationship between the genomic effects of T and the establishment of male-typical regulatory pathways. Developmental processes linked to female-typical systems are an open issue, although it may well be that the absence of masculinization and defeminization represent sufficient conditions.

Far more is known about hormonal processes and the expression of conspecific aggression during adulthood. Studies in rodents and birds, for example, have established the importance of hormone metabolism. Aromatization and 5α-reduction of T in males and the 3β hydroxylation of the neurosteroid DHEA to androstenedione in females represent important mechanistic steps. A critical role for steroid receptors as transcription factors is obvious. Although some of the major target neurochemical systems have been identified, it is again the case that substantial work is needed to identify the full range of cellular processes that are affected, as well as the genomic and nongenomic mechanisms that mediate these effects. Progress in this area is essential for characterizing the neuromodulation of neurochemical function by gonadal hormones and neurosteroids. It represents an essential step in developing a systems model that eventually should encompass gene regulation, functional circuitry, behavioral expression, and adaptation.

The neuromodulator hypothesis can provide an integrative conceptual framework that broadly accounts for the hormonal contribution to sex-typical offensive aggression. Figure 16 depicts these effects based on the examples presented in this chapter. Although an emphasis on neuromodulation provides an overarching construct, an interesting feature of the model is that it produces opposite effects in each sex. In males the net effect of gonadal steroids is facilitative, whereas in females neurosteroids are inhibitory. The hypothesis raises a host of substantive research questions that can be best addressed through concepts that emphasize integration and a systems approach. From this perspective, continuing arguments for direct causal effects of hormones in either males or females seem to be limited in their capacity to advance the field.

There is much that remains to be defined. Gaps exist concerning neuroanatomical circuitry in males. An understanding of neuroanatomical substrates in females is essentially nonexistent. Whether this form of offensive aggression is elicited or inhibited by olfactory stimuli is unknown. The characterization of cellular and molecular mechanisms is in its early stages. In males, critical studies defining the molecular interface between T, its metabolites, and components of the 5-HT and AVP/AVT (and no doubt other) systems are required. In females, defining the nongenomic and genomic processes through which the neurosteroid DHEA modulates $GABA_A$ receptor is an essential step. This is only a partial list based on the representative systems covered in this chapter. In the aggregate, efforts to fully characterize the hormonal contribution to the development and expression of offensive aggression will require defining multiple effects covering both genomic and membrane-level actions. These must be elucidated in complex neurobiological circuits and the relevance of any particular mechanistic process may well vary by neuroanatomical site. This point emphasizes the value of a systems perspective.

Finally, it must be acknowledged that it was not possible to cover all aspects of hormone function in offensive aggression; a decision was made to focus on gonadal steroids in males and neurosteroidal effects in females. Other areas of interest are the effects of corticosteroids and interactions between the serotonin and vasopressin systems (Ferris, *et al.,* 1996; Haller *et al.,* 2000a,b). Reasons for not covering these areas were that much of the work on the HPA axis has been in the context of stress and subordination and that potential hormonal contributions to the 5-HT–AVP interface have been explored (e.g. Fuchs and Flügge, 1998; Blanchard *et al.,* 1993, 1995).

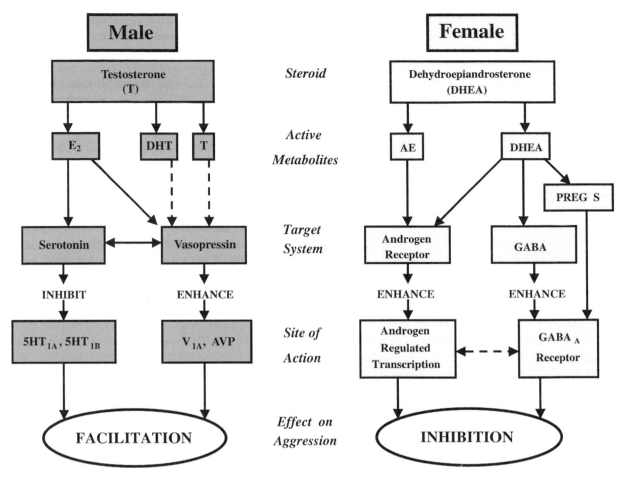

FIGURE 16 A summary of hormonal modulation of representative neurochemical systems in the regulation of conspecific offensive aggression in males and females. The principal steroids and key metabolites are shown. Known effects are indicated by solid lines (———), potential effects by dashed lines (– – –).

And what of the bridge to humans? Research with animal models demonstrates the complex nature of hormonal modulation and, perhaps even more important, the need for increasingly refined models when assessing endocrine contributions to human behavior. There has been progress in definitions. Looking at hostility, irritability, impulsivity, and other attributes, for example, is an improvement over grouping very different behaviors under "aggression." Basic research also indicates that focusing on a single genetic or physiological marker as a cause of aggression is very difficult. A systems perspective again is required, one that recognizes when hormones may have a role; that the physiological effects are modulatory; and that social structure, life events, and subsequent adaptions are reflected in alterations in cellular signaling pathways and neuroanatomical circuits.

Acknowledgments

The preparation of this chapter was supported in part by NIH grant 1 R01 MH59300 to NGS. In addition, studies reported from the author's laboratory have been supported in the past by NSF, NIH, and the H.F. Guggenheim Foundation. I am indebted to the many students and colleagues who contributed their time and energy over the years, particularly S. Lu, S. McKenna, A. Cologer-Clifford, S. Hu, R.E. Whalen, and R. Gandelman.

References

Adamec, R.E. (1997). Transmitter systems involved in neural plasticity underlying increased anxiety and defense—implications for understanding anxiety following traumatic stress. *Neurosci. Biobehav. Rev.* **21**, 755–765.

Maruyama, K., Endoh, H., Saski-Iwaoka, H., Kanou, H., Shimaya, E., Hashimoto, S., Kato, S., and Kawashima, H. (1998). A novel isoform of rat estrogen receptor beta with 18 amino acid insertion in the ligand binding domain as a putative dominant negative regulator of estrogen action. *Biochem. Biophys. Res. Commun.* **246**, 142–147.

Masonis, A.E.T., and McCarthy, M.P. (1995). Direct effects of the anabolic/androgenic steroids, stanozolol and 17α-methyltestosterone, on benzodiazepine binding to the γ-aminobutyric acid$_A$ receptor. *Neurosci. Lett.* **189**, 35–38.

Masonis, A.E.T., and McCarthy, M.P. (1996). Effects of the androgenic/anabolic steroid stanozolol on GABA$_A$ receptor function: GABA-stimulated ^{36}Cl influx and [^{35}S] TBPS binding. *J. Pharmacol. Exp. Ther.* **279**, 186–193.

Matter, J., Ronan, P., and Summers, C. (1998). Central monoamines in free-ranging lizards: Differences associated with social roles and territoriality. *Brain Behav. Evol.* **51**, 23–32.

Matthews, R. (1979). Testosterone levels in aggressive offenders. *In* "Psychopharmacology of Aggression" (M. Sandler, ed.), pp. 123–130.

Maurice, T., Phan, V.L., Urani, A., Kamei, H., Noda, Y., and Nabeshima, T. (1999). Neuroactive neurosteroids as endogenous effectors for the sigma1 (sigma1) receptor: Pharmacological evidence and therapeutic opportunities. *Jpn. J. Pharmacol.* **81**, 125–155.

Maxson, S.C. (1996). Issues in the search for candidate genes in mice as potential animal models of human aggression. *Ciba Found. Symp.* **194**, 21–35.

Maxson, S.C. (1998). Homologous genes, aggression and animal models. *Dev. Neuropsych.* **14**, 143–156.

Mazur, A., and Booth, A. (1998). Testosterone and dominance in men. *Behav. Brain Sci.* **21**, 353–363.

Mazur, A., Susman, E., and Edelbrock, S., (1997). Sex differences in testosterone response to a video game competition. *Evol. Human Behav.* **18**, 317–326.

McCarthy, M.M. (1995). Functional significance of steroid modulation of GABAergic neurotransmission: Analysis at the behavioral, cellular, and molecular levels. *Horm. Behav.* **29**, 131–140.

McCarthy, M.M., Corrini, H., Schumacher, M., Johnson, A.E., Pfaff, D.W., Schwartz-Giblin, S., and McEwen, B.S. (1992). Steroid regulation and sex differences in [^{3}H]muscimol binding in hippocampus, hypothalamus and midbrain in rats. *J. Neuroendocrinol.* **4**, 393–399.

McCaul, K.D., Claude, B.A., and Joppa, M. (1992). Winning, losing, mood, and testosterone. *Horm. Behav.* **26**, 486–504.

McEwen, B., Davis, P., Parsons, B., and Pfaff, D. (1979). The brain as a target for steroid hormone action. *Annu. Rev. Neurosci.* **2**, 65–112.

McGregor, A., and Herbert, J. (1992). Differential effects of excitotoxic basolateral and corticomedial lesions of the amygdala on the behavioural and endocrine responses to either sexual or aggression-promoting stimuli in the male rat. *Brain Res.* **574**, 9–20.

McKenna, S.E., Simon, N.G., and Cologer-Clifford, A. (1992). An assessment of agonist/antagonist effects of tamoxifen in the female mouse brain. *Horm. Behav.* **26**, 536–544.

McKenna-Repsher, S.E., and Simon, N.G. (1994). Estrogen receptor interactions with nuclear matrix of limbic tissue in the female mouse. *Soc. Neurosci. Abst.* **20**, 376.

McKenna-Repsher, S.E., and Simon, N.G. (1995). Immunodetection of estrogen receptor in nuclear matrix of the female mouse brain. *Soc. Neurosci. Abst.* **21**, 191.

McKittrick, C.R., Magarinos, A.M., Blanchard, D.C., Blanchard, R.J., McEwen, B.S., and Sakai, R.R. (2000). Chronic social stress reduces dendritic arbor in CA3 of hippocampus and decreases binding to serotonin transporter sites. *Synapse* **36**, 85–94.

McQueen, J.K., Wilson, H., Sumner, B.E.H., and Fink, G. (1999). Serotonin transporter (SERT) mRNA and binding site densities in male rat brain affected by sex steroids. *Brain Res. Mol. Brain Res.* **63**, 241–247.

Meek, L.R., Romeo, R.D., Novak, C.M., and Sisk, C.L. (1997). Actions of testosterone in prepubertal and postpubertal male hamsters: Dissociation of effects on reproductive behavior and androgen receptor immunoreactivity. *Horm. Behav.* **31**, 75–88.

Mehta, A.K., and Ticku, M.K. (1999). An update on GABA$_A$ receptors. *Brain Res.* **29**, 196–217.

Melcangi, R.C., Poletti, A., Cavarretta, I., Celotti, F., Colciago, F., Magnaghi, V., Motta, M., Negri-Cesi, P., and Martini, L. (1998). The 5alpha-reductase in the central nervous system: Expression and modes of control. *J. Steroid Biochem. Mol. Biol.* **65**, 295–299.

Melcher, T., Maas, S., Herb, A., Sprengel, R., Seeburg, P.H., and Higuchi, M. (1996). A mammalian RNA editing enzyme. *Nature (London)* **379**, 460–464.

Melloni, R.H., Connor, D.F., Phunong, T., Hang, P., Harrison, R.J., and Ferris, C.F. (1997). Anabolic-androgenic steroid exposure during adolescence and aggressive behavior in golden hamsters. *Physiol. Behav.* **61**, 359–364.

Menard, C.S., and Harlan, R.E. (1993). Up-regulation of androgen receptor immunoreactivity in the rat brain by androgenic-anabolic steroids. *Brain Res.* **622**, 226–236.

Mendelson, S., and Gorzalka, B. (1985). 5-HT$_{1A}$ receptors: Differential involvement in female and male sexual behavior in the rat. *Physiol. Behav.* **37**, 345–351.

Mendelson, S.D., and McEwen, B.S. (1990a). Chronic testosterone propionate treatment decreases the concentration of

[³H]quipazine binding at 5-HT₃ receptors in the amygdala of the castrated male rat. *Brain Res.* **528**, 339–343.

Mendelson, S., and McEwen, B. (1990b). Testosterone increases the concentration of [³H]8-hydroxy-2-(di-n-propylamino) tetralin binding at 5-HTlA receptors in the medial preoptic nucleus of the castrated male rat. *Eur. J. Pharmacol.* **181**, 329–331.

Mengod, G., Vilaro, T., Raurich, A., Lüopez-Gimüenez, F., Cortües, R., and Palacios, J. (1996). 5-HT receptors in mammalian brain: Receptor autoradiography and in situ hybridization studies of new ligands and newly identified receptors. *Histochem. J.* **11**, 747–758.

Metzger, D.A., Curtis, S., and Korach, K.S. (1991). Diethylstilbestrol metabolites and analogs: Differential ligand effects on estrogen receptor interactions with nuclear matrix. *Endocrinology (Baltimore)* **128**, 1785–1791.

Meyer-Bahlburg, H.F.L., Nat, P., Boon, D.A., Sharma, M., and Edwards, J.A. (1974). Aggressiveness and testosterone measures in man. *Psychosom. Med.* **36**, 269–274.

Miczek, K.A. (1999). Aggressive and social stress responses in genetically modified mice: From horizontal to vertical strategy. *Psychopharmacology* **147**, 17–19.

Miczek, K.A., Weerts, E., Haney, M., and Tidey, J. (1994). Neurobiological mechanisms controlling aggression: Preclinical developments and pharmacotherapeutic interventions. *Neurosci. Biobehav. Rev* **18**, 97–110.

Miczek, K.A., DeBold, J.F., van Erp, A.M., and Tornatzky, W. (1997). Alcohol, GABA_A-benzodiazepine receptor complex, and aggression. *Recent Dev. Alcohol* **13**, 139–171.

Middlemiss, D., and Hutson, P. (1990). The 5-HT1B receptors. *Ann. N.Y. Acad. Sci.* **600**, 132–148.

Miquel, M., Doucet, E., Riad, M., Adrien, J., Verge, D., and Hamon, M. (1992). Effect of the selective lesion of serotoninergic neurons on the regional distribution of 5HT₁A receptor mRNA in the rat brain. *Mol. Brain Res.* **14**, 357–362.

Mize, A.L., and Alper, R.H. (2000). Acute and long-term effects of 17β-estradiol on G_{i/o} coupled neurotransmitter receptor function in the female rat brain as assessed by agonist-stimulated [³⁵S]GTPγS binding. *Brain Res.* **859**, 326–333.

Mohr, E., Meyerhof, W., and Richter, D. (1995). Vasopressin and oxytocin: Molecular biology and evolution of the peptide hormones and their receptors. *Vitam. Horm. (N.Y.)* **51**, 235–266.

Monaghan, E., and Glickman, S. (1992). Hormones and aggressive behavior. *In* "Behavioral Endocrinology" (J. Becker, S. Breedlove, and D. Crews, eds.), pp. 261–285. MIT Press, Cambridge, MA.

Monsma, F.J., Jr., Shen, Y., Ward, R.P., Hamblin, M.W., and Sibley, D.R. (1993). Cloning and expression of a novel serotonin receptor with high affinity for tricyclic psychotropic drugs. *Mol. Pharmacol.* **43**, 320–327.

Moore, F.L., Richardson, C., and Lowry, C.A. (2000). Sexual dimorphism in numbers of vasotocin-immunoreactive neurons in brain areas associated with reproductive behaviors in the rough skin newt. *Gen. Comp. Endocrinol.* **117**, 281–298.

Mora, G.R., Prins, G.S., and Mahesh, V.B. (1996). Autoregulation of androgen receptor protein and messenger RNA in rat ventral prostrate is protein synthesis dependent. *J. Steroid Biochem. Mol. Biol.* **58**, 539–549.

Mosselman, S., Polman, J., and Dijkema, R. (1996). ERβ: Identification and characterization of a novel human estrogen receptor. *FEBS Lett.* **392**, 49–53.

Motelica-Heino, I., Edwards, D.A., and Roffi, J. (1993). Intermale aggression in mice: Does hour of castration after birth influence adult behavior? *Physiol. Behav.* **53**, 1017–1019.

Moyer, K.E. (1974). Sex differences in aggression. *In* "Sex Differences in Behavior" (R. Friedman, R. Richart, and R. Van de Wiele, eds.), pp. 335–372. Wiley, New York.

Mugford, R.A., and Nowell, N.W. (1970). Pheromones and their effect on aggression in mice. *Nature (London)* **226**, 967–968.

Muldoon, T.G. (1980). Regulation of steroid hormone receptor activity. *Endocr. Rev.* **1**, 339–364.

Muramatsu, M., and Inoue, S. (2000). Estrogen receptors: How do they control reproductive and nonreproductive functions? *Biochem. Biophys. Res. Commun.* **270**, 1–10.

Murasawa, S., Matsubara, H., Kijma, K., Maruyama, K., and Yasukiyo, M. (1995). Structure of the rat V1a vasopressin receptor gene and characterization of its promoter region and complete cDNA sequence of the 3′-end. *J. Biol. Chem.* **270**, 20042–20050.

Negri-Cesi, P., Poletti, A., and Celotti, F. (1996). Metabolism of steroids in the brain: A new insight into the role of 5-alpha-reductase and aromatase in brain differentiation and functions. *J. Steroid Biochem. Mol. Biol.* **58**, 455–466.

Nelson, R.J. (1995). "An Introduction to Behavioral Endocrinology." Sinaur Assoc., Sunderland, MA.

Nelson, R.J. (1997). The use of genetic "knockout" mice in behavioral endocrinology research. *Horm. Behav.* **31**, 188–196.

Nelson, R.J., and Young, K.A. (1998). Behavior in mice with targeted disruption of single genes. *Neurosci. Biobehav. Rev.* **22**, 453–462.

Nett, S.T., Jorge-Rivera, J.C., Myers, M., Clark, A.S., and Henderson, L.P. (1999). Properties and sex-specific differences of GABA_A receptors in neurons expressing gamma1 subunit mRNA in the preoptic area of the rat. *J. Neurophysiol.* **81**, 192–203.

Newman, S.W. (1999). The medial extended amygdala in male reproductive behavior. A node in the mammalian social behavior network. *Ann. N.Y. Acad. Sci.* **29**, 242–257.

Nielsen, D.A., Virkkunen, M., Lappalainen, J., Eggert, M., Brown, G.L., Long, J.C., Goldman, D., and Linnoila, M.

(1998). A tryptophan hydroxylase gene marker for suicidality and alcoholism. *Arch. Gen. Psychiatry* **55**, 593–602.

Oesterreich, S., Zhang, Q., Hopp, T., Fuqua, S.A., Michaelis, M., Zhao, H.H., Davie, J.R., Osborne, C.K., and Lee, A.V. (2000). Tamoxifen-bound estrogen receptor (ER) strongly interacts with the nuclear matrix protein HET/SAF-B, a novel inhibitor of ER-mediated transactivation. *Mol. Endocrinol.* **14**, 369–381.

Ogawa, S., Lubahn, D.B., Korach, K.S., and Pfaff, D.W. (1997). Behavioral effects of estrogen receptor gene disruption in male mice. *Proc. Natl. Acad. Sci. U.S.A.* **94**, 1476–1481.

Ogawa, S., Inoue, S., Watanabe, T., Hiroi, H., Orimo, A., Hosoi, T., Ouchi, Y., and Muramatsu, M. (1998a). The complete primary structure of human estrogen-β and its heterodimerization with estrogen receptor-α in vivo and in vitro. *Biochem. Biophys. Res. Commun.* **243**, 122–126.

Ogawa, S., Washburn, T.F., Lubahn, D.B., Korach, K.S., and Pfaff, D.W. (1998b). Modifications of testosterone-dependent behaviors by estrogen receptor-alpha gene disruption in male mice. *Endocrinology (Baltimore)* **139**, 5058–5069.

Ogawa, S., Chan, J., Chester, A.E., Gustafsson, J., Korach, K., and Pfaff, D. (1999). Survival of reproductive behaviors in estrogen receptor β gene-deficient (βERKO) male and female mice. *Neurobiology* **96**, 12887–12892.

Ohno, S., Geller, L.N., and Lai, E.V. (1974). TfM mutation and masculinization versus feminization of the mouse central nervous system. *Cell.* **3**, 235–242.

Olivier, B., and Mos, J. (1990). Serenics, serotonin and aggression. *Prog. Clin. Biol. Res.* **361**, 203–230.

Olivier, B., Mos, J., Raghoebar, M., de Koning, P., and Mak, M. (1994). Serenics. *Prog. Drug Res.* **42**, 169–248.

Olivier, B., Mos, J., Van Oorschot, R., and Hen, R. (1995). Serotonin receptors and animal models of aggressive behavior. *Pharmacopsychiatry* **28**, 80–90.

Olweus, D., Mattsson, Å., Schalling, D., and Löw, H. (1980). Testosterone, aggression, physical, and personality dimensions in normal adolescent males. *Psychosom. Med.* **42**, 253–269.

Olweus, D., Mattsson, Å., Schalling, D., and Löw, H. (1988). Circulating testosterone levels and aggression in adolescent males: A causal analysis. *Psychosom. Med.* **50**, 261–272.

Osterlund, M.K., Halldin, C., and Hurd, Y.L. (2000). Effects of chronic 17beta-estradiol treatment on the serotonin 5-HT(1A) receptor mRNA and binding levels in the rat brain. *Synapse* **35**, 39–44.

Ota, Y., Ando, H., Ueda, H., and Urano, A. (1999). Differences in seasonal expression of neurohypophysial hormone gene in ordinary and precocious male masu salmon. *Gen. Comp. Endocrinol.* **116**, 40–48.

Owen, K., Peters, P., and Bronson, F. (1974). Effects of intracranial implants of testosterone propionate on intermale aggression in castrated mice. *Horm. Behav.* **5**, 83–92.

Paech, K., Webb, P., Kuiper, G.G.J.M., Nilsson, S., Gustaffsson, J.-Å., Kushner, P.J., and Scanlan, T.S. (1997). Differential ligand activation of estrogen receptors ERα and ERβ at AP1 sites. *Science* **277**, 1508–1510.

Paige, L.A., Christensen, D.J., Crøn, H., Norris, J.D., Gottlin, E.B., Padilla, K.M., Chang, C., Ballas, L.M., Hamilton, P.T., McDonnell, D.P., and Fowlkes, D.M. (1999). Estrogen receptor (ER) modulators each induce distinct conformational changes in ERα and ERβ. *Proc. Natl. Acad. Sci. U.S.A.* **96**, 3999–4004.

Palacios, J., Waeber C., Hoyer, D., and Mengod, G. (1990). Distribution of serotonin receptors. *Ann. N.Y. Acad. Sci.* **600**, 36–52.

Panzica, G.C., Castagna, C., Viglietti-Panzica, C., Grossmann, R., and Balthazart, J. (1999a). Effects of testosterone on sexually dimorphic parvocellular neurons expressing vasotocin mRNA in the male quail brain. *Brain Res.* **850**, 55–62.

Panzica, G.C., Castagna, C., and Viglietti-Panzica, C. (1999b). Gonadal steroid-dependent neuronal circuitries in avian limbic and preoptic regions. *Eur. J. Morphol.* **37**, 112–116.

Parks, C., Robinson, P., Sibille, E., Shenk, T., and Toth, M. (1998). Increased anxiety of mice lacking the serotonin$_{1A}$ receptor. *Genetics* **95**, 10734–10739.

Paroli, E., Pantaleoni, G.C., Valeri, P., Nencini, P., and Jame, R. (1972). Inhibitory effect of dehydroepiandrosterone on aggressive behavior. *Arch. Intl. Pharmacodyn. Ther.* **196**, 147–150.

Pazos, A., and Palacios, J.M. (1985). Quantitative autoradiographic mapping of serotonin receptors in the rat brain. I. Serotonin-l receptors. *Brain Res.* **346**, 205–230.

Pecins-Thompson, M., and Bethea, C.L. (1998). Ovarian steroid regulation of 5-HT1A autoreceptor messenger ribonucleic acid expression in the dorsal raphe of rhesus macaques. *Neuroscience* **89**, 267–277.

Pennie, W.D., Aldridge, T.C., and Brooks, A.N. (1998). Differential activation by xenoestrogen of ERα and ERβ when linked to different response elements. *J. Endocrinol.* **158**, R11–R14.

Perché, F., Young, J. Robel, P., Simon, N.G., and Haug, M. (2000). Prenatal testosterone treatment potentiates the aggression-suppressive effect of the neurosteroid dehydroepiandrosterone in female mice. *Aggressive Behav.* **27**, 130–138.

Peroutka, S. (1991). The molecular pharmacology of 5-hydroxytryptamine receptor subtypes. *Recep. Biochem. Methods.* **15**, 65–80.

Peroutka, S. (1992). Phylogenic tree analysis of G-protein-coupled 5-HT receptors: Implications for receptor nomenclature. *Neuropharmacology* **31**, 609–613.

Peroutka, S.J. (1994). 5-Hyroxytryptamine receptors in vertebrates and invertebrates: Why are there so many? *Neurochem. Int.* **25**, 533–536.

Peroutka, S.J., and Howell, T.A. (1994). The molecular evolution of G protein-coupled receptors: Focus on 5-hydroxytryptamine receptors. *Neuropharmacology* **33**, 319–324.

Peroutka, S.J., Schmidt, A.W., Sleight, A.J., and Harrington, M.A. (1990). Serotonin receptor "families" in the central nervous system: An overview. *Ann. N.Y. Acad. Sci.* **600**, 104–112.

Persky, H., Smith, K.D., and Basu, G.K. (1971). Relation of psychologic measure of aggression and hostility to testosterone production in man. *Psychosom. Med.* **33**, 265–277.

Persky, H., Dreisbach, L. Miller, W.R., O'Brien, C.P., Khan, M.A., Lief, H.I., Charney, N., and Strauss, D. (1982). The relation of plasma androgen levels to sexual behaviors and attitudes of women. *Psychosom. Med.* **44**, 305–319.

Petterson, K., Grandien, K., Kuiper, G.G.J.M., and Gustafsson, J.-Å. (1997). Mouse estrogen receptor β forms estrogen response element-binding heterodimers with estrogen receptor α. *Mol. Endocrinol.* **11**, 1486–1496.

Pope, H.G., Jr., and Katz, D.L. (1990). Homicide and near-homicide by anabolic steroid users. *J. Clin. Psychiatry* **51**, 28–31.

Pope, H.G., Jr., Kouri, E.M., Powell, K.F., Cambell, C., and Katz, D.L. (1996). Anabolic-androgenic steroid use among 123 prisoners. *Compr. Psychiatry* **37**, 322–327.

Pope, H.G., Jr., Kouri, E.M., and Hudson, J.I. (2000). Effects of supraphysiologic dose of testosterone on mood and aggression in normal men: A randomized controlled trial. *Arch. Gen. Psychiatry* **57**, 133–140.

Potegal, M., and Ferris, C.F. (1990). Intraspecific aggression in male hamsters is inhibited by intrahypothalamic VP receptor antagonist. *Aggressive Behav.* **15**, 311–320.

Prins, G.S., and Birch, L. (1993). Immunocytochemical analysis of androgen receptor along the ducts of the separate rat prostate lobes after androgen withdrawal and replacement. *Endocrinology (Baltimore)* **132**, 169–178.

Quigley, C.A., De Bellies, A., Marschke, K.B., el-Awady, M.K., Wilson, E.M., and French, F.S. (1995). Androgen receptor defects: Historical, clinical, and molecular perspectives. *Endocr. Rev.* **16**, 271–321.

Raap, D.K., DonCarlos, L., Garcia, F., Muma, N., Wolf, W.A., Battaglia, G., and Van de Kar, L.D. (2000). Estrogen desensitizes 5-HT$_{1A}$ receptors and reduces levels of G$_Z$, G$_{i1}$ and G$_{i3}$ proteins in the hypothalamus. *Neuropharmacology* **39**, 1823–1832.

Raboch, J., Cerna, H., and Zemek, P. (1987). Sexual aggressivity and androgens. *Br. J. Psychiatry.* **151**, 398–400.

Rada, R.T., Laws, D.R., Kellner, R., Stravastava, L., and Peake, G. (1983). Plasma androgens in violent and nonviolent sex offenders. *Bull. Am. Acad. Psychiat. Law* **11**, 149–158.

Ramboz, S., Saudou, F., Amara, D.A., Belzung, C., Segu, L., Misslin, R., Bubot, C., and Hen, R. (1996). 5-HT$_{1B}$ receptor knockout—behavioral consequences. *Behav. Brain Res.* **73**, 305–312.

Ramboz, S., Oosting, R., Amara, D.A., Kung, H., Blier, P., Mendelson, M., Mann, J., Brunner, D., and Hen, R. (1998). Serotonin receptor 1A knockout: An animal model of anxiety-related disorder. *Proc. Natl. Acad. Sci. U.S.A.* **95**, 14476–14481.

Rasika, S., Alveraz-Buylla, A., and Nottebohm, F. (1999). BDNF mediates the effects of testosterone on the survival of new neurons in an adult brain. *Neuron* **22**, 53–62.

Rastegar, A., Ciesielisk, L., Simler, S., Messripour, M., and Mandel, P. (1993). Brain monoamines following castration of aggressive muricidal rats. *Neurochem. Res.* **18**, 471–477.

Rhen, T., and Crews, D. (2000). Organization and activation of sexual and agonistic behavior in the leopard gecko, *Eublepharis mascularius. Neuroendocrinology* **71**, 252–261.

Rines, J.P., and Vom Saal, F.S. (1984). Fetal effects on sexual behavior and aggression in young and old female mice treated with estrogen and testosterone. *Horm. Behav.* **18**, 117–129.

Robel, P., and Baulieu, E.E. (1995). Dehydroepiandrosterone (DHEA) is a neuroactive neurosteroid. *Ann. N.Y. Acad. Sci.* **774**, 82–110.

Robel, P., Young, J., Corpéchot, C., Mayo, W., Perché, F., Haug, M., Simon, H., and Baulieu, E.E. (1995). Biosynthesis and assay of neurosteroids in rats and mice: Functional correlates. *J. Steroid Biochem. Mol. Biol.* **53**, 355–360.

Ropartz, P. (1968). The relation between olfactory stimulation and aggressive behavior in mice. *Anim. Behav.* **16**, 97–100.

Rose, R.M. (1975). Consequences of social conflict on plasma testosterone levels in rhesus monkeys. *Psychosom. Med.* **37**, 50.

Ross, J. (1996). Control of messenger RNA stability in higher eukaryotes. *Trends Genet.* **12**, 171–175.

Rotondo, A., Schuebel, K., Bergen, A., Aragon, R., Virkkunen, M., Linnoila, M., Goldman, D., and Nielson, D. (1999). Identification of four variants in the tryptophan hydroxylase promotor and association to behavior. *Mol. Psychiatry* **4**, 360–368.

Rowe, F.A., and Edwards, D.A. (1971). Olfactory bulb removal: Influences on the aggressive behaviors of male mice. *Physiol. Behav.* **7**, 889–892.

Rubinow, D.R., Schmidt, P.J. (1996). Androgens, brain, and behavior. *Am. J. Psychiatry.* **153**, 974–984.

Ruby, D.E. (1978). Seasonal changes in the territorial behavior of the iguanid lizard *Sceloporus jarrovi. Copeia,* pp. 430–438.

Rupprecht, R. (1997). The neuropsychopharmacological potential of neuroactive steroids. *J. Psychiat. Res.* **31**, 297–314.

Rupprecht, R., and Holsboer, F. (1999). Neuroactive steroids: Mechanisms of action and neuropsychopharmacological perspectives. *Trends Neurosci.* **22**, 410–416.

Rupprecht, R., Reul, J.M.H.M., Trapp, T., van Steensel, B., Wetzel, C., Damm, K., Zieglgansberger, W. and Holsboer, F. (1993). Progesterone receptor-mediated effects of neuroactive steroids. *Neuron* **11**, 523–530.

Sachs, A.B. (1993). Messenger RNA degradation in eukaryotes. *Cell (Cambridge Mass.)* **74**, 413–421.

Salvador, A., Suay, F., Martinez-Sanchis, S., Simon, V.M., and Brain, P.F. (1999). Correlating testosterone and fighting in male participants in judo contests. *Physiol. Behav.* **68**, 205–209.

Sasano, H., Takashashi, K., Satoh, F., Nagura, H., and Harada, N. (1998). Aromatase in the human central nervous system. *Clin. Endocrinol.* **48**, 325–329.

Saudou, F., Amara, D.A., Dierich, A., LeMeur, M., Ramboz, S., Segu, L., Buhot, M.C., and Hen, R. (1994). Enhanced aggressive behavior in mice lacking 5-HT$_{1B}$ receptor. *Science* **265**, 1875–1878.

Scaramella, T.J., and Brown, W.A. (1978). Serum testosterone and aggressiveness in hockey players. *Psychosom Med.* **40**, 262–265.

Scearce-Levie, K., Chen, J.P., Gardner, E., and Hen, R. (1999). 5-HT receptor knockout mice: Pharmacological tools or models of psychiatric disorders. *Ann. N.Y. Acad. Sci.* **868**, 701–715.

Schechter, D., Howard, S.M., and Gandelman, R. (1981). Dihydrotestosterone promotes fighting behavior of female mice. *Horm. Behav.* **15**, 233–237.

Schlegel, M.L., Spetz, J.F., Robel, P. and Haug, M. (1985). Studies on the effects of dehydroepiandrosterone and its metabolites on attacks by castrated mice on lactating intruders. *Physiol. Behav.* **34**, 867–870.

Schlinger, B.A., (1997). The activity and expression of aromatase in songbird. *Brain Res. Bull.* **44**, 359–364.

Schlinger, B.A., and Callard, G.V. (1990a). Aromatization mediates aggressive behavior in quail. *Gen. Comp. Endocrinol.* **79**, 39–53.

Schlinger, B.A., and Callard, G.V. (1990b). Aggressive behavior in birds: An experimental model for studies of brain-steroid interactions. *Comp. Biochem. Physiol. A* **97**, 307–316.

Schmidt, B.M.W., Gerdes, D., Feuring, M., Falkenstein, E., Christ, M., and Wehling, M. (2000). Rapid, nongenomic steroid actions: A new age? *Front. Neuroendocrinol.* **21**, 57–94.

Schwabe, J.W., Chapman, L., and Rhodes, D. (1995). The oestrogen receptor recognizes an imperfectly palindromic response element through an alternative side-chain conformation. *Structure* **15**, 201–213.

Scott, J.P. (1966). Agonistic behavior of mice and rats: A review. *Am. Zool.* **6**, 683–701.

Segovia, S., and Guillamon, A. (1993). Sexual dimorphism in the vomeronasal pathway and sex differences in reproductive behaviors. *Brain Res. Brain Res. Rev.* **18**, 51–74.

Segovia, S., Guillamon, A., Del Cerro, M.C., Ortega, E., Perez-Laso, C., Rodriguea-Zafra, M., and Beyer, C. (1999). The development of brain sex differences: A multisignaling process. *Behav. Brain Res.* **105**, 69–80.

Shaikh, M.B., and Siegel, A. (1994). Neuroanatomical and neurochemical mechanisms underlying amygdaloid control of defensive rage behavior in the cat. *Braz. J. Med. Biol. Res.* **27**, 2759–2779.

Shapiro, R.A., Xu, C., and Dorsa, D.M. (2000). Differential transcriptional regulation of rat vasopressin gene expression by estrogen receptor alpha and beta. *Endocrinology (Baltimore)* **141**, 4056–4064.

Sheridan, P.J. (1978). Localization of androgen- and estrogen-concentrating neurons in the diencephalon and telencephalon of the mouse. *Endocrinology (Baltimore)* **103**, 1328–1334.

Shibata, H., Spencer, T.E., Oñate, S.A., Jenster, G., Tsai, S.Y., Tsai, M., and O'Malley, B.W. (1997). Role of co-activators and co-repressors in the mechanism of steroid/thyroid receptor action. *Recent Prog. Horm. Res.* **52**, 141–165.

Shih, J.C., Chen, K., and Ridd, M.J. (1999). Monoamine oxidase: From genes to behavior. *Annu. Rev. Neurosci.* **22**, 197–217.

Shughrue, P.J., Komm, B., and Merchenthaler, I. (1996). The distribution of estrogen receptor-β mRNA in the rat hypothalamus. *Steroids* **61**, 678–681.

Shughrue, P.J., Lane, M.V., and Merchenthaler, I. (1997). Comparative distribution of estrogen receptor-α and β mRNA in the rat central nervous system. *J. Comp. Neurol.* **388**, 507–525.

Shughrue, P.J., Lane, M.V., Scrimo, P.J., and Merchenthaler, I. (1998). Comparative distribution of estrogen receptor-α (ER-α) and β (ER-β) mRNA in the rat pituitary, gonad and reproductive tract. *Steroids* **63**, 498–504.

Shupnik, M.A., and Rosenzweig, B.J. (1990). Identification of an estrogen-responsive element in the rat LH beta gene. DNA-estrogen receptor interactions and functional analysis. *Biol. Chem.* **266**, 17084–17091.

Sibille, E., Pavlides, C., Benke, D., and Toth, M. (2000). Genetic inactivation of the serotonin$_{1A}$ receptor in mice results in downregulation of major GABA$_A$ receptor α subunits, reduction of GABA$_A$ receptor binding, and benzodiazepine-resistant anxiety. *J. Neurosci.* **20**, 2758–2765.

Siegel, A., Schubert, K.L., and Shaikh, M.B. (1997). Neurotransmitters regulating defensive rage behavior in the cat. *Neurosci. Biobehav. Rev.* **21**, 733–742.

Siegel, A., Roeling, T.A., Gregg, T.R., and Kruk, M.R. (1999). Neuropharmacology of brain-stimulation-evoked aggression. *Neurosci. Biobehav. Rev.* **23**, 359–389.

Sijbesma, H., Schipper, J., and de Kloet, E. (1990). The anti-aggressive drug eltoprazine preferentially binds to 5-HT$_{1A}$ and 5-HT$_{1B}$ receptor subtypes in rat brain: Sensitivity to guanine nucleotides. *Eur. J Pharmacol.* **187**, 209–223.

Sijbesma, H., Schipper, J., de Kloet, E., Mos, J., van Aken, H., and Olivier, B. (1991). Postsynaptic 5-HT$_1$ receptors and offensive aggression in rats: A combined behavioral and auto-radiographic study with eltoprazine. *Pharmacol. Biochem. Behav.* **38**, 447–458.

Silverin, B., Baillien, M., Foidart, A., and Balthazart, J. (2000). Distribution of aromatase activity in the brain and peripheral tissues of passerine and nonpasserine avian species. *Gen. Comp. Endocrinol.* **117**, 34–53.

Simerly, R.B. (1995). Hormonal regulation of limbic and hypothalamic pathways. In P.E. Micevych and J. Hammer Jr. (eds.). *Neurobiological Effects of Sex Steroid Hormones.* Cambridge University Press, Cambridge, pp. 85–114.

Simerly, R.B. (1998). Organization and regulation of sexually dimorphic neuroendocrine pathways. *Behav. Brain Res.* **92**, 195–203.

Simerly, R.B., Chang, C., Muramatsu, M., and Swanson, L.W. (1990). Distribution of androgen and estrogen receptor mRNA-containing cells in the rat brain: An in situ hybridization study. *J. Comp. Neurol.* **294**, 76–95.

Simon, N.G. (1979). The genetics of intermale aggression in mice: Recent research and alternative strategies. *Neurosci. Biobehav. Rev.* **3**, 97–106.

Simon, N.G. (1981). Hormones and human aggression: A comparative perspective. *Int. J. Ment. Health* **10**, 60–74.

Simon, N.G., and Coccaro, E.F. (1999). Human aggression: What's animal research got to do with it. *H.F. Guggenheim Found. Rev.* **3**, 13–20.

Simon, N.G., and Cologer-Clifford, A. (1991). In utero contiguity to males does not influence morphology, behavioral sensitivity to testosterone, or hypothalamic androgen binding in CF-1 female mice. *Horm. Behav.* **25**, 518–530.

Simon, N.G., and Gandelman, R. (1978). Aggression-promoting and aggression eliciting properties of estrogens in male mice. *Physiol. Behav.* **21**, 161–164.

Simon, N.G., and Masters, D.B. (1987). Activation of male-typical aggression by testosterone but not its metabolites in C57BL/6J female mice. *Physiol. Behav.* **41**, 405–407.

Simon, N.G., and Masters, D.B. (1988). Activation of intermale aggression by combined androgen-estrogen treatment. *Aggressive Behav.* **14**, 291–295.

Simon, N.G., and Perry, M. (1988). Medroxyprogesterone acetate and tamoxifen do not decrease aggressive behavior in CF-1 male mice. *Pharmacol., Biochem. Behav.* **30**, 829–833.

Simon, N., and Whalen, R. (1986). Hormonal regulation of aggression: Evidence for a relationship among genotype, receptor binding, and behavioral sensitivity to androgen and estrogen. *Aggressive Behav.* **12**, 255–266.

Simon, N., and Whalen, R. (1987). Sexual differentiation of androgen-sensitive and estrogen-sensitive regulatory systems for aggressive behavior. *Horm. Behav.* **21**, 493–500.

Simon, N.G., Gandelman, R., and Howard, S.M. (1981). MER-25 does not inhibit the activation of aggression by testosterone in adult Rockland-Swiss mice. *Psychoneuroendocrinology* **6**, 131–137.

Simon, N.G., Gray, J.L., and Gandelman, R. (1983). An empirically derived scoring system for intermale aggression in mice. *Aggressive Behav.* **9**, 157–166.

Simon, N.G., Whalen, R.E., and Tate, M.P. (1985). Induction of male-like aggression by androgens but not by estrogens in adult female mice. *Horm. Behav.* **19**, 204–212.

Simon, N.G., Lu, S.F., McKenna, S.E., Chen, X., and Clifford, A.C. (1993). Sexual dimorphisms in regulatory systems for aggression. *In* "The Development of Sex Differences and Similarities in Behavior" (M. Haug *et al.*, eds.), pp. 389–408. Kluwer Academic Publishers, Amsterdam.

Simon, N., McKenna, S., Lu, S., and Cologer-Clifford, A. (1996). Development and expression of hormonal systems regulating aggression. *Ann. N.Y. Acad. Sci.* **794**, 8–17.

Simon, N.G., Cologer-Clifford, A., Lu, S.F., McKenna, S.E., and Hu, S. (1998). Testosterone and its metabolites modulate 5HT1A and 5HT1B agonist effects on intermale aggression. *Neurosci. Biobehav. Rev.* **23**, 325–336.

Slotnick, B., and McMullen, M. (1972). Intraspecific fighting in albino mice with septal forebrain lesions. *Physiol. Behav.* **8**, 333–337.

Sluyter, F., van Oortmerrsen, G.A., de Ruiter, A.J., and Koolhaas, J.M. (1996). Aggression in wild house mice: Current state of affairs. *Behav. Genet.* **26**, 489–496.

Smith, J.W. (1977). "The Behavior of Communicating: An Ethological Approach." Harvard University Press, Cambridge, MA.

Sohrabji, F., Miranda, R.C.G., and Toran-Allerand, C.D. (1995). Identification of a putative estrogen response element in the gene encoding brain-derived neurotrophic factor. *Proc. Natl. Acad. Sci. U.S.A.* **92**, 11110–11114.

Soler, H., Vinayak, P., and Quadagno, D. (2000). Biosocial aspects of domestic violence. *Psychoneuroendocrinology* **25**, 721–739.

Soma, K.K., Sullivan, K., and Wingfield, J. (1999). Combined aromatase inhibitor and antiandrogen treatment decreases territorial aggression in a wild songbird during the nonbreeding season. *Gen. Comp. Endocrinol.* **115**, 442–453.

Stavisky, R.C., Register, T.C., Watson, S.L., Weaver, D.S., and Kaplan, J.R. (1999). Behavioral responses to ovariectomy and chronic anabolic steroid treatment in female cynomolgus macaques. *Physiol. Behav.* **66**, 95–100.

Stenoien, D.L., Mancini, M.G., Patel, K., Allegretto, E.A., Smith, C.L., and Mancini, M.A. (2000). Subnuclear trafficking of estrogen receptor-alpha and steroid receptor coactivator-1. *Mol. Endocrinol.* **14**, 518–534.

Stevenson, P.A., Hofmann, H.A., Schoch, K., and Shildberger, K. (2000). The fight and flight responses of crickets depleted of biogenic amines. *J. Neurobiol.* **43**, 107–120.

Studer, L.H., Reddon, J.R., and Siminoski, K.G. (1997). Serum testosterone in adult sex offenders: A comparison between Caucasians and North American Indians. *J. Clin. Psychol.* **53**, 375–385.

Suay, F., Salvador, A., González-Bono, E., Sanchís, C., Martínez-Sanchis, S., Simón, V.M., and Montoro, J.B. (1999). Effects of competition and its outcome on serum testosterone, cortisol and prolactin. *Psychoneuroendocrinology* **24**, 551–566.

Sullivan, A. (2000). The he hormone. *N.Y. Times Mag.,* April 2, pp. 46–56.

Summers, C.H., and Greenberg, N. (1995). Activation of central biogenic amines following aggressive interaction in male lizards, *Anolis carolinensis. Brain Behav. Evol.* **45**, 339–349.

Sumner, B.E.H., Grant, K.E., Rosie, R., Hegele-Hartung, C., Fritzemeier, K.H., and Fink, G. (1999). Effects of tamoxifen on serotonin transporter and 5-hydroxytryptamine$_{2A}$ receptor binding sites and mRNA levels in the brain of ovariectomized rats with or without acute estradiol replacement. *Mol. Brain Res.* **73**, 119–128.

Sun, J., Meyers, M., Fink, B.E., Rajendran, R., Katzenellenbogen, J.A., and Katzenellenbogen, B.S. (1999). Novel ligands that function as selective estrogens or antiestrogens for estrogen receptor-α or estrogen receptor-β. *Endocrinology (Baltimore)* **140**, 800–804.

Svare, B.B. (1983). "Hormones and Aggressive Behavior." Plenum Press, New York.

Tecott, L.H., and Barondes, S.H. (1996). Genes and aggressiveness. Behavioral genetics. *Curr. Biol.* **6**, 238–240.

Tetel, M.J. (2000). Nuclear receptor coactiavtors in neuroendocrine function. *J. Neuroendocrinol.* **12**, 927–932.

Thiblin, I., Runeson, B., and Rajs, J. (1999). Anabolic androgenic steroids and suicide. *Ann. Clin. Psychiatry* **11**, 223–231.

Tirassa, P., Thiblin, I., Agren, G., Vigneti, E., Aloe, L., and Stenfors, C. (1997). High-dose anabolic androgenic steroids modulate concentrations of nerve growth factor and expression of its low affinity receptor (p75-NGFr) in male rat brain. *J. Neurosci. Res.* **47**, 198–207.

Tokarz, R.R. (1986). Hormonal regulation of male reproductive behavior in the lizard Anolis sagrei: A test of the aromatization hypothesis. *Horm. Behav.* **20**, 364–377.

Tokarz, R.R. (1987). Effects of the antiandrogens cyproterone acetate and flutamide on male reproductive behavior in a lizard (*Anolis sagrei*). *Horm. Behav.* **21**, 1–16.

Tora, L., Gaub, M.P., Mader, S., Dierich, A., Bellard, M., and Chambon, P. (1988). Cell-specific activity of a GGTCA half-palindromic oestrogen-responsive element in the chicken ovalbumin gene promoter. *EMBO J.* **7**, 3771–3778.

Torand-Allerand, C.D. (2000). Novel sites and mechanisms of oestrogen action in the brain. *Novartis Found. Symp.* **230**, 56–73.

Torand-Allerand, C.D., Singh, M., and Setalo, G., Jr. (1999). Novel mechanisms of oestrogen action in the brain: New players in an old story. *Front. Neuroendocrinol.* **20**, 97–121.

Tremblay, G.B., Tremblay, A., Copeland, N.G., Gilbert, D.J., Jenkins, N.A., Labrie, F., and Giguère, V. (1997). Cloning, chromosomal localization and functional analysis of the murine estrogen receptor β. *Mol. Endocrinol.* **11**, 353–365.

Tremblay, G.B., Tremblay, A., Labrie, F., and Giguère, V. (1999). Dominant activity of activation function 1 (AF-1) and differential stoichiometric requirements for AF-1 and -2 in the estrogen receptor alpha-beta heterodimeric complex. *Mol. Cell. Biol.* **19**, 1919–1927.

Trevino, A., Wolf, A., Jackson, A., Price, T., and Uphouse, L. (1999). Reduced efficacy of 8-OH-DPAT's inhibition of lordosis behavior by prior estrogen treatment. *Horm. Behav.* **35**, 215–223.

Tribollet, E., Audigier, S., Dubois-Dauphin, M., and Dreifuss, J.J. (1990). Gonadal steroids regulate oxytocin receptors but not vasopressin receptors in the brain of male and female rats. An autoradiographical study. *Brain Res.* **511**, 129–140.

Tribollet, E., Arsenijevic, Y., and Barberis, C. (1998). Vasopressin binding sites in the central nervous system: Distribution and regulation. *Prog. Brain Res.* **119**, 45–55.

Truss, M., Candau, R., Chavez, S., and Beato, M. (1995). Transcriptional control by steroid hormones: The role of chromatin. *Ciba Found. Symp.* **191**, 7–17.

Tsai, M.J., and O'Malley, B.W. (1994). Molecular mechanisms of action of steroid/thyroid receptor superfamily members. *Annu. Rev. Biochem.* **63**, 451–486.

Tzukerman, M.T., Esty, A., Sansito-Mere, D., Danielian, P., Parker, M.G., Stein, R.B., Pike, J.W., and McDonnell, D.P. (1994). Human estrogen receptor transactivational capacity determined by both cellular and promoter context and mediated by two functionally distinct intramolecular regions. *Mol. Endocrinol.* **8**, 21–30.

Uphouse, L., Caldarola-Pastuszka, M., and Montanez, S. (1992). Intra-cerebral action of the 5-HT$_{1A}$ agonists, 8OH-DPAT and buspirone, and of the 5-HT$_{1A}$ partial agonist/antagonist, NAN-190, on female sexual behavior. *Neuropharmacology* **31**, 969–981.

van den Bergh, J.G. (1994). Pheromones and mammalian reproduction. In E. Knobil and J.D. Neill (eds.). *The Physiology of Reproduction.* Raven Press, New York. pp. 343–349.

van Goozen, S.H., Wiegant, V.W., Endert, E., Helmond, F.A., and van de Poll, N.E. (1997). Psychoendocrinological assessment of the menstrual cycle: The relationship between hormones, sexuality, and mood. *Arch. Sex. Behav.* **26**, 359–382.

van Honk, J., Tuiten, A., Verbaten, R., van den Hout, M., Koppeschaar, H., Thijsen, J., and de Haan, E. (1999). Correlations among salivary testosterone, mood, and selective attention to threat in humans. *Horm. Behav.* **36**, 17–24.

Van Kesteren, R.E., and Geraerts, W.P. (1998). Molecular evolution of ligand-binding specificity in the vasopressin/oxytocin receptor family. *Ann. N.Y. Acad. Sci.* **15**, 25–34.

van Oortmerssen, G.A., and Sluyter, F. (1994). Studies on wild house mice. V. Aggression in lines selected for attack latency and their Y-chromosomal congenics. *Behav. Genet.* **24**, 73–78.

Vernier, P., Phillipe, H., Samama, P., and Mallet, J. (1993). Bioamine receptors: Evolutionary and functional variations of a structural leitmotif. *EXS* **63**, 297–337.

Virgin, C.E., Jr., and Sapolsky, R.M. (1997). Styles of male social behavior and their endocrine correlates among low-ranking baboons. *Am. J. Primatol.* **42**, 25–39.

Virkkunen, M., Rawlings, R., Tokola, R., Poland, R.E., Guidotti, A., Nemeroff, C., Bissette, G., Kalogeras, K., Karonen, S.L., and Linnoila, M. (1994). CSF biochemistries, glucose metabolism, and diurnal activity rhythms in alcoholic violent offenders, fire setters, and healthy volunteers. *Arch. Gen. Psychiatry* **51**, 20–27.

Virkkunen, M., Goldman, D., and Linnoila, M. (1996). Serotonin in alcoholic violent offenders. *Ciba Found. Symp.* **194**, 168–177.

vom Saal, F.S. (1979). Prenatal exposure to androgen influences morphology and aggressive behavior in male and female mice. *Horm. Behav.* **12**, 1–11.

vom Saal, F.S. (1981) Variation in phenotype due to random intrauterine positioning of male and female fetuses in rodents. *J. Reprod. Fertil.* **62**, 633–650.

vom Saal, F.S. (1983) Variation in infanticide and parental behavior in male mice due to prior intrauterine proximity to female fetuses: Elimination by prenatal stress. *Physiol. Behav.* **30**, 675–681.

vom Saal, F.S. (1984). The intrauterine position phenomenon: Effects on physiology, aggressive behavior and population dynamics in house mice. *Prog. Clin. Biol. Res.* **169**, 135–179.

vom Saal, F.S. (1989). Sexual differentiation in litter-bearing mammals: Influence of sex of adjacent fetuses in utero. *J. Anim. Sci.* **67**, 1824–1840.

vom Saal, F.S., and Bronson, F.H. (1980). Sexual characteristics of adult female mice are correlated with their blood testosterone levels during prenatal development. *Science* **208**, 597–599.

vom Saal, F.S., and Moyer, C.L. (1985). Prenatal effects on reproductive capacity during aging in female mice. *Biol. Reprod.* **32**, 1116–1126.

vom Saal, F.S., Svare, B.B., and Gandelman, R. (1976). Time of neonatal androgen exposure influences length of testosterone treatment required to induce aggression in adult male and female mice. *Behav. Biol.* **17**, 391–397.

von Engelhardt, N., Kappeler, P.M., and Heistermann, M. (2000). Androgen leveles and female social dominance in Lemur catta. *Proc. R. Soc. London, Ser. B* **267**, 1533–1539.

Vukmirovic, O.G., and Tilghman, S.M. (2000). Exploring genome space. *Nat. Insight* **405**, 820–822.

Wallman, J. (1999). Serotonin and impulsive aggression: Not so fast. *H.F. Guggenheim Found. Rev.* **3**, 21–29.

Wang, Z., and De Vries, G.J. (1995). Androgen and estrogen effects on vasopressin messenger RNA expression in the medial amygdaloid nucleus in male and female rats. *J. Neuroendocrinol.* **7**, 827–831.

Wang, Z., Young, L.J., De Vries, G.J., and Insel, T.R. (1998). Voles and vasopressin: A review of molecular, cellular, and behavioral studies of pair bonding and paternal behaviors. *Prog. Brain Res.* **119**, 483–499.

Wang, Z.X., Smith, W., Major, D.E., and De Vries, G.J. (1994). Sex and species differences in the effects of cohabitation on vasopressin messenger RNA expression in the bed nucleus of the stria terminalis in prairie voles (*Microtus ochrogaster*) and meadow voles (*Microtus pennsylvanicus*). *Brain Res.* **650**, 212–218.

Watanabe, T., Inoue, S., Ogawa, S., Ishii, Y., Hiroi, H., Ikeda, K., Orimo, A., and Muramatsu, M. (1997). Agonistic effect of tamoxifen is dependent on cell type, ERE-promoter context, and estrogen receptor subtype: Functional difference between estrogen receptors α and β. *Biochem. Biophys. Res. Commun.* **236**, 140–145.

Watters, J.J., Poulin, P., and Dorsa, D.M. (1998). Steroid hormone regulation of vasopressinergic neurotransmission in the central nervous system. *Prog. Brain Res.* **119**, 247–261.

Webb, P., Lopez, G.N., Uht, R.M., and Kushner, P.J. (1995). Tamoxifen activation of the estrogen receptor/AP-1 pathway: Potential origin for the cell-specific estrogen-like effects of antiestrogens. *Mol. Endocrinol.* **9**, 443–456.

Webb, P., Nguyen, P., Valentine, C., Lopez, G.N., Kwok, G.R., McInerney, E., Katzenellenbogen, B.S., Enmark, E., Gustafsson, J.A., Nilson, S., and Kushner, P.J. (1999). The estrogen receptor enhances AP-1 activity by two distinct mechanisms with different requirements for receptor transactivation functions. *Mol. Endocrinol.* **13**, 1672–1685.

Wheling, M. (1997). Specific, nongenomic actions of steroid hormones. *Annu. Rev. Physiol.* **59**, 365–393.

Whitfield, G.K., Jurutka, P.W., Haussler, C.A., and Hausler, M.R. (1999). Steroid hormone receptors: Evolution, ligands and molecular basis of biologic function. *J. Cell Biochem., Suppl.* 32–33, 110–122.

Wieland, S.J., and Fox, T.O. (1981). Androgen receptors from rat kidney and brain: DNA-binding properties of wild-type and tfm mutant. *J. Steroid Biochem.* **14**, 409–414.

Wingfield, J.C. (1994). Control of territorial aggression in a changing environment. *Psychoneuroendocrinology* **19**, 709–721.

Wingfield, J.C., Henger, R.F., Dufty, A.M.J., and Ball, G.F. (1990). The challenge hypothesis: Theoretical implications for patterns of testosterone secretion, mating systems and breeding strategies. *Am. Nat.* **136**, 829–846.

Wingfield, J.C., Jacobs, J., and Hillgarth, N. (1997). Ecological constraints and the evolution of hormone-behavior interrelationships. *Ann. N.Y. Acad. Sci.* **807**, 22–41.

Wittenberger, J.F. (1981). "Animal Social Behavior." Duxbury Press, Boston.

Wolf, D.A., Herzinger, T., Hermking, H., Blaschke, D., and Horz, W. (1993). Transcriptional and posttranscriptional regulation of human androgen receptor expression by androgen. *Mol. Endocrinol.* **7**, 924–936.

Wolffe, A.P., and Guschin, D. (2000). Chromatin structural features and targets that regulate transcription. *J. Struct. Biol.* **129**, 102–122.

Wong, D.T., Bymaster, F.P., and Engelman, E.A. (1995). Presynaptic regulation of extracellular serotonin concentrations in brain. *In* "Serotonin in the Central Nervous System and Periphery" (A. Takada and G. Curzon eds.), pp. 3–15. Elsevier, Amsterdam.

Wood, R.I., and Newman, S.W. (1993). Intracellular partitioning of androgen receptor immunoreactivity in the brain of the male Syrian hamster: Effects of castration and steroid replacement. *J. Neurobiol.* **24**, 925–938.

Wright, D.E., Seroogy, K.B., Lundgren, K.H., Davis, B.M., and Jennes, L. (1995). Comparative localization of serotonin$_{1A, 1C}$ and $_2$ receptor subtype mRNAs in rat brain. *J. Comp. Neurol.* **351**, 357–373.

Yang, L.Y., and Arnold, A.P. (2000). Interaction of BDNF and testosterone in the regulation of adult perineal motoneurons. *J. Neurobiol.* **44**, 308–319.

Yates, W.R., Perry, P., and Murray, S. (1992). Aggression and hostility in anabolic steroid users. *Biol. Psychiatry* **31**, 1232–1234.

Yesalis, C., Kennedy, N., Kopstein, A., and Bahrke, M. (1993). Anabolic androgenic steroid use in the United States. *JAMA, J. Am. Med. Assoc.* **270**, 1217–1221.

Young, J., Corpechot, C., Haug, M., Gobaille, S., Baulieu, E.E., and Robel, P. (1991). Suppressive effects of dehydroepiandrosterone and 3β-methyl-androst-5-en-17-one on attack towards lactating female intruders by castrated male mice. II. Brain neurosteroids. *Biochem. Biophys. Res. Commun.* **174**, 892–897.

Young, J., Corpéchot, C., Perché, F., Haug, M., Baulieu, E.E., and Robel, P. (1995). Neurosteroids: Pharmacological effects of a 3β-hydroxy-steroid dehydrogenase inhibitor. *Endocrine* **2**, 505–509.

Young, J., Corpéchot, C., Perché, F., Eychenne, B., Haug, M., Baulieu, E.E., and Robel, P. (1996). Neurosteroids in the mouse brain: Behavioral and pharmacological effects of a 3β-hydroxysteroid dehydrogenase inhibitor. *Steroids* **61**, 144–149.

Young, L.J., Wang, Z., and Insel, T.R. (1998). Neuroendocrine bases of monogamy. *Trends Neurosci.* **21**, 71–75.

Young, L.J., Nilsen, R., Waymire, K.G., MacGregor, G.R., and Insel, T.R. (1999). Increased affiliative response to vasopressin in mice expressing the V1a receptor from a monogamous vole. *Nature (London)* **400**, 766–768.

Zhou, L., Blaustein, J.D., and De Vries, G.J. (1994). Distribution of androgen receptor immunoreactivity in vasopressin and oxytocin-immunoreactive neurons in male rats. *Endocrinology (Baltimore)* **134**, 2622–2627.

Zhou, A., Marschke, K.B., Arnold, K.E., Berger, E.M., Fitzgerald, P., Mais, D.E., and Allegretto, E.A. (1999). Estrogen receptor beta activates the human retinoic acid receptor alpha-1 promoter in response to tamoxifen and other estrogen antagonists, but not in response to estrogen. *Mol. Endocrinol.* **13**, 418–430.

Zhuang, X., Gross, C., Santarelli, L., Compan, V., Trillat, A.C., and Hen, R. (1999). Altered emotional states in knockout mice lacking 5-HT1A or 5 HT1B receptors. *Neuropsychopharmacology* **21**, 52S–60S.

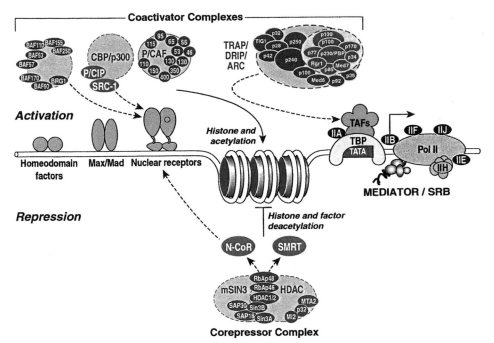

CHAPTER 5, FIGURE 2 A general model depicting the role of coactivator and corepressor complexes in nuclear receptor (NR) transcription. Coactivator complexes include SWI/SNF, CBP/SRC-1/p/CAF, and TRAP/DRIP/ARC. The SWI/SNF complex has ATP-dependent chromatin remodeling activities, whereas CBP and p/CAF complexes possess histone acetyltransferase activities. These complexes may act in concert to relieve chromatin-mediated repression, with the TRAP/DRIP/ARC complex functioning to recruit core transcription factors. Corepressor complexes include the SIN3/HDAC complex, which may be recruited via the NR corepressors N-CoR or SMRT. This complex possesses histone deacetylase activity and is thought to reverse actions of histone acetyltransferase-containing complexes. (Reprinted with permission from Glass, C.K., and Rosenfeld, M.G. The coregulator exchange in transcriptional functions of nuclear receptors. *Genes and Development* **14**, 121-141. © 2000 Cold Spring Harbor Laboratory Press.)

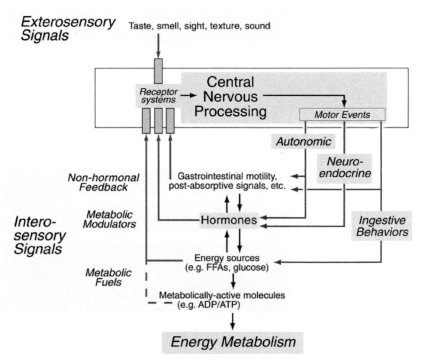

CHAPTER 7, FIGURE 2 A schematic representation of the exterosensory and interosensory signals for the motor events that control energy balance. Motor outputs are shown in red, sensory inputs in blue. Interosensory inputs can be categorized as non-hormonal feedback signals (e.g., gastric distension), hormones (metabolic modulators), and metabolic fuels. Autonomic motor actions regulate gastrointestinal, adrenal medullary, and pancreatic functions; neuroendocrine motor output controls glucocorticoid, thyroid, and growth hormones; and behavioral motor actions mediate eating, drinking, and specialized appetites. ADP, adenosine diphosphate; ATP, adenosine triphosphate; CART, cocaine and amphetamine regulated transcript; CRH, corticotropin-releasing hormone; FFA, free-fatty acid.

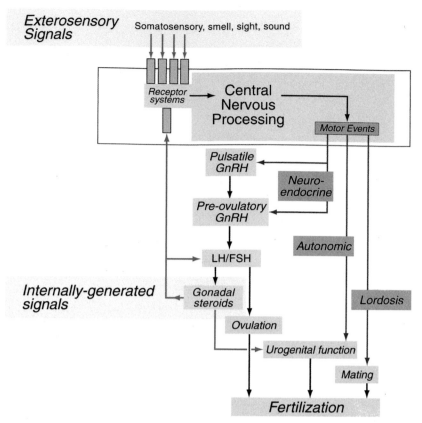

CHAPTER 7, FIGURE 3 A schematic representation of the exterosensory and internally generated signals for the motor events that control female reproductive functions in the rat. Motor outputs are shown in red, internal signals in blue. Somatosensory and olfactory inputs are key exterosensory inputs, whereas sight and sound play more subsidiary roles. Gonadal steroids are the internal modulators rather than triggers for behavior. Autonomic motor actions regulate urogenital functions; neuroendocrine motor output controls gonadotropin secretion from the anterior pituitary; and behavioral motor actions mediate lordosis. FSH, follicle-stimulating hormone; GnRH, gonadotropin-releasing hormone; LH, luteinizing hormone.

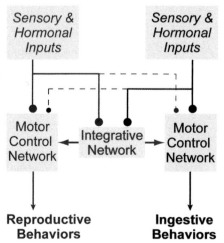

CHAPTER 7, FIGURE 8 The same array of metabolic sensory signals and hormonal modulators influences both the reproductive and the ingestive behavior systems. First, the diversity of hormone receptor expression shows that hormonal information that appears to be primarily directed at one control network can influence the other. The expression of gonadal steroid receptors is illustrated as red dots, and leptin, insulin, and glucocorticoid receptors are shown as black dots. Second, there are neural projections from an intermediate set of integrative nuclei that are responsive to both gonadal steroids and the other hormones concerned with energy balance. In turn, the neural outputs of this integrative network target both the reproductive and the ingestive behavior control networks. Neural inputs from other parts of the brain concerned with more general functions target both the motor control networks and the intermediate integrative neurons.

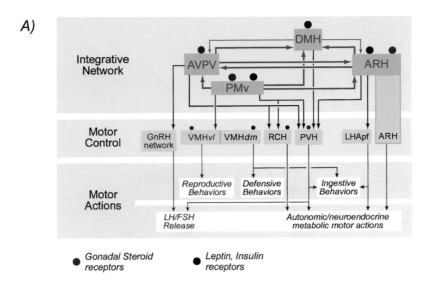

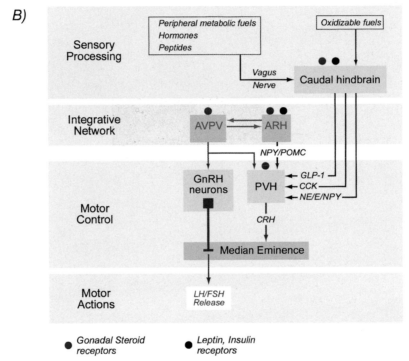

CHAPTER 7, FIGURE 9   (A) A schematic diagram of an integrative network and the associated motor control networks for a variety of motor actions for reproductive and ingestive behaviors. Sets of neurons in the gonadotropin-releasing hormone (GnRH) network, ventromedial nucleus (VMH), retrochiasmatic area (RCH), paraventricular (PVH), perifornical part of the lateral hypothalamic area (LHApf), and arcuate nucleus (ARH) provide direct control of reproductive or energy balance motor functions. In turn, the ventrolateral part (vl) of the VMH controls female reproductive behaviors, while the dorsomedial (dm) part of the VMH appears to control defensive and some aspects of ingestive behavior. Collectively all these motor control cell groups are then regulated by inputs from a higher-level integrative network. The receptor expression patterns and the connections from some neurons in the arcuate (ARH), anteroventral periventricular (AVPV), dorsomedial (DMH), and the ventral premammillary (PMv) nuclei provide evidence that they make up such an integrating network that can influence in a divergent manner the neurons in the reproductive and energy balance motor control networks. Functions concerned with integrative actions are shown in blue, those with reproductive function in red, and those with ingestive behavior and energy balance in black. (B) The sensory processing, integrative, and motor control networks for one of the motor actions described above, LH/FSH release. Sensory processing of information about metabolic fuel availability is thought to occur in the hindbrain and to be projected to forebrain areas via catecholaminergic and other neurons (CCK, cholecystokinin; E, epinephrine; GLP-1, glucagon-like peptide-1; NE, norepinephrine; NPY, neuropeptide Y; POMC, pro-opiomelanocortin). Some evidence suggests that both estrogen receptors and corticotropin-releasing hormone (CRH) neurons might influence GnRH neurons directly. Modulation by hormones such as estrogen (red dots), or leptin and insulin (black dots), might occur in the areas shown.

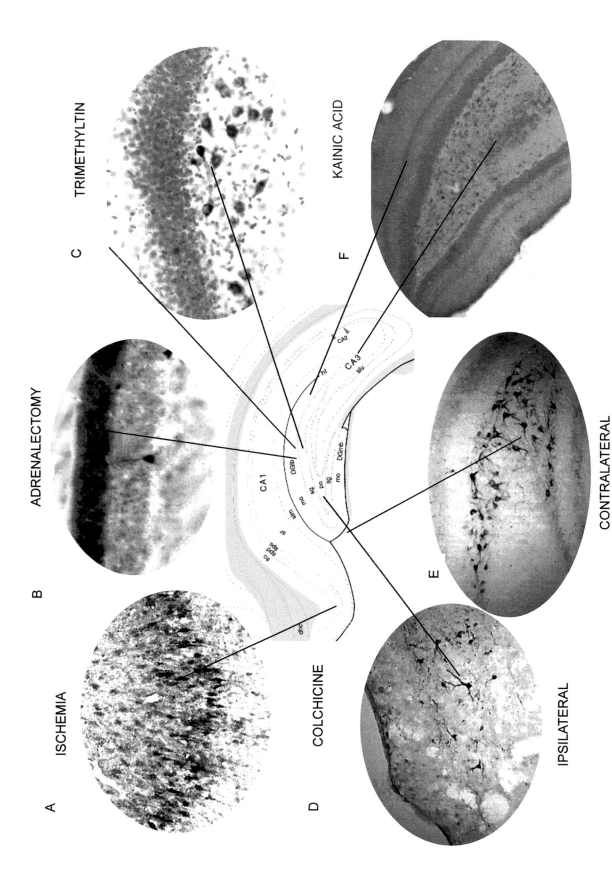

CHAPTER 14, FIGURE 4 (A) Interneurons display CGRP-IR following ischemia (Bulloch et al., 1998). (B) CGRP-IR following adrenalectomy. Note the heavy increase of immunoreactivity in the intermolecular layer of the dentate gyrus (Bulloch et al., 1996b). (C) CGRP-IR following trimethyltin treatment in mossy cells of the dentate gyrus. (D and E) CGRP-IR in mossy cells following colchicine injections into the hippocampus (Bulloch et al., 1996b). (F) Dentate gyrus with a decrease of CGRP-IR in the intermolecular layer following treatment with kainic acid (Bulloch et al., 1997).

6

Hormonal Basis of Social Conflict and Communication

H. Elliott Albers

Center for Behavioral Neuroscience
Departments of Biology and Psychology
Georgia State University
Atlanta, Georgia 30303

Kim L. Huhman

Center for Behavioral Neuroscience
Department of Psychology
Georgia State University
Atlanta, Georgia 30303

Robert L. Meisel

Department of Psychological Sciences
Purdue University
West Lafayette, Indiana 47907

I. INTRODUCTION

Social conflict and communication are necessary for successful reproduction, for the formation and maintenance of stable social relationships and optimal spacing, and for the defense of resources. Engaging in social conflict is necessary for the formation of social structure, and communication is essential for its maintenance (Archer, 1988). Animals communicate in many different ways. When animals are not in close proximity, they often communicate with distal signals that may be chemical, visual, or auditory. However, when animals are in close physical contact, proximate events such as acts of aggression or postural changes can communicate important information. Therefore, it is not surprising that the changing levels of hormones that occur in association with social conflict and reproduction can have a dramatic effect on communicative behavior. There is a substantial body of data on the interactions among hormones, reproductive behavior, and communicative behavior. However, significantly less is known about how hormones regulate social conflict and the communicative behaviors that are involved in influencing social relationships. This chapter focuses on the hormonal regulation of social conflict and communi-

nication in Syrian (sometimes called golden) hamsters (*Mesocricetus auratus*).

Social behavior and its hormonal regulation has been studied in Syrian hamsters since the 1950s. Unlike many other species, both male and female hamsters are highly aggressive and the behaviors engaged in during social conflict are readily observable and easily quantified. The severity of these encounters (in terms of bites or tissue damage) is usually quite low, and dominance relationships are often formed with relatively little overt aggression. These relationships are usually established very rapidly and remain stable over time (Lerwill and Makings, 1971). Hamsters also exhibit a variety of communicative behaviors that are easily quantified and that have been investigated extensively (Johnston, 1985). As such, hamsters represent a comparatively simple animal model for the study of social conflict and communication.

II. BEHAVIORS EXHIBITED DURING SOCIAL CONFLICT

The term agonistic behavior refers to all behaviors related to social conflict between conspecifics. Agonistic behavior includes those actions considered aggressive such as threat, attack, and pursuit, as well as other behaviors that can occur at high levels during social interactions including defense or submission and various forms of communication. Many factors contribute to the type and frequency of agonistic behavior observed in individuals of different species. Species that live in large groups where social contact is nearly continuous display agonistic behavior in different circumstances than do species that live in more solitary social environments. However, regardless of the type of social organization displayed by a species, agonistic behavior is critical to the formation and maintenance of those social relationships.

A. Aggression

One of the most important and well-studied forms of agonistic behavior is aggression. Aggression is a complex phenomenon that has been classified in a variety of different ways. One of the most commonly used classifications of aggression was devised by Moyer (1971), who defined the different forms of aggression based on the social situation in which the aggression occurred (e.g., predatory or territorial). Another approach to classifying aggression has been to simply divide aggression into defensive and offensive behaviors (Blanchard and Blanchard, 1988). Offensive behavior consists of behaviors used in attack; defensive behaviors lack an active approach to the opponent. No matter which classification of aggression is used, it is clear that hormones can have very different effects in different situations. Although the physiological regulation of some forms of aggression may have common neural and endocrine mechanisms, it is also clear that not all forms of aggression are controlled by the same neural or endocrine mechanisms.

B. Defensive or Submissive Behaviors

In addition to aggression, animals display a wide variety of other agonistic behaviors during social conflict. Another class of behaviors observed during social conflict is defensive or submissive in nature. These behaviors include flight and the display of defensive or submissive postures. The majority of research on agonistic behavior has focused on different forms of offensive aggression so much less is known about the physiological factors regulating defensive or submissive behaviors (Siegel *et al.*, 1999).

C. Communication

Another type of behavior that is frequently observed during social conflict is communicative behavior. Communication plays a critical role in the formation and maintenance of social relationships between individual animals, as well as in more complex social organizations. Mammals communicate with conspecifics in many different ways.

One of the most common forms of communication in mammals is scent marking (Johnson, 1973; Vandenbergh, 1994; Yahr, 1983). Mammals scent mark by depositing odors in the environment in their urine and feces and through the use of specialized glands. Scent marking is used to communicate many different types of social information. It can be used to find a mate, define a territory, or to broadcast the presence of an individual. One advantage of scent marking over other forms of communication is that odors can persist for long periods. This allows animals to communicate even though they may not be present at the same time. Hamsters scent mark in at least two ways. One form of scent marking used by hamsters is called flank marking (Dieterlen, 1959; Johnston, 1975a,b,c). The flank glands are darkly pigmented sebaceous glands located on the dorsal flank region. The glands are significantly larger and more darkly pigmented in males than in females, and the size and activity of the glands are regulated by testosterone in both males and females (Hamilton and Montagna, 1950; Vandenbergh, 1973). In males, castration reduces the size of the glands and administration of testosterone restores the size of the glands. In females, ovariectomy does not alter the size or pigmentation of the glands, but administration of testosterone can increase the size of the glands to that seen in males. Hamsters flank mark by arching their backs and rubbing the glands against objects in the environment (Johnston, 1975a,c, 1977). Grooming of the flank glands and other regions, which normally occurs in association with marking, may be a way of mixing flank gland secretions with chemical signals from other sources such as the harderian glands. Flank marking is thought to broadcast the presence of an individual to other hamsters (Johnston, 1985), but can also communicate specific types of information in different social settings (discussed later). A second form of scent marking used by hamsters is vaginal marking (Johnston, 1977). Female hamsters deposit vaginal secretions in the environment by pressing their genital area against the ground and moving forward. The primary role of vaginal marking is in attracting males just prior to the female's coming into sexual receptivity and being prepared to mate (Johnston, 1985). Vaginal discharge may also play some role in the inhibition of aggression in males during a potential mating opportunity because the presence of vaginal discharge inhibits aggression even in highly aggressive male hamsters (Murphy, 1976a). Salivary and urine odors also appear to be capable of communicating socially important information in hamsters (Friedle and Fischer, 1984; White *et al.,* 1984, 1986). Female hamsters can discriminate the salivary and urinary odors of dominant and subordinate male hamsters. Females also appear to be able to predict a male's dominance status from his urinary odors (White *et al.,* 1984).

Auditory signals are another way hamsters communicate. The most thoroughly studied form of auditory communication in hamsters is ultrasonic vocalizations (Floody and Pfaff, 1977b,c,d). Many rodents emit high-frequency calls, and these signals may be used for a number of social functions such as attracting and locating sexual partners. Ultrasonic communication has been studied most fully during mating and in young rodents. It is not known if ultrasonic communication plays an important role during social conflict. It may be that less is known about the function of ultrasonic communication during social conflict because it can only be observed with the use of specialized equipment. Another auditory signal produced by hamsters is tooth chattering. This sound, which is produced by the rapid closing of the jaw when the upper and lower incisors are aligned, occurs frequently during nearly all interactions between male hamsters, but in less than half of the interactions between female hamsters. It has been suggested (Johnston, 1985) that the amount of tooth chattering is related to the level of agonistic tension or arousal, although little is known about its possible functions.

Finally, and probably most important, hamsters communicate through their behavior. Most of what is known about the functions of these behaviors comes from descriptive analyses of social encounters between two hamsters (discussed later).

III. HOW IS AGONISTIC BEHAVIOR STUDIED?

Agonistic behaviors, by definition, are social behaviors that are expressed in the presence of another conspecific. Studies of the mechanisms controlling social behavior are inherently more complex than the investigation of behavior that occurs when animals are alone. Experimental manipulations such as castration cannot only affect the social behavior of the experimental animal, but they can also affect that animal's stimulus properties (e.g., scent). If a manipulation alters the stimulus properties of an experimental animal, it has the potential to alter how other animals will respond to it. When other animals change their response to the experimental animal, the experimental animal may in turn change its social behavior. For example, manipulation of hormone levels might change the chemical signals emitted by an experimental animal. This change in the scent of the experimental animal could then trigger a reduction in aggression by other animals and therefore a reduction in defensive or submissive behaviors in the experimental animal. As a result, it can be difficult to determine whether a manipulation alters a specific behavior by directly influencing the mechanisms controlling that behavior or indirectly by changing an animal's behavior in response to a change in how other animals respond to it.

Agonistic behavior has been studied extensively using a variety of different paradigms in the field as well as in the laboratory. The use of so many different experimental paradigms combined with the number and complexity of the behaviors studied makes comparisons across the different approaches difficult. A number of different laboratory paradigms have been developed specifically for studying different types of aggression (Miczek, 1983). Some of these paradigms have used artificial stimuli (e.g., electrical shock or brain lesions) to induce aggression, whereas others have attempted to study aggression in situations that more closely mimic conflict situations found in nature (Blanchard and Blanchard, 1988). One commonly used approach is the resident–intruder paradigm, wherein an intruder animal is introduced into the home cage of the resident animal. Another commonly used approach has been to place two animals in a neutral environment. One limitation of these approaches as they are typically employed is that the test chambers are usually relatively small and do not give animals the opportunity to flee. As discussed later, the effects of hormones on aggression may differ depending on the paradigm used. Most of the laboratory paradigms that have been employed for studying agonistic behavior have focused on interactions between pairs of animals. However, studies examining group interactions have provided important new data in species that have more complex social organizations (e.g., Blanchard *et al.,* 1995).

One difficulty in studying agonistic behavior is that animals express different types of behavior during social encounters. Numerous approaches have been employed to record and analyze agonistic behavior (Simon, 1983). One approach has been to employ a discrete scoring system where one or more behaviors are measured and analyzed separately. Using this approach, the investigator monitors and scores separate behaviors such as the number of bites, the latency to attack, or the number of flees. Although this approach has been used extensively, it can create a complicated set of data when large numbers of behaviors are measured, and it can miss important behavioral events when only a limited number of behaviors are monitored.

Another approach has been to use composite scoring systems that combine multiple measures of behavior into one score. One composite system that has proven useful in studying agonistic behavior in hamsters measures all behaviors expressed during social encounters and classifies them into four general categories: (1) aggressive, (2) social, (3) nonsocial, and (4) defensive or submissive (Huhman *et al.,* 1990). For example, aggressive behaviors include upright and side offense, attack, bites, and chase; social behavior consists of attend, approach, investigate, sniff, and nose touch; nonsocial behaviors include locomotor or exploratory, self-groom, nesting, feeding, and sleeping; and defensive or submissive behaviors are flee, upright and side defense, tail-up, flee, and tooth chatter. By quantifying the duration of each of these four classes of behavior, it is possible to gain a more comprehensive view of the nature of each individual's behavior during social interactions. A strength of this approach is that it is possible to determine whether manipulations affect specific

types of behavior or all behaviors as a whole. However, one weakness of this approach is that it does not provide a category that specifically measures communicative behavior.

IV. SOCIAL INTERACTION AND COMMUNICATION IN HAMSTERS

Although there are very little field data on the behavior of Syrian hamsters, it is thought that they live a primarily solitary existence (Murphy, 1977). If both male and female hamsters live in isolation, both sexes are expected to be aggressive to defend their home burrows against intruders. If this social structure is the basis for agonistic behavior in hamsters, several other predictions about their behavior logically follow. First, hamsters should be more aggressive in a familiar territory than in an unfamiliar territory. Second, isolated hamsters should be more aggressive than are group-housed hamsters. Finally, males and females should attack one another except when opportunities for reproduction exist. As described later, there is a substantial body of evidence obtained in the laboratory to confirm each of these predictions.

The behaviors that occur during social encounters between Syrian hamsters have been described in detail in both males and females (Floody and Pfaff, 1977a; Grant and Mackintosh, 1962; Kislak and Beach, 1955; Lerwill and Makings, 1971; Payne and Swanson, 1970; Siegel, 1985; Takahashi and Lisk, 1984) (see Table 1 and Fig. 1). During a first encounter, hamsters exhibit a series of somewhat stereotyped agonistic behaviors that include behaviors related to social investigation. Shortly following initial investigations, high levels of aggression are observed unless one of the hamsters is a sexually receptive female. Attacks are observed significantly more frequently during initial encounters between hamsters that are unfamiliar with one another than during subsequent encounters (Ferris *et al.,* 1987). The most complete analysis of agonistic behavior was conducted in female hamsters. Floody and Pfaff (1977a) filmed aggressive encounters and analyzed the behaviors from individual frames of these films. The general sequence of behaviors seems to be the same regardless of the aggressive experience of individual animals. Still, there are some changes in the probability that certain behaviors will occur as the number of aggressive encounters

TABLE 1

Behaviors Frequently Observed in Male and Female Hamsters during Social Conflict

Behavior	Description	Possible function
Nose-to-nose	Noses of two individuals in close proximity; investigation of face	Provides initial information on the sex and state of other hamster
Circle, mutual sniff	Hamsters circle each other sniffing genital area and other body regions	Provides more detailed information on the state of the other hamster
Sparring	One hamster attempts to attack while the other fends off the attempt	Mild form of aggression
Upright and side postures	Hamster is standing on rear paws when upright or on three paws when side oriented toward its opponent	Used both offensively to initiate attack and defensively to ward off an attack
Paw up or defensive sideways	Hamster lifts paw and turns away from approaching opponent	Fends off attacks
Attack	A bite that occurs from upright posture or while hamsters is on all four paws; often the opponent is held with the front paws	Intense form of aggression
Rolling fight	Both animals attempting to bite the opponent while holding on and rolling around the ground	Intense form of aggression
Flee or flight (fly away)	Explosive movement of one hamster away from the other, usually displayed after the loss of a fight	Escape
Full submissive posture	Hamster lies unmoving on back with limbs spread; sometimes continues after opponent has moved away	Inhibits attacks
Stretch-attend	Cautious approach with body stretched and lowered, eyes on opponent, sniffing	Risk assessment by subordinate
Tail-up move or tail-up freeze	Tail is raised and back arched while moving away from opponent or while freezing	Inhibits attacks[a]
Walk away	Hamster walks away from opponent	Disengages from opponent; most frequently occurs during early stages of encounter
Flank marking	Hamster arches side and rubs flank region against objects	Communication

[a] Only observed in male hamsters.

increase (Floody and Pfaff, 1977a). Initially, nose-to-nose leads to upright postures, and then either directly to an attack or an attack after some period of following (also termed chase). Circling is not generally seen in inexperienced females. As females engage in more fights, uprights and following alternate, with attacks predominantly coming after an upright. On-back attacks occur frequently at all stages of experience, although with more aggressive encounters on-back attacks lead to rolling fights. Studies in females who are not sexually receptive have shown that the frequency of aggressive behavior diminishes and the sequencing of agonistic behavior changes significantly over a series of encounters, even in hamsters that are paired together for only brief periods in which dominant or subordinate relationships are not formed (i.e. 3-minute encounters) (Floody and Pfaff, 1977a). Similar patterns of agonistic behaviors are observed in male hamsters. Males also exhibit high levels of aggression during initial encounters, aggression declining over time (Ferris *et al.*, 1987). However, males display significantly less aggression toward females than toward other males.

A. Factors Responsible for Initiating Social Conflict

The factors that are responsible for stimulating the high levels of aggression seen in hamsters during initial encounters are not fully understood. There is evidence that olfactory signals are important for the initiation of

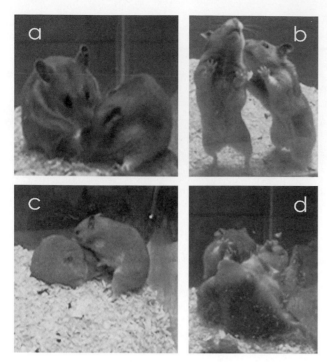

FIGURE 1 Photographs of a behavioral sequence during an aggressive encounter between two females. (a) Initially the females investigate one another with nose to nose contact. (b) This investigation is followed by an upright posture in which the intruder is looking upward and the resident animal's attention is directed toward the intruder. (c) The resident female then begins the attack with a characteristic perpendicular approach. (d) The sequence culminates with a biting attack.

aggression because centrally or peripherally induced olfactory impairment substantially reduces at least some forms of aggression (Devor and Murphy, 1973; Murphy, 1976a). Bilateral olfactory bulbectomy significantly reduces the aggression of a resident hamster toward an intruder, but does not reduce the amount of aggression displayed in response to an attack by another hamster. The effects of the olfactory bulbectomy on aggression appear to due to olfactory impairment because peripheral blocking of olfaction has similar effects on aggression. Vaginal secretions are one type of odor that can alter levels of aggression and submission (Fischer and Brown, 1993). Significantly higher levels of aggression are seen between males in arenas scented with vaginal secretions from a diestrous female than in clean arenas.

There is also evidence that visual signals may play a role in agonistic activity. Hamsters have prominent black markings on their chests. It has been proposed that these markings serve as a threat because of evidence that they are displayed during offensive postures and hidden during defensive postures (Grant and Mackintosh, 1962). However, other studies found that subordinate hamsters displayed the markings more completely than did dominants (Johnston, 1976). Other studies found that darkening and enlarging the marks in one animal resulted in a significant increase in flight behavior of the opponent and a significant increase in aggressive behavior in the marked hamster (Grant *et al.,* 1970). However, these studies were conducted initially in the home cage of the marked hamster, which increases the likelihood of victory. Other investigators have failed to repeat the findings that intensifying these markings increased success in weight-matched hamsters tested in a neutral arena (Johnston, 1985). Other evidence in support of a role for visual cues in regulating aggression has come from studies of blinded hamsters (Murphy, 1976a,b). Over four aggression tests, blinded hamsters spent significantly longer times attacking a nonaggressive hamster than did sighted hamsters, although there was no difference between sighted and blinded hamsters in the initiation of attacks. Although these data support the hypothesis that visual cues may be important in the cessation of aggression, they should be viewed with some caution. Blinding not only blocks the ability to see the opponent, it also begins the seasonal transition to the winter-like reproductive state in hamsters. High levels of aggression are observed in the winter-like state that is produced by exposure to short photoperiods or blinding (discussed later). Another factor that appears to influence the expression of agonistic behavior is the time of day (Landau, 1975a; Lerwill and Makings, 1971). Hamsters exhibit the highest levels of both offensive and defensive behavior shortly after the onset of darkness. The day–night difference is striking with about a threefold increase in the frequency of offensive and defensive behaviors between animals tested shortly after dark onset versus those tested during the early light phase.

B. Relationship between Agonistic Behavior and the Formation of Dominant–Subordinate Relationships

Agonistic behaviors displayed during successive encounters change dramatically in association with the formation of dominant–subordinate relationships (Boice *et al.*, 1969; Drickamer *et al.*, 1973; Drickamer and Vandenbergh, 1973; Ferris *et al.*, 1987; Johnston, 1975a,c). When two or more hamsters are placed together, they rapidly form stable dominant–subordinate relationships. The relationship between agonistic behavior and the formation of dominant–subordinate relationships has been studied in several ways. Some studies have allowed pairs or larger groups of hamsters to live together in relatively large arenas and then have scored their agonistic behavior at specific intervals (Drickamer *et al.*, 1973; Drickamer and Vandenbergh, 1973; Johnston, 1975c). Other studies have housed hamsters separately and examined their agonistic behavior for short test intervals (Ferris *et al.*, 1987; Johnston, 1975a). The relationship between the expression of agonistic behavior and the formation of dominance–subordinate behavior is very similar in the different testing conditions. In one example, pairs of male hamsters were housed separately, but tested together for 15 min per day on five consecutive days (Fig. 2A). During an initial encounter between

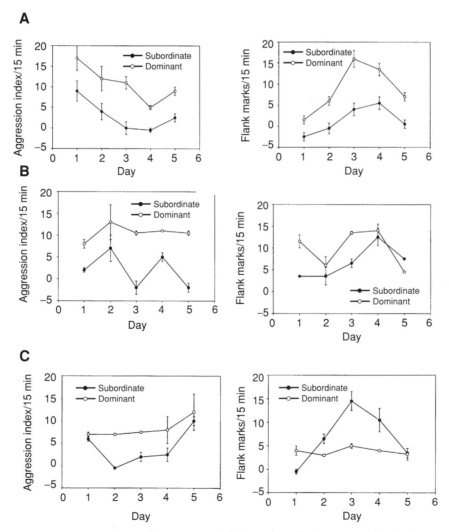

FIGURE 2 Mean amount of aggression and flank marking for dominant and subordinate members of pairs of male hamsters with intact flank glands (A), pairs in which one member was flank glandectomized and its partner sham operated (B), and pairs in which both members were flank glandectomized (C). Redrawn from Ferris *et al.* (1987).

two males, aggression levels are high in both animals, although the levels of aggression are significantly greater in the male that subsequently becomes dominant. After the initial encounter, the levels of agonistic behavior significantly decline in both hamsters during subsequent encounters; however, the dominant animal continues to exhibit higher levels of aggression than does the subordinate (see Fig. 2A). As the levels of aggression decline over successive days, the levels of flank marking significantly increase in the dominant hamster. In one study (Ferris *et al.*, 1987), the amount of flank marking was also found to increase in the subordinate hamster, but to a much lesser extent than seen in dominant hamsters. However, in other studies the flank marking levels in subordinate hamsters tended to be quite low (Johnston, 1975a). In pairs of hamsters living in large arenas with multiple compartments, subordinate hamsters mark only in their home nest, whereas dominant hamsters mark throughout the apparatus including in its opponent's home nest (Johnston, 1975c). In experiments in which groups of males or groups females were housed together continuously, a significant reduction in aggression was observed within 3 days (Drickamer *et al.*, 1973; Drickamer and Vandenbergh, 1973); however, whether there was a corresponding increase in the amount of flank marking was not reported. In these social hierarchies, dominant animals flank marked significantly more than did subordinates and there was a suggestion that the levels of flank marking correlated with social rank (Table 2). In summary, stable dominant–subordinate relationships are characterized by low levels of aggression and high levels of communication (i.e., flank marking).

The function of the flank gland in maintaining stable dominant–subordinate relationships has been tested in studies in which flank glands have been surgically removed in one or both hamsters prior to their social interaction (Ferris *et al.*, 1987). When flank glands are removed from one or both hamsters, aggression levels do not decline and flank marking levels do not increase over successive encounters, as they do in hamsters with their flank glands intact (Fig. 2,B,C). However, in the majority of cases, one hamster consistently displays higher levels of aggression, suggesting that the same individual is dominant-during each social encounter. In addition, there appears to be no relationship between whether a hamster has intact flank glands and whether it is dominant or subordinate. Thus, the presence of flank glands does not appear to be critical for determining who will be dominant, but their presence does appear to be critical for reducing aggression in both dominant and subordinate hamsters who have formed a stable social relationship. These data have led to the hypothesis that the chemical signals produced and disseminated by marking with the flank gland are different for the dominant and subordinate animals, and that these signals are essential for maintaining the dominant–subordinate relationship despite a dramatic reduction in aggression. There is also evidence that hamsters can discriminate between flank gland secretions from dominant and subordinate hamsters (Montgomery-St. Laurent *et al.*, 1988). Thus, it appears that the dominant hamster emits a chemical signal that conveys its dominance and the subordinate hamster emits a chemical signal that acknowledges its subordinate status. However, the chemical signals produced

TABLE 2
Correlates of Social Rank in Four Groups of Male Hamsters[a]

Social rank	Mean body weight (±1 SE)	Mean flank gland Index (±1 SE)	Mean percentage wins (±1 SE)	Mean flank marks (±1 SE)
1	107 (1)	619 (17)	95.3 (2.5)	113 (15)
2	106 (1)	589 (11)	36.7 (5.8)	48 (27)
3	105 (3)	541 (5)	22.6 (5.5)	20 (6)
4	106 (1)	531 (9)	8.3 (1.7)	8 (4)
Probability	NS	0.01	0.01	0.025

[a] NS, not significant.
Modified from Drickamer *et al.*, 1973.

by dominant hamsters does not appear to be aversive because subordinate hamsters will spend considerable amounts of time exploring areas that are scented with it (Fullenkamp *et al.*, 1987; Solomon and Glickman, 1977).

C. Factors That Influence the Outcome of Social Conflict

1. Gender

In most species, males engage in higher levels of agonistic behavior than do females. However, in hamsters, females exhibit more of these behaviors than males. During social encounters between male and sexually unreceptive female hamsters, females are more aggressive and usually become dominant over males (Marques and Valenstein, 1977; Payne and Swanson, 1970; Tiefer, 1970). Some studies have found higher levels of aggression during male–male encounters than during female–female encounters (Drickamer and Vandenbergh, 1973), but others have not (Payne and Swanson, 1970). Females can also exhibit higher levels of other agonistic behaviors. Females flank mark at significantly higher levels than do males in response to male odors (Albers and Prishkolnik, 1992). However, during social encounters between males and females, males appear to mark more frequently than do females (Payne and Swanson, 1970; Takahashi and Lisk, 1983).

2. Flank Gland Size and Pigmentation

Perhaps the best predictor of success during social encounters is the size and pigmentation of the flank glands. Studies in groups of four male hamsters housed together for 3 days have found that success in agonistic encounters (as measured by quantifying several agonistic behaviors) to be highly correlated ($r = 0.82$) with an index of the size and pigmentation of the flank glands (Drickamer *et al.*, 1973). Even in experiments in which the weight of the hamsters is held constant, there is a strong correlation ($r = 0.77$) between the size and pigmentation of the glands and success in social conflict (Table 2). Because the size of the flank gland is testosterone-dependent, these data suggest that testosterone may be critical in determining the outcome of social conflict. Although females have a much smaller flank gland than do males, there appears to be a similar relationship between the size and pigmentation of the gland and the outcome of social conflict (Drickamer and Vandenbergh, 1973). In groups of four females, there was a strong correlation ($r = 0.78$) between size and pigmentation of the flank gland and the success in agonistic encounters. Dominance hierarchies were formed quickly in the females (in 4 hours or less) and remained stable over the 8 days of testing.

3. Body Weight

Another important determinate of the outcome during social conflict is body weight. There is a strong positive correlation ($r = 0.66$–0.76) between body weight and success during agonistic encounters in males (Drickamer *et al.*, 1973; Payne and Swanson, 1970; Vandenbergh, 1971). In females fighting other females, there is an even stronger positive correlation between body weight and success ($r = 0.74$–0.91) (Drickamer and Vandenbergh, 1973; Payne and Swanson, 1970). Because female hamsters generally weigh more than do males, this difference in body weight may contribute to the observation that females are usually victorious over males. However, even in encounters between weight-matched opponents, females win more frequently than do males (Marques and Valenstein, 1977). Females that weigh significantly less than males are dominant in approximately 50% of the cases. Another exception to the relationship between body weight and dominance is found in hamsters that have experienced testicular regression as the result of exposure to short photoperiods. These hamsters defeated heavier males that had defeated them prior to their exposure to the short photoperiod (Garrett and Campbell, 1980).

4. Social Experience

An individual's prior social experience is also an important factor in determining success in social conflict. One of the simplest manipulations of social history is to allow an individual to interact with other conspecifics or to eliminate that interaction by housing it alone. As with other rodent species (Brain and Benton, 1983), when male hamsters are socially isolated aggression levels can increase and the expression of submissive behavior can occur at greater distances (Brain, 1972; Grelk *et al.*, 1974; Huang and Hazlett, 1974; Payne *et al.*, 1984, 1985; Wise, 1974). Similarly, female hamsters housed individually seem to be more aggressive than are females housed in groups (Brain, 1972; Grelk *et al.,* 1974; Wise, 1974). In these studies, female hamsters were maintained in the laboratory either one per cage or in groups of four (Grelk *et al.,* 1974; Wise, 1974) or ten (Brain, 1972) per cage for from 6 to 9 weeks. The number of females per cage has not been systematically manipulated, although it could be argued that housing female hamsters in groups is unnatural and stressful (Fritzsche *et al.,* 2000), so that the particular size of the groups does not matter. Also not examined systematically is the development of aggressiveness across the isolation period. Wise (1974) found that females were less aggressive when tested after 14–29 days of isolation than they were after 30–46 days. Again, the assumption is that isolation represents the normal social condition for these animals and that group housing produces an abnormal reduction in aggression. One consequence of this manipulation is that group-housed hamsters become a good source of stimulus animals for aggression tests because they rarely initiate fights themselves (e.g., Brain, 1972; Meisel *et al.,* 1988).

A dramatic example of how social experience can influence subsequent behavior during social conflict is a phenomenon called *conditioned defeat.* Conditioned defeat occurs when a hamster has been defeated in the home cage of a larger, more aggressive male and is characterized by the complete absence of normal territorial defense of the home cage following this brief defeat experience. When hamsters who have experienced conditioned defeat are paired in their home cage with a smaller nonaggressive male (a younger group-housed animal), they display no aggressive behavior but instead display defensive and submissive behaviors such as flee, tail lift, tooth chatter, and defensive postures (Potegal *et al.,* 1993). Conditioned defeat can persist for at least 1 month and can be induced during a single 15-minute encounter. Interestingly, predatory aggression does not appear to be affected in hamsters that had been severely defeated (Polsky, 1976).

5. Environment

Another factor that may influence agonistic behavior and the outcome of social conflict is the environment where the conflict occurs. Because the assumption is that animals engage in aggression to defend some resource, it follows that animals should be less aggressive in a neutral arena than in a familiar environment or their home territory. There is evidence that resident hamsters have an advantage over opponents in their home cage (Murphy, 1976a; Murphy and Schneider, 1970; however, see also Lerwill and Makings, 1971). Still, hamsters can also be aggressive when tested outside of their home cage (Payne and Swanson, 1970). Another approach that has been taken is to house animals in a large arena separated by a partition. Once the partition is removed, the location of fights can then be scored. In one study in which females were housed on both sides of the partition, aggressive interactions occurred in both compartments, although there was a tendency for females to be more dominant in the home area (Takahashi and Lisk, 1984). A similar division of aggression occurs when a male and female are housed on both sides of the partition (Lisk *et al.,* 1983). In all but a few experiments of hamster social behavior, the testing arena was sufficiently small that it would be difficult for the animals to avoid one another. There are no systematic studies of the effects of providing space for animals to avoid others or to flee the encounter entirely, and there are some data suggesting the pattern of social behavior observed can change depending on the size of the testing arena (Takahashi and Lisk, 1984).

In females, the presence of vaginal marks in the environment is a powerful determinant of the outcome of a conflict (Fischer and McQuiston, 1991). Female hamsters prefer areas that do not contain vaginal marks, when given a choice between a clean area and an area marked by another female. In addition, females will vaginal mark significantly more often in the clean area than in the scented area. When a testing arena is scented with the vaginal secretions of a female prior to a test with another female, the donor is significantly more aggressive and less submissive. In addition, the donor does all the vaginal marking and most of the flank marking. Not only can the existence of vaginal marks determine the outcome of a social interaction, it can actually reverse recently established dominant–subordinate relationships. When vaginal secretions from the subordinate hamster were applied to the testing arena prior to a second 30-min social interaction, the subordinate hamster became dominant in two-thirds of the pairs that were studied (Fischer and McQuiston, 1991).

6. *Characteristics of the Opponent*

Another significant variable in social conflict is the characteristics of the opponent. As previously discussed, the interactions between two animals can be very complex and difficult to understand. Attempts have been made to simplify the social conflicts with the use of opponents that respond minimally to the agonistic behavior of the experimental animal. Some studies have used small group-housed opponents, whereas others have used hamsters with bilateral olfactory bulbectomy as nonaggressive intruders (Murphy, 1976a). In one study, hamsters with bilateral olfactory bulbectomies were also muzzled and restrained to serve as a target for the experimental animal and to reduce the consequences of their behavior on the outcome of the experiment (Potegal *et al.,* 1980a). Still other studies have combined the use of a muzzle with the administration of sedatives (Potegal *et al.,* 1980b).

V. HORMONAL REGULATION OF SOCIAL CONFLICT AND COMMUNICATION

Hormones can influence agonistic behavior in a number of ways. Hormones can act directly on the neural circuits that regulate specific behaviors to change the functioning of those circuits and thereby change the expression of behavior. In addition, hormones can have less direct effects on the stimulus properties of an individual that may also significantly influence agonistic behaviors. For example, hormones can alter body weight, which can increase the likelihood that an individual will be victorious in a social conflict. It is also important to recognize that social encounters can regulate the levels of various hormones. For example, some animals defeated during conflict have lower levels of circulating testosterone than do the victors. In short, social behavior and the endocrine system interact in a complex bidirectional fashion.

The effects of hormones on behavior can occur at different stages of development. Early in development, hormones can exert organizational effects that serve to permanently change the neural circuits that control behavior. In adults, hormones are thought to have primarily activational effects, in which the functioning of the neural circuits controlling behavior are transiently

modified. There is a large literature on both the organizational and activational effects of hormones on agonistic behaviors. This chapter focuses on the activational effects of hormones and their interaction with the neural circuits controlling agonistic behavior in adults.

There are two major approaches providing evidence that gonadal hormones regulate agonistic behavior. The first approach has been to experimentally manipulate hormones; the second approach has been to correlate the levels of agonistic behavior with naturally occurring changes in hormone levels. Most of the evidence that gonadal hormones influence agonistic behavior has come from studies in which the effects of gonadectomy on specific agonistic behaviors have been examined. Many of these studies have gone on to examine the effects of the replacement of gonadal hormones in the gonadectomized animals. This classic endocrine approach has provided valuable data on the importance of these hormones in regulating social behavior. However, in nature, changes in the levels of gonadal hormones such as those produced by castration rarely, if ever, occur. Nevertheless, there can be significant changes in the levels of gonadal hormones in animals as the result of seasonal variations, social experience, puberty, and aging. It is important to determine whether these naturally occurring changes in gonadal hormones are sufficient to alter the levels of social conflict and communication. Unfortunately, there is still much we need to learn about the magnitude of the changes that occur in gonadal hormones in the hamster.

A. Effects of Gonadal Hormones on Agonistic Behavior in Males

1. *Testicular Hormones*

Testosterone appears to be the major androgen secreted from the hamster testis (Lau *et al.,* 1978; Terada *et al.,* 1980). Circulating levels of testosterone vary from approximately 0.5 to 6 ng/ml, depending on age, season, social status, and the characteristics of the assay used to measure it. As in many species (Bartke *et al.,* 1973; Ellis and Desjardins, 1982), male hamsters exhibit a pulsatile pattern of testosterone release from the testis (Bartke, 1985). Although there are significant changes in the physiological levels of circulating testosterone in hamsters as well as in other rodents, there are surprisingly few studies that have investigated the functional significance of these changes.

2. Agonistic Behavior

a) Developmental Changes   Hamsters reach puberty at 45–60 days of age and probably become fertile at approximately 50–55 days of age (Festing, 1972). During the first 30 days of life, testosterone levels remain low (approximately 0.5–1.0 ng/ml) and then increase rapidly until adult levels occur at approximately 50 days of age (Vomachka and Greenwald, 1979). There may be a slight reduction in testosterone levels following day 50. Testosterone levels then remain relatively constant even into advanced age in males that have been continuously housed (e.g., 31 months) in long photoperiods in the laboratory (Swanson *et al.*, 1982). There is only a very limited amount of data with which to compare the developmental changes in testosterone with developmental changes in agonistic behavior. One study examined the development of aggressive behavior in pairs of male hamsters from day 30 to adulthood (Whitsett, 1975). The increase in aggression in the pairs correlates well with the increasing levels of testosterone that are secreted during this interval. Aggression increases from day 30 and begins to level off at days 50–60. However, it seems unlikely that testosterone is responsible for the increase in aggression because the same developmental pattern was seen in pairs of hamsters that were castrated, as well as in pairs that were gonadally intact. Thus, it seems unlikely that the increasing level of aggression during the prepubertal period requires increasing levels of circulating testosterone during this period.

b) Seasonal Changes   Hamsters display dramatic seasonal changes in reproductive capacity (Bartness and Goldman, 1989). Seasonal changes in hamsters are regulated by photoperiod length and can be easily manipulated in the laboratory. Exposure to short photoperiod (<12.5 hr per day) for 6–8 weeks induces the nonbreeding condition that is characterized by dramatic changes in the regulation of the reproductive function by the hypothalamic-pituitary-gonadal axis. During the winter nonbreeding condition, testosterone levels are reduced to approximately 0.5 ng/ml, testis size is dramatically reduced, and there are major changes in the release of pituitary hormones.

After approximately 5 months, the reproductive system spontaneously begins to transform back into a functional state. This phenomenon, called spontaneous testicular recrudescence, actually begins prior to the occurrence of long summer-like photoperiods. Testicular recrudescence results in an increase in circulating testosterone levels beginning about 24 weeks after the initial exposure to short photoperiod. In summary, the seasonal changes produced by photoperiodic mechanisms in the hamster result in large changes in testosterone that range from some of the lowest to some of the highest levels seen in intact male hamsters.

In many species, aggression occurs at high levels during the breeding season when testosterone levels are high and at low levels in the nonbreeding season when testosterone levels are low. In contrast, Syrian hamsters exhibit a dramatically different seasonal pattern of aggression. Following induction of the nonbreeding condition by exposure to short photoperiod, the levels of aggression rise dramatically (Garrett and Campbell, 1980) (Fig. 3). These behavioral effects occur despite significant reductions in circulating levels of testosterone (Albers *et al.*, 1991; Turek *et al.*, 1975). In addition, when the breeding condition was reinstated by either exposure to a long photoperiod or by the development of spontaneous testicular recrudescence,

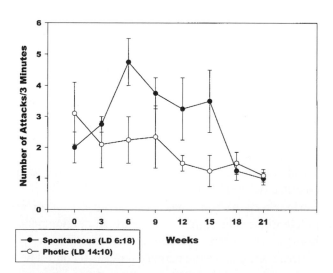

FIGURE 3   Mean number of attacks during 3-min aggression trials by male hamsters exposed to either a long photoperiod (LD, light:dark, 14:10) or a short photoperiod (LD 6:18). Redrawn from Garrett and Campbell (1980).

aggression levels declined. Thus, exposure to short photoperiods produces a dramatic uncoupling of the levels of testosterone from the levels of aggression. Little is known about the neural and endocrine factors that may mediate the increased levels of aggression seen in short photoperiods. One mechanism might be an enhanced sensitivity to testosterone in short-photoperiod-exposed hamsters. There is evidence that short photoperiods increases the sensitivity of some tesosterone-dependent events to testosterone, but not others (Campbell *et al.,* 1978; Morin and Zucker, 1978; Turek and Ellis, 1981).

The effects of photoperiod on agonistic behavior raises questions about the findings of a number of studies completed before these effects were recognized. Many of the studies examining the effects of castration and testosterone replacement on aggression either did not specify the lighting conditions in which the hamsters were housed or housed hamsters in LD (light:dark) 12:12, which acts as a short photoperiod to induce nonbreeding conditions (Evans and Brain, 1974; Payne, 1973, 1974; Payne and Swanson, 1971a,b, 1972a). As a result, it is not certain whether these experiments examined the effects of testosterone on aggression in hamsters in the breeding state, in the nonbreeding condition, or during the transition between the breeding and nonbreeding conditions. If we consider only the experiments in which it was explicitedly stated that hamsters were maintained in LD cycles that maintain the breeding state (i.e., LD cycles with more than 12.5 hr light per day), some studies provide evidence that testosterone influences hamster aggression (Drickamer *et al.,* 1973; Vandenbergh, 1971), but others do not (Tiefer, 1970; Whitsett, 1975).

c) Effect of Social Experience

Studies in a variety of species have shown that social experience can significantly alter the physiological levels of circulating testosterone (Harding, 1981; Katangole *et al.,* 1971; Sanford *et al.,* 1974). These changes can be transient or long-lasting, depending on the duration and nature of the social stimuli or interaction. In male hamsters, a significant increase in circulating testosterone occurs when males interact with female hamsters that are sexually receptive or when they are exposed to vaginal secretions from females that are sexually receptive. However, vaginal secretions are not required

for the estrous-female-induced increase in testosterone because it persists when males are exposed to estrous females that had their vaginas removed (Macrides *et al.,* 1974; Pfeiffer and Johnston, 1992). Males that were allowed to interact, but not fight, with another male did not exhibit a significant increase in testosterone (Pfeiffer and Johnston, 1992). However, when social interactions between males are maintained over a more extended interval, some types of social stimuli can produce long-lasting changes in testosterone levels. For example, when two male hamsters are allowed to interact for short intervals over several days, one hamster becomes dominant and the other subordinate. In association with the development of this relationship is a significant change in testosterone levels. The levels of testosterone are reduced in the subordinate by approximately 60% (Huhman *et al.,* 1991); they remain unchanged in the dominant hamster. In summary, the existing data, although very limited, indicate that social experience can produce significant changes in the physiological levels of circulating testosterone in hamsters.

There is surprisingly little data available on whether changes in testosterone of the magnitude and duration produced by social stimuli can affect any type of social behavior in rodents. Studies in rats and hamsters have found no correlation between changes in testosterone induced by social stimuli and several measures of sexual behavior (Damassa *et al.,* 1977; Pfeiffer and Johnston, 1992). However, studies in four different strains of mice found a significant positive correlation between the onset of mounting and the circulating levels of testosterone in each strain, but no significant correlation between testosterone and ejaculation latency in any strain (Batty, 1978). In intact rats, a positive correlation has been reported between baseline levels of testosterone and aggression (Schuurman, 1980). Another approach to studying this question has been to determine the behavioral effects of experimentally manipulating testosterone levels within the physiological range by providing different concentrations of testosterone in constant-release capsules. Studies in rats have found that when constant-release capsules containing testosterone producing five different levels of testosterone were implanted in castrate rats (0.2, 0.5, 0.8, 1.8, and 3.1 ng/ml) the levels of aggression were dose-dependent. In contrast, there was no relationship between the magnitude of male sexual behavior and the levels of circulating testosterone (Albert *et al.,* 1990; Damassa *et al.,* 1977). Less than 10% (0.2 ng/ml) of the peak physiological levels (3 ng/ml) of testosterone were required for the full expression of male sex behavior, whereas the amount of aggression was found to be proportional to the levels of testosterone up to peak physiological levels. However, there was no further increase in the frequency of aggression when supraphysiological concentrations of testosterone were administered. In summary, the limited amount of data available suggests that changes in circulating levels of testosterone such as those produced by social experience can be functionally significant. However, changes in testosterone levels within the physiological range may affect some testosterone-dependent behaviors but not others, and these relationships may differ among species. The very limited amount of data available, which comes exclusively from studies in rats, suggests that physiological changes in testosterone may affect aggression but not sex behavior in males.

d) *Effects of Castration and Hormone Replacement*

Most of the data on the effects of castration and hormone replacement has examined the effects of these treatments on aggression and not other forms of agonistic behavior. However, one study that looked at the effects gonadal hormones on defensive or submissive behavior found no differences in the amount of defensive or submissive behavior in castrates given oil or three different forms of androgens, including testosterone (Payne, 1974) In contrast, there is a substantial body of evidence that castration and the administration of gonadal hormones to castrates can significantly influence the expression of aggression in hamsters (Drickamer *et al.,* 1973; Grelk *et al.,* 1974; Payne, 1973, 1974; Payne and Swanson, 1971b, 1972a; Potegal *et al.,* 1980a; Vandenbergh, 1971). In some of these studies the effects of castration and testosterone therapy on several measures of aggression are substantial, but in other studies the effects are quite limited. In still other studies, castration and gonadal hormones were not found to influence any measure of aggression (Evans and Brain, 1974; Garrett and Campbell, 1980; Tiefer, 1970; Whitsett, 1975). It is not clear why there are such large differences among these studies, although it seems likely that many of these differences result from

the differences in experimental protocols. Basic variables such as the time since castration and the duration of hormone administration varied widely among these studies. Another factor is that these studies have used a variety of different measures of aggression, and it has been suggested that gonadal hormones may influence only some measures of aggression (e.g., latency) but not others (e.g., duration of aggression) (Payne, 1973; Potegal *et al.,* 1980a). Other factors that may contribute to the differences are discussed next.

Studies in which testosterone has been administered have also examined the relationship between testosterone, the size of the flank gland, and the outcome of social conflict. Because the size and pigmentation of the flank gland is very sensitive to the levels of circulating testosterone, the effects of administration of different concentrations of testosterone on flank gland size and on social encounters were determined. After a short period for recovery from surgery, castrated hamsters were injected with oil or 0.1, 0.5, or 1.0 mg testosterone for 3 weeks and then housed in a large arena for 3 days. The two highest doses of testosterone had very similar effects on both the flank gland and the outcome of the social interactions. Hamsters that received either 0.5 or 1.0 mg of testosterone had flank glands of the same size and pigmentation and ranked either first or second in the group. The hamsters that received 0.1 mg testosterone had glands that were significantly smaller than in the hamsters receiving higher levels of testosterone and were always ranked third in the group of four. The castrates that received no testosterone replacement had significantly smaller and less pigmented glands and consistently ranked last in the group. Another study examined the effects of manipulating the size of the flank gland with topically administered testosterone (Rowe and Swanson, 1977). Castrated hamsters that received topical administration of testosterone to the flank gland exhibited similar patterns of dominance–submission as intact hamsters and castrate hamsters that received systemic injections of testosterone. In contrast, castrates not receiving any form of testosterone had higher levels of submission and lower levels of dominance behaviors. Although the dose of testosterone that was topically administered maintained the size of the flank gland but not the sex accessory glands, the possibility that testosterone had behavioral effects in the brain cannot be excluded.

As discussed earlier, body weight is one of the best predictors of which animal will win a social conflict. This raises the interesting question of whether the increased body weight that occurs following castration influences aggression. The only experiment in which aggression levels were compared in gonadally intact hamsters and castrates that were significantly heavier than the intacts found no significant differences in levels of aggression (Whitsett, 1975). In many of the experiments in which castrated hamsters were found to be less aggressive than gonadally intact hamsters, the body weights of the animals were selected to be similar (Garrett and Campbell, 1980; Payne, 1973, 1974; Payne and Swanson, 1972a). Thus, castration may have a dual effect on aggression. The increase in body weight produced by castration may increase the probability of success in agonistic encounters, while reducing the probability of agonistic success by reducing testosterone levels. Group-housed hamsters tend to be significantly heavier than socially isolated hamsters (Borer *et al.*, 1988; Fritzsche *et al.*, 2000; Meisel *et al.*, 1990b), which is interesting because they also tend to be less aggressive.

One way that social experience may alter social behavior is by changing the circulating levels of hormones. It is also possible that hormones might have different effects depending on an individual's prior social experience. Although there is evidence to suggest that testosterone levels may be elevated in isolated males, it is not known if testosterone is responsible for the increased levels of aggression. However, some support for this possibility comes from studies in castrated hamsters. No differences were found in aggression between castrated hamsters that had been single- or group-housed for approximately 1 month and tested with another castrate (Grelk *et al.*, 1974). Unfortunately, this study did not include a positive control such as a sham-castrate group to demonstrate that gonadally intact, single-housed hamsters are more aggressive than castrates. Thus, although it is likely that social experience is a key element in determining the effects of gonadal hormones on aggression, the effects of social experience in hamsters is not well understood. This lack of information also raises serious questions about the interpretation of much of the existing data on the role of testosterone in hamster aggression. Nearly every study examining the effects of testosterone on aggression in

hamsters that has been conducted has used multiple behavioral tests. As we have seen with conditioned defeat, each social interaction has the potential to produce significant long-term changes in an individual's subsequent social behavior.

There is a limited amount of data in hamsters that gonadal hormones can alter an individual's stimulus properties and thereby alter how other animals respond to it. When castrated hamsters are given testosterone or progesterone, there is a significant reduction in the amount of aggression displayed by their intact opponents (Payne and Swanson, 1972a). In another study, castrated males were found to be attacked significantly less frequently than intact males by opponents that were trained fighters (Evans and Brain, 1974).

Testosterone is one of a number of circulating androgens with potent effects on behavior. The majority of studies that have examined the effects of androgens on aggression in hamsters have administered testosterone. However, one experiment compared the effects of three androgens on aggression in long-term castrates and found androstenedione to be the most potent in restoring aggression, followed by testosterone propionate and dihydrotestosterone (Payne, 1974). There is also some evidence on the effects of ovarian hormones on aggression in male hamsters. Implantation of ovarian tissue into castrated males produced significantly higher levels of aggression than in castrates not receiving the tissue implants (Payne and Swanson, 1971b). Studies on the effects of estrogens on aggression in castrated male hamsters have had mixed results (Payne and Swanson, 1972a; Tiefer, 1970; Vandenbergh, 1971). The administration of progesterone to castrated males increased aggression when their opponents were females but not when they were males (Payne and Swanson, 1972a). However, progesterone administered to castrated males reduced the aggression and overall agonistic behavior displayed by intact males with which they interacted.

3. Communicative Behavior

The form of communication that appears to be most important during social conflict in hamsters is flank marking. Flank marking occurs frequently during social interactions and appears to communicate different types of information. Flank marking can occur at high levels during social interactions, but can also be stimulated by the odors of other hamsters when individuals are alone.

a) Developmental Changes In pairs of intact male hamsters or pairs of castrated male hamsters, flank marking during social interactions increased two- to three- fold from day 35 to approximately day 50–60 and then appeared to level off (Whitsett, 1975). An investigation of the development of odor-stimulated flank marking found that marking first developed between days 18 and 22 (Ferris *et al.*, 1996), which corresponds to an interval when circulating testosterone levels are quite low. Taken together, these data suggest that the development of flank marking behavior is not dependent on the developmental increase in circulating testosterone.

b) Seasonal Changes The levels of odor-stimulated flank marking do not vary in a seasonal pattern (Garrett and Campbell, 1980) despite the dramatic reduction in testosterone that occurs following exposure to short photoperiods. No differences were observed in the number of odor-induced flank marks in animals that had experienced short-photoperiod-induced testicular regression, or exposure to long-photoperiod or spontaneous testicular recrudescence. Short photoperiod does appear to affect another form of communication in hamsters, ultrasonic vocalizations (Matochik *et al.*, 1986). Intact males and castrates exposed to short photoperiods had significantly higher ultrasonic calling rates when exposed to a sexually receptive female than did males housed in long photoperiods and exposed to a sexually receptive female. The functional significance of this seasonal change in ultrasonic calling rates is not known.

c) Effects of Social Experience At present, there has been no investigation of whether changes in circulating testosterone stimulated by social stimuli are capable of altering the levels of flank marking.

d) Effects of Castration and Hormone Replacement The effects of castration and administration of testosterone have been studied for both odor-stimulated flank marking and flank marking that occurs during social encounters. Following castration, flank marking in response to the odors of other males declines

slowly over 4–5 weeks and administration of testosterone restores precastration levels of flank marking in 4–5 weeks (Albers *et al.*, 1992; Albers and Prishkolnik, 1992; Johnston, 1981). The effects of testosterone on flank marking that occurs during social encounters is less clear. One study found that the frequency of flank marking is significantly lower in castrated males during 5-minute social encounters with intact males in a neutral arena (Vandenbergh, 1971) and that the administration of testosterone for 11–14 days increased flank marking (Vandenbergh, 1971). However, another study (Payne, 1974) found no difference in the amount of flank marking between groups of castrated hamsters administered oil, testosterone, dihydrotestosterone, or androstenedione for 8 days during a 10-minute social encounter in their home cage with an intact intruder. In addition, pairs of castrated hamsters flank mark at the same levels during brief social encounters as do pairs of intact hamsters (Whitsett, 1975). However, when hamsters from the castrated pairs were tested with hamsters from the intact pairs, the intact hamsters flank marked significantly more frequently than did the castrates. Thus, although, testosterone appears to be important for flank marking, castrated animals can flank mark at high levels.

B. Effects of Gonadal Hormones in Females

1. Ovarian Hormones

Saidapur and Greenwald (1978) measured estradiol and progesterone levels through the female hamster's estrous cycle (Fig. 4). Levels of both of these hormones are low during estrus and on the first day of diestrus. Estradiol levels begin to increase on diestrous day 2, with peak levels of approximately 175 pg estradiol/ml of serum early in proestrus. Later on in proestrus, serum estradiol levels fall coincident with a rise in progesterone. Progesterone is elevated for approximately 10 hr during proestrus, with peak levels of almost 20 ng/ml of serum. Ovulation occurs early on the day of vaginal estrus.

2. Agonistic Behavior

a) Changes over the Estrous Cycle Female hamsters have a consistent 4-day ovulatory cycle. Proestrus is defined as the day during which the females are

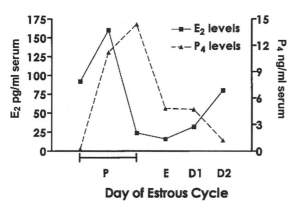

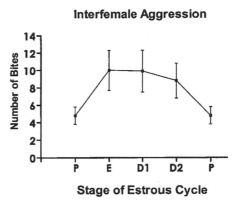

FIGURE 4 Fluctuations in serum estradiol (E₂) and progesterone (P₄) levels during the estrous cycle of a female Syrian hamster. A single sample is illustrated for estrus (E), the first day of diestrus (D1) and the second day of diestrus (D2). The sampling time for proestrus (P) is expanded to illustrate the progesterone surge. Redrawn from Saidapur and Greenwald (1978).

FIGURE 5 Average number of biting attacks across days of the estrous cycle for a group of female hamsters. Pairs of females were permitted to interact for 1 hour each day. The day of proestrus (P) is plotted twice to illustrate a complete cycle. E–estrus, D1–first day of diestrus, D2–second day of diestrus. Redrawn from Takahashi and Lisk (1983).

sexually responsive, followed by estrus and then two diestrous days. On proestrus, female hamsters respond to the presence of both male and female hamsters with the expression of the sexually receptive posture, lordosis (Ciaccio *et al.*, 1979; Fischer and Brown, 1993; Floody and Pfaff, 1977a; Kislak and Beach, 1955; Lisk *et al.*, 1983; Marques and Valenstein, 1977; Steel, 1979; Takahashi and Lisk, 1983, 1984; Vandenbergh, 1971; Wise, 1974). With one exception (Giordano *et al.*, 1986), there is agreement that levels of agonistic behavior toward male and female opponents vary during the estrous cycle (Fig. 5). Despite this agreement, there are differences in the specific measures of aggression that fluctuate and when these fluctuations occur.

b) Seasonal Changes Seasonal patterns of reproduction are the result of photoperiodic mechanisms in female hamsters just as they are in male hamsters. In females housed in short photoperiods (less than 12.5 hr of light per day) for 6–8 weeks, the 4-day estrous cycle ceases, estradiol levels significantly decline, and large daily surges in progesterone are observed (Jorgenson and Schwartz, 1985; Moline, 1981). The estrous cycle resumes spontaneously (i.e., without having to be exposed to long photoperiods) after approximately 5 months. Like males, female hamsters housed in short photoperiods have higher levels of aggression than females housed in long photoperiods.

However, following ovariectomy short-photoperiod-exposed hamsters had levels of aggression similar to females housed in long photoperiods (Elliott and Nunez, 1992; Fleming *et al.*, 1998). If ovariectomized female hamsters were given sequential administrations of estradiol and progesterone, females housed in short photoperiods had higher levels of aggression than did females housed in long photoperiods (Badura and Nunez, 1989; Elliott and Nunez, 1992; Fleming *et al.*, 1998; Honrado *et al.*, 1991). Honrado *et al.* (1991) examined the time course of the development of enhanced aggression in short photoperiods and observed that the increase in aggression occurred between 4 and 14 weeks (the two closest time periods tested). Further, the levels of aggression returned to their initial levels by weeks 20, indicating that there was a spontaneous reversal of the effects of the short photoperiod. It appears that short photoperiods do not necessarily produce elevated levels of aggression in female hamsters but, rather, that animals housed under these conditions lose their responsiveness to the inhibitory actions of estradiol and progesterone on aggression.

If photoperiod has the net effect of elevating aggression in female hamsters, what is the mechanism underlying this phenomenon? With most physiological and behavioral end points, the effects of photoperiod are mediated by regulation of the pineal gland (Bartness and Goldman, 1989). Indeed, removal of the pineal gland eliminated the differences in aggression between female hamsters maintained in long and short photoperiods (Badura and Nunez, 1989; Fleming *et al.*, 1998). Further, removal of the pineal gland would be expected to eliminate the source of melatonin, a hormone secreted during darkness (Bartness and Goldman, 1989). To test the role of melatonin in mediating photoperiod effects on aggression, female hamsters maintained in long photoperiods were given daily injections of melatonin for 7 weeks (Fleming *et al.*, 1998). As early as 2 weeks after the start of melatonin injections, gonadally intact female hamsters showed elevations of aggression compared with control animals. The effects of melatonin were maintained when the females were tested at 4 weeks, the last test given. The principal effects of photoperiod (i.e., increasing the duration of melatonin secretion) seem to be to reduce the sensitivity of the females to estradiol and progesterone. An unanswered question in this research area is whether the melatonin acts directly on the neurons responsive to estradiol and progesterone or indirectly in some manner on other sites in the neural pathway regulating the expression of aggression.

c) Effects of Ovariectomy and Hormone Replacement.
One approach that has been taken to identify the hormonal basis for the estrous cycle variations in aggression has been to remove the female's ovaries and to exogenously administer estradiol and progesterone in a pattern that approximates the temporal release of these hormones during the estrous cycle. In this way the effects of estradiol and progesterone on aggression, either alone or in combination, can be isolated.

For estradiol, acute treatments have ranged from 1 to 3 days of estradiol treatment. Lisk and Nachtingall (1988) gave ovariectomized female hamsters Silastic implants of estradiol for 3 days. Different groups of females were initially tested 6, 12, or 24 hr after Silastic implantation and then again at 24-hr intervals. Combining the behavioral responses for these animals produced a record of aggression at 6- to 12-hr intervals during 3 days of estradiol treatment. In this study, there was an initial decrease in attacks and chases between 24 and 48 hrs after estradiol treatment. The frequency of attacks and chases increased between 54 and 72 hrs after estradiol implantation to levels equivalent to those measured prior to hormone treatment. This time course

is consistent with the inhibition of aggression on the second diestrous day of the female's cycle, when estradiol levels are high, compared with estrus when estradiol levels are the lowest (Saidapur and Greenwald, 1978). Unfortunately, most studies have not measured aggression until at least 2 days after estradiol treatment. The common finding in these studies is that estradiol does not alter aggression parameters in either males or females compared with levels of aggression following ovariectomy (Floody and Pfaff, 1977a; Kislak and Beach, 1955; Meisel *et al.*, 1990a; Meisel and Sterner, 1990; Vandenbergh, 1971).

When female hamsters are ovariectomized, a single injection of progesterone has no effect on the expression of aggression (Meisel *et al.*, 1988). In contrast, a progesterone injection following 2 days of estradiol treatment essentially eliminates aggression of female hamsters toward both male and female opponents (Floody and Pfaff, 1977a; Kislak and Beach, 1955; Meisel *et al.*, 1990a; Meisel and Sterner, 1990). It appears that progesterone has a biphasic action on aggression, however (Ciaccio *et al.*, 1979; Meisel and Sterner, 1990). For example, if female hamsters are given 2 days of estradiol, the first injection of progesterone eliminates aggression, but an injection of progesterone on the following day increases aggression to levels higher than those seen prior to the initial progesterone treatment (Fig. 6). Removing

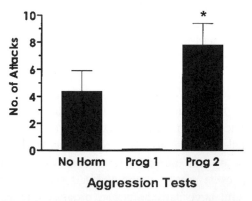

FIGURE 6 Ovariectomized female hamsters without hormone replacement (No Horm) are aggressive toward female intruders. A series of injections of estradiol and progesterone (Prog 1) eliminates aggression. When an additional injection of progesterone is given the following day (Prog 2), aggression is elevated to a level that is significantly higher (*) than prior to hormone treatment.

progesterone returns the female's level of aggression to that seen in the estradiol-only condition, reinforcing the idea that there are biphasic effects of progesterone that depend on the duration of progesterone exposure (Ciaccio *et al.,* 1979). In intact cycling females there is an enhancement of aggression at the end of the sexually receptive period (e.g., Lisk *et al.,* 1983), and a progesterone surge as a result of mating may control this reversion to the aggressive state.

The cellular mechanisms through which progesterone acts to inhibit aggression are largely unknown. One of these mechanisms may be through the production of metabolites that have activity at specific neurotransmitter receptor sites. Progesterone seems to be metabolized in the brain to neurosteroids that have an affinity for modulatory sites on the GABA$_A$ receptor and act as GABA agonists (Baulieu, 1997). Peripheral injection of metabolites of progesterone produced in the brain (e.g., either tetrahydrodeoxycorticosterone or allopregnanolone) do not affect aggression in estradiol–treated female hamsters (Kohlert and Meisel, 2001). The same is true if the injection of allopregnanolone is made directly into the ventricular system of the brain. Yet, if a low dose of progesterone, which has no behavioral effects of its own, is given systemically, the neurosteroid tetrahydrodeoxycorticosterone delivered to the brain's ventricular system will inhibit aggression. The suggestion here is that one mechanism through which progesterone inhibits aggression is through interactions with GABA$_A$ receptors (see also Canonaco *et al.,* 1990; Potegal, 1986), although other cellular actions triggered by progesterone itself are also needed.

In addition to acute treatments with estradiol and progesterone, some studies have investigated the effects of chronic treatment with these hormones. The biological significance of these studies may seem limited, although there are several ways in which this experimental approach is valuable. One application of these studies is to uncover dynamic changes in aggression during estradiol exposure. Because the elevation in estradiol during the estrous cycle occurs for only a few days, chronic estradiol treatment can increase the time period during which animals can be tested. A perhaps less artificial application of these studies extends to modeling hormone changes during pregnancy and the consequent effects on aggression. Based on a rather small literature, it seems that female hamsters are more

aggressive during pregnancy than they are during their estrous cycle (Giordano *et al.,* 1986; Wise, 1974). This appears to be true for all elements of aggressive behavior. Giordano *et al.* (1986) made systematic observations of aggression for the first 15 days of pregnancy (the gestation period for Syrian hamsters is 16 days) and found an increase in aggression between days 4 to 12. Attacks and rolling fights actually peaked on day 6 of pregnancy and then declined to a low on day 15, with following (termed chases in this study) maintaining relatively high levels between days 6 and 13 and then declining on day 15. Aggression on day 15 of pregnancy (the day prior to birth) declined significantly to a level equivalent to the first day of pregnancy in this study. Certainly estradiol and progesterone levels are rapidly changing during the estrous cycle; yet these hormones are elevated for much longer durations during pregnancy (Baranczuk and Greenwald, 1973). Therefore, it is useful to examine aggression in ovariectomized females given several weeks of exposure to these hormones.

There are several studies in which estradiol treatments were administered for 10 to 15 days. When aggression was tested between females over this time period, there were no changes in measures of aggression compared to control conditions without hormone treatment (Fraile *et al.,* 1987; Meisel *et al.,* 1988; Vandenbergh, 1971). When female hamsters given chronic estradiol exposure were tested with male hamsters, there was generally a decrease in aggression by the females (Carter *et al.,* 1973; Meisel *et al.,* 1988; Payne and Swanson, 1971a). It is difficult to interpret this loss of aggression because females typically showed sexual behavior (lordosis) directed toward the males.

The effect of chronic progesterone on aggression in females appears to be dependent on whether females are tested with male or female hamsters. If females are given progesterone for 4 consecutive days, there is a consistent decrease in attacks and rolling fights in tests with other females (Fraile *et al.,* 1987, 1988). When tested with males, 10 days of progesterone treatment increased the levels of aggression in female hamsters (Payne and Swanson, 1971a; 1972b). In this case, the females did not display lordosis, although the levels of aggression in the males were decreased by the hormone treatments to the females. It may be that the progesterone treatment altered the sensory quality of the female, which altered the aggressive response of the male. Because the primary measure of aggression in these studies was which animal won the fight, the decrease in male aggression could have led indirectly to increases in the female's level of aggression. These effects of progesterone on aggression may explain some of the changes in aggression during pregnancy because aggression is initially low during pregnancy and then rises and this pattern superficially coincides with the effects of 4 and 10 days of progesterone treatment. Perhaps more systematic studies designed to manipulate hormone levels in a way that is consistent with the changes in estradiol and progesterone during pregnancy would address this issue directly.

3. Communicative Behavior

The levels of flanking marking seen in female hamsters varies significantly across the estrous cycle (Fig. 7). In response to the odors of male hamsters, females flank mark at lower levels on the day of sexual receptivity than on any other day of the estrous cycle (Albers and Rowland, 1989; Takahashi and Lisk, 1984). A similar relationship between flank marking and the estrous cycle is seen during social encounters (Tiefer, 1970).

Ovariectomy reduces the amount of flank marking in response to odors or during social encounters (Albers and Rowland, 1989; Takahashi and Lisk, 1984; Vandenbergh, 1971). The administration of estradiol

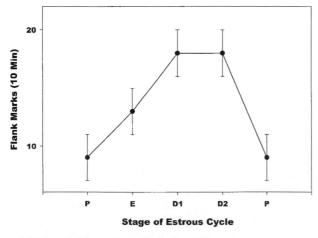

FIGURE 7 The amount of odor-stimulated flank marking observed over the estrus cycle. Abbreviations: P, proestrus; E, estrus; D1, diestrus 1; D2, diestrus 2. Redrawn from Albers and Rowland (1989).

to ovariectomized hamsters restores precastration levels of marking behavior (Albers and Rowland, 1989; Takahashi and Lisk, 1984; Vandenbergh, 1971). The injection of progesterone in ovariectomized females significantly reduces flank marking in estradiol-primed females, but has no effect in ovariectomized females without significant levels of circulating estradiol. These data suggest that the changing levels of ovarian hormones over the estrous cycle are responsible for the 4-day rhythm in flank marking levels that occurs in females with estrous cycles. One interesting feature of the effects of gonadal hormones on flank marking is the time course of their effects. Three weeks appear to be required for the full expression of the reduction of flank marking produced by ovariectomy and for the full restoration of precastration levels of flank marking by estradiol (Albers and Rowland, 1989). These data suggest that the effects of estradiol on flank marking may not be sufficiently rapid to account for the 4-day rhythm of flank marking during the estrous cycle. It seems more likely that the large rise in progesterone that occurs prior to the reduction in flank marking is responsible for the 4-day rhythm in flank marking. Progesterone injected into ovariectomized females administered estradiol significantly reduces flank marking when tested 6 hours later (Albers and Rowland, 1989).

The effects of testosterone on flank marking in females have been examined (Albers and Prishkolnik, 1992; Vandenbergh, 1971). Studies of odor–stimulated marking and marking that occurs during social encounters with other females have found ovariectomized females flank mark at high levels when they are administered testosterone.

C. Effects of Adrenal Hormones

1. Adrenal Hormones

Although adrenal glands are larger in female rats than in males, this sex difference is reversed in hamsters (Gaskin and Kitay, 1970). Male hamsters have larger adrenal glands, a higher secretion of glucocorticoids from the adrenals *in vivo* and *in vitro*, a higher concentration of plasma glucocorticoids, and greater hepatic metabolism of adrenal steroids *in vitro* than do female hamsters. Each of these sex differences is opposite that observed in rats. Pituitary–adrenal function in hamsters is influenced by the gonads, but again in a different manner than in rats. Whereas estrogen stimulates adrenal function in rats, testosterone stimulates adrenocortical function in hamsters and estrogen appears to be of minimal importance. Another interesting feature is that hamster adrenals secrete both cortisol and corticosterone, as do adrenals in humans, and not primarily corticosterone as in rats and mice. In addition, cortisol appears to be the more labile hormone in terms of circadian rhythmicity (Albers *et al.*, 1985) and stress responsivity (Huhman *et al.*, 1990).

2. Agonistic Behavior

There are data in rodents supporting a role for the hormones of the pituitary–adrenocortical axis in the modulation of agonistic behavior, although what that role is remains unclear (for review, see Brain, 1972, 1979; Haller *et al.*, 1998; Leshner, 1980, 1983). Much of the discrepancy probably results from the difficulty in examining the effects of either glucocorticoids or adrenocorticotropin (ACTH) without altering levels of the other hormone concurrently. Any manipulation probably also alters brain levels of corticotropin-releasing hormone (CRH). In addition, any experimental manipulation that alters gonadal hormone levels will also have an impact on the pituitary–adrenocortical hormones. The time course of treatments may be critical as well, and there appear to be important differences in the effects of these hormones depending on whether they are given acutely or chronically (Brain, 1979; Haller *et al.*, 1998). In general, it appears that in rats that glucocorticoids facilitate aggression, whereas ACTH (particularly long-term) treatment decreases aggression (Haller *et al.*, 2000; Leshner, 1983). In male hamsters, there is a marked circadian rhythm in agonistic behavior with the peak frequency of this behavior occurring just after lights out (Landau, 1975a). This rhythm appears to be at least partially independent of rhythms in other social behaviors and in locomotor activity. It is unlikely that the circadian rhythm in agonistic behavior depends on gonadal hormones because these hormones do not show a pronounced rhythm in hamsters. However, this rhythm in agonistic behavior does appear to depend on adrenal hormones because it is abolished by adrenalectomy (Landau, 1975b). In adrenalectomized hamsters given cortisol, aggression is significantly higher than in hamsters without cortisol

replacement or in sham-adrenalectomized hamsters, indicating that cortisol may increase aggressiveness in male hamsters.

It has been hypothesized that ACTH facilitates the acquisition of submissive or defensive responses in subordinate animals, which then might, in turn, decrease the amount of overt fighting produced (Leshner, 1980). Social defeat, or becoming subordinate, is associated with increases in pituitary–adrenocortical hormones in hamsters (Figs. 8 and 9) (Huhman *et al.*, 1990, 1991). The importance of pituitary–adrenocortical hormones in the maintenance of subordinate behaviors is unclear, however. A recent experiment examining the role of CRH in the expression of conditioned defeat in hamsters used a peripherally administered CRH receptor antagonist for the CRH-R1 receptor subtype. Blockade of this receptor did not alter the subsequent agonistic behavior of these hamsters, but the usual ACTH response to the social interaction was completely attenuated (Jasnow *et al.*, 1999). This indicates that ACTH is not necessary for the production of submissive and defensive behaviors in a subordinate hamster and is in agreement with earlier work indicating that ACTH does not alter agonistic behavior in male or female hamsters (Evans and Brain, 1974; Floody and Pfaff, 1977a). In conclusion, the data are somewhat sparse in hamsters, but there appears to be little support for an important role of pituitary–adrenocortical hormones in the control of agonistic behavior.

D. Conclusion

Hamsters provide a comparatively simple model with which to study social conflict and communication. Because hamsters appear to live predominately solitary lifestyles, it seems likely that when they encounter one another they either fight, flee, or mate. Because of the absence of field data and because most of the research on social conflict in hamsters has used small testing arenas, we do not know how often social interactions are terminated by flight. If hamsters do not mate or flee when they encounter another hamster, social conflict typically occurs. During social conflict, hamsters can engage in a range of different behaviors that are investigative, aggressive, or defensive or submissive. Social conflict rapidly results in the formation of dominant–subordinate relationships. These relationships, which

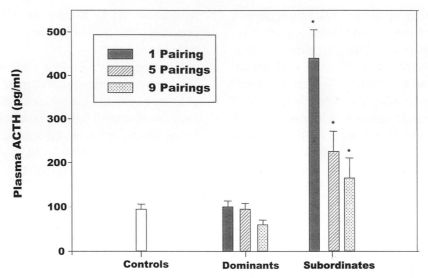

FIGURE 8 Mean plasma adrenocorticotropin (ACTH) in home cage controls and in dominant and subordinate male hamsters following one, five, and nine exposures to social conflict. Redrawn from Huhman *et al.* (1991).

remain remarkably stable, are characterized by relatively low levels of conflict. Communication (e.g., flank marking) is at least one of the reasons for the reduction in conflict and the maintenance of these stable relationships. However, even though this pattern of social behavior in hamsters is relatively simple when compared to the patterns of social behavior seen in many other species, investigating the mechanisms underlying the control of these behaviors remains extremely challenging.

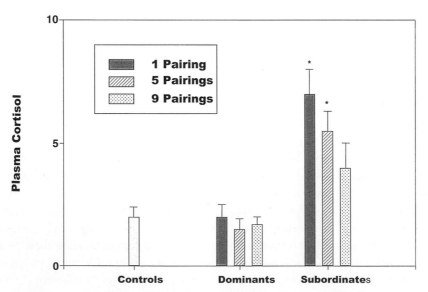

FIGURE 9 Mean plasma cortisol in home cage controls and in dominant and subordinate male hamsters following one, five, and nine exposures to social conflict. Redrawn from Huhman *et al.* (1991).

Despite a large literature, there remains much to be learned about the role of hormones in regulating social conflict and communication. One of the most important questions that remains to be answered fully is whether the changes in the circulating levels of hormones that occur naturally are sufficient to influence these behaviors. For female hamsters the answer to this question is "yes." Although the effects of fluctuations in estradiol during the estrous cycle on aggression seem to be minimal, the sequential release of estradiol and progesterone results in a consistent inhibition of aggression. Whether natural fluctuations in androgens regulate aggression in males is more ambiguous. One of the most long-lasting and dramatic changes in hormones in hamsters, as well as many other species, occur seasonally. In species that have seasonal patterns of breeding there are large seasonal changes in gonadal hormones. In many species, agonistic behaviors such as aggression increase in association with the seasonal increase in testosterone (Wingfield *et al.,* 1994). However, in hamsters an opposite relationship is seen between aggression and the seasonal pattern of testosterone. When testosterone levels are at their lowest during the year, aggression levels are at their highest. The expression of some other agonistic behaviors also appears to be unrelated to the seasonal changes in circulating testosterone (e.g., flank marking). A similar inverse relationship between circulating levels of testosterone and aggression over the year has been reported in another species of hamsters as well (Jasnow *et al.,* 2000). There are other examples in which the levels of aggression appear to be unrelated to seasonal changes in testosterone (Wingfield *et al.,* 1994). Therefore, seasonal changes in gonadal hormones appear to be important in influencing the expression of agonistic behavior in some species, but these hormones do not play a universal role in regulating these behaviors. At present, there is little evidence that naturally occurring changes in hormones are responsible for changes in agonistic behavior in hamsters. For example, although the prepubertal increase in agonistic behavior in intact animals correlates with the increasing levels of testosterone, the same developmental increase in agonistic behavior occurs in castrated hamsters. To our knowledge there are only a limited number of examples in which naturally occurring changes in hormones may be responsible for changes in agonistic behavior or communication in hamsters.

There is good evidence that the changing levels of ovarian hormones over the estrous cycle are responsible for changing the expression of aggression and flank marking, and the circadian rhythm in adrenal hormones may be responsible for the circadian rhythm seen in aggression. In summary, before hormones can be considered to be functionally significant in controlling agonistic and communicative behaviors, it must be demonstrated that changes in hormone levels that occur naturally produce changes in the expression of these behaviors.

The results obtained from studies of the effects of castration and androgen replacement on agonistic behavior and communicative behavior in hamsters have not always been consistent. It is not clear why some studies have found little or no effect of androgens on agonistic behavior and others have found large effects. At least some of these differences would seem to be the result of differences in experimental methods. One significant problem in interpreting the results of the majority of these experiments is that either the environmental lighting conditions were not specified or the hamsters were housed in a short photoperiod (12 h light per day). As a result, it is impossible to know if these animals were in the breeding condition, in nonbreeding condition, or in some transition period between these conditions. Because androgens may have very different effects on behavior under these different conditions, interpretation of the data form these studies is difficult. Another important methodological issue is the use of repeated testing. During an initial encounter, a winner and a loser are often quickly defined. In at least some cases, losing a single encounter is sufficient to produce dramatic and long-lasting effects on subsequent social behavior, as is the case in conditioned defeat. How the experience of previously winning or losing a conflict or a series of conflicts might alter the effects of hormones on agonistic or communicative behavior is not well understood. In short, much remains to be learned about the role of androgens in the control of agonistic behavior in male hamsters. Although there is clear evidence that androgens can influence at least some components of agonistic behavior including aggression, androgens do not always influence these behaviors. It is important to point out that despite popular lore, there does not appear to be a linear relationship between the circulating levels of androgens and aggression, and, in fact, there is good evidence that androgens do not affect at least some forms of aggression in a number of species (e.g., Christenson *et al.*, 1972; Demas *et al.*, 1998; Gottreich *et al.*, 2001).

Social experience may be one of the factors that contribute to determining whether androgens influence agonistic behavior. There is a substantial body of evidence on the interactions between social experience and the levels of circulating gonadal hormones. The challenge hypothesis, which was developed from elegant field studies in birds, states that periods of social instability, such as increases in male–male interactions, increases aggression and testosterone (Wingfield *et al.*, 1987, 1990). The increase in testosterone in response to these challenges does not activate aggression but supports a period of heightened aggression. There is considerable support for this hypothesis, although it does not appear to hold in all cases (Klukowski and Nelson, 1998; Wingfield *et al.*, 1987). Another example in which social experience is important in determining the effects of androgens on agonistic behavior occurs in laboratory rats. In the absence of certain types of social experience, gonadal hormones are relatively ineffective in activating aggression in male rats (Albert *et al.*, 1992). Male rats that cohabitate with a female or compete for limited food exhibit significantly higher levels of aggression in response to testosterone than those than do not have these experiences. In summary, evidence from a number of species indicates that social experience may be a critical variable in understanding how androgens influence social conflict and communication.

VI. NEURAL MECHANISMS CONTROLLING SOCIAL CONFLICT AND COMMUNICATION

A. Flank Marking

Neuropeptides from the vasopressin–oxytocin family of peptides play important roles in the social behavior in many vertebrate species. One of the first demonstrations of a role of these peptides in the control social behavior was the finding that arginine-vasopressin (AVP) injected into the rostral hypothalamus stimulated flank marking in hamsters (Ferris *et al.*, 1984; see Albers *et al.*, 1992; Ferris, 1992, for reviews). Subsequent studies demonstrated that AVP stimulated flank marking in

a dose-dependent manner (Albers *et al.*, 1986, 1991; Ferris *et al.*, 1988) and that AVP antagonists significantly inhibited flank marking stimulated by AVP, the odors of other hamsters, or social interaction (Albers *et al.*, 1986; Ferris *et al.*, 1985, 1986a). Furthermore, AVP–stimulated flank marking was not found to require peripheral feedback from the flank gland because AVP stimulated flank marking in hamsters following gland removal (Albers and Ferris, 1986). Anatomical studies revealed that the AVP-responsive region contains a significant number of AVP immunoreactive (IR) fibers (Albers *et al.*, 1991; Dubois Dauphin *et al.*, 1990; Ferris *et al.*, 1989) and AVP binding sites (Dubois-Dauphin *et al.*, 1990; Ferris *et al.*, 1993; Johnson *et al.*, 1995). Structure activity studies and data obtained with selective AVP antagonists indicated that a V_{1a}-like AVP receptor mediates the effects of AVP on flank marking (Albers *et al.*, 1986). In addition, lesions of the medial preoptic area (MPOA) have been found to significantly reduce the levels of flank marking during social encounters (Hammond and Rowe, 1976).

One of the interesting features of AVP's ability to stimulate flank marking is that the AVP-responsive region extends in a relatively long zone from the posterior MPOA and posterior lateral preoptic area to the posterior medial and lateral aspects of the anterior hypothalamus (AH) (referred to here as MPOA-AH). This region was localized using unilateral injections of AVP in a small volume of vehicle (10–100 nl) to minimize its spread (Fig. 10). Lesion studies indicated that the destruction of a relatively small part of this zone was sufficient to significantly reduce flank marking (Ferris *et al.*, 1986b). In addition, stimulation of flank marking by unilateral injection of AVP was blocked by lesions of the contralateral anterior hypothalamus (Ferris *et al.*, 1994). Taken together these data suggest that the expression of flank marking requires the recruitment of a relatively large number of neurons in the AVP-responsive region of the MPOA-AH; however, stimulation of a subpopulation of these neurons with AVP can activate the circuitry controlling the behavior and initiate its expression.

The AVP-responsive region of the MPOA-AH contains significant numbers of AVP-IR fibers and receives afferent input from a variety of central nervous system (CNS) sites (Albers *et al.*, 1992). The location of the neurons that regulate the expression of flank marking by

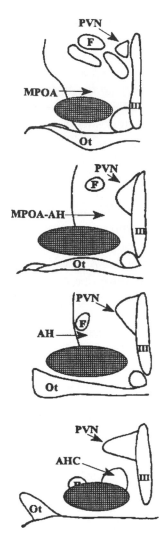

FIGURE 10 Approximate boundaries of the zone in the medial preoptic aspect of the anterior hypothalamus where small-volume injections of arginine-vasopressin stimulate flank marking. Abbreviations: PVN, paraventricular nucleus; F, fornix; MPOA, medial preoptic area; III, third ventricle; Ot, optic chiasm; AH, anterior hypothalamus. From Albers and Bramshad (1998).

releasing AVP in the AVP-responsive region has not been defined. The distribution, projection, and regulation of AVP-IR neurons in hamsters differs in a number of ways from those of other rodents and even other species of hamsters (Bamshad *et al.*, 1993; Bittman *et al.*, 1991; Buijs *et al.*, 1986; De Vries,1990). For example, several populations of parvocellular neurons that express AVP-IR in rats are absent in Syrian hamsters

(Albers *et al.*, 1991; Ferris *et al.*, 1995). The magnocellular AVP system of hamsters also differs in important ways from that of rats. Unlike rats, AVP-IR magnocellular neurons in hamsters do not project exclusively to the posterior pituitary (Ferris *et al.*, 1991; Mahoney *et al.*, 1990), so it is possible that AVP magnocellular neurons could be involved in the control of flank marking. The destruction of the magnocellular AVP neurons that form the hypothalamo-neurohypophysial system produces the expected decreases in plasma AVP levels and the resultant increases in water intake and urine output, but does not eliminate the expression of flank marking. It has been estimated that approximately 30% of the neurons in and around the AVP-responsive region of the MPOA-AH do not project to the neurohypophysis. The AVP-IR neurons that do not project to the neurohypophysis are found primarily in parts of the supraoptic nuclei, paraventricular nucleus, and nucleus circularis. It has been proposed that at least some of the AVP-IR cell bodies important in the regulation of flank marking are in the supraoptic nucleus. Unilateral kainic acid lesions of neurons in the supraoptic nucleus significantly reduce flank marking stimulated by the odors of other hamsters (Ferris *et al.*, 1990a). It appears that these lesions disrupt the input to the AVP-responsive region and not its efferent system because they do not eliminate the ability of AVP to stimulate flank marking when injected into the MPOA-AH. In contrast, lesions of neurons in the paraventricular nucleus do not significantly reduce odor-stimulated flank marking or marking induced by the injection of AVP into the MPOA-AH. Other studies also indicate that neurons in the supraoptic nucleus are important in flank marking (M. Bamshad and H. E. Albers, unpublished data). Double-labeling studies have shown that neurons from the supraoptic nucleus that project to the AVP-responsive region of the MPOA-AH exhibit more Fos-IR after the induction of flank marking by injection of AVP into the MPOA-AH than in saline-injected controls. Although these data support the overall hypothesis that neurons in the supraoptic nucleus that project to the AVP-responsive region are important in the control of flank marking, it is not clear why they are activated in response to flank marking stimulated by AVP injected into the MPOA-AH. More data are required to define whether projections from the supraoptic nucleus release AVP into the AVP-responsive region and thereby stimulate flank marking as part of the normal control of the behavior.

Neuroanatomical studies have also shown that the AVP-responsive region in the MPOA-AH is connected to several other sites that appear to be involved in the regulation of flank marking by AVP. For example, neuroanatomical tracing studies have shown that the AVP-responsive region in the MPOA-AH is reciprocally connected with the lateral septum (LS), the bed nucleus of the stria terminalis (BNST) and the periaqueductal gray (PAG) (Albers *et al.,* 1992; Ferris *et al.,* 1990b). AVP receptor binding is found in the LS, BNST, and PAG (Ferris *et al.,* 1993; Johnson *et al.,* 1995), and microinjection of AVP into these regions stimulates flank marking (Hennessey *et al.,* 1992; Irvin *et al.,* 1990). Additional support for a role of these sites in the control of flank marking comes from studies employing Fos-IR (Bamshad and Albers, 1996). The stimulation of flank marking by the injection of AVP into the AVP-responsive region of the MPOA-AH increases the number of cells expressing Fos-IR in the LS, BNST, and PAG. An unexpected finding was that higher levels of Fos-IR were found in the central nucleus of the amygdala (Ce) in hamsters that flank marked in response to AVP than in controls. The possible role of the Ce in flank marking has been supported further by the finding that lesions of the Ce reduce flank marking stimulated by AVP injected into the AVP-responsive region of the MPOA-AH (Bamshad *et al.,* 1996b). It is interesting, however, that although substantial levels of AVP receptor binding exists in the Ce (Ferris *et al.,* 1993; Johnson *et al.,* 1995), AVP injected into this region does not stimulate flank marking (Bamshad *et al.,* 1996b). Lesions of the corticomedial amygdala essentially eliminate odor-stimulated flank marking and flank marking during female–female encounters, but not during female–male encounters (Petrulis and Johnston, 1999; Takahashi and Gladstone, 1988), and electrical stimulation of this region stimulates flank marking in males (Potegal *et al.,* 1996a). The main olfactory system and not the vomeronasal system appear to be of primary importance for odor-stimulated flank marking (Johnston, 1992; Johnston and Mueller, 1990; Petrulis *et al.,* 1999a,b). In summary, several of the sites involved in regulation of flank marking are anatomically interconnected and may represent essential components of the neural circuit controlling the behavior.

It seems likely that AVP interacts with other neurochemical signals in the MPOA-AH to regulate the expression of flank marking. Glutamate is an excitatory neurotransmitter that appears to mediate fast synaptic neurotransmission in the hypothalamus (van den Pol and Trombley, 1993). To investigate whether AVP interacts with excitatory amino acid neurotransmitters to regulate flank marking, AVP was injected in combination with either NMDA or non-NMDA antagonists (Bamshad *et al.,* 1996a). Both NMDA and non-NMDA glutamate antagonists were found to inhibit the ability of AVP to stimulate flank marking in the MPOA-AH. Thus, excitatory amino acid neurotransmitters may interact with AVP in regulating flank marking in the AVP-responsive region of the MPOA-AH.

There is also evidence that other neurotransmitters may serve to inhibit the behavioral effects of AVP in the MPOA-AH. In female hamsters, injection of norepinephrine (NE) in combination with AVP into the MPOA-AH produces a dose-dependent inhibition of AVP-induced flank marking (Whitman *et al.,* 1992). In contrast, the combined injection of either serotonin, dopamine, or neuropeptide Y with AVP does not diminish the levels of AVP-induced flank marking. The injection of epinephrine (EPI) also has inhibitory effects on AVP-induced flank marking in females, although these effects are less consistent than those of NE. The similar effects of NE and EPI may be due to the ability of both NE and EPI to activate α and β noradrenergic receptors. The AVP-responsive region of the MPOA-AH contains fibers that exhibit tyrosine hydroxylase-IR and dopamine β-hydroxylase-IR (Vincent, 1988), suggesting that NE could have a physiological role in altering the response of this region to AVP. One very interesting feature of the effects of NE is that it only inhibits AVP-induced flank marking in female hamsters. In males, the combined injection of AVP and NE produces no inhibition of AVP-stimulated flank marking.

In male hamsters, serotonin (5-HT) in the AH also appears to play an important role in modulating AVP-induced flank marking. There is a dense field of AVP-IR and 5-HT-IR fibers in the AH that are in the same region as AVP and 5-HT binding sites in male hamsters (Ferris *et al.,* 1997). AVP-induced flank marking is inhibited when 5-HT or the 5-HT$_{1A/7}$ agonist DPAT is combined with AVP and injected into the AH (Ferris and Delville,

1994). Similarly, the systemic administration of the 5-HT reuptake inhibitor, fluoxetine, inhibits flank marking stimulated by injection of AVP into either the AH or the ventrolateral hypothalamus (VLH) (Ferris and Delville, 1994). As previously discussed, flank marking was not inhibited in female hamsters following the combined injection of AVP and 5-HT in other experiments (Whitman *et al.*, 1992). Thus, it is possible that there is a sex difference in the ability of 5-HT to inhibit flank marking.

Data indicate that galanin can inhibit AVP-induced flank marking in the MPOA-AH. When combined with AVP, galanin inhibited flank marking in a dose-dependent manner in male hamsters (Ferris *et al.*, 1999). Galanin binding is found in the AVP-responsive zone in the MPOA-AH, as well as in other sites where AVP stimulates flank marking such as the central gray and LS. Thus, galanin may be another important modulator of flank marking by its actions in several CNS sites.

There is also some data that oxytocin can influence flank marking under certain circumstances. Oxytocin (OXT) stimulates little or no flank marking in hamsters tested in solitary conditions (Albers and Ferris, 1986; Ferris *et al.*, 1984). However, in at least some social conditions, OXT is capable of stimulating flank marking (Harmon *et al.*, 1996). In female hamsters that have established dominant–subordinate relationships, injection of OXT into the MPOA-AH of the dominant female stimulates high levels of flank marking when she is tested during a social encounter with a subordinate, but OXT stimulates little or no flank marking when she is tested alone. The ability of OXT to stimulate flank marking is not simply the result of testing the hamster with another individual. When OXT is injected into the MPOA-AH of a female tested with another female with whom she has not previously interacted, little or no flank marking is observed. These data suggest the possibility that social history or context can alter the behavioral response of these brain regions to OXT.

B. Aggression

AVP appears to play an important role in regulating aggression in hamsters. The injection of AVP into the AH stimulates offensive aggression by a resident males who had previously been trained to fight toward a male intruder, and the injection of a selective V_{1a} AVP receptor antagonist into the AH causes a dose-dependent reduction in this aggression (Ferris *et al.*, 1997; Ferris and Potegal, 1988). In addition, the injection of a V_{1a} AVP receptor antagonist also inhibits aggression of trained fighters in a neutral arena (Potegal and Ferris, 1989). It is not known if AVP and AVP antagonists influence aggression in hamsters that are not trained fighters. The region where AVP influences aggression appears to at least partially overlap the zone where AVP stimulates flank marking; however, it is not known if the same neurons are involved in controlling both behaviors. Concentrations of AVP above 0.9 M injected into the AH stimulate flank marking in resident hamsters even when intruders are placed in their home cage. However, injection of 0.09 μM AVP into the AH, which typically produces little or no flank marking, increases the aggression of resident hamsters toward male intruders (Ferris *et al.*, 1997). Thus, AVP appears to be able to stimulate both aggression and flank marking when injected into an overlapping region of the AH, but the behavior elicited depends on the concentration of AVP administered.

A number of other hypothalamic regions have also been implicated in the regulation of aggression in hamsters. The injection of AVP into the VLH facilitates offensive aggression in males who were trained fighters (Fig. 11) (Delville *et al.*, 1996). However, it is not known if the inhibition of AVP activity in the VLH inhibits the normal expression of aggression. There is also evidence that AVP-IR neurons in the nucleus circularis and the medial supraoptic nucleus are involved in offensive aggression. Fos-IR was significantly higher in these regions in male hamsters that engaged in offensive aggression than in control hamsters that were exposed to a wood block that carried the odor of an intruder. In another study, Fos mRNA was also found to be significantly greater in the supraoptic nucleus in dominant hamsters than in subordinate hamsters or controls. The effects of lesions of the MPOA and the AH on agonistic behavior in females during social encounters with other females (Hammond and Rowe, 1976) have also been investigated. Lesions of the MPOA significantly reduced aggression but increased submissive behavior. These lesions had no effect on investigative behaviors. Lesions of the AH were reported to significantly reduce low intensity aggression; however, the site of the lesion

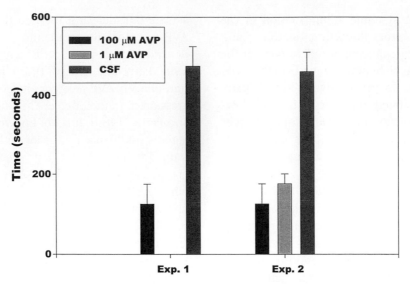

FIGURE 11   Mean latency to bites in male hamsters exposed to an intruder placed in their home cage. The subjects were tested after microinjection of arginine-vasopressin (1 μM or 100 μM) or artificial CSF into the ventrolateral hypothalamus. In experiment 1 the subjects were gonadally intact experienced fighters and in experiment 2 they were experienced fighters that had been castrated and implanted with Silastic capsules containing testosterone. Redrawn from Delville *et al.* (1996).

as illustrated in this paper is well outside of the area referred to as the AH by most authors.

There is considerable evidence that 5-HT can inhibit aggression in a variety of species (Eichelman, 1990), and there is evidence in male hamsters that 5-HT may inhibit aggression facilitated by AVP—systemic injection of fluoxetine inhibits offensive aggression stimulated by injection of AVP in either the AH or VLH (Ferris and Delville, 1994). No studies have been conducted in females to indicate whether AVP and 5-HT interact to regulate aggression. However, recent studies suggest that there is an important sex difference in the role of the 5-HT system in regulating aggression (Joppa *et al.*, 1997). In males, an intracerebroventricular injection of a 5-HT agonist significantly reduced intermale offensive aggression, but did not reduce offensive aggression in females. It will be interesting to determine whether the inability of 5-HT agonists to inhibit aggression in females is the result of the inability of 5-HT to inhibit the facilitatory effects of AVP on aggression in the AH. There is also some evidence that there are differences in GABA binding in the brains of aggressive and nonaggressive hamsters (Potegal *et al.*, 1982). GABA binding in

limbic, striatal, and diencephalic structures, but not cortex, pons, or medulla, was found to be significantly greater in female hamsters that displayed high levels of aggressiveness when compared to nonaggressive females.

There are several lines of evidence that the septum is involved in regulating aggression in hamsters. Septal lesions increase aggression in both male and female hamsters; however, changes in a number of other behaviors have also been observed (e.g., nest building and hoarding) (Johnson *et al.*, 1972; Sodetz *et al.*, 1967; Sodetz and Bunnell, 1970; however, see also Shipley and Kolb, 1977). Destruction of the anteroventral septum dramatically increases aggression toward other males and even toward sexually receptive females (Potegal *et al.*, 1981a). Electrical stimulation of the septum reduces aggression with the lowest threshold for the reduction of attacks in the mid- and ventral septum (Potegal *et al.*, 1981b). Interestingly, however, no differences in Fos-IR were found in the septum between males engaged in offensive aggression and controls (Delville *et al.*, 2000).

There is evidence that several other limbic structures are also involved in the regulation of aggression.

Lesions of the amygdala appear to reduce both aggression and flight behavior, as well as the total amount of social interaction (Bunnell *et al.,* 1970; Shipley and Kolb, 1977). The destruction of the medial amygdala also significantly reduces aggression in female hamsters (Takahashi and Gladstone, 1988), and electrical stimulation of the corticomedial amygdala stimulates aggression in males (Potegal *et al.,* 1996a). The medial amygdala also contained higher levels of Fos-IR in male and female hamsters engaged in offensive aggression than in controls (Delville *et al.,* 2000; Potegal *et al.,* 1996b). In these studies, control animals were either trained to pursue blocks of wood or were simply exposed to blocks of wood that contained another hamster's scent. Another study also found the medial amygdala to contain higher levels of Fos-IR in females during an aggressive encounter than in nontested controls. However, the same high levels of Fos-IR were observed in the medial amygdala of another group of females that did not display aggression during the social encounter (Joppa *et al.,* 1995). So, activation of Fos-IR in the medial amygdala may be the result of some aspect of social interaction other than the display of aggression.

C. Defensive or Submissive Behavior

Comparatively little is known about the neural mechanisms involved in controlling defensive or submissive behavior in hamsters. However, data on the distribution of Fos in the brains of dominant and subordinate male hamsters have provided new information on the CNS sites that may be involved in defensive or submissive behavior. An initial study comparing Fos-IR in dominant and subordinate hamsters found no differences in the number of Fos-IR neurons (Kollack-Walker and Newman, 1997). However, in a subsequent study in which the hamsters were habituated to handling and novel environments, significant differences were observed (Kollack-Walker *et al.,* 1997). Subordinate hamsters were found to have significantly more Fos mRNA in the central amygdala, dorsal raphe, locus coeruleus, and BNST. In addition, a number of hypothalamic regions such as the MPOA, AH, ventromedial hypothalamus, and paraventricular nucleus (PVN) also exhibited significant increases in Fos mRNA levels in defeated hamsters.

D. Dominant–Subordinate Relationships

As already described, aggressive behavior and flank marking play important roles in the establishment and maintenance of dominant–subordinate relationships in hamsters. The injection of a V_{1a} AVP receptor antagonist into hamsters that have not previously interacted prevents the formation of a dominant–subordinate relationship (Ferris, 1992). The inability to form such a relationship may be the result of the inhibition of aggressive behavior. In hamsters that have established a dominant–subordinate relationship, the injection of AVP and AVP antagonists can also significantly alter the amount of flank marking displayed by both the dominant and subordinate hamster (Ferris *et al.,* 1986a). The injection of AVP into the MPOA-AH of the subordinate hamster stimulates high levels of flank marking despite the presence of the dominant hamster. The injection of an AVP antagonist into the dominant hamster significantly reduces flank marking despite the presence of the subordinate hamster. The effects of AVP and AVP antagonists appear to be primarily on flank marking and not on the dominant–subordinate relationship because injection of these substances does not reverse the basic dominant–subordinate relationship of these hamsters even when given over three consecutive days (Fig. 12).

The development of dominant–subordinate relationships appears to alter specific components of the hamster AVP system (Ferris *et al.,* 1989). Subordinate hamsters in well-established dominant–subordinate relationships were found to have lower levels of AVP-IR in the AH, but not other regions, compared to dominant hamsters or to socially isolated controls. Immunohistochemical analysis also indicated that there were fewer AVP-IR fibers in the AH and lower numbers of AVP-IR cell bodies in the nucleus circularis in subordinates compared to dominant hamsters or controls. These data raise the interesting possibility that the formation of dominant–subordinate relationships alter the amount of AVP and that the differences in AVP levels may account for at least some of the differences in the levels of flank marking and aggression seen between dominant and subordinate hamsters.

There is also some evidence that norepinephrine may be involved in controlling agonistic behaviors in stable dominant–subordinate relationships. Following the establishment of dominant–subordinate relationships in

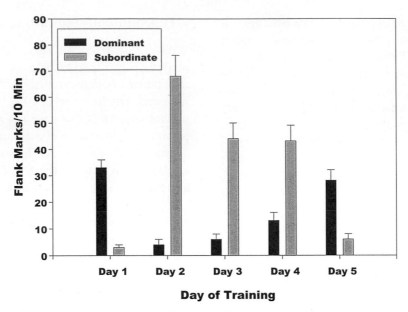

FIGURE 12 Mean flank marking in pairs of dominant–subordinate male hamsters following microinjection of a V_{1a} arginine-vasopressin antagonist and arginine-vasopressin, respectively, into the medial preoptic aspect of the anterior hypothalamus over three consecutive days (day 2–4). Injection of the antagonist inhibits flank marking in the dominant hamster and injection of vasopressin stimulates flank marking in the subordinate on all 3 days of treatment. Note that on day 5, when no treatments were given, the dominant hamsters flank mark significantly more than the subordinate hamsters, as they did on day 1. Redrawn from Ferris *et al.* (1986a).

female hamsters, the injection of NE into the MPOA-AH responsive region significantly reduces the numbers of attacks and bites displayed by dominant hamsters (Harmon *et al.*, 1995).

E. Gonadal Hormones

1. Flank Marking

There is considerable evidence that the MPOA-AH mediates at least some of the effects of gonadal hormones on a number of different behaviors. The finding that AVP in the MPOA-AH is a critical neurochemical signal for flank marking has provided the opportunity to test the hypothesis that gonadal hormones influence flank marking by altering the signaling capacity of AVP in this region. Specifically, gonadal hormones could influence flank marking by altering the amount of AVP released or by altering the sensitivity or response to AVP. It might be anticipated that gonadal hormones influence flank marking by altering the amount of AVP

in neurons controlling flank marking because gonadal hormones have been shown to have dramatic effects on AVP-IR in a number of limbic structures in other species (De Vries *et al.*, 1985). However, in hamsters, gonadal hormones produce no detectable alterations in AVP-IR in the MPOA-AH or in a variety of other structures probably involved in the control of flank marking (Albers *et al.*, 1991; Hennessey *et al.*, 1994; Huhman and Albers, 1993). Although the possibility that gonadal hormones influence flank marking by altering AVP release cannot be excluded, these data provide little support for this hypothesis. Instead, gonadal hormones appear to influence flank marking by altering the sensitivity or response of the MPOA-AH to AVP. In males, testosterone significantly increases the amount of flank marking induced by AVP microinjected into the MPOA-AH (Fig. 13) (Albers *et al.*, 1988). These data suggest the possibility that gonadal hormones influence the amount of AVP-induced flank marking in the MPOA-AH by altering AVP binding. This hypothesis is

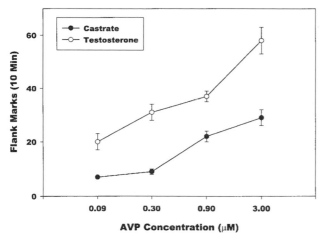

FIGURE 13 Dose-dependent stimulation of flank marking by microinjection of arginine-vasopressin (AVP) into the medial preoptic aspect of the anterior hypothalamus of castrated hamsters or hamsters with physiological levels of circulating testosterone. Redrawn from Albers *et al.* (1988).

supported by the finding that castration reduces V_{1a} receptor binding in the posterior lateral preoptic–anterior hypothalamic continuum and that administration of testosterone restores it (Johnson *et al.,* 1995; Young *et al.,* 2000). The effects of testosterone have also been studied on V_{1a} mRNA levels. Unlike V_{1a} binding, V_{1a} mRNA is detected primarily in the medial preoptic nucleus (MPN) which is in the anterior part of the AVP-responsive zone. This discrepancy between V_{1a} binding and mRNA distribution was also found in several other areas of brain and suggests the possibility of receptor transport. Nevertheless, V_{1a} mRNA levels in the MPN but not other CNS sites are regulated by testosterone in a manner similar to that seen for V_{1a} binding (Fig. 14). In summary, these data indicate that the MPOA-AH is an important site in mediating the effects of gonadal hormones on flank marking and suggest that gonadal hormones may modulate flank marking by altering the biosynthesis of the V_{1a} AVP receptors, at least in male hamsters.

It is not known if gonadal hormones influence behavior by acting in a parallel manner at multiple CNS sites or if gonadal hormones have a primary site of action in controlling specific behaviors. There is evidence that gonadal hormones act at multiple CNS sites to influence at least some behaviors, for example, mating behavior in male hamsters and androgen recep-

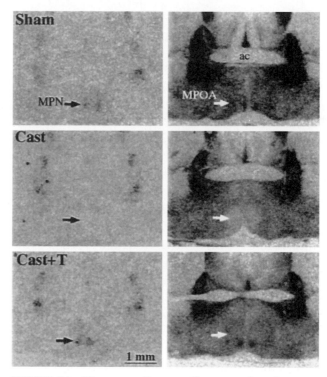

FIGURE 14 Film autoradiograms illustrating the relative intensities of V_{1a} receptor mRNA (left) and binding (right) signals in adjacent sections of the medial preoptic nucleus (MPN) and medial preoptic area (MPOA) in sham-operated (Sham), castrated (Cast), and testosterone-treated castrated (Cast + T) male hamsters. Note that the hybridization signal in the ventromedial aspect of the MPN is nearly eliminated in castrated hamsters, while binding is reduced in a much larger area. ac, anterior commissure. From Young *et al.* (2000).

tors have been localized to many of the structures involved in controlling flank marking (Clancy *et al.*, 1994; Wood and Newman, 1993). However, gonadal hormones may influence flank marking by acting primarily in the MPOA-AH (Albers and Cooper, 1995) because gonadal hormones have only small effects on the ability of AVP to stimulate flank marking in the LS, BNST, and PAG. At present, the simplest hypothesis is that the MPOA-AH is the primary site where gonadal hormones influence flank marking. Nevertheless, it seems unlikely that gonadal hormones act exclusively in the MPOA-AH to influence the behavior.

Where ovarian hormones act in the brain to influence flank marking is not known. Several studies have examined whether implantation of estradiol into hypothalamic sites in ovariectomized females can restore the levels of flank marking seen prior to ovariectomy (Takahashi *et al.*, 1985; Takahashi and Lisk, 1985, 1987). Estradiol implants in either the MPOA or AH for 1 week were not found to restore preovariectomy levels of flank marking. One explanation for finding that estradiol implants did not restore flanking might be that systemically administered estradiol to ovariectomized hamsters requires approximately 3 weeks to restore preovariectomy levels of flank marking (Albers and Rowland, 1989).

Ovarian hormones influence the amount of flank marking stimulated by AVP injected into the MPOA-AH. The amount of flank marking stimulated by AVP injected into the MPOA-AH varies as a function of the estrous cycle (Albers *et al.*, 1996), with the lowest levels of AVP-stimulated flank marking occurring on the day of sexual receptivity. The alterations in response to AVP over the estrous cycle appear to result from the changing levels of ovarian hormones over the estrous cycle. Estradiol administered to ovariectomized hamsters increases the amount of AVP-stimulated flank marking, and progesterone given to estradiol-treated hamsters reduces AVP-induced marking (Huhman and Albers, 1993). It will be interesting to determine if gonadal hormones influence the biosynthesis of the V_{1a} receptor in females as well as in males.

2. Aggression

The role of AVP in mediating some of the effects of gonadal hormones on aggression in hamsters has only been investigated in males. It is not known whether testosterone influences the facilitation of aggression by AVP injected into the AH. However, because castration reduces AVP binding in this region (Johnson *et al.*, 1995) it seems possible that castration could reduce AVP-induced aggression. There is evidence that gonadal hormones influence the effects of AVP on aggression in the VLH (Delville *et al.*, 1996). AVP receptor binding is also reduced in the VLH following castration, and precastration levels of binding can be restored by testosterone. AVP injected into the VLH facilitates aggression in intact males and castrated males given testosterone, but does not facilitate aggression in castrated controls. Thus, the regulation of AVP binding in the VLH may explain why AVP is unable to stimulate aggression in castrated males when injected into this region.

In females, a number of studies have examined the sites where ovarian hormones act to influence

aggression. The strategy taken to determine these steroid sites of action has been to give either systemic estradiol treatment followed by an intracranial progesterone implant or the reverse, in which estradiol is applied to specific brain sites and progesterone is injected systemically. Commonly, the hypothalamus has been the primary target for these implant studies, based on the most abundant sites of intracellular estradiol and progestin receptors in hamster brain (Krieger *et al.*, 1976; Munn *et al.*, 1983).

For estradiol implant studies, females were given a baseline test followed by the application of estradiol to the MPOA, AH, or ventromedial hypothalamus, generally for 3–4 days. When tested with either males or females, there were no consistent effects of intracranial estradiol on measures of aggression for any of the sites tested (Sterner *et al.*, 1992; Takahashi *et al.*, 1985; Takahashi and Lisk, 1985, 1987). In some of these studies, there was an effect of repeated testing that apparently was not related to a particular hormone treatment (Takahashi *et al.*, 1985; Takahashi and Lisk, 1985, 1987). The injection of progesterone produced a general decrement in aggression in tests with males, particularly those elements of aggression related to attack (Sterner *et al.*, 1992; Takahashi *et al.*, 1985; Takahashi and Lisk, 1985, 1987). These effects of estradiol implants in conjunction with progesterone injection were seen consistently with estradiol implants in the anterior and ventromedial hypothalamus (Sterner *et al.*, 1992; Takahashi *et al.*, 1985; Takahashi and Lisk, 1985, 1987) and to a somewhat lesser degree with implants in the MPOA (Takahashi *et al.*, 1985). A similar reduction in attacks was observed in one study following estradiol implants in the medial nucleus of the amygdala (Sterner *et al.*, 1992). One problem with the interpretation of these results is that these hormone treatments typically induced the expression of sexual behavior. There may have been a direct inhibition of aggression or an indirect reduction in aggression due to behavioral competition with sexual behavior. In one study, females implanted with estradiol and injected with progesterone were tested with female hamsters (Sterner *et al.*, 1992). In this case, there were reliable reductions in attacks with estradiol implants in either the anterior or ventromedial hypothalamus, but not with implants in the medial amygdala.

Complementary studies have been done with female hamsters receiving estradiol injections followed by implants of either progesterone (Takahashi and Lisk, 1985) or the synthetic progestin, promegestone (Meisel *et al.*, 1990a). In these studies, the most effective inhibition of aggression came when the implants were placed in the ventromedial hypothalamus (Meisel *et al.*, 1990a; Takahashi and Lisk, 1985, 1986) and to a lesser extent in the MPOA (Takahashi and Lisk, 1985). There were no effects of progestin implants in the AH on aggression (Meisel *et al.*, 1990a; Takahashi and Lisk, 1985).

It is interesting that although hormone implants in the MPOA, ventromedial hypothalamus, and medial amygdala all act to inhibit aggression, lesions of these brain areas yield different outcomes. Lesions of the MPOA (Hammond and Rowe, 1976) or medial amygdala (Takahashi and Gladstone, 1988) reduce aggressive response in female hamsters. In contrast, lesions of the ventromedial hypothalamus enhance aggression in female hamsters (Malsbury *et al.*, 1977). What these results suggest is that estradiol and progesterone produce different effects on neural activity in these areas, increasing activity in the ventromedial hypothalamus, but decreasing activity in the MPOA and medial amygdala.

F. Sex Differences

Hamsters display unusual sex differences in the expression of flank marking and aggression in many but not all situations (Albers and Prishkolnik, 1992; Payne and Swanson, 1970). Unlike most species, female hamsters scent mark at higher levels than do males and exhibit higher levels of aggressive behavior. It seems somewhat unlikely that the sex differences in these behaviors are the result of sex differences in the vasopressinergic system. Examination of AVP-IR in a variety of limbic regions in male and female hamsters has not revealed the sex differences that have been reported in other rodent species (Delville *et al.*, 1994; Hennessey *et al.*, 1994). The only evidence for a sex difference in AVP-IR in hamsters comes from one study (Delville *et al.*, 1994) that reported a sex difference in AVP-IR— males had 50% more AVP-IR in the supraoptic nucleus than females. However, another study (Hennessey *et al.*, 1994) found no sex differences in AVP-IR in the supraoptic nucleus. There is also no evidence that sex differences in the amount of flank marking result from sex differences in the response to AVP because the amount of flank marking stimulated by the injection of several different concentrations of AVP into the

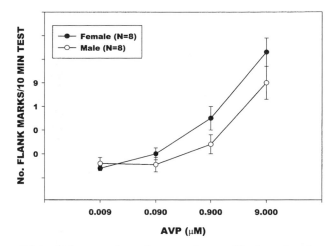

FIGURE 15 Dose-dependent stimulation of flank marking by microinjection of arginine-vasopressin (AVP) into the medial preoptic aspect of the anterior hypothalamus of male and female hamsters. No sex differences were observed. Redrawn from Hennessey *et al.* (1994).

MPOA-AH was similar in male and female hamsters (Fig. 15) (Hennessey *et al.*, 1994). Although the possibility that sex differences in flank marking and aggression result from sex differences in the vasopressinergic system cannot be excluded, the existing data do not provide strong support for this hypothesis. It seems more likely that the sex differences observed in these behaviors are the result of sex differences in the effects of NE or 5-HT or both on the release of or response to AVP. There is considerable evidence that sex differences exist in the functioning of NE and 5-HT systems in the MPOA-AH of a number of rodent species (De Vries, 1990); however, it is important to examine whether sex differences in these systems also occur in hamsters.

Acknowledgments

The original research presented was supported by grants NS37232 and IBN-9742370 to H. E. A., NS34896 to K. L. H., and IBN-9723876 and a grant from the Guggenheim Foundation to R. L. M.

References

Albers, H. E., and Bramshad, M. (1998). Role of vasopressin and oxytocin in the control of social behavior in Syrian hamsters. *Prog. Brain Res.* **119**, 395–408.

Albers, H. E., and Cooper, T. T. (1995). Effects of testosterone on the behavioral response to arginine vasopressin microinjected into the central gray and septum. *Peptides (N.Y.)* **16**, 269–273.

Albers, H. E., and Ferris, C. F. (1986). Role of the flank gland in vasopressin induced scent marking behavior in the hamster. *Brain Res. Bull.* **17**, 387–389.

Albers, H. E., and Prishkolnik, J. (1992). Sex differences in odor–stimulated flank marking behavior in the Golden hamster (*Mesocricetus auratus*). *Horm. Behav.* **26**, 229–239.

Albers, H. E., and Rowland, C. M. (1989). Ovarian hormones influence odor stimulated flank marking in the hamster (*Mesocricetus auratus*). *Physiol. Behav.* **45**, 113–117.

Albers, H. E., Yogev, L., Todd, R. B., and Goldman, B. D. (1985). Adrenal corticoids in hamsters: Role in circadian timing. *Am. J. Physiol.* **248**, R434–R438.

Albers, H. E., Pollock, J., Simmons, W. H., and Ferris, C. F. (1986). A V1-like receptor mediates vasopressin-induced flank marking behavior in hamster hypothalamus. *J. Neurosci.* **6**(7), 2085–2089.

Albers, H. E., Liou, S. Y., and Ferris, C. F. (1988). Testosterone alters the behavioral response of the medial preoptic-anterior hypothalamus to microinjection of arginine vasopressin in the hamster. *Brain Res.* **456**, 382–386.

Albers, H. E., Rowland, C. M., and Ferris, C. F. (1991). Arginine-vasopressin immunoreactivity is not altered by photoperiod or gonadal hormones in the Syrian hamster (*Mesocricetus auratus*). *Brain Res.* **539**, 137–142.

Albers, H. E., Hennessey, A. C., and Whitman, D. C. (1992). Vasopressin and the regulation of hamster social behavior. *Ann. N. Y. Acad. Sci.* **652**, 227–242.

Albers, H. E., Karom, M., and Whitman, D. C. (1996). Ovarian hormones alter the behavioral response of the medial preoptic anterior hypothalamus to arginine-vasopressin. *Peptides (N.Y.)* **17**, 1359–1363.

Albert, D. J., Jonik, R. H., Watson, N. V., Gorzalka, B. B., and Walsh, M. L. (1990). Hormone-dependent aggression in male rats is proportional to serum testosterone concentration but sexual behavior is not. *Physiol. Behav.* **48**, 409–416.

Albert, D. J., Jonik, R. H., and Walsh, M. L. (1992). Hormone dependent aggression in male and female rats: Experimental, hormonal, and neural foundations. *Neurosci. Biobehav Rev.* **16**, 177–192.

Archer, J. (1988). "The Biology of Aggression." Cambridge University Press, Cambridge, UK.

Badura, L. L., and Nunez, A. A. (1989). Photoperidodic modulation of sexual and aggressive behavior in female golden hamsters (*Mesocricetus auratus*): Role of the pineal gland. *Horm. Behav.* **23**, 27–42.

Bamshad, M., and Albers, H. E. (1996). Neural circuitry controlling vasopressin-stimulated scent marking in Syrian hamsters (*Mesocricetus auratus*). *J. Comp. Neuro.* **369**, 252–263.

Bamshad, M., Novak, M. A., and De Vries, G. J. (1993). Sex and species differences in the vasopressin innervation of sexually naive and parental prairie voles, *Microtus ochrogaster* and meadow voles, *Microtus pennsylvanicus*. *J. Neuroendocrinol.* **5**, 247–255.

Bamshad, M., Cooper, T. T., Karom, M., and Albers, H. E. (1996a). Glutamate and vasopressin interact to control scent marking in Syrian hamsters (*Mesocricetus auratus*). *Brain Res.* **731**, 213–216.

Bamshad, M., Karom, M., Pallier, P., and Albers, H. E. (1996b). Role of the central amygdala in social communication in Syrian hamsters (*Mesocricetus auratus*). *Brain Res.* **744**, 15–22.

Baranczuk, R., and Greenwald, G. S. (1973). Peripheral levels of estrogen in the cyclic hamster. *Endocrinology (Baltimore)* **92**, 805–812.

Bartke, A., Steele, R. E., Musto, N., and Caldwell, B. V. (1973). Fluctuations in plasma testosterone levels and stimulates testicular growth in hamsters exposed to short day-length. *Endocrinology (Baltimore)* **97**, 1601–1604.

Bartke, A. J. (1985). Male hamster reproductive endocrinology. *In* "The Hamster: Reproduction and Behavior," pp. 74–98. Plenum Press, New York.

Bartness, T. J., and Goldman, B. D. (1989). Mammalian pineal melatonin: A clock for all seasons. *Experientia* **45**, 939–945.

Batty, J. (1978). Acute changes in plasma testosterone levels and their relation to measures of sexual behavior in the male house mouse (*Mus musculus*). *Anim. Behav.* **26**, 349–357.

Baulieu, E. E. (1997). Neurosteroids: Of the nervous system, by the nervous system, for the nervous system. *Prog. Brain Res.* **52**, 1–32.

Bittman, E. L., Bartness, T. J., Goldman, B. D., and De Vries, G. J. (1991). Suprachiasmatic and paraventricular control of photoperiodism in Siberian hamsters. *Am. J. Physiol.* **260**, R90–R101.

Blanchard, D. C., and Blanchard, R. J. (1988). Ethoexperimental approaches to the biology of emotion. *Annu. Rev. Psychol.* **39**, 43–68.

Blanchard, D. C., Blanchard, R. J., McEwen, B., and Sakai, R. R. (1995). Visible burrow system as a model of chronic social stress: Behavioral and neuroendocrine correlates. *Psychoneuroendocrinology* **20**, 117–134.

Boice, R., Hughes, D., and Cobb, C. J. (1969). Social dominance in gerbils and hamsters. *Psychon. Sci.* **16**, 127–128.

Borer, K. T., Pryor, A., Conn, C. A., Bonna, R., and Kielb, M. (1988). Group housing accelerates growth and induces obesity in adult hamsters. *Am. J. Physiol.* **255**, R128–R133.

Brain, P. F. (1972). Effects of isolation/grouping on endocrine function and fighting behavior in male and female golden hamsters (*Mesocricetus auratus* Waterhouse). *Behav. Biol.* **7**, 349–357.

Brain, P. F. (1979). Effects of the hormones of the pituitary-adrenal axis on behavior. *Chem. Influences Behav.* pp. 331–372.

Brain, P. F., and Benton, D. (1983). Conditions of housing, hormones, and aggressive behavior. *In* "Hormones and Aggressive Behavior" (B. B. Svare, ed.), pp. 351–372. Plenum Press, New York.

Britton, K., Lee, G., Vale, W., River, J., and Koob, G. F. (1986). Corticotropin releasing factor antagonists block activating and 'anxiogenic' actions of CRF in the rat. *Brain Res.* **369**, 303–306.

Buijs, R. M., Pevet, P., Masson-Pevet, M., Pool, C. W., De Vries, G. J., Canguilhem, B., and Vivien-Roels, B. (1986). Seasonal variation in vasopressin innervation in the brain of the European hamster (*Cricetus cricetus*). *Brain Res.* **371**, 193–196.

Bunnell, B. N., Sodetz, F. J., and Shalloway, D. I. (1970). Amygdaloid lesions and social behavior in the golden hamster. *Physiol. Behav.* **5**, 153–161.

Campbell, C. S., Finkelstien, J. S., and Turek, F. W. (1978). The interaction of photoperiod and testosterone on the development of copulatory behavior in castrated male hamsters. *Physiol. Behav.* **21**, 409–415.

Canonaco, M., Valenti, A., and Maggi, A. (1990). Effects of progesterone on [35 S] t-butylbicyclophosphorothinate binding in some forebrain areas of the female rat and its correlation to aggressive behavior. *Pharmacol., Biochem. Behav.* **37**, 433–438.

Carter, C. S., Michael, S. J., and Morris, A. H. (1973). Hormonal induction of female sexual behavior in male and female hamsters. *Horm. Behav.* **4**, 129–141.

Christenson, T., Wallen, K., Brown, B., and Glickman, S. E. (1972). Effects of castration, blindness and anosmia on social reactivity in the male Mongolian gerbil (*Meriones ungulstus*). *Physiol. Behav.* **10**, 989–994.

Ciaccio, L. A., Lisk, R. D., and Reuter, L. A. (1979). Prelordotic behavior in the hamster: A hormonally modulated transition from aggression to sexual receptivity. *J. Comp. Physiol. Psychol.* **93**, 771–780.

Clancy, A. N., Whitman, D. C., Michael, R. P., and Albers, H. E. (1994). Distribution of androgen receptor-like immunoreactivity in the brains of intact and castrated male hamsters. *Brain Res. Bull.* **33**, 325–332.

Damassa, D. A., Smith, E. A., Tennent, B., and Davidson, J. M. (1977). The relationship between circulating testosterone levels and male sexual behavior in rats. *Horm. Behav.* **8**, 275–286.

Delville, Y., Koh, E. T., and Ferris, C. F. (1994). Sexual differences in the magnocellular vasopressinergic system in golden hamsters. *Brain Res. Bull.* **33**, 535–540.

Delville, Y., Mansour, K. M., and Ferris, C. F. (1996). Testosterone facilitates aggression by modulating vasopressin receptors in the hypothalamus. *Physiol. Behav.* **60**, 25–29.

Delville, Y., De Vries, G. J., and Ferris, C. F. (2000). Neural connections of the anterior hypothalamus and agonistic behavior in golden hamster. *Brain Behav. Evol.* **55**, 53–76.

Demas, G. E., Moffatt, C. A., Drazen, D. L., and Nelson, R. J. (1998). Castration does not inhibit aggressive behavior in adult male prairie voles (*Microtus ochrogaster*). *Physiol. Behav.* **66**, 59–62.

Devor, M., and Murphy, M. R. (1973). The effect of peripheral olfactory blockade on the social behavior of the male golden hamster. *Behav. Biol.* **9**, 31–42.

De Vries, G. J. (1990). Sex differences in neurotransmitter systems. *J. Neuroendocrinol.* **2**(1), 1–13.

De Vries, G. J., Buijs, R. M., van Leeuwen, F. W., Caffe, A. R., and Swaab, D. F. (1985). The vasopressinergic innervation of the brain in normal and castrated rats. *J. Comp. Neurol.* **233**, 236–254.

Dieterlen, F. (1959). Das Verhalten des syrischen Goldhamsters (*Mesocricdtus auratus* Waterhouse). *Z. Tierpsychol.* **16**, 47–103.

Drickamer, L. C., and Vandenbergh, J. G. (1973). Predictors of social dominance in the adult female golden hamster (*Mesocricetus auratus*). *Anim. Behav.* **21**, 564–570.

Drickamer, L. C., and Vandenbergh, J. C., and Colby, D. R. (1973). Predictors of dominance in the male golden hamster (*Mesocricetus auratus*). *Anim. Behav.* **21**, 557–563.

Dubois-Dauphin, M., Pevet, P., Tribollet, E., and Dreifuss, J. J. (1990). Vasopressin in the brain of the golden hamster: The distribution of vasopressin binding sites and of immunoreactivity to the vasopressin-related glycopeptide. *J. Comp. Neurol.* **300**, 535–548.

Eichelman, B. S. (1990). Neurochemical and pschopharmacologic aspects of aggressive behavior. *Annu. Rev. Med.* **41**, 149–158.

Elliott, A. S., and Nunez, A. A. (1992). Photoperiod modulates the effects of steriods on sociosexual behaviors of hamsters. *Physiol. Behav.* **51**, 1189–1193.

Ellis, G. B., and Desjardins, C. (1982). Male rats secrete luteinizing hormone and testosterone episodica. *Endocrinology (Baltimore)* **110**, 1618–1627.

Evans, C. M., and Brain, P. F. (1974). Some studies on endocrine influences on aggressive behavior in the golden hamster (*Mesocrietus auratus* Waterhouse). *Prog. Brain Res.* **41**, 473–480.

Ferris, C. F. (1992). Role of vasopressin in aggressive and dominant/subordinate behaviors. *Ann. N. Y. Acad. Sci.* **652**, 212–226.

Ferris, C. F., and Delville, Y. (1994). Vasopressin and serotonin interactions in the control of agonistic behavior. *Psychoneuroendocrinology* **19**, 593–601.

Ferris, C. F., and Potegal, M. (1988). Vasopressin receptor blockade in the anterior hypothalamus suppresses aggression in hamsters. *Physiol. Behav.* **44**, 235–239.

Ferris, C. F., Albers, H. E., Wesolowski, S. M., Goldman, B. D., and Leeman, S. E. (1984). Vasopressin injected into the hypothalamus triggers a complex stereotypic behavior in Golden hamsters. *Science* **224**, 521–523.

Ferris, C. F., Pollock, J., Albers, H. E., and Leeman, S. E. (1985). Inhibition of flank-marking behavior in Golden hamsters by microinjection of a vasopressin antagonist into the hypothalamus. *Neurosci. Lett.* **55**, 239–243.

Ferris, C. F., Meenan, D. M., Axelson, J. F., and Albers, H. E. (1986a). A vasopressin antagonist can reverse dominant/subordinate behavior in hamsters. *Physiol. Behav.* **38**, 135–138.

Ferris, C. F., Meenan, D. M., and Albers, H. E. (1986b). Microinjection of kainic acid into the hypothalamus of Golden hamsters prevents vasopressin-dependent flank-marking behavior. *Neuroendocrinology* **44**, 112–116.

Ferris, C. F., Axelson, J. F., Shinto, L. H., and Albers, H. E. (1987). Scent marking and the maintenance of dominant/subordinate status in male Golden hamsters. *Physiol. Behav.* **40**, 661–664.

Ferris, C. F., Singer, E., Meenan, D. M., and Albers, H. E. (1988). Inhibition of vasopressin-stimulated flank marking behavior by V1-receptor antagonists. *Eur. J. Pharmacol.* **154**, 153–159.

Ferris, C. F., Axelson, J. F., Martin, M., and Robrege, L. F. (1989). Vasopressin immunoreactivity in the anterior hypothalamus is altered during the establishment of dominant/subordinate relationships between hamsters. *Neuroscience* **29**, 675–683.

Ferris, C. F., Irvin, R. W., Potegal, M., and Axelson, J. F. (1990a). Kainic acid lesion of vasopressinergic neurons in the hypothalamus disrupts flank marking behavior in golden hamsters. *J. Neuroendocrinol.* **2**, 123–129.

Ferris, C. F., Gold, L., De Vries, G. J., and Potegal, M. (1990b). Evidence for a functional and anatomical relationship between the lateral septum and the hypothalamus in the control of flank marking behavior in Golden hamsters. *J. Comp. Neurol.* **293**, 476–485.

Ferris, C. F., Pilapil, C. G., Hayden-Hixson, D., Wiley, R. G., and Koh, E. T. (1991). Functionally and anatomically distinct populations of vasopressinergic magnocellular neurons in the female golden hamster. *J. Neuroendocrinol.* **4**, 193–205.

Ferris, C. F., Delville, Y., Grzonka, Z., Luber-Narod, J., and Insel, T. R. (1993). An iodinated vasopressin (V1) antagonist blocks flank marking and selectively labels neural binding sites in golden hamsters. *Physiol. Behav.* **54**, 737–747.

Ferris, C. F., Delville, Y., Irvin, R. W., and Potegal, M. (1994). Septo-hypothalamic organization of a stereotyped behavior controlled by vasopressin in golden hamsters. *Physiol. Behav.* **55**, 755–759.

Ferris, C. F., Delville, Y., Miller, M. A., Dorsa, D. M., and De Vries, G. J. (1995). Distribution of small vasopressinergic neurons in golden hamsters. *J. Comp. Neuro.* **360**, 589–598.

Ferris, C. F., Delville, Y., Brewer, J. A., Mansour, K., Yules, B., and Melloni, R. H. (1996). Vasopressin and developmental onset of flank marking behavior in Golden hamsters. *J. Neurobiol.* **30**, 192–204.

Ferris, C. F., Melloni, R. H., Jr., Koppel, G., Perry, K. W., Fuller, R. W., and Delville, Y. (1997). Vasopressin/serotonin interactions in the anterior hypothalamus control aggressive behavior in golden hamsters. *J. Neurosci.* **17**, 4331–4340.

Ferris, C. F., Delville, Y., Bonigut, S., and Miller, M. A. (1999). Galanin antagonizes vasopressin-stimulated flank marking in male golden hamsters. *Brain Res.* **832**, 1–6.

Festing, M. F. W. (1972). Hamsters. *In* "The UFAW Handbook on the Care and Management of Laboratory Animals," pp. 242–256. Williams & Wilkins, Baltimore, MD.

Fischer, R., and Brown, P. (1993). Vaginal secretions increase the likelihood of intermale aggression in Syrian hamsters. *Physiol. Behav.* **54**, 213–214.

Fischer, R. B., and McQuiston, J. (1991). A possible role for syrian hamster, *Mesocricetus auratus,* vaginal secretion in interfemale competition. *Anim. Behav.* **42**, 949–954.

Fleming, A. S., Phillips, A., Rydall, A., and Levesque, L. (1998). Effects of photoperiod, the pineal gland and the gonads on agonsitic behavior in female golden hamsters (*Mesocricetus auratus*). *Physiol. Behav.* **44**, 227–234.

Floody, O. R., and Pfaff, D. W. (1977a). Aggressive behavior in female hamsters: The hormonal basis for fluctuations in female aggressiveness correlated with estrous state. *J. Comp. Physiol. Psychol.* **91**, 443–464.

Floody, O. R., and Pfaff, D. W. (1977b). Communication among hamsters by high-frequency acoustic signals: I. Physical characteristics of hamster calls. *J. Comp. Physiol. Psychol.* **91**, 794–806.

Floody, O. R., and Pfaff, D. W. (1977c). Communication among hamsters by high-frequency acoustic signals: II. Determinants of calling by females and males. *J. Comp. Physiol. Psychol.* **91**, 807–819.

Floody, O. R., and Pfaff, D. W. (1977d). Communication among hamsters by high-frequency acoustic signals: III. Responses evoked by natural and synthetic ultrasounds. *J. Comp. Physiol. Psychol.* **91**, 820–829.

Fraile, I. G., McEwen, B. S., and Pfaff, D. W. (1987). Progesterone inhibition of aggressive behaviors in hamsters. *Physiol. Behav.* **39**, 225–229.

Fraile, I. G., McEwen, B. S., and Pfaff, D. W. (1988). Comparative effects of progesterone and alphaxalone on aggressive, reproductive and locomotor behaviors. *Pharmacol., Biochem. Behav.* **30**, 729–735.

Friedle, R., and Fischer, R. (1984). Discrimination of salivary olfactants by male *Mesocricetus auratus. Psychol. Rep.* **55**, 67–70.

Fritzsche, P., Reik, M., and Gattermann, R. (2000). Effects of social stress on behavior and corpus luteum in female golden hamsters (*Mesocricetus auratus*). *Physiol. Behav.* **68**, 625–630.

Fullenkamp, A. M., Fischer, R. B., and Vance, R. A. (1987). A lack of avoidance of flank gland secretions by male Syrian hamsters. *Physiol. Behav.* **39**, 73–76.

Garrett, J. W., and Campbell, C. S. (1980). Changes in social behavior of the male golden hamster accompanying photoperiodic changes in reproduction. *Horm. Behav.* **14**, 303–318.

Gaskin, J., and Kitay, J. (1970). Adrenocortical function in the hamster: Sex differences and effects of gonadal hormones. *Endocrinology (Baltimore)* **87**, 779–786.

Giordano, A. L., Siegel, H. I., and Rosenblatt, J. S. (1986). Intrasexual aggression during pregnancy and the estrous cycle in golden hamsters (*Mesocrietus auratus*). *Aggressive Behav.* **12**, 213–222.

Gottreich, A., Zuir, I., Hammel, I., and Terkel, J. (2001). Noninvolvement of testosterone in aggressive defense behavior in the male blind mole rat *Spalax ehrenbergi. Aggress. Behav.* **27**, 64–72.

Grant, E. C., and Mackintosh, J. H. (1962). A comparison of the social postures of some common laboratory rodents. *Unknown,* pp. 246–259.

Grant, E. C., Mackintosh, J. H., and Lerwill, C. J. (1970). The effect of a visual stimulus on the agonistic behavior of the golden hamster. *Z. Tierpsychol.* **27**, 73–77.

Grelk, D. F., Papson, B. A., Cole, J. E., and Rowe, F. A. (1974). The Influence of caging conditions and hormone treatments on fighting in male and female hamsters. *Horm. Behav.* **5**, 355–366.

Haller, J., Halasz, J., Makara, G., and Kruk, M. (1998). Acute effects of glucocorticoids: Behavioral and pharmacological perspectives. *Neurosci. Biobehav. Rev.* **23**, 337–344.

Haller, J., Millar, S., Van de Schraaf, J., De Kloet, R. E., and Kruk, M. R. (2000). The active phase-related increase in corticosterone and aggression are linked. *J. Neuroendocrinol.* **12**, 431–436.

Hamilton, J. B., and Montagna, W. (1950). The sebaceous glands of the hamster: I. Morphological effects of androgens on integumentary structures. *Am. J. Anat.* **86**, 191–233.

Hammond, M. A., and Rowe, F. A. (1976). Medial preoptic and anterior hypothalamic lesions: Influences on aggressive behavior in female hamsters. *Physiol. Behav.* **17**, 507–513.

Harding, C. F. (1981). Social modulation of circulating hormones in the male. *Am. Zool.* **21**, 223–232.

Harmon, A. C., Huhman, K. L., Moore, T. O., and Albers, H. E. (1995). Microinjectin of norepinephrine (NE) into the medial preoptic-anterior hypothalamus (MPOA-AH) regulates agonistic behavior in female Syrian hamsters. *Soc. Neurosci.* **21**, 2091.

Harmon, A. C., Huhman, K. L., Lee, K. N., and Albers, H. E. (1996). Social relationships alter the ability of oxytocin (OXT) to stimulate flank marking in female Syrian hamsters. *Soc. Neurosci.* **26**, 2070.

Hennessey, A. C., Whitman, D. C., and Albers, H. E. (1992). Microinjection of arginine-vasopressin into the periaqueductal gray stimulates flank marking in Syrian hamsters (*Mesocricetus auratus*). *Brain Res.* **569**, 136–140.

Hennessey, A. C., Huhman, K. L., and Albers, H. E. (1994). Vasopressin and sex differences in hamster flank marking. *Physiol. Behav.* **55**, 905–911.

Honrado, G. I., Paclik, L., and Fleming, A. S. (1991). The effects of short day exposure on seasonal and circadian reproductive rhythms of female golden hamsters. *Physiol. Behav.* **50**, 357–363.

Huang, D., and Hazlett, B. A. (1974). Submissive distance in the golden hamster *Mesocrietus auratus. Anim. Behav.* **22**, 467–472.

Huhman, K. L., and Albers, H. E. (1993). Estradiol increases the behavioral response to arginine vasopressin (AVP) in the medial preoptic-anterior hypothalamus. *Peptides (N.Y.)* **14**, 1049–1054.

Huhman, K. L., Bunnell, B. N., Mougey, E. H., and Meyerhoff, J. L. (1990). Effects of social conflict on POMC-derived peptides and glucocorticoids in male golden hamsters. *Physiol. Behav.* **47**, 949–956.

Huhman, K. L., Moore, T. O., Ferris, C. F., Mougey, E. H., and Meyerhoff, J. L. (1991). Acute and repeated exposure to social conflict in male golden hamsters: Increases in plasma POMC-peptides and cortisol and decreases in plasma testosterone. *Horm. Behav.* **25**, 206–216.

Irvin, R. W., Szot, P., Dorsa, D. M., Potegal, M., and Ferris, C. F. (1990). Vasopressin in the septal area of the Golden hamster controls scent marking and grooming. *Physiol. Behav.* **48**, 693–699.

Jasnow, A. M., Banks, M. C., Owens, E. C., and Huhman, K. L. (1999). Differential effects of two corticotropin-releasing factor antagonists on conditioned defeat in male Syrian hamster (*Mesocricetus auratus*). *Brain Res.* **846**, 122–128.

Jasnow, A. M., Huhman, K. L., Bartness, T. J., and Demas, G. E. (2000). Short-day increases in aggression are inversely related to circulating testosterone concentrations in male siberian hamsters (*Phodopus sungorus*). *Horm Behav.* **38**, 102–110.

Johnson, A. E., Barberis, C., and Albers, H. E. (1995). Castration reduces vasopressin receptor binding in the hamster hypothalamus. *Brain Res.* **674**, 153–158.

Johnson, D. A., Poplawsky, A., and Bieliauskas, L. (1972). Alterations of social behavior in rats and hamsters following lesions of the septal function. *Psychon. Sci.* **26**, 19–20.

Johnson, R. P. (1973). Scent marking in mammals. *Anim. Behav.* **21**, 521–535.

Johnston, R. E. (1975a). Scent marking by male Golden hamsters (*Mesocricetus auratus*). I. Effects of odors and social encounters. *Z. Tierpsychol.* **37**, 75–98.

Johnston, R. E. (1975b). Scent marking by male golden hamsters (*Mesocricetus auratus*). II. The role of the flank gland scent in the causation of marking. *Z. Tierpsychol.* **37**, 138–144.

Johnston, R. E. (1975c). Scent marking by male Golden hamsters (*Mesocricetus auratus*). III. Behavior in a seminatural environment. *Z. Tierpsychol.* **37**, 213–221.

Johnston, R. E. (1976). The role of dark chest patches and upright postures in the agonistic behavior of male hamsters, *Mesocricetus auratus*. *Behav. Biol.* **17**, 161–176.

Johnston, R. E. (1977). The causation of two scent-marking behaviour patterns in female hamsters (*Mesocricetus auratus*). *Anim. Behav.* **25**, 317–327.

Johnston, R. E. (1981). Testosterone dependence of scent marking by male hamster (*Mesocricetus auratus*). *Behav. Neural Biol.* **310**, 96–99.

Johnston, R. E. (1985). Communication. *In* "The Hamster: Reproduction and Behavior" (H. I. Seigel, ed.), pp. 121–149. Plenum Press, New York.

Johnston, R. E. (1992). Vomeronasal and/or olfactory mediation of ultrasonic calling a scent marking by female golden hamsters. *Physiol. Behav.* **51**, 437–438.

Johnston, R. E., and Mueller, U.G. (1990). Olfactory but not vomeronasal mediation of scent marking by golden hamsters. *Physiol. Behav.* **48**, 701–706.

Joppa, M. A., Meisel, R. L., and Garber, M. A. (1995). c-Fos expression in female hamster brain following sexual and aggressive behaviors. *Neuroscience* **68**, 783–792.

Joppa, M. A., Rowe, R. K., and Meisel, R. L. (1997). Effects of serotonin 1A or 1B receptor agonists on social aggression in male and female Syrian hamsters. *Pharmacol., Biochem. Behav.* **58**, 349–353.

Jorgenson, K. L., and Schwartz, N. B. (1985). Shifts in gonadotropin and steroid levels that precede anestrus female in golden hamsters exposed to a short photoperiod. *Biol. Reprod.* **32**, 611–618.

Katangole, L. B., Naftolin, F., and Short, R. V. (1971). Relationship between blood levels of luteinizing hormone and testosterone in bulls, and the effects of sexual stimulation. *J. Endocrinol.* **50**, 457–466.

Kislak, J. W., and Beach, F. A. (1955). Inhibition of aggressiveness by ovarian hormones. *Endocrinology (Baltimore)* **56**, 684–692.

Klukowski, M., and Nelson, C. E. (1998). The challenge hypothesis and seasonal changes in aggression and steroids in male northern fence lizards (*Sceloporus undulatus* hyacinthinus). *Horm. Behav.* **33**, 197–204.

Kohlert, J. G., and Meisel, R. L. (2001). Inhibition of aggression by progesterone and its metabolites in female Syrian hamsters. *Aggress. Behav.* **27**, 372–381.

Kollack-Walker, S., and Newman, S. W. (1997). Mating and agonistic behavior produce different patterns of Fos immunolabeling in the male Syrian hamster brain. *Neuroscience* **66**, 721–736.

Kollack-Walker, S., Watson, S. J., and Akil, H. (1997). Social stress in hamsters: Defeat activates specific neurocircuits within the brain. *J. Neurosci.* **17**, 8842–8855.

Krieger, M. S., Morrell, J. I., and Pfaff, D. W. (1976). Autoradiographic localization of estradiol–concentrating cells in the female hamster brain. *Neuroendocrinology* **22**, 193–205.

Landau, I. T. (1975a). Light-dark rhythms in aggressive behavior of the male golden hamster. *Physiol. Behav.* **14**, 767–774.

Landau, I. T. (1975b). Effects of adrenalectomy on rhythmic and non-rhythmic aggressive behavior in the male golden hamster. *Physiol. Behav.* **14**, 775–780.

Lau, I. F., Saksena, S. K., Dahlgren, L., and Chang, M. C. (1978). Steroids in the blood serum and testis of cadmium choloride treated hamsters. *Biol. Reprod.* **19**, 886–889.

Lerwill, C. J., and Makings, P. (1971). The agonistic behavior of the golden hamster *Mesocricetus auratus* (Waterhouse). *Anim. Behav.* **19**, 714–721.

Leshner, A. (1980). The interaction of experience and neuroendocrine factors in determining behavioral adaptations to aggression. *Prog. Brain Res.* **53**, 427–438.

Leshner, A. (1983). Pituitary-adrenocortical effects on intermale agonistic behavior. *Horm. Aggressive Behav.,* pp. 27–38.

Lisk, R. D., and Nachtingall, M. J. (1988). Estrogen regulation of agonistic and proceptive responses in the golden hamster. *Horm. Behav.* **22**, 35–48.

Lisk, R. D., Ciaccio, C. L., and Catanzaro, C. C. (1983). Mating behavior of the golden hamster under seminatural conditions. *Anim. Behav.* **31**, 659–666.

Macrides, F., Bartke, A., Fernandez, F., and D'Angelo, W. (1974). Effects of exposure to vaginal odor and receptive females on plasma testosterone levels in the male hamster. *Neuroendocrinology* **15**, 355–364.

Mahoney, P. D., Koh, E. T., Irvin, R. W., and Ferris, C. F. (1990). Computer-aided mapping of vasopressin neurons in the hypothalamus of the male golden hamster: Evidence of magnocellular neurons that do not project to the neurophysis. *J. Neuroendocrinol.* **2**, 113–122.

Malsbury, C. W., Kow, L. M., and Pfaff, D. W. (1977). Effects of medial hypothalamic lesions on the lordosis response and other behaviors in female Golden hamsters. *Physiol. Behav.* **19**, 223–237.

Marques, D. M., and Valenstein, E. S. (1977). Individual differences in aggressiveness of female hamsters: Response to intact and castrated males and to females. *Anim. Behav.* **25**, 131–139.

Matochik, J. A., Miernicki, M., Powers, J. B., and Bergondy, M. L. (1986). Short photoperiods increase ultraasonic vocalization rates among male Syrian hamsters. *Physiol. Behav.* **38**, 453–458.

Meisel, R. L., and Sterner, M. R. (1990). Progesterone inhibition of sexual behavior is accompanied by an activation of aggression in female Syrian hamsters. *Physiol. Behav.* **47**, 415–417.

Meisel, R. L., Sterner, M. R., and Diekman, M. A. (1988). Differential hormonal control of aggression and sexual behavior in female Syrian hamsters. *Horm. Behav.* **22**, 453–466.

Meisel, R. L., Fraile, I. G., and Pfaff, D. W. (1990a). Hypothalamic sites of progestin action on aggression and sexual behavior in female Syrian hamsters. *Physiol. Behav.* **47**, 219–223.

Meisel, R. L., Hays, T. C., Del Paine, S. N., and Luttrell, V. R. (1990b). Induction of obesity by group housing in female Syrian hamster. *Physiol. Behav.* **47**, 815–817.

Miczek, K. A. (1983). Ethopharmacology of aggression, defense, and defeat. *In* "Aggressive Behavior: Genetic and Neural Approaches," pp. 147–166. Erbaum, Hillsdale, NJ.

Moline, M. L. (1981). Luteinizing hormone rhythms in female golden hamsters: Circadian, photoperiodic and endocrine interactions. Ph.D. Thesis, Harvard Medical School, Cambridge, MA.

Montgomery-St. Laurent, T., Fullenkamp, A., and Fischer, R. (1988). A role for the hamster's flank gland in heterosexual communication. *Physiol. Behav.* **44**, 759–762.

Morin, L. P., and Zucker, I. (1978). Photoperiodic regulation of copulatory behavior in the male hamster. *J. Endocrinol.* **77**, 249–258.

Moyer, K. E. (1971). "The Physiology of Hostility." Markham, Chicago.

Munn, A. R., Sar, M., and Stumpf, W. E. (1983). Topographic distribution of progestin target cells in hamster brain and pituitary after injection of [3H]R5020. *Brain Res.* **274**, 1–10.

Murphy, M. R. (1976a). Olfactory stimulation and olfactory bulb removal: Effects on territorial aggression in male Syrian golden hamsters. *Brain Res.* **113**, 95–110.

Murphy, M. R. (1976b). Blinding increases territorial aggression in male syrian golden hamsters. *Behav. Biol.* **17**, 139–141.

Murphy, M. R. (1977). Intraspecific sexual preferences of female hamsters. *J. Comp. Physiol. Psychol.* **91**, 1337–1346.

Murphy, M. R., and Schneider, G. (1970). Olfactory bulb removal eliminates mating behavior in the male golden hamster. *Science* **167**, 302–304.

Payne, A. P. (1973). A comparison of the aggressive behaviour of isolated intact and castrated male golden hamsters towards intruders introduced into the home cage. *Physiol. Behav.* **10**, 629–631.

Payne, A. P. (1974). A comparison of the effects of androstenedione, dihydrotestosterone and testosterone propionate on aggression in the castrated male golden hamster. *Physiol. Behav.* **13**, 21–26.

Payne, A. P., and Swanson, H. H. (1970). Agonistic behavior between pairs of hamsters of the same and opposite sex in a neutral observation area. *Behaviour* **36**, 259–269.

Payne, A. P., and Swanson, H. H. (1971a). Hormonal control of aggressive dominance in the female hamster. *Physiol. Behav.* **6**, 355–357.

Payne, A. P., and Swanson, H. H. (1971b). The effect of castration and ovarian implantation on aggressive behavior of male hamsters. *J. Endocrinol.* **51**, 217–218.

Payne, A. P., and Swanson, H. H. (1972a). The effect of sex hormones on the agonistic behavior of the male golden hamster (*Mesocricetus auratus* Waterhouse). *Physiol. Behav.* **8**, 687–691.

Payne, A. P., and Swanson, H. H. (1972b). The effect of sex hormones on the aggressive behavior of the female golden hamster (*Mesocricetus auratus* Waterhouse). *Anim. Behav.* **20**, 782–787.

Payne, A. P., Andrews, M. J., and Wilson, C. A. (1984). Housing, fighting and biogenic amines in the midbrain and hypothalamus of the golden hamster. *In* "Ethopharmacological Aggression Research" (K. A. Miczek, K. Menno, and O. Berend, eds.), pp. 227–247. Liss, New York.

Payne, A. P., Andrews, M. J., and Wilson, C. A. (1985). The effects of isolation, grouping and aggressive interactions on in. *Physiol. Behav.* **34**, 911–916.

Petrulis, A., and Johnston, R. E. (1999). Lesions centered on the medial amygdala impair scent-marking and sex-odor recognition but spare discrimination of individual odors in female golden hamsters. *Behav. Neurosci.* **113**, 345–357.

Petrulis, A., Peng, M., and Johnston, R. E. (1999a). Lateral olfactory tract transections impair discrimination of individual odors, sex odor preferences, and scent marking in female golden hamsters (*Mesocricetus auratus*). *In* "Advances in Chemical Signals in Vertebrates" (R. E. Johnston, D. Müller Schwarze, and P. Sorensen, eds.), pp. 549–561. Kluwer Academic/Plenum, New York.

Petrulis, A., Peng, M., and Johnston, R. E. (1999b). Effects of vomeronasal organ removal on individul odor discrimination, sex-odor preference, and scent marking by female hamsters. *Physiol. Behav.* **66**, 73–83.

Pfeiffer, C. A., and Johnston, R. E. (1992). Socially stimulated androgen surges in male hamsters: The roles of vaginal secretions, behavioral interactions, and housing conditions. *Horm. Behav.* **26**, 283–293.

Polsky, R. H. (1976). Conspecific defeat, isolation/grouping and predatory behavior in golden hamsters. *Psychol. Rep.* **38**, 571–577.

Potegal, M. (1986). Differential effects of ethyl (R,S)-nipecotate on the behaviors of highly and minimally aggressive female golden hamsters. *Psychopharmacology* **89**, 444–448.

Potegal, M., and Ferris, C. F. (1989). Intraspecific aggression in male hamsters is inhibited by intrahypothalamic vasopressin-receptor antagonist. *Aggress. Behav.* **15**, 311–320.

Potegal, M., Blau, A. D., Black, M., and Glusman, M. (1980a). Effects of castration of male golden hamsters on their aggression toward a restrained target. *Behav. Neural Bio.* **29**, 315–330.

Potegal, M., Blau, A., Black, M., and Glusman, M. (1980b). A technique for the study of intraspecific aggression in the golden hamster under conditions of reduced target variability. *Psychol. Rec.* **30**, 191–200.

Potegal, M., Blau, A., and Glusman, M. (1981a). Inhibition of intraspecific aggression in male hamsters by septal stimulation. *Physiol. Psychol.* **9**, 213–218.

Potegal, M., Blau, A., and Glusman, M. (1981b). Effects of anteroventral septal lesions on intraspecific aggression in male hamsters. *Physiol. Behav.* **26**, 407–412.

Potegal, M., Perumal, A. S., Barkai, A. I., Cannova, G. E., and Blau, A. D. (1982). GABA binding in the brains of aggressive and non-aggressive female hamster. *Brain Res.* **247**, 315–324.

Potegal, M., Huhman, K., Moore, T., and Meyeroff, J. (1993) Conditioned defeat in the Syrian golden hamster (*Mesocricetus auratus*). *Behav. Neural Biol.* **60**, 93–102.

Potegal, M., Herbert, M., DeCoster, M., and Meyerhoff, J. L. (1996a). Brief, high-frequency stimulation of the corticomedial amygdala induces a delayed and prolonged increase of aggressiveness in male syrian hamsters. *Behav. Neurosci.* **110**, 401–412.

Potegal, M., Ferris, C. F., Hebert, M., Meyerhoff, J., and Skaredoff, L. (1996b). Attack priming in female Syrian golden hamsters is associated with a c-fos-coupled process within the cortico-medial amygdala. *Neuroscience* **75**, 869–880.

Rowe, E. A., and Swanson, H. H. (1977). A comparison of central and peripheral effects of testosterone propionate on social interactions inthe male golden hamster. *J. Endocrinol.* **72**, 39P–40P.

Saidapur, S. K., and Greenwald, G. S. (1978). Peripheral blood and ovarian levels of sex steroids in the cyclic hamster. *Biol. Reprod.* **18**, 401–408.

Sanford, L. M., Palmer, W. M., and Howland, B. E. (1974). Influence of sexual activity on serum levels of LH and testostrone in the ram. *Can. J. Anim.* **54**, 579–585.

Schuurman, T. (1980). Hormonal correlates of agonistic behavior in adult male rats. *Prog. Brain Res.* **53**, 415–420.

Shipley, J. E., and Kolb, B. (1977). Neural correlates of species-typical behavior in the Syrian golden hamster. *J. Comp. Physiol. Psychol.* **91**, 1056–1073.

Siegel, A., Roeling, T. A. P., Gregg, T. R., and Kruk, M. R. (1999). Neuropharmacology of brain-stimulation-evoked aggression. *Neurosci. Biobehav. Rev.* **23**, 359–389.

Siegel, H. I. (1985). Male sexual behavior. *In* "The Hamster: Reproduction and Behavior" (H. I. Siegel, ed.), pp. 191–204. Plenum Press, New York.

Simon, N. G. (1983). New strategies for aggression research. *In* "Aggressive Behavior: Genetic and Neural Approaches," pp. 19–36. Erlbaum, Hillsdale, NJ.

Sodetz, F. J., and Bunnell, B. N. (1970). Septal ablation and the social behavior of the golden hamster. *Physiol. Behav.* **5**, 79–88.

Sodetz, F. J., Matalka, E. S., and Bunnell, B. N. (1967). Septal ablation and effective behavior in the golden hamster. *Psychon. Sci.* **7**, 189–190.

Solomon, J. A., and Glickman, S. E. (1977). Attraction of male golden hamster (*Mesocricetus auratus*) to the odors of male conspecifics. *Behav. Biol.* **2**, 367–376.

Steel, E. (1979). Male-female interaction throughout the oestrous cycle of the Syrian hamster (*Mesocricetus auratus*). *Anim. Behav.* **27**, 919–929.

Sterner, M. R., Meisel, R. L., and Diekman, M. A. (1992). Forebrain sites of estradiol-17B activation sexual behavior and aggression in female Syrian hamsters. *Behav. Neurosci.* **106**, 162–171.

Swanson, L. J., Desjardins, C., and Turek, F. W. (1982). Aging of the reproductive system in the male hamster: Behavioral and endocrine patterns. *Biol. Reprod.* **26**, 757–764.

Takahashi, L. K., and Gladstone, C. D. (1988). Medial amygdala lesions and the regulation of sociosexual behavioral patterns across the estrous cycle in female golden hamsters. *Behav. Neurosci.* **102**, 268–275.

Takahashi, L. K., and Lisk, R. D. (1983). Organization and expression of agonistic and socio-sexual behavior in golden hamsters over the estrous cycle and after ovariectomy. *Physiol. Behav.* **31**, 477–482.

Takahashi, L. K., and Lisk, R. D. (1984). Intrasexual interactions among female golden hamsters (*Mesocricetus auratus*) over the estrous cycle. *J. Comp. Psychol.* **98**, 267–275.

Takahashi, L. K., and Lisk, R. D. (1985). Estrogen action in anterior and ventromedial hypothalamus and the modulation of heterosexual behavior in female golden hamsters. *Physiol. Behav.* **34**, 233–239.

Takahashi, L. K., and Lisk, R. D. (1986). Intracranial site regulating the biphasic action of progesterone in estrogen-primed golden hamsters. *Endocrinology (Baltimore)* **119**, 2744–2754.

Takahashi, L. K., and Lisk, R. D. (1987). Diencephalic organization of estradiol sensitive sites regulation sociosexual behavior in female golden hamsters: Contralateral versus ipsalateral activation. *Brain Res.* **425**, 337–345.

Takahashi, L. K., Lisk, R. D., and Burnett, A. L. (1985). II Dual estradiol action in diencephalon and the regulation of sociosexual behavior in female golden hamsters. *Brain Res.* **359**, 194–207.

Terada, N., Sato, B., and Matsumoto, K. (1980). Formation of 5b- and 5a-products as major C_{19} -steroids from progestrone *in vitro* in immature golden hamster testis. *Endocrinology (Baltimore)* **101**, 1554–1561.

Tiefer, L. (1970). Gonadal hormones and mating behavior in the adult golden hamster. *Horm. Behav.* **1**, 189–202.

Turek, F. W., and Ellis, G. B. (1981). Steroid-dependent and steroid-independent aspects of the photoperiodic control od seasonal reproductive cycles in male hamsters. *In* "Biological Clocks in Seasonal Reproductive Cycles," pp. 251–260. Wright, Bristol.

Turek, F. W., Elliott, J., Alvis, J., and Menaker, M. (1975). Effects of prolonged exposure to nonstimulatory photoperiods on the activity of the neuroendocrine-testicular axis of golden hamsters. *Biol. Reprod.* **13**, 475–481.

Vandenbergh, J. G. (1971). The effects of gonadal hormones on the aggressive behavior of adult Golden hamsters (*Mesocricetus auratus*). *Anim. Behav.* **19**, 589–594.

Vandenbergh, J. G. (1973). Effects of gonadal hormones on the flank gland of the golden hamster. *Horm. Res.* **4**, 28–33.

Vandenbergh, J. G. (1994). Pheromones and mammalian reproduction. *In* "The Physiology of Reproduction" (E. Knobil and J. D. Neill, eds.), 2nd ed., pp. 343–359. Raven Press, New York.

van den Pol, A. N., and Trombley, P. Q. (1993). Glutamate neurons in hypothalamus regulate excitatory transmission. *J. Neurosci.* **13**, 2829–2836.

Vincent, S. R. (1988). Distributions of tyrosin hydroxylase-, dopamine-beta-hydroxylase, and Phenylethanolamine-N-methyltransferase-immunoreactive neurons in the brain of the hamster. *J. Comp. Neurol.* **268**, 584–599.

Vomachka, A. J., and Greenwald, G. S. (1979). The development of gonadotropin and steroid hormone patterns in male and female hamsters from birth to puberty. *Endocrinology (Baltimore)* **105**, 960–966.

White, P., Fischer, R., and Meunier, G. (1984). The ability of females to predict male status via urinary odors. *Horm. Behav.* **18**, 491–494.

White, P., Fischer, R., and Meunier, G. (1986). Female discrimination of male dominance by urine odor cues in hamsters. *Physiol. Behav.* **37**, 273–277.

Whitman, D. C., Hennessey, A. C., and Albers, H. E. (1992). Norepinephrine inhibits vasopressin-stimulated flank marking in the Syrian hamster by acting within the medial preoptic-anterior hypothalamus. *J. Neuroendocrinol.* **4**(5), 541–546.

Whitsett, J. M. (1975). The development of aggressive and marking behavior in intact and castrated male hamsters. *Horm. Behav.* **6**, 47–57.

Wingfield, J. C., Ball, G. F, Dufty, A. M., Hegner, R. E., and Ramenofsky, M. (1987). Testosterone and aggression in birds. *Am. Sci.* **75**, 602–608.

Wingfield, J. C., Hegner, R. E., Dufty, A. M. J., and Ball, G. F. (1990). The "challenge hypothesis": Theoretical implications for patterns of testosterone secretion, mating systems, and breeding strategies. *Am. Natu.* **136**, 829–846.

Wingfield, J. C., Whaling, C. S., and Marler, P. (1994). Communication in vertebrate aggression and reproduction: The role of hormones. *In* "The Physiology of Reproduction" (E. Knobil and J. D. Neill, eds.) 2nd ed. pp. 303–342. Raven Press, New York.

Wise, D. A. (1974). Aggression in the female golden hamster: Effects of reproductive state and social isolation. *Horm. Behav.* **5**, 235–250.

Wood, R. I., and Newman, S. W. (1993). Mating activates androgen receptor-containing neurons in chemosensory pathways of the male Syrian hamster brain. *Brain Res.* **614**, 65–77.

Yahr, P. (1983). Hormonal influences on territorial marking behavior. *In* "Hormones and Aggressive Behavior" (B. B. Svare, ed.), pp. 145–175. Plenum Press, New York.

Young, L. J., Wang, Z., Cooper, T. T., and Albers, H. E. (2000). Vasopressin receptor (V1a) in the hamster brain: Synthesis, transport and transcriptional regulation by androgen. *J. Neuroendocrinol.* **12**, 1179–1185.

7

Energy Balance, Ingestive Behavior, and Reproductive Success

Jill E. Schneider

Department of Biological Sciences
Lehigh University
Bethlehem, Pennsylvania 18015

Alan G. Watts

Department of Biological Sciences
University of Southern California
Los Angeles, California 90089

I. INTRODUCTION

The neuroendocrine mechanisms that control energy balance have reciprocal links to all physiological systems, including the reproductive system. This chapter focuses on the mechanisms that influence ingestive behavior, body weight, body fat content, body fat distribution, energy expenditure, and fuel homeostasis. Reproductive processes are an important part of the energy balancing system because evolutionary adaptation involves not only survival, but also differential reproductive success. Mechanisms that control ingestive behavior and energy balance did not evolve specifically to ensure a set point for body weight or body composition or to prevent clinical syndromes, such as obesity or diabetes, but rather to increase survival and optimize reproductive success.

A biological perspective on this problem begins with the observation that living cells expend energy constantly and thus require a continuous supply of fuels for energy metabolism. A constant supply of glucose as a metabolic substrate is particularly critical for cells in the central nervous system. Food ingestion, digestion, and metabolism are the primary means by which these energetic requirements are met, but food availability and energetic demands fluctuate in most habitats, and most organisms do not eat continuously. All but the most

primitive organisms engage in a variety of activities that preclude eating for varying periods of time; they rest, sleep, forage, exercise, hibernate, compete, court, mate, parent, work, play, or engage in intense research and scholarship. Ingested fuels are either used for intracellular oxidation or stored in internal reservoirs in the form of glycogen in tissue such as liver and muscle or in the form of triglycerides in adipose tissue. When the digestive tract is empty, the body relies on fuels and nutrients from internal (e.g., body fat) and external reservoirs (e.g., food hoards). The ability to store significant quantities of energy in the form of glycogen and lipids in adipose tissue and to defer ingestion allows organisms more time for activities that improve reproductive success. The ability to monitor internal and external energy availability allows animals to prioritize their behavioral options.

Conversely, during energetic challenges, energetically costly activities are curtailed in order to conserve energy for those activities that are essential for immediate survival. For example, during harsh winters when thermoregulatory demands are high, members of some species become gonadally regressed and sexually inactive. Even in species that breed year round, reproductive processes are inhibited when food availability is low or when increased energy demands are not met by compensatory food intake. A survey of the link between energy availability and reproduction in representatives of all mammalian orders prompted Franklin Bronson to declare "of all the environmental factors that affect reproduction, food availability must be accorded the most important role" (1989, p. 88). When food is plentiful and energy requirements are low, energy is available for all of the immediately essential processes necessary for life: thermoregulation, locomotion, foraging, ingestion, digestion, and intracellular processes. The surplus can be used for long-term energetic investment or stored as lipid in adipose tissue. When energy availability is scarce or energy requirements high, the physiological mechanisms that partition energy into various activities tend to favor processes that ensure the survival of the individual over processes that promote growth, longevity, and reproduction. Physiological processes that are primarily dedicated to reproduction tend to be low on the energy priority list relative to essential processes such as cellular respiration and thermoregulation because reproductive processes are energetically expensive and can be delayed when the survival of the individual is in jeopardy (Bronson, 1989, 2000). Many aspects of reproductive behavior and physiology are influenced by factors such as food intake, body fat content, exercise, and ambient temperature because all of these influence the availability of energy for cellular oxidation.

When food and stored fuels are plentiful and energy demands are low, the immune system protects organisms from infections that might be fatal if left unchecked for long periods. The immune system, however, is also an energetically costly affair and is not always necessary for survival during acute emergencies. Immune function is inhibited when energy must be diverted to other processes (reviewed by Nelson and Klein, 2000). When ambient temperatures drop, the typical response of most homeothermic animals is to increase metabolic rate and heat production, and to suppress immune function. Thermoregulatory behaviors, such as nesting and huddling, help to conserve energy by preventing heat loss. Members of some species engage in still more extreme energy-conserving adaptations during energetically challenging winter conditions. Some species hibernate; that is, they initiate a regulated decrease in heart rate and body temperature that is sustained for varying duration depending on the species. In some temperate-zone mammals, these re-

sponses occur in anticipation of the cold winter season because they are initiated by changes in day length. In some species, the change in day length actually prevents the suppression of immune function that is normally brought on by cold ambient temperatures (Nelson and Klein, 2000). This chapter is not concerned specifically with immune function, thermoregulation, or even reproduction per se. Rather, this chapter has relevance for understanding the mechanisms that prioritize and coordinate these activities in the service of maintaining fuel homeostasis under fluctuating energetic conditions and optimizing reproductive success.

This integrative systems perspective on energy balance is valuable in economic, agricultural, and medical contexts. Widespread obesity poses a complex medical, economic, and sociological conundrum. At the beginning of this millennium, approximately 40 million Americans were categorized as "obese" (defined as a body-mass-to-height index that is at least 30% over the ideal). Although obesity is common, it is highly stigmatized and associated with highly publicized adverse health consequences (reviewed by Kopelman, 2000). Lack of awareness is clearly not the problem. Diet and exercise books are ubiquitous on the best-seller lists. Several billion dollars are spent each year on various diet products, low-fat or low-calorie foods and beverages, and on expensive high-risk liposuction procedures performed for both medical and purely cosmetic reasons. Still more money is spent on the development of various drugs that influence food intake, body weight, and composition. At the same time, the prevalence of eating disorders, such as anorexia nervosa, is increasing among both men and women of the more affluent segments of society, as well as in lower income and minority populations. Decreased appetite and food intake influence mortality associated with cancer, inflammatory diseases, and autoimmune diseases. Women at both extremes of the body weight distribution and those with diabetes are at risk for various reproductive neuroendocrine disorders associated with low circulating levels of gonadal steroids. Low levels of these hormones, in turn, are associated with osteoporosis and impaired cognitive function. This chapter has relevance for understanding nutritional infertility, amenorrhea, anovulation, and diminished libido associated with decreased food intake or with increased energy expenditure that is not offset by compensatory food intake. Because of the multiple reciprocal links among energy availability, the hypothalamic-pituitary-gonadal (HPG) system, osteoporosis, and cognitive function, research in this field will have an impact on setting standards for nutritional and caloric intake appropriate for men and women in athletic or combat training. It is clear that diet and training must be balanced for optimal physical and mental performance and to minimize injuries (reviewed by Otis *et al.*, 1997). In addition, this research will provide relevant information for animal scientists interested in improving feed efficiency, breeding, and lactation in dairy and meat animals; and for conservation and fisheries biologists interested in improving the breeding success of various species. As mentioned previously, coordination of energy partitioning has relevance for understanding the immune system. In the past, behavioral neuroscientists tended to categorize ingestive behaviors as homeostatic, and reproductive and maternal behaviors as nonhomeostatic. The reproductive, gastrointestinal, metabolic, and immune systems were studied independently by separate groups of investigators with very little cross-collaboration. In contrast, more recent work at the interface of these fields has initiated a new synthetic line of research aimed at understanding seasonal adaptation, reproduction, and immune function in the context of energy homeostasis (Loffreda *et al.*, 1998; reviewed in Wallen and Schneider, 2000).

This chapter begins with a historical perspective from which to view the more recent developments in this interdisciplinary field of research. Next, we introduce the major components of energy economy (intake, storage, and expenditure), emphasizing the reciprocal relationships among them. We then summarize current understanding of the neural effectors for control of intake, storage, and expenditure. Next, we discuss how they are controlled by gustatory, gastric, and metabolic sensory stimuli. We then illustrate how these sensory signals are mediated or modulated by hormones and other chemical messengers. The subsequent section concerns the neural effectors, sensory stimuli, and hormonal mediators that control reproductive processes. Finally, we discuss integration of the systems that control energy intake and reproduction.

II. HISTORICAL PERSPECTIVE ON REGULATION OF ENERGY BALANCE

Processes related to fuel homeostasis have captured the interests of the most prominent scientists in history. Charles Darwin (1809–1882) was acutely aware of the importance of food availability as an environmental factor controlling reproduction. This concept was pivotal to the theory of evolution by natural selection. Darwin noticed that lack of food and hard living influenced the fertility of free-living relatives of domestic animals. He reasoned that animals must "struggle for their food, at least during certain seasons" and that "individuals of the same species, having slightly different constitutions or structure" would reproduce differentially under what he termed "natural selection" (Darwin, 1859, p. 96). Darwin included behavior along with all of the other structural phenotypes, thus building the foundation for the sciences of behavioral biology (ethology, physiological psychology, behavior endocrinology, and the neurosciences). Another source of differential reproductive success is that individuals with the same food availability vary in the efficiency with which their bodies use fuel derived from ingested food. Differential feed efficiency explains the remarkable reproductive success observed in organisms adapted for harsh environments in which food availability is low. For example, in rural subsistence farming villages of Keneba, Gambian women work on their farms and simultaneously gestate and nurse several consecutive children, all the while consuming an average of only 1500 calories per day. Pregnancy outcome and lactational performance in these women ranks as "good," despite the fact that the caloric intake is ranked significantly lower than international standards (Prentice *et al.*, 1981; Roberts *et al.*, 1982).

Claude Bernard (1813–1878), one of the founders of physiology and Darwin's contemporary, suggested that an organism's physiological systems existed to maintain a favorable "milieu interieur," the internal environment in which cells carry out their functions. According to Bernard (1856), the internal factors to be optimized included the internal availability of calories and nutrients. Thus, Bernard used experimental techniques to demonstrate the formation and breakdown of liver glycogen in service of maintaining what came to be known as glucose homeostasis. The word "homeostasis" was coined later by the prominent neurologist, Walter Cannon (1871–1945), who thought that organisms were goaded into regulatory behaviors, such as eating, by uncomfortable conditions (e.g., stomach contractions or dry mouth) that occur whenever homeostasis is not maintained within optimal limits (Cannon, 1932). It is now well recognized that homeostatic inclinations originate with peripheral sensory signals that in turn control behavior, and this notion can be traced to Bernard and Cannon.

The focus on behavior as a pivotal factor in the maintenance of homeostasis is largely due to the diverse contributions of Curt Richter (1943), who proposed the notion of "self-regulatory" behaviors. Richter's contributions were in the same tradition as the experiments of Berthold (1849), the nineteenth century physiologist who first used organ removal and hormone replacement to demonstrate the influence of testicular secretions on sex behavior. For example, Richter (1936) used adrenalectomy and corticosteroid replacement to help establish the importance of the peripheral secretions in control of sodium consumption. Richter was also one of the first to recognized that energy balancing systems are directly related to reproductive success and to examine the mechanisms that change energy and fluid balance during pregnancy and lactation.

During the 1930s and 1940s, the interests of many behavioral scientists were temporarily diverted away from physiological psychology toward animal learning, largely due to the theories of Watson and Skinner. Meanwhile Karl Lashley and his expositor, Charles T. Morgan, continued and finally reestablished the study of the appetitive or motivational aspects of behavior that originally derived from the ideas of early ethologists, such as Wallace Craig, Konrad Lorenz and Niko Tinbergen. The motivational aspect of ingestive behavior referred to the innate or instinctive drive state of hunger or thirst measurable by the subjects' approach to food or water, tendency to perform an operant task for food or water reward, or consumption of unpalatable substances. Furthermore, Lashley and Morgan attributed the motivational state to the brain. Morgan, noting that insulin treatment stimulated eating, postulated that the hormone changed the internal milieu, thereby causing an arousal of the brain mechanisms responsible for motivated behavior. He also put forth the

notion of satiation, a reduction in the central arousing neural event or hormone by ingestion of food or water, thereby ushering in the discovery of different neural events that govern the termination of meals. The language and concepts of Lashley and Morgan are still apparent in the literature, particularly with regard to the neuroanatomical underpinnings of ingestion.

Although Lashley's primary focus was not on hormones, his students went on to lay the foundations of behavioral endocrinology. For example, his student, Frank A. Beach (1911–1988), elucidated the hormonal control of sexual motivation and behavior, wrote the first text on hormones and behavior, and is generally agreed to be the father of the modern era of behavioral endocrinology (Beach, 1948). The distinction between the appetitive and consummatory aspects of behavior used by Beach and his colleagues to study sex behavior continue to provide heuristic value and testable predictions for understanding neural control of ingestive and other behaviors. These ideas provide an important context for understanding the function of neuropeptides such as neuropeptide Y and hormones such as leptin (Ammar *et al.*, 2000; Seeley *et al.*, 1995).

The early brain-lesion studies of Lashley and Morgan also paved the way for the methodological breakthrough and watershed findings of S. W. Ranson's laboratory group. Within this modern framework built of hormones, brain, and motivated behavior, Ranson's group reintroduced the use of stereotaxic surgery (the technique developed at the turn of the century by Horsley and Clark) to begin the new era of functional neuroanatomy. They made bilateral electrolytic lesions in specific brain areas to determine which areas were critical for control of food intake and body mass. Specifically, lesions of the ventromedial hypothalamus (VMH) led to overeating (Hetherington and Ranson, 1940; Teitelbaum, 1955; Reeves and Plum, 1969), whereas lesions of the lateral hypothalamic area (LHA) led to decreased food intake and body weight and to eventual starvation (Anand and Brobeck, 1951b; Teitelbaum and Stellar, 1954). Based on these and other similar experiments, Stellar (1954) articulated the dual center hypothesis, a model for control of food intake by the interactions of two brain areas—a feeding center located in the LHA and a satiety center located in the VMH.

The value of the dual center hypothesis was that it provided both a methodology and a theoretical model that could be falsified by clear experimental outcomes. Subsequent experiments falsified both the dual and the center aspects of the hypothesis. First, it is clear that there are more than two critical areas for control of food intake. Second, the idea of a brain center that controls one particular behavior was not supported by data demonstrating that hormone implants into particular brain areas influence several types of behaviors (e.g., sex, maternal, aggressive) and physiological processes (e.g., pituitary, gonadal, pancreatic, and adrenal secretion, peripheral fuel metabolism, and thermogenesis). The neural circuits that control sex behavior contain brain areas that are also part of the circuits that control maternal, aggressive, affiliative, and ingestive behaviors (Newman, 1999). Furthermore, the original VMH lesions produced changes in peripheral hormones and metabolism that indirectly affected food intake and body weight. The legacy of the dual center hypothesis is the concept of stimulatory and inhibitory drive networks that control ingestion. This language and the focus on the hypothalamus dominate the current literature concerning the neuroanatomy of ingestion.

It has been noted that those parts of the hypothalamus lesioned by Hetherington and Ranson contain chemical messengers and receptors that stimulate (e.g., orexin in the LHA) or inhibit (leptin receptors in the ARH) food intake (Elmquist *et al.*, 1999). However, it would be a mistake to view these findings as support for the dual center hypothesis. The effects of orexin on food intake are secondary to its effects on sleep patterns and arousal (Lubkin *et al.*, 1998; Willie *et al.*, 2001). Furthermore, elevated levels of endogenous leptin fail to induce satiety in obese individuals. In the 1960s to 1980s a variety of experimental outcomes overturned the dual center hypothesis and revitalized Bernard and Cannon's notion of peripheral stimuli that control homeostatic behaviors.

After Hetherington and Ranson (1940), subsequent experiments focused on postingestive stimuli and the location of their detectors. For example, the glucostatic (Mayer, 1955) and lipostatic (Kennedy, 1953) hypotheses posited that food intake was controlled by detectors of plasma glucose and body fat content, respectively. Kennedy reasoned that the response to low food availability was multifaceted and involved not only the stimulation of mechanisms that increase food procurement,

but also the inhibition of energetically costly activities, such as those associated with reproduction. He was one of the first physiologists to recognize that elucidation of the peripheral signals that increase food intake would reveal the signals that inhibit reproductive processes (Kennedy and Mitra, 1963a,b). Around this same time, Russek proposed that receptors in the liver detect signals derived from glucose oxidation and convey this information to brain mechanisms that control food intake (Russek, 1963). A common thread among these theories was the idea that internal metabolic cues are used to couple food intake to energy expenditure. There is disagreement about the importance of specific postingestive stimuli, yet it is widely accepted that information from orosensory receptors and metabolic fuel detectors are integrated with central effector systems. The metabolic perspective led to the observation that the original VMH lesions produced profound changes in peripheral hormone secretion and metabolism that indirectly influenced food intake. Such VMH lesions actually encompassed regions of the paraventricular nucleus of the hypothalamus (PVH) that influence autonomic control of gastric motility (Saper *et al.*, 1976; Swanson and Kuypers, 1980) and may have damaged PVH projections that influence insulin secretion (VMH projections to the pancreas have yet to be identified using a variety of tract-tracing methods). Subdiaphragmatic vagotomy prevented VMH lesion-induced hyperphagia and obesity (Inoue and Bray, 1977; Berthoud and Jeanrenaud, 1979; Gold *et al.*, 1980; Bray *et al.*, 1981; Cox and Powley, 1981; Sclafani *et al.*, 1981), adding further support to the notion that the alterations in food intake characteristic of the VMH syndrome are most likely a consequence of peripheral influences rather than a change in centrally controlled motivation. The lesions induced an abnormal state of energy partitioning that was severely biased toward energy storage, which, in turn, left an insufficient supply of fuels available for essential cellular processes. Thus, the primary cause of hunger and hyperphagia was the lack of oxidizable fuels due to excessive energy storage, rather than damage to a purported center for hunger motivation. Mark Friedman expressed this idea by stating that "an animal with VMH lesions may not increase its food intake in order to gain weight, but because it is gaining weight" (Friedman and Stricker, 1976). Some of these peripheral metabolic effects are probably mediated, in part, by the peptide systems known to reside in the LHA and VMH-PVH areas.

Subsequent work has focussed attention on brain areas outside the hypothalamus. The basic orofacial reflexes associated with acceptance or rejection of sapid substances are organized in the hindbrain to control meal size (Grill and Kaplan, 1990). Furthermore, circadian input derives from the suprachiasmatic nucleus (SCH) (Buijs *et al.,* 1998; Saeb-Parsy *et al., 2000;* Watts, 1991). Peripheral metabolic and gastric stimuli provide essential input to the central mechanisms that control food intake. Food intake is controlled by mechanisms that integrate information about the oxidation of different metabolic substrates (i.e., glucose and free fatty acids), and these controls are located peripherally, possibly in the liver (reviewed by Friedman, 1998). Consequently, it was established that any model of the control of food intake must extend beyond the dual center hypothesis to include several interconnected nodes of both metabolic and neural integration.

These discoveries of the 1970s and 1980s provide an important context for new discoveries in the molecular neurobiology of ingestive behavior. In 1994 positional cloning was used to identify the *ob* protein, leptin, and its receptors in the arcuate nucleus (ARH) and elsewhere in the hypothalamus. These studies opened the door to subsequent discoveries of new orexigenic peptides in the LHA and anorexic peptides in the lateral ARH and a revitalized interest in hypothalamic control of food intake. Techniques for localization of changes in gene expression, tract-tracing using viruses transported transneuronally, markers for neural activation such as c-*fos* and suppressors of cytokine signaling, gene therapies, DNA microarrays, and genetic knockouts are now used to elucidate inhibitory and stimulatory hypothalamic circuits that are influenced by fasting, feeding, and treatment with hormonal mediators such as leptin, insulin, and glucocorticoids. Sawchenko (1998) has suggested that the efficiency in elucidating the underpinnings of motivated behaviors will be greater if, "in the design and interpretation of our experiments, we attend carefully to the lessons of the past" (p. 440). Some of these lessons of the past are:

1. Motivated behaviors are subject to distributed neural control. Peptide receptors in the cerebral hemispheres and hypothalamus are often duplicated (and

may have originated during evolution) in the caudal brainstem.

2. Critical sensory inputs link intracellular oxidizable fuel availability to food intake. Experimental manipulations of hormones and central neural circuits result in peripheral metabolic effects that indirectly influence behavior.

3. Identified neural circuits that purportedly control intake might influence the consummatory and appetitive aspects of ingestion differentially. The same or overlapping neural circuits influence more than one type of behavior (including reproductive, maternal, or aggressive) and, when viewed in an ecologically relevant social context, it becomes clear that these circuits increase the probability of the occurrence of one behavior over another.

Thus, with the identification of each new potential satiety or hunger circuit in the hypothalamus it should be expected that:

1. These hypothalamic circuits are likely to interact with inputs from the caudal hindbrain and periphery and might well have interactions with the cerebral hemispheres.

2. Intracerebroventricular (ICV) treatments with particular peptides are likely to produce changes in peripheral energy expenditure or partitioning that indirectly influences motivated behavior, or both.

3. Prior to declaring a neural circuit feeding stimulatory or feeding inhibitory, both the consummatory and appetitive aspects of ingestion must be examined in an ecologically relevant social context.

This chapter retains important aspects of all of these historical contributions. Much of the organization of the central nervous system (CNS) circuitry involved in energy balance has been studied in terms of the inhibitory and stimulatory circuits, the theoretical origin of which is the dual center hypothesis. This view must be modified, however, when the consummatory and appetitive aspects of ingestion are dissected and when behavior is studied in a social context. From this perspective, the putative feeding-stimulatory circuits simply direct attention toward food procurement, whereas actual intake decreases, remains unchanged, or is increased by indirect effects of those central circuits on peripheral metabolism. Conversely, feeding-inhibitory circuits increase the likelihood of engaging in behaviors unrelated to food procurement (e.g., mate searching, courtship, and copulation). In addition, this chapter emphasizes that peripheral sensory events influence motivation by controlling the activity of these circuits. In the final analysis, actual food intake, storage, and expenditure are determined by sensory systems that link fuel deficits to ingestion. Understanding the nature of these metabolic sensory stimuli and their detectors is imperative for understanding food intake and reproduction.

III. ENERGY ECONOMY

This section provides basic information about the three primary components of energy economy—intake, expenditure, and storage. These components are interrelated such that fuels from food intake and internal storage (glycogen, protein, and fat), along with oxygen, are converted to carbon dioxide, water, and energy expenditure (heat and work).

A. Intake

Food intake has been studied from a variety of different perspectives, each of which emphasizes different levels of biological organization. First, the study of central effector systems arose from the dual center hypothesis and the related notion of drive networks located in the brain. Second, primary sensory stimuli refer to extero- and interosensory cues. Exterosensory systems are the senses associated with the taste, smell, and texture of food, as well as with social, temporal, and spatial contextual cues. Interosensory systems are related to stimuli such as those detected by mechanoreceptors receptors in the gut and to stimuli generated by changes in metabolic fuel oxidation. Third, input that arises from hormones and neuropeptides secreted peripherally (insulin or cholecystokinin, CCK) are classified as hormonal mediators or modulators, not as metabolic signals. The secretion of some of these substances is linked to energy availability, and thus the level of these hormones can provide information about energy availability to central effector systems. Hormones and peripherally secreted peptides inform the brain about the energetic status and reproductive state of the animal,

thereby enhancing the occurrence of behavioral and metabolic adjustments that are appropriate for the environmental, reproductive, and energetic conditions. In most cases, the animal has the option to ignore the hormonal information if more urgent needs arise related to survival and reproduction. In addition, hormones and peripherally secreted peptides can alter or modulate the metabolic stimulus. For example, some chemical messengers actually alter the availability of oxidizable fuels (the primary metabolic sensory stimulus) and, thus, have indirect effects on the central effector systems.

The central effector system for food intake comprises at least two separate eating-stimulatory and eating-inhibitory neural circuits that reside in the hypothalamus (reviewed by Watts, 2000) and act via the final common motor neurons that function as the central pattern generator for rhythmic ingestion patterns in the caudal hindbrain (reviewed by Grill and Kaplan, 1990). For example, part of the putative stimulatory circuit for ingestive behavior involves the synaptic release of neuropeptide Y (NPY) and agouti-related protein (AgRP) from the terminals of neurons whose cell bodies are located in the ARH. In contrast, a putative feeding-inhibitory circuit involves increased expression of proopiomelanocortin (POMC) and its cleavage to α-melanocortin-stimulating hormone (α-MSH), another peptide synthesized in the lateral ARH that acts at melanocortin 4 (MC-4) receptors expressed by neurons in the LHA and PVH (reviewed by Elmquist *et al.*, 1998b, 1999). The lateral part of the ARH also contains neurons that express cocaine- and amphetamine-related transcript (CART). In studies that measured the amount of food eaten, ICV treatment with NPY/AgRP and α-MSH/CART increased and decreased the amount of food eaten, respectively. Factors that increase food intake, such as a period of food deprivation, are associated with activation of the NPY/AgRP network and suppression of the α-MSH/CART network. Antagonists to NPY receptors decrease food intake, and antagonists for the MC receptors increase food intake.

In addition to these two circuits, a vast array of other neuropeptides have been shown to influence food intake. A fraction of these are listed in Table 1. Corticotropin-releasing hormone (CRH) and the closely related peptide, urocortin, might also have a role in the control of food intake. CRH agonists decrease

TABLE 1
Effects of Various Factors on Food Intake, the Sympathetic Nervous System, and Reproductive Processes[a]

	Food intake	Sympathetic nervous system and/or energy availability	Reproduction
Sensory stimuli			
Food deprivation	↑	↓	↓
2DG	↑	↓	↓
MP/MA	↑	↓	↓
2,5-AM	↑	↓	↓
Central peptides			
AgRP	↑	↓	↓
α-MSH	↓	↑	- - -↑
Bombesin-like peptides	↓	↑	↑
β-endorphin	↑	↓	↓
CART	↓	↑	↑
CCK	↓	↑	↑
CRH	↓	↑	↓
Galanin	↑	↓	↑ ↓
Glucagon-like peptide	↓	↓	↑
MCH	↑	↓	↓ ↑
Motilin	↑	- - -	↓
NPY	↑	↓	↓ ↑
Orexin	↑	↑	↓ ↑
TRH	↓	↑	↑
Urocortin	↓	- - -	↓
Vasopressin	↓	↑	↓
Peripheral hormones			
CCK	↓	↑	↑
Glucagon	↓	↑	↓ ↑
Glucocorticoids	↑	↓	↓
Insulin (high doses)	↑	↓	↓
Insulin (low doses ICV)	↓	- - -	↑
Leptin	↓	↑	↑
Thyroid hormone	↑	↑	↑ ↓

[a] Most of the factors that influence food intake also affect sympathetic activity, the availability of oxidizable metabolic fuels, and reproductive processes. Up arrows indicate increased food intake, increased sympathetic outflow to brown adipose tissue, increased availability of oxidizable metabolic fuels, or facilitation of LH pulses or sex behavior. Down arrows indicate a decrease. Peptides that increase food intake, such as NPY, galanin, MCH and, orexin, have both inhibitory and facilitory effects on pulsatile LH secretion depending on the dose and steroid mileau. The information was compiled from a variety of review articles (Bray and York, 1999; Crawley, 1999; Geary, 1999; Glass *et al.*, 1999; Heinrichs and Richard, 1999; I'Anson *et al.*, 1991; Kalra *et al.*, 1998; Langhans and Hrupka, 1999; Merali *et al.*, 1999; Ritter *et al.*, 1999; G. P. Smith, 1999; Tritos and Maratos-Flier, 1999; Van Dijk and Thiele, 1999; Schneider and Wade, 2000; Schneider *et al.*, 2000b), and from research articles (MacLusky *et al.*, 2000; Parent *et al.*, 2000; Pinski *et al.*, 1992; Pu *et al.*, 1998; Tsukamura *et al.*, 2000; J.-L. Wang *et al.*, 2000; Whitley *et al.*, 2000).

food intake in a wide variety of species, including sheep, pigs, mice, rats, guinea pigs, birds, and fish (reviewed by Heinrichs and Richard, 1999). CRH has two identified receptor subtypes, CRHr1 and CRHr2. CRH gene expression is increased by leptin treatment and decreased by glucocorticoid treatment (Mercer *et al.*, 1996). CRH-induced reductions in food intake are also accompanied by anxiogenesis, other stress-associated responses, and formation of conditioned taste aversion. The more recently discovered CRF-family ligand, urocortin, however, reduces food intake at doses that do not produce anxiogenic effects and also fails to support a conditioned taste aversion (Benoit *et al.*, 2000). Urocortin-like immunoreactivity in the supraoptic nucleus is decreased after 48 hr of food deprivation and increased after water deprivation (Hara *et al.*, 1997). Thus, it has been suggested that urocortin might be more specifically involved in normal control of satiety.

The vast majority of research on the molecular biology of these peptides examines the amount of food eaten (food intake), but does not distinguish between consumption of food and the drive to eat (the appetitive or motivational aspects of eating). Furthermore, the subject animals are housed singly, removed from any social context. Other data, however, support the idea that central NPY influences only appetitive aspects of behavior. In experiments designed to distinguish between these two aspects of ingestion, food deprivation and its associated increase in NPY release or treatment with NPY increases behaviors related to food procurement without changing consummatory aspects of ingestive behavior (e.g., Ammar *et al.*, 2000; Bartness and Clein, 1994; Seeley *et al.*, 1995). Furthermore, NPY treatment in rats increases behaviors related to food procurement and results in inhibited sex behavior in the presence of a palatable liquid (Ammar *et al.*, 2000). Conversely, the putative inhibitory circuits, such as those mediated by the adipocyte hormone leptin, increases the probability of choosing sex behavior over food searching, again without decreasing the consummatory aspects of ingestive behavior (Ammar *et al.*, 2000). In order to understand the function of each of the central peptides related to ingestive behavior, it is necessary to examine both the appetitive and consummatory aspects of behavior as well as ingestive behavior within a social context.

The adaptive significance of a putative feeding-stimulatory circuit is obvious. It brings metabolic fuels, nutrients, water, salt, and other minerals into the digestive tract and serves to maintain salt and water balance, maintain cell structure, promote tissue growth and differentiation, and maintain a supply of energy for cellular processes, movement, and thermogenesis. These functions are critical for survival, but these functions alone do not lead to the perpetuation of the species and evolutionary adaptation. Given that adaptation is defined in terms of differential reproductive success, the critical function of food intake is to optimize reproductive success under fluctuating energetic conditions. In many species, food intake is positively correlated with the energetic demands associated with reproductive activity. Reproduction is energetically expensive relative to other activities, due to the structural and energetic needs of the developing offspring, as well as those of the mother and her own growing and differentiating reproductive organs. In mammals, the energetic demands of lactation are the most costly in the females' repertoire, and hyperphagia during lactation is common, even in species that do not show increases in food intake at other times. In small mammals that bear multiple rapidly developing offspring, food intake triples at its peak during lactation relative to prepregnant intake. Even in birds, reproduction incurs critical energetic costs due to their high metabolic rate and other costs related to their volant lifestyle (reviewed by Ball and Bentley, 2000). In many bird species, the cost of feeding young chicks with crop milk or captured food is so high that it requires the full participation of both parents. In this respect, it is interesting that the anabolic peptide NPY, a neuropeptide whose synthesis and secretion are elevated during lactation and other energetic challenges, has been one of the most evolutionarily conserved peptides for its size in the animal kingdom (Larhammar, 1996).

It is commonly presumed that food intake is inhibited in order to avoid obesity. The increase in obesity associated with a release from energetic challenges (such as harsh ambient temperatures, low food availability, and requirements for physical work) argue against this hypothesis. Other considerations suggest that inhibitory controls are more closely related to other aspects of survival and reproduction. Once food procurement and intake have taken place so as to meet the present energy demand and to build a supply of stored energy (body fat or food caches), food intake must be inhibited in order to take advantage of these stored fuels. In some species, these activities take place between daily mealtimes. In other species such as elephant seals and emperor penguins, ingested food is used, the excess stored as fat, and then food intake is inhibited for up to 3 months of competition for mates and breeding (reviewed by Groscolas, 1990; Mrosovsky and Sherry, 1980). Food intake resumes at the end of the breeding period when stored fuels are all but exhausted. When ground squirrels encounter cold ambient temperatures accompanied by low food availability and short day length, food intake is inhibited during an extended period of hibernation (Mrosovsky and Sherry, 1980). On awakening from hibernation, these animals are predisposed toward courtship and mating, despite being at the nadir of body-fat content. The evidence to date suggests that hibernators share similarities in the feeding-stimulatory and -inhibitory neural circuits, such as those mediated by NPY and galanin (Boswell *et al.*, 1993). These similarities do not explain the behavioral differences between hibernators and nonhibernators. Thus, it must be postulated that still other circuits play a dominant role in control of reproduction and food intake in hibernating species. When water availability is limiting, food intake is inhibited to conserve water and salt balance. Dehydration-induced anorexia nevertheless results in a fall in plasma leptin and stimulates the central neural circuits (e.g., neurons that synthesize and secrete neuropeptide Y) that under normal circumstances induce hunger and initiate food ingestion. The continued anorexia in the face of low leptin levels and increased NPY gene expression and secretion is due to an additional neural pathway that inhibits eating by overriding NPY and other feeding-stimulatory circuits (Watts, 2000, 2001b). If we wish to understand inhibition of food intake, progress might be facilitated by more attention to the mechanisms that are most closely linked to survival and reproductive success.

Primary sensory stimuli arise from the taste, smell, and texture of food; gastric distension and contraction; or stimuli generated by the oxidation of metabolic fuels. An episode of eating, a meal, is initiated in part by orosensory stimuli and the learned context in which food has previously been presented. These stimuli are sufficient to start a meal, presumably in the absence of postingestive cues (Weingarten, 1983), although the

efficacy of orosensory and contextual cues in meal initiation has not been tested using every conceivable measure of endogenous energy status. The effects of orosensory stimuli can be observed by looking at changes in ingestive behavior (e.g., the number of licks per unit time) that occur prior to postingestive events (digestion, absorption, etc.). For example, when different concentrations of sucrose are offered to rats and the lick rate is measured for 30 seconds, the number of licks per 30-second period is significantly positively correlated with the concentration of the sucrose solution, suggesting that gustatory, rather than postingestive, sensations are responsible for the concentration-dependent changes in behavior (reviewed by J. C. Smith, 2000). New methods of studying the microstructure of the ingestion of foods with varying degrees of palatability over the long term promise new insights into the interactions between orosensory, postingestive, and circadian signals.

The size of the meal or the termination of the meal is thought to be controlled in part by a sensory system that detects the presence or absence of food in the gastrointestinal tract. Afferent fibers in the gastrointestinal tract are sensitive to a variety of sensory events, such as mechanical distention of the lumen or gut contraction and chemical properties of the luminal contents, and these are mediated via the vagus nerve (for a particularly thorough review, see G. J. Schwartz, 2000). Gastric loads confined to the stomach suppress meal size as a function of volume, independent of nutrient content. For the most part, these signals affect only meal size. Food intake, however, is a function of the size of the meal as well as the number of meals per unit time. The mechanisms that control food intake serve the need to maintain fuels adequate for survival and reproduction, and thus it follows that a sensory system monitors some aspect of energy metabolism and conveys this information to the effector system or motor program that controls ingestion. Primary metabolic sensory stimuli result from the oxidation of glucose and free fatty acids (FFAs). Both of these metabolic pathways contribute to the formation of adenosine triphosphate (ATP), the energy currency of cells. Mounting evidence suggests that changes in food intake result from metabolic sensory stimuli generated by changes in this final common pathway in oxidative metabolism (reviewed by Friedman, 1998). As discussed later in this chapter, these postingestive gastric and metabolic stimuli are thought to be detected peripherally in liver and conveyed by the vagus nerve (G. J. Schwartz, 2000; Tordoff *et al.,* 1991; Ritter *et al.,* 1994; Ritter and Taylor, 1989) or detected in the CNS (Levin *et al.,* 1999; Ritter and Taylor, 1989).

In contrast to these primary sensory events, hormones and other peptides secreted into the bloodstream are categorized as mediators because their levels in plasma change in response to the sensory stimuli. Thus, plasma levels of these chemical messengers convey information from sensory events to the effector system. The chemical messengers that influence food intake, like those that influence sex behavior, do not act as triggers or terminators of behavior. Rather, they provide a milieu or context that changes the probability that a particular behavior will occur by modulating metabolic stimuli, altering the perception of sensory stimuli, or acting at various nodes of integration in the CNS.

Sex hormones illustrate the contrast between hormonal modulators and hormonal triggers. For example, male-typical levels of testosterone do not trigger male copulatory behavior. They simply increase the probability that mating will occur in the presence of a sexually motivated female. In some species, but not all, elevated levels of sex hormones are critical for the occurrence of sex behavior. Copulatory behavior continues even after gonadectomy in sexually experienced individuals of many different species. Thus, the sex drive exists without hormonal stimulation. In many species, the hormones that control fertility, such as the ovarian steroids, have become coopted during evolution to increase the probability that sex behavior occurs during the time when fertilization is likely to be successful. For example, in rodents, the hormones that are critical for ovulation, estradiol and progesterone, also increase female sexual motivation and the incidence of mating behavior. Furthermore, the specific hormones that facilitate the occurrence of female-typical sex behavior differ among species. In some species estradiol and progesterone are critical, whereas in others androgens or glucocorticoids are critical for the synchronization of sex behavior and ovulation (Rissman *et al.,* 1990). Similarly, male-typical sex behavior is influenced by either estrogens, androgens, or progesterone, or by none of these steroids, depending on the species. During evolution, progesterone has been coadapted to facilitate male-typical behavior in certain species that lack testosterone (reviewed by Crews, 2000). In addition, mammalian sex behavior

is influenced by a vast array of other hormones, neuropeptides, and neuromodulators.

Similarly, the reproductive hormones have been coadapted to modulate ingestive behavior in service of survival and subsequent reproductive success. Hormones increase the probability of eating when fuels are needed, but the drive exists apart from hormones. The motivation to eat can be elicited directly by changes in fuel availability without changes in hormones. The hormones differ from species to species. In at least some species, the hormones of pregnancy and lactation have been coadapted to facilitate increases in food intake. For example, circulating levels of progesterone rise dramatically during pregnancy and estradiol levels rise to a lesser extent. Lactation, in contrast, is characterized by high levels of the anterior pituitary hormone, prolactin. In ovariectomized female rats, treatment with moderate levels of estradiol and high levels of progesterone increases food intake. Furthermore, there is a dose-dependent increase in food intake with prolactin treatment in ovariectomized females primed with estradiol (Gerardo-Gettens *et al.,* 1989a,b). Changes in levels of hormones, however, do not fully account for the changes in food intake. The increases in food intake during lactation are of a greater magnitude than those induced by exogenous hormone treatment. These hormones influence food intake when microinfused directly into the brain, and yet no one would argue that they are the primary sensory signals for energy availability and oxidation. Rather, they inform the brain about the reproductive state of the animal, and enhance the occurrence of behavioral and metabolic adjustments that are appropriate for that phase of reproduction in that particular species. During lactation, when vast amounts of energy are diverted toward milk production, powerful interosensory signals arise directly from changes in energy status in the mother's central nervous or periphery, and these are more likely to account for the dramatic increases in food intake. The hormones of pregnancy act in concert with or accentuate the primary metabolic sensory signals that arise from the energetic demands of reproduction. What's more, the metabolic sensory signals and the hormonal mediators affect not only food intake, but also the partitioning of stored energy, and there are species differences in the way these hormones modulate food intake, storage and, expenditure (reviewed by Wade and Schneider, 1992).

In addition to the reproductive hormones, chemical messengers secreted in the periphery that modulate ingestive behavior include amylin, catecholamines, CCK, glucagon, glucocorticoids, insulin, leptin, thyroid hormone, and many others. Some of these are secreted in response to gastric distension or nutrient contact with the gut (reviewed by G. J. Schwartz, 2000). Others, such as leptin and insulin, are secreted in response to the availability of oxidizable fuels or to adipocyte filling or both (Levy *et al.,* 2000; Matschinsky, 1996; Mueller *et al.,* 1998; Newgard and McGarry, 1995; J. Wang *et al.,* 1998). Because their synthesis is coupled to substrate metabolism, it can be argued that the levels of these peptides are in a position to inform the brain about fuel that is available for oxidation and as well as the amount of fuel in storage, thus allowing the animals to set priorities for behavioral activities. Whether the animal makes use of this information depends on the species, the season, the phase of reproduction, and whether there are more pressing needs related to survival (Schneider *et al.,* 1998; Schneider and Zhou, 1999a).

It has been demonstrated that shifts in metabolic fuel use can trigger the central effector system directly without affecting the hormonal mediators. For example, the hyperphagia and increased NPY secretion that is typical of diabetic rats can be ameliorated by a shift from carbohydrate to FFA use by feeding diabetic rats a high-fat diet (Chavez *et al.,* 1998; Ji and Friedman, 2000). The lack of diabetic hyperphagia in high-fat-fed rats is more closely associated with changes in hepatic energy status than with changes in plasma leptin (Ji and Friedman, 2000). These experiments demonstrate that metabolic sensory stimuli can override the effects of hormones and neuropeptides on ingestive behavior. Virtually every diet aid or antiobesity treatment on the market eventually leads to a plateau in body weight, after which no more weight can be lost, and body weight is usually regained after the termination of the treatment. Thus, attention to mechanisms that override or counteract the effects of chemical messengers is imperative for understanding the control of daily food intake and obesity.

Investigators from the Bourne Laboratory have suggested that it might be useful to classify factors that influence food intake as either direct or indirect controls, that is, direct or indirect with respect to the feed-

ing motor program contained in the caudal hindbrain (G. P. Smith, 1999). The putative direct controls (e.g., CCK and gastric distension) induce changes in the feeding motor program in the decerebrate animal, whereas the indirect controls (e.g., learned cues) require intact connections between the hindbrain and the rest of the brain. This anatomical distinction might have heuristic value because it emphasizes the importance of the caudal hindbrain in control of food intake. However, the terminology is most certainly counterproductive. The terms "direct" and "indirect" are useful only when they are defined with respect to a particular locus in the brain and body, just as the terms "afferent" and "efferent" are meaningful only when qualified with respect to a particular locus. For example, important questions arise as to whether various hormones influence feeding by acting directly on receptors in a particular hypothalamic nucleus or indirectly by changing peripheral hormone secretion or fuel metabolism. Whether the hindbrain is involved or not, the term "direct" is used to describe action on any part of the brain or body. Thus, in this chapter, the terms "direct" and "indirect," like the terms "afferent" and "efferent," will be used as needed with respect to many different specific loci, not just the caudal hindbrain.

Still other investigators have categorized factors that influence food intake as long term or short term. Stimuli generated by gastric distension, increased intracellular fuel oxidation, and hepatic energy status are the putative short-term signals. In contrast, changes in hormonal mediators are categorized as long-term signals that allow the regulation of food intake in service of maintaining a particular level of adiposity. This terminology might be misleading because the short duration of the increase in food intake in response to metabolic inhibitors might be an artifact of these experimental treatments (for further discussion, see Friedman, 1990). As we discuss later, some data suggest that these so-called short-term metabolic signals contribute to long-term body-weight regulation (Ji and Friedman, 2000; Levin *et al.,* 1999), demonstrating that metabolic sensory signals have long-term consequences. The distinction between long term and short term might be a stumbling block if it deters the investigation of a particular class of stimuli simply because exogenous treatments used to mimic these stimuli change food intake for hours instead of weeks.

The following sections illustrate that food intake is reciprocally linked to energy storage and expenditure. If the fundamental sensory stimuli that control food intake are generated by changes in the oxidation of metabolic fuels, then any internal secretion that influences energy expenditure and storage indirectly influences food intake. In this context, it is imperative to note that nearly every internal secretion that influences food intake also influences the sympathetic nervous system and, hence, the digestive process, fuel partitioning, fuel oxidation, or energy expenditure, including the energy expended for reproductive processes (Table 1). Even when these substances are microinfused directly to CNS nuclei, they influence autonomic function, which in turn influences peripheral hormone secretion, fuel metabolism, gut emptying and energy expenditure. For example, central treatment with NPY increases food intake in sated rats and also results in elevated corticosteroid and insulin secretion, two events that promote energy storage as fat. A predisposition toward energy storage is a condition that can result in a deficit in the availability of oxidizable metabolic fuels, and this, in turn, might produce a deficit in ATP for cellular work. A deficit in liver ATP is a potent stimulus for hyperphagia, and rats with diet-induced obesity show a lower hepatic energy status than obesity-resistant rats. This is just one example of an experimental treatment (ICV NPY) that appears to induce obesity by stimulating the feeding motor program directly, but which in fact probably influences both food intake and body weight indirectly, via peripheral effects on energy storage. One of the greatest challenges in studying ingestive behavior is differentiating between the effects that occur by the direct action of chemical messengers on effector systems and the effects that occur by changing peripheral fuel metabolism, which then feeds back on the central effector system. Furthermore, the hypotheses developed using single-gene mutants, genetic knockout animals and DNA microarrays must be tested in ecologically relevant social contexts and with regard to both the consummatory and appetitive aspects of ingestion.

B. Storage

The three most important energy storage compartments in mammals are the gastrointestinal tract, the adipose tissue depot, and tissues such as liver and muscle.

The gastrointestinal tract is a relatively short-term storage compartment and accounts for only a small amount of the energy in the body relative to the adipose tissue depots. Food is emptied from the gut in a matter of hours in most species. After a meal, excess fuels from the digestive tract are rapidly sequestered as glycogen in the liver and muscle and as triglycerides in adipose tissue. In many species, the stomach has emptied by the end of the sleep period, at the start of the daily activity period. The exceptions are the ruminants and certain other animals that use gut fermentation as a source of metabolic fuel. In these animals, intestinal flora living in special gut compartments use the carbohydrates ingested by the host in a fermentation process. These bacteria release medium-chain fatty acids as a by-product of fermentation. The fatty acids are absorbed by the gut, enter the host's circulation, and are either oxidized or stored. Thus, depletion of the gastrointestinal store of metabolic fuels may be prolonged in members of fermenting species.

When the gastrointestinal tract is empty, the body must rely on metabolic fuels stored in liver, muscle, and fat as reserve energy sources. The principal fuels used by most monogastric vertebrates including human beings are glucose, FFAs, and ketone bodies. Lactate, pyruvate, and amino acids play important roles in intermediate metabolism. Muscle glycogen is metabolized primarily in support of local muscle energy expenditure, whereas the breakdown of liver glycogen helps maintain levels of circulating glucose for all tissues, but in particular for cells in the CNS. Liver glycogen is also considered a short-term energy source because it can be depleted in less than a day in most species in the absence of food intake. Glycogen turnover in the brain is more rapid than in the periphery; however, glycogen turnover in the brain is enhanced in areas where adjacent neural activity is increased. In these short time periods (one-half hour to 1 hour), it has been suggested that glycogen supplies fuels to brain cells when glucose is in short supply (Swanson *et al.*, 1992). Neurons grown in astrocyte cultures are impaired less severely by glucose withdrawal than neurons grown in cultures without astrocytes (Swanson and Choi, 1993). Evidence suggests that astrocyte glycogen content effects the neurophysiolgical function of axons in the absence of glucose (Wender *et al.*, 2000).

The fat component is by far the largest energy storage depot. For example, adult men contain on the average 140,000 kcal energy in total body fat, six times the kilocalories stored as protein and almost 200 times the energy stored as carbohydrate (including carbohydrates stored as tissue glycogen and circulating glucose). Survival during food deprivation or anorexia requires that FFAs and glycerol be hydrolyzed from triglycerides in the lipid components of adipocytes. FFAs are transported into mitochondria, where they are used as fuels via β-oxidation in a variety of peripheral tissues (e.g., muscle, pancreas, and brown adipose tissue). FFAs are also mobilized to the liver where they are either oxidized or used in the formation of ketone bodies. A significant increase in plasma ketone bodies results from food deprivation or even mild food restriction. During prolonged starvation, lean mass is metabolized, and amino acids and glycerol are used in gluconeogenesis, the synthesis of new glucose. Most peripheral cells require insulin for glucose uptake, whereas most cells in the CNS do not require the presence of insulin. Thus, during fasting peripheral cells tend to use FFAs, whereas CNS cells tend to use glucose. During prolonged food deprivation, the brain can adjust to chronically low glucose availability by the use of ketone bodies (acetoacetate and β-hydroxy-butyrate) for as much as 50–60% of its energy requirements. The shift to ketone use requires prolonged exposure to these substrates.

A variety of chemical messengers influence the deposition and breakdown of white adipose tissue (WAT) by acting in either the brain or periphery. Epinephrine from the adrenal medulla acts as a plasma hormone to stimulate WAT blood flow and lipolysis of WAT triglycerides. It has been convincingly demonstrated, however, that lipolysis in WAT is controlled by both epinephrine and norepinephrine (NE) acting as neurotransmitters from sympathetic nerves. For example, in rats exposed to cold ambient temperatures, WAT NE turnover and plasma FFA concentrations increase, and these responses are not blocked by adrenal demedullation (Garofalo et al., 1996). In addition, plasma FFAs and glucose are increased in response to treatment with drugs that inhibit fuel oxidation. Adrenalectomy in dogs and adrenal demedullation in rats fail to block increases in lipolysis mediated by metabolic inhibitors (Goldfien et al., 1966; Teixeira et al., 1973). Mechanisms in the hypothalamus and caudal hindbrain are involved. WAT receives substantial cholaminergic input from the caudal brain stem, which is directly influenced by projections from the midbrain and hypothalamic areas, and WAT innervation is critical for changes in adiposity that occur in response to hormones, circadian rhythms, and environmental changes (Bamshad et al., 1998; Lazzarini and Wade, 1991; reviewed by Bartness and Bamshad, 1998). The hyperglycemic response to inhibitors of glucose oxidation occur in animals in which the caudal hindbrain has been surgically disconnected from the rest of the brain, and the application of inhibitors of glucose oxidation directly into specific nuclei in the caudal hindbrain trigger compensatory sympathoadrenal response and consequent hyperglycemia (DiRocco and Grill, 1979). The results emphasize that role of a metabolic sensory system that monitors fuel availability and controls the mobilization of fuels from storage.

Four subtypes of adrenergic receptors are involved in the control of lipolysis by catecholamines—α_2- and β_{1-3}-adrenoreceptors (reviewed by Lafontan, 1994a; Lafontan and Berlan, 1995; Lafontan et al., 1995). Both epinephrine and NE act as agonists to the adrenoreceptors. In experiments using specific receptor agonists, the activation of the three β-adrenoreceptor subtypes stimulates lipolysis, whereas the activation of the α_2-adrenoreceptor inhibits it. The roles of the three β-adrenoreceptors vary with species, sex, and the particular location of WAT depots. It is thought that, in response to natural secretion of catecholamines, lipolysis is stimulated when β-adrenoreceptor activation predominates, whereas lipolysis is inhibited when α_2-adrenoreceptor activation predominates.

Lipids are stored in discrete depots distributed throughout the body, and there are sex differences in WAT distribution. Women are more likely to store WAT in the lower body in subcutaneous depots of the hips, thighs, and buttocks. Changes in the balance of α- and β-adrenoreceptors predispose subcutaneous WAT toward triglyceride synthesis in response to the hormones of pregnancy and toward hydrolization and mobilization of FFAs and glycerol in response to the hormones of lactation (Rebuffe-Scrive et al., 1987). In addition, there are species differences in the responsiveness of WAT lipolysis to the hormones of pregnancy and lactation (reviewed by Wade and Schneider, 1992).

In contrast to the female pattern of fat distribution, men tend to store more fat in the upper body, particularly in the intraabdominal visceral area. Of these two patterns of fat storage, only upper-body intraabdominal obesity is associated with cardiovascular disease, insulin resistance, and late-onset diabetes in both men and women with this pattern (Kissebah and Krakower, 1994). Differences in WAT sensitivity to catecholamines are thought to play a role in obesity. For example, women with male-typical intraabdominal and visceral obesity show an attenuated sensitivity to epinephrine in upper-body but not in lower-body subcutaneous WAT, and this results in significantly lower whole-body lipolytic sensitivity to epinephrine (Horowitz and Klein, 2000).

Hormones play an important role in fuel partitioning during and after meals. During the preabsorptive phase of a meal, the sight, smell, and taste of food triggers a neural reflex that results in insulin and glucagon release during the first few minutes of a meal. This cephalic phase of insulin secretion declines unless the meal continues. Subsequent to the cephalic phase, the absorptive phase of eating is characterized by further insulin release facilitated by increased plasma glucose levels and the secretion of gut peptides (e.g., CCK, gastrin, and secretin), released in response to the arrival of nutrients.

Most of the chemical messengers that influence food intake also influence energy storage. In general, those that increase food intake are anabolic (i.e., they result in a net increase in energy storage). Those present in the central effector system include AgRP, GHRH, MCH, NPY, opiates, and orexin. For example, central treatment with NPY results in reduced sympathetic activity to peripheral tissues involved in energy expenditure and elevation of the levels of hormones that promote energy storage. ICV NPY treatment increases glucocorticoid and insulin secretion (Zarjevski *et al.*, 1993). A predisposition toward energy storage is a condition that can result in a deficit in the availability of oxidizable metabolic fuels, and this, in turn, might produce a deficit in ATP for cellular work. A deficit in liver ATP is a potent stimulus for hyperphagia, and rats with diet-induced obesity show a lower hepatic energy status than obesity resistant rats (Ji and Friedman, 2000). This is just one example of an experimental treatment (ICV NPY) that was originally thought to induce obesity by stimulating the feeding motor program directly, but which in fact probably influences body weight indirectly, via peripheral effects on energy storage.

Anabolic peripheral hormones include insulin when this hormone is administered peripherally in high doses. Conversely, those central peptides that decrease food intake are catabolic, including α-MSH, bombesin, CCK, CRH, glucagon-like peptide (GLP-1), serotonin, somatostatin, and thyrotropin-releasing hormone TRH. Adipocyte leptin is a peripherally secreted catabolic hormone that increases the oxidation of metabolic fuels and prevents triglyceride formation. The catabolic action of leptin occurs in peripheral tissues, such as the pancreas, liver, and skeletal muscle. However, the application of leptin to the brain (especially the VMH) also increases peripheral thermogenesis and fuel oxidation.

Insulin, glucagon, somatostatin, and leptin are hormones that govern energy partitioning. Insulin, secreted when plasma glucose levels are high, promotes uptake of glucose from circulation in peripheral tissues. Glucagon, secreted when plasma glucose is low, is important for hydrolyzation and mobilization of metabolic fuels from storage depots, whereas somatostatin inhibits the secretion of both insulin and glucagon. The *ob* protein, leptin, is synthesized in and secreted from adipocytes along with insulin when plasma glucose is high. More accurately, stimulus-secretion coupling in pancreas and adipocytes occurs in response to an increase in levels of intracellular glucose oxidation (Levy *et al.*, 2000; Matschinsky, 1996; Mueller *et al.*, 1998; Newgard and McGarry, 1995; J. Wang *et al.*, 1998). Insulin is essential for glucose uptake and triglyceride formation in all peripheral tissues (e.g., WAT, liver, pancreas, and muscle), and thus its main function is to move glucose to where it is used or stored. However, the unopposed accumulation of lipid in nonadipose tissue would rapidly lead to insulin resistance. This adverse consequence of lipid accumulation is not due to triglycerides per se but rather the intracellular excess of acyl-CoA that is thought to provide substrate for potentially destructive nonoxidative pathways such as *de novo* ceramide formation and lipid peroxidation. To prevent the toxic effects of lipid accumulation in nonadipose tissue, leptin is secreted along with insulin to inhibit triglyceride formation and increase β-oxidation and thermogenesis (Unger, 2000).

It has been suggested that insulin and leptin inform the CNS of the size of adipose tissue depots (Campfield *et al.,* 1995; Kaiyala *et al.,* 1995; Schwartz *et al.,* 1991). Contrary to this notion, obesity occurs in many populations of animals without mutations in the genes that encode either the protein or receptor, and these obese individuals show elevated endogenous levels of insulin, leptin, and glucocorticoids that apparently fail to induce satiety and prevent obesity. It is unlikely that the adaptive function of these hormones is to prevent obesity (adaptive function is defined as the trait that confers differential reproductive success). It is more likely that these hormones increase the availability of fuels in tissues where they are oxidized and prevent the accumulation of fuels in tissues where they would promote insulin resistance. In addition, the sex hormones estradiol and progesterone act in both brain and periphery to influence lipolysis and triglyceride synthesis (reviewed by Wade and Schneider, 1992). Again, the primary role of these hormones is not to prevent obesity, but to optimize reproductive success.

Many species show a remarkable ability to defend overall body adiposity in response to diets and surgical treatments that decrease adiposity. For example, after the surgical excision of specific WAT depots (lipectomy), animals reliably regain their presurgery level of adiposity by increasing food intake or decreasing metabolic rate or both (Fried *et al.,* 1986; Hamilton and Wade, 1988; Mauer and Bartness, 1995; Weber *et al.,* 2000). It is tempting to speculate that the mechanisms that control food intake operate in service of maintaining an optimal body weight or body fat content, a putative set point. The utility of this set point hypothesis is limited, however, because it fails to generate testable hypotheses (i.e., there is no outcome that falsifies the hypothesis). Any factor that increases adiposity is usually said to raise the set point; thus there is no outcome of any experimental manipulation that falsifies the existence of the set point. It is more useful to examine the regrowth of adipose tissue in terms of testable hypotheses that can be used to guide medical and cosmetic treatments for obesity. One such testable idea is that subcutaneous WAT might be protective against lipoprotein abnormalities associated with insulin resistance (Terry *et al.,* 1991). For example, when subcutaneous WAT depots are removed from healthy Syrian hamsters, compensatory growth occurs in visceral and abdominal WAT depots. Lipectomized hamsters develop hypertriglyceridemia and insulin resistance on

regaining their previous body weight and fat content in the visceral area. The disturbing conclusion is that after subcutaneous lipectomy in hamsters (and perhaps liposuction in women), whole-body adiposity is restored, with a redistribution toward visceral-abdominal obesity, the phenotype most closely linked to cardiovascular disease, insulin resistance, and late-onset diabetes (Weber *et al.,* 2000).

Over one-third, and by some estimates up to 50%, of adults in the United States, Canada, and the western European countries are obese, having a BMI of 25 kg/m^2. In some population subgroups, the percentage of individuals who are obese is more than 70% (Flegal *et al.,* 1998). The prevalence of overweight individuals seems less surprising from an evolutionary perspective. According to the idea of evolution by natural selection, the optimal range of body weights is defined by the minimum and maximum body weights that allow reproductive success. In many species, reproduction is adversely affected only at the extremes of body weight, as long as individuals can use energy from their diets or from their energy stores. If during evolutionary history there has been little reproductive consequence to maintenance of a particular body weight, it is not surprising that body weight varies considerably among individuals within the population. Given that subcutaneous fat is stored in response to the hormones of pregnancy, the fuels from these depots are used during lactation, and these depots protect against insulin-resistance, it is no wonder that human females are predisposed toward subcutaneous lipid accumulation. Furthermore, after individuals have raised reproductively competent offspring, there is virtually no selection pressure to maintain a particular body weight or fat content. Evolutionary considerations predict that the narrow range of ideal or healthy body weight, as defined by medical professionals or fashion designers, will not be maintained, especially by individuals who have survived beyond their reproductive years.

One of the evolutionary advantages of the maintenance of heritable variation within populations or within species is that it allows adaptation to fluctuating environmental conditions (as far as natural selection leads to changes in gene frequency of populations). During ages when energy availability is low and energetic demands high, selection might be expected to favor individuals who are fuel efficient and able to store what little energy is available as body fat. When energy availability is high and demand low, reproductive success would be compromised only if the excessive body weight were so extreme that it precluded some aspect of reproduction or survival, such as predator avoidance or migration. For example, large fat depots are maladaptive in birds that fly (e.g., arctic terns) compared to those that do not (e.g., penguins). In many populations, a large degree of heritable variance in body weights has been essential for adaptation to fluctuating energetic conditions. It has been observed that in laboratory rodents, domestic animals, and human beings body weight is a quantitative trait (i.e., it displays continuous variation characteristic of a trait influenced by many genes). Modern molecular analysis of quantitative trait loci (QTLs) has estimated that there are approximately 70 independent loci that influence body weight in mice, and thus there are likely to be many genes in which allelic variation can account for body weight differences (Barsh *et al.,* 2000). Environmental factors acting throughout development of the individual interact with these genetic factors. In some species, body weight and adiposity change reliably with changes in photoperiod (daylength) and these changes in body weight are achieved by changes in food intake, metabolism, or both. In keeping with a biological perspective, this chapter is concerned primarily with mechanisms that allow differential reproductive success and not with purported mechanisms that maintain body weight set point.

As mentioned in Section IIIA, changes in energy storage cause changes in body weight and adiposity, and these changes generate stimuli that influence food intake. If some types of obesity result from a propensity toward fuel storage, it might be accompanied by deficits in the availability of fuels for intracellular oxidation, and low intracellular energy status would generate signals that increase hunger and food intake. Unlike the hypothesis that obesity increases the body weight set point, the hypothesis that obesity results from a deficit in oxidizable metabolic fuels is testable (the hypothesis would be falsified if obesity-prone individuals had normal energy status in peripheral tissues). Consistent with this hypothesis, rats prone toward diet-induced obesity show lower baseline hepatic energy status than rats resistant to diet-induced obesity (Ji and Friedman, 2000). Furthermore, when individuals exhibit an extreme pre-

disposition toward energy storage, the availability of metabolic fuels for oxidation might be compromised to the extent that energetically costly processes such as reproductive and immune function are compromised. This is exemplified by anestrus induced by insulin treatment in hamsters that are limited to the food intake of saline-treated controls, but not induced in insulin-treated hamsters that are allowed to overeat (Wade *et al.,* 1991). More research should be aimed at the effects of fuel partitioning and metabolic energy deficits on food intake. In general, research on hyperphagia, obesity, and reproduction must consider the reciprocal interactions between energy, storage, and energy intake.

C. Expenditure

Very few of the experimental treatments and natural stimuli that increase body weight and adiposity do so without affecting energy expenditure. A long list of lesions and neuropeptide and hormone treatments that increase food intake also increase body weight and adiposity, even when the increase in food intake is prevented (Himms-Hagen, 1989). Conversely, animals treated with anorexic agents often lose more body weight and adiposity than can be accounted for by the decrease in food intake. Changes in energy storage in the face of stable food intake must be mediated by changes in energy expenditure. This section introduces the various aspects of energy expenditure.

In most animals, fuels and oxygen are converted to carbon dioxide, water, heat, and work on the environment. The heat and work that result from this conversion make up the animal's total energy expenditure. Thermogenesis, the generation of heat, is due to exothermic chemical reactions involved in metabolism (obligatory thermogenesis) plus the thermogenesis required to maintain body temperature (cold-induced thermogenesis) and the thermogenesis incurred by diet (diet-induced thermogenesis). Cold- and diet-induced thermogenesis are often collectively referred to as adaptive or facultative thermogenesis. When an organism is at rest, not performing work on the environment, energy expenditure is directly measured as thermogenesis. Resting energy expenditure is often measured indirectly as the amount of oxygen consumed.

When animals encounter food shortages, they increase work related to the procurement of food and conserve energy by decreasing their metabolic rate at rest. Food deprivation reduces sympathetic activity and consequently reduces blood pressure, heart rate, and basal metabolic rate (Daly *et al.,* 1992; Ernsberger and Nelson, 1988; Landsberg and Young, 1981; Overton *et al.,* 1997; Saris, 1995; VanNess *et al.,* 1997; Young and Landsberg, 1977). The significant reduction in blood pressure, heart rate, and energy expenditure occurs during both the light and dark phases and is independent of changes in eating, drinking, and locomotor activity (T. D. Williams *et al.,* 2000). Decreased metabolic rate is an evolutionary adaptation that conserves energy in environments with unpredictable food supplies, but is also an obstacle to successful dieting. It is not surprising then that reduced resting metabolic rate is a predictor of future obesity. Age-matched individuals whose resting metabolic rate per kilogram lean body mass is below normal are at a significantly higher risk for becoming obese during a subsequent 4-year period (Ravussin *et al.,* 1988). Formerly obese women who have lost body fat content through calorie restriction exhibit resting metabolic rates per kilogram lean body mass approximately 15% lower than women who have never been overweight (Geissler *et al.,* 1987). Many (but not all) of the factors that increase food intake also inhibit sympathetic activity (e.g., food deprivation, treatment with inhibitors of metabolic fuel oxidation, VMH lesions, treatment with NPY, NE, and β-endorphin), whereas factors that decrease food intake also increase sympathetic activity (e.g., treatment with bomesin, CCK, CRH, and leptin) (reviewed by Bray and York, 1999). It has been suggested that food intake is actually controlled (increased or decreased) directly by changes in sympathetic activity, which in turn influence the secretion of CRH (Bray and York, 1999). However, food intake and sympathetic activity are dissociated in some circumstances. The fact that food intake is increased at cold ambient temperatures, when sympathetic activity is elevated, suggests that food intake is directly controlled by signals other than decreased sympathetic activity. Thermoregulation at cold ambient temperatures demands increased energy expenditure, and thus it is most likely that increases in food intake in the cold is related to signals generated by the need for oxidizable metabolic fuels. Although it is generally agreed that a low rate of energy expenditure, reduced sympathetic activity, and high energy

efficiency contribute to obesity, clinical treatments that increase sympathetic activity have not been widely accepted for long-term treatment of obesity due to the potentially adverse effects on cardiac function.

The thermic effect of food increases metabolic rate by 25–40% (Shibala and Bukowiecki, 1987). If animals are chronically hyperphagic, thermogenesis is increased to the extent that weight gain is less than would be expected based on the energetic cost of digestion and fat deposition. This increase in thermogenesis in chronically hyperphagic animals is termed diet-induced thermogenesis. Contrary to the notion that diet-induced thermogenesis evolved to maintain a set point for body weight, a clearly important effect of diet-induced thermogenesis is that it acts to prevent triglyceride accumulation in nonadipose tissues, which, in turn, is thought to lead to impairment of pancreatic β-cells and myocardium and to insulin resistance (Unger, 2000).

It has been suggested that differences in diet-induced thermogenesis account for differences in the propensity to become obese. Progress in understanding thermogenesis has been facilitated by studying small mammals for which thermogenesis is critical, due to their high surface-area-to-volume ratio. Thermogenesis is augmented in rodents and other small animals by the proliferation and increased activity of specialized adipocytes that convert calories derived from ingested food directly into heat. These adipocytes differ from WAT cells in that they have a greater number of more highly developed mitochondria, the source of their brown appearance. Brown adipose tissue (BAT) cells have an especially pronounced ability to use metabolic fuels due to the high concentration of mitochondria and their ability to synthesize a specific protein that allows controlled uncoupling of the mitochondrial respiratory chain. Uncoupled oxidative phosphorylation results in more energy dissipated as heat. In BAT, mitochondrial uncoupling is dependent on uncoupling proteins. Uncoupling protein number 1 (UCP-1, also known as thermogen) and UCP-2 are found in BAT (Klaus *et al.,* 1991; Ricquier *et al.,* 1991). In rodents, nonshivering thermogenesis in BAT plays a critical role in survival at low ambient temperatures and in the energy economy. For example, nonshivering thermogenesis in BAT accounts for as much as 40% of the total energy available from food intake (Himms-Hagen, 1985).

In food-restricted or food-deprived rats, sympathetic activity and BAT thermogenesis are decreased and energy efficiency is increased. β_3-adrenoreceptors are expressed on BAT, and treatment with β-adrenergic agonists doubles thermogenesis (Himms-Hagen *et al.*, 1994). BAT thermogenesis is further increased by an increase in the availability of FFAs, the primary substrate for fuel oxidation in BAT. The availability of metabolic fuels and other effects of the environment on BAT might also be mediated by the CNS. BAT receives extensive sympathetic innervation from the CNS (Bamshad *et al.*, 1999), and sympathetic activity to BAT is reduced in many rodent models of obesity (Himms-Hagen, 1989). Thus, BAT thermogenesis is an important mechanism involved in adaptive changes in energy efficiency in rodents. UCP-1, -2, and -3 are present in neonates of most mammalian species in which it has been examined, including rodents, carnivores, ruminants, and primates. In many species, such as human beings and ruminants, BAT is present in significant quantities only for a limited period of neonatal life, whereas it is present in larger quantities in adults of a variety of small rodents (reviewed by Himms-Hagen, 1990). In those animals for which BAT is not the source of nonshivering thermogenesis, other uncoupling proteins might play a role. UCP-2 is an uncoupling protein expressed in most tissues at varying levels, whereas UCP-3 is present in skeletal muscle (Fleury *et al.*, 1997; Boss *et al.*, 1997; Vidal-Puig *et al.*, 1997).

Hormones play a variety of roles in mediating changes in energy expenditure. Glucocorticoids decrease, and thyroid hormone and leptin increase, sympathetic activity and thermogenesis. High levels of glucocorticoids are necessary for most types of experimental obesity. The development of obesity of *ob/ob* and *db/db* mice, mice that overexpress agouti protein, and *fa/fa* fatty rats is prevented by adrenalectomy (Saito and Bray, 1984; Yukimura *et al.*, 1978; Shimomura *et al.*, 1987; Shimizu *et al.*, 1989). It is possible that elevated glucocorticoids contribute to obesity by inhibiting the release of the catabolic peptide CRH. ICV CRH treatment increases sympathetic activity in nerves to BAT (Holt and York, 1989) and prevents body-weight gain in obese (fa/fa) rats (Rohner-Jeanrenaud *et al.*, 1989). Increased TRH secretion from the PVH leads to the increased synthesis and secretion of pituitary thyroid-stimulating hormone (TSH), which in turn stimulates

the synthesis and release of the thyroid secretions, triiodothyronine (T_3) and thyroxine (T_4). In addition, a family of deiodinases metabolizes the less active T_4 to the more active T_3. Elevated plasma levels of T_3 lead to increased metabolic rate, thermogenesis, and energy expenditure and thus are critical for survival at cold ambient temperatures (Silva, 1995). The adipocyte hormone leptin, secreted in response to increased availability of oxidizable glucose, increases energy expenditure and produces tissue-specific increases in fuel oxidation. For example, leptin increases the availability and oxidation of glucose (Kamohara *et al.*, 1997; Zhou *et al.*, 1998) and FFAs (Bai *et al.*, 1996; Y. T. Zhou *et al.*, 1997). Leptin or NE treatment augments weight loss and thermogenesis in adrenalectomized animals, but has no effect in thyroidectomized animals, suggesting that thyroid hormone is permissive in the control of thermogenesis. Thyroid hormone, leptin, and glucocorticoids have synergistic effects. The change in glucocorticoids, T_3, and thermogenesis are prevented by treatment with leptin (Ahima *et al.*, 1996; Legradi *et al.*, 1997). These effects of leptin are assumed to be via neuroendocrine action; however, it is possible that leptin attenuates the fasting-induced increases in glucocorticoids and thyroid hormone by increasing fuel availability and oxidation. An increase in fuel availability and oxidation would be expected to counteract the metabolic stimulus for secretion of glucocorticoids and thyroid hormone (e.g., see Schneider *et al.*, 1998). Furthermore, the reason leptin fails to influence fuel oxidation in the absence of thyroid hormone might be due to a lack of available metabolic fuels that accompanies conditions in which the levels of plasma thyroid hormone are low.

Chronic treatment with NPY results in significant increases body weight and body-fat content (Stanley *et al.*, 1986), and, although some of these effects are related to increased food intake, changes in energy expenditure and storage play a role. Direct application of NPY to the PVH also inhibits sympathetic activity in projections to both WAT and BAT, and this is part of the mechanism whereby NPY inhibits energy expenditure and increases energy storage (Billington *et al.*, 1991). The inhibited sympathetic activity and fuel oxidation in NPY-treated animals might in turn generate a metabolic sensory signal that further increases food intake. These peripheral metabolic influences of NPY, as well as of other peptides, explain the effects of these peptides on food intake that do not occur in temporal synchrony with the presence of these peptides in the brain.

Other than thermoregulation, the most energetically expensive activity in the female repertoire is reproduction, especially lactation. Thus, it is not surprising that mechanisms exist to conserve energy by the inhibition of reproduction when energy demands are high but food is in short supply. Later in the chapter, the metabolic sensory signals and hormonal and neuropeptide mediators and effectors for fasting-induced anestrus are discussed.

It has been demonstrated that certain immune responses are energetically costly and are routinely inhibited during metabolic challenges, such as harsh winter conditions. Cold induces increases in thyroid hormone secretion and its effects on steroid-facilitated transcription might also mediate these effects. In some species that are highly adapted to living in cold winter environments, changes in photoperiod (day length) trigger mechanisms that prevent immune function from being compromised on short-day winter photoperiods (Nelson and Klein, 2000).

The study of the effects of hormones and neuropeptides on food intake must be accompanied by attention to the effects of these molecules on energy expenditure. Because all of the substance in Table 1 influence aspects of intake, storage, and expenditure, these are often categorized in terms of their overall effect on energy economy rather than in terms of their effect on food intake or expenditure alone. Thus, treatment with anabolic substances, such as NPY and galanin, tend to increase energy intake and storage and to decrease energy expenditure and reproductive processes, such as sex behavior and luteinizing hormone (LH) secretion in rats (e.g., Kalra and Kalra, 1996). Treatment with catabolic substances, such as leptin, decrease food intake and body weight and increase energy expenditure, sex behavior, and LH secretion in rats (e.g., Ahima *et al.,* 1996; Ammar *et al.,* 2000; Eckel *et al.,* 1998). Most of the peptides in Table 1 fit into this pattern, with a few exceptions, such as orexin, which increases both food intake and energy expenditure by increasing general arousal and preventing a normal sleep period (Lubkin *et al.,* 1998; Willie *et al.,* 2001). Some of these hormonal effects differ depending on their level of synthesis and secretion. For example, high plasma

concentrations of thyroid hormone tend to increase energy expenditure, but might also inhibit sex behavior by interfering with steroid-receptor-facilitated gene transcription. Increased secretion of thyroid hormone at cold temperatures interferes with estrogen-receptor-facilitated transcription in hypothalamic neurons important for sex behavior (Dellovade *et al.,* 1995; Zhu *et al.,* 1996, 1997), and thus thyroid hormone binding in the CNS might underlie the decreased expression of sex behavior.

The consequence of reciprocal interactions among intake, storage, and expenditure is that a change in one requires a compensatory change by the others. Evolutionary processes have produced species that vary from one another in the pattern of intake, storage, and expenditure. This is abundantly clear with regard to the changes in energy balance during a reproductive cycle. Pregnancy and especially lactation are energetically costly in all mammalian species; however, species differ in the energetic strategies they use to meet these energetic demands (reviewed by Wade and Schneider, 1992). During pregnancy, females of some species increase energy intake in excess of the demands of the growing conceptus, thereby bolstering their own maternal energy stores in anticipation of the energetic demands of lactation. In contrast, females of other species, such as Syrian hamsters, show no change whatsoever in food intake during pregnancy but instead mobilize their own fat stores to meet the demands of the growing conceptus and increase hoarding behavior to fortify external energy depots (Wade *et al.,* 1986). During pregnancy, Siberian hamsters also fail to increase food intake and, as a consequence, lose internal energy stores (body fat) (Schneider and Wade, 1987), but at the same time increase food hoarding, increasing external energy stores (Bartness, 1997). Unlike rats and other species, female hamsters enter lactation in a state of internal negative energy balance and meet the energetic demands of lactation by increasing food intake, thereby taking advantage of their externally stored food. Females of other species, such as Grey seals, fast during lactation, drawing on their maternal fat stores and using metabolic adjustments to direct energy toward milk production (reviewed by Wade and Schneider, 1992). These examples illustrate that various species use a variety of energetic strategies, with different patterns of intake, storage, and expenditure, in order to meet their energetic requirements for reproductive success.

IV. HUNGER, FOOD PROCUREMENT, AND FOOD INTAKE

Research on the molecular neuroendocrinology of ingestive behavior is focused primarily on food intake (i.e., the amount of food eaten, meal size, and other aspects of meal patterns). This research is summarized here with regard to the central effector systems, primary sensory stimuli, and the hormonal mediators and modulators. In addition, a few experiments have been designed to distinguish between the appetitive and the consummatory aspects of ingestion. For example, hormonal, neuropeptide, and reproductive states have been shown to influence food hoarding, approach to food, and operant performance for food reward. This chapter emphasizes the importance of motivation as well as the social and environmental context. Finally, the central, sensory, and hormonal control of food intake are compared and contrasted to control of reproduction.

It has been suggested that the various sensory and hormonal inputs on central networks are not temporally equal when it comes to regulating motor events. Some exteroreceptive stimuli act immediately in a reflex manner to control the moment-to-moment actions in a meal (e.g., the processing of gustatory and oropharyngeal information in the hindbrain). In contrast, postingestive stimuli from gut distension and metabolic fuel availability have often been categorized as short-term signals. Changes in body fat content are relatively slow compared to the changes in circulating and intracellular metabolic fuel availability, and thus hormonal modulators associated with body-fat content (e.g., insulin and leptin) are commonly referred to as long-term signals. As we have stated in earlier, these hormones are not themselves sensory events, but at times they are in a position to provide the brain with information about sensory events. The hormones should not be mistaken for the sensory stimuli that they represent.

It can also be argued that short-term signals have been misclassified. Metabolic inhibitors typically increase food intake for hours, rather than days, but this might be attributable to the experimental treatments rather than to the capacity of the interorecep-

tors themselves to sustain feeding-stimulatory effects (for further discussion, see Friedman, 1990). Furthermore, chronic diet-induced obesity can be attributed to interoreceptors that sense deficits in hepatic energy status (Ji *et al.*, 2000) and to differences in glucose sensitivity in specific brain areas (Levin *et al.*, 1999), suggesting that metabolic sensory signals have long-term consequences. Finally, labeling the hormonal mediators, such as insulin and leptin, long-term signals is counterproductive if it discourages the investigation of how hormones that fluctuate wildly in a single day are translated into a signal that purportedly regulates food intake over several days or weeks. It would be unfortunate if these labels masked the importance of metabolic sensory signals for understanding obesity and disorders of energy partitioning.

A. Effector Systems

Figure 1 provides a schema of the brain circuits responsible for mediating the motor actions of ingestive behaviors and illustrates that a wide variety of neural components must be involved with controlling motivated behaviors. At the simplest level, the brain contains four broad-ranging neural systems concerned with controlling motivated behaviors: those involved with the transduction and processing of sensory signals, those that control behavioral state and circadian timing, those that process the types of information concerned with processing neural representations of sensory objects, and those involved with motor control. Sets of motor feedback and hormonal signals interact with many different levels of the brain to influence behavioral, autonomic, and neuroendocrine motor actions. In particular, central pattern generators for the rhythmic neural patterns that underlie licking, masticating, and swallowing are located in the caudal hindbrain, and it is likely that hypothalamic circuits ultimately influence food intake by modulating the function of the central pattern generators. Furthermore, a plethora of the same hormones and peptides that have been studied in the hypothalamus are also released at terminals in the caudal hindbrain where abundant receptors for these peptides are found.

Sensory stimuli can be defined either as interosensory signals encoding internal state or exterosensory inputs that encode features of the goal object such

a)   b)

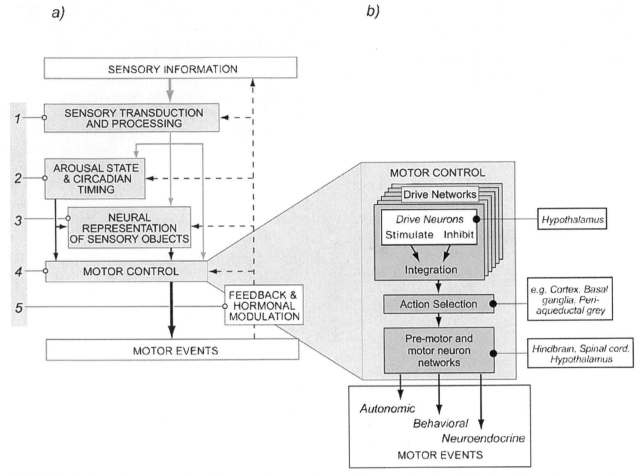

FIGURE 1 A schematic representation of the interacting neural systems that control motivated behaviors. Sensory inputs are shown in grey, central neural connections in black, and hormonal and feedback signals as dashed lines. Five functional components and their interactions are illustrated. (a) Four subsystems can be categorized as neural components concerned with (1) transduction and processing of sensory information, (2) regulating behavioral state and circadian timing, (3) generating neural representations of objects in sensory space, and (4) controlling motor actions. A final system (5) consists of feedback and hormonal signals that can interact act with the neural components located at all levels of the schema. (b) An exploded schematic view of the components that make up motor control networks. Motor control networks are organized at three levels: drive networks that can either stimulate or inhibit motor actions, action selection networks that integrate the outputs of drive networks with those of other systems, and executive premotor and motor neuron networks that generate the motor actions. The location of the some of the neural components in the motor control module is shown on the right.

as smell, taste, temperature, tactile properties, and visual appearance. Each of these sensory modalities has specific receptors, transduction mechanisms, and labeled-line access to central processing networks located throughout the brain (system 1, Fig. 1a). Although important sensory processing occurs in the telencephalon, particularly the sensory cortex, the sensory processing that occurs subcortically has important effects on motivated behaviors. For example, al-

tered sensitivity to the taste of sodium occurs in the hindbrain of hyponatremic animals and is an important adjunct to increased sodium appetite. Another example is the differential interpretation by the hindbrain of somatosensory information responsible for lordosis depending on the day of the estrous cycle. In addition, integration of signals from separate metabolic pathways, such as those for glucose and FFA oxidation, occurs intracellularly (Friedman and Tordoff, 1986). It has been suggested that some sensory signals and hormonal mediators can directly access drive networks (Fig. 1b). For example, drinking can be initiated by either increasing plasma osmolality or angiotensin II (A-II). It has been suggested that food intake is influenced by inhibitors of metabolic fuel oxidation or by hormonal mediators (e.g., leptin or insulin), particularly when low plasma levels of these hormones reflect a deficit in energy availability and storage. There are receptors for these hormones in some hypothalamic areas, suggesting that a decrease in binding of hormones to these receptors can increase food intake (Elmquist *et al.*, 1999; Flier, 1998).

Anticipation and behavioral timing are distinguishing features of motivated behaviors (reviewed by Boulos and Terman, 1980; Mistlberger, 1994). These features are notably absent from decorticate animals (Grill and Kaplan, 1990), showing that the neural processing required for anticipation resides the forebrain. To enable motor control networks to generate anticipatory behaviors, two distinct but interacting sets of neural circuits either provide circadian timing information or control behavioral state (system 2, Fig. 1a). The circadian timing system originates in the hypothalamic SCH and generates the timing signal that entrains virtually all neural activity within the limits determined by the prevailing photoperiod (Moore, 1997). On the other hand, those networks controlling behavioral state include neurons in the reticular nucleus of the thalamus, catecholamine cell groups in the hindbrain (e.g., the locus coeruleus), cholinergic neurons in the basal forebrain, the ventrolateral preoptic nucleus, histaminergic neurons in the tuberomammillary nucleus, and the hypocretin-orexin neurons in the LHA (McCormick and Bal, 1997; Semba, 2000; Sherin *et al.*, 1998; Willie *et al.*, 2001). In addition, entrainment of food-anticipatory activity is mediated by an endogenous circadian clock (or feeding-entrainable oscillator) that is anatomically distinct from the light-entrainable oscillator in the SCH (Stephan *et al.*, 1979). The feeding-entrainable oscillator is set by sensory stimuli generated by changes in the availability of oxidizable fuels (Stephan, 1997), and entrainment requires nonvagal gut–brain communication (Comperatore and Stephan, 1990; Davidson and Stephan, 1998; Stephan, 1997). The location of the meal-entrainable oscillator is unknown, but it is predicted to be in close proximity to the sensory detectors of metabolic fuels, consistent with the notion that clocks are located near their zeitgebers (Davidson and Stephan, 1999a).

The brain contains a wide range of circuits that process sensory information in such a way that objects are represented neurally in sensory space (system 3, Fig. 1a). This highly complex cognitive processing effectively interprets, prioritizes, stores, and retrieves information collected by the sensory systems. Parts of the forebrain also produce emotional appraisals of this sensory information (LeDoux, 1996). Collectively, these systems are responsible for a series of functions that are critical for controlling motivational behaviors and include learning and memory mechanisms in the telencephalon and cerebellum; reward–aversion systems in the midbrain ventral tegmentum, parts of the basal forebrain (particularly the nucleus accumbens) the amygdala, and parts of the cortex, particularly prefrontal regions; and systems in the hippocampus, parts of the parietal cortex, and other regions of the brain containing place and head-direction neurons responsible for allocentric and egocentric spatial representation (Maguire *et al.*, 1998; Rolls, 1999b; Taube, 1998). A great deal of exterosensory information is collectively processed through these networks, parts of which assign what has been called incentive value to a particular goal object (Toates, 1986). Neural pathways mediating the interactions between sensory object representation and motor networks are not fully understood, but sets of bidirectional connections between the hypothalamus and cortical structures, such as the prefrontal cortex and hippocampus, and subcortical regions, such as the amygdala, septal nuclei, bed nuclei of the stria terminalis, and basal ganglia, are all likely to be critical for the integrative operations that designate and coordinate these aspects of motivated behaviors (Öngür and Price, 2000; Saper, 1985; Swanson, 2000; Swanson and Petrovich, 1998).

The three systems we have just described process information in a way that in many respects is not goal-specific—their neural circuits are involved to some degree with all motivated behaviors. For example, the SCH provides circadian timing information for all neural functions. Similarly, an animal processes information for spatial navigation in essentially the same parts of the telencephalon, irrespective of whether it is looking for food, a mate, or shelter. On the other hand, some of the components in the motor control systems (system 4, Fig. 1a) involve neurons that are concerned with functions that are relatively goal-specific and are responsible for controlling particular aspects of individual goal-associated functions. For example, neurons in parts of the hypothalamus are concerned specifically with food procurement, ingestion, or sexual behavior, but not with agonistic or thermoregulatory behaviors. Finally, interactions among different networks, particularly in the hypothalamus, are of paramount importance. For example, the effects of a negative energy balance are not limited to simply increasing the drive to eat; they also suppress reproductive neuroendocrine function, behavioral motivation, and performance (Ammar *et al.,* 2000; Schneider *et al.,* 2000a; Wade *et al.,* 1996). Similarly, dehydration leads to severe anorexia as well as increasing the drive to drink (Watts, 2001a). This cross-behavioral coordination is part of the mechanism that not only selects those motor actions with the highest behavioral priority, but also suppresses those actions that might exaggerate energetic deficits. This coordination involves sensory and hormonal modulation acting together with the divergent neuroanatomic outputs from individual drive networks (see Section VI).

Most of the neuroanatomical work since the 1950s has concentrated on the role of efferent hypothalamic networks, together with the premotor and motor neuron networks in the hindbrain that control food intake. Less attention has been paid to those parts of the telencephalon involved with the more complex processing responsible for anticipation, reward assignment, foraging, and motor programs selection (see Rolls, 1999b). Ultimately however, these systems might play a key role in the etiology of, for example, human eating disorders.

The cloning of the genes that encode leptin and the leptin receptor, and the subsequent discovery of leptin's effects on the NPY and melanocortin system created a resurgence of interest in the hypothalamus as a major component in the networks that control ingestive behavior. So far, the bulk of this work has highlighted a restricted number of hypothalamic cell groups that appear to be intimately involved with regulating the motor responses to altered energy balance. These are the ARH, VMH, dorsomedial nucleus (DMH), PVH, retrochiasmatic (RCH), and LHA areas (Elmquist *et al.,* 1999; Schwartz *et al.,* 2000). Other investigators note

that these networks must act in concert with the feeding motor program in the caudal brain stem (Grill *et al.,* 2000; Watts, 2000). These networks are illustrated in Figure 9 and are discussed at the end of this chapter with regard to their role in food intake, energy balance, and reproduction.

1. Arcuate Nucleus

The ARH contains a variety of neural networks that are responsive to fasting and eating and to hormonal modulators of food intake. For example, the ARH is a major target for the binding of leptin and insulin to the signaling forms of their respective receptors. Many ARH neurons express leptin and insulin receptors, and experimental manipulation of circulating leptin alters the expression of neuropeptide genes in the ARH (Marks *et al.,* 1990; Sahu, 1998; Schwartz *et al.,* 1997).

Substantial evidence implicates many of the neuropeptides expressed by ARH neurons as critical determinants in the homeostatic aspects of eating behavior; some of these stimulate eating, whereas others inhibit it. The watershed experiments of Clark and coworkers in 1984 demonstrated that ICV NPY treatment stimulates eating in rats, and subsequently a variety of other investigators further characterized the behavioral effects of NPY (Clark *et al.,* 1985; Stanley and Leibowitz, 1985; Stanley *et al.,* 1993), and this NPY probably originates in the ARH. Elevated NPY immunoreactivity, mRNA, or both occurs in the ARH following food restriction, food deprivation, and dehydration, and during lactation and vigorous exercise (Abizaid *et al.,* 1997; Brady *et al.,* 1990; Lewis *et al.,* 1993; Smith, M. S., 1993; Wilding *et al.,* 1997; Woods *et al.,* 1998; Watts *et al.,* 1999), and central treatment with Y receptor antagonists blocks the feeding effects of NPY (Dube *et al.,* 1994; Balasubramaniam, 1997; Crop *et al.,* 2001). The endogenous MC-4 receptor antagonist, AgRP, is colocalized with NPY in the ARH and stimulates food intake when administered intraventricularly (Rossi *et al.,* 1998). Furthermore, AgRP mRNA increases following starvation (Mizuno and Mobbs, 1999; Wilson *et al.,* 1999), and targeted disruption of the MC-4 receptor is associated with obesity and hyperphagia (Huszar *et al.,* 1997; Marsh *et al.,* 1999). In summary, several different lines of evidence support the notion that the NPY plays a central role in the control of energy balance. However, it is surely not the only peptide system that does so. Mice that lack NPY show normal food intake and body weight (Erickson *et al.*, 1996a,b), suggesting that other physiological systems (perhaps AgRP) can compensate for a lack of NPY during development and perhaps play important roles during normal feeding.

Contrary to modern variants of the dual center hypothesis, the ARH is not exclusively stimulatory with regard to food intake. ARH neurons also express neuropeptides that can inhibit food intake when administered directly into the brain. Two of them, α-MSH (a peptide derived from POMC) and cocaine- and amphetamine-regulated transcript (CART), are coexpressed in the ARH (Elias *et al.*, 1998a), and the expression of both their genes decreases following starvation (Brady *et al.*, 1990; Kristensen *et al.*, 1998). Similarly, neurotensin is an anorexigenic peptide contained in ARH neurons whose gene expression is reduced during negative energy balance (Watts *et al.*, 1999). Based on their neuropeptide content, ARH neurons probably contribute to the stimulatory and inhibitory networks.

The ARH also contains a population of growth-hormone-releasing-hormone (GHRH) neurons, some of which coexpress neurotensin (Sawchenko *et al.*, 1985). GHRH and somatostatin regulate the secretion of growth hormone and influence peripheral metabolism. In this manner, the ARH can be considered part of the neuroendocrine motor neuron network.

NPY and AgRP-containing ARH neurons project both to the PVH (O'Donohue *et al.*, 1985) and to neurons containing melanin-concentrating hormone (MCH) in the LHA (Broberger *et al.*, 1998a; Elias *et al.*, 1998b; Li *et al.*, 2000). ARH projections to the LHA may provide a link between neurons directly engaged by hormones that signal changes in energy balance and neurons in the LHA projecting to those parts of the brain involved with the planning and execution of motivated behaviors (Elmquist *et al.*, 1999; Risold *et al.*, 1997; Sawchenko, 1998). Based on the presence of AgRP-immunoreactive fibers, ARH efferent connections apparently also target other parts of the brain implicated in regulating autonomic and behavioral aspects of feeding: the lateral septal (LS) nuclei, some parts of the bed nuclei of the stria terminalis (BST), and the amygdala, the parabrachial nucleus, and the medulla (Bagnol *et al.*,

1999; Broberger *et al.*, 1998b; Haskell-Luevano *et al.*, 1999).

2. Paraventricular Nucleus

The PVH is a critical hypothalamic cell group that regulates many motor aspects of energy balance. It contains a prominent population of neuroendocrine CRH motor neurons that ultimately control glucocorticoid secretion (Watts, 1996; Whitnall, 1993), as well as groups of TRH and somatostatin neuroendocrine neurons that are all positioned to regulate endocrine control of metabolism (Swanson, 1987). Central treatment with CRH decreases food intake and body weight in a wide variety of organisms (reviewed by Heinrichs and Richard, 1999; Rothwell, 1990; Spina *et al.*, 1996).

The PVH is one of the most sensitive brain areas for the feeding-stimulatory effects of microinjections of NPY (Stanley *et al.*, 1986). As previously discussed and reviewed by Walker (1999), injections of NPY or NE into the PVH stimulate feeding. Chronic treatment with NPY results in increased body weight and body-fat content. Food restriction increases NPY expression and synthesis in the ARH and release in the PVH. NPY receptors are abundant in the PVH. Of the 6 NPY Y receptors, Y1 and Y5 have been implicated in control of food intake (reviewed by Walker, 1999). Central application of antisense oligonucleotides to the NPY Y1 or Y5 receptors decreases food intake (Lopez-Valpuesta *et al.*, 1996; Schaffhauser *et al.*, 1997). At least three different antagonists for the Y1 receptor reverse the effects of NPY on food intake and decrease food intake in free-feeding animals that are not treated with NPY (Kanatani *et al.*, 1996; Morgan *et al.*, 1998; Wieland *et al.*, 1998). Treatment with an antagonist for the Y5 receptor subtype, CGP 71683A, inhibits NPY-induced and deprivation-induced food intake in lean and obese Zucker rats, and also significantly inhibits food intake in 24-hour food-deprived and streptozotocin-induced diabetic rats (Criscione *et al.*, 1998). Longer-term treatment with this Y5 antagonist results in significant loss of body weight and body fat content (Criscione *et al.*, 1998). The treatment with antagonists to specific NPY receptor subtypes confirms that NPY affects food intake by acting on either the Y1 or Y5 receptors in Syrian hamsters (Corp *et al.*, 2001). NPY treatment also inhibits sympathetic nervous system (SNS) activity in projections to both

WAT and BAT, and this is part of the mechanism whereby NPY inhibits energy expenditure and increases energy storage (Billington *et al.,* 1991; Bray, 1992). These peripheral effects, in turn, might be essential to the long-term effects of NPY on food intake.

NPY increases behaviors related to finding and procuring a carbohydrate solution, without increasing intake of an orally infused solution (Seeley *et al.,* 1995; Ammar *et al.,* 2000). These results suggest that NPY can influence the motivational aspects of ingestion, without influencing the consummatory aspects. These results also suggest that the increased intake in earlier studies in which chronic NPY treatment increased food intake might be due to the metabolic or hormonal signals that result when NPY decreases peripheral energy expenditure and fuel oxidation.

The mechanisms that control the motivation to eat most likely involve the extensive descending PVH projections to the periaqueductal gray (PAG), parabrachial nucleus (PB), dorsal vagal complex, and preautonomic neurons in the hindbrain and spinal cord. In turn, the PVH receives leptin- and insulin-related viscerosensory information from the ARH and the DMH, and from ascending (predominantly monoaminergic) inputs that relay the vagally mediated information from the viscera critical for coordinating feeding responses with peripheral requirements (Risold and Swanson, 1997; Swanson, 1987).

3. Lateral Hypothalamic Area

Of all the hypothalamic cell groups implicated in controlling ingestive behaviors, the multiple and complex roles of the LHA have probably been the most difficult to define. It is a large, generally ill-defined, and heterogeneous collection of neurons that has connections extending throughout the brain. Its neurons project to and receive extensive inputs from the telencephalon, including parts of the cortex and hippocampus, nucleus accumbens and substantia innominata, nuclei of the septal complex, amygdala, and BST (Öngür and Price, 2000; Risold and Swanson, 1997; Risold *et al.,* 1997; Saper, 1985; Swanson, 1987). In turn, it also has strong projections to the PAG, PB, dorsal medulla (Moga *et al.,* 1990b; Kelly and Watts, 1998; Swanson, 1987), and to some parts of the PVH that control neuroendocrine output (Larsen *et al.,* 1994; Watts

et al., 1999; Swanson, 1987). These connections place the LHA in a prime position for incorporating the motivational aspects of ingestive behaviors into the motor patterns organized by the hypothalamus.

Under conditions of unrestricted feeding, the integrated output of LHA neurons tends to stimulate eating (Elmquist *et al.,* 1999), the substrate of which probably includes the large population of MCH-containing neurons that have extensive projections throughout the brain (Bittencourt *et al.,* 1992; Shimada *et al.,* 1998). However, its overall function is clearly not mandatory but, apparently, has more of a subtle and modulatory nature (Bernardis and Bellinger, 1996; Sawchenko, 1998; Winn, 1995). This notion is supported by the fact that excitotoxic lesions in those parts of the LHA most closely related to feeding cause only mild hypophagia and do not impede compensatory responses following food or water deprivation (Winn, 1995). It is interesting that these same LHA lesions markedly attenuate compensatory ingestive responses to deficits originating internally, that is, those that do not have the exterosensory components present with deprivation but instead are generated by direct manipulation of homeostatic variables (e.g., 2-deoxy-D-glucose treatment or colloid-induced hypovolemia) (Winn, 1995). Thus, the LHA might act to coordinate signals derived from internal state variables (e.g., those originating the ARH, see Section IV.A.1) with those mechanisms originating in the telencephalon that are responsible for motivated anticipatory action (Elmquist *et al.,* 1999; Winn, 1995).

Additional support for the LHA's complex role derives from the presence of at least two neuropeptides, neurotensin and CART, that inhibit eating if exogenously applied into the brain of fed animals (Kristensen *et al.,* 1998; Levine *et al.,* 1983). In addition, during the development of dehydration–anorexia, levels of CRH (a known anorexic neuropeptide) and neurotensin increase in a subpopulation of LHA neurons that projects to the PB (Kelly and Watts, 1998; Watts *et al.,* 1999). From this perspective, it has been suggested that the diverse neuropeptidergic output of the LHA—like that of the ARH—contributes to both the stimulatory and inhibitory networks, is differentially modulated by its array of afferents (Kelly and Watts, 1996; Swanson, 1987), and has the capacity to regulate feeding in a wide variety of circumstances.

4. Ventromedial Nucleus

Perhaps the most difficult nucleus to fit into a scheme accounting for ingestive behaviors is the VMH. This large medial zone cell group consists of two well-defined subdivisions—the dorsomedial (dm) and ventrolateral parts (vl)—separated by a smaller central part. As discussed in Section II, lesion studies in the 1950s identified the VMH as a pivotal component of the circuit that controlled eating behavior. The VMH was considered to be satiety center because large electrolytic lesions produced hyperphagia and obesity. The validity of these findings was questioned a few years later (Gold, 1973) on the grounds that more restricted lesions did not produce these effects and that lesions in the vicinity of the VMH may have compromised descending PVH projections that regulate autonomic functions leading to increased feeding (Inoue and Bray, 1977; Berthould and Jeanrenaud, 1979; Gold *et al.*, 1980; see Grossman, 1979, for review). Since that time, neuron-specific excitotoxic lesions have failed to clarify the role of the VMH in the behavioral aspects of energy balance.

Most studies have reported that the VMH does not send significant projections to the PVH and sends only sparse projections to the DMH (Canteras *et al.*, 1994; Luiten *et al.*, 1987; Sawchenko and Swanson, 1983; Thompson and Swanson, 1998). Furthermore, results from methods that trace neural projections across one or more synapses using transneuronal viruses have raised serious doubts about the notion that neurons located in the VMH contribute to the sympathetic motor command circuit postulated by Strack *et al.* (1989) to control energy metabolism. Experiments using this technique have consistently failed to label VMH neurons following viral injections into peripheral targets concerned with energy balance, such as the pancreas, stomach wall, or BAT and WAT (Bamshad *et al.*, 1999; Jansen *et al.*, 1997; Rinaman *et al.*, 2000; Strack *et al.*, 1989).

It is clear that the VMHdm contains a significant number of leptin receptors and that some of these neurons project to parts of the hypothalamus concerned with circadian timekeeping (Elmquist *et al.*, 1998a,b). One of the most striking effects of temporary inactivation of the VMH is a disruption of circadian-dependent spontaneous feeding, such that diurnal, but not nocturnal, food intake increases (Choi *et al.*, 1998; Choi and Dallman, 1999). Finally, the VMH contains glucose-sensing neurons that may contribute to a wider central glucose-sensing network (Levin *et al.*, 1999). Collectively these data suggest that one function of VMH neurons might be to consolidate the circadian feeding rhythm in the face of feedback from leptin and glucose alterations following a normal meal. Based on the evidence of its neural connections and its high levels of ER receptors, the VMH is clearly involved with regulating social behaviors, including agonistic and female-typical sex behaviors. In rodents, the binding of estradiol to VMH estrogen receptors is necessary and sufficient for induction of progestin receptors and female sex behavior in response to a sexually experienced male. As we discuss later, aspects of steroid-induced sex behavior are compromised by metabolic challenges such as food deprivation, cold exposure, and exercise that is not offset by compensatory increases in food intake (reviewed by Wade *et al.*, 1996). The VMH is thus a potential site for the integration of energy balance with the reproductive system.

5. Caudal Hindbrain

The central pattern generators for the stereotyped rhythmic movements of eating reside in the hindbrain, suggesting that the central effector circuits previously described influence ingestive behavior via descending projections. In addition, the caudal hindbrain contains detectors of intracellular fuel oxidation, receives numerous afferent inputs from peripheral sensory detectors, and is capable of integrating sensory inputs from the mouth, stomach, and small intestine into ingestive patterns that regulate meal size (Grill and Kaplan, 1990). This was convincingly demonstrated by chronic supracollicular decerebration, a surgical procedure that disconnects the caudal hindbrain from the more rostral parts of the brain, including the hypothalamus. Food was infused into the oral cavity and orofacial movements associated with acceptance or rejection of the infused food were measured. Decerebrate rats either licked, masticated, and allowed food to enter the digestive tract or passively rejected the infused food; the size of the meals varied as a function of both orosensory and postingestive stimuli (Grill and Norgren, 1978a,b). Thus, the caudal hindbrain shows the capacity to integrate sensory information into the ingestive motor program, thereby modulating meal size. In addition, the chronic decerebrate responds to a cerebral metabolic emergency triggering a sympathoadrenal response and consequent hyperglycemia (DiRocco and Grill, 1979), indicating that the detection of metabolic deficits and homeostatic responses to those deficits are possible without the forebrain. Because the hindbrain contains these reflexive motor programs and is evolutionarily older than the forebrain, it follows that the forebrain circuits most likely act through the hindbrain to influence ingestive behavior. Furthermore, the caudal hindbrain has the potential to respond to a wide variety of peptides, hormones, and pharmacological agents by changes in meal size. Chronically decerebrate rats increase food intake in response to insulin treatment (Flynn and Grill, 1983) and decrease food intake in response to treatment with CCK, bombesin, d-fenfluramine, mCPP, or apomorphine (Grill and Smith, 1988; Flynn and Robillard, 1992; Grill *et al.,* 1997; Kaplan *et al.,* 1998; Kaplan and Södersten, 1994). Chemical messengers that influence food intake when infused directly into hindbrain nuclei or into the fourth cerebral ventricle include insulin, leptin, urocortin, and melanocortin receptor ligands (Grill *et al.,* 1998, 2000; D. L. Williams *et al.,* 2000), hindbrain receptors for these peptides are abundant (Hoggard *et al.,* 1997; Mountjoy *et al.,* 1994; Mercer *et al.,* 1998b; Skofitsch *et al.,* 1985; Unger *et al.,* 1991b). Chronic decerebrate animals lack the capacity to find and procure food, learn a conditioned taste aversion, or respond to metabolic deficits (such as those incurred by food deprivation) by altering food intake and body weight, and thus these abilities might be mediated via peripheral gastric and metabolic signals that are integrated with the forebrain peptide circuits already described (reviewed by G. P. Smith, 1999). Neural projections from the caudal hindbrain to the hypothalamic stimulatory and inhibitory circuits are discussed later in the chapter, particularly with regard to sensory detection of metabolic fuels.

B. Sensory Systems

Sensory inputs are categorized as either interosensory and exterosensory signals generated by ingestive behaviors and subsequent postingestive events. All the exterosensory modalities contribute to the organization of ingestive behaviors (Fig. 2), but their relative importance varies depending on the species and the situation. Intero- and exterosensory receptors or detectors relay information to the brain about internal states that are used to control neuroendocrine, autonomic, and behavioral motor events.

1. Orosensory Stimuli

All exterosensory modalities, but particularly gustatory and olfactory information, play key roles in organizing foraging behavior and food selection (Risold *et al.,* 1997; Spector, 2000). Before exterosensory information can affect the ingestive-behavior motor networks it must be processed by those parts of the brain—particularly the cortex—that assign reward value to a particular food item, learn and remember its location in the environment, and engage the appropriate navigational strategies for getting there (Rolls, 1999a). Gustatory inputs from taste receptors in the tongue first enter the brain through the facial, glossopharyngeal, and vagus nerves and synapse in the rostral zone of the medial nucleus of the solitary tract (NTS), but the trajectory of gustatory projections from the NTS depends on the species examined (Norgren, 1984). There are two major patterns in mammals. First, the gustatory part of the rat NTS projects to the PB, particularly to its medial part, from which two ascending gustatory pathways originate (Norgren, 1984). The first pathway projects to some of the BST and to the medial part of the central nucleus of the amygdala (CEAm). After processing in the amygdala, gustatory information can then modulate hypothalamic function by way of projections back to the BST, particularly its fusiform and oval nuclei (Dong *et al.,* 2001). The oval nucleus of the BST might also be an important point for the subcortical processing of information from main olfactory inputs (Dong *et al.,* 2001). The second pathway from the PB projects to the parvicellular part of the ventral posteriormedial nucleus of the thalamus, which then projects to the prefrontal cortex, particularly the agranular insular cortex. The second major pattern is found in primates; here gustatory-related pathways avoid the PB and project directly from the NTS to the thalamus and from there to the insular cortex. Gustatory information also reaches the orbitofrontal cortex, where it is integrated with other types of sensory information and with reward-related signals (Rolls, 2000; Schultz *et al.,*

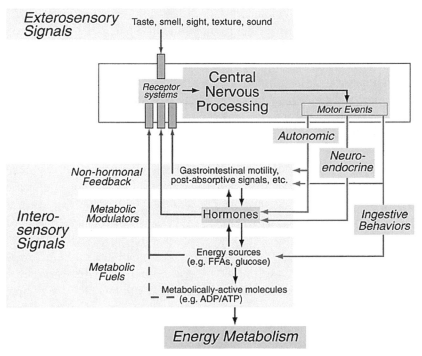

FIGURE 2   A schematic representation of the exterosensory and interosensory signals for the motor events that control energy balance. Motor outputs are shown in red, sensory inputs in blue. Interosensory inputs are categorized as nonhormonal feedback signals (e.g., gastric distension), hormones (metabolic modulators), and metabolic fuels. Autonomic motor actions regulate gastrointestinal, adrenal medullary, and pancreatic functions; neuroendocrine motor output controls glucocorticoid, thyroid, and growth hormones; and behavioral motor actions mediate eating, drinking, and specialized appetites. ADP, adenosine diphosphate; ATP, adenosine triphosphate; CART, cocaine and amphetamine regulated transcript; CRH, corticotropin-releasing hormone; FFA, free-fatty acid. **See insert for a color version of this figure.**

2000). In both primate and rat, these cortical regions project back to the amygdala and hypothalamus, particularly the LHA (Ongur and Price, 2000; Swanson, 2000), which might offer a substrate for the incorporation of cortically processed gustatory information into those parts of the ingestive-behavior drive networks located in the hypothalamus.

2. Gastrointestinal Stimuli

The presence of nutrients in the gastrointestinal tract has measurable effects on meal termination and meal size. Meal size is dramatically increased by sham feeding, an experimental treatment in which ingested nutrients are emptied from the stomach prior to their absorption by the small intestine (Young *et al.*, 1974). Measured volumes infused into the stomach over a physiological range (termed gastric loads) increase the firing rate of vagal mechanosensitive nerve fibers and decrease meal size in a dose-dependent fashion independent of nutrient content (Mathis *et al.*, 1998; Rinaman *et al.*, 1988; Schwartz *et al.*, 1991; Phillips and Powley, 1996). Meal ingestion increases neural activation in the area postrema (AP) and medial NTS where these vagal afferents terminate, and this affect is attenuated in sham-fed animals (Rinaman *et al.*, 1988). Furthermore, the effects of gastric load on meal size are prevented by total bilateral subdiaphragmatic vagotomy, sensory vagotomy, and capsaicin treatment (Phillips and Powley, 1998). Similar studies have revealed the effects of vagally mediated mechanical and nutrient stimuli in the small intestine (duodenum, jejunum, and ileum) (reviewed by G. J. Schwartz, 2000).

This sensory system has been elegantly elucidated by Powley *et al.* (1992). Mechanical (luminal touch, stretch, and contraction) and chemical feedback from the gastrointestinal tract can control food intake via a sensory–motor lattice comprising the vagal efferent motor neurons from the dorsal motor vagal nucleus (DMN) and vagal afferent terminations in the NTS. This feedback involves particular intramuscular arrays of putative mechanoreceptors, cell-types particularly well suited to detect muscle contraction and tension (Powley *et al.,* 1992). In addition to these vagally mediated negative feedback signals, the role of nonvagal splanchnic extrinsic gut afferent innerveration is unknown and requires exploration (G. J. Schwartz, 2000).

3. Metabolic Stimuli

Signals generated by the oxidation of metabolic fuels act as sensory stimuli to the brain following their transduction into neurally coded information, either by peripherally located receptors that generate vagal inputs to the NTS (Hevener *et al.,* 2000) or by direct actions on central neurons (Levin *et al.,* 1999). Compared to what is known about mechanoreceptors and chemoreceptors in the gut, very little is certain about the sensory detectors for metabolic fuel availability and oxidation. There is evidence for metabolic sensory detectors in both the brain and periphery, and it has been suggested that they detect changes in the oxidation of a single substrate, either glucose or FFAs, or in metabolic events related to the oxidation of fuels in general.

Even without knowledge of the specific nature of metabolic sensory detectors, their existence can be demonstrated experimentally by measuring changes in ingestive behavior in response to metabolic substrates and pharmacological agents that inhibit specific metabolic pathways. For example, 2-deoxy-D-glucose (2DG) and 5-thio-glucose (5TG) are transported into cells, are phosphorylated, and then compete with glucose-6-phosphate at the phosphohexoseisomerase step, inhibiting glycolysis (Brown, 1962). Systemic treatment with 2DG or 5TG induces robust increases in food intake in rats and other mammals (with only a few exceptions, one of which is Syrian hamsters). Concurrent with the inhibition of glucose utilization, 2DG and 5TG induce hyperglycemia (increased levels of plasma glucose) by triggering the sympathoadrenal response. Systemic treatment with high

doses of insulin causes decreased levels of plasma glucose and, like 2DG, induces robust increases in food intake in rats, hamsters, and other mammals. It is important to note that systemic insulin and 2DG stimulate food intake, but have opposite effects on plasma glucose, demonstrating that food intake is responsive to decreased glucose oxidation or its metabolic sequelae, not to levels of plasma glucose per se. Furthermore, there is no evidence that these detectors are sensitive only to events related to glycolysis. For example, food intake is increased by treatments that decrease FFA oxidation, such as methyl palmoxirate (MP) or mercaptoacetate (MA). MP binds irreversibly to carnitine palmitoyltransferase I (CPT-I), the enzyme necessary for transport of long-chain FFAs into mitochondria (Tutwiler *et al.,* 1985). Thus, treatment with MP inhibits FFA oxidation, with a consequent reduction in the formation of ketone bodies (Tutwiler *et al.,* 1985; Schneider *et al.,* 1988), and increases food intake (Friedman and Tordoff, 1986; Friedman *et al.,* 1986; reviewed by Scharrer, 1999). MA, another inhibitor of FFA oxidation treatment, acts by blockade of mitochondrial acyl-CoA-dehydrogenases (Bauche *et al.,* 1983), and peripheral, but not central, treatment with MA increases food intake (Langhans and Scharrer, 1987; Ritter and Taylor, 1989; Scharrer and Langhans, 1986). MP treatment is more effective in animals that are predisposed toward the use of fat fuels. For example, MP treatment results in larger increases in food intake in rats that have been previously food deprived, that have been fed a high-fat diet, or that have been treated with 2DG (Friedman and Tordoff, 1986; Friedman *et al.,* 1986). These studies illustrate that information related to the availability of specific metabolic substrates is integrated, perhaps at the levels of intracellular metabolism. It has been suggested that the sensory detectors are responsive to FFA oxidation per se (reviewed by Scharrer, 1999); however, other evidence indicates that inhibitors of FFA oxidation influence food intake because they decrease the general availability of metabolic fuels. More specifically, treatment with metabolic inhibitors decreases liver ATP content, the ATP-to-ADP ratio, and the phophorylation potential (Friedman *et al.,* 1998).

In addition, food intake is stimulated in a dose-dependent manner by treatment with 2,5-anhydro-D-mannitol (2,5-AM), a fructose analog that inhibits gluconeogenesis and glycogenolysis in the liver and causes mild hypoglycemia without reaching the brain in appreciable quantities (Tordoff *et al.*, 1988). MP and 2,5-AM have a synergistic effect on food intake (Friedman and Rawson, 1995). The effects of 2,5-AM on food intake are prevented by hepatic vagotomy. Rats initiate meals sooner and eat more food during hepatic-portal than jugular infusion of 2,5-AM. After such infusions of radiolabeled 2,5-AM, significant quantities were found in liver but not in brain. Unlike previous work that used jugular and hepatic-portal infusion of 2DG and a variety of metabolic substrates (e.g., fructose and glucose), these results using 2,5-AM and MP provide clear evidence for detection of fuel oxidation in liver (Tordoff *et al.*, 1991).

Further work determined that the primary sensory stimulus was related to liver energy status as measured by the availability of ATP, the ADP-to-ATP ratio, or the phosphorylation potential. Administration of fructose and the fructose analog 2,5-AM traps inorganic phosphates with a resulting decrease in ATP synthesis. Doses of 2,5-AM that increase food intake produce a significant depletion of hepatic ATP. In keeping with the idea that 2,5-AM increases food intake by trapping inorganic phosphates with consequent depletion of hepatic ATP, the effects of 2,5-AM on food intake are reversed by the infusion of sodium phosphate solution into the liver (Rawson and Friedman, 1994; Rawson *et al.*, 1994; Friedman, 1995). Hepatic energy status decreases after fasting and increases after refeeding (Ji and Friedman, 1999). Finally, rats prone to diet-induced obesity show significantly lower hepatic energy status than obesity-resistant rats (Ji and Friedman, 2000). Obesity-prone rats appear to have a defect in energy partitioning such that ingested energy is preferentially stored, thereby creating a deficit in oxidizable substrates and continued hyperphagia. Together these results provide a strong case for the importance of hepatic energy status for the control of daily food intake and as a mechanism that underlies diet-induced obesity.

Other investigators have emphasized the sensory detection of fuel availability in the brain. Glucoprivic treatments stimulate food intake for short time periods when restricted to the hindbrain, but not the forebrain (Ritter *et al.*, 1981), and when 2DG is microinjected into more discreet areas in the caudal hindbrain that contain catecholaminergic projections to the forebrain (Ritter *et al.*, 2000). Short-term 2DG-induced increases in food intake are attenuated in rats with lesions of the AP and the medial NTS, that leave the DMN intact (Bird *et al.*, 1983; Contreras *et al.*, 1982; Hyde and Miselis, 1983; Ritter and Taylor, 1990). These results provide evidence that the hindbrain is one area that receives sensory input from peripheral detectors of fuel availability and also might be an area where sensory detectors of fuel availability are located.

Glucoprivic signals that increase food intake are detected in the hindbrain and then projected to forebrain areas by catecholaminergic cells. In support of this model, central treatment with NE or E is sufficient to increase food intake (Ritter and Epstein, 1975), and catecholamine neurons are necessary for 2DG-induced increases in food intake (Ritter *et al.*, 2001). PVH injections of the immunotoxin saporin conjugated to an antibody against dopamine-β-hydroxylase (DSAP), which targets NE and E neurons selectively, prevent increases in food intake in response to 2DG treatment. These DSAP lesions do not prevent increases in food intake in response to food deprivation or MA treatment. The same DSAP lesions severely reduced tyrosine hydroxylase immunoractivity (TH-IR) (a marker for catecholaminergic cells) in hindbrain neurons known to be glucoresponsive. TH-IR was reduced in the A2, C2, C3, and A6 cell groups and was almost completely eliminated in the area of the A1/C1 overlap (Ritter *et al.*, 2001).

Glucoprivic treatments that increase food intake also produce a cerebral metabolic emergency, as evidenced by sympathoadrenal activation and compensatory hyperglycemia (in contrast to the experiments with 2,5-AM that induce only a mild decrease in plasma glucose). Thus, experiments that use glucoprivic treatments might be more relevant to pathological metabolic deficits that are acute and severe, such as those that occurs in individuals with uncontrolled glucose homeostasis (e.g., diabetics). Putative glucose-sensitive brain areas might be sensitive to events related directly to glycolysis or to sequelae of subsequent metabolic events. For example, ATP-sensitive potassium channels mediate the effects of glucose on the firing rate of glucose-sensitive neurons in the brain, and the source of ATP might be from local glycolysis or mitochondrial metabolism (reviewed by Levin *et al.*, 1999).

In contrast to the detectors, the neural substrates involved in metabolic control of food intake are well known and include the AP-NTS, lateral PB, CEAm, and PVH. Treatment with MA, 2,5-AM, and 2DG increase food intake and FOS-li in the AP-NTS, and the increase in response to MA and 2,5-AM, but not 2DG, is prevented by total, bilateral subdiaphragmatic vagotomy (Ritter *et al.*, 1994). 2DG-induced, insulin-induced, and MA-induced increases in food intake also are prevented or attenuated by AP-NTS lesions. Both electrolytic and excitotoxic lesions centered in the dorsal and central lateral PB prevent the effects of MA, but not 2DG, on food intake and on FOS-li. Electrolytic but not cytotoxic lesions in the external and superior lateral PB prevent MA-induced eating, suggesting that fibers of passage, but not cell bodies involved in lipoprivic eating, are located in these subnuclei (Calingasan and Ritter, 1993). These results led to the suggestion that the dorsal and central lateral PB function specifically to control lipoprivic food intake. It should be noted, however, that ibotenic acid lesions of the lateral PB prevented the effects of 2,5-AM on 4-hour food intake (Grill *et al.*, 1995) and treatment with 2,5-AM increase FOS-li in the PB. 2,5-AM treatment increases eating via effects on hepatic energy status, and thus it might be suggested that the PBN is important for integration of signals from hepatic energy status. Contrary to this notion, 2,5-AM-induced FOS-li in the PB is absent in decerebrate rats, indicating that the PB is activated by descending input from the forebrain.

Bilateral electrolytic lesions of the CEAm significantly attenuated both MA-induced and 2DG-induced increases in food intake and in FOS-li (Tordoff *et al.*, 1982; Ritter and Calingasan, 1994). The fact that this area projects to the PVH suggests at least one mechanism whereby metabolic sensory systems impart drive to the feeding-stimulatory and feeding-inhibitory circuits. MA and 2DG treatment increase FOS-li in the PVH, and PVH DSAP lesions prevent 2DG-induced increased in food intake. Thus, it is surprising that electrolytic lesions that obliterate the PHV bilaterally fail to attenuate increases in food intake induced by either gluco- or lipoprivation. These results suggest that the PVH might participate in food intake, but that PVH involvement is not necessary. It is possible that hindbrain catecholamine neurons involved in glucoprivic food intake send collateral processes to areas other than PVH.

Another central effector mechanism common to virtually all of these metaboli challenges is an increase in hypothalamic NPY content with fuel deficits and a decrease in NPY content with fuel surplus (Chavez *et al.*, 1998). At least some of the NPY neurons that are sufficient for food intake induced by glucoprivation might originate in brain areas other than PVH (such as the DMH).

C. Hormone Mediators and Modulators

Fuel partitioning and intake are influenced by a wide variety of hormones and other chemical messengers. This can be demonstrated by exogenous application of these agents. It is more difficult to know which of these hormones controls behavior under natural circumstances. Glucagon was one of the first hormones proposed as a peripheral satiety signal in 1957. Pancreatic insulin and glucagon are secreted during the early stages of a meal, and hepatic-portal treatment with either of these proteins decreases meal size, but not water intake (reviewed by Geary, 1999). The feeding-inhibitory effects of glucagon are prevented by hepatic branch vagotomy, whereas the effects of intraperitoneal insulin treatment are attenuated by subdiaphragmatic vagotomy (Weatherford and Ritter, 1988). Other pancreatic hormones that decrease food intake include GLP-1 and enterostatin. In addition, epinephrine, leptin, and glucocorticoid have received a great deal of attention with regard to food intake. The secretion of these hormones is determined to a large extent by two sets of control mechanisms—the autonomic and neuroendocrine motor systems, and the stimuli generated by intracellular oxidation of metabolic fuels in endocrine secretory cells. However, at any particular time the relative importance of the neural and peripheral control systems for each of these hormones is determined by a wide variety of factors, including the availability of fuels for oxidation and the time of day. To affect the three categories of motor actions (see Fig. 2), insulin, leptin, and glucocorticoid all target specific receptors expressed by restricted sets of neurons, particularly in the hypothalamus and hindbrain (Porte *et al.*, 1998; Schwartz *et al.*, 2000).

1. Insulin and Food Intake

High doses of insulin increase food intake in a wide variety of species. The feeding-stimulatory effects of insulin treatment have already been discussed because high doses of insulin affect food intake indirectly, via increased fuel storage and a consequent deficit in the availability of oxidizable fuels. Thus, insulin treatment has been used as a tool to examine the sensory detection of fuel availability. In contrast, low doses of insulin administered ICV have the opposite effect on food intake—they decrease it. The hypothesis that insulin can target the brain directly to regulate feeding and metabolism was proposed in the 1970s (Woods *et al.,* 1979). Although its mechanism of action has not been elucidated, that ICV insulin reduces food intake and the identification of an active insulin transport mechanism across the blood–brain barrier (Schwartz *et al.,* 1991) and of specific insulin receptors in the brain, particularly in the ARH (Baskin *et al.,* 1987; Marks *et al.,* 1990; Unger *et al.,* 1991a), all support the idea that insulin acts centrally to influence food intake. Evidence demonstrated that a targeted disruption of the neural insulin receptor gene (NIRKO), but not the peripheral insulin receptor gene, is associated with increased body-fat deposition and hyperphagia (at least in females), in keeping with the idea that insulin might act directly in the brain to regulate food intake and metabolism (Brüning *et al.,* 2000). It has been difficult to reconcile this hypothesis with the well-known hyperphagia that occurs when plasma insulin is elevated. Furthermore, plasma insulin has long been known to fluctuate dramatically during the course of a day (with meals), and a theoretical and empirical framework is needed to understand how these dynamic patterns of hormone secretion might influence food intake over long periods of time. As we explain with regard to leptin (next), the chronically elevated insulin levels in obese individuals fail to induce satiety and reduce food intake.

2. Leptin and Food Intake

The actions of leptin in the brain have been the focus of intense investigation since 1995. In the 1960s, single-gene mutant obesity syndromes were identified and characterized. Mice homozygous for the recessive *ob* allele located on chromosome 6 were found to develop hyperphagia, hyperglycemia, hyperinsulinemia, and obesity. A remarkably similar syndrome was observed in mice homozygous for a recessive mutation in the *db* allele located on chromosome 4 (Hummel *et al.,* 1966). Clues to the nature of these mutations were ob-

tained by parabiosis experiments in which a small proportion of circulating blood was exchanged between pairs of mice that were surgically joined. When obese *ob/ob* mice were parabiosed with lean partners, the *ob/ob* partner failed to show their characteristic body weight gain relative to singly housed *ob/ob* mice or *ob/ob* mice paired with *ob/ob* partners (Haessler and Crawford, 1965; Chlonverakis, 1972). In contrast, when obese *db/db* mice were paired with lean partners, the *db/db* mice continued to gain weight and did not differ significantly from singly housed *db/db* mice or *db/db* mice paired with *db/db* partners (Coleman and Hummel, 1969). When *ob/ob* mice were paired with *db/db* mice, the *ob/ob* mice again failed to gain body weight, whereas the *db/db* mice attained a body weight characteristic of the genotype. From these observations came the notion that hyperphagia and obesity in *ob/ob* mice are due to the absence of a circulating satiety factor, whereas the same traits in *db/db* mice are due to decreased sensitivity to this satiety factor. The development of modern molecular techniques led to positional cloning of the *ob* gene and to the discovery of the *ob* protein leptin (from Greek *leptos,* "thin, small") (Zhang *et al.,* 1994). Subsequently, recombinant leptin was examined for behavioral and neuroendocrine effects. Treatment with leptin (systemically or intracerebrally) reduces food intake in both wild-type and *ob/ob* mice, but not in *db/db* mice that lack the functional leptin receptor (Campfield *et al.,* 1995). Leptin treatment, either peripherally or systemically, decreases food intake (selectively reducing meal size) in wild-type (nonmutant) rodents (Eckel *et al.,* 1998) and sheep (Henry *et al.,* 1999). Leptin is secreted from WAT cells. In populations of well-fed animals, leptin is highly positively correlated with body adiposity. Plasma leptin concentrations change within hours of fasting or refeeding, prior to any change in adiposity. A similar pattern is found in adipocytes in culture; baseline leptin secretion is proportional to adipocyte cell size, and leptin secretion is more acutely regulated by the availability of metabolic fuels (Levy *et al.,* 2000). Thus, it appears that changes in leptin might inform the brain about peripheral energy status.

In support of the notion that leptin controls body weight and adiposity, chronic leptin administration reduces food intake and increases energy expenditure (Campfield *et al.,* 1995); its plasma concentration increases following feeding in rats (Ahima *et al.,* 1998),

ICV leptin (and insulin) treatment decreases NPY gene expression (Mercer *et al.*, 1996), and the overexpression of NPY in *ob/ob*, but not *db/db*, mice is attenuated by leptin treatment (Schwartz *et al.*, 1996; Stephens *et al.*, 1995).

Many investigators have taken these data as support for the lipostatic hypothesis, which suggests that adipocyte filling increases leptin synthesis and secretion, which in turn act as a short-term satiety factor to prevent further lipocyte filling. A great deal of data do not fit this model (Flier, 1998; Unger, 2000; Levy *et al.*, 2000). Leptin fluctuates rapidly with changes in the availability of oxidizable fuels when levels of adiposity are unchanging, and thus it is unlikely that leptin provides an accurate measure of adiposity (Schneider *et al.*, 2000b). Obese animals that lack mutations for either leptin or for the leptin receptor with high endogenous concentrations of plasma leptin are not sated by their own high endogenous levels of circulating leptin (Flier, 1998). Furthermore, the transport of leptin across the blood–brain barrier is saturated in all but the leanest individuals, and thus only relatively lean animals are responsive to changes in plasma leptin that are within the physiological range (Levy *et al.*, 2000). Consequently, it is unlikely that changes in leptin secretion are detected by the brain unless leptin is already at low concentrations. If changes in leptin secretion play a role in control of food intake, it is more likely to do so when dietary fuels, glycogen, and fat stores are severely depleted. At such times, a deficit in leptin binding in the ARH might provide one of many stimuli to increase food intake by increasing the activity of NPY or AgRP neurons and decreasing activity in the POMC or CART neurons. Each of these systems acts, at least in part, by way of downstream NPY and MC-4 receptor mechanisms in the LHA and PVH (Cowley *et al.*, 1999; Elmquist *et al.*, 1999; Marsh *et al.*, 1999; Schwartz *et al.*, 2000).

Other investigators have noted that leptin transport across the blood–brain barrier is decreased by fasting and increased by refeeding (Levy *et al.*, 2000). These data suggest that adipocyte filling and the consequent plasma levels of the hormone are not the primary determinant of central leptin binding. Rather, entry of leptin into the brain is controlled by as yet unknown stimuli that result from fasting and refeeding. Changes in leptin entry to the brain might influence food intake (and reproduction), but the original question still remains unanswered: What is the sensory stimulus that links energy deficits to changes in the blood–brain barrier? If the integrity of the blood–brain barrier is controlled by yet another hormone that informs the brain about energy status, what is the metabolic stimulus that influences the secretion of that hormone? Thus, the largest gap in our understanding of control of food intake concerns the primary sensory stimuli that influence hormonal mediators, and future research should be aimed at elucidating the nature of these stimuli and their detectors. Adding more hormones and peptides to the list of controls for ingestion and reproduction will not determine the nature of the metabolic stimulus.

The strongest evidence in support of the idea that a particular hormone binding to its receptor in a particular brain area is necessary and sufficient for a particular behavior is the demonstration of a change in behavior in response to localized treatment with an antagonist that acts at a specific receptor for that peptide. To date, the idea that hunger and eating are triggered by falling leptin has not been tested directly because an antagonist to the leptin receptor has not been developed. Furthermore, systemic treatment with leptin has not proven reliable as an intervention for obesity in human beings, except in one subject with a mutation in the human gene that codes for leptin (Farooqi *et al.*, 1999; Montague *et al.*, 1997). Other data demonstrate that central NPY can be influenced by deficits in metabolic fuel availability even when plasma leptin levels are high or unchanging (Chavez *et al.*, 1998; Ji and Friedman, 2000). Together, these data show that leptin is not the only important mediator of metabolic effects on food intake.

Species differences in the response to falling leptin indicate that increased food intake is not a universal response to decreased circulating concentrations of this protein. In Syrian hamsters, plasma leptin levels fall sharply during food deprivation (Schneider *et al.*, 2000b), yet Syrian hamsters fail to show post-fast hyperphagia (Schneider *et al.*, 1988). This phenomenon might be explained by attention to social context and by studying both consummatory and appetitive aspects of behaviors. For example, if low plasma leptin levels divert attention away from sex and toward food procurement, it would be predicted that food deprivation and falling plasma leptin might result in increased food searching or hoarding and decreased sex behavior in response to a sexually experienced partner in Syrian hamsters. Conversely, leptin treatment might decrease fasting-induced hoarding and facilitate sex behavior (Schneider and Buckley, 2001). In one study of ovariectomized hamsters brought into heat with estradiol and progesterone treatments, leptin treatment increased lordosis duration in fed, but not in fasted, hamsters (Wade *et al.*, 1997). The effects of leptin on Syrian hamsters have not been tested in a social context in which the subject is allowed to choose among food, hoarding, and sex. When male rats were presented with a sexually receptive female and a bottle of a palatable sucrose solution simultaneously, the number of intromissions and ejaculations increased, whereas the consumption of sucrose decreased in leptin-treated males relative to vehicle-treated controls (Ammar *et al.*, 2000). These results are consistent with the notion that leptin promotes sexual motivation as long as hunger motivation is not elevated. Thus, it might be predicted that when stored energy is depleted and the availability of oxidizable fuels is low, the fall in plasma leptin might promote appetitive aspects of ingestion, such as food hoarding and foraging.

3. CCK, Other Chemical Messengers, and Food Intake

The glucocorticoid hormones have long been known to have important effects on metabolism. They regulate glucose utilization, and during negative energy balance can increase gluconeogenesis by increasing protein catabolism. Glucocorticoids can also affect many functions in the brain and are intimately involved with modulating the neural responses to stress (Sapolsky *et al.*, 2000; Watts, 1996). These effects are mediated by two types of receptor—mineralocorticoid (MR) high-affinity low-capacity receptors, and glucocorticoid (GR) lower-affinity high-capacity receptors (de Kloet *et al.*, 1998). With regard to the neural networks regulating ingestive behavior, elucidating how glucocorticoids are by themselves able to regulate ingestive behavior and metabolism has been confounded by the complex interrelationships among glucocorticoids, leptin, and insulin (Porte *et al.*, 1998). Certainly the GR is expressed by virtually all nuclei implicated in controlling metabolism. Adrenalectomy attenuates most forms of obesity and hyperphagia, and these effects are reversed by central, but not peripheral, treatment with glucocorticoids (Green *et al.*, 1992). The fact that glucocorticoids increase NPY levels in diabetic rats that lack insulin and leptin (Strack *et al.*, 1995) suggests that glucocorticoids can act both by themselves and with insulin and leptin as important modulators of ingestive behavior (Dallman *et al.*, 1993).

Feeding and digestion result in the release of peptides that act as putative satiety factors when administered systemically. These include CCK, bombesin, gastrin-releasing peptide, and neuromedin B (Gibbs *et al.*, 1973; Gibbs and Smith, 1988; Muurahainen *et al.*, 1993; Kirkham *et al.*, 1995). CCK was one of the first studied gastrointestinal peptides and remains the most studied. Antagonists to CCK administered peripherally increase meal size (Reidelberger and O'Rourke, 1989). Treatment with the CCK agonist, CCK-8, inhibits food intake in a dose-dependent manner without supporting a conditioned taste aversion. CCK-8 treatment in conjunction with gastric distension, produces satiating effects that are greater than either CCK-8 treatment or gastric distension alone (Schwartz *et al.*, 1993). It is hypothesized that the entry of food into the stomach increases the firing rate of gastric stretch receptors and activates CCK secretion from duodenum. Both of these negative feedback signals are thought to act synergistically to target neurons in the hindbrain and other brain sites to inhibit feeding and regulate associated autonomic motor actions.

Peptides such as CCK decrease meal size; yet, when administered chronically, CCK-treated animals eat more meals and thus do not reduce body weight or body-fat content. This suggests that the signal for meal size is distinct from the signal that balances food intake relative to energy expenditure. Other sensory signals, such as those that result from a deficit in hepatic energy status, link food intake to energy storage and expenditure. CCK treatment has a synergistic interaction with sensory stimuli related to gut distention or other chemical cues from nutrients in the gut (reviewed by G. J. Schwartz, 2000). In addition, the effect of CCK on meal size is potentiated by coadministration of either insulin or leptin, suggesting that hormonal modulators can interact with meal-terminating peptides to affect intake (Figlewicz *et al.*, 1986; reviewed by Ritter *et al.*, 1999). The investigation of such interactions will be emphasized in future research on ingestive behavior.

Several lines of evidence suggest that metabolic sensory stimuli that are detected in either the periphery or the caudal hindbrain might interact with hormonal modulators to influence food intake. Information from the hindbrain might reach the forebrain effectors via a number of known pathways. Early candidates for the projection of these signals from the caudal hindbrain to the forebrain included catecholaminergic projections to the PVH and DMH (Ritter *et al.*, 1998). It has been noted that CCK neurons in the AP and GLP-1 neurons in the caudal NTS project to the PVH and DMH. In keeping with a role for CCK-ergic and GLP-1-ergic control of food intake, CCK and GLP-1 when administered directly into the third cerebral ventricle reduce meal size (Turton *et al.*, 1996), and ICV treatment with antagonists to the CCK and GLP-1 receptors produce reliable increases in meal size. One difference between CCK and GLP-1 treatment is that third-ventricular CCK, but not GLP-1, treatment decreases food intake without the formation of a conditioned taste aversion. However, GLP-1 might influence food intake directly via action in the PVH. Central microinfusions of GLP-1 directly into the PVH reduces short-term food intake without the formation of a conditioned taste aversion. Bilateral lesions of the PVH prevent the effects of third-ventricular GLP-1 infusion on food intake, but do not influence the formation of a conditioned taste aversion by the same treatment. Together, these data suggest that information of interoreceptors regarding the availability of oxidizable fuels or peripheral CCK secretion might be received in the hindbrain and might reach the central feeding inhibitory centers via NE, CCK, or GLP-1 projections to PVH.

D. Behavioral State

Behavioral state has profound influence on motivated behaviors. The animal's behavioral state is controlled by sets of neural systems whose cell bodies are located throughout the hindbrain, hypothalamus, and basal forebrain. These include cholinergic neurons in the basal forebrain, monoaminergic cell groups in the hindbrain (e.g., the noradrenergic locus coeruleus and the serotonergic raphe nuclei), and histaminergic neurons in the tuberomammillary nucleus. One set of neurons that has gained prominence in this respect are those in the lateral hypothalamus containing orexin. Identi-

fied almost simultaneously by two independent groups (De Lecea *et al.*, 1998; Sakurai *et al.*, 1998), these neurons express prominent amounts of two related peptides, orexin A and B, and are distributed quite extensively in the LHA. Initial studies showed that orexin A and B are excitatory (De Lecea *et al.*, 1998) and increase food intake when injected ICV (Sakurai *et al.*, 1998). Certainly, stimuli that lead to a negative energy balance and significant hypoglycemia increase orexin mRNA levels (Cai *et al.*, 1999; Griffond *et al.*, 1999; Moriguchi *et al.*, 1999). However, other data have strongly implicated the orexins in the control of behavioral state (Willie *et al.*, 2001). The fact that orexin neurons project strongly to the locus coeruleus and the tuberomammilary nucleus is consistent with this notion (Peyron *et al.*, 1998). Finally, three observations support the idea that orexin neurons might form a link between the systems controlling behavioral state and energy balance (Willie *et al.*, 2001). First, an orexigenic peptide (dynorphin) is also synthesized in orexin neurons (Chou *et al.*, 2001); second, a knock-out of the orexin gene leads to narcolepsy (Chemelli *et al.*, 1999); third, the destruction of orexin neurons generates narcolepsy, hypophagia, and obesity (Hara *et al.*, 2001).

V. REPRODUCTION

Many of the factors that increase hunger or food intake also inhibit reproductive processes. This dual function can be ascribed to many of the sensory stimuli, the neuropeptides that are part of the neural effector systems, and the hormonal mediators and modulators that have already been discussed (Table 1).

The hypothalamic-pituitary-gonadal (HPG) system controls ovulation and lactation, influences the behavioral acts associated with copulation, and influences the complex social interactions of courtship and parental behaviors. The HPG system is integrated with sensory inputs and motor output in other parts of the brain and periphery (see Fig. 3). Energetic challenges inhibit reproduction by acting at many levels, including, hypothalamic control of gonadotropin-releasing hormone (GnRH) pulses, hypothalamic and pituitary control of the LH surge, gonadal steroid secretion, and neural steroid receptors that control sex behavior (reviewed by Wade *et al.*, 1996).

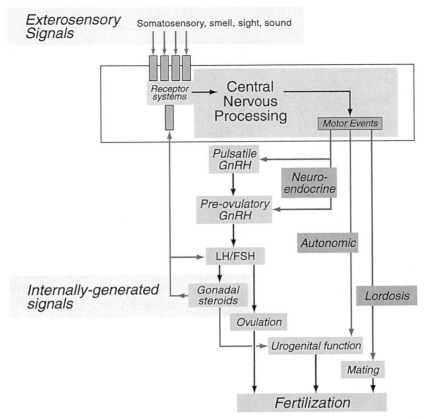

FIGURE 3   A schematic representation of the exterosensory and internally generated signals for the motor events that control female reproductive functions in the rat. Motor outputs are shown in red, internal signals in blue. Somatosensory and olfactory inputs are key exterosensory inputs, whereas sight and sound play more subsidiary roles. Gonadal steroids are the internally generated modulators rather than triggers for behavior. Autonomic motor actions regulate urogenital functions; neuroendocrine motor output controls gonadotropin secretion from the anterior pituitary; and behavioral motor actions mediate lordosis. FSH, follicle-stimulating hormone; GnRH, gonadotropin-releasing hormone; LH, luteinizing hormone. **See insert for a color version of this figure.**

LH pulsatility, the LH surge, and lordosis (the female postural reflex essential for successful mating) have been studied most extensively in rodents, and therefore our discussion focuses on the interaction of these mechanisms with those that control energy balance. In addition, it is important to remember that not all mammals show spontaneous ovulatory cycles. In many species, female-typical sex behavior and ovulation are induced by tactile and olfactory cues from adult males; energy availability and oxidation have profound effects on reproduction in these species as well (e.g., Gill and Rissman, 1997; Temple and Rissman, 2000a). Furthermore, most spontaneous ovulators do not typi-

cally experience a succession of ovulatory cycles in nature. Most experience a series of pregnancies followed by a period of anestrus and anovulation during lactation (this period is termed lactational diestrus). The period of lactational diestrus is lengthened by energetic challenges (Woodside *et al.*, 1998). Thus in many species living in their natural habitats, the most ecologically meaningful point of interaction between energy and reproduction occurs during lactation. In addition to the effects of energy on reproduction, the reverse is also true. Reproductive processes have important influences on energy intake, storage, and expenditure that are beyond the scope of this review, but are discussed elsewhere (Wade and Schneider, 1992).

A. Effector Systems

1. Pulsatile LH Secretion

The temporal release pattern of secretion of LH, like that of many hormones, is pulsatile rather than constant. The frequency of these pulses is between 20 and 30 minutes in female rats. In males, the interpulse interval is longer and the amplitude higher, but the mechanisms are essentially the same for both sexes. The timing of LH pulsatility derives directly from the firing patterns of neuroendocrine motor neurons that produce a pulsatile release pattern of GnRH from their terminals in the median eminence (ME). This has been elegantly revealed in sheep, in which it is possible to collect blood simultaneously from the hypophysial and systemic vasculatures (Clarke and Cummins, 1982). Pulses of GnRH in hypophysial blood correlate very closely with pulses of LH in the general circulation (Figs. 4A and 4B).

A number of models have been proposed to explain the neural basis of pulsatile LH release, but the precise neural mechanisms remain controversial. In one model, the soma of GnRH neurons and the pulse generator are distinct entities located at different hypothalamic locations (Bourguignon *et al.*, 1997a,b; Maeda *et al.*, 1995). Other evidence suggests that the pulse generator involves the soma of GnRH motor neurons. A prototypical pulsatile GnRH release pattern is exhibited by cultured neurons transfected with the GnRH gene (Wetsel *et al.*, 1992) and by more physiologically derived *in vitro* preparations (Terasawa *et al.*, 1999). More data are needed to determine whether the innate pulses from cultured GnRH cells are sufficient to mimic the species-specific pulse pattern required for follicular development. It is more likely that the species-specific pattern of pulsatility necessary for follicular development emerges from the interactions of a neuronal network comprising GnRH motor neurons that have the ability to generate simple secretory oscillations coordinated by proximal, possibly GABAergic and glutamatergic, premotor neurons (see Fig. 5A) (Brown *et al.*,

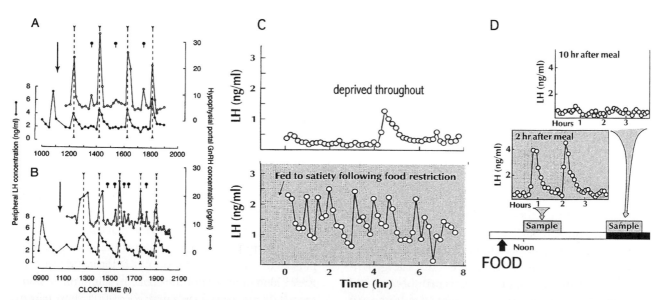

FIGURE 4   (A and B) Luteinizing hormone (LH) and gonadotropin releasing hormone (GnRH) profiles taken simultaneously from peripheral (LH) and hypophysial portal (GnRH) blood from two sheep. Dashed lines indicate coincidental episodes of GnRH and LH secretion; dots indicate GnRH episodes without coincidental LH secretion. The arrows indicate the start times of hypophysial portal blood sampling. Adapted from Clark and Cummins (1982), *Endocrinology* **111**, 1737–1739, © The Endocrine Society. (C) The frequency of LH pulses is significantly reduced in food restricted gilts (top) and is restored within two hours of a single meal (bottom). Adapted by G. N. Wade from Cosgrove *et al.* (1991). (D) Rapid induction of LH pulses after a single meal in female rats in which puberty has been delayed by chronic food restriction. Adapted by G. N. Wade (Wade *et al.*, 1996) from Bronson and Heideman (1990).

A   *B*

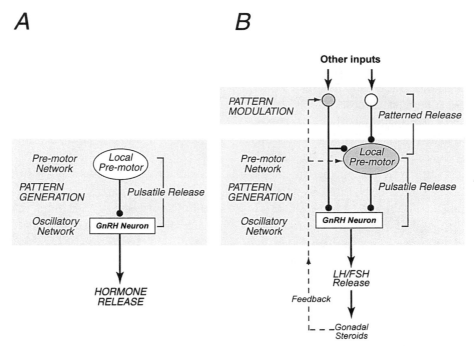

FIGURE 5   Two schematic diagrams illustrating the organization of the neural elements that control (A) pulsatile and (B) more complex patterned gonadotropin secretion. (A) Pulsatile hormone release can be generated by the interaction of an oscillatory network consisting of the neuroendocrine motor neurons and local premotor neurons. (B) More complex patterned release is generated by modulating pulsatile release by way of inputs from other sets of premotor neurons whose projections are directed either at the more local premotor neurons or at the local premotor neurons and the GnRH neurons. Some of these inputs are estrogen-sensitive (gray) and are more distal from the GnRH neurons. FSH, follicle-stimulating hormone; GnRH, gonadotropin-releasing hormone; LH luteinizing hormone.

1994; Bourguignon *et al.,* 1997a,b; Leng and Brown, 1997; Herbison, 1998).

A variety of different transmitter systems, including catecholamines, opiates, CCK, NPY, and CRH have been implicated in the regulation of LH secretion in normal animals that are not energetically challenged (Kimura *et al.,* 1983; Kalra *et al.,* 1997; McDonald, 1990). Collectively, these inputs target both local premotor neurons and GnRH neurons to alter LH pulsatility (Fig. 5B) (Brown *et al.,* 1994; Herbison, 1998). Many, but not all, of these premotor neurons are estrogen-sensitive and are critical for mediating the effects of gonadal steroids on the GnRH network (Herbison, 1998). Central treatment with either an antibody raised against NPY or antisense oligonucleotides for NPY mRNA suppresses pulsatile LH secretion in free-feeding ovariectomized rats, suggesting that NPY at

normal physiological levels has an excitatory influence on GnRH secretion (Xu *et al.,* 1996; Kasuya *et al.,* 1998). In addition, α-MSH, an antagonist to the melanocortin receptor, is inhibitory, whereas MCH is stimulatory for LH secretion in ovariectomized estradiol-treated rats (Gonzalez *et al.,* 1997). As discussed later, fasting-induced increases in NPY, but not α-MSH, are implicated in the inhibitory effects of leptin on LH pulsatility.

a) Energetic Challenges   The primary locus whereby energetic challenges inhibit reproduction is the GnRH pulse generator, and these effects are similar in males and females (reviewed by Bronson, 2000). Pulsatile LH secretion, follicle development, and ovulation can be reinstated by treatment with species-specific pulses of GnRH in fasted rats, sheep, pigs, cows, monkeys, and humans (Bronson, 1986; Cameron, 1996; Day *et al.*, 1986; Foster and Olster, 1985; Kile *et al.*, 1991; Manning and Bronson, 1991; Cameron and Nosbisch, 1991; Nillius *et al.*, 1975; Armstrong and Britt, 1987). Food deprivation and treatments with inhibitors of the oxidation of glucose inhibit GnRH secretion (Foster and Bucholtz, 1995) and decrease FOS-like immunoreactivity in GnRH-containing forebrain neurons (Berriman *et al.*, 1992). In spontaneous ovulators, it is unlikely that a negative energy balance affects GnRH synthesis because, in at least a few species, GnRH mRNA, GnRH content, and the number of GnRH immunoreactive neurons are not decreased and, in some cases, are increased by energetic challenges (I'Anson *et al.*, 1991; Ebling *et al.*, 1990; McShane *et al.*, 1993). In sheep and rats, energetic challenges fail to decrease pituitary LH and follicle-stimulating hormone (FSH) content or message (Bronson, 1988; Beckett *et al.*, 1997). However, GnRH mRNA is inhibited by food deprivation in male rats (Gruenewald and Matsumoto, 1993), and GnRH transcription or translation might be expected to be an important locus of effect in birds and in mammalian species that are induced-ovulators. There is precedence for environmental regulation at this level. In birds, indirect evidence suggests that environmental cues (e.g., photoperiod) control reproduction via changes in the expression of genes for GnRH. Specifically, environmental cues regulate the GnRH peptide content and the content of the pro-GnRH peptide (the unprocessed peptide), implicating photoperiodic regulation of pro-GnRH gene transcription. However, direct evidence for the environmental control of gene expression has not been established because the GnRH gene has not been subcloned in these particular species (reviewed by Ball and Bentley, 2000).

Due to the rapid effects of metabolic fuel availability on pulsatile LH secretion, it is generally agreed that metabolic signals produce neural signals that inhibit pulsatile GnRH secretion. Food deprivation decreases the frequency of LH pulses, and these pulses are reinstated within hours of refeeding in rats, gilts, and male monkeys (Figs. 4C and 4D) (Armstrong and Britt, 1987; Cosgrove *et al.*, 1991; Bronson, 1986, 1988; Bronson and Heideman, 1990; Cameron, 1996; Cameron and Nosbisch, 1991; Clark *et al.*, 1990; Schreihofer *et al.*, 1993). Changes in adiposity and resulting changes in

periheral hormones are presumably slower than these rapid changes in GnRH and LH secretion.

Mounting evidence supports the idea that some metabolic challenges inhibit GnRH pulses by increasing hypothalamic sensitivity to estradiol. LH pulses are not inhibited by food deprivation or by low ICV doses of 2DG in ovariectomized rats, unless they are treated with estradiol (Cagampang *et al.*, 1990; Murahashi *et al.*, 1996).

Given the well-known feedback of steroids on GnRH secretion, it was surprising that initial studies failed to find functional estrogen receptors (ER) on GnRH neurons *in vivo*. GnRH neurons express mRNA and estrogen receptor immunoreactivity (ER-IR) for both ERα and ERβ, although whether these are translated into functional proteins remains controversial (Butler *et al.*, 1999; Hrabovszky *et al.*, 2000; Skynner *et al.*, 1999). Future experiments must examine the role of ERβ or the ratio of ERα to ERβ as potential mediators of the effects of energetic challenges on GnRH secretion.

Several lines of evidence suggest that metabolic challenges increase steroid negative feedback in brain areas with projections to GnRH neurons. It has been suggested that increased sensitivity to steroids might be due to increases in receptors for those steroids. Consistent with this idea, metabolic challenges are associated with increased ER-IR in the medial preoptic area (mPOA) in Syrian hamsters (H.-Y. Li *et al.*, 1994), and in the PVH in hamsters and rats (Estacio *et al.*, 1996; H.-Y. Li *et al.*, 1994). These brain areas contain either GnRH neurons or nuclei that project to GnRH neurons. It has been suggested that the essential estradiol negative feedback occurs in the PVH because ER-IR are increased in the PVH in fasted rats (Estacio *et al.*, 1996) and the microinfusion of estradiol into the PVH accentuates fasting-induced suppression of pulsatile LH secretion in ovariectomized rats (Nagatani *et al.*, 1994). It has been suggested that some metabolic challenges, particularly glucoprivic challenges, inhibit pulsatile LH secretion by increasing catecholaminergic input from the NTS to the PVH (Cagampang *et al.*, 1992; Maeda *et al.*, 1994; Nagatani *et al.*, 1994). The effect of steroid binding in the PVH is thought to increase the secretion of CRH in neurons that project to the vicinity of GnRH neurons (Maeda *et al.*, 1994; Tsukamura *et al.*, 1999). Although CRH is one component of the HPA, or stress system, it would be incorrect to state that the effects of metabolic challenges act via the stress response, as has been demonstrated by Hilton and Loucks (2000). CRH inhibits GnRH pulse generator activity, and these results are probably not mediated by adrenocorticotropic hormone (ACTH) or glucocorticoids (Xiao and Ferin, 1988; Xiao *et al.*, 1989). It has long been thought that CRH inhibits LH by direct action on GnRH terminals (Petraglia *et al.*, 1987; MacLusky *et al.*, 1988). In addition, the microinfusion of estradiol into the A2 region of the NTS also accentuates fasting-induced suppression of pulsatile LH secretion in ovariectomized rats (Nagatani *et al.*, 1994). Thus, estradiol might also influence the brainstem projections to the PVH by binding in the NTS (Nagatani *et al.*, 1994).

In addition to effects on steroid negative feedback, energetic challenges can inhibit LH secretion via steroid-independent effects in sheep and rats (Foster and Olster, 1985; Nagatani *et al.*, 1996b; Bronson, 1988; Murahashi *et al.*, 1996). Severe energetic challenges also alter pituitary sensitivity to GnRH (Day *et al.*, 1986; Booth, 1990; Beckett *et al.*, 1997; I'Anson *et al.*, 1991), resulting in decreased secretion of LH and FSH. For example, estradiol treatment enhances the pituitary GnRH receptor as well as mRNA for the receptor in well-fed and moderately food-restricted sheep, but this estradiol-induced enhancement is absent in severely food-restricted sheep (Beckett *et al.*, 1997).

NPY has different effects on the HPG system, depending on the steroid milieu and level of NPY secretion. For example, NPY is a stimulatory factor in the generation of LH pulses in fed animals. However, in a variety of experimental models, the high sustained levels of NPY associated with fasting are inhibitory for LH secretion, particularly when circulating levels of ovarian steroids are low. Third-ventricular treatment with NPY inhibits LH pulse frequency and amplitude in ovariectomized rats, and this effect is reversed when GnRH is administered (McDonald *et al.*, 1989). Chronic third-ventricular NPY treatment also inhibits the HPG system in male rats (Pierroz *et al.*, 1996). In food-restricted, lactating, anovulatory rats, elevated NPY immunoreactivity in the ARH persists for 10 days after return to *ad libitum*-feeding. In keeping with a role for NPY in prolonged suppression of the HPG system by food restriction, plasma LH is inhibited in food-restricted rats during lactation, and LH does not increase to fed levels until 10 days after the return to *ad libitum* feeding

(Abizaid *et al.*, 1997). Treatment with a Y5 receptor agonist lengthens the duration of lactational diestrus, whereas treatment with a Y5 receptor antagonist attenuates the effects of fasting on the duration of lactational diestrus (Walker *et al.*, 2000).

As previously mentioned, CRH has inhibitory influences on LH secretion, and treatment with antagonists to CRH prevents the effects of fasting on LH pulses in ovariectomized steroid-treated rats (Maeda *et al.*, 1994). The gut peptide CCK is secreted as a neuropeptide in the CNS in regions containing gonadal steroid receptors and GnRH neurons, such as the mPOA (Simerly *et al.*, 1986). GnRH-containing neurons in the mPOA are thought to receive projections from CCK fibers (Simerly *et al.*, 1986), and CCK implanted in this area has both stimulatory and inhibitory influences on LH secretion (Hashimoto and Kimura, 1986; Kimura *et al.*, 1983). In addition, treatment with another gut peptide, GLP-1, increases the secretion of LH within 5 minutes of injection in male rats (Beak *et al.*, 1998). GLP-1, like CCK, is also secreted in the CNS. Furthermore, a 48-hour fast decreases hypothalamic GLP-1 content compared to that of fed rats. CCK neurons in the AP and GLP-1 neurons in the caudal NTS project to the PVH, one area where it is thought that food deprivation increases sensitivity to steroid negative feedback on the GnRH pulse generator.

2. LH Surge

The LH surge is the culmination of a gradual increase in the amplitude and frequency of LH pulses on the afternoon of proestrus. The LH surge and ovulation depend on the superimposition of a phasic pattern of release on the underlying pulsatility (Fox and Smith, 1985; Hoeger *et al.*, 1999). In response to increases in circulating estrogen and progesterone, rat GnRH neurons are activated during the afternoon of proestrus to initiate a massive increase in GnRH release into the portal vasculature (Fig. 6), which in turn is necessary for the rupture of the mature follicle (Sarkar *et al.*, 1976). This patterning requires a circadian signal from the SCH that interacts in an estrogen-dependent manner with the network that generates pulsatility. Two sets of inputs are important for controlling the preovulatory LH surge, which in turn might be modulated by energy balance (Fig. 7) (Briski and Sylvester, 1998). First, premotor inputs from catecholaminergic, opiate,

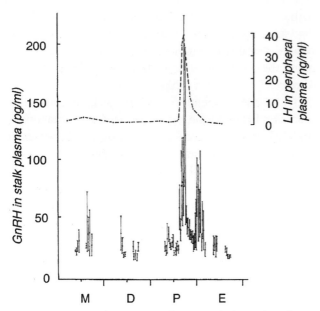

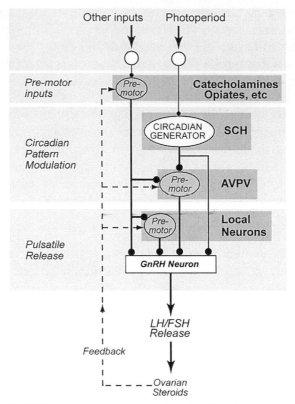

FIGURE 6 Preovulatory surge of GnRH in the hypophysial portal blood in cycling female rats is coincidental with the LH surge. D, diestrus; E, estrus; GnRH, gonadotropin-releasing hormone; LH, luteinizing hormone; M, metestrus; P, proestrus. Adapted from Sarkar *et al.* (1976), *Nature* **264**, 461–463, with permission.

FIGURE 7 A schematic diagram based on Fig. 5 showing the organization of the neural components that are thought to mediate the pre-ovulatory LH surge in rats. The pulsatile LH release generated by the GnRH network in Fig. 5A is modulated by more complex sets of neural inputs to generate the surge, some of which are estrogen-sensitive (gray). These inputs include a circadian signal from the suprachiasmatic nucleus (SCH). The SCH projects to GnRH neurons and the anteroventral periventricular nucleus (AVPV), which, unlike the SCH, contains estrogen receptors. Other groups of premotor neurons are both proximal (e.g., local GABAergic neurons) and distal (e.g., catecholaminergic neurons in the hindbrain or opiate neurons in the arcuate nucleus) to GnRH neurons, some of which are estrogen-sensitive. Inputs that mediate the effects of energy balance on the pre-ovulatory surge might do so by way of these premotor neurons.

and other peptidergic neurons are vital for the preovulatory surge and may well convey a variety of different types of information, including energy status, to the GnRH network. These inputs derive from a variety of sources in the forebrain and hindbrain, and target both GnRH neurons as well as other more local premotor neurons (Fig. 7) (Herbison, 1998; Simonian *et al.*, 1999). By themselves, however, these inputs are not sufficient to generate the preovulatory LH surge. A second set of inputs influences preovulatory GnRH secretion by providing circadian timing signals from the SCH (Brown-Grant and Raisman, 1977; Wiegand *et al.*, 1980; Wiegand and Terasawa, 1982). There is evidence that the SCH provides a vasoactive intestinal peptide (VIP)-ergic input directly to GnRH neurons (van der Beek *et al.*, 1997), and this projection might provide important environmental input into the GnRH secretory pattern. Lesion data show that the estrogen-stimulated LH surge in female rats requires both the SCH and a small group of neurons in the preoptic area called the anteroventral periventricular nucleus (AVPV) to which the SCH projects quite heavily (Watson *et al.*, 1995; Watts, 1991). The AVPV is sexually dimorphic

in terms of its size, patterns of neuropeptide expression, and the density of its innervation from parts of from the BST (Simerly, 1998; Simerly *et al.*, 1988). Critically, the AVPV also contains a large number of estrogen and progesterone receptors, which is not the case for the SCH (Herbison, 1998). Two sets of data suggest that the AVPV acts as a premotor neuroendocrine motor pattern generator of the type illustrated in Fig. 5. First, it projects directly to GnRH neurons (Gu and Simerly, 1997). Second, small lesions of the AVPV as well as the region between the SCH and AVPV block both the preovulatory and the SCH-dependent release of LH (Wiegand *et al.*, 1980; Wiegand and Terasawa, 1982). By virtue of its bidirectional neural connections with the ARH and the PVH, the AVPV might be important for mediating some effects of changes in reproductive function on energy balance and vice versa.

NPY appears to be involved in the normal LH surge, an event driven by positive feedback from estradiol. When high levels of estradiol and progesterone are exerting positive feedback effects on GnRH secretion, NPY is released into the pituitary portal circulation along with GnRH, and the NPY action on Y1 receptors potentiates the effects of GnRH on the LH surge (Leupen *et al.*, 1997; Urban *et al.*, 1996).

a) Metabolic Challenges Metabolic challenges alter the GnRH and LH surge, independent of their effects on pulsatile LH secretion. Effects on the neural mechanisms that control the LH surge can be demonstrated by measuring plasma LH levels in ovariectomized (OVX) animals treated with surge-inducing doses of estradiol. For example, food-deprived rats and Syrian hamsters show heightened sensitivity to estradiol positive feedback (Mangels *et al.*, 1996; Sprangers and Piacsek, 1997). This is consistent with the potentiation of LH secretion that occurs when GnRH is released in concert with elevated levels of NPY (Leupen *et al.*, 1997; Urban *et al.*, 1996). The potentiation of the LH surge does not explain anovulation in response to energetic challenges, unless the increased sensitivity to estradiol induces a premature LH surge that dissociates the surge from the occurrence of mature follicles or from mating. An additional or alternative reason for anovulation might be the suppression of the FSH surge that occurs in food-restricted rats (Sprangers and Piacsek, 1997). Reduced or suppressed FSH surges may be at least one contributor to retarded follicular development and anestrus (Schwartz, 1974; Hirshfield and Midgley, 1978). Still other experiments show that systemic treatment with inhibitors of glucose oxidation and treatment with high hypoglycemia-inducing doses of insulin can attenuate estradiol-induced LH surges in rats (Briski and Sylvester, 1998; Crump *et al.*, 1982; Howland,

1980; Medina *et al.*, 1998). These experiments imply that different metabolic challenges might work on different levels of the HPG system. Specifically, metabolic signals generated by food deprivation inhibit pulsatile LH secretion, decreases the FSH surge, and facilitate the LH surge, whereas signals generated by treatment with insulin or inhibitors of glucose oxidation inhibit the LH surge.

The role of the SCH and AVPV in mediating metabolic effects on the GnRH should be examined more closely. SCH contains neurons responsive to glucose availability (Hall et al., 1997). Thus, it is possible that deficits in fuel availability affect GnRH and LH secretion by disrupting the circadian input from the SCH to the AVPV or to GnRH neurons directly. The first ovulation after lactational diestrus is associated with the return of the circadian-timed LH surge without a prior increase in pulsatile LH secretion. Thus, AVPV and SCH might be expected to play an important rule in mediating lactational diestrus prolonged by energetic challenges.

3. Sex Behavior

Sex behavior differs among females of various species, but has been studied most intensively in rats, in which sex behavior is characterized by a stereotypical arched-back posture called lordosis. Lordosis is an estrogen-gated reflex that is essential for penile intromission. It is triggered by the somatosensory stimulation generated as the male mounts the female and is perhaps the best-characterized motivated behavioral event (Pfaff, 1980, 1999). Because it is a reflex event, much of the sensory processing takes place in hindbrain and spinal motor pattern generators. However, estrogen-induced progesterone receptors and progesterone action on these receptors in the VMH are necessary and sufficient for the occurrence of lordosis in response to a sexually experienced male (Pfaff, 1980, 1999). It has been known since the 1970s that the VMH contains abundant ER and estrogen-induced progesterone receptors (PR), and that these are concentrated in its ventrolateral subdivision (Pfaff, 1980; Simerly *et al.*, 1990; LaFlamme *et al.*, 1998; Shughrue *et al.*, 1997). Projections of the VMH to the PAG (Canteras *et al.*, 1994) form part of the system that mediates estrogen's effects on lordosis. Sex behavior in males rats is facilitated by testosterone acting in a variety of brain areas, particularly the mPOA.

a) Metabolic Challenges   Many of the metabolic stimuli and hormonal modulators that increase the drive to eat also inhibit sex behavior. Inhibited HPG function precludes the display of steroid-induced sex behavior in many species. In addition, inhibitory effects of metabolic challenges on sex behavior are independent of the inhibitory effects of these challenges on GnRH, LH, FSH, follicle development, and gonadal steroid secretion in Syrian hamsters (H.-Y. Li *et al.*, 1994; Dickerman *et al.*, 1993; Panicker *et al.*, 1998; Panicker and Wade, 1998; Siegel and Wade, 1979). For example, in ovariectomized Syrian hamsters brought into estrus with estradiol and progesterone treatment, the duration of lordosis is decreased by food deprivation (Dickerman *et al.*, 1993). Changes in the behavioral responsiveness to steroids might be related to the decrease in ER in areas critical for estrous behavior, such as the VMH (H.-Y. Li *et al.*, 1994; Panicker and Wade, 1998; Roemmich *et al.*, 1997; Estacio *et al.*, 1996). Although most metabolic challenges fail to increase food intake in Syrian hamsters (Silverman and Zucker, 1976; DiBattista, 1983), they do increase hunger motivation (Dibattista and Bedard, 1987; Schneider *et al.*, 1988), and thus it would be predicted that various metabolic challenges would divert attention away from sex behavior and toward food hoarding and other appetitive behaviors in this species.

NPY is a good candidate for a central mediator of the effects of metabolic challenges on sex behavior. For example, ICV treatment with NPY antisera attenuates food intake and body weight gain, and increases the display of sex behavior in obese Zucker female rats (Marin-Bivens *et al.*, 1998). NPY agonists increase food intake and decrease lordosis duration in ovariectomized Syrian hamsters brought into estrus with ovarian steroid treatment (Corp *et al.*, 2001). The effects of NPY treatment on lordosis duration are most likely mediated by Y2 receptors, whereas the effects of NPY treatment on food intake in rats and Syrian hamsters are most likely mediated by Y5 receptors, with some influence also exerted via Y1 receptors (Corp *et al.*, 2001; Kalra *et al.*, 1992; Raposinho *et al.*, 1999). The dual effects of NPY allow individuals to take advantage of mating opportunities as long as fuel availability is not a problem and to forgo mating in favor of foraging when there is a fuel deficit. For example, in fed male rats, ingestion of a palatable sucrose solution is inhibited by the presence of a sexually receptive female. The converse is not true—the sex behavior of fed males is not influenced by the presence of a bottle of sucrose (Saito *et al.*, 1999). In male rats treated with NPY, however, the latency to intromission and ejaculation is prolonged (Clark *et al.*, 1985; Poggioli *et al.*, 1990), and this effect is exaggerated by the presence of a bottle of sucrose (Ammar *et al.*, 2000). NPY-treated males make more trips to and drink more from a bottle of sucrose than do saline-treated males, regardless of the presence of a sexually receptive female. The effects of NPY appear to influence the appetitive or motivational, rather than the consummatory, aspects of both behaviors. NPY treatment shifts attention toward eating and away from sex without affecting erectile or ejaculatory function (Clark *et al.*, 1985; Kalra and Kalra, 1996). Similarly, NPY increases drinking from a bottle, but does not increase ingestion of a solution infused into the oral cavity (Ammar *et al.*, 2000; Seeley *et al.*, 1995). The role of NPY in the inhibition of the HPG system and sex behavior and in increasing food intake is seen in species as diverse as rodents, fish, and snakes (Ammar *et al.*, 2000; Morris and Crews, 1990; Narnaware *et al.*, 2000). Together these data support the idea that neurotransmitters allow animals to set priorities by influencing the motivation to engage in particular behaviors.

Other central peptides that we have discussed with regard to ingestive behavior influence sex behavior. CRH secretion increases in response to food deprivation, and CRH infusion into the mesencephalic central gray, ARH-VMH, or mPOA inhibits sex behavior as well as food intake in both males and females (Sirinathsinghji *et al.*, 1983; Sirinathsinghji, 1987). It is well known that CRH is secreted under life-threatening conditions that require either a fight or flight response, at a time when neither eating nor sex are high priorities. Vertebrates respond to many emergency situations, such as habitat destruction or inclement weather, with a characteristic set of adaptations that include and increase in locomotor activity and suppression of reproductive behavior (Wingfield *et al.*, 2000). In a variety of stressful situations, CRH initiates the HPA system, which rapidly mobilizes oxidizable metabolic fuels, increases heart rate and blood circulation, inhibits digestion, and orchestrates a whole host of responses that increase survival. CRH is also anxiogenic and increases memory retrieval and social affiliations. The effects of

CRH extend to the motivational aspects of ingestion. For example, CRH-induced decreases in food intake are accompanied by decreases in food hoarding in rats (Cabanac and Richard, 1995). CRH inhibits the HPG axis by direct action on GnRH secretion, as mentioned previously (Petraglia *et al.,* 1987; MacLusky *et al.,* 1988), and this effect has secondary effects on ovulation, estrous cyclicity, and sex behavior. Although it is clear that CRH affects copulatory performance, we are not aware of studies that examine the direct effects of CRH or the related urocortins, on sexual motivation.

Another aspect of the stress response that also inhibits reproductive processes is the release of endogenous opiates, particularly β-endorphin. In female obese Zucker rats, treatment with an opioid antagonist attenuated obesity and improved sexual performance (Marin-Bivens and Olster, 1999). In nonobese rats and in white-crowned sparrows, treatment with opiates or opioid agonists inhibits sex behavior, including motivational aspects of sex behavior such as ear wiggling, presentations, and courtship vocalizations (Maney and Wingfield, 1998; Wiesner and Moss, 1986), whereas treatment with opioid antagonists facilitates sex behavior (Allen *et al.,* 1985; Maney and Wingfield, 1998). In both rats and white-crowned sparrows, the inhibitory effects of CRH are blocked by simultaneous treatment with antisera to β-endorphin or to opiate antagonists, and thus it has been suggested that CRH inhibits sex behavior by increasing release of β-endorphin (Maney and Wingfield, 1998; Sirinathsiinghji *et al.,* 1983). The effects of β-endorphin on sex behavior have not been replicated consistently in rats or in other species (e.g., Jones *et al.,* 2001; Sirinathsinghji, 1986; Torii *et al.,* 1995). It is possible that some of these discrepancies are due to differences in the time of testing relative to the time of treatment (Torii *et al.,* 1999). Another POMC cleavage product, α-MSH, decreases food intake and increases sex behavior (Gonzalez *et al.,* 1993; Scimonelli *et al.,* 2000). More work is needed to determine whether these peptides are involved in the normal expression of sex behavior, or whether they mediate the effects of energetic challenges on sex behavior, or both.

CCK is a gut peptide that has been implicated in meal termination; however, CCK is abundant in the brain, and the binding of CCK to CCK-A receptors is critical for estradiol-induced lordosis behavior in rats (Holland *et al.,* 1997). It would not be surprising to find that central CCK release is involved in the effects of metabolic fuel availability on GnRH secretion (Perera *et al.,* 1993) and on sex behavior. In contrast, peripherally secreted CCK does not appear to mediate the effects of fasting on sex behavior in Syrian hamsters. Progress in understanding the effects of various chemical messengers on sex behavior will be facilitated by examining both motivated (e.g., foraging, consumption of an unpalatable diet, hoarding, and overcoming obstacles to performing operant tasks to obtain food) and consummatory aspects of behavior in species-specific social contexts.

In the CNS, there are a number of hypothalamic nuclei involved in both reproductive behavior and energy balance that could facilitate information flow between these two systems (Fig. 8). The GnRH neurons in the caudal preoptic area and those in the mediobasal

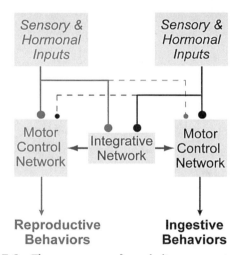

FIGURE 8   The same array of metabolic sensory signals and hormonal modulators influences both the reproductive and the ingestive behavior systems. First, the diversity of hormone receptor expression in response to changes in metabolic fuel availability shows that hormonal information that appears to be primarily directed at one control network can influence the other. The expression of gonadal steroid receptors is illustrated as red dots, and leptin, insulin, and glucocorticoid receptors are shown as black dots. Second, there are neural projections from an intermediate set of integrative nuclei that are responsive to both gonadal steroids and the other hormones traditionally associated with energy balance. In turn, the neural outputs of this integrative network target both the reproductive and the ingestive behavior control networks. Neural inputs from other parts of the brain concerned with more general functions target both the motor control networks and the intermediate integrative neurons. **See insert for a color version of this figure.**

hypothalamus of some species are obvious candidates. Other areas deserve more attention by virtue of the presence of receptors for various hormones and neuropeptides and their projection sites. Four hypothalamic cell groups seem particularly well placed to function in this manner (Fig. 9): the DMH, AVPV, ARH, and the ventral premammalary nucleus (PMv). Of these, the ARH and PMv express both gonadal steroid receptors and leptin or insulin receptors (LaFlamme *et al.*, 1998; Elias *et al.*, 2000; Marks *et al.*, 1990; Simerly *et al.*, 1990). Neurons in these nuclei are potentially regulated by the sets of hormones associated with reproduction and energy balance. On the other hand, neurons in the AVPV (e.g., gonadal steroid) and DMH (e.g., leptin) contain a significant number of only one type of receptor, but they have afferent and efferent projection patterns that allow strong neural interactions with the more receptor-diverse ARH and PMv (Fig. 9). Critically, each of these nuclei also has strong connections with other cell groups such as the PVH or the GnRH network, responsible for controlling specific reproductive or metabolic motor actions.

B. Sensory Systems

As are the networks controlling energy balance, those neural networks important for ovulation are influenced by internal and external sensory stimuli (Fig. 3). Research in this area has a long and distinguished history and has brought forth many of the central principles of behavioral neuroendocrinology (Beach, 1948; Marshall, 1936; Pfaff, 1980; Tinbergen 1951).

1. Exterosensory Stimuli

Virtually all sensory modalities play critical roles in organizing reproductive behaviors. In rodents, olfaction plays a significant role in initiating sequences of reproductive events, whereas visual signals are clearly important in species that have complex courtship behaviors. Somatosensory signals are important for triggering postural reflexes, of which lordosis in rats is the best understood, and these have been reviewed elsewhere in exquisite detail (Pfaff, 1980, 1999). In temperate-zone animals with the facultative reproductive strategy, cues from ambient temperature and day length control reproductive function. In mammalian species, the HPG system is inhibited by short day lengths and sponta-

neously recrudesces in time for spring. In birds, the HPG system is stimulated by long days and becomes refractory to long days in time for winter migration. The inhibitory effects of short-day photoperiods are mediated through photoreceptors, either the eye or other specialized organs that detect day length, and these have fascinating interactions with energetic and social cues (reviewed by Ball, 2000; Lee and Gorman, 2000).

2. Interosensory Stimuli

Based on the theory that there is a sensory system that monitors fuel availability and influences food intake, it was suggested that this same sensory system controls reproduction (reviewed in Wade and Schneider, 1992; Wade *et al.*, 1996; Schneider and Wade, 2000). According to this idea, the GnRH pulse generator and sex behavior are influenced by the minute-to-minute availability of oxidizable metabolic fuels. In support of this theory, the effects of metabolic challenges on LH pulsatility occur far more rapidly than changes in body-fat content in a wide variety of species (Figs. 4C and 4D) (Armstrong and Britt, 1987; Bronson, 1986, 1988; Bronson and Heideman, 1990; Cameron, 1996; Cameron and Nosbisch, 1991; Clarke *et al.*, 1990; Schreihofer *et al.*, 1993; reviewed by Wade et al., 1996).

The lipostatic (or adipostatic) hypothesis, in which reproduction is controlled by body-fat stores (Kennedy and Mitra, 1963a,b; Frisch, 1990), has been repeatedly rejected in favor of the metabolic hypothesis for a number of reasons. First, the lipostatic hypothesis and related ideas concerning the adipocyte protein leptin cannot account for the rapid increases in pulsatile LH secretion that occur within 60 minutes of refeeding (Figs. 4C and 4D). Second, the lipostatic hypothesis or the critical body fat hypothesis held that females should delay ovulation until their energy reserves reach some critical level that ensures survival of the offspring should the mother face a food shortage during lactation. This, however, is inconsistent with the life histories of representative species of three of the most populous orders of mammals—rodents, insectivores, and marsupials. Most of these mammalian species are relatively small and their fat stores amount to only a small fraction of the energy needed for a full fertile cycle of pregnancy and lactation. Furthermore, these species tend to have short life spans and, thus, cannot afford the luxury of postponing reproductive attempts until their energy

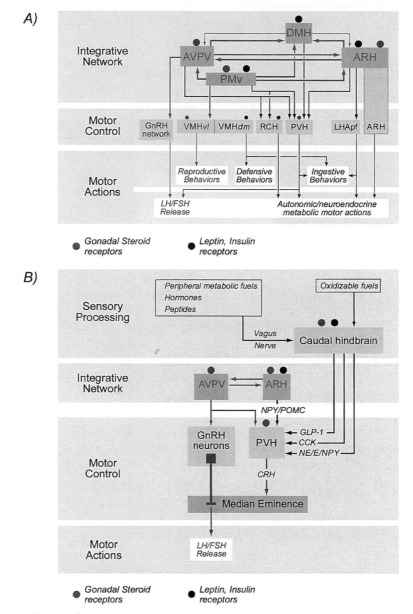

FIGURE 9 (A) A schematic diagram of an integrative network and the associated motor control networks for a variety of motor actions for reproductive and ingestive behaviors, LH/FSH release, and autonomic and neuroendocrine effects on energy expenditure and metabolism. Sets of neurons in the gonadotropin-releasing hormone (GnRH) network, ventromedial nucleus (VMH), retrochiasmatic area (RCH), paraventricular nucleus (PVH), perifornical part of the lateral hypothalamic area (LHApf), and arcuate nucleus (ARH) control reproductive or energy balance motor functions directly. In turn, the ventrolateral part of the VMH (VMHvl) controls female reproductive behaviors, while the dorsomedial part of the VMH (VMHdm) appears to control defensive and some aspects of ingestive behavior. Collectively all these motor control cell groups are then regulated by inputs from a higher-level integrative network. The receptor expression patterns and the connections from some neurons in the ARH, anteroventral periventricular nucleus (AVPV), dorsomedial nucleus (DMH), and the ventral premammillary nucleus (PMv) provide evidence that they make up an integrating network that can influence the neurons in the reproductive and energy balance motor control networks in a divergent manner. Functions concerned with the integrative actions are shown in blue, those with reproductive function in red, and those with ingestive behavior and energy balance in black. (B) The sensory processing, integrative, and motor control networks for one of the motor actions described above, LH/FSH release. Sensory processing of information about metabolic fuel availability is thought to occur in the hindbrain and to be projected to forebrain areas via catecholaminergic and other neurons (CCK, cholecystokinin; E, epinephrine; GLP-1, glucagon-like peptide-1; NE, norepinephrine; NPY, neuropeptide Y; POMC, pro-opiomelanocortin). Some evidence suggests that both estrogen receptors and corticotropin-releasing hormone (CRH) neurons might influence GnRH neurons directly. Modulation by hormones such as estrogen (red dots), or leptin and insulin (black dots) might occur in the areas shown. **See insert for a color version of this figure.**

stores are adequate to ensure reproductive success. Abundant examples demonstrate that females ovulate whenever oxidizable metabolic fuels are available despite the fact that their energy reserves are insufficient to ensure the successful production of offspring in the event of a food shortage (reviewed by Bronson, 2000). Finally, an extensive body of experimental evidence fails to support the lipostatic hypothesis (Bucholtz *et al.,* 1996; Bronson and Manning, 1991; Cameron and Nosbisch, 1991; reviewed by Wade and Schneider, 1992; Wade *et al.,* 1996).

Body-fat content, caloric intake, ambient temperature, and exercise interact to control reproductive function. For example, food deprivation can inhibit estrous cyclicity, but only after glycogen and fat stores have been sufficiently depleted. For instance, a 48-hour period of food deprivation inhibits estrous cycles in lean, but not in fat, Syrian hamsters (Schneider and Wade, 1989). Factors that increase energy expenditure, such as prolonged exercise or cold exposure, can inhibit estrous cyclicity, but only when the increase in energy expenditure is not offset by increased caloric intake or use of oxidizable fuels mobilized from adipose tissue. For example, reports of menstrual irregularities, amenorrhea (the cessation of menstrual cycles), diminished sexual desire and activity, and infertility are common in athletes and dancers, but usually only in those who fail to increase their food intake to compensate for the unusual energetic demands of their training schedules. When the training schedule is relaxed, menstrual cycles resume without a significant increase in body weight (Abraham *et al.,* 1982). In Syrian hamsters, increased exercise and prolonged housing at cold ambient temperatures both require increased energy expenditure. Both of these energetic challenges inhibit estrous cycles only when the increased energy expenditure is not offset by increased intake (Powers *et al.,* 1994; Schneider and Wade, 1990b). Wild populations of mice (*Mus musculus*) breed successfully on sub-Antarctic islands and in frozen-food lockers where an abundant food supply is continuously available (Berry and Peters, 1975; Laurie, 1946). In laboratory mice (*Mus domesticus*), estrous cycles and uterine weight are adversely affected by housing at cold ambient temperatures (7°C), but only in those mice that are not allowed to increase their food intake (Manning and Bronson, 1990).

Metabolic sensory control of reproduction is remarkably similar to metabolic sensory control of food intake. Systemic treatment with 2DG increases food intake in rats, inhibits estrous cycles in hamsters, and inhibits pulsatile LH secretion in rats and ewes, despite the fact that these treatments have negligible effects on body-fat content (Bucholtz *et al.,* 1996; Foster and Bucholtz, 1995; Friedman and Tordoff, 1986; Friedman *et al.,* 1986; Howland, 1980; Murahashi *et al.,* 1996; Nagatani *et al.,* 1996; Schneider and Wade, 1989, 1990a; Schneider *et al.,* 1993). Consistent with the idea that estrous cycles are inhibited by 2DG's competitive inhibition of glycolysis, the effects of 2DG on estrous cycles in Syrian hamsters can be overcome by pretreatment with an equal dose of glucose or fructose (Schneider *et al.,* 1997b). In this regard, it is notable that treatment with glucose prevents the fall in plasma leptin; however, treatment with fructose does not (Suga *et al.,* 2000)—yet estrous cycles continue when fructose is provided.

Reproductive processes, like food intake, are also sensitive to changes in FFA oxidation, especially when animals are predisposed toward the use of fat fuels. Fat hamsters do not show fasting-induced anestrus, but MP treatment inhibits estrous cyclicity in fat fasted Syrian hamsters (Schneider *et al.,* 1988; Schneider and Wade, 1989). Food intake in rats and estrous cycles in hamsters are affected by treatments that block FFA oxidation only in animals that are predisposed toward FFA oxidation. For example, MP and 2DG have synergistic effects on food intake in rats and on estrous cyclicity in hamsters fed *ad libitum* (Friedman and Tordoff, 1986; Friedman *et al.,* 1986; Schneider and Wade, 1989, 1990a; Schneider *et al.,* 1997a). In ovariectomized hamsters treated with estradiol and progesterone, lordosis duration and ER-IR in the VMH are decreased in hamsters treated simultaneously with 2DG and MP, but not with either drug alone (H.-Y. Li *et al.,* 1994). During fasting, caloric homeostasis is maintained by hydrolysis of triglycerides to FFAs and glycerol. FFAs are mobilized to various peripheral tissues where they are preferentially oxidized, thereby sparing glucose for oxidation in the CNS. According to the metabolic hypothesis, estrous cycles continue in fat fasted hamsters because their large adipose tissue depots are a source of FFAs for cellular oxidation during food deprivation. In fat MP-treated hamsters, MP blocks FFA oxidation, thereby neutralizing the advantage of a high body-fat content. Similarly, in MP-treated hamsters fed *ad libitum,* carbohydrates can be used as an alternative fuel source to maintain estrous cyclicity. When the use of both fuels is blocked by simultaneous treatment with MP and 2DG, anestrus is induced. The metabolic signal may be related to one or several metabolic events, or to a common final metabolic event, such as the formation of ATP (Friedman, 1998).

It might be suggested that these systemic metabolic inhibitors inhibit the GnRH neurons directly. This is not the case. Just as AP lesions attenuate the feeding-stimulatory effects of 2DG and insulin, AP lesions block the inhibitory effects of 2DG or high doses of insulin on estrous cycles in hamsters, ER-IR in VMH and ARH, lordosis induced by exogenous hormone treatment in ovariectomized hamsters, and LH pulses in rats (Cates and O'Byrne, 2000; H.-Y. Li *et al.,* 1994; Schneider and Zhu, 1994; Panicker *et al.,* 1998).

The effects of acute glucoprivation on both food intake and reproduction might be detected in areas of the caudal brain stem. Slow microinfusion of 2DG into the fourth ventricle in rats increases food intake, elicits the sympathoadrenal hyperglycemic response, and inhibits pulsatile LH secretion (Ritter *et al.,* 1981; Murahashi *et al.,* 1996). The microinfusion of 0.5 M 5TG into the fourth ventricle at a rate of 1 μl/hr over days 1 and 2 of the estrous cycle inhibits ovulation and sex behavior in Syrian hamsters fed *ad libitum* (Zhou and Schneider, 2000). However, higher doses were required to induce anestrus than were required to induce a sympathoadrenal hyperglycemic response, suggesting that these two responses are dissociable. Collectively, these data provide strong evidence for a neural circuitry whereby information about fuel availability is detected or integrated in the hindbrain and influences glucose homeostatic mechanisms, food intake, and the HPG system. The sensory stimulus, although related to glucose oxidation, might actually be generated by changes in the availability of other substrates in intracellular and mitochondrial metabolism. It is not yet known whether the sensory stimulus for control of GnRH secretion is the same as that for the control of food intake or control of the sympathoadrenal response to glucoprivation.

Hindbrain catecholamine cell groups and their projections to the forebrain are involved in the metabolic control of reproduction (Nagatani *et al.,* 1996; Estacio *et al.,* 2001), just as they are involved in glucoprivic

control of food intake (Ritter *et al.,* 2001). Some of the same cell groups and their projections that have been implicated in the control of food intake (e.g., A1 and A2) have also been implicated in the hypothalamic steroid negative feedback that results from metabolic challenges (Nagatani *et al.,* 1996; Estacio *et al.,* 2001). In addition, the A1 cell group shows ER-IR (Heritage *et al.,* 1980), projects to the POA (Wright and Jennes, 1993), and influences GnRH secretion (Conde *et al.,* 1995, 1996). It remains to be determined whether reproduction and food intake are controlled by the exact same fuel detecting neurons and by the same catecholaminergic projections.

The role of the vagus nerve might be a point of divergence for the neural pathways that control food intake and reproduction. Earlier in this chapter we note that food intake is controlled by peripheral sensory signals mediated by the vagus nerve. Vagotomy and capsaicin treatment have demonstrated a role for peripheral detectors of fuel oxidation in control of food intake. In contrast, evidence for the vagal mediation of metabolic signals for reproduction is equivocal. In Syrian hamsters, anestrus is not induced by treatment with 2,5-AM, the fructose analog that increases food intake by reducing hepatic energy status in rats (Schneider, 1997). Furthermore, total bilateral subdiaphragmatic vagotomy fails to prevent anestrus, reduced lordosis duration, and reduced ER-IR in the VMH induced by fasting or metabolic inhibitors (Schneider *et al.,* 1997a,b; H.-Y. Li *et al.,* 1994). However, negative results of vagotomy must be regarded with caution because the vagus nerve can regenerate after surgery. Data in rats also fail to implicate peripheral control of LH pulses. 2DG infused at 250 mg/kg is equally effective when infused into either the hepatic portal or jugular vein. A lower dose of 50 mg/kg is not effective when infused into the hepatic portal vein. This dose was never infused into the jugular; nevertheless, these results were taken to suggest that peripheral detectors of glucoprivation are not important for the control of LH pulses. Although these results should be regarded with caution, they suggest that critical signals for control of reproduction (unlike those for control of food intake) are not generated peripherally and mediated by the vagus nerve.

Other data, however, support a role for vagally mediated metabolic stimuli in control of reproduction. Fasting-induced suppression of pulsatile LH secretion in rats, as well as increases in PVH ER-IR in both rats and increases in mPOA ER-IR in hamsters, are reversed by total subdiaphragmatic vagotomy (Cagampang *et al.*, 1992; Estacio *et al.*, 1996; H.-Y. Li *et al.*, 1994). Inhibition and resinstatement of the cycle might be under separate controls. That is, reproductive processes might be inhibited by mechanisms that detect central deficits in fuel availability, but estrous cycles might be reinstated by vagally mediated peripheral signals. In addition, the neural mechanisms that inhibit sex behavior, unlike those that inhibit LH pulses, might be unrelated to input from the vagus.

C. Hormonal Mediators and Modulators

In general, hormone treatments at doses that increase food intake tend to inhibit reproductive processes. For example, insulin given systemically at doses sufficient to cause hypoglycemia has a suppressive effect on LH secretion and estrous cyclicity, while at the same time increasing food intake and body-fat content (Wade *et al.*, 1991; Medina *et al.*, 1998). Conversely, insulin treatment at low doses administered intracerebrally tend to decrease food intake and have a permissive effect on pulsatile LH secretion (Dong *et al.*, 1991; Miller *et al.*, 1995; Arias *et al.*, 1992). Leptin treatments given either systemically or ICV inhibit food intake and prevent the effects of fasting on LH pulses and estrous cyclicity. The central neuropeptides mentioned earlier show a similar pattern. Putative satiety peptides released from the gut tend to stimulate GnRH and LH secretion when injected systemically. Intravenous injection of CCK stimulates GnRH release in male monkeys (Perera *et al.*, 1993), whereas motilin inhibits pulsatile LH secretion in rats and ewes (Tsukamura *et al.*, 2000). Taken altogether, these results support that idea that when fuels are in short supply, a number of hormonal factors conspire (either directly or indirectly) to increase food procurement and to conserve energy for the processes necessary for immediate survival.

1. Insulin and Reproduction

Insulin has been a useful tool for demonstrating that hormones act indirectly via effects on metabolic fuel disposition to influence both reproduction and food intake. The inhibitory effects of insulin on reproduction (e.g., insulin-induced hyperphagia) are not due to

insulin per se but rather to the effects of insulin on the disposition of metabolic fuels. Insulin treatment inhibits estrous cycles in Syrian hamsters that are limited to the food intake of the saline-treated control hamsters, but the same dose of insulin fails to inhibit estrous cycles when the hamsters are allowed to overeat to compensate for increased energy storage (Wade *et al.*, 1991). These data are in keeping with the metabolic hypothesis and not with the adipostatic hypothesis. The adipostatic hypothesis predicts that both the *ad libitum*–fed and the food-limited insulin-treated hamsters will show normal estrous cycles because both groups gain body fat. To the contrary, insulin inhibits estrous cyclicity only in the food-limited hamsters, although causing both groups to gain body fat. The metabolic hypothesis predicts that insulin will only inhibit estrous cycles when it promotes energy storage with a net loss of fuels available for intracellular oxidation. Consistent with this idea, insulin treatment inhibits estrous cycles only when its stimulatory effects on energy storage are not offset by increased caloric intake in the food-limited hamsters. Insulin treatment induces significant increases in plasma leptin levels in both *ad libitum*–fed and food-limited hamsters, indicating that the inhibitory effects of insulin on estrous cycles are not mediated by falling leptin (Blum *et al.*, 2000). This phenomenon is not limited to Syrian hamsters. For example, in female rats and ewes pulsatile LH secretion is inhibited by insulin infusion, but not when the metabolic effects of insulin are offset by simultaneous glucose infusion (Clarke *et al.*, 1990; He *et al.*, 1999; Rodriguez *et al.*, 1999).

Insulin treatment at low doses intracerebrally tends to decrease food intake and has a permissive effect on pulsatile LH secretion (Dong *et al.*, 1991; Miller *et al.*, 1995; Arias *et al.*, 1992). First, in male sheep, streptozotocin-induced diabetes reduces the frequency of LH pulses (Bucholtz *et al.*, 2000), but this can be reinstated by ICV treatment with insulin at doses that affect neither peripheral insulin or glucose concentrations (Tanaka *et al.*, 2000). Second, mice that have functional disruption of the insulin receptor gene when it is expressed in the brain (NIRKO) but not the periphery show hypothalamic hypogonadism. The effects on food intake and on LH levels are exaggerated in females (Brüning *et al.*, 2000). Insulin receptors are expressed by neurons in the ARH, however, the location of the receptors responsible for these actions is unknown. In any case, these data suggest that a total absence of insulin is incompatible with LH pulsatility and fertility. One possibility that has not been explored is whether or not the permissive effects of central insulin are due to the direct action of insulin on brain circuitry for the GnRH pulse generator or are secondary to the effects of insulin on glucose uptake.

The role of natural fluctuations in plasma insulin in control of reproduction has not been clarified. In Syrian hamsters, estrous cycles are inhibited by a 48-hr, but not a 24-hr fast. The normal estrous cyclicity in the 24-hr-fasted hamster cannot be explained by changes in plasma leptin because plasma leptin levels plummet by 12 hours after the start of fasting and do not increase to fed levels until at least 48 hours after the start of refeeding. In contrast to leptin, plasma insulin concentrations are already increased by 12 hours after refeeding, consistent with a role for this hormone in control of estrous cycles in Syrian hamsters (Schneider *et al.*, 2000b). Conversely, a critical role for natural fluctuations in plasma insulin is not supported by studies demonstrating that meal-induced increases in insulin are not necessary for the meal-induced increases in pulsatile LH secretion (Williams *et al.*, 1996).

2. Leptin and Reproduction

A great deal of circumstantial evidence supports the idea that reproductive processes are controlled by changes in the secretion of the adipocyte protein leptin (although other data do not support this hypothesis). Treatment with leptin, at doses that decrease food intake, also prevents the effects of underfeeding on several aspects of reproduction in both lean and obese laboratory rodents (Ahima *et al.*, 1996, 1997, 1999; Barash *et al.*, 1996; Chehab *et al.*, 1996, 1997; Cheung *et al.*, 1997; Gruaz-Gumowski *et al.*, 1998; Schneider *et al.*, 1998; Wade *et al.*, 1997). Exogenous leptin treatment in rodents reverses the effects of food restriction or food deprivation on aspects of reproduction, including the onset of puberty (Aubert *et al.*, 1998; Chehab *et al.*, 1997; Ahima *et al.*, 1997; Barash *et al.*, 1996; Apter, 1997; Gruaz-Gumowski *et al.*, 1998), the length of the estrous cycle (Chehab *et al.*, 1996; Schneider *et al.*, 1998), the length of lactational diestrus (Woodside *et al.*, 1998), gonadotropin and gonadal steroid levels (Ahima *et al.*, 1996; Yu *et al.*, 1997a,b), and pulsatile

LH secretion (Finn *et al.*, 1998; Nagatani *et al.*, 1998) in mice, rats, hamsters, and nonhuman primates. Earlier studies used large, possibly pharmacological, doses of leptin. In a later study, investigators estimated the dose of mouse leptin that results in plasma concentrations of total leptin estimated to be within the physiological range of rats (Watanobe *et al.*, 1999b). This dose of mouse leptin partially, but not fully, reverses the effects of food deprivation on estradiol-induced LH and prolactin surges in rats (Watanobe *et al.*, 1999b). In another study, subcutaneous infusions of mouse leptin that maintain plasma levels of total leptin within the physiological range of rats prevent fasting-induced changes in neuroendocrine function and in NPY, POMC, and CART mRNA levels in the ARH in rats (Ahima *et al.*, 1999). Leptin treatment fails to reverse the effects of fasting on gonadotropin secretion in male rhesus macaques (Lado-Abeal *et al.*, 1999, 2000).

How might leptin influence the GnRH pulse generator or the LH surge? In rats, leptin receptors (Ob-R) are not found on GnRH neurons per se. Most the GnRH perikarya are in areas rostral to the areas that are rich in Ob-R. Leptin receptor mRNA is found on GT1–7 cells in culture using gene amplification, and GT1–7 cells secrete GnRH in response to the addition of leptin to the media (Magni *et al.*, 1999). The discrepancy between the *in vivo* and *in vitro* findings might be an artifact of the vast number of cells in GT1–7 cultures compared to the sparsely located GnRH cells *in vivo*. There are, however, both hypothalamic and extrahypothalamic areas rich in Ob-R that project to areas that contain GnRH neurons, as well as to areas implicated in control of food intake (reviewed in Cunningham *et al.*, 1999; Friedman and Halaas, 1998; Benoit *et al.*, 2000). Leptin receptors are strongly expressed by the PMv and the ARH, both of which have strong connections to the GnRH network and so may affect GnRH release patterning. In addition, both nuclei project to the AVPV (Fig. 9) and are so are in a position to exert leptin-sensitive effects on the preovulatory GnRH surge. Whether leptin-receptor-containing neurons from the PMv or ARH specifically contribute to these projections has not been examined directly.

A fall in leptin might be one factor that increases hunger or food intake and inhibits reproduction. One point of divergence between mechanisms that control food intake and those that control reproduction is that leptin influences food intake via melanocortinergic pathways, whereas the effects of leptin on LH pulsatility and estrous cyclicity appear to be independent of the melanocortin system (Hohmann *et al.,* 2000; Zhou and Schneider, 2000). For example, in *ob/ob* mice, ICV treatment with SHU9119 reverses the effects of leptin on food intake, but not on gonadotropin levels or seminal vesicle weight (Hohmann *et al.,* 2000). Similarly, in Syrian hamsters, ICV treatment with SHU9119 reverses the effects of leptin on food intake, but does not attenuate the ability of leptin treatment to reverse fasting-induced anestrus and does not induce anestrus in hamsters fed *ad libitum* (Zhou and Schneider, 2000). Furthermore, the failure of SHU9119 to reverse the effects of leptin on fasting-induced anestrus was not explained by the hyperphagia in SHU9119-treated hamsters. SHU9119 treatment did not reverse the effects of leptin on estrous cyclicity even when the hamsters were limited to the food intake of the vehicle-treated controls (Zhou and Schneider, 2000). Finally, mutant individuals (both mice and human beings) that lack MC-4 receptor show moderate to severe obesity with no disturbance of the HPG systems and normal fertility (reviewed by Barsh *et al.,* 2000).

Despite adequate neuroanatomical structures necessary for leptin control of GnRH, there are several unanswered questions about the mechanisms of leptin's effects. Most investigators studying leptin have claimed that leptin provides an accurate estimate of body-fat content. To the contrary, changes in plasma leptin concentrations and *ob* gene expression change more rapidly than do body-fat levels in response to a variety of energetic challenges such as fasting and refeeding and cold exposure in rats, mice, hamsters, and human beings (Boden *et al.,* 1996; Frederich *et al.,* 1995; Thompson, 1996; Harris *et al.,* 1996; Saladin *et al.,* 1995; Levy *et al.,* 1997; Rentsch *et al.,* 1995; Trayhurn *et al.,* 1995; Trayhurn and Rayner, 1996; Ahren *et al.,* 1997; Kolaczynski *et al.,* 1996; Schneider *et al.,* 2000b). It has been established that reproduction is responsive to short-term changes in the availability of oxidizable metabolic fuels. Perhaps leptin provides an estimate of metabolic fuel availability and thereby mediates the effects of oxidizable fuel availability on reproductive function. In keeping with this hypothesis, plasma leptin secretion is directly dependent on the availability of oxidizable fuels (Levy *et al.,* 2000; J. Wang *et al.,* 1998).

Some data are not consistent with the notion that a particular plasma level of leptin is necessary for normal estrous cycles. In Syrian hamsters, anestrus is induced by a 48-hr, but not a 24-hr, period of food deprivation. In fasted–refed hamsters, plasma leptin levels do not increase to fed levels at 3, 6, 12, or 24 hours after the start of refeeding, and these hamsters show normal estrous cycles despite their fasting levels of plasma leptin (Schneider *et al.,* 2000b). Thus, the normal estrous cycles of 24-hr fasted hamsters cannot be explained by an increase in plasma leptin after refeeding. Consistent with the hypothesis that leptin synthesis and secretion are controlled by the availability of oxidizable metabolic fuels (Levy *et al.,* 2000; J. Wang *et al.,* 1998), it might be that the slow restoration of plasma leptin concentration in hamsters is due to the lack of postfast hyperphagia in this species (Silverman and Zucker, 1976). Thus, although plasma leptin levels are an approximate reflection of fuel availability, they cannot account for metabolic control of reproduction. These data run contrary to the hypothesis that leptin levels mediate energetic effects on reproduction.

More work is needed to understand what role, if any, is played by plasma leptin in control of reproduction. It is possible that discrete pulses of leptin influence the HPG system (Licinio *et al.,* 1997, 1998). Alternatively leptin levels might change in tissues at times when changes in plasma leptin are undetectable. In Syrian hamsters, leptin levels rise more rapidly in peripheral tissues than in plasma in response to refeeding (Owzar *et al.,* 2000). Thus, it is possible that these more rapid changes are detected peripherally and sent to the brain via peripheral afferent neurons. However, the neural pathways whereby changes in tissue leptin might influence reproduction are unknown.

As mentioned with regard to food intake, leptin transport across the blood–brain barrier is decreased by fasting and increased after refeeding. Thus, in contrast to predictions of the adipostatic hypothesis, the entry of leptin into the brain is controlled by as yet unknown stimuli that result from fasting and refeeding in the absence of changes in adipocyte filling. This provides an explanation of how leptin might influence reproduction and food intake. However, it also brings us back to the same question: What are the primary sensory stimuli that result from fasting that decrease hormone transport across the blood–brain barrier?

Despite initial excitement over the discovery of leptin, mounting evidence supports the idea that a variety of other factors are critical in control of reproduction. First, the metabolic control of fertility occurs in the complete absence of leptin. For example, when the *ob/ob* mutation, which was maintained on the C57BL/6J inbred mouse strain, is placed on a different genetic background (C57BL/6J-BALB/cJ), the *ob/ob* mice are fertile despite a lack of leptin and morbid obesity and hyperglycemia or hyperinsulinemia (Ewart-Toland *et al.,* 1999). Second, when *ob/ob* mice also lack NPY (e.g., the *ob*/NPY double-knockout mouse) they are more fertile than *ob/ob* mice that have a functional gene for NPY (Erickson *et al.,* 1996b). Thus, the infertility in *ob/ob* mice is not due to a lack of leptin binding directly to the neural circuits that underlie the GnRH pulse generator, but due to NPY-induced inhibition of LH. Other data demonstrate that central NPY can be influenced by deficits in metabolic fuel availability even when plasma leptin levels are high or unchanging (Chavez *et al.,* 1998; Ji and Friedman, 2000). Together, these data show that leptin is not the only important mediator of metabolic effects on reproduction (and food intake).

In the final analysis, an antagonist specific to the leptin receptor and methods for measuring pulsatile leptin secretion are required to determine whether or not an above-fasting level of leptin is necessary for normal reproduction. An alternative explanation is that there are at least two separate signals—an inhibitory signal related to falling plasma leptin and a facilitory signal related to more rapid signals from realimentation (e.g., signals from gut distension, CCK, or metabolic fuel availability). In addition, the importance of leptin for reproduction might vary with the age, species, and other more pressing sensory inputs. Experiments are underway to determine whether or not levels of plasma leptin are critical for the onset of puberty.

A vast amount of data suggests that reproductive processes are responsive to the minute-to-minute availability of metabolic fuels. For example, pulsatile LH secretion is inhibited by food deprivation, but is restored within minutes or hours on refeeding in a wide variety of species (Armstrong and Britt, 1987; Bronson, 1986, 1988; Bronson and Heideman, 1990; Cameron, 1996; Cameron and Nosbisch, 1991; Clarke *et al.,* 1990; Schreihofer *et al.,* 1993). One obvious question that has not been answered is whether or not the restoration of LH pulses are preceded by an increase in plasma leptin or insulin. This is a critical question that must be answered if we wish to fully understand the relative importance of hormones as modulators of reproduction. Single-gene mutants (such as *ob/ob* mice) cannot be used to answer these questions because the mechanisms that account for reproductive abnormalities in mutants with no circulating leptin may be quite different from those mechanisms that switch the ovulatory cycle on and off during feast and famine or summer and winter, when plasma leptin levels fluctuate within measurable physiological ranges.

If leptin is a permissive factor for normal HPG function, it is not the only factor. In outbred nonmutant animals, above-fasting levels of leptin are not sufficient for normal estrous cyclicity. For example, leptin can fully reverse the effects of fasting on puberty in rats restricted to 80% of their *ad libitum* food intake, but not in rats restricted to 70% of their *ad libitum* intake (Cheung *et al.,* 1997). Similarly, in ovariectomized hamsters brought into estrus by estradiol and progesterone treatment, leptin increases the duration of lordosis in *ad libitum*–fed, but not in food-deprived hamsters (Dickerman *et al.,* 1993). Furthermore, leptin can shorten the duration of lactational diestrus in rats exposed to acute food deprivation, but not in rats exposed to prolonged chronic food restriction (Woodside *et al.,* 2000). Leptin treatment can attenuate, but cannot fully overcome, the effects of fasting on the estradiol-induced LH and prolactin surges in rats (Watanobe *et al.,* 1999a). In Syrian hamsters, fasting-induced anestrus was reversed and normal sex and social behavior and ovulation rate were restored in hamsters injected either intraperitoneally (IP) with 5 mg/kg leptin every 12 hours or continuously infused ICV with 1 μg/day leptin during fasting on days 1 and 2 of the estrous cycle. However, fasting-induced anestrus is not significantly attenuated by either IP or ICV leptin treatment when each injection of leptin is preceded by an injection of 2DG or MP, even though these doses of MP and 2DG did not induce anestrus in hamsters fed *ad libitum* (Schneider *et al.,* 1998; Schneider and Zhou, 1999a). Finally, insulin treatment induces anestrus in hamsters limited to the food intake of saline-treated controls, even though this treatment increases, rather than decreases plasma leptin levels (Blum *et al.,* 2000). Together these experiments provide strong evidence that high concentrations of leptin in brain or in plasma are not sufficient for normal estrous cyclicity and argue against the idea that leptin is a simple metabolic gate for the onset of reproduction (reviewed by Schneider *et al.*, 2000a).

3. CCK, Other Chemical Messengers, and Reproduction

Hormones that are released in response to the presence of food in the digestive tract have stimulatory effects on various aspects of reproduction. For example, the intestinal peptide motilin is secreted in the presence of nutrients in the gut. Peripheral administration of motilin increases the frequency of LH pulses (Tsukamura *et al.*, 2000). As noted earlier, CCK treatment has facilitory influences on sex behavior in rats and primates. Glucocorticoids and adrenal catecholamines are secreted in response to food deprivation, generalized stress, and cerebral metabolic emergency, and these hormones have inhibitory effects of reproductive processes. For example, the effects of food deprivation on LH secretion require an intact adrenal gland (Cagampang *et al.*, 1999). These effects are probably mediated via the caudal brain stem (Cates and O'Bryne, 2000).

VI. INTEGRATION OF MECHANISMS THAT CONTROL FOOD INTAKE AND REPRODUCTION

Mechanisms that control ingestive behavior and energy balance function to increase survival and optimize reproductive success. They did not evolve to prevent clinical syndromes such as obesity and diabetes. Rather, moderate obesity is more likely a consequence of thousands of years of adaptation to environments in which food availability fluctuated seasonally or unpredictably. In such environments, selection would be expected to favor mechanisms that can respond to food shortages by increasing metabolic efficiency and storage, which would be likely to increase the probability of survival and reproductive success during subsequent shortages. Environmental factors interact with the inherited propensity to eat and store energy. Modern life is characterized by decreased physical labor, passive means of transportation, an increasingly sedentary lifestyle, an almost constant easy access to snack foods and high-calorie drinks, a sea of synthetic and xenobi-

otic estrogens, and a wide range of pollutants in the air and water. Many of these factors might tend to promote obesity, and the effect might differ according to genetic predisposition. However, obesity per se is not the disease. Obesity is correlated with increased incidence of diabetes, insulin resistance, and cardiovascular disease and is socially stigmatized. Not all obese individuals develop these clinical problems. This perspective allows scientists in academia and industry to focus on understanding the mechanisms whereby the various factors that lead to obesity and the consequences of some particular types of obesity might lead to insulin resistance, cardiovascular disease, and psychological problems. This perspective will be more productive than a search for putative mechanisms that would, in so-called normal individuals, regulate body weight at a healthy and fashionable set point.

For biologists, this perspective suggests a variety of testable hypotheses concerning the mechanisms that control the consummatory and motivational aspects of sex behavior and ingestion in a natural or seminatural context in which the animals have choices between food and sex. The enormous variety of central neuropeptides, sensory stimuli, and hormonal mediators and modulators conspire to direct attention and action toward behaviors that optimize reproductive success. During energetic challenges, deficits in the oxidizable fuels detected by sensory receptors, falling insulin and leptin, and increased neuropeptides such as NPY tend to initiate processes that (1) save energy by decreasing resting metabolic rate and inhibiting the HPG and immune systems, and (2) ensure adequate food intake by increasing the motivation to forage and hoard food. These same factors conspire to decrease the motivation to engage in sex-related behaviors. When food is plentiful and the primary sensory detectors send information indicating that the demand for oxidizable fuels has been met increases in peripheral hormones, such as CCK and leptin, and decreases in neuropeptides, such as NPY, tend to increase the motivation to engage in sex-related activities. Thus, the animal will ignore palatable food when in the presence of a sexually interested opposite-sex conspecific. The remainder of the chapter examines the points of convergence and divergence in the mechanisms that control food-related behaviors, sex-related behaviors, and HPG function. Many of the sensory stimuli, hormones, and neuropeptides are the same for food intake and for reproduction, although there are a few differences. In addition, there are several points of divergence with regard to the brain areas where the hormones and neuropeptides act and with regard to that specific receptor subtypes that are activated.

A. Integration at the Level of the Central Nervous System

1. Dorsomedial Nucleus

The DMH is a somewhat poorly defined nucleus that can be considered part of the periventricular zone of the hypothalamus (Thompson and Swanson, 1998). It has long been associated with controlling ingestive behaviors (Bernardis and Bellinger, 1987, 1998) and appears to play an important role in the circadian control of corticosterone secretion (Buijs *et al.*, 1998). With regard to reproductive function, electrical stimulation of the DMH lesions blocks pulsatile LH release (Gallo, 1981), and it is associated with some patterns of prolactin secretion (Gunnet and Freeman, 1985). The organization of both afferent and efferent DMH connections (Fig. 9) suggests that it is well placed to act as a visceromotor (including neuroendocrine) motor pattern controller (Risold *et al.*, 1997; Thompson and Swanson, 1998). Its major efferent connections are intrahypothalamic and, for energy balance and reproduction, target the AVPV, PVH, and ARH (Li *et al.*, 1998; Luiten *et al.*, 1987; Thompson *et al.*, 1996). But the densest and best-characterized DMH projection in terms of function is to the PVH. NPY neurons in the DMH are activated during lactation and project to the PVH (Li *et al.*, 1998). Furthermore, DMH is critical for mediating circadian effects on glucocorticoid secretion and may be responsible for some of leptin's actions on PVH function (Elmquist *et al.*, 1998c). As discussed previously, the PVH is thought to be an important site for the fasting-induced increase in sensitivity to steroid negative feedback (Nagatani *et al.*, 1994). Also, PVH is thought to be the principal site of action whereby estradiol decreases food intake. Dilute implants of estradiol decrease food intake when implanted into the PVH, but not the VMH in rats (Butera and Beikirch, 1989). Furthermore, lesions of the PVH, but not the VMH, block the effects of systemic estradiol treatment on food intake (Butera *et al.*, 1992). By virtue of these connections to the PVH, the DMH should receive more attention in the future.

2. Anteroventral Periventricular Nucleus

As we have discussed earlier, the AVPV is a small periventricular nucleus located in the preoptic region. It projects directly to GnRH neurons (Gu and Simerly, 1997), contains abundant ER and PR, and shows sexual dimorphic expression of peptide and neurotransmitters (Simerly, 1998; Simerly *et al.*, 1988); it thus plays a critical role in regulating the preovulatory gonadotropin surge (see Section V). However, three sets of efferent projections may help mediate the influences of gonadal steroids on the ingestive behavior control networks (Fig. 9) (Gu and Simerly, 1997). First, the AVPV provides strong atrial natriuretic peptide and neurotensin-containing projections to the PVH, particularly to its parvicellular parts (Moga and Saper, 1994; Standaert and Saper, 1988). Both of these neuropeptides can affect ingestive behavior and those PVH-regulated systems concerned with energy balance (Oliveira *et al.*, 1997; Watts, 2001b; Wiedemann *et al.*, 2000). Second, the AVPV projects to the DMH and, finally, to the ARH. The significance of these AVPV projections in metabolic control of reproduction is unclear and represents an inviting avenue of research.

3. Arcuate Nucleus

We have already described how the NPY, AgRP, and α-MSH projections from the ARH to the PVH and LHA are important for mediating hormonal effects on ingestive behaviors and might also be important for influencing reproduction (see Section VI.A.1). In addition, the ARH has long been implicated in the regulation of ovulation, and at least some of the effects of altered energy balance on GnRH release might be mediated by ARH neurons. First, both NPY and β-endorphin (a cleavage product of the POMC protein) are elevated by energetic challenges (Abizaid *et al.*, 1997; Brady *et al.*, 1990; Lewis *et al.*, 1993; M. S. Smith, 1993; Woods *et al.*, 1998; Watts *et al.*, 1999) and have major actions on GnRH and LH release (Goodman *et al.*, 1995; Herbison, 1998; Kalra *et al.*, 1997; McDonald *et al.*, 1989; Pierroz *et al.*, 1996; Walker *et al.*, 2000). Second, POMC- and NPY-containing neurons in the ARH express leptin receptors (Elmquist *et al.*, 1999). Third, some NPY- and β-endorphin-containing neurons in the ARH project to the PVH where there are abundant opiate, Y1, and Y5 receptors (Gerald *et al.*, 1996; Glass *et al.*,

1999). Finally, some NPY- and β-endorphin-containing neurons project directly to the vicinity of GnRH terminals in the ME, where numerous GnRH nerve fibers and terminals were colocalized with Y1 receptor immunoreactivity (Li et al., 1999; Simonian et al., 1999). Given their diverse connections to the GnRH network, it is possible that these circuits represent one means by which signals generated by changes in metabolic fuel availability can affect reproductive competence.

In response to energetic challenges such as low food availability and lactation, central peptides that increase food intake also decrease resting energy expenditure and inhibit reproductive processes (sex behavior and GnRH and LH secretion). Mechanisms that control food intake and reproduction in service of energy balance share in common up-sregulated NPY gene transcription and protein synthesis in the DMH and ARH and release of NPY into the PVH. Divergence of these circuits then occurs postsynaptically. For example, NPY increases food intake and decreases sympathetic activity in BAT by acting primarily on Y1 or Y5 receptors in the PVH (Van Dijk et al., 1994), whereas NPY inhibits sex behavior (at least in Syrian hamsters) via NPY Y2 receptors (Corp et al., 2001) and these Y2 receptors are thought to be located elsewhere in the hypothalamus or hindbrain (Dumont et al., 1993). In addition, the Y1 and Y5 receptors on or near GnRH fibers in the ME have been implicated in the effects of NPY on LH secretion. Alternatively, or in addition, some of the effects of NPY on food intake and reproduction are due to effects of NPY on peripheral endocrine and metabolic activity. These peripheral effects are via the adrenal gland, but the effects on food intake diverge from those on reproduction. The effects of food-deprivation-induced elevations in NPY on food intake are mediated via adrenal glucocorticoids (Sainsbury et al., 1997; Stanley et al., 1989), and food-deprivation effects on LH might be mediated via adrenal catecholamines (Cagampang et al., 1999). A great deal more work is needed to understand the different roles of these specific ligands and their receptors with regard to the motivational and consummatory aspects of ingestive behavior and sex behavior.

4. Ventral Premammillary Nucleus

The PMv is located in the caudal part of the hypothalamus immediately ventral to the fornix and lateral to the ARH and expresses both gonadal steroid and leptin receptors (Elmquist et al., 1998a; Simerly et al., 1990; LaFlamme et al., 1998). The PMv projects heavily to the PVH and ARH (Canteras et al., 1992; Luiten et al., 1987), placing it in a position to mediate some of the effects of gonadal steroids on energy balance and negative feedback effects on pulsatile LH secretion. Its other major projections are to the VMHvl and the AVPV (Fig. 9) (Canteras et al., 1992; Luiten et al., 1987), which implicate it the control of sex behavior and ovulation. In turn, the PMv receives strong projections from the posterior dorsal part of the medial amygdala and the principal nucleus of the BST, both of which contain high levels of gonadal steroid receptors and are heavily implicated in olfactory-driven reproductive behaviors (Canteras et al., 1995; Risold et al., 1997). The fact that leptin receptors are found in both the PMv and the VMH (albeit in rather lower numbers in the VMHvl than the VMHdm; Elmquist et al., 1998a) suggests that these two nuclei are able to mediate the effects of energy balance on reproductive behaviors (Fig. 9). In ovariectomized Syrian hamsters brought into heat with estradiol and progesterone treatment, lordosis duration is decreased by fasting or treatment with metabolic inhibitors. This effect is accompanied by a decrease in ER-IR in the VMH (and an increase in ER-IR in the PVH and mPOA). Treatment with leptin increases the duration of lordosis in fed, but decreases lordosis duration in fasted, ovariectomized females brought into heat with estradiol and progesterone treatment (Wade et al., 1997). The effects of leptin on lordosis duration occur without changes in ER-IR in the VMH, but ER-IR in the PMv have not been published.

B. Integration at the Level of the Primary Sensory Systems

Both food intake and reproduction are responsive to stimuli resulting from the availability of oxidizable metabolic fuels. Treatments that block glucose oxidation (and subsequent metabolic events leading to the formation of ATP) also increase food intake and inhibit reproductive processes, including sex behavior. High doses of insulin administered peripherally increase food intake and inhibit reproductive process, and these effects are reversed by simultaneous treatment with glucose or fructose. Thus, the effects of insulin are not due to neuroendocrine effects of the hormone per se but rather to indirect effects on fuel metabolism. GnRH and LH secretion and estrous cyclicity are inhibited by these treatments, which also cause a cerebral metabolic emergency. Effects of inhibitors of glucose oxidation and insulin on food intake and reproduction are attenuated in animals with lesions of the AP (and minor damage to the medial NTS).

Hindbrain catecholamine projections, possibly to PVH, have been implicated in glucoprivic control of food intake and in general metabolic control of reproductive processes. It has been clearly demonstrated that catecholamine neurons are essential for glucoprivic control of food intake. At least some catecholamine cell groups have been reported to be essential for the increase in ER-IR in the PVH in rats (Estacio *et al.,* 2001). More work is needed to determine whether catecholamine projections are essential for the effects of specific metabolic deficits on reproductive processes such as estrous cycles or pulsatile LH secretion.

Signals from a deficit in glucose utilization might be one part of the system that influences food intake and reproduction, but other signals also play a role during naturally occurring metabolic challenges. For example, in sharp contrast to the effects of either hypoglycemia or inhibitors of glucose oxidation, the effects of food deprivation on subsequent food intake and estrous cycles are not prevented by AP/NTS lesions, suggesting a role for signals other than those related to glucoprivation.

There is no doubt that food intake is controlled by hepatic energy status, as represented by the ATP-to-ADP ratio or the phosphorylation potential and that these effects are mediated by the vagus nerve. Similar evidence is not available for reproductive processes. One study showed that treatment with 2,5-AM failed to inhibit estrous cyclicity, but this useful metabolic inhibitor, which decreases hepatic energy status by trapping inorganic phosphates, has not been used in other species to our knowledge. The effects of metabolic inhibitors on reproductive processes were not prevented by total bilateral subdiaphragmatic vagotomy. This has led to the idea that reproduction is particular sensitive to events related to central glucose oxidation. However, more careful work is necessary to fully understand the role of peripheral energy status on reproductive function. In one elegant study, pulsatile LH secretion was inhibited in fasted rats, but was restored by acute gastric

vagotomy. Similar work has not be replicated in other species with other pharmacological inhibitors and gastric stimuli. One hypothesis that should be tested is that there might be particular signals for the inhibition of pulsatile LH secretion and different signals for reinitiation of the pulse generator or rescue of the ovarian follicle.

The nature of the metabolic signal for both food intake and reproduction are still unknown. However, a metabolic sensory system controls the secretion of chemical messengers such as insulin and leptin as well as the transport of these hormones across the blood–brain barrier. A complete understanding of energy balance is impossible until we characterize this pivotal sensory system. Similarly, sensory signals that detect the availability and oxidation of metabolic fuels control the immune system, hibernation, and probably entrain the feeding-entrainable circadian oscillator.

C. Integration at the Level of Hormonal Mediators and Modulators

Low doses of insulin and leptin administered ICV decrease food intake and increase reproductive function in the presence of a minimum of metabolic fuels. These effects are taken as evidence for direct endocrine action of these hormones. The results are certainly consistent with the notion that hormones conspire to create a physiological milieu in which mating can occur without regard to foraging or food hoarding. It is also clear that these hormones only facilitate reproduction when sufficient metabolic fuels are available. Treatment with leptin can fully reverse the effects of fasting on puberty in rats restricted to 80% of their *ad libitum* food intake, but not in rats restricted to 70% of their *ad libitum* intake (Cheung *et al.,* 1997). Systemic leptin increases the duration of lordosis in *ad libitum*–fed, but not in food-deprived, hamsters (Wade *et al.,* 1997). Leptin treatment can shorten the duration of lactational diestrus in rats exposed to acute food deprivation, but not in rats exposed to prolonged chronic food restriction (Woodside *et al.,* 2000). Fasting-induced anestrus is not significantly attenuated by either IP or ICV leptin treatment when each injection of leptin is preceded by an injection of 2DG or MP, even though these doses of MP and 2DG did not induce anestrus in hamsters fed *ad libitum* (Schneider *et al.,* 1998; Schneider and

Zhou, 1999a). Insulin treatment induces anestrus in hamsters limited to the food intake of saline-treated controls, even though this treatment increases, rather than decreases, plasma leptin levels (Blum *et al.,* 2000). Both insulin and leptin have metabolic effects on a variety of tissues. Leptin increases glucose and FFA oxidation, whereas insulin promotes uptake of glucose in peripheral cells and in some CNS cells. One testable hypothesis is that even in the CNS, insulin and leptin increase the activity of the GnRH pulse generator by increasing *in situ* fuel oxidation.

A number of interactions might occur between hormones and metabolic sensory stimuli. One possibility that should be considered in more detail is that these hormonal and metabolic signals interact intracellularly at the level of mitochondrial metabolism. For example, fasting-induced anestrus is prevented by leptin, but not when each dose of leptin is preceded by a low dose of an inhibitor of glucose oxidation (e.g., 2DG) or FFA oxidation (e.g., MP) (Schneider *et al.,* 1998). These results might reflect an interaction between leptin and metabolic inhibitors at the level of intracellular fuel oxidation, although interactions at other levels are possible. Leptin increases the availability and oxidation of glucose (Kamohara *et al.,* 1997; Ceddia *et al.,* 2001), whereas 2DG has the opposite effect (Brown, 1962). Leptin increases the intracellular availability and oxidation of FFAs, possibly via the inhibition of acetyl CoA decarboxylase and consequent disinhibition of CPT-I (Bai *et al.,* 1996; Y. T. Zhou *et al.,* 1997), whereas MP has the opposite effects, irreversibly binding CPT-I and preventing the transport of FFAs into mitochondria (Tutwiler *et al.,* 1985). Because MP is not thought to reach the brain in appreciable quantities, it might be that the interaction between leptin and MP occurs peripherally.

Direct effects of hormonal mediators and metabolic signals on GnRH neurons in the ARH are under investigation. GnRH neurons in culture have been shown to express leptin receptor mRNA and are also glucose sensitive. It should be noted, however, that the effects of insulin-induced hypoglycemia, and glucoprivation on GnRH secretion *in vivo* are abolished by lesions of the AP and medial NTS, and thus there can be no doubt that these metabolic stimuli do not affect GnRH neurons directly.

1. Caudal Hindbrain

Deficits in metabolic fuel availability and oxidation block or attenuate the facilitory effects of leptin on reproduction. Future work must examine the integration of hormonal modulators and primary metabolic sensory stimuli. One possibility is that these signals are integrated in the caudal hindbrain. As previously noted, the AP is essential for the effects of glucoprivation on reproduction and food intake. In addition, leptin receptors are present in the caudal hindbrain, in areas such as the AP and NTS (Grill *et al.,* 2000). Lesions of the AP and medial NTS block glucoprivic and hypoglycemic effects on estrous cycles in hamsters, pulsatile LH secretion in rats, ER-IR in VMH and ARH, and lordosis induced by exogenous hormone treatment in ovariectomized hamsters (Cates and O'Byrne, 2000; H.-Y. Li *et al.,* 1994; Schneider and Zhu, 1994; Panicker *et al.,* 1998). However, AP/medial NTS lesions fail to block food-deprivation-induced anestrus, and, thus, if the effects of fasting are mediated by falling leptin, the AP/NTS are not critical for these effects. The slow microinfusion of 2DG into the fourth ventricle in rats inhibits pulsatile LH secretion (Murahashi *et al.,* 1996), whereas the slow microinfusion of 5TG inhibits estrous cycles in Syrian hamsters (Zhou and Schneider, 2000). In Syrian hamsters, fasting-induced anestrus is reversed by slow infusion of leptin into either the third or fourth ventricle, suggesting that leptin can influence reproduction by action in the hindbrain (Zhou and Schneider, 1999, 2000). Collectively, these results suggest at least one mechanism whereby changes in leptin secretion might interact with changes in metabolic fuel availability to influence reproduction. Leptin receptor mRNA is found in the caudal NTS in mice and Syrian hamsters (Mercer *et al.,* 1998b). Direct catecholaminergic projections from the NTS to the GnRH cell bodies in the mPOA might mediate metabolic effects on the GnRH surge (Castaneyra-Perdomo *et al.,* 1992). Furthermore, information from the NTS might reach the forebrain steroid-concentrating nuclei or the GnRH neurons indirectly via the lateral parabrachial nucleus (LPBN) (Lowey, 1990) or via catecholaminergic projections to the PVH (Maeda *et al.,* 1994). Leptin receptors in the hindbrain are found in close proximity to GLP-1 and CCK neurons. As noted earlier with regard to food intake, CCK neurons in the AP and GLP-1 neurons in the caudal NTS project to the PVH and DMH. The PVH is one area where it is thought that food deprivation increases sensitivity to steroid negative feedback on the GnRH pulse generator. Evidence shows that treatment with GLP-1 increases GnRH secretion in GT1–7 cells in culture and increases the secretion of LH within 5 minutes of injection in male rats (Beak *et al.,* 1998). Furthermore, a 48-hour fast decreased hypothalamic GLP-1 content compared to that of fed rats. One testable hypothesis is that metabolic and hormonal stimuli that are detected or integrated in the hindbrain act on the GnRH pulse generator via catecholaminergic, GLP-1, or CCK neurons that originate in the hindbrain.

The similarity between this putative pathway for control of GnRH and the pathway for control of reproduction is striking. It has become increasingly apparent that the study of ingestive behavior can be facilitated by attention to the methodologies and theoretical considerations from the field of reproduction and vice versa, as first suggested by Wade and Schneider (1992).

Acknowledgments

We express our thanks to Mark I. Friedman, Antonio A. Nunez, and Timothy J. Bartness for insightful suggestions, and to Deanna Scott, Pamela Little, Carol Buckley, Robert Blum, Dan Zhou, and Laura Szymanski for invaluable help with the preparation of the manuscript. This work was supported by research grant IBN9723938 from the National Science Foundation and DK53402 from the National Institutes of Diabetes and Digestive and Kidney Diseases, by Career Development Award MH 01096 from the National Institute of Mental Health (J.E.S.), and by NS 29728 from the National Institute of Neurological Disorder and Stroke (A.G.W.).

References

Abizaid, A., Walker, C. D., and Woodside, B. (1997). Changes in neuropeptide Y immunoreactivity in the arcuate nucleus during and after food restriction in lactating rats. *Brain Res.* **761**, 306–312.

Abraham, S. F., Beumont, P. J. V., Fraser, I. S., and Llewellyn-Jones, D. (1982). Body weight, exercise and menstrual status among ballet dancers in training. *Br. J. Obstet. Gynec.* **89**, 507–510.

Ahima, R. S., Prabakaran, D., Mantzoros, C., Qu, D., Lowell, B., Maratos-Flier, E., and Flier, J. (1996). Role of leptin in the neuroendocrine response to fasting. *Nature (London)* **382**, 250–252.

Ahima, R. S., Dushay, J., Flier, S. N., Prabakaran, D., and Flier, J. S. (1997). Leptin accelerates the onset of puberty in normal female mice. *J. Clin. Invest.* **99**, 391–395.

Ahima, R. S., Prabakaran, D., and Flier, J. S. (1998). Postnatal leptin surge and regulation of circadian rhythm of leptin by feeding. Implications for energy homeostasis and neuroendocrine function. *J. Clin. Invest.* **101**, 1020–1027.

Ahima, R. S., Kelly, J., Elmquist, J. K., and Flier, J. S. (1999). Distinct physiologic and neuronal responses to decreased leptin and mile hyperleptinemia. *Endocrinology (Baltimore)* **140**, 4923–4931.

Ahren, B., Mansson, S., Gingerrich, R., and Havel, P. J. (1997). Regulation of plasma leptin in mice: Influence of age, high-fat diet, and fasting. *Am. J. Physiol.* **273**, R113–R120.

Allen, D. L., Renner, K. J., and Luine, V. N. (1985). Naltrexone facilitation of sexual receptivity in the rat. *Horm. Behav.* **19**, 98–103.

Ammar, A. A., Sederholm, F., Saito, T. R., Scheurink, A. J. W., Johnson, A. E., and Sodersten, P. (2000). NPY-leptin: Opposing effects on appetitive and consummatory ingestive behavior and sexual behavior. *Am. J. Physiol.* **278**, R1627–R1633.

Anand, B. K., and Brobeck, J. R. (1951b). The localization of a feeding center in the hypothalamus. *Proc. Soc. Exp. Biol. Med.* **77**, 323–324.

Anderson, S. S., and Fedak, M. A. (1987). The energetics of sexual success of grey seals and comparison with the costs of reproduction in other pinnipeds. *In* "Reproductive Energetics in Mammals" (A. S. I. Loudon and P. A. Racey, eds.), pp. 319–341. Oxford Scientific Publications, Oxford.

Apter, D. (1997). Leptin in puberty. *Clin. Endocrinol.* **47**, 175–176.

Arias, P., Rodriguez, M., Szwarcfarb, B., Sinay, I. R., and Moguilevsky, J. A. (1992). Effect of insulin on LHRH release by perfused hypothalamic fragments. *Neuroendocrinology* **56**, 415–418.

Bagnol, D., Lu, X.-Y., Kaelin, C. B., Day, H. E. W., Ollmann, M., Gantz, I., Akil, H., Barsh, G. S., and Watson, S. J. (1999). Anatomy of an endogenous antagonist: Relationship between agouti-related protein and proopiomelanocortin in brain. *J. Neurosci.* **19**, 1–7.

Bai, Y., Zhang, S., Kim, K.-S., Lee, J.-K., and Kim, K.-H. (1996). Leptin inhibits acetyl CoA carboxylase in 313 pre-adipocytes. *J. Biol. Chem.* **271**, 13939–13942.

Balasubramaniam, A. (1997). Neuropeptide Y family of hormones: Receptor subtypes and antagonists. *Peptides (N.Y.)* **18**, 445–457.

Ball, G. F., and Bentley, G. E. (2000). Neuroendocrine mechanisms mediating photoperiodic and social regulation of seasonal reproduction in birds. *In* "Reproduction in Context: Social and Environmental Influences on Reproduction"

(K. Wallen and J. E. Schneider, eds.), pp. 129–158. MIT Press, Cambridge, MA.

Bamshad, M., Aoki, V. T., Adkinson, M. G., Warren, W. S., and Bartness, T. J. (1998). Central nervous system origins of the sympathetic nervous system outflow to white adipose tissue. *Am. J. Physiol.* **275**, R291–R299.

Bamshad, M., Song, C. K., and Bartness, T. J. (1999). CNS origins of the sympathetic nervous system outflow to brown adipose tissue. *Am. J. Physiol.* **276**, R1569–R1578.

Barash, I. A., Cheung, C. C., Weigle, D. S., Ren, H., Kabigting, E. B., Kuijper, J. L., Clifton, D. K., and Steiner, R. A. (1996). Leptin is a metabolic signal to the reproductive system. *Endocrinology (Baltimore)* **137**, 3144–3147.

Barnett, S. A. (1973). Maternal processes in the cold-adaptation of mice. *Biol. Rev. Cambridge Philos. Soc.* **48**, 477–508.

Barsh, G. S., Farooqi, I. S., and O'Rahilly, S. (2000). Genetics of body-weight regulation. *Nature (London)* **404**, 644–651.

Bartness, T. J. (1997). Food hoarding is increased by pregnancy, lactation, and food deprivation in Siberian hamsters. *Am. J. Physiol.* **272**, 118–125.

Bartness, T. J., and Bamshad, M. (1998). Innervation of mammalian white adipose tissue: Implications for the regulation of total body fat. *Am. J. Physiol.* **275**, R1399–R1411.

Bartness, T. J., and Clein, M. R. (1994). Effects of food deprivation and restriction, and metabolic blockers on food hoarding in Siberian hamsters. *Am. J. Physiol.* **266**, R1111–R1117.

Bartness, T. J., Demas, G. E., and Song, C. K. (2000a). Central nervous system innervation of white adipose tissue. *In* "Adipose Tissue" (S. Klaus, ed.), pp. 201–229. Landes Bioscience, Georgetown, TX.

Baskin, D. G., Figlewicz, D. P., Woods, S. C., Porte, D., Jr., and Dorsa, D. M. (1987). Insulin in the brain. *Annu. Rev. Physiol.* **49**, 335–347.

Bauche, F., Sabourault, D., Giudicelli, Y., Nordmann, J., and Nordmann, R. (1983). Inhibition in vitro of acyl-CoA dehydrogenase by 2-mercaptoacetate in rat liver mitochondria. *Biochem. J.* **215**, 457–464.

Bauer-Dantoin, A. C., McDonald, J. K., and Levine, J. E. (1992). Neuropeptide Y potentiates luteinizing hormone (LH)-releasing hormone-induced LH secretion only under conditions leading to preovulatory LH surges. *Endocrinology (Baltimore)* **131**, 2946–2952.

Beach, F. A. (1948). "Hormones and Behavior" Hoeber, New York.

Beak, S. A., Heath, M. M., Small, C. J., Morgan, D. G., Ghateim M. A., Taylor, A. D., Buckingham, J. C., Bloom, S. R., and Smith, D. M. (1998). Glucagon-like peptide-1 stimulates luteinizing hormone-releasing hormone secretion in a rodent hypothalamic neuronal cell line. *J. Clin. Invest.* **101**, 1334–1341.

Beckett, J. L., Sakurai, H., Adams, B. M., and Adams, T. E. (1997). Moderate and severe nutrient restriction has divergent effects on gonadotroph function in orchidectomized sheep. *Biol. Reprod.* **57**, 415–419.

Bennett, P. A., Lindell, K., Karlsson, C., Robinson, I. C., Carlsson, L. M., and Carlsson, B. (1998). Differential expression and regulation of leptin receptor isoforms in the rat brain: Effects of fasting and oestrogen. *Neuroendocrinology* **67**, 29–26.

Benoit, S., Schwartz, M., Baskin, D., Woods, S. C., and Seeley, R. (2000). CNS Melanocortin system involvement in the regulation of food intake and body weight. *Horm. Behav.* **37**, 299–305.

Bergendahl, M., Iranmanesh, A., Evans, W. S., and Veldhuis, J. D. (2000). Short-term fasting selectively suppresses leptin pulse mass and 24-hour rhythmic leptin release in healthy midluteal phase women without disturbing leptin pulse frequency or its entropy control (pattern orderliness). *J. Clin. Endocrinol. Metab.* **85**, 207–213.

Bernard, C. (1856). "Leçons de physiologie expérimentale appliquée á lá médicine faites au Collége de France." Bailliére, Paris.

Bernard, J. F., and Bandler, R. (1998). Parallel circuits for emotional coping behavior: New pieces in the puzzle. *J. Comp. Neurol.* **401**, 429–436.

Bernard, J. F., Alden, M., and Besson, J. M. (1993). The organization of the efferent projections from the pontine parabrachial area to the amygdaloid complex: A Phaseolus vulgaris leucoagglutinin (PHA-L). study in the rat. *J. Comp. Neurol.* **329**, 201–229.

Bernard, J. F., Dallel, R., Raboisson, P., Villanueva, L., and Le Bars, D. (1995). Organization of the efferent projections from the spinal cervical enlargement to the parabrachial area and periaqueductal gray: A PHA-L study in the rat. *J. Comp. Neurol.* **353**, 480–505.

Bernardis, L. L., and Bellinger, L. L. (1987). The dorsomedial hypothalamic nucleus revisited: 1986 update. *Brain Res.* **434**, 321–381.

Bernardis, L. L., and Bellinger, L. L. (1996). The lateral hypothalamic area revisited: Ingestive behavior. *Neurosci. Biobehav. Rev.* **20**, 189–287.

Bernardis, L. L., and Bellinger, L. L. (1998). The dorsomedial hypothalamic nucleus revisited: 1998 update. *Proc. Soc. Exp. Biol. Med.* **218**, 284–306.

Berriman, S. J., Wade, G. N., and Blaustein, J. D. (1992). Expression of Fos-like proteins in gonadotropin-releasing hormone neurons of Syrian hamsters: Effects of estrous cycles and metabolic fuels. *Endocrinology (Baltimore)* **131**, 2222–2228.

Berry, R. J., and Peters, J. (1975). Macquarie Island house mice: A genetical isolate on a sub-Antarctic island. *J. Zool.* **176**, 375–389.

Berthold, A. A. (1849). "Transplantation of Testis" (translation by D. P. Quiring). *Bull. Hist. Med.* **16**, 42–46 (1944).

Berthoud, H.-R., and Jeanrenaud, B. (1979). Acute hyperinsulinemia and its reversal by vagotomy after lesions of the ventromedial hypothalamus in anesthetized rats. *Endocrinology (Baltimore)* **105**, 146–151.

Berthoud, H.-R., and Powley, T. L. (1992). Vagal afferent innervation of the rat fundic stomach: Morphological characterization of the gastric tension receptor. *J. Comp. Neurol.* **319**, 261–276.

Bester, H., Besson, J. M., and Bernard, J. F. (1997). Organization of efferent projections from the parabrachial are to the hypothalamus: A *Phaseolus vulgaris*-leucoagglutinin study in the rat. *J. Comp. Neurol.* **383**, 245–281.

Bester, H., Bourgeais, L., Villanueva, L., Besson, J. M., and Bernard, J. F. (1999). Differential projections to the intralaminar and gustatory thalamus from the parabrachial area: A PHA-L study in the rat. *J. Comp. Neurol.* **405**, 421–449.

Billington, C. J., Briggs, J. E., Grace, M., and Levine, A. S. (1991). Effects of intracerebroventricular injection of neuropeptide Y on energy metabolism. *Am. J. Physiol.* **260**, R321–R327.

Bird, E., Cardone, C. C., and Contreras, R. J. (1983). Area postrema lesions disrupt food intake induced by cerebroventricular infusions of 5-thioglucose in the rat. *Brain Res.* **270**, 193–196.

Bittencourt, J. C., and Sawchenko, P. E. (2000). Do centrally administered neuropeptides access cognate receptors? An analysis in the central corticotropin-releasing factor system. *J. Neurosci.* **20**, 1142–1156.

Bittencourt, J. C., Presse, F., Arias, C., Peto, C., Vaughan, J., Nahon, J. L., Vale, W., and Sawchenko, P. E. (1992). The melanin-concentrating hormone system of the rat brain—an immunization and hybridization histochemical characterization. *J. Comp. Neurol.* **319**, 218–245.

Blessing, W. W. (1997). "The Lower Brainstem and Bodily Homeostasis." Oxford University Press, New York.

Blum, R. M., and Schneider, J. E. (2000). Fasting-induced anestrus is associated with low, while insulin-induced anestrus is associated with high plasma leptin concentrations. *Society for Neurosciences* (Abstract.).

Boden, G., Chen, X., Mozzoli, M., and Ryan, I. (1996). Effect of fasting on serum leptin in normal human subjects. *J. Clin. Endocrinol. Metab.* **81**, 3419–3423.

Borer, K. T., Campbell, C. S., Tabor, J., Jorgenson, K., Kandarian, S., and Gordon, L. (1983). Exercise reverses photoperiodic anestrus in Golden hamsters. *Biol. Reprod.* **29**, 38–47.

Boss, O., Samec, S., Paoloni-Giacobino, A., Rossier, C., Dulloo, A., Seydoux, J., Muzzin, P., and Giacobino, J. P. (1997). Uncoupling protein-3: A new member of the mitochondrial carrier family with tissue-specific expression. *FEBS Lett.* **408**, 39–42.

Boswell, T., Richardson, R. D., Schwartz, M. W., D'Alessio, D. A., Woods, S. C., Sipols, A. J., Baskin, D. G., and Kenagy, G. J. (1993). NPY and galanin in a hibernator: Hypothalamic gene expression and effects on feeding. *Brain Res. Bull.* **32**, 379–384.

Boswell, T., Richardson, R. D., Seeley, R. J., Ramenofsky, M., Wingfield, J. C., Friedman, M. I., and Woods, S. C. (1995). Regulation of food intake by metabolic fuels in white-crowned sparrows. *Am. J. Physiol.* **269**, R1462–R1468.

Boulos, Z., and Terman, M. (1980). Food availability and daily biological rhythms. *Neurosci. Biobehav. Rev.* **4**, 119–132.

Bourguignon, J. P., Gerard, A., Purnelle, G., Czajkowski, V., Yamanaka, C., Lemaitre, M., Rigo, J. M., Moonen, G., and Franchimont, P. (1997a). Duality of glutamatergic and GABAergic control of pulsatile GnRH secretion by rat hypothalamic explants: I. Effects of antisense oligodeoxynucleotides using explants including or excluding the preoptic area. *J. Neuroendocrinol.* **9**, 183–191.

Bourguignon, J. P., Gerard, A., Purnelle, G., Czajkowski, V., Yamanaka, C., Lemaitre, M., Rigo, J. M., Moonen, G., and Franchimont, P. (1997b). Duality of glutamatergic and GABAergic control of pulsatile GnRH secretion by rat hypothalamic explants: II. Reduced NR2C- and GABAA-receptor mediated inhibition at initiation of sexual maturation. *J. Neuroendocrinol.* **9**, 193–199.

Brady, L. S., Smith, M. A., Gold, P. W., and Herkenham, M. (1990). Altered expression of hypothalamic neuropeptide mRNAs in food-restricted and food-deprived rats. *Neuroendocrinology* **52**, 441–447.

Bray, G. A., and York, D. A. (1999). The MONA LISA hypothesis in the time of leptin. *Recent Prog. Horm. Res.* **53**, 95–117.

Bray, G. A., and York, D. A. (1999). Reciprocal relation of food intake and sympathetic activity: The MONALISA Hypothesis. *In* "Nutrition, Genetics and Obesity" (G. A. Bray and D. H. Ryan, eds.), pp. 122–143. Louisiana State University Press, Baton Rouge.

Bray, G. A., Inoue, S., and Nishizawa, Y. (1981). Hypothalamic obesity. The antonomic hypothesis and the lateral hypothalamus *Diabetologia* **20**, 366–377.

Briski, K. P., and Sylvester, P. W. (1998). Role of endogenous opiates in glucoprivic inhibition of the luteinizing hormone surge and fos expression by preoptic gonadotropin-releasing hormone neurones in ovariectomized steroid-primed female rats. *J. Neuroendocrinol.* **10**, 769–776.

Broberger, C., De Lecea, L., Sutcliffe, J. G., and Hokfelt, T. (1998a). Hypocretin/orexin- and melanin-concentrating hormone-expressing cells form distinct populations in the rodent lateral hypothalamus: Relationship to the neuropeptide Y and agouti gene-related protein systems. *J. Comp. Neurol.* **402**, 460–474.

Broberger, C., Johansen, J., Johansson, C., Schalling, M., and Hokfelt, T. (1998b). The neuropeptide Y/agouti gene-related protein (AGRP). Brain circuitry in normal, anorectic and monosodium glutamate-treated mice. *Proc. Natl. Acad. Sci. U.S.A.* **95**, 15043–15048.

Bronson, F. H. (1986). Food-restricted, prepubertal female rats: Rapid recovery of luteinizing hormone pulsing with excess food, and full recovery of pubertal development with gonadotropin-releasing hormone. *Endocrinology (Baltimore)* **118**, 2483–2487.

Bronson, F. H. (1987). Puberty in female rats: Relative effect of exercise and food restriction. *Am. J. Physiol.* **252**, R140–R144.

Bronson, F. H. (1988). Effect of food manipulation on the GnRH-LH-estradiol axis of young female rats. *Am. J. Physiol.* **254**, R616–R621.

Bronson, F. H. (1989). "Mammalian Reproductive Biology." University of Chicago Press, Chicago and London.

Bronson, F. H. (2000). Puberty and energy reserves: A walk on the wild side. *In* "Reproduction in Context: Social and Environmental Influences on Reproduction" (K. Wallen and J. E. Schneider, eds.), pp. 15–34. MIT Press, Cambridge, MA.

Bronson, F. H., and Heideman, P. D. (1990). Short-term hormonal responses to food intake in peripubertal female rats. *Am. J. Physiol.* **259**, R25–R31.

Bronson, F. H., and Manning, J. M. (1991). The energetic regulation of ovulation: A realistic role for body fat. *Biol. Reprod.* **44**, 945–950.

Brown, D., Herbison, A. E., Robinson, J. E., Marrs, R. W., and Leng, G. (1994). Modelling the luteinizing hormone-releasing hormone pulse generator. *Neuroscience* **63**, 869–879.

Brown, J. (1962). Effects of 2-deoxy-D-glucose on carbohydrate metabolism: Review of the literature and studies in the rat. *Metab., Clin. Exp.* **11**, 1098–1112.

Brown-Grant, K., and Raisman, G. (1977). Abnormalities in reproductive function associated with the destruction of the suprachiasmatic nuclei in female rats. *Proc. R. Soc. London. Ser. B* **198**, 279–296.

Brüning, J. C., Gautam, D., Burks, D. J., Gillette, J., Schubert, M., Orban, P. C., Klein, R., Krone, W., Müller-Wieland, D., and Kahn, C. R. (2000). Role of brain insulin receptor in control of body weight and reproduction. *Science* **289**, 2122–2125.

Bryson, J., Phuyal, J., Swan, V., and Caterson, I. D. (1999). Leptin has acute effects on glucose and lipid metabolism in both lean and gold thioglucose-obese mice. *Am. J. Physiol.* **277**, E417–E422.

Bucholtz, D. C., Vidwans, N. M., Herbosa, C. G., Schillo, K. K., and Foster, D. L. (1996). Metabolic interfaces between growth and reproduction. V. Pulsatile luteinizing hormone secretion is dependent on glucose availability. *Endocrinology (Baltimore)* **137**, 601–607.

Bucholtz, D. C., Chiesa, A., Pappano, W. N., Nagatani, S., Tsukamura, H., Maeda, K. I., and Foster, D. L. (2000). Regulation of pulsatile luteinizing hormone secretion by insulin in the diabetic male lamb. *Biol. Reprod.* **62**, 1248–1255.

Buijs, R. M., Hermes, M. H., and Kalsbeek, A. (1998). The suprachiasmatic nucleus-paraventricular nucleus interactions: A bridge to the neuroendocrine and autonomic nervous system. *Prog. Brain Res.* **119**, 365–382.

Buijs, R. M., Wortel, J., Van Heerikhuize, J. J., Feenstra, M. G., Ter Horst, G. J., Romijn, H. J., and Kalsbeek, A. (1999). Anatomical and functional demonstration of a multisynaptic suprachiasmatic nucleus adrenal (cortex) pathway. *Eur. J. Neurosci.* **11**, 1535–1544.

Butera, P. C., and Beikirch, R. J. (1989). Central implants of diluted estradiol: Independent effects on ingestive and reproductive behaviors of ovariectomized rats. *Brain Res.* **491**, 266–273.

Butera, P. C., and Czaja, J. A. (1984). Intracranial estradiol in ovariectomized guinea pigs: Effects on ingestive behaviors and body weight. *Brain Res.* **322**, 41–48.

Butera, P. C., Willard, D. M., and Raymond, S. A. (1992). Effects of PVN lesions on the responsiveness of female rats to estradiol. *Brain Res.* **576**, 304–310.

Butler, J. A., Sjöberg, M., and Coen, C. W. (1999). Evidence for oestrogen receptor alpha-immunoreactivity in gonadotrophin-releasing hormone-expressing neurons. *J. Neuroendocrinol.* **11**, 331–335.

Cabanac, M., and Richard, D. (1995). Acute intraventricular CRF lowers the hoarding threshold in male rats. *Physiol. Behav.* **57**, 705–710.

Cagampang, F. R. A., Maeda, K.-I., Yokoyama, A., and Ota, K. (1990). Effect of food deprivation on the pulsatile LH release in the cycling and ovariectomized female rat. *Horm. Metab. Res.* **22**, 269–272.

Cagampang, F. R. A., Maeda, K.-I., and Ota, K. (1992). Involvement of the gastric vagal nerve in the suppression of pulsatile luteinizing hormone release during acute fasting in rats. *Endocrinology (Baltimore)* **130**, 3003–3006.

Cagampang, F. R. A., Strutton, P. H., Goubillon, M. L., and Coen, C. W. (1999). Adrenomedullectomy prevents the suppression of pulsatile luteinizing hormone release during fasting in female rats. *J. Neuroendocrinol.* **1**, 429–433.

Cai, X. J., Widdowson, P. S., Harrold, J., Wilson, S., Buckingham, R. E., Arch, J. R., Tadayyon, M., Clapham, J. C., Wilding, J., and Williams, G. (1999). Hypothalamic orexin expression: Modulation by blood glucose and feeding. *Diabetes* **48**, 2132–2137.

Calingasan, N. Y., and Ritter, S. (1993). Lateral parabrachial subnucleus lesions abolish feeding induced by mercaptoacetate by not by 2-deoxy-D-glucose. *Am. J. Physiol.* **265**, R1168–R1178.

Cameron, J. L. (1996). Regulation of reproductive function in primates by short-term changes in nutrition. *Rev. Reprod.* **1**, 117–126.

Cameron, J. L., and Nosbisch, C. (1991). Suppression of pulsatile luteinizing hormone and testosterone secretion during short term food restriction in the adult male rhesus monkey (*Macaca mulatta*). *Endocrinology (Baltimore)* **128**, 1532–1540.

Campbell, C. S., and Davis, J. D. (1974). Peripheral control of food intake: Interaction between test diet and postingestive chemoreception. *Physiol. Behav.* **12**, 377–384.

Campfield, L. A., and Smith, F. J. (1990). Transient declines in blood glucose signal meal initiation. *Int. J. Obes.* **14**, 16–31.

Campfield, L. A., Smith, F. J., Guisez, Y., Devos, R., and Burn, P. (1995). Recombinant mouse ob protein: Evidence for a peripheral signal linking adiposity and central neural networks. *Science* **269**, 546–549.

Campfield, L. A., Smith, F. J., and Burn, P. (1996). The OB protein (leptin) pathway-A link between adipose tissue mass and central neural networks. *Horm. Metab. Res.* **28**, 619–632.

Cannon, W. B. (1932). "The Wisdom of the Body." W.W. Norton and Co., New York.

Canteras, N. S., Simerly, R. B., and Swanson, L. W. (1992). Projections of the ventral premammillary nucleus. *J. Comp. Neurol.* **324**, 195–212.

Canteras, N. S., Simerly, R. B., and Swanson, L. W. (1994). Organization of projections from the ventromedial nucleus of the hypothalamus: A Phaseolus vulgaris-leucoagglutinin study in the rat. *J. Comp. Neurol.* **348**, 41–79.

Canteras, N. S., Simerly, R. B., and Swanson, L. W. (1995). Organization of projections from the medial nucleus of the amygdala: A PHAL study in the rat. *J. Comp. Neurol.* **360**, 213–245.

Canteras, N. S., Chiavegatto, S., Valle, L. E., and Swanson, L. W. (1997). Severe reduction of rat defensive behavior to a predator by discrete hypothalamic chemical lesions. *Brain Res. Bull.* **44**, 297–305.

Cao, G. Y., Considine, R. V., and Lynn, R. B. (1997). Leptin receptors in the adrenal medulla of the rat. *Am. J. Physiol.* **273**, E448–E452.

Carlsson, B., Carlsson, B., Lindell, K., Gabrielsson, B., Karlsson, C., Bjarnason, R., Westphal, O., Karlsson, U., Sjöstrom, L., and Carlsson M. S. (1997). Serum leptin concentrations in relation to pubertal development. *Arch. Dis. Child.* **77**, 396–400.

Carr, K. D., Kutchukhidze, N., and Park, T. H., (1999). Differential effects of mu and kappa opioid antagonists on Fos-like immunoreactivity in extended amygdala. *Brain Res.* **822**, 34–42.

Carro, E., Pinilla, L., Seoane, L. M., Considine, R. V., Aguilar, E., Casanueva, F. F., and Dieguez, C. (1997). Influence of endogenous leptin tone on the estrous cycle and luteinizing hormone pulsatility in female rats. *Neuroendocrinology* **66**, 375–377.

Castaneyra-Perdomo, A., Perez-Delgado, M. M., Montagnese, C., and Coen, C. W. (1992). Brainstem projections to the medial preoptic region containing the luteinizing hormone-releasing hormone perikarya in the rat. An immunohistochemical and retrograde transport study. *Neurosci. Lett.* **139**, 135–139.

Cates, P., and O'Bryne, K. (2000). The area postrema mediates insulin hypoglycaemia-induced suppression of pulsatile LH secretion in the female rat. *Brain Res.* **853**, 151–155.

Ceddia, R. B., William, W. N., Jr., and Curi, R. (2001). The response of skeletal muscle to leptin. *Front. Biosci.* **6**, D90–D97.

Cerda-Reverter, J.-M., Sorbera, L.-A., Carrillo, M., and Zunuy, S. (1999). Energetic dependence of NPY-induced LH secretion in teleost fish (*Dicentrarchus labrax*). *Am. J. Physiol.* **227**, R1627–R1634.

Chalmers, D. T., Lovenberg, T. W., and De Souza, E. B. (1995). Localization of nobel corticotropin-releasing factor receptor (CRF2) mRNA expression to specific subcortical nuclei in rat bran: Comparison with CRF1 receptor mRNA expression. *J. Neurosci.* **15**, 6340–6350.

Chappell, P. E., and Levine, J. E. (2000). Stimulation of gonadotropin-releasin hormone surges by estrogen. I. Role of hypothalamic progesterone receptors. *Endocrinology (Baltimore)* **141**, 1477–1485.

Chavez, M., Seeley, R. J., Havel, P. J., Friedman, M. I., Matson, C. A., Woods, S. C., and Schwartz, M. W. (1998). Effect of a high-fat diet on food intake and hypothalamic neuropeptide gene expression in streptozotocin diabetes. *J. Clin. Invest.* **102**, 340–346.

Chehab, F. F. (1997). The reproductive side of leptin. *Nat. Med.* **3**, 952–953.

Chehab, F. F., Lim, M. B., and Lu, R. (1996). Correction of the sterility defect in homozygous obese female mice by treatment with the human recombinant leptin. *Nat. Genet.* **12**, 318–320.

Chehab, F. F., Mounzih, K., Lu, R., and Lim, M. E. (1997). Early onset of reproductive function in normal female mice treated with leptin. *Science* **275**, 88–90.

Chemelli, R. M., Willie, J. T., Sinton, C. M., Elmquist, J. K., Scammell, T., Lee, C., Richardson, J. A., Williams, S. C., Xiong, Y., Kisanuki, Y., Fitch, T. E., Nakazato, M., Hammer, R. E., Saper, C. B., and Yanagisawa, M. (1999). Narcolepsy in orexin knockout mice: Molecular genetics of sleep regulation. *Cell (Cambridge, Mass.)* **98**, 437–451.

Chen, G., Koyama, K., Yuan, X., Lee, Y., Zhou, Y. T., O'Doherty, R., Newgard, C. B., and Unger, R. H. (1996). Disappearance of body fat in normal rats induced by adenovirus-mediated leptin gene therapy. *Proc. Natl. Acad. Sci. U.S.A.* **93**, 14795–14799.

Chen, H., Charlat, O., Tartaglia, L. A., Woolf, E. A., Weng, X., Ellis, S. J., Lakey, N. D., Culpepper, J., Moore, K. J., Breitbart, R. E., Duyk, G. M., Tepper, R. I., and Morgenstern, J. P. (1996). Evidence that the diabetes gene encodes the leptin receptor: Identification of a mutation in the leptin receptor gene in db/db mice. *Cell (Cambridge, Mass.)* **84**, 491–495.

Chen, Y., and Heiman, M. (2000). Chronic leptin administration promotes lipid utilization until fat mass is greatly reduced preserves lean mass of normal female rats. *Regul. Pept.* **92**, 113–119.

Cheung, C. C., Thornton, J. E., Kuijper, J. L., Weigle, D. S., Clifton, D. K., and Steiner, R. A. (1997). Leptin is a metabolic gate for the onset of puberty in the female rat. *Endocrinology (Baltimore)* **138**, 855–858.

Chlonverakis, C. (1972). Insulin resistance of parabiotic ob/ob. *Horm. Metab. Res.* **4**, 143–148.

Choi, S., and Dallman, M. F. (1999). Hypothalamic obesity: Multiple routes mediated by loss of function in medial cell groups. *Endocrinology (Baltimore)* **140**, 4081–4088.

Choi, S., Wong, L. S., Yamat, C., and Dallman, M. F. (1998). Hypothalamic ventromedial nuclei amplify circadian rhythms, do they contain a food-entrained endogenous oscillator? *J. Neurosci.* **18**, 3843–3852.

Chou, T. C., Lee, C. E., Lu, J., Elmquist, J. K., Hara, J. Willie, J. T., Beuckmann, C. T., Chemelli, R. M., Sakurai, T., Yanagisawa, M., Saper, C. B., and Scammell, T. E. (2001). Orexin (hypocretin) neurons contain dynorphin. *J. Neurosci.* **21**, RC168.

Chua, S. C., Chung, W. K., Wu-Peng, X. S., Zhang, Y., Liu, S., Tartaglia, L. A., and Leibel, R. L. (1996). Phenotypes of mouse diabetes and fat fatty due to mutations in the OB (leptin) receptor. *Science* **271**, 994–996.

Cioffi, J. A., Shafer, A. W., Zupancic, T. J., Smith-Gbur, J., Mikhail, A., Platika, D., and Snodgrass, H. R. (1996). Novel B219/OB receptor isoforms: Possible role of leptin in hematopoiesis and reproduction. *Nat. Med.* **2**, 585–589.

Clark, J. T., Kalra, P. S., Crowley, W. R., and Kalra, S. P. (1984). Neuropeptide Y and human pancreatic polypeptide stimulate feeding behavior in rats. *Endocrinology (Baltimore)* **115**, 427–429.

Clark, J. T., Kalra, P. S., and Kalra, S. P. (1985). Neuropeptide Y stimulates feeding but inhibits sexual behavior in rats. *Endocrinology (Baltimore)* **117**, 2435–2442.

Clarke, I. J., and Cummins, J. T. (1982). The temporal relationship between gonadotropin releasing hormone (GnRH) and luteinizing hormone (LH) secretion in ovariectomized ewes. *Endocrinology (Baltimore)* **111**, 1737–1739.

Clarke, I. J., and Henry, B. A. (1999). Leptin and reproduction. *Rev. Reprod.* **4**, 48–55.

Clarke, I. J., Horton, R. J. E., and Doughton, B. W. (1990). Investigation of the mechanism by which insulin-induced hypoglycemia decreases luteinizing hormone secretion in ovariectomized ewes. *Endocrinology (Baltimore)* **127**, 1470–1476.

Coleman, D. L. (1973). Effects of parabiosis of obese with diabetes and normal mice. *Diabetologia* **9**, 294–298.

Coleman, D. L., and Hummel, K. (1969). Effects of parabiosis of normal with genetically diabetic mice. *Am. J. Physiol.* **217**, 1298–1304.

Comperatore, C. A., and Stephan, F. K. (1990). Effects of vagotomy on the entrainment of activity rhythms to food access. *Physiol. Behav.* **47**, 671–678.

Conde, G. L., Bicknell, R. J., and Herbison, A. E. (1995). Changing patterns of Fos expression in brainstem catecholaminergic neurons during the rat oestrous cycle. *Brain Res.* **672**, 68–76.

Conde, G. L., Herbison, A. E., Fernandez-Galaz, C., and Becknell, R. J. (1996). Estrogen uncouples noradrenergic activation of Fos expression in the female rat preoptic area. *Brain Res.* **735**, 197–207.

Contreras, R. J., Fox, E., and Drugovich, M. L. (1982). Area postrema lesions produce feeding deficits in the rat: Effects of preoperative dieting and 2-deoxy-D-glucose. *Physiol. Behav.* **29**, 875–884.

Corp, E. S., Greco, B., Powers, J. B., Bivens, C. L., and Wade, G. N. (2001). Neuropeptide Y inhibits estrous behavior and stimulates feeding via separate receptors in Syrian hamsters. *Am. J. Physiol.* **280**, R1061–R1068.

Cosgrove, J. R., Booth, P. J., and Foxcroft, G. R. (1991). Opioidergic control of gonadotropin secretion in the prepubertal gilt during restricted feeding and realimentation. *J. Reprod. Fertil.* **91**, 277–284.

Cowley, M. A., Pronchuk, N., Fan, W., Dinulescu, D. M., Colmers, W. F., and Cone, R. D. (1999). Integration of NPY, AGRP, and melanocortin signals in the hypothalamic paraventricular nucleus, evidence of a cellular basis for the adipostat. *Neuron* **24**, 155–163.

Cox, J. E., and Powley, T. L. (1981). Prior vagotomy blocks VMH obesity in pair-fed rats. *Am. J. Physiol.* **240**, E573–E583.

Craig, W. (1918). Appetites and aversions as constituents of instincts. *Biol. Bull. (Woods Hole, Mass.)* **34**, 91–107.

Crawley, J. N. (1999). The role of galanin in feeding behavior. *Neuropeptides* **33**, 369–375.

Crews, D. (2000). Sexuality: The environmental organization of phehotypic plasticity. *In* "Reproduction in Context: Social and Environmental Influences on Reproduction" (K. Wallen and J. E. Schneider, eds.), pp. 473–500. MIT Press, Cambridge, MA.

Criscione, L., Rigollier, P., Batzl-Hartmann, C., Rueger, H., Stricker-Krongrad, A., Wyss, P., Brunner, L., Whitebread, S., Yamaguchi, Y., Gerald, C., Heurich, R. O., Walker, M. W., Chiesi, M., Schilling, W., Hofbauer, K. G., and Levens, N. (1998). Food intake in free-feeding and energy-deprived lean rats is mediated by the neuropeptide Y5 receptor. *Clin. Invest.* **102**, 2136–2145.

Crump, A. D., Lomax, M. A., and Rodway, R. G. (1982). Oestradiol-induced luteinizing hormone (LH) release is inhibited by 2-deoxyglucse infusion in sheep. *J. Physiol. (London)* **330**, 93P–94P.

Cunningham, M. J., Clifton, D. K., and Steiner, R. A. (1999). Leptin's actions on the reproductive axis: Perspectives and mechanisms. *Biol. Reprod.* **60**, 216–222.

Dallman, M. F., Strack, A. M., Akana, S. F., Bradbury, M. J., Hanson, E. S., Scribner, K. A., and Smith, M. (1993). Feast and famine: Critical role of glucocorticoids with insulin in daily energy flow. *Front. Neuroendocrinol.* **14**, 303–347.

Daly, P. A., Young, J. B., and Landsberg, L. (1992). Effect of cold exposure and nutrient intake on sympathetic nervous system activity in rat kidney. *Am. J. Physiol.* **263**, F586–F593.

Darwin, C. (1859/1985). "The Origin of Species." Penguin, London.

Davidson, A. J., and Stephan, F. K. (1998). Circadian food anticipation persists in capsaicin deafferented rats. *J. Biol. Rhythms* **13**, 422–429.

Davidson, A. J., and Stephan, F. K. (1999a). Plasma glucagons, glucose, insulin, and motilin in rats anticipating daily meals. *Physiol. Behav.* **66**, 309–315.

Davidson, A. J., and Stephan, F. K. (1999b). Feeding-entrained circadian rhythms in hypophysectomized rats with suprachiasmatic nucleus lesions. *Am. J. Physiol.* **277**, R1376–R1384.

Davis, J. D., and Campbell, C. S. (1973). Peripheral control of meal size in the rat: Effect of sham feeding on meal size and drinking rate. *J. Comp. Physiol. Psychol.* **83**, 379–387.

Day, M. L., Imakawa, K., Zalesky, D. D., Kittok, R. J., and Kinder, J. E. (1986). Effects of restriction of dietary energy intake during the prepubertal period on secretion of luteinizing hormone and responsiveness of the pituitary to luteinizing hormone-releasing hormone in heifers. *J. Anim. Sci.* **62**, 1641–1647.

de Kloet, E. R., Vreugdenhil, E., Oitzl, M. S., and Joels, M. (1998). Brain corticosteroid receptor balance in health and disease. *Endocr. Rev.* **19**, 269–301.

De Lecea, L., Kilduff, T. S., Peyron, C., Gao, X., Foye, P. E., Danielson, P. E., Fukuhara, C., Battenberg, E. L., Gautvik, V. T., Bartlett, F. S., 2nd, Frankel, W. N., van den Pol, A. N., Bloom, F. E., Gautvik, K. M., and Sutcliffe, J. G. (1998). The hypocretins: Hypothalamus-specific peptides with neuroexcitatory activity. *Proc. Natl. Acad. Sci. U.S.A.* **95**, 322–327.

Dellovade, T. L., Zhu, Y. S., and Pfaff, D. W. (1995). Potential interactions between estrogen receptor and thyroid receptors relevant for neuroendocrine systems. *J. Steroid Biochem. Mol. Biol.* **53**, 27–31.

Demerath, E. W., Towne, B., Wisemandle, W., Blangero, J., Chumlea, W. C., and Siervogel, R. M. (1999). Serum leptin concentration, body composition, and gonadal hormones during puberty. *Int. J. Obes. Relat. Metab. Disord.* **23**, 678–685.

Deutsch, J. A. (1990). Food intake: Gastric factors. *In* "Handbook of Behavioral Neurobiology" (E. M. Stricker, ed.), Vol. 10, pp. 151–182. Plenum Press, New York.

Diano, S., Kalra, P. S., Sakamoto, H., and Horvath, T. L. (1998). Leptin receptors in estrogen receptor-containing neurons of the female rat hypothalamus. *Brain Res.* **812**, 256–259.

DiBattista, D. (1983). Food deprivation and insulin-induced feeding in the hamster. *Physiol. Behav.* **30**, 683–687.

DiBattista, D., and Bedard, M. (1987). Effects of food deprivation on hunger motivation in Golden hamsters (Mesocricetus auratus). *J. Comp. Psychol.* **101**, 183–189.

Dickerman, R. W., Li, H.-Y., and Wade, G. N. (1993). Decreased availability of metabolic fuels suppresses estrous behavior in Syrian hamsters. *Am. J. Physiol.* **264**, R568–R572.

DiRocco, R. J., and Grill, H. J. (1979). The forebrain is not essential for sympathoadrenal hyperglycemic response to glucoprivation. *Science* **204**, 1112–1114.

Dong, H.-W., Petrovich, G. D., Watts, A. G., and Swanson, L. W. (2001). The basic organization of the efferent projections of the oval and fusiform nuclei of the bed nuclei of the stria terminalis in the adult rat brain. *J. Comp. Neurorol.* **436**, 430–455.

Dong, Q., Lazarus, R. M., Wong, L. S., Vellios, M., and Handelsman, D. J. (1991). Pulsatile LH secretion in streptozotocin-induced diabetes in the rat. *J. Endocrinol.* **131**, 49–55.

Dube, M. G., Xu, B., Crowley, W. R., Kalra, P. S., and Kalra, S. P. (1994). Evidence that neuropeptide Y is a physiological signal for normal food intake. *Brain Res.* **646**, 341–344.

Dueck, C. A., Matt, K. S., Manore, M. M., and Skinner, J. S. (1996). Treatment of athletic amenorrhea with a diet and training intervention program. *Int. J. Sport Nutr.* **6**, 24–40.

Dumont, Y., Satoh, H., Cadieux, A., Taoudi-Benchekroun, M., Pheng, L. H., St-Pierre, S., Fournier, A., and Quirion, R. (1993). Evaluation of truncated neuropeptide Y analogues with modifications of the tyrosine residue in position 1 on Y1, Y2 and Y3 receptor sub-types. *Eur. J. Pharmacol.* **238**, 37–45.

Ebling, E. J., Wood, R. I., Karsch, F. J., Vannerson, L. A., Suttie, J. M., Bucholtz, D. D., Schall, R. E., and Foster, D. L. (1990). Metabolic interfaces between growth and reproduction. III. Central mechanisms controlling pulsatile luteinizing hormone secretion in the nutritionally growth-limited female lamb. *Endocrinology* **126**, 2719–2727.

Eckel, L. A., Langhans, W., Kahler, A., Campfield, L. A., Smith, F. J., and Geary, N. (1998). Chronic administration of OB protein decreases food intake by selectively reducing meal size in female rats. *Am. J. Physiol.* **275**, R186–R193.

Elias, C. F., Lee, C., Kelly, J., Aschkenasi, C., Ahima, R. S., Couceyro, P. R., Kuhar, M. J., Saper, C. B., and Elmquist, J. K. (1998a). Leptin activates hypothalamic CART neurons projecting to the spinal cord. *Neuron* **21**, 1375–1385.

Elias, C. F., Saper, C., Maratos-Flier, E., Tritos, N. A., Lee, C., Kelly, J., Tatro, J. B., Hoffman, G. E., Ollmann, M. M., Barsh, G. S., Sakurai, T., Yanagisawa, M., and Elmquist, J. K. (1998b). Chemically defined projections linking the mediobasal hypothalamus and the lateral hypothalamic area. *J. Comp. Neurol.* **402**, 442–459.

Elias, C. F., Kelly, J. F., Lee, C. E., Ahima, R. S., Drucker, D. J., Saper, C. B., and Elmquist, J. K. (2000). Chemical characterization of leptin-activated neurons in the rat brain. *J. Comp. Neurol.* **423**, 261–281.

Elmquist, J. K., Ahima, R. S., Maratos-Flier, E., Flier, J. S., and Saper, C. B. (1997). Leptin activates neurons in ventrobasal hypothalamus and brainstem. *Endocrinology (Baltimore)* **138**, 839–842.

Elmquist, J. K., Bjorbaek, C., Ahima, R. S., Flier, J. S., and Saper, C. B. (1998a). Distributions of leptin receptor mRNA isoforms in the rat brain. *J. Comp. Neurol.* **395**, 535–547.

Elmquist, J. K., Maratos-Flier, E., Saper, C. B., and Flier, J. S. (1998b). Unraveling the central nervous system pathways underlying responses to leptin. *Nat. Neurosci.* **1**, 445–450.

Elmquist, J. K., Ahima, R. S., Elias, C. F., Flier, J. S., and Saper, C. B. (1998c). Leptin activates distinct projections from the dorsomedial and ventromedial hypothalamic nuclei. *Proc. Natl. Acad. Sci. U.S.A.* **95**, 741–746.

Elmquist, J. K., Elias, C. F., and Saper, C. B. (1999). From lesions to leptin: Hypothalamic control of food intake and body weight. *Neuron* **22**, 221–232.

Emilsson, V., Liu, Y. L., Cawthorne, M. A., Morton, N. M., and Davenport, M. (1997). Expression of the functional leptin receptor mRNA in pancreatic islets and direct inhibitory action of leptin on insulin secretion. *Diabetes* **46**, 313–316.

Erickson, J. C., Clegg, K. E., and Palmiter, R. D. (1996a). Sensitivity to leptin and susceptibility to seizures of mice lacking neuropeptide Y. *Nature (London)* **381**, 415–421.

Erickson, J. C., Hollopeter, G., and Palmiter, R. D. (1996b). Attenuation of the obesity syndrome of ob/ob mice by the loss of neuropeptide Y. *Science* **274**, 1704–1707.

Ernsberger, P., and Nelson, D. O. (1988). Effects of fasting and refeeding on blood pressure are determined by nutritional state not by body weight change. *Am. J. Hypertens.* **1**, 153S–157S.

Estacio, M. A., Yamada, S., Tsukamura, H., Hirunagi, K., and Maeda, K. (1996a). Effect of fasting and immobilization stress on estrogen receptor immunoreactivity in the brain in ovariectomized female rats. *Brain Res.* **717**, 55–61.

Estacio, M. A. C., Tsukamura, H., Yamada, S., Tsukahara, S., Hirunagi, K., and Maeda, K. (1996). Vagus nerve mediates the increase in estrogen receptors in the hypothalamic paraventricular nucleus and nucleus of the solitary tract during fasting in ovariectomized rats. *Neurosci. Lett.* **208**, 25–28.

Estacio, M. A. C., Tsukamura, H., Reyes, B. A. S., and Maeda, K. I. (2001). Noradrenergic inputs to the paraventricular nucleus (PVN) is involved in estrogen receptor a expression in the PVN of 48-h fasted and 2DG-injected female rats. *Soc. Neurosci. Abstracts.* Vol. 27, Program No. 409.6.

Ewart-Toland, A., Mounzih, K., Qiu, J., and Chehab, F. F. (1999). Effect of the genetic background on the reproduction of leptin-deficient obese mice. *Endocrinology (Baltimore)* **140**, 732–738.

Falconer, D. S., and Mackay, T. F. C. (1995). "Introduction to Quantitative Genetics." Addison-Wesley, Harlow.

Farooqi, I. S. *et al.* (1999). Effects of recombinant leptin therapy in a child with congenital leptin deficiency. *N. Engl. J. Med.* **341**, 879–884.

Fedak, M. A., and Anderson, S. S. (1982). The energetics of lactation: Accurate measurements from a large wild mammal, the Grey seal (*Halichoerus grypus*). *J. Zool.* **198**, 473–479.

Fei, H., Okano, H. J., Li, C., Lee, G. H., Zhao, C., Darnell, R., and Friedman, J. M. (1997). Anatomic localization of alternatively spliced leptin receptors (Ob-R) in mouse brain and other tissues. *Proc. Natl. Acad. Sci. U.S.A.* **94**, 7001–7005.

Figlewicz, D. P., Stein, L. J., West, D., Porte, D., Jr., and Woods, S. C. (1986). Intracisternal insulin alters sensitivity to CCK-induced meal suppression in baboons. *Am. J. Physiol.* **250**, R856–R860.

Finn, P. D., Cunningham, M. J., Pau, K. Y., Spies, H. G., Clifton, D. K., and Steiner, R. A. (1998). The stimulatory effect of leptin on the neuroendocrine reproductive axis of the monkey. *Endocrinology (Baltimore)* **139**, 4652–4662.

Fitzsimons, J. T. (1998). Angiotensin, thirst and sodium appetite. *Physiol. Rev.* **78**, 583–686.

Flanagan, L. M., Blackburn, R. E., Verbalis, J. G., and Stricker, E. M. (1992). Hypertonic NaCl inhibits gastric motility and food intake in rats with lesions in the rostral AV3V region. *Am. J. Physiol.* **263**, R9–R14.

Flegal, K. M., Carroll, M. D., Kuczmarski, R. J., and Johnson, C. L. (1998). Overweight and obesity in the United States: Prevalence and trends, 1960–1994. *Int. J. Obesity* **22**, 39–47.

Fleury, C., Neverova, M., Collins, S., Raimbault, S., Champigny, O., Levi-Meyrueis, C., Bouillaud, F., Seldin, M. F., Surwit, R. S., Ricquier, D., and Warden, C. H. (1997). Uncoupling protein-2: A novel gene linked to obesity and hypoinsulinemia. *Nat. Genet.* **15**, 269–272.

Flier, J. S. (1998). What's in a name? In search of leptin's physiologic role. *J. Clin. Endocrinol. Metab.* **83**, 1407–1413.

Flynn, F. W., and Grill, H. J. (1983). Insulin elicits ingestion in decerebrate rats. *Science* **221**, 188–190.

Flynn, F. W., and Robillard, L. (1992). Inhibition of ingestive behavior following 4th ventricle bombesin injection in chronic decerebrate rats. *Behav. Neurosci.* **106**, 1011–1014.

Foster, D. L., and Bucholtz, D. C. (1995). Glucose as a possible metabolic cue timing puberty. *In* "Serono International Symposium on Puberty: Basic and Clinical Aspects" (C. Bergada and J. A. Moguilevsky, eds.), pp. 319–332. Ares-Serono Symposia, Rome, Italy.

Foster, D. L., and Nagatani, S. (1999). Physiological perspectives on leptin as a regulator of reproduction: Role in timing puberty. *Biol. Reprod.* **60**, 205–215.

Foster, D. L., and Olster, D. H. (1985). Effect of restricted nutrition on puberty in the lamb: Patterns of tonic luteinizing hormone (LH) secretion and competency of the LH surge system. *Endocrinology* **116**, 375–381.

Fox, A. S., Foorman, A., and Olster, D. H. (2000). Effects of intracerebroventricular leptin administration on feeding and sexual behaviors in lean and obese female Zucker rats. *Horm. Behav.* **37**, 377–387.

Fox, S. R., and Smith, M. S. (1985). Changes in the pulsatile pattern of luteinizing hormone secretion during the rat estrous cycle. *Endocrinology (Baltimore)* **116**, 1485–1492.

Frederich, R. C., Lollmann, B., Hamann, A., Napolitano-Rosen, A., Kahn, B. B., Lowell, B. B., and Flier, J. S. (1995). Expression of ob mRNA and its encoded protein in rodents. *J. Clin. Invest.* **96**, 1658–1663.

Fried, S. K., Born, M., Vasselli, J. R., Haraczkiewicz, E., and Kral, J. G. (1986). Effects of total subcutaneous lipectomy (LPS) in female rats fed a high fat diet. *Fed. Proc., Fed. Am. Soc. Exp. Biol.* **45**, 350.

Friedman, J. M., and Halaas, J. L. (1998). Leptin and the regulation of body weight in mammals. *Nature (London)* **395**, 763–770.

Friedman, M. I. (1978). Hyperphagia in rats with experimental diabetes mellitus: A response to a decreased supply of utilizable fuels. *J. Comp. Physiol. Psychol.* **92**, 109–117.

Friedman, M. I. (1990). Making sense out of calories. *In* "Handbook of Behavioral Neurobiology" (E. M. Stricker, ed.), Vol. 10, pp. 513–529. Plenum Press, New York.

Friedman, M. I. (1991). Metabolic control of calorie intake. *In* "Chemical Senses: Appetite and Nutrition" (M. I. Friedman,

M. G. Tordoff, and M. R. Kare, eds.), Vol. 4, pp. 19–38. Dekker, New York.

Friedman, M. I. (1995). Control of energy intake by energy metabolism. *Am. J. Clin. Nutr.* **62**(Suppl.), 1096S–1100S.

Friedman, M. I. (1997). An energy sensor for control of energy intake. *Proc. Nutr. Soc.* **56**, 41–50.

Friedman, M. I. (1998). Fuel partitioning and food intake. *Am. J. Clin. Nutr.* **67**, S513–S518.

Friedman, M. I., and Rawson, N. E. (1995). Fuel metabolism and appetite control. *In* "Appetite and Body Weight Regulation," pp. 63–76. CRC Press, Boca Raton, FL.

Friedman, M. I., and Stricker, E. M. (1976). The physiological psychology of hunger: A physiological perspective. *Psychol. Rev.* **83**, 409–431.

Friedman, M. I., and Tordoff, M. G. (1986). Fatty acid oxidation and glucose utilization interact to control food intake in rats. *Am. J. Physiol.* **251**, R840–R845.

Friedman, M. I., Tordoff, M. G., and Ramirez, I. (1986). Integrated metabolic control of food intake. *Brain Res. Bull.* **17**, 855–859.

Frisch, R. E. (1990). Body fat, menarche, fitness and fertility. *In* "Adipose Tissue and Reproduction" (R. E. Frisch, ed.), pp. 1–26. Karger, Basel.

Fujii, T., Inoue, S., Hagai, K., and Nakagawa, H. (1989). Involvement of adrenergic mechanism in hyperglycemia due to SCN stimulation. *Horm. Metab. Res.* **21**, 643–645.

Fulton, S., Woodside, B., and Shizgal, P. (2000). Modulation of brain reward circuitry by leptin. *Science* **287**, 125–128.

Gallagher, M., McMahan, R. W., and Schoenbaum, G. (1999). Orbitofrontal cortex and representation of incentive value in associative learning. *J. Neurosci.* **19**, 6610–6614.

Gallo, R. V. (1981). Effect of electrical stimulation of the dorsomedial hypothalamic nucleus on pulsatile LH release in ovariectomized rats. *Neuroendocrinology* **32**, 134–138.

Garofalo, M. A. R., Kettelhut, I. C., Roselino, J. E. S., and Migliorini, R. H. (1996). Effect of acute cold exposure on norepinephrine turnover rates in rate white adipose tissue. *J. Auton. Nerv. Syst.* **60**, 206–208.

Geary, N. (1999). Effects of glucagon, insulin, amylin and CGRP on feeding. *Neuropeptides* **33**, 400–405.

Gehlert, D. R. (1999). Role of hypothalamic neuropeptide Y in feeding and obesity. *Neuropeptides* **33**, 329–338.

Geissler, C. A., Miller, D. S., and Shah, M. (1987). The daily metabolic rate of the post-obese and the lean. *Am. J. Clin. Nutr.* **45**, 914–920.

Gerald, C., Walker, M. W., Criscione, L., Gustafson, E. L., Batzl-Hartmann, C., Smith, K. E., Vaysse, P., Durkin, M. M., Laz, T. M., Linemeyer, D. L., Schaffhauseer, A. O., Whitebread, S., Hofbauer, K. G., Taber, R. I., Branchek, T. A., and Weinshank, R. L. (1996). A receptor subtype involved in neuropeptide-Y-induced food intake. *Nature (London)* **382,** 168–171.

Gerardo-Gettens, T., Moore, B. J., Stern, J. S., and Horwitz, B. A. (1989a). Prolactin stimulates food intake in a dose-dependent manner. *Am. J. Physiol.* **256,** R276–R280.

Gerardo-Gettens, T., Moore, B. J., Stern, J. S., and Horwitz, B. A. (1989b). Prolactin stimulates food intake in the absence of ovarian progesterone. *Am. J. Physiol.* **256,** R701–R706.

Gibbs, J., and Smith, G. P. (1988). The actions of bombesin-like peptides on food intake. *Ann. N.Y. Acad. Sci.* **547,** 210–216.

Gibbs, J., Young, R. C., and Smith, G. P. (1973). Cholecystokinin decreases food intake in rats. *J. Comp. Physiol. Psychol.* **84,** 488–495.

Gill, C. J., and Rissman, E. F. (1997). Female sexual behavior is inhibited by short- and long-term food restriction. *Physiol. Behav.* **61,** 387–394.

Glass, M. J., Billington, C. J., and Lewis, A. S. (1999). Opioids and food intake: Distributed functional neural pathways? *Neuropeptides* **33,** 360–366.

Gold, R. M. (1973). Hypothalamic obesity: The myth of the ventromedial nucleus. *Science* **182,** 488–490.

Gold, R. M., Sawchenko, P. E., DeLuca, C., Alexander, J., and Eng, R. (1980). Vagal mediation of hypothalamic obesity but not of supermarket dietary obesity. *Am. J. Physiol.* **238,** R447–R453.

Goldfien, A., Gullixson, K. S., and Hargrove, G. (1966). Evidence for centers in the central nervous system that regulate fat mobilzation in dogs. *J. Lipid Res.* **7,** 357–367.

Gonzalez, M. I., Baker, B. I., and Wilson, C. A. (1997). Stimulatory effect of melanin-concentrating hormone on luteinising hormone release. *Neuroendocrinology* **66,** 254–262.

Gonzalez, M. I., Celis, M. E., Hole, D. R., and Wilson, C. A. (1993). Interaction of oestradiol, alpha-melanotrophin and noradrenaline within the ventromedial nucleus in the control of female sexual behaviour. *Neuroendocrinology* **58,** 218–226.

Goodman, R. L., Parfitt, D. B., Evans, N. P., Dahl, G. E., and Karsch, F. J. (1995). Endogenous opioid peptides control the amplitude and shape of gonadotropin-releasing hormone pulses in the ewe. *Endocrinology (Baltimore)* **136,** 2412–2420.

Goubillon, M.-L., and Thalabard, J.-C. (1996). Insulin-induced hypoglycemia decreases luteinizing hormone secretion in the castrated male rat: Involvement of opiate peptides. *Neuroendocrinology* **64,** 49–56.

Green, P. K., Wilkinson, C. W., and Woods, S. C. (1992). Intraventricular corticosterone increases the rate of body weight gain in underweight adrenalectomized rats. *Endocrinology* **130,** 269–275.

Griffond, B., Risold, P. Y., Jacquemard, C., Colard, C., and Fellmann, D. (1999). Insulin-induced hypoglycemia in-

creases preprohypocretin (orexin) mRNA in the rat lateral hypothalamic area. *Neurosci. Lett.* **262,** 77–80.

Grill, H. J., and Kaplan, J. M. (1990). Caudal brainstem participates in the distributed neural control of feeding. *In* "Handbook of Behavioral Neurobiology" (E. M. Stricker, ed.), Vol. 10, pp. 125–150. Plenum Press, New York.

Grill, H. J., and Norgren, R. (1978a). Chronically decerebrate rats demonstrate satiation but not bait-shyness. *Science* **201,** 267–269.

Grill, H. J., and Norgren, R. (1978b). The taste reactivity test. II. Mimetic responses to gustatory stimuli in chronic thalamic and chronic decerebrate rats. *Brain Res.* **143,** 281–897.

Grill, H. J., and Smith, G. P. (1988). Cholecystokinin decreases sucrose intake in chronic decerebrate rats. *Am. J. Physiol.* **254,** R853–R856.

Grill, H. J., Friedman, M. I., Norgren, R., Scalera, G., and Seeley, R. (1995). Parabrachial nucleus lesions impair feeding response elicited by 2,5-anhydro-D-mannitol. *Am. J. Physiol.* **268,** R676–R682.

Grill, H. J., Donahey, J. C. K., King, L., and Kaplan, J. M. (1997). Contribution of caudal brainstem to *d*-fenfluramine anorexia. *Psychopharmacology* **130,** 375–381.

Grill, H. J., Ginsberg, A. B., Seeley, R. J., and Kaplan, J. M. (1998). Brainstem application of melanocortin receptor ligands produces long-lasting effects on feeding and body weight. *J. Neurosci.* **18,** 10128–10135.

Grill, H. J., Markison, S., Ginsberg, A., and Kaplan, J. M. (2000). Long-term effects on feeding and body weight after stimulation of forebrain or hindbrain CRH receptors with urocortin. *Brain Res.* **867,** 19–28.

Groscolas, R. (1990). Metabolic adaptations to fasting in emperor and king penguins. *In* "Penguin Biology" (L. S. Davis and J. T. Darby, eds.), pp. 269–296. Academic Press, San Diego, CA.

Grossman, S. P. (1979). The biology of motivation. *Annu. Rev. Psychol.* **30,** 209–242.

Grossman, S. P. (1990). "Thirst and Sodium Appetite." Academic Press, San Diego, CA.

Gruaz, N. M., Pierroz, D. D., Rohner-Jenrenaud, F., Sizonenko, P. C., and Aubert, M. L. (1993). Evidence that neuropeptide Y could represent a neuroendocrine inhibitor of sexual maturation in unfavorable metabolic conditions in the rat. *Endocrinology (Baltimore)* **133,** 1891–1894.

Gruaz, N. M., Lalaoui, M., Pierroz, D. D., Englaro, P., Sizoneko, P. C., Blum, W. F., and Aubert, M. L. (1998). Chronic administration of leptin into the lateral ventricle induces sexual maturation in severely food-restricted female rats. *J. Neuroendocrinol.* **10,** 627–633.

Gruaz-Gumowski, N. M., Lalaoui, M., Pierroz, D. D., Englaro, P., Sizonenko, P. C., Blum, W. F., and Aubert, M. L. (1998).

Chronic administration of leptin into the lateral ventricle induces sexual maturation in severely food-restricted female rats. *J. Neuroendocrinol.* **10**, 627–633.

Gruenewald, D. A., and Matsumoto, A. M. (1993). Reduced gonadotropin-releasing hormone gene expression with fasting in the male rat brain. *Endocrinology (Baltimore)* **132**, 480–482.

Gu, G. B., and Simerly, R. B. (1997). Projections of the sexually dimorphic anteroventral periventricular nucleus in the female rat. *J. Comp. Neurol.* **384**, 142–164.

Gunnet, J. W., and Freeman, M. E. (1985). The interaction of the medial preoptic area and the dorsomedial-ventromedial nuclei of the hypothalamus in the regulation of the mating-induced release of prolactin. *Neuroendocrinology* **40**, 232–237.

Haessler, H. A., and Crawford, J. D. (1965). Alterations in fatty acid composition of depot fat associated with ob. *Ann. N.Y. Acad. Sci.* **131**, 476–484.

Hakansson, M. L., Hulting, A., and Meister, B. (1996). Expression of leptin receptor mRNA in the hypothalamic arcuate nucleus-relationship with NPY neurons. *NeuroReport* **7**, 3087–3092.

Hakansson, M. L., Brown, H., Ghilardi, N., Skoda, R. C., and Meister, B. (1998). Leptin receptor immunoreactivity in chemically defined target neurons of the hypothalamus. *J. Neurosci.* **18**, 559–572.

Halaas, J. L., Gajiwala, K. S., Maffei, M., Cohen, S. L., Chait, B. T., Rabinowitz, D., Lallone, R. L., Burley, S. K., and Friedman, J. M. (1995). Weight-reducing effects of the plasma protein encoded by the obese gene. *Science* **269**, 543–546.

Hall, A. C., Hoffmaster, R. M., Stern, E. L., Harrington, M. E., and Bickar, D. (1997). Suprachiasmatic nucleus neurons are glucose sensitive. *J. Biol. Rhythms* **12**, 388–400.

Hamilton, J. M., and Wade, G. N. (1988). Lipectomy does not impair fattening induced by short photoperiods or high fat diets in female Syrian hamsters. *Physiol. Behav.* **43**, 85–92.

Hara, Y., Ueta, Y., Isse, T., Kabashima, N., Shibuya, I., Hattori, Y., and Yamashita, H. (1997). Increase of urocortin-like immunoreactivity in the rat supraoptic nucleus after dehydration but not food deprivation. *Neurosci. Lett.* **229**, 65–68.

Hara, J., Beuckmann, C., Nambu, T., Willie, J., Chemelli, R., Sinton, C., Sugiyama, F., Yagami, K., Goto, K., Yanagisawa, M., and Sakurai, T. (2001). Genetic ablation of orexin neurons in mice causes a sleep disorder similar to human narcolepsy, hypophagia, and obesity. *Neuron* **30**, 345–354.

Harris, R. (1997). Loss of body fat in lean parabiotic partners of *ob/ob* mice. *Am. J. Physiol.* **272**, R1809–R1815.

Harris, R. (1999). Parabiosis between *db/db* and *ob/ob* or *db/+* mice. *Endocrinology (Baltimore)* **140**, 138–145.

Harris, R., Ramsay, T. G., Smith, S. R., and Bruch, R. C. (1996). Early and late stimulation of ob mRNA expression in meal-fed and overfed rats. *J. Clin. Invest.* **97**, 2020–2026.

Hashimoto, R., and Kimura, F. (1986). Inhibition of gonadotropin secretion induced by cholecystokinin implants in the medial preoptic area by the dopamine receptor blocker, pimozide, in the rat. *Neuroendocrinology* **42**, 32–37.

Haskell-Luevano, C., Chen, P., Li, C., Chang, K., Smith, M. S., Cameron, L. J., and Cone, R. D. (1999). Characterization of the neuroanatomical distribution of agouti-related protein immunoreactivity in the rhesus monkey and the rat. *Endocrinology (Baltimore)* **140**, 1408–1415.

He, D., Funabashi, T., Sano, A., Uemura, T., Minaguchi, H., and Kimura, F. (1999). Effects of glucose and related substrates on the recovery of the electrical activity of gonadotropin-releasing hormone pulse generator which is decreased by insulin-induced hypoglycemia in the estrogen-primed ovariectomized rat. *Brain Res.* **820**, 71–76.

Heinrichs, S. C., and Richard, D. (1999). The role of corticotropin-releasing factor and urocortin in the modulcation of ingestive behavior. *Neuropeptides* **33**, 350–359.

Henry, B. A., Godong, J. W., Alexander, W. S., Tilbrook, A. J., Canny, B. J., Dunshea, F., Rao, A., Mansell, A., and Clarke, I. J. (1999). Central administration of leptin to ovariectomized ewes inhibits food intake without affecting the secretion of hormones from the pituitary gland: Evidence for a dissociation of effects on appetite and neuroendocrine function. *Endocrinology (Baltimore)* **140**, 1175–1182.

Herbert, H., Moga, M. M., and Saper, C. B. (1990). Connections of the parabrachial nucleus with the nucleus of the solitary tract and the medullary reticular formation in the rat. *J. Comp. Neurol.* **293**, 540–580.

Herbison, A. E. (1998). Multimodal influence of estrogen upon gonadotropin-releasing hormone neurons. *Endocr. Rev.* **19**, 302–330.

Heritage, A. S., Stumpf, W. E., Sar, M., and Grant, L. D. (1980). Brainstem catecholamine neurons are target sites for sex steroid hormones. *Science* **207**, 1377–1379.

Hess, W. R. (1954). "Diencephalon: Autonomic and Extrapyramidal Function." Grune & Stratton, New York.

Hetherington, A. W., and Ranson, S. W. (1940). Hypothalamic lesions and adiposity in the rat. *Anat. Rec.* **78**, 149–172.

Hevener, A. L., Bergman, R. N., and Donovan, C. M. (2000). Portal vein afferents are critical for the sympathoadrenal response to hypoglycemia. *Diabetes* **49**, 8–12.

Hilton, L. K., and Loucks, A. B. (2000). Low energy availability, not exercise stress, suppresses the diurnal rhythm of leptin in healthy young women. *Am. J. Physiol.* **278**, E43–E49.

Himms-Hagen, J. (1985). Brown adipose tissue metabolism and thermogenesis. *Annu. Rev. Nutr.* **5**, 69–94.

Himms-Hagen, J. (1989). Brown adipose tissue thermogenesis and obesity. *Prog. Lipid Res.* **28**, 67–115.

Himms-Hagen, J. (1990). Brown adipose tissue thermogenesis: Interdisciplinary studies. *FASEB J.* **4**, 2890–2898.

Himms-Hagen, J., Cui, J., Danforth, E., Jr., Taatjes, D. J., Lang, S. S., Waters, B. L., and Claus, T. H. (1994). Effect of CL-316,243, a thermogenic beta 3-agonist, on energy balance and brown and white adipose tissue in rats. *Am. J. Physiol.* **266**, R1371–R1382.

Hinde, R. A. (1970). "Animal Behaviour. A Synthesis of Ethology and Comparative Psychology." McGraw-Hill, New York.

Hirshfield, A. N., and Midgley, A. R., Jr. (1978). The role of FSH in the selection of large ovarian follicles in the rat. *Biol. Reprod.* **19**, 606–611.

Hoeger, K. M., Kolp, L. A., Strobl, F. J., and Veldhuis, J. D. (1999). Evaluation of LH secretory dynamics during the rat proestrous LH surge. *Am. J. Physiol.* **276**, R219–R225.

Hoggard, N., Mercer, J. G., Rayner, V., and Moar, K. (1997). Localization of leptin receptor mRNA splice variants in murine peripheral tissues by RT-PCR and in situ hybridization. *Biochem. Biophys. Res. Commun.* **232**, 383–387.

Hohmann, J. G., Teal, T. H., Clifton, D. K., Davis, J., Hruby, V. J., Han, G., and Steiner, R. A. (2000). Differential role of melanocortins in mediating leptin's central effects on feeding and reproduction. *Am. J. Physiol.* **278**, R50–R59.

Holland, K. L., Popper, P., and Micevych, P. E. (1997). Infusion of CCK-A receptor mRNA antisense oligodeoxynucleotides inhibits lordosis behavior. *Physiol. Behav.* **62**, 537–543.

Holt, S. J., and York, D. A. (1989). The effects of adrenalectomy corticotropin-releasing hormone and vasopressin on the sympathetic firing rate of nerves to interscapular brown adipose tissue in the zucker rat. *Physiol. Behav.* **45**, 1123–1129.

Horn, C. C., and Friedman, M. I. (1998). Metabolic inhibition increase feeding and brain Fos-like immunoreactivity as a function of diet. *Am. J. Physiol.* **275**, R448–R459.

Horn, C. C., Kaplan, J. M., Grill, H. J., and Friedman, M. I. (1998). Brain fos-like immunoreactivity in chronic decerebrate and neurologically intact rats given 2,5-anhydro-D-mannitol. *Brain Res.* **801**, 107–115.

Horn, C. C., Addis, A., and Friedman, M. I. (1999). Neural substrate for an integrated metabolic control of feeding behavior. *Am. J. Physiol.* **276**, R113–R119.

Horowitz, J. F., and Klein, S. (2000). Whole body and abdominal lipolytic sensitivity to epinephrine is suppressed in upper body obese women. *Am. J. Physiol.* **278**, E1144–E1152.

Howland, B. E. (1980). Effect of glucoprivation induced by 2-deoxy-D-glucose on serum gonadotropin levels, pituitary response to GnRH and progesterone-induced release of luteinizing hormone in rats. *Horm. Metab. Res.* **12**, 520–523.

Hoyle, C. H. V. (1999). Neuropeptide families and their receptors: Evolutionary perspectives. *Brain Res.* **848**, 1–25.

Hrabovsky, E., Shughrue, P. J., Merchenthaler, I., Hajszan, T., Carpenter, C. D., Liposits, Z., and Petersen, S. L. (2000). Detection of estrogen receptor-beta messenger ribonucleic acid and 125I-estrogen binding sites in luteinizing hormone-releasing hormone neurons of the rat brain. *Endocrinology (Baltimore)* **141**, 3506–3509.

Huang, X. F., Koutcherov, I., Lin, S., Wang, H. Q., and Storlien, L. (1996). Localization of leptin receptor mRNA expression in mouse brain. *NeuroReport* **7**, 2635–2638.

Hulsey, M. G., Lu, H., Wang, T., Martin, R. J., and Baile, C. A. (1998). Intracerebroventricular (i.c.v.) administration of mouse leptin in rats: Behavioral specificity and effects on meal patterns. *Physiol. Behav.* **65**, 445–455.

Hummel, K. P., Dickie, M. M., and Coleman, D. L. (1966). Diabetes a new mutation in the mouse. *Science* **153**, 1127–1128.

Huszar, D., Lynch, C. A., Fairchild-Huntress, V., Dunmore, J. H., Fang, Q., Berkemeier, L. R., Gu, W., Kesterson, R. A., Boston, B. A., Cone, R. D., Smith, F. J., Campfield, L. A., Burn, P., and Lee, F. (1997). Targeted disruption of the melanocortin-4 receptor results in obesity in mice. *Cell (Cambridge, Mass.)* **88**, 131–141.

Hwa, J. J., Ghibaudi, L., Compton, D., Fawziand, A. B., and Strader, C. D. (1996). Intracerebroventricular injection of leptin increases thermogenesis and mobilizes fat metabolism in ob/ob mice. *Horm. Metab. Res.* **28**, 659–663.

Hyde, T. M., and Miselis, R. R. (1983). Effects of area postrema/caudal medial nucleus of solitary tract lesions on food intake and body weight. *Am. J. Physiol.* **244**, R577–R587.

I'Anson, H., Foster, D. L., Foxcroft, C. R., and Booth, P. J. (1991). Nutrition and reproduction. *Oxford Rev. Reprod. Biol.* **13**, 239–311.

Inoue, S., and Bray, G. A. (1977). The effects of subdiaphragmatic vagotomy in rats with ventromedial hypothalamic obesity. *Endocrinology (Baltimore)* **100**, 108–104.

Jansen, A. S., Hoffman, J. L., and Loewy, A. D. (1997). CNS sites involved in sympathetic and parasympathetic control of the pancreas: A viral tracing *Brain Res.* **766**, 29–38.

Ji, H., and Friedman, M. I. (1999). Compensatory hyperphagia after fasting tracks recovery of liver energy status. *Physiol. Behav.* **68**, 181–186.

Ji, H., and Friedman, M. I. (2000). Differences in postabsorptive metabolism in rats prone to diet-induced obesity. *Appetite* **35**, 293.

Ji, H., Graczyk-Milbrandt, G., and Friedman, M. I. (2000). Metabolic inhibitors synergistically decrease hepatic energy status and increase food intake. *Am. J. Physiol.* **278**, R1579–R1582.

Johnson, A. K., and Thunhorst, R. L. (1997). The neuroendocrinology of thirst and salt appetite: Visceral sensory signals and mechanisms of central integration. *Front. Neuroendocrinol.* **18**, 292–353.

Jones, J. E., Corp, E. S., and Wade, G. N. (2001). Effects of naltrexone and CCK on estrous behavior and food intake in Syrian hamsters. *Peptides (N.Y.)* **22**, 601–606.

Ju, G., and Swanson, L. W. (1989). Studies on the cellular architecture of the bed nuclei of the stria terminalis in the rat. I. Cytoarchitecture. *J. Comp. Neurol.* **280**, 587–602.

Ju, G., Swanson, L. W., and Simerly, R. B. (1989). Studies on the cellular architecture of the bed nuclei of the stria terminalis in the rat. II. Chemoarchitecture. *J. Comp. Neurol.* **280**, 603–621.

Kaiyala, K. J., Woods, S. C., and Schwartz, M. W. (1995). New model for the regulation of energy balance and adiposity by the central nervous system. *Am. J. Clin. Nutr.* **62**, 1123A–1134S.

Kakizaki, Y., Watanobe, H., Kohsaka, A., and Suda, T. (1999). Temporal profiles of interleukin-1b, interleukin-6, and tumor necrosis factor-a in the plasma and hypothalamic paraventricular nucleus after intravenous or intraperitoneal administration of lipopolysaccharide in the rat: Estimation by push-pull perfusion. *Endocr. J.* **46**, 487–496.

Kalra, P. S., Dube, M. G., and Kalra, S. P. (2000). Effects of centrally administered antisense oligodeoxynucleotides on feeding behavior and hormone secretion. *Methods Enzymol.* **314**, 184–200.

Kalra, S. P., and Kalra, P. S. (1996). Nutritional infertility: The role of interconnected hypothalamic neuropeptide Y-galanin-opioid network. *Front. Neuroendocrinol.* **17**, 371–401.

Kalra, S. P., Dube, M. G., Sahu, A., Phelps, C. P., and Kalra, P. S. (1991). Neuropeptide Y secretion increases in the paraventricular nucleus in association with increased appetite for food. *Proc. Natl. Acad. Sci. U.S.A.* **88**, 10931–10935.

Kalra, S. P., Fuentes, M., Fournier, A., Parker, S. L., and Crowley, W. R. (1992). Involvement of the Y-1 receptor subtype in the regulation of luteinizing hormone secretion by neuropeptide Y in rats. *Endocrinology (Baltimore)* **130**, 3323–3330.

Kalra, S. P., Horvath, T., Naftolin, F., Xu, B., Pu, S., and Kalra, P. S. (1997). The interactive language of the hypothalamus for the gonadotropin releasing hormone (GNRH) system. *J. Neuroendocrinol.* **9**, 569–576.

Kamohara, S., Burcelin, R., Halaas, J. L., Friedman, J. M., and Charron, M. J. (1997). Acute stimulation of glucose metabolism in mice by leptin treatment. *Nature (London)* **389**, 374–377.

Kanatani, A., Ishihara, A., Asahi, S., Tanaka, T., Ozaki, S., and Ihara, M. (1996). Potent neuropeptide Y Y1 receptor antagonist 1229U91: Blockade of neuropeptide Y-induced and physiological food intake. *Endocrinology (Baltimore)* **137**, 3177–3182.

Kaplan, J. M., and Södersten, P. (1994). Apomorphine supp-

resses ingestive behaviour in chronic decerebrate rats. *NeuroReport* **5**, 1839–1840.

Kaplan, J. M., Seeley, R. J., and Grill, H. J. (1993). Daily caloric intake in intact and chronic decerebrate rats. *Behav. Neurosci.* **107**, 876–881.

Kaplan, J. M., Song, S., and Grill, H. J. (1998). Serotonin receptors in the caudal brainstem are necessary and sufficient for the anorectic effect of peripherally administered mCPP. *Psychopharmacology* **137**, 43–49.

Kaplan, J. M., Roitman, M., and Grill, H. J. (2000). Food deprivation does not potentiate glucose taste reactivity responses of chronic decerebrate rats. *Brain Res.* **870**, 102–108.

Kasuya, E., Mizuno, M., Watanabe, G., and Terasawa, E. (1998). Effects of an antisense oligodeoxynucleotide for neuropeptide Y mRNA on in vivo luteinizing hormone-releasing hormone release in ovariectomized female rhesus monkeys. *Regul. Pept.* **75–76**, 319–325.

Kay-Nishiyama, C., and Watts, A. G. (1998). CRH in dehydration-induced anorexia: CRH immunoreactivity in non-colchicine treated rats, and CRH R2 receptor mRNA levels in the ventromedial hypothalamic nucleus. *Soc. Neurosci. Abstr.* **24**, 449.

Kay-Nishiyama, C., and Watts, A. G. (1999). Dehydration modifies somal CRH immunoreactivity in the rat hypothalamus: An immunocytochemical study in the absence of colchicine. *Brain Res.* **822**, 251–255.

Keisler, D. H., Daniel, J. A., and Morrison, C. D. (1999). The role of leptin in nutritional status and reproductive function. *J. Reprod. Fertil., Suppl.* **54**, 425–435.

Kelly, A. B., and Watts, A. G. (1996). The mediation of dehydration-induced peptidergic gene expression in the rat lateral hypothalamic area by forebrain afferent projections. *J. Comp. Neurol.* **370**, 231–246.

Kelly, A. B., and Watts, A. G. (1998). The region of the pontine parabrachial nucleus is a major target of dehydration-sensitive CRH neurons in the rat lateral hypothalamic area. *J. Comp. Neurol.* **394**, 48–63.

Kennedy, G. C. (1953). The role of depot fat in the hypothalamic control of food intake in the rat. *Proc. R. Soc. London* **140**, 578–592.

Kennedy, G. C., and Mitra, J. (1963a). Hypothalamic control of energy balance and the reproductive cycle in the rat. *J. Physiol. (London)* **166**, 395–407.

Kennedy, G. C., and Mitra, J. (1963b). Body weight and food intake as initiating factors for puberty in the rat. *J. Physiol. (London)* **166**, 408–418.

Kieffer, T. J., Heller, R. S., and Habener, J. F. (1996). Leptin receptors expressed on pancreatic beta-cells. *Biochem. Biophys. Res. Commun.* **224**, 522–527.

Kiess, W., Blum, W. F., and Aubert, M. L. (1998). Leptin, puberty and reproductive function: Lessons from animal studies and observations in humans. *Eur. J. Endocrinol.* **138**, 26–29.

Kile, J. P., Alexander, B. M., Moss, G. E., Hallford, D. M., and Nett, T. M. (1991). Gonadotropin-releasing hormone overrides the negative effect of reduced dietary energy on gonadotropin synthesis and secretion in ewes. *Endocrinology* **128**, 843–849.

Kimura, F., Hashimoto, R., and Kawakami, M. (1983). The stimulatory effect of cholecystokinin implanted in the medial preoptic area on luteinizing hormone secretion in the ovariectomized estrogen-primed rat. *Endocrinol. Jpn.* **30**, 305–309.

Kirkham, T. C., Perez, S., and Gibbs, J. (1995). Prefeeding potentiates anorectic actions of neuromedin B and gastrin releasing peptide. *Physiol. Behav.* **58**, 1175–1179.

Kissebah, A. A., and Krakower, G. R. (1994). Regional adiposity and morbidity. *Physiol. Rev.* **74**, 761–811.

Klaus, S., Casteilla, L., Bouillaud, F., and Riquier, D. (1991). The uncoupling protein UCP: A membraneous mitochondrial ion carrier exclusively expressed in brown adipose tissue. *Int. J. Biochem.* **23**, 791–801.

Kolaczynski, J. W., Considine, R. V., Ohannesian, J., Marco, C., Opentanova, I., Nyce, M. R., Myint, M., and Caro, J. F. (1996). Responses of leptin to short-term fasting and refeeding in humans. *Diabetes* **45**, 1511–1515.

Kopelman, P. G. (2000). Obesity as a medical problem. *Nature (London)* **404**, 634–643.

Kral, J. G. (1976). Surgical reduction of adipose tissue in the male Sprague-Dawley rat. *Am. J. Physiol.* **231**, 1090–1096.

Kristensen, P., Judge, M. E., Thim, L., Ribel, U., Christjansen, K. N., Wulff, B. S., Clausen, J. T., Jensen, P. B., and Madsen, O. D. (1998). Hypothalamic CART is a new anorectic peptide regulated by leptin. *Nature (London)* **393**, 72–76.

Lado-Abeal, J., Lukyanenko, Y. O., Swamy, S., and Hermida, R. C. (1999). Short-term leptin infusion does not affect circulating levels of LH, testosterone or cortisol in food-restricted pubertal male rhesus macaques. *Clin. Endocrinol. (Oxford)* **51**, 41–51.

Lado-Abeal, J., Hickox, J. R., Cheung, T. L., Veldhuis, J. D., Hardy, D. M., and Norman, R. L. (2000). Neuroendocrine consequences of fasting in adult male macaques: Effects of recombinant rhesus macaque leptin infusion. *Neuroendocrinology* **71**, 196–208.

LaFlamme, N., Nappi, R. E., Drolet, G., Labrie, C., and Rivest, S. (1998). Expression and neuropeptidergic characterization of estrogen receptors (ERalpha and Erbeta) throughout the rat brain: Anatomical evidence of distinct roles of each subtype. *J. Neurobiol.* **36**, 357–378.

Lafontan, M. (1994a). Adrenergic regulation of lipolysis and vascularization of the adipose tissue. *Rev. Prat.* **44**, 19–23.

Lafontan, M. (1994b). Differential recruitment and differential regulation by physiological amines of fat cell beta-1, beta-2 and beta-3 adrenergic receptors expressed in native fat cells and in transfected cell lines. *Cell. Signal.* **6**, 363–392.

Lafontan, M., and Berlan, M. (1995). Fat cell alpha 2-adrenoceptors: The regulation of fat cell function and lipolysis. *Endocr. Rev.* **16**, 716–738.

Lafontan, M., and Langin, D. (1995). Cellular aspects of fuel mobilization and selection in white adipocytes. *Proc. Nutr. Soc.* **54**, 49–63.

Lafontan, M., Bousquet-Melou, A., Galitzky, J., Barbe, P., Carpene, C., Langin, D., Valet, P., Casta, I., Bouloumie, A., and Saulnier-Blanche, J. S. (1995). Adrenergic receptors and fat cells: Differential recruitment by physiological amines and homologous regulation. *Obes. Res.* **3**, 507S–514S.

Lambert, P. D., Wilding, J. P. H., Aldokhayel, A. A. M., Gilbey, S. G., Ghatei, M. A., and Bloom, S. R. (1994). Naloxone-induced anorexia increases neuropeptide-Y concentrations in the dorsomedial hypothalamus—Evidence for neuropeptide-Y opioid interactions in the control of food-intake. *Peptides (N.Y.)* **15**, 657–660.

Landsberg, L., and Young, J. B. (1981). Diet and the sympathetic nervous system: Relationship to hypertension. *Int. J. Obes.* **5**(Suppl. 1), 79–91.

Langhans, W., and Scharrer, E. (1987). Evidence for vagally mediated satiety signal derived from hepatic fatty acid oxidation. *J. Auton. Nerv. Sys.* **18**, 13–18.

Larhammar, D. (1996). Evolution of neuropeptide Y, peptide YY and pancreatic polypeptide. *Regul. Pept.* **62**, 1–11.

Larsen, P. J., Hay-Schmidt, A., and Mikkelsen, J. D. (1994). Efferent connections from the lateral hypothalamic region and the lateral preoptic area to the hypothalamic paraventricular nucleus of the rat. *J. Comp. Neurol.* **342**, 299–319.

Laurie, E. M. O. (1946). The reproduction of the house mouse (*Mus musculus*) living in different environments. *Proc. R. Soc. London* **133**, 248–281.

Lazzarini, S. J., and Wade, G. N. (1991). Role of sympathetic nerves in effects of estradiol on rat white adipose tissue. *Am. J. Physiol.* **260**, R47–R51.

Leak, R. K., Card, J. P., and Moore, R. Y. (1999). Suprachiasmatic pacemaker organization analyzed by viral transynaptic transport. *Brain Res.* **819**, 23–32.

Lebrethon, M. C., Vandersmissen, E., Gerard, A., Parent, A. S., Junien, J. L., and Bourguignon, J. P. (2000). In vitro stimulation of the prepubertal rat gonadotropin-releasing hormone pulse generator by leptin and neuropeptide Y through distinct mechanisms. *Endocrinology (Baltimore)* **141**, 1464–1469.

Leclereq-Meyer, L., Considine, R. V., Sener, A., and Malaisse, W. J. (1996). Do leptin receptors play a functional role in the endocrine pancreas? *Biochem. Biophys. Res. Commun.* **229**, 794–798.

LeDoux, J. (1996). "The Emotional Brain." Simon & Schuster, New York.

Lee, T. M., and Gorman, M. R. (2000). Timing of reproduction by the integration of photoperiod with other seasonal signals. *In* "Reproduction in Context: Social and Environmental Influences on Reproduction" (K. Wallen and J. E. Schneider, eds.), pp. 191–218. MIT Press, Cambridge, Massachusetts.

Lee, G. H., Proenca, R., Montez, J. M., Carroll, K. M., Darvishzadeh, J. G., Lee, J. I., and Friedman, J. M. (1996). Abnormal splicing of the leptin receptor in diabetic mice. *Nature (London)* **379**, 632–635.

Lee, M. D., Aloyo, V. J., Fluharty, S. J., and Simansky, K. J. (1998). Infusion of the serotonin 1B (5-HT1B) agonist CP-93,129 into the parabrachial nucleus potently and selectively reduces food intake in rats. *Psychopharmacology (Berlin)* **136**, 304–307.

Lee, Y., Wang, M.-Y., Kakuma, T., Wang, Z. W., Babcock, E., McCorkle, K., Higa, M., Zhou, Y. T., and Unger, R. H. (2001). Liporegulation in diet-induced obesity: The antisteatotic role of hyperleptinemia. *J. Biol. Chem.* **276**, 5629–5635.

Legradi, G., Emerson, C. H., Ahima, R. S., Flier, J. S., and Lechan, R. M. (1997). Leptin prevents fasting-induced syppression of prothyrotropin-releasing hormone messenger ribonucleic acid in neurons of the hypothalamic paraventricular nucleus. *Endocrinology (Baltimore)* **138**, 2569–2576.

Leibowitz, S. F. (1978). Paraventricular nucleus: A primary site mediating adrenergic stimulation of feeding and drinking. *Pharmacol., Biochem. Behav.* **8**, 163–175.

Leng, G., and Brown, D. (1997). The origins and significance of pulsatility in hormone secretion from the pituitary. *J. Neuroendocrinol.* **9**, 493–513.

Leupen, S. M., Bescke, L. M., and Levine, J. E. (1997). Neuropeptide Y Y1-receptor stimulation is required for physiological amplification of preovulatory luteinizing hormone surges. *Endocrinology (Baltimore)* **138**, 2735–2739.

Levin, B. E., and Routh, V. H. (1996). Role of the brain in energy balance and obesity. *Am. J. Physiol.* **271**, R491–R500.

Levin, B. E., Dunn-Meynell, A. A., and Routh, V. H. (1999). Brain glucose sensing and body energy homeostasis: Role in obesity and diabetes. *Am. J. Physiol.* **276**, R1223–R1231.

Levine, A. S., Kneip, J., Grace, M., and Morley, J. E. (1983). Effect of centrally administered neurotensin on multiple feeding paradigms., *Pharmacol., Biochem. Behav.* **18**, 19–23.

Levy, J. R., LeGall-Salmon, E., Santos, M., Pandak, W. M., and Stevens, W. (1997). Effect of enteral versus parenteral nutrition on leptin gene expression and release into the circulation. *Biochem. Biophys. Res. Commun.* **237**, 98–102.

Levy, J. R., Gyarmati, J., Lesko, J. M., Adler, R., and Stevens, W. (2000). Dual regulation of leptin secretion: Intracellular

energy and calcium dependence of regulated pathway. *Am. J. Physiol. Endocrinol. Metab.* **278**, R892–R901.

Lewis, D. E., Shellard, L., Koeslag, D. G. *et al.* (1993). Intense exercise and food restriction cause similar hypothalamic neuropeptide Y increases in rats. *Am. J. Physiol.* **264**, E279–E284.

Li, C., Chen, P., and Smith, M. S. (1998). Neuropeptide Y (NPY) neurons in the arcuate nucleus (ARH) and dorsomedial nucleus (DMH), areas activated during lactation, project to the paraventricular nucleus of the hypothalamus (PVH). *Regul. Pept.* **75**, 93–100.

Li, C., Chen, P., and Smith, M. S. (1999). Morphological evidence for direct interaction between arcuate nucleus neuropeptide Y (NPY) neurons and gonadotropin-releasing hormone neurons and the possible involvement of NPY Y1 receptors. *Endocrinology (Baltimore)* **140**, 5382–5390.

Li, C., Chen, P. L., and Smith, M. S. (2000). Corticotropin releasing hormone neurons in the paraventricular nucleus are direct targets for neuropeptide Y neurons in the arcuate nucleus: An anterograde tracing study. *Brain Res.* **854**, 122–129.

Li, H.-Y., Wade, G. N., and Blaustein, J. D. (1994). Manipulations of metabolic fuel availability alter estrous behavior and neural estrogen-receptor immunoreactivity in Syrian hamsters. *Endocrinology (Baltimore)* **135**, 240–247.

Li, H.-Y., Wang, L. L., and Yeh, R. S. (1999). Leptin immunoreactivity in the central nervous system in normal and diabetic rats. *NeuroReport* **10**, 437–442.

Li, S., Hong, M., Fournier, A., St.-Pierre, S., and Pelletier, G. (1994). Role of neuropeptide Y in the regulation of gonadotropin-releasing hormone gene expression in rat preoptic area. *Mol. Brain Res.* **26**, 69–73.

Licinio, J., Montzoros, C., Negrao, A. B., Cizza, G., Wong, M. L., Bongiomo, P. B., Chrousos, G. P., Karp, B., Allen, C., Flier, J. S., and Gold, P. W. (1997). Human leptin levels are pulsatile and inversely related to pituitary-adrenal function. *Nat. Med.* **3**, 575–579.

Licinio, J., Negrão, A. B., Mantzoros, C., Kaklamani, V., Wong, L., Bongiorno, P. B., Mulla, A., Cearnal, L., Veldhuis, J. D., Flier, J. S., McCann, S. M., and Gold, P. W. (1998). Synchronicity of frequently samples, 24-h concentrations of circulating leptin luteinizing hormone, and estradiol in healthy women. *Proc. Natl. Acad. Sci. U.S.A.* **95**, 2541–2546.

Loffreda, S., Yang, S. Q., Lin, H. Z., Karp, C. L., Brengman, M. L., Wang, D. J., Klein, A. S., Bulkley, G. B., Bas, C., Noble, P. W., Lane, M. D., and Diehl, A. M. (1998). Leptin regulates proinflammatory immune responses. *FASEB J.* **12**, 57–65.

Lopez-Valpuesta, F. J., Nyce, J. W., and Myers, R. D. (1996). NPY-Y1 receptor antisense injected centrally in rats causes hyperthermic and feeding. *NeuroReport* **7**, 2781–2784.

Loucks, A. B., Heath, E. M., Verdun, M., and Watts, J. R. (1994). Dietary restriction reduces luteinizing hormone (LH) pulse frequency during waking hours and increases LH pulse amplitude during sleep in young menstruating women. *J. Clin. Endocrinol. Metab.* **78**, 910–915.

Loucks, A. B., Verdun, M., and Heath, E. M. (1998). Low energy availability, not stress of exercise, alters LH pulsatility in exercising women. *J. Appl. Physiol.* **84**, 37–46.

Louis-Sylvestre, J., and LeMagnen, J. (1980). Fall in blood glucose level precedes meal onset in free-feeding rats. *Neurosci. Biobehav. Rev.* **4**, 13–15.

Lubkin, M., Stricker, E. M., and Krongrad, A. (1998). Independent feeding and metabolic actions of orexins in mice. *Biochem. Biophys. Res. Commun.* **253**, 241–245.

Luiten P. G., Horst, G. J., and Steffens, A. B. (1987). The hypothalamus: Intrinsic connections and outflow pathways to the endocrine system in relation to feeding and metabolism. *Prog. Neurobiol.* **28**, 1–54.

Lynn, R. B., Cao, G., Considine, R.V., Hyde, T. M., and Caro, J. F. (1996). Autoradiographic localization of leptin binding in the choroid plexus of ob/ob and db/db mice. *Biochem. Biophys. Res. Commun.* **219**, 884–889.

MacDonald, M. J. (1990) Elusive proximal signals of beta-cells for insulin secretion. *Diabetes* **39**, 1461–1466.

MacLusky, N. J., Naftolin, F., and Leranth, C. (1988). Immunocytochemical evidence for direct synaptic connections between corticotroppin-releasing factor (CRF) gonadotropin-releasing hormone (GnRH)-containing neurons in the preoptic area of the rat. *Brain Res.* **439**, 391–395.

Maeda, K.-I., Cagampang, F. R. A., Coen, C. W., and Tsukamura, H. (1994). Involvement of the catecholaminergic input to the paraventricular nucleus and of corticotropin-releasing hormone in the fasting-induced suppression of luteinizing hormone release in female rats. *Endocrinology (Baltimore)* **134**, 1718–1722.

Maeda, K.-I., Tsukamura, H., Ohkura, S., Kawakami, S., Nagabukuro, H., and Yokoyama, A. (1995). The LHRH pulse generator: A mediobasal hypothalamic location. *Neurosci. Biobehav. Rev.* **19**, 427–437.

Maeda, K.-I., Nagatani, S., Estacio, M. A., and Tsukamura, H. (1996). Novel estrogen feedback sites associated with stress-induced suppression of luteinizing hormone secretion in female rats. *Cell. Mol. Neurobiol.* **16**, 311–324.

Maffei, M., Halaas, J., Ravussin, E., Pratley, R. E., Lee, G. H., Zhang, Y., Fei, H., Kim, S., Lallone, R., Ranganathan, S., Kern, P. S., and Friedman, J. M. (1995). Leptin levels in human and rodent: Measurement of plasma leptin and ob RNA in obese and weight-reduced subjects. *Nat. Med.* **1**, 1155–1161.

Magni, P., Vettor, R., Pagano, C., Calcagno, A., Beretta, E., Messi, E., Zanis, M., Martini, L., and Motta, M. (1999). Expression of a leptin receptor in immortalized gonadotropin-releasing hormone-secreting neurons. *Endocrinology (Baltimore)* **140**, 1581–1585.

Maguire, E. A., Burgess, N., Donnett, J. G., Frackowiak, R. S., Frith, C. D., and O'Keefe, J. (1998). Knowing where and getting there: A human navigation network. *Science* **280**, 921–924.

Maldonado-Irizarry, C. S., Swanson, C. J., and Kelley, A. E. (1995). Glutamate receptors in the nucleus accumbens shell control feeding behavior via the lateral hypothalamus. *J. Neurosci.* **15**, 6779–6788.

Maney, D. L., and Wingfield, J. C. (1998). Neuroendocrine suppression of female courtship in a wild passerine: Corticotropin-releasing factor and endogenous opioids. *J. Neuroendocrinol.* **10**, 593–599.

Mangels, R. A., Jetton, A. E., Powers, J. B., and Wade, G. N. (1996). Food deprivation and the facilitory effects of estrogen in female hamsters: The LH surge and locomotor activity. *Physiol. Behav.* **60**, 837–843.

Manning, J. M., and Bronson, F. H. (1990). The effects of low temperature and food intake on ovulation in domestic mice. *Physiol. Zool.* **63**, 938–948.

Manning, J. M., and Bronson, F. H. (1991). Suppression of puberty in rats by exercise: Effects on hormone levels and reversal with GnRH infusion. *Am. J. Physiol.* **260**, R717–R723.

Mantzoros, C. S., Qu, D., Frederich, R. C., Susulic, V. S., Lowell, B. B., Maratos-Flier, E., and Flier, J. S. (1996). Activation of beta(3) adrenergic receptors suppresses leptin expression and mediates a leptin-independent inhibition of food intake in mice. *Diabetes* **45**, 909–914.

Marin-Bivens, C. L., and Olster, D. H. (1999). Opiod receptor blockade promotes weight loss and improves the display of sexual behaviors in obese Zucker femal rats. *Pharmacol., Biochem. Behav.* **63**, 515–520.

Marin-Bivens, C. L., Kalra, S. P., and Olster, D. H. (1998). Intraventricular injection of neuropeptide Y antisera curbs weight gain and feeding, and increases the display of sexual behaviors in obese Zucker female rats. *Regul. Pept.* **75–76**, 327–334.

Marin-Bivens, C. L., Jones, J. E., Lubbers, L. S., and Wade, G. N. (2000). Acute fasting decreases sexual receptivity and estrogen receptor alpha immunoreactivity in adult female rats. *Soc. Neurosci. Annu. Meet.* **26**, 472–477.

Marks, J. L., Porte, D., Jr., Stahl, W. L., and Baskin, D. G. (1990). Localization of insulin receptor mRNA in rat brain by in situ hybridization. *Endocrinology (Baltimore)* **127**, 3234–3236.

Marsh, D. J., Hollopeter, G., Huszar, D., Laufer, R., Yagaloff, K. A., Fisher, S. L., Burn, P., and Palmiter, R. D. (1999). Response of melanocortin-4 receptor-deficient mice to anorectic and orexigenic peptides. *Nat. Genet.* **21**, 119–122.

Marshall, F. H. A. (1936). Sexual periodicity and the causes which determine it. *Philos. Trans. R. Soc. London* **226**, 423–456.

Marti, A., Berraondo, B., and Martinez, J. A. (1999). Leptin: Physiological actions. *J. Physiol. Biochem.* **55**, 43–49.

Martinez, V., Barrachina, M. D., Wang, L., and Tache, Y. (1999). Intracerebroventricular leptin inhibits gastric emptying of a solid nutrient meal in rats. *NeuroReport* **10**, 3217–3221.

Masuzaki, H., Ogawa, Y., Sagawa, N., Hosoda, K., Matsumoto, T., Mise, H., Nishimura, H., Yoshimasa, Y., Tanaka, I., Mori, T., and Nakao, K. (1997). Nonadipose tissue production of leptin: Leptin as a novel placenta-derived hormone in humans. *Nat. Med.* **3**, 1029–1033.

Matarasso, A., Kim, R. W., and Kral, J. G. (1998). The impact of liposuction on body fat. *Plast. Reconstr. Surg.* **102**, 1686–1689.

Mathis, C., Moran, T. H., and Schwartz, G. J. (1998). Load-sensitive rat gastric vagal afferents encode volume but not gastric nutrients. *Am. J. Physiol.* **274**, R280–R286.

Matschinsky, F. M. (1996). A lesson in metabolic regulation inspired by the glucokinase glucose sensor paradigm. *Diabetes* **45**, 223–241.

Mauer, M. M., and Bartness, T. J. (1995). A role for testosterone in the maintenance of seasonally appropriate body mass but not in lipectomy-induced body fat compensation in Siberian hamsters. *Obes. Res.* **3**, 31–41.

Mayer, J. (1955). Regulation of energy intake and the body weight. The glucostatic theory and the lipostatic hypothesis. *Ann. N. Y. Acad. Sci.* **63**, 15–43.

McCormick, D. A., and Bal, T. (1997). Sleep and arousal: Thalamocortical mechanisms. *Annu. Rev. Neurosci.* **20**, 185–215.

McDonald, J. K. (1990). Role of neuropeptide Y in reproductive function. *Ann. N. Y. Acad. Sci.* **611**, 258–272.

McDonald, J. K., Lumpkin, M. D., and De Paolo, L. V. (1989). Neuropeptide Y suppresses pulsatile secretion of luteinizing hormone in ovariectomized rats: Possible site of action. *Endocrinology (Baltimore)* **125**, 186–191.

McShane, T. M., Petersen, S. L., McCrone, S., and Keisler, D. H. (1993). Influence of food restriction on neuropeptide-Y, proopiomelanocortin, and luteinizing hormone-releasing hormone gene expression in sheep hypothalami. *Biol. Reprod.* **49**, 831–839.

Medina, C. L., Nagatani, S., Darling, T. A., Bucholtz, D. C., Tsukamura, H., Maeda, K., and Foster, D. L. (1998). Glucose availability modulates the timing of the luteinizing hormone surge in the ewe. *J. Neuroendocrinol.* **10**, 785–792.

Meglasson, M. D., and Matschinsky, F. M. (1986). Pancreatic islet glucose metabolism and regulation of insulin secretion. *Diabetes/Metab. Rev.* **2**, 163–214.

Merali, Z., McIntosh, J., and Anisman, H. (1999). Role of bombesin-related peptides in the control of food intake. *Neuropeptides* **33**, 376–386.

Mercer, J. G., Hoggard, N., Williams, L. M., Lawrence, C. B., Hannah, L. T., and Trayhurn, P. (1996). Localization of leptin receptor mRNA and the long form splice variant (Ob-Rb) in mouse hypothalamus and adjacent brain regions by in situ hybridization. *FEBS Lett.* **387**, 113–116.

Mercer, J. G., Beck, B., Burlet, A., Moar, K. M., Hoggard, N., Atkinson, T., and Barrett, P. (1998a). Leptin (ob) mRNA and hypothalamic NPY in food-deprived/refed Syrian hamsters. *Physiol. Behav.* **64**, 191–195.

Mercer, J. G., Moar, K. M., and Hoggard, N. (1998b). Localization of leptin receptor (Ob-R) messenger ribonucleic acid in the rodent hind brain. *Endocrinology (Baltimore)* **139**, 29–34.

Miller, D. W., Blache, D., and Martin, G. B. (1995). The role of intracerebral insulin in the effect of nutrition on gonadotropin secretion in mature male sheep. *J. Endocrinol.* **147**, 321–329.

Miller, K. K., Parulekar, M. S., Schoenfeld, E., Anderson, E., Hubbard, J., Klibanski, A., and Grinspoon, S. K. (1998). Decreased leptin levels in normal weight women with hypothalamic menorrhea: The effects of body composition and nutritional intake. *J. Clin. Endocrinol. Metab.* **83**, 2309–2312.

Minami, S., Kamegai, J., Sugihara, H., Suzuki, N., Higuchi, H., and Wakabayashi, I. (1995). Central glucoprivation evoked by administration of 2-deoxy-D-glucose induces expression of the c-fos gene in a subpopulation of neuropeptide Y neurons in the rat hypothalamus. *Mol. Brain Res.* **33**, 305–310.

Minokoshi, Y., Haque, M. S., and Shimazu, T. (1999). Microinjection of leptin into the ventromedial hypothalamus increases glucose uptake in peripheral tissues in rats. *Diabetes* **48**, 287–291.

Mistlberger, R. E. (1994). Circadian food-anticipatory activity: Formal models and physiological mechanisms. *Neurosci. Biobehav. Rev.* **18**, 171–195.

Mitsugi, N., Hashimoto, R., Yoshida, K., Arita, J., and Kimura, F. (1988). Effects of preoptic injection of glucagon on luteinizing hormone secretion in ovariectomized rats with or without estrogen priming. *Exp. Clin. Endocrinol.* **91**, 135–142.

Mizuno, T. M., and Mobbs, C. V. (1999). Hypothalamic agouti-related protein messenger ribonucleic acid is inhibited by leptin and stimulated by fasting. *Endocrinology (Baltimore)* **140**, 814–817.

Mizuno, T. M., Bergen, H., Kleopoulos, S., Bauman, W. A., and Mobbs, C. V. (1996). Effects of nutritional status and aging on leptin gene expression in mice: Importance of glucose. *Horm. Metab. Res.* **28**, 679–684.

Moga, M. M., and Saper, C. B. (1994). Neuropeptide-immunoreactive neurons projecting to the paraventricular hypothalamic nucleus in the rat. *J. Comp. Neurol.* **346**, 137–150.

Moga, M. M., Saper, C. B., and Gray, T. S. (1989). Bed nucleus of the stria terminalis: Cytoarchitecture, immunohistochemistry, and projection to the parabrachial nucleus in the rat. *J. Comp. Neurol.* **283**, 315–332.

Moga, M. M., Herbert, H., Hurley, K. M., Yasui, Y., Gray, T. S., and Saper, C. B. (1990a). Organization of cortical, basal forebrain, and hypothalamic afferents to the parabrachial nucleus in the rat. *J. Comp. Neurol.* **295**, 624–661.

Moga, M. M., Saper, C. B., and Gray, T. S. (1990b). Neuropeptide organization of the hypothalamic projection to the parabrachial nucleus in the rat. *J. Comp. Neurol.* **295**, 662–682.

Mogenson, G. J. (1977). "The Neurobiology of Behavior: An Introduction." Erlbaum, Hillsdale, NJ.

Mogenson, G. J., Jones, D. L., and Yim, C. Y. (1980). From motivation to action: Functional interface between the limbic system and the motor system. *Prog. Neurobiol.* **14**, 69–97.

Montague, C. T., Farooqi, S. I., Withehead, J. P. *et al.* (1997). Congenital leptin deficiency is associated with severe early-onset obesity in humans. *Nature (London)* **387**, 903–908.

Moore, R. Y. (1997). Circadian rhythms: Basic neurobiology and clinical applications. *Annu. Rev. Med.* **48**, 253–266.

Moore, R. Y., and Silver, R. (1998). Suprachiasmatic nucleus organization. *Chronobiol. Int.* **15**, 475–487.

Morgan, D. G. A., Small, C. J., Abusnana, S. *et al.* (1998). The NPY Y1 receptor antagonist BIBP 3226 blocks NPY induced feeding via a non-specific mechanism. *Regul. Pept.* **75-76**, 377–382.

Moriguchi, T., Sakurai, T., Nambu, T., Yanagisawa, M., and Goto, K. (1999). Neurons containing orexin in the lateral hypothalamic area of the adult rat brain are activated by insulin-induced acute hypoglycemia. *Neurosci. Lett.* **264**, 101–104.

Morris Y. A., and Crews, D. (1990). The effects of exogenous neuropeptide Y on feeding and sexual behavior in the red-sided garter snake (*Thamnophis sirtalis parietalis*). *Brain Res.* **530**, 339–341.

Mountjoy, K. G., Mortrud, M. T., Low, M. J., Simerly, R. B., and Cone, R. D. (1994). Localization of the melanocortin-4 receptor (MC4-R) in neuroendocrine and autonomic control circuits in the brain. *Mol. Endocrinol.* **8**, 1298–1308.

Mrosovsky, N., and Sherry, D. F. (1980). Animal anorexias. *Science* **207**, 837–842.

Mueller, W. M., Grégoire, F. M., Stanhope, K. L., Mobbs, C. V., Mizuno, T. M., Warden, C. H., Stern, J. S., and Havel, P. J. (1998). Evidence that glucose metabolism regulates leptin secretion from cultured rat adipocytes. *Endocrinology (Baltimore)* **139**, 551–558.

Muoio, D. M., Dohn, G. L., Fiedork, F. T., Tapscott, E. B., and Coleman, R. A. (1997). Leptin directly alters lipid partitioning in skeletal muscle. *Diabetes* **46**, 1360–1363.

Murahashi, K., Bucholtz. D. C., Nagatani, S., Tsukahara, S., Tsukamura, H., Foster, D. L., and Maeda, K.-I. (1996). Suppression of luteinizing hormone pulses by restriction of glucose availability is mediated by sensors in the brain stem. *Endocrinology (Baltimore)* **137**, 1171–1176.

Murakami, T., Yamashita, T., Iida, M., Kuwajima, M., and Shima, K. (1997). A short form of leptin receptor performs signal transduction. *Biochem. Biophys. Res. Commun.* **231**, 26–29.

Murray, J. F., Adan, R. A., Walker, R., Baker, B. I., Thody, A. J., Nijenhuis, W. A., Yukitake, J., and Wilson, C. A. (2000). Melanin-concentrating hormone, melanocortin receptors and regulation of luteinizing hormone release. *J. Neuroendocrinol.* **12**, 217–223.

Muurahainen, N. E., Kissileff, H. R., and Pi-Sunyer, F. X. (1993). Intravenous infusion of bombesin reduces food intake in humans. *Am. J. Physiol.* **264**, R350–R354.

Nagatani, S., Bucholtz, D. C., Murahashi, K., Estacio, M. A. C., Tsukamura, H., Foster, D. L., and Maeda, K.-I. (1996a). Reduction of glucose availability suppresses pulsatile LH release in female and male rats. *Endocrinology (Baltimore)* **137**, 1166–1170.

Nagatani, S., Tsukamura, H., Murahashi,K., Bucholtz, D. C., Foster, D. L., and Maeda, K. (1996b). Paraventricular norepinephrine release mediates glucoprivic suppression of pulsatile luteinizing hormone secretion. *Endocrinology* **137**, 3183–3186.

Nagatani, S., Tsukamura, H., Murahashi, K., and Maeda, K. I. (1996c). A rapid suppressive effect of estrogen in the paraventricular nucleus on pulsatile LH release in fasting-ovariectomized rats. *J. Neuroendocrinol.* **8**, 267–273.

Nagatani, S., Tsukamura, H., and Maeda, K.-I. (1994). Estrogen feedback needed at the paraventricular nucleus or A2 to suppress pulsatile luteinizing hormone release in fasting female rats. *Endocrinology (Baltimore)* **135**, 870–875.

Nagatani, S., Guthikonda, P., Thompson, R. C., Tsukamura, H., Maeda, K., and Foster, D. L. (1998). Evidence for GnRH regulation by leptin: Leptin administration prevents reduced pulsatile LH secretion during fasting. *Neuroendocrinology* **67**, 370–376.

Nagatani, S., Guthikonda, P., and Foster, D. L. (2000). Appearance of a nocturnal peak of leptin during puberty. *Horm. Behav.* **37**, 345–352.

Narnaware, Y. K., Peyon, P. P., Lin, X., and Peter, R. E. (2000). Regulation of food intake by neuropeptide Y in goldfish. *Am. J. Physiol.* **279**, R1025–R1034.

Nazian, S. J., and Cameron, D. F. (1999). Temporal relation between leptin and various indices of sexual maturation in the male rat. *J. Androl.* **20**, 487–491.

Nelson, R. J., and Klein, S. (2000). Environmental and social influences on seasonal breeding and immune function. *In*

"Reproduction in Context: Social and Environmental Influences on Reproduction" (K. Wallen and J. E. Schneider, eds.), pp. 219–256. MIT Press, Cambridge, MA.

Newgard, C. B., and McGarry, J. D. (1995). Metabolic coupling factors in pancreatic B-cell signal transduction. *Annu. Rev. Biochem.* **64**, 689–719.

Newman, S. W. (1999). The medial extended amygdala in male reproductive behavior. *Ann. N. Y. Acade. Sci.* **877**, 424–257.

Nillius, S. J., Fries, H., and Wide, L. (1975). Successful induction of follicular maturation and ovulation by prolonged treatment with LH-releasing hormone in women with anorexia nervosa. *Am. J. Obstet. Gynecol.* **122**, 921–928.

Nishiyama, M., Makino, S., Asaba, K., and Hashimoto, K. (1999). Leptin effects on the expression of type-2 CRH receptor mRNA in the ventromedial hypothalamus in the rat. *J. Neuroendocrinol.* **11**, 307–314.

Norgren, R. (1976). Taste pathways to hypothalamus and amygdala. *J. Comp. Neurol.* **166**, 17–30.

Norgren, R. (1984). Taste: Central neural mechanisms. *In* "Handbook of the Physiology: The Nervous System III-Sensory Processes" (I. Darien-Smith, ed.), pp. 1087–1128. American Physiological Society, Washington, DC.

Norgren, R., and Leonard, C. M. (1973). Ascending central gustatory pathways. *J. Comp. Neurol.* **150**, 217–237.

Novin, D., VanderWeele, D. A., and Rezek, M. (1973). Infusion of 2-deoxy-D-glucose into the hepatic-portal system causes eating: Evidence for peripheral glucoreceptors. *Science* **181**, 858–860.

Nye, E. J., Borstein, S. R., Grice, J. E., Tauchnitz, R., Hockings, G. I., Strakosch, C. R., Jackson, R. V., and Torpy, D. J. (2000). Interactions between the stimulated hypothalamic-pituitary-adrenal axis and leptin in humans. *J. Nueroendocrinol.* **12**, 141–145.

Oates, M., Woodside, B., and Walker, C.-D. (2000). Chronic leptin administration in developing rats affects energy balance and stress responsiveness independently of changes in maternal behavior. *Horm. Behav.* **37**, 366–376.

O'Donohue, I. L., Chronwall, B. M., Pruss, R. M. *et al.* (1985). Neuropeptide Y and peptide YY in neuronal and endocrine systems. *Peptides (N.Y.)* **6**, 755–768.

Oliveira, M. H., Antunes-Rodrigues, J., Gutkowska, J., Leal, A. M., Elias, L. L., and Moreira, A. C. (1997). Atrial natriuretic peptide and feeding activity patterns in rats. *Braz. J. Med. Biol. Res.* **30**, 465–469.

Öngür, D., and Price, J. L. (2000). The organization of networks within the orbital and medial prefrontal cortex of rats, monkeys and humans. *Cereb. Cortex* **10**, 206–219.

Öngür, D., An, X., and Price, J. L. (1998). Prefrontal cortical projections to the hypothalamus in macaque monkeys. *J. Comp Neurol.* **401**, 480–505.

Orskov, C., Poulen, S. S., and Mollen, M. (1996). Glucagon-like peptide-1 receptors in the subfornical organ and the area psotrema are accessible to circulating glucagons-like peptide-1. *Diabetes* **45**, 832–835.

Otis, C. L., Drinkwater, B., Johnson, M., Loucks, A., and Wilmore, J. (1997). American college of sports medicine position stand. The female athlete triad. *Med. Sci. Sports Exercise* **29**, i–ix.

Owzar, K., Goldner, J., Blum, R. M., and Little, P. (2000). Leptin concentrations increase after refeeding in adipose tissue but not in plasma. *Soc. Neurosci. Abstract.* Vol. 26, Program No. 540.18.

Overton, J. M., VanNess, J. M., and Casto, R. M. (1997). Food restriction reduces sympathetic support of blood pressure in spontaneously hypertensive rats. *J. Nutr.* **127**, 655–660.

Palmert, M. R., Radovick, S., and Boepple, P. A. (1998). Leptin levels in children with central precocious puberty. *J. Clin. Endocrinol. Metab.* **83**, 2260–2265.

Palmiter, R. D., Erickson, J. C., Hollopeter, G., Baraban, S. C., and Schwartz, M. W. (1998). Life without neuropeptide Y. *Recent Prog. Horm. Res.* **53**, 163–199.

Panicker, A. K., and Wade, G. N. (1998). Insulin-induced repartitioning of metabolic fuels inhibits hamster estrous behavior: Role of area postrema. *Am. J. Physiol.* **274**, R1094– R1098.

Panicker, A. K., Mangels, R. A., Powers, J. B., Wade, G. N., and Schneider, J. E. (1998). AP lesions block suppression of estrous behavior, but not estrous cyclicity, in food-deprived Syrian hamsters. *Am. J. Physiol.* **275**, R158–R164.

Parent, A. S., Lebrethon, M. C., Gerard, A., Vandersmissen, E., and Bourguignon, J. P. (2000). Leptin effects on pulsatile gonadotropin releasing hormone secretion from the adult rat hypothalamus and interaction with cocaine and amphetamine regulated transcript and neuropeptide Y. *Regul. Pept.* **92**, 17–24.

Patchev, V. K., and Almeida, O. F. (1996). Gonadal steroids exert facilitating and "buffering" effects on glucocorticoid-mediated transcriptional regulation of corticotropin-releasing hormone and corticosteroid receptor genes in rat brain. *J. Neurosci.* **16**, 7077–7084.

Patchev, V. K., Hayashi, S., Orikasa, C., and Almeida, O. F. (1995). Implicationss of estrogen-dependent brain organization for gender differences in hypothalamo-pituitary-adrenal regulation. *FASEB J.* **9**, 419–423.

Pelleymounter, M. A., Cullen, M. J., Baker, M. B., Hecht, B., Winters, D., Boone, T., and Collins, F. (1995). Effects of the obese gene product on body weight regulation in ob/ob mice. *Science* **269**, 540–549.

Pelleymounter, M. A., Baker, M. B., and McCaleb, M. (1999). Does estradiol mediate leptin's effects on adiposity and body weight? *Am. J. Physiol.* **276**, E955–E963.

Perera, A. D., Veralis, J. G., Mikuma, N., Majumdar, S. S., and Plant, T. M. (1993). Cholecystokinin stimulates gonadotropin-releasing hormone release in the monkey *(Macaca mulatta)*. *Endocrinology (Baltimore)* **132**, 1723–1728.

Perrigo, G., and Bronson, F. H. (1983). Foraging effort, food intake, fat deposition and puberty in female mice. *Biol. Reprod.* **29**, 455–463.

Petraglia, F., Sutton, S., Vale, W., and Plotsky, P. (1987). Corticotropin-releasing factor decreases plasma luteinizing hormone levels in female rats by inhibiting gonadotropin-releasing hormone release into hypophysial-portal circulation. *Endocrinology (Baltimore)* **120**, 1083–1088.

Petrovich, G. D., and Swanson, L. W. (1997). Projections from the lateral part of the central amygdalar nucleus to the postulated fear conditioning circuit. *Brain Res.* **763**, 247–254.

Peyron, C., Tighe, D. K., van den Pol, A. N., de Lecea, L., Heller, H. C., Sutcliffe, J. G., and Kilduff, T. S. (1998). Neurons containing hypocretin (orexin) project to multiple neuronal systems. *J. Neurosci.* **18**, 9996–10015.

Pfaff, D. W. (1980). "Estrogens and Brain Function." Springer-Verlag. New York.

Pfaff, D. W. (1982). Motivational concepts: Definitions and distinctions. *In* "The Physiological Mechanisms of Motivation" (D. W. Pfaff, ed.), pp. 3–24. Springer-Verlag. New York.

Pfaff, D. W. (1999). "Drive. Neurobiological and Molecular Mechanisms of Sexual Motivation." MIT Press, Cambridge, MA.

Phillips, D. L., Rautenberg, W., Rashotte, M. E., and Stephan, F. K. (1993). Evidence for a separate food-entrainable circadian oscillator in the pigeon. *Physiol. Behav.* **53**, 1105–1113.

Phillips, R. J., and Powley, T. L. (1996). Gastric volume rather than nutrient content inhibits food intake. *Am. J. Physiol.* **271**, R766–R769.

Phillips, R. J., and Powley, T. L. (1998). Gastric volume detection after selective vagotomies in rats. *Am. J. Physiol.* **274**, R1626–R1638.

Pieper, D. R., Ali, H. Y., Benson, L., Shows, M., Lobocki, C. A., and Subramanian, M. G. (1995). Voluntary exercise increases gonadotropin secretion in male golden hamsters. *Am. J. Physiol.* **269**, R179–R185.

Pierroz, D. D., Catzeflis, C., Aeby, A. C., Rivier, J. E., and Aubert, M. L. (1996). Chronic administration of neuropeptide Y into the lateral ventricle inhibits both the pituitary-testicular axis and growth hormone and insulin-like growth factor I secretion in intact adult male rats. *Endocrinology (Baltimore)* **137**, 3–12.

Pinski, J., Yano, T., and Schally, A. V. (1992). Inhibitory effects of the new bombesin receptor antagonist RC-3095 on the luteinizing hormone release in rats. *Neuroendocrinology* **56**, 831–837.

Poggioli, R., Bergoni, A. V., Marrama, D., Giuliani, D., and Bertolini A. (1990). NPY-induced inhibition of male copulatory activity is direct behavioural effect. *Neuropeptides* **16**, 169–172.

Pomonis, J. D., Levine, A. S., and Billington, C. J. (1997). Interaction of the hypothalamic paraventricular nucleus and central nucleus of the amygdala in naloxone blockade of neuropeptide Y-induced feeding revealed by c-fos expression. *J. Neurosci.* **17**, 5175–5182.

Porte, D., Jr., Seeley, R. J., Woods, S. C., Baskin, D. G., Figlewicz, D. P., and Schwartz, M. W. (1998). Obesity, diabetes and the central nervous system. *Diabetologia* **41**, 863–881.

Powers, J. B., Jetton, A. E., and Wade, G. N. (1994). Interactive effects of food deprivation and exercise on reproductive function in female hamsters. *Am. J. Physiol.* **267**, R185–R190.

Powley, T. L., Berthoud, H.-R., Fox, E. A., and Laughton, W. (1992). The dorsal vagal complex forms a sensory-motor lattice: The circuitry of gastrointestinal reflexes. *In* "Neuroanatomy and Physiology of Abdominal Vagal Afferents" (S. Ritter, R. C. Ritter, and C. D. Barnes, eds.), pp. 57–107. CRC Press, Boca Raton, FL.

Prentice, A. M., Whitehead, R. G., Roberts, S. B., and Paul, A. A. (1981). Long-term energy balance in child-bearing Gambian women. *Am. J. Clin. Nutr.* **34**, 2790–2799.

Prevost, J. (1961). "Ecologie du Manchot empereur." Hermann, Paris.

Pu, S., Jain, M. R., Kalra, P. S., and Kalra, S. P. (1998). Orexins, a novel family of hypothalamic neuropeptides, modulate pituitary luteinizing hormone secretion in an ovarian steroid-dependent manner. *Regul. Pept.* **78**, 133–136.

Quinton, N. D., Smith, R. F., Clayton, P. E., Gill, M. S., Shalet, S., Justice, S. K., Simon, S. A., Walters, S., Postel-Vinay, M. C., Blakemore, A. I., and Ross, R. J. (1999). Leptin binding activity changes with age: The link between leptin and puberty. *J. Clin. Endocrinol. Metab.* **84**, 2336–2341.

Raposinho, P. D., Broqua, P., Pierroz, D. D., Hayward, A., Dumont, Y., Quirion, R., Junien, J. L., and Aubert, M. L. (1999). Evidence that the inhibition of luteinizing hormone secretion exerted by central administration of neuropeptide Y (NPY) in the rat is predominantly mediated by the NPY-Y5 receptor subtype. *Endocrinology (Baltimore)* **140**, 4046–4055.

Rascher, W., Meffle, H., and Gross, F. (1985). Hemodynamic effects of arginine vasopresin in conscious water-deprived rats. *Am. J. Physiol.* **249**, H29–H33.

Ravussin, E., Lillioja, S., Knowler, W. C., Christin, L., Freymond, D., Abbott, W. G., Boyce, V., Howard, B. V., and Bogardus, C. (1988). Reduced rate of energy expenditure as a risk factor for body-weight gain. *N. Engl. J. Med.* **318**, 467–472.

Rawson, N. E., and Friedman, M. I. (1994). Phosphate loading prevents the decrease in ATP and increase in food intake produced by 2,5-anhydro-D-mannitol. *Am. J. Physiol.* **266**, R1792–R1796.

Rawson, N. E., Blum, H., Osbakken, M. D., and Friedman, M. I. (1994). Hepatic phosphate trapping, decreased ATP, and increased feeding after 2,5-anhydro-D-mannitol. *Am. J. Physiol.* **266**, R112–R117.

Rawson, N. E., Ulrich, P. M., and Friedman, M. I. (1996). Fatty acid oxidation modulates the eating response to fructose analogue 2,5-anhydro-D-mannitol. *Am. J. Physiol.* **271**, R144–R148.

Rebuffe-Scrive, M., Lonnroth, P., Marin, P., Wesslau, C., Bjorntorp, P., and Smith, U. (1987). Regional adipose tissue metabolism in men and postmenopausal women. *Int. J. Obes.* **11**, 347–355.

Reeves, A. G., and Plum, F. (1969). Hyperphagia, rage, and dementia accompanying a ventromedial hypothalamic neoplasm. *Arch. Neurol. (Chicago)* **20**, 616–624.

Reidelberger, R. D., and O'Rourke, M. F. (1989). Potent cholecystokinin antagonist L 364718 stimulates food intake in rats. *Am. J. Physiol.* **257**, R1512–R1518.

Reidy, S. P., and Weber, J. (2000). Leptin: An essential regulator of lipid metabolism. *Comp. Biochem. Physiol. A* **125**, 285–298.

Reilly, S. (1999). The parabrachial nucleus and conditioned taste aversion. *Brain Res. Bull.* **48**, 239–254.

Reis, D. J., and Cuenod, M. (1965). Central regulation of carotid baroreceptor reflexes in the cat. *Am. J. Physiol.* **209**, 1267–1277.

Rentsch, J., Levens, N., and Chiesi, M. (1995). Recombinant ob-gene product reduces food intake in fasted mice. *Biochem. Biophys. Res. Commun.* **214**, 131–136.

Richter, C. P. (1922). A behavioristic study of the activity of the rat. *Comp. Psychol. Monogr.* **1**, 1–55.

Richter, C. P. (1936). Increased salt appetite in adrenalectomized rats. *Am. J. Physiol.* **115**, 115–61.

Richter, C. P. (1943). Total self-regulatory functions in animals and human beings. *Harvey Lec.* **38**, 63–103.

Richter, C. P. (1956). Self-regulatory functions during gestation and lactation. *In* "Gestation" (C. A. Vilee, ed.), pp. 11–93. Josiah Macy, Jr. Found., New York.

Richter, C. P., and Barelare, B. (1938). Nutritional requirements of pregnant and lactating rats studied by the self selection method. *Endocrinology (Baltimore)* **23**, 15–24.

Ricquier, D., Casteilla, L., and Bouillaud, F. (1991). Molecular studies of the uncoupling protein. *FASEB J.* **5**, 2237–2242.

Rinaman, L., Baker, E. A., Hoffman, G. E., Stricker, E. M., and Verbalis, J. G. (1988). Medullary c-Fos activation in rats after ingestion of a satiating meal. *Am. J. Physiol.* **275**, R262-.

Rinaman, L., Levitt, P., and Card, J. P. (2000). Progressive postnatal assembly of limbic-autonomic circuits revealed by central

transneuronal transport of pseudorabies virus. *J. Neurosci.* **20**, 2731–2741.

Risold, P. Y., and Swanson, L. W. (1997). Connections of the rat lateral septal complex. *Brain Res. Rev.* **24**, 115–195.

Risold, P. Y., Thompson, R. H., and Swanson, L. W. (1997). The structural organization of connections between hypothalamus and cerebral-cortex. *Brain Res. Rev.* **24**, 197–254.

Rissman, E. F., Clendenon, A. L., and Krohmer, R. W. (1990). Role of androgens in the regulation of sexual behavrio in the female musk shrew. *Neuroendocrinology* **51**, 468–473.

Ritter, R. C., Slusser, P. G., and Stone, S. (1981). Glucoreceptors controlling feeding and blood glucose are in the hindbrain. *Science* **213**, 451–453

Ritter, R. C., Covasa, M., and Matson, C. A. (1999). Cholecystokinin: Proofs and prospects for involvement in control of food intake and body weight. *Neuropeptides* **33**, 387–399.

Ritter, S., and Calingasan, N. Y. (1994). Neural substrates for metabolic controls of feedng. *In* "Nutritional and Central Nervous Systems Function" (J. Fernstrom and G. Miller, eds.), pp. 77–94. CRC Press, Boca Raton, FL.

Ritter, S., and Dinh, T. T. (1994). 2-Mercaptoacetate and 2-deozy-D-glucose induce Fos-like immunoreactivity in rat brain. *Brain Res.* **641**, 111–120.

Ritter, S., and Taylor, J. S. (1989). Capsaicin abolishes lipoprivic but not glucoprivic feeding in rats. *Am. J. Physiol.* **256**, R1232–1239.

Ritter, S., and Taylor, J. S. (1990). Vagal sensory neurons are required for lipoprivic but not glucoprivic feeding in rats. *Am. J. Physiol.* **258**, R1395–R1401.

Ritter, S., Ritter, R. C., Barnes, C. D., eds. (1992a). "Neuroanatomy and Physiology of Abdominal Vagal Afferents." CRC Press, Boca Raton, FL.

Ritter, S., and Calingasan, N. Y., Hutton, B., and Dinh, T. T. (1992b). Cooperation of vagal and central neural systems in monitoring metabolic events controlling feeding behavior. *In* "Neuroanatomy and Physiology of Abdominal Vagal Afferents" (S. Ritter, R. C. Ritter, and C. D. Barnes, eds.), pp. 249–277. CRC Press, Boca Raton, FL.

Ritter, S., Dinh, T. T., and Friedman, M. I. (1994). Induction of Fos-like immunoreactivity (Fos-li) and stimulation of feeding by 2,5-anhydro-D-mannitol (2,5-AM) require the vagus nerve. *Brain Res.* **646**, 53–64.

Ritter, S., Llewellyn-Smith, I., and Dinh, T. T. (1998). Subgroups of hindbrain catecholamine neurons are selectively activated by 2-deoxy-D-glucose induced metabolic challenge. *Brain Res.* **805**, 41–54.

Ritter, S., Dinh, T. T., and Zhang, Y. (2000). Localization of hindbrain glucoreceptive sites controlling food intake and blood glucose. *Brain Res.* **856**, 37–47.

Ritter, S., Bugarith, K., and Dinh, T. T. (2001). Immunotoxic destruction of distinct catecholamine subgroups produces selective impairment of glucoregulatory responses and neuronal activation. *J. Comp. Neurol.* **432**, 197–216.

Roberts, S. B., Paul, A. A., Cole, T. J., and Whitehead, R. G. (1982). Seasonal changes in activity, birth weight and lactation performance in rural Gambian women. *Trans. R. Soc. Trop. Med. Hyg.* **76**, 668–678.

Robin, J.-P., Frain, M., Sardet, C., Groscolas, R., and Le, Y. (1988). Protein and lipid utilization during long-term fasting in emperor penguins. *Am. J. Physiol.* **254**, R61–R68.

Robin, J.-P., Boucontet, L., Pascal, C., and Groscolas, R. (1998). Behavioral changes in fasting emperor penguins: Evidence for a "refeeding signal" linked to a metabolic shift. *Am. J. Physiol.* **274**, R746–R753.

Rodriguez, M., Arias, P., Refojo, D., Feleder, C., and Moguilevsky, J. (1999). Arrest of pulsatile luteinizing hormone (LH) secretion during insulin-induced hypoglycemia (IIH): improvement by intrahypothalamic perfusion with glucose. *Exp. Clin. Endocrinol. Diabetes* **107**, 257–261.

Roemmich, J. N., Li, X., Rogol, A. D., and Rissman, E. F. (1997). Food availability affects neural estrogen receptor immunoreactivity in prepubertal mice. *Endocrinology* **138**, 5366–5373.

Rohner-Jeanrenaud, F., Walker, C. D., Greco-Perotto, R., and Jeanrenaud, B. (1989). Central corticotropin-releasing factor administration prevents the excessive body weight gain of genetically obese (fa/fa) rats. *Endocrinology (Baltimore)* **124**, 733–739.

Rolls, B. J., and Rolls, E. T. (1982). "Thirst." Cambridge University Press, Cambridge, UK.

Rolls, E. T. (1999a). "The Brain and Emotion." Oxford University Press, Oxford.

Rolls, E. T. (1999b). Spatial view cells and the representation of place in the primate hippocampus. *Hippocampus* **9**, 467–480.

Rolls, E. T. (2000). The orbitofrontal cortex and reward. *Cereb. Cortex* **10**, 284–294.

Rossetti, L., Massillon, D., Barzilai, N., Vuguin, P., Chen, W., Hawkins, M., Wu, J., and Wang, J. (1997). Short term effects of leptin on hepatic gluconeogenesis and in vivo insulin action. *J. Biol. Chem.* **272**, 27758–27763.

Rossi, M., Kim, M. S., Morgan, D. G., Small, C. J., Edwards, C. M., Sunter, D., Abusnana, S., Goldstone, A. P., Russell, S. H., Stanley, S. A., Smith, D. M., Yagaloff, K., Ghatei, M. A., and Bloom, S. R. (1998). A C-terminal fragment of Agouti-related protein increases feeding and antagonizes the effect of alpha-melanocyte stimulating hormone *in vivo*. *Endocrinology (Baltimore)* **139**, 4428–4431.

Rothwell, N. J. (1990). Central effects of CRF on metabolism and energy balance. *Neurosci. Biobehav. Rev.* **14**, 263–271.

Rowland, N. (1982). Failure of deprived hamsters to increase their food intake: Some behavioral and physiological determinants. *J. Comp. Physiol. Psychol.* **96**, 591–603.

Ruffin, M. P., Caulliez, R., and Nicolaidis, S. (1995). Parallel metabolic and feeding responses to lateral hypothalamic stimulation. *Brain Res.* **700**, 121–128.

Russek, M. (1963). Participation of hepatic glucoreceptors in the control of intake of food. *Nature (London)* **197**, 79–80.

Saeb-Parsy, K., Lombardelli, S., Khan, F. Z., McDowall, K., Au-Yong, I. T., and Dyball, R. E. (2000). Neural connections of hypothalamic neuroendocrine nuclei in the rat. *J. Neuroendocrinol.* **12**, 635–648.

Sahu, A. (1998). Evidence suggesting that galanin (GAL), melanin-concentrating hormone (MCH), neurotensin (NT), proopiomelanocortin (POMC) and neuropeptide Y (NPY) are targets of leptin signaling in the hypothalamus. *Endocrinology (Baltimore)* **139**, 795–798.

Sahu, A. (2000). Evidence suggesting that the potentiating action of neuropeptide Y on luteinizing hormone (LH)-releasing hormone-induced LH release remains unaltered in aged female rats. *J. Neuroendocrinol.* **12**, 495–500.

Sahu, A., and Kalra, S. P. (1998). Absence of increased neuropeptide Y neuronal activity before and during the luteinizing hormone (LH) surge may underlie the attenuated preovulatory LH surge in middle-aged rats. *Endocrinology (Baltimore)* **139**, 696–702.

Sainsbury, A., Cusin, I., Rohner-Jeanrenaud, F., and Jeanrenaud, B. (1997). Adrenalectomy prevents the obesity syndrome produced by chronic central neuropeptide Y infusion in normal rats. *Diabetes* **46**, 209–214.

Saito, M., and Bray, G. A. (1984). Adrenalectomy and food restriction in the genetically obese (ob/ob) mouse. *Am. J. Physiol.* **246**, R20–R25.

Saito, T. R., Moritani, N., Hashimoto, H., Arkin, A., and Takahashi, K. W. (1999). Simultaneous observation of ingestive and copulatory behavior of the male rat. *Exp. Anim.* **48**, 285–288.

Sakurai, T., Amemiya, A., Ishii, M., Matsuzaki, I., Chemelli, R. M., Tanaka, H., Williams, S. C., Richardson, J. A., Kozlowski, G. P., Wilson, S., Arch, J. R., Buckingham, R. E., Haynes, A. C., Carr, S. A., Annan, R. S., McNulty, D. E., Liu, W. S., Terrett, J. A., Elshourbagy, N. A., Bergsma, D. J., and Yanagisawa, M. (1998). Orexins and orexin receptors: A family of hypothalamic neuropeptides and G protein-coupled receptors that regulate feeding behavior. *Cell (Cambridge, Mass.)* **92**, 573–585.

Saladin, R., de Vos, P., Guerre-Millo, M., Leturque, A., Girard, J., Staels, B., and Auwerx, J. (1995). Transient increase in obese gene expression after food intake or insulin administration. *Nature (London)* **377**, 527–529.

Saper, C. B. (1985). Organization of cerebral cortical afferent systems in the rat. II. Hypothalamocortical projections. *J. Comp. Neurol.* **237**, 21–46.

Saper, C. B., Loewy, A. D., Swanson, L. W., and Cowan, W. M. (1976). Direct hypothalamo- autonomic connections. *Brain Res.* **117**, 305–312.

Sapolsky, R. M., Romero, L. M., and Munck, A. U. (2000). How do glucocorticoids influence stress responses? Integrating permissive, suppressive, stimulatory, and preparative actions. *Endocr. Rev.* **21**, 55–89.

Sar, M., Sahu, A., Crowley, W. R., and Kalra, S. P. (1990). Localization of neuropeptide-Y immunoreactivity in estradiol-concentrating cells in the hypothalamus. *Endocrinology (Baltimore)* **127**, 2752–2756.

Saris, W. H. (1995). Effects of energy restriction and exercise on the sympathetic nervous system. *Int. J. Obes. Relat. Metab. Disord.* **7**, S17–S23.

Sarkar, D. K., Chiappa, S. A., Fink, G., and Sherwood, N. M. (1976). Gonadotropin-releasing hormone surge in prooestrous rats. *Nature (London)* **264**, 461–463.

Sarmiento, E., Benson, B., Kaufman, S., Ross, L., Qi, M., Scully, S., and DiPalma, C. (1997). Morphologic and molecular changes induced by recombinant human leptin in the white and brown adipose tissue of C57BL/6 mice. *Lab. Invest.* **77**, 243–256.

Satio, T. R., Moritani, N., Haskimoto, H., Arkin, A., and Takahaski, K. W. (1999). Simultaneous observation of ingestive and copulatory behavior of the male rat. *Exp. Anim.* **48**, 285–288.

Sawchenko, P. E. (1998). Toward a new neurobiology of energy balance, appetite, and obesity: The anatomists weigh in. *J. Comp. Neurol.* **402**, 435–441.

Sawchenko, P. E., and Swanson, L. W. (1983). The organization of forebrain afferents to the paraventricular and supraoptic nuclei of the rat. *J. Comp. Neurol.* **218**, 121–144.

Sawchenko, P. E., Swanson, L. W., Rivier, J., and Vale, W. W. (1985). The distribution of growth hormone releasing factor (GRF) immunoreactivity in the central nervous system of the rat: An immunohistochemical study using antisera directed against rat hypothalamic GRF. *J. Comp. Neurol.* **237**, 100–115.

Scarpace, P. J., Matheny, M., Pollock, B. H., and Tumer, N. (1997). Leptin increases uncoupling protein expression and energy expenditure. *Am. J. Physiol.* **273**, E226–E230.

Schaffhauser, A. O., Stricker-Krongrad, A., Brunner, L. *et al.* (1997). Inhibition of food intake by neuropeptide Y Y5 receptor antisense oligodeoxynucleuotides. *Diabetes* **46**, 1792–1798.

Scharrer, E. (1999). Control of food intake by fatty acid oxidation and ketogenesis. *Nutrition* **9**, 704–714.

Scharrer, E., and Langhans, W. (1986). Control of food intake by fatty acid oxidation. *Am. J. Physiol.* **250**, R1003–R1006.

Schneider, J. E. (1997). Effects of the fructose analog, 2,5-anhydro-d-mannitol, on food intake and estrous cyclicity in Syrian hamsters. *Am. J. Physiol.* **272**, R935–R939.

Schneider, J. E., and Buckley, C. A. (2001). Leptin attenuates the effects of food deprivation on hoarding in Syrian hamsters. *Soc. Neurosci. Abstracts.* Vol. 27, Program No. 635.1.

Schneider, J. E., and Wade, G. N. (1987). Body composition, food intake, and brown fat thermogenesis in pregnant Djungarian hamsters. *Am. J. Physiol.* **253**, R314–R320.

Schneider, J. E., and Wade, G. N. (1989). Availability of metabolic fuels controls estrous cyclicity of Syrian hamsters. *Science* **244**, 1326–1328.

Schneider, J. E., and Wade, G. N. (1990a). Decreased availability of metabolic fuels induces anestrus in Golden hamsters. *Am. J. Physiol.* **258**, R750–R755.

Schneider, J. E., and Wade, G. N. (1990b). Effects of diet and body fat content on cold-induced anestrus in Syrian hamsters. *Am. J. Physiol.* **259**, R1198–R1204.

Schneider, J. E., and Wade, G. N. (1991). Effects of ambient temperature and body fat content on maternal litter reduction in Syrian hamsters. *Physiol. Behav.* **49**, 135–139.

Schneider, J. E., and Wade, G. N. (2000). Inhibition of reproduction in service of energy balance. *In* "Reproduction in Context: Social and Environmental Influences on Reproduction" (K. Wallen and J. E. Schneider, eds.), pp. 35–82. MIT Press, Cambridge, MA.

Schneider, J. E., and Zhou, D. (1999a). Interactive effects of central leptin and peripheral fuel oxidation on estrous cyclicity. *Am. J. Physiol.* **277**, R1020–R1024.

Schneider, J. E., and Zhou, D. (1999b). Treatment with SHU9119 increases food intake but does not induce anestrus in Syrian hamsters fed *ad libitum*. *Soc. Neurosci. Abstr.* p. 415.

Schneider, J. E., and Zhu, Y. (1994). Caudal brain stem plays a role in metabolic control of estrous cycles in Syrian hamsters. *Brain Res.* **661**, 70–74.

Schneider, J. E., Lazzarini, S. J., Friedman, M. I., and Wade, G. N. (1988). Role of fatty acid oxidation in food intake and hunger motivation in Syrian hamsters. *Physiol. Behav.* **43**, 617–623.

Schneider, J. E., Friedenson, D. G., Hall, A., and Wade, G. N. (1993). Glucoprivation induces anestrus and lipoprivation may induce hibernation in Syrian hamsters. *Am. J. Physiol.* **264**, R573–R577.

Schneider, J. E., Finnerty, B. C., Swann, J. M., and Gabriel, J. M. (1995). Glucoprivic treatments that induce anestrus, but do not affect food intake, increase FOS-like immunoreactivity in the area postrema and nucleus of the solitary tract in Syrian hamsters. *Brain Res.* **698**, 107–113.

Schneider, J. E., Hall, A. J., and Wade, G. N. (1997a). Central vs. peripheral metabolic control of estrous cycles in Syrian hamsters. I. Lipoprivation. *Am. J. Physiol.* **272**, R400–R405.

Schneider, J. E., Goldman, M. D., Leo, N. A., and Rosen, M. E. (1997b). Central vs. peripheral metabolic control of estrous cycles in Syrian hamsters. II. Glucoprivation. *Am. J. Physiol.* **272**, R406–R412.

Schneider, J. E., Goldman, M. D., Tang, S., Bean, B., Ji, H., and Friedman, M. I. (1998). Leptin indirectly affects estrous cycles by increasing metabolic fuel oxidation. *Horm. Behav.* **33**, 217–228.

Schneider, J. E., Zhou, D., and Blum, R. M. (2000a). Leptin and metabolic control of reproduction. *Horm. Behav.* **37**, 306–326.

Schneider, J. E., Blum, R. M., and Wade, G. N. (2000b) Metabolic control of food intake and estrous cycles in Syrian hamsters: I. Plasma insulin and leptin. *Am. J. Physiol.* **278**, R476–R485.

Schreihofer, D. A., Amico, J. K. A., and Cameron, J. L. (1993). Reversal of fasting-induced suppression of luteinizing hormone (LH) secretion in male rhesus monkeys by intragastric nutrient infusion: Evidence for rapid stimulation of LH by nutritional signals. *Endocrinology (Baltimore)* **132**, 1890–1897.

Schultz, W. (1998). Predictive reward signal of dopamine neurons. *J. Neurophysiol.* **80**, 1–27.

Schultz, W., Tremblay, L., and Hollerman, J. R. (2000). Reward processing in primate orbitofrontal cortex and basal ganglia. *Cereb. Cortex* **10**, 272–283.

Schwartz, N. B. (1974). The role of FSH and LH and of their antibodies on follicle growth and on ovulation. *Biol. Reprod.* **10**, 236–272.

Schwartz, G. J. (2000). The role of gastrointestinal vagal afferents in the control of food intake: Current prospects. *Nutrition* **16**, 866–873.

Schwartz, M. W., Bergman, R. N., Kahn, S. E., Taborsky, G. J., Jr., Fisher, L. D., Sipols, A. J., Woods, S. C., Steil, G. M., and Porte, D., Jr. (1991). Evidence for entry of plasma insulin into cerebrospinal fluid through an intermediate compartment in dogs. Quantitative aspects and implications for transport. *J. Clin. Invest.* **88**, 1272–1281.

Schwartz, M. W., Baskin, D. G., Bukowski, T. R., Kuijper, J. L., Foster, D., Lasser, G., Prunkard, D. E., Porte, D. Jr., Woods, S. C., Seeley, R. J., and Weigle, D. S. (1996). Specificity of leptin action on elevated blood glucose levels and hypothalamic neuropeptide Y gene expression in ob/ob mice. *Diabetes* **45**, 531–535.

Schwartz, M. W., Ballman, M. F., and Woods, S. C. (1995). Hypothalamic response to starvation: Implications for the study of wasting disorders. *Am. J. Physiol.* **269**, R949–R957.

Schwartz, M. W., Seeley, R. J., Woods, S. C., Weigle, D. S., Campfield, L. A., Burn, P., and Baskin, D. G. (1997). Leptin increases hypothalamic proopiomelanocortin messenger-

RNA expression in the rostral arcuate nucleus. *Diabetes* **46**, 2119–2123.

Schwartz, M. W., Woods, S. C., Porte, D., Jr., Seeley, R. J., and Baskin, D. G. (2000). Central nervous system control of food intake. *Nature (London)* **404**, 661–671.

Scimonelli, T., Medina, F., Wilson, C., and Celis, M. E. (2000). Interaction of alpha-melanotropin (alpha-MSH) and nora-drenaline in the median eminence in the control of female sexual behavior. *Peptides* **21**, 219–223.

Sclafani, A., Aravich, P. F., and Landman, M. (1981). Vagotomy blocks hypothalamic hyperphagia in rats on a chow diet and sucrose solution, but not on a palatable mixed diet. *J. Comp. Physiol. Psychol.* **95**, 720–734.

Seeley, R. J., and Schwartz, M. W. (1999). Neuroendocrine regulation of food intake. *Acta Paediatr., Suppl.* **88**, 58–61.

Seeley, R. J., Grill, H. J., and Kaplan, J. M. (1994). Neurological dissociation of gastrointestinal and metabolic contributions to meal size control. *Behav. Neurosci.* **108**, 347–352.

Seeley, R. J., Payne, C. J., and Woodes, S. C. (1995). Neuropeptide Y fails to increase intraoral intake in rats. *Am. J. Physiol.* **268**, R423–R427.

Seeley, R. J., Van Dijk, G., Campfield, L. A., Smith, F. J., Burn, P., Nelligan, J. A., Bell, S. M., Baskin, D. G., Woods, S. C., and Schwartz, M. W. (1996). Intraventricular leptin reduces food intake and body weight of lean rats but not obese Zucker rats. *Horm. Metab. Res.* **28**, 664–668.

Semba, K. (2000). Multiple output pathways of the basal forebrain: Organization, chemical heterogeneity, and roles in vigilance. *Behav. Brain Res.* **115**, 117–141.

Sherin, J. E., Elmquist, J. K., Torrealba, F., and Saper, C. B. (1998). Innervation of histaminergic tuberomammillary neurons by GABAergic and galaninergic neurons in the ventrolateral preoptic nucleus of the rat. *J. Neurosci.* **18**, 4705–4721.

Shibala, H., and Bukowiecki, L. J. (1987). Regulatory alterations of daily energy expenditure induced by fasting or overfeeding in unrestrained rats. *J. Appl. Physiol.* **63**, 465–470.

Shimabukuro, M., Koyama, K., Chen, G., Wang, M. Y., Trieu, F., Lee, Y., Newgard, C. B., and Unger, R. H. (1997). Direct antidiabetic effect of leptin through triglyceride depletion of tissues. *Proc. Natl. Acad. Sci. U.S.A.* **94**, 4637–4641.

Shimada, M., Tritos, N. A., Lowel, B. B., Flier, J. S., and Maratos-Flier, E. (1998). Mice lacking melanin-concentrating hormone are hypophagic and lean. *Nature (London)* **396**, 670–674.

Shimada, S., Inagaki, S., Kibota, Y., Ogawa, N., Shibaski, T., and Takagi, H. (1989). Coexistence of peptides (corticotropin releasing factor/neurotensin and substance P/Somatostatin) in the bed nucleus of the stria terminalis and central amygdaloid nucleus of the rat. *Neuroscience* **30**, 377–383.

Shimizu, H., Shargill, N. S., and Bray, G. A. (1989). Adrenalectomy and response to corticosterone and MSH in the genetically obese yellow mouse. *Am. J. Physiol.* **256**, R494–R500.

Shimizu, H., Ohshima, K., Bray, G. A., Peterson, M., and Swerdloff, R. S. (1993). Adrenalectomy and castration in the genetically obese (*ob/ob*) mouse. *Obes. Res.* **1**, 377–383.

Shimomura, Y., Bray, G. A., and Lee, M. (1987). Adrenalectomy and steroid treatment in obese (ob/ob) and diabetic (*db/db*) mice. *Horm. Metab. Res.* **19**, 295–299.

Shughrue, P. J., Lane, M. V., and Merchenthaler, I. (1997). Comparative distribution of estrogen receptor alpha and -beta mRNA in the rat central nervous. *J. Comp. Neurol.* **388**, 507–525.

Siegel, L. I., and Wade, G. N. (1979). Insulin withdrawal impair sexual receptivity and retention of brain cell nuclear estrogen receptors in diabetic rats. *Neuroendocrinology* **29**, 200–206.

Sierra-Honigmann, M. R., Nath, A. K., Murkami, C., Garcia-Cardena, G., Papaetropoulos, A., Sessa, W. C., Madge, L. A., Schechner, S., Schwabb, M. B., Polverin, P. J., and Flores-Riveros, J. R. (1998). Biological action of leptin as an angiogenic factor. *Science* **281**, 1686–1689.

Silva, J. E. (1995). Thyroid hormone control of thermogenesis and energy balance. *Thyroid* **5**, 481–492.

Silverman, H. J., and Zucker, I. (1976). Absence of post-fast food compensation in the Golden hamster (*Mesocricetus auratus*). *Physio. Behav.* **17**, 271–285.

Simerly, R. B. (1998). Organization and regulation of sexually dimorphic neuroendocrine pathways. *Behav. Brain Res.* **92**, 195–203.

Simerly, R. B., and Swanson, L. W. (1987). The distribution of neurotransmitter-specific cells and fibers in the anteroventral periventricular nucleus: Implications for the control of gonadotropin secretion in the rat. *Brain Res.* **400**, 11–34.

Simerly, R. B., Gorski, R. A., and Swanson, L. W. (1986). Neurotransmitter specificity of cells and fibers in the medial preoptic nucleus: An innumohistochemical study in the rat. *J. Comp. Neurol.* **246**, 343–363.

Simerly, R. B., McCall, L. D., and Watson, S. J. (1988). Distribution of opioid peptides in the preoptic region: Immunohistochemical evidence for a steroid-sensitive enkephalin sexual dimorphism. *J. Comp. Neurol.* **276**, 442–459.

Simerly, R. B., Chang, C., Muramatsu, M., and Swanson, L. W. (1990). Distribution of androgen and estrogen receptor mRNA-containing cells in the rat brain: An in situ hybridization study. *J. Comp. Neurol.* **294**, 76–95.

Simonian, S. X., Spratt, D. P., and Herbison, A. E. (1999). Identification and characterization of estrogen receptor alpha-containing neurons projecting to the vicinity of the gonadotropin-releasing hormone perikarya in the rostral preoptic area of the rat. *J. Comp. Neurol.* **411**, 346–358.

Sirinathsinghji, D. J. (1985). Modulation of lordosis behavior in the female rat by corticotropin releasing factor, beta-endorphin and gonadotropin releasing hormone in the mesencephalic central gray. *Brain Res.* **336**, 45–55.

Sirinathsinghji, D. J. (1986). Regulation of lordosis behavior in the femal rat by corticotropin-releasing factor, beta-endorphin/corticotropin and luteinizing hormone-releasing hormone neuronal systems in the medial preoptic area. *Brain Res.* **375**, 49–56.

Sirinathsinghji, D. J. (1987). Inhibitory influence of corticotropin-releasing factor on components of sexual behavior in the male rat. *Brain Res.* **407**, 1885–1888.

Sirinathsinghji, D. J., Rees, L. H., Rivier, J., and Vale, W. (1983). Corticotropin-releaing factor is a potenti inhibitor of sexual receptivity in the female rat. *Nature (London)* **305**, 232–235.

Skofitsch, G., Insel, T. R., and Jacobwitz, D. M. (1985). Binding sites for corticotropin releasing factor in sensory areas of the rat hindbrain and spinal cord. *Brain Res. Bull.* **15**, 519–522.

Skynner, M. J., Sim, J. A., and Herbison, A. E. (1999). Detection of estrogen receptor alpha and beta messenger ribonucleic acids in adult gonadotropin-releasing hormone neurons. *Endocrinology (Baltimore)* **140**, 5195–5201.

Smedh, U., Hakansson, M. L., Meister, B., and UvnasMoberg, K. (1998). Leptin injected into the fourth ventricle inhibits gastric emptying . *NeuroReport* **9**, 297–301.

Smith, G. P. (1999). Introduction to the reviews on peptides and the control of food intake and body weight. *Neuropeptides* **33**, 323–328.

Smith, G. P. (2000). The controls of eating: A shift from nutritional homeostasis to behavioral neuroscience. *Nutrition* **16**, 814–820.

Smith, J. C. (2000). Microstructure of the rat's intake of food, sucrose and saccharin in 24-hour tests. *Neurosi. Biobehav. Rev.* **24**, 199–212.

Smith, M. S. (1993). Lactation alters neuropeptide-Y and proopiomelanocortin gene expression in the arcuate nucleus of the rat. *Endocrinology (Baltimore)* **133**, 1258–1265.

Spector, A. C. (2000). Linking gustatory neurobiology to behavior in vertebrates. *Neurosci. Biobehav. Rev.* **24**, 391–416.

Spiegelman, B. M., and Flier, J. S. (1996). Adipogenesis and obesity—Rounding out the big picture. *Cell (Cambridge, Mass.)* **87**, 377–389.

Spina, M., Merlo-Pick, E., and Chan, R. K. W. (1996). Appetite-suppressing effects of urocortin, a novel CRF-related neuropeptide. *Science* **273**, 1561–1564.

Sprangers, S. A., and Piacsek, B. E. (1997). Chronic underfeeding increases the positive feedback efficacy of estrogen on gonadotropin secretion. *Proc. Soc. Exp. Biol. Med.* **216**, 398–403.

Standaert, D. G., and Saper, C. B. (1988). Origin of the atriopeptin-like immunoreactive innervation of the paraventricular nucleus of the hypothalamus. *J. Neurosci.* **8**, 1940–1950.

Stanley, B. G., and Leibowitz, S. F. (1985). Neuropeptide Y injected in the paraventricular hypothalamus: A powerful stimulant of feeding behavior. *Proc. Natl. Acad. Sci. U.S.A.* **82**, 3940–3943.

Stanley, B. G., Kyrkouli, S. E., Lampert, S., and Leibowitz, S. F. (1986). Neuropeptide Y chronically injected into the hypothalamus: A powerful neurochemical inducer of hyperphagia and obesity. *Peptides (N.Y.)* **7**, 1189–1192.

Stanley, B. G., Lanthier, D., Chin, A. S., and Leibowitz, S. F. (1989). Suppression of neuropeptide Y-elicited eating by adrenalectomy or hypophysectomy: Reversal with corticosterone. *Brain Res.* **501**, 32–36.

Stanley, B. G., Magdalin, W., Seirafi, A., Thomas, W. J., and Leibowitz, S. F. (1993). The perifornical area—the major focus of (a) patchy distributed hypothalamic neuropeptide Y-sensitive feeding system(s). *Brain Res.* **604**, 304–317.

Stellar, E. (1954). The physiology of motivation. *Psychol. Rev.* **61**, 5–22.

Stellar, E. (1994). The physiology of motivation. *Psychol. Rev.* **101**, 301–311.

Stephan, F. K. (1983). Circadian rhythm dissociation induced by periodic feeding in rats with suprachiasmatic lesions. *Behav. Brain Res.* **7**, 81–98.

Stephan, F. K. (1997). Calories affect zeitgeber properties of the feeding entrained circadian oscillator. *Physiol. Behav.* **62**, 995–1002.

Stephan, F. K., and Davidon, A. J. (1998). Glucose, but not fat, phase shifts the feeding-entrained circadian clock. *Physiol. Behav.* **65**, 277–288.

Stephan, F. K., Swann, J. M., and Sisk, C. L. (1979). Anticipation of 24-hr feeding schedules in rats with lesions of the suprachiasmatic nucleus. *Behav. Neural Biol.* **25**, 346–363.

Stephens, T. W., Basinski, M., Bristow, P. K., Bue-Valleskey, J. M., Burgett, S. G., Craft, L., Hale, J., Hoffmann, J., Hsiung, H. M., Kriauciunas, A. *et al.* (1995). The role of neuropeptide Y in the antiobesity action of the obese gene product. *Nature* **377**, 530–532.

Strack, A. M., Sawyer, W. B., Hughes, J. H., Platt, K. B., and Loewy, A. D. (1989). A general pattern of CNS innervation of the sympathetic outflow demonstrated by transneuronal pseudorabies viral infections. *Brain Res.* **491**, 156–162.

Strack, A. M., Sebastian, R. J., Schwartz, M. W., and Dallman, M. F. (1995). Glucocorticoids and insulin: Reciprocal signals for energy balance. *Am. J. Physiol.* **268**, R142–R149.

Stratford, T. R., and Kelley, A. E. (1997). GABA in the nucleus accumbens shell participates in the central regulation of feeding behavior. *J. Neurosci.* **17**, 4434–4440.

Stratford, T. R., Kelley, A. E., and Simansky, K. J. (1999). Blockade of GABAA receptors in the medial ventral pallidum elicits feeding in satiated rats. *Brain Res.* **825**, 199–203.

Stricker, E. M. (1983). Brain neurochemistry and control of food intake. *In* Handbook of Behavioral Neurobiology (E. Satinoff and P. Teitelbaum, eds.), Vol. 6, pp. 329–366. Plenum Press, New York.

Stricker, E. M. (1990). Homeostatic origins of ingestive behavior. *In* "Handbook of Behavioral Neurobiology" (E. M. Stricker, ed.), Vol. 10, pp. 45–60. Plenum Press, New York.

Strobel, A., Issad, T., Camoin, L., Ozata, M., and Strosberg, A. D. (1998). A leptin missense mutation associated with hypogonadism and morbid obesity. *Nat. Genet.* **18**, 213–215.

Suga, A., Hirano, T., Kageyama, H., Osaka, T., Namba, Y., Tsuji, M., Miura, M., Adachi, M., and Inoue, S. (2000). Effects of fructose and glucose on plasma leptin, insulin and insulin resistance in leave and VMH-lesioned obese rats. *Am. J. Physiol.* **278**, E677–E683.

Swanson, L. W. (1987). The hypothalamus. *In* "Handbook of Chemical Neuroanatomy" (A. Bjorklund, T. Hökfelt, and L. W. Swanson, eds.), Vol. 5, pp. 1–124. Elsevier, Amsterdam.

Swanson, L. W. (1992). Spatiotemporal patterns of transcription factor gene expression accompanying the development and plasticity of cell phenotypes in the neuroendocrine system. *Prog. Brain Res.* **92**, 91–113.

Swanson, L. W. (2000). Cerebral hemisphere regulation of motivated behavor. *Brain Res.* **886**, 113–164.

Swanson, L. W., and Kuypers, H. G. (1980). The paraventricular nucleus of the hypothalamus: Cytoarchitectonic subdivisions and organization of projections to the pituitary, dorsal vagal complex, and spinal cord as demonstrated by retrograde fluorescence double-labeling methods. *J. Comp. Neurol.* **94**, 555–570.

Swanson, L. W., and Mogenson, G. J. (1981). Neural mechanisms for the functional coupling of autonomic, endocrine and somatomotor responses in adaptive behavior. *Brain Res.* **228**, 1–34.

Swanson, L. W., and Petrovich, G. D. (1998). What is the amygdala? *Trends Neurosci.* **21**, 323–331.

Swanson, R. A., and Choi, D. W. (1993). Glial glycogen stores affect neuronal survival during glucose deprivation *in vitro*. *J. Cereb. Blood Flow Metab.* **13**, 162–169.

Swanson, R. A., Morton, M. M., Sagar, S. M., and Sharp, F. R. (1992). Sensory stimulation induces local cerebral glycogenolysis: Demonstration by autoradiography. *Neuroscience* **51**, 451–461.

Tanaka, T., Nagatani, S., Bucholtz, D. C., Ohkura, S., Tsukamura, H., Maeda, K., and Foster, D. L. (2000). Central action of insulin regulates pulsatile luteinizing hormone secretion in the diabetic sheep model. *Biol. Reprod.* **62**, 1256–1261.

Tartaglia, L., Dembski, M., Weng, X., Deng, N., Culpepper, J. K., Devos, R., Richards, G., and Campfield, L. (1995). Identification and expression cloning of a leptin receptor, OB-R. *Cell (Cambridge, Mass.)* **83**, 1263–1271.

Taube, J. S. (1998). Head direction cells and the neurophysiological basis for a sense of direction. *Prog. Neurobiol.* **55**, 225–256.

Teirmaa, T., Luukkaa, V., Rouru, J., Koulu, M., and Huupponen, R. (1998). Correlation between circulating leptin and luteinizing hormone during the menstrual cycle in normal-weight women. *Eur. J. Endocrinol.* **139**, 190–194.

Teitelbaum, P. (1955). Sensory control of hypothalamic hyperphagia. *J. Comp. Physiol. Psychol.* **48**, 156–163.

Teitelbaum, P., and Epstein, A. (1962). The lateral hypothalamic syndrome: Recovery of feeding and drinking after lateral hypothalamic lesions. *Psychol. Rev.* **69**, 74–90.

Teitelbaum, P., and Stellar, E. (1954). Recovery from failure to eat produced by hypothalamic lesions. *Science* **120**, 894–895.

Teitelbaum, P., and Stricker, E. (1994). Compound complementarities in the study of motivated behavior. *Psychol. Rev.* **101**, 312–317.

Teixeira, V. L., Antunes-Rodrigues, J., and Migliorini, R. H. (1973). Evidence for centers in the central nervous system that selectively regulate fat mobilization in the rat. *J. Lipid Res.* **14**, 672–677.

Temple, J. L., and Rissman, (2000a). Acute re-feeding reverses food restriction-induced hypothalamic-pituitary gonadal axis deficits. *Biol. Reprod.* **63**, 1721–1726.

Temple, J. L., and Rissman, E. F. (2000b). Brief re-feeding restores reproductive readiness in food restricted female mush shrews (*Suncus murinus*). *Horm. Behav.* **38**, 21–28.

Terasawa, E., Keen, K. L., Mogi, K., and Claude, P. (1999). Pulsatile release of luteinizing hormone releasing hormone (LHRH) in cultured LHRH neurons derived from the embryonic olfactory placode of the rhesus monkey. *Endocrinology (Baltimore)* **140**, 1432–1441.

Terry, R. B., Stefanick, M. L., Haskell, W. L., and Wood, P. D. (1991). Contributions of regional adipose tissue depots to plasma lipoprotein concentrations in overweight men and women: Possible protective effects of thigh fat. *Metab., Clin. Exp.* **40**, 733–740.

Thompson, M. P. (1996). Meal-feeding specifically induces obese mRNA expression. *Biochem. Biophys. Res. Commun.* **224**, 332–337.

Thompson, R. H., and Swanson, L. W. (1998). Organization of inputs to the dorsomedial nucleus of the hypothalamus: A reexamination with Fluorogold and PHAL in the rat. *Brain Res. Rev.* **27**, 89–118.

Thompson, R. H., Canteras, N. S., and Swanson, L. W. (1996). Organization of projections from the dorsomedial nucleus of the hypothalamus—a PHA-L study in the rat. *J. Comp. Neurol.* **376**, 143–173.

Thong, F. S., and Graham, T. E., (1999). Leptin and reproduction: Is it a critical link between adipose tissue, nutrition, and reproduction? *Can. J. Appl. Physiol.* **24**, 317–336.

Tinbergen, N. (1951). "The Study of Instinct." Oxford University Press. Oxford.

Toates, F. (1986). "Motivational Systems." Cambridge University Press, Cambridge, UK.

Toates, F. (1994). Comparing motivational systems—an incentive motivation perspective. *In* "Appetite: Neural and Behavioral Bases" (C. R. Legg and D. A. Booth, eds.). Oxford University Press, New York.

Tordoff, M. G., Geiselman, P. J., Grijalva, C. V., Kiefer, S. W., and Novin, D. (1982). Amygdaloid lesions impair ingestive responses to 2-deoxy-D-glucose but not insulin. *Am. J. Physiol.* **242**, R129–R135.

Tordoff, M. G., Rafka, R., Dinovi, M. J., and Friedman, M. I. (1988). 2,5-Anhydro-D-mannitol: A frutose analogue that increases food intake in rats. *Am. J. Physiol.* **254**, R150–R153.

Tordoff, M. G., Rawson, M. I., and Friedman, M. I. (1991). 2,5-Anhydro-D-mannitol acts in liver to initiate feeding. *Am. J. Physiol.* **261**, R283–R288.

Torii, M., Kubo, K., and Sasaki, T. (1995). Naloxone and initial estrogen action to induce lordosis in ovariectomized rats: The effect of a cut between the septum and preoptic area. *Neurosci. Lett.* **195**, 167–170.

Torii, M., Kubo, K., and Sasaki, T. (1999). Facilitatory and inhibitory effects of beta-endorphin on lordosis in female rats: Relation to time of administration. *Horm. Behav.* **35**, 271–278.

Trayhurn, P., and Rayner, D. V. (1996). Hormones and the ob gene product (leptin) in the control of energy balance. *Biochem. Soc. Trans.* **24**, 565–570.

Trayhurn, P., Duncan, J. S., and Rayner, D. V. (1995). Research communication acute cold-induced suppression of ob (obese) gene expression in white adipose tissue of mice: Mediation by the sympathetic system. *Biochem. J.* **311**, 729–733.

Tremblay, L., and Schultz, W. (1999). Relative reward preference in primate orbitofrontal cortex. *Nature (London)* **398**, 704–708.

Tritos, N. A., and Maratos-Flier, E. (1999). Two important systems in energy homeostasis: Melanocortins and melanin-concentrating hormone. *Neuropeptides* **33**, 339–349.

Tsukamura, H., Tsukamura, S., Maekawa, F., Moriyama, R., Reyes, B. A., Sakai, T., Niwa, Y., and Foster, D. L. (2000). Peripheral or central administration of motilin suppresses LH release in female rats: A novel role for motilin. *J. Neuroendocrinol.* **12**, 403–408.

Tsukamura, S., Tsukamura, H., Foster, D. L., and Maeda, K.-I. (1999). Effect of corticotropin- releasing hormone antagonist on oestrogen-dependent glucoprivic suppression of luteinizing hormone secretion in female rats. *J. Neuroendocrinol.* **11**, 101–105.

Turton, M. D., O'Shea, D., Gunn, I., Beak, S. A., Edwards, C. M., Meeran, K., Choi, S. J., Taylor, G. M., Heath, M. M., Lambert, P. D., Wilding, J. P., Smith, D. M., Ghatei, M. A., Herbert, J., and Bloom, S. R. (1996). A role for glucagons-like peptide-1 in the central regulation of feeding. *Nature (London)* **379**, 69–72.

Tutwiler, G. F., Brentzel, H. J., and Kiorpes, T. C. (1985). Inhibition of mitochondrial carnitine palmitoyl transferase A in vivo with methyl 2-tetradecylglycidate (methyl palmoxirate) and its relationship to ketonemia and glycemia. *Proc. Soc. Exp. Biol. Med.* **178**, 288–296.

Ueyama, T., Krout, K. E., Nguyen, X. V., Kollert, A., Mettenleiter, T. C., and Loewy, A. D. (1999). Suprachiasmatic nucleus: A central autonomic clock. *Nat. Neurosci.* **2**, 1051–1053.

Unger, J. W., Livingston, J. N., and Moss, A. M. (1991a). Insulin receptors in the central nervous system: Localization, signalling mechanisms and functional aspects. *Prog. Neurobiol.* **36**, 343–362.

Unger, J. W., Moss, A. M., and Livingston, J. N. (1991b). Immunohistochemical localization of insulin receptors and phosphotyrosine n the brainstem of the adult rat. *Neuroscience* **42**, 853–861.

Unger, R. H. (2000). Leptin physiology: A second look. *Regul Pept.* **92**, 87–95.

Unger, R. H., Zhou, Y. T., and Orei, L. (1999). Regulation of fatty acid homeostasis in cells: Novel role of leptin. *Proc. Natl. Acad. Sci. U.S.A.* **96**, 2327–2332.

Urban, J. H., Das, I., and Levine, J. E. (1996). Steroid modulation of neuropeptide Y-induced luteinizing hormone releasing hormone release for median eminence fragments from male rats. *Neuroendocrinology* **63**, 112–119.

van der Beek, E. M., Horvath, T. L., Wiegant, V. M., Van den Hurk, R., and Buijs, R. M. (1997). Evidence for a direct neuronal pathway from the suprachiasmatic nucleus to the gonadotropin-releasing hormone system: Combined tracing and light and electron microscopic immunocytochemical studies. *J. Comp. Neurol.* **384**, 569–579.

Van Dijk, G., and Thiele, T. E. (1999). Glucagon-like peptide-1 (7–36) amide: A central regulator of satiety and interoceptive stress. *Neuropeptides* **33**, 406–414.

Van Dijk, G., Scheurink, G. A., Ritter, S., and Steffens, A. (1995). Glucose homeostasis and sympathoadrenal activity in mercaptoacetate-treated rats. *Physiol. Behav.* **57**, 759–764.

Van Dijk, G., Seeley, R. J., Thiele, T. E., Friedman, M. I., Ji, H., Wilkinson, C. W., Burn, P., Campfield, L. A., Tenenbaum, R., Baskin, D., Woods, S. C., and Schwartz, M. W. (1999). Metabolic, gastrointestinal, and CNS neuropeptide effects of brain leptin administration in the rat. *Am. J. Physiol.* **276**, R1425–1433.

VanItallie, T. B., and Kissileff, H. R. (1990). Human obesity: A problem in body energy economics. *In* "Handbook of Behavioral Neurobiology" (E. M. Stricker, ed.), Vol. 10, pp. 207–240. Plenum Press, New York.

VanNess, J. M., Casto, R. M., and Overton, J. M. (1997). Antihypertensive effects of food-intake restriction in aortic coarctation hypertension. *J. Hypertens.* **15**, 1253–1562.

Vasselli, J. R., Chu, K., Kissileff, H. R., and Maggio, C. A. (1998). Resistance to the feeding and body weight inhibitory effects of peripherally-injected leptin (rMuLep) in Zucker obese and lean rats. *Soc. Neurosci. Abst.* **28**, 449.

Viau, V., Chu, A., Soriano, L., and Dallman, M. F. (1999). Independent and overlapping effects of corticosterone and testosterone on corticotropin-releasing hormone and arginine vasopressin mRNA expression in the paraventricular nucleus of the hypothalamus and stress-induced adrenocorticotropic hormone release. *J. Neurosci.* **19**, 6684–6693.

Vidal-Puig, A., Solanes, G., Grujic, D., Flier, J. S., and Lowell, B. B. (1997). UCP3: An uncoupling protein homologue expressed preferentially and abundantly in skeletal muscle and brown adipose tissue. *Biochem. Biophys. Res. Commun.* **235**, 79–82.

Wade, G. N. (1972). Gonadal hormones and behavioral regulation of body weight. *Physiol. Behav.* **8**, 523–534.

Wade, G. N., and Schneider, J. E. (1992). Metabolic fuels and reproduction in female mammals. *Neurosci. Biobehav. Rev.* **16**, 235–272.

Wade, G. N., Jennings, G., and Trayhurn, P. (1986). Energy balance and brown adipose tissue thermogenesis during pregnancy in Syrian hamsters. *Am. J. Physiol.* **250**, R845–R850.

Wade, G. N., Schneider, J. E., and Friedman, M. I. (1991). Insulin-induced anestrus in Syrian hamsters. *Am. J. Physiol.* **260**, R148–R152.

Wade, G. N., Schneider, J. E., and Li, H.-Y. (1996). Control of fertility by metabolic cues. *Am. J. Physiol.* **270**, E1–E19.

Wade, G. N., Lempicki, R. L., Panicker, A. K., Frisbee, R. M., and Blaustein, J. D. (1997). Leptin facilitates and inhibits sexual behavior in female hamsters. *Am. J. Physiol.* **272**, R1354–R1358.

Walczewska, A., Yu, W. H., Karanth, S., and McCann, S. M. (1999). Estrogen and leptin have differential effects on FSH and LH release in female rats. *Proc. Soc. Exp. Biol. Med.* **222**, 170–177.

Walker, M. W. (1999). NPY and feeding: Finding a role for the Y5 receptor subtype. *In* "Pennington Center Nutrition Series Vol. 9, Nutrition, Genetics, and Obesity" (G. A. Bray and D. H. Ryan, eds.). Louisiana State University Press, Baton Rouge, LA.

Walker, C. D., Toufexis, D. J., Abizaid, A., Junien, J. L., and Woodside, B. (2000). Neuropeptide Y Y5 receptor stimulation lengthens the duration of lactational diestrus: Possibly through inhibition of luteinizing hormone release. *Soc. Neurosci. Abstr.,* p. 413.

Wallen, K., and Schneider, J. E., eds. (2000). "Reproduction in Context: Social and Environmental Influences on Reproduction." MIT Press, Cambridge, MA.

Wang, J., Liu, R., Hawkins, M., Barzilai, N., and Rossetti, L. (1998). A nutrient-sensing pathway regulates leptin gene expression in muscle and fat. *Nature (London)* **393**, 684–688.

Wang, J.-L., Chinookoswong, N., Yin, S., and Shi, Z.-Q. (2000). Calorigenic actions of leptin are additive to, but not dependent on, those of thyroid hormones. *Am. J. Phys.* **279**, E1278–E1285.

Wang, M. Y., Lee, Y., and Unger, R. H. (1999). Novel form of lipolysis induced by leptin. *J. Biol. Chem.* **274**, 1741–1744.

Wang, T. L., Hartzell, D. L., Flatt, W. P., Martin, R. J., and Baile, C. A. (1998). Responses of lean and obese Zucker rats to centrally administered leptin. *Physiol. Behav.* **65**, 333–341.

Wang, T. L., Hartzell, D. L., Rose, B. S., Flatt, W. P., Hulsey, M. G., Menon, N. K., Makula, R. A., and Baile, C. A. (1999). Metabolic responses to intracerebroventricular leptin and restricted feeding. *Physiol. Behav.* **65**, 839–848.

Wang, Y., Kuropatwinski, K. K., White, D. W., Hawley, T. S., Hawley, R. G., Tartaglia, L. A., and Baumann, H. (1997). Leptin receptor action in hepatic cells. *J. Biol. Chem.* **272**, 16216–16223.

Ward, D. T., Hammond, T. G., and Harris, H. W. (1999). Modulation of vasopressin-elicited water transport by trafficking of awuaporin2-containing vesicles. *Annu. Rev. Physiol.* **61**, 683–697.

Watanobe, H., and Suda, T. (1999). A detailed study of the role of sex steroid milieu in determining plasma leptin concentrations in adult male and female rats. *Biochem. Biophys. Res. Commun.* **259**, 56–59.

Watanobe, H., Nasushita, R., Sasaki, S., and Suda, T. (1998). Evidence that a fast, rate-sensitive negative feedback effect of corticosterone is not a principal mechanism underlying the indomethacin inhibition of interleukin—1B-induced adrenocorticotropin secretion in the rat. *Cytokine* **10**, 377–381.

Watanobe, H., Schioth, H. B., Wikberg, J. E., and Suda, T. (1999a). The melanocortin 4 receptor mediates leptin stimulation of luteinizing hormone and prolactin surges in steroid-primed ovariectomized rats. *Biochem. Biophys. Res. Commun.* **257**, 860–864.

Watanobe, H., Suda, T., Wikberg, J. E. S., and Schioth, H. B. (1999b). Evidence that physiological levels of circulating leptin exert a stimulatory effect on luteinizing hormone and pro-

lactin surges in rats. *Biochem. Biophys. Res. Commun.* **263**, 162–165.

Watson, R. E., Jr., Langub, M. C., Jr., Engle, M. G., and Maley, B. E. (1995). Estrogen-receptive neurons in the anteroventral periventricular nucleus are synaptic targets of the suprachiasmatic nucleus and peri suprachiasmatic region. *Brain Res.* **689**, 254–264.

Watts, A. G. (1991). The efferent projections of the suprachiasmatic nucleus. Anatomical insights into the control of circadian rhythms. *In* "The Suprachiasmatic Nucleus: The Mind's Clock" (D. Klein, R. Y. Moore, and S. M. Reppert, eds.), pp. 75–104. Oxford University Press, New York.

Watts, A. G. (1996). The impact of physiological stimulation on the expression of corticotropin-releasing hormone and other neuropeptide genes. *Front. Neuroendocrinol.* **17**, 281–326.

Watts, A. G. (1999). Dehydration-associated anorexia: Development and rapid reversal. *Physiol. Behav.* **65**, 871–878.

Watts, A. G. (2000). Understanding the neural control of ingestive behaviors: Helping to separate cause from effect with dehydration-associated anorexia. *Horm. Behav.* **37**, 261–283.

Watts, A. G. (2002). Motivation, neural substrates. *In* "The Handbook of Brain Theory and Neural Networks" (M. Arbib, ed.). MIT Press, Cambridge, MA (in press).

Watts, A. G. (2001b). Neuropeptides and the integration of motor responses to dehydration. *Annu. Rev. Neurosci.* **24**, 357–384.

Watts, A. G., and Sanchez-Watts, G. (1995a). A cell-specific role for the adrenal gland in regulating CRH mRNA levels in rat hypothalamic neurosecretory neurons after cellular dehydration. *Brain Res.* **687**, 63–70.

Watts, A. G., and Sanchez-Watts, G. (1995b). Region-specific regulation of neuropeptide mRNAs in rat limbic forebrain neurons by aldosterone and corticosterone. *J. Physiol. (London)* **484**, 721–736.

Watts, A. G., Kelly, A. B., and Sanchez-Watts, G. (1995). Neuropeptides and thirst: The temporal response of corticotropin-releasing hormone and neurotensin/neuromedin N gene expression in rat limbic forebrain neurons to drinking hypertonic saline. *Behav. Neurosci.* **109**, 1146–1157.

Watts, A. G., Sanchez-Watts, G., and Kelly, A. B. (1999). Distinct and similar patterns of neuropeptide gene expression are present in rat hypothalamus following dehydration-induced anorexia or paired food restriction. *J. Neurosci.* **19**, 6111–6121.

Weatherford, S. C., and Ritter, S. (1988). Lesion of vagal afferent terminals impairs glucagons- induced suppression of food intake. *Physiol. Behav.* **43**, 645–650.

Weber, R. V., Buckley, M. C., Fried, S. K., and Kral, J. G. (2000). Subcutaneous lipectomy causes a metabolic syndrome in hamsters. *Am. J. Physiol.* **279**, R936–R943.

Weigle, D. S., Bukowski, T., Foster D., Holderman, S., Kramer, J., Lasser, G., Lofton-Day, C., Prunkard, D., Raymond, C., and Kuijper, J. (1995). Recombinant ob protein reduces feeding and body weight in the ob/ob mouse. *J. Clin. Invest.* **96**, 2065–2070.

Weigle, D. S., Hutson, A. M., Kramer, J. M., Fallon, M. G., Lehner, J. M., Lok, S., and Kuijper, J. L. (1998). Leptin does not fully account for the satiety activity of adipose tissue-conditioned medium. *Am. J. Physiol.* **275**, R976–985.

Weingarten, H. P. (1983). Conditioned cues elicit feeding in sated rats: A role for learning in meal initiation. *Science* **220**, 431–433.

Wender, R., Brown, A. M., Fern, R., Swanson, R. A., Farrell, K., and Ransom, B. R. (2000). Astrocytic glycogen influences axon function and survival during glucose deprivation in central white matter. *J. Neurosci.* **20**, 6804–6810.

Wetsel, W. C., Valenca, M. M., Merchenthaler, I., Liposits, Z., Lopez, F. J., Weiner, R. I., Mellon, P. L., and Negro-Vilar, A. (1992). Intrinsic pulsatile secretory activity of immortalized luteinizing hormone releasing hormone-secreting neurons. *Proc. Natl. Acad. Sci. U.S.A.* **89**, 4149–4153.

Whitley, N. C., Barb, C. R., Kraeling, R. R., Barrett, J. B., Rampacek, G. B., Carroll, J. A., and Keisler, D. H. (2000). Feed intake and serum GH, LH and cortisol in gilts after intracerebroventricular or intravenous injection of urocortin. Domestic animal. *Endocrinology (Baltimore)* **19**, 209–221.

Whitnall, M. H. (1993). Regulation of the hypothalamic corticotropin-releasing hormone neurosecretory system. *Prog. Neurobiol.* **40**, 573–629.

Wiedemann, K., Jahn, H., and Kellner, M. (2000). Effects of natriuretic peptides upon hypothalamo pituitary-adrenocortical system activity and anxiety behaviour. *Exp. Clin. Endocrinol. Diabetes.* **108**, 5–13.

Wiegand, S. J., and Terasawa, E. (1982). Discrete lesions reveal functional heterogeneity of suprachiasmatic structures in regulation of gonadotropin secretion in the female rat. *Neuroendocrinology* **34**, 395–404.

Wiegand, S. J., Terasawa, E., Bridson, W. E., and Goy, R. W. (1980). Effects of discrete lesions of preoptic and suprachiasmatic structures in the female rat. Alterations in the feedback regulation of gonadotropin secretion. *Neuroendocrinology* **31**, 147–157.

Wieland, H. A., Engel, W., Eberlein, W., Rudolf, K., and Doods, H. N. (1998). Subtype selectivity of the novel nonpeptide neuropeptide Y Y1 receptor antagonist BIBO 3304 and its effect on feeding in rodents. *Br. J. Pharmacol.* **125**, 549–555.

Wiesner, G., Vaz, M., Collier, G., Seals, D., Kaye, D., Jennings, G., Lambert, G., Wilkinson, D., and Ester, M. (1999). Leptin is released from the human brain: Influence of adiposity and gender. *J. Clin. Endocrinol. Metab.* **84**, 2270–2274.

Wiesner, J. B., and Moss, R. L. (1986a). Suppression of receptive and proceptive behavior in ovariectomized, estrogen-progesterone-primed rats by intraventricular beta-endorphin: Studies of behavioral specificity. *Neuroendocrinology* **43**, 57–62.

Wiesner, J. B., and Moss, R. L. (1986b). Behavioral specificity of beta-endorphin suppression of sexual behavior: Differential receptor antagonism. *Pharmacol. Biochem. Behav.* **24**, 1235–1239.

Williams, D. L., Kaplan, J. M., and Grill, H. J. (2000). The role of the dorsal vagal complex and the vagus nerve in feeding effects of melanocortin-3/4 receptor stimulation. *Endocrinology (Baltimore)* **141**, 1332–1337.

Williams, N. I., Lancas, M. J., and Cameron, J. L. (1996). Stimulation of luteinizing hormone secretion by food intake: Evidence against a role for insulin. *Endocrinology (Baltimore)* **137**, 2565–2571.

Williams, T. D., Chambers, J. B., May, O. L., Henderson, R. P., Rashotte, M. E., and Overton, J. M. (2000). Concurrent reductions in blood pressure and metabolic rate during fasting in the unrestrained SHR. *Am. J. Physiol.* **278**, R255–R262.

Willie, J. T., Chemelli, R. M., Sinton, C. M., and Yanagisawa, M. (2001). To eat or sleep? The role of orexin in coordination of feeding and arousal. *Annu. Rev. Neurosci.* **24**, 429–458.

Wilson, B. D., Bagnol, D., Kaelin, C. B., Ollmann, M. M., Gantz, I., Watson, S. J., and Barsh, G. S. (1999). Physiological and anatomical circuitry between Agouti-related protein and leptin signaling. *Endocrinology (Baltimore)* **140**, 2387–2397.

Wingfield, J. C., Jacobs, J. D., Tramontin, A. D., Perfito, N., Meddle, S., Maney, D. L., and Soma, K. (2000). Toward an ecological basis of hormone-behavior interactions in reproduction of birds. *In* "Reproduction in Context: Social and Environmental Influences on Reproduction" (K. Wallen and J. E. Schneider, eds.), pp. 85–158. MIT Press, Cambridge, MA.

Winn, P. (1995). The lateral hypothalamus and motivated behavior: An old syndrome reassessed and a new perspective gained. *Curr. Dir. Psychol. Sci.* **4**, 182–187.

Wood, A. D., and Bartness, T. J. (1996a). Caloric density affects food hoarding and intake by Siberian hamsters. *Physiol. Behav.* **59**, 897–903.

Wood, A. D., and Bartness, T. J. (1996b). Food deprivation-induced increases in hoarding by Siberian hamsters are not photoperiod-dependent. *Physiol. Behav.* **60**, 1137–1145.

Wood, A. D., and Bartness, T. J. (1997). Partial lipectomy, but not PVN lesions, increases food hoarding by Siberian hamsters. *Am. J. Physiol.* **272**, R783–R792.

Woods, S. C., Lotter, E. C., McKay, L. D., and Porte, D., Jr. (1979). Chronic intracerebroventricular infusion of insulin reduces food intake and body weight of baboons. *Nature (London)* **282**, 503–505.

Woods, S. C., Seeley, R. J., Porte, D., Jr., and Schwartz, M. W. (1998). Signals that regulate food intake and energy homeostasis. *Science* **280**, 1378–1383.

Woodside, B., Abizaid, A., and Jafferali, S. (1998). Acute food deprivation lengthens lactational infertility in rats and this effect is reduced by systemic leptin administration. *Am. J. Physiol.* **274**, R16553–R1658.

Woodside, B., Abizaid, A., and Walker, C. (2000). Changes in leptin levels during lactation: Implications for lactational hyperphagia and anovulation. *Horm. Behav.* **37**, 353–365.

Woodward, C. J., Hervey, G. R., Oakey, R. E., and Whitaker, E. M. (1991). The effects of fasting on plasma corticosterone kinetics in rats. *Br. J. Nutr.* **66**, 117–127.

Wright, D. E., and Jennes, L. (1993). Origin of noradrenergic projections to GnRH perikarya-containing areas in the medial septum-diagonal band and preoptic area. *Brain Res.* **621**, 272–278.

Xiao, E., and Ferin, M. (1988). The inhibitory action of corticotropin-releasing hormone on gonadotropin secretion in the ovariectomized rhesus monkey is not mediated by adrenocorticotropic hormone. *Biol. Reprod.* **38**, 763–767.

Xiao, E., Luckhaus, J., Niemann, W., and Ferin, M. (1989). Acute inhibition of gonadotropin secretion by corticotropin-releasing hormone in the primate: Are the adrenal glands involved? *Endocrinology (Baltimore)* **124**, 1632–1637.

Xu, B., Pu, S., Kalra, P. S., Hyde, J. F., Crowley, W. R., and Kalra, S. P. (1996). An interactive physiological role of neuropeptide Y and galanin in pulsatile pituitary luteinizing hormone secretion. *Endocrinology* **137**, 5297–5302.

Yamamoto, H., Nagai, K., and Nakagawa, H. (1985). Lesions involving the suprachiasmatic nucleus eliminate the glucagons response to intracranial injection of 2-deoxy-D-glucose. *Endocrinology (Baltimore)* **117**, 468–473.

Yoneda, N., Saito, S., Kimura, M., Yamada, N., Iida, M., Murakami, T., Irahara, M., Shima, K., and Aono, T. (1998). The influence of ovariectomy on ob gene expression in rats. *Horm. Metab. Res.* **30**, 263–265.

Young, J. B., and Landsberg, L. (1977). Suppression of sympathetic nervous sytem during fasting. *Science* **196**, 1473–1475.

Young, R. C., Gibbs, J., Antin, J., and Smith, G. P. (1974). Absence of satiety during sham feeding in the rat. *J. Comp. Phsyiol. Psychol.* **87**, 795–800.

Yu, W. H., and McCann, S. M. (1991). Feedback of follicle-stimulating hormone to inhibit luteinizing hormone and stimulate follicle-stimulating hormone release in ovariectomized rats. *Neuroendocrinology* **53**, 453–459.

Yu, W. H., Kimur, M., Walczewska, A., Karanth, S., and McCann, S. M. (1997a). Role of leptin in hypothalamic-pituitary function. *Proc. Natl. Acad. Sci. U.S.A.* **94**, 1023–1028.

Yu, W. H., Walczewska, A., Karanth, S., and McCann, S. M. (1997b). Nitric oxide mediates leptin-induced luteinizing hormone-releasing hormone (LHRH) and LHRH and leptin-induced LH release from the pituitary gland. *Endocrinology (Baltimore)* **138**, 5055–5058.

Yukimura, Y., Bray, G. A., and Wolfsen, A. R. (1978). Some effects of adrenalectomy in the fatty rat. *Endocrinology (Baltimore)* **103**, 1924–1928.

Yura, S., Ogawa, Y., Sagawa, N., Masuzaki, H., Itoh, H., Ebihara, K., Aizawa-Abe, M., Fuji, S., and Nakao, K. (2000). Accelerated puberty and late-onset hypothalamic hypogonadism in female transgenic skinny mice overexpressing leptin. *J. Clin. Invest.* **105**, 749–755.

Zamorano, P. L., Mahesh, V. B., De Sevilla, L. M., Chorich, L. P., Bhat, G. W., and Brann, D. W. (1997). Expression and localization of the leptin receptor in endocrine and neuroendocrine tissues of the rat. *Neuroendocrinology* **65**, 223–228.

Zarjevski, N., Cusin, I., Vettor, R., Rohner-Jeanrenaud, F., and Jeanrenaud, B. (1993). Chronic intracerebroventricular neuropeptide-Y administration to normal rats mimics hormonal and metabolic changes of obesity. *Endocrinology (Baltimore)* **133**, 1753–1758.

Zhang, Y., Proenca, R., Maffei, M., Barone, M., Leopold, L., and Friedman, J. M. (1994). Positional cloning of the mouse Obese gene and its human homologue. *Nature (London)* **372**, 425–431.

Zhou, D., and Schneider, J. E. (1999). Fourth ventricular leptin prevents fasting-induced anestrus in Syrian hamsters. *Soc. Neurosci. Abstr.,* p. 414.

Zhou, D., and Schneider, J. E. (2000). Impairment of the sympathoadrenal response to glucoprivation is not necessary for anestrus induced by glucoprivation. *Soc. Neurosci. Abstr.,* p. 215.

Zhou, Y. T., Shimabukuro, M., Koyama, K., Lee, Y., Wang, M. Y., Trieu, F., Newgard, C. B., and Unger, R. H. (1997). Induction by leptin of uncoupling protein-2 and enzymes of fatty acid oxidation. *Proc. Natl. Acad. Sci. U.S.A.* **94**, 6386–6390.

Zhu, Y. S., Yen, P. M., Chin, W. W., and Pfaff, D. W. (1996). Estrogen and thyroid hormone interaction on regulation of gene expression. *Proc. Natl. Acad. Sci. U.S.A.* **93**, 12587–12592.

Zhu, Y. S., Dellovade, T., and Pfaff, D. W. (1997). Gender-specific induction of pituitary RNA by estrogen and its modification by thyroid hormone. *J. Neuroendocrinol.* **9**, 395–403.

8

Neuroendocrinology of Body Fluid Homeostasis

Steven J. Fluharty

Department of Animal Biology and Pharmacology
Institute of Neurological Sciences
University of Pennsylvania
Schools of Medicine and Veterinary Medicine
Philadelphia, Pennsylvania 19104

I. INTRODUCTION

The maintenance of body fluid homeostasis is a continual challenge for mammals. Since evolving from sea-dwelling creatures millions of years ago, the subsequent commitment to terrestrial life required the establishment of mechanisms to procure water and electrolytes from the environment and to regulate the composition and distribution of fluids in the organism. Because the fluid matrix of the body supports the circulation and metabolic processes in all cells, physiological functions depend on the proper volume and electrolyte content of the intracellular and extracellular fluids. However, water and electrolyte loss is continual in mammals, owing to renal excretion of soluble waste products, respiratory loss, and thermoregulatory needs, as well as more severe challenges such as diarrhea, vomiting, hemorrhage, lactation in females, and prolonged deprivation of water. In order to defend body fluid homeostasis in the face of so many challenges, elaborate neural and endocrine controls have evolved. Their dynamic interplay, in both minimizing water loss and maximizing gain through thirst and mineral appetites, is the subject of this chapter. Before proceeding, however, it is first necessary to review the distribution and com-position of body fluids in mammals and the physiological variables that influence this delicate balance (cf. Guyton, 1991).

II. PHYSIOLOGY OF BODY FLUID HOMEOSTASIS

A. Distribution and Composition of Body Fluids

Although the old adage is "You are what you eat," in fact "You are what you drink" would be a more accurate statement. In the typical adult, approximately 60% of total body mass reflects the water content of the body. This percentage is somewhat lower and more variable in females and obese individuals because the water composition of fat is the lowest of any tissue. The majority of total body water, approximately two-thirds, is found in cells and is referred to as the intracellular fluid (ICF). The ICF contains potassium and bicarbonate as well as glucose and several amino acids. The presence of these ions and other molecules in the ICF results in an osmolality of approximately 300 mOsm. The generation of this osmotic pressure is the key to understanding the dynamic balance between the ICF and the other main compartment of body water, the extracellular fluid (ECF).

The ECF accounts for the remaining one-third of total body water. Actually, the ECF is further subdivided into the fluid in the circulation (blood plasma) and the surrounding cells (but not contained in blood vessels), referred to as the interstitial fluid (ISF). The plasma is the smallest compartment, accounting for 7–8% of total body water, whereas the ISF represents 26%; together the plasma and the ISF add up to the 33% that makes up the ECF. As was true for the ICF, the ECF also contains several solutes, principally the ions sodium and chloride. One of the unique properties of water as the principal solvent of the ECF is that a significant majority of sodium and chloride dissolved in the ECF remains as separable ions and does not exclusively form electroneutral NaCl complexes. This insures that these ions, especially sodium, carry electrochemical charges when transported across cell membranes, an event which is the foundation of the action potential and neural excitability.

B. Forces Governing Fluid Exchange—Osmotic and Starling Equilibrium

Although the volume and composition of the ICF and ECF differ, the total number of solutes dissolved per unit volume of water is actually equal in the two compartments. Hence, we refer to the ICF and ECF as being in osmotic equilibrium with an optimal value of 300 mOsm; most cellular reactions are dependent on the maintenance of this equilibrium. But like any equilibrium, this condition is subject to sudden and substantial changes. In this regard, the ECF is the interface between the cells and the external environment. Thus, any perturbations of osmotic equilibrium initially affect the ECF, and this change in their immediate aqueous environment subsequently forces the cells to adapt. For instance, an increase in the solute concentration of the ECF, as occurs during the ingestion of a meal (particularly one high in salt), or following the preferential loss of water from the ECF, usually due to respiratory and thermoregulatory factors (i.e., sweating), increases the osmotic pressure of the ECF. In order to restore osmotic equilibrium, albeit at a new higher osmolality, water flows from the cells into the ECF because the

movement of ions across the cell membranes is generally restricted. The net result of this shift in water distribution is to increase the ICF osmolality and dilute that of the ECF until both are once again equal. However, the movement of water from the ICF creates a condition known as cellular dehydration. As discussed in more detail later, cellular dehydration is a powerful stimulus for renal conservation of water and the arousal of thirst, and these responses are ultimately responsible for restoring body fluid osmolality to normal (Gilman, 1937; Verney, 1946, 1947; Wolf, 1950, 1958).

The two main compartments of the ECF, the plasma and ISF, are also in a dynamic equilibrium wherein two opposing forces govern their exchange of fluids (Starling, 1896). One of these forces is a specialized form of osmotic pressure known as oncotic pressure. Oncotic pressure develops because the ISF is actually a protein-free filtrate of the plasma; thus, the exclusive presence of proteins in the plasma represents a concentration-dependent force that tends to attract and retain fluids and electrolytes in the plasma and away from the ISF. The second important factor that contributes to fluid exchange between the plasma and ISF of the ECF is the variable hydrostatic pressure that exists on the arterial and venous sides of all capillary beds. On the arterial side, the hydrostatic pressure is at its highest due to its relative proximity to the heart. However, as the distance between the heart and the capillary bed increases, the hydrostatic pressure progressively dampens and reaches its lowest point on the venous side of the circulation. In contrast, the ISF has negligible hydrostatic pressure throughout most capillary beds.

The balance of oncotic and hydrostatic forces, referred to as Starling equilibrium, governs fluid exchange between the plasma and the ISF. More specifically, on the arterial side of the circulation, the hydrostatic pressure exceeds the oncotic pressure and water (and ions) are forced out of the plasma and into the surrounding ISF. On the venous side, however, the relative strength of these opposing forces is reversed because the constancy of the oncotic pressure now exceeds the dampened hydrostatic pressure, leading to a net movement of fluid back into the plasma. This dynamic interplay of hydrostatic (outward) and oncotic (inward) forces insures that tissues are adequately perfused as nutrient-laden plasma bathes cells on the arterial side and then is returned to the circulation for replenishment on the venous side. This arrangement also permits the larger ISF to act as a reservoir for the plasma should its volume decline. This condition, known as hypovolemia, occurs whenever there is an absolute reduction in blood volume most commonly associated with hemorrhage. Because there is no change in the osmolality of the ECF, cells do not provide the much needed water and extracellular dehydration results. On the other hand, the hypovolemia also can produce a drop in blood pressure that lowers hydrostatic pressure, allowing more fluid to enter from the ISF and more of it to remain in the circulation. However, this shift in Starling equilibrium is not sufficient to fully repair hypovolemia and therefore, like cellular dehydration, extracellular depletion is a stimulus for renal conservation of fluids and thirst (Fitzsimons, 1961; Gauer and Henry, 1963; Stricker, 1966). Unlike cellular dehydration, hypovolemia is also a stimulus for salt appetite because the blood loss is isoosmotic and sodium is the major electrolyte of the ECF (Fitzsimons, 1979; Stricker, 1971, 1981; Stricker and Wolf, 1966).

C. Summary

Osmotic and Starling equilibrium both illustrate an important point. When perturbations in body fluid homeostasis occur, transient shifts in the compartmentalization of body water provide temporary and incomplete relief—a complete restoration of homeostasis requires the ingestion of additional fluids as well as continued renal conservation. These complementary physiological and behavioral responses are controlled by neural and endocrine mechanisms. We now turn our attention to a discussion of these regulatory systems.

III. OSMOTIC REGULATION AND HOMEOSTASIS

A. Vasopressin and Osmoregulation

The osmotic equilibrium that exists between the ICF and ECF is one of the most tightly regulated variables in physiology. In most healthy individuals, deviations as little as 1–2% from the optimal value of 300 mOsm elicit compensatory mechanisms. Such extreme sensitivity is critical because many physiological processes are influenced by osmolality, most notably

neural excitability. Of principal importance in this regard is the release of the arginine vasopressin (AVP), a neurohypophysial hormone that acts on the most distal regions of the nephron to promote water reabsorption. This hormone-induced antidiuresis, when coupled with sodium excretion and thirst, restores body fluid osmolality to normal.

AVP is one of two peptide hormones that are synthesized in the hypothalamus and subsequently transported to and released from the posterior pituitary or neurohypophysis. Both AVP and the other hormone, oxytocin, contain nine amino acids that differ in only two locations. Indeed, they appear to have evolved from a common ancestral precursor, vasotocin, that is still found in some nonmammalian vertebrates (Fitzsimons, 1979). The important role of the pituitary gland in body fluid homeostasis was first noted in the early 1900s when it was observed that exogenous administration of a pituitary extract decreased urine flow. Within 10 years this extract became one of the principal treatments for diabetes insipidus, a disease associated with excessive diuresis, in most cases resulting from substantial damage to hypothalamic projections to the neurohypophysis that significantly impairs or abolishes the production of AVP (Verbalis *et al.*, 1984); less commonly the disease results from genetic mutations in the AVP gene (Robertson, 1995; Schmale and Richter, 1984) or defects in AVP receptors that mediate its renal action (Fugiwara *et al.*, 1995). Although it would take some 50 years, the discovery of AVP as the antidiuretic hormone released from the pituitary provided an effective replacement therapy for the clinical management of most patients with diabetes insipidus.

AVP and oxytocin are synthesized in specialized magnocellular neurons found in two hypothalamic nuclei, the supraoptic (SON) and paraventricular (PVN) (cf. Robertson, 1986). These magnocellular neurons possess long axons that project deep into the posterior pituitary, where they synapse on capillaries. The cytology of these cells is among the most remarkable of those found in any other region of the nervous system, with numerous structural features that facilitate massive hormone release. There are approximately 20,000 magnocellular neurons in the hypothalamus, and they give rise to over 5 million nerve terminals in the posterior pituitary gland that are densely packed with secretory granules (over 98% of the terminal surface area) that store more than a week's supply of the hormone. AVP is synthesized in the soma of these hypothalamic neurons and transported down the axons associated with a family of carrier molecules known as neurophysins. When neural activity is increased in these magnocellular neurons, the synthesis and transport of AVP is facilitated and the peptide is released from the bulbous axon terminals into the pituitary and systemic circulation. This is a classic example of neurosecretion in which the hypothalamus controls the level of AVP in the plasma and its subsequent ability to promote renal conservation of water (Stricker and Verbalis, 1999).

Although AVP release is responsive to both intracellular and extracellular dehydration, the first demonstration of the mechanism(s) that couple its release to perturbations in body fluid homeostasis was provided by E. B. Verney's classic studies of osmotic control of AVP (Verney, 1946, 1947; Jewell and Verney, 1957). In these landmark investigations, Verney used anesthetized dogs that had been preloaded with an intragastric gavage of water. In a normally hydrated dog, this water load produces a pronounced water diuresis. Verney then examined the ability of intravenous or intracarotid infusion of various hyperosmotic solutes to reduce urine flow. This physiological measure served as Verney's bioassay for AVP release because he conducted nearly all of his experimentation prior to the development of radioimmunoassay for plasma AVP levels. Verney discovered that intracarotid infusions of hyperosmotic solutions that were excluded from cells (e.g., NaCl, sucrose, and mannitol) produced an antidiuresis. In contrast, solutes such as urea that raised ECF osmolality but could equilibrate across cell membranes did not alter urine flow. Hence, an increase in effective osmotic pressure of the ECF, not simply osmolality, with the resultant cellular dehydration was viewed as the adequate stimulus for AVP release. Moreover, intracarotid infusions of solutes were significantly more effective than intravenous administration, indicating a central site of action, and these antidiuretic effects were abolished by pituitary damage, which is consistent with stimulation of AVP release. In subsequent years, following the development of a radioimmunoassay for AVP, all of Verney's original findings were confirmed and it was determined that AVP release had the expected sensitivity to hyperosmolality (1–2% threshold) and that increases in plasma AVP were linearly related to increased ECF osmolality over a very broad range (Dunn *et al.,* 1973; Robertson, 1986).

After completing his experimentation, Verney and his colleagues proceeded to develop a hypothetical model through which changes in plasma osmolality could regulate the pituitary release of AVP. It was in this context that the power of his deductive reasoning was most apparent. Verney proposed the existence of specialized receptor cells in the forebrain, referred to as osmoreceptors, that functioned as interoceptive detectors of plasma osmolality. When ECF osmolality is elevated, these cells lose water to the surrounding ISF and shrink. This decrease in cell volume subsequently activates vasopressinergic neurons, which release the peptide into the circulation. More recent anatomical and electrophysiological research has helped confirm and extend Verney's original hypothesis. The osmoreceptors appear to be innervated by inhibitory interneurons that project to the vasopressinergic neurons in the SON and PVN of the hypothalamus (Verbalis, 1993). These interneurons appear to function as mechanoreceptors whose dendritic processes wrap around the osmoreceptors. The firing rate of the mechanoreceptors is sensitive to osmoreceptor cell volume and inversely proportional to plasma osmolality. More specifically, when plasma osmolality and osmoreceptor cell volume are normal, sustained neural activity in the mechanoreceptors inhibits vasopressinergic neurons, whereas when osmolality increases and the osmoreceptors shrink, the firing rate of the mechanoreceptors declines, the vasopressinergic neurons are released from tonic inhibition, and the peptide hormone is released. Aside from this postulated mechanism of tonic inhibition, there is also evidence of numerous synaptic inputs on magnocellular neurons that regulate AVP release primarily by excitation (Verbalis, 1993).

Although the central transduction mechanism that relates plasma osmolality to vasopressin release from magnocellular neurons is fairly well understood, there is continuing controversy surrounding the location(s) of osmoreceptors and their associated mechanoreceptors. Initially there appeared to be several hypothalamic and extrahypothalamic nuclei that possess neurons whose firing rates were altered by changes in plasma osmolality or, in some cases, the sodium concentration of the ECF, a major determinant of plasma osmolality (c.f. McKinley *et al.,* 1978; Weiss and Almli,

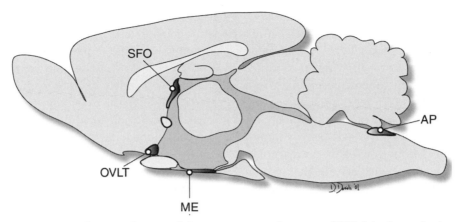

FIGURE 1 Schematic diagram of the circumventricular organs (CVOs) in the rat brain, depicted in the saggital plane. AP, area postrema; ME, median eminence; OVLT, organum vasculosum of the lamina termanilis; SFO, subfornical organ.

1975). However, other research has focused on a family of structures known as the circumventricular organs (CVOs; see Fig. 1). The CVOs are located around the circumference of the cerebral ventricles, exposing their ependymal surface to cerebrospinal fluid. They are highly vascularized structures with fenesterated capillaries, resulting in a very weak blood–brain barrier. This latter quality has resulted in the suggestion that they function as windows through which events in the plasma can alter brain function (McKinley *et al.,* 1990), as would be required of candidate osmoreceptors. In Verney's original experiments (1946, 1947), he noted that urea was not an adequate stimulus for AVP release. At first glance, this observation was viewed as consistent with Verney's hypothesis of effective osmotic pressure and the resultant cellular dehydration as the critical event; urea crosses cell membranes and equilibrates in the ICF and ECF without necessitating a cellular efflux of water. However, urea does not cross the blood–brain barrier. Consequently, when it is administered into the circulation, water flows from the cerebral ISF into the hyperosmotic plasma. This selective loss of water increases the osmolality of the cerebral ISF that, in turn, draws water out of cells in the brain. Thus, osmoreceptors that reside in the blood–brain barrier would dehydrate and, this event should subsequently activate AVP release. Because urea is such a poor stimulus for AVP release, it has been suggested that osmoreceptors may reside in CVOs, where the weak blood–brain barrier would allow urea to cross the epithelial membrane

of the capillaries, enter the surrounding ISF, and then move into cells without producing any cellular dehydration (Thrasher *et al.,* 1982b). Among the CVOs, the organum vasculosum of the lamina termanilis (OVLT) has best fulfilled the criteria for an osmoreceptor, including direct projects from intrinsic cells in the OVLT to the magnocellular neurons of the SON and PVN (Oldfield *et al.,* 1994; Verbalis *et al.,* 1995) that could serve as the postulated mechanoreceptors; changes in neuronal firing and expression of the immediate early gene c-fos during hyperosmolality (Oldfield *et al.,* 1994; Verbalis *et al.,* 1995); and the observation that lesions that include the OVLT and surrounding tissue substantially impair osmotic control of vasopressin release, resulting in a syndrome of chronic hypernatremia (Buggy and Johnson, 1977; Johnson and Buggy, 1978; Thrasher *et al.,* 1982b). It is important to emphasize, however, that osmoreceptors may be more widely distributed outside the OVLT and within adjacent tissue in the anterior wall of the third ventricle, including other CVOs such as the subfornical organ (SFO) and in the median preotic (MPO) nucleus, and that some magnocellular neurons are intrinsically sensitive to hyperosmolality.

Once released into the circulation, AVP travels to the kidney where it acts on AVP receptors located on the basal membrane of the peritubular epithelial cells that line the late distal tubule and collecting duct regions of the nephron. Under conditions of normal osmotic equilibrium, this region is impermeable to water, which results in the continuing dilution of luminal fluid and its excretion as urine. However, when AVP acts on its membranous receptors, it dramatically reverses the permeability of this region to water, allowing for its rapid reabsorption. This shift in membrane permeability begins with occupancy of an AVP receptor subtype, the V_2 receptor, which is a member of the superfamily of G-protein-coupled receptors (GPCR). These receptors are coupled to GTP-binding proteins wherein agonist stimulation initiates a biochemical cascade that results in the formation of intracellular second messengers. In the case of AVP, the V_2 receptor is coupled to Gs and the subsequent activation of adenylyl cyclase, resulting in the generation of cAMP in the peritubular epithelial cells. This second messenger increases the catalytic activity of protein kinase A, which phosphorylates structural and apical membrane proteins, allowing water to flow from the lumen of the nephron across the peritubular epithelial cells to be reabsorbed by the surrounding capillary network. Although AVP is required for this process to begin, the force that actually attracts the water is the extreme hypertonicity of the interstitum-surrounding medullary nephrons (cf. Guyton, 1991), and the reabsorptive capacity of the capillaries is due to their high intrinsic oncotic pressure (i.e., Starling equilibrium; see Section II.B).

B. Natriuretic Hormones

Although it is widely recognized that the antidiuretic activity of AVP is the most important hormonal regulator of renal function during hyperosmolality, it has been proposed that natriuretic hormones could also facilitate this restorative process. A postulated role for hormone-dependent natriuresis is particularly attractive since the reduction in urine volume induced by AVP necessarily limits the ability of the kidney to excrete excess solutes. In this regard, oxytocin the other neurohypophysial peptide hormone, has been shown to increase sodium excretion by interfering with several ion transport mechanisms throughout the nephron. As in the case of AVP, this action is dependent on the occupancy of an oxytocin receptor that is coupled to GTP-binding proteins, resulting in the generation of inositol triphosphate (InsP3) and the subsequent mobilization of intracellular calcium, as well as a reduction of cAMP levels (Flanagan-Cato and Fluharty, 1995). The central

mechanism mediating oxytocin release from hypothalamic magnocellular neurons during hyperosmolality is presumably similar to that proposed for AVP (Stricker and Verbalis, 1986), although oxytocin release is responsive to a variety of other stimuli as well (Verbalis, 1990). Although the physiological significance of these renal actions of oxytocin during hyperosmolarity has been questioned, the kidney is as sensitive to the natriuretic effect of oxytocin as it is to the antidiuretic effects of AVP (Verbalis *et al.,* 1991).

Another hormone that can regulate renal sodium excretion is atrial natriuretic peptide (ANP). It had long been postulated that the atria of the heart were the source of a humoral substance that could stimulate natriuresis. It was referred to as a third factor to distinguish it from two well-established regulators of sodium excretion, glomerular filtration rate and the adrenal steroid aldosterone (DeBold *et al.,* 1981; De Wardner *et al.,* 1961). In the 1980s this atrial factor was identified as ANP. ANP is a large polypeptide that contains a 33-amino-acid C-terminal fragment that possesses most of the native hormone's biological activity (Cantin and Genest, 1985; Geller *et al.,* 1984; Misono *et al.,* 1984). It is synthesized and released from cardiac myocytes (Cantin *et al.,* 1980), although it is also found in the brain (Jacobowitz *et al.,* 1984; Tanaka *et al.,* 1984) along with receptors for the peptide (Quirion *et al.,* 1984). Although the principal stimulus for ANP release appears to be volume expansion, there is also evidence indicating that hyperosmolality can elicit its release from myocytes (cf. Cantin and Genest, 1985). The major physiological effects of ANP include vasodilation, antagonism of the renin-angiotensin system, inhibition of aldosterone actions, and natriuretic properties (Chartier *et al.,* 1984; Kleinert *et al.,* 1984).

Although the direct renal actions of ANP that promote sodium excretion are not fully understood, it appears to involve receptor-mediated activation of a particulate guanylyl cyclase and the subsequent generation of the intracellular second messenger, cGMP, in peritubular epithelial cells in the proximal and distal tubular regions of the nephron (Hamet *et al.,* 1984). Similar to AVP, this elevation in cyclic nucleotide production alters membrane permeability, although in this case the change impedes sodium reabsorption from the lumen across the epithelial cells and into the surrounding capillaries. Activation of ANP receptors is also associated with the production of nitric oxide, a freely diffusible molecule with powerful vasodilatory effects previously known as endothelial-derived relaxing factor (Winquist *et al.*, 1984). Thus, the natriuretic response to ANP is augmented by increased renal hemodynamics, enhanced glomerular filtration rate, and blockade of aldosterone-induced sodium retention (see Section IV.C). However, although the natriuretic action of ANP is substantial, its constellation of cardiovascular and renal effects, as well as the relative potency of stimuli that release this peptide, suggest that it may play a more important role in volume regulation than as a compensatory response to hyperosmolality (see Section IV.D).

C. Contribution of Thirst to Osmoregulation

The importance of thirst to osmoregulation was first recognized when it was discovered that renal adaptations (i.e, antidiuresis and natriuresis) took entirely too long to correct even minor bouts of hyperosmolality. In striking similarity to Verney's (1946, 1947) pioneering work on AVP release, Gilman and colleagues (Gilman, 1937) demonstrated that ingestion of water greatly facilitates the restoration of osmotic homeostasis and discovered that the signal for the initiation of drinking was cellular dehydration, as had been noted previously for AVP release (Wolf, 1950, 1958; see Section III.A). However, most early investigations of thirst were dominated by Cannon's (1918) persuasive view that peripheral signals associated with dehydration, such as dryness of the oropharyngeal region, were the critical interoceptive stimuli that aroused this motivated behavior. This viewpoint significantly delayed identification and hampered the analysis of neural and endocrine stimuli that are integrated in the brain. Attention shifted to the central nervous system when Andersson reported that the intracerebroventricular (ICV) infusion of hypertonic solutions rapidly aroused thirst in conscious goats (Andersson, 1953, 1978). His work also suggested that such integrative mechanisms resided in the basal forebrain, perhaps in periventricular tissue bathed by the solutes that had been administered into the cerebral ventricles.

The contemporary setting for research on the neurological mechanisms of osmoregulatory thirst has relied heavily on the success of the strategies employed during investigations of neurohypophysial function. Thus, it was imagined that osmoreceptors might serve as interoceptive sensors that activate neural circuits to arouse thirst in response to hyperosmolality. In one of the first studies designed to localize the osmoreceptors for thirst, it was found that large lesions of the basal hypothalamus anterior to the optic chiasm attenuated drinking induced by systemic hypertonic sodium chloride, but not the thirst induced by hypovolemia (Blass, 1968). The specificity of this lesion-induced deficit for osmoregulatory thirst was essential; no previous lesions in any area of the forebrain had produced a singular deficit but had instead impaired all drinking behavior; this result was not consistent with the selective loss of osmoreceptors but instead a more generalized behavioral deficit. The most noteworthy example of these more global behavioral deficits was observed following large bilateral lesions of the lateral hypothalamus. Initially, this area was thought to contain critical neural centers for both hunger and thirst (Stellar, 1954). Consistent with this view, lesions of this area produced aphagia and adipsia (Teitelbaum and Epstein, 1962). However, subsequent analysis of these lesioned animals revealed that these deficiencies of ingestive behavior were due to severe sensorimotor impairments that compromised all goal-directed behavior, presumably due in part to damage of ascending dopaminergic neurons (cf. Ungerstedt, 1974; Stricker, 1976; Stricker and Zigmond, 1976).

The initial lesions that attenuated osmoregulatory thirst were quite large and it required the use of electrophysiological techniques to more precisely identify circumscribed areas in the preoptic region of the hypothalamus that might represent the neural circuitry that regulates this behavior. In this regard, several laboratories reported the presence of osmosensitive neurons in a much smaller, lateral area of the preoptic zone in both rats and rabbits (Peck and Novin, 1971). As interest continued to focus on this region, Blass and Epstein (1971) completed a series of experiments that appeared to unequivocally establish the presence of osmoreceptors for thirst in the lateral preoptic area (LPO) of rats. These experiments were elegantly designed and thorough in their behavioral analysis and, although their conclusions have been challenged, there is little doubt that their work established one of the benchmarks for the proper analysis of the neural substrates of any motivated behavior.

The landmark work of Blass and Epstein (1971) began with a replication of the earlier studies by demonstrating that lesions in a much smaller more lateral region of the preoptic area (LPO) produced the same selective attenuation of osmotic but not volemic thirst, as had been observed previously following much larger lesions. Much more than a lesion study, however, these experiments also included intracranial injections into the LPO. In one series of experiments, they demonstrated that direct injection of hypertonic solutions into the LPO elicited a rapid and robust thirst response despite the fact that the cellular dehydration was limited to the brain regions immediately under the tip of the guide cannula. The results of these experiments established that cellular dehydration limited to the LPO, and perhaps immediately adjacent tissue, was sufficient to arouse thirst. These cannulae were then use for a second series of experiments whose results complemented those obtained with selective dehydration of the LPO. In these studies, Blass and Epstein demonstrated that selective rehydration of the LPO during infusions of water significantly reduced the thirst elicited by systemic administration of hypertonic saline. The implications of these findings are far reaching—even though putative osmoreceptors located throughout the CNS and periphery, such as hepatic sensors (Baertschi and Vallet, 1981; Sawchenko and Friedman, 1979), are active during systemic cellular dehydration, those in the LPO must be necessary for behavioral expression because when they are quiescent due to rehydration with water the thirst is inhibited. In order to demonstrate that the water infusions did not generally impair ingestive behavior, they demonstrated that drinking in response to exogenous renin was unaffected (see Section IV.E). Collectively, this comprehensive analysis of the LPO involving the use of both lesions and direct intracranial injections not only suggested the presence of osmoreceptors in this brain region, but also appeared to assign them a primary, if not exclusive, role in the interoceptive control of osmotic thirst.

Although it initially appeared that the LPO established and fulfilled all of the criteria for behaviorally relevant osmoreceptors, several experiments conducted over the next few years began to challenge the exclusivity of this brain region for osmoregulatory thirst. The first serious challenge arose from a reinvestigation of the effects of LPO lesions on thirst (Coburn and Stricker, 1978). As would be required of any credible reevaluation of previously published work, their research began by replicating the earlier finding that LPO lesions abolished drinking in response to very high doses of intraperitoneal (IP) hypertonic saline (i.e. 2 ml 2-M NaCl) during a 2-hour behavioral test. However, in many lesioned animals it was observed that the animals increased their water intake much later, usually during the overnight hours, in a delayed effort to behaviorally compensate for the earlier cellular dehydration. These observations were reminiscent of those reported after other types of hypothalamic damage in which the severity of the homeostatic imbalance (e.g., cellular dehydration) could produce profound sensorimotor impairments in brain-damaged animals that prohibited the expression of organized behavior during short-term tests; once the sensorimotor deficits had abated, however, the lesioned animals exhibited some goal-directed behavior, albeit delayed (Stricker *et al.*, 1979). Applying the same reasoning to LPO-lesioned animals, Coburn and Stricker (1978) found that these rats reliably responded to hyperosmotic challenges if they were administered in a fashion that produced less sudden and severe homeostatic imbalances, for instance, by slow intravenous infusion or by increasing the sodium content of the diet. Moreover, the drinking response elicited by a more severe hyperosmotic stimuli was always greater if the lesioned animals were permitted a longer time to respond to the challenge; neurologically intact animals rarely exhibited these delayed behavioral responses. The major implication of these findings, and of some that had been reported previously (Rowland, 1976), was to seriously question the necessity of osmoreceptors in the LPO for the arousal of thirst, clearly, if animals could respond to a variety of osmotic challenges even after destruction of the LPO, some other population(s) of osmoreceptors must be activated.

It is probably fair to say that the initial lesion studies of the LPO were the foundation on which the osmoreceptor theory for thirst was constructed. Because the validity of the interpretation was seriously challenged, the results of other experiments involving intracranial injections were subjected to closer scrutiny and eventual reinterpretation. For instance, although it is true that selective dehydration of the LPO and surrounding tissue does elicit thirst responses, the amount of water consumed is never as large as that produced by more widespread systemic dehydration or even ICV infusions of hyperosmotic solutes. Moreover, rehydration of the LPO reduces drinking in response to systemic dehydration but never eliminates it. Neither of these interpretations is consistent with the exclusive localization of osmoreceptors for thirst in the LPO; if this localization of function were true then equivalent hyperosmotic activation of the LPO should mimic thirst induced by peripheral manipulations and replenishment of their cellular water should completely inhibit thirst. Instead, the partial efficacy of dehydration and rehydration of the LPO led investigators to propose alternative locations for the osmoreceptors of thirst.

The original conception of osmoreceptors for thirst was derived from the success of experiments investigating the osmotic control of neurohypophysial function (see Section III.A). It is not surprising, then, that the search for alternative osmoreceptors was greatly facilitated by previous studies that had identified sites that regulate AVP release. In this regard, the relative ineffectiveness of urea in releasing AVP was pivotal. Although urea can equilibrate across cell membranes and will not produce osmotic withdraw of water when in the immediate interstitial fluid, it does not cross the blood–brain barrier and will dehydrate the brain when urea levels rise in the vasculature. This property led to the proposal of osmoreceptors in areas that lack a blood–brain barrier, and this was confirmed with the subsequent identification of such neurons in the CVOs (see Fig. 1 and Section III.A). Urea is also a very poor dipsogen despite the fact that dehydration of putative osmoreceptors residing in areas that possess a blood–brain barrier, such as the LPO, should provide a sufficient stimulus for thirst. Alternatively, if osmoreceptors for thirst, like their counterparts for AVP release, were located in CVOs, then the ineffectiveness of urea is understandable—these regions would not be experiencing any change in effective osmotic pressure (cf. Ramsay and Thrasher, 1990). Subsequent research that focused on the CVOs proved very profitable. The combination of lesion studies with iontophoretic application of very small volumes of osmotically active solutes identified osmosensitive neurons regulating thirst in these highly vascularized structures (cf. Oldfield, 1991). In some structures, such as the OVLT,

osmoreceptors for thirst and AVP release were colocalized (Thrasher *et al.*, 1982b), although in general those regulating thirst appeared to be less circumscribed and more distributed along the entire dorsal–ventral continuum of the anterior wall of the third ventricle (Oldfield *et al.*, 1994), including additional structures such as the SFO (Hosutt *et al.*, 1981) and MPO, both of which are reciprocally connected to the OVLT. Collectively, these anterior CVOs are ideally positioned to monitor events in the ECF, especially the plasma, and are presumably innervated by mechanoreceptive neurons that activate descending pathways controlling the appetitive phase of thirst.

Although several lines of converging evidence have shifted attention away from the LPO and onto a postulated role for the CVOs, many of the lessons learned from the research on the LPO are applicable to any study that attempts to link a given brain structure to the control of motivated behavior. In this regard, it is likely that the early lesions that appeared so promising suffered from at least two confounding variables. First, the size of these lesions was such that they probably directly encroached on the anterior wall of the third ventricle or, alternatively, damaged efferent projections from the CVOs in this region to other hypothalamic sites and brain-stem structures necessary for the arousal of osmoregulatory thirst (Miselis, 1981). Second, as the work of Coburn and Stricker (1978) suggested, these lesions may also have damaged ascending projections coursing throughout the hypothalamus known to be important in sensorimotor integration, this damage creating a susceptibility to severe homeostatic stress (i.e., extreme hyperosmotic stimuli) that resulted in gross behavioral impairments in brief tests. The experiments involving direct intracranial injections were also beset with technical and interpretational difficulties indicative of the times. For instance, the volume of injected solutions was relatively large and no control experiments were conducted to ascertain the distance the fluid may have diffused beyond the intended LPO site. This is particularly worrisome when injections are made in close proximity to the ventricles because if the injecta enters the CSF, it is rapidly transported throughout the ventricular system allowing for ependymal activation of CVOs such as the OVLT (Johnson and Epstein, 1975; see Section IV.C). Indeed, this dilution of the hyperosmotic solution by the cerebospinal fluid (CSF) might well explain why water intake elicited by LPO injections is never as large as that evoked by direct dehydration of parenchymal tissue in the anteroventral third-ventricle region or systemic injections of hypertonic saline. The necessity for solutions to diffuse from the LPO to some other more distant site could also explain the inability of water to completely inhibit thirst aroused by systemic dehydration. Equipped with the benefit of hindsight, it is not difficult to discern how the apparent importance of the LPO to osmoregulatory thirst was misinterpreted.

D. Summary

Hyperosmolality can develop for a variety of reasons, some of them naturally occurring events such as the ingestion of a salty meal and others inventions of the laboratory such as central or peripheral injections of osmotically active solutes. In each case, compensatory adaptations begin immediately with the transient efflux of water from cells into the surrounding ECF. This osmotic withdraw of water establishes a new osmotic equilibrium between the ICF and ECF, albeit at a level higher than the optimal value of 300 mOsm. This cellular dehydration and not the hyperosmolality is the critical stimulus that activates renal and behavioral mechanisms that are essential for the complete restoration of the original equilibrium. Under the direct influence of the neurohypophysial hormone AVP, the kidney begins to conserve water and excrete a very concentrated urine; a process that may be facilitated by the release of natriuretic hormones such as oxytocin and ANP. However, renal adaptations alone are not sufficient to rapidly restore osmotic equilibrium, because this requires the ingestion of water. The arousal of thirst in response to cellular dehydration has numerous parallels with the control of AVP release, although each of these events appears to be controlled by separable but overlapping neural circuitry. In each case the cellular dehydration is initially detected by osmosensitive neurons that are contained in CVOs, and this interoceptive signal is then transduced into neural changes, apparently by mechanoreceptor neurons, thus ensuring that complementary behavioral and physiological adaptations act concurrently in the defense of osmotic homeostasis.

IV. VOLUME REGULATION AND HOMEOSTASIS

A. Control of Vasopressin by Hypovolemia

The neurohypophysial release of AVP in response to a hyperosmotic stimulus is governed by a single interoceptive mechanism. There is a simple linear relationship between plasma osmolality and elevated plasma AVP levels. However, the relationship between blood volume and AVP is somewhat more complicated. At low levels of blood loss that do not produce hypotension (i.e., less than 10% of blood volume) increases in plasma AVP levels are very small. In contrast, when hypovolemia is large enough to compromise blood pressure, AVP levels are dramatically increased and continue to rise with further reductions in blood volume. Gauer and Henry (1963) were the first investigators to delineate some of the mechanisms that contribute to the biphasic relationship between AVP release and blood volume. Their work demonstrated that baroreceptors provide an important neural control of AVP release during hypovolemia.

Baroreceptors are specialized nerves endings that innervate parts of the vasculature, particularly in the thoracic cavity, atria of the heart, aortic arch, and carotid silnus. Their afferent projections to the central nervous system (CNS) are part of the sensory component of the autonomic nervous system. Baroreceptor activity is directly related to the pressure exerted by the circulation on the inner wall of blood vessels, which is generally a reliable index of blood volume and vascular filling. Consequently, when plasma volume is normal or even expanded, elevated neural activity in the afferent projections of the baroreceptors activates a number of CNS-mediated responses designed to maintain cardiovascular homeostasis, such as reflexive bradycardia, vasodilation, and ANP release (cf. Guyton, 1991; see Section III.B). Conversely, when plasma volume is low, reductions in the baroreceptor firing rate produce the opposite spectrum of cardiovascular responses, including atria tachycardia, vasoconstriction, and activation of the renin-angiotensin system (see Section IV.B).

The neurohpophysial release of AVP is regulated by two separate populations of baroreceptors whose differential contributions are, in part, responsible for the biphasic relationship between plasma volume and AVP levels. Low levels of hypovolemia that do not affect blood pressure are detected primarily by baroreceptors located in the low pressure, or venous side, of the circulation such as the great pulmonary vessels and left atria, usually referred to as cardiopulmonary baroreceptors. Their activation during nonhypotensive hypovolemia is not surprising because veins are thin-walled, highly distentible vessels and therefore are responsive to small decrements in blood volume. Indeed, this physical property of veins, referred to as venous compliance, is one of the most important intrinsic controls of the cardiovascular system because it ensures that after moderate blood loss veins collapse, redistributing blood to arteries and preserving arterial pressure (cf. Guyton, 1991). However, although this initial phase of AVP release during hypovolemia exhibits a low threshold for activation, it is also a very low-amplitude response, with decreases in blood volume of 10% producing only slight increases in plasma AVP levels. As plasma volume deficits worsen, high-pressure baroreceptors located on the arterial side of the circulation such as the carotid sinus and aortic arch begin to respond and contribute to the elevation of AVP release. Although the threshold for activation of the arterial baroreceptors is high, requiring plasma volume deficits in excess of 10% that in addition produce a decline in mean arterial blood pressure, the magnitude of the AVP response is substantially greater as well.

Both low- and high-pressure baroreceptors send their afferent projections into the brain stem where they synapse on neurons in the nucleus of the solitary tract (NTS). The NTS is a longitudinal nucleus that is loosely segregated into discrete regions that subserve a variety of visceral functions involved in gustatory, gastrointestinal, and cardiovascular regulation. The baroreceptors synapse on intrinsic NTS neurons that are located in the medial NTS adjacent to the area postrema (AP) (see Fig. 4). These NTS neurons subsequently project predominantly to A1 catecholaminergic neurons in the ventrolateral medulla or to a lesser extent to other areas, such as the parabrachial nucleus (PBN). The A1 and PBN neurons ultimately synapse on vasopressinergic neurons in the SON and PVN (Verbalis *et al.*, 1995). Neural activity in the interneurons of these circuits is apparently proportional to plasma volume; when volume is normal, activity is high and tonically inhibits AVP release; when volume declines, firing rate is re-

duced and the inhibition of AVP release is removed. Although the differential threshold of the high- and low-pressure baroreceptors results from the adequate stimuli (i.e., pressure and volume) in their sensory fields (arterial and venous circulation, respectively) this pattern of central innervation is probably responsible for the varying amplitudes of these two responses. More specifically, the NTS neurons that arise from the high-pressure baroreceptors ultimately innervate a larger population of hypothalamic magnocellular neurons through their multisynaptic connections and thus are capable of mobilizing a much larger AVP response when activated.

An abundance of experimental and clinical data support the view that osmotic and volemic controls are separable pathways for the regulation of AVP release. One particularly illustrative example of this separation is a condition referred to as essential hypernatremia. Patients who suffer from this disease do not release AVP in response to osmotic signals, and plasma sodium levels rise (hypernatremia); in contrast, they exhibit a normal rise in AVP levels during hypovolemia (Bayliss and Thompson, 1988). However, electrophysiological evidence has demonstrated that both osmotic mechanoreceptors and volemic baroreceptors innervate the same population of SON and PVN vasopressinergic neurons in the hypothalamus (cf. Robertson, 1986). Under most perturbations of body fluid homeostasis, such as water deprivation, this pattern of innervation ensures that individual AVP neurons can maximize hormone release during concurrent osmotic and volemic stimuli. However, in some conditions such as hyponatremia with concurrent volume depletion, baroreceptor innervation of AVP neurons would tend to stimulate AVP release, whereas the decline in plasma sodium and osmolality normally would inhibit it. Because SON and PVN neurons are dually innervated by both inputs, these neurons have to integrate these conflicting stimuli. When such conflicts arise, osmotic control overrides that exerted by volemic mechanisms and AVP release is inhibited despite the presence of hypovolemia (Stricker and Verbalis, 1986). The primacy of osmotic control may result from the synaptic innervation of vasopressin neurons by OVLT or other osmotically sensitive projection neurons, and the baroreceptor inputs arising from the NTS, PBN, and A1 cell group. More specifically, it seems likely that the projection neurons mediating the baroreceptor signal primarily synapse on the most distal dendrites, whereas the mechanoreceptors that arise from the osmoreceptors synapse in the immediate vicinity of the axon hillock of the magnocellular neurons. In this way osmotic inputs can establish a zone of shunting inhibition that prevents any baroreceptor activation of AVP release. This example illustrates the integrative capacity of SON and PVN neurons as well as the fact that AVP is more important for osmotic than volemic regulation, presumably because there are many additional factors that participate in the defense of ECF volume and composition. While this includes intrinsic controls of GFR and renal excretion, of principal importance in this regard are the adrenal steroid, aldosterone, and the renin-angiotensin system.

B. Aldosterone

During hyperosmolality, the reabsorption of water promoted by the actions of AVP is the principal renal adaptation that corrects this homeostatic imbalance; enhanced reabsorption of electrolytes such as sodium exacerbates the hypertonicity of the ECF. However, during hypovolemia the restoration of body fluid homeostasis is critically dependent on the kidney's ability to conserve water and sodium. Since the 1930s, it has been known that adrenal cortical extracts decrease sodium excretion and that surgical removal of the adrenal glands (adrenalectomy) results in extreme and uncontrollable sodium loss (Richter, 1936). These antinatriuretic effects of adrenal cortical extracts are mediated by the actions of the adrenal steroid hormone, aldosterone.

The adrenal glands are paired organs that sit atop the kidneys. Each adrenal is a duplex gland consisting of an inner medullary region that synthesizes and releases catecholamines into the circulation and an outer or cortical region. The adrenal cortex consists of three discrete layers, the zona glomerulosa, the zona fasiculata, and the zona reticularsis. The last two zones contain glucocorticoids, whereas the first is the site of aldosterone synthesis and release. Zona glomerulosa cells release aldosterone in response to a variety of stimuli, although, surprisingly, hyponatremia (a decrease in plasma sodium levels) is not a very potent stimulus for aldosterone release (Cade and Perenich, 1965). Instead, the zona glomerulosa cells are more responsive to an increase in plasma potassium levels (hyperkalemia), which is usually a very reliable index of the severity of sodium depletion (cf. Guyton, 1991). A rise in plasma potassium levels as small as 1 mEq/liter, which can occur while an individual eats a meal rich in potassium, results in a significant increase in aldosterone release. Moreover, hyperkalemia can produce the largest and most sustained increases in aldosterone and is known to interact with other stimuli for aldosterone release, particularly the renin-angiotensin system (see Section IV.C).

In the kidney, aldosterone acts on Type I (mineralocorticoid, MR) corticosteroid receptors that are located in the cytoplasm of peritubular epithelial cells in the late distal tubule and collecting duct of the nephron (Eisen and Harmon, 1986). These receptors have equally high affinity for corticosterone and aldosterone (Sheppard and Funder, 1987), but the high levels of the glucocorticoids (GRs) are inactivated by an enzyme 11-β hydroxy-steroid dehydrogenase, allowing the lower levels of aldosterone to occupy the receptor (Funder, 1990; Jellinek *et al.,* 1993; Monder and Lakshmi, 1990; Lakshmi *et al.,* 1991). Once aldosterone binds to this receptor, the complex is translocated to the nucleus, where it acts to increase gene transcription and protein synthesis (Dallman *et al.,* 1991). In the kidney, these genomic events increase the efficiency of sodium reabsorption at the expense of potassium, whose excretion is correspondingly increased. Evidence has suggested that aldosterone may additionally interact with heterodimers of Type I (MR) and Type II (GR) receptors (see Chapter 53), and that some of its metabolites may interact with membrane excitability proteins, such as ligand-gated ion channels or G-protein-coupled receptors, to induce more rapid nongenomic effects that may contribute to renal sodium conservation (Baulieu, 1978; Wehling *et al.,* 1992). In addition to the kidney, aldosterone can also act on other target organs, such as sweat glands, salivary glands, and the gastrointestinal tract to facilitate sodium transport, the heart where it may participate in tissue remodeling after myocardial infarction, and the brain to regulate salt ingestion (see Section IV.F and Chapter 53).

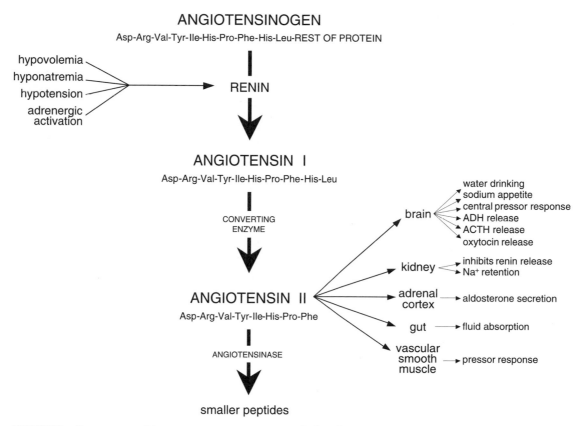

FIGURE 2 Components of the renin-angiotensin system including the major stimuli for renin release and the diverse target organs and actions of AngII. Modified from Fluharty and Sakai (1995).

C. Renin-Angiotensin System

At the turn of century Tigerstedt and Bergmann (1897) demonstrated that injections of renal extracts into normotensive animals elevated blood pressure. The implications of this work were far reaching; this was the first suggestion that the kidney, long recognized as an exocrine organ, might also possess endocrine functions important in the regulation of cardiovascular and body fluid homeostasis. Tigerstedt and Bergmann coined the term "renin" to refer to the biologically active substance isolated from the kidney, but it took almost 50 years to delineate the details of this important hormonal system. The critical fist step in this research was the demonstration that renin was in fact an enzyme that acted on a large plasma protein to generate a circulating peptide hormone that became known as angiotensin II (AngII) (see Fig. 2; Peach, 1977).

The rate-limiting step in the synthesis of AngII is the release of the proteolytic enzyme renin from the justaglomerular (JG) cells of the kidney (Catanzaro *et al.*, 1983). Renin is stored as a larger protein, prorenin, that is released constitutively from the Golgi apparatus and converted to the active enzyme, probably by the protease cathepsin B, an enzyme that is colocalized with renin in both immature and mature secretory granules (Matsuba *et al.*, 1989; Taugner *et al.*, 1985). Renin acts on a plasma α-globulin protein, referred to as angiotensinogen that is primarily synthesized in the liver, but is also found in other tissues including the brain (Dzau *et al.*, 1986; Healy and Printz, 1984; Lynch *et al.*, 1987). The amino terminus of angiotensinogen contains a tetra-decapeptide that is the actual substrate for renin whose action cleaves a biologically inactive decapeptide known as angiotensin I (AngI). AngII is subsequently produced from AngI by a dipeptide carboxypeptidase called angiotensin-converting enzyme (ACE), which removes two amino acids from the carboxy terminus of AngI to generate AngII in the plasma. Large amounts of ACE are present in the endothelial cells of the pulmonary vasculature, although equally high levels are found elsewhere, particularly in the brain, heart, and salivary glands (Ganong, 1994; Ganten and Speck, 1978). ACE, although the name implies otherwise, is not specific to the renin-angiotensin system and is in fact identical with kininase II, an enzyme responsible for the inactivation of bradykinin and kallidin. Despite this fact, blockade of ACE is a very effective way to decrease circulating AngII levels, which is therapeutically beneficial in the treatment of hypertension and congestive heart failure.

Once generated, AngII acts on two distinct cell surface receptors referred to as AT_1 and AT_2, both of which are G-protein-coupled receptors (GPCR) (see Fig. 3) (Bumpus *et al.*, 1991; Chiu *et al.*, 1989; Reagan *et al.*, 1990; Speth and Kim, 1990; Tsutumi and Saavedra, 1991a). The diverse array of physiological, endocrinological, and behavioral effects of AngII that act cooperatively to maintain cardiovascular and body fluid homeostasis are primarily the result of AT_1-receptor activation (cf. Fluharty and Sakai, 1995). Finally, AngII is inactivated by a variety of extracellular amino-, carboxy-,

and endo-peptidases located in close proximity to its target organs. The presence of angiotensinogen, renin, ACE, and immunoreactive AngII in many tissues has led to the proposal of intrinsic renin-angiotensin system (RAS) in a variety of tissues, such as the brain, heart, salivary gland, kidney, and specific vascular beds (Ganten and Speck, 1978; Ganten *et al.*, 1983; Ganong, 1994; Phillips *et al.*, 1979, 1993). The interaction of these putative systems with the more classic circulating hormonal cascade and their physiological importance remains a subject of intense experimental investigation.

As the rate-limiting step in the production of AngII, renin activity is regulated by a variety of stimuli all of which signal that cardiovascular and body fluid homeostasis have been compromised (cf. Peach, 1977; Zehr *et al.*, 1980). Renin is produced and secreted from JG cells in the kidney. These cells are located at the transition between the ascending loop of Henle and the convoluted distal tubule of the nephron in direct contact with glomeurlar, vascular, and luminal tissues (cf. Guyton, 1991). This specialized anatomical positioning provides for the mechanisms that regulate renin release. For instance, during hypovolemia renal perfusion pressure declines and this is probably detected by intrarenal baroreceptors located on afferent and efferent arterioles, which trigger renin release from a subpopulation of JG cells. Similarly, during sodium depletion specialized cells in the macula densa detect a decline in the delivery of sodium and chloride from the loop of Henle to the distal tubule and stimulate renin release from JG cells that are probably distinct from but overlapping with those that are volume sensitive. Some studies have additionally suggested that JG cells may be directly responsive to ions and stretch.

JG cells are innervated by postganglionic neurons of the sympathetic nervous system, which, when activated during hypotensive hypovolemia, release norepinephrine that stimulates β-receptors on the JG cells to release renin. Indeed, this appears to be one of the reasons why β-adrenergic antagonists are effective antihypertensives. The JG cells also respond to circulating catecholamines released from the adrenal medullary chromaffin cells during sympathetic arousal. The ability of the sympathoadrenal system to regulate the release of renin is just one example of the many interactions between the RAS and autonomic nervous system,

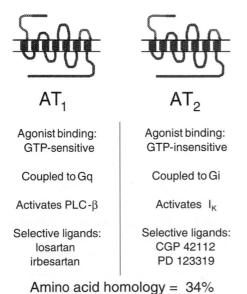

AT_1   **AT_2**

Agonist binding: Agonist binding:
GTP-sensitive   GTP-insensitive

Coupled to Gq   Coupled to Gi

Activates PLC-β Activates I_K

Selective ligands: Selective ligands:
losartan   CGP 42112
irbesartan   PD 123319

Amino acid homology = 34%

FIGURE 3 Structural and functional features of the two major AngII receptors, AT_1 and AT_2.

which act cooperatively to regulate cardiovascular function (discussed later). The collective effects of hypovolemia, hypotension, and sodium depletion on renin release ensure that circulating AngII levels are elevated during distortions of the ECF and can act to restore homeostasis.

The first physiological action of AngII to be described was its ability to stimulate the synthesis and release of the antinatriuretic hormone aldosterone from the zona glomerulosa cells of the adrenal cortex (Aguilera and Marusic, 1971; Catt *et al.*, 1987). In this regard, AngII is known to interact with other stimuli for aldosterone release, including hyponatremia and hyperkalemia in order to acheive a more pronounced aldosterone release. The interaction with elevated plasma potassium levels is particularly important because it has helped resolve a continuing controversy concerning the physiological significance of AngII in the regulation of aldosterone release. Intravenous (IV) infusions of AngII in normovolemic animals produces a significant but relatively transient elevation in aldosterone levels, leading some investigators to conclude that the contribution of AngII to adrenal steroidogenesis during hypovolemia or sodium depletion is minor. However, when AngII is administered during or even after hyperkalemia, intended to mimic the normal electrolyte environment of sodium deprivation, much lower doses of AngII produce greater and more sustained increases in aldosterone release. The mechanism for this enhancement involves an upregulation of AngII receptors on the zona glomerulosa cells (Catt *et al.*, 1987). This example of hormonal sensitization illustrates two very important principles. First, exogenous administration of hormones in normal animals rarely reveals their full biological efficacy because they are acting isolated from the many other variables that are present in animals experiencing perturbations in body fluid homeostasis. Second, these contemporaneous signals frequently sensitize cells to the action of hormones and the resultant effect is usually greater than simply additive. This concept of hormonal synergies has proven to be very useful in understanding several actions of AngII, particularly the control of ingestive behavior (see Sections IV.D, IV.E; Fluharty and Sakai, 1995).

The cardiovascular system is also an important target organ for the actions of AngII. Circulating AngII acts directly on most vascular smooth muscle to produce vasoconstriction and an increase in total peripheral resistance (cf. Morgan, 1987; Peach, 1977). In fact, it is approximately four times more potent than catecholamines (CAs), the other major contributor to vascular tone, although AngII and CAs appear to mutually facilitate the pressor actions of each other. In the kidney, the vasoconstrictive activity of AngII results in an increase in glomerular filtration rate that contributes to tubuloglomerular autoregulatory feedback mechanisms (Loudon *et al.*, 1983; Navar and Rosivall, 1984). AngII also increases cardiac contractility, but there is little or no change in cardiac output because the substantial pressor response activates baroreceptor reflexes that cause a vagally mediated decline in chronotropic and ionotropic activity. The hemodynamic profile of AngII has been implicated in the pathogenesis of hypertension, and this disorder can be treated with ACE inhibitors and with antagonists of the AT_1 receptor subtype. Interestingly, these drugs lower blood pressure even when plasma renin activity is normal, suggesting that both the sensitivity of vascular tissue to AngII and the hormone's level in the plasma are important determinants of high blood pressure.

In addition to its many peripheral target organs, AngII also has important actions within the nervous system. As mentioned previously, sympathetic innervation of JG cells is a major stimulus for renin release during hypotensive hypovolemia. But once its levels rise in the circulation, AngII facilitates adrenergic neurotransmission in several ways. First, AngII can increase the synthesis of CAs in the brain and autonomic nervous system apparently by promoting phosphorylation and induction of the rate-limiting enzyme tyrosine hydroxylase (Peach, 1977). Second, AngII has been reported to increase norepinephrine release from sympathetic postganglionic neurons (Levens *et al.*, 1981a; Malik and Nasjletti, 1976), as well as adrenal medullary release of epinephrine (Vollmer *et al.*, 1990). Third, AngII appears to inhibit the reuptake and inactivation of norepinephrine that enhances the activity of CAs (Levens *et al.*, 1981b; Peach, 1977). Finally, AngII can augment the sensitivity of vascular smooth muscle to adrenergic activation, particularly during sodium depletion (Vollmer *et al.*, 1988). Because AngII does not alter the density of adrenergic receptors in vascular smooth muscle, this effect is probably mediated by a postreceptor modification that results in increased

CA-stimulated phosphoinositide hydrolysis and the attendant mobilization of intracellular calcium. Collectively, these many actions of AngII enhance the contributions of the sympathoadrenal system to the maintenance of cardiovascular function during perturbations of body fluid homeostasis.

Although as a circulating peptide hormone AngII does not readily cross the blood–brain barrier, it is widely recognized that AngII elicits a variety of physiological, endocrinological, and behavioral responses by acting on the CNS (Phillips, 1978). These actions are mediated by AT_1 receptors located on neurons in the CVOs (see Fig. 4), highly vascularized structures whose fenestrated capillaries permit the entry of peptides into the brain (Gehlert *et al.*, 1991; Obermuller *et al.*, 1991; Song *et al.*, 1992; Steckelings *et al.*, 1992; Tsutsumi and Saavedra, 1991b). For instance, AngII acts directly on neurons in the SFO, and perhaps indirectly in the OVLT and PVN, to stimulate the release of AVP from the neurohypophysis (Bealer *et al.*, 1979; Keil *et al.*, 1975; Ferguson and Renaud, 1986; Shoji *et al.*, 1989). This centrally mediated response occurs primarily during hypotensive blood loss and is additive with the stimulation provided by afferent baroreceptor input on magnocellular neurosceretory cells and plasma osmolarity (Sterling *et al.*, 1980).

AngII also regulates adenohypophysial function, particularly the release of prolactin and adrenocorticotropin (ACTH). These effects are probably mediated by AT_1 receptors located on neurons that project into the median eminence and hypothalamic hypophysial portal system, although an additional effect of AngII directly on lactotrophs and corticotrophs has not been ruled out (Aguilera *et al.*, 1995; Kucharezyk *et al.*, 1987; Peach, 1977; Phillips, 1978). The stimulatory effect of AngII on ACTH release is the probable mechanism that allows AngII to directly stimulate aldosterone release from zona glomerulosa cells as it simultaneously promotes the continued synthesis of this steroid. Collectively, the effects of AngII on both divisions of the pituitary gland ensure that it promotes and sustains antidiuresis and antinatriuresis during severe hypovolemia.

The complex effects of AngII on cardiovascular regulation include actions that are mediated by the CNS. Of principal importance is the central pressor response elicited by AngII, which is known to be separable from and complementary to the peripheral effects of the hormone on total peripheral resistance. In a classic set of experiments, Buckley and his colleagues (Bickerton and Buckley, 1961; Smookler *et al.*, 1966) developed a cross-circulation procedure in dogs to convincingly demonstrate that blood-borne AngII was able to act in the brain to induce an increase in blood pressure. Further investigations revealed that this response occurred when AngII interacted with receptors in the AP (see Fig. 4) (Joy, 1971; Joy and Lowe, 1970), a CVO located in the brain stem at the obex of the fourth ventricle, although more rostral CVOs and their connectivity to the PVN are probably involved in this response as well (Hoffman and Phillips, 1976; Jensen *et al.*, 1992; Mangiapane and Simpson, 1980). Moreover, stimulation of the AP and other CVOs by blood-borne AngII increases AVP release from the hypothalamus and activates descending control of the sympathetic nervous system, and both of these responses contribute to the magnitude of the centrally mediated increment in blood pressure (Falcon *et al.*, 1978; Scholkens *et al.*, 1982; Unger *et al.*, 1981). Indeed, the importance of AVP to the maintenance of arterial blood pressure is widely accepted (Liard, 1984). Finally, it has also been suggested that AngII may act in the dorsal motor nucleus of the vagus to modulate parasympathetic tone (Casto and Phillips, 1984; Diz *et al.*, 1984; Rettig *et al.*, 1986). Although the central pressor response and the endocrine effects of AngII are likely to contribute to the maintenance of cardiovascular and body fluid homeostasis, the behavioral effects of AngII represent the best understood actions of this hormone in the CNS.

D. Neuroendocrine Controls of Hypovolemic Thirst

1. Baroreceptors and Thirst

The search for the interoceptive mechanisms that mediate the arousal of thirst during hypovolemia has been greatly influenced by an understanding of the regulation of endocrine and autonomic responses that are activated during this condition. Because most of the early investigations of hypovolemic thirst occurred prior to the discovery of the dipsogenic action of AngII

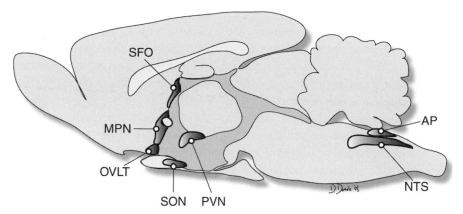

FIGURE 4 Distribution of AT$_1$ receptors in CVOs and elsewhere in the rat brain known to be involved in thirst and body fluid homeostasis. AP, area postrema; MPN, medial preoptic nucleus; NTS, nucleus of the solitary tract; OVLT, organum vasculosum of the lamina termanilis; SFO, subfronical organ; SON, supraoptic nucleus.

they focused on neural signals, particularly baroreceptors and the autonomic nervous system. Distortions of ECF volume are detected by baroreceptors and these interoceptive signals are conveyed to the CNS. This produces widespread activation of the sympathetic nervous system, subsequently orchestrating vascular, cardiac, and renal responses that collectively begin to defend ECF homeostasis (cf. Guyton, 1991). It was tempting to propose that these same afferent signals acted in the brain to arouse thirst.

In order to produce hypovolemia in animals, these earlier studies employed a variety of procedures that had in common the ability to produce blood loss. However, although the cardiovascular and renal compensations under these conditions were easily amenable to study, the behavioral analysis of thirst was frequently hampered by some of the debilitating effects of hemorrhage and anemia. In order to produce a more controlled and less severe form of hypovolemia, Fitzsimons (1961) developed a new, much more benign procedure that involved the use of hyperoncotic colloids. Peripheral administration (e.g., intraperitoneal) of these colloids, such as polyethylene glycol (PEG), increased the oncotic pressure of the ISF and thereby disrupted Starling equilibrium (see Section II.B). As a result, as plasma was filtered on the arterial side of capillaries, its return to the vascular space was impeded by the colloid and therefore sequestered in the ISF. In short, this procedure produced a redistribution and reduction in plasma volume without actual blood loss. Moreover, a broad range

of plasma volume deficits could be produced by use of these colloids and the resultant hypovolemia was both reproducible and reversible. Soon after its initial description, the use of PEG and the related technique of dialysis (Falk, 1966) became the preferred paradigm for the production of hypovolemia and the experimental analysis of thirst (Stricker, 1968).

Most of the early evidence that implicated baroreceptors in the control of thirst during hypovolemia was based largely on correlative evidence. For instance, the arousal of thirst induced by PEG treatment or other volume-depleting procedures occurs soon after the onset of hypovolemia, is quantitatively related to the severity of the plasma volume deficit (Fitzsimons, 1961; Stricker, 1966), and is most pronounced when the blood loss is sufficiently large as to produce moderate hypotension as well (Hosutt *et al.*, 1978; Hosutt and Stricker, 1981); curiously, severe hypotension appears to inhibit thirst. These and other observations led Stricker (1966) to propose that two distinct classes of baroreceptors mediate the arousal of thirst, as is true for the activation of the autonomic and endocrine responses to hypovolemia and hypotension (see Section IV.C). When plasma deficits are relatively small and nonhypotensive it was suggested that the drinking primarily results from activation of cardiopulmonary baroreceptors located on the venous side of the circulation in the great veins and atria (Kaufman, 1984; Stricker, 1966). However, when plasma volume deficits are larger and result in arterial hypotension, the thirst may in addition be stimulated by arterial baroreceptors primarily found in the carotid sinus and aortic arch.

Experimental support for baroreceptors in the control of hypovolemic thirst has relied on a variety of techniques designed to directly manipulate afferent neural activity in these autonomic reflexes. For instance, procedures that decrease venous return to the heart, such as inflation of a ballon in or placement of a constrictive cuff around the vena cava, decrease mean arterial blood pressure and stimulate thirst (Fitzsimons and Moore-Gillon, 1980; Thrasher *et al.,* 1982a). The water intake is attenuated by surgical denervation of cardiopulmonary or sinoarotic baroreceptors and is abolished by denervation of both in dogs (Quillen *et al.,* 1988). Similarly, crushing the left atria appendage decreases thirst during nonhypotensive hypovolemia in sheep, although this procedure causes a small but significant increase in spontaneous water intake (Zimmerman *et al.,* 1981). In contrast, activation of cardiopulmonary baroreceptors by inflation of a ballon placed at the junction between the great pulmonary vessels and left atrium inhibits thirst, although these effects are not limited to hypovolemic thirst and a decrease in spontaneous water intake has also been observed (Moore-Gillon and Fitzsimons, 1982; Kaufman, 1984). Collectively, these studies have revealed that the relationship between baroreceptor activity and thirst is not as simple as originally envisioned and involves both stimulatory and inhibitory components. In a normovolemic animal, baroreceptor activity responsive to both volume and pressure inhibits thirst. As plasma volume decreases, the decline in baroreceptor afferent input stimulates thirst, but some afferent activity must remain because surgical denervation or destruction of baroreceptor sensory fields eliminates the water intake. Presumably the integrative centers of the brain that mediate the arousal of thirst are monitoring the dynamic change between the baseline baroreceptor firing rate and its subsequent decline during the development of hypovolemia and hypotension. Conversely, an increase in the baroreceptor firing rates signals to the brain the restoration of normal ECF volume or the occurrence of volume expansion, and hence thirst is inhibited.

2. Renin-Angiotensin System and Thirst

Although it is now clear that cardiopulmonary and arterial baroreceptors make an important contribution to the arousal of drinking behavior during perturbations of ECF homeostasis, the suggestion that AngII might also act in the brain to control thirst represented the first proposal that this behavior might have an endocrine basis. The discovery of the dipsogenic action of AngII began innocently enough with a few early studies suggesting that exogenous administration of renal extracts could under some conditions elicit drinking in nondeprived rats (Ascher and Anson, 1963; Linazasoro *et al.,* 1954; Nairn *et al.,* 1956). However, it was the meticulous research of James Fitzsimons that firmly established a role for the RAS in the behavioral regulation of body fluid homeostasis. In an initial series of experiments, he demonstrated that the surgical removal of the kidneys (nephrectomy) significantly reduced drinking in response to the hypovolemia induced by caval ligation (Fitzsimons, 1969). To prove that this effect was due to removal of the kidneys from the circulation and not anuria, he demonstrated that bladder puncture and uretheric ligation did not reduce the thirst response. On the basis of these results and those involving injections of renal extracts, he proposed that hypotension and hypovolemia released renin into the circulation (see Section IV.C) and that the subsequent generation of blood-borne AngII acted in the brain to arouse thirst. In support of this hypothesis, Fitzsimons and many of his colleagues demonstrated that intravenous infusion of AngII or direct injection of the peptide into the brain elicited thirst in rats (Epstein *et al.,* 1970; Fitzsimons and Simons, 1969; Hsaio *et al.,* 1977) and many other mammals (cf. Fitzsimons, 1979).

However, although the diposgenic potency of the exogenous administration of AngII was quite compelling, these results initially presented a paradox—how could a circulating peptide hormone penetrate the blood–brain barrier to gain access to structures in the CNS involved in the arousal of thirst? Although the answer seems obvious now with the discovery of CVOs that lack a blood–brain barrier (see Fig. 1), the research that ultimately focused on these structures as loci for the dipsogenic action of AngII is both interesting and informative. While investigating the central sites at which the application of AngII would produce thirst, Johnson and Epstein (1975) noted that most of the responsive parenchymal locations in the basal forebrain were located either in close proximity to the cerebral ventricles or in regions where the cannula shaft transversed a ventricular space in route to the intended injection site. By using radiolabeled AngII, they further discovered that in both locations the injected peptide diffused away from the cannulae tip and effluxed up the shaft, thus gaining access to the cerebral ventricles. Moreover, diffusion of the AngII into the CSF was critical for its dipsogenic action because if the cannulae were angled in such a way as to avoid diffusion of the injecta into the ventricles animals would not drink. Subsequently, they demonstrated that direct ICV injection of AngII elicited thirst at doses equal to or lower that those required in the parenchymal sites, implicating ependymal tissue surrounding the ventricles in this behavioral response.

Working almost simultaneously with Johnson's analysis of the importance of the ventricles, Simpson and Routtenberg (1973, 1975) reported that the SFO, a CVO located in the dorsal third ventricle just under the fornix, contained high concentrations of aceylcholinesterase. Because the central administration of the cholinomimetic carbachol was known to stimulate drinking in rats (Lehr *et al.,* 1967), they proposed the SFO as a likely site for this action. Consistent with this hypothesis, they demonstrated that direct application of carbachol into the ventricles or the SFO elicited drinking and that this response was enhanced by coadministration of physotigmine, a cholinesterase inhibitor. With the emerging interest in AngII as a centrally acting hormone that might participate in the regulation of hypovolemic thirst, they also investigated whether the SFO was responsive to AngII. In the first papers published that suggested a CVO as a central site for the dispogenic action of AngII, Simpson and Routtenberg (1973, 1975) reported that lesions of the SFO attenuated water intake elicited by administration of AngII in the periphery or elsewhere in the brain.

Although these early results were encouraging, Simpson went on to complete a much more comprehensive analysis of the SFO and AngII-induced thirst when he joined Alan Epstein's laboratory at the University of Pennsylvania (Simpson *et al.,* 1978). Initially, they replicated the finding that lesions of the SFO abolished drinking stimulated by IV infusion of AngII, but did not impair drinking elicited by IV hypertonic saline. However, they were not content to let their analysis rely solely on the vagueness and interpretational difficulties of lesion studies (cf. Hosutt *et al.,* 1981; Buggy and

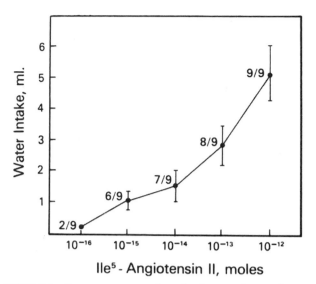

FIGURE 5 Dose–response analysis for the stimulation of water intake by AngII administered into the SFO of rats. From Simpson *et al.* (1978).

Johnson, 1977; see Section III.C). Instead, they complemented the lesion studies by using the technique of direct intracranial injection of AngII into the SFO, an extremely small structure that is difficult to insert a cannula into without destruction of the underlying tissue, to painstakingly demonstrate the unique sensitivity of this structure to AngII. In these studies, AngII was shown to arouse drinking after application to the SFO of doses several orders of magnitude lower than those necessary in surrounding tissues or in the ventricles (see Fig. 5). Moreover, they found that infusion of nonselective AngII receptor antagonists into the SFO decreased substantially, or in some cases completely eliminated, drinking in response to IV AngII; administration of the antagonists in surrounding brain regions did not produce this pharmacological blockade. These behavioral studies were being completed just as several laboratories reported that iontophoretic application of AngII activated neurons in the SFO (Felix and Schelling, 1982; Jhamandas *et al.,* 1989) and that the SFO contained specific membrane–associated AngII receptors, later identified as the AT_1 subtype (Gehlert *et al.,* 1991; Song *et al.,* 1992; Tsutsumi and Saavedra, 1991b). Collectively these studies strongly support the hypothesis that elevated levels of circulating AngII stimulate AT_1 receptors in the SFO and activate efferent projections to the hypothalamus, including the PVN

(Lind and Johnson, 1982; Lind *et al.,* 1982; Miselis *et al.,* 1979) and brain stem, that mediate drinking behavior (Miselis, 1981). Although it has become clear than other CVOs are probably involved (e.g., OVLT and MPO; c.f. Phillips and Hoffman, 1976), the basic premise of this model has not really been challenged.

Despite the magnitude and reliably of the water intake elicited by exogenous AngII, attempts to quantify the contribution of the endogenously generated hormone to most models of hypovolemic thirst has remained a source of continuing controversy and debate (Pawloski and Fink, 1990; Stricker *et al.,* 1976; Stricker, 1977; Van Eckelen and Phillips, 1988). Although a variety of procedures have been used to assess the physiological role of AngII in the control of thirst, most have attempted to study this issue by disrupting AngII function during experimental manipulations that produce thirst. These approaches have included surgical procedures such as nephrectomy to remove the main source of renin (Fitzsimons, 1969, Houpt and Epstein, 1971; Fitzsimons and Stricker, 1971) or ablation of CVOs that contain central AngII receptors (Mangiapane *et al.,* 1983; Simpson and Routtenberg, 1975; Simpson *et al.,* 1978; Thunhorst *et al.,* 1987), pharmacological treatments designed to reduce the formation of AngII in the plasma (e.g., ACE inhibitors; Lehr *et al.,* 1973) or block the activation of AngII receptors by the use of high-affinity nonselective or AT_1-specific antagonists (Fregly and Rowland, 1991; Kirby *et al.,* 1992; Rowland *et al.,* 1992); and the use of antisense oligonucleotides to attenuate AngII receptor expression in brain (Gyurko *et al.,* 1993; Sakai *et al.,* 1994; Sakai *et al.,* 1995). In general the results of these experiments have suffered from numerous interpretational difficulties. For instance, most of the pharmacological manipulations are limited in efficacy by factors such as accessibility to the CNS after peripheral administration, partial agonist activity of some antagonists, and the likelihood of spare receptors. Much more troublesome is that the fact that any approach that prevents AngII from mobilizing autonomic and endocrine responses during hypotensive hypovolemia, can exacerbatic this condition, resulting in arterial hypotension so severe as to debilitate the animal and nonspecifically interfere with drinking behavior. Depending on your perspective, these results could be used to conclude that AngII only plays a permissive role during thirst by supporting

adequate cardiovascular function necessary for behavioral competence (Evered, 1992; Mann *et al.,* 1987; Stricker, 1977) or, alternatively, to a gross overestimate of the contribution of AngII to experimentally induced thirst by inferring that the observed behavior is completely dependent on AngII because its removal eliminates the drinking response (Houpt and Epstein, 1971).

As an alternative approach, several investigators have attempted to quantify the precise relationship between elevated plasma AngII levels and the magnitude of the thirst response elicited by a variety of experimental procedures (Johnson *et al.,* 1981; Leenen and Stricker, 1974; Mann *et al.,* 1980; Pawloski and Fink, 1990; Stricker, 1977; Stricker *et al.,* 1976; Van Eekelen and Phillips, 1988). The initial phase of these experiments usually involves the generation of a dose–effect curve relating water intake to plasma AngII levels after intravenous infusion of the hormone in normal rats. Measurements of plasma AngII levels under these conditions is very important because the steady-state level of the hormone is dependent not only on the amount exogenously infused, but also on its summation with endogenous levels and their combined degradation by angiotensinases. These values are then compared to the plasma AngII levels in animals subjected to experimental manipulations such as water deprivation, caval ligation, isoproterenol-induced hypotension, and PEG-induced hypovolemia, all of which produce varying amounts of water intake (see Fig. 6).

Interestingly, the results of these experiments have been praised both by friend and foe of AngII. Those who favor a physiological role for AngII in thirst argue that the plasma AngII levels in hypovolemic animals that exhibit drinking typically exceed the dipsogenic threshold (200 pg/ml) for the hormone as determined in normovolemic animals (Hsaio *et al.,* 1977; Johnson *et al.,* 1981). On the other hand, the critics acknowledge that the AngII levels are high enough to contribute to the observed thirst, but are quick to point out that the hypovolemic animals actually drink substantially more water than predicted by extrapolation from the dose–effect curve generated in normal animals. Hence, they maintain that AngII makes a relatively minor contribution and that baroreceptors probably account for the majority of the thirst aroused during hypovolemia and hypotension (Stricker *et al.,* 1976; Stricker, 1977; Van Eekelen and Phillips, 1988). The problem that plagues

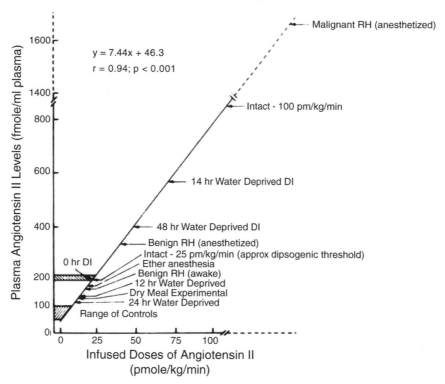

FIGURE 6 Linear relationship between infused doses of AngII and plasma levels of the hormone in rats. Also depicted on the graph are the levels of AngII generated during dehydration and several other experimental manipulations. From Johnson *et al.* (1981).

both interpretations is that the experimental design is flawed insofar as it relies on observations made in normal animals to make inferences about the behavioral potency of plasma AngII in hypovolemic animals. In fact, AngII is a very potent pressor agent when administered to normal animals and the rise in arterial blood pressure activates baroreceptors that simultaneously reduce thirst elicited by the peptide (Evered, 1992); prevention of this rise in blood pressure with hypotensive agents increases the amount of water consumed during IV infusion of AngII (Evered *et al.,* 1988; Robinson and Evered, 1987). The blunting of the dipsogenic response to AngII by the pressor response in water-replete animals results in an underestimate of the hormone's contribution to thirst in hypovolemic animals because the rise in blood pressure does not occur. In fact, evidence suggests that the unloading of baroreceptors during hypovolemia does not just remove an inhibitory brake on AngII-induced thirst, but may actually sensitize the brain to the peptide's dipsogenic action (Thunhorst and Johnson, 1993; Thunhorst *et al.,* 1993).

In addition to an interaction with neural afferents, it has also been suggested that the behavioral actions of AngII may be regulated by steroid hormone action in the CNS. There is ample evidence that adrenal steroids, particularly glucocorticoids, potentiate the ability of AngII to stimulate salt appetite (Fluharty and Epstein, 1983; Fluharty and Sakai, 1995; see Section IV.F and Chapter 53), although a similar effect on thirst remains controversial (Fluharty and Epstein, 1983; Ganesan and Sumners, 1989; Sumners *et al.,* 1991; Wilson *et al.,* 1986). On the other hand, the ovarian steroid estrogen has a profound effect on the ability of AngII to elicit thirst and is an illustrative example of the importance of steroid–peptide interactions in the hormonal control of behavior.

It is a common observation that when estrogen levels are high during pregnancy or at proesterus, female rats drink less water, particularly in response to hypovolemic challenges that involve activation of the RAS (Findlay *et al.,* 1979; Vijande *et al.,* 1977, 1978). Earlier studies demonstrated that chronic administration of high doses of estrogen to ovarectomized rats decreased drinking stimulated by central or peripheral administration of AngII, but not hypertonic saline (Fregly, 1980; Fregly et al., 1985; Fregly and Thrasher, 1978). In subsequent experiments, it was shown that implantation of crystalline estrogen into the preoptic area of the hypothalamus of ovarectomized female rats similarly reduced AngII-induced water intake, although the use of exceedingly high doses of the steroid continued (Jonklass and Buggy, 1985).

In an effort to establish that this antagonism of AngII represents an important contribution of estrogen to the physiology of body fluid homeostasis, a hormone replacement paradigm that mimics the plasma profile of the estrogen peak during the estrus cycle (Butcher et al., 1974; Wooley and McEwen, 1993) was used to investigate its effect on the dipsogenic action of AngII (Kisley et al., 1999). In these studies it was demonstrated that 2 days of estrogen administration to ovarectomized female rats decreased water intake stimulated by ICV administration of AngII (see Fig. 7). In contrast, equivalent drinking responses elicited by the cholinomimetic carbachol were unaffected. Moreover, this antidipsogenic action of estrogen was dose-dependent with a threshold dose that is comparable to that required to reinstate lordosis behavior after removal of the ovaries, the classic physiological action of this steroid hormone in female rats (cf. Pfaff, 1980). On the other hand, there was no evidence that estrogen interacted with progesterone in the control of water intake, a result that is distinctly different from the neuroendocrine controls of female reproductive behavior. Perhaps most significantly, the ability of estrogen to inhibit AngII-induced water intake was prevented by prior treatment with the estrogen antagonist, CI628. This compound has been investigated for its antitumor properties and is known to block the genomic actions of estrogen. Since CI628 can reverse the inhibition of thirst produced by estrogen, the effect probably involves transcriptional control of central pathways that mediate the dipsogenic action of AngII.

Estrogen has been reported to increase plasma renin activity and angiotensinogen levels (Healy et al., 1992), yet surprisingly this hyperangiotensinergic condition rarely results in hypertension in women, whose prevalence of cardiovascular disease is much less than that of males. Although there appear to be several reasons for this cardioprotection, including decreased ACE activity, a reduction in the expression or sensitivity of AngII receptors in some of its target organs may also contribute. Because estrogen attenuates thirst induced by the exogenous administration of AngII, a decrease in the brain's sensitivity to this behavioral action is the most parsimonious explanation, and this desensitization could be mediated by decreased AT_1 receptors, reduced signal transduction, or both. In fact, some earlier studies suggested that estrogen treatment could cause a small decrease in AngII receptors in the diencephalon (Chen et al., 1982; Fregly et al., 1985; Jonklass and Buggy, 1985), but the exact location and relative contribution of each of the AngII receptor subtypes, AT_1 and AT_2, to this decrement was not determined. Using quantitative receptor autoradiography, researchers investigated the effects of systemic estrogen on AngII receptor expression in all the forebrain nuclei known to involved in body fluid homeostasis including CVOs, such as the OVLT, MPO, SFO, and median eminence, as well as the PVN and SON of the hypothalamus (Kisley et al., 1999b). Although all these regions contained AT_1 receptors (see Fig. 4), the population in the SFO was the only one significantly decreased by estrogen replacement in ovarectomized female rats (see Fig. 8). Moreover, these same investigators used a new approach to analyze gene expression, antisense RNA expression profiling (Phillips and Eberwine, 1996), a technique especially well suited for the analysis of low abundance genes in the brain (Kisley et al., 1999a). These studies

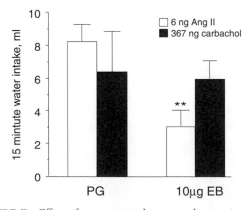

FIGURE 7 Effect of estrogen replacement therapy in ovarectomized rats on water intake elicited by intracerebroventricular injection of AngII or carbachol. EB, estradiol benzoate; PG, progesterone. From Kisley et al. (1999).

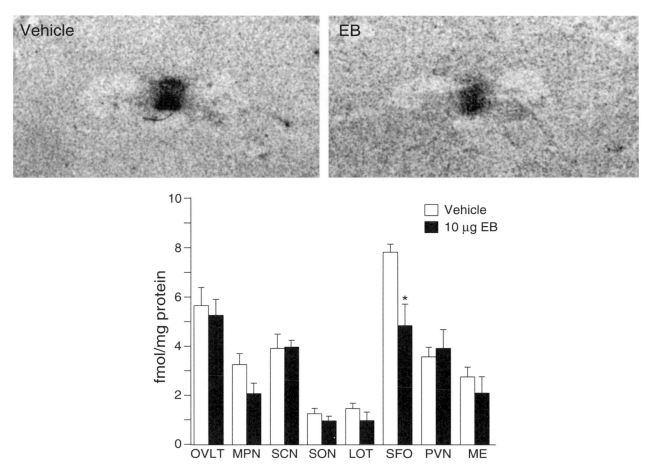

FIGURE 8 Effect of estrogen on AT_1 receptor expression in rat brain. (A) Autoradiogram of the SFO. (B) Summary of AT_1 levels in several locations following estrogen treatment. From Kisley *et al.* (1999). ME, median eminence; MPN, medial preoptic nucleus; OVLT, organum vaculosum of the lamina terminalis; SCN, suprachiasmatic nucleus; SFO, subfronical organ; SON, supraoptic nucleus.

confirmed that the decrease in AT_1 receptor protein expression in the SFO was associated with a comparable reduction in the levels of AT_1 receptor mRNA. Thus, it would appear that the estrogen attenuation of AngII induced water intake results from decreased AT_1 receptor expression in the SFO, a CVO known to mediate many of the central actions of the peptide hormone.

A major challenge in behavioral neuroendocrinolgy is determining how changes in receptor levels and gene expression translate into changes in neuronal activity that, in turn, may influence behavior. In this regard, the analysis of estrogen modulation of AngII-induced thirst has proven quite useful. These studies have relied on the use of immunohistochemistry and c-fos as a marker of the pattern of neuronal activation induced by AngII (Herbert *et al.,* 1992; Lebrun *et al.,* 1995;

Mahon *et al.,* 1995; Rowland *et al.,* 1994b, 1996). The marker c-fos is an immediate early gene whose mRNA levels increase within minutes of neuronal activation; subsequently, the c-fos protein appears in the nucleus, where it dimerizes with other transcription factors to regulate cell function (Dragunow and Fraull, 1989; Hoffman *et al.,* 1993; Sagar *et al.,* 1988; Sheng and Greenberg, 1990). The central administration of AngII induced intense c-fos immunoreactivity in the SFO as well as many of its efferent targets, including the OVLT, MPO, SON, and PVN. Surprisingly, estrogen actually increased AngII-induced c-fos expression, but in only one of these targets, the lateral magnocellular neurons of the PVN. The SFO innervates only two types of neurons in this zone of the PVN, oxytocinergic and vasopressinergic neurons, and double-labeling

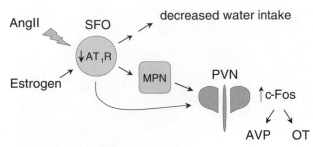

FIGURE 9 Schematic model summarizing the many actions of estrogen that may regulate body fluid homeostasis. From Kisley *et al.* (2000).

studies revealed that the increased c-fos immunoreactivity was limited to the vasopressin population (Kisley *et al.*, 2000). At first glance it is not obvious how a decrease in AT_1 receptors in the SFO produced by estrogen could result in an increase in neural activity in one of its target nuclei that is a critical part of the efferent circuitry of thirst. The most likely explanation is that the decrease in receptor binding causes a decrease in an inhibitory GABAergic pathway originating from interneurons of the SFO and projecting to vasopressinergic neurons in the lateral magnocellular zone of the PVN (Rowland *et al.*, 1994a; Verbalis, 1993). These increases in neuronal activation could explain the previously discussed estrogen modulation of AngII-induced thirst by enhancing inhibitory pressor responses, as well as by increasing plasma AVP to maintain plasma osmolarity at a time when ingestive behavior is reduced in the interests of successful mating and reproduction (see Fig. 9).

E. Salt Appetite and Volume Homeostasis

In contrast to osmoregulatory thirst, hypovolemic animals need to ingest both water and NaCl to properly restore the volume and composition of the ECF. Most scientists believe that life began in a salty marine environment, and even after abandonment of that ecological niche NaCl remains the principal component of the fluid matrix in which the cells of mammals are now immersed. The motivation to search for and ingest sodium-containing foods and fluids is apparently innate (Epstein and Stellar, 1955; Nachman and Valentino, 1966) and is generally referred to as salt appetite. From a behavioral perspective, the appetite consists of the natural preference for isotonic NaCl

solutions that most mammals display and a willingness to ingest very concentrated NaCl solutions, which are normally avoided, when sodium deficiency develops (Richter, 1936). Although thirst and hunger have been extensively studied in animals, salt appetite has received much less attention, perhaps because sodium deficiency is not a common occurrence or even a recognizable sensation in most humans due to the high abundance of NaCl in our diet (Thorn *et al.*, 1942). Most traditional approaches to the study of salt appetite have been influenced by the successful analysis of the neural and endocrine substrates of hypovolemic thirst (see Section IVD). As such, these investigations have focused on the involvement of baroreceptors and activation of the renin-angiotensin-aldosterone hormonal axis. An additional role for low plasma sodium levels (hyponatremia) has recently emerged as a candidate for the inhibitory control of salt consumption (discussed later).

Hypovolemia, presumably detected by afferent baroreceptor input to the caudal brain stem, was one of the first interoceptive stimuli for salt appetite to be investigated (Stricker, 1966, 1971; Stricker and Wolf, 1966). Evidence consistent with a role for neural input arising from hypovolemia includes the observation that stimulation of atrial baroreceptors by inflation of a balloon positioned in the junction of the superior vena cava and right atrium of rats, presumably mimicking volume expansion, inhibits salt intake; this is also true of thirst (Toth *et al.*, 1987). However, several other studies have challenged this by demonstrating a clear temporal dissociation both between the onset and duration of hypovolemia and salt ingestion that is not consistent with the view that this behavior is regulated by neural signals. For instance, hypovolemia produced by the hyperoncotic colloid PEG induces rapid increases in water intake, whereas salt ingestion does not begin for several more hours (Stricker, 1966; Stricker and Wolf, 1966), and this lengthy delay is not dependent on the severity of the hypovolemia (Stricker, 1980). Moreover, once salt consumption begins it continues long after the restoration of the volume of the ECF (Stricker, 1980). One particularly striking example of this clear separation between hypovolemia and salt intake involved the use of IP dialysis against glucose (Falk, 1966; Falk and Lipton, 1967). As in the use of PEG, this procedure produces an immediate thirst and a delayed salt appetite. In these studies, a few hours after the dialysis, when salt ingestion would not normally have begun, even though the hypovolemia was quite substantial, intragastic intubation of isotonic saline was used to completely restore plasma volume. Despite the successful restoration of extracellular fluids, the animals still developed a salt appetite several hours later. These results demonstrate that salt ingestion, in contrast to thirst, is not directly linked to the status of the ECF and further suggest that hypovolemia may initiate stimulatory events that, once engaged, function independent of plasma volumes; likely candidates are the endocrine consequences of ECF depletion (discussed later).

The delay in the arousal of salt appetite during hypovolemia has been one of the most significant challenges to the involvement of cardiopulmonary and arterial baroreceptors in the regulation of this behavior. In contrast to thirst, it would appear that the arousal of the salt appetite is simply too slow to be mediated by a rapidly generated neural signal. However, Stricker and colleagues (Stricker, 1981, 1983; Stricker *et al.*, 1979, 1987) have demonstrated that this delayed onset after PEG treatment can be eliminated if the rat's diet is changed from the standard high-sodium, laboratory chow to a sodium-deficient diet 2–4 days previously. Rats maintained on this deficient diet have reduced plasma volume and plasma sodium concentrations and increased basal plasma renin activity and aldosterone levels, as well as enhanced levels of these hormones and hypotension after PEG treatment. They also exhibit reduced pituitary secretion of oxytocin due to the reduced plasma sodium concentration. The more rapid appearance of enhanced salt ingestion may be due to these normonal changes, in that AngII and aldosterone have been implicated in the stimulation of this behavior (cf. Fluharty and Sakai, 1995; see also Chapter 53), and reduced oxytocin may disinhibit salt ingestion (R. E. Blackburn *et al.*, 1992, 1995; R. F. Blackburn *et al.*, 1992; Stricker and Verbalis, 1986, 1996; Verbalis *et al.*, 1993).

An alternative explanation for the rapid and robust salt ingestion, while not excluding a role for hormonal changes, focuses instead on the hypotension and subsequent activation of baroreceptors. In support of this view, other investigators have used various procedures that rapidly produce salt appetite even in rats maintained on standard laboratory chow. For instance, the combination of a systemic diuretic (e.g., furosemide) and low dose of the ACE-inhibitor captopril have been reported to produce a rapid thirst and salt appetite in rats that appears to be dependent on the generation of very high levels of AngII acting on AT_1 receptors in the CVOs of the brain (Fitts and Masson, 1989, 1990; Thunhorst and Johnson, 1994). In fact, the salt intake after this combined treatment is much greater than the simple addition of the intakes produced by either the diuretic-induced hypovolemia or the high levels of AngII generated by ACE inhibition when each is given alone. In searching for interactive mechanims that could explain this apparent synergy, Thunhorst and Johnson reported that decreases in mean arterial blood pressure, and not hypovolemia per se, were most predictive of the enhanced appetite, suggesting a role for arterial baroreceptors (Thunhorst and Johnson, 1994; Johnson and Thunhorst, 1995); however, more severe hypotension has been reported to inhibit salt appetite (Fitzsimons and Stricker, 1971; Hosutt and Stricker, 1981; Stricker, 1971). Moreover, they demonstrated that denervation of carotid sinus and aortic arch baroreceptors significantly reduced salt intake during sodium depletion and the continued enhancement of the appetite with repeated episodes of sodium deficiency (Thunhorst *et al.*, 1994). The latter result is particularly striking because this progressive escalation of salt intake is also partially dependent on elevated AngII levels (DeLuca *et al.*, 1992; Sakai *et al.*, 1987, 1989). Collectively, these studies emphasize that the concept of baroreceptor involvement in the control of salt appetite does not view these afferent neural signals in isolation from other interoceptive mechanisms, but instead focuses on their interactions with ongoing physiological and endocrine changes, a perspective that has been equally illuminating in the analysis of hypovolemic thirst (see Sections IV.D and IV.E).

The numerous difficulties and inconsistencies encountered in early attempts to link baroreceptor function to the control of salt appetite no doubt provided some of the impetus for a different orientation to this problem, focusing on the hormonal consequences of sodium deficiency rather than the physiological disturbances that result from such deficiency (cf. Schulkin and Fluharty, 1993; Fluharty and Sakai, 1995). In view of the fact that AngII and aldosterone are critically involved in the maintenance of ECF volume and renal conservation of water and sodium (see Sections IVB and IV.C), it seemed natural to investigate the involvement of these hormonal systems in salt appetite. However, the results of early studies of these hormones were not always encouraging and frequently were more controversial than convincing.

The involvement of aldosterone in the control of salt appetite first received experimental attention with the demonstration that the exogenous administration of mineralocorticoids to normal or adrenalectomized rats would increase salt intake (Fregley and Waters, 1966; McEwen *et al.*, 1986b; Wolf, 1965). It is now well established that aldosterone can act in the brain to arouse salt appetite when animals are sodium deficient and these data are reviewed extensively in Chapter 53. Briefly, it appears that this behavioral action of the mineralocorticoids is mediated by two separate mechanisms (cf. Fluharty and Sakai, 1995). On the one hand, aldosterone acts at cytosolic Type I (MR) receptors to induce genomic changes that probably include the regulation of AngII and oxytocin action in the brain. This mechanism requires 1–2 days for its full expression

and is enhanced by glucocorticoid activation of Type II (GR) adrenal steroid receptors. It has become clear that aldosterone can also induce more rapid increases in salt intake through an action at the cell surface. This nongenomic effect requires the conversion of aldosterone to its tetrahydro metabolites, which then interact with membrane-associated ligand-gated ion channels (Sakai *et al.*, 2000). These two distinct modes of action allow the adrenal steroids to participate in both the short- and long-term control of salt appetite (see Fig. 10; Flanagan-Cato and Fluharty, 1997).

On the other hand, these postulated actions of aldosterone are not necessary for the development of salt appetite. The most striking example of this independence from the action of adrenal steroids is the adrenalectomized animal that develops a robust life-sustaining increase in sodium ingestion in the absence of any aldosterone (Richter, 1936). Similarly, PEG-induced hypovolemia elicits both thirst and salt appetite even when aldosterone levels are prevented from rising by adrenalectomy with low-level mineralocorticoid replacement therapy to maintain renal conservation of

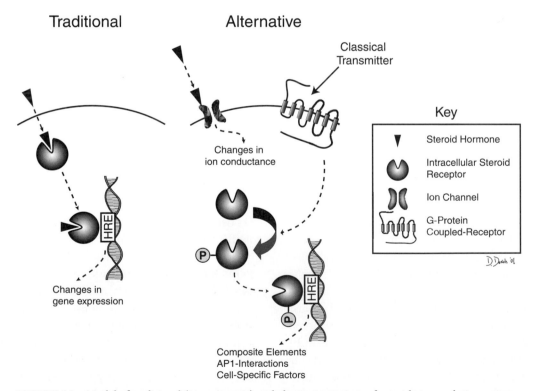

FIGURE 10 Model of traditional (i.e., genomic) and alternative actions of steroids in regulating nervous system function and behavior. From Flanagan-Cato and Fluharty (1997).

sodium (Stricker, 1980; Stricker and Wolf, 1968); although these animals were given even larger doses of exogenous glucocorticoids that could potentially interact with other stimuli for the induction of the appetite (described below). Finally, antagonism of cerebral Type I (MR) adrenal steroids receptors with high-affinity antagonists (Sakai *et al.*, 1986) or the blockade of their expression with antisense oligonucleotides (Sakai *et al.*, 1996; Sakai *et al.*, 1997, 2000) at doses that completely suppress deoxycorticosterone (DOCA)-induced salt intake only partially reduce the appetite elicited by dietary deprivation. Thus, although it is clear that adrenal steroids participate in the control of salt appetite, it is equally apparent that other endocrine and neural components are required for the full expression of the appetite during hypovolemia and sodium deficiency.

The stimulatory effect of AngII on salt ingestion was first suggested by two independent reports that brief infusions of large doses of AngII into the cerebral ventricles or surrounding tissue of the anterior forebrain increased the intake of dilute NaCl solutions (Buggy and Fisher, 1974; Chiaraviglio, 1976). In subsequent work, Epstein and his colleagues (Bryant *et al.*, 1980) and Fitzsimon's laboratory at Cambridge University (Avrith and Fitzsimons, 1980) simultaneously demonstrated that more prolonged elevations of AngII in the brain elicited substantial intake of both water and strong salt solutions steadfastly avoided by animals not receiving AngII. These studies involved continuous infusions of AngII into the anterior portion of the third ventricle, and the hormone was therefore broadcast widely in the brain, undoubtedly gaining access to the CVOs and to the ECF and parenchyma of the brain wherever the cannulae pentrated the ependyma (Johnson and Epstein, 1975). In subsequent work, more localized infusions of AngII into the antero-ventral portion of the third ventricle in the immediate vicinity of the OVLT, elicited both water and salt ingestion, whereas similar infusions into the SFO only increased water intake (Fitts and Masson, 1990), indicating that the AngII receptor populations controlling thirst and salt appetite may have distinct but overlapping distributions.

The physiological significance of many of these early results, however, was obscured by two problems (cf. Fitzsimons and Stricker, 1971). First, very high concentrations of AngII were necessary to stimulate salt ingestion, in most cases approximately 10-fold those

required for the arousal of thirst. Second, when such high doses were administered, a significant natriuresis developed, probably due to the elevated blood pressure, and the temporal pattern and magnitude of the salt intake that developed appeared directly related to and in compensation for the renal sodium excretion and ensuing negative sodium balance (Findlay and Epstein, 1980; Fluharty and Manaker, 1983). These problems continued to plague the acceptance of hormonal controls for salt appetite until it was recognized that the normal physiological setting for AngII and aldosterone is one in which both hormones are elevated concurrently (Stricker *et al.*, 1979) and thus can interact, which led to the birth of the synergy hypothesis.

Because both AngII and adrenal steroids separately stimulate salt ingestion, it was suggested that they might work cooperatively to elicit a salt appetite when elevated concurrently, as is the case during hypovolemia and sodium depletion (Epstein, 1982, 1984; Fluharty and Epstein, 1983; Fluharty and Sakai, 1995; Fregly and Rowland, 1985; Sakai, 1986; Sakai *et al.*, 1986; see also Chapter 53). In support of this hypothesis, exogenous doses of the mineralocorticoids, DOCA, or aldosterone, and ICV AngII, that were insufficient to elicit salt intake, did produce a robust salt appetite when given together (see Fig. 11; Fluharty and Epstein, 1983; Sakai, 1986). This effect was much greater than additive over a broad range of doses of each hormone, specific for salt intake, and not secondary to excessive renal sodium excretion. It was further demonstrated that blockade of AngII or aldosterone action alone resulted in a partial reduction in the appetite elicited by dietary deprivation, whereas the simultaneous inhibition or both hormones in the brain (Sakai *et al.*, 1986), but not in the periphery (Sakai and Epstein, 1990), abolished it. Collectively, these experiments with agonists and antagonists appeared to confirm the validity of the synergy hypothesis in situations in which the appetite was associated with elevated endogenous levels of AngII and aldosterone (Stricker, 1983).

Although the synergy hypothesis originally focused attention on an interaction between mineralocorticoids and AngII, most perturbations of the ECF associated with the arousal of salt appetite increase glucocorticoid levels as well (Stricker *et al.*, 1979). Despite the emphasis of earlier studies on mineralocorticoids, glucocorticoids also modulate the actions of AngII.

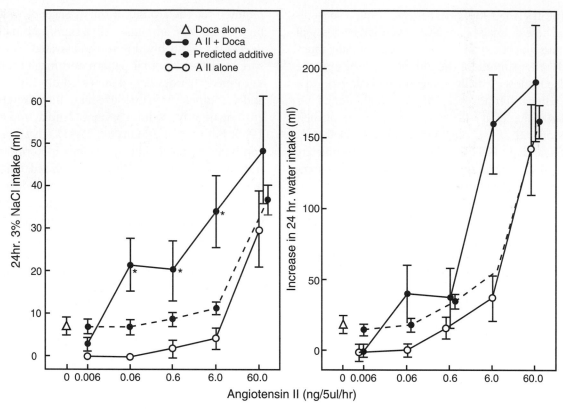

FIGURE 11 Synergistic interaction between the adrenal steroid, deoxycorticosterone (DOCA) and central AngII on (A) salt appetite but (B) not thirst in rats. From Fluharty and Epstein (1983).

For example, glucocorticoids increase the expression of brain angiotensinogen (Bunnemann *et al.,* 1993; Deschepper and Flaxman, 1990; Riftina *et al.,* 1995; Ryan *et al.,* 1997), which may generate more ligand to activate AngII receptors. In addition, glucocorticoids can increase AngII receptors (Ganesan and Sumners, 1989; Sumners *et al.,* 1991; Shelat *et al.,* 1999a) and enhances its cellular signaling (Sato *et al.,* 1992; Shelat *et al.,* 1999b). Finally, glucocorticoids stimulate the expression of Type I (MR) receptors, which may explain how glucocorticoids augment DOCA-induced salt appetite (Ma *et al.,* 1993) and why DOCA, a mixed adrenal steroid agonist, is a better syngery partner with AngII than aldosterone (Fluharty and Epstein, 1983; Sakai, 1986). Thus, the revision of the synergy hypothesis includes an important role for glucocorticoids and Type II (GR) adrenal steroid receptors (Fluharty and Sakai, 1995; see also Chapter 53).

Initially, the analysis of the possible cellular events underlying the synergy focused on the fact that adrenal steroids can increase AngII receptor expression, thus sensitizing the brain to the behavioral actions of AngII. In fact, there is an increase in AngII receptor binding in homogenates from brain tissue (King *et al.,* 1988; Wilson *et al.,* 1986), specific brain nuclei (DeNicola *et al.,* 1993; Gutkind *et al.,* 1988), and neuronal cultures (Fluharty and Sakai, 1995; Sumners and Fregly, 1989) when adrenal steroids are elevated. In all of these previous studies, the identity of the AngII receptor subtype altered by steroids was not known. Further research has examined these changes with greater anatomical resolution and revealed that the combination of glucocorticoids and mineralocorticoids caused a substantial increase in the density of AT$_1$ receptors in the SFO and a similar but much smaller change in the PVN and AP (see Fig. 12, Shelat *et al.,* 1999). Conversely, the absence of adrenal steroids decreases AT$_1$ receptors in the SFO (Shelat *et al.,* 1999a). In almost all cases except the *in vitro* studies, the increase in AngII receptor expression induced

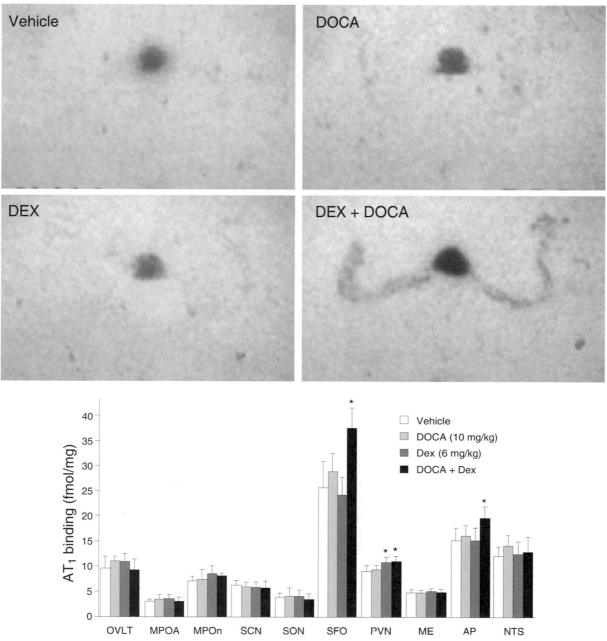

FIGURE 12 Effect of adrenal steroids on AT_1 receptor expression in rat brain. Autoradiogram of SFO. (B) Summary of AT_1 levels in several locations following steroid treatments. AP, area postrema; DEX, dexamethasone; ME, median eminence; MPOA, medial preoptic area; MPOn, medial preoptic nucleus; NTS, nucleus of the solitary tract; OVLT, organum vaculosum of the lamina terminalis; PVN, paraventricular nucelus; SCN, suprachiasmatic nucleus; SFO, subfronical organ; SON, supraoptic nucleus. From Shelat *et al.* (1999a).

by corticosteroids was correlated with increased salt intake.

Several converging lines of evidence suggest that adrenal steroids act genomically to modulate the ex-pression of AT_1 receptors. First, the promoter region of the AT_1 receptor contains an active glucocorti-coid response element (Guo *et al.,* 1995; Pearce and Yamamoto, 1993). Second, the time course of the receptor up-regulation induced by the steroids in a variety of cells (Fluharty and Sakai, 1995; Provencher *et al.*, 1995; Shelat *et al.*, 1999b; Wintersgill *et al.*, 1995) is consistent with a genomic mechanism of action (Carson-Jurica *et al.*, 1990; Tsai and O'Malley, 1994). Third, the steroid effects can be abolished with inhibitors of protein synthesis (Fluharty and Sakai, 1995; Ullian *et al.*, 1992). Last, adrenal steroid effects on AT_1 binding are accompanied by parallel increases in AT_1 mRNA levels (Aguilera *et al.*, 1995; Sato *et al.*, 1994) and injection of RNA isolated from steroid-treated neuroblastoma cells into oocytes increased AT_1 receptor expression (Fluharty and Sakai, 1995).

The enhancement of AngII-induced salt appetite by adrenal steroids implies that the increase in AT_1 receptor expression must amplify some of the cellular actions of the peptide in the brain (cf. Fluharty and Sakai, 1995). The AT_1 receptor is a protypical GPCR (see Fig. 3; cf. Bottari *et al.*, 1993) that is coupled to various G-proteins and multiple signal transduction pathways (see Fig. 13). One of these pathways, phosphoinositide hydrolysis and the attendant mobilization of intracellular calcium (Berridge, 1993), has been implicated in the neuronal actions of AngII (Carrithers *et al.*, 1990; Hay *et al.*, 1993; Mah *et al.*, 1992; Monck *et al.*,

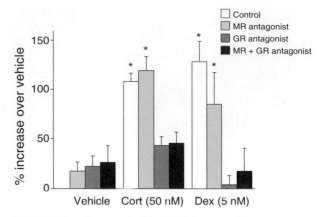

FIGURE 14   Glucocorticoids (GRs) increase AT_1 receptor expression in cultured cells and this up-regulation is blocked by GR-specific antagonists. Cort, corticosterone; Dex, dexamethasone. From Shelat *et al.* (1999b).

1990; Tallent *et al.*, 1991), and there were earlier suggestions that adrenal steroids could augment this cellular response (Fluharty and Sakai, 1995), especially in vascular smooth muscle (Sato *et al.*, 1992; Schiffrin *et al.*, 1984; Ullian *et al.*, 1992).

In order to explore the cellular basis of glucocorticoid and mineralocorticoid regulation of AT_1 receptors and their function, we used a homogenous cell line that expresses corticosteroid receptors (McEwen *et al.*, 1986a) and a high density of AT_1 receptors coupled to phosphoinositide hydrolysis (Bokkala and Joseph, 1997). This study demonstrated that corticosterone and dexamethasone increased the expression of AT_1 receptors and this effect was mediated by activation of the Type II (GR) receptor (see Fig. 14). In contrast, only high doses of aldosterone or DOCA increased AT_1 receptors, and this effect was apparently mediated by the cross-reactivity of these steroids with the Type II (GR) receptor (Reul and de Kloet, 1985) because GR, but not MR, antagonists prevented the up-regulation. Glucocorticoids also enhanced AngII-stimulated InsP3 production, including maximal responses to the peptide, and this effect was probably attributable to the receptor changes because the expression of the G-protein (Gq) that couples AT_1 receptors to a phosphoinositide-specific phospholipase C (Fluharty and Sakai, 1995; Siemens *et al.*, 1991; Taylor *et al.*, 1990) was unaffected. The effects of the mineralocorticoid aldosterone on the intracellular generation of InsP3 were more complex. At low doses of AngII, the response was increased,

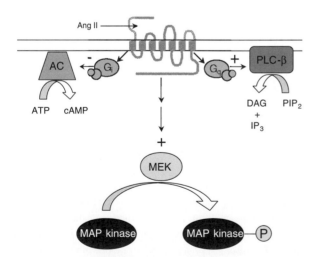

FIGURE 13   Pathways of AT_1-mediated signal transduction in the central nervous system. AC, adenylyl cyclase; ATP, andenosine triphosphate; PLC-β, phospholipase C-β; cAMP, cyclic adenosine monophosphate; DAG, diacylglycerol; IP_3, inositol trisphosphate; MAP kinase, mitogen activated protein kinase; MEK, MAP extracellular signal related kinase; PIP_2, phosphatidylinositol 4, 5 bisphosphate.

but as the dose of AngII approached maximal stimulation this augmentation disappeared, a result reminiscent of pervious observations in neuroblastoma cells (Fluharty and Sakai, 1995). This apparent increase occurred without any change in AT_1 receptor or Gq expression, raising the possibility that agonist-dependent stimulation of phospholipase C or some other aspect of this signal transduction pathway may have been altered (Campbell *et al.,* 1990).

Most of the research motivated by the synergy hypothesis has focused on the hypothesis that the delayed appearance of salt appetite relative to thirst represents the gradual strengthening of an excitatory stimulus (i.e., AngII) by the genomic actions of the adrenal steroids. Alternatively, it has been suggested that this delay is caused by the gradual disappearance of an inhibitory stimulus for salt appetite (Stricker and Verbalis, 1999). The historical foundation of this idea can be traced to a very early observation made in hypovolemic animals that hyponatremia or osmotic dilution inhibits thirst and potentiates salt ingestion (Stricker, 1980, 1981; Stricker *et al.,* 1987; Stricker and Verbalis, 1987, 1988). This reciprocal relationship was used to explain the immediate thirst and delayed salt appetite commonly observed in hypovolemic animals. According to this view, at the onset of hypovolemia the combination of afferent baroreceptor input and elevated AngII levels (see Sections IV.D and IV.E) stimulates thirst, but these inputs are insufficient to arouse salt appetite due to a prevailing unidentified inhibitory stimulus. As the thirst proceeds, the animals dilute their body fluids because the ingested water cannot repair the volume deficit or be readily excreted to prevent the reduction in plasma osmolality. Consequently, as the osmotic dilution intensifies, it inhibits thirst and disinhibits salt appetite. The salt intake raises plasma osmolality, temporarily reinstating thirst and diminishing salt appetite. The continuation of this pattern of alternating fluid consumption permits the animals to ingest the appropriate amounts of water and salt to maintain body fluids near isotonicity.

The fact that osmotic dilution inhibits thirst is well established and the mechanism is quite sensitive— a 5% reduction in plasma osmolality is sufficient to cause complete cessation of water intake despite persistent and severe hypovolemia (cf. Stricker and Verbalis, 1999). However, two central questions continue to spark debate about the hypothesis of a long latency, inhibitory stimulus for salt appetite. First, what is the evidence that reduced plasma osmolality or hyponatremia participates in the control of salt appetite? Second, what is the identity of this putative inhibitory stimulus or stimuli?

One of the first systematic investigations of the role of hyponatremia in the control of salt appetite involved acute sodium loss produced by subcutaneous injection of formalin. Formalin produces severe hypovolemia that is accompanied by significant hyponatremia because local damage to capillaries and ionic pumps permits sodium to accumulate inside of cells. In marked contrast to other procedures such as PEG, that produce equivalent hypovolemia, formalin produces an immediate thirst and a very rapid salt appetite (Jalowiec and Stricker, 1970a). Moroever, when formalin-treated rats are permitted to drink water but not salt so as to exacerbate the hyonatremia, they exhibit a much greater salt appetite when the saline is made available (Jalowiec and Stricker, 1970b). Although these results emphasis the importance of hyponatremia to salt appetite, others do not. For instance, because thirst occurs very rapidly after PEG and the salt intake is delayed, as previously discussed, it has been suggested that the ingestion of water produces a slowly developing hyponatremia in hypovolemic animals that is subsequently responsible for the arousal of salt appetite. However; PEG-treated rats denied access to water and salt for 24 hr drink both fluids as soon as they are available, even though no period of dilutional hyponatremia preceded the salt ingestion (Stricker and Wolf, 1966). Moreover, acute or chronic osmotic dilution produced by intragastric water gavage does not produce salt appetite (Stricker and Wolf, 1966; Bryant *et al.,* 1980). Therefore, hyponatremia appears neither necessary nor sufficient for the arousal of salt appetite. Equally clear, however, is that the presence of hyponatremia in hypovolemic animals, as is usually the case due to the dilution of body fluids by immediate thirst, potentiates salt appetite when other excitatory neural and endocrine signals are of sufficient magnitude to arouse this behavior.

The identification of the signal(s) associated with hyponatremia that might act in the brain to potentiate salt appetite has focused on several candidates. Simplest of these is the sodium ion itself; it has been suggested that a consequence of hyponatremia may be reduced delivery of sodium to a critical set of neurons in the brain (Stricker, 1980; Weisinger *et al.,* 1982). This neural circuit, or an interacting one, may respond to reduced sodium by the activation of the cerebral renin-angiotensin system, and this locally generated AngII could facilitate the stimulatory effects of the circulating hormone (Fluharty and Sakai, 1995; Sakai and Epstein, 1990; Thornton and Nicolaidis, 1994). Although both of these stimuli would presumably act in a stimulatory fashion, the most compelling evidence has favored an important inhibitory role for the neurohypophysial hormone oxytocin in the central control of salt appetite. In this view, hyponatremia potentiates salt appetite during hypovolemia because it removes this inhibitory stimulus (Stricker and Verbalis, 1986; Stricker *et al.,* 1987).

The initial suggestion that the oxytocin might function as the inhibitory stimulus for salt appetite was based on the inverse relationship between salt intake and plasma oxytocin levels consistently observed under a variety of physiological conditions (Stricker and Verbalis, 1987, 1988, 1990, 1999; Stricker *et al.,* 1987). In order to directly test this hypothesis, oxytocin was infused intravenously into hypovolemic rats. Suprisingly, this infusion did not decrease salt ingestion as expected, nor did a similar infusion of an oxytocin receptor antagonist increase saline intake. At first glance, these results did not support this proposed role for oxytocin; then it was recognized that pituitary secretion of peptide into the plasma paralleled its release from neurons projecting from the PVN to elsewhere in the brain. Hence, the hypothesis was revised to propose an inhibitory role for centrally released oxytocin.

The proposal of a central inhibitory role for oxytocin in the control of salt appetite has gained wide acceptance because it is strongly supported by numerous studies; other putative inhibitory peptides, or biogenic amines, such as ANP (Fitts *et al.,* 1985; Schulkin and Fluharty, 1993), tachykinis (Massi *et al.,* 1988), or serotonin (Johnson *et al.,* 1998) have received less attention. For instance, ICV administration of oxytocin inhibited salt, but not water, intake in hypovolemic animals (Stricker and Verbalis, 1987). Presumably this route of administration permits sufficiently high concentrations of the peptide to interact with critical receptor populations in a way that peripheral administration of the hormone does not. In addition, the systemic administration of the opioid antagonist naloxone, which disinhibits oxytocin secretion in the brain, similarly in-

hibited salt appetite and this effect was prevented by the prior central injection of an oxytocin receptor antagonist (R. F. Blackburn *et al.,* 1992). Moreover, salt ingestion elicited by hypovolemia or ICV AngII was enhanced by the antagonism or destruction of oxytocin receptors (R. E. Blackburn *et al.,* 1992; Verbalis *et al.,* 1995), as well a variety of treatments—all of which inhibit the secretion of oxytocin (cf. Stricker and Verbalis, 1988, 1990, 1997, 1999). Most notable in this impressive list of manipulations is the peripheral administration of DOCA (Stricker and Verbalis, 1999) because it suggests that the adrenal steroids may dually regulate salt appetite by enhancing excitatory stimuli (i.e., AngII) and diminishing inhibitory ones. Indeed, although adrenal steroids do not down-regulate oxytocin receptor expression in the brain (Shelat *et al.,* 1998), they do decrease its release, particularly in response to AngII (Stricker and Verbalis, 1999).

F. Summary

Hypovolemia presents a distinctly different challenge for body fluid homeostasis than does hyperosmolality. In hyperosmolality, body fluid osmolality is elevated by dehydration and restored to normal by renal conservation and ingestion of water. The complex composition of the ECF and its pivotal role in cardiovascular function necessitates more elaborate control mechanisms. During blood loss or hypovolemia, the autonomic nervous system is activated and mediates several cardiovascular reflexes and renal adaptations that minimize the impact of the ECF loss on the maintenance of blood pressure. In addition, endocrine responses including the pituitary release of AVP, aldosterone release from the adrenal cortex, and the generation of AngII in the plasma, act in the kidneys to ensure isotonic conservation of water and sodium. AngII has several additional actions within other target organs that contribute to the regulation of body fluid homeostasis, including the brain where it participates in the control of thirst and salt appetite.

The motivated behaviors of thirst and salt appetite complement the neural, endocrine, and renal responses to hypovolemia. Thirst appears to be stimulated by a cooperative interaction between the unloading of baroreceptors and the action of AngII in CVOs of the brain. The stimuli for salt appetite include these same

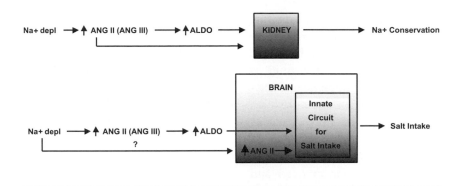

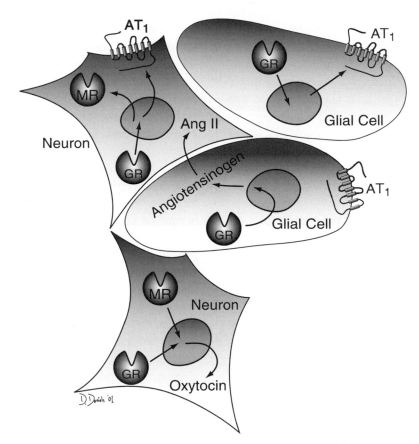

FIGURE 15 Schematic model and proposed cellular mechanisms of the synergy between adrenal steroids and peptides in the central control of salt appetite. (A) Summary of the initial model based on behavioral studies. (B) Cellular interactions. ALDO, aldosterone; MR, mineralocorticoid type I receptor; GR, glucocorticoid type II receptor; AT$_1$, Ang II type 1 receptor.

neural and endocrine interactions, but also include additional hormonal synergies. Of principal importance in this regard are the interactions between the corticosteroids and AngII. The genomic actions of these steroids increase the density of AngII receptors and amplify the cellular singaling mechanisms that transduce the binding of AngII into behavioral actions (see Fig. 15). But there is also a prominent role for an inhibitory peptide oxytocin. Hypovolemia stimulates neurohypophyseal secretion of oxytocin, which is decreased by hyponatremia and adrenal steroids. Thus, during the early stages of hypovolemia prior to the genomic actions of the steroids, thirst predominates under the influence of AngII and baroreceptors because AngII is not yet a sufficient stimulus for salt appetite and oxytocin inhibits it. This initial ingestion of water produces osmotic dilution that reduces oxytocin levels and its inhibitory action on salt intake. As the slowly developing genomic actions of the steroids are established, the oxytocin-mediated inhibition is further removed, and the brain is sensitized to the excitatory action of AngII on salt appetite.

V. CONCLUSION

Body fluid homeostasis requires the successful integration of the complementary physiological mechanisms of conservation and behavioral controls of ingestion. The regulation of these diverse homeostatic processes involves the coordination of neural and endocrine signals. The neural machinery is appropriately attuned to the changing composition of body fluids—osmosensitive neurons monitor plasma osmolality reflective of sodium levels and afferent baroreceptor input detects changes in vascular volume and arterial blood pressure that accompany ECF depletion. But hormones also serve as important interoceptive stimuli that apprise the brain of alterations in body fluid homeostasis. In some cases these chemical signals are generated in peptidergic neurons of the brain (e.g., oxytocin), but in other cases they are circulating hormones (e.g., AVP and AngII) for which the CNS is one of their many target organs. In these instances, the receptors for these hormones are located in CVOs that are uniquely structured to respond to the changes in body fluids during dehydration. Neural mechanisms that monitor the ECF are also localized in these highly specialized structures. And although it is generally accepted that the nervous system controls hormonal secretions, it is equally important that these hormones frequently modulate the impact of neural events.

Another general principle that has emerged from the study of body fluid homeostasis is that the genomic actions of steroids function as longer-term signals that regulate the more rapid behavioral actions of peptides. With regard to the stimulation of salt appetite, a major

hormonal system regulated by adrenal steroids is the renin-angiotensin system. The steroids increase AngII receptor expression and enhance the peptide's production of intracellular second messengers. This augmentation of the cellular actions of AngII is necessary for the arousal of salt appetite and prepares the brain to respond to future episodes of sodium deficiency. The central actions of oxytocin, an important inhibitory control of salt appetite during hypovolemia, are also regulated by corticosteroids. In this case, the regulation is achieved by reducing the neuronal release of oxytocin, thus disinhibiting salt ingestion at a time when the excitatory actions of AngII have been enhanced. Eventually, the combined intakes of salt and water restore the isotonicity of body fluids.

The best testimony regarding the generalities and importance of the neuroendocrine principles that govern body fluid homeostasis is the increasing evidence that similar processes subserve hunger and energy homeostais. The study of feeding behavior is undergoing a revolution with the discovery of several new neurochemical systems (cf. Sawchenko, 1998). Emerging from this research is the realization that some of these hormones act as long-term signals directly (e.g., leptin) or indirectly (e.g., insulin and corticosteroids) related to adiposity and metabolism. Moreover, these peripheral hormones act in the brain and regulate the activity of peptides in the hypothalamus and elsewhere known to be involved in the control of eating behavior. Some of these peptides are excitatory, such as neuropeptide Y, whereas others are inhibitory, most notably the melanocortins. Still other peptides are the more classic circulating hormones (e.g., cholecystokinin) whose behavioral actions are dependent on an interaction with neural signals, particularly vagal afferents that monitor gastric distension (Schwartz and Moran, 1998). The obvious analogies to the mechanisms regulating body fluid osmolality and volume are inescapable, and it is clear that the study of body fluid homeostasis has been invaluable in elucidating the neuroendocrinology of motivated behavior.

Acknowledgments

I thank Drs. Derek Daniels, John Hines, Jon Roth, and Dan Yee for very helpful comments on several earlier versions of this chapter; I am additionally indebted to Derek Daniels for his design of many of the original figures. I am also grateful to Kerry Moore and Deborah Lastowka for their expertise and patience during the preparation of the manuscript. The original research reviewed here was supported, in part, by NIH grants MH43787, NS23986, and DK52018.

References

Aguilera, G., and Marusic, E. T. (1971). Role of the renin-angiotensin system in the biosynthesis of aldosterone. *Endocrinology (Baltimore)* **89**, 1524–1529.

Aguilera, G., Young, W. S., Kiss, A., and Bathia, A. (1995). Direct regulation of hypothalamic corticotropin releasing hormone neurons by angiotensin II. *Neuroendocrinology* **61**, 437–444.

Andersson, B. (1953). The effect of injections of hypertonic NaCl-solutions into different parts of the hypothalamus of goats. *Acta Physiol. Scand.* **28**, 188–201.

Andersson, B. (1978). Regulation of water intake. *Physiol. Rev.* **58**, 582–603.

Ascher, A. W., and Anson, S. G. (1963). A vascular permeability factor of renal origin. *Nature (London)* **198**, 1097–1099.

Avirth, D. B., and Fitzsimons, J. T. (1980). Increased sodium appetite in the rat induced by intracranial administration of components of the renin-angiotensin system. *J. Physiol. (London)* **301**, 349–364.

Baertschi, A. J., and Vallet, P. G. (1981). Osmosensitivity of the hepatic portal vein area and vasopressin release in rats. *J. Physiol. (London)* **315**, 217–230.

Baulieu, E. F. (1978). Cell membrane, a target for steroid hormones. *Mol. Cell. Endocrinol.* **12**, 247–254.

Baylis, P. H., and Thompson, C. J. (1988). Osmoregulation of vasopressin secretion and thirst in health and disease. *Clin. Endocrinol. (Oxford)* **29**, 549–576.

Bealer, S. L., Phillips, M. I., Johnson, A. K., and Schmid, P. G. (1979). Anteroventral third ventricle lesions reduce antidiuretic responses to angiotensin II. *Am. J. Physiol.* **236**, E610–E615.

Berridge, M. J. (1993). Inositol triphosphate and calcium signaling. *Nature (London)* **361**, 315–325.

Bickerton, R. K., and Buckley, J. B. (1961). Evidence for a central mechanism in angiotensin induced hypertension. *Proc. Soc. Exp. Biol. Med.* **106**, 834–836.

Blackburn, R. E., Demko, A. D., Hoffman, G. E., Stricker, E. M., and Verbalis, J. G. (1992). Central oxytocin inhibition of angiotensin induced salt appetite in rats. *Am. J. Physiol.* **263**, R1347–R1353.

Blackburn, R. E., Samson, W. K., Fulton, R. J., Stricker, E. M., and Verbalis, J. G. (1995). Central oxytocin and atrial natriuretic peptide receptors mediate osmotic inhibition of salt appetite in rats. *Am. J. Physiol.* **269**, R245–R251.

Blackburn, R. E., Stricker, E. M., and Verbalis, J. G. (1992). Central oxytocin mediates inhibition of sodium appetite by naloxone in hypovolemic rats. *Neuroendocrinology* **156**, 255–263.

Blass, E. M. (1968). Separation of cellular and extracellular controls of drinking in rats by frontal brain damage. *Science* **162**, 1501–1503.

Blass, E. M., and Epstein, A. N. (1971). A lateral preoptic osmosensitive zone for thirst in the rat. *J. Comp. Physiol. Psych.* **76**, 378–394.

Bokkala, S., and Joseph, S. K. (1997). Angiotensin II-induced down-regulation of inositol triphosphate receptors in WB rat liver epithelial cells. *J. Cell. Biochem.* **272**, 12454–12461.

Bottari, S. P., de Gasparo, M., Steckelings, U. M., and Levens, N. R. (1993). Angiotensin II receptor subtypes: Characterization, signaling mechanism, and possible physiological implications. *Front. Neuroendocrinol.* **14**, 123–171.

Bryant, R. W., Epstein, A. N., Fitzsimons, J. T., and Fluharty, S. J. (1980). Arousal of a specific sodium appetite in the rat with continuous intracerebroventricular infusion of angiotensin II. *J. Physiol. (London)* **301**, 365–382.

Buggy, J., and Fisher, A. E. (1974). Evidence for a dual central role for angiotensin in water and sodium intake. *Nature (London)* **250**, 735.

Buggy, J., and Johnson, A. K. (1977). Preoptic-hypothalamic penventricular lesions: Thirst deficits and hypernatremia. *Am. J. Physiol.* **233**, R44–R52.

Bumpus, F. M., Catt, K. J., Chiu, A. T., de Gasparo, M., Goodfriend, T., Husain, A., Peace, M. J., Taylor, D. G., Jr., and Timmermans, P. B. (1991). Nomenclature for angiotensin receptors. A report of the Nomenclature Committee of the Council for High Blood Pressure Research. *Hypertension* **17**, 720–721.

Bunnemann, B., Lippoldt, A., Aguirre, J. A., Cintra, A., and Metzger, R. (1993). Glucocorticoid regulation of angiotensinogen gene expression in discrete areas of the male rat brain. *Neuroendocrinology* **57**, 856–862.

Butcher, R. L., Collins, W. E., and Fugo, N. W. (1974). Plasma concentration of LH, FSH, prolactin, progesterone, and estradiol-17β throughout the 4-day estrous cycle of the rat. *Endocrinology (Baltimore)* **94**, 1704–1708.

Cade, R., and Perenich, T. (1965). Secretion of aldosterone by rats. *Am. J. Physiol.* **208**, 1026–1030.

Campbell, M. D., Subramaniam, S., Kotlikoff, M. I., Williamson, J. R., and Fluharty, S. J. (1990). Cyclic AMP modulates inositol polyphosphate production and calcium mobilization in neuroblastoma x glioma hybrid NG108-15 Cells. *Mol. Pharmacol.* **38**, 282–288.

Cannon, W. B. (1918). The physiological basis of thirst. *Proc. R. Soc. London* **90**, 283–301.

Cantin, M., and Genest, J. (1985). The heart and the atrial natriuretic factor. *Endocr. Rev.* **6**, 107–127.

Cantin, M., Tautu, C., Ballak, M., Yung, L., Benchimol, S., and Beuzeron, J. (1980). Ultrastructural cytochemistry of atrial muscle cells. IX. Reactivity of specific granules in cultured cardiocytes. *J. Mol. Cell. Cardiol.* **12**, 1033.

Carrithers, M. D., Raman, V. K., Masuda, S., and Weyhenmeyer, J. A. (1990). Effect of angiotensin II and III on inositol polyphosphate production in differentiated NGI08-15 hybrid cells. *Biochem. Biophys. Res. Commun.* **167**, 1200–1205.

Carson-Jurica, M. A., Schrader, W. T., and O'Malley, B. W. (1990). Steroid receptor family: Structure and functions. *Endoc. Rev.* **11**, 210–220.

Casto, R., and Phillips, M. I. (1984). Cardiovascular actions of microinjections of angiotensin II in the brain stem of rats. *Am. J. Physiol.* **246**, R811–R816.

Catanzaro, D. F., Mullins, J. J., and Morris, B. J. (1983). The biosynthetic pathway of renin in mouse submandibular gland. *J. Biol. Chem.* **258**, 7364–7368.

Catt, K. J., Carson, M. C., Hausdorff, W. P., Leach-Harper, C. M., Baukal, A. J., Guillemette, G., Balla, T., and Aguilera, G. (1987). Angiotensin II receptors and mechanisms of action in adrenal glomerulosa cells. *J. Steroid Biochem.* **27**(4–6), 915–927.

Chartier, L., Schiffrin, E. L., Thibault, G., and Garcia, R. (1984). Atrial natriuretic factor inhibits the effect of angiotensin II, ACTH and potassium on aldosterone secretion in vitro and angiotensin II-induced steroidogenesis in vivo. *Endocrinology (Baltimore)* **115**, 2026.

Chen, F. M., Hawkins, R., and Printz, M. P. (1982). Evidence for a functional, independent brain-angiotensin system: Correlation between regional distribution of brain angiotensin receptors, brain angiotensinogen, and drinking during the estrus cycle of rats. *Exp. Brain Res., Suppl.* **4**, 157–168.

Chiaraviglio, E. (1976). Effect of the renin-angiotensin system on sodium intake. *J. Physiol. (London)* **255**, 57–66.

Chiu, A. T., Herblin, W. F., McCall, D. E., Ardecky, R. J., Carmni, D. J., Duncia, J. V., Pease, L. J., Wong, P. C., Wexler, R. R., Johnson, A. L., and Timmermans, P. B. M. W. M. (1989). Identification of angiotensin 11 receptor subtypes. *Biochem. Biophy. Res. Commu.* **165**, 196–203.

Coburn, P. C., and Stricker, E. M. (1978). Osmoregulatory thirst in rats after lateral preoptic lesions. *J. Comp. Physiol. Psychol.* **92**, 350–361.

Dalman, M. F., Scherrer, F. C., and Taylor, L. (1991). Localization of the HSP90 binding site within the hormone binding domain of the glucocorticoid receptor by peptide competition. *J. Biol. Chem.* **266**, 3482–3490.

DeBold, A. J., Borenstein, H. B., Veress, A. T., and Sonnenberg, H. (1981). A rapid and potent natriuretic response to intravenous injection of atrial myocardial extract in rats. *Life Sci.* **28**, 89–94.

DeNicola, A. F., Seltzer, A., Tsutsumi, K., and Saavedra, J. M. (1993). Effects of deoxycorticosterone acetate (DOCA) and aldosterone on Sar1-angiotensin II binding sites in the brain. *Cell. Mol. Neurobiol.* **13**, 529–539.

Deschepper, C. F., and Flaxman, M. (1990). Glucocorticoid regulation of rat diencephalons angiotensinogen production. *Endocrinology (Baltimore)* **126**, 963–970.

De Wardener, H. E., Mills, I. H., Clapham, W. F., and Hayter, C. J. (1961). Studies on the efferent mechanism of the sodium diuresis which follows the administration of intravenous saline in the dog. *Clin. Sci.* **21**, 249–258.

Diz, D. I., Barnes, K. L., and Ferrario, C. M. (1984). Hypotensive actions of microinjections of angiotensin II into the dorsal motor nucleus of the vagus. *J. Hypertens.* **2**(Suppl. 3), 53–56.

Dragunow, M., and Fraull, R. (1989). The use of c-Fos as a metabolic marker in neuronal pathway tracing. *J. Neurosci. Methods* **29**, 261–265.

Dunn, F. L., Brennan, T. J., Nelson, A. E., and Robertson, G. L. (1973). The role of blood osmolality and volume in regulating vasopressin secretion in the rat. *J. Clin. Invest.* **52**, 3212–3219.

Dzau, V. J., Ingelfinger, J., Pratt, R. E., and Ellison, K. E. (1986). Identification of renin and angiotensinogen messenger RNA sequences in mouse and rat brains. *Hypertension* **8**, 544–548.

Eisen, L. P., and Harmon, J. M. (1986). Activation of the rat kidney mineralocorticoid receptor. *Endocrinology (Baltimore)* **119**, 1419–1426.

Epstein, A. N. (1982). Mineralocorticoids and cerebral angiotensin may act together to produce sodium appetite. *Peptides (Fayetteville, NY)* **3**, 493–494.

Epstein, A. N. (1984). The dependence of the salt appetite of the rat on the hormonal consequences of sodium deficiency. *J. Physiol. (Paris)* **79**, 496–498.

Epstein, A. N., and Stellar, E. (1955). The control of salt preference in the adrenalectomized rat. *J. Comp. Physiol. Psychol.* **48**, 167–172.

Epstein, A. N., Fitzsimons, J. T., and Rolls, B. J. (1970). Drinking induced by injection of angiotensin into the brain of the rat. *J. Physiol. (London)* **210**, 457–474.

Evered, M. D. (1992). Investigating the role of angiotensin II in thirst: Interactions between arterial pressure and the control of drinking. *Can. J. Physiol. Pharmacol.* **70**, 791–797.

Evered, M. D., Robinson, M. M., and Rose, P. A. (1988). Effect of arterial pressure on drinking and urinary responses to angiotensin II. *Am. J. Physiol.* **254**, R67–R74.

Falcon, J. C., II, Phillips, M. I., Hoffman, W. E., and Brody, M. J. (1978). Effects of intraventricular angiotensin II mediated by the sympathetic nervous system. *Am. J. Physiol.* **235**, H392–H399.

Falk, J. L. (1966). Serial sodium depletion and NaCI solution intake. *Physiol. Behav.* **1**, 75–77.

Falk, J. L., and Lipton, J. M. (1967). Temporal factors in the genesis of NaCI appetite by intraperitoneal dialysis. *J. Comp. Physiol. Psychol.* **63**, 247–251.

Felix, D., and Schelling, P. (1982). Increased sensitivity of neurons to angiotensin II in SHR as compared to WKY rats. *Brain Res.* **252**, 63–69.

Ferguson, A. V., and Renaud, L. P. (1986). Systemic angiotensin acts at subfornical organ to facilitate activity of neurohypophysial neurons. *Am. J. Physiol.* **251**, R721–R717.

Findlay, A. L. R., and Epstein, A. N. (1980). Increased sodium intake is somehow induced in rats by intravenous angiotensin II. *Horm. Behav.* **14**, 86–92.

Findlay, A. L. R., Fitzsimmons, J. T., and Kucharczyk, J. (1979). Dependence of spontaneous and angiotensin-induced drinking in the rat upon the oestrous cycle and ovarian hormones. *J. Endocrinol.* **82**, 215–225.

Fitts, D. A., and Masson, D. B. (1989). Forebrain sites of action for drinking and salt appetite to angiotensin or captopril. *Behav. Neurosci.* **103**, 865–872.

Fitts, D. A., and Masson, D. B. (1990). Preoptic angiotensin and salt appetite. *Behav. Neurosci.* **104**, 643–650.

Fitts, D. A., Thunhorst, R. L., and Simpson, J. B. (1985). Natriuresis and reduction of salt appetite by lateral ventricular infusion of atriopeptin II. *Brain Res.* **348**, 118–124.

Fitzsimons, J. T. (1961). Drinking by rats depleted of body fluid without increase in osmotic pressure. *J. Physiol. (London)* **159**, 297–309.

Fitzsimons, J. T. (1969). The role of a renal thirst factor in drinking induced by extracellular stimuli. *J. Physiol. (London)* **201**, 349–368.

Fitzsimons, J. T. (1979). "The Physiology of Thirst and Sodium Appetite." Cambridge University Press, Cambridge, UK.

Fitzsimons, J. T., and Moore-Gillon, M. J. (1980). Drinking and antidiuresis in response to reductions in venous return in the dog: Neural and endocrine mechanisms. *J. Physiol. (London)* **308**, 403–416.

Fitzsimons, J. T., and Simons, B. J. (1969). The effect on drinking in the rats of intravenous angiotensin, given alone or in combination with other stimuli of thirst. *J. Physiol. (London)* **203**, 45–57.

Fitzsimons, J. T., and Stricker, E. M. (1971). Sodium appetite and the renin-angiotensin system. *Nature (London). New Biol.* **231**, 58–60.

Flanagan-Cato, L. M., and Fluharty, S. J. (1995). Guanine nucleotide regulation and cateon sensitivity of agonist binding to rat brain oxytocin receptors. *Brain Res.* **701**, 75–80.

Flanagan-Cato, L. M., and Fluharty, S. J. (1997). Emerging mechanisms of the behavioral effects of steroids. In "Current Opinions in Neurobiology" (D. Sparks and R. Harris-Warwick, eds.), Vol. 7, pp. 844–848. Current Biology.

Fluharty, S. J., and Epstein, A. N. (1983). Sodium appetite elicited by intraceribroventricular infusion of angiotensin II in the rat: II Synergistic interaction with systemic mineralcorticoids. *Behav. Neurosci.* **97**, 746–758.

Fluharty, S. J., and Manaker, S. (1983). Sodium appetite elicited by intracerebroventricular infusion of angiotensin II in the rat: I. Relation to urinary sodium excretion. *Behav. Neurosci.* **97**, 738–745.

Fluharty, S. J., and Sakai, R. R. (1995). Behavioral and cellular analysis of adrenal steroid and angiotensin interactions mediating salt appetite. In "Progress in Psychobiology and Physiological Psychology" Vol. 16 (S. J. Fluharty, A. R. Morrison, J. M. Sprague and E. Stellar, eds.), pp. 177–212. Academic Press, New York.

Fregly, M. J. (1980). Effect of chronic treatment with estrogen on the dipsogenic response of rats to angiotensin. *Pharmacol., Biochem. Behav.* **12**, 131–136.

Fregly, M. J., and Rowland, N. E. (1985). Role of renin-angiotensin-aldosterone system in NaCl appetite of rats. *Am. J. Physiol.* **248**, R1–R11.

Fregly, M. J., and Rowland, N. E. (1991). Effect of nonpeptide angiotensin II receptor antagonist, DUP7S3, on angiotensin-related water intake in rats. *Brain Res. Bull.* **27**, 97–100.

Fregly, M. J., and Thrasher, T. N. (1978). Attenuation of angiotensin II-induced water intake in estrogen-treated rats. *Pharmacol., Biochem. Behav.* **9**, 509–514.

Fregly, M. J., and Waters, I. W. (1966). Effect of mineralocorticoids on spontaneous sodium chloride appetite of adrenalectomized rats. *Physiol. Behav.* **1**, 65–74.

Fregly, M. J., Rowland, N. E., Sumners, C., and Gordon, D. B. (1985). Reduced dipsogenic responsiveness to intracerebroventricularly administered angiotensin II in estrogen-treated rats. *Brain Res.* **338**, 115–121.

Fugiwara, T. M., Morgan, K., and Bichet, D. G. (1995). Molecular biology of diabetes insipidus. *Annu. Rev. Med.* **46**, 331–343.

Funder, J. W. (1990). 1 β-Hydroxysteroid dehydrogenase and the meaning of life. *Mol. Cell. Endocrinol.* **68**, C3–C5.

Galaverna, O., Deluca, L. A., Schulkin, J., Yao, S. Z., and Epstein, A. N. (1992). Deficits in NaCl ingestion after damage to the central nucleus of the amygdala. *Brain Res. Bull.* **28**, 89–98.

Ganesan, R., and Sumners, C. (1989). Glucocorticoids potentiate the dispogenic action of angiotensin II. *Brain Res.* **499**, 121–130.

Ganong, W. F. (1994). Origin of the angiotensin II secreted by cells. *Proc. Soc. Exp. Biol. Med.* **205**, 213–219.

Ganten, D., and Speck, G. (1978). The brain renin-angiotensin system: A model for the synthesis of peptides in the brain. *Biochem. Pharmacol.* **27**, 2379–2389.

Ganten, D., Hermann, K., Bayer, C., Unger, T., and Lang, R. E. (1983). Angiotensin synthesis in the brain and increased turnover in hypertensive rats. *Science* **221**, 869–871.

Gauer, O. H., and Henry, J. P. (1963). Circulatory basis of fluid volume control. *Physiol. Rev.* **43**, 423–481.

Gehlert, D. R., Gackenheimer, S. L., and Schober, D. A. (1991). Autoradiographic localization of subtypes of angiotensin II antagonist binding in the rat brain. *Neuroscience* **44**, 501–514.

Geller, D. M., Currie, M. C., Wakitani, K., Cole, B. R., Adams, S. P., Fok, K. F., Siegel, N. R., Eubanks, S. R., Galluppi, G. R., and Needleman, P. (1984). Atriopeptins: A family of potent biologically active peptides derived from mammalian atria. *Biochem. Biophys. Res. Commun.* **120**, 133.

Gilman, A. (1937). The relation between blood osmotic pressure, fluid distribution and voluntary water intake. *Am. J. Physiol.* **120**, 323–328.

Guo, D. F., Uno, S., Ishihata, A., Nakamura, N., and Inagami, T. (1995). Identification of a *cis*-acting glucocorticoid responsive element in the rat angiotensin II type 1A promotor. *Circ. Res.* **77**, 249–257.

Gutkind, J. S., Kurihara, M., and Saavedra, J. M. (1988). Increased angiotensin II receptors in brain nuclei of DOCA-salt hypertensive rats. *Am. J. Physiol.* **255**, H646–H650.

Guyton, A. C. (1991). "Textbook of Medical Physiology," 8th ed. Saunders, Philadelphia.

Gyurko, R., Wielbo, D., and Phillips, M. I. (1993). Antisense inhibition of AT_1 receptor mRNA and angiotensinogen mRNA in the brain of spontaneously hypertensive rats reduces hypertension of neurogenic origin. *Regul. Pept.* **49**, 167–174.

Hamet, P., Tremblay, J., Pang, S. C., Carrier, F., Thibault, G., Gutkowska, J., Cantin, M., and Genest, J. (1984). Effect of native and synthetic atrial natriuretic factor on cyclic GMP. *Biochem. Biophys. Res. Commun.* **123**, 515.

Hay, M., Edwards, U. L., Lindsley, K., Murphy, S., Shamia, R. V., Bhalla, R. C., and Johnson, A. K. (1993). Increases in cytosolic $Ca^{2~}$ in rat area postrema/inNTS neurons produced by angiotensin II and arginine-vasopressin. *Neurosci. Lett.* **151**, 121–125.

Healy, D. P., and Printz, M. P. (1984). Distribution of immunoreactive angiotensin II, angiotensin I, angiotensinogen, and renin in the central nervous system of intact and nephrectomized rats. *Hypertension* **6**(Suppl I), I-130–I-136.

Healy, D. P., Ye, M. Q., Yuan, L. X., and Schachter, B. S. (1992). Stimulation of angiotensinogen mRNA levels in rat pituitary by estradiol. *Am. J. Physiol.* **263**, E355–E361.

Herbert, J., Forsling, M. L., Howes, S. R., Stacey, P. M., and Shiers, H. M. (1992). Regional expression of c-Fos antigen in the basal forebrain following intraventricular infusions of angiotensin and its modulation by drinking either water or saline. *Neuroscience* **51**, 867–882.

Hoffman, G. E., Smith, M. S., and Verbalis, J. G. (1993). C-Fos and related immediate early gene products as markers of activity in neuroendocrine systems. *Front. Neuroendocrinol.* **14**, 173–213.

Hoffman, W. E., and Phillips, M. I. (1976). Regional study of cerebral ventricle sensitive sites to angiotensin II. *Brain Res.* **110**, 313–330.

Hosutt, I. A., and Stricker, E. M. (1981). Hypotension and thirst in rats after phentolamine treatment. *Physiol. Behav.* **27**, 463–468.

Hosutt, J. A., Rowland, N., and Stricker, E. M. (1978). Hypotension and thirst in rats after isoproterenol treatment. *Physiol. Behav.* **21**, 593–598.

Hosutt, J. A., Rowland, N., and Stricker, E. M. (1981). Impaired drinking responses of rats with lesions of the subfornical organ. *J. Comp. Physiol. Psych.* **95**, 104–113.

Houpt, K. A., and Epstein, A. N. (1971). The complete dependence of beta-adrenergic drinking on the renal dipsogen. *Physiol. Behav.* **7**, 897–902.

Hsaio, S., Epstein, A. N., and Camardo, J. S. (1977). The dipsogenic potency of peripheral angiotensin II. *Horm. Behav.* **8**, 129–140.

Jacobowitz, D. M., Skofisch, G., Keiser, H. R., Eskay, R. L., and Zamir, N. (1984). Evidence for the existence of atrial natriuretic factor-containing neurons in rat brain. *Neuroendocrinology* **40**, 92.

Jalowiec, J.-E., and Stricker, E. M. (1970a). Restoration of body fluid balance following acute sodium deficiency in rats. *J. Comp. Physiol. Psychol.* **70**, 94–102.

Jalowiec, J. E., and Stricker, E. M. (1970b). Sodium appetite in rats after apparent recovery from acute sodium deficiency. *J. Comp. Physiol. Psychol.* **73**, 238–244.

Jellinek, P. H., Monder, C., McEwen, B. S., and Sakai, R. R. (1993). Differential inhibition of 11 β-hydroxysteroid dehydrogenase by carbenoxolone in rat brain regions and peripheral tissues. *J. Steroid Biochem.* **46**, 209–213.

Jensen, L. L., Harding, J. W., and Wright, J. W. (1992). Role of paraventricular nucleus in control of blood pressure and drinking in rats. *Am. J. Physiol.* **262**, F1068–F1075.

Jewell, P. A., and Verney, E. B. (1957). An experimental attempt to determine the site of the neurohypophysial osmoreceptors in the dog. *Philos. Trans. R. Soc. London, Ser. B* **240**, 197–324.

Jhamandas, J. H., Lind, R. W., and Renaud, L. P. (1989). Angiotensin II may mediate excitatory neurotransmission from the subfornical organ to the hypothalamic supraoptic nucleus: An anatomical and electrophysiological study in the rat. Brain Res. 487, 52–61.

Johnson, A. K., and Buggy, J. (1978). Periventricular preoptic-hypothalamus is vital for thirst and normal water economy. Am. J. Physiol. 234, R122–R125.

Johnson, A. K., and Epstein, A. N. (1975). The cerebral ventricles as the avenue for the dipsogenic action of intracranial angiotensin. Brain Res. 68, 399–418.

Johnson, A. K., Mann, J. F. E., Rascher, W., Johnson, J. K., and Ganten, D. (1981). Plasma angiotensin II concentrations and experimentally induced thirst. Am. J. Physiol. 240, R229–R234.

Johnson, A. K., and Thunhorst, R. L. (1995). Sensory mechanisms in the behavioral control of body fluid balance: Thirst and salt appetite. In "Progress in Psychobiology and Physiological Psychology" Vol. 16 (S. J. Fluharty, A. R. Morrison, J. M. Sprague, and E. Stellar, eds.), pp. 145–176. Academic Press, New York.

Jonklaas, J., and Buggy, J. (1985). Angiotensin-estrogen central interaction: Localization and mechanism. Brain Res. 326, 239–249.

Joy, M. D. (1971). The intramedullary connections of the area potrema involved in the central cardiovascular response to angiotensin II. Clin. Sci. 41, 89–100.

Joy, M. D., and Lowe, R. D. (1970). The site of cardiovascular action of angiotensin II in the brain. Clin. Sci. 39, 327–336.

Kaufman, S. (1984). Role of right atrial receptors in the control of drinking in the rat. J. Physiol. (London) 349, 389–396.

Keil, L. C., Summy Long, J., and Severs, W. B. (1975). Release of vasopressin by angiotensin II. Endocrinology (Baltimore) 96, 1063–1065.

King, S. J., Harding, J. W., and Moe, K. E. (1988). Elevated salt appetite and brain binding of angiotensin II in mineralocorticold-treated rats. Brain Res. 448, 140–149.

Kirby, R. F., Thunhorst, R. L., and Johnson, A. K. (1992). Effects of a non-peptide angiotensin receptor antagonist on drinking and blood pressure responses to centrally administered angiotensins in the rat. Brain Res. 576, 348–350.

Kisley, L. R., Sakai, R. R., Ma, Y. Y., and Fluharty, S. J. (1999a). Ovarian steroid hormone regulation of angiotensin II induced water intake in the rat. Am. J. Physiol. 276, R90–R96.

Kisley, L. R., Sakai, R. R., and Fluharty, S. J. (1999b). Estrogen regulation of gene expression in the pituitary and central renin-angiotensin systems. Brain Res. 844, 34–42.

Kisley, L. R., Sakai, R. R., Ma, L. Y., Flanagan-Cato, L. M., and Fluharty, S. J. (2000). Estrogen-induced changes in c-fos expression in forebrain following central angiotensin II. Neuroendocrinology 72, 306–317.

Kleinert, H. D., Maack, T., Atlas, S. A., Januszewicz, A., Sealey, J. E., and Laragh, J. H. (1984). Atrial natriuretic factor inhibits angiotensin-, norepinephrine-, and potassium-induced vascular contractility. Hypertension 6, 1.

Kucharezyk, J., Cowan, J., and Layberry, R. (1987). Pressor inhibition of angiotensin-induced ACTH secretion. Can. J. Physiol. Pharmacol. 65, 2308–2312.

Laird, J. F. (1984). Vasopressin in cardiovascular control: Role of circulating vasopressin. Clin. Sci. 67, 473–481.

Lakshmi, V., Sakai, R. R., McEwen, B. S., and Monder, C. (1991). Regional distribution of 11 β-hydroxysteroid dehydrogenase in rat brain. Endocrinology (Baltimore) 128, 1741–1748.

Lebrun, C. J., Blume, A., Herdegen, T., Seifert, K., Bravo, R., and Unger, T. (1995). Angiotensin II induces a complex activation of transcription factors in the rat brain: Expression of Fos, Jun, and Krox proteins. Neuroscience 65, 93–99.

Leenen, F. H. H., and Sticker, E. M. (1974). Plasma renin activity and thirst following hypovolemia or caval ligation in rats. Am. J. Physiol. 226, 1238–1242.

Lehr, D., Mallow, J., and Krukowski, M. (1967). Copious drinking and simultaneous inhibition of urine flow elicited by β-adrenergic stimulation and contrary effect of colinergic stimulation. J. Pharmacol. Exp. Ther. 158, 150–163.

Lehr, D., Goldman, H. W., and Casner, P. (1973). Renin-angiotensin role in thirst: Paradoxical enhancement of drinking by angiotensin convening enzyme inhibitor. Science 182, 1031–1034.

Levens, N. R., Peach, M. J., and Carey, R. M. (1981a). Interactions between angiotensin peptides and the sympathetic nervous system mediating intestinal sodium and water absorption in the rat. J. Clin. Invest. 67, 1197–1207.

Levens, N. R., Peach, M. J., Carey, R. M., Poat, J. A., and Munday, K. A. (1981b). Response of the rat jejunum to angiotensin II: Role of norepinephrine and prostaglandins. Am. J. Physiol. 240, G17–G24.

Linazasoro, J. M., Jimenez Diaz, C., and Castro Mendoza, H. (1954). The kidney and thirst regulation. Bull. Inst. Med. Res. 7, 53–61.

Lind, R. W., and Johnson, A. K. (1982). Subfornical organ-median preoptic connections and drinking and pressor responses to angiotensin II. J. Neurosci. 2, 1043–1051.

Lind, R. W., Van Hoesen, G. W., and Johnson, A. K. (1982). An HRP study of the connections of the subfonical organ of the rat. J. Comp. Neurol. 210, 265–277.

Loudon, M., Bing, R. F., Thurston, H., and Swales, J. D. (1983). Arterial wall uptake of renal renin and blood pressure control. Hypertension 5, 629–634.

Lynch, K. R., Hawelu-Johnson, C. L., and Guyenet, P. G. (1987). Localization of brain angiotensinogen mRNA by hybridization histochemistry. *Mol. Brain Res.* **2**, 149–158.

Ma, L. Y., McEwen, B. S., Sakai, R. R., and Schulkin, J. (1993). Glucocorticoids facilitate mineralocorticoid-induced sodium intake in the rat. *Horm. Behav.* **27**, 240–250.

Mah, S. J., Ades, A. M., Mir, R., Siemens, I. R., Williamson, J. R., and Fluharty, S. J. (1992). Association of solubilized angiotensin II receptors with phospholipase C in murine neuroblastoma NIE-I 15 cells. *Mol. Pharmacol.* **42**, 428–437.

Mahon, J. M., Allen, M., Herbert, J., and Fitzsimmons, J. T. (1995). The association of thirst, sodium appetite, and vasopressin release with c-Fos expression in the forebrain of the rat after intracerebroventricular injection of angiotensin II, angiotensin-(1–7), or carbachol. *Neuroscience* **69**, 199–208.

Malik, K. U., and Nasjletti, A. (1976). Facilitation of adrenergic transmission by locally generated angiotensin II in rat mesenteric arteries. *Circ. Res.* **38**, 26–30.

Mangiapane, M. L., and Simpson, J. B. (1980). Subfornical organ: Forebrain site of pressor and dipsogenic action of angiotensin II. *Am. J. Physiol.* **239**, R382–R389.

Mangiapane, M. L., Thrasher, T. N., Keil, L. C., Simpson, J. B., and Ganong, W. F. (1983). Deficits in drinking and vasopre- ssin secretion after lesions of nucleus medianus. *Neuroendocrinology* **37**, 73–77.

Mann, J. F. E., Johnson, A. K., and Ganten, D. (1980). Plasma angiotensin II: Dipsogenic levels and angiotensin-generating capacity of renin. *Am. J. Physiol.* **238**, R372–R377.

Mann, J. F. E., Johnson, A. K., Ganten, D., and Ritz, E. (1987). Thirst and the renin-angiotensin system. *Kidney Int.* **32**(Suppl. 21), 527–534.

Massi, M., Polidori, C., Gentili, L., Perfumi, M., de Caro, G., and Maggi, C. A. (1988). The tachykinin NH$_2$-senktide, a selective neurokinin B receptor agonist, is a very potent inhibitor of salt appetite in the rat. *Neurosci. Lett.* **92**, 341–346.

Masson, D. B., and Fitts, D. A. (1989). Subfornical organ connectivity and drinking to captopril or carbachol in rats. *Behav. Neurosci.* **103**, 873–880.

Matsuba, H., Watanabe, T., Watanabe, M., Ishii, Y., Waguri, S., Kominami, E., and Uchiyama, Y. (1989). Immunohistochemical localization of prorenin, renin and cathepsins B, H, and L in juxtaglomerular cells of the rat kidney. *J. Histochem. Cytochem.* **37**, 1689–1697.

McEwen, B. S., de Kloet, E., and Rostene, W. (1986a). Adrenal steroid receptors and actions in the nervous system. *Physiological Rev.* **66**, 1121–1188.

McEwen, B. S., Lamdin, L. T., Rainbow, T. C., and DeNicola, A. F. (1986b). Aldosterone effects on salt appetite in adrenalectomized rats. *Neuroendocrinology* **43**, 38–43.

McKinley, M. J., Denton, D. A., and Weisinger, R. S. (1978). Sensors for antidiuresis and thirst-osmoreceptors or CSF sodium detectors. *Brain Res.* **141**, 89–103.

McKinley, M. J., McAllen, R. M., Mendelsohn, F. A. O., Allen, A. M., Chai, S. Y., and Oldfield, B. J. (1990). Circumventricular organs: Neuroendocrine interfaces between the brain and the humoral milieu. *Front. Neuroendocrinol.* **11**, 91–127.

Miselis, R. R. (1981). The efferent projections of the subfornical organ of the rat: A circumventricular organ within a neural network subserving water balance. *Brain Res.* **230**, 1–23.

Miselis, R. R., Shapiro, R. E., and Hand, P. J. (1979). Subfornical organ efferents to neural systems for control of body water. *Science* **205**, 1022–1025.

Misono, R. S., Fukumi, H., Grammer, R. T., and Inagami, T. (1984). Rat atrial natriuretic factor: Complete amino acid sequence and disulfide linkage essential for biological activity. *Biochem. Biophys. Res. Commun.* **120**, 981–988.

Monck, J. R., Williamson, R. E., Rogulja, I., Fluharty, S. J., and Williamson, J. R. (1990). Angiotensin II effects on the cytosolic free Ca^2 concentration in NIE-1 15 neuroblastoma cells: Kinetic properties of the Ca^2 transient measured in single fura-2-loaded cells. *J. Neurochem.* **54**, 278–287.

Monder, C., and Lakshmi, V. (1990). Corticosteroid 11 β-hydrogenase of rat tissues: Immunological studies. *Endocrinology (Baltimore)* **126**, 2435–2443.

Moore-Gillon, M. I., and Fitzsimons, J. T. (1982). Pulmonary vein-atrial junction stretch receptors and the inhibition of drinking. *Am. J. Physiol.* **242**, R452–R457.

Morgan, K. G. (1987). Calcium and smooth muscle tone. *Am. J. Med.* **82**(Suppl. 3B), 9–15.

Nachman, M., and Valentino, D. A. (1966). Roles of taste and postingestional factors in the satiation of sodium appetite in rats. *J. Comp. Physiol. Psychol.* **62**, 280–283.

Nairn, R. C., Masson, G. M. C., and Corcoran, A. C. (1956). The production of serous effusions in nephrectomized animals by the administration of renal extracts and renin. *J. Pathol. Bacteriol.* **71**, 151–163.

Navar, L. G., and Rosivall, L. (1984). Contribution of the renin-angiotensin system to the control of intrarenal hemodynamics. *Kidney Int.* **25**, 857–868.

Obermuller, N., Unger, T., Gohlke, P., de Gasparo, M., and Bottari, S. P. (1991). Distibution of angiotensin II receptor subtypes in rat brain nuclei. *Neurosci. Lett.* **132**, 11–15.

Oldfield, B. J. (1991). Neurochemistry of the circuitry subserving thirst. *In* "Thirst. Physiological and Psychological Aspects" (D. J. Ramsay and D. Booth, eds.), pp. 176–193. Springer-Verlag, London.

Oldfield, B. J., Badoer, E., Hards, D. K., and McKinley, M. J. (1994). Fos production in retrogradely labeled neurons of the lamina terminalis following intravenous infusion of either hypertonic saline or angiotensin II. *Neuroscience* **60**, 255–262.

Pawloski, C. M., and Fink, G. D. (1990). Circulating angiotensin II and drinking behavior in rats. *Am. J. Physiol.* **259**, R531–R538.

Peach, M. J. (1977). Renin-angiotensin system: Biochemistry and mechanism of action. *Physiol. Rev.* **57**, 313–370.

Pearce, D., and Yamamoto, K. R. (1993). Mineralocorticoid and glucocorticoid receptor activities distinguished by nonreceptor factors at a composite response element. *Science* **259**, 1161–1165.

Peck, J. W., and Novin, D. (1971). Evidence that osmoreceptors mediating drinking in rabbits are in the lateral preoptic area. *J. Comp. Physiol. Psych.* **74**, 134–147.

Pfaff, D. W. (1980). "Estrogens and brain function: Neural analysis of a hormone-controlled mammalian reproductive behavior." Springer-Verlag, New York.

Phillips, J., and Eberwine, J. H. (1996). Antisense RNA amplification: A linear amplification method for analyzing the mRNA population from single living cells. *Methods: Companion to Methods Enzymol.* **10**, 283–288.

Phillips, M. I. (1978). Angiotensin in the brain. *Neuroendocrinology* **25**, 354–377.

Phillips, M. I., and Hoffman, W. E. (1976). Sensitive sites in the brain for blood pressure and drinking responses to angiotensin II. *In* "Central Actions of Angiotensin and Related Hormones" (F. P. Buckley and C. Ferrario, eds.), pp. 325–356. Pergamon Press, New York.

Phillips, M. I., Weyhenmeyer, D., and Ganten, D. (1979). Evidence for an endogenous brain renin angiotensin system. *Fed. Proc., Fed. Am. Soc. Exp. Biol.* **38**, 2260–2266.

Phillips, M. I., Speakman, E. A., and Kimura, B. (1993). Levels of angiotensin and molecular biology of the tissue renin angiotensin systems. *Regul. Pept.* **43**, 1–20.

Provencher, P. H., Saltis, J., and Funder, J. W. (1995). Glucocorticoids but not mineralocorticoids modulate endothelin-1 and angiotensin II binding in SHR vascular smooth muscle cells. *J. Steroid Biochem. Mol. Biol.* **52**, 219–225.

Quillen, F. W., Jr., Reid, I. A., and Keil, L. C. (1988). Cardiac and arterial baroreceptor influences on plasma vasopressin and drinking. *In* "Vasopressin: Cellular and Integrative Functions" (A. W. Cowley, J.-F. Laird, and D. A. Ausiello, eds.), pp. 405–411. Raven Press, New York.

Quirion, R., De Léan, A., Gutkowska, J., Cantin, M., and Genest, J. (1984). Receptors/acceptors for the atrial natriuretic factor (ANF) in brain and related structures. *Peptides (N.Y.)* **5**, 1167.

Ramsay, D. J., and Thrasher, T. N. (1990). Thirst and water balance. *In* "Handbook of Behavioral Neurobiology" (E. M. Stricker, ed.), Vol. 10, pp. 353–386. Plenum Press, New York.

Reagan, L. P., Ye, X. H., Mir, R., DePalo, L. R., and Fluharty, S. J. (1990). Up-regulation of angiotensin II receptors by in vitro differentiation of murine N1E-115 neuroblastoma cells. *Mol. Pharmacol.* **38**, 878–886.

Rettig, R., Healy, D. P., and Printz, M. P. (1986). Cardiovascular effects of microinjections of angiotensin II into the nucleus tractus solitarii. *Brain Res.* **364**, 233–240.

Reul, J. M. H. M., and de Kloet, E. R. (1985). Two receptor systems for corticosterone in rat brain: Microdistribution and differential occupation. *Endocrinology (Baltimore)* **133**, 1941–1950.

Richter, C. P. (1936). Increased salt appetite in adrenalectomized rats. *Am. J. Physiol.* **115**, 155–161.

Riftina, F., Angulo, J., Pompei, P., and McEwen, B. S. (1995). Regulation of angiotensinogen gene expression in the rat forebrain by adrenal steroids and relation to salt appetite. *Mol. Brain Res.* **33**, 201–208.

Robertson, G. L. (1986). Posterior pituitary. *In* "Endocrinology and Metabolism" (P. Felig, J. Baxter, and L.-A. Frohman, eds.), pp. 338–385. McGraw-Hill, New York.

Robertson, G. L. (1995). Diabetes insipidus. *Clin. Endocrinol. Metab.* **24**, 549–572.

Robinson, M. M., and Evered, M. D. (1987). Pressor action of intravenous angiotensin II reduces drinking response in rats. *Am. J. Physiol.* **252**, R754–R759.

Rowland, N. (1976). Circadian rhythms and the partial recovery of regulatory drinking in rats after lateral hypothalamic lesions. *J. Comp. Physiol. Psych.* **90**, 382–393.

Rowland, N. E., Rozelle, A., Riley, P. J., and Fregly, M. J. (1992). Effect of nonpeptide angiotensin receptor antagonists on water intake and salt appetite in rats. *Brain Res. Bull.* **29**, 389–393.

Rowland, N. E., Li, B. H., Rozelle, A. K., Fregly, M. J., Garcia, M., and Smith, G. C. (1994a). Localization of changes in immediate early genes in brain in relation to hydromineral balance: Intravenous angiotensin II. *Brain Res. Bull.* **33**, 427–436.

Rowland, N. E., Li, B. H., Rozelle, A. K., and Smith, G. C. (1994b). Comparison of Fos-like immunoreactivity induced in rat brain by central injection of angiotensin II and carbachol. *Am. J. Physiol.* **267**, R792–R798.

Rowland, N. E., Fregly, M. J., Li, B. H., and Han, L. (1996). Angiotensin-related induction of immediate early genes in rat brain. *Regul. Pept.* **66**, 25–29.

Ryan, M. C., Shen, P. J., and Gundlach, A. L. (1997). Angiotensinogen and natriuretic peptide mRNAs in rat brain: Localization and differential regulation by adrenal steroids in hypothalamus. *Peptides (N.Y.)* **18**, 495–504.

Sagar, S. M., Sharp, F. R., and Curran, T. (1988). Expression of c-Fos protein in brain: Metabolic mapping at the cellular level. *Science* **240**, 1328–1331.

Sakai, R. R. (1986). The hormones of renal sodium conservation act synergistically to arouse sodium appetite in the rat. *In* "Thirst and Sodium Appetite" (G. de Caro, A. N. Epstein, and M. Massi, eds.), pp. 425–430. Plenum Press, New York.

Sakai, R. R., and Epstein, A. N. (1990). Peripheral angiotensin II is not the cause of sodium appetite in the rat. *Appetite (London)* **15**, 161–170.

Sakai, R. R., Nicolaidis, S., and Epstein, A. N. (1986). Salt appetite is suppressed by interference with angiotensin II and aldosterone. *Am. J. Physiol.* **251**, R762–R768.

Sakai, R. R., Frankman, S. P., Fine, W. B., and Epstein, A. N. (1987). Salt appetite is enhanced by one prior episode of sodium depletion in the rats. *Behav. Neurosci.* **101**, 724–731.

Sakai, R. R., Frankman, S. P., Fine, W. B., and Epstein, A. N. (1989). Prior episodes of sodium depletion increase need-free sodium intake of the rat. *Behav. Neurosci.* **103**, 186–192.

Sakai, R. R., He, P. F., Yang, X. D., Ma, L. Y., Guo, Y. F., Reilly, J. J., Moga, C. N., and Fluharty, S. J. (1994). Intracerebroventricular administration of AT_1 receptor antisense oligonucleotides inhibits the behavioral actions of angiotensin II. *J. Neurochem.* **62**, 2053–2056.

Sakai, R. R., Ma, L. Y., He, P. F., and Fluharty, S. J. (1995). Effect of intracerebroventricular administration of angiotensin type 1 (AT_1) receptor antisense oligonucleotides on thirst in the rat. *Reg. Peptides* **59**, 183–192.

Sakai, R. R., Ma, L. Y., Zhang, D. M., McEwen, B. S., and Fluharty, S. J. (1996). Antisense oligonucleotides inhibit mineralocorticoid receptor expression and function in the brain. *Neuroendocrinology* **64**, 425–429.

Sakai, R. R., Ma, L. Y., Zhang, D. M., Itharat, P., and Fluharty, S. J. (1997). Intracerebroventricular administration of mineralocorticoid receptor antisense oligonucleotides attenuates salt appetite in the rat. *Stress* **21**, 37–50.

Sakai, R. R., McEwen, B. S., Fluharty, S. J., and Ma, L. Y. (2000). The amygdala: Site of genomic and non-genomic arousal of oldosterone-induced sodium intake. *Kidney Int.* **57**, 1337–1345.

Sato, A., Suzuki, H., Iwaita, Y., Nakazato, Y., Kato, H., and Saruta, T. (1992). Potentiation of inositol triphosphate production by dexamethasone. *Hypertension* **19**, 109–115.

Sato, A., Suzuki, H., Murakami, M., Nakazato, Y., Iwaita, Y., and Saruta, T. (1994). Glucocorticoid increases angiotensin II type 1 receptor and its gene expression. *Hypertension* **23**, 25–30.

Sawchenko, P. E. (1998). Toward a new neurobiology of energy balance, appetite, and obesity: The anatomists weigh in. *J. Comp. Neurol.* **402**, 435–441.

Sawchenko, P. E., and Friedman, M. I. (1979). Sensory functions of the liver—a review. *Am. J. Physiol.* **236**, RS–R20.

Schiffrin, E. L., Gutkowska, J., and Genest, J. (1984). Effect of angiotensin II and deoxycorticosterone infusion on vascular angiotensin II receptors in rats. *Am. J. Physiol.* **246**, H608–H614.

Schmale, H., and Richter, D. (1984). Single base deletion in the vasopressin gene is the cause of diabetes insipidus in Brattleboro rats. *Nature (London)* **308**, 705–709.

Scholkens, B. A., Jung, W., Rascher, W., Dietz, R., and Ganten, D. (1982). Intracerebroventricular angiotensin II increases arterial blood pressure in rhesus monkeys by stimulation of pituitary hormones and the sympathetic nervous system. *Experientia* **38**, 469–470.

Schulkin, J., and Fluharty, S. J. (1993). Neuroendocrinology of sodium hunger: Angiotensin corticosteroids, and atrial natriuretic hormone. *In* "Hormonally Induced Changes in Mind and Brain" (J. Schulkin, ed.), pp. 13–49. Academic Press, New York.

Schwartz, G. J., and Moran, T. H. (1998). Integrative gastro intestinal actions of the brain-gut peptide cholecystokinin in satiety. *In* "Progress in Psychobiology and Physiological Psychology" (A. R. Morrison and S. J. Fluharty, eds.), Vol. 17, pp. 1–34. Academic Press, New York.

Shelat, S. G., Fluharty, S. J., and Flanagan-Cato, L. M. (1998). Adrenal steroid regulation of central angiotensin II receptor subtypes and oxytocin receptors in rat brain. *Brain Res.* **807**, 135–146.

Shelat, S. G., King, J. L., Flanagan-Cato, L. M., and Fluharty, S. J. (1999a). Mineralocorticoids and glucocorticoid interactions on salt appetite and angiotensin II binding in rat brain and pituitary. *Neuroendocrinology* **272**, 92–105.

Shelat, S. G., Flanagan-Cato, L. M., and Fluharty, S. J. (1999b). Glucocorticoid and mineralocorticoid regulation of angiotensin II type I receptor binding and phosphoinositide hydrolysis in WB cells. *Endocrinology* **162**, 381–391.

Sheng, M., and Greenberg, M. E. (1990). The regulation and function of c-Fos and other immediate early genes in the nervous system. *Neuron* **4**, 477–485.

Sheppard, K. E., and Funder, J. W. (1987). Equivalent affinity of alderstone and corticosterone for type I receptors in kidney and hippocampus: Direct binding studies. *J. Steroid Biochem.* **28**, 737–742.

Shoji, M., Share, L., and Crofton, J. T. (1989). Effect on vasopressin release of microinjection of angiotensin II into the paraventricular nucleus of conscious rats. *Neuroendocrinology* **50**, 327–333.

Siemens, I. R., Adler, H. J., Addya, K., Mah, S. J., and Fluharty, S. J. (1991). Biochemiscal analysis of solubilized angiotensin II receptors from murine neuroblastoma NIE-1 15 cells by covalent cross-linking and affinity purification. *Mol. Pharmacol.* **40**, 717–726.

Simpson, J. B., and Routtenberg, A. (1973). Subfornical organ: Site of drinking elicitation by angiotensin II. *Science* **181**, 1172–1174.

Simpson, J. B., and Routtenberg, A. (1975). Subfornical lesions reduce intravenous angiotensin-induced drinking. *Brain Res.* **88**, 154–161.

Simpson, J. B., Epstein, A. N., and Camardo, J. S., Jr. (1978). Localization of receptors for the dipsogenic action of angiotensin II in the subfomical organ of rat. *J. Comp. Physiol. Psychol.* **92**, 581–608.

Smookler, H. H., Severs, W. B., Kinnard, W. J., and Buckley, J. P. (1966). Centrally mediated cardiovascular effects of angiotensin II. *J. Pharmacol. Exp. Ther.* **153**, 485–494.

Song, K., Allen, A. M., Paxinos, G., and Mendelsohn, F. A. O. (1992). Mapping, of angiotensin II receptor subtype heterogeneity in rat brain. *J. Comp. Neurol.* **316**, 467–484.

Speth, R. C., and Kim, K. H. (1990). Discrimination of two angiotensin II receptor subtypes with a selective agonist analogue of angiotensin II. *Biochem. Biophys. Res. Commun.* **169**, 997–1006.

Starling, E. H. (1896). On the absorption of fluids from the connective tissue spaces. *J. Physiol. (London)* **19**, 312–326.

Steckelings, U. M., Bottari, S. P., and Unger, T. (1992). Angiotensin receptor subtypes in the brain. *Trends Pharmacol. Sci.* **13**, 365–368.

Stellar, E. (1954). The physiology of motivation. *Psychol. Rev.* **61**, 5–22.

Sterling, G. H., Chee, O., Riggs, R. V., and Keil, L. C. (1980). Effect of chronic intracerebroventricular angiotensin II infusion on vasopressin release in rats. *Neuroendocrinology* **31**, 182–188.

Stricker, E. M. (1966). Extracellular fluid volume and thirst. *Am. J. Physiol.* **211**, 232–238.

Stricker, E. M. (1968). Some physiological and motivational properties of hypovolemic stimulus for thirst. *Physiol. Behav.* **3**, 379–385.

Stricker, E. M. (1971). Effects of hypovolemia and/or caval ligation on water and NaCI solution drinking by rats. *Physiol. Behav.* **6**, 299–305.

Stricker, E. M. (1976). Drinking by rats after lateral hypothalamic lesions: A new look at the lateral hypothalamic syndrome. *J. Comp. Physiol. Psychol.* **90**, 127–143.

Stricker, E. M. (1977). The renin-angiotensin system and thirst: A reevaluation. II. Drinking elicited in rats by caval ligation and isoproterenol. *J. Comp. Physiol. Psychol.* **91**, 1220–1231.

Stricker, E. M. (1980). The physiological basis of sodium appetite: A new look at the "depletion-repletion" model. *In* "Biological and Behavioral Aspects of Salt Intake" (M. R. Kare, M. J. Fregley, and R. A. Bernard, eds.), pp. 185–204. Academic Press, New York.

Stricker, E. M. (1981). Thirst and sodium appetite after colloid treatment in rats. *J. Comp. Physiol. Psychol.* **95**, 1–25.

Stricker, E. M. (1983). Thirst and sodium appetite after colloid treatment in rats: Role of the renin angiotensin-aldosterone system. *Behav. Neurosci.* **97**, 725–737.

Stricker, E. M., and Verbalis, J. G. (1986). Interaction of osmotic and volume stimuli in regulation of neurohypophyseal secretion in rats. *Am. J. Physiol.* **250**, R267–R275.

Stricker, E. M., and Verbalis, J. G. (1987). Central inhibitory control of sodium appetite in rats: Correlation with pituitary oxytocin secretion. *Behav. Neurosci.* **101**, 560–567.

Stricker, E. M., and Verbalis, J. G. (1988). Hormones and behavior: The biology of thirst and sodium appetite. *Am. Sci.* **76**, 261–267.

Stricker, E. M., and Verbalis, J. G. (1996). Central inhibition of salt appetite by oxytocin in rats. *Regul. Pept.* **66**, 83–85.

Stricker, E. M., and Verbalis, J. G. (1999). Water intake and body fluids. *In* "Fundamental Neuroscience," pp. 1111–1127. Academic Press, San Diego, CA.

Stricker, E. M., and Zigmond, M. J. (1976). Recovery of function after damage to central catecholamine containing neurons: A neurochemical model for the lateral hypothalamic syndrome. *In* "Progress in Psychobiology and Physicological Psychology," Vol. 6 (J. M. Sprague and A. N. Epstein, eds.), pp. 121–188. Academic Press, New York.

Stricker, E. M., and Verbalis, J. G., eds. (1999). Thirst and salt appetite. *In* "Handbook of Behavioral Neurobiology" (E. M. Stricker, ed.), Plenum Press, New York.

Stricker, E. M., and Wolf, G. (1966). Blood volume and tonicity in relation to sodium appetite. *J. Comp. Physiol. Psychol.* **62**, 275–279.

Stricker, E. M., Bradshaw, W. U., and McDonald, R. H., Jr. (1976). The renin-angiotensin system and thirst: A reevaluation. *Science* **194**, 1169–1171.

Stricker, E. M., Cooper, P. H., Marshall, J. F., and Zigmond, M. J. (1979). Acute homeostatic imbalances reinstate sensoramotor dysfunctions in rats with lateral hypothalamic lesions. *J. Comp. Physiol. Psychol.* **93**, 512–521.

Stricker, E. M., Vagnucci, A. H., McDonald, R. H., Jr., and Leenen, F. H. (1979). Renin and aldosterone secretions during hypovolemia in rats: Relation to NaCI intake. *Am. J. Physiol.* **237**, R45–R51.

Stricker, E. M., Hosutt, J. A., and Verbalis, J. G. (1987). Neurohypophyseal secretion in hypovolemic rats: Inverse relation to sodium appetite. *Am. J. Physiol.* **252**, R889–R896.

Sumners, C., and Fregly, M. J. (1989). Modulation of angiotensin II binding sites in neuronal cultures by mineralocorticoids. *Am. J. Physiol.* **256**, C121–C129.

Sumners, C., Gault, T. R., and Fregly, M. J. (1991). Potentiation of angiotensin II-induced drinking by glucocorticoids is a glucocorticoid type II receptor (GR)-mediated event. *Brain Res.* **552**, 283–290.

Tallant, E. A., Diz, D. I., Khosla, M. C., and Ferrario, C. M. (1991). Identification and regulation of angiotensin II receptor subtypes on NGIO8-15 cells. *Hypertension* **17**, 1135–1143.

Tanaka, I., Misono, K. S., and Inagami, T. (1984). Atrial natriuretic factor in rat hypothalamus, atria and plasma: Determination by specific radioimmunoassay. *Biochem. Biophys. Res. Commun.* **124**, 663–668.

Taugner, R., Buhrle, C. P., Boling, R., and Kirschke, H. (1985). Coexistence of renin and cathepsin in epithelial cell secretory granules. *Histochemistry* **83**, 103–108.

Taylor, S. J., Smith, J. A., and Exton, J. H. (1990). Purification from bovine liver membranes of a guanine nucleotide dependent activator of phosphoinositide-specific phospholipase C. *J. Biol. Chem.* **265**, 17150–17156.

Teitelbaum, P., and Epstein, A. N. (1962). The lateral hypothalamic syndrome: Recovery of feeding and drinking following lesions in the lateral hypothalamus. *Psychol. Rev.* **69**, 74–90.

Thorn, G. W., Dorrance, S. S., and Day, E. (1942). Addison's disease: Evaluation of synthetic desoxycorticosterone acetate therapy in 158 patients. *Ann. Int. Med.* **16**, 1053–1096.

Thornton, S. N., and Nicolaidis, S. (1994). Long-term mineralocorticoid-induced changes in rat neuron properties plus interaction of aldosterone and Ang II. *Am. J. Physiol.* **266**, R564–R571.

Thrasher, T. N., Keil, L. C., and Ramsay, D. J. (1982a). Hemodynamic, hormonal, and drinking responses to reduced venous return in the dog. *Am. J. Physiol.* **243**, R354–R362.

Thrasher, T. N., Keil, L. C., and Ramsay, D. J. (1982b). Lesions of the laminar terminalis (OVLT) attenuate osmotically-induced drinking and vasopressin secretion in the dog. *Endocrinology* **110**, 1837–1839.

Thunhorst, R. L., and Johnson, A. K. (1993). Effects of arterial pressure on drinking and urinary responses to intracerebroventricular angiotensin II. *Am. J. Physiol.* **264**, R211–R217.

Thunhorst, R. L., and Johnson, A. K. (1994). Renin-angiotensin, arterial blood pressure, and salt appetite in rats. *Am. J. Physiol.* **266**, R458–R465.

Thunhorst, R. L., Fitts, D. A., and Simpson, J. B. (1987). Separation of captopril effects on salt and water intake by subfornical organ lesions. *Am. J. Physiol.* **252**, R409–R418.

Thunhorst, R. L., Lewis, S. J., and Johnson, A. K. (1993). Role of arterial baroreceptor input on thirst and urinary responses to intracerebroventricular angiotensin II. *Am. J. Physiol.* **265**, R591–R595.

Thunhorst, R. L., Lewis, S. J., and Johnson, A. K. (1994). Effects of sinoaortic baroreceptor denervadon on depletion-induced salt appetite. *Am. J. Physiol.* **267**, R1043–R1049.

Tigerstedt, R., and Bergman, P. G. (1898). Niere and Kreislauf. *Skand. Archiv Physiol.* **8**, 223–271.

Toth, E., Stelfox, J., and Kaufman, 5. (1987). Cardiac control of salt appetite. *Am. J. Physiol.* **252**, R925–R929.

Tsai, M. J., and O'Malley, B. W. (1994). Molecular mechanisms of steroid/thyroid receptor superfamily members. *Ann. Rev. Neurosci.* **63**, 451–486.

Tsutsumi, K., and Saavedra, J. M. (1991a). Characterization and development of angiotensin II receptor subtypes (AT$_1$ and AT$_2$) in rat brain. *Am. J. Physiol.* **261**, R209–R216.

Tsutsumi, K., and Saavedra, J. M. (1991b). Quantitative autoradiography reveals different angiotensin II receptor subtypes in selected rat brain nuclei. *J. Neurochem.* **56**, 348–351.

Ullian, M. E., Schelling, J. R., and Linas, S. L. (1992). Aldosterone enhances angiotensin II receptor binding and inositol phosphate responses. *Hypertension* **20**, 67–73.

Unger, T., Rascher, W., Schuster, C., Pavlovitch, R., Schomig, A., Dietz, R., and Ganten, D. (1981). Central blood pressure effects of substance P and angiotensin II: Role of the sympathetic nervous system and vasopressin. *Eur. J. Pharmacol.* **71**, 33–42.

Van Eckelen, J. A. M., and Phillips, M. I. (1988). Plasma angiotensin II levels at moment of drinking during angiotensin II intravenous administration. *Am. J. Physiol.* **255**, R500–R506.

Verbalis, I. G. (1990). Clinical aspects of body fluid homeostasis in humans. *In* "Handbook of Behavioral Neurobiology" (E. M. Stricker, ed.), Vol. 10, pp. 421–462. New York: Plenum.

Verbalis, J. G. (1993). Osmotic inhibition of neurohypophysial secretion, *Ann. N. Y. Acad. Sci.* **22**, 146–160.

Verbalis, J. G., Robinson, A. G., and Moses, A. M. (1984). Postoperative and post-traumatic diabetes insipidus. *In* "Diabetes Insipidus in Man" (P. Czernichow and A. G. Robinson, eds.), pp. 247–265. Karger, Basel.

Verbalis, J. G., Mangione, M. P., and Stricker, E. M. (1991). Oxytocin produces natriuresis in rats at physiological plasma concentrations. *Endocrinology* **128**, 1317–1322.

Verbalis, J. G., Blackburn, R. E., Olsen, B. R., and Stricker, E. M. (1993). Central oxytocin inhibition of food and salt ingestion: A mechanism for intake regulation of solute homeostasis. *Regul. Pept.* **45**, 149–154.

Verbalis, J. G., Hoffman, G. E., and Sherman, T. G. (1995). Use of immediate early genes as markers of oxytoxin and vasopressin neuronal function. *Curr. Opin. Endocrinol. Metab.* **2**, 157–168.

Verney, E. B. (1946). Absorption and excretion of water. *Lancet* **251**, 739–744.

Verney, E. B. (1947). The antidiuretic hormone and the factors which determine its release. *Proc. R. Soc. London, Ser. B* **135**, 25–106.

Vijande, M., Costales, M., Schiaffini, O., and Martin, B. (1977). Sex differences in polyethylene glycol-induced thirst. *Experientia* **34**, 742–743.

Vijande, M., Costales, M., Schiaffini, O., and Martin, B. (1978). Angiotensin-induced drinking: Sexual differences. *Pharmacol., Biochem. Behav.* **8**, 753–755.

Vollmer, R. R., Corey, S. P., and Fluharty, S. J. (1988). Angiotensin II facilitation of pressor responses to adrenal field stimulation in pithed rats. *Am. J. Physiol.* **254**, R95–R101.

Vollmer, R. R., Corey, S. P., Meyers, S. A., Stricker, E. M., and Fluharty, S. J. (1990). Angiotensin augments epinephrine release in pithed rats sed a low sodium diet. *Am. J. Physiol.* **258**, R187–R192.

Wehling, M., Christ, M., and Theisen, K. (1992). Membrane receptors for aldosterone: A novel pathway for mineralocorticoid action. *Am. J. Physiol.* **263**, E974–E979.

Weisinger, R. S., Considine, P., Denton, D. A., Leksell, L., McKinley, M. J., Mouw, D. R., Muller, A. F., and Tarjan, F. (1982). Role of sodium concentration of the cerebrospinal fluid in the salt appetite of sheep. *Am. J. Physiol.* **242**, R51–R53.

Weiss, C. S., and Almli, R. (1975). Lateral preoptic and lateral hypothalamic units: In search of the osmoreceptors for thirst. *Physiol. Behav.* **15**, 713–722.

Wilson, K. M., Sumners, C., Hathaway, S., and Fregly, M. J. (1986). Mineralocorticoids modulate central angiotensin II receptors in rats. *Brain Res.* **382**, 87–96.

Winquist, R. J., Faison, E. P., Waldman, S. A., Schwartz, K., Murad, F., and Rapoport, R. M. (1984). Atrial natriuretic factor elicits an endothelium-independent relaxation and activates particulate guanylate cyclase in vascular smooth muscle. *Proc. Natl. Acad. Sci. U.S.A.* **81**, 7661.

Wintersgill, H. P., Warburton, P., Bryson, S. E., Ball, S. G., and Balmforth, A. J. (1995). Glucocorticoids regulate the expression of angiotensin AT1 receptors in the human hepatoma cell line, PLC-PRF-5. *Eur. J. Pharmacol.* **288**, 365–371.

Wolf, A. V. (1950). Osmometric analysis of thirst in man and dog. *Am. J. Physiol.* **161**, 75–86.

Wolf, A. V. (1958). "Thirst." Thomas, Springfield, IL.

Wolf, G. (1965). Effect of deoxycorticosterone on sodium appetite of intact and adrenalectomized rats. *Am. J. Physiol.* **208**, 1281–1285.

Wooley, C. S., and McEwen, B. S. (1993). Roles of estradiol and progesterone in regulation of hippocampal dendritic spine density during the estrous cycle in the rat. *J. Comp. Neurol.* **336**, 293–306.

Zehr, J. E., Kurz, K. D., Seymour, A. A., and Schultz, H. D. (1980). Mechanisms controlling renin release. *Adv. Exp. Med. Biol.* **130**, 135–170.

Zimmerman, M. B., Blaine, E. H., and Stricker, E. M. (1981). Water intake in hypovolemic sheep: Effects of crushing the left atrial appendage. *Science* **211**, 489–491.

9

Corticotropin-Releasing Factor, Corticosteroids, Stress, and Sugar: Energy Balance, the Brain, and Behavior

Mary F. Dallman, Victor G. Viau, Seema Bhatnagar, Francisca Gomez, Kevin Laugero, and M. E. Bell

Department of Physiology
University of California at San Francisco
San Francisco, California 94143-0444

I. INTRODUCTION

The myriad effects of glucocorticoids on brain and behavior are best understood in the context of the state of the organism. The effects of and requirements for glucocorticoids are very different depending both on whether the animal is under a condition of low (basal) or high (stressed) central corticotropin-releasing factor (CRF) drive and which central neural pathways are, in consequence, predominantly activated.

Under basal nonstressed conditions, there is generally a low central CRF drive, and the glucocorticoids have critically important effects on energy balance and metabolism and maintain (possibly through this means) normal CRF levels. Caloric supply appears to be critical to the regulation of the hypothalamic-pituitary-adrenal (HPA) axis under basal conditions, and the activity of the axis can be shown to be determined by sucrose ingestion.

CRF is both the neurotransmitter and neurohormone that orchestrates the state manifestations of stress in the brain and body. Under conditions of stress, CRF alters perception, behavior, learning and memory, autonomic outflow, and neuroendocrine activity. Moreover, inputs to the brain that are activated by chronic or intermittent repeated stressors form a memory that apparently emphasizes the use of limbic and monoaminergic pathways, which are usually not so prominently involved under ordinary nonstressful conditions. To a large extent, we believe that the activation of the central CRF network in response to chronic stressors serves to maintain life under adverse circumstances. The glucose-mobilizing and behavioral effects of glucocorticoids modify the effects of CRF, allowing the prolongation of life.

Below, we first discuss the adrenocortical system and the role of glucocorticoids under basal conditions, in the absence of stressors. This part deals extensively with the role of adrenal steroids on energy balance through their actions on both the body and brain. Next, we discuss the impact of chronic sustained or repeated stressors on energy balance and the responsivity of the stressed brain to new stimuli. This section includes a discussion of inputs that are emphasized by the state of chronic stress and the requirement for high glucocorticoids in the implementation of this state. We next provide evidence that supports the CRF system as a primary activator of the stress state and discuss specific sites in brain that are activated by stress and CRF and that interact with corticosteroids. We then discuss the adaptation to repeated stressors and the paraventricular thalamus. Finally, we discuss how the CRF-glucocorticoid axis is modulated by interactions with the gonadal axis. This part delineates the major effects of sex hormones on both energy balance and function in the HPA axis.

II. CORTICOSTEROID ACTIONS UNDER NONSTRESSFUL CONDITIONS—ENERGY BALANCE

A. Introduction to the Hypothalamic-Pituitary-Adrenal Axis

The synthesis and secretion of corticosteroids from the adrenal cortex is primarily mediated by the action of adrenocorticotropin (ACTH) on melanocortin-2 receptors integral to cortical cell membranes (Mountjoy *et al.*, 1992). Adrenal sensitivity to ACTH changes as a function of the time of day (Jasper and Engeland, 1994; Kaneko *et al.*, 1980); this may result from neural input driven by the suprachiasmatic nuclei (Buijs *et al.*, 1993, 1997, 1999; Kalsbeek *et al.*, 1993). Nonetheless, the action of ACTH on glucocorticoid-secreting cells is essential for glucocorticoid synthesis and secretion. Usually ACTH concentrations in the circulation are in the low picomolar range (e.g., Dallman *et al.*, 1987). At these concentrations, ACTH has effects specific to the adrenals, but has few extraadrenal actions. It is important to note, however, that the glucocorticoid response to ACTH saturates at low circulating ACTH concentrations and that the maximal adrenal response at higher concentrations integrates the ACTH concentrations over time and simply persists longer (Fig. 1).

ACTH secretion from the anterior pituitary is usually entirely controlled by the secretory activity of CRF- and

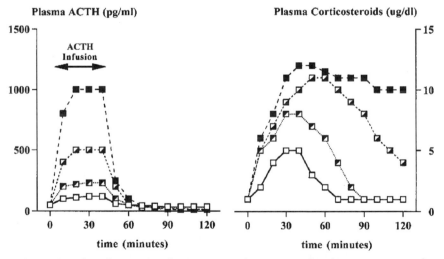

FIGURE 1 Adrenals integrate the ACTH signal over time after the acute capacity for adrenal steroidogenesis is achieved. Four rates of ACTH were infused into dogs between 0 and 40 min. Plasma ACTH (left) and corticosteroids (a combination of 75% cortisol and 25% corticosterone, right) were measured for 2 hours. The maximal adrenal response occurs at <300 pg/ml ACTH; thereafter, the duration of the adrenal response continues until the amount of ACTH infused is represented by the amount of glucocorticoid secreted (integrated adrenal response). The integrated corticosteroid response correlates >95% with the ACTH infused. Because adrenal steroidogenic capacity is reached within the first third of the dynamic range of ACTH, plasma corticosteroid concentrations are a more sensitive measure of HPA activity in this range and plasma ACTH concentrations are a more sensitive measure in the higher ranges. The data are approximate and were taken from Keller-Wood *et al.* (1983).

arginine vasopressin (AVP)-containing neurons in the medial parvocellular portion of the paraventricular nuclei of the hypothalamus (PVN). Thus, under normal conditions, ACTH serves as a slave that links activity of CRF/AVP neurons to adrenal glucocorticoid secretion. The normal regulation of glucocorticoid secretion by hypothalamic CRF/AVP secretion may occasionally be short-circuited as a consequence of the action of infection-induced cytokines acting on the anterior pituitary corticotrope cells to directly cause ACTH secretion (Makara *et al.,* 1970). However, this seems to be a specific exception, not the rule, and may simply represent an emergency booster to the known effects of cytokines on the stimulation of CRF/AVP secretion by the hypothalamus (Richard, 1993; Rivest and Laflamme, 1995; Rivest *et al.,* 1995). Thus, circulating concentrations of ACTH and corticosteroids normally reflect precisely the prior secretion of CRF/AVP by the hypothalamic median eminence (Alexander *et al.,* 1996).

Although CRF is required to stimulate ACTH synthesis and secretion from the pituitary, AVP, itself a weak secretogog, interacts with CRF to potentiate the secretion of ACTH from the corticotrope (Antoni, 1986, 1993; Gillies *et al.,* 1982). The CRF/AVP ratio in parvocellular neurons of the PVN changes under various conditions and in this way can control the amount of ACTH released in response to stimulation of the PVN (Antoni, 1993).

B. Feedback Regulation of Corticotropin-Releasing Factor and Arginine Vasopressin by Corticosteroids

The efficacy of hypothalamic CRF/AVP secretion on adrenal function is monitored and responded to through the feedback actions of the circulating concentrations of free corticosteroids. There is little, if any basal feedback by corticosteroids at the pituitary (Cole *et al.,* 2000b), in large part because the corticotropes are enriched in transcortin, which binds much of the free steroid that reaches the cells (Koch *et al.,* 1974). In the brain, the corticosteroids act through two corticosteroid receptors—a high-affinity low-capacity type I or mineralocorticoid receptor (MR), and a lower-affinity high-capacity type II or glucocorticoid receptor (GR). The activation of both receptors by endogenous corticosteroids serves to control the subsequent CRF/AVP

secretion from the PVN (Bradbury *et al.,* 1994; Dallman *et al.,* 1987, 1989b, 1992; de Kloet, 1991; Dodt *et al.,* 1993; McEwen *et al.,* 1986; Ratka *et al.,* 1989; Spencer *et al.,* 1998).

The distribution of MR is more discrete than that of GR and is probably best shown in early experiments in which adrenalectomized rats were injected intravenously with approximately 3 nM highly labeled corticosterone. This quantity of labeled corticosterone is sufficient to associate with MR, but too low to occupy GR appreciably. Brains collected over time after injections revealed by autoradiographic analysis highly selective uptake and retention of the label (Birmingham *et al.,* 1984; McEwen *et al.,* 1986). The greatest area of concentration of the steroid, reflecting MR binding, was in the hippocampal formation (Krowzowski and Funder, 1983). High expression of MR in hippocampus has subsequently been shown in humans and nonhuman primates (Rupprecht *et al.,* 1993; Sanchez *et al.,* 2000). Although the high concentrations of MR in hippocampus have attracted most experimental attention, MR are also distributed in the amygdala, prefrontal cortex, lateral septum, and a variety of motor neurons in the brain stem (Birmingham *et al.,* 1984). There appear to be few MR localized in the hypothalamus (Ahima *et al.,* 1991; Reul and de Kloet, 1985), supporting the notion that feedback inhibition on CRF through the actions of corticosteroid-activated MR are indirect (Dallman *et al.,* 1987; Herman and Cullinan, 1997; Levine *et al.,* 1988).

In contrast to MR, GR are broadly distributed throughout the brain and pituitary (Cintra *et al.,* 1991; Gustafsson *et al.,* 1987). There is dense GR staining in hypothalamus, limbic brain, cortex, and brain stem. Of considerable interest for understanding the effects of corticosteroids on brain is that most neurons that synthesize and secrete monoamines contain GR (Ceccatelli *et al.,* 1989; Cintra *et al.,* 1991; Fuxe *et al.,* 1985; Harfstrand *et al.,* 1986; Honkaniemi *et al.,* 1992; Kainu *et al.,* 1993).

The sites in brain at which corticosteroid feedback acts to inhibit basal ACTH secretion remain unclear. That basal feedback does occur in the brain has been most compellingly demonstrated by the increase in ACTH and corticosterone that occurs in rats in which very small doses of MR and GR antagonists are infused into a cerebral ventricle under basal conditions (Ratka *et al.,* 1989; Van Haarst *et al.,* 1996). However, the delineation of the specific sites in brain that directly inhibit CRF/AVP secretion from the PVN has been difficult to come by. A requirement that must be met for a feedback site is that delivery of the steroid to that site should reduce CRF, ACTH, and corticosterone synthesis or secretion. Moreover, if the feedback site is one that regulates the endogenous system, the natural glucocorticoid (either cortisol or corticosterone) must induce the inhibition. Using these criteria, it does not appear that there is a marked degree of feedback at the PVN itself. Bilateral implants of the potent synthetic glucocorticoid, dexamethasone did inhibit CRF and AVP expression in the PVN and decreased ACTH (Kovacs et al., 1986; Kovacs and Mezey, 1987; Sawchenko, 1987); however, corticosterone implants did not (Kovacs and Makara, 1988). Bilateral implants of corticosterone in the amygdala, septum, and hippocampus were effective in reducing ACTH secretion in adrenalectomized rats (Kovacs and Makara, 1988), suggesting that these sites may subserve basal feedback regulation in the HPA axis. However, the action of the steroid in these limbic sites may also be secondary to their more direct effects on behavior and metabolism.

C. Circadian Rhythms in Glucocorticoid Concentrations

In most species there is a circadian rhythm in circulating corticosteroid concentrations. The rhythm is more marked and easier to detect in plasma from species such as most primates, rats, and mice, which have high concentrations of corticosteroid-binding globulin (transcortin), but Less obvious rhythms exist in other species as well. This is because the measurement of corticosteroids usually encompasses both protein-bound and free moieties. However, it is the free steroid that can diffuse into the extracellular fluid and act at its receptors in target cells (Gala and Westhal, 1965). Those species with high concentrations of transcortin may take advantage of the variable permeability of blood vessels to high-molecular-weight compounds to bathe liver or fat cells (Penicaud et al., 2000), for example, with higher concentrations of corticosteroids than the brain, at the same total plasma steroid concentrations (Pardridge, 1981).

In rats, and probably in humans, the amplitude of the circadian variation in free corticosteroid concentrations

has been estimated to be as much as 200-fold (Dallman et al., 1989a). During the trough of the rhythm, at the end of the period of activity, and during the early hours of inactivity, free corticosteroid concentrations are sufficient to occupy the high-affinity MR, but are normally too low to occupy the GR (see Dallman et al., 2000). Thus, both systemically and in the brain, under basal conditions GR are only occupied for a portion of each day.

In all species tested so far, the circadian rhythm in corticosteroids peaks at the onset of the daily activity cycle under *ad libitum* feeding conditions. In both rats and humans, at the trough of the rhythm, ACTH concentrations are very low and appear to represent constitutive secretion from the pituitary corticotropes; at the peak of the rhythm, hypothalamic CRF secretion is required (reviewed in Dallman et al., 1995). The anticipatory rise in corticosteroids to circulating concentrations appropriate for GR occupancy appears to prime the organism for the increased metabolic requirements of the active period of the circadian cycle (e.g., Nagai and Nakagawa, 1992; Steffens et al., 1993; van Cauter et al., 1994). Through GR occupancy, glucocorticoids stimulate enzyme synthesis in the liver, increasing the capacity for gluconeogenesis, and act on fat and muscle to effect the mobilization of small molecules that can be transported to the liver to serve as substrates for glucose synthesis (Felig et al., 1995).

The importance of normal energy-intake patterns on the circadian rhythm in corticosteroids is clear in rats and humans. Even short-term starvation activates the HPA axis so that GRs are occupied throughout the day and night (Beer et al., 1989; Dallman et al., 1999; Fichter and Pirke, 1984; Friedl et al., 2000; Horrocks et al., 1990; Schwartz et al., 1995). Conversely, sustained constant feeding reduces the amplitude of the rhythm in cortisol (Saito et al., 1989). Moreover, when the expression of CRF mRNA is measured in the PVN of rats fed *ad libitum*, CRF peaks just prior to the time of feeding and falls dramatically within 90 min of lights out (Kwak et al., 1992); this is not a consequence of the high concentrations of corticosterone at this time of day because the same pattern is observed in adrenalectomized rats (Kwak et al., 1993). Similarly, bilaterally adrenalectomized rats fasted overnight exhibit marked ACTH secretion, which is damped when rats are fed calories by gavage during this time (Hanson et al., 1994). Thus, it appears that a major portion of the basal circadian rhythm in the HPA axis is driven by the state of body energy.

D. Restricted Feeding and Rhythms in the Hypothalamic-Pituitary-Adrenal Axis

When rats are trained for a task by working for food, they are exposed to a restricted feeding paradigm and are usually maintained at 80–90% of normal body weight. Under these conditions, the peak of the circadian corticosterone rhythm shifts to occur just prior to the onset of feeding (Honma *et al.*, 1983a; Krieger, 1974; Levine *et al.*, 1979; Wilkinson *et al.*, 1979). However, if the duration of food allowance is sufficiently prolonged that the rats have normal food intake and body weights, the corticosterone rhythm is normal and peaks just prior to the usual nocturnal period of activity (Honma *et al.*, 1983b).

Norepinephrine secretion into the PVN normally peaks during the dark period in rats fed *ad libitum,* but changes its rhythm to peak just prior to the time of feeding in rats adapted to a restricted feeding cycle (Mitome *et al.*, 1994). Further study of this phenomenon has suggested that the control of the timing of circadian peaks in activity, temperature, and corticosterone is removed from the circadian clock in the

suprachiasmatic nuclei and is provided by the hypothalamic ventromedial nuclei (Choi and Dallman, 1998; Krieger, 1979, 1980). Using a transgenic rat with a per-1 promotor expressing luciferase, Reppert and colleagues have shown that the acrophase of the luciferase rhythm in livers of rats under restricted-feeding conditions shifts by 10 hours toward the new time of onset of feeding within 2 days of the new schedule (Stokkan *et al.*, 2001). This result, which shows a faster shift than either shifts in activity or the HPA axis, suggests that the shifts in timing of the circadian peaks in activity, temperature and corticosterone are regulated by circadian clocks in the periphery and transmitted through visceral afferent inputs to the brain and ventromedial nuclei. Thus, under restricted-feeding conditions, it appears that signals from the periphery supersede those from the circadian clock in the suprachiasmatic nuclei and cause the new phase of rhythms in autonomic, neuroendocrine, and behavioral outflows.

From this, it seems clear that the normal circadian rhythm in glucocorticoid secretion is highly regulated by energy intake and balance. The daily peaks in the activity of the HPA axis provide the energetic basis for the continuing bouts of energy expenditure in the absence of certain evidence that exogenous substrate will be forthcoming. This point is reinforced by the data shown in Fig. 2. When rats were allowed to drink

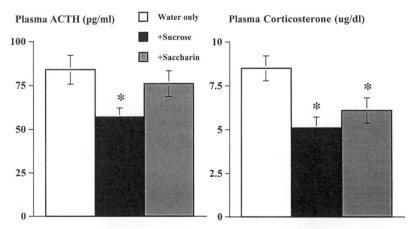

FIGURE 2   Sucrose drinking decreases the circadian increase in plasma ACTH (left) and corticosterone (right). Rats were provided with *ad libitum* sucrose or saccharin the previous night and then given sucrose or saccharin 4 hours before lights out and sampled 1–2 hours before lights out, at the time of the circadian peak in ACTH and corticosterone. *Indicates significantly less than control group given water only at both times. From M. F. Dallman and P. K. Siiteri (upublished results).

sucrose toward the end of the light cycle, the normal rise in plasma ACTH and corticosterone concentrations was diminished (M. F. Dallman and P. K. Siiteri, unpublished).

E. Glucocorticoids and Insulin

However, in combination with sufficient insulin, glucocorticoids also have a profound effect on the deposition of body fat stores (Akana *et al.*, 1996; Dallman *et al.*, 1993; Rebuffe-Scrive *et al.*, 1992; Rohner-Jeanrenaud, 1995; Strack *et al.*, 1995b). In otherwise unstressed rats, the implantation of pellets of corticosterone that raise the daily duration and degree of GR occupancy stimulates plasma insulin concentrations and fat deposit weight in a dose-related manner (Akana *et al.*, 1992; Rebuffe-Scrive *et al.*, 1992). At high concentrations, in the presence of abnormally elevated corticosterone and insulin, frank obesity occurs (Freedman *et al.*,1985; Rebuffe-Scrive *et al.*, 1992; Strack *et al.*, 1995b; see Dallman and Bhatnagar, 2001), partly as a consequence of the inhibition of sympathetic outflow by glucocorticoids (e.g., Bray *et al.*, 1990; Brown and Fisher, 1986). This potentiating effect of glucocorticoids on insulin and fat storage may explain the apparently contradictory finding that meals are also associated with increased glucorticoid secretion in both humans and rats (Follenius *et al.*, 1982; Shiraishi *et al.*, 1984). Moreover, in rats provided with preferred food after a brief fast, CRF secretion from the central nucleus of the amygdala occurs (Merali *et al.*, 1998), in addition to the presumptive secretion of CRF from the PVN (Shiraishi *et al.*, 1984). However, insulin secretion also occurs when meals are ingested. Thus, it seems likely that the corticosteroid secretion that occurs in combination with meal-associated insulin secretion serves the function of reinforcing the storage of calories in fat.

In summary, under basal conditions, corticosteroids serve metabolism. They insure that energy is available as glucose for potential need during the active portion of the circadian rhythm, and when feeding occurs in combination with insulin secretion they also appear to ensure that there are plentiful energy reserves. This hypothesis is perhaps most clearly exemplified by the analysis of the effects of bilateral adrenalectomy.

F. Adrenalectomy

1. Low to Normal Corticosteroids

Adrenalectomy removes all endogenous corticosteroids—the salt-retaining hormone, aldosterone, and the glucose-active hormones, corticosterone—in rats. In all of the experiments discussed here adrenalectomized rats were provided with saline to drink, which allows physiological replacement for the loss of aldosterone.

Loss of glucocorticoids, either through surgical or pharmacological means, results in greatly increased PVN CRF expression and induction of AVP expression, increased secretion of both neuropeptides, and markedly increased ACTH synthesis and secretion from the corticotrope cells (e.g., Akana and Dallman, 1997; Jacobson *et al.*, 1989; Kovacs *et al.*, 2000; Plotsky, 1987; Plotsky and Sawchenko, 1987). In the absence of hypothalamic drive, increased ACTH synthesis and secretion does not occur in adrenalectomized rats (Dallman *et al.*, 1985; Levin *et al.*, 1988). CRF mRNA expression is also reduced in the central nucleus of the amygdala in adrenalectomized rats (Makino *et al.*, 1994a; Schulkin *et al.*, 1994; Viau *et al.*, 2001). However, the absence of glucocorticoids through adrenalectomy does not alter CRF mRNA expression in the bed nuclei of the stria terminalis (BNST) (Viau *et al.*, 2001; Watts and Sanchez-Watts, 1995). Moreover, the decrease in CRF mRNA in amygdala that follows adrenalectomy does not occur, and the CRF mRNA content is not affected when corticosteroids are replaced in adrenalectomized rats that also have lesions in the PVN (Palkovits, 1999). These results suggest strongly that under control conditions of no stress, the lack of glucocorticoids after adrenalectomy is responded to only by CRF-synthesizing neurons in the PVN. By contrast, glucocorticoid concentrations in the stress range strongly increase CRF expression in both the amygdala and the BNST (Makino *et al.*, 1994a,b, 1995; Shepard *et al.*, 2000; Swanson and Simmons, 1989; Watts and Sanchez-Watts, 1995). Thus, there appears to be a distinct difference in the mechanisms of responses in CRF cell groups to subnormal and supranormal concentrations of glucocorticoids (see Section III).

In addition to changes in CRF expression and secretion that occur after adrenalectomy, adrenalectomized rats have a characteristic reduction in energy consumption and storage. Food intake is reduced by about 20%, growth rate is reduced, insulin concentrations are decreased, and sympathetic activity and energy expenditure are increased, although in the absence of stressors the rats fare well and appear healthy (e.g., Akana *et al.,* 1999; Bhatnagar *et al.,* 2000a). The reduction in insulin secretion in adrenalectomized rats may in part be due to the loss of Y1 and Y5 receptors, which occurs specifically in the ventromedial hypothalamus; although adrenalectomized rats feed normally in response to neuropeptide Y (NPY) infused into the cerebral ventricles, they no longer respond with increased insulin secretion (Wisialowski *et al.,* 2000). The lack of normal insulin secretion in response to NPY may account in part for the characteristic leanness of adrenalectomized rats. Many of the other metabolic consequences of adrenalectomy may result from the central changes in CRF synthesis and secretion. The central effects of injected CRF include anorexia (Gosnell *et al.,* 1983), increased sympathetic outflow (Brown and Fisher, 1985, 1986; Fisher *et al.,* 1982), excitation of activity in thermogenic brown adipose tissue (BAT) (Holt and York, 1989; Rothwell, 1989) and reduction in white adipose tissue (WAT) mass (Richard, 1993).

Both central behavioral and metabolic changes induced by adrenalectomy are restored to normal by the systemic provision of corticosterone (e.g., Akana and Dallman, 1997; Bhatnagar *et al.,* 2000a; Watts and Sanchez-Watts, 1995). However, corticosteroids may act primarily to cure the metabolic effects of adrenalectomy, or they may act primarily to inhibit CRF synthesis and secretion. For instance, adrenalectomy increases the basal firing rate and stressor-induced responses of neurons in the locus coeruleus (LC), and this appears to be a consequence of increased CRF secretion on (LC) neurons, which is abolished in a dose-related fashion by the direct infusion of CRF antagonists (Pavcovich and Valentino, 1997). Thus, it is not possible at this point to determine whether the changes in central CRF drive cause the metabolic effects observed after adrenalectomy, or vice versa.

Another set of behavioral effects of adrenalectomy in addition to decreased food intake includes the decreased consumption of normally preferred sweet solutions and drug seeking (Bell *et al.,* 2000; Bhatnagar *et al.,* 2000a; Richter *et al.,* 1941; Seidenstadt and Eaton, 1978; Adamec and McKay, 1993; Beck and

Fibiger, 1995; Deroche *et al.,* 1995; Goldstein *et al.,* 1996; Marinelli *et al.,* 1994; Meerlo *et al.,* 1996; Piazza *et al.,* 1993; Silva, 1977). In preliminary experiments, we confirm that another prefered behavior, wheel-running, is markedly reduced in adrenalectomized rats, compared to sham-adrenalectomized rats (Moberg and Clark, 1976; K. D. Laugero, R. Kapur, and M. F. Dallman, unpublished results). All of these diminished behaviors, which are reversed by treatment with glucocorticoids, may be subsumed under the rubric of pleasurable activities. The absence of glucocorticoid concentrations in the range of the circadian maximum markedly reduces these behaviors, suggesting a strong effect of GR occupancy on hedonic pursuits under basal nonstressed conditions.

2. Sucrose

There have been sporadic reports that allowing adrenalectomized rats to drink nutritive carbohydrates tends to restore the reduced food intake, body weight, and metabolic derangements to normal (Kang *et al.,* 1992; Richter *et al.,* 1941). We have begun to reexplore this phenomenon. Although adrenalectomized rats do not voluntarily drink as much 30% sucrose as normal rats, they do drink approximately 40% of the normal amount (Bell *et al.,* 2000; Laugero *et al.,* 2001).

Moreover, rats that are allowed 9 days of access to sucrose during the first 14 days after adrenalectomy exhibit normal caloric intake, body weight gain, caloric efficiency, thermogenic uncoupling protein content in BAT, and body fat content, compared to sham-adrenalectomized rats; this is different from adrenalectomized rats offered equally sweet saccharin (Bell *et al.,* 2000; Bhatnagar *et al.,* 2000a) (see Fig. 3).

Circulating hormone concentrations, including ACTH and insulin, were also normalized by sucrose drinking. As we anticipated from the remarkably low ACTH concentrations observed in the sucrose-drinking rats, we have also found that CRF mRNA expression in their brains is also normal in both the hypothalamus and amygdala (Fig. 4).

When adrenalectomized rats drink an adequate amount of calorically rich sucrose and saline, there are few, if any, deficits caused by removal of the corticosteroids. We have confirmed these results in 5-day adrenalectomized rats provided with saline only and with saccharin or sucrose, compared with

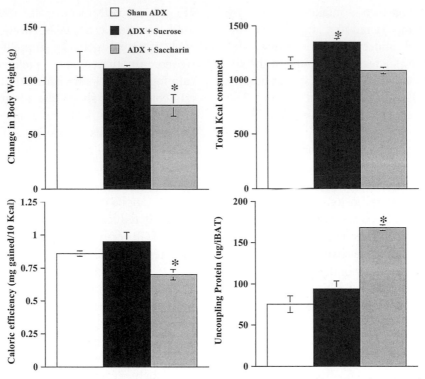

FIGURE 3 Voluntarily drinking sucrose, but not saccharin, restores adrenalectomized rats to normal energy balance. *Indicates different from sham-adrenalectomized rats. Data from Bell *et al.* (2000); Bhatnagar *et al.* (2000a).

sham-adrenalectomy, in a single experiment (Laugero *et al.*, 2001). Furthermore, adrenalectomized rats drinking sucrose do not have evidence of increased activity in the LC compared to adrenalectomized rats drinking saline ± saccharin (Laugero *et al.*, 2001), suggesting that normalizing metabolism or CRF by sucrose reduces the increased basal neuronal firing rate in the LC found after adrenalectomy (Pavcovich and Valentino, 1997). Moreover, rats given sucrose exhibit at least twice as many *fos*-positive neurons in the medial central nucleus of the amygdala as rats given saccharin (Yamamoto *et al.*, 1997).

These unexpected and novel findings suggest that under basal conditions the role of glucocorticoids is to normalize energy balance. They may do this entirely through central actions on CRF and, thus, food intake (Dallman, 1984; Dallman *et al.*, 1993, 1995; Strack *et al.*, 1995a) or through their well- known actions on tissue metabolism (Felig *et al.*, 1995). However, it is clear that the provision of calories as a sweet drink also results, as does glucocorticoid replacement, in the reversal of the effects of adrenalectomy on energy balance

and CRF expression. These results provide the underpinnings of a new scheme for the regulation of the HPA axis under basal conditions that takes into account our findings on the effects of sucrose (Fig. 5).

In summary, under basal conditions when there are no stressors to contend with, the function of glucocorticoids is the regulation of energy stores. Glucocorticoids act directly in the periphery and either directly or indirectly on brain to maintain energy, both available and stored, for use as glucose. We consider adrenalectomized rats in the category of unstressed animals; the ingestion of sucrose by adrenalectomized rats entirely remediates the loss of corticosterone. These results suggest strongly that in the absence of stress corticosteroid feedback may be exerted through the effects of the steroids on metabolism. The marked central neuropeptidergic responses to bilateral adrenalectomy result from the metabolic derangement, rather than the loss of glucocorticoids per se. Thus, Fig. 5a shows the usual schematic of control in the HPA axis, but includes effects of both corticosteroids and sympathetic outflow on elements

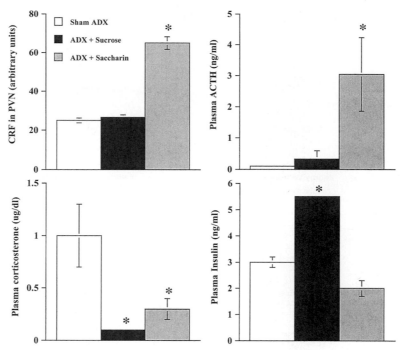

FIGURE 4 Voluntarily drinking sucrose, but not saccharin, restores adrenalectomized rats to normal hormonal balance. *Indicates different from sham-adrenalectomized rats. Note that despite the lack of a corticosterone feedback signal, rats drinking sucrose exhibit normal CRF mRNA expression in the PVN and normal ACTH concentrations in plasma. Data from Bell *et al.* (2000); Bhatnagar *et al.* (2000a).

of energy balance. After adrenalectomy (Fig. 5b), sympathetic outflow is markedly increased, possibly as a consequence of increased central CRF drive, and there is a marked reduction in variables that promote energy stores. Adrenalectomized rats that drink sucrose (Fig. 5c) exhibit normal energetic variables and also normal CRF and ACTH. Thus, in the intact organism (Fig. 5d), corticosteroid feedback on CRF may be indirectly mediated through the effects of the steroids on metabolism, yielding a basal brain-glucocorticoid-metabolic feedback system. The specific metabolic feedback signal to the brain requires identification.

III. CHRONIC AND REPEATED INTERMITTANT STRESSORS—GLUCOCORTICOIDS AND STATE-DEPENDENT CHANGES IN BRAIN

Generally, life does not consist of only basal unprovoked conditions. The "slings and arrows of outrageous fortune" attack both frequently and unpredictably throughout an organism's life span, and all organisms are evolutionarily designed to deal with stressors (e.g., Johnston, 1999). In mammals, either a very intense single stimulus (Bruijnzeel *et al.*, 1999; van Dijken *et al.*, 1993) or more modest sustained or repeated stimuli (Akana and Dallman, 1997; Akana *et al.*, 1996; Bhatnagar and Dallman, 1998a,b; Bhatnagar *et al.*, 1995, 1998; de Boer *et al.*, 1990; Kant *et al.*, 1985; Lilly *et al.*, 1983; Ottenweller *et al.*, 1989, 1992; Scribner *et al.*, 1991, 1993) alter brain function to deal, in some fashion, with what is coming next. It has become clear that a major means of preparing the brain for altered neuroendocrine, autonomic, and behavioral responses after stressors is the activation of the central CRF neuronal system (Brown *et al.*, 1981, 1982; Sutton *et al.*, 1982; reviewed in Dunn and Berridge, 1990; Koob, 1999; Owens *et al.*, 1990). A consistent component of the physiological response to stressors is the acutely increased activity of the HPA axis and its subsequently altered regulation.

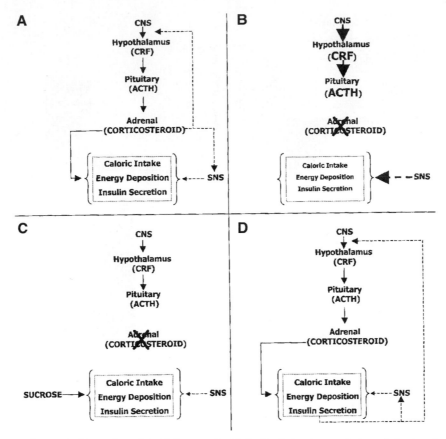

FIGURE 5 Revised model of glucocorticoid feedback in the regulation of the basal HPA axis. (A) Glucocorticoid feedback effects have been assumed to be exerted by a direct action of the steroids on the brain. Under basal conditions, glucocorticoids are also required for normal sympathetic nervous system (SNS) and energetic regulation. (B) Removal of the adrenal steroids by adrenalectomy increases the activity of the HPA and SNS axes and reduces metabolic function. (C) However, drinking sucrose prevents all of these adrenalectomy-induced neuroendocrine, autonomic, and energetic disruptions. (D) The suppressive effects of glucocorticoids on basal HPA and SNS function may be due to the metabolic effects of the steroids in the periphery (i.e., there is an adrenal-metabolism-brain feedback loop). Input to each level in the model is shown by an arrow. The size of the arrow indicates the net drive. Solid lines are stimulatory; dashed lines are inhibitory. **X** indicates adrenalectomy.

Under conditions of chronic stress, glucocorticoids, through direct actions on the brain as well as on metabolism, play a major role in the neuroendocrine, autonomic, and behavioral responses that occur to new stimuli.

We first address the effects of acute stress and corticosteroid feedback and then the neural pathways that are excited by acute stress, citing papers that use the immediate early gene *c-Fos* as a marker of neural activity (Morgan and Curran, 1989, 1991) to determine

groups of activated cells. Next we discuss the effects of chronic stress on the regulation of the HPA axis and central catecholaminergic sites after subsequent novel (heterotypic) stress. With repetition or persistence of the chronic stressor, the specificities of the activated neural systems change toward the activation of a circuit containing a common set of central monoaminergic, and limbic structures. It is the activation of this circuit, probably regulated by the activation of CRF-containing cell groups, that appears to sensitize behavioral, neuroendocrine, and autonomic activity in the state of chronic stress (Section IV). Next (Section V), we discuss the effects of CRF and catecholamines on these central sites. In addition, we mention briefly the effects of chronic stressors on the mesolimbic system, which probably is also a part of the stressor-sensitized response system. High concentrations of glucocorticoids play a major role in this. We discuss in detail (Section VI) adaptation, the effects of repeated stressors on the nth HPA response, and the role of the thalamic paraventricular nucleus as a recognition site for the state of chronic stress. In Section VII, we describe some of the effects of sucrose on neuroendocrine, autonomic, and behavioral responses to imposed stressors.

A. Acute Stressors and Glucocorticoid Feedback

The pretreatment of animals or humans with glucocorticoids results in the potent and dose-related inhibition of responses to subsequently applied stressors by the HPA axis (e.g., Dallman *et al.*, 1987, 1989a; Dallman and Jones, 1973; Gaillet *et al.*, 1993; Garcia-Belenguer *et al.*, 1993; Keller-Wood and Dallman, 1984; Kling *et al.*, 1993; Kovacs *et al.*, 2000; Nicholson *et al.*, 1987; Weidenfeld *et al.*, 1997; Wilkinson *et al.*, 1997). The feedback effects appear to require the occupancy of both MR and GR (Bradbury *et al.*, 1994; de Kloet *et al.*, 1999; Jacobson and Sapolsky, 1993; Korte *et al.*, 1996; Ratka *et al.*, 1989; Spencer *et al.*, 1990, 1991, 1993, 1998; Young *et al.*, 1990, 1998).

B. Acute Stressors and *c-Fos* Responses

It is clear that there are many central neural circuits used to activate the motor CRF neurons of the HPA axis by various stressors. Neural information about hypoglycemia, volume depletion, hypotension, intraperitoneally injected lipopolysaccharide, conditioned taste aversion, and pain paradigms enters the central nervous system (CNS) through autonomic afferents with a first synaptic relay at the nucleus of the tractus solitarius (NTS) (Buller *et al.*, 1999; Cullinan *et al.*, 1995; Cullinan and Zaborsky, 1991; Monnikes *et al.*, 1997; Navarro *et al.*, 2000; Pan *et al.*, 1997; Pezzone *et al.*, 1993; Rivest and Laflamme, 1995; Sawchenko *et al.*, 1993; Tkacs and Strack, 1995;

Wan *et al.*, 1993). At this site, they have immediate access to the long axons of the noradrenergic cell group (A2) that make monosynaptic connections with CRF neurons in the PVN and stimulate CRF secretion (Liposits *et al.*, 1987; Pacak *et al.*, 1995, 1996; Plotsky, 1989, 1991; Plotsky *et al.*, 1989; Szafarczyk *et al.*, 1988).

In general, lesions of the afferent input to the NTS, catecholamine cell groups, or the upstream catecholaminergic pathways either block or strongly reduce HPA responses to these stimuli (Darlington *et al.*, 1986; Gaillet *et al.*, 1993; Li and Rowland, 1995; Li *et al.*, 1998; Pacak *et al.*, 1996; Pan *et al.*, 1997; Plotsky *et al.*, 1989). Clearly, therefore, these major inputs from the viscera are important to at least HPA stress responses. Similarly, inputs from the circumventricular organs sensing osmolality and volume are directly linked to the PVN and are required for its stimulation after osmolar and volume stressors (Kovacs and Sawchenko, 1993).

On the other hand, stressors that can be characterized as more psychological, such as footshock, restraint, immobilization, and establishing social hierarchies appear to use limbic inputs as the initiating source of their primary stimulus to the PVN (see Chung *et al.*, 1999; Herman and Cullinan, 1997; Herman *et al.*, 1996b; Palkovits *et al.*, 1998; Sawchenko *et al.*, 2000). However, glucocorticoid antagonists injected into the NTS interfere with stress-induced memory involving amygdalar function (Roozendaal *et al.*, 1999).

Two reviews have made excellent attempts to distinguish between types of stressors and the pathways they use to activate CRF cells in the PVN. (Herman *et al.*, 1996c; Herman and Cullinan, 1997) distinguish between direct or systemic stressors that activate direct, frequently monosynaptic inputs to the PVN and processive stressors that require cognition and arise in cortical limbic sites that have polysynaptic input to the PVN; processive stressors appear to cause stimulation through the inhibition of tonic inhibitory tone on CRF cells, which is mediated by γ-aminobutyric acid (GABA) (Bowers *et al.*, 1998). Sawchenko *et al.*, (2000) distinguish between systemic stressors that usually serve to move variables away from their regulated setpoints, are not perceived, and "are transduced by a manageably small number of peripheral or central receptors"; and neurogenic stressors that "involve manipulations whose effective stimuli are less easily specified, often rely upon somatosensory or nociceptive pathways for their initial transduction, and involve a distinct cognitive and/or affective component." Both analyses are very useful; however, they deal primarily with the issue of the most direct inputs to the PVN provided by a specific stimulus rather than common central stress pathways that are activated in response to the stressor.

There is a fairly large set of brain-cell groups that responds to acute stress, whether or not their activity is required for activity in the HPA axis. These have been thoroughly documented (e.g., Cullinan *et al.*, 1995; Honkaniemi, 1992; Kovacs, 1998; Li *et al.*, 1996; Melia *et al.*, 1994). That not all stressor-activated *fos*-positive groups are required for the activation of the PVN was shown most elegantly by Li *et al.* (1996). Nonetheless, there appears to be a common group that expresses *fos*-like activity after any acute stressor (see Bhatnagar and Dallman, 1998a; Bruijnzeel *et al.*, 1999; Chowdhury *et al.*, 2000; Chung *et al.*, 1999; Kollack-Walker *et al.*, 1999; Kovacs, 1998). These include the frontal, cingulate, and pyriform cortex; hippocampus (sometimes, not always); lateral septum; BNST; medial, basolateral and central nuclei of the amygdala; nucleus accumbens; parvocellular PVN; periaqueductal gray; LC; lateral parabrachial nucleus; dorsal raphe nucleus; NTS, and ventrolateral medulla (see Fig. 6).

In summary, there is a broad set of neural structures that are activated by acute stressors. Only some of these stress circuits may be required to activate the HPA axis, depending on the specific stimulus. However, the aminergic, visceral, limbic, and cortical cell groups are quite uniformly activated by stressors, and it is these groups that probably act to prepare the organism for further onslaughts through coordinated behavioral, autonomic, and neuroendocrine changes. Three sites that are usually activated contain CRFergic cells: the PVN, the central nucleus of the amygdala (CeA) and the BNST. A fourth CRF-containing cell group in the brain stem, Barrington's nucleus, may also be important for readying the animal for further stress. This nucleus has been shown to project to sympathetic premotor neurons in the spinal cord (Cano *et al.*, 2000), suggesting that it may play a role in autonomic adjustments to chronic or repeated stress.

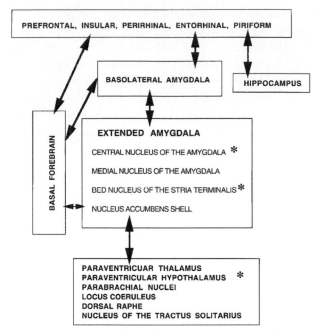

FIGURE 6 Central stress pathways and cell groups. The indicated cell groups have been included if there is activation of *c-Fos* induced by chronic stress, presentation of a heterotypic stressor by intracerebroventricular infusions of CRF, and modification of *c-Fos* activity after adaptation to homotypic stress. *Indicates CRF-synthesizing neurons. All of the named sites are innervated by CRF immunoreactive fibers. Most of the brain-stem, hypothalamic and thalamic inputs have separate inputs to the other sites in the limbic brain and need not enter these structures through sites in the extended amygdala.

C. Chronic Stressors on New Hypothalamic-Pituitary-Adrenal Responses

1. Facilitation (Heterotypic Stimuli)

One stimulus followed by another appears to have no effect on the responsivity of the HPA axis. Because the initial stressor stimulates corticosteroid secretion, we expect the amplitude of the second response to be damped because of the inhibitory feedback effects of the steroids. Although it is very easy to demonstrate experimentally the strong inhibitory effects of glucocorticoids on stressor-induced ACTH secretion when treatment precedes the application of a stressor (see previous discussion), this does not occur after a period of chronic stress. Even though chronic stress results in quantities of corticosteroid secretion that are adequate to suppress acute HPA responses, when exposed to a novel stressor the HPA axis either responds with normal or increased amplitude (e.g., Akana and Dallman, 1997; Bhatnagar and Meaney, 1995; Dallman and Jones, 1973; Lilly *et al.*, 1983, 1986a,b, 2000; Makino *et al.*, 1995; Plotsky, 1987; Scribner *et al.*, 1991, 1993; Young *et al.*, 1990; reviewed in Dallman and Bhatnagar, 2001). Facilitated ACTH responses to heterotypic stimuli have been shown to be blocked by lesions of the amygdala (Beaulieu *et al.*, 1986; Lilly *et al.*, 2000; Van de Kar *et al.*, 1991), suggesting strongly that activity in the CeA is required for the expression of facilitation. However, lesions of the CeA that block facilitated HPA responses to novel stressors in chronically stressed rats do not alter the timing or magnitude of HPA responses to the same stimuli in naïve rats exposed only to the novel stimulus. Although a functional amygdala is required for full HPA responses to some stimuli, it is not necessary for some responses (e.g., hemorrhage, cold, and ether) or for restraint stress alone (Prewitt and Herman, 1997). In these cases, the amygdala participation in the HPA response is state-dependent and requires prior stress.

2. High Concentrations of Glucocorticoids

Facilitated ACTH responses do not occur in previously stressed rats exposed to a new stressor if they are adrenalectomized and have not had corticosteroid replacement. In the absence of corticosterone, there are smaller than usual CRF and ACTH responses to a new stimulus in previously stressed rats (Akana and Dallman, 1997; Marti *et al.*, 1999; Murakami *et al.*, 1997; Tanimura and Watts, 1998, 2000). Although occupancy of both GR and MR is important for the control of ACTH responses to repeated stressors (Cole *et al.*, 2000a), high plasma corticosteroid concentrations are required to demonstrate the facilitation of ACTH secretion in previously stressed rats (Fig. 7) (Akana and Dallman, 1997; Murakami *et al.*, 1997; Tanimura and Watts, 1998, 2000). Thus, although glucocorticoid concentrations must be normal, and not low, for the appropriate regulation of the HPA axis under basal conditions, high concentrations are required for an adequate response to new stress in chronically stressed animals.

Because lesions of the amygdala inhibit facilitated HPA responses and there are plentiful GR in the amygdala, we tested whether corticosterone-containing implants directly in the CeA would restore facilitation in adrenalectomized rats. High concentrations of corticosterone in the CeA did not alter the amplitude of

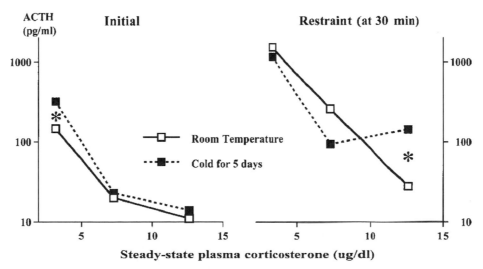

FIGURE 7 Facilitation of ACTH secretion in chronically stressed rats requires high glucocorticoid concentrations. Although plasma ACTH concentrations are negatively related to steady-state corticosterone concentrations under initial conditions in adrenalectomized rats at both room temperature and in cold, the concentrations of ACTH 30 min after the heterotypic stressor of restraint demonstrate facilitation only at the highest corticosterone concentrations in the cold-exposed rats. At room temperature (no chronic stress), the inhibition of the ACTH response to restraint is inversely related to the concentrations of corticosterone. From Akana and Dallman (1997), *Endocrinology* **138**, 3249–3258.

the ACTH response to restraint in either control or cold-exposed rats (Akana *et al.,* 2001). Thus, the amygdala are required, but are not sufficient for facilitatory responses to new stressors that occur in the state of chronic stress.

Together, these results show that chronic or prior stressors cause plasticity in the neural pathways to the HPA axis, thus changing its control characteristics to new stimuli markedly. Clearly the amygdala are involved in these state-dependent pathways, as is the LC (Gaillet *et al.,* 1993; Ziegler *et al.,* 1999). Furthermore, acute stressors administered to chronically stressed animals increase norepinephrine secretion in the PVN and other brain structures (Finlay *et al.,* 1995; Goldstein *et al.,* 1996; Nissenbaum *et al.,* 1991; Pacak *et al.,* 1995; Pavcovich *et al.,* 1990; Quirce and Maickel, 1981; Serova *et al.,* 1999). Similarly, chronic stressors (also defined as surgical manipulation of the rat within the previous 2 days) followed by acute stimuli increase dopamine secretion in the nucleus accumbens and prefrontal cortex (Deroche *et al.,* 1995; Erb and Stewart, 1999; Finlay *et al.,* 1995; Floresco *et al.,* 1998; Florino and Phillips, 1999; Garris *et al.,* 1999; Highfield *et al.,* 2000; Kalivas and Stewart, 1991; Louilot and Besson, 2000; Wu *et al.,* 2000).

In summary, chronic or prior stress results in state-dependent changes in the brain such that subsequent responses in the HPA axis as well as in catecholaminergic target sites in brain hyperrespond to new stimuli. These state-dependent changes require high glucocorticoid concentrations and probably account for the autonomic, neuroendocrine, and behavioral changes that accompany chronic stress.

IV. CORTICOTROPIN-RELEASING FACTOR AS THE CENTRAL ORGANIZER OF NEUROENDOCRINE, AUTONOMIC, AND BEHAVIORAL RESPONSES TO STRESS

A. Evidence That Corticotropin-Releasing Factor Is a Major Player in Responses to Persistent Stressors

When the common central structures that respond to stressors are activated (Fig. 6), it seems clear that the activation of CRF neurons plays a large role in the subsequent responses of the organism. This has been shown by comparing *fos*-positive structures that are elicited by central infusions of CRF and stressors (e.g., Arnold *et al.,* 1992; Imaki *et al.,* 1993; Parkes *et al.,* 1993); measuring changes in CRF content in brain after the administration of chronic stressors (Chappell *et al.,* 1986; Stout *et al.,* 2000); and testing the autonomic, neuroendocrine, and behavioral effects of CRF injected into the cerebral ventricles (e.g., Bovetto *et al.,* 1996; Dunn and Berridge, 1987; Linthorst *et al.,* 1997; Pellymounter *et al.,* 2000; Sutton *et al.,* 1982; Wiersma *et al.,* 1998; reviewed in Dunn and Berridge, 1990; Heinrichs and De Souza, 2001; Koob, 1999; Owens and Nemeroff, 1991; Weninger and Majzoub, 2001). The demonstration that CRF antagonists block many of the typical responses to repeated or chronic stressors unequivocally documents the fact that the central CRF system is critical to changes resulting from stressors (e.g., Bianchi and Panerai, 1995; Chang and Opp, 2000; Curtis *et al.,* 1997; Goeders and Guerin, 2000; Heinrichs and Richard, 1999; Jezova *et al.,* 1999; Kawahara *et al.,* 2000; Macey *et al.,* 2000; Melia and Duman, 1991; Morimoto *et al.,* 1993; Okuyama *et al.,* 1999; Rivier *et al.,* 1986; Schulz and Lehnert, 1996; Shaham *et al.,* 1998; Smagin *et al.,* 1998; reviewed in Heinrichs and De Souza, 2001; Weninger and Majzoub, 2001).

Some of the similar effects of chronic stress that are mediated by CRF (or its near-cousin urocortin; Behan *et al.,* 1996; Kozicz *et al.,* 1998; Wong *et al.,* 1996) injected into the brain include anorexia (Krahn *et al.,* 1986, 1990; Ohata *et al.,* 2000; Pellymounter *et al.,* 2000; Smagin *et al.,* 1998), decreased caloric efficiency (Smagin *et al.,* 1999), increased sympathetic and decreased parasympathetic outflow to the cardiovascular system (Brown and Fisher, 1983; Buwalda *et al.,* 1997, 1998; Habib *et al.,* 2000; Linthorst *et al.,* 1997; Nijsen *et al.,* 2001), decreased activity in the hypothalamic-pituitary-gonadal (HPG) axis (see Section VIII), and alterations in a variety of behaviors such as learning and memory, fear, and drug seeking (Heinrichs and De Souza, 2001; Koob, 1999; Smagin and Dunn, 2000; Weninger and Majzoub, 2000). These effects are all modulated by the actions of corticosteroids, apparently either through the alteration of CRF activity or by interactions with monoaminergic systems that are primarily responsible for effecting the changes (e.g., Koob, 1999; Koob and Le Moal, 2001).

B. Distribution of Corticotropin-Releasing-Factor-Responsive Neurons and Receptors

From a relatively small number of cell groups, there is wide distribution of CRF fibers identified by immunocytochemistry throughout the brain (Swanson et al., 1983). By following fos immunolocalization of cells activated by intraventricularly injected CRF, the loss of this fos activation by coinjection of CRF receptor antagonists, and the distribution of CRF receptors 1 and 2, Bittencourt and Sawchenko (2000) have mapped brain sites affected by CRF. Similar to the common groups of cells activated by stress (see previous discussion; Li and Sawchenko, 1998), there were increases of similar magnitude after CRF injection, with the effective blockade by CRF receptor antagonist, in fos cell numbers in the prefrontal cortex; septum; amygdala; BNST; paraventricular nuclei of the thalamus; dorsomedial, arcuate, and paraventricular nuclei of the hypothalamus; periaqueductal gray; LC parabrachial nuclei; raphe nuclei; and NTS (see Fig. 6). Many, if not all of these brain sites, particularly in the brain stem and subcortical regions, are well known to be strongly affected by feeding and input from visceral autonomic receptors and provide the sites that control motor, autonomic, and neuroendocrine outflow. Thus, the central CRF-activated system is poised to modulate energy acquisition and use under stressful conditions.

C. Effects of Stress on Corticotropin-Releasing-Factor Expression in Limbic Sites

Chronic stressors in combination with high (but not low-normal) concentrations of glucocorticoids increase CRF mRNA and peptide concentrations in the amygdala, the extended amygdala (Gray and Bingaman, 1996), and the BNST (Kasckow et al., 1999; Makino et al., 1994a,b, 1995; Shepard et al., 2000; Watts and Sanchez-Watts, 1995). Stress also increases CRF concentrations in dialysis fluid of probes over the amygdala (Merali et al., 1998; Pich et al., 1993). Lesions of both structures damp or abolish HPA responses to re-

peated stressors (Bohus et al., 1996; Gray et al., 1993; Herman et al., 1996a; Lilly et al., 2000; Van de Kar et al., 1991).

V. SOME SITES OF THE STATE-DEPENDENT CHANGES THAT RESULT FROM CHRONIC STRESS

A. Amygdala, Glucocorticoids, Norepinephrine, and Stress

Studies of the effects of the amygdala on fear-conditioned behavior have restored the study of emotion to the central curriculum of neuoscience. Four laboratories, LeDoux, Davis, Fanselow, and McGaugh, have caused this structure to yield many secrets (see Davis, 1998; Davis and Whalen, 2001; Fanselow and Le Doux, 1999; Ferry et al., 1999; LeDoux, 1994; McGaugh et al., 1996; Roozendaal and McGaugh, 1997b). Moreover, the anatomy and connectivity of the amygdala have become clearer (Broadle-Biber et al., 1993; Moga and Gray, 1985; Moga et al., 1990; Petrovich et al., 1996; Petrovich and Swanson, 1997; Pikkarainen et al., 1999; Pitkanen et al., 1997; Swanson and Petrovich, 1998; Wilensky et al., 2000; Yamamoto et al., 1997). By definition, fear-conditioned behavior represents the responses of animals in a state of chronic stress exposed to a heterotypic stressor. The paradigm provides inescapable shock paired with a tone or distinctive environment, followed by testing fear behaviors in novel settings or after having transported the previously shocked rats to the distinctive environment.

Elegant studies on fear-conditioned behavior have shown that inputs to the lateral amygdala are forwarded to the CRF-containing structures, the CeA, and the BNST (Davis, 1998; LeDoux, 1998). However, increasing emphasis is now being placed on another output of the lateral amygdala to the nucleus accumbens and limbic cortices in response to treatments that demand vigilance, but not necessarily fear (Davis and Whalen, 2001; Holland and Gallagher, 1999). The stimulation of the basolateral amygdala increases extracellular dopamine in the nucleus accumbens through a glutamate-mediated mechanism that does not depend on increased dopamine secretion from the ventrotegmental area (VTA) (Floresco et al., 1998). Initiated by input to the lateral nucleus of the amygdala, outputs from the CeA and BNST, the nucleus accumbens, and limbic cortex can all fairly directly influence the activity of neurons in the neuroendocrine hypothalamus, periaqueductal gray (behavior) and monoaminergic cell groups, parabrachial nuclei, and dorsal vagal nuclei, and premotor sympathetic neurons in the interomediolateral cord (autonomic responses) (see Fig. 6).

Stress inevitably excites *fos*-expression in the amygdala; frequently in the lateral, basolateral, central, and medial subnuclei. Stress-induced activity of the amygdala has been shown to affect conditioned fear behavior and learning and memory, among other effects (e.g., Cahill *et al.*, 1995; Cahill and McGaugh, 1996; Davis, 1998; Davis and Whalen, 2001; de Quervqin *et al.*, 1998; LeDoux, 1998; Quirarte *et al.*, 1997). Moreover, the actions of both norepinephrine and glucocorticoids are required for appropriate learning and memory to occur after the administration of the conditioning-shock bout (e.g., McGaugh *et al.*, 1996; Roozendaal and McGaugh, 1997a,b). High glucocorticoid concentrations *in vivo* also strongly modulate the inhibitory effects exerted by serotonin on afferent glutaminergic input to the lateral amygdala (Stutzmann *et al.*, 1998), and there is good evidence that a stimulatory effect of glucocorticoids is exerted on serotonin synthesis in the dorsal raphe nuclei (Azmitia, 1999; Azmitia and McEwen, 1969, 1974).

1. Locus Coeruleus, Stress, and Corticotropin-Releasing Factor

Although the expression of CRF R1 or R2 was not found in the LC (Bittencourt and Sawchenko, 2000), both CRF and urocortin induce *fos* staining in the LC, as does stress (Bittencourt and Sawchenko, 2000; Li and Sawchenko, 1998). It seems clear that both CRF and CRF antagonists injected directly into the LC affect activity in noradrenergic neurons (Curtis *et al.*, 1997; Lehnert *et al.*, 1998; Melia and Duman, 1991; Pavcovich and Valentino, 1997; Schulz and Lehnert, 1996; Smagin *et al.*, 1995; Valentino *et al.*, 1983, 1992; Van Bocksdale *et al.*, 1999). Norepinephrine is secreted as a consequence of CRF-induced activation of the LC throughout the brain, and it may play an extremely important part in the organized responses to chronic stressors (Chang *et al.*, 2000; Curtis *et al.*, 1995, 1997; Finlay *et al.*, 1995; Kawahara *et al.*, 2000; Melia and Duman, 1991; Nissenbaum and Abercrombie, 1992;

Nissenbaum *et al.*, 1991; Pavcovich *et al.*, 1990; Smagin *et al.*, 1995). There is only a small direct input to the PVN from the LC (Cunningham and Sawchenko, 1990; Pacak *et al.*, 1995; Sawchenko and Swanson, 1982); however, lesions of the LC markedly inhibit ACTH and corticosterone responses to stress (Gaillet *et al.*, 1993; Ziegler *et al.*, 1999). In addition, unilateral pontine-mesencephalic denervation of rats does not abolish the secretion of norepinephrine in the ipsilateral PVN in response to stress (Palkovits *et al.*, 1999). These results suggest that, either through its slight direct input to the PVN or through its strong inputs to the amygdala and BNST, the LC is important not only for behavioral and autonomic responses, but also for HPA-axis responses to chronic stress.

B. Mesolimbic System, Stress, and Glucocorticoids

The VTA is connected through the medial forebrain bundle to the nucleus accumbens. The shell of the accumbens, in particular, appears to engage or provide salience to feelings of pleasure for the animal (Franklin and Druhan, 2000; King *et al.*, 1997; Pennartz *et al.*, 1994; reviewed in Berridge and Robinson, 1998; Robbins and Everitt, 1996; Wise and Rompre, 1989). This system is activated in its various parts by feeding, copulation, sweet drinks, and drugs. It appears to have a good deal to do with relating salience (or wanting) to incoming stimuli; a rat with an electrode implanted in any of these structures self-stimulates the electrode and ignores food and drink. Drugs delivered to either the VTA or to the nucleus accumbens stimulate dopamine secretion, and the amount of this secretion is strongly dependent on the glucocortioid environment (Koob, 1999; Koob and Le Moal, 2001; Piazza *et al.*, 1993, 1996; Piazza and Le Moal, 1997, 1998). The site of action of glucocorticoids on stimulated dopamine secretion into the nucleus accumbens is unclear. However, repeated stress, like repeated drug administration, increases tyrosine hydroxylase protein content in the VTA and cyclic adenylyl-monophosphate (AMP)-dependent protein kinase activity in the nucleus accumbens (Ortiz *et al.*, 1995), suggesting that the action of the steroids at both sites may be important.

We have tested the effects of glucocorticoids on the amount of saccharin ingested by adrenalectomized rats, compared to sham-adrenalectomized controls. There was a strict positive relationship between the amount of saccharin solution ingested and the replacement doses of corticosterone in adrenalectomized rats (Bhatnagar *et al.*, 2000a). Adrenalectomized rats, although they consistently drank a few milliliters, did not drink much saccharin at all, which correlates well with the finding that adrenalectomy markedly reduces dopamine secretion in the shell of the accumbens (Barrot *et al.*, 2000; Goeders and Guérin, 1996; Nakahara *et al.*, 2000; Shoaib and Shippenberg, 1996). Moreover, it required high concentrations of corticosterone in adrenalectomized rats for them to ingest amounts of either saccharin (Bhatnagar *et al.*, 2000a) or sucrose (Bell *et al.*, 2000) that were equal to controls. In our work, we have found that intact rats or adrenalectomized rats with high concentrations of corticosterone replacement respond to cold stress with increases in sucrose consumption above their own room-temperature control values. By contrast, adrenalectomized rats with a lower dose of corticosterone replacement do not drink more sucrose in the cold than at room temperature (M. E. Bell, unpublished). This result suggests strongly that stress-induced increases in corticosterone concentrations increase the salience of the sweet solution to a greater extent than even normal corticosterone concentrations.

The results of these experiments testing the interaction of corticosteroids and ingestion of sweet solutions resemble closely the effects of stress on drug relapse. Both CRF and glucocorticoids have been strongly associated with drug seeking and relapsing behaviors (Erb *et al.*, 1998; Erb and Stewart, 1999; Koob and Le Moal, 2001; Marinelli *et al.*, 1998; Shaham *et al.*, 1997, 1998).

In summary, there are plastic changes that occur in the brain under conditions of chronic stress that are probably orchestrated by changes in the activity of the central CRF neuronal system (Fig. 6). Highly interconnected limbic structures that are associated with emotion are activated by the combination of stress and high glucocorticoids. Monoaminergic cell groups (serotonin, norepinephrine, and dopamine) increase their responsivity to acute stressors under the state of chronic stress and are probably in part responsible for the increased activity observed in the sensitive limbic structures (Tanaka *et al.*, 2000). A further layer of control, represented by increased activity in the limbic cortex that results from chronic stress via the same trans-

mitters, has been ignored here, although it is clearly important. The total effect of stress- and glucocorticoid-induced use of these pathways results in the behavioral, autonomic, and neuroendocrine changes that result in chronically stressed animals and humans. These changes, which occur with high concentrations of glucocorticoids together with stress, have marked and obvious implications for the understanding of psychiatric disease.

VI. REPEATED HOMOTYPIC STRESS (ADAPTATION) AND THE PARAVENTRICULAR THALAMUS

A. Repeated Stress

Repeated exposure to the same (homotypic) stressor can lead to a decrement in the HPA response to the renewed application of that stressor. This decrement, termed adaptation, is evidenced by decreased HPA responses to the nth exposure to a stressor compared to the first exposure to that stressor. It is important to note that there are no reports of animals exhibiting a complete lack of response to a homotypic stressor. That is, there is always an HPA response to a homotypic stressor that is above baseline values, regardless of how many days the homotypic stressor has been administered.

The adaptation of ACTH to repeated restraint or immobilization (30 min up to 2.5 hr; 6–16 days) has been consistently demonstrated (Cole *et al.*, 2000a; Garcia *et al.*, 2000; Giralt and Armario, 1989; Hauger *et al.*, 1990; Viau and Sawchenko, 1995). In addition, adaptation is also observed after repeated cold (Bhatnagar and Meaney, 1995), noise (Armario *et al.*, 1986), water immersion (de Boer *et al.*, 1990), and handling (Dobrakova *et al.*, 1993). Presumably, this adaptation of HPA responses to repeated exposure to the same stressor has adaptive value for the animal. When the occurrence and stimulus characteristics become predictable and familiar, it makes sense for the animal to decrease its response to that stressful stimulus. Thus, the adaptation of the HPA axis occurs in response to many types of stressful stimuli that differ in their intensity and duration.

However, adaptation is not always observed, even though the stressor has presumably become familiar.

Plasma corticosterone concentrations were the same during the eighth exposure to 60-min footshock as they were during the first exposure (Pittman *et al.,* 1990). Similarly, no adaptation was seen in animals exposed to 10 days of footshock (Kant *et al.,* 1985) or 10 days of forced running (Kant *et al.,* 1985). There are indications that although the ACTH response to repeated stressors adapts, corticosterone does not always adapt (Bhatnagar *et al.,* 1995; Giralt and Armario, 1989; Hauger *et al.,* 1990; Lachuer *et al.,* 1994). However, this may be a function of the duration or timing of blood sampling after stress (see Fig. 1), or it may be that the adrenal becomes more sensitive to circulating ACTH after exposure to some types of repeated stressors. Therefore, corticosterone measurements alone may mistakenly suggest no adaptation when, in fact, adaptation is occurring in brain sites and at the pituitary. There is some evidence indicating that early environmental events, such as maternal separation, may alter adaptation to chronic stress (Bhatnagar and Meaney, 1995). Thus, whether adaptation to chronic stress occurs may be a function of the specific chronic stressor itself, as well as of the characteristics of the individual exposed to that chronic stress.

B. Changes in the Paraventricular Nucleus

Repeated exposure to restraint or immobilization (Imaki *et al.,* 1991; Makino *et al.,* 1999; Mamalaki *et al.,* 1992; Prewitt and Herman, 1997) or to a variable-stress paradigm (Prewitt and Herman, 1997) increases CRF mRNA in the parvocellular paraventricular nuclei (pPVN). Repeated psychosocial stress increases the resting levels of AVP in the external zone of the median eminence (de Goeij *et al.,* 1992a) and increases the colocalization of AVP in CRF-containing neurons in the pPVN (de Goeij *et al.,* 1992b). These and other studies demonstrate an activation of either or both ACTH secretagogs, CRF and AVP, in the pPVN as a result of exposure to repeated stress. Whether one or both of the secretagogs increase may depend on the type of repeated stressor in question; nonetheless, results suggest the presence of strong excitatory afferent input to the pPVN with repeated stress exposure. The pPVN receives afferents from a wide variety of sources as described earlier. We describe here two categories of inputs, from brain-stem amine groups and from limbic structures, and their pos-

sible involvement in the adaptation to chronic-stress-induced HPA activity. First, however, the potential role of glucocorticoid negative feedback effects in mediating adaptation are discussed.

C. Negative Feedback Effects of Glucocorticoids

The release of glucocorticoids by repeated exposure to the homotypic stressor produces negative feedback effects on subsequent HPA activity. These negative feedback effects are balanced or overcome when the animal is exposed to a novel stressor. However, can negative feedback effects underlie the adaptation to a homotypic stressor? There is evidence to suggest that adaptation can occur, in part, through negative feedback effects exerted by glucocorticoids. Spencer and colleagues have shown that peripheral injections of an MR antagonist or a combination of MR and GR antagonists block the adaptation of corticosterone to repeated restraint (Cole *et al.,* 2000a). Therefore, adaptation involves, in part, glucocorticoids released by daily exposure to stress, and these glucocorticoids act on MR as well as GR to exert negative feedback effects on HPA activity. The specific sites at which glucocorticoids may exert their negative feedback effects to inhibit subsequent responses to a homotypic stressor have not been identified. Potential candidates include the frontal cortex, septum, and hippocampus, based primarily on their involvement in negative feedback effects under acute stress (Cole *et al.,* 2000a; Herman *et al.,* 1996c). The possibility that the paraventricular thalamus may be such a site under chronic stress conditions is discussed in Section VI.D.

1. Brain-Stem Amine Groups

A number of studies have found changes in neuronal firing rates or catecholamine-synthesizing-enzyme levels in brain-stem regions following exposure to repeated stress. Tyrosine hydroxylase mRNA in the LC is increased by repeated immobilization (Mamalaki *et al.,* 1992) and chronic social subordinance (Watanabe *et al.,* 1995), and tryptophan hydroxylase mRNA is increased in the dorsal raphe by repeated immobilization (Chamas *et al.,* 1999). Increased rates in neuronal firing of LC neurons are also observed in repeatedly immobilized rats (Pavcovich *et al.,* 1990).

Lowry *et al.* (2000) have demonstrated that CRF-induced stimulation of a subpopulation of serotonin-containing neurons in the dorsal raphe is enhanced in rats that have been repeatedly exposed to restraint. Together, as in chronic stress, these studies suggest that activity in brain-stem amine groups that provide afferent inputs to both the PVN and limbic structures that regulate HPA activity is altered by repeated stress exposure.

Lachuer *et al.* (1994) have examined adaptation of HPA activity in concert with changes in concentrations of the catecholamine metabolite dihydroxy phenyl acetic acid (DOPAC) at different times during 10 days of repeated restraint exposure. They found that DOPAC levels in the A1-C1 brain-stem catecholamine groups decreased in parallel with ACTH levels with repeated exposure to restraint. However, when repeatedly restrained animals were exposed to the novel stress of ether, both HPA responses and DOPAC levels were enhanced. The authors suggest that because brain-stem catecholamine groups change their activity depending on the specific stressor (homotypic or heterotypic), these changes are secondary to the control by limbic structures that regulate behavioral adaptation to the homotypic stressor. Thus, it may be that brain-stem sensory inputs to limbic regions produce behavioral adaptation and descending inputs from these limbic structures produce adaptation in brain-stem catecholaminergic nuclei. These descending inputs can be inhibitory or provide a smaller stimulatory signal to brain-stem nuclei. In any case, the net effect is that there is decreased stimulatory sensory input to the PVN and adapted HPA responses. When adapted animals are exposed to the novel stress of ether, there may be the activation of brain-stem inputs to the limbic structures, and the descending inputs from the limbic structures to both the brain stem and PVN are stimulatory, the net result being enhanced activity in the PVN (Lachuer *et al.*, 1994). In this model, activity in brain-stem nuclei that provide afferent inputs to the PVN can be directly modified by descending inputs from limbic structures. Although direct empirical support for this hypothesis is necessary, there is some evidence suggesting that changes in activity of brain-stem catecholamine cell groups can be a result of descending modulatory inputs and only secondary to the stress exposure itself (Li *et al.*, 1996).

2. Limbic Structures

A number of limbic sites, including the prefrontal cortex, hippocampus, and amygdala are known to regulate HPA responses to acute stressors and represent reasonable candidates for brain regions that may regulate adaptation and facilitation to repeated stress (see previous discussion). In the amygdala, the central, basolateral, and basomedial subdivisions exhibit increased neuronal activity (fos protein) in rats exposed to restraint after 7 days of 4 hours of repeated cold (Bhatnagar and Dallman, 1998a). However, lesions of the CeA did not alter CRH or AVP mRNA in the pPVN in rats exposed to a variable stressor paradigm (Prewitt and Herman, 1997), although the effects on the adaptation or facilitation of ACTH and B levels are not known. Thus, a clear role for a specific amygdaloid subnucleus in adaptation to repeated chronic stressors has not been demonstrated.

D. Paraventricular Thalamus

We have been examining the role of the paraventricular thalamic nucleus (PVTh) in both the facilitation and adaptation of HPA activity in repeatedly stressed rats. The posterior division of the PVTh (pPVTh) exhibits increased neuronal activity (fos protein) in rats exposed to restraint after repeated cold (Bhatnagar and Dallman, 1998a). Lesions of the PVTh enhance ACTH and corticosterone responses to restraint in repeated cold-stressed rats, but not control rats, suggesting that normally the PVTh inhibits acute stress-induced activity on HPA-axis activity in stressed rats (Bhatnagar and Dallman, 1998a). The PVTh may also inhibit some of the effects of stressors on metabolism because such lesions also block the normal stress-induced reduction in feeding and body temperature rhythms and augment subcutaneous fat deposit weight (Bhatnagar and Dallman, 1999). These inhibitory effects of the PVTh on HPA activity in repeatedly stressed rats involve, in part, the activation of ascending cholecystokinin-(CCK-) containing inputs to the PVTh from the dorsal raphe, ventrolateral periaqueductal gray, and lateral parabrachial nucleus (Bhatnagar *et al.*, 2000b).

We have found that the inhibition of HPA activity by the PVTh extends to conditions of homotypic stress. Repeatedly restrained (7 days) rats exhibit an adaptation of ACTH and corticosterone that is blocked by lesions of the posterior PVTh (S. Bhatnagar, unpublished results). Again posterior PVTh lesions did not alter ACTH and corticosterone responses to acute restraint. Adaptation may be due to negative feedback effects of glucocorticoids released by repeated exposure to the stressor (as previously discussed) and we are testing whether the pPVTh is a site of negative feedback effects of glucocorticoids. Adaptation may also be the result of an active inhibitory pathway that includes the PVTh. By no means are these two possible mechanisms for adaptation mutually exclusive. Thus, the functional PVTh inhibits both the facilitation and adaptation of HPA activity in repeatedly stressed rats. The unique feature of the PVTh, which distinguishes it from many other limbic structures that regulate HPA activity, is that the PVTh does not alter HPA responses to acute stress. The function of the PVTh in modulating HPA responses to acute stress appears to be strictly dependent on the state of chronic stress.

It is important to note that both heterotypic and homotypic stressors increase the number of *fos*-expressing neurons in the PVTh in chronically stressed rats (Bhatnagar and Dallman, 1998a; Li and Sawchenko, 1998). However, the number of *fos*-expressing cells in brain stem, limbic sites, and PVN are increased in response to a heterotypic stressor (Bhatnagar and Dallman, 1998a) and are decreased in response to a homotypic stressor (Li and Sawchenko, 1998). Thus, evidence indicates that the PVTh registers chronic stress and generally inhibits HPA function after both heterotypic and homotypic stressors.

The pPVTh receives afferent inputs from brain-stem amine cell groups in which activity is altered by chronic stress exposure. For example, the PVTh contains serotonin immunoreactive fibers (Freedman and Cassell, 1994) and retrograde tracer studies have demonstrated direct afferent input from the dorsal raphe to the PVTh (Eberhart *et al.*, 1985; Otake and Nakamura, 1995; Otake *et al.*, 1994, 1995; Otake and Ruggerio, 1995). In addition, the PVTh receives afferent input from brainstem catecholamine-synthesizing cell bodies. Thus, the PVTh may act in concert with the brain-stem regions already described to regulate both facilitation and adaptation to repeated or chronic stress.

The pPVTh projects specifically to the CeA, basomedial basolateral amygdala, and nucleus accumbens (Freedman and Cassell, 1994; Moga *et al.*, 1995; Su

and Bentivoglio, 1990; Turner and Herkenham, 1991), and prefrontal cortex (Bubser and Deutch, 1998). The PVTh has very few direct projections to the PVN, and its effects on HPA activity are likely to involve either upstream limbic or downstream brain-stem structures that, in turn, project to the PVN. The involvement of limbic regions such as the amygdala seems critical for the evaluation of a stressful stimulus that is required so that a decision can be made regarding its familiarity and relevance. That is, the sensory characteristics of the stressor must be compared to a memory for those characteristics in order to decide whether the stressor is novel or familiar. If the stressor is novel, facilitation results; if the stressor is familiar, adaptation may result. In this proposal, the PVTh is a critical site for the transmission of information between the brain-stem and limbic structures and, therefore, one part of a larger circuit that may regulate both adaptation and facilitation.

In summary, unlike heterotypic stressors imposed on chronically stressed animals, there is adaptation to the *n*th presentation of a homotypic stressor, with reduced neuroendocrine, autonomic, and behavioral responses. Limbic and brain-stem structures that exhibit more *fos*-positive neurons after heterotypic stressors, accompanied by increased autonomic, HPA, and behavioral responsivity, show fewer *fos*-positive neurons after repeated presentation of homotypic stressors, accompanied by decreased autonomic, HPA, and behavioral responses. Of interest is the finding that in chronically stressed rats there are an increased number of *fos*-positive neurons in the PVTh when either heterotypic or homotypic stressors are applied. The PVTh appears to be a structure that integrates the memory of prior stress with new stressors and is generally inhibitory to its downstream structures.

VII. SUCROSE AND CHRONIC STRESS

A. Chronic Stress and Energy Balance

Chronic stress reduces food intake and increases energy use (reviewed in Dallman and Bhatnagar, 2001). Most of these effects of chronic stress are probably mediated by central actions of CRF (e.g., Gosnell *et al.*, 1983; Smagin *et al.*, 1999; see Section IV), although many may be mediated by the elevated concentrations of corticosteroids and decreased concentrations of insulin as well (Akana *et al.*, 1999). It has been argued that decreases in body-weight gain, food intake, and caloric efficiency are among the most sensitive measurements for detecting imposed stress in mammals; in rodents these are equally if not more sensitive than measurements of ACTH and corticosterone (Dallman, 2001).

B. Effects of Sucrose and Other Carbohydrates on Responses to Chronic Stress

There is a considerable literature in humans and rats on the effects of carbohydrate ingestion on sensitivity to pain and opioids (e.g., Carbajal *et al.*, 1999; D'Anci, 1999; D'Anci *et al.*, 1997; Kanarek and Homoleski, 2000; Kanarek *et al.*, 1997, 2000; Mercer and Holder, 1997). Both the perception of pain and autonomic and behavioral responses to it are diminished when carbohydrates are provided before the painful stimulus. Although pain also stimulates activity in the HPA axis (Palkovits *et al.*, 1999), we are not aware of any reports on the effects of carbohydrate ingestion on the HPA responses to pain specifically.

Similar to the stressor of pain, in athletes undergoing high-level prolonged exercise carbohydrate ingestion reduces the perception of effort, increases post-exercise maximal effort, and reduces responsivity in the ACTH and cortisol to high-level exertion (Febbraio *et al.*, 2000a,b; Kraemer *et al.*, 1998; MacLaren *et al.*, 1999; Murray *et al.*, 1991; Sadamoto *et al.*, 2000; Utter *et al.*, 1999; Whitley *et al.*, 1998).

Finally, in the psychiatric literature, there are some findings that suggest that carbohydrate ingestion may be important for self-treatment of depression. Patients with unipolar depression must meet five of nine criteria set out in the Diagnostic and Statistical Manual of Mental Disorders (DSM-IV) 1994 Diagnostic Manual of the American Psychiatric Society. Weight loss or weight gain, decreased or increased food intake, hypo- or hypersomnolence, hyperarousal or apathy are included in the nine criteria. Because chronic stress is often associated with depression (e.g., Holsboer, 2000) and the effects of chronic stress in animals resemble markedly the effects of melancholic depression in humans, there has been considerable effort to apply stressed-animal models to the study of depression in humans. Patients with melancholic unipolar depression as described by Wong *et al.* (2000) exhibit weight loss, decreased food intake, sleeplessness, hyperarousal, and hyperactivity in brain norepinephrine and the HPA axis. Moreover, as do chronically stressed animals, patients with chronic depression who have committed suicide have been found to express increased CRF and AVP in their hypothalamic PVN (Purba *et al.*, 1996; Raadsheer *et al.*, 1994) and increased tyrosine hydroxylase in their LC (Zhu *et al.*, 1999). It is melancholic depressives who generally demonstrate hyperactivity in their HPA axes and abnormal dexamethasone suppression tests (Holsboer, 2000).

By contrast, some people with atypical depression may gain weight, increase food intake, sleep more, and be apathetic. Moreover, there is the syndrome of night eating described by Strunkard *et al.* (1995) in which people under chronic stress have elevated plasma ACTH and cortisol concentrations and eat most of their daily food after the usual dinner time, 70% as carbohydrate (Birketvedt *et al.*, 1999). It seems possible that both atypical depressives and night eaters may be self-treating with food in order to make themselves feel better (Damasio, 1999). It also seems possible, but highly speculative, that there is an effect of sucrose ingestion on brain catecholamines and CRF in chronically stressed individuals (like the effect of sucrose in adrenal electomized rats) that may mediate the behavioral effects of sucrose or other carbohydrates.

We have begun to test the effects of sucrose ingestion on responses to chronic stress. Rats allowed sucrose and water to drink during 5 days of chronic cold (5°C) lose similar amounts of body weight as do rats drinking only water. However, sucrose-drinking rats in cold have heavier fat stores and lower uncoupling protein-1 content in BAT. Moreover, caloric efficiency is improved and plasma ACTH and corticosterone concentrations are decreased in sucrose-drinking rats compared to water-drinking controls (Bell *et al.*, 2002). We do not yet have information about the expression of catecholamines and CRF in the brains in these rats. However, at this point, the experiments suggest that rats voluntarily drink more sucrose under the stress of chronic cold and that many of the usual consequences of cold on autonomic and HPA function are decreased when rats drink sucrose.

Rats trained in a learned helplessness paradigm are given uncontrollable shock on one day and then tested behaviorally on later days. Rats provided with uncontrollable shock eat less and lose weight over the subsequent days, but if given the choice prefer sucrose to saccharin (Dess and Choe, 1994; Dess *et al.,* 1998; Dess and Eidelheit, 1998). In a striking experiment, it was shown that, if after inescapable shock the rats drank dextrose during the 24 hours between the conditioning shock and the shuttlebox test, there was neither a loss in weight nor the usual deficit in shuttlebox behavior the next day (Minor and Saade, 1997). Clearly, this is an example of the behavioral and autonomic effects of a major stress that are relieved by the ingestion of a carbohydrate. Again, we are unaware of any brain neuropeptide or neuroendocrine data for experiments such as these. However, we predict that catecholamine synthesis in (and secretion from) neurons in the LC and CRF expression in the amygdala, and possibly the BNST and PVN are reduced in the group of rats drinking dextrose.

In summary, increased carbohydrate ingestion alters perception, pain thresholds, autonomic activity, and HPA activity under conditions of stress in humans and rats. It seems plausible to suppose that sucrose acts both metabolically and, through signals of improved metabolism, on the brain to alter activity in the common CRF and monoaminergic pathways that are activated by stress. A fairly large number of studies demonstrate the positive effects (or potential effect) of carbohydrate ingestion on autonomic, behavioral, and endocrine responses to stress. However, the studies are scattered among disciplines, and no single study that we know of has examined all aspects of the role (or mechanism) of carbohydrate ingestion on ameliorating responses to stressors. This is an important area of study for the future.

VIII. INTERACTIONS BETWEEN THE GONADAL AND ADRENAL AXES WITH STRESS

Stressors affect the activity of many neuroendocrine systems in addition to the HPA axis, and some of the autonomic, behavioral, and neuroendocrine effects of the state of stress may be determined by responses of these other endocrine systems. Here we examine some aspects of the effects of stress-induced changes in concentrations of gonadal steroid hormones on metabolism and neuropeptide expression in brain.

A. Stress, Sex Hormones, and Energy Balance

It is generally agreed that activation of the HPA axis is a necessary response for the adaptation of the organism to a stressor. Thus, fuel mobilization is promoted and anabolic processes are inhibited until the emergency is over. Stress inhibits reproduction by inhibiting the activity of the HPG axis at different levels. These actions result in decreased circulating sex hormones and alterations in behavioral and cognitive aspects of reproduction. The inhibitory effects of stress-induced HPA axis activity on the HPG axis and the reciprocal interaction between them are further discussed later. Here we focus on the effects of sex hormones on some peripheral and central aspects of the regulation of energy balance. We question how stress-induced changes in sex hormone concentrations directly or indirectly modulate energetic responses to stress.

Many studies in rodents using the classic approaches of endocrinectomy and sex hormone replacement have shown that sex hormones modify basal (nonstress) energy balance, affecting both energy intake and expenditure. Moreover, it is clear that developmental and reproductive states such as puberty, adulthood, pregnancy, lactation, and menopause modify basal metabolic demands of the organism in important ways.

1. Gonadectomy, Estrogens, Progesterone, and Androgens

Female rats that are ovariectomized (OVX) increase food intake (FI) and body weight (BW), mainly through increased fat weight, and concomitantly decrease voluntary physical activity and thermogenesis (Wade and Gray, 1979). These effects are reversed by the administration of estradiol (E), the principal ovarian steroid that regulates energy balance. Progesterone (P) plays a secondary role, increasing adiposity and FI only when E is present. The fluctuations in these hormones in rats (and women) during the estrous (or menstrual) cycle and pregnancy correlate with fluctuations in FI, BW, and physiological and behavioral thermoregulation.

In most male adult mammals, gonadectomy (GDX) decreases BW gain and FI (Wade, 1976). In adult males, testosterone (T) is the main circulating sex hormone. However, apart from acting directly as an androgen, T also serves as a pro-hormone. In many tissues, T is metabolized to E by the T-sensitive enzyme aromatase cytochrome P450 and to dihydrotestosterone (DHT), a nonaromatizable androgen, by the action of the enzyme 5α-steroid reductase. Many of the effects of T on peripheral tissues and brain are mediated by the actions of its metabolites exerted in combination with estrogen or androgen receptors. The decrease in FI and BW after GDX can be reversed by treatment with T, but this action is strongly dose-dependent. Although low concentrations of T restore metabolism in GDX rats to normal, higher doses of T decrease BW gain and FI (Gentry and Wade, 1976; Hervey and Hutchinson, 1973). The effects of physiological levels of T on BW gain are due to its anabolic action on the lean mass of the somatic tissues. The loss of BW, induced by high doses of T, primarily results from loss of body fat content (Gentry and Wade, 1976; Hervey and Hutchinson, 1973). It has been suggested that the effects of high doses of T on FI, fat content loss, and decreased BW gain might be due to the aromatization of T to E. The facts that T stimulates aromatase and that the administration of high doses of (nonaromatizable) DHT do not have the same effects as high doses of T support this hypothesis.

2. Voluntary Physical Activity

Voluntary physical activity is a behavior that modifies energy expenditure. OVX reduces running-wheel activity and E reverses the effect in female rats (Wade, 1972), whereas P administration inhibits running activity (Axelson *et al.*, 1986). These effects are in agreement with changes in physical activity during the estrous cycle (Butcher *et al.*, 1974). However, in intact rats the inhibition of ovarian and estrous activity cycles by P does not override the stimulatory effects of E on running behavior (Axelson *et al.*, 1986). In women, the loss of ovarian function after menopause is related to decreased physical activity, and estrogen therapy increases activity levels and improves exercise capacity (Poehlman and Tchernof, 1998; Redberg *et al.*, 2000).

In GDX male rats T, but not DHT, increases running activity, although E is much more effective than T (Roy and Wade, 1975). Moreover, male aromatase-deficient (aromatase knockout, ArKO) mice with high serum T concentrations that cannot be aromatized to E have reduced spontaneous physical activity (Jones *et al.*, 2000), supporting the role of aromatization and the action of E on the regulation of physical activity. The direct effects of E at the level of the hypothalamic medial preoptic area have been shown to increase voluntary physical activity (Fahrbach *et al.*, 1985). However, it is likely that changes induced by E on adiposity, glucose metabolism, and bone density, among others, can also affect physical activity.

3. Sex Hormones and Adipose Tissue Regulation

a) Brown Adipose Tissue and Thermogenesis

BAT is present in neonatal humans and in rodents throughout life. BAT is activated in rodents that have been placed in cold or ingest palatable high-calorie diets. BAT is involved in the control of body composition and responds to cold or excess energy through increasing the rate of nonshivering thermogenesis. However, in adult humans in whom BAT mass is low, its contribution may be of lesser importance (Himms-Hagen, 1990).

The thermogenic characteristic of BAT is due to the presence of uncoupling protein 1 (UCP-1), an inner mitochondrial membrane transporter that uncouples the process of mitochondrial respiration from oxidative phosphorylation, thus diminishing ATP production and generating heat. UCP-1 is uniquely found in BAT and not elsewhere (Himms-Hagen, 1990). Changes in BAT activity are mediated by the outflow of the sympathetic nervous system. The importance of UCP-1 activity is shown by the BAT-deficient UCP-promoter-driven diphtheria toxin A (UCP-DTA) mice, which develop obesity as a result of both decreased energy expenditure and, later, hyperphagia (Lowell and Flier, 1996; Mantzoros *et al.*, 1998). Furthermore, these phenomena are accompanied by alterations in peripheral and central hypothalamic regulation of energy balance (Tritos *et al.*, 1988).

In rats, ovarian hormones decrease cold-induced thermogenesis by reducing norepinephrine- (NE-) induced UCP-1 synthesis (Puerta *et al.*, 1993) and cytochrome-c oxidase activity in brown adypocites (Abelenda and Puerta, 1999). The effect of NE on thermogenic activity is mainly mediated by β-adrenoreceptors that are regulated by T but not by DHT (Cardinali *et al.*, 1982; Xu *et al.*, 1990, 1991).

However, high concentrations of E dissociate the thermogenic activity of BAT from its sympathetic activation (Nava *et al.,* 1994). The possible effects of sex hormones on uncoupling activity mediated by UCP-2 and UCP-3 are unknown.

b) White Adipose Tissue   WAT is the main compartment for energy storage and many studies support the contribution of adipose tissue, via its secretion of hormones (including leptin) to the regulation of energy balance and whole-body homeostasis (Kim and Moustaid-Moussa, 2000). Moreover, WAT also stores, converts, and releases sex hormones; the fatty pool of sex steroids appears to be greater than the plasma pool (Basdevant *et al.,* 1986).

Changes induced by sex hormones on BW are not always directly related to changes in feeding behavior, but may be related to changes at the level of fat deposits. It is still unknown whether the effects of sex hormones on adipose tissue mass are directly mediated via interactions with sex hormone receptors in fat cells or secondary to the effects exerted by sex hormones on central sites that regulate BW and energy expenditure. Nevertheless, the receptors and enzymes necessary to convert androgens to estrogens are present in adipose tissue.

Both human and rodent studies suggest that estrogen plays an important role in WAT regulation. Gender differences in the distribution of WAT in humans, the decrease in WAT stores in postmenopausal women using estrogen replacement therapy (Poehlman and Tchernof, 1998), and the already mentioned effects of OVX and estrogen replacement in rats are some examples. Studies have shown: (1) E treatment of OVX rats reduces lipoprotein-lipase activity in WAT, fatty acid synthesis, and uptake (Edens and Wade, 1983; Hamosh and Hamosh, 1975); (2) T, but not DHT, stimulates lipolysis in rat adipocytes by increasing the number of β-adrenoreceptors, and (3) both T and DHT increase the activity of the adenylate cyclase through uncertain mechanisms (Cardinali *et al.,* 1982; Xu *et al.,* 1990, 1991). Studies of (ArKO) and estrogen-receptor knockout (ERKO) mice unequivocally reveal a very important role for estrogens in the regulation of WAT in both male and female mice.

Two types of estrogen receptors (ER), ERα and ERβ, and aromatase are found in male and female adipose tissue (Crandall *et al.,* 1998; Pedersen *et al.,* 1991,

1996; Wade and Gray, 1979). The characterization of the phenotypes of ArKO, α-ER and β-ER knockout (αERKO and βERKO, respectively), and double-ER knockout (DERKO) mice has been an extraordinary tool (Couse and Korach, 1999; Heine *et al.,* 2000; Jones *et al.,* 2000; Ohlsson *et al.,* 2000). In αERKO male and female mice, WAT depots are significantly heavier than in control wild-type mice and the difference increases with age. The increased WAT weight is accounted for by increases in the number and size of the adipocytes. Similar results have been obtained with male and female ArKO mice, in which the administration of exogenous 17β-E reversed the phenotype, resulting in decreased fat deposit weights comparable to those in wild-type mice. The adult DERKO mouse has a phenotype similar to that observed in ArKO and αERKO mice; however, the βERKO mice do not differ from wild-type mice. Therefore, the data strongly support a role for estrogen action mediated by ERα in adipocyte physiology in both males and females.

c) Leptin: Signal of Adiposity   Leptin, the *obese* (*ob*) gene product, is the long-sought hormone synthesized and secreted by adipocytes. Leptin has important effects on many aspects of energy-balance regulation as well as reproduction. Concentrations of leptin in the circulation correlate highly to both the degree of adiposity and adipocyte size in humans and rodents. The *ob/ob* knockout mouse, totally deficient in leptin and the *db/db* knockout mouse, lacking the long form of the leptin receptor (OB-Rb), exhibit hyperphagia, massive obesity, and infertility (Pellymounter *et al.,* 1995; Swerdloff *et al.,* 1976). Chronic treatment with exogenous leptin of *ob/ob* mice not only restores normal FI and BW, but also fertility (Chehab *et al.,* 1996, 1997; Cunningham *et al.,* 1999; Mounzih *et al.,* 1997). The function of leptin in the control of reproduction appears to be very important, supporting the idea that critical BW and adipose tissue mass are necessary for the onset of puberty (Cunningham *et al.,* 1999).

B. Hypothalamus, Neuropeptide Y, and Melanocortins in Regulation of Energy Balance

The hypothalamus is the target of many peripheral signals (including leptin) and neural pathways that control energy balance and BW. In the 1990s, the number of neuropeptides known to be involved in energy-balance regulation and the understanding of their mechanisms of action have increased enormously. Many reviews have focused on the hypothalamic regulation of energy balance and the interaction with peripheral signals (Baskin et al., 1999); (Cowley et al., 1999; Elmquist et al., 1998; Inui, 2000; Woods et al., 1998). Here, we restrict ourselves to the discussion of only four hypothalamic neuropeptides involved in the regulation of feeding and energy expenditure: the functions and effects of sex hormones on the neuropeptide Y (NPY)- and proopiomelanocortin (POMC)-synthesizing cells in the arcuate (ARC) hypothalamus, and the CRF-synthesizing cells in the PVN. NPY and POMC neurons in the ARC project to important appetite-regulating nuclei, including the PVN (Baker and Herkenham, 1995). At the PVN, NPY and POMC-derived peptides such as α-melanocyte-stimulating hormone (α-MSH) and β-endorphins (β-END) innervate CRF neurons (Liposits et al., 1988) and exert major effects on FI and energy expenditure.

NPY stimulates food intake, CRF synthesis and secretion (Haas and George, 1987, 1989; Heinrichs et al., 1992, 1993; Suda et al., 1993; Tsagarakis et al., 1989), and insulin secretion (Marks et al., 1996; van Dijk et al., 1994; Wisialowski et al., 2000), and it inhibits sympathetic outflow to BAT (Egawa et al., 1991; Hwa, et al., 1999). NPY injected into the PVN is the most potent central orexigenic factor known. NPY inhibits thermogenesis and increases energy storage in WAT (Billington et al., 1991, 1994; Egawa et al., 1991; Jolicoeur et al., 1994; Scarpace et al., 1997). Therefore, repeated administration of NPY induces the rapid development of obesity (Stanley et al., 1986). NPY increases FI, with a significant preference for carbohydrate intake. The inhibition of thermogenesis is mediated by the suppression of sympathetic outflow to BAT, decreasing UCP mRNA and lipoprotein lipase mRNA (Scarpace et al., 1997). The effects of NPY are mediated by at least five types of receptors, the Y5 appearing to be the one involved in regulation of feeding (Duhault et al., 2000; Gerald et al., 1996; Hwa et al., 1999).

CRF is an anorectic neuropeptide that mediates stress-induced hypophagia and also inhibits caloric efficiency and affects locomotor activity. Two distinct CRF receptor (CRFR) subtypes, CRFR1 and CRFR2, are thought to mediate CRF actions on the central nervous system. Studies comparing the effects of CRF Administration in locomotor activity and feeding in CRFR1-deficient mice and wild-type mice suggest an important role for CRFR1 in mediating CRF-induced locomotor activation, whereas other receptor subtypes, probably CRFR2, may mediate the appetite-suppressing effects of CRF-like peptides (Contarino et al., 2000).

A cleavage product of the POMC protein is α-MSH, which produces anorexia. α-MSH acts through melanocortin receptors, primarily MCR-3 and MCR-4. The central administration of α-MSH decreases energy storage and FI even in starved rats (Vergoni and Bertolini, 2000). Furthermore, centrally administered melanocortin receptor agonists also inhibit basal insulin release and alter glucose tolerance, supporting the role of the central melanocortin receptor system also in processes related to energy partitioning (Fan et al., 2000). The major role played by the melanocortin system is also reflected by POMC knockout mice, which develop hyperphagia and obesity with a time course and severity comparable to that in MC4-R knockout mice. In the POMC knockout mouse, the daily administration of a stable α-MSH analog reverses the metabolic effects (Zemel and Shi, 2000).

Another cleavage product of the POMC protein is the endogenous opioid, β-END, which increases the rewarding properties of food. When injected intracerebroventricularly, β-END affects the voluntary approach to food (perhaps altering its salience) more than it increases consummatory behavior. Supporting the interpretation that β-END affects stimulus salience rather than consummatory behavior is the finding that the administration of the opioid antagonist naloxone exerts major anorectic effects on preferred diets compared to less preferred diets. Moreover, in rodents and humans, naltrexone alters the pleasant properties of sweet and salty solutions.

1. Effects of Leptin on Neuropeptide Y, α-Melanocyte-Stimulating Hormone, and Corticotropin-Releasing Factor

Leptin-sensitive neurons must express the long form of the Ob receptor, Ob-Rb. Ob-Rb are found in NPY-, POMC- and CRF-expressing neurons, among others (Baskin et al., 1995; Elmquist et al., 1998; Thornton et al., 1997). Leptin serves as a negative feedback signal from fat cells to the hypothalamus and inhibits feeding and increases energy expenditure resulting in resistance to obesity.

NPY mRNA levels in the ARC are decreased by leptin injected into a cerebral ventricle, whereas the injection of NPY into the PVN reduces the effects of leptin on food intake (Kotz *et al.*, 1998). The *ob/ob* mice have increased NPY mRNA levels that are decreased by the peripheral administration of leptin.

POMC gene expression is suppressed in *ob/ob* and *db/db* mice and in fasted rats. The administration of leptin stimulates POMC gene expression in *ob/ob* mice and fasted rats. However, is not known whether POMC mRNA regulation by leptin is reflected by equimolar or differential posttranscriptional increases in POMC-derived peptides.

The effects of leptin on CRF synthesis and secretion are controversial, as is the mechanism. Studies *in vitro* support stimulatory (Costa *et al.*, 1997) or inhibitory effects (Heiman *et al.*, 1997) of leptin on CRF release. Studies *in vivo* support both effects of leptin on CRF as well (Heiman *et al.*, 1997; Huang *et al.*, 1998; Jang *et al.*, 2000). It has been shown that leptin reduces the plasma ACTH and corticosterone responses to restraint *in vivo*. Moreover, it has been suggested that leptin might have a dual effect on CRF in adult rats—a rapid effect that decreases the CRF storage pool and a second effect that inhibits CRF synthesis. It has also been shown that the administration of leptin to *ob/ob* mice prevents the induction of CRF synthesis and the activation of CRF-ergic neurons in response to food deprivation.

Urocortin, a CRF-related neuropeptide, is a more potent suppressor of FI than leptin or CRF when injected peripherally. It has been shown that leptin might contribute to the potent satiety effects of urocortin by the acute modulation of an inert transport system at the level of brain–blood barrier (Kastin *et al.*, 2000).

C. Sex Hormones and Central Aspects of Control of Energy Balance

Interestingly, most of the neuropeptides involved in regulation of feeding and energy expenditure have effects on the regulation of activity in the HPG axis. Furthermore, most of them are modulated by sex hormones. The direct effects of sex hormones at the hypothalamic level cannot be excluded because αER,

progesterone receptors, androgen receptors (Handa *et al.*, 1994a; Simerly *et al.*, 1990; Yokosuka *et al.*, 1997), aromatase (Sanghera *et al.*, 1991; Wagner and Morrell, 1997), and 5α-reductase (Poletti and Martini, 1999) exist in many hypothalamic neurons.

NPY mRNA levels throughout the ARC are modulated by T in male rats. GDX decreases NPY mRNA levels and this effect is reversed by T. A marked regional sex difference exists in the distribution of NPY-mRNA-containing cells in the caudal extremity of the ARC. Male rats have higher NPY mRNA levels than do females (Urban *et al.*, 1993). Estrogen deficiency is known to increase NPY expression (Baskin *et al.*, 1995). Increased levels of hypothalamic NPY have been also observed with pubertal development and it has been suggested that NPY may have a role in the onset of puberty (Lebrethon *et al.*, 2000; Sutton *et al.*, 1988). Moreover, it has been shown that the stimulatory effect of hypothalamic NPY, via the Y5 receptor subtype, on gonadotrophin-releasing-hormone (GnRH) secretion before puberty results in increased GnRH pulsatility (Lebrethon *et al.*, 2000). The Y5 receptor is also involved in the effects of NPY on feeding (Hwa *et al.*, 1999) and insulin secretion (Wisialowski *et al.*, 2000). However, the inhibition of the gonadal axis by NPY has also been shown to be mediated by Y5 receptors (e.g., evidence that the inhibition of luteinizing hormone secretion exerted by the central administration of NPY in the rat is predominantly mediated by the NPY Y5 receptor subtype; Raposinho *et al.*, 1999).

The central administration of NPY to prepubertal rats can indefinitely delay sexual maturation by inhibiting GnRH secretion, an effect thought to be mediated by the Y1 receptor (Pralong *et al.*, 2000). Moreover, in OVX rats, treatment with E results in increased Y1 receptor mRNA. These observations support the idea that E increases the sensitivity of GnRH neurons to NPY through stimulation of Y1 gene expression, and that E's actions are mediated by the induction and subsequent activation of progesterone receptors (Xu *et al.*, 2000).

Testosterone stimulates POMC gene expression in a select group of cells located in the rostral portion of the ARC (Chowen-Breed *et al.*, 1989). GDX decreases POMC mRNA, whereas T and E (but not DHT) replacement (Chowen-Breed *et al.*, 1990) reverses the effect and eliminates the POMC mRNA variation over the 24-hr day (Steiner *et al.*, 1994). Increased hypothalamic

POMC mRNA has been also observed in the male rat during pubertal development (Kerrigan *et al.,* 1991, 1992; Wiemann *et al.,*1989). Moreover, the effects of T on POMC mRNA appear to be parallel to that observed in β-END (Matera and Wardlaw, 1994), which has been related to the inhibition of GnRH (Chowen-Breed *et al.,* 1989; Wiemann *et al.,* 1989). However, in male sheep and golden hamsters, T treatment during a long-day photoperiod reduces POMC mRNA in the ARC nucleus (Bittman *et al.,* 1999; Hileman *et al.,* 1998). The administration of gonadal steroids can alter the content of hypothalamic α-MSH and influence the diurnal variations of the peptide (Scimonelli and Celis, 1987). The effects of androgens and estrogens on pPVN CRF are discussed later in the context of the interactions between the HPA and HPG axes.

Thus, the effects of sex hormones on feeding and energy stores could be a direct consequence of the output from central autonomic pathways or from neuroendocrine cascades, or they could be secondary to changes induced in BW, adiposity or changes in metabolism. Either way, the complexity of the regulation of energy balance suggests that sex hormones act simultaneously and by multiple mechanisms at both the central and peripheral levels. However, neither female nor male ArKO mice (with high T levels) nor αERKO mice are hyperphagic, suggesting that feeding behavior is tightly regulated by other factors.

1. Sex Hormones and Leptin

Factors such as fasting and feeding (Pellymounter *et al.,* 1995), insulin (Fehmann *et al.,* 1997; Hardie *et al.,* 1996), glucocorticoids (Russell *et al.,* 1998; Wabitsch *et al.,* 1996), and catecholamines (Hardie *et al.,* 1996; Trayhurn *et al.,* 1995) have regulatory effects on leptin. Growing evidence also suggests a role for sex hormones in the regulation of leptin. There are strong gender differences in circulating leptin concentrations in humans and rodents. After normalization by age, weight, and body-fat mass, the circulating levels of leptin before, during, and after puberty are higher in females than in males (Frederich *et al.,* 1995; Havel *et al.,* 1996; Rosenbaum *et al.,* 1996; Watanobe and Suda, 1999). *In vivo* and *in vitro* studies support the stimulatory effects of estrogens and inhibitory effects of androgens on leptin synthesis and secretion. OVX decreases leptin mRNA in adipose tissue and circulating leptin con-

centrations; both effects are reversed after E replacement. In human women, fluctuations in leptin correlate positively with E concentration, but not with P, and it appears that P has no effects on leptin (Lavoie *et al.,* 1999; Stock *et al.,* 1999). *In vitro,* fat from females with functioning gonads is more responsive to the stimulatory effects of E and dexamethasone on leptin release (Kristensen *et al.,* 1999). In males, circulating T is negatively associated with leptin (Luukkaa *et al.,* 1998). The effects of estrogen and androgen appear to be mediated by sex-steroid-receptor-dependent mechanisms. However, there are also other studies in humans and rodents suggesting that factors other than sex hormones may account for the gender differences observed in leptin concentrations.

2. Stress and Sex Steroids: Immediate as Well as Long-Term Effects

Chronic stress has been consistently associated with decreased circulating sex hormones in adults, a finding that has been generally interpreted as a physiological mechanism that puts reproduction on hold in the face of an immediate emergency. However, after a brief review of some of the important effects of sex hormones on energy balance, it is also likely that stress-induced changes in sex hormones have major effects on metabolic and behavioral responses to stress. Gonadal-hormone concentrations are not consistently reported to be decreased by stress, particularly in pubertal male rats (Akana *et al.,* 1999; Almeida *et al.,* 1998; Gomez and Dallman, 2001). Throughout puberty in males, there is a progressive increase in basal T secretion that continues until adulthood is achieved. This period is characterized by many changes—a very rapid growth rate, as well as physiological and behavioral maturation in systems more directly related to changes in reproductive competence.

In the male rat just entering puberty, stress-inhibiting gonadal hormones do not make intuitive sense. The physiological value of expending effort on controlling a still nonfunctional reproductive system under stress is not clear. Rather, it is likely that during the onset of puberty, basal and stress-induced metabolic demands, as well as the effects of stress on a still nonfunctional reproductive system, might differ from those in adult rats. Perhaps because of preconceived notions that link sexual hormones to reproduction, stress to the inhibition of reproduction, stress to glucocorticoids, and glucocorticoids to metabolism, the importance of sexual hormones on energy balance as an important and integral part of the stress response has been underexplored. We have begun to study this aspect of the regulation of metabolism by stress-induced changes in other neuroendocrine systems.

The stress of cold for 5 days does not decrease median circulating T concentrations in pubertal male rats and the relationships between corticosterone, FI, and fat stores are different from those observed in adult male rats, which do exhibit a cold-induced reduction in T (Akana *et al.*, 1999). These data suggested that, during puberty, the interaction among glucocorticoids, stress, and sex hormones might be strongly related to the regulation of energy balance. To test this hypothesis, we forced pubertal and adult male rats to maintain experimentally manipulated androgen levels in chronic cold (Gomez and Dallman, 2001). Our data demonstrate that in pubertal and adult male rats, androgens have few significant effects under basal conditions (in room temperature). However, pubertal male rats in chronic cold are at risk in terms of energy balance in their responses to androgen concentrations. Low T promoted survival by increasing FI and BW gain, whereas higher T resulted in decreased FI and BW and relative abdominal obesity. ARC NPY mRNA levels were increased in stressed pubertal male rats treated with high T (F. Gomez and M. F. Dallman, unpublished observations), suggesting: (1) a role for aromatization in the effects of T on ARC NPY-mRNA expression; (2) possible interactions between aromatase and stress, and (3) possible inhibition of thermogenesis induced by NPY, which could account for the failing rats in the high-T group that had to be removed from the experiment.

Chronic cold significantly reduced ARC POMC mRNA only in control (low-T) and GDX (no-T) pubertal male rats. There were no effects observed in adult rats either at room temperature or in cold. However, pubertal rats treated with medium and high doses of T and DHT did not have changes in POMC (F. Gomez and M. F. Dallman, unpublished observations). These data suggest: (1) the effects of androgens on ARC POMC mRNA are age-dependent; (2) T does not appear to require aromatization, and (3) there are complex interactions among dose-dependent effects of sex hormones on the central regulation of energy balance and stress.

In summary, we have briefly reviewed some of the interactions between sex hormones and the regulation of energy balance, as well as some of our own results that bear on the topic. It appears that under conditions of stress in male rats entering puberty that a tightly controlled regulation of sex hormones is required not for just inhibiting reproduction in the future, but for helping to shift the survival priorities from the species to the individual.

D. Central Interactions of the Hypothalamic-Pituitary-Gonadal and the Hypothalamic-Pituitary-Adrenal Axes

Countless studies have shown that stress and HPA activation inhibit reproductive function and behavior. This relationship is by no means unidirectional because reproductive status and gender impact heavily on both basal and stress-induced HPA activity. This indicates that the gonadal and adrenal systems are intimately entwined, due in large part to the interactive effects of sex steroids and glucocorticoids. These very interactions have made it difficult to approach the central bases by which the gonadal steroids act to regulate the HPA axis. This question is important, considering gender-based differences in neuropathology associated with HPA dysregulation. Several excellent surveys exist with respect to the mechanisms by which stress disrupts reproductive function (Rivier and Rivest, 1991; Tilbrook *et al.*, 2000). Here we examine the flip side of this relationship by focusing on the mechanisms by which sex steroids regulate the HPA axis, working toward developing newer approaches to studying how the gonadal and adrenal systems act and interact in the central nervous system.

1. *Basic Hypothalamic-Pituitary-Adrenal and Hypothalamic-Pituitary-Gonadal Interactions*

Drawing from several studies, Fig. 8 provides a simplified overview of the bidirectional interactions of the HPA and HPG systems, both in the brain and in the periphery. The stress-induced inhibition of reproduction, in the very least, is mediated via the direct inhibitory effects of CRF on luteinizing-hormone-releasing-hormone (LHRH) synthesis and release (Rivier *et al.*, 1986). The central and peripheral administration of ACTH also alters plasma luteinizing

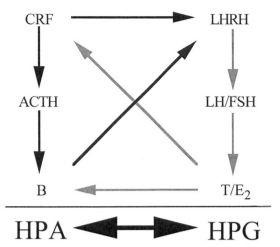

FIGURE 8 Bidirectional interactions between the HPA and HPG systems. These interactions have made it difficult to explore whether the stimulatory and inhibitory effects of estrogen and testosterone, respectively, are caused by direct effects on the HPA axis or indirectly via alterations in glucocorticoid feedback. Although estrogen appears to act on both CRF and AVP expression in the PVN, testosterone effects on the system appear selective to AVP. B, corticosterone; E2, estradiol; HPA, hypothalamo-pituitary-adrenal; HPG, hypothalamo-pituitary-gonadal; T, testosterone.

hormone (LH) concentrations. However, the direction of this response is gender- and sex-steroid-dependent (Mann *et al.,* 1986; Putnam *et al.,* 1991; reviewed in Brann and Mahesh, 1991; Mahesh and Brann, 1992). Plasma LH increases in females and decreases in males after ACTH administration. Estrogen priming in females enhances the stimulatory effects of ACTH on LH release. Finally, stress and elevated glucocorticoid concentrations disrupt all aspects of the HPG system, ultimately inhibiting sex-steroid synthesis and release. Interesting exceptions have been noted, however. For example, the inhibitory effects of stress and exogenous glucocorticoids on the HPG system in male rats depend on the sexual activity of the animal at the time of glucocorticoid delivery and stress exposure (see Lemaire *et al.,* 1997). These and other issues of how sex and sex steroid status modulate HPG responses to stress have been extensively reviewed elsewhere (see Tilbrook *et al.,* 2000). However, it is now becoming clear that sex steroids play a major role in modifying HPA function directly.

Figure 8 also shows that the very same elements of the gonadal axis that are subject to adrenal and stress in-

fluences, in turn, exert reciprocal effects on the adrenal axis. Central (intracerebroventriculer) LHRH administration stimulates plasma cortisol concentrations in ewes (Porter *et al.,* 1989). In the rodent brain, a subset of LHRH-expressing neurons in the medial preoptic area are not neurosecretory (Merchenthaler *et al.,* 1984, 1989). CRF-immunoreactive (CRF-ir) neurons have been shown to contact LHRH-expressing medial preoptic neurons (MacLusky *et al.,* 1988). Thus, the central stimulatory effects of LHRH on cortisol release may reflect the existence of reciprocal LHRH-CRF contacts. Finally, several functional studies indicate that sex steroids exert their effects at all levels of the HPA axis, including the feed-forward and feedback elements explored later (Fig. 9). Both corticosteroid receptor subtypes, as well as progesterone and androgen receptors, can recognize and function at a common DNA site (Chen *et al.,* 1997; Minor and Yamamoto, 1991; Nelson *et al.,* 1999; Otten *et al.,* 1988). Moreover, androgen and glucocorticoid receptors are capable of interacting at the transcriptional level by physically interacting to form heterodimers (Chen *et al.,* 1997).

Sex differences in both basal and stressed HPA activity are apparent in a variety of species, including rodents, humans, and nonhuman primates (Handa *et al.,* 1994a; Seeman *et al.,* 1995; Young, 1995, 1996). Compared to males, females secrete higher levels of ACTH and glucocorticoids under basal conditions and in response to stress. This has been attributed to the inhibitory effects of T in males, and, for the most part, to stimulatory effects of estrogen in females. Thus, sex differences in HPA stress responsivity are abolished by GDX in males, and OVX in females. In rodents, adult females secrete more ACTH and corticosterone in response to a variety of stimuli, including ether, immobilization, restraint, footshock, and novelty. Note that in both rodents and humans, females secrete higher levels of corticosteroid-binding globulin (CBG) (reviewed in Rosner, 1990). Higher CBG concentrations in females effectively reduce the free or biologically active component of total circulating glucocorticoids to concentrations comparable to those in males.

Whereas sex differences in HPA function are reflected by the stimulatory effects of estrogen in females, androgens exert inhibitory effects in males. The earliest reports reflecting the inhibitory effects of T were first considered at the level of the adrenal gland

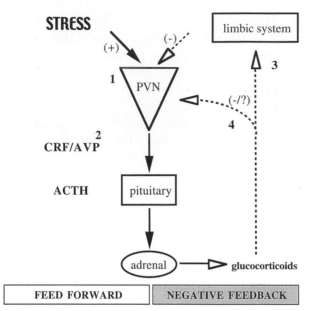

STRESS

CRF/AVP

ACTH

FEED FORWARD   **NEGATIVE FEEDBACK**

FIGURE 9 Basic features of the HPA axis and where testosterone and estrogen intersect on this design. Feed forward: Stress activates (+) the HPA axis, stimulating the release of corticotropin-releasing factor (CRF) and arginine vasopressin (AVP) from the paraventricular nucleus of the hypothalamus (PVH). CRF and AVP stimulate the release of adrenocorticotropin (ACTH) from the anterior pituitary. At the adrenal gland, ACTH stimulates the synthesis and release of glucocorticoids (corticosterone in the rat, cortisol in humans and nonhuman primates). Negative feedback: In addition to their physiological effects, glucocorticoids exert inhibitory (−) effects on the axis, either directly at the level of the PVN or upstream in several elements of the limbic system. Key features: 1. Androgen and estrogen receptors are not present in ACTH-regulating neurons of the PVN, but are distributed in several brain nuclei, including the limbic system and converging input to the PVH (see Fig. 4). 2. Androgen effects on the axis appear selective to AVP synthesis and release, whereas estrogen acts on both CRF and AVP. 3. Both estrogen and testosterone interact on glucocorticoid feedback. Testosterone interacts with corticosterone at the level of the MPOA, which communicates with the PVN directly and indirectly via converging limbic input (see Figs. 10, 12). 4. The dual possibilities indicated for feedback at the PVN result from disagreement between the authors on conclusions drawn from results in the literature.

(Sencar-Cupovic and Milkovic, 1976). Sex differences in adrenal morphology and in adrenal weight and stress responsiveness (greater in females) appear at 40 days of age in the rat and are maximal by day 55, near the time of sexual maturity in this rodent. These sex dif-

ferences are offset by GDX in males. In humans, sex differences are clearly indicated in young adults; adult females show a higher pulse frequency in basal ACTH release and greater cortisol responses to ACTH (Ho *et al.,* 1987; Horrocks *et al.,* 1990; Roelfsema *et al.,* 1993) than males. However, no clear sex differences in the pattern of ACTH release are apparent in children (Ho *et al.,* 1987; Wallace *et al.,* 1991). Studies indicate greater departures in HPA activity among older men and women (>65 years), where ACTH and glucocorticoid responses to stress are found to be consistently higher in women (Seeman *et al.,* 1995). Thus, sex-dependent differences in HPA function in humans are clearly evident and are associated with the development and maturation of the HPG axis. There are excellent overviews of some of the earlier developmental and aging studies with respect to sex differences in HPA function (Goya *et al.,* 1989; Nikicicz *et al.,* 1984; Schoenfeld *et al.,* 1980; Seeman *et al.,* 1995; Sencar-Cupovic and Milkovic, 1976).

2. Estrogen, Progesterone, and Hypothalamic-Pituitary-Adrenal Function

Ovarian regulation of HPA function is indicated by cyclic variations in basal and stress HPA activity (Atkinson and Waddell, 1997; Viau and Meaney, 1991). As plasma estrogen increases during the follicular phase in women (and about the time of proestrous in rats), so do basal plasma ACTH and glucocorticoid concentrations. Likewise, HPA responses to stress and immune challenge in cycling females are also greatest during periods of elevated estrogen levels (Atkinson and Waddell, 1997; Nappi and Rivest, 1995; Viau and Meaney, 1991). At the level of the hypothalamic PVN, these cyclic variations in HPA function can be explained by variations in the synthesis and release of CRF and AVP (Bohler *et al.,* 1990; Greer *et al.,* 1986; Haas and George, 1989; Nappi and Rivest, 1995; Van Tol *et al.,* 1988; Watts and Swanson, 1989). Although the majority of studies examining the effects of estrogen on HPA function in females indicate stimulatory effects on ACTH and glucocorticoid release, several others have identified inhibitory effects (discussed in Dyas *et al.,* 2000; Viau and Meaney, 1991). It is now clear that the direction of the HPA response to estrogen (and its lack of response) depends on the age of the subject, the length of OVX prior to steroid replacement, and both the dose and duration of estrogen exposure. In short, OVX rats with chronic (or static) high-estrogen-level replacement show enhanced basal and stressed HPA function compared to OVX rats without replacement (Burgess and Handa, 1992). On the other hand, OVX rats with chronic low-estrogen-level replacement have reduced HPA responses to stress compared to rats without replacement (Dyas *et al.,* 2000). However, we have also discovered what Mother Nature was trying to tell us all along—acute steroid priming in OVX females, with estrogen alone, fails to stimulate the HPA axis. Another key, and often avoided, steroid plays a critical role in females—elevations in estrogen can provoke acute stimulatory effects on HPA function only against a background of low P levels (Viau and Meaney, 1991). Moreover, this stimulatory effect of estrogen is blocked or delimited by elevations in P (Viau and Meaney, 1991), as would normally occur in the intact cycling rat during the later phases of estrus and early diestrus (or the luteal phase in humans). An inhibitory effect of P on estrogen-induced CRF mRNA in the PVN has been shown in the female rhesus monkey (Roy *et al.,* 1999). Thus, acute and dual estrogen-progesterone steroid replacement is the most appropriate way of modeling cyclic variations in HPA function. Chronic replacement with low estrogen concentrations (≤ 25 pg/ml) in the OVX rat is a more suitable endocrinological approximation of postmenopausal women on estrogen replacement therapy (ERT). Both ERT in women and low estrogen replacement in the OVX rat suppress HPA responses to stress (Dyas *et al.,* 2000; Lindheim *et al.,* 1992, 1994).

At this point, how estrogen and P act and interact to regulate HPA responses to stress bears consideration. Borrowing from how estrogen and P operate in the HPG axis, P has been shown to oppose the regulatory actions of estrogen by suppressing estrogen receptor expression and activity (reviewed in Mahesh and Brann, 1998; Zanisi and Messi, 1991; see also Brown and MacLusky, 1994). Thus, a similar interaction between P and estrogen receptors may be occurring in the HPA axis. The interplay between estrogen and P on HPA activity is further revealed by a marvellous series of studies by Stern and Levine (1974) on stress and HPA activity in lactating rats. The ovarian output of P is elevated and estrogen is significantly reduced during lactation. Interestingly, HPA responses to a va-

riety of stressful stimuli are reduced in lactating rats compared to virgin rats. This HPA resistance to stress is sustained by suckling and reversed by pup removal. Moreover, as long as the pups are present, the HPA axis of lactating rats remain refractory to estrogen doses that would normally stimulate HPA activity in OVX or intact females. Stress-induced increases in CRF and AVP mRNA in the PVN are also blunted in lactating rats vs virgin rats (Lightman and Young, 1989). Thus, HPA refractoriness to stress during lactation appears to be associated with a reduction in drive to the PVN motor neurons, that is, in part, produced by a reduction in circulating estrogen levels and sustained by suckling-induced elevations in P.

Several *in vitro* and *in vivo* experiments have indicated direct effects of estrogen and P on HPA function (see Buckingham, 1982; Patchev and Almeida, 1996, 1998; Paulmyer-Lacroix *et al.,* 1996). Several other studies suggest that part of the stimulatory and interactive effects of estrogen and P on ACTH release involve alterations in glucocorticoid feedback efficacy (reviewed in Young, 1995). P can act as a GR and MR antagonist *in vitro* (Chou and Lüttge, 1988; Rupprecht *et al.,* 1993). However, there is little evidence to suggest that it functionally antagonizes glucocorticoid feedback inhibition of ACTH *in vivo*. The acute administration of P under basal conditions inhibits stress-induced ACTH release in ewes (Keller-Wood *et al.,* 1988). Moreover, chronic P treatment in ewes enhances the suppressive effects of cortisol on ACTH release (Keller-Wood, 1998). In OVX rats with chronic estrogen replacement, P appears to disrupt fast-feedback inhibition of ACTH (Redei *et al.,* 1994). Reduced HPA responses to stress during the luteal phase in women and following proestrus in the female rat (when P levels are rising) all argue against P antagonizing glucocorticoid feedback.

Sex differences in glucocorticoid feedback potency have been remarked on for years. Thus, males and females consistently show differences in the degree of suppression by exogenous corticosterone and dexamethasone (DEX) on ACTH under basal and stress conditions (Almeida *et al.,* 1997; Young *et al.,* 1996). However, attempts to relate these functional differences to sex differences and estrogen effects on MR and GR mRNA expression, binding affinity, and capacity have remained inconsistent (Ahima *et al.,* 1992; Burgess and Handa, 1992, 1993; Carey *et al.,* 1995; Ferrini and De

Nicola, 1991; Turner, 1992, 1997). Although MR and GR binding capacity are tightly associated with glucocorticoid feedback sensitivity, sex differences in glucocorticoid feedback regulation of the HPA axis may be more subtle or dynamic. In the rat hippocampus, sex differences in the regional and cellular distribution of GR-ir are evident in response to adrenalectomy (ADX) and corticosterone replacement (Ahima *et al.*, 1992). Thus, sex-steroid-dependent differences in glucocorticoid feedback could potentially be revealed by regional differences in GR-ir localization (or occupancy) in response to stress. In response to GDX + ADX, male rats show a more rapid recovery in hippocampal cytoplasmic MR binding than do females (MacLusky *et al.*, 1996). Because conventional corticosteroid cytosolic binding assays involve surgical ADX, MacLusky *et al.* (1996) has argued that sex differences in MR binding may be masked by higher corticosterone responses to the adrenal surgery in females. This notion could be tested, perhaps, in binding experiments that employ less stressful pharmacological or slow corticosterone removal procedures (see Jacobson *et al.*, 1989).

Although several of the earliest studies on gender differences in HPA function were attributed to sex steroid actions on corticosteroid-synthesizing enzymes in the adrenal gland (Kitay *et al.*, 1965, 1966), it soon became clear that sex differences in glucocorticoid release are produced by central effects on ACTH release (Colby and Kitay, 1972, 1974). Thus, the PVN has become an important crossroad in this design. Gender differences in basal and stimulated ACTH release are now explained by increased synthesis and secretion of CRF in females (Hiroshige *et al.*, 1973; Watts and Swanson, 1989). Moreover, the stimulatory effects of estrogen on ACTH release are paralleled by elevations in both CRF and AVP expression in the PVN (Bohler *et al.*, 1990; Viau and Meaney, 1992).

The CRF gene contains several estrogen-receptor-response elements (Vamvakopoulos and Chrousos, 1993, 1994). Only a sparse number of medial parvocellular CRF-ir neurons in the PVN, however, contain either α-ER or β-ER mRNA (Alves *et al.*, 1998; Laflamme *et al.*, 1998; Shughrue *et al.*, 1997; Simerly *et al.*, 1990). In fact, a clear majority of CRF ER-positive cells in the PVN appear to be in autonomic neurons. Thus, estrogenic regulation of the neuroendocrine ACTH-regulating arm of the HPA axis does not appear to reside in the PVN. Several alternate sites of action for estrogen (as well as for P) regulation of the HPA axis in females are suggested by the distribution of gonadal steroid receptors in several hypothalamic and extrahypothalamic nuclei that are functionally and anatomically connected to the PVN. Likely candidates in this case include the hippocampus, the CeA and medial nucleus of the amygdala, the medial preoptic nucleus, and the BNST. CRF- and ER-expressing cell groups overlap in the CeA and the BNST (Sawchenko *et al.*, 1993; Sawchenko and Swanson, 1989). Thus, estrogen could regulate parvocellular CRF indirectly, via CRF-related pathways to the PVN.

There has been a remarkable and important increase in the number of studies examining the neuroprotective effects of sex steroids. However, despite gender differences in HPA function and the neuropathology associated with hypercortisolemia and HPA hyperdrive, how gonadal steroids operate in the central nervous system to regulate PVN function has received little attention. Only a handful of studies have explored gender- and estrogen-based differences in stress-induced patterns of neuronal activity and drive to the PVN. Major sex differences in stress-induced patterns of neural activation have been revealed by quantitative 2-deoxyglucose autoradiography (Brown *et al.*, 1996). Thus, in response to restraint combined with forelimb formalin injection, female rats show higher rates of glucose metabolism in several brain regions than do males. This sex difference was evident in several sex-steroid-sensitive regions, including the medial amygdala, medial preoptic nucleus, ventromedial nucleus, ARC, and various subfields of the hippocampus. As previously discussed, ACTH responses to auditory stress and immune challenge are reduced in OVX rats with chronic low-estrogen replacement. This reduced HPA reactivity to stress is also associated with a suppression in stress-induced Fos protein expression in the medial parvocellular zone of the PVN, the CeA, and the medullary catecholaminergic cell groups (Dyas *et al.*, 2000). These findings are consistent with an upstream effect of estrogen on pathways controlling PVN activity and provide an encouraging indication that immediate early genes can be used to approach the central effects of estrogen and sex steroids in general on HPA function.

3. Testosterone and Hypothalamic-Pituitary-Adrenal Function

Studies examining the role of androgens in HPA function have been relatively less problematic than the interactive and dynamic effects of ovarian steroids in females, but no less complex. As previously discussed, a variety of earlier *in vitro* and *in vivo* studies indicate that T can act at the level of the adrenal gland to inhibit glucocorticoid synthesis and adrenocortical responses to ACTH. *In vivo,* the inhibitory effects of T are clearly indicated at the level of the anterior pituitary. Marked elevations in pituitary weight and ACTH content occur in response to GDX, and these changes are reversible with T replacement (Kitay, 1963). Note that anterior pituitary corticotrophs express few if any androgen receptors and minimal aromatase activity (McEwen, 1980; Thieulant and Duval, 1985). Thus, sex differences in ACTH release do not reflect direct T effects at the level of the pituitary in males.

In contrast to the marked effects of OVX and estrogen on basal ACTH and corticosterone in females, testicular influences on basal HPA function in males are not readily indicated by single measurements of ACTH and corticosterone during the circadian trough in basal HPA activity (Lesniewska *et al.,* 1990; Sillence and Rodway, 1990). In male rhesus monkeys, blood sampling over a 24-hr period revealed a loss in the circadian periodicity in circulating cortisol levels in response to GDX (Smith and Norman, 1987). This was most apparent during the active phase of the HPA cycle, seen as a protracted increase in circulating cortisol. Although it may be construed that the bulk of studies examining HPA function are performed in males because they represent or possess a more stable gonadal environment, numerous reports indicate that this is not the case. In fact, T levels in males fluctuate just as dynamically as does estrogen in females. Moreover, T levels in males vary in a manner that is reciprocal to the diurnal rhythm in plasma glucocorticoids in rodents, humans, and nonhuman primates (Bartke *et al.,* 1973; Kalra and Kalra, 1977; Plymate *et al.,* 1989; Smith and Norman, 1987; Winters *et al.,* 1991). Thus, basal HPA activity is subject to gonadal influence in males, at least during the active phase of the HPA rhythm.

Naturally occurring variations in T levels also play an important role in determining the magnitude of the HPA response to stress. We found that basal T levels vary considerably in gonadally intact male rats (0.8–6.2 ng/ml) and are negatively correlated with plasma ACTH and corticosterone responses to restraint stress (Viau and Meaney, 1996). A similar relationship was found in GDX males with the same range of T replacement. DHT, the nonaromatizable form of T, also exerts inhibitory effects on novelty- and footshock-induced ACTH release, indicating mediation by androgen receptors rather than ER (Handa *et al.,* 1994b). Thus, HPA reactivity to stress in males is explainable as a function of individual differences in circulating T levels. These findings may very well underlie the relationship frequently seen between social status and HPA function in numerous species, in which subordinates show increased glucocorticoid levels under basal and stress conditions or decreased gonadal function (reviewed in Blanchard *et al.,* 1993; Saltzman *et al.,* 1998; Sapolsky, 1982, 1987). Plasma corticosterone responses to stress are substantially higher in subordinate male rats, which also have decreased T levels (Blanchard *et al.,* 1995; Monder *et al.,* 1994). The opposite relationship occurs in dominant rats. Whereas decreased gonadal function is often thought to reflect the inhibitory effects of social subordination and social stress on the HPG axis, sex steroid levels probably play an active role in sustaining HPA status once a dominance hierarchy is formed (see Saltzman *et al.,* 1998).

The dose-related inhibitory effects of T on stress-induced ACTH release proved fortunate for us in exploring how androgens act in the brain to regulate the HPA axis. Building on those findings, we first examined the extent to which the inhibitory effects of T on stress-induced ACTH are reflected in resting-state levels of CRF and AVP content in the median eminence (Viau and Meaney, 1996). We found that the dose-related inhibitory effects of T on ACTH varied as a function of AVP, but not CRF, content in the median eminence. Although these findings are in keeping with an inhibitory effect of T on hypophysial AVP, chronic DHT treatment has been shown to reverse the stimulatory effect of GDX on CRF-ir cell numbers in the PVN (Bingaman *et al.,* 1994b). The degree to which this is reflected specifically in medial parvocellular neurons needs to be resolved because CRF is also produced by autonomic neurons of the PVN. Note that androgen receptors are not colocalized with medial parvocellular CRF-ir neurons and appear to be restricted to autonomic-related neurons in the PVN (Bingaman *et al.*, 1994a; Simerly *et al.*, 1990; Zhou *et al.*, 1994). As with estrogen, T regulation of the HPA axis must be operating outside or upstream from the PVN. As with ER, androgen receptors in the brain are also contained in several forebrain, hypothalamic, limbic, and medullary structures supplying direct and indirect (multisynaptic) input to the PVN.

Our discovery of the medial preoptic area (MPOA) as a critical site mediating corticosterone and T interactions on HPA activity followed a fortuitous route. We initially wondered whether the dose-related effects of T replacement on ACTH responses to stress could be reflected, in turn, by dose-related effects on GR and MR binding capacity in the brain (Viau and Meaney, 1996). Despite one previous study showing no effect of chronic DHT replacement on GR binding in the hippocampus, hypothalamus, and pituitary (Handa *et al.*, 1994b), we nonetheless extended our analysis to include the MPOA because of its concentrations of glucocorticoid and androgen receptors and its role in regulating reproduction and social behavior. No effect of T was found except for GR levels in the MPOA, where GR binding capacity showed a graded and positive response to plasma T levels. Corticosterone and T implants in the MPOA inhibited ACTH responses to restraint stress. Interestingly, and similar with respect to the peripheral effects of T, the inhibitory effects of these MPOA implants on stress-induced ACTH was strongly correlated, in turn, with resting-state median eminence levels of AVP, but not CRF (see Fig. 10). Finally, lesioning the MPOA blocked the inhibitory effects of high peripheral T levels on ACTH responses to stress.

Anatomically, the MPOA (and its androgen-sensitive subnuclei) is in a position to modify the PVN and the HPA axis directly or indirectly (Cullinan *et al.*, 1993; Risold *et al.*, 1997; Simerly and Swanson, 1988; Swanson, 1976, 1987). In addition to sending direct projections to the PVN, the MPOA receives and reciprocates input from the BNST and amygdala. These structures, in turn, express high concentrations of both glucocorticoid and androgen receptors. Thus, although our findings place the MPOA in an important position to mediate the central inhibitory effects of T on stress HPA stress activity, it probably represents one of many obligatory relays. In this regard, lesioning the MPOA has been shown to inhibit the corticosterone re-

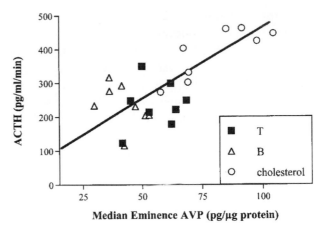

FIGURE 10 Both corticosterone and T act at the level of the MPOA to inhibit ACTH responses to stress and resting-state levels of AVP in the median eminence. The strong negative correlation between stress-induced ACTH levels and median eminence AVP in individual animals receiving corticosterone (B) and testosterone (T) implants in the MPOA suggests that androgen and glucocorticoid inhibition of ACTH release in males involves hypophysial AVP. Viau and Meaney (1996).

sponse to electrical stimulation of the medial amygdala (Feldman and Weidenfeld, 1998).

As further inroads are made into the central actions of sex steroids on HPA function, we must not stray too far from the very interactive nature of the adrenal and gonadal systems. As already discussed, this is indicated by sex differences in glucocorticoid feedback inhibition of ACTH (Almeida *et al.*, 1997; Young, 1996), and by sex differences and sex steroid effects on GR, MR, and CRH mRNA responses to adrenalectomy (Patchev, 1996, 1998). Inherent to this interaction, of course, is that manipulating one system has effects on the other. Thus, adrenalectomy, stress, and glucocorticoid administration alter gonadotropin and sex steroid secretion in males and females. Conversely, the normal daily rhythm in circulating glucocorticoids is disrupted by GDX and OVX. Given this functional cross talk, how can we assume, for example, that glucocorticoid feedback inhibition of the HPA axis occurs independently of the gonadal axis and gonadal steroid release? By the same token, to what extent do sex steroids regulate the HPA axis independently of the glucocorticoids?

Given the shared inhibitory characteristics by which the glucocorticoids and T regulate the HPA axis in males, suggesting an overlap in their signalling

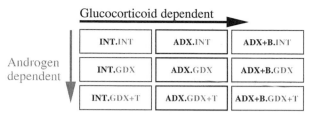

Glucocorticoid dependent

Androgen dependent

INT.INT	ADX.INT	ADX+B.INT
INT.GDX	ADX.GDX	ADX+B.GDX
INT.GDX+T	ADX.GDX+T	ADX+B.GDX+T

FIGURE 11 Schematic describing how we distinguish glucocorticoid- (left to right) from androgen-dependent (top to bottom) effects on HPA function. Building on the central limb of this design, we subsequently examined the glucocorticoid-independent effects of androgens on CRF and AVP mRNA expression in known forebrain effectors of the HPA axis (Viau *et al.,* 1999, 2001).

pathways to the PVN, we have explored the extent to which T exerts independent and glucocorticoid-dependent effects on basal and stress HPA activity (Viau *et al.,* 1999). This was achieved by manipulating the gonadal and adrenal endocrine systems simultaneously, so that the interactive and independent effects of corticosterone and testosterone on the HPA axis could be distinguished (see Fig. 11). Two important characteristics were revealed. First, CRF biosynthesis in the PVN under basal conditions is dominated by glucocorticoid-dependent effects, whereas AVP is regulated by testosterone-dependent effects. Second, restraint-induced HPA activity, indicated by concentrations of plasma ACTH and Fos protein induction in medial parvocellular PVN neurons, is determined by the interactive effects of corticosterone and T on drive to the PVN.

In keeping with these findings, subordinate males show elevations in AVP-ir, but not CRF-ir in the external (hypophysiotropic) zone of the median eminence (Albeck *et al.,* 1997; de Goeij *et al.,* 1992a). Hierarchical differences in stress-induced ACTH are not always apparent, however. In the presence of a dominant male, subordinates hypersecrete ACTH and show a selective depletion of AVP from the median eminence, provided this social encounter occurs in a novel environment (Romero *et al.,* 1995). Consequently, the inhibitory actions of T on stress-induced ACTH cannot be fully explained as a function of CRF and AVP synthesis in the PVN but appear to depend in larger part on T regulation of the neurogenic drive to the PVN. The degree to which corticosterone and T interact to modulate this drive ap-

pears to be situation-specific. Along these lines, DHT replacement has been shown to reverse the stimulatory effects of GDX on novelty-induced Fos mRNA expression in the PVN and, interestingly, in the hippocampus (Yukhananov and Handa, 1997).

At this point, it appears that T has the potential to operate on several forms of converging forebrain, hypothalamic, and limbic input to the PVN. Thus, another level of problem, beyond T and glucocorticoid interactions at the PVN, is how to begin exploring where T acts in the brain to integrate reproductive, social, and HPA function. Androgen receptors are notably distributed in CRF- and AVP-expressing cell groups of the amygdala and BNST, all of which send multimodal information to the PVN and regulate basal and stress HPA activity (reviewed in Herman and Cullinan, 1997; Lopez *et al.,* 1999). Building on one limb of our previous design (see Fig. 11), we have extended our analysis of the glucocorticoid-independent effects of T to these CRF- and AVP-expressing cell groups (Viau *et al.,* 2001). This design revealed independent and stimulatory effects of T on CRF mRNA in the fusiform nuclei of the anterior BNST and on AVP mRNA in the posterior BNST. Moreover, in the central and medial amygdala, T does not act alone, but interacts with corticosterone on CRF and AVP mRNA expression. Common to our earlier findings, these effects were paralleled by alterations in AVP, but not CRF mRNA, expression in medial parvocellular PVN neurons.

Several connectional and functional studies indicate that direct projections from the amygdala to the medial parvocellular zone of the PVN are sparse and that the BNST acts as an obligatory relay (Canteras *et al.,* 1995; Dyas *et al.,* 1999; Gray, 1993; Mulders *et al.,* 1997; Prewitt and Herman, 1998; Sanchez *et al.,* 1995; Sawchenko and Swanson, 1983; Silverman *et al.,* 1981). Thus, the upstream and selective effects of T on medial parvocellular AVP may involve amygdala projections relayed to and through CRF- and AVP-expressing neurons in the BNST. There is evidence to suggest that distinct regions of the BNST differentially regulate CRF and AVP expression in the PVN. Posterior BNST lesions, encompassing AVP-expressing neurons, tend to increase AVP in the parvocellular PVN (Herman *et al.,* 1994). Anterior BNST lesions, encompassing CRF-expressing neurons, decrease parvocellular CRF mRNA expression in the PVN (Herman *et al.,* 1994).

The PVN is, indeed, a recipient of CRF-ir input originating from the fusiform nucleus, and the posterior BNST projects massively and preferentially to the parvocellular zone of the PVN (Champagne *et al.*, 1998; Moga and Saper, 1994). Thus, the effects of T on CRF and AVP expression in the BNST may have a bearing on the selective nature by which T regulates AVP expression in the PVN.

Another important subsystem in the brain involves the accessory olfactory bulb (AOB). In addition to regulating social and reproductive behavior by virtue of its projections to and through the MPOA, medial amygdala, and posterior aspects of the BNST, the AOB can ultimately regulate the endocrine arm of the PVN (see Kelly *et al.*, 1997; Risold *et al.*, 1997). Interestingly, olfactory bulbectomy increases AVP-ir, but not CRF-ir, in the external zone of the median eminence and potentiates the ACTH response to ether exposure (Marcilhac *et al.*, 1999a,b). These findings collectively implicate androgen-sensitive neurons of the BNST and their extended circuitries as important integrators of social behavior, reproduction, and HPA function. Although androgen- (and estrogen-)receptor-expressing cell groups in the brain have yet to be systematically localized to PVN-projecting neurons, phenotyped, and functionally tested by direct steroid application, we now have a means with which to begin constructing and segregating androgen-sensitive pathways from glucocorticoid-sensitive pathways in the brain (see Fig. 12).

In summary, studies examining the central effects of gonadal steroids on HPA activity have been lacking and somewhat fragmented. A major obstacle to this central approach is that sex steroids act, interact, and vary as a function of development, reproductive status, and social status. Moreover, independent and glucocorticoid-overlapping pathways to the PVN mediate sex steroid regulation of the HPA axis. However, as we have discussed here, these obstacles can be overcome by using appropriate steroid replacement regimens that simultaneously control gonadal and adrenal hormonal status. Future studies employing this steroid replacement strategy, both under acute and repeated stress conditions, should prove revealing. Although depression is associated with HPA hyperactivity, clinical evidence now supports an involvement of sex steroids in the development of depression in both men and women

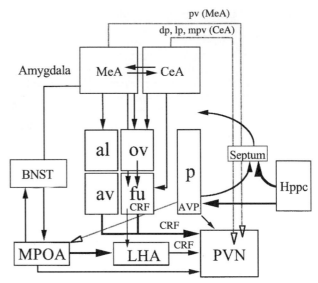

FIGURE 12 Based on results from anatomical and functional studies from many labs together with our current findings, several possible routes through which the actions of androgens on brain could regulate the HPA axis are illustrated. Both the anterior and posterior aspects of the BNST should prove to be critical components in this scheme, considering their sensitivity to androgens, communication with the PVN, and connectivity with several forebrain regulators of the HPA axis, including the amygdala, medial preoptic area, and converging hippocampal (ventral subicular) input. Androgen and estrogen receptors are embedded in most, if not all, of these structures. al, anterolateral; av, anteroventral; AVP, arginine-vasopressin; BNST, bed nuclei of the stria terminalis; CeA, central amygdala; dp, dorsal parvocellular; fu, fusiform; LHA, lateral hypothalamic area; lp, lateral posterior; MeA, medial amygdala; MPOA, medial preoptic area; mpv, medioventral parvocellular; ov, oval; pBNST, posterior bed nucleui of the stria terminalis (encompassing AVP-expressing neurons); pv, periventricular; PVN, paraventricular nucleus of the hypothalamus. Based on Canteras *et al.* (1995); Dyas *et al.* (1999); Gray (1993); Herman *et al.* (1994); Moga and Saper (1994); Mudlers *et al.* (1997); Prewitt and Herman (1998); Sanchez *et al.* (1995); Sawchenko and Swanson (1983); Silverman *et al.* (1981); Risold *et al.* (1997); Viau *et al.* (2001); Watts (2000).

(reviewed in Piccinelli and Wilkinson, 2000; Seidman and Walsh, 1999; Young and Korzun, 1998). Moreover, emerging basic and clinical studies indicate potential therapeutic effects of sex steroid replacement therapy in depression (Bernardi *et al.*, 1998a,b; Bloch *et al.*, 2000; Kornstein and McEnany, 2000; Kornstein *et al.*, 2000a,b; Seidman and Rabkin, 1998). Thus, where and how sex steroids, stress, and depression intersect in the brain remains an important question.

Acknowledgments

We gratefully acknowledge NIH grant DK28172 for support of the work from our lab that is described here. The chapter also draws heavily on the work of others who are or have been in the lab; we have built on the work of Drs. Susan Akana, Takenori Sato, Charles Wilkinson, Bill Engeland, Masanori Kaneko, Maureen Keller-Wood, Dan Darlington, Lauren Jacobson, Margaret Bradbury, Alison Strack, Simon Hanson, Shuso Suemaru, SuJean Choi, and the many summer students whose help and enthusiasm have been essential to our understanding of rhythms, feeding, and stress. Dr. Alison Strack was the person who first strongly recognized the potentially interesting interaction between drinking sucrose and the regulation of function in the HPA axis, and we thank her.

References

Abelenda, M., and Puerta, M. (1999). Dual control of cytocrome-c oxidase activity by female sex steroids. *Eur. J. Endocrinol.* **141**, 630–636.

Adamec, R. E., and McKay, D. (1993). Amygdala, kindling, anxiety, and corticotrophin-releasing factor (CRF). *Physiol. Behav.* **54**, 423–431.

Ahima, R. S., Krowzowski, Z. S., and Harlan, R. E. (1991). Type I corticosteroid receptor-like immunoreactivity in the rat CNS: Distribution and regulation by corticosteroids. *J. Comp. Neurol.* **313**, 522–538.

Ahima, R. S., Lawson, A. N., Osei, S. Y., and Harlan, R. E. (1992). Sexual dimorphism in regulation of type II corticosteroid receptor immunoreactivity in the rat hippocampus. *Endocrinology (Baltimore)* **131**, 1409–1416.

Akana, S. F., and Dallman, M. F. (1997). Chronic cold in adrenalectomized, corticosterone (B)-treated rats: Facilitated corticotropin responses to acute stress emerge as B increases. *Endocrinology (Baltimore)* **138**, 3249–3258.

Akana, S. F., Scribner, K. A., Bradbury, M. J., Strack, A. M., Walker, C.-D., and Dallman, M. F. (1992). Feedback sensitivity of the rat hypothalamic-pituitary adrenal axis and its capacity to adjust to exogenous corticosterone. *Endocrinology (Baltimore)* **131**, 585–594.

Akana, S. F., Hanson, E. S., Horsley, C. J., Strack, A. M., Bhatnagar, S., Bradbury, M. J., Milligan, E. D., and Dallman, M. F. (1996). Clamped corticosterone (B) reveals the effect of endogenous B on both facilitated responsivity to acute restraint and metabolic responses to chronic stress. *Stress* **1**, 33–49.

Akana, S. F., Strack, A. M., Hanson, E. S., Horsley, C. J., Milligan, E. D., Bhatnagar, S., and Dallman, M. F. (1999). Interactions among chronic cold, corticosterone and puberty on energy intake and deposition. *Stress* **3**, 131–146.

Akana, S. F., Chu, A., Soriano, L., and Dallman, M. F. (2001). Corticosterone exerts site-specific and state-dependent effects in prefrontal cortex and amygdala on regulation of insulin and fat depots. *J. Neuroendocrinol.* **13**, 625–637.

Albeck, D. S., McKittrick, C. R., Blanchard, D. C., Blanchard, R. J., Nikulina, J., McEwen, B. S., and Sakai, R. R. (1997). Chronic social stress alters levels of corticotropin-releasing factor and arginine vasopressin mRNA in rat brain. *J. Neurosci.* **17**, 4895–4903.

Alexander, S. L., Irvine, C. H. G., and Donald, R. A. (1996). Dynamics of the regulation of the hypothalamo-pituitary-adrenal (HPA) axis determine using a non-surgical method for collecting pituitary venous blood from horses. *Front. Neuroendocrinol.* **17**, 1–50.

Almeida, O. F., Canoine, V., Ali, S., Holsboer, F., and Patchev, V. K. (1997). Activational effects of gonadal steroids on hypothalamo-pituitary-adrenal regulation in the rat disclosed by response to dexamethasone suppression. *J. Neuroendocrinol.* **9**, 129–134.

Almeida, S. A., Anselmo-Franci, J. A., Rosa e Silva, A. A., and Carvalho, T. L. (1998). Chronic intermittent immobilization of male rats throughout sexual development: A stress protocol. *Exp. Physiol.* **83**, 701–704.

Alves, S. E., Lopez, V., McEwen, B. S., and Weiland, N. G. (1998). Differential colocalization of estrogen receptor beta (ERbeta) with oxytocin and vasopressin in the paraventricular and supraoptic nuclei of the female rat brain: An immunocytochemical study. *Proc. Nat. Acad. Sci. U.S.A.* **95**, 3281–3286.

Antoni, F. A. (1986). Hypothalamic control of adrenocorticotropin secretion: Advances since the discovery of 41-residue corticotropin-releasing factor. *Endocr. Rev.* **7**, 351–378.

Antoni, F. A. (1993). Vasopressinergic control of pituitary adrenocorticotropin comes of age. *Front. Neuroendocrinol.* **14**, 76–122.

Armario, A., Lopez-Calderon, A., Jolian, T., and Balasch, J. (1986). Response of anterior pituitary hormones to chronic stress. *Neurosci. Biobehav. Rev.* **10**, 245–250.

Arnold, F. J. L., de Lucas Bueno, M., Shiers, H., Hancock, D. C., Evan, G. I., and Herbert, J. (1992). Expression of c-fos in regions of the basal limbic forebrain following intracerebroventricular corticotropin-releasing factor in unstressed or stressed male rats. *Neuroscience* **51**, 377–390.

Atkinson, H. C., and Waddell, B. J. (1997). Circadian variation in basal plasma corticosterone and adrenocorticotropin in the rat: Sexual dimorphism and changes across the estrous cycle. *Endocrinology (Baltimore)* **138**, 3842–3848.

Axelson, J. F., Zoller, L. C., Tomassone, J. E., and Collins, D. C. (1986). Effects of silastic progesterone implants on activity cycles and steroid levels in ovariectomized and intact female rats. *Physiol. Behav.* **38**, 879–885.

Azmitia, E. C. (1999). Serotonin neurons, neuroplasticity, and homeostasis of neural tissue. *Neuropsychopharmacology* **21**, 33S–45S.

Azmitia, E. C., and McEwen, B. S. (1969). Corticosterone regulation of tryptophan hydroxylase in midbrain of rat. *Science* **166**, 1274–1276.

Azmitia, E. C., and McEwen, B. S. (1974). Adrenalcortical influence on rat brain tryptophan-hydroxylase activity. *Brain Res.* **78**, 291–302.

Baker, R. A., and Herkenham, M. (1995). Arcuate nucleus neurons that project to the hypothalamic paraventricular nucleus: Neuropeptidergic identity and consequences of adrenalectomy on mRNA levels in the rat. *J. Comp. Neurol.* **358**, 518–530.

Barrot, M., Marinelli, M., Abrous, D. N., Rouge-Pont, F., Le Moal, M., and Piazza, P. V. (2000). The dopaminergic hyper-responsiveness of the shell of the nucleus accumbens is hormone-dependent. *Eur. J. Neurosci.* **12**, 973–979.

Bartke, A., Steele, R. E., Musto, N., and Caldwell, B. V. (1973). Fluctuations in plasma testosterone levels in adult male rats and mice. *Endocrinology (Baltimore)* **92**, 1223–1228.

Basdevant, A., Raison, J., De Lignieres, B., and Guy-Grand, B. (1986). Metabolism of sex hormones and adipose tissue. *J. Gynecol. Obstet. Biol. Reprod.* **15**, 147–152.

Baskin, D. G., Norwood, B. J., Schwartz, M. W., and Koerker, D. J. (1995). Estradiol inhibits the increase of hypothalamic neuropeptide Y messenger ribonucleic acid expression indced by weight loss in ovariectomized rats. *Endocrinology (Baltimore)* **136**, 5547–5554.

Baskin, D. G., Figlewicz Latteman, D. P., Seeley, R. J., Woods, S. C., Porte, D., Jr., and Schwartz, M. W. (1999). Insulin and leptin: Dual adiposity signals to the brain for the regulation of food intake and body weight. *Brain Res.* **848**, 114–123.

Beaulieu, S., Di Paolo, T., and Barden, N. (1986). Control of ACTH secretion by the central nucleus of the amygdala: Implication of the serotoninergic system and its relevance to the glucocorticoid delayed negative feedback mechanism. *Neuroendocrinology* **44**, 247–254.

Beck, C. H. M., and Fibiger, H. C. (1995). Conditioned fear-induced changes in behavior and in expression of the immediate early gene c-fos with and without diazepam pretreatment. *J. Neurosci.* **15**, 709–720.

Beer, S. F., Bircham, P. M. M., Bloom. S. R., Clark, P. M., Hales, C. N., Hughes, C. M., Jones, C. T., Marsh, D. R., Raggatt, P. R., and Findlay, A. L. R. (1989). The effect of a 72-h fast on plasma levels of pituitary, adrenal, thyroid, pancreatic and gastrointestinal hormones in healthy men and women. *J. Endocrinol.* **120**, 337–350.

Behan, D. P., Grigoriadis, D. E., Lovenberg, T., Chalmers, D., Heinrichs, S., Liaw, C., and De Souza, E. B. (1996). Neurobiology of corticotropin releasing factor (CRF) receptors and CRF-binding protein: Implications for the treatment of CNS disorders. *Mol. Psychiatry* **1**, 265–277.

Bell, M. E., Bhatnagar, S., Liang, J., Soriano, L., Nagy, T. R., and Dallman, M. F. (2000). Voluntary sucrose ingestion, like corticosterone replacement, prevents the metabolic deficits of adrenalectomy. *J. Neuroendocrinol.* **12**, 461–470.

Bernardi, M., Genedani, S., Tagliavini, S., and Bertolini, A. (1989a). Effect of castration and testosterone on experimental models of depression in mice. *Behav. Neurosci.* **103**, 1148–1150.

Bernardi, M., Vergoni, A. V., Sandrini, M., Tagliavini, S., and Bertolini, A. (1989b). Influence of ovariectomy, estradiol and progesterone on the behavior of mice in an experimental model of depression. *Physiol. Behav.* **45**, 1067–1068.

Berridge, K. C., and Robinson, T. E. (1998). What is the role of dopamine in reward: Hedonic impact, reward learning, or incentive salience? *Brain Res. Rev.* **28**, 309–369.

Bhatnagar, S., and Dallman, M. F. (1998a). Neuroanatomical basis for facilitation of hypothalamic-pituitary-adrenal responses to a novel stressor after chronic stress. *Neuroscience* **84**, 1025–1039.

Bhatnagar, S., and Dallman, M. F. (1999). The paraventricular nucleus of the thalamus alters rhythms in core temperature and energy balance in a state-dependent manner. *Brain Res.* **851**, 66–75.

Bhatnagar, S., and Meaney, M. J. (1995). Hypothalamic-pituitary-adrenal function in chronic intermittently cold-stressed neonatally handled and non handled rats. *J. Neuroendocrinol.* **7**, 97–108.

Bhatnagar, S., Mitchell, J. B., Betito, K., Boksa, P., and Meaney, M. J. (1995). Effects of chronic intermittent cold stress on pituitary adrenocortical and sympathetic adrenomedullary functioning. *Physiol. Behav.* **57**, 633–639.

Bhatnagar, S., Dallman, M. F., Roderick, R. E., Basbaum, A. I., and Taylor, B. K. (1998). The effects of prior chronic stress on cardiovascular responses to acute restraint and formalin injection. *Brain Res.* **797**, 313–320.

Bhatnagar, S., Bell, M. E., Liang, J., Soriano, L., Nagy, T. R., and Dallman, M. F. (2000a). Corticosterone facilitates saccharin intake in adrenalectomized rats. Does corticosterone increase stimulus salience? *J. Neuroendocrinol.* **12**, 453–460.

Bhatnagar, S., Viau, V., Chu, A., Soriano, L., Meijer, O. C., and Dallman, M. F. (2000b). A cholecystokinin-mediated pathway to the paraventricular thalamus is recruited in chronically stressed rats and regulates hypothalamic pituitary adrenal function. *J. Neurosci.* **20**, 5564–5573.

Bianchi, M., and Panerai, A. (1995). CRH and the noradrenergic system mediate the antinociceptive effect of central interleukin-1 in the rat. *Brain Res. Bull.* **36**, 113–117.

Billington, C. J., Briggs, J. E., Grace, M., and Levine, A. S. (1991). Effects of intracerebroventricular injeciton of neuropeptide Y on energy metabolism. *Am. J. Physiol.* **260**, R321–R327.

Billington, C. J., Briggs, J. E., Harker, S., Grace, M., and Levine, A. S. (1994). Neuropeptide Y in hypothalamic paraventricular nucleus: A center coordinating energy metabolism. *Am. J. Physiol.* **266**, R1765–R1770.

Bingaman, E. W., Baeckman, L. M., Yracheta, J. M., and Handa, R. J. (1994a). Localization of androgen receptor within peptidergic neurons of rat forebrain. *Brain Res. Bull.* **35**, 379–382.

Bingaman, E. W., Magnuson, D. J., Gray, T. S., and Handa, R. J. (1994b). Androgen inhibits the increases in hypothalamic corticotropin-releasing hormone (CRH) and CRH-immunoreactivity following gonadectomy. *Neuroendocrinology* **59**, 228–234.

Birketvedt, G. S., Florholmen, J., Sundsfjord, J., Osterud, B., Dinges, D., Bilker, W., and Stunkard, A. (1999). Behavioral and neuroendocrine characteristics of the night-eating syndrome. *JAMA, J. Am. Med. Assoc.* **282**, 657–663.

Birmingham, M. K., Sar, M., and Stumpf, W. E. (1984). Localization of aldosterone and corticosterone in the central nervous system, assessed by quantitative autoradiography. *Neurochem. Res.* **9**, 333–350.

Bittencourt, J. C., and Sawchenko, P. E. (2000). Do centrally administered neuropeptides access cognate receptors?: An analysis in the central corticotropin-releasing factor system. *J. Neurosci.* **20**, 1142–1156.

Bittman, E. L., Tubbiola, M. L., Foltz, G., and Hegarty, C. M. (1999). Effects of photoperiod and androgen on proopiomelanocortin gene expression in the arcuate nucleus of golden hamsters. *Endocrinology (Baltimore)* **140**, 197–206.

Blanchard, D. C., Sakai, R. R., McEwen, B. S., Weiss, S. M., and Blanchard, R. J. (1993). Subordination stress: Behavioral, brain and neuroendocrine correlates. *Behav. Brain Res.* **58**, 113–121.

Blanchard, D. C., Spencer, R. L., Weiss, S. M., Blanchard, R. J., McEwen, B. S., and Sakai, R. R. (1995). Visible burrough system as a model of chronic social stress: Behavioral and neuroendocrine correlates. *Psychoneuroendocrinology* **20**, 117–134.

Bloch, M., Schmidt, P. J., Danaceau, M., Murphy, J., Nieman, L., and Rubinow, D. R. (2000). effects of gonadal steroids in women with a history of post-partum depression. *Am. J. Psychiatry* **157**, 924–930.

Bohler, H. C., Jr., Zoeller, R. T., King, J. C., Rubin, B. S., Weber, R., and Merriam, G. R. (1990). Corticotropin releasing hormone mRNA is elevated on the afternoon of proestrus in the parvocellular paraventricular nuclei of the female rat. *Mol. Brain Res.* **8**, 259–262.

Bohus, B., Koolhaas, J. M., Luiten, P. G. M., Korte, S. M., Roosendaal, B., and Wiersma, A. (1996). The neurobiology of the central nucleus of the amygdala in relation to neuroendocrine and autonomic outflow. *Prog. Brain Res.* **107**, 447–460.

Bovetto, S., Rouillard, C., and Richard, D. (1996). Role of CRH in the effects of 5-HT-receptor agonists on food intake and metabolic rate. *Am. J. Physiol.* **271**, R1231–R1238.

Bowers, G., Cullinan, W. E., and Herman, J. P. (1998). Region-specific regulation of glutamic acid decarboxylase (GAD) mRNA expression in central stress circuits. *J. Neurosci.* **18**, 5938–5947.

Bradbury, M. J., Akana, S. F., and Dallman, M. F. (1994). Roles of type I and II corticosteroid receptors in regulation of basal activity in the hypothalamo-pituitary-adrenal axis during the diurnal trough and the peak: Evidence for a nonadditive effect of combined receptor occupation. *Endocrinology (Baltimore)* **134**, 1286–1296.

Brann, D. W., and Mahesh, V. B. (1991). Role of corticosteroids in female reproduction. *FASEB, J.* **5**, 2691–2698.

Bray, G. A., Fisler, J., and York, D. A. (1990). Neuroendocrine control of the development of obesity: Understanding gained from studies of experimental animal models. *Front. Neuroendocrinol.* **11**, 128–181.

Broadle-Biber, M. C., Singh, V. B., Corley, K. C., Phan, T.-H., and Dilts, R. P. (1993). Evidence that coricotropin-releasing factor within the extended amygdala mediates the activation of tryptophan hydroxylase produced by sound stress in rats. *Brain Res.* **628**, 105–114.

Brown, L. L., Siegel, H., and Etgen, A. M. (1996). Global sex differences in stress-induced activation of cerebral metabolism revealed by 2-deoxyglucose autoradiography. *Horm. Behav.* **30**, 611–617.

Brown, M. R., and Fisher, L. A. (1983). Central nervous system effects of corticotropin-releasing factor in the dog. *Brain Res.* **280**, 75–79.

Brown, M. R., and Fisher, L. A. (1985). Corticotropin-releasing factor: Effects on the autonomic nervous system and visceral systems. *Fed. Proc. Fed. Am. Soc. Exp. Biol.* **44**, 243–248.

Brown, M. R., and Fisher, L. A. (1986). Glucocorticoid suppression of the sympathetic nervous system and adrenal medulla. *Life Sci.* **39**, 1003–1012.

Brown, M. R., Fisher, L. A., Rivier, J., Spiess, J., Rivier, C., and Vale, W. (1981). Corticotropin-releasing factor: Effects on the sympathetic nervous system and oxygen consumption. *Life Sci.* **30**, 207–210.

Brown, M. R., Fisher, L. A., Spiess, J., Rivier, C., Rivier, J., and Vale, W. (1982). Corticotropin-releasing factor: Actions on the sympathetic nervous system and metabolism. *Endocrinology (Baltimore)* **111**, 928–931.

Brown, T. J., and MacLusky, N. J. (1994). Progesterone modulation of estrogen receptors in microdissected regions of rat hypothalamus. *Mol. Cell. Neurosci.* **5**, 283–290.

Bruijnzeel, A. W., Stam, R., Compaan, J. C., Croiset, G., Akkermans, L. M. A., Olivier, B., and Wiegent, V. M. (1999). Long-term sensitization of Fos-responsivity in the rat central nervous system after a single stressful experience. *Brain Res.* **819**, 15–22.

Bubser, M., and Deutch, A. Y. (1998). Thalamic paraventricular nucleus neurons collateralize to innervate the prefrontal cortex and nucleus accumbens. *Brain Res.* **787**, 304–310.

Buckingham, J. C. (1982). Effects of adrenocortical and gonadal steroids on the secretion in vitro of corticotrophin and its hypothalamic releasing factor. *J. Endocrinol.* **93**, 123–132.

Buijs, R. M., Kalsbeek, A., van der Woude, T. P., van Heerikhuize, J. J., and Shinn, S. (1993). Suprachismatic nucleus lesion increases corticosterone secretion. *Am. J. Physiol.* **264**, R1186–R1192.

Buijs, R. M., Wortel, J., van Heerikhuize, J. J., and Kalsbeek, A. (1997). Novel environment induced inhibition of corticosterone secretion: Physiological evidence for a suprachiasmatic nucleus mediated neuronal hypothalamo-adrenal cortex pathway. *Brain Res.* **758**, 229–236.

Buijs, R. M., Wortel, J., van Heerikhuize, J. J., Feenstra, M. G. P., Ter Horst, G. J., Romijn, H. J., Kalsbeek, A. (1999). Anatomical and functional demonstration of a multisynaptic suprachiasmatic nucleus adrenal (cortex) pathway. *Eur. J. Neurosci.* **11**, 1535–1544.

Buller, K. M., Smith, D. W., and Day, T. A. (1999). Differential recruitment of hypothalamic neuroendocrine and ventrolateral medulla catecholamine cells by non-hypotensive and hypotensive hemorrhages. *Brain Res.* **834**, 42–54.

Burgess, L. H., and Handa, R. J. (1992). Chronic estrogen-induced alterations in adrenocorticotropin and corticosterone secretion, and glucocorticoid receptor-mediated functions in female rats. *Endocrinology (Baltimore)* **131**, 1261–1269.

Burgess, L. H., and Handa, R. J. (1993). Estrogen-induced alterations in the regulation of mineralcorticoid and glucocorticoid receptor messenger RNA expression in the female rat anterior pituitary gland and brain. *Mol. Cell. Neurosci.* **4**, 191–198.

Butcher, R. L., Collins, W. E., and Fugo, N. W. (1974). Plasma concentrations of LH, FSH, prolactin, progesterone and estradiol 17ß throughout the 4-day estrous cycle of the rat. *Endocrinology (Baltimore)* **94**, 1704–1708.

Buwalda, B., de Boer, S. F., Van Kalkeren, A. A., and Koolhaas, J. M. (1997). Physiological and behavioral effects of chronic intracerebroventricular infusion of corticotropin-releasing factor in the rat. *Psychoneuroendocrinology* **22**, 297–309.

Buwalda, B., Van Kalkeren, A. A., de Boer, S. F., and Koolhaas, J. M. (1998). Behavioral and physiological consequences of repeated daily intracerebroventricular injection of corticotropin-releasing factor in the rat. *Psychoneuroendocrinology* **23**, 205–218.

Cahill, L., and McGaugh, J. L. (1996). Modulation of memory storage. *Curr. Opin. Neurobiol.* **6**, 237–242.

Cahill, L., Babinsky, R., Markowitsch, H. J., and McGaugh, J. L. (1995). The amygdala and emotional memory. *Nature (London)* **377**, 295–296.

Cano, G., Card, J. P., Rinaman, L., and Sved, A. (2000). Connections of Barrington's nucleus to the sympathetic nervous system in rats. *J. Auton. Nerv. Syst.* **79**, 117–128.

Canteras, N. S., Simerley, R. B., and Swanson, L. W. (1995). Organization of projections from the medial nucleus of the amygdala: A PHAL study in the rat. *J. Comp. Neurol.* **360**, 213–245.

Carbajal, R., Chauvet, X., Couderc, S., and Olivier-Martin, M. (1999). Randomized trial of analgesic effects of sucrose, glucose and pacifiers in term neonates. *Br. Med. J.* **319**, 1393–1397.

Cardinali, D. P., Ritta, M. N., and Gejman, P. V. (1982). norepinephrine stimulates testosterone aromatization and inhibits 5 alpha reduction via beta-adrenoreceptors in rat pineal gland. *Mol. Cell. Endocrinol.* **28**, 199–209.

Carey, M. P., Deterd, C. H., de Koning, J., Helmerhorst, F., and de Kloet, E. R. (1995). The influence of ovarian steroids on hypothalamic-pituitary-adrenal regulation in the female rat. *J. Endocrinol.* **144**, 311–321.

Ceccatelli, S., Cintra, A., Hokfelt, T., Fuxe, K., Wikstrom, A.-C., and Gustafsson, J. Å. (1989). Coexistence of glucocorticoid receptor-like immunoreactivity with neuropeptides in the hypothalamic paraventricular nucleus. *Exp. Brain Res.* **78**, 33–42.

Chamas, F., Serova, L., and Sabban, E. L. (1999). Tryptophan hydroxylase mRNA levels are elevated by repeated immobilization stress in rat raphe nuclei but not in pineal gland. *Neurosci. Lett.* **267**, 157–160.

Champagne, D., Beaulieu, J., and Drolet, G. (1998). CRFergic innervation of the paraventricular nucleus of the rat hypothalamus: A tract-tracing study. *J. Neuroendocrinol.* **11**, 119–131.

Chang, F.-C., and Opp, M. R. (2000). IL-1 is a mediator of increases in slow-wave sleep induced by CRH-receptor blockade. *Am. J. Physiol.* **279**, R793–R802.

Chang, M.-S., Sved, A., Zigmond, M. J., and Austin, M. C. (2000). Increased transcription of the tyrosine hydroxylase gene in individual locus coeruleus neurons following foot-shock stress. *Neuroscience* **101**, 131–139.

Chappell, P. B., Smith, M. A., Kilts, C. D., Bissette, G., Ritchie, J., Anderson, C., and Nemeroff, C. B. (1986). Alterations in corticotropin-releasing factor-like immunoreactivity in discrete brain regions after acute and chronic stress. *J. Neurosci.* **6**, 2908–2914.

Chehab, F. F., Lim, M. E., and Lu, R. (1996). Correction of the sterility defect in homozygous obese female mice by treatment with human recombinant leptin. *Nat. Genet.* **12**, 318–320.

Chehab, F. F., Mounzih, K., Ronghua, L., and Lim, M. E. (1997). Early onset of reproductive function in normal female mice treated with leptin. *Science* **275**, 88–90.

Chen, S.-Y., Wang, J., Yu, G.-Q., Liu, W., and Pearce, D. (1997). Androgen and glucocorticoid receptor heterodimer formation. A possible mechanism for mutual inhibition of transcriptional activity. *J. Biol. Chem.* **272**, 14087–14092.

Choi, S., and Dallman, M. F. (1998). The hypothalamic ventromedial nuclei amplify circadian rhythms: Do they contain a food-entrained oscillator? *J. Neurosci.* **18**, 3843–3852.

Chou, Y. C., and Lüttge, W. G. (1988). Activated type II receptors in brain cannot rebind glucocorticoids: Relationship to progesterone's antiglucocorticoid actions. *Brain Res.* **440**, 67–78.

Chowdhury, G. M. I., Fujioka, T., and Nakamura, S. (2000). Induction and adaptation of Fos expression in the rat brain by two types of acute restraint stress. *Brain Res. Bull.* **52**, 171–182.

Chowen-Breed, J. A., Clifton, D. K., and Steiner, R. A. (1989). Regional specificity of testosterone regualtion of proopiomelanocortin gene expression in the arcuate nucleus of the male rat brain. *Endocrinology (Baltimore)* **124**, 2875–2881.

Chowen-Breed, J. A., Argente, J., Vician, L., Clifton, D. K., and Steiner, R. A. (1990). Pro-opiomelanocortin messenger RNA in hypothalamic neurons is increased by testosterone through aromatization to estradiol. *Neuroendocrinology* **52**, 581–588.

Chung, K. K. K., Martinez, M., and Herbert, J. (1999). c-fos experession, behavioural, endocrine and autonomic responses to acute social stress in male rats after chroniuc restraint: Modulation by serotonin. *Neuroscience* **95**, 453–463.

Cintra, A., Fuxe, K., Solfrini, V., Aganati, L. F., Tinner, B., Wikstrom, A.-C., Staines, W., Okret, S., and Gustafsson, J. A. (1991). Central peptidergic neurons as targets for glucocorticoid action. Evidence for the presence of glucocorticoid receptor immunoreactivity in various types of classes of peptidergic neurons. *J. Steroid Biochem. Mol. Biol.* **40**, 93–103.

Colby, H. D., and Kitay, J. I. (1972). Interaction of testosterone and ACTH in the regulation of adrenal corticosterone secretion in the male rat. *Endocrinology (Baltimore)* **91**, 1247–1252.

Colby, H. D., and Kitay, J. I. (1974). Interaction of estradiol and ACTH in the regulation of adrenal corticosterone production in the rat. *Steroids* **24**, 527–536.

Cole, M. A., Kalman, B. A., Pace, T. W. W., Topczewski, F., Lawrey, M. J., and Spencer, R. L. (2000a). Selective blockade of the mineralocorticoid receptor impairs hypothalamic-pituitary-adrenal axis expression of habituation. *J. Neuroendocrinol.* **12**, 1034–1042.

Cole, M. A., Kim, P. J., Kalman, B. A., and Spencer, R. L. (2000b). Dexamethasone suppression of corticosteroid secretion: Evaluation of the site of action by receptor measures and functional studies. *Psychoneuroendocrinology* **25**, 151–167.

Contarino, A., Dellu, F., Koob, G. F., Smith, G. W., Lee, K. F., Vale, W. W., and Gold, L. H. (2000). Dissociation of locomotor activation and suppression of food intake induced by CRF in CRFR1-deficient mice. *Endocrinology (Baltimore)* **141**, 2698–2702.

Costa, A., Poma, A., Martignoni, E., Nappi, G., Ur, E., and Grossman, A. (1997). Stimulation of corticotropin-releasing hormone release by the obese (ob) gene product, leptin, from hypothalamic explants. *NeuroReport* **8**, 1131–1134.

Couse, J. F., and Korach, K. S. (1999). Estrogen receptor null mice: What have we learned and where will they lead us. *Endocr. Rev.* **20**, 358–417.

Cowley, M. A., Pronchuk, N., Fan, W., Dinulescu, D. M., Colmers, W. F., and Cone, R. D. (1999). Integration of NPY, AGRP, amd melanocortin signals in the hypothalamic paraventricular nucleus: Evidence of a cellular basis for the adipostat. *Neuron* **24**, 155–163.

Crandall, D. L., Busler, D. E., Novak, T. J., Weber, R. V., and Kral, J. G. (1998). Identification of estrogen receptor beta RNA in human breast and abdominal subcutaneous adipose tissue. *Biochem. Biophys. Res. Commun.* **248**, 523–526.

Cullinan, W. E., and Zaborsky, L. (1991). Organization of ascending hypothalamic projections to the rostral forebrain with special reference to the innervation of cholinergic projection neurons. *J. Comp. Neurol.* **306**, 631–667.

Cullinan, W. E., Herman, J. P., and Watson, S. J. (1993). Ventral subicular interaction with the hypothalamic paraventricular nucleus: Evidence for a relay in the bed nucleus of the stria terminalis. *J. Comp. Neurol.* **332**, 1–20.

Cullinan, W. E., Herman, J. P., Battaglia, D. F., Akil, H., and Watson, S. J. (1995). Pattern and time course of immediate early gene expression in rat brain following acute stress. *Neuroscience* **64**, 477–505.

Cunningham, E. T., Jr., and Sawchenko, P. E. (1990). Anatomical specificity of noradrenergic inputs to the paraventricular and supraoptic nuclei of the rat hypothalamus. *J. Comp. Neurol.* **274**, 60–76.

Cunningham, M. J., Clifton, D. K., and Steiner, R. A. (1999). Leptin's actions on the reproductive axis: Perspectives and mechanisms. *Biol. Reprod.* **60**, 216–222.

Curtis, A. L., Pavcovich, L. A., Grigoriadis, D. E., and Valentino, R. J. (1995). Previous stress alters corticotropin-releasing factor neurotransmission in the locus coeruleus. *Neuroscience* **65**, 541–550.

Curtis, A. L., Lechner, S. M., Pavcovich, L. A., and Valentino, R. J. (1997). Activation of the locus coeruleus noradrenergic system by intracoerulear microinfusion of corticotropin-releasing factor: Effects on discharge rate, cortical norepinephrine levels and cortical electroencephalographic activity. *J. Pharmacol. Exp. Ther.* **281**, 163–172.

Dallman, M. F. (1984). Viewing the ventromedial hypothalamus from the adrenal gland. *Am. J. Physiol.* **246**, R1–R12.

Dallman, M. F. (2001). "Stress, and Sickness Decrease Food Intake and Body Weight: How Does this Happen?" Free University of Berlin, Berlin.

Dallman, M. F., Bhatnagar, S. (2001). "Chronic Stress and Energy Balance: Role of the Hypothalamo-Pituitary-Adrenal Axis." Oxford University Press, New York.

Dallman, M. F., and Jones, M. T. (1973). Corticosteroid feedback control of ACTH secretion on subsequent stress responses in the rat. *Endocrinology (Baltimore)* **92**, 1367–1375.

Dallman, M. F., Makara, G. B., Roberts, J. L., Levin, N., and Blum, M. (1985). Corticotrope response to removal of releasing factors and corticosteroids in vivo. *Endocrinology (Baltimore)* **117**, 2190–2197.

Dallman, M. F., Akana, S. F., Cascio, C. S., Darlington, D. N., Jacobson, L., and Levin, N. (1987). Regulation of ACTH secretion: Variations on a theme of B. *Recent Prog. Horm. Res.* **43**, 113–173.

Dallman, M. F., Akana, S. F., Levin, N., Jacobson, L., Cascio, C. S., Darlington, D. N., Suemaru, S., and Scribner, K. (1989a). Corticosterone (B) replacement in adrenalectomized rats: Insights into the regulation of ACTH secretion. *In* "The Control of the Hypothalamic-Pituitary-Adrenocortical Axis" (F. C. Rose, ed.), pp. 95–116. International Universities Press: London.

Dallman, M. F., Levin, N., Cascio, C. S., Akana, S. F., Jacobson, L., and Kuhn, R. W. (1989b). Pharmacological evidence that the inhibition of diurnal adrenocorticotropin secretion by corticosteroids is mediated by tupe I corticosterone-preferring receptors. *Endocrinology (Baltimore)* **124**, 2844–2850.

Dallman, M. F., Akana, S. F., Scribner, K. A., Bradbury, M. J., Walker, C.-D., Strack, A. M., and Cascio, C. S. (1992). Stress, feedback and facilitation in the hypothalamo-pituitary-adrenal axis. *J. Neuroendocrinol.* **4**, 517–526.

Dallman, M. F., Strack, A. M., Akana, S. F., Bradbury, M. J., Hanson, E. S., Scribner, K. A., and Smith, M. (1993). Feast and famine: Critical role of glucocorticoids with insulin in daily energy flow. *Front. Neuroendocrinol.* **14**, 303–347.

Dallman, M. F., Akana, S. F., Strack, A. M., Hanson, E. S., and Sebastian, R. J. (1995). The neural network that regulates energy balance is responsive to glucocorticoids and insulin and also regulates HPA axis responsivity at a site proximal to CRF neurons., *In* "Stress: Basic Mechanisms and Clinical Implications" (G. P. Chrousos, R. McCarty, K. Pacak, G. Cizza, E. Sternberg, P. W. Gold, and R. Kvetnansky, eds.), pp. 730–742. N. Y. Acad. Sci., New York.

Dallman, M. F., Akana, S. F., Bell, M. E., Bhatnagar, S., Choi, S., Chu, A., Horsley, C., Levin, N., Meijer, O. C., Strack, A. M., Soriano, L., and Viau, V. (1999). Starvation: Early signals, sensors and sequelae. *Endocrinology (Baltimore)* **140**, 4015–4023.

Dallman, M. F., Akana, S. F., Bhatnagar, S., Bell, M. E., and Strack, A. M. (2000). Bottomed out: Metabolic significance of the circadian trough in glucocorticoid concentrations. *Int. J. Obes.* **24**, S40–S46.

Damasio, A. R. (1999). "The Feeling of What Happens: Body and Emotion in the Making of Consciousness." Harcourt Brace, New York.

D'Anci, K. E. (1999). Tolerance to morphine-induced antinociception is decreased by chronic sucrose or polycose intake. *Pharmacol. Biochem. Behav.* **63**, 1–11.

D'Anci, K. E., Kanarek, R. B., and Marks-Kaufman, R. (1997). Beyond sweet taste: Saccharin, sucrose, and polycose differ in their effects upon morphine-induced analgesia. *Pharmacol. Biochem. Behav.* **56**, 341–345.

Darlington, D. N., Shinsako, J., and Dallman, M. F. (1986). Medullary lesions eliminate the ACTH response to hemorrhage. *Am. J. Physiol.* **251**, R106–R115.

Davis, M. (1998). Are different parts of the extended amygdala involved in fear versus anxiety? *Biol. Psychiatry* **44**, 1239–1247.

Davis, M., and Whalen, P. J. (2001). The amygdala: Vigilance and emotion. *Mol. Psychiatry* **6**, 13–34.

de Boer, S. F., Koopmans, S. J., Slangen, J. L., and Van Der Gugten, J. (1990). Plasma catecholamine, corticosterone and glucose responses to repeated stress in rats: Effect of interstressor interval length. *Physiol. Behav.* **47**, 1117–1124.

de Goeij, D. C. E., Dijkstra, H., and Tilders, F. J. H. (1992a). Chronic psychosocial stress enhances vasopressin, but not corticotropin-releasing factor in the external zone of the median eminence of male rats: Relationship to subordinate status. *Endocrinology (Baltimore)* **131**, 847–893.

de Goeij, D. C. E., Jezova, D., and Tilders, F. J. H. (1992b). Repeated stress enhances vasopressin synthesis in corticotropin releasing factor neurons in the paraventricular nucleus. *Brain Res.* **577**, 165–168.

de Kloet, E. R. (1991). Brain corticosteroid receptor balance and homeostatic control. *Front. Neuroendocrinol.* **12**, 95–164.

de Kloet, E. R., Oitzl, M. S., and Joels, M. (1999). Stress and cognition: are corticosteroids good or bad guys? *Trends Neurosci.* **22**, 422–426.

de Quervqin, E.-F., Roozendaal, B., and McGaugh, J. L. (1998). Stress and glucocorticoids impair retrieval of long-term spacial memory. *Nature (London)* **394**, 787–790.

Deroche, V., Marinelli, M., Maccari, S., Le Moal, M., Simon, H., and Piazza, P. V. (1995). Stress-induced sensitization and glucocorticoids. I. Sensitization of dopamine-dependent locomotor effects of amphetamine and morphine depends on stress-induced corticosterone secretion. *J. Neurosci.* **15**, 7181–7188.

Dess, N. K., and Choe, S. (1994). Stress selectively reduces sugar + saccharin mixture intake but increases proportions of calories consumed as sugar by rats. *Psychobiology* **22**, 77–84.

Dess, N. K., and Eidelheit, D. (1998). The bitter with the sweet: The taste/stress/temperament nexus. *Biol. Psychol.* **48**, 103–119.

Dess, N. K., Choe, S., and Minor, T. R. (1998). The interaction of diet and stress in rats: High-energy food and sucrose treatment. *J. Exp. Psychol. Anim. Behav. Processes* **24**, 60–71.

Dobrakova, M., Kvetnansky, R., Oprsalova, Z., and Jezova, D. (1993). Specificity of the effect of repeated handling on sympathetic-adrenomedullary and pituitary-adrenocortical activity in rats. *Psychoneuroendocrinology* **18**, 163–174.

Dodt, C., Kern, W., Fehm, H. L., and Born, J. (1993). Antimineralocorticoid canrenoate enhances secretory activity of the hypothalamus-pituitary-adrenocortical (HPA) axis in humans. *Neuroendocrinology* **58**, 570–574.

Duhault, J., Boulanger, M., Chamorro, S., Boutin, J. A., Della Zuana, O., C. D., Fauchere, J.-L., Feletou, M., Germain, M., Husson, B., Vega, A. M., Renard, P., and Tisserand, F. (2000). Food intake regulation in rodents: Y5 or Y1 NPY receptors or both? *Can. J. Physiol. Pharmacol.* **78**, 173–185.

Dunn, A. J., and Berridge, C. W. (1990). Physiological and behavioral responses to corticotropin-releasing factor administration: Is CRF a mediator of anxiety or stress responses? *Brain Res. Rev.* **15**, 71–100.

Dunn, A. J., and Berridge, C. W. (1987). Corticotropin-releasing factor elicits a stress-like activation of cerebral catecholaminergic systems. *Pharmacol., Biochem. Behav.* **27**, 685–691.

Dyas, C. V., Buller, K. M., and Day, T. A. (1999). Neuroendocrine response to an emotional stressor: Evidence for involvement of the medial but not the central amygdala. *Eur. J. Neurosci.* **11**, 2312–2322.

Dyas, C. V., Xu, Y., Buller, K. M., and Day, T. A. (2000). Effects of chronic oestrogen replacement on stress-induced activation of hypothalamic-pituitary-adrenal axis control pathways. *J. Neuroendocrinol.* **12**, 784–794.

Eberhart, J. A., Morell, J. I., Krieger, M. S., and Pfaff, D. W. (1985). An autoradiographic study of projections ascending from the midbrain central gray, and from the region lateral to it, in the rat. *J. Comp. Neurol.* **241**, 285–310.

Edens, N. K., and Wade, G. N. (1983). Effects of estradiol on tissue distribution of newly-synthesized fatty acids in rats and hamsters. *Physiol. Behav.* **31**, 703–709.

Egawa, M., Yoshimatsu, H., and Bray, G. A. (1991). Neuropeptide Y suppresses sympathetic activity to interscapular brown adipose tissue in rats. *Am. J. Physiol.* **260**, R328–R334.

Elmquist, J. K., Maratos-Flier, E., Saper, C. B., and Flier, J. S. (1998). Unraveling the central nervous system pathways underlying responses to leptin. *Nat. Neurosci.* **1**, 445–450.

Erb, S., and Stewart, J. (1999). A role for the bed nucleus of the stria terminalis, but not the amygdala, in the effects of corticotropin-releasing factor on stress-induced reinstatement of cocaine seeking. *J. Neurosci.* **19**(1–6), RC35.

Erb, S., Shaham, Y., and Stewart, J. (1998). The role of corticotropin-releasing factor and corticosterone in stress- and cocaine-induced relapse to cocaine seeking in rats. *J. Neurosci.* **18**, 5529–5536.

Fahrbach, S. E., Meisel, R. L., and Pfaff, D. W. (1985). Preoptic implants of estradiol increase wheel running but not the open field activity of female rats. *Physiol. Behav.* **35**, 985–992.

Fan, W., Dinulescu, D. M., Butler, A. A., Zhou, J., Marks, D. L., and Cone, R. D. (2000). The central melanocortin system can directly regulate serum insulin levels. *Endocrinology (Baltimore)* **141**, 3072–3079.

Fanselow, M. S., and Le Doux, J. E. (1999). Why we think plasticity underlying Pavlovian fear conditioning lies in the basolateral amygdala. *Neuron* **23**, 229–232.

Febbraio, M. A., Keenan, J., Angus, D. J., Campbell, S. E., and Garnham, A. P. (2000a). Preexercise carbohydrate ingestion, glucose kinetics, and muscle glycogen use: Effect of glycemic index. *J. Appl. Physiol.* **89**, 1845–1851.

Febbraio, M. A., Chiu, A., Angus, D. J., Arkinstall, M. J., and Hawley, J. A. (2000b). Effects of carbohydrate ingestion before and during exercise on glucose kinetics and performance. *J. Appl. Physiol.* **89**, 2220–2226.

Fehmann, H.-C., Peiser, C., Bode, H.-P., Stamm, M., Staats, P., Hedetoft, C., Lang, R. E., and Goke, B. (1997). Leptin: A potent inhibitor of insulin secretion. *Peptides (N.Y.)* **18**, 1267–1273.

Feldman, S., and Weidenfeld, J. (1998). The excitatory effects of the amygdala on hypothalamo-pituitary-adrenocortical responses are mediated by hypothalamic norepinephrine, serotonin and CRF-41. *Brain Res. Bull.* **45**, 389–393.

Felig, P., Baxter, J. D., and Frohman, L. A. (1995). "Endocrinology and Metabolism." McGraw-Hill, San Francisco.

Ferrini, M., and De Nicola, A. F. (1991). Estrogens up-regulate type I and type II glucocorticoid receptors in brain regions from ovariectomized rats. *Life Sci.* **48**, 2593–2601.

Ferry, B., Roozendaal, B., and McGaugh, J. L. (1999). Role of norepinephrine in mediating stress hormone regulation of long-term memory storage: A critical involvement of the amygdala. *Biol. Psychiatry* **46**, 1140–1152.

Fichter, M. M., and Pirke, K. M. (1984). Hypothalamic pituitary function in starving healthy subjects. *In* "The Psychobiology of Anorexia Nervosa" (K. M. Pirke and D. Ploog, eds.), pp. 124–135. Springer-Verlag, Berlin.

Finlay, J. M., Zigmond, M. J., and Abercrombie, E. D. (1995). Increased dopamine and norepinephrine release in medial prefrontal cortex induced by acute and chronic stress: Effects of diazepam. *Neuroscience* **64**, 619–628.

Fisher, L. A., Rivier, J., Rivier, C., Spiess, J., Vale, W., and Brown, M. R. (1982). Corticotropin-releasing factor: Effects on the autonomic nervous system and visceral systems. *Endocrinology (Baltimore)* **110**, 2222–2224.

Floresco, S. B., Yang, C. R., Phillips, A. G., and Blaha, C. D. (1998). Basolateral amygdala stimulation evokes glutamate receptor-dependent dopamine efflux in the nucleus accumbens of the anesthetized rat. *Eur. J. Neurosci.* **10**, 1241–1251.

Florino, D. F., and Phillips, A. G. (1999). Facilitation of sexual behavior and enhanced dopamine efflux in the nucleus accumbens of male rats after D-amphetamine-induced behavioral sensitization. *J. Neurosci.* **16**, 456–463.

Follenius, M., Brandenburger, G., and Hetter, B. (1982). Diurnal cortisol peaks and their relationship to meals. *J. Clin. Endocrinol. Metab.* **55**, 757–761.

Franklin, T. R., and Druhan, J. P. (2000). Expression of Fos-related antigens in the nucleus accumbens and associated regions following exposure to a cocaine-paired environment. *Eur. J. Neurosci.* **12**, 2097–2106.

Frederich, R., Lollmann, B., Hamann, A., Napolitano-Rosen, A., Kahn, B. B., Lowell, B. B., and Flier, J. S. (1995). Expression of ob mRNA and its encoded protein in rodents: Impact of nutrition and obesity. *J. Clin. Invest.* **96**, 1658–1663.

Freedman, L. J., and Cassell, M. D. (1994). Relationship of thalamic basal forebrain projection neurons to the peptidergic innervation of the midline thalamus. *J. Comp. Neurol.* **348**, 321–342.

Freedman, M. R., Castonguay, T. W., and Stern, J. S. (1985). Effect of adrenalectomy and glucocorticoid replacement on development of obesity. *Am. J. Physiol.* **250**, R595–R607.

Friedl, K. E., Moore, R. J., Hoyt, R. W., Marchitelli, L. J., Martinez-Lopez, L. E., and Askew, W. (2000). Endocrine markers of semistarvation in healthy lean men in a multi-stressor environment. *J. Appl. Physiol.* **88**, 1820–1830.

Fuxe, K., Wikström, A.-C., Okret, S., Agnati, L. F., Härfstrand, A.,

Yu, Q.-Y., Granholm, L., Zoli, M., Vale, W., and Gustafsson, J.-A. (1985). Mapping of glucocorticoid receptor immunoreactive neurons in the rat tel- and diencephalon using a monoclonal antibody against rat liver glucocorticoid receptor. *Endocrinology (Baltimore)* **117**, 1803–1812.

Gaillet, S., Alonso, G., Le Borgne, R., Barbanel, G., Malaval, F., Assenmacher, I., and Szafarczyk, A. (1993). Effects of discrete lesions in the ventral noradrenergic ascending bundle on the corticotropic stress response depend on the site of the lesion and on the plasma levels of adrenal steroids. *Neuroendocrinology* **58**, 408–419.

Gala, R. R., and Westhal, U. (1965). Corticosteroid-binding globulin in the rat: Studies on the sex differences. *Endocrinology (Baltimore)* **77**, 841–851.

Garcia, A., Marti, O., Valles, A., Dal-Zotto, S., and Armario, A. (2000). Recovery of the hypothalamic-pituitary-adrenal response to stress. *Neuroendocrinology* **72**, 114–125.

Garcia-Belenguer, S., Oliver, C., and Mormede, P. (1993). Facilitation and feedback in the hypothalamo-pituitary-adrenal axis during food restriction in rats. *J. Neuroendocrinol.* **5**, 663–668.

Garris, P. A., Kilpatrick, M., Bunin, M. A., Michael, D., Walker, Q. D., and Wrightman, R. M. (1999). Dissociation of dopamine release in the nucleus accumbens from intracranial self-stimulation. *Nature (London)* **398**, 67–69.

Gentry, R. T., and Wade, G. N. (1976). Androgenic control of food inatke and body weight in male rats. *J. Comp. Physiol. Psychol.* **96**, 18–25.

Gerald, C., Walker, M. W., Criscione, L., Gustafson, E. L., Batzl-Hartmann, C., Smith, K. E., Vaysse, P., Durkin, M. M., Laz, T. M., Linemeyer, D. L., Schaffhauser, A. O., Whitebread, S., Hofbauer, K. G., Taber, R. I., Branchek, T. A., and Weinshank, R. L. (1996). A receptor subtype involved in neuropeptide-Y-induced food intake. *Nature (London)* **382**, 168–171.

Gillies, G., Linton, E. A., and Lowry, P. (1982). Corticotropin releasing activity of the new CRF is potentiated several times by vasopressin. *Nature (London)* **299**, 355–357.

Giralt, M., and Armario, A. (1989). Individual housing does not influence the adaptation of the pituitary-adrenal axis and other physiological variables to chronic stress in adult male rats. *Physiol. Behav.* **45**, 477–481.

Goeders, N. E., and Guérin, G. F. (1996). Effects of surgical and pharamacological adrenalectomy on the initiation and maintenance of intravenous cocaine self-administraiton. *Brain Res.* **722**, 145–152.

Goeders, N. E., and Guérin, G. F. (2000). Effects of the CRH receptor antagonist CP[154–526] on intravenous cocaine self-administration in rats. *Neuropsychopharmacology* **23**, 577–586.

Goldstein, L. E., Rasmussen, A. M., Bunney, B. S., and Roth, R. H. (1996). Role of the amygdala in the coordination of behavioral, neuroendocrine, and prefrontal cortical monoamine responses to psychological stress in the rat. *J. Neurosci.* **16**, 4787–4798.

Gomez, F., and Dallman, M. F. (2001). Manipulation of androgens causes different energetic responses to cold in 60- and 40-day-old rats. *Am. J. Physiol.* **280**, R262–R273.

Gosnell, B. A., Morley, J. E., and Levine, A. S. (1983). A comparison of the effects of corticotropin-releasing factor and sauvagine on food intake. *Pharmacol. Biochem. Behav.* **19**, 771–775.

Goya, R. G., Castro, M. G., and Sosa, Y. E. (1989). Diminished diurnal secretion of corticosterone in aging female but not male rats. *Gerontology* **35**, 2311–2318.

Gray, T. S. (1993). Amydgaloid CRF pathways. Role in autonomic, neuroendocrine, and behavioral responses to stress. *N. Y. Acad. Sci.* **697**, 53–60.

Gray, T. S., and Bingaman, E. W. (1996). The amygdala: Corticotropin-releasing fator, steroids and stress. *Crit. Rev. Neurobiol.* **10**, 155–168.

Gray, T. S., Piechowski, R. A., Yracheta, J. M., Rittenhouse, P. A., Bethea, C. L., and Van de Kar, L. D. (1993). Ibotenic acid lesions in the bed nucleus of the stria terminalis attenuate conditioned stress-induced increases in prolactin, ACTH and corticosterone. *Neuroendocrinology* **57**, 517–524.

Greer, E. R., Caldwell, J. D., Johnson, M. F., Prange, A. J., Jr., and Pederson, C. A. (1986). Variations in concentrations of oxytocin and vasopressin in the paraventricular nucleus of the hypothalamus during the estrous cycle in rats. *Life Sci.* **38**, 2311–2318.

Gustafsson, J.-A., Carlstedt-Due, J., Poellinger, L., Okret, S., Wikstrom, A.-C., Bronnegard, M., Gillner, M., Dong, Y., Fuxe, K., Cintra, A., Harfstrand, A., and Agnati, L. (1987). Biochemistry, molecular biology, and physiology of the glucocorticoid receptor. *Endocr. Rev.* **8**, 185–234.

Haas, D. A., and George, S. R. (1987). Neuropeptide Y administration acutely increases hypothalamic corticotropin-releasing factor immunoreactivity: Lack of effect in other rat brain regions. *Life Sci.* **41**, 2725–2731.

Haas, D. A., and George, S. R. (1989). Neuropeptide Y-induced effects on hypothalamic corticotropin-releasing factor content and release are dependent on noradrenergic/adrenergic neurotransmission. *Brain Res.* **498**, 333–338.

Habib, K. E., Weld, K. P., Rice, K. C., Pushkas, J., Champoux, M., Listwak, S., Webster, E. L., Atkinson, A. J., Schulkin, J., Contoreggi, C., Chrousos, G. P., McCann, S. M., Suomi, S. J., Higley, J. D., and Gold, P. W. (2000). Oral administration of a corticotropin-releasing hormone receptor antagonist significantly attenuates behavioral, neuroendocrine and autonomic responses to stress in primates. *Proc. Nat. Acad. Sci. U.S.A.* **97**, 6079–6084.

Hamosh, M., and Hamosh, P. (1975). The effect of estrogen on the lipoprotein lipase activity of rat adipose tissue. *J. Clin. Invest.* **55**, 1132–1135.

Handa, R. J., Burgess, L. H., Kerr, J. E., and O'Keefe, J. A. (1994a). Gonadal steroid hormone receptors and sex differences in the hypothalamo-pituitary-adrenal axis. *Horm. Behav.* **28**, 464–466.

Handa, R. J., Nunley, K. M., Lorens, S. A., Louie, J. P., McGivern, R. F., and Bollnow, M. R. (1994b). Androgen regulation of adrenocorticotropin and corticosterone secretion in the male rat following novelty and foot shock stressors. *Physiol. Behav.* **55**, 117–124.

Hanson, E. S., Bradbury, M. J., Akana, S. F., Scribner, K. S., Strack, A. M., and Dallman, M. F. (1994). The diurnal rhythm in adrenocorticotropin responses to restraint in adrenalectomized rats is determined by caloric intake. *Endocrinology (Baltimore)* **134**, 2214–2220.

Hardie, L. J., Rayner, D. V., Holmes, S., and Trayhurn, P. (1996). Circulating leptin levels are modulated by fasting, cold exposure and insulin administration in lean but not Zucker (fa/fa) rats as measured by ELISA. *Biochem. Biophys. Res. Commun.* **223**, 660–665.

Harfstrand, A., Fuxe, K., Cintra, A., Agnati, L. F., Zini, I., Wikstrom, A.-C., Okret, S., Yu, Z.-Y., Goldstein, M., Steinbusch, H., Verhofstad, A., and Gustafsson, J.-Å. (1986). Glucocorticoid receptor immunoreactivity in monoaminergic neurons of rat brain. *Proc. Nat. Acad. Sci. U.S.A.* **83**, 9779–9783.

Hauger, R. L., Lorang, M., Irwin, M., and Aguilera, G. (1990). CRF receptor regulation and sensitization of ACTH responses to acute ether stress during chronic intermittent immobilization stress. *Brain Res.* **532**, 34–40.

Havel, P. J., Kasim-Karakas, S., Dubic, G. R., Mueller, W., and Phinney, S. D. (1996). Gender differences in plasma leptin concentration. *Nat. Med.* **2**, 949–950.

Heiman, M. L., Ahima, R. S., Craft, L. S., Schoner, B., Stephens, T. W., and Flier, J. S. (1997). Leptin inhibition of the hypothalamic-pituitary-adrenal axis in response to stress. *Endocrinology (Baltimore)* **138**, 3859–3863.

Heine, P. A., Taylor, J. A., Iwamoto, G. A., Lubahn, D. B., and Cooke, P. S. (2000). Increased adipose tissue in male and female estrogen receptor-α knockout mice. *Proc. Nat. Acad. Sci. U.S.A.* **97**, 12729–12734.

Heinrichs, S. C., and De Souza, E. B. (2001). Corticotropin-releasing factor in brain: Executive gating of neuroendocrine and functional outflow. (B. S. McEwen, ed.), pp. 125–137.

Heinrichs, S. C., and Richard, D. (1999). The role of corticotropin-releasing factor and urocortin in the modulation of ingestive behavior. *Neuropeptides* **33**, 350–359.

Heinrichs, S. C., Cole, B. J., Pich, E. M., Menzaghi, F., Koob, G. F., and Hauger, R. L. (1992). Endogenous corticotropin-releasing factor modulates feeding induced by neuropeptide Y or a tail-pinch stressor. *Peptides (N.Y.)* **13**, 879–884.

Heinrichs, S. C., Menzaghi, F., Pich, E. M., Hauger, R. L., and Koob, G. F. (1993). Corticotropin-releasing factor in the paraventricular nucleus modulates feeding induced by neuropeptide Y. *Brain Res.* **611**, 18–24.

Herman, J. P., and Cullinan, W. E. (1997). Neurocircuitry of stress: Central control of the hypothalamo-pituitary-adrenocortical axis. *Trends Neurosci.* **20**, 78–83.

Herman, J. P., Cullinan, W. E., and Watson, S. J. (1994). Involvement of the bed nucleus of the stria terminalis in tonic regulation of paraventricular hypothalamic CRH and AVP mRNA expression. *J. Neuroendocrinol.* **6**, 433–442.

Herman, J. P., Dolgas, C. M., and Carlson, S. L. (1996a). Ventral subiculum regulates hypothalamo-pituitary-adrenocortical and behavioral responses to cognitive stressors. *Neuroscience* **86**, 449–459.

Herman, J. P., Prewitt, C. M., and Cullinan, W. E. (1996b). Neuronal circuit regulation of the hypothalamo-pituitary-adrenocortical stress axis. *Crit. Rev. Neurobiol.* **10**, 1–24.

Herman, J. P., Prewitt, C. M.-F., and Cullinan, W. E. (1996c). Neuronal circuit regulation of the hypothalamo-pituitary-adrenocortical stress axis. *Crit. Rev. Neurobiol.* **10**, 371–394.

Hervey, G. R., and Hutchinson, I. (1973). The effects of testosterone on body weight and composition in the rat. *Proc. Soc. Endocrinol.* **57**, 24–25.

Highfield, D., Clements, A., Shalev, U., McDonald, R., Featherstone, R., Stewart, J., and Shaham, Y. (2000). Involvement of the medial septum in stress-induced relapse to heroin seeking in rats. *Eur. J. Neurosci.* **12**, 1705–1713.

Hileman, S. M., Kuehl, D. E., and Jackson, G. L. (1998). Photoperiod affects the ability of testosterone to alter proopiomelanocortin mRNA, but not luteinizing hormone-releasing hormone mRNA, levels in male sheeps. *J. Neuroendocrinol.* **10**, 587–592.

Himms-Hagen, J. (1990). Brown adipose tissue thermogenesis: Role in thermoregulation, energy regulation and obesity. *In* "Thermoregulation: Physiology and Biochemistry" (E. Schonbaum and P. Lomax, eds.), pp. 327–414. Pergamon Press, New York.

Hiroshige, T., Abe, K., Wada, S., and Kaneko, M. (1973). Sex difference in circadian periodicity of CRF activity in the rat hypothalamus. *Neuroendocrinology* **11**, 306–320.

Ho, K. Y., Evans, W. S., Blizzard, R. M., Veldhuis, J. D., Merriam, G. R., Samojlik, E., Furlanetto, R., Rogol, A. D., Kaiser, D. L., and Thorner, M. O. (1987). Effects of sex and age on the 24-hour profile of growth hormone secretion in man: Im-

portance of endogenous estradiol concentrations. *J. Clin. Endocrinol. Metabol.* **64**, 51–58.

Holland, P. C., and Gallagher, M. (1999). Amygdala circuitry in attentional and representational processes. *Trends Cogniti. Sci.* **3**, 65–73.

Holsboer, F. (2000). The corticosteroid receptor hypothesis of depression. *Neuropsychopharmacology* **23**, 477–501.

Holt, S. J., and York, D. A. (1989). The effects of adrenalectomy, corticotropin releasing factor and vasopressin on the sympathetic firing rate of nerves to interscapular brown adipose tissue in the Zucker rat. *Physiol. Behav.* **45**, 1123–1129.

Honkaniemi, J. (1992). Colocalization of peptide- and tyrosine hydroxylase-like immunoreactivities with Fos-immunoreactive neurons in rat central amygdaloid nuclei after immobilization stress. *Brain Res.* **598**, 107–113.

Honkaniemi, J., Pelto-Huikko, M., Rechardt, L., Isola, J., Lammi, A., Fuxe, K., Gustafsson, J.-A., Wilkstrom, A.-C., and Hokfelt, T. (1992). Colocalization of peptide and glucocorticoid receptor immunoreactivities in rat central amygdaloid nucleus. *Neuroendocrinology* **55**, 452–459.

Honma, K.-I., von Goetz, C., and Aschoff, J. (1983a). Effects of restricted daily feeding on freerunning circadian rhythm in rats. *Physiol. Behav.* **30**, 905–913.

Honma, K.-I., Honma, S., and Hiroshige, T. (1983b). Critical role of food amount for prefeeding corticosterone peak in rats. *Am. J. Physiol.* **245**, R339–R344.

Horrocks, P. M., Jones, A. F., Ratcliffe, W. A., Holder, G., White, A., Holder, R., Ratchiffe, J. G., and London, D. R. (1990). Patterns of ACTH and cortisol pulsatility over twenty-four hours in normal males and females. *Clin. Endocrinol. (Oxford)* **32**, 127–134.

Huang, Q., Rivest, R., and Richard, D. (1998). Effects of leptin on corticotropin- releasing factor (CRF) synthesis and CRF neuron activation in the paraventricular hypothalamic nucleus of obese (ob/ob) mice. *Endocrinology (Baltimore)* **139**, 1524–1532.

Hwa, J. J., B, W. M., P, W., Ghibaudi, L., Gao, J., Salisbury, B. G., Mullins, D., Hamud, F., Strader, C. D., and Parker, E. M. (1999). Activation of the NPY Y5 receptor regulates both feeding and energy expentiture. *Am. J. Physiol.* **277**, R1428–R1434.

Imaki, T., Nahan, J. L., Rivier, C., Sawchenko, P. E., and Vale, W. W. (1991). Differential regulation of corticotropin-releasing factor mRNA in rat brain regions by glucocorticoids and stress. *J. Neurosci.* **11**, 585–599.

Imaki, T., Shibasaki, T., Hotta, M., and Demura, H. (1993). Intracerebroventricular administration of corticotropin-releasing factor induces c-fos mRNA expression in brain regions related to stress responses: Comparison with pattern of c-fos mRNA induction after stress. *Brain Res.* **616**, 114–125.

Inui, A. (2000). Transgenic approach to the study of body weight regulation. *Pharmacol. Rev.* **52**, 35–61.

Jacobson, L., and Sapolsky, R. (1993). Augmented ACTH responses to stress in adrenalectomized rats replaced with constant physiological levels of corticosterone are partially normalized by acute increases in corticosterone. *Neuroendocrinology* **58**, 420–429.

Jacobson, L., Akana, S. F., Cascio, C. S., Scribner, K., Shinsako, J., and Dallman, M. F. (1989). The adrenocortical system responds slowly to the removal of corticosterone in the absence of stress. *Endocrinology (Baltimore)* **124**, 2144–2152.

Jang, M., Mistry, A., Swick, A. G., and Romsos, D. R. (2000). Leptin rapidly inhibits hypothalamic neuropeptide Y secretion and stimulates corticotropin-releasing hormone secretion in adrenalectomized mice. *J. Nutri.* **130**, 2813–2820.

Jasper, M. S., and Engeland, W. C. (1994). Splanchnic neural activity modulates ultradian and circadian rhythms in adrenocortical secretion in awake rats. *Neuroendocrinology* **59**, 97–109.

Jezova, D., Ocheldalski, T., Glickman, M., Kiss, A., and Aguilera, G. (1999). Central corticotropin-releasing hormone receptors modulate hypothalamic-pituitary-adrenocortical and sympathoadrenal activity during stress. *Neuroscience* **94**, 797–802.

Johnston, M. (1999). Feasting, fasting and fermentation. *Trends Genet.* **15**, 29–33.

Jolicoeur, F. B., Bouali, S. M., Fournier, A., and St. Pierre, S. (1994). Mapping of hypothalamic sites involved in the effects of NPY on body temperature and food intake. *Brain Res. Bull.* **36**, 125–129.

Jones, M. E. E., Thorburn, A. W., Britt, K. L., Hewitt, K. N., Wreford, N. G., Proietto, J., Oz, O. K., Leury, B. J., Robertson, K. M., Yao, S., and Simpson, E. R. (2000). Aromatase-deficient (ArKO) mice have a phenotype of increased adiposity. *Proc. Nat. Acad. Sci. U.S.A.* **97**, 12735–12740.

Kainu, T., Honkaniemi, J., Gustafsson, J.-A., Rechardt, L., and Pelto-Huikko, M. (1993). Co-localization of peptide-like immunoreactivities with glucocorticoid receptor- and Fos-like immunoreactivities in the rat parabrachial nucleus. *Brain Res.* **615**, 245–251.

Kalivas, P. W., and Stewart, J. (1991). Dopamine transmission in the initiation and expression of drug- and stress-induced sensitization of motor activity. *Brain Res. Rev.* **16**, 223–244.

Kalra, P. S., and Kalra, S. P. (1977). Circadian periodicities of serum androgens, progesterone, gonadotropins and luteinizing hormone-releasing hormone in male rats: The effects of hypothalamic deafferentation. *Endocrinology (Baltimore)* **101**, 1821–1827.

Kalsbeek, A., Teclemariam-Mesbah, R., and Pevet, P. (1993). Efferent projecions of the suprachiasmatic nucleus in the golden hampster (*Mesocricetus auratus*). *J. Comp. Neurol.* **332**, 293–314.

Kanarek, R. B., and Homoleski, B. A. (2000). Modulation of morphine-induced antinociception by palatable solutions in male and female rats. *Pharmacol. Biochem. Behav.* **66**, 653–659.

Kanarek, R. B., Przypek, J., D'Anci, K. E., and Marks-Kaufman, R. (1997). Dietary modulation of mu and kappa opiod receptor- mediated analgesia. *Pharmacol. Biochem. Behav.* **58**, 43–49.

Kanarek, R. B., Homoleski, B. A., and Wiatr, C. (2000). Intake of a palatable sucrose solution modifies the actions of spiradone, a kappa opioid receptor agonist on analgesia and feeding behavior in male and female rats. *Pharmacol. Biochem. Behav.* **65**, 97–104.

Kaneko, M., Hiroshige, T., Shinsako, J., and Dallman, M. F. (1980). Diurnal changes in amplification of hormone rhythms in the adrenocortical system. *Am. J. Physiol.* **239**, R309–R316.

Kang, J.-S., Pilkington, J. D., Ferguson, D., Kim, H.-K., and Romsos, D. R. (1992). Dietary glucose and fat attenuate effects of adrenalectomy on energy balance in ob/ob mice. *J. Nutr.* **122**, 895–905.

Kant, G. J., Eggleston, T., Landman-Roberts, L., Kenion, G. G., Driver, G. C., and Meyerhoff, J. L. (1985). Habituation to repeated stress is stressor specific. *Pharmacol., Biochem. Behav.* **22**, 631–634.

Kasckow, J. W., Regmi, A., Mulchahey, J. J., Plotsky, P. M., and Hauger, R. L. (1999). Changes in brain corticotropin-releasing factor messenger RNA expression in aged Fischer 344 rats. *Brain Res.* **822**, 228–230.

Kastin, A. J., Akerstrom, V., and Pan, W. (2000). Activation of urocortin transport into brain by leptin. *Peptides (N.Y.)* **21**, 1811–1817.

Kawahara, H., Kawahara, Y., and Westerink, B. H. C. (2000). The role of afferents to the locus coeruleus in the handling stress-induced increase in the release of noradrenaline in the medial prefrontal cortex: A dual-probe microdialysis study. *Eur. J. Pharmacol.* **387**, 279–286.

Keller-Wood, M. E. (1998). ACTH responses to hypotension and feedback inhibition of ACTH are increased by chronic progesterone treatment. *Am. J. Physiol.* **274**, R81–R87.

Keller-Wood, M. E., and Dallman, M. F. (1984). Corticosteroid inhibition of ACTH secretion. *Endocr. Rev.* **5**, 1–24.

Keller-Wood, M. E., Shinsako, J., and Dallman, M. F. (1983). Integral as well as proportional adrenal responses to ACTH. *Am. J. Physiol.* **245**, R53–R59.

Keller-Wood, M. E., Silbiger, J., and Wood, C. E. (1988). Progesterone attenuates the inhibition of adrenocorticotropin responses by cortisol in nonpregnant ewes. *Endocrinology (Baltimore)* **123**, 647–651.

Kelly, J. P., Wrynn, A. S., and Leonard, B. E. (1997). The olfactory bulbectomized rat as a model of depression: An update. *Pharmacol. Ther.* **74**, 299–316.

Kerrigan, J. R., Paul, M. M., Krieg, R. J., Queen, T. A., Monahan, P. E., and Rogol, A. D. (1991). Augmented hypothalamic proopiomelanocortin gene expression with pubertal development in the male rats: Evidence for an androgen receptor-independent action. *Endocrinology (Baltimore)* **128**, 1029–1035.

Kerrigan, J. R., Krieg, R. J., and Rogol, A. D. (1992). Exogenous androgen does not alter hypothalamic proopiomelanocortine gene transcript levels in the sexually immature male rat. *Neuroendocrinology* **56**, 264–270.

Kim, S., and Moustaid-Moussa, N. (2000). Secretory, endocrine and Autocrine/Paracrine function of the adipocyte. *J. Nutr.* **130**, 3110–3115.

King, D., Zigmond, M. J., and Finlay, J. M. (1997). Effects of dopamine depletion in the medial prefrontal cortex on the stress-induced increase in extracellular dopamine in the nucleus accumbens core and shell. *Neuroscience* **97**, 141–153.

Kitay, J. I. (1963). Pituitary adrenal function in the rat after gonadectomy and gonadal hormone replacement. *Endocrinology (Baltimore)* **73**, 253–260.

Kitay, J. I., Coyne, M. D., Newsom, W., and Nelson, R. (1965). Relation of the ovary to adrenal corticosterone production and adrenal enzyme activity in the rat. *Endocrinology (Baltimore)* **77**, 902–908.

Kitay, J. I., Coyne, M. D., Nelson, R., and Newsom, W. (1966). Relation of the testis to adrenal enzyme activity and adrenal corticosterone production in the rat. *Endocrinology (Baltimore)* **78**, 1061–1066.

Kling, M. A., Demitrack, M. A., Whitfield, H. J. J., Kalogeros, K. T., Listwack, S. J., DeBellis, M. D., Chrousos, G. P., Gold, P. W., and Brandt, H. A. (1993). Effects of the glucocortioid antagonist RU 486 on pituitary-adrenal function in patients with anorexia nervosa and healthy volunteers: Enhancement of plasma ACTH and cortisol secretion in underweight patients. *Neuroendocrinology* **57**, 1082–1091.

Koch, B., Bucher, B., and Mialhe, C. (1974). Pituitary nuclear retention of dexamethasone and ACTH biosynthesis. *Neuroendocrinology* **15**, 365–375.

Kollack-Walker, S., Don, C., Watson, S. J., and Akil, H. (1999). Differential expression of c-fos mRNA within neurocircuits of male hamsters exposed to acute or chronic defeat. *J. Neuroendocrinol.* **11**, 547–559.

Koob, G. F. (1999). Corticotropin-releasing factor, norepinephrine and stress. *Biol. Psychiatry* **46**, 1167–1180.

Koob, G. F., and Le Moal, M. (2001). Drug addiction, dysregulation of reward, and allostasis. *Neuropsychopharmacology* **24**, 97–129.

Kornstein, S. G., and McEnany, G. (2000). Enhancing pharmacologic effects in the treatment of depression in women. *J. Clin. Psychiatry* **61** (Suppl. 11), 18–27.

Kornstein, S. G., Schatzberg, A. F., Thase, M. E., Yonkers, K. A., McCullough, J. P., Keitner, G. I., Gelenberg, A. J., Davis, S. M., Harrison, M., and Keller, M. B. (2000a). Gender differences in treatment response to sertaline versus imipramine in chronic depression. *Am. J. Psychiatry* **157**, 1445–1452.

Kornstein, S. G., Schatzberg, A. F., Thase, M. E., Yonkers, K. A., McCullough, J. P., Keitner, G. I., Gelenberg, A. J., Ryan, C. E., Hess, A. L., Harrison, M., Davis, S. M., and Keller, M. B. (2000b). Gender differences in chronic major and double depression. *J. Affect. Disord.* **60**, 1–11.

Korte, S. M., Korte-Bouws, G. A. H., Koob, G. F., de Kloet, E. R., and Bohus, B. (1996). Mineralocorticoid and glucocorticoid receptor antagonists in animal models of anxiety. *Physiol. Behav.* **54**, 261–267.

Kotz, C. M., Briggs, J. E., Pomonis, J. D., Grace, M. K., Levine, A. S., and Billington, C. J. (1998). Neural site of leptin influence on neuropeptide Y signaling pathways altering feeding and uncoupling protein. *Am. J. Physiol.* **275**, R478–R484.

Kovacs, K. (1998). c-Fos as a transcription factor: A stresssful (re)view from a functional map. *Neurochem. Int.* **33**, 287–297.

Kovacs, K., and Makara, G. B. (1988). Corticosterone and dexamethasone act at different brain sites to inhibit adrenalectomy-induced adrenocorticotropin secretion. *Brain Res.* **474**, 205–210.

Kovacs, K., Kiss, J. Z., and Makara, G. B. (1986). Glucocorticoid implants around the hypothalamic paraventricular nucleus prevent the increase of corticotropin-releasing factor and arginine vasopressin caused by adrenalectomy. *Neuroendocrinology* **44**, 229–234.

Kovacs, K. J., and Mezey, E. (1987). Dexamethasone inhibits corticotropin-releasing factor gene expression in the rat paraventricular nucleus. *Neuroendocrinology* **46**, 365–368.

Kovacs, K. J., and Sawchenko, P. E. (1993). Mediation of osmoregulation influences on neuroendocrine corticotropin-releasing factor expression by the ventral lamina terminalis. *Proc. Natt. Acad. Sci. U.S.A.* **90**, 7681–7685.

Kovacs, K. J., Foldes, A., and Sawchenko, P. E. (2000). Glucocorticoid negative feedback selectively targets vasopressin transcription in parvocellular neurosecretory neurons. *J. Neurosci.* **20**, 3843–3852.

Kozicz, T., Yanihara, H., and Arimura, A. (1998). Distribution of urocortin-like immunoreactivity in the central nervous system of the rat. *J. Comp. Neurol.* **391**, 1–10.

Kraemer, W. J., Volek, J. S., Bush, J. A., Putukian, M., and Sebastianelli, W. J. (1998). Hormonal responses to consecutive days of heavy-resistance exercise with or without nutritional supplementation. *J. Appl. Physiol.* **85**, 1544–1555.

Krahn, D. D., Gosnell, B. A., Grace, M., and Levine, A. S. (1986). CRF antagonist partially reverses CRF- and stress-induced effects on feeding. *Brain Res. Bull.* **17**, 285–289.

Krahn, D. D., Gosnell, B. A., and Majchrzak, M. J. (1990). The anorectic effects of CRH and restraint stress decrease with repeated exposures. *Biol. Psychiatry* **27**, 1094–1102.

Krieger, D. T. (1974). Food and water restriction shifts corticosterone, temperature, activity and brain amine periodicity. *Endocrinology (Baltimore)* **95**, 1195–1201.

Krieger, D. T. (1979). Central nervous system disease. *Clin. Endocrinol. Metab.* **8**, 467–485.

Krieger, D. T. (1980). Ventromedial hypothalamic lesions abolish food-shifted circadian adrenal and temperature rhythmicity. *Endocrinology (Baltimore)* **106**, 649–654.

Kristensen, K., Pedersen, S. B., and Richelsen, B. (1999). Regulation of leptin by steroid hormones in rat adipose tissue. *Biochem. Biophy. Res. Commun.* **259**, 624–630.

Krowzowski, Z. S., and Funder, J. W. (1983). Renal mineralocorticoid receptors and hippocampal corticosterone binding species have identical intrinsic steroid specificity. *Proc. Nat. Acad. Sci. U.S.A.* **80**, 6056–6060.

Kwak, S. P., Young, E. A., Morano, I., Watson, S. J., and Akil, H. (1992). Diurnal corticotropin-releasing factor mRNA variation in the hypothalamus exhibits a rhythm distinct fom that of plasma corticosterone. *Neuroendocrinology* **55**, 74–83.

Kwak, S. P., Morano, M. I., Young, E. A., Watson, S. J., and Akil, H. (1993). Diurnal CRH mRNA rhythm in the hypothalamus: Decreased expression in the evening is not dependent on exogenous glucocorticoids. *Neuroendocrinology* **57**, 96–105.

Lachuer, J., Delton, I., Buda, M., and Tappaz, M. (1994). The habituation of brainstem catecholaminergic cell groups to chronic daily stress is stress specific like that of the hypothalamo-pituitary-adrenal axis. *Brain Res.* **638**, 196–202.

Laflamme, N., Nappi, R. E., Drolet, G., Labrie, C., and Rivest, S. (1998). Expression and neuropeptidergic characterization of estrogen receptors (ERa and ERb) throughout the rat brain: Anatomical evidence of distinct roles of each subtype. *J. Neurobiol.* **36**, 357–378.

Laugero, K. D., Bell, M. E., Bhatnagar, S., Soriano, L., and Dallman, M. F. (2001). Sucrose ingestion normalizes central expresion of corticotropin-releasing factor mRNA and energy balance in adrenalectomized rats: A glucocorticoid-metabolic-brain axis? *Endocrinology (Baltimore)* **142**, 2796–2804.

Lavoie, H. B., Taylor, A. E., Sharpless, J. L., Anderson, E. J., Strauss, C. C., and Hall, J. E. (1999). Effects of short term hormone replacement on serum leptin levels in postmenopausal women. *Clin. Endocrinol. (Oxford)* **51**, 415–422.

Lebrethon, M. C., Vandersmissen, E., Gerard, A., Parent, A. S., Junien, J. L., and Bourguignon, J. P. (2000). In vitro stimulation of the prepubertal rat gonadotropin-releasing hormone pulse generator by leptin and neuropeptide Y trough distinct mechanisms. *Endocrinology (Baltimore)* **141**, 1464–1469.

LeDoux, J. E. (1998). Fear and the brain: Where have we been and where are we going? *Biol. Psychiatry* **44**, 1229–1238.

LeDoux, J.E. (1994). The Amygdala: Contributions to fear and stress. *Semin. Neurosci.* **6**, 231–237.

Lehnert, H., Schultz, C., and Dieterich, K. (1998). Physiological and neurochemical aspects of corticotropin-releasing factor actions in the brain: The role of the locus coeruleus. *Neurochem. Res.* **23**, 1039–1052.

Lemaire, V., Taylor, G.T., and Mormede, P. (1997). Adrenal axis activation by chronic social stress fails to inhibit gonadal function in male rats. *Psychoneuroendocrinology* **22**, 563–573.

Lesniewska, B., Nowak, M., and Malendowicz, L. K. (1990). Sex differences in adrenocortical structure and function. XXVIII. ACTH and corticosterone in intact, gonadectomized and gonadal hormone replaced rats. *Horm. Metab. Res.* **22**, 378–381.

Levin, N., Shinsako, J., and Dallman, M. F. (1988). Corticosterone acts on the brain to inhibit adrenalectomy-induced adrenocorticotropin secretion. *Endocrinology (Baltimore)* **122**, 694–704.

Levine, S., Weinberg, J., and Brett, L. P. (1979). Inhibition of pituitary-adrenal activity as a consequence of consummatory behavior. *Psychoneuroendocrinology* **4**, 275–286.

Li, B.-H., and Rowland, N.E. (1995). Effects of vagotomy on cholecystokinin- and dexfenfluramine-induced Fos-like immunoreactivity in the rat brain. *Brain Res. Bull.* **37**, 589–593.

Li, H., Weiss, S. R. B., Chuang, D.-M., Post, R. M., and Rogawski, M. A. (1998). Bidirectional synaptic plasticity in the rat basolateral amygdala: Characterization of an activity-dependent switch sensitive to the presynaptic metabotropic glutamate receptor antagonist 2S-a-ethylglutamic acid. *J. Neurosci.* **18**, 1662–1670.

Li, H.-Y., and Sawchenko, P. E. (1998). Hypothalamic effector neurons and extended circuitries activated in "neurogenic" stress: A comparison of footshock effects exerted acutely, chronically, and in animals with controlled glucocorticoid effects. *J. Comp. Neurol.* **393**, 244–266.

Li, H.-Y., Ericsson, A., and Sawchenko, P. E. (1996). Distinct mechanisms underlie activation of hypothalamic neurosecretory neurons and their medullary catecholaminergic afferents in categorically different stress paradigms. *Proc. Nat. Acad. Sci. U.S.A.* **93**, 2359–2364.

Lightman, S. L., and Young, W. S., III. (1989). Lactation inhibits stress-mediated secretion of corticosterone and oxytocin and hypothalamic accumulation of corticotropin-releasing factor and enkephalin messenger ribonucleic acids. *Endocrinology (Baltimore)* **124**, 2358–2364.

Lilly, M. P., Engeland, W. C., and Gann, D. S. (1983). Responses of cortisol secretion to repeated hemorrhage in the anesthetized dog. *Endocrinology (Baltimore)* **112**, 681–688.

Lilly, M. P., Engeland, W. C., and Gann, D. S. (1986a). Adrenal medullary responses to repeated hemorrhage in conscious dogs. *Am. J. Physiol.* **251**, R1193–R1199.

Lilly, M. P., Engeland, W. C., and Gann, D. S. (1986b). Pituitary-adrenal responses to repeated small hemorrhage in conscious dogs. *Am. J. Physiol.* **251**, R1200–R1207.

Lilly, M. P., Putney, D. J., and Carlson, D. E. (2000). Potentiated responses of corticotropin (ACTH) to repeated moderate hemorrhage requires amygdalar neuronal processing. *Neuroendocrinology* **71**, 88–98.

Lindheim, S. R., Legro, R. S., Bernstein, L., Stanczyk, Z. F., Vijod, M. A., Presser, S. C., and Lobo, R. A. (1992). Behavioral stress responses in premenopausal women and the effects of estrogen. *Am. J. Obstet. Gynecol.* **167**, 1831–1836.

Lindheim, S. R., Lergo, R. S., Morris, R. S., Wong, I. L., Tran, D. Q., Vijod, M. A., Stanczyk, F. Z., and Lobo, R. A. (1994). The effect of progestins on behavioral stress responses in postmenopausal women. *J. Soc. Gynecol. Invest.* **1**, 79–83.

Linthorst, A. C., Falachskamm, C., Hopkins, S. J., Hoadley, M. E., Labeur, M. S., Holsboer, F., and Reul, J. M. (1997). Long-term intracerebroventricular infusion of corticotropin-releasing hormone alters neuroendocrine, neurochemical, autonomic, behavioral and cytokine responses to systemic cytokine challenge. *J. Neurosci.* **17**, 4448–4460.

Liposits, Z., Phelix, C., and Paull, W. K. (1987). Electron microscopic analysis of tyrosine hydroxylase, dopamine-B-hydroxylase and phenylethanolamine-N-methyl transferase immunoreactive innervation of the hypohtalamic paraventricular nucleus in the rat. *Histochemistry* **84**, 105–120.

Liposits, Z., Sievers, L., and Paull, W. K. (1988). Neuropeptide Y- and ACTH-ximmunoactive innervation of corticotropin releasing factor (CRF)-synthesizing neurons in the hypothalamus of the rat. *Histochemistry* **88**, 227–234.

Lopez, J. F., Akil, H., and Watson, S. J. (1999). Neural circuits mediating stress. *Biol. Psychiatry* **46**, 1461–1471.

Louilot, A., and Besson, C. (2000). Specificity of amygdalostriatal interactions in the involvement of mesencephalic dopaminergic neurons in affective perceptions. *Neuroscience* **96**, 73–82.

Lowell, B., and Flier, J. S. (1996). Brown adipose tissue, beta3-adrenergic receptors and obesity. *Ann. Rev. Medi.* **48**, 307–316.

Lowry, C. A., Rodda, J. E., Lightman, S. L., and Ingraham, C. D. (2000). Corticotropin-releasing factor increases in vitro firing rates of serotoninergic neurons in the rat dorsal raphe nucleus: Evidence for activation of a topograhically organized mesolimbic serotoninergic system. *J. Neurosci.* **20**, 7728–7736.

Luukkaa, V., Pesonen, U., Huhtaniemi, I., Lehtonen, A., Tilvis, R., Tuomilehto, J., Koulu, M., and Huupponen, R. (1998). Inverse correlation between serum testosterone and leptin in men. *J. Clin. Endocrinol. Metab.* **83**, 3243–3246.

Macey, D. J., Koob, G. F., and Markou, A. (2000). CRF and urocortin decreased brain stimulation reward in the rat: Reversal by a CRF receptor antagonist. *Brain Res.* **866**, 82–91.

MacLaren, D. P. M., Reilly, T., Campbell, I. T., and Hopkin, C. (1999). Hormonal and metabolic responses to maintained hyperglycemia during prolonged exercise. *J. Appl. Physiol.* **87**, 124–131.

MacLusky, N. J., Naftolin, F., and Leranth, C. (1988). Immunocytochemical evidence for direct synaptic connections between corticotrophin-releasing factor (CRF) and gonadotrophin-releasing hormone (GnRH)-containing neurons in the preoptic area of the rat. *Brain Res.* **439**, 391–395.

MacLusky, N. J., Yuan, H., Elliott, J., and Brown, T. J. (1996). Sex differences in corticosteroid binding in the rat brain: An in vitro autoradiographic study. *Brain Res.* **708**, 71–81.

Mahesh, V. B., and Brann, D. W. (1992). Interaction between ovarian and adrenal steroids in the regulation of gonadotropin secretion. *J. Steroid Biochem. Mol. Biol.* **41**, 495–513.

Mahesh, V. B., and Brann, D. W. (1998). Neuroendocrine mechanisms underlying the control of gonadotropin secretion by steroids. *Steroids* **63**, 252–256.

Makara, G. B., Stark, E., and Palkovits, M. (1970). Afferent pathways of stressful stimuli: Corticotrophin release after hypothalamic deafferentation. *J. Endocrinol.* **47**, 411–416.

Makino, S., Gold, P. W., and Schulkin, J. (1994a). Corticosterone effects on corticotropin-releasing hormone mRNA in the central nucleus of the amygdala and the parvocellular region of the paraventricular nucleus of the hypothalamus. *Brain Res.* **640**, 105–112.

Makino, S., Gold, P. W., and Schulkin, J. (1994b). Effects of corticosterone on CRH mRNA and content in bed nucleus of the stria terminalis; comparison with the effects in the bed nucleus of the amygdala and the paraventricular nucleus of the hypothalamus. *Brain Res.* **657**, 141–149.

Makino, S., Schulkin, J., Smith, M. A., Pacak, K., Palkovits, M., and Gold, P. W. (1995). Regulation of corticotropin-releasing hormone receptor messenger ribonucleic acid in the rat brain and pituitary by glucocorticoids and stress. *Endocrinology (Baltimore)* **136**, 4517–4525.

Makino, S., Asaba, K., Nishiyama, M., and Hashimoto, S. (1999). Decreased type 2 corticotropin-releasing hormone receptor mRNA expression in the ventromedial hypothalamus during repeated immobilization stress. *Neuroendocrinology* **70**, 160–167.

Mamalaki, E., Kvetnansky, R., Brady, L. S., Gold, P. W., and Herkenham, M. (1992). Repeated immobilization stress alters tyrosine hydroxylase, corticotropin-releasing hormone and corticosteroid receptor messenger ribonucleic axis levels in rat brain. *J. Neuroendocrinol.* **4**, 689–699.

Mann, D. R., Evans, D. C., Jacobs, V. L., and Collins, D. C. (1986). Influence of acute intracerebroventricular (i.c.v.) administration of corticotrophin (ACTH) on LH secretion in male rats: Effect of pretreatment with ACTH antiserum on the serum LH responses to an acute ether stress. *J. Endocrinol.* **108**, 275–280.

Mantzoros, C. S., Frederich, R. C., Qu, D., Lowell, B. B., Maratos-Flier, E., and Flier, J. S. (1998). Severe leptin resistance in brown fat-deficient uncoupling protein promoter-driven diptheria toxin A mice despite suppression of hypothalamic neuropeptide Y and circulating corticosterone concentrations. *Diabetes* **47**, 230–238.

Marcilhac, A., Anglade, G., Héry, F., and Siaud, P. (1999a). Effects of bilateral olfactory bulbectomy on the anterior pituitary corticotropic cell activity in male rats. *Horm. Metab. Res.* **31**, 399–401.

Marcilhac, A., Anglade, G., Héry, F., and Siaud, P. (1999b). Olfactory bulbectomy increases vasopressin but not corticotropin-releasing hormone, content in the external layer of the median eminence of male rats. *Neurosci. Lett.* **262**, 89–92.

Marinelli, M., Piazza, P. V., Deroche, V., Maccari, S., Le Moal, M., and Simon, H. (1994). Corticosterone circadian secretion differentially facilitates dopamine-mediated psychomotor effect of cocaine and morphine. *J. Neurosci.* **14**, 2724–2731.

Marinelli, M., Aouizerate, B., Barrot, M., Le Moal, M., and Piazza, P. V. (1998). Dopamine-dependent responses to morphine depend on glucocorticoid receptors. *Proc. Natl. Acad. Sci. U.S.A.* **95**, 7742–7747.

Marks, J. L., Waite, K., and Davies, L. (1996). Intracerebroventricular Neuropeptide Y produces hyperinsulinemia in the presence and absence of food. *Physiol. Behav.* **60**, 685–692.

Marti, O., Harbuz, M. S., Andres, R., Lightman, S. L., and Armario, A. (1999). Activation of the hypothalamic-pituitary axis in adrenalectomized rats: Potentiation by chronic stress. *Brain Res.* **831**, 1–7.

Matera, C., and Wardlaw, S. L. (1994). Aromatization is not required for androgen induced changes in proopiomelanocortin gene expression in the hypothalamus. *Brain Res. Mol. Brain Res.* **27**, 275–280.

McEwen, B. S. (1980). Binding and metabolism of sex steroids by the hypothalamic-pituitary unit: Physiological implications. *Ann. Rev. Physiol.* **42**, 97–110.

McEwen, B. S., de Kloet, E. R., and Rostene, W. (1986). Adrenal steroid receptors and actions in the central nervous system. *Physiol. Rev.* **66**, 1121–1188.

McGaugh, J. L., Cahill, L., and Roozendaal, B. (1996). Involvement of the amygdala in memory storage: Interaction with other brain systems. *Proc. Natl. Acad. Sci. U.S.A.* **93**, 13508–13514.

Meerlo, P., Overkamp, G. J. F., Dann, S., Van den Hoofdakker, R. H., and Koolhaas, J. M. (1996). Changes in behavior and body weight following a single or double social defeat in rats. *Stress* **1**, 21–32.

Melia, K. R., and Duman, R. (1991). Involvement of corticotropin-releasing factor in chronic stress regulation of the brain noradrenergic system. *Proc. Natl. Acad. Sci. U.S.A.* **88**, 8382–8386.

Melia, K. R., Ryabinin, A. E., Schroeder, R., Bloom, F. E., and Wilson, M. C. (1994). Induction and habituation of immediate early gene expression in rat brain by acute and repeated restraint stress. *J. Neurosci.* **14**, 5929–5938.

Merali, Z., McIntosh, J., Kent, P., Michaud, D., and Anisman, H. (1998). Aversive and appetitive events evoke the release of corticotropin-releasing hormone and bombesin-like peptides at the central nucleus of the amygdala. *J. Neurosci.* **18**, 4758–4766.

Mercer, M. E., and Holder, M. D. (1997). Antinociceptive effects of palatable sweet ingesta on human responsivity to pressure pain. *Physiol. Behav.* **61**, 311–318.

Merchenthaler, I., Gorcs, T., Setalo, G., Petrusz, P., and Flerko, B. (1984). Gonadotropin-releasing hormone (GnRH) neurons and pathways in the rat brain. *Cell. Tissue Res.* **237**, 15–29.

Merchenthaler, I., Culler, M. D., Petrusz, P., Flerko, B., and Negro-Vilar, A. (1989). Immunocytochemical localization of the gonadotropin-releasing hormone-associated peptide portion of the LHRH precursor in hypothalamus and extrahypothalamic regions of the rat central nervous system. *Cell. Tissue Res.* **155**, 5–14.

Minor, J. N., and Yamamoto, K. R. (1991). Regulatory crosstalk at composite response elements. *Trends Biochem. Sci.* **16**, 423–426.

Minor, T. R. and Saade, S. (1997). Postsstress glucose mitigates behavioral impairment in rats in the "learned helplessness" model of psychopathology. *Biol. Psychiatry* **42**, 324–334.

Mitome, M., Honma, S., Yoshihara, T., and Honma, K.-I. (1994). Prefeeding increase in paraventricular NE release is regulated by a feeding-associated rhythm in rats. *Am. J. Physiol.* **266**, E606–E611.

Moberg, G. P., and Clark, C. R. (1976). Effect of adrenalectomy and dexamethasone treatment on circadian running in the rat. *Physio. Behav.* **4**, 617–619.

Moga, M. M., and Gray, T. S. (1985). Evidence for corticotropin-releasing factor, neurotensin and somatostatin in the neural pathway from the central nucleus of the amygdala to the parabrachial nucleus. *J. Comp. Neurol.* **241**, 275–284.

Moga, M. M., and Saper, C. B. (1994). Neuropeptide-immunoreactive neurons projecting to the paraventricular hypothalamic nucleus in the rat. *J. Comp. Neurol.* **346**, 137–150.

Moga, M. M., Herbert, H., Hurley, K. M., Yasui, Y., Gray, T. S., and Saper, C. B. (1990). Organization of cortical, basal forebrain, and hypothalamic afferents to the parabrachial nucleus in the rat. *J. Comp. Neurol.* **295,** 624–661.

Moga, M. M., Weis, R. P., and Moore, R. Y. (1995). Efferent projections of the paraventricular thalamic nucleus of the rat. *J. Comp. Neurol.* **359,** 221–238.

Monder, C., Sakai, R. R., Miroff, Y., Blanchard, D. C., and Blanchard, R. J. (1994). Reciprocal changes in plasma corticosterone and testosterone in stressed male rats maintained in a visible burrow system: Evidence for a mediating role of testicular 11-beta-hydroxysteroid dehydrogenase. *Endocrinology (Baltimore)* **134,** 1193–1198.

Monnikes, H., Lauer, G., Bauer, C., Tebbe, J., Zittel, T. T., and Arnold, R. (1997). Pathways of Fos expression in locus coeruleus, dorsal vagal complex and PVN in response to intestinal lipid. *Am. J. Physiol.* **273,** R2059–R2071.

Morgan, J. I., and Curran, T. (1989). Stimulus-transcription coupling in neurons: Role of cellular immediate-early genes. *Trends Neurosci.* **12,** 459–462.

Morgan, J. I., and Curran, T. (1991). Stimulus-transcription coupling in the nervous system: Involvement of the inducible proto-oncogenes fos and jun. *Ann. Rev. Neurosci.* **14,** 421–451.

Morimoto, A., Nakamori, T., Morimoto, K., Tan, N., and Murakami, N. (1993). The central role of corticotropin-releasing factor (CRF1-41) in psychological stress in rats. *J. Physiol. (London)* **460,** 221–229.

Mountjoy, K. G., Robbins, L. S., Mortrud, M. T., and Cone, R. D. (1992). The cloning of a family of genes that encode the melanocortin receptors. *Science* **257,** 1248–1251.

Mounzih, K., Lu, R., and Chehab, F. F. (1997). Leptin treatment rescues the sterility of genetically obese ob/ob males. *Endocrinology (Baltimore)* **138,** 1190–1193.

Mulders, W. H. A. M., Meek, J., Hafmans, T. G. M., and Cools, A. R. (1997). Plasticity in the stress-regulating circuit: Decreased input from the bed nucleus of the stria terminalis to the hypothalamic paraventricular nucleus in Wistar rats following adrenalectomy. *Eur. J. Neurosci.* **9,** 2462–2471.

Murakami, K., Akana, S. F., and Dallman, M. F. (1997). Corticosteroid feedback inhibition of dopamine-B-hydroxylase, and facilitation of acute stress responses. *J. Neuroendocrinol.* **9,** 601–608.

Murray, R., Paul, G. L., Seifert, J. G., and Eddy, D. E. (1991). Response to varying rates of carbohydrate ingestion during exercise. *Med. Sci. Sports Exercise* **23,** 713–718.

Nagai, K., and Nakagawa, H. (1992). "Central Regulation of Energy Metabolism with Special Reference to Circadian Rhythm." CRC Press, Boca Raton, FL.

Nakahara, D., Nakamura, M., Oki, Y., and Ishida, Y. (2000). Lack of glucocorticoids attenuates the self-stimulation-induced increase in the in vivo synthesis rate of dopamine but not serotonin in the rat nucleus accumbens. *Eur. J Neurosci.* **12,** 1495–1500.

Nappi, R. E., and Rivest, S. (1995). Ovulatory cycle influences the stimulatory effect of stress on the expression of corticotropin-releasing factor receptor messenger ribonucleic acid in the paraventricular nucleus of the female rat hypothalamus. *Endocrinology (Baltimore)* **136,** 4073–4083.

Nava, M. P., Fernandez, A., Abelenda, M., and Puerta, M. (1994). Dissociation between brown adipose tissue thermogenesis and sympathetic activity in rats with high plasma levels of oestradiol. *Pfluegers Arch.* **426,** 40–43.

Navarro, M., Spray, K. J., Cubero, M., Thiele, T. E., and Bernstein, I. L. (2000). cFos induction during conditioned taste aversion expression varies with aversion strength. *Brain Res.* **887,** 450–453.

Nelson, C. C., Hendy, S. C., Shukin, R. J., Cheng, H., Bruchovsky, N., Koop, B. F., and Rennie, P. S. (1999). Determinants of DNA sequence specificity of the androgen, progesterone, and glucocorticoid receptors: Evidence for differential steroid receptor response elements. *Mol. Endocrinol.* **13,** 2090–2107.

Nicholson, S. A., Campbell, E. A., Gillham, B., and Jones, M. T. (1987). Recovery of the components of the hypothalamo-pituitary-adrenocortical axis in the rat after chronic treatment with prednisolone. *J. Endocrinol.* **113,** 239–247.

Nijsen, M. J. M. A., Croiset, G., Diamont, M., De Wied, D., and Weigent, V. M. (2001). CRH signalling in the bed nucleus of the stria terminalis is involved in stress-induced cardiac vagal activation in conscious rats. *Neuropsychopharmacology* **24,** 1–10.

Nikicicz, H., Kasprzak, A., and Malendowicz, L. K. (1984). Sex differences in adrenocortical structure and function. XIII. Stereologic studies on adrenal cortex of maturing male and female hamsters. *Cell. Tissue Res.* **235,** 459–462.

Nissenbaum, L. K., and Abercrombie, E. D. (1992). Enhanced tyrosine hydroxylation in hippocampus of chronically stressed rats upon exposure to a novel stressor. *J. Neurochem.* **58,** 276–281.

Nissenbaum, L. K., Zigmond, M. J., Sved, A. F., and Abercrombie, E. D. (1991). Prior exposure to chronic stress results in enhanced synthesis and release of hippocampal norepinephrine in response to a novel stress. *J. Neurosci.* **11,** 1478–1484.

Ohata, H., Suzuki, K., Oki, Y., and Shibasaki, T. (2000). Urocortin in the ventromedial hypothalamic nucleus acts as an inhibitor of feeding behavior in rats. *Brain Res.* **861,** 1–7.

Ohlsson, C., Hellberg, N., Parini, P., Vidal, O., Bohlooly, M., Rudling, M., Lindberg, M. K., Warner, M., Angelin, B., and

Gustafsson, J.-A. (2000). Obesity and disturbed lipoprotein profile in estrogen receptor-α-deficient male mice. *Biochem. Biophys. Res. Commun.* **278**, 640–645.

Okuyama, S., Chaki, S., Kawashima, N., Suzuki, Y., Ogawa, S.-I., Nakazato, A., Kumagai, T., Okubo, T., and Tomisawa, K. (1999). Receptor binding, behavioral and electrophysiological profiles of nonpeptide corticotropin-releasing factor subtype 1 receptor antagonists CRA1000 and CRA 1001. *J. Pharmacol. Exp. Ther.* **289**, 926–935.

Ortiz, J., Decaprio, J. L., Kosten, T. A., and Nestler, E. J. (1995). Strain-selective effects of corticosterone on locomotor sensitization to cocaine and on levels of tyrosine hydroxylase and glucocorticoid receptor in the ventral tegmental area. *Neuroscience* **67**, 383–397.

Otake, K., and Nakamura, Y. (1995). Sites of origin of corticotropin-releasing factor-like immunoreactive projection fibers to the paraventricular thalamic nucleus in the rat. *Neurosci. Lett.* **201**, 84–86.

Otake, K., and Ruggerio, D. A. (1995). Monoamines and nitric oxide are employed by afferents engaged in midline thalamic regulation. *J. Neurosci.* **15**, 1891–1911.

Otake, K., Reis, D. J., and Ruggiero, D. A. (1994). Afferents to the midline thalamus issue collaterals to the nucleus tractus solitarii: An anatomical basis for thalamic and visceral reflex integration. *J. Neurosci.* **14**, 5694–5707.

Otake, K., Ruggerio, D. A., and Nakamura, Y. (1995). Adrenergic innervation of forebrain neurons that project to the paraventricular thalamic nucleus in the rat. *Brain Res.* **697**, 17–26.

Otten, A. D., Sanders, M. M., and McKnight, G. S. (1988). The MMTV LTR promoter is insuced by progesterone and dihydrotestosterone but not by estrogen. *Mol. Endocrinol.* **2**, 143–147.

Ottenweller, J. E., Natelson, B. H., Pitman, D. L., and Drastal, S. D. (1989). Adrenocortical and behavioral responses to repeated stressors: Toward an animal model of chronic stress and stress-related mental illness. *Biol. Psychiatry* **26**, 829–841.

Ottenweller, J. E., Servatius, R. J., Tapp, W. N., Drastal, S. D., Bergen, M. T., and Natelson, B. H. (1992). A chronic stress state in rats: Effects of repeated stress on basal corticosterone and behavior. *Physiol. Behav.* **51**, 689–698.

Owens, M. J., and Nemeroff, C. B. (1991). Physiology and pharmacology of corticotropin-releasing factor. *Pharmacol. Rev.* **43**, 425–473.

Owens, M. J., Bartolome, J., Schanberg, S. M., and Nemeroff, C. B. (1990). Corticotropin-releasing factor concentrations exhibit an apparent diurnal rhythm in hypothalamic and extrahypothalamic brain regions: Differential sensitivity to corticosterone. *Neuroendocrinology* **52**, 626–631.

Pacak, K., Palkovits, M., Kopin, I. J., and Goldstein, D. S. (1995). Stress-induced norepinephrine release in hypothalamic par-

aventricular nucleus and pituitary-adrenocortical and sympathoadrenal activity: *In vivo* microdialysis studies. *Front. Neuroendocrinol.* **16**, 89–150.

Pacak, K., Palkovits, M., Makino, S., Kopin, I. J., and Goldstein, D. S. (1996). Brainstem hemisection decreases corticotropin-releasing hormone mRNA in the paraventricular nucleus but not in the central amygdaloid nucleus. *J. Neuroendocrinol.* **8**, 543–551.

Palkovits, M. (1999). Interconnections between the neuroendocrine hypothalamus and the central autonomic system. *Front. Neuroendocrinol.* **20**, 270–295.

Palkovits, M., Young, W. S., III, Kovacs, K., Toth, T., and Makara, G. B. (1998). Alterations in corticotropin-releasing hormone gene expression of central amygdaloid neurons following long-term paraventricular lesions and adrenalectomy. *Neuroscience* **85**, 135–147.

Palkovits, M., Baffi, J. S., and Pacak, K. (1999). The role of ascending neuronal pathways in stress-induced release of norepinephrine in the hypothalamic-paraventricular nucleus of rats. *J. Neuroendocrinol.* **11**, 529–539.

Pan, B., Castro-Lopes, J. M., and Coimbra, A. (1997). Chemical sensory deafferentation abolishes hypothalamic-pituitary activation induced by noxious stimulation or electroacupuncture, but only decreases that caused by immobilization stress. A c-fos study. *Neuroscience* **78**, 1059–1068.

Pardridge, W. M. (1981). Transport of protein-bound hormones into tissues *in vivo*. *Endocr. Rev.* **2**, 103–123.

Parkes, D., Rivest, K., Lee, S., Rivier, C., and Vale, W. (1993). Corticotropin-releasing factor activates c-fos, NGFI-B and CRF gene expression within the paraventricular nucleus of the rat hypothalamus. *Mol. Endocrinol.* **7**, 1357–1367.

Patchev, V. K., and Almeida, O. F. (1996). Gonadal steroids exert facilitating and "buffering" effects on glucocorticoid-mediated transcriptional regulation of corticotropin-releasing hormone and corticosteroid receptor genes in rat brain. *J. Neurosci.* **16**, 7077–7084.

Patchev, V. K., and Almeida, O. F. (1998). Gender specificity in the neural regulation of the response to stress: New leads from classical paradigms. *Mol. Biol.* **16**, 63–77.

Paulmyer-Lacroix, O., Hery, F., Mugeat, M., and Grino, M. (1996). The modulatory role of estrogens on corticotropin-releasing factor gene expression in the hypothalamic paraventricular nucleus of ovariectomized female rats: Role of the adrenal gland. *J. Neuroendocrinol.* **8**, 515–519.

Pavcovich, L. A., and Valentino, R. J. (1997). Regulation of a putative neurotransmitter effect of corticotropin-releasing factor: Effects of adrenalectomy. *J. Neurosci.* **17**, 401–408.

Pavcovich, L. A., Cancela, L. M., Volosin, M., Molina, V. A., and Ramirez, O. A. (1990). Chronic stress-induced changes in locul coeruleus neuronal activity. *Brain Res. Bull.* **24**, 293–296.

Pedersen, S. B., Borglum, J. D., Eriksen, E. F., and Richelsen, B. (1991). Nuclear estradiol binding in rat adipocytes. Regional variations and regulatory influences of hormones. *Biochim. Biophys. Acta* **1093**, 80–86.

Pedersen, S. B., Fuglsig, S., Sjögren, P., and Richelsen, B. (1996). Identification of steroid receptors in human adipose tissue. *Eur. J. Clin. Invest.* **26**, 1051–1056.

Pellymounter, M. A., Cullen, M. J., Baker, M. B., Hecht, R., Winters, D., Boone, T., and Collins, F. (1995). Effects of the obese gene product on body weight regulation in ob/ob mice. *Science* **269**, 540–543.

Pellymounter, M. A., Joppa, M., Carmouche, M., Cullen, M. J., Brown, B., Murphy, B., Grigoriadis, D. E., Ling, N., and Foster, A. C. (2000). Role of corticotropin-releasing factor (CRF) receptors in the anorexic syndrome induced by CRF. *J. Pharmacol. Exp. Ther.* **293**, 799–806.

Penicaud, L., Cousin, B., Leloup, C., Lorsignol, A., and Casteilla, L. (2000). The autonomic nervous system, adipose tissue plasticity, and energy balance. *Nutrition* **16**, 903–908.

Pennartz, C. M. A., Groenewegen, H. J., and Lopes da Silva, F. H. (1994). The nucleus accumbens as a complex of functionally distinct neuronal ensembles: An integration of behavioural and anatomical data. *Prog. Neurobiol.* **42**, 719–761.

Petrovich, G. D., and Swanson, L. W. (1997). Projections of the lateral part of the central amygdalar nucleus to the postulated fear conditioning circuit. *Brain Res.* **763**, 247–254.

Petrovich, G. D., Risold, P. Y., and Swanson, L. W. (1996). Organization of projections from the basomedial nucleus of the amygdala: A PHAL study in the rat. *J. Comp. Neurol.* **374**, 387–420.

Pezzone, M. A., Lee, W.-S., Hoffman, G. E., Pezzone, K. M., and Rabin, B. S. (1993). Activation of brainstem catecholaminergic neurons by conditioned and unconditioned aversive stimuli as revealed by c-Fos immunoreactivity. *Brain Res.* **608**, 310–318.

Piazza, P. V., and Le Moal, M. (1997). Glucocorticoids as a biological substrate of reward: Physiological and pathophysiological implications. *Brain Res. Rev.* **25**, 359–372.

Piazza, P. V., and Le Moal, M. (1998). The role of stress in drug self-administration. *Trends Pharmacol. Sci.* **19**, 67–74.

Piazza, P. V., Deroche, V., Deminiere, J.-M., Maccari, S., Le Moal, M., and Simon, H. (1993). Corticosterone in the range of stress-induced levels possesses reinforcing properties: Implications for sensation-seeking behaviors. *Proc. Natl. Acad. Sci. U.S.A.* **90**, 11738–11742.

Piazza, P. V., Rouge-Pont, F., Derche, V., Maccari, S., and Simon, H., Le Moal, M. (1996). Glucocorticoids have state-dependent stimulant effects on the mesencephalic dopamin-

ergic transmission. *Proc. Natl. Acad. Sci. U.S.A.* **93**, 8716–8720.

Piccinelli, M., and Wilkinson, B. (2000). Gender differences in depression. *Br. J. Psychiatry* **177**, 486–492.

Pich, E. M., Koob, G. F., Heilig, M., Menzaghi, F., Vale, W., and Weiss, F. (1993). Corticotropin-releasing factor release from the mediobasal hypothalamus of the rat as measured by microdialysis. *Neuroscience* **55**, 695–707.

Pikkarainen, M., Ronkko, S., Savander, V., Insausti, R., and Pitkanen, A. (1999). Projections from the lateral, basal and accessory basal nuclei of the amygdala to the hippocampal formation in the rat. *J. Comp. Neurol.* **403**, 229–260.

Pitkanen, A., Savander, V., and LeDoux, J. E. (1997). Organization of intra-amygdaloid circuitries in the rat: An emerging framework for understanding functions of teh amygdala. *Trends Neurosci.* **20**, 517–523.

Pittman, D. L., Ottenweller, J. E., and Natelson, B. H. (1990). Effect of stressor intensity on habituation and sensitization of glucocorticoid responses in rats. *Behav. Neurosci.* **104**, 28–36.

Plotsky, P. M. (1987). Facilitation of immunoreactive corticotropin-releasing factor secretion into the hypophysial-portal circulation after activation of catecholaminergic pathways or central norepinephrine injection. *Endocrinology (Baltimore)* **121**, 924–930.

Plotsky, P. M. (1989). Regulation of the adrenocortical axis: Hypophysiotropic coding, catecholamines and glucocorticoids. *In* "The Control of the Hypothalamo-Pituitary-Adrenocortical Axis" (F. C. Rose, ed.), pp. 131–146.

Plotsky, P. M. (1991). Pathways to the secretion of adrenocorticotropin: A view from the portal. *J. Neuroendocrinol.* **3**, 1–9.

Plotsky, P. M., and Sawchenko, P. E. (1987). Hypophysial-portal plasma levels, median eminence content and immunohistochemical staining of corticotropin-releasing factor, arginine vasopressin and oxytocin after pharmacological adrenalectomy. *Endocrinology (Baltimore)* **120**, 1361–1369.

Plotsky, P. M., Cunningham, E. T., Jr., and Widmaier, E. P. (1989). Catecholaminergic modulation of corticotropin-releasing factor and adrenocorticotropin secretion. *Endocr. Rev.* **10**, 437–458.

Plymate, S. R., Tenover, J. S., and Bremner, W. J. (1989). Circadian variation in testosterone, sex hormone binding globulin, and calculated non-sex hormone binding globlin bound testosterone in healthy young and elderly men. *J. Androl.* **10**, 366–371.

Poehlman, E. T., and Tchernof, A. (1998). Traversing the menopause: Changes in energy expenditure and body composition. *Coronary Artery Dis.* **9**, 799–803.

Poletti, A., and Martini, L. (1999). Androgen-activating enzymes in the central nervous system. *J. Steroid Biochem. Mol. Biol.* **69**, 117–122.

Porter, D. W., Lincoln, D. W., and Naylor, A. M. (1989). Plasma cortisol is increased during the inhibition of LH secretion by central LHRH in the ewe. *Neuroendocrinology* **51**, 705–712.

Pralong, F. P., Voirol, M., Giacomini, M., Gaillard, R. C., and Grouzmann, E. (2000). Acceleration of pubertal development following central blockade of the Y1 subtype of neuropeptide Y receptors. *Regul. Pept.* **95**, 47–52.

Prewitt, C. M., and Herman, J. P. (1997). Hypothalamo-pituitary-adrenocortical regulation following lesions of the central nucleus of the amygdala. *Stress* **4**, 263–279.

Prewitt, C. M., and Herman, J. P. (1998). Anatomical interactions between the central amygdaloid nucleus and the hyptohalamic paraventricular nucleus of the rat: A dual tract-tracing analysis. *J. Chem. Neuroanat.* **15**, 173–185.

Puerta, M., Abelenda, M., Nava, M. P., and Fernandez, A. (1993). Reduced noradrenaline responsivensess of brown adypocites isolated from estradiol-treated rats. *Can. J. Physiol. Pharmacol.* **71**, 858–861.

Purba, J. S., Hoogendijk, W. J. G., Hofman, M. A., and Swaab, D. F. (1996). Increased number of vasopressin- and oxytocin-expressing neurons in the paraventricular nucleus of the hypothalamus in depression. *Arch. Gen. Psychiatry* **53**, 137–143.

Putnam, C. D., Brann, D. W., and Mahesh, V. B. (1991). Acute activation of the adrenocorticotropin-adrenal axis: Effect on gonadotropin and prolactin secretion in the female rat. *Endocrinology (Baltimore)* **128**, 2558–2566.

Quirarte, G. L., Roozendaal, B., and McGaugh, J. L. (1997). Glucocorticoid enhancement of memory storage involves noradrenergic activation in the basolateral amygdala. *Proc. Natl. Acad. Sci. U.S.A.* **94**, 14048–14053.

Quirce, C. M., and Maickel, R. P. (1981). Alterations of biochemical parameters by acute and repetitive stress situations in mice. *Psychoneuroendocrinology* **6**, 91–97.

Raadsheer, F. C., Hoogendijk, W. J. G., Stam, F. C., Tilders, F. H. J., and Swaab, D. F. (1994). Increased numbers of corticotropin-releasing hormone expressing neurons in the hypothalamic paraventricular nucleus of depressed patients. *Neuroendocrinology* **60**, 433–436.

Raposinho, P. D., Broqua, P., Pierroz, D. D., Hayward, A., Dumont, Y., Quirion, R., Junien, J. L., and Aubert, M. L. (1999). Evidence that the inhibition of luteinizing hormone secretion exerted by central adminstration of neuropeptide Y (NPY) in the rat is predominantly mediated by the NPY-Y5 receptor subtype. *Endocrinology (Baltimore)* **140**, 4046–4055.

Ratka, A., Sutanto, W., Bloemers, M., and de Kloet, E. R. (1989). On the role of brain mineralocorticoid (type I) and glucocorticoid (type II) receptors in neuroendocrine regulations. *Neuroendocrinology* **50**, 117–123.

Rebuffe-Scrive, M., Walsh, U. A., McEwen, B., and Rodin, J. (1992). Effect of chronic stress and exogenous glucocorticoids on regional fat distribution and metabolism. *Physiol. Behav.* **52**, 583–590.

Redberg, R. F., Nishino, M., McElhinney, D. B., Dae, M. W., and Botvinick, E. H. (2000). Long-term estrogen replacement therapy is associated with improved excercise capacity in postmenopausal women without known coronary artery disease. *Am. Heart J.* **139**, 739–744.

Redei, E., Li, L., Halasz, I., McGivern, R. F., and Aird, F. (1994). Fast glucocorticoid feedback inhibition of ACTH secretion in the ovariectomized rat: Effect of chronic estrogen and progesterone. *Neuroendocrinology* **60**, 113–123.

Reul, J. M. H. M., and de Kloet, E. R. (1985). Two receptor systems for corticosterone in rat brain: Microdistribution and differential occupation. *Endocrinology (Baltimore)* **117**, 2505–2511.

Richard, D. (1993). Involvement of corticotropin-releasing factor in the control of food intake and energy expenditure. *Ann. N. Y. Acad. Sci.* **697**, 155–172.

Richter, C. P., Bunch, G. H. J., and Wooden, H. E. J. (1941). Sodium chloride and dextrose appetite of untreated and treated adrenalectomized rats. *Endocrinology (Baltimore)* **29**, 115–125.

Risold, P. Y., Thompson, R. H., and Swanson, L. W. (1997). The structural organization of connections between hypothalamus and cerebral cortex. *Brain Res. Rev.* **24**, 197–224.

Rivest, S., and Laflamme, N. (1995). Neuronal activity and neuropeptide gene transcription in brains of immune-challenged rats. *J. Neuroendocrinol.* **7**, 501–525.

Rivest, S., Laflamme, N., and Nappi, R. E. (1995). Immune challenge and immobilization stress induce transcription of the gene encoding the CRF receptor in selective nuclei of the hypothalamus. *J. Neurosci.* **15**, 2680–2695.

Rivier, C., and Rivest, S. (1991). Effect of stress on the activity of the hypothalamo-pituitary-gonadal axis: Peripheral and central mechanisms. *Biol. Reprod.* **45**, 523–532.

Rivier, C., Rivier, J., and Vale, W. (1986). Stress-induced inhibition of reproductive functions: Role of endogenous corticotropin-releasing factor. *Science* **231**, 607–609.

Robbins, T. W., and Everitt, B. J. (1996). Neurobehavioural mechanisms of reward and motivation. *Curr. Opin. Neurobiol.* **6**, 228–236.

Roelfsema, F., van der Berg, G., Frolich, M., Veldhuis, J. D., van Eijk, A., Buurman, M. M., and Etman, B. H. (1993). Sex-dependent alteration in cortisol response to endogenous adrenocorticotropin. *J. Clin. Endocrinol. Metab.* **77**, 234–240.

Rohner-Jeanrenaud, F. (1995). A neuroendocrine reappraisal of the dual-centre hypothesis: Its implications for obesity and insulin resistance. *Int. J. Obes.* **19**, 517–534.

Romero, L. M., Levine, S., and Sapolsky, R. M. (1995). Patterns of adrenocorticotropin secretagog release in response to social interactions and various degrees of novelty. *Psychoneuroendocrinology* **20**, 183–191.

Roozendaal, B., and McGaugh, J. L. (1997a). Basolateral amygdala lesions block the memory-enhancing effect of glucocorticiod administration in the rat. *Eur. J. Neurosci.* **9**, 76–83.

Roozendaal, B., and McGaugh, J. L. (1997b). Glucocorticoid receptor agonist and antagonist administration into the basolateral but not central amygdala modulates memory storage. *Neurobiol. Learn. Mem.* **67**, 176–179.

Roozendaal, B., Williams, C. L., and McGaugh, J. L. (1999). Glucocorticoid receptor activation in the rat nucleus of the solitary tract facilitates memory consolidation: Involvement of the basolateral amygdala. *Eur. J. Neurosci.* **11**, 1317–1323.

Rosenbaum, M., Nocolson, M., Hirsh, J., Heymsfield, S. B., Gallagher, D., Chu, F., and Leibel, R. L. (1996). Effects of gender, body composition and menopause on plasma concentrations of leptin. *J. Clin. Endocrinol. Metab.* **81**, 1344–1347.

Rosner, W. (1990). The functions of corticosteroid-binding globulin and sex hormone-binding globulin: Recent advances. *Endoc. Rev.* **11**, 80–91.

Rothwell, N. J., (1989). CRF is involved in the pyrogenic and thermogenic effects of interleukin 1beta in the rat. *Am. J. Physiol.* **256**, E111–E115.

Roy, B. N., Reid, R. L., and Van Vugt, D. A. (1999). The effects of estrogen and progesterone on corticotropin-releasing hormone and arginine vasopressin messenger ribonucleic acid levels in the paraventricular nucleus and supraoptic nucleus of the rhesus monkey. *Endocrinology (Baltimore)* **140**, 2191–2198.

Roy, E. J., and Wade, G. N. (1975). Role of estrogens in androgen induced spontaneus activity in male rats. *J. Comp. Physiol. Psychol.* **89**, 573–579.

Rupprecht, R., Reul, J. M., van Steensel, B., Spengler, D., M. S., Berning, B., Holsboer, F., and Damm, K. (1993). Pharmacological and functional characterization of human mineralocorticoid and glucocorticoid receptor ligands. *Eur. J. Pharmacol.* **247**, 145–154.

Russell, C. D., Petersen, R. N., Rao, S. P., Ricci, M. R., and Prasad, A. (1998). Leptin expression in adipose tissue from obese humans: Depot-specific reguation by insulin and dexamethasone. *Am. J. Physiol.* **275**, E507–E515.

Sadamoto, T., Kusano, M., and Yamagiwa, T. (2000). Attenuated cardiovascular adjustment to sustained static exercise after carbohydrate loading. *J. Auton. Nerv. Syst.* **80**, 175–182.

Saito, M., Nishimura, K., and Kato, H. (1989). Modification of circadian cortisol rhythm by cyclic and continuous enteral nutrition. *J. Nutr. Sci. Vitaminol.* **35**, 639–647.

Saltzman, W., Schultz-Darken, N. J., Wegner, F. H., Wittwer, D. J., and Abbott, D. H. (1998). Suppression of cortisol levels in subordinate female marmosets: Reproductive and social contributions. *Horm. Behav.* **33**, 58–74.

Sanchez, M. M., Aguado, F., Sanchez-Toscano, F., and Saphier, D. (1995). Adrenalectomy alters the response of neurons in the bed nucleus of the stria terminalis to electrical stimulation of the medial amygdala. *Brain Res. Bull.* **36**, 63–69.

Sanchez, M. M., Young, L. J., Plotsky, P. M., and Insel, T. R. (2000). Distribution of corticosteroid receptors in the rhesus brain: Relative absence of glucocorticoid receptors in the hippocampal formation. *J. Neurosci.* **20**, 4657–4668.

Sanghera, M. K., Simpson, E. R., McPhaul, M. J., Kozlowski, G., Conley, A. J., and Lephart, E. D. (1991). Immunocytochemical distribution of aromatase cytochrome P450 in the rat brain using peptide-generated polyclonal antibodies. *Endocrinology (Baltimore)* **129**, 2834–2844.

Sapolsky, R. M. (1982). The endocrine stress-response and social status in the wild baboon. *Horm. Behav.* **16**, 279–292.

Sapolsky, R. M. (1987). "Stress, Social Status and Reproductive Physiology in Free-living Baboons." Prentice-Hall, Englewood Cliffs, NJ.

Sawchenko, P. E. (1987). Evidence for a local site of action for glucocorticoids in inhibiting CRF and vasopressin expression in the paraventricular nucleus. *Brain Res.* **403**, 213–224.

Sawchenko, P. E., and Swanson, L. W. (1982). The organization of noradrenergic pathways from the brainstem to the paraventricular and supraoptic nuclei in the rat. *Brain Res. Rev.* **4**, 275–325.

Sawchenko, P. E., and Swanson, L. W. (1983). The organization of forebrain afferents to the paraventricular and supraoptic nuclei of the rat. *J. Comp. Neurol.* **218**, 121–144.

Sawchenko, P. E., and Swanson, L. W. (1989). Organization of CRF immunoreactive cells and fibers in the rat brain: Immunohistochemical studies. In "CRC Critical Reviews in Corticotropin-releasing Factor: Basic and Clinical Studies of a Neuropeptide" pp. 29–51. CRC Press, Boca Raton, FL.

Sawchenko, P. E., Imaki, T., Potter, E., Kovacs, K., J. L., and Vale, W. (1993). The functional neuroanatomy of corticotropin-releasing factor. *Ciba Found. Symp.* **172**, 5–21.

Sawchenko, P. E., Li, H.-Y., and Ericsson, A. (2000). Circuits and mechanisms governing hypothalamic responses to stress: A tale of two paradigms. *Prog. Brain Res.* **122**, 61–78.

Scarpace, P. J., Matheny, M., Pollock, B. H., and Tumer, N. (1997). Leptin increases uncoupling protein expression and energy expenditure. *Am. J. Physiol.* **273**, E226–E230.

Schoenfeld, N. M., Leatham, J. H., and Rabii, J. (1980). Maturation of adrenal stress responsiveness in the rat. *Neuroendocrinology* **31**, 101–105.

Schulkin, J., McEwen, B. S., and Gold, P. W. (1994). Allostasis, amygdala, and anticipatory angst. *Neurosci. Biobehav. Rev.* **18**, 385–396.

Schulz, C., and Lehnert, H. (1996). Activation of noradrenergic neurons in the locus coeruleus by corticotropin-releasing factor. *Neuroendocrinology* **63**, 454–458.

Schwartz, M. W., Dallman, M. F., and Woods, S. C. (1995). The hypothalamic response to starvation: Implications for the study of wasting disorders. *Am. J. Physiol.* **269**, R949–R957.

Scimonelli, T. N., and Celis, M. E. (1987). Effect of gonadectomy and reposition of gonadal steroids on alpha-menalocyte-stimulating hormone concentration in discrete hypothalamic areas during a 24-h period. *Neuroendocrinology* **45**, 441–445.

Scribner, K. A., Walker, C.-D., Cascio, C. S., and Dallman, M. F. (1991). Chronic streptozotocin diabetes in rats facilitates the acute stress response without altering pituitary or adrenal responsiveness to secretagogues. *Endocrinology (Baltimore)* **129**, 99–108.

Scribner, K. A., Akana, S. F., Walker, C.-D., and Dallman, M. F. (1993). Streptozotocin-diabetic rats exhibit facilitated adrenocorticotropin responses to acute stress, but normal sensitivity to feedback by corticosteroids. *Endocrinology (Baltimore)* **133**, 2667–2674.

Seeman, T. E., Singer, B., and Charpentier, P. (1995). Gender differences in patterns of HPA axis response to challenge: Macarthur suties of successful aging. *Psychoneuroendocrinology* **20**, 711–725.

Seidenstadt, R. W., and Eaton, K. E. (1978). Adrenal and ovarian regulation of salt and sucrose consumption. *Physiol. Behav.* **21**, 313–316.

Seidman, S. N., and Rabkin, J. G. (1998). Testosterone replacement therapy for hypogonadal men with SSRI-refractory depression. *J. Affect. Disord.* **48**, 157–161.

Seidman, S. N., and Walsh, B. T. (1999). Testosterone and depression in aging men. *Am. J. Geriat. Psychiatry* **7**, 18–33.

Sencar-Cupovic, I., and Milkovic, S. (1976). The development of sex differences in the adrenal morphology and responsiveness in stress of rats from birth to the end of life. *Mech. Ageing Dev.* **5**, 1–19.

Serova, L., Danailov, E., Chamas, F., and Sabban, E. L. (1999). Nicotine infusion modulates immobilization stress-triggered induction of gene expression of rat catecholamine biosynthetic enzymes. *J. Pharmacol. Exp. Ther.* **291**, 884–892.

Shaham, Y. S. E., Funk, D., Erb, S., Brown, T. J., Walker, C.-D., and Stewart, J. (1997). Corticotropin-releasing factor, but not corticosterone, is involved in stress-induced relapse to heroin seeking in rats. *J. Neurosci.* **17**, 2605–2614.

Shaham, Y. S. E., Leung, S., Buczek, Y., and Stewart, J. (1998). CP-154,526, a selective non-peptide antagonist of the corticotropin-releasing factor1 receptor attenuates stress-induced relapse to drug seeking in cocaine- and heroin-treated rats. *Psychopharmacology* **137**, 184–190.

Shepard, J. D., Barron, K. W., and Myers, D. A. (2000). Corticosterone delivery to the amygdala increases corticotropin-releasing factor mRNA in the central amygdaloid nucleus and anxiety-like behavior. *Brain Res.* **861**, 288–295.

Shiraishi, I., Honma,K.-I., Honma, S., and Hiroshige, T. (1984). Ethosecretogram: Relation of behavior to plasma corticosterone in freely moving rats. *Am. J. Physiol.* **247**, R40–R45.

Shoaib, M., and Shippenberg, T. S. (1996). Adrenalectomy attenuates nicotine-induced dopamine release and locomotor activity in rats. *Psychopharmacology* **128**, 343–350.

Shughrue, P. J., Lane, M. V., and Merchenthaler, I. (1997). Comparative distribution of estrogen receptor-alpha and -beta mRNA in the rat central nervous system. *J. Comp. Neurol.* **388**, 507–525.

Sillence, M. N., and Rodway, R. G. (1990). Effects of trenbolone acetate and testosterone on growth and on plasma concentrations of corticosterone and ACTH in rats. *J. Endocrinol.* **126**, 461–466.

Silva, T. A. (1977). Saccharin aversion in the rat following adrenalectomy. *Physiol. Behav.* **19**, 239–244.

Silverman, A. J., Hoffman, D. L., and Zimmerman, E. A. (1981). The descending afferent connections of the paraventricular nucleus of the hypothalamus (PVN). *Brain Res. Bull.* **6**, 47–61.

Simerly, R. B., and Swanson, L. W. (1988). Projections of the medial preoptic nucleus: A *Phaseolus vulgaris* leucoagglutinin anterograde tract-tracing study in the rat. *J. Comp. Neurol.* **270**, 209–242.

Simerly, R. B., Chang, C., Muramatsu, M., and Swanson, L. W. (1990). Distribution of androgen and estrogen receptor mRNA-containing cells in the rat brain: And in situ hybridization study. *J. Comp. Neurol.* **294**, 76–95.

Smagin, G. N., and Dunn, A. J. (2000). The role of CRF receptor subtypes in stress-induced behavioral responses. *Eur. J. Pharmacol.* **405**, 199–206.

Smagin, G. N., Swiergiel, A. H., and Dunn, A. J. (1995). corticotropin-releasing factor administered into the locus coeruleus, but not the parabrachial nucleus, stimulates norepinephrine release in the prefrontal cortex. *Brain Res. Bull.* **36**, 71–76.

Smagin, G. N., Howell, L. A., Ryan, D. H., De Souza, E. B., and Harris, R. B. (1998). The role of CRF2 receptors in corticotropin-releasing factor- and urocortin-induced anorexia. *NeuroReport* **9**, 1601–1606.

Smagin, G. N., Howell, L. A., Redmann, S., Jr., Ryan, D. H., and Harris, R. B. H. (1999). Prevention of stress-induced weight loss by third ventricular CRF receptor antagonist. *Am. J. Physiol.* **268**, R1461–R1469.

Smith, C. J., and Norman, R. L. (1987). Circadian periodicity in circulating cortisol is absent after orchidectomy in rhesus macaques. *Endocrinology (Baltimore)* **121**, 2186–2191.

Spencer, R. L., Young, E. A., Choo, P. H., and McEwen, B. S. (1990). Adrenal steroid type I and type II receptor binding: Estimates of in vivo receptor number, occupancy, and activation with varying level of steroid. *Brain Res.* **514**, 37–48.

Spencer, R. L., Miller, A. H., Stein, M., and McEwen, B. S. (1991). Corticosterone regulation of type I and type II adrenal steroid receptors in brain, pituitary, and immune tissue. *Brain Res.* **549**, 236–246.

Spencer, R. L., Miller, A. H., Moday, H., Stein, M., and McEwen, B. S. (1993). Diurnal differences in basal and acute stress levels of type I and type II adrenal steroid activation in neural and immune tissues. *Endocrinology (Baltimore)* **133**, 1941–1950.

Spencer, R. L., Paul, J. K., Kalman, B. A., and Cole, M. A. (1998). Evidence for mineralocorticoid receptor facilitation of glucocorticoid receptor-dependent regulation of hypothalamo-pituitary-adrenal activity. *Endocrinology (Baltimore)* **139**, 2718–2736.

Stanley, B. G., Kyrkouli, S. E., Lampert, S., and Leibowitz, S. F. (1986). Neuropeptide Y chronically injected into the hypohtalamus: A powerful neurochemical inducer of hyperphagia and obesity. *Peptides (N.Y.)* **7**, 1189–1192.

Steffens, A. B., Strubbe, J. H., and Scheurink, A. J. W. (1993). Circadian rhythmicity in autonomic nervous system functioning. *In* "New Functional Aspects of the Suprachiasmatic Nucleus of the Hypothalamus" (H. Nakagawa, Y. Oomura, and K. Nagai, eds.), pp. 241–247. John Libbey Press, London.

Steiner, R. A., Kabigting, E. B., Lent, K., and Clifton, D. K. (1994). Diurnal rhythm in proopiomelanocortin mRNA in the arcuate nucleus of the male rat. *J. Neuroendocrinol.* **6**, 603–608.

Stern, J. M., and Levine, S. (1974). Psychobiological aspects of lactation in rats. *Prog. Brain Res.* **41**, 433–444.

Stock, S. M., Saude, E. M., and Bremme, K. A. (1999). Leptin levels vary significantly during the menstrual cycle, preganancy, and in vitro fertilization treatment: Possible relation to estradiol. *Fertil. Steril.* **72**, 657–662.

Stokkan, K.-A., Yamazaki, S., Tei, H., Sakai, Y., and Menaker, M. (2001). Entrainment of the circadian clock in the liver by feeding. *Science* **291**, 490–493.

Stout, S. C., Mortas, P., Owens, M. J., Nemeroff, C. B., and Moreau, J.-L. (2000). Increased corticotropin-releasing factor concentrations in the bed nucleus of the stria terminalis of anhedonic rats. *Eur. J. Pharmacol.* **401**, 39–46.

Strack, A. M., Sebastian, R. J., Schwartz, M. W., and Dallman, M. F. (1995a). Glucocorticoids and insulin: Reciprocal signals for energy balance. *Am. J. Physiol.* **268**, R142–R149.

Strack, A. M., Horsley, C. J., Sebastian, R. J., Akana, S. F., and Dallman, M. F. (1995b). Glucocorticoids and insulin: Complex interaction on brown adipose tissue. *Am. J. Physiol.* **268**, R1209–R1216.

Strunkard, A. J., Grace, W. J., and Wolff, H. G. (1955). The night eating syndrome: A pattern of food intake among certain obese patients. *Am. J. Med.* **19**, 78–86.

Stutzmann, G. E., McEwen, B. S., and LeDoux, J. E. (1998). Serotonin modulation of sensory inputs to the lateral amygdala: Dependency on corticosterone. *J. Neurosci.* **18**, 9529–9538.

Su, H.-S., and Bentivoglio, M. (1990). Thalamic midline cell populations projecting to the nucleus accumbens, amygdala and hippocampus in the rat. *J. Comp. Neurol.* **297**, 582–593.

Suda, T., Tozawa, F., Iwai, I., Sato, Y., Sumitomo, T., Nakano, Y., Yamada, M., and Demura, H. (1993). Neuropeptide Y increases the corticotropin-releasing factor messenger ribonucleic acid level in the rat hypothalamus. *Mol. Brain Res.* **18**, 311–315.

Sutton, R. E., Koob, G. F., Le Moal, M., Rivier, J., and Vale, W. (1982). Corticotropin-releasing factor (CRF) produces behavioral activation in rats. *Nature (London)* **297**, 331–333.

Sutton, S. W., Mitsugi, N., Plostky, P. M., and Sarkar, D. K. (1988). Neuropeptide Y (NPY): A possible role in the initiation of puberty. *Endocrinology (Baltimore)* **123**, 2152–2154.

Swanson, L. W. (1976). An autoradiographic study of efferent connections of the preoptic region in the rat. *J. Comp. Neurol.* **167**, 227–256.

Swanson, L. W. (1987). "The Hypothalamus." Am. Elsevier, New York.

Swanson, L. W., and Petrovich, G. (1998). What is the amygdala? *Trends Neurosci.* **21**, 323–331.

Swanson, L. W., and Simmons, D. M. (1989). Differential steroid hormone and neural influences on peptide mRNA levels in CRH cells of the paraventricular nucleus: A hybridization histochemical study in the rat. *J. Comp. Neurol.* **285**, 413–435.

Swanson, L. W., Sawchenko, P. E., Rivier, J., and Vale, W. W. (1983). Organization of ovine corticotropin-releasing factor immunoreactive cells and fibers in the rat brain: An immunohistochemical study. *Neuroendocrinology* **36**, 165–186.

Swerdloff, R. S., Batt, R. A., and Bray, G. A. (1976). Reproductive hormonal function in the genetically obese (ob/ob) mouse. *Endocrinology (Baltimore)* **98**, 1359–1364.

Szafarczyk, A., Guillaume, V., Conte-Devolx, B., Alonso, G., Malaval, P., Pares-Herbute, N., Oliver, C., and Assenmacher, I. (1998). Central catecholaminergic system stimulates secretion of CRH at different sites. *Am. J. Physiol.* **255**, E436–E468.

Tanaka, M., Yoshida, M., Emoto, H., and Ishii, H. (2000). Noradrenaline systems in the hypothalamus, amygdala and locus coeruleus are involved in the provocation of anxiety: Basic studies. *Eur. J. Pharmacol.* **405**, 397–406.

Tanimura, S. M., and Watts, A. G. (1998). Corticosterone can facilitate as well as inhibit corticotropin-releasing hormone gene expression in the rat hypothalamic paraventricular nucleus. *Endocrinology (Baltimore)* **139**, 3830–3836.

Tanimura, S. M., and Watts, A. G. (2000). Adrenalectomy dramatically modifies the dynamics of neuropeptide and c-fos gene responses to stress in the hypothalamic paraventricular nucleus. *J. Neuroendocrinol.* **12**, 715–722.

Thieulant, M. L., and Duval, J. (1985). Differential distribution of androgen and estrogen receptors in rat pituitary cell populations separated by centrifugal elutriation. *Endocrinology (Baltimore)* **116**, 1299–1303.

Thornton, J. E., Cheung, C. C., Clifton, D. K., and Steiner, R. A. (1997). Regulation of hypothalamic proopiomelanocortin mRNA by leptin in ob/ob mice. *Endocrinology (Baltimore)* **138**, 5063–5066.

Tilbrook, A. J., Turner, A. I., and Clarke, I. J. (2000). Effects of stress on reproduction in non-rodent mammals: The role of glucocorticoids and sex differences. *Rev. Reprod.* **5**, 105–113.

Tkacs, N. C., and Strack, A. M. (1995). Systemic endotoxin induces Fos-like immunoreactivity in rat spinal sympathetic regions. *J. Auton. Nerv. Syst.* **51**, 1–7.

Trayhurn, P., Duncan, J. S., and Rayner, D. V. (1995). Acute cold-induced supression of ob (obese) gene expression in white adipose tissue of mice: Mediation by the sympathetic system. *Biochem. J.* **311**, 729–733.

Tritos, N. A., Elmquist, J. K., Mastaitis, J. W., Flier, J. S., and Maratos-Flier, E. (1988). Characterization of expression of hypothalamic appetite-regulating peptides in obese hyperleptinemic brown adipose tissue-deficient (uncoupling protein-promoter-driven diphtheria toxin A) mice. *Endocrinology (Baltimore)* **139**, 4634–4641.

Tsagarakis, S., Rees, L. H., Besser, G. M., and Grossman, A. (1989). Neuropeptide-Y stimulates CRF-41 release from rat hypothalami in vitro. *Brain Res.* **502**, 167–170.

Turner, B. B. (1992). Sex differences in the binding of Type I and Type II corticosteroid receptors in rat hippocampus. *Brain Res.* **581**, 229–236.

Turner, B. B. (1997). Influence of gonadal steroids on brain corticosteroid receptors: A minireview. *Neurochem. Res.* **22**, 1375–1385.

Turner, B. H., and Herkenham, M. (1991). Thalamoamygdaloid projections in the rat: A test of the amygdala's role in sensory processing. *J. Comp. Neurol.* **313**, 295–325.

Urban, J. H., Bauer-Dantoin, A. C., and Levine, J. E. (1993). Neuropeptide Y gene expression in the arcuate nucleus: Sexual dimorphism and modulation by testosterone. *Endocrinology (Baltimore)* **132**, 139–145.

Utter, A. C., Kang, J., Nieman, D. C., Williams, F., Robertson, R. J., Henson, D. A., Davis, J. M., and Butterworth, D. F.

(1999). Effect of carbohydrate ingestion and hormonal responses on ratings of perceived exertion during prolonged cycling and running. *Eur. J. Appl. Physiol.* **80**, 92–99.

Valentino, R. J., Foote, S. L., and Aston-Jones, G. (1983). Corticotropin-releasing factor activates noradrenergic neurons of the locus coeruleus. *Brain Res.* **270**, 363–367.

Valentino, R. J., Page, M., Van Bockstaele, E. J., and Aston-Jones, G. (1992). Corticotropin-releasing factor innervation of the locus coeruleus region: Distribution and sources of input. *Neuroscience* **48**, 689–705.

Vamvakopoulos, N. C., and Chrousos, G. (1993). Evidence of direct estrogenic regulation of human corticotropin-releasing hormone gene expression. Potential implications for the sexual dimorphism of the stress response and immune/inflammatory reaction. *J. Clin. Invest.* **92**, 1896–1902.

Vamvakopoulos, N. C., and Chrousos, G. (1994). Hormonal regulation of corticotrpin-releasing hormone gene expression: Implications for the stress response and immune/inflammatory reaction. *Endocr. Rev.* **15**, 409–420.

Van Bockstaele, E. J., Peoples, J., and Valentino, R. J. (1999). Anatomic basis for differential regulation of the rostrolateral peri-locus coeruleus region by limbic afferents. *Biol. Psychiatry* **46**, 1352–1363.

van Cauter, E., Polonsky, K. S., Blackman, J. D., D., R., Sturis, J., Byrne, M. M., and Scheen, A. J. (1994). Abnormal temporal patterns of glucose tolerance in obesity: Relationship to sleep-related growth hormone secretion and circadian cortisol rhythmicity. *J. Clin. Endocrinol. Metab.* **79**, 1797–1805.

Van de Kar, L. D., Piechowski, R. A., Rittenhouse, P. A., and Gray, T. S. (1991). Amygdaloid lesions: Differential effect on conditioned stress and immobilization-induced increases in corticosterone and renin secretion. *Neuroendocrinology* **54**, 89–95.

van Dijk, G., Bottone, A. E., Strubbe, J. H., and Steffens, A. B. (1994). Hormonal and metabolic effects of paraventricular hypothalamic administration of neuropeptide Y during rest and feeding. *Brain Res.* **660**, 96–103.

van Dijken, H. H., de Goeij, D. C. E., Sutano, W., Mos, J., de Kloet, E. R., and Tilders, F. J. H. (1993). Short inescapable stress produces long-lasting changes in the brain-pituitary-adrenal axis of adult male rats. *Neuroendocrinology* **58**, 57–64.

Van Haarst, A. D., Oitzl, M. S., Workel, J. O., and de Kloet, E. R. (1996). Chronic brain glucocorticoid receptor blockade enhances the rise in circadian and stress-induced pituitary-adrenal activity. *Endocrinology (Baltimore)* **137**, 4935–4943.

Van Tol, H. H., Bolwerk, E. L., Liu, B., and Burbach, J. P. (1988). Oxytocin and vasopressin gene expression in the hypothalamo-neurohypophyseal system of the rat during the estrous cycle, pregnanacy and lactation. *Endocrinology (Baltimore)* **122**, 945–951.

Vergoni, A. V., and Bertolini, A. (2000). Role of melanocortins in the central control of feeding. *Eur. J. Pharmacol.* **405**, 25–32.

Viau, V., and Meaney, M. J. (1991). Variations in the hypothalamo-pituitary-adrenal response to stress during the estrous cycle in the rat. *Endocrinology (Baltimore)* **129**, 2503–2511.

Viau, V., and Meaney, M. J. (1992). Regulation of ACTH co-secretagogues during the estrous cycle in the rat. *Soc. Neurosci. Abstr.* **18.**

Viau, V., and Meaney, M. J. (1996). The inhibitory effect of testosterone on hypothalamic-pituitary-adrenal responses to stress is mediated by the medial preoptic area. *J. Neurosci.* **16**, 1866–1876.

Viau, V., and Sawchenko, P. E. (1995). The pattern of cellular activation seen in response to acute restraint suggests commonalities among neurogenic stress models. *Soc. Neurosci. Abstr.*

Viau, V., Chu, A., Soriano, L., and Dallman, M. F. (1999). Independent and overlapping effects of corticosterone and testosterone on corticotropin-releasing hormone and arginine vasopressin mRNA expression in the paraventricular nucleus of the hypothalamus and stress-induced adrenocorticotropic hormone release. *J. Neurosci.* **19**, 6684–6693.

Viau, V., Soriano, L., and Dallman, M. F. (2001). Androgens alter corticotropin- releasing hormone and vasopressin mRNA within forebrain sites known to regulate activity in the hypothalamic-pituitary-adrenal axis. *J. Neuroendocrinol.* **13**, 442–452.

Wabitsch, M., Jensen, P. B., Blum, W. F., Christoffersen, C. T., Englaro, P., Heinze, E., Rascher, W., Teller, W., Tornqvist, H., and Hauner, H. (1996). Insulin and cortisol promote leptin production in cultured human fat cells. *Diabetes* **45**, 1435–1438.

Wade, G. N. (1972). Gonadal hormones and behavioral regualtion of body weight. *Physiol. Behav.* **8**, 523–534.

Wade, G. N. (1976). Sex hormones, regulatory behaviors, and body weight. *In* "Advances in the Study of Behavior" (J. S. Rosenblatt, R. A. Hinde, E. Shaw, and C. G. Beer, eds.), pp. 201–279. Academic Press, New York.

Wade, G. N., and Gray, J. M. (1979). Gonadal effects on food intake and adiposity: A metabolic hypothesis. *Physiol. Behav.* **22**, 583–593.

Wagner, C. K., and Morrell, J. I. (1997). Neuroanatomical distribution of aromatase mRNA in the rat brain: Indications of regional regulation. *J. Steroid Biochem. Mol. Biol.* **61**, 307–314.

Wallace, W. H., Crowne, E. C., Shalet, S. M., Moore, C., Gibson, S., Littley, M. D., and White, A. (1991). Episodic ACTH and cortisol secretion in normal children. *Clin. Endocrinol. (Oxford)* **34**, 215–221.

Wan, W., Janz, L., Vriend, C. Y., Sorensen, C. M., Greenberg, A. H., and Nance, D. M. (1993). Differential induction of

c-Fos immunoreactivity in hypothalamus and brain stem nuclei following central and peripheral administration of endotoxin. *Brain Res. Bull.* **32**, 581–587.

Watanabe, Y., McKitterick, C. R., Blanchard, D. C., Blanchard, R. J., McEwen, B. S., and Sakai, R. R. (1995). Effects of chronic social stress on tyrosine hydroxylase mRNA and protein levels. *Mol. Brain Res.* **32**, 176–180.

Watanobe, H., and Suda, T. (1999). A detailed study on the role of sex steroid millieu in determining plasma leptin concentrations in adult male and female rats. *Biochem. Biophy. Res. Commun.* **259**, 56–59.

Watts, A. G. (2000). Understanding the neural control of ingestive behaviors: Helping to separate cause from effect with dehydration-associated anorexia. *Horm. Behav.* **37**, 261–283.

Watts, A. G., and Sanchez-Watts, G. (1995). Region-specific regulation of neuropeptide mRNAs in rat limbic forebrain neurones by aldosterone and corticosterone. *J. Physiol. (London)* **484**, 721–736.

Watts, A. G., and Swanson, L. W. (1989). Durnal variations in the content of preprocorticotropin-releasing hormone messenger ribonucleic acids in the hypothalamic paraventricular nucleus of rats of both sexes as measured by in situ hybridization. *Endocrinology (Baltimore)* **125**, 1734–1738.

Weidenfeld, J., Itzik, A., and Feldman, S. (1997). Effect of glucocorticoids on the adrenocortical axis repsonse to electrical stimulation of the amygdala and the ventral noradrenergic bundle. *Brain Res.* **754**, 187–194.

Weninger, S. C., and Majzoub, J. A. (2001). Regulation and actions of corticotropin-releasing hormone. (B. S. McEwen, ed.), pp. 103–124.

Whitley, H. A., Humphreys, S. M., Campbell, I. T., Keegan, M. A., Jayanetti, T. D., Sperry, I. A., MacLaren, D. P., Reilly, T., and Frayn, R. N. (1998). Metabolic and performance responses during endurance exercise after high-fat and high-carbohydrate meals. *J. Appl. Physiol.* **85**, 418–424.

Wiemann, D. K., Clifton, D. K., and Steiner, R. A. (1989). Pubertal changes in gonadotropin-releasing hormone and proopiomelanocortin gene expression in the brain of the male rat. *Endocrinology (Baltimore)* **124**, 1760–1767.

Wiersma, A., Konsman, J. P., Knollema, S., Bohus, B., and Koolhaas, J. M. (1998). Differential effects of CRH infusion into the central nucleus of the amygdala in the roman high-avoidance and low-avoidance rats. *Psychoneuroendocrinology* **23**, 261–274.

Wilensky, A. E., Schafe, G. E., and Le Doux, J. E. (2000). The amygdala modulates memory consolidation of fear-motivated inhibitory avoidance learningbut not classical fear conditioning. *J. Neurosci.* **20**, 7059–7066.

Wilkinson, C. W., Shinsako, J., and Dallman, M. F. (1979). Daily rhythms in adrenal responsiveness to adrenocorticortopin are determined primarily by the time of feeding in the rat. *Endocrinology (Baltimore)* **104**, 350–359.

Wilkinson, C. W., Peskind, E. R., and Raskind, M. A. (1997). Decreased hypothalamic-pituitary-adrenal axis sensitivity to cortisol feedback inhibition in human aging. *Neuroendocrinology* **65**, 79–90.

Winters, S. J., Medhamurthy, R., Gay, V. L., and Plant, T. M. (1991). A comparison of moment to moment and diurnal changes in circulating inhibin and testosterone concentrations in male rhesus monkeys (*Macaca mulatta*). *Endocrinology (Baltimore)* **129**, 1755–1761.

Wise, R. A., and Rompre, P.-P. (1989). Brain dopamine and reward. *Annu. Rev. Psychol.* **40**, 191–225.

Wisialowski, T., Parker, R., Preston, E., Sainsbury, A., Kraegen, E., Herzog, H., and Cooney, G. (2000). Adrenalectomy reduces neuropeptide Y-induced insulin release and NPY receptor expression in the rat ventromedial nucleus. *J. Clin. Invest.* **105**, 1253–1259.

Wong, M.-L., Al-Shekhlee, A., Bongiorno, P. B., Esposito, A., Khatri, P., Sternberg, E. M., Gold, P. W., and Licinio, J. (1996). Localization of urocortin messenger RNA in rat brain and pituitary. *Mol. Psychiatry* **1**, 307–312.

Wong, M.-L., Kling, M. A., Munson, A. J., Listwak, S., Licinio, J., Prolo, P., Karp, B., McCutcheon, I. E., Geracioti, T. D., Jr., DeBellis, M. D., Rice, K. C., Goldstein, D. S., Veldhuis, J. D., Chrousos, G., Oldfield, E. H., McCann, S. M., and Gold, P. W. (2000). Pronounced and sustained central hypernoradrenergic function in major depression with melancholic features: Relation to hypercortisolism and corticotropin-releasing hormone. *Proc. Natl. Acad. Sci. U.S.A.* **97**, 325–330.

Woods, S. C., Seeley, R. J., Porte, D., and Schwartz, M. W. (1998). Signals that regulate food intake and energy homeostasis. *Science* **280**, 378–1383.

Wu, Y., Pearl, S. M., Zigmond, M. J., and Michael, A. C. (2000). Inhibitory glutamineergic regulation of evoked dopamine release in striatum. *Neuroscience* **96**, 65–72.

Xu, M., Urban, J. H., Hill, J. W., and Levine, J. E. (2000). Regulation of hypothalamic neuropeptide Y Y1 receptor gene expression during the estrous cycle: Role of progesterone receptors. *Endocrinology (Baltimore)* **141**, 3319–3327.

Xu, X., De Pergola, G., and Bjorntorp, P. (1990). The effects of androgens on the regulation of lipolysis in adipose precursor cells. *Endocrinology (Baltimore)* **126**, 1229–1234.

Xu, X., De Pergola, G., and Bjorntorp, P. (1991). Testosterone increases lipolysis and the number of beta-adrenoreceptors in male rat adipocytes. *Endocrinology (Baltimore)* **128**, 379–382.

Yamamoto, T., Sako, N., Nobuyuki, S., and Iwafune, A. (1997). Gustatory and visceral inputs to the amygdala of the rat: Conditioned taste aversion and induction of c-fos-like immunoreactivity. *Neurosci. Lett.* **226**, 127–130.

Yokosuka, M., Okamura, H., and Hayashi, S. (1997). Postnatal development and sez difference in neurons containing estrogen receptor-a immunoreactivity in the preoptic brain, the diencephalon, and the amygdala in the rat. *J. Comp. Neurol.* **389**, 81–93.

Young, E. A. (1995). The role of gonadal steroids in hypothalamic-pituitary-adrenal axis regulation. *Crit. Rev. Neurobiol.* **9**, 371–381.

Young, E. A. (1996). Sex differences in response to exogenous corticosterone: A rat model of hypercortisolemia. *Mol. Psychiatry* **1**, 313–319.

Young, E. A., and Korzun, A. (1998). Psychoneuroendocrinology of depression. Hypothalamic-pituitary-gonadal axis. *Psychiat. Clin. North Am.* **21**, 309–323.

Young, E. A., Akana, S. F., and Dallman, M. F. (1990). Decreased sensitivity to glucocorticoid fast feedback in chronically stressed rats. *Neuroendocrinology* **51**, 536–542.

Young, E. A., Lopez, J. E., Murphy-Weinberg, V., Watson, S. J., and Akil, H. (1998). The role of mineralocorticoid receptors in hypothalamic-pituitary-adrenal regulation in humans. *J. Clin. Endocrinol. Meta.* **83**, 3339–3345.

Yukhananov, R. Y., and Handa, R. J. (1997). Estrogen alters proenkephalin RNAs in the paraventricular nucleus of the hypothalamus following stress. *Brain Res.* **764**, 109–116.

Zanisi, M., and Messi, E. (1991). Sex steroids and the control of LHRH secretion. *J. Steroid Biochem. Mol. Biol.* **40**, 155–163.

Zemel, M. B., and Shi, H. (2000). Pro-opiomelanocortin (POMC) deficiency and peripheral melanocortins in obesity. *Nutr. Rev.* **58**, 177–180.

Zhou, L., Blaustein, J. D., and De Vries, G. J. (1994). Distribution of androgen receptor immunoreactivity in vasopressin- and oxytocin-immunoreactive neurons in the male rat brain. *Endocrinology (Baltimore)* **134**, 2622–2627.

Zhu, M.-Y., Klimek, V., Dilley, G. E., Heycock, J. W., Stockmeier, C., Overholser, J. C., Meltzer, H. Y., and Ordway, G. A. (1999). Elevated levels of tyrosine hydroxylase in the locus coeruleus in major depression. *Biol. Psychiatry* **46**, 1275–1286.

Ziegler, D. R., Cass, W. A., and Herman, J. P. (1999). Excitatory influence of the locus coeruleus in hypothalamic-pituitary-adrenocortical axis responses to stress. *J. Neuroendocrinol.* **11**, 361–369.

10

Hormonal Modulation of Central Motivational States

Jay Schulkin

Department of Physiology and Biophysics
Georgetown University School of Medicine
Washington, D.C. 20007

I. INTRODUCTION

Motivational states are generated by the brain. Thirst is a state of the brain (Epstein *et al.*, 1973). The acceptance of concepts such as motivation, however, has been in decline in some intellectual traditions (but not all) that traditionally were focused on motivation and brain function. The concept of motivation warrants resurrection particularly in the context of the hormonal regulation of behavior.

The chapter begins with a discussion of the concept of motivation, its relationship to the central nervous system function, and specific hormonal systems. I suggest that the behavioral expression of central motive states is coded, in part, by neuropeptide expression in the brain and is regulated by steroids.

II. THE CONCEPT OF MOTIVATION

The concept of motivation has figured in the explanation of human behavior since recorded history. Perhaps it is a cognitive category selected to facilitate the prediction and explanation of goal-directed behavior (e.g., Aristotle, 1968).

Freud (1924/1960) understood that the concept of drive, or libido, generated by the brain was fundamental to explain behavior. But both his drive reduction model and his obsession with sexual behavior limited his purview. And although he started out studying the brain to help explain motivated behavior, he had left that behind by the turn of the century.

The concept of motivation and drive were fundamental in the scientific lexicon of psychology and ethology (Lashley, 1938; Hebb, 1949; Tinbergen, 1951, 1969). Unfortunately, however, motivational systems have always had a tendency to multiply like instincts. However, that is no different from the unrestrained multiplication of the newest peptide receptors sites. [How many serotonin, angiotensin, corticotropin-releasing hormone (CRH) receptor sites are there now?]

Here are some questions to consider:

1. The concept is bedeviled by questions such as, How many kinds of motivational explanations are there? There are several. They are not necessarily mutually exclusive. They include drive reduction or homeostatic theories, incentive theories, hedonic theories. Of course, when food is attractive it can be attractive because (a) the animal is hungry (internally pushed—hunger for sodium; Wolf, 1969); (b) the food is interesting and salient (externally pulled toward an object—incentive motivation; Young, 1941, 1966); or (c) the food itself is pleasing and hedonic and attractive (sea water tastes good to the sodium-deficient animal, see Toates, 1986).

2. Is there a family of core motivational states? Yes. There are core motivational states that subserve the health and reproductive fitness of the animal (Pfaff, 1999; Schulkin, 1999). Such central states of the brain are biologically based and serve a wide variety of functions both in terms of short-term (hunger, thirst, fear) and long-term significance (reproduction).

3. When is it legitimate to invoke a motivational explanation? The concept of motivation provides a definite context and legitimate scientific function when the goals and direction of behavior are being discerned in the explanation of animal and human behavior (Tolman, 1932; Hebb, 1949).

Eliot Stellar (1954) formulated a view held by a generation of investigators about the general mechanism that underlies motivational states. Stellar's view

put forward in the classic paper "The Physiology of Motivation" was that the hypothalamus played a fundamental role in the regulation of excitatory and inhibitory central states (Stellar, 1954; see also Hebb, 1949). The framework was one in which both internal physiological changes and sensory detection mediated by central hypothalamic sites resulted in behavioral adaptation. Although often construed as merely under hypothalamic control, other regions of the brain are obviously involved in the expression of motivated behaviors (Fig. 1).

Experiments using electrical (Olds, 1958) and chemical self-stimulation of the hypothalamus and other forebrain sites (Grossman, 1968; Miller, 1957) suggested specific systems in the brain that could result in the expression of specific behavior. This later result was subsequently challenged with the set of findings

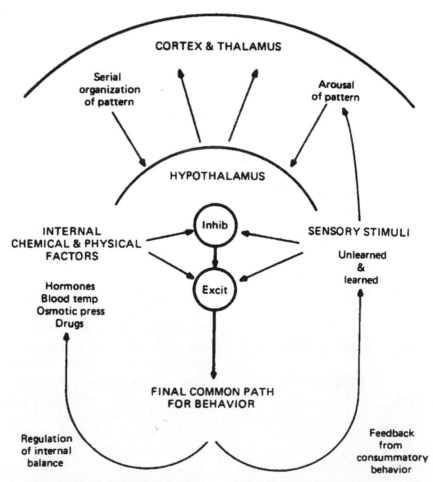

FIGURE 1   The physiological control of motivated behavior (Stellar, 1954).

that the same site in the hypothalamus when stimulated could elicit a range of behaviors depending upon the context (Valenstein, 1973; Valenstein *et al.,* 1970). The same stimulation in regions of the hypothalamus could elicit thirst, hunger, or sex drive depending upon the context (see also Wise, 1971). One reasonable explanation for the electrical self-stimulation effects on behavior is that the stimulation increases the salience of environmental stimuli (Berridge and Valenstein, 1991). In retrospect, the expression of behavior by the activation of neural circuits depends upon the context or ecological conditions. Behavior does not exist in a vacuum.

But the idea that there are not specific signals for the elicitation of behavior also does not hold. There are both general and specific mechanisms that underlie motivated behaviors (Pfaff, 1999; Toates, 1986; Stellar, 1954; Fig. 2).

What mechanisms underlie the legitimate use of the term? They include psychological, biological, and neuroscientific levels of analysis (Miller, 1957, 1959; Gallistel, 1980; Swanson, 1988; Nader *et al.,* 1997). My principal focus will be on the neuroendocrine mechanisms that underlie central motive states.

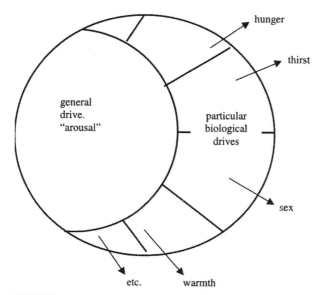

FIGURE 2 Drive, or motivation, has at least two components: a component necessary for the *energization* of behavior—arousal—that is general across motivational states; and mechanisms that respond to humoral and other particular physiological signals arising from specific biological needs, such as hunger, thirst, sex hormones, temperature changes, and the like. This second component gives *direction* to motivated behavior (Pfaff, 1999).

Neuropeptides, for example, play specific roles in the expression of motivated behaviors (see Pfaff, 1999; Schulkin, 1999; Watts, 2000). Neuropeptides play diverse roles in both physiological and behavioral regulation in which there are specific functions (e.g., angiotensin, oxytoxin, vasopressin; see Herbert, 1993; Hoebel, 1988; Carter *et al.,* 1999).

Consider the peptide oxytocin: Oxytocin plays multiple roles in the facilitation of physiological regulation of milk letdown during lactation and water homeostasis (Fitzimons, 1979). But oxytocin (or vasopressin; see, e.g., Young *et al.,* 1999) expression in the brain underlies behavioral functions such as attachment (see, e.g., Insel, 1992; Carter, 1992; Carter *et al.,* 1999). Oxytocin is both a pituitary peptide linked to milk letdown and a neuropeptide linked to a variety of central states in which behavior serves physiological regulation and reproductive fitness. The central motivational state that underlies parental behavior is rich and behaviorally diverse (Hinde, 1970; Marler and Hamilton, 1966).

Or consider angiotensin: A peptide produced in both the brain and periphery, angiotensin also has a major impact on the cravings for both water and sodium (Epstein *et al.,* 1968; Denton, 1982). Injected centrally, angiotensin II increases both water intake and sodium intake (see Fitzsimons, 1979, 1999). The behavior of water and sodium ingestion complements the regulatory effects of angiotensin at the level of the kidney and other systemic organ systems (e.g., heart) linked to body fluid homeostasis.

Thus, motivational states should be characterized as the readiness to behave in suitable environments (Hinde, 1968, 1970). The behavior is best understood in the context of being directed in a certain trajectory (Tinbergen, 1951, 1969). Neural systems potentiate or depotentiate the readiness for behavioral expression (Gallistel, 1980; von Holst and von St. Paul, 1963). But also note that the thirst that the animal is trying to quench at the water hole is in the context of fear of possible predation, detection of danger signals, and hunger that may be related to a specific nutrient or mineral. Motivational explanations are perhaps never totally isolated. Motivational systems compete for expression (see McFarland, 1991; Shettleworth, 1998).

Depicted in Fig. 3 is one of the ways in which Miller and his colleagues and students understood the concept

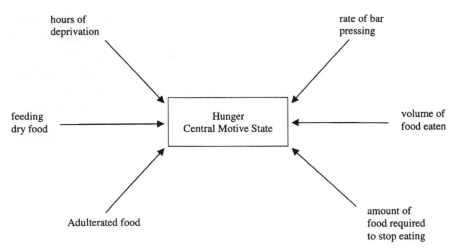

FIGURE 3 The instrumental way in which Neal Miller characterized drive states (Miller, 1959; Toates, 1986).

of motivation (Miller, 1957, 1959). For Miller, motivation was an essential category in the experimental design; the physiological and neural levels of analysis were linked to the behavioral level of analysis. The behaviors in the laboratory often reflect the degree of deprivation (food), ability to undergo travail to approach or avoid a set of environmental conditions, and attractiveness of the food source.

At a psychological level of analysis, motivational states can reflect behavioral flexibility to attain a goal—the range of behavioral options that could be employed toward an end by a motivated animal (e.g., Teitelbaum, 1967, 1977; Epstein, 1982; Tinbergen, 1951, 1969). The representation of goal objects and behavioral flexibility figure importantly in understanding motivational states.

The concept of motivation is linked to that of drive and energy (e.g., Freud, 1924/1960; Hull, 1943; Lorenz, 1981). The concept of motivation is hydraulic in nature; no doubt the degree of food deprivation, the degree of decreases in glucose levels results in the search and instrumental behaviors to procure the required nutrients. The homeostasis model, linked to depletion and repletion of energy and the use of energy, is part of the consideration of a motivational state; but it is neither a necessary nor sufficient condition (Toates, 1986). Of course the ingestion of food depends upon a number of factors, including the palatability of the food (Young, 1941, 1966) and the assessment of danger in the environment in which food is located.

The strict drive reduction model of learning is an impoverished conception of what underlies behavior. Many animals can learn about where sources of food or water or salt are at a time when they may not be in any of these central states. One example will suffice: Rats can learn, for example, where salt was and how to acquire it at a time in which the rat is not hungry for sodium (Krieckhaus and Wolf, 1968). Information processing about objects at locations, how to acquire a substance, and even what time of day a particular nutrient might appear (Rosenwasser *et al.,* 1988) occurs with or without having sodium hunger at a particular time. Two points stand out from these observations: Central motivate states are a larger class than simple drive-reinforcement categorization (see also Tolman, 1932); the simple drive reduction models of learning (cf. Hull, 1943; Miller, 1959) were placed in a larger behavioral context in which learning about objects was much broader (Shettleworth, 1998).

In fact, Miller (1959) helped introduce an information-processing model to the study of animal learning, thereby broadening the narrow behavioristic conception that had limited the study of animal behavior. Predicting events is essential to cognitive and behavioral adaptation (see also Dickinson, 1980). Some years later behavioristic studies would themselves become part of the cognitive revolution that eventually swept through psychology, including behaviorism (e.g., Dickinson, 1980).

What is clear from these discussions is that information-processing systems that represent objects are integral to motivational systems, complex or simple. The brain is an information-processing organ; motivation represented in neural circuits coded by neuropeptides or neurotransmitters is no different (Schulkin, 1999; Pfaff, 1999; Herbert, 1993).

Thus, the concept of motivation is tied to function and evolution and plays an important epistemological role in the explanation of behavior. That is the logical status of motivation in our scientific lexicon (Pfaff, 1999).

III. CENTRAL MOTIVE STATES

The concept of a central state is relatively modern. It is clearly stated in the works of Lashley (1938), Tinbergen (1951, 1969), Hinde (1970), Hebb (1949), Morgan (1957), Beach (1942), and Stellar (1954). A central motive state is a state of the brain (Lashley, 1938; Beach, 1942) that is often expressed in terms of two central tendencies toward objects: one that is attractive and approached, and one that is aversive and withdrawn from (Konorski, 1967; Schneirla, 1959).

There are two prominent features, for example, of the central motive state of hunger. The first is the appetitive phase (the search for the desired entity) and the second is the consummatory phase (actually ingesting the desired item or otherwise fulfilling a need). This distinction was expressed early on by the American nat-

uralist Wallace Craig (1918) and later by the pragmatist philosopher John Dewey (1925/1989). Within a short time it was incorporated within ethology (Tinbergen, 1951, 1969; Hinde, 1970; Marler and Hamilton, 1966) and psychobiology (Beach, 1942) or physiological psychology (Stellar, 1954; Hebb, 1949). Table 1 (adapted and expanded from Swanson, 1988) describes some of the features that are essential to central motive states.

Consider an example: Appetite for sodium, as I indicated above, is a good model of a motivational system (see Wolf, 1969; Denton, 1982; Schulkin, 1991a). On the appetitive side, salt-hungry rats or sheep will bar press for salt with a frequency that is related to the strength of the degree of sodium need (Denton, 1982; Quartermain and Wolf, 1967). Salt-hungry rats are also willing to run down an alley for very small quantities of salt (about 0.1 ml for each run; Schulkin *et al.*, 1991; Zhang *et al.*, 1984). Moreover, the intensity of running, for example, is related to the strength of the sodium hunger induced by mineralocorticoids alone, or by the combination of angiotensin and mineralocorticoid hormones (Fig. 4).

Now consider the consummatory phase: The infusions into the oral cavity reveal a pattern of facial responses for ingestion and rejection (Grill and Norgren, 1978a) that are, in fact, governed by the caudal brainstem (Grill and Norgren, 1978b). A sweet taste usually, though not always, elicits an ingestive sequence; a bitter taste, a rejection sequence. Hypertonic NaCl elicits a mixed ingestive-rejection sequence in the rat that

TABLE 1
Features That Are Essential to Central Motive States[a]

Initiation phase	Procurement phase	Consummatory phase	Competition for behavioral expression
Deficit signals	Arousal (general)	Programmed motor responses	Multiple motivational states
Exteroceptive sensory information	Foraging behavior	Discriminatory factors	Environmental Factors
Cognitive information (conditioning, anticipatory)	Locomotion Sensory integration	Satiety mechanisms Reinforcement	
Circadian influences	Previous experience	Hedonic	
Long-term memory	Short-term memory		
	Incentives		
	Maintenance of homeostasis (visceral integration)		

[a] Adapted and expanded from Swanson (1989).

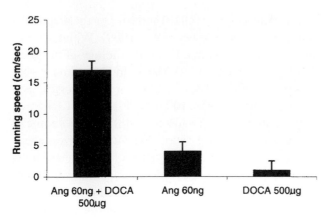

FIGURE 4 Running speed for 3% NaCl of a group of rats that was treated with both DOCA and angiotensin, only angiotensin, or with only DOCA (deoxycorticosterone) (Zhang *et al.*, 1984).

reflects sodium balance. But when rats are salt hungry, the oral-facial response to NaCl is changed. The response is now largely ingestive; the rejection response decreases (Berridge *et al.*, 1984; Berridge and Schulkin, 1989). This effect, at least in rats, is specific (Fig. 5).

Other tastants (e.g., HCl) that elicit equally mixed ingestive-aversive responses are not changed when the rat is salt hungry (Berridge *et al.*, 1984). Moreover, the oral-facial change to intraoral infusion of hypertonic NaCl is not dependent upon experience. The first time rats are sodium depleted, they demonstrate the phenomena (Berridge *et al.*, 1984).

Palatability information processing, in this case of hypertonic sodium (seawater), underlies central motive states such as the tendency to ingest sodium (Berridge *et al.*, 1984; Berridge and Schulkin, 1989). The behavioral and neural mechanisms that underlie palatability are unconscious (Berridge, 1996).

Allesthesia is a physiological term that has been used (Cabanac, 1971, 1979) to depict the regulatory role of hedonics in behavior. Like the example above with regard to sodium hunger, shifts in everything from temperature to sexual attraction underlie hedonic judgments. In fact, one of the more interesting examples is the motivational behaviors that are revealed with regard to cooling the brain; rats will bar press to alter their brain temperature (e.g., Stellar and Corbit, 1973). Key features of central states are the appetitive behaviors and their diverse expression and consummatory behaviors.

But central states are again wider than this class. The ingestion of sodium, like the attraction to a number

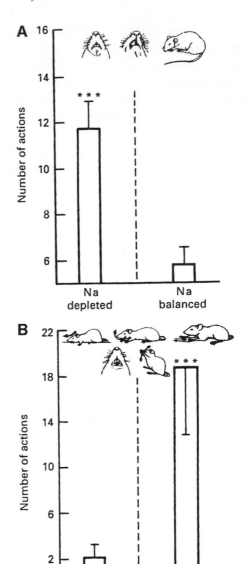

FIGURE 5 Taste-reactivity profiles of rats to intraoral infusions of hypertonic NaCl when the hormones of sodium homeostasis were elevated (Na depleted) and when they were not (Na balanced). (A) Combined mean (±SEM) number of ingestive actions (rhythmic tongue protrusions, and paw licks). (B) Combined mean (±SEM) number of aversive actions (chin rubs, headshakes, paw treads, gapes, face washes, and forelimb flails) (Berridge and Schulkin, 1989; Berridge *et al.*, 1984).

of appetitive and subsequent consummatory objects, are determined by salience, interests, (Bindra, 1969, 1978; Berridge, 1996), hedonic attractiveness (Beeb-Center, 1932; Young, 1959), and sensory stimulation

(Schneirla, 1959, 1965). The ingestion literature distinguishes preference from appetite (Young, 1959), liking from wanting (Berridge, 1996). The concept of central motive state functions as an umbrella term that accounts for a number of functions. In other words, central motive states reflect the interactions among the state of the animal, its prior associations, drive state, hedonic judgements about events, and the incentives that are evaluated in suitable environmental contexts (Bindra, 1969; Toates, 1986; Mook, 1987; Bolles, 1975). To the sodium-hungry animal the hypertonic salt stands out and is hedonically positive; sources where sodium was located are recalled in memory, and objects associated with sodium are salient (Krieckhaus and Wolf, 1968; Schulkin, 1991a).

Similar scenarios describe the courses of most hormonally induced central motive states. Such motivational states result in behaviors that include the craving for and ingestion of food and water, sex behavior, as well as social attachments (including parental behavior), fear, or addictive drug use (see Koob *et al.,* 1989).

The advantage of studying simple motivational systems is that they are tractable at many levels of analysis (Wolf, 1969), that is part of the excitement of studying phenomenon such as sodium hunger or thirst, which are less "sexy" than sex behavior, parental behavior, drug cravings, etc. All these behaviors result from central motive states induced and sustained by humoral mechanisms (see below). They all feature appetitive as well as consummatory phases of motivation and include salience or interest in various objects. The behaviors linked to hormonal effects on neuropeptides or neurotransmitters is particularly amenable to analysis of the central mechanisms underlying motivated behavior (Swanson, 1988, 2000; Denton *et al.,* 1996; Pfaff, 1999).

The roots of motivational systems are found within a biological perspective (Sober and Wilson, 1998). Behavior evolved to serve animal reproductive ability and fitness. Motivational states are designed to maintain internal stability and navigate external circumstances (see Gallistel, 1980, 1985).

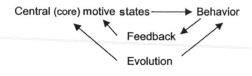

But the issue of flexibility as the cardinal feature of a motivational system may not be correct (James, 1890; Epstein, 1982). That is, I suspect the contrast between motivation and instinct (Epstein, 1982) is somewhat misleading. In this view, instinct is blind and dumb; motivation, by contrast, is replete with representations of objects and their importance and behavioral options to attain the goal. Surely the concept of representation that figures importantly in understanding the brain as an information-processing system is independent of whether the animal is limited in its behavioral options. Something can be instinctual and be fixed, and something can be motivated and be fixed. They are not exclusive. But the intuition that Epstein adumbrated was that motivational systems are flexible, opportunistic, and resourceful in the achievement of a goal. This no doubt captures an important element of central motive states.

In debates about the usefulness of the concept of motivation, it was noted that representations of goal objects are neither necessary nor sufficient for motivated behavior (cf. Dethier, 1966, 1982; Stellar, 1960; Toates, 1986; Wise, 1987). The hungry fly may be a machine, narrow in purpose, with few behavioral options and still have representations of goal objects.

IV. NEURAL CIRCUITS UNDERLYING MOTIVATIONAL STATES

The reticular formation was envisioned to underlie arousal, as was later the activation of catecholamines. We now know that a number of neurotransmitter systems (e.g., serotonin, dopamine) that project widely throughout brain both arouse and placate neuronal systems that underlie central motive states (e.g., Hoebel, 1988; Swanson, 2000).

Consider the central gustatory–visceral system in the brain in which a wide variety of neuropeptides are synthesized. C. Judson Herrick (1905), at the turn of the twentieth century, described a pathway in the catfish from the solitary nucleus to the amygdala which later Pfaffmann and his colleagues (1977) and others (see Spector, 2000) thought might underlie motivated behavior. The seventh, nineth, and tenth cranial nerves transmit visceral information to the central nervous system and terminate in the rostral portion of the solitary nucleus. Gustatory and other visceral information are then transmitted to the medial region of the parabrachial nucleus (Norgren, 1984, 1995). From this region there are two main projection systems: a dorsal projection to the ventral basal thalamus and insular cortex, and a ventral projection that courses through the lateral hypothalamus into the central nucleus of the amygdala, in addition to the bed nucleus of the stria terminalis (Norgren, 1984). It was suggested (Pfaffmann *et al.,* 1977) that the sensory evaluation of a food or fluids—whether sweet or salty—is made by the dorsal projection, and that the organization of the drive, and the hedonic value of the stimulation, is made by the ventral projection. It is interesting that many of the neuropeptides, or their receptor sites, and steroid receptor sites that are linked to central states are localized within these regions.

Angiotensin, and its receptor sites, is one peptide that is localized in many of the regions of this visceral pathway in the brain (see Lind *et al.,* 1984). In addition, oxytocin, vasopressin, prolactin, neuropeptide Y, and corticotrophin releasing factor (CRH) are also distributed along the central visceral axis (Fig. 6). This axis includes the central nucleus of the amygdala, the bed nucleus of the stria terminalis, the paraventricular nucleus of the hypothalamus, and brain stem sites such as the parabrachial and solitary nuclei (Gray *et al.,* 1986; Swanson and Mogenson, 1981). This is the same pathway that organizes motivated behaviors in general (Pfaffmann *et al.,* 1977; Stellar and Stellar, 1985). It is part of the neural system—described by Herrick (1905, 1948) and expanded upon by Nauta (1961; also see Norgren, 1995)—that underlies central excitatory states.

Nauta noted that the concept of the limbic system should include motor regions of the basal ganglia (see Mogenson and Huang, 1973; Mogenson and Yang, 1991). The basal ganglia forms an essential link in translating motivational signals from the amygdala and hypothalamus into the organization of action (Swanson and Mogenson, 1981; Swanson, 2000; Kelley, 1999) via the activation of brain stem sites (e.g., Pfaff, 1999; lordosis).

Since Nauta's (1963) original suggestion research has substantiated that regions of the basal ganglia do in fact seem to underlie a variety of motivated behaviors (addiction; Koob, 2000) perhaps via changes in dopaminergic transmission. The nucleus acumbens via glutamate receptors within the acumbens may underlie appetitive instrumental learning and may be an important link in translating limbic functions into functional action (Kelley, 1999).

Let's now turn to several model systems in the hormonal regulation of motivational states.

V. INDUCTION OF NEUROPEPTIDES BY STEROIDS AND CENTRAL STATES

Steroids, by facilitating neuropeptide expression and regulation in the brain, increase the likelihood of motivational states, sustain them, and decrease their expression (e.g., Herbert, 1993; Pfaff, 1999; Schulkin, 1999).

By influencing central states, hormones and their actions in the brain prepare an animal to perceive stimuli and behave in certain characteristic ways; they increase the likelihood of responding to environmental signals (e.g., Gallistel, 1980; Mook, 1987).

There are a variety of contexts in which steroids and peptides interact to regulate behavior (Herbert, 1993; Hoebel, 1988). These contexts range from ingestion of food, water, and sodium to maternal behavior, fear, and aggression. These states, in turn, generate behaviors that, through both anticipatory and reactive mechanisms, help the organism maintain internal stability and external coherence to internal demands (Herbert, 1993; Schulkin, 1999). Steroids and peptides or neuropeptides interact to influence behavior by their actions in the brain. There are many examples in which hormones that serve to maintain physiological stability also affect behaviors that serve the same goal.

Steroid hormones such as estrogen, progesterone, aldosterone, corticosterone, testosterone, and Vitamin 1,25D3 are widely distributed in the brain (e.g., Pfaff, 1980; Stumpf and O'Brien, 1987; McEwen, 1995). They have profound effects, for example, on the induction or inhibition of neuropeptide gene expression and subsequent central states and behavioral output (Herbert, 1993).

A. Mineralocorticoids, Glucocorticoids, and Angiotensin

As noted above, mineralocorticoid hormones increase sodium ingestion (Richter, 1943; Wolf, 1964;

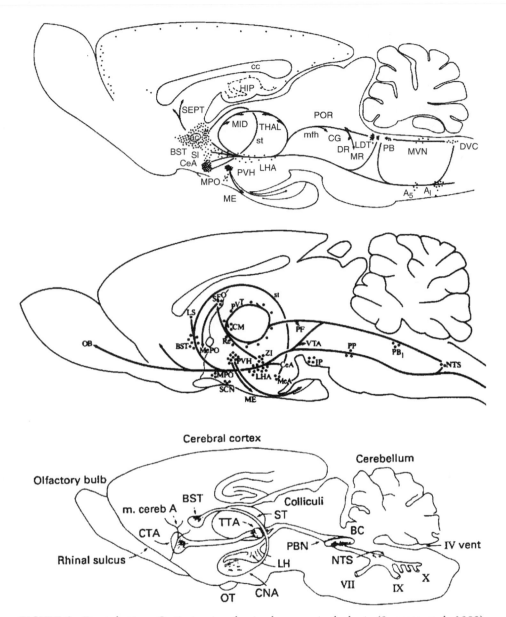

FIGURE 6 Top to bottom: Corticotropin-releasing hormone in the brain (Swanson *et al.*, 1983), angiotensin sites in the brain (Lind *et al.*, 1984), and the central gustatory neural axis (Norgren, 1995). Note that many of the peptide sites overlap with gustatory sites in the brain.

Fig. 7). Mineralocorticoids increase angiotensin-II receptors in the brain and in cell-line cultures. The same treatment is known to increase angiotensin mRNA in cell-line cultures, in addition to mobilizing intracellular calcium and second-messenger systems (S. J. Fluharty, unpublished observations; Fluharty and Sakai, 1995). Mineralocorticoids also potentiate angiotensin-II-induced sodium intake (Fluharty and Epstein, 1983; Massi and Epstein, 1990).

Elevated glucocorticoids potentiate angiotensin-II-induced drinking (Fig. 7). The background of glucocorticoids that are normally elevated following depletion of the body's fluids induces angiotensin-II cells, thereby potentiating the hormone's dipsogenic (Fregly *et al.*, 1979; Sumners *et al.*, 1991) and natriorexegenic actions. This interaction generates the central states of thirst and sodium hunger, in which both appetitive and consummatory behaviors are expressed. The behavior

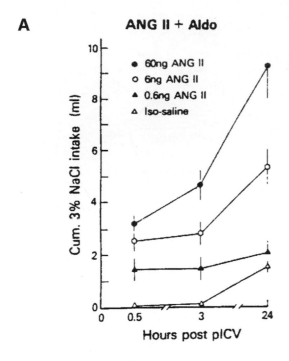

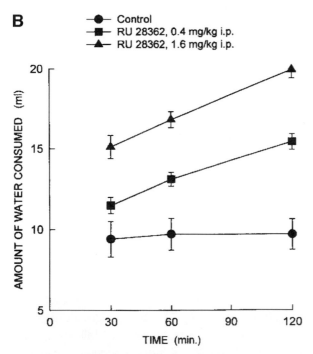

FIGURE 7 (A) Sodium ingestion in rats following daily injections of aldosterone (40 μg) followed by central injection of angiotensin (Sakai, 1986). (B) Water ingestion following systemic daily injections of the glucocorticoid agonist followed by a central injection of angiotensin II (10n) (Sumners *et al.,* 1991).

serves the same end point as the renin-angiotensin-aldosterone system, namely, the body's fluid homeostasis (e.g., Fitzsimons, 1999; Johnson and Thunhorst, 1997; Blair-West *et al.,* 1998).

B. Glucocorticoids and Neuropeptide Y

At low doses, corticosterone also stimulates food intake, and it appears to do so, in part, through activation of neuropeptide Y in the brain (Leibowitz, 1995; Wang *et al.,* 1999; Fig. 8). Produced in gastrointestinal sites as well as the central nervous system (Gray *et al.,* 1986), neuropeptide Y is activated in the arcuate nucleus and the paraventricular nucleus by food deprivation and corticosterone (Brady *et al.,* 1990; Dallman *et al.,* 1995; Lambert *et al.,* 1995). This increase in food intake depends on an intact adrenal gland, and perhaps from activation of type-2 corticosteroid receptors (Tempel and Leibowitz, 1994).

Low doses of glucocorticoids can potentiate neuropeptide-Y-induced food ingestion (Heinrichs *et al.,* 1993). Specifically, corticosterone and neuropeptide Y generate carbohydrate ingestion, or fast energy pickups (Bhatnagar *et al.,* 2000; Morley *et al.,* 1987; Kalra *et al.,* 1991; see also Seeley *et al.,* 1995). This steroid and neuropeptide hormone facilitate the central motive state of craving carbohydrates. Adrenalectomy abolishes these effects, and corticosterone will restore them. But without a suitable context in which other concerns are made prevalent in the information-processing systems in the brain (predator detection, conflict with conspecifics), eating or drinking may or may not take place.

C. Estrogen, Oxytocin, and Prolactin

A paradigmatic example of steroids and peptides acting together to generate central motive states that underlie successful reproduction is that of estrogen-primed rats given progesterone and oxytocin to induce sexual receptivity (Pfaff, 1980; Pfaff, 1999). A variety of animals treated with systemic estrogen and then with progesterone demonstrate similar sexual receptivity. Estrogen increases oxytocin expression in cells in the ventral medial hypothalamus. Without sufficient estrogen, oxytocin expression declines, and is restored only when estrogen is again elevated (e.g., Schumacher

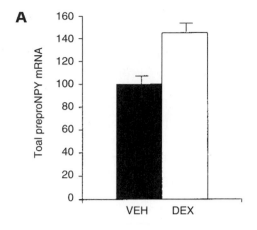

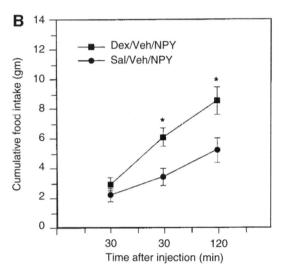

FIGURE 8 (A) Total hybridization preproneuropeptide Y (preproNPY) mRNA in the arcuate nucleus in vehicle-injected controls (VEH) and hamsters injected daily for 28 days with dexamethasone (DEX). (Adapted from Mercer *et al.,* 1996.) (B) Cumulative food intake following pretreatment with dexamethasone (100 μg/kg) or vehicle followed 6 hours later by central injection of a vehicle or neuropeptide Y (500 ng Heinrichs *et al.,* 1993).

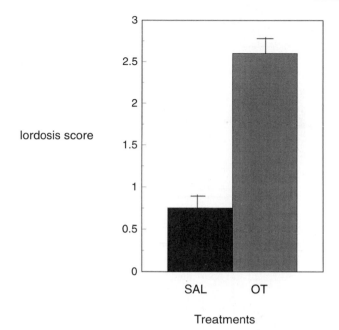

FIGURE 9 Estrogen-facilitated oxytocin-induced lordosis behavior (adapted from Schumacher *et al.,* 1990). SAL, saline; OT, oxytocin.

In other words, by facilitating the expression of neuropeptides (e.g., oxytocin) or receptor sites (e.g., progestin), the gonadal steroid hormones lower the threshold at which a sexual response to environmental stimuli will be elicited by inducing central states in the brain (e.g., Pfaff, 1999; Wade and Crews, 1991). And in this context well-known appetitive and consummatory expression of central states occurs (see Beach, 1942, 1947; Everitt, 1990). But the behavioral expression is not axiomatic and varies with the environmental circumstances and the competition with other internal needs. Motivation figures in determining the direction that behavior will take.

But one should also note and consider the multiple effects of estrogen on neuropeptides and neurotransmitters in the brain (Pfaff, 1999), in addition to progesterone, adrenergic and muscarinic receptors, enkephalin, gonadotrophin-releasing hormone (GnRH), and oxytocin.

Now consider the relationship among estrogen, and prolactin and maternal behavior: Like oxytocin and a number of other peptides, prolactin is a pituitary hormone and a neuropeptide with a diversity of functions. Central infusions of prolactin facilitate maternal behavior (Bridges and Freemack, 1995), but only if

et al., 1990). Oxytocin infused within this region of the brain elicits sexual receptivity, and in estrogen- and progesterone-primed rats the dose of oxytocin needed to elicit the behavior is decreased. Thus, by increasing oxytocin expression in the brain's ventral medial hypothalamus, estrogen facilitates the likelihood of sexual motivation and receptivity (Fig. 9).

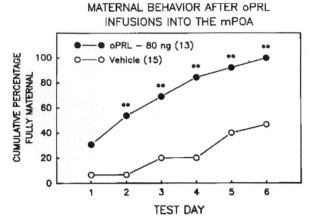

FIGURE 10 Maternal behaviors after bilateral infusions of 40 ng of prolactin (PRL) into the medial preoptic nucleus in estrogen-treated and nontreated rats (from Bridges *et al.,* 1990).

there is a sufficient level of background estrogen. In other words, as the case with oxytocin, estrogen facilitates the likelihood of maternal behavior by increasing prolactin expression in the brain (Bridges *et al.,* 1990). Changes in prolactin expression in the brain alter maternal behavior (Lucas *et al.,* 1998; McCarthy *et al.,* 1994). Prolactin stimulates maternal central states through both physiologic and behavioral mechanisms (Fig. 10).

D. Gonadal Steroids and Vasopressin or Vasotocin

Testosterone concentrations vary with the seasons (e.g., Wingfield, 1993, 1994). One testosterone-mediated behavior linked to territorial behavior, scent marking, occurs via the gonadal steroid's activation of vasopressin in the brain, particularly in the bed nucleus of the stria terminalis. Infused into this region, vasopressin facilitates the expression of scent marking. A background treatment of testosterone enhances this response (Albers *et al.,* 1988). The same holds for male parental behavior among prairie voles. Presumably, testosterone facilitates this behavior by sustaining and increasing central vasopressin or vasotocin synthesis (De Vries, 1995; see also Moore *et al.,* 1992). But the central state is not in a vacuum and competes internally for expression.

Without testosterone, vasopressinergic neurons are severely depleted in specific regions of the brain that underlie parental behavioral and territorial aggression

(De Vries *et al.,* 1985; De Vries, 1995). For example, regions of the medial preoptic and anterior hypothalamic region (Albers and Rawls, 1989) and medial amygdala are importantly involved in flank-marking behavior and aggressive behaviors (e.g., Ferris *et al.,* 1989, 1997); testosterone facilitates flank marking via the induction of vasopressin expression in the medial amygdala. The removal of the gonadal steroids reduce vasopressin gene expression in this region of the brain and reduces flank marking behavioral expressions (Fig. 11).

E. Glucocorticoids and Central CRH

Corticotropin-releasing hormone (CRH) plays a fundamental role in the regulation of the pituitary-adrenal axis by increasing secretion of pituitary adrenocorticotropin hormone (ACTH), which in turn stimulates glucocorticoids such as corticosterone from the adrenal glands. Corticosterone then regulates its own production by decreasing CRH output from the paraventricular nucleus of the hypothalamus and ACTH output from the pituitary gland (Munck *et al.,* 1984; Dallman *et al.,* 1995).

Glucocorticoids increase CRH gene expression in regions of the brain (central nucleus of the amygdala and lateral bed nucleus of the stria terminalis) (Watts and Watts-Sanchez, 1995: Swanson and Simmons, 1989; Makino *et al.,* 1994a,b; Thompson *et al.,* 2000; Fig. 12). By contrast, corticosterone decreases CRH expression in the parvocellular region of the paraventricular nucleus (Swanson and Simmons, 1989; Makino *et al.,* 1994; Watts and Watts-Sanchez, 1995).

Corticosterone and central CRH are in fact elevated during conditions of adversity (e.g., Kalin and Shelton, 1989; Koob, 2000; Nemeroff *et al.,* 1984). Corticosterone can potentiate fear-induced freezing behavior (Coordimas *et al.,* 1994; Jones *et al.,* 1998; Pugh *et al.,* 1997; Takahashi, 1995) perhaps via the expression of central CRH. Moreover, corticosterone can facilitate CRH-induced startle response (Lee *et al.,* 1994). In fact, corticosterone increased the expression of CRH gene expression, which facilitated contextual fear conditioning (Thompson *et al.,* 2000; Fig. 13).

Central infusions of corticosterone directly into the central nucleus of the amygdala not only increases CRH gene expression but also reduces the behavior of

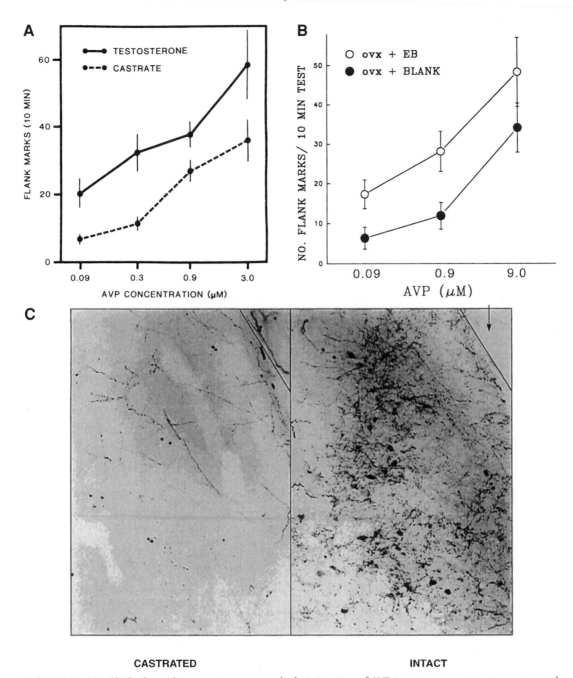

CASTRATED   INTACT

FIGURE 11 (A, B) Flank-marking reaction to central administration of AVP in estrogen or testosterone-treated (EB) and nontreated (BLANK) ovariectomized (ovx) female hamsters (Albers *et al.,* 1988; Huhman and Albers, 1993). (C) Vasopressin-immunoreactive cells and fibers in the medial nucleus of the amygdala in castrated rats (courtesy of De Vries, 1995).

exploration of open field (one measure of fear or anxiety) (Shepard *et al.,* 2000). Interference with CRH expression in the brain reduced fear-related behavioral responses (e.g., Habib *et al.,* 2000).

Together, the steroid and the peptide sustain the central motive state of fear; the appetitive phase is avoiding the fearful situation, and the consummatory phase is the relief that comes from being out

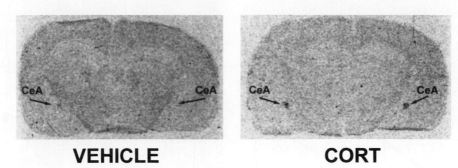

VEHICLE   **CORT**

FIGURE 12   Digitized images of CRH mRNA in the central nucleus of the amygdala (CeA) in corticosterone (4 mg) or vehicle treated rats (after Thompson *et al.,* 2000).

of danger. The central state of fear is replete with expectations.

It is interesting that among primates elevated cortisol levels are associated with being more likely to be inhibited and fearful (e.g., Kagan *et al.,* 1988; Gunnar *et al.,* 1989; Kalin *et al.,* 2000; Habib *et al.,* 2002), demonstrating exaggerated startle responses when presented with acoustic stimuli (Schmidt *et al.,* 1997), and showing fear of social context (Schmidt *et al.,* 1999; Schmidt and Schulkin, 1999). A subset of fearful macaques, for example, who have higher central CRH expression, demonstrate exaggerated fearful responses (Kalin *et al.,* 2000). Perhaps they are prepared (temperamentally) to see the world in fearful ways because of cortisol's action in the brain to induce CRH gene expression (Swanson and Simmons, 1989; Makino *et al.,* 1994a,b).

Finally, consider corticosterone and CRH and the self-administration of psychotropic agents (Piazza and

Le Moal, 1997; Koob, 2000). Addiction to drugs is a paradigmatic example of central motive states that obviously has no evolutionary or adaptive relevance. It is an aberration of normal function. Appetitive and consummatory behaviors pervade addictive behaviors, with positive and negative states pervasive (Koob, 2000). Both high levels of corticosterone and central CRH have been linked to addictive behavior. For example, CRH infusions into the lateral ventricle facilitate amphetamine-induced self-administration (Sarnyai *et al.,* 1993). Corticosterone levels are known to influence the expression of amphetamine self-administration (Cador *et al.,* 1993; Piazza *et al.,* 1991). Systemic injections of corticosterone increase the likelihood of amphetamine self-administration, as do stressful events (Maccari *et al.,* 1991), which increase both corticosterone and central CRH (Heinrichs *et al.,* 1993). Individual differences in levels of corticosterone

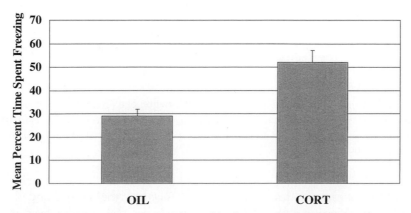

FIGURE 13   Freezing responses (seconds) of rats in the retention test in corticosterone treated (5 mg per day for four days) or vehicle treated (Thompson *et al.,* 2000).

are correlated with amphetamine self-administration; the higher the level, the greater the self-administration (Piazza *et al.,* 1991).

Corticosterone levels have also been shown to influence dopamine-dependent psychomotor effects of both morphine and cocaine self-administration (Deroche *et al.,* 1995). Corticosterone is known to influence self-administration of cocaine; the greater the degree of corticosterone that circulates, the greater the probability of self-administration of cocaine (Goeders and Guerin, 1996).

Corticotropin-releasing hormone in the brain has been linked to the anxiety associated with heroin, morphine, cocaine, tobacco, and alcohol withdrawal (e.g., Sarnyai *et al.,* 1995; Pich *et al.,* 1995; Richter Rodriguez di Fonseca *et al.,* 1997; C. P. Richter *et al.,* unpublished; Zhou *et al.,* 1996); all result in elevated levels of CRH in the central nucleus of the amygdala (Fig. 14).

Reducing CRH expression in the amygdala reduces morphine withdrawal symptoms (Heinrich *et al.,* 1995). And inhibiting corticosterone synthesis by metyrapone decreases the vulnerability of relapse to cocaine self-administration (Piazza and Le Moal, 1997). Corticotropin-releasing hormone expression within the bed nucleus of the stria terminalis is linked to stress-facilitated vulnerability to relapse. For example, central infusions of CRH into the bed nucleus of the stria terminalis results in greater ingestion of psychotropic drugs by rats. Interference with CRH decreases this behavioral response (Shaham *et al.,* 2000). Perhaps by

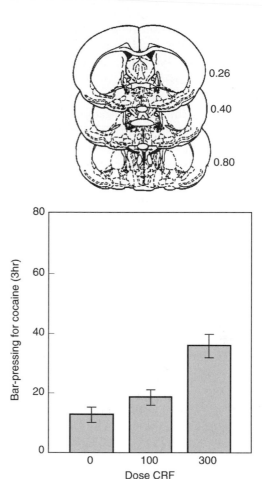

FIGURE 15 Vulnerability to relapse for cocaine seeking in rats injected into the bed nucleus of the stria terminalis with corticotropin-releasing hormone (CRF, which is the same as CRH) (adapted from Erb and Stewart, 1999).

increasing or decreasing CRH gene expression by corticosterone and the central states of being fixed on an addicted object, these rats are more vulnerable to self-administration of these psychotropic drugs (Fig. 15).

In each of the conditions in which glucocorticoids and central CRH are elevated, it is not axiomatic that the animal will be fearful or be in state of withdrawal. In characterizing the state of the animal, its motivational state, one needs to understand the environmental context and the internal competition for expression.

VI. CONCLUSION

To explain animal behavior, motivation figures importantly in our science. Motivation functions to

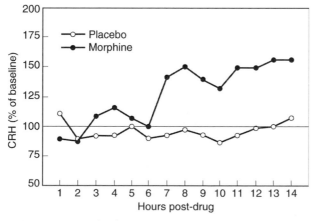

FIGURE 14 Levels of corticotropin-releasing hormone (CRH) measured by dialysis following withdrawl from morphine (C. P. Richter, J. Schulkin, and Weiss, unpublished observations).

orchestrate the direction of goal-directed behaviors. Motivation is fundamental to a theory of the direction of behavior (Lakoff and Johnson, 1999; but also cf. Wise, 1987; Grossman, 1968, 1979; Oatley, 1970). Core motivational states are biological functions that serve the animal in the organization of behavior and the adaptation to changing environmental demands. In other words, a full account of motivated behavior will include behavioral-psychological, neural, physiological, and molecular levels of explanations and be placed within an evolutionary context.

The concept of central motivational states is tied to characterizing functional states of the brain. Steroids, by facilitating neuropeptides or neurotransmitters or receptor sites, can influence central states that are typically, though not exclusively, linked to functional requirements. As I have indicated in this chapter, and as is well represented in this book, there are a number of examples in which steroid hormones act in the brain in a feedforward fashion to sustain or induce neuropeptide gene expression that have functional consequences; they range from thirst and sodium appetite to hunger to sexual motivation to territorial defense to fear, etc (Schulkin, 1999).

But the behavioral state does not exist in a vacuum; it depends upon the environment and other cognitive and physiological events. Nonetheless, functional circuits in the brain underlie both specific and nonspecific aspects of motivational states. Steroids, by the induction and regulation of neuropeptides, constitute one mechanism that plays an essential role in the expression of motivational states.

References

Albers, H. E., and Rawls, S. (1989). Coordination of hamster lordosis and flank marking behavior: Role of arginine vasopressin within the medial preoptic-anterior hypothalamus. *Brain Res. Bull.* **23**, 105–109.

Albers, H. E., Liou, S. Y., and Ferris, C. F. (1988). Testosterone alters the behavioral response of the medial preoptic-anterior hypothalamus to microinjection of arginine vasopfessin in the hamster. *Brain Res.* **456**, 382–386.

Alberts, A. C., Jackintell, L. A., and Phillips, J. A. (1994). Effects of chemical and visual exposure to adults on growth, hormones, and behavior of juvenile green iguanas. *Physiol. Behav.* **55**(6), 897–892.

Alexander, G. M., Packard, M. G., and Hines, M. (1994). Testos-

terone has rewarding affective properties in male rats: Implications for the biological basis of sexual motivation. *Behav. Neurosci.* **108**, 424–428.

Aristotle (1968). "DeAnima" (D. W. Hamlyn, transl.). "Clarendon Aristotle Series" (J. L. Ackrill, gen. ed.). Clarendon Press, Oxford.

Arnold, M. B. (1969). Emotion, motivation, and the limbic system. *Ann. N. Y. Acad. Sci.* **159**, 1041–1058.

Balleine, B. W., and Dickinson, A. (1998). Goal-directed instrumental action: Contingency and incentive learning and their cortical substrates. *Neuropharmocology* **37**, 407–419.

Balthazart, J., Reid, J., Absil, P., Foidart, A., and Ball, G. F. (1995). Appetitive as well as consummatory aspects of male behavior in quail are activated by androgens and estrogens. *Behav. Neurosci.* **109**(3), 495–501.

Beach, F. A. (1942). Central nervous mechanisms involved in the reproductive behavior of vertebrates. *Psychol. Bull.* **39**, 200–206.

Beach, F. A. (1947). A review of physiological and psychological studies of sexual behavior in mammals. *Physiol. Rev.* **27**, 240–307.

Beeb-Center, J. G. (1932). "The Psychology of Pleasantness and Unpleasantness." Van Nostrand, New York.

Berridge, K. C. (1996). Food reward: Brain substrates of wanting and liking. *Neurosci. Biobehav. Rev.* **20**, 1–35.

Berridge, K. C. (2000). Reward learning: Reinforcement, incentives and expectations. *In* "The Psychology of Learning and Motivation" (D. L. Medin, ed.). Academic Press, New York.

Berridge, K. C., and Schulkin, J. (1989). Palatability shift of a salt associated incentive drive associated during sodium depleteion. *Q. J. Exp. Psychol.* **41**, 121–138.

Berridge, K. C., and Valenstein, E. S. (1991). What psychological process mediates feeding evoked by electricial stimulation of the lateral hypothalamus. *Behav. Neurosci.* **105**, 3–14.

Berridge, K. C., Flynn, F. W., Schulkin, J., and Grill, H. J. (1984). Sodium depletion enhances salt palatability in rats. *Behav. Neurosci.* **98**, 652–660.

Bhatnagar, S., Bell, M. E., Liang, J., Soriano, L., Nagy, T. R., and Dallman, M. F. (2000). Corticosterone facilitates saccharin intake in adrenalectomized rats; does corticosterone increase stimulus salience. *J. Endocrinol.* **12**, 453–460.

Bindra, D. (1969). A unified inerpretation of emotions and motivation. *Ann. N. Y. Acad. Sci.* **159**, 1071–1083.

Bindra, D. (1978). How adaptive behavior is produced: A perceptual-motivational alternative to response reinforcement. *Behav. Brain Sci.* **1**, 41–91.

Blair-West, J. R., Carey, K. D., Denton, D. A., Weisinger, R. S., and Shade, R. E. (1998). Evidence that brain aniotensin II is involved in both thirst and sodium appetite in baboons. *Am. J. Physiol.* **275**, R1639–R1646.

Bolles, R. C. (1975). "Theories of Motivation." Harper & Row, New York.

Bolles, R. C., and Fanselow, M. S. (1980). A perceptual-defensive-recuperative model of fear and pain. *Behav. Brain Sci.* **3**, 291–323.

Boring, E. G. (1942). "Sensation and Perception in the History of Experimental Psychology." Appleton Century, New York.

Brady, L. S., Smith, M. A., Gold, P. W., and Herkenham, M. (1990). Altered expression of hypothalamic neuropeptide mRNAs in food restricted and food-deprived rats. *Neuroendocrinology* **52**, 441–447.

Bridges, R. S., and Freemark, M. S. (1995). Human placental lactogen infusions into the medial preoptic area stimulate maternal behavior in steroid-primed, nulliparous female rats. *Horm. Behav.* **29**, 216–226.

Bridges, R. S., Numan, M., Ronsheim, P. M., Mann, P. E., and Lupini, C. E. (1990). Central prolactin infusions stimulate maternal behavior in steroid-treated, nulliparous female rats. *Proc. Natl. Acad. Sci. U.S.A.* **87**, 8003–8007.

Cabanac, M. (1971). Physiological role of pleasure. *Science* **173**, 1103–1107.

Cabanac, M. (1979). Sensory pleasure. *Q. Rev. Biol.* **54**, 1–29.

Cador, M., Dulluc, J., and Mormede, D. P. (1993). Modulation of the locomotor response to amphetamine by corticosterone. *Neuroscience* **56**, 981–988.

Campeau, S., Falls, W. A., Cullinan, W. E., Helmreich, D. L., Davis, M., and Watson, S. J. (1997). Elicitation and reduction of fear: Behavioral and neuroendocrine indices and brain induction of the immediate-early gene C-FOS. *Neuroscience* **78**, 1087–1104.

Cannon, W. B. (1927). The James-Lange theory of emotions: A critical examination and an alternative theory. *Am. J. Physiol.* **39**, 106–124.

Carter, C. S. (1992). Oxytocin and sexual behavior. *Neurosci. Biobehav. Rev.* **16**, 131–144.

Carter, C. S., Lederhendler, I. L., and Kirkpatrick, B. (1999). "The Integrative Neurobiology of Affiliation." MIT Press, Cambridge, Mass.

Cassell, M. D., Gray, T. S., and Kiss, J. Z. (1986). Neuronal architecture in the rat central nucleus of the amygdala: A cytological, hodological, and immunocytochemical study. *J. Comp. Neurol.* **246**, 478–499.

Cho, K., and Little, H. J. (1999). Effects of corticosterone on excitatory amino acid responses in dopamine-sensitive neurons in the ventral tegmental area. *Neuroscience* **88**, 837–845.

Cole, B. J., and Koob, G. F. (1989). Low doses of corticotropin-releasing factor potentiate amphetamine-induced stereotyped behavior. *Psychopharmacology* **99**, 27–33.

Cox, V. C., and Valenstein, E. S. (1965). Attenuation of aversive properties of peripheral shock by hypothalamic stimulation. *Science* **149**, 323–325.

Craig, W. (1918). Appetites and aversions as constituents of instinct. *Biol. Bull. (Woods Hole, Mass.)* **34**, 91–107.

Crenshaw, B. J., De Vries, G. J., and Yahr, P. (1992). Vasopressin innervation of sexually dimorphic structures of the gerbil forebrain under various hormonal conditions. *J. Comp. Neurol.* **322**, 589–598.

Dallman, M. F., Akana, S. F., Strack, A. M., Hanson, E. S., and Sebastian, R. J. (1995). The neural network that regulates energy balance is responsive to glucocorticoids and insulin and also regulates HPA axis responsivity at a site proximal to CRF neurons. *Ann. N. Y. Acad. Sci.* **771**, 730–742.

Darwin, C. (1872/1965). "The Expression of the Emotions in Man and Animals." Murray, London.

Delville, Y., Mansour, K. M., and Ferris, C. F. (1996). Testosterone facilitates aggression by modulating vasopressin receptors in the hypothalamus. *Physiol. Behav.* **60**, 25–29.

Dennett, D. C. (1978). "Brainstorms." Bradford Books, New York.

Dent, G. W., Okimoto, D. K., and Smith, M. A. (2000). Stress-induced alterations in corticotropin-releasing hormone and vasopressin gene expression in the paraventricular nucleus during ontogeny. *Neuroendocrinology* **71**, 333–342.

Denton, D. A. (1982). "The Hunger for Salt." Springer-Verlag, New York.

Denton, D. A., McKinley, M. J., and Weisinger, R. S. (1996). Hypothalamic integration of body fluid regulation. *Proc. Nat. Acad. Sci. U.S.A.* **93**, 7397–7304.

Deroche, V., Marinelli, M., Macccari S. *et al.* (1995). Stress-induced sensitization and glucocorticoids. 1. Sensitization of Dopamine-dependent locomotor effects of amphetamine and morphine depends on stress-induced corticosterone secretion. *J. Neurosci.* **15**(11), 7181–7188.

Dethier, V. G. (1966). Insects and the concept of motivation. *Nebr. Symp. Motivation* **14**, 105–136.

Dethier, V. G. (1982). The contribution of insects to the study of motivation. *In* "Changing Concepts in the Nervous System" (A. R. Morrison and P. L. Strick, eds.), pp. 445–455. Academic Press, New York.

Dethier, V. G., and Stellar, E. (1961). "Animal Behavior." Prentice-Hall, Englewood Cliffs, NJ.

De Quervain, D. J. F., Roozendaal, B., and McGaugh, J. L. (1998). Stress and glucocorticoids impair retrieval of long-term spatial memory. *Nature (London)* **394**, 787–790.

Deutsch, J. A. (1960). "The Structural Basis of Behavior." University of Chicago Press, Chicago.

De Vries, G. J. (1995). Studying neurotransmitte systems to understand the development and function of sex differences in the brain; the case of vasopressin. *In* "Neurobiological Effects of Sex Steriod Hormone" (P. E. Micevych and R. P. Hamer, Jr., eds.). Cambridge University Press, Cambridge, UK.

De Vries, G. J., Van Leeuwen, B. F. W., Caffe, A. R., and Swaab, D. F. (1985). The vasopressinergic innervation of the brain in normal and castrated rats. *J. Comp. Neurol.* **233**, 236–254.

Dewey, J. (1925/1989). "Experience and Nature." Open Court Press, LaSalle, Il.

Dickinson, A. (1980). "Contemporary Animal Learning." Cambridge University Press, Cambridge, UK.

Eagle, D. M., Humby, T., Dunnett, S. B., and Robbins, T. W. (1999). Effects of regional striatal lesions on motor, motivational, and executive aspects of progressive-ration performance in rats. *Behav. Neurosci.* **113**(4), 718–731.

Edwards, D. A., and Einhorn, L. C. (1986). Preoptic and midbrain control of sexual motivation. *Physiol. Behav.* **37**, 329–335.

Ekman, P. (1982). "Emotion and the Human Face." Cambridge University Press, Cambridge, UK.

Epstein, A. N. (1982). Instinct and motivation as explanations for complex behavior. *In* "The Physiological Mechanisms of Motivation" (D. W. Pfaff, ed.), pp. 25–58. Springer-Verlag, New York.

Epstein, A. N., Fitzsimons, J. T., and Simons, B. J. (1968). Drinking caused by the intracranial injection of angiotensin into the rat. *J. Physiol. (London)* **200**, 98P–100P.

Epstein, A. N., Kissileff, H. R., and Stellar, E. eds. (1973). "The Neuropsychology of Thirst." Winston, Washington, DC.

Erb, S., and Stewart, J. (1999). A role for the bed nucleus of the stria terminalis, but not the amygdala, in the effects of corticotropin-releasing factor on stress-induced reinstatement of cocaine seeking. *J. Neurosci.* **19**, 1–6.

Erb, S., Shaham, Y., and Stewart, J. (1996). Stress reinstates cocaine-seeking behavior affter prolonged extinction and a drug-free period. *Psychopharmacology* **128**, 408–412.

Erb, S., Shaham, Y., and Stewart, J. (1998). The role of corticotropin-releasing factor and corticosterone in stress and cocaine-induced relapse to cocaine seeking rats. *J. Neurosci.* **18**, 5529–5536.

Everitt, B. J. (1990). Sexual motivation: A neural and behavioral analysis of the mechanisms underlying appetitive and copulatory responses of male rats. *Neurosci. Biobehav. Rev.* **14**, 217–232.

Everitt, B. J., and Herbert, J. (1975). The effects of implanting testosterone propionate into the central nervous system on the sexual behavior of adrenalectomized female rhesus monkeys. *Brain Res.* **86**, 109–120.

Ferris, C. F., Axelson, J. F., Martin, A. M., and Roberge, I. F. (1989). Vasopressin immunoreactivity in the anterior hypothalamus is altered during the establishment of dominant/

subordinate relationships between hamsters. *Neuroscience* **29**(3), 675–683.

Ferris, C. F., Melloni, R. H., Koppel, G., Perry, K. W., Fuller, R. W., and Delville, Y. (1997). Vasopressin/serotonin interactions in the anterior hypothalamus control aggressive behavior in Golden hamsters. *J. Neurosci.* **17**(11), 4331–4340.

Fitzsimons, J. T. (1979). "The Physiology of Thirst and Sodium Appetite." Cambridge University Press, Cambridge, UK.

Fitzsimons, J. T. (1999). Angiotesnin, thirst and sodium appetite. *Physiol. Rev.* **76**, 585–686.

Fitzsimons, J. T., and Le Magnen, J. (1969). Eating as a regulatory control of drinking. *J. Comp. Physiol. Psychol.* **67**, 273–283.

Fluharty, S. J., and Epstein, A. N. (1983). Sodium appetite elicited by interacerebroventricular infusion of angiotensin II in the rat: II. Synergistic interaction with systemic mineralocorticoids. *Behav. Neurosci.* **97**, 746–758.

Fluharty, S. J., and Sakai, R. R. (1995). Behavioral and cellular studies of corticosterone and angiotensin interaction in brain. *Prog. Psychobiol. Physiol. Psychol.* Academic Press, San Diego CA.

Flynn, J. P. (1972). Patterning mechanisms, patterned reflexes, and attack behavior in cats. *Nebr. Symp. Motivation* **20**, 125–153.

Fregly, M. J., Katovich, M. J., and Barney, C. C. (1979). Effect of chronic treatment with desoxycorticosterone on the dipsogenic response of rats to isoproterenol and angiotensin. *Pharmacology* **19**, 165–172.

Freud, S. (1924/1960). "A General Introduction to Psychoanalysis" (J. Riviere, ed. and transl.). Washington Square Press, New York.

Gallistel, C. R. (1975). Motivation as central organizing process: The psychophysical approach to its functional and neurophysiological analysis. *Nebr. Symp. Motivation* **22**, 182–125.

Gallistel, C. R. (1980). "The Organization ot Action—A New Synthesis." Erlbaum, Hillsdale, NJ.

Glickman, S. E., and Schiff, B. B. (1967). A biological theory of reinforcement. *Psycho. Rev.* **74**, 81–109.

Goeders, N. E., and Guerin, G. F. (1996). Role of corticosterone in intravenous cocaine self-administration in rats. *Neuroendocrinology* **64**, 337–348.

Gray, T. S., O'Donohue, T. L., and Magnuson, D. J. (1986). Neuropeptide Y innervation of amygdaloid and hypothalamic neurons that project to the dorsal vagal complex in rat. *Peptides* **7**, 341–349.

Gray, T. S., Piechowski, R. A., Yracheta, J. M., Rittenhouse, P. A., Bethea, C. L., and Van de Kar, L. D. (1993). Ibotenic acid lesions in the bed nucleus of the stria terminalis attenuate conditioned stress-induced increases in prolactin, ACTH and corticosterone. *Neuroendocrinology* **57**, 517–524.

Grill, H. J., and Norgren, R. (1978a). The taste reactivity test. I. Oral-facial responses to gustatory stimuli in neurologically normal rats. *Brain Res.* **143**, 263–279.

Grill, H. J., and Norgren, R. (1978b). The taste reactivity test. II. Mimetic responses to gustatory stimuli in chronic thalamic and chronic decerebrate rats. *Brain Res.* **143**, 281–297.

Grossman, S. P. (1968). The physiological basis of specific and nonspecific motivational processes. *Nebr. Symp. Motivation* **16**, 1–46.

Grossman, S. P. (1979). The biology of motivation. *Annu. Rev. Psychol.* **30**, 209–242.

Gubernick, D. J., and Nelson, R. J. (1989). Prolactin and paternal behavior in the biparental california mouse, *Peromyscus californicus. Horm. Behav.* **23**, 203–210.

Gunnar, M. R., Mangelsdorf, S., Larson, M., and Hertsgaard, L. (1989). Attachment, temperament, and adrenocortical activity in infancy: A study of psychoendocrine regulation. *Dev. Psychol.* **25**, 355–363.

Habib, K. E., Weld, K. P., Rice, K. C., Pushkas, J., Champoux, M., Listwak, S., Webster, E. L., Atkinson, A. J., Schulkin, J., Contoreggi, C., Chrousos, G. P., McCann, S. M., Suomi, S. J., Higley, J. D., and Gold, P. W. (2000). Oral administrator of a corticotropin-releasing hormone receptor antagonist significantly attenuates behavioral, neuroendocrine, and autonomic responses to stress in primates. *Proc. Natl. Acad. Sci. U.S.A.* **97**, 6079–6084.

Habib, K. E., Pushkas, J. P., Chrousos, G. P., Champoux, M., Rice, K. C., Schulkin, J., Erickson, K., Ronsaville, D., McCann, S. M., Suomi, S. J., Gold, P. W., and Higley, J. D. (2002). Sensitization of brain corticotropin releasing hormone after maternal deprivation and peer separation in juvenile primates. *Proc. Natl. Acad. Sci. U.S.A.* (in press).

Hebb, D. O. (1949). "The Organization of Behavior: A Neuropsychological Theory." Wiley, New York.

Hebb, D. O. (1955). Drives and the conceptual nervous system. *Psychol. Rev.* **62**, 243–254.

Heinrichs, S. C., Menzaghi, F., Pich, E. M., Hauger, R. L., and Koob, G. F. (1993). Corticotropin-releasing factor in the paraventricular nucleus modulates feeding induced by neuropeptide Y. *Brain Res.* **611**, 18–24.

Herbert, J. (1993). Peptides in the limbic system: Neurochemical codes for coordinated adaptive responses to behavioral and physiological demand. *Neurobiology* **41**, 723–791.

Herman, J. P. (1993). Regulation of adrenocorticosteroid receptor mRNA expression in the central nervous system. *Cell. Mol. Neurobiol.* **13**, 349–372.

Herrick, C. J. (1948). "The Brain of the Tiger Salamander." University of Chicago Press, Chicago, IL.

Hinde, R. A. (1968). Critique of energy models of motivation. *In* "Motivation" (D. Bindra and J. Stewart, eds.). Penguin Books, Baltimore, MD.

Hinde, R. A. (1970). "Animal Behavior—A Synthesis of Ethology and Comparative Psychology," 2nd. ed. McGraw-Hill, New York.

Hoebel, B. (1988). Neuroscience of motivation: Peptides and pathways that define motivational systems. *In* "Handbook of Experimental Psychology" (S. S. Stevens, ed.). Wiley, New York.

Huhman, K. L., Babagbemi, T. O., and Ablers, H. E. (1995). Bicuculline blocks neuropeptide Y-induced phase advances when microinjected in the suprachiasmatic nucleus of Syrian hamsters. *Brain Res.* **675**, 333–336.

Hull, C. L. (1943). "Principles of Behavior." Appleton-Century-Crofts, New York.

Ikemoto, S., and Panksepp, J. (1999). The role of the nucleus acumbens dopamine in motivated behavior: A unifying interpretation with special reference to reward-seeking. *Brain Res. Rev.* **31**, 6–41.

Insel, T. R. (1992). Oxytocin—a neuropeptide for affiliation—evidence from behavioral and receptor autoradiographic and comparative studies. *Psychoneuroendocrinology* **17**, 3–35.

Jackson, J. H. (1958). The Croonian lectures on evolution and dissolution of the nervous system. *In* "Selected Writings of John Hughlings Jackson" (J. Taylor ed.). Staples Press, London; reprinted from *Br. Med. J.* **1**, 591–593, 660–663, 703–707 (1884).

Jaeger, T. V., and van der Kooy, D. (1996). Separate neural substrates mediate the motivating and disctiminative properties of morphine. *Behav. Neurosci.* **110**, 181–201.

James, W. (1890). "Principles of Psychology." Holt, New York.

Jennings, H. S. (1906). "Behavior of the Lower Organism." Columbia University Press, New York.

Johnson, A. E., Barberis, C., and Albers, H. E. (1995). Castration reduces vasopressin receptor binding in the hamster hypothalamus. *Brain Res.* **673**, 153–159.

Johnson, A. K., and Thunhorst, R. L. (1997). The neuroendocrinology of thirst and salt appetite: Visceral sensory signals and mechanisms of central integration. *Front. Neuroendocrinol.* **18**, 292–353.

Jones, R. B., Beuving, G., and Blokhuis, H. J. (1988). Tonic immobility and heterophil/lymphocyte responses of the domestic fowl to corticosterone infusion. *Physiol. Behav.* **47**, 249–253.

Kagan, J., Reznick, J. T., and Snidman, N. (1988). Biological basis of childhood shyness. *Science* **240**, 167–171.

Kalin, N. H., and Shelton, S. E. (1998). Asymmetric frontal brain ontogeny and stability of separation and threat-induced defensive behaviors in rhesus monkeys during the first year of life. *Am. J. Primatol.* **44**, 125–135.

Kalin, N. H., Shelton, S. E., and Davidson, R. J. (2000). Cerebrospinal fluid corticotropin-releasing hormone levels are elevated in monkeys with patterns of brain activity associated with fearful temperament. *Biol. Psychiatry* **47**, 579–585.

Kalra, S. P., Dube, M. G., Sahu, A., Phelps, C. P., and Kalra, P. S. (1991). Neuropeptide Y secretion increases in the paraventricular nucleus in association with increased appetite for food. *Proc. Natl. Acad. Sci. U.S.A.* **88**, 10931–10935.

Karil, P. (1968). The limbic system and the motivation process. *J. Physiol. (Paris)* **60**(Suppl. 1), 3–48.

Kelley, A. E. (1999). Neural integrative activites of nucleus accumbens subregions in relation to learning and motivation. *Psychobiology* **27**, 198–213.

Konorski, J. (1967). "Integrative Activity, of the Brain: An Interdisciplinary Approach." University of Chicago Press, Chicago.

Koob, G. F. (2000). Neurobiology of addiction. *Ann. N. Y. Acad. Sci.* **909**, 170–185.

Koob, G. F., Stinus, L., Le Moal, M., and Bloom, F. E. (1989). Opponent process theory of motivation: Neurobiological evidence from studies of opiate dependence. *Neurosci. Biobehav. Rev.* **13**, 135–140.

Koob, G. F., Caine, B., Markou, A., Pulvirenti, L., and Weiss, F. (1994). Role for the mesocortical dopamine system in the motivating effects of cocaine. *NIDA Res. Monogr.* **145**, 1–18.

Krieckhaus, E. E., and Wolf, G. (1968). Acquisition of sodium by rats: Interaction of innate mechanisms and latent learning. *J. Comp. Physiol. Psychol.* **65**, 197–201.

Lakoff, G., and Johnson, M. (1999). "Philosophy in the Flesh." Basic Books, New York.

Lambert, P. D., Phillips, P. J., Wilding, J. P. H., Bloom, S. R., and Herbert, J. (1995). C-fos expression in the paraventricular nucleus of the hypothalamus following intracerebroventricular infusions of neuropeptide Y. *Brain Res.* **670**, 59–65.

Lane, J. M., Herbert, J., and Fitzsimons, J. T. (1997). Increased sodium appetite stimulates C-FOS expression in the organum vasculosum of the lamina terminalis. *Neuroscience* **78**, 1167–1176.

Lang, P. J. (1995). The emotion probe. *Am. Psychol.* **50**, 372–385.

Lashley, K. S. (1938). An experimental analysis of instinctive behavior. *Psychol. Rev.* **45**, 445–471.

Lashley, K. S. (1951). The problem of serial order in behavior. *In* "Cerebral Mechanisms in Behavior" (L. A. Jeffres, ed.), pp. 506–528. Wiley, New York.

Lashley, K. S. (1966). Drive as facilitation of specific neural mechanisms. *In* "Motivation" (D. Bindra and J. Stewart, eds.), pp. 60–62. Penguin Books, Baltimore, MD.

Lee, Y., Schulkin, J., and Davis, M. (1994). Effect of corticosterone on the enhancement of the acoustic startle reflex by corticotropin releasing hormone. *Brain Res.* **666**, 93–98.

Leibowitz, S. F. (1995). Brain peptides and obesity: Pharmacological treatment. *Obes. Res.* **3**, 573–589.

Le Magnen, J. (1985). "Hunger." Cambridge University Press, Cambridge, UK.

Lind, R. W., Swanson, L. W., and Ganten, D. (1984). Organization of angiotensin II immunoreactive cells and fibers in the rat central nervous system. *Neuroendocrinology* **40**, 2–24.

Lorenz, K. (1981). "The Foundations of Ethology." Springer, New York.

Louch, C. D., and Higginbotham, M. (1967). The relation between social rank and plasma corticosterone levels in mice. *Gen. Comp. Endocrinol.* **8**, 441–444.

Lucas, B. K., Ormandy, C. J., Binart, N., Bridges, R. S., and Kelly, P. A. (1998). Null mutation of the prolactin receptor gene produces a defect in maternal behavior. *Endocrinology (Baltimore)* **139**, 4102–4107.

Maccari, S., Piazza, P. V., Deminiere, J. M. *et al.* (1991). Life events-induced decrease of coticosteroid type 1 receptors in associated with reducede corticosterone feedback and enhanced vulnerability to amphetamine self-administration. *Brain Res.* **547**, 7–12.

Mahon, J. M., Allen, M., Herbert, J., and Fitzsimons, J. T. (1995). The association of thirst, sodium appetite and vasopressin release with c-fos expression in the forebrain of the rat after intracerebroventricular injection of angiotensin II, angiotensin-(1-7) or carbachol. *Neuroscience* **69**, 199–208.

Makino, S., Gold, P. W., and Schulkin, J. (1994a). Corticosterone effects on corticotropin-releasing hormone mRNA in the central nucleus of the amygdala and the parvocellular region of the paraventricular nuclues of the hypothalamus. *Brain Res.* **640**, 105–112.

Makino, S., Gold, P. W., and Schulkin, J. (1994b). Effects of corticosterone on CRH mRNA and content in the bed nucleus of the amygdala and the paraventricular nucleus of the hypothalamus. *Brain Res.* **657**, 141–149.

Marler, C. A., Chu, J., and Wilczynski, W. (1995). Arginine vasotocin injection increases probability of calling in cricket frogs, but causes call changes characteristic of less aggressive males. *Horm. Behav.* **29**, 554–570.

Marler, C. A., Boyd, S. K., and Wilczynski, W. (1999). Forebrain arginine vasotocin correlates of alternative mating strategies in cricket frogs. *Horm. Behav.* **36**, 53–61.

Marler, P., and Hamilton, W. J. (1966). "Mechanisms of Animal Behavior." Wiley, New York.

Maslow, A. H. (1954). "Motivation and Personality." Harper & Row, New York.

McCarthy, M. M., Curran, G. H., and Siegel, H. I. (1994). Evidence for the involvement of prolactin in the maternal behavior of the hamster. *Physiol. Behav.* **55**, 181–184.

McClelland, D. C., Atkinson, J. W., Clark, R. W., and Lowell, E. L. (1976). "The Achievement Motive," 2nd ed. Irvington, New York.

McEwen, B. S. (1995). Neuroendocrine interactions. *In* "Psychopharmacology: The Fourth Generation of Progress" (F. E. Bloom and D. J. Kupfer, eds.). Raven Press, New York.

McFarland, D. (1991). Defining motivation and cognition in animals. *Int. Stud. Philos. Sci.* **5**, 153–170.

McGaugh, J. L. (2000). Memory—a century of consolidation. *Science* **287**, 248–251.

Menzaghi, F., Heinrichs, S. C., Pick, E. M., Tilders, F. J. H., and Koob, G. F. (1993). Functional impairment of hypothalamic corticotropin-releasing factor neurons with immunotargeted toxins enhances food intake induced by neuropeptide Y. *Brain Res.* **618**, 76–82.

Meyer, R. E., and Mirin, S. M. (1979). "The Heroin Stimulus." Plenum Press, New York.

Miller, N. (1965). Chemical coding of behavior in the brain. *Science* **148**, 328–338.

Miller, N. E. (1957). Experiments of motivation. Studies combining psychological, physiological, and pharmacological techniques. *Science* **126**, 1271–1278.

Miller, N. E. (1959). Liberalization of basic S-R concepts: Extensions to conflict behavior, motivation and social learning. *In* "Psychology: A Study of a Science" (S. Koch, ed.), Vol. 2, pp. 196–292. McGraw-Hill, New York.

Milner, P. M. (1991). Brain-stimulation reward: A review. *Can. J. Psychol.* **45**, 1–36.

Mitchell, J. B., and Gratton, A. (1994). Involvement of mesolimbic dopamine neurons in sexual behaviors: Implications for the neurobiology of motivation. *Rev. Neurosci.* **5**, 317–329.

Moga, M. M., Saper, C. B., and Gray, T. S. (1989). Bed nucleus of the stria terminalis: Cytoarchitecture, immunohistochemistry, and projection to the parabrachial nucleus in the rat. *J. Comp. Neurol.* **283**, 315–332.

Mogenson, G. J., and Huang, Y. H. (1973). The neurobiology of motivated behavior. *Prog. Neurobiol.* **1**, 52–83.

Mogenson, G. J., and Yang, C. R. (1991). The contribution of basal forebrain to limbic-motor integration and the mediation of motivation to action. *Adv. Exp. Med. Biol.* **295**, 267–290.

Mook, D. (1987). "Motivation." Norton Press, New York.

Moore, F. L., Wood, R. E., and Boyd, S. K. (1992). Sex steroids and vasotocin interact in a female amphibian (*Taricha granulosa*) to elicit female-like egg-laying behavior or male-like courtship. *Horm. Behav.* **26**, 156–166.

Morall, Z., McINtosh, J., Kent, P., Michaud, D., and Anisman, H. (1998). Aversive and appetitive events evoke the release of corticotropin-releasing hormone and bombesin-like peptides at the central nuclues of the amygdala. *J. Neurosci.* **18**, 4758–4766.

Morgan, C. T. (1966). The central motive state. *In* "Motivation" (D. Bindra and J. Stewart, eds.), pp. 88–83. Penguin Books, Baltimore, MD.

Morgan, C. T., and Stellar, E. (1950). "Physiological Psychology." 2nd ed. McGraw-Hill, New York.

Morley, J. E., Levine, A. S., Gosnell, B. A., Kneip, J., and Grace, M. (1987). Effect of neuropeptide Y on ingestive behaviors in the rat. *Am. J. Physiol.* **252**, R599–R609.

Nader, K., and van der Kooy, D. (1997). Deprivation state switches the neurobiological substrates mediating opiate reward in the ventral tegmental area. *J. Neurosci.* **17**, 383–390.

Nader, K., Bechara, A., and van der Kooy, D. (1997). Neurobiological constraints on behavioral models of motivation. *Annu. Rev. Psychol.* **48**, 85–114.

Nauta, W. J. H. (1961). Fibre degeneration following lesions of the amygdaloid complex in the monkey. *J. Anat.* **95**(4), 516–531.

Nauta, W. J. H. (1963). Central nervous organization and the endocrine motor system. *In* "Advances in Neuroendocrinology" (A. V. Nalbandov, ed.), pp. 5–27. University of Illinois Press, Urbana.

Nederkoorn, C., Smulders, F. T. Y., and Jansen, A. (2000). Cephalic phase responses, craving and food intake in normal subjects. *Appetite* **35**, 45–55.

Nelson, R. J. (1997). The use of genetic "kockout" mice in behavioral endocrinology research. *Horm. Behav.* **31**, 188–196.

Nemeroff, C. B., Widerlov, E., Bissette, G., Wallens, H., Karlsson, I., Ekluud, K., Kilts, C. D., Loosen, P. T., and Vale, W. (1984). Elevated concentrations of CSF corticotropin releasing factor-like immunoreactivity in depressed outpatients. *Science* **26**, 1342–1344.

Norgren, R. (1984). Central neural mechanisms of taste. *In* "Handbook of Physiology and the Nervous System. Vol. 3: Sensory Processes," pt. 2.1 (J. M. Brookhart and V. B. Mountcastle, eds.), pp. 1087–1128. American Physiological Society, Bethesda, MD.

Norgren, R. (1995). Gustatory system. *In* "The Rat Nervous System" (G. Paxinos, ed.). Academic Press, San Diego, CA.

Norgren, R., and Leonard, C. M. (1973). Ascending central gustatory pathways. *J. Comp. Neurol.* **150**, 217–238.

Oatley, K. (1970). Brain mechanisms and motivation. *Nature (London)* **225**, 797–801.

Olds, J. (1958). Self-stimulation of the brain: Its use to study local effects of hunger, sex, and drugs. *Science* **127**, 315–324.

Olds, M. E., and Forbes, J. L. (1981). The central basis of motivation: Intracranial self-stimulation studies. *Annu. Rev. Psychol.* **32**, 523–574.

Owens, M. J., Bartolome, J., Schanberg, S. M., and Nemeroff, C. B. (1990). Corticotropin-releasing factor concentrations exhibit an apparent diurnal rhythm in hypothalamic and extrahypothalamic brain regions: Differential sensitivity to corticosterone. *Neuroendocrinology* **52**, 626–631.

Pacak, K., Armando, I., Fukuhara, K., Kvetnansky, R., Palkovits, M., Kopin, I. J., and Goldstein, D. S. (1992). Noradrenergic activation in the paraventricular nucleus during acute and chronic immobilization stress in rats: An in vivo microdialysis study. *Brain Res.* **589**, 91–96.

Panksepp, J. (1998). "Affective Neuroscience: The Foundations of Human and Animal Emotions." Oxford University Press, New York.

Panzica, G. C., Viglietti-Panzica, C., and Balthazart, J. (1996). The sexually dimorphic medial preoptic nucleus of quail: A key brain area mediating steroid action on male sexual behavior. *Front. Neuroendocrinol.* **17**, 51–125.

Papez, J. W. (1937). A proposed mechanism of emotion. *Archi. Neurol. Psychiatry* **38**, 725–744.

Paut-Pagano, L., Roky, R., Valatx, J. L., Kitahama, K., and Jouvet, M. (1993). Anatomical distribution of prolactin-like immunoreactivity in the rat brain. *Neuroendocrinology* **58**, 682–695.

Pavlov, I. P. (1927). "Conditional Reflexes. An Investigation of the Physiological Activity of the Cerebral Cortex." Oxford University Press, London.

Pfaff, D. W. (1980). "Estrogens and Brain Function." Springer-Verlag, New York.

Pfaff, D. W. (1982). Neurobiological mechanisms of sexual motivation. *In* "The Physiological Mechanisms of Motivation" (D. W. Pfaff, ed.), Springer-Verlag, New York.

Pfaff, D. W. (1999). "Drive." MIT Press, Cambridge, MA.

Pfaffmann, C. (1960). The pleasures of sensation. *Psychol. Rev.* **67**, 253–268.

Pfaffmann, C. (1982). Taste: A model of incentive motivation. *In* "The Physiological Mechanisms of Motivation" (D. W. Pfaff, ed.), pp. 61–97. Springer-Verlag, New York.

Pfaffmann, C., Norgren, R., and Grill, H. J. (1977). Sensory affect and motivation. *In* "Topic Function of Sensory Systems" (B. M. Wenzel and H. P. Ziegler, eds.). New York Academy of Sciences, New York.

Piazza P. V., and Le Moal, M. (1997). Glucocorticoids as a biological substrate of reward: Physiological and pathophysiological implications. *Brain Res. Rev.* **25**, 359–372.

Piazza, P. V., Maccari, S., Deminiere, J. M., Le Moal, M., Mormede, P., and Simon, H. (1991). Corticosterone levels determine individual vulnerability to amphetamine self-administration. *Neurobiology* **88**, 2088–2092.

Pugh, C. R., Tremblay, D., Fleshner, M., and Rudy, J. W. (1997). A selective role for corticosterone in contextual-fear conditioning. *Behav. Neurosci.* **111**, 503–5111.

Quartermain, D., and Wolf, G. (1967). Drive properties of mineralocorticoid-induced sodium appetite. *Physiol. Behav.* **2**, 261–263.

Quirarte, G. L., Roozendaal, B., and McGaugh, J. L. (1997). Glucocorticoid enhancement of memory storage involves nonadrenergic activation in the basolateral amygdala. *Proc. Natl. Acad. Sci. U.S.A.* **94**, 14048–14053.

Rescorla, R. A. (1988). Pavlovian conditioning: It's not what you think it is. *Am. Psychol.* **43**, 151–160.

Richter, C. P. (1943). Total self-regulatory functions in animals and human beings. *Harvey Lect.* **38**, 63–103.

Richter, R. M., Pich, E. M., Koob, G. F., and Weiss, F. (1995). Sensitization of cocaine-stimulated increase in extracellular levels of corticotropin-releasing factor from the rat amygdala after repeated administration as determined by intracranial microdialysis. *Neurosci. Lett.* **187**, 169–172.

Richter, R. M., and Weiss, F. (1999). In vivo CRF release in rat amygdala is increased during cocaine withdrawal in self-administering rats. *Synapse* **32**, 254–261.

Rolls, B. J., Rolls, E. T., and Rave, E. A. (1982). The influence of variety on human food selection and intake. *In* "The Psychobiology of Human Food Selection" (L. M. Barker, ed.), pp. 101–122. AVI Publ., Westport, CT.

Rosenwasser, AM., Schulkin, J., and Adler, N. T. (1988). Anticipatory appetitive behavior of adrenalectomized rats under circadian salt-access schedules. *Anim. Learn. Behav.* **16**, 324–329.

Sakai, R. R. (1986). The hormones of renal sodium conservation act synergistically to arouse a sodium appetite in the rat. *In* "The Physiology of Thirst and Sodium Appetite," (G. de Caro, A. N. Epstein, and M. Massi, eds.). Plenum, New York.

Salamone, J. D. (1994). The involvement of nucleus accumbens dopamine in appetitive and aversive motivation. *Behav. Brain Res.* **61**, 117–133.

Sarnyai, Z., Biro, E., Gardi, J., Vecsernyes, M. *et al.* (1993). Alterations of corticotropin-releasing factor-like immunoreactivity in different brain regions after acute cocaine administration in rats. *Brain Res.* **616**, 315–319.

Sarnyai, Z., Biro, E., Gardi, J., Vecsernyes, M. *et al.* (1995). Brain corticotropin-releasing factor mediates 'anxiety-like' behavior induced by cocaine withdrawal in rats. *Brain Res.* **675**, 89–97.

Schmidt, L. A., and Schulkin, J. (1999). "Extreme Fear, Shyness, and Social Phobia." Oxford University Press, Oxford.

Schmidt, L. A., Fox, N. A., Rubin, K. H., Sternberg, E. M., Gold, P. W., Smith, C. C., and Schulkin, J. (1997). Behavioral and neuroendocrine responses in shy children. *Dev. Psychobiol.* **36**, 127–140.

Schmidt, L. A., Fox, N. A., Sternberg, E. M., Gold, P. W., Smith, C. C., and Schulkin, J. (1999). Adrenocortical reactivity and social competence in seven year-olds. *Pers. Individ. Differ.* **26**, 977–985.

Schneirla, T. C. (1959). An evolutionary and developmental theory of biphasic processes underlying approach and withdrawal. *In* "The Nebraska Symposium on Motivation" (M. R. Jones, ed.), pp. 1–43. University of Nebraska Press, Lincoln.

Schneirla, T. C. (1965). Aspects of stimulation and organization in approach/withdrawal processes underlying vertebrate behavioral development. *In* "Advances in the Study of Behavior" (D. Lehrman, R. Hindle, and E. Shaw, eds.), pp. 1–74. Academic Press, New York.

Schulkin, J. (1991a). "Sodium Hunger." Cambridge University Press, Cambridge, UK.

Schulkin, J. (1991b). Hedonic consequences of salt hunger. *In* "The Hedonics of Taste" (R. C. Bolles, ed.), Erlbaum, Hillsdale, NJ.

Schulkin, J. (1999). "The Neruroendocrine Regulation of Behavior." Cambridge University Press, Cambrige, UK.

Schulkin, J. (2001). "Biological and Behavioral Regulation of Calcium Ingestion." Cambridge University Press, Cambrige, UK.

Schulkin, J., McEwen, B. S., and Gold, P. W. (1994). Allostasis, amygdala and anticipatory angst. *Neurosci. Biobehav. Rev.* **18**, 385–396.

Schulkin, J., Gold, P. W., and McEwen, B. S. (1998). Induction of corticotropin releasing hormone gene expression by glucocorticoids. *Psychoneuroendocrinology*.

Schumacher, M., Coirini, H., Pfaff, D. W., and McEwen, B. S. (1990). Behavioral effects of progesterone associated with rapid modulation of oxytocin receptors. *Science* **250**, 691–694.

Seeley, R. J., Payne, C. J., and Woods, S. C. (1995). Neuropeptide Y fails to increase intraoral intake in rats. *Am. J. Physiol.* **268**, R423–R427.

Shaham, Y., Erb, S., and Stewart, J. (2000). Stess-induced relapse to heroin and cocaine seeking in rats: A review. *Brain Res. Rev.* **33**, 13–33.

Shepard, J. D., Barron, K. W., and Myers, D. A. (2000). Corticosterone delivery to the amygdala increases CRH in the central nucleus of the amygdala and anxiety-like behavior. *Brain Res.* (in press).

Shettleworth, S. J. (1998). "Cognition, Evolution and Behavior." Oxford University Press, Oxford.

Skinner, B. F. (1938). "The Behavior of Organisms." Appleton-Century, New York.

Smith, G. W., Aubry, J. M., Dellu, F. *et al.* (1998) Corticotropin releasing factor receptor 1-deficient mice display decreased anxiety, impaired stress response, and aberrant neuroendocrine development. *Neuron* **20**, 1093–1102.

Sober, E., and Wilson, D. S. (1998). "Unto Others: The Evolution and Psychology of Unselfish Behavior." Harvard University Press, Cambridge, MA.

Solomon, R. L. (1980). The opponent process theory of acquired motivation. *Am. Psychol.* **35**, 691–712.

Spector, A. C. (2000). Linking gustatory neurobiology to behavior in vertebrates. *Neurosci. Biobehav. Rev.* **24**, 391–416.

Stellar, E. (1954). The physiology of motivation. *Psychol. Rev.* **61**, 5–22.

Stellar, E. (1960). Drive and motivation. *In* "Handbook of Physiology" (H. W. Magoun, ed.), Vol. 3, Sect. 1. American Physiological Society, Washington, DC.

Stellar, E., and Corbit, J. D. (1973). Neural control of motivated behavior. *Neurosci. Res. Program Bull.* **11**, 295–410.

Stellar, J. R., and Stellar, E. (1985). "The Neurobiology of Motivation and Reward." Springer-Verlag, New York.

Stricker, E. M., and Wolf, G. (1969). Behavioral control of intravascular fluid volume: Thirst and sodium appetite. *Ann. N. Y. Acad. Sci.* **157**, 553–568.

Stricker, E. M., and Zigmond, M. J. (1974). Effects on homeostasis of intraventricular injections of 6-hydroadopamine in rats. *J. Comp. Physiol. Psychol.* **86**, 973–974.

Stumpf, W. E., and O'Brien, L. P. (1987). 1,25 (OH) vitamin D sites of action in the brain. *Histochemistry* **87**, 393–406.

Sudakov, K. V. (1996). Motivation and reinforcement in the systemic mechanisms of behavior: Dynamic reinforcement engrams. *Neurosci. Behav. Physiol.* **26**, 445–453.

Sumners, C., Gault, T. R., and Fregly, M. J. (1991). Potentiation of angiotensin II-induced drinking by glucocorticoids is a specific glucocorticoid Type II receptor (GR)-mediated event. *Brain Res.* **552**, 283–290.

Suomi, S. J. (1997). Early determinants of behavior: Evidence from primate studies. *Bri. Med. J.* **53**, 170–184.

Swanson, L. W. (1988). The neural basis of motivated behavior. *Acta Morphol. Neurol. Scand.* **26**, 165–176.

Swanson, L. W. (2000). Cerebral hemisphere regulation of motivated behavior. *Brain Res. Rev.* **886**, 113–164.

Swanson, L. W., and Mogenson, G. J. (1981). Neural mechanisms for the functional coupling of autonomic, endocrine and somatomotor responses in adaptive behavior. *Brain Res.* **228**, 1–34.

Swanson, L. W., and Simmons, D. M. (1989). Differential steroid hormone and neural influences on peptide mRNA levels in corticotropin-releasing hormone cells of the paraventricular nucleus: A hybridization histochemical study in the rat. *J. Comp. Neurol.* **285**, 413–435.

Swanson, L. W., Sawchenko, P. E., Rivier, J., and Vale, W. W. (1983). Organization of ovine corticotropin releasing hormone immunoreactive cells and fibers in the rat brain: An immunohistochemical study. *Neuroendocrinology* **36**, 165–186.

Takahashi, L. K. (1995). Glucocorticoids, the hippocampus, and behavioral inhibition in the preweanling rat. *J. Neurosci.* **15**, 6023–6034.

Teitelbaum, P. (1967). The biology of drive. *In* "The Neurosciences: A Study Program" (G. Quarton, T. Melnechuk, and F. D. Schmidt, eds.), Rockefeller University Press, New York.

Teitelbaum, P. (1971). The encephalization of hunger. *Prog. Physiol. Psychol.* **4**, 319–350.

Teitelbaum, P. (1977). Levels of integration of the operant. *In* "Handbook of Operant Behavior" (W. K. Honig and J. E. R. Staddon, eds.), pp. 7–27. Prentice-Hall, Englewood Cliffs, NJ.

Tempel, D. L., and Leibowitz, S. F. (1994). Adrenal steroid receptors: Interactions with brain neuropeptide systems in relation to nutrient intake and metabolism. *J. Neuroendocrinol.* **6**, 479–501.

Thompson, B. L., Schulkin, J., and Rosen, J. B. (2000). Repeated administration of corticosterone facilitates contextual fear conditioning and CRH mRNA expression in the amygdala. *Neurosci. Abstr.*

Thorndike, E. L. (1911). "Animal Intelligence." Macmillan, New York.

Tinbergen, N. (1951/1969). "The Study of Instinct." Oxford University Press, Oxford.

Toates, F. (1986). "Motivational Systems." Cambridge University Press, Cambridge, UK.

Tolman, E. C. (1932). "Purposive Behavior in Animals and Men." The Century Co., New York.

Tolman, E. C., and Gleitman, H. (1949). Studies in learning and motivation. I. Equal reinforcements in both end-boxes, followed by shock in one end-box. *J. Exp. Psychol.* **39**, 810–819.

Valenstein, E. S. (1973). History of brain stimulation: Investigations into the physiology of motivation. *In* "Brain Stimulation and Motivation: Research and Commentary" (E. S. Valenstein, ed.). Scott, Foresman, Glenview, IL.

Valenstein, E. S., Cox, V. C., and Kakolewski, J. K. (1970). Reexamination of the role of the hypothalamus in motivation. *Psychol. Rev.* **77**, 16–31.

Vanderwolf, C. H., Kelly, M. E., Kraemer, P., and Streather, A. (1988). Are emotion and motivation localized in the limbic system and nucleus accumbens? *Behav. Brain Res.* **27**, 45–58.

von Holst, E., and von St. Paul, U. (1963). On the functional organization of drives. *Anim. Behav.* **11**, 1–20; reprinted in von Holst (1973).

Wade, J., and Crews, D. (1991). The effects of intracranial implantation of estrogen on receptivity in sexually and asexually reproducing female whiptail lizards, *Cnemidophorus inomatus* and *Cnemidophorus uniparens*. *Horm. Behav.* **25**, 342–353.

Wahlestedt, C., Pich, E. M., Koob, G. F., Yee, F., and Heilig, M. (1993). Modulation of anxiety and neuropeptide Y-Y1 receptors by antisense oligodeoxynucleotides. *Science* **259**, 528–531.

Wang, J., Dourmashkin, J. T., Yun, R., and Leibowitz, S. F. (1999). Rapid changes in hypothalamic neuropeptide Y produced by carbohydrate-rich meals that enhance corticosterone and glucose levels. *Brain Res.* **848**, 124–136.

Wang, Z., Smith, W., Major, D. E., and De Vries, G. J. (1994). Sex and species differences in the effects of cohabitation on vasopressin messenger RNA expression in the bed nucleus of the stria terminalis in prairie voles (*Microtus ochrogaster*) and meadow voles (*Microtus pennsylvanicus*). *Brain Res.* **650**, 212–218.

Watts, A. G. (2000). Understanding the neural control of ingestive behaviors: Helping to separate case from effect with dehydration-associated anorexia. *Horm. Behav.* **37**, 261–283.

Watts, A. G., and Watts-Sanchez, G. (1995). Region specific regulation of neuropeptidem RNA's in rat limbic forebrain neurons by aldosterone and corticosterone. *Brain Res.* **484**, 63–70.

Weninger, S. C., Dunn, A. J., Muglia, L. J. *et al.* (1999). Stress-induced behaviors require the corticotropin-releasing hormone (CRH) receptor, but not CRH. *Proc. Natl. Acad. Scl. U.S.A.* **96**, 8283–8299.

Wingfield, J. C. (1993). Control of testicular cycles in the song sparrow, Melospiza melodia melodia: Interaction of photoperiod and an endogenous program? *Gen. Comp. Endocrinol.* **92**, 388–401.

Wingfield, J. C. (1994). Control of territorial aggression in a changing environment. *Psychoneuroendocrinology* **19**, 709–721.

Winslow, J. T., Hastings, N., Carter, C. S. *et al.* (1993). A role for central vasopressin in pair bonding in monogamous prairie voles. *Nature (London)* **365**, 545–548.

Wise, R. A. (1971). Individual differences in effects of hypothalamic stimulation: The role of stimulation locus. *Physiol. Behav.* **6**, 569–572.

Wise, R. A. (1987). Sensorimotor modulation and the viable action patter: Toward a noncircular definition of drive and motivation. *Psychobiology* **15**, 7–20.

Wise, R. A., and Rompre, P. P. (1989). Brain dopamine and reward. *Annu. Rev. Psychol.* **40**, 191–225.

Wolf, G. (1964). Sodium appetite elicited by aldosterone. *Psychon. Sci.* **1**, 211–212.

Wolf, G. (1969). Innate mechanisms for regulation of sodium appetite. *In* "Olfaction and Taste" (C. Pfaffmann, ed.). Rockefeller University Press, New York.

Young, L. J., Nilsen, R., Waymore, K. G., MacGregor, G. R., and Insel, T. R. (1999). Increased affiliative response to vasopressin in mice expressing the Vla receptor from a monogamous vole. *Nature (London)* **400,** 766–768.

Young, P. T. (1941). The experimental analysis of appetite. *Psychol. Bull.* **38,** 129–164.

Young, P. T. (1959). The role of affective processes in learning and motivation. *Psychol. Rev.* **66,** 104–125.

Young, P. T. (1966). "Motivation and Emotion." Wiley, New York.

Zhang, D.-M., Stellar, E., and Epstein, A. N. (1984). Together intracranial angiotensin and systemic mineralocorticoid produce avidity for salt in the rat. *Physiol. Behav.* **32,** 677–681.

Zhou, Y., Spangler, R., LaForge, K. S., Maggos, C. E., Ho, A., and Kreek, M. J. (1996). Modulation of CRF-R1 mRNA in rat anterior pituitary by dexamethasone: correlation with POMC mRNA. *Peptides* **17,** 435–441.

11

Neurochemical Coding of Adaptive Responses in the Limbic System

Joe Herbert

Department of Anatomy
Cambridge University
Cambridge CB2 3BY, United Kingdom

Jay Schulkin

Department of Physiology and Biophysics
Georgetown University School of Medicine
Washington, DC 20007

I. INTRODUCTION

A. Behavior as Adaptation

Studies on the hormonal basis of behavior in the laboratory tend to focus on a single behavioral category. There are good reasons for this. Behavior is so complex, the neural mechanisms controlling it are so difficult to define, and the intellectual, technical, and financial resources of a single research worker and his or her laboratory so limited, that anything else seems the path to chaos, superficiality, and lack of precision. And there are the demands of a career: To be categorized as an "expert" in a defined field is the desiderata for many, and reasonably so. The other chapters in this book are witness to the success of this "reductionist" approach; reducing the complex world of an animal, such as the rat, to a single experimental setup and the study of a single behavior. For example, nearly all of what we know about the neuroendocrine regulation of eating, drinking, and sexual and maternal behavior comes from such studies, and they continue to yield important information based on careful and clever experiments. Yet this is not, and cannot be, the whole story. If we are to consider an animal as a biological entity—that is, a successful survivor—then we must ask ourselves how behaviors that together represent the adaptive repertory interact with each other. Are there similarities between the neuroendocrine mechanisms underlying these apparently diverse behaviors? How does an animal select the most appropriate behavioral response in the constantly changing world in which it lives?

In this chapter we focus on only some of the behaviors, and hope that their diversity will be sufficient for the points we want to make even considering only a limited agenda. We will discuss principally some selected aspects of the neuroendocrine regulation of sexual, maternal, and ingestive behaviors, considering similarities and differences, paradoxes and divergencies, always remembering that success in a competitive world implies success in all of these behaviors, however different their neuro-hormonal control might seem to be at first sight, and that the brain must contain not only the means for expressing each behavior, but also some means of deciding priority and appropriateness of distinct behavioral patterns (Herbert, 1993; Schulkin, 1999).

B. Homeostasis, Allostasis, and Adaptation

Discussions of behaviors that increase fitness logically begin with homeostasis (Bernard, 1878; Cannon, 1914), though, as we will see, homeostatic mechanisms cannot account completely for adaptive behavior. At its simplest, homeostasis has three components: the necessity to confine some physiological parameter within defined limits (e.g. blood volume, plasma sodium, blood glucose, body temperature), a mechanism to detect when these limits are exceeded (a state of demand or stress), and the means to deploy concerted behavioral and physiological processes to rectify this incipient or actual demand (Goldstein, 2000). Differences between species, or between genetic makeup, previous experience, or current physiological state of individuals within a species may all alter the set-point of homeostatic mechanisms or their tolerated range; nevertheless, any discussion of adaptive behavior, and the essential role played in such behavior by neuroendocrine mechanisms, must begin with homeostasis.

However, there are behaviors that, though adaptive, have no clear set-point, and that may anticipate, rather than respond to, current demand: These processes are termed *allostasis* (Sterling and Eyer, 1981; Schulkin *et al.,* 1994). Both homeostatic and allostatic demand represent forms of stress, and the response to stress, even if it is apparently successful (that is, it meets current or anticipated demand), may involve metabolic, behavioral, or pathological costs (Schulkin *et al.,* 1994; McEwen, 1998). Furthermore, the price of failure to meet homeostatic or allostatic demand is likely to be injury or death and a significant decrease in fitness.

Though the physiological environment is, rightly, the milieu on which homeostasis is usually discussed, all animals (we are really referring to mammals) live in a social environment. This adds two additional but crucial factors: First, the social environment regulates, to a greater or lesser degree, the animals' attempts to compensate for homeostatic or allostatic threats. This is because the resources needed (e.g., food, water, salt, shelter) are themselves the subjects of intra- and interspecific competition or sharing (Denton, 1982). Individuals therefore need to regulate their personal environment in the context of others attempting to do the same but competing for limited resources. But again the social environment can also facilitate the responses to homeostatic or allostatic regulation (Herbert, 1993). Second, the social environment itself is a persistent feature of most animals' lives (including man) and also has optimal or suboptimal qualities, which are also adaptive and need to be detected and responded to if the individual is to make the best use of its social environment or is not to be put at risk by the behavior of others. Demands from the social environment can be in some species a second source of stress, and (we will argue)

coping with these is not only an essential part of adaptation, but the neural and endocrine mechanisms that are involved overlap and resemble those that are associated with the more traditional examples of homeostasis.

Therefore, a major function of that part of the brain known as the limbic system is just this: to enable an individual to detect departures from the range of physiological or social homeostatic or allostatic states, energize the appropriate set of responses to this challenge, and assess the efficacy of the result. At this point, it might be thought that this definition would have difficulty in including reproductive behavior, but we will try to show that there is compelling neuroendocrine and theoretical evidence to suggest that reproduction, though it has distinctive features, is nevertheless based on generalized mechanisms associated with conventional homeostatic and allostatic responses.

II. RECOGNIZING DEMAND STATES

A. Information Flow

Our intention in this chapter is not, therefore, to repeat the detailed information set out elsewhere in this book but to draw on that information. We begin by considering the neuroendocrine mechanisms involved in ingestive behavior (that is, water, salt, and food), to see whether there are common features in the control of these behaviors, and also show how an individual selects, from the environment, the appropriate response to a defined demand state. Each of these behaviors depends, to some degree, on the reception and decoding of two sets of afferent information. The first signals the demand itself: In the case of salt and water, there are volume receptors that signal decreased blood volume or osmoreceptors that indicate changes in plasma osmolality (Fitzsimons, 1979, 1998; Denton, 1982). Feeding depends on more complex afferent information, though falls in blood glucose and signals from the liver are involved (Gibbs *et al.,* 1993; Kupfermann, 1994). The second information flow, much more complex even than these, involves the detection and recognition of appropriate means of rectifying the demand set up by the primary afferent signals: for example, in the case of water deficits, recognition of a water source, or the way to access one; for salt deficits, the ability to detect and ingest salt; for low energy states, the means to acquire and ingest suitable food.

The relative complexity of these two sets of signals is reflected in the way they are coded. The demand state is signaled by a chemical input, often associated with a receptor-mediated afferent neural input. In the case of blood volume, neural input from the stretch receptors of the vasculature and release of the peptide angiotensin II within the blood are sufficient to initiate the adaptive responses (Stricker, 1990; Fitzsimons, 1998). If sodium deficiency is severe, then the release of the steroid aldosterone acts as an additional specific peripheral signal (as well as osmolality) and helps to initiate sodium appetite as it acts in the brain (Schulkin, 1991). In the case of energy deficits, if glucose levels drop sharply, or ATP-rich compounds from the liver decrease, this acts as a signal acting directly on neurons sensitive to these factors; but there are also endocrine signals, including the peptide leptin, released largely from white fat, that may play a role in initiating or terminating the response to food, as well as more direct input from the afferent nerves from the gastrointestinal tract (Kupfermann, 1994; Bray, 2000).

It is important to point out that peripheral factors may be involved not only on the initiation of adaptive responses, but also in their termination. Overhydration, for example, has been associated with the release of another peptide (atrial natriuretic factor: ANP), which terminates drinking (McCann *et al.*, 1989; Szczepanska-Sadowska *et al.*, 1992), and there are a variety of gastrointestinal peptides, including cholecystokinin (CCK), that can terminate feeding (Smith, 1997).

Different demand states are encoded, quite specifically, by a combination of signals that are either directly related to the state itself (i.e., low plasma sodium, increased osmolality, changes in blood glucose) or as chemical signals that carry specific information about the nature of the demand state [e.g. mineralocorticoids registering the need for sodium, angiotensin and vasopressin signaling hypovolaemia (Richter, 1936; Wolf, 1958; Epstein and Sakai, 1987; Fitzsimons, 1998)]. The second set is also, of course, part of the adaptive process: That is, these chemical signals, as well as conveying information to the brain, act on peripheral receptors (e.g., on blood vessels, kidneys, endocrine glands) that mediate physiological responses that contribute to

adaptation. The peripheral endocrine signals thus have two functions: They are part of the adaptive process itself [e.g., argininine-vasopressin (AVP) and angiotensin act on the peripheral vasculature and on the kidney in situations of salt or water imbalance]; and they are part of the signaling process to the parts of the brain that are concerned with homeostatic regulation and responses (Fitzsimons, 1998).

Thus the afferent sensory system, so capable of carrying somatic information, is supplemented in a visceral context by additional, endocrine signals. These signals are decoded by areas of the brain (e.g., hypothalamus) that respond both directly to the homeostatic parameter (e.g., glucostats, osmoreceptors) and to the endocrine chemical signals (Ramsay and Booth, 1991). They are also decoded by afferent information from peripheral nerves (e.g., in the vagal-associated brain stem nuclei such as the solitary nucleus or the parabrachial nucleus), as well as by catecholaminergic and serotonergic input from brain stem nuclei. The hypothalamus and related areas are responsive to endocrine signals via a number of mechanisms: these include steroid receptors [e.g., mineralocorticoid (MR) receptors], circumventricular receptors to peripheral peptides (e.g., angiotensin II), or to peptides that are transported into the brain by carrier mechanisms (e.g., leptin, insulin), again largely in the hypothalamus (Dubey *et al.*, 1983; Schwartz *et al.*, 1990; Dallman *et al.*, 1992; Elmquist *et al.*, 1998; Woods *et al.*, 1996).

B. Reproduction as Demand

It is in the central state of the brain in which these afferent codes are translated into demand states and hence coordinated patterns of response. Before considering these in more detail, we should discuss whether or not reproductive behaviors fit into this general pattern. Reproduction is not, of course, a response to a metabolic or physiological demand in the usual sense. However, it is axiomatic that a successful reproductive strategy is essential for maximal fitness. Reproduction is also a demand in the sense that it imposes on the individual the need to compete successfully for a mate (in many species, this is particularly marked for the males, and may involve aggression-related risks) and, principally for the mother, the metabolic and behavioral demands of parenting (Dixson, 1998).

The secretion of gonadal steroids can be considered as an afferent signal, in the sense that they initiate a series of behavioral (and somatic) responses that are related to reproductive success (Herbert, 1996a). As we will see, the neural mechanisms responsible for activation of sexual responses, and the selection of a mate, are in many ways comparable to those associated with other, if distinct, adaptive responses (Pfaus, 1999). It seems likely, therefore, that similar neural mechanisms are used for this set of adaptively important responses as for others. The steroid signal from the gonads, therefore, acts as a peripheral "demand" signal to initiate sexuality, just as other, equally specific peripheral signals (e.g., aldosterone) act to signal other demand conditions (e.g., salt depletion). Sexual demand is only satisfied by the presence of a potential sexual partner, which initiates the stereotyped mating behavior observed in all mammalian species. The recognition and response to potential partners requires the same high-level processing that is also needed to identify and respond to other demand-related stimuli (Pfaff, 1980) (e.g., food sources). The function of gonadal and placental steroids in the initiation and regulation of maternal behavior is less clear-cut than for sexual behavior, though they clearly have a role (Bridges *et al.,* 1997). Their contribution to establishing parental behavior can, to this extent, also be compared to a "demand" state, one that is only satisfied by the recognition of the presence of an appropriate young, and the consequent set of adaptive responses to it.

III. RECOGNIZING THE SOLUTION

We must now consider, in more detail, the higher-level processing associated with recognizing the solution to a demand state. This second set of afferent information is quite different from that signaling the demand state. This source may not be concerned with signaling the nature of the demand or homeostatic or allostatic challenge but with locating the means to defend the individual's integrity. Whereas the afferent information about the nature of the stress (whether endocrine or physiological) addresses neural mechanisms in the hypothalamus and brainstem as part of the function of these parts of the brain in monitoring the internal environment, information about the external environ-

ment requires additional, and more elaborate, neural processing (Nieuwenhuys, 1996). Areas of the brain such as the amygdala are responsive to both internal and external signals (Schulkin *et al.,* 1994), along with more analytic areas of the brain, such as the cerebral neocortex: These areas are highly specialized to recognize complex patterns of information (e.g., visual scenes, complex auditory input).

Detailed discussion of their roles in these processes is not only outside the scope of this chapter but unnecessary, since we can assume that their function in the context of adaptive behavior is no different from any other in which the individual needs to recognize objects or events in the environment and relate these to previous experience (Mesulam, 1998; Gazzaniga, 2000). Identifying a pool of water for what it is, or recognizing that a tap will give water, or that water may be obtained in a given situation or following a learned procedure, are all examples of this second system. The important points, in the context of the present discussion, are that this process requires additional neural machinery over that signaling the demand state and, more pertinently, a means whereby that state is brought into relation with other sources of information essential for behavioral adaptation. That is, the first set of signals will not only encode the demand state, but will also enable the individual to match information from the external environment (either current or residing in memory) with the current nature of the homeostatic demand. In short, there must be a mechanism for allowing the current demand state to impinge on the animals' analysis of the external environment. There must also be the converse process: Relevant information from the external environment is analyzed by mechanisms that can be "matched" with current physiological needs. At a descriptive level, this is reflected by the changes in motivational and emotional state that are induced by homeostatic or allostatic demands. Basically, it seems that the afferent signals encoding the demand set up specific motivational states, and these are then brought into conjunction with the information being received from the animal's external environment, or drawn into working memory from data about that environment previously stored in longer-term memory.

The function of the second set of afferent information, relying as it does on elaborate processing of the external environment, is particularly important in the animal's assessment of its social environment. An animal's social environment not only regulates its access to adaptive resources, but also can itself be the source of psycho-social stress and endangerment (e.g., the receipt of aggression from other members of the group, or from other groups) (Herbert and Martinez, 2001). Analysis of complex social relations depends, of course, on the allocortical and neocortical systems that have been already discussed in relation to the decoding of other complex external environmental stimuli. However, the assessment of the value of these social events, particularly those that signal potential or actual danger, needs the same neural mechanism that is also used to attach value to motivationally important features from the environment. This attribution, as we have seen, is dependent on the animal's current demand state. An assessment of the social limitations to any evident homeostatic solution is, therefore, required. This is no different from the "cost-benefit" analysis known in other areas of inquiry (economics). It is, of course, particularly evident in the context of reproductive behavior (Hinde, 1974; Wilson, 1975).

This rather general overview suggests strongly that the neuroendocrine systems responsible for coordinated adaptive responses must have the following features:

1. They must be able to decode specific physiological or endocrine demand signals derived from the periphery.
2. They must be able to relate this information to other information derived from the external environment.
3. They must be able to organize (encode) a coordinated behavioral response, and this has to include both endocrine and autonomic components.
4. They must be able to prioritize an animal's response, so that the most immediate and urgent demands are dealt with over those that can wait, or be subjugated until the principal challenge has either passed or been effectively dealt with.
5. They must be able to assess the efficacy of the adaptive response.
6. They must take into account constraints from the animal's external environment, in particular that deriving from its social group.

All these considerations suggest that the neural systems responsible will be both distributed (because each adaptive response has several components) and overlapping (because different adaptive responses nevertheless have common features: e.g., cardiovascular activation, corticoid secretion) (Fig. 1).

Our hypothesis is that neurochemical coding within the limbic system is essentially involved in the integration and coordination of behavioral adaptation; behavior is turned on, other behaviors are inhibited, priorities are established, conflict and partial resolution are endured (Herbert, 1993; Schulkin, 1999). Let's turn to the brain.

IV. GENE EXPRESSION IN THE BRAIN IN DEMAND STATES: IMMEDIATE-EARLY GENES

There are a number of ways to measure activity in the nervous system and thus to detect changes in its state. These include recording electrical activity, measuring metabolic activity, assessing changes in enzyme levels, measuring the release of putative transmitters, and detecting alterations in gene expression. Each has its strengths and limitations. However, to detect activity in a distributed system does require a method that allows wide scanning of the CNS, and the expression of immediate-early genes (IEGs) (Sheng and Greenberg, 1990; Smith *et al.*, 1992)—such as c-fos, but including many other IEGs—has been particularly useful in studying neural systems implicated in adaptation. This is because the expression of c-fos and other IEGs makes no assumption about the phenotype of the neurons concerned (Herrera and Robertson, 1996), and also because it is possible to scan the whole brain by using quite routine immunocytochemical or *in situ* hybridization methods, now well established for many other genes. However, there are drawbacks: First, although it is well-established that the c-fos protein and that of other IEGs act as transcription regulators (as do many other peptides), we do not yet know on which genes they operate in the brain under specified circumstances; in other words, no direct functional interpretation is possible. Second, although increased expression of these genes is usually assumed to indicate increased activity, there is no guarantee that this is an essential requirement; that is, absence of expression may not

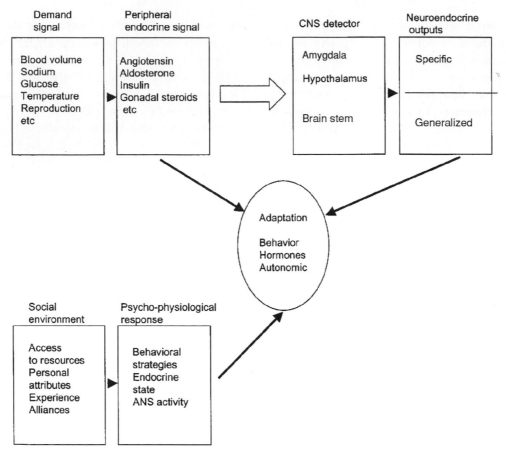

FIGURE 1 Diagrammatic representation of the process involved in the recognition and response to physiological and psychological demand. The scheme emphasizes the interaction between internal and external signals in detecting and coping with a defined demand state and the distinction between "specific" and "generalized" responses to demand (stress).

indicate absence of activity. Finally, though most studies have focused on c-fos, there are a large number of associated IEGs, and it is not yet clear whether differential expression of a range of IEGs has physiological importance in adaptive processes in the brain (Stamp and Herbert, 1999).

Whatever its limitations, the principle of using the IEG technique to map distributed systems involved in defined adaptive responses is clear enough. The requisite state is induced (i.e., water deprivation, salt-depletion, food deprivation, sexual readiness, or maternal behavior), and the effect this has on IEG expression is mapped throughout the brain (McKinley *et al.,* 1994; Rowland *et al.,* 1994; Baum and Everitt, 1992; Lin *et al.,* 1998; Wang *et al.,* 1999). Of course, there are precautions: to ensure that the state induced

is the intended one, to take account of the severity or duration of the demand or stress, to know the ability of the animal to resolve the demand (e.g., the availability of appropriate resources), and so on. There are also the problems associated with quantifying the changes in IEG expression (different for *in situ* or immunocytochemical procedures). Nevertheless, this method has given us, for the first time, some indication of the identity, distribution, and distinctive characteristics of the systems responsive to the various demands listed above, though it cannot, of course, tell us much about their role in adaptation itself.

If a rat is deprived of water for 24 hours, its brain shows a characteristic pattern of increased c-fos expression. There is a prominent group of c-fos-positive neurons surrounding the anterior border of the third ventricle extending upward toward the subfornical organ, which is also positive, and down toward the OVLT, another site of increased expression (Rowland *et al.*, 1994). This area, the AV3V region, has long been known to be concerned with thirst and is essential for the dipsogenic response to water deprivation (Buggy and Johnson, 1977; Johnson, 1985): For examples, lesions here interfere with drinking responses, and local infusions of Ang II stimulate them. So the pattern of c-fos expression in this part of the hypothalamus following this demand confirms the findings of very different experimental approaches (e.g., the effects of lesions or local infusions of dipsogenic substances (Herbert, 1996b). But c-fos expression is not limited to this area. There is increased expression in both the magnocellular and parvicellular regions of the hypothalamic paraventricular nucleus (PVN), in the central nucleus of the amygdala, and in the brain stem; the parabrachial nucleus, and the solitary nucleus are among those areas that express increased c-fos. Since it is known that the endocrine response to water deprivation is largely orchestrated by the PVN, that thirst is dependent on the AV3V, and that the cardiovascular reaction is regulated (in part) by the solitary and parabrachial nuclei, the distribution of c-fos in this demand state relates well to what is known from other experimental approaches. This method allows the distributed population of neurons responsive to water deprivation to be mapped (Fig. 2). Sodium depletion by itself gives a similar but not identical picture. The major difference is that the OVLT seems to be particularly responsive to this procedure, which correlates with experimental evidence suggesting that it has a special role in sodium balance (Lane *et al.*, 1997; Franchini and Vivas, 1999).

Food deprivation results in a different pattern. Fos expression is increased in the parvicellular PVN in unfed rats and sheep, as following water deprivation, but also in the ventromedial, dorsomedial, and lateral hypothalamic nuclei and the lateral septum (Chaillou *et al.*, 2000; Carr *et al.*, 1998). Increased expression in the central nucleus of the amygdala and bed nucleus of the stria terminalis (BNST) has been recorded. Sites in the brain stem include the solitary nucleus, the ventral tegmental area, and the parabrachial nuclei (Fig. 2). It is clear that even at a descriptive level, one can define distributed networks of limbic neurons that are selectively activated in the context of defined demand states; it is also evident that in some cases (e.g., the PVN) there may be overlap between these networks, a facet that requires explanation.

Although we have suggested that the secretion of gonadal steroids can act as a surrogate demand signal in the context of sexual behavior, in fact treating castrated animals with such steroids, though they induce sexual readiness, does not result in a definable pattern of fos expression in the brain. At first sight this might seem incompatible with the inclusion of sexual behavior and its control by gonadal steroids in the more general pattern of adaptive behavior. If, however, a testosterone-treated male rat is placed in the presence of a sexually receptive female (or even in the context in which previous sexual interaction has taken place), a striking pattern of c-fos expression is invoked (Baum and Everitt, 1992; Pfaus *et al.*, 1993; Kollack-Walker and Newman, 1995) (Fig. 2). Sexual interaction itself also induces c-fos in a variety of species, though most of these findings, it has to be said, have been made on males. It is clear that c-fos expression in sexually active males is the response to the female, not to the presence of testosterone, but only if the steroidal environment (in this case, testosterone) is appropriate. Yet a coherent explanation of the effects of this hormone must include anticipation: Testosterone-treated males, after all, will work for a female or seek one out under natural conditions; there must be a neural mechanism that corresponds to this observed feature. It would be easy to suggest that, perhaps, the study of a different IEG might reveal something about this central state, but there is no rationale for such a statement.

There is, as yet, no reliable way of demonstrating sexual motivation (in the absence of an appropriate partner) by objective changes in the brain's activity. However, the fos experiments may tell us something interesting about the role of the brain in sexuality. It seems that the areas of the limbic brain that are concerned with sexual behavior are only activated by the immediate prospect or actuality of sexual interaction (Pfaus *et al.*, 1993). The important point is that although parts of the hypothalamus, amygdala, and brain stem express c-fos under these conditions, they are not the same areas as are observed after either water or food deprivation (Herbert, 1996a). In males, the medial POA in the hypothalamus is activated, which relates well

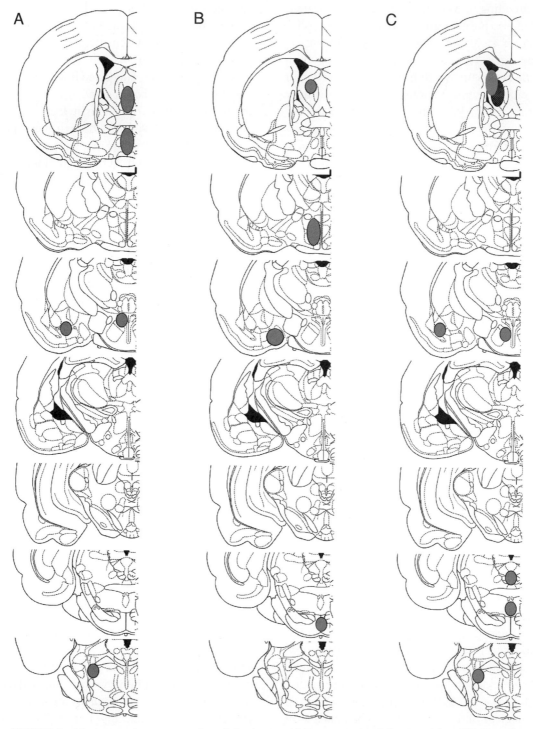

FIGURE 2   Diagrammatic representation of the pattern of Fos expression following either (A) water deprivation, (B) sexual stimulation, (C) psychological (restraint) stress. In each case the pattern is distributed but distinctive for the nature of the demand state. The pattern after water deprivation is reproduced by icv angiotensin infusions, and that after restraint by CRF (or AVP) infusions.

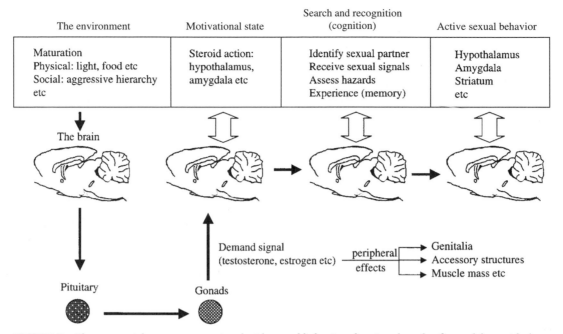

FIGURE 3   The sequential processes associated with sexual behavior, showing the role of gonadal steroids (e.g., testosterone) as a "demand" signal. The differential role of the brain at each stage is also illustrated.

to the known involvement of this part of the brain in masculine patterns of sexual behavior (Baum, 1995). In the amygdala, it is the corticomedial nuclei that express c-fos, areas that receive prominent olfactory input, long known to be important in (rodent) sexual behavior. An area in the ventral tegmentum is also activated; although this has been associated with sexual behavior, its role is less defined than the others.

The results of examining c-fos expression in the context of sexual behavior also tells us something interesting about the relation between internal signals (in this case, testosterone) and external ones (the presence of a sexually receptive female), and reinforces the suggestion, made above, that there has to be a close and coordinated interaction between these two sources of afferent information. Unfortunately, less has been done on this aspect of adaptive behavior in the context of other demand states. The important point, however, is that whereas parts of three of the major areas of the limbic system express c-fos in association with sexual behavior, these are again distinct from those activated by other states, such as water or food deprivation. Taken together, these findings suggest a local specialization within the major divisions of the limbic system, corresponding to individual demand.

There are three main conclusions to be drawn from this limited comparative survey of c-fos expression in the brain during defined demand states. Each state evokes a distributed pattern of c-fos; this is distinctive in that the overall form of the pattern differs between states; there are certain regions (e.g., the parvicellular PVN, the central amygdala nucleus) that seem to react to a variety of demand states (Fig. 3) and this may represent more general characteristics of the adaptive process, comparable, in some ways, to Selye's concept of the "generalized" stress response (Selye, 1936, 1978).

V. THE CONCEPT OF THE LIMBIC SYSTEM

A. Its Role in Adaptation

If behavioral adaptation is an essential and definable characteristic of mammals (in our context), then there must be a corresponding neural mechanism. The concept of the limbic system has been considerably modified since Broca (1878) first introduced the term, and this needs no rehearsal here. There are even those who suggest that the definition is too vague or the concept too unnecessary for the idea of a limbic system to be sustainable (Kotter and Meyer, 1992; Blessing, 1997). We contend that the limbic system is as definable as any other part of the brain, and adaptation, allostasis, and homeostasis are the intrinsic and essential functions of this system. Indeed, it is not possible to understand the brain's function in a biological context without invoking the existence of a limbic system (MacLean, 1990; Nieuwenhuys, 1996). Contemporary views on the function of the limbic system derive from the major and well-known insight by Papez (1937), who first suggested a coherent function for this part of the brain. However, Papez also introduced two problems: The first, equally well-known, is that he excluded the amygdala, now recognized to be an intrinsic part of this system (Davis, 1992; LeDoux, 1992; Swanson and Petrovich, 1998). This omission has long since been rectified, though there are still theoretical treatments of emotion that leave it out (Gray, 1982). The second, which still persists, is that the function of the limbic system is "emotion." There is no doubt that the expression of emotion is an intrinsic role of the limbic system (MacLean, 1955; LeDoux, 1998). There is also no doubt that this is only part of what it does, and to limit discussion of the limbic system to the origin and display of emotionality is both too restrictive and misleading, since it undervalues the real role of this part of the brain.

The concept of neural "systems" is well established and recognizes the anatomical fact that there are parts of the brain that specialize in defined subsets of overall neural function. Nobody has problems about accepting the concept, or reality, of the motor, somatosensory, or visual systems. A wealth of anatomical and physiological data show that these areas are activated during the associated functional state, and that damage to parts of any particular system will result in deficits in corresponding abilities. A brief consideration of even these well-defined systems, however, shows that they are, in fact, less distinct that might be supposed. For example, all agree that there are three cortical areas (precentral, postcentral, and calcharine), which, together with their associated thalamic nuclei, represent parts of these three systems. But closer inspection of how that information is processed in these systems shows that the boundaries between them are highly indistinct. For example, visual information is processed progressively by more anterior regions of the cortex; these blend into other areas that process other categories of sensory information (e.g., in the temporal lobe) (Zeki, 1993). The motor system (Kuypers, 1987) also includes the basal ganglia, though these structures also have functions that lie outside the usual definition of "motor" (e.g., cognition). The cerebellum, usually classified as part of the motor system, has a huge afferent (sensory) input and recently has also been implicated in cognitive functions of various kinds. Within the thalamus, there are nuclei (the "association" group) that seem to straddle different functional categories. The conclusion is that there is no point trying to draw precise and clear-cut boundaries around neural "systems"; all must interact, and there will always be both functional and anatomical areas of blending between them. So it is with the limbic system. Although there are areas that everyone might agree must be included in such a definition (e.g., the amygdala, the hypothalamus, the septum), there are other parts that have both "limbic" and other functions (e.g., the hippocampus), and yet others in which blending of limbic and other functions occurs (e.g., in the frontal cortex, or the brain stem) (Swanson and Mogenson, 1981; Nieuwenhuys, 1996). Yet there is no other part of the brain that is clearly devoted to adaptive functions, and this, we believe, is not only the defining feature of the limbic system, but also one that has substantial experimental support.

Most people would recognize the hypothalamus, amygdala, septum, hippocampus, BNST, anterior thalamic nuclei, cingulate, and orbito-frontal cortex as components of the limbic system (though, as we have said, opinions have differed over the years), together with a variety of brain stem nuclei, which have included the parabrachial nuclei, the solitary nuclei, and even the raphe and other aminergic structures (Everitt *et al.,* 1983; Price *et al.,* 1987; Nieuwenhuys, 1996). The caveat about the indistinct nature of boundaries between systems needs to be recalled. As we have seen, the use of c-fos, together with experimental approaches that include local lesions, implantation of hormones, or electrical or chemical stimulation, have indicated as much for the hypothalamus. The preoptic area (POA), for example, is clearly involved in masculine patterns of sexual behavior but also in maternal behavior: Are the same neuronal pools used for both behaviors, or are there different patterns of activity in the POA, not visible by the current techniques, but which represent specific pools of neurons? The areas involved in feeding (e.g., ventromedial and dorsomedial nuclei, VMN, DMN) seem distinct from those implicated in male sexual behavior (but, for example, feminine patterns of sexual behavior are known to be associated with VMN; see Pfaus, 1999)

B. The Modular Limbic System

Labeling different components of the limbic system (e.g., hypothalamus, septum, hippocampus, ventral striatum, and amygdala) as anatomical entities clearly indicates one view of how this part of the brain is organized. If we assume that anatomical definitions are associated with equally distinct functional ones, we arrive at a *modular* view of the limbic system. This is a system that comprises a number of interconnected, anatomically circumscribed units, each with a particular contribution to make to the function of the system as a whole. The hypothalamus might be said to be concerned with the organization or expression of motivated behavioral and endocrine responses, or the amygdala proposed as the area in which emotional or affective qualities are attributed to motivationally relevant stimuli, and the septum and nucleus accumbens as part of a mechanism for inhibiting or selecting behavioral responses. Within each area there may be further anatomically based functional subdivisions; for example, within the hypothalamus are anatomically recognizable nuclei or divisions, such as the preoptic area or the paraventricular, suprachiasmatic, and arcuate nuclei (Everitt and Hökfelt, 1986). Within each structure there may be further subdivisions: For example, the paraventricular nucleus is divided into a number of subnuclei (Kiss *et al.*, 1991) and so on. The assumption is that an anatomically defined area will have a correspondingly discrete functional role. This is reflected in the standard neuroanatomical approach to the analysis of function, which is based heavily on observing the effects of localized lesions. Lesions in the amygdala, for example, have different effects on, say, male sexual behavior than lesions in the hypothalamus. The first disturbs the male's gathering and processing of information about an estrous female, whereas the second interferes with the organization of the sexual response to such a stimulus (Hansen *et al.*, 1984; McGregor and Herbert, 1992a). Within the amygdala, different nuclei

may have definable roles in emotion-related learning (Parkinson *et al.*, 2000). So there is evidence for regional subdivision of function within the limbic system. However, a second viewpoint on how the limbic system is organized depends on its neurochemical architecture.

VI. NEUROCHEMICAL CODING OF ADAPTIVE RESPONSES

Although it is legitimate to consider how different parts of the limbic system contribute to adaptive responses, and whether within each area there are subregions with additional specificities, this anatomical (regional) architectural approach is not the only one possible. The limbic system is distinguished by the range and concentration of its chemical transmitters (some of which may be termed neuromodulators). The chemical architecture of the limbic system may also offer clues about its organization and the relevance of this to the way the brain differentiates between different demands or stresses and adapts to them.

A. Amino-Acid Transmitters

To simplify the argument, we will limit the discussion to four classes of such chemicals (Fig. 4). Amino acids, such as glutamate and γ-amino-butyric acid (GABA), represent the simplest. They are used throughout the brain as transmitters (together with a few other candidates, such as glycine and possibly others); there is nothing special about their actions in the limbic system, so far as we know at present, though they clearly play a significant role here as elsewhere. Their apparent chemical simplicity is complicated by a profusion of receptors and post-receptor cellular events; but this, again, is common to other parts of the brain and enables amino-acid transmitters to act as chemical switches in the neural networks, characteristic, for example, of the cortex as well as in longer-term changes such as those underlying some forms of learning. In the limbic system, it is likely that neural "processing" (which may be site-dependent) relies upon the frequency and spatial distribution of electrochemical coding; this has been extensively studied in the neocortex and in so-called "simpler" (nonmammalian) nervous systems, but has received less attention in the

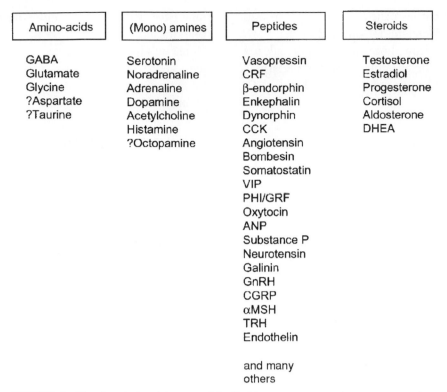

Amino-acids	(Mono) amines	Peptides	Steroids
GABA	Serotonin	Vasopressin	Testosterone
Glutamate	Noradrenaline	CRF	Estradiol
Glycine	Adrenaline	β-endorphin	Progesterone
?Aspartate	Dopamine	Enkephalin	Cortisol
?Taurine	Acetylcholine	Dynorphin	Aldosterone
	Histamine	CCK	DHEA
	?Octopamine	Angiotensin	
		Bombesin	
		Somatostatin	
		VIP	
		PHI/GRF	
		Oxytocin	
		ANP	
		Substance P	
		Neurotensin	
		Galinin	
		GnRH	
		CGRP	
		αMSH	
		TRH	
		Endothelin	
		and many others	

FIGURE 4 The chemical architecture of the limbic system: comparisons among amino acids, amines, peptides, and steroids as components of the chemical codes underlying adaptive responses.

limbic system, though there are exceptions. However, the conclusion is that there may be nothing special about the function of the amino-acid transmitters in the limbic system, other than their site of action. However, it does seem that glutamate and GABA are particularly useful in the brain under circumstances where there are clear topographical arrangements of information flow (that is, a spatial "code") (Trimmer, 1999). For example, the corticostriatal pathways and the thalamocortical projections have a clear topographical organization: Such arrangements are a consistent theme of many cortically associated neural systems. We suggest that this feature is much less prominent in the limbic system: Here, as we will try to show, functional specificity is encoded by a rather different mechanism from that established for neocortical systems (see Herbert, 1993).

B. Peptides as Coding Agents

Peptides are altogether more complex chemically than amino-acids, and there are dozens (perhaps hun-

dreds) known to be released in the brain. Here they act as elsewhere in the body—as complex intercellular signals (Acher, 1980). The limbic system has the highest concentration of peptides in the brain, though they are found in most other parts. The development of immunohistochemistry and related techniques has altered our view of the way the limbic system is organized. Peptide-containing neurons are found in all parts, though the distribution is not even (Swanson, 1987; Herbert, 1993). In some cases a local group supplies terminals to a wide area (e.g., proopiomelanocorticotropin-expressing neurons: POMC). In others, neurons and terminals are found in several, relatively dispersed areas (e.g., those containing corticotropin-releasing factor: CRF) (Palkovits and Brownstein, 1985; Palkovitz *et al.*, 1985). The neurochemical view of the limbic system suggests a series of parallel or complementary pathways, each distinguished from the others by its specific content of peptides (Fig. 5). These differ from other neurochemicals (such as the monoamines) in that their behavioral

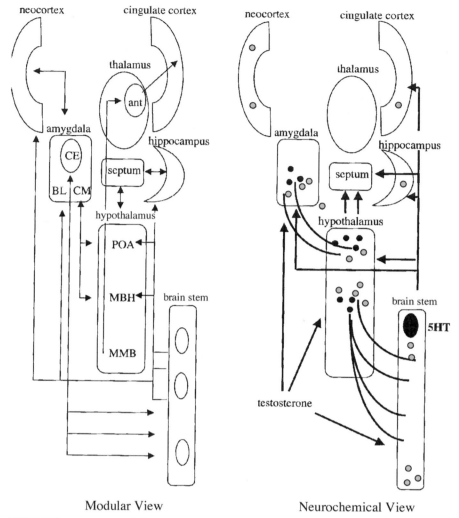

Modular View   Neurochemical View

FIGURE 5 Two views of the organization of the limbic system. On the left, the modular view, emphasizing the different structures that make up the limbic system and the close anatomical connections between them. On the right, examples of a neurochemical view, in which the typical distribution of two peptides (Ang II, black circles, and CRF, grey circles) are shown (with both similarities and differences), together with one monoamine (5-HT) and the input from peripheral steroids (e.g., testosterone).

effects can be quite specific. It seems plausible that peptides represent the neurochemical codes by which specific adaptive responses are organized (Mayer and Baldi, 1991).

This conclusion follows from the following premise: Peptides initiate or regulate relatively specific patterns of behavior. They do more than this: They also enable a related set of physiological (endocrine, autonomic) responses that, together with the behavior, represent the adaptive response. This differentiates them from some other neurochemicals, particularly the amines (sero-

tonin, dopamine, noradrenaline, acetylcholine); the latter seem able to alter a wide spectrum of behavior; that is, their function, though important, is less specific. Some examples of the roles of peptides support this idea.

C. Angiotensin and Adaptation to Water Loss

It has been known for years that an icv infusion of angiotensin II (Ang II) initiates robust drinking within a few minutes, even in water-replete animals, and an equally robust salt appetite some hours later (Epstein *et al.*, 1970; Fitzsimons, 1979). But Ang II does more than this: It also acts as a powerful pituitary secreto-gogue, releasing vasopressin and ACTH, and activates central autonomic brain stem centers regulating blood pressure (Mangiapane *et al.*, 1983). Injection of pico-molar amounts of Ang II into a number of brain stem sites, including the solitary nucleus (nucleus tractus solitarius: NTS) and area postrema, have hyperten-sive and cardio-accelerator effects. This is the adap-tive response expected in the context of reduced blood volume (Chan *et al.*, 1991).

Both central and peripheral Ang II are released under such conditions, and it appears likely that this peptide can initiate the requisite adaptation to that homeostatic emergency. Icv infusion of Ang II also induces a pattern of c-fos that closely resembles that seen after water de-

privation (Herbert *et al.*, 1992a). Other behaviors (e.g., eating, sexual activity, thermoregulation) are not acti-vated by Ang II. This is not to say that Ang II is the only peptide concerned with drinking. It is no surprise that other peptides are dipsogenic when one recalls that drinking occurs in many contexts and for many reasons (e.g., prandial, schedule-driven, opportunistic). There are also other peptidergic signals that release both vaso-pressin and ACTH; this is similarly not unexpected, for there are many other contexts that require the secretion of the pituitary hormones (particularly ACTH). Neither is Ang II "the" cardiovascular peptide. Many other pep-tides have been shown to have cardiovascular actions following either icv or local infusions into the limbic system or brainstem. These include the opioid pep-tides, vasopressin, substance P, oxytocin, neuropeptide Y (NPY), CRF, and ANP (Reid and Rubin, 1987; Share, 1988) (Fig. 6).

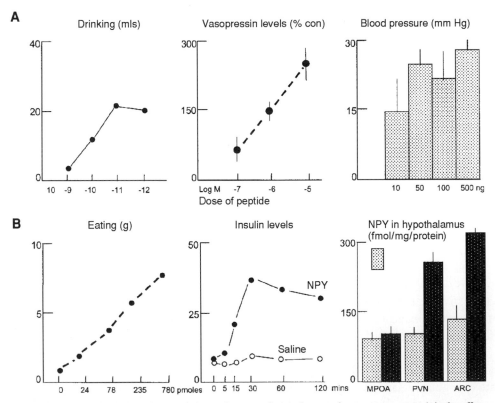

FIGURE 6 Two examples of the coordinated action of peptides on adaptive responses. (A) The effect of icv angiotensin II on drinking, vasopressin levels in the blood, and blood pressure (Fitzsimons, 1979; Schiavone *et al.*, 1988; Hoffman and Phillips, 1976). (B) The effects of NPY on eating and on insulin levels in the blood and the effects of food deprivation of hypothalamic NPY (MPOA, medial preoptic area; PVN, paraventricular nucleus; ARC, hypothalamic arcuate nucleus) (Stanley *et al.*, 1992; Moltz and McDonald, 1985; Kalra and Kalra, 1990).

This does not diminish the case for a specific role for Ang II: Specificity is not the same as exclusivity. Just as drinking can occur in situations other than hypovolaemia and be controlled by other (possibly peptidergic) factors, so changes in cardiovascular activity are part of many adaptive responses, and therefore many peptidergic systems have been implicated in the control of heart rate and blood pressure centrally as well as peripherally (Turner *et al.*, 1986; Share, 1988). In the case of cardiovascular regulation, this interpretation is supported by the existence of numerous parallel pathways between rostral structures controlling cardiovascular activity—such as the hypothalamus and central amygdala—and those in the brainstem, including the NTS and areas of the ventrolateral medulla (Spyer, 1989). If we postulate chemical coding of adaptive responses by peptides, then a behavior that occurs in different contexts, though it may be behaviorally similar, will have different controls. Furthermore, Ang II is not the only peptide concerned with hypovolaemia. Peripheral endocrine responses to haemorrhage, for example, include a wide range of hormones, including adrenocorticotropin (ACTH), arginine vasopressin (AVP), cortisol, and aldosterone, as well as Ang II; this suggests activation of several corresponding intracerebral systems, including CRF. The specificity of a peptide system therefore lies in the pattern of response (i.e., behavioral, endocrine, and autonomic outputs) it evokes and the context in which this pattern occurs, not in the nature of individual outputs. But the role of Ang II in adaptive coordination can be reasonably clearly defined. Can this idea be extended to other peptide-containing systems?

If there are peptides coding for initiating adaptive responses, there may also be others signaling the reverse. In the case of hypovolaemic drinking, atriopeptin (atrial natriuretic factor: ANP) may fulfil this function: Hypervolaemia seems to increase its release, and infusions antagonize the effects of angiotensin II (Steele *et al.*, 1991; Szczepanska-Sadowska *et al.*, 1992).

It is not yet clear exactly how Ang II (and other peptides) are released in the brain: that is, whether there is a classical synaptic mechanism (which has been questioned), or whether peptides are released locally and act by local diffusion, rather in the manner of local neuroendocrine agents. This "volume" hypothesis is supported by the lack of synaptic structures in some peptidergic endings, the lack of a re-uptake mecha-

nism (which would encourage local diffusion) (Fuxe *et al.*, 1991), a supposed "mismatch" between peptidergic endings and receptors (Herkenham, 1987, 1991), and the low concentration (high affinity) at which many peptides are effective (Bloom, 1980). If this is a general feature of limbic peptides, then it suggests that this part of the brain operates on a principle somewhat different from some others (e.g., the cerebral cortex, the striatum), but one more resembling a classical neuroendocrine system. The release of peptides into the pituitary portal system is, then, simply a special instance of a more general phenomenon.

D. The Peptidergic Control of Energy Balance

Eating demonstrates these principles further. Icv infusion of NPY reliably induces feeding in satiated rats and other species, even after repeated administration (Clark *et al.*, 1984; Morley *et al.*, 1987; Kalra and Kalra, 1990). NPY, the most powerful orexigen known, causes rats to work for food and reduces their avoidance of adulterated food, results that indicate increased motivation to eat (Flood and Morley, 1991). Motivational effects are an intrinsic part of adaptive responses, so it is not surprising that peptides have powerful motivational roles. NPY (and NPY mRNA) is increased in the hypothalamus following food deprivation and decreased by eating (Sahu *et al.*, 1988; Dallman *et al.*, 1993). Rats, like many other species, show a marked diurnal rhythm in eating behavior, and NPY levels in the various regions of the hypothalamus (including the suprachiasmatic nucleus: SCN) are higher during the dark phase of the daily light cycle (when rats feed) (Hastings, 1995), thus suggesting that NPY may play a part in the circadian control of food intake (Jhanway-Unilay *et al.*, 1990; McKibbin *et al.*, 1991). Rats infused with NPY show marked preference for carbohydrate, rather than protein or fat (Leibowitz, 1992). This strongly suggests that NPY is activating a differentiated ingestive response. There is increasing evidence that NPY, like other peptides, has other actions, thereby suggesting that it is concerned not simply with regulating carbohydrate intake, but also with a more general mechanism, such as carbohydrate (glucose) homeostasis. Like other peptides implicated in adaptive responses, NPY has associated neuroendocrine actions: in this case, a prominent interaction with insulin, which reinforces its efficacy as a carbohydrate regulator (Moltz and McDonald, 1985).

The role of NPY in food intake in response to energy deficit allows us to consider some other aspects of the peptidergic control of adaptive responses. NPY is found in many parts of the brain; for example, in the cerebral cortex and the intergeniculate leaflet (IGL) of the lateral geniculate body (De Quidt and Emson, 1986). Its function in these situations may not be related to food intake, or even energy homeostasis, though the postulated role of IGL-derived NPY in phase shifts may have an impact on diurnal feeding patterns (Biggs and Prosser, 1999). However, peptides in different parts of the brain may have unrelated functions: The "coding" depends on site of release. Like most other neurotransmitters, NPY has several distinct receptors. The specificity of the orexigenic effects of NPY may thus be dependent both on site of action and on receptor subtype (Leibowitz and Alexander, 1991; Brooks et al., 1994). There are several other peptides that have orexigenic actions, including agouti-related protein (AGRP), melanocyte-concentrating hormone (MCH), galinin, the orexins (perhaps), and gherelin (Ahima and Flier, 2000; Cowley et al., 1999; Claycombe et al., 2000). Food intake (like water balance) is such an important, if behaviorally heterogeneous, activity, it is not surprising that there are several chemical systems that can regulate it, though exactly how they interact and the contexts in which they operate are still not very clear. Some, for example, may be concerned with short-term energy deficits, others (e.g., leptin) with adaptation to longer-term starvation. Perhaps more surprising, there seem to be as many peptides that terminate or reduce food intake than stimulate it, including leptin, GLP-1, bombesin, α-melanocyte stimulating hormone (α-MSH), cocaine- and amphetamine-regulated transcript (CART), CRF and other peptides, many acting on the melancortin-4 receptor (Gibbs et al., 1993; Jegou et al., 2000; Kamegai et al., 2000). This is an apparent paradox for those who suggest that the prevalence of human obesity is based on a lack of suppressive mechanisms for food intake, since, it is proposed, most animals habitually live in conditions of food shortage rather than food bounty. All these considerations apply to other peptide systems implicated in adaptive responses. Peptides, however, are not only implicated in adaptive responses, but also in the prioritization of these responses. So it is fitting that peptides may stimulate (or inhibit) one set of responses, while having the opposite effect on another. For example, NPY (and other agents acting on appetite, such as leptin) have marked effects on reproduction (NPY inhibits sexual behavior), which is well-known to be sensitive to current energy levels and to be associated, in some species, with marked changes in food intake (Kalra et al., 1988).

Perhaps the most important lesson is that to focus on only one peptide is to underestimate both the complexity of adaptive responses and the neural mechanisms underlying them. The plethora of peptides associated with eating shows that not only are there many inputs to putative "appetite-controlling circuits," but that there may be chains of peptidergic systems that, together form the controlling mechanism. The action of peripheral leptin on the central mechanism controlling food intake through a secondary action on NPY, and other peptides associated with energy intake illustrate the point (Ahima and Flier, 2000). Within the brain there may also be chains of peptidergic neurons. Another good example is the interaction between CRF and POMC-expressing neurons in the PVN and arcuate nuclei of the hypothalamus (Almeida et al., 1992).

E. Is There a Peptidergic Code for Sexual Behavior?

The apparent anomaly represented by sexual behavior has already been mentioned in the context of c-fos expression and gonadal steroids. It is now almost 30 years since it was suggested that GnRH (LHRH) might activate sexual behavior in female rats (Pfaff, 1973), an idea that fitted well with its pituitary role: Many peptides have related behavioral and endocrine functions. However, the intervening years have not seen the establishment of this peptide as a major controlling factor for sexual behavior, though there have been persistent attempts to do so. This is all the more remarkable since the cellular actions of steroids as transcriptional regulators, together with the time needed to activate sexual behavior, point to some intermediate (protein or peptide) mediator. Much attention has been focused on the mechanisms for inducing reproduction at times or in conditions that are the most propitious for success and that carry the least risk.

A considerable number of other peptides have been proposed as important for sexual behavior. The model most frequently used is that based on the estrogen-treated female rat (Pfaff, 1982). Under standard laboratory conditions, an ovariectomized, estrogen-treated female rat requires additional progesterone to show full and reliable sexual receptivity. Substituting progesterone by a number of peptides, including oxytocin, TRH, and substance P, can increase receptivity measures (Pfaus, 1999). However, the requirement for postestrogenic progesterone is peculiar to female rodents with short, nonluteal cycles and there are a large number of other substances that have a similar action to progesterone; that is, facilitation of the behavioral effects of estrogen does seem rather nonspecific. So whether these experiments indicate a general role for some or all of these peptides in sexual behavior remains arguable. However, in the case of some of them (e.g., oxytocin), a role in sexual interaction may plausibly be part of a larger one in affiliative behavior (see below), a significant element in the social mechanisms of adaptation.

Less attention has been given to equally important mechanisms that ensure that reproduction is inhibited at other times, and yet such mechanisms must exist. Reproduction is behaviorally hazardous and metabolically expensive. It is as important to prevent reproduction at inappropriate times in the life span as to initiate it. It is thus noteworthy that many adaptively significant peptides inhibit sexual behavior. These include those associated with stress responses (CRF), alternative patterns of adaptation (NPY), and inappropriate environmental conditions (β-endorphin) (Herbert, 1992, 1996a). The role of β-endorphin is particularly interesting (Fig. 7). This peptide has a markedly inhibitory effect on sexual behavior after icv infusion. β-endorphin is one member of a cluster of peptides that are produced by posttranslational metabolism of the POMC precursor, a process that itself varies in different tissues (Taylor and Kaiser, 1986). Other members of this family (e.g., α-MSH) have notable (depressive) actions on eating (Cowley *et al.,* 1999). ACTH is also produced from the same precursor, though whether this peptide has an intracerebral behavioral role is still unknown. At the level of the pituitary, CRF activates the release of β-endorphin (along with ACTH), and a similar action has been suggested in the hypthala-

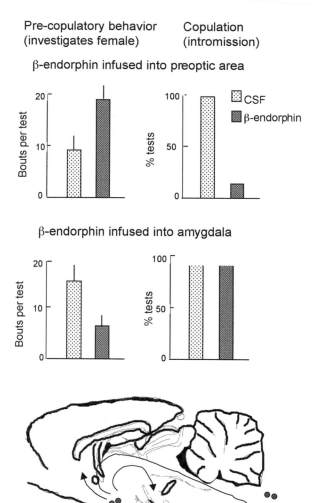

β-endorphin in rat brain

FIGURE 7 The regional effects of β-endorphin on sexual behavior. Above: the inhibitory effects of β-endorphin infused into the POA in copulation in the male rat, but the absence of effect on pre-copulatory (investigative) behavior. Middle: the converse results following β-endorphin infused into the amygdala. Below: the distribution of β-endorphin in the rats brain.

mus. Here, CRF is expressed largely in the parvicellular PVN, whereas POMC is found mostly in the arcuate nucleus (Nalaver *et al.,* 1979; Palkovits and Brownstein, 1985). From this nucleus, peptidergic fibers are carried to many other parts of the limbic system, a feature common to other peptides. Sexual behavior is attenuated in many species during pregnancy, when β-endorphin levels in the hypothalamus are increased (Bridges and Ronsheim, 1987). The photoperiod, operating through the pineal gland, acts as a powerful brake on reproduction in some species (e.g., the hamster, ferret, and sheep) (Hastings and Herbert, 1986) and is also associated with increased β-endorphin. The social structure of the group in which the animal lives also inhibits reproduction (Herbert, 1987). For example, subordinate members of groups of monkeys show low levels of both sexual behavior and fertility compared to more dominant ones, and have higher levels of β-endorphin in their cerebrospinal fluid (CSF). β-endorphin inhibits not only sexual behavior, but also GnRH release (Wardlaw and Frantz, 1983) and hence gonadal function: Suppressed gonadal activity is a prominent feature of animals that are chronically stressed, including humans. Of course in species in which affiliation is an adaptation, encouraged during reproduction, or in general in response to duress, one should expect different sorts of endocrine signals (Insel and Harbaugh, 1989; Carter et al., 1992).

F. Site-Specific Actions of Peptides: Reconciling Anatomical and Chemical Coding

Since peptides form distributed networks of neurons and fibers throughout the limbic system, the same peptide may be active within distinct regions. The behavioral actions of β-endorphin are one example. β-endorphin may be released within the hypothalamus, but also within the amygdala. This suggests there may be an interaction between the site of release and the chemical identity of the neurotransmitter: That is, both anatomical and chemical specificities may contribute to the behavioral action of a given peptide. There has been rather little work on this point, but the effects of local infusions of β-endorphin into these two areas on sexual behavior illustrate it. After bilateral infusions of as little as 10 or 40 pmoles into the POA, male rats continue to pursue and investigate an estrous female in the usual way, vigorously and repeatedly, so that an observer unaware of their treatment would expect that at any moment the expected sequence of mounting and intromission would begin. After a while it becomes apparent that mounting does not occur; the animals seem restricted to the precopulatory part of their interaction with the female and unable to proceed to the next, copulatory (consummatory), stage of their

sequence (Hughes et al., 1987). This behavior recalls that described following bilateral electrolytic or neurochemical lesions of the POA (Hansen et al., 1984). The effects of infusions into the amygdala are quite different: Bilateral infusions of β-endorphin into the amygdala (but not the nearby caudate-putamen) had a consistent and specific effect on the sexual behavior of male rats (McGregor and Herbert, 1992b). Investigation of the female was reduced greatly, but not abolished. Eventually β-endorphin-treated males started to copulate, though the time they took to do so (the intromission latency) was much prolonged. However, once they had started to copulate, their behavior became indistinguishable from males receiving control (CSF) infusions. So, unlike infusions into the POA, β-endorphin in the amygdala selectively interfered with the precopulatory (appetitive) part of sexual interaction. These results suggest that peptides acting within different parts of the limbic system may alter distinct components of adaptive behaviors.

There is some limited evidence for similar features for other peptides. For example, CRF within either the amygdala or hypothalamus seems to have distinct roles in stress. Hypothalamic CRF is contributes to the endocrine and autonomic response to stress (thought the latter may also depend on brainstem CRF), whereas the behavioral component (Koob and Bloom, 1985; Berridge and Dunn, 1986; De Goeij et al., 1991) (e.g., anxiety or fearful responses) is more related to the action of CRF within the amygdala (Elkabir et al., 1990). Within the amygdala, CRF is not evenly distributed: For example, the central nucleus has profuse CRF-expressing neurons (Moga and Gray, 1995). It is also significant that the feedback actions of corticosterone on CRF-expression in the hypothalamus and amygdala are not the same, thus suggesting that there is also differential endocrine control over peptide expression in the two areas of the brain (Swanson and Simmons, 1989; Makino et al., 1994; Watts, 1996). All these findings point to regionally specific effects of peptides in given adaptive contexts (Schulkin, 1999). A complication in the interpretation of some of these findings is that urocortin may be responsible for some of the effects formerly attributed to CRF (Van Pett et al., 2000); the relative roles of these two peptides is still not well defined. Nevertheless, is does appear that CRF has regionally specific roles within the brain that need to be understood if we are to define its role in adaptation fully.

It is interesting that although the amygdala has been clearly implicated in salt appetite (Nitabach *et al.,* 1989), there has been little exploration of the role of angiotensin II in either dipsogenic responses or sodium intake. Most of the work on the results of Ang II infusions into the amygdala have been focused on other types of behavior: for example, its anxiogenic effects (Okuyama *et al.,* 1999). These, of course, may be relevant to its role in adaptation. However, it does seem that more exploration of the role of this (and other) peptides in the amygdala in ingestion might be very fruitful. These include NPY, already discussed as a member of the plethora of peptides regulating food intake. NPY, as pointed out, is found in many areas of the brain—in contrast to some other peptides. It is unlikely that the NPY found in all sites is directly concerned with food intake: More probable is the supposition, firmly found for some other transmitters (e.g., acetylcholine) that function may vary with location. Even in the hypothalamus, NPY found within some nuclei (e.g., the arcuate) responds to fasting or hyperglycemia, whereas that in other parts does not (Williams *et al.,* 1988). However, bearing in mind the contribution of various parts of the limbic system to food intake and food choice (e.g., the amygdala), it is surprising that more work has not been done on the effects of local infusions or antagonism of NPY on feeding behavior. Like some of the other peptides implicated in metabolic regulation, NPY also has effects on anxiety (anxiolytic) (Thorsell *et al.,* 1999), which again raises functional questions about the relation of this emotional state to demand situations.

G. Maternal Behavior

Unlike sexual behavior, there is substantial evidence that maternal behavior is regulated by peptides. Icv infusions of oxytocin evoke maternal behavior in nonparturient ewes and female rats (Kendrick *et al.,* 1987, 1993). Oxytocin mRNA increases in the hypothalamus in mothers at birth and lesions of the major source of oxytocin (the PVN) prevent the normal display of maternal behavior (Insel, 1990; Numan, 1988). The release of peripheral oxytocin from the posterior pituitary has long been known to be associated with successful parturition and milk ejection, so this is another exam-

ple of the coordinated action of central and peripheral peptides in an adaptive response (others include angiotensin II, vasopressin, and the release of various gut peptides in the control of eating). Various lines of evidence suggest that the POA is important in the control of maternal behavior (Numan *et al.,* 1998): This further suggests that if oxytocin acts within this site, this may the chemical signal that enables this part of the brain (also concerned with other behaviors, such as masculine patterns of sexual behavior) to function in an appropriate way. But oxytocin may not be the only peptide important in maternal behavior, thus again illustrating the point that adaptive behavior is regulated by multiple peptides. Furthermore, there are those who suggest that the apparent role of oxytocin in maternal behavior is only a special case of a more general function: to facilitate "bonding" behavior, a feature not only of maternal but also of sexual and other affiliative behaviors (Carter *et al.,* 1992; Kendrick, 2000). If this is so, then peptides such as oxytocin may have more general functions, particularly in the social regulation of adaptation.

Other peptides, as expected, are also implicated in maternal behavior. Prolactin is particularly interesting. This large peptide, long known to be released from the anterior pituitary as an essential component of successful lactation, now seems also to have a central role (Bridges *et al.,* 2001). Prolactin, like other pituitary peptides, is also found in limbic neurons, as are its receptors; the latter are found in many areas of the hypothalamus, amygdala, and in certain areas of the brain stem (Bakowska and Morrell, 1997; Pi and Voogt, 2000). Central infusions of prolactin increase maternal behavior (though this may also need appropriate levels of gonadal steroids, in the rat at least), as well as food intake, a coordinated action that fits it well for a role central to the demands of maternity (Bridges and Freemark, 1995).

H. Adapting to a Changing Environment: Stress

Any demand represents a potential stress (McEwen, 1998) The term is a generic one: that is, there are many events that can be classified as "stress"; their common feature is that they threaten physiological or environmental (including social) conditions and demand an appropriate behavioral and physiological response.

Stressors can be acute, persistent, or repeated. In the case of the latter two, it is likely that the individual's response to the continuing stress may change with time, as the result of a number of underlying or associated processes. These are referred to as "adaptation" in the experimental literature (Chen and Herbert, 1995) and as "coping" in psychosocial investigation on man (Dantzer, 1993). These are likely to result in autonomic activation, including increased heart rate, raised blood pressure, and catecholamine secretion. These observations show that there is a coordinated, targeted response to a stress across both behavioral and physiological domains. The secretion of glucocorticoids is one prominent endocrine feature of many demand states or stresses.

The borderline between the stressed and unstressed condition will always remain indefinite. The newer findings on the neuroendocrine responses to specific stressors do not exclude more generalized responses to stress: Corticoids (and perhaps peripheral catecholamines) may be released under all these conditions. ACTH, a peripheral peptide deriving from the anterior pituitary, is released by a range of central peptides, including CRF, AVP, and Ang II, and there is growing evidence that each may contribute differentially to ACTH control as conditions vary (Whitnall, 1989). ACTH is released under many different conditions, including stressors of various categories, and this must be why there are multiple peptide pathways available for its control (Jones and Gillham, 1988; Plotsky, 1991). Other pituitary hormones, such as prolactin and growth hormone, are also released in response to different demands; the plurality of peptides coding for their release is also explicable on these grounds.

A variety of studies suggest that CRF-containing cerebral systems play an important role in the general response to stress. CRF is expressed in neurons and terminals throughout the limbic system, in a number of cell groups in the brain stem associated with autonomic function (such as the parabrachial nucleus, locus coeruleus, and dorsal vagal complex), as well as in many areas of the cortex, particularly limbic regions (Merchenthaler and Gorzalka, 1982). There are also high-affinity binding sites for CRF scattered throughout those areas containing terminals (Thatcher-Britton *et al.*, 1986). Icv CRF infusions seem able to recreate both behavioral and physiological responses that

closely resemble those to (acute) stress (Cole *et al.*, 1990; Monnikes *et al.*, 1992; Harbuz *et al.*, 1993). CRF has anxiogenic effects in experimental tests of anxiety; it enhances responses both to acoustic startle and to conditioned fear and enhances the behavioral responses of male rats to other, unfamiliar males. Blockage of CRF type-1 receptors, or breeding mice that lack the CRF1 receptor, reduces responses to fear or anxiety-provoking stimuli (Habib, 2000). In addition to the well-known action on pituitary ACTH release, infusing CRF intracerebroventricularly (icv) invokes a range of autonomic responses, including enhanced catecholamine secretion, alterations in gastrointestinal activity, and increased blood pressure and heart rate. Icv CRF also induces a pattern of c-fos expression in the brain that closely resembles that seen after exposing an animal to a fearful stimulus (Arnold *et al.*, 1992).

However, the role of CRF may differ according to, among other factors, the duration of the stress. Changes in response to a stress across time is an important feature of adaptation. An acute stress stimulates the transcription of CRF in the parvicellular PVN. By contrast, the expression of AVP, which is coexpressed in some parvicellular neurons, is not markedly elevated (Ma *et al.*, 1997). Repeatedly stressing the animal changes this pattern: CRF is no longer so markedly elevated, whereas AVP is greatly increased. It should be recalled that CRF and AVP have synergistic actions on both endocrine and behavioral stress-like responses (Gillies *et al.*, 1982).

This modified pattern in "late" gene expression is mirrored by parallel ones in IEGs. C-fos in the PVN, for example, though greatly increased after an acute stress, is much less evident after a persistent one (Chen and Herbert, 1995; Martinez *et al.*, 1998). However, in other areas of the limbic system, such as the lateral septum, c-fos may persist. The pattern of other IEGs, such as Fos-B, are different (Stamp and Herbert, 1999). These results show that habituation to a stress, or adaptation across time, is associated with changing patterns of gene expression in the brain. Time is another parameter to set alongside the differentiated patterns associated with the nature of the demand itself.

In the brain, there are also common features of demand states. These include changes in gene expression (both IEG and "late" response genes) in the parvicellular PVN, an area well-known to be concerned with the regulation of pituitary POMC and hence the levels of adrenal glucocorticoids (Plotsky, 1991). Activation of autonomic centers in the brain stem (e.g., the solitary nucleus) is also a consistent feature of stressful demands. It is now known that there are interactions between glucocorticoids and both IEGs and "late"-response genes such as CRF and AVP. For example, the induction of *c-fos* mRNA and protein in stress-related circuitry overlaps considerably with the distribution of glucocorticoid receptors (GR) and MR in the rat brain, and in some areas colocalization of the two has been observed (Wei and Vedeckis, 1997). This is particularly relevant, since some AP-1 constituents (binding sites for some IEGs) can dimerize with the GR and inhibit binding to the glucocorticoid response element (GRE). Dimerization of Fos or Jun with the GR inhibits the ability of the GRC (i.e., GR bound by hormone) to bind to the GRE (Gottlicher *et al.,* 1998). It is likely that the GRC and AP-1 DNA binding regions couple and neutralize each others' transcriptional ability. Therefore, the changes in glucocorticoids and receptors during stress might alter the downstream effects of AP-1 proteins, and vice versa.

This survey leads to strong support for the idea that peptides are the "words" of a neurobiological "language" that specifies the form of the adaptive response (Hoebel, 1988; Mayer and Baldi, 1991). As in a true language, a single peptide has limited meaning, but the actions of many together, in a varied pattern, may account for much of what can be observed, at a phenomenological level, of the coordinated behavioral, endocrine, and autonomic response to demand.

VII. INTERACTIONS AMONG AMINES, PEPTIDES, AND STEROIDS

Just as peptides do not operate independently of each other, they also interact with other chemical elements of the limbic system, particularly steroids and amines. Some roles of steroids have already been discussed, particularly their contribution to afferent information (though, of course, they also act as effectors of the adaptive process). There are many instances of steroids interacting with peptides, besides the obvious ones of acting as feedback signals regulating the pituitary. Salt intake is stimulated both by mineralo-corticoids as well as cen-

tral and perpheral peptides (Epstein and Sakai, 1987); maternal behavior is dependent on placental and ovarian steroids as well as central peptides (Rosenblatt *et al.,* 1979); eating is stimulated by glucocorticoids, as well as by other peripheral and central signals (Dallman *et al.,* 1993); gonadal steroids regulate reproductively important peptides such as β-endorphin (Wardlaw *et al.,* 1982). Steroids have no delivery-based "anatomical" address system; that is, they access all parts of the brain. Their action, of course, is limited by the anatomical distribution of their receptors or, as seems the case for at least some steroids, direct nongenomic actions on the neuronal cell membrane. Receptors are, of course, equally as important for peptides, and there is increasing evidence (e.g., from knockouts) that receptor deletions have greater and more predictable behavioral effects that those of their parent peptides. Steroids may be one set of factors regulating the level of peptide receptors.

VIII. THE (MONO)AMINERGIC SYSTEMS

The amines represent a family of systems that have pervasive effects on adaptive behavior. Serotonin, noradrenaline, dopamine, and acetylcholine are all amines that have both anatomical and chemical features distinguishing them from peptides (as well as other classes of chemical transmitters).

Their distinguishing anatomical features are that the neurons expressing these amines are all located in comparatively small groups in the basal brain (either brain stem, midbrain, or basal forebrain). From these rather restricted sources, a wide network of fibers spreads to many parts of the brain. However, an equally prominent feature is that these networks, though individually extensive, are also distinct, in that they overlap only partially. Functionally, therefore, activation of one member of this family will induce a distributed pattern of response in the brain that is widespread but not identical to that induced by other members. It is important to note that although the limbic system, however defined, has a rich aminergic innervation, other parts of the brain (e.g., the cerebral cortex) also receive a plentiful supply. So activation of an aminergic system is likely to have effects that are not limited to the limbic system. It is also important to recall that in some

of the social context (involving, perhaps, considerable amounts of neocortical processing) to more basic considerations, such as the strength or urgency of the current demand state. The complexity of aggression—the behavior pattern, the contexts in which it occurs, and the uses to which it is put—means that there can never be a single, definable neural system underlying this behavior. Neither can those neural systems implicated in aggression be clearly separated from those more closely associated with other behaviors. However, no theoretical treatment of the neural basis of adaptation can be satisfactory without taking aggressive interactions into account.

X. CONCLUSIONS

Behavioral adaptation and the chemical codes in the limbic system that underlie adaptation are set in ecological contexts in which there are tradeoffs between competing desires—food, water, mates, safety, etc. Balancing the set of biological needs is an endless task; homeostatic and allostatic mechanisms are recruited to balance both short- and long-term needs.

The limbic system contains both specific and nonspecific mechanisms to achieve internal stability. Peptides within the limbic system are contained in both specific and nonspecific neural systems. Afferent signals (demand or deficit signals-peripheral signals) act to invoke coordinating behavioral responses. The limbic system has a unique role in adjusting the requirements of the internal milieu to the demands of the external world. Appraisal mechanisms to facilitate and coordinate behavior are responsive to a wide range of demands, including recognition of need states, assessment of danger, coordination of drive demands, etc.

Increased flexibility is the unique contribution of limbic mediation to whole body physiology by coordinating responses to diverse demands. The key feature of successful adaptation in the short-term is stability; for the long-term it is viability (reproduction). Limbic systems are not just the coordinated response to adversity but to opportunity, anticipating future rewards.

Chemical codes within the limbic system play diverse roles. Peptides, amines, and steroids each have their role: They interact but they are not the same. For example, CRF in the hypothalamus is tied intimately to systemic physiological regulation; CRF in the amygdala

and bed nucleus of the stria terminalis is tied to behavioral demands. Angiotensin in one region of the brain may be more responsive to thirst, in another to sodium appetite. Both complement each other in the maintenance of extracellular fluid volume. The limbic system may be distinct from other, phylogenetically more recent, parts of the brain in that its function is coded in chemical terms, rather than in neuronal networks characteristic of neocortical systems.

References

Acher, R. (1980). Molecular evolution of biologically active polypeptides. *Proc. R. Soc. London, Ser. B* **210,** 21–43.

Ahima, R. S., and Flier, J. S. (2000). Leptin. *Annu. Rev. Physiol.* **62,** 413–437.

Almeida, O. F. X., Hassan, A. H. S., Harbuz, M. S., Linton, E. A., and Lightman, S. L. (1992). Hypothalamic corticotropin-releasing hormone and opioid peptide neurons: Function changes after adrenalectomy and/or castration. *Brain Res.* **571,** 189–198.

Arnold, F. J. L., De Lucas Bueno, M., Shiers, H., Hancock, D. C., Evan, G. I., and Herbert, J. (1992). Expression of *c-fos* in regions of the basal limbic forebrain following intra-cerebroventricular corticotropin-releasing factor (CRF) in unstressed or stressed male rats. *Neuroscience* **51,** 377–390.

Attili, G., and Hinde, R. A. (1986). Categories of aggression and their motivatonal heterogeneity. *Ethol. Sociobiol.* **7,** 17–27.

Bakowska, J. C., and Morrell, J. I. (1997). Atlas of the neurons that express mRNA for the long form of the prolactin receptor in the forebrain of the female rat. *J. Comp. Neurol.* **386,** 161–177.

Baum, M. J. (1995). Reassessing the role of medial preoptic area/anterior hypothalamic neurons in appetitive aspects of masculaine sexual behavior. *In* "The Pharmacology of Sexual Function and Dysfunction" (J. Bancroft, ed.), pp. 133–142. Excerpta Medica, Amsterdam.

Baum, M. J., and Everitt, B. J. (1992). Increased expression of c-fos in the medial preoptic area after mating in male rats: Role of afferent inputs from the medial amygdala and midbrain central tegmental field. *Neuroscience* **50,** 627–646.

Becker, J. B. (1999). Gender differences in dopaminergic function in striatum and nucleus accumbens. *Pharmacol., Biochem. Behav.* **64,** 803–812.

Bernard, C. (1878). "Lecons sur les phénomeñes de la vie communs aux animaux et aux végetaux." Bailliere, Paris.

Berridge, C. V., and Dunn, A. J. (1986). Corticotropin-releasing factor elicits naloxone-sensitive stress-like alterations in exploratory behaviour in mice. *Regul. Pept.* **16,** 83–93.

Biggs, K. R., and Prosser, R. A. (1999). Neuropeptide Y blocks GABAB-induced phase-shifts of the suprachiasmatic circadian clock in vitro. *Brain Res.* **821,** 461–466.

Blessing, W. W. (1997). Inadequate frameworks for understanding bodily homeostasis. *Trends Neurosci.* **20,** 235–239.

Bloom, F. E., ed. (1980). "Peptides. Integrators of Cell and Tissue Function." Raven Press, New York.

Brady, K. T., and Sonne, S. C. (1999). The role of stress in alcohol use, alcoholism treatment, and relapse. *Alcohol Res. Health* **23,** 263–271.

Bray, G. A. (2000). Afferent signals regulating food intake. *Proc. Nutr. Soc.* **59,** 373–384.

Bridges, R. S., and Freemark, M. S. (1995). Human placental lactogen infusions into the medial preoptic area stimulate maternal behavior in steroid-primed, nulliparous female rats. *Horm. Behav.* **29,** 216–226.

Bridges, R. S., and Ronsheim, P. M. (1987). Immunoreactive beta-endorphin concentrations in brain and plasma during pregnancy in rats: Possible modulation by progesterone and estradiol. *Neuroendocrinology* **45,** 381–388.

Bridges, R. S., Robertson, M. C., Siu, R. P., Sturgis, J. D., Henriquez, B. M., and Mann, P. E. (1997). Central lactogenic regulation of maternal behavior in rats: Steroid dependence, hormone specificity and behavioral potencies of rat prolactin and rat placental lactogen I. *Endocrinology (Baltimore)* **138,** 2.

Bridges, R. S., Rigero, B. A., Byrnes, E. M., Yang, L., and Walker, A. M. (2001). Central infusions of the recombinant human prolactin receptor antagonist, S179D-PRL, delay the onset of maternal behavior in steroid-primed, nulliparous female rats. *Endocrinology (Baltimore)* **142,** 730–739.

Broca, P. (1878). Anatomie comparée des circonvolutions cérébrales. Le grand lobe limbique et la scissure limbique dans le série des mammifères. *Rev. Anthropol.* **1,** 385–498.

Brooks, A. N., Howe, D. C., Porter, D. W. F., and Naylor, A. M. (1994). Neuropeptide-Y stimulates pituitary-adrenal activity in fetal and adult sheep. *J. Neuroendocrinol.* **6,** 161–166.

Buggy, J., and Johnson, A. K. (1977). Preoptic-hypothalamic periventricular lesions: Thirst deficits and hypernatremia. *Am. J. Physiol.* **233,** R44–R52.

Bunin, M. A., and Wightman, R. M. (1999). Paracrine neurotransmission in the CNS: Involvement of 5-HT. *Trends Neurosci.* **22,** 377–382.

Caggiula, A. R., Herndon, J. G., Scanlon, R., Greenstone, D., Bradshaw, W., and Sharp, D. (1979). Dissociation of active from immobility components of sexual behavior in female rats by central 6-hydroxydopamine: Implications for CA involvement in sexual behavior and sensorimotor responsiveness. *Brain Res.* **172,** 505–520.

Cannon, W. B. (1914). The emergency function of the adrenal medulla in pain and the major emotions. *Am. J. Physiol.* **39,** 356–372.

Carr, K. D., Park, T. H., Zhang, Y., and Stone, E. A. (1998). Neuroanatomical patterns of Fos-like immunoreactivity induced by naltrexone in food-restricted and ad libitum fed rats. *Brain Res.* **779,** 26–32.

Carter, S. C., Williams, J. R., Witt, D. M., and Insel, T. R. (1992). Oxytocin and social bonding. *Ann. N. Y. Acad. Sci.* **652,** 204–211.

Chaillou, E., Baumont, R., Tramu, G., and Tillet, Y. (2000). Effect of feeding on fos protein expression in sheep hypothalamus with special reference to the supraoptic and paraventricular nuclei: An immunohistochemical study. *Eur. J. Neurosci.* **12,** 4515–4524.

Chan, R. K. W., Chan, Y. S., and Wong, T. M. (1991). Responses of cardiovascular neurons in the rostral ventrolateral medulla of the normotensive Wistar Kyoto and spontaneously hypertensive rats to iontophoretic application of angiotensin II. *Brain Res.* **556,** 145–150.

Chen, X., and Herbert, J. (1995). Regional changes in c-fos expression in the basal forebrain and brainstem during adaptation to repeated stress: Correlations with cardiovascular, hypothermic and endocrine responses. *Neuroscience* **64,** 675–685.

Chung, K. K. K., Martinez, M., and Herbert, J. (1999). Central serotonin depletion modulates the behavioural, endocrine and physiological responses to repeated social stress and subsequent *c-fos* expression the brains of male rats. *Neuroscience* **92,** 613–625.

Clark, J. T., Kalra, P. S., Crowley, W. R., and Kalra, S. P. (1984). Neuropeptide Y and human pancreatic polypeptide stimulate feeding in rats. *Endocrinology (Baltimore)* **115,** 427–429.

Claycombe, K. J., Xue, B. Z., Mynatt, R. L., Zemel, M. B., and Moustaid-Moussa, N. (2000). Regulation of leptin by agouti. *Physiol. Genom.* **2,** 101–105.

Cole, B. J., Cador, M., Stinus, L., Rivier, J., Vale, W., Koob, G. F., and Le Moal, M. (1990). Central administration of a CRF antagonist blocks the development of stress-induced behavioral sensitization. *Brain Res.* **512,** 343–346.

Cowley, M. A., Pronchuk, N., Fan, W., Dinulescu, D. M., Colmers, W. F., and Cone, R. D. (1999). Integration of NPY, AGRP and melanocortin signals in the hypothalamic paraventricular nucleus: Evidence of a cellular basis for the adipostat. *Neuron* **24,** 155–163.

Dallman, M. F., Akana, S. F., Scribner, K. A., Bradbury, M. J., Walker, C.-D., Strack, A. M., and Cascio, C. S. (1992). Stress, feedback and facilitation in the hypothalamo-pituitary-adrenal axis. *J. Neuroendocrinol.* **4,** 517–526.

Dallman, M. F., Strack, A. M., Akana, S. F., Bradbury, M. J., Hanson, E. S., Scribner, K. A., and Smith, M. (1993). Feast and famine: Critical role of glucocorticoids with insulin in daily energy flow. *Front. Neuroendocrinol.* **14,** 303–347.

Dantzer, R. (1993). Coping with stress. In "Stress: From Synapse to Syndrome" (S. C. Stanford and P. Salmon, eds.), pp. 167–189. Academic Press, London.

Davis, M. (1992). The role of the amygdala in fear and anxiety. Annu. Rev. Neurosci. **15**, 353–375.

De Goeij, D. C. E., Kvetnansky, R., Whitnall, M. H., Jesova, D., Berkenbosch, F., and Tilders, F. J. H. (1991). Repeated stress-induced activation of corticotropin-releasing factor neurons enhances vasopressin stores and colocalization with corticotropin-releasing factor in the median eminence of rats. Neuroendocrinology **53**, 150–159.

Denton, D. A. (1982). "The Hunger for Salt." Springer-Verlag, Berlin.

De Quidt, M. E., and Emson, P. C. (1986). Distribution of neuropeptide Y-loke immunoreactivity in the rat central nervous system II. Immunohistochemical analysis. Neuroscience **18**, 545–618.

Dixson, A. F. (1998). "Primate Sexuality." Oxford University Press, Oxford.

Dougherty, D. M., Moeller, F. G., Bjork, J., and Marsh, D. M. (1999). Plasma L-tryptophan depletion and aggression. Adv. Exp. Med. Biol. **467**, 57–65.

Dubey, A. K., Herbert, J., Martensz, N. D., Beckford, U., and Jones, M. T. (1983). Differential penetration of three pituitary peptide hromones into the cerebrospinal fluid of rhesus monkey. Life Sci. **32**, 1857–1863.

Elkabir, D. R., Wyatt, M. E., Vellucci, S. V., and Herbert, J. (1990). The effects of separate or combined infusions of corticotropin-releasing factor and vasopressin either intraventricularly or into the amygdala on aggressive and investigative behavior in the rat. Regul. Pept. **28**, 199–214.

Elmquist, J. K., Maratos-Flier, E., Saper, C. B., and Flier, J. S. (1998). Unraveling the central nervous system pathways underlying responses to leptin. Nat. Neurosci. **1**, 445–450.

Epstein, A. N., and Sakai, R. R. (1987). Angiotensin-aldosterone synergy and salt intake. In "Brain Peptides and Catecholamines in Cardiovascular Regulation" (C. M. Ferraria and J. P. Buckley, eds.), pp. 337–345. Raven Press, New York.

Epstein, A. N., Fitzsimons, J. T., and Rolls, B. J. (1970). Drinking induced by injection of angiotensin into the brain of the rat. J. Physiol. (London) **210**, 457–474.

Everitt, B. J., and Hökfelt, T. (1986) Neuroendocrine anatomy of the hypothalamus. In "Neuroendocrinology" (S. C. Lightman and B. J. Everitt, eds.), pp. 5–31. Blackwell, Oxford.

Everitt, B. J., Herbert, J., and Keverne, E. B. (1983). The neuroendocrine anatomy of the limbic system: A discussion with special reference to steroid responsive neurons, neuropeptides and monoaminergic systems. Prog. Anat. **3**, 235–260.

Feenstra, M. G. (2000). Dopamine and noradrenaline release in the prefrontal cortex in relation to unconditioned and conditioned stress and reward. Prog. Brain Res. **126**, 133–163.

Fitzsimons, J. T. (1979). "The Physiology of Thirst and Sodium Appetite." Cambridge University Press, Cambridge, UK.

Fitzsimons, J. T. (1998). Angiotensin, thirst and sodium appetite. Physiol. Rev. **78**, 583–686.

Flood, J. F., and Morley, J. E. (1991). Increased food intake by neuropeptide Y is due to an increased motivation to eat. Peptides (N.Y.) **12**, 1329–1332.

Franchini, L. F., and Vivas, L. (1999). Distribution of Fos immunoreactivity in rat brain after sodium consumption induced by peritoneal dialysis. Am. J. Physiol. **276**, R1180–R1187.

Fuxe, K., Agnati, L. F., Aguirre, J. A., Bjelke, B., Tinner, B., Pich, E. M., and Eneroth, P. (1991). On the existence of volume transmission in the central neuropeptide Y neuronal systems. Studies on tranmitter receptor mismatches and on biological effects of neuropeptide Y fragments. In "Volume Transmission in the Brain: Novel Mechanisms for Neural Transmission" (K. Fuxe and L. F. Agnati, eds.), pp. 105–130. Raven Press, New York.

Gazzaniga, M. S., ed. (2000). "The New Cognitive Neurosciences," 2nd ed. MIT Press, Cambridge, MA.

Gibbs, J., Geary, N., and Smith, G. P. (1993). Peptide signals for satiety. In "Growth Factors Peptides and Receptors," pp. 435–443. Plenum Press, New York.

Gillies, G. E., Linton, E. A., and Lowry, P. J. (1982). Corticotropin releasing activity of the new CRF is potentiated several times by vasopressin. Nature (London) **299**, 355–357.

Goldstein, D. S. (2000). "The Autonomic Nervous System in Health and Disease." Dekker, New York.

Gottlicher, M., Heck, S., and Herrlich, P. (1998). Transcriptional cross-talk, the second mode of steroid hormone receptor action. J. Mol. Med. **76**, 480–489.

Gray, J. P. (1982). "The Neuropsychology of Anxiety." Oxford University Press, Oxford.

Groenewegen, H. J., Berendse, H. W., Meredith, G. E., Haber, S. N., Voorn, P., Wolters, J. G., and Lohman, A. H. M. (1991). Functional anatomy of the ventral, limbic system-innervated striatum. In "The Mesolimbic Dopamine System: From Motivation to Action" (P. W. Scheel-Kruger, ed.), pp. 19–59. Wiley, Chichester.

Habib, K. E. et al. (2000). Oral administration of a corticotropin-releasing hormone receptor antagonist significantly attenuates vehavioral, neuroendocrine and autonomic responses to stress in primates. Proc. Natl. Acad. Sci. U.S.A. **97**, 6079–6084.

Hansen, S., Drake, A. F., and Hagelsrum, J. K. (1984). Emergence of displacement activities in the male rat following thwarting of sexual behavior. Behav. Neurosci. **98**, 868–883.

Harbuz, M. S., Chalmers, J., De Souza, L., and Lightman, S. L. (1993). Stress-induced activation of CRF and c-fos mRNAs in the paraventricular nucleus are not affected by serotonin depletion. *Brain Res.* **609**, 167–173.

Hastings, M. H. (1995). Circadian rhythms: Peering into the molecular clockwork. *J. Neuroendocrinol.* **7**, 331–340.

Hastings, M. H., and Herbert, J. (1986). Endocrine rhythms. *In* "Neuroendocrinology" (B. J. Everitt and S. L. Lightman, eds.), pp. 49–102. Blackwell, Oxford.

Herbert, J. (1987). Neuroendocrine responses to social stress. *In* "Neuroendocrinology of Stress. Clinical Endocrinology and Metabolism" (A. Grossman, ed.), Bailliere, London. pp. 467–490.

Herbert, J., Forsling, M. L., Howes, S. R., Stacey, P. M., and Shiers, H. M. (1992a). Regional expression of c-fos antigen in the basal forebrain following intraventricular infusions of angiotensin and its modulation by drinking either water or saline. *Neuroscience* **51**, 867–882.

Herbert, J. (1992b). Proopiomelanocortin peptides and reproduction: An integrated endocrine and behavioural system. *In* "Clinical Perspectives in Endogenous Opioid Peptides" (M. Negri, ed.), pp. 185–218. Wiley, Chichester.

Herbert, J. (1993). Peptides in the limbic system: Neurochemical codes for co-ordinated adaptive responses to behavioral and physiological demand. *Prog. Neurobiol.* **41**, 723–791.

Herbert, J. (1996a). Sexuality, stress, and the chemical architecture of the brain. *Annu. Rev. Sex Res.* **7**, 1–43.

Herbert, J. (1996b). Studying the central actions of angiotensin using the expression of immediate-early genes: Expectations and limitations. *Regul. Pept.* **66**, 13–18.

Herbert, J., and Martinez, M. (2001). Neural mechanisms underlying aggressive behaviour. *In* "Conduct Disorders in Childhood and Adolescence" (J. Hill and B. Mauchan, eds.), pp. 67–102. Cambridge University Press, Cambridge, UK.

Herkenham, M. (1987). Mismatches between neurotransmitter and receptor localizations in brain: Observations and implications. *Neuroscience* **23**, 1–38.

Herkenham, M. (1991). Mismatches between neurotransmitter and receptor localizations: Implications for endocrine function in brain. *In* "Volume Transmission in the Brain: Novel Mechanisms for Neural Transmission" (K. Fuxe and L. F. Agnati, eds.), pp. 63–87. Raven Press, New York.

Herrera, D. G., and Robertson, H. A. (1996). Activation of c-fos in the brain. *Prog. Neurobiol.* **50**, 83–107.

Hinde, R. A. (1974). "Biological Bases of Human Behavior." McGraw-Hill, New York.

Hoebel, B. G. (1988). Neuroscience and motivation: Pathways and peptides that define motivational systems. *In* "Stevens' Handbook of Experimental Psychology" (R. C. Atkinson, R. J.

Herrnstein, G. Lindzey, and R. D. Luce, eds.), 2nd ed., pp. 547–625. Wiley, New York.

Hoffman, W. E., and Phillips, M. I. (1976). Regional study of cerebral ventricle sensitive sites to angiotensin II. *Brain Res.* **110**, 313–330.

Hollerman, J. R., and Schultz, W. (1998). Dopamine neurons report an error in the temporal prediction of reward during learning. *Nat. Neurosci.* **1**, 304–309.

Hughes, A. M., Everitt, B. J., and Herbert, J. (1987). Selective effects of β-endorphin infused into the hypothalamus, preoptic area and bed nucleus of the stria terminalis. *Neuroscience* **23**, 1063–1073.

Hull, E. M., Du, J., Lorrain, D. S., and Matuszewich, L. (1997). Testosterone, preoptic dopamine, and copulation in male rats. *Brain Res. Bull.* **44**, 327–333.

Insel, T. R. (1990). Regional changes in brain ocytocin receptors post-partum: Time course and relationship to maternal behavior. *J. Neuroendocrinol.* **2**, 1–7.

Insel, T. R., and Harbaugh, C. R. (1989). Lesions of the hypothalamic paraventricular nucleus disrupt the initiation of maternal behavior. *Ann. N. Y. Acad. Sci.* **652**, 122–141.

Jegou, S., Boutelet, I., and Vaudry, H. (2000). Melanocortin-3 receptor mRNA expression in pro-opiomelanocortin neurones of the rat arcuate nucleus. *J. Neuroendocrinol.* **12**, 501–505.

Jhanway-Unilay, M., Beck, B., Burlet, C., and Leibowitz, S. F. (1990). Diurnal rhythm of neuropeptide Y-like immunoreactivity in the suprachiasmatic, arcuate and paraventricular nuclei and other hypothalamic sites. *Brain Res.* **536**, 331–334.

Johnson, A. K. (1985). The periventricular anteroventral third ventricle 9AV3V: Its relationship with the subfornical organ and neural systems involved in m aintaining body fluid homeostasis. *Brain Res. Bull.* **15**, 595–601.

Jones, M. T., and Gillham, B. (1988). Factors involved in the regulation of adrenocorticotropic hormone/β-lipotropic hormone. *Phys. Rev.* **68**, 743–818.

Kalra, S. P., and Kalra, P. S. (1990). Neuropeptide Y: A novel peptidergic signal for the control of feeding behavior. *In* "Behavioral Aspects of Neuroendocrinology" (D. Ganter and D. W. Pfaff, eds.), pp. 191–221. Springer, Berlin.

Kalra, S. P., Clark, J. T., Sahu, A., Dube, M. G., and Kalra, P. S. (1988). Control of feeding and sexual behaviors by neuropeptide Y: Physiological implications. *Synapse* **2**, 254–257.

Kamegai, J., Tamura, H., Shimizu, T., Ishii, S., Sugihara, H., and Wakabayashi, I. (2000). Central effect of ghrelin an endogenous growth hormone secretagogue on hypothalamic peptide gene expression. *Endocrinology (Baltimore)* **141**, 4797–4800.

Kendrick, K. M. (2000). Oxytocin, motherhood and bonding. *Exp. Physiol.* **85**, 111S–124S.

Kendrick, K. M., Keverne, E. B., and Baldwin, B. A. (1987). Intracerebroventricular oxytocin stimulates maternal behavior in the sheep. *Neuroendocrinology* **46**, 56–61.

Kendrick, K. M., Fabre-Nys, C., Blache, D., Goode, J. A., and Broad, K. D. (1993). The role of oxytocin release in the mediobasal hypothalamus of the sheep in relation to female sexual receptivity. *J. Neuroendocrinol.* **5**, 13–21.

Kiss, J. Z., Martos, J., and Palkovits, M. (1991). Hypothalamic paraventricular nucleus: A quantitative analysis of cytoarchitecture subdivisions in the rat. *J. Comp. Neurol.* **313**, 563–573.

Kollack-Walker, S., and Newman, S. W. (1995). Mating and agonistic behavior produce different patterns of fos immunolabeling in the male Syrian hamster brain. *Neuroscience* **66**, 721–736.

Koob, G. F., and Bloom, F. E. (1985). Corticotropin-releasing hormone and behavior. *Fed. Proc., Fed. Am. Soc. Exp. Biol.* **44**, 259–263.

Kotter, R., and Meyer, N. (1992). The limbic system: A review of its empirical foundation. *Behav. Brain Res.* **52**, 105–127.

Kupfermann, I. (1994). Neural control of feeding. *Curr. Opin. Neurobiol.* **4**, 869–876.

Kuypers, H. G. J. M. (1987). Some aspects of the organization of the output of the motor cortex. *In* "Motor Areas of the Cerebral Cortex," pp. 63–82. Wiley, Chichester.

Lane, J. M., Herbert, J., and Fitzsimons, J. T. (1997). Increased sodium appetite stimulates c-fos expression in the organum vasculosum of the lamina terminalis. *Neuroscience* **78**, 1167–1176.

LeDoux, J. E. (1992). Emotion and the amygdala. *In* "The Amgdala: Neurobiological Aspects of Emotion, Memory and Mental Dysfunction" (J. P. Aggleton, ed.), pp. 339–351. Wiley-Liss, New York.

LeDoux, J. E. (1998). "The Emotional Brain." Weidenfeld & Nicolson, London.

Lefebvre, H., Contesse, V., Delarue, C., Vaudry, H., and Kuhn, J. M. (1998). Serotonergic regulation of adrenocortical function. *Horm. Metab. Res.* **30**, 398–403.

Leibowitz, S. F. (1992). Neurochemical-neuroendocrine systems in the brain controlling macromutrient intake and metabolism. *Trends Neurosci.* **15**, 491–497.

Leibowitz, S. F., and Alexander, J. T. (1991). Analysis of neuropeptide Y-induced feeding: Dissociation of Y1 and Y2 receptor efects on natural meal patterns. *Peptides (N.Y.)* **12**, 1251–1260.

Leibowitz, S. F., and Alexander, J. T. (1998). Hypothalamic serotonin in control of eating behavior, meal size, and body weight. *Biol. Psychiatry* **44**, 851–864.

Le Moal, M., and Simon, H. (1992). Mesolimbic dopaminergic network: Functional and regulatory roles. *Physiol. Rev.* **71**, 155–234.

Lin, S. H., Miyata, S., Weng, W., Matsunaga, W., Ichikawa, J., Furuya, K., Nakashima, T., and Kiyohara, T. (1998). Comparison of the expression of two immediate early gene proteins, FosB and Fos in the rat preoptic area, hypothalamus and brainstem during pregnancy parturition and lactation. *Neurosci. Res.* **32**, 333–341.

Lopez, H. H., and Ettenberg, A. (2000). Haloperidol challenge during copulation prevents subsequent increase in male sexual motivation. *Pharmacol., Biochem. Behav.* **67**, 387–393.

Lucas, L. R., Pompei, P., and McEwen, B. S. (2000). Salt appetite in salt-replete rats: Involvement of mesolimbic structures in deoxycorticosterone-induced salt craving behavior. *Neuroendocrinology* **71**, 386–395.

Ma, X., Levy, A., and Lightman, S. L. (1997). Emergence of an isolated arginine vasopressin (AVP) response to stress after repeated restraint: A study of both AVP and corticotropin-releasing hormone messeger ribonucleic acid (RNA) and heteronuclear RNA. *Endocrinology (Baltimore)* **138**, 4351–4357.

MacLean, P. D. (1955). The limbic system ("visceral brain") and emotional behavior. *Arch. Neurol. Psychiatry* **73**, 130–134.

MacLean, P. D. (1990). "The Triune Brain in Evolution: Role in Paleocerebral Function." Plenum Press, New York.

Makino, S., Gold, P. W., and Schulkin, J. (1994). Corticosterone effects on corticotropin-releasing hormone nRNA in the central nucleus of the amygdala and the parvocellular region of the paraventricular nucleus of the hypothalamus. *Brain Res.* **640**, 105–112.

Mangiapane, M. L., Thrasher, T. N., Keil, L. C., Simpson, J. B., and Ganong, W. F. (1983). Deficits in drinking and vasopressin secretion after lesions of the nucleus medianus. *Neuroendocrinology* **37**, 73–77.

Martinez, M., Phillips, P. J., and Herbert, J. (1998). Adaptation in patterns of c-fos expression in the brain associated with exposure to either single or repeated social stress in male rats. *Eur. J. Neurosci.* **10**, 20–33.

Mayer, E. A., and Baldi, J. P. (1991). Can regulatory peptides be regarded as words of a biological language? *Am. J. Physiol.* **261**, G171–G184.

McCann, S. M., Franci, C. R., and Antunes-Rodrigues, J. (1989). Hormonal control of water and electrolyte intake and output. *Acta. Physiol. Scand.* **136**, 97–104.

McEwen, B. S. (1998). Protective and damaging effects of stress mediators. *N. Engl. J. Med.* **338**, 171–179.

McGregor, A., and Herbert, J. (1992a). Differential effects of excitotoxic basolateral or corticomedial lesions of the amygdala on the behavioral and endocrine responses to either sexual or aggression-provoking stimuli in the male rat. *Brain Res.* **574**, 9–20.

McGregor, A., and Herbert, J. (1992b). Specific effects of β-endorphin infused into the amygdala on sexual behavior in the male rat. *Neuroscience* **46**, 165–172.

McKibbin, P. E., Roger, P., and Williams, G. (1991). Increased neuropeptide Y concentrations in the lateral hypothalamic area of the rat after the onset of darkness: Possible relevance to the circadian periodicity of feeding behavior. *Life Sci.* **48**, 2527–2533.

McKinley, M. J., Hards, D. K., and Oldfield, B. J. (1994). Identification of neural pathways activated in dehydrated rats by means of Fos-immunohistochemistry and neural tracing. *Brain Res.* **653**, 305–314.

Meguid, M. M., Fetissov, S. O., Blaha, V., and Yang, Z. J. (2000). Dopamine and serotonin VMN release is related to feeding status in obese and lean Zucker rats. *NeuroReport* **14**, 2069–2072.

Merchenthaler, V. I., and Gorzalka, B. B. (1982). Immunocytochemical localization of corticotrophin-releasing factors 9CRF in the rat brain. *Am. J. Anat.* **165**, 385–396.

Mesulam, M.-M. (1998). From sensation to cognition. *Brain* **121**, 1013–1052.

Miczek, K. A., Weerts, E. M., Vivian, J. A., and Barros, H. M. (1995). Aggression, anxiety and vocalizations in animals: GABAA and 5-HT anxiolytics. *Psychopharmaclogy* **121**, 38–56.

Moga, M. M., and Gray, T. S. (1995). Evidence for corticotropin-releasing factor, neurotensin and somatostatin in the neural pathway from the central nucleus of the amygdala to the parabrachial nucleus. *J. Comp. Neurol.* **241**, 275–284.

Moltz, J. H., and McDonald, J. K. (1985). Neuropeptide Y: Direct and indirect action on insulin secretion in the rat. *Peptides (N.Y.)* **6**, 1155–1159.

Monnikes, H., Schmidt, B. G., Raybould, H. E., and Tache, Y. (1992). CRF in the paraventricular nucleus mediates gastric and colonic motor response to restraint stress. *Am. J. Physiol.* **262**, G137–G143.

Moore, R. Y., Bloom, F. E. (1978). Central catecholamine neuron systems: Anatomy and physiology of the dopamine systems. *Annu. Rev. Neurosci.* **1**, 129–169.

Morley, J. E., Levine, A. S., Gosnell, B. A., Kneip, J., and Grace, M. (1987). Effect of neuropeptide Y on ingestive behaviors in the rat. *Am. J. Physiol.* **252**, R599–R609.

Nalaver, G., Zimmerman, E. A., Defendini, R., Liotta, A. S., Krieger, D. T., and Brownstein, M. J. (1979). Adrenocorticotrophin and β-lipotropin in the hypothalamus. *J. Cell Biol.* **81**, 50–58.

Nieuwenhuys, R. (1996). The greater limbic system, the emotional motor system and the brain. *Prog. Brain Res.* **107**, 551–580.

Nitabach, M. N., Schulkin, J., and Epstein, A. N. (1989). The medial amygdala is part of a mineralocorticoid-sensitive circuit controlling NaCl intake in the rat. *Behav. Brain Res.* **35**, 127–134.

Numan, M. (1988). Maternal behavior. *In* "The Physiology of Reproduction" (E. Knobil and J. D. Neill, eds.), pp. 1569–1645. Raven Press, New York.

Numan, M., Numan, M. J., Marzella, S. R., and Palumbo, A. (1998). Expression of c-fos, fos B, and egr-1 in the medial preoptic area and bed nucleus of the stria terminalis during maternal behavior in rats. *Brain Res.* **792**, 348–352.

Okuyama, S., Sakagawa, T., Chaki, S., Imagawa, Y., Ichiki, T., and Inagami, T. (1999). Anxiety-like behavior in mice lacking the angiotensin II type-2 receptor. *Brain Res.* **821**, 150–159.

Pal, P., Raj, S. S., Mohan, M., and Pal, G. K. (2000). Modulation of feeding and drinking behavior by catecholamines injected into nucleus accumbens in rats. *Indian J. Physiol. Pharmacol.* **44**, 24–32.

Palkovits, M., and Brownstein, M. J. (1985). Distribution of neuropeptides in the central nervous system using biochemical micromethods. *In* "Handbook of Chemical Neuroanatomy" (A. Björklund and T. Hökfelt, eds.), pp. 1–71. Elsevier, Amsterdam.

Palkovitz, M., Brownstein, M. J., and Vale, W. (1985). Distribution of corticotropin-releasing factor in rat brain. *Fed. Proc., Fed. Am. Soc. Exp. Boil.* **44**, 215–219.

Papez, J. W. (1937). A proposed mechanism of emotion. *Arch. Neurol. Psychiatry* **79**, 217–224.

Parkinson, J. A., Robbins, T. W., and Everitt, B. J. (2000). Dissociable roles of the central and basolateral amygdala in appetitive emotional learning. *Eur. J. Neurosci.* **12**, 405–413.

Pfaff, D. W. (1973). Luteinizing hormone releasing factor (LRF) potentiates lordosis behavior in hypophysectomised ovariextomized female rats. *Science* **182**, 1148–1149.

Pfaff, D. W. (1980). "Estrogens and Brain Function." Springer-Verlag, New York.

Pfaff, D. W. (1982). Neurobiological mechanisms of sexual motivation. *In* "The Physiological Mechanisms of Motivation" (D. W. Pfaff, ed.), pp. 287–317. Springer, New York.

Pfaff, D. W. (1999). "Drive." MIT Press, Cambridge, MA.

Pfaus, J. G. (1999). Neurobiology of sexual behavior. *Curr. Opin. Neurobiol.* **9**, 751–758.

Pfaus, J. G., Kleopoulos, S. P., Mobbs, C. V., Gibbs, R. B., and Pfaff, D. W. (1993). Sexual stimulation activates c-fos within estrogen-containing regions of the female rat forebrain. *Brain Res.* **624**, 253–267.

Pi, X., and Voogt, J. L. (2000). Effect of suckling on prolactin receptor immunoreactivity in the hypothalamus of the rat. *Neuroendocrinology* **71**, 308–317.

Plotsky, P. M. (1991). Pathways to the secretion of adrenocorticotrophin: A view from the portal. *J. Neuroendocrinol.* **3**, 1–9.

Price, J. L., Russchen, F. T., and Amaral, D. G. (1987). The
limbic region II: The amygdaloid complex. *In* "Handbook of
Chemical Neuroanatomy" (A. Björklund, T. Hökfelt, and L. W.
Swanson, eds.), pp. 279–388. Elsevier, Amsterdam.

Ramsay, D. J., and Booth, D. A. (1991). "Thirst: Physiological
and Psychological Aspects." Springer-Verlag, London.

Rehman, J., Kaynan, A., Christ, G., Valcic, M., Maayani, S., and
Melman, A. (1999). Modification of sexual behavior of Long-
Evans male rats by drugs acting on the 5-HT1A receptor. *Brain
Res.* **821**, 414–425.

Reid, J. L., and Rubin, P. C. (1987). Peptides and central neural
reglation of the circulation. *Physiol. Rev.* **64**, 725–749.

Richter, C. P. (1936). Increased salt appetite in adrenalectomized
rats. *Am. J. Physiol.* **115**, 155–161.

Rosenblatt, J. S., Siegel, H. I., and Mayer, A. D. (1979). Progress in
the study of maternal behavior in the rat: Hormonal, nonhormonal, sensory and developmental aspects. *Adv. Study Behav.*
10, 225–311.

Rowland, N. E., Li, B.-H., Rozelle, A. K., Fregley, M. J., Garcia, M.,
and Smith, G. C. (1994). Localization of changes in immediate early genes in brain in relation to hydromineral balance:
Intravenous angiotensin II. *Brain Res. Bull.* **33**, 427–436.

Rowland, N. E., Marshall, M., and Roth, J. D. (2000). Comparison of either norepinephrine-uptake inhibitors or phenter-
mine combined with serotoninergic agents on food intake in
rats. *Psychopharmacology* **149**, 77–83.

Sahu, A., Kalra, P. S., and Kalra, S. P. (1988). Food deprivation
and ingestion induce reciprocal changes in neuropeptide Y
concentrations in the paraventricular nucleus. *Peptides (N.Y.)*
9, 83–86.

Schiavone, M. T., Santos, R. A. S., Brosnihan, K. B., Khosla, M. C.,
and Ferrario, C. M. (1988). Release of vasopressin from the rat
hypothalmo-neurohypophysial system by angiotensin (1–7)
heptapeptide. *Proc. Natl. Acad. Sci. U.S.A.* **85**, 4095–4098.

Schulkin, J. (1991). "Sodium Hunger". Cambridge University
Press, Cambridge, UK.

Schulkin, J. (1999). "The Neuroendocrine Regulation of Behavior." Cambridge University Press, Cambridge, UK.

Schulkin, J., McEwen, B. S., and Gold, P. W. (1994). Allostasis,
amygdala and the anticipatory angst. *Neurosci. Behav. Rev.* **18**,
385–396.

Schwartz, M. W., Sipols, A., Kahn, S. E., Lattemann, D. F.,
Taborsky, G. J., Bergman, R. N., Woods, S. C., and Porte,
D. (1990). Kinetics and specificity of insulin uptake from
plasma into cerebrospinal fluid. *Am. J. Physiol.* **259**, E378–
E383.

Scimonelli, T., Medina, F., Wilson, C., and Celis, M. E. (2000).
Interaction of alpha-melanotropin (alpha-MSH) and nora-

drenaline in the median eminence in the control of female
sexual behavior. *Peptides (N.Y.)* **21**, 219–223.

Selye, H. (1936). A syndrome produced by diverse nocuous
agents. *Nature* **138**, 32–33.

Selye, H. (1978). "The Stress of Life." McGraw-Hill, New York.

Share, L. (1988). Role of vasopressin in cardiovascular regulation. *Physiol. Rev.* **68**, 1248–1284.

Sheng, M., and Greenberg, M. E. (1990). The regulation and
function of c-fos and other immediate early genes in the nervous system. *Neuron* **4**, 477–485.

Smith, G. P. (1997). "Satiation from Gut to Brain." Oxford University Press, Oxford.

Smith, M. A., Banerjee, S., Gold, P. W., and Glowa, J. (1992).
Induction of c-fos and other immediate-early genes in the
nervous system. *Neuron* **4**, 477–485.

Spanagel, R., and Weiss, F. (1999). The dopamine hypothesis of
reward: Past and current status. *Trends Neurosci.* **22**, 521–527.

Spyer, K. M. (1989). Neural mechanisms involved in cardiovascular control during affetive behaviour. *Trends Neurosci.* **12**,
506–513.

Stamp, J. A., and Herbert, J. (1999). Multiple immediate-early
gene expression during physiological and endocrine adaptation to repeated stress. *Neuroscience* **94**, 1313–1322.

Stanley, B. G., Magdalin, W., Seiafi, A., Nguyen, M. M., and
Leibowitz, S. F. (1992). Evidence for neuropeptide Y mediation of eating produced by food deprivation and for a variant
of the Y$_1$ receptor mediating this peptide's effect. *Peptides* **13**,
581–587.

Steele, M. K., Gardner, D. G., Xie, P., and Schultz, H. D. (1991).
Interactions between ANP and ANG II in regulating blood
pressure an sympathetic outflow. *Am. J. Physiol.* **260**, R1145–
R1151.

Sterling, P., and Eyer, J. (1981). Allostasis: A new paradigm to
explain arousal pathology. *In* "Handbook of Life Stress, Cognition and Health" (S. Fisher and J. Reason, eds.), pp. 629–652.
Wiley, New York.

Stricker, E. M. (1990). Homeostatic origins of ingestive behavior.
In "Neurobiology of Food and Fluid Intake." (E. M. Stricter,
ed.), pp. 287–324. Plenum Press, New York.

Swanson, L. W. (1987). The hypothalamus. *In* "Handbook of
Chemical Neuroanatomy" (A. Björklund, T. Hökfelt, and L. W.
Swanson, eds.), pp. 1–124. Elsevier, Amsterdam.

Swanson, L. W., and Mogenson, G. J. (1981). Neural mechanisms for the functional coupling of autonomic, endocrine
and somatomotor responses in adaptive behavior. *Brain Res.
Rev.* **3**, 1–34.

Swanson, L. W., and Petrovich, G. D. (1998). What is the amygdala? *Trends Neurosci.* **21**, 323–331.

Swanson, L. W., Simmons, D. M. (1989). Differential steroid
hormone and neural influences on peptide m RNA levels

in corticotropin releasing hormone cells of the paraventricular nucleus: A hybridization histochemical study in the rat. *J. Comp. Neurol.* **285**, 413–435.

Szczepanska-Sadowska, E., Opperman, C. S., Simon, E., Gray, D., Plashka, K., and Szczypaczewska, M. (1992). Central ANP administration in conscious dogs responding to dehydration and hypovolemia. *Am. J. Physiol.* **262**, R746–R753.

Szczypka, M., Rainey, M. A., Kim, D. S., Alaynick, W. A., Marck, B. T., Matsumoto, A. M., and Palmiter, R. D. (1999). Feeding behavior in dopamine-deficient mice. *Proc. Natl. Acad. Sci. U.S.A.* **96**, 12138–12143.

Taylor, J. W., and Kaiser, E. T. (1986). The structural characterization of β-endorphin and related peptide hormones and neurotransmitters. *Pharmacol. Rev.* **38**, 291–319.

Thatcher-Britton, K., Lee, G., Vale, W., Rivier, J., and Koob, G. F. (1986). Corticotropin-releasing factor (CRF) receptor antagonist blocks activating and 'anxiogenic' actions of DRF in the rat. *Brain Res.* **369**, 303–306.

Thorsell, A., Carlsson, K., Ekman, R., and Heilig, M. (1999). Behavioral and endocrine adaptation, and up-regulation of NPY expression in rat amygdala following repeated restraint stress. *NeuroReport* **10**, 3003–3007.

Trimmer, B. A. (1999). The messenger is not the message; or is it? *In* "Beyond Neurotransmission" (P. S. Katz, ed.), p. 391. Oxford University Press, Oxford.

Turner, S. A., Stock, G., and Ganten, D. (1986). Cardiovascular regulation. *In* "Neuroendocrinology" (B. J. Everitt, ed.), pp. 331–359. Blackwell, Oxford.

Tzschentke, T. M. (2001). Pharmacology and behavioral pharmacology of the mesocortical dopamine system. *Prog. Neurobiol.* **63**, 241–320.

van den Buuse, M. (1998). Role of the mesolimbic dopamine system in cardiovascular homeostasis. Stimulation of the ventral tegmental area modulates the effect of vasopressin on blood pressure in conscious rats. *Clin. Exp. Pharmacol. Physiol.* **25**, 661–668.

Van Pett, K., Viau, V., Bittencourt, J. C., Chan, R. K., Li, H. Y., Arias, C., Prins, G. S., Perrin, M., Vale, W., and Sawchenko, P. E. (2000). Distribution of mRNAs encoding CRF receptors in brain and pituitary of rat and mouse. *J. Comp. Neurol.* **428**, 191–212.

Wang, H., Storlien, L. H., and Huang, X. F. (1999). Influence of dietary fats on c-Fos-like immunoreactivity in mouse hypothalamus. *Brain Res.* **843**, 184–192.

Wardlaw, S. L., and Frantz, A. G. (1983). Brain β-endorphin during pregnancy, parturition and the post-partum period. *Endocrinology (Baltimore)* **113**, 1664–1668.

Wardlaw, S. L., Thoron, L., and Frantz, A. G. (1982). Effects of sex steroids on brain β-endorphin. *Brain Res.* **245**, 327–331.

Watts, A. G. (1996). The impact of physiological stimuli on the expression of corticotropin-releasing hormone (CRH) and other neuropeptide genes. *Front. Neuroendocrinol.* **17**, 281–326.

Wei, P., and Vedeckis, W. V. (1997). Regulation of the glucocorticoid receptor gene by the AP-1 transcription factor. *Endocrine* **7**, 303–310.

Wellman, P. J. (2000). Norepinehrine and the control of food intake. *Nutrition* **16**, 837–842.

Wersinger, S. R., and Rissman, E. F. (2000). Dopamine activates masculine sexual behavior independent of the estrogen receptor alpha. *J. Neurosci.* **20**, 4248–4254.

Whitnall, M. H. (1989). Stress selectively activates the vasopressin-containing subset of corticotropin-releasing hormone neurons. *Neuroendocrinology* **50**, 702–707.

Williams, G., Steel, J. H., Cardoso, H., Ghatei, M. A., Lee, Y. C., Gill, J. S., Burrin, J. M., Polak, J. M., and Bloom, S. R. (1988). Increased hypothalamic neuropeptide Y concentrations in diabetic rats. *Diabetes* **37**, 763–772.

Wilson, E. O. (1975). "Sociobiology. The New Synthesis." Harvard University Press, Cambridge, MA.

Wolf, A. V. (1958). "Thirst: Physiology of the Urge to Drink and Problems of Water Lack." Thomas, Springfield, IL.

Woods, S. C., Chavez, M., Partk, C. R., Riedy, C., Kaiyala, K., Richardson, R. D., Filgewicz, D. P., Schwartz, M. W., Porte, D., and Seeley, R. J. (1996). The evaluation of insulin as a metabolic signal influencing behavior via the brain. *Neurosci. Biobehav. Rev.* **20**, 139–144.

Zeki, S. (1993). "A Vision of the Brain." Blackwell Scientific Publications, Oxford.

12

Stress, Opioid Peptides, and Their Receptors

Ryszard Przewłocki

Department of Molecular Neuropharmacology
Institute of Pharmacology
Polish Academy of Sciences
and Department of Applied Psychology
Jagiellonian University
Kraków, Poland

I. INTRODUCTION: THE CONCEPT OF STRESS

Stress is mental or bodily tension resulting from the factors (stressors) that tend to alter exsistent homeostasis, the integrity or health of the body. A stress response is the compensatory reaction of the body to the disturbance caused by a stressor, i.e. a physical or psychological event creating direct physical threat or an event that challenges our existent equilibrium not because it is physically threatening but because of how the organism perceives it (Lovallo, 1997).

Understanding of the mechanisms by which an organism responds to environmental disturbances and threats began with the concept of an internal environment that must be maintained to preserve life. Claude Bernard suggested that functions of living organisms are determined by the external and internal environment. Keeping the internal environment constant while the external environment changes is critical for preserving life. Physical challenges to the integrity of an organism provoke responses to counteract those threats. Bernard's idea of the mechanisms that keep internal fluid stability and support body cells was further expanded by Walter Cannon (1939). He introduced the term homeostasis to describe physiological reactions that maintain the steady state of the organism in the face of external stimuli. He has suggested that homeostasis is a process of maintaining the internal stability of an organism facing environmental change(s). He has noted that the brain plays an important role in maintaining homeostasis as it communicates with the rest of the body via specialized sensory nerves to recognize the external threats and detect the internal state of the body. Finally, the brain is able to activate multiple mechanisms to compensate the disturbed nonequilibrium states. Cannon also observed that psychological as well as physiological disturbances could elicit the responses from the sympathetic nervous system and adrenals.

The concept of stress was formulated first by Selye in 1936. He observed that irrespective of the nature (or identity) of the stressor(s), the physiological changes were relatively similar and were primarily mediated by the hypothalamo-pituitary-adrenal (HPA) axis. He termed the physiological response "stress." He also introduced a term, "stressor," to describe the cause or source of threat such as heat, cold, or toxic and infectious agents. He discovered that exposure to stressors caused enlargement of the adrenal cortex, reduction of weight of the thymus and lymph glands, and induction of stomach ulcers. Selye described the process in terms of a three-stage model called the General Adaptation

Syndrome (GAS). The first adaptive reaction to external challenge is likely to be flight or fight. To make this reaction effective, the heart rate increases, pupils dilatate, digestion ceases, muscles tense, and adrenals are activated. This is the so-called alarm stage. If this reaction is unsuccesful, the body continues to function above the homeostatic arousal level. This is the resistance stage. The organism has adapted to stress and copes with it but requires additional resources, thus depleting original stores necessary for normal body functioning. The third stage occurs when the threat has not been removed and the organism proceeds to the exhaustion stage. Eventually death may occur.

Former theories of stress emphasized the physiological responses, but more recent ones have pointed out the involvement of emotional and psychological factors. Mason (1971) showed that stressors unaccompanied by an emotional component resulted in a minimal physiological response. Munck *et al.* (1984) suggested that the initial psychological response was specific to a particular stressor. This response aims at maintaining homeostasis, disturbed by the stressor. The subsequent and slower response of the HPA axis is not a reaction to the stressor per se, but to the initial psychological response.

Kopin *et al.* (1988) characterized stress as a state in which expectations did not match current or anticipated perceptions of the internal or external environment. The usually unconscious adjustment in the activity of several systems may result in homeostasis. The failure to maintain homeostasis leads to a distress response associated with emotional components such as fear or anxiety. However, the distinction between physical and psychological stress appears to be arbitrary because all physical stressors have a psychological component (Lovallo, 1997), and physiological and psychological factors are equally important in stress response.

The main response of an organism to a stressor involves the activation of HPA, which results in the secretion of proopiomelanocortin-derived peptides such as adrenocorticotropic hormone (ACTH) and opioid peptide β-endorphin, as well as corticotropin-releasing factor (CRF) and glucocorticoids. This reaction is accompanied by autonomic response, activation of the sympathetic nervous system, and release of noradrenaline from sympathetic nerve endings and adrenaline from adrenal medulla. The released

hormones alter cardiovascular and immune system functioning.

New concepts of stress developed as a result of recent research into the physiology, pharmacology, and molecular biology of the endogenous opioid peptides (EOPs). Stress and accompanying emotions may affect body functions, and severe stress may induce long-term alterations in the activity of various opioid neuronal systems, function of the brain, and eventually alterations of behavior, such as motor activity, nociceptive threshold, feeding, sexual behavior, etc. Several behavioral responses to stressors can be augmented or antagonized by opioid receptor antagonists. Therefore, the involvement of EOPs have been propounded. There are numerous data implicating EOPs in the effects of stress on blood pressure and in pathogenesis of hypertension. Further, several lines of evidence indicate that stressful stimuli may influence the immune system, which is altered through the interrelations among the central opioidergic pathways, neuroendocrine system, and the sympathetic nervous system. Furthermore, extensive evidence suggests that the opioid influences on the immune response are mediated through opioid receptors on the surface of immune cells. EOPs can also alter immune activity through interactions with the neuroendocrine and the nervous systems. Thus, it appears that EOP systems play an important role in the interaction of the organism with different stress factors by fulfilling essentially stress-protective and stress-limiting functions.

In this chapter, I will discuss the possible involvement of opioids in mediating physiological as well as psychological reactions to stress. Further, I will focus on the neurobiological mechanisms underlying interactions of EOP systems with other stress-conveying pathways. Finally, I will discuss alternations in EOP systems and multiple opioid receptors that occur as a result of the organism's reaction and adaptation to stressful stimuli.

II. OPIOID SYSTEMS

A. Multiple Opioid Peptides

Over the last two decades, considerable advance has been made in our understanding of the biogenesis of various EOPs, their anatomical distribution, and the characteristics of the multiple receptors with which they interact. It has been shown that EOPs derive from three precursor proteins: proopiomelanocortin (POMC), prodynorphin (PDYN), and proenkephalin (PENK), which were cloned in the late 1970s and early 1980s (Nakanishi *et al.,* 1979; Kakidani *et al.,* 1982; Noda *et al.,* 1982). The details concerning discoveries regarding EOPs, their body and brain distribution and properties, have been reviewed elsewhere (Höllt, 1990). The main groups derived from PENK, PDYN, and POMC are enkephalins, dynorphins, and β-endorphin, respectively. PENK is the source of Met- and Leu-enkephalins and several longer peptides. EOPs such as dynorphin A, dynorphin B, α- and β-neoendorphin, and several larger molecules can be generated from PDYN. POMC is the precursor of β-endorphin, α-endorphin, and several nonopioid peptides. Recently, a novel group of peptides has been discovered in the brain and named endomorphins, endomorphin-1 (Tyr-Pro-Trp-Phe-NH$_2$) and endomorphin-2 (Tyr-Pro-Phe-Phe-NH$_2$). They are unique in comparison with other EOPs, having characteristic structure and high selectivity toward μ-opioid receptors (Zadina *et al.,* 1997). Anatomical studies have demonstrated a distinct anatomical distribution of endomorphins and their synthesis in separated cellular systems.

The EOP-containing neurons have been found to be represented in the regions involved in the stress response, e.g., the hypothalamus, pituitary, and adrenals. Similarly, the autonomic nervous system centers have been shown to be innervated by central and peripheral opioidergic neurons. Further, they are widely distributed in various brain areas associated with emotional components of stress. It is important to note that most EOPs are not usually tonically active, and hence opioid antagonists have little or no effect in the state of homeostasis. On the other hand, they are activated by stressful stimuli and influence certain physiological effects of such stimuli. EOPs are closely associated with "classical" stress hormones such as ACTH, CRF, and adrenaline. ACTH and β-endorphin are produced from the same prohormone molecule POMC, and they are co-secreted from pituitary corticotrophs and neurons in the brain. Adrenaline is coreleased with enkephalins from adrenals, while dynorphins are costored with CRF in the hypothalamic neurons.

B. Multiple Opioid Receptors

Three members of the opioid receptor family were cloned in the early 1990s, beginning with the mouse δ (DOR1) opioid receptor (Evans *et al.,* 1992; Kieffer *et al.,* 1992) and followed by cloning of the μ (MOR1) opioid receptor (Chen *et al.,* 1993a; Fukuda *et al.,* 1993; Thompson *et al.,* 1993) and the κ (KOR1) opioid receptor (Chen *et al.,* 1993b; Li *et al.,* 1993; Meng *et al.,* 1993; Minami *et al.,* 1993; Nishi *et al.,* 1993). These three receptors belong to the family of seven transmembrane G-protein coupled receptors, and they share extensive structural homologies. There is also some affinity of EOPs for the different opioid receptors. The cloned μ receptor is a morphine-like receptor, and endomorphins can be its endogenous ligands. The enkephalins bind to the δ opioid receptor with great affinity and, therefore, they are considered to be endogenous δ-receptor agonists. The affinity of β-endorphin binding to μ and δ receptors was found to be similar. Dynorphins bind to κ-opioid receptor and therefore they appear to function as its endogenous ligands.

Several subtypes of the opioid receptors (μ_1, μ_2; δ_1, δ_2; κ_1, κ_2, κ_3) have been postulated on the basis of pharmacological studies. Molecular attempts to identify subtypes of opioid receptors have not been successful so far, although the existence of several variants of opioid receptors has been suggested (Koch *et al.,* 1998; Uhl *et al.,* 1999; Abbadie *et al.,* 2000; Pasternak and Pan, 2000).

III. DISTRIBUTION OF OPIOID PEPTIDES AND RECEPTORS IN THE STRESS NETWORK

A. Proopiomelanocortin System

β-Endorphin and related peptides are present in the nucleus arcuatus of the mediobasal hypothalamus (Khachaturian *et al.,* 1985; Bugnon *et al.,* 1979; Sofroniew, 1979). An extensive nerve fiber system originating in the arcuate nucleus terminates in many areas of the brain that have been implicated in the stress response, e.g., the hypothalamic nuclei, limbic and raphe nuclei, and some pontine nuclei. In addition, some of these structures might also be innervated by POMC neurons located in the nucleus tractus solitarii (NTS) of the caudal medulla, which project laterally and which also enter the spinal cord (Bronstein *et al.,* 1992; Maley, 1996). Endocrine cells of the intermediate lobe of the pituitary, cells of some peripheral tissues, and immunocytes also contain, synthesize, and release POMC peptides (Blalock *et al.,* 1985; Bloom *et al.,* 1978). These systems are involved in the peripheral responses to stress.

B. Proenkephalin System

PENK neurons are widespread throughout the central and peripheral nervous systems. They are localized predominantly in interneurons, some of which form local longer tract projections. PENK neurons are abundant in the paraventricular nucleus and the nucleus arcuatus of the hypothalamus. A number of PENK neurons exist in limbic system structures, e.g., the hippocampus, septum, and bed nucleus of the stria terminalis. Septal PENK neurons project directly to the amygdala. PENK fibers extend throughout the bed nucleus of the stria terminalis and project from there to the paraventricular nucleus and median eminence. PENK neurons have been found in the spinal cord, cranial sensory systems, and in the major pain-signaling network. A variety of PENK-containing cells are present in the adrenal medulla (Viveros *et al.,* 1979).

C. Prodynorphin System

PDYN neurons are widely distributed in the brain areas associated with stress (Watson *et al.,* 1981; Khachaturian *et al.,* 1985). Dynorphin and related peptides are present in the magnocellular neurons of the paraventricular nucleus of the hypothalamus, where they are costored with vasopressin. In addition, these peptides have been found in the NTS, an area usually associated with the regulation of vagal and other autonomic functions. Further, PDYN neurons occur in the limbic system and in areas of the spinal cord involved in the transmission of nociceptive stimuli. Cells expressing PDYN mRNA are also present in a subpopulation of anterior lobe gonadotrophs (Khachaturian *et al.,* 1985), in the intermediate lobe melanotrophs colocalized with POMC mRNA (Day *et al.,* 1993) as well as in neuronal terminals in the posterior pituitary pituicytes, and in the adrenals, predominantly in the adrenal cortex (Day *et al.,* 1991).

D. Endomorphins

Endomorphins are endogenous peptides recently isolated from the bovine and human brain (Zadina *et al.,* 1997; Hackler *et al.,* 1997). These peptides differ in their amino acid sequences from other known EOPs in which the Tyr residue is followed by Gly, while endomorphins are related to the family of the previously discovered opioid peptides containing Tyr-Pro residues such as morphiceptin, hemorphin, and casomorphins. Endomorphins are localized in neuronal circuits involved in processing nociceptive information and also in many regions of the nervous system containing μ-opioid receptors implicated in stress response and autonomic functions (Zadina *et al.,* 1999).

E. Opioid Receptors

Opioid receptors are differentially distributed in the neuronal stress axis. Dense μ- and κ-opioid receptor binding and high expression are present in most of the hypothalamic nuclei of monkey (Mansour *et al.,* 1988) and man, respectively (Peckys and Landwehrmeyer, 1999). However, those areas of the rat brain contained little (or no) μ-receptor binding (Mansour *et al.,* 1987). Hypothalamic nuclei also showed little δ-receptor binding. Low-density binding was observed in the ventromedial nucleus in the rat. In contrast, dense δ-receptor binding was detected in the median eminence of the monkey. All three opioid receptors are present in the median eminence of the monkey, whereas the κ receptor predominates in the rat median eminence, a finding that is consistent with the distribution of opioid receptors in the posterior lobe of pituitary of the monkey and rat (Mansour *et al.,* 1988). Localization of opioid receptors in the hypothalamic nuclei is in line with the effects of opioids on the neuroendocrine system. Moderate density of μ- and κ-opioid receptor binding sites has been seen in the periaqueductal grey, locus coeruleus, substania nigra, ventral tegmental area, raphe nuclei, and NTS, whereas low δ-opioid receptor binding is present in the substantia nigra and NTS. Further, opioid-receptor containing neurons occur in the limbic system, where they may mediate the emotional component of stress, and in areas of the spinal cord involved in the transmission of nociceptive stimuli. Opioid receptors have also been found in the peripheral nervous system (Wittert *et al.,* 1996; Hedner and Cassuto, 1987; Bechara and van der Kooy, 1985). In addition, they are expressed by various immune cells (Wybran *et al.*, 1979; Blalock *et al.*, 1985; Sibinga and Goldstein, 1988; Carr *et al.*, 1988, 1989; Stein *et al.*, 1990; Gaveriaux *et al.*, 1995; Chuang, 1995; Peterson *et al.*, 1998).

IV. INVOLVEMENT OF OPIOIDS IN SOME BEHAVIORAL AND PHYSIOLOGICAL RESPONSES TO STRESS

A. Motor Activity

Stresses such as restraint (Zurita and Molina, 1999), tail pinch pressure (Amir, 1986), foot shock (Van den Berg *et al.*, 1998), and forced swimming (Abel, 1993; Overstreet *et al.*, 1986; Walker *et al.*, 1981) were found to produce a decrease in motor and investigatory behavior. These motor effects of stress were modified by the opiate antagonist naloxone. Blockade of opioid receptors by opioid antagonists had either no effect on motor behavior (Rodgers and Deacon, 1981) or decreased motor activity (Arnsten and Segal, 1979; Katz, 1979; Walker *et al.*, 1981; Roth *et al.*, 1981; Kavaliers and Innes, 1987). Naloxone treatment produced a decrease in locomotor activity and rearing in rats exposed to an open field (Rodgers and Deacon, 1979; Walker *et al.*, 1981), and potentiated the effect of immobilization stress (acute and chronic) on locomotor activity after amphetamine (Diaz-Otanez *et al.*, 1997). The results may suggest the activation of EOP systems, which underlies some of the changes in investigatory behavior evoked by exposure to stress. The restraint stress enhanced the immobility time in the forced swimming test, and this effect was blocked by naloxone (Zurita and Molina, 1999). Emotional stimulus (forced perception of another rat receiving foot shocks) induced a transient decrease in ambulation and rearing immediately after the last session, but an increase in ambulation, rearing, and sniffing was observed in the period from half an hour until at least 15 days after the stimulus experience. Naloxone also inhibited both emotional motor effects of stress, thus suggesting the involvement of EOPs in the behavioral responses (Van den Berg *et al.*, 1998). In contrast, the same research group demonstrated that foot shock stress (10-minute session for five consecutive days) induced a decrease in ambulation, rearing,

and sniffing and an increase in immobility in the small open field, and these effects were not antagonized by naloxone (Van den Berg *et al.*, 1998). Thus, various kinds of stress may induce changes in motor activity, which may or may not involve EOP systems.

It is interesting that naloxone potentiated stress-evoked freezing in male rats (Klein *et al.*, 1998). In contrast, in females naloxone did not affect freezing, regardless of stress conditions. These results reveal a sex difference in the effects of naloxone on freezing behavior and suggest that sex differences may exist with respect to the role of endogenous opioids under stress. Furthermore, the restraint stress elicited an increase in locomotor activity in one population of mice, while significantly decreased the activity of other animals (Kavaliers and Innes, 1987). The stress-induced increases in locomotor activity of the mainland deer mice were blocked by the δ-opioid antagonist, ICI 154,129, whereas the decreases in locomotion in the insular animal were inhibited by naloxone, thereby indicating differential involvement of specific opioid receptor types δ and possibly μ, respectively, in the behavioral responses to stress (Kavaliers and Innes, 1987). These results demonstrate that there are marked population differences in the stress-induced, opioid-mediated responses of animals, and that various responses to stress may be mediated by various EOPs and their receptors.

Exposure to stressful situations has also been shown to change the effects of opiates. Both exogenous opioids and EOPs have been observed to exert bidirectional (depending on the dose) effects on motor activity. In general, low doses produced an arousal and increase in activity, whereas higher ones caused decrease in motor activity, leading to sedation, stupor, or catalepsy. Morphine enhanced the immobility time induced by forced swimming in rat (Zurita and Molina, 1999). The fact that this effect was blocked by naloxone suggests the involvement of an endogenous opioidergic process in this response. Further, stress is able to alter the locomotor stimulatory effects of morphine in rats, a phenomenon called stress-induced behavioral sensitization to morphine. The augmentation of the locomotor effects of low but not high doses of morphine was seen after repeated, but not after single stress events. The enhancement of morphine-induced stimulation of locomotor activity was observed in response to the repeated application (three times) of such stressors as restraint, handling, and social defeat (Stohr *et al.,* 1999). The corticosterone release under stress seems to be involved in stress-induced behavioral sensitization to morphine (Stohr *et al.,* 1999). Moreover, restraint stress increased the locomotor response to morphine, but not in the rats in which stress-induced corticosterone secretion was suppressed. These results suggest that corticosterone secretion may be one of the mechanisms by which repeated stress amplifies motor responses to morphine (Deroche *et al.,* 1992).

It is interesting that morphine elicited hyperactivity in the hamsters habituated to handling, whereas in nonhabituated animals morphine evoked hypoactivity. The effects of handling diminished across test days, so on the last test day, morphine elicited hyperactivity in both habituated and nonhabituated animals (Schnur *et al.,* 1988). The results are in line with the suggestion that stress induces the release of EOPs, which summate with exogenous opiates to exert the final effect. Mice exhibit marked suppression of motility when they are placed in the same cage in which they had previously received electric shock. This suppression of motility was associated with a decrease in Met-enkephalinergic activity in the striatum of the conditioned suppression group (Nabeshima *et al.,* 1986). Inhibition of Met-enkephalin degradation by thiorphan and bestatin attenuated the conditioned suppression of motility, and this effect was mediated by an opioid receptor, since it was antagonized by naloxone. These results suggest that thiorphan- and bestatin-evoked attenuation of the conditioned suppression of motility may be directly proportional to the increases in endogenous Met-enkephalin contents in the striatum (Nabeshima *et al.,* 1988). Injection of enkephalin analog D-Ala^2-Met^5-enkephalinamide into the ventral tegmental area of rats has been shown to increase spontaneous motor activity, whereas daily D-Ala^2-Met^5-enkephalinamide injection into the ventral tegmental area resulted in a progressive enhancement in the motor stimulant effect. Furthermore, rats receiving daily foot-shock stress for a few days exhibited a significantly greater motor stimulant response to intraventral tegmental area injection with D-Ala^2-Met^5-enkephalinamide than control rats. Thus, it is possible that the endogenous enkephalin system in the ventral tegmental area may participate in motor sensitization to subsequent environmental stress (Kalivas and Abhold, 1987).

In rats subjected to a social stress, there was no depression of locomotor behavior in the dominant rats in response to a selective δ-opioid receptor agonist SNC-80 as compared to subdominant and singly housed rats. Dominant rats displayed stimulant rather than depressant responses to δ-opioid receptor activation and, therefore, dominance may increase the excitatory effects of δ-receptor agonists (Pohorecky *et al.,* 1999). The effects of the κ-opioid receptor agonists tifluadom, bremazocine, and U50,488H on locomotor activity were assessed in C57BL/6 and DB/2 mice. The drug administration resulted in locomotor activity depression in both strains, and the effect was enhanced by immobilization stress (Castellano *et al.,* 1988). Thus, various opioid receptors appear to be differentially involved in the modulation of stress-induced alteration of motor activity. It is also likely that stress-induced motor suppression may be mediated or potentiated by PDYN and the κ-receptor system, while PENK and δ receptors may act to attenuate the response.

B. Place Preference, Reward, and Self-Administration

Morphine (Katz and Gormezano, 1979; Mucha and Iversen, 1984; Mucha and Herz, 1986; van der Kooy *et al.,* 1982), EOPs (Bals-Kubik *et al.,* 1993) and various μ- and δ-opioid receptor agonists (Spanagel *et al.,* 1992) elicit conditioned place preference; e.g., animals are inclined to choose an initially nonpreferred environment associated with previous administration of an opioid. On the contrary, opioid antagonist naloxone (Mucha and Iversen, 1984; Mucha and Herz, 1986) and κ-opioid receptor agonists (Iwamoto, 1985; Mucha and Herz, 1985) evoke place aversion. It appears that stress influences place preference conditioned by opioids. The inescapable shock enhanced morphine-conditioned place preference when tested 24 hours thereafter (Will *et al.,* 1998). This effect was developed even when conditioning was delayed for several days following the stressor. Acute emotional stress induced by forcing mice to witness another mouse being subjected to acute physical stress caused an increase in the sensitivity to the rewarding effects of morphine (Kuzmin *et al.,* 1996). The exposure to mild intermittent stress appeared to enhance the reinforcing efficacy of heroin in rats (Shaham and Stewart, 1994; Shaham *et al.,* 2000; Spanagel *et al.,* 1998). It is interesting that foot shock influenced heroin-induced drug reinstatement behavior (Shaham *et al.,* 1997; Spanagel *et al.,* 1998). The foot-shock stressor reliably reinstated the previously extinguished heroin-taking behavior, thereby suggesting that stress may be a critical factor leading to relapse in opiate addicts. Pretreatment with CRF-receptor antagonist significantly attenuated the reinstatement effect of the stressor in heroin-trained rats, thus indicating the involvement of CRF in the phenomenon (Shaham *et al.,* 1998). Stress has been shown to reduce self-stimulation from ventral tegmental area that was attenuated by intracerebral administration of opioid peptides (Zacharko *et al.,* 1998). Stress appears also to influence self-administration of opiates. The mild foot shock applied before each of self-administration session evoked higher rates of lever pressing for heroin in rats exposed to foot shock (Shaham *et al.,* 1997). However, the physical stress (e.g., acute foot shock) did not significantly affect self-administration (Kuzmin *et al.,* 1996).

C. Nociception: Stress-Induced Analgesia

One year after the discovery of enkephalins in 1976, Akil and her colleagues were the first to report that exposure to foot-shock stress caused potent antinociception in rats. Furthermore, they found that naloxone partially reversed this analgesia, a result that suggests an involvement of EOPs. A number of later studies showed that various kinds of stress such as exposure to novel stimuli (Kavaliers and Innes, 1988), inescapable footshocks (De Vries *et al.,* 1979; Hemingway and Reigle, 1987; Lewis *et al.,* 1980; Rosecrans *et al.,* 1986; Terman *et al.,* 1984), restraint (Kelly and Franklin, 1987, Kurumaji *et al.,* 1987), food deprivation (Konecka *et al.,* 1985; Wideman *et al.,* 1996), forced swimming (Terman *et al.,* 1986a; Cooper and Carmody, 1982; Suaudeau and Costentin, 2000), cold water stress (Bodnar *et al.,* 1979; Girardot and Holloway, 1985b), burn injury (Osgood *et al.,* 1987), learned helplessness (Maier *et al.,* 1983; Hemingway and Reigle, 1987), social isolation (Konecka and Sroczynska, 1990), food deprivation (Hodgson and Bond, 1996; Konecka *et al.,* 1985), pregnancy (Baron and Gintzler, 1984, 1987), conditioned fear in animals and man (exposure to a stimulus resembling an original traumatic event in-duced naloxone-reversible analgesia in the patients with posttraumatic stress disorder) (Fanselow, 1986; Przewlocka *et al.,* 1990; Levine *et al.,* 1984; Pitman *et al.,* 1990), handling stress (Fanselow and Sigmundi, 1986), mild social stress (Kulling *et al.,* 1988; Pohorecky *et al.,* 1999), defeat stress (Miczek *et al.,* 1982), stressful odors (Fanselow and Sigmundi, 1986), and even consequences of exposure to biting flies in domestic and wild animals (Colwell and Kavaliers, 1992) resulted in antinociception, which under certain conditions appeared to be mediated by endogenous opioids, e.g., naloxone-sensitive stress-induced analgesia (Akil *et al.,* 1984, 1986; Girardot and Holloway, 1985a). The analgesic opioid effects were comparable with the stress effects induced in rodents by analgesic doses of morphine (5–10 mg/kg), but the former were usually faster and shorter-lasting. In rodents, usually mild stressors produced opioid-dependent analgesia, whereas severe stressors induced analgesia independent of opioids (Hamm and Knisely, 1987; Hawranko *et al.,* 1994; Izumi *et al.,* 1983; Mogil *et al.,* 1996). Stress severity plays an important role in determining the neurochemical basis of stress-induced analgesia. Increasing severity (duration or intensity) of stress causes a shift from an opioidergic to a nonopioidergic mechanism in mediation of the resultant analgesia. For example, more severe conditions of swimming (longer duration or lower water temperature) produced stress-induced analgesia insensitive to the opiate antagonist, naltrexone, whereas less severe swimming conditions produced analgesia significantly attenuated by this drug (Terman *et al.,* 1986b). Opioid or nonopioid stress analgesia could be evoked by changing only the intensity of foot shock applied to either front or hind paws when duration and temporal pattern were held constant (Cannon *et al.,* 1984). It is interesting that the stress-induced analgesia is followed by a period of hyperalgesia with a series of symptoms characteristic of the exogenous opioid abstinence syndrome (Cristea *et al.,* 1993). Some studies have indicated that there are substantial sex and population differences in the novelty-induced analgesia displayed by various populations of deer mice (Kavaliers and Innes, 1987, 1988). Exposure to a new environment elicited significant, naloxone-reversible analgesic responses in three populations of deer mice, but male deer mice displayed significantly greater levels of analgesia than females (Kavaliers and

Innes, 1987, 1988). Furthermore, Marek *et al.* (1989) also have found that opioidergic forms of analgesia following stress in mice depended on genetic factor(s). Thus, these results suggest that the activation of opioid analgesic systems by stress is both sex and strain dependent (Mogil *et al.*, 1997).

Some findings suggest an early evolutionary development and phylogenetic continuity of stress responses to aversive stimuli mediated by opioidergic and nonopioidergic mechanisms (Kavaliers, 1987). Exposure to either cold or warm stress increased the thermal nociceptive thresholds of the terrestrial snail *Cepaea nemoralis*. The warm stress-induced analgesia was blocked by opiate antagonists whereas cold stress-induced analgesia was unaffected. Exposure to tail-pinch stress increased the thermal nociceptive thresholds (which was antagonized by naloxone) of the slug, *Limax maximus* (Kavaliers and Hirst, 1986). These results indicate that this mollusc displays both opioidergic and nonopioidergic forms of stress-induced analgesia in a manner anaus to that reported in mammals.

The development of tolerance to the analgesia induced by repeated forced intermittent cold water swim has been reported (Girardot and Holloway, 1985b). Naltrexone antagonized the adaptive aspect of all those analgesia forms. Thus, EOPs may play a functional role in the behavioral adaptation to aversive, stressful environmental situations. A series of studies in humans has shown that physical exercise leds to temporary hypoalgesia. Reduced sensitivity to pain is demonstrable after long-distance exercise (such as a marathon run) but also after intensive physical exercise. Pain threshold elevation is most pronounced during maximal exertion, but hypoalgesia persists also after exercise has stopped, thus demonstrating that a systemic analgesic effect is induced by the exercise process (Droste, 1992).

Exposure to acute stress potentiates the magnitude and duration of analgesia following both the peripheral and intracerebroventricular administration of several opioid agonists as compared to nonstressed controls (Calcagnetti *et al.*, 1992). Both supraspinal and spinal analgesic opioidergic mechanisms significantly contribute to the enhanced analgesic potency of opioids in the subjects exposed to various types of stress. Opioid-treated rats exposed to restraint stress showed potentiation of the magnitude and duration of opioid

analgesia (Woolfolk and Holtzman, 1995; Calcagnetti and Holtzman, 1992; Calcagnetti *et al.*, 1990). However, rats given agonists with high intrinsic activity at the μ receptor displayed the most potent and consistent potentiation of analgesia compared to the unrestrained controls. Thus, the results suggest that the activation of the μ receptor is of primary importance for restraint to potentiate analgesia (Calcagnetti *et al.*, 1990, 1992). Naloxone or naltrexone at low doses antagonized certain kinds of stress-induced analgesia. However, neither antagonist is selective toward the μ-opioid receptor, and this experiment demonstrates only the involvement of an opioid receptor in the phenomena. A few studies have authenticated the above conclusion by using the more specific μ receptor antagonists, β-FNA and CTOP (Fanselow *et al.*, 1989). The octapeptide CTOP dose-dependently reversed fear-induced conditional analgesia in rats when administered intraventricularly in rats (Fanselow *et al.*, 1989). More recently, the authors have demonstrated that CTOP suppressed stress-induced analgesia when injected into the periaqueductal gray (Wiedenmayer and Barr, 2000). Thus, the μ-opioid receptor system localized in the midbrain periaqueductal gray appears to be involved in opioid stress-induced analgesia.

Fields (2000) recently has described the neuronal pain-modulating circuit, which includes the periaqueductal gray, amygdala, and raphe nuclei in the brain stem. Through descending projections, this circuit controls both the spinal and trigeminal dorsal horn pain-transmitting neurons. This system may be activated by acute stress and mediates stress analgesia in animals and humans. An interesting finding is that prolonged chronic stress such as repeated cold swim, in contrast to acute stress, decreases sensitivity to antinociceptive effects of morphine. Chronically stressed mice were hyposensitive to μ-opioid receptor-mediated antinociception (Omiya *et al.*, 2000). Rats exposed to the stress of repeated exposure to a noxious heat exhibited stress-induced analgesia but antinociception was reduced (detected using the tail-flick test) after the administration of β-endorphin into the periaqueductal gray region of the brain (Hawranko *et al.*, 1999).

Several studies demonstrated potential involvement of δ-opioid receptor in stress-induced analgesia (Hart *et al.*, 1983, 1985; Kitchen and Pinker, 1990; Killian *et al.*, 1995). The studies showed that naltrindole and ICI 174874 inhibited analgesia induced by warm water (20°C) swim stress both in adult and young rats (Kitchen and Pinker, 1990). Also, cold water swim stress (5°C) was antagonized by the δ-receptor antagonist ICI 174,864. This antinociceptive response was antagonized by prior administration of the δ_2-opioid receptor antagonist, naltriben, but not by the δ_1 receptor antagonist, 7-benzylidenenaltrexone, in mice (Killian *et al.*, 1995). An other study showed that the cold water swim stress response was selectively antagonized by naltrindole, but not by the δ_1 antagonist, [D-Ala^2-Leu^5-Cys^6]enkephalin, the μ receptor antagonist, β-funaltrexamine, or by the κ antagonist, nor-binaltorphimine (Vanderah *et al.*, 1993). These studies suggest that cold water swim stress analgesia is mediated by δ_2-opioid receptors. However, the selective δ-opioid receptor antagonist naltrindole had no influence on the psychological stress-induced analgesia (Takahashi *et al.*, 1990), indicating the specific involvement of δ-opioid receptors in certain kinds of stress, such as swim stress.

The involvement of κ receptors in stress-induced analgesia has also been demonstrated. Early studies suggested that the κ-opioid receptor antagonist reversed nonopioid stress-induced analgesia, whereas the μ-opioid receptor might mediate opioid analgesia (Panerai *et al.*, 1984, 1987). More recently it was demonstrated that nor-binaltorphimine, a selective κ-receptor antagonist, blocked the foot-shock, stress-induced analgesia when administered systemically or intrathecally in rats (Menendez *et al.*, 1993). Further, the stress analgesia induced by exposure to psychological stress was also antagonized by pretreatment with nor-binaltorphimine and Mr2266 (Takahashi *et al.*, 1990). Furthermore, chronic cold swim stress increased the antinociceptive response via the κ-opioid receptor (Omiya *et al.*, 2000). The antinociceptive activity of U50,488H was demonstrated in mice subjected to the repeated cold stress. It is interesting that the antinociceptive activity of μ agonist DAMGO was attenuated by stress. These results suggest that spinal κ-opioid receptors may be responsible for endogenous analgesia induced by some types of stress.

The potential involvement of the brain POMC and β-endorphin systems in stress-induced analgesia has to be widely considered. Early evidence showed that hypothalamic and midbrain β-endorphin levels were

changed upon foot-shock stress, possibly due to the enhanced release of this peptide (Przewłocki *et al.*, 1987). Conditioned stress evoked naloxone-sensitive analgesia and a marked decrease in the β-endorphin level in the hypothalamus and both lobes of the pituitary, together with an increase in the peptide level in plasma (Przewłocka *et al.*, 1990). However, β-endorphin was increased in the periaqueductal gray matter, where terminals of β-endorphinergic neurons are located (Kulling *et al.*, 1989; Nakagawasai *et al.*, 1999), and in the arcuate nucleus of the medial basal hypothalamus after exposure of rats to mild social stress (aggressive confrontation) and forced walking stress (Nakagawasai *et al.*, 1999), respectively. Lesions of the arcuate nucleus reduced the opioid-mediated stress-induced analgesia, but it is interesting that they enhanced a form of foot-shock stress-induced analgesia that was not blocked by injections of the opiate receptor blocker, naltrexone (Kelsey *et al.*, 1986). Thus, the arcuate lesions led to compensatory changes in the nonopioid analgesic system, resulting in the enhanced nonopiate-mediated, stress-induced analgesia. Further, naloxone injections into the periaqueductal grey area and arcuate nucleus blocked analgesia in defeated mice (Miczek *et al.*, 1985). Furthermore, microinjections of antibodies against β-endorphin into the midbrain periaqueductal gray attenuated the antinociception elicited by electro-acupuncture (Xie *et al.*, 1983). Another study suggested the potential role of β-endorphinergic cells within the NTS in stress-induced analgesia. Electrical stimulation of this structure evoked opioid-mediated analgesia in the rat (Lewis *et al.*, 1987). Such results may indicate that β-endorphin-containing neuronal cells, at least partly, may be involved in this phenomenon.

There are some suggestions that stress-induced analgesia may also depend on peripheral pools of β-endorphin. It is not clear whether pituitary pools of β-endorphin play a role in the phenomenon, since some kinds of stress induce peptide release into the blood without affecting nociception. Some studies suggest that although the integrity of the adenohypophysis is essential for the manifestation of stress-induced analgesia, an adenohypophyseal mechanism, probably involving neither ACTH nor β-endorphin, is essential for the development of the analgesia that accompanies stress (Millan *et al.*, 1980, 1981a). Lim *et al.* (1982) have suggested that plasma levels of β-endorphin do not reflect changes in pain threshold, and β-endorphin levels in the anterior pituitary, neurointermediate lobe, and plasma probably are not causally related to stress effects such as foot-shock-induced analgesia. Some results suggest that the stress of labor causes an increase in the maternal secretion of β-endorphin that is not related to the degree of pain itself (Jouppila *et al.*, 1983). The mean level of β-endorphin in cerebrospinal fluid was significantly greater in the patients with posttraumatic stress disorder compared with normal value. Thus, the increased endorphinergic activity in the central nervous system may exist in patients with posttraumatic stress disorder, and hypersecretion of opioids might constitute an adaptive response to traumatic experience (Baker *et al.*, 1997). However, there is poor correlation between cerebrospinal fluid and plasma β-endorphin level when measured in combat veterans with posttraumatic stress disorder (Baker *et al.*, 1997). The recent study on mice with a selective deficiency of β-endorphin clearly demonstrated the critical role of β-endorphin in stress-induced analgesia. In these mice, the lack the opioid-dependent naloxone-reversible analgesia was observed in response to mild swim stress (Rubinstein *et al.*, 1996). The mice exhibited normal analgesia in response to morphine, indicating the presence of functional μ-opioid receptors. Mutant mice also displayed significantly greater nonopioid analgesia in response to cold water swim stress compared with the controls, and displayed paradoxical naloxone-induced analgesia. These changes may reflect compensatory up-regulation of alternative opioid-independent pain inhibitory mechanisms.

There is some evidence suggesting a role of the brain PENK-derived peptides in stress-induced analgesia (Kurumaji *et al.*, 1987). Exposure of mice to forced swim in cold water produced opioid analgesia that was blocked by intrathecal pretreatment with antiserum to Met-enkephalin, but not to Leu-enkephalin, β-endorphin, or dynorphin (Mizoguchi *et al.*, 1997). The study suggests that the swim stress-induced analgesia is mediated by spinal Met-enkephalin. The inhibition of PENK peptide degradation has been reported to potentiate this phenomena when applied intraventricularly in mice (Chipkin *et al.*, 1982; Christie and Chesher, 1983). Enkephalinase inhibitor thiorphan evoked a dose-related potentiation of both the peak

effect and the duration of the stress-induced analgesia after exposure of rats to inescapable foot shock (Chipkin *et al.*, 1982). Moreover, it was shown that adrenal demedullation abolished the analgesic response (Lewis *et al.*, 1982), thereby suggesting the participation of circulating PENK peptides. Unexpectedly, however, enkephalin-deficient knockout mice exhibited normal stress-induced analgesia (Konig *et al.*, 1996).

The involvement of the PDYN system in the mediation of stress remains unclear. A recent study in mice demonstrated that psychological stress-induced analgesia was fully antagonized by the selective κ-opioid receptor antagonist nor-binaltorphimine, although this compound was without any effect on foot-shock- and swim-induced antinociception (Takahashi *et al.*, 1990). Further, Starec *et al.* (1997) demonstrated that dynorphin exerted an analgesic effect in mice when combined with a stressor. Such results provide evidence that the PDYN system, as well as κ receptors, may be involved in the mechanisms of certain kinds of stress. However, it appears that some kinds of stress may inhibit, rather than activate, the brain PDYN system. For example, it has been shown that the *in vitro* hypothalamic release of α-neoendorphin, a peptide derived from PDYN, is lowered in rats subjected to conditioned fear-induced stress, which itself is accompanied by naloxone-reversible analgesia (Przewłocka *et al.*, 1990). Further, a rise in the content of dynorphin in the hypothalamus after foot-shock stress has been reported, thus suggesting a suppression of dynorphin release (Millan *et al.*, 1981b). It is interesting that the stress-induced opioid-mediated responses were modified in CB1 canabinoid receptor knockouts. Indeed, these mutants did not exhibit antinociception following a forced swim in warm water. However, absence of the CB1 cannabinoid receptor did not modify the antinociceptive effects induced by different opioid agonists. These results indicate that a physiological interaction between the opioid and cannabinoid systems is necessary to allow the development of opioid-mediated responses to stress (Valverde *et al.*, 2000).

Experimental data clearly demonstrate that opioids are able to inhibit nociception arising in inflamed tissue by a local peripheral action, presumably via the terminal region of the sensory nerves. Similar effects are observed when endogenous opioid peptides are released under stress conditions from immune cells present in the inflamed tissue (Stein *et al.*, 1990; Przewłocki *et al.*, 1992; Herz, 1995, 1996). Immunoreactive β-endorphin and enkephalins, processed in these cells, seem to be the relevant peptides in this respect. Although the mechanism of stress-induced release of opioid peptides from the immunocytes is presently not clear, there is indication that this process involves cytokines and CRF.

Thus, whether or not EOPs play a role in the antinociception depends on the kind of stress and variables studied. Some stressors activate the EOP systems but others do not. Moreover, when EOPs are involved there is frequently interaction with other neuronal systems. Therefore, the analgesic effects of stress are complex and difficult to characterize. Nevertheless, the reaction to certain kinds of stress have been shown to be mediated by specific neuronal opioid systems, since they are known to cause release of these opioid peptides and may be modulated by opiates.

D. Thermoregulation: Stress-Induced Hyperthermia

Several forms of stress have been shown to cause hyperthermia in the rat. Foot-shock stress produced hyperthermia, the degree of which was found to be a function of current intensity (Pechnick and Morgan, 1987). Restraint stress and novelty stress also produced hyperthermia (Vidal *et al.*, 1984). Naloxone (Vidal *et al.*, 1984; Kapas *et al.*, 1989) slightly reduced restraint and "novelty" hyperthermias (Vidal *et al.*, 1984) or emotional hyperthermia (Blasig *et al.*, 1978). These effects suggest that endogenous opioids are not significantly involved in the thermal effects of the stressors. They may play only a minor role in the regulation of basal temperature (Vidal *et al.*, 1984). Peak rise in temperature following foot-shock stress was not affected by naltrexone or chronic morphine administration; however, the rate of return to baseline temperature was slowed by these treatments. Thus, the endogenous opioidergic system appears to be involved in the return to normal body temperature following foot shock, but not in the foot-shock-induced rise in temperature (Pechnic and Morgan, 1987).

Restraint stress affects the changes in body temperature induced by morphine and opioid peptides administered either systemically or intracerebroventricularly (icv) in rats. The unstressed group of rats responded to all doses of morphine, DAMGO, DADLE, and D-Met^2-Pro^5-enkephalin with an increase in core temperature. In contrast, restrained rats showed a decrease in core temperature following the injection of opioids (Appelbaum and Holtzman, 1986; Spencer *et al.*, 1985; Szikszay *et al.*, 1983). An interesting finding is that administration of cholecystokinin reduced the hypothermic response to systemic morphine in restrained rats, but hyperthermia elicited by administration of morphine to freely moving rats was not diminished by cholecystokinin pretreatment. These results support the hypothesis that cholecystokinin may contribute to the regulation of the endogenous opioid system (Kapas *et al.*, 1989).

There is indirect evidence of involvement of opioid peptide β-endorphin in the hypothalamic mechanisms of the development of fever and stress-induced hyperthermia. In the unanesthetized rabbits, microinjection of β-endorphin in the preoptic-anterior hypothalamus resulted in the elevation of body temperature. It has been suggested that β-endorphin reduces sensitivity of hypothalamic neurons to high ambient temperature, and that this reduction leads to the increased peripheral vasoconstriction, inhibition of evaporative heat loss, and modification of behavioral thermoregulation, resulting in the elevation of body temperature (Gordon *et al.*, 1984).

Plasma β-endorphin response under three exercise-thermoregulatory stress conditions was measured in humans during stationary upright cycling. The β-endorphin response pattern closely paralleled rectal temperature changes in all conditions. These data suggest that conditions of increasing thermoregulatory stress caused by exercise are associated with rising peripheral β-endorphin concentration (Kelso *et al.*, 1984).

It has been previously reported that sauna-induced fevers result in a rise in β-endorphin levels in normal volunteers. This report describes also the changes in plasma β-endorphin in cancer patients suffering from whole body hyperthermia. The presented results show that there is a linear relationship between thermal stress—defined in terms of core temperature, duration of hyperthermia, or both—and the quantitative rise in plasma β-endorphin levels.

E. Feeding Behavior

Stress is known to influence feeding. Some kinds of stress augment feeding in animals, and opioid antagonists appear to abolish it (Antelman and Rowland, 1981; Holtzman 1974; Teskey and Kavaliers, 1988). Stress produced by pinching the tail has been shown to compel satiated animals to eat and display oral stereotypes. Eating induced by the tail pinch was reduced by microinjections of naloxone and the μ-selective antagonist CTOP into the substantia nigra, thereby indicating the selective involvement of μ-opioid receptors. In fact, the stress-induced eating did occur after the treatment with κ- and δ-opioid receptor antagonists (Hawkins *et al.*, 1994). Opioid peptides may determine partly the rewarding aspects of eating. Mercer and Holder (1997) argue that the altered EOP activity may elicit food cravings that, in turn, may influence food consumption. Support for this opioidergic theory of food cravings is provided by various clinical conditions (bulimia nervosa, anorexia nervosa, Prader-Willi syndrome, and eating-induced obesity) that are associated with altered EOP levels, intensified food cravings, and increased or decreased food intake (Morley *et al.*, 1982, 1983).

Furthermore, food deprivation results in alterations of EOP levels in the brain and pituitary of the rat (Majeed *et al.*, 1986; Tsuji *et al.*, 1987) similar to those induced by chronic stress. The data support the notion that EOPs, in particular dynorphin, and the μ-opioid receptor appear to play a role in the modulation of food intake by stress. EOP activity altered by stress may elicit food craving, which than may influence food consumption (Mercer and Holder, 1997).

F. Cardiovascular Effects

Cardiovascular responses to stress include the increased catecholamine secretion, tachycardia due to the elevated cardiac sympathetic and reduced vagal efferent activity, peripheral vasoconstriction in certain vascular beds, arrhythmia, and hypertension. Some data suggest the involvement of particular EOP systems in these processes. EOPs are present in the cerebrospinal fluid and the cerebrovascular bed, and opioid receptors have been found in cerebral perivascular nerves. Their activation may modulate the function of vasoreg-

ulatory mechanisms that are involved in the control of the cerebrovascular tone. Under resting conditions, EOPs do not appear to play an important role in the regulation of the cardiovascular system, but they become important under stress (Benyo and Wahl, 1996). Restraint stress evoked an increase in heart rate, blood pressure, and plasma catecholamine levels in rats. Pretreatment with β-funaltrexamine partially attenuated the increase in heart rate in response to stress (Houdi *et al.*, 1996). During μ-opioid receptor activation by DAMGO, restraint stress resulted in bradycardia. Psychosocial stress appears to elevate blood pressure via an opioid-dependent mechanism in normotensive rats, since naloxone has been demonstrated to attenuate or reverse the elevation in blood pressure in both renovascular and spontaneous hypertension (Szilagyi, 1991).

During periods of severe stress, opioid blockade increased ambulatory blood pressure in humans. These observations suggest that opioidergic mechanisms inhibit ambulatory blood pressure responses during naturally occurring stress (McCubbin *et al.*, 1998). The results of another study indicated that relaxation training reduced the diastolic pressure response to mental arithmetic stress. Opioid receptor blockade with naltrexone antagonized the effects of relaxation training. The study suggests that some of the physiological effects of relaxation training are mediated by augmentation of inhibitory opioid mechanisms (McCubbin *et al.*, 1998). Thus, an endogenous opioid mechanism appears to inhibit the cardiovascular response to stress. In the brain, the POMC neurons are involved in the control of the function of the NTS, the structure known to participate in the control of cardiac function. Intravenous or intracerebroventricular administration, as well as the injection into the NTS of β-endorphin, has been shown to decrease blood pressure (Hassen *et al.*, 1982; Sitsen *et al.*, 1982). The localization of enkephalins in the paraventricular nucleus of the hypothalamus, a brain region important for the regulation of the stress response, further substantiates the involvement of the opioid system in the modulation of stress-induced hypertension. The studies on the cardiovascular responses to centrally administered PENK products are contradictory so far and provide little insight into the physiological role of central PENK in cardiovascular functions. However, adrenal PENK peptides, released by the stimulation of the splanchnic nerve, may induce bradycardia and hypotension as shown in reserpinized dogs (Hanbauer *et al.,* 1982).

Dynorphin decreases blood pressure and produces bradycardia when applied intravenously or into the cisterna magna (Laurent and Schmitt, 1983). In contrast, application of dynorphin into the NTS or cerebral ventricles does not alter cardiovascular function (Hassen *et al.,* 1982; Glatt *et al.,* 1987). Prodynorphin peptides appear to modulate the release of vasopressin from the posterior lobe and may regulate diuresis in this way. κ-Opioid receptor agonists are powerful diuretics (Leander, 1982). Therefore, prodynorphin peptides and κ receptors may thereby influence the cardiovascular system. In humans, mental stress affects blood pressure and increases various opioid peptides in plasma. Subjects responding to stress with a low increase in blood pressure had high levels of β-endorphin, whereas those who reacted with a high stress-induced blood pressure had elevated levels of dynorphin and Met-enkephalin. Pretreatment with naloxone enhanced blood pressure in low responders but not in high-blood-pressure responders (Fontana *et al.,* 1997). It is interesting that naloxone decreased blood pressure response in hypertensive subjects with acute stress-induced increase in blood pressure, a result that suggests pressor effects of some EOPs, possibly dynorphins or PENK-derived peptides, in hypertensive patients (Fontana *et al.,* 1997).

Therefore, it is likely that some EOPs may, under some circumstances, counteract the cardiovascular effect of moderate stress—e.g., tachycardia and increased blood pressure—whereas some others may be involved in hypertensive pathology. In contrast, EOPs appear to mediate cardiovascular depression that occurs in response to severe stress. In fact, a number of studies have demonstrated that naloxone reverses the hypotension induced by most cardiovascular shock states (Vargish *et al.,* 1980; Reynolds *et al.,* 1980; Feuerstein *et al.,* 1981).

G. Respiration

Is well documented that opioids and EOPs influence respiration (McQueen, 1983), and stress may modulate respiration. Rats exposed to inescapable footshock displayed an increase in respiratory rate, and naloxone potentiated the footshock-induced increase in ventila-

tion (Isom and Elshowihy, 1982). Chronic footshock stress attenuated both the respiratory stimulation produced by acute footshock and the potentiation induced by naloxone. These results strongly suggest that stress can influence respiratory function through the activation of endogenous opioid systems and release of the endogenous opioids as a compensatory reaction that prevents excessive stimulation of respiration (Isom and Elshowihy, 1982).

H. Reproduction

Stress is frequently accompanied by an impairment of reproductive functions (Calogero *et al.,* 1998). Stressors generally induce a depression of the hypothalamus-pituitary-testis system, mediated by the activated HPA, which results in a fall in plasma luteinizing hormone (LH) and testosterone levels (Petralgia *et al.,* 1986). There is accumulating evidence that CRF is a critical stress factor that exerts inhibitory actions upon sexual behavior and secretion of gonadotropins. However, CRF may inhibit hypothalamic neurons producing gonadotropin-releasing hormone—most likely via endogenous opioidergic pathways, although direct effects of CRF on gonadotrophin-releasing hormone neurons are also likely to occur (Almeida *et al.,* 1989). Endogenous opioids, originating through CRF-independent mechanisms in the brain or even the pituitary, may also influence gonadotropin production (Chatterton, 1990). Acute opioid administration decreases plasma LH levels due to an inhibitory modulation of gonadotrophin releasing hormone discharge from the hypothalamic neurons (Briski *et al.,* 1984; Domanski *et al.,* 1989; Ferin and Vande, 1984; Genazzani *et al.,* 1993; Petralgia *et al.,* 1986). EOPs released from the hypothalamus inhibit LH secretion, resulting in inhibition of ovulation and termination of pregnancy. Data suggesting the involvement of EOPs in the direct control of the neuroendocrine mechanism modulating gonadotrophin secretion have been reported.

In stress, the presence of low plasma LH levels and an abnormal LH pulsatile secretion have been related to increased opioidergic activity, thus supporting the role of opioids in the integration of hormonal and neuronal systems of the brain (Genazzani *et al.,* 1993). Inhibitory effects of foot-shock stress on LH release were found to be antagonized by μ and κ (but not δ) receptor antagonists as well as by antibodies against both β-endorphin and dynorphin (but not Met-enkephalin) (Petralgia *et al.*, 1986). Therefore, this study may suggest the involvement of POMC and PDYN (but not PENK) neurons in the control of LH release during stress. Restraint stress reduced plasma testosterone levels in the control rats; reduction was blocked by naloxone (Akinbami *et al.*, 1994; Akinbami and Mann, 1996).

Testicular steroidogenesis may also be locally inhibited by opioid peptides via peripheral opioid receptors (Kostic *et al.*, 1998), in particular β-endorphin secreted into plasma and secreted locally by the Leydig cells (Eskeland *et al.*, 1989, 1992; Fabbri *et al.*, 1988). However, estrogen treatment enhanced PENK gene expression in the ventromedial hypothalamus (Quinones-Jenab *et al.*, 1996) and PENK expression therein can be associated with estrogen as well as progesteron concentration during the estrous cycle (Funabashi *et al.*, 1995). Stress and estrogen appear to have specific effects on PENK expression in the hypothalamic neurons (Priest *et al.*, 1997). A recent study demonstrated an increase in the μ-opioid receptor mRNA in the ventromedial nucleus and arcuate nucleus of hypothalamus after the administratioon of 17-β-estradiol in ovariectomized females, which indicates the estrogenic regulation of μ-opioid receptor in the hypothalamus (Quinones-Jenab *et al.*, 1997). The μ-opioid receptor involvement in sexual function was recently observed in μ-receptor knockout mice. Male homozygotes showed unexpected changes in sexual function as shown by reduced mating activity, a decrease in sperm count and motility, and smaller litter size (Tian *et al.*, 1997).

V. INVOLVEMENT OF OPIOIDS IN MODULATION OF THE HYPOTHALAMO-PITUITARY-ADRENAL AXIS

A. Corticotropin-Releasing Factor System

Stress from various origins may induce secretion of CRF and enhance its synthesis in neurons of the paraventricular nucleus of hypothalamus (Haas and George, 1988; de Goeij *et al.*, 1991; Bartanusz *et al.*, 1993; Imaki *et al.*, 1996). CRF appears to be a po-

tent secretagogue of the three major endogenous opioid peptides (β-endorphin, Met-enkephalin, and dynorphin) acting via specific CRF receptors (Nikolarakis *et al.*, 1986), and stimulating opioidergic neurons in the hypothalamus (Almeida *et al.*, 1993). It is interesting that CRF neurons appear to control EOP release tonically, since the application of the CRF receptor antagonist, α-helical CRF$_{9-41}$, lowered the rate of the basal release of both β-endorphin and Met-enkephalin from the hypothalamus. However, EOPs may act on CRF neurons to modulate CRF secretion, but this remains less clear. Enkephalins as well as low doses of β-endorphin were shown to stimulate CRF release from the hypothalamus *in vitro* in a naloxone-reversible fashion (Buckingham, 1986). An increase in CRF mRNA levels in the paraventricular nucleus as well as the increased plasma ACTH concentration were observed *in vivo* after the intraventricular injection of moderate doses of β-endorphin in rats (Wang *et al.*, 1996). Both effects were mediated via the opioid receptors. The effect of β-endorphin on ACTH release was inhibited by intravenous injection of anti-CRF antiserum. These results suggest, on one hand, that the injection of β-endorphin increases the neuronal activity and the biosynthesis of CRF in the paraventricular nucleus, and a rise in CRF secretion stimulates the secretion of ACTH. On the other hand, higher doses of β-endorphin administered intraventricularly inhibited both basal and acetylcholine- and serotonine-stimulated CRF release (Buckingham, 1986). Furthermore, intraventricular administration of both β-endorphin and dynorphin induced a dose-related inhibition of CRF secretion into the hypophysial portal circulation of rats (Plotsky, 1986), and the effect was antagonized by naltrexone, thus suggesting the involvement of opioid receptors. Centrally administered EOPs inhibited hypoglycemia-induced CRF gene expression in the hypothalamus and supressed CRF release, which in consequence led to a decrease in ACTH secretion and POMC mRNA levels in the anterior pituitary (Suda *et al.*, 1992). Further, both κ- and μ-opioid (but not δ) receptor agonists inhibited the stimulated release of CRF from rat hypothalamus *in vitro* (Tsagarakis *et al.*, 1990), the effects being specifically reversed by opioid antagonists. It is interesting that naltrindole, which is a selective antagonist of δ-opioid receptors, clearly enhanced basal and stimulated

CRF release. Thus, a complex relationship between the EOP and CRF systems appears to exist. It is possible that depending on circumstances, EOP systems act directly on CRF neurons or indirectly via other neuronal systems.

B. Vasopressin and Oxytocin Systems

Stress activates the neuronal and hormonal vasopressin system of animals (Knepel *et al.*, 1985; Vellucci and Parrott, 1997). In humans, anticipation of novelty seems to be a human-specific stress stimulus for a sustained elevation of plasma vasopressin in men (Ehrenreich *et al.*, 1996). Vasopressin released upon stress appears to affect EOP systems. Subcutaneous administration of arginine vasopressin to conscious rats induced a dose-dependent increase in plasma β-endorphin levels (Mormede *et al.*, 1986). This effect seems to be mediated via both arginine vasopressin V1- and V2-receptors (Kjaer *et al.*, 1993a). Further, passive immunization with antivasopressin antibodies inhibited stress-induced secretion of POMC-derived peptides (Linton *et al.*, 1985). The vasopressin system may directly contribute to the regulation of POMC-derived peptide release from the pituitary. *In vitro,* vasopressin was shown to release both β-endorphin and ACTH from anterior pituitary (Arimura *et al.*, 1969; Przewłocki *et al.*, 1979; Vale *et al.*, 1978). Thus, vasopressin acts synergistically with CRF both *in vitro* and *in vivo* (Gillies *et al.*, 1982; Rivier *et al.*, 1984). Recent studies have shown that vasopressin is a potent secretogogue of hypothalamic β-endorphin *in vitro* and *in vivo* (Barna *et al.*, 1990; Burns *et al.*, 1989). An interesting finding is that vasopressin receptor blockade reduced CRF-induced β-endorphin release *in vitro*. Therefore, vasopressin appears to participate in the effects of CRF. The significance of this control of the mechanism of β-endorphin release remains to be established. An interesting possibility is that CRF tonically activates some central β-endorphin neurons (as well as PENK and, to some extent, PDYN cells) and controls basal release of these peptides. However, in stress, vasopressin may participate in the mediation of opioid release. Hypothalamic vasopressinergic neurons, appear to be an essential mediator of CRF effect, thereby suggesting the occurrence of CRF synapses on or in the vicinity of vasopressinergic neurons (Almeida *et al.*, 1993). Thus, it appears that vasopressin might be an important modulator of POMC-derived peptide secretion, and it has to be considered an important factor in the mediation of stress reactions.

However, EOPs appear to participate in the control of vasopressinergic neurons in the hypothalamus and posterior pituitary. Some evidence suggests that EOPs might exert an inhibitory control over vasopressin release in response to stressors such as foot shock and immobilization (Knepel *et al.*, 1985). EOPs interact with the magnocellular vasopressinergic (and oxytocinergic) neurons at several levels to inhibit the release of these hormones in response to various physiological stimuli (Knepel and Reimann, 1982). These results suggest lack of tonic inhibition of vasopressin release by EOPs. EOPs appear to inhibit excitatory input to vasopressinergic and oxytocinergic neurons via μ-opioid receptors (Q. S. Liu *et al.*, 1999). Knepel and Reimann (1982) showed that morphine and β-endorphin inhibited the electrical field-stimulated release of vasopressin from the mediobasal hypothalamus *in vitro*.

The inhibition of secretion can occur both at the level of the terminals and in cell bodies of magnocellular cells. In fact, their activity is modulated by presynaptic inhibition of afferent inputs to magnocellular cells by opioids as well as direct effects of afferent input cells on the cell bodies (Brown *et al.*, 2000). Systemic administration of morphine to rats reduced vasopressin release into the pituitary stalk blood. This effect was antagonized by naloxone, which itself was without any effect. But the inhibition of vasopressin release from posterior lobe terminals appears to be mediated through κ- rather than μ- or δ-opioid receptors. The κ-selective agonists as well as dynorphin A_{1-13} inhibited secretion of vasopressin, and this effect was antagonized by naloxone and the selective κ-receptor antagonist nor-binaltophimine (Zhao *et al.*, 1988; Bondy *et al.*, 1988). κ-Opioid receptors may also directly modulate activity and release of vasopressin (but not oxytocin) in the hypothalamic magnocellular neurosecretory neurons (Brown and Leng, 2000). Furthermore, the κ-receptor might be an autoreceptor in this system because of a high degree of colocalization of κ-opioid receptors, dynorphin, and vasopressin in magnocellular nerve terminals (Shuster *et al.*, 2000).

VI. STRESS-INDUCED ALTERATIONS IN ENDOGENOUS OPIOIDERGIC SYSTEMS

A. Hypothalamo-Pituitary-Adrenal Axis

1. Proopiomelanocortin System

Acute and chronic stress appears to influence the activity of EOP systems in the brain. Evidence indicates that releasable pools of β-endorphin exist within the hypothalamus. It was previously demonstrated that β-endorphin might be released from hypothalamic slices *in vitro* (Osborne *et al.*, 1979). An early *in vivo* study showed that a short-term foot-shock stress caused depletion of β-endorphin in the hypothalamus, septum, and periaqueductal gray of rats (Millan *et al.*, 1981a; Przewłocki *et al.*, 1982; Rossier *et al.*, 1977), indicating an enhanced release of the peptide therefrom. It is interesting that conditioned fear-induced stress markedly decreased hypothalamic content of β-endorphin (Przewłocka *et al.*, 1990). This result is in line with the previous observation that there is a measurable decrease in β-endorphin levels in the midbrain when chronically stressed rats are acutely restressed (Akil *et al.*, 1986). The later data indicated that either enhanced releasability of β-endorphin or an increase in the releasable pool of this peptide occurred following repeated exposure to stress. However, cold swim stress increased β-endorphin levels in the hypothalamus (Vaswani *et al.*, 1988). But more severe stress, i.e., acute prolonged intermittent foot shock, induced no alternation in the hypothalamic and midbrain levels of the peptide (Akil *et al.*, 1986; Przewłocki *et al.*, 1987). Thus, the stress-induced decrease in hypothalamic β-endorphin levels might be detectable only after mild, short-term stress. Various kinds of chronic stress (repeated foot shock, repeated electroconvulsive shock) did not induce substantial alterations in the brain β-endorphin levels (Lasoń *et al.*, 1987; Przewłocki *et al.*, 1987), though social isolation of adult gerbils increased levels of the peptide in the hypothalamus and amygdala (Raab *et al.*, 1985). It is noteworthy that tissue levels of neuropeptides are influenced by several processes, such as release, biosynthesis, and axonal transport. Hence, a likely explanation of the apparently unchanged β-endorphin levels in the hypothalamus is that high-intensity or long-term stress induces rapid stimulation of POMC biosynthesis in the brain, which, in turn, may prevent depletion of POMC-derived peptides. Furthermore, the POMC gene appears to be under negative control of adrenal steroids, since adrenalectomy induces an increase in hypothalamic POMC mRNA levels, which may contribute to the adaptive processes (Beaulieu *et al.*, 1988). Acute, one-hour restraint stress increased the levels of POMC mRNA in the arcuate nucleus slightly but significantly (Larsen and Mau, 1994). Water restriction had no effect on POMC mRNA levels in the hypothalamus (Zhou *et al.*, 1999), whereas the level of POMC mRNA in the nucleus arcuatus decreased following repeated immobilization (Makino *et al.*, 1999). Another study demonstrated that food deprivation also decreased the POMC mRNA levels in the hypothalamus (Gayle *et al.*, 1999). Following restraint, POMC mRNA increased in the mediobasal hypothalamus in pigs (Vellucci and Parrott, 1997). In fact, chronic stress may lead to an increase in the biosynthesis of β-endorphin, since the levels of the peptide in the cerebrospinal fluid were significantly greater in the patients with posttraumatic stress disorder when compared with normal values (Baker *et al.*, 1997). Thus, hypersecretion of β-endorphin in the brain might constitute an adaptive response to stress. Nevertheless, additional studies of POMC biosynthesis and release in the hypothalamus and extrahypothalamic structures are necessary before the effects of stress on the activation of the brain POMC systems can be fully understood.

Stress leads to a substantial release of β-endorphin into blood in animals and humans. β-Endorphin-containing cells, corticotrophs in the anterior pituitary lobe, react to different types of acute stress, such as electrical foot shock (Guillemin *et al.*, 1977; Millan *et al.*, 1981a; Przewłocki *et al.*, 1982; Rossier *et al.*, 1977), swim stress (Young *et al.*, 1993a; Przewłocka *et al.*, 1988; Vaswani *et al.*, 1988), burn injury (Osgood *et al.*, 1987), immobilization (Forman and Estilow, 1988; Larsen and Mau, 1994; Kjaer *et al.*, 1993b), cold stress (Forman *et al.*, 1988), food (Majeed *et al.*, 1986) and water deprivation (Zhou *et al.*, 1999), labor (McLean *et al.*, 1994; Pancheri *et al.*, 1985), electroacupuncture (Pan *et al.*, 1996), and stress produced during simulated combat military flight (Leino *et al.*, 1998) by enhancing the release of β-endorphin as well as ACTH. The release increases the rate of POMC synthesis and processing in the anterior lobe (Harbuz and Lightman, 1989; Akil *et al.*, 1982; Zhou *et al.*, 1999; Höllt *et al.*, 1986).

The intermediate lobe of the pituitary responds to stress in a similar way (Akil *et al.*, 1985; Berkenbosch *et al.*, 1983; Przewłocki *et al.*, 1982; Young *et al.*, 1993b), thus leading to the elevation in POMC products in the plasma. Acute exposure to a 30-minute swim stress at room temperature caused a several-fold increase in the β-endorphin level in plasma, which derived from the intermediate lobe (Young, 1990; Young *et al.*, 1993b). The effect was completely blocked by apomorphine, thus indicating the involvement of dopaminergic receptors. Acute ether stress followed by one-hour restraint stress also increased POMC mRNA in the intermediate lobe cells, which appeared to be mediated by tonic activity of serotoninergic system (Garcia-Garcia *et al.*, 1998) POMC-containing cell types in both anterior and intermediate pituitary lobes are derived from a single embryonic rudiment and synthesize the same hormone precursor, POMC, but differ in the pattern of precursor processing and regulation of peptide secretion. The predominant EOP released by stress was β-endorphin$_{1-31}$, originating from the anterior pituitary (Young and Akil, 1985). Yet stress also induced a slight increase in N-acetyl-β-endorphin content deriving from intermediate lobe pools. This peptide is devoid of opioidergic activity, but it contributes to the changes in the circulating β-endorphin levels (Akil *et al.*, 1985; Young, 1990). The secretion of POMC-derived peptides from the anterior lobe and intermediate lobe is differentially regulated, and the relative contributions of the lobes may vary with the stimulus. For example in response to restraint stress, β-endorphin and ACTH are secreted equally from the anterior lobe and intermediate lobe, whereas the intermediate lobe was the most important source of β-endorphin and α-MSH in response to ether stress (Kjaer *et al.*, 1995).

Chronic stress leads to a substantial increase in β-endorphin levels in both the anterior and the intermediate lobe of the pituitary (Akil *et al.*, 1985; Höllt *et al.*, 1986; Przewłocki *et al.*, 1987). Prolonged stress decreases the proportion of β-endorphin in the releasable pool of the anterior lobe corticotropes. Chronic foot shock releases proportionaly more β-lipotropin than β-endorphin in the rat (Young *et al.*, 1993b). Repeated immobilization (Skultetyova and Jezova, 1999; Marti *et al.*, 1999; Lopez-Calderon *et al.*, 1991), water restriction (Zhou *et al.*, 1999), repeated injection of hypertonic saline (Kiss and Aguilera, 1993), and adjuvant-induced inflammation (Aguilera *et al.*, 1997; Harbuz and Lightman, 1992) significantly increased POMC mRNA in the anterior lobe. The level of POMC mRNA increased selectively in the anterior but not in the intermediate lobe after repeated foot shock (Höllt *et al.*, 1986). This finding suggests a selective activation of POMC synthesis in the anterior lobe only in response to chronic stress. In contrast, other studies have indicated that rats subjected to chronic foot shock or forced swim stress demonstrate an increase in POMC mRNA levels in the intermediate lobe of the pituitary (Kesley *et al.*, 1984). Therefore, it is likely that specific chronic stress such as swim stress may stimulate POMC biosynthesis in the intermediate lobe. In fact, chronic swim stress results in the increased plasma levels of N-acetyl-β-endorphin (Young, 1990).

2. Proenkephalin System

Stressful stimuli strongly activate the PENK system within the hypothalamus. Early studies demonstrated that foot-shock stress (McGivern *et al.*, 1983; Rossier *et al.*, 1978) and social isolation (Raab *et al.*, 1985) induced a decrease in the hypothalamic content of PENK-derived peptides. In contrast, other studies reported no obvious effect of immobilization, foot-shock, or cold swim stress upon PENK peptide levels and its mRNA in the rat hypothalamus (Millan *et al.*, 1981a; Przewłocki *et al.*, 1987; Takayama *et al.*, 1986; Vaswani *et al.*, 1988; Vellucci and Parrott, 1997). However, a plethora of further studies clearly indicated that stressful stimuli enhanced PENK gene expression in the cells localized in the parvocellular part of the hypothalamic paraventricular nucleus (Harbuz and Lightman, 1989; Lightman and Young, 1989; Garcia-Garcia *et al.*, 1998; Larsen and Mau, 1994; Priest *et al.*, 1997). Stress induced by the injection of hypertonic saline increased PENK mRNA levels in the paraventricular nucleus, and the effects were blocked by the administration of RU-486 (Garcia-Garcia *et al.*, 1998). Levels of PENK mRNA also increased within the medial parvocellular subset of the hypothalamic paraventricular nucleus after one-hour restraint stress (Larsen and Mau, 1994). Novelty or the injection of hypertonic saline also elevated levels of PENK mRNA and c-fos mRNA in the paraventricular nucleus, whereas estrogen attenuated the elevation of PENK mRNA in that structure (Yukhananov and Handa, 1997). Social deprivation (14 to 20 days) in rats was also associated with an activation of the central PENK opioid system. The deprivation increased the levels of PENK mRNA and Met-enkephalin immunoreactivity in the hypothalamus (Iglesias *et al.*, 1992). Interesting studies were performed in transgenic mice with human PENK-β-galactosidase fusion transgene. It was shown that the transgene determined correct phenotypic expression and appropriate stress regulation within the hypothalamus of transgenic mice. Acute osmotic stress and hypovolemia induced transgene expression in neurons within both the paraventricular and supraoptic nuclei (Borsook *et al.*, 1994a,c). Chronic osmotic stress resulted in dramatic induction of transgene expression in both nuclei (Borsook *et al.*, 1994a,b). Thus, the activation of hypothalamic, in particular paraventricular and supraoptic, PENK neurons may play a significant role in the response to both acute and prolonged stress. Levels of PENK mRNA increased also in the nucleus caudatus after restraint stress in pigs (Vellucci and Parrott, 1997). In the forebrain, proenkephalin mRNA levels were found to be transiently decreased by 29% in the anterior and medial aspects of the caudate putamen and the nucleus accumbens after 7 or 14 days of isolation stress, but the levels returned to control levels after 28 days of isolation (Angulo *et al.*, 1991).

There are some data on the influence of stress on the pituitary PENK system. Zhu and Desiderio (1994) observed that space flight stress diminished the Met-enkephalin level in in the posterior pituitary of rats and suggested that posterior pituitary enkephalinergic system may respond to this type of unique stress. Further, the same group of authors demonstrated that the level of Met-enkephalin significantly increased 10 days after head injury in rats (Grigoriants *et al.*, 1995).

Lewis *et al.* (1982) demonstrated the role of adrenal medullary PENK opioids in some behavioral responses to stress. The exposure of rats to short, intermittent foot shock caused a decrease in the adrenal medullary content of PENK-derived peptides (Lewis *et al.*, 1982),

thus pointing to an enhanced release of these opioids. Levels of PENK peptides in the adrenal medulla were decreased after acute stress but returned to the control levels in chronically stressed rats. PENK mRNA levels increased several-fold over control after hypoglycemic stress (Kanamatsu *et al.*, 1986).

A recent study in humans demonstrated biphasic changes in the plasma level of peptide F, the peptide derived from PENK, in response to heavy exercise. Initially the level of peptide F decreased but significantly increased during recovery period (Bush *et al.*, 1999). This result suggests that the biosynthetic activity of adrenal PENK cells increases upon prolonged stress, thus compensating for the enhanced peptide release into the blood. However, Van Loon *et al.* (1990) suggested that plasma Met-enkephalin in rats derived from sympathetic peripheral neurons and not only from the adrenals. Repeated daily exposure to restraint stress resulted in an adaptive loss of the plasma Met-enkephalin response. Repeated immobilization stress increased, however, the PENK mRNA in sympathetic neurons of the rat cervical and stellate ganglia (Nankova *et al.*, 1996). Thus, it seems that in the periphery, both adrenal opioidergic cells and sympathetic neurons contribute to stress response. In addition, it is likely that different types of stress selectively activate different pools of PENK peptides.

3. Prodynorphin System

Dynorphin levels in the hypothalamus remain unchanged in stress conditions (Morley *et al.*, 1982; Przewłocki *et al.*, 1987). But the hypothalamic levels of PDYN-derived peptides significantly increased after acute swim stress and starvation (Przewłocki *et al.*, 1983a, 1988a), thereby probably indicating an inhibition of their release. In contrast, a pronounced fall in hypothalamic dynorphin levels was observed in rats subjected to electroconvulsive shocks, cold swim stress, or two-hour exposure to 4°C (Lason *et al.*, 1987; Morley *et al.*, 1982; Vaswani *et al.*, 1988). This finding may indicate the enhancement of PDYN-derived peptide release during seizures and extreme stress. In contrast, repeated electroconvulsive shock markedly increased dynorphin content and PDYN mRNA levels in the hypothalamus (Hong *et al.*, 1985; Lason *et al.*, 1987). Thus, hypothalamic PDYN neurons appear to by particularly sensitive to seizures. There is no evidence that chronic stress, e.g., recurrent foot shock (Przewłocki *et al.*, 1987) or conditioned fear-induced stress (Przewłocka *et al.*, 1990), influences the hypothalamic PDYN system. Also, no evidence of the changes in PDYN biosynthesis has been found in hippocampal dentate neurons after chronic restraint stress (Watanabe *et al.*, 1995). However, isolation induced a significant accumulation of PDYN mRNA selectively in the paraventricular nucleus, but no changes were noted in mRNA content within the supraoptic nucleus (Matthews *et al.*, 1993). No significant differences were observed in the level of PDYN mRNA in the nucleus accumbens between low and high responders to novelty stress in rats (Hooks *et al.*, 1994). On the contrary, profound increase in the PDYN mRNA has been demonstrated in the brain, in particular in the nucleus accumbens, during intake and withdrawal from several drugs of abuse (Wang *et al.*, 1999; Przewłocka *et al.*, 1996; Trujillo *et al.*, 1995). The hypothalamic PDYN system clearly responded to dehydration and water deprivation, as was evidenced by an increase in the hypothalamic PDYN-derived peptides (Przewłocki *et al.*, 1983b; Höllt *et al.*, 1981; Majeed *et al.*, 1986) and PDYN mRNA levels (Sherman *et al.*, 1986). Dehydration significantly increased PDYN mRNA in the magnocellular neurons of the paraventricular and supraoptic nucleus (Matthews *et al.*, 1993).

Intermittent foot shock and swim stress produced no alternations in PDYN-derived peptide content in the anterior pituitary (Przewłocki *et al.*, 1987; Vaswani *et al.*, 1988). Another study showed that dynorphin levels in the posterior pituitary (containing dynorphin neuronal terminals) were not altered after acute foot shock (Przewłocki *et al.*, 1987). Thus, the above mentioned observations do not provide clear indications whether stress activates PDYN peptide biosynthesis and release in the pituitary.

The data also strengthen the notion that dynorphin might play a role in reproductive functions. PDYN mRNA levels in the posterior pituitary melanotrophs were up-regulated three- to four-fold in the intermediate lobes of postpartum females as compared to pregnant or nonpregnant female rats (Day *et al.*, 1993). Further, dynorphin, which is coexpressed with vasopressin in the magnocellular neurons of the paraventricular and supraoptic nuclei, was coregulated with vasopressin in

response to hyperosmolality and appeared to inhibit vasopressin and oxytocin release from the posterior pituitary (Young and Lightman, 1992).

B. Opioid Receptors

Several studies have been conducted to assess stress-induced alterations in opioid receptors. The presumptive mild stress of handling was sufficient to decrease μ- or δ-receptor binding in several investigated brain regions, including the frontal cortex and olfactory tubercle, when compared to unhandled control animals (Stein *et al.*, 1992).

Fear-induced stress was shown to cause a decrease in [^{3}H]Leu-enkephalin binding to the rat brain (Chance *et al.*, 1978; Sumova and Jakoubek, 1989). Similar results were obtained in rats after exposure to forced swimming (Christie *et al.*, 1981). Low-affinity [^{3}H]Leu-enkephalin binding to brain homogenates at low temperature was significantly reduced in mice exposed to forced acute and chronic swim trials. It is likely that the reduced binding reflects the increased *in vivo* occupation of opioid-binding sites by EOPs (Christie and Chesher, 1983). Seeger *et al.* (1984) reported that either prolonged intermittent foot shock or forced swimming caused a significant reduction in [^{3}H]diprenorphine binding in the hypothalamus and other brain structures, as measured by autoradiography. A single 20-minute foot shock resulted in the diminished [^{3}H]DAMGO binding in the septum (Stein *et al.*, 1992). A decrease in high-affinity [^{3}H]etorphine binding after restraint stress in rat brain membranes (Hnatowich *et al.*, 1986) and a drop in the number of μ-opioid receptors in the midbrain after inescapable shock (Stuckey *et al.*, 1989) have also been documented. Thus, acute stress appears to decrease the binding of opioid receptor ligands, a finding that suggests a persistent activation of opioid receptors due to an enhanced release of EOPs.

Chronic, recurrent stress induced by repetitive electroconvulsive shocks has been shown to cause down-regulation of both δ- and μ-opioid receptors in some structures of the rat brain (Nakata *et al.*, 1985). The sleep deprivation-induced stress decreased B_{max} of δ- and μ-opioid receptors in the limbic system (Fadda *et al.*, 1991, 1992). It is reasonable to assume that the effect may constitute an adaptive response to the enhanced release of EOPs during stress. Rank-related stress has been shown to change responsiveness of the δ-opioid receptor system, and dominance could increase the excitatory effects of δ-receptor agonists indicating enhanced sensitivity of the receptor in dominant rats in comparison to nondominant ones (Pohorecky *et al.*, 1999). In line with these findings, Holaday *et al.* (1982) reported an up-regulation of δ-opioid receptors in response to repeated electroconvulsive shock treatments. Further, an increase in the number of δ-opioid receptors in the corpus striatum was reported after repeated immobilization stress (Zeman *et al.*, 1988). Moreover, another study showed that stressors such as intermittent foot shock and four days of water deprivation induced an increase in δ- and μ-binding sites in the rat limbic system. 90-hour water deprivation induced increases in [^{3}H]DAMGO binding in the septum as well as increases in [^{3}H]DSTLE binding in the caudate and accumbens nuclei (Stein *et al.*, 1992). Offspring from prenatally stressed female rats showed increases in μ-opioid receptors in some brain areas such as the striatum, lateral amygdala, and pyriform nucleus (Insel *et al.*, 1990). Further, mice selectively bred for high swim stress–induced analgesia were found to have significantly higher μ-receptor density in the whole brain than those with low analgesic response to stress (Mogil *et al.*, 1994). In contrast, defeat stress was without effect on the expression of μ-opioid receptor-encoding mRNA in the substantia nigra (Nikulina *et al.*, 1999). Howeve, Lewis *et al.* (1987) were unsuccessful in demonstrating any changes in the number or affinity of δ-, κ- and μ-sites in various brain and spinal cord regions of rats exposed to chronic stress.

Some recent studies have analyzed the changes in the biosynthesis of opioid receptors as a result of stress. A novelty stress increased the levels of κ-opioid receptor mRNA in the ventral zone of the medial parvocellular part but not in the lateral parvocellular part of the paraventricular nucleus, claustrum, nucleus accumbens, or the nucleus of the lateral olfactory tract (Yukhananov and Handa, 1996). Within 30 minutes after social defeat stress, the level of μ-opioid receptor-encoding mRNA increased in the lateral ventral tegmental area, as detected and quantified by *in situ* hybridization histochemistry, and the level remained increased for at least

6 hours. These data suggest that stress-induced alteration of μ-opioid receptor-encoding mRNA expression in the ventral tegmental area may be involved in the consequences of social defeat stress (Nikulina *et al.*, 1999).

Evidently, the results of the studies are discrepant and sometimes contradictory. Clearly, more studies are needed before the influence of stress on specific opioid receptors can be elucidated.

VII. MULTIPLE NEUROCHEMICAL INTERACTIONS WITH OPIOID SYSTEM IN CONSEQUENCE OF STRESS

A. Dopaminergic System

Stress has been shown to activate selectively the mesolimbic dopaminergic system located in the nucleus accumbens, the prefrontal cortex, and the ventral tegmental area region (Deutch *et al.*, 1985; Scatton *et al.*, 1988; George *et al.*, 2000; Cuadra *et al.*, 1999; Fadda *et al.*, 1993), whereas the nigrostriatal dopaminergic neurons seem not to be affected by such stimuli (Kalivas and Abhold, 1987). Further, dopamine turnover in the mesolimbic system is accelerated by cues that have been associated with a previously applied stressor (Deutch *et al.*, 1985). This observation may suggest that fear and anxiety accompanying stress are involved in evoking the biochemical changes.

Stress-induced variations in activity of the central dopaminergic system can be altered by opioids. The administration of opioids into the ventral tegmental area has been shown to enhance dopamine turnover in the nucleus accumbens septi and the prefrontal cortex (Spanagel *et al.*, 1992; Leone *et al.*, 1991; Noel and Gratton, 1995), as well as the motor stimulant effect of foot-shock stress (Kalivas and Abhold, 1987). However, the administration of opioid antagonists prevented stress-induced variations in dopamine turnover (Kalivas and Abhold, 1987). Further, repeated immobilization stress enhanced sensitivity to dopamine agonists as a result of hyperactivity of opioidergic systems. In fact, Kalivas and his colleagues (1988) have shown that daily exposure to mild foot-shock stress enhanced the motor stimulatory effect of DAMGO injected into the ventral tegmental area. But daily intraventral tegmental area administration of this enkephalin analogue potentiated the capacity of acute foot shock to elevate dopamine metabolism in the nucleus accumbens. Furthermore, it was shown that daily pretreatment with naltrexone prior to stress prevented augmentation of the effects of DAMGO when both substances were administered into the ventral tegmental area, thus indicating the involvement of EOPs released locally into the structure during stress. Microinjection of enkephalin analogues into the ventral tegmental area produced an increase in spontaneous motor activity, and this effect was antagonized by intra-accumbens or peripheral administration of dopamine receptor antagonists (Broekkamp *et al.*, 1979; Kelley *et al.*, 1980). Systemic administration or microinjection of morphine onto dopamine cells in the ventral tegmental area excited dopaminergic neurons in the rat (Gysling and Wang, 1983; Mattews and German, 1984). The enkephalin-evoked increase in motor activity was associated with an increase in dopamine metabolism in the mesolimbic system and appeared to be mediated through the μ-opioid receptor (Latimer *et al.*, 1987). These receptors are most likely localized on local GABA-ergic interneurons in the ventral tegmental area, since DAMGO-induced effects can be antagonized by GABA antagonists (Kalivas *et al.*, 1990). The δ- and κ-opioid receptors appear also to be involved in modulation of activity of the ventral tegmental area dopaminergic neurons. The activation of the δ- (but not κ) opioid receptor in the ventral tegmental area appears to facilitate a brain reward system (Jenck *et al.*, 1987) and dopamine release therein (Devine *et al.*, 1993). However, the administration of the κ-opioid receptor agonist U50,488H and the stable dynorphin analogue E 2078 into this structure induced dose-dependent aversion in the place-conditioning procedure (Bals-Kubik *et al.*, 1993). Thus, it is interesting that the aversive effects of κ-opioid receptor agonists observed following their peripheral or intraventricular administration may be mediated at least partly by the modulation of dopaminergic cell activity. The effect of exogenous or endogenous opioids appears to be mediated through local GABA interneurons, e.g., via disinhibition of the GABA neurons, thereby releasing the dopamine neurons from tonic GABA inhibition. Under nonstress conditions, the tonic activity of EOPs is minimal or absent, allowing profound GABA inhibition; however, during stress, EOPs inhibit GABA interneurons, resulting in an activation of dopaminergic transmission. But EOP-containing terminals provide a direct synaptic input to dopaminergic neurons in the ventral tegmental area and may directly modulate activity of dopaminergic neurons during stress (Sesack and Pickel, 1992). EOPs may also influence the activity of the mesolimbic dopaminergic system in the nucleus accumbens by altering the activity of dopaminergic terminals. It is known that the release of dopamine from the nucleus accumbens is enhanced by some opioids (Di Chiara and Imperato, 1988; Spanagel *et al.*, 1990). This effect appears to be mediated by μ- as well as δ-opioid receptors (Spanagel *et al.*, 1990). In contrast, κ-opioid receptor agonists inhibit dopamine release from this structure (Di Chiara and Imperato, 1988; Spanagel *et al.*, 1990).

The restraint stress induced dopamine release in the frontal cortex *in vivo*, and this response was further sensitized in chronically stressed rats. Naloxone pretreatment normalized this sensitized response. This result indicates that endogenous opioidergic mechanisms in the frontal cortex, presumably activated during chronic stress, may be involved in the development of such sensitization process (Cuadra *et al.*, 1999). The interaction of hypothalamic tuberoinfundibular dopaminergic neurons with EOPs may be of some importance in stress. The hypothalamic tuberoinfundibular dopaminergic neurons localized in the nucleus arcuatus are inhibited by opiates (Haskins *et al.*, 1981). The inhibition of dopamine release into the portal vessels during stress, as a consequence of enhanced release of EOPs (most likely β-endorphin), may promote the release of POMC peptides and vasopressin from the intermediate lobe and posterior lobe of pituitary, respectively. However, an intrinsic dopaminergic system exerts an inhibitory control on POMC peptide release via D2 dopaminergic receptors (Tiligada and Wilson, 1990; Tong and Pelletier, 1992; Yamaguchi *et al.*, 1996). It is apparent from the preceding paragraph that the opioidergic network in both the ventral tegmental area and nucleus accumbens is critically involved in the regulation of dopaminergic neuron activity during stress.

Opioids modulate activity of the mesocorticolimbic dopaminergic system, and this interaction appears to underlie major aspects of stress-copying behaviors, motor response to stress, and reward and drug seeking.

B. Adrenergic System

It is well established that under stressful conditions adrenergic system activity is increased in several brain structures (Tanaka, 1999; Tsuda *et al.*, 1986). Psychological stress and conditioned fear cause increases in noradrenaline release in the hypothalamus as well as in the amygdala and locus coeruleus (Tanaka, 1999). Locus coeruleus neurons have been suggested to regulate states of attention and vigilance as well as activity of the sympathetic nervous system. These neurons have also been implicated not only in the actions of stress but also as a critical target for opioid action. Some data indicate that CRF release upon stress stimulates brain systems by triggering the activity of catechoalminergic neurons (Emoto *et al.*, 1993; Otagiri *et al.*, 2000) and opioidergic systems. However, opioids influence catecholaminergic neurons. Several *in vitro* studies have documented that the activation of μ- (but not κ- and δ-) receptors inhibits the [^{3}H]noradrenaline release from rat brain cortical slices (Illes, 1989). In hypothalamic and neostriatal slices of rats, morphine also depresses the evoked secretion of [^{3}H]noradrenaline, again suggesting the involvement of μ-presynaptic inhibitory receptors (Diaz-Guerra *et al.*, 1986; Schoffelmeer *et al.*, 1988), although in contrast, other studies suggest that the activation of μ- and κ-opioid receptors does not modulate noradrenaline release from the basal hypothalamus (Heijna *et al.*, 1990). μ-Receptors also seem to activate noradrenaline release from the rat hippocampus (Jackisch *et al.*, 1988). On the contrary, presynaptic κ-opioid receptors appear to inhibit noradrenergic transmission in the rabbit hippocampus (Jackisch *et al.*, 1988).

Microinjections of morphine suppressed the activity of noradrenergic neurons from the locus coeruleus in freely moving cats (Abercrombie *et al.*, 1988). Iontophoretic application of μ- (but not κ- and δ-) receptor agonists caused a marked and naloxone-reversible inhibition of locus coeruleus cell activity *in vitro* due to an increase in K$^+$ conductance and subsequent hyperpolarization (for review, see North, 1986). This observation suggests that μ-opioid receptors may influence

excitatory transmission to the locus coeruleus. Thus, the majority of current data suggest that the noradrenergic system may remain under the inhibitory control of an opioidergic network in several structures of the central nervous system. The enhanced opioidergic activity occurring during stress seems to modulate the function of the noradrenergic system.

How do EOPs communicate with catecholaminergic neurons upon stress, and what is the evidence for such interaction? An early study reported that naloxone administration enhanced stress-induced increases in noradrenaline turnover in the rat brain (Tanaka *et al.*, 1983). It has been demonstrated that the stressor-induced conditioning of locus coeruleus unit activity was profoundly potentiated by systemic naloxone administration in freely moving cats (Abercrombie *et al.*, 1988). In line with the previous reports is the observation that immobilization stress increased noradrenaline release from the hypothalamus, amygdala, and thalamus, which was attenuated by morphine and enhanced by naloxone (Tanaka *et al.*, 1983, 1988, 1991). The intraventricular administration of Met-enkephalin during the early phase of stress attenuated the stress-induced increase in noradrenaline turnover in several brain structures (Tanaka *et al.*, 1985, 1989). These studies suggest that various kinds of stress activate noradrenergic neurons in the brain, and EOPs counteract this enhanced activity. The coactivation of the EOP system, which inhibits the activity of the locus coeruleus and lateral tegmental noradrenergic neurons, would favor adaptive behavioral coping in response to the emotional elements of stress. An interesting study of Tanaka's group demonstrated that psychological stress, experienced by rats exposed to emotional responses displayed by other electrically shocked rats, significantly increased the activity of noradrenergic neuron in some brain regions, which was attenuated by morphine (Tanaka *et al.*, 1991). These findings suggest that psychological stress, in which an emotional factor is predominantly involved, causes increases in noradrenaline release that are independent of opioid modulation.

C. Autonomic Nervous System

Stress results in a broad spectrum of autonomic effects. They include (a) elevation of plasma catecholamine levels due to the enhanced adrenomedullary and sympathetic outflow; (b) an increase in mean arterial pressure and tachycardia (Fisher, 1989); (c) stress-induced intestinal effects (Tache *et al.,* 1990); and (d) immunosuppression (Glaser *et al.,* 1987; Blazar *et al.,* 1986; Fujiwara *et al.,* 1999). Further, stress mobilizes the release of β-endorphin from the pituitary gland and PENK peptides from the adrenomedullary cells and sympathetic nerves (Matthews and Challis, 1995; Nankova *et al.,* 1996; Jarry *et al.,* 1985; Farrell *et al.,* 1983). Little is known about the effect of stress on peripheral PDYN-derived peptides. A source of these peptides in the periphery could also be the gastrointestinal tract, since it has been shown that they are released from the duodenum *in vitro* (Majeed *et al.,* 1986).

Circulating EOPs released from pituitary and adrenals, as well as those released from the postganglionic nerves, may modulate the effects of stress. These EOPs may inhibit sympathetic outflow via the action on peripheral sympathetic nerves. This suggestion is supported by several observations. It has been shown that tachycardia induced by the stimulation of the accelerans nerve was reduced by ethylketocyclazocine, a preferential κ-opioid receptor agonist. The chronotropic effect of noradrenaline was not changed by this compound, and μ- and δ-opioid receptor agonists were without effect. Therefore, Starke *et al.* (1985) have concluded that postganglionic sympathetic neurons innervating the sinus node of the rabbit heart may have presynaptic κ-opioid receptor. Further, it has been shown that κ- and δ-opioid receptor types (but not μ-) are localized on sympathetic nerves in the isolated guinea pig atria (Ledda *et al.,* 1985). In several isolated arteries, κ- and δ-opioid receptor agonists depressed the response to sympathetic stimulation. Agonists of the κ-opioid receptor decreased noradrenaline release from postganglionic neurons into the blood. But EOPs and opiates may stimulate the sympathetic nervous system. Intracerebroventricularly administration of β-endorphin to rats increased plasma noradrenaline and adrenaline (Yamauchi *et al.,* 1997) via opioid receptors. However, the increase in catecholamine levels by restraint stress was not inhibited by anti-β-endorphin antisera but was clearly diminished by naloxone. The results suggest that some EOPs other than β-endorphin are involved in restrain stress–induced activation of the autonomic nervous system. In fact, immobilization stress activated

enkephalin neurons in the ventral medulla paragigantocellularis and lateral reticular nuclei, which might be involved in autonomic response to stress (Mansi *et al.,* 2000). Exposure to stress increased sympathetic nervous system activity by inducing an elevation of plasma noradrenaline, and might disturb glucose homeostasis. I. M. Liu *et al.* (1999) found that a hypoglycemic effect was produced in the rats with streptozotocin-induced diabetes after cold exposure, and the effect was reversed by naloxone. It was suggested that the hypoglycemia was mediated by β-endorphin, since the increase in the plasma concentration was observed upon stress. Moreover, intravenous injection of β-endorphin in the rats with streptozotocin-induced diabetes produced a lowering of plasma glucose level. Therefore, β-endorphin appears to be responsible for the induction of hypoglycemic effects in diabetic rats after cold stress. In rats, post-exercise peak of insulin in response to glucose was markedly reduced when compared to resting controls, and the administration of naloxone further decreased the insulin response. These results suggest that EOPs may participate in the physiological adaptation to exercise stress by maintaining post-exercise insulin response to glucose (Bouix *et al.,* 1996).

An other study in humans provided evidence that δ-opioid receptors and possibly enkephalins might influence autonomic sympathetic reactivity. The selective δ-opioid receptor agonist deltorphin failed to modify basal plasma levels of noradrenaline in control rats but completely suppressed the insulin-evoked elevation of noradrenaline and the release of both noradrenaline and adrenaline elicited by cold stress. These findings provide evidence that δ-opioid receptors and possibly enkephalins may modify the autonomic sympathetic output (degli Uberti *et al.,* 1993).

The lymphoid organs, like many others, are also innervated by the autonomic nervous system, and there is a growing body of evidence that this system can have immunomodulatory effects. Noradrenergic postganglionic nerve fibers are found in the thymus, spleen, lymph nodes, and gut-associated lymphoid tissue, where they can make direct contact with immunocytes (Ader *et al.,* 1990). It would appear that opioids may influence peripheral noradrenergic nerves and noradrenergic innervation of lymphoid organs. However, there is evidence that cells of the immune system produce EOPs (Blalock *et al.,* 1985). Therefore, it is likely that in situations such as inflammation, immunocytes may release EOPs under stress and through paracrine or direct synaptic-like communication mediate the peripheral effects of stress (Stein *et al.,* 1990; Przewłocki *et al.,* 1992; Herz, 1995).

D. Immune System

A variety of stressors have been found to alter immune functions in animals and to affect pathological processes in humans. EOPs released in stress may interact with the immune system by modulating immune responses to various factors (Moynihan *et al.,* 2000; Jodar *et al.,* 1994; Sacerdote *et al.,* 1994; Shavit *et al.,* 1985). Some *in vitro* studies suggested that EOPs enhanced immune responses (Plotnikoff and Miller, 1983; Wybran, 1985; Gatti *et al.,* 1993), while others led to the opposite conclusion (Greenberg *et al.,* 1984; Shavit *et al.,* 1986; Ben-Eliyahu *et al.,* 1990). In fact, stress can suppress immune function in rats and decrease their resistance to tumor challenge. Greenberg *et al.* (1984) have found that stress induced by tail shock suppressed natural killer cell cytotoxicity, and this effect was blocked by naltrexone. Furthermore, subsequent studies showed that inescapable foot-shock stress (Shavit *et al.,* 1986) and forced swimming (Ben-Eliyahu *et al.,* 1990) decreased natural killer cell activity and finally reduced the resistance of rats to a mammary ascites tumor (Shavit *et al.,* 1984). An other study demonstrated that heat stress-induced immunosupression during pregnancy was mediated by the opioid system, most likely by placental β-endorphin release into blood (Nakamura *et al.,* 1998). The effect was inhibited by naloxone, thus indicating the involvement of opioid receptors. Overnight restraint stress of mice decreased concanavalin A-driven lymphocyte proliferation, plaque-forming cell response to sheep red blood cells, and natural killer cell activity in the spleen, but the phagocytic activity was enhanced (Marotti *et al.,* 1996). It is interesting that the injection of Met-enkephalin before restraint stress abolished these changes (except for the natural killer cell activity) and attenuated the stress-induced elevation of glucocorticoids, although Met-enkephalin itself affected the immune responses to stress: It decreased natural killer cell activity and the plaque-forming cell response and enhanced phagocytic activity. Further study revealed that the concentra-

tions of β-endorphin in splenocytes, peripheral blood mononuclear cells, and lymph node cells were significantly increased after the exposure to inescapable intermittent foot shock for 20 minutes (Sacerdote *et al.,* 1994). In contrast, the exposure to a continuous foot shock for three minutes did not affect the concentrations of the opioid peptide (Sacerdote *et al.,* 1994). Recent studies have indicated that the brain produced interferon-α (IFN-α) in response to inflammatory stress, and the effect was inhibited by naloxone. Central administration of IFN-α inhibited natural killer cytotoxicity. Further study revealed that IFN-α decreased the activity of hypothalamic neurons via opioid receptors, which in turn resulted in the activation of CRF neurons, thereby suppressing natural killer cytotoxicity through the activation of the splenic sympathetic nerves in splenocytes (Hori *et al.,* 1998).

EOPs are synthesized and released under stress conditions from immune cells present in the inflamed tissue (Herz, 1995; Stein *et al.,* 1990; Przewłocki *et al.,* 1992). The majority of studies indicated that the effects of stress on immune response were blocked by opioid-receptor antagonists, thus indicating that they were mediated by endogenous EOPs mobilized during stress. However, some kinds of stress, such as foot shock, that induce nonopioid analgesia may cause immunosupression insensitive to naloxone (Ben-Eliyahu *et al.,* 1990).

VIII. OPIOIDERGIC CONTROL OF STRESS RESPONSES: CONCLUSIONS

The reviewed data strongly suggest the involvement of EOPs in the modulation of stress responses. EOP systems appear to play an important role in the interaction of an organism with different stress factors by fulfilling stress-limiting and stress-protective functions. Though relatively quiescent in the resting state, these peptides are released during intense stimulation and modify, in a number of ways, disturbed homeostasis. The acute, mild, short-lasting stressors appear to mobilize EOPs, which may in turn act to oppose stress-precipitated reactions and, in concert with other factors, can counteract the initial response. Stress is accompanied by the changes in the contents of opioid peptides, mRNAs encoding their precursors, and opioid-receptor binding in the brain. Considerable progress has been made in accumulating data in an attempt to answer the questions of which particular EOPs are released by stressor(s) and which specific EOP or receptor types are involved in certain stress effects. Further characterization of the involvement of particular EOPs in stress-induced behavioral effects is desirable and possible.

Systemic stressors act via hypothalamic factors, e.g., CRF, which in concert with arginine vasopressin and other substances activate the release of ACTH and β-endorphin, or directly activate pituitary cells to release ACTH, which in turn results in the release of glucocorticoids and adrenaline. EOPs appear to modulate HPA. They attenuate the stress-induced rise in plasma catecholamine levels in stressed rats (Nakamura *et al.,* 1989). EOPs can thus limit the HPA axis response to stress by dampening the adrenocortical system in stress and uncoupling the adrenal gland from hypothalamo-pituitary stimulation. However, interactions of EOPs with the brain catecholaminergic systems, i.e., the noradrenergic system originating in the locus coeruleus and the dopaminergic mesolimbic system derived from the ventral tegmental area, appear to influence the ability of an organism to cope with stress. It has been proposed that stressors activate the coeruleus neurons that generate fear and anxiety. Coactivation of the EOP system (most likely β-endorphin) inhibits the activity of the locus coeruleus, which favors adaptive behavioral coping. However, EOPs derived from POMC and possibly from PENK may enhance the activity of the mesolimbic dopaminergic system during stress, thereby resulting in the reinforcement of positive emotional state, a decrease in anxiety, and better adaptation. In contrast, PDYN peptides may have an opposite effect on the dopaminergic system in stress.

It is now clear that numerous stressors modulate behavior that involves EOPs. However, a number of studies have indicated that the type of stress employed, its length, the frequency of stressor action, age and animal species, former stress experience, housing conditions, etc. are important variables determining character of the response and EOP involvement. Various stressors produce a wide range of behavioral responses, such as motor suppression and catalepsy, that are sensitive to opioid receptor antagonists. Several studies have shown that analogues of enkephalins attenu-

ated whereas dynorphin (Katoh *et al.,* 1990, 1991) and naloxone (Lester and Fansalow, 1986) potentiated stress-induced immobility. Thus, it is likely that the endogenous PDYN system may act upon motor and emotional aspects of the stress response in a manner oposite that of POMC and PENK systems.

Stress, via different pathways, appears to activate endogenous nociceptive systems. Furthermore, various kinds of stress elicit antinociception, which, under certain conditions, appears to be mediated by EOPs. EOPs participate in analgesic mechanisms stimulated by pregnancy (Iwasaki and Namiki, 1997). Several studies have also suggested that these EOP systems mediate analgesia evoked by placebo treatment (Gracely *et al.,* 1983; Gross, 1984). Placebo analgesia is apparently reversed by the opioid antagonist, naloxone. Further, exposure to stress potentiates the magnitude and duration of analgesia following both the peripheral and intracerebroventricular administration of several opioid agonists. The critical involvement of the μ-opioid receptor in stress-induced analgesia has been postulated, although κ- and δ-opioid sites also might be involved in analgesia after certain kinds of stress. The recent study on knockout mice has pointed to a role of the endogenous β-endorphin system in stress-induced analgesia (Rubinstein *et al.,* 1996), whereas unexpectedly, enkephalins seem to play a minor role, since enkephalin-deficient knockout mice exhibit normal stress-induced analgesia (Konig *et al.,* 1996).

Several results of animal studies indicate that there are close links between EOPs and feeding behavior upon stress. A number of studies have aimed at elucidating the link among stress, EOP systems, the central mechanism of feeding modulation, and the pathogenesis of certain eating disorders, including eating-induced obesity, anorexia nervosa, bulimia, and Prader-Willi syndrome (Johnson, 1995). Williams *et al.* (1988) demonstrated that neither adrenal- nor pituitary-derived EOPs were responsible for mediating the effects of stress upon feeding behavior. This observation points to the involvement of central pools of EOPs in these effects. It is also evident that various stress paradigms initiate inhibition of gastric, small intestine, and colonic transit. However, only a limited number of stressors, such as cold restraint or septic shock stress, appear to induce those gastric effects via EOPs (Gue *et al.,* 1988; Williams and Burks, 1989).

Bechara, A., and van der Kooy, D. (1985). Opposite motivational effects of endogenous opioids in brain and periphery. *Nature (London)* **314**, 533–534.

Ben-Eliyahu, S., Yirmiya, R., Shavit, Y., and Liebeskind, J. C. (1990). Stress-induced suppression of natural killer cell cytotoxicity in the rat: A naltrexone-insensitive paradigm. *Behav. Neurosci.* **104**, 235–238.

Benyo, Z., and Wahl, M. (1996). Opiate receptor-mediated mechanisms in the regulation of cerebral blood flow. *Cerebrovasc. Brain Metab. Rev.* **8**(4), 326–357.

Berkenbosch, F., Tilders, R. J. H., and Vermes, I. (1983). (3-Adrenoceptor activation mediates stress-induced secretion of β-endorphin-related peptides from the intermediate but not anterior pituitary. *Nature (London)* **305**, 237–239.

Blalock, J. E., Harbour-McMenamin, D., and Smith, E. M. (1985). Peptide hormones shared by the neuroendocrine and immunologic systems. *J. Immunol.* **135**, 858–861.

Blasig, J., Höllt, V., Bauerle, U., and Herz, A. (1978). Involvement of endorphins in emotional hyperthermia of rats. *Life Sci.* **23**, 2525–2531.

Blazar, B. A., Rodrick, M. L., O'Mahony, J. B., Wood, J. J., Bessey, P. Q., Wilmore, D. W., and Mannick, J. A. (1986). Suppression of natural killer-cell function in humans following thermal and traumatic injury. *J. Clin. Immunol.* **6**(1), 26–36.

Bloom, F. E., Battenberg, E., Rossier, J., Ling, N., and Guillemin, R. (1978). Neurons containing β-endorphin in rat brain exist separately from those containing enkephalin: Immunocytochemical studies. *Proc. Natl. Acad. Sci. U.S.A.* **75**, 1591–1595.

Bodnar, R. J., Glusman, M., Brutus, M., Spiaggia, A., and Kelly, D. D. (1979). Analgesia induced by cold-water stress: Attenuation following hypophysectomy. *Physiol. Behav.* **23**, 53–62.

Bohus, M. J., Landwehrmeyer, G. B., Stiglmayr, C. E., Limberger, M. F., Bohme, R., and Schmahl, C. G. (1999). Naltrexone in the treatment of dissociative symptoms in patients with borderline personality disorder: An open-label trial. *J. Clin. Psychiatry* **60**(9), 598–603.

Bondy, C. A., Gainer, H., and Russell, J. T. (1988). Dynorphin A inhibits and naloxone increases the electrically stimulated release of oxytocin but not vasopressin from the terminals of the neural lobe. *Endocrinology (Baltimore)* **122**(4), 1321–1327.

Borsook, D., Falkowski, O., Burstein, R., Strassman, A., Konradi, C., Dauber, A., Comb, M., and Hyman, S. E. (1994a). Stress-induced regulation of a human proenkephalin-beta-galactosidase fusion gene in the hypothalamus of transgenic mice. *Mol. Endocrinol.* **8**, 116–125.

Borsook, D., Falkowski, O., Rosen, H., Comb, M., and Hyman, S. E. (1994b). Opioids modulate stress-induced proenkephalin gene expression in the hypothalamus of transgenic mice: A

model of endogenous opioid gene regulation by exogenous opioids. *J. Neurosci.* **14**, 7261–7271.

Borsook, D., Konradi, C., Falkowski, O., Comb, M., and Hyman, S. E. (1994c). Molecular mechanisms of stress-induced proenkephalin gene regulation: CREB interacts with the proenkephalin gene in the mouse hypothalamus and is phosphorylated in response to hyperosmolar stress. *Mol. Endocrinol.* **8**, 240–248.

Bouix, O., Najimi, A., Lenoir, V., Kerdelhue, B., and Orsetti, A. (1996). Endogenous opioid peptides stimulate post-exercise insulin response to glucose in rats. *Int. J. Sports Med.* **17**, 80–84.

Briski, K. P., Quigley, K., and Meites, J. (1984). Endogenous opiate involvement in acute and chronic stress-induced changes in plasma LH concentrations in the male rat. *Life Sci.* **34**, 2485–2493.

Broekkamp, C. L., Phillips, A. G., and Cools, A. R. (1979). Facilitation of self stimulation behavior following intracerebral microinjection of opioid into the ventral tegmental area. *Pharmacol., Biochem. Behav.* **11**, 289–295.

Bronstein, D. M., Schafer, M. K., Watson, S. J., and Akil, H. (1992). Evidence that beta-endorphin is synthesized in cells in the nucleus tractus solitarius: Detection of POMC mRNA. *Brain Res.* **587**(2), 269–275.

Brown, C. H., and Leng, G. (2000). In vivo modulation of postspike excitability in vasopressin cells by kappa-opioid receptor activation. *J. Neuroendocrinol.* **12**(8), 711–714.

Brown, C. H., Russell, J. A., and Leng, O. (2000). Opioid modulation of magnocellular neurosecretory cell activity. *Neurosci. Res.* **36**(2), 97–120.

Brown, S. L., and Van Epps, D. E. (1985). Suppression of T lymphocyte chemotactic factor production by the opioid peptides beta-endorphin and met-enkephalin. *J. Immunol.* **134**(5), 3384–3390.

Buckingham, J. C. (1986). Stimulation and inhibition of corticotropin releasing factor secretion by β-endorphin. *Neuroendocrinology* **42**, 148–152.

Bugnon, C., Bloch, B., Lenys, D., Gouget, A., and Fellmann, D. (1979). Comparative study of the neuronal populations containing beta-endorphin, corticotropin and dopamine in the arcuate nucleus of the rat hypothalamus. *Neurosci. Lett.* **14**(1), 43–48.

Burns, G., Almeida, O. F. X., Passarelli, F., and Herz, A. (1989). A two-step mechanism by which corticotropin-releasing hormone releases hypothalamic β-endorphin: The role of vasopressin and G-proteins. *Endocrinology (Baltimore)* **125**, 1365–1372.

Bush, J. A., Kraemer, W. J., Mastro, A. M., Triplett-McBride, N. T., Volek, J. S., Putukian, M., Sebastianelli, W. J., and Knuttgen, H. G. (1999). Exercise and recovery responses of adrenal medullary neurohormones to heavy resistance exercise. *Med. Sci. Sports Exercise* **31**, 554–559.

Calcagnetti, D. J., and Holtzman, S. G. (1992). Potentiation of morphine analgesia in rats given a single exposure to restraint stress immobilization. *Pharmacol., Biochem. Behav.* **41**(2), 449–453.

Calcagnetti, D. J., Fleetwood, S. W., and Holtzman, S. G. (1990). Pharmacological profile of the potentiation of opioid analgesia by restraint stress. *Pharmacol., Biochem. Behav.* **37**, 193–199.

Calcagnetti, D. J., Stafinsky, J. L., and Crisp, T. (1992). A single restraint stress exposure potentiates analgesia induced by intrathecally administered DAGO. *Brain Res.* **592**, 305–309.

Calogero, A. E., Bagdy, G., and D'Agata, R. (1998). Mechanisms of stress on reproduction. Evidence for a complex intrahypothalamic circuit. *Ann. N. Y. Acad. Sci.* **851**, 364–370.

Cannon, J. T., Terman, G. W., Lewis, J. W., and Liebeskind, J. C. (1984). Body region shocked need not critically define the neurochemical basis of stress analgesia. *Brain Res.* **323**, 316–319.

Cannon, W. B. (1939). "The Wisdom of the Body." Norton, New York.

Carr, D. J., Kim, C. H., deCosta, B., Jacobson, A. E., Rice, K. C., and Blalock, J. E. (1988). Evidence for a delta-class opioid receptor on cells of the immune system. *Cell. Immunol.* **116**(1), 44–51.

Carr, D. J., deCosta, B. R., Kim, C. H., Jacobson, A. E., Guarcello, V., Rice, K. C., and Blalock, J. E. (1989). Opioid receptors on cells of the immune system: Evidence for delta- and kappa-classes. *J. Endocrinol.* **122**, 161–168.

Castellano, C., Ammassari-Teule, M., Libri, V., and Pavone, F. (1988). Effects of kappa-opioid receptor agonists on locomotor activity and memory processes in mice. *Pol. J. Pharmacol. Pharm.* **40**, 507–513.

Chance, W. T., White, A. C., Krynock, G. M., and Rosecrans, J. A. (1978). Conditional fear-induced decrease in the binding of H-N-leu-enkephalin to rat brain. *Brain Res.* **141**, 371–374.

Chatterton, R. T. (1990). The role of stress in female reproduction: Animal and human considerations. *Int. J. Fertil.* **35**, 8–13.

Chen, Y., Mestek, A., Liu, J., Hurley, J. A., and Yu, L. (1993a). Molecular cloning and functional expression of a mu-opioid receptor from rat brain. *Mol. Pharmacol.* **44**(1), 8–12.

Chen, Y., Mestek, A., Liu, J., and Yu, L. (1993b). Molecular cloning of a rat kappa opioid receptor reveals sequence similarities to the mu and delta opioid receptors. *Biochem. J.* **295**(Pt. 3), 625–628.

Chipkin, R. E., Latranyi, M. B., and Iorio, L. C. (1982). Potentiation of stress-induced analgesia (SIA) by thiorphan and its block by naloxone. *Life Sci.* **31**, 1189–1192.

Christie, M. J., and Chesher, G. B. (1983). [3H]Leu-enkephalin binding following chronic swim-stress in mice. *Neurosci. Lett.* **36**, 323–328.

Christie, M. J., Chesher, G. B., and Bird, K. D. (1981). The correlation between swim-stress induced antinociception and [3H] leu-enkephalin binding to brain homogenates in mice. *Pharmacol., Biochem. Behav.* **15**, 853–857.

Chuang, R. Y. (1995). Mu opioid receptor gene expression in immune cells. *Biochem. Biophys. Res. Commun.* **216**(3), 922–930.

Colwell, D. D., and Kavaliers, M. (1992). Evidence for activation of endogenous opioid systems in mice following short exposure to stable flies. *Med. Vet. Entomol.* **6**, 159–164.

Cooper, K. and Carmody, J. (1982). The characteristics of the opioid-related analgesia induced by the stress of swimming in the mouse. *Neurosci. Lett.* **31**, 165–170.

Cristea, A., Restian, A., and Vaduva, G. (1993). Endogenous opioid abstinence syndrome. *Rom. J. Physiol.* **30**, 241–247.

Cuadra, G., Zurita, A., Lacerra, C., and Molina, V. (1999). Chronic stress sensitizes frontal cortex dopamine release in response to a subsequent novel stressor: Reversal by naloxone. *Brain Res. Bull.* **48**, 303–308.

Day, R., Schafer, M. K., Collard, M. W., Watson, S. J., and Akil, H. (1991). A typical prodynorphin gene expression in corticosteroid-producing cells of the rat adrenal gland. *Proc. Natl. Acad. Sci. U.S.A.* **88**, 1320–1324.

Day, R., Schafer, M. K., Collard, M. W., Weihe, E., and Akil, H. (1993). Prodynorphin gene expression in the rat intermediate pituitary lobe: Gender differences and postpartum regulation. *Endocrinology (Baltimore)* **133**(6), 2652–2659.

de Goeij, D. C., Kvetnansky, R., Whitnall, M. H., Jezova, D., Berkenbosch, F., and Tilders, F. J. (1991). Repeated stress-induced activation of corticotropin-releasing factor neurons enhances vasopressin stores and colocalization with corticotropin-releasing factor in the median eminence of rats. *Neuroendocrinology* **53**(2), 150–159.

degli Uberti, E. C., Ambrosio, M. R., Vergnani, L., Portaluppi, F., Bondanelli, M., Trasforini, G., Margutti, A., and Salvadori, S. (1993). Stress-induced activation of sympathetic nervous system is attenuated by the delta-opioid receptor agonist deltorphin in healthy man. *J. Clin. Endocrinol. Metab.* **77**(6), 1490–1494.

Deroche, V., Piazza, P. V., Casolini, P., Maccari, S., Le Moal, M., and Simon, H. (1992). Stress-induced sensitization to amphetamine and morphine psychomotor effects depend on stress-induced corticosterone secretion. *Brain Res.* **598**(1–2), 343–348.

Deutch, A. Y., Tam, S. Y., and Roth, R. H. (1985). Footshock and conditioned stress increase DOPAC in the ventral tegmental area but not substantia nigra. *Brain Res.* **333**, 143–146.

Devine, D. P., Leone, P., Pocock, D., and Wise, R. A. (1993). Differential involvement of ventral tegmental mu, delta and kappa opioid receptors in modulation of basal mesolimbic dopamine release: In vivo microdialysis studies. *J. Pharmacol. Exp. Ther.* **266**(3), 1236–1246.

De Vries, G. H., Chance, W. T., Payne, W. R., and Rosecrans, J. A. (1979). Effect of autoanalgesia on CNS enkephalin receptors. *Pharmacol., Biochem. Behav.* **11**, 741–744.

Diaz-Guerra, F. J., Augood, S., Emson, P. C., and Dyer, R. G. (1986). Morphine inhibits electrically stimulated noradrenaline release from slices of rat medial preoptic area. *Neuroendocrinology* **43**, 89–91.

Diaz-Otanez, C. S., Capriles, N. R., and Cancela, L. M. (1997). D1 and D2 dopamine and opiate receptors are involved in the restraint stress-induced sensitization to the psychostimulant effects of amphetamine. *Pharmacol., Biochem. Behav.* **58**(1), 9–14.

Di Chiara, G., and Imperato, A. (1988). Opposite effects of p- and K-opiate agonists on dopamine release in the nucleus accumbens and in the dorsal caudate of freely moving rats. *J. Pharmacol. Exp. Ther.* **244**, 1067–1081.

Domanski, E., Przekop, F., Chomicka, L., and Ostrowska, A. (1989). Effect of stress on the course of oestrous cycle and the release of luteinizing hormone; the role of endorphin in these processes. *Acta Physiol. Pol.* **40**, 64–73.

Droste, C. (1992). Transient hypoalgesia under physical exercise—relation to silent ischaemia and implications for cardiac rehabilitation. *Ann. Acad. Med. Singapore* **21**, 23–33.

Ehrenreich, H., Stender, N., Gefeller, O., tom Dieck, K., Schilling, L., and Kaw, S. (1996). A novelty-related sustained elevation of vasopressin plasma levels in young men is not associated with an enhanced response of adrenocorticotropic hormone (ACTH) to human corticotropin releasing factor (hCRF). *Res. Exp. Med.* **196**(5), 291–299.

Emoto, H., Koga, C., Ishii, H., Yokoo, H., Yoshida, M., and Tanaka, M. A. (1993). CRF antagonist attenuates stress-induced increases in NA turnover in extended brain regions in rats. *Brain Res.* **627**(1), 171–176.

Eskeland, N. L., Lugo, D. I., Pintar, J. E., and Schachter, B. S. (1989). Stimulation of beta-endorphin secretion by corticotropin-releasing factor in primary rat Leydig cell cultures. *Endocrinology (Baltimore)* **124**(6), 2914–2919.

Eskeland, N. L., Molineaux, C. J., and Schachter, B. S. (1992). Regulation of beta-endorphin secretion by corticotropin-releasing factor in the intact rat testis. *Endocrinology (Baltimore)* **130**(3), 1173–1179.

Evans, C. J., Keith, D. E., Jr., Morrison, H., Magendzo, K., and Edwards, R. H. (1992). Cloning of a delta opioid receptor by functional expression. *Science* **258**, 1952–1955.

Fabbri, A., Knox, G., Buczko, E., and Dufau, M. L. (1988). Beta-endorphin production by the fetal Leydig cell: Regulation and implications for paracrine control of Sertoli cell function. *Endocrinology (Baltimore)* **122**(2), 749–755.

Fadda, P., Tortorella, A., and Fratta, W. (1991). Sleep deprivation decreases mu and delta opioid receptor binding in the rat limbic system. *Neurosci. Lett.* **129**, 315–317.

Fadda, P., Martellotta, M. C., De Montis, M. G., Gessa, G. L., and Fratta, W. (1992). Dopamine D1 and opioid receptor binding changes in the limbic system of sleep deprived rats. *Neurochem. Int.* **20**(Suppl.), 153S–156S.

Fadda, P., Martellotta, M. C., Gessa, G. L., and Fratta, W. (1993). Dopamine and opioids interactions in sleep deprivation. *Prog. Neuropsychopharmacol. Biol. Psychiatry* **17**, 269–278.

Faden, A. J., Molineauks, C. J., Rosenberg, J. G., Jacobs, T. P., and Cox, B. M. (1985). Endogenous opioid immunoreactivity in rat spinal cord following traumatic injury. *Ann. Neurol.* **17**, 368–390.

Fanselow, M. S. (1986). Conditioned fear-induced opiate analgesia: A competing motivational state theory of stress analgesia. *Ann. N. Y. Acad. Sci.* **467**, 40–54.

Fanselow, M. S., and Sigmundi, R. A. (1986). Species-specific danger signals, endogenous opioid analgesia, and defensive behavior. *J. Exp. Psychol., Anim. Behav. Processes* **12**, 301–309.

Fanselow, M. S., Calcagnetti, D. J., and Helmstetter, F. J. (1989). Role of mu and kappa opioid receptors in conditional fear-induced analgesia: The antagonistic actions of nor-binaltorphimine and the cyclic somatostatin octapeptide, Cys2Tyr3Orn5Pen7-amide. *J. Pharmacol. Exp. Ther.* **250**(3), 825–830.

Farrell, L. D., Harrison, T. S., and Demers, L. M. (1983). Immunoreactive met-enkephalin in the canine adrenal; response to acute hypovolemic stress. *Proc. Soc. Exp. Biol. Med.* **173**(4), 515.

Ferin, M., and Vande, W. R. (1984). Endogenous opioid peptides and the control of the menstrual cycle. *Eur. J. Obstet. Gynecol. Reprod. Biol.* **18**, 365–373.

Ferri, S., Arrigo-Reina, R., Candeletti, S., Cost, G., Murari, G., Speroni, E., and Scoto, G. (1983). Central and peripheral sites of action for the protective effect of opioids of the rat stomach. *Pharmacol. Res. Commun.* **15**, 409–418.

Feuerstein, G., Chiueh, C. C., and Kopin, I. J. (1981). Effect of naloxone on the cardiovascular and sympathetic response to hypovolemic hypotension in the rat. *Eur. J. Pharmacol.* **75**(1), 65–69.

Fields, H. L. (2000). Pain modulation: Expectation, opioid analgesia and virtual pain. *Prog. Brain Res.* **122**, 245–253.

Fisher, L. A. (1989). Corticotropin-releasing factor: Endocrine and autonomic integration of responses to stress. *Trends Pharmacol. Sci.* **10**, 189–193.

Fontana, F., Bernardi, P., Pich, E. M., Boschi, S., De Iasio, R., Spampinato, S., and Grossi, G. (1997). Opioid peptide modulation of circulatory and endocrine response to mental stress in humans. *Peptides (N.Y.)* **18**, 169–175.

Forman, L. J., and Estilow, S. (1988). Estrogen influences the effect of immobilization stress on immunoreactive β-endorphin levels in the female rat pituitary. *Proc. Soc. Exp. Biol. Med.* **187**, 190–196.

Forman, L. J., Estilow, S., Mead, J., and Vasilenko, P. (1988). Eight weeks of streptozotocin-induced diabetes influences the effects of cold stress on immunoreactive beta-endorphin levels in female rats. *Horm. Metab. Res.* **10**, 555–558.

Fujiwara, R., Shibata, H., Komori, T., Yokoyama, M. M., Okazaki, Y., and Ohmori, M. (1999). The mechanisms of immune suppression by high-pressure stress in mice. *J. Pharm. Pharmacol.* **51**(12), 1397–1340.

Fukuda, K., Kato, S., Mori, K., Nishi, M., and Takeshima, H. (1993). Primary structures and expression from cDNAs of rat opioid receptor delta- and mu-subtypes. *FEBS Lett.* **327**(3), 311–314.

Funabashi, T., Brooks, P. J., Kleopoulos, S. P., Grandison, L., Mobbs, C. V., and Pfaff, D. W. (1995). Changes in pre-proenkephalin messenger RNA level in the rat ventromedial hypothalamus during the estrous cycle. *Brain Res. Mol. Brain Res.* **28**(1), 129–134.

Garcia-Garcia, L., Harbuz, M. S., Manzanares, J., Lightman, S. L., and Fuentes, J. A. (1998). RU-486 blocks stress-induced enhancement of proenkephalin gene expression in the paraventricular nucleus of rat hypothalamus. *Brain Res.* **786**, 215–218.

Gatti, G., Masera, R. G., Pallavicini, L., Sartori, M. L., Staurenghi, A., Orlandi, F., and Angeli, A. (1993). Interplay in vitro between ACTH, beta-endorphin, and glucocorticoids in the modulation of spontaneous and lymphokine-inducible human natural killer (NK) cell activity. *Brain Behav. Immunol.* **7**, 16–28.

Gaveriaux, C., Peluso, J., Simonin, F., Laforet, J., and Kieffer, B. (1995). Identification of kappa- and delta-opioid receptor transcripts in immune cells. *FEBS Lett.* **369**(2–3), 272–276.

Gayle, D., Ilyin, S. E., and Plata-Salaman, C. R. (1999). Feeding status and bacterial LPS-induced cytokine and neuropeptide gene expression in hypothalamus. *Am. J. Physiol.* **277**(4, Pt. 2), R1188–R1195.

Genazzani, A. R., Genazzani, A. D., Volpogni, C., Pianazzi, F., Li, G. A., Surico, N., and Petraglia, F. (1993). Opioid control of gonadotrophin secretion in humans. *Hum. Reprod.* **8**(Suppl. 2), 151–153.

George, T. P., Verrico, C. D., Xu, L., and Roth, R. H. (2000). Effects of repeated nicotine administration and footshock stress on rat mesoprefrontal dopamine systems: Evidence for opioid mechanisms. *Neuropsychopharmacology* **23**, 79–88.

Gillies, G. E., Linton, E. A., and Lowry, P. J. (1982). Corticotropin-releasing activity of new CRF is potentiated several times by vasopressin. *Nature (London)* **299**, 355–357.

Girardot, M. N., and Holloway, F. A. (1985a). Effect of age and long-term stress experience on adaptation to stress analgesia in mature rats: Role of opioids. *Behav. Neurosci.* **99**, 411–422.

Girardot, M. N., and Holloway, F. A. (1985b). Naltrexone antagonizes the biobehavioral adaptation to cold water stress in rats. *Pharmacol., Biochem. Behav.* **22**, 769–779.

Giuffre, K. A., Udelsman, R., Listwak, S., and Chrousos, G. P. (1988). Effects of immune neutralization of corticotropin releasing hormone, adrenocorticotropin, and β-endorphin in the surgically stressed rat. *Endocrinology (Baltimore)* **122**, 306–310.

Glaser, R., Rice, J., Sheridan, J., Fertel, R., Stout, J., Speicher, C., Pinsky, D., Kotur, M., Post, A., Beck, M. *et al.* (1987). Stress-related immune suppression: Health implications. *Brain Behav. Immunol.* **1**(1), 7–20.

Glatt, C. E., Kenner, J. R., Long, J. B., and Holaday, J. W. (1987). Cardiovascular effects of dynorphin A1-13 in conscious rats and its modulation of morphine bradycardia over time. *Peptides (N.Y.)* **8**, 1089–1092.

Gordon, C. J., Rezvani, A. H., and Heath, J. E. (1984). Role of beta-endorphin in the control of body temperature in the rabbit. *Neurosci. Biobehav. Rev.* **8**, 73–82.

Gracely, R. H., Dubner, R., Wolskee, P. J., and Deeter, W. R. (1983). Placebo and naloxone can alter post-surgical pain by separate mechanisms. *Nature (London)* **306**, 264–265.

Greenberg, A., Dyck, D., and Sandler, L. (1984). Opponent processes, neurohormones and neural resistance. *In* "Impact of Psychoendocrine in Cancer and Immunity" (B. Fox and B. Newberry, eds.), p. 225. Hogrefe, Toronto.

Grigoriants, O. O., Pravdenkova, S. V., Andersen, B. J., and Desiderio, D. M. (1995). Alteration of opioid peptide concentrations in the rat pituitary following survivable closed head injury. *Neurochem. Res.* **20**(7), 827–823.

Gross, F. (1984). Placebo—the universal drug. *Methods. Inf. Med.* **23**, 176–182.

Gue, M., Pascaud, X., Honde, C., Junien, J. L., and Bueno, L. (1988). CNS blockade of acoustic stress-induced gastric motor inhibition by kappa-opiate agonists in dogs. *Am. J. Physiol.* **254**, 802–807.

Guillemin, R., Vargo, T., Rossier, J., Minick, S., Ling, N., Rivier, C., Vale, W., and Bloom, F. (1977). β-endorphin and adrenocorticotropin are secreted concomitantly by the pituitary gland. *Science* **197**, 1367–1369.

Gysling, K., and Wang, R. Y. (1983). Morphine-induced activation of A10 dopamine neurons in the rat. *Brain Res.* **277**, 119–127.

Haas, D. A., and George, S. R. (1988). Single or repeated mild stress increases synthesis and release of hypothalamic corticotropin-releasing factor. *Brain Res.* **461**(2), 230–237.

Hackler, L., Zadina, J. E., Ge, L. J., and Kastin, A. J. (1997). Isolation of relatively large amounts of endomorphin-1 and endomorphin-2 from human brain cortex. *Peptides (N.Y.)* **18**(10), 1635–1639.

Hamm, R. J., and Knisely, J. S. (1987). Ontogeny of an endogenous, nonopioid and hormonally mediated analgesic system. *Dev. Psychobiol.* **20**, 539–548.

Hanbauer, I., Govoni, F., Majane, E., Yang, H.T., and Costa, E. (1982). In vivo regulation of the release of met enkephalin-like peptides from dog adrenal medulla. *Adv. Biochem. Psychopharmacol.* **33**, 63–69.

Harbuz, M. S., and Lightman, S. L. (1989). Responses of hypothalamic and pituitary mRNA to physical and psychological sterss in rat. *J. Endocrinol.* **122**, 705–711.

Harbuz, M. S., and Lightman, S. L. (1992). Stress and the hypothalamo-pituitary-adrenal axis: Acute, chronic and immunological activation. *J. Endocrinol.* **134**(3), 327–339.

Hart, S. L., Slusarczyk, H., and Smith, T. W. (1983). The involvement of opioid delta-receptors in stress induced antinociception in mice. *Eur. J. Pharmacol.* **95**, 283–285.

Hart, S. L., Slusarczyk, H., and Smith, T. W. (1985). The effects of selective opioid delta-receptor antagonists on stress-induced antinociception and plasma corticosterone levels in mice. *Neuropeptides* **5**, 303–306.

Haskins, J. T., Gudelsky, G. A., Moss, R. L., and Porter, J. C. (1981). Iontophoresis of morphine into the arcuate nucleus effects on dopamine concentrations in hypophysial portal plasma and serum prolactin concentrations. *Endocrinology (Baltimore)* **108**, 767–771.

Hassen, A. K., Feuerstein, G. Z., and Faden, A. I. (1982). Cardiovascular responses to opioid agonists injected into the nucleus of the tractus solitarius of anaesthetized cats. *Life Sci.* **31**, 2193–2196.

Hawkins, M. F., Fuller, R. D., Baumeister, A. A., and McCallum, M. D. (1994). Effects in the rat of intranigral morphine and DAGO on eating and gnawing induced by stress. *Pharmacol., Biochem. Behav.* **49**, 737–740.

Hawranko, A. A., Monroe, P. J., and Smith, D. J. (1994). Repetitive exposure to the hot-plate test produces stress induced analgesia and alters beta-endorphin neuronal transmission within the periaqueductal gray of the rat. *Brain Res.* **667**, 283–286.

Hawranko, A. A., Serafini, M., and Smith, D. J. (1999). Antianalgesia and reduced antinociception from supraspinally administered beta-endorphin in stressed rats: Dependence on spinal cholecystokinin via cholecystokinin B receptors. *Neurosci. Lett.* **267**, 101–104.

Hedner, T., and Cassuto, J. (1987). Opioids and opioid receptors in peripheral tissues. *Scand J. Gastroenterol., Suppl.* **130**, 27–46.

Heijna, M. H., Hogenboom, F., Schoffelmeer, A. N. M, and Mulder, A. H. (1990). Opioid receptormediated inhibition of dopamine release from rat basal hypothalamus slices; involvement of both p and K receptors. *Eur. J. Pharmacol.* **183**, 2334–2335.

Hemingway, R. B., and Reigle, T. G. (1987). The involvement of endogenous opiate systems in learned helplessness and stress-induced analgesia. *Psychopharmacology (Berlin)* **93**, 353–357.

Hernandez, D. E., Nemeroff, C. B., Orlando, R. C., and Prange, A. J. (1983). The effect of centrally administered neuropeptides on the development of stress-induced gastric ulcers in rats. *J. Neurosci. Res.* **9**, 145–157.

Herz, A. (1995). Role of immune processes in peripheral opioid analgesia. *Adv. Exp. Med. Biol.* **373**, 193–199.

Herz, A. (1996). Peripheral opioid analgesia-facts and mechanisms. *Prog. Brain Res.* **110**, 95–104.

Hnatowich, M. R., Labella, F. S., Kiernan, K., and Glavin, G. B. (1986). Cold-restraint stress reduces (3H) etorphine binding to rat brain membranes: Influence of acute and chronic morphine and naloxone. *Brain Res.* **380**, 107–113.

Hodgson, D. M., and Bond, N. W. (1996). The role of hypophyseal and adrenal mechanisms in the hypoalgesic response to non-contingent food delivery in the rat. *Behav. Brain Res.* **80**, 27–32.

Holaday, J. W. (1983). Cardiovascular effects of endogenous opiate systems. *Annu. Rev. Pharmacol. Toxicol.* **23**, 541–594.

Holaday, J. W., Hitzeman, R. J., Curell, I., Tortella, F. C., and Belenky, G. I. (1982). Repeated electroconvulsive shock or chronic morphine treatment increases the number of 3H-D-Ala2-D-Leu5-enkephalin binding sites in the rat rain membranes. *Life Sci.* **31**, 2359–2362.

Höllt, V. (1990). Regulation of opioid peptides gene expression. *In* "Opioids I" (A. Herz, ed.), pp. 307–333. Springer-Verlag.

Höllt, V., Haarmann, I., Seizinger, B. R., and Herz, A. (1981). Levels of dynorphin-(1-13) immunoreactivity in rat neurointermediate pituitaries are concomitantly altered with those of leucine enkephalin and vasopressin in response to various endocrine manipulations. *Neuroendocrinology* **33**(6), 333–339.

Höllt, V., Przewłocki, R., Haarmann, I., Almeida, O. F. X., Kley, N., Millan, M. J., and Herz, A. (1986). Stress-induced alterations in the levels of messenger RNA coding for proopiomelanocortin and prolactin in rat pituitary. *Neuroendocrinology* **43**, 277–282.

Holtzman, S. G. (1974). Behavioral effects of separate and combined administration of naloxone and amphetamine. *J. Pharmacol. Exp. Ther.* **189**, 51–60.

Hong, J. S., Yoshikawa, K., Kanamatsu ,T., McGinty, J. F., and Sabol, S. L. (1985). Effects of repeated electroconvulsive shock on the biosynthesis of enkephalin and concentration of dynorphin in the rat brain. *Neuropeptides* **5**, 557–560.

Hooks, M. S., Sorg, B. A., and Kalivas, P. W. (1994). The relationship between MRNA levels and the locomotor response to novelty. *Brain Res.* **663**, 312–316.

Hori, T., Katafuchi, T., Take, S., and Shimizu, N. (1998). Neuroimmunomodulatory actions of hypothalamic interferon-alpha. *Neuroimmunomodulation* **5**(3–4), 172–177.

Houdi, A. A., Marson, L., Davenport, K. E., and Van Loon, G. R. (1996). Effects of beta-FNA on sympathoadrenal, cardiovascular, and analgesic responses to DAMPGO at rest and during stress. *Pharmacol., Biochem. Behav.* **53**, 927–933.

Iglesias, T., Montero, S., Otero, M. J., Parra, L., and Fuentes, J. A. (1992). Preproenkephalin RNA increases in the hypothalamus of rats stressed by social deprivation. *Cell. Mol. Neurobiol.* **6**, 547–555.

Illes, P. (1989). Modulation of transmitter and hormone release by multiple neuronal opioid receptors. *Rev. Physiol. Biochem. Pharmacol.* **112**, 140–233.

Imaki, T., Naruse, M., Harada, S., Chikada, N., Imaki, J., Onodera, H., Demura, H., and Vale, W. (1996). Corticotropin-releasing factor up-regulates its own receptor mRNA in the paraventricular nucleus of the hypothalamus. *Brain Res. Mol. Brain Res.* **38**(1), 166–170.

Insel, T. R., Kinsley, C. H., Mann, P. E., and Bridges, R. S. (1990). Prenatal stress has long term effects on brain opiate receptors. *Brain Res.* **511**, 93–97.

Isom, G. E., and Elshowihy, R. M. (1982). Interaction of acute and chronic stress with respiration: Modification by naloxone. *Pharmacol., Biochem. Behav.* **16**, 599–603

Iwamoto, E. T. (1985). Place-conditioning properties of mu, kappa, and sigma opioid agonists. *Alcohol. Drug Res.* **6**(5), 327–339.

Iwasaki, H., and Namiki, A. (1997). [A review of pregnancy-induced analgesia]. *Masui* **46**, 598–606.

Izumi, R., Takahashi, M., and Kaneto, H. (1983). Involvement of different mechanisms, opioid and non-opioid forms, in the analgesia induced by footshock (FS) and immobilized-water immersion (IW) stress. *Jpn. J. Pharmacol.* **33**, 1104–1106.

Jackisch, R., Geppert, M., Lupp, A., Huang, H. Y., and Illes, P. (1988). Types of opioid receptors modulating neurotransmitter release in discrete brain regions. *In* "Regulatory Roles of Opioid Peptides" (P. Illes and C. Farsang , eds.), pp. 240–258. VCH, Weinheim.

Jarry, H., Duker, E. M., and Wuttke, W. (1985). Adrenal release of catecholamines and Met-enkephalin before and after stress as measured by a novel in vivo dialysis method in the rat. *Neurosci. Lett.* **60**(3), 273–278.

Jenck, F., Gratton, A., and Wise, R. A. (1987). Opioid receptor subtypes associated with ventral tegmental facilitation of lateral hypothalamic brain stimulation reward. *Brain Res.* **423**, 34–38.

Jodar, L., Takahashi, M., and Kaneto, H. (1994). Trends in physiological role of opioids in psychoneuroendocrine-immune network. *Yakubutsu Seishin Kodo* **14**, 195–214.

Johnson, R. D. (1995). Opioid involvement in feeding behavior and the pathogenesis of certain eating disorders. *Med. Hypotheses* **45**, 491–497.

Jouppila, R., Jouppila, P., Karlqvist, K., Kaukoranta, P., Leppaluoto, J., and Vuolteenaho, O. (1983). Maternal and umbilical venous plasma immunoreactive beta-endorphin levels during labor with and without epidural analgesia. *Am. J. Obstet. Gynecol.* **147**, 799–802.

Kakidani, H., Furutani, Y., Takahashi, H., Noda, M., Morimoto, Y., Hirose, T., Asai, M., Inayama, S., Nakanishi, S., and Numa, S. (1982). Cloning and sequence analysis of cDNA for porcine beta-neo-endorphin/dynorphin precursor. *Nature (London)* **298**, 245–249.

Kalivas, P. W., and Abhold, R. (1987). Enkephalin release into the ventral area in response to stress: Modulation of mesocorticolimbic dopamine. *Brain Res.* **414**, 339–348.

Kalivas, P. W., Duffy, P., Dilts, R., and Abhold, R. (1988). Enkephalin modulation of A10 dopamine neurons: A role in dopamine sensitization. *Ann. N. Y. Acad. Sci.* **537**, 405–414.

Kalivas, P. W., Duffy, P., and Eberhardt, H. (1990). Modulation of A10 dopamine neurons by gamma-aminobutyric acid antagonists. *J. Pharmacol. Exp. Ther.* **253**, 858–866.

Kanamatsu, T., Unsworth, C. D., Diliberto, E. J. J., Viveros, O. H., and Hong, J. S. (1986). Reflex splanchnic nerve stimulation increases levels of proenkephalin A mRNA and proenkephalin A related peptides in the rat adrenal medulla. *Proc. Natl. Acad. Sci. U.S.A.* **83**, 9245–9249.

Kapas, L., Benedek, G., and Penke, B. (1989). Cholecystokinin interferes with the thermoregulatory effect of exogenous and endogenous opioids. *Neuropeptides* **14**, 85–92.

Katoh, A., Nabeshima, T., and Kameyama, T. (1990). Behavioral changes induced by stressful situations: Effects of enkephalins, dynorphin, and their interactions. *J. Pharmacol. Exp. Ther.* **253**, 600–607.

Katoh, A., Nabeshima, T., and Kameyama, T. (1991). Interaction between enkephalinergic and dopaminergic systems in stressful situations. *Eur. J. Pharmacol.* **193**, 95–99.

Katz, R. J. (1979). Opiate stimulation increases exploration in the mouse. *Int. J. Neurosci.* **9**(4), 213–215.

Katz, R. J., and Gormezano, G. A. (1979). Rapid and inexpensive technique for assessing the reinforcing effects of opiate drugs. *Pharmacol., Biochem. Behav.* **11**(2), 231–233.

Kavaliers, M. (1987). Evidence for opioid and non-opioid forms of stress-induced analgesia in the snail, *Cepaea nemoralis*. *Brain Res.* **410**, 111–115.

Kavaliers, M., and Hirst, M. (1986). Naloxone-reversible stress-induced feeding and analgesia in the slug Limax maximus. *Life Sci.* **38**, 203–209.

Kavaliers, M., and Innes, D. (1987). Stress-induced opioid analgesia and activity in deer mice: Sex and population differences. *Brain Res.* **425**, 49–56.

Kavaliers, M., and Innes, D. G. (1988). Novelty-induced opioid analgesia in deer mice (*Peromyscus maniculatus*): Sex and population differences. *Behav. Neural Biol.* **49**, 54–60.

Kelly, S. J., and Franklin, K. B. (1987). Role of peripheral and central opioid activity in analgesia induced by restraint stress. *Life Sci.* **41**, 789–794.

Kelley, A. E., Stinus, L., and Iversen, S. D. (1980). Interactions between D-Ala-Met-enkephalin, A10 dopaminergic neurons, and spontaneous behavior in the rat. *Behav. Brain Res.* **1**, 3–24.

Kelsey, J. E., Hoerman, W. A., Kimball, L. D., Radack, L. S., and Carter, M. V. (1986). Arcuate nucleus lesions reduce opioid stress-induced analgesia (SIA) and enhance non-opioid SIA in rats. *Brain Res.* **382**, 278–290; published erratum: *Ibid.* **407**(2), 412 (1987).

Kelsey, S. J., Watson, S. J., and Akil, H. (1984). Changes in pituitary POMC mRNA levels. *Soc. Neurosci. Abstr.* **10**, 359.

Kelso, T. B., Herbert, W. G., Gwazdauskas, F. C., Goss, F. L., and Hess, J. L. (1984). Exercise-thermoregulatory stress and increased plasma beta-endorphin/beta-lipotropin in humans. *J. Appl. Physiol.* **57**, 444–449.

Khachaturian, H., Lewis, M. E., Schafer, M. K.-H., and Watson, S. J. (1985). Anatomy of CNS opioid systems. *Trends Neurosci.* **8**, 111–119.

Kieffer, B. L., Befort, K., Gaveriaux-Ruff, C., and Hirth, C. G. (1992). The delta-opioid receptor: Isolation of a cDNA by expression cloning and pharmacological characterization. *Proc. Natl. Acad. Sci. U.S.A.* **89**(24), 12048–12052.

Killian, P., Holmes, B. B., Takemori, A. E., Portoghese, P. S., and Fujimoto, J. M. (1995). Cold water swim stress- and delta-2 opioid-induced analgesia are modulated by spinal gamma-aminobutyric acidA receptors. *J. Pharmacol. Exp. Ther.* **274**(2), 730–734.

Kiss, A., and Aguilera, G. (1993). Regulation of the hypothalamic pituitary adrenal axis during chronic stress: Responses to repeated intraperitoneal hypertonic saline injection. *Brain Res.* **630**(1–2), 262–270.

Kitchen, I., and Pinker, S. R. (1990). Antagonism of swim-stress-induced antinociception by the delta-opioid receptor antagonist naltrindole in adult and young rats. *Br. J. Pharmacol.* **100**(4), 685–668.

Kjaer, A., Knigge, U., Vilhardt, H., Bach, F. W., and Warberg, J. (1993a). Involvement of vasopressin V1- and V2-receptors in histamine- and stress-induced secretion of ACTH and beta-endorphin. *Neuroendocrinology* **57**, 503–509.

Kjaer, A., Knigge, U., Bach, F. W., and Warberg, J. (1993b). Permissive, mediating and potentiating effects of vasopressin in the ACTH and beta-endorphin response to histamine and restraint stress. *Neuroendocrinology* **58**, 588–596.

Kjaer, A., Knigge, U., Bach, F. W., and Warberg, J. (1995). Stress-induced secretion of pro-opiomelanocortin-derived peptides in rats: Relative importance of the anterior and intermediate pituitary lobes. *Neuroendocrinology* **61**, 167–172.

Klein, L. C., Popke, E. J., and Grunberg, N. E. (1998). Sex differences in effects of opioid blockade on stress-induced freezing behavior. *Pharmacol., Biochem. Behav.* **61**(4), 413–417.

Knepel, W., and Reimann, W. (1982). Inhibition by morphine and (β-endorphin of vasopressin release evoked by electrical stimulation of the rat medial basal hypothalamus in vitro. *Brain Res.* **238**, 484–488.

Knepel, W., Przewłocki, R., and Herz, A. (1985). Foot shock stress-induced release of vasopressin in adenohypophysectomized and hypophysectomized rats. *Endocrinology (Baltimore)* **117**, 292–299.

Koch, T., Schulz, S., Schroder, H., Wolf, R., Raulf, E., and Höllt, V. (1998). Carboxyl-terminal splicing of the rat mu opioid receptor modulates agonist-mediated internalization and receptor resensitization. *J. Biol. Chem.* **273**(22), 13652–13657.

Konecka, A. M., and Sroczyńska, I. (1990). Stressors and pain sensitivity in CFW mice. Role of opioid peptides. *Arch. Int. Physiol. Biochim.* **98**, 245–252.

Konecka, A. M., Sroczyńska, I., and Przewłocki, R. (1985). The effect of food and water deprivation on post-stress analgesia in mice and levels of beta-endorphin and dynorphin in blood plasma and hypothalamus. *Arch. Int. Physiol. Biochim.* **93**(4), 279–284.

Kong, L. Y., McMillian, M. K., Hudson, P. M., Jin, L., and Hong, J. S. (1997). Inhibition of lipopolysaccharide-induced nitric oxide and cytokine production by ultralow concentrations of dynorphins in mixed glia cultures. *J. Pharmacol. Exp. Ther.* **280**(1), 61–66.

Konig, M., Zimmer, A. M., Steiner, H., Holmes, P. V., Crawley, J. N., Brownstein, M. J., and Zimmer, A. (1996). Pain responses, anxiety and aggression in mice deficient in preproenkephalin. *Nature (London)* **383**, 535–538.

Koob, G. F., and Le Moal, M. (1997). Drug abuse: Hedonic homeostatic dysregulation. *Science* **278**, 52–58.

Kopin, I. J., Eisenhofer, G., and Goldstein, D. (1988). Sympathomedullary system and stress. *In* "Mechanisms of Physical and Emotional Stress" (G. P. Chrousos, D. L. Loriaux, and W. Gold, eds.), pp. 11–23. Plenum Press, New York.

Kostic, T., Andric, S., Maric, D., and Kovacevic, R. (1998). The effect of acute stress and opioid antagonist on the activity of NADPH-P450 reductase in rat Leydig cells. *J. Steroid Biochem. Mol. Biol.* **66**(1–2), 51–54.

Kulling, P., Frischknecht, H. R., Pasi, A., Waser, P. G., and Siegfried, B. (1988). Social conflict-induced changes in nociception and beta-endorphin-like immunoreactivity in pituitary and discrete brain areas of C57BL/6 and DBA/2 mice. *Brain Res.* **450**, 237–246.

Kulling, P., Siegfried, B., Frischknecht, H. R., Messiha, F. S., and Pasi, A. (1989). Beta-endorphin-like immunoreactivity levels in the hypothalamus, the periaqueductal grey and the pituitary of the DBA mouse: Determination by ELISA and relationship to nociception. *Physiol. Behav.* **46**, 25–28.

Kurumaji, A., Takashima, M., and Shibuya, H. (1987). Cold and immobilization stress induced changes in pain responsiveness and brain met-enkephalin-like immunoreactivity in the rat. *Peptides (N.Y.)* **8**, 355–359.

Kuzmin, A., Semenova, S., Zvartau, E. E., and Van Ree, J. M. (1996). Enhancement of morphine self-administration in drug naive, inbred strains of mice by acute emotional stress. *Eur. Neuropsychopharmacol.* **6**(1), 63–68.

Larsen, P. J., and Mau, S. E. (1994). Effect of acute stress on the expression of hypothalamic messenger ribonucleic acids encoding the endogenous opioid precursors preproenkephalin A and proopiomelanocortin. *Peptides (N.Y.)* **15**, 783–790.

Lasoń, W., Przewłocka, B., Stala, L., and Przewłocki, R. (1983). Changes in hippocampal immunoreactive dynorphin and neoendorphin content following intra-amygdalar kainic acid-induced seizures. *Neuropeptides* **3**(5), 399–404.

Lasoń, W., Przewłocka, B., and Przewłocki, R. (1987). Single and repeated electroconvulsive shock differentially affects the prodynorphin and proopiomelanocortin system in the rat. *Brain Res.* **403**, 301–307.

Latimer, L. G., Duffy, P., and Kalivas, P. W. (1987). Mu opioid receptor involvement in enkephalin activation of dopamine neurons in the ventral tegmental area. *J. Pharmacol. Exp. Ther.* **241**, 328–337.

Laurent, S., and Schmitt, H. (1983). Central cardiovascular effects of kappa agonists dynorphin-(1-13) and ethylketocyclazocine in the anaesthetized rat. *Eur. J. Pharmacol.* **96**, 165–169.

Leander, J. D. (1982). A kappa opioid effects increased urination in the rat. *J. Pharmacol. Exp. Ther.* **224**, 89–94.

Ledda, F., Mantelli, L., and Corti, V. (1985). Sensitivity to dynorphin1-13 of the presynaptic inhibitory opiate receptors of the guinea-pig heart. *Eur. J. Pharmacol.* **117**, 377–380.

Leino, T. K., Leppaluoto, J., Ruokonen, A., and Kuronen, P. (1998). Pro-opiomelanocortin activation and simulated interceptor combat flight. *Aviat. Space Environ. Med.* **69**, 486–490.

Leone, P., Pocock, D., and Wise, R. A. (1991). Morphine-dopamine interaction: Ventral tegmental morphine increases nucleus accumbens dopamine release. *Pharmacol., Biochem. Behav.* **39**(2), 469–472.

Lester, L. S., and Fanselow, M. S. (1986). Naloxone's enhancement of freezing: Modulation of perceived intensity or memory processes? *Physiol. Psychol.* **14**, 5–10.

Levine, J. D., Feldmesser, M., Tecott, L., Lane, S., and Gordon, N. C. (1984). The role of stimulus intensity and stress in opioid-mediated analgesia. *Brain Res.* **304**, 265–269.

Lewis, J. W., Cannon, J. T., and Liebeskind, J. C. (1980). Opioid and nonopioid mechanisms of stress analgesia. *Science* **208**, 623–625.

Lewis, J. W., Tordoff, M. G., Sherman, J. E., and Liebeskind, J. C. (1982). Adrenal medullary enkephalin-like peptides may mediate opioid stress analgesia. *Science* **217**, 557–559.

Lewis, J. W., Mansour, A., Khachaturian, H., Watson, S. J., and Akil, H. (1987). Opioids and pain regulation. *In* "Neurotransmitters and Pain Control" (H. Akil and J. W. Lewis, eds.), pp. 129–159. Karger, Basel.

Li, S., Zhu, J., Chen, C., Chen, Y. W., Deriel, J. K., Ashby, B., and Liu-Chen, L. Y. (1993). Molecular cloning and expression of a rat kappa opioid receptor. *Biochem. J.* **295**(Pt. 3), 629–633.

Lightman, S. L., and Young, W. S. (1989). Influence of steroids on the hypothalamic corticotropin-releasing factor and preproenkephalin mRNA responses to stress. *Proc. Natl. Acad. Sci. U.S.A.* **86**, 4306–4310.

Lim, A. T., Wallace, M., Oei, T. P., Gibson, S., Romas, N., Pappas, W., Clements, J., and Funder, J. W. (1982). Foot shock analgesia. Lack of correlation with pituitary and plasma immunoreactive-beta-endorphin. *Neuroendocrinology* **35**, 236–241.

Linton, E. A., Tilders, F. J. H., Hodgkinson, S., Berkenbosch, F., Vermes, I., and Lowry, P. J. (1985). Stress-induced secretion of adrenocorticotropin in rats is inhibited by antisera to ovine corticotropin-releasing factor and vasopressin. *Endocrinology (Baltimore)* **116**, 966–970.

Liu, I. M., Niu, C. S., Chi, T. C., Kuo, D. H., and Cheng, J. T. (1999). Investigations of the mechanism of the reduction of plasma glucose by cold-stress in streptozotocin-induced diabetic rats. *Neuroscience* **92**, 1137–1142.

Liu, Q. S., Han, S., Jia, Y. S., and Ju, G. (1999). Selective modulation of excitatory transmission by mu-opioid receptor activation in rat supraoptic neurons. *J. Neurophysiol.* **82**(6), 3000–3005.

Lopez-Calderon, A., Ariznavarreta, C., Gonzalez-Quijano, M. I., Tresguerres, J. A., and Calderon, M. D. (1991). Stress induced changes in testis function. *J. Steroid Biochem. Mol. Biol.* **40**, 473–479.

Lovallo, W. L. (1997). "Stress and Health. Biological and Psychological Interactions." Sage Publ., Thousand Oaks, CA.

Maier, S. F., Sherman, J. E., Lewis, J. W., Terman, G. W., and Liebeskind, J. C. (1983). The opioid/nonopioid nature of stress-induced analgesia and learned helplessness. *J. Exp. Psychol., Anim. Behav. Processes* **9**, 80–90.

Majeed, N. H., Lasoń, W., Przewłocka, B., and Przewłocki, R. (1986). Brain and peripheral opioids after changes in ingestive behavior. *Neuroendocrinology* **42**, 267–272.

Makino, S., Asaba, K., Nishiyama, M., and Hashimoto, K. (1999). Decreased type 2 corticotropin-releasing hormone receptor mRNA expression in the ventromedial hypothalamus during repeated immobilization stress. *Neuroendocrinology* **70**(3), 160–167.

Maley, B. E. (1996). Immunohistochemical localization of neuropeptides and neurotransmitters in the nucleus solitarius. *Chem. Senses* **21**(3), 367–376.

Mansi, J. A., Laforest, S., and Drolet, G. (2000). Effect of stress exposure on the activation pattern of enkephalin-containing perikarya in the rat ventral medulla. *J. Neurochem.* **74**, 2568–2575.

Mansour, A., Khachaturian, H., Lewis, M. E., Akil, H., and Watson, S. J. (1987). Autoradiographic differentiation of mu, delta, and kappa opioid receptors in the rat forebrain and midbrain. *J. Neurosci.* **7**(8), 2445–264.

Mansour, A., Khachaturian, H., Lewis, M. E., Akil, H., and Watson, S. J. (1988). Anatomy of CNS opioid receptors. *Trends Neurosci.* **11**(7), 308–314.

Marek, P., Yirmiya, R., Panocka, I., and Liebeskind, J. C. (1989). Genetic influences on brain stimulation-produced analgesia in mice. I. Correlation with stress-induced analgesia. *Brain Res.* **489**, 182–184.

Marotti, T., Gabrilovac, J., Rabatic, S., Smejkal-Jagar, L., Rocic, B., and Haberstock, H. (1996). Met-enkephalin modulates stress-induced alterations of the immune response in mice. *Pharmacol., Biochem. Behav.* **54**, 277–284.

Marti, O., Harbuz, M. S., Andres, R., Lightman, S. L., and Armario, A. (1999). Activation of the hypothalamic-pituitary axis in adrenalectomised rats: Potentiation by chronic stress. *Brain Res.* **821**(1), 1–7.

Mason, J. W. (1971). A re-valuation of the concept of nonspecificity in stress theory. *J. Psychiatr. Res.* **8**, 323–333.

Matthews, R. T., and German, D. C. (1984). Electrophysiological evidence for excitation of rat ventral tegmental area

dopamine neurons by morphine. *Neuroscience* **11**, 617–625.

Matthews, S. G., and Challis, J. R. (1995). Developmental regulation of preproenkephalin mRNA in the ovine paraventricular nucleus: Effects of stress and glucocorticoids. *Brain Res. Dev. Brain Res.* **86**(1–2), 259–267.

Matthews, S. G., Parrott, R. F., and Sirinathsinghji, D. J. (1993). Isolation- and dehydration-induced changes in neuropeptide gene expression in the sheep hypothalamus. *J. Mol. Endocrinol.* **11**, 181–189.

McCubbin, J. A., Bruehl, S., Wilson, J. F., Sherman, J. J., Norton, J. A., and Colclough, G. (1998). Endogenous opioids inhibit ambulatory blood pressure during naturally occurring stress. *Psychosom. Med.* **60**, 227–231.

McGivern, R. F., Mousa, S., Couri, D., and Berntson, G. G. (1983). Prolonged intermittent footshock stress decreases met- and leu-enkephalin levels in brain with concomitant decreases in pain threshold. *Life Sci.* **33**, 47–54.

McLean, M., Thompson, D., Zhang, H. P., Brinsmead, M., and Smith, R. (1994). Corticotrophin-releasing hormone and beta-endorphin in labour. *Eur. J. Endocrinol.* **131**, 167–172.

McQueen, D. S. (1983). Opioid peptide interactions with respiratory and circulatory systems. *Br. Med. Bull.* **39**(1), 77–82.

Menendez, L., Andres-Trelles, F., Hidalgo, A., and Baamonde, A. (1993). Involvement of spinal kappa opioid receptors in a type of footshock induced analgesia in mice. *Brain Res.* **611**(2), 264–271.

Meng, F., Xie, G. X., Thompson, R. C., Mansour, A., Goldstein, A., Watson, S. J., and Akil, H. (1993). Cloning and pharmacological characterization of a rat kappa opioid receptor. *Proc. Natl. Acad. Sci. U.S.A.* **90**(21), 9954–9958.

Mercer, M. E., and Holder, M. D. (1997). Food cravings, endogenous opioid peptides, and food intake: A review. *Appetite* **29**, 325–352.

Miczek, K. A., Thompson, M. L., and Shuster, L. (1982). Opioid-like analgesia in defeated mice. *Science* **215**, 1520–1522.

Miczek, K. A., Thompson, M. L., and Shuster, L. (1985). Naloxone injections into the periaqueductal grey area and arcuate nucleus block analgesia in defeated mice. *Psychopharmacology (Berlin)* **87**, 39–42.

Millan, M. J., Przewłocki, R., and Herz, A. (1980). A non-beta-endorphinergic adenohypophyseal mechanism is essential for an analgetic response to stress. *Pain* **8**, 343–353.

Millan, M. J., Przewłocki, R., Jerlicz, M. H., Gramsch, C., Höllt, V., and Herz, A. (1981a). Stress induced release of brain pituitary β-endorphin: Major role of endorphin in generation of hyperthermia, not analgesia. *Brain Res.* **208**, 325–328.

Millan, M. J., Tsang, Y. F., Przewłocki, R., Höllt, V., and Herz, A. (1981b). The influence of footshock stress upon brain pituitary and spinal cord pools of immunoreactive dynorphin in rats. *Neurosci. Lett.* **24**, 75–79.

Minami, M., Toya, T., Katao, Y., Maekawa, K., Nakamura, S., Onogi, T., Kaneko, S., and Satoh, M. (1993). Cloning and expression of a cDNA for the rat kappa-opioid receptor. *FEBS Lett.* **329**(3), 291–295.

Mizoguchi, H., Narita, M., Kampine, J. P., and Tseng, L. F. (1997). [Met5]enkephalin and delta2-opioid receptors in the spinal cord are involved in the cold water swimming-induced antinociception the mouse. *Life Sci.* **61**(7), PL81–PL86.

Mogil, J. S., Marek, P., O'Toole, L. A., Helms, M. L., Sadowski, B., Liebeskind, J. C., and Belknap, J. K. (1994). Mu-opiate receptor binding is up-regulated in mice selectively bred for high stress-induced analgesia. *Brain Res.* **653**(1–2), 16–22.

Mogil, J. S., Sternberg, W. F., Balian, H., Liebeskind, J. C., and Sadowski, B. (1996). Opioid and nonopioid swim stress-induced analgesia: A parametric analysis in mice. *Physiol. Behav.* **59**, 123–132.

Mogil, J. S., Richards, S. P., O'Toole, L. A., Helms, M. L., Mitchell, S. R., Kest, B., and Belknap, J. K. (1997). Identification of a sex-specific quantitative trait locus mediating nonopioid stress-induced analgesia in female mice. *J. Neurosci.* **17**(20), 7995–8002.

Morley, J. E., Elson, M. K., Levine, A. S., and Shafer, R. B. (1982). The effects of stress on central nervous system concentrations of the opioid peptide, dynorphin. *Peptides (N.Y.)* **3**, 901–906.

Morley, J. E., Levine, A. S., Yim, G. K., and Lowy, M. T. (1983). Opioid modulation of appetite. *Neurosci. Biobehav. Rev.* **7**, 281–305.

Mormede, P., Vincent, J. D., and Kerdelhue, B. (1986). Vasopressin and oxytocin reduce plasma prolactin levels of conscious rats in basal and stress conditions. Study of the characteristics of the receptor involved. *Life Sci.* **39**, 1737–1743.

Moynihan, J. A., Karp, J. D., Cohen, N., and Ader, R. (2000). Immune deviation following stress odor exposure: Role of endogenous opioids. *J. Neuroimmunol.* **102**, 145–153.

Mucha, R. F., and Herz, A. (1985). Motivational properties of kappa and mu opioid receptor agonists studied with place and taste preference conditioning. *Psychopharmacology (Berlin)* **86**(3), 274–280.

Mucha, R. F., and Herz, A. (1986). Preference conditioning produced by opioid active and inactive isomers of levorphanol and morphine in rat. *Life Sci.* **38**(3), 241–249.

Mucha, R. F., and Iversen, S. D. (1984). Reinforcing properties of morphine and naloxone revealed by conditioned place preferences: A procedural examination. *Psychopharmacology (Berlin)* **82**(3), 241–247.

Munck, A., Guyre, P. M., and Holbrook, N. J. (1984). Physiological functions of glucocorticoids in stress and their relation to pharmacological actions. *Endocr. Rev.* **5**, 25–44.

Nabeshima, T., Katoh, A., Hiramatsu, M., and Kameyama, T. (1986). A role played by dopamine and opioid neuronal systems in stress-induced motor suppression (conditioned suppression of motility) in mice. *Brain Res.* **398**, 354–360.

Nabeshima, T., Katoh, A., and Kameyama, T. (1988). Inhibition of enkephalin degradation attenuated stress-induced motor suppression (conditioned suppression of motility). *J. Pharmacol. Exp. Ther.* **244**, 303–309.

Nakagawasai, O., Tadano, T., Tan, N. K., Niijima, F., Sakurada, S., Endo, Y., and Kisara, K. (1999). Changes in beta-endorphin and stress-induced analgesia in mice after exposure to forced walking stress. *Methods Find. Exp. Clin. Pharmacol.* **21**, 471–476.

Nakamura, H., Nagase, H., Yoshida, M., Ogino, K., Seto, T., Hatta, K., and Matsuzaki, I. (1998). Opioid peptides mediate heat stress-induced immunosuppression during pregnancy. *Am. J. Physiol.* **274**, 672–676.

Nakamura, M., Kamata, K., Inoue, H., and Inaba, M. (1989). Effects of opioid peptides administered in conscious rats on the changes in blood adrenaline levels caused by immobilization stress. *Jpn. J. Pharmacol.* **50**, 354–356.

Nakanishi, S., Inoue, A., Kita, T., Nakamura, M., Chang, A. C., Cohen, S. N., and Numa, S. (1979). Nucleotide sequence of cloned cDNA for bovine corticotropin-beta-lipotropin precursor. *Nature (London)* **278**, 423–427.

Nakata, Y., Chang, K. J., Mitchell, C. L., and Hong, J. S. (1985). Repeated electroconvulsive shock down regulates the opioid receptors in rat brain. *Brain Res.* **346**, 160–163.

Nankova, B., Kvetnansky, R., Hiremagalur, B., Sabban, B., Rusnak, M., and Sabban, E. L. (1996). Immobilization stress elevates gene expression for catecholamine biosynthetic enzymes and some neuropeptides in rat sympathetic ganglia: Effects of adrenocorticotropin and glucocorticoids. *Endocrinology (Baltimore)* **137**(12), 5597–5604.

Nikolarakis, K. E., Almeida, O. F., and Herz, A. (1986). Stimulation of hypothalamic (3-endorphin and dynorphin release by corticotropin releasing factor (in vitro). *Brain Res.* **399**, 152–155.

Nikulina, E. M., Hammer, R. P., Jr., Miczek, K. A., and Kream, R. M. (1999). Social defeat stress increases expression of mu-opioid receptor mRNA in rat ventral tegmental area. *NeuroReport* **10**(14), 3015–3019.

Nishi, M., Takeshima, H., Fukuda, K., Kato, S., and Mori, K. (1993). cDNA cloning and pharmacological characterization of an opioid receptor with high affinities for kappa-subtype-selective ligands. *FEBS Lett.* **330**(1), 77–80.

Noda, M., Furutani, Y., Takahashi, H., Toyosato, M., Hirose, T., Inayama, S., Nakanishi, S., and Numa, S. (1982). Cloning and sequence analysis of cDNA for bovine adrenal preproenkephalin. *Nature (London)* **295**, 202–206.

Noel, M. B., and Gratton, A. (1995). Electrochemical evidence of increased dopamine transmission in prefrontal cortex and nucleus accumbens elicited by ventral tegmental mu-opioid receptor activation in freely behaving rats. *Synapse* **21**(2), 110–122.

Nordin, M., Morat, P., and Zainora, M. (1987). The effect of endogenous opioids on blood pressure during stress. *Clin. Exp. Pharmacol. Physiol.* **14**, 303–308.

North, R. A. (1986). Opioid receptor types and membrane ion channels. *Trends Neurosci.* **9**, 144–177.

Omiya, Y., Goto, K., Ishige, A., and Komatsu, Y. (2000). Changes in analgesia-producing mechanism of repeated cold stress loading in mice. *Pharmacol., Biochem. Behav.* **65**, 261–266.

Osborne, H., Przewłocki, R., Höllt, V., and Herz, A. (1979). Release of β-endorphin from rat hypothalamus in vitro. *Eur. J. Pharmacol.* **55**, 425–428.

Osgood, P. F., Murphy, J. L., Carr, D. B., and Szyfelbein, S. K. (1987). Increases in plasma beta-endorphin and tail flick latency in the rat following burn injury. *Life Sci.* **40**, 547–554.

Otagiri, A., Wakabayashi, I., and Shibasaki, T. (2000). Selective corticotropin-releasing factor type 1 receptor antagonist blocks conditioned fear-induced release of noradrenaline in the hypothalamic paraventricular nucleus of rats. *J. Neuroendocrinol.* **12**(10), 1022–1026.

Overstreet, D. H., Janowsky, D. S., Gillin, J. C., Shiromani, P. J., and Sutin, E. L. (1986). Stress-induced immobility in rats with cholinergic supersensitivity. *Biol. Psychiatry* **21**(7), 657–664.

Pan, B., Castro-Lopes, J. M., and Coimbra, A. (1996). Activation of anterior lobe corticotrophs by electroacupuncture or noxious stimulation in the anaesthetized rat, as shown by colocalization of Fos protein with ACTH and beta-endorphin and increased hormone release. *Brain Res. Bull.* **40**, 175–182.

Pancheri, P., Zichella, L., Fraioli, F., Carilli, L., Perrone, G., Biondi, M., Fabbri, A., Santoro, A., and Moretti, C. (1985). ACTH, beta-endorphin and met-enkephalin: Peripheral modifications during the stress of human labor. *Psychoneuroendocrinology* **10**, 289–301.

Panerai, A. E., Martini, A., Sacerdote, P., and Mantegazza, P. (1984). Kappa-receptor antagonist reverse 'non-opioid' stress-induced analgesia. *Brain Res.* **304**(1), 153–156.

Panerai, A. E., Bianchi, M., Brini, A., and Sacerdote, P. (1987). Endogenous opioids and their receptors in stress-induced analgesia. *Pol. J. Pharmacol. Pharm.* **39**, 597–607.

Pasternak, G. W., and Pan, Y. X. (2000). Antisense mapping: Assessing functional significance of genes and splice variants. *Methods Enzymol.* **314**, 51–60.

Pechnick, R. N., and Morgan, M. J. (1987). The role of endogenous opioids in foot shock-induced hyperthermia. *Pharmacol., Biochem. Behav.* **28**, 95–100.

Peckys, D., and Landwehrmeyer, G. B. (1999). Expression of mu, kappa, and delta opioid receptor messenger RNA in the human CNS: A 33P in situ hybridization study. *Neuroscience* **88**(4), 1093–1135.

Peterson, P. K., Molitor, T. W., and Chao, C. C. (1998). The opioid-cytokine connection. *J. Neuroimmunol.* **83**(1–2), 63–69.

Petralgia, F., Vale, W., and Rivier, C. (1986). Opioids act centrally to modulate stressinduced decrease in luteinizing hormone in the rat. *Endocrinology (Baltimore)* **119**, 2445–2450.

Pitman, R. K., van der Kolk, B. A., Orr, S. P., and Greenberg, M. S. (1990). Naloxone-reversible analgesic response to combat-related stimuli in posttraumatic stress disorder. A pilot study. *Arch. Gen. Psychiatry* **47**, 541–544.

Plotnikoff, N. P., and Miller, G. C. (1983). Enkephalins as immunomodulators. *Int. J. Immunopharmacol.* **5**, 437–441.

Plotsky, P. M. (1986). Opioid inhibition of immunoreactive corticotropin-releasing factor secretion into the hypophysial-portal circulation of rats. *Regul. Pept.* **16**, 235–242.

Pohorecky, L. A., Skiandos, A., Zhang, X., Rice, K. C., and Benjamin, D. (1999). Effect of chronic social stress on delta-opioid receptor function in the rat. *J. Pharmacol. Exp. Ther.* **290**, 196–206.

Priest, C. A., Borsook, D., and Pfaff, D. W. (1997). Estrogen and stress interact to regulate the hypothalamic expression of a human proenkephalin promoter-beta-galactosidase fusion gene in a site-specific and sex-specific manner. *J. Neuroendocrinol.* **9**(4), 317–326.

Przewłocka, B., Vetulani, J., Lasoń, W., Dziedzicka, M., Silberring, J., Castellano, C., and Przewłocki, R. (1988). The difference in stress-induced analgesia in C57BL/6 and DBA/2 mice: A search for biochemical correlates. *Pol. J. Pharmacol. Pharm.* **40**, 497–506.

Przewłocka, B., Sumova, A., and Lasoń, W. (1990). The influence of anticipation stress on opioid systems in rat. *Pharmacol., Biochem. Behav.* **37**, 661–666.

Przewłocka, B., Turchan, J., Lasoń, W., and Przewłocki, R. (1996). The effect of single and repeated morphine administration on the prodynorphin system activity in the nucleus accumbens and striatum of the rat. *Neuroscience* **70**(3), 749–754.

Przewłocki, R., Höllt, V., Voight, K. H., and Herz, A. (1979). Modulation of in vitro release of (3-endorphin from the separate lobes of the rat pituitary. *Life Sci.* **24**, 1601–1608.

Przewłocki, R., Millan, J., Gramsch, C., Millan, M. H., and Herz, A. (1982). The influence of selective adeno-neurointermedio-hypophysectomy upon plasma and brain levels of

β-endorphin and their response to stress in rats. *Brain Res.* **242**, 107–117.

Przewłocki, R., Lasoń, W., Konecka, A., Gramsch, C., Herz, A., and Reid, L. (1983a). Theopioid peptide dynorphin, circadian rhythms, and starvation. *Science* **219**, 71–73.

Przewłocki, R., Shearman, G. T., and Herz, A. (1983b). Mixed opioid/nonopioid effects of dynorphin and dynorphin-related peptides after their intrathecal injection in rats. *Neuropeptides* **3**, 233–239.

Przewłocki, R., Lasoń, W., Höllt, V., Silberring, J., and Herz, A. (1987). The influence of chronic stress on multiple opioid peptide systems in the rat: Pronounced effects upon dynorphin in spinal cord. *Brain Res.* **413**, 213–219.

Przewłocki, R., Majeed, N. H., Wędzony, K., and Przewłocka, B. (1988a). The effect of stress on the opioid peptide systems in the rat nucleus accumbens. *In* "Stress: Neurochemical and Humoral Mechanisms" (R. Kvetnansky, G. R. Van Loon, R. McCarty, and J. Axelrod, eds.), pp. 155–161. Gordon & Breach, New York.

Przewłocki, R., Haarmann, I., Nikolarakis, K., Herz, A., and Höllt, V. (1988b). Prodynorphin gene expression in spinal cord is enhanced after traumatic injury in the rat. *Mol. Brain Res.* **4**, 37–41.

Przewłocki, R., Hassan, A. H., Lasoń, W., Epplen, C., Herz, A., and Stein, C. (1992). Gene expression and localization of opioid peptides in immune cells of inflamed tissue: Functional role in antinociception. *Neuroscience* **48**(2), 491–500.

Quinones-Jenab, V., Ogawa, S., Jenab, S., and Pfaff, D. W. (1996). Estrogen regulation of preproenkephalin messenger RNA in the forebrain of female mice. *J. Chem. Neuroanat.* **12**(1), 29–36.

Quinones-Jenab, V., Jenab, S., Ogawa, S., Inturrisi, C., and Pfaff, D. W. (1997). Estrogen regulation of mu-opioid receptor mRNA in the forebrain of female rats. *Brain Res. Mol. Brain Res.* **47**(1–2), 134–138.

Raab, A., Seizinger, B. R., and Herz, A. (1985). Continuous social defeat induces an increase of endogenous opioids in discrete brain areas of the mongolian gerbil. *Peptides (N.Y.)* **6**, 387–391.

Ray, A., Henke, P. G., and Sullivan, R. M. (1988). Opiate mechanisms in the central amygdala and gastric stress pathology in rats. *Brain Res.* **442**, 195–198.

Reynolds, D. G., Gurll, N. J., Vargish, T., Lechner, R. B., Faden, A. I., and Holaday, J. W. (1980). Blockade of opiate receptors with naloxone improves survival and cardiac performance in canine endotoxic shock. *Circ. Shock* **7**(1), 39–44.

Rivier, C., Rivier, J., Mormede, P., and Vale, W. (1984). Studies on the nature of the interaction between vasopressin and corticotropin-releasing factor on adrenocortin release in the rat. *Endocrinology (Baltimore)* **115**, 882–886.

Rodgers, R. J., and Deacon, R. M. (1979). Effect of naloxone on the behaviour of rats exposed to a novel environment. *Psychopharmacology (Berlin)* **65**(1), 103–105.

Rodgers, R. J., and Deacon, R. M. (1981). Footshock-analgesia: Prevention by behavioral manipulation but not by naloxone. *Physiol. Behav.* **26**(2), 183–187.

Rosecrans, J. A., Robinson, S. E., Johnson, J. H., Mokler, D. J., and Hong, J. S. (1986). Neuroendocrine, biogenic amine and behavioral responsiveness to a repeated footshock-induced analgesia (FSIA) stressor in Sprague-Dawley (CD) and Fischer-344 (CDF) rats. *Brain Res.* **382**, 71–80.

Rossier, J., French, E. D., Rivier, C., Ling, N., Guillemin, R., and Bloom, F. E. (1977). Foot-shock induced stress increases beta-endorphin levels in blood but not brain. *Nature (London)* **270**, 618–620.

Rossier, J., Guillemin, R., and Bloom, F. E. (1978). Foot-shock induced stress decreases Leu-enkephalin immunoreactivity in rat hypothalamus. *Eur. J. Pharmacol.* **48**, 465–466.

Roth, K. A., Katz, R. J., Schmaltz, K., and Sibel, M. (1981). Reduced behavioral activity due to opiate blockade: Relations to stress. *Int. J. Neurosci.* **12**, 59–62.

Rubinstein, M., Mogil, J. S., Japon, M., Chan, E. C., Allen, R. G., and Low, M. J. (1996). Absence of opioid stress-induced analgesia in mice lacking beta-endorphin by site-directed mutagenesis. *Proc. Natl. Acad. Sci. U.S.A.* **93**, 3995–4000.

Sacerdote, P., Manfredi, B., Bianchi, M., and Panerai, A. E. (1994). Intermittent but not continuous inescapable footshock stress affects immune responses and immunocyte beta-endorphin concentrations in the rat. *Brain Behav. Immunol.* **8**(3), 251–260.

Scatton, B., D'Angio, M., Driscoll, P., and Serrano, A. (1988). An in vitro voltametric study of the response of mesocortical and mesoaccumbens dopaminergic neurons to environmental stimuli in strains of rats with differing levels of emotionality. *Ann. N.Y. Acad. Sci.* **537**, 124–137.

Schnur, P., Martinez, Y., and Hang, D. (1988). Effects of stress on morphine-elicited locomotor activity in hamsters. *Behav. Neurosci.* **102**(2), 254.

Schoffelmeer, A. N. M., Hogenboom, F., and Mulder, A. H. (1988). Sodium dependent; H-noradrenaline release from rat neocortical slices in the absence of extracellular calcium: Presynaptic modulation by p-opioid receptor and adenylate cyclase activation. *Naunyn-Schmiedebergs Arch. Pharmacol.* **338**, 548–552.

Seeger, T. F., Sforzo, G. A., Pert, C. B., and Pert, A. (1984). In vivo autoradiography: Visual-ization of stress induced changes in opiate receptor occupancy in the rat brain. *Brain Res.* **305**, 303–311.

Selye, H. (1936). A syndrome produced by diverse nocuous agents. *Nature (London)* **138**, 32.

Sesack, S. R., and Pickel, V. M. (1992). Dual ultrastructural localization of enkephalin and tyrosine hydroxylase immunoreactivity in the rat ventral tegmental area: Multiple substrates for opiate-dopamine interactions. *J. Neurosci.* **12**, 1335–1350.

Shaham, Y., and Stewart, J. (1994). Exposure to mild stress enhances the reinforcing efficacy of intravenous heroin self-administration in rats. *Psychopharmacology (Berlin)* **114**(3), 523–527.

Shaham, Y., Funk, D., Erb, S., Brown, T. J., Walker, C. D., and Stewart, J. (1997). Corticotropin-releasing factor, but not corticosterone, is involved in stress-induced relapse to heroin-seeking in rats. *J. Neurosci.* **17**(7), 2605–2614.

Shaham, Y., Erb, S., Leung, S., Buczek, Y., and Stewart, J. (1998). CP-154,526, a selective, non-peptide antagonist of the corticotropin-releasing factor1 receptor attenuates stress-induced relapse to drug seeking in cocaine- and heroin-trained rats. *Psychopharmacology (Berlin)* **137**(2), 184–190.

Shaham, Y., Erb, S., and Stewart, J. (2000). Stress-induced relapse to heroin and cocaine seeking in rats: A review. *Brain Res. Brain Res. Rev.* **33**(1), 13–33.

Shavit, Y., Lewis, J. W., Terman, G. W., Gale, R. P., and Liebeskind, J. C. (1984). Opioid peptides mediate the suppressive effect of stress on natural killer cell cytotoxicity. *Science* **223**, 188–190.

Shavit, Y., Terman, G. W., Martin, F. C., Lewis, J. W., Liebeskind, J. C., and Gale, R. P. (1985). Stress, opioid peptides, the immune system, and cancer. *J. Immunol.* **135**, 834s–837s.

Shavit, Y., Lewis, J. W., Terman, G., Gale, R. P., and Liebeskind, C. (1986). Stress, opioid peptides and immune function. *In* "Neuroregulation of Autonomic Endocrine and Immune Systems" (R. C. A. Frederickson, J. N. Hendrie, and H. C. Hingtgen, eds.), p. 343. Nijhoff, Boston.

Sherman, T. G., Civelli, O., Douglas, J., Herbert, E., and Watson, S. J. (1986). Coordinate expression of hypothalamic pro dynorphin and pro-vasopressin mRNA with osmotic stimulation. *Neuroendocrinology* **44**, 222–228.

Shuster, S. J., Riedl, M., Li, X., Vulchanova, L., and Elde, R. (2000). The kappa opioid receptor and dynorphin colocalize in vasopressin magnocellular neurosecretory neurons in guinea-pig hypothalamus. *Neuroscience* **96**(2), 373–383.

Sibinga, N. E., and Goldstein, A. (1988). Opioid peptides and opioid receptors in cells of the immune system. *Annu. Rev. Immunol.* **6**, 219–249.

Sitsen, J. M., Van Ree, J. M., and De Jong, W. (1982). Cardiovascular and respiratory effects of beta-endorphin in anesthetized and conscious rats. *J. Cardiovasc. Pharmacol.* **4**(6), 883–838.

Skultetyova, I., and Jezova, D. (1999). Dissociation of changes in hypothalamic corticotropin-releasing hormone and pituitary proopiomelanocortin mRNA levels after prolonged stress exposure. *Brain Res. Mol. Brain Res.* **68**(1–2), 190–192.

Sofroniew, M. V. (1979). Immunoreactive beta-endorphin and ACTH in the same neurons of the hypothalamic arcuate nucleus in the rat. *Am. J. Anat.* **154**(2), 283–289.

Spanagel, R., Herz, A., and Schippenberg, T. S. (1990). The effects of opioid peptides on dopamine release in the nucleus accumbens: An in vivo microdialysis study. *J. Neurochem.* **55**, 1734–1740.

Spanagel, R., Herz, A., and Shippenberg, T. S. (1992). Opposing tonically active endogenous opioid systems modulate the mesolimbic dopaminergic pathway. *Proc. Natl. Acad. Sci. U.S.A.* **89**(6), 2046–2050.

Spanagel, R., Sillaber, I., Zieglgansberger, W., Corrigall, W. A., Stewart, J., and Shaham, Y. (1998). Acamprosate suppresses the expression of morphine-induced sensitization in rats but does not affect heroin self-administration or relapse induced by heroin or stress. *Psychopharmacology (Berlin)* **139**(4), 391–401.

Spencer, R. L., Ayres, E. A., and Burks, T. F. (1985). Temperature responses in restrained and unrestrained rats to the selective mu opioid agonist, DAGO. *Proc. West. Pharmacol. Soc.* **28**, 107–110.

Starec, M., Nejedly, A., Malek, J., Rosina, J., Gojisova, E., and Krsiak, M. (1997). Exposure to stress alters the effects of dynorphins in the hot plate test. *Physiol. Res.* **46**, 451–457.

Starke, K., Schoffel, E., and Illes, P. (1985). The sympathetic axons innervating the sinus node of the rabbit possess presynaptic opioid x-, but not lx- or S-receptors. *Naunyn-Schmiedebergs Arch. Pharmacol.* **329**, 206–209.

Stein, C., Hassan, A. H., Przewlocki, R., Gramsch, C., Peter, K., and Herz, A. (1990). Opioids from immunocytes interact with receptors on sensory nerves to inhibit nociception in inflammation. *Proc. Natl. Acad. Sci. U.S.A.* **87**(15), 5935–5939.

Stein, E. A., Hiller, J. M., and Simon, E. J. (1992). Effects of stress on opioid receptor binding in the rat central nervous system. *Neuroscience* **51**, 683–690.

Stohr, T., Almeida, O. F., Landgraf, R., Shippenberg, T. S., Holsboer, F., and Spanagel, R. (1999). Stress- and corticosteroid-induced modulation of the locomotor response to morphine in rats. *Behav. Brain Res.* **103**(1), 85–93.

Straub, R. H., Westermann, J., Scholmerich, J., and Falk, W. (1998). Dialogue between the CNS and the immune system in lymphoid organs. *Immunol. Today* **19**(9), 409–413.

Stuckey, J., Marra, S., Minor, T., and Insel, T. R. (1989). Changes in mu opiate receptors following inescapable shock. *Brain Res.* **476**, 167–169.

Suaudeau, C., and Costentin, J. (2000). Long lasting increase in nociceptive threshold induced in mice by forced swimming: Involvement of an endorphinergic mechanism. *Stress* **3**(3), 221–227.

Suda, T., Sato, Y., Sumitomo, T., Nakano, Y., Tozawa, F., Iwai, I., Yamada, M., and Demura, H. (1992). Beta-endorphin inhibits hypoglycemia-induced gene expression of corticotropin-releasing factor in the rat hypothalamus. *Endocrinology (Baltimore)* **130**(3), 1325–1330.

Sumova, A., and Jakoubek, B. (1989). Analgesia and impact induced by anticipation stress: Involvement of the endogenous opioid peptide system. *Brain Res.* **13**, 273–280.

Sun, K., Lin, B. C., Zhang, C., Wang, C. H., and Zhu, H. N. (1989). Possible involvement of (3-endorphin in the deteriorating effect of arginine vasopressin on burn shock in rats. *Circ. Shock* **29**, 167–174.

Szikszay, M., Benedek, G., and Szekely, J. I. (1983). Thermoregulatory effects of D-met2-pro5-enkephalinamide. *Neuropeptides* **3**, 465–475.

Szilagyi, J. E. (1991). Psychosocial stress elevates blood pressure via an opioid dependent mechanism in normotensive rats. *Clin. Exp. Hypertens. A* **13**, 1383–1394.

Tache, Y., Garrick, T., and Raybould, H. (1990). Central nervous system action of peptides to influence gastrointestinal motor function. *Gastroenterology* **98**, 517–528.

Takahashi, M., Senda, T., Tokuyama, S., and Kaneto, H. (1990). Further evidence for the implication of kappa opioid receptor mechanism in the production of the stress induced analgesia. *Jpn. J. Pharmacol.* **53**, 487–494.

Takayama, H., Ota, Z., and Ogawa, N. (1986). Effect of immobilization stress on neuro-peptides and their receptors in rat central nervous system. *Regul. Pept.* **15**, 239–248.

Tanaka, M. (1999). Emotional stress and characteristics of brain noradrenaline release in the rat. *Ind. Health* **37**(2), 143–156.

Tanaka, M., Kohno, Y., Tsuda, A., Nakagawa, R., Ida, Y., Iimori, Y., Hoaki, Y., and Nagasaki, N. (1983). Differential effect of morphine on noradrenaline release in brain regions of stressed and non-stressed rats. *Brain Res.* **275**, 105–115.

Tanaka, M., Tsuda, A., Ida, Y., Ushijima, I., Tsujimaru, S., and Nagasaki, N. (1985). Methionine-enkephalin inhibits stress-induced increases in noradrenaline turnover in brain regions of rats. *Jpn. J. Pharmacol.* **37**, 117–119.

Tanaka, M., Ida, Y., and Tsuda, A. (1988). Naloxone, given before but not after stress exposure, enhances stress-induced increases in regional brain noradrenaline release. *Pharmacol., Biochem. Behav.* **29**(3), 613–616.

Tanaka, M., Ida, Y., Tsuda, A., Tsujimaru, S., Shirao, I., and Oguchi, M. (1989). Met-enkephalin, injected during the early phase of stress, attenuates stress-induced increases in noradrenaline release in rat brain regions. *Pharmacol., Biochem. Behav.* **32**, 791–795.

Tanaka, M., Tsuda, A., Yokoo, H., Yoshida, M., Mizoguchi, K., and Shimizu, T. (1991). Psychological stress-induced increases in noradrenaline release in rat brain regions are attenu-

ated by diazepam, but not by morphine. *Pharmacol., Biochem. Behav.* **39**(1), 191–195.

Terman, G. W., Shavit, Y., Lewis, J. W., Cannon, J. T., and Liebeskind, J. C. (1984). Intrinsic mechanisms of pain inhibition: Activation by stress. *Science* **226**, 1270–1277.

Terman, G. W., Lewis, J. W., and Liebeskind, J. C. (1986a). Two opioid forms of stress analgesia: Studies of tolerance and cross-tolerance. *Brain Res.* **368**, 101–106.

Terman, G. W., Morgan, M. J., and Liebeskind, J. C. (1986b). Opioid and non-opioid stress analgesia from cold water swim: Importance of stress severity. *Brain Res.* **372**, 167–171.

Teskey, G. C., and Kavaliers, M. (1988). Effects of opiate agonists and antagonists on aggressive encounters and subsequent opioid-induced analgesia, activity and feeding responses in male mice. *Pharmacol., Biochem. Behav.* **31**, 43–52.

Thompson, R. C., Mansour, A., Akil, H., and Watson, S. J. (1993). Cloning and pharmacological characterization of a rat mu opioid receptor. *Neuron* **11**(5), 903–913.

Tian, M., Broxmeyer, H. E., Fan, Y., Lai, Z., Zhang, S., Aronica, S., Cooper, S., Bigsby, R. M., Steinmetz, R., Engle, S. J., Mestek, A., Pollock, J. D., Lehman, M. N., Jansen, H. T., Ying, M., Stambrook, P. J., Tischfield, J. A., and Yu, L. (1997). Altered hematopoiesis, behavior, and sexual function in mu opioid receptor-deficient mice. *J. Exp. Med.* **185**(8), 1517–1522.

Tiligada, E., and Wilson, J. F. (1990). Ionic, neuronal and endocrine influences on the proopiomelanocortin system of the hypothalamus. *Life Sci.* **46**, 81–90.

Till, M., Gati, T., Rabai, K., Szombath, D., and Szekely, J. I. (1988). Effect of [D-Met2, Pro-enkeph, alinamide on gastric ulceration and transmucosal potential difference. *Eur. J. Pharmacol.* **15**, 325–330.

Tong, Y., and Pelletier, G. (1992). Role of dopamine in the regulation of proopiomelanocortin (POMC) mRNA levels in the arcuate nucleus and pituitary gland of the female rat as studied by in situ hybridization. *Brain Res. Mol. Brain Res.* **15**(1–2), 27–32.

Trujillo, K. A., Bronstein, D. M., Sanchez, I. O., and Akil, H. (1995). Effects of chronic opiate and opioid antagonist treatment on striatal opioid peptides. *Brain Res.* **698**(1–2), 69–78.

Tsagarakis, S., Rees, L. H., Besser, N., and Grossman, A. (1990). Opiate receptor subtype regulation of CRF-41 release from hypothalamus in vitro. *Neuroendocrinology* **51**, 599–605.

Tsuda, A., Tanaka, M., Ida, Y., Tsujimaru, S., Ushijima, I., and Nagasaki, N. (1986). Effects of preshock experience on enhancement of rat brain noradrenaline turnover induced by psychological stress. *Pharmacol., Biochem. Behav.* **24**(1), 115–119.

Tsuji, S., Nakai, Y., Fukata, J., Nakaishi, S., Takahashi, H., Usui, T., and Imura, H. (1987). Effects of food deprivation and high fat diet on immunoreactive dynorphin A(1-8) levels in brain regions of Zucker rats. *Peptides (N.Y.)* **8**, 1075–1078.

Uhl, G. R., Sora, I., and Wang, Z. (1999). The mu opiate receptor as a candidate gene for pain: Polymorphisms, variations in expression, nociception, and opiate responses. *Proc. Natl. Acad. Sci. U.S.A.* **96**(14), 7752–7755.

Vale, W., Rivier, C., Yang, L., Minick, S., and Guillemin, R. (1978). Effects of purified hypothalamic corticotropin releasing factor and other substances on the secretion of adrenocorticotropin and β-endorphin immunoreactivities in vitro. *Endocrinology (Baltimore)* **103**, 1911–1915.

Valverde, O., Ledent, C., Beslot, F., Parmentier, M., and Roques, B. P. (2000). Reduction of stress-induced analgesia but not of exogenous opioid effects in mice lacking CB1 receptors. *Eur. J. Neurosci.* **12**, 533–539.

Van den Berg, C. L., Lamberts, R. R., Wolterink, G., Wiegant, V. M., and Van Ree, J. M. (1998). Emotional and footshock stimuli induce differential long-lasting behavioural effects in rats; involvement of opioids. *Brain Res.* **799**, 6–15.

Vanderah, T. W., Wild, K. D., Takemori, A. E., Sultana, M., Portoghese, P. S., Bowen, W. D., Hruby, V. J., Mosberg, H. I., and Porreca, F. (1993). Modulation of morphine antinociception by swim-stress in the mouse: Involvement of supraspinal opioid delta-2 receptors. *J. Pharmacol. Exp. Ther.* **267**(1), 449–455.

van der Kooy, D., Mucha, R. F., O'Shaughnessy, M., and Bucenieks, P. (1982). Reinforcing effects of brain microinjections of morphine revealed by conditioned place preference. *Brain Res.* **243**(1), 107–117.

Van Loon, G. R., Picrzchala, K., Houdi, A. A., Kvetnansky, R., and Zeman, P. (1990). Tolerance and cross-tolerance to stress-induced increases in plasma metenkephalin in rats with adaptively increased resting secretion. *Endocrinology (Baltimore)* **126**, 2196–2204.

Vargish, T., Reynolds, D. G., Gurll, N. J., Lechner, R. B., Holaday, J. W., and Faden, A. I. (1980). Naloxone reversal of hypovolemic shock in dogs. *Circ. Shock* **7**(1), 31–38.

Vaswani, K. K., Richard, C. W., and Tejwani, G. A. (1988). Cold swim stress-induced changes in the levels of opioid peptides in the rat CNS and peripheral tissues. *Pharmacol., Biochem. Behav.* **29**, 163–168.

Vellucci, S. V., and Parrott, R. F. (1997). Vasopressin and oxytocin gene expression in the porcine forebrain under basal conditions and following acute stress. *Neuropeptides* **31**, 431–438.

Vidal, C., Suaudeau, C., and Jacob, J. (1984). Regulation of body temperature and nociception induced by non-noxious stress in rat. *Brain Res.* **297**, 1–10.

Viveros, D. H., Diliberto, E. J., Jr., Hazum, E., and Chang, K. J. (1979). Opiate-like materials in the adrenal medulla:

Evidence for storage and secretion with catecholamines. *Mol. Pharmacol.* **16**, 1101–1108.

Walker, J. M., Berntson, G. G., Paulucci, T. S., and Champney, T. C. (1981). Blockade of endogenous opiates reduces activity in the rat. *Pharmacol., Biochem. Behav.* **14**, 113–116.

Wang, X. M., Zhou, Y., Spangler, R., Ho, A., Han, J. S., and Kreek, M. J. (1999). Acute intermittent morphine increases preprodynorphin and kappa opioid receptor mRNA levels in the rat brain. *Brain Res. Mol. Brain Res.* **66**(1–2), 184–187.

Wang, X. Q., Imaki, T., Shibasaki, T., Yamauchi, N., and Demura, H. (1996). Intracerebroventricular administration of beta-endorphin increases the expression of c-fos and of corticotropin-releasing factormessenger ribonucleic acid in the paraventricular nucleus of the rat. *Brain Res.* **707**(2), 189–195.

Watanabe, Y., Weiland, N. G., and McEwen, B. S. (1995). Effects of adrenal steroid manipulations and repeated restraint stress on dynorphin mRNA levels and excitatory amino acid receptor binding in hippocampus. *Brain Res.* **680**, 217–225.

Watson, S. J., Akil, H., Ghazarossian, V. E., and Goldstein, A. (1981). Dynorphin immunocytochemical localization in brain and peripheral nervous system: Preliminary studies. *Proc. Natl. Acad. Sci. U.S.A.* **78**(2), 1260–1263.

Wideman, C. H., Murphy, H. M., and McCartney, S. B. (1996). Interactions between vasopressin and food restriction on stress-induced analgesia. *Peptides (N.Y.)* **17**(1), 63–66.

Wiedenmayer, C. P., and Barr, G. A. (2000). Mu opioid receptors in the ventrolateral periaqueductal gray mediate stress-induced analgesia but not immobility in rat pups. *Behav. Neurosci.* **114**, 125–136.

Will, M. J., Watkins, L. R., and Maier, S. F. (1998). Uncontrollable stress potentiates morphine's rewarding properties. *Pharmacol., Biochem. Behav.* **60**(3), 655–664.

Williams, C. L., and Burks, T. (1989). Stress, opioids and gastrointestinal transit. In "Neuropeptides and Stress" (Y. Taché, J. E. Morley, and M. R. Brown, eds.), p. 175. Springer, Berlin.

Williams, C. L., Villar, R. G., Peterson, J. M., and Burks, T. F. (1988). Stress-induced changes in intestinal transit in the rat: A model for irritable bowel syndrome. *Gastroenterology* **94**, 611–621.

Wittert, G., Hope, P., and Pyle, D. (1996). Tissue distribution of opioid receptor gene expression in the rat. *Biochem. Biophys. Res. Commun.* **218**(3), 877–881.

Woolfolk, D. R., and Holtzman, S. G. (1995). Rat strain differences in the potentiation of morphine-induced analgesia by stress. *Pharmacol., Biochem. Behav.* **51**(4), 699–703.

Wybran, E. (1985). Enkephalins and endorphins as modifiers of the immune system: Present and future. *Fed. Proc., Fed. Am. Soc. Exp. Biol.* **44**, 92–96.

Wybran, J., Appelboom, T., Famaey, J. P., and Govaerts, A. (1979). Suggestive evidence for receptors for morphine and methionine-enkephalin on normal human blood T lymphocytes. *J. Immunol.* **123**(3), 1068–1070.

Xie, G. X., Han, J. S., and Höllt, V. (1983). Electroacupuncture analgesia blocked by micro-injection of anti-beta endorphin antiserum into periaqueductal grey in rabbit. *Int. J. Neurosci.* **18**, 287–292.

Yamaguchi, H., Aiba, A., Nakamura, K., Nakao, K., Sakagami, H., Goto, K., Kondo, H., and Katsuki, M. (1996). Dopamine D2 receptor plays a critical role in cell proliferation and proopiomelanocortin expression in the pituitary. *Genes Cells* **1**(2), 253–268.

Yamauchi, N., Shibasaki, T., Wakabayashi, I., and Demura, H. (1997). Brain beta-endorphin and other opioids are involved in restraint stress-induced stimulation of the hypothalamic-pituitary-adrenal axis, the sympathetic nervous system, and the adrenal medulla in the rat. *Brain Res.* **777**, 140–146.

Young, E. A. (1990). Induction of the intermediate lobe proopiomelanocortin system with chronic swim stress and β-adrenergic modulation of this induction. *Neuroendocrinology* **52**, 405–414.

Young, E. A., and Akil, H. (1985). Corticotropin-releasing factor stimulation of adrenocorticotropin and β-endorphin release: Effect of acute and chronic stress. *Endocrinology (Baltimore)* **117**, 23–30.

Young, E. A., Bronstein, D., and Akil, H. (1993a). Dopamine regulation of swim stress induction of the pituitary intermediate lobe proopiomelanocortin system. *Neuroendocrinology* **58**, 294–302.

Young, E. A., Przewłocki, R., Patel, P., Watson, S. J., and Akil, H. (1993b). Altered ratios of beta-endorphin: Beta-lipotropin released from anterior lobe corticotropes with increased secretory drive. I. Effects of diminished glucocorticoid secretion. *J. Neuroendocrinol.* **5**, 115–120.

Young, W. S., and Lightman, S. L. (1992). Chronic stress elevates enkephalin expression in the rat paraventricular and supraoptic nuclei. *Brain Res. Mol. Brain Res.* **13**, 111–117.

Yukhananov, R. Y., and Handa, R. J. (1996). Alterations in kappa opioid receptor mRNA levels in the paraventricular nucleus of the hypothalamus by stress and sex steroids. *NeuroReport* **7**(10), 1690–1694.

Yukhananov, R. Y., and Handa, R. J. (1997). Estrogen alters proenkephalin RNAs in the paraventricular nucleus of the hypothalamus following stress. *Brain Res.* **764**, 109–116.

Zacharko, R. M., Maddeaux, C., Hebb, A. L., Mendella, P. D., and Marsh, N. J. (1998). Vulnerability to stressor-induced disturbances in self-stimulation from the dorsal and ventral A10 area: Differential effects of intraventricular D-Ala2-Met5-enkephalinamide, D-Ala2, N-Me-Phe4, Gly-Ol5-enkephalin, and D-Pen2, D-Pen5-enkephalin administration. *Brain Res. Bull.* **47**, 237–248.

Zadina, J. E., Hackler, L., Ge, L. J., and Kastin, A. J. (1997). A potent and selective endogenous agonist for the mu-opiate receptor. *Nature (London)* **386**, 499–502.

Zadina, J. E., Martin-Schild, S., Gerall, A. A., Kastin, A. J., Hackler, L., Ge, L. J., and Zhang, X. (1999). Endomorphins: Novel endogenous mu-opiate receptor agonists in regions of high mu-opiate receptor density. *Ann. N. Y. Acad. Sci.* **897**, 136–144.

Zeman, P., Alexandrova, M., and Kvetnansky, R. (1988). Opioid lx and b and dopamine receptor number changes in rat striatum during stress. *Endocrinol. Exp.* **22**, 59–66.

Zhao, B. G., Chapman, C., and Bicknell, R. J. (1988). Functional kappa-opioid receptors on oxytocin and vasopressin nerve terminals isolated from the rat neurohypophysis. *Brain Res.* **462**(1), 62–66.

Zhou, Y., Spangler, R., Maggos, C. E., Wang, X. M., Han, J. S., Ho, A., and Kreek, M. J. (1999). Hypothalamic-pituitary-adrenal activity and pro-opiomelanocortin mRNA levels in the hypothalamus and pituitary of the rat are differentially modulated by acute intermittent morphine with or without water restriction stress. *J. Endocrinol.* **163**(2), 261–267.

Zhu, X., and Desiderio, D. M. (1994). Effects of space flight stress on proopiomelanocortin, proenkephalin A, and tachykinin neuropeptidergic systems in the rat posterior pituitary. *Life Sci.* **55**, 347–350.

Zurita, A., and Molina, V. (1999). Prior morphine facilitates the occurrence of immobility and anhedonia following stress. *Physiol. Behav.* **65**(4–5), 833–837.

13

Effects of Social Stress on Hormones, Brain, and Behavior

D. Caroline Blanchard
Pacific Biomedical Research Center, and
Department of Genetics and Molecular Biology
John A. Burns School of Medicine
Honolulu, Hawaii 96822

Christina R. McKittrick
Center for Molecular and Behavioral
Neuroscience
Rutgers University
Newark, New Jersey 07102

Matthew P. Hardy
The Population Council
New York, New York 10021

Robert J. Blanchard
Department of Psychology
University of Hawaii
Honolulu, Hawaii 96822

I. WHY STUDY EFFECTS OF SOCIAL STRESS?

A. Differences in Effects of Different Stressors

Although stress has long been conceptualized in terms of a generic pattern of physiological responses, some recent work indicates that different types of stressful events may produce qualitatively different patterns of effects in both behavior and physiology: Electric foot shock and repeated social defeat have been reported to produce opposite effects on systolic blood pressure and mean arterial blood pressure in male rats, with enhancement in the former situation and decrements in the latter (Adams *et al.*, 1987). Whereas fear of a previously received foot shock produced both bradycardia and immobility in almost all rat subjects, fear of a dominant rat produced bradycardia in about 50% of subjects, and immobility primarily in the others (Roozendal *et al.*, 1990). Similarly, though water deprivation had a duration-dependent anxiolytic effect in the elevated

plus maze, one-hour restraint was anxiogenic in the same situation (McBlane and Handley, 1994). Social defeat produced a significant decrease in variability indexes for a number of cardiac electrical activity parameters, whereas three nonsocial stressors (restraint, shock-probe test, and swimming) either failed to change or increased these indices (Sgoifo *et al.*, 1999). Although a variety of stressors tend to elicit self-grooming in the rat, the time course, form, and magnitude of these are different with different stressors (van Erp *et al.*, 1994).

B. Social Stress as a Chronic or Recurrent Factor in Evolution

Differences in response to specific stressors suggest the advisability of focusing research involving the biobehavioral consequences of stress on the types of stressors that are most likely to be broadly represented across mammalian species, including humans. In contrast to many of the stressful manipulations used in laboratory studies, social stress is a chronic or recurring factor in the lives of virtually all higher animal species.

Disputes over resources, including access to a sexual or reproductive partner or in the process of setting up and maintaining territoriality or dominance relationships, may involve agonistic behaviors that result in wounding, exhaustion, and sometimes even death. Even for species in which individuals are solitary except for mating and rearing of young, spacing is based on the agonistic or avoidant behaviors that are seen when conspecific encounters occur. Because social stress effects are both common and powerful, they, along with response to predators, have provided much of the impetus for the evolution of stress mechanisms. These include both behavioral and physiological adaptations, potentially differing for acute as opposed to chronic situations, that may potentially influence virtually every area of an animal's life.

C. Effects of Social Stress in People

Social stress is viewed as a major (Nakao *et al.,* 1998) factor in the etiology of a variety of psychopathologies such as depression and anxiety (e.g., Kessler, 1997; Patten, 1999), in addition to its effects on male (e.g., McGrady, 1984) and female (Wasser and Barash, 1983) reproduction, immune functioning (Ader *et al.,* 1999), heart disease (Hemingway and Marmot, 1998), and the like. Social stress in people is often evaluated in terms of the number and magnitude of life events that an individual experiences, and a general conclusion from this approach is that a plethora of moderately stressful events can have as great an impact as a few major events (Dohrenwend, 1973). Another important index, strongly associated with the number of stressful events that are likely to be experienced, is social status. Low social status is regarded as having an impact on almost every area of the individual's life, with implications for access to resources, safe living conditions, and health care. What is particularly interesting, however, is that these material differences do not appear to account entirely for social status effects. The ranking difference itself, and the meaning assigned by the individual to his or her status with reference to others, may provide stress that is additional to (or interactive with) the material consequences of low status (de Ridder, 2000).

II. ANIMAL MODELS OF SOCIAL STRESS

Animal models of social stress involve single, intermittent, or chronic exposure of a subject animal to a conspecific, other member of the same species. The results of such exposure may be expected to vary with the subject species and the age, gender, and previous history of the individual, as well as the circumstances in which the exposure takes place. Most laboratory studies of social stress effects use rodents, typically laboratory rats or mice. However, hamsters, a variety of mouse species in addition to the domesticated laboratory mouse, and other rodents have also been used, albeit less frequently. Primates also serve as subjects of laboratory investigation of social stress effects, but their social and stress-related behaviors are more commonly observed under natural or seminatural conditions.

Adult males are the subjects of a great majority of social stress studies, as indeed they appear to be for work on animal models of stress-related psychopathologies in general (D. C. Blanchard *et al.,* 1995). With reference to social stress effects, this may reflect that in most mammalian species males tend to create a dominance hierarchy that is much more visible than are the dominance relationships of females, as the male hierarchy influences a wider range of behaviors of the hierarchical animals. In addition, for many species individual male dyadic confrontations, particularly when these occur in the home cage or living area of one of the males, reliably produce fighting, in which the resident has a major advantage. This phenomenon provides a fast and reliable method of ensuring defeat in the intruder, while enabling researchers to quantify social stress in terms of the characteristics of the fight and its parameters (e.g., number and duration of sessions).

A. Laboratory Models of Social Stress

1. Social Defeat

In general, two types of social stress situations are used in laboratory studies. The first type uses individual confrontations, typically separated by longer periods in which the stressed intruder is returned to its home cage or to a neutral site. These are typically labeled "social defeat" tests, and, in order to reduce wounding and other physical concomitants of the encounter, they may be followed by an additional period in which the defeated animal is left in the resident's home cage but protected by a barrier such as a wire mesh cage. These protected exposures may be repeated, with or without actual physical contact of the two animals, on successive test days.

2. Colony, or Chronic Defeat Models

The other type of social stress situation involves chronic exposure of animals maintained in groups or colonies. The physical and social environments and other parameters of these groups vary considerably from seminatural habitats with tunnels and burrow systems including both male and female animals to standard animal cages in which multiple animals of only one sex are housed. The strength of agonistic interaction within these groups also appears to vary considerably; housing with females and provision of larger and more natural habitats tend to produce higher levels of fighting. Various indices of both the agonistic interactions and other behaviors manifested by individual animals may be used to infer a dominance hierarchy.

3. Intermittent Defeat

Other variants tend to fall between these two protocols. One frequently used variant involves caging two animals, usually male, in adjacent areas such that they are chronically exposed to the sight, smell, and sound of the other, but with tactile contact precluded. At intervals the barriers between the enclosures are removed and the two animals allowed to interact directly. In these encounters, one animal may be an experienced fighter, and the other naive, such that it is very predictable that the naive male will be defeated. In other variants, both males are naive, but they quickly establish a victor and a defeated or submissive member of the pair. Although this has much in common with the "social defeat" model, i.e. punctuated physical encounters, typically involving fighting, the defeated animal is left in chronic sensory (except for tactile) contact with the victor, such that its exposure to this psychosocial stress is chronic rather than intermittent.

All the above models are capable of providing animals with a history of victory and a history of defeat, both of which potentially may be compared to controls. For some of these, winners and losers are directly comparable with reference to housing conditions and prior social experience, while for others, notably the resident-intruder type social defeat models, the social disruption models, and those intermittent defeat models in which

an experienced animal is paired with one that is naive, the winners typically have much more social experience and in a different arena (i.e., their own home area rather than that of the other animal for social defeat, and in a variety of locations for the social disruption models) than do the losers. The colony dominant-subordinate, intermittent defeat using initially naive animals, and the social instability models all involve some opportunities for agonistic interactions among animals with initially equivalent experience. However, for those models winning and losing may reflect factors of individual differences between the two animals, such that comparisons following victory or defeat experience must also take into account the possibility of preexisting differences.

4. Social Instability

Social instability models involve setting up social groups and later mixing them. Since intruders into an established home area are typically attacked more strongly than are subordinates within a stable social grouping, this procedure would be expected to involve a very high level of agonistic behavior. However, like crowding, this procedure does blur the distinction between dominant and subordinate, or victorious and defeated animals, in that animals with only experience of victory, or only experience of defeat, are unlikely to emerge from these procedures. Moreover, the protocol may or may not attempt to measure agonistic interactions for each animal.

5. Social Disruption

Social disruption is achieved by introducing a selected high aggressive male or a succession of high aggressive males into a stable social group (Padgett *et al.*, 1998). As with social instability models, this procedure produces animals that are all likely to have been defeated in several of their agonistic interactions, those involving the highly aggressive male intruders. However some of the grouped subjects may also have experience of victory, either in within-group fights, or, on occasion, in agonistic encounters with the high aggressive male intruders. Thus, for both social disruption and social instability models, although there is the possibility of dividing subjects into categories based on their own specific history of victory and defeat, it should be recognized that these experiences are likely to be less polarized than those of the first three paradigms given above.

6. *Crowding*

Additional variants of laboratory social stress models include crowding and social isolation. Properly speaking, crowding should refer only to studies in which animals are placed together in housing situations such that each has less than a standard amount of space. This may mean three rats in a cage meant for one, or 21 rats in a cage meant for seven. Since there is little information on what are the optimum or even reasonable space requirements for most animal species, the definition of crowding is necessarily somewhat arbitrary. In addition, the two examples given above illustrate than "crowding" measured as animals per unit area may be quite different from "crowding" as number of interacting animals per housing unit, and it might be expected that these two aspects of crowding would have differential effects. Crowding also implies that the mechanism of social stress is proximity, rather than agonistic interaction per se, and crowding stress studies may or may not involve attempts to measure agonistic reactions, and to identify dominant and subordinate animals within the groups.

7. *Social Isolation*

It might be thought contradictory that both social grouping and social isolation may be stressful, since this differentiation seems to leave no "normal" situation to serve as a minimal stress control. However, such a view does not take into account differences in social organization between species, or, between sexes within the same species. Thus although social grouping appears to be more stressful for male rats, female rats are more stressed by isolation (Brown and Grunberg, 1995; Haller *et al.,* 1999). In addition, conditions within a particular paradigm such as isolation or grouping can be manipulated to produce more or less stress. The choice of which to consider the stressor, isolation or grouping, may in some cases be based on associated behavioral changes rather than endocrine response (e.g., Haller and Hallasz, 1999).

B. Naturalistic or Field Studies of Social Stress Effects

Since a major focus of this chapter is on brain and endocrine effects of social stress, and these are much more difficult to evaluate in animals in their natural environment, it will be laboratory models such as the above that are emphasized. However, some field studies also involve sampling of blood, feces, and other tissues to provide indices of relevant hormone levels. In these studies, the social stresses are typically inferred from the subject animal's position within the group dominance hierarchy, or, more precisely, from its recent activities with reference to moving up or down in that hierarchy. Although naturalistic studies do provide a wider and more elaborate range of behaviors for which social stress effects might be described, and an expanded analysis of the conditions under which social agonistic behaviors generate little or great magnitude of stress, they generally lack a minimal stress control group for purposes of comparison. Such studies typically compare animals that are high or low in a dominance hierarchy, are moving up or down in the hierarchy, or that show certain patterns of endocrine levels or functioning. In field studies it is particularly difficult to measure physiological changes as a function of time following agonistic interaction or other stressful experience.

C. Studies of Effects of Social Stress in Females

As noted above, the vast majority of social stress studies involve male subjects, as females of most species show relatively little within-sex fighting. In addition, even when fighting between males and females is common, the females may appear to be rather little stressed by it, in terms of measures such as wounding or subsequent avoidance of the male (R. J. Blanchard *et al.,* 2001b). This may reflect that in many of the more commonly used subject species male attack on females is inhibited and does little damage. Female-female fighting may become more intense under some circumstances, e.g., during the week or so following parturition. In addition, selection of highly aggressive males, or of attackers subjected to physiological manipulations such as to make them more likely to show intense attack, can be used to ensure a strong attack on females. These studies, while very interesting, tend to be cumbersome to run. Also, they may not permit clear interpretation of male-female differences in response to attack, since serious attack by males on females in species such as rats that show sexual dimorphism in size must either involve high-magnitude size differences or the use of very small (young?) males.

In addition, females of many mammalian species show a relatively specific inhibition of ovulation or other reduced reproductive functioning while in social groups containing a dominant (reproductively active) female. These nonreproductive females may show few other signs of stress or distress. Nonetheless, the rapidity with which they may begin to cycle following removal of the dominant female makes it clear that this suppression is a response, albeit a very specific one, to the social hierarchy.

D. Social Stress Mechanisms and Markers

This plethora of techniques for producing social stress suggests the need for ways to evaluate whether subjects have indeed experienced an adequate degree of social stress. One approach may be to evaluate the specific experiences that are regarded as mechanisms in the stress experience. Another is to examine behaviors or physiological changes that may serve as relatively specific markers or indices of stress.

With the possible exception of crowding, the major mechanism by which social experience is regarded as producing stress is agonistic behavior. For laboratory mice and rats, the most commonly used subjects of laboratory research on social stress, this agonistic behavior is a very obvious component of most social grouping studies. It may be measured directly, in terms of fighting within each specific male dyad within a group, or indirectly, in terms of wounds on the combatants. Both techniques provide a good indication of dominant or subordinate status, since offensive attack, as is seen on the part of the dominant or the experienced victor, is aimed toward a different target site on the body of its opponent than are the attack bites of the defensive subordinate or experienced loser (Blanchard and Blanchard, 1977). Measures of agonistic behavior that do not take into account crucial specifics, e.g., a score that is summed for all fighting within a group regardless of which animals fight, or overall wounding scores regardless of wound location, do not permit an analysis in terms of dominant-subordinate or winners as opposed to losers. All animals within such a group may be compared to controls without agonistic experience, but it is to be supposed that a good deal of analytic precision is lost when this information is not available. Exceptions are females—for whom overt fighting tends to be uncommon, except for a few species such as hamsters and spotted hyaenas, in which females are dominant to males and female-female fighting is common—and established or stable social groups, as may be the case in many field studies.

With reference to indices or markers of stress, the prototypical stress marker is activity of the hypothalamic pituitary adrenal axis, typically measured as the level of cortisol or corticosterone in the plasma, saliva, or feces. As will be seen, although this marker is very consistent for most laboratory studies, there are some exceptions to the general rule of high values for stressed subjects. Other commonly used indices of stress are changes in relevant organs (e.g., increased adrenal weight) and weight loss during the putatively stressful period. When all of these plus direct measures of agonistic experience are taken, they often covary consistently. Although not all such measures are taken in every study, they provide very useful indications that social stress was indeed a factor in the experimental conditions imposed or a clear variate in the nonexperimental situation in which observations were made.

E. Scope of This Chapter

This chapter will attempt to cover three broad aspects of the effects of social stress: first, behavior; second, changes in brain systems; and third, endocrine changes. Some recent work on social stress effects has tended to examine these factors together, for example, asking whether animals that show a particular pattern of endocrine changes also show changes in behavior or in brain systems. Such approaches are aimed at determining the mechanisms of interaction of these domains, and we will attempt to sketch out these interactive effects whenever possible. Our focus will be on changes in each of these domains following social stress to relatively normal animals (e.g., not lesioned, drugged, or with genetic modifications); we examine them largely in the context of laboratory research, although field studies will also be considered.

We will not attempt to deal with a range of other stress-responsive systems that are also interesting and potentially important but are covered in other chapters in this volume. These include analgesia, cardiovascular changes, autonomic functions, seizure manifestations, immune response, lipoprotein cholesterol, circadian rhythms, body temperature, and electrophysiological correlates.

III. BEHAVIORAL CONSEQUENCES OF SOCIAL STRESS

A. Agonistic Behaviors: Aggression and Defense

The immediate behavioral consequences of decisive agonistic interactions are comprised in two groups of behaviors, one that may be used to infer victory, the other, defeat. These have been intensively described in laboratory rodents, beginning with the studies of Grant and his colleagues (Grant and Chance, 1958; Grant, 1963; Grant and MacKintosh, 1963), with further analyses in rats (e.g., Blanchard and Blanchard, 1977) and mice (e.g., Grimm, 1980). Such studies identified components such as lateral attack, chase, and standing on top of as aggressive elements, and flight-avoidance, defensive upright, and lying on the back as defensive elements. For mice, in particular, the defensive upright is typically regarded as a "submissive" posture and is widely used to indicate defeat, as it tends to coincide with a cessation of aggressive behaviors and to recur as a conditioned response in situations in which the animal has previously been attacked (Siegfried *et al.*, 1984). "Submissive" behaviors have traditionally (Lorenz, 1966) been interpreted as serving as a cut-off for further attack, but they appear not to be particularly effective in this role, except by concealing body areas that are the target for attack by the offensive animal (Blanchard and Blanchard, 1977). Their inability to halt conspecific attack is illustrated by the fact that virtually all uses of social defeat models attempt to provide some protection for the loser, which would not be necessary if its "submissive" postures were effective in terminating physical attack.

The prevalence of defensive upright as a criterion for determining that the defensive animal has "lost" the fight may also reflect the situation in which most such encounters occur. These tend to be small and relatively featureless spaces in which escape is impossible and flight dangerous, since it exposes the back of the fleeing animal, a primary target for offensive biting attack in a number of rodent species (Pellis and Pellis, 1992). When escape is made possible through the provision of larger habitats with side tunnels and chambers, such defensive upright behaviors are relatively rare, and avoidance and flight are more prevalent among subordinate males (Blanchard and Blanchard, 1989). In such situations the determination of dominants and subordinates reflects changes that may occur over a day or so of interactions, with subordinates gradually showing less and less aggressive behavior, while the dominant continues to be aggressive.

Table 1 presents findings for changes in aggression and defensive behaviors on a relatively long-term basis (i.e., longer than within a single session of agonistic interaction). These indicate a very consistent reduction in aggression over days for subordinate male rats in a Visible Burrow System, along with increases in avoidance of the open area (which is typically patrolled by the dominant); immobility, crouching, or freezing; and risk assessment (Blanchard and Blanchard, 1989; D. C. Blanchard *et al.*, 1995; R. J. Blanchard *et al.*, 2001a,b). This last category, risk assessment, involves information-gathering activities concerning potential threat, and includes scanning as well as the assumption of low back postures while cautiously approaching a threat stimulus (D. C. Blanchard *et al.*, 1991a). These changes in aggressive and defensive behavior may be further enhanced in a subset of subordinate rats in a semi-natural Visible Burrow System (VBS) that show a sharply reduced corticosterone (CORT) response to restraint stress (see Section IV.A.2 below) (D. C. Blanchard *et al.*, 1995; R. J. Blanchard *et al.*, 2001a).

Most of the same changes are seen in subordinate tree shrews. Although the testing conditions (they are paired with highly experienced fighters such that they are quickly and easily defeated) are such as to minimize any aggressive behaviors, they show the increased avoidance, immobility (measured as locomotor activity in their home cage situation, in all but tactile contact with the dominant), and risk assessment (Fuchs *et al.*, 1996; Kramer *et al.*, 1999; Van Kampen *et al.*, 2000). Increases in particular defensive behaviors such

TABLE 1
Behavioral Effects of Social Stress: Aggression and Defense in Social Situations[a]

Effects	Experimental animal	References
Aggression		
VBS submissives show ↓ over time in colonies	Long-Evans rats	Blanchard *et al.* (2001a)
VBS submissives show ↓ over time in colonies	Long-Evans rats	Blanchard *et al.* (1995)
Stress nonresponsive submissives show least aggression	Long-Evans rats	Blanchard *et al.* (1995)
Avoidance		
VBS submissives show ↑ avoidance of surface area	Long-Evans rats	Blanchard *et al.* (1995)
Corticosterone nonresponsive submissives ↑ avoidance	Long-Evans rats	Blanchard *et al.* (1995)
Submissives show ↑	Tree shrews	Van Kampen *et al.* (2000)
Submissives show ↑	Tree shrews	Kramer *et al.* (1999)
Defensive behaviors (various)		
Defeat increases submissive postures	Mice	Frischknecht *et al.* (1982)
DBA mice show analgesia to attack, fail to change defense as function of attack experience. C57BL/6 (no analgesia) show ↑ defensive upright and immobility after attack	Mice	Kulling *et al.* (1987)
VBS colony submissives show ↑ defense to a predator	Long-Evans rats	Blanchard and Blanchard (1989)
VBS colony submissives show ↑ "tunnel guarding"	Long-Evans rats	Blanchard *et al.* (2001b)
Immobility, crouching		
VBS corticosterone nonresponding submissives show ↓ lying and ↑ crouching, compared to responding submissives	Long-Evans rats	Blanchard *et al.* (2001a)
Social defeat ↑ crouching	Rat	Chung *et al.* (1999)
Submissives show ↓ locomotor act. in presence of dom	Tree shrew	Fuchs *et al.* (1996)
Risk assessment (RA)		
Submissives show ↑ fearful scanning	Cynomolgous females	Shively *et al.* (1997a,b)
Dom males show ↑ scanning	Sugar glider	Mallick *et al.* (1994)
Submissives show ↑ RA but clomipramine normalizes	Tree shrew	Fuchs *et al.* (1996)

[a]Abbreviations for this and all following tables: Dom = dominant, also variously referred to as alpha or winner; Sub = submissive, subordinate, subdominant, non-alpha, or loser; Con = unstressed control.

as the upright "submissive" posture have also been reported after defeat in both rats and mice, as has risk assessment for subordinate Cynomolgous monkey females (R. J. Blanchard *et al.,* 2001a; Chung *et al.,* 1999; Siegfried *et al.,* 1984; Kulling *et al.,* 1987; Shively *et al.,* 1997a,b). One potentially anomalous finding is that enhanced scanning within a mixed-sex group has been reported for sugar glider dominants (Mallick *et al.,* 1994). However, as the dominant males were moved to other groups, where they became subordinates, scanning increased. This may reflect that scanning has functions in addition to localization-identification of threat sources, and that without more specific behavioral in-

dications such as stretched postures, it may not reflect defensive risk assessment.

B. Emotional Behaviors Measured Outside the Agonistic Context

Because of the strong association between stress and an array of emotional disorders (e.g., Mineka and Zinbarg, 1996), a major emphasis of social stress studies of animals has been to evaluate emotionality. Table 2 presents studies involving socially stressed animals run in tasks designed to measure anxiety, as well as a number of other defensive behaviors; the latter are

742 I. *Mammalian Hormone-Behavior Systems*

Behavioral Effects of Social Stress: Emotionality Outside Agonistic Context[a]

Effects	Experimental animal	References
Anxiety		
Doms, aggressive isolates show ↑ +-maze anxiety	Mouse	Ferrari *et al.* (1998)
Social defeat ↑ +-maze anxiety	C57BL/6J mice	Avgustinovich *et al.* (1997)
Social defeat ↑ +-maze anxiety	"Wild-type" rats	Ruis *et al.* (1999)
Social defeat ↑ +-maze anxiety	Rats	Menzaghi *et al.* (1994, 1996)
Social defeat ↑ +-maze anxiety	Rats	Heinrichs *et al.* (1992, 1994)
Social defeat ↑ +-maze anxiety	Rats	Berton *et al.* (1998, 1999)
Social victory ↓ +-maze anxiety	Rats	Haller and Halasz (2000)
Isolation anxiogenic, social stress normalizes	Rats	Haller and Halasz (1999)
Submissives in "minimal" physical contact social defeat procedure show ↑ anxiety in black white test	NMRI mice	Keeney and Hogg (1999)
Submissives in social defeat with chronic exposure show: ↓ # of squares crossed in open field ↑ immobility, Porsolt's test	C57BL/6J mice	Kudryavtseva *et al.* (1991a,b)
Immobility, crouching		
No change for submissives in "minimal" physical contact social defeat procedure (forced swim test)	NMRI mice	Keeney and Hogg (1999)
Sub mice show ↑ "catatonic-like immobility"	C57BL/6J mice	Kudryavtseva *et al.* (1991a,b)
Stress nonresponsive VBS subordinates show ↑ to handling	Long-Evans rats	Blanchard *et al.* (2001a)
Social defeat ↑ immobility to "sudden silence"	"Wild-type" rats	Ruis *et al.* (1999)
Risk assessment (RA)		
Aggressive isolates and dom grouped males ↑ RA on +-maze	Swiss mice	Ferrari *et al.* (1998)
Social defeat ↓ "peepings" in +-maze	C57BL/6J mice	Avgustinovich *et al.* (1997)
Submissives show ↑ (to social odors, in home cage)	Male mice	Garbe and Kemble (1994)
Two of 3 VBS groups (dominants, nonresponsive submissives) show ↑ stretched attend on stretch attend apparatus	Long-Evans rats	Blanchard *et al.* (2001a)
Ultrasonic vocalizations (USV)		
Social defeat ↑ USV to startle stimuli	Long-Evans rats	Vivian and Miczek (1998, 1999)
Social defeat ↑ USV to startle stimuli	Long-Evans rats	Tornatsky and Miczek (1994)

[a]See Table 1 for abbreviations.

differentiated from those presented in Table 1 in that they are measured outside the initiating agonistic situation. The anxiety test most commonly used in conjunction with socially stressed animals is the elevated plus-maze. For subordinate rats, plus-maze findings tend to be extremely consistent, with a number studies showing that subordinates show more anxiety-like behaviors on this test, while social victory decreases anxiety-like plus-maze behavior (Heinrichs *et al.*, 1992, 1994;

Menzaghi *et al.*, 1994, 1996; Ruis *et al.*, 1999; Haller and Halasz, 2000). One interesting study, however, found that mild social stress normalizes the anxiety-like response of social isolates in the plus-maze task (Haller and Hallasz, 1999).

Data from mouse studies was somewhat more varied. Avgustinovich *et al.* (1997) reported that c57BL/6J mice show enhanced plus-maze anxiety after social defeat. However, Ferrari *et al.* (1998) found that among isolates, the more aggressive males showed higher plus-maze anxiety, as did dominant males among group-housed animals. The plus-maze anxiety measures of the Ferrari *et al.* (1998) test included risk assessment measures, and the aggressive isolates and grouped dominants also showed enhanced risk assessment, in addition to avoidance of open arms, the classical anxiety measure of the elevated plus-maze test. This potential rat-mouse difference may reduce to a difference in procedure, in that the rat studies compared socially stressed (defeated) rats to controls, whereas the Ferrari *et al.* studies compared aggressive or dominant mice to controls. Possibly both winner and loser animals are more anxious than those that have not had aggressive experience. Other anxiety tasks that have been shown to be responsive to social stress effects are the black-white test (enhanced anxiety after social defeat; Keeney and Hogg, 1999), open field, and Porsolt's test (reduced number of squares crossed and enhanced immobility, respectively; Kudryavtseva *et al.*, 1991a).

After social defeat, immobility to a "sudden silence" was enhanced (Ruis *et al.*, 1999). Similarly, VBS subordinates nonresponsive to restraint stress show reduced activity, including righting, to handling (R. J. Blanchard *et al.*, 2001a) than controls, dominants, or stress responsive subordinates. However a "minimal" physical contact social defeat procedure failed to alter immobility for mice in the forced swim test (Keeney and Hogg, 1999). Risk assessment is a pivotal defensive behavior that decreases with both high levels of defensiveness or when defensiveness declines toward a normal, nondefensive state (D. C. Blanchard *et al.*, 1991a). It is very sensitive to subordination or defeat, but the direction of change is different for different situations, perhaps depending on the level of threat experienced in the test situation. The Ferrari *et al.* (1998) findings that aggressive and dominant mice show the highest levels of risk assessment on the elevated plus-maze are compatible with a report by Avgustinovich *et al.* (1997) that social defeat in mice may reduce "peepings" in this test if the defensiveness of the latter, but not the former, is so great as to reduce risk assessment. Subordinate mice show enhanced risk assessment to social odors in their own home cage, as do two of three VBS groups (dominants and nonresponsive subordinates) in a stretch attend apparatus (Garbe and Kemble, 1994; R. J. Blanchard *et al.*, 2001a).

Social defeat has also been consistently reported to increase ultrasonic vocalizations to startle stimuli such as strong air puffs in rats (Vivian and Miczek, 1998, 1999), as well as to the situation in which the animal has previously been defeated (Tornatsky and Miczek, 1994, 1995).

C. Effects of Social Stress on Drinking and Drug-Taking Behaviors

Social stress is also viewed as an important factor in drug abuse and alcoholism, to studies of this relationship have been undertaken in animal models. Table 3 presents a number of such studies, also including some studies of the effects of social stress on eating and drinking, as well as consumption of normally hedonic but not addictive substances such as sucrose. Studies in mice, rats, and monkeys provide a relatively consistent finding of enhanced alcohol intake for socially stressed animals (R. J. Blanchard *et al.*, 1987; Higley *et al.*, 1991, 1998; Hilakivi-Clarke and Lister, 1992; Weisinger *et al.*, 1989). This effect does appear to be somewhat variable for different strains of mice (Kudryavtseva *et al.*, 1991b), however, and with "minimal" physical contact social defeat procedures (Keeney and Hogg, 1999). The Wolfgramm and Heyne (1991) study found that dominant rats show less alcohol intake even when isolated, as well as in a contact housing situation that exposed subjects to other animals but precluded direct physical contact. In partial contrast, the R. J. Blanchard *et al.* (1992) study found no difference between animals that subsequently became dominant or subordinate prior to grouping, but that subordinates increased alcohol intake after grouping while dominants did not. Similarly, Hilakivi-Clarke and Lister (1992) found no differences in alcohol intake between dominant mice and controls. It might also be noted that the social stress in the monkey studies was motherless rearing, whereas in the rat and mouse studies it involved some type of social agonistic experience.

Similarly, social defeat was consistently reported to increase cocaine self-administration (Haney *et al.*, 1995; Lemaire *et al.*, 1994; Miczek and Mutschler, 1996; Tidey and Miczek, 1997). This fits well with findings that social stress effects generalize to both those of psychomotor stimulants, e.g., amphetamine (Miczek *et al.*, 1999), and pentylenetetrazole (Vivian *et al.*, 1994)

TABLE 3

Effects of Social Stress on Ingestion and Drug-Taking Behaviors[a]

Effects	*Experimental animal*	*References*
Alcohol consumption		
No change for submissives in "minimal" physical contact social defeat procedure	NMRI mice	Keeney and Hogg (1999)
Sub C57BL/6J but not CBA/lac showed ↑	Mice	Kudryavtseva *et al.* (1991b)
"Severely wounded" submissives	Mice	Hilakivi-Clarke and Lister (1992)
VBS colony submissives show ↑ alcohol intake	Long-Evans rats	Blanchard *et al.* (1987)
VBS colony doms and submissives show alcohol intake differences prior to grouping, but submissives > doms after grouping	Long-Evans rats	Blanchard *et al.* (1992)
Doms take less alcohol intake while isolated, or contact housed	Wistar rats	Wolffgramm and Heyne (1991)
Pair-caged rats show ⇑ alcohol intake consumption	Rats	Weisinger *et al.* (1989)
Mother-deprived monkeys ⇑ alcohol consumption	Rhesus monkeys	Higley *et al.* (1998)
Mother-deprived monkeys ⇑ alcohol consumption and isolation ⇑ alcohol intake in controls	Rhesus monkeys	Higley *et al.* (1991)
Isolation stress ⇑ alcohol intake	Aged rats	Nunez *et al.* (1999)
Isolation stress ⇑ alcohol intake	Rats	Roske *et al.* (1994)
Diazepam consumption		
Submissives take ↑ Dzp	Wistar rats	Wolffgramm and Heyne (1991)
Drug self-administration		
Social stress ↑ cocaine self-administration	M&F rats	Haney *et al.* (1995)
Social defeat ↑ acquisition of cocaine self-administration	Long-Evans rats	Tidey and Miczek (1997)
Social stress ↑ cocaine self-administration	Long-Evans rats	Miczek and Mutschler (1996)
Social instability ⇓ the ↑ in amphetamine self-administration seen when males cohabit with females	Rats	Lemaire *et al.* (1994)
Eating and drinking		
VBS colony submissives show ↓	Long-Evans rats	Blanchard and Blanchard (1989)
Generalization of social stress to drug cues		
d-Amphetamine	Long-Evans rats	Miczek *et al.* (1999)
Pentylenetetrazole	Long-Evans rats	Vivian *et al.* (1994)
Sucrose intake		
No difference between dom and sub in intake	CD-1 mice females	Mole and Cooper (1995)

[a]See Table 1 for abbreviations.

in drug-discrimination tests, in that such similarities may enable the social stressor to serve as a drug-cue. Diazepam consumption is also increased in subordinate rats (Wolffgramm and Heyne, 1991). One potentially anomalous finding is that social instability reduces the increase in amphetamine self-administration seen when males cohabit with females (Lemaire *et al.*, 1994).

These increases in alcohol and drug (diazepam as well as cocaine) taking stand in contrast to the lack of effect (for sucrose intake; Mole and Cooper, 1995) or reduction (in eating lab chow and drinking water; Blanchard and Blanchard, 1989) reported for subordinate mice and rats, respectively. The latter finding may be confounded by the presence of the dominant, since in that study food and water were located in an area that the dominant tended to patrol during the lights-off period when most consumption occurs. However, later variants of the VBS provided food and water in each chamber and still found a reduction in subordinate weight, thereby suggesting that food intake, at least, may still be reduced for these animals (D. C. Blanchard *et al.,* 1998).

D. Effects of Social Stress on Sexual Behavior

Social stress has relatively consistent effects on male sexual behavior. Studies in laboratory mice (D'Amato, 1988), deer mice (Dewsbury, 1988), laboratory rats (Blanchard and Blanchard, 1989), and lemurs (Perret, 1992) indicate that subordinates show reduced sexual behavior. It should be noted that this reduction may also, at least in part, reflect the conditions under which the observations in several of these studies were made— groups or colonies such that the dominant is or has recently been present. Given the degree to which proximity to a dominant animal influences subordinate behavior (see Section III.E below) and the existence of "sneaker" strategies for male mating (Plaistow and Tsubaki, 2000), it is possible that subordinate males' sexual behavior is better described as transiently suppressed by the dominant. Although dominant males do appear to disproportionately father young in some studies, in others this is not the case, findings that may reflect the existence of female mate selection strategies (e.g., Gagneux *et al.,* 1999), as well as male "sneaker" strategies and a host of post-mating factors. Subordinates also show reductions, and dominants increases, in scent marking (Flügge *et al.,* 1998; Fuchs *et al.,* 1996; Mallick *et al.,* 1994), which may be related to attraction of females as well as other aspects of territory marking.

Sexual behavior of subordinate females also appears to be inhibited, and this may occur in conjunction with, or independently of, suppression of ovulation (Saltzman *et al.,* 1997). The suppression of ovulation in subordinate females is found in a range of rodent and primate species (naked mole rats, Faulkes *et al.,*

TABLE 4
Social Stress Effects on Sexual Behaviors[a]

Effects	Experimental animal	References
Suppression of ovulation		
Sub females	Naked mole rats	Faulkes *et al.* (1990)
Pair housing with sister	Djungarian hamsters	Gudermuth *et al.* (1992)
Females exposed to female groups	Mice	Marchlewska-Koj *et al.* (1994)
Sub females	Damaraland mole-rats	Bennett *et al.* (1996)
Sub females	Marmosets	Saltzman *et al.* (1997)
Sub females	Black tufted-ear marmosets	Smith and French (1997)
Sub females out of contact w dom ovulated in 10 days; but in contact w dom scent, ovulated in 30 days	Marmosets	Barrett *et al.* (1990)
Sexual behavior		
Sub males show ↓ sexual behavior	Albino mice	D'Amato (1988)
Sub males show ↓ sexual behavior	Deer mice	Dewsbury (1988)
Sub males show ↓ sexual behavior	Long-Evans rats	Blanchard and Blanchard (1989)
Sub males show ↓ sexual behavior	Lesser mouse lemurs	Perret (1992)
Scent marking		
Dom males show ↑	Sugar gliders	Mallick *et al.* (1994)
Submissives show ↓ but T replacement normalizes	Tree shrews	Flügge *et al.* (1998)
Submissives show ↓ but clomipramine normalizes	Tree shrews	Fuchs *et al.* (1996)

[a]See Table 1 for abbreviations.

1990; hamsters, Gudermuth *et al.,* 1992; Damaraland mole-rat, Bennett *et al.,* 1996; mice, Marchlewska-Koj *et al.,* 1994; marmosets, Barrett *et al.,* 1990; Saltzman *et al.,* 1997). It is not clear to what degree this suppression might be ascribed to social stress, as it may persist in response to particular pheromones given off by the dominant female, otherwise not present (Saltzman *et al.,* 1997). As will be seen later (Section VI.B), these subordinate females frequently have lower, rather than higher, plasma glucocorticoid values, thus further complicating the issue of whether stress is involved.

E. Effects of Social Stress on Other Social Behaviors

As might be expected, subordinates, socially defeated males, and dominants transferred from one group to another (where they are very likely to become subordinate) show reduced affiliativeness and social contact (rat, Blanchard and Blanchard, 1989; Meerlo *et al.,* 1996a; female cynomolgus monkeys, Shively *et al.,* 1997a,b). Socially stressed animals appear to show considerable sensitivity to relevant physical and behavioral features of other animals; subordinate male mice prefer the odors of familiar dominants to those of unfamiliar dominants (Rawleigh *et al.,* 1993), whereas subordinate female vervet monkeys show a pattern of behavior changes in response to the menstrual cycle of the dominant female, a feature that modulates the dominant's defensiveness.

Changes in behavior in response to the presence and proximity of a dominant have been shown for both rodent and primate species. Some of these changes appear to involve efforts to become less behaviorally

---

TABLE 5
Social Stress Effects on Other Social Behaviors[a]

Effects	Experimental animal	References
Access to resources		
Submissives, and doms transferred to another colony have ↓ access to a variety of resources	Sugar gliders	Mallick *et al.* (1994)
Affiliativeness		
Sub show ↓ affiliativeness and ↑ avoidance	Cynomolgus females	Shively *et al.* (1997a,b)
Odor preferences (conspecific)		
Doms prefer odor of familiar antagonist; submissives prefer unfamiar females but familiar dominants	Mice	Rawleigh *et al.* (1993)
Performance changes in presence of dominant		
Dom and sub show no learning differences when tested individually but submissives "play dumb" when tested together	*Macaca mulatta*	Drea and Wallen (1999)
Presence of dom ↓ SS brain (reward) in sub	Hamsters	Kureta and Watanabe (1996)
Submissives lose "tug of war" for food with 30 cm but not with 100 cm separation from dom	Long-tailed macaques	Schaub (1995)
Responsivity to dom female's menstrual cycle		
Sub females show ↑ agg and ↓ social activity during Dom females late luteal phase (when dom is more defensive)	Vervet monkeys	Rapkin *et al.* (1995)
Social contact		
VBS subordinates show ↓ social contact	Long-Evans rats	Blanchard and Blanchard (1989)
Social defeat ↓	Rats	Meerlo *et al.* (1996a)

[a]See Table 1 for abbreviations.   SS = self-stimulation.

provocative, e.g., selectively losing a tug of war for food when the competing dominant is close by (Long-tailed macaque, Schaub, 1995). In another intriguing finding, subordinate rhesus macaques showed no learning deficiencies compared to dominants when tested individually but "played dumb" when tested together (Drea and Wallen, 1999). The presence of a dominant appears to produce anhedonia with reference to rewards (hamster, Kureta and Watanabe, 1996), a phenomenon that may or may not entirely account for the performance deficiencies seen in such situations.

F. Effects of Social Stress on Nonsocial Behaviors

The degree to which social experience can result in serious, indeed lethal, stress was shown in pioneering studies by Barnett (1963), who reported that intruders into wild rat colonies often died over a period of several days. Such "stress deaths" have been reported in a number of other rodent species (blind mole rats, Zuri *et al.*, 1998; naked mole rats, Margulis *et al.*, 1995; mice, Ebbesen *et al.*, 1991), as well as for subordinates in laboratory rat VBS colonies (Blanchard and Blanchard, 1989). Other species, such as lions (Schaller, 1972), hyaenas (Kruuk, 1972), and chimpanzees (Wrangham and Peterson, 1996), also show lethal intraspecific fighting, but in these cases the death typically results directly from physical trauma rather than from stress per se. Weight loss and a reduction in weight gain are also commonly associated with subordination in rodents (Blanchard and Blanchard, 1989; D. C. Blanchard *et al.*, 1995; R. J. Blanchard *et al.*, 2001a,b) and following social defeat (Haller *et al.*, 1999; Meerlo *et al.*, 1996a, 1997). Although these may in part reflect eating reductions, they may also reflect enhanced metabolic demands associated with stress.

Decreases in locomotion, exploration, and celerity of movement are a very consistent finding with subordinate or socially defeated animals, including rats (Blanchard and Blanchard, 1989; R. J. Blanchard 2001a,b; Meerlo *et al.*, 1996a,b, 1997; Ruis *et al.*, 1999; Tornatsky and Miczek, 1994), tree shrews (Fuchs *et al.*, 1996; Kramer *et al.*, 1999; Van Kampen *et al.*, 2000), and sugar gliders (Mallick *et al.*, 1994).

Memory deficits associated with social stress appear to be those involving hippocampal mediation (Ohl and Fuchs, 1999). These deficits do not appear in close correspondence with alternating cycles of glucocorticoid elevation, thus suggesting a longer-term or indirect effect of stress on memory processes (Ohl and Fuchs, 1998). A very intriguing finding is that social stress may influence learning functions through mechanisms other than or in addition to glucocorticoid increases, as exogenous administration of these, to match the elevation seen with the social stressor, failed to produce so profound or lasting a disruption of learning (Krugers *et al.*, 1997; Ohl *et al.*, 2000).

G. Summary of Effects of Social Stress on Behavior

Social stress appears to be capable of altering a very wide range of behaviors. It facilitates the expression of anxiety-like behaviors in tests such as the elevated plus maze and produces a pattern in VBS subordinate male rats that is very similar to many of the target symptoms of depression (D. C. Blanchard *et al.*, 1995). Social stress also increases substance-taking and may enhance responsivity to drugs of abuse. These changes and other indications of compromised social and sexual functioning in socially stressed animals provide a potential link to behavioral dysfunctions from stress in humans.

IV. HORMONAL ASPECTS OF SOCIAL STRESS: HYPOTHALAMIC-PITUITARY-ADRENAL AXIS FUNCTION

The activity of the hypothalamic pituitary-adrenal (HPA axis) has been studied in a several animal species in a variety of models of psychosocial stress. Not surprisingly, the majority of studies indicate that the HPA axis is activated in low-ranking animals in hierarchical social groups and in animals that have been defeated by a conspecific. However, activity and reactivity of the HPA axis has been shown to be modulated by a variety of different factors, including the species, gender, and behavioral style of the individuals.

A. Corticotropin and Adrenal Steroids

1. Basal Secretion
Most studies of dominance hierarchies in rodents, guinea pigs, and nonhuman primates have found

TABLE 6
Social Stress Effects on Nonsocial Behaviors[a]

Effects	Experimental animal	References
Activity		
Submissives show ↓ locomotion and movement celerity	Long-Evans rat	Blanchard and Blanchard (1989); R. J. Blanchard et al. (2001a,b)
Social defeat ↓ exploratory and motor behavior	Long-Evans rat	Tornatsky and Miczek (1994)
Social defeat ↓ activity	"Wild-type" rat	Ruis et al. (1999)
Social defeat ↓ activity	Laboratory Rat	Meerlo et al. (1996a)
Social defeat ↓ activity	Laboratory Rat	Meerlo et al. (1996b)
Social defeat ↓ activity in Roman low and high avoiders	RLA, RHA rat	Meerlo et al. (1997)
Submissives show ↓ locomotion, and scent marking	Tree shrew	Van Kampen et al. (2000)
Submissives show ↓ scent marking	Tree shrew	Kramer et al. (1999)
Dom males show ↑ activity, celerity, and scent marking (home cage or colony)	Sugar glider	Mallick et al. (1994)
Submissives show ↓ activity (clomipramine normalizes)	Tree shrew	Fuchs et al. (1996)
Death		
After exposure to vibrations or odors of neighboring males, on long-term basis	Blind mole rats	Zuri et al. (1998)
In intruders into colonies	Wild rats	Barnett (1963)
In mixed-sex colonies, submissives show ↑ mortality	Long-Evans rats	Blanchard and Blanchard (1990)
In groups of 3, dom live longer than submissives; in groups of 9, no rank order, die earlier than groups of 3	Mice	Ebbesen et al. (1991)
When queen removed from colony, 3 previously submissive females fought, 2 died	Naked mole rat	Margulis et al. (1995)
Learning		
Prolonged psychosocial stress ↓ spatial learning similar but artificial elevation of corticosterone only mild effect on spatial memory performance	Laboratory rat	Krugers et al. (1997)
Memory		
Submissives show ↓ hippocampus-mediated memory	Tree shrew	Ohl et al. (2000)
Submissives show ↓ but not in temporal sequence with corticosterone increase in alternating stress-no stress periods	Tree shrew	Ohl and Fuchs (1998)
Submissives show ↓ in hippocampus-dependent but not hippocampus-independent memory with alternating stress periods	Tree shrews	Ohl and Fuchs (1999)
Weight loss or reduced weight gain		
VBS submissives show weight loss	Long-Evans rats	Blanchard and Blanchard (1989); D. C. Blanchard et al. (1995); R. J. Blanchard et al. (2001a,b)
Social defeat and instability ↓ weight gain	Male rats	Haller et al. (1999)
Social defeat ↓ weight gain	Male rats	Meerlo et al. (1996a)
Social defeat ↓ weight gain in Roman low and high avoiders	RHA, RLA rats	Meerlo et al. (1997)

[a]See Table 1 for abbreviations.

TABLE 7
Effects of Social Status on Baseline Glucocorticoid Levels[a]

Species	Gender	Paradigm	Basal glucocorticoid levels	Reference
Mice	Male	Single-sex groups	Sub > Dom = Con	Louch and Higginbotham (1967)
			Sub = Dom = Con	Hilakivi *et al.* (1989)
			Sub = Dom > Con (both adapted with time, Dom faster than Sub)	Bronson (1973)
		Mixed-sex groups	Sub > Dom = Con at early time points; Sub = Dom > Con at later time points	Ely and Henry (1978)
	Female	Single-sex groups	Sub > Dom	Schuhr (1987)
Rats	Male	Single-sex groups	Sub > Dom	Popova and Naumenko (1972)
			Sub > Con (but Sub adapted with time)	Krugers *et al.* (1997)
		Mixed-sex groups	Sub > Con (Dom not sampled)	de Goeij *et al.* (1992)
			Sub > Dom = Con	Blanchard *et al.* (1993, 1995); McKittrick *et al.* (1995)
			Sub > Dom	Ely *et al.* (1997)
			Sub > Dom > Con	Dijkstra *et al.* (1992)
		Resident-intruder dyads	Sub > Dom = Con	Raab *et al.* (1986)
Syrian hamsters	Male	Housing in proximity to established dominant (no physical contact)	Sub > Dom = Con	Huhman *et al.* (1992)
Guinea pigs	Male	Long-term mixed-sex groups	Sub = Dom	Sachser (1987); Sachser *et al.* (1998)
		Male dyads with one female	Sub (losers) > Dom (winners) = Con	Sachser and Lick (1989)
African wild dogs	Male + female	Field studies of social groups (fecal corticosterone)	Dom > Sub (effect most pronounced in females)	Creel *et al.* (1996)
Dwarf mongoose	Female	Field studies of social groups (urinary cortisol)	Dom > Sub	Creel *et al.* (1996)
Tree shrews	Male	Housing in proximity to established dominant (no physical contact)	Sub > Con (Dom not sampled)	von Holst (1977); Fuchs and Flügge (1995)
Black tufted-ear marmosets	Female	Single-sex groups	Dom (ovulatory) = Sub (anovulatory)	Smith and French (1997)
Common marmosets	Male + female	Mixed-sex groups	Females: Dom > Sub Males: Sub = Dom	Johnson *et al.* (1996)
	Female	Mixed-sex groups	Dom (ovulatory) > Sub (anovulatory)	Saltzman *et al.* (1994, 1998)
Squirrel monkeys	Male	Mixed-sex groups	Sub > Dom	Manogue *et al.* (1975)
		Single and mixed-sex groups	Dom > Sub in mixed-sex groups only	Mendoza *et al.* (1979)
		Single-sex pairs	Dom > Sub	Coe *et al.* (1979)

continues

Continued

Species	Gender	Paradigm	Basal glucocorticoid levels	Reference
Vervet monkeys	Male	Mixed-sex groups	Sub = Dom in stable groups; Dom > Sub in newly formed or reconstituted groups	McGuire *et al.* (1986)
Cynomolgus macaques	Female	Single-sex groups	Sub > Dom	Shively *et al.* (1997a,b); Shively (1998)
	Male	Single-sex groups	Sub = Dom	Botchin *et al.* (1994)
Olive baboons	Male	Field studies of social groups	Sub > Dom	Sapolsky (1983); Virgin and Sapolsky (1997)

[a]Except where noted, glucocorticoids were measured in blood. See Table 1 for abbreviations.

elevated basal glucocorticoid secretion in subordinate animals compared to dominants. Subordination has been shown to increase corticosterone levels in mice, rats, and hamsters (Louch and Higginbotham, 1967; Popova and Naumenko, 1972; Ely and Henry, 1978; Raab *et al.,* 1986; Schuhr, 1987; Huhman *et al.,* 1992; de Goeij *et al.,* 1992; D. C. Blanchard *et al.,* 1993; Ely *et al.,* 1997), corticosterone and cortisol levels in guinea pigs and tree shrews (von Holst, 1977; Sachser and Lick, 1989), and cortisol levels in squirrel monkeys, cynomolgous macaques, and olive baboons (Manogue *et al.,* 1975; Coe *et al.,* 1979; Sapolsky, 1983; Shively *et al.,* 1997a,b). The increased glucocorticoid levels are often accompanied by weight loss, thymus involution, or adrenal hypertrophy (von Holst, 1977; Raab *et al.,* 1986; Sachser and Lick, 1989; de Goeij *et al.,* 1992; D. C. Blanchard *et al.,* 1993), or a combination thereof. Corticotropin (ACTH) may also be elevated in the subordinates (Huhman *et al.,* 1991, 1992), although that is not always the case (de Goeij *et al.,* 1992).

Although in most social stress models it is the subordinates that appear to be most severely stressed, in many cases the dominant animals show evidence of HPA axis activation as well. In our VBS model of chronic social stress, for example, both dominant and subordinate male rats have elevations in plasma corticosterone in blood sampled immediately after removal from the burrow system (D. C. Blanchard *et al.,* 1993, 1995; McKittrick *et al.,* 1995). In addition, all animals housed in the VBS show some degree of thymus involution and adrenal hypertrophy, although these effects are much more pronounced in the subordinate animals. This suggests that both the dominants and the subordinates are stressed within the context of the VBS. However,

if blood is sampled after the animals have been allowed to rest in individual cages for one hour after removal from the VBS, corticosterone remains high in the subordinates but returns to control levels in the dominants, thus indicating more efficient regulation of the HPA axis in these animals (McKittrick *et al.,* 2000). Similarly, group housing of previously isolated mice increases plasma corticosterone in both subordinate and dominants, but the glucocorticoid concentrations return to control levels more rapidly in dominants than in subordinates (Bronson, 1973). In studies using other models of social stress, dominants as well as subordinates had higher corticosterone levels, decreased thymus weight, and increased adrenal weights compared to single- or pair-housed controls; the effects were generally more pronounced in the subordinate animals (Louch and Higginbotham, 1967; Dijkstra *et al.,* 1992).

In contrast to the above studies, dominant animals have been found to have higher levels of basal glucocorticoids in social groups of dwarf mongoose, wild dogs, and marmosets (Saltzman *et al.,* 1994; Creel *et al.,* 1996). These effects are observed primarily in females and may be related to ovulatory cyclicity. In marmoset populations, low-ranking females are often anovulatory and also have lower levels of cortisol than a normally cycling female of higher rank; in newly formed mixed-sex groups, cortisol levels increase if the female achieves dominant status but decrease if the animal becomes an anovulatory subordinate (Saltzman *et al.,* 1994). Cortisol levels in anovulatory subordinates are also lower than in ovariectomized animals, thereby suggesting factors other than ovarian hormones contribute to the regulation of cortisol in these animals (Saltzman *et al.,* 1998). This relationship between rank and cortisol level does not hold true for all primate species, however, since subordinate female cynomolgus monkeys have higher cortisol levels than their dominant counterparts (Shively, 1998). In addition, a study of female cotton-top tamarins showed no difference in cortisol levels between high-ranking cycling and low-ranking non-cycling postpubertal females in the same natal group, although cortisol levels were higher in newly cycling females, reflective of a change of social status (Ziegler *et al.,* 1995). Similar findings were obtained for black tufted-ear marmosets; dominant and subordinate females in natal family groups showed similar levels of cortisol, regardless of the cycling status (ovulatory or anovulatory) of the latter. Cortisol levels did, however, increase following conflicts within the family group (Smith and French, 1997).

Several other studies have indicated that the stability of social status and housing conditions influences baseline HPA axis activity. For example, housing marmosets in unstable peer groups led to an increase in morning cortisol measures in both males and females, although in both sexes, cortisol levels fell as the peer groups stabilized (Johnson *et al.,* 1996). In olive baboon populations, rank predicted cortisol levels only in stable hierarchies; in unstable hierarchies, cortisol increased with frequency with which the animal was challenged by lower-ranking individuals but was not altered when the individual challenged other animals of higher rank (Sapolsky, 1992a). Similarly, plasma cortisol levels increased as squirrel monkeys were moved from individual housing to male peer groups to male-female group (Mendoza *et al.,* 1979). The effects were most pronounced in the higher-ranking males, again suggesting increased HPA activity as a result of repeated challenges by lower-ranking animals. In rats, one complex model uses a combination of mixed-sex housing and frequent colony reorganization to induce a variety of physiological changes indicative of HPA activation, including increased basal corticosterone, decreased thymus weight, and increased adrenal size (Klein *et al.,* 1992). However, social instability may have less predictable effects in other scenarios, as in one study with rhesus monkeys inoculated with the simian immunodeficiency virus, which showed that animals that met daily in unstable groups had lower plasma cortisol levels than those that interacted within stable groups, despite the fact that the animals in the unstable condition

showed behavioral signs of stress, as well as altered immune function and shorter survival time (Capitanio *et al.,* 1998). Therefore, although social instability is generally viewed as stressful, the effects on basal HPA function and other stress-related parameters may vary considerably with the experimental condition.

2. Reactivity and Feedback Control of HPA Axis

Socially subordinate animals are generally equally or more reactive to a novel stressor compared to their dominant counterparts, as shown in social groups of mice (Ely and Henry, 1978), rats (Dijkstra *et al.,* 1992), hamsters (Huhman *et al.,* 1992), guinea pigs (Haemisch, 1990), squirrel monkeys (Coe *et al.,* 1979), and olive baboons (Sapolsky, 1983). However, under some circumstances, subordinate animals have been shown to have less robust response to stress than dominants (Manogue *et al.,* 1975; de Goeij *et al.,* 1992). Indeed, this is what we found in our VBS model of chronic social stress. The subordinate animals have a blunted corticosterone response to a novel restraint stressor; this effect is attributable to a subpopulation of subordinates that has little or no corticosterone increase following stressor exposure (D. C. Blanchard *et al.,* 1995). These stress-nonresponsive subordinates appear to be the most highly stressed in this model, showing greater decrements in insulin, glucose, testosterone, and CBG compared to the stress-responsive subordinates (McKittrick, 1996).

Similar subgroups of subordinates were also identified in social groups of olive baboons. Subordinates that had a high number of consortships, a behavior more typical of high-ranking animals, also had large HPA responses to stress, accompanied by higher basal levels of cortisol (Virgin and Sapolsky, 1997). In contrast, the HPA response to an acute stressor was blunted in another group of subordinates, and basal cortisol levels were also somewhat lower. Finally, a third group of particularly aggressive subordinates had no elevation in basal cortisol; it is postulated that the initiation of aggressive actions played a role in attenuating glucocorticoid secretion (Virgin and Sapolsky, 1997).

The HPA axis response to an agonistic interaction appears to depend, in part, on the outcome of the encounter. After fighting between rats, corticosterone goes up more and stays higher longer in the losers compared to the winners (Koolhaas *et al.,* 1983); a similar study showed that an animal that submits to a challenger exhibits an increased plasma corticosterone, whereas plasma corticosterone declines if the other animal submits (Haller *et al.*, 1996). The gender of the animal may also influence the magnitude of the stress response, as illustrated in wild dwarf mongooses, where male subordinates had higher stress responses than male dominants, whereas in the females, the dominant was more responsive (Creel *et al.*, 1996).

Social stress has also been show to alter HPA axis responsiveness to ACTH, corticotropin-releasing factor (CRF), and its secretagogues, as well as affecting the feedback mechanisms regulating the termination of the HPA axis response. For example, in olive baboons, although the cortisol response to an acute stressor did not differ with social status, low-ranking males had a decreased ACTH response to exogenous CRF and impaired negative feedback following dexamethasone (DEX) administration (Sapolsky, 1983, 1989). Conversely, ACTH leads to a more pronounced increase in glucocorticoid levels in subordinate compared to dominant mice (Ely and Henry, 1978) and female cynomolgous macaques (Shively, 1998). Social defeat enhanced the ACTH but not the corticosterone response to iv CRF (Buwalda *et al.*, 1999). Housing conditions after defeat appear to modulate the consequences of defeat, as rats housed individually had greater ACTH responses to CRF administration and larger adrenals and smaller thymus weights than animals housed in a group of familiar conspecifics (Ruis *et al.*, 1999). The individually housed animals also had impaired DEX suppression of ACTH and corticosterone.

Administration of DEX reveals deficits in feedback inhibition of the HPA axis in other social stress models as well. In addition to the olive baboons and rats mentioned above, subordinate female cynomolgous monkeys had less efficient DEX suppression compared to dominants (Shively, 1998), and marmosets housed in social groups had a blunted cortisol response to DEX when compared to pair-housed animals (Johnson *et al.*, 1996). Analysis of DEX-suppression in male cynomolgous macaques indicated that those animals that were DEX-resistant were also more than twice as likely to have come from unstable rather than stable social groups. However, this result is in contrast to another study of rhesus macaques, in which animals exposed to unstable social groupings showed enhanced DEX suppression of cortisol, compared to animals exposed

to stable social conditions (Capitanio *et al.*, 1998). It should be noted that in the latter experiment, animals were grouped together for only 100 minutes per day, rather than being housed continuously in social groups; the differences in experimental design may account, in part, for the seemingly contradictory results.

B. Corticosteroid Receptors and Corticosteroid-Binding Globulin

The biological effects of circulating glucocorticoids can be modulated by alterations in the availability of intracellular steroid receptors and in circulating levels of corticosteroid-binding globulins (CBG). In both the VBS and tree shrew models of social stress, chronic subordination led to a decrease in the expression of glucocorticoid receptor (GR) mRNAs in hippocampus. In the tree shrew, 13 days of psychosocial stress led to a decline in GR mRNA levels in CA1 and CA3 of hippocampus in subordinates compared to unstressed control subordinates (Johren *et al.*, 1994). Similarly, subordinate rats housed in a VBS had lower mRNA levels of GR and mineralocorticoid receptor (MR) mRNA levels were lower in CA1 (Chao *et al.*, 1993). This downregulation of gene expression does not appear to translate into a corresponding change in GR binding in hippocampus, hypothalamus, or pituitary of the subordinates, although it is likely that subtle differences in binding in selective hippocampal subfields may not be detectable in homogenates of whole brain regions (D. C. Blanchard *et al.*, 1995). However, another group did find decreased GR binding within hippocampus and hypothalamus, but not pituitary, in rats killed one week after social defeat; by three weeks post-defeat, GR binding had returned to control levels in all brain regions, but by that time, hippocampal MR binding had declined significantly (Buwalda *et al.*, 1999). A study of rats housed in stable mixed-sex groups also demonstrated a decrease in hippocampal MR binding, which was proposed to be associated with impaired feedback control of the HPA axis response in these animals (Maccari *et al.*, 1991). The apparent stress-induced down-regulation of hippocampal glucocorticoid and mineralocorticoid receptors may reflect a compensatory response to higher levels of circulating glucocorticoids.

The effects of chronic social stress on plasma levels of CBG have also been examined in the VBS model. Since glucocorticoids bound to CBG in blood are unable to cross membranes in order to interact with their intracellular receptors, alterations in CBG concentrations may play an important role in regulating the bioavailability of circulating CORT. Compared to controls, all VBS-housed animals had decreased circulating levels of CBG: this effect was greater in the subordinates than in the dominants, and was most pronounced in the stress-nonresponsive subgroup of subordinates (McKittrick, 1996; Spencer *et al.,* 1996). The observed decreases in CBG, particularly in the nonresponders, combined with increased CORT levels may lead to higher levels of free bioactive corticosterone. This hypothesis is supported by the observation that the concentration of plasma CBG was significantly correlated with the number of available (unoccupied) glucocorticoid receptors in the spleens of the VBS animals (Spencer *et al.,* 1996). The increases in free CORT may be short-lived in the animals with low CBG concentrations, however, as low CBG levels are correlated with an increased rate of glucocorticoid clearance (Bright, 1995), most likely because CBG-bound CORT is not accessible to degradative enzymes.

C. Summary

The above data indicate, not surprisingly, that social subordination and defeat appear to be stressful and lead to HPA axis activation. Chronic social stress can lead to long-term changes in HPA activity, including persistent elevations in basal glucocorticoids, abnormal responses to subsequent stressors, and impaired feedback regulation. For the most part, these effects are seen most clearly in subordinate animals housed in stable social groups; however, similar responses have observed in dominant animals in such groups, and also in animals of all ranks in unstable social groupings. In addition to altering the levels of circulating glucocorticoids, social stress may also lead to changes in central glucocorticoid receptor populations and in peripheral regulation of CBG, which may, in turn, modulate the biological effectiveness of these steroids.

V. INTERACTIONS BETWEEN HORMONES AND BRAIN SYSTEMS IN SOCIAL STRESS

The effects of psychosocial stressors on the brain is a topic of considerable interest to many researchers for several reasons. First of all, unlike many laboratory stressors, the stressfulness of social conflict tends to be primarily of psychological, rather than physical, origin. Although some wounding may occur in social dominance or defeat paradigms, in most cases, a full-blown stress response can be generated in a subordinate or defeated animal merely through visual and/or olfactory contact with the previously encountered animal. The nonphysical nature of social stressors makes them useful in generating models of stress-related illnesses in humans, since relatively few people in modern society experience severe physical stressors in their lifetimes, while psychological stressors are relatively commonplace. Stressful life events have been associated with several mental illnesses, including depression and other affective disorders; many of these disorders, in turn, appear to be linked to various neurochemical imbalances in the brain. Determining the effects of social stress on neuronal transmission may provide clues to how stress alters behavior and physiology in animals and humans alike.

A. Neurotransmitter Systems

1. Monoamines

a) Serotonin The transmitter system most widely studied in the context of social stress is the serotonergic system. Serotonin neurotransmission has been shown to be altered by a variety of laboratory stressors, and serotonin (5-hydroxytryptamine; 5-HT) also plays a role in mediating many of the behaviors that contribute to and are affected by social status, including aggression and sexual behavior. The majority of studies suggest that 5-HT systems are activated in response to social stress. Examination of tissue concentrations of 5-HT and its metabolite, 5-hydroxyindole acetic acid (5-HIAA) have shown elevated concentrations of 5-HIAA and/or increased 5-HIAA/5-HT ratios in various brain regions of subordinate rats and mice, suggesting increased serotonergic activity. In the VBS model of social stress, levels of 5-HIAA are higher in subordinates than in dominants and controls in limbic areas of the brain such as preoptic area, hippocampus, and amygdala (D. C. Blanchard *et al.,* 1991b). Similarly, submissive mice had increased 5-HIAA in hypothalamus, hippocampus, and brainstem (Hilakivi *et al.,* 1989), whereas repeated, but not single, social defeat increased the midbrain 5-HIAA to 5-HT ratio

TABLE 8
Effects of Social Stress on Central Serotonergic Systems

Type of measurement	Outcome	Reference
Monoamine content in tissue homogenates	↑ 5-HIAA in limbic areas in subordinate mice and rats	Hilakivi *et al.* (1989); Blanchard *et al.* (1991b)
	↑ 5-HIAA/5-HT ratio in midbrain of defeated Lewis rats	Berton *et al.* (1998)
5-HT innervation	↑ 5-HT immunoreactive fibers in lateral septum and anterior hypothalamus of defeated hamsters	Delville *et al.* (1998)
Monoamines in CSF	↑ 5-HIAA in CSF of subordinate talapoin monkeys	Yodyingyuad *et al.* (1985)
Receptor binding	↑ 5-HT$_{2A}$ binding in cortex and ↓ 5-HT$_{1A}$ binding in hippocampus of subordinate rats and tree shrews	Flügge (1995); McKittrick *et al.* (1995); Berton *et al.* (1998)
	↓ 5-HT$_{1A}$ binding in median raphe of subordinate rats	McKittrick (1996)
	↓ 5-HT transporter binding in hippocampus of subordinate and dominant rats; also after single social defeat	Berton *et al.* (1999); McKittrick *et al.* (2000)
Response to receptor agonists	↓ Corticosterone response to 5-HT$_{1A}$ agonist in defeated rats	Korte *et al.* (1995)
	↓ Behavioral response to 5-HT$_{2A}$ agonist in defeated rats	Benjamin *et al.* (1993)
	No difference between subordinate and dominant cynomolgus monkeys in response to fenfluramine (5-HT releaser)	Botchin *et al.* (1994); Shively (1998)

in defeated Lewis rats (Berton *et al.*, 1998, 1999). In addition, adult golden hamsters that had been socially defeated during puberty had increased 5-HT innervation of lateral septum and anterior hypothalamus, thus suggesting that defeat led to an increase in the capacity to release 5-HT in these areas (Delville *et al.*, 1998).

In addition to these rodent studies, various serotonergic parameters have been examined in nonhuman primates. Subordinate talapoin monkeys had elevated levels of 5-HIAA in their cerebrospinal fluid; this is believed to reflect increased 5-HT neurotransmission in the brain (Yodyingyuad *et al.*, 1985). In cynomolgous macaques, the stability of the social group appeared to be more important than rank, as animals that had previously been housed in unstable social groups had lower 5-HIAA and 5-HT concentrations in prefrontal cortex compared to animals maintained in social groups; however, these changes may have reflected adaptive responses following termination of the stressor, since the level of 5-HT in these animals was lower in those that had been housed in unstable colonies more recently (Fontenot *et al.*, 1995). One interesting study

showed that high levels of 5-HT in the blood was associated with dominant status in vervet monkeys, with 5-HT levels increasing or decreasing as the animal experienced a corresponding rise or fall in rank (Raleigh *et al.*, 1984). The relevance of these findings to central 5-HT neurotransmission is unclear, however, since it is likely that peripheral and central serotonergic systems are regulated independently.

Both pre- and postsynaptic receptors and transporters for 5-HT have been shown to be altered by social stress. Perhaps the most consistent findings are a stress-related increase in binding to 5-HT$_{2A}$ receptors in cortex and a corresponding decrease in 5-HT$_{1A}$ receptors in hippocampus (McKittrick *et al.*, 1995; Flügge, 1995; Berton *et al.*, 1998). In addition, in the VBS model, binding to presynaptic 5-HT$_{1A}$ autoreceptors is preferentially down-regulated in the median raphe of subordinate animals (C. R. McKittrick unpublished observations). Further examination of the down-regulation of 5HT$_{1A}$ receptors in hippocampus and elsewhere indicates that in the tree shrew, this receptor subtype is regulated not only by increased glucocorticoid levels in the subordinates but also by stress-induced suppression of testosterone, as binding was returned to control levels in most brain regions by exogenous administration of testosterone (Flügge *et al.*, 1998).

A single social defeat also led to a decrease in binding to the 5-HT transporter in hippocampus (Berton *et al.*, 1999). The relationship of the 5-HT transporter response to the severity of social stress is unclear, however, since in our model, all VBS-housed animals show a similar decrease in 5HT transporter binding, with the most pronounced effects occurring in the dominant animals (McKittrick *et al.*, 2000). The dominant animals do appear to be somewhat stressed compared to the pair-housed controls, thus suggesting that the down-regulation of 5-HT transporters may be part of an adaptive response to mild social stress; conversely, the decrease in binding may occur simply as a result of agonistic interactions between the animals without regard to the relative stressfulness of these encounters.

The functional effects of the changes in 5-HT receptors are unclear. Defeated rats exhibit a blunted corticosterone response to the 5-HT$_{1A}$ agonist 8-OH-DPAT, thereby suggesting a functional subsensitivity of these receptors, a result that corresponds well with the observed decrease in receptor number (Korte *et al.*, 1995). In contrast, whereas an enhanced response to 5-HT$_{2A}$ stimulation might be expected, the behavioral response to a 5-HT$_2$ agonist was decreased, rather than increased, in defeated rats (Benjamin *et al.*, 1993). It should be noted, however, that in this particular experiment the behavioral response was measured after a single social defeat, which does not lead to a measurable change in 5-HT$_2$ binding capacity (Berton *et al.*, 1999), thus suggesting that the desensitization may occur through changes in receptor-linked signal transduction pathways or some other mechanism. Finally, in cynomolgous monkeys, the hormonal responses to the 5-HT-releaser fenfluramine did not differ between dominant and subordinate animals, thereby indicating no differences in postsynaptic sensitivity to nonselective stimulation of 5-HT transmission (Botchin *et al.*, 1994; Shively, 1998).

b) Norepinephrine   The effects of chronic social stress on both pre- and postsynaptic elements of noradrenergic neurotransmission have been studied in rat and tree shrew models of psychosocial stress.

Messenger mRNA levels of tyrosine hydroxylase, the rate-limiting enzyme in catecholamine synthesis, were shown to be selectively increased in noradrenergic, but not dopaminergic, brain regions; in some cases, the increased mRNA levels in locus coeruleus were accompanied by a corresponding increase in immunoreactive tyrosine hydroxylase protein (Brady *et al.*, 1994; Watanabe *et al.*, 1995). Since several different stress paradigms have shown that the locus coeruleus noradrenergic system is activated by stress, the changes in tyrosine hydroxylase probably reflect an up-regulation of synthetic capacity as a result of increased neuronal activity and transmitter release.

Functional alterations in noradrenergic systems are also a consequence of social stress. Following three days of social crowding, male rats exhibited a blunted corticosterone response to both isoprenaline, a β-adrenergic receptor agonist, and clonidine, an α_2-adrenergic antagonist; the hypothalamic histamine response to these two drugs was also attenuated (Bugajski *et al.*, 1993). However, crowding had little effect on the corticosterone response to the α_1-adrenoceptor agonist phenylephrine, thus suggesting that the various adrenergic receptor populations are differentially regulated as a result of social crowding.

Adrenergic receptor subtypes are affected by subordination stress as well, as shown in the tree shrew model. After 10 days of social stress, α_2-adrenoceptor binding was down-regulated in the subordinates compared to dominants in several brain regions, including periaqueductal gray (PAG), the perifornical region of hypothalamus, medial amygdala, the nucleus of the solitary tract (STN), and the dorsal motor nucleus of the vagus (DMV); in addition, low-affinity binding sites were present in the STN, PAG, and medial amygdala of the dominants but not the subordinates (Flügge *et al.*, 1992). Time course studies indicate that these receptors have different temporal patterns of regulation within individual brain regions. For example, in locus coeruleus and DMV, binding was decreased after only two days of psychosocial stress and remained low throughout the period of subordination (Flügge, 1996). Binding in STN was similarly downregulated, although these changes were not apparent until day 21. In contrast, the response of α_2-receptors in the prefrontal cortex was biphasic, with a transient decrease in binding at day 10, followed by a return to control values by day

21 and a subsequent increase in binding at day 28. In addition, binding affinity of various α_2-adrenoceptor subtypes was altered in temporal and regional patterns distinct from the changes in receptor number.

β-adrenergic receptors are also regulated in a similarly complex manner in this model. Both β_1 and β_2-adrenoceptors are transiently down-regulated in prefrontal cortex after two days of subordination and up-regulated in the pulvinar nucleus after 10 and 28 days, respectively; however, β_1-adrenoceptors are also decreased in parietal cortex and hippocampus at 28 days (Flügge *et al.*, 1997). In addition, the affinity for β-adrenergic receptors was decreased in cortex and hippocampus following 21 days of psychosocial stress. These complex changes in regional populations of adrenergic receptor subtypes indicate that the function of various noradrenergic circuits may be differentially regulated in response to chronic stress; furthermore, this regulation may occur via changes in receptor turnover, synthesis, and conformation.

c) Dopamine   Unlike serotonin and norepinephrine, dopamine has only recently been considered to be a stress-responsive neurotransmitter. As a result, studies focusing on the effects of social stress on dopaminergic systems are relatively rare. Although in one mouse study dominants did have lower brain stem dopamine content than subordinate or control animals (Hilakivi *et al.*, 1989), in monkey and rat social hierarchies, tissue content of dopamine and its metabolites was unaffected by rank (D. C. Blanchard *et al.*, 1991b; Fontenot *et al.*, 1995). A similar lack of effect was observed on the regulation of tyrosine hydroxylase in dopaminergic nuclei, in contrast to the increase in tyrosine hydroxylase mRNA and protein seen in noradrenergic nuclei (Watanabe *et al.*, 1995).

Dopaminergic neurotransmission is not completely unaffected by social stress, however. Exposing previously defeated rats to the threat of defeat elicits an increase in extracellular dopamine content in both the prefrontal cortex and the nucleus accumbens, as measured using *in vivo* microdialysis (Tidey and Miczek, 1996; 1997), a result indicating that these limbic areas are responsive to stimuli associated with social stressors. In addition, binding and function of the D_2 dopamine receptor subtype has been shown to be de-

creased in socially subordinate female cynomolgous monkeys. These animals have decreased D_2 receptor binding capacity in the basal ganglia, as indicated by PET scanning after injection with [18]fluoroclebopride; in addition, the subordinates exhibited a blunted prolactin response to the D_2 antagonist, haloperidol, indicating a functional subsensitivity of these receptors (Shively *et al.*, 1997a,b; Shively, 1998).

2. Amino Acid Transmitters

Very few studies have examined the effects of social stress on components of excitatory amino acid neurotransmission. However, Krugers *et al.* (1993) found that a single social defeat was sufficient to lead to changes in the ratio of N-methyl-D-aspartate (NMDA) and α-amino-3-hydroxy-5-methyl-4-isoxazoleproprionic acid (AMPA) receptors in the CA3 area hippocampus of rats: Specifically, binding of [3H]CGP39653 to NMDA receptors was increased in stratum radiatum of CA3, while [3H]CNQX binding to AMPA receptors was decreased in this and other areas of hippocampus.

There also appear to be alterations in $GABA_A$ receptors following defeat in mice. Northern blot analysis of both α_1 and γ_2 $GABA_A$ subunits has shown that mRNA levels of both subunits are increased in cortex at four hours post-defeat and remain elevated for at least 72 hours before falling to control levels after seven days (Kang *et al.*, 1991). Subunit mRNA levels were unchanged in cerebellum and hippocampus, and no changes were observed in any region in the brains of the resident animals that defeated the intruder mice. The increase in subunit expression is likely to reflect a general up-regulation of the $GABA_A$ receptor but it may also indicate changes in the subunit composition, and thus the electrical and pharmacological properties, of the receptors.

3. Neuropeptides

a) CRF and Vasopressin   Corticotropin-releasing factor (CRF) and arginine-vasopressin (AVP) are known to be involved in the initiation and modulation of HPA axis activity; in addition, extrahypothalamic CRF and AVP circuits have been implicated in the mediation of stress-related and social behaviors, respectively. As a result, the effect of social stressors on the expression and release of these two neuropeptides has been studied in

TABLE 9
Effects of Social Stress on CRF and AVP

Type of measurement	Outcome	Reference
Tissue content or immunoreactive peptide	↑ in AVP immunoreactivity in anterior hypothalamus of defeated hamsters	Ferris *et al.* (1989); Delville *et al.* (1998)
	↓ AVPir in median eminence of subordinate rats; no change with defeat after colchicine treatment to block transport	de Goeij *et al.* (1992)
	↓ AVPir in median eminence after single defeat in colchicine-treated rats	de Goeij *et al.* (1992)
Extracellular levels	↓ AVP in PVN after social defeat in rats (measured with *in vivo* microdialysis)	Wotjak *et al.* (1996)
mRNA	No differences in AVP in PVN	Albeck *et al.* (1996)
	↓ AVP mRNA in medial amygdala of subordinate rats	
	↑ CRF mRNA in PVN of dominant and stress-responsive subordinate rats	Albeck *et al.* (1996)
	↓ CRF mRNA in PVN of non-stress-responsive subordinate rats	
	↑ CRF mRNA in central amygdala of all subordinate rats	
Receptor binding	↓ CRF receptor binding in anterior pituitary and hippocampus of subordinate tree shrews	Fuchs and Flügge (1995)
	↑ CRF receptor binding in cortex, amygdala, and choroid plexus in conjuction with decreased conjuction with decreased binding affinity	

a variety of animal models. Social subjugation either in adulthood or in puberty led to reduction in AVP stores in anterior hypothalamus of hamsters as determined by both fiber immunostaining and radioimmunoassay (RIA) of extracts from tissue micropunches, a result that suggests increased AVP release within this brain region, which is involved in aggressive behavior in this species (Ferris *et al.*, 1989; Delville *et al.*, 1998). Similarly, measurement of AVP in samples collected via *in vivo* microdialysis indicates that social defeat enhances release of this peptide in another area of the hypothalamus, the paraventricular nucleus (PVN), where it is believed to play a role in modulation of the HPA axis response (Wotjak *et al.*, 1996). Conversely, AVP immunostaining was increased in the zona externa of the median eminence (ZEME), a projection area of neurons originating in the PVN, in subordinate colony-housed male rats (de Goeij *et al.*, 1992). Inescapable interaction with the dominant after administration of the neuronal transport blocker, colchicine, did not alter the AVP immunoreactivity in ZEME in subordinate rats, however, suggesting that the encounter with the dominant did

not lead to AVP release in this area. In contrast, AVP content was reduced in colchicine-treated animals following a single defeat, thus indicating that AVP release and content are regulated differentially following acute and chronic social stress.

We used the VBS model to investigate the effects of chronic social stress on mRNA for AVP and CRF. Messenger RNA levels for AVP were unaffected by social stress in the PVN but were significantly decreased in the medial amygdala, whereas CRF mRNA was increased in the central amygdala (Albeck *et al.*, 1996). The changes in CRF mRNA in the PVN were a bit more complex. Mixed-sex housing in the VBS increased CRF mRNA content in PVN in both dominant and subordinate males compared to pair-housed controls, but only in those animals that retained relatively normal corticosterone responses to an acute stressor. In the stress-nonresponsive subordinates (described above), CRF mRNA content was significantly lower than in any other group, suggesting that the inability of these animals to mount a sufficient HPA axis response may be due to dysfunction at the level of the hypothalamic CRF neurons.

I. Mammalian Hormone-Behavior Systems

The receptors for CRF have been shown to be differentially regulated in the tree shrew model of social stress. After 24 days of psychosocial stress, subordinates show a down-regulation of CRF receptors in brain regions involved in HPA axis regulation, including the anterior pituitary, dentate gyrus, and CA1–CA3 of hippocampus; binding was also decreased in the superior colliculus (Fuchs and Flügge, 1995). Conversely, both the number of binding sites and the affinity of CRF receptors was increased in other areas of the brain, including the frontal and cingulate cortex, the claustrocortex, the central and lateral nucleus of amygdala, and the choroid plexus. However, in all regions except the claustrocortex and the central amygdala, this increase was partially offset by a decrease in binding affinity.

Overall, it appears that social stress activates the AVP and CRF neuropeptide circuits that are directly associated with activation and regulation of the HPA axis; an apparent increase in presynaptic activity is accompanied by a corresponding down-regulation of the postsynaptic elements, at least in the case of CRF. In contrast, evidence from both hamsters and rats indicates that subordination and defeat inhibit the extrahypothalamic AVP circuits involved in aggressive and sexual behavior. Finally, although CRF mRNA is up-regulated in extrahypothalamic areas, the net effect of social stress on CRF neurotransmission in these areas is less clear, since the number and affinity of the postsynaptic receptors are altered in a complex manner.

b) Other The regulation of other stress-related peptides has been investigated in our VBS model of chronic social stress. Galanin, a 29-amino acid neuropeptide, can be found in approximately 80% of the tyrosine-hydroxylase containing neurons in the locus coeruleus. Chronic social stress leads to an increase in mRNA levels of preprogalanin in the locus coeruleus of the subordinate animals (Holmes *et al.,* 1995). The levels of mRNA were positively correlated with the number of wounds per animal and negatively correlated with body weight gain, a result suggesting that the degree of galanin gene expression was associated by the severity of the stress. The increase in preprogalanin mRNA in the subordinate animals parallels that observed in tyrosine hydroxylase mRNA (see above), thereby indicating that the two mRNAs may be up-regulated in tandem as

a result of a stress-induced increase in the activity of locus coeruleus neurons.

In addition, mRNA levels of proopiomelanocortin (POMC), the precursor to ACTH and β-endorphin, were increased in the anterior pituitary of subordinate rats (Brady *et al.,* 1994). Again, the magnitude of the response correlated with wounding and weight loss, and also adrenal weight, thus suggesting that the POMC response reflected stressor severity.

B. Immediate Early Gene Expression

Expression of immediate early genes, such as *c-fos,* is often used as an identifier of neural circuits activated by a given stimulus. The effect of social defeat on *c-fos* expression has been studies in several different species. In mice, defeat has been shown to increase *c-fos*-like immunoreactivity in limbic and sensory relay areas such as cingulate cortex, lateral septum, bed nucleus of the stria terminalis (BNST), hippocampus, hypothalamus, amygdala, periaqueductal gray, dorsal raphe, locus coeruleus, and several brain stem sensory nuclei (Matsuda *et al.,* 1996; Nikulina *et al.,* 1998). After a single defeat, *c-fos* expression returned to baseline levels within 24 hours, but with chronic defeat, a more prolonged increase was observed (Matsuda *et al.,* 1996). In contrast, although similar circuits were activated in rats following single defeat, the *c-fos* response in these animals adapted with repeated defeat, so that *c-fos* expression was increased only in BNST, periventricular nucleus of hypothalamus (PVN), medial amygdala, and the medial and dorsal raphe nuclei (Martinez *et al.,* 1998). Similarly, in male Syrian hamsters, the *c-fos* response to repeated defeat habituated in the supraoptic nucleus, lateral septum, central amygdala and amygdalohippocampal area but remained high in the anterior and ventromedial hypothalamic nuclei, dorsal periaqueductal gray, and dorsal raphe (Kollack-Walker *et al.,* 1999). However, the response in PVN adapted with chronic defeat but remained significant in the locus coeruleus in hamsters, whereas the converse was true in rats. These variations may be related not only to differences among experimental protocols, but also to species-specific differences in the behavioral and cognitive response to social defeat.

C. Neuronal Structure and Survival

Several studies have indicated that chronic stress affects neurons in the hippocampal formation in a variety of ways, leading to alterations in dendritic morphology, cell survival, and neurogenesis. A recent examination of morphology of hippocampal neurons has found significant shrinkage of the apical dendritic arbors of CA3 pyramidal neurons is seen in all animals in the VBS (McKittrick *et al.*, 2000). There is a decrease in arbor complexity (branch points) in both dominants and subordinates, and dominants have a reduction in total dendritic length as well. The observation that these changes occur to a similar (or greater) extent in dominants as well as in the more severely stressed subordinates suggests that dendritic remodeling may be a common response to chronic activation of the HPA axis but does not vary significantly with the severity of the stress. This conclusion is supported by data showing similar degrees of dendritic atrophy in animals subjected either to the relatively mild stressor of repeated restraint or to a more severe, chronic variable-stress regimen (Magariños and McEwen, 1995; Magariños *et al.*, 1996).

A study of tree shrews has shown similar dendritic atrophy in subordinates compared to unstressed controls, although pyramidal cell morphology in dominant animals was not examined (Magariños *et al.*, 1996). In addition to dendritic atrophy, chronic social stress also led to a time-dependent increase in the staining intensity of the nucleoplasm of CA1 and CA3 pyramidal cells, indicating alterations in nuclear chromatin structure, but these changes were not accompanied by signs of neuronal degeneration or cell loss (Fuchs *et al.*, 1995; Vollmann-Honsdorf *et al.*, 1997). However, the number of bromodeoxyuridine-labeled cells was decreased within the dentate gyrus of subordinate tree shrews compared to controls, thus indicating that neurogenesis in this part of the hippocampus is inhibited by chronic social stress (Gould *et al.*, 1997).

Far more pronounced pathological changes were found in the hippocampus of vervet monkeys that died spontaneously at a primate center in Kenya. These animals exhibited signs of severe stress, such as gastric ulcers and enlarged adrenals, and several also showed evidence of social conflict, such as bite marks. When compared to animals euthanized for other reasons, the stressed monkeys showed evidence of neurodegeneration in Ammon's horn, especially CA3, including reduced perikarya size, dispersed Nissl bodies, increased vesicle number, and decreased dendritic width (Uno *et al.*, 1989). However, it must be noted these animals are presumed to have died from stress-related causes, which indicates a severity of stress much greater than that seen in most other social stress paradigms.

D. Summary

As described above, social stress leads to many changes in the brain, affecting neuronal structure and survival as well as neurochemical transmission. Overall, social stress, like other stressors, seems to induce a net stimulation of serotonergic and noradrenergic neurons, although the functional outcome of increased transmitter release is likely to be modulated by region- and time-specific in receptor populations. Few studies have been conducted to examine the effects of social stress on other classical transmitter systems, although social stress has been shown to modify various aspects of dopaminergic, GABAergic, and excitatory amino acid transmission. In neuropeptide systems, CRF and AVP pathways involved in the HPA axis response appear to be activated by social stress, whereas extrahypothalamic AVP and CRF are inhibited and stimulated, respectively. Chronic social stress can alter the morphology of hippocampal neurons, which may affect learning and memory processes in these animals. Finally, although the effects on hippocampal pyramidal cell survival are currently equivocal, chronic subordination has been shown to retard neurogenesis within the dentate gyrus. Together, these results indicate that social stress can have profound consequences on the brain; further study is needed to determine which of these changes are adaptive and which can lead to pathological changes in brain function and behavior.

VI. REPRODUCTIVE ASPECTS OF SOCIAL STRESS: HYPOTHALAMIC-PITUITARY-GONADAL AXIS

It is well established that stress suppresses reproductive function (Rose and Sachar, 1981; Selye, 1950; Bliss *et al.*, 1972). The concept of stress, however, embraces a large range of diverse phenomena, and further subdivision of terms is helpful for the sake of clarity. Stressors are the aversive conditions or stimuli that provoke responses in animals that, in total, are termed the stress response. The stress response was first called the general adaptation syndrome by its discoverer, Hans Selye (1946), in reference to physiological adjustments made to compensate for the stressor and preserve the internal milieu in the body. The adjustments, though adaptive in the short term, can have harmful effects in the chronic setting (Shanks *et al.*, 1998). The postulated adaptive value of the stress response traces its evolutionary origin to the "flight or fight" cascade of neuroendocrine events that ensue when an animal confronts a potential predator (Sapolsky, 1992b). In the threatened animal, the sequential rapid release of corticotropin-releasing hormone (CRH) from hypothalamic neurons and adrenocorticotropic hormone (ACTH) by the pituitary stimulates a massive outpouring of glucocorticoid from the adrenal gland, which serves to mobilize glucose in the blood for needed energy (Hers, 1986; Munck and Guyre, 1986). Simultaneously, heightened sympathetic nervous system activity and release of epinephrine and norepinephrine increase the heart rate, and secretion of endorphins blunts the sensation of pain should tissue injury be inflicted (Hedman *et al.*, 1990). It is thought that the stress response is survival related in the presence of a predator but harmful when it occurs inappropriately and is prolonged.

A. Stress from Crowding and Social Dominance

Evidence from studies of numerous animal species has shown that suppression of reproductive function is associated with the stress response. Here the adaptive significance may lie in the preservation of the species, with the stress response providing a physiological cue that external conditions are unfavorable for reproduction (Handelsman and Dong, 1992). Naturally occurring social stressors, the focus of this chapter, appear to fall broadly into two categories: crowding (e.g., in snowshoe hares; Boonstra and Singleton, 1993) and subordinate status in social dominance hierarchies (which will be termed *social stress*). In both cases, competition for food or access to a mate leads to

aggressive encounters between individuals that, when repeated and unpredictable, become an aversive stimulus or stressor. Stress-induced elevations in glucocorticoids have been implicated as the principal mediators of the inhibition in reproductive function, both directly through reductions in the gonadal responsiveness to gonadotrophins (Charpenet *et al.*, 1981; Orr and Mann, 1992) and indirectly through inhibition of the gonadotrophins themselves (Sapolsky, 1985; Norman and Smith, 1992; Akinbami *et al.*, 1994).

B. Stress and Reproductive Functioning

The association between social stress and glucocorticoid-mediated inhibition of reproductive function has been established for both sexes (Marchlewska-Koj, 1997) but is defined more clearly for males compared to females. This is attributable to the higher levels of testosterone in males relative to females, and the role of testosterone in promoting the aggressive behavior that leads to stressful attacks (Monaghan and Glickman, 1992). Female hyenas, which are unusually aggressive due to high levels of androgen production by the adrenal gland, are an exception to the rule (Jenks *et al.*, 1995). In females, there is abundant evidence that social interactions can play a role in suppressing reproductive function, including both reductions in sexual behavior and suppression of ovulation (Saltzman *et al.*, 1994). As noted under Section IV.A.1, alterations in ovulation and changes in HPA activity are both associated with social stratification in females of a number of primate species, but the relationships among these factors appear to be complex and to differ from one species to another.

In males, the ability to impose social stress on a subordinate is one mechanism of sexual selection. If the dominant male suppresses reproductive function in the subordinate males, his exclusive access to females ensures preferential perpetuation of the dominant's genes. Consistent with this hypothesis, crowding experiments have provided a dramatic demonstration of the consequences of social stress (reviewed by Bronson, 1989). At the start of such experiments one or two breeding pairs of mice are put into a large, physically complex cage and allowed to breed. Aggression between males increases as the population size, and its density, increase. Eventually, the population size within the cage self-regulates, at which point reproduction by all but a few adult animals, the dominants, stops entirely.

In populations where there is social stratification among individuals, low-ranking animals generally have lower reproductive fitness and engage in fewer sexual encounters than high-ranking individuals (Calhoun, 1962; von Holst, 1977; Sapolsky, 1982; Blanchard and Blanchard, 1990). The stressful nature of subordination is likely to play a role in the inhibition of male reproductive function in these situations. Subordinate males often have lower testosterone titers compared to dominants, particularly during establishment of social hierarchies (Rose *et al.*, 1971; Coe *et al.*, 1979; Mendoza *et al.*, 1979; von Holst *et al.*, 1983; Sachser and Pröve, 1986; Sachser and Lick, 1989; Dijkstra *et al.*, 1992). Defeat by a conspecific can lead to a rapid decline of plasma testosterone (Rose *et al.*, 1975; von Holst, 1977; Schuurman, 1980; Sachser and Lick, 1989, 1991), whereas social victories may lead to an increase in testosterone levels in dominants (Coe *et al.*, 1982; Bernstein *et al.*, 1983; Sachser and Pröve, 1986). In addition, subordinate animals also have a larger and more prolonged inhibition of testosterone and gonadotrophins following exposure to other, nonsocial stressors, while dominants may have a smaller decline or a transient rise in testosterone (Bronson, 1973; Sapolsky, 1986).

1. Androgen Levels in Dominant Males

Aggressiveness has been found to be positively correlated with testosterone levels in primates. However, increased aggression is not necessarily correlated with dominance in these populations (Sapolsky, 1982; Bernstein *et al.*, 1983). In rodents, castration decreases aggressive behaviors, an effect that can be reversed by testosterone replacement (Brain, 1983). Clamping testosterone levels by castration and steroid replacement has been shown to have no behavioral effect on competitive interactions and agonistic behavior. In primates, social defeat seems to play a role in perpetuating the difference in testosterone levels between dominant and subordinate animals, as the differences are most prominent during hierarchy formation but may disappear when the hierarchy has stabilized and aggressive encounters become less frequent (Rose *et al.*, 1971; Sapolsky, 1982; Coe *et al.*, 1982). In situations where there is continued fighting in social groups, how-

ever, the difference in testosterone between social ranks is maintained (Sachser and Pröve, 1986). Although the majority of agonistic encounters in the VBS occur within the first few days of colony formation, there is still a low, but significant, degree of fighting throughout the remainder of the housing period (D. C. Blanchard *et al.*, 1995).

2. Androgen Levels in Subordinate Males

In rats housed in the VBS, chronic social stress leads to declines in circulating levels of testosterone in subordinate males, as compared to dominants and control rats housed in standard rat cages with a female (D. C. Blanchard *et al.*, 1993). Similar reductions in testicular androgen production have been shown for other animal populations with hierarchical social structures (Mendoza *et al.*, 1979; Coe *et al.*, 1979; von Holst *et al.*, 1983; Sachser and Pröve, 1986). Repeated agonistic encounters may play a role in maintaining the low testosterone levels in the subordinate animals. In a wide variety of rodent models, laboratory stressors have been shown to lead to a rapid suppression of testosterone secretion (Gray *et al.*, 1978; Taché *et al.*, 1980; Charpenet *et al.*, 1981; Collu *et al.*, 1984b; Armario and Castellanos, 1984; Bidzinska *et al.*, 1993; Srivastava *et al.*, 1993). Similarly, stress leads to a decline in plasma testosterone levels in primates, including man (Aakvaag *et al.*, 1978; Coe *et al.*, 1978; Wheeler *et al.*, 1984; Sapolsky, 1985; Norman and Smith, 1992). In addition, stress may decrease androgen levels through glucocorticoid-independent mechanisms (Gray *et al.*, 1978; Taché *et al.*, 1980; Rivest and Rivier, 1991).

3. Endocrine Mechanisms of Social Stress in Males

Regulation of testosterone secretion in socially stressed animals is complex, as both stress and glucocorticoids have been shown to affect testosterone synthesis and secretion at several different levels. ACTH and CRH have been shown to inhibit testosterone secretion in animals and man (Schaison *et al.*, 1978; Vreeburg *et al.*, 1984; Rivier and Vale, 1985; Mann *et al.*, 1987), with a concomitant decrease in LH in some cases (Vreeburg *et al.*, 1984; Rivier and Vale, 1985). These effects can be blocked by adrenalectomy (Vreeburg *et al.*, 1984; Rivier and Vale, 1985; Mann *et al.*, 1987) or inhibition of cortisol synthesis with metyrapone (Schaison *et al.*, 1978), thus suggesting a primary role of glucocorticoids. In rats and humans, glucocorticoid administration leads to a reduction in testosterone levels (Doerr and Pirke, 1976; Schaison *et al.*, 1978; Mann *et al.*, 1987; Urban *et al.*, 1991); glucocorticoid receptors on the Leydig cells in the testis provide an possible anatomical substrate for this effect (Stalker *et al.*, 1989). Glucocorticoids act directly on the testes by inhibiting Leydig cell sensitivity to gonadotropins. Dexamethasone and corticosterone treatment reduces basal testosterone levels and decreases binding to testicular LH/human chorionic gonadotropin (hCG) receptors (Bambino and Hsueh, 1981; Mann *et al.*, 1987). The functional significance of the decrease in LH receptor is shown by the blunted androgenic response to hCG in glucocorticoid-treated animals and humans (Bambino and Hsueh, 1981; Mann *et al.*, 1987; Schaison *et al.*, 1978). Incubation with various natural and synthetic glucocorticoids leads to a similar decrease in steroidogenesis in cultured testicular cells, an effect that can be reversed by the Type II glucocorticoid receptor antagonist mefipristone (RU 486) (Bambino and Hsueh, 1981; Orr and Mann, 1992).

In contrast to exogenous glucocorticoids, the decrease in testosterone synthesis following stress does not appear to be mediated by alterations in LH/hCG receptor binding (Taché *et al.*, 1980; Orr and Mann, 1990). The responses of testes from stressed animals to gonadotropin stimulation is blunted, however, both *in vivo* (Charpenet *et al.*, 1981; Sapolsky, 1985) and *in vitro* (Charpenet *et al.*, 1981; Collu *et al.*, 1984a; Orr and Mann, 1990). Testosterone synthesis following incubation of Leydig cells with hCG, dibutyryl cAMP, or choleratoxin is decreased in stressed rats, despite comparable levels of cellular cAMP production; similarly, basal cAMP content in Leydig cells are comparable between stressed and unstressed rats (Charpenet *et al.*, 1981). This finding suggests that the stress-induced impairment in testicular sensitivity to gonadotropins occurs at a site distal to second messenger production, perhaps at the level of second messenger-effector coupling. Changes in coupling, in turn, may affect the synthetic capacity of the testes, since stress has been shown to decrease the activities (Vmax) of 17β-hydroxylase-17,20-lyase and 3β-hydroxysteroid dehydrogenase, which are all involved in testosterone steroidogenesis (Srivastava *et al.*, 1993; Akinbami *et al.*, 1994). Similar inhibition of androgen

synthetic enzyme activity has been induced by glucocorticoids *in vitro* (Welsh *et al.*, 1982; Hales and Payne, 1989; Agular *et al.*, 1992).

The inhibitory effects of glucocorticoids on testosterone synthesis may also be regulated by changes in the bioavailability of corticosterone to the testes. Testicular Leydig cells contain high concentrations of 11β-hydroxysteroid dehydrogenase (11βHSD), an enzyme that oxidatively inactivates corticosterone. It has been postulated that this enzyme serves to modulate the effects of corticosterone by regulating intracellular glucocorticoid concentrations (Monder *et al.*, 1994b). In the VBS, subordinate rats were shown to have lower testicular 11βHSD activity than dominants and controls (Monder *et al.*, 1994a). Thus, an additional mechanism by which chronic social stress may lead to decreased testosterone production is through a decrease in the protective effects of 11βHSD within the testes, leading to elevated intracellular levels of corticosterone. The glucocorticoid-independent mechanisms of stress-induced testosterone suppression are not clear but may involve endogenous opiates or nitric oxide or both (Kostic *et al.*, 1998, 1999).

Although stress has been shown to decrease LH secretion in some instances (Bronson, 1973; Gray *et al.*, 1978; Taché *et al.*, 1980; Sapolsky, 1985; Rivier *et al.*, 1986; López-Calderón *et al.*, 1991; Rivest and Rivier, 1991; Norman and Smith, 1992), a decrease in testosterone is not always accompanied by a concomitant decrease in plasma LH (Puri *et al.*, 1981; Charpenet *et al.*, 1981; Mann and Orr, 1990; Akinbami *et al.*, 1994; Orr and Mann, 1992). Decreases in LH, when observed, appear to be a result of decreased hypothalamic GnRH stimulation (Coe *et al.*, 1982; Bidzinska *et al.*, 1993) and increased opioid-mediated inhibition of central LH release (Sapolsky and Krey, 1988; Bidzinska *et al.*, 1993; Akinbami *et al.*, 1994). The inhibitory effects of the opioid system appear to be mediated primarily through μ- and κ-receptor subtypes (Sapolsky and Krey, 1988). Stress-induced testosterone suppression can also be blocked by peripheral opioid receptor antagonism.

The exact mechanism of testosterone suppression in the VBS animals is not known. Further studies will be necessary to elucidate the temporal progression of the changes in testosterone and the testicular synthetic capacity and responsiveness to gonadotropin. It is likely that the stress-related changes in testosterone secretion involve a combination of the central and peripheral effects of stress and glucocorticoids described above, including central inhibition of GnRH and LH, decreased testicular responsiveness to LH, and decreased testicular degradation of corticosterone.

VII. GENERAL SUMMARY

Social stress effects are currently evaluated in a variety of laboratory models. These may differ considerably in the intensity of the stress produced and in the degree to which they afford dominant and subordinate or victorious and defeated animals that can legitimately be compared with each other, as well as with controls. Although HPA axis activity is strongly associated with social as with other stressors, it does not always differentiate dominant from subordinate animals. Moreover, some social stressors appear to produce effects in addition to those that are mediated by HPA axis activity.

In general, there is good agreement between findings with respect to behavioral, neurochemical, and hormonal sequellae of social stress in animal models, as compared to the range of behavioral and medical conditions involving similar changes in highly stressed people. This provides some degree of validation for social stress paradigms and strengthens the need for finer analysis of social stress effects and mechanisms in animal models. Nonetheless, it is not clear that laboratory animal models of social stress, necessarily providing only a restricted range of behavioral options and opportunities for both winners and losers, afford the same range of stress response and stress reduction mechanisms that may appear in the same species under more natural conditions (Sachser *et al.,* 1998). This emphasizes the value of attempts to incorporate enhanced social and environmental complexity into laboratory models, suggesting that these may provide a more complete range of behavioral and physiological stress effects, including both destructive and ameliorative mechanisms. More generally, however, the complex interplay of behavioral and physiological mechanisms in social stress suggests that research using only nonsocial stressors is unlikely to illuminate many of the stress mechanisms operative in human populations.

Acknowledgments

The authors acknowledge the participation of Randall Sakai and Bruce McEwen in the Visible Burrow System work reported here. This work was supported by NSF IBN 28543.

References

Aakvaag, A., Sand, R., and Opstad, P. K. (1978). Hormonal changes in serum in young men during prolonged physical strain. *Eur. J. Appl. Physiol.* **39,** 283–291.

Adams, N., Lins, M. D., and Blizard, D. A. (1987). Contrasting effects of social stress and foot-shock on acute cardiovascular response in salt-sensitive rats. *Behav. Neural Biol.* **48**(3), 368–381.

Ader, R., Felten, D. L., and Cohen, N., eds. (1999). "Psychoneuroimmunology," 3rd ed. Academic Press, New York.

Agular, B. M., Vinggaard, A. M., and Vind, C. (1992). Regulation by dexamethasone of the 3-hydroxysteroid dehydrogenase activity in adult rat Leydig cells. *J. Steroid Biochem. Mol. Biol.* **43,** 565–571.

Akinbami, M. A., Taylor, M. F., Collins, D. C., and Mann, D. R. (1994). Effect of a peripheral and a central acting opioid antagonist on the testicular response to stress in rats. *Neuroendocrinology* **59,** 343–348.

Albeck, D. S., McKittrick, C. R., Blanchard, D. C., Blanchard, R. J., Nikulina, J., McEwen, B. S., and Sakai, R. R. (1996). Chronic social stress alters expression of corticotropin-releasing factor and arginine-vasopressin mRNAs in rat brain. *J. Neurosci.* **17,** 4895–4903.

Armario, A., and Castellanos, J. M. (1984). A comparison of corticoadrenal and gonadal responses to acute immobilization stress in rats and mice. *Physiol. Behav.* **32,** 517–519.

Avgustinovich, D. F., Gorbach, O. V., and Kudryavtseva, N. N. (1997). Comparative analysis of anxiety-like behavior in partition and plus-maze tests after agonistic interactions in mice. *Physiol. Behav.* **61**(1), 37–43.

Bambino, T. H., and Hsueh, A. J. W. (1981). Direct inhibitory effect of glucocorticoids upon testicular luteinizing hormone receptor and steroidogenesis *in vivo* and *in vitro. Endocrinology (Baltimore)* **108,** 2142–2148.

Barnett, S. A. (1963). "The Rat: A Study in Behavior." Aldine, Chicago.

Barrett, J., Abbott, D. H., and George, L. M. (1990). Extension of reproductive suppression by pheromonal cue in subordinate female marmoset monkeys, *Callithrix jacchus. Reprod. Fertil.* **90**(2): 411–418.

Benjamin, D., Knapp, D. J., and Pohorecky, L. A. (1993). Ethanol prevents desensitization of 5-HT$_2$ receptor-mediated responses consequent to defeat in territorial aggression. *J. Stud. Alcohol., Suppl.* **11,** 180–184.

Bennett, N. C., Faulkes, C. G., and Molteno, A. J. (1996). Reproductive suppression in subordinate, non-breeding female Damaraland mole-rats: Two components to a lifetime of socially induced infertility. *Proc. R. Soc. London, B Ser.* **263**, 1599–1603.

Bernstein, I. S., Gordon, T. P., and Rose, R. M. (1983). The interaction of hormones, behavior, and social context in nonhuman primates. *In* "Hormones and Aggressive Behavior" (B. B. Svare, ed.), pp. 535–561. Plenum Press, New York.

Berton, O., Aguerre, S., Sarrieau, A., Mormede, P., and Chaouloff, F. (1998). Differential effects of social stress on central serotonergic activity and emotional reactivity in Lewis and spontaneously hypertensive rats. *Neuroscience* **82**, 147–159.

Berton, O., Durand, M., Aguerre, S., Mormede, P., and Chaouloff, F. (1999). Behavioral, neuroendocrine and serotonergic consequences of single social defeat and repeated fluoxetine pretreatment in the Lewis rat stain. *Neuroscience* **92**, 327–341.

Bidzinska, B., Petraglia, F., Angioni, S., Genazzani, A. D., Criscuolo, M., Ficarra, G., Trentini, G. P., and Genazzani, A. R. (1993). Effect of different chronic intermittent stressors and acetyl-*l*-carnitine on hypothalamic β-endorphin and GnRH and on plasma testosterone levels in male rats. *Neuroendocrinology* **57**, 985–990.

Blanchard, D. C., and Blanchard, R. J. (1990). Behavioral correlates of chronic dominance-subordination relationships of male rats in a seminatural situation. *Neurosci. Biobehav. Rev.* **14**, 455–462.

Blanchard, D. C., Blanchard, R. J., and Rodgers, R. J. (1991a). Risk assessment and animal models of anxiety. *In* "Animal Models in Psychopharmacology" (B. Olivier, J. Mos, and J. L. Slangen, eds.), pp. 117–134. Birkhauser, Basel.

Blanchard, D. C., Cholvanich, P., Blanchard, R. J., Clow, D. W., Hammer, R. P., Jr, Rowlett, J. K., and Bardo, M. T. (1991b). Serotonin, but not dopamine, metabolites are increased in selected brain regions of subordinate male rats in a colony environment. *Brain Res.* **568**, 61–66.

Blanchard, D. C., Sakai, R. R., McEwen, B. S., Weiss, S. M., and Blanchard, R. J. (1993). Subordination stress: Behavioral, brain and neuroendocrine correlates. *Behav. Brain Res.* **58**, 113–121.

Blanchard, D. C., Spencer, R., Weiss, S. M., Blanchard, R. J., McEwen, B. S., and Sakai, R. R. (1995). The visible burrow system as a model of chronic social stress: Behavioral and neuroendocrine correlates. *Psychoendocrinology* **20**, 117–134.

Blanchard, D. C., Hebert, M. A., Yudko, E., Sakai, R. R., McKittrick, C., McEwen, B. S., and Blanchard, R. J. (1998). Disruption of HPA axis function in subordinate, socially stressed, rats not attributable to changes in food intake. *Soc. Neurosci. Abstr.* **2**, 1378.

Blanchard, R. J., and Blanchard, D. C. (1977). Aggressive behavior in the rat. *Behav. Biol.* **21**, 197–224.

Blanchard, R. J., and Blanchard, D. C. (1989). Anti-predator defensive behaviors in a visible burrow system. *J. Comp. Psychol.* **103**, 70–82.

Blanchard, R. J., Hori, K., Tom, P., and Blanchard, D. C. (1987). Social structure and ethanol consumption in the laboratory rat. *Pharmacol., Biochem. Behav.* **28**(4), 437–442.

Blanchard, R. J., Flores, T., Magee, L., Weiss, S., and Blanchard, D. C. (1992). Pregrouping aggression and defense scores influence alcohol consumption for dominant and subordinate rats in visible burrow systems. *Aggressive Behav.* **18**, 459–467.

Blanchard, R. J., Yudko, E., Dulloog, L., and Blanchard, D. C. (2001a). Defense changes in stress-nonresponsive subordinate males in a visible burrow system. *Physiol. Behav.* **72**, 635–642.

Blanchard, R. J., Dulloog, L., Markham, C., Nishimura, O., Compton, J. N., Jun, A., Han, C., and Blanchard, D. C. (2001b). Sexual and aggressive interactions in a visible burrow system with provisioned burrows. *Physiol. Behav.* **72**, 245–254.

Bliss, E. L., Frishat, A., and Samuels, L. (1972). Brain and testicular function. *Life Sci.* **11**, 231–238.

Boonstra, R., and Singleton, G. R. (1993). Population declines in the snowshoe hare and the role of stress. *Gen. Comp. Physiol.* **91**, 126–143.

Botchin, M. B., Kaplan, J. R., Manuck, S. B., and Mann, J. J. (1994). Neuroendocrine responses to fenfluramine challenge are influenced by exposure to chronic social stress in adult male cynomolgus macaques. *Psychoneuroendocrinology* **19**, 1–11.

Brady, L. S., Blanchard, R. J., and Blanchard, D. C. (1994). Chronic social stress increases mRNA expression of tyrosine hydroxylase in the locus coeruleus and pro-opiomelanocortin in the anterior pituitary in rats. *Soc. Neurosci. Abstr.* **20**(Pt. I), 646.

Brain, P. F. (1983). Pituitary-gonadal influences on social aggression. *In* "Hormones and Aggressive Behavior" (B. B. Svare, ed.), pp. 3–25. Plenum Press, New York.

Bright, G. M. (1995). Corticosteroid-binding globulin influences kinetic parameters of plasma cortisol transport and clearance. *J. Clin. Endocrinol. Metab.* **80**, 770–775.

Bronson, F. H. (1973). Establishment of social rank among grouped male mice: Relative effects on circulating FSH, LH, and corticosterone. *Physiol. Behav.* **10**, 947–951.

Bronson, F. H. (1989). "Mammalian Reproductive Biology." University of Chicago Press, Chicago.

Brown, K. J., and Grunberg, N. E. (1995). Effects of housing on male and female rats: Crowding stresses male but calm females. *Physiol. Behav.* **58**(6), 1085–1089.

Bugajski, J., Gadek-Michalska, A., and Borycz, J. (1993). Social crowding stress diminishes the pituitary-adrenocortical and hypothalamic histamine response to adrenergic stimulation. *J. Physiol. Pharmacol.* **44**, 447–456.

Buwalda, B., de Boer, S. F., Schmidt, E. D., Felszeghy, K., Nyakas, C., Sgoifo, A., Van der Vegt, B. J., Tilders, F. J., Bohus, B., and Koolhaas, J. M. (1999). Long-lasting deficient dexamethasone suppression of hypothalamic-pituitary-adrenocortical activation following peripheral CRF challenge in socially defeated rats. *J. Neuroendocrinol.* **11**, 513–520.

Calhoun, J. B. (1962). "The Ecology and Sociology of the Norway Rat," U.S. Department of Health, Education, and Welfare, Bethesda, MD.

Capitanio, J. P., Mendoza, S. P., Lerche, N. W., and Mason, W. A. (1998). Social stress results in altered glucocorticoid regulation and shorter survival in simian acquired immune deficiency syndrome. *Proc. Natl. Acad. Sci. U.S.A.* **95**, 4714–4719.

Chao, H. M., Blanchard, D. C., Blanchard, R. J., McEwen, B. S., and Sakai, R. R. (1993). The effect of social stress on hippocampal gene expression. *Mol. Cell. Neurosci.* **4**, 543–548.

Charpenet, G., Taché, Y., Forest, M. G., Haour, F., Saez, J. M., Bernier, M., Ducharme, J. R., and Collu, R. (1981). Effects of chronic intermittent immobilization stress on rat testicular androgenic function. *Endocrinology (Baltimore)* **109**, 1254–1258.

Chung, K. K., Martinez, M., and Herbert, J. (1999). Central serotonin depletion modulates the behavioural, endocrine and physiological responses to repeated social stress and subsequent c-fos expression in the brains of male rats. *Neuroscience* **92**(2), 613–625.

Coe, C. L., Mendoza, S. P., Davidson, J. M., Smith, E. R., Dallman, M. F., and Levine, S. (1978). Hormonal response to stress in the squirrel monkey (*Saimiri sciureus*). *Neuroendocrinology* **26**, 367–377.

Coe, C. L., Mendoza, S. P., and Levine, S. (1979). Social status constrains the stress response in the squirrel monkey. *Physiol. Behav.* **23**, 633–638.

Coe, C. L., Franklin, D., Smith, E. R., and Levine, S. (1982). Hormonal responses accompanying fear and agitation in the squirrel monkey. *Physiol. Behav.* **29**, 1051–1057.

Collu, R., Gibb, W., Bichet, D. G., and Ducharme, J. R. (1984a). Role of arginine-vasopressin (AVP) in stress-induced inhibition of testicular steroidogenesis in normal and in AVP-deficient rats. *Endocrinology (Baltimore)* **115**, 1609–1615.

Collu, R., Gibb, W., and Ducharme, J. R. (1984b). Effects of stress on the gonadal function. *J. Endocrinol. Invest.* **7**, 529–537.

Creel, S., Creel, N. M., and Monfort, S. L. (1996). Social stress and dominance. *Nature (London)* **379**, 212.

D'Amato, F. R. (1988). Effects of male social status on reproductive success and on behavior in mice (*Mus musculus*). *J. Comp. Psychol.* **102**(2), 146–151.

de Goeij, D. C. E., Dijkstra, H., and Tilders, F. J. H. (1992). Chronic psychosocial stress enhances vasopressin, but not corticotropin-releasing factor, in the external zone of the median eminence of male rats: Relationship to subordinate status. *Endocrinology (Baltimore)* **131**, 847–853.

Delville, Y., Melloni, R. H., Jr., and Ferris, C. F. (1998). Behavioral and neurobiological consequences of social subjugation during puberty in golden hamsters. *J. Neurosci.* **18**, 2667–2672.

de Ridder, D. (2000). Social status and stress. *In* "Encyclopedia of Stress." (G. Fink, ed.), Vol. 3, pp. 468–473. Academic Press, San Diego, CA.

Dewsbury, D. A. (1988). Kinship, familiarity, aggression, and dominance in deer mice (*Peromyscus maniculatus*) in seminatural enclosure. *J. Comp. Psychol.* **102**(2), 124–128.

Dijkstra, H., Tilders, F. J. H., Hiehle, M. A., and Smelik, P. G. (1992). Hormonal reactions to fighting in rat colonies: Prolactin rises during defence, not during offence. *Physiol. Behav.* **51**, 961–968.

Doerr, P., and Pirke, K. M. (1976). Cortisol-induced suppression of plasma testosterone in normal adult males. *J. Clin. Endocrinol. Metab.* **43**, 622–629.

Dohrenwend, B. S. (1973). Social status and stressful life events, *H. Pers. Soc. Psychol.* **28**(2), 225–235.

Drea, C. M., and Wallen, K. (1999). Low-status monkeys "play dumb" when learning in mixed social groups. *Proc. Natl. Acad. Sci. U.S.A.* **96**(22), 12965–12969.

Ebbesen, P., Villadsen, J. A., Villadsen, H. D., and Heller, K. E. (1991). Effect of subordinance, lack of social hierarchy, and restricted feeding on murine survival and virus leukemia. *Exp. Gerontol.* **26**(5), 479–486.

Ely, D. L., and Henry, J. P. (1978). Neuroendocrine response patterns in dominant and subordinate mice. *Horm. Behav.* **10**, 156–169.

Ely, D., Caplea, A., Dunphy, G., and Smith, D. (1997). Physiological and neuroendocrine correlates of social position in normotensive and hypertensive rat colonies. *Acta Physiol. Scand., Suppl.* **640**, 92–95.

Faulkes, C. G., Abbott, D. H., and Jarvis, J. U. (1990). Social suppression of ovarian cyclicity in captive and wild colonies of naked mole-rats, *Heterocephalus glaber. J. Reprod. Fertil.* **88**(2), 559–568.

Ferrari, P. F., Palanza, P., Parmigiani, S., and Rodgers, R. J. (1998). Interindividual variability in Swiss male mice: Relationship between social factors, aggression, and anxiety. *Physiol. Behav.* **63**(5), 821–827.

Ferris, C. R., Axelson, J. F., Martin, A. M., and Roberge, L. F. (1989). Vasopressin immunoreactivity in the anterior hypothalamus is altered during the establishment of dominant/subordinate relationships between hamsters. *Neuroscience* **29**(3), 675–683.

Flügge, G. (1995). Dynamics of central nervous 5-HT$_{1A}$-receptors under psychosocial stress. *J. Neurosci.* **15**, 7132–7140.

Flügge, G. (1996). Alterations in the central nervous alpha 2-adrenoceptor system under chronic psychosocial stress. *Neuroscience* **75**, 187–196.

Flügge, G., Johren, O., and Fuchs, E. (1992). [^{3}H]Rauwolscine binding sites in the brains of male tree shrews are related to social status. *Brain Res.* **597**, 131–137.

Flügge, G., Ahrens, O., and Fuchs, E. (1997). Beta-adrenoceptors in the tree shrew brain. II. Time-dependent effects of chronic psychosocial stress on [125I]iodocyanopindolol bindings sites. *Cell. Mol. Neurobiol.* **17**, 417–432.

Flügge, G., Kramer, M., Rensing, S., and Fuchs, E. (1998). 5-HT$_{1A}$-receptors and behavior under chronic stress: Selective counteraction by testosterone. *Eur. J. Neurosci.* **10**(8), 2685–2693.

Fontenot, M. B., Kaplan, J. R., Manuck, S. B., Arango, V., and Mann, J. J. (1995). Long-term effects of chronic social stress on serotonergic indices in the prefrontal cortex of adult male cynomolgus macaques. *Brain Res.* **705**, 105–108.

Fuchs, E., and Flügge, G. (1995). Modulation of binding sites for corticotropin-releasing hormone by chronic psychosocial stress. *Psychoneuroendocrinology* **20**, 33–51.

Fuchs, E., Uno, H., and Flügge, G. (1995). Chronic psychosocial stress induces morphological alterations in hippocampal pyramidal neurons of the tree shrew. *Brain Res.* **673**, 275–282.

Fuchs, E., Kramer, M., Hermes, B., Netter, P., and Hiemke, C. (1996). Psychosocial stress in tree shrews: Clomipramine counteracts behavioral and endocrine changes. *Pharmacol., Biochem. Behav.* **54**(1), 219–228.

Gagneux, P., Boesch, C., and Woodruff, D. S. (1999). Female reproductive strategies, paternity and community structure in wild West African chimpanzees. *Anim. Behav.* **57**(1), 19–32.

Garbe, C. M., and Kemble, E. D. (1994). Effects of prior agonistic experience on risk assessment and approach behavior evoked by familiar or unfamiliar conspecific odors. *Aggressive Behav.* **20**(2), 143–149.

Gould, E., McEwen, B. S., Tanapat, P., Galea, L. A., and Fuchs, E. (1997). Neurogenesis in the dentate gyrus of the adult tree shrew is regulated by psychosocial stress and NMDA receptor activation. *J. Neurosci.* **17**, 2492–2498.

Grant, E. C. (1963). An analysis of the social behavior of the male laboratory rat. *Behaviour* **21**, 260–281.

Grant, E. C., and Chance, M. R. A. (1958). Rank order in caged rats. *Anim. Behav.* **6**, 183–194.

Grant, E. C., and MacKintosh, J. H. (1963). A comparison of the social postures of some common laboratory rodents. *Behaviour* **21**, 246–259.

Gray, G. D., Smith, E. R., Damassa, D. A., Ehrnekranz, J. R. L., and Davidson, J. M. (1978). Neuroendocrine mechanisms mediating the suppression of circulating testosterone levels associated with chronic stress in male rats. *Neuroendocrinology* **25**, 247–256.

Grimm, V. E. (1980). The role of submissiveness in isolation induced intermale fighting in mice. *Int. J. Neurosci.* **11**(2), 115–120.

Gudermuth, D. F., Butler, W. R., and Johnston, R. E. (1992). Social influences on reproductive development and fertility in female Djungarian hamsters (*Phodopus campbelli*). *Horm. Behav.* **26**(3), 308–329.

Haemisch, A. (1990). Coping with social conflict, and short-term changes of plasma cortisol titers in familiar and unfamiliar environments. *Physiol. Behav.* **47**, 1265–1270.

Hales, D. B., and Payne, A. H. (1989). Glucocorticoid-mediated repression of P450$_{scc}$ mRNA and *de novo* synthesis in cultured Leydig cells. *Endocrinology (Baltimore)* **124**, 2099–2104.

Haller, J., and Halasz, J. (1999). Mild social stress abolishes the effects of isolation on anxiety and chlordiazepoxide reactivity. *Psychopharmacology (Berlin)*, **144**(4), 311–315.

Haller, J., and Halasz, J. (2000). Anxiolytic effects of repeated victory in male Wistar rats. *Aggressive Behav.* **26**(3), 257–261.

Haller, J., Kiem, D. T., and Makara, G. B. (1996). The physiology of social conflict in rats: What is particularly stressful? *Behav. Neurosci.* **110**, 353–359.

Haller, J., Fuchs, E., Halasz, J., and Makara, G. B. (1999). Defeat is a major stressor in males while social instability is stressful mainly in females: Towards the development of a social stress model in female rats. *Brain Res. Bull.* **50**(1), 33–39.

Handelsman, D. J., and Dong, Q. (1992). Ontogenic regression: A model of stress and reproduction. *In* "Stress and Reproduction" (K. E. Sheppard, J. H. Boublik, and J. W. Funder, eds.), pp. 333–346. Raven Press, New York.

Haney, M., Maccari, S., Le Moal, M., Simon, H., and Piazza, P. V. (1995). Social stress increases the acquisition of cocaine self-administration in male and female rats. *Brain Res.* **98**(1–2), 46–52.

Hedman, A., Hjemdahl, P., Nordlander, R., and Astrom, H. (1990). Effects of mental and physical stress on central haemodynamics and cardiac sympathetic nerve activity during QT interval-sensing rate-responsive and fixed rate ventricular inhibited pacing. *Eur. Heart J.* **11**, 903–915.

Heinrichs, S. C., Pich, E. M., Miczek, K. A., Britton, K. T., and Koob, G. F. (1992). Corticotropin-releasing factor antagonist reduces emotionality in socially defeated rats via direct neurotropic action. *Brain Res.* **581**(2), 190–197.

Heinrichs, S. C., Menzaghi, F., Pich, E. M., Baldwin, H. A., Rassnick, S., Britton, K. T., and Koob, G. F. (1994). Anti-stress action of a Corticotropin-Releasing Factor antagonist on behavioral reactivity to stressors of varying type and intensity. *Neuropsychopharmacology* **11**(3), 179–186.

Hemingway, H., and Marmot, M. (1998). Psychosocial factors in the primary and secondary prevention of coronary heart disease: A systematic review. *In* "Evidence Based Cardiology" (S. Yusuf, J. A. Cairns, A. J. Camm, E. L. Fallen, and B. J. Gersh, eds.), pp. 269–285. BMJ Books, London.

Hers, H. G. (1986). Effects of glucocorticoids on carbohydrate metabolism. *Agents Actions* **17**, 248–254.

Higley, J. D., Hasert, M., Suomi, S., and Linnoila, M. (1991). Nonhuman primate model of alcohol abuse: Effects of early experience, personality, and stress on alcohol consumption. *Proc. Natl. Acad. Sci. U.S.A.* **88**(16), 7261–7265.

Higley, J. D., Hasert, M., Suomi, S., and Linnoila, M. (1998). The serotonin uptake inhibitor sertraline reduces excessive alcohol consumption in nonhuman primates: Effect of stress. *Neuropsychopharmacology* **18**(6), 431–443.

Hilakivi, L. A., Lister, R. G., Durcan, M. J., Ota, M., Eskay, R. L., Mefford, I., and Linnoila, M. (1989). Behavioral, hormonal and neurochemical characteristics of aggressive a-mice. *Brain Res.* **502**, 158–166.

Hilakivi-Clarke, L., and Lister, R. G. (1992). Social status and voluntary alcohol consumption in mice: Interaction with stress. *Psychopharmacology (Berlin)* **108**(3), 276–282.

Holmes, P. V., Blanchard, D. C., Blanchard, R. J., Brady, L. S., and Crawley, J. N. (1995). Chronic social stress increases levels of preprogalanin mRNA in the rat locus coeruleus. *Pharmacol., Biochem. Behav.* **50**, 655–660.

Huhman, K. L., Moore, T. O., Ferris, C. F., Mougey, E. H., and Meyerhoff, J. L. (1991). Acute and repeated exposure to social conflict in male Golden hamsters: Increases in plasma POMC-peptides and cortisol and decreases in plasma testosterone. *Horm. Behav.* **25**, 206–216.

Huhman, K. L., Moore, T. O., Moughey, E. H., and Meyerhoff, J. L. (1992). Hormonal responses to fighting in hamsters: Separation of physical and psychological causes. *Physiol. Behav.* **51**, 1083–1086.

Jenks, S., Weldele, M., Frank, L., and Glickman, S. (1995). Acquisition of matrilineal rank in captive spotted hyenas: Emergence of a natural social system in peer-reared animals and their offspring. *Anim. Behav.* **50**, 893–904.

Johnson, E. O., Kamilaris, T. C., Carter, C. S., Calogero, A. E., Gold, P. W., and Chrousos, G. P. (1996). The biobehavioral consequences of psychogenic stress in a small, social primate *(Callithrix jacchus jacchus)*. *Biol. Psychiatry* **40**, 317–337.

Johren, O., Flügge, G., and Fuchs, E. (1994). Regulation of hippocampal glucocorticoid receptor gene expression by psychosocial conflict. *Ann. N. Y. Acad. Sci.* **746**, 429–430.

Kang, I., Thompson, M. L., Heller, J., and Miller, L. G. (1991). Persistent elevation in GABA$_A$ receptor subunit mRNAs following social stress. *Brain Res. Bull.* **26**, 809–812.

Keeney, A. J., and Hogg, S. (1999). Behavioral consequences of repeated social defeat in the mouse: Preliminary evaluation of a potential animal model of depression. *Behav. Pharmacol.* **10**(8), 753–764.

Kessler, R. C. (1997). The effects of stressful life events on depression. *Annu. Rev. Psychol.* **48**, 191–214.

Klein, F., Lemaire, V., Sandi, C., Vitiello, S., Van der Logt, J., Laurent, P. E., Neveu, P., Le Moal, M., and Mormede, P. (1992). Prolonged increase of corticosterone secretion by chronic social stress does not necessarily impair immune functions. *Life Sci.* **50**, 723–731.

Kollack-Walker, S., Don, C., Watson, S. J., and Akil, H. (1999). Differential expression of c-fos mRNA within neurocircuits of male hamsters exposed to acute or chronic defeat. *J. Neuroendocrinol.* **11**, 547–559.

Koolhaas, J. M., Schuurman, T., and Fokkema, D. S. (1983). Social behavior of rats as a model for the psychophysiology of hypertension. *In* "Biobehavioral Bases of Coronary Heart Disease" (T. H. Schmidt, T. M. Dembroski, and G. Blümchen, eds.), pp. 391–400. Karger, Basel.

Korte, S. M., Buwalda, B., Meijer, O., de Kloet, E. R., and Bohus, B. (1995). Socially defeated male rats display a blunted adrenocortical response to a low dose of 8-OH-DPAT. *Eur. J. Pharmacol.* **272**, 45–50.

Kostic, T. S., Andric, S. A., Maric, D., and Kovacevic, R. (1998). The effect of acute stress and opioid antagonist on the activity of NADPH-P450 reductase in rat Leydig cells. *J. Steroid Biochem. Mol. Biol.* **66**, 51–54.

Kostic, T. S., Andric, S. A., Maric, D., Stojilkovic, S. S., and Kovacevic, R. (1999). Involvement of inducible nitric oxide synthase in stress-impaired testicular steroidogenesis. *J. Endocrinol.* **163**, 409–416.

Kramer, M., Hiemke, C., and Fuchs, E. (1999). Chronic psychosocial stress and antidepressant treatment in tree shrews: Time-dependent behavioral and endocrine effects. *Neurosci. Biobehav. Rev.* **23**(7), 937–947.

Krugers, H. J., Koolhaas, J. M., Bohus, B., and Korf, J. (1993). A single social stress-experience alters glutamate receptor-binding in rat hippocampal CA3 area. *Neurosci. Lett.* **154**, 73–77.

Krugers, H. J., Douma, B. R., Andringa, G., Bohus, B., Korf, J., and Luiten, P. G. (1997). Exposure to chronic psychosocial stress and corticosterone in the rat: Effects on spatial discrimination learning and hippocampal protein kinase Cgamma immunoreactivity. *Hippocampus* **7**(4), 427–436.

Kruuk, H. (1972). "The Spotted Hyena: A Study of Predation and Social Behavior." University of Chicago Press, Chicago.

Kudryavtseva, N. N., Bakshtanovskaya, I. V., and Koryakina, L. A. (1991a). Social model of depression in mice of C57BL/6J strain. *Pharmacol., Biochem. Behav.* **38**(2), 315–320.

Kudryavtseva, N. N., Madorskaya, I. A., and Bakshtanovskaya, I. V. (1991b). Social success and voluntary ethanol consumption in mice of C57BL/6J and CBA/Lac strains. *Physiol. Behav.* **50**(1), 143–146.

Kulling, P., Frischknecht, H. R., Pasi, A., Waser, P. G., and Siegfried, B. (1987). Effects of repeated as compared to single aggressive confrontation on nociception and defense behavior in C57BL/6 and DBA/2 mice. *Physiol. Behav.* **39**(5), 599–605.

Kureta, Y., and Watanabe, S. (1996). Influence of social dominance of self-stimulation behavior in male golden hamsters. *Physiol. Behav.* **59**(4–5), 621–624.

Lemaire, V., Deminiere, J. M., and Mormede, P. (1994). Chronic social stress conditions differentially modify vulnerability to amphetamine self-administration. *Brain Res.* **649**(1–2), 348–352.

López-Calderón, A., Ariznavarreta, C., González-Quijano, M. I., Tresguerres, J. A. F., and Calderón, M. D. (1991). Stress induced changes in testis function. *J. Steroid Biochem. Mol. Biol.* **40**, 473–479.

Lorenz, K. (1966). "On Aggression." MJF Books, New York.

Louch, C. D., and Higginbotham, M. (1967). The relation between social rank and plasma corticosterone levels in mice. *Gen. Comp. Endocrinol.* **8**, 441–444.

Maccari, S., Piazza, P. V., Deminiere, J. M., Lemaire, V., Mormede, P., Simon, H., Angelucci, L., and Le Moal, M. (1991). Life events-induced decrease of corticosteroid type I receptors is associated with reduced corticosterone feedback and enhanced vulnerability to amphetamine self-administration. *Brain Res.* **547**, 7–12.

Magariños, A. M., and McEwen, B. S. (1995). Stress-induced atrophy of apical dendrites of hippocampal CA3c neurons: Comparison of stressors. *Neuroscience* **69**, 83–88.

Magariños, A. M., McEwen, B. S., Flügge, G., and Fuchs, E. (1996). Chronic psychosocial stress causes apical dendritic atrophy of hippocampal CA3 pyramidal neurons in subordinate tree shrews. *J. Neurosci.* **16**, 3534–3540.

Mallick, J., Stoddart, D. M., Jones, I., and Bradley, A. J. (1994). Behavioral and endocrinological correlates of social status in the male sugar glider (*Petaurus breviceps* Marsupialia: Petauridae). *Physiol. Behav.* **55**(6), 1131–1134.

Mann, D. R., and Orr, T. E. (1990). Effects of restraint stress on gonadal proopiomelanocortin peptides and the pituitary-testicular axis in rats. *Life Sci.* **46**, 1601–1609.

Mann, D. R., Free, C., Nelson, C., Scott, C., and Collins, D. C. (1987). Mutually independent effects of adrenocorticotropin on luteinizing hormone and testosterone secretion. *Endocrinology (Baltimore)* **120**, 1542–1550.

Manogue, K. R., Leschner, A. I., and Candland, D. K. (1975). Dominance status and adrenocortical reactivity to stress in squirrel monkeys (*Saimiri sciureus*). *Primates* **16**, 457–463.

Marchlewska-Koj, A. (1997). Sociogenic stress and rodent reproduction. *Neurosci. Biobehav. Rev.* **21**, 699–703.

Marchlewska-Koj, A., Pochron, E., Galewicz-Sojecka, A., and Galas, J. (1994). Suppression of estrus in female mice by the presence of conspecifics or by foot shock. *Physiol. Behav.* **55**(2), 317–321.

Margulis, S. W., Saltzman, W., and Abbott, D. H. (1995). Behavioral and hormonal changes in female naked mole-rats (heterocephalus glaber) following removal of the breeding female from a colony. *Horm. Behav.* **29**(2), 227–247.

Martinez, M., Phillips, P. J., and Herbert, J. (1998). Adaptation in patterns of c-fos expression in the brain associated with exposure to either single or repeated social stress in male rats. *Eur. J. Neurosci.* **10**, 20–33.

Matsuda, S., Peng, H., Yoshimura, H., Wen, T. C., Fukuda, T., and Sakanaka, M. (1996). Persistent c-fos expression in the brains of mice with chronic social stress. *Neurosci. Res.* **26**, 157–170.

McBlane, J. W., and Handley, S. L. (1994). Effects of two stressors on behavior in the elevated X-maze; preliminary investigation of their interaction with 8-OH-DPAT. *Psychoparmacology (Berlin)* **116**(2), 173–182.

McGrady, A. V. (1984). Effects of psychological stress on male reproduction: A review. *Arch. Androl.* **13**, 1–7.

McGuire, M. T., Brammer, G. L., and Raleigh, M. J. (1986). Resting cortisol levels and the emergence of dominant status among male vervet monkeys. *Horm. Behav.* **20**(1), 106–117.

McKittrick, C. R. (1996). "Physiological, Endocrine and Neurochemical Consequences of Chronic Social Stress." Rockefeller University Press, New York.

McKittrick, C. R., Blanchard, D. C., Blanchard, R. J., McEwen, B. S., and Sakai, R. R. (1995). Serotonin receptor binding in a colony model of chronic social stress. *Biol. Psychiatry* **37**, 383–393.

McKittrick, C. R., Magariños, A. M., Blanchard, D. C., Blanchard, R. J., McEwen, B. S., and Sakai, R. R. (2000). Chronic social stress reduces dendritic arbors in CA3 of hippocampus and decreases binding to serotonin transporter sites. *Synapse* **36**(2), 85–94.

Meerlo, P., Overkamp, G. J., Daan, S., Van den Hoofdakker, R. H., and Koolhaas, J. M. (1996a). Changes in behavior and body weight following a single or double social defeat in rats. *Stress* **1**(1), 21–32.

Meerlo, P., Overkamp, G. J., Benning, M. A., Koolhaas, J. M., and Van den Hoofdakker, R. H. (1996b). Long-term changes in open field behavior following a single social defeat in rats can be reversed by sleep deprivation. *Physiol. Behav.* **60**(1), 115–119.

Meerlo, P., Overkamp, G. J., and Koolhaas, J. M. (1997). Behavioral and physiological consequences of a single social defeat in Roman high- and low-avoidance rats. *Psychoneuroendocrinology* **22**(3), 155–168.

Mendoza, S. P., Coe, C. L., Lowe, E. L., and Levine, S. (1979). The physiological response to group formation in adult male squirrel monkeys. *Psychoneuroendocrinology* **3**, 221–229.

Menzaghi, F., Howard, R. L., Heinrichs, S. C., Vale, W., Rivier, J., and Koob, G. F. (1994). Characterization of a novel and potent corticotropin-releasing factor antagonist in rats. *J. Pharmacol. Exp. Ther.* **269**(2), 564–572.

Menzaghi, F., Heinrichs, S. C., Vargas-Cortes, M., Goldstein, G., and Koob, G. F. (1996). IRI-514, a synthetic peptide analogue of thymopentic, reduces the behavioral response to social stress in rats. *Physiol. Behav.* **60**(2), 397–401.

Miczek, K. A., and Mutschler, N. H. (1996). Activational effects of social stress on IV cocaine self-administration in rats. *Psychopharmacology (Berlin)* **128**(3), 256–264.

Miczek, K. A., Mutschler, N. H., van Erp, A. M., Blank, A. D., and McInerney, S. C. (1999). d-amphetamine "cue" generalizes to social defeat stress: Behavioral sensitization and attenuated accumbens dopamine. *Psychopharmacology (Berlin)* **147**(2), 190–199.

Mineka, S., and Zinbarg, R. (1996). Conditioning and ethological models of anxiety disorder: Stress-in-dynamic-context anxiety models. *Nebr. Symp. Motivation* **43**, 135–210.

Mole, A., and Cooper, S. J. (1995). Opioid modulation of sucrose intake in CD-1 mice: Effects of gender and housing conditions. *Physiol. Behav.* **58**(4), 791–796.

Monaghan, E., and Glickman, S. (1992). Hormones and aggressive behavior. *In* "Behavioral Endocrinology" (J. Becker, M. Breedlove, and D. Crews, eds.), pp. 261–285. MIT Press, Cambridge, MA.

Monder, C., Sakai, R. R., Miroff, Y., Blanchard, D. C., and Blanchard, R. J. (1994a). Reciprocal changes in plasma corticosterone and testosterone in stressed male rats maintained in a visible burrow system: Evidence for a mediating role of testicular 11?-hydroxysteroid dehydrogenase. *Endocrinology (Baltimore)* **134**, 1193–1198.

Monder, C., Marandici, A., and Hardy, M. P. (1994b). 11?-hydroxysteroid dehydrogenase alleviates glucocorticoid-mediated inhibition of steroidogenesis in rat Leydig cells. *Endocrinology (Baltimore)* **134**, 1199–1204.

Munck, A., and Guyre, P. M. (1986). Glucocorticoid physiology, pharmacology and stress. *Adv. Exp. Med. Biol.* **196**, 81–96.

Nakao, M., Nomura, S., Yamanaka, G., Kumano, H., and Kuboki, T. (1998). Assessment of patients by DSM-III-R and DSM-IV in a Japanese psychosomatic clinic. *Psychother. Psychosom.* **67**, 43–49.

Nikulina, E. M., Marchand, J. E., Kream, R. M., and Miczek, K. A. (1998). Behavioral sensitization to cocaine after a brief social stress is accompanied by changes in fos expression in the murine brainstem. *Brain Res.* **810**(1–2), 200–210.

Norman, R. L., and Smith, C. J. (1992). Restraint inhibits luteinizing hormone and testosterone secretion in intact male rhesus macaques: Effects of concurrent naloxone administration. *Neuroendocrinology* **55**, 405–415.

Nunez, M. J., Riviero, P., Becerra, M. A., De Miguel, S., Quintans, M. R., Nunez, L. A., Legazpi, M. P., Mayan, J. M., Rey-Mendez, M., Varela, M., and Freire-Garabal, M. (1999). Effects of alprazolam on the free-choice ethanol consumption induced by isolation stress in aged rats. *Life Sci.* **64**(20), 213–217.

Ohl, F., and Fuchs, E. (1998). Memory performance in tree shrews: Effects of stressful experiences. *Neurosci. Biobehav. Rev.* **23**(2), 319–323.

Ohl, F., and Fuchs, E., (1999). Differential effects of chronic stress on memory processes in the tree shrew. *Brain Res. Cogn. Brain Res.* **7**(3), 379–387.

Ohl, F., Michaelis, T., Vollmann-Honsdorf, G. K., Kirschbaum, C., and Fuchs, E. (2000). Effect of chronic psychosocial stress and long-term cortisol treatment on hippocampus-mediated memory and hippocampal volume: A pilot-study in tree shrews. *Psychoneuroendocrinology* **25**(4), 357–363.

Orr, T. E., and Mann, D. R. (1990). Effects of restraint stress on plasma LH and T concentrations, Leydig cell LH/HCG receptors, and *in vitro* testicular steroidogenesis in adult rats. *Horm. Behav.* **24**, 324–341.

Orr, T. E., and Mann, D. R. (1992). Role of glucocorticoids in the stress-induced suppression of testicular steroidogenesis in adult male rats. *Horm. Behav.* **26**, 350–363.

Padgett, D. A., Sheridan, J. F., Dorne, J., Berntson, G. G., Candelora, J., and Glaser, R. (1998). Social stress and the reactivation of latent herpes simplex virus type 1. *Proc. Natl. Acad. Sci. U.S.A.* **95**(12), 7231–7235.

Patten, S. B. (1999). Depressive symptoms and disorders, levels of functioning and psychosocial stress and integrative hypothesis. *Med. Hypotheses* **53**(3), 210–216.

Pellis, S. M., and Pellis, V. C. (1992). Analysis of the targets and tactics of conspecific attack and predatory attack in northern grasshopper mice *Onychomys leucogaster. Aggressive Behav.* **18**, 301–316.

Perret, M., (1992). Environmental and social determinants of sexual function in the male lesser mouse lemur (*Microcebus murinus*). *Folia Primatol.* **59**(1), 1–25.

Plaistow, S. J., and Tsubaki, Y. (2000). A selective trade-off for territoriality and non-territoriality in the polymorphic damselfly *Mnais costalis. Proc. R. Soc. London, B Ser.* **267**, 969–975.

Popova, N. K., and Naumenko, E. V. (1972). Dominance relations and the pituitary-adrenal system in rats. *Anim. Behav.* **20**, 108–111.

Puri, C. P., Puri, V., and Anand Kumar, T. C. (1981). Serum levels of testosterone, cortisol, prolactin and bioactive luteinizing hormone in adult male rhesus monkeys following cage-restraint or anaesthetizing with ketamine hydrochloride. *Acta Endocrinol. (Copenhagen)* **97**, 118–124.

Raab, A., Dantzer, R., Michaud, B., Mormede, P., Taghzouti, K., Simon, H., and Le Moal, M. (1986). Behavioral, physiological and immunological consequences of social status and aggression in chronically coexisting resident-intruder dyads of male rats. *Physiol. Behav.* **36**, 223–228.

Raleigh, M. J., McGuire, M. T., Brammer, G. L., and Yuwiler, A. (1984). Social and environmental influences on blood serotonin concentrations in monkeys. *Arch. Gen. Psychiatry* **41**, 405–410.

Rawleigh, J. M., Kemble, E. D., and Ostrem, J. (1993). Differential effects of prior dominance or subordination experience on conspecific odor preferences in mice. *Physiol. Behav.* **54**(1), 35–39.

Rivest, S., and Rivier, C. (1991). Influence of the paraventricular nucleus of the hypothalamus in the alteration of neuroendocrine functions induced by intermittent footshock or interleukin. *Endocrinology (Baltimore)* **129**, 2049–2057.

Rivier, C., and Vale, W. (1985). Effect of the long-term administration of corticotropin-releasing factor on the pituitary-adrenal and pituitary-gonadal axis in the male rat. *J. Clin. Invest.* **75**, 689–694.

Rivier, C., Rivier, J., and Vale, W. (1986). Stress-induced inhibition of reproductive functions: Role of endogenous corticotropin-releasing factor. *Science* **231**, 607–609.

Roozendaal, B., Koolhaas, J. M., and Bohus, B. (1990). Differential effect of lesioning of the central amygdala on the bradycardiac and behavioral response of the rat in relation to conditioned social and solitary stress. *Behav. Brain Res.* **41**(1), 39–48.

Rose, R. M., Bernstein, I. S., and Holaday, J. W. (1971). Plasma testosterone, dominance rank and aggressive behavior in a group of male rhesus monkeys. *Nature (London)* **231**, 366–368.

Rose, R. M., Gordon, T. P., and Bernstein, I. S. (1975). Consequences of social conflict on plasma testosterone levels in rhesus monkeys. *Psychosom. Med.* **37**, 50–61.

Rose, R. R., and Sachar, E. (1981). Psychoendocrinology. *In* "Textbook of Endocrinology" (R. H. Williams, ed.), 6th ed., pp. 645–671. Saunders, Philadephia.

Roske, I., Baeger, I., Frenzel, R., and Oehme, P. (1994). Does a relationship exist between the quality of stress and the motivation to ingest alcohol? *Alcohol* **11**(2), 113–124.

Ruis, M. A., te Brake, J. H., Buwalda, B., De Boer, S. F., Meerlo, P., Korte, S. M., Blokhuis, H. J., and Koolhaas, J. M. (1999). Housing familiar male wildtype rats together reduces the long-term adverse behavioral and physiological effects of social defeat. *Psychoneuroendocrinology* **24**, 285–300.

Sachser, N. (1987). Short-term responses of plasma norepinephrine, epinephrine, glucocorticoid and testosterone titers to social and non-social stressors in male guinea pigs of different social status. *Physiol. Behav.* **39**(1), 11–20.

Sachser, N., and Lick, C. (1989). Social stress in guinea pigs. *Physiol. Behav.* **46**, 137–144.

Sachser, N., and Lick, C. (1991). Social experience, behavior, and stress in guinea pigs. *Physiol. Behav.* **50**, 83–90.

Sachser, N., and Pröve, E. (1986). Social status and plasma-testosterone-titers in male guinea pigs (*Cavia aperia f. porcellus*). *Ethology* **71**, 103–114.

Sachser, N., Durschlag, M., and Hirzel, D. (1998). Social relationships and the management of stress. *Psychoneuroendocrinology* **23**, 891–904.

Saltzman, W., Schultz-Darken, N. J., Scheffler, G., Wegner, F. H., and Abbott, D. H. (1994). Social and reproductive influences on plasma cortisol in female marmoset monkeys. *Physiol. Behav.* **56**, 801–810.

Saltzman, W., Severin, J. M., Schultz-Darken, N. J., and Abbott, D. H. (1997). Behavioral and social correlates of escape from suppression of ovulation in female common marmosets housed with the natal family. *Am. J. Primatol.* **41**(1), 1–21.

Saltzman, W., Schultz-Darken, N. J., Wegner, F. H., Wittwer, D. J., and Abbott, D. H. (1998). Suppression of cortisol levels in subordinate female marmosets: Reproductive and social contributions. *Horm. Behav.* **33**, 58–74.

Sapolsky, R. M. (1982). The endocrine stress-response and social status in the wild baboon. *Horm. Behav.* **16**, 279–292.

Sapolsky, R. M. (1983). Individual differences in cortisol secretory patterns in the wild baboon: Role of negative feedback sensitivity. *Endocrinology (Baltimore)* **113**, 2263–2267.

Sapolsky, R. M. (1985). Stress-induced suppression of testicular function in the wild baboon: Role of glucocorticoids. *Endocrinology (Baltimore)* **116**, 2273–2278.

Sapolsky, R. M. (1986). Stress-induced elevation of testosterone concentrations in high ranking baboons: Role of catecholamines. *Endocrinology (Baltimore)* **118**, 1630–1635.

Sapolsky, R. M. (1989). Hypercortisolism among socially subordinate wild baboons originates at the CNS level. *Arch. Gen. Psychiatry* **46**, 1047–1051.

Sapolsky, R. M. (1992a). Cortisol concentrations and the social significance of rank instability among wild baboons. *Psychoneuroendocrinology* **17**, 701–709.

Sapolsky, R. M. (1992b). In "Stress and the Aging Brain, and the Mechanisms of Neuron Death." MIT Press, Cambridge, MA.

Sapolsky, R. M., and Krey, L. C. (1988). Stress-induced suppression of luteinizing hormone concentrations in wild baboons: Role of opiates. *J. Clin. Endocrinol. Metab.* **66**, 722–726.

Schaison, G., Durand, F., and Mowszowicz, I. (1978). Effect of glucocorticoids on plasma testosterone in men. *Acta Endocrinol. (Copenhagen)* **89**, 126–131.

Schaller, G. B. (1972). "The Serengeti Lion: A Study of Predator-prey Relations." University of Chicago Press, Chicago.

Schaub, H. (1995). Dominance fades with distance: An experiment on food competition in long-tailed macaques (*Macaca fascicularis*). *J. Comp. Psychol.* **109**(2), 196–202.

Schuhr, B. (1987). Social structure and plasma corticosterone level in female albino mice. *Physiol. Behav.* **40**, 689–693.

Schuurman, T. (1980). Hormonal correlates of agonistic behavior in adult male rats. *Prog. Brain Res.* **53**, 415–420.

Selye, H. (1946). The general adaptation syndrome and the disease of adaptation. *J. Clin. Endocrinol.* **6**, 117–230.

Selye, H. (1950). "Stress: A Treatise Based on the Concepts of the General-Adaptation-Syndrome and the Diseases of Adaptation." Acta, Montreal.

Sgoifo, A., Koolhaas, J. M., Musso, E., and De Boer, S. F. (1999). Different sympathovagal modulation of heart rate during social and nonsocial stress episodes in wild-type rats. *Physiol. Behav.* **67**(5), 733–738.

Shanks, N., Harbuz, M. S., Jessop, D. S., Perks, P., Moore, P. M., and Lightman, S. L. (1998). Inflammatory disease as chronic stress. *Ann. N.Y. Acad. Sci.* **840**, 599–607.

Shively, C. A. (1998). Social subordination stress, behavior, and central monoaminergic function in female cynomolgus monkeys. *Biol. Psychiatry* **44**, 882–891.

Shively, C. A., Grant, K. A., Ehrenkaufer, R. L., Mach, R. H., and Nader, M. A. (1997a). Social stress, depression, and brain dopamine in female cynomolgus monkeys. *Ann. N.Y. Acad. Sci.* **807**, 574–577.

Shively, C. A., Laber-Laird, K., and Anton, R. F. (1997b). Behavior and physiology of social stress and depression in female cynomolgus monkeys. *Biol. Psychiatry* **41**(8), 871–882.

Siegfried, B., Frischknecht, H. R., and Waser, P. G. (1984). Defeat, learned submissiveness, and analgesia in mice: Effect of genotype. *Behav. Neural Biol.* **42**(1), 91–97.

Smith, T. E., and French, J. A. (1997). Social and reproductive conditions modulate urinary cortisol excretion in black tufted-ear marmosets (*Callithrix Kuhli*). *Am. J. Primatol.* **42**(4), 253–267.

Spencer, R. L., Miller, A. H., Moday, H., McEwen, B. S., Blanchard, R. J., Blanchard, D. C., and Sakai, R. R. (1996). Chronic social stress produces reductions in available splenic type II corticosteroid receptor binding and plasma corticos-

teroid binding globulin levels. *Psychoneuroendocrinology* **21**, 95–109.

Srivastava, R. K., Taylor, M. F., and Mann, D. R. (1993). Effect of immobilization stress on plasma luteinizing hormone, testosterone, and corticosterone concentrations and on 3?-hydroxysteroid dehydrogenase activity in the testes of adult rats. *Proc. Soc. Exp. Biol. Med.* **204**, 231–235.

Stalker, A., Hermo, L., and Antakly, T. (1989). Covalent affinity labeling, radioautography, and immunocytochemistry localize the glucocorticoid receptor in rat testicular Leydig cells. *Am. J. Anat.* **386**, 369–377.

Taché, Y., Ducharme, J. R., Haour, F., Saez, J., and Collu, R. (1980). Effect of chronic intermittent immobilization stress on hypophyso-gonadal function of rats. *Acta Endocrinol. (Copenhagen)* **93**, 168–174.

Tidey, J. W., and Miczek, K. A. (1996). Social defeat stress selectively alters mesocorticolimbic dopamine release: An in vivo microdialysis study. *Brain Res.* **721**, 140–149.

Tidey, J. W., and Miczek, K. A. (1997). Acquisition of cocaine self-administration after social stress: Role of accumbens dopamine. *Psychopharmacology (Berlin)* **130**(3), 203–212.

Tornatzky, W., and Miczek, K. A. (1994). Behavioral and autonomic responses to intermittent social stress: Differential protection by clonidine and metoprolol. *Psychopharmacology (Berlin)* **116**(3), 346–356.

Tornatzky, W., and Miczek, K. A. (1995). Alcohol, anxiolytics and social stress in rats. *Psychopharmacology (Berlin)* **121**(1), 135–144.

Uno, H., Tarara, R., Else, J., Suleman, M., and Sapolsky, R. (1989). Hippocampal damage associated with prolonged and fatal stress in primates. *J. Neurosci.* **9**, 1705–1711.

Urban, J. H., Miller, M. A., and Dorsa, D. M. (1991). Dexamethasone-induced suppression of vasopressin expression in the bed nucleus of the stria terminalis and medial amygdala is mediated by changes in testosterone. *Endocrinology (Baltimore)* **128**, 109–116.

van Erp, A. M., Kruk, M. R., Meelis, W., and Willekens-Bramer, D. C. (1994). Effect of environmental stressors on time course, variability and form of self-grooming in the rat: Handling, social contact, defeat, novelty, restraint and fur moistening. *Behav. Brain Res.* **65**(1), 47–55.

Van Kampen, M., Schmitt, U., Hiemke, C., and Fuchs, E. (2000). Diazepam has no beneficial effects on stress-induced behavioral and endocrine changes in male tree shrews. *Pharmacol., Biochem. Behav.* **65**(3), 539–546.

Virgin, C. E., Jr., and Sapolsky, R. M. (1997). Styles of male social behavior and their endocrine correlates among low-ranking baboons. *Am. J. Primatol.* **42**(1), 25–39.

Vivian, J. A., and Miczek, K. A. (1998). Effects of mu and delta opioid agonists and antagonists on affective vocal and reflexive pain responses during social stress in rats. *Psychopharmacology (Berlin)* **139**(4), 364–375.

Vivian, J. A., and Miczek, K. A. (1999). Interactions between social stress and morphine in the periaqueductal gray: Effects on affective vocal and reflexive pain responses in rats. *Psychopharmacology (Berlin)* **146**(2), 153–161.

Vivian, J. A., Weerts, E. M., and Miczek, K. A. (1994). Defeat engenders pentylenetetrazole-appropriate responding in rats: Antagonism by midazolam. *Psychopharmacology (Berlin)* **116**(4), 491–498.

Vollmann-Honsdorf, G. K., Flügge, G., and Fuchs, E. (1997). Chronic psychosocial stress does not affect the number of pyramidal neurons in tree shrew hippocampus. *Neurosci. Lett.* **233**, 121–124.

von Holst, D. V. (1977). Social stress in tree shrews: Problems, results and goals. *J. Comp. Physiol. Psychol.* **120**, 71–86.

von Holst, D., Fuchs, E., and Stöhr, W. (1983). Physiological changes in *Tupaia belangeri* under different types of social stress. *In* "Biobehavioral Bases of Coronary Heart Disease" (T. H. Schmidt, T. M. Dembrowski, and G. Blümchen, eds.), pp. 382–390. Karger, Basel.

Vreeburg, J. T. M., de Greef, W. J., Ooms, M. P., van Wouw, P., and Weber, R. F. A. (1984). Effects of adrenocorticotropin and corticosterone on the negative feedback action of testosterone in the adult male rat. *Endocrinology (Baltimore)* **115**, 977–983.

Wasser, S. K., and Barash, D. P. (1983). Reproductive suppression among female mammals: Implications for biomedicine and sexual selection theory. *Q. Rev. Biol.* **58**, 513–538.

Watanabe, Y., McKittrick, C. R., Blanchard, D. C., Blanchard, R. J., McEwen, B. S., and Sakai, R. R. (1995). Effects of chronic social stress on tyrosine hydroxylase mRNA and protein levels. *Mol. Brain Res.* **32**, 176–180.

Weisinger, R. S., Denton, D. A., and Osborne, P. G. (1989). Voluntary ethanol intake of individually- or pair-house rats: Effect of ACTH or dexamethasone treatment. *Pharmacol., Biochem. Behav.* **33**(2), 335–341.

Welsh, T. H., Bambino, T. H., and Hsueh, A. J. W. (1982). Mechanism of glucocorticoid-induced suppression of testicular androgen biosynthesis *in vitro. Biol. Reprod.* **27**, 1138–1146.

Wheeler, G. D., Wall, S. R., and Belcastro, A. N. (1984). Reduced serum testosterone and prolactin levels in male distance runners. *JAMA, J. Am. Med. Assoc.* **252**, 514–516.

Wolffgramm, J., and Heyne, A. (1991). Social behavior, dominance, and social deprivation of rats determine drug choice. *Pharmacol., Biochem. Behav.* **38**(2), 389–399.

Wotjak, C. T., Kubota, M., Liebsch, G., Montkowski, A., Holsboer, F., Neumann, I., and Landgraf, R. (1996). Release of vasopressin within the rat paraventricular nucleus in response to emotional stress: A novel mechanism of regulating adrenocorticotropic hormone secretion? *J. Neurosci.* **16**, 7725–7732.

Wrangham, R., and Peterson, D. (1996). "Demonic Males: Apes and the Origin of Human Violence." Houghton Mifflin, Boston, and New York.

Yodyingyuad, Y., de la Riva, C., Abbott, D. H., Herbert, J., and Keverne, E. B. (1985). Relationship between dominance hierarchy, cerebrospinal fluid levels of amine transmitter metabolites (5-hydroxyindoleacetic acid and homovanillic acid) and plasma cortisol in monkeys. *Neuroscience* **16**, 851.

Ziegler, T. E., Scheffler, G., and Snowdon, C. T. (1995). The relationship of cortisol levels to social environment and reproductive functioning in female cotton-top tamarins, *Saguinus oedipus. Horm. Behav.* **29**, 407–424.

Zuri, I., Gottreich, A., and Terkel, J. (1998). Social stress in neighboring and encountering blind mole-rats (*Spalax ehrenbergi*). *Physiol. Behav.* **64**(5), 611–620.

14

Regulation of the Injury-Immune Response in the Central Nervous System

Allostasis and Allostatic Load in Immunity

Karen Bulloch and Bruce S. McEwen

Laboratory of Neuroendocrinology
Rockefeller University
New York, New York 10021

I. INTRODUCTION

This article deals with the paradox of the protective yet damaging responses of the nervous system to challenge. The initial response to a psychological or physical stressor, a pathogen or a physical insult, activates a process we term *allostasis* (McEwen and Stellar, 1993; Sterling and Eyer, 1988). This is the process of adaptation that helps the body maintain *homeostasis*, which is defined here as those aspects of physiology (pH, oxygen tension, and body temperature) that are essential for life. Prolonged and aggravated activation of allostasis can lead to tissue damage initiated by the imbalance in the activities of the mediators of allostasis. This damage is the price the body pays for being forced to adapt repeatedly to stressors or other environmental challenges. We term this erosive process of wear and tear *allostatic load* (McEwen and Stellar, 1993; McEwen, 1998). Thus the same mechanisms that help tissues and organs adapt to the external or internal environment can also turn against those organs when they are not turned off when not needed, or are otherwise in a state of imbalance and hyperactivity (McEwen, 1998).

Common examples of such allostatic load can be seen in the cardiovascular system (e.g., blood pressure responses to acute challenge that can accelerate atherosclerosis when repeatedly active over long periods) and the hypothalamic pituitary adrenal (HPA) axis (e.g., the glucocorticoid responses to stressors that acutely mobilize energy, enhance memory for emotionally charged events, and promote movement of immune cells to sites where they are needed). Yet when "activated over extended periods of time," HPA hyperactivity can promote obesity, brain cell atrophy, and impaired immune function.

Less understood, but of utmost importance to the integrity of central nervous system (CNS) function, is the impact of allostatic load on the long-term injury-healing response within the CNS. Although the brain has been regarded as an organ largely inaccessible to the peripheral immune system, we now know that the activation of the acute phase response in the CNS plays an important role in determining how the immune-injury response within the brain reacts to pathogens or trauma. The brain's primary immune cells, microglia and astroglia, are activated following insults to the CNS. It is clear that there are circumstances under which the normal adaptive role of these cells in regulating other immune cells in responses to repeated or severe challenge can give rise to an allostatic load. This includes the very processes that are activated to promote adaptation to a physical challenge that, if not contained, can lead to damage beyond that of the original insult.

This chapter reviews this emerging area of research after first summarizing the key concepts and describing the systems that are involved. In order to understand the role of the injury-immune-healing responses (IIHR) to trauma in the CNS, we first must have a clear understanding of the mechanisms underlying regional regulation of IIHR and the relationship between adaptive responses of the body to challenge and exacerbation of the IIHR that leads to pathophysiology. To fully appreciate this paradox, we will first consider the concepts of allostasis and allostatic load in more detail.

II. PROTECTIVE AND DAMAGING EFFECTS OF BIOLOGICAL MEDIATORS OF ADAPTATION

A. Allostasis: The Process of Adaptation

When the body is challenged by unexpected or threatening events, or is simply adjusting to the day-night rhythm of sleep and activity as well as food consumption, it reacts physiologically in an adaptive manner in order to maintain homeostasis. This process is called *allostasis,* literally "maintaining stability through change" (Sterling and Eyer, 1988). Systemically, it involves, but is not confined to, the production or release, or both, of physiological mediators such as adrenalin from the adrenal medulla and glucocorticoids from the adrenal cortex. These mediators produce adaptive responses in tissues throughout the body that lead to the enhancement of memory, mobilization and replenishment of energy, and trafficking of immune cells to places in the body where they are needed to fight an infection.

1. Allostasis and Excitatory Amino Acids

Allostasis is an organizing principle applicable to many systems of the body that are involved in adaptation. In the nervous system, for example, neurotransmitters released by neuronal activity produce effects locally that either propagate or inhibit neural activity. Neurotransmitters and hormones are usually released during a discrete period of activation and then are shut off, and the mediators themselves are removed from the

intracellular space by reuptake or metabolism in order not to prolong their effects (McEwen, 2000). In the CNS, a classic example of allostasis and allostatic load is the role of excitatory amino acid (EAA) neurotransmitters that are released when excitatory synapses in the hippocampus and many other brain regions become active (McEwen, 2000). Over the short run, EAAs transfer information via synapses to other nerve cells and participate in synaptic plasticity and learning and memory formation (Eichenbaum and Harris, 2000). EAAs also are involved in adaptive structural plasticity of brain regions that also involve regulation by circulating hormones: estrogen-induced synapse formation (Woolley and McEwen, 1994), remodeling of dendrites of hippocampal neurons with stress, and regulation of neurogenesis of dentate gyrus granule neurons (McEwen, 1999). However, EAAs are also involved in damage processes: ischemic damage, seizure damage, pathophysiological processes such as are found in Huntington's disease, Parkinson's disease, and Alzheimer's disease; they are also suspected to play a role in damage from head trauma (Sapolsky, 1992). Finally, EAAs are believed to play a role in gradual impairment of cognitive function with aging, a process in which glucocorticoids may play a catalytic role in both aging and in the effects of damaging agents (Sapolsky, 1992). In resolving the other factors involved in these processes, the management of calcium homeostasis and the production and destruction of free radicals appear to play a central role in distinguishing between adaptation (allostasis) and damage (allostatic load) (Landfield and Eldridge, 1994; Mattson, 1997).

2. Glucocorticoids and Catecholamines in Allostasis

Other examples of allostasis involve hormones associated with stress. Like the example for the excitatory amino acids, glucocorticoids have protective effects in the short run and yet can have damaging effects over longer time intervals if there are many adverse life events or if the hormonal secretion is disregulated (McEwen, 1998). Acutely, glucocorticoids stimulate locomotor activity and food intake but chronically promote obesity and contribute to insulin resistance (Leibowitz and Hoebel, 1997; McEwen *et al.,* 1993; Brindley and Rolland, 1989). Moreover, for the cardiovascular system, there is a similar paradox where catecholamines acutely help the system adjust to increased demand but chronically contribute to accelerated atherosclerosis (Manuck *et al.,* 1991, 1995; Sterling and Eyer, 1988). In the brain, both catecholamines and glucocorticoids acutely facilitate memories for emotionally charged events (Cahill *et al.,* 1994; Roozendaal, 2000), but glucocorticoids secreted during repeated stress participate in remodeling of pyramidal neurons in the hippocampus and shutdown of ongoing neurogenesis in the dentate gyrus (McEwen, 1999). Glial cell reduction may also be involved (Rajkowska *et al.,* 1999). Moreover, after very prolonged and severe stress, pyramidal neurons may actually die (Uno *et al.,* 1989). Through some or all of these processes, the hippocampus undergoes an atrophy, and this is detected in the human brain by structural MRI and has been reported in such conditions as recurrent depressive illness, Cushing's syndrome, posttraumatic stress disorder, mild cognitive impairment in aging and schizophrenia (McEwen, 1997; Sapolsky, 1996).

3. Allostasis in the Immune Response

In response to a local infection or minor damage, regional mechanisms can activate an injury-immune healing response (IIHR) that is appropriate to contain the contamination or injury and initiate the healing response. In the case of a severe infection or trauma, allostasis is maintained by the activation of an acute phase response (APR). The APR is a *systemic* response involving the activation of innate immune cells and the production of local and systemic mediators (e.g., acute phase reactive proteins and cytokines) that activate the cellular and humoral immune responses while at the same time initiating neuroendocrine responses that promote redistribution of immune cells to where they are needed. In the normal resolution of the acute phase response, mediators are also released that limit or "contain" the inflammatory and the HPA responses (Baumann and Gauldie, 1994).

Hormones and other systemic mediators produced during the onset of the APR are similar to those produced by acute stressors and can act to enhance certain types of immunity (McEwen *et al.,* 1997). Exacerbation of these hormones by acute (restraint) stress during a delayed-type hypersensitivity reaction can further enhance the magnitude of this response (Dhabhar and McEwen, 1999). It is also known (Dhabhar and McEwen, 1999; Spencer *et al.,* 2000) that these effects are mediated, at least in part, by glucocorticoids and catecholamines that act to promote movement, or trafficking, of immune cells to places in the body where they are required to fight an infection or other challenge.

B. Allostatic Load: The Price of Adaptation

Protection and damage can be caused by the same mediators of allostasis released in different temporal patterns. Here we consider the characteristics of the overactivity of these mediators that leads to pathophysiology and damage. Figure 1 presents a number of alternative patterns of the hormonal stress response that illustrate what is called "allostatic load" (McEwen, 1998). As noted above, *allostasis* refers to the process of adaptation to return the body to a state of homeostasis. In the case of an acute stressor, this involves the output of stress hormones that act in the ways described above to restore homeostasis in the face of a challenge (McEwen and Stellar, 1993; Sterling and Eyer, 1988). *Allostatic load* refers to the price the body pays for being forced to adapt to adverse psychosocial or physical situations over extended periods, or in some cases to certain individuals, and in situations that are horrific; e.g., rape, the extreme terrors of a battlefield. The physiological manifestations of allostatic load result in either the presence of too much of the mediators or an inefficient operation of the allostasis response systems (see top panel in Figure 1).

In Figure 1, the top left panel refers to chronic stress. Chronic stress is manifested by the frequent turning on of the production of mediators of adaptation by novel events. The negative consequences of chronic stress arise from the overexposure to these mediators, which results in various types of pathophysiology and excessive wear and tear on certain target organs described above. People who have had excessive stress in their lives, as measured by multiple periods of poverty level income, show earlier aging, more depression, and an earlier decline of both physical and mental functioning (Lynch *et al.,* 1997). Moreover, individuals who have been abused as children suffer an increased risk for depression, suicide, substance abuse, and earlier mortality and morbidity from a wide range of diseases (Felitti *et al.,* 1998).

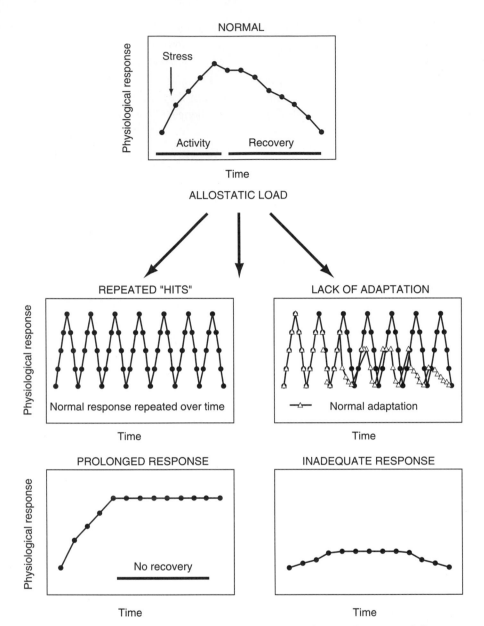

FIGURE 1   Four types of response patterns of allostatic mediators. The top panel illustrates the normal allostatic response, in which a response is initiated by a stressor, sustained for an appropriate interval, and then turned off. The remaining panels illustrate four conditions that lead to allostatic load: (1) Repeated "hits" from multiple novel stressors, which may or may not change the response profiles of the mediators, leading to an allostatic state. (2) An example of an allostatic state involving lack of adaptation of the mediator to repeated presentations of the same situation. (3) Example of an allostatic state involving a prolonged response due to delayed shut down of the mediator in the aftermath of a stress or failure to show a normal diurnal rhythm. (4) An example of an allostatic state involving the inadequate response of one mediator that leads to compensatory hyperactivity of other mediators: e.g., inadequate secretion of glucocorticoid, resulting in increased levels of cytokines that are normally counter-regulated by glucocorticoids. Figure drawn by Dr. Firdaus Dhabhar, Rockefeller University. Reprinted from McEwen (1998), *N. Engl. J. Med.* **338**, 171–179.

Yet there are circumstances in which the number of stressful events may not be excessive but in which the body fails to manage the hormonal response after stress or during the diurnal rhythm, and these are illustrated in the three remaining panels in Figure 1. The top right panel illustrates a failure to habituate to repeated stressors of the same kind. Measurement of cortisol in a repeated public speaking challenge has revealed individuals who do not habituate, and these individuals, who lack self-confidence and self-esteem, are undoubtedly overexposing their bodies to stress hormones under many circumstances in daily life that do not overtly disturb other individuals (Kirschbaum et al., 1995).

The bottom left panel of Figure 1 refers to failure to turn off efficiently the response of the mediators of allostasis. One example of this is seen for individuals with two parents who are hypertensive and who, as a result, show prolonged elevation of blood pressure after a psychological stressor (Gerin and Pickering, 1995). Another example, in the realm of the diurnal rhythm, is the hypersecretion of cortisol in the evening in people who have been sleep deprived (Leproult et al., 1997; Spiegel et al., 1999), as well as in depressed individuals (Michelson et al., 1996; Young et al., 1994). One reason that evening elevation of cortisol is bad is that it has a greater effect in causing a delayed hyperglycemic state than does cortisol elevation in the morning (Plat et al., 1999). And chronic elevation of glucocorticoids in the diurnal rhythm has other effects: e.g., in depression, loss of bone mineral density has been reported and this can be related to the diurnally elevated levels of glucocorticoids (Michelson et al., 1996).

However, allostatic load can also result from the inadequate production of the mediators of allostasis. The bottom right panel of Figure 1 describes a situation in which the response of mediators of allostasis is inadequate to the needs of the individual genotype. This results in excessive activity of other allostatic systems, such as the inflammatory cytokines, which are normally contained by elevated levels of cortisol and catecholamines. The Lewis rat illustrates this condition, having less corticosterone than the virtually syngenic Fischer rat. Lewis rats are vulnerable to inflammatory and autoimmune disturbances, which are not found in Fischer rats, and these can be corrected by administering exogenous glucocorticoids (Sternberg, 1997). Comparable human disorders in which lower-than-needed cortisol may play a role include atopic dermatitis fibromyalgia and chronic fatigue syndrome (Buske-Kirschbaum et al., 1997; Crofford et al., 1994; Heim et al., 2000; Poteliakhoff, 1981; Ur et al., 1992).

To gain a better understanding of how an allostatic load has an impact on the immune response and in particular the IIHR response in the CNS, we next consider the extrinsic mechanisms of allostasis that are superimposed upon and sometimes override the intrinsic regulatory mechanism of the immune system.

III. ALLOSTASIS AND THE INJURY-IMMUNE HEALING RESPONSE: REGIONAL REGULATION

Any comprehensive discussion of allostasis of IIHR must take into consideration the interaction of the immune system with the autonomic and the neuroendocrine systems. We will first review the individual and interactive components of the endocrine, autonomic nervous system and immune systems and their roles in allostasis. This discussion will pave the way for a detailed discussion of allostatic load during the regional regulation of the injury-immune response in the CNS.

A. The Neuroendocrine System

The neuroendocrine system plays a vital regulatory role in modulating the injury-immune response (McEwen et al., 1997; Risdon et al., 1991). Indeed, virtually every hormone in the body has been reported to have some influence on immune function (McEwen et al., 1997). Particularly important are the catecholamines and glucocorticoids, which influence the trafficking of immune cells (Spencer et al., 2000), and these will be discussed below. These same hormones also regulate the types of immune responses by modulating cytokine production and cytokine receptors (Munck et al., 1984; Sapolsky et al., 2000). They can do this either by direct modulation of the immune cells or by their interaction with neurons and the modulation of neurally generated molecules that affect the IIHR (McEwen et al., 1997). The aspects of the endocrine system that are dealt with in this chapter will focus primarily on glucocorticoid interactions with immunocytes involved in regional regulations of immune or trauma responses within the primary, secondary, and tertiary lymphoid tissues.

B. Autonomic Nervous System

The autonomic nervous system (ANS) is divided anatomically into three components: the parasympathetic, with cranial and sacral connections; the sympathetic, with central nervous connections in the thoracic and lumbar segments of the spinal cord; and the enteric nervous system, which innervates the digestive system. The sensory nervous system should also be included in any discussion of neuroendocrine-immune interaction, since its input into the ANS can initiate changes in autonomic tone and can alert the brain to changes or challenges from the external environment as well as help set the stage for the response to these stimuli (Levine, 1968; Loewy, 1990).

The CNS centers for ANS control lie within the cortex, brain stem, spinal cord, and especially the hypothalamus. The ANS functionally overlaps with both sensory and motor systems and, together with the limbic system and cerebral cortex, is critical for memory and learning (Bannister, 1988) and for allostasis. Parasympathetic and sympathetic nerves transmit signals from the CNS to visceral organs after the brain integrates information from sensory nerves regarding the status of an organ.

1. Parasympathetic

Parasympathetic signals leave these brain stem centers and are distributed to peripheral organs and tissues, including those of the immune system. The vagus nerve is the largest component of the parasympathetic nervous system and carries both efferent and afferent nerve fibers. Two vagal components have evolved in the mammalian CNS to regulate peripheral parasympathetic functions. The dorsal motor complex (DMC) controls parasympathetic function below the level of the diaphragm, while the ventral vagal complex (VVC), composed of nucleus ambiguus and nucleus retrofacial in the brain stem, controls organs above the diaphragm, such as the heart, thymus, and lungs, as well as other glands and tissues of the neck and upper chest, and spe-

cialized muscles such as those of the esophageal complex. The VVC is very important in allostasis and is often activated in potentially stressful situations (Porges, 1992) prior to sympathetic activation. Vagal activation is also an essential component of the normal resolution of the body's response to stressful situations by turning off or toning down the effects of sympathetic activation.

The ability of the vagal systems to shift priorities rapidly by regulating metabolic output while fostering motor and psychological processes associated with appropriate social engagement and disengagement with the physical and emotional environment is an intrinsic component of allostasis. We are now just beginning to realize that the disruption of these mechanisms by either "overexposure" to external or internal environmental cues or the breakdown of ANS regulation can lead to allostatic load, which can ultimately extract a severe toll on health (Sloan *et al.*, 1999).

2. Sympathetic

The sympathetic nervous system is the main immediate response system to acute environmental sensors. Catecholamines are the other major mediators of allostasis besides glucocorticoids, and they have effects that in some cases synergize with, and in other cases oppose, the actions of glucocorticoids. Glucocorticoids potentiate the actions of catecholamines while at the same time containing their release, and in the adrenal medulla glucocorticoids promote epinephrine synthesis by regulating the key enzyme, phenylethanolamine N methyl transferase or PNMT (Goldstein and Pacak, 2000; Sapolsky *et al.*, 2000). At the same time, catecholamines help maintain normal HPA function, since adrenergic input to the adrenal cortex facilitates ACTH-induced steroidogenesis (Young and Landsberg, 2000).

One of the most important distinctions is between norepinephrine release by the dispersed sympathetic nerves and epinephrine release by the adrenal medulla (Goldstein and Eisenhofer, 2000; Young and Landsberg, 2000). For example, in girls with chronic fatigue syndrome, morning resting epinephrine levels are elevated, whereas norepinephrine levels are not, compared to age-matched controls (Kavelaars *et al.*, 2000). Whereas norepinephrine release is particularly important for the discrete regulation of blood vessel constriction and blood flow, redistributing and influencing a host of organs such as the heart, spleen, and pancreas, epinephrine release is important for skeletal muscles that do not have extensive sympathetic innervation. One of the important actions of epinephrine in muscle is to retard the degradation of proteins by working against the catabolic actions of glucocorticoids (Young and Landsberg, 2000). Epinephrine release is also more closely related to emotional distress, whereas norepinephrine release is more related to physical exertion.

3. Sensory and Enteric Nervous System

The sensory nervous system is composed of strategically placed sensory neurons and their terminals, which convey information about the internal and external environment back to CNS autonomic centers for processing and reactions. The enteric nervous system component occupies the digestive system and participates in digestion and motility. It is somewhat independent from the ANS but is still subject to its regulation and to the process of adaptation to environmental stressors. It, too, is a target of allostatic load.

The neurons from the aforementioned "divisions" of the ANS innervate the tissues and organs of the immune system in developmentally discrete and diverse ways. A brief review of immune system and the innervation in the primary, secondary, and teriary immune tissues will provide a background for understanding the basis of the IIHR within the CNS.

C. The Immune System: Mobile and Structural Cellular Constituents

Immunologists have long recognized that the pathways by which an antigen-pathogen gains entry into the body as well as the age or physical state of the individual at the time of the infection can influence the class, type, and magnitude of an immune response (Bulloch, 1982, 1985). It is also well known that some pathogens escape effective immune clearance such as observed in leprosy, syphilis, and AIDS. Unfortunately, the mechanisms utilized by either the body or the pathogen for these differences have not been adequately explained, but they undoubtedly relate to the fact that the immune system is a diffuse system throughout the body with primary, secondary, and tertiary tissues and movement (or

"trafficking"; see Spencer *et al.,* 2000) of immune cells between these tissues as well as coordination and regulation via nerves and hormones (McEwen *et al.,* 1997).

1. Mobile Cellular Components of the Immune System

The cells of the immune system are classified into two functional groups. The first group of immunocytes constitutes the phylogenetically older *innate* immune system, of which natural killer cells and accessory cells, i.e., macrophages and eosinophils, are components. The second group, the *adaptive* or specific immune system, consists of T and B cells, which require antigen recognition in the presence of the specific immune cell receptors [the major histocompatibility complex (MHC)] and chemical messengers (cytokines) in order to carry out their function.

2. Stromal Lymphoid Tissues: Stationary Structures of the Immune System

Immunocytes of the innate and adaptive immune systems are cells derived from and educated in primary lymphoid tissues that are stationary (Paul, 1993), e.g., the thymus and bone marrow, fetal liver and fetal spleen. The immunocytes then take up residence in the secondary, stationary stromal lymphoid tissues, such as the spleen and lymph nodes. Spleen cells filter and concentrate pathogens from the blood, while cells within the strategically placed lymph nodes filter pathogens that drain them from the lymph. These stationary, secondary immune tissues thus provide the major specialized environments where many immune responses are generated (Bulloch, 1985; Paul, 1993).

3. Tertiary Immune Tissues

In some areas of the body that lack a formal secondary lymphatic structure, local cells take on adjunct roles and produce factors that sequester immunocytes to regulate the injury-immune response following injury or pathogenic attack. These areas are referred to as tertiary immune tissues and are present in the gut, skin, and brain. Following an injury to these regions, the immediate effects of these local mechanisms is to promote allostasis, and one of the most important forms of allostasis in the injury/immune response is to control the initiation and resolution of the systemic acute phase response·(APR) in response to more severe injuries.

4. *Neuroanatomy of the Immune System*

The major goal of the immune system is to protect against the invasion and destruction of tissue by pathogens. It is now quite clear that the neuroendocrine system and ANS work together to regulate immunocyte activation as well as to provide a series of checks and balances to contain the destructive properties of each response. This occurs both at the level of the immunocytes (T and B lymphocytes and their accessory cells) and within the stationary stroma of lymphoid tissues (Saposky *et al.*, 2000). It is the cooperation between these systems that constitutes the basis of allostasis in immunity. One of the key aspects of allostasis is the role of innervation of stationary immune tissues.

Research in neuroanatomy and neuroendocrine immunology during the past three decades has changed the concepts governing the regulation of the immune system. Most important are the studies showing the innervation of the immune system by the autonomic nervous system and the potent effects that ANS neuroactivation molecules, i.e., neurotransmitters, neuropeptides, growth factors, etc., alone and in combination with endocrine hormones, can exert a profound effect on the IIHR via the expression of specific neural and endocrine receptors on the constituent cells of the immune system (immunocytes). Figure 2 is a schematic representation of innervation of immune organs and tissues by the ANS.

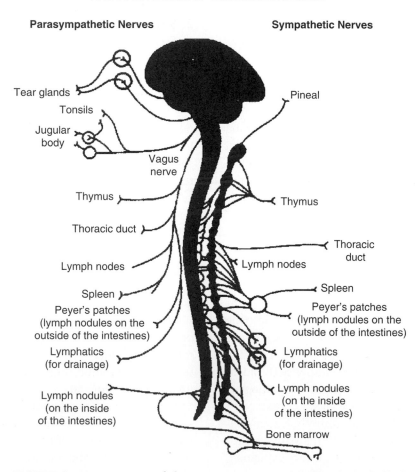

FIGURE 2 Neuroanatomy of the immune system innervation. From Bulloch (2000), in "Handbook of Physiology," Vol. IV, pp. 353–379, © 2000 by Oxford University Press.

The ANS influence on immune tissues begins during the development of the embryo. Early in embryonic development, nerves derived from the vagus complex penetrate the developing thymus gland and delineate the boundaries between the cortex and the medulla. Sympathetic fibers arrive later in embryonic development and are found primarily in association with the vasculature. The neurotransmitters released by the vagal parasympathetic innervation is thought to be involved initially with the maturation of the gland and later in the adult with the thymus' endocrine and immune function (Bulloch, 1985, 2000).

The innervation of other primary immune tissues such as bone marrow also occurs in embryonic development, and like the thymus, the innervation of these other structures is discretely distributed and is involved in both prenatal and postnatal immune functions (Calvo, 1968; Bulloch, 2000).

The largest secondary immune tissue in the juvenile and the adult is the spleen. Its innervation, which is primarily sympathetic in origin in rodents and humans, occurs later in development than the thymus. This rich sympathetic innervation is maintained throughout puberty but slowly declines with age in some but not all strains of rats (Felten *et al.*, 1987). Experimental data suggest that norepinephrine has an inhibitory or containing effect on the "virgin" lymphoid cells that reside in the spleen (Madden *et al.*, 1994) and this inhibition may be one way the nervous system operates to regulate regionally the immune response in the periphery.

For example, monocytes, which are nonactivated accessory cells of the innate immune system, express many β-adrenergic receptors. These innate immune cells are the primary regulators of acquired immunity by processing and presenting antigen and secreting cytokines. *In vitro*, they can be induced by certain agents to become macrophages. During this inducion, their β-adrenergic receptors are down-regulated. However, if they are first treated with norepinephrine (NE), transformation into macrophages is blocked. However, once it has occurred, the activation of the mature macrophage is not reversed by NE, probably due to the reduction of β-adrenergic receptors (Radojcic *et al.*, 1991). These data are but one of many examples showing that NE regulation of immunocytes is one of containment of nonactivated cells and is permis-

sive for those that are committed to an activated function. Thus the role of the sympathetic innervation of the spleen appears to be one that is devoted to modulating the fine-tuning of the immune response. This makes good biological sense, given the pattern and intensity of innervation by catecholamines in this tissue.

Sensory innervation, which we include as part of the ANS circuitry, relays information concerning conditions within the periphery back to the brain with terminations in the nucleus tractus solitarius. The enteric nervous system also has been shown to innervate the secondary and tertiary lymphoid structures of the gut and plays a major role in regulating inflammatory trafficking and responses that occur (Theodorou *et al.*, 1996).

D. Trafficking of Immune Cells among Primary, Secondary, and Tertiary Immune Tissues

Another important role of ANS neuroregulators and circulating steroid hormones is to facilitate the movement, or trafficking, of immune cells between the bloodstream and primary, secondary, and tertiary immune tissues. Studies in animal stress models and limited data in human subjects undergoing stress show that glucocorticoid elevations during stress cause leukocytes to leave the blood stream and concentrate in organs or marginate on blood vessels (Dhabhar *et al.*, 1996; Spencer *et al.*, 2000). The biological rationale for this phenomena is the mobilization of immunocytes for immediate response to an injury. This is demonstrated most eloquently in a classic model of delayed-type hypersensitivity (DTH), in which studies of the actions of catecholamines and glucocorticoids on the movement of immune cells into a site of challenge shows that these hormones facilitate the margination of immune cells to blood vessels in many parts of the body (Dhabhar and McEwen, 1999; Dhabhar *et al.*, 2000; Spencer *et al.*, 2000). When there is a local challenge by a pathogen or other antigen, regional factors are activated, such as interferon gamma, that help recruit and bring additional immune cells into the tissue (Dhabhar *et al.*, 2000). If the damage to the region is severe, then the stage is set for a systemic reaction, which is mediated by the acute phase response.

E. Acute Phase Response

What is an acute phase response (APR) and what does it do? Following an insult that involves physical trauma, or breaching of either skin or mucosal protective barriers by pathogens, the first action by the host is generally to mount a local defense response at the site of the injury. If the magnitude of the insult is too great and a regional response is insufficient to contain or eliminate the source of damage caused by the injury, major metabolic changes occur that initiate a systemic and inflammatory response. This response constitutes a form of allostasis and is called the *acute phase response*. The APR is pivotal in determining the resolution of the trauma and is composed of a series of events that leads to a systemic mobilization of endocrine, nervous, and immune system factors to contain, eliminate, or suppress an invading pathogen or as a response to surgical, mechanical, or even emotional trauma such as shock (Baumann and Gauldie, 1994).

Physiological events that constitute the APR involve (1) a change in the set point of the hypothalamic febrile centers, (2) an increase in granulocyte numbers in the blood and at the site of injury, (3) endocrine changes involving release of ACTH, cortisol, adrenal catecholamines, growth hormones, thyroid hormone, aldosterone, and vasopressin, and (4) cardiovascular changes (Gallin *et al.*, 1992). In addition, metabolic changes occur primarily in the liver and lead to the activation of many genes that increase gluconeogenesis, protein catabolism, decrease of nitrogen balance, and a marked increase in acute phase proteins (Young *et al.*, 1991; Steel and Whitehead, 1994).

1. First Phase of the APR

Sensory pain pathways and other neural and endocrine mediators are activated in response to the trauma (Anisman *et al.*, 1996a,b). Vascular tone changes as a result of both local and neurogenic factors causing dilation of blood vessels particularly in postcapillary venules that eventually lead to extravasation and apparent redness. At the primary site of trauma, several cellular events occur that have the potential of generating either local or systemic consequences. When mucosal or cutaneous barriers are initially breached by pathogens or trauma, sensory C fibers are stimulated, and neuropeptides such as substance P (SP), calcitonin gene related peptide (CGRP), and other mediators are released from sensory nerve terminals. One of the primary targets of these mediators is the mast cells, and these peptides aid in their degranulation. Mast cell factors, in turn, cause platelet aggregation and changes in vascular permeability that lead to swelling and redness, extravasation, and the accumulation of neutrophils and macrophages at the site of the trauma (Berczi *et al.*, 1996). The neutrophils that are generally the first immunocytes to arrive at the site of injury are gradually replaced by macrophages (Baumann and Gauldie, 1994).

The regional macrophages are pivotal in initiating the first wave of the APR. These cells release a series of factors such as tumor necrosis factor-α (TNFα) that stimulate stromal cells to release migratory factors such as intracellular adhesion molecules (ICAM). The release and consequent action of these factors constitute the initiation of the second wave of the APR. Additional TNF and interleukin-1 (IL-1) release leads to the accumulation of leukocytes. The presence of IL-1 further stimulates regional fibroblasts to make interleukin-6 (IL-6) and chemotaxic peptides and adhesion molecules (Baumann and Gauldie, 1994; Perry and Gordon, 1988).

2. Activation of a Systemic APR

Failure by the local milieu to contain the injury response or the pathogenic attack leads to systemic activation of the hypothalamic pituitary adrenal (HPA) axis. This activation can result in a febrile response and the release of ACTH from the pituitary and glucocorticoids from the adrenal cortex. Glucocorticoids increase the systemic mobilization of the APR by directly stimulating the synthesis of acute phase proteins (APP) in the liver. However, the principal action of glucocorticoids is to enhance, synergistically, the effects of IL-1 and IL-6 type on many APP. The production of APP acts in concert with the immune system to contain, eliminate, and repair the damage caused by the trauma (Baumann and Gauldie, 1994).

Mobilization of the systemic response constitutes the hallmark of the APR and sets up the stage for the type (i.e., cellular verses humoral) and magnitude of the adaptive or specific immune response. Activated macrophages will consume and process the pathogen and carry it to the regional lymph nodes. Here a series of factors are released that lead to the proliferation and maturation of pathogenic-specific immune cells, which return to the injury site and expand their immune repertoire to deal with and eliminate the trauma.

3. Containment and Resolution of the APR

The resolution of the APR generally occurs over a 24–48 hour period after the initial insult, and there are several factors that contribute to its down-regulation. One factor is the short half-life of cytokines and another more important event is the feedback shut down of stromal and macrophage by glucocorticoids (Baumann and Gaulde, 1994; Gallin and Paul, 1993).

Thus, within these tissues, the normal sequence of events from the initiation of the APR to the activation of the *type* (cellular verses humoral), *class* (subtypes of humoral immunity, e.g., IgG verses IgA), and *magnitude* of adaptive immunity is tailored to fit the environment rather than the type of injury or pathogen (Steel and Whitehead, 1994).

F. Allostatic Load and the Dysfunction of the APR

Although not fully appreciated or understood, it is now clear that underlying many chronic illnesses is the failure of the HPA axis to regulate glucocorticoids and shutdown of the APR. An inadequate glucocorticoid response can occur in a variety of physiological and psychological conditions that lead to a form of allostatic load and thus undermine the immune-healing process. Specifically, in this type of allostatic load, the inflammatory responses may not be adequately shut down by the HPA, thereby leading to chronic inflammation or other immune dysfunctions (Sapolsky *et al.*, 2000).

IV. THE INJURY-IMMUNE HEALING RESPONSE IN THE BRAIN

A. Allostasis vs Allostatic Load

Superimposed upon the ANS hardwiring and the hormonal neuroendocrine influence on the organs and tissues of the immune system are other physiological events that can exert a profound influence on the immune response and, with prolonged exacerbation, lead ultimately to allostatic load. These events are the hormonal and neural actions that vary with the developmental history, genetic makeup, and physiologic state of individuals. These variations, in turn, can be compounded by external influences such as seasonal and diurnal rhythms and exaggerated stressful experiences.

The ability of the immune system to adjust to these internal and external environmental cues is another example of allostasis and affects the competence of the immunocytes' effector functions. Specifically, the immune system mediators of allostasis promote trafficking of lymphocytes, regional containment of the magnitude of the immune responses, control of the class or type of immune response (i.e., cellular verses humoral immunity), and help maintain the developmental integrity of immune tissues (McEwen *et al.*, 1997; Blalock, 1989; Bulloch, 1982; Sirinek and O'Dorisio, 1991). In addition, regional neural and endocrine mechanisms are now known to fine-tune the systemic acute phase response (APR) and control the outcome of immune responses.

This is particularly true in primary immune tissues and tertiary immune tissues, such as endocrine glands, skin, and the central nervous system (CNS). Here neuroendocrine factors can influence the progression of an APR and set the stage for the type and magnitude of the adaptive immune response. The result of this fine-tuning may not be entirely beneficial from the point of view of elimination of pathogens from the body. Indeed, a normal T-cell antiviral attack may be down-regulated in certain regions, e.g., CNS or critical endocrine tissues, in favor of a less effective B-cell response. The regulatory override mechanisms of immune allostasis employed by the cells within the primary and tertiary tissues most likely have evolved to protect tissues that are critical to life from self-destruction by the cellular immune response in favor of a less effective immune response. This type of regional regulation might be viewed as one kind of an allostatic load for the immune system, with the ultimate cost being the buildup of certain viruses (e.g., slow viruses or herpes viruses) within the body over time, until a disease state is finally manifested that cannot be controlled by the dominating immune response.

B. Allostasis and the IIHR in the CNS

Excessive challenges as well as a failure in adequately activating the HPA axis, as noted above, can lead to an allostatic load that compromises intrinsic mechanisms, which in turn can cause damage beyond that of the initial challenge. It now appears that similar

IIHR mechanisms operate within the CNS. Although the understanding of the IIHR within the CNS is still in its infancy, particularly when compared to our understanding of peripheral responses, there have been recent advances in neuroimmunology that have begun to shed light on these events and dispel many of the myths concerning the ability of the brain to protect itself against pathogens and other traumas.

For years the brain was considered an immune, privileged tissue. This was due, primarily, to the perception that the blood brain barrier (BBB) is an impenetrable structure to cellular elements and large molecules, and, secondarily, to the lack of formal lymphoid structures within the brain. However, recent advances in studies of immune cell migration between blood and brain and in our understanding of the BBB have modified this view, as will now be discussed.

Although the understanding of the IIHR within the CNS is still in its infancy, neuroimmunology clearly demonstrates that the CNS is capable of mounting an effective IIHR subject to the rules of allostasis. This response is unique from that observed outside the brain's boundaries, and there are even differences within specific regions of the brain. What is special about the CNS IIHR, in contrast to a systemic immune response, is the regulation of the sequence, timing, magnitude and type of acute phase response–adaptive immune response that can occur. This uniqueness is due to several factors.

1. Lymphoid Structures Associated with the CNS

Although no formal lymphoid structure resides within the CNS, it is now clear that the brain does have primitive afferent lymphatic pathways that are capable of draining fluid and pathogens to the cervical lymph nodes and thus can provide the stimulus and environment for generating an adaptive immune response (Weller *et al.*, 1996). Specifically, the retropharnygeal lymph glands also have been shown to receive fluid drainage from the CNS via the cribriform plate in the nasal cavity in animals (Bradbury *et al.*, 1981; Weller *et al.*, 1996) as well as in man (Lowhagen *et al.*, 1994). Aside from these lymphoid structures, there are other lymphoid structures surrounding the brain's perimeter that contain immunocytes (Cogburn and Glick, 1981). The pineal gland is one such structure (Cogburn and Glick, 1981), and the Harderian glands—

sebaceous glands associated with the eye of many amphibians, reptiles, birds, and some mammals—are another (Campbell and Gibbson, 1970; Quay, 1965; Kappers, 1969; Romieu and Jullien, 1942; Spiroff, 1958). The Harderian glands are believed to provide a front-line defense by supplying immunoglobulins to combat pathogens that invade the eye (Bang and Bang, 1968; Walcott, 1983).

2. Immunocyte Access to the CNS

Not only do these primitive lymphoid tissues exist, but it is also evident that both innate and adaptive immunocytes can readily gain access to the central nervous system. The recent seminal work on the access of the CNS to peripheral immunocytes clearly demonstrates that the nervous system is not as privileged an immune site as initial dogma would have had us believe. Within the last two decades, research has proven that the CNS is accessible to the migration of bone marrow-derived microglia (MG), macrophages (Eglitis and Mezey, 1997), and lymphocytes (Williams and Hickey, 1995). There is even a demonstration that these bone marrow-derived stem cells can give rise to some types of neuronal precursors (Mezey *et al.*, 2000; Woodbury *et al.*, 2000).

The entry of hematopoietic cells into the CNS is likely due, in part, to the venules of the CNS endothelial beds, for new data show that they bear a strong functional resemblance to peripheral high endothelial venules. Like their peripheral counterparts, the endothelial cells of the CNS venules can express accessory or adhesion molecules and are receptive to peripheral cellular trafficking (Male *et al.*, 1995; Grau *et al.*, 1997; Kielian and Hickey, 2000). Furthermore, it is now clear that in addition to immunocyte and precursor cells, plasma electrolytes, hormones, and other molecules that compose the cerebrospinal fluid (CSF), cytokines, can gain entrance through the seven regions of the brain that lack a BBB (Williams *et al.*, 1994), collectively called the "circumventricular organs," i.e., area postrema, median eminence, pituitary neural lobe, organum vasculosum lamina terminalis, pineal gland, subcommisural organ, and subfornical organ (Oldfield and McKinley, 1995).

Recent studies of the brain's response to injury demonstrate quite clearly that in addition to sequestering immunocytes and stem cells in the CNS, regions of the brain can act as tertiary immune tissues, and cells of both neuronal and glial origin can be induced to make molecules that serve to modulate allostasis in normal brain function as well as during the IIHR.

3. Microglia: A Major Cellular Constituent of Allostasis in the CNS

Microglia (MG) are the major vehicles for immune allostasis in the CNS. MG are a type of macrophage derived from bone marrow, like other hematopoietic cells, that migrate into the CNS during embryogenesis (Eglitis and Mezey, 1997). During this migration they undergo a series of transitions into MG. This transition is not unique to the brain, for cells of the macrophage family can vary markedly in phenotype and function according to the region of the body and the microenvironment (Perry and Gordon, 1988; Qiao *et al.,* 1996). Even within the CNS the function of MG varies with their distribution (Perry and Gordon, 1988; Williams and Hickey, 1995; Raivich *et al.,* 1999) MG are more similar to the Langerhans cell in the skin (Perry and Gordon, 1988), another macrophage-like cell, than to peritoneal macrophages.

Best known for their role in CNS damage, MG have an important role in allostasis within the normal CNS that is related to their functions in the injured brain. Understanding the relationship between the MG role in normal and in the injured CNS is key to the understanding of neuroimmune-based diseases and the development of therapies addressing allostatic load in the CNS. Here we examine the role of microglia in CNS noninflammatory structural remodeling.

a) Synaptic Stripping MG, together with astrocytes, have a less well-characterized nonimmune housekeeping role in the CNS (Mor *et al.,* 1999). For example, studies on CNS motor neuron regeneration following axotomy demonstrate that MG are involved in removing morphologically intact synaptic terminals from neuronal surface membranes, a process called *synaptic stripping*, before the neurons show demonstrable signs of damage. This removal is most likely secondary to a primary signal that loosens the synaptic contact (Blinzinger and Kreutzberg, 1968). Several molecules such as CD 44 (HCAM) (Jones *et al.,* 1997) have been associated with this phenomenon, but a full understanding of this process has yet to be elucidated.

Indeed, there are many events in the CNS involving structural remodeling of neurons that do not involve injury, and these events are under hormonal regulation and respond to environmental changes. Recent evidence shows that neuronal turnover and synaptic and dendritic remodeling are modulated during normal physiological events such as chronic stress (Gould *et al.,* 1990) and the estrous cycle (Woolley *et al.,* 1990).

What remains unclear is how these events occur, or what prevents an inflammatory response to these cellular modifications within the CNS. It is possible that the dendritic spines may be removed or remodeled by the target neuron itself, but it is also quite possible that the pre- and postsynaptic elements are removed by a rapidly responding cell type such as the MG. Evidence that reinforces this view is suggested by the experimental model in which ligation of entorhinal cortex projections to the parvalbumin neurons of the hippocampus produces dissociation of presynaptic terminals and shrinkage of the dendrites. This response is totally blocked when MG are inhibited (Eyupoglu *et al.,* 2000).

By stripping or disconnecting the terminals from neural processes and possibly also providing signal molecules to induce dendritic shrinkage, activated MG would engulf and process the elements of the pre- and postsynaptic terminal without presenting any "novel antigens" that were masked within the synaptic structure. In fact, such a process is not unique to MG function, since anergy, the blocking of an inflammatory response, is a documented role of the activated MG-macrophages in resolving the injury response in the CNS (Raivich *et al.,* 1999). Closely linked to its remodeling role is the role of the MG during regeneration or restructuring of neurons (Mor *et al.,* 1999).

b) Production of Trophic Factors by MG and Other Reactive Cells Transforming growth factor $\beta 1$ (TGF-$\beta 1$), a multifunctional peptide growth factor that plays a role in the response of the CNS to trauma and SR is expressed by MG (Morgan *et al.,* 1993; Nichols *et al.,* 1991). Adrenal steroids down-regulate TGF-$\beta 1$ in MG, thereby raising the possibility that the expression of this growth factor following injury might be mediated directly through glucocorticoid receptors, since cultured MG have been shown to express both GR and MR (Tanaka *et al.,* 1997). However, in the event that

MG do not express detectable GR or MR in the resting stage, glucocorticoids may indirectly modulate their action through the modulation of neuropeptides, such as CGRP, that target MG (Reddington *et al.*, 1995).

c) Glia Involvement in Hormone Release Pituicytes and MG in the pituitary may influence hormone secretion by regulating neurovascular contacts, and astroglia in the hypothalamus regulate the synaptic inputs from specific neuronal populations involved in pituitary hormone release (McQueen, 1994; Garcia-Segura and Chowen, 1996). MG, tanycytes, and astrocytes in the arcuate nucleus and median eminence also release trophic factors that regulate hormone secretion by hypothalamic neurons (Garcia-Segura and Chowen, 1996), as well as secrete cytokines such as IL-6.

Reactive glial cells produce a variety of cytokines and trophic factors that are key to coordination of the cellular response to injury (Norenberg, 1994). They also have receptors for insulin and insulin-like growth factors (IGF-I and IGF-II) (Guthrie *et al.*, 1995). Cytokines such as IL-1β, β-FGF, and IGF-I, which are expressed in the deafferented hippocampus, have been shown to promote glial proliferation (Chernausek, 1993) and hypertrophy (Friedman *et al.*, 1983; Toran-Allerand and Bentham, 1991) and thus may participate as paracrine or autocrine factors directing glial responses to trauma or pathological insult (Berninger *et al.*, 1995).

d) MG and the CNS Response to Damage In response to a trauma, injury, or pathogenic attack, certain cell types within the brain such as MG, astrocytes, and even neurons can serve as tertiary immune tissues. They synthesize and respond to cytokines and other neuroimmune molecules and thereby take on the role of becoming the "in-resident" immune modulators of CNS allostasis (Lassmann and Hickey, 1993; Ford *et al.*, 1995; Perry and Gordon, 1988; Hickey *et al.*, 1991). In addition, both adhesion molecules specific for immunocytes and factors of the complement pathway (Pasinetti *et al.*, 1992) are expressed within the brain by both resident and migratory cells following trauma. However, it is the control of the APR within the brain by resident brain tissue that will ultimately determine what response will occur to trauma or pathogenic attack. In this regard, the MG, like its peripheral counterpart, the macrophage, and to a lessor degree the as-

trocyte, are pivotal in initiating and maintaining allostasis in the IIHR in the CNS.

Following acute injury to the CNS, MG and astrocytes are the primary immune cells of the brain, activation of which initiates a network of morphological and metabolic changes leading to repair of tissue damage and protection against infectious agents. Neuronal cells rapidly change gene expression and stimulate adjacent cells in response to injury. MG are the first cells to respond to injured neurons. Their activation in response to an injury of any type is weighted and stereotypic (Raivich *et al.*, 1999). This includes the graded production of proinflammatory cytokines, functional changes in brain vascular endothelia, and recruitment of immune cells into the injured tissue. The stereotypic responses of glia to injury reflects a program, conserved by evolution, in the preservation and repair of damaged neurons. There are graded activation stages (Fig. 3) associated with CNS injury blunt trauma, neurotoxins, and severe immune responses within the CNS such as viral, bacterial, parasite infection, or autoimmune-mediated inflammation. They have receptors for complement fragments, such as the FC region of IgG (FCγ) which endows them with highly specific binding for low levels of immunoglobulin in brain (Cunningham *et al.*, 1998; Weller *et al.*, 1996; Fishman and Savitt, 1999; Liu *et al.*, 1995). Other MG functional markers are derived from a number of molecules such as neurotransmitter receptors i.e., β-adrenergic receptors, CGRP receptors (Reddington *et al.*, 1995) or cytokines, e.g., IL1, IL2, IL6, TNF-β (Garcia-Segura and Chowen,

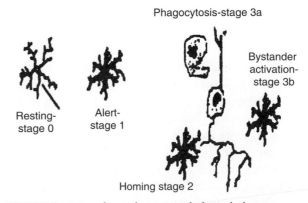

FIGURE 3 Microglia undergo morphological changes corresponding to their stage of activation (Raivich *et al.*, 1999). See text for description of stages of activation.

1996), to which MG are responsive to or which MG secrete in order to affect other cells.

More recently, factors underlying metabolic processes occurring in these different morphological stages have been identified and reflect differences in expression of molecules for adhesion, cytoskeletal organization, antigen presentation, induction of cell proliferation, and phagocytosis (Raivich *et al.,* 1999).

V. THE HIPPOCAMPUS: A MODEL FOR REGIONAL IMMUNE ALLOSTASIS AND ALLOSTATIC LOAD

One of the regions of the brain that undergoes extensive structural remodeling is the hippocampus. It is particularly interesting because these changes have been directly linked to changes in behavior and memory. The hippocampus is a sensitive and vulnerable region of the brain that undergoes morphological remodeling in adult life and is also sensitive to damage from stroke, seizures, physical trauma, and stress (Sapolsky, 1992; McEwen *et al.,* 1995). Recently Kim *et al.* (2000) has shown that the vulnerability of the hippocampus is indicated by the high concentration of MG present in this structure that relates to the functional changes that are occurring.

Hippocampal function declines with age (Sapolsky, 1992; Landfield and Eldridge, 1994), more so in some individuals than in others (Meaney *et al.,* 1988; S. Lupien *et al.,* 1994; Seeman *et al.,* 1997; S. J. Lupien *et al.,* 1998), and it is suspected that a elevated secretion of adrenal steroids may contribute to age-related increases in vulnerability to insults and loss of function (Sapolsky, 1992; McEwen, 1995; Lupien *et al.,* 1998). Adrenal hormones thus play a large role in hippocampal function during the life span, as will be summarized below.

A. Adrenal Steroids

The hippocampal formation is rich in receptors for adrenal steroids (McEwen *et al.,* 1968). This finding, first in rats and later in primates (Gerlach *et al.,* 1976) and birds (Rhees *et al.,* 1972), suggested that the adrenal cortex must have a far-reaching influence on this region of the brain. In the past decade research has eluci-

dated the multiple hormonal influences in hippocampal structure and function, ranging from adaptive plasticity (allostasis) to severe pathophysiological changes (allostatic load).

The hippocampal formation plays an important role in spatial and declarative memory as well as in contextual memory (Smriga *et al.,* 1996) and is vulnerable to processes during aging, correlated with elevated cortisol levels, that decrease hippocampal volume and produce memory impairments in declarative and spatial memory (Lupien *et al.,* 1998). In addition, there are degeneration-enhancing effects of glucocorticoids in response to ischemia, seizures, and head trauma (Sapolsky, 1992; Landfield and Eldridge, 1994; Lowenstein *et al.,* 1994).

B. Importance of NMDA Receptors

Many of the above-mentioned hormone effects on morphology and function of the hippocampus do not occur alone but rather in the context of ongoing neuronal activity. In particular, excitatory amino acids and NMDA receptors play an important role in the adaptive functional and structural changes produced in the hippocampal formation by steroid hormones. This includes the effects of adrenal steroids to produce atrophy of CA3 pyramidal neurons (McEwen *et al.,* 1995), as well as the actions of adrenal steroids to contain dentate gyrus (DG) neurogenesis (Cameron *et al.,* 1998; Cameron and Gould, 1996).

At the same time, excitatory amino acids and NMDA receptors are involved in the destructive actions of stress and trauma on the hippocampus (Cameron and Gould, 1996) and one of the challenges is to understand whether there is a transition from adaptive plasticity to permanent damage and what mechanisms underlie it. One of the more interesting aspects of structural remodeling in the hippocampus is the glucocorticoid and glutamate–NMDA regulated neurogenesis and neuronal cell death that occur in the adult DG.

C. Neurogenesis and Cell Death of Granule Neurons

Adrenalectomy induces an increase in DG granule neuron apoptosis and neurogenesis, and this process is suppressed by adrenal steroid replacement, a result indicating that the HPA axis plays an important regulatory role. DG neuronal cell birth and death seem to be simultaneous processes during development (Gould and Cameron, 1996; Gould *et al.*, 1991), which continues in the adult of several species, including humans (Bayer, 1980; Cameron *et al.*, 1993; Eriksson *et al.*, 1998; Gould *et al.*, 1997; Gould *et al.*, 1999; Kaplan and Hinds, 1977; Kempermann *et al.*, 1997; Kornack and Rakic, 1999). The cells that give rise to these granule cell neurons are derived from precursors located in the innermost region of the granule cell layer (Kaplan and Bell, 1984) Although it is known that the proliferation and differentiation of these precursors into these newly generated neurons are modulated by the NMDA type of glutamate receptor (Cameron *et al.*, 1998a,b; Cameron and Gould, 1995; Cameron *et al.*, 1995), the exact cell types and mechanisms involved in initiating cell division and cell removal still remain unknown.

D. Calcitonin Gene Related Peptide, Structural Remodeling, and the IIHR in the Hippocampus

The neuroimmune peptide calcitonin gene related peptide (CGRP) is one of the most diverse, influential immunoregulators of the periphery. This important neuropeptide has multiple functions, including its actions as a potent vasodilator (Drossman, 1994), an immune modulator (Hosoi *et al.*, 1993; Nong *et al.*, 1989; Foremen, 1987; Umeda and Arisawa, 1989; Bulloch *et al.*, 1991, 1994, 1998a; McGillis *et al.*, 1991; Lombardi *et al.*, 1998; Sirinek and O'Dorisio, 1991; Pincelli *et al.*, 1993; Mullins *et al.*, 1993), a neural and immune developmental molecule (Bulloch *et al.*, 1998b; Noble *et al.*, 1993; Griffiths *et al.*, 1993; Arii *et al.*, 1993), a modulator of hormone release involved in growth and development (Fahim *et al.*, 1990; Netti *et al.*, 1989), a stimulator of sympathetic outflow (Fisher *et al.*, 1983), which is mediated by CRF (Kovacs *et al.*, 1995), and an inducer of apoptosis (Bulloch *et al.*, 1995, 1998a; Sakuta *et al.*, 1996). Some of the different functional roles for CGRP may not be independent but may be part of a cascade of events that constitute the healing response to injury. We (Bulloch *et al.*, 1996a,b, 1997) and others (Galeazza *et al.*, 1993) have shown that CGRP is expressed following various kinds of trauma and plays an important role in the acute phase response that may be of particular relevance to the outcome of the

regional injury response in the central nervous system (Berczi *et al.*, 1996).

In recent studies, the expression of CGRP within the hippocampus increases in five separate models of CNS injury: adrenalectomy (Bulloch *et al.*, 1996b), ischemia (Bulloch *et al.*, 1998b), intrahypocampal colchicine injections (Bulloch *et al.*, 1996b), trimetheyltin ingestion, and kainic acid injections (Saria *et al.*, 1989; Bulloch *et al.*, 1997). In each case, the expression of this peptide was limited to the specific region of damage and in association with the surviving neuronal population (Figure 4). Although the up-regulation of CGRP may be solely associated with neuronal cell survival (Wang *et al.*, 1993), other studies have shown that both microglia and astrocytes express CGRP receptors and that exposure to physiological levels of CGRP induces c-fos in microglia and astrocytes and increases plasminogen activators (Reddington *et al.*, 1995). The plasminogen activator system has been shown to be involved in neuronal cell migration, dendritic remodeling (Nakajima *et al.*, 1993) in the CNS during injury (Moonen *et al.*, 1982), and the final phases of apoptosis (Kataoka *et al.*, 1999).

E. Adrenal Steroid Effects and Receptors in Microglia

There is a link between CGRP and other, systemic mediators of allostasis and allostatic load, namely, catecholamines and glucocorticoids. Not only does CGRP stimulate sympathetic outflow through CRF release (Kovacs *et al.*, 1995), but this peptide is negatively regulated by adrenal steroids (Smith *et al.*, 1991) in some tissues. Yet the exact site and mechanism of glucocorticoid actions on MG are unclear.

As noted above, under physiological conditions, the actions of agents like CGRP or circulating adrenal steroids on MG may have important consequences for neuronal development, metabolism, and activity for the formation and plasticity of synaptic connections (Schumacher and Robel, 1996). MG undergo activation in response to physical and chemical insults, aging, and neurodegenerative diseases, and this is often associated with elevated levels of stress hormones. In addition, steroid hormones may affect regenerative processes in neurons by modulating glial responses following injury (Norenberg, 1994).

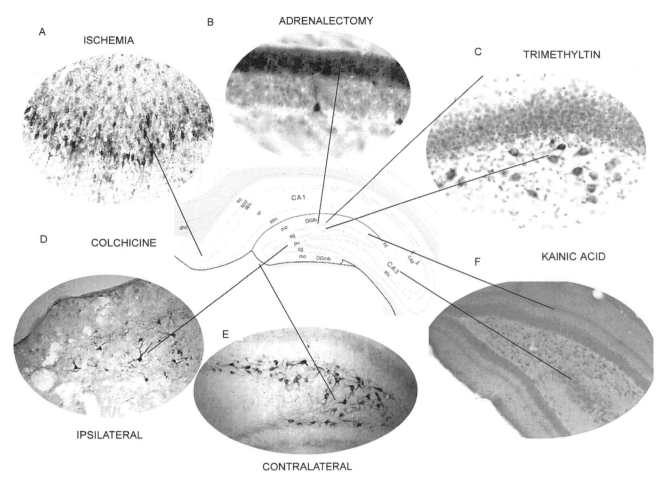

FIGURE 4 (A) Interneurons display CGRP-IR following ischemia (Bulloch *et al.*, 1996a). (B) CGRP-IR following adrenalectomy. Note the heavy increase of immunoreactivity in the intermolecular layer of the dentate gyrus (Bulloch *et al.*, 1996b). (C) CGRP-IR following trimethyltin treatment in mossy cells of the dentate gyrus. (D/E) CGRP-IR in mossy cells following colchicine injections into the hippocampus (Bulloch *et al.*, 1996b). (F) Dentate gyrus with a decrease of CGRP-IR in the intermolecular layer following treatment with kainic acid (Bulloch *et al.*, 1997). **See insert for a color version of this figure.**

VI. CONCLUSIONS

We have seen that allostasis in the immune system is mediated by systemic and local tissue mediators involving, on the one hand, circulating adrenal steroids, catecholamines, and other hormones and, on the other hand, local tissue mediators such as CGRP. The trafficking of immune cells in and out of stationary immune tissues and in and out of tissues where pathogens or damage have taken place constitutes another mechanim of allostasis in the immune system, along with the acute phase response. Overreactions of the acute phase response due to inadequate counterregulation by glucocorticoids and catecholamines constitutes a major form of immune system allostatic load in many tissues, including the central nervous system.

The central nervous system is not at all isolated from the immune system. Rather, it should be viewed as a tertiary immune tissue, and the elements of immune system function in the CNS play an important role in the IIHR as well as in normal adaptation and plasticity. The neuropeptide CGRP appears to be a particularly potent local tissue mediator of the IIHR in the central nervous system. Immune cell trafficking into brain may be one mechanism for responding to damage and even, perhaps, to normal physiological processes. In addition, there are indications that immune-system-derived stem cells may give rise to neurons and glial cells. At the same time, the resident microglial cells in brain turn out to have multiple potential roles not only in conditions involving brain damage but also for adaptive plasticity in the normal brain.

References

Anisman, H., Baines, M. G., Berczi, I., Bernstein, C. N., Blennerhassett, M. G., Gorczynski, R. M., Greenberg, A. H., Kisil, F. T., Mathison, R. D., Nagy, E., Nance, D. M., Perdue, M. H., Pomerantz, D. K., Sabbadini, E. R., Stanisz, A., and Warrington, R. J. (1996a). Neuroimmune mechanisms in health and disease: 1. Health. *Canadian Med. Assoc. J.* **155**, 867–874.

Anisman, H., Baines, M. G., Berczi, I., Bernstein, C. N., Blennerhassett, M. G., Gorczynski, R. M., Greenberg, A. H., Kisil, F. T., Mathison, R. D., Nagy, E., Nance, D. M., Perdue, M. H., Pomerantz, D. K., Sabbadini, E. R., Stanisz, A., and Warrington, R. J. (1996b). Neuroimmune mechanisms in health and disease: 2. Disease. *Can. Med. Assoc. J.* **155**, 1075–1082.

Arii, Y., Kawai, H., Sato, K., Yamaguchi, H., and Saito, S. (1993). Effects of calcitonin gene-related peptide on muscle cell differentiation and development. *Rinsho Shinkeigaku* **33**, 595–599.

Bang, B. G., and Bang, F. B. (1968). Localized lymphoid tissue and plasma cells in paraocular and paranasal organ systems in chickens. *Am. J. Pathol.* **53**, 735–751.

Bannister, R. (1988). Introduction and classification. *In* "Autonomic Failure: A Texbook of Clinical Disorders of the Autonomic Nervous System" (R. Bannister, ed.), pp. 1–22.

Baumann, H., and Gauldie, J. (1994). The acute phase response. *Immunol. Today* **15**, 74–80.

Bayer, S. (1980). Development of the hippocampal region in the rat. I. Neurogenesis examined with 3H thymidine autoradiography. *J. Comp. Neurol.* **190**, 87–114.

Berczi, I., Chalmers, I. M., Nagy, E., and Warrington, R. J. (1996). The immune effects of neuropeptides. *Baillieres Clin. Rheumatol.* **10**, 227–257.

Berninger, B., Marty, S., Zafra, F., da Penha Berzaghi, M., Thoenen, H., and Lindholm, D. (1995). GABAergic stimulation switches from enhancing to repressing BDNF expression in rat hippocampal neurons during maturation in vitro. *Development* **121**, 2327–2325.

Blalock, J. E. (1989). A molecular basis for bidirectional communication between the immune and neuroendocrine systems. *Physiol. Rev.* **69**, 1–32.

Blinzinger, K., and Kreutzberg, G. (1968). Displacement of synaptic terminals from regenerating motoneurons by microglial cells. *Z. Zellforsch. Mikrosk. Anat.* **85**, 145–157.

Bradbury, W. B., Cserr, H. F., and Westrop, J. (1981). Drainage of cerebral interstitial tissue fluid into deep cervical lymph of the rabbit. *Am. J. Physiol.* **240**, F329–F336.

Brindley, D. N., and Rolland, Y. (1989). Possible connections between stress, diabetes, obesity, hypertension and altered lipoprotein metabolism that may result in atherosclerosis. *Clin. Science* **77**, 453–461.

Bulloch, K. (1982). "Neuroendocrine-immune Circuitry Pathways Included with the Induction and Persistence of Humoral Immunity." University Microfilm International, Ann Arbor, MI.

Bulloch, K. (1985). Neuroanatomy of lymphoid tissue: A review. *In* "Neural Modulation of Immunity" (R. Guillemin *et al.*, eds.), pp. 111–141. Raven Press, New York.

Bulloch, K. (2000). Regional neural regulation of immunity: Anatomy and function. *In* "Handbook of Physiology" (B. S. McEwen, ed.), Sec. 7, Vol. IV, pp. 353–379. Oxford University Press, Oxford.

Bulloch, K., Radojcic, T., Yu, R., Hausman, J., Lenhard, L., and Baird, S. (1991). The distribution and function of calcitonin gene-related peptide in the mouse thymus and spleen. *Psycho Neuro Endocrin Immunology* **4**, 186–194.

Bulloch, K., McEwen, B., Diwa, A., Radojcic, T., Hausman, J., and Baird, S. (1994). The role of calcitonin gene related peptide (CGRP) in the mouse thymus revisited. *Ann. N.Y. Acad. Sci.* **741**, 129–136.

Bulloch, K., Diwa, A., and McEwen, B. S. (1995). Calcitonin gene related peptide (CGRP) induced apoptosis in vitro murine thymocytes via receptor insensitive to the antagonist CGRP 8-27 with a potency similar to that induced by glucocorticoid. *Inflammopharmacology* **3**, 75–76.

Bulloch, K., Milner, T. A., Reagan, L. P., Weiland, N. G., Buzsaki, G., and McEwen, B. S. (1996a). Calcitonin gene related peptide-immunoreactivity (CGRP-IR) expression in hippocampal CA1 neurons following ischemia may suppress inflamatory immune response to dying pryamidal cells. *Soc. Neurosci. Abstr.* **22**, 1455.

Bulloch, K., Prasad, A., Conrad, C. D., McEwen, B., and Milner, T. A. (1996b). Calcitonin gene-related peptide level in the rat dentate gyrus increases after damage. *NeuroReport* **7**, 1036–1040.

Bulloch, K., Milner, T. A., Pierce, J., and McEwen, B. S. (1997). Kainic Acid induction of CGRP-LI in the hippocampal formation of rats: Regional regulation of the CNS injury/immune response. *Neurosci. Abstr.* **23**, 716.

Bulloch, K., McEwen, B. S., Norberg, J., Diwa, A., and Baird, S. (1998a). Selective regulation of T cell development and function by calcitonin gene related peptide (CGRP) in the thymus and spleen: An example of regional regulation of immunity by the neuroendocrine system. *Ann. N.Y. Acad. Sci.* **840**, 551–562.

Bulloch, K., Milner, T. A., Prasad, A., Hsu, M., Buzsaki, G., and McEwen, B. S. (1998b). Calcitonin gene related peptide-like immunoreactivity in hippocampal neurons following ischemia: A putative regional modulator of the CNS/injury response. *Exp. Neurol.* **150**, 195–205.

Buske-Kirschbaum, A., Jobst, S., Wustmans, A., Kirschbaum, C., Rauth, W., and Hellhammer, D. H. (1997). Attenuated free cortisol response to psychosocial stress in children with atopic dermatitis. *Psychosom. Med.* **59**, 419–426.

Cahill, L., Prins, B., Weber, M., and McGaugh, J. L. (1994). Beta-adrenergic activation and memory for emotional events. *Nature (London)* **371**, 702–704.

Calvo, W. (1968). The innervation of the bone marrow in laboratory animals. *Am. J. Anat.* **123**, 315–328.

Cameron, H. A., and Gould, E. (1996). The control of neuronal birth and survival. *In* "Receptor Dynamics in Neural Development" (C. A. Shaw, ed.), pp. 141–157. CRC Press, New York.

Cameron, H. A., McEwen, B. S., and Gould, E. (1995). Regulation of adult neurogenesis by excitatory input and NMDA receptor activation in the dentate gyrus. *J. Neurosci.* **15**, 4687–4692.

Cameron, H. A., Tanapat, P., and Gould, E. (1998a). Adrenal steroids and N-methyl-D-aspartate receptor activation regulate neurogenesis in the dentate gyrus of adult rats through a common pathway. *Neuroscience* **82**, 349–354.

Cameron, H. A., Hazel, T. G., and McKay, R. D. (1998b). Regulation of neurogenesis by growth factors and neurotransmitters. *J. Neurobiol.* **36**, 287–306.

Campbell, E., and Gibbson, M. A. (1970). A histological and histochemical study of the development of the pineal gland in the chick. *Galleus domesticus. Can. J. Zool.* **48**, 1321–1328.

Chernausek, S. D. (1993). Insulin-like growth factor-1 (IGF-1) production by astroglial cells: Regulation and importance for epidermal growth factor-induced cell replication. *J. Neurosci.* **34**, 189–197.

Cogburn, L. A., and Glick, B. (1981). Lymphopoiesis in the chicken pineal gland. *Am. J. Anat.* **162**, 131–142.

Crofford, L. J., Pillemer, S. R., Kalogeras, K., Cash, J. M., Michelson, D., Kling, M. A., Sternberg, E. M., Gold, P. W., Chrousos, G. P., and Wilder, R. L. (1994). Hypothalamic-pituitary-adrenal axis perturbations in patients with fibromyalgia. *Arthritis Rheum.* **37**, 1583–1592.

Cunningham, T. J., Hodge, L., Speicher, D., Reim, D., Tyler-Polsz, C., Levitt, P., Eagleson, K., Kennedy, S., and Wang, Y. (1998). Identification of a survival-promoting peptide in medium conditioned by oxidatively stressed cell lines of nervous system origin. *J. Neurosci.* **18**, 7047–7060.

Dhabhar, F. S., and McEwen, B. S. (1999). Enhancing versus suppressive effects of stress hormones on skin immune function. *Proc. Natl. Acad. Sci. U.S.A.* **96**, 1059–1064.

Dhabhar, F. S., Miller, A. H., McEwen, B. S., and Spencer, R. L. (1996). Stress-Induced changes in blood leukocyte distribution: Role of adrenal steroid hormones. *J. Immunol.* **157**, 1638–1644.

Dhabhar, F. S., Satoskar, A. R., Bluethmann, H., David, J. R., and McEwen, B. S. (2000). Stress-induced enhancement of skin immune function: A role for interferon. *Proc. Natl. Acad. Sci. U.S.A.* **97**, 2846–2851.

Drossman, D. A. (1994). Irritable bowel syndrome. *Gastroenterologist* **2**, 315–326.

Eglitis, M. A., and Mezey, E. (1997). Hematopoietic cells differentiate into both microglia and macroglia in the brains of adult mice. *Proc. Nat. Acad. Sci. U.S.A.* **94**, 4080–4085.

Eichenbaum, H., and Harris, K. (2000). Toying with memory in the hippocampus. *Nat. Neurosci.* **3**, 205–206.

Eriksson, P. S., Permlieva, E., Bjork-Eriksson, T., Alborn, A.-M., Nordborg, C., Peterson, D. A., and Gage, F. H. (1998). Neurogenesis in the adult human hippocampus. *Nat. Med.* **4**, 1313–1317.

Eyupoglu, I. Y., Bechmann, I., and Nitsch, R. (2000). Microglial activity modulates dendritic changes following partial deafferentiation. *Soc. Neurosci. Abstr.* **26**(Pt. 1. 414.3), 1098.

Fahim, A., Rettori, V., and McCann, S. M. (1990). The role of calcitonin gene-related peptide in the control of growth hormone and prolactin release. *Neuroendocrinology* **51**, 688–693.

Felitti, V. J., Anda, R. F., Nordenberg, D., Williamson, D. F., Spitz, A. M., Edwards, V., Koss, M. P., and Marks, J. S. (1998). Relationship of childhood abuse and household dysfunction to many of the leading causes of death in adults. The adverse childhood experiences (ACE) study. *Am. J. Prev. Med.* **14**, 245–258.

Felten, S. Y., Bellinger, D. L., Collier, T. J., Coleman, P. D., and Felten, D. L. (1987). Decreased sympathetic innervation of spleen in aged Fischer 344 rats. *Neurobio. Aging* **8**, 159–165.

Fisher, L., Kikkawa, D., Rivier, J., Amara, S., Evans, R., Rosenfeld, M., Vale, W., and Brown, M. (1983). Stimulation of noradrenergic sympathetic outflow by calcitonin gene-related peptide. *Nature (London)* **305**, 534–536.

Fishman, P. S., and Savitt, J. M. (1989). Selective localization by neuroglia of immunoglobulin G in normal mice. *J. Neuropath. Exp. Neurol.* **48**, 212–220.

Ford, A. L., Goodsall, A. L., Hickey, W. F., and Sedgwick, J. D. (1995). Normal adult ramified microglia separated from other central nervous system macrophages by flow cytometric sorting. Phenotypic differences defined and direct ex vivo antigen presentation to myelin basic protein-reactive CD4+ T cells compared. *J. Immunol.* **154**, 4309–4321.

Foremen, J. (1987). Substance P and calcitonin gene-related peptide: Effects on mast cells in human skin. *Int. Arch. Allergy Appl. Immunol.* **82**, 366.

Friedman, W., McEwen, B. S., Toran-Allerand, C. D., and Gerlach, J. (1983). Perinatal development of hypothalamic and cortical estrogen receptors in mouse brain: Methodological aspects. *Dev. Brain Res.* **11**, 19–27.

Galeazza, M. T., Garry, M. G., and Seybold, V. S. (1993). Analysis of mRNA levels for CGRP and SP in dorsal root ganglia and release of these peptides from spinal cord in a rat model of peripheral inflammation. *Soc. Neurosci. Abstr.* **19**.

Gallin, J. I., and Paul, W. E. (1993). "Inflammation: Fundamental Immunology," 3rd ed., pp. 1015–1032. Raven Press, New York.

Gallin, J. I., Goldstein, I. M., and Snyderman, R. (1992). "Inflammation: Basic Principles and Clinical Correlates." Raven Press, New York.

Garcia-Segura, L. M., and Chowen, J. A. (1996). Endocrine glia—roles of glial-cells in the brain actions of steroid and thyroid-hormones and in the regulation of hormone secretion. *Front. Neuroendocrinol.* **17**, 180–211.

Gerin, W., and Pickering, T. G. (1995). Association between delayed recovery of blood pressure after acute mental stress and parental history of hypertension. *J. Hypertens.* **13**, 603–610.

Gerlach, J., McEwen, B. S., Pfaff, D. W., Moskovitz, S., Ferin, M., Carmel, P., and Zimmerman, E. (1976). Cells in regions of rhesus monkey brain and pituitary retain radioactive estradiol, corticosterone and cortisol differently. *Brain Res.* **103**, 603–612.

Goldstein, D. S., and Eisenhofer, G. (2000). Sympathetic nervous system physiology and pathophysiology in coping with the environment. *In* "Coping with the Environment: Neural and Endocrine Mechanisms." Oxford University Press, New York.

Goldstein, D. S., and Pacak, K. (2000). Catecholamines in the brain and responses to environmental challenges. *In* "Coping with the Environment: Neural and Endocrine Mechanisms" (B. S. McEwen, ed.), pp. 45–60. Oxford University Press, New York.

Gould, E., and Cameron, H. A. (1996). Regulation of neuronal birth, migration and death in the rat dentate gyrus. *Dev. Neurosci.* **18**, 22–35.

Gould, E., Allan, M., and McEwen, B. S. (1990). Dendritic spine density of adult hippocampal pyramidal cells is sensitive to thyroid hormone. *Brain Res.* **525**, 327–329.

Gould, E., Woolley, C. S., and McEwen, B. S. (1991). Naturally occurring cell death in the developing dentate gyrus of the rat. *J. Comp. Neurol.* **304**, 408–418.

Gould, E., McEwen, B. S., Tanapat, P., Galea, L. A. M., and Fuchs, E. (1997). Neurogenesis in the dentate gyrus of the adult tree

shrew is regulated by psychosocial stress and NMDA receptor activation. *J. Neurosci.* **17**, 2492–2498.

Gould, E., Tanapat, P., McEwen, B. S., Flugge, G., and Fuchs, E. (1998). Proliferation of granule cell precursors in the dentate gyrus of adult monkeys is diminished by stress. *Proc. Natl. Acad. Sci. U.S.A.* **95**, 3168–3171.

Gould, E., Reeves, A. J., Fallah, M., Tanapat, P., and Gross, C. G. (1999). Hippocampal neurogenesis in adult Old World primates. *Proc. Natl. Acad. Sci. U.S.A.* **96**, 5263–5267.

Grau, V., Herbst, B., van der Meide, P. H., and Steiniger, B. (1997). Activation of microglial and endothelial cells in the rat brain after treatment with interferon-gamma in vivo. *Glia* **19**, 181–189.

Griffiths, A. L., Middlesworth, W., Goh, D. W., and Hutson, J. M. (1993). Exogenous calcitonin gene-related peptide causes gubernacular development in neonatal (Tfm) mice with complete androgen resistance. *J. Pediatr. Surg.* **28**, 1028–1030.

Guthrie, K. M., Nguyen, T., and Gall, C. M. (1995). Insulin-like growth factor-1 mRNA is increased in deafferented hippocampus: Spatiotemporal correspondence of a trophic event with axon sprouting. *J. Comp. Neurol.* **352**, 147–160.

Heim, C., Ehlert, U., and Hellhammer, D. H. (2000). The potential role of hypocortisolism in the pathophysiology of stress-related bodily disorders. *Psychoneuroendocrinology* **25**, 1–35.

Hickey, W. F., Hsu, B. L., and Kimura, H. (1991). T-lymphocyte entry into the central nervous system. *J. Neurosci. Res.* **28**, 254–260.

Hosoi, J., Murphy, G. F., Egan, C. L., Lerner, E. A., Grabbe, S., Asahina, A., and Granstein, R. D. (1993). Regulation of Langerhans cell function by nerves containing calcitonin gene-related peptide. *Nature (London)* **363**, 159–163.

Jones, L. L., Kreutzberg, G. W., and Raivich, G. (1997). Regulation of CD44 in the regenerating mouse facial motor nucleus. *Eur. J. Neurosci.* **9**, 1854–1863.

Kaplan, M., and Bell, D. (1984). Mitotic neuroblasts in the 9-day-old and 11-month-old rodent hippocampus. *J. Neurosci.* **4**, 1429–1441.

Kalpan, M. S., and Hinds, J. W. (1977). Neurogenesis in the adult rat: Electron microscopic analysis of light radioautographs. *Science* **197**, 1092–1094.

Kappers, J. A. (1969). The mammalian pineal organ. *J. Neurovisceral Relation, Suppl.* **9**, 140–184.

Kataoka, K., Asai, T., Taneda, M., Ueshima, S., Matsuo, O., Kuroda, R., Carmeliet, P., and Collen, D. (1999). Nigral degeneration following striato-pallidal lesion in tissue type plasminogen activator deficient mice. *Neurosci. Lett.* **266**, 220–222.

Kavelaars, A., Kuis, W., Knook, L., Sinnema, G., and Heijnen, C. J. (2000). Disturbed neuroendocrine-immune interactions in chronic fatigue syndrome. *J. Clin. Endocrinol. Metab.* **85,** 692–696.

Kempermann, G., Kuhn, H. G., and Gage, F. H. (1997). Genetic influence on neurogenesis in the dentate gyrus of adult mice. *Proc. Natl. Acad. Sci. U.S.A.* **94,** 10409–10414.

Kielian, T., and Hickey, W. F. (2000). Proinflammatory cytokine, chemokine, and cellular adhesion molecule expression during the acute phase of experimental brain abscess development. *Am. J. Pathol.* **157,** 647–658.

Kim, W. G., Mohney, R. P., Wilson, B., Jeohn, G. H., Liu, B., and Hong, J. F. (2000). Regional difference in susceptibility to lipopolysaccharide-induced neurotoxicity in the rat brain: Role of microglia. *J. Neurosci.* **20,** 6309–6316.

Kirschbaum, C., Prussner, J. C., Stone, A. A., Federenko, I., Gaab, J., Lintz, D., Schommer, N., and Hellhammer, D. H. (1995). Persistent high cortisol responses to repeated psychological stress in a subpopulation of healthy men. *Psychosom. Med.* **57,** 468–474.

Kornack, D., and Rakic, P. (1999). Continuation of neurogenesis in the hippocampus of the adult macaque monkey. *Proc. Nat. Acad. Sci. U.S.A.* **96,** 5768–5773.

Kovacs, A., Biro, E., Szeleczky, I., and Telegedy, G. (1995). Role of endogenous CRF in the mediation of neuroendocrine and behavioral responses to calcitonin gene-related peptide in rats. *Neuroendocrinology* **62,** 418–424.

Landfield, P. W., and Eldridge, J. C. (1994). Evolving aspects of the glucocorticoid hypothesis of brain aging: Hormonal modulation of neuronal calcium homeostasis. *Neurobiol. Aging* **15,** 579–588.

Lassmann, H., and Hickey, W. F. (1993). Radiation bone marrow chimeras as a tool to study microglia turnover in normal brain and inflammation. *Clin. Neuropathol.* **12,** 284–285.

Leibowitz, S. F., and Hoebel, B. G. (1997). Behavioral neuroscience of obesity. *In* "Handbook of Obesity" (G. A. Bray, C. Bouchard, and W. P. T. James, eds.), pp. 313–358. Dekker, New York.

Leproult, R., Copinschi, G., Buxton, O., and Van Cauter, E. (1997). Sleep loss results in an elevation of cortisol levels the next evening. *Sleep* **20,** 865–870.

Levine, S. (1968). Hormones and conditioning. *In* "Nebraska Symposium on Motivation" (W. Arnold, ed.), pp. 85–101. University of Nebraska Press, Lincoln.

Liu, L., Tornqvist, E., Mattsson, P., Eriksson, N. P., Persson, J. K., Morgan, B. P., Aldskogius, H., and Svensson, M. (1995). Complement and clusterin in the spinal cord dorsal horn and gracile nucleus following sciatic nerve injury in the adult rat. *Neuroscience* **68,** 167–179.

Loewy, A. S. M. (1990). Central regulation of autonomic function. *In* "Anatomy of the Autonomic Nervous System: An Overview" (A. Loewy, ed.), pp. 3–16. Oxford University Press, Oxford and New York.

Lombardi, V. R., Garcia, M., and Cacabelos, R. (1998). Microglial activation induced by factor(s) contained in sera from Alzheimer-related ApoE genotypes. *J. Neurosci. Res.* **54,** 539–553.

Lowenstein, D. H., Gwinn, R. P., Seren, M. S., Simon, R. P., and McIntosh, T. K. (1994). Increased expression of mRNA encoding calbindin—D228K, the glucose-regulated proteins, or the 72 kDa heat-shock protein in three models of acute CNS injury. *Brain Res.* **22,** 299–308.

Lowhagen, P., Johansson, B. B., and Norgborg, C. (1994). The nasal route of cerebrospinal fluid drainage in man. A light-microscopic study. *Neuropathol. Appl. Neurobiol.* **20,** 543–550.

Lupien, S. J., Lecours, A. R., Lussier, I., Schwartz, G., Nair, N. P. V., and Meaney, M. J. (1994). Basal cortisol levels and cognitive deficits in human aging. *J. Neurosci.* **14,** 2893–2903.

Lupien, S. J., de Leon, M. J., De Santi, S., Convit, A., Tarshish, C., Nair, N. P. V., Thakur, M., McEwen, B. S., Hauger, R. L., and Meaney, M. J. (1998). Cortisol levels during human aging predict hippocampal atrophy and memory deficits. *Nat. Neurosci.* **1,** 69–73.

Lynch, J. W., Kaplan, G. A., and Shema, S. J. (1997). Cumulative impact of sustained economic hardship on physical, cognitive, psychological, and social functioning. *N. Engl. J. Med.* **337,** 1889–1895.

Madden, K. S., Felten, S. Y., Felten, D. L., Hardy, C. A., and Livnat, S. (1994). Sympathetic nervous system modulation of the immune system. II. Induction of lymphocyte proliferation and migration in vivo by chemical sympathectomy. *J. Neuroimmunol.* **49,** 67–75.

Male, D., Rahman, J., Linke, A., Zhao, W., and Hickey, W. (1995). An interferon-inducible molecule on brain endothelium which controls lymphocyte adhesion mediated by integrins. *Immunology* **84,** 453–460.

Manuck, S. B., Kaplan, J. R., Muldoon, M. F., Adams, M. R., and Clarkson, T. B. (1991). The behavioral exacerbation of atherosclerosis and its inhibition by propranolol. *In* "Stress, Coping and Disease" (P. M. McCabe, N. Schneiderman, T. M. Field, and J. S. Skyler, eds.), pp. 51–72. Erlbaum, Hove and London.

Manuck, S. B., Kaplan, J. R., Adams, M. R., and Clarkson, T. B. (1995). Studies of psychosocial influences on coronary artery atherosclerosis in cynomolgus monkeys. *Health Psychol.* **7,** 113–124.

Mattson, M. P. (1997). Calcium as sculptor and destroyer of neural circuitry. *Exp. Gerontol.* **27,** 29–49.

McEwen, B. S. (1995). Stressful experiences, brain and emotions: Developmental, genetic and hormonal influences. *In* "Cognitive Neurosciences" (M. S. Gazzaniga, ed.), pp. 1117–1135. MIT Press, Cambridge, MA.

McEwen, B. S. (1997). Possible mechanisms for atrophy of the human hippocampus. *Mol. Psychiatry* **2**, 255–262.

McEwen, B. S. (1998). Protective and damaging effects of stress mediators. *N. Engl. J. Med.* **338**, 171–179.

McEwen, B. S. (1999). Stress and hippocampal plasticity. *Annu. Rev. Neurosci.* **22**, 105–122.

McEwen, B. S. (2000). "Protective and Damaging Effects of Stress Mediators: Central Role of the Brain," pp. 25–34. Elsevier, Amsterdam.

McEwen, B. S., and Stellar, E. (1993). Stress and the Individual: Mechanisms leading to disease. *Arch. Intern. Med.* **153**, 2093–2101.

McEwen, B. S., Weiss, J., and Schwartz, L. (1968). Selective retention of corticosterone by limbic structures in rat brain. *Nature (London)* **220**, 911–912.

McEwen, B. S., Sakai, R. R., and Spencer, R. L. (1993). Adrenal steroid effects on the brain: Versatile hormones with good and bad effects. *In* "Hormonally-Induced Changes in Mind and Brain" (J. Schulkin, ed.), pp. 157–189. Academic Press, San Diego, CA.

McEwen, B. S., Albeck, D., Cameron, H., Chao, H. M., Gould, E., Hastings, N., Kuroda, Y., Luine, V., Magarinos, A. M., McKittrick, C. R., Orchinik, M., Pavlides, C., Vaher, P., Watanabe, Y., and Weiland, N. (1995). Stress and the brain: A paradoxical role for adrenal steroids. *In* "Vitamins and Hormones" (G. D. Litwack, ed.), pp. 371–402. Academic Press, San Diego, CA.

McEwen, B. S., Biron, C. A., Brunson, K. W., Bulloch, K., Chambers, W. H., Dhabhar, F. S., Goldfarb, R. H., Kitson, R. P., Miller, A. H., Spencer, R. L., and Weiss, J. M. (1997). The role of adrenocorticoids as modulators of immune function in health and disease: Neural, endocrine and immune interactions. *Brain Res. Rev.* **23**, 79–133.

McGillis, J. P., Humphreys, S., and Reid, S. (1991). Characterization of functional calcitonin gene-related peptide receptors on rat lymphocytes. *J. Immunol.* **147**, 3482–3489.

McQueen, J. K. (1994). Glial cells and neuroendocrine function. *J. Endocrinol.* **143**, 411–415.

Meaney, M., Aitken, D., Berkel, H., Bhatnager, S., and Sapolsky, R. (1988). Effect of neonatal handlng of age-related impairments associated with the hippocampus. *Science* **239**, 766–768.

Mezey, E., Chandross, K. J., Harta, G., Maki, R. A., and McKercher, S. R. (2000). Turning blood into brain: Cells bearing neuronal antigens generated in vivo from bone marrow. *Science* **290**, 1779–1782.

Michelson, D., Stratakis, C., Hill, L., Reynolds, J., Galliven, E., Chrousos, G., and Gold, P. (1996). Bone mineral den-

sity in women with depression. *N. Engl. J. Med.* **335**, 1176–1181.

Moonen, G., Grau-Wagemans, M. P., and Selak, I. (1982). Plasminogen activator-plasmin system and neuronal migration. *Nature (London)* **298**, 753–755.

Mor, G., Nilsen, J., Horvath, T., Bechmann, I., Brown, S., Garcia-Segura, L. M., and Naftolin, F. (1999). Estrogen and microglia: A regulatory system that affects the brain. *J. Neurobiol.* **40**, 484–496.

Morgan, T. E., Nichols, N. R., Pasinetti, G. M., and Finch, C. E. (1993). TGF-beta 1 mRNA increases in macrophage/microglial cells of the hippocampus in response to deafferentation and kainic acid-induced neurodegeneration. *Exp. Neurol.* **120**, 291–301.

Mullins, M. W., Ciallella, J., Rangnekar, V., and McGillis, J. P. (1993). Characterization of a calcitonin gene-related peptide (CGRP) receptor on mouse bone marrow cells. *Regul. Pept.* **49**, 65–72.

Munck, A., Guyre, P. M., and Holbrook, N. (1984). Physiological functions of glucocorticoids is stress and their relation to pharmacological actions. *Endocr. Rev.* **5**, 25–44.

Nakajima, K., Nagata, K., Hamanoue, M., Takemoto, N., and Kohsaka, S. (1993). Microglia-derived elastase produces a low-molecular-weight plasminogen that enhances neurite outgrowth in rat neocortical explant cultures. *J. Neurochem.* **61**, 2155–2163.

Netti, C., Guidobono, F., Sibilia, V., Pagani, F., Braga, P. C., and Pecile, A. (1989). Evidence of a central inhibition of growth hormone secretion by calcitonin gene-related peptide. *Neuroendocrinology* **49**, 242–247.

Nichols, N. R., Laping, N. J., Day, J. R., and Finch, C. E. (1991). Increases in transforming growth factor-B mRNA in hippocampus during response to entorhinal cortex lesions in intact and adrenalectomized rats. *J. Neurosci. Res.* **28**, 134–139.

Noble, B. S., McMillan, D. N., and Maltin, C. A. (1993). Calcitonin gene related peptide stimulates differentiation of neonatal rat myogenic cultures. *Growth Regul.* **3**, 245–248.

Nong, Y., Titus, N., Ribeiro, R. J., and Remold, H. (1989). Peptides encoded by calcitonin gene inhibit macrophage function. *J. Immunol.* **143**, 45.

Norenberg, M. D. (1994). Astrocyte responses to CNS injury. *J. Neuropathol. Exp. Neurol.* **53**, 213–220.

Oldfield, B. J., and McKinley, M. J. (1995). Circumventricular organs. *In* "The Rat Nervous System" (G. Paxinos, ed.), pp. 391–403. Academic Press, San Diego, CA.

Pasinetti, G. M., Johnson, S. A., Rozovsky, M., Lampert-Etchells, M., Morgan, D. G., Gordon, M. N., Morgan, T. E., Willoughby, D. A., and Finch, C. E. (1992). Complement C1qB and C4 mRNAs responses to lesioning in rat brain. *Exp. Neurol.* **118**, 117–125.

Paul, W. E. (1993). "Fundamental Immunology." Raven Press, New York.

Perry, V. H., and Gordon, S. (1988). Macrophages and microglia in the nervous sytetem. *Trends Neurosci.* **11**, 273–277.

Pincelli, C., Fantini, F., and Giannetti, A. (1993). Neuropeptides and skin inflammation. *Dermatology* **187**, 153–158.

Plat, L., Leproult, R., L. Hermite-Baleriaux, M., Fery, F., Mockel, J., Polonsky, K. S., and Van Cauter, E. (1999). Metabolic effects of short-term elevations of plasma cortisol are more pronounced in the evening than in the morning. *J. Clin. Endocrinol. Metab.* **84**, 3082–3092.

Porges, S. W. (1992). Vagal tone: A physiologic marker of stress vulnerability. *Pediatrics* **90**, 498–504.

Poteliakhoff, A. (1981). Adrenocortical activity and some clinical findings in acute and chronic fatigue. *J. Psychosom. Res.* **25**, 91–95.

Qiao, L., Braunstein, J., Golling, M., Schurmann, G., Autschback, F., Moller, P., and Meuer, S. (1996). Differential regulation of human T cell responsiveness by mucosal versus blood monocytes. *Eur. J. Immunol.* **26**, 922–927.

Quay, W. B. (1965). Histological structure and cytology of the pineal organ in birds and mammals. *Prog. Brain Res.* **10**, 49–86.

Radojcic, T., Baird, S., Darko, D., Smith, D., and Bulloch, K. (1991). Changes in B-Adrenergic receptor distribution on immunocytes during differentiation: An analysis of T cells and macrophages. *J. Neurosci. Res.* **30**, 328–335.

Raivich, G., Bohatschek, M., Kloss, C. U. A., Werner, A., Jones, L. L., and Kreutzberg, G. W. (1999). Neuroglial activation repertoire in the injured brain: Graded response,molecular mechanisms and cues to physioligical function. *Brain Res. Rev.* **30**, 77–105.

Rajkowska, G., Miguel-Hidalgo, J. J., Wei, J., Dilley, G., Pittman, S. D., Meltzer, H. Y., Overholser, J. C., Roth, B. L., and Stockmeier, C. A. (1999). Morphometric evidence for neuronal and glial prefrontal cell pathology in major depression. *Biol. Psychiatry* **45**, 1085–1098.

Reddington, M., Priller, J., Treichel, J., Haas, C., and Kreutzberg, G. W. (1995). Astrocyte and microglia as potential targets for calcitonin gene related peptide in the CNS. *Can. J. Physiol. Pharmacol.* **73**, 1047–1049.

Rhees, R., Abel, J., and Haack, D. (1972). Uptake of tritiated steroids in the brain of the duck (*Anas platyrhynchos*). An autoradiographic study. *Gen. Comp. Endocrinol.* **18**, 292–300.

Risdon, G., Kumar, V., and Bennett, M. (1991). Differential effects of dehydroepiandrosterone (DHEA) on murine lymphopoiesis and myelopoiesis. *Exp. Hematol.* **19**, 128–131.

Romieu, M., and Jullien, G. (1942). Sur l'existence d'une formation lymphoide dans l'épiphyse des galliances. *C.R. Seances Soc. Biol. Ses Fil.* **136**, 626–628.

Roozendaal, B. (2000). Glucocorticoids and the regulation of memory consolidation. *Psychoneuroendocrinology* **25**, 213–238.

Sakuta, H., Inaba, K., and Muramatsu, S. (1996). Calcitonin gene-related peptidide enhances apoptosis of thymocytes. *J. Neuroimmunol.* **67**, 103–109.

Sapolsky, R. (1992). "Stress, the Aging Brain and the Mechanisms of Neuron Death." MIT Press, **1**, 423. Cambridge, MA.

Sapolsky, R. M. (1996). Why stress is bad for your brain. *Science* **273**, 749–750.

Sapolsky, R. M., Romero, L. M., and Munck, A. U. (2000). How do glucocorticoids influence stress responses? Integrating permissive, suppressive, stimulatory, and preparative actions. *Endocr. Rev.* **21**, 55–89.

Saria, A., Marksteiner, J., Humpel, C., and Sperk, G. (1989). Pronounced increases in brain levels of calcitonin gene-related peptide after kainic acid induced seizures. *Regul. Pept.* **26**, 215–223.

Schumacher, M., and Robel, P. (1996). Development and regeneration of the nervous system—a role for neurosteroids. *Dev. Neurosci.* **18**, 6–21.

Seeman, T. E., McEwen, B. S., Singer, B. H., Albert, M. S., and Rowe, J. W. (1997). Increase in urinary cortisol excretion and memory declines: MacArthur Studies of Successful Aging. *J. Clin. Endocrinol. Metab.* **82**, 2458–2465.

Sirinek, L. P., and O'Dorisio, M. S. (1991). Modulation of immune function by intestinal neuropeptides. *Acta Oncol.* **30**, 509–517.

Sloan, R. P., Shapiro, P. A., Bagiella, E., Myers, M. M., and Gorman, J. M. (1999). Cardiac autonomic control buffers blood pressure variability responses to challenge: A psychophysiology model of coronary artery disease. *Psychosomatic Med.* **61**, 58–68.

Smith, G. D., Seckl, J. R., Sheward, W. J., Bennie, J. G., Carroll, S. M., Dick, H. *et al.* (1991). Effect of adrenalectomy and dexamethasone on neuropeptide content of dorsal root ganglia in the rat. *Brain Res.* **564**, 27–30.

Smriga, M., Saito, H., and Nishiyama, N. (1996). Hippocampal long-and short-term potentiation is modulated by adrenalectomy and corticosterone. *Neuroendocrinology* **64**, 35–41.

Spencer, R. L., Kalman, B. A., and Dhabhar, F. S. (2000). Role of endogenous glucocorticoids in immune system function: Regulation and counterregulation. *In* "Coping with the Environment: Neural and Endocrine Mechanisms" (B. S. McEwen, ed.), pp. 381–423. Oxford University Press, New York.

Spiegel, K., Leproult, R., and Van Cauter, E. (1999). Impact of sleep debt on metabolic and endocrine function. *Lancet* **354**, 1435–1439.

Spiroff, B. E. N. (1958). Embryonic and post-hatching development of the pineal body of the domestic fowl. *Am. J. Anat.* **103**, 375–401.

Steel, D., and Whitehead, A. S. (1994). The major acute phase reactants: C-reactive protein, serum amyloid P component and serum amyloid protein. *Immunol. Today* **15**, 81–88.

Sterling, P., and Eyer, J. (1988). Allostasis: A new paradigm to explain arousal pathology. *In* "Handbook of Life Stress, Cognition and Health" (S. Fisher and J. Reason, eds.), pp. 629–649. Wiley, New York.

Sternberg, E. M. (1997). Neural-immune interactions in health and disease. *J. Clin. Invest.* **100**, 2641–2647.

Tanaka, J., Fujita, H., Matsuda, S., Toku, K., Sakanaka, M., and Maeda, N. (1997). Glucocorticoid- and mineralocorticoid receptors in microglial cells: The two receptors mediate differential effects of corticosteroids. *Glia* **20**, 23–37.

Theodorou, V., Fioramonti, J., and Bueno, L. (1996). Integrative neuroimmunology of the digestive tract. *Vet. Res.* **27**, 427–442.

Toran-Allerand, C. D., and Bentham, W. (1991). Insulin influences the morphology and glial fibrillary acidic protein (GFAP) expression in organotypic cultures. *Brain Res.* **558**, 296–304.

Umeda, Y., and Arisawa, M. (1989). Inhibition of natural killer activity by calcitonin gene-related peptide. *Immunopharmacol. Immunotoxicol.* **11**, 309.

Uno, H., Ross, T., Else, J., Suleman, M., and Sapolsky, R. (1989). Hippocampal damage associated with prolonged and fatal stress in primates. *J. Neurosci.* **9**, 1709–1711.

Ur, E., White, P. D., and Grossman, A. (1992). Hypothesis: Cytokines may be activated to cause depressive illness and chronic fatigue syndrome. *Eur. Arch. Psychiatry Clin. Neurosci.* **241**, 317–322.

Walcott, B. (1983). Innervation of a lacrimal gland. *Soc. Neurosci. Abstr.* **8**, 116.

Wang, F. Z., Feng, C. H., and Liu, Z. P. (1993). The role of Ca in changes of membrane function and the protection of CGRP in hippocampal slice during hypoxia. *Soc. Neurosci.* **16**, No. 479.93.

Weller, R. O., Engelhardt, B., and Phillips, M. I. (1996). Lymphocytes targeting of the central nervous system: A review of afferent and efferent CNS-immune pathways. *Brain Pathol.* **6**, 275–288.

Williams, K. C., and Hickey, W. F. (1995). Traffic of hematogenous cells through the central nervous system. *Curr. Top. Microbiol. Immunol.* **202**, 221–245.

Williams, K. C., Ulvestad, E., and Hickey, W. F. (1994). Immunology of multiple sclerosis. *Clin. Neurosci.* **2**, 229–245.

Woodbury, D., Swartz, E. J., Prockop, D. J., and Black, I. (2000). Adult human bonemarrow stromal cells differentiate into neurons. *J. Neurosci. Res.* **61**, 364–370.

Woolley, C., and McEwen, B. S. (1994). Estradiol regulates hippocampal dendritic spine density via an N-methyl-D-aspartate receptor dependent mechanism. *J. Neurosci.* **14**, 7680–7687.

Woolley, C., Gould, E., Frankfurt, M., and McEwen, B. S. (1990). Naturally occurring fluctuation in dendritic spine density on adult hippocampal pyramidal neurons. *J. Neurosci.* **10**, 4035–4039.

Young, B., Gleeson, M., and Cripps, A. W. (1991). C-reactive protein: A critical review. *Pathology* **23**, 118–124.

Young, E. A., Haskett, R. F., Grunhaus, L., Pande, A., Weinberg, M., Watson, S. J., and Akil, H. (1994). Increased evening activation of the hypothalamic-pituitary-adrenal axis in depressed patients. *Arch. Gen. Psychiatry.* **51**, 701–707.

Young, J. B., and Landsberg, L. (2000). "Synthesis, Storage and Secretion of Adrenal Medullary Hormones: Physiology and Pathophysiology." Oxford University Press, New York.

15

Pheromones, Odors, and Vasanas: The Neuroendocrinology of Social Chemosignals in Humans and Animals

Martha K. McClintock

Department of Psychology
Institute for Mind and Biology
University of Chicago
Chicago, Illinois 60637

I. OVERVIEW

In 1949, Frank Beach first demonstrated scientifically that odors, hormones, and sexual behavior are linked in mammals. He reported that male beagles could determine whether a female was in heat simply from the odor of her urine (Beach and Gilmore, 1949). Since the publication of this seminal paper, there has been a dramatic transformation of the field of hormones and behavior, paralleled by an equally dramatic transformation in our understanding of olfaction and the discovery of pheromones.

When Beach's paper was published, olfaction was still thought to play a limited role in animals that had evolved an elaborate neocortex (Broca, 1878, 1979; reviewed by Bourliere, 1955; Harrington and Rosario, 1992; Hediger, 1951). This bias was reinforced by cultural beliefs that humans are microsmatic, with an olfactory system that is virtually vestigial in terms of shaping human behavior (Bieber and Friedman, 1992). Indeed Freud's (1895) view that normal psychosexual development required repressing awareness of odors from bodily functions prevailed, supported by Ellis (1929) and Kraft-Ebing (1965). Neuroanatomists were just beginning to recognize that the "visceral" or "limbic" brain was not simply for olfactory processing, but also contained neural structures underlying emotion (MacLean, 1949; Papez, 1937). Electrical activity in the olfactory receptor epithelium was about to be measured for the first time (Beidler and Tucker, 1955; Hodgson *et al.*, 1955; Ottoson, 1956). Pheromones had yet to be discovered, even in insects.

Fifty years later, in 2000, it was known that there are not a small set of "primary receptors," but rather a thousand olfactory receptor types (Amoore, 1977; Buck and Axel, 1991). There are 12 million olfactory epithelial cells in humans (Moran *et al.*, 1982) and in rodents 50 million project to 1800 gomeruli (Meisami and Safari, 1981; Mombaerts *et al.*, 1996). An astonishingly diverse array of hormones appear to serve as neurotransmitters within the olfactory bulb (Halasz, 1990). Nonlinear dynamics is the current model for neural processing of odors (Laurent, 1999; Mori *et al.*, 1999). It is well established that odors play a major role in the reproductive behavior of many mammals (Halpin, 1986; Johnston, 2000) and are strongly linked to emotions, memory, and social behavior (Breipohl, 1982; Doty, 1984; Ehrlichman and Bastone, 1992; Getchell, 1991). These interactions are modulated by hormones and can alter endocrine function as well.

In 1959, the term "pheromone" was proposed for social chemosignals that are produced by one member of a species and regulate the endocrine function, behavior, or development of another member of the same species. Their functional definition also emphasized "the principle of minute amounts being effective" (Karlson and Lüscher, 1959). They were first discovered in insects and, more recently, in a broad spectrum of species ranging across kingdoms from yeast to humans.

Current research calls for a reconceptualization of the endocrine and behavioral function of pheromones and odors. Chemical signals are not only single compounds, but also blends and mosaics. In mammals, these signals serve cognitive functions involving categorization, memory, and emotional functions that modulate reactions to the environment. They also act as classic pheromones and trigger specific behaviors and long-term neuroendocrine changes. In between these extremes, however, there is a previously unrecognized functional class, for which we have used the Sanskrit term "vasana." This functional category is most readily studied in humans because it comprises chemosignals that change emotional state and modulate preferences without their being identified verbally as having an odor—a verbal distinction based on levels of consciousness that is nonetheless applicable to nonhuman species.

Over the course of the past 50 years, the term "pheromone" has acquired many meanings, implications, and connotations that are not supported by empirical research. Therefore, we call for a return to definitions of pheromones and chemosignals based on function. We will show that other attributes, previously used to define pheromones, are no longer appropriate. These include the simplicity of the chemical signal, neural mechanisms mediating their transduction and processing, innateness and the role of learning, and evolutionary specialization, that is, the evolution of a specific compound associated with a unique response.

In sum, we designed this chapter to provide a theoretical synthesis and foundation for defining a common vocabulary and deriving an empirical framework

for future research on the neuroendocrinology of social chemosignals. We recognize that humans are animals and therefore insights on the principles of neuroendocrine mechanisms derived from animals will enable us to leap ahead in the study of human chemosensory systems. We also presume that mammals are capable of some, albeit not all, of the percepts, cognitive processes, and emotional responses experienced by humans. Thus the clinical and human research can make strong contributions to organizing a conceptual framework for the plethora of animal work that has accumulated in the past 50 years since Frank Beach's seminal article (Beach and Gilmore, 1949; Shafik, 1997).

II. PRIMER AND MODULATOR PHEROMONES

A. Definitions

1. Pheromones Versus Odors

Various terms have been proposed for social chemosignals that are not odors. These include pheromone, pheromone blends, mosaic signals, chemosignal, semiochemical, vomodor, and vomeropherin (Beauchamp *et al.*, 1976; but see revision: Beauchamp, 2000; Albone, 1984; Brown, 1979; Burghardt, 1980; Johnston, 2000; Katz and Shorey, 1979; Martin, 1980; McClintock, 1998a, 2001; Sachs, 1999).

"Vomeromodulin" is the term proposed for the glycoprotein secreted by the lateral nasal gland of the rat, which carries compounds of low volatility to the vomeronasal organ (Khew-Goodall *et al.*, 1991). "Pheromaxein" has been proposed for the pheromone binding protein for 5α-androst-16-en-3-one, as well as other 16-androstenes, first isolated from the parotid gland and saliva of the Göttingen minature boar (Booth and White, 1988). There are many other pheromone-binding proteins in species such as the elephant, mouse, rat, and hamster, which have not been given such specialized names (Lazar *et al.*, 2000; Rasmussen *et al.*, 1998).

The meaning of these myriad terms have evolved over the past 50 years, as data have accumulated, limiting their usefulness. The following section is an effort to define and standardize terms for further work in the burgeoning field of social chemosignals and neuroendocrinology. It is based on detailed discussions presented elsewhere, which lay out the benefits of using function as the basis for distinguishing between odors and pheromones, not the other multitudinous characteristics that have been proposed, and are, in fact, independent of function. These characteristics are chemical identity, receptor organs, neuroendocrine mechanisms, developmental trajectory or species specificity (Jacob *et al.,* 2002; McClintock, 2001).

Insect researchers introduced the term "pheromone" to distinguish chemosignals with a specific social function. In the current insect literature, however, "pheromone" is used interchangeably with "odor" (Mafra-Neto and Cardé, 1994; Vickers and Baker, 1994) as it is in the mammalian literature (e.g., Kelliher *et al.,* 1999; Thornhill and Gangestad, 1999, among many others). Using "pheromone" and "odor" interchangeably is confusing because "odor" already has a distinct meaning describing olfaction in humans, mammals, and other vertebrates (see Section III). An odor is the percept caused by any olfactory chemosignal. Thus, it requires at least the capacity for attention and awareness, if not conscious experience, which pheromones, by definition, do not require for their functional effects (although the compound may also have an odor).

As mammalian researchers applied the term "pheromone" to behaviorally more complex organisms, they made explicit the functional distinction between pheromones and odors. Pheromones have clear and obvious behavioral or physiological effects that are shaped minimally by their odor qualities. For example, taste aversions can be conditioned to body odors of mice, but only minimally to pheromones that elicit male mating behavior (Kay and Nyby, 1992).

In addition, pheromones do not function like odors in terms of sensory adaptation or stimulus generalization. Behavioral responses to odorants adapt relatively quickly. Pheromonal responses take much longer to adapt, if at all. For example, a gilt living next to a boar adapts to his sight and sound but not to his mating pheromone, androstenone (the common word for 5α-androst-16-en-3-one; Tilbrook and Hemsworth, 1990). This behavioral finding is consistent with recent neurophysiological evidence that neurons binding a specific pheromone in the mouse vomeronasal epithelium, and that are then activated via phospholipase C, do not adapt with prolonged exposure to

the pheromone (Holy *et al.,* 2000). In addition, olfactory receptor neurons bind a variety of odorants, thus contributing to the generalization and cross-adaptation within classes of odorants (Todrank *et al.,* 1991). In contrast, VNO neurons bind only one of the identified mouse primer pheromones (Leinders-Zufall *et al.,* 2000). Although the degree of cross-adaptation between pheromone receptors awaits study, it is already clear both from the behavioral data and the new receptor binding data that the time and space constraints for these two types of chemosensory transduction systems are quite different.

In addition, contemporary chemosensory scientists have also developed a daunting array of other criteria for pheromones (Beauchamp *et al.,* 1976; but see revised discussion: Beauchamp, 2000). Taken as a whole, however, this large set of criteria virtually precludes use of the term "pheromone," risking leaving the field without an appropriate term to describe social chemosignals that are not odors. We call for a return to simple functional criteria to define "pheromone."

The typical and universally accepted definition of a pheromone is a chemical signal that is secreted by one individual of a species and triggers a specific behavioral, neuroendocrine, or developmental response in another individual of the same species. This is the first half of the original functional definition that Karlson and Lüscher published in *Nature* (Karlson and Lüscher, 1959). They created this new term to designate a group of "active substances" that were similar to but that could not be called hormones because they were not the products of endocrine glands (Karlson and Lüscher, 1959).

Pheromones are also distinct from hormones because they are inherently social. Hormones function within an individual. Pheromones are a specialized communication system using chemosignals that enables one individual to change the behavior or physiology of another. For example, the female tobacco budworm moth (*Heliothis virescens*) helps a male find her by releasing a mixture of six molecules (Vickers and Baker, 1994). This pheromone functions as a sex attractant; the male alternates between specific neural programs to fly upwind to find the female (Mafra-Neto and Cardé, 1994; Vickers and Baker, 1994).

There is, however, a second part of the original definition of "pheromone," which has typically been omitted from the recent literature: "The principle of minute amounts being effective holds" (Karlson and Lüscher, 1959).

This second functional criterion for defining a pheromone is as important as the first, especially for distinguishing pheromones from odors. The principle that minute amounts are sufficient to produce large functional effects has been borne out by recent research demonstrating the high sensitivity (detecting concentrations of 10^{-11} M) and specificity of pheromone receptor neurons in the vomeronasal organ of the mouse (Leinders-Zufall *et al.*, 2000). Indeed, 10^{-7} ml of male mouse urine, presented only once a day, is sufficient to stimulate reproductive maturation in prepubescent mice (Vandenbergh, 1994). This criteria is also met by our findings, described below, that nanomole quantities of steroid chemosignals, comparable to amount secreted in one-hundredth of a drop of human sweat, can affect both the neural, physiological and psychological states of other people, even when the steroids cannot be consciously discerned as odors (Jacob *et al.*, 2001a,b; Stern and McClintock, 1998).

At this point in the discovery process, these few functional criteria are necessary and sufficient for distinguishing odors and pheromones. Indeed, all the additional proposed criteria have since been shown to be inappropriate for some species.

1. Pheromone responses are not independent of experience. The social experience of preweanling female mice modulates their subsequent response to the male primer pheromone that accelerates female puberty (Mucignat-Caretta *et al.*, 1995).

2. Not all pheromones are mediated by the vomeronasal system. The main olfactory system, as well as the accessory olfactory system, mediates responses to pheromones not only in rabbits (Hudson and Distel, 1986), but also in at least six other species (see Section V.).

3. Behavioral pheromones do not always release stereotyped behavior. In humans, steroid chemosignals, which are undetectable as odors, modulate emotional responses to social interactions, and then only in particular contexts (Jacob *et al.*, 2001a). Similar modulatory effects and context dependence are also found in animal species (see Section III.C.).

4. Pheromones need not be a single compound. Indeed, pheromone blends have multiple components in

which it is the precise ratio that signals information (Johnston, 2000).

5. Finally, as the chemical structures of pheromones have been identified, we have discovered that pheromones are not species-specific. The Asian elephant and several butterfly and moth species (*Lepidoptera*) all use (Z)-7dodecen-1-yl acetate as a sex attractant (Rasmussen *et al.*, 1996).

2. Four Classes of Pheromones

Pheromones are divided into four classes based on their functional effects, all of which are distinct from odors.

a) Releasers   The first, and possibly most familiar, class of pheromones is the releaser pheromones, which trigger or "release" stereotyped behavior. This class of pheromones was first distinguished by Wilson and Bossert (1963). They operate quickly, triggering within seconds to minutes changes in the nervous system that release or facilitate relatively stereotyped behavior patterns or sets of functionally related behaviors.

The stimulus may be in response to the pheromone itself, as in insects flying up concentration gradients of a sex attractant, or to another stimulus, such as flank stimulation, which would not normally trigger the response. A few molecules of androstenol in the breath of a boar immobilizes estrous gilts in a mating stance that allows the boar to mount (Gower, 1972). The pheromone alone is sufficient to trigger behavior, or it can potentiate a response to flank stimulation. This is the same compound, purported to be a sex attractant in humans, which the media and marketing by the fragrance industry treat inappropriately as prototypical human pheromones.

Releaser pheromones have been studied intensively in the context of sexual attraction and mating behavior and have also been extensively reviewed (Fernandez-Fewell and Meredith, 1994; French and Schaffner, 2000; Halpin, 1986; Rasmussen and Schulte, 1999; Stacey, 1987; Wood and Swann, 2000). Less often studied, but probably equally important for social structures, are pheromones that modulate aggression among males (Drickamer and Martan, 1992; Estes *et al.*, 1982; Shanas and Terkel, 1997) or that enhance the salubrious effects of living in female groups (Clarke *et al.*, 1992;

Kappeler, 1998; LeFevre and McClintock, 1991; Restall *et al.*, 1995; Stockley, 1996; Wright *et al.*, 1994).

A recent study in rats elegantly demonstrates that a releaser pheromone can be detected and processed by the main olfactory system and not the vomeronasal nasal organ (even though the VNO does mediate other pheromonal effects in this species). Airborne compounds from estrous females are both necessary and sufficient to quickly release spontaneous penile erections and stereotyped thrusting without any tactile stimulation (Sachs, 1997; Sachs *et al.*, 1994). Male rats that respond to airborne compounds with noncontact erections manifest increases in neuronal c-fos in projections from the main olfactory projection system, without increases in c-fos activity in five nuclei of the olfactory bulb that typically process odor information. The main olfactory projections are to the nucleus accumbens, the medial amygdala, the bed nucleus of the stria terminalis, and the medial preoptic nucleus. These areas also receive projections from the vomernasal system in response to other pheromones from estrous females, particularly those requiring direct contact with urine. Taken together these data support the hypothesis that there are reciprocal interactions between the main and accessory olfactory systems in the processing of pheromones (see reviews by Johnston, 1998; Shipley and Ennis, 1996).

b) Primers The second class is primer pheromones, which stimulate a long-term regulatory or developmental neuroendocrine change in the receiving individual (Wilson and Bossert, 1963). This pheromone class has many neuroendocrine effects, and so is covered in detail below (see Section III.B.). These include pheromonal regulation of ovarian function at various points in the life span: puberty, the ovarian cycle, pregnancy, and reproductive senescence. In addition, primer pheromones regulate male gonadal function as well as other endocrine systems in both sexes, including the adrenal axis and neuropeptides such as oxytocin.

That function must be used to define and classify a pheromone, rather than chemical identity, is illustrated dramatically by the 16-androstenes used by pigs. The same steroid can function both as a releaser pheromone in the female, triggering the mating stance, and as a primer pheromone, accelerating puberty in immature female pigs (Booth, 1984; Kirkwood *et al.*, 1983).

c) Signalers The third class of pheromones is signaler pheromones, which indicate or "signal" to other members of the same species such attributes of the sender as identity or reproductive status. The recipient may or may not act on this information and thus, in contrast to releaser pheromones, signaler pheromones do not have a prepotent effect on behavior (Bronson and Marsden, 1964). That is, the pheromone influences behavior by providing information but is not necessarily associated with a particular response. Rather, the responses depend on other cues, the social context, motivational state, and the experiences of the recipient.

Signaler pheromones operate in an intermediate time course and promote less stereotyped responses. For example, female hamsters typically live alone and will aggressively oust male intruders. When in heat or estrus, however, the female marks the perimeter of her territory with copious vaginal secretions to signal the male that she is aggressive no longer but indeed is sexually receptive (Fiber and Swann, 1996; Johnston, 1975). The male may or may not act on this information to enter the female's territory and mate with her.

Robert Johnston has conducted a comprehensive body of work in this area, utilizing comparisons of many different species. He has demonstrated that social class, roles, and status can be signaled in a variety of ways, as well as kinship, individual identity, and nutritional status (see reviews by Ferkin *et al.*, 1997; Johnston, 1998, 2000). A major contribution of his work is establishing that a pheromonal signal between mammals, as between insects, can be a single compound, a blend of a small number of components, in which the precise ratio signals the information, or mosaics, which are a mixture of a large number of components in which the precise ratio is not important.

Signaling pheromones also carry genetic information. For example, in addition to functioning in cell-cell interactions and regulating immune responses, the major histocompatibility complex (MHC) is a source of unique individual body odors in animals (Beauchamp *et al.*, 1985; Yamaguchi *et al.*, 1981; Yamazaki *et al.*, 1979). Among inbred strains of rodents, differences at MHC loci, against an otherwise identical genetic background, enable MHC-based olfactory recognition, mating preferences, and selective block of pregnancy (Brown *et al.*, 1986; Egid and Brown, 1989; Eklund *et al.,* 1991; Yamazaki *et al.,* 1976, 1983). In seminatural populations of mice, mating preferences and nesting patterns are influenced by MHC genotypes (Manning *et al.,* 1992; Potts *et al.,* 1991). Pregnant females signal the MHC type of the sire of their litter through expression of MHC-mediated fetal odor types (Beauchamp *et al.,* 2000). Males can learn to discriminate these odors, which influence their social behavior toward the pregnant female.

The possibility of such signaling systems in humans has been suggested by Ober's observation that married couples in an isolated religious community are less likely than random to share more than 5 out of 10 HLA alleles (the human MHC; Ober *et al.,* 1997, 1998). Disassortative mating based on HLA was not found in a population of South American Indians (Hedrick and Black, 1997), but this group had a small sample size and significantly more HLA types, a situation that does not provide the power for detecting a nonrandom pattern.

Whether marriage partner selection based on similarity of HLA genes could be influenced by signaling pheromones has yet to be determined. It is interesting that the pleasantness of body odor is weakly associated negatively with the number of HLA matches between smellers and odor donors (mean $r = -0.14$; Wedekind and Füri, 1997; Wedekind *et al.,* 1995), although this study did not measure mating partner preferences, as is implied by the article's title. Indeed, the function of HLA odor choice may be more broadly social, including kin recognition and choice of social networks. Women chose odors from men who had a few HLA matches over those with none, based on matches with the HLA genes they had inherited from their fathers, but not their mothers (Jacob *et al.,* 2002).

d) Modulators We have recently proposed a fourth class of pheromones, modulator pheromones (McClintock, 2000). This class of behavioral pheromones was discovered during human research on the psychological effects of two steroid chemosignals (described later in this chapter; see Section III.C.). This new class of modulating pheromones may also be applicable to animal pheromone systems. Their recognition may help resolve some debates over the definition of what constitutes a pheromonal system in mammals by making explicit a class intermediate between releasers and signalers (Beauchamp *et al.,* 1976; Katz and Shorey, 1979; Martin, 1980).

Modulator pheromones modulate ongoing behavior or a psychological reaction to a particular context without triggering specific behaviors or thoughts. They change stimulus sensitivity, salience, and sensory-motor integration. They do not have a prepotent effect on behavior, and their effects are less dramatic than releaser pheromones. However, they do more than simply convey information about the sender and are more specific than primer or signaler pheromones.

B. Neuroendocrine Responses to Priming Pheromones

1. Ovarian Function

Priming pheromones from females and males regulate ovarian function throughout the reproductive life span. Thus they operate in many different endocrine and behavioral contexts by (1) regulating spontaneous ovarian cycles and the timing of mating, (2) turning on the cyclicity of the hypothalamic-pituitary-ovarian axis in puberty or in anovulatory adults, (3) coordinating the birth cycle of pregnancy and lactation with supportive environments, and (4) modulating the length of the reproductive life span, ended by senescence of the ovarian axis (McClintock, 1981a,b, 1987, 2000). Recent work in mice elegantly demonstrates that some of these different functions are served by different chemical compounds (Leinders- Zufall *et al.,* 2000). Whether this is the case in other species, such as the rat and human, awaits identification of the compounds, as has been accomplished so skillfully in mice (Jemiolo *et al.,* 1989; Novotny *et al.,* 1990, 1999). The following focuses on Norway rats and humans in order to illustrate the principles of primer pheromone systems, and compares them with other mammalian species.

a) Animal
i) Ovarian cycle.
Preovulatory LH surge. Female rats produce primer pheromones that regulate the spontaneous ovarian cycles of other females with whom they live. During follicular development and the concomitant increase in estrogen levels, Sprague-Dawley females produce pheromones that accelerate the timing of the preovulatory LH surge in other females. This effect is observed when the pheromones are presented continuously for days to other females that have spontaneous ovarian cycles (McClintock, 1978). This is a phase-advancing

pheromone and ovarian cycles are shortened. Estrogen, unopposed by progesterone, may be part of the endocrine mechanism producing a phase-advancing pheromone. Females during early follicular development, as well as ovariectomized estrogen-primed females, produce a pheromone that induces an LH surge in other ovariectomized estrogen-primed females (Beltramino and Taleisnik, 1983). This LH response is virtually immediate, detected in blood within three to four hours of exposure.

Later in the cycle, during the LH surge itself, when there is also a surge of progesterone and estrogen levels are high, females produce a pheromone that has the opposite effect when presented continuously, delaying the LH surge and prolonging the cycles of other females (McClintock, 1978). This is a phase-delaying pheromone for spontaneous ovarian cycles.

Guinea pigs are similar to rats in that they produce different pheromones at different phases of their ovarian cycle (Jesel and Aron, 1976). Urine collected during the late follicular and ovulatory phase shortened the life span of the corpus luteum but did not affect ovulation. In contrast, pheromones from the luteal phase increased the number of ova shed, without affecting the corpus luteum.

These primer pheromones are in marked contrast to those of house mice, which only phase-delay the estrous cycle. Thus, groups of female mice living together have longer cycles and more pseudopregnancies (classically termed the Lee-Boot effect; reviewed by Vandenbergh, 1994). Moreover, their time of maximal pheromone sensitivity or production is after ovulation on estrus, during formation of the corpus luteum (see Figure 1; Ryan and Schwartz, 1977). In rats this sensitive period is hypothesized to be around ovulation (Schank and McClintock, 1992; but see Schank and McClintock, 1997). Thus, species differ in whether they produce phase-advance pheromones, phase-delay pheromones, or both. They also differ in the timing of maximal sensitivity and the neuroendocrine mechanisms that are regulated (species differences reviewed by McClintock, 1983c,d).

Group dynamics. A computer simulation of the dynamic interactions among five spontaneously cycling "rats," producing phase-advance and phase-delay pheromones at the appropriate phases of the estrous cycle, yielded an ovarian cycle-length distribution that matched empirical data (Schank and McClintock,

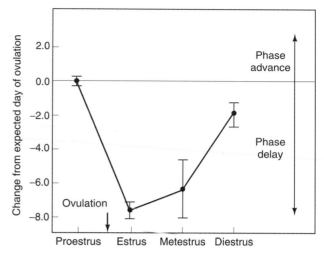

FIGURE 1 A phase response curve for the effect of ovarian pheromones on the degree of estrus suppression of female laboratory mice living in social groups (Ryan and Schwartz, 1977; redrawn in McClintock, 1983c).

1992). In this model, each female produces a pulse of the phase-advancing pheromone followed immediately by a pulse of phase-delay pheromone, and then has two days without pheromone production. This is the expected temporal pattern of production during spontaneous ovarian cycles. Moreover, the model assumes that females' sensitivity to pheromones is similar to that of odorants. Thus, rats have marked individual differences in sensitivity and variation in sensitivity during the ovarian cycle, peaking around ovulation (see Section III.A.2.a).

Simulations with this coupled-oscillator model reveal that under specific initial conditions, the ovarian cycles of five interacting "rats" are synchronized. That is, after seven cycles, rats are more likely to be at the same phase of their ovarian cycles at the same time. This simulation outcome matches the empirical data, expressed as the average level of ovarian synchrony obtained by groups of five Norway rats (Schank and McClintock, 1992). Thus, the dynamic computer model matches biological data at three levels of analysis: the pattern of the group of cycles from rats living together, the ovarian cycle lengths of individual rats, and the neuroendocrine events that produce the ovarian cycle.

The model helped us reconceptualize the phenomenon. It revealed that synchrony of ovarian cycles is but one outcome of these pheromonal interactions with a group. Under other initial conditions, the females' cycles became more asynchronous, i.e., overdistributed in time. Finally, there was a particular initial condition that was unusually stable, i.e. the state was more likely to be maintained than it was during Monte Carlo simulations without pheromonal interactions.

This stable state was synchrony within asynchrony. There were two subsets of rats in the group: Each that had LH surges at the same time but was asynchronous with respect to the other set. These patterns of asynchrony and cycle stability are also seen among Sprague-Dawley rats living in groups of five. In retrospect, finding various outcomes of a dynamic system should not have been surprising. Indeed, other species, such as ringtailed lemurs, manifest dynamic blends of synchrony and asynchrony of ovarian cycles within social groups (Pereira, 1991).

Thus, the most parsimonious description of the effect of primer pheromones is at the level of the individual, particularly the timing of the LH surge, rather than at the group level and the multifaceted phenomena of group dynamics. At the level of the group, the model demonstrates that social regulation of ovulation is highly sensitive to context and initial conditions, as well as to the individual differences in responsiveness to ovarian pheromones (Schank and McClintock, 1992).

Analyzing synchrony and other dynamic patterns is complex, and prone to error when quantized as phases of a cycle (Schank, 1997). These insights informed the design and interpretation of our experiment demonstrating ovarian pheromones in women (see Section II.B.1.b), and may be profitably applied to the social and pheromonal mechanisms of other species that manifest synchronized ovarian cycles (including chimpanzees and other primates; Wallis, 1989; Wallis *et al.,* 1986; reviewed by McClintock, 1983c,d; Schank, 1997), as well as other forms of social regulation of fertility (e.g., in cows; Hradecky, 1989).

Partial LH surges. The model also led us to discover a new neuroendocrine mechanism regulating the length of ovarian cycles. We obtain realistic simulation results only when the model incorporates partial LH surges, which restart follicular development without inducing ovulation (Schank and McClintock, 1992). Indeed, repeated blood sampling with jugular cannulation revealed that prolonged eight-day cycles had a partial LH surge at midcycle, four to five days after a full preovulatory surge of LH and four days before the next (Gans

and McClintock, 1993). Pheromones may create these partial LH surges, lengthening the ovarian cycle, not just by one day, but by several days—the time required to develop a new set of follicles.

Partial LH surges may be dynamically similar to the phenomenon of "silent estrus" observed in seasonally anestrous sheep exposed to a ram and his pheromones (Signoret, 1991). In this species, an LH surge occurs without full ovulation and mating. Immediately after exposure to the ram's primer pheromone, LH rises partially, but not enough to constitute a full preovulatory surge of LH and ovulation. To have this effect, the male must remain present for a day. Even when he does, the subsequent corpus luteum is short lived and the cycle short. Moreover, progesterone priming is insufficient to induce mating activity, hence the term 'silent' estrus. Ovulation with an overt estrus does not occur until the second or third ovarian cycle when progesterone priming has fully developed (reviewed in Signoret, 1991).

Context sensitivity. The insight that ovarian pheromones are context sensitive was strongly reinforced by discovering that ovulatory pheromones have the opposite effect when presented to females living in olfactory isolation, either continuously or as a single pulse (Schank and McClintock, 1997). Under these conditions of extreme olfactory isolation (pheromone isolation delivery system, PIDS) (Schank *et al.,* 1995), ovulatory pheromones shorten, not lengthen, the recipients' spontaneous cycles.

This study underscores the context dependence of this pheromone system and an essential factor in pheromonal systems of other species (reviewed in Bronson, 2000; McClintock, 1983c,d; K. Mori *et al.,* 1999; Y. Mori *et al.,* 1990; Signoret, 1991). Primer pheromones from ovulatory females may have had the opposite effect in this study because extreme olfactory isolation, which is undoubtedly unusual if not stressful, changed the recipient's neuroendocrine state (see context dependent effects in humans; Jacob *et al.,* 2001a, 2002). Alternatively, the compound(s) themselves may have been different because frequent bedding changes, done to create olfactory isolation, precluded the bacterial action that is necessary for production of characteristic pheromones or odors in other rodents and humans (Sipos *et al.,* 1995; Zeng *et al.,* 1992, 1996; Wysocki and Preti, 2000).

Genetics. Finally, genetic differences may be a source of the different effects, thus setting the stage for molecular genetics that can identify the genes involved in mediating the effects of pheromones on ovarian function. For example, during the 1980s and early 1990s, Sprague-Dawley rats were subjected to strong artificial selection of the hypothalamic-pituitary-ovarian axis, which increased the number of regular four-day cycles, increased litter size, and accelerated the age of reproductive senescence (Gans and McClintock, 1993). The change in response to ovulatory odor came after selective breeding of the modified Charles-River Sprague-Dawley strain using rats with five-day cycles (Gans and McClintock, 1993). This may explain production of a phase-advance, rather than the phase-delay, pheromone on proestrus (Gans and McClintock, 1993; Schank and McClintock, 1997). It remains to be determined, however, whether this constitutes a shift from production during diestrus (Beltramino and Taleisnik, 1983; McClintock, 1984a) or potentially the loss altogether of the phase-delay pheromone. A loss of the delay signal, or a shift in the time of its production relative to sensitivity, might preclude development of estrous synchrony, asynchrony, and cycle stasis (Schank and McClintock, 1992).

Wistar rats, a different genetic strain, have different primer pheromones and ovarian function. Wistar females have both four- and five-day cycles and the effect of female urine in these strains is simply to increase the proportion of four-day cycles (Aron, 1979; Aron *et al.,* 1971; Chateau *et al.,* 1972). In a wild rat species, *Bandicota bengalensis,* the net effect of female urine is also shortening of the cycle (Sahu and Ghosh, 1982).

Different genetic breeds of sheep also have different responses to pheromones. In Merino sheep, the male can induce ovulation and estrus throughout seasonal anestrus, whereas in European breeds this can happen only at the end of the season (Signoret and Lindsey, 1982). An interesting finding is that partial surges of LH can be induced by males of all breeds, thus reinforcing the concept that there are different neuroendocrine mechanisms for partial and full LH surges.

Neuroendocrine mechanisms. Ovarian pheromones are mediated by the vomeronasal organ in the rat (Beltramino and Taleisnik, 1983; for reviews see Meredith and Fernandez-Fewell, 1994; Chapters 4, 16, and 17). However, it is noteworthy that the VNO does not mediate all primer pheromone effects in the mouse (Marchlewska-Koj *et al.,* 1998) or in a variety of other mammals, notably rats, sheep, pigs, rabbits, guinea pigs, and lemurs (see Section V.A; also reviews on this point by Dorries *et al.,* 1997; Johnston, 1998; Signoret, 1991).

Sprague-Dawley rats that respond to ovulatory pheromones with shorter cycles have low levels of prolactin on estrus (Gans and McClintock, 1993; see Chapter 4 by Carter and Keverne for a review of dopamine-prolactin systems in mice and other species). Prolactin acts on the corpus luteum to maintain levels of progesterone and prolong the cycle (Sanchez-Criado *et al.,* 1986). Thus, as expected, females that responded to the pheromone with low prolactin on estrus also had low progesterone on metestrus, as did Wistar rats responding to rat urine with cycle shortening (Chateau *et al.,* 1976). This is similar to the luteolytic effects of bovine cervical mucus and urine (Izard, 1983).

Individual differences. Prolactin may not be the only neuroendocrine mechanism mediating effects of ovarian cycle pheromones. When Argentinian rats of an unidentified strain were ovariectomized and estrogen primed, they responded immediately to urine from females in the early follicular phase with an increase in LH pulses, followed by a full surge of LH (Beltramino and Taleisnik, 1983). Thus, ovarian pheromones in the rat are an excellent model for studying the interaction within a species of two different neuroendocrine mechanisms for social regulation of ovulation: GnRH-pituitary LH-follicle and dopamine-prolactin-corpus luteum. These represent the two main anatomical events determining the ovarian cycle: time required for follicular development and the life span of the corpus luteum.

Individual differences are the hallmark of pheromonal regulation (reviewed by McClintock, 1983a,c). This is a biological characteristic that our computer simulation demonstrated was necessary for the type of dynamic interactions seen within groups of rats. Most striking in both studies were the individual differences in strength of response, including complete insensitivity (Chateau *et al.,* 1976; Gans and McClintock, 1993). In rats, responsiveness is enhanced in those individuals that are isolated socially from other females (Aron, 1979). Even the classic phenomenon of estrous suppression by other females occurs only in a subset of mice (Lamond, 1959). Those mice that are responsive were less androgenized by developing *in utero* immediately next to their brothers (Vom Saal, 1989). In addition, genetic similarity of the male and female plays a role (Barkley *et al.,* 1993; DeLeon and Barkley, 1987).

Male pheromones. Male primer pheromones stimulate luteinizing hormone-releasing hormone (GnRH) in a variety of species, triggering a preovulatory surge of LH and ovulation (e.g., prairie vole; Dluzen *et al.,* 1981; Djungarian hamster, Erb *et al.,* 1993; review by Meredith, 1991a, and Chapter 4 by Carter and Keverne). In other species, there is a phase-response curve to male pheromones. For example, when females are in the luteal phase, male urine shortens the cycles of woolly opossums (Perret and Benmbarek, 1991), lengthens it when they are in the follicular phase, and has no effect when the females are already in the ovulatory phase.

In ovariectomized estrogen-primed rats, male pheromones stimulate the preovulatory LH surge by binding at the vomeronasal organ. There are genetic differences in male primer pheromone production. Male Sprague-Dawley rats do not have urine that shortens the ovarian cycles as do Wistar male rats (M. K. McClintock, unpublished observations). This strain difference may reflect VNO receptor defects, because Sprague-Dawley male urine does not stimulate VNO receptors as does Wistar male urine (Inamura *et al.,* 1999).

Male urinary pheromones act through at least three pathways to stimulate an LH surge in ovariectomized estrogen-primed female rats. In intact females, these three neuroendocrine mechanisms are likely to have similar effects, mediating shortening of spontaneous estrous cycles ((Mora *et al.,* 1985; Sanchez-Criado, 1982) and inducing ovulation in anestrous females (Johns *et al.,* 1978).

1. Male bedding induces c-fos reactivity in the accessory olfactory bulb and other central accessory olfactory structures (Dudley *et al.,* 1992). Information is then relayed via an uncrossed pathway to the premammillary nucleus before reaching the medial basal hypothalamus and triggering GnRH pulses (Beltramino and Taleisnik, 1983; classic review by Aron, 1979).

2. Male bedding increases axonal transport of GnRH for intracerebral release (Moss and Dudley, 1984; Wooten *et al.,* 1975; review by Meredith, 1991a).

3. In the olfactory bulb, male urine reverses estrogenic inhibition of GABA synthesis (Becerra *et al.,* 1996).

In a different context, male urine did not increase fos-immunoreactivity in GnRH cell bodies (Rajendren *et al.,* 1993). In this particular study, females were exposed to bedding only briefly and in an unnatural paradigm: three to six blocks of 15 minutes in a cage with soiled bedding. The more natural and effective type of exposure is application of urine directly to the nares (Johns *et al.,* 1978). This mimics what happens during social investigation, when the male is spraying the female and she is sniffing him. Normally, the sight and sounds of a male are present to enhance pheromonal action (Beauchamp *et al.,* 1985; Beltramino and Taleisnik, 1983; deCatanzaro *et al.,* 1999).

Thus, the effects of male primer pheromones on females are as context dependent as are the effects of female primers. Context dependence is mediated by cortical and subcortical pathways processing nonpheromonal stimuli from the male as well as motor systems within the female. In rats, their effect is disinhibition, if not potentiation, of multiple pheromonal pathways. Evidence for a peripheral mechanism for context dependence comes from mice. The vomeronasal organ is ennervated by neurons releasing norepinepherine (Keverne, 1999). Norepinepherine may act locally to increase sensitivity of the sensory epithelium or change glandular secretions of pheromone transporter proteins, as well as the vasculature, which effects the pumping action of the VNO. In rats, circadian rhythms gate the main olfactory system so that male pheromones can only affect estrogen-dependent GABA synthesis in the morning (Becerra *et al.,* 1996).

ii) Puberty. In mice, adult females inhibit puberty onset of juvenile females with whom they live. In the laboratory, puberty inhibition occurs primarily during the fall and winter months. In the field, it occurs during high-population densities, thus providing an effective mechanism for regulating population dynamics (reviewed by Drickamer, 1984; Vandenbergh, 1994). The puberty delay pheromone in female mouse urine is 2,5-dimethlypyrazine (Leinders-Zufall *et al.,* 2000; Ma *et al.,* 1998). The juvenile females most susceptible to this pheromone are those that have not been prenatally androgenized by developing *in utero* next to their male sibs (Vom Saal, 1989). Individual differences among rats may have the same origin, since prenatal androgens sexually differentiate the vomeronasal system (see review by Segovia and Guillamon, 1993; Zehr *et al.,* 2001).

Inhibition of female puberty is observed in species as diverse as house, prairie, deer, and hopping mice, Mongolian gerbils, marmosets, and tamarins, although its context dependence has not been explicated as elegantly as in mice. In primates, social dominance plays an important role in determining which individuals will be inhibited, as well as which will produce inhibitory pheromones. For example, subordinate females also experience morphological changes in their scent gland and produce less pheromonal secretions (see reviews by Abbott, 1984; Baker *et al.,* 1999; French *et al.,* 1984; Molina *et al.,* 2000; Saltzman *et al.,* 1998; Snowdon, 1983). In nonprimate species, social dominance may also be more important than pheromonal or odor cues in reproductive suppression (e.g., naked mole-rat; T. E. Smith *et al.,* 1997).

A genetic basis for individual differences in response to puberty-inhibiting pheromones is evidenced in rats. Female Holtzman rats living with a group of females and a male achieve puberty later than those just living with a male (Vandenbergh and Post, 1976). In contrast, puberty in Wistar rats is not inhibited by living with other females (Slob *et al.,* 1985). The Wistar strain is notable because puberty occurs much later than it does in other strains (Tomasino, 2000). This suggests that there are genes in common with pheromonal responsiveness and the neuroendocrine regulation of the ovarian axis during puberty.

In contrast to the effect of female pheromones on puberty, males typically accelerate puberty and enhance hormonal stimulation of ovulation (Zarrow *et al.,* 1972; reviewed by Bronson and Rissman, 1986; Schank and Alberts, 2000; Vandenbergh, 1994). In mice, the effect is strongest in the laboratory during the spring and summer months (Drickamer, 1984) but occurs in all seasons and population densities in the field (Vandenbergh, 1994).

Again, the females most sensitive to pheromones are those who were not androgenized by their brothers *in utero* (Vom Saal, 1989); see review of sexual differentiation of the vomeronasal system in the rat (Segovia

and Guillamon, 1993). Postnatal experience also plays a role. Preweanling females reared with their fathers react more readily to the puberty-accelerating effects of adult male urine than do females reared only with other females (Mucignat-Caretta *et al.,* 1995). The interaction of prenatal hormones and postnatal experience could be modulating the female's behavior toward the pheromones, rather than her pheromonal sensitivity. Female mice choose to spend time near puberty-delaying pheromones until they reach their first estrus, whereupon they change to sitting near male pheromones that will continue accelerating their puberty (Drickamer, 1992).

Puberty acceleration by male pheromones is mediated by the vomeronasal system in mice and Dungarian hamsters (Lomas and Keverne, 1982; Reasner *et al.,* 1993; see reviews by Meredith, 1991a, and Chapter 4 by Carter and Keverne). Moreover, mice do not express V1r and V2r, pheromone receptor genes in the wild-type VNO, if they are missing p73, a gene whose RNA is most highly expressed in the neuroepithelium of the vomeronasal organ, as well as the accessory olfactory bulb, the amygdala, and hypothalamus (Yang *et al.,* 2000). This gene may be the same one discovered phenotypically, 30 years before molecular genetics were feasible (Eleftheriou *et al.,* 1972). Genetic factors are also functionally implicated by strain differences in rats, where Holtzmann females respond to male puberty-accelerating pheromones, and Wistar females do not (Slob *et al.,* 1985; Vandenbergh, 1976).

Male urine and preputial gland secretions contain several compounds that accelerate puberty: 2-sec-butyl-4,5-dihydrothiazole, 3,4-dehydro-exo-brevicomin, α- and β-farnasenes, and 6-hydroxy-6-methyl-3-heptanone (Novotny *et al.,* 1999). Each of these compounds stimulates neural activity in a unique, nonoverlapping subset of vomeronasal neurons (Leinders-Zufall *et al.,* 2000). Moreover, in contrast to olfactory neurons, the VNO neurons, activated via phospholipase C, do not adapt with prolonged exposure to the pheromone (Holy *et al.,* 2000). It is noteworthy that these mouse pheromones each have a distinct odor to humans but are bound at the mouse VNO and clearly are processed differently in mice than is an odor percept in humans. Moreover, they are effective in miniscule concentrations, 10^{-11}, in accordance with the definition of pheromone.

iii) Pregnancy. The metabolic demands of pregnancy and lactation are great (Leon and Woodside, 1983) and thus must be coordinated with a supportive physical and social environment. A female may benefit by altering the timing of her fertility in response to signals from other reproductively active females so that she ovulates, mates, and gives birth at the same time as do females of her social group (McClintock, 1998b). In Norway rats, doing so increases the probability of conceiving (McClintock, 1984b), reduces infanticide by males and other females (Mennella and Moltz, 1988, 1989), permits sharing of the lactational burden, avoids inter-litter competition, a source of high infant mortality (Mennella *et al.*, 1990), and enables sex-ratio biasing of offspring (Blumberg *et al.*, 1992). Breeding synchrony can also swamp the capacity of predators (Ims, 1990).

Many other species also exhibit socially facilitated breeding synchrony: root voles (Johannesen *et al.*, 2000), Townsend voles (Lambin, 1993), common shrews (Stockley, 1996), Australian cashmere goats (Restall *et al.*, 1995), sable antelope (Thompson, 1991, 1995), European wild boar (Delcroix *et al.*, 1990), cats (Michel, 1993), beef-cows (Wright *et al.*, 1994), ring-tailed lemurs (Pereira, 1991), squirrel monkeys (Schiml *et al.*, 1996), golden lion tamarins (French, 1987), and lion-tailed macaques (Clarke *et al.*, 1992).

The coordination of birth cycles within a population can be achieved by pheromones from pregnant or lactating females regulating ovulation in recipients. In rats, pheromones from pregnant females enhance or phase-advance ovulation in spontaneously cycling females (McClintock, 1983b). In mice, urine from pregnant and lactating house mice also accelerates ovulation during puberty (Drickamer and Hoover, 1979).

In pregnant mice, male pheromones can terminate a female's pregnancy so that she comes into heat and mates again with a new intruding male (Bruce, 1959). Although this has obvious benefits for the intruding male, why would vulnerability to male pheromones evolve in females, particularly when it appears to reduce fitness? The answer lies in the social context in which pregnancy-disrupting pheromones operate.

A female mouse develops a protective memory of the male with whom she mates so that his pheromones do not disrupt her pregnancy. Strikingly, the female will do this only if the male has remained with her for at least four to five hours after mating (Rosser and Keverne, 1985). Presumably, such behavior indicates he is not just a transient male, but instead is likely to remain close by and provide paternal care, especially by provisioning food for the female (Brown, 1993; Wright and Brown, 2000). Her memory for the sire of her litter lasts for 50 days (Brennan *et al.*, 1990), precisely the time it takes for the female to carry her pregnancy to term and raise her offspring to weaning.

The female can terminate her pregnancy in response to a newly arrived male and afford herself the opportunity to re-conceive with him. The female must be in direct contact with the new male's urine, and she is targeted and sprayed with urine from both males during intense inter-male competition (deCatanzaro, 1999; deCatanzaro *et al.*, 1996, 1999). She can thus use pheromonal cues from males to benefit from male-male competition and "choose" a good sire for her offspring.

She does this, however, only when she has made a minimal investment in her current pregnancy. Pregnancy termination can occur only during the first three days post conception, prior to implantation of the blastocysts, and incurs only a minimal delay in conceiving offspring, i.e., similar to that incurred during a spontaneous ovarian cycle.

The protective memory of a steadfast mate does not depend on cognitive recognition or memory of the odor but is mediated by processes within the vomeronasal system, perhaps by using information from the sire's major histocompatability loci to determine his individual identity (H2; Lloyd-Thomas and Keverne, 1982; Selway and Keverne, 1990; Yamazaki *et al.*, 1983). Likewise, termination of the pregnancy is mediated by the vomeronasal system. The new male's pheromone must be present during the surges of prolactin that maintain the corpus luteum in order to terminate the pregnancy (Rosser *et al.*, 1989). The genetic, molecular, and neuroendocrine mechanisms of this remarkable pheromone system have been worked out in elegant detail and are reviewed in Chapter 4 by Carter and Keverne. It remains to be determined whether similar mechanisms mediate other forms of pregnancy disruption, such as that triggered by other females in red-backed voles (Kawata, 1987).

iv) Lactation. Pheromones from lactating rats and their pups prolong and increase the variability of the recipients' ovarian cycles (McClintock, 1983b,d). This signal is particularly potent in suppressing postpartum estrus and may come from fetuses *in utero* late in pregnancy (Gudermuth *et al.,* 1984). This form of fertility suppression may serve to delay conception by other females in the social group, until the nursing female is herself ready to conceive. Doing so, would promote the birth synchrony that enables communal nursing and is so beneficial for pup survival in this socially breeding species reviewed in McClintock, 1983d, 2000.

In addition, maternal pheromones from lactating female rats enhance maternal care and survival of the pup. After nursing for 14 days, when their pups are first becoming mobile, production of a maternal pheromone by lactating rats is at its peak (Lee and Moltz, 1984; Moltz, 1984; Moltz and Lee, 1981; Moltz and Leon, 1973; Schumacher and Moltz, 1982). The maternal pheromone is produced in the liver under the control of prolactin and is secreted in the mother's feces (Lee *et al.,* 1982). Rat pups are attracted to maternal feces, are coprophagic and thereby receive nutrients that promote mylenization of their nervous systems. They also populate the flora of their gut appropriately, in anticipation of beginning to eat the solid food in their environment, significantly reducing their risk of fatal gut infections (Lee and Moltz, 1984).

v) Reproductive senescence. As female rats age, approximately half of them enter an anovulatory state without spontaneous ovarian cycles called "constant estrus," a misnomer (LeFevre and McClintock, 1988). Females living in social isolation from other females are more likely to stop ovulating and do so at a younger stage than do group-housed females, which are more likely to maintain ovarian cycles, albeit irregular ones (LeFevre and McClintock, 1991, 1992). A similiar anovulatory state can be induced in young females by exposing them to light 24 hours a day. These prematurely aged females produce pheromones that disrupt the cyclicity of young rats and inhibit ovulation (McClintock and Adler, 1978).

Aging anovulatory female rats can resume ovulation in response to pheromones from young males (Mora *et al.,* 1994; M. K. McClintock, unpublished observations). Young males stimulate progesterone secretion from the adrenal and the ovary and a full luteinizing hormone (LH) surge, followed by ovulation (Day *et al.,* 1988). The female then mates with the young male (LeFevre and McClintock, 1992). Likewise, male urine

can trigger an LH surge in young females that are in light-induced constant estrus (Johns *et al.,* 1978). In mice, the potency of this stimulatory male pheromone declines from 2 to 30 months of age, similar to reproductive senescence in the female (Wilson and Harrison, 1983). Thus, it is primarily young males that have the pheromonal capacity to stimulate fertility in older and anovulatory females.

In sum, both female and male pheromones regulate the rate and state of reproductive senescence, thus affecting the reproductive life span of female rats. The reproductive life span capacity to extend reproductive life span is one of the most significant variables in determining the life time fitness of many animal species. Therefore this trait and associated neuroendocrine mechanisms would be under a strong positive selection pressure in most environments (McClintock, 1981b).

b) Human Women produce ovarian pheromones that regulate the timing of the preovulatory surge of luteinizing hormone (LH) in other women (McClintock, 1998a, 1999, 2000; Whitten, 1999). When presented daily throughout two menstrual cycles, axillary compounds from the follicular phase of the menstrual cycle shorten the follicular phase and advance the preovulatory LH surge of recipient women. In contrast, daily exposure to periovulatory compounds lengthens the follicular phase and delays the preovulatory LH surge (Fig. 2). These compounds have no effect on the duration of menstruation, or on the life span of the corpus luteum, thus indicating that they affect the neuroendocrine mechanisms of follicular development and the timing of the preovulatory LH surge.

As predicted, axillary compounds from the follicular phase are reported to accelerate pulses of LH in recipient women, whereas ovulatory phase compounds slow them (Shinohara *et al.,* 1999). 3α-Androstenol (5α-androst-16-en-3α-ol) is detectable in female axillary secretions that influence the timing of women's menstrual cycles (Preti *et al.,* 1987) and may be a compound contributing to the phase-delay effect of human pheromones. Indeed, this steroid slows the pulsatile release of LH in women (Shinohara *et al.,* 2000). Moreover, women who synchronize their menstrual cycles are more sensitive to androstenol (5α-androst-16-en-3α-ol) applied directly under their noses than women

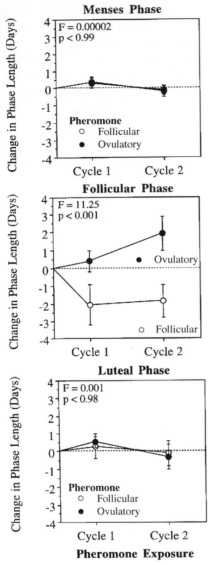

FIGURE 2 Effect of ovarian pheromones on the follicular phase of women (from Stern and McClintock, 1998, *Nature* **392**, 177–179).

who do not. There is no such differential sensitivity to androstenone (5α-androst-16-en-3-one) or to pyridine (Morofushi et al., 2000).

It is not clear why sensitivity to an odor predicts a primer pheromone effect (see also Pierce et al., 1993; Stevens and O'Connell, 1995, 1996). Further work is needed to identify what chemical compounds are both necessary and sufficient. The neuroendocrine mechanisms of the human system may profitably be studied with an *in vivo* model. Secretion of GnRH by

primary cultures of human olfactory cells is increased a thousand-fold by steroids and an odorant, l-carvone (Barni *et al.*, 1999), and thus might serve as such a model system.

These two distinct ovarian-cycle pheromones are functionally similar to those produced by female rats (McClintock, 1978; see Section II.B.1.a.). This parallel suggested that humans, as well as rats and mice, might also produce primer pheromones during the birth cycle of pregnancy and lactation. Indeed, breast-feeding pheromones from lactating women and their infants increase the variability of the ovarian cycle in women who are exposed to them daily for two months (Spencer *et al.*, 2000).

Only trace amounts of compounds are necessary to exert their effects, and they are effective without being consciously detected as an odor. In the case of ovarian-cycle compounds, women did not report detecting any body odor on the pads (Stern and McClintock, 1998). In the study of breastfeeding compounds, the frequency of odor detection was indistinguishable for pads containing breastfeeding compounds and the carrier-control pads containing potassium phosphate buffer solution. When asked to describe the pads with breastfeeding compounds, women used a wide variety of odor descriptors. The most common categories were fragrance (19%) and body odor (17%). Nonetheless, an increased rate of detection of body odor was not associated with ovarian responses to the breastfeeding compounds (Bullivant *et al.*, 2000).

In both experiments, human axillary compounds had been collected on cotton pads, frozen, and thawed before being wiped just under the recipient's nose. Freezing axillary secretions on cotton reduces the detection of body odors, which do become detectable again if the compounds are chemically extracted from the pad (G. Preti, personal communication). Thus, the fact that odors were detected on only 53% of the pads demonstrates that odor perception is not necessary for the compounds' pheromonal function, but does not imply that fresh axillary or breastfeeding compounds are without a distinct odor (e.g., Fleming *et al.*, 1993; Mennella and Beauchamp, 1991; Mennella *et al.*, 2002; Schaal and Marlier, 1998; Wysocki and Preti, 2000).

These pheromones are a likely mechanism for menstrual synchrony, the phenomenon in which women within a social group become more likely to menstruate at the same time than random groups of women (McClintock, 1971; Preti, 1987; Preti *et al.,* 1986; Russell et al., 1980; Wilson, 1987; reviews by M. K. McClintock, 1983c, 1998b, 2000; A. Weller and Weller, 1993; L. Weller *et al.,* 1995). As in rats, synchrony has the opportunity to develop only when all the females in the group have interacted for at least seven consecutive ovulatory cycles, and even then occurs only under specific initial conditions (Schank and McClintock, 1992). Other potential forms of the social control of ovulation in women are asynchrony, regularization of the cycle, or changes in the rate of ovulatory cycles.

Many studies have been done that document conditions under which synchrony does occur and those in which it does not (for more extensive reviews, see Graham, 1991; McClintock, 1983, 2000; Rogel, 1978; Stern and McClintock, 1998; A. Weller and Weller, 1993; L. Weller and Weller, 1995, 1997). The conditions under which social synchronization occurs include women who are (1) living together in small groups, (2) close friends, (3) sharing activities, (4) coworkers, particularly those with high job interdependency but low stress, or (5) mothers and daughters (Goldman, 1987; Graham and McGrew, 1980, 1992; Little *et al.,* 1989; Matteo, 1987; Quadagno *et al.,* 1981; Shinohara *et al.,* 2000; Skandhan *et al.,* 1979; A. Weller and Weller, 1992, 1993, 1995a,b; L. Weller *et al.,* 1995, 1999a,b).

Those in which menstrual synchrony did not occur include groups of women who are (1) without the opportunity to synchronize (i.e., have too few concurrent cycles that are both consecutive and ovulatory), (2) lesbian couples with prolonged intense contact, (3) members of multiple groups, or (4) people with particular personality traits (Jarett, 1984; Strassmann, 1997; Trevathan *et al.,* 1993; A. Weller and Weller, 1995b, 1998b; Wilson *et al.,* 1991).

A variety of statistical methods for detecting synchrony has been critically evaluated (Arden and Dye, 1998; Graham, 1991; McClintock, 1998b; Schank, 1997; A. Weller and Weller, 1997, 1998a), although inaccurately in some cases because of an inadequate understanding of interacting oscillating systems or an incomplete literature review (Doty, 1981; Graham, 1993; Rhine, 1995; Strassmann, 1999; Wilson, 1992, 1993). Excellent and accessible discussions of dynamic inter-

actions between oscillating systems have been written by Glass and Mackey (1988), Strogatz and Stewart (1993), and Winfree (1980, 1987).

It has been suggested that menstrual synchrony simply reflects a reporting bias caused by the "wishful thinking" of close friends (Strassmann, 1999). Yet at the time of the original study (McClintock, 1971), women were reticent about casually discussing their menstrual periods with their friends; 47% reported that they did not know when their friends were menstruating, and among those that were aware, 48% were only "vaguely aware." All women kept menstrual calendars, were interviewed individually, and were blind to the hypothesis being tested. Thus, reporting bias by the subjects is an unlikely explanation for the scientific data.

Finally, there are various reports in the anthropological and historical literature, which although not verifiable statistically are nonetheless interesting, particularly because they predate the scientific literature. For example, a heratic ostracon from Ramesside Egypt in 1200 B.C. describes synchronized menstruating women (Wilfong, 1998). A myth from Karok Native Americans living near the Klamath River describes the Pleides constellation as synchronized menstruating women (Buckley, 1988; Harrington, 1931). A traditional string figure depicting menstrual synchrony is made by Yolngu, an Australian Aboriginal group (McCarthy, 1960). Unfortunately, menstrual synchrony has been narrowly conceived in the anthropological literature, rather than focusing broadly on social regulation of ovulation. Moreover, its ubiquity has been overstated. It has even been suggested to contribute to the origins of culture (Knight, 1991).

Although menstrual synchrony was the first manifestation of human pheromones to be reported in the scientific literature, it is not likely to be the most important biological manifestation. First, from an evolutionary perspective, having many consecutive ovulatory menstrual cycles is a social artifact, not a species trait. Both ovulation and consecutive cycles are necessary for this dynamic interaction of oscillating systems (Schank and McClintock, 1992). Women have begun having spontaneous ovulatory menstrual cycles during the majority of their adult lives only with the advent of reliable contraception. Historically, women with many consecutive menstrual cycles were probably relatively rare. A notable exception is Roman Egypt, when customs and law did enable divorced women to live independently during their fertile years (based on census data; Bagnall and Frier, 1994).

Typically, because contraception was inadequate or not practiced, women in their fertile years were less likely to have menstrual cycles than they were to have birth cycles of pregnancy and lactation. Indeed, in agrarian and hunter-gather populations, ovulatory menstrual cycles occur on average no more than three times in two years (Eaton *et al.*, 1994; Strassmann, 1997). This is also true for most mammals with spontaneous ovulatory cycles because the function of spontaneous cycles is to create repeated opportunities for the female mammal to conceive, which they do when ecological conditions afford them adequate nutritional and physical resources (Bronson, 2000; Schneider and Wade, 2000).

As soon as conception occurs, menstrual cycles are suspended until infants are successfully weaned, typically for three to four years, unless there is miscarriage or the infant dies. Thus, the neuroendocrine mechanisms of ovulation and the menstrual cycle evolved as an interlude within the much longer birth cycle: puberty with only occasional ovulatory cycles, is followed by conception, pregnancy, lactation, and then resumption of menstrual cycles only until the next conception. Therefore, as in rodents (see Section II.B.1.a), ovarian and breastfeeding pheromones likely evolved to regulate ovulation and ovarian function in a variety of reproductive and environmental contexts, such as initiation of ovulatory cycles at puberty, after lactational anovulation, and at the beginning of reproductive senescence, around 35 years of age.

Animal pheromones often operate only in seasons optimal for raising offspring and even then only in specific social contexts (e.g., Mori *et al.*, 1999; see Section II.B). In socially breeding species of birds and lemurs, social signals tighten with a social group the coordination of birth peak stimulated by cues from a supportive environment (reviewed in McClintock, 1981b, 1983c; Pereira, 1991). This may also be the context in which human primer pheromones evolved. Humans evidence seasonal rhythms in ovulation and births. Even modern-day women living in artificial environments manifest a seasonal rhythm in their LH surge. In the spring, LH surges begin later in the day than they do during the rest of the year (Casper *et al.*, 1988; Edwards

et al., 1980; Testart *et al.*, 1982; see review by Stern and McClintock, 1996). More dramatically, hunter gatherers living in the arid environment of the Kalahari desert have sharp annual peaks in conceptions and births that are coordinated with the rainy season and food availability (Van der Welt *et al.*, 1978). Some years, rains fail and conceptions are rare altogether, thus indicating a lack of ovulatory cycles. Seasonality of births also occurs among the Lese, subsistence farmers in the Ituri Forest of Zaire (Bailey *et al.*, 1992). Therefore, future human work may profitably focus on the effects of ovarian pheromones and other social signals as ovulation regulators under stressful environmental or social conditions.

Humans may have male primer pheromones as well. Women in an all-women college who were in social proximity with men three or more times a week had shorter and more regular cycles than women who saw men less often (McClintock, 1971). This cycle pattern is associated with ovulation (Treloar *et al.*, 1967; Vollman, 1977; review by Stern and McClintock, 1996). When women lived where there were always men in their social environment, there was no association between spending social time with a man and menstrual cycle length (Quadagno *et al.*, 1981). However, women who slept in the same bed with a man more than once in a 40 day period were more likely to ovulate than were women who did not (Veith *et al.*, 1983). In this study, sexual intercourse was unrelated to likelihood of ovulation or menstrual cycle length, although such associations have been reported by others (Cutler *et al.*, 1980, 1985; Stanislaw and Rice, 1987).

The association between ovulation and interacting with men may not reflect direct causality. Women who are socially isolated in general have irregular anovulatory cycles (Harrison, 1997), and psychosocial stressors such as a stepfather in the family accelerate a daughter's pubertal maturation (Ellis and Garber, 2000; Ellis *et al.*, 1999). Nonetheless, increased ovulation in the presence of men could be mediated by male primer pheromones, as it is in other mammals (see Section II. B.2.a). Indeed, in a small sample of women with a high frequency of aberrant cycles, those exposed to an extract of men's axillary compounds were more likely to have normal cycles (Cutler *et al.*, 1986; see Wilson, 1988, for revised statistics, and Cutler, 1988).

2. Testicular Function

a) Animal   Primer pheromones from estrous females stimulate male LH and testosterone production in a variety of mammalian species (Dluzen and Ramirez, 1987; Kamel *et al.,* 1977; Purvis and Haynes, 1978; Signoret, 1991; Wysocki *et al.,* 1983; reviewed in Breipohl, 1982, and Wood, 1997). Sometimes this effect is detected only when males are not gonadally active, such as during the nonmating season in sheep, and even then only at sunrise, when the frequency of LH pulses is low (Gonzalez *et al.,* 1988). In other species, such as the hamster, testosterone modulates the male's behavioral sensitivity to female pheromones, and both are necessary for mating. Testosterone is hypothesized to promote synaptic connections, thereby gating transmission of chemosensory information to the preoptic area and hypothalamus (Wood, 1997; Wood and Newman, 1995).

In primates, there are several phenomena that could be explained by similar pheromonal mechanisms, although data indicate that social interactions are more prepotent than pheromonal communication (Abbott, 1984; Belcher *et al.,* 1986; Clark, 1981; Doty, 1984; Goldfoot, 1981; Hennessy *et al.,* 1978; Michael *et al.,* 1976; Savage *et al.,* 1988; Ziegler, 1990; Ziegler *et al.,* 1993). The prepotence of social suppression of fertility is also seen in some nonprimate species (e.g., in guinea pigs, mothers suppress their sons' fertility; Maken and Hennessy, 1999). Because social mechanisms are prepotent, the neuroendocrine mechanisms for primer pheromones in male primates remain understudied.

In male mice, an intact vomeronasal organ is necessary for hormonal responses to female primer pheromones (Wysocki *et al.,* 1983). In male rats, exposure to estrous bedding increases the number of c-fos-immunoreactive neurons at each level of the vomeronasal projection circuit (Bressler and Baum, 1996). This pathway is also essential in the hamster (Wood, 1997, 1998), where c-fos expression is increased throughout the vomeronasal pathways (Fernandez-Fewell and Meredith, 1994; Meredith and Fernandez-Fewell, 1994).

In rats, it is the olfactory bulb that mediates recognition of the presence of an estrous female (Dluzen and Ramirez, 1989), as well as GnRH responses within the olfactory bulb to the female primer pheromones.

In voles, the vomeronasal system mediates similar responses (see Chapter 4 by Carter and Keverne). In contrast, an intact olfactory system is not necessary for testicular responses in sexually experienced rams, as anosmia does not prevent stimulation of testosterone production by estrous ewes (Gonzalez *et al.,* 1991; Signoret, 1991).

When prepubescent male rats are living together in a group, puberty is accelerated by pheromones from adult males or females. Accelerated reproductive maturity is indicated by a reduction in hypothalamic aromatase and 5-α-reductase activity as well as higher levels of testosterone and estradiol in plasma (Dessi-Fulgheri and Lupo, 1982). In mice, however, urine from adult males has the opposite effect and delays puberty (Vandenbergh, 1994). Similarly, urine or scent marks from a dominant male prosimian, *Microcebus murinus,* increases prolactin and reduces testosterone levels in recipient adult males, even when they have never met the odor donor (Perret and Schilling, 1987, 1995; Schilling *et al.,* 1984). These compounds are airborne urinary chemosignals mediated by the main olfactory system, not the vomeronasal system, which requires direct contact with urine (Schilling *et al.,* 1990). There is relatively little research on the role of primer pheromones in interactions among males. This domain has been neglected in favor of studying heterosexual interactions, and we cannot yet know the full extent of pheromonal effects among males on a variety of different hormonal systems set in diverse social contexts.

b) Human   For men, no studies have tested the hypothesis that there are male primer pheromones that affect other men. There is only inconclusive evidence that female primer pheromones affect testicular function.

A field researcher reported that his beard grew more when he left an isolated island and spent time with his mistress (Anonymous, 1970). Although he verified that his beard growth was a bioassay for his testosterone levels, he reported that his beard started growing prior to leaving the island, thus indicating that the cause was not necessarily pheromonal but could have been anticipation (Anonymous, 1970). However, testosterone does not rise in anticipation of sexual intercourse in stable heterosexual couples, only afterwards (Dabbs and Mohammed, 1992).

An unidentified compound, termed "armpitin," is reported to temporarily induce male sterility (Greenstein, 1965), and a synthetic steroid, pregna-4,20-diene-3,6-dione, applied directly to the VNO, reduces the pulsatility of follicle stimulating hormone (FSH) and LH and decreases testosterone in serum (Monti-Bloch et al., 1998). Although these authors have conceptualized their work in terms of heterosexual interactions and sex specificity, both effects indicate reduced testicular function and are more consistent with inter-male competition, in which a male signal reduces GnRH function and the fertility of another male.

Men may also respond to olfactory or pheromonal cues from their pregnant wives and children. Men who are responsive to olfactory and other cues from newborn infants have higher prolactin levels and larger drops in testosterone following the birth of their child than do nonresponsive men. Their hormone profiles are also correlated with that of their partner (Storey et al., 2000). These responses in men are similar to males of other mammalian species in which paternal care is important (Wynne-Edwards and Reburn, 2000).

3. Adrenal Function

Adrenal pheromones have been studied only in animals. In female mice, the adrenal gland is necessary for the production of urinary pheromones that suppress ovulation and estrus of other females, classically termed the Lee-Boot effect (Ma et al., 1998). The adrenal controls production of 2,5-dimethylpyrazine, a compound both necessary and sufficient for the mutual suppression of ovarian function in crowded groups of females. It is secreted along with four other adrenal dependent compounds, which do not counteract its potency, and may serve other functions (2-heptanone, trans-5-hepten-2-one, trans-4-hepten-2-one, pentyl acetate and cis-2-penten-1-yl acetate; Novotny et al., 1986). This elegant work is a culmination of a longer series of studies on the adrenal dependence of estrus suppression pheromones in the house mouse (Christian, 1955; Drickamer and McIntosh, 1980; Drickamer et al., 1978; Lee and van der Boot, 1955; Southwick and Bland, 1959; Vandenbergh, 1994).

It will be important to determine whether dimethylpyrazine regulates only the hypothalamic-pituitary-ovarian axis or also the adrenal axis (Marchlewska-Koj and Zacharczuk-Kakietek, 1990). To date, there are no studies testing this hypothesis. There is a striking paucity of mammalian research on primer pheromones that regulate hormones other than GnRH and affect either the adrenal or nonreproductive endocrine systems.

Pheromones do acutely increase plasma corticosterone in mice and in the prosimian, Microcebus murinus (Marchlewska-Koj and Zacharczuk-Kakietek, 1990; Schilling et al., 1984). In addition, several studies have used the terms "alarm pheromones" and even "funeral odors," some of which increase corticosterone levels (Mackay-Sim and Laing, 1980, 1981a,b; Pinel et al., 1981; Stevens and Koster, 1972; Valenta and Rigby, 1968, 1974). Nonetheless, more work is required to determine whether these are true primer pheromones or odors that are detectable and reliable signals that the sender is alarmed or distressed (see Sections II.A.2.c and III.A.5).

The best evidence is from rats, where exocrine glands near the eye produce the active compound and the odor of hormonal metabolites in urine or feces have been rule out. Rats that are stressed by swimming produce a pituitary-dependent low-molecular-weight compound that prevents other rats from relaxing and floating when they become tired (Abel, 1994; Abel and Bilitzke, 1990). This compound may be that produced by exocrine glands under the regulation of melanocortin peptides (Chen et al., 1997). The recipient's response could be mediated by the adrenal axis, the ANS, or direct effects on neural circuits.

Mice may also have alarm pheromones. Both male and female mice avoid airborne chemosignals from a mouse stressed by injections of hypertonic saline. It is interesting that the excretion of urine or feces by the stressed animal is not necessary for the production of the chemosignal, thus suggesting that a specialized gland may be involved (Rottman and Snowdon, 1972). Moreover, airborne chemosignals from a mouse stressed by foot shock cannot be used to condition taste aversion, as can many other odors; these particular compounds may have more specificity than do odors (Zalaquett and Thiessen, 1991).

C. Modulator Pheromones

1. Human

a) Modulators Not Releasers   Two steroids, Δ4, 16-androstadien-3-one (common name androstadienone) and 1,3,5,(10),16-estratetraen-3-ol (common name estratetraenol), have been claimed to be human pheromones that stimulate specific social cognitions and motivations: increased well-being, friendliness, and sociability, particularly feeling at ease for women and self-confidence for men (Kodis *et al.,* 1998; press releases and interview quotations from industry-associated scientists: Berliner, 1994, 1996; Blakeslee, 1993; Taylor, 1994).

Behavioral and psychological data, however, do not support these strong claims for releaser pheromones, but indicate instead that these steroids are either modulator pheromones or vasanas (see Sections II.A.2.d and IV.A. for definitions, as well as extended reviews upon which this section is based (Jacob *et al.,* 2002; McClintock, 2000; McClintock *et al.,* 2001). The primary effect of both steroids is to change an underlying tone or valence for perceiving external stimuli—in other words, a mood. These effects are measurable with well-validated measures of human mood: Profile of Mood States (POMS), Positive and Negative Affective States (PANAS), Addiction Research Center Inventory (ARCI), and Visual Analog Scales (VAS). They have also been replicated in three independent studies (Jacob and McClintock, 2000; Jacob *et al.,* 2001a).

Neither behavior, motivation, nor cognition are reflexively associated with exposure to these steroids, as is the case for classic releaser pheromones. In the context of everyday life in and around a university or within a laboratory setting, these steroids do not act as simple releasers of social behavior, thoughts, or mental-states—specifically, feeling more social, self-confident, or friendly (Jacob and McClintock, 1999, contra Kodis *et al.,* 1998).

Nonetheless, in both settings, they do affect general emotional and arousal states even when presented in nanomolar quantities (Jacob and McClintock, 1999, 2000). Indeed, an effective dose of androstadienone was 9 nanomoles, placed just under the nose on the upper lip; the amount contained in 1/100th of a drop of male sweat. Because the steroids were presented outside the nose, even less reached the nasal cavity. This amount was not consciously perceived as an odor (Jacob *et al.,* 2002; Lundstrom *et al.,* 2000) and indeed is well below the odor threshold of most compounds by at least four orders of magnitude (Devos *et al.,* 1990), although threshold for androstadienone is 0.96 ppb (Amoore, 1977). Mood effects were obtained both with a weak olfactory mask, the carrier substance propylene glycol,

and with a strong mask, created with clove oil. Therefore, these steroids meet one of the functional criteria for a pheromone—that they are effective in minute quantities. They also do not depend on their odor properties for their functional effects.

b) Absence of Sex Specificity   The actions of these steroids are not sex specific; both men and women responded to each steroid. Women in the late follicular phase of their menstrual cycles responded more strongly and positively to both steroids than did men. In contrast, men actually felt worse after exposure to the steroids, as compared to their control sessions. This was especially true in response to estratetraenol, directly refuting the hypothesis that estratetraenol might serve as a female sex attractant for men.

Thus, when measured with well-validated measures of psychological state (POMS, PANAS, ARCI, and VAS scales), there is no evidence to date that supports the simple hypothesis that the primary role of these steroids is limited to sex-specific effects on interpersonal and sexual interactions between men and women. For example, estratetraenol, the "female" steroid produced by the placenta in pregnant women (Knuppen and Breuer, 1963), immediately affects women by increasing their positive mood (Jacob and McClintock, 1999). Moreover, after two hours of exposure, their negative mood is reduced. Women feel less anxiety and are less "down" than during exposure only to the carrier solution.

The effect of androstadienone on women is similar to that of estratetraenol. This last finding, that androstadienone reduces negative mood, has been corroborated via a 70-item modification of the DeRogatis Inventory (Grosser *et al.,* 2000). It is noteworthy that the ovary produces androstadienone as does the testis. Moreover, androstadienone levels are not correlated with testosterone production in men (Gower and Ruparelia, 1992). Indeed, it is synthesized in the axillae of some men and women by resident coryneform bacteria, rather than being excreted by apocrine glands (see section IV.B; Rennie *et al.,* 1990).

c) Autonomic Nervous System   Androstadienone and estratetraenol also modulate classic indicators of autonomic nervous system (ANS) tone (Jacob *et al.,* 2001a). Without being verbally detected as odors, both steroids raise the skin temperature of men's hands and lower it in women. Likewise, each steroid increases

ANDROSTADIENONE

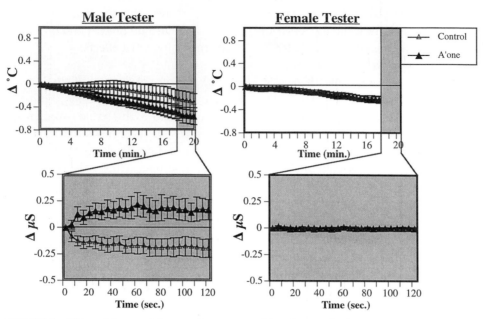

FIGURE 3 Effect of the sex of the experimenter on subjects' sympathetic nervous system responses to human modulator pheromones: androstadienone and estratetraenol (from Jacob *et al.,* 2001a, *Physiol. Behav.* **74**, 15–27, © Elsevier Science).

skin conductance, with a significantly greater effect on women than on men. Consistent, albeit weaker, findings have also been reported among women who reported themselves to be in the periovulatory portion of their cycle (Lundstrom *et al.,* 2000). Skin conductance is a "pure" indicator of sympathetic tone because the eccerine sweat glands are innervated only by the sympathetic and not the parasympathetic system (Hugdahl, 1995).

These data address previous conflicting results. Preliminary data suggested an increase in sympathetic tone (Monti-Bloch and Grosser, 1991). In contrast, it was later reported that androstadienone has a sympatholytic and parasympathomimetic effect in women (Grosser *et al.,* 2000). The interpretation of ANS effects in the latter report, however, was supported only by cardiorespiratory measures and was not consistent with the reported increase in skin conductance. Given potential uncoupling of the two autonomic branches, as well as multidetermination of the classic ANS indicators (Berntson *et al.,* 1994), the effects of these steroids are likely not interpretable within a classic "flight or flight" paradigm.

d) Context Dependence Both psychological and physiological responses are dependent on the socioexperimental context, again providing evidence that these compounds are not simply behavioral releasers. The social conditions of the experiment determine whether a response is detected or not. Women respond to the steroids only in the sessions run by a male tester, an effect that may or may not be solely attributable to tester gender (see Fig. 3; Jacob *et al.,* 2001a). Men's responses, in contrast, are not affected by this difference in socioexperimental context. Similarly, women experience an immediate increase in a positive mood only in the presence of the male tester, whereas men's responses are unaffected, at least in the social context of this particular study.

e) Individual Differences Up to this point, we have discussed the average response to androstadienone and estratetraenol. It is essential to recognize, however, that we also documented marked individual differences in the strength and valence of the mood response (McClintock *et al.,* 2001). For example, in women, androstadienone typically prevents the deterioration of positive mood often seen during the mild demands of a testing session. However, a few atypical women have marked negative responses and do not enjoy this ameliorative effect. Further research is needed to determine whether these response differences are inborn (e.g., women missing a gene for a particular pheromone or receptor; Rodriguez *et al.*, 2000) or whether they arise with experience (exposure to the steroid in different social contexts).

f) Natural Sources   Both steroids occur naturally in humans. Androstadienone, a 16-ene-steroid without androgenic activity, has been measured in peripheral plasma of men at .01–.06 μg/100 ml unconjugated, .05–.1 μg/100 ml sulphate-conjugated (Brooksbank *et al.*, 1969), 98 ng/100 ml (Brooksbank *et al.*, 1972), and 2.05 pmol/ml (Fukushima *et al.*, 1991). It is also found in men's sweat (Labows, 1988), semen (Kwan *et al.*, 1992), and axillary hair (Nixon *et al.*, 1988; Rennie *et al.*, 1990). In women, androstadienone is measurable in plasma at 36 ng/100 ml (Brooksbank *et al.*, 1972), and estratetraenol has been isolated from the urine of pregnant women in the third trimester (Thysen *et al.*, 1968).

Fragrance manufacturers claim to have isolated the steroids from skin cells (Kodis *et al.*, 1998), but there is no peer-reviewed publication stating how they were extracted, isolated, or identified (Preti and Wysocki, 1999). We do not know whether the sloughed epithelial cells were obtained from men and women or whether there are sex differences in their steroid profile. The hypothesis that skin could be a pheromone source is certainly appealing and has been explicated by Cohn (1994).

Androstadienone has several sources in humans (reviewed by Smals and Weusten, 1991). In the testis it is synthesized in a single step from pregnenolone (via 16-ene-synthetase; see Figure 4). It can also be synthesized from progesterone, albeit in small amounts in the testis, and more likely in the ovary or placenta. It is also produced by the adrenals of both men and women in response to ACTH stimulation (Smals and Weusten, 1991). Androstadienone is further metabolized into the 16-androstenes, which in humans takes place only in peripheral tissue (see Section IV.B.).

Estratetraenol is synthesized from androstadienone in a single step (as studied in the supernatant of hu-

man placental homogenate (see Figure 4; Knuppen and Breuer, 1963). Note that the previous literature on these putative human pheromones used the vague term "estratetraene," which refers to a large class of steroids. Estratetraenol is a more accurate common name, indicating the ketone at the third carbon position.

2. Animal

Animal pheromones also function as modulators but have been described in the literature without the benefit of a term to distinguish them from releaser pheromones. Many pheromones work only in specific contexts, and operate by modulating perception of specific stimuli or behavioral responses. Signoret (1991) has made this point most eloquently in describing the context sensitivity of behavioral and primer pheromones in sheep. The important contexts determining responsiveness are both social and photoperiodic, as they are in other species such as lesser mouse lemurs and meadow voles (Ferkin and Gorman, 1992; Perret and Schilling, 1995; Wayne *et al.*, 1989). In the rat, the prepotence of photoperiod and pheromones are reversed. Pheromonal systems override and inhibit the effect of seasonal day length on testicular function (Nelson *et al.*, 1985).

In female rats, pheromones modulate the lordosis response to a male's mount, but are insufficient by themselves to trigger the reflex (Rajendren *et al.*, 1993). Olfactory stimuli in the rat also modulate the female's approach to males (Romero *et al.*, 1990) and maternal responses to tactile stimuli from the pups, although they are neither necessary nor sufficient for either sexual or maternal behavior (Fleming *et al.*, 1992; Malenfant *et al.*, 1991). Goldfoot (1981) pointed out that "copulins," short-chain aliphatic acids isolated from the vaginal secretions of rhesus monkeys, do not "release" male sexual behavior unless the male and female are in a small restrictive enclosure (Michael *et al.*, 1976). In open spaces, typical of this species' ecology, copulins play a more subtle, modulating role.

In the pig, androstenone (the common name for 5α-androst-16-en-3-one) and androstenol (5α-androst-16-en-3α-ol) are classic examples of releaser pheromones. During artificial insemination, only an aerosol spray of the pheromones and hand pressure are

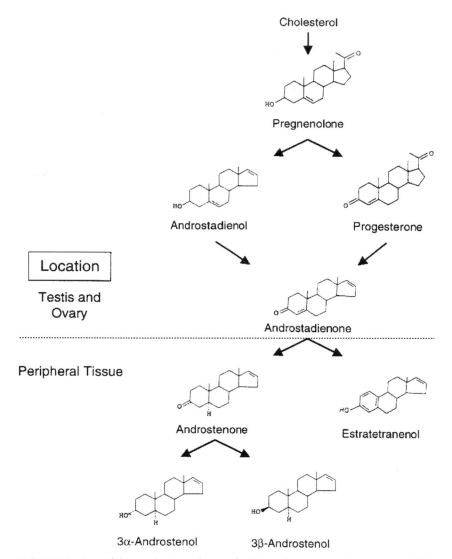

FIGURE 4 Steroid biosynthetic pathways for 16-androstenes and estratetraenol in humans (Dorfman and Ungar, 1965; Gower and Ruparelia, 1992; Smals and Weusten, 1991). The common names are defined here with steroid nomenclature to avoid ambiguity: androstadienol (Δ5,16-androstadien-3β-ol), androstadienone (Δ4,16, androstadien-3-one), androstenone (5α-androst-16-en-3-one), 3α-androstenol (5α-androst-16-en-3α-ol; this is the steroid to which "androstenol" typically refers), 3β-androstenol (5α-androst-16-en-3β-ol), and estratetraenol (1,3,5(10), 16-estratetraen-3-ol; this is the steroid to which the common name "estratetraene" typically refers).

needed to immediately elicit the mating stance from a gilt in estrus, thus evidencing their releaser function (Melrose *et al.,* 1971). But it must be recognized that the response does not always occur. Normally, the releaser pheromone operates in the context of other stimuli from the boar because the female approaches the male's pen and stands near him. Nonolfactory

cues from the nearby boar enhance the effectiveness of the pheromone, so that it is virtually 100% effective (Tilbrook and Hemsworth, 1990).

Does this interaction with the context mean that these classic releaser pheromones are misclassified and are in fact modulators? Experimental manipulations can determine which classification is appropriate by determining whether the pheromone is stimulating the behavior (a releaser) or serving as a context for more prepotent stimuli (a modulator). For example, when a gilt lives continuously next to a boar, she adapts to his visual and auditory cues, but his pheromones are still 75% effective. She does not ever adapt to the pheromone itself, only to other cues of the boar's presence. Thus, in this case, the pheromone is a releaser and the other stimuli from the male function as contextual cues.

III. SOCIAL ODORS AND CHEMOSIGNALS

Odors, smells, and scents are defined as chemosignals that are encoded and processed by olfactory receptors, the main olfactory system, and primary and secondary olfactory cortices. In humans, they are the percepts produced by molecules binding at the receptors of the olfactory epithelium. These percepts are accessible to conscious awareness, emotions, attention, recognition, and memory as well as classification and identification. They are thereby capable of acquiring meaning or significance by association, and can be used as an unconditioned stimulus in paired associations.

Odorants are the molecules that produce odors. It is often stated, incorrectly, that odorants must be volatile. Volatile compounds are those that evaporate, turning from a liquid to a gas at normal temperatures and pressures. There are, however, many volatile compounds that are odorless, such as H_2O. Likewise, many strong odorants are not volatile compounds. Steroid hormones are an excellent example. Androstenone is a steroid produced copiously by boars, and it has such a strong odor that it depresses the mood of people living near pig farms (Schiffman *et al.*, 1995c).

More correctly, odorants must be vagile, that is, capable of being dispersed, and reach the olfactory epithelium. Nonvolatile odorants can be airborne as aerosols, carried on dust motes, or in aqueous solutions bound to carrier proteins.

At the beginning of the nineteenth century, it was widely accepted in Europe that odors played an essential role in sexuality and social interactions (Harrington and Rosario, 1992). By the end of the century, that view was still held primarily by evolutionary biologists for sexual selection in animals (Darwin, 1871). For humans, however, civilization was equated with deodorizing the environment on the one hand, and adding back sophisticated scents and perfumes on the other (Corbin, 1986). Freud was an exemplar, believing that attractiveness of body odors, urine, and feces had to be repressed for normal psychosexual development (Freud, 1895, p. 269). Needless to say, this view is not characteristic of other modern and sophisticated cultures, such as those in India (Arimondi *et al.*, 1993). And in the United States, body odors from women are generally judged "pleasant" while men's body odors are "musky" (Russell, 1976).

A. Hormonal Modulation of Responses to Odors

The primary role of hormones is to modulate the sensory properties of odors or to change the responses to them, including emotional responses and meaning. They can also be odorants themselves. We now know that an odorant is encoded by the integration of information generated by binding at multiple olfactory receptors. Thus, it is no longer appropriate to make generalizations about hormonal modulation of general olfactory acuity when studies have tested but two or three compounds (Dorries, 1992, contra the argument for a concept of "general olfactory acuity" in humans; Doty *et al.*, 1994; Yoshida, 1984).

Instead, it will be more productive to look at hormonal modulation of responses to specific compounds that serve known social functions. It would be an efficient research strategy to take advantage of evolved systems (i.e., focus on the odorants that evolved to serve social functions) and to study the hormonal mechanisms involved in their sensory processing and integration with social behavior (McClintock, 1981a,b, 1983d). Dramatic progress following this strategy has been achieved elegantly in the mouse, hamster, domestic pig, and elephant (Johnston, 2000; Rasmussen and Schulte, 1999; Signoret, 1991; Vandenbergh, 1994).

In addition, because "neutral" odors in the environment can take on social meaning, particularly when associated with food, territory, other individuals, or social roles, it is likely that hormones play a role in the process of learned associations. Yet there is a surprising paucity of behavioral information about olfactory animals (with the exception of a few species; Eeckman and Freeman, 1991; Kay and Laurent, 1999). The recent discovery of hormone receptors and their gene expression throughout the olfactory system of animals indicates that this will be a fruitful area to study. The human literature is much richer, both conceptually and factually.

1. Sex Differences

In the few laboratory rodents studied to date, males have greater olfactory sensitivity to nonsocial odorants, such as cyclopentanone and eugenol (clove), than do females, except when the females are in the periovulatory phase of their ovarian cycle (Kumar *et al.,* 1999; Pietras and Moulton, 1974; Schmidt and Schmidt, 1980). But the range of nonsocial odorants studied in mammals is extremely limited. Moreover, even when studying social odors, such as urine, the early studies used only a motivated behavior, such as time spent investigating a smell, to measure sex differences or effects of hormonal manipulations. Use of such limited behavioral repertoire cannot determine whether hormones are affecting the sensory acuity for a specific odorant (Doty, 1989) or its meaning without itself affecting acuity (Pfaff and Pfaffman, 1969).

This distinction has been made in research on humans. In contrast to the few laboratory rodents studied, women of all ages in many different cultures have greater olfactory sensitivity than do men, e.g., detecting and naming over 10,000 odors (Brand and Millot, 2001; Cain, 1982; Deems and Doty, 1987; Doty, 1989; Doty *et al.,* 1984a,b, 1985; Evans *et al.,* 1995; Gilbert *et al.,* 1989; Koelega, 1994; Koelega and Köster, 1974; Jones *et al.,* 1995; Shipley and Ennis, 1996; Velle, 1987; Wysocki and Gilbert, 1989). Women are also better able to perceive differences in odor quality than are men, although they do not differ on their verbal descriptors of the odors (Gilbert *et al.,* 1989). These sex differences are found midlife, after menopause and the concomitant decline in ovarian hormones, as well as in old age, when testosterone drops in men. Therefore, this sex difference in acuity for a variety of nonsocial odors may well result from organizational effects of hormones during brain development. In contrast, women's ability to become dramatically more sensitive to odors (6 log units) is seen only during their reproductive years (Dalton *et al.,* 2002). Girls and postmenopausal women, like men, do

not have this ability, suggesting an activational role for hormones.

Parallel sex differences are seen in brain function associated with olfactory processing. Women have larger evoked potentials in response to amyl acetate (banana oil), particularly the N1 to P2 peak amplitude (the major signal component), even when there was no detectable difference in odor identification or threshold (Evans *et al.,* 1995). Women have eight times more activation of their frontal and temporal lobes in response to eugenol (clove), phenylethyl alcohol, and hydrogen sulfide (rotten eggs) than do men (Yousem *et al.,* 1999). The authors argue that this sex difference was specific to olfaction, because comparable sex differences were not seen with photic stimulation of the occipital cortex (Levin *et al.,* 1998; Ross *et al.,* 1997). Women are more sensitive to the steroid androstenone, a social odor produced by men (Bradley, 1984; see reviews in Section IV.B). Women, in contrast to men, report that body odor is the single most important variable in choice of a sexual partner and the sense most likely to reduce sexual desire (Herz and Cahill, 1997).

These findings dramatically raise the issue of the role of the meaning and emotional reactions in detection of odors. Olfaction does not occur in disembodied isolation but functions in a rich social and environmental context. It becomes interwoven with other sensory inputs and mental states to create experiences that are far richer and more complex than an artificially isolated system (Johnston, 2000; McClintock, 2000, 2001, 1981a; Wilson and Leon, 1988; Wood, 1997).

Neural evidence for this context dependence is dramatic in rats. Over 90% of the mitral cells in the olfactory bulb—cells that are but one synapse away from the sensory epithelial cells—are in fact driven by the meaning of the odorant (i.e., signaling a sweet drink or not) rather than by its chemical identity (i.e., vanilla vs almond; Kay and Laurent, 1999). This provides powerful evidence for constant downward regulation of sensory information by higher subcortical and cortical processes (Freeman and Kozma, 2000; Kay and Freeman, 1998; Kay *et al.,* 1996; Kay and Laurent, 1999). Perhaps, then, psychophysical tests of olfactory acuity should not be considered evidence for sex differences just in the primary steps of odor processing, independent of meaning encoded in other parts of the brain.

In an olfactory memory task, only women respond differentially to experimental instructions to make either an analytic or emotional responses to odor (Herz and Cupchick, 1992). However, when men and women were told that there was an odor in the room that might affect performance on a simple clerical task, men performed significantly worse, whereas women performed better (Gilbert *et al.*, 1997). These phenomena were interpreted as "women are more susceptible to suggestion." An alternative interpretation would be that women use social information about odor meaning in a positive way, to improve their performance, in contrast to men, who experience a performance deficit when told that odors might be affecting them. In either case, both findings are evidence for a sex difference in the dynamic interactions between the detection of odors and their meaning in a social context.

2. Ovarian Cycle Hormones

a) Animal   The extant data point to an increase in olfactory sensitivity to neutral odors around the time of ovulation in wild and laboratory rodents (Barraclough and Cross, 1963; Kumar and Archunan, 1999; Kumar *et al.*, 1999; Phillips and Vallowe, 1975; Pietras and Moulton, 1974; Rittner and Schmidt, 1982). This effect is likely mediated by estradiol (see Fig. 5; Pietras and Moulton, 1974). Testosterone has similar effects on females (Phillips and Vallowe, 1975), but the studies were conducted before techniques were available to determine whether estradiol or androgen receptors in the brain mediated the effects of testosterone. In con-

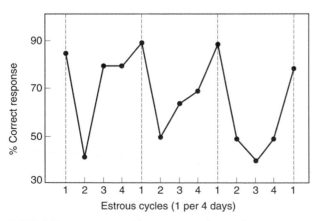

FIGURE 5   Variation in olfactory acuity during the ovarian cycle of the laboratory rat (*Rattus norvegicus;* Pietras and Moulton, 1974). The odorant was cyclopentanone at a concentration of 10^{-3} of vapor saturation. Males have olfactory sensitivity enabling performance of 75% correct. From Pietras and Moulton (1974), *Physiol. Behav.* **12**, © Elsevier Science.

trast, progesterone and pseudopregnancy decrease olfactory sensitivity of female rats, suppressing it below that of ovariectomized females (Phillips and Vallowe, 1975; Pietras and Moulton, 1974). Some of the neuroendocrine mechanisms for effects of ovarian steroids on the olfactory system have been elucidated, especially recent discoveries of gene identification for steroid receptors expressed in the olfactory system (Gu *et al.*, 1999; O'Connor *et al.*, 1988; Shughrue *et al.*, 1997a,b; Stumpf and Sar, 1982; see Section V).

Becerra and colleagues (1996) provide an elegant example of the dynamic interaction among hormones, odors, pheromones, and circadian rhythms. Estrogen, either alone or in combination with progesterone, reduces glutamic acid decarboxylase, the enzyme that synthesizes the neurotransmitter gamma-aminobutyric acid (GABA) in the rat olfactory bulb. These hormonal effects can be reversed by male pheromones, but only when presented during the morning phase of the enzyme's circadian rhythm, not during the afternoon.

b) Human   Le Magnen's first study of the menstrual cycle and olfactory acuity (1952) detected changes in sensitivity only to a synthetic musk, exaltolide, and not to safrol, pyridine, or guaiacol. For a time, the most frequently studied olfactants were musks, particularly androstenone, because of speculation that such musks might serve as a human pheromone as they do in animals (Amoore *et al.*, 1975; Good *et al.*, 1976; Kloek, 1961; Köster, 1975; Vierling and Rock, 1967). More recently, it has been determined that the menstrual cycle affects sensitivity to other nonsocial olfactants, such as citral (Pause *et al.*, 1996).

The perception of odor changes over the course of the human menstrual cycle (for early reviews, see Doty, 1976; Messent, 1976; Rogel, 1978). Inadequate measures of the menstrual cycle, as well as failure to use standard definitions of menstrual cycle phase, make it difficult to interpret most of this literature in terms of specific hormonal or neuroendocrine mechanisms. For example, effects reported to occur during "the ovulatory period" are in fact likely to occur just after ovulation in one study, when progesterone has already risen [i.e., the day of the rise in basal body temperature (Pause *et al.*, 1996), but just prior to the preovulatory LH surge in others (Gangestad and Thornhill, 1998)].

Because the hormone profiles are so dramatically different at these times, the field needs to conduct studies that do measure precisely the changes in ovarian cycle hormones. This can be achieved by anchoring peri-ovulatory effects to the preovulatory LH surge (Stern and McClintock, 1996) rather than to ovulation. Ovulation is at best an estimated anatomical event, with only an indirect connection to the brain, that is mediated by a change in ovarian hormones. Estrogen, for example, which is highest for several days before ovulation, increases olfactory sensitivity of hypogonadal and normal women (Good *et al.*, 1976; Schneider *et al.*, 1958), whereas testosterone, which also rises a small amount just prior to ovulation, lowers olfactory thresholds (Schneider *et al.*, 1958). Moreover, ovulation itself is not necessary for cyclic changes in sensitivity, as women taking birth control pills to create anovulatory menstrual cycles also show cyclic variation (Doty *et al.*, 1981, 1982).

Nonetheless, it is now firmly established that the menstrual cycle does alter the perception of some odorants, as it does other chemosensory systems such as the taste of sugar (Than *et al.*, 1994). It is interesting that in contrast to earlier reports, the effects on threshold sensitivity to neutral odors are relatively minor, especially when measured with sophisticated methods (Doty *et al.*, 1975, 1981, 1982; Graham *et al.*, 2000; Herberhold *et al.*, 1982; Hummel *et al.*, 1991; Mair *et al.*, 1978; Wysocki and Beauchamp, 1984). Rather, it is the richness and complexity of the perception, and the emotional valence that changes more dramatically (Gangestad and Thornhill, 1998; Grammer, 1993; Hummel *et al.*, 1991; Pause *et al.*, 1996). For example, in the preovulatory phase, the emotional profile of citral was less complex, with 50% fewer descriptors, than the postovulatory phase (Pause *et al.*, 1996), a difference paralleled by recordings of event related potentials (P3-1). Thus effects of hormones on meaning and emotional associations are not limited to androstenone, as others have surmised (Hummel *et al.*, 1991). However, the use of different odors in different studies again means that this question is far from answered, e.g., Herberhold *et al.* (1982) examined the effect's of "primary odors," now an outmoded concept (Amoore, 1977).

Hormones may also have a gating or permissive effect of odors on psychological state, such as mood. It is primarily during the "ovulatory phase" that women are more likely to report feeling more submissive and less aggressive in response to androstenone (Benton, 1982). Around the time of ovulation, women prefer the scent of men with symmetrical bodies (Gangestad and Thornhill, 1998) and sexually are more readily aroused in the presence of masculine ("fresh fougere") or feminine odors ("aladehydic floral") (Graham *et al.*, 2000). Androstenone, the component of male sweat that smells urinous, like boar-taint, is rated as unattractive by women, except when they are in the ovulatory phase of their cycle, when it becomes emotionally neutral (Grammer, 1993).

Most psychological measures to date have obviously been constrained by the assumption of a pheromone-like scenario, in which the odorant triggers specific social thoughts and emotions linked to heterosexual and sexual interactions. Nonetheless, they do establish the principle that ovarian hormones can regulate emotional responses to odors. It remains to be determined whether these effects are limited to biosocial odors, or whether they extend to neutral odors as well. That they do is indicated by Schiffman's finding that estrogen replacement therapy enhances the anger-reducing effects of pleasant floral and fruity odors, whereas estrogen plus progesterone does not (Schiffman *et al.*, 1995c).

Several mechanisms have been proposed for menstrual cycle effects on olfaction, including structural changes in the olfactory epithelium (Arimondi *et al.*, 1993), which has more meitotic activity in the preovulatory phase, with irregular basal cells and protruding supporting cells—morphological changes that disappear after ovulation. Other potential anatomical mechanisms are changes in the viscosity of the olfactory mucus, which would affect the transport of odorant molecules (Mair *et al.*, 1978), leading to greater cyclic variation in acuity for volatile than nonvolatile compounds. Patency of the nasal passages are hormonally modulated (Schneider and Wolf, 1960). Increases in sensitivy around menses (Doty *et al.*, 1981, 1982) could be mediated by the changes in cholinergic activity, phagocytosis, and vascularity in the nasal mucosa of some menstruating women (Toppozada *et al.*, 1981). Centrally, there are changes in LHRH and estrogen within the olfactory system (Breipohl, 1982; Stumpf and Sar, 1982) as well as nonspecific changes in attention (Asso, 1986; Parlee, 1983; Patkai *et al.*, 1974; Wright and Badia, 1999).

These insights from humans permit a richer interpretation of the animal literature. Hormones are unlikely to simply change sensitivity at the periphery, as they can do for behavioral reflexes (Adler *et al.,* 1977; Bradshaw and Berkley, 2000). But rather, they change motivational and emotional systems in the brain, which then down-regulate neural activity in the periphery of the olfactory system. Although not hormonal, this principle has been demonstrated by Kay (Kay and Laurent, 1999), who showed that 90% of mitral cell neurons, only one synapse from the receptors, are driven by the meaning of an odor rather than its chemical identity.

3. Testicular Hormones

a) Animal In rats, gonadectomy of males does not affect olfactory sensitivity to neutral nonsocial odors (Carr and Caul, 1962; Carr *et al.,* 1965; Le Magnen, 1952; Phillips and Vallowe, 1975; Pietras and Moulton, 1974). What testicular function does affect is the rat's behavioral sensitivity to biologically meaningful odors, such as the urine of estrous females (Carr and Caul, 1962). Differential response to the odor of estrous females is also not mediated by absolute olfactory detection thresholds (Carr *et al.,* 1962). Rather, it is mediated by central action of hormones on motivational and emotional processes, such as the preoptic nucleus (Pfaff and Pfaffman, 1969).

This early work has been confirmed and extended to demonstrate that testosterone augments neural c-fos expression within the projection pathways of the vomeronasal organ: the accessory olfactory bulb, posterior-dorsal medial amygdala, intermediate portion of the posterior bed nucleus of the stria terminalis (BNST), and then to the lateral subdivision of the medial preoptic area (Paredes *et al.,* 1998). This pathway is sexually dimorphic, with androgen and estrogen receptors along the way (reviewed by Segovia and Guillamon, 1993). There are also direct projections from the vomeronasal organ to the mPOA and hypothalamus (Larriva-Sahd *et al.,* 1993). There may also be a role for neurosteroids in rats. In male mice, the neurosteroid pregnenolone sulfate modulates *N*-methly-D-aspartate (NMDA) receptors to reduce the male's interest or preference for estrous urine (Kavaliers and Kinsella, 1995).

Similar systems have been elegantly described in hamsters (Fiber and Swann, 1996; Gomez and Newman, 1992; Swann, 1997; for reviews, see Scalia and Winans, 1975; Wood, 1997). The primary difference between these species is that both the main and accessory olfactory systems are involved in male responses to vaginal secretions, whereas only the accessory olfactory system mediates the male rat's responses to urine and feces of periovulatory females. Thus, what appears to be testicular modulation of the male rat's detection of the smell, i.e. responses to an odor, is in fact primarily mediated by a releaser pheromone acting exclusively via the accessory olfactory system (see Section V.).

In contrast, testosterone in the hamster does modulate the male's sense of smell of vaginal secretions, a biologically meaningful odorant processed by the main olfactory pathway. This is in addition to affecting his behavioral responses to a releaser pheromone. It will be interesting to determine how these pheromonal experiences, which are modulated by testosterone, change the odor perception of the urine, a psychological process that is not directly affected by testosterone in the rat but may be in the hamster.

As data accumulate in other species (e.g., meadow voles; Ferkin and Gorman, 1992), it will be possible to understand how ecological and social variables selected and shaped hormonal regulation of olfactory systems. Ferrets are carnivores and show both similarities and differences to rodents in the role of the main olfactory system in response to social odors. Both male and female ferrets increase their sniffing when they are placed on bedding, even when they are gonadectomized, indicating that they smell an odorant (Kelliher *et al.,* 1998). Therefore, a change in sniffing behavior cannot explain the increase in neural activity (c-fos expression) of the main olfactory bulb produced by testosterone. Because the main olfactory bulb projects to the hypothalamus in this species, testosterone appears to modulate detection and modulation of social odors that may be pheromones (see Section II.B.2.a).

Other behavioral domains need to be elucidated, such as the role of hormones in social recognition. Individual recognition of juveniles is complex and dependent on learning, memory, and multiple odor cues from the animal and its environment. This ability, therefore, is likely to be modulated by a variety of endocrine factors. For example, male rats spend more time investigating juvenile pups than do females, although they are less interested in them and do not recognize them when presented again two hours later. Castration of the males abolishes this sex difference, so that the males become more interested, spend less time sniffing, and can remember the identity of the pup for over three hours (Bluthé *et al.*, 1990; Gheusi *et al.*, 1994). Vasopressin and cholecystokininergic neurons are also involved (Bluthé *et al.*, 1993).

b) Human   In men, by using a signal detection paradigm to control for motivational effects, Doty (Doty and Ferguson-Segall, 1989) concluded that there were no effects of castration in men on threshold sensitivity to ethyl acetate, although there was an effect on task performance. Whether this generalizes to other odorants remains to be determined for a wide array of social and nonsocial odors (Breipohl, 1982; Doty, 1986a,b). For example, many boys become anosmic to the steroid androstenone during puberty, an odorant that is certainly a social odor (see Section IV.B). Quantitative threshold values were determined in addition to eliciting both descriptive and emotional responses (Dorries *et al.*, 1989). The threshold for the detection of androstenone rose significantly between ages of 14 and 20, the number of anosmic boys increased from 10 to 40%, and the percentage of boys labeling the odor as bad dropped from 65% to 30%. No such changes were found for the nonsocial odors of pyridine (a "masculine" odor found in wood oil, coffee, and tobacco) or phenylethlmethylethylcarbinol (a "feminine" floral odor).

Thus, by adulthood, many men have developed a specific anosmia to androstenone (Griffith and Patterson, 1970; Koelega and Köster, 1974). Interestingly, this adult anosmia is both genetic (Wysocki and Beauchamp, 1984) and reversible with repeated exposure (Wysocki and Beauchamp, 1984). Taken together, these data suggest two possible phenotypes for the genetic predisposition: (1) loss of sensitivity during the pubertal rise of androgens or (2) an inability to acquire and maintain sensitivity with experience.

4. Pregnancy and Lactation
a) Animal   The olfactory sensitivity of mice to nonsocial odors is reported to increase just prior to parturition (Schmidt *et al.*, 1982). However, neither the psychological nor the neuroendocrine mechanisms of this phenomenon have been identified. In rats, progesterone and the state of pseudopregnancy dramati-

cally decreases detection of a nonsocial odor, cyclopentanone, thus suggesting that the increase in sensitivity prior to parturition may result from the drop in progesterone at the same time. In other words, olfactory sensitivity may actually be returning to normal, rather than increasing.

With parturition and lactation, many mammals do have increased olfactory sensitivity to the social odors of their own offspring, thus enabling them to distinguish their offspring from the other neonates in their environment. Bats living in caves provide a dramatic example. Maternal colonies of Mexican free-tailed bats can have several million adult females living in one cave, with tens of thousands of newborn pups kept together in a large crèche. The mothers roost separately, and come twice a day to find and nurse their pups (Davis *et al.*, 1962). Using odor cues, they are able to discriminate pups they have nursed from those they have not. They use odorants secreted from glands around their own muzzles, with which they have marked their pups during a previous nursing, as well as the pup's own odor (Bradbury, 1977; Gustin and McCracken, 1987; Loughry and McCracken, 1991). This exquisitely discriminate nursing is the norm in most, albeit not all, species of bats (de Fanis and Jones, 1995, 1996).

Mice depend mainly on olfaction for behaving maternally toward their pups (Smotherman *et al.*, 1974; reviews by Numan, 1988; Rosenblatt, 1985, 1990). The physiological context of parturition plays an essential role in the female mouse's ability to learn the odor of her pups, although ovarian steroids are not the key mechanism. Rather, oxytocin is a more likely candidate, triggered by vaginal cervical stimulation and facilitating dopaminergic systems in the olfactory bulbs (Calamandrei and Keverne, 1992; Ferguson *et al.*, 2000).

The specific neuroendocrine mechanisms for the effects of oxytocin on olfactory bulb function have been elegantly worked out in detail by Keverne and colleagues by studying sheep and goats (Brennan and Keverne, 1997; Kendrick *et al.*, 1997). When ewes smell the airborne odors of their lambs within a few hours of birth, they form a fleeting memory, which then becomes consolidated, enabling them to selectively recognize the odor of their offspring for life. Oxytocin may contribute to selective olfactory recognition by modulating noradrenergic release within the main olfactory bulb and not the vomeronasal system (Lévy *et al.*,

1995a). Estrogen and progesterone during pregnancy do not play a direct role in the olfactory learning, although these ovarian steroids may serve an essential primer function by regulating the production of oxytocin and its receptors (Kendrick *et al.*, 1997).

In contrast, the hormones of pregnancy do modulate the female rat's response to her pups' odors, in addition to other sensory cues (Fleming *et al.*, 1992; Fleming and Sarker, 1990; also see reviews by Bridges, 1990; Fleming, 1986). Virgin females become responsive to pup odors more quickly if they are primed with the hormones of pregnancy. Moreover, maternal responsiveness to pups is enhanced and retained longer if the dams interact with pups during the pregnancy. It is not yet determined, however, whether these hormones: (1) increase the salience or emotional meaning of the pups' odors, (2) facilitate learning their association with other somatosensory aspects of the pups, or (3) function as a state-dependent signal for positive interactions with the smell of pups (Fleming *et al.*, 1989; Fleming and Korsmit, 1996).

In any event, both the main olfactory system and the vomeronasal organ are necessary for maternal olfactory recognition in the rat, in contrast to the sheep (Brouette-Lahlou *et al.*, 1992; Fleming *et al.*, 1992). An interesting finding is that projections to the cingulate, medial amygdala, and prefrontal cortex mediate habituation to the normally aversive pup stimuli. But retention of memories of those stimuli is mediated only by the prefrontal cortex (Fleming and Korsmit, 1996).

Oxytocin also plays a role, and the olfactory bulb is a critical site of action, particularly the mitral and granule cells (Yu *et al.*, 1996a,b). There it depresses inhibitory effects of GABA transmission (Osako *et al.*, 2000). Male rats, which typically find pups aversive and will kill them, do not express mRNA for the oxytocin receptor in the plexiform layer of the olfactory bulb, although they do elsewhere in the brain (Vaccari *et al.*, 1998).

b) Human   Early in pregnancy, many women report an aversion to specific strong odors, an effect whose function has been attributed to avoiding teratagens during organogensis in the fetus. In addition, sensitivity to musk increases late in pregnancy (Good *et al.*, 1976). However, when overall odor sensitivity is measured with both odor-detection threshold-paradigms and intensity ratings, pregnant women are not significantly different from other women (Gilbert and

Wysocki, 1991; Laska *et al.*, 1996). Nonetheless, they do experience significant changes for specific odors. They are more sensitive to eugenol (clove), perceive amyl acetate (bananas) and mercaptans (skunk, cabbage) as more intense, but are less sensitive to androstenone (urine; Doty, 1986a; Gilbert and Wysocki, 1991). Thus, if pregnancy hormones modulate nonsocial odors, they are likely to affect the meaning or emotional reactions to the odors, not olfactory acuity. There is also little known about the sensitivity of lactating women to olfactants, another time in when the mother's food intake has a profound effect on the development of her child (Mennella and Beauchamp, 1991; Mennella *et al.*, 1995, 2002).

Only six hours after giving birth, mothers can readily distinguish the odor of their own infant from that of other infants (Russell *et al.*, 1983; reviews by Corter and Fleming, 1995). Moreover, mothers find more pleasant the body odors of their newborns, including urine and feces, than do other women or men. In striking parallel with animal behavior, mothers who later report that their infant's odors are pleasant are those who had body contact with their infants within a few minutes of delivery and nursed them within a few hours (Fleming *et al.*, 1993). This contrasts sharply with mothers who had delayed contact with their infants and subsequently found their infant's odors unpleasant.

The dynamics of progesterone and estradiol during late pregnancy and the postpartum levels of cortisol may play a role in a mother's ability to develop or maintain olfactory discrimination of her infant and positive emotional responses to their odors (Fleming *et al.*, 1997a,b). Women with high cortisol levels postpartum are more attracted to their own infant's odor and better able to recognize it. These hormones, however, are likely to play only a facilitatory role, as they do in animals. Women without children and the hormonal priming of pregnancy can learn to identify infants by their odor if they are given the chance to hold the infants for just one hour (Kaitz and Eidelman, 1992).

5. Adrenal Function

The olfactory regulation by hormones from the hypothalamic-pituitary-adrenal axis has been understudied. Fortunately, there is a growing collection of tantilizing research. The most coherent is on olfactory regulation of catecholamines (adrenaline and noradrenaline; reviewed by Haller *et al.*, 1998).

Adrenalectomized rats become more sensitive to pyridine, an effect that is reversed by corticosterone. However, corticosterone administered to intact animals has no effect (Sakellaris, 1972). Recently, CRF has been localized within the neurons projecting from the olfactory bulb of the rat (Imaki et al., 1989) and two monkey species, *Saimiri sciureus* and *Macaca fascicularis* (Basset et al., 1992). It is interesting that neuronal activity indicated by early gene expression (c-fos) corresponds more closely with a CRF binding protein, which is a ligand inhibitor, rather than the receptor (Chan et al., 2000). Whether these systems are modulated at all by the animal's adrenal state is unknown, nor have any behavioral correlates been identified.

In humans, evidence for adrenal effects on olfactory function comes from the positive correlation between cortisol levels and olfactory sensitivity for the right nostril of women. The right nostril's ipselateral connections may play a larger role in odor processing than do those of the left nostril (Gilbert et al., 1989; Pause et al., 1996; Zatorre et al., 1992). Likewise, mothers with high cortisol are better able to discriminate odors of their infants and to rate them positively (Fleming et al., 1993, 1997a,b; Steiner et al., 1986).

Human adrenal syndromes, however, suggest the opposite relationship between cortisol and olfactory sensitivity. Patients with Cushing syndrome and excessive cortisol production have low olfactory sensitivity, whereas those with Addison's disease and low levels of cortisol have high olfactory sensitivity (reviewed by Henkin, 1975; Henkin and Bartter, 1966; Mackay-Sim, 1991). Such associations, however, are not necessarily neural and could result mechanically from changes in swelling of nasal tissue and epithelium produced by the antiinflammatory effects of corticosteroids (Mott, 1991).

6. Broad Range of Endocrine Effects

There are a variety of endocrine syndromes associated with disrupted olfactory function or anosmia, suggesting that a broad range of hormones may affect olfactory function (see reviews by Breipohl, 1982; Deems et al., 1991; Getchell, 1991; Mackay-Sim, 1991; Schiffman and Gatlin, 1993). For example, patients with hypothyroidism have odor recognition thresholds that are 10 times that of normal subjects, a deficit that can be reversed with thyroid treatment. Little is known about the possible mediating neuroendocrine mecha-

nisms, although the high regeneration rate of olfactory glomeruli make it an ideal system for study.

Diabetics also experience high olfactory thresholds, a deficit that has been assumed to reflect peripheral neuropathy from vascular disease (Settle, 1991; Weinstock et al., 1993). Recently, however, insulin receptors have been discovered in high density in the rat olfactory bulb, implicating insulin and its receptors in olfactory processing (see review by Schulingkamp et al., 2000). Corresponding behavioral research in the rat has yet to be done.

Some hormones regulate olfactory function in multiple contexts. Oxytocin's effects on maternal recognition of their offspring's odors is well documented (Lévy et al., 1995a), and mice lacking the oxytocin gene have social amnesia (Ferguson et al., 2000). In addition, oxytocin affects olfaction in the context of thirst. Electrical stimulation of the parvoventricular nucleus and intracerebroventricular infusion of oxytocin inhibits mitral cells in the olfactory bulbs as well as granule cells (Chou et al., 1995; Hatton and Yang, 1990; Yu et al., 1996a,b).

There are some endocrine syndromes that are associated with olfactory deficits but do not indicate direct hormonal action on the olfactory epithelium or central olfactory system. Rather, they have an indirect anatomical association mediated by developmental anomalies. For example, Kallmann syndrome is associated with anosmia, hypogonadism, and disrupted GnRH function. It was thought that low gonadal steroids might produce anosmia, as is the case in animal species. We now know that these two correlated traits do not cause one another, but share a common cause during fetal development (Dellovade et al., 1998; Parhar et al., 1995). Kallman syndrome is associated with a genetic deficit for the structural proteins that enable olfactory neurons containing GnRH to penetrate the olfactory placode during fetal development (Schwanzel-Fukuda and Pfaff, 1991). Without these proteins, neither the olfactory system nor the hypothalamic structures develops normal function.

Likewise, pseudo-hypoparathyroidism is associated with olfactory deficits and deficiency of the Gs alpha protein of adenylyl cyclase. It was therefore hypothesized that G-coupled protein played an important role in olfactory transduction. However, the discovery of olfactory deficits in patients with intact Gs alpha protein activity, but similar developmental deficits, indicates that the olfactory impairment results from a constellation of skeletal deficits (Doty *et al.*, 1997), potentially caused by deficiency in G-coupled protein and not a direct effect of parathyroid hormone on olfactory function.

B. Sources of Social Odors and Chemosignals

Many social odors and chemosignals are under endocrine control, originating from various parts of the body. Some body odors originate from body fluids such as urine, feces, and saliva, which serve various other physiological functions. Others originate from specialized exocrine glands, evolved solely for social communication. Table 1 provides exemplars of this diversity, with references to excellent reviews of the broad animal literature.

Less well known to behavioral endocrinologists are the human data, which derive from the chemosensory, clinical, and industrial literature. Not only do humans have endocrine-based body odors that serve social functions, but there is growing evidence that environmental odors can regulate neuroendocrine function and acquire social meaning. Examples of such human social odors are also provided in Table 1, along with citations of the classic papers and comprehensive literature reviews.

Typically, the animal and human literatures to do not cross-reference each other. In this chapter, the animal and human literatures have been juxtaposed in the service of two goals. First, to encourage further work on human social odors that will have the same multilevel and neuroendocrine analyses that have been applied to many animal species. Second, to encourage further animal work that includes a psychological as well as behavioral perspective, elegant psychophysics, and sensitivity to the importance of social context evidenced in the human research.

IV. VASANAS AND LEVELS OF AWARENESS

A. An Appropriate Term Needed for "Unconscious Odors"

Human studies have enabled us to tackle the question of conscious and unconscious processing of odors and social chemosignals. In the case of animals, this distinction must be inferred from species-typic orienting or attentional behaviors, sniffing, digging for a hidden odor source, or through use of conditioned or unconditioned stimuli in an operant paradigm (Bluthé *et al.*, 1990; Gheusi *et al.*, 1994; Kay and Freeman, 1998; Kelliher *et al.*, 1998; Wallace and Rosen, 2000). Ethologists in the European tradition have skillfully inferred from such data species differences in types of conscious experience (e.g., Griffin, 2001; von Uexküll, 1937), but it will always be an inference. In humans, however, direct verbal reports and the techniques of psychophysics and cognitive psychology have enabled direct measurement of distinct levels of awareness.

A strong odor, such as that of androstenone or clove, is a percept that drives attention and whose existence can be verbally reported. Although many people find the quality of odors more difficult to articulate than those of visual features, there are many successful studies using multidimensional scaling to quantify descriptors (e.g., Doty, 1997; Doty *et al.*, 1994; Russell *et al.*, 1993). Eugenol, the major component of clove oil, is described with high consensus as "spicy" by almost 90% of American respondents. This is true both among individuals of the same age, and throughout the life span (Russell *et al.*, 1993). Androstenone, in contrast, is described with very little consensus among individuals, most often as "floral," "musky," "spicy," "woody," "urinous," or "other." Moreover, its odor description changes with age. More than 40% of people have a specific anosmia and cannot detect its odor at all.

Weak odors, in contrast, are percepts detectable only when a person's attention is focused on trying to detect the presence of an odor or to identify it. For example, people can be in a room that has a weak orange odor. They do not report smelling orange until they are asked to return to the room and determine whether or not an orange smell is present, whereupon they are accurate. There are a variety of psychophysical methods that can be used to quantify odor strength or intensity, such as signal detection theory. For example, people trying to detect weak odors have a small (d'). Weak odors are those with concentrations within one standard deviation of the background noise (Lawless *et al.*, 1995; Meilgaard *et al.*, 1991).

Subliminal or implicit odors are those not consciously accessible to verbal description. Nonetheless, given a forced choice paradigm, people's verbal

TABLE 1
Sources of Social Odors in Animals and Humans

Information carried	Body source	Gender and age of producer	Species	Biological system modifying odor production	Compound identity	References
Alarm, fear, stress	Exocrine gland	Males	Rat, *Rattus norvegicus*	Pituitary	Melanocortin peptides	Abel (1994); Abel and Bilitzke (1990); Chen et al. (1997)
Alarm, fear, stress	Urine	Adults	Mice, *Mus musculus*	Adrenal		Carr et al. (1970); Rottman and Snowdon (1972); Thiessen and Coke (1990); Zalaquett and Thiessen (1991)
Alarm, fear, stress	Urine and body odors	Adult males	Rat	Adrenal		Mackay-Sim and Laing (1980, 1981a,b); Stevens and Koster (1972); Valenta and Rigby (1968)
Alarm, fear, stress	Scent marks, sebaceous glands	Adult males and females	Nonhuman primate review	Adrenal		Epple (1976, 1980)
Alarm, fear, stress	Urine	Young and adult females	Domestic pig, *Sus scrofa*	Adrenal		Vieuille-Thomas and Signoret (1992)
Attractiveness	Chest and axillae	Men	Humans	Not yet identified		Gangestad and Thornhill (1998); Herz and Cahill (1997); Thornhill and Gangestad (1999)
Death	Whole body	Adult males	Rat	Tissue decomposition	Cadaverine and putrescine	Pinel et al. (1981)
Emotional state, gender, age	Axillae	Young and old adults	Humans	Not yet identified		Chen and Haviland-Jones (1999); Chen et al. (1997)
Gender	Glandular scent marks	Adults	Nonhuman primate review	Gonads		Epple (1976, 1980)
Gender, identity	Chest	Children and adults	Humans	Not yet identified		Spielman et al. (1995)
Gender, identity	Genital, vaginal	Children and adults	Humans	Reproductive		Huggins and Preti (1976, 1981); Spielman et al. (1995)
Gender, identity	Mouth, breath, saliva	Children and adults	Humans	Not yet identified		Preti et al. (1995); Tonzetich (1971); Torzetich et al. (1978)
Gender, identity	Sloughed epithelial cells	Children and adults	Humans	Steroids		Berliner et al. (1991); Roberts and Marks (1980)

Gender, stress, activity	Male apocrine gland	Adult males	Humans	Gonads	Aqueous soluble precursor to E- and Z-3-Methyl-2-hexanoic acid	Zeng et al. (1992)
Identity	Amniotic fluid	Fetus	Humans, rats	Pregnancy		Hepper (1987); Marlier et al. (1998); Schaal and Marlier (1998); Schaal et al. (1998); Varendi et al. (1998)
Identity	Feet	Children and adults	Humans	Not yet identified		Kanda et al. (1990)
Identity	Glandular scent marks	Adults	Nonhuman primate review	Not yet identified		Epple (1976, 1980)
Identity	Scalp, hair	Children and adults	Humans	Not yet identified		Labows et al. (1979)
Identity	Skin, urine, torso	Young and adults	Review of humans, mice, rats	Immune, MHC		Bartoshuk and Beachamp (1994); Wedekind and Penn (2000); Jacob et al. (2002)
Identity of mother	Breast	Adult women	Humans	Lactation		MacFarlane (1975); Makin and Porter (1989); Marlier et al. (1997, 1998); Schaal (1986)
Identity of newborn	Torso	Neonates	Humans	Not yet identified		Russell et al. (1983)
Illness	Feet	Children and adults	Humans	Not yet identified		Kanda et al. (1990)
Illness	Scent marks, urine	Adults	House mouse, Mus musculus	Parasite load		Kavaliers et al. (1998); Penn and Potts (1998); Rich and Hurst (1998)
Illness	Urine	Children and adults	Humans	Inborn errors of metabolism, infectious and degenrative diseases		Preti et al. (1997); Rizzo and Roth (1994); Sastry et al. (1980); Wysocki and Preti (2000)

(continued)

TABLE 1
(continued)

Information carried	Body source	Gender and age of producer	Species	Biological system modifying odor production	Compound identity	References
Illness, schizophrenia	Urine, sweat	Adults	Humans	Central nervous system		Weiner (1967)
Nutritional status	Feces	Children and adults	Humans	Diet		Moore et al. (1984)
Nutritional status	Various	Young and adults	Rats, mice, domestic animals	Diet		Broom (1999); Schellinck et al. (1992)
Reproductive and adrenal status	Axillae and microflora	Adult males and females	Humans	Gonads	C6 to C11 normal branced and unsaturated aliphatic acids	Leyden et al. (1991); Preti et al. (1997); Rikowski and Grammer (1999); Russell (1976); Spielman et al. (1995, 1998); Zeng et al. (1991, 1992)
Reproductive and adrenal status	Sebaceous glands	Young and adults	Humans	Gonads and adrenal		Greene et al. (1970); Montagna and Parakkal (1974); Strauss et al. (1983)
Reproductive and social status	Circumgenital scent marks	Adult females	Tamarin Sanguinus fusicicollis and cotton top, guinea pig	Ovarian cycle		Smith and Abbott (1998)
Reproductive and social status	Periorbital and lip glands	Adult males	Warthog Phacochoerus aethiopicus and domestic pig	Testes, adrenal		Drickamer and Martan (1992); Estes et al. (1982)
Reproductive status	Glandular scent marks	Adult females	Nonhuman primate	Ovarian cycle		Epple (1976, 1980)
Reproductive status	Milk	Adult females	Holstein cow, horse	Ovarian cycle	36 of 80 volatile compounds; di-n-propyl phthalate; 1-iodoundecane	Kumar et al. (2000); Ma and Klemm (1997a)
Reproductive status	Preputial gland	Adult males	Rat, Rattus norvegicus	Testes		Merkx et al. (1988)
Reproductive status	Sebaceous glands, urine	Young and adults	Mammalian	Gonadal and adrenal		Shorey (1976); Stoddart (1976)

Function	Source	Sex/age	Species	Origin	Chemical	References
Reproductive status	Sweat	Adult women	Humans	Ovarian cycle	Androstenol	Preti et al. (1987); Wysocki and Preti (2000)
Reproductive status	Urine	Adult females	Horse	Ovarian cycle	Various identified	Ma and Klemm (1997b)
Reproductive status	Urine	Adult females	Dog, rat	Ovarian cycle		Beach and Gilmore (1949); Chateau et al. (1972); Kavaliers and Kinsella (1995); Pfaff and Pfaffman (1969); Shafik (1997)
Reproductive status	Urine	Adult males, androgenized females	Rat, house mouse, woolly opossum caluromys-philander, horse	Testes, androgenization		Carr et al. (1962); Hurst (1989); McDonnell et al. (1988); Perret and Benmbarek (1991)
Reproductive status	Urine, sweat, saliva, plasma, coryneform bacteria	Adult males	Humans, pig	Testes	Androstenol, androstenone, androstadienone, androstadienol	Gower (1981); Gower et al. (1985, 1988, 1994); Gower and Ruparelia (1992); Louveau et al. (1991); Pause et al. (1999a); Smals and Weusten (1991)
Reproductive status	Urine, temporal gland, breath	Adult males and females	Asian and African elephant Elephas maximus and African elephant Loxodonta africana	Gonadal	Cyclohexanone, ketones, frontalin, farnsols	Doty (1984); Rasmussen et al. (1996, 1997a,b); Rasmussen and Schulte (1999)
Reproductive status	Vaginal secretions	Adult females	Holstein cow	Ovarian cycle	Acetaldehyde	Ma et al. (1996)
Reproductive status	Vaginal secretions	Adult females	Nonhuman primate	Ovarian cycle	Aliphatic acids	Epple (1976, 1980)
Social status	Scent marks	Adults	Mammals	Adrenal and gonads		Kappeler (1998); Rich and Hurst (1998)
Submission	Urine	Juveniles	Pig	Adrenal		McGlone (1984)
Territory	Feces	Adults	Dorcas gazelle, ungulgate	Gonads		Essghaier and Johnson (1981); Grau (1976)
Territory	Facial glands	Adult males	Warthog	Testes		Estes et al. (1982)

responses that an odor is present are relatively accurate and nonrandom, even though they believe themselves to be guessing and do not report smelling or detecting an odor (Comette-Muniz and Cain, 1998; Dravnieks *et al.,* 1984; Kline *et al.,* 2000; Köster and Degel, 2000; Meilgaard *et al.,* 1991; Wysocki and Preti, 2000). Subliminal odors appear to be encoded by a different type of memory than are verbally described odors (Lehrner *et al.,* 1999; Degel *et al.,* 1999, 2001).

Finally, there are compounds that alter psychological states such as mood and arousal but do not require being detectable to have these effects. For example, the synthetic steroid, estratetraenyl acetate, modulates brain function without detection even as a subliminal odor (Sobel *et al.,* 1999) as do various nonsteroickel compounds (Lorig *et al.,* 1990, 1991). Likewise, low concentrations of androstadienone and estratetraenol cannot be discerned verbally when masked by clove oil or even presented alone in propylene glycol, yet they modulate people's emotional responses to being tested (Jacob and McClintock, 2000). Thus, these steriods are social chemosignals, but they are not odors. And while they are presented in the section above as putative modulator pheromones, they may ultimately fail to fulfill all the necessary functional criteria to be classified as such. For example, they may not be present at high enough concentrations during social interactions. If so, what should such unconscious social chemosignals be called?

The phrase "unconscious odor" is an oxymoron. Therefore, we have proposed "vasana" as an appropriate term for those unconscious social chemosignals that are neither odors nor pheromones (McClintock, 2001). This is an existing Sanskrit noun derived from the verb "vas," which means "to perfume." The primary definition of "vasana" is "the impression of anything left unconsciously in the mind" (Monier-Williams, 1899). The term is used to explain why a person has a tendency to react to a situation in a particular way. We find it useful to adopt this philosophical term in our classification of human social chemosignals because both its etymology and its functional definition are so close to the findings from our empirical psychological data. It is equally applicable to other "unconscious odors" which are not social, such as galoxolide (Lorig and Schwartz, 1988; Lorig *et al.,* 1990, 1991).

Vasanas are a class of social odors intermediate between odors and pheromones. They are distinguishable along two functional dimensions (see Fig. 6). The first dimension is the concentration at which the compounds have functional effects. Pheromones operate at the lowest concentrations, vasanas at intermediate levels, and odors at the highest concentrations. The second dimension is the level of consciousness necessary for

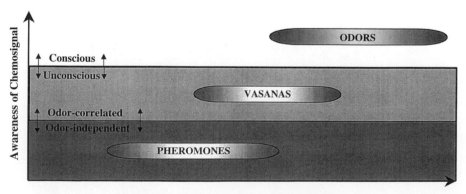

FIGURE 6   Odors, vasanas and pheromones are distinguished by the concentration and levels of consciousness needed for their functional effects (McClintock *et al.,* 2001).

their functional effects. Odors are perceptions and require conscious detection and description. Vasanas operate below the threshold of detection, although their effects are associated with odor properties when perceived at higher concentrations and consciously detected. Finally, the functions of pheromones are independent of their odor properties.

B. 16-Androstenes

The vasana concept may bring order to research on the effects of androstenone and androstenol on human psychological state and behavior. Humans are, to date, the only species other than the pig that produces significant levels of these nonandrogenic 16-androstenes. Androstadienone is virtually absent in the testis of other species studied: rat, guinea pig, cat, rabbit, hamster, dog, rhesus macaques, and crab eating macaque, although some 16-androstene production is reported in *Macaca fascicularis* and gorilla (Smals and Weusten, 1991; Weusten, 1989; Weusten *et al.,* 1990; review by Gower, 1972; Gower and Ruparelia, 1992).

In the boar testis, androstadienone is converted by 5α-reductase to androstenone, a musky odorant, which is readily stored in fat and the parotid gland. There, some of it is converted to 5α-androst-16-en-3β-ol, and after puberty, less to the 3α-ol form. These androstenols are the urinous odorants identified as "boar taint" (Patterson, 1968; Prelog and Ruzicka, 1944). A mixture of androstenone and the androstenols serve as boar mating pheromones (Melrose *et al.,* 1971; see Section II.A.2).

In humans, androstadienone is found in the testis and the ovary. However, the conversion to androstenone does not occur in the testis, as it does it the boar, but in peripheral tissue abundant with 5-α-reductase, such as the skin, axillary sweat glands, and salivary glands (see Figure 4; reviewed by Smals and Weusten, 1991). There, another enzyme, 3-ketosteroid-oxidoreductase, metabolizes it into the musky, and more pleasant, 5α-androst-16-en-3α-ol (and less to the 3β-ol). The adrenal also produces these 16-androstenes in humans, as ACTH increases their production in both men and women. Through this pathway, androstenol becomes measurable in urine of men and women as well as men's sweat (Brooksbank *et al.,* 1974; Brooksbank and Haslewood, 1961).

These steroids have been categorized inappropriately as human sex attractant pheromones both in the scientific literature and by a plethora of fragrance manufactures for marketing purposes. Indeed, calling them "sex attractants" is a conceptual stretch given that their behavioral effect on a gilt is not to attract her to the boar, but to render her catatonic so that he can mount. Moreover, few studies have actually measured sexual behavior (Cutler *et al.,* 1998; but see Wysocki and Preti, 1998). Instead, research has tested their effects on use of bathroom stalls and seat choice in dentist offices and theaters (reviewed by Gower and Ruparelia, 1992; see Table 2).

The designs of all but a few psychological experiments fail to appreciate the species differences between androstenone and 3α-androstenol excreted in urine, sweat, and saliva. Androstenone ("boar taint") is more common in boars and has a strong urinous odor (Labows and Wysocki, 1984; Prelog and Ruzicka, 1944). Seventy percent of women find it "repellent," in marked contrast to 15% of men (Gower *et al.,* 1985; Griffith and Patterson, 1970). In humans, it is 3α-androstenol that is the most predominant 16-androstene excreted in urine, axillary and back sweat, saliva, and seminal fluid (Brooksbank and Haslewood, 1961; Kwan *et al.,* 1992; Mallet *et al.,* 1988; Preti *et al.,* 1987; Watson *et al.,* 1988). It has a more pleasant musky, rather than a urinous, odor (Ohloff *et al.,* 1983), particularly for those anosmic to urinous components (Amoore *et al.,* 1975; Labows and Wysocki, 1984).

There are actually three, if not four, forms of androstenol excreted in humans (Brooksbank, 1970; Brooksbank and Gower, 1964; Gower and Ruparelia, 1992). There are both 3α and 3β forms of 5α-androstenol, as well as a $5\beta,3\alpha$ form (see Table 2 notes). The 5β-3β form has not been reported, although it is a stable steroid (Steraloids, Inc., Providence, Rhode Island, personal communication). Thus "androstenol" is an ambiguous common name, but usually refers to the 5α-3α form. For complete precision, chemists at Steraloids, Inc. named the 5α-3α form "achlaisterol," which they derived from Scottish Gaelic for armpit "achlais." To further complicate matters, androstenone quickly converts, in small amounts, to 3α-androstenol when it is exposed to air (Gower and Ruparelia, 1992). Therefore, the behavioral effects in Table 2 attributed

TABLE 2
Human Psychological Responses to the Odor of Steroids, Body Odors, and Environmental Odors

Compound	Significant psychological response	Context	Smellers	Individual differences?	Hormone modulation of response	Concentration	Detected as an odor?	Potential vasana?	Reference
STEROIDS									
Androstenone	Chose seats in waiting room and theater	Daily life	Men, women	Yes	W > M, men avoided them?	32 μgm; •	Yes	Yes	Clark (1978); Kirk-Smith and Booth (1980)
Androstenone	Detection	Daily life	Men, women	Yes	W > M	•	Yes	Yes	Gilbert and Wysocki (1987); Labows and Wysocki (1984)
Androstenone	None	Daily life	Men, women	No	No	Boar-Mate™	Yes	No	McCollough et al. (1981)
Androstenone	Sexiness of people in photographs	Laboratory	Men, women	Yes	Sex differences	•	Yes	Yes	Filsinger et al. (1984, 1985)
Androstenone	Feel less sexy	Laboratory	Men, women	Yes	Women only	•	Yes	Yes	Filsinger et al. (1984)
Androstenone	Sleep EEG, dreams	Laboratory	Men, women	•	•	•	No	Yes	Boecker and Badia (1992)
Androstenone	Detection	Laboratory	Men, women	Yes	W > M	•	Yes	Yes	Griffith and Patterson (1970); Kloek (1961)
Androstenone	Detection	Laboratory	Women	Yes	Greatest periovulatory	4000-fold variation	Yes	Yes	Cowley et al. (1977); Labows and Wysocki (1984)
Androstenone	Less unpleasant	Laboratory	Women	Yes	Periovulatory	•	Yes	Yes	Grammer (1993); Hummel et al. (1991)
Androstenone	Chemosensory event-related potentials	Laboratory	Women	Yes	Greatest periovulatory	≤1.25 mg/ml	Yes/no	Yes	Pause et al. (1999b)
Androstenone	Photos of men less sexy, attractive, intelligent, erotic, interesting	Laboratory	Women	Yes	Greatest periovulatory	Only in ethanol	Yes	Yes	Maiworm and Langthaler (1992, 1998)
Androstenol	Photos of men less sexy	Laboratory	Women	•	Menstrual cycle	•	Yes	Yes	Maiworm and Langthaler (1992, 1998)
Androsten-3α-ol	Avoid bathroom stalls	Daily life	Men, women	Yes	Men only	•	Yes	Yes	Gustavson et al. (1987)

Androsten-3α-ol	Social exchanges with men	Daily life	Women	Yes	Greatest periovulatory	1 mg/ml	Yes	Yes	Cowley et al. (1991)
Androstenol	None on social exchanges with men or women	Daily life	Men	•	•	1 mg/ml	Yes	No	Cowley et al. (1991)
Androstenol	Mood	Daily life	Women	•	Menstrual cycle	•	Yes	Yes	Benton (1982)
Androsten-3α-ol	Favorable assessments of people	Laboratory	Men, women	Yes	Only women's judgements of men	Face mask	Yes	Yes	Cowley et al. (1977)
Androsten-3α-ol	Women in photos more attractive and sexy	Laboratory	Men, women	Yes	M = W	Face mask	Yes	Yes	Kirk-Smith et al. (1978)
Androsten-3α-ol	No effect of attractivness of people	Laboratory	Men, women	•	•	Dab on neck	Yes	No	Black and Biron (1982 vs. Benton, 1982)
Androsten-3α-ol	None on sexual arousal	Laboratory	Men, women	•	•	Face mask	Yes	No	Benton and Wastell (1986)
Androsten-3α-ol	Sexiness/attractiveness of people in photographs	Laboratory	Men, women	Yes	Increased men's ratings of men, decreased women's rating of men	•	•	Yes	Filsinger et al. (1984, 1985)
Androsten-3α-ol	Submissive mood increased	Laboratory	Women	•	Greatest periovulatory	150 μgm on upper lip	No	Yes	Black and Biron (1982 vs. Benton, 1982)
Androsten-3α-ol	Irritability increased	Laboratory	Women	•	Only during menses	Face mask	Yes	Yes	Cowley et al. (1980)
Androsterone	Did not avoid bathroom stalls	Daily life	Men, women	Yes	Men only	•	•	•	Gustavson et al. (1987)
Androsterone	Photos of men warmer, friendlier, less sexy	Laboratory	Women	•	•	•	Yes	Yes	Maiworm and Langthaler (1992, 1998)

BODY ODORS

Axillae	Discriminate emotional state and age	Laboratory	Men, women	Yes	•	•	Yes	Yes	Chen and Haviland-Jones (1999)

(continued)

TABLE 2
(continued)

Compound	Significant psychological response	Context	Smellers	Individual differences?	Hormone modulation of response	Concentration	Detected as an odor?	Potential vasana?	Reference
Axillae and chest	Pleasantness	Laboratory	Men, women	Yes	Periovulatory highest	●	Yes	Yes	Wedekind and Füri (1997); Wedekind et al. (1995)
Axillae, back, and chest	Choice preference	Meeting room	Women	Yes	●	●	Yes	Yes	Jacob et al. (2002)
Axillae	Chemosensory event-related potentials	laboratory	Women	Yes	Menstrual cycle	●	Yes/no	Yes	Pause et al. (1999b)
Axillae, back, and chest	Faster CS-ERP to self than non-self odors	Laboratory	Men, women	Yes	●	●	Yes	Yes	Pause et al. (1999a)
Vaginal secretions	Unpleasantness and intensity	Laboratory	Men	Yes	●	●	Yes	Yes	Doty et al. (1975); Huggins and Preti (1981); Preti et al. (1979)
Fatty acids in vaginal secretions	No effect on social exchanges	Daily life	Men, women	●	●	.25 ml of 1% solution	Yes	Yes	Cowley et al. (1991)

ENVIRONMENTAL ODORANTS

Compound	Significant psychological response	Context	Smellers	Individual differences?	Hormone modulation of response	Concentration	Detected as an odor?	Potential vasana?	Reference
Eugenol	Negative emotional response to dentist	Daily life	Men, women	●	●	●	Yes	Yes	Robin et al. (1999)
Swine	Depression, tension, anger, vigor, fatigue confusion	Daily life	Men, women	●	●	●	Yes	Yes	Schiffman et al. (1995c)
Anise	Preference	Daily life	Newborns	●	●	●	Yes	Yes	Schaal et al. (2000)
Fragrances	Tension, depression, confusion, anger vigor, fatigue	Laboratory	Men	Race	●	●	Yes	Yes	Schiffman et al. (1995b)
Baby powder, chocolate	Positive emotion, health	Laboratory	Men, women	Yes	●	●	Yes	Yes	Knasko (1995)
Dimethylsulfide	Negative mood not arousal	Laboratory	Men, women	●	●	●	Yes	Yes	Knasko (1992)

836

Odorant	Effect	Setting	Subjects						Reference
Eugenol	Stress increase, ANS	Laboratory	Men, women	•	•		Yes	Yes	Robin et al. (1999)
Eugenol, vanillin, menthol, methylmethacrylate, propionic acid	Emotion and ANS	Laboratory	Men, women	Yes	Various		Yes	Yes	Alaoui-Ismaïli et al. (1997)
Feigned odorant	Pleasure, not dominance or arousal	Laboratory	Men, women	•	•		No	•	Knasko et al. (1990)
Nutmeg	Stress reduction, blood pressure	Laboratory	Men, women	•	•		Yes	Yes	Lorig and Schwartz (1988); Warren et al. (1987)
Pemenone, isovaleric acid	Disgust	Laboratory	Men, women	Yes	100 mM		Yes	Yes	O'Connell et al. (1989); Stevens and O'Connell (1995, 1996)
Peppermint	Sleep, ANS	Laboratory	Men, women	•	.26 mg/liter		No	Yes	Badia et al. (1990)
Peppermint, lavandin grosso	Sleep, dreams	Laboratory	Men, women	•	•		No	Yes	Boecker and Badia (1992)
Various reviewed	Emotions, mood, health	Laboratory	Men, women	•	Yes		Yes	Yes	Ehrlichman and Bastone (1992)
Various reviewed	Language processing	Laboratory	Men, women	•	•		Yes	Yes	Lorig (1999)
Artificial milk, lavendar	Stress reduction, cortisol	Laboratory	Newborns	•	•		Yes	Yes	Kawakami et al. (1997)
Aldhydic floral, fresh fougere	Sexual arousal	Laboratory	Women	Yes	Menstrual cycle		Yes	Yes	Graham et al. (2000)
Fragrances	Tension, depression, confusion	Laboratory	Women	•	Estrogen progesterone		Yes	Yes	Schiffman et al. (1995a)

Androstenone: 5α-androst-16-en-3-one (strongly urinous, boar taint).

Androstenol: Three different compounds, often not distinguished in literature reviews: 5α-androst-16-en-3α-ol; androsten-3α-ol or 3α-androstenol (musky); 5α-androst-16-en-3β-ol; androsten-3β-ol or 3β-androstenol 5β-androst-16-en-3α-ol.

Androsterone: 3α-hydroxy-5α-androstan-17-one (urinous/musky; not found in human sweat).

to androstenone could in fact have been mediated by minute amounts of 3α-androstenol. None of the studies in Table 2 compared the four forms of androstenol described above. Future psychological work is needed to correct this confusion of chemical imprecision.

Although these experiments are tantalizing, their designs are based on the premise that androstenol and androstenone would have releasing effects on behavior, much like pheromonal responses of the gilt or male insects' responses to female sex attractants. Indeed, the introductions of many articles create a sex attractant context by stating that these steroids are "testosterone metabolites" or "structurally related to testosterone," implying androgenic activity. Neither of these statements is true. This literature could profitably be revisited from the perspective of a broader social context than sex attractants and the potential for modulatory effects of steroids, similar to those demonstrated for their precursor, androstadienone.

Theoretically, in terms of determining whether these particular 16-androstenes function as odors, vasanas, or modulatory pheromones, it will be essential first to determine whether they do have behavioral effects when presented at concentrations below conscious detection. If they do not, they are simply social odors that are strong, weak, or subliminal (see Section III). If they do function without being consciously detected as odors, the next question is whether their effects are predicted by a person's psychological response to them at higher concentrations when they are consciously perceived.

If there is a predictive relationship between detectable odor and unconscious effects, then they appropriately would be termed vasanas. For example, women's olfactory sensitivity to androstenone does predict the strength of chemosensory event-related potential response to male body odor (Pause *et al.*, 1999b). However, if no predictive relationship exists then they would be appropriately termed modulator pheromones. Even more powerful evidence for being a human pheromone would be the demonstration that the 40% of humans with a specific anosmia to 16-androstenes (Labows and Wysocki, 1984) nonetheless manifest psychological or physiological responses to these compounds (see Table 2).

C. Environmental Odorants

The vasana concept is also applicable to environmental compounds that alter performance or mood without being verbally detected as an odor. For example, subliminal concentrations of orange in a testing room improves vigilance and and calculating ability (Köster and Degel, 2000). The strength of this effect is predicted by a person's ability to detect orange odor and not by how pleasant they judged the odor to be.

The term "vasana" could also be applied to unconscious odors that merge with unconscious tastes or other stimuli to produce a detectable percept (Dalton *et al.*, 2000; Gadlin and Fiss, 1967; Laska and Teubner, 1999). For example, the relationship between the threshold for detection and perceived intensity rates for odors has been demonstrated for *l*-carvone (Lawless *et al.*, 1995). If *l*-carvone had similar effects on mood or behavior, both above and below threshold, then it would be termed a "vasana" when it functions below the threshold of conscious detection and an "odor" when it functions above the threshold of detection.

Odors are so intimately linked with emotion and memory in humans (Dodd, 1988; Ehrlichman and Bastone, 1992; Lorig and Schwartz, 1988; Warren *et al.*, 1987) that such effects are plausible and testable. Table 2 presents environmental odors that are reported to affect mood and performance, and may also do so in social interactions when they are presented in low concentrations, below the level of conscious detection.

V. ROUTES OF ACTION IN HUMANS

We now know from animal research that a pheromone cannot be defined by its receptor organ (reviewed by Johnston, 1998, 2000; McClintock, 2001). Pheromones can act via the main olfactory system, the vomeronasal system, or skin absorption. In principle, therefore, there are several routes by which human pheromones could exert their effects. However, anatomical evidence for a specialized pheromone system in humans is currently ambiguous. The following draws from more detailed reviews by McClintock and colleagues (McClintock, 2001; Wysocki and Preti, 2000).

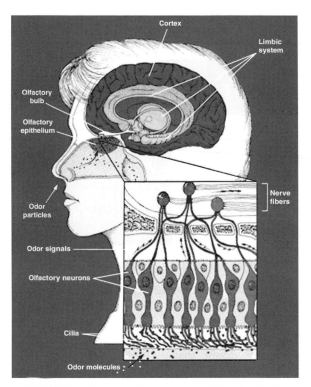

FIGURE 7 Human olfactory system (Kibiuk, 1995).

A. Main Olfactory System

Human primer and modulator pheromones may act via the main olfactory epithelium as do some other mammalian pheromones. The main olfactory system mediates the pheromonal effects of (1) male urine in rats, particularly on the lordosis reflex (Becerra *et al.,* 1996; Pfaus *et al.,* 1994), (2) mating behavior in male hamsters (Fiber and Swann, 1996), (3) sex attractants and puberty acceleration in the pig (Dorries *et al.,* 1990), (4) release of suckling in newborn rabbits (Coureaud and Schaal, 2000; Hudson and Distel, 1983, 1986; Mykytowycz, 1979), (5) the ram effect in sheep (Aujard, 1997; Lévy *et al.,* 1995b), (6) reduction of testosterone in male lesser mouse lemurs by dominant male urine (Schilling *et al.,* 1990), and (7) ovarian suppression in mice (Marchlewska-Koj *et al.,* 1998). This important theoretical point has been reviewed by Johnston (1998, 2000), Perret and Schilling (1987), and Preti and Wysocki (1999).

Indeed, the human V1RL1 gene, homologous with rodent pheromone V1r receptor genes, is expressed in human olfactory epithelium, although the full distribu-tion of receptor cells has yet to be reported (Rodriguez *et al.,* 2000). Moreover, the human olfactory system is dynamically linked with the limbic system, cortex, and cerebellum, and so provides the functional neuroanatomy necessary to mediate effects of both modulator and primer pheromones as well as vasanas (see Fig. 7; Dade *et al.,* 1998; Kay, 1979; Kline *et al.,* 2000; Oureshy *et al.,* 2000; Royet *et al.,* 2001; Savic *et al.,* 2000; Sobel *et al.,* 1998, 1999; Zald *et al.,* 1998; see Chapter 17).

B. VNO System

1. Vomeronasal Organ

The presence of a vomeronasal organ (VNO) in human adults has been quite controversial. Reports of the population-wide incidence of vomeronasal organs are inconsistent (Zbar *et al.,* 2000) and range from 39% of people examined (Johnson *et al.,* 1985) to 100% (Moran *et al.,* 1991). Some report adult structures larger than those of fetuses (Jahnke and Merker, 2000), while others report a small structure rarely detected bilaterally (Zbar *et al.,* 2000).

and Dulac, 1997; Keverne, 1999; Matsunani and Buck, 1997; and Winans, Chapter 17).

The functionality of the human structure remains debatable, as it is in catarrhine monkeys and apes (Molina *et al.*, 2000; Preti and Wysocki, 1999; Smith *et al.*, 1999). Most have concluded that the structure has a function only to guide neurogenesis of LHRH-containing neurons in the fetus (Rugarli, 1999; Schwanzel-Fukuda and Pfaff, 1991) and none in the adult (Trotier *et al.*, 2000; Wysocki and Preti, 2000).

Recent claims that the human vomeronasal organ is functional rest only on evidence from the recording of surface potential changes from VNO epithelium during exposure to steroidal compounds (Berliner *et al.*, 1996) or "vomeropherins," which are compounds left unidentified for commercial protection (Moran *et al.*, 1995). However, interpreting these results as proof of neural function has been criticized appropriately (Preti and Wysocki, 1999). Definitive evidence for neural function must include demonstration of receptor potentials and neural transmission to the brain.

Furthermore, attempts to locate genes for receptors in the human vomeronasal epithelium have yielded pseudogenes with stop codons (Herrada and Dulac, 1997; Linman *et al.*, 1999; Tirindelli *et al.*, 1998; Giorgi *et al.*, 2000). Recently, however, a human gene V1RL1 has been isolated from "nasal epithelium" (Rodriguez *et al.*, 2000), and its role in pheromone receptors in rodents and other mammals suggests a similar function in humans. It has yet to be determined whether this gene is expressed specifically in the vomeronasal epithelium or other olfactory regions.

2. Nasopalatine Duct

In addition to the vomeronasal organ, the vomeronasal system has another half, the nasopalatine duct (NPD). In many vertebrates, the nasopalatine duct passes from the mouth to the nose through the incisive canal, providing direct communication between the oral and nasal cavities. Male elephants, for example, bypass their long trunks by directly transferring urine from the female or other substances to the bilateral nasopalatine ducts at the roof of their mouths (Rasmussen and Schulte, 1999). Pheromones, bound to and then released by a series of different carrier proteins, travel a much shorter distance to the vomeronasal organ through the incisive canal, rather than up the en-

tire length of the trunk (Lazar *et al.*, 2000; Rasmussen *et al.*, 1998).

Although the nasopalatine duct plays an essential role in chemical signaling in other vertebrates, no one studying either human chemosenses or biomedical aspects of the human nasal septum had attempted to locate it in humans. Recently, we rediscovered this piece of human anatomy (Jacob *et al.*, 2000). In adults, the nasal opening of the nasopalatine duct lies at the junction of the nasal floor and septum and is both inferior and posterior to the vomeronasal organ. It turned out that this was just where it was described by French anatomists a century ago (see Fig. 8; Jacob *et al.*, 2000; Potiquet, 1891).

The close proximity of the two structures may have caused some investigators to mistakenly identify the nasal opening of the nasopalatine duct as a vomeronasal organ. Such confusion may account for contradictory reports of detection frequency and location of the vomeronasal organ (reviewed in Jacob *et al.*, 2000). For example, many articles have described the human VNO as located "at the base of the nasal septum" or "2 mm above the floor of the nasal cavity." This is the location of the NPD. The VNO is 0.5 to 1.8 cm above the nasal floor (Abolmaali *et al.*, 2001).

Complete patency between the mouth and nose in humans is rare and has been noticed only in the dental literature, which regards it as a form of oral pathology. Buccal nasopalatine duct openings in the premaxilla area are usually discovered only when they present with troublesome symptoms such as pain and swelling or discharge from the roof of the mouth (reviewed by Jacob *et al.*, 2000).

Half a century ago, reports of nasopalatine duct patency agreed that an obvious patent canal does not exist between the oral and nasal cavities in human adults, although they did not agree upon the point during development at which the duct becomes obstructed (Bellairs, 1951; Noyes, 1935; Roper-Hall, 1941). To our knowledge, however, there has been no recent, systematic investigations of nasopalatine duct patency utilizing more modern techniques to determine definitively whether stable patency exists on a microscopic or molecular level, undetectable with the large, simple probes used during maxillofacial exams and previous studies. Doing so would elucidate the potential pathways involved in mediating social and other chemosignals in humans. Moreover, it may be a binding site for putative pheromones, e.g. V1LR1 (Rodriguez *et al.*, 2000), or a well vascularized absorption site. Conversely, it may exist anatomically but not play a functional role, as is the case in hamsters (Meredith, 1991b).

C. Unexplored Chemosensory Systems

Finally, to complicate matters, vertebrates have a number of other olfactory mechanisms, variants of which might be present or functional in humans (for review, see McClintock, 2000, 2001). Examples include the nervus terminalis or terminal nerve (Fuller and Burger, 1990; Wirsig-Wiechmann, 1993; Schwanzel-Fukuda and Pfaff, 1995) and the septal organ of Masera (Vandenbergh, 1988). Very little is known about the roles these subsystems may play in mammalian, let alone human, chemosensation and social behavior.

In addition, putative pheromones could be absorbed through nasal mucosa or the skin if presented at sufficiently high concentrations. When doses of 17β-estradiol exceed 300 micrograms a day, an intranasal spray is an effective route of administration for alleviating menopausal symptoms and regulating insulin-like growth factor I (Garnerio *et al.*, 1999; Studd *et al.*, 1999). Steroids and musks can also permeate the skin (Hood *et al.*, 1996; Johnson *et al.*, 1995; Sitruk-Ware, 1988), although they typically act over days to weeks and require occlusion, carrier substances, and relatively high doses. None of these attributes characterized presentation of human primer and modulator pheromones studied to date (Jacob and McClintock, 2000; Spencer *et al.*, 2000; Stern and McClintock, 1998). Nonetheless, further study is needed to determine whether absorption is an effective route of action for any human social chemosignal.

VI. SUMMARY OF CONCEPTUAL ISSUES

Social chemosignals are not simply vestigial. Rather they are the oldest sensory system for coordinating social and reproductive behavior. Because they are evolutionarily conserved, they are a parsimonious system for integrating social interactions, emotions, and motivation in a variety of physical contexts and endocrine states. Hormones play a role in three ways.

1. They change the meaning of an odorant, often without changing sensitivity or acuity. This can be accomplished by gating the relationship between stimuli, cortical function, and behavior. They also alter brain circuits that down-regulate olfactory processing in the periphery.

2. Hormones are regulated by social odors and pheromones.

3. Hormones are social chemosignals themselves, functioning as odors, pheromones, and vasanas.

Including humans in the comparative psychology and neuroendocrinology of social chemosignals provides animal research with a rich framework for addressing the relationship among perception, psychological responses, and levels of awareness. The animal literature brings precise insights about neuroendocrine mechanisms of production and response. It also brings a heightened appreciation for the diversity of ways that the same social function can be achieved.

Defining social chemosignals in terms of their function, that is, their effects on other individuals, is an unambiguous way of distinguishing among odors, the four classes of pheromones, and vasanas. Functional criteria are powerful because they resolve the confusion and controversies caused by the fact that one compound can be two types of social chemosignal. For example, androstenone is a releaser pheromone among pigs (Gower and Ruparelia, 1992) but also is an odor consciously perceived by humans, causing depression in people living near pig farms (Schiffman *et al.*, 1995c). Conversely, a single function for social chemosignals, such as puberty acceleration by male mice, can be produced by several different pheromone compounds, any one of which is sufficient (Novotny *et al.*, 1999; Leinders-Zufall *et al.*, 2000). Using functional definitions, and not overly constraining them by adding other independent criteria—such as chemical identity, receptors, neural mechanisms, developmental pathways or evolved species specificity—gives the terms the flexibility necessary to capture the complex characteristics of naturally evolved systems for social communication.

Context is essential for the function of each type of social chemosignal. For example, male pheromones stimulate estrus in female mice, but primarily when they have been living together in all female groups (McClintock, 1983c; Whitten *et al.*, 1968).

Androstadieone modulates the tone of women's sympathetic nervous system, but only in the psychosocial context created by a male tester (Jacob *et al.*, 2001a). The odor of human vaginal secretions is unpleasant in the laboratory (Doty *et al.*, 1975) but pleasant in a sexual context (Herz and Cahill, 1997).

Context dependence is undoubtedly mediated by centrifugal regulation of the periphery by cortical and subcortical systems, as are the mitral cells in the rat (Kay and Laurent, 1999) or the vomeronasal organ, which noradrenalin may regulate by changing sensitivity of the sensory epithelium or glandular secretion of pheromone transporters (Keverne, 1999). Nonetheless, the bias toward viewing sensory systems as processing information only from the periphery to the cortex remains, and so context is still an understudied aspect of the neural and endocrine mechanisms of social chemosignals.

Because context is an essential mechanism for social chemosignals, behavioral and hormonal responses to them are graded. Some always elicit a specific response, provided that the hormonal environment is appropriate. For example, in rats and in dogs, the odor of female urine is sufficient to stimulate penile erections in males without any physical stimulation (Sachs, 1997; Shafik, 1997). In contrast, other social chemosignals simply modulate the probability of an event that occurs on its own, such as ovarian primer pheromones that modulate the timing of the preovulatory LH surges during spontaneous ovarian cycles (McClintock, 1983d). Even the releaser pheromone, androstenone, is not 100% effective in eliciting the gilt's mating stance, and its effectiveness is modulated by other social cues in the environment (Tilbrook and Hemsworth, 1990). Finally, some social chemosignals simply create a context that enables other behavior, such as MHC or kin odors that enable parental responses to pups, but do not cause them (Beauchamp *et al.*, 2000).

The new term, "modulator pheromone" covers those behavioral pheromones that modulate the probability of behavior without directly eliciting it. They also function by modulating mood, emotional tone, stimulus salience, or attentional processes. Androstadienone is a putative modulator pheromone in humans because it modulates an individual's emotional reaction to the social situation of being in a psychological experiment. This modulating function is similar to that of hormones,

operating within an individual. For example, testosterone modulates the meaning of estrous urine, and the interest shown it by a male rat, without changing his olfactory acuity or ability to detect its odor.

Likewise, the term "modulator pheromone" is applicable in animals to behavioral pheromones that are not releasers. There are many examples of "releases" pheromones in the behavioral literature whose description makes it clear that they are not actually releasers, but have been so labeled because an appropriate term has been unavailable until now. For example, male pheromones modulate the rat's lordosis response to a male's mount, but are not sufficient by themselves to trigger the reflex (Rajendren *et al.*, 1993). Copulins, rhesus monkey pheromones, modulate, but do not release, male sexual behavior in natural environments (Goldfoot, 1981; Michael *et al.*, 1976).

"Vasana" is the new term for social chemosignals that operate at concentrations below the level of conscious detection as odors, yet nonetheless modulate psychological state and behavior (McClintock *et al.*, 2001). The concept was derived from human research where verbal reports could verify their existence; that is, that they are not dectable as odors (Jacob and McClintock, 2000; Jacob *et al.*, 2001b, 2002). There also is every reason to expect that they operate in animals, even without benefit of verbal reports. Vasanas in animals could be demonstrated, for example, by determining that an environmental odorant changes the probability of an animal's behavior, yet when presented does not elicit sniffing, investigative behavior, or any orienting responses typically seen in response to odors (e.g., Bluthé *et al.*, 1990; Gheusi *et al.*, 1994; Kay and Freeman, 1998; Kelliher *et al.*, 1998; Wallace and Rosen, 2000). It is likely that in time, vasanas will be distinguished from odors by the type and level of their olfactory processing.

Finally, given the chemical isolation and identification of a wide variety of social odors and pheromones, it is now clear that there is not a unique set of chemical compounds that each species uses uniquely as social chemosignals, even though their evolved function is species-specific. For example, 100 lepidoptera species utilize only 20 compounds as sex pheromones (Kaisling, 1996). Urine and feces from the common spiny mouse suppress ovulation in the coexisting golden spiny mouse (van Aarde and Haim, 1999). Goat urine induces ovulation in sheep (Signoret and

Lindsey, 1982). Hamster vaginal secretions regularize the cycles of rats, even though the two species did not evolve sharing the same territory (Inamura *et al.,* 1999; Weizenbaum *et al.,* 1977). The compound, (Z)-7-dodecenyl acetate, is a sex attractant used both by elephants and by *lepidoptera* (Kelly, 1996; Rasmussen *et al.,* 1997b). A yeast sex attractant pheromone triggers GnRH release from the rat pituitary (Loumaye *et al.,* 1982). This later cross-species effect operates across kingdoms and is strong support for the recent discovery of three gene families encoding GnRH, which have evolved along separate trajectories from a time that predates vertebrates, perhaps 500 million years ago (Fernald and White, 1999).

Thus, it is clear that the production of new compounds is not evolving as rapidly as are species. Rather, coaptation has occurred and cross-species effects should no longer be surprising. As the genetics of receptors for social chemosignals unfolds, we should expect to find similar receptor and transduction systems across species. Indeed, this redundancy across species can be capitalized upon to advance the discovery of receptor and neuroendocrine mechanisms, which will have general significance beyond the species in which they are first elucidated.

A final example illustrates the rich interplay between all types of social chemosignals, and involves interactions of species ranging across kingdoms, from fungi to animalia. In this example, steroid social chemosignals mediate interactions between human culture and natural ecosystems.

Truffles are a European culinary delicacy. The fruiting bodies of this fungus, *Tuber melanosporum Vitt.,* contain 3α-androstenol; a musky steroid, at concentration as high as those produced by mature boars (Claus *et al.,* 1981; Karg, 1988). Italians can therefore use pigs to locate their white Italian truffles growing deep underground. But the pigs are difficult to handle, because the truffles are so attractive that the pigs often trample or eat them. So, the French use dogs to locate the odor of their black Périgord truffles, which they can do only after giving the dogs extensive olfactory-discrimination training. It has been discovered, however, that the trained dogs do not actually respond to the odor of androstenol, as do pigs, but to dimethly sulfide, another odorant produced by the truffles (Talou *et al.,* 1990). This compound, incidentally one sulfide group less than a hamster sex attractant (Briand *et al.,* 2000), is a social territorial odor used by flies (genus *Suillia*) to congregate and lay their eggs together as a social group. Finally, truffles also contain small amounts of androstenone, the more urinous compound produced by boars, as do parsnips and celery root, "the poor man's truffles" (Claus and Hoppen, 1979). Androstenone is synthesized directly from androstadienone, a modulator pheromone, or perhaps a vasana, which unconsciously modulates human emotional responses to social interactions (Jacob and McClintock, 2000; Jacob *et al.,* 2001a).

References

Abbott, D. H. (1984). Behavioral and physiological suppression of fertility in subordinate marmoset monkeys. *Am. J. Primatol.* **6,** 169–186.

Abel, E. L. (1994). The pituitary mediates production or release of an alarm chemosignal in rats. *Horm. Behav.* **28**(2), 139–145.

Abel, E. L., and Bilitzke, P. J. (1990). A possible alarm substance in the forced swimming test. *Physiol. Behav.* **48**(2), 233–239.

Abolmaali, N. D., Kuhnau, D., Knecht, M., Kohler, K., Huttenbrink, K. B., and Hummel, T. (2001). Imaging of the human vomeronasal duct. *Chem. Senses* **26**(1), 35–39.

Adler, N. T., Davis, P. G., and Komisaruk, B. R. (1977). Variation in the size and sensitivity of a genital sensory field in relation to the estrous cycle in rats. *Horm. Behav.* **9**(3), 334–344.

Alaoui-Ismaïli, O., Robin, O., Rada, H., Dittmar, A., and Vernet-Maury, E. (1997). Basic emotions evoked by odorants: Comparison between autonimic responses and self-evaluation. *Physiol. Behav.* **62**(4), 713–720.

Albone, E. (1984). "Mammalian Semiochemistry: The Investigation of Chemical Signals between Mammals." Wiley, New York.

Amoore, J. E. (1977). Specific anosmia and the concept of primary odors. *Chem. Senses* **2,** 267–281.

Amoore, J. E., Popplewell, J. R., and Whissell-Buechy, D. (1975). Sensitivity of women to musk odor: No menstrual variation. *J. Chem. Ecol.* **1,** 291–297.

Anonymous (1970). Effects of sexual activity on beard growth in man. *Nature (London)* **226,** 869–870.

Arden, M. A., and Dye, L. (1998). The assessment of menstrual synchrony: Comment on Weller and Weller (1997). *J. Comp. Psychol.* **112,** 323–324.

Arimondi, C., Vannelli, G. B., Mathe, F., and Mrowinski, D. (1993). Importance of olfaction in the sexual life: Morphofunctional and psychological studies in man. *Biomed. Res. (India)* **4,** 43–52.

Aron, C. (1979). Mechanisms of control of the reproductive function by olfactory stimuli in female mammels. *Physiol. Rev.* **59**, 229–284.

Aron, C., Roos, J., and Roos, M. (1971). Olfactory stimuli and their function in the regulation of the duration of the oestrous cycle in the rat. *J. Interdiscip. Cycle Res.* **2**, 239–246.

Asso, D. (1986). The relationship between menstrual cycle changes in nervous system activity and psychological, behavioural and physical variables. *Biol. Psychol.* **23**, 53–64.

Aujard, F. (1997). Effect of vomeronasal organ removal on male socio-sexual responses to female in a prosimian primate (*Microcebus murinus*). *Physiol. Behav.* **62**, 1003–1008.

Badia, P., Wesenstcn, N., Lammer, W., Culpepper, J., and Harsh, J. (1990). Responsiveness to olfactory stimuli presented in sleep. *Physiol. Behav.* **48**, 87–90.

Bagnall, R. S., and Frier, B. W. (1994). "The Demography of Roman Egypt." Cambridge University Press, Cambridge, UK.

Bailey, R. C., Jenike, M. R., Ellison, P. T., Bentley, G. R., Harrigan, A. M., and Peacock, N. R. (1992). The ecology of birth seasonality among agriculturalists in central Africa. *J. Biosoc. Sci.* **24**, 393–412.

Baker, J. V., Abbott, D. H., and Saltzman, W. (1999). Social determinants of reproductive failure in male common marmosets housed with their natal family. *Anim. Behav.* **58**, 501–513.

Barkley, M., DeLeon, D. D., and Weste, R. (1993). Pheromonal regulation of the mouse estrous cycle by a heterogenotypic male. *J. Exp. Zool.* **265**, 558–566.

Barni, T., Maggi, M., Fantoni, G., Granchi, S., Mancina, R., Gulisano, M., Marra, F., Macorsini, E., Luconi, M., Rotella, C., Serio, M., Balboni, G. C., and Vannelli, G. B. (1999). Sex steroids and odorants modulate gonadotropin-releasing hormone secretion in primary cultures of human olfactory cells. *J. Clin. Endocrinol. Metab.* **84**, 4266–4273.

Barraclough, C. A., and Cross, B. A. (1963). Unit activity in the hypothalamus of the cyclic female rat: Effect of genital stimuli and progesterone. *J. Endocrinol.* **26**, 339–359.

Bartoshuk, L. M., and Beachamp, G. K. (1994). Chemical senses. *Annu. Rev. Psychol.* **45**, 419–449.

Basset, J. L., Shipley, M. T., and Foote, S. L. (1992). Localization of corticotropin-releasing factor-like immunoreactivity in monkey olfactory-bulb and secondary olfactory areas. *J. Comp. Neurol.* **316**, 348–362.

Beach, F. A., and Gilmore, R. W. (1949). Reponse of male dogs to urine from females in heat. *J. Mammal.* **30**, 391–392.

Beauchamp, G. K. (2000). Defining pheromones. *In* "The Monell Connection" (L. J. Stein, ed.), Fall 2000, p. 2. Monell Chemical Senses Center, Philadelphia.

Beauchamp, G. K., Doty, R. L., Moulton, D. G., and Mugford, R. A. (1976). The pheromone concept in mammalian chemical communication: A critique. *In* "Mammalian Olfaction, Reproductive Processes, and Behavior" (R. L. Doty, ed.), pp. 144–157. Academic Press, New York.

Beauchamp, G. K., Yamazaki, K., Wysocki, C. J., Slotnick, B. M., Thomas, L., and Boyse, E. A. (1985). Chemosensory recognition of mouse major histocompatibility types by another species. *Proc. Natl. Acad. Sci. U.S.A.* **82**, 4186–4188.

Beauchamp, G. K., Curran, M., and Yamazaki, K. (2000). MHC-mediated fetal odourtypes expressed by pregnant females influence male associative behavior. *Anim. Behav.* **60**, 289–295.

Becerra, N. N., Grigorjev, C., and Munaro, N. (1996). Glutamic acid decarboxylase in rat olfactory bulb: Effect of ovarian steriods or male pheromones. *Eur. J. Pharmacol.* **312**, 83–87.

Beidler, L. M., and Tucker, D. (1955). Response of nasal epithelium to odor stimulation. *Science* **122**, 76.

Belcher, A. M., Smith, A. B., Jurs, P. C., Lavine, B., and Epple, G. (1986). Analysis of chemical signals in a primate species (*Saguinus fuscicollis*): Use of behavioral, chemical, and pattern recognition methods. *J. Chem. Ecol.* **12**, 513–531.

Bellairs, A. A. (1951). Observations on the incisive canaliculi and nasopalatine ducts. *Br. Dent. J.* **91**, 281–286.

Beltramino, C., and Taleisnik, S. (1983). Release of LH in the female rat by olfactory stimuli. *Neuroendocrinology* **36**, 53–58.

Benton, D. (1982). The influence of androstenol—a putative human pheromone—on mood throughout the menstrual cycle. *Biol. Psychol.* **15**, 249–256.

Benton, D., and Wastell, V. (1986). Effects of androstenol on human sexual arousal. *Biol. Psychol.* **22**, 141–147.

Berliner, D. L. (1996). Awakening the world's sixth sense through human pheromone technology. *In* "Erox Annual Report." 4034 Clipper Court, Fremont, California.

Berliner, D. L., Monti-Bloch, L., Jennings-White, C., and Diaz-Sanchez, V. (1996). The functionality of the human vomeronasal organ (VNO): Evidence for steroid receptors. *J. Steroid Biochem. Mol. Biol.* **58**, 259–265.

Berliner, D. L. (1994). Fragrance compositions containing human pheromones. U.S. Pat. 5,278,141.

Berliner, D. L., Jennings-White, C., and Lavker, R. M. (1991). The human skin: Fragrances and pheromones. *J. Steroid Biochem. Mol. Biol.* **39**, 671–679.

Berntson, G. G., Cacioppo, J. T., Quigley, K. S., and Farbo, V. T. (1994). Autonomic space and psychophysiological response. *Psychophysiology* **31**, 44–61.

Bieber, I., B., B. T., and Friedman, R. C. (1992). Olfaction and human sexuality: A psychoanalytic approach. *In* "Science of Olfaction" (M. J. Serby and K. L. Chobor, eds.), pp. 396–409. Springer-Verlag, New York.

Black, S. L., and Biron, C. (1982). Androstenol as a human pheromone: No effect on perceived physical attractiveness. *Behav. Neural Biol.* **34**, 326–330.

Blakeslee, S. (1993). Human nose may hold an additional organ for a real sixth sense. *N.Y. Times.* Sept. 7, 1993. Sec. C, p. 3.

Blumberg, M., Mark, S., Mennella, J. A., Moltz, J. A., and McClintock, M. K. (1992). Facultative sex-ratio adjustment in Norway rats: Litters born asynchronously are female biased. *Behav. Ecol. Sociobiol.* **31**, 401–408.

Bluthe, R. M., Schoenen, J., and Dantzer, R. (1990). Androgen-dependent vasopressinergic neurons are involved in social recognition in rates. *Brain Res.* **519**, 150–157.

Bluthe, R. M., Suarez, S., Fink, G., Roques, B., and Dantzer, R. (1993). Social recognition in mice is modulated by androgen-dependent vasopressinergic and cholecystokininergic neurotransmission. *Soc. Neurosci. Abstr.* **19**, 173.

Boecker, M., and Badia, P. (1992). The effects of the odor androstenone on sleep. *Sleep Res.* **21**, 142.

Boehm, N., and Gasser, B. (1993). Sensory receptor-like cells in the human foetal vomeronasal organ. *NeuroReport* **4**, 867–870.

Boehm, N., Ross, H., and Gasser, B. (1994). Luteinizing hormone-releasing hormone (LHRH)-expressing cells in the nasal sptum of human fetuses. *Brain Res. Dev.* **82**, 867–870.

Booth, W. D. (1984). Sexual dimorphism involving steroidal pheromones and their binding protein in the submaxillary salivary gland of the Gottingen miniature pig. *J. Endocrinol.* **100**, 195–202.

Booth, W. D., and White, C. A. (1988). The isolation, purification and some properties of pheromaxein, the pheromonal steroid-binding protein, in procine submaxillary glands and saliva. *J. Endocrinol.* **128**, 47–57.

Bossy, J. (1980). Development of olfactory and related structures in staged human embryos. *Anat. Embryol.* **161**, 225–236.

Bourliere, F. (1955). "The Natural History of Mammals." Harrap, London.

Bradbury, J. W. (1977). Social organization and communication. *In* "Biology of bats" (W. A. Wimsatt, ed.), Vol. 3, pp. 1–72. Academic Press, New York.

Bradley, E. A. (1984). Olfactory acuity to a pheromonal substance and psychotic illness. *Biol. Psychiatry* **19**, 899–905.

Bradshaw, H. B., and Berkley, K. J. (2000). Estrous changes in responses of rat gracile nucleus neurons to stimulation of skin and pelvin viscera. *J. Neurosci.* **20**, 7722–7727.

Brand, G., and Millot, J. L. (2001). Sex differences in human olfaction: Between evidence and enigma. *Q. J. Exp. Psychol. B* **54**, 259–270.

Breipohl, W. (1982). "Olfaction and Endocrine Regulation." IRL Press, London.

Brennan, P., Kaba, H., and Keverne, E. B. (1990). Olfactory recognition: A simple memory system. *Science* **250**, 1223–1226.

Brennan, P. A., and Keverne, E. B. (1997). Neural mechanisms of mammalian olfactory learning. *Prog. Neurobiol.* **51**, 457–481.

Bressler, S. C., and Baum, M. J. (1996). Sex comparison of neuronal fos immunoreactivity in the rat vomeronasal projection circuit after chemosensory stimulation. *Neuroscience* **4**, 1063–1072.

Briand, L., Huet, J. C., Perez, V., Lenoir, C., Nespoulous, C., Boucher, Y., Trotier, D., and Pernollet, J. C. (2000). Odorant and pheromone binding by aphrodisin, a hamster aphrodisiac protein, a hamster aphrodisiac protein. *FEBS Lett.* **476**, 179–185.

Bridges, R. S. (1990). Endocrine regulation of parental behavior in rodents. *In* "Mammalian Parenting: Biochemical, Neurobiological, and Behavioral Determinants" (N. A. Krasnegor and R. S. Bridges, eds.), pp. 93–117. Oxford University Press, New York.

Broca, P. (1878). Le grand lobe limbique et la scissure limbique. *Rev. Anthropol.* **1**, 385–498.

Broca, P. (1979). Anatomie du lobe olfactif. *Bull. Soc. Anthropol.* Ser. **4**, pp. 596–598.

Bronson, F. H. (2000). Puberty and energy reserves: A walk on the wild side. *In* "Reproduction in Context" (K. Wallen and J. E. Schneider, eds.), pp. 15–33. MIT Press, Cabridge, MA.

Bronson, F. H., and Marsden, H. M. (1964). Male induced synchrony of estrus in deermice. *Gen. Comp. Endocrinol.* **4**, 634–637.

Bronson, F. H., and Rissman, E. F. (1986). The biology of puberty. *Biol. Rev. Cambridge Philos. Soc.* **61**, 157–195.

Brooksbank, B. W., Wilson, D. A., and MacSweeney, D. A. (1972). Fate of androsta-4,16-dien-3-one and the origin of 3-hydroxy-5-androst-16-ene in man. *J. Endocrinol.* **52**, 239–251.

Brooksbank, B. W. (1970). Labelling of steriods in axillary sweat after administration of 3H-D5-pregnenolone and 14C-progesterone to a healthy man. *Experientia* **26**, 1012–1014.

Brooksbank, B. W., and Gower, D. B. (1964). The use of thin-layer and gas-liquid chormatography in the idenfication of 5β-androsten-16-en-3α-ol and androsta-5,16-dien-3β-ol in human urine. *Steroids* **4**, 787–800.

Brooksbank, B. W., and Haslewood, G. A. D. (1961). The estimation of androt-16-en-3α-ol in human urine: Partial synthesis of androstenol and of its β-glucosiduronic acid. *Biochem. J.* **80**, 488–496.

Brooksbank, B. W., Cunningham, A. E., and Wilson, D. A. (1969). The detection of androsta-4,16-dien-3-one in peripheral plasma of adult men. *Steroids* **13**, 29–50.

Brooksbank, B. W., Brown, R., and Gustafsson, J. A. (1974). The detection of 5a-androst-16-en-3a-ol in human male axillary sweat. *Experientia* **30**, 864–865.

Broom, D. M. (1999). Social transfer of information in domestic animals. *Symp. Zool. Soc. London* **72**, 158–168.

Brouette-Lahlou, I., Vernet-Maury, E., Godinot, F., and Chanel, J. (1992). Vomeronasal organ sustains pups' anogenital licking in primiparous rats. *In* "Chemical Signals in Vertebrates" (R. L. Doty and D. Müller-Schwarze, eds.), Vol. 6, pp. 551–555. Plenum Press, New York.

Brown, R. E. (1979). Mammalian social odors: A critical review. *Adv. Study Behav.* **10,** 103–162.

Brown, R. E. (1993). Hormonal and experiential factors influencing parental behavior in male rodents—an integrative approach. *Behav. Processes* **30,** 1–28.

Brown, R. E., Singh, P. B., and Roser, B. (1986). The major histocompatibility complex and the chemosensory recognition of individuality in rats. *Physiol. Behav.* **40,** 65–73.

Bruce, H. M. (1959). An exteroceptive block to pregnancy in the mouse. *Nature (London)* **184,** 105.

Buck, L., and Axel, R. (1991). A novel multigene family may encode odorant receptors: A molecular basis for odor recognition. *Cell (Cambridge, Mass.)* **65,** 175–187.

Buckley, T. (1988). Menstruation and the power of yurok women. *In* "Blood Magic" (T. Buckley and A. Gottlieb, eds.), pp. 187–209. University of California Press, Berkeley.

Bullivant, S. B., Spencer, N. A., Jacob, S., Sellegren, S. A., Mennella, J. A., and McClintock, M. K. K. (2000). Odor characteristics of breastfeeding chemosignals. *Chem. Senses* **25,** 613.

Burghardt, G. M. (1980). Behavioural and stimulus correlates of vomeronasal functioning in reptiles: Feeding, grouping, sex and tongue use. *In* "Chemical Signals in Vertebrates and Aquatic Animals" (D. Müller-Schwarze and R. M. Silverstein, eds.), pp. 275–301. Plenum Press, New York.

Cain, W. S. (1982). Odor identification by males and females: Prediction vs. performance. *Chem. Senses* **7,** 129–142.

Calamandrei, G., and Keverne, E. B. (1992). Maternal experience increases c-fos expression in the olfactory and hypothalamic areas of female mouse cns. *Eur. J. Neurosci., Suppl.* **5,** 41.

Carr, W. J., and Caul, W. F. (1962). The effect of castration in the rat upon discrimination of sex odors. *Anim. Behav.* **10,** 20–27.

Carr, W. J., Solberg, B., and Pfaffmann, C. (1962). The olfactory threshold for oestrous female urine in normal and castrated male rats. *J. Comp. Psychol.* **55,** 415–417.

Carr, W. J., Loeb, L. S., and Dissinger, M. L. (1965). Response of rats to sex odors. *J. Comp. Psychol.* **59,** 370–377.

Carr, W. J., Martorono, R. D., and Krames, L. (1970). Responses of mice to odors associated with stress. *J. Comp. Physiol. Psychol.* **71,** 223–228.

Casper, R. F., Erskine, H. J., Armstrong, D. T. *et al.* (1988). In vitro fertilization: Diurnal and seasonal variation in luteinizing hormone surge onset and pregnancy rates. *Fertil. Steril.* **49,** 644–647.

Chan, R. K., Vale, W. W., and Sawchenko, P. E. (2000). Paradoxical activational effects of a corticotropin-releasing factor-binding protein "ligand inhibitor" in rat brain. *Neuroscience* **101,** 115–129.

Chateau, D. J., Roos, J., and Aron, C. (1972). Effect of male or female urine from normal or castrated rats on the duration of the estrus cycle in femal rats. *C. R. Hebd. Seances Soc. Biol. Ses Fil.* **166,** 1110–1113.

Chateau, D. J., Roos, J., Plaf-Roser, S., Roos, M., and Aron, C. (1976). Hormonal mechanisms involved in the control of oestrous cycle duration by the odour of urine in the rate. *Acta Endocrinol. (Copenhagen)* **82,** 426–435.

Chen, D., and Haviland-Jones, J. (1999). Rapid mood change and human odors. *Physiol. Behav.* **68,** 241–250.

Chen, W. B., Kelly, M. A., OpitzAraya, X., Thomas, R. E., Low, M. J., and Cone, R. D. (1997). Exocrine gland dysfunction in MC5-R-deficient mice: Evidence for coordinated regulation of exocrine gland function by melanocortin peptides. *Cell (Cambridge, Mass.)* **91,** 789–798.

Chou, C. L., DiGiovanni, S. R., Mejia, R., Nielsen, S., and Knepper, M. A. (1995). Oxytocin as an antidiuretic hormone. I. Concentration dependence of action. *Am. J. Physiol.* **269,** F70–F77.

Christian, J. J. (1955). Effect of population size on the adrenal glands and reproductive male mice in populations of fixed size. *Am. J. Physiol.* **182,** 282–300.

Clark, A. B. (1981). Olfactory communication, *Galago crassicaudatus,* and the social life of prosimians. *In* "Recent Advances in Primatology" (D. J. Chivers and K. A. Joysey, eds.), pp. 109–117. Academic Press, London.

Clark, T. (1978). Whose pheromone are you? *World Med.,* pp. 21–23.

Clarke, A. S., Harvey, N. C., and Lindberg, D. G. (1992). Reproductive coordination in a nonseasonally breeding primate species, *Macaca silenus. Ethology* **91,** 46–58.

Claus, R., and Hoppen, H. D. (1979). The boar-pheromone steroid identified in vegetables. *Experientia* **35,** 1674–1675.

Claus, R., Hoppen, H. D., and Karg, H. (1981). The secret of truffles: A steroidal pheromone? *Experientia* **37,** 1178–1179.

Cohn, B. A. (1994). In search of human pheromones. *Arch. Dermatol.* **130,** 1048–1051.

Comette-Muniz, J. E., and Cain, W. S. (1998). Trigeminal and olfactory sensitivity: Comparison of modalities and methods of measurement. *Int. Arch. Occup. Environ. Health* **71,** 105–110.

Corbin, A. (1986). "The Foul and the Fragrant: Odor and the French Social Imagination." Harvard University Press, Cambridge, MA.

Corter, C. M., and Fleming, A. S. (1995). Psychobiology of maternal behavior in human beings. *In* "Handbook of Parenting"

(M. H. Bornstein, ed.), Vol. 2, pp. 87–116. Erlbaum, Toronto.

Coureaud, G., and Schaal, B. (2000). Attraction of newborn rabbits to abdominal odors of adult conspecifics differing in sex and physiological state. *Dev. Psychobiol.* **36**, 271–281.

Cowley, J. J., Johnson, A. L., and Brooksbank, B. W. L. (1977). The effect of two odorous compounds on performance in an assessment-of-people test. *Psychoneuroendocrinology* **2**, 159–172.

Cowley, J. J., Harvey, F., Johnson, A. T., and Brooksbank, B. W. L. (1980). Irritability and depression during the menstrual cycle—possible role for an exogenous pheromone? *Ir. J. Psychol.* **3**, 143–156.

Cowley, J. J., Johnson, A. L., and Brooksbank, B. W. L. (1991). Human exposure to putative pheromones and changes in aspects of social behavior. *J. Steroid Biochem. Mol. Biol.* **39**, 647–659.

Cutler, W. B. (1988). Reply to wilson. *Horm. Behav.* **22**, 272–277.

Cutler, W. B., Garcia, C. R., and Krieger, A. M. (1980). Sporadic sexual behavior and menstrual cycle length in women. *Horm. Behav.* **14**, 163–172.

Cutler, W. B., Preti, G., Huggins, G. R., Erickson, B., and Garcia, C. R. (1985). Sexual behavior frequency and biphasic ovulatory type menstrual cycles. *Physiol. Behav. 34*, 805–810.

Cutler, W. B., Preti, G., Krieger, A., Huggins, G. R., Garcia, C. R., and Lawley, H. J. (1986). Human axillary secretions influence women's menstrual cycles: The role of donor extract from men. *Horm. Behav.* **20**, 463–473.

Cutler, W. B., Friedman, E., and McCoy, N. L. (1998). Pheromonal influences on sociosexual behavior in men. *Arch. Sex. Behav.* **27**, 1–13.

Dabbs, J. M., and Mohammed, S. (1992). Male and female salivary testerone concentration before and after sexual activity. *Physiol. Behav.* **52**, 195–197.

Dade, L. A., Jones-Gotman, M. J., Zatorre, R. J., and Evans, A. C. (1998). Human brain function during odor encoding and recognition. A PET activation study. *Ann. N.Y. Acad. Sci.* **30**, 572–574.

Dalton, P., Doolittle, N., Nagata, H., and Breslin, P. A. (2000). The merging of the senses: Integration of subthreshold taste and smell. *Nat. Neurosci.* **3**, 431–432.

Dalton, P., Doolittle, N., and Breslin, P. A. S. (2002). Gender-specific induction of enhanced sensitivity to odors. *Nat. Neurosci.* **5**, 199–200.

Darwin, C. (1871). "The Descent of Man and Selection in Relation to Sex." A. L. Burt, New York.

Davis, R. B., Herreid, C. F., II, and Short, H. L. (1962). Mexican free-tailed bats in Texas. *Ecol. Monogr.* **32**, 311–346.

Day, J. R., Morales, T. H., and Lu, J. K. H. (1988). Male stim-

ulation of luteinizing hormone surge, progesterone secretion and ovulation in spontaneously persistent-estrous, aging rats. *Biol. Reprod.* **38**, 1019–1026.

deCatanzaro, D. (1999). "Motivation and Emotion: Evolutionary, Physiological, Development, and Social Perspectives." Prentice Hall, Upper Saddle River, NJ.

deCatanzaro, D., Zacharias, R., and Muir, C. (1996). Disruption of early pregnancy by direct and indirect exposure to novel males in mice: Comparison of influences of preputialectomized and intact males. *J. Reprod. Fertil.* **106**, 269–274.

deCatanzaro, D., Muir, C., Sullivan, C., and Boissy, A. (1999). Pheromones and novel male-induced pregnancy disruptions in mice: Exposure to conspecifics is necessary for urine alone to induce an effect. *Physiol. Behav.* **66**, 153–157.

Deems, D. A., and Doty, R. L. (1987). Age-related changes in the phenyl ethyl alcohol odor detection threshold. *Trans.—Pa. Acad. Ophthalmol. Otolaryngol.* **39**, 646–650.

Deems, D. A., Doty, R. L., Settle, R. G., Moore-Gillon, V., Shaman, P., Mester, A. F., Kimmelman, C. P., Brightman, V. J., and Snow, J. B., Jr. (1991). Smell and taste disorders, a study of 750 patients from the university of pennsylvania smell and taste center. *Arch. Otolaryngol.-Head Neck Surg.* **117**, 519–528.

de Fanis, E., and Jones, G. (1995). Post-natal growth, mother-infant interactions and development of vocalizations in the vespertilionid bat *Plectuos auritus*. *J. Zool.* **235**, 85–97.

de Fanis, E., and Jones, G. (1996). Allomaternal care and recognition between mothers and young in pipistrelle bats (*Pipistrellus pipistrellus*). *J. Zool.* **240**, 781–787.

Degel, J., and Koster, E. P. (1999). Odors: Implicit memory and performance effects. *Chem. Senses* **24**, 317–325.

Degel, J., Piper, D., and Koster, E. P. (2001). Implicit learning and implicit memory for odors: The influence of odor identification and retention time. *Chem. Senses* **26**, 267–280.

Delcroix, I., Mauget, R., and Signoret, J. P. (1990). Existence of synchronization or reproduction at the level of the social group of the European wild boar (*Sus-scrofa*). *J. Reprod. Fertil.* **89**, 613–617.

DeLeon, D. D., and Barkley, M. (1987). Male and femal genotype mediate pheromonal regulation of the mouse estrous cycle. *Biol. Reprod.* **37**, 1066–1074.

Dellovade, T., Schwanzel-Fukuda, M., Gordan, J., and Pfaff, D. (1998). Aspects of GnRH neurobiology conserved across vertebrate forms. *Gen. Comp. Endocrinol.* **112**, 276–282.

Dessi-Fulgheri, F., and Lupo, C. (1982). Odour of male and female rats changes hypothalamic aromatase and 5a-reductase activity and plasma sex steroid levels in unisexually reared male rats. *Physiol. Behav.* **28**, 231–235.

Devos, M., Patte, F., Rouault, J., Laffort, P., and Van Gemert, L. J. (1990). "Standardized Human Olfactory Thresholds." Oxford University Press, New York.

Dluzen, D. E., and Ramirez, V. D. (1987). Involvement of olfactory bulb catecholamines and luteinizing hormone-releasing hormone in response to social stimuli mediating reproductive functions. *Ann. N.Y. Acad. Sci.* **519**, 252–268.

Dluzen, D. E., and Ramirez, V. D. (1989). Receptive female rats stimulate norepinephrine release from olfactory bulbs of freely behaving male rats. *Neuroendocrinology* **49**, 28–32.

Dluzen, D. E., Ramirez, V. D., Carter, C. S., and Getz, L. L. (1981). Male vole urine changes luteinizing hormone-releasing hormone and norepinephrine in female olfactory bulb. *Science* **212**, 573–575.

Dodd, G. H. (1988). The molecular dimension in perfumery. *In* "Perfumery: The Psychology and Biology of Fragrance" (S. Van Toller and G. H. Dodd, eds.), pp. 19–46. Chapman & Hall, New York.

Dorfman, R. I., and Ungar, F. (1965). "Metabolism of Steroid Hormones." Academic Press, New York.

Dorries, K. M. (1992). Sex differences in olfaction in mammals. *In* "Science of Olfaction" (M. J. Serby and K. L. Chobor, eds.), pp. 245–275. Springer-Verlag, New York.

Dorries, K. M., Schmidt, H. J., Beauchamp, G. K., and Wysocki, C. J. (1989). Changes in sensitivity to the odor of androstenone during adolescence. *Dev. Psychol.* **22**, 423–435.

Dorries, K. M., Adkins-Regan, E., and Halpern, B. P. (1990). Domestic pig: Possible model for study of specific anosmia to androstenone. *Chem. Senses* **15**, 567.

Dorries, K. M., Adkins-Regan, E., and Halpern, B. P. (1997). Sensitivity and behavioral responses to the pheromone androstenone are not mediated by the vomeronasal organ in domestic pigs. *Brain, Behav. Evol.* **49**, 53–62.

Doty, R. L. (1976). Reproductive endocrine influences upon human nasal chemoreception: A review. *In* "Mammalian Olfaction, Reproductive Processes, and Behavior" (R. L. Doty, ed.), pp. 295–321. Academic Press, New York.

Doty, R. L. (1981). Olfactory communication in humans. *Chem. Senses* **6**, 351–376.

Doty, R. L. (1984). "Social Odours in Mammals." Clarendon Press, Oxford.

Doty, R. L. (1986a). Gender and the endocrine-related influences on human olfactory preception. *In* "Clinical Measurements of Taste and Smell" (H. L. Meiselman and R. S. Rivlin, eds.), pp. 377–413. Macmillan, New York.

Doty, R. L. (1986b). Reproductive endocrine influences upon olfactory perception: A current perspective. *J. Chem. Ecol.*

Doty, R. L. (1989). Influence of age and age-related diseases on olfactory function. *Ann. N.Y. Acad. Sci.* **561**, 76–86.

Doty, R. L. (1997). Studies of human olfaction from the University of Pennsylvania Smell and Taste Center. *Chem. Senses* **22**, 565–586.

Doty, R. L., and Ferguson-Segall, M. (1989). Influence of adult

castration on the olfactory sensitivity of the male rat: A signal detection analysis. *Behav. Neurosci.* **103**, 691–694.

Doty, R. L., Ford, M., Preti, G., and Huggins, G. R. (1975). Changes in the intensity and pleasantness of human vaginal odors during menstrual cycle. *Science* **190**, 1316–1318.

Doty, R. L., Snyder, P. J., Huggins, G. R., and Lowry, L. D. (1981). Endocrine, cardiovascular, and psychological correlated of olfactory sensitivity changes during the human menstrual cycle. *J. Comp. Physiol. Psychol.* **95**, 45–60.

Doty, R. L., Hall, J. W., Flickinger, G. L., and Sondheimer, S. J. (1982). Cyclical changes in olfactory and auditory sensitivity during the menstrual cycle: No attenuation by oral contraceptive medication. *In* "Olfaction and Endocrine Regulation" (W. Breiphol, ed.), pp. 285–297. IRL Press, London.

Doty, R. L., Shaman, P., Applebaum, S. L., Giberson, R., Sikorski, L., and Rosenberg, L. (1984a). Smell identification ability: Changes with age. *Science* **226**, 1441–1443.

Doty, R. L., Shaman, P., and Dann, M. (1984b). Development of the University of Pennsylvania smell identification test: A standardized microencapsulated test of olfactory function. *Physiol. Behav.* **32**, 489–502.

Doty, R. L., Applebaum, S., Zusho, H., and Settle, R. G. (1985). Sex differences in odor identification ability: A cross-cultural analysis. *Neuropsychologia* **23**, 667–672.

Doty, R. L., Smith, R., McKeown, D. A., and Raj, J. (1994). Tests of human olfactory function: Principal components analysis suggests that most measure a common source of variance. *Perception Psychophys.* **56**, 701–707.

Doty, R. L., Fernandez, A. D., Levine, M. A., Moses, A. M., and McKeown, D. A. (1997). Olfactory dysfunction in pseudohypoparathyroidism: Dissociation from G5α protein deficiency. *J. Clin. Endocrinol. Metab.* **82**, 247–250.

Døving, K. B., and Trotier, D. (1998). Review. Structure and function of the vomeronasal organ. *J. Exp. Biol.* **201**, 2913–2925.

Dravnieks, A., Masurat, T., and Lamm, R. A. (1984). Hedonics of odors and odor descriptors. *J. Air Pollut. Control Assoc.* **34**, 752–755.

Drickamer, L. C. (1984). Seasonal variation in acceleration and delay of sexual maturation in female mice by urinary chemosignals. *J. Reprod. Fertil.* **72**, 55–58.

Drickamer, L. C. (1992). Behavioral selection of odor cues by young female mice affects age of puberty. *Dev. Psychobiol.* **25**, 461–470.

Drickamer, L. C., and Hoover, J. E. (1979). Effects of urine from pregnant and lactating female house mice on sexual maturation of juvenile females. *Dev. Psychobiol.* **12**, 545–551.

Drickamer, L. C., and Martan, J. (1992). Odor discrimination and dominance in male domestic guinea-pigs. *Behav. Processes* **27**, 187–194.

Drickamer, L. C., and McIntosh, T. K. (1980). Effects of adrenalectomy on the presence of a maturation-delaying pheromone in the urine of female mice. *Horm. Behav.* **14**, 146–152.

Drickamer, L. C., McIntosh, T. K., and Rose, E. A. (1978). Effects of ovariectomy on the presence of a maturation-delaying pheromone in the urine of female mice. *Horm. Behav.* **11**, 131–137.

Dudley, C. A., Rajendren, G., and Moss, R. L. (1992). Induction of fos immunoreactivity in central accessory olfactory structures of the female rat following exposure to conspecific males. *Mol. Cell. Neurosci.* **3**, 360–369.

Eaton, S. B., Pike, M. C., Short, R. V., Lee, N. C., Trussell, J., Hatcher, R. A., Wood, J. W., Worthman, C. M., Jones, N. G. B., Konner, M. J., Hill, K. R., Bailey, R., and Hurtado, A. M. (1994). Women's reproductive cancers in evolutionary context. *Q. Rev. Biol.* **69**, 353–367.

Edwards, R. G., Steptoe, P. C., Fowler, R. E. *et al.* (1980). Observations on preovulatory human ovarian follicles and their aspirates. *Br. J. Obstet. Gynaecol.* **87**, 769–779.

Eeckman, F. H., and Freeman, W. J. (1991). Asymmetric sigmoid nonlinearity in the rat olfactory system. *Brain Res.* **557**, 13–21.

Egid, K., and Brown, J. L. (1989). The major histocompatibility complex and female mating preferences in mice. *Anim. Behav.* **38**, 4186–4188.

Ehrlichman, H., and Bastone, L. (1992). Olfaction and emotion. *In* "Science of Olfaction" (M. J. Serby and K. L. Chobor, eds.), pp. 410–438. Springer-Verlag, New York.

Eklund, A., Egid, K., and Brown, J. L. (1991). The major histocompatibility complex and matin preferences of male mice. *Anim. Behav.* **42**, 693–694.

Eleftheriou, B. E., Bailey, D. W., and Zarrow, M. X. (1972). A gene controlling male pheromonal facilitation of PMSG-induced ovulation in mice. *J. Reprod. Fertil.* **31**, 155–158.

Ellis, B. J., and Garber, J. (2000). Psychosocial antecedents of variation in girls' pubertal timing: Maternal depression, stepfather presence, and marital and family stree. *Child Dev.* **71**, 485–501.

Ellis, B. J., McFadyen-Ketchum, S., Dodge, K. A., Pettit, G. A., and Bates, J. E. (1999). Quality of early family relationships and individual differences in the timing of pubertal maturation in girls: A longitudinal test of an evolutionary model. *J. Pers. Soc. Psychol.* **77**, 387–401.

Ellis, H. (1929). "Studies in the Psychology of Sex," Vol. 2, pp. 44–112. Random House, New York.

Epple, G. (1976). Chemical communication and reproductive processes in nonhuman primates. *In* "Mammalian Olfaction, Reproductive Processes, and Behavior" (R. L. Doty, ed.), pp. 257–282. Academic Press, London.

Epple, G. (1980). Relationships between aggression, scent mark-ing, and gonadal state in a primate, the tamarin *Saguinus fascicollis*. *In* "Chemical Signals, Vertebrates and Aquatic Invertebrates" (D. Müller-Schwarze and R. M. Silverstein, eds.), pp. 87–50. Plenum Press, New York.

Erb, G. E., Edwards, H. E., Jenkins, K. L., Mucklow, L. C., and Wynne-Edwards, K. E. (1993). Induced components in the spontaneous ovulatory cycle of the Djungarian hamster (*Phodopus campbelli*). *Physiol. Behav.* **54**, 955–959.

Essghaier, M. F. A., and Johnson, D. R. (1981). Distribution and use of dung heaps by Dorcas gazelle in western Libya. *Mammalia* **45**, 152–155.

Estes, R. D., Cumming, D. H. M., and Hearn, G. W. (1982). New facial glands in domestic pig and warthog. *J. Mammal.* **63**, 618–624.

Evans, W. J., Cui, L., and Starr, A. (1995). Olfactory event-related potentials in normal human subjects: Effects of age and gender. *Electroencephalogr. Clin. Neurophysiol.* **95**, 293–301.

Ferguson, J. N., Young, L. J., Hearn, E. F., Matzuk, M. M., Insel, T. R., and Winslow, J. T. (2000). Social amnesia in mice lacking the oxytocin gene. *Nat. Genet.* **3**, 284–288.

Ferkin, M. H., and Gorman, M. L. (1992). Photoperiod and gonadal hormones influence odor preferences of the male meadow vole, *Microtus pennsylvanicus*. *Physiol. Behav.* **51**, 1087–1091.

Ferkin, M. H., Sorokin, E. S., and Johnston, R. E. (1997). Effect of prolactin on the attractiveness of male odors to females in meadow voles: Independent and additive effects with testosterone. *Horm. Behav.* **31**, 55–63.

Fernald, R. D., and White, R. B. (1999). Gonadotropin-releasing hormone genes: Phylogeny, structure and functions. *Front. Neuroendocrinol.* **20**, 224–240.

Fernandez-Fewell, G. D., and Meredith, M. (1994). C-fos expression in vomeronasal pathways of mated or pheromone-stimulated male golden hamsters: Contributions from vomeronasal sensory input and expression related to mating performance. *J. Neurosci.* **14**, 3643–3654.

Fiber, J. M., and Swann, J. M. (1996). Testosterone differentially influences sex-specific pheromone-stimulated fos expression in limbic regions of Syrian hamsters. *Horm. Behav.* **30**, 455–473.

Filsinger, E. E., Braun, J. J., Monte, W. C., and Linder, D. E. (1984). Human (*Homo sapiens*) response to the pig (*Sus scrofa*) sex pheromone 5-alpha-androst-16-en-3-one. *J. Comp. Psychol.* **98**, 219–222.

Filsinger, E. E., Braun, J. J., and Monte, W. C. (1985). An examination of the effects of putative pheromones on human judgments. *Ethol. Sociobiol.* **6**, 227–236.

Fleming, A. S. (1986). Psychobiology of rat maternal behavior: How and where hormones act to promote maternal behavior at parturition. *Ann. N.Y. Acad. Sci.* **474**, 234–251.

852 I. Mammalian Hormone-Behavior Systems

Fleming, A. S., and Korsmit, M. (1996). Plasticity in the maternal circuit: Effects of maternal experience on fos-lir in hypothalamic, limbic, and cortical structures in the postpartum rat. *Behav. Sci.* **110**, 567–582.

Fleming, A. S., and Sarker, J. (1990). Experience-hormone interactions and maternal behavior in rats. *Physiol. Behav.* **47**, 1165–1173.

Fleming, A. S., Cheung, U., Myhal, N., and Kessler, Z. (1989). Effects of maternal hormones on 'timity' and attraction to pup-related odors in femal rats. *Physiol. Behav.* **46**, 449–453.

Fleming, A. S., Gavarth, K., and Sarker, J. (1992). Effects of transections to the vomeronasal nerves or to the main olfactory bulbs on the initiation and long-term retention of maternal behavior in primiparous rats. *Behav. Neural Biol.* **57**, 177–188.

Fleming, A. S., Corter, C., Franks, P., Schneider, B., and Steiner, M. (1993). Postpartum factors related to mother's attraction to newborn infant odors. *Dev. Psychobiol.* **26**, 115–132.

Fleming, A. S., Ruble, D., Krieger, H., and Wong, P. Y. (1997a). Hormonal and experiential correlates of maternal responsiveness during pregnancy and the puerperium in human mothers. *Horm. Behav.* **31**, 145–158.

Fleming, A. S., Steiner, M., and Corter, C. (1997b). Cortisol, hedonics, and maternal responsiveness in human mothers. *Horm. Behav.* **32**, 85–98.

Freeman, W. J., and Kozma, R. (2000). Local-global interactions and the role of mesoscopic (intermediate-range) elements in brain dynamics. *Behav. Brain Sci.* **23**, 401–408.

French, J. A. (1987). Synchronization of ovarian cycles within and between social-groups in golden lion tamarins (leontopithecus-rosalia). *Am. J. Primatol.* **12**, 469–478.

French, J. A., and Schaffner, C. M. (2000). Contextual influences on sociosexual behavior in monogamous primates. *In* "Reproduction in Context: Social and Environmental Influences in Reproduction" (K. Wallen and J. E. Schneider, eds.), pp. 325–420. MIT Press, Cambridge, MA.

French, J. A., Abbott, D. H., and Snowdon, C. T. (1984). The effect of social and environment on estrogen excretion, scent marking, and sociosexual behavior in tamarins (*Saguinus oedipus*). *Am. J. Primatol.* **6**, 155–167.

Freud, S. (1895). Project for a scientific psychology. *In* "Standard Edition of the Complete Psychological Works of Sigmund Freud" (J. Strachey, ed.), Vol. 1. Hogarth Press, London.

Fukushima, S., Akane, A., Matsubara, K., and Shiono, H. (1991). Simultaneous determination of testosterone and androstadienone (sex attractant) in human plasma by gas chromatography-mass spectrometry with high-resolution selected-ion monitoring. *J. Chromatogr.* **565**, 35–44.

Fuller, G., and Burger, P. (1990). Nervus terminalis (cranial nerve zero) in the adult human. *Clin. Neuropathol.* **9**, 279–283.

Gaafar, H. A., Tantawy, A. A., Melis, A. A., Hennawy, D. M., and Shehata, H. M. (1998). The vomeronasal (Jacobson's) organ in adult humans: Frequency of occurrence and enzymatic study. *Acta Oto-Laryngol.* **118**, 409–412.

Gadlin, W., and Fiss, H. (1967). Odor as a facilitator of the effects of subliminal stimulation. *J. Pers. Soc. Psychol.* **7**, 95–100.

Gangestad, S. W., and Thornhill, R. (1998). Menstrual cycle variation in women's preferences for the scent of symmetrical men. *Proc. R. Soc. London* **265**, 927–933.

Gans, S. E., and McClintock, M. K. (1993). Individual differences among rats in the timing of the preovulatory LH surge are predicted by lordosis reflex intensity. *Horm. Behav.* **27**, 403–417.

Garcia-Velasco, J., and Mondragon, M. (1991). The incidence of the vomeronasal organ in 1000 human subjects and its possible clinical significance. *J. Steroid Biochem. Mol. Biol.* **39**, 561–563.

Garnerio, P., Tsouderos, Y., Marton, I., Pelissier, C., Varin, C., and Delmas, P. D. (1999). Effects of intranasal 17β-estradiol on bone turnover and serum insulin-like growth factor I in postmenopausal women. *J. Clin. Endocrinol. Metab.* **84**, 2390–2397.

Getchell, T. V. (1991). "Smell and Taste in Health and Disease," pp. 817–827. Raven Press, New York.

Gheusi, G., Bluthe, R.-M., Goodall, G., and Dantzer, R. (1994). Social and individual recognition in rodents: Methodological aspects and neurobiological bases. *Behav. Processes* **33**, 59–88.

Gilbert, A. N., and Wysocki, C. J. (1987). The National Geographic smell survey: Effects of age are heterogenous. *Ann. NY Acad. Science* **561**, 12–28.

Gilbert, A. N., and Wysocki, C. J. (1991). Quantitative assessment of olfactory experience during pregnancy. *Psychosom. Med.* **53**, 693–700.

Gilbert, A. N., Greenberg, M. S., and Beachamp, G. K. (1989). Sex, handedness and side of nose modulate human odor perception. *Neuropsychologia* **27**, 505–511, 1313.

Gilbert, A. N., Knasko, S. C., and Sabini, J. (1997). Sex differrences in task performance associated with attention to ambient odor. *Arch. Environ. Health* **52**, 195–199.

Giorgi, D., Friedman, C., Trask, B. J., and Rouquier, S. (2000). Characterization of nonfunctional VIR-like pheromone receptor sequences in human. *Genome Res.* **10**, 1979–1985.

Glass, L., and Mackey, M. C. (1988). "From Clocks to Chaos." Princeton University Press, Princeton, NJ.

Goldfoot, D. A. (1981). Olfaction, sexual behavior, and the pheromone hypothesis in rhesus monkeys: A critique. *Am. Zool.* **21**, 153–164.

Goldman, S. E. (1987). Menstrual synchrony: Social and personality factors. *J. Soc. Behav. Pers.* **2**, 243–250.

Gomez, D. M., and Newman, S. W. (1992). Differential projections of the anterior and posterior regions of the medial amygdaloid nucleus in the Syrian hamster. *J. Comp. Neurol.* **317**, 195–218.

Gonzalez, R., Orgeur, P., and Signoret, J. P. (1988). Luteinizing hormone, testosterone and cortisol responses in rams upon presentation of oestrous females in the non-breeding season. *Theriogenology* **30**, 1075–1086.

Gonzalez, R., Levý, F., Orgeur, P., and Poindron, P. (1991). Female effect in sheep. II. Role of volatile substances from the sexually receptive female; implication of the sense of smell. *Reprod. Nutr. Dev.* **31**, 103–109.

Good, P. R., Geary, N., and Engen, T. (1976). The effect of estrogen on odor detection. *Chem. Senses* **2**, 45–50.

Gower, D. B. (1972). 16-unsaturated C19 steroids. A review of their chemistry, biochemistry and possible physiological role. *J. Steroid Biochem.* **3**, 45–103.

Gower, D. B. (1981). The biosynthesis and occurrence of 16-androstenes in man. *In* "Hormones in Normal and Abnormal Human Tissues" (K. Fotherby and S. B. Pal, eds.), Vol. 1, pp. 1–27. de Gruyter, Berlin.

Gower, D. B., and Ruparelia, B. A. (1992). Olfaction in humans with special reference to odorous 16-androstenes: Their occurrence, perception and possible social, psychological and sexual impact. *J. Endocrinol.* **137**, 167–187.

Gower, D. B., Bird, S., Sharma, P., and House, F. R. (1985). Axillary 5α-androst-16-en-3-one in men and women: Relationship with olfactory acuity to odorous 16-androstenes. *Experientia* **41**, 1134–1136.

Gower, D. B., Nixon, A., and Mallet, A. I. (1988). The significance of odorous steroids in axillary odour. *In* "Perfumery: The Psychology and Biology of Fragrance" (S. Van Toller and G. H. Dodd, eds.), pp. 47–76. Chapman & Hall, London.

Gower, D. B., Holland, K. T., Mallet, A. I., Rennie, P. J., and Watkins, W. J. (1994). Comparison of 16-androstene steroid concentrations in sterile apocrine sweat and axillary secretions: Interconversions of 16-androstenes by the axillary microflora-a mechanism for axillary odour production in man? *J. Steroid Biochem. Mol. Biol.* **48**, 409–418.

Graham, C. A. (1991). Menstrual synchrony: An update and review. *Hum. Nat.* **2**, 293–311.

Graham, C. A. (1993). Letter to the editor. *Psychoneuroendocrinology* **18**, 533–534.

Graham, C. A., and McGrew, W. C. (1980). Menstrual synchrony in female undergraduates living on a coeducational campus. *Psychoneuroendocrinology* **5**, 245–252.

Graham, C. A., and McGrew, W. C. (1992). Social factors and menstrual synchrony in a population of nurses. *In* "Menstrual Health in Women's Lives" (A. J. Dan and L. L. Lewis, eds.), Chapter 23, pp. 246–253. University of Illinois Press, Chicago.

Graham, C. A., Janssen, E., and Sanders, S. (2000). Effects of fragrance on female sexual arousal and mood across the menstrual cycle. *Psychophysiology* **37**, 76–84.

Grammer, K. (1993). 5-α-androst-16-en-3α-on: A male pheromone? A brief report. *Ethol. Sociobiol.* **14**, 201–207.

Grau, G. A. (1976). Olfaction and reproduction in ungulates. *In* "Mammalian Olfaction, Reproductive Processes, and Behavior" (R. L. Doty, ed.), pp. 219–241. Academic Press, London.

Greene, R. S., Downing, D. T., Pochi, P. E., and Strauss, J. S. (1970). Anatomical variation in the composition of human skin surface lipid. *J. Invest. Dermatol.* **54**, 240–247.

Greenstein, J. S. (1965). Armpitin. *Can. Med. Assoc. J.* **93**, 1351.

Griffin, D. R. (2001). "Animal Minds: Beyond Cognition to Consciousness." University of Chicago Press, Chicago.

Griffith, N. M., and Patterson, R. L. S. (1970). Human olfactory responses to 5x-androst-16-en-3-one-principal component of boar taint. *J. Sci. Food Agric.* **21**, 4–6.

Grosser, B. I., Monti-Bloch, L., Jennings-White, C., and Berliner, D. L. (2000). Behavioral and electrophysiological effects of androstadienone, a human pheromone. *Psychoneuroendocrinology* **25**, 289–299.

Gu, J., Dudley, C., Su, T., Spink, D. C., Zhang, Q. Y., Moss, R. L., and Ding, X. (1999). Cytochrome P450 and steroid hydroxylase activity in mouse olfactory and vomeronasal mucosa. *Biochem. Biophys. Res. Commun.* **266**, 262–267.

Gudermuth, D. F., McClintock, M. K. K., and Moltz, H. (1984). Suppression of postpartum fertility in pairs of female rats sharing the same nesting environment. *Physiol. Behav.* **33**, 257–260.

Gustavson, A. R., Dawson, M. E., and Bonett, D. G. (1987). Androstenol, a putative human pheromone, affects human (Homo sapiens) male choice performance. *J. Comp. Psychol.* **101**, 210–212.

Gustin, M. K., and McCracken, G. F. (1987). Scent recognition between females and pups in the bat *Tadarida brasiliensis mexicana. Anim. Behav.* **35**, 13–19.

Halasz, N. (1990). "The Vertebrate Olfactory System. Chemical Neuroanatomy, Function and Development." Akadémiai Kiadó, Budapest.

Haller, J., Makara, G. B., and Kruk, M. R. (1998). Catecholaminergic involvement in the control of aggression: Hormones, the peripheral sympathetic, and central noradrenergic systems. *Neurosci. Biobehav. Rev.* **22**, 85–67.

Halpin, Z. T. (1986). Individual odors among mammals: Origins and functions. *Adv. Study Behav.* **16**, 39–70.

Harrington, A., and Rosario, V. (1992). Olfaction and the primitive: Nineteenth-century medical thinking on olfaction. *In*

"Science of Olfaction" (M. J. Serby and K. L. Chobor, eds.), pp. 3–27. Springer-Verlag, New York.

Harrington, J. P. (1931). Karuk texts. *Int. J. Am. Linguistics* **6**, 121–161, 194–226.

Harrison, V. (1997). Family emotional process, reactivity, and patterns of ovulation. *Fam. Syst.* **4**, 49–62.

Hatton, G. I., and Yang, Q. Z. (1990). Activation of excitatory amino acid inputs to supraoptic neurons. I. Induced increases in dye-coupling in lactating, but not virgin or male rats. *Brain Res.* **513**, 264–269.

Hediger, H. (1951). "Observations sur la psychologie animale dans les Parcs Nationaux du Congo Belge." Institut des Parcs Nationaux du Congo Belge, Brussels.

Hedrick, P. W., and Black, F. L. (1997). HLA and mate selection: No evidence in South Amerindians. *Am. J. Hum. Genet.* **61**, 505–511.

Henkin, R. I. (1975). The role of adrenal corticosteroids in sensory processes. *In* "Handbook of Physiology" (R. O. Greep and E. B. Astwood, eds.), Sect. 7, pp. 209–230. American Physiological Society, Washington, DC.

Henkin, R. I., and Bartter, F. C. (1966). Studies on olfactory threshold in normal man and in patients with adrenal cortical insufficiency: The role of adrenal cortical steroids and of serum sodium concentration. *J. Clin. Invest.* **45**, 1631–1639.

Hennessy, M. B., Coe, C. L., Mendoza, S. P., Lowe, E. L., and Levine, S. (1978). Scent-marking and olfactory investigatory behavior in the squirrel monday (*Saimiri sciureus*). *Behav. Biol.* **24**, 57–67.

Hepper, P. G. (1987). The amniotic fluid: An important priming role in kin recognition. *Anim. Behav.* **35**, 1343–1346.

Herberhold, C., Genkin, H., Brändle, L. W., Leitner, H., and Wöllmer, W. (1982). Olfactory threshold and hormone levels during the human menstrual cycle. *In* "Olfaction and Endocrine Regulation" (W. Breipohl, ed.), pp. 343–351. IRL Press, London.

Herrada, G., and Dulac, C. (1997). A novel family of putative pheromone receptors in mammals with a topographically organized and sexually dimorphic distribution. *Cell (Cambridge, Mass.)* **90**, 763–773.

Herz, R., and Cahill, E. (1997). Differential use of sensory information in sexual behavior as a function of gender. *Hum. Nat.* **8**, 275–289.

Herz, R. S., and Cupchick, G. C. (1992). An experimental characterization of odor-evoked memories. *Chem. Senses* **17**, 519–528.

Hodgson, E. S., Lettvin, J. Y., and Roeder, K. D. (1955). Physiology of a primary chemoreceptor unit. *Science* **122**, 417–418.

Holy, T. E., Dulac, C., and Meister, M. (2000). Responses of vomeronasal neurons to natural stimuli. *Science* **289**, 1569–1572.

Hood, H. L., Wickett, R. R., and Bronaugh, R. L. (1996). In vitro percutaneous absorption of the fragrance ingredient musk xylol. *Food Chem. Toxicol.* **34**, 483–488.

Hradecky, P. (1989). Possible induction by estrous cos of pheromone production in penmates. *J. Chem. Ecol.* **15**, 1067–1076.

Hudson, R., and Distel, H. (1983). Nipple location by newborn rabbits: Behavioral evidence for pheromonal guidance. *Physiol. Behav.* **85**, 260–275.

Hudson, R., and Distel, H. (1986). Pheromonal release of suckling in rabbits does not depend on the vomeronasal organ. *Physiol. Behav.* **37**, 123–128.

Hugdahl, K. (1995). "Psychophysiology: The Mind-Body Perspective." Harvard University Press, Cambridge, MA.

Huggins, G. R., and Preti, G. (1976). Volatile constituents of human vaginal secretions. *Am. J. Obstet. Gynecol.* **126**, 129–136.

Huggins, G. R., and Preti, G. (1981). Vaginal odors and secretions. *Clin. Obstet. Gynecol.* **24**, 355–377.

Hummel, T., Gollisch, R., Wildt, G., and Kobal, G. (1991). Changes in olfactory perception during the menstrual cycle. *Experientia* **47**, 712–715.

Humphrey, T. (1940). The development of the olfactory and the accessory formations in human embryos and fetuses. *J. Comp. Neurol.* **73**, 431–468.

Hurst, J. L. (1989). The complex network of olfactory communication in populations of wild house mice *Mus domesticus*: Rutty-urine marking and investigation with family groups. *Anim. Behav.* **37**, 705–725.

Imaki, T., Nahon, J. L., Sawchenko, P. E., and Vale, W. W. (1989). Widespread expression of corticotripin-releasing factor messenger-RNA and immunoreactivity in the rat olfactory-bult. *Brain Res.* **496**, 35–44.

Ims, R. A. (1990). On the adaptive value of reproductive synchrony as a predator-swamping strategy. *Am. Natt.* **136**, 485–498.

Inamura, I., Matsumoto, Y., Kashiwayanagi, M., and Kurihara, K. (1999). Laminar distribution of pheromone-receptive neurons in rat vomeronasal epithelium. *J. Physiol. (London)* **517**, 731–739.

Izard, M. K. (1983). Pheromones and reproduction in domestic animals. *In* "Pheromones and Reproduction in Mammals" (J. G. Vandenbergh, ed.), pp. 253–285. Academic Press, New York.

Jacob, S., and McClintock, M. K. (1999). Volatile human steroids: What they do and don't do. *Aroma Chol. Rev.* **7**(4), 1–2.

Jacob, S., and McClintock, M. K. (2000). Psychological state and mood effects of steroidal chemosignals in women and men. *Horm. Behav.* **37**, 57–58.

Jacob, S., Zelano, B., Gungor, A., Abbott, D., Naclerio, R., and McClintock, M. K. (2000). Location and gross morphology of the nasopalatine duct in human adults. *Arch. Otolaryngol. Head Neck Surg.* **126**, 741–748.

Jacob, S., Hayreh, D. J. S., and McClintock, M. K. (2001a). Context-dependent effects of steroid chemosignals on human physiology and mood. *Physiol. Behav.* **74**, 15–27.

Jacob, S., Kinnunen, L. H., Metz, J., Cooper, M., and McClintock, M. K. (2001b). Sustained human chemosignal unconsciously alters brain function. *NeuroReport* **12**, 2391–2394.

Jacob, S., Zelano, B., Hayreh, D., and McClintock, M. K. (2002). Assessing putative human pheromones. *In* "Cognition and Olfaction" (C. Rouby, ed.). Cambridge University Press, Cambridge, UK.

Jacob, S., McClintock, M. K., Zelano, B., and Ober, C. (2002). Paternally inherited HLA alleles are associated with women's choice of male odor. *Nat. Gen.* **30**, 175–179.

Jacobson, L. (1813). "Anatomical Description of a New Organ in the Nose of Domesticated Animals" (D. Trotier and K. B. Doving, transl.). *Chem. Senses* **23**, 743–754 (1998).

Jahnke, V., and Merker, H.-J. (2000). Electron microscopic and functional aspects of the human vomeronasal organ. *Am. J. Rhinol.* **14**, 63–67.

Jarett, L. R. (1984). Psychological and biological influences on menstruation: Synchrony, cycle length and regularity. *Psychoneuroendocrinology* **9**, 21–28.

Jemiolo, B., F., A., Xie, T. M. *et al.* (1989). Puberty-affecting synthetic analogs of urinary chemosignals in the house mouse, *Mus-domesticus. Physiol. Behav.* **46**, 293–298.

Jesel, L., and Aron, C. L. (1976). The role of pheromones in the regulation of estrous cycle duration in the guinea pig. *Neuroendocrinology* **20**, 97–109.

Johannesen, E., Andreassen, H. P., and Ims, R. A. (2000). The effect of patch isolation on repductive synchrony in the root vole. *Oikos* **89**, 37–40.

Johns, M. A., Feder, H. H., Komisaruk, B. R., and Mayer, A. D. (1978). Urine-induced reflex ovulation in anovulatory rats may be a vomeronasal effect. *Nature (London)* **272**, 446–448.

Johnson, A., Josephson, R., and Hawke, M. (1985). Clinical and histological evidence for the presence of the vomeronasal (Jacobson's) organ in adult humans. *J. Otolaryngol.* **14**, 71–79.

Johnson, E. W. (1998). CaBPs and other immunohistochemical markers of the human vomeronasal system: A comparison with other mammals. *Microsc. Res. Tech.* **41**, 530–541.

Johnson, M. E., Blankschtein, D., and Langer, R. (1995). Permeation of steroids through human skin. *J. Pharm. Sci.* **84**, 1144–1146.

Johnston, R. E. (1975). Sexual excitation function of hamster vaginal secretion. *Anim. Learn. Behav.* **3**, 161–166.

Johnston, R. E. (1998). Pheromones, the vomeronasal system, and communication: From hormonal responses to individual recognition. *Ann. N.Y. Acad. Sci.* Olfaction and Taste XII **855**, 333–348.

Johnston, R. E. (2000). Chemical communication and pheromones: The types of chemical signals and the role of the vomeronasal system. *In* "The Neurobiology of Taste and Smell" (T. E. Finger, W. L. Silver, and D. Restrepo, eds.), pp. 101–127. Wiley-Liss, New York.

Jones, R. E., Brown, C. C., and Ship, J. A. (1995). Odor identification in young and elderly African-Americans and Caucasians. *Spec. Care Dentist* **15**, 138–143.

Kaisling, K.-F. (1996). Peripheral mechanisms of pheromone reception in moths. *Chem. Senses* **21**, 257–268.

Kaitz, M., and Eidelman, A. I. (1992). Smell-recognition of newborns by women who are not mothers. *Chem. Senses* **17**, 225–229.

Kamel, F., Wright, W. W., Mock, E. J., and Frankel, A. I. (1977). The influence of mating and related stimuli on plasma levels of inteinizing hormone prolactin and testosterone in the male rat. *Endocrinology (Baltimore)* **101**, 421–429.

Kanda, F., Yagi, E., Fukuda, M., Nakajima, K., Ohta, T., and Nakata, O. (1990). Elucidation of chemical compounds responsible for foot malodour. *Br. J. Dermatol.* **122**, 771–776.

Kappeler, P. M. (1998). To whom it may concern: The transimission and function of chemical signals in *Lemur catta. Behav. Ecol. Sociobiol.* **42**, 411–421.

Karg, H. (1988). Pheromones in mammals with special emphasis on the boar scent steroids, also occurring in humans and truffles. *Verh.—K. Akad. Geneeskd. Belg.* **50**, 121–138.

Karlson, P., and Lüscher, M. (1959). 'Pheromones': A new term for a class of biologically active substances. *Nature (London)* **183**, 55–56.

Katz, R. A., and Shorey, H. H. (1979). In defense of the term "pheromone." *J. Chem. Ecol.* **5**, 299–301.

Kavaliers, M., and Kinsella, D. M. (1995). Male preference for the odors of estrous female mice is reduced by the neruosteroid pregnenolone sulfate. *Brain Res.* **5**, 222–226.

Kavaliers, M., Colwell, D. D., and Choleris, E. (1998). Parasitized female mice display reduced aversive responses to the odours of infected males. *Proc. R. Soc. London* **265**, 1111–1118.

Kawakami, K., Takai-Kawakami, K., Okazaki, Y., Kurihara, H., Shimizu, Y., and Yanaihara, T. (1997). The effect of odors on human newborn infants under stress. *Infant Behav. Dev.* **20**, 531–535.

Kawata, M. (1987). Pregnancy failure and suppression by female-female interaction in enclosed populations of the red-backed vole, *Clethrionomys-rufocanus-Bedfordiae. Behav. Ecol. Sociobiol.* **20**, 89–97.

Kay, E., and Nyby, J. (1992). LiCl Aversive-conditioning has transitory effects on pheromonal responsiveness in male house mice (*Mus domesticus*). *Physiol. Behav.* **53**, 105–113.

Kay, L. M., and Freeman, W. J. (1998). Bidirectional processing in the olfactory-limbic axis during olfactory. *Behav. Sci.* **112**, 541–553.

Kay, L. M., and Laurent, G. (1999). Odor- and context-dependent modulation of mitral cell activity in behaving rats. *Nat. Neurosci.* **2**, 1003–1009.

Kay, L. M., Lancaster, L. R., and Freeman, W. J. (1996). Reaference and attractors in the olfactory system during odor recognition. *Int. J. Neural Syst.* **7**, 489–495.

Kay, M. M. B. (1979). The thymus: Clock for immunologic aging? *J. Invest. Dermatol.* **73**, 29–38.

Kelliher, K. R., Chang, Y.-M., Wersinger, S. R., and Baum, M. J. (1998). Sex difference and testosterone modulation of pheromone-induced neuronal fos in the ferret's main olfactory bulb and hypothalamus. *Biol. Reprod.* **59**, 1454–1463.

Kelliher, K. R., Liu, Y. C., Baum, M. J., and Sachs, B. D. (1999). Neuronal fos activation in olfactory bulb and forebrain of male rats having erections in the presence of inaccessible estrous femals. *Neuroscience* **92**, 1025–1033.

Kelly, D. R. (1996). When is a butterfly like an elephant? *Chem. Biol.* **3**, 595–602.

Kendrick, K. M., DaCosta, A. P. C., Broad, K. D. *et al.* (1997). Neural control of maternal behavior and olfactory recognition of offspring. *Brain Res. Bull.* **44**, 383–395.

Keverne, E. B. (1999). The vomeronasal organ. *Science* **286**, 716–720.

Khew-Goodall, Y., Grillo, M., Getchell, M. L., Danho, W., Getchell, T. V., and Margolis, F. L. (1991). Vomeromodulin, a putative pheromone transporter: Cloning, characterization, and cellular localization of a novel glycoprotein of lateral nasal gland. *Fed. Proc., Fed. Am. Soc. Exp. Biol.* **5**, 2976–2982.

Kibiuk, L. (1995). http://www.sfn.org/briefings/smell.

Kirk-Smith, M., and Booth, D. A. (1980). Effect of androstenone on choice of location in others' presence. *In* "Olfaction and Taste VII" (H. Van der Starre, ed.), pp. 397–400. IRL Press, London.

Kirk-Smith, M., Booth, D. A., Carroll, D., and Davies, P. (1978). Human social attitudes affected by androstenol. *Res. Commun. Psychol., Psychiatry Behav.* **3**, 379–384.

Kirkwood, R. N., Hughes, P. E., and Booth, W. D. (1983). The influence of boar-related odours on puberty attainment in gilts. *Anim. Prod.* **36**, 131–136.

Kjær, I., and Fischer-Hansen, B. (1996). Luteinizing hormone-releasing hormone and innervation pathways in human prenatal nasal submucosa: Factors of importance in evaluating Kallmann's syndrome. *Acta Pathol. Microbiol. mmunol. Scand.* **104**, 680–688.

Kline, J. P., Schwartz, G. E., Dikman, Z. V., and Bell, I. R. (2000). Electroencephalagraphic registration of low concentrations of isoamyl acetate. *Consciousness Cogn.* **9**, 50–65.

Kloek, J. (1961). The smell of some steroid sex-hormones and their metabolites. Reflections and experiments concerning the significance of smell for the mutual relation of sexes. *Psychiatr. Neurol. Neurochir.* **64**, 309–344.

Knasko, S. C. (1992). Ambient odor's effects on creativity, mood, and perceived health. *Chem. Senses* **17**, 27–35.

Knasko, S. C. (1995). Pleasant odors and congruency: Effects on approach behavior. *Chem. Senses* **20**, 479–487.

Knasko, S. C., Gilbert, A. N., and Sabini, J. (1990). Emotional state, physical well-being and performance in the presence of feigned ambient odor. *J. Appl. Physiol.* **20**, 1345–1357.

Knight, C. (1991). "Blood Relations. Menstruation and the Origins of Culture." Yale University Press, New Haven, CT.

Knuppen, R., and Breuer, H. (1963). Biogenese von Östratetraenol Biem Menschen. *Acta Endocrinol. (Capenhagen)* **42**, 129–134.

Kodis, M., Moran, D., and Houy, D. (1998). "Love Scents." Dutton, New York.

Koelega, H. S. (1994). Sex differences in olfactory sensitivity and the problem of the generality of smell acuity. *Percept. Mot. Skills* **78**, 203–213.

Koelega, H. S., and Köster, E. P. (1974). Some experiments on sex differences in odor perception. *Annu. N.Y. Acad. Sci.* **237**, 234–246.

Köster, E. P. (1975). Human psychophysics in olfaction. *In* "Methods in Olfactory Research" (D. G. Moulton, A. Turk, and J. W. J. Johnston, eds.), pp. 345–374. Academic Press, London.

Köster, E. P., and Degel, J. (2000). Performance effects of subconsciously perceived odors: The influence of pleasantness, familiarity and odor identification. *Chem. Senses* **25**, 622.

Kraft-Ebing, R. (1965). "Psychopathia Sexualis," p. 21. Bell Publ., New York.

Kreutzer, E. W., and Jafek, B. W. (1980). The vomeronasal organ of Jacobson in the human embryo and fetus. *Otolaryngol. Head Neck Surg.* **88**, 119–123.

Kumar, K. R., and Archunan, G. (1999). Influence of the state of the cycle on olfactory sensitivity in laboratory mice. *Indian J. Exp. Biol.* **37**, 317–318.

Kumar, K. R., Kannan, S., and Archunan, G. (1999). Estrus phase appears to be maximum sensitive in olfactory memory of mouse. *Biol. Notes* **1**, 33.

Kumar, K. R., Archunan, G., Jeyaraman, R., and Narasimhan, S. (2000). Chemical characterization of bovine urine with special reference to oestrus. *Vet. Res. Commun.* **24**, 445–454.

Kwan, T. K., Trafford, D. J., Makin, H. L. J., Mallet, A. I., and Gower, D. B. (1992). GC-MS studies of 16-androstenes and other C19 steroids in human semen. *J. Steroid Biochem. Mol. Biol.* **43**, 549–556.

Labows, J. N. (1988). Odor detection, generation and etiology in the axilla. *In* "Antiperspirants and Deodorants" (C. Felger and K. Laden, eds.), pp. 321–343. Dekker, New York.

Labows, J. N., and Wysocki, C. J. (1984). Individual differences in odor perception. *Perfumer Flavorist* **9**, 21–26.

Labows, J. N., McGinley, K. J., Webster, G., and Leyden, J. J. (1979). Characteristic gamma-lactone production of the genus pityrosporum. *Appl. Environ. Microbiol.* **38**, 412–415.

Lambin, X. (1993). Determinants of the synchrony of reproduction in Townsend voles, *Microtus townsendii. Oikos* **67**, 107–113.

Lamond, D. R. (1959). Effect of stimulation derived from other animals of the same species on oestrus cycles in mice. *J. Endocrinol.* **18**, 343–349.

Larriva-Sahd, J., Rondan, A., Orozco-Estevez, H., and Sanchez-Robles, M. R. (1993). Evidence of a direct projection of the vomeronasal organ to the medial preoptic nucleus and hypothalamus. *Neurosci. Lett.* **163**, 45–49.

Laska, M., and Teubner, P. (1999). Olfactory discrimination ability for homologous series of aliphatic alcohols and aldehydes. *Chem. Senses* **24**, 263–270.

Laska, M., Kich, B., Heid, B., and Hudson, R. (1996). Failure to demonstrate systematic changes in olfactory perception in the course of pregnancy: A longitudinal study. *Chem. Senses* **21**, 567–571.

Laurent, G. (1999). A systems perspective on early olfactory coding. *Science* **286**, 723–728.

Lawless, H. T., Thomas, C. J., and Johnston, M. (1995). Variation in odor thresholds for 1-carvone and cineole and correlations with suprathreshold intensity ratings. *Chem. Senses* **20**, 9–17.

Lazar, J., Prestwich, G. D., and Rasmussen, L. E. L. (2000). Urinary and trunk mucus protein carriers of (Z)-7-dodecenyl acetate, the sex pheromone of the Asian elephant. *Chem. Senses* **25**, 603.

Lee, S., and van der Boot, L. (1955). Spontaneous pseudopregnancy in mice. *Acta Physiol. Pharmacol. Neerl.* **4**, 442–443.

Lee, T. M., Halpern, B., Lee, C., and Moltz, H. (1982). Reduced prolactin binding to liver membranes during pheromonal emission in the rat. *Pharmacol., Biochem. Behav.* **17**, 1149–1154.

Lee, T. M., and Moltz, H. (1984). The maternal pheromone and deoxycholic-acid in relation to brain myelin in the preweanling rat. *Physiol. Behav.* **33**, 931–935.

LeFevre, J., and McClintock, M. K. K. (1988). Reproductive senescence in female rats: A longitudinal study of individual differences in estrous cycles and behavior. *Biol. Reprod.* **38**, 780–789.

LeFevre, J., and McClintock, M. K. K. (1991). Isolation accelerates reproductive senescence and alters its predictors in female rats. *Horm. Behav.* **25**, 258–272.

LeFevre, J., and McClintock, M. K. K. (1992). Social modulation of behavioral reproductive senescence in female rats. *Physiol. Behav.* **52**, 603–608.

Lehrner, J. P., Walla, P., Laska, M., and Deecke, L. (1999). Different forms of human odor memory: A developmental study. *Neurosci. Lett.* **272**, 17–20.

Leinders-Zufall, T., Lane, A. P., Puche, A. C., Ma, W., Novotny, M. V., Shipley, M. T., and Zufall, F. (2000). Ultrasensitive pheromone detection by mammalian vomeronasal neurons. *Nature (London)* **405**, 792–796.

Le Magnen, J. (1952). Les phénomènes olfacto-sexuels chez le rat blanc. *Arch. Sci. Physiol.* **6**, 295–331.

Leon, M., and Woodside, B. (1983). Energetic limits on reproduction: Maternal food intake. *Physiol. Behav.* **30**, 945–957.

Levin, J. M., Ross, M. H., Mendelson, J. H., Mello, N. K., Cohen, B. M., and Renshaw, P. F. (1998). Sex differences in blood-oxygenation-level-dependent functional MRI with primary visual stimulation. *Am. J. Psychiatry* **155**, 434–436.

Lévy, F., Kendrick, K. M., Goode, J. A., Guevara-Guzman, R., and Keverne, E. B. (1995a). Oxytocin and vasopressin release in the olfactory bulb of parturient ewes: Changes with maternal experience and effects on acetylcholine y-aminobutyric acid, glutamate and noradrenaline release. *Brain Res.* **669**, 197–206.

Lévy, F., Locatelli, A., Piketty, V., Tillet, Y., and Poindron, P. (1995b). Involvement of the main but not the accessory olfactory system in maternal behavior of primiparous and multiparous ewes. *Physiol. Behav.* **57**, 97–104.

Leyden, J. J., Nordstrom, K. M., and McGinley, K. J. (1991). Cutaneous microbiology. *In* "Physiology, Biochemistry and Molecular Biology of the Skin" (L. A. Goldsmith, ed.), pp. 1403–1424. Oxford University Press, New York.

Linman, E. R., Corey, D. P., and Dulac, C. (1999). TRP2: A candidate transduction channel for mammalian pheromone sensory signaling. *Proc. Natl. Acad. Sci. U.S.A.* **96**, 5791–5796.

Little, B. B., Guzick, D. S., Malina, R. M., and Rocha Ferreira, M. D. (1989). Environmental influences cause menstrual synchrony, not pheromones. *Am. J. Hum. Biol.* **1**, 53–57.

Lloyd-Thomas, A., and Keverne, E. B. (1982). Role of the brain and accessory olfactory system in the block to pregnancy in mice. *Neuroscience* **7**, 907–913.

Lomas, D. E., and Keverne, E. B. (1982). Role of the vomeronsal organ and prolactin in the acceleration of puberty in female mice. *J. Reprod. Fertil.* **66**, 101–107.

Lorig, T. S. (1999). On the similarity of ododr and language preception. *Neurosci. Biobehav. Rev.* **23**, 391–398.

Lorig, T. S., and Schwartz, G. E. (1988). Brain and odor: I. Alteration of human EEG by odor administration. *Psychobiology* **16**, 281–284.

Lorig, T. S., Herman, K. B., Schwartz, G. E., and Cain, W. S. (1990). EEG activity during the administration of low concentration odors. *Bull. Psychonom. Soc.* **28**, 405–408.

Lorig, T. S., Huffman, E., DeMartino, A., and DeMarco, J. (1991). The effects of low concentration odors on EEG activity and behavior. *Psychophysiology* **5**, 69–77.

Loughry, W. J., and McCracken, G. F. (1991). Factors influencing female-pup scent recognition in Mexican free-tailed bats. *J. Mammal.* **72**, 624–626.

Loumaye, E., Thorner, J., and Catt, K. J. (1982). Yeast mating pheromone activates mammalian gonadotrophs: Evolutionary conservation of a reproductive hormone? *Science* **218**, 1323–1325.

Louveau, I., Bonneau, M., and Gower, D. B. (1991). Biosynthesis of 16-androstene steroids and testosterone by porcine testis tissue in vitro: Effect of age and relationships with fat 5α-androstenone levels in vivo. *Acta Endocrinol. (Copenhagen)* **125**, 526–531.

Lundstrom, N. J., Olsson, M. J., and Larsson, M. (2000). Effects of the putative pheromone 4,16-androstadien-3-one on psychological and psychophysiological variables: Weak evidence. *Chem. Senses* **25**, 613.

Ma, W., and Klemm, W. R. (1997a). Bovine milk volatiles as related to reproductive cycle. *J. Dairy Sci.* **80**, 3227–3233.

Ma, W., and Klemm, W. R. (1997b). Variations of urinary volatiles during the equine estrous cycle. *Vet. Res. Commun.* **21**, 437–446.

Ma, W., Clement, B. A., and Klemm, W. R. (1996). Cyclic changes in volatile constituents of bovine vaginal secretions. *J. Chem. Ecol.* **21**, 1895–1906.

Ma, W., Zhongshan, M., and Novotny, M. V. (1998). Role of the adrenal gland and adrenal-mediated chemosignals in suppression of estrus in the house mouse: The lee-boot effect revisted. *Biol. Reprod.* **59**, 1317–1320.

MacFarlane, A. (1975). Olfaction in the development of social preferences in the human neonate. *Ciba Found. Symp.* **33**, 103–117.

Mackay-Sim, A. (1991). Changes in smell and taste function in thyroid, parathyroid, and adrenal disease. *In* "Smell and Taste in Health and Science" (T. V. Getchell, R. L. Doty, L. M. Bartoshuk, and Snow, J. B., JR., eds.), pp. 817–827. Raven Press, New York.

Mackay-Sim, A., and Laing, D. G. (1980). Discrimination of odors from stressed rates by nonstressed rats. *Physiol. Behav.* **24**, 699–704.

Mackay-Sim, A., and Laing, D. G. (1981a). Rats' responses to blood and body odors of stressed and non-stressed conspecifics. *Physiol. Behav.* **27**, 503–510.

Mackay-Sim, A., and Laing, D. G. (1981b). The sources of odors from stressed rats. *Physiol. Behav.* **27**, 511–513.

MacLean, P. D. (1949). Psychosomatic disease and the "visceral brain": Recent developments bearing on the Papez theory of emotion. *Psychosom. Med.* **11**, 338–353.

Mafra-Neto, A., and Cardé, R. (1994). Fine-scale stucture of pheromone plumes modulates upwind orientation of flying moths. *Nature (London)* **369**, 142.

Mair, R. G., Bouffard, J. A., Engen, T., and Morton, T. H. (1978). Olfactory sensitivity during the menstrual cycle. *Sens. Processes* **2**, 90–98.

Maiworm, R. E., and Langthaler, W. U. (1992). Influence of androstenol and androsterone on the evaluation of men of varying attractiveness levels. *In* "Chemical Signals in Vertebrates" (D. Müller-Schwarze and R. L. Doty, eds.), Vol. 6, pp. 575–579. Plenum Press, New York.

Maiworm, R. E., and Langthaler, W. U. (1998). Communication by odor—the influence of body odor on the attractiveness of men. *In* "Fragrances: Beneficial and Adverse Effects" (P. J. Frosch, J. D. Johanse, and I. R. White, eds.), pp. 28–35. Springer, Berlin.

Maken, D. S., and Hennessy, M. B. (1999). Rehousing periadolescent male guinea pigs (*Cavia porcellus*) apart from their mothers for 24 hours increases maternally directed sexual behavior and plasma testosterone. *J. Comp. Psychol.* **113**, 435–442.

Makin, J. W., and Porter, R. H. (1989). Attractiveness of lactating females' breast odors to neonates. *Child Dev.* **60**, 803–810.

Malenfant, S. A., Barry, M., and Fleming, A. S. (1991). Effects of cyclohexamide on the retention of olfactory learning and experience effects in postpartum rats. *Physiol. Behav.* **49**, 289–294.

Mallet, A. I., Nixon, A., Ruparelia, B. A., and Gower, D. B. (1988). Analysis of odourous 16-androstene steroids in human axillary hair and saliva. *In* "Advances in Steroid Analysis" (S. Gorog, ed.), pp. 287–291. Akadémiai Kiadó, Budapest.

Manning, C. J., Wakeland, E. K., and Potts, W. K. (1992). Communal nesting patterns in mice implicate MHC genes in kin recognition. *Nature (London)* **360**, 581–583.

Marchlewska-Koj, A., and Zacharczuk-Kakietek, M. (1990). Acute increase in plasma corticosterone level in female mice evoked by pheromones. *Physiol. Behav.* **48**, 577–580.

Marchlewska-Koj, A., Kruczek, M., Olejniczak, P., and Pochron, E. (1998). Involvement of main and vomeronasal systems in modification of oestrous cycle in female laboratory mice. *Acta Theriol.* **43**, 235–240.

Marlier, L., Schaal, B., and Soussignan, R. (1997). Orientation responses to biological odours in the human newborn. Initital pattern and postnatal plasticity. *Neuroscience* **320**, 999–1005.

Marlier, L., Schaal, B., and Soussignan, R. (1998). Neonatal responsiveness to the odor of amniotic and lacteal fluids: A test of perinatal chemosensory continuity. *Child Dev.* **69**, 611–623.

Martin, I. G. (1980). "Homeochemic," intraspecific chemical signal. *J. Chem. Ecol.* **6**, 517–519.

Matsunani, H., and Buck, L. B. (1997). A multigene family encoding a diverse array of putative pheromone receptors in mammals. *Cell (Cambridge, Mass.)* **90**, 775–784.

Matteo, S. (1987). The effect of job stress and job interdependency on menstrual cycle length, regularity and synchrony. *Psychoneuroendocrinology* **12**, 467–476.

McCarthy, F. D. (1960). The string figures of Yirrkalla. *In* "Records of the American-Australian Scientific Expedition to Arnhem Land. Anthropology and Nutrition" (C. P. Mountford, ed.), Vol. 2. Melbourne University Press, Melbourne.

McClintock, M. K. (2000). Human pheromones: Primers, releasers, signalers or modulators? *In* "Reproduction in Context" (K. Wallen and J. E. Schneider, eds.), pp. 355–420. MIT Press, Cambridge, MA.

McClintock, M. K. (1971). Menstrual synchrony and suppression. *Nature (London)* **229**, 244–245.

McClintock, M. K. (1978). Estrous synchrony in the rat and its mediation by airborne chemical communication (*Rattus norvegicus*). *Horm. Behav.* **11**, 414–418.

McClintock, M. K. (1981a). Simplicity from complexity: A naturalistic approach to behavior and neuroendocrine function. *In* "New Directions for Methodology of Social and Behavioral Science" (I. Silverman, ed.), Vol. 8, pp. 1–19. Jossey-Bass, San Francisco.

McClintock, M. K. (1981b). Social control of the ovarian cycle and the function of estrous synchrony. *Am. Zool.* **21**, 243–256.

McClintock, M. K. (1983a). The behavioral endocrinology of rodents: A functional analysis. *BioScience* **33**, 574–577.

McClintock, M. K. (1983b). Modulation of the estrous cycle by pheromones from pregnant and lactating rats. *Biol. Reprod.* **28**, 823–829.

McClintock, M. K. (1983c). Pheromonal regulation of the ovarian cycle: Enhancement, suppression, and synchrony. *In* "Pheromones and Reproduction in Mammals" (J. G. Vandenbergh, ed.), pp. 113–149. Academic Press, New York.

McClintock, M. K. (1983d). Synchronizing ovarian and birth cycles by female pheromones. *In* "Chemical Signals in Vertebrates" (D. Müller-Schwarze and R. Silverstein, eds.), pp. 159–178. Plenum Press, New York.

McClintock, M. K. (1984a). Estrous synchrony: Modulation of ovarian cycle length by female pheromones. *Physiol. Behav.* **32**, 701–705.

McClintock, M. K. (1984b). Group mating in the domestic rat as a context for sexual selection: Consequences for analysis of sexual behavior and neuroendocrine responses. *Adv. Study Behav.* **14**, 1–50.

McClintock, M. K. (1987). "A Functional Approach to the Behavioral Endocrinology of Rodents." Prentice-Hall, New York.

McClintock, M. K. (1998a). On the nature of mammalian and human pheromones. *Ann. N.Y. Acad. Sci.* **855**, 390–392.

McClintock, M. K. (1998b). Whither menstrual synchrony? *Annu. Rev. Sex. Res.* **9**, 77–95.

McClintock, M. K. (1999). Pheromones and the regulation of ovulation. *Nature (London)* **401**, 232–233.

McClintock, M. K., and Adler, N. T. (1978). Induction of persistent estrus by airborne chemical communication among female rats. *Horm. Behav.* **11**, 414–418.

McClintock, M. K., Jacob, S., Zelano, B., and Hayreh, D. J. S. (2001). Pheromones and vasanas: The functions of social chemosignals. *In* "Evolutionary Psychology and Motivation" (J. A. French, A. C. Kamil, and D. W. Leger, eds.), Vol. 48, pp. 75–112. University of Nebraska Press, Lincoln.

McCollough, P. A., Owen, J. W., and Pollak, E. I. (1981). Does androstenol [sic] affect emotion? *Ethol. Sociobiol.* **2**, 85–88.

McDonnell, S. M., Hinrichs, K., Cooper, W. L., and Kenney, R. M. (1988). Use of an androgenized mare as an aid in detection of estrus in mares. *Theriogenology* **30**, 547–553.

McGlone, J. J. (1984). Olfactory cues and pig agonistic behavior: Evidence for a submissive pheromone. *Physiol. Behav.* **34**, 195–198.

Meilgaard, M., Civille, G. V., and Carr, B. T. (1991). "Sensory Evaluation Techniques." CRC Press, Boca Raton, FL.

Meisami, E., and Bathnager, K. P. (1998). Structure and diversity in mammalian accessory olfactory bulb. *Microsc. Res. Tech.* **43**, 476–499.

Meisami, E., and Safari, L. (1981). A quantitative study of the effects of early unilateral olfactory deprivation on the number and distribution of mitral and tufted cells and of glomeruli in the rat olfactory bulb. *Brain Res.* **221**, 81–107.

Melrose, D. R., Reed, H. C., and Patterson, R. L. S. (1971). Androgen steriods associated with boar odour as an aid to the detection of oestrus in pig artificial insemination. *Br. Vet. J.* **127**, 497–502.

Mennella, J. A., Blumberg, M., McClintock, M. K., and Moltz, H. (1990). Inter-litter competition and communal nursing among Norway rats: Advantages of birth synchrony. *Behav. Ecol. Sociobiol.* **27**, 183–190.

Mennella, J. A., and Beauchamp, G. K. (1991). The transfer of alcohol to human milk. *N. Engl. J. Med.* **325**, 981–985.

Mennella, J. A., and Moltz, H. (1988). Infanticide in the male rat—the role of the vomeronasal organ. *Physiol. Behav.* **42**, 303–306.

Mennella, J. A., and Moltz, H. (1989). Pheromonal emission by pregnant rats protects against infanticide by nulliparous conspecifics. *Physiol. Behav.* **46**, 591–595.

Mennella, J. A., Johnson, A. L., and Beauchamp, G. K. (1995). Garlic ingestion by pregnant women alters the odor of amniotic fluid. *Chem. Senses* **20**, 207–209.

Mennella, J. A., Jagnow, C., and Beauchamp, G. K. (2001). Prenatal and postnatal flavor learning by human infants. *Pediatrics* **107**(6), E88.

Meredith, M. (1991a). Sensory processing the main and accessory olfactory systems: Comparisons and contrasts. *J. Steroid Biochem. Mol. Biol.* **39**, 601–614.

Meredith, M. (1991b). Vomeronasal damage not nasopalatine duct damage causes behavior deficits In male hamsters. *Chem. Senses* **16**, 155–168.

Meredith, M., and Fernandez-Fewell, G. (1994). Vomeronasal system, LHRH, and sex behaviour. *Psychoneuroendocrinology* **19**, 657–72.

Merkx, J., Slob, A. K., and Bosch, J. J. V. D. W. T. (1988). The role of the preputial glands in sexual attractivity of the female rat. *Physiol. Behav.* **42**, 59–64.

Messent, P. R. (1976). Female hormones and behavior. *In* "Exploring Sex Differences" (B. Lloyd and J. Archer, eds.), pp. 185–212. Academic Press, London.

Michael, R. P., Bonsall, R. W., and Zumpe, D. (1976). Letters to the editor: "Lack of effects of vaginal fatty acids, etc." A reply to Goodfoot *et al. Horm. Behav.* **7**, 365–367.

Michel, C. (1993). Induction of estrus in cats by photoperiodic manipulations and social-stimuli. *Lab. Anim.* **27**, 278–280.

Molina, A. L. C., Ceballos, R. M., and Sanchez, V. D. (2000). Chemical communication in primates. *Salud Ment.* **23**, 25–32.

Moltz, H. (1984). Commentary—the maternal pheromone, not maternal odors, as an innate stimulus for the preweanling rat—a reply. *Dev. Psychobiol.* **17**, 325–326.

Moltz, H., and Lee, T. M. (1981). The maternal pheromone of the rat: Identity and functional significance. *Physiol. Behav.* **26**, 301–306.

Moltz, H., and Leon, M. (1973). Stimulus control of the maternal pheromone in the lactating rat. *Physiol. Behav.* **10**, 69–71.

Mombaerts, P., Wang, F., Dulac, C., Chao, S. K., Nemes, A., Mendelsohn, M., Edmondson, J., and Axel, R. (1996). Visualizing an olfactory sensory map. *Cell (Cambridge, Mass.)* **87**, 675–686.

Monier-Williams, M. (1899). "A Sanskrit-English Dictionary." Oxford University Press, Oxford.

Montagna, W., and Parakkal, P. F. (1974). "The Structure and Function of Skin." Academic Press, New York.

Monti-Bloch, L., and Grosser, B. I. (1991). Effect of putative pheromones on the electrical activity of the human vomeronasal organ and the olfactory epithelium. *J. Steroid Biochem. Mol. Biol.* **39**, 573–582.

Monti-Bloch, L., Jennings-White, C., Dolber, D. S., and Berliner, D. L. (1994). The human vomeronasal system. *Psychoneuroendocrinology* **19**, 673–686.

Monti-Bloch, L., Diaz-Sanchez, V., Jennings-White, C., and Berliner, D. L. (1998). Modulation of serum testosterone and autonomic function through stimulation of the male human vomeronasal organ (VNO) with pregna-4,20-diene-3,6-dione. *J. Steroid Biochem. Mol. Biol.* **65**, 237–242.

Moore, J. G., Krotoszynski, B. K., and O'Neill, H. J. (1984). Fecal odorgrams. A method for partial reconstruction of ancient and modern diets. *Dig. Dis. Sci.* **29**, 907–911.

Mora, O. A., Sanchez-Criado, J. E., and Guisado, S. (1985). Role of the vomeronasal organ on the estral cycle reduction of pheromones in the rat. *Rev. Espe. Fisiol.* **41**, 305–310.

Mora, O. A., Cabrera, M. M., and Sanchez-Criado, J. E. (1994). Hormonal pattern of the pheromonal restoration of cyclic activity in aging irregularly cycling and persistent-estrus female rats. *Biol. Reprod.* **51**, 920–925.

Moran, D. T., Rowley, J. C., III, Jafek, B. W., and Lowell, M. A. (1982). The fine structure of the olfactory mucosa in man. *J. Neurocytol.* **11**, 721–746.

Moran, D. T., Jafek, B. W., and Rowley, J. C., III. (1991). The vomeronasal (Jacobson's) organ in man: Ultrastructure and frequency of occurence. *J. Steroid Biochem. Mol. Biol.* **39**, 545–552.

Moran, D. T., Monti-Bloch, L., Stensaas, L. J., and Berliner, D. L. (1995). Structure and function of the human vomeronasal organ. *In* "Handbook of Olfaction and Gustatation" (R. L. Doty, ed.), Vol. 36, pp. 793–820. Dekker, New York.

Mori, K., Nagao, H., and Yoshihara, Y. (1999). The olfactory bulb: Coding and processing of odor molecule information. *Science* **286**, 711–715.

Mori, Y., Shimizu, K., and Hoshino, K. (1990). Melatonin but not the ram-effect reactivates quiescent ovarian activity of midanestrous ewe. *Jpn. J. Vet. Res.* **52**, 773–779.

Morofushi, M., Shinohara, K., Funabashi, T., and Kimura, F. (2000). Positive relationship between menstrual synchony and ability to smell 5α-androst-16-en-3α-ol. *Chem. Senses* **25**, 407–411.

Moss, R. L., and Dudley, C. A. (1984). The challenge of studying the behavioral effects of neuropeptides. *In* "Handbook of Psychopharmacology" (L. L. Iversen and S. D. Iversen, eds.), Vol. 18, pp. 397–454. Plenum Press, New York.

Mott, A. E. (1991). Topical corticosteroid therapy for nasal polyposis. *In* "Smell and Taste in Health and Disease" (T. V. Getchell, R. L. Doty, L. M. Bartoshuk, and J. B. Snow, eds.), pp. 553–572. Raven Press, New York.

Mucignat-Caretta, C., Caretta, A., and Cavaggioni, A. (1995). Pheromonally accelerated puberty is enhanced by previous experience of the same stimulus. *Physiol. Behav.* **57**, 901–903.

Mykytowycz, R. (1979). Some difficulties in the study of the function and composition of semiochemicals in mammals, particularly wild rabbits, Orycotolagus cuniculus. *In* "Chemical Ecology: Odour Communication in Animals" (F. J. Ritter, ed.), pp. 105–115. Elsevier/North-Holland Biomedical Press, Amsterdam.

Nelson, R. J., Fleming, A. S., Wysocki, C. J., Shinder, T. W., and Zucker, I. (1985). Chemosensory and neural influences on photoperiodic responsiveness of laboratory rats. *Neuroendocrinology* **40**, 288–290.

Nixon, A., Mallet, A., and Gower, D. (1988). Simultaneous quantification of 5 odorous steroids (16-androstenes) in the axillary hair of men. *J. Steroid Biochem.* **29**, 505–510.

Novotny, M., Memiolo, B., Harvey, S., Wiesler, D., and Marchlewska-Koj, A. (1986). Adrenal-mediated endogenous metabolites inhibit puberty in female mice. *Science* **231**, 722–725.

Novotny, M., Harvey, S., and Jemiolo, B. (1990). Chemistry of male-dominance in the house mouse, mus-domesticus. *Experientia* **46**, 109–113.

Novotny, M. V., Ma, W., Weisler, D., and Zidek, L. (1999). Positive identification of the puberty-accelerating pheromone of the house mouse: The volatile ligands associating with the major urinary protein. *Proc. R. Soc. London, Ser. B* **266**, 2017–2022.

Noyes, H. J. (1935). Naso-palatine duct and Jacobson's organ in new-born infants. *J. Dent. Res.* **15**, 155–156.

Numan, M. (1988). Maternal behavior. *In* "The Physiology of Reproduction" (K. Knobil and J. Neil, eds.), pp. 1529–1645. Raven Press, New York.

Ober, C., Weitkamp, L. R., Cox, N., Dytch, H., Kostyu, D., and Elias, S. (1997). HLA and mate choice in humans. *Am. J. Hum. Genet.* **61**, 497–504.

Ober, C., Hyslop, T., Elias, S., Weitkamp, L. R., and Hauck, W. W. (1998). Human leukocyte antigen matching and fetal loss: Results of a 10-year prospective study. *Hum. Reprod.* **13**, 33–38.

O'Connell, R. J., Stevens, D. A., Akers, R. P., Coppola, D. M., and Grant, A. J. (1989). Individual differences in the quantitative and qualitative responses of human subjects to various odors. *Chem. Senses* **14**, 293–302.

O'Connor, L. H., Nock, B., and McEwen, B. S. (1988). Regional specificity of gamma-aminobutryric acid receptor regulation by estradiol. *Neuroendocrinology* **47**, 473–481.

Ohloff, G., Maurer, B., Winter, B., and Giersch, W. (1983). Structural and configurational dependence of the sensory process in steroids. *Helv. Chim. Acta* **66**, 192–217.

Ortmann, R. (1989). Über Sinneszellen am fetalen vomeronasalen Organ des Menschen. *H.N.O.* **37**, 191–197.

Osako, Y., Otsuka, T., Taniguchi, M., Oka, T., and Kaba, H. (2000). Oxytocin enhances postsynaptic glutamatergic transmission between rat olfactory bulb neurones in culture mechanism. *Neurosci. Lett.* **299**, 65–8.

Ottoson, D. (1956). Analysis of the electrical activity of the olfactory epithelium. *Acta Physiol. Scand.* **35**, 1–83.

Oureshy, A., Kawashima, R., Imran, M. B., Sugiura, M., Goto, R., Okada, K., Inoue, K., Itoh, M., Schormann, T., and Zilles, K. (2000). Functional mapping of human brain in olfactory processing: A PET study. *J. Neurophysiol.* **84**, 1656–1666.

Papez, J. W. (1937). A proposed mechanism of emotion. *Arch. Neurol. (Chicago)* **38**, 725–743.

Paredes, R. G., Lopez, M. E., and Baum, M. J. (1998). Testosterone augments neuronal fos responses to estrous odors throughout the vomeronasal projection pathway of gonadectomized male and female rats. *Horm. Behav.* **33**, 48–57.

Parhar, I., Pfaff, D., and Schwanzelfukuda, M. (1995). Genes and behavior as studied through gonadotropin-releasing-hormone (GNRH) neurons—comparative and functional-aspects. *Cell. Mol. Neurobiol.* **15**, 107–116.

Parlee, M. B. (1983). Menstrual rhythms in sensory processes: A review of fluctuations in vision, olfaction, audition, taste and touch. *Psychol. Bull.* **93**, 539–548.

Patkai, P., Johannson, G., and Post, B. (1974). Mood, alertness and sympathetic-adrenal medullary activity during the menstrual cycle. *Psychosom. Med.* **36**, 503–512.

Patterson, R. L. S. (1968). 5x-androst-16-ene-3-one: Compound responsible for taint in boar fat. *J. Sci. Food Agric.* **19**, 31–38.

Pause, B. M., Sojka, B., Krauel, K., Fehm-Wolfsdorf, G., and Ferstl, R. (1996). Olfactory information processing during the course of the menstrual cycle. *Biol. Psychol.* **44**, 31–54.

Pause, B. M., Krauel, K., Sojka, B., and Ferstl, R. (1999a). Body odor evoked potentials: A new method to study the chemosensory perception of self and non-self in humans. *Genetica* **104**, 285–294.

Pause, B. M., Rogalski, K. P., Sojka, B., and Ferstl, R. (1999b). Sensitivity to androstenone in female subjects is associated with an altered brain response to male body odor. *Physiol. Behav.* **68**, 129–137.

Pearlman, S. M. (1934). Jacobson's organ (organon vomeronasale, Jacobsoni): Its anatomy, gross, microscopic and comparative, with some observations as well on its function. *Ann. Otol., Rhinol., Laryngol.* **43**, 739–768.

Penn, D., and Potts, W. K. (1998). Chemical signals and parasite-mediated sexual selection. *Trends Ecol. Evol.* **13**, 391–396.

Pereira, M. E. (1991). Asynchrony within estrous synchrony among ringtailed lemurs (primates: lemuridae). *Physiol. Behav.* **49**, 47–52.

Perret, M., and Benmbarek, S. (1991). Male influence on estrous cycles in female woolly opossum *(Caluromys philander).*
J. Reprod. Fertil. **91**, 557–566.

Perret, M., and Schilling, A. (1987). Role of prolactin in a
pheromone-like sexual inhibition in the male lesser mouse
lemur. *J. Endocrinol.* **114**, 279–287.

Perret, M., and Schilling, A. (1995). Sexual responses to urinary chemosignals depond on photoperiod in a male primate.
Physiol. Behav. **58**, 633–639.

Pfaff, D., and Pfaffman, C. (1969). Behavioral and electrophys-
iological responses of male rats to female rat urine odors.
In "Olfaction and Taste" (C. Pfaffmann, ed.), pp. 260–267.
Rockefeller University Press, New York.

Pfaus, J. G., Jakob, A., Kleopoulos, S. P., Gibbs, R. B., and Pfaff,
D. W. (1994). Sexual stimulation induces Fos immunoreactivity within GnRH neurons of the female rat preoptic area: Interaction with steroid hormones. *Neuroendocrinology* **60**, 283–
290.

Phillips, P. D., and Vallowe, H. H. (1975). Cyclic fluctuations in
odor detection by female rats and the temporal influences of
exogenous steriods on ovariectomized rats. *Proc. Pea. Acad.
Sci.* **49**, 160–164.

Pierce, J. D., Wysocki, C. J., and Aronov, E. V. (1993). Mutual
cross-adaptation of the volatile steroid androstenone and a
non-steroid perceptual analog. *Chem. Senses* **15**, 245–255.

Pietras, R. J., and Moulton, D. G. (1974). Hormonal influences
on odor detection in rats: Changes associated with the estrous
cycle, pseudopregnancy, ovariectomy, and administration of
testosterone propionate. *Physiol. Behav.* **12**, 475–491.

Pinel, J. P. J., Gorzalka, B. B., and Ladak, F. (1981). Cadaverine
and putrescine initiate the burial of dead conspecifics by rats.
Physiol. Behav. **27**, 819–824.

Potiquet, M. (1891). Le Canal Jacobson. *Rev. Larygol., Otol., Rhinol.* **2**, 737–753.

Potts, W. K., Manning, C. J., and Wakeland, E. K. (1991). Mating
patterns in seminatural populations of mice influenced by
MHC genotype. *Nature (London)* **352**, 619–621.

Prelog, V., and Ruzicka, L. (1944). Untersuchungen uber Or-
ganextrakte. 5. Mitteilung: Uber zwei muschusartig riechende
Steroide aus Schweines-testes-extracten. *Hev. Chim. Acta* **27**,
61–66.

Preti, G. (1987). Reply to Wilson. *Horm. Behav.* **21**, 547–550.

Preti, G., and Wysocki, C. J. (1999). Human pheromones:
Releasers or primers. *In* "Advances in Chemical Signals in Vertebrates" (R. E. Johnston, D. Müller-Schwarze,
and P. W. Sorensen, eds.), Vol. 8, pp. 315–331. Kluwer
Academic/Plenum Press, New York.

Preti, G., Huggins, G. R., and Silverberg, G. D. (1979). Alterations in the organic compounds of vaginal secretions caused
by sexual arousal. *Fertil. Steril.* **32**, 47–54.

Preti, G., Cutler, W. B., Garcia, C. R., Huggins, G. R. *et al.* (1986).
Human axillary secretions influence women's menstrual cycles: The role of donor extract of females. *Horm. Behav.* **20**,
474–482.

Preti, G., Cutler, W. B., Christensen, C. M., Lawley, H. J.,
Huggins, G. R., and Garcia, C.-R. (1987). Human axillary extracts: Analysis of compounds from samples which
influence menstrual timing. *J. Chem. Ecol.* **13**, 717–
731.

Preti, G., Lawley, H. J., Hormann, C. A., Cowart, B. J., Feldman,
R. S., Lowry, L. D., and Young, I.-M. (1995). Non-oral and
oral aspects of oral malodor. *In* "Bad Breath: Research Perspectives" (M. Rosenberg, ed.), pp. 149–173. Ramot Publishing,
Tel-Aviv.

Preti, G., Spielman, A. I., and Wysocki, C. J. (1997). Vomeronasal
organ and human chemical communication. *Encycl. Hum. Biol.*
8, 769–783.

Purvis, K., and Haynes, N. B. (1978). Effect of the odour of female
rat urine on plasma testosterone concentrations in male rat.
J. Reprod. Fertil. **53**, 63–65.

Quadagno, D. M., Shubeita, H. H., Deck, J., and Francoeur, D.
(1981). Influence of male social contracts, exercise and all-
female living conditions on the menstrual cycle. *Psychoneuroendocrinology* **6**, 239–244.

Rajendren, G., Dudley, C. A., and Moss, R. L. (1993). Influence
of male rats on the luteinizing hormone-releasing hormone
neuronal system in female rats: Role of the vomeronasal organ.
Neuroendocrinology **57**, 898–906.

Rasmussen, L. E. L., and Schulte, B. A. (1999). Ecological and
biochemical constraints on pheromonal signaling systems in
Asian elephants and their evolutionary implications. *In* "Advances in Chemical Signals in Vertebrates" (R. E. Johnston,
D. Müller-Schwarze, and P. W. Sorensen, eds.), Vol. 8, pp.
315–331. Kluwer Academic/Plenum Press, New York.

Rasmussen, L. E. L., Lee, T. D., Roelofs, W. L., Zhang, A., and
Daves, G. D., Jr. (1996). Asian elephants and Lepidoptera
have a common sex pheromone. *Nature (London)* **379**, 684.

Rasmussen, L. E. L., Gunawardena, R., and Rasmussen, R. A.
(1997a). Do Asian elephants, especially males in musth,
chemically signal via volatile compounds in breath? *Chem.
Senses* In press.

Rasmussen, L. E. L., Lee, T. D., Zhang, A., Roelofs, W. L., and
Daves, G. D., Jr. (1997b). Purification, identification, concentration and bioactivity of (Z)-7dodecen-1-yl acetate: Sex
pheromone of the female Asian elephant, *Elephas maximus.*
Chem. Senses **4**, 417–37.

Rasmussen, L. E. L., Greenwood, D., Feng, L., and Prestwich,
G. (1998). Initial characterizations of secreted proteins from
Asian elephants that bind the sex pheromone (Z)-7-dodecenyl
acetate.

Reasner, D. S., Johnston, R. E., and DeVoogd, T. J. (1993). Alteration of the bed nucleus of the stria terminalis (BNST) in young female djungarian hamsters (*Phodopus campbelli*) exposed to adult males. *Behav. Neural Biol.* **60**, 251–258.

Rennie, P. J., Holland, K. T., Mallet, A. I., Watkins, W. J., and Gower, D. B. (1990). 16-androstene content of apocrine sweat and microbiology of the human axilla. *In* "Chemical Signals in Vertebrates" (D. W. MacDonald, D. Müller-Schwarze, and S. N. Natynczuk, eds.), pp. 55–60. Oxford University Press, Oxford.

Restall, B. J., Restall, H., and WalkdenBrown, S. W. (1995). The induction of ovulation in anovulatory goats by oestrous females. *Anim. Reprod. Sci.* **40**, 299–303.

Rhine, R. J. (1995). quantifying synchrony among reproductive or other states. *Am. J. Primatol.* **36**, 201–212.

Rich, T. J., and Hurst, J. L. (1998). Scent marks as reliable signals of the competitive ability of mates. *Anim. Behav.* **56**, 727–735.

Rikowski, A., and Grammer, K. (1999). Human body odour, symmetry and attractiveness. *Proc. R. Soc. London* **266**, 869–874.

Rittner, M., and Schmidt, U. (1982). The influence of the sexual cycle on the olfactory sensitivity of wild female house mice (*Mus musculus domesticus*). *Z. Säugetierkud.* **47**, 47–50.

Rizzo, W. B., and Roth, K. S. (1994). On 'being led by the nose.' *Arch. Pediatr. Adolesc. Med.* **148**, 869–872.

Roberts, D., and Marks, R. (1980). The determination of regional and age variations in the rate of desquamation: A comparison of four techniques. *J. Invest. Dermatol.* **74**, 13–17.

Robin, O., Alaoui-Ismaïli, O., Dittmar, A., and Vernet-Maury, E. (1999). Basic emotions evoked by eugenol odor differ according to the dental experience: A neurovegetative analysis. *Chem. Senses* **24**, 327–335.

Rodriguez, I., Greer, C. A., Mok, M. Y., and Mombaerts, P. (2000). A putative pheromone receptor gene expressed in human olfactory mucosa. *Nat. Genet.* **26**, 18–19.

Rogel, M. J. (1978). A critical evaluation of the possibility of higher primate reproductive and sexual pheromones. *Psychol. Bull.* **85**, 810–830.

Romero, P. R., Beltramino, C. A., and Carrer, H. F. (1990). Participation of the olfactory system in the control of approach behavior of the female rat to the male. *Physiol. Behav.* **47**, 685–690.

Roper-Hall, H. T. (1941). Patent incisive canal. *Br. Dent. J.* **71**, 306–309.

Rosenblatt, J. S. (1985). Maternal behavior among the nonprimate mammals. *In* "Handbook of Behavioral Neurobiology" (N. T. Adler, D. Pfaff, and R. W. Goy, eds.), Vol. 7, pp. 229–298. Plenum Press, New York.

Rosenblatt, J. S. (1990). Landmarks in the physiological study of maternal behavior with special reference to the rat. *In* "Mammalian Parenting: Biochemical, Neurobiological, and Behavioral Determinats" (N. A. Krasnegor and R. S. Bridges, eds.), pp. 40–60. Oxford University Press, New York.

Roslinski, D., Bhatnagar, K. P., Burrows, A. M., and Smith, T. (2000). Comparative morphology and histochemistry of glands associated with vomeronasal organ in humans, mouse lemurs and voles. *Anat. Rec.* **260**, 92–101.

Ross, M. H., Yurgelun-Todd, D. A., Renshaw, P. F., Maas, L. C., Mendelson, J. H., Mello, N. K., Cohen, B. M., and Levin, J. M. (1997). Age-related reduction in functional MRI response to photic stimulation. *Neurology* **48**, 173–176.

Rosser, A. E., and Keverne, E. B. (1985). The importance of central noradrenergic neurones in the formation of an olfactory memory in the prevent of pregnancy block. *Neuroscience* **16**, 1141–1147.

Rosser, A. E., Remfry, C. J., and Keverne, E. B. (1989). Restricted exposure of mice to primer pheromones coincident with prolactin surges blocks pregnancy by changing hypothalamic dopamine release. *J. Reprod. Fertil.* **87**, 553–559.

Rottman, S. J., and Snowdon, C. T. (1972). Demonstration and analysis of an alarm pheromone in mice. *J. Comp. Physiol. Psychol.* **81**, 483–90.

Royet, J. P., Hudry, J., Zald, D. H., Godinot, D., Grégoire, M. C., Lavenne, F., Costes, N., and Holley, A. (2001). Functional neuroanatomy of different olfactory judgments. *NeuroImage* **13**, 506–519.

Rugarli, E. I. (1999). Human genetics '99: Sexual development. *Am. J. Hum. Genet.* **65**, 943–948.

Russell, M. J. (1976). Human olfactory communication. *Nature (London)* **260**, 520–522.

Russell, M. J., Switz, G. M., and Thompson, K. (1980). Olfactory influences on the human menstrual cycle. *Pharmacol., Biochem. Behav.* **13**, 737–738.

Russell, M. J., Mendelson, T., and Peeke, H. V. S. (1983). Mothers' identification of their infact's odors. *Ethol. Sociobiol.* **4**, 29–31.

Russell, M. J., Cummings, B. J., Profitt, B. F., Wysocki, C. J., Gilbert, A. N., and Cotman, C. W. (1993). Life span changes in the verbal categorization of odors. *J. Gerontol.: Psychol. Sci.* **48**, 49–53.

Ruysch, F. (1703). "Thesaurus Anatomicus tertius." Amsterdam.

Ryan, K. D., and Schwartz, N. B. (1977). Grouped female mice: Demonstration of pseudopregnancy. *Biol. Reprod.* **17**, 578–583.

Sachs, B. D. (1997). Erection evoked in male rats by airborne scent from estrous females. *Physiol. Behav.* **62**, 921–924.

Sachs, B. D. (1999). Airborne aphrodisiac odor from estrous rats: Implication for pheromonal classification. *In* "Advances in Chemical Signals in Vertebrates" (R. E. Johnston, ed.), pp. 333–342. Plenum Press, New York.

Sachs, B. D., Akasofu, K., Citron, J. H., Dainiels, S. B., and Natoli, J. H. (1994). Noncontact stimulation from estrous females evokes penile erection in rats. *Physiol. Behav.* **55**, 1073–1079.

Sahu, A., and Ghosh, A. (1982). Effect of grouping and sex on the estrous regulation of a wild rat, *Bandicota bengalensis. Biol. Reprod.* **27**, 1023–1025.

Sakellaris, P. C. (1972). Olfactory thresholds in normal and adrenalectomized rats. *Physiol. Behav.* **9**, 495–500.

Saltzman, W., Schultz-Darken, N. J., Wegner, F. H., Wittwer, D. J., and Abbot, D. H. (1998). Suppression of cortisol levels in subordinate female marmosets: Reproductive and social contributions. *Horm. Behav.* **33**, 58–74.

Sánchez-Criado, J. E. (1982). Involvement of the vomeronasal system in the reproductive physiology of the rat. *In* "Olfaction and Endocrine Regulation" (W. Breipohl, ed.), pp. 209–221. IRL Press, London.

Sánchez-Criado, J. E., Lopez, F., and Aguilar, E. (1986). Pituitary regulation of corpus luteum progesterone secretion in cyclic rats. *Endocrinology (Baltimore)* **119**, 1083–1088.

Sastry, S. D., Buck, K. T., Janak, J., Dressler, M., and Preti, G. (1980). Volatiles emitted by humans. *In* "Biochemical Applications of Mass Spectrometry" (G. R. Waller and O. C. Dermer, eds.), First supplementary, pp. 1085–1129. Wiley, New York.

Savage, A., Ziegler, T. E., and Snowdon, C. T. (1988). Sociosexual development, pair bond formation, and mechanisms of fertility suppression in female cotton-top tamarins (*Saguinus oedipus oedipus*). *Am. J. Primatol.* **14**, 345–359.

Savic, I., Guylas, B., Larsson, M., and Roland, P. (2000). Olfactory functions are mediated by parallel and hierarchical processing. *Neuroendocrinology* **26**, 735–745.

Scalia, F., and Winans, S. S. (1975). The differential projections of the olfactory bulb and accessory olfactory bulb in mammals. *J. Comp. Neurol.* **161**, 31–56.

Schaal, B. (1986). Presumed olfactory exchanges between mother and neonate in humans. *In* "Ethology and Psychology" (J. L. Camus and J. Conler, eds.), pp. 101–10. Privat IEC, Toulouse, France.

Schaal, B., and Marlier, L. (1998). Maternal and paternal perception of individual odor signatures in human amniotic fluid—potential role in early bonding? *Biol. Neonate* **74**, 266–273.

Schaal, B., Marlier, L., and Soussignan, R. (1998). Olfactory function in the human fetus: Evidence from selective neonatal responsiveness to the odor of amniotic fluid. *Behav. Neurosci.* **112**, 1438–1449.

Schaal, B., Marlier, L., and Soussignan, R. (2000). Human foetuses learn odours from their pregnant mother's diet. *Chem. Senses* **25**, 729–737.

Schank, J., and McClintock, M. K. K. (1992). A coupled-oscillator model of ovarian-cycle synchrony among female rats. *J. Theor. Biol.* **157**, 317–362.

Schank, J., and McClintock, M. K. K. (1997). Ovulatory pheromone shortens ovarian cycles of female rats in olfactory isolation. *Physiol. Behav.* **62**, 899–904.

Schank, J. C. (1997). Problems with dimensionless measurement models of synchrony in biological systems. *Am. J. Primatol.* **41**, 65–85.

Schank, J. C., and Alberts, J. R. (2000). Effects of male rat urine on reproductive and developmental parameters in the dam and her female offspring. *Horm. Behav.* **38**, 130–136.

Schank, J. C., Tomasino, C. I., and McClintock, M. K. K. (1995). The development of a pheromone isolation and delivery (PID) system for small mammals. *J. Inst. Anim. Technol.* **46**, 103–113.

Schellinck, H. M., West, A. M., and Brown, R. E. (1992). Rats can discriminate between the urine odors of genetically identical mice maintained on different diets. *Physiol. Behav.* **51**, 1079–1082.

Schiffman, S. S., and Gatlin, C. A. (1993). Clinical physiology of taste and smell. *Annu. Rev. Nutr.* **13**, 405–436.

Schiffman, S. S., Sattely-Miller, E. A., Suggs, M. S., and Graham, B. G. (1995a). The effect of pleasant odors and hormone status on mood of women at midlife. *Brain Res. Bull.* **36**, 19–29.

Schiffman, S. S., Suggs, M. S., and Sattely-Miller, E. A. (1995b). Effect of pleasant odors on mood of males at midlife: Comparison of African-American and European-American men. *Brain Res. Bull.* **36**, 31–37.

Schiffman, S. S., Miller, E. A. S., Suggs, M. S., and Graham, B. G. (1995c). The effect of environmental odors emanating from commercial swine operations on the mood of nearby residents. *Brain Res. Bull.* **37**, 369–375.

Schilling, A., Perret, M., and Predine, J. (1984). Sexual inhibition in a prosimian primate: A pheromone-like effect. *J. Endocrinol.* **102**, 143–151.

Schilling, A., Serviere, J., Gendrot, G., and Perret, M. (1990). Vomeronasal activation by urine in the primate *Microcebus murinus*: A 2 DG study. *Exp. Brain Res.* **81**, 609–618.

Schiml, P. A., Mendoza, S. P., Saltzman, W., Lyons, D. M., and Mason, W. A. (1996). Seasonality in squirrel monkeys (*Saimiri sciureus*), social facilitation by females. *Physiol. Behav.* **60**, 1105–1113.

Schmidt, C., and Schmidt, U. (1980). Changes in the olfactory sensitivity during the estrus cycle in female laboratory mice. *Chem. Senses* **5**, 359–365.

Schmidt, U., Schmidt, C., and Breipohl, W. (1982). Olfactory sensitivity changes during the estrous cycle, gestation and lactation in mice. *In* "Olfaction and Endocrine Regulation" (W. Breipohl, ed.), pp. 323–332. IRL Press, London.

Schneider, J. E., and Wade, G. N. (2000). Inhibition of reproduction in service of energy balance. *In* "Reproduction in Context: Social and Environmental Influences on Reproductive

Physiology and Behavior" (K. Wallen and J. E. Schneider, eds.), pp. 35–82. MIT Press, Cambridge, MA.

Schneider, R. A., and Wolf, S. (1960). Relation of olfactory acuity to nasal membrane function. *J. Appl. Physiol.* **15**, 914–920.

Schneider, R. A., Costiloe, J. P., Howard, R. P., and Wolf, S. (1958). Olfactory preception thresholds in hypogonadal women: Changes accompanying administration of androgen and estrogen. *J. Clin. Endocrinol. Metab.* **18**, 379–390.

Schulingkamp, R. J., Pagano, T. C., Hung, D., and Raffa, R. B. (2000). Insulin receptors and insulin action in the brain: Review and clinical implications. *Neurosci. Biobehav. Rev.* **24**, 855–872.

Schumacher, S. K., and Moltz, H. (1982). The maternal pheromone of the rat as an innate stimulus for pre-weanling young. *Physiol. Behav.* **28**, 67–71.

Schwanzel-Fukuda, M., and Pfaff, D. (1991). Migration of LHRH-immunoreactive neurons from the olfactory placode rationalizes olfacto-hormonal relationships. *J. Steroid Biochem. Mol. Biol.* **39**, 565–572.

Schwanzel-Fukuda, M., and Pfaff, D. (1995). Structure and function of the *Nervus terminalis. In* "Handbook of Olfaction and Taste" (R. L. Doty, ed.), pp. 835–864. Dekker, New York.

Segovia, S., and Guillamon, A. (1993). Sexual dimorphism in the vomeronasal pathway and sex differences in reproductive behaviors. *Brain Res. Rev.* **18**, 51–74.

Selway, R., and Keverne, E. B. (1990). Hippocampal lesions are without effect on olfactory memory formation in the context of pregnancy block. *Physiol. Behav.* **47**, 249–252.

Settle, R. G. (1991). The chemical senses in diabetes mellitus. *In* "Smell and Taste in Health and Disease" (T. V. Getchell, ed.), pp. 829–843. Raven Press, New York.

Shafik, A. (1997). Olfactory-corporeal reflex: Description of a new reflex and its role in the erectile process. *Eur. Urol.* **32**, 105–109.

Shanas, U., and Terkel, J. (1997). Mole-rat harderian gland secretions inhibit aggression. *Anim. Behav.* **54**, 1255–1263.

Sherwood, R. J., MacLachlan, J. C., Aiton, J. F., and Scarborough, J. (1999). The vomeronasal organ in the human embryo, studied by means of three-dimensional computer reconstruction. *J. Anat.* **195**, 413–418.

Shinohara, K., Morofushi, M., and Kimura, F. (1999). Effects of human pheromones on pulsatile luteinizing hormone secretions. *Neurosci. Res., Suppl.* **23**, S233.

Shinohara, K., Morofushi, M., Funabashi, T., Mitsushima, D., and Kimura, F. (2000). Effect of 5α-androst-16-en-3α-ol on the pulsatile secretion of luteinizing hormone in human females. *Chem. Senses* **25**, 465–467.

Shipley, M. T., and Ennis, M. (1996). Functional organization of the olfactory system. *J. Neurobiol.* **30**, 123–176.

Shorey, H. H. (1976). "Animal Communication by Pheromones." Academic Press, New York.

Shughrue, P., Scrimo, P., Lane, M., Askew, R., and Merchenthaler, I. (1997a). The distribution of estrogen receptor-beta mRNA in forebrain regions of the estrogen receptor-alpha knockout mouse. *Endocrinology (Baltimore)* **128**, 5649–5652.

Shughrue, P. J., Lane, M. V., and Merchenthaler, I. (1997b). Comparative distribution of estrogen receptor-alpha and-beta mRNA in the rat central nervous system. *J. Comp. Neurol.* **388**, 507–25.

Signoret, J. P. (1991). Sexual pheromones in the domestic sheep: Importance and limits in the regulation of reproductive physiology. *J. Steriod Biochem. Mol. Biol.* **39**, 639–646.

Signoret, J. P., and Lindsey, D. R. (1982). The male effect in domestic mammals: Effect on LH-secretion and ovulation; importance of olfactory clues. *In* "Olfaction and Endocrine Regulation" (W. Breipohl, ed.). pp. 63–72. IRL Press, London.

Sipos, M. L., Alterman, L., Perry, B., Hyby, J. G., and Vandenbergh, J. G. (1995). An ephemeral pheromone of female house mice: Degradation by oxidation. *Anim. Behav.* **50**, 113–120.

Sitruk-Ware, R. (1988). Transdermal delivery of steroids. *Contraception* **39**, 1–20.

Skandhan, K. P., Pandya, A. K., Skandhan, S., and Mehta, Y. B. (1979). Synchronization of menstruation among intimates and kindreds. *Panminerva Med.* **21**, 131–134.

Slob, A. K., van Es, G., and van der Werff ten Bosch, J. J. (1985). Social factors and puberty in female rats. *J. Endocrinol.* **104**, 309–313.

Smals, A. G. H., and Weusten, J. J. A. M. (1991). 16-ene-steroids in the human testis. *J. Steroid Biochem.* **40**, 587–592.

Smith, T. D., and Bhatnagar, K. P. (2001). The human vomeronasal organ. Part III: Prenatal development from infancy to the ninth decade. *J. Anat.* **199**, 289–302.

Smith, T. D., Siegel, M. I., Mooney, M. P., Burdi, A. R., Burrows, A. M., and Todhunter, J. S. (1996). Vomeronasal organ growth and development in normal and cleft lip and palate human fetuses. *Cleft Palate-Craniofacial J.* **33**, 385–394.

Smith, T. D., Siegel, M. I., Mooney, M. P., Burdi, A. R., Burrows, A. M., and Todhunter, J. S. (1997). Prenatal growth of the human vomeronasal organ. *Anat. Rec.* **248**, 447–455.

Smith, T. D., Siegel, M. I., Burrows, A. M., Mooney, M. P., Burdi, A. R., Fabrizio, P. A., and Clemente, F. R. (1998). Searching for the vomeronasal organ of adult humans: Preliminary findings on location, structure, and size. *Microsc. Res. Tech.* **41**, 483–491.

Smith, T. D., Siegel, M. I., Burrows, A. M., Mooney, M. P., Burdi, A. R., Fabrizio, P. A., and Clemente, F. R. (1999). Histological changes in the fetal human vomeronasal epithelium during volumetric growth of the vomeronasal organ. *In* "Advances in

Chemical Signals in Vertebrates" (R. E. Johnston, D. Müller-Schwarze, and P. W. Sorensen, eds.), Vol. 8, pp. 583–591. Kluwer Academic/Plenum Press, New York.

Smith, T. E., and Abbott, D. H. (1998). Behavioral discrimination between circumgenital odor from peri-ovulatory dominant and anovulatory female common marmosets (*Callithrix jacchus*). *Am. J. Primatol.* **46**, 265–284.

Smith, T. E., Faulkes, C. G., and Abbott, D. H. (1997). Combined olfactory contact with the parent colony and direct contact with nonbreeding animals does not maintain suppression of ovulation in female naked mole-rats (*Heterocephalus glaber*). *Horm. Behav.* **31**, 277–288.

Smotherman, W. P., Bell, R. W., Starzec, J., and Elias, J. (1974). Maternal responses to infant vocalizations and olfactory cues in rats and mice. *Behav. Biol.* **12**, 55–66.

Snowdon, C. T. (1983). Ethology, comparative psychology, and animal behavior. *Annu. Rev. Psychol.* **34**, 63–94.

Sobel, N., Prabhakaran, V., Desmond, J. E., Glover, G. H., Goode, R. L., Sullivan, E. V., and Gabrieli, J. D. (1998). Sniffing and smelling: Separate subsystems in the human olfactory cortex. *Nature (London)* **392**, 282–286.

Sobel, N., Prabhakaran, V., Hartley, C. A., Desmond, J. E., Glover, G. H., Sullivan, E. V., and Gabrieli, J. D. E. (1999). Blind smell: Brain activation induced by an undetected airborne chemical. *Brain Res.* **122**, 209–217.

Southwick, C. H., and Bland, V. P. (1959). Effect of population density on adrenal glands and reproductive organs of CWF mice. *Am. J. Physiol.* **197**, 111–114.

Spencer, N. A., Jacob, S., Sellegren, S. A., Bullivant, S. B., Mennella, J. A., and McClintock, M. K. K. (2000). Effects of breastfeeding chemosignals on the human menstrual cycle. *A. Chem. S. Absts.* No. 236.

Spielman, A. I., Zeng, X.-N., Leyden, J. J., and Preti, G. (1995). Proteinaceous precursors of human axillary odor: Isolation of two novel odor-binding proteins. *Experientia* **51**, 40–47.

Spielman, A. I., Sunavala, G., Harmony, J. A., Stuart, W. D., Leyden, J. J., Turner, G., Vowels, B. R., Lam, W. C., Yang, S., and Preti, G. (1998). Identification and immunohistochemical localization of protein precursors to human axillary odors in apocrine glands and secretions. *Arch. Dermatol.* **134**, 813–818.

Stacey, N. E. (1987). Roles of hormones and pheromones in fish reproductive behavior. *In* "Psychobiology of Reproductive Behavior. An Evolutionary Perspective" (D. Crews, ed.), pp. 28–60. Prentice-Hall, Englewood Cliffs, NJ.

Stanislaw, H., and Rice, F. (1987). Acceleration of the menstrual cycle by intercourse. *Psychophysiology* **2**, 714–717.

Steiner, M., Fleming, A. S., Anderson, V., Monkhouse, E., and Boulter, G. E. (1986). A psychoneuroendocrine profile for postpartum blues? *In* "Hormones and Behavior" (L.

Dennerstein and J. Fraser, eds.), pp. 327–335. Elsevier, Amsterdam.

Stensaas, L., Lavker, R. M., Monti-Bloch, L., Grosser, B., and Berliner, D. (1991). Ultrastructure of the human vomeronasal organ. *J. Steroid Biochem. Mol. Biol.* **39**, 553–560.

Stern, K. N., and McClintock, M. K. K. (1996). Individual variation in biological rhythms. *In* "Psychopharmacology and Women. Sex, Gender, and Hormones" (M. F. Jensvold, U. Halbreich, and J. A. Hamilton, eds.), pp. 393–407. American Psychiatric Press, Washington, DC.

Stern, K., and McClintock, M. K. (1998). Regulation of ovulation by human pheromones. *Nature (London)* **392**, 177–179.

Stevens, D. A., and Koster, E. P. (1972). Open-field responses of rats to odors from stressed and non-stressed predecessors. *Behav. Biol.* **7**, 519–525.

Stevens, D. A., and O'Connell, R. J. (1995). Enhanced sensitivity to androstenone following regular exposure to pemenone. *Chem. Senses* **20**, 413–419.

Stevens, D. A., and O'Connell, R. J. (1996). Pemenone and androstenone do not cross-adapt reciprocally. *Chem. Senses* **21**, 711–717.

Stockley, P. (1996). Synchrony of estrus in common shrews. *J. Mammal.* **77**, 383–387.

Stoddart, D. M. (1976). "Mammalian Odours and Pheromones." Arnold, London.

Storey, A. E., Walsh, C. J., Quinton, R. L., and Wynne-Edwards, K. E. (2000). Hormonal correlates of paternal responsiveness in new and expectant fathers. *Evol. Hum. Behav.* **21**, 79–95.

Strassmann, B. I. (1997). The biology of menstruation in Homo sapiens: Total lifetime menses, fecundity, and nonsynchrony in a natural fertility population. *Curr. Anthropol.* **38**, 123–129.

Strassmann, B. I. (1999). Menstrual synchrony pheromones: Cause for doubt. *Hum. Reprod.* **14**, 579–580.

Strauss, J. S., Downing, D. T., and Ebling, F. J. (1983). Sebaceous glands. *In* "Biochemistry and Physiology of the Skin" (L. A. Goldsmith, ed.), pp. 569–595. Oxford University Press, New York.

Strogatz, S., and Stewart, L. (1993). Coupled oscillators and biological synchronization. *Sci. Am.* **269**, 68–75.

Studd, J., Pornel, B., Marton, I., Bringer, J., Varin, C., Tsouderos, Y., and Christiansen, C. (1999). Efficacy and acceptability of intranasal 17β-oestradiol for menopausal symptoms: Randomised dose-response study. *Lancet* **353**, 1574–1578.

Stumpf, W. E., and Sar, M. (1982). Central aspects of olfacto-endocrine interactions. *In* "Olfaction and Endocrine Regulation" (W. Breipohl, ed.), pp. 11–21. IRL Press, London.

Swann, J. M. (1997). Gonadal steroids regulate behavioral responses to pheromones by actions on a subdivision of the medial preoptic nucleus. *Brain Res.* **750**, 189–194.

Takami, S., Getchell, M. L., Chen, Y., Monti-Bloch, L., Berliner, D. L., Stensaas, L. J., and Getchell, T. V. (1993). Vomeronasal epithelial cells of the adult human express neuron-specific molecules. *NeuroReport* **4**, 375–378.

Talou, T., Gaset, A., Delmas, M., Kulifaj, M., and Montant, C. (1990). Dimethyl sulphide: The secret for black truffle hunting by animals? *Mycol. Res.* **94**, 277–278.

Taylor, R. (1994). Brave new nose: Sniffing out human sexual chemistry. *J. NIH Res.* **6**, 47–51.

Testart, J., Frydman, R., and Roger, M. (1982). Seasonal influence of diurnal rhythms in the onset of the plasma luteinizing hormone surge in women. *J. Clin. Endocrinol. Metab.* **55**, 374–377.

Than, T. T., Delay, E. R., and Maier, M. E. (1994). Sucrose threshold variation during the menstrual cycle. *Physiol. Behav.* **56**, 237–239.

Thiessen, D., and Coke, R. (1990). Alarm odors suppress the immune system. *In* "Chemical Signls in Vertebrates" (D. Müller-Schwartz, ed.), Vol. 5, pp. 507–518. Plenum Press, New York.

Thompson, K. V. (1991). Flehmen and social-dominance in captive female sable antelope, *Hippotragus niger. Appl. Anim. Behav. Sci.* **29**, 121–133.

Thompson, K. V. (1995). Flehmen and birth synchrony among female sable antelope, *Hippotragus niger. Anim. Behav.* **50**, 475–484.

Thornhill, R., and Gangestad, S. W. (1999). The scent of symmetry: A human sex pheromone that signals fitness? *Evol. Hum. Behav.* **20**, 175–201.

Thysen, B., Elliott, W. H., and Katzman, P. A. (1968). Identification of estra-1, 3, 5, (10), 16-tetraen-3-ol (estratetraenol) from the urine of pregnant women. *Steroids* **11**, 73–87.

Tilbrook, A. J., and Hemsworth, P. H. (1990). Detection of oestrus in gilts housed adjacent or opposite boars or exposed to exogenous boar stimuli. *Appl. Anim. Behav. Sci.* **28**, 233–245.

Tirindelli, R., Mucignat-Caretta, C., and Ryba, N. J. P. (1998). Molecular aspects of pheromonal communication via the vomeronasal organ of mammals. *Trends Neurosci.* **21**, 482–486.

Todrank, J. T., Wysocki, C. J., and Beauchamp, G. K. (1991). The effects of adaptation on the perception of similar and dissimilar odors. *Chem. Senses* **16**, 467–482.

Tomasino, C. I. (2000). Pubertal traits of risk factors for mammary cancer in the female Norway rat. Doctorial Disseration, University of Chicago, Department of Organismal Biology and Anatomy, Chicago.

Tonzetich, J. (1971). Direct gas chromatographic analysis of sulphur compounds in mouth air in man. *Arch. Oral Biol.* **16**, 587–597.

Tonzetich, J., Preti, G., and Huggins, G. R. (1978). Changes in concentration of volatile sulfur compounds of mouth air during the menstrual cycle. *J. Int. Med. Res.* **6**, 245–254.

Toppozada, H., Michaels, L., Toppozada, M., El-Ghazzawai, E., Talaat, A., and Elwany, S. (1981). The human nasal mucosa in the menstrual cycle. *J. Laryngol. Otol.* **95**, 1237–1247.

Treloar, A. E., Boynton, R. E., Behn, D. G., and Brown, B. W. (1967). Variation of the human menstrual cycle through reproductive life. *Int. J. Fertil.* **12**, 77–126.

Trevathan, W. R., Burleson, M. H., and Gregory, W. L. (1993). No evidence for menstrual synchrony in lesbian couples. *Psychoneuroendocrinology* **18**, 425–435.

Trotier, D., Eloit, C., Wassef, M., Talmain, G., Bensimon, J. L., Doving, K. B., and Ferrand, J. (2000). The vomeronasal cavity in adult humans. *Chem. Senses* **25**, 269–380.

Vaccari, C., Lolait, S. J., and Ostrowski, N. L. (1998). Comparative distribution of vasopressin V1b and oxytocin receptor messenger ribonucleic acids in brain. *Endocrinology (Baltimore)* **139**, 5015–5033.

Valenta, J. G., and Rigby, M. K. (1968). Discrimination of the odor of stressed rats. *Science* **161**, 599–600.

Valenta, J. G., and Rigby, M. K. (1974). Stress-generated rat odors: Chemical isolation. *NTIS Rep. AD/A* **3**, 331.

van Aarde, R., and Haim, A. (1999). The influence of urinary and fecal odors on ovarian function in coexisting Acomys species. *Isr. J. Zool.* **45**, 261–265.

Vandenbergh, J. G. (1976). Acceleration of sexual maturation in female rats by male stimulation. *J. Reprod. Fertil.* **46**, 451–453.

Vandenbergh, J. G. (1988). Pheromones and mammalian reproduction. *In* "The Physiology of Reproduction" (E. Knobil and J. D. Neill, eds.), Vol. 2, pp. 1679–1696. Raven Press, New York.

Vandenbergh, J. G. (1994). Pheromones and mammalian reproduction. *In* "The Physiology of Reproduction" (E. Knobil and J. D. Neill, eds.), 2nd ed., pp. 343–359. Raven Press, New York.

Vandenbergh, J. G., and Post, W. (1976). Endocrine coordination in rhesus monkeys: Female responses to the male. *Physiol. Behav.* **17**, 979–984.

Van der Welt, L. A., Wilmsen, E. N., and Jenkins, T. (1978). Unusual sex hormone patterns among desert-dwelling hunter-gatherers. *J. Clin. Endocrinol. Metab.* **46**, 658–663.

Varendi, H., Christensson, K., Porter, R. H., and Winberg, J. (1998). Soothing effect of amniotic fluid smell in newborn infants. *Early Hum. Dev.* **51**, 47–55.

Veith, J. L., Buck, M., Getzlaf, S., Van Dalfsen, P., and Slade, S. (1983). Exposure to men influences the occurrence of ovulation in women. *Physiol. Behav.* **31**, 313–315.

Velle, W. (1987). Sex differences in sensory functions. *Perspect. Biol. Med.* **30**, 490–522.

Vickers, N. J., and Baker, T. C. (1994). Reiterative responses to single strands of odor promote sustained upwind flight and odor source location by mothes. *Proc. Natl. Acad. Sci. U.S.A.* **91**, 5756–5760.

Vierling, J. S., and Rock, J. (1967). Variations in olfactory sensitivity to exaltolide during the menstrual cycle. *J. Appl. Physiol.* **22**, 311–315.

Vieuille-Thomas, C., and Signoret, J. P. (1992). Pheromonal transmission of an aversive experience in domestic pig. *J. Chem. Ecol.* **18**, 1551–1557.

Vollman, R. (1977). The menstrual cycle. *Major Probl. Obstet. Gynecol.* **7**, 1–193.

Vom Saal, F. S. (1989). The production of and sensivity to cues that delay puberty and prolong subsequent oestrous cycles in female mice are influenced by prior intrauterine position. *J. Reprod. Fertil.* **86**, 457–471.

von Uexküll, J. (1937). A stroll through the worlds of animals and men. *In* "Instinctive Behavior. The Development of a Modern Concept" (C. H. Schiller, ed.), pp. 5–80. International Universitites Press, New York.

Wallace, K. J., and Rosen, J. B. (2000). Predator odor as an unconditioned fear stimulus in rats: Elicitation of freezing by trimethylthiazoline, a component of fox feces. *Behav. Neurosci.* **114**, 912–922.

Wallis, H. (1989). Synchrony of menstrual cycles in captive group-living baboons (*Papio cynocephalus* and *P. anubis*). *Am. J. Primatol.* **18**, 167–168.

Wallis, J., King, B. J., and Roth-Meyer, C. (1986). The effect of female proximity and social interaction on the menstrual cycle of crab-eating monkeys (*Macaca fascicularis*). *Primates* **27**, 83–94.

Warren, C. B., Munteanu, M. A., Schwartz, G. E., Benaim, C., Walter, H. G., Leight, R. S., Withycombe, D. A., Mookberjee, B. D., and Trenkle, R. W. (1987). Method of causing the reduction of physiological and/or subjective reactivity to stress in humans being subjected to stress conditions. U.S. Patents 4671959, 4670463, 4670264.

Watson, D., Murray, S., Taylor, G. W., Gower, D. B., Ruparelia, D. B., Vinson, G. P., and Anderson, E. (1988). Gas chromatography-Electron capture mass spectrometry of steroids of human origin. *Biochem. Soc. Trans.* **16**, 737–758.

Wayne, N. L., Malpaux, B., and Karsch, F. J. (1989). Social cues can play a role in the timing onset of the breeding-season of the ewe. *J. Reprod. Fertil.* **87**, 707–713.

Wedekind, C., and Füri, S. (1997). Body odour preferences in men and women: Do they aim for specific MHC combinations or simply heterozygosity? *Proc. R. Soc. London* **264**, 1471–1479.

Wedekind, C., and Penn, D. (2000). MHC genes, body odours and odour preferences. *Nephrol. Dial. Transplan.* **15**, 1269–1271.

Wedekind, C., Seebeck, T., Bettens, F., and Paepke, A. J. (1995). MHC-dependent mate preferences in humans. *Proc. R. Soc. London* **260**, 245–249.

Weiner, H. (1967). External chemical messengers. III. Mind and body in schizophrenia. *N.Y. State J. Med.* **67**, 1287–1311.

Weinstock, R. S., Wright, H. N., and Smith, D. U. (1993). Olfactory dysfunction in diabetes mellitus. *Physiol. Behav.* **53**, 17–21.

Weizenbaum, F., McClintock, M. K., and Adler, N. T. (1977). Decreases in vaginal acyclicity of rats when house with female hamsters. *Horm. Behav.* **8**, 342–347.

Weller, A., and Weller, L. (1992). Menstrual synchrony in female couples. *Psychoneuroendocrinology* **17**, 171–177.

Weller, A., and Weller, L. (1993). Menstrual synchrony between mothers and daughters and between roommates. *Physiol. Behav.* **53**, 943–949.

Weller, A., and Weller, L. (1995a). The impact of social interaction factors on menstrual synchrony in the workplace. *Psychoneuroendocrinology* **20**, 21–31.

Weller, A., and Weller, L. (1995b). Examination of menstrual synchrony among women basketball players. *Psychoneuroendocrinology* **20**, 613–622.

Weller, A., and Weller, L. (1997). Menstrual synchrony under optimal condtions: Bedouin families. *J. Comp. Physiol. Psychol.* **111**, 1430–151.

Weller, A., and Weller, L. (1998a). Assessment of the state of menstrual synchrony: Reply to comment by Arden and Dye (1998). *J. Comp. Psychol.* **112**, 325–326.

Weller, A., and Weller, L. (1998b). Prolonged and very intensive contact may not be conducive to menstrual synchrony. *Psychneuroendocrinology* **23**, 19–32.

Weller, L., and Weller, A. (1995). Menstrual synchrony: Agenda for future research. *Psychneuroendocrinology* **20**, 377–383.

Weller, L., and Weller, A. (1997). Menstrual variability and the measurement of menstrual synchrony. *Psychoneuroendocrinology* **22**, 115–128.

Weller, L., Weller, A., and Avinir, O. (1995). Menstrual synchrony: Only in roommates who are close friends? *Physiol. Behav.* **58**, 883–889.

Weller, L., Weller, A., Koresh-Kamin, H., and Ben-Shoshan, R. (1999a). Menstrual synchrony in a sample of working women. *Psychoneuroendocrinology* **24**, 449–459.

Weller, L., Weller, A., and Roizman, S. (1999b). Human menstrual synchrony in families and among close friends: Examining the importance of mutual exposure. *J. Comp. Physiol. Psychol.* **113**, 261–268.

Weusten, J. J. A. M. (1989). "Biochemical Pathways in Human Testicular Steroidogenesis." University of Nijmegen, Nijmegen.

Weusten, J. J. A. M., van der Wouw, M. P. M. E., Smals, A. G. H., Hofman, J. A., Kloppenborg, P. W. C., and Benraad, T. J. (1990). Differential metabolism of pregnenolone by testicular homogenates of humans and two species of Macaques. *Horm. Metab. Res.* **22**, 619–621.

Whitten, W. K. (1999). Pheromones and the regulation of ovulation. *Nature (London)* **401**, 232–233.

Whitten, W. K., Bronson, F. H., and Greenstein, J. A. (1968). Estrus-inducing pheromone of male mice: Transport by movement of air. *Science* **161**, 584–585.

Wilfong, T. G. (1998). Menstrual synchrony and the "place of women" in ancient Egypt. *In* "Gold of Praise: Studies on Ancient Egypt in Honor of Edward F. Wente" (E. Teeter and J. Larson, eds.), pp. 419–434. Oriental Institute Press, Chicago.

Wilson, D. A., and Leon, M. (1988). Spatial patterns of olfactory bulb single-unit responses to learned olfactory cues in young rats. *J. Neurophysiol.* **59**, 1770–1782.

Wilson, E. O., and Bossert, W. H. (1963). Chemical communication among animals. *Recent Prog. Horm. Res.* **19**, 673–710.

Wilson, H. C. (1987). Female axillary secretions influence women's menstrual cycles: A critique. *Horm. Behav.* **21**, 536–546.

Wilson, H. C. (1988). Male axillary secretins influence women's menstrual cycles: A critique. *Horm. Behav.* **22**, 266–277.

Wilson, H. C. (1992). A critical review of menstrual synchrony research. *Psychoneuroendocrinology* **17**, 565–591.

Wilson, H. C. (1993). Reply to letter by graham. *Psychoneuroendocrinology* **18**, 535–539.

Wilson, H. C., Kiefhaber, S. H., and Gravel, V. (1991). Two studies of menstrual synchrony: Negative results. *Psychneuroendocrinology* **16**, 353–359.

Wilson, M. C., and Harrison, D. E. (1983). Decline in male mouse pheromone with age. *Biol. Reprod.* **29**, 81–86.

Winfree, A. T. (1980). "The Geometry of Biological Time." Springer-Verlag, Berlin.

Winfree, A. T. (1987). "When Time Breaks Down." Princeton University Press, Princeton, NJ.

Wirsig-Wiechmann, C. R., and Jennes, L. (1993). Gonadotropin-releasing hormone agonist binding in tiger salamander nasal cavity. *Neurosci. Lett.* **160**, 201–204.

Wood, R. I. (1997). Thinking about networks in the control of male hamster sexual behavior. *Horm. Behav.* **32**, 40–45.

Wood, R. I. (1998). Integration of chemosensory and hormonal input in the male Syrian hamster brain. *Ann. N.Y. Acad. Sci.* **855**, 362–372.

Wood, R. I., and Newman, S. W. (1995). Integration of chemosensory and hormonal cues is essential for mating behavior in the male Syrian hamster. *J. Neurosci.* **15**, 7261–7269.

Wood, R. I., and Swann, J. M. (2000). Neuronal integration of chemosensory and hormonal signals in the control of male sexual behavior. *In* "Reproduction in Context: Social and Environmental Influences on Reproductive Physiology and Behavior" (K. Wallen and J. E. Schneider, eds.), pp. 423–444. MIT Press, Cambridge, MA.

Wooten, G. F., Kopin, I. J., and Axelrod, J. (1975). Effects of colchicine and vinoblastine on axonal transport and transmitter release in sympathetic nerves. *Ann. N.Y. Acad. Sci.* **253**, 528.

Wright, I. A., Rhind, S. M., Smith, A. J., and Whyte, T. K. (1994). Female-female influences on the duration of the postpartum anestrous period in beef-cows. *Anim. Prod.* **59**, 49–53.

Wright, K. P., and Badia, P. (1999). Effects of menstrual cycle phase and oral contraceptives on alertness, cognitive performance, and circadian rhythms during sleep deprivation. *Behav. Brain Res.* **103**, 185–194.

Wright, S. L., and Brown, R. E. (2000). Maternal behavior, paternal behavior, and pup survival in CD-1 albino mice (*Mus musculus*) in three different housing conditions. *J. Comp. Psychol.* **114**, 183–192.

Wynne-Edwards, K. E., and Reburn, C. J. (2000). Behavioral endocrinology of mammalian fatherhood. *Trends Ecol. Evol.* **15**, 464–468.

Wysocki, C. J., and Beauchamp, G. K. (1984). Ability to smell androstenone is genetically determined. *Proc. Natl. Acad. Sci. U.S.A.* **81**, 4899–902.

Wysocki, C. J., and Gilbert, A. N. (1989). National Geographic Smell Survey: Effects of age are heterogenous. *Annu. N.Y. Acad. Sci.* **561**, 12–28.

Wysocki, C. J., and Preti, G. (1998). Pheromonal influences. *Arch. Sex. Behav.* **27**, 627–629.

Wysocki, C. J., and Preti, G. (2000). Human body odors and their perception. *Jpn. J. Taste Smell Res.* **7**, 19–42.

Wysocki, C. J., Katz, Y., and Bernhard, R. (1983). Male vomeronasal organ mediates female-induced testosterone surges in mice. *Biol. Reprod.* **28**, 917–922.

Yamaguchi, M., Yamazaki, K., Beauchamp, G. K., Bard, J., Thomas, L., and Boyse, E. A. (1981). Distinctive urinary odors governed by the major histocompatibility complex. *Proc. Natl. Acad. Sci. U.S.A.* **78**, 5817–5820.

Yamazaki, K., Boyse, E. A., Mike, V., Thaler, H. T., Mathieson, B. J., Abbot, J., Boyse, J. *et al.* (1976). Control of mating preferences in mice by genes in the major histocompatibility complex. *J. Exp. Med.* **144**, 1324–1335.

Yamazaki, K., Yamaguchi, M., Baranoski, L., Bard, J., Boyse, E. A., and Thomas, L. (1979). Recognition among mice: Evidence from the use of a Y-maze differentially scented by congenic mice of different major histocompatibility types. *J. Exp. Med.* **150**, 755–760.

Yamazaki, K., Beauchamp, G. K., Wysocki, C. J., Bard, J., Thomas, L., and Boyse, E. A. (1983). Recognition of H-2 types in relation to the blocking of pregnancy in mice. *Science* **221**, 186–188.

Yang, A., Walker, N., Bronson, R., Kaghad, M., Oosterwegel, M., Bonnin, J., Vagner, C., Bonnet, H., Dikkes, P., Sharpe, A., McKeon, F., and Caput, D. (2000). p73-deficient mice have neurological, pheromonal and inflammatory defects but lack spontaneous tumours. *Nature (London)* **404**, 99–103.

Yoshida, M. (1984). Correlation analysis of detection threshold data for 'standard test' odors. *Bull. Fac. Sci. Eng., Chuo. Univ.* **27**, 343–353.

Yousem, D. M., Maldjian, J. A., Siddiqi, F., Hummel, T., Alsop, D. C., Geckle, R. J., Bilker, W. B., and Doty, R. L. (1999). Gender effects on odor-stimulated functional magnetic resonance imaging. *Brain Res.* **818**, 480–487.

Yu, G. Z., Kaba, H., Okutani, F., Takahashi, S., Higuchi, T., and Seto, K. (1996a). The action of oxytocin originating in the hypothalamic paraventricular nucleus on mitral and granule cells in the rat main olfactory bulb. *Neuroscience* **72**, 1073–1082.

Yu, G. Z., Kaba, H., Okutani, F., Takahashi, S., and Higuchi, T. (1996b). The olfactory bulb: A critical site of action for oxytocin in the induction of maternal behaviour in the rat. *Neuroscience* **72**, 1083–1088.

Zalaquett, C., and Thiessen, D. (1991). The effects of odors from stressed mice on conspecific behavior. *Physiol. Behav.* **50**, 221–227.

Zald, D. H., Donndelinger, M. J., and Pardo, J. V. (1998). Elucidating dynamic brain interactions with across-subjects correlational analyses of positron emission tomographic data: The functional connectivity of the amygdala and orbitofrontal cortex during olfactory tasks. *J. Cereb. Blood Flow Metab.* **18**, 896–905.

Zarrow, M. X., Elefthériou, B. E., and Denenberg, V. H. (1972). Pheromonal facilitation of HCG-induced ovulation in different strains of immature mice. *Biol. Reprod.* **6**, 277–280.

Zatorre, R. J., Jones-Gotman, M. J., Evans, A. C., and Meyer, E. (1992). Functional localization and lateralization of human olfactory cortex. *Nature (London)* **360**, 339–340.

Zbar, R. I. S., Zbar, L. I., Dudley, C., Trott, S. A., Rohrich, R. J., and Moss, R. L. (2000). A classification schema for the vomeronasal organ in humans. *Plast. Reconstr. Surg.* **105**, 1284–1288.

Zehr, J. L., Gans, S. E., and McClintock, M. K. (2001). Variation in reproductive traits is associated with short anogenital distance in female rats. *Dev. Psychobiol.* **38**, 229–238.

Zeng, X.-N., Leyden, J. J., Lawley, H. J., Sawano, K., Nohara, I., and Preti, G. (1991). Analysis of characteristic odors from human male axillae. *J. Chem. Ecol.* **17**, 1469–1492.

Zeng, X.-N., Leyden, J. J., Brand, J. G., Spielman, A. I., McGinley, K. J., and Preti, G. (1992). An investigation of human apocrine gland secretion for axillary odor precursors. *J. Chem. Ecol.* **18**, 1039–1055.

Zeng, X.-N., Leyden, J. J., Spielman, A. I., and Preti, G. (1996). Analysis of characteristic human female odors: Qualitative comparison to males. *J. Chem. Ecol.* **22**, 237–257.

Ziegler, T. E. (1990). "Socioendocrinology of Primate Reproduction." Wiley-Liss, New York.

Ziegler, T. E., Epple, G., Snowdon, C. T., Porter, T. A., Belcher, A. M., and Kuederling, I. (1993). Detection of the chemical signals of ovulation in the cotton top tamarin, *Saguinus oedipus. Anim. Behav.* **45**, 313–322.

ISBN 0-12-532105-8

90038

ISBN 0-12-532105-8